Britain's High Speed Train– a promise fulfilled.

Some years ago British Rail promised its Inter-City travellers an improved deal in terms of speed and comfort. Today the High Speed Train has fulfilled this promise and revolutionised rail travel on a number of major routes.

Available to the world's railways through BRE-Metro Ltd., the High Speed Train concept incorporates the best in B.R.'s design and engineering know-how supported by BRE-Metro's proven record of quality and reliability which are appreciated worldwide.

The H.S.T. has brought new standards to Britain's Inter-City travellers and in the first five years of operation, 5·8 thousand million passenger miles were covered by these trains with journey times being reduced by up to 20%. With its cost effectiveness proved in one of the most demanding travel environments in the world, a close look at the H.S.T. is essential when considering updating your Inter-City services.

Very sensible people Britain's Inter-City Travellers.

BRE-METRO WORLDWIDE ◯

Shaping the future.

General Manager, BRE-Metro Limited, Railway Technical Centre, Derby DE2 8UP. Telephone: 0332 49211. Telex: 37367.

JANE'S WORLD RAILWAYS 1983-84

Jane's Publishing Company Limited, 238 City Road, London EC1V 2PU, England
Jane's Publishing Inc, 13th Floor, 135 West 50th Street, New York, NY 10020, USA

thousands
of sacm engines
on the
railway tracks

H+H Publicité - Photo Alsthom Atlantique

BBC
BROWN BOVERI

competent · dependable · worldwide

Brown Boveri Group

The name BBC Brown Boveri links production facilities,
sales companies, technical offices, branches and agencies in about
140 countries, to form a worldwide enterprise employing
some 100 000 persons and having a consolidated annual sales
of about 10 000 million Swiss francs (equivalent to about
5 billion US dollars).

Products, systems and installations for the generation,
distribution and utilization of electrical energy,
including the associated automation, protection and control,
form the backbone of the BBC production range.

Traction

Modern intercity train of the Norwegian State Railways.
BBC supplied the complete electrical equipment for the locomotives
and the passenger coaches. The locomotives have three-phase
asynchronous traction motors.

Design, supply and installation of complete sets of electrical equipment for all traction fields

Main-line, local and industrial railways,
including railways running at very high speeds
Surface, elevated or underground mass transit
systems, including suburban and urban
commuter trains, light rail vehicles, trams
and trolleybuses
Funiculars and rack railways
New, unconventional means of transport

Supply of components

Electric machines
Equipment for conversion and distribution
of electricity
Protective and control systems
Lighting, heating, ventilating and air
conditioning equipment for railway coaches
Substations for a.c. and d.c. supply
Overhead contact wire installations

Charging systems for diesel engines

Turbochargers, pressure-wave superchargers

For further information please consult your local BBC agency or write to: **Switzerland:** BBC Brown, Boveri & Company, Ltd., P.O. Box 58, CH-5401 Baden;
Fed. Republic of Germany: Brown, Boveri & Cie. Aktiengesellschaft, Postfach 351, D-6800 Mannheim 1; **Austria:** Oesterreichische Brown Boveri-Werke AG,
Postfach 184, A-1101 Vienna; **Brazil:** Indústria Elétrica Brown Boveri S.A., Caixa Postal 975, 06000 Osasco (SP); **Canada:** Brown Boveri Canada Ltd., 4000 Trans-
Canada Highway, Pointe Claire P.Q. H 9R 1B2; **Italy:** Tecnomasio Italiano Brown Boveri S.p.A., Casella postale 10225, I-20100 Milano; **Norway:** A/S Norsk Elektrisk
& Brown Boveri, Postboks 1174, Sentrum, Oslo 1; **Spain:** Brown Boveri de España S.A., Apartado 36127, E-Madrid 16; **USA:** Brown Boveri Corp., 1460 Livingston
Ave., North Brunswick NJ 08902; **Other countries:** Brown Boveri International Group, P.O. Box 58, CH-5401 Baden, Switzerland.   507608 · VI

Alphabetical list of advertisers

Don't let 300 million clips mislead you

It's true that for over 20 years Pandrol has produced probably the most versatile, most cost-effective and inherently safe resilient track fastening system in the world – a system built around a unique concept – the Pandrol Clip.

But Pandrol is also a company ready to undertake customized design and manufacture of fastenings capable of meeting the most demanding of non-standard specifications.

A company with a wealth of expertise in all aspects of track technology, with extensive investment in research and development; in modern manufacturing techniques; in up-to-the-minute instrumented test facilities.

Investment and know-how that has led to the introduction of the 'e' Series – a new range of clips with even more than 300 million-plus potential, designed for automatic high-speed installation on the tracks of tomorrow.

For your next track project contact Pandrol Limited, 1 Vincent Square, London, SW1P 2PN, England. Telephone 01-834 2255. Telex 21474.

We won't mislead you.

PANDROL®
GETTING TO GRIPS WORLDWIDE

[5]

Breda's solution to the problems of mass rail transit...

COMMUTER TRAIN
Italian State Railways

ELECTRIC MOTO COACH
Rome Underground - Italy

LIGHT RAIL VEHICLE
GCRTA - Cleveland - USA

RAPID TRANSIT CAR
WMATA - Washington DC - USA

BREDA COSTRUZIONI FERROVIARIE SpA
Via Ciliegiole - 51100 Pistoia - Italy
Sofer - Officine Ferroviarie - Pozzuoli
Avis - Castellammare di Stabia
Omeca - Reggio Calabria
Ferrosud - Matera
Imesi - Carini (PA)
Cometra - Giammoro (ME)

GRUPPO
EFIM

AVIOFER
BREDA

Classified list of advertisers

The companies advertising in this publication have informed us that they are involved in the fields of manufacture indicated below:

Access control systems
Thorn EMI Electronics

Air brake equipment
Davies & Metcalfe
Mecanoexportimport
New York Air Brake
Oerlikon-Bührle
SAB Nife

Air-conditioned carriages
BRE-Metro
Daewoo Heavy Industries
Hyundai
MAN
Mecanoexportimport
SOCIMI

Air-conditioning equipment
BBC Brown, Boveri
Hyundai
Pintsch Bamag
Toshiba

Air filters
Davies & Metcalfe

Air springs
Hyundai

Aluminium semis
Hyundai

Area traffic control systems
GEC-Traffic Automation

Articulated light rail vehicles
Bombardier

Automatic couplers
AEG-Telefunken
BBC Brown, Boveri
Davies & Metcalfe
Daewoo Heavy Industries
Hyundai
Mecanoexportimport
SOCIMI

Automatic fare collection systems
GEC-Traffic Automation

Automatic vehicle monitoring equipment
GEC-Traffic Automation

Automatic wagon identification
AEG-Telefunken

Autopilots for trams, underground railways, etc
AEG-Telefunken
Ansaldo
BBC Brown, Boveri
Hyundai

Auxiliary motors
AEG-Telefunken
BBC Brown, Boveri
Mecanoexportimport
SOCIMI

Auxiliary vehicles
Daewoo Heavy Industries
Zweiweg Fahrzeug

Axle-box liner plates
Daewoo Heavy Industries
Mecanoexportimport

Axle-boxes & bearings
Kolmex
Mecanoexportimport

Axle-boxes & cylindrical roller bearings
Hyundai
Mecanoexportimport

Axle drive for diesel hydraulic locomotives
Ganz Mávag
Hyundai
Mecanoexportimport
Swiss Locomotive

Axle gears
GEC Traction
Hyundai
Mecanoexportimport
Swiss Locomotive

Axles, railway
Kolmex
Mecanoexportimport

Ballast wagons
Daewoo Heavy Industries
Hyundai
Mecanoexportimport

Barriers & access control equipment
Thorn EMI Electronics

Battery electric vehicles
Daewoo Heavy Industries
Hyundai
Wickham, D

Bearings, plain
Mecanoexportimport

Bearings, roller
Mecanoexportimport

Bogies
Breda
BRE-Metro
Daewoo Heavy Industries
FIREMA Consortium
Hyundai
Kolmex
Leo Gottwald
MAN
Socimi
Swiss Locomotive
Toshiba
Wickham, D

Bogies, especially air suspension type
Breda
BRE-Metro
Daewoo Heavy Industries
FIREMA Consortium
Hyundai
MAN
SOCIMI

Boxes, battery
Breda
Daewoo Heavy Industries
Mecanoexportimport

Brake equipment
Davies & Metcalfe
Hyundai
Kolmex
Mecanoexportimport
New York Air Brake
Oerlikon-Bührle
SAB Nife
SOCIMI

Brake equipment (hydraulic disc)
New York Air Brake
SAB Nife

Brake equipment (hydrodynamic braking system)
New York Air Brake

Brake slack adjusters
Davies & Metcalfe
Mecanoexportimport
SAB Nife

Brake units for disc brakes
Davies & Metcalfe
Hyundai
Mecanoexportimport
New York Air Brake
SAB Nife
SOCIMI

Brake units for tread brakes
Davies & Metcalfe
Hyundai
Mecanoexportimport
New York Air Brake
SAB Nife

Breakdown cranes
Takraf

Buffers
Kolmex
Mecanoexportimport

Buffers, friction
Hyundai
Mecanoexportimport

Buffers, rubber
Mecanoexportimport

Cables, electric
AEG-Telefunken
Hyundai
Mecanoexportimport

Car body tilting equipment
Breda
BRE-Metro
Hyundai
Mecanoexportimport

Carriages & wagons
Breda
BRE-Metro
CIMT
Daewoo Heavy Industries
FIREMA Consortium
Ganz-Mávag
Hyundai
Mecanoexportimport
MAN
Messerschmitt-Bölkow-Blohm

Castings, aluminium & aluminium alloy
BRE-Metro
Mecanoexportimport

Castings, iron
Daewoo Heavy Industries
Mecanoexportimport
New York Air Brake
SACM
Wickham, D

Coach heaters
AEG-Telefunken
Daewoo Heavy Industries
Pintsch Bamag

Coal wagons
BRE-Metro
FIREMA Consortium
Hyundai
Kolmex
Mecanoexportimport

Commuter railcars
Bombardier

ACCESS AND REVENUE CONTROL

In addition to automatic systems for car parking control involving barrier and pay & display facilities for which the company is UK market leader, *THORN EMI* also offers a range of ticket issuing, ticket vending and barrier systems for railways and other mass transportation systems.

The company supplies advanced microprocessor-based systems to local authorities, British Rail and London Transport. Other products include information systems – such as computer-controlled *LED* displays –

and the application of watermark magnetics in stored value and access control systems.

Can we tell you more about our extensive capability? Write today for further information giving details of your particular requirement.

Leadership in Access & Revenue Control

 THORN EMI Electronics

THORN EMI Electronics Limited Communications Division
Wookey Hole Road. Wells Somerset BA5 1AA England
telephone 0749-72081 telex 44254

A THORN EMI Company

Compressed motors
Hyundai

Compressors
Daewoo Heavy Industries
Davies & Metcalfe
Ganz-Mávag
Hyundai
Mecanoexportimport
New York Air Brake

Computer controlled district control centres & marshalling yards
AEG-Telefunken
Ansaldo

Computerised railway operation & maintenance systems
AEG-Telefunken
Ansaldo
Gibbs & Hill
Vickers Design & Projects

Computerised ticket issuing machines
Thorn EMI Electronics

Concrete sleepers/manufacturing plant & equipment
Monier

Concrete sleepers/ties
Monier

Consulting systems
GEC-Traffic Automation

Containers
Breda
Kolmex
Mecanoexportimport

Control equipment, locomotive
AEG-Telefunken
Ansaldo
BBC Brown, Boveri
BRE-Metro
Deuta-Werke
Hyundai
Mecanoexportimport
New York Air Brake
Toshiba

Control equipment, signal etc
AEG-Telefunken
Ansaldo
BRE-Metro
Field & Grant
GEC-Traffic Automation
Tyer
Zone-Controls

Conveyors for ballast
Wickham, D

Couplings
AEG-Telefunken
BRE-Metro
Daewoo Heavy Industries
Kolmex
Mecanoexportimport
SOCIMI
Toshiba
Wickham, D

Cranes, electric
Hyundai
MAN
Takraf

Crankshafts
Mecanoexportimport

Crew-carrying vehicles
Daewoo Heavy Industries
Zweiweg Fahrzeug

Crossings
BBC Brown, Boveri

Current collectors
AEG-Telefunken
BRE-Metro
Hyundai
Toshiba

Diesel-electric cars
Ansaldo
Breda
Daewoo Heavy Industries
FIREMA Consortium
Hyundai
Kolmex
Messerschmitt-Bölkow-Blohm
SOCIMI
Wickham, D

Diesel-electric cars, shunting & transfer
AEG-Telefunken
Breda
Daewoo Heavy Industries
Hyundai
MAN
SOCIMI

Diesel-electric locomotives
Ansaldo
Bombardier
Breda
BRE-Metro
Daewoo Heavy Industries
Energomachexport
Fiat
FIREMA Consortium
Ganz-Mávag
Hyundai
Krauss-Maffei
Krupp MaK
Mecanoexportimport
SOCIMI
Swiss Locomotive
Toshiba

Diesel-electric railcars
Ansaldo
Breda
BRE-Metro
CIMT
Daewoo Heavy Industries
FIREMA Consortium
Ganz-Mávag
Hyundai
MAN
Mecanoexportimport
Messerschmitt-Bölkow-Blohm
SOCIMI
Toshiba
Wickham, D

Diesel engine parts
Mecanoexportimport
Ruston Diesels
SACM
SEMT-Pielstick

Diesel engines
Alsthom-Atlantique
Bombardier
Daewoo Heavy Industries
Energomachexport
Ganz-Mávag
General Motors Corporation
Hyundai
Isotta Fraschini
MAN
Mecanoexportimport
Motoren -und Turbinen-Union
Ruston Diesels
SACM
SEMT-Pielstick

Diesel-hydraulic coaches
Breda
Daewoo Heavy Industries
FIREMA Consortium
Ganz-Mávag
Hyundai
MAN
Mecanoexportimport
Messerschmitt-Bölkow-Blohm
SOCIMI

Diesel-hydraulic locomotives
Breda
BRE-Metro
Daewoo Heavy Industries
Ganz-Mávag
Krupp MaK
SOCIMI
Swiss Locomotive

Diesel-hydraulic railcars
Breda
Daewoo Heavy Industries
FIREMA Consortium
Ganz-Mávag
MAN
Mecanoexportimport
Messerschmitt-Bölkow-Blohm
SOCIMI
Wickham, D

Diesel-hydraulic self-propelled railcars
Krupp MaK

Diesel locomotives
Breda
BRE-Metro
Cockerill
Daewoo Heavy Industries
Energomachexport
FIREMA Consortium
Ganz-Mávag
Kolmex
Krauss-Maffei
Mecanoexportimport
SOCIMI
Swiss Locomotive

Diesel-mechanical railcars
Breda
Daewoo Heavy Industries
FIREMA Consortium
Hyundai
MAN
Mecanoexportimport
SOCIMI
Wickham, D

Diesel passenger railbuses (trolleys)
Breda
BRE-Metro
Ganz-Mávag
Hyundai
MAN
Mecanoexportimport
SOCIMI
Wickham, D

Diesel railcars
Breda
BRE-Metro
Daewoo Heavy Industries
FIREMA Consortium
Ganz-Mávag
Hyundai
MAN
Mecanoexportimport
Wickham, D

Disc brake equipment for trams, locomotives, etc
Davies & Metcalfe
Hyundai
Mecanoexportimport
New York Air Brake
Oerlikon-Bührle
SAB Nife
SOCIMI

Disc brakes
Daewoo Heavy Industries
Davies & Metcalfe
Hyundai
Mecanoexportimport
New York Air Brake
SAB Nife
SOCIMI

Discharge gates
Daewoo Heavy Industries
Mecanoexportimport

57 nations choose world leader.

Because it's the most reliable locomotive ever built.

Because it's the most easily maintained locomotive in the world.

Because it's backed up by the number one parts and service network in the industry.

Because it comes with free service assistance for life.

Because virtually every part in it has been proven over and over again, year after year in some of the most grueling conditions anywhere.

And because people everywhere feel better about ordering equipment they can trust, GM-powered locomotives are the most sought-after locomotives sold on the planet.

Contact us at the Electro-Motive Division, La Grange, Illinois 60525, U.S.A., to find out more.

In a world where two nations often have trouble agreeing on anything, it's nice to see 57 nations choosing one thing. We're glad it's us.

GM-powered locomotives are produced in La Grange, Illinois, U.S.A. and at wholly-owned subsidiaries in Canada and South Africa.

We have a branch in Argentina and associates and licensees in Australia, Belgium, Brazil, West Germany, South Korea, Spain, Sweden, the United Kingdom and Yugoslavia.

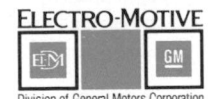

ELECTRO-MOTIVE

Division of General Motors Corporation

Door & window fittings
Daewoo Heavy Industries
Hyundai
Mecanoexportimport

Door control equipment
AEG-Telefunken
Deuta-Werke
Hyundai
Mecanoexportimport
Pintsch Bamag
SOCIMI

Double-deck coaches
FIREMA Consortium
Mecanoexportimport

Double-deck diesel train-set
FIREMA Consortium

Double-deck electric train-set
Ansaldo
FIREMA Consortium

Draught (draw) gears
Davies & Metcalfe
Mecanoexportimport

Draw & buffer device with rubber shock absorbers
Davies & Metcalfe
Hyundai

Draw springs
BRE-Metro
Mecanoexportimport

Driver's safety and vigilance equipment
AEG-Telefunken
Ansaldo
Davies & Metcalfe
Deuta-Werke

Electric couplers
AEG-Telefunken
Davies & Metcalfe
New York Air Brake
Toshiba

Electric locomotive equipment
AEG-Telefunken
Ansaldo
BBC Brown, Boveri
Cockerill
Energomachexport
GEC Traction
Hyundai
Mecanoexportimport
SOCIMI
Swiss Locomotive
Toshiba

Electric propulsion equipment
AEG-Telefunken
Ansaldo
BBC Brown, Boveri
GEC Traction
Hyundai
SOCIMI

Electric railcars
AEG-Telefunken
Ansaldo
Breda
BRE-Metro
CIMT
Daewoo Heavy Industries
Energomachexport
FIREMA Consortium
Ganz-Mávag
GEC Traction
MAN
Mecanoexportimport
Messerschmitt-Bölkow-Blohm
SOCIMI
Toshiba

Electric subway cars
AEG-Telefunken
Ansaldo
Breda
BRE-Metro
CIMT
Daewoo Heavy Industries
FIREMA Consortium
Ganz-Mávag
GEC Traction
Hyundai
MAN
Mecanoexportimport
Messerschmitt-Bölkow-Blohm
SOCIMI

Electric tractors
AEG-Telefunken
Daewoo Heavy Industries

Electric trailer cars
AEG-Telefunken
Breda
BRE-Metro
Daewoo Heavy Industries
FIREMA Consortium
Ganz-Mávag
SOCIMI
Toshiba

Electric transmission systems
BBC Brown, Boveri
Energomachexport
GEC Traction
Gibbs & Hill
Mecanoexportimport

Electrical equipment
AEG-Telefunken
Ansaldo
BBC Brown, Boveri
Energomachexport
Field & Grant
GEC Traction
Hyundai
Mecanoexportimport
Pintsch Bamag
SOCIMI
Toshiba
Tyer
Zone-Controls

Electric traction equipment
Ansaldo
BBC Brown, Boveri
Daewoo Heavy Industries
Energomachexport
GEC Traction
Hyundai
Mecanoexportimport
SOCIMI

Electro pneumatic brakes
AEG-Telefunken
Davies & Metcalfe
Hyundai
Mecanoexportimport
New York Air Brake
Oerlikon-Bührle
SAB Nife
SOCIMI

Electromagnetic rail brakes
AEG-Telefunken
Davies & Metcalfe
New York Air Brake
Oerlikon-Bührle
SOCIMI

Electronic control systems for diesel locomotives including adaptation for radio control
AEG-Telefunken
BBC Brown, Boveri
Deuta-Werke
Gibbs & Hill
Krauss-Maffei
New York Air Brake

Electronic protection equipment for rail vehicles (slip & spin protection)
AEG-Telefunken
Ansaldo
BBC Brown, Boveri
Davies & Metcalfe
Deuta-Werke
GEC Traction
Hyundai
Krauss-Maffei
New York Air Brake
Oerlikon-Bührle

Electronic seat reservation
Toshiba

Electronic testing equipment
AEG-Telefunken
BRE-Metro

Engine parts, diesel
Energomachexport
Mecanoexportimport
Ruston Diesels
SACM
SEMT-Pielstick

Engine testing equipment
AEG-Telefunken

Engine testing equipment for governors
Ruston Diesels

Exhaust motors
AEG-Telefunken
Hyundai

Exhausters
Davies & Metcalfe

Fail-safe warning systems
AEG-Telefunken
Deuta-Werke
Gibbs & Hill
Hyundai
Pintsch Bamag

Fareboxes
GEC-Traffic Automation

Filters (air)
Davies & Metcalfe
Hyundai

Filters (oil)
Davies & Metcalfe

Flameproof mining locomotives
GEC Traction
Ganz-Mávag

Flatcars
Daewoo Heavy Industries
MAN
Mecanoexportimport
SOCIMI

Flexible couplings (rubber)
Mecanoexportimport

Fluorescent lighting
AEG-Telefunken
Hyundai
Mecanoexportimport
Pintsch Bamag

Forgings, steel
BRE-Metro
Daewoo Heavy Industries
Mecanoexportimport

Freight cars
Bombardier
Breda
BRE-Metro
Daewoo Heavy Industries
FIREMA Consortium
Hyundai
Mecanoexportimport
SOCIMI

They're happiest when on the move.

SLM rail vehicles don't hold much with standing still. They want to be off,
earning their keep. Which they are specially calculated, designed and built for.
They are not overweight and are kind to the track. With a temperament
and constitution suited to their tasks: fast, easy-running, easy-climbing,
manœuvrable and rugged. SLM main line and shunting locomotives as well
as rack railcars and locomotives are proving their worth all over the world.
Whether with electric or diesel-electric drive. They need very little attention
and perform untiringly to their owners' content. Get in touch with us;
we like to get things moving.

Friction control pedestal suspension
Daewoo Heavy Industries
Mecanoexportimport

Gang warning systems
Pintsch Bamag

Gears & gearboxes
AEG-Telefunken
Ganz-Mávag
GEC Traction

Generators
AEG-Telefunken
BBC Brown, Boveri
Daewoo Heavy Industries
GEC Traction
Hyundai
Mecanoexportimport
Pintsch Bamag
SOCIMI
Toshiba

Generators, portable
Plasser & Theurer

Gondola-wagons
Daewoo Heavy Industries
Hyundai
Mecanoexportimport
SOCIMI

Hand brakes
Daewoo Heavy Industries
Davies & Metcalfe
Hyundai
Mecanoexportimport

Heat exchangers
Pintsch Bamag

Heating equipment (switch)
AEG-Telefunken
Energomachexport
Pintsch Bamag

Hoists
MAN

Hopper cars
Breda
BRE-Metro
Daewoo Heavy Industries
FIREMA Consortium
Hyundai
Mecanoexportimport
SOCIMI

Hose & couplings
Davies & Metcalfe
Mecanoexportimport
New York Air Brake

Hydraulic & profile-clearing rail pullers
Elektro-Thermit

Hydraulic pumps
New York Air Brake

Hydraulic shearing devices
Elektro-Thermit

Hydraulic working platforms
Zweiweg Fahrzeug

Industrial gas turbine
BBC Brown, Boveri
Energomachexport

Inspection, track
Plasser & Theurer
Wickham, D

Instruments
AEG-Telefunken
BBC Brown, Boveri

Insulated rail joins
Energomachexport

Insulation, electric
AEG-Telefunken
Hyundai

Intercity high-speed systems
Bombardier

Intercommunication equipment
AEG-Telefunken
BBC Brown, Boveri
GEC-Traffic Automation
Hyundai
Mecanoexportimport
Toshiba

Interlocking signalling equipment
AEG-Telefunken
Energomachexport
Field & Grant
Tyer
Zone-Controls

Iron ore wagons
Daewoo Heavy Industries
Hyundai
Mecanoexportimport

Level crossing barriers, automatic & manual
Field & Grant
GEC-Traffic Automation
Pintsch Bamag
SAB Nife
Tyer
Zone-Controls

Light rail vehicles
AEG-Telefunken
Ansaldo
Breda
BRE-Metro
Daewoo Heavy Industries
FIREMA Consortium
Ganz-Mávag
GEC Traction
MAN
SOCIMI
Wickham, D

Lighting equipment, locomotives
AEG-Telefunken
BBC Brown, Boveri
Hyundai
Mecanoexportimport
Pintsch Bamag

Lighting equipment, trains
AEG-Telefunken
BBC Brown, Boveri
Hyundai
Mecanoexportimport
Pintsch Bamag
SAB Nife

Load braking devices
Davies & Metcalfe
Oerlikon-Bührle
SAB Nife

Locomotive equipment
AEG-Telefunken
Cockerill
GEC Traction
Mecanoexportimport
Toshiba

Locomotive equipment, electric
AEG-Telefunken
Ansaldo
BBC Brown, Boveri
Cockerill
GEC Traction
Mecanoexportimport
SOCIMI
Toshiba

Locomotives, diesel
Ansaldo
Breda
BRE-Metro
Daewoo Heavy Industries
Ganz-Mávag
Swiss Locomotive

Locomotives, diesel-electric
AEG-Telefunken
Breda
BRE-Metro
Cockerill
Daewoo Heavy Industries
Fiat
FIREMA Consortium
Ganz-Mávag
Hyundai
Kolmex
Krauss-Maffei
Mecanoexportimport
SOCIMI
Swiss Locomotive
Toshiba

Locomotives, diesel-hydraulic
Breda
BRE-Metro
Cockerill
Daewoo Heavy Industries
FIREMA Consortium
Ganz-Mávag
Hyundai
Krauss-Maffei
Mecanoexportimport
SOCIMI
Swiss Locomotive
Wickham, D

Locomotives, diesel-mechanical
Cockerill
FIREMA Consortium
Hyundai
Mecanoexportimport
Swiss Locomotive

Locomotives, electric
AEG-Telefunken
Ansaldo
Breda
BRE-Metro
Cockerill
Daewoo Heavy Industries
Fiat
FIREMA Consortium
Ganz-Mávag
GEC Traction
Hyundai
Kolmex
Krauss-Maffei
Mecanoexportimport
SOCIMI
Swiss Locomotive
Toshiba

Locomotives, industrial & mining
AEG-Telefunken
Cockerill
Daewoo Heavy Industries
Ganz-Mávag
GEC Traction
Krauss-Maffei

Locomotives, tilting body
Fiat

Locomotives, washing equipment
Wickham, D

Loudspeakers
AEG-Telefunken

Low-noise wheels
SAB Nife

Maintenance facilities
GEC-Traffic Automation

NEW FROM GANZ-MÁVAG
Saves energy - provides comfort

This attractive articulated railbus combines the prime characteristics of a train and a bus.
It was jointly developed by Ganz-Mávag and Ikarus

DRIVING MOTOR TYPE:	Cummins NTA 855 R or Ganz-Mávag 6KH 15/16
OUTPUT:	250 kW
TRANSMISSION:	Twin Disk TAC 22 hydromechanical or Voith T 211 hydrodynamic
GAUGE:	1435 mm
DESIGNED SPEED:	100 km/h
SEATS:	86
TOTAL PASSENGER CAPACITY:	160
EMPTY MASS ABT:	28 t
MAX AXLE LOAD:	10 t
TOTAL LENGTH:	25200 mm

Ganz Mávag
BUDAPEST

Locomotive and Railway Carriage
Manufacturers, Mechanical Engineers
Budapest VIII, Könyves Kálmán krt 76
H-1967 Budapest, P.O. Box 136
Telex: 22-5575
Phone: 335-950
Cable: Ganzmávag Budapest

[16]

**Only good brakes
make a train safe
– OERLIKON BRAKES –**

Rectifiers, silicon
AEG-Telefunken
Ansaldo
BBC Brown, Boveri
Toshiba

Refrigerated equipment
BBC Brown, Boveri
Breda
Hyundai
Pintsch Bamag

Refrigerated wagons
AEG-Telefunken
Breda
Daewoo Heavy Industries
FIREMA Consortium
Mecanoexportimport
SOCIMI

Registering & non-registering fareboxes & turnstiles
GEC-Traffic Automation

Regulations, ballast
Mecanoexportimport
Pintsch Bamag

Remote control equipment
AEG-Telefunken
Ansaldo
BBC Brown, Boveri
Toshiba

Remote control equipment for diesel engines
BBC Brown, Boveri
Ruston Diesels

Research & development
GEC-Traffic Automation

Resilient wheels
SAB Nife
SOCIMI
Wickham, D

Revenue collection
Thorn EMI Electronics

Road-rail shunting units
Hyundai
Zweiweg Fahrzeug

Roller bearing axle-boxes
Daewoo Heavy Industries
Mecanoexportimport

Rolling stock, railway
Breda
BRE-Metro
Daewoo Heavy Industries
Energomachexport
FIREMA Consortium
Ganz-Mávag
Hyundai
Kolmex
MAN
Mecanoexportimport
SOCIMI
Swiss Locomotive
Toshiba

Sanding devices
Davies & Metcalfe
New York Air Brake

Seats, passenger
BRE-Metro
Mecanoexportimport

Self-propelled gallery cars
Bombardier

Signalling systems & apparatus
AEG-Telefunken
Ansaldo
Energomachexport
Field & Grant
GEC-Traffic Automation
Tyer

Simulation methodologies
Ansaldo

Sleepers
Mecanoexportimport
Monier
SOCIMI

Sliding side wagons
Daewoo Heavy Industries
FIREMA Consortium
Hyundai
Mecanoexportimport

Special purpose self-propelled railway vehicles
Mecanoexportimport
Pandrol

Speed control devices
AEG-Telefunken
Ansaido
BBC Brown, Boveri
Deuta-Werke

Speed control devices, diesel engines
Ruston Diesels

Speed indications
AEG-Telefunken
Deuta-Werke

Standby diesel generators
AEG-Telefunken
Alsthom-Atlantique
MAN
Ruston Diesels
SOCIMI

Steam heating apparatus
Energomachexport
Mecanoexportimport

Steel castings
BRE-Metro
Daewoo Heavy Industries
Mecanoexportimport

Steel structures
BRE-Metro
Daewoo Heavy Industries
Hyundai

Stored-value currency cards
Thorn EMI Electronics

Surface & underground battery & trolley locomotives
AEG-Telefunken
BRE-Metro
GEC Traction

Surface trolley locomotives
Energomachexport

Suspension components
Mecanoexportimport

Switch heaters
Pintsch Bamag

Switchgear, electric
AEG-Telefunken
Ansaldo
BBC Brown, Boveri
Field & Grant
Pintsch Bamag
Toshiba
Tyer
Zone-Controls

Tank cars
Breda
BRE-Metro
Daewoo Heavy Industries
Energomachexport
FIREMA Consortium
Hyundai
Mecanoexportimport
SOCIMI

Telecommunications
AEG-Telefunken
BBC Brown, Boveri
Gibbs & Hill
Toshiba

Thyristors & thyristor equipment
AEG-Telefunken
Ansaldo
BBC Brown, Boveri
GEC Traction
Hyundai
Toshiba

Ticket dispensers
GEC-Traffic Automation
Thorn EMI Electronics

Toilets, flushing
Hyundai
Mecanoexportimport

Tower vehicles
Zweiweg Fahrzeug

Track analyser
Hyundai
Plasser & Theurer

Track-cleaning machines
Plasser & Theurer
Zweiweg Fahrzeug

Track inspection cars
Hyundai
Mecanoexportimport
Plasser & Theurer
Wickham, D

Track laying train
Hyundai
Plasser & Theurer

Track liners
Plasser & Theurer

Track machines
Energomachexport

Track maintenance equipment
Leo Gottwald
Monier
Pandrol
Plasser & Theurer
Vickers Design & Projects

Track measuring vehicle (cars & coaches)
Plasser & Theurer

Track renewal train (gantry cranes)
Plasser & Theurer

Track undercutters
Plasser & Theurer

Traffic control systems
AEG-Telefunken
Ansaldo
Deuta-Werke
GEC-Traffic Automation
Gibbs & Hill
Hyundai
Toshiba

Trailers
Breda
Daewoo Heavy Industries
FIREMA Consortium
Ganz-Mávag
Hyundai
Messerschmitt-Bölkow-Blohm
SOCIMI
Wickham, D

HYUNDAI RUNS THE FUTURE

Hyundai manufactures a full range of railway rolling stock, as well as Diesel Electric Locomotives.

Now we are only happy to hear that those manufactured by us are running satisfactorily on their rails, both domestic and abroad.

Also, we are the only manufacturer in Asia that builds locomotives under technical licence agreement with GM/EMD in U.S.A.

Please find your satisfaction from our goods.

▲HYUNDAI
ROLLING STOCK CO.,LTD.

Head Office: (Works)
621 Deokjeong-Dong, Changwon, Kyungnam, Korea
TEL.: (1551) 82-1341/50 TLX.: K3744 HDHEAVY

Seoul Office: (Sales & Marketing)
KPO Box 1677, Seoul, Korea TEL.: 725-7591/5
TLX.: K23720 HDROLLS

OVERSEAS BRANCH OFFICES
*Tokyo TEL: 03-211-0851/4 TLX: J28548 HDT *Jakarta TEL: 511332, 511772 TLX: 44287 HDSS JKT, IA *Singapore TEL: 2221937 TLX: RS21923 HYUNDAI *Sydney TEL: 02-2336517 TLX: AA70700 *London TEL: 01-741-1531 TLX: 938270 HD LDNG *Lagos TEL: 614992 TLX: 21097 HDLGS *New York TEL: (201) 592-7766 TLX: 6853396 HDC NJ *Chicago TEL: 312-980-5454/6 TLX: 206251 SEL INTL ENGR *Santiago TEL: 88160, 726807 TLX: 340451 HDCORP CK

Tramcars
AEG-Telefunken
Ansaldo
Breda
FIREMA Consortium
Ganz-Mávag
Hyundai
Kolmex
Mecanoexportimport
SOCIMI

Transformers
AEG-Telefunken
BBC Brown, Boveri
Energomachexport
Gibbs & Hill
Toshiba

Trucks
Breda
BRE-Metro
Daewoo Heavy Industries
Hyundai
SOCIMI

Turbo-generators
AEG-Telefunken
BBC Brown, Boveri
Energomachexport
Hyundai

Two-way vehicles
Breda
SOCIMI
Wickham, D
Zweiweg-Fahrzeug

Tyres, railway
Kolmex
Mecanoexportimport
Nikex

Ultrasonic testing equipment
BRE-Metro
Hyundai

Underground supplies vehicles
Ansaldo
Hyundai

Valves, pneumatic
Davies & Metcalfe
Mecanoexportimport
New York Air Brake
Oerlikon-Bührle

Ventilation equipment
BBC Brown, Boveri
Hyundai
Toshiba

Ventilators
Hyundai
Mecanoexportimport

Wagons & carriages
Breda
BRE-Metro
Daewoo Heavy Industries
FIREMA Consortium
Ganz-Mávag
Hyundai
MAN
Mecanoexportimport
SOCIMI

Water heaters
Energomachexport

Welded fabrications
Breda
BRE-Metro
Daewoo Heavy Industries
Mecanoexportimport
Wickham, D

Welding equipment & accessories
Elektro-Thermit

Wheel and axle testing equipment
BRE-Metro
Hyundai

Wheel-rail-technique
Hyundai

Wheels and axles
Energomachexport
Kolmex
Mecanoexportimport
SOCIMI
Valdunes

Windscreen wipers
Mecanoexportimport

Workshops, complete
Ansaldo
Hyundai
MAN
Mecanoexportimport
Vickers Design & Projects

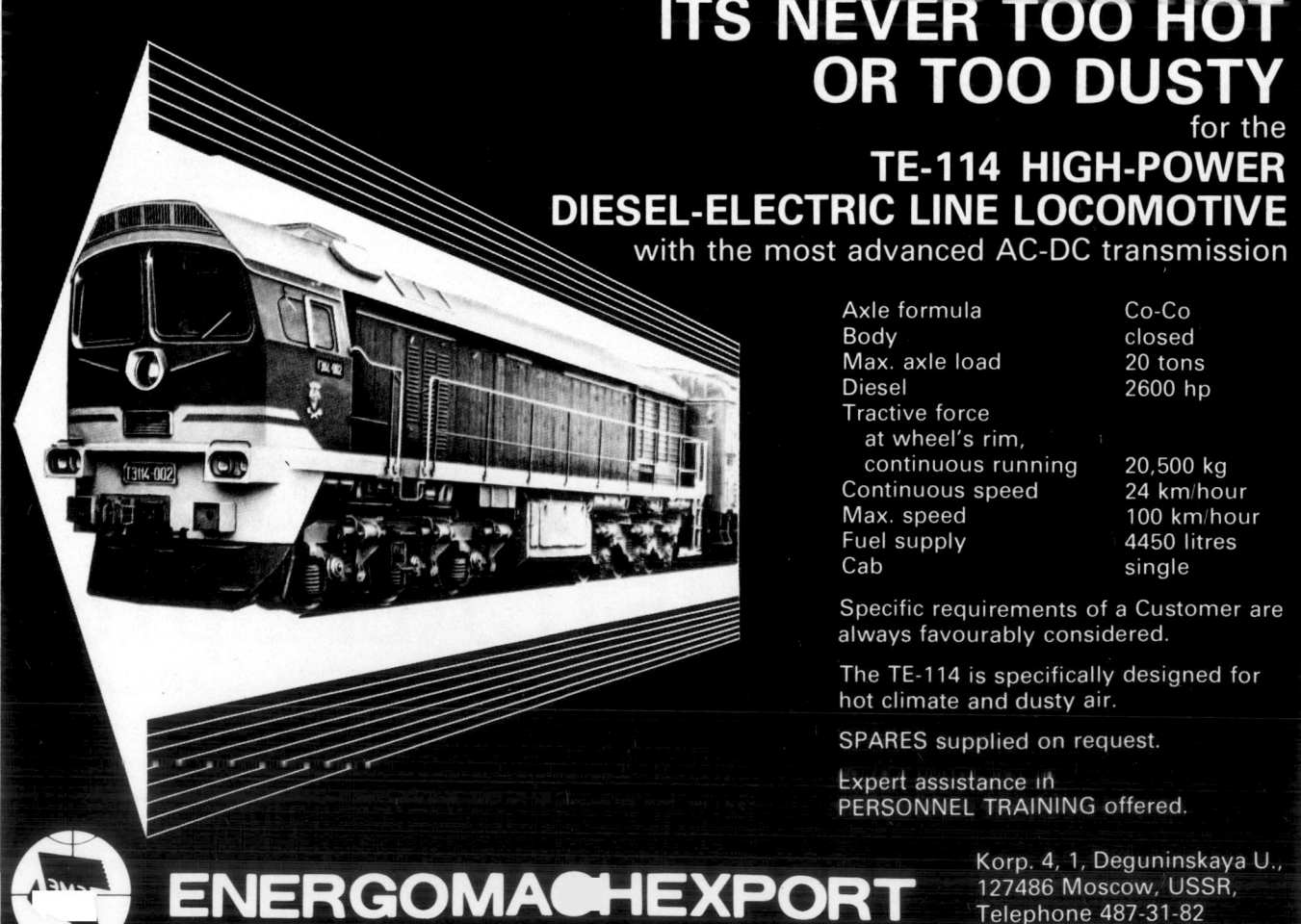

[23]

High performance diesel engines and power systems

Years in the forefront of technology and constant involvement with the specific requirements of our traditional customers have given us the leading edge and the widest experience in the field.

The MTU package

Traction units and peripheral equipment	**Diesel Engines** for rail traction and train electricity **Couplings** resilient or torsionally rigid models **Electronics** electronic monitoring and control systems
Systems engineering	Engineering services for project definition, project handling, field installation and start-up, as well as locomotive re-engining
Product support	Worldwide product support organization with field technicians and mechanics, maintenance and repair facilities, and parts inventories; operator training; workshop planning service

Power ratings

Railroad applications

Diesel engine series

		Shunting
		and Industrial
396	525 - 1180 kW	**Locomotives**

Diesel engine series

396	525 - 1570 kW	**Multi-purpose**
		Locomotives

Diesel engine series

396	1050 - 1570 kW	
652	1800 kW	**Main Line**
956/1163	2460 - 4100 kW	**Locomotives**

Diesel engine series

		Mountain Railroad
		and Narrow-
396	525 - 1180 kW	**Gauge Railroads**

Diesel engine series

396	525 - 1180 kW	
for continuous-duty		
generator sets, 50 Hz or 60 Hz		**Train Electricity**

Motoren- und Turbinen-Union Friedrichshafen GmbH
P. O. Box 2040 · D-7990 Friedrichshafen/W. Germany

◆MONIER
Prestressed concrete sleeper manufacturing systems

The name Monier Limited is synonymous with prestressed concrete sleeper manufacture. More than 25 years of innovative development in Australia has established Monier's manufacturing system as being one of the most efficient and economical in the world today.

Monier Limited is now offering opportunities that will allow its manufacturing system to be used internationally.

Through either a licensee or joint venture agreement, Monier Limited will provide a complete service from the design of the sleeper and sleeper-making machinery to the planning and operation of the factory.

Monier Limited will provide all patented machinery and knowhow to help ensure successful operation.

The Monier manufacturing system is unique. It combines a low capital cost with low labour in production while maintaining a high product quality and high output.

The system is versatile allowing economic production at different rates to meet variable demand.

Monier's system is suitable for all fastening systems and all track gauges.

If you would like further details, please write or telex Monier Limited at its head office in Australia.

◆MONIER
Concrete Sleepers

Head Office:
Monier Limited, 6 Thomas Street,
CHATSWOOD N.S.W. 2067 Australia

International Phone 612 411 9611
Telex MONIER AA 26673

International Locations: Canada ● Indonesia ● Japan ● Malaysia ● New Zealand ● Papua New Guinea ● Philippines ● Thailand ● United States of America.

WICKHAM

engineers' cars

All engineering departments needing personnel transport or service vehicles will find at least one specially designed car or trolley in the Wickham range to suit their requirements.

Rugged, hard working cars that will repay their cost over and over again; from a simple 'pump' trolley, through a wide range of powered trolleys and cars to the specially built types for catenary inspection, ambulance duties and emergency track repair work. You name it; we'll send you details. . . or be ready to modify one of our standard models for you.

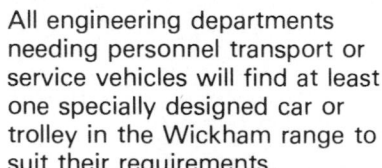

D. Wickham & Company Limited,
Ware, Hertfordshire, England.   Tel: Ware 2491/7.   Cables: Wickham Ware.   Telex: 81340

Our experiences date from the past century – our perspectives reach into the next millenium.

AEG and railways – cooperation by system.

Eversince the construction of our first electrical railway drive in 1889, railway technology has undergone complete changes. Economy was improved immensely, safety increased considerably and, thus, reliability has grown. Main points of all considerations were easy operating of systems and passenger comfort. An end of the development is not yet to be seen.
AEG-TELEFUNKEN plans, builds and supplies electrical plants, systems and components for a future-oriented railway technology. This includes the complex field of railway automation, together with its operation control, yard technology, interlocking and train control technology, as well as passenger service systems, traction power supply and distribution, electrical equipment for locomotives and traction

Magnetic Levitation Railway
– a new rapid transit system.

vehicles of all railway systems, plus passenger coaches. And we are producing automatic car couplings with the same meticulousness and precision as we do electrical components for buses.
The train radio communication system which we developed means applied safety, with information being transmitted like a flash and without interference. Nowadays, we are already working on solutions for tomorrow to reduce travel and transport time even more, to still improve economy and to increase passenger safety and comfort. Our customers allover the world are our partners in the search for such solutions. Only by such a cooperation by system, most effective problem solutions may be generated for main line and rapid transit systems of the future.
Railway technology is just one example of the efficiency and the innovative power of AEG-TELEFUNKEN. We gladly inform you in more detail on the many potentialities and the decisive advantages of a cooperation with AEG-TELEFUNKEN. Please, just write us.

AEG-TELEFUNKEN
Railway Systems

I am interested in receiving further information on railway technology from AEG-TELEFUNKEN.

Name: _____

Company: _____

Department: _____

Address: _____

To AEG-TELEFUNKEN
Attn. Mr. Hübner A 3 V7 P, Hohenzollerndamm 150, D-1000 Berlin 33

A 3.-1708 E

FOR A SPEEDY, SAFE AND ECONOMIC TRANSPORT

MECANOEXPORTIMPORT

offers:

- diesel-hydraulic locomotives, range of power between 450HP and 2400 HP, standard and wide gauge.
- diesel-hydraulic locomotives, range of power between 180 HP and 1100 HP, narrow, standard and wide gauge.
- diesel-electric locomotives, range of power between 1100 HP and 4000 HP
- electric locomotives of 5100 kW, 25 kV, 50 Hz
- locomotive components and equipment
- articulated and double-articulated tramcars, motor waggon and trailer
- interurban electric trains
- technical assistance, equipment and spare parts for refitting and repairing your locomotives fleet.
- faultless service during and after the guarantee period.

For detailed information apply to
MECANOEXPORTIMPORT
Specialized Foreign Trade Company
79522 Bucharest-Romania
10, M.Eminescu St.
P.O.B.: 22-107
Telephone: 12 46 00
Telex: 10269

Our greatest strength is our economy.

Since 1835, Cockerill has been building locomotives that are designed to work hard in the toughest conditions but still be simple to service.

Our engineering concept of high "component modularity" is what makes our new shunting locomotive so special.

Its unique design makes it easy to service as well as economical to run.

Plus the improved suspension means the locomotive tracks better and gives a much more comfortable ride. And an ergonomically controlled dashboard allows easier operator control.

Rugged CMI shunting locomotives are currently hard at work worldwide in railway networks, harbours, mines and in many industries such as steel, glass and chemicals.

Call us, or write to the address below for more information.

You'll find the low running costs and competitive initial price add up to unbeatable value.

Cockerill Mechanical Industries, Sector Locomotives, B-4100 Seraing (Belgium). Tel.: (32.41) 36.60.00 Telex: 41225.

The New CMI Shunting Locomotive.

Specifications

Axles - 2, 3, 4 and 6.
Weight - 24 to 120 tons.
Power - 200 to 2000 HP.
All tracks and gauges available.

Our new dashboard.

COCKERILL
MECHANICAL
INDUSTRIES

Shunting locomotives
Diesel engines
Boilers
Nuclear installations
General Mechanical Equipment
Metallurgical material
Defence

Facts tell in our favour

- ○ Export of 34,000 passenger coaches in three decades

- ○ Experience in all climatic zones

- ○ Most up-to-date technical equipment for energy supply, air-conditioning, running gear

- ○ Large variety of types by application of standardized assemblies

- ○ Highly economical in service and maintenance

Two locomotives for the sight of one.

ECO/83

D. 145 INLOC inverter locomotive for the Italian FS

One locomotive, two services Rail transport faces ever more demanding challenges in terms of technology, functional efficiency, and economy. Fiat Ferroviaria has a concrete answer ready to hand in its INLOC 1000-1500 hp diesel-electric "inverter" locomotive, which can be used for both heavy shunting and goods or passenger lines.
From its starting (tractive effort 22,000 kg) to its maximum speed (100 kph), its capacity is designed for continuous use and overloading is impossible.

High technology hand in hand with top performance and low running costs The INLOC is powered by two 700 hp diesels, which can be used separately as well. These are mass-produced engines from Fiat Iveco's truck range, with all the advantages this means with regard to economy, maintenance, and reliabil-

ity. On the electrical side, too, there are equivalent payoffs thanks to the static "inverter" that makes it possible to use asynchronous three-phase a.c. traction motors of varying frequency and voltage.

There's a lot more than meets the eye in this locomotive A world of research, design, and construction. The Fiat Ferroviaria world. Since 1917, Fiat Ferroviaria has been working for the progress of rail transport, both urban and intercity. From the "Littorina" of yesteryear to the TEE, the "Pendolino", the ALn 668, the jumbo tram, and the Eurofima bogie. Whistle stops, these, not final destinations, because for Fiat Ferroviaria the journey through progress knows no end of the line.

FIAT *FERROVIARIA SAVIGLIANO*

A journey through progress

GEC
CARD TECHNOLOGY DIVISION

Shake Rattle & Roll

No problem with GEC Card Transport systems, our 'one-piece'*
unit has had all the problems shaken out of it already, making it the
ideal on-board transport ticketing systems for companies going
somewhere.

*The single large diameter wheel drive has proved itself in extensive
environmental tests including vibration and shock. Ask for details, we're way out
in front with Intelligent Card Transports.

Ask GEC about card technology systems. We've put profitability into the stripe.

**GEC TRAFFIC AUTOMATION LTD.,
ELSTREE WAY, BOREHAMWOOD, HERTS., WD6 1RX
TEL 01-953 2030 TELEX 22777**

30.000.000 HP
WORLDWIDE

World leader in medium speed diesel,
engines, SEMT-PIELSTICK have maintained
over the years their international reputation
through 27 licencees located in most industrial
countries all over the world.
SEMT-PIELSTICK's experience combined with their
research and development resources have been a major
contributory factor to the company's success as an innovator
in diesel technology.
Trust plays a large part in selecting a particular brand of diesel
engine, whether the application be merchant or naval shipping,
diesel electric power stations or rail traction.
Users of SEMT-PIELSTICK diesel engines trust us.
... And they are right. Because our second to none knowledge
of the diesel engine is right where they want it... At their service.

**ALSTHOM
ATLANTIQUE**

mécanique

groupe diesel

2, quai de Seine
93203 Saint-Denis - France
Téléphone : 820.61.91
Télex : 620333 F. Motla

E 120: The multi-purpose electrical locomotive.

The new E 120 three-phase universal locomotive of the Deutsche Bundesbahn. One of the most advanced and efficient locomotive types world-wide.

The E 120 combines all aspects expected nowadays from a modern locomotive: the speed necessary to operate fast passenger trains, the traction effort demanded for heavy freight train service, the reliability required for continous operation, the costeffectiveness for a maximum of rationalization. In short: the versatility of a genuinely universal locomotive.

The development (electrical part by BBC, Mannheim) and manufacture of prototypes were performed by a consortium of the three top German producers of locomotives, under the prime contractorship of Krauss-Maffei and in close cooperation with the Deutsche Bundesbahn.

The results achieved not only make us proud, but give evidence of the know-how and confidence acquired by Krauss-Maffei by suppliing more than 20.000 locomotives world-wide.

Our know-how is available to you as well and your experts will give you all detailed information you may request. Drop us a line or call us.

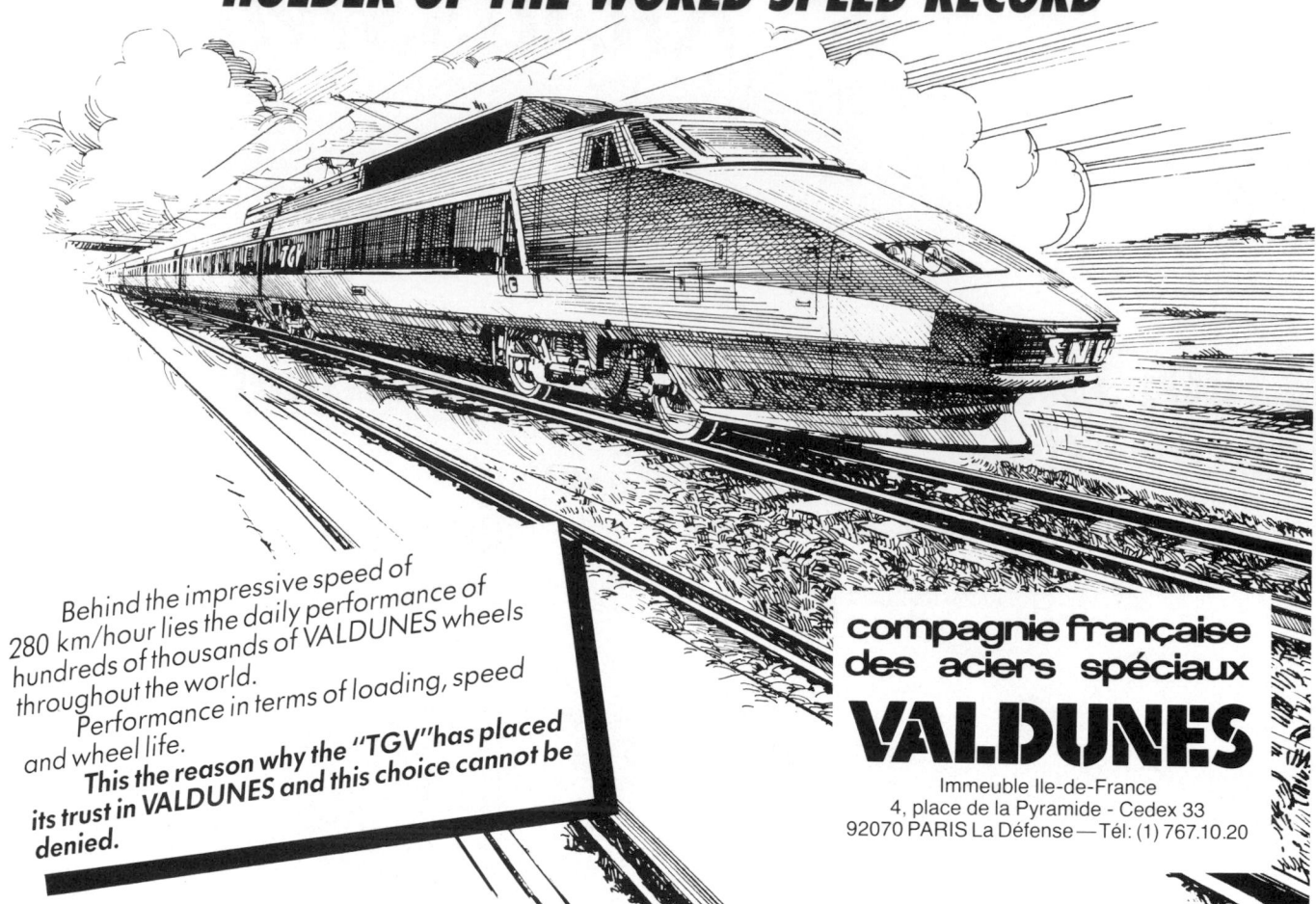

rolling stock for railways and mass transits

second class intercity coach for Italian State Railways

3 kV d.c., 4.400 kW locomotive for
Italian State Railways

750 V motor coach for
Milan Transport Authority

FIREMA Consortium

Corso di Porta Romana, 63 - 20122 Milano Italy - Tel. (02) 5465708-588936 - Telex: 322255 FIREMA I

OUR GOAL IS THE SAME AS YOURS:
to roll out on the open "track" of the market

Why not meet together in a mutually
favourable co-operation?

We have more than 30 years' experience in the
manufacture and supply of complete railway
wheelsets as well as tyres, discs and axles for:
>wagons
>carriages
>locomotives
>special railway vehicles

Manufacturers: Diósgyöri Gépgyár
>H-3544 Miskolc
>HUNGARY

Our possibilities offer possibilities for you too.

Should you have a specific inquiry for our
wheelsets we'll be pleased to give you a
detailed quotation.
Free brochure is available on request.

Exporters: NIKEX
>H-1016
>Budapest
>Mészáros u. 48-54
>HUNGARY

1st Class Traction Power

![Diesel-electric standard locomotive type DE 1002 with three-phase current power transmission](image)

Diesel-electric standard locomotive type DE 1002 with three-phase current power transmission

Krupp MaK manufactures:

- Diesel-electric locomotives with three-phase current power transmission above 500 kW engine output.
- Diesel-hydraulic locomotives above 250 kW engine output.

- Diesel-hydraulic self-propelled railcars.
- Rail-going container reloading systems for horizontal handling of containers and loading areas for varying cargo.

⊛ KRUPP MaK Maschinenbau GmbH

P.O.Box 90 09 · 2300 Kiel 17 · Germany (West)
Phone (-431) 38 11 · Cable mak kiel · Telex 02 99 877 mak d

All reflections on economy lead to Diesel-Hydraulic

As yet, there is no more reliable and economical power transmission for shunting locomotives than the diesel-hydraulic system with the Voith turbo-reversing transmission.

economical shunting

Voith have been manufacturing power drive components for locomotives and railcars for a great many years, earning a worldwide reputation in the process and developing of a highly specialist knowledge of the locomotive industry. And for shunting locomotives there are the special reversing transmissions with purely hydrodynamic reversing.
We are thoroughly familiar with the engineering problems posed by

difficult operational conditions. Our aim is to achieve compatibility between engine, transmission, cardan shafts, axle drive and cooling unit. Voith's comprehensive service embraces all necessary calculation work and assistance in control system design through to advice, training and after-sales service, and is available througout the world.

J.M. Voith GmbH
Div. Power Transmissions Engineering
P.O. Box 1940, D-7920 Heidenheim

VG 8310 e/1

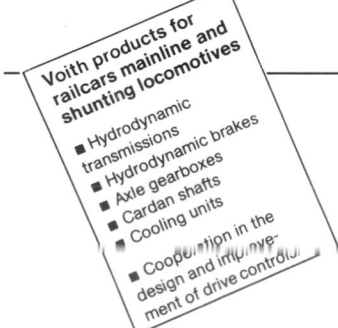

Voith products for railcars mainline and shunting locomotives

■ Hydrodynamic transmissions
■ Hydrodynamic brakes
■ Axle gearboxes
■ Cardan shafts
■ Cooling units
■ Cooperation in the design and influyement of drive controul

VOITH

...economical shunting

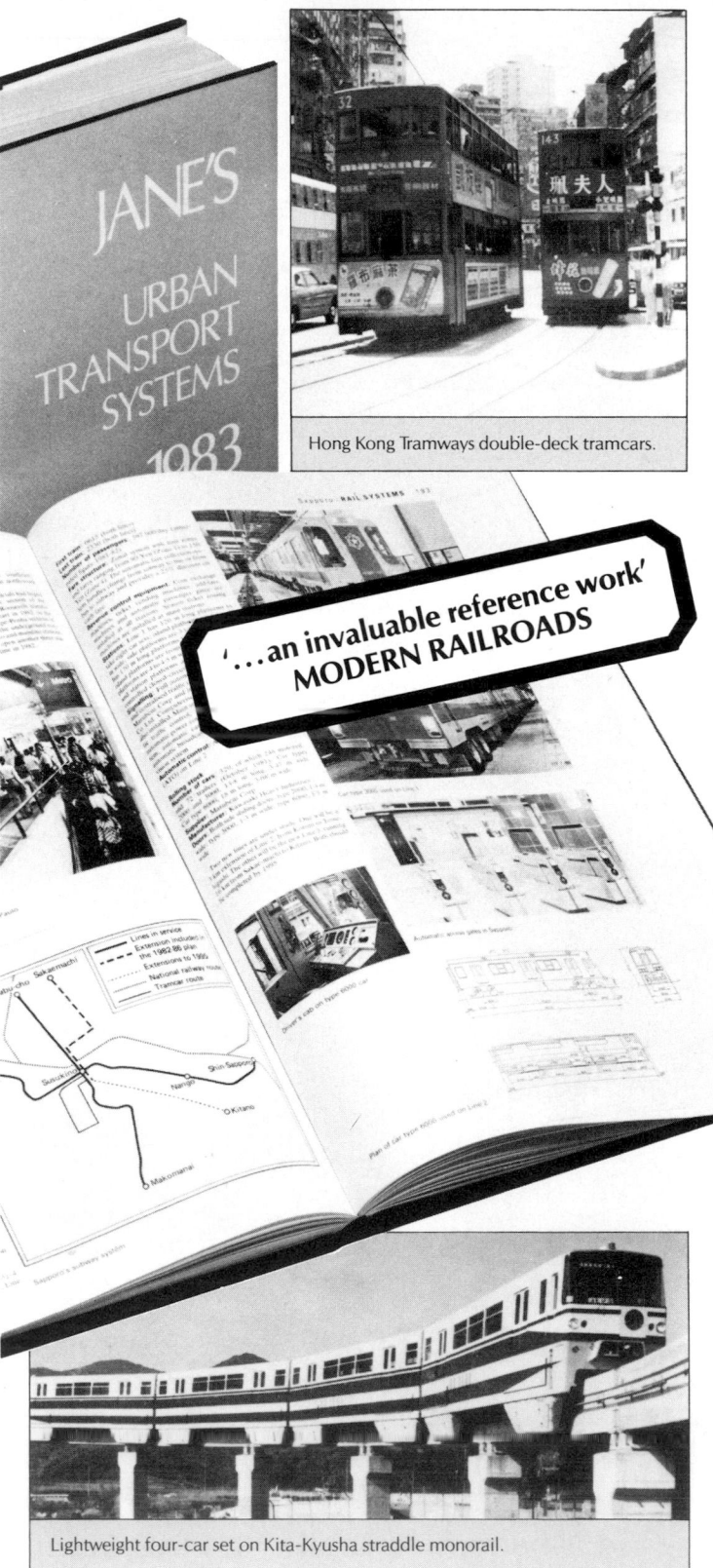

Meeting tough demands

Extreme topographical conditions with steep gradients of up to 70‰ as well as high traffic level and varying platform heights were only some of the exacting specifications to be met for this service.

Our solution: the DT8, a close-coupled two-car train unit with all 8 axles driven, designed for multiple unit working, provided with amply sized doorways and movable steps and – last but not least – modern styling.

A 316.52 e ze

M·A·N

CIMT

CIMT LORRAINE
60 YEARS OF TECHNICAL PROGRESS
AND EXPERIENCE IN THE FIELD OF PASSENGER
TRANSPORT AT YOUR SERVICE.

MASS TRANSIT
AND COMMUTER TRAINS

DOUBLE DECK TRAINS

PASSENGER COACHES

DIESEL RAILCARS

CABLE CARS

GANG CARS

PRELIMINARY STUDIES
OF COMPLETE SYSTEMS

MANAGEMENT
OF INDUSTRIAL
CONSORTIUMS

Paris mass transit

Marseilles mass transit

Ivory coast railcar

Mexico City mass transit

Paris suburban double deck coaches

Trolleybus

LORRAINE

COMPAGNIE INDUSTRIELLE DE
MATÉRIEL DE TRANSPORT

42, AV. RAYMOND-POINCARÉ,
75116 PARIS - TÉL. : 505.14.00
TELEX : CIMTRAM 610119 F.

continuous

**action
tamping machine**

09-CSM

The new
tamping technology
Non-stop-Tamping

Continuous motion
cyclic tamping

Compared to conventional machines **only 20% of the total mass of the machine is accelerated and braked** because only the actual work units – tamping, lifting and lining units – positioned on a separate underframe, are moved in work cycle from sleeper to sleeper. The main frame of the machine, which carries operator's cabin, power supply and drive for the entire machine, moves forward continuously.

This means:

- **30% higher tamping output**
  better utilisation of train intervals
- **a new level of working comfort**
  no acceleration pull
  no braking jolt
  no vibration in the cabin
- **energy savings**
  lower acceleration of mass
- **less strain of drive, brakes and main frame**
  no jolting strain
  reduction of wear

= cost savings and comfort

Plasser & Theurer

Head Office: A - 1010 Vienna, Johannesgasse 3
Great Britain: Plasser Railway Machinery (G.B.) Ltd.
Manor Road, West Ealing, London W 13

Progress is our tradition

TOSHIBA Air-Conditioners

With Capacities Ranging from 2,250 kcal/h (0.7 ton) to 42,000 kcal/h (14 tons)

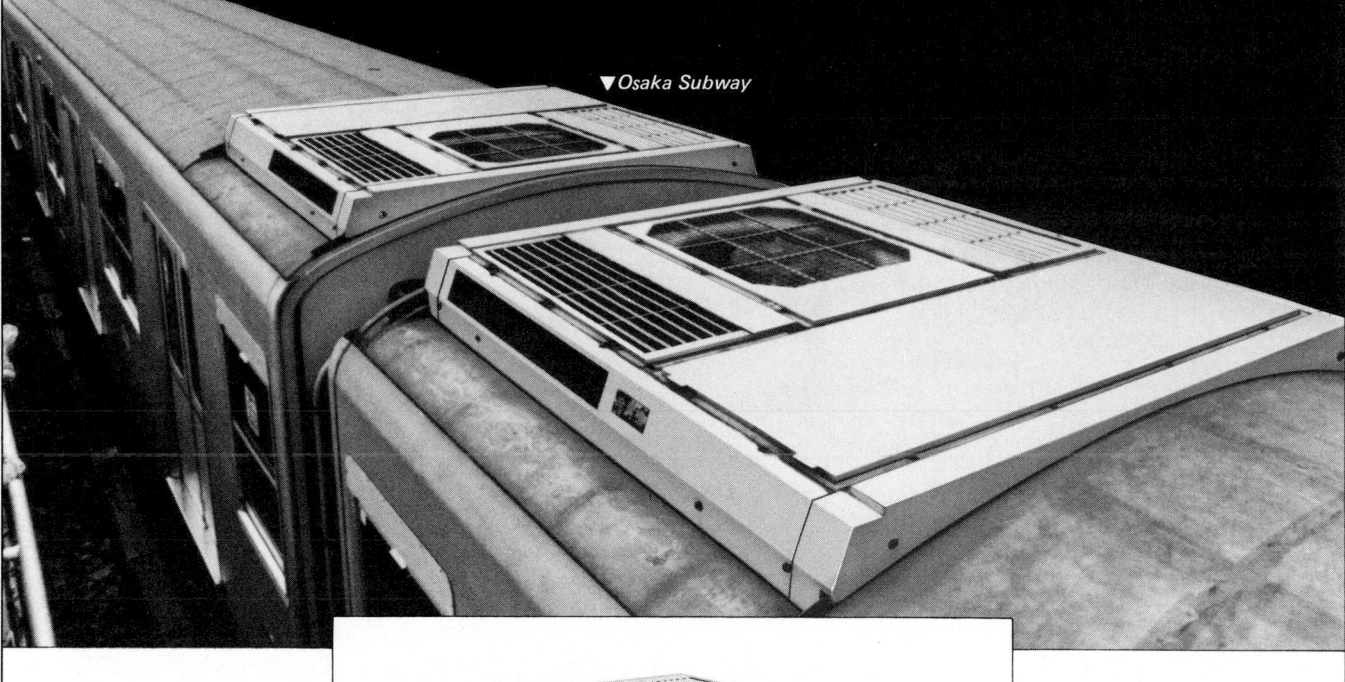

▼Osaka Subway

20,000 kcal/h Unit

TOSHIBA offers air-conditioners in a wide range of cooling and heating capacities to meet the demands of all types of rolling stock for railway and subway transportation. More than 72,000 units are being used throughout the world.

Major advantages that TOSHIBA air-conditioning equipment offers include:
- Hermetic compressors that prevent gas leakage
- Compactness and lightweight
- Minimal maintenance
- Energy-saving

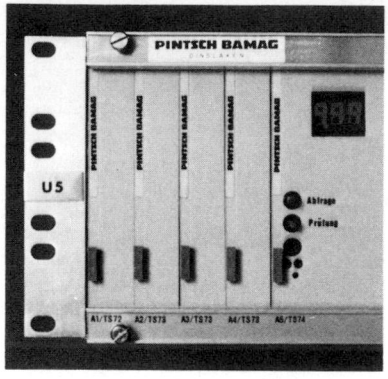

By WARD for B.R. at COLTON

Designed for 200 km/h traffic on this major re-route by B.R., this large installation is just one example of Ward's capability in the manufacture of advanced trackwork. Ward expertise – in demand throughout the world.

A 208 metre double junction to by-pass Selby coalfield

The plan

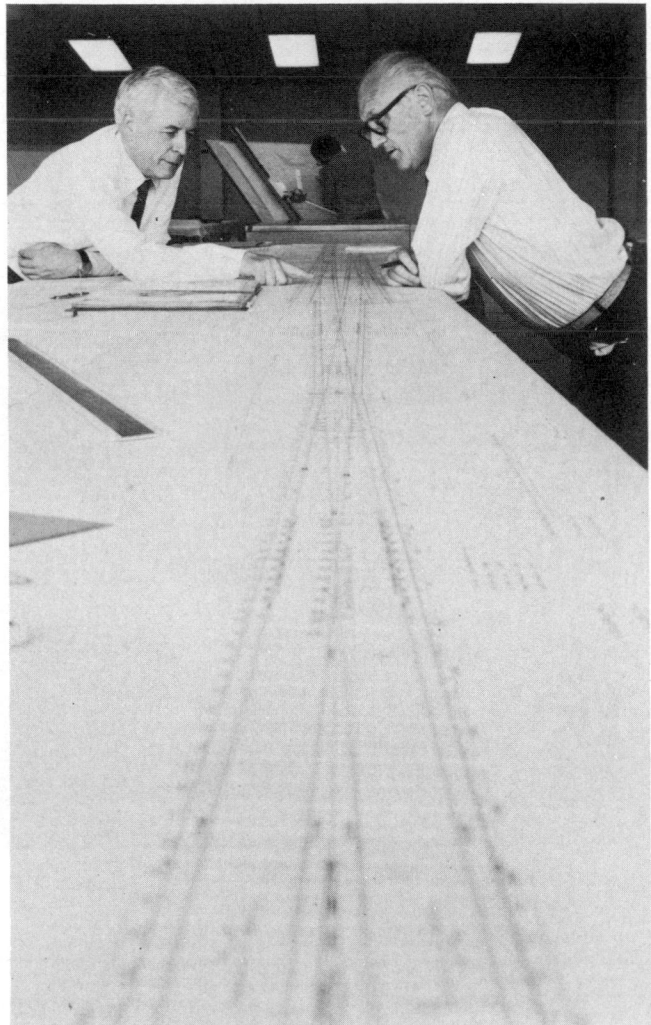

The practicality

by courtesy of British Rail

Thos. W. Ward (Railway Engineers) Ltd

Midland Foundry, Osmaston Street, Sandiacre, NOTTINGHAM NG10 5AN.
Tel: 0602 390125   Telex: 37256 REWARD G

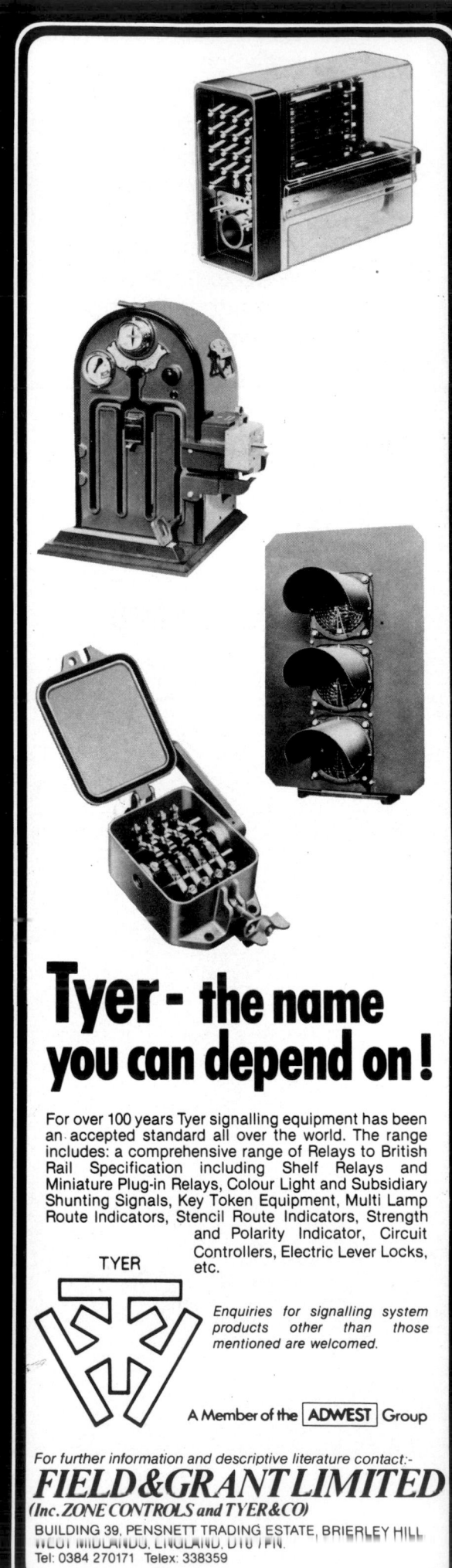
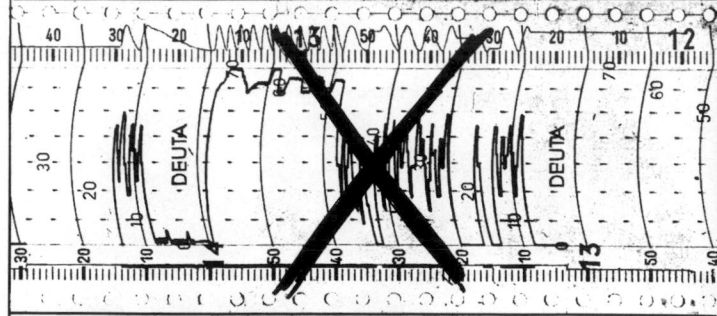

![SOCIMI logo]

Socimi for design testing and production

The Socimi concern is active in design, testing and production of railway, subway and tramway rolling stocks with relative components, buses, trolley buses and relative components for body and chassis assemblies.

Within the Company's organization, the engineering section has first line space and importance; its job is to research, identify and test new more advanced solutions, better to answer the various demands of the vast field of public transport, both on rail and on road.

Planners and style designers, who are leading men in this sector, are supported by specialized technicians and design experts in transport systems, structures and technical drawing etc.

These men are constantly in touch with other important design centres, both in Italy and abroad. Socimi also manufactures under licence of several European and North American companies who are leaders in their respective fields.

Socimi can boast an exceptional technical background in the design and manufacture of railway and road traction components.

It is certain of offering to the market the best rolling stocks and components, to best meet the specific demands of the user bodies (commuter transport, subway transport, tramways, bus and trolley-bus transport etc.).

Socimi is a market oriented Company which knows that a product no longer stands alone, but only as a product/service compound.

The Company is willing to characterize its image as a comprehensive organization which sells, together with its qualified production, all the necessary services.

SOCIMI

Società Costruzioni Industriali Milano s.p.a.
Management and offices
Via San Calimero n. 3
20122 Milan – Italy
Telephone (02) 5465251/5
Telex 310331

'An industry of new growth of jobs and progress carrying your people and their goods to brighter horizons and a better life . . . .
This industry has turned around, it's getting stronger, the payoff is more jobs and opportunities and that's darn good news.'
US President Ronald Reagan speaking in the City Auditorium, Omaha, Nebraska, October 1982

JANE'S
WORLD RAILWAYS

TWENTY-FIFTH EDITION

EDITED BY
GEOFFREY FREEMAN ALLEN

1983-84

ISBN 0 7106-0777-6

JANE'S YEARBOOKS

''Jane's'' is a registered trade mark

Railway Cars: Proven concepts. We extend them to new requirements.

MBB

Partner in international programs

- ☐ High speed trainsets for Intercity Traffic
- ☐ Underground and suburban trains
- ☐ Passenger coaches for all purposes
- ☐ High comfort tourist trains
- ☐ Sleeping-, dining- and couchette cars
- ☐ Electrically and diesel driven trainsets
- ☐ Special railway cars for service and maintenance

Messerschmitt-Bölkow-Blohm GmbH
Helicopter and Transport Division
Plant Donauwörth
Postfach 13 53
D-8850 Donauwörth/Germany
Telex 51 843, Telephone 71208

Contents

Foreword

A depressing year, 1982, though no more so for most railways than for the world's business in general. And for most railways, if not for many of their suppliers hard-hit by investment cutbacks, it could have been worse.

In diminished and much more sharply contested passenger and freight markets railways generally managed at least to defend their shares of earlier and easier years. And there was a significant mark of improved operating economy and efficiency in that the American recession hit rock-bottom at the year's end without any major private enterprise railroad in the dire financial distress that 1982's steep plunges in carloadings would have caused a decade earlier.

On the other hand, some national railways came under intensified pressure either to reduce their calls on public money or, in the Third World, to protract capital improvements because of their countries' urgent need to brake demands for foreign currency and loans. In Europe Italy, the Netherlands and Norway were among countries where governments compelled the railways to order swingeing passenger fare increases to reduce the level of state subsidy. But in Italy at least the government was not showing any inclination to back out of massive financial commitments to the railways' long-overdue re-equipment, though in mid-1983, sadly, RENFE's ambitious ten-year plan was ditched as unrealistic by Spain's new government, which demanded a new four year-based plan. Other projects seriously affected by financial difficulties included Mexico's big electrification and new railway plan, Nigeria's start on a standard-gauge network and Indonesia's Jabotabek urban railway scheme.

Three particularly harassed giants of the world railway scene were the national systems of Japan, the Federal Republic of Germany and Britain. Unconvinced that the drastic retrenchment in Japanese National Railways (JNR) staffing and scale of operation legislated in 1981 will have the full planned effect, or fearing maybe that like earlier economy plans it will be baulked at local political level or by the labour unions, Japan's major political parties, with the pure Socialist exception, have fallen for a new nostrum. Now the size of JNR is branded the root of its ills, on the simplistic ground that any enterprise employing more than 60 000 is constitutionally incapable of unitary management.

Government and a majority in the Japanese Diet apparently believes that the stopper can be clapped on JNR's barely imaginable accumulated deficit of 12 250 000 million yen — for which, of course, past political vote-seeking in pegging fares at absurdly low levels, fostering uneconomic rural line-building and side-stepping effective capital reconstruction is partly culpable — by carving JNR up into seven separate systems. Hiving off two of the three outer island networks may have arguable point. The putative break-up of the Shinkansen network implied in the creation of four separate railways in Honshu and Kyushu, on the other hand, can only be counter-productive.

The ultimate aim is seemingly to sell the separate parts of JNR to private enterprise, though how they can possibly be transmuted into saleable properties without deep financial and physical surgery is baffling. True, Japan has a number of private enterprise railway models with a positive operating ratio, but almost all are commuter or short-haul. It is nowhere near as simple to extract a surplus from an all-purpose national railway as from a compact conurbation passenger network where, to cite the Seibu Railway as an example, track capacity is exploited to extreme limit by running a 1½-minute evening peak train service out of Tokyo with an *average* load factor of 234 per cent. (Starting from a 100 per cent base, which represents full occupation of a train-set's specified seated and standing capacity, Seibu measures a 150 per cent load factor as leaving just enough room to cope with magazine reading, 200 per cent as restricting reading matter manoeuvre to a pocket book, 250 per cent as preventing any limb movement.)

Similar commuter passivity in the West would ease the financial anxieties of some major railways and rapid transit authorities a trifle. But it would barely ripple the surface of the problems besetting, for instance, the German Federal Railway (DB).

Hard hit by the recession in heavy industry, where its traffics were 11 per cent down in 1982, the DB has been driven to budget for a deficit climbing higher yet to almost DM 5000 million in 1983 (though it hopes to do better in practice). This loss is of course struck after most of the various forms of Federal support and compensations have been accounted as revenue, and they aggregated almost DM 9240 million in 1982. At the end of 1982 the DB bent under an accumulated deficit of DM 36 000 million.

Up to mid-1983 neither a change of government in Bonn nor a new DB directorate had to outward appearances contributed much to a solution of the DB's central problems except a new intensity of debate. Withdrawals of a thousand or two trains a week and of passenger services on a handful of branches only scratch the surface of critical difficulties, such as the greatly over-sized DB infrastructure in the country at large, and persistence with a rural train operating and pricing framework that meets only 28 per cent of its costs.

Just a little of the dynamism which, across the Atlantic, has all but halved Conrail's labour force in six years, got rid of over 15 per cent of its route-mileage in 1982 and dumped Conrail's commuter train — and commuter train-crew — responsibilities on to state authorities, would serve Federal Germany and the DB well. Conrail's turnaround from a US$243 million loss in 1976 to a net income of $130 million in 1982 is surely an achievement to rank with any latter-day technological triumph, such as France's LGV. Continental European sensitivities to railway change are much more tender. Out in the Federal Republic's Länder any slimming-down of the rural DB, or fairer apportionment of its running costs, will doubtless be resisted as staunchly as it has been in the past: while at the same time, probably, the irrational environmental objections to the DB's *Neubaustrecke* routeing plans will go on protracting the DB's desperately-needed trunk network reshaping.

To put its recent performance in a more acceptable public light, the DB has been promoting a reframed version of its accounts. This presents separate profit-and-loss balances for the operation of solely commercial passenger and freight services, for the operation of socially-supported train services, and for infrastructure. From it the commercial sector emerges with a healthy surplus on direct costs; the social services (support included in revenue) with a modest shortfall; and the infrastructure, inevitably, with a heavy deficit of cost over Federal subventions and what appears a very modest contribution from DB revenue.

As so far published in very summary form, this revised DB balance sheet looks crude and begs many questions. But the basic idea is logical.

The DB's point is, of course, that national rail infrastructure should be accounted as much of a public, permanent asset as roads or waterways. Sensibly, the DB does not revive the concept of a straight Federal infrastructure takeover, debated and rejected in Bonn a year or two ago; so it has more recently in Sweden, where the preference is for an as yet vaguely-defined assumption of political responsibility for major infrastructure development. State charge of infrastructure could so easily lead to the embedding of all railway management in a Ministerial bureaucracy, with the dire results so long experienced in Italy.

Whether any or all of a national, multi-purpose railway's infrastructure cost is visibly covered out of public funds is not necessarily an issue. What is decades overdue is parity of rail treatment with other modes in measuring the effect of infrastructure costs on transport performance and economy, however the infrastructure bills may be met.

It makes no difference to a road operator's balance sheet if one of his lorries is the sole daily user of a road, the rest part of a milling motorway herd. So long as all are under load and on a paying transit, there will be little, if any, variation in the vehicles' operating ratios. Why should a railway's performance be judged finally on the productivity of its fixed as well as its mobile assets? And particularly so in a global recession, when its competitors are immune to the financial consequences of under-utilisation of their infrastructure?

RUSTON RAIL TRACTION POWER

Low maintenance costs and low fuel consumption plus a proved compact design from a large manufacturing group with a long history of locomotive engineering, make Ruston diesel power the logical choice for modern rail traction demands – including the outstanding Type 58 Freight Locomotive entering service with British Rail.

Type 58 Freight Locomotive. Reproduced by courtesy of British Rail Engineering Ltd.

After more than 150 years of railways, with their enduring role in inter-urban and urban transport accepted by all seriously-regarded opinion — except, conceivably, in Mrs Thatcher's Britain — and with capitalist, let alone mixed-economy nations committed to freedom of transport choice, it is high time railways were assessed essentially on their efficiency in running and filling trains in response to market or publicly sponsored demand. The cost of providing, maintaining or expanding the trains' thoroughfares should be accounted and considered as a separate business. Amongst other things, that would make superfluous the perennial duelling with dubious statistics to prove that this or that type of transport is getting away with a substandard share of its true road costs.

This is not to argue that all existing rail infrastructure is sacrosanct (though to destroy traders' confidence by publishing academic exercises in network truncation and leaving them in Damoclean suspense over a railway, as was done in Britain under Beeching and has just been repeated in the shoddy Serpell Report, is deplorable). Where new technology or method makes assets dispensable, they should go. Budgetary disciplines there must be, perhaps externally imposed. Admittedly, cogent cases may exist for closing routes, but the decision to shut down must be clearly political, likewise the assignment of financial responsibility if retention on social grounds is ordered.

So long as rival transport is taxed without direct reference to this infrastructure cost—or, in the case of some north-west European inland water transport, gets virtually a free ride—there are few benchmarks for rational intermodal comparison. Is it beyond modern ingenuity to devise a basic taxation formula for all forms of overland transport, public and private, based on unit weight, capacity, maximum speed and any other elements influencing infrastructure costs which would secure parity of treatment and economic appraisal? And which could be applied to individual trains as a fair measure of the infrastructure expense each incurs?

What is inequitable is that a railway's economic performance should be judged by its bottom line after, for example, its whole rail activity has had to share the costs of extra track and signalling capacity to cope with metropolitan peak-hour commuter surges. Or that in a severe recession a railway should be driven to trim its infrastructure just for a better short-term balance between fixed costs and income, regardless of whether the extra capacity may be badly needed when the upturn comes.

The divorce of infrastructure management and accounting from the running and marketing of trains makes more sense still if it is allied to the kind of profit-centred management structure which British Rail is developing. The division of BR's rail business into five product sectors, each accountable for the assets it exclusively or primarily uses and for the size of contribution to total costs generated with them, has some teething problems yet to resolve. (And there is conceivably a case for a sixth business sector—passenger stations, combining commercial development and operational management.) But one major benefit is already patent: infrastructure departments are getting more precise, realistic specifications of what is needed to accommodate and efficiently operate traffic currently and prospectively on offer.

Another gain of separate, detailed infrastructure accounting in respect of each business sector should be that public authorities contributing to the total costs of socially-supported passenger services would see clearly whether or not they were getting value for money. Misgivings that some of their cash was being sucked into an all-system upkeep fund should be given a conclusive quietus.

August 1983

G Freeman Allen

[60]

MANUFACTURERS

LOCOMOTIVES AND ROLLING STOCK

ACEC
Ateliers de Constructions Electriques de Charleroi SA

BP 4, 6000 Charleroi 1, Belgium

Telephone: 3271 44 21 11
Telegrams: ACEC, Charleroi
Telex: 51.227

President: P Uytdenhoef
Managing Director: J L Dalcq
Director, Transport Division: P Dayez
Marketing Director, export: R Schneidesh
  Belgium: A Leriche

Products: Electrical equipment for locomotives and railcars (1.5 and 3 kV dc; 25 kV ac): starting apparatus either rheostatic, with individual contactor or cam control, or by thyristor choppers, with rheostatic or regenerative braking, or both simultaneously; nose- or fully-suspended motors; various electronic devices, including wheel-slip detectors and programmed speed controllers; electrical control gear for auxiliary circuits; (25 or 50 kV, 50 or 60 Hz ac, single-phase) silicon diode rectifiers, with voltage adjustment by transformer tapping switch; silicon diode and thyristor rectifiers, with voltage adjustment by thyristor; rheostatic or regenerative braking; electrical equipments for multi-voltage rolling stock (3 kV dc and 25 kV ac 50 Hz; 3 kV dc, 1.5 kV dc and 25 kV ac 50 Hz; 3 kV dc, 1.5 kV dc, 25 kV ac 50 Hz and 15 kV ac 16⅔ Hz) as above. For diesel-electric locomotives: multiple-circuit dc generators, or ac generators with diode rectifier; dc motors; simultaneous control of fuel injection, generator output and battery charging by transistorised circuitry. For single or articulated light rail vehicles: controller with 99 or 135 positions; parallel or series-parallel starting with electronic control of starting current; rheostatic braking with thyristor chopper control for mixed regenerative and rheostatic braking. For metro cars with one or two motors per bogie: thyristor chopper control for mixed regenerative and rheostatic braking.

ACEC has supplied the electrical equipment for the latest Belgian National Railways (SNCB) Type 27 4180 kW electric locomotives, which have been designed for mixed traffic use on 600-tonne passenger trains and 800-tonne freight trains. With the latter the Type 27 can sustain 80 km/h up the SNCB's maximum main-line gradient (1.8 per cent). The four Type LE921S traction motors are controlled by choppers with Vernier thyristors and rheostatic braking is fitted. Similar equipment is in process of design and manufacture for SNCB Type 21 3150 kW 3 kV dc mixed traffic locomotives and for the dual-voltage types (3 kV dc/1.5 kV dc and 3 kV dc/25 kV ac) to be derived from the Type 21.

Constitution: Founded 1904.

ACEC chopper equipment for LRV

Chopper equipment for SNCB Class 80 emu

SNCB Class 27 3 kV dc Bo-Bo

Chopper equipment for SNCB Class 27

SNCB Class 80 3 kV dc emu

Latest SNCB traction equipped by ACEC

Class	Wheel arrangement	Line voltage	Rated output (kW) continuous/one-hour	Max speed km/h	Weight tonnes	No in service	Year first built	Builders Mechanical parts	Builders Electrical equipment
Type 27	Bo-Bo	3 kV dc	4180/4380	160	85	30	1982	BN	ACEC
Type 21	Bo-Bo	3 kV dc	3150/3320	160	85	—	1983	BN	ACEC

Electric multiple-units equipped by ACEC

Class	Cars per unit	Line voltage	Motor cars per unit	Motored axles per motor car	Rated output (kW) per motor	Max speed km/h	Weight tonnes per set	Total seating capacity	Length per set mm	No in service	Rate of acceleration m/s²	Year first built	Builders Mechanical parts	Builders Electrical equipment
AM.80	2	3 kV dc	1	4	310	160	126	171	25 075	40	0.75	1981	BN	ACEC

ACF
ACF Industries, Incorporated
Amcar Division
Shippers Car Line Division

Head office: 750 Third Avenue, New York, New York 10017, USA

Amcar Division: Main & Clark Streets, St Charles, Missouri 63301
Telephone: (314) 724 7850

Shippers Car Line Division: 620 N Second Street, St Charles, Missouri 63301
Telephone: (314) 723 9600

President: Ivan A Burns
Amcar General Manager: James C O'Hara
Shipper Car Line General Manager: Bruce A Gustafsen

Products: Amcar designs and builds freight cars for railroads, industrial shippers, and Shippers Car Line's lease fleet. Amcar also produces railway car parts, piggyback trailer hitches and mixing bowls. Recent products include the ACF Pressureaide covered hopper car, which has been developed specially for the transport of flour and similar commodities. A pressure differential car with a capacity of 141.6 m³ (5000 ft³), it operates with internal pressures of up to 14.5 psi, which allows both faster unloading of the product, and also unloading at a greater distance from receiving bins than with previous models.

Shippers Car Line leases and sells special-purpose railroad freight and tank cars to industrial corporations and provides maintenance for cars in the service lease fleet at seven plants.

ACF Pressureaide covered hopper wagon

Aebi
Robert Aebi AG

Head office: Uraniastrasse 31-33, 8023 Zurich, Switzerland

Telephone: (01) 211 09 70
Telegrams: Aebi, Zurich
Telex: 813 795

Works: Regensdorf

Telephone: 840 25 50
Telex: 55557

Products: Diesel-hydraulic and diesel-mechanical locomotives.

Aeckerle
Hugo Aeckerle

Bredenbekstrasse 12, 2000 Hamburg 66 (Ohlstedt), Federal Republic of Germany

Telephone: 6 05 01 69
Telegrams: Unilok, Hamburg
Telex: 02-12359

Products: Unilok road/rail shunting locomotives.

AEG-Telefunken
Geschäftsbereich Bahntechnik

Head office: Hohenzollerndamm 150, 1000 West Berlin 33, Federal Republic of Germany

Telephone: (030) 828-1
Telegrams: Elektron Bahnen, Berlin
Telex: 185 498

Products: Electrical equipment for ac/dc/undulatory-current and three-phase locomotives, railcars, multiple-units including diesel-electric vehicles for main-line and branch-line services, mining and industrial locomotives, transit stock for suburban and underground railways, trams and trolleybuses.

Recent traction vehicle work has included participation with the 50 c/s Group in the equipment of Costa Rica State Railways' 12 two-frequency four-axle locomotives with diode rectifiers and tapchanger. The company has acquired the former German Federal Railway (DB) dual-voltage locomotive No 182001-8 and re-equipped it as test-bed for three-phase current traction technology. The

Dual-frequency Bo-Bos with diode rectifiers and tapchanger for Costa Rica State Railways

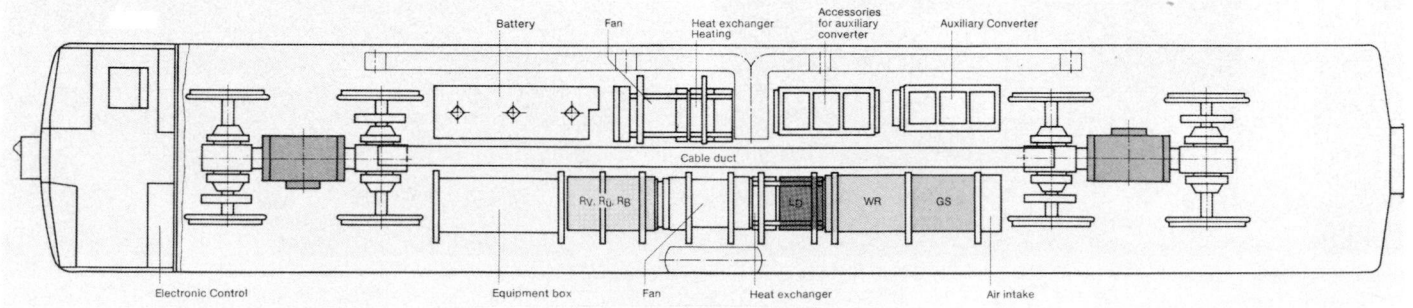

Underfloor layout of BVG Type F79.3 emu K-car

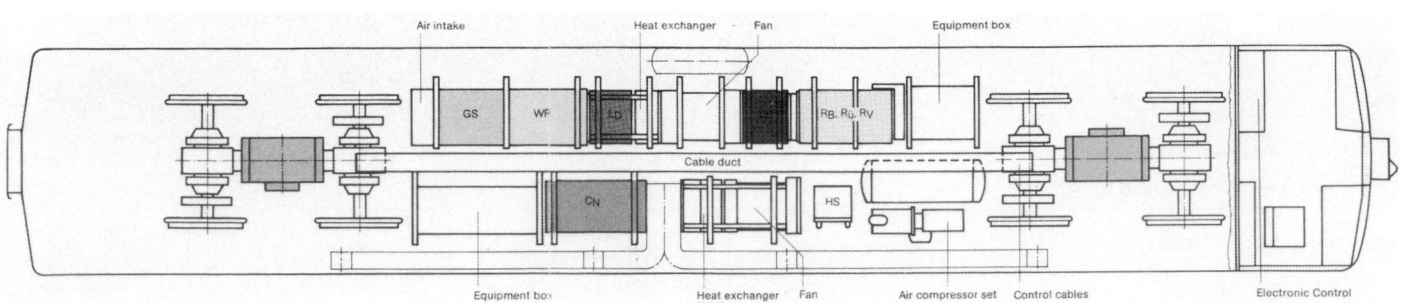

Underfloor layout of BVG Type F79.3 emu S-car

company is developing a system suitable for export to railways operating with a 50-60 Hz ac supply.

Current activities in the field of suburban traffic systems are equipment for light rapid transit vehicles for Melbourne, Oslo, Frankfurt, Kassel and Stuttgart, metros at Buenos Aires, Calcutta, Madrid, Oslo and Vienna as well as the complete automation system for the Amsterdam Metro. In the 100 cars for the Melbourne & Metropolitan Tramways Board (MMTB), being built by Commonwealth Engineering (Vic) Pty Ltd, AEG-Telefunken is employing equipment including chopper-controlled Type ABS 3322 motors of a type supplied to the Hanover public transport authority, USTRA.

AEG-Telefunken is also furnishing three-phase traction equipment for 39 Type F79.3 two-car metro emus being built by Waggon-Union for the West Berlin authority, Berliner Verkehrs-Betriebe (BVG). All components are underfloor-mounted and accessible from both sides of the car, and from a longitudinal central space. Each car has its own self-sufficient traction unit for two twin motors. In the S-car there are in addition the main circuit-breaker HS and the common line filter (LN and CN), as well as the air-compressor set, while the K-car accommodates the auxiliary power supply. A prefabricated central cable duct running the length of the car contains all the control cables, which are connected to the appropriate control gear by means of multi-pole connectors. The electronic control equipment is mounted in the rear wall of the driver's cab. The compactness of the three-phase induction motor allows use of individual axle-drives from a longitudinally-located twin motor, despite the increased power rating of 89 kW per axle compared to the 70 kW of conventional BVG trains. Moreover, the bogie wheelbase has been shortened from 1900 to 1800 mm.

To simplify the maintenance and trouble-shooting of the electronic equipment, the complete control system has been designed for application of diagnostic devices. By using special testing connectors a computer-aided functional test can be made. The electronic control equipment is housed in a dustproof cubicle, with a separately-cooled heat-exchanger at the rear wall ensuring permanently clean operating conditions.

In mixed emu stock operation the speed/torque characteristics of the three-phase emu will automatically adapt to the performance characteristics of a conventional dc cam controller-operated set, though maximum speed will be limited to 70 km/h. Regenerative and rheostatic braking is fitted, with compressed air to cover loss of line voltage in the low-speed range, electrical brake failures, emergencies and to hold units at rest.

BVG Type F79.3 three-phase metro emus
Gauge: 1435 mm
Length of unit over couplers: 32.1 m

Type BAS 5638/6D three-phase twin motor used in BVG Type F79.3 emu

Distance between bogie pivots: 9.5 m
Bogie wheelbase: 1.8 m
Body width: 2.65 m
Height above rail: 3.425 m
New wheel diameter: 850 mm
Gear ratio: 6.625:1
Two-car unit tare weight: 42.8 tonnes
Seating/crush capacity: 72/320
Power output at rim, 30 km/h and over: 700 kW
Tractive effort at rim, 30 km/h and over: 84 kN
Braking power at rim, 60 km/h and over: 1400 kN
  up to 60 km/h: 184 kN
Max speed: 80 km/h
Max starting acceleration, empty: 1.8 m/s^2
Max braking deceleration, empty: 1.8 m/s^2
Supply: 750 V dc
Motors per two-car set: 8 arranged as longitudinal twin-motors
Continuous motor output: 89 kW
Max operational motor speed: 3600 rpm

Constitution: Manufacture of traction equipment started in 1889. AEG-Telefunken has been concerned with the development of generation, distribution, and consumption of electric power for all purposes.

Two-car underground emu, Type F79.3, with three-phase drive for BVG, West Berlin

Tram with chopper control for MMTB, Melbourne, Australia

AFNE
Astilleros y Fabricas Navales del Estado

Corrientes 672, 1043 Buenos Aires, Argentina

Telephone: 45 7031/39
Telegrams: AFNE
Telex: 17924

Products: Diesel-hydraulic locomotives, rolling stock and bogies, including Ride Control bogies for freight wagons manufactured under licence from Amsted; locotractors manufactured under licence from Cockerill.

Alcan
Alcan Canada Products Ltd

Box 269, Toronto-Dominion Centre, Toronto, Ontario M5K 1K1, Canada

Telephone: (416) 366 7211
Telegrams: Alcan, Toronto
Telex: 06-22641

Products: More than 30 years of experience designing lightweight aluminium rolling stock for both freight and passenger service. Supplies aluminium sheet, plate, and extrusions for rail transport applications of all kinds.

All-aluminium LRC locomotive and cars in service with VIA Rail Canada are designed jointly by Alcan, Bombardier-MLW, and Dofasco. A total of 2424 aluminium covered hopper cars for grain are in service in Canada for the Canadian Wheat Board: tare, 20.2 tonnes; payload, 79.6 tonnes; cubic capacity, 125 m^3. Construction: 7004, 6351 extrusions; 5083 plate, steel stub sills and bolsters.

Aluminium grain hopper by Alcan

LRC power car and trailer

Alna Koki
Alna Koki Company Ltd

Head office and works: No 4-5, 1-chome, Hgashinaniwa-cho, Amagasaki-City, Hyogo Pref, Japan

Telephone: (06) 401 7281
Telex: 5242782

Chairman: Kenichi Hibi
President: Setsuro Tanabe

Managing Director: Shinichi Ishizuka
Directors: Yoshiharu Araki, Kiyoyuki Yamagami

Products: Electric railcars; passenger coaches; LRVs; general purpose freight wagons; low floor wagons; tank wagons; dump wagons. Major sales in 1980-82 included 110 electric railcars for Hankyu Corporation, 100 electric railcars for Tobu Railways, and 24 LRVs, 63 coaches and special-purpose railcars and 159 remodelled railcars for other Japanese private railways.

Constitution: Established in 1947 by Hankyu Electric Railways Ltd under the name of Naniwa Koki Company Ltd; became Alna Koki Co Ltd in 1970. Capacity is just over 20 passenger cars and 50 freight wagons a month.

Series 7300 aluminium-bodied emu for Hankyu Corporation

Series 700 light rail vehicle for Hiroshima Electric Railway Co

Alna Koki electric railcars or multiple-units

Class	No of cars per unit	Line voltage	Motor cars per unit	Motored axles per motor car	Rated output (kW) per motor	Service speed km/h	Weight tonnes per car (M-motor T-trailer)	Total seating capacity	Length per car mm (M-motor T-trailer)	No of units in service	Rate of acceleration m/s^2	Year first built	Builders Mechanical parts	Builders Electrical equipment
Hankyu Corp 7300 series (aluminium)	8	1.5 kV	4	4	150	110	M 32.9 T 21.8	436	M 18 350 T 18 300	2	0.78	1982	Alna Koki Co Ltd	Toyo Denki Seizo KK
Hankyu Corp 7300 series (steel)	8	1.5 kV	4	4	150	110	M 36.4 T 25.3	436	M 18 350 T 18 300	3	0.78	1981	Alna Koki Co Ltd	Toyo Denki Seizo KK
Hiroshima 700 series (LRV)	1	600 V	1	2	52	40	19	37	13 500	4		1982	Alna Koki Co Ltd	Toyo Denki Seizo KK
Nagasaki 1200 series (LRV)	1	600 V	1	2	46	40	15.5	28	11 700	5		1982	Alna Koki Co Ltd	Mitsubishi Electric Corporation

Alsthom-Atlantique

Member of Traction Export

Head office: 38 avenue Kléber, 75784 Paris, France

Telephone: 502 14 13
Telegrams: Alsthom, Paris
Telex: 27672

Rail Transport Materials Division: Tour Neptune, 72086 Paris La Défense (Cedex 20)

Works: Belfort
　　Telephone: (84) 22 82 40
　　Tarbes
　　Telephone: (62) 93 02 97
　　Aytré-La Rochelle
　　Telephone: (46) 53 30 42

Chairman: Pierre Loygue
General Director: Roger Chalvon Demersay
Export Sales Director: Paul De Lieven
Railway Division Manager: Franck Vaingnedroye
Counsellor to Management for Railway Matters: Jacques Bedel De Buzareingues

Products: Electric, diesel-electric, industrial and mining locomotives; electric, diesel and gas-turbine railcars; electric and diesel multiple-units; rail transit cars and rolling stock; passenger coaches; automatic couplers; electrical equipment and transmissions; railway electrification; signalling systems and apparatus.
　Alsthom-Atlantique, with Francorail, heads a consortium of French manufacturers which is establishing a new company, TGV Inc, to promote French TGV/LGV high-speed technology in the USA.

Altai

Altai Wagon Works

Head office: Altai, USSR
Exports: Energomachexport, Deguninskaya Str 1, Korp 4, 127486 Moscow

Telephone: 147 21 77
Telex: 7565

Products: Freight wagons.

Alusuisse

Swiss Aluminium Ltd

Head office: Buckhauserstrasse 11, 8048 Zurich, Switzerland

Telephone: (01) 497 44 22
Telex: 822 333
Telegrams: Alusuisse

Main works: Walz- und Presswerk, 3965 Chippis

Technical Director: Jurg Zehnder
Marketing Manager: H A Christen

Principal subsidiaries
Aluminium-Walzwerke Singen GmbH
7700 Singen/Hohentwiel, Federal Republic of Germany

Consolidated Aluminum Corporation
PO Box 14448, St Louis, Missouri 63141, USA
Alusuisse France SA
Route de Tonnerre, 89600 St-Florentin, France

Products: Design of aluminium freight cars, underground and suburban coaches, long-distance passenger coaches and components; supply of aluminium semis.
　In 1982 Alusuisse and Portec signed a licensing agreement whereby Portec gained exclusive western hemisphere rights to manufacture and market the Algola aluminium coal gondola car, of which a prototype has run over 233 000 km in revenue service on the Santa Fe and Burlington Northern Railroads, USA. The prototype has 10 per cent more payload capacity than a standard US steel gondola.

Algola gondola car for coal transport, designed to Alusuisse large extrusion technique; tare weight 18.44 tonnes, payload 101 tonnes

Norwegian State Railways (NSB) Type B7 coach designed to Alusuisse large extrusion technique, built by Strømmens Vaerksted A/S

Amherst

Amherst Industries, Inc

Port Amherst, Charleston, West Virginia 25306, USA

Telephone: (304) 925 1171

Products: Freight wagons; interior linings for tank and hopper wagons.

Ammendorf

VEB Waggonbau Ammendorf

Ammendorf, German Democratic Republic

Telephone: 4650
Telex: 04216

Head office: Merseburger Strasse 89, 4011 Halle
Exports: Schienenfahrzeuge Export-Import Volkseigener Aussenhandelsbetrieb der DDR, Otztaler Strasse 5, 1100 East Berlin

Products: Long-distance passenger and restaurant cars. Output for Soviet Railways (SZD) since 1976 has totalled over 7300 vehicles, including 1250 restaurant cars and 1290 air-conditioned vehicles. In 1982 the works completed the 20 000th long-distance car supplied to the USSR by VEB Kombinat Schienenfahrzeugbau.
　Among recent products is the Type SK/k restaurant car for SZD, fully air-conditioned and equipped with a hot-water heating system that can be operated either electrically or with solid fuel. The all-welded, box-frame steel body is mounted on Type KWS-ZNII bogies with primary and secondary helical springing that interacts with friction and hydraulic shock absorbers. The 48-seat saloon

SZD restaurant car Type SK/k

is finished internally in plastics. The kitchen range is designed for firing either with solid fuels or oil, a 14-day supply of which can be carried in the car, but in a further development an all-electric kitchen is planned.

The latest development in couchette cars for SZD is the Type K/rki, which incorporates nine four-berth compartments, a radio compartment, a service compartment with kitchen and two toilets. It is fitted for either solid fuel or electric heating and air-conditioned, with power supplied from a 28 kW generator that is driven by cardan shaft from an axle. In the K/rki as in earlier models particular attention has been paid to fire precautions; four fire-resistant dividing walls have been built into the body and all wiring is protected by armoured steel piping. Prepared, like preceding production for SZD, to operate in ambient temperatures ranging from −50 to +50°C, the 56-tonne K/rki is designed for operation at up to 160 km/h.

Constitution: Originating as a carriage works in 1823, the plant took up tramcar, bus and narrow-gauge passenger car construction in 1945, but from the early 1950s it developed as a specialised coachbuilder for SZD, to which it has now delivered 20 000 vehicles. A member of Vereinigter Schienenfahrzeugbau der DDR eV.

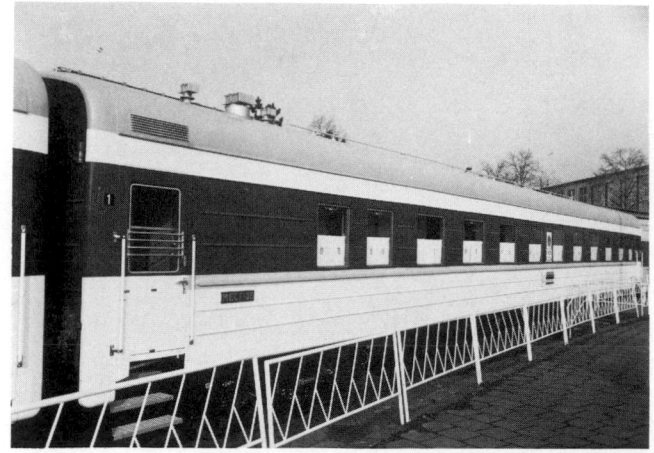

SZD couchette car Type K/rki

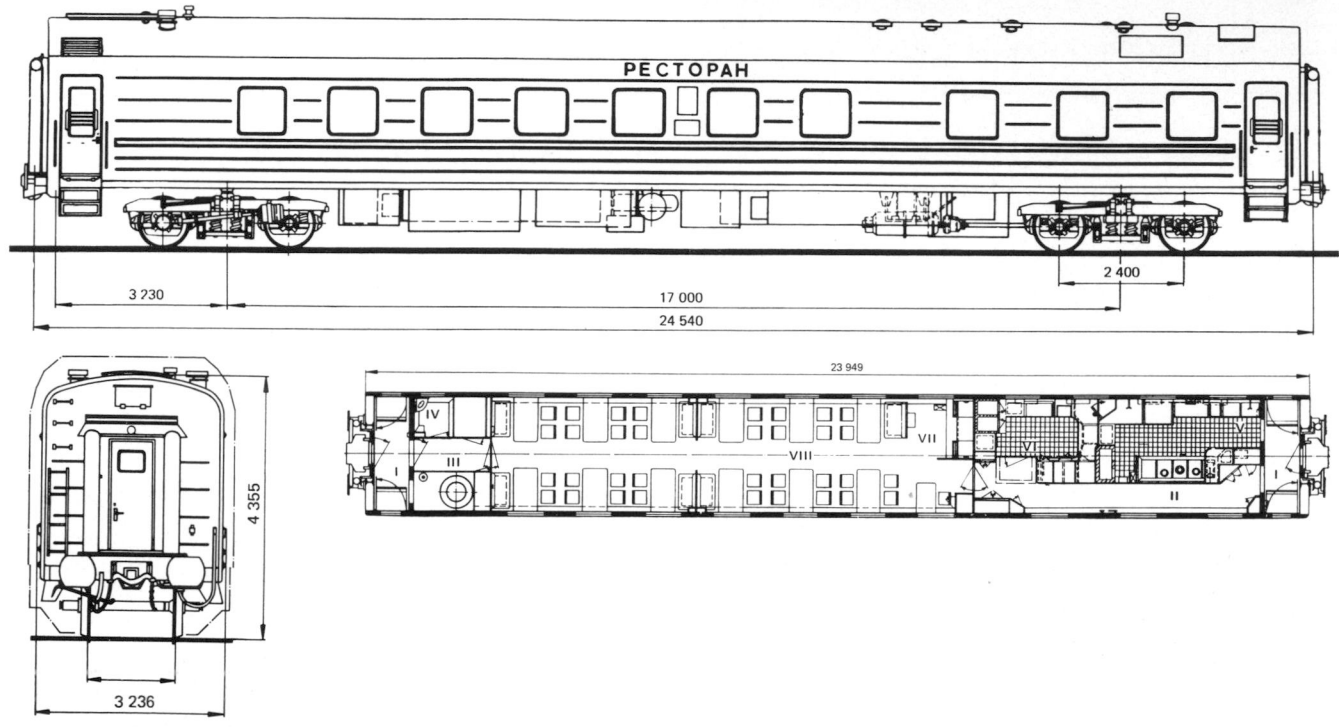

Layout of SZD restaurant car Type SK/k

Anbel
The Anbel Group

2323 South Voss Road, Houston, Texas 77057, USA

Telephone: (713) 977 9737
Telex: 910-881-1168

President: Kenneth Roy Nichols

Vice-President: Alan R Cripe
Administration Manager: B L Dowdy
Field Services: H Rendon
Chief Sales Director: G A Brichford
Export Sales: R A Huber

Products: Diesel-hydraulic locomotives (300 to 1500 hp; remanufacture only of diesel-electric locos to 3000 hp); freight wagons.

ANF-Industrie
Société ANF-Industrie

Tour Aurore, Place des Reflets, 92080 Paris-Défense (Cedex 5), France

Telephone: 778 62 62
Telex: 610 817

Works: 59154 Blanc-Misseron, 59770 Marly-les-Valenciennes

Sales: GIE Francorail (passenger vehicles)
GIE Norfer (freight wagons)

Chairman: Jean Pelabon
General Manager: Pierre Vachel

Products: Turbotrains, diesel railcar units, railcars, light alloy trailers for railcars; passenger coaches; double-deck electric power cars; metro and mass transit vehicles; all kinds of standard and special-purpose freight wagons; all types of power and trailer bogies.

Recent products include three 10-car gas turbine-powered trains for Egyptian Railways, to operate at up to 160 km/h over the 208 km Cairo-Alexandria route. Each 26.2-metre end power car has a Turmo XIIC 1200 kW traction turbine driving a Voith hydraulic transmission and two Astazou IV turbines to power the auxiliaries (only three of each train-set's four are run simultaneously, the fourth

Type X2100 440-kW, 56-seat diesel railcar for French Railways (SNCF), mixed first- and second-class accommodation, weight 44 tonnes, max speed 140 km/h, 50 ordered

being held in reserve). The power car bogies are equipped with orthodox clasp and electromagnetic rail brakes, the trailer bogies with disc brakes; as on French Railways' Type RTG turbine-powered sets, from which the design is derived, the power bogies are Type Y223, the trailer bogies Type Y224.

The power car cab ends, which include a concealed screw coupling and buffers so that a set can be hauled, have been designed after fresh aerodynamic research. They incorporate roof level deflectors to keep exhaust clear of trailing cars. A Siemens cab signalling system, activated by track-mounted beacons, employs a micro-processor which obtains an automatic brake application if prescribed maximum speed is exceeded by 3 km/h and emergency braking if the excess is more than 10 km/h.

Each set comprises two power cars including 36 second-class seats, three each of 56-seat first-class and 80-seat second-class trailers and two grill-bar cars each including 60 second-class seats. All seats are reversible and each row has

its own window. The grill-bar cars are equipped with refrigeration cabinets from which pre-prepared tray meals are served at seats, which are fitted with chair-back folding tables. The whole unit is air-conditioned, including the driving cabs, and special care has been taken to protect the ventilation system and the car interiors from the ingress of sand. Each trailer is 25.91 metres long. Total tare weight of a 10-car set is 457 tonnes.

Double-deck electric power cars are being manufactured by ANF-Industrie together with CIMT, TCO and Jeumont-Schneider for Type Z2N emus for French Railways' Paris suburban network. Each emu is composed of two motor cars and two or three trailers and up to three emus can be operated in multiple. The power car is manufactured in 1.5 kV dc and dual-current (1.5 kV dc and 25 kV ac) versions, with a maximum speed of 140 km/h.

The double-deck design achieves a passenger capacity of 344 in a power car and 1700 in a four-vehicle emu.

Driving motor car for French Railways Type Z2N bi-level emus

Liquefied gas wagon for Iraqi Republican Railways Organisation

Turbotrain for Egyptian Railways

ANF-Industrie diesel railcars or multiple-units and turbotrains

Class	Cars per unit	Motor cars per unit	Motored axles per motor car	Trans-mission	Rated power (kW) per motor	Max speed km/h	Weight tonnes per car (M-motor T-trailer)	Total seating capacity	Length per car m (M-motor T-trailer)	No in service	Year first built	Builders Mechanical parts	Builders Engine & type	Builders Trans-mission
SNCF X 4300	2	1	2	Hydro-kinetic	330	120	M & T 60	100/150	21	425	1962	ANF	Saurer	Voith
SNCF X 4700	2	1	2	Hydro-kinetic	440	140	M & T 60	100/150	21	425	1967	ANF	Saurer	Voith
SNCF X 4900	3	2	2	Hydro-kinetic	330 × 2	140	M & T 106	154	M 20.3 T 20.2	13	1975	ANF	Saurer	Voith
SNCF ETG (Turbo)	4	2	2	Hydro-kinetic	Turmo III: 860 Diesel: 330	160	M & T 163	188	87.2	14	1970	ANF	Turbomeca; Saurer	Voith
SNCF RTG (Turbo)	5	2	2	Hydro-kinetic	Turmo XII: 1200 Turmo III: 850	200	M & T 225	280	M & T 129	39	1973	ANF	Turbomeca	Voith
Turbotrain (Iran)	5	2	2	Hydro-kinetic	Turmo III: 850	160	M & T 225	280	M & T 129	4	1973/1974	ANF	Turbomeca	Voith
Turbotrain (USA)	5	2	2	Hydro-kinetic	Turmo III: 850	160	M & T 281	276	M & T 129	7 (+6 Type SNCF)	1973/1974	ANF	Turbomeca	Voith
Turbotrain (Egypt)	10	2	2	Hydro-kinetic	Turmo XII: 1200	160	M & T 465	600	M & T 260	(1983) 3 units	1982	ANF	Turbomeca	Voith

ANF-Industrie electric railcars or multiple-units

Class	Cars per unit	Line voltage	Motor cars per unit	Motored axles per motor car	Rated output (kW) per motor	Max speed km/h	Weight tonnes per car (M-motor T-trailer)	Total seating capacity	Length per car mm (M-motor T-trailer)	No in service	Rate of acceleration m/s²	Year first built	Builders Mechanical parts	Builders Electrical equipment
SNCF Z2N	4 or 5	1.5 kV or 25 kV	2	4	350	140	M 66-70 T 42	166/220	M 25 100 T 24 280	T 40	0.9	1982	ANF + CIMT; TCO (M)	TCO; Jeumont-Schneider

Ansaldo
Ansaldo Trasporti SpA

Head office and main works: Via Nuova delle Brecce 260, 80147 Naples, Italy

Telephone: (081) 7810 111
Telex: 710131

Offices: Via Bergognone 34, 20144 Milan
Telephone: 02 42441
Telex: 332192, 314337
Via N Lorenzi 8, 16152 Genoa
Telephone: 010 41051
Telex: 270098

Chairman: Gio Batta Clavarino
Managing Director: David Panzeri
Commercial Director: Vincenzo Magro
Technical Director: Carlo Rizzi

Products: Electric propulsion equipments, either rheostatic or electric, for railway, urban and suburban vehicles with ac and dc motors; electronic converters and controls; auxiliary apparatus; components for power and signal electronics; power supply plants for electrified transport with central control of electrification networks; automation and signalling for railway, underground and surface transport systems; planning, designing and management methodologies for public transport; sale, components and auxiliary apparatus for power supply and automation plants; installation, start-up and servicing.

Recent orders have included the electrical equipments for Italian State Railways (FS) locomotives of the following types: 71 Class E633 electric, the first fully chopper-controlled FS type, a 4200 kW B-B-B with three T850 motors; 89 Class E656 Bo-Bo-Bo; and 95 Class DE445 diesel-electric. Chopper-controlled traction units together with driving trailers have been supplied to Ferrovie Nord Milano. The company is also the main contractor for the FS ac electrification in Sardinia (see entry under Electrification equipment).

Constitution: Ansaldo dates from 1853 and is now a holding company controlling 11 factories (15 000 employees) grouped in three joint-stock companies according to their product lines. Ansaldo Trasporti groups four traction equipment manufacturers: Asgen of Genoa, Italtrafo of Naples, CGE and Breda of Milan.

Driving cab of FS Class E633 B-B-B electric locomotive

FS Class E633 B-B-B electric locomotive

Arad
Arad Car and Passenger Coach Bogies
Member of the Wagon Manufacture Enterprises Group

Avenue Aurel Vlaicu 41-43, 2900 Arad, Romania

Telephone: 966 37020/30520
Telegrams: Vagoane Arad
Telex: 76256

Products: Sleeping and dining cars; first, second or third class coaches; saloon coaches; train-heating cars; brake and luggage vans; power generating cars; mail vans; observation and conference saloons; lounge coaches; four- and multi-axled freight cars, covered high-board open, flat with or without side and front walls and stanchions, tipping of 40 or 25 metres³, gondola, grain transport, pellet, etc; four- and six-axle dumpers; flat cars on four, six, 10, 12 or 20 axles for heavy transport; ore transport cars; sliding-roof or side-wall cars, etc, for any gauge from 900 to 1676 mm.

Constitution: MecanoExportImport supplier.

Arbel
Arbel Industrie

194 boulevard Faidherbe, 59506 Douai, France

Telephone: (27) 88 33 11
Telegrams: Indarbel, Douai
Telex: 130 036

President and General Manager: Conrad Bernstein
Managing Director, Wagons Dept: Jacky Laurent

Licensing agreements: Italy: Omeca (Reggio Calabria)
                                        Ferrosud (Matera)
                               Spain: CAF (Beasain)
                                        Ateinsa (Madrid)

Tipping wagon with air-operated body

Type Fads hopper

Products: Covered and open freight wagons, tank wagons, wagons for bulk transport of cement and powdered chemicals, mineral wagons, container wagons and bogies.

Recent major orders have included new types of wagons to meet market demands, notably:

500 Type LDS two-axle wagons for the transport of vehicles for French Railways (SNCF); 13.6 metres long with a tare weight of 14.3 tonnes, they can carry a load of 21.5 tonnes at a maximum speed of 120 km /h;

500 Type Kils two-axle wagons with mechanically-operated sheeting for French Railways (SNCF);

160 four-bogie tank wagons for transport of superphosphoric acid for Techmashimport (USSR); capacity is 63 m³, overall length 16 metres, and gross laden weight 176 tonnes. The tank is fabricated in Uranus Type B6 stainless steel and is heat-insulated.

Type Kils wagon with mechanically-operated sheet for SNCF

Superphosphoric acid tank wagon for Techmashimport, USSR

ASEA AB

Transport Division
721 83 Västeras, Sweden

Telephone: 46 21 10 00 00
Telex: 40720

Chairman: Curt Nicolin
President: Percy Barnovik
Vice President, Marketing: Arne Bennborn
General Manager, Transport Division: Åke Nilsson
Traction Sales Manager: Lars Olof Nilsson

Products: Electric ac and dc locomotives; commuter and intercity trains; subway cars; trams; electrical equipment for railway electrification and all types of rail vehicles; mining and industrial locomotives and wagons.

During 1982 Swedish State Railways (SJ) ordered a further 40 thyristor locomotives of Class Rc5 valued at approximately £30 million. Deliveries will continue up to the autumn of 1985. ASEA already had an order from SJ for 20 locomotives of this type and the first unit was commissioned in July 1982. The fresh order will take the SJ fleet of thyristor-controlled Rc locomotives well beyond 300. The Rc5 is a further development of the Rc4 series and with several important improvements, including more powerful thyristors and a microcomputer-based indication system with memory and display to monitor equipment and advise the driver in plain text about the state of the locomotive as well as instructions on dealing with faults. The hundred most recent fault indications are stored in the memory, thus giving detailed information to the depot when the locomotive comes in for maintenance and repairs. The driver also has a better working environment with an air-conditioned and ergonomically

Artist's impression of Type GF6C Co-Co for British Columbia Railway

Convertor for one motor of a Type Rc5

Newly-developed traction motor for Type Rc5

designed cab, with a completely new console. Other improvements include: new type of traction motor with fully laminated stator; fewer and simpler components, thus providing some space in the machinery compartment and facilitating maintenance; and a new disc braking system, based partly on electro-pneumatic control of the main brake-line pressure. The locomotive has also been prepared for future installation of electrodynamic braking.

Norwegian State Railways (NSB) placed an order for seven more Class El 16 electric locomotives, valued at approximately £6.5 million for delivery beginning at the end of 1983. The locomotives have a continuous rating of 4400 kW and are equipped with electrical braking rated 4 × 600 kW and static frequency convertors for supply of all auxiliary power equipment. In the winter of 1981-82 an El 16 was successfully tested on the Salzburg-Innsbruck line of the Austrian Federal Railways (ÖBB).

The co-operation with General Motors, initiated by collaboration with the GM Electromotive Division in manufacturing the 47 Class AEM-7 high-speed locomotives for Amtrak, has been consolidated by two further joint venture contracts for thyristor-controlled Co-Co locomotives. One is for 30 locomotives ordered by South African Transport Services; they will have a rating of 3780 kW, fed from a 25 kV 50 Hz system and are intended for heavy coal haulage.

The second is for seven locomotives for the British Columbia Railway Company, Canada, for use in the North-Eastern Coal Project, one of Canada's largest industrial developments; delivery was to commence at the end of 1983. They were to be Class GF6C, a full-width Co-Co producing 6000 hp diesel equivalent (4400 kW) operating from a 50 kV 60 Hz ac supply. Each locomotive was to be 20.7 metres long and weigh 178 tonnes. They were being manufactured at the Diesel Division of Canadian General Motors, with electric traction equipment, including transformers, thyristor convertors and controls, supplied by ASEA. The locomotives will haul trains of 98 118-tonne hopper cars over a new electrified branch line from the Quintette and Bullmoose Mines to the BC Rail main line at Anzac, which is programmed to transport 7.6 million tonnes of coal annually until the mid-1990s from the mines to Prince Rupert for export to Japan.

A contract for the supply of 30 660-volt light rail vehicles was obtained from the city of Gothenburg with an option for an additional 50 units. Gothenburg plans to modernise its network and it is estimated that a total of about 200 vehicles will be required by the end of the century. In collaboration with AB Hägglund & Söner, an ASEA Group company, the ASEA Transport Division has developed a completely new type of vehicle of six-axle articulated design to accommodate 60 seated and up to 90 standing passengers. It weighs 26.5 tonnes and is powered by four 75 kW traction motors fed from a dc chopper unit incorporating a two-phase main chopper and an overvoltage/braking chopper. The propulsion system is designed to provide acceleration at a maximum of 1.3 m/s² up to a speed of 30 km/h with top speed of 80 km/h. A combined electrical and mechanical braking system provides maximum utilisation of electrodynamic braking almost to a standstill. Emergency braking is by disc and electromagnetic track brakes. The action of the braking chopper returns an average of 400 kW to the supply network during retardation from 80 to 40 km/h. A microcomputer-based control system is used for operation, control and fault indication.

Constitution: The company was founded in 1883 and built its first dc locomotive in 1891. Its first complete railway electrification project was for a 25 Hz single-phase emu system and was carried out in 1907.

Cab of Type Rc5 Bo-Bo

Radio-controlled Atuloc 503 of 48 tonnes weight and 10 tonnes max tractive effort, built by ASEA SA of Persan, France, delivered to Redland Aggregates Ltd, England

ASEA electric locomotives

Class	Wheel arrangement	Line voltage	Rated output (kW) IEC 349	Max speed km/h	Weight tonnes	No in service	Year first built	Builders Mechanical parts	Builders Electrical equipment
Rc 2	Bo-Bo	15 kV/16⅔ Hz	3600	135	77	100	1969	ASEA	ASEA
Rc 3	Bo-Bo	15 kV/16⅔ Hz	3600	135	77	10	1970	ASEA	ASEA
Rc 4	Bo-Bo	15 kV/16⅔ Hz	3600	135	78	130	1975	ASEA	ASEA
Rc 5	Bo-Bo	15 kV/16⅔ Hz	3600	135	78	1	1982	ASEA	ASEA
Rm	Bo-Bo	15 kV/16⅔ Hz	3600	100	92	6	1977	ASEA	ASEA
1043	Bo-Bo	15 kV/16⅔ Hz	3600	135	78	4	1971		ASEA
1043	Bo-Bo	15 kV/16⅔ Hz	4000	135	82	6	1973		ASEA
El 16	Bo-Bo	15 kV/16⅔ Hz	4440	140	80	10	1977	ASEA	ASEA
GM6C	Co-Co	11 kV/25 Hz 12.5-25 kV/60 Hz	4200	74	165	1	1975	GM-EMD	ASEA/GM
GM10B	Bo-Bo-Bo	11 kV/25 Hz 12.5-25 kV/60 Hz	6210	60	180	1	1976	GM-EMD	ASEA
AEM7	Bo-Bo	11 kV/25 Hz 12.5-25 kV/60 Hz	4320	200	91	47	1979	GM-EMD	ASEA
40-700	Bo-Bo	25 kV/50 Hz	3600	100	80	8	1982	ASEA	ASEA

ASEA electric railcars or multiple-units

Class	Cars per unit	Line voltage	Motor cars per unit	Motored axles per motor car	Rated output (kW) per motor continuous	Max speed km/h	Weight tonnes per set	Total seating capacity	Length per set mm	No in service	Rate of acceleration m/s²	Year first built	Builders Mechanical parts	Builders Electrical equipment
SJ X10	2	15 kV 16⅔ Hz	1	4	285	140	101	184	49 868	8	0.9 (with full load)	1982	ASEA	ASEA
FC-MC	4	1.65 kV (dc)	2	4	200	120	161.2	240	81 200	2	0.85	1979	Scandia-Randers	ASEA
Queensland Rlys emu	3	25 kV/50 Hz	2	4	135	100	119.4	248	119 400	35	0.775 (with 490 pass)	1979	Walkers Ltd	ASEA

Norwegian State Railways Type El 16 on 1981-82 winter test by Austrian Federal Railways at Badgastein, on Tauern transalpine route

One of 40 Type 700 thyristor Bo-Bos for Iranian State Railways

Swedish State Railways Type Rc5 Bo-Bo

First of 34 Type X10 emus delivered to Swedish State Railways in 1983

Astarsa
Astilleros Argentinos Rio de la Plata SA

Head office: Tucumàn 1438, 1050 Buenos Aires, Argentina

Telephone: 40 7014
Telegrams: Astarsa, Baires
Telex: 21692

Works: Calle Solis Y Rio Lujan, 1648 Tigre, Prov Buenos Aires

Telephone: 749 1071 78

Associated company: General Motors Corporation

Products: Diesel-electric locomotives.

Licences: MTE and Alsthom (France)

ATEINSA
Aplicaciones Tecnicas Industriales SA

Head office: Zurbano 70, Madrid 10, Spain

Telephone: 419 95 50
Telegrams: Ateinsa, Madrid
Telex: 22055

Works: Factoria de Villaverde, Carretera Villaverde, Vallecas 18, Madrid 21

President: Manuel Costales Gòmez-Olea

Products: Locomotives, electric and diesel-electric; diesel railcars; rolling stock: passenger carriages; goods wagons, mineral wagons, ballast wagons, special-purpose freight cars for steel works and other industries.

Export Sales: Inirail, C/Rosario Pino 14-16, Pta 15, Madrid 20

Constitution: ATEINSA was set up in 1973 to take over the railway rolling stock production of Astilleros Españoles, SA. Owned by Instituto Nacional de Industria (INI).

August, 23
"23 August" Works
Member of MecanoExportImport

B-dul Muncii 256, Bucharest, Romania

Telephone: 28 30 10; 28 20 10
Telex: 10344

Products: Diesel-hydraulic locomotives of 150-2600 hp and diesel-electric locomotives of 1000-1500 hp for shunting, secondary and main-line duties, under licence from Sulzer, Alco, MTU, MAN, Voith, Clark, Brown Boveri, Gelenkwellen, Oerlikon, Knorr-Bremse and others.

Constitution: The "23 August" Works started production of 150-1500 hp diesel-hydraulic locomotives for shunting and secondary line duties in 1964. A MecanoExportImport supplier.

Babcock & Wilcox Española
Sociedad Española de Construcciones Babcock & Wilcox

Alameda de Recalde, 27 Bilbao 9, Spain

Telephone: 4415700
Telegrams: Babcock, Bilbao
Telex: 32776

Chairman and Managing Director: Angel Simon
Chief Sales Director: Julio Larrea
Export Sales Director: D Luis Moreno

Branch office: Lagasca 88, Madrid 1

Telephone: 4018300
Telex: 27657

Export Sales: Inirail, C/Rosario Pino 14-16, Pta 15, Madrid 20

Products: Passenger and freight cars, electric train units, main-line diesel-electric and hydraulic units, shunting locomotives, main-line locomotives, railway rolling stock for steel industries, railway slewing cranes, truck axle for automatic shift, reduction units and traction gears, metro train-sets.
For Spanish Railways the company has recently manufactured passenger coaches, narrow-gauge electric train units, diesel-electric locomotives for steel industries, torpedo ladle wagons, reduction units and traction gears. Exports have featured diesel-electric locomotives for Colombia, Guatemala and numerous African railways.

Constitution: Owned by Instituto Nacional de Industria (INI).

Badoni
Antonio Badoni SpA

Corso Matteotti 7, 22053 Lecco, Italy

Telephone: 341 364306
Telegrams: Badoni, Lecco
Telex: 380086

Chairman: Gualberto Lesi

Managing Director and Sales Director: Giuseppe R Kramer Badoni

Products: Diesel-hydraulic shunting locomotives; radio-controlled shunters; hydrostatic transmission; railway wagons.
The company supplies radio-controlled shunting locomotives whenever high temperature or hazardous conditions advise against control from the driver's cab. The portable battery-fed control equipment is fitted with a dead-man control that stops the shunting locomotive should the driver be suddenly incapacitated. It is also possible to lock the shunting locomotive controls by pushing an emergency button on both sides of the driver's cab.

Baguley-Drewry
Baguley-Drewry Ltd

Uxbridge Street, Burton-on-Trent, Staffordshire DE14 3JT, England

Telephone: 0283 66751
Telegrams: Baguley, Burton-on-Trent

Chairman: W R Souster

Products: Diesel-mechanical, diesel-hydraulic, diesel-electric, industrial and mining locomotives (battery and trolley); diesel-mechanical and diesel-hydraulic railcars.

Barclay
Andrew Barclay, Sons & Co Ltd

Caledonia Works, Kilmarnock, Ayrshire KA1 2QD, Scotland

Telephone: 0563 23573/4/5/6
Telegrams: Barclayson, Kilmarnock
Telex: 778497

Chairman: P J Alcock
Managing Director: S E H Kewney

Products: Diesel-hydraulic, diesel-electric locomotives (30 to 1000 hp); steam, fireless and crane locomotives; boilers and locomotive components; general engineering and fabrications; iron castings, SG iron castings and non-ferrous castings.

280 hp 0-6-0 flameproof diesel-hydraulic locomotive built for BP Chemical Works at Grangemouth, England

Barlows
Barlows Heavy Engineering Ltd
Rolling Stock Division

PO Box 183, Benoni 1500, Transvaal, South Africa

Telephone: (011) 54 7511
Telegrams: Swivel, Benoni
Telex: 80559

Chairman: K C Comins

Managing Director: A L Snell
Sales Manager (Rolling Stock Division): G M Kew

Products: Freight wagons; end-of-car and sliding sill hydraulic cushioning; underframes for locomotives and passenger coaches.

Constitution: Barlows Heavy Engineering Ltd (the major engineering subsidiary of the Barlow Group) is one of the largest companies of its kind in South Africa. The company was founded in 1889.
In October 1956 the company entered the rolling stock manufacturing field when the Rolling Stock Division was formed.

Batiruhr

54 rue Santos-Dumont, 75015 Paris, France

Telephone: 531 87 49
Telegrams: Batiruhr, Paris

Products: Diesel-hydraulic, diesel-mechanical, mining and industrial locomotives; electric and diesel personnel coaches for industrial and mining operations.

Bautista Buriasco
Bautista Buriasco E Hijos Ltda SA

Av Bautista Buriasco s/n, 2445 Maria Juana, Province Santa Fe, Argentina

Telephone: 91 214/414

Products: Freight wagons; welded steel bogies.

Bautzen
VEB Waggonbau Bautzen

Neuesche Promenade 920, 8600 Bautzen, German Democratic Republic

Telephone: 5350
Telex: 0287225

Exports: Schienfahrzeuge Export-Import Volkseigener Aussenhandelsbetrieb der DDR, Otztaler Strasse 5, 1100 East Berlin

Products: Passenger, couchette, restaurant and baggage cars. Recent deliveries have included 20 restaurant cars for Uganda Railways Corporation. Iranian Railways have been supplied with 100 second-class cars of mixed compartment and open configuration, 40 first-class couchette cars and 25 restaurant cars, all of Type X. A further 20 restaurant cars of Type X have been built for Bulgarian State Railways (BDZ) and deliveries to Hungarian State Railways (MAV) have included 75 Type Y passenger cars and 30 restaurant cars.
At the start of 1983 the works was engaged on a Syrian State Railways (CFS) order comprising 100 air-conditioned first-class, 80 second-class, 20 air-conditioned restaurant and 10 mail/baggage cars of Type X.

Restaurant car for MAV

Since the 1960s the works has specialised in RIC-specification cars and in 1980 it launched its Type X series to the UIC 567-1 pattern. Comprising nine-compartment first-class cars which are adaptable to couchette use, 11-compartment second-class cars and restaurant cars, the series is designed for 160 km/h operation. The 26.4 metre-long vehicles, built in all-welded lightweight steel, have underfloor air-conditioning arranged to maintain an interior temperature of up to 24°C in ambients ranging from −25 to +50°C. Two brushless three-phase generators in each car, axle-driven via cardan shafts, have a total output of 40 kW at 110 volts, but when the car is at rest the auxiliaries can be fed from a shore supply. The Görlitz VI K-Mg bogies are equipped with electro-magnetic as well as shoe brakes, but are adaptable to other systems in international use. Cars can be fitted for 200 km/h operation with Type GP 200 bogies incorporating disc, shoe and electromagnetic brakes.

Constitution: Opened as an iron foundry and machinery plant in 1846, the works took up tram manufacture in 1897. After 1945 it developed from passenger and freight vehicle repair into construction of a wide variety of vehicles from long-haul passenger cars to railbuses and freight wagons, but has latterly specialised in passenger cars. A member of Vereinigter Schienenfahrzeugbau der DDR eV.

First-class coach for Syrian State Railways (CFS)

Interior of MAV restaurant car

Interior of CFS first-class car

BBC Brown Boveri
BBC Brown, Boveri & Company Ltd

Postfach 58, 5401 Baden, Switzerland

Telephone: (056) 75 11 11
Telegrams: Brownbover Baden
Telex: 558214

Chairman, Group Managing Committee: Piero Hummel
Member of Group Managing Committee, General Manager, Brown Boveri International: Erwin Bielinski
Group Marketing Manager, Power Transmission, Distribution and Utilisation: Sparre Pedersen
Group Marketing Manager, Traction: Ernst Isler

Group companies (with substantial railway activity)
Austria
Oesterreichische Brown Boveri-Werke AG
Postfach 184, 1101 Vienna
Telephone: (0222) 62810
Telegrams: Brownbover Wien
Telex: 131760

Brazil
Industria Elétrica Brown Boveri SA
CP 5528, 01000 São Paulo
Telephone: (011) 802 2111
Telegrams: Brownbover São Paulo
Telex: 33446

Canada
Brown Boveri Canada Ltd
4000 Trans-Canada Highway, Pointe Claire, Quebec H9R 1B2
Telephone: (514) 697 6210
Telegrams: Brownbover Montreal
Telex: 05 821 542

Federal Republic of Germany
Brown, Boveri & Cie Aktiengesellschaft
Postfach 351, 6800 Mannheim 1
Telephone: (0621) 381-1
Telegrams: Brownbover Mannheim
Telex: 462411 122

Class DE500 diesel-electric shunter with BBC three-phase drive

Three-car emu of Bern-Lötschberg-Simplon Railway with BBC Brown Boveri equipment

Italy
Tecnomasio Italiano Brown Boveri SpA (TIBB)
Casella postale 10225, 20100 Milan
Telephone: (02) 5797.1
Telegrams: Tecnomasio Milano
Telex: 310153

Norway
A/S Norsk Elektrisk & Brown Boveri (NEBB)
Postboks 1174 Sentrum, Oslo 1
Telephone: (02) 43 90 50
Telegrams: NEBB Oslo
Telex: 71268

Spain
Brown Boveri de España SA (BBE)
Apartado 36127, Madrid 16
Telephone: (01) 270 54 04
Telex: 43236/27572

Switzerland
BBC Aktiengesellschaft Brown, Boveri & Cie
Postfach 58, 5401 Baden
Telephone: (056) 75 11 11
Telegrams: Brownbover Baden
Telex: 558211

USA
Brown Boveri Corporation
1460 Livingston Avenue, North Brunswick, New Jersey 08902
Telephone: (201) 932 6000
Telegrams: Brownbover North Brunswick New Jersey
Telex: 844 464/5

Krupp-MaK Class DE1002 diesel-electric locomotive with BBC three-phase drive

Class 250 general-duty 4552 kW locomotive with BBC equipment for RENFE

Class EL 17 electric locomotive with asynchronous squirrel-cage motors for NSB

Products: Electrical equipment for electric, diesel-electric traction vehicles (locomotives and powered railcars) of all types and for all applications, surface and underground, main-line, suburban and mass transit, and for light rail vehicles, streetcars and trolleybuses; electric propulsion equipment for rack railways, aerial tramways and unconventional transport systems; complete vehicle propulsion systems for all types of dc or ac supply voltages with electro-mechanical or electronic controls; equipment and components from the vehicle power supply take-off through to and including the traction motor and auxiliaries; electrical equipment for railway passenger coaches; complete systems for passenger comfort with power supply, lighting, heating and air-conditioning.

Among substantial orders from various countries in Europe and overseas, the most significant has been the decision of the Danish State Railway (DSB) to use Brown Boveri three-phase drive technology for locomotives in their 25 kV 50 Hz main-line electrification programme. DSB foresees the need to procure about 120 electric locomotives by the year 2000. The design will be based on the system technology developed for the German Federal Railway Class E 120. Three-phase drive systems are now being acknowledged as promising solutions for a varied range of traction vehicles, by public transport administrations, by industrial companies with their own rail networks, and by a number of other electrical equipment suppliers with their own designs. Since the commissioning of the first locomotive with BBC three-phase drive in 1971, Brown Boveri has received orders for 240 locomotives equipped with this drive technology; 114 of them had been commissioned by the end of 1982.

Recent deliveries of electrical equipment by the Brown Boveri Group have included:

Swiss company for domestic customers: a total of 20 power cars, 16 driving and 16 intermediate trailers for the BLS, BT, GFM and RVT standard-gauge private railways; two shuttle trains, each with power car and driving trailer, to the metre-gauge Gornergrat rack railway; four prototype phase-angle controlled Class Re 4/4 IV locomotives to the Swiss Federal Railways (SBB); 19 articulated trolleybuses to Public Transport Geneva; 80 Type EW IV first-class passenger coaches and 15 Class Re 4/4 II locomotives to SBB.

Swiss company exports with participation by the local BBC company: 25 phase-angle controlled power cars and 25 driving trailers to the Norwegian State Railways (NSB); 35 inter-city passenger coaches to NSB; 100 trolleybuses to Edmonton, Canada; a prototype trolleybus to Johannesburg, South Africa; and a prototype articulated light rail vehicle to Toronto, Canada.

With participation by the Swiss Locomotive Works (SLM): six diesel-electric locomotives for mixed rack-and-adhesion operation to Indonesian State Railways.

BBC Mannheim: 20 (out of a total of 37 ordered) Class ME diesel-electric locomotives with three-phase transmission to the DSB; further three-phase drive systems to four West German locomotive builders for Class DE 500 diesel-electric shunters; first of four Class DE 1100 diesel-electric locomotives with three-phase drive to Krupp-MaK; further light rail vehicles, with chopper controls, to various city transport administrations in the Federal Republic of Germany (over 100 such chopper controls have been ordered from BBC since 1978).

Oesterreichische Brown Boveri-Werke AG: more Class 1044 locomotives for Austrian Federal Railways (ÖBB); two Class 4020 power cars for ÖBB; first of five Class 1063 shunting locomotives with three-phase drive for ÖBB; four driving trailers for Steiermark railways in Austria; 18 drive systems for diesel-electric shunters (with three-phase drive) by Krupp-MaK, Krauss-Maffei and Thyssen-Henschel; four sets of generators and motors for narrow-gauge diesel-electric power cars for FEVE, Spain.

BBC-Sécheron SA
BBC-Sécheron Ltd
Company of the Brown Boveri Group

14 avenue de Sécheron, 1211 Geneva 21, Switzerland

Telephone: 022 32 67 50
Telegrams: Electricité, Geneva
Telex: 22130

General Manager: H J Froidevaux
Sales Manager: A Reymond
Manager, Traction Division: R Kratzer
Deputy Manager, Traction Division: H Hintze

Products: Complete electrical equipment for trolleybuses; electronic control systems for electric and diesel-electric traction vehicles of all kinds; components for locomotives and rolling stock including wheel flange lubricators, earthing brushes, manual and automatic couplers, dc circuit breakers; complete dc substations.

BBC-Sécheron has now supplied more than 2000 electronic control systems for locomotives, train-sets, tramways, underground railways, LRVs and trolleybuses as well as components and couplers for all rolling stock types, dc substations (particularly to Egypt) and trolleybuses world-wide.

Type UR dc circuit-breakers

Type	UR 12	UR 26	UR 36
Highest permissible operating voltage (V)	1000 2000 4000	1000 2000 4000	1000 2000
Continuous current (A)	1200	2600	3600
Breaking current range (kA)	0.6-2.4	1.25-5	2-10
Braking capability for t = 10 ms (circuit time constant) 1 kV	30 kA	45 kA	100 kA
2 kV	30 kA	40 kA	75 kA
4 kV	20 kA	35 kA	
Installation	Vertical or horizontal	Vertical or horizontal	Vertical
Applications	Motor-coaches for tramways, underground railways and main-line railways; small locomotives	Motor-coaches for under-ground and main-line railways; locomotives	Locomotives

Constitution: Company of the Brown Boveri Group. The company was founded as A de Meuron & Cuenod for the manufacture of electrical equipment.

Beijing
Beijing 'Feb 7th' Locomotive Works

Chang Xindian, Beijing, People's Republic of China

Telephone: 818408, 818269
Telegrams: 9927

Member of China National Machinery Import & Export Corporation
Erhtikou, Hsi Chiao, Beijing

Telex: 22328, 22242

Products: Diesel locomotives; diesel engines; hydraulic transmissions; fuel injectors; fuel injection pumps; cardan shafts; bogies.

The BJ series of diesel-hydraulic locomotive is produced in 2700 hp B-B and 5400 hp C-C versions. The B-B has been in series production since 1975. Both types employ the Type 12240 1100 rpm 12-cylinder engine which is also manufactured in the plant. The B-B weighs 92 tonnes, has a starting tractive effort of 23.7 tonnes, a continuous tractive effort of 16.27 tonnes at 24.3 km/h and a maximum speed of 120 km/h.

The works also manufactures the Type Dong Feng 7 diesel-electric Co-Co for heavy shunting. It is fitted with a four-stroke 12-cylinder Vee engine of Type 12240-1, exhaust turbo-charged with intermediate air-cooling, which has a rating of 2200 hp at 1000 rpm. The transmission is ac/dc alternator, employing silicon rectifiers.

Weight in working order: 135 tonnes ± 2%
Max axle-load: 22.5 tonnes ± 3%
Max designed speed: 80 km/h
Starting tractive effort: 41.14 tonnes
Continuous tractive effort: 30.15 tonnes at 12.7 km/h
Length overall: 18.8 m
Width overall: 3.37 m
Height overall: 4.75 m

Type BJ (Beijing) 2700 hp diesel-hydraulic B-B locomotive

Type Dong Feng 7 2200 hp diesel-electric Co-Co locomotive

BEML
Bharat Earth Movers Ltd
Railcoach Division

Unity Buildings, J C Road, Bangalore 560 002, India

Chairman and Managing Director: Maj Gen S N Bhaskar
General Manager: J M Swaminathan
Deputy General Manager: Lt Col A R Sharma
Senior Manager (R & D): K S Jagannatha

Products: Integral passenger coaches in steel; welded lightweight stock such as second class coaches, brake and luggage vans, sleeping coaches; heavy-duty road trailers and earth-moving equipment.

Constitution: The Railcoach Division of Bharat Earth Movers Ltd was the first factory in India to take up manufacture, in 1947, of all-metal broad-gauge coaches, steel, welded, lightweight passenger coaches, postal vans, parcel vans, brake and luggage vans, day-cum-sleeper coaches, motor-cum-parcel coaches. The Division has since supplied over 7400 coaches of different types for Indian Railways. Coaches have also been exported to Bangladesh and Sri Lanka.

Coach assembly shop

Interior of second-class day coach

Berwick
Berwick Forge and Fabricating

PO Box 188, West Ninth Street, Berwick, Pennsylvania 18603, USA

Telephone: (717) 752 2784

Products: Freight wagons and railroad forgings.

134.5 m³ (4750 ft³) capacity covered hopper

15.24 m (50 ft) box car as supplied to several US railroads

Bethlehem Steel
Bethlehem Steel Corporation

Bethlehem, Pennsylvania 18016, USA

Telephone: (215) 694 2424

Chairman: D H Trautlein

Sales: J D Dougherty
Vice-Chairmen: R F Schubert
                  R M Smith

Foreign agents: Brettenham House, Lancaster Place, London WC2E 7EN, England

Products: Freight wagons; components; axles; rails and track accessories.

Bi-Modal
Bi-Modal Corporation
Subsidiary of North American Car Corporation, a Tiger International Company

Head office: 200 Railroad Avenue, PO Box 767, Greenwich, Connecticut 06830, USA

Telephone: (203) 629 4692
Telex: H1282825 (HOMforNYK)

Main works: 109 Willowbrook Lane, West Chester, Pennsylvania 19380
Telephone: (215) 692 5990

President: Robert S Reebie
Senior Vice President, Operations: Eugene Hindin
Vice Presidents
  Engineering: Alan R Cripe
  Marketing and Sales: Henry A Fahl
  Manufacturing: James H Fahy Jr
  Leasing: Melvin Garner
  Administration and Finance: James C Louney

Spread-tandem Model 2200 RoadRailer in rail mode

Spread-tandem layout locates rail axle between RoadRailer's road axles

Products: The Bi-Modal Corporation produces the RoadRailer, a dedicated bi-modal freight vehicle which can be pulled by a road tractor or by locomotives in railway trains. The RoadRailer product line in 1983 included 45-foot dry van units, a single-axle container chassis with or without highway gear, an AutoVan capable of carrying under cover up to five cars and used for general merchandise on the return, as well as a refrigerated van. RoadRailers are available for sale or lease together with a full service maintenance programme.

Each Bi-Modal RoadRailer has two sets of running gear: a set of tandem axle rubber tyres for highway operation and a single-axle with steel wheels for rail operation. Each set of wheels is locked into a running or stored position depending upon the desired mode of operation. Each running gear is mounted with its own braking system and air suspension system, and the rail set includes an automatic hot box detector. The air suspension system provides a smooth ride in each mode, as well as accomplishing the mode-to-mode transfer operation, for which only a hard standing is needed at the terminal. The current dry van RoadRailer, 13.72 metres (45 feet) long, 4.11 metres (13.5 feet) high, and 2.44 metres (8 feet) wide provides an excess of 85 cubic metres (3000 cubic feet) for loading. The front end of the AdapterRailer unit is equipped with a Type F tight-lock coupler and rail air lines, compatible with road locomotives equipped with an MREP air supply. The air suspension system, slack-free articulated couplers and a two-line air brake system give the loaded goods a passenger train quality of ride as well as the maintenance of high speed, operated as dedicated unit trains.

The van structure is of semi-monocoque design, with extruded aluminium upper and lower longitudinal rails, aluminium and steel cross members, extruded heavy aluminium posts and aluminium skin.

During 1982 the undercarriage was redesigned in what is termed a spread tandem arrangement, which locates the rail axle between the pair of road axles, to overcome problems of laden weight distribution when RoadRailers are operating in the rail mode. This has generally raised the dry van's permissible load capacity under US interstate highway legislation by 3000 to 5000 lb. The modified RoadRailer has a tare weight of 16 800 lb (16 500 lb with optional duplex tyres) and a maximum load capacity of 43 200 lb (43 500 lb with duplex

tyres), subject to local highway regulations. Payloads of over 45 000 lb have been legally carried over road on the recently-introduced Empire State Xpress RoadRailer service between New York and Buffalo.

Empire State Xpress is a five times-weekly overnight service marketed by a newly-formed Bi-Modal subsidiary, Road-Rail Transportation (RRTC), which also manages its terminals; the trains are run under contract over Conrail tracks with Conrail locomotives and train crews. RRTC has been granted full deregulated rail carrier status by the Interstate Commerce Commission. Terminals, called 'Railports', have been leased from Conrail at Buffalo and Rochester; and at South Bronx, New York, from the New York State Department of Transportation.

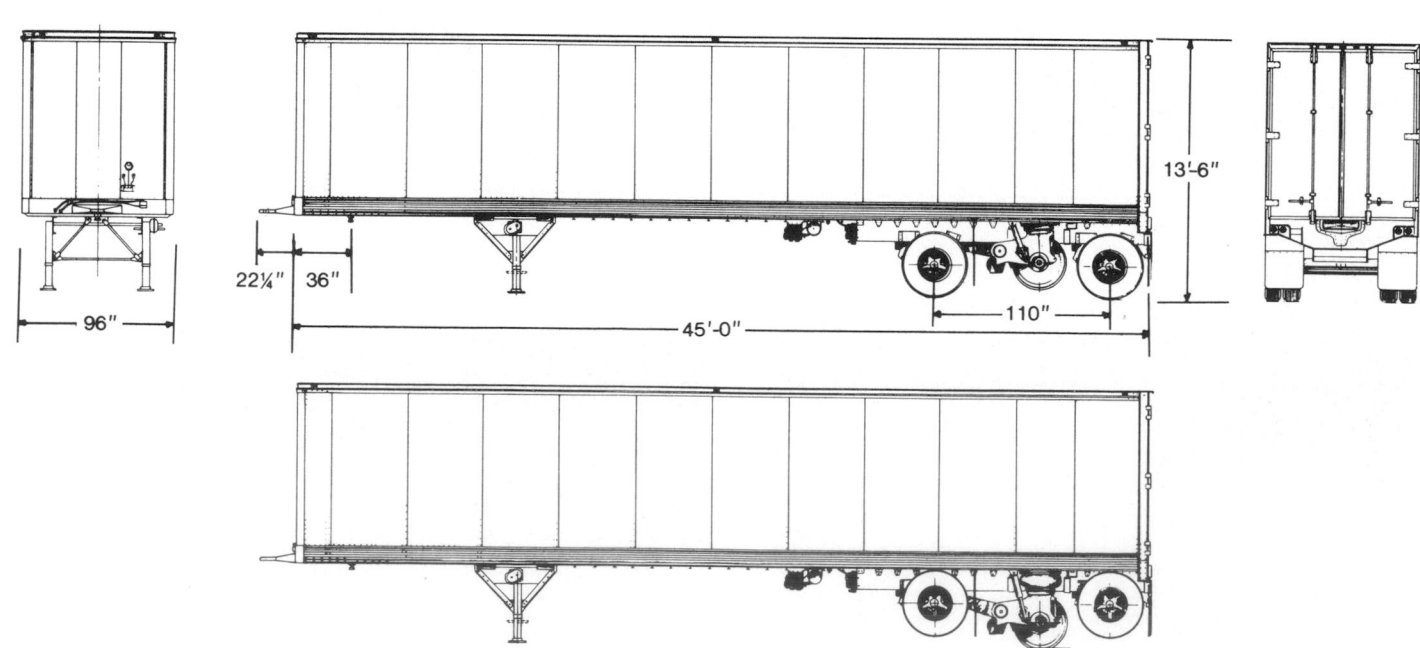
Spread-tandem Model 2200 RoadRailer

In 1983 Inter-Rail Express Corporation (IREX) of New York was to take delivery of a fleet of 100 refrigerated RoadRailers to start a 30-hour transit operation of fruit and vegetable trains from the Orlando-Sebring area of Florida to a Hunts Point Market terminal in the Bronx; the RoadRailer meets the restricted Hudson River Tunnel clearances, which have hitherto forced rail freight for New York City to make a lengthy detour or else to complete the journey by road or barge. The refrigerated RoadRailers were to backhaul merchandise from New York to Florida.

The auto-carrying RoadRailer, the AutoVan, is also multi-purpose. Four of the five vehicles it can carry are slung on the slant, locked on to tracks let down at one end from the ceiling and which when not in use can be retracted to free the whole cube for dry cargo. The AutoVan has been successfully tested with a load of autos from Chicago to Seattle and back.

Based on exhaustive evaluation of RoadRailer performance in tests or daily commercial operation of the RoadRailer over 10 US railroads, the company claims the economic advantages for the RoadRailer over various types of traditional and new lightweight equipment in US intermodal use given in the accompanying tables.

Excesses over RoadRailer per trailer/container in domestic dry freight use (%)

| | 89 ft flatcar | TOFC piggyback | | | COFC containers | |
		4-Runner	Impack	Lo-Pac	Frame car	Stacked
Operating tare weight	173	138	109	153	87	81
Train resistance, 2% grade	66	50	39	59	34	25
level, 112 km/h	118	107	84	82	64	119
Fuel consumption, 88.5 km/h average	104	89	70	75	56	93
Rail axles, maintenance cost	100	100	120	133	100	140
Investment, vehicle fleet	21	24	21	20	3	13
terminals	36	36	36	36	36	36

Linehaul cost per unit-trip of 1000 miles ($)

	RoadRailer	Impack	89 ft flatcar
Maintenance of way	37.62	49.12	56.26
Train operations	108.80	108.80	108.80
Locomotive ownership and operation	98.22	167.56	198.25
Terminal	30.92	43.84	43.92
Vehicle ownership/maintenance	136.30	130.28	81.94
Administration/loss and damage	57.56	77.58	85.20
Total	469.62	577.18	574.37
RoadRailer saving (%)	—	19	18

BN

Constructions Ferroviaires et Métalliques 'BN' SA
Spoorwegmateriel en Metaalconstructies 'BN' NV

Rue Montoyer 10, 1040 Brussels, Belgium

Telephone: 2 511 39 60
Telegrams: Brunag
Telex: 61 736

Chairman: A Dubuisson
Managing Director: O J Bronchart
General Manager: M Simonart
Manager, General Transport Division: J Olivier
Export Manager, Transport Division: J Cuylits

Products: Diesel-electric, diesel-hydraulic and electric locomotives, passenger coaches, freight wagons, LRV and metro stock; emus; containers; industrial equipment.

Orders under construction in 1982 included: 105 LRVs for Charleroi and the Belgian coast; 100 LRVs for The Hague (Netherlands); 90 6th series Type M4 coaches, 105 2nd and 3rd series Type AM 80 electric two-car units, 30 2nd series Type 27, 30 3000 kW Type 21 electric locomotives and 400 TADS wagons for Belgian National Railways (SNCB); 90 flat wagons for container transport for National Railways of Zaire (ONATRA); and 64 eight-axle LRVs for the Manila elevated light rail line, of which the first vehicle was shipped to Manila in October 1982 for an exhibition of urban mass transit equipment.

Orders gained in 1982 included: 130 flat wagons for container transport for Netherlands Railways; 35 7th series M4 coaches for the SNCB; modernisation of 16 four-axle vehicles and construction of three new ones for Marseilles; and eight three-car units to a design derived from the SNCB Class AM 80 emus for Moroccan Railways (ONCF). The ONCF units are for operation in six-car train-sets.

SNCB Class 27 electric Bo-Bo
Gauge: 1435 mm
Traction motors: 4
Weight: 85 tonnes
Power, one-hour rating: 4380 kW at 88.6 km/h
continuous rating: 4180 kW at 88.2 km/h

Tractive effort at wheels, one-hour: 177.5 kN
continuous: 166.3 kN
Max starting effort: 234 kN
Effort at 160 km/h: 78 kN
Max catenary current demand: 1700 A
Max speed: 160 km/h* (200)
Half-worn wheel diameter: 1215 mm
Gear ratio: 1 : 2.829
Rated voltage: 3 kV
* pending SNCB track modifications

Electrical and traction equipment: Maximum adhesion due to transmission of the traction effort via a low-slung traction system; traction effort and speed regulation by means of thyristor choppers; reduced effort between wheels and track by use of fully suspended motors and transverse adjustment device for axles.

Braking: Rheostatic braking electronically-coupled with pneumatic braking.

Aluminium: Non-load bearing parts such as the doors, partitions, facings and roofing are made of extruded aluminium.

Modularity: A modular design of the cab and of the electrical and pneumatic equipment located in the body reduces maintenance time. An integrated pneumatic board allows units to be fitted and removed without interfering with piping.

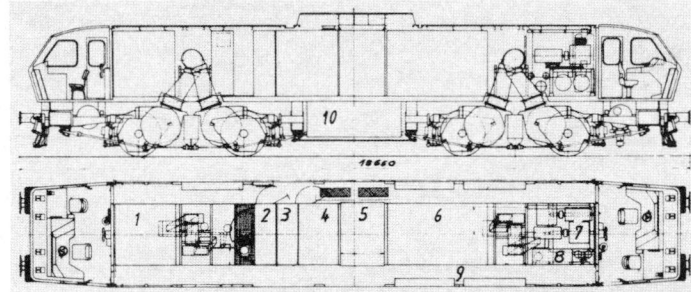

SNCB Class 27 electric Bo-Bo (1) static convertors (2) low voltage cubicle (3) high voltage cubicle (4) high-speed circuit-breaker (5) braking resistors (6) choppers (7) motor-compressor sets (8) pneumatic equipment (9) batteries (10) filter and smoothing reactors

Type AM80 two-car emu for SNCB; design to be adapted for Moroccan Railways three-car emus

Type 27 4150-kW Bo-Bo electric locomotive for Belgian National Railways (SNCB)

Manila eight-axle LRVs
Gauge: 1435 mm
Body length: 29.28 m
Total width: 2.5 m
Floor height: 900 mm
Height, rail to roof: 3.272 m
Wheel diameter: 660 mm
Doors: 5 double (on both sides)
  type: BN swing outboards plug
  opening: 1.3 m
Weight empty: 41 tonnes
Capacity: Total 374; 81 seated; 293 standing (7/m²)
Max service speed: 60 km/h
Acceleration: 1 m/s²
Average service deceleration: 1.3 m/s²
Average emergency deceleration: 2.08 m/s²
Minimum horizontal radius: 25 m
Articulation: 2 BN patented articulations with access passage of 1.66 m, full passenger protection, and anti-vandalism design
Bogies: 2 BN monomotor bogies at car ends; 2 BN trailer bogies under the articulations
Nominal line voltage: 750 V
Motor power: 2 × 217.7 kW
Traction equipment with chopper control for regeneration of energy (ACEC Belgium)
Brake equipment: Electro-dynamic (rheostatic) brakes as service brake;
2 disc brakes per motor bogie as emergency and substitution brake;
2 disc brakes per trailer bogie as service brake;
2 electromagnetic track brakes per bogie for emergency use.
Initially the vehicles will operate in trains of two units (748 passengers) providing the line with a transport capacity of 20 000 passengers per hour in each direction.

Constitution: Present style of the BN company dates from July 1977 when La Brugeoise et Nivelles absorbed Constructions Ferroviaires du Centre.

SNCB Class AM80 emu second-class saloon

Manila LRV interior

Eight-axle LRV for Manila, designed for twin-unit operation

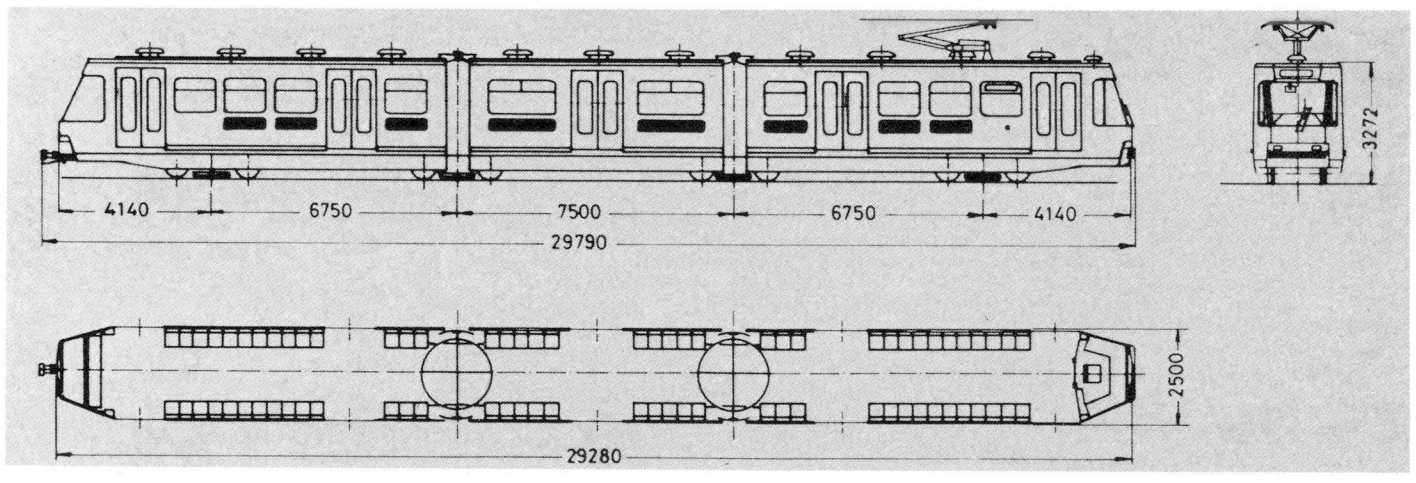
Layout of Manila LRV

SNCB Class AM 80 emu

Cars per unit	Line voltage	Motor cars per unit	Motored axles per motor car	Rated output (kW) per motor	Max speed kmlh	Weight tonnes per set	Total seating capacity	Length per set mm	Rate of acceleration mls²	Year first built	Builders Mechanical parts	Builders Electrical equipment
2	3 kV	1	4	1240	160	105	171	25 075	0.75	1982	BN	ACEC

Bombardier
Bombardier Inc

Rail and Diesel Products Division

1505 Dickson Street, Montreal, Quebec H1N 2H7, Canada

Telephone: (514) 253 7333
Telex: 05 828841

President: Gérard L Lepage

Vice President, Sales and Service: Ian B Crowe
Director, International Sales: Mohan N Wadhwani

Mass Transit Division

1350 Nobel, Boucherville, Montreal, Quebec J4V 1A1

Telephone: (514) 655 6121
Telex: 05 13486

President: Raymond Royer
Vice President, Marketing and Sales: Carl Mawby

Products, Rail and Diesel Products Division: Bombardier manufactures the original 'M' series, now termed the HRC line, of diesel-electric locomotives for domestic use and the 'MX', 'DL' and 'MXS' series for the international market. The four-cycle turbocharged model 251 diesel engine provides power for all Bombardier locomotives. It has a growing variety of marine and stationary applications in its full range of five sizes with 6, 8, 12, 16 or 18 cylinders and power ratings from 875 to 4500 hp.

Bombardier locomotives are designed for world-wide applications offering optimum accommodation to geographical and climatic conditions; limited axle loads from approximately 26 455 to 55 000 lb (12-24.95 tonnes); and configuration to all UIC, African and other reduced-clearance structure gauges. High-adhesion bogies, which maximise effective adhesive weight, can be offered, as can idle pilot axles to spread weight.

A feature of the HRC series is the CGE Constant Kilowatt Excitation and Micro-limit Wheelslip control system. Combined with 'Hi-Ad' high-adhesion bogies or Zero Weight Transfer (ZWT) bogies, this is claimed to achieve a 20 per cent improvement in adhesion capability. New auxiliary equipment designs include more efficient radiator fans, ventilated dynamic braking equipment and panel filters in place of mechanical filters. Another innovation offers the operator ability to adjust each notch horsepower setting independently, to tailor the notch schedule to optimal fuel efficiency at every engine speed setting. This not only checks excessive fuel consumption, but also eliminates vibrations and shock caused by sudden changes between notch selections.

Diesel locomotive orders secured in 1982 included one worth C$13.4 million for the supply of ten MX620 2400 hp locomotives and related spare parts to the National Railways of Cameroon. This order, financed by loans from the Export Development Corp (EDC) and the Canadian International Development Agency (CIDA), followed a similar order for 20 Bombardier locomotives already in service in Cameroon. An order from Tunisian National Railways Corporation (SNCFT) worth C$26 million covered 13 MXS624 2200 hp locomotives for metre gauge and 9 MXS620 locomotives of 2400 hp for standard gauge. A contract worth C$52 million was won for the supply of engines, parts and supervision for the rebuilding of 84 locomotives for RFFSA, Brazil.

Deliveries in 1982 included: 20 3200 hp Type HR616 locomotives for Canadian

Bombardier LRC 3500 bhp locomotive in service with VIA-Canada

National; 12 Type MX624 2400 hp locomotives for Bangladesh Railways; 10 Type MX620 2000 hp locomotives for the 914 mm-gauge Ferrocarriles de Guatemala and four Type DL535E 1200 hp locomotives for the narrow-gauge White Pass line of the British Yukon Railway.

In 1982 the company won a repeat order from VIA Rail Canada worth C$100 million for 10 locomotives and 50 cars of its LRC ('Light Rapid Comfortable') equipment. The LRC cars are equipped with an active automatic body-tilt system. Each bogie is fitted with an accelerometer and associated electronic servo valve that activate the banking mechanism, which is a modified swing linkage. The system senses lateral motion only and disregards any vertical motion ensuing from superelevation or imperfect track; it compensates for excess of

Bombardier diesel locomotives

Class	Wheel arrangement	Electric transmission	Rated power (hp)	Max speed km/h	Total weight tonnes	No in service	Year first built	Builders		
								Mechanical parts	Engine & type	Transmission
LRC	Bo-Bo 2-axle bogie	ac-dc	2600	200	102	23	Prototype 1972 Amtrak 1978 VIA Rail 1978	Bombardier Rail & Diesel Products Div	Bombardier 251 diesel engine 16 cyl	Canadian General Electric
HR406	Bo-Bo	ac-dc	900	108	118	—	—	Bombardier Rail & Diesel Products Div	Bombardier 251 diesel engine 6 cyl	Canadian General Electric
HR412	Bo-Bo	ac-dc	1800	107	109 127	10	1978	Bombardier Rail & Diesel Products Div	Bombardier 251 diesel engine 12 cyl	Canadian General Electric
HR416	Bo-Bo	ac-dc	2250	107	116 127	—	—	Bombardier Rail & Diesel Products Div	Bombardier 251 diesel engine 16 cyl	Canadian General Electric
HR616	Co-Co 3-axle bogie	ac-dc	2400	107	172.4 190.5	20	1980	Bombardier Rail & Diesel Products Div	Bombardier 251 diesel engine 16 cyl	Canadian General Electric
HR618	Co-Co	ac-dc	2700	107	176 190.5	—	—	Bombardier Rail & Diesel Products Div	Bombardier 251 diesel engine 18 cyl	Canadian General Electric
M-630	Co-Co	ac-dc	2250	107	172.4 190.5	28	1972	Bombardier Rail & Diesel Products Div	Bombardier 251 diesel engine 16 cyl	Canadian General Electric
DL-532	Bo-Bo	dc-dc	900	115	69	113	1958	Bombardier Rail & Diesel Products Div	Bombardier 251 diesel engine 6 cyl	Canadian General Electric
DL-535	Co-Co	dc-dc	900	115	85.7	182	1973	Bombardier Rail & Diesel Products Div	Bombardier 251 diesel engine 6 cyl	Canadian General Electric
DL-536	Bo-Bo	dc-dc	900	115	85.7	20	1976	Bombardier Rail & Diesel Products Div	Bombardier 251 diesel engine 6 cyl	Canadian General Electric
MX-615	Co-Co	dc-dc	1100	115	72	74	1971	Bombardier Rail & Diesel Products Div	Bombardier 251 diesel engine 8 cyl	Canadian General Electric
MX-620	Co-Co	ac-dc/dc-dc	1500	115	96	154	1970	Bombardier Rail & Diesel Products Div	Bombardier 251 diesel engine 12 cyl	Canadian General Electric
MX-624	Co-Co	ac-dc	1800	115	111	62	1974	Bombardier Rail & Diesel Products Div	Bombardier 251 diesel engine 12 cyl	Canadian General Electric
MX-636	Co-Co	ac-dc	2700	108	120	18	1973	Bombardier Rail & Diesel Products Div	Bombardier 251 diesel engine 16 cyl	Canadian General Electric
MXS-620	Co-Co	dc-dc	1500	115	105	61	1973	Bombardier Rail & Diesel Products Div	Bombardier 251 diesel engine 12 cyl	Canadian General Electric
MXS-624	Co-Co	—	1800	115	94.8	—	1982	Bombardier Rail & Diesel Products Div	Bombardier 251 diesel engine 12 cyl	Canadian General Electric
MXS-627	Co-Co	ac-dc	2000	120	120	13	1978	Bombardier Rail & Diesel Products Div	Bombardier 251 diesel engine 16 cyl	Canadian General Electric

superelevation at low speed as well as cant deficiency. In the event of a malfunction, hydraulic pressure in the servo valve locks the linkage affected and centres the coach body. The car bodies are of aluminium-skinned, monocoque construction and the vehicles have passed AAR 800 000 lb buff load compression tests.

The LRC locomotive is not fitted with tilting mechanism. To secure comparable curving performance orthodox twin H-beam framing has been discarded in favour of a depressed, fabricated underframe in which the 3500 hp 16-cylinder Type 251 engine is cradled between twin 1000-gallon fuel tanks. Centre of gravity is about 1.2 metres above the rails. Tilting mechanism apart, the locomotive bogies are similar to those of the passenger cars; two large conical spring coils on each bogie compensate for the additional lateral motion of the engine block, compressing to help centralise the engine in place. Maximum designed speed is 200 km/h.

Bombardier also offers its clients application studies, technical assistance, technical training, spare parts supply, overhaul and repair service. The company maintains a continuing programme of diesel engine research and development with emphasis on improvement of existing equipment. In Montreal, Bombardier operates the only privately-owned medium-speed diesel laboratory in Canada.

Constitution: Founded in 1902 as the Locomotive and Machine Co of Montreal Ltd, the company was purchased in 1904 by the American Locomotive Company (later renamed Alco Product Inc) and later renamed Montreal Locomotive Works (MLW).

By the early 1950s over 4000 locomotives had been manufactured at the Montreal location. In 1948 Dominion Engineering Works Limited began manufacturing Alco diesel engines to be incorporated into Alco locomotives, produced by Montreal Locomotive Works. MLW introduced the first diesel-electric locomotive in Canada in the early 1950s. In 1969 Alco Products Inc stopped locomotive production and sold the locomotive designs to Montreal Locomotive Works. The company also took over service responsibility for more than 8000 Alco diesel-electric locomotives world-wide. In 1969 the company expanded internationally, acquiring licences in Argentina, India, Australia and Spain. Bombardier has since added Brazil and West Germany to the list (a long-term licensing agreement for manufacture of Bombardier-designed

locomotives in West Germany by the Transportation Systems Division of Krauss-Maffei AG was concluded in 1982). In 1975 Bombardier purchased Montreal Locomotive Works Ltd.

Products, Mass Transit Division: Rubber-tyred metro cars, articulated light rail vehicles, commuter railcars.

An important order won in 1982 was for the supply of 825 Type R-62 metro cars to the New York Metropolitan Transportation Authority, to be assembled at the company's Barre, Vermont, plant with 40 per cent US-made components. The order was worth US $662.9 million.

In mid-1982 Bombardier shipped a first train of nine rubber-tyred metro cars for Mexico City. This was the start of delivery of an order for 180 cars granted to Bombardier in 1981 by the Mexican company Constructora Nacional de Carros de Ferrocarril (CNCF). Three-car sets are coupled semi-permanently to form a nine-car consist comprising six power and three trailer cars. The cars will run both underground and above, with a maximum gradient of 6.5 to 8 degrees, in temperatures varying from −5 to +45°C.

Type MX-636 Co-Co supplied to Greek Railways

Type MXS-627 Co-Co supplied to Portuguese Railways

Cab of LRC power car

Braine-le-Comte
Usines de Braine-le-Comte SA

Rue des Frères Dulait, 7490 Braine-le-Comte, Belgium

Telephone: (067) 55 31 07
Telegrams: Usines, Braine-le-Comte
Telex: 57458

Chairman: Pol Boël
Director and Manager: Jaques Preud'homme

Products: Freight wagons.

Braithwaite
Braithwaite & Co Ltd

Head office: 5 Hide Road, Calcutta 700 043, India

Telephone: 45 9901
Telegrams: Bromkirk, Calcutta
Telex: CA 7910

Branch office: Bharat Yuvak Bhawan, 1 Jai Singh Road, New Delhi 110 001

Works: Clive Works, 5 Hide Road, Calcutta 700 043
Angus Works, Angus PO, Hooghly, West Bengal

Chairman and Managing Director: R Datta
Director, Production, Planning and Control: S Venkata Raman
General Manager, Clive Works: H K Chatterjee
  Angus Works: P K Dasgupta
Commercial Manager, Clive Works: T K Bhowmick
  Angus Works: B P Rakshit

Products: Railway wagons, bridges, buildings for factories, power houses and steel plants, overhead electric travelling cranes, wharf cranes, railway breakdown cranes, container cranes, portal cranes, tower cranes, hammerhead

Bogie open wagon for Viet-Nam; tare 15.6 tonnes, carrying capacity 40.4 tonnes, length 13.7 m, gauge 1000 mm

cranes, diesel-electric cranes, trailers, coal and other material handling plants, jute mill machinery, pressed steel tanks, iron castings, steel forgings.

Constitution: Braithwaite is a Government of India undertaking, and has successfully executed orders for equipment from undertakings abroad in Bahrain, Burma, Ghana, Hong Kong, Iraq, the Republic of Korea, Kenya, Kuwait, Malaysia, Maldives, Nepal, New Zealand, Philippines, Sudan, Sri Lanka, Taiwan, Uganda, the United Arab Emirates, Viet-Nam, Yugoslavia and Zambia.

24-axle 250-tonne special wagon for Bhilai Steel Plant; tare 199 tonnes, carrying capacity 250 tonnes, length 46.77 m, gauge 1676 mm

Sulphuric acid tank wagon for Zambia, Class ICC 103-AW; tare 20 tonnes, carrying capacity 41 tonnes, length 9.86 m, gauge 1067 mm

Heavy duty wagons for Bhilai Steel Plant; tare 45.9 tonnes, carrying capacity 76 tonnes, length 11.98 m, gauge 1676 mm

Bogie covered wagons for Uganda with full side-width doors; tare 18.8 tonnes, carrying capacity 34 tonnes, length 13.7 m, gauge 1000 mm

Bratstvo

Preduzece Sinskih Vozila Subotica, Yugoslavia

Telephone: 23 762 5
Telegrams: Vagoni, Yugoslavia
Telex: 15138

Products: Freight wagons and three-axle double-deck articulated automobile carriers. The auto-carrier, 24.8 metres long over buffers, is designed for operation at up to 120 km/h and has estimated load capacities of 12 Mp on the lower deck, 8 Mp on the upper. It can convey a total of 21 cars which are individually within 3.3 × 1.38 metres dimensional limits, or the equivalent in larger vehicles. The front part of the upper deck can be inclined at an angle of 17 degrees by a hydraulic mechanism for ease of loading.

Articulated three-axle auto-carrier

Breda
Breda Costruzioni Ferroviarie SpA

Via Ciliegiole, 51100 Pistoia, Italy

Telephone: (0573) 367801
Telegrams: Ferbreda, Pistoia
Telex: 570186

Chairman: Giuseppe Capuano
General Manager: Corrada Fici
Vice General Manager: Alberto Bracco

Products: Passenger coaches, light alloy or steel electric train-sets for long distances, for rapid transit of commuters and for underground lines.
Recent designs have included the Pendolare four-car emu designed for regional commuter service which, though adopted for series production by Italian

Pendolare emu power car

SFSM, Naples, three-car 1.5 kV dc LRV unit, tare weight 50 tonnes, continuous rating 700 kW

Shaker Heights light rail vehicles delivered in 1980 by Breda to Cleveland, USA

State Railways (FS), is adaptable to other operators' requirements. The Pendolare is conceived to work with equal facility in short-haul services, where stops are closely spaced and load variations significant, and on longer-distance operations where stops are less frequent and load fluctuations less marked. A special feature of the design is the depth of the passenger doors and the fitment of folding steps so that the unit is compatible with different platform levels. Key factors influencing the design were: achievement of fast start-to-stop average speeds; reduction of energy consumption and operating costs; good acceleration and deceleration rates, plus efficient braking, all under automatic control to the maximum extent feasible; and an interior layout combining high passenger comfort quality with fast handling of passengers at stops.

The weight-saving body, of modular design to simplify variation of seating layout, service areas and number of power-operated doors, is chiefly fabricated from large welded extrusions and sheeting in light alloy. Airplane-type seating in 1.6-metre modules leaves 800 mm between seats. Most of the equipment is underfloor in easily demountable modular housings.

The first emu in Italian service to be fitted with full chopper control, the Pendolare has two power cars with a combined continuous rating of 1760 kW at 3 kV dc, giving it a starting acceleration rate of 1 m/s² and an average of 0.66 m/s² up to 100 km/h; maximum speed is 140 km/h and average braking rate from that 1 m/s². Length and tare weight of the power car are respectively 25.65 metres and 53 tonnes, of the trailer 23.9 metres and 29 tonnes. A total seating capacity in each four-car set of 856 is possible.

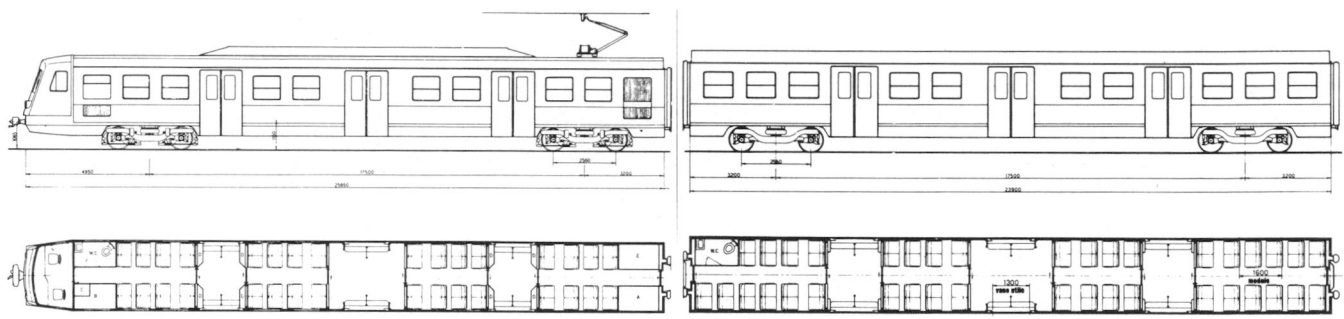

General arrangement of Pendolare emu

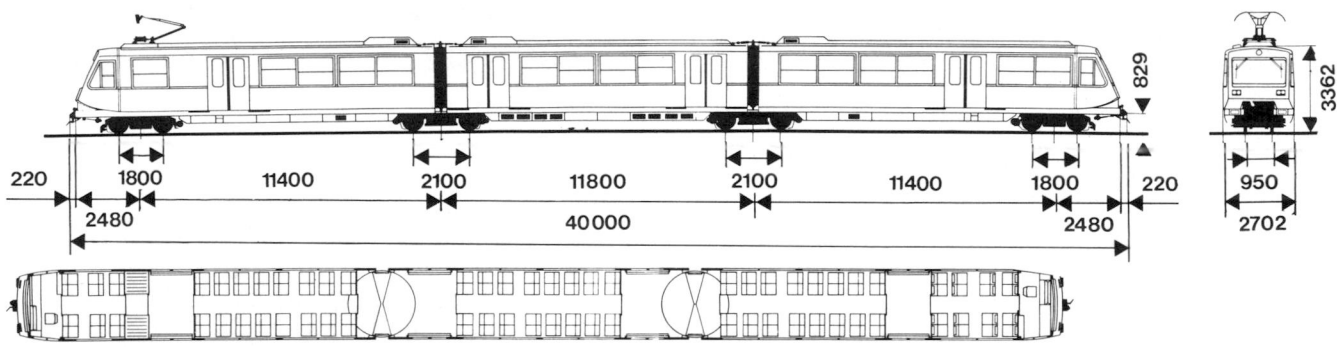

Naples three-car LRV unit

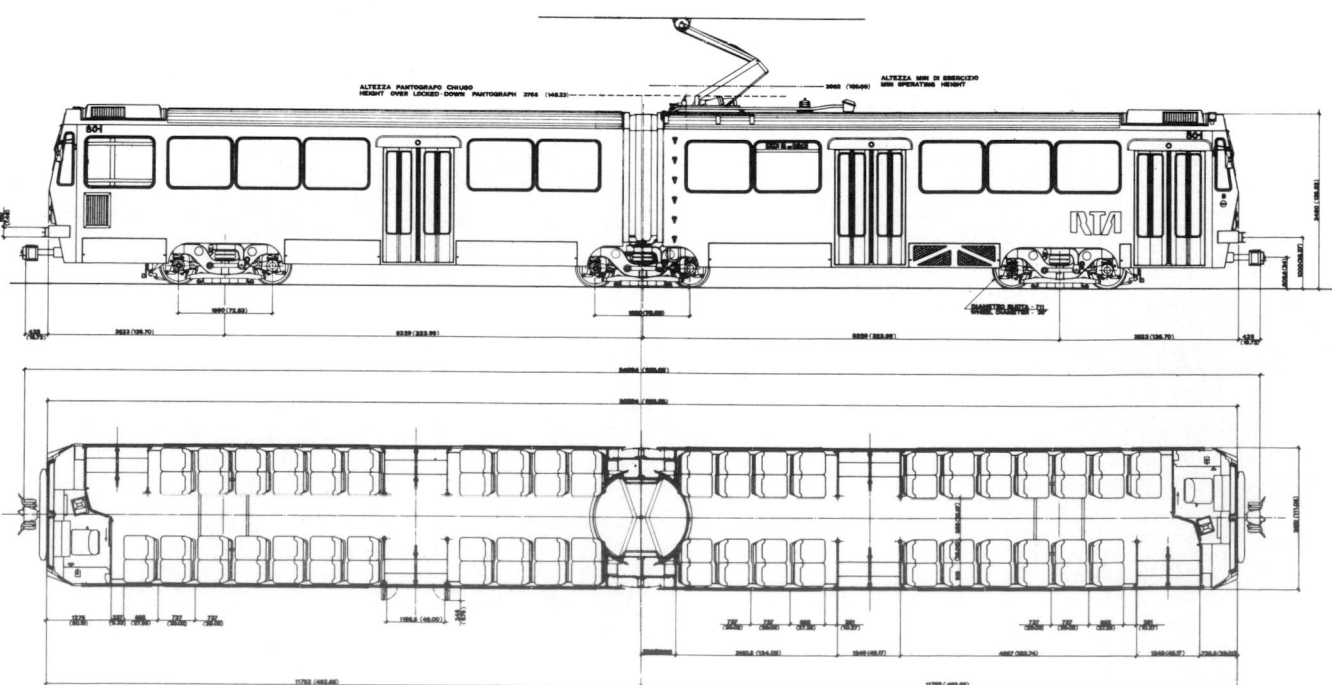

General arrangement of LRV unit for Cleveland

BREL
British Rail Engineering Ltd

Railway Technical Centre, London Road, Derby DE2 8UP, England

Telephone: 0332 49211
Telex: 37367

Chairman: J G Urquhart
Managing Director: P A Norman
Production Director: G M James
Financial Director: C R Wood

Products: Diesel and electric locomotives and multiple-units; passenger coaches; freight wagons; bogies; steel, iron and non-ferrous castings; coil and laminated springs; crane machinery.

Recent sales to British Rail have featured the Class 58 'Rail freight' Co-Co locomotive, of which 36 are to be built; objectives of the design are: economy in construction; ease of maintenance, and minimum overall costs; adaptation to export applications with minimum modifications.

BR rating: 2460 kW
Max speed: 130 km/h
Engine: Ruston RK3ACT 12 cyl
Traction motor: Brush TM 73-62
Gauge: 1435 mm
Wheel arrangement: Co-Co
Length over buffers: 19 130 mm
Total wheelbase: 14 860 mm
Distance between bogie centres: 10 800 mm
Max height: 3950 mm
Width over bodysides: 2720 mm
Wheel diameter (new): 1120 mm
Weight (with full supplies): 130 tonnes
Max axle load: 21.6 tonnes

The underframe is designed to carry all the static loads imposed by the equipment and those arising from dynamic forces when in operation. In addition, the underframe is designed to take an end load of 200 tons at buffer height and to allow lifting of the complete locomotive at the centre pivots without permanent deformation of the members.

The area between the driving cabs is divided into four sections. The first houses the radiator equipment, and one electrically-driven traction motor blower. The radiator mountings, ducting, fan cowls and fan motor supports are incorporated in one complete removable module. The second section houses the power unit, and compressors; access to each side of the power unit is afforded by bodyside doors. The third section houses the turbocharger air inlet and electrical equipment. The fourth section houses the electrical control equipment cabinet, the main rectifier, the second electrically-driven traction motor blower, and the brake equipment.

The monobloc-wheel bogies are designated BR CP3 and each is fitted with three driven axles. The main bogie frame is of welded construction consisting of two main longitudes of box construction incorporating substantial castings connected by cross-members which are castings/fabrications. The bogie frame is supported from the axleboxes by the primary suspension consisting of helical springs in the vertical plane and 'silentbloc' parallel rubber bushes in the lateral/longitudinal plane. Traction motors are axle-hung nose-suspended by links and rubber bushes. Secondary suspension is by Flexicoils, with three springs per side, fitted into pockets in the underframe.

The centrally located diesel engine is a Ruston RK3ACT charge air cooled 12-cylinder engine continuously rated at 2610 kW at 1000 rpm having a BMEP at this rating of 16.9 bar although as fitted in the Class 58 it is de-rated to 2460 kW (15.9 bar BMEP). It is of the four stroke turbo-charged type with a cylinder bore of 254 mm, a piston stroke of 305 mm with a mean piston speed of 10.2 m/s and arranged in two banks with an included angle of 45 degrees. The engine is of monobloc construction and is completely enclosed.

The alternators are specially designed for traction requirements, with particular attention to interchangeability, ease of maintenance, life of wearing parts and selection of insulating materials. The set comprises a main and auxiliary alternator each having its own brushless exciter. The main alternator rotor is built on a hollow hub which is solidly coupled to the engine crankshaft through a coupling adaptor. A solid flanged shaft extension which forms the auxiliary alternator rotor and carries both exciter rotors is bolted to the main alternator hub and is supported at its outer end by a roller bearing.

Class 58 'Railfreight' diesel-electric Co-Co locomotive

Class 317 emu for London St Pancras-Bedford suburban electrification

Mk III sleeping car

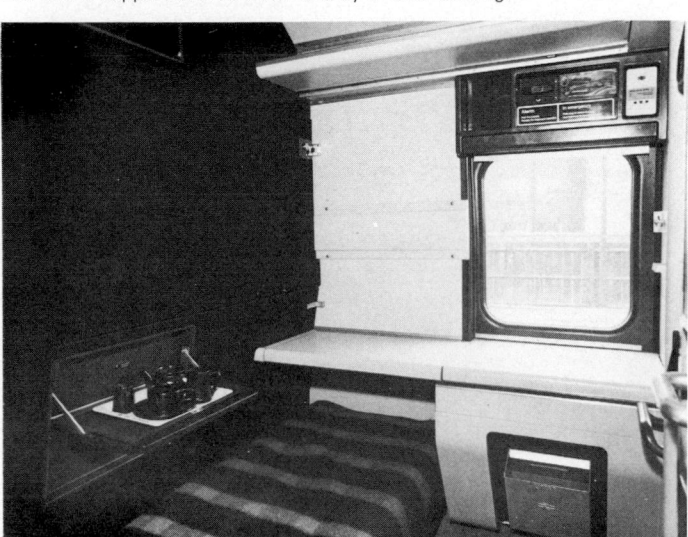
Mk III sleeping car compartment, convertible to one- or two-berth occupation

High-Speed Train built by BREL at Derby and Crewe *(Brian Morrison)*

Type HBA 32-tonne capacity hopper, one of 10 000 built for British Rail

27-tonne load capacity Type VGA full side-access van

The Brush-designed traction motors, designated TM 73-62 are derivatives of those used on the British Rail Class 45 and 56 locomotives.

The locomotives are fitted with slow speed control at 0.5 mph for BR's 'merry-go-round' automatic coal discharge services. In slow speed the six traction motors are connected in series to better match the alternator characteristic. The engine speed is constant and at present is set at idling (450 rpm). The driver can select one of four speed settings, locomotive speed being sensed at two traction motors. The train speed is then automatically controlled, the driver simply controlling the brake if necessary (eg during downhill loading). Electronic wheelslip detection operates on the principle of comparing traction motor currents. When a wheelslip is detected the traction alternator excitation volts are rapidly removed, thus cutting the tractive effort. At the same time the load demand signal is driven down. When wheelslip has ceased the tractive effort is restored to a level lower than that pre-set before wheelslip, the reduction being proportional to the time for which wheelslip lasted, and gradually restored to its former level under control of the governor. The locomotive is exclusively air-braked. Up to three Class 58 can be driven in multiple.

Other recent deliveries to BR have included:

Further 200 km/h High Speed Trains, comprising two diesel-electric power cars each fitted with a Paxman diesel engine giving an output of 1680 kW, and Mk III passenger coaches with full air-conditioning, double glazed windows and automatic internal doors;

Four-car electric multiple-units of Classes 317 and 455 for London Midland and Southern Regions. These units, based on the Mk III coach, incorporate modern seating, and passenger-operated sliding doors. They are capable of operating at 160 km/h and are designed for medium-distance commuter services;

Air-conditioned Mark III sleeping cars, of which 210 are being built, incorporate extensive soundproofing and the most advanced fire and safety precau-

tions. They are currently being phased into service on Anglo-Scottish night trains;

46-tonne glw two-axle coal hopper wagons carrying coal from collieries to power stations on BR's merry-go-round system, the latest design of which is capable of 96 km/h operation;

44-tonne glw two-axle full side-access van with two sliding door panels on each side, for general merchandise and palletised goods;

46-tonne glw two-axle open wagons for bulk materials;

40-tonne capacity bogie hopper wagons used by the Director of Civil Engineering to transport ballast, discharged via wide bottom doors;

Long-welded rail-carrying wagons, forming an 11-wagon train, used by civil engineers; each vehicle designed to carry 32 rails of 183 metres individual length.

Recent production for private buyers has included:

51-tonne glw two-axle bulk powder tank wagons incorporating aeration equipment for rapid pressure-assisted discharge into overhead silos;

70-tonne glw bogie flat wagon built to convey armoured vehicles, but capable of conveying a wide variety of loads at high speed;

Cross-braced freight bogies designed to overcome the traditional problems of instability and excessive wheel-flange wear. These bogies, with an excellent curving performance and high design speed, are suitable for all standard- and narrow-gauge applications.

Constitution: The company was formed in January 1970 as a subsidiary of the British Railways Board to manage the 13 main railway works. It undertakes all types of railway engineering work both for British Rail and private companies. Exports are handled chiefly by BRE-Metro Limited, the joint export sales company of British Rail Engineering Ltd and Metro-Cammell Ltd. BREL has also announced a new lightweight rail passenger vehicle built in association with Leyland Vehicles Ltd, the BRE-Leyland Railbus.

BRE-Leyland

Railway Technical Centre, London Road, Derby DE2 8UP, England

Telephone: 0332 49211
Telex: 37367

Leyland Vehicles
Railbus Dept, Leyland Bus, Preston, Lancashire PR5 1SN
Telephone: 07744 24241
Telex: 67515

Products: The BRE-Leyland Railbus is a lightweight rail vehicle which combines road and rail technology to provide inexpensive urban and rural transport. Mounting a specially adapted Leyland National bus body of integral steel on a simple rail underframe incorporating a two-axle, high-performance suspension system, the design has produced a highly adaptable vehicle which combines the advantages of a low initial purchase price with equally modest operating and maintenance costs.

The railbus can be built either as a single car with driving positions at both ends or as a twin-car set. Both types are equipped for multiple-unit operation and each car can carry up to 100 passengers (64 seated). A Leyland 218 bhp engine mounted under the floor of each car supplies power to one axle via a fully automatic gearbox and final drive unit. Fuel consumption is about 4 km/litre and maximum speed is 120 km/h. Interior equipment and decor can be fitted to meet individual customer's requirements and the railbus concept can also be applied

to mail and parcels traffic, dual passenger and light freight operations or to vehicles fitted out as maintenance and crew accommodation cars.

Constitution: Joint export venture by British Rail Engineering Ltd and Leyland Vehicles.

BRE-Leyland Railbus

Bremer
Bremer Waggonbau GmbH

Postfach 110 109, Pfalzburger Strasse 251, 2800 Bremen 11, Federal Republic of Germany

Telephone: 45 40 11
Telegrams: Bremer Waggonbau, Bremen
Telex: 024 4423

Managing Director: Peter Müller
Export Sales: Uhr Trahm

Products: Diesel and electric multiple-units; passenger coaches; freight wagons, in particular repair and renovation.

Constitution: The company was formed in December 1975. The works occupy the site of the former Hansa Waggon AG.

BRE-Metro

Offices
14 Melbury Terrace, London NW1 6JU, England
Railway Technical Centre, London Road, Derby DE2 8UP
(Registered office): PO Box 248, Leigh Road, Washwood Heath, Birmingham B8 2YJ

Telephone: (Derby) 0332 49211
             (Birmingham) 021-327 4777
Telex: (Derby) 37367
        (Birmingham) 33401

Chairman: J G Urquhart
General Manager: F D Pinto
Sales and Contracts Manager: C E Band
Chief Sales and Contracts Engineer: R W Kelly
Senior Sales and Contracts Engineers: T Robson
                                           R J Champion
                                           A E Andrews

Products: Diesel and electric locomotives; multiple-unit trains; passenger coaches; freight wagons; rapid transit stock; and a wide range of bogies.

Recent sales have included 110 bogie hopper wagons to Kenya Railways; coaches (first- and second-class, comprising 40 sleeping cars, and 10 restaurant cars) and four types of bogie wagon (low-sided, high-sided, covered with sliding doors and brake vans) to the Tanzanian Railways Corporation; two types of bogie covered wagon (broad-gauge and narrow-gauge) to Bangladesh Railways; high-capacity ferry vans (80 tonnes glw, 26 tonnes tare) to Danzas SA of Switzerland; cross-braced freight bogies, which offer marked improvements in wheel flange and rail life where routes are tortuous and axle loads are high, to the Malayan Railway Administration; and bogies to Kalmar Verkstads AB of Sweden.

Contracts have recently been secured to supply passenger coaches to Córas Iompair Éireann, Ireland, and Kenya Railways while passenger coaches and freight wagons are to be built for the Congo-Ocean Railway in West Africa.

Current projects include the design of a new locomotive and coach specifically for the export market, the production of a rapid transit cross-braced (self-steering) bogie, and the continuous development of existing designs of all types of rolling stock and bogies for individual customers.

Constitution: Joint export sales company of British Rail Engineering Ltd and Metro-Cammell Ltd.

36.8-tonne load capacity sliding-door van for Tanzanian Railways Corporation

Bogie hopper wagon supplied to Kenya Railways

High-capacity ferry van for Danzas SA

Passenger coach for Tanzanian Railways Corporation

Briggs & Turivas
Briggs & Turivas, Inc

Box 270, 310 Grant Street, Dennison, Ohio 44621, USA

Telephone: (614) 922 5994

President: P B Paull
Vice-President: G Kaswinkel
Vice-President, Sales: C A Vaughn

Products: Freight wagons.

Brookville
Brookville Locomotive

PO Box 130, Pickering Street, Brookville, Pennsylvania 15825, USA

Telephone: (814) 849 7321
Telegrams: Broloc
Telex: 866729

Vice President, Marketing: Dalph S McNeil
Sales Engineer: Larry Conrad

Products: Four- to 30-ton diesel locomotives with mechanical, torque converter, power shift or hydrostatic transmissions. Final drives are cardan shaft or chain and sprocket and suspension is chevron or journals and springs. Used above ground as industrial switchers, yard locomotives and in steel and concrete factories; and underground for tunnel construction and hardrock mining. The latest 914 mm (3 foot) high 'Low Pro' has been passed for use in gaseous coal mines.

'Low Pro', approved for use in coal mines

Brush

Brush Electrical Machines Ltd (Traction Division)
Member of the Hawker Siddeley Group

Falcon Works, Loughborough, Leicestershire LE11 1HJ, England

Telephone: 0509 63131
Telegrams: Brush, Loughborough
Telex: 341091

Chairman: J M Durber
Managing Director: A R Creswick
Traction Director: B G Sephton
Manager, Traction Sales and Projects: D R Minkley
  Traction Engineering: P Duerden
  Traction Service: D B Roe
  Contracts: P Markham
Chief Tendering Engineer: R J Gardener

Products: Main-line diesel-electric and electric locomotives; diesel-electric transfer and shunting locomotives; power equipments including alternators, generators, motors, and auxiliary machines, transformers, rectifiers, invertors, electronic and conventional control gear equipment for diesel-electric and electric locomotives, diesel railcars, diesel and electric multiple-unit trains; complete electrical propulsion equipment for rapid transit trains.

The wide range of traction equipment recently supplied includes main-line passenger locomotives, power equipment for the successful British Rail High Speed Train and New South Wales State Rail Authority's XPT, high-power freight locomotives and power equipments in the 1250 to 3500 hp range for both home and overseas railways. The company has also provided power equipment for 25 kV electric traction, including British Rail's APT, and complete equipment packages for rapid transit systems.

Shunting and transfer locomotives of 400 to 1000 hp have been supplied world-wide. The company's latest orders have covered supply of 1000 hp Bo-Bo main-line mixed traffic locomotives to Sri Lanka Government Railways and Bo-Bo shunting locomotives to Turkish Iron & Steel Company.

Constitution: Brush Electrical Ltd was formed in 1889 with the acquisition of the Falcon Engine and Car Works in Loughborough, and has been involved in electric traction since then. Falcon Works' history of rail traction building began in 1875, with the manufacture of steam locomotives. Originally producing tram-cars in large numbers, Brush entered the diesel-electric field in 1948 and has been a major supplier of main-line and shunting locomotives and power equipment, also emu and rapid transit equipment.

Brush-built 1000 hp Bo-Bo diesel for Sri Lanka Government Railways

Thyristor-controlled Class 315 emu of British Rail's 25 kV 50 Hz network, with Brush power equipment

---

Budd

The Budd Company
Railway Division

Head office: Red Lion & Verree Roads, Philadelphia, Pennsylvania 19115, USA

Telephone: (215) 673 1020
Telegrams: Lionred
Telex: 710 670 9970

Works: Red Lion Plant, Red Lion & Verree Roads, Philadelphia, Pennsylvania 19115

Chairman: G F Richards
President and Chief Executive: Rene H Vansteenkiste
General Manager, Railway Division: W I Wilson Sr
Marketing Manager, Railway Division: J B Darrah
International Sales Manager, Railway Division: R H Behrend

Export sales: International Activities, Philadelphia, Pennsylvania 19115

Foreign Agent Europe: 9 rue de l'Industrie, 92000 Courbevoie, France

Telephone: 333 58 60
Telex: 842 61061

Products: Stainless-steel passenger coaches and components, fabricated passenger coach bogies and components.

The company has formed a Transit Group to stress its concern for railway and transit products. The Transit Group's head, Rene H Vansteenkiste, is in charge of Budd's Railway Division in Philadelphia, together with Budd interests in Carel Fouché Languepin, a French railcar builder partly owned by Budd, and Universal Mobility, Inc, a Salt Lake City-based manufacturer of people mover systems. Budd is working with UMI to provide a monorail transit system for the Miami Metrozoo. The Transit Group is concentrating on international markets, particularly pursuit of railcar orders in South America, South Korea and the Far East. Emphasis is also being placed on marketing the Lo-Pac 2000 low-profile intermodal freight car, and technical developments such as a steerable bogie and tilt suspension system have been accorded high priority.

Recent orders obtained in the USA include one from Chicago Transit Authority for 300 additional stainless steel rapid transit cars, value approximately $134

Recess in Lo-Pac 2000's well avoids need to retract trailer landing gear after loading

Low-profile loading of TOFC trailers on Lo-Pac 2000 (right) compared with conventional flatcar (extreme left)

million, with delivery expected in 1986, and one from New York MTA for 316 emu cars for Long Island and ex-NYC 700-volt dc third-rail routes. The company has also built a fleet of Amfleet II cars for Amtrak.

The company has made its first move into the freight car manufacturing field with its deep-well, multi-unit articulated Lo-Pac 2000, which can be used to convey either 40-foot containers or road trailers of up to 13.72 metres (45 feet) length. Its most important features, however, are that it achieves low-profile loading, reducing the overhead clearance of a piggyback trailer load by as much as 762 mm, so that loaded trailer or container combinations of up to 4.11 metres height will clear the most restrictive loading gauges on US Class I railroads; and that through improved aerodynamic packing of a loaded train and the Lo-Pac 2000's economical tare weight, energy saving on the rail transit is considerable.

A two-unit, 33.83-metre (111-ft) long articulated Lo-Pac 2000 weighs approximately the same as an orthodox TOFC/COFC 27.13-metre (89-ft) trailer, but weight advantage rises as the number of units in a Lo-Pac 2000 is increased, so that less energy is expended in hauling a six-unit bearing six 45-foot road trailers than in moving five conventional flatcars carrying five trailers. The Lo-Pac 2000 is easily convertible from bogies with 70 tons' total payload capacity to 100 tons for higher load performance; in either case the fully-laden units can negotiate 53.34-metre (175-ft) radius curves. With a fully loaded car, fully worn wheels and solid springs, minimum vertical curvature is 304 metres (1000 ft).

Constitution: In April 1978 Budd became a US-based operation of Thyssen AG of the Federal Republic of Germany.

Burn Standard Co Ltd
A Government of India Enterprise

Head office: 10-C Hungerford Street, Calcutta 700 017, India

Telephone: 44-1067, 1762, 1772, 1788
Telegrams: Burnwagon Calcutta
Telex: 021 2795

Works: Howrah and Burnpur; and Raniganj, Durgapur, Ondal, Gulfarbari, Jabalpur, Niwar and Salem

Chairman and Managing Director: Prasanta Chandra Sen

Products: Railway rolling stock and components; centre buffer couplers and components; points and crossings; crossing sleepers; casting-steel, grey iron, S G iron and alloy steel; forging, stamping and pressing; railway sleepers and fishplates; springs for railway and automotive industry; automatic bottom-door discharge wagons; tramcars.

Constitution: Burn Standard Company Ltd, a Government of India undertaking, is successor to Burn and Co Ltd and The Indian Standard Wagon Co, Ltd. The company came into existence following the nationalisation of the undertakings of the two companies in 1975. The company has two engineering units located at Howrah and Burnpur in West Bengal and seven refractory and ceramic units spread over different parts of the country.

Established in 1874, the Howrah Works was the first manufacturer of rolling stock in India and pioneers in foundry practice and structural steel fabrications of a wide range including bridge construction. The Works have extensive facilities for manufacture of railroad equipment such as crossing sleepers, switches and crossings. The Burnpur Works manufactures prototypes of almost all new types of wagon introduced by the Indian Railways and has guided the Railway Board in design and manufacture of wagons for use in the country and also for export. It specialises in production of springs for coaches, locomotives, wagons and automobiles and for various other uses. The Burnpur Works also deals in heavy die forgings, material handling structurals and equipment for the mining industry.

The company has produced about 163 000 wagon units for Indian Railways and exported more than 1150 wagons.

Cadoux
Établissements Cadoux

7 rue Galilée, 75116 Paris, France

Telephone: 723 61 52
Telex: 610091

Products: Freight wagons. The company's latest products include a bogie container flatcar, of which 100 have been supplied or are on order. Mounted on Type Y25Css bogies, it has a tare weight of 18.5 tonnes and is designed for load capacities of up to 61.5 tonnes; it can traverse a minimum curve radius of 75 metres.

Bulk grain wagon, tare weight 21.2 tonnes, load capacity 95 m³ and 58.8 tonnes

Clinker wagon for Guinea, tare weight 16.8 tonnes, load capacity 27 m³ and 40.2 tonnes

18.5-tonne tare container wagon

Metre-gauge car transporter for RAN

CAF
Construcciones y Auxiliar de Ferrocarriles SA
Member of Servicio de Exportacion de Material Ferroviario

Padilla 17, Madrid 6, Spain

Telephone: 225 11 00
Telegrams: Cafauxiliar, Madrid
Telex: 23197

President: José I Cangas
Chairman: Pedro Ardaiz

General Manager: Juan José Anza

Products: Electric, diesel-electric and diesel-mechanical locomotives; electric and diesel-electric railcars; passenger coaches; rapid transit stock; freight wagons; rolling stock components.

Recent traction products have included, for Spanish National Railways (RENFE), the 6235 hp Class 251 B-B-B electric locomotive and the Class 444 inter-city emu. The Class 251, built under Mitsubishi licence, is a 129-tonne machine with chopper control and monomotor bogies affording alternative gearings for 100 and 160 km/h maximum speeds.

The Stone-Carrier air-conditioned Class 444 emu is designed for normal operation as a three-car unit comprising 1160 kW power car, trailer and driving trailer, with scope for operation of up to 12 cars in multiple (using either three-car or power-plus-trailer two-car sets). Car-body width is 2.95 metres, maximum height 4.2 metres. Primary suspension is coil springs with oil damping,˙ and secondary suspension Sumiride pneumatic. The power car has dynamic braking, the trailers air braking.

Recent rolling stock products include Type T-2 sleeping cars on Minden-Deutz bogies for RENFE operation; and telescopic-hood steel coil, twin-deck auto-carrier and sliding side-wall bogie freight cars for RENFE. The sliding-wall cars have four panels each side, built of aluminium-section frame members and sheet. Length over buffers is 21.7 metres, tare weight approximately 30 tonnes and payload capacity 50 tonnes. Designed for international circulation, the vehicles are mounted on Type Y21Css bogies.

Constitution: The present company, Construcciones y Auxiliar de Ferrocarriles, SA, was formed by the merger of Material Movil y Construcciones, SA (MMC) into Compania Auxiliar de Ferrocarriles, SA (CAF) retaining the initials CAF. It is the largest manufacturer of railway rolling stock in Spain. It was established in 1917 when deliveries started for RENFE.

RENFE Class 251 B-B-B electric locomotive

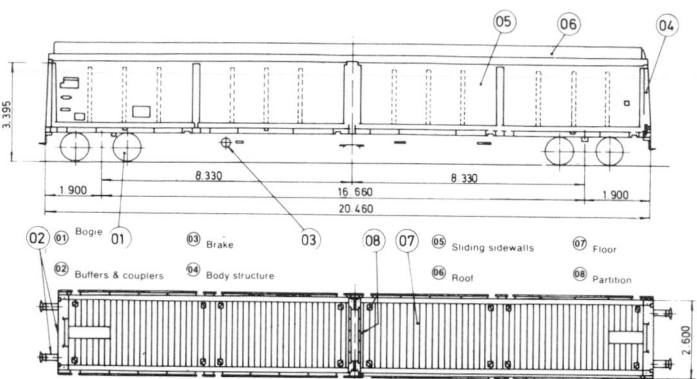
Layout of sliding-wall van

Sliding wall van

RENFE Class 444 emu

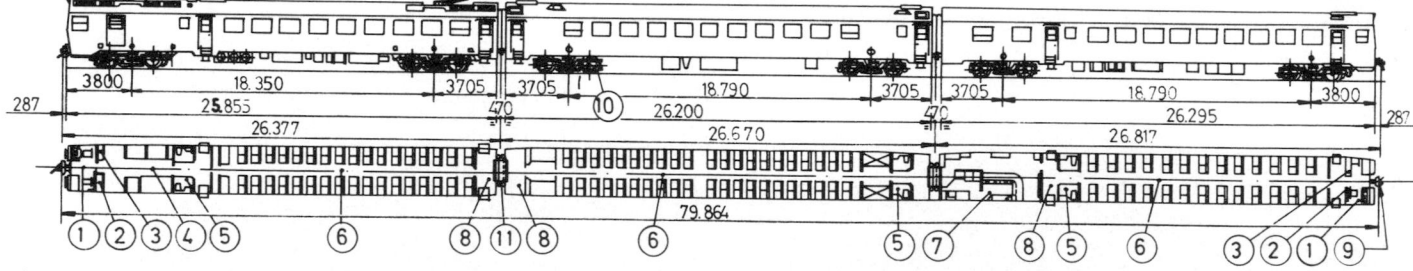
Class 444 emu (**1**) driving cab (**2**) LT cabinet (**3**) HT cabinet (**4**) baggage compartment (**5**) toilet (**6**) passenger compartment (**7**) cafeteria-bar (**8**) access vestibules (**9**) Scharfenberg automatic coupler (**10**) bogie (**11**) intercommunication

---

Cafici
Cafici (International) SA

PO Box 298, 1211 Geneva 11, Switzerland

Telephone: 038 25 62 68

Products: Diesel- and electric-powered double-deck railcars. A demonstration diesel prototype to UIC gauge parameters has been derived from the design built for locomotive push-pull train-set operation in Paris by CIMT and for the Italian State (FS) and Nord Milano (FNM) Railways by CIMT's licensee, Casaralta SpA, and which has also been developed in electric multiple-unit format.

In the diesel-powered car the engine compartment occupies an area of three seating bays' size at one end of the lower saloon. The latter is therefore accessible only from one of the two entrance vestibules, from both of which staircases lead to the upper saloon. Consequently the vestibule adjoining the engine compartment needs only a single-leaf, 900 mm-wide entrance, which in turn makes room for a 13-seat compartment over the bogie at that end; the compartment adjoining the driving cab at the opposite end has only four seats. Total

Cafici bi-level diesel railcar

lower floor seating capacity is 65, mostly in a 3 + 2 arrangement, that on the upper floor 60, mostly in a 2 + 2 layout. Heating-ventilation is assured by two units, each of which serves a central compartment and a side compartment together with associated platforms and driver's cab. The system consists of a blower fan, a recycling flap and a water-air heater exchanger for heating. The air is blown through ducts which run along the bottom of each compartment side. Fresh air is drawn into each unit (through ducts and filters) through a side intake in the driver's cab. During heating, water directed to the water-air exchanger on each unit is supplied by a boiler located in the engine compartment. Heat regulation is automatic. An auxiliary air-cooling device may be installed in the platform ceilings for more intensive cooling of the upper deck in summer. Lighting is fluorescent, with fittings recessed in the underside of the aircraft locker-like luggage racks.

The prototype is fitted with a standard Fiat IVECO 828 SRI 8-V 90-degree four-stroke, turbocharged engine with a 316 kW rating at 2200 rpm, driving through a five-speed synchromesh gearbox with a fluid clutch and via cardan shafts to both axles on one bogie; the inboard axle includes reverse in its gearing. A bigger 525 kW engine can be used and electric transmission is also an option. The vehicle is proposed for multiple-unit as well as single car operation, in a three-car format with two power cars enclosing a trailer, or in a four-car format with two inner trailers, hence the offer of higher power, for which the compartment has adequate space. The configuration of the engine enables it to be lowered through a floor well for overhaul.

The Fiat bogie serves for both powered and trailing axles, and is fitted with two-stage vertical and one-stage horizontal suspension. Primary suspension is through four variable rate springs which rest on the axleboxes with rigid stops to limit vertical movement. The secondary suspension is equipped with two air springs, each containing a rubber spring acting as vertical bumper block that permits vehicle travel in case of compressed air failure. Transverse suspension is assured by the secondary suspension springs, together with auxiliary cushioned check blocks. Suspension components are completed by hydraulic dampers and an anti-roll bar. Body-bogie connection is by means of rubber springs interposed between a bolted pivot on the load cross-member and the central bogie frame cross-member. Bogies are equipped with shoe brakes acting on tyres and also disc brakes.

For electric traction each power car can be arranged for a continuous output of 1200-1400 kW, at a tare weight of 62 tonnes. Its seating capacity is 120, that of a

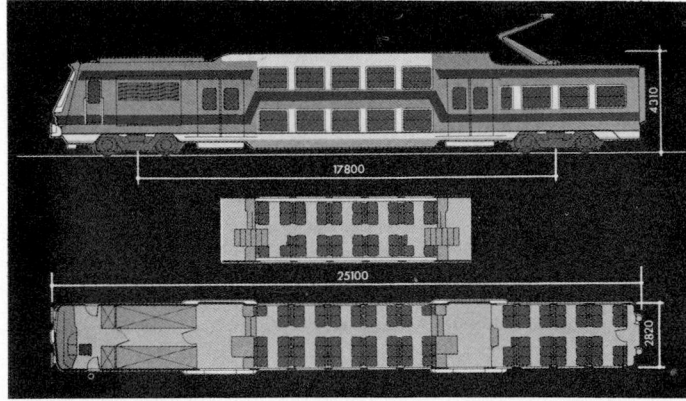

Bi-level emu power car

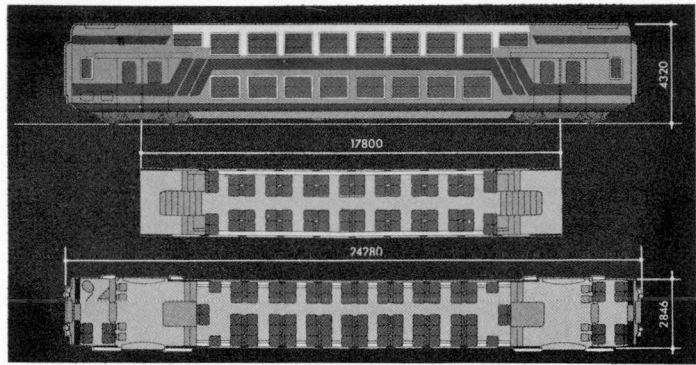

Bi-level emu intermediate trailer

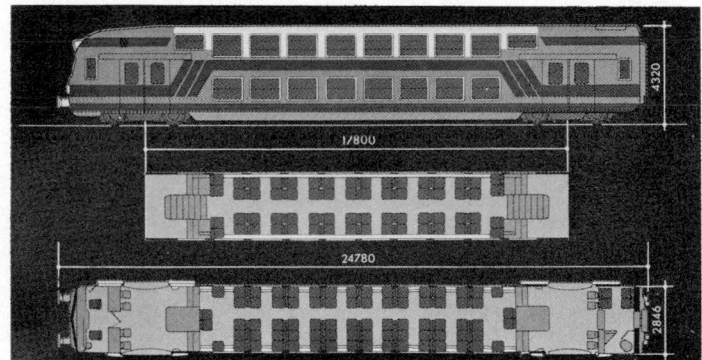

Bi-level emu driving trailer

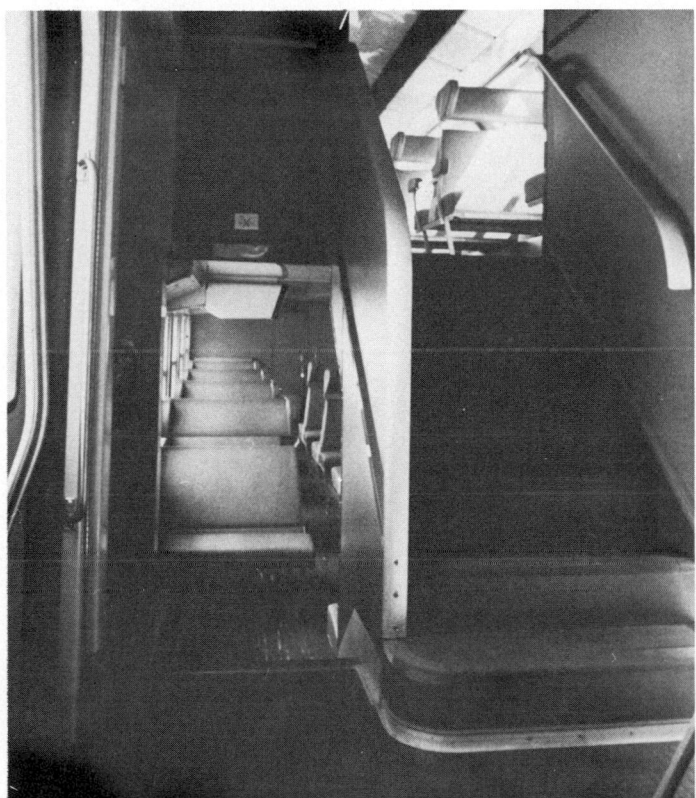

Vestibule of bi-level diesel railcar

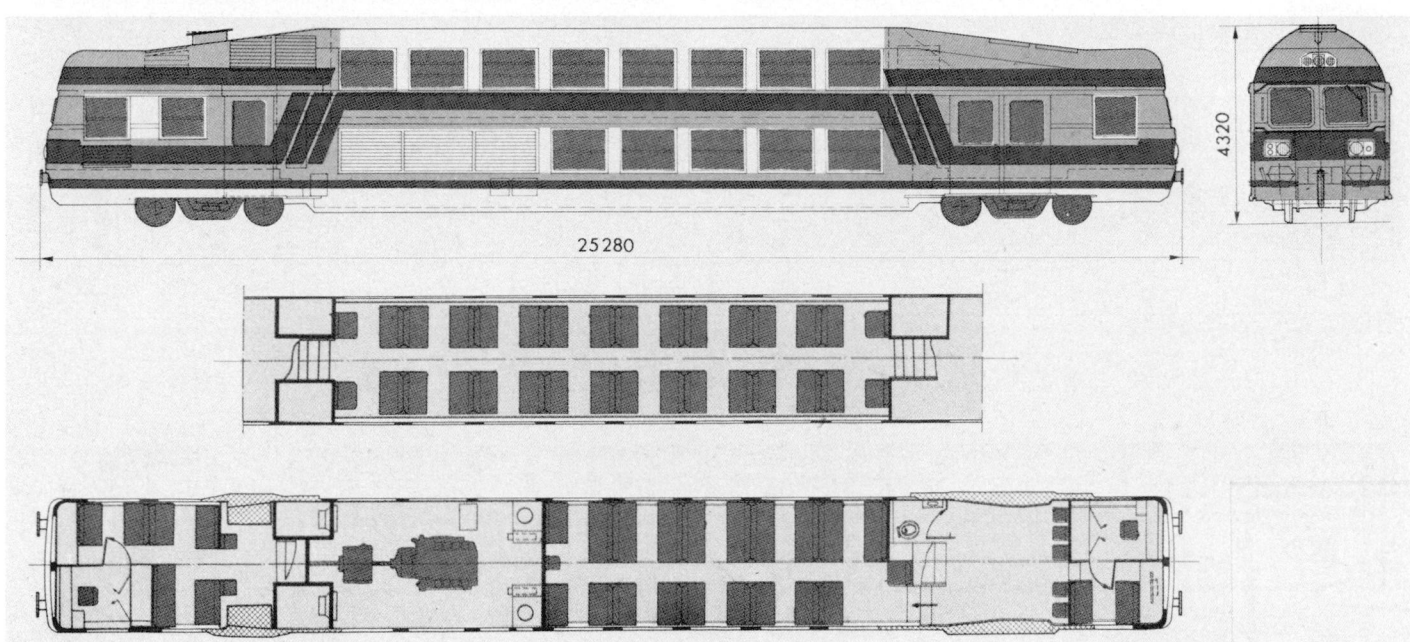

Bi-level diesel railcar layout

42 tonnes-tare intermediate trailer 150, and of a 43 tonnes-tare driving trailer 142. Maximum speed of a double-deck emu is 140 km/h.

Constitution: The consortium is a partnership of CIMT-Lorraine SA of Paris, Casaralta SpA of Bologna, Italy, and Fiat Ferroviaria Savigliano of Turin, Italy, formed principally to market diesel-powered double-deck railcars based on the design of the double-deck passenger vehicles now widely used by French Railways (SNCF).

Upper deck of bi-level diesel railcar

Cafici diesel railcars

Cars per unit	Motor cars per unit	Motored axles per motor car	Transmission	Rated power (kW) per motor	Max speed km/h	Weight tonnes per car (M-motor T-trailer)	Total seating capacity	Length per car mm (M-motor T-trailer)	No in service	Year first built	Builders		
											Mechanical parts	Engine & type	Transmission
1	1	2	Mechanical	316	115	M 55	133	M 25 280	1	1982	CIMT-Fiat Casaralta	Fiat-IVECO	Fiat
3	1	2	Mechanical	316	115	M 55 T 42	283	M 25 280 T 24 280	1	1982	CIMT-Fiat Casaralta	Fiat-IVECO	Fiat
4	2	2	Mechanical	316	115	M 55 T 42	576	M 25 280 T 24 280	1	1982	CIMT-Fiat Casaralta	Fiat-IVECO	Fiat

Callegari
José Callegari E Hijos

Rivadavia y Peru, Zarate, Prov Buenos Aires, Argentina

Telephone: 2800 3228

President: Pablo A A Callegari
Director General: Clara Mandelli Vda de Callegari
Sales and Export Director: Eduardo Rivas

Products: Freight wagons.

Canton Motive Power
Canton Motive Power Machinery Works

Canton, Kwangtung, People's Republic of China

Products: Steam locomotives.

Carel Fouché
Carel Fouché SA

Head office: BP 86, 27940 Aubevoye, France

Telephone: 16 (32) 530840
Telegrams: Caremo, Gaillon
Telex: 180665

Works: BP 86, 27940 Aubevoye
2 rue du Miroir, 72006 Le Mans Cedex

Sales organisation: Francorail-MTE
33 quai du Dion Bouton, 92814 Puteaux Cedex

President: R Juchs
Commercial Manager: M Jennequin

Products: Railway passenger cars of stainless steel and conventional design.
As well as supplying stainless steel rolling stock to French National Railways, Carel Fouché is now manufacturing railcars for Saudi Arabia (SGRO), Egyptian National Railways, Venezuela (IAAFE) and Brazil. Recently, Francorail signed a contract for the supply of 225 stainless steel metro motor coaches for New York City Transit Authority; Carel Fouché is the carbody builder concerned.

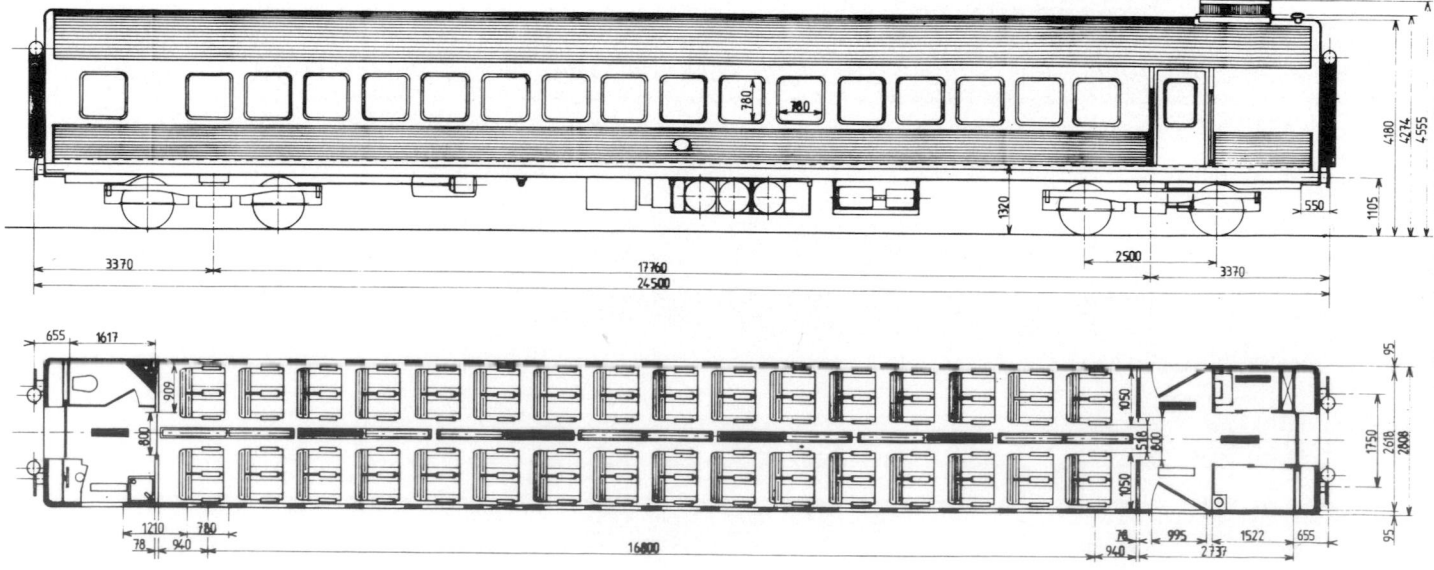

Layout of air-conditioned second-class car for Egyptian National Railways on Minden 6/82 bogies, weight 39 tonnes

Constitution: Created in 1968 through the merger of Carel-Fouché et cie (established 1875) and la Soudre Electrique Languepin (established 1912), the company owns two factories, in Aubevoye (staffed by 700) and Le Mans (staffed by 500), and produces passenger vehicles in stainless steel. By the end of 1982 a total of 5800 passenger coaches (4100 with stainless steel bodies) had been produced.

In August 1973, together with the companies Creusot-Loire, De Dietrich, Jeumont-Schneider and MTE, Carel Fouché created a *Groupement d'Intérêt Economique* under the name of Francorail-MTE, chiefly to promote export sales.

First class air-conditioned car for Egyptian National Railways

Casaralta
Officine di Casaralta SpA

Via Ferrarese 205, 40128 Bologna, Italy

Telephone: 35 84 54
Telegrams: Rotabili, Bologna
Telex: 511068

President: Aldo Farina
Chairman: Giorgio Regazzoni
General Manager: Carlo Farina

Products: Electric locomotives and railcars; single- and double-deck passenger coaches; freight wagons.

In the latest development of double-deck commuter rolling stock the company, in conjunction with Fiat Ferroviaria Savigliano of Turin and CIMT-Lorraine of Paris, has completed a prototype bi-level electric power car.

Bi-level driving trailer for Italian State Railways (FS)

CAT
Compañia Auxiliar de Transportes SA

Avenida José Antonio 20, Apartado 358, Madrid 14, Spain

Telephone: 2 22 0414
Telegrams: Autrans, Madrid

Works: Carretera du Andalucia, Villaverde

Telephone: 797 91 00

President: D Miguel Igartua Losa
Sales Director: D José Ma Oteiza

Products: Freight wagons.

Cattaneo
Ferriere Cattaneo SA

6512 Giubiasco, Switzerland

Telephone: 092 27 31 31/32/33/34
Telegrams: Ferrum
Telex: 79392

Managing Directors: Aleardo Cattaneo
　　　　　　　　　　Serenella Graf-Cattaneo

Products: Freight wagons, carbon and alloy steel die forgings.

Constitution: Established 1870.

Cement-carrying wagon by Cattaneo; length 13.2 m, tare 24.5 tonnes, load capacity 56 tonnes

Cegielski
Cegielski Locomotive and Wagon Works
Zaklady Przemyslu Metalowego H Cegielski

ul Dzierzynskiego 223/229, 61-485 Poznan, Poland

Telephone: 212 31
Telex: 0415343

Export sales: Kolmex, 49 Mokotowska, 00-542 Warsaw

Products: Diesel locomotives of 1700 hp and above, passenger coaches (including couchette cars and bar coaches) for 1435 mm gauge, passenger coaches for 1520 mm gauge, diesel railcars.

Constitution: Cegielski is the largest rolling stock works in Poland, building 300 to 400 passenger coaches annually for export alone.

CEM
CEM-Cie Electro-Mécanique

37 rue du Rocher, 75383 Paris (Cedex 08), France

Telephone: (01) 522 9840
Telegrams: Electranic Paris
Telex: 650 398; 290 381

(For further details see CIMT-Lorraine and TCO.)

CFD
Compagnie de Chemins de Fer Départementaux

Head office: 10 avenue Friedland, 75008 Paris, France

Telephone: 561 97 34
Telex: 660 955

Main works: 51210 Montmirail

President: F de Coincy
General Manager: P Grau
Sales Manager: J L Quillet
Service Manager: A Lapiczak

Two Type 2300 metre-gauge railcars operating as multiple-unit in Portugal

Products: Diesel-electric and diesel-hydraulic railcars and locomotives for all track gauges; industrial and mining locomotives; and bogies.
  Among the company's recent deliveries have been four diesel-hydraulic 550 hp vehicles specially created for catenary maintenance on French National Railways' (SNCF's) 260 km/h Paris-Lyons LGV. Weighing 40 tonnes, with a top speed of 90 km/h and 40 km/h capability on a 40 per cent gradient, each vehicle is mounted on air-suspension bogies and has an underfloor Poyaud 6C520 340 hp, 2500 rpm engine and CFD Power Shift automatic transmission. Controlled slow running between 0 and 10 km/h is possible . Each vehicle has three driving positions and its equipment includes a Sietam work platform.
  Other products have included two 425 hp diesel-hydraulic railcars for Corsican Railways, industrial diesel-hydraulic shunters and bogies for Speno International.

1500 hp Type BB 1500 diesel-hydraulic locomotive

CFMF
Compagnie Française de Matériel Ferroviaire

40 boulevard Henri-Sellier, 92150 Suresnes, France

Telephone: 506 15 74
Telegrams: Fauvgir
Telex: 611 486

President: Jacques Dambrine
Assistant General Managers: Jacques Martin
                                Georges Reille
Commercial Director: Joachim Lagall

Products: Freight wagons; tank wagons.

CFMF tank wagon

Changchow Diesel Locomotive Factory

Changchow, Jiangsu, People's Republic of China

Telegrams: Equipex, Peking

Products: Diesel-hydraulic locomotives ranging from 60 to 500 hp including type NY380 built for forestry, mine, industrial and shunting operations. Available in all gauges and rated at 380 hp, it weighs from 24 to 40 tonnes

NY380 version for 1435 mm gauge operations

Changchun Locomotive Works

Changchun, Jilin, People's Republic of China

Products: Steam locomotives.

Changchun Passenger Car Works

Changchun, Jilin, People's Republic of China

Products: Lightweight passenger coaches for high-speed (160 km/h) operations, sleeping cars, metro railcars.
  Recent products have included 23.6-metre all-steel second-class sleeping and day cars. The sleeping cars are divided into eight four-berth compartments and have a tare weight of 43.5 tonnes; the day cars seat 118 and have a tare weight of 43 tonnes. An all-steel two-car metro railcar, operating by third-rail collection at 750 volts dc, mounted on air-sprung bogies, has a tare weight of 34 tonnes. Four traction motors, each with a 76 kW hourly rating, give a 0.9 m/s acceleration rate to a top speed of 80 km/h.

Two-car metro unit

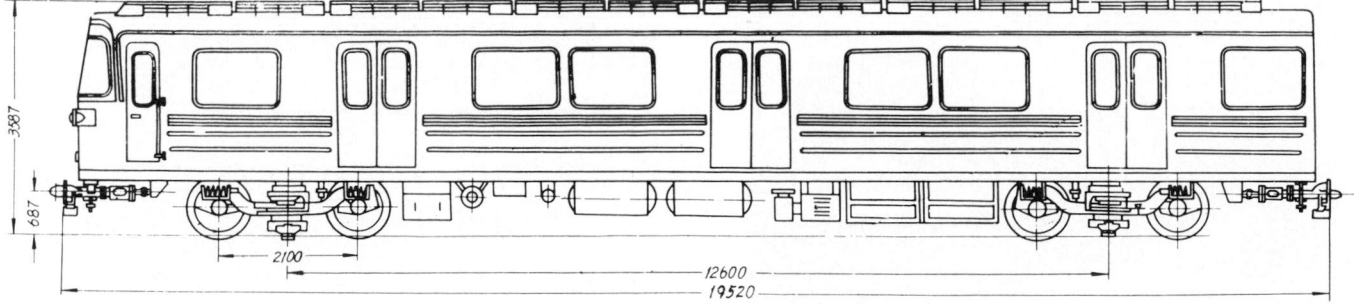

Metro railcar general arrangement

Chiangan Rolling Stock
Chiangan Rolling Stock Plant

Chiangan, Wuhan, Hubei, People's Republic of China

Products: Freight wagons and passenger coaches.

China National Railway Locomotive and Rolling Stock Industry Corporation

10 Fu Xing Road, Beijing, People's Republic of China

Telephone: 86 45245; 86 42685
Telegrams: Machimpex, Beijing
Telex: 22328

Products: Diesel-electric and diesel-hydraulic locomotives with various ratings; electric locomotives; steam locomotives; box cars, gondola, flat cars, various

kinds of special freight cars; passenger coaches; subway electric railcars; rail travelling cranes; various types of medium and high-speed diesel engines with different ratings (Models 16 240ZB, 12 240Z, 8 240Z, 12 180ZL, 16 200Z, 6L 207E); a variety of component parts, such as roller bearings, turbochargers, governors, pistons, piston rings, fuel injectors, air compressors, water pumps, springs of all sizes; coupler and buffer gear; brake equipments; traction alternator and motor sets; electric control systems; instruments; silicon rectifiers for diesel and electric locomotives; forklift trucks; storage battery cars; refrigerating equipment; and castings and forgings of all sizes.

Constitution: The Corporation handles the affairs of China's 33 railway supply plants and four scientific research departments.

Chishuyen Rolling Stock
Chishuyen Rolling Stock Plant

Changchou, Jiangsu, People's Republic of China

Products: Diesel-electric and diesel-hydraulic locomotives.

Cimmco International

ECE House, 28A Kasturba Gandhi Marg, New Delhi 110 001, India

Telephone: 44381
Telegrams: Cimwag, New Delhi
Telex: 031-3618

Central India Machinery Manufacturing Co Ltd

Head office: Birla Nagar (Gwalior)

Main works: (Wagon & Structural Division), Bharatpur (Rajasthan)

Chairman: D P Mandelia
President, Cimmco International: D K Goyal

Products: Design and manufacture of freight vehicles including special-purpose wagons; wagon components and spares. The company has pioneered the Indian development of bottom-door discharge hopper wagons for the transport of coal in connection with the country's Super Thermal Power projects; these vehicles have been built under licence from Ortner Freight Car Co and are similar to the US company's well-known 'Rapid Discharge' wagons. The company has also devised lineside apparatus to trigger the opening and closing of the hopper doors, thus permitting automatic discharge to any pre-programmed sequence.
Recent production has featured: for Indian Railways, 600 bogie vans, 700 bogie open wagons, 730 four-wheel tank wagons and 410 bogie brake-vans; for National Thermal Power Corporation Ltd, New Delhi, 120 bottom-door coal hoppers; for UP State Electricity Board, Lucknow, 22 bottom-door coal hoppers; for MP State Electricity Board, Jabalpur, 50 bogie coal hoppers; for Viet-Nam Railways, 125 bogie vans and 40 coal hoppers; for Nigerian Railway Corporation, 50 bogie vans; and for Bangladesh Railway Board, 50 bogie vans.

Fertiliser wagon with stainless steel lining for Bangladesh Railway Board

Bottom-door coal hopper for National Thermal Power Corporation Ltd

CIMT-Lorraine
Compagnie Industrielle de Matériel de Transport

42 avenue Raymond Poincaré, 75116 Paris, France

Telephone: 505 14 00
Telex: 610 119

President: Franck Vaingnedroye
Director General: Francis Horvilleur
Commercial Manager: Paul Dagan

Products: Diesel-electric and electric train-sets; passenger coaches; freight wagons.
Since 1973 the company has built more than 800 double-deck cars of different internal configurations for the inner and outer suburban Paris services of French National Railways (SNCF); its Italian licensee Casaralta SpA has undertaken production of 324 cars of the same pattern for Italian State Railways (FS) and the Nord Milano Railway (FNM). In late 1982 CIMT-Lorraine began delivery of the first pre-series models of an SNCF emu version, Class Z5600; the full order comprises 132 power cars and 132 trailers, and ANF-Industrie, TCO and Jeumont-Schneider are co-operating with CIMT-Lorraine in the production. The power cars, all of 1.5 kV dc, each have a 1400 kW rating, weigh 67 tonnes and seat

Caracas Metro air-conditioned cars

Mass transit cars for Marseilles Metro

Mexico City Metro train-set

Interior of VAL Lille train-set

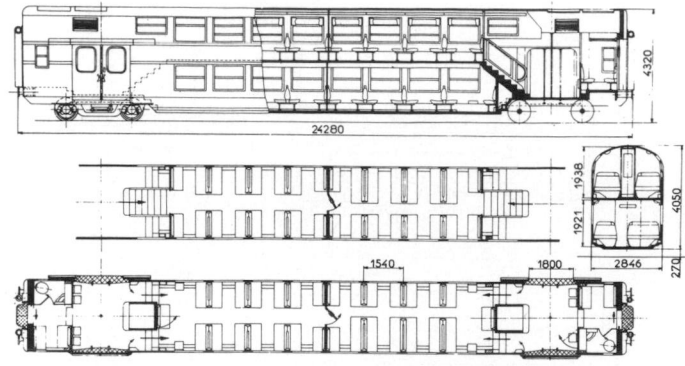

Layout of double-deck Type ABe first/second-class trailer

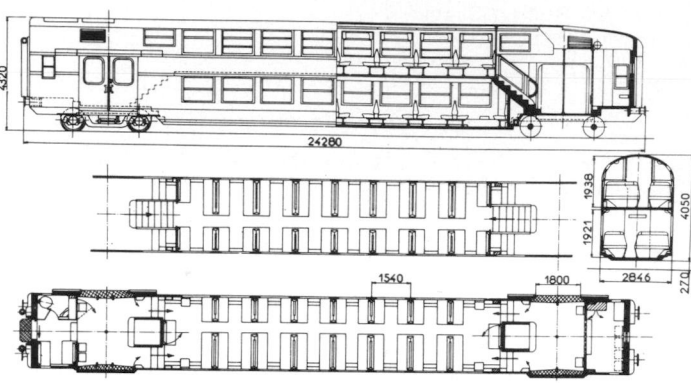

Layout of double-deck Type BDe second-class car with baggage compartment

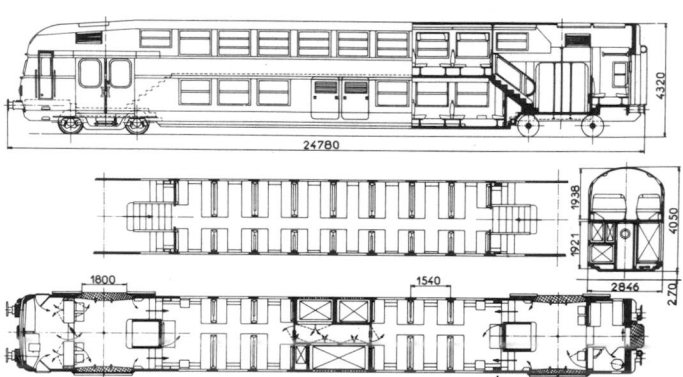

Layout of double-deck Type Bxe second-class driving trailer

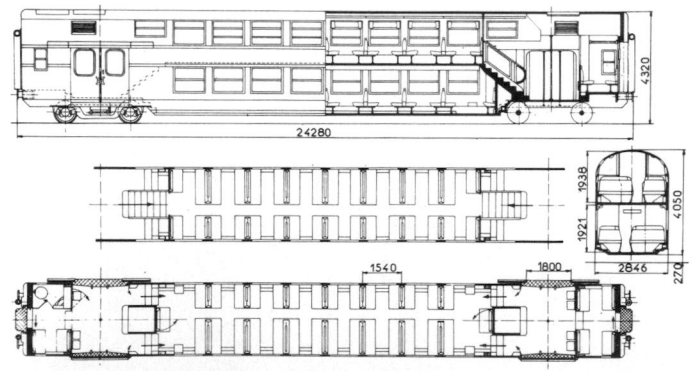

Layout of double-deck Type Be second-class trailer

Driving cab of Type Bxe double-deck driving trailer

118; a set of two motor cars and two trailers has a seating capacity of 550. During 1983 16 units of two power cars and three trailers each were to be introduced into Paris-Melun service, followed in 1984 by 50 sets of two power cars and two trailers apiece for Paris RER Line C. Also to appear in 1984 is a dual-voltage 1.5 kV dc/25 kV ac version (Class Z8800); it is expected that 50 four-car sets will be ordered for 1985-87 delivery for Paris RER Line D, between Orry and Châtelet.

CIMT, Casaralta SpA and Fiat Ferroviaria Savigliano have formed the Cafici partnership to promote a diesel railcar version of the double-deck design.

Recent metro contracts have included:

VAL rapid transit system, Lille: Joint venture with TCO and Matra, electrical equipment supplied by TCO, vehicle built by CIMT. Completely automated operation by two-car units with normal passenger load of 150 at a minimum headway of one minute;

Mexico City Metro: Initial order of 247 cars jointly with Alsthom. Additional 225 under construction, also with Alsthom;

Caracas Metro: 140 cars, all motored with air-conditioned aluminium bodies, in collaboration with Alsthom, for first Propatria-Chacaico line, opening 1983; 102 for extension to Palo Verde, opening 1984; 136 for second line from Las Adjuntas to Silencio;

Marseilles: 66 power cars and 15 trailers.

SNCF non-powered double-deck cars

	Bxe	Be	ABe	BDe
Length overall between coupler faces (mm)	24 780	24 280	24 280	24 280
Width overall (mm)	2846	2846	2846	2846
Height (m)	4.32	4.32	4.32	4.32
Centre to centre of bogies (mm)	17 800	17 800	17 800	17 800
Y 30 P bogie wheelbase (mm)	2400	2400	2400	2400
Wheel diameter (mm)	840	840	840	840
Height of floors above rail,				
lower level (mm)	365	365	365	365
upper level (mm)	2342	2342	2342	2342
door threshold (mm)	970	970	970	970
Height under ceiling,				
lower compartment (mm)	1921	1921	1921	1921
upper compartment (mm)	1938	1938	1938	1938
Door type and width		sliding 1.8 m		
Seats	134	164	74 + 70	156
Folding seats	11	11	11	9
Seated (5 passengers/m²) and standees	257	296	268	283
Tare weight (tonnes)	47.5	41	42	40.5

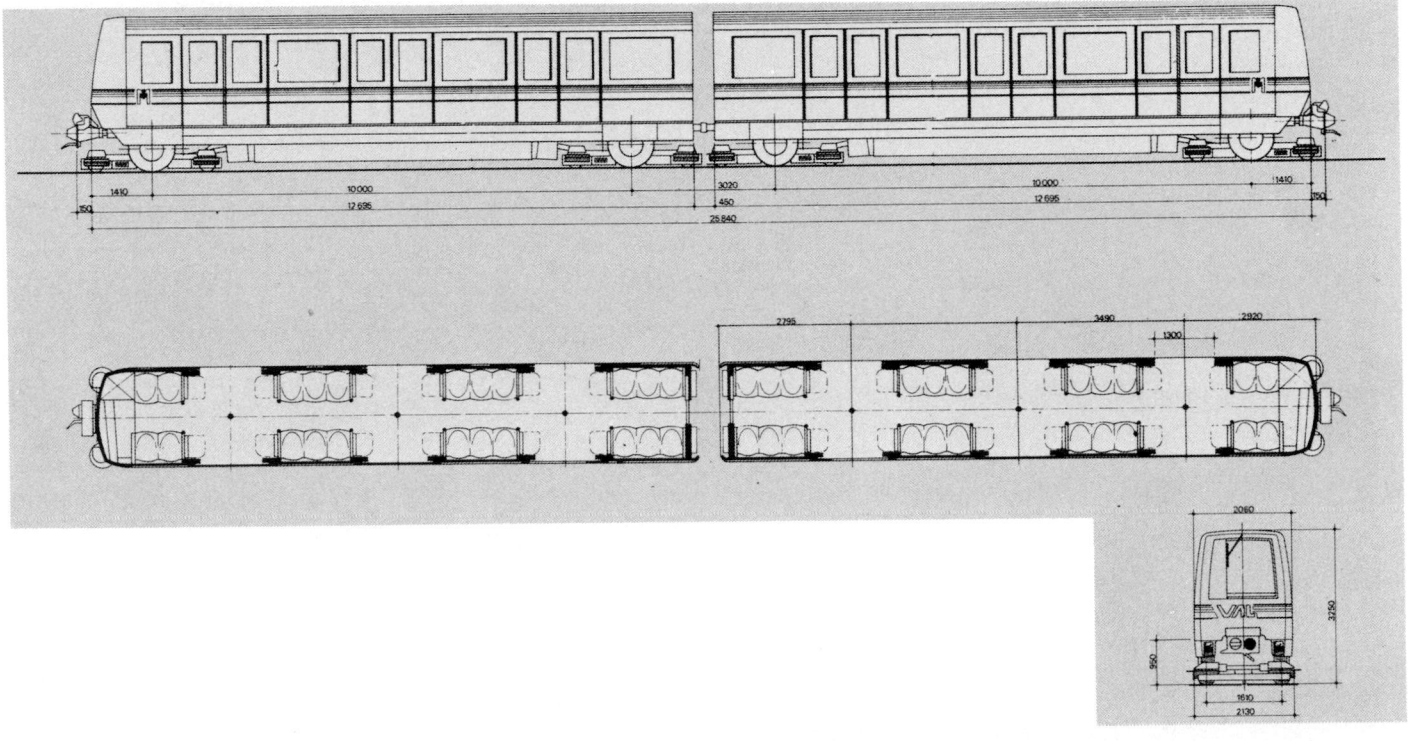

VAL two-car 750 V dc rubber-tyred set, with four 140 kW motors, total capacity 68 seats and standing room for 56

CKD
CKD Praha
Member of Czechoslovakia's Pragoinvest diesel locomotive exporting group

Head office: U Kolbenky 159, Prague 9, Czechoslovakia

Telephone: 83 13 54
Telegrams: CKD, Prague
Telex: 01 1160; 01 1229

Export sales: Pragoinvest, Ceskomoravská 23, 18 056 Prague 9, Czechoslovakia

Products: Diesel-electric locomotives; diesel engines.

Clayton Equipment
NEI Mining Equipment Ltd

Hatton, Derby DE6 5EB, England

Telephone: 0283 812382
Telegrams: Clayquip, Derby
Telex: 341828

Director: R A Boast

Products: Battery, trolley and diesel locomotives with electric, hydraulic or mechanical transmissions; electric and battery driven industrial and mining locomotives; special-purpose internal combustion engine or electric powered rail vehicles, including flameproof machines for coal-mine use.

Constitution: Clayton Equipment, now part of NEI Mining Equipment Ltd, was incorporated in 1931 by S R Devlin to carry on the manufacture of locomotives, rail cars, transfer cars and general engineering products.

CLW
Chittaranjan Locomotive Works

Chittaranjan, Burdwan District, West Bengal, India

Telephone: Asansol 2021/2022/2023
Telegrams: Locoworks

General Manager: K S Ramaswamy

Products: Electric locomotives; diesel shunters; narrow-gauge diesel locomotives.

Typical recent products for Indian Railways have included:
Class WAM-4 mixed traffic electric locomotive: Co-Co; 3640 hp; axleload 18.8 tonnes; voltage supply 25 kV; weight 112.8 tonnes; rheostatic braking; max service speed 120 km/h;

Class WAM-4 mixed traffic electric locomotive

Class WCG-2 dc freight locomotive: Co-Co; 4200 hp; axleload 22 tonnes; voltage supply 1.5 kV dc; weight 132 tonnes; max speed 120 km/h; rheostatic braking.

Constitution: This motive power plant, a production unit of Indian Railways, started production in January 1950.

Class WCG-2 dc freight locomotive

Clyde
The Clyde Engineering Company Pty Ltd

Head office: PO Box 73, Factory Street, Granville, New South Wales 2142, Australia

Telephone: 682 2111
Telegrams: Cydeengco, Sydney
Telex: 21647

Branches (workshops): Sydney Road, Bathurst, New South Wales. Neptune Terrace, Rosewater, South Australia. Links Avenue, Eagle Farm, Queensland

Chairman: J E Thomson
Sales Manager: Kevin C Thomson

Products: Diesel-electric and diesel-hydraulic locomotives; rapid transit stock.

Constitution: In 1948, by arrangement with General Motors Corporation, the company started to build diesel-electric locomotives to GM design incorporating Electromotive power equipment.

CMI
Cockerill Mechanical Industries

Head office: quai Greiner 1, 4100 Seraing, Belgium

Telephone: 3241 36 60 00
Telex: 41225

Works: CMI, Dept Locomotives et Moteurs Marins, 4100 Seraing

Products: Shunting locomotives of 200 to 2000 hp, on two, three or four axles, for all gauges and types of track. Recent orders have come chiefly from Belgium, Argentina (130 locomotives), Republic of Korea, Zaïre, Peru, France, Angola, Portugal, Algeria, Luxembourg and Taiwan. In 1982 the company's shunter design was completely re-appraised from both technological and ergonomic standpoints. The company has also developed a range of 300 to 600 kW electric locomotives, powered either by a main supply conductor or by batteries affording at least two hours' operation without recharging; these locomotives are conceived especially for underground applications where avoidance of pollution is critical. The company is also pursuing high-security remote radio control of shunting locomotives in a system adaptable to all types of locomotive.

Constitution: The present company is the product of a 1981 merger of SA Cockerill and SA Hainaut-Sambre. Cockerill-Sambre employs more than 40 000 people and has 150 subsidiaries around the world. The present company, CMI-Cockerill Mechanical Industries, is the former Division Construction Mécanique of Cockerill Sambre, which became an independent subsidiary in December 1982. CMI employs more than 2000 people, and specialises in products for heavy industry including locomotives. It has produced thousands of locomotives of all types and power for both main-line and shunting work and is a leading manufacturer of diesel-hydraulic shunting locomotives.

New CMI 450 hp, 40-tonne 0-4-0 shunter with remote radio control

670 hp 040A-040A traction unit for Minero Peru

Standard three-axle diesel-hydraulic shunter, available with 300-750 bhp ratings and 17-25 tonne axleloads

One of 130 040 diesel-hydraulic shunters supplied to FA of Argentina; available in various gauges, 225-500 bhp outputs and 12-25-tonne axleloads

CNCFSA
Constructora Nacional de Carros de Ferrocarril SA

San Lorenzo 925 5° Piso, Col de Valle, Mexico 12, DF, Mexico

Telephone: 30700
Telegrams: Concarril, Mexico City

Director-General: Enrique Ollivier Guibaudet
Subdirector, Sales: César Mota Aguilar
Subdirector, Marketing: Sergio Camargo Piñuela

Works: Cd Sahagún, Hidalgo

Telephone: 585 05 42

Products: Box cars of 70- or 100-ton capacity, outside post, nailable steel floor; covered hopper cars of 70- or 100-ton capacity, without centre sill, with centre discharges, all steel, welded with outside post or open top hopper; open top gondola cars with fixed ends solid bottom floor, 70- or 100-ton capacity for general service; 70-ton airside dump cars; bulk commodity gondolas of 100-ton capacity; tank cars to carry 20 000 gallons of non-hazardous materials; flat cars of 70-ton capacity for general service equipped with hydraulic and pneumatic absorption device; flat cars (piggyback) equipped to carry trailer-bodies or containers; top cupola cabooses equipped with oil heaters, toilets, water tanks and standard features; lightweight subway cars for 162/165 passengers with fully automatic controls; and passenger cars equipped with fabricated bogies and all-steel body for 68 persons.

Cobrasma Sumaré SA
Subsidiary of Cobrasma SA

Head office: Rua da Estacão 523, Osasco, São Paulo, Brazil

Telephone: (011) 801 8000
Telex: (011) 33330

Works: Km 104 Via Anhanguera, Sitio São João, Distrito de Hortolândia, Sumaré, São Paulo

Telephone: (0192) 65 1711
Telex: (019) 1926

President: Luis Eulalio de Bueno Vidigal
Vice-Presidents: Marcos V Xavier da Silveira
　　　　　　　　Luis Eulalio de Bueno Vidigal Filho
Managing Director: Eduardo Luiz Pinto e Silva
Directors: Mário Melo Torres
　　　　　　Paulo Darcy Cantuária de Araujo
Assistant Directors: Rubens Cerdá Soares
　　　　　　　　　Sylvio Giordano
　　　　　　　　　Antonio Augusto de Azevedo Antunes

Products: Freight wagons; passenger coaches; metro cars; LRVs.
The company has lately delivered 16 emus to Ferrovia Paulista SA (FEPASA) for the São Paulo suburban system and a further 14 to Brazilian Federal Railways (RFFSA) for the Rio de Janeiro suburban network, together with the first of the light rail vehicles ordered by Companhia do Metropolitano do Rio de Janeiro.
Recent products include a covered, gravity-discharge hopper for 1600 mm gauge with a load capacity of 72 tonnes or 103 metres^3 of citric pellets or bulk grain. The three hoppers in the vehicle have a 45-degree slope and the hatch covers are continuous. Internal length is 16.85 metres, internal width 3.06 metres and height 4.64 metres.

Constitution: Founded in 1944, the company has the capacity to produce 3000 freight wagons and 300 passenger coaches, emus, metro and pre-metro cars annually.

LRV for Companhia do Metropolitano do Rio de Janeiro

Prototype bulk covered hopper car with 72-tonne payload capacity

Comeng
Comeng Holdings Ltd

41 Berry Street, Granville, New South Wales 2142, Australia

Telephone: 02 682 3677
Telegrams: Comhold, Sydney
Telex: 24572

Chairman: D A Pratten
Managing Director: K P McInerney
Executive Director: I Silink

Products: Electric, diesel-electric, diesel-hydraulic locomotives; railcars; passenger coaches, light rail vehicles, trains; freight wagons; containers; Miner draftgear; track equipment.
Prominent among the company's recent products is the InterCity XPT for New South Wales State Rail Authority (NSW-SRA), which Commonwealth Engineering (NSW) Pty Ltd designed in conjunction with British Rail under a technical licence agreement. The order, valued at A$68 million, was for four train-sets each comprising two power cars and five trailers, plus two spare power cars. The power car, incorporating a Paxman Valenta engine rated at 1492 kW to suit Australian climatic and operating conditions, is a redesign of BR's High Speed Train vehicle that is 2.5 tonnes lighter; changes include a driving cab fashioned in moulded laminate fibreglass. The traction equipment is geared for a high tractive effort to allow for the NSW system's steep gradients; hence maximum speed is limited to 160 km/h. The 24.2-metre long trailers are a new design. Constructed in stainless steel, they employ a standard bodyshell formed of two-metre modules to obtain variations of interior accommodation. On preliminary trials the first power car was run up to 183 km/h on NSW Southern Line track.
In 1982 the Inter City XPT equipment was introduced on services from Sydney to Kempsey (504 km), Albury (654 km) and Orange (321 km). Their schedules on these routes were respectively, with former best times between the same points in brackets: 6 hours 42 minutes (8 hours 28 minutes); 7 hours 25 minutes (9 hours 3 minutes); and 4 hours 44 minutes (5 hours 7 minutes).
Also for NSW-SRA, Commonwealth Engineering (NSW) Pty Ltd is constructing a further 50 1.5 kV dc 2700 kW electric locomotives. Similar to the ten Class 85 locomotives already supplied, the new units are designated Class 86.
Under an initial contract, six of Hamersley Iron's 3900 hp Comeng Alco diesel-electric locomotives have been remanufactured. This has entailed substantial redesign, a conspicuous product of which is a spacious new cab spe-

NSW-SRA Class 86 1.5 kV dc 2700 kW electric locomotive

cially treated to reduce interior noise. Further remanufacturing orders are anticipated.
Passenger vehicle orders have included 10 long-distance day and 10 roomette sleeping cars for Queensland Government Railways, constructed by Commonwealth Engineering (Qld) Pty Ltd. Commonwealth Engineering (Vic) Pty Ltd has produced 200 emu power cars and 100 emu trailers for VicRail.

Constitution: Comeng Holdings Ltd and its subsidiary companies comprise the largest rolling stock manufacturing group in the southern hemisphere with manufacturing plants in all Australian States, including: Commonwealth Engineering (NSW) Pty Ltd; Commonwealth Engineering (Queensland) Pty Ltd; Commonwealth Engineering (Victoria) Pty Ltd; Comeng Western Australia; Comeng Aresco Pty Ltd, South Australia; Mittagong Engineering Pty Ltd (New South Wales).

Melbourne Class Z3 tramcar supplied by Commonwealth Engineering (Vic) Pty Ltd

Three-car emu of VicRail

NSW-SRA Class 85 1.5 kV dc 2700 kW electric locomotives

NSW-SRA InterCity XPT power car

Interior of Queensland long-distance day coach

Long-distance day coach for Queensland Government Railways

Comeng electric locomotives

Class	Wheel arrangement	Line voltage	Rated output (kW) continuous/ one-hour	Max speed km/h	Weight tonnes	No in service	Year first built	Builders	
								Mechanical parts	Electrical equipment
85	Co-Co	1.5 kV dc	2700/3050	130	122	10	1979	Comeng	Mitsubishi
86	Co-Co	1.5 kV dc	2700/3050	130	116	50 on order; deliveries started 1983	1983	Comeng	Mitsubishi

Cometal
Cometal-Mometal SARL

PO Box 1041, Maputo, Mozambique

Telephone: 752124/5/6/7/8
Telegrams: Cometal, Maputo
Telex: 6-267

Products: Freight wagons; inspection cars.

Cometarsa
Cometarsa SAIC

LN Alem 1067, Piso 25, 1001 Buenos Aires, Argentina

Telephone: 31 6277
Telegrams: Cometarsa, Baires

Works: Campana, Prov Buenos Aires

Products: Diesel-electric, diesel-hydraulic locomotives; freight wagons.

Costamasnaga
Costamasnaga SpA

Viale 4 Novembre, Costamasnaga (Como), Italy

Telephone: 031 855 192
Telegrams: Costamasnagaspa
Telex: 380184

Chairman: Claudio Marina
Director General: Gino Giuliani
Sales Director: Ida Magni

Products: Freight wagons.
  Recent orders from the Italian State Railways include one for a further 500 Type Sdkmmss intermodal transporters. This carrier, with a tare weight of 16 tonnes, is of the fixed recess or 'pocket' type, for conveyance of road semi-trailers, demountable bodies or containers; each vehicle can accommodate a single 37-tonne road semi-trailer or up to two containers or demountable bodies. Also ordered by the FS for 1983 delivery were 50 Type Saadss twin-unit intermodal cars for semi-trailer piggybacking; and 400 Type Vrtz two-axle wagons for transport of 144 metre-long rails.

4-axle covered wagon with sliding roof

33.5-tonne bogie tank wagon for compressed gas transport, load capacity 46.5 tonnes, carrying capacity 93 m³

Gantry cranes and Type Sdkmmss transporters

Coelferf
Costruzioni Elettromeccaniche Ferroviare Fiorentino di Ezio Pecchioli

Via Renato Bruschi 156, Sesto Fiorentino, Florence, Italy

Telephone: 4491241
Telegrams: Coelferf, Sesto Fiorentino

Works: Via Petrosa 11/13/15, Sesto Fiorentino, Florence

Products: Freight cars including refrigerator wagons.

Creusot-Loire
Société Creusot-Loire
Traction Division

31/32 quai de Dion Bouton, 92806 Puteaux, France

Telephone: 776 41 62
Telex: 610425

President: M Pineau-Valencienne
Director: Henry Jullien

Products: Diesel-electric, diesel-hydraulic locomotives and railcars; mechanical equipment; bogies. Powered bogies are a speciality; the company produces B type bogies for SNCF's BB 15000 and BB 7200 locomotives, C type bogies for the French CC 6500 locomotives, and bogies for the 260 km/h TGV train-sets.

Constitution: Established in 1782, Creusot-Loire has been building locomotives since 1838. A member of Francorail.

Czechoslovak Wagon Works
Československé Vagónky
(Member of Strojexport, Foreign Trade Co Ltd, Prague)

Nám Dukelskych hrdinu 95/41, 058 01 Poprad, Czechoslovakia

Telephone: 25242
Telex: 078 348

Works: Vagónka Studénka, 742 13 Studénka
      Vagónka Poprad, 058 80 Poprad
      Vagónka Česka Lipa, 470 79 Česka Lipa

Chairman: Stefan Tužinsky
Managing Director: Jan Hlavačik
Sales Director: Karol Košik

Products: Type M152 light steel diesel railcars and trailers; passenger coaches; freight wagons of types Faccs, Falls, Es, Eas, Gbs, Res/Nas, Zts, Zacs/Ra, Zags/Ra, Zagkks/Ra and Zae.

Two-axle light steel railcar M 152 for secondary lines, shown in Czechoslovak State Railways' (CSD) livery

Daewoo
Daewoo Heavy Industries Ltd

PO Box 7955, Seoul, Republic of Korea

Telephone: Seoul 779 1031. Anyang 3 6171
Telegrams: Dhiltdincheon
Telex: 23301/28473

Chairman: Woo Choong Kim
President: Young Suk Yoon
Executive Vice President: Myun Hoo Hong
Rolling Stock Division Director: Jae Ho Kim
Export Sales Manager: Soon Hyuck Park

Products: Passenger coaches, freight wagons, locomotives, railcars, electric multiple-unit and car components.

Recent achievements include a contract, secured jointly with GEC Transportation Projects Ltd of the UK, to supply Lines 3 and 4 of the Seoul Subway with 402 Type Mc emu cars; electrical equipment for the vehicles is to be produced by

Explosion-proof 600 hp diesel-hydraulic locomotive for Korea General Chemical Corporation

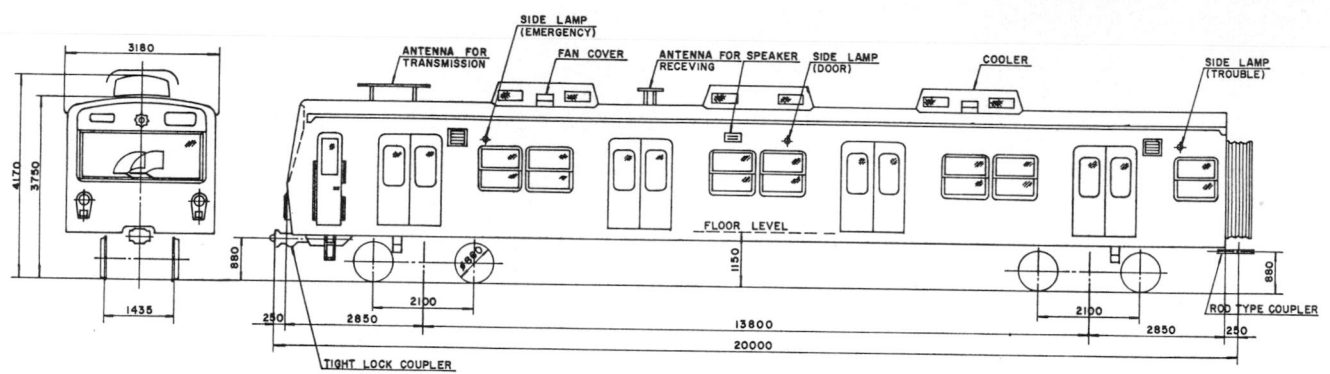

Type Mc power car

Daewoo diesel multiple-units

Cars per unit	Motor cars per unit	Motored axles per motor car	Transmission	Rated power (kW) per motor	Max speed km/h	Weight tonnes per car (M-motor T-trailer)	Total seating capacity	Length per car m	No in service	Year first built	Builders Mechanical parts	Engine & type	Transmission
5	2	4	Elec	84	110	PM: 58.5 M: 42.8 T: 38.5	192	21	2	1979	Daewoo	Cummins KTA-1150L	Elec

Daewoo diesel locomotives

Class	Wheel arrangement	Transmission	Rated power (kW)	Max speed km/h	Total weight tonnes	No in service	Year first built	Builders Mechanical parts	Engine & type	Transmission
Shunting	0-4-0	Hyd	176	60	18.3	11	1978	Daewoo	Daewoo-MAN (D2156HM)	NICO (Japan)
Hazardous area shunting	0-4-0	Hyd	176	32	25	1	1982	Daewoo	Daewoo-MAN (D2156HM)	NICO (Japan)
Shunting	B-B	Hyd	2 × 185	35	35	1	1982	Daewoo	Daewoo-MAN (D2156MT)	NICO (Japan)
Hazardous area shunting	B-B	Hyd	447	27	55	1	1981	Daewoo	Niigata (DMF31SB1)	NICO (Japan)
Shunting	B-B	Hyd	447	23	75	1	1982	Daewoo	Niigata (DMF31SB1)	NICO (Japan)

Daewoo electric railcars or multiple-units

Class	Cars per unit	Line voltage	Motor cars per unit	Motored axles per motor car	Rated output (kW) per motor	Max speed km/h	Weight tonnes per car (M-motor T-trailer)	Total seating capacity (M-motor T-trailer)	Length per car m	No of cars in service	Rate of acceleration km/h/s	Year first built	Builders Mechanical parts	Electrical equipment
Commuter	4, 6, 8 or 10	25 kV ac or 1500 V dc	2, 4 or 6	4	120	110	Tc: 34.5 M: 43.5 M': 46.5	T: 48 M: 54 M': 54	20	212	2.5	1976	Daewoo	Daewoo & Hitachi (Japan)
Commuter	4, 6, 8 or 10	1500 V dc	4 or 6	4	150	100	MC: 41.5 M1: 40.5 M2: 40.5	MC: 48 M1: 54 M2: 54	20	32	3.0		Daewoo	Hitachi
Commuter	4, 6, 8 or 10	1500 V dc	2, 4 or 6	4	150	100	Tc: 33.0 M1: 42.2 M2: 41.8 T: 31.7	Tc: 48 M1: 54 M2: 54 T: 54	20	402 (under manufacture)	3.0	1983	Daewoo	GEC Traction
Inter-city	10	25 kV ac	6	4	120	100	Tc: 43.5 M: 51.5 M': 51.0 Tb: 40.0 Ts: 37.5	561	20	20	2.0	1979	Daewoo	Daewoo & Hitachi

GEC Traction Co. Worth US$300 million, the order is scheduled for completion by the end of 1984. These six-car units, operating on a 1435 mm gauge system electrified at 1.5 kV dc, comprise four power car each taring 42.2 or 41.8 tonnes and two trailers each taring 33 tonnes, with seats for 312 passengers and room for 624 standing. The units feature chopper control of motors and regenerative as well as air braking. Their rate of acceleration is 3.0 km/h/s and rate of deceleration, 3.5 km/h/s (service) and 4.5 km/h/s (emergency).

Affiliated companies

Daewoo International [America] Corp
100 Daewoo Place, Carlstadt, New Jersey 07072, USA
Tel: (201) 935 8700

Daewoo International Co [Montreal] Ltd
540 Beauharnios, 2nd Floor, Montreal H2N 1L2, Canada
Tel: (514) 381 4431/3

Daewoo International [Panama] SA
Edificio 25, Colon Free Zone, Colon, Republic of Panama
Tel: (47) 6823/7003, 23 8144

Daewoo Handels GmbH
71-Niederrad, Saonestrasse 1, 6000 Frankfurt/Main, Federal Republic of Germany
Tel: 0611 666011/5

Daewoo Industrial Co [UK] Ltd
11th Floor, Bastion House, 140 London Wall, London EC2, England
Tel: 01-588 0081/7

Daewoo France
Centre Seine T41, 23 rue Linois, 75015 Paris, France
Tel: 575 15 30

Daewoo Industrial Co [HK] Ltd
Room 1901-5, Lane Crawford House 19/F, 64-70A Queen's Road Central, Hong Kong
Tel: 5-230825/230589

Constitution: Originating in 1937, the present company was formed to create a major South Korean rolling stock industry in 1973. From manufacture of passenger cars and freight wagons it progressed to construction of complete multiple-unit trains, including long-haul air-conditioned diesel (Type DEC) and electric (Type EEC) sets for Korean National Railroad. Major export markets for passenger vehicles and freight wagons have been created in Bangladesh, Malaysia, New Zealand, Indonesia and elsewhere. Following technical agreements with MAN of West Germany in 1970 and with several Japanese manufacturers, the company offers a wide range of marine, automotive and industrial diesel engines, and is now expanding into the construction of diesel locomotives and railcars, and also of electric locomotives.

Type Mc emu for Seoul Subway

Air-conditioned electric Type EEC train-set for Korean National Railroad

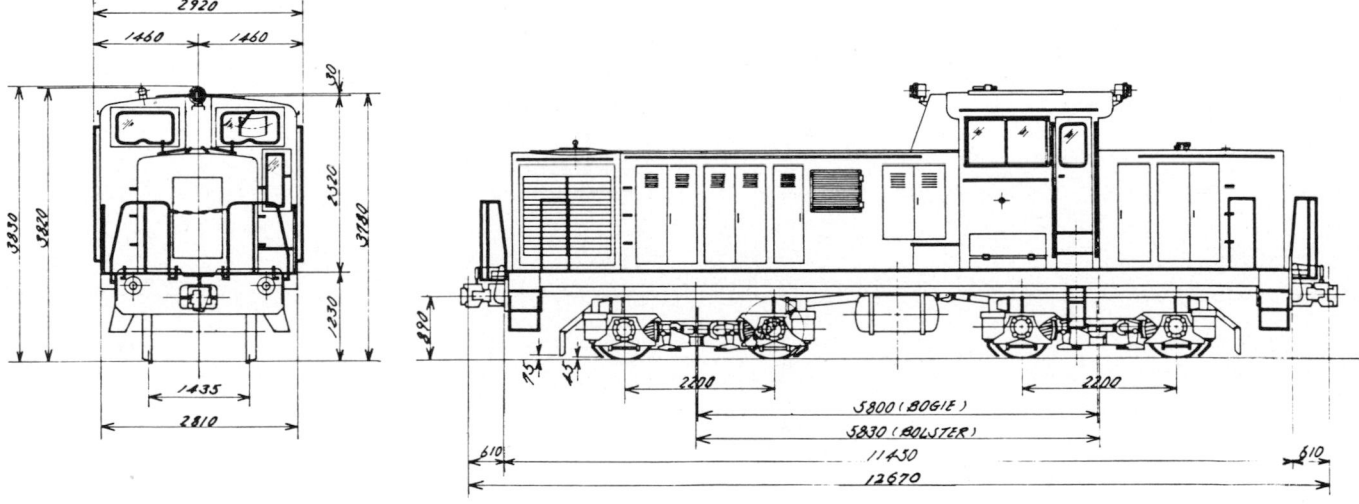

600 hp diesel-hydraulic locomotive general arrangement

Dalian Locomotive and Rolling Stock Works
Member of China National Machinery Import and Export Corporation

Dalian, Liaoning, People's Republic of China

Telegrams: Dallocwks, Dalian

Products: Diesel locomotives; freight wagons.
    In production is the 3300 hp Type Dong Feng 4 Co-Co diesel locomotive with ac-dc electric transmission with silicon rectifiers. It has a 23-tonne axleload and is geared for a top speed of 120 km/h as a passenger unit, or 100 km/h in freight service. Powered by a Type 16240Z diesel engine and Type TQFR3000 generator, it weighs 138 tonnes and measures 5.851 × 1.79 × 2.994 metres. It has a possible continuous rating of 3600 hp at 1100 rpm. In September 1982 a total of 541 were operating on the Chinese People's Republic Railways. The transmission is manufactured by the Yong Ji Electric Machinery Works.

Type Dong Feng 4 diesel locomotive

Bogie of Type Dong Feng 4 diesel-electric Co-Co

Type 62A wagon, tare weight 60 tonnes, payload capacity 60 tonnes and 71.6 m³, length over couplers 13.49 m

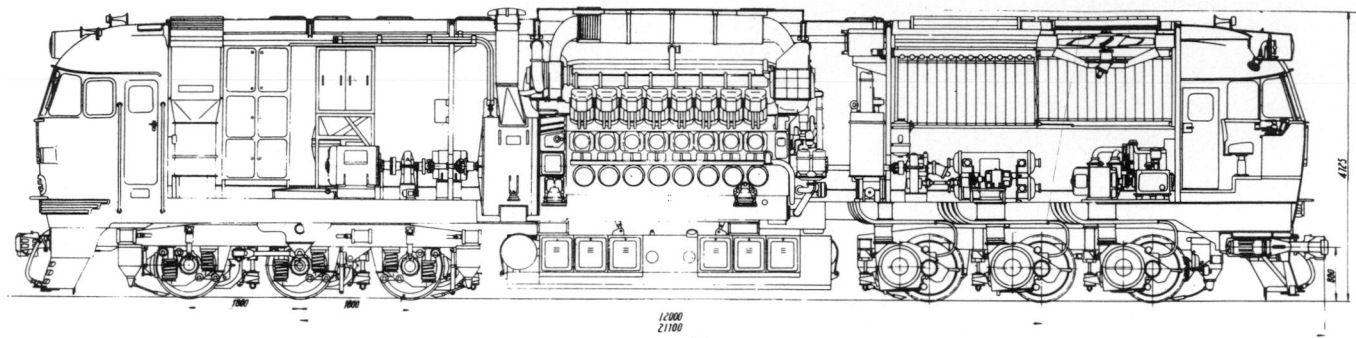

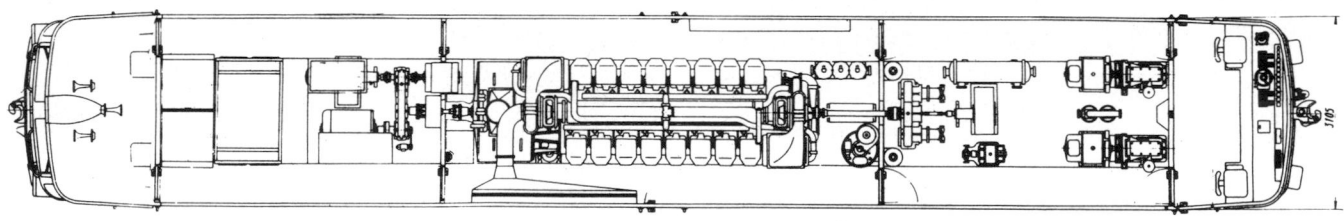

Layout of 3300 hp Type Dong Feng 4 Co-Co diesel locomotive

Datong Locomotive Works

Datong, People's Republic of China

Products: China Railroad 2-10-2 (Type Qian Jin) steam locomotive for freight service.

Class QJ 2-10-2

Loco type	QJ8WT	QJ12WT
Wheel arrangement	2-10-2	
Max speed	80 km/h	
Power at wheel tread	2980 hp	
Minimum radius	145 m	
Gauge	1435 mm	
Weight, engine in working order	133 tonnes	
on front bogie	13 tonnes	
on driving wheel	100 tonnes	
on trailing bogie	20 tonnes	

Boiler steam pressure		15 kgf/cm²
Tube number and diameter		80 × 51 mm
Flue number and diameter		69 × 133 mm
Grate area		6.8 m²
Combustion chamber length		1200 mm
Boiler barrel diameter, inside		2100 mm
Cylinders (2), diameter and stroke		650 × 800 mm
Driving wheel diameter		1500 mm

	4-wheel tender	6-wheel tender
Coal capacity	14.5 tonnes	21.5 tonnes
Water capacity	40 tonnes	50 tonnes
Stoker	Type C-3	
Coal pusher	To customer's request	
Engine and tender, max width	3375 mm	3375 mm
max height	4790 mm	4790 mm
max length	26 023 mm	29 181 mm
Fuel	Coal	

Davis
W H Davis & Sons Ltd

Langwith Junction, Mansfield, Nottingham NG20 9RZ, England

Telephone: 0623 74 2621
Telex: 37657

Chairman: W H T Davis

Directors: C W Davis
           D Sharpe
Secretary: J Cowling
Sales Manager, Rolling Stock: M S Burge
  Containers: D G Bradley
  Trailers: M E Price

Products: Freight wagons; specialised stock for industry.

Constitution: The company was formed in 1900.

Conversion of existing flat wagon with concrete mixer for London Transport

Hopper bogie wagon for Bangladesh Railways

Two-axle hopper wagon for UK operations

Bitumen tank wagon of 51 tonnes glw for Shell (UK) Oil Ltd

50-tonne capacity palletised UKF fertiliser wagon

51 tonnes glw hopper for conveyance of dry and wet sand, capacity 28.7 m³

De Dietrich
De Dietrich & Cie

Reichshoffen, 67110 Niederbronn-les-Bains, France

Telephone: (88) 09 16 66
Telegrams: Dietriwagons
Telex: 870 850

Sales organisation: Francorail (for railway rolling stock)
De Dietrich & Cie (for other equipment)

President: Gilbert de Dietrich
Director, Rolling Stock Division: Maurice Canioni

Products: Passenger coaches; high-speed bogies; special wagons for steel shipments (torpedo ladle wagons).
Sales during 1982 included the supply to French Railways (SNCF) of further

De Dietrich Type C80 metre-gauge bogie for passenger cars

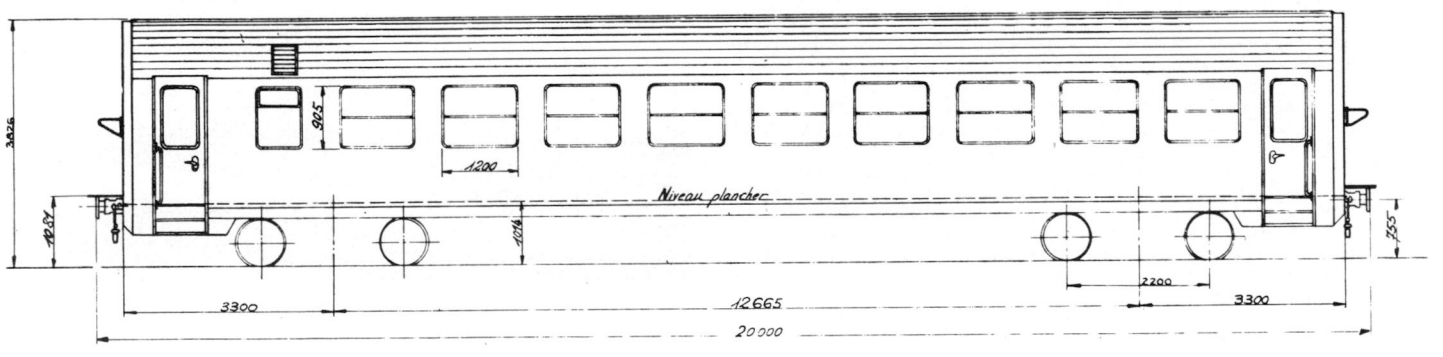

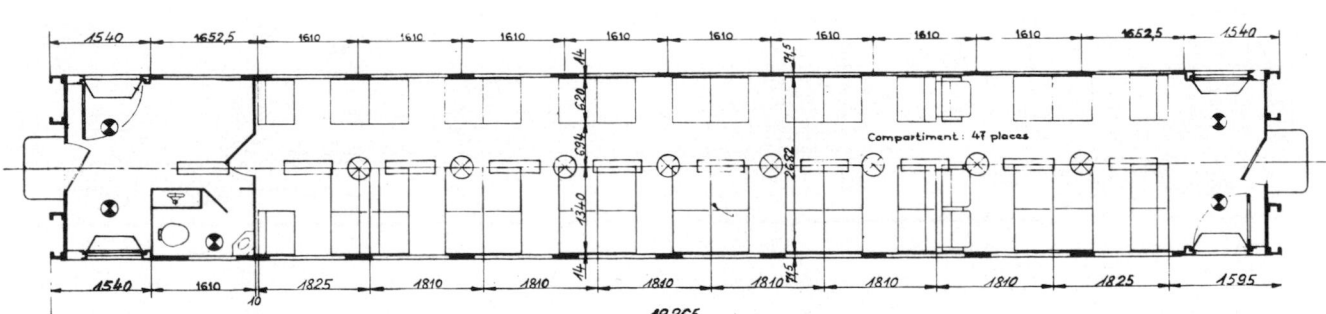

Layout of first-class inter-city car for ONCFG

passenger cars for the Paris-Lyons TGV train-sets, locomotive-hauled Corail passenger cars, new Type Z2 emus and ambulance cars. The company also produced Type Y32 high-speed bogies for SNCF and Netherlands Railways (NS), diesel-electric locomotive bodies for other systems, special wagons for the steel industry, and passenger cars and bogies for metre-gauge systems.

Constitution: Established in 1684, the company commenced railway rolling stock production in the mid-19th century. Since 1973 it has been part of the Groupement d'Intérêt Economique Francorail, which also includes the ANF-Industrie, Carel Fouché, Creusot-Loire, Jeumont-Schneider and MTE companies. In conjunction with Francorail the company handles manufacture of self-propelled coaching stock, and also manufactures UIC-pattern and other types of passenger car and high-speed bogie for SNCF and railways abroad. In addition to rolling stock, the company makes and markets other railway-related equipment such as special steel-industry wagons, points and crossings for surface and sub-surface railways, and signalling equipment.

Ambulance car for French Railways (SNCF)

Type B6 Dux air-conditioned push-pull driving trailer with baggage compartment for French Railways (SNCF)

Second-class inter-city passenger car for metre-gauge Guinea Railways (ONCFG)

Interior of ONCFG second-class inter-city car

Dessau
VEB Waggonbau Dessau

Joliot-Curie-Strasse 48, 4500 Dessau, German Democratic Republic

Telephone: 7510
Telex: 0488241

Products: Mechanically-refrigerated wagons and trains; ice-cooled wagons.

Recent production has been dominated by 600 two-axle covered and 211 four-axle open goods wagons for Syrian Railways, and by 650 refrigerated five-wagon sets of Type ZB5 and 2150 four-axle, 21-metre mechanically-refrigerated wagons of Type MK4 for Soviet Railways (SZD); from 1981 to 1985 the plant was committed to manufacture of 6450 further refrigerated vehicles, either in single wagons or in sets, for SZD. The Type MK4 wagon was developed specifically to suit the climatic and operating conditions of SZD. The bodywork employs a 'sandwich' technique, enclosing polyurethane foam, which combines a tare weight reduction to 42.5 tonnes with increased load capacity of 110 cubic metres and 44 tonnes and which also improves cooling efficiency. In 1983 the works produced the 30 000th refrigerator wagon built in the German Democratic Republic for SZD.

Type MK4 mechanically-refrigerated vehicle for SZD

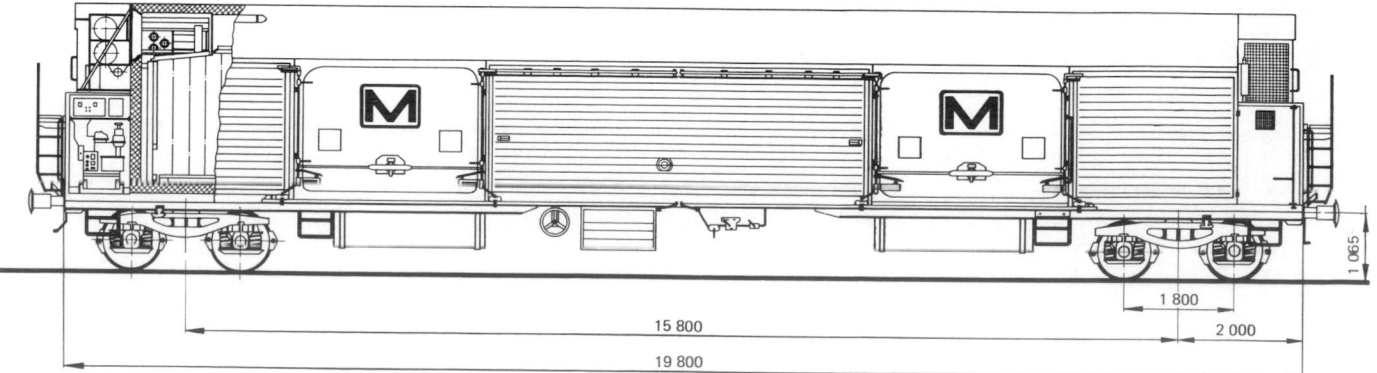

Type MK4 wagon

A similar constructional technique has been adopted in the latest four-axle mechanically-refrigerated wagon with service compartment, of which 67 have been manufactured for the Czechoslovak food industry. This vehicle, 18.74 metres long over buffers, tares 34 tonnes and has a load capacity of 64 cubic metres and 38 tonnes. The underfloor fuel tanks have a 700-litre capacity, sufficient for seven days' normal operation; the electrical apparatus can be connected to a shore supply if required. The attendant's compartment features a folding seat and bunk, toilet facilities, electric cooker, refrigerator, boiler and heater, and folding table.

Ten refrigerator trains were supplied to Romania in 1982. Each consists of eight refrigerator cars and a power supply car including compartments for personnel. Each train has a payload capacity of 332 tonnes. The temperatures of the cargo loading chambers or rooms can be regulated from −20 to +14°C.

Constitution: The works began special-purpose goods wagon manufacture when it resumed production in 1945. In 1948 it began construction of ice-cooled wagons and from 1957 mechanically-refrigerated vehicles, and turned out its 37 000th vehicle in 1980. A member of Vereinigter Schienenfahrzeugbau der DDR eV.

Exports: Schienenfahrzeuge Export-Import Volkseigener Aussenhandelsbetrieb der DDR, Otztaler Strasse 17, 1100 East Berlin

Mechanically-refrigerated vehicle with attendant's compartment for Czechoslovakia

Refrigerator train for Romanian State Railways

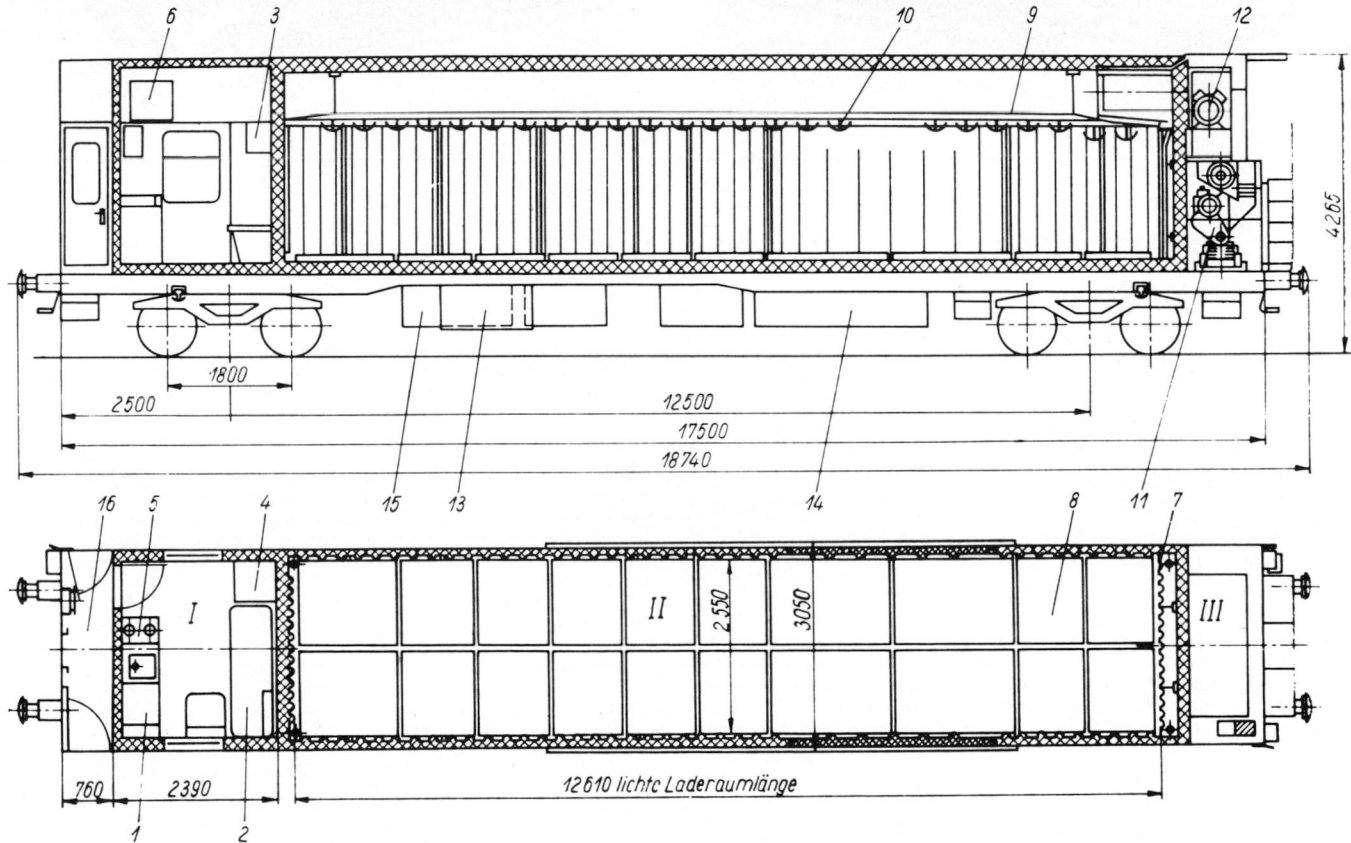

Czechoslovak mechanically-refrigerated vehicle. (I) attendant's compartment (II) loading space (III) machinery compartment (1) refrigerator (2) bunk (3) switch cabinet (4) closet (5) electric hotplate (6) water tank (7) ventilator (8) floor grilles (9) upper space (10) meat carriers (11) diesel-electric plant (12) cooling plant (13) oil-burning plant (14) fuel tank (15) lighting battery (16) entrance lobby

---

Diema
Diema Diepholzer Maschinenfabrik Fritz Schoettler GmbH

Diemastrasse 11, Postfach 1170, 2840 Diepholz 1, Federal Republic of Germany

Telephone: 0 54 41 30 41/43
Telegrams: Diema, Diepholz
Telex: 0941 222

Managing Director: Peter Benzien
Sales Director: Klaus Fuhrmann

Self-propelled Type GT10 transporter

Products: Standard and broad-gauge diesel shunting locomotives, narrow-gauge diesel mine locomotives, narrow-gauge industrial locomotives, hydraulic tippers and motorised work trolleys.
Variants include:
Diesel shunters: outputs 10-300 bhp, weights 1-36 Mp, all gauges available, eg Type DVL;
Diesels for underground use: outputs 10-300 bhp, weights 1-30 Mp, eg Type DTL;
Flameproof mining diesels: outputs 28-100 bhp, weights 3.5-14 Mp, eg Type DGL30;
Self-propelled transporters: units up to 10 cubic metres capacity, eg Type GT10.

Motorised work trolley by Diema

Type DGL30 flameproof mining diesel

Type DVL diesel shunter

Difco
Difco Inc

PO Box 238, Findlay, Ohio 45840, USA

Telephone: (419) 422 0525
Telegrams: Difco, Findlay

Chairman: D F Flowers
Managing Director: Fred F Flowers
Chief Sales Director: Robert J Ward

Products: Air side-dump wagons.
The double fulcrum principle is employed on all Difco air dump cars. The dump body is supported in stable equilibrium on widely-spaced fulcrums (trunnions or pivots) which prevent rocking or swaying of the body during transport. No locking mechanism is needed, which reduces down time, saves maintenance and prevents all possibility of accidental dumping. The vehicle

dumps to either side with equal facility. Operation of a small valve handle is all that is required to dump the car. This apparatus may be arranged so that an entire train can be dumped from a locomotive or any one car in the train. Large, telescoping air cylinders rapidly raise the dump body to the full, 50 degree dumping angle. The end of the dumping stroke is cushioned by air trapped in cylinders. Doors open and close automatically as the body tips and returns to central position. Only the door on the dumping side opens; the upper door remains positively closed. The door-operating mechanism is underfloor and protected at all times from dirt and damage. The mechanism is so constructed that the door will 'float' without injury on any obstruction during dumping. One-piece floors are solidly welded to closely-spaced floor beams to withstand the heaviest loading punishment.
Bogies are AAR ride control and roller bearing-equipped and feature a long-travel spring arrangement. A maximum capacity spring package consisting of 63 mm travel outer, 95 mm travel inner and 86 mm travel helper springs is available as an option for heavy industrial and mining applications.

Constitution: Founded in 1915 for the production of heavy and light industrial railway rolling stock and mine haulage equipment.

77-ton, 50 yd³ payload capacity Difco air side-dump wagon for Texas Utilities Generating Co boiler ash and sludge disposal

100-ton, 50 yd³ payload capacity Difco air side-dump wagon for Missouri Pacific Railroad track maintenance work

DLW
Diesel Locomotive Works

Varanasi 221 004 (UP), India

Telephone: 64451-55
Telegrams: Dieseloco
Telex: 054-230

General Manager: M G Verma
Chief Mechanical Engineer: K B Kapur
Chief Design Engineer: K L Vagale

Products: Diesel engines 1400-2600 hp; diesel generating sets; diesel-electric locomotives of metre, standard and broad gauges and components for diesel locomotives.

Constitution: DLW is a unit of the Indian Railways.

Class WDM2 diesel-electric locomotive for Indian Railways

Dorbyl
Dorbyl Railway Products (Pty) Ltd

PO Box 229, Boksburg 1460, South Africa

Telephone: (011) 52-8276
Telegrams: Dorlonsa, Johannesburg
Telex: 8-8024

Chairman: K N Jenkins

Managing Director, Railway Products: D B Mostert
Executive Directors, Railway Products: J C de Beer
M E Gravenor

Products: Diesel-electric locomotives, electric (25 kV 50 Hz ac) locomotives, industrial locomotives, freight wagons, guards' vans, steam heat vehicles, cast steel wheels and axles. (See also Addenda).

Constitution: The company is a subsidiary of Dorbyl Ltd, which was established in South Africa as Wade & Dorman Ltd, Structural Engineers in 1909. The manufacture of rolling stock was begun in 1944.

Type XNJ-7 anhydrous ammonia tank wagon; tare 32 tonnes, load 41.8 tonnes, capacity 74 370 litres

Type FSLJ-2 general purpose covered wagon; tare 25.25 tonnes, load 45 tonnes, capacity 64.6 m³

Type SCL-4 motor vehicle transport wagon; tare 25.24 tonnes, load 11.36 tonnes

Type XBJ-11 bulk powder wagon; tare 25.3 tonnes, 48.7 tonnes, capacity 47 m³

Dorbyl-built diesel locomotives

Class	Wheel arrangement	Transmission	Rated power (kW)	Max speed km/h	Total Weight tonnes	No in service	Year first built	Builders Mechanical parts	Builders Engine & type	Builders Transmission
U10B	B-B	Elec	671	103	49.9	67	1965	GE	Caterpillar D-398	4/GE 761
SG10B	B-B	Elec	895	103	69.8	124	1975	GE	GE FDL-8	4/GE 761
U15C	C-C	Elec	1230	103	81.6	232	1971	GE	GE FDL-8	6/GE 761
U26C	C-C	Elec	2050	103	95.3	316	1975	GE	GE FDL-12	6/GE 761

Duro Daković
Duro Daković Industries

PO Box 63, 55001 Slavonski Brod, Yugoslavia

Telephone: 055 231-011
Telegrams: Lokomotive, Slavonski Brod
Telex: 23421/23424

Products: Diesel-electric (610-1840 kW), diesel-hydraulic (150-1176 kW) and diesel-mechanical locomotives; light rail vehicles and trams; diesel railcars and train-sets; passenger coaches; freight wagons; hopper wagons with lateral discharge for bulk cargoes, tank wagons, granular hopper wagons, cereal hopper wagons, flat wagons, container wagons.

Constitution: Duro Daković was founded in 1921 as the first Yugoslav locomotive and wagon manufacturer. Diesel locomotives have been produced since 1954.

Duewag Aktiengesellschaft
Werk Düsseldorf

Königsberger Strasse 100, 4000 Düsseldorf, Federal Republic of Germany

Telephone: 211 73431
Telegrams: Duewag
Telex: 08582722

Products: Streetcars; light rail vehicles; pre-metro cars; subway cars; bogies of bi- and mono-motor type; car components of fibre-glass; H-Bahn type people mover system.

Electroputere
Electroputere Works, Craiova 1100, Jud Dolj

Calea București 144, 1100 Craiova, Romania

Telephone: 941 44494/42077
Telex: 41234

Alco-engined 3000 hp diesel-electric Co-Co for Romanian Railways (CFR)

Products: Diesel-electric Co-Co locomotives from 2100 to 4000 hp; electric Co-Co locomotives of 7350 hp.

Since 1960 the works has built 2100 hp diesel-electric locomotives under a Sulzer/Brown Boveri licence. Over 2000 of this type have been built for Romanian Railways and systems in other countries, among them Polish State Railways (402), the Railways Administration in the People's Republic of China (183), and Bulgarian State Railways (120). Powered by a twin-bank 12-cylinder 12 LDA 28 type diesel engine developing a maximum 2300 hp (under UIC conditions), the locomotive is intended for both passenger and freight service; it has dc/dc transmission and Knorr braking. The first Romanian Railways locomotives of this type have run over 3 million km.

A later unified series of Electroputere locomotives is based on Alco engines with power outputs between 1500 and 4000 hp, manufactured by Reșița Works under Alco licence. The 3000 and 4000 hp locomotives so far produced are locally designed. They are intended for mixed traffic and have common features. Engines are four-stroke, pressure-charged with direct injection, at a nominal speed of 1100 rpm, and charge air-cooled. The number of cylinders is 12 in the 3000 hp and 16 in the 4000 hp model. Both have self-supporting superstructures, with cabs at each end, and Flexicoil bogie suspension. All axles are powered with compensated dc, nose-suspended, series excitation traction motors. Transmission is ac/dc in both, and braking equipment is Knorr. Electroputere has already won an order for 10 4000 hp locomotives from Greece.

The demand for haulage of heavier trains resulted in the development of the most powerful locomotive ever constructed in Romania, a 5100 kW Co-Co electric, which is manufactured under ASEA licence. The first units of this type were delivered to Romanian Railways in 1967 and have since recorded over 2.5 million km in service. To date over 700 electric locomotives have been manufactured and delivered by Electroputere, including 105 exported to Yugoslavia and China.

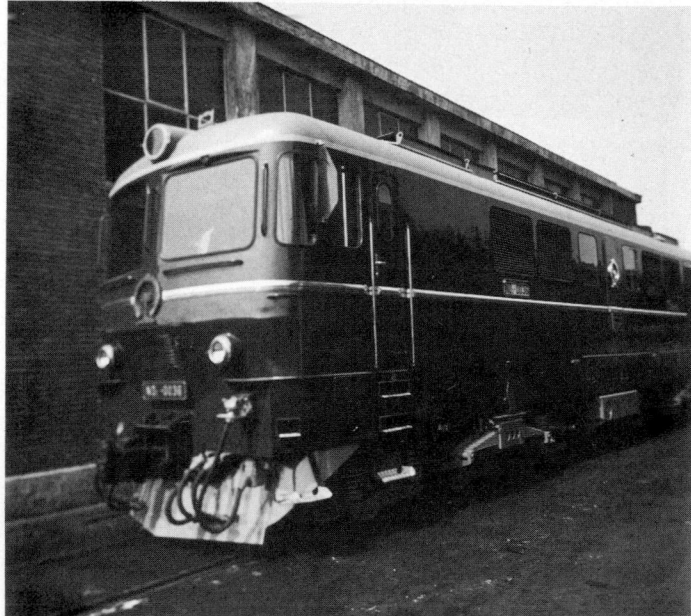
Sulzer-engined 2100 hp diesel-electric Co-Co for China

Alco-engined 4000 hp diesel-electric Co-Co for Hellenic Railways (CH)

Electroputere diesel-electric locomotives

Wheel arrangement	Transmission	Rated power (kW)	Starting tractive effort kN	Continuous tractive effort/speed kN/km/h	Max speed km/h	Total weight tonnes	Year first built	Builders		
								Mechanical parts	Engine & type	Transmission
Co-Co	dc/dc	1200	320 285	200/21.5 172/25.2	100/120	117	1960	Electroputere	Sulzer 12LDA 28	Electroputere
Co-Co	ac/dc	2235	422 350 304	257/24 213/29 185/33.3	105-115 140 140-160	120	1980	Electroputere	Alco 12R-251	Electroputere
Co-Co	ac/dc	2980	350	200/40	140	126	1980	Electroputere	Alco 12R-251	Electroputere

Electroputere co-operates with a large number of other factories in Romania supplying auxiliary machines and apparatus, the braking system control and supply equipment, metering equipment lamps, etc. Diesel engines are manufactured by ICM Reşiţa and bogies by ICM Caransebes.

Constitution: A MecanoExportImport supplier. Electroputere Craiova is the largest manufacturer of industrial electrical equipment in Romania. In 1955-59 the works manufactured for the passenger transport enterprise of Bucharest 161 tramcars, which were the beginning of its rolling stock construction.

Electroputere electric locomotives

CFR class	Wheel arrangement	Line voltage	Rated output (kW) continuous/one-hour	Max tractive effort (kN)	Max speed km/h	Weight tonnes	No in service	Year first built	Builders Mechanical parts	Electrical equipment
40	Co-Co	25 kV ac	5100/5400	412	120	126	440	1965	Electroputere-ASEA	Electroputere-ASEA
41	Co-Co	25 kV ac	5100/5400	304	160	126		1965	Electroputere-ASEA	Electroputere-ASEA

Emaq
Emaq-Engenharia e Máquinas SA

Rodovia BR116, Km 121.5, Estrada Rio-Teresópolis 25.900, Magé, Rio de Janeiro, CP 09, Brazil

Telephone: (021) 733 1446/1467/1566
Telegrams: Emalita
Telex: 2123363

Products: Locomotives; rolling stock. The company has licences from MLW, Montreal for diesel-electric locomotive manufacture; from MTE, France for electric locomotives; and from Alco Power Inc of the USA for the EMAQ-251 diesel engine.
Recent contracts include an order from Ferrovia Paulista SA (FEPASA) for 80 electric locomotives, to be delivered 1984-86.

Emaq electric locomotives for FEPASA

Class	Wheel arrangement	Line voltage	Rated output (kW) continuous one-hour	Max speed km/h	Weight tonnes	Builders Mechanical parts	Electrical equipment
EC 362	Bo-Bo	3 kV dc	260	90	100	Emaq	Various

Emaq diesel locomotives

Class	Wheel arrangement	Transmission	Rated power (kW)	Max speed km/h	Total weight tonnes	No in service	Year first built	Builders Mechanical parts	Engine & type	Transmission
MX 620	Co-Co	Electric	1490	103	96	71	1980	Emaq	Alco Model EC 251	GE

Energomachexport
V/O Energomachexport

Deguninskaya Str 1, Korp 4, 127486 Moscow, USSR

Telephone: 14/ 21 //
Telegrams: Energoexport
Telex: 411926; 411965

Chairman: V Pavlov

Sales Directors: V Slabejko
V Tsvetkov

Products: Soviet exports of diesel and electric locomotives; electric train-sets; passenger coaches; freight wagons; railway interlocking equipment; signalling and block systems; metro stock; track machines and mechanisms.

Constitution: The company was formed to handle all railway equipment exports from the Soviet Union. Principal partners include the Ludinovo, Novocherkassk, and Voroshilovgrad locomotive works.

Ercole Marelli Group
Ercole Marelli Elettromeccanica Generale SpA

Viale Edison 50, 20099 Sesto San Giovanni, Milan, Italy

Telephone: (02) 2494
Telegrams: Marelgen Sesto S Giovanni
Telex: 310043, 320575

General Manager: Umberto Lugo
Traction Division: Mario Pastorelli

Products: Main traction and auxiliary electrical equipment for locomotives, railcars and LRVs.
Recent Italian State Railways (FS) rolling stock for which the company has

supplied electrical equipment includes the 3 kV dc Pendolare four-car emus, a prototype six-set production of which was soon followed by an FS order for 90 power cars and 150 trailers. Ferrovie Nord Milano also ordered 12 power cars. Each set has two power cars with all axles individually motored for a total continuous rating of 1760 kW; full chopper control is coupled with regenerative braking. In addition the company offers chopper control systems for 750 volt and 1.5 kV dc rapid transit units. Ercole Marelli has also provided 240T165 traction motors and complete electrical apparatus for 60 Class ALe801 emu power cars of the FS and participated in the FS Class E656 3860 kW Bo-Bo-Bo electric locomotive programme.

Constitution: Ercole Marelli & C, the holding and parent company, was founded in 1891. In January 1980 the former Plant and Systems Division became an autonomous company registered as Ercole Marelli Elettromeccanica Generale SpA (EMG).

ESW
Export Association of Swiss Rolling Stock Manufacturers

Member companies: SIG Swiss Industrial Company; Swiss Car & Elevator Manufacturing Corp Ltd; Schindler Carriage & Wagon Co Ltd

Products: Electric and diesel railcars; urban, inter-urban and suburban train units; LRV/tramcars; passenger coaches; dining cars; sleeping cars; mail/luggage vans; rack and pinion rolling stock; goods wagons; motor and trailer bogies; high speed bogies; inter-car gangway crossovers; miscellaneous components for all kind of rail vehicles etc.

Fablok
Locomotive Works Fablok

Ul F Dzierżyńskiego 3, 32-500 Chrzanow, Poland

Telephone: 22 31
Telegrams: Fablok, Chrzanow
Telex: 032256

Export sales: Kolmex, 49 Mokotowska, 00-542 Warsaw

Products: Diesel-electric, diesel-hydraulic and diesel-mechanical locomotives; brake equipment.

Fauvet-Girel
Établissements Fauvet-Girel

40 boulevard Henri Sellier, 92150 Suresnes, France

Telephone: 506 15 74
Telegrams: Fauvgir
Telex: 611 486

President: Jacques Dambrine

Assistant General Managers: Jacques Martin
Georges Reille
Commercial Director: Joachim Lagall

Products: Hopper wagons, tank wagons, special wagons, semi-trailers, containers, diesel-electric and diesel-hydraulic shunting locomotives from 150 to 1600 bhp.

Constitution: The company was formed in 1918 and has two main wagon-building plants at Arras and Lille.

FAVYS SAIC
Fabrica Argentina de Vagones y Silos

Maipo 726, 3er piso, 1006 Buenos Aires, Argentina

Telephone: 392 2736

Works: Av Lastra y La Porteña, Chascomús, Prov Buenos Aires

Telephone: 2305

Products: Rolling stock.

Ferrostaal
Ferrostaal AG

PO Box 10 12 65, Hohenzollernstrasse 24, 4300 Essen, Federal Republic of Germany

Telephone: 0201 20141
Telegrams: Ferrostaal, Essen
Telex: 0857100

Directors: Dr Hans Singer
Wilhelm Haverkamp
Wilhelm Lüttenberg
Dr Klaus von Menges
Gerhard Thulmann
Hans-Ulrich Gruber

Products: Diesel-electric, diesel-hydraulic, diesel-mechanical, diesel mining locomotives; diesel railcars; railbuses; diesel multiple-units; LRVs; passenger coaches; freight wagons; rail maintenance trucks and cranes; track materials.

Ferrostaal lightweight three-car diesel train-set

Ferrosud
Ferrosud SpA

PO Box 94, Via Appia Antica Km 13, 75100 Matera, Italy

Telephone: PBX 212114
Telegrams: TF 212114 Ferrosud
Telex: 760025

Chairman: Giuseppe Capuano
Vice-Chairman: Renato Piccoli
Managing Director: Angelo Mangone

Products: Electric and diesel locomotives; railcars and trailers for electric and diesel trains; passenger coaches; freight wagons; bogies.
The company's recent orders from Italian State Railways (FS) have included: 100 Type Bc air-conditioned couchette cars on high-speed F79 bogies, arranged for four-berth first-class or six-berth second-class compartment occupation; 680 further bogies of the Fiat F79 design; 350 vans of Type Gabs on Type Y25Cs2 bogies; 250 each of Type Gbhs and Gbs two-axle covered vans; 100 sliding-wall Type Habfis vans on Type Y25Cs2 bogies; and a further 20 Type WR self-service cafeteria cars.

Constitution: Ferrosud was set up in 1963 for the manufacture and marketing of railway and tramway rolling stock. Production began in 1968. Export sales are handled through Fiat and Breda Costruzioni Ferroviarie; 50 per cent of the company is controlled by Fiat Ferroviaria Savigliano and 50 per cent by EFIM.

Type Bc couchette car for Italian State Railways (FS)

Type WRz cafeteria car

Interior of Type WRz self-service cafeteria car

Sliding-wall Type Habfis van for FS

Type Gabs van for FS

FFA
FFA Flug- und Fahrzeugwerke AG

9423 Altenrhein, Switzerland

Telephone: (071) 43 01 01
Telegrams: FFA, Rorschach
Telex: 77 230

Chairmen: Dr C Caroni and Dr L Caroni
Sales Director: R Séquin

Products: Passenger cars, powered, trailer or driving trailer, of lightweight steel and aluminium alloy design for all gauges; bogies for all types of car; streetcars; tram bogies; postal, goods and container wagons. Special constructions for all purposes; designs; understructure; modification; and individual components and sub-assemblies.

FFA is one of three groups involved in manufacture of Swiss Federal Railways' (SBB) Mk IV passenger cars for internal inter-city service. Fully air-conditioned, the vehicles are built to standard UIC 26.4-metre length in welded all-steel on an orthodox underframe meeting UIC end-loading specifications. Weight is 43 tonnes, seating capacity 60 and a new design of SIG bogie, equipped with disc and electro-magnetic rail brakes, fits the vehicle for 200 km/h: with SBB subject at present to a 140 km/h limit, as yet only one bogie per car is being fitted with electro-magnetic rail brakes. Electro-pneumatically operated sliding plug doors are of an 800 mm wide single-leaf Kiekert-pattern type. The automatic air-conditioning demands up to 35 kW of power for cooling and 42 kW for heating, but economises on energy by mixing fresh air with recirculated air from non-smoking seating areas.

FFA manufactured the integral all-welded lightweight steel bodies and, under licence, the Wegmann disc-braked trailer bogies with secondary air suspension for the Bodensee-Toggenburg Railway's new three-car emus.

Constitution: FFA was founded in 1925 as Flug- und Fahrzeugwerke AG Altenrhein (FFA). During 1931-35 the first funiculars and suspension cars were built, and the rail carriage department began in 1945-47. FFA supplies rolling stock for the SBB (Swiss Federal Railways) as well as for a large number of private and municipal railway undertakings.

SBB Mk IV coach first-class seating

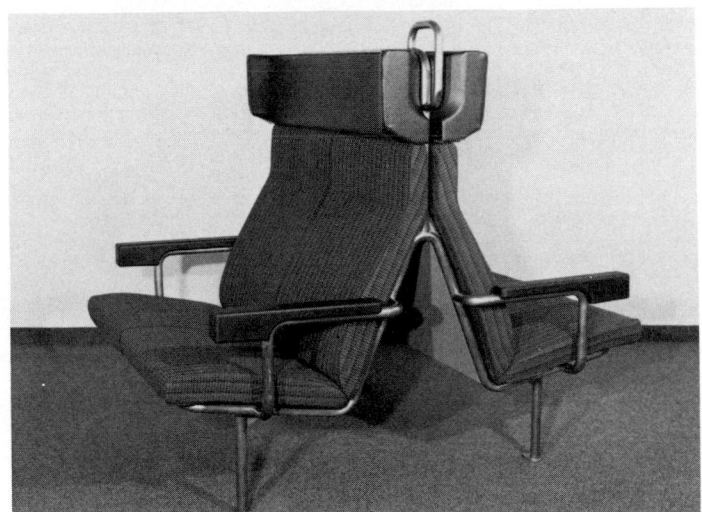

SBB Mk IV coach second-class seating

Type LDG80-Z metre-gauge trailer bogie for mixed adhesion and rack working supplied to St Gallen-Gais-Appenzell Railway

Wegmann type FFA bogie fitted to BT emu trailers

Bodensee-Toggenburg Railway (BT) three-car emu

Swiss Federal (SBB) Mk IV inter-city coach

Type BDt driving trailer supplied to Rhaetian Railways

Fiat
Fiat Ferroviaria Savigliano SpA

Works: 4 Piazza Galateri, 12038 Savigliano (Cuneo), Italy

Telephone: (0172) 366791
Telex: 21234

Chairman: Vittorino Chiusano
Managing Director: Renato Piccoli
Works Director: Franco Bergamasco
Sales Managers: Vincenzo Milanesio
Aldo Della Morte

Products: Electric, diesel-electric locomotives; electric and diesel railcars; multiple-units; passenger coaches (sleeping cars, self service cars, restaurant coaches, saloon cars, TEE coaches); freight wagons; bogies and components.

A recent product is the Type D145 centre-cab diesel-electric locomotive for shunting and light mixed traffic work, of which ten have been delivered to the Italian State Railways (FS). Developed by Fiat in conjunction with Elettromeccanica Parizzi, the D145 is also known as the Inloc because of its inverter and three-phase variable voltage frequency ac motor transmission. The Inloc also pursues recent Fiat practice in adapting heavy road vehicle diesel engines to rail traction, as in the modified ALn 668 railcars supplied to Swedish Railways (SJ), which embodied two such engines rather than a single special-purpose rail traction engine of greater cost and complexity. The two IVECO 12-cylinder 2100 rpm Vee engines in the Inloc have been developed from road vehicle diesels and give the locomotive a rating of 1000 to 1500 hp; continuous tractive effort is 24 000 kg at a top speed of 100 km/h, 18 000 kg at a maximum of 120 km/h. Length over buffers is 14.8 metres, bogie wheelbase 2.2 metres and maximum axle-loading 17.5 tonnes, but the FS Type D145's total weight of 70 tonnes is capable of optional reduction to 64 tonnes.

Constitution: The activity of Fiat in the field of railway rolling stock began in 1917 with the manufacture of passenger and freight cars. In 1931 Fiat put the first diesel railcars into service before beginning production of diesel multiple-units and locomotives, progressing to the tilting body electric 'Pendolino' train (see main entry for Italian State Railways). In 1960 production of standardised light railcars powered by petrol engines began, diesel engines having been introduced in 1934.

By the end of 1975 all the activities of Fiat concerning design and manufacture of railway rolling stock were entrusted to Fiat Ferroviaria Savigliano SpA, the company which now controls Fiat Materfer SAA (Cordoba, Argentina), O.ME.CA. (Reggio Calabria, Italy) and Ferrosud (Matera, Italy).

ALn 668.3000 series railcar in FS service on Cuneo-Ventimille run at Tonde *(John S Baker)*

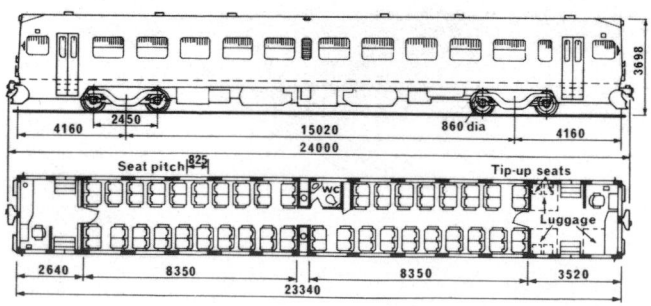

Type D145 diesel-electric for FS

Modified Aln 668 for Swedish Railways (SJ)

Modified ALn 668 redesigned by Fiat for Swedish Railways

Fiat electric locomotives

Class	Wheel arrangement	Line voltage	Rated output (kW) continuous one-hour	Max speed km/h	Weight tonnes	No in service	Year first built	Builders Mechanical parts	Electrical equipment
E.444	Bo-Bo	3 kV dc	4420	200	80	74	1970	Fiat	Asgen-F Marelli
E.632	B-B-B	3 kV dc	4500	130	98	1	1977	Fiat	TIBB
E.633	B-B-B	3 kV dc	4500	160	98	4	1977	Fiat	TIBB
E.632	B-B-B	3 kV dc	4500	130	105	15	1981	Fiat	Ansaldo-E Marelli-TIBB
E.633	B-B-B	3 kV dc	4500	160	105	75	1981	Fiat-TIBB-SOFER	Ansaldo-E Marelli-TIBB

Fiat diesel railcars or multiple-units since 1960

Class	Cars per unit	Motor cars per unit	Motored axles per motor car	Transmission	Rated power (kW) per motor	Max speed km/h	Weight tonnes per car (M-motor T-trailer)	Total seating capacity	Length per car mm (M-motor T-trailer)	No in service	Year first built	Builders Mechanical parts	Engine & type	Trans-mission
—	2	1	2	Hyd	485	117	M 51 / T 34	M 86 / T 102	M 26 040 / T 25 700	M 108 / T 102	1960	Fiat-OM	Fiat-OM	Fiat-OM
—	3	2	2	Mech	107	92	M 37 / T 24	M 80 / T 51	M 22 350 / T 17 700	M 30 / T 15	1960	Fiat	Fiat	Fiat
ALn668	2	1	2	Mech	110	88	M 34 / T 20	M 71 / T 67	M 22 110 / T 17 700	M 10 / T 7	1961	Fiat	Fiat	Fiat
ALn668 (1400)	1	1	2	Mech	110	114	34	71	22 110	10	1961	Fiat	Fiat	Fiat
—	1	1	2	Mech	177	95	51	76	25 200	10	1962	Fiat	Fiat	Fiat
ALn668	2	1	2	Mech	110	88	M 34 / T 20	M 71 / T 67	M 22 110 / T 17 700	M 1 / T 1	1962	Fiat	Fiat	Fiat
ALn668	1	1	2	Mech	110	88	34	87	22 110	2	1962	Fiat	Fiat	Fiat
—	2	1	2	Hyd	570	120	51	80	26 380	60	1962	Fiat-OM	Fiat-OM	Fiat-OM
ALn668 (1500)	1	1	2	Mech	114	114	35	71	22 110	50	1963	Fiat	Fiat	Fiat
ALn668	1	1	2	Mech	158	130	34	68	23 250	2	1968	Fiat	Fiat	Fiat
ALn668 (1600)	1	1	2	Mech	158	114	40	71	22 110	33	1968	Fiat	Fiat	Fiat
ALn668 (1800)	1	1	2	Mech	114	114	41	71	22 110	77	1968	Fiat	Fiat	Fiat
—	1	1	2	Mech	143	109	48	Saloon	24 270	1	1970	Fiat	Fiat	Fiat
ALn668	1	1	2	Mech	114	88	36	87	22 110	2	1970	Fiat	Fiat	Fiat
ALn668	1	1	2	Mech	114	114	36	71	22 110	1	1970	Fiat	Fiat	Fiat
ALn668	1	1	2	Mech	114	114	37	68	23 540	2	1970	Fiat	Fiat	Fiat
ALn668	1	1	2	Mech	114	114	38	68	23 540	2	1970	Fiat	Fiat	Fiat
—	1	1	2	Mech	172	100	52	Bar 60	24 300	1	1971	Fiat	Fiat	Fiat
—	1	1	2	Mech	172	100	52	76	24 300	1	1971	Fiat	Fiat	Fiat
ALn668	1	1	2	Mech	147	96	36	71	22 110	7	1971	Fiat	Fiat	Fiat
ALn668	1	1	2	Mech	147	103	36	71	22 110	12	1971	Fiat	Fiat	Fiat
ALn668	1	1	2	Mech	114	114	41	71	22 110	28	1971	Fiat	Fiat	Fiat
—	2	2	2	Mech	143	131	38	M 71 / T 95	23 730	66	1972	Fiat	Fiat	Fiat
ALn668 (1000)	1	1	2	Mech	147	131	38	68	23 540	162	1972	Fiat	Fiat	Fiat
—	1	1	2	Hyd	170	130	50	66 / Bar 60	25 600	5 / 5	1973	Fiat-OM	Fiat	Fiat-OM
—	1	1	2	Hyd	184	108	52	Bar 60	26 150	50	1974	Fiat-OM	Fiat	Fiat-OM
ALn668	1	1	2	Mech	184	131	38	68	23 812	1	1975	Fiat	Fiat	Fiat
ALn668	1	1	2	Mech	147	96	38	68	23 540	15	1977	Fiat	Fiat	Fiat
ALn668 (1200)	1	1	2	Mech	121	114	38	69	23 540	60	1977	Fiat	Fiat	Fiat
ALn668 (3000)	1	1	2	Mech	147	131	38	69	23 540	40	1979	Fiat	Fiat	Fiat
Y1 (SJ)	1	1	2	Hyd	147	133	42	68	24 400	100	1979	Fiat	Fiat	Fiat
ALn668	1	1	2	Mech	147	131	38	68	23 540	5	1978	Fiat	Fiat	Fiat
ALn668	1	1	2	Mech	114	88	38	82	23 540	5	1978	Fiat	Fiat	Fiat
ALn668	1	1	2	Mech	176	95	37	68	23 540	2	1978	Fiat	Fiat	Fiat
ALn668	1	1	2	Mech	114	88	37	69	23 540	2	1978	Fiat	Fiat	Fiat
ALn668	1	1	2	Mech	147	91	37	91	23 540	3	1980	Fiat	Fiat	Fiat
ALn668 (3100)	1	1	2	Mech	147	131	37	69	23 540	80	1980	Fiat	Fiat	Fiat
ALn668 (3200)	1	1	2	Mech	169	130	38	69	23 540	25	1980	Fiat	Fiat	Fiat
ALn668	1	1	2	Mech	147	91	38	73	23 540	3	1981	Fiat	Fiat	Fiat
ALn668	1	1	2	Mech	168	124	38	69	23 540	5	1982	Fiat	Fiat	Fiat
ALn663 (1000)	1	1	2	Mech	169	110/130	40	63	23 540	120	1982	Fiat	Fiat	Fiat
A2n	1	1	2	Mech	316	114	60	125	25 280	1	1982	Casaralta-Fiat-CIMT	Fiat	Fiat
ALn668 (3400/3500)	1	1	2	Mech	169	110/130	38	69	23 540	80	1981	Fiat	Fiat	Fiat

Fiat diesel locomotives since 1960
Italian State Railways (FS)

Class	Wheel arrangement	Transmission	Rated power (kW)	Max speed km/h	Total weight tonnes	No in service	Year first built	Builders		
								Mechanical parts	Engine & type	Transmission
D.341	Bo-Bo	Elec	1029	110	65	40	1960	Fiat	Fiat	Fiat-TIBB
D.461	Co-Co	Elec	1617	150	97	1	1960	Fiat	Fiat	Fiat-Alsthom
—	B-B	Elec	478	37	68	5	1961	Fiat	Fiat	Fiat
DE.101	B-B	Elec	551	85	49	1	1962	Fiat	Fiat-OM	Fiat-CGE
D.443	B-B	Elec	1397	130	70	50	1970	Fiat	Fiat	TIBB-E Marelli-Breda
—	Co-Co	Elec	1470	85	84	1	1965	Fiat	Fiat	Fiat-E Marelli
—	Bo-Bo	Elec	706	85	53	42	1965	Fiat	Fiat	Fiat-E Marelli
—	Bo-Bo	Elec	1103	100	66	1	1966	Fiat	Fiat	Fiat-E Marelli
D.445	B-B	Elec	1103	130	72	35	1974	Fiat	GMT	Fiat-E Marelli
D.445	B-B	Elec	1558	130	75	20	1981	Fiat	GMT	Fiat-Ansaldo
D.145	Bo-Bo	Elec	735	1000	64	10	1981	Fiat	Fiat	Fiat-Parizzi-AEG

Fiat electric railcars or multiple-units since 1960

Class	Cars per unit	Line voltage	Motor cars per unit	Motored axles per motor car	Rated output (kW) per motor	Max speed km/h	Weight tonnes per car (M-motor T-trailer)	Total seating capacity	Length per car mm (M-motor T-trailer)	No in service	Year first built	Builders	
												Mechanical parts	Electrical equipment
—	3	1.5 kV dc	2	Bo-Bo	90	90	30	M 200 T 227	M 17 145 T 17 110	M 27 T 13	1970	Fiat-TIBB-Breda	Asgen-TIBB-E Marelli
—	3	750 V dc	2	Bo-Bo	110	80	30	208	M 17 740 T 17 740	M 54	1974	Fiat-OM-TIBB	Asgen-E Marelli-Breda
Y0160	1	3 kV dc	1	1A+A1	350	250	40	—	28 700	1	1970	Fiat	Fiat-Ansaldo
ETR401	4	3 kV dc	4	1A+A1	250	250	45	171	M 27 350 T 25 350	1	1975-76	Fiat	Fiat-Ansaldo
—	2	3 kV dc	1	B-B	180	130	M 66 T 55	162	25 805	20	1972-73	Fiat	EE-AEI Traction
—	4	3 kV dc	4	1A+A1	250	190	50	167	M 27 785 T 25 800	1		Fiat-CAF	Fiat-Ansaldo
Jumbo Tram	1	550 V dc	1	B+2+2+B	125	60	32	251	29 200	100	1976	Fiat	Fiat-Asgen
—	1	600 V dc	1	B+2+B	210	75	40	290	29 494	40	1982	Fiat	AEG
—	1	600 V dc	1	B+2+B	210	75	40	301	29 494	60	1983	Fiat	Ansaldo

---

Fiat-Materfer
Fiat-Materfer SA

Cerrito 740, Piso 19 (CP 1309), Buenos Aires, Argentina

Telephone: 35 8112/3478/9562
Telex: 9155

Chairman: Angelo Ridolfo

Products: Diesel-electric, diesel-hydraulic, diesel-mechanical locomotives (locotractors); railcars; passenger coaches; metro cars; special wagons; mail vans.

Recent products include two-car emus for the Buenos Aires metro with full chopper control and regenerative braking. The sets are in service on lines A, C, D, and E of the railway and are compatible with existing rolling stock. All axles are powered. Each car has a driver's cab at one end. The passenger compartment has 15 single and 13 double seats with room for 129 standing passengers (6 per square metre). Each coach has four electro-pneumatic sliding doors on each side which are controlled automatically, although they can be controlled manually in an emergency. The driver's cab has its own mechanical sliding plug-in door, but may also be entered through a sliding door from the car. Standard Scharfenberg automatic couplings facilitate operation of up to three loaded sets in multiple, more when units are empty. The air-suspension bogies have joints with spherical bearings for easy negotiation of sharp curves. Longitudinal mounting of the 750 volt dc, 185 kW motors, one per bogie with drives at both ends of the shaft to gearboxes and universal joints, enables simultaneous driving of both bogie axles and enhances adhesion. Electrical equipment is by Siemens.

Constitution: Fiat-Materfer began production of railway rolling stock in 1960. Owned by Fiat Ferroviaria Savigliano, Italy.

Fiat-Materfer Buenos Aires metro train-sets

Cars per unit	Line voltage	Motors cars per unit	Motored axles per motor car	Rated output (kW) per motor	Max speed km/h	Weight tonnes per car	Total seating capacity	Length per car mm	No in service	Rate of acceleration m/s²	Year first built	Builders	
												Mechanical parts	Electrical equipment
2	1.5 kV dc	2	4	185	80	32.07 31.69	41	17 770	40	0.8	1980	Fiat-Materfer	Siemens AEG

Fiat-Materfer diesel-hydraulic railcars for long-distance service

Cars per unit	Motor cars per unit	Motored axles per motor car	Transmission	Rated power (kW) per motor	Max speed km/h	Weight tonnes per car (M-motor T-trailer)	Total seating capacity (M-motor T-trailer)	Length per car m	No in service	Year first built	Builders		
											Mechanical parts	Engine & type	Transmission
1-4	1	2	Hyd	186.5	108	M 52.19 T 44.23	M 64 T 72	25.7	100	1975	Fiat-Materfer	Fiat IVECO	Fiat OM Brescia

Electric multiple-unit for Buenos Aires metro

First-class diesel railcar for Cuban Railways

Interior of Buenos Aires metro emu

Serving area of self-service cafeteria car for Cuban Railways; length 25.56 m, tare weight 50 tonnes

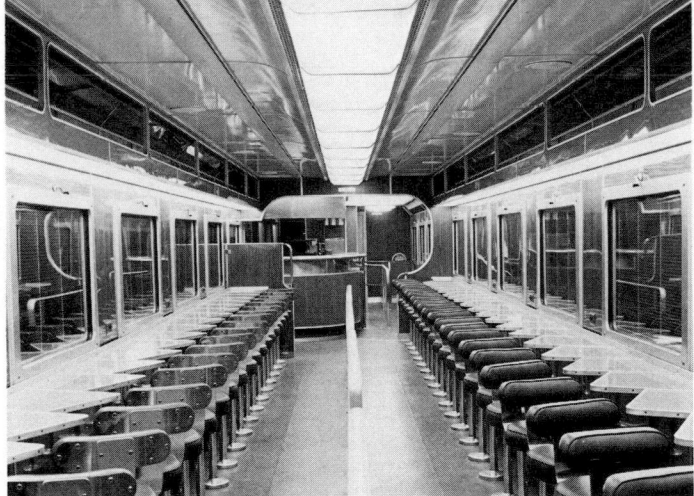

Seating area of Cuban Railways cafeteria car, with provision for hot food service

Interior of Cuban Railways first-class diesel railcar

Firema Consortium

Head office: Corso di Porta Romana 63, 20122 Milan, Italy

Telephone: (02) 5465708; (02) 588936

President: Dr Ing Giorgio Regazzoni
General Manager: Prof Ing Francesco Perticaroli

Member companies
Officine di Cittadella SpA
Via Rometta all 'Olmo 5, 35013 Cittadella (Padua)
Telephone: 049 591966
Telex: 430854

Officina Meccanica della Stanga SpA
Corso Stati Uniti 3, 35100 Padua
Telephone: 049 760488
Telex: 430218

Casaralta SpA
Via Ferrarese 205, 40128 Bologna
Telephone: 051 358454
Telex: 511068

Class Le724 emu driving trailer for FS

Fiore SpA
General Management: 81020 S Nicola La Strada (Caserta)
Telephone: 0823 467677
Telex: 720387
Works: Zona Industriale, 81020 S Nicola La Strada (Caserta)
  Via Gabella del Pesce 23, 80056 Ercolano (Naples)

Officine Casertane SpA
81020 S Nicola La Strada (Caserta)
Telephone: 0823 467499
Telex: 720458

To co-ordinate and develop studies in the design and manufacture of powered and trailer rolling-stock the Firema Group has founded:

Firema Engineering SRL
Corso di Porta Romana 63, 20122 Milan
Telephone: 02 5465708, 588936
Telex: 322255

Products: Locomotives, multiple-units, railcars, underground rolling stock, light rail vehicles, passenger and freight cars.

With Italian State Railways (FS) set to order 1250 new open saloon cars for its inter-city operations in 1982, Officine di Cittadella manufactured to FS designs a prototype car built to standard UIC 26.4-metre length. Weighing 36 tonnes tare and fitted with plug end doors, the vehicle seats 84. It is equipped with forced air ventilation, not air-conditioning, and is not fitted with electro-magnetic track brakes, so that its top operating speed is limited to 160 km/h. Its appearance followed commitment to production of 350 of the Type nBz car with pairs of centrally-located double doors and entrance vestibules for FS medium-distance services. This air-conditioned vehicle is 26.4 metres long overall, tare 35.4 tonnes and seats 82 in a strikingly styled saloon interior.

The Group's recent deliveries to FS have included 30 light-alloy driving trailers of Class Le724, from its member Officina Meccanica della Stanga of Padua. To be employed with the latest FS chopper-controlled 3 kV dc power cars, each trailer has 72 seats and standing room for 102 within a tare weight of 30.9 tonnes and length of 24.78 metres; it is designed for 140 km/h maximum speed.

In 1982 the Group received orders from FS for the mechanical parts for 60 more Class E656 3 kV dc 3860 kW Bo-Bo-Bo electric locomotives. Of this total 20 were to be assembled by Casaralta (with electrical equipment by Retam); and 40 by Officina Casertane (with electrical equipment for 33 by Metalmeccanica Lucana, for the remainder by Ansaldo).

FS inter-city open saloon

FS inter-city open saloon interior

Type nBz car for FS medium-distance operation

Benevento-Cancello Railway 80-seat 3 kV dc railcar

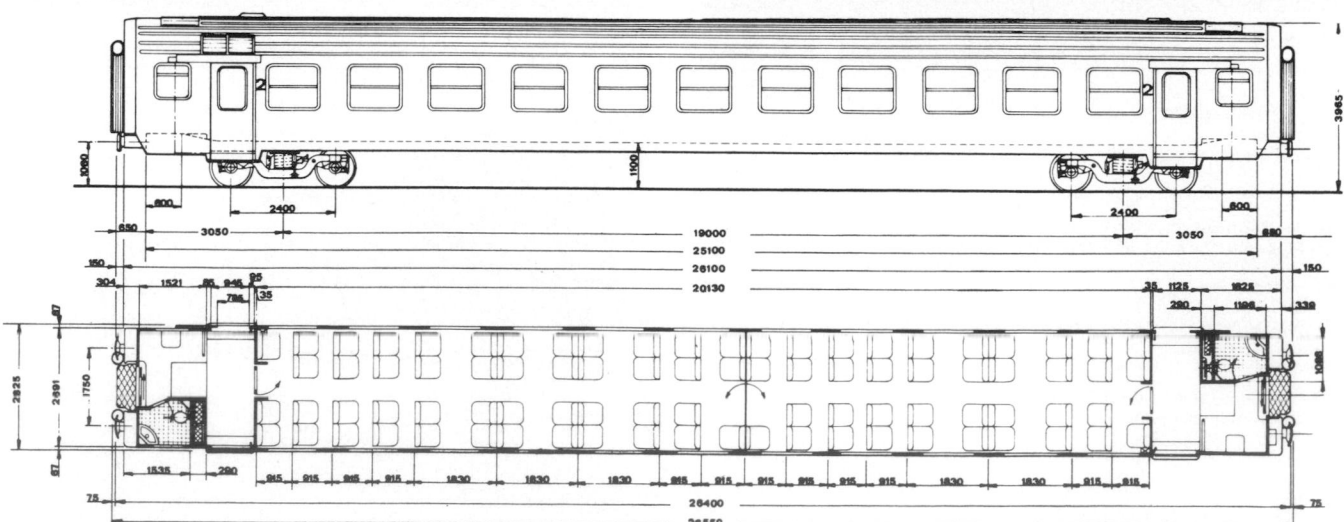
FS inter-city open saloon layout

FMC

FMC Corp

Marine and Rail Equipment Division

4700 NW Front Avenue, PO Box 3616, Portland, Oregon 97208, USA

Telephone: (503) 228 9281
Telex: 36 0672

President: John E Carroll Jr
Chief Engineer: R J Landregan
Chief Sales Officer: William R Galbraith

Products: Freight wagons.
FMC's new high volume 30-ton box-car is designed for light density cargoes,
such as tissue paper, insulation, plastic bottles, etc. It has a 50 per cent greater inside capacity than a 'standard' 50-foot boxcar, yet its 57 000 lb empty weight is about the same as that of a 'standard' car. Weight-saving features include a box girder-designed corrugated end, permitting the use of a lighter weight steel without sacrifice of strength and a wooden floor. The car's leading dimensions are: length, inside 18.59 m; width, inside 2.9 m; height, inside at eaves 3.96 m; door opening (clear), width 3.05 m, height 3.78 m; length over coupler pulling faces 20.34 m; bogie centres 14.1 m; bogie wheelbase 1.68 m; total wheelbase 15.77 m; width, extreme 3.25 m; height, top of rail to top of roof 5.16 m; cubic capacity 213.3 m^3; gross rail load 54 431 kg; tare weight 25 855 kg.

FMC's 4000 cubic foot 100-ton open top gondola is designed for unit-train operation utilising rotary dump service. The gondola's leading particulars are: length, inside 14.3 m; over pulling face of couplers 16.18 m; bogie centres 12.34 m; width, inside 2.97 m, extreme 3.25 m; bogie wheelbase 1.78 m; total wheelbase 14.12 m; gross rail load 119 295 kg; estimated tare weight 28 077 kg.

FMC high-volume 30-ton boxcar with 213 m^3 load capacity

FMC high-side coal gondola with 113.3 m^3 capacity

FNV

Veiculos e Equipamentos S/A

Avenida Maria Coelho Aguiar n° 215, Block A, 8th floor, 05804 São Paulo, Brazil

Telephone: 011 545 3610, 011 545 5089
Telegrams: Fabriva
Telex: 01121901

President: José Burlamaqui de Andrade
Superintendent Director: José Antonio P de Andrade
Industrial Director: Waldemar Fonseca
Railway Equipments Division: Antonio Cleubis de Campos
Foundry Division: José Carlos Zebral

Products: Freight wagons; passenger coaches; electric train-sets; Barber stabilised bogies; draftgears; couplers; cast steel wheels and components.
Major contracts recently fulfilled have been with: RFFSA, Brazil, for 50 platform wagons, 1600 mm gauge, maximum gross weight 100 tons, length 18.3 m; and 10 platform wagons, metre gauge, maximum gross weight 80 tons, length 13.8 m; Ciminas, Brazil, for 115 bulk cement bogie wagons, metre gauge, capacity 50 metres^3, maximum gross weight 80 tons, equipped with low-pressure discharge system; and with Enafer, Peru, for 60 hopper wagons, 1435 mm gauge, 23 cubic metre capacity, maximum gross weight 72 tons, bottom unloading by means of two longitudinal doors (800 × 3048 mm) with adjustable opening device to provide material flow control.

Constitution: The company was formed in 1943 to manufacture freight wagons. The plant covers an area of over 80 000 metres^2 and has diversified to include production of couplers, yokes, bogies and cast wheels among its railway industry range.

Hopper wagon for calcareous stones, metre gauge, 21 m^3 capacity, glw 64 tons, delivered to Cemento El Melon, Chile, in 1982

Iron ore gondola wagons, 1600 mm gauge, for car-dumper unloading operation, 45 m^3 capacity, glw 119 tons, delivered to RFFSA in 1982

Box wagon for fertilisers, bottom-unloading, metre gauge, 74 m^3 capacity, glw 80 tons, delivered to Nitrofertil, Brazil, in 1982

Bulk cement bogie wagon for Ciminas, Brazil

Francorail

33 quai de Dion Bouton, 92814 Puteaux Cedex, France

Telephone: 776 43 64
Telex: 630 756

Managing Director: H Jullien (General Manager, Société MTE)
Directors: J Pelabon (President, ANF-Industrie)
R Juchs (President, Carel Fouché)
G De Dietrich (President, De Dietrich & Cie)
J Lerebours-Pigeonnière (President, Société MTE)
Sales Manager: H Dhaussy

Products: Main-line electric and diesel-electric locomotives; high-speed TGV trains; turbotrains; shunting locomotives and other tractive stock; electric and diesel multiple-units; railcars; metro cars; passenger coaches and other rolling stock; bogies; constituent sub-assemblies of the above-mentioned equipment; advanced vehicles and transport systems; metropolitan rapid transit systems; suburban transport systems.

The Group's recent orders have included 72 2648 kW (3600 hp) diesel-electric Co-Co locomotives for the Baghdad-Hussaiba line under construction by Iraqi Republic Railways (IRRO). General design is by MTE. The engine is an Alco 16-cylinder turbo-charged Type 251F, which is linked to an ac/dc transmission feeding nose-suspended traction motors via a silicon rectifier. The locomotives are produced in passenger and freight haulage variants, the former with a gross weight of 126 tonnes, the latter with a gross weight of 135 tonnes and a maximum axle-loading of 22.5 tonnes. An order for six locomotives of the same type was awarded to Francorail by Saudi Government Railways (SGRO); these machines were delivered in 1982.

ANF's plant at Crespin is currently producing 236 modern air-conditioned passenger coaches of six different types for IRRO as well as three gas turbine train-sets of 10 vehicles each, plus eight stand-by vehicles, for Egyptian Railways (ER). (For details see under ANF-Industrie.)

3600 hp diesel-electric for Saudi Government Railways (SGRO)

Carel-Fouché's plant at Aubevoye is currently producing 153 stainless steel passenger coaches for ER.

Francorail has been awarded an order for 225 power cars for the New York City Transit Authority. The manufacture of these stainless steel cars will involve most of Francorail's production plants.

Francorail, with Alsthom-Atlantique, is a leader of the consortium of French manufacturers which is establishing a new company, TGV Inc, to market TGV/LGV technology in the USA.

Francorail diesel locomotives

Class	Wheel arrangement	Transmission	Rated power (kW)	Max speed km/h	Total weight tonnes	No in service	Year first built	Builders		
								Mechanical parts	Engine & type	Transmission
18 000	A1A-A1A	ac/dc	1325	119	96	25	1980	Creusot-Loire	Alsthom-Atlantique 12PA4185	Jeumont-Schneider
3600	Co-Co	ac/dc	2650	140 160	126	87 (deliveries in progress)	1982	Creusot-Loire De Dietrich ANF	Alco 251	Jeumont-Schneider
900	Bo-Bo	dc/dc	661	80	68	20	1981	Alsthom Creusot-Loire	Poyaud	Alsthom Jeumont-Schneider

(For diesel railcars, multiple-units and turbotrains, see under ANF-Industrie)

Francorail electric railcars or multiple units

Class	Cars per unit	Line voltage	Motor cars per unit	Motored axles per motor car	Rated output (kW) per motor	Max speed km/h	Weight tonnes per car (M-motor T-trailer)	Total seating capacity	Length per car mm (M-motor T-trailer)	No in service	Rate of acceleration m/s²	Year first built	Builders	
													Mechanical parts	Electrical equipment
SNCF Z 7300	2	1.5 kV	1	4	325	160	M 63 T 39.5	159	M 25 100 T 25 100	90		1980	Carel Fouché De Dietrich ANF	Jeumont-Schneider Alsthom TCO
SNCF Z 9500	2	1.5 kV/ 25 kV	1	4	325	160	M 65 T 50	159	M 25 100 T 25 100	56		1982	Carel Fouché De Dietrich ANF	Jeumont-Schneider Alsthom TCO
	4	3 kV	2	4	281.5	90	M 58 T 44	264	M 22 235 T 22 000	25 on order	0.8	(Delivery to begin 1984)	Francorail Cobrasma	Francorail TCO IEBB
SNCF Z2N	4 or 5	1.5 kV or 25 kV	2	4	350	140	M 66-70 T 42	166/220	M 25 100 T 24 280	40	0.9	1982	ANF & CIMT TCO (M)	TCO & Jeumont-Schneider

Francorail electric locomotives

Class	Wheel arrangement	Line voltage	Rated output (kW) continuous one-hour	Max speed km/h	Weight tonnes	No in service	Year first built	Builders	
								Mechanical parts	Electrical equipment
SNCF BB22220	Bo-Bo	1.5 kV/25 kV	4400	200	89	10 (Nos BB 22351-60)	1976	Alsthom Creusot-Loire	Jeumont-Schneider Alsthom
SNCF BB22220	Bo-Bo	1.5 kV/25 kV	4400	100	80	20 (Nos BB 22361-80)	1976	Alsthom Creusot-Loire	Jeumont-Schneider Alsthom
SNCF BB7400	Bo-Bo	1.5 kV	4400	180	85	30 (Nos BB 7411-40)	1976	Alsthom Creusot-Loire	Jeumont-Schneider Alsthom
FEPASA 2200	Bo-Bo	3 kV	2540	90	100	80 (on order)	(Delivery to begin 1984)	MTE Alsthom-Atlantique	MTE Alsthom-Atlantique Siemens AEG ACEC BBC

Freighter
Freighter Industries Ltd

Ashley House, 409 St Kilda Road, Melbourne, Victoria 3004, Australia

Telephone: 03 267 3888
Telegrams: Escor, Melbourne
Telex: 32148

Products: Hy-Rail road-rail conversion vehicle; all-steel containers. Hy-Rail equipment is designed to enable a conventional road vehicle to be converted to run on railway lines with a minimum of effort and time. The basic principle is the use of small flanged rail wheels which come in contact with the rail line and take a percentage of the vehicle weight. These act as guides preventing the road wheels from running off the track. The traction for acceleration and braking is provided in the normal manner by the road tyres being in contact with the line.

Hy-Rail can be fitted to nearly all road vehicles provided tyre track is compatible with or can be safely modified to suit the particular rail gauge required. Hy-Rail can be built to suit all gauges and uses its patented over-centre principle to lock the rail wheels into their on-rail mode. The same method is used in locking down aircraft undercarriages.

Hy-Rail for road/rail conversion

Kosan Frichs
Kosan Frichs A/S

Soren Frichsvej 38, 8100 Aarhus C, Denmark

Telephone: (06) 15 85 55
Telegrams: Frichs, Aarhus
Telex: 64373

Director: E F Hyldahl

Products: Diesel locomotives and railcars; diesel and electric railcars and multiple-units; centrifugally-cast cylinder liners for diesel engines.

Constitution: Founded as a general engineering company in 1854; the manufacture of diesel locomotives started in 1925. The company was incorporated into Kosan in January 1980.

Fuji
Fuji Heavy Industries Ltd
Rolling Stock Division

7-2 1-chome Nishishinjuku 1-chome, Shinjuku-ku, Tokyo 160, Japan

Telephone: 03 347 2436
Telegrams: Fujiheavy, Tokyo
Telex: 0 232 2268

Chairman: Eiichi Ohara

President: Sadamachi Sasaki
Executive Director: Sukemitsu Irie
Director and General Manager: Masami Suwabe
Manager, Rolling Stock Sales: Eiichi Sano

Products: Electric and diesel train-sets; passenger coaches; freight wagons; works vehicles.

Constitution: Fuji Heavy Industries stems from the Nakajima Aircraft Company. The Nakajima Company was dissolved in 1945, but in 1953 it was reorganised as Fuji Heavy Industries, specialising in building SUBARU automobiles, buses, rolling stock and aircraft.

Crane car for New York City Transit Authority, USA

Model K1HA 183 KEI diesel railcar for Japanese National Railways

Maintenance and line cars for Greater Cleveland Regional Transit Authority, USA

Revolving platform car for Japanese National Railways

Fuji Car
Fuji Car Manufacturing Co Ltd

383 Sayamacho, Minamikawachigun, Osaka 589, Japan

Telephone: (Sakai) 0722 (36) 5761
Telegrams: Fujcar, Sakai
Telex: 05374487

Chairman: Kanichi Nakayasu
Senior Managing Director: Junnich Takano
Export Sales: Hisashi Okumura

Products: Passenger coaches; freight wagons; bogies.
In co-operation with Japan Oil Transportation Ltd (JOT), the company has

developed a prototype covered hopper wagon capable of two-way loading with different commodities without risk of contamination. Adulteration is prevented by the use of rubber membranes running the full length of the body interior, attached at the top and bottom; the membranes' position can be varied by altering the position of inversion plates running along the bottom of the car. When the plates are open, the membranes line the car walls; when they are closed, the membranes are moved to meet and form an inner wall along the centre of the car, the body of which is then converted into chambers. Hopper-top covers are arranged to provide for easy loading in both configurations. The device ensures that a commodity loaded in one configuration does not touch any surfaces with which a commodity loaded in the alternative configuration comes in contact. The vehicle is fitted with air-operated discharge for one mode, and bottom side-doors for discharge in the alternative loading mode.

Constitution: The company was formed in 1924. In 1945 the name was changed in order to specialise in the manufacture of rolling stock.

Funkey
C H Funkey & Co (Pty) Ltd

PO Box 183, Barnsley Road, Industrial Sites, Benoni 1500, South Africa

Telephone: 845 1256
Telex: 4 20955

Managing Director: Gerald Steyn
Marketing Director: Ray Dalcher
Director, Spares and Logistics: John Galloway

Products: Mining battery locomotives, mining diesel locomotives, inspection trolleys, 22-man gang trolleys and industrial shunting locomotives from 10 to 65 tonnes.

Constitution: C H Funkey is now a wholly-owned subsidiary of the Barlow Rand Group. For closer connection with the Benoni plant of Barlows Heavy Engineering the company has moved to new premises in Benoni.

Funkey 65-ton Type F60 diesel-hydraulic Bo-Bo

Funkey 30-ton Type F40 diesel-hydraulic 0-4-0

Funkey 6-ton battery mining locomotive

Funkey industrial locomotives

Type	Diesel-hydrostatic					Diesel-hydrokinetic				Diesel-electric	
Model	F10	F14	F17	F20	F30	F40	F45	F50	F60	TH75	F80
Duty	Light yard shunt	Light siding shunt	Short-haul shunt	Short-haul shunt	Shunt and branch line	Shunt and branch line	Shunt and branch line	Branch line	Branch line	Long-haul, branch line and ultra low-speed	Long-haul branch line
Weight (tonnes)	7.5-10	12-15	16-18	18-22	23-40	33-44	40-60	50	55-65	75	50-80
Power (kW)	44	62	113	170	200-270	340-480	340-480	340-480	500-750	500-750	900
Transmission	Variable displacement axial pump Fixed displacement radial motor	Variable displacement axial pump Fixed displacement radial motor	Clark torque converter and 3-speed power shift transmission	Clark torque converter and 3-speed power shift transmission	Allison converter and 3-speed converter transmission	Twin Disc or Clark torque converter and 4-speed power shift transmission	Twin Disc or Clark torque converter and 4-speed power shift transmission	Twin Disc or Clark torque converter and 4-speed power shift transmission	Clark torque converter and 4-speed power shift transmission	Brown Boveri alternator; ac axle-hung motors	Brown Boveri alternator; dc axle-hung motors
Gearbox	—	—	Axle-mounted worm and wheel gearbox	Axle-mounted spiral bevel input, straight tooth pinion and gear output	Axle-mounted spiral bevel input, straight tooth pinion and gear output	Axle-mounted spiral bevel input, straight tooth pinion and gear output	Axle-mounted spiral bevel input, straight tooth pinion and gear output	Axle-mounted heavy duty spiral bevel input, single helical output on each axle	Axle-mounted heavy duty spiral bevel input, single helical output on each axle	—	—
Final drive	Heavy duty chain	Heavy duty chain	Cardan shafts	Cardan shafts	Cardan shafts	Cardan shafts	Cardan shafts	Cardan shafts	Cardan shafts	—	—
Brakes	Dynamic and parking (mechanical)	Dynamic and parking Train-vacuum	Loco-air Train-vacuum	Loco-air Train-vacuum	Loco-air Train-vacuum	Loco-air Train-vacuum	Loco-air Train-vacuum	Loco-air Train-vacuum	Loco-air Train-vacuum	Loco-air Train-vacuum	Loco-air Train-vacuum
Speed (km/h)	0-10	0-13.5	0-25	0-30	0-30/50	0-50	0-50	0-50	0-50	0-60	0-70
Starting tractive effort (kN) at 27% adhesion	20-26	32-40	42-48	48-58	61-85	87-117	106-159	132	146-172	316 (43%)	162-259 (33%)
Wheel arrangement	0-4-0	0-4-0	0-4-0	0-4-0	0-4-0	0-4-0	0-6-0	Bo-Bo	Bo-Bo	0-6-0	Bo-Bo

Optional extras: Train air brake equipment, tandem/multiple operation, deadman/vigilance control, tinted windows, air-conditioned cab, overhead power pick-up (on diesel-electric units) to replace diesel engine
Standard features: 6 mm steel plate body. Weatherproof/heat insulated cab, large-capacity exhauster and compressor, high-technology soft ride suspension

Gallinari
A Gallinari SpA

Viale Ramazzini 37, 42100 Reggio Emilia, Italy

Telephone: 31 641
Telegrams: Gallinari, Reggio Emilia
Telex: 530601

Products: Passenger coaches; flat and covered wagons, tank wagons, baggage and mail cars.

Ganz
Ganz Electric Works

Lövőház utca 39, Budapest 1024, Hungary

Telephone: 158 210
Telegrams: Alterno, Budapest
Telex: 225363

General Manager: György Papp
Deputy General Manager: László Zatykó
Export Sales Manager: Sándor Csernock

Products: Electric main-line locomotives; railcars and train-sets; trams and metros; electric components for trolleybuses and diesel-electric vehicles; railway signalling and interlocking equipments; complete power transmission equipments; complete substations.

Series production of Class V43 2200 kW (3000 hp) locomotives with diode rectifier for Hungarian State Railways (MÁV) started in 1964 under licence from the 50 c/s Group. By the end of 1982 about 380 locomotives had been manufactured. As early as 1967 Ganz Electric Works began tests of thyristor control with equipment supplied by Siemens. The next experiment was the manufacture of a 2200 kW series locomotive with thyristor control, for which the thyristor rectifier and control equipment were supplied by AEG. From experience gained GEW developed and manufactured two prototype six-axle thyristor controlled 3600 kW locomotives which were put into service in 1974 and 1975. Since 1981 five of these locomotives have been in operation on MÁV and 19 more are being manufactured for MÁV.

Among recent products is a three-car 25 kV 50 Hz commuter emu for Yugoslav Railways (JZ). The centre car only is powered and carries most of the electrical equipment under its floor. Its four compound-excited, ripple-current dc motors

have a combined continuous rating of 1200 kW and one of 1750 kW for acceleration from rest to 100 km/h; maximum speed is 120 km/h. Motor control is stepless by means of two series-connected, half-controlled thyristor rectifiers. Train speed control is automatic when a pre-set value is attained and is secured by the rheostatic braking fitted in addition to Oerlikon air brakes; rate of acceleration from rest to approximately 60 km/h is 0.5 m/s². Auxiliary motors are three-phase squirrel-cage asynchronous machines. A full three-car unit is 72.4 metres in length and weighs 145.5 Mp tare; when designed exclusively for second-class use, with centrally-located entrance doors in each car, it has a total of 236 seats. An initial delivery of 46 units has been followed by an order for four more, to be delivered in 1983 for service during the Winter Olympics at Sarajevo in 1984.

Constitution: This enterprise developed from the electrical department started by Ganz and Co in 1878.

Alternative first-class saloon design for three-car emu

3680 kW 160 km/h 25 kV 50 Hz locomotive for Hungarian State Railways (MÁV)

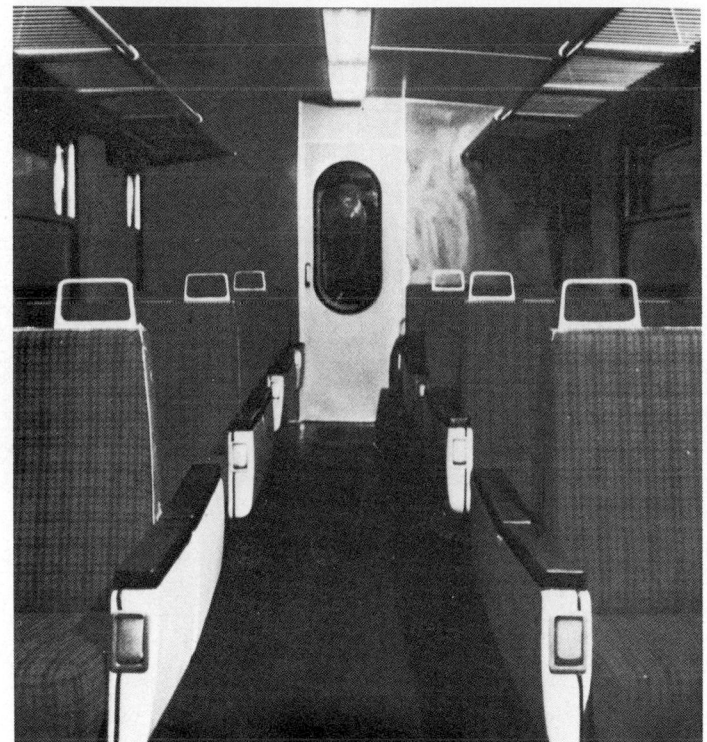

Three-car 25 kV 50 Hz commuter emu for Yugoslav Railways (JZ)

Second-class saloon interior of three-car JZ emu

Ganz electric locomotives

MÁV	Wheel arrangement	Line voltage	Rated output (kW) continuous	Max speed km/h	Weight tonnes	No in service	Year first built	Builders Mechanical parts	Electrical equipment
V 63	Co-Co	25 kV 50 Hz	3680	160	116	7	1980	Ganz-Màvag	Ganz Electric
V 43	B-B	25 kV 50 Hz	2200	130	80	380	1964	Ganz-Màvag	Ganz Electric

Ganz electric multiple-units for JZ

Cars per unit	Line voltage	Motor cars per unit	Motored axles per motor car	Rated output (kW) per motor	Max speed km/h	Weight per set (M-motor (T-trailer)	Total seating capacity	Length per set m (M-motor T-trailer)	No in service	Rate of acceleration first m/s²	Year first built	Builders Mechanical parts	Electrical equipment
3	25 kV	1	4	combined 1200-1750	120	143.5 Mp T+M+T	236	72.41 T+M+T	46	0.5	1976	Ganz-Màvag	Ganz Electric

Ganz-Mávag
Ganz-Mávag Locomotive and Railway Carriage Manufacturers and Mechanical Engineers

PO Box 136, Könyves Kálmán krt 76, Budapest VIII, Hungary

Telephone: 335-950, 137-020
Telegrams: Ganzrnávag, Budapest
Telex: 22 5575, 22 5576

Chairman and General Director: Dr András Dunajszki
Commercial Director: Dr Antal Fleck
Sales Manager, Railway Rolling Stock: Tibor Trompler

Products: Diesel-electric, diesel-hydraulic locomotives (250 to 2200 kW); diesel railcars, multiple-units, electric multiple-units and rapid-transit vehicles.
The first of a fleet of 44 two-car 1.5 kV dc emus for the Wellington area of New Zealand Railways (NZR) has lately been delivered under a contract placed in

1979. Each vehicle is mounted on air-sprung bogies constructed under licence from SIG, Switzerland and the single power car has four nose-suspended GEC Type G316AZ traction motors with a total continuous rating of 400 kW; this motor is derived from the Type G310AZ widely employed in British Rail's most recent emus, with modifications to suit NZR's 1067 mm gauge. Rate of acceleration is 0.75 m/s² up to 40 km/h, or an average of 0.44 m/s² from rest to 80 km/h, the emus' limit on NZR, though they are designed for a top speed of 100 km/h; they have also been prepared to sustain 80 km/h up the 0.9 per cent climb in tunnel between Wellington and Tawa, one of several steep inclines in the operating area. Rheostatic and electro-pneumatic disc braking are blended in a six-stage system, designated Westcode 3+3, produced by Westinghouse Brake & Signal Co of Australia, which achieves a maximum retardation rate of 1 m/s² and will halt a unit from 100 km/h within 460 metres. Seating capacity of a two-car unit is 148.

Constitution: Ganz Railway Carriage Manufacturers and Mechanical Engineers, and Mávag Locomotive and Machine Works were merged in 1959 to form Ganz-Mávag.

Type DHM11 1325 kW diesel-hydraulic locomotive for Tunisian Railways

Two-car suburban emu for Wellington area of New Zealand Railways

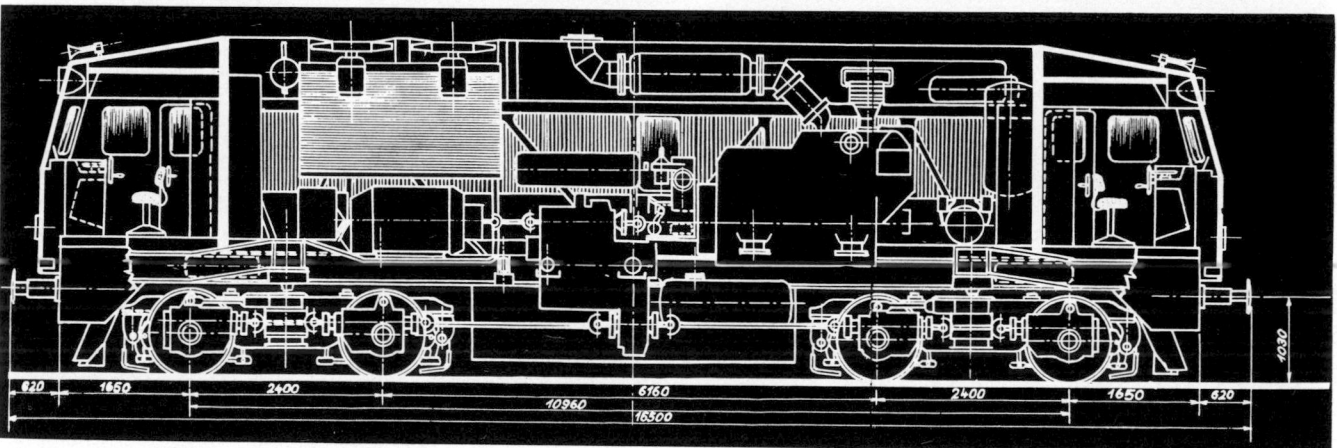

Type DHM7 diesel-hydraulic locomotive rated at 1325 kW

Garrett Railroad Car & Equipment
Garrett Railroad Car & Equipment, Inc

PO Box 2208, East Cherry Street, Newcastle, Pennsylvania 16102, USA

Telephone: (412) 658 9061

President: F J Garrett

President, Southern Division: J E Lands
Vice President, Railroad Car Division: R E Krause
Marketing Manager, Rebuilt Equipment: H J Reed
Marketing Manager, New Equipment: J R Garrett

Products: New and rebuilt freight wagons for revenue and industrial use; freight wagon repairs; and special steel fabrication of rolling stock components and related parts.

Garrett Railroad Car Parts Corporation

PO Box 34, Darlington, Pennsylvania 16115, USA

Telephone: (412) 827 8121

President: D E Needler

Assistant to President: J W Shearer
Vice President: M A Sitarik
Operations Manager: B Donohue
Materials Manager: E D Garrett

Products: New, reconditioned and used rolling stock parts; complete air brake repair facility; rebuilt or specially modified rolling stock parts and equipment.

GEC Australia
GEC Australia Ltd

Evans Road, Rocklea, Queensland 4106, Australia

Telephone: 07 2771611
Telegrams: Geched, Brisbane
Telex: 40167

Divisional Managing Director: J B Torrance

Products: Electric and diesel-electric locomotives; rolling stock; electric and diesel-electric traction power and control equipment.

GEC Traction
GEC Traction Ltd

Head office: PO Box 134, Manchester M60 1AH, England

Telephone: 061 872 2431
Telegrams: Assocelect, Manchester
Telex: 667152

UK works: Trafford Park, Manchester; Preston and Sheffield

Directors: J Legg (Managing)
K Appelbee
F Marley
D R Love
K Gunary
C Salt
A L Fairbrother
R L McNaughton
P A Heron

Products: Complete electric and diesel-electric locomotives; multiple-unit trains and power cars; propulsion equipments for all types mentioned. The product range includes equipment for all standard electrification voltages from 600 to 3000 volts dc plus 25 and 50 kV ac, as well as covering the complete spectrum of axleloads, track gauges and speeds.

The company's major projects at the start of 1983 included:
Australia: Propulsion equipment for 380 emu power cars for the 1.5 kV Melbourne suburban services of VicRail, built by Comeng. The majority will have camshaft control but a number will have chopper control. Manufacture is being split between the UK and Australia.
Brazil: Propulsion equipments for 65 3 kV suburban emu trains. The prototype vehicles were built in West Germany and the production trains in Brazil. The manufacture of electrical equipment has also been split between Brazil and the UK.
Brazil: 35 180-tonne Co-Co heavy freight locomotives. The complete locomotives are being designed by GEC Traction in the UK but will be built in Brazil. Electrification is at 25 kV, 60 Hz.
Hong Kong: A total of 470 power cars for the 1.5 kV Mass Transit Railway had been ordered. A second order had been placed for the 25 kV suburban trains of the Kowloon-Canton Railway.
Ireland: Equipment of 40 1.5 kV chopper trains for Dublin suburban service. The vehicles are being built in West Germany.
Republic of Korea: A total of 134 three-car trains were being equipped for Lines 3 and 4 of the Seoul metro. They will include regenerative chopper equipments and some manufacture of electrical equipment will take place in South Korea together with that of the vehicles themselves.
South Africa: Latest orders for the Class 6E1 mixed traffic locomotives bring the total for this one class to 1045, the largest single class of electric locomotive in the world. A further six complete Class 9E locomotives have been supplied for the world's largest application of 50 kV electrification. Work was in hand for equipment for a further 203 of the 3 kV Class 5M2A suburban emu trains.
UK: Work was well advanced on equipment for BR Southern Region's 117 Class 455 suburban emu trains.

Smaller projects in hand included equipment for diesel locomotives for Iraq and Saudi Arabia, trolleybuses for South Africa and the USA, and trams for India.

Constitution: GEC Traction traces its railway history back to the Robert Stephenson Company which, in 1823, was the first company in the world to be established specifically to build locomotives. The company has been continuously in the railway traction business for 160 years, longer than any other manufacturer in the world. The company now incorporates the traction activities of many other locomotive and electric traction manufacturers, notably AEI, BTH, Dick Kerr, English Electric, GEC, Metro-Vickers, Siemens (UK) and the Vulcan Foundry.

GEC Traction is the United Kingdom's largest exporter of electric traction propulsion equipment.

Sales of more than 35 000 electric and diesel locomotives and equipments have been made to 71 countries since 1890. The locomotives and equipments have operated in widely differing conditions from tropical heat throegh dsert to the Arctic; in altitudes ranging from below sea level to the world's highest railway (over 15 000 feet); on slow freight and high-speed inter-city services; and on mass transit systems. The production range includes thyristor control for the world's standard electrification voltages: 25 and 50 kV at 50 and 60 Hz; 3000, 1500, 750 and 600 volts dc and battery.

The company is presently involved in contracts for railways in eight overseas countries in addition to several projects in the UK. This work involves mechanical parts builders in eight countries. Similarly the company's manufacturing base is in the UK but there are also close links with overseas factories; its products are built under licence in four countries overseas.

Two 3 kV suburban emus for Brazil

Artist's impression of heavy freight locomotives in manufacture for Brazil

1.5 kV suburban emu for VicRail, Australia

25 kV suburban emu for Kowloon-Canton Railway

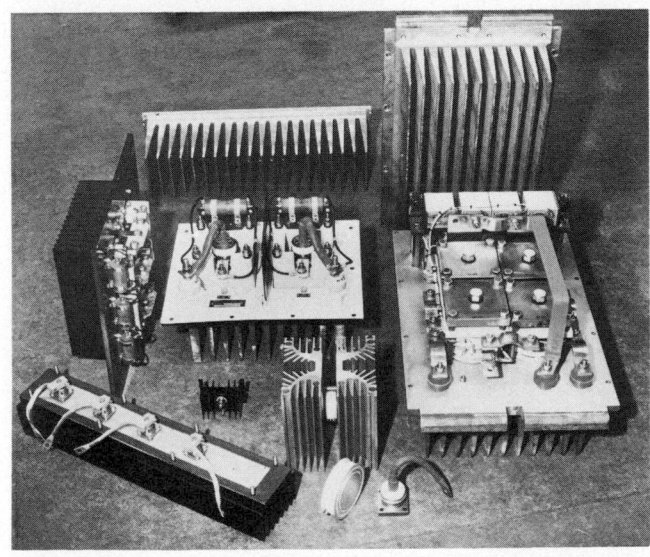
GEC semi-conductor devices and their mounting/cooling arrangements

1.5 kV regenerative chopper equipment for Dublin emus undergoing full load combined testing at GEC Traction's Preston works

GEC-equipped 1.5 kV dc emu for Wellington suburban services, New Zealand

GEC-equipped, third-rail dc Class 455 emu for British Rail Southern Region

General Electric
General Electric Company
Transportation Systems Business Operations

2901 East Lake Road, Erie, Pennsylvania 16531, USA

Telephone: 875 2794
Telegrams: Geco 14 Eri

Export Office: International Region, GE Co, 570 Lexington Avenue, New York, New York 10022

Vice-President and General Manager, Locomotive Marketing Division: John C Dwyer
Manager, Locomotive Marketing: R C McIntyre
Manager, Renewal Parts Marketing: L E Ewell

Products: Diesel-electric and electric locomotives; switching and mining locomotives.

The company's latest domestic diesel-electric locomotive, the 3600 bhp Type C36-7, is a six-axle complement to the four-axle B36-7 of the same output introduced in 1980. Claimed to offer a potential 11.4 per cent fuel saving by comparison with earlier high-tonnage freight units on typical US freight duty cycles, the C36-7 employs the GE four-stroke diesel engine with GE 1616B4 turbocharger. A main feature of the latter is an improved turbocharger seal system that has reduced the amount of compressed air needed to prevent carbon build-up and subsequent seal failure; its further benefit is improvement of fuel system efficiency as a result of a reduction in the air compressor duty cycle. Moreover, the turbocharger's lower operating temperature obviates the need to modify the engine speed schedule to permit acceleration to higher speed when traction load is comparatively low; this too lowers fuel consumption, since the auxiliary load, all mechanically driven, is proportionately lowered by reversion to a standard speed schedule. Besides these and other fuel

Type C30-7 locomotive

GE Type SL 80 switching locomotive

Export models

Locomotive types	U10B	U11B	U15C	U22C*	U18C	U26C	U30C
Gross hp	1050	1100	1650	2300	1950	2750	3200
Hp for traction	950	1000	1550	2165	1820	2600	3000
Number of axles	4	4	6	6	6	6	6
Track gauge	All gauges from 914 to 1676 mm						
Couplers	To suit railway requirements						
Tractive effort at continuous motor rating (kN)	161	161	241	241	265	265	265
Max speed (km/h)	103	103	103	103	103	103	103
Minimum weight (kg)	49 700	49 700	80 500	88 900	80 500	96 200	96 200
Electrical system	dc/dc	dc/dc	dc/dc	dc/dc	ac/dc	ac/dc	ac/dc
Engine	CAT	CAT	GE	GE	GE	GE	GE
	D379	D398	FDL8	FDL12	FDL8	FDL12	FDL12
Traction gen/alt	GT 601	GT 601	GT 581	GT 581	GTA11	GTA11	GTA11
Traction motors	GE761	GE761	GE761	GE761	GE761	GE761	GE761

*Streamlined dual cab design available

economy improvements, the locomotive has enhanced haulage capability through use of Sentry Adhesion Control and the higher tractive effort rating of the GE-752AF motor.

Early in 1983 the company announced that it had completed and was testing two 'Dash 8' prototypes, successors of the 'Dash 7' models of its New Series described above, which was inaugurated in 1977. Pre-production models of the 'Dash 8' line were scheduled for 1984 and series production of its five planned models, B23-8, B30-8, C30-8, B36-8 and C36-8, from 1985 onwards. A main feature of the 'Dash 8' series will be extended use of electronics technology. A closed loop control system employing microprocessors will monitor performance of the locomotive and its components continuously, and to optimise the in-built diagnostic capability of the apparatus in reducing downtime most of the control equipment will be grouped in modules designed for ease of replacement. To improve fuel efficiency, the radiator fan, traction motor cooling and dynamic brake systems will have electrical instead of mechanical drives. To improve compressor reliability and cut costs of its maintenance by reducing its running time, a clutch is being added to the drive shaft from engine to compressor. A tractive effort increase of 10 per cent is expected from the 'Dash 8' models as a result of improved motor insulation and current carrying capacity.

In addition to its contract to supply National Railways of Mexico (NdeM) with 1000 diesel-electric locomotives or kits over a 10-year period, GE has won a $65 million order to supply 39 electric locomotives for NdeM's Queretaro Division. The type to be delivered is the E60C, a development of the design currently in service in the USA. (See also Addenda)

Licence agreements: General Electric (USA) has locomotive manufacturing agreements with the following:
Australia: A Goninan & Co
Brazil: General Electric do Brasil
Federal Republic of Germany: Krupp
South Africa: Dorbyl

GE 'New Series' Type C36-7 high adhesion diesel-electric locomotive

Electric locomotives

	E60C	E42C	E25B
Rail hp, continuous	5900	3750	2125
Voltage, kV	25/50	25	25
Frequency	50/60	60	60
Number of axles	6	6	4
Minimum weight			
lb	331 000	198 000	240 000
kg	150 000	90 000	109 100
Max speed			
mph	70	68	70
km/h	113	110	113
Continuous tractive effort			
lb	82 000	44 000	55 000
kg	37 200	20 000	25 000
Track gauges			
in	56·5/66	39·4/42	56·5/66
mm	1435/1676	1000/1067	1435/1676
Major equipment			
Traction motors	GE752	GE761	GE752
Line breaker	Vacuum circuit breaker		
Transformer	Sealed design-FOA		
Power converter	Forced air-cooled thyristors		
Ventilating system	Single blower, self-cleaning filters		

Type U26C locomotive

Type B36-7 locomotive

General Electric Type E42C 25 kV electric locomotive

Domestic general purpose models

Model	B18-7	B23-7	B30-7A	C30-7A	B36-7	C36-7
Wheel arrangement	B-B	B-B	B-B	C-C	B-B	C-C
Engine data						
No of engines (all turbocharged) and hp	1 × 1800	1 × 2250	1 × 3000	1 × 3000	1 × 3600	1 × 3600
No of cylinders	8	12	12	12	16	16
Model	GE FDL-8	GE FDL-12	GE FDL-12	GE FDL-12	GE FDL-16	GE FDL-16
rpm	1050	1050	1050	1050	1050	1000
Dimensions						
Length (m)	16.97	18.64	18.64	20.5	18.64	20.5
Height (m)	4.68	4.68	4.68	4.68	4.68	4.68
Width (m)	3.1	3.1	3.1	3.1	3.1	3.1
Bolster centres (m)	9.35	11.18	11.18	12.47	11.18	12.47
Bogie wheelbase (m)	2.74	2.74	2.74	4.14	2.74	4.14
Minimum track curvature (radians or degrees)						
for single unit	150' or 39°	150' or 39°	150' or 39°	273' or 21°	150' or 39°	273' or 21°
for mu or coupled to train	250' or 23°	250' or 23°	250' or 23°	273' or 21°	250' or 23°	273' or 21°
Weight on drivers minimum and max (lb)	230 600/268 000	253 000/280 000	253 600/280 000	359 000/420 000	259 800/280 000	366 600/420 000
Tractive effort						
Starting at 25% adhesion for minimum and max weight (lb)	57 650/67 000	63 250/70 000	63 250/70 000	89 750/105 000	64 950/70 000	91 650/105 000
Continuous tractive effort (lb) and speed (mph) on gear ratio indicated	61 000/8.4	61 000/10.7	64 600/12.0*	96 900/8.8	64 600/12.0*	96 900/11.0
Gear ratio and max speed mph (specimen)	83/20-70	83/20-70	83/20-70	83/20-70	83/20-70	83/20-70

*Power match   Note: All units equipped with roller bearing journals.

Switching locomotives

Model	SL80	SL110	SL144
Wheel arrangement	B-B	B-B	B-B
Engine data (all turbocharged)			
No of engines and hp	2 × 300	2 × 300	2 × 550
No of cylinders	6	6	6
Model	Cummins NT-855L4	Cummins NT-855L4	Cummins KTA-1150-L
rpm	2100	2100	2100
Dimensions			
Length (m)	11.58	12.5	13.72
Height (m)	3.92	3.92	4.04
Width (m)	2.9	2.9	2.9
Bolster centres (m)	6.1	6.71	7.62
Bogie wheelbase (m)	2.36	2.36	2.59
Minimum track curvature (radians or degrees)	75' or 77°	75' or 77°	100' or 57°
Weight on drivers minimum and max (lb)	130 000/160 000	170 000/220 000	230 000/288 000
Tractive effort			
Starting at 30% adhesion for minimum and max weight (lb)	39 000/48 000	51 000/66 000	69 000/86 400
Continuous tractive effort (lb) and speed (mph)	31 600/6.4	31 600/6.4	61 560/5.5
Gear ratio and max speed (mph)	20.9/1-21	20.9/1-21	10.52/1-35

General Electric do Brasil
General Electric do Brasil SA

Head offices: Rua Antonio de Godoy 88, São Paulo, Brazil

Telephone: 222 1177
Telex: 011 24018

Works: Estrada Campinos-Monte Mor Km 103, 13100 Campinos, São Paulo

Telephone: 41 1944
Telegrams: Ingenetric Campinos
Telex: 019 1168/1112

Chairman: J R Stonesifer
President: J B A Amorim
Manager, Heavy Apparatus Sector: F A Walsh
Manager, Marketing Operations: L C Mascarenhas
Railroad Operation, Enterprise, Transportation and Electrification: Guilhermo Marin

Products: Electric, diesel-electric locomotives.
 Recent contracts cover supply of 23 2387 kW, 180-tonne diesel-electric locomotives to Carajás, Brazil (1600 mm gauge); and of 20 1492 kW, 96-tonne diesel-electric locomotives to Mozambique State Railways (1067 mm gauge).

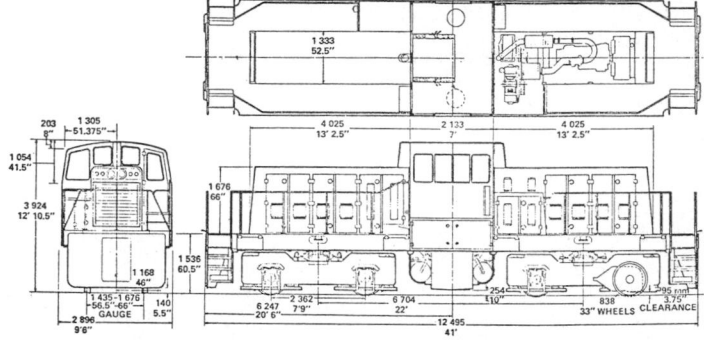

General arrangement of Type SL-110 switcher

448 kW Type SL-110 diesel-electric Bo-Bo switcher

1492 kW diesel-electric Co-Co for 1067 mm gauge Mozambique State Railways (CFM)

3 kV dc 3820 kW Co-Co electric locomotive by General Electric do Brasil

2685 kW diesel-electric Co-Co for National Railways of Mexico

670 hp B-B diesel-electric locomotive for 1600 mm gauge

570 hp B-B metre-gauge diesel-electric shunter

General Electric do Brasil diesel locomotives

Type	Wheel arrangement	Transmission	Rated power (kW)	Max speed kmlh	Total weight tonnes	No in service	Year first built	Builders		
								Mechanical parts	Engine & type	Transmission
Switcher	B-B	Elec	448	35	91	37	1966	GE	Cummins NT-855L2	GE
Switcher	B-B	Elec	388	35	73	57	1970	GE	Cummins NT-855L1	GE
Shunter	B-B	Elec	671	103	60	80	1971	GE	Caterpillar D398	GE
Road	C-C	Elec	1680	103	165/180	170	1972	GE	GE FDL12	GE
Switcher	B-B	Elec	98	35	25	3	1974	GE	Cummins H-6 Bl	GE
Road	C-C	Elec	1492	103	93/108	384	1974	GE	GE FDL12	GE
Switcher	B-B	Elec	671	35	100/127	23	1975	GE	Caterpillar D398	GE
Switcher	B-B	Elec	216	35	45	6	1977	GE	Cummins NT-855L3	GE
Switcher	B-B	Elec	388	35	60	19	1979	GE	Cummins NT-855L1	GE
Shunter	B-B	Elec	477	103	50	1	1979	GE	Caterpillar D379	GE
Road	C-C	Elec	1716	103	130	13	1979	GE	GE FDL12	GE
Road	C-C	Elec	2685	103	120	15	1979	GE	GE FDL16	GE
Road	C-C	Elec	1940	103	95	6	1980	GE	GE FDL12	GE

General Electric do Brasil electric locomotives

Type	Wheel arrangement	Line voltage	Rated output (kW) continuous	Max speed kmlh	Weight tonnes	No in service	Year first built	Builders	
								Mechanical parts	Electrical equipment
Road	C-C	3 kV dc	3820	125	144	10	1967	GE	GE
Road	B-B	3 kV dc	1620	100	73	30	1967	GE	GE

General Motors
Electro-Motive Division

Head office and main works: 9301 West 55th Street, La Grange, Illinois 60525, USA

Telephone: (312) 387 6543
Telegrams: Elmodiv, La Grange
Telex: 270041
TWX: 910 691 2186/2187/2188

General Manager: Peter K Hoglund
Director of Sales and Service: Warren A Fox
General Sales Manager, Domestic Locomotives: R E Hill
General Sales Manager, Export Locomotives and Associates: Frank J Babel

General Service Manager: William E Becker
General Parts Manager: Lutz W Elsner

Licensees: General Motors has locomotive manufacturing licence agreements with the following companies:
Clyde Engineering Co Pty Ltd, Granville, NSW, Australia
BN, Nivelles, Belgium
Material y Construcciones SA (MACOSA), Valencia, Spain
Kalmar Verkstad, Kalmar, Sweden
Duro Dakovic, Slavonski Brod, Yugoslavia
Thyssen-Henschel, Kassel, Federal Republic of Germany
Equipamentos Villares SA, São Paulo, Brazil
Hyundai Rolling Stock Co, Seoul, Republic of Korea

Supply agreement: General Motors has a supply agreement with Brush Electrical Machines Ltd, Loughborough, England

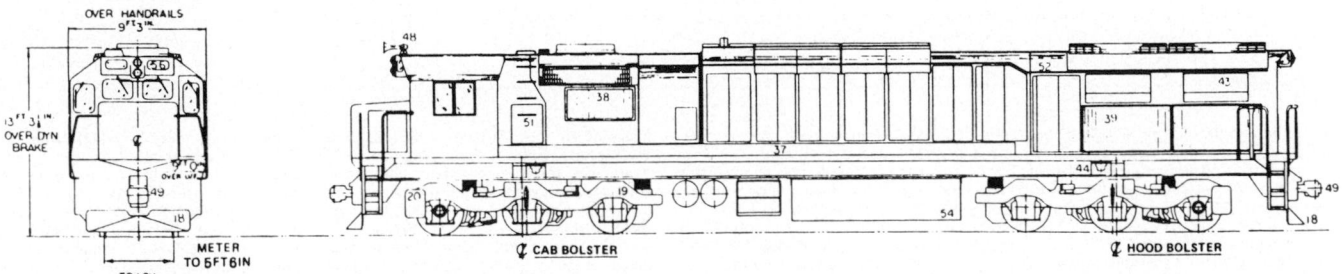

Layout of GT26C locomotive

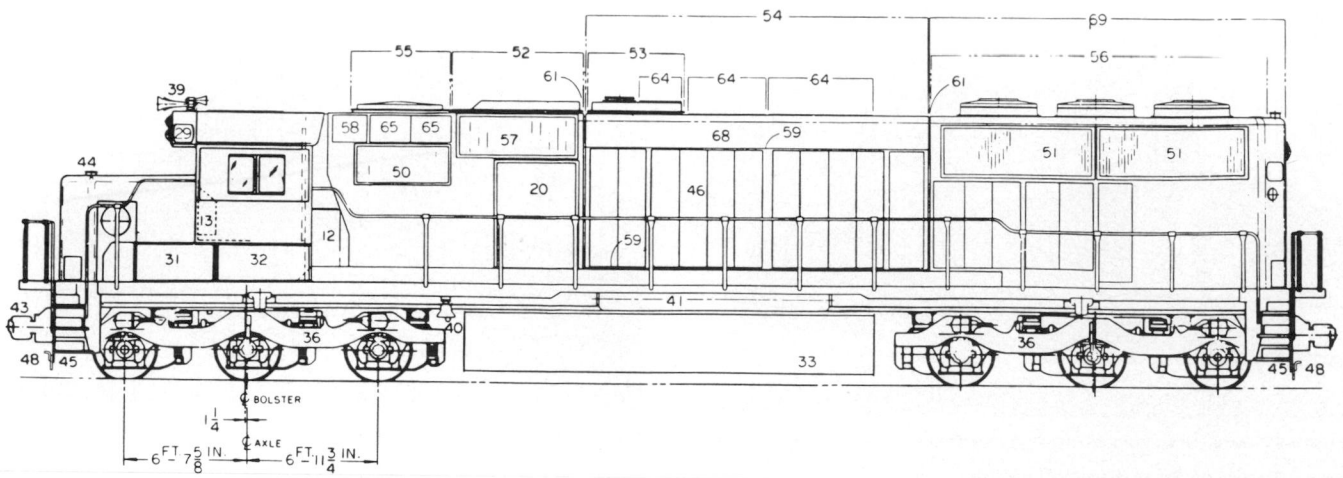

Layout of SD50 locomotive

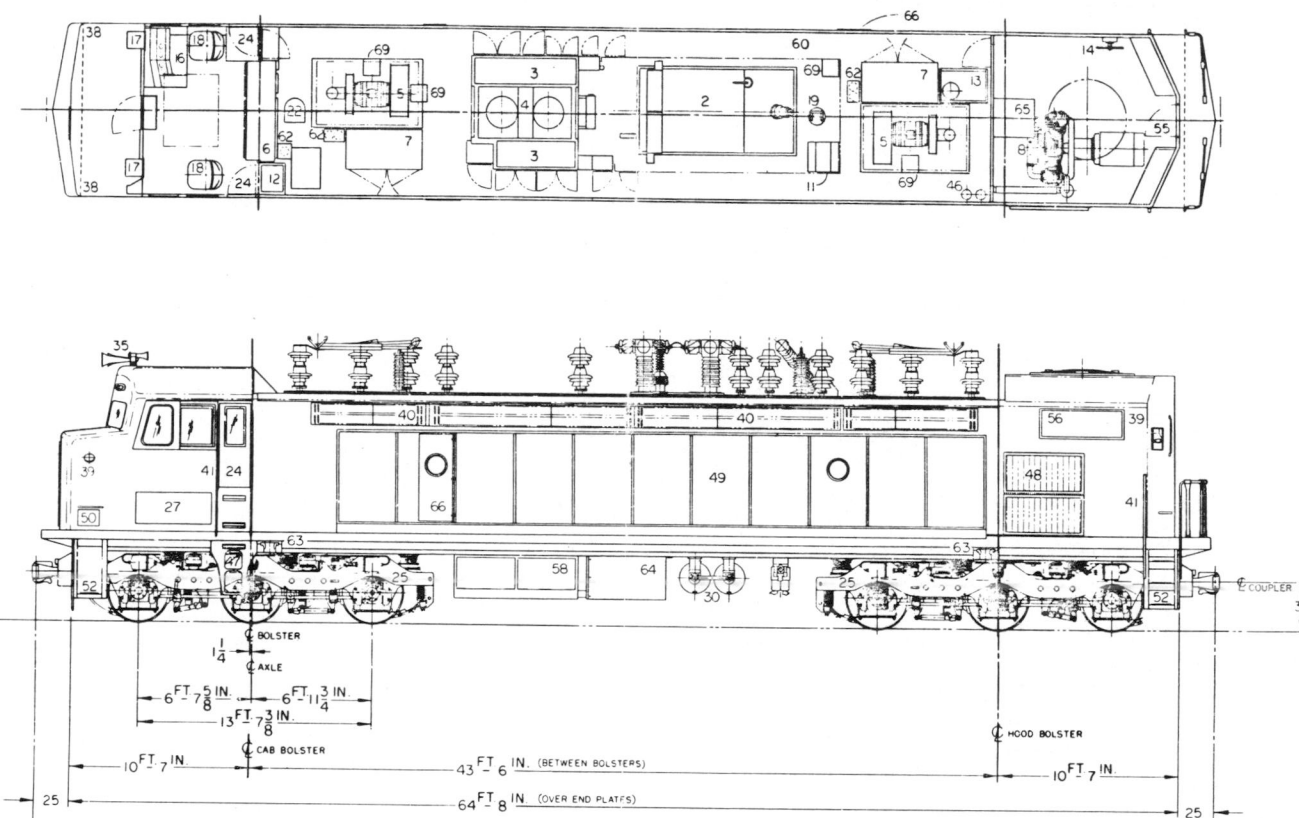

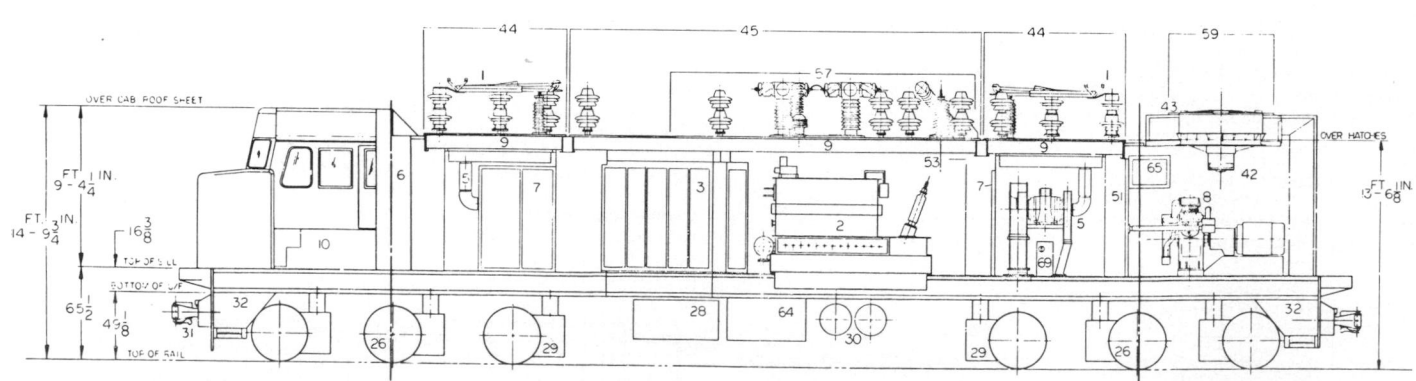

General arrangement of Type GF6C electric locomotive **(1)** Brecknell, Willis pantographs **(2)** main transformer with smoothing reactor **(3)** thyristor convertor cabinet **(4)** oil cooler blower **(5)** traction motor blower modules (2) **(6)** electrical control cabinet **(7)** contactor cabinet **(8)** air compressor (WXO) with ac motor (60 hp, 30/60 Hz at 900 rpm) **(9)** air plenum **(10)** main air brake equipment **(11)** auxiliary transformer **(12)** refrigerator/water cooler **(13)** auxiliary compressor and air dryer rack **(14)** handbrake **(15)** short hood access **(16)** driver's console **(17)** cab heaters **(18)** cab seats **(19)** grounding transformer **(20)** radio equipment **(21)** ladder **(22)** toilet (bag type) **(23)** cab windshields **(24)** cab door **(25)** bogie, 3-axle HTC type **(26)** wheels, diameter 42 in **(27)** air brake equipment access **(28)** battery box, underfloor **(29)** traction motor, 6 × E88 **(30)** main reservoirs, underfloor **(31)** coupler, E-type **(32)** draftgear, NC 391 **(34)** number box **(35)** horn **(36)** headlight **(37)** classification lights **(38)** sandboxes, 20.6 ft³ end max **(39)** sandbox fillers **(40)** air inlets **(41)** handrails **(42)** dynamic brake fan, diameter 54 in **(43)** dynamic brake grids, radial type **(44)** equipment removal hatches **(45)** thyristor cooling compartment and main transformer removal hatch **(46)** fire extinguisher, automatic **(47)** boarding step **(48)** air inlet and shutters, manual **(49)** side panels, batten type structure **(50)** sand trap access **(51)** machine room partition **(52)** steps **(53)** high voltage bushing **(55)** long hood access **(56)** dynamic brake air inlet **(57)** high voltage equipment, roof mounted **(58)** capacitor box, underfloor **(59)** dynamic brake hatch **(60)** corridor **(61)** high voltage access door **(62)** electrical-electronic cabinet air filters **(63)** jacking pads **(64)** filter reactor box, underfloor **(65)** dynamic brake contactor cabinet **(66)** personnel door (2) **(67)** nose door **(68)** ditch lights **(69)** heater, 4 × 4.5 kW **(70)** windshield wipers

Overseas manufacturing: General Motors has overseas locomotive facilities in the following countries:
Diesel Division, General Motors of Canada, London, Ontario, Canada
Electro-Motive Division of South Africa, Port Elizabeth, South Africa
General Motors Interamerica Corporation, Buenos Aires, Argentina

Products: Diesel-electric and electric locomotives; remanufacturing services.

Recent export diesel locomotive orders

Quantity	Description	Country
35	GT22LC-2	Zimbabwe
10	JT22LC-2	Sudan
4	GP15-1	Venezuela
2	G26CW-2	Israel
6	SDL50	Saudi Arabia
5	SW1001	Saudi Arabia
5	G22CU	Taiwan
100	GT26M2C	South Africa
51	SW1002	South Africa
6	SW1003	South Africa
6	SDL40-2	Mauritania
3	GP38-2	Mexico
8	GP40-2	Mexico

Recent domestic diesel locomotive orders

Quantity	Description	Railway
58	B-B	Amtrak
24	Electric	Amtrak
40	B-B	ATSF
68	C-C	ATSF
165	C-C	BN
40	B-B	BN
46	B-B	Chessie
10	B-B	Chi/Southern Shore
50	B-B	C&NW
18	B-B	Conrail
16	C-C	Denver & Rio Grande
32	C-C	Family Lines
16	C-C	KCS
10	B-B	Kennecott Copper
17	B-B	L&N
32	C-C	L&N
10	C-C	Missouri-Kansas-Texas
125	B-B	Mopac
30	C-C	Mopac
17	B-B	N J DoT
19	C-C	N&W
10	B-B	St Louis & SF
70	C-C	SP
85	B-B	SP
87	B-B	Southern
150	C-C	UP
10	B-B	WP
24	B-B	Chicago RTA

3500/3800 hp GP50 general purpose locomotive

3500/3800 hp SD50 special duty locomotive

Single-cab SDL50 locomotive with solid state modular controls and ac-dc transmission

Type GP15 diesel-electric locomotive for Venezuela

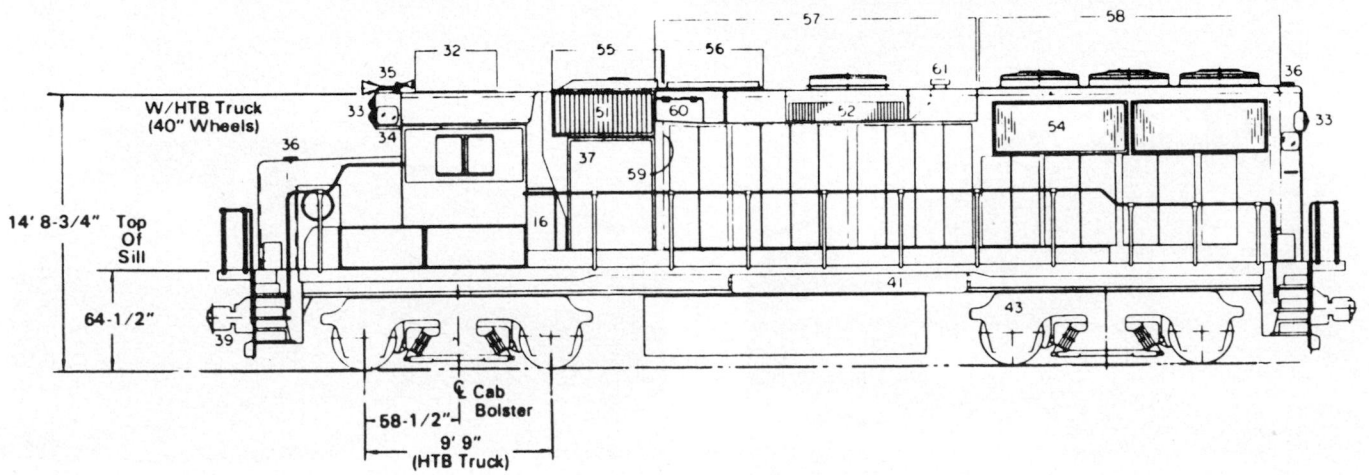

Layout of GP50 locomotive

In 1981, GM-EMD introduced the turbocharged 645F3 engine. This new power plant features a number of improvements, including a refined turbine blade, strengthening of the turbine wheel and the addition of higher capacity gearing to the planetary gear train. The crankcase contains features which strengthen the main bearing support frame connection to the crankcase base rail and air box structures. The cylinder head retainer system has been redesigned and strengthened in order to increase bolting load. A new fuel injector features a 12.7 mm (½ in) diameter plunger, which provides an increased injection for excellent combustion. The material in the camshaft has been upgraded to provide increased strength and reliability.

GM-EMD also introduced in 1981 the Super Series Adhesion Control System. This obtains greater tractive effort through more effective use of the available friction between the wheel and the rail. 33 per cent more tonnage can be hauled than with locomotives with conventional slip correction systems. The Super Series system uses a ground speed radar allied to the traction motor characteristics and the motor current to set a constantly changing voltage limit; this controls the allowable wheel creep to achieve the high adhesion level.

Domestic models (diesel-electric)

		Switchers		General purpose B-B locomotives		Special duty C-C locomotives		
Model number		SW1001	MP15	GP38-2	GP40-2	GP50	SD40-2	SD50
Engine type		8-645E	12-645E	16-645E	16-645E3B	16-645F3	16-645E3B	16-645F3
Turbocharged		No	No	No	Yes	Yes	Yes	Yes
Rated hp		1100/1000	1650/1500	2200/2000	3300/3000	3800/3500	3300/3000	3800/3500
Wheel diameter and gear ratio		40 in 62:15	40 in 62:15	40 in 62:15	40 in 62:15	40 in 70:17	40 in 62:16	40 in 70:17
Continuous tractive	lb	41 700	46 800	55 400	55 400	64 200	83 100	96 300
	kg	18 910	21 228	25 130	25 130	29 121	37 690	43 682
Continuous speed	mph	6.7	9.3	10.8	11.3	9.8	11.1	9.8
	km/h	10.8	15	10.4	18.2	16	17.9	16
Max speed	mph	65	65	65	65	70	65	70
	km/h	105	105	105	105	113	105	113
Weight	lb	230 000	248 000	250 000	256 000	260 000	368 000	368 000
	kg	104 330	112 490	113 400	116 120	117 936	166 920	166 925
Overall length		44 ft 8 in	47 ft 8 in	59 ft 2 in	59 ft 2 in	59 ft 2 in	68 ft 10 in	71 ft 2 in
		13.61 m	14.52 m	18.03 m	18.03 m	18.03 m	20.98 m	21.69 m
Overall height		14 ft 3 in	15 ft	15 ft 4 in	15 ft 4 in	15 ft 5⅞ in	15 ft 7 in	15 ft 7⅛ in
		4.34 m	4.57 m	4.67 m	4.67 m	4.69 m	4.75 m	4.75 m
Overall width		10 ft	10 ft	10 ft 4 in	10 ft 4 in	10 ft 3⅛ in	10 ft	10 ft 3⅛ in
		3.05 m	3.05 m	3.15 m	3.15 m	3.12 m	3.05 m	3.12 m

Export models (diesel-electric)

		B-B locomotives		C-C locomotives				
Model number		G-18U	G-22U	G-22CW	G-26CW	GT-22CW	JT22LC-2	GT-26CW-2
Engine type		8-645-E	12-645-E	12-645-E	16-645-E	12-645-E3	12-645-E3B	16-645-E3
Turbocharged		No	No	No	No	Yes	Yes	Yes
Rated hp		1100/1000	1650/1500	1650/1500	2200/2000	2475/2250	2412/2190	3300/3000
Wheel diameter and gear ratio		40 in 63:14	40 in 63:14	40 in 62:15	40 in 62:15	40 in 62:15	36 in 57:16	40 in 62:15
Continuous tractive	lb	33 600	33 360	58 200	57 960	57 840	44 196	67 220
	kg	15 240	15 130	26 400	26 290	26 240	20 047	30 490
Continuous speed	mph	8.6	13.5	7.2	10.3	12.1	15.8	14.1
	km/h	13.8	21.7	11.6	16.6	19.5	25	22.7
Max speed	mph	60	60	65	65	65	68.6	65
	km/h	97	97	105	105	105	110	105
Weight	lb	143 800	63 560	196 800	209 400	219 750	192 195	255 400
	kg	65 230	74 190	89 270	94 980	99 690	87 178	115 850
Overall length		38 ft	46 ft 6 in	46 ft 6 in	51 ft 9 in	57 ft	61 ft 10½ in	64 ft
		11.58 m	14.17 m	14.17 m	15.76 m	17.37 m	18.86 m	19.51 m
Overall height		12 ft 3 in	12 ft 7 in	12 ft 7 in	12 ft 7 in	13 ft 3 in	13 ft 4½ in	13 ft 6 in
		3.73 m	3.88 m	3.83 m	3.83 m	4.04 m	4.07 m	4.11 m
Overall width		9 ft 8 in	9 ft 3 in	9 ft 3 in	9 ft 3 in	9 ft 3 in	10 ft 3 in	9 ft 3 in
		2.95 m	2.82 m	2.82 m	2.82 m	2.82 m	3.12 m	2.82 m

Electric models

Model number		J4FC	GF6C	JF6C	AEM-7
Rated hp		4000	6000	6000	7000
Wheel diameter and gear ratio		40 in 76:19	40 in 70:17	40 in 70:17	51 in 1:3.31
Continuous tractive	lb	67 446	95 180	95 180	NA
	kg	30 593	43 175	43 175	NA
Continuous speed	mph	22	10.3	10.3	NA
	km/h	35	16.52	16.52	NA
Max speed	mph	62	68	68	125
	km/h	100	110	110	201
Weight	lb	275 000	330 000	330 000	199 500
	kg	124 740	149 688	149 688	90 493
Overall length		62 ft 10 in	68 ft 10 in	70 ft 8 in	51 ft 5¹³/₁₆ in
		19.15 m	20.98 m	21.53 m	15.70 m
Overall height		13 ft 7⅞ in	15 ft 4½ in	15 ft 4½ in	14 ft 6 in
		4.16 m	4.68 m	4.68 m	4.42 m
Overall width		9 ft 11½ in	10 ft 7¹³/₁₆ in	10 ft 7¹³/₁₆ in	10 ft
		3.03 m	3.24 m	3.24 m	3.05 m

Export model GT26C locomotive

Turbocharged model GT22LC-2 locomotive for National Railways of Zimbabwe with high adhesion bogie

1650/1500 hp export model G22 locomotive

Export model 2412/2190 hp turbocharged JT22LC-2 for Sudan Railways

Model SW1002 shunter by Electro-Motive Division of South Africa for South African Transport Services

Electric model AEM-7 for Amtrak

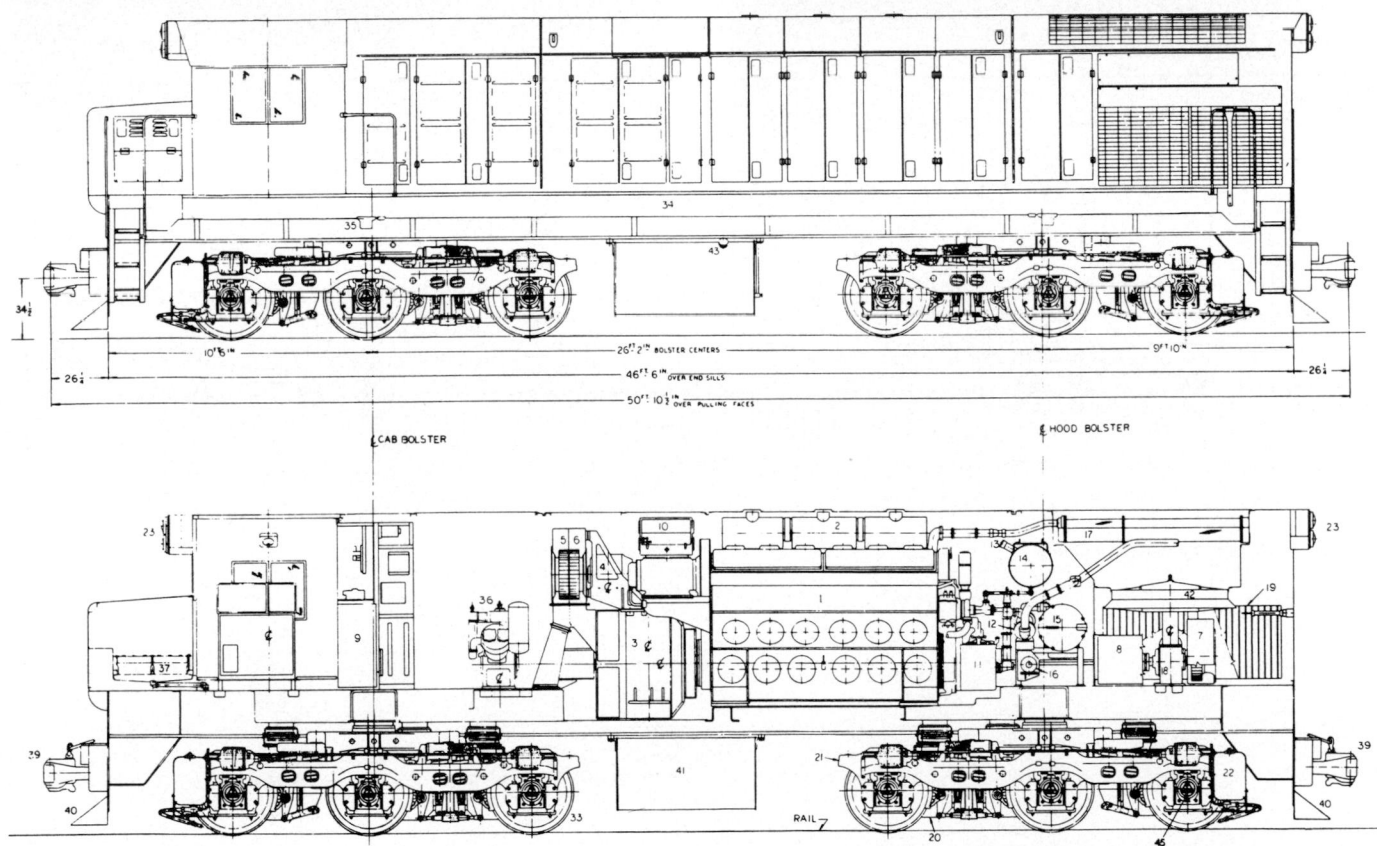

Export model G22 diesel-electric locomotive

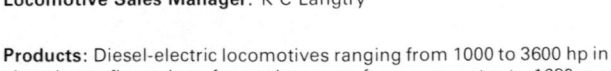

General Motors of Canada
Diesel Division, General Motors of Canada Limited

PO Box 5160, London, Ontario N6A 4N5, Canada

Telephone: (519) 452 5274
Telegrams: Gemodiesel
Telex: 064 7231

General Manager: J C Larmond
General Sales Manager: J W Jarrell
Locomotive Sales Manager: K C Langtry

Products: Diesel-electric locomotives ranging from 1000 to 3600 hp in four- and six-axle configurations for track gauges from one metre to 1680 mm.

Type GP38-2 2000 hp locomotive for Cape Breton Development Corporation

Recent sales have included: 26 Model GT26CW to Algerian National Railways (SNTF); 143 Model G22W(AC) to Egyptian Railways (ER); four Model GP38-2 to Cape Breton Development Corp (DEVCO), Canada; 26 Model GT22LC 2 to Zimbabwe Railways; and two Model GT26CW-2 to ENAFER-Peru.

Type GT26CW 3000 hp locomotive for Algerian Railways

Type GT22LC-2 2250 hp locomotive for National Railways of Zimbabwe

Type G22W (AC) 1500 hp locomotive for Egyptian State Railways

Type SD40-2 3000 hp locomotive for British Columbia Railway

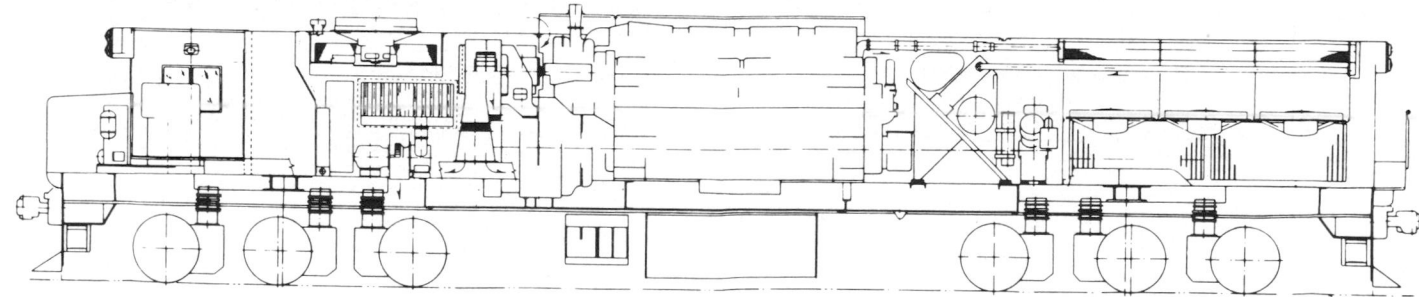

Type GT26CW layout

Locomotive models currently available

Model†	Engine	Tractive (hp)	Axles	Continuous tractive effort (kg)	Axle weight (kg)	Gauge (mm)	Gear ratio*
G-18U	8-645E	1000	4	15 240	15 218	1000-1676	63:14
G-18W	8-645E	1000	4	17 600	16 307	1435-1676	62:15
G-22U	12-645E	1500	4	15 132	18 030	1000-1676	63:14
G-22W	12-645E	1500	4	17 600	18 552	1435-1676	62:15
G-22CU	12-645E	1500	6	22 969	14 061	1000-1676	63:14
G-22CW	12-645E	1500	6	26 399	14 878	1435-1676	62:15
GL-22C	12-645E	1500	6	20 194	12 738	1000-1676	57:16
G-26CU	16-645E	2000	6	22 861	15 599	1000-1676	63:14
G-26CW	16-645E	2000	6	26 290	16 310	1435-1676	62:15
GL-26C	16-645E	2000	6	19 976	13 562	1000-1676	57:16
GT-22CU	12-645E3	2250	6	22 793	16 677	1000-1676	63:14
GT-22CW	12-645E3	2250	6	26 237	18 227	1435-1676	62:15
GT-22LC	12-645E3	2250	6	20 047	14 303	1000-1676	57:16
GT-26CU	16-645E3	2700	6	24 900	17 585	1000-1676	63:14
GT-26CW	16-645E3	3000	6	30 490	19 818	1435-1676	62:15

NOTE: *Other gear ratios available. †'T' signifies turbocharged engine

Gestesa
Groupo Español Suizo de Trenes Electricos SA

Calle Felipe IV, 10-1° Dcha, Madrid, Spain

Telephone: 28 52 36
Telegrams: Gestren, Madrid

Products: Electric multiple-units.

Constitution: This group comprises La Maquinista Terrestre y Maritima; Material y Construcciones SA; Industrias Aguirena SA.

Gloucester
Gloucester Railway Carriage & Wagon Co Ltd
Subsidiary of Babcock International plc

Bristol Road, Gloucester GL1 5RS, England

Telephone: 0452 25104/5
Telegrams: Railcar, Gloucester
Telex: 4 37173

Chairman: E A Madenski
Managing Director: J S P Phillips

Sales Director: R A Clark
Engineering Director: R S Morris

Products: Freight wagon designs; bogies; suspension systems; Miner doorgear.

Constitution: First known as the Gloucester Wagon Co Ltd, the company was formed in 1860 and two years later built the first iron wagon in the United Kingdom. Since 1969 the company has concentrated on the design of railway wagons and the design and manufacture of bogies and vehicle suspensions. Gloucester is a licensee for Miner Enterprise Inc for doorgears and discharge systems.

Goninan
A Goninan & Co Ltd

PO Box 21, Broadmeadow, New South Wales 2292, Australia

Telephone: 049 699 299
Telegrams: Platinum, Newcastle
Telex: 28061

General Manager: E W Eddy
Assistant General Manager, Broadmeadow Works: J G Fitzgerald
Engineering Manager: A Rice
Sales Manager: K Moss

Products: Diesel-electric locomotives; freight wagons; passenger coaches; diesel-hydraulic and electric passenger railcars, and fabricated rail bogies.

The company's recent production has included 92 double-deck, stainless steel passenger cars for the State Rail Authority of New South Wales, for service on the Sydney metropolitan network. A new contract worth A$83 million, for 100 double-deck passenger cars, was won in November 1982. The company has also successfully tendered for the manufacture of 13 diesel-electric main-line locomotives for the Queensland Railways. These were to be diesel-electric Co-Cos of General Electric USA Type U22C, with a rating of 1716 kW and a service speed of 80 km/h; weight was to be 97.6 tonnes. Goninan was to build the mechanical parts, employing GE Type FDL 12 engines and GE transmissions with GE Type 761 traction motors. The locomotive type is new to Australia.

Goninan is also turning out the first fabricated steel bogie to be produced in Australia, the GPS. To be used on NSW coal wagons, it is suitable for other kinds of freight rolling stock. The bogie is of the fabricated one piece rigid-frame type. Main features of the GPS bogie are: inherent strength to weight ratio; ability to operate under 100-tonne wagons at speeds up to 100 km/h, which is achieved by two-stage primary suspension, load-sensitive friction dampers, a hemispherical centre pivot and resilient sidebearers coupled with the rigid H-frame; an all-welded H-frame design incorporating improved welding procedures, which assures a high fatigue life; rigid frame construction which will not lozenge in curves or tangent track, a performance characteristic which, together with low unsprung mass, reduces wear on both wheel and rail. The model in production is the GPS 25 with a 25-tonne axleload rating. Higher capacities are available up to 32-tonne axleload rating.

Constitution: Engaged in the manufacturing field since 1900, this company has extended its licence agreement with General Electric, USA, for diesel-electric locomotives, and entered into a licence agreement with Pullman Standard Division, USA, for rail passenger coaches. It has a licence agreement with Gloucester Railway Carriage & Wagon Co Ltd, UK, for primary suspension bogies.

Double-deck suburban car for Sydney metropolitan network, New South Wales

Type GPS 25 fabricated steel bogie

Goodwin
A E Goodwin Ltd

863-871 Bourke Street, Waterloo, New South Wales 2017, Australia

Telephone: 698 1163
Telegrams: Goodwineng
Telex: 22656

Chief Executive: D W Chambers

Products: Freight wagons; draftgear; track construction and equipment.

Görlitz
VEB Waggonbau Gorlitz

Brunnenstrasse 11, 8900 Gorlitz, German Democratic Republic

Telephone: 690
Telegrams: Waggonbau, Gorlitz
Telex: 286227

Products: Passenger coaches; sleeping cars; double-deck coaches; bogies.

The works now specialises in sleeping cars conforming to RIC requirements and with berths of similar character to those of Western European vehicles, convertible to one-, two- or three-bed use. Since 1976 it has constructed over 365 cars of this type for both 1435 mm and 1520 mm-gauge networks of Soviet Railways (SZD), which can employ them on international workings to such points as Paris, Tehran and Pyongyang, as well as on domestic services, where necessary via frontier stations with bogie-changing facilities for break of gauge. Recent orders for other Comecon countries have included 180 similar cars for PKP in Poland, 60 for BDZ in Bulgaria and 55 for CSD in Czechoslovakia. A forward building programme up to 1985 features a further 290 cars of RIC pattern for SZD. Other recent production has featured 40 couchette and 32 saloon passenger cars for Chinese Railways.

The works' latest development of its RIC-pattern sleeping car is the Type WLx, designed for operation at up to 200 km/h. The welded all-metal body is mounted on bogies of the new Type GP200, which has been created jointly by Gorlitz and

Narrow-gauge Uganda Railways (UR) passenger cars designed for African environmental conditions

the Rail Vehicle Institute of Prague, and which is arranged for fitment of electromagnetic rail brakes as well as disc or shoe brakes. In this bogie wheel-set guidance is provided by means of axle guide-rods of glass fibre reinforced plastic, which are arranged unilaterally towards the bogie centre. The car is equipped with a single-channel underfloor air-conditioning system and each of its 11 compartments has individual temperature control. The power supply incorporates an automatic voltage selector that enables the car to operate at all UIC voltages. Tare weight is approximately 52 tonnes.

A basic passenger car model has been devised for African conditions and the first 40 third-class coaches and 10 second-class couchettes to this pattern have been supplied to Uganda Railways (UR). These metre-gauge cars are designed for a maximum speed of 80 km/h. Bogies without axle guards of the Görlitz V type are employed, modified for metre gauge; they can also be adapted to 1067 mm gauge. The coaches are of welded lightweight construction, with optimum protection against corrosion. All are equipped with MCA/DA central buffer coupling, with provision for subsequent mounting of a jaw-clutch coupling. The coaches are equipped with independent air-operated shoe brakes plus a hand brake at each end. Special emphasis has been paid to heat insulation and sound-proofing: all internal surfaces of the sheeting are treated with an anti-

noise compound, and floor, front walls, lateral walls and roof are insulated with finest glass wool which is welded in foil packages. The upward-opening windows have thermo-panes of safety glass. All coaches are provided with cold running water (hydraulic main supply) and a drinking water system which is connected with a steriliser. The electric power supply includes a 3 kW motor alternator-generator which is directly driven through an axlebox drive. All control and switching systems are accommodated in a cabinet near the entrance. Static fans are fitted in the roof and ceiling-type ventilators in the passenger saloons.

Constitution: After resuming production in 1945 as a manufacturer of special-purpose freight wagons, the plant switched to broad-gauge restaurant and couchette cars in 1949. In 1952 it took up production of double-deck commuter passenger cars and electric and diesel multiple-units, but since 1970 it has specialised in long-haul passenger cars, principally sleeping cars. A member of Vereinigter Schienenfahrzeugbau der DDR eV.

Exports: Schienenfahrzeuge Export-Import Volkseigener Aussenhandelsbetrieb der DDR, Otztaler Strasse 17, 1100 East Berlin

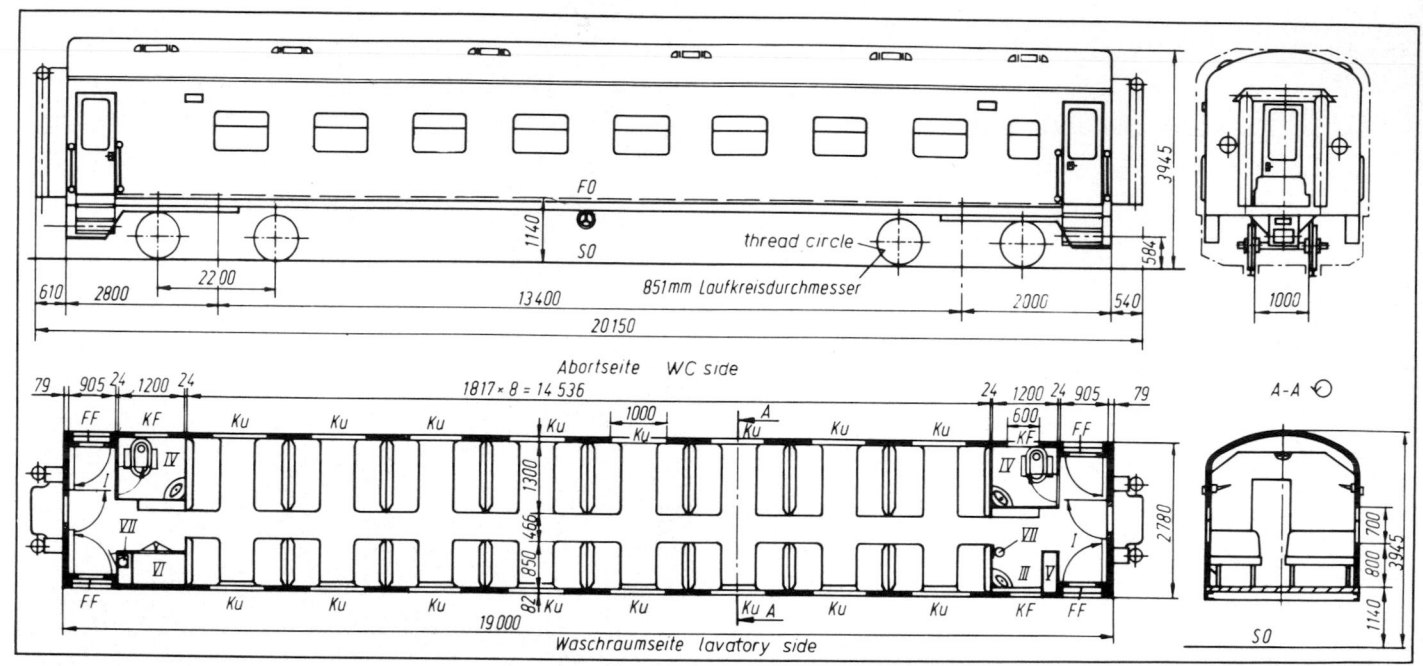

General arrangement of third-class UR coach

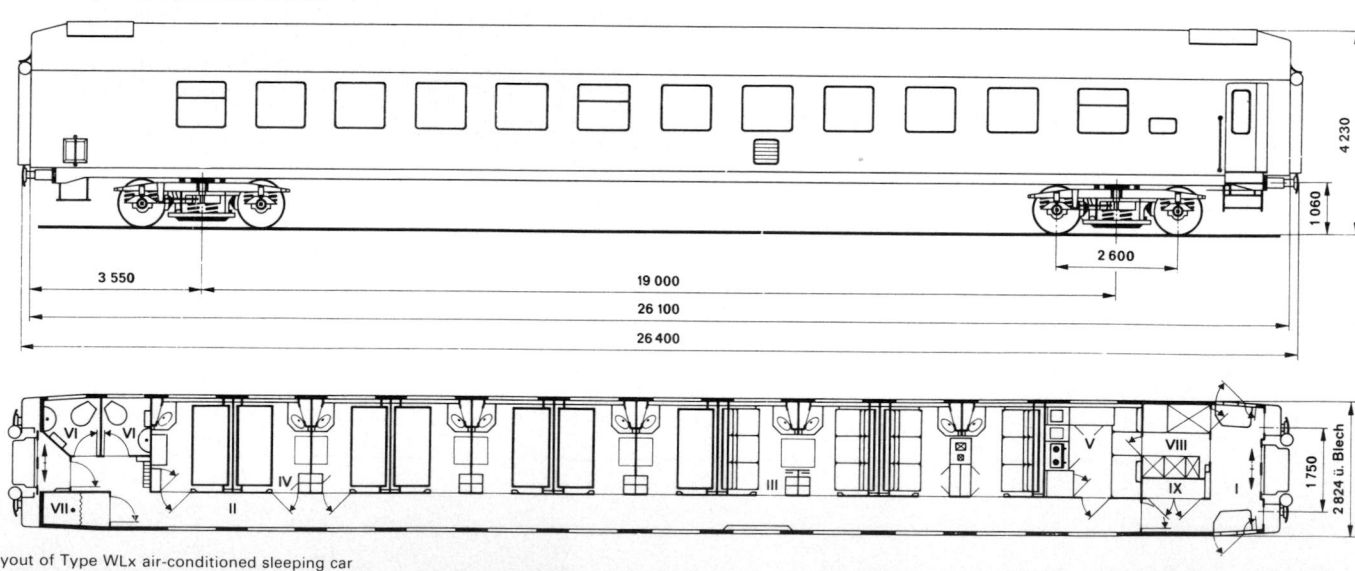

Layout of Type WLx air-conditioned sleeping car

Type WLx air-conditioned sleeping car

GOŠA
SOUR Industrija GOŠA

Head office: Industrijska 1, 11 420 Smederevska Palanka, Yugoslavia
Sales office: Nemanjina 4, 11 000 Belgrade

Telephone: 011 831 022
Telegrams: Gosa Smederevska Palanka
Telex: 11 684
Telex (sales): 11568

Chairman: Tihoslav Tosić
Managing Director: Srba Trajković
Sales Director: Slavko Djorić
Export Sales: Slavko Ivanović

Products: Passenger coaches; diesel and electric train-sets; tank wagons; refrigerated cars; and special-purpose wagons.

International 'Y' type first-class passenger coach for Yugoslav Railways

---

Graaff
Graaff Kommanditgesellschaft

Postfach 160/180, 3210 Elze 1, Federal Republic of Germany

Telephone: 05068 180
Telegrams: Graffwaggon, Elze
Telex: 0927168

Managing Director: Dipl Ing Wolfgang Graaff

Products: Containers; railroad rolling stock; road vehicles; plywood van bodies; sandwich panels.

Constitution: Founded in 1914.

Greenbat
Greenbat (Engineering) Ltd
Part of Hunslet (Holdings) Ltd

Albion Works, Armley Road, Leeds LS12 2TP, England

Telephone: 0532 442933
Telegrams: Greenbat, Leeds
Telex: 55468

Chief Executive: P J O Alcock
Sales Director: G Derrett-Smith
Sales Manager: K G Wainwright

Products: Battery, trolley, trolley/battery and pantograph locomotives up to 30 tonnes in weight; coke car locomotives; motor transmission and control units.
  The company is the supplier of trains for London's unique Post Office Underground Railway, the automatically-operated system which threads 10.5 km of tunnel under the city. Its unmanned trains transfer some 40 000 bags of mail daily between main London sorting centres served by its seven stations. The equipment includes 34 train-sets.

Constitution: Greenbat (Engineering) Ltd became part of Hunslet (Holdings) Ltd in 1980 in order to provide a wider range of mining and surface locomotives.

Licensing agreement: Mining and Allied Machinery Corporation Ltd, West Bengal, India

London Post Office Railway train-set

Greenville Steel Car Company
Subsidiary of Ampco-Pittsburgh Corporation

Greenville, Pennsylvania 16125, USA

Telephone: (412) 588 7000
Telegrams: Greencar

Chairman: M L Berkman
President: L O Richards, Jr
Vice-President, Sales: J T Egbert

Products: Railroad freight cars.

Constitution: Formed in 1910 as the Greenville Metal Products Co, the present name was adopted in 1914 when the company first undertook repair of freight wagons. In 1916 the first new wagons were built and this has been the major activity since, combined with extensive repair work and supply of replacement parts.

Quadruple-hopper coal car with 100-short ton (91-tonne) capacity

Triple-tub coal car with 103-short ton (93.4-tonne) capacity

The Gregg Company, Ltd

15 Dyatt Place, PO Box 430, Hackensack, New Jersey 07602, USA

Telephone: (201) 489 2440
Telegrams: Greggcar Hackensack NJ
Telex: 219216; 134320

Main works: Gregg/Equimetal Empresa Fabril de Equipamentos Metalicos, SARL, 7521 Sines Codex, Portugal

Chairman: W K Gregg
President: R T Gregg
Executive Vice-President: H Ross

Products: Covered and open wagons, mineral wagons, refrigerator wagons, tank wagons, wagons for transport of road vehicles, container wagons, bulk powder wagons, flat wagons, ballast and aluminium wagons, bogies for freight and passenger vehicles.

Groupement 50 Hz
50 c/s Group

Lowenstrasse 29, PO Box 433, 8021 Zurich 1, Switzerland

Telephone: (01) 221 1744
Telegrams: Coordinat, Zurich
Telex: 813 954

Products: Provision and erection of complete railway electrification equipment.

Constitution: The Group comprises ACEC of Belgium, Alsthom-Atlantique of France, Société MTE of France, AEG-Telefunken and Siemens AG of the Federal Republic of Germany and BBC Brown Boveri & Co Ltd of Switzerland.

Recent contracts

	No of units	Motive power units	Year introduced	Gauge (mm)	Weight (tonnes)	Continuous rating (kW)	Continuous/max speed (km/h)	
Portuguese Railways (CP)	18	Three-car units, Class 2100	1977	1665	161.4	1200	64.5/120	Series motors for pulsating dc current, lv tap changer, silicon rectifier, rheostatic braking
	15	Three-car units, Class 2100	1982	1665	161.4	1200	64.5/120	Series motors for pulsating dc current, lv tap changer, silicon rectifier, rheostatic braking
Turkish Railways (TCDD)	40	Electrical equipments for three-car units	1978	1435		1020	64.5/120	Series motors for pulsating dc current, semi-controlled silicon rectifiers, rheostatic braking
South African Railways (SAR)	100	Freight locos, Class 7E	1978	1065	123.5	2925	35/100	Motors for pulsating dc current with mixed excitation, semi-controlled silicon rectifiers with turn-off circuits, rheostatic braking
	25	Freight locos, Class 7E2	1981	1065	126	2925	35/100	
	40	Freight locos, Class 7E2	1982	1065	126	2925	35/100	
Ferrocarriles de Costa Rica SA (FECOSA)	12	Dual frequency mixed-traffic locos	1981	1067	64	1270	32/80	Silicon rectifier, lv tap changer, rheostatic braking
National Railways of Zimbabwe (NRZ)	30	Freight locos	1982	1067	114	2466	32/100	Motors for pulsating dc current with mixed excitation, semi-controlled silicon rectifiers with turn-off circuits, rheostatic braking

GSI
General Steel Industries Inc, Engineering Division

PO Box 2396, 8400 Midland Boulevard, St Louis, Missouri 63114, USA

Telephone: (314) 423 6500

President: Keith L Jackson

Vice-President, Sales: Thomas P Taylor
Manager of Engineering: Eugene L Benner

Products: Design of cast steel rapid transit, coach and locomotive bogies.

Constitution: GSI was founded in 1904 by General Steel Castings Corp and became Castings Division, GSI, in 1964, and Engineering Division in 1973.

Hägglunds
AB Hägglund & Soner

PO Box 600, 891 01 Örnskoldsvik, Sweden

Telephone: 0660 80000
Telegrams: Hagglundsoner
Telex: 6051

Chairman: Bert-Olof Svanholm
Managing Director: Bo Sodersten

Sales Director: Hans Wikstrom

Products: Electric locomotives; Type X10 emus with ASEA electrical equipment for Swedish State Railways (SJ); rapid transit surface and underground cars; street (tram) cars; bogies; mining and construction equipment; heavy trucks; bus bodies; hydraulic motors.

Constitution: Hagglunds was founded in 1899 and is one of the largest engineering companies in northern Sweden. In 1972 it became a subsidiary company of ASEA of Vasteras. In 1973 Hagglunds acquired the railcar and locomotive division of ASJ of Linkoping and production was transferred to Örnskoldsvik.

Hawker Siddeley
Hawker Siddeley Canada Inc

Head office: 7 King Street East, Toronto, Ontario M5C 1A3, Canada
Main works
(Passenger equipment): Canadian Car Division, Thunder Bay, Ontario
(Freight equipment): Trenton Works Division, Trenton, Nova Scotia

Sales offices
(Passenger equipment): PO Box 67, Station F, Thunder Bay, Ontario P7C 4V6
            PO Box 6001, Toronto AMF, Ontario L5P 1B3
(Freight equipment): Suite 1515, 800 Dorchester Boulevard West, Montreal, Quebec H3B 1X9

Telephone: (416) 362 2941
Telegrams: Hawsidcan, Toronto
Telex: 06 217711

Chairman: Sir Arnold Hall
President and Chief Executive Officer: R F Tanner
Export Manager (Freight Wagons): R C Frost
Director of Marketing: R L McCallum
Sales Managers,
  Freight Equipment: C W Smith
  Passenger Equipment: K G Chapman

Coiled steel covered hopper car for CP Rail

40-tonne ballast car for Zambia Railways

Products: Railway freight cars of all types; subway, commuter and inter-city passenger coaches; light rail vehicles; wheels and axles; bogies; railway castings.

Recent contracts have included:
CP Rail, Canada: 500 × 100-short ton (90.7-tonne) coiled steel covered hopper cars;
National Railways of Mexico (FNdeM): 201 × 70-short ton (63.5-tonne) twin hopper cars;
Chemins de Fer du Togo: 92 × 37-tonne clinker cars and 12 × 11 300-US gallon (42 770-litre) tank cars;
Zambia Railways: 50 × 40-tonne dropside gondolas and 189 × 40-tonne ballast cars;
Tanzania Railways Corporation: 100 × 40-tonne cattle cars;
Toronto Area Transit Operating Authority (GO Transit): 71 bi-level passenger cars.

GO Transit bi-level cars
Gauge: 1435 mm
Length over couplers: 25 908 mm
Distance between bogie centres: 19 507 mm
Bogie wheelbase: 2591 mm
Wheel diameter, new: 838 mm
Overall width: 2997 mm
Roof height above rail level: 4851 mm
Floor height above rail: 635 mm
Door height: 1981 mm
Interior height, lower and upper deck: 2007 mm
　intermediate deck: 2133 mm
Height of coupler centre above rail: 876 mm
Entrance door width: 1321 mm
Vestibule door width: 711 mm
Seating capacity, lower deck: 54
　intermediate deck: 36
　upper deck: 72
　total: 162
Crush capacity: 438
Weight: 48 989 kg
Design buffing strength: 3558 kN
Minimum curve radius: 76 m
Minimum vertical curve: 610 m
High-voltage system: 575 V ac 3-phase 60 Hz
Low-voltage system: 32 V dc
Body construction,
　underframe: welded low alloy, high tensile steel
　side sills: extruded aluminium
　side walls and roof: welded aluminium extrusions, riveted aluminium skin
　interior finish: Melamine panelling, vinyl trim, fibreglass, ABS mouldings
　exterior finish: polyurethane paint

Constitution: The Eastern Car Company Ltd, one of the original predecessors of this company, started in the railway freight car business in 1913. Hawker Siddeley Group Ltd, UK, has a 59 per cent interest in the company; the remaining interest is held by public shareholders.

Bi-level commuter cars of GO Transit entering Union station, Toronto

Bi-level cars under construction at Canadian Car Division of Hawker Siddeley Canada Inc

Hawker Siddeley Canada electric metro multiple-units

Class	Cars per unit	Line voltage	Motor cars per unit	Motored axles per motor car	Rated output (kW) per motor	Max speed km/h	Weight per car tonnes	Total seating capacity	Length per car mm	No in service	Rate of acceleration m/s²	Year first built	Builders Mechanical parts	Electrical equipment
MBTA 4	2	600 V	2	4	82	105	27.295	42	14 884	70	1.11	1978	H-5—C-1	General Electric
MBTA 12	2	600 V	2	4	82	105	30.75	58	19 913	120	1.11	1980	H-5—C-1	General Electric
TTC H-5	2	580 V	2	4	85	88	29.699	76	22 790	134	1.12	1976	H-5—C-1	Garrett AiResearch Manufacturing Co

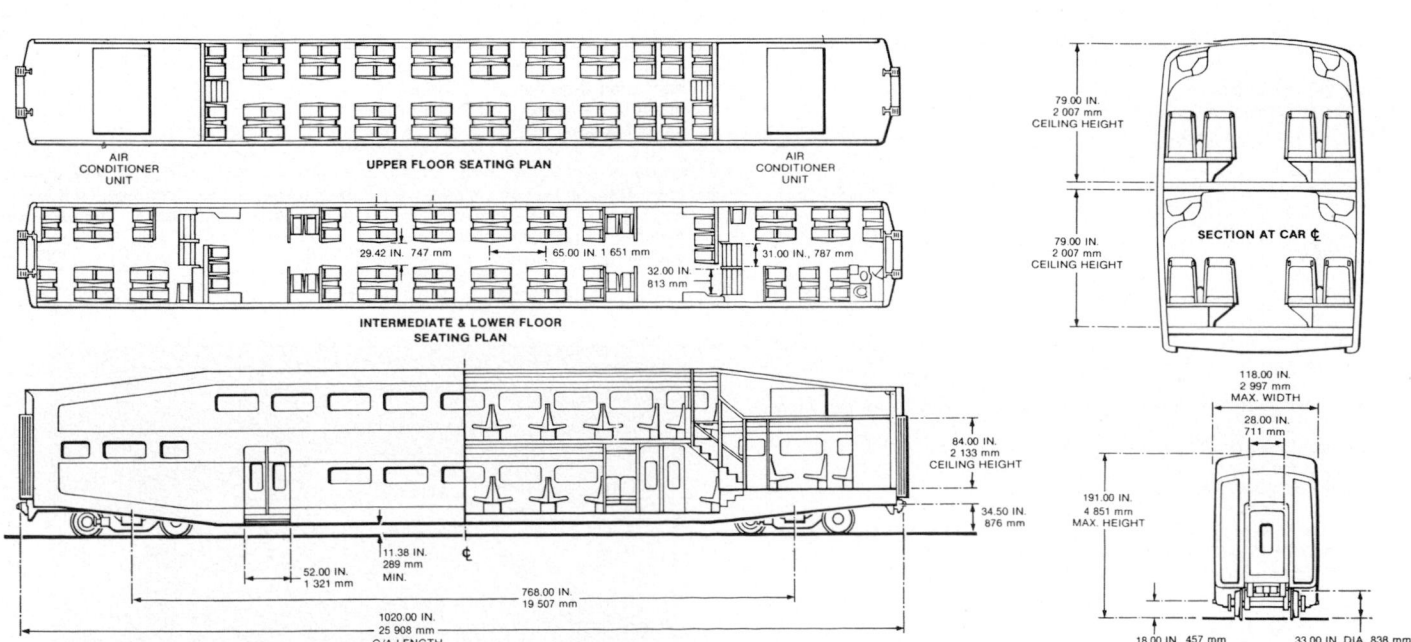
Layout of bi-level passenger car for GO Transit

Bi-level commuter car lower level

Bi-level commuter car upper level

Bi-level commuter car washroom

Bi-level commuter car stairs to upper level

Head Wrightson
Head Wrightson Teesdale Ltd
A Davy Corporation company

PO Box 10, Stockton-on-Tees, Cleveland TS17 6AZ, England

Telephone: 0642 62241
Telex: 58533

Managing Director: J G Wood
Marketing Director: D I R Featonby
Sales Manager: B Preece

Products: Rolling stock for ironworks: ore transfer wagons, scale wagons, hot metal transfer wagons, slag ladle wagons, torpedo ladle wagons (100-300 tonnes capacity); for steelworks: hot metal transfer wagons, slag ladle transfer wagons, ingot casting wagons; for non-ferrous works: slag ladle wagons (air/hydraulic tipped).

Hitachi
Hitachi Ltd

6-2 Nippon Building, Otemachi 2-chome, Chiyoda-ku, Tokyo 100, Japan

Telephone: (03) 270 2111
Telegrams: Hitachy, Tokyo
Telex: 22395, 22432, 24491, 26375

President and Representative Director: Hirokichi Yoshiyama
Executive Vice President and Director: Masafumi Misu
Executive Managing Director: Kiyoshi Shimai

2400 kW Bo-Bo-Bo electric locomotive for Zaire

Products: Electric, diesel-electric, diesel-hydraulic locomotives; electric and diesel railcars; passenger and freight cars; industrial rolling stock.

Constitution: Fabrication and assembly of railcars takes place at the Kasada works while locomotives are assembled at Mito.

3000 kW Co-Co electric locomotive in Morocco

Hitachi standard diesel-hydraulic locomotives

Model	HG-20/25B	HG-30/35BB	HG-45/50BB	HG-55/60BB
Type	Gear drive	Gear drive	Gear drive	Gear drive
	End cab type	Semi centre-cab type	Centre-cab type	Centre-cab type
Axle arrangement	B	B-B	B-B	B-B
Weight in working order (tonnes)	20/25	30/35	45/50	55/60
Engine	Cummins NH220BI X 1 set	Cummins NRT0-6 X 1 set	Cummins KT1150L X 1 set	Cummins KTA 1150L X 1 set
	190 hp/2100 rpm	335 hp/2100 rpm	450 hp/2100 rpm	550 hp/2100 rpm
Converter	Nico (twin disc type)	Nico (twin disc type)	Nico (twin disc type)	Nico (twin disc type)
	CB 100	CBS 115	CBS 115	CBS 115-2
Starting tractive effort (kg)	5000/6250	7500/8750	11 250/12 500	13 750/15 000
Continuous tractive force (kg)	4600-1360	7000-2800	10 300-3000	12 900-3700
Continuous speed (km/h)	5.6-20.0	4.8-19.3	5.9-20.7	5.8-21.2
Max height above rail (mm)	3620	3745	3745	3745
Max width overall (mm)	2600	2700	2700	2700
Max length over end frames (mm)	5800	10 900	10 900	10 900
Wheel diameter (mm)	860	860	860	860
Driving stand	Single	Single	Single	Single
Brake system	Straight air brake (locomotive only)	Straight air brake (locomotive only)	Straight air brake (locomotive only)	Straight air brake (locomotive only)

Holec
Holec Machines & Systems Group
Smit Slikkerveer BV
Traction Group

Head office: PO Box 4050, 2980 AB Ridderkerk, Netherlands

Telephone: 01804 13633
Telex: 20377

Works: Ringdijk 390, Ridderkerk

Managing Director: K C Hoogendijk

Commercial Director: P P Lagache
Manager Traction Group: Ir J C D van Altenburg
Technical Director: Ir A Verhoef

Principal subsidiary: Holec Machines & Systems Group, Heemaf BV, Hengelo

Products: Manufacturers of electrical equipment for locomotives and rolling stock, offering design, manufacture and commissioning of complete traction systems following conventional designs or designs based on power electronics for vehicles to operate on main-line, inter-urban, urban rapid transit, underground, tramway or trolleybus systems; traction power supply equipment; electric transmissions for electric railway, tramway and road vehicles; and electrical equipment for dc substations.

Modular Holec chopper installation in tramway car of The Hague

Rotterdam metro train-set with Holec electrical equipment

Pneumatically-powered Holec dc switches for resistor control in Rotterdam car

The Hague tramway car with Holec chopper control

Hsiangtan
Hsiangtan Electric Generator Plant

Hunan, People's Republic of China

Products: Electric locomotives. The plant produced China's first electric CC locomotive in the 1950s, a 4900 hp unit based on the Soviet-designed N-60s; numbered 6-Y-1.

Hudson (Raletrux)
Robert Hudson (Raletrux) Limited

PO Box 4, Morley, Leeds LS27 8TG, England

Telephone: 0532 534931
Telegrams: Raletrux, Morley
Telex: 55133

Chairman: M J Bradford

Managing Director: C R Whyte

Products: Industrial rolling stock, including special cars for mine main haulage, quarries and estates; complete narrow-gauge railway systems for all applications.

Constitution: Manufacturing facilities were established in 1865, and the company exports to hard-rock mining operations throughout the world. Robert Hudson (Raletrux) Ltd is now part of the Firsteel Group of companies.

Hudson (South Africa)
Robert Hudson & Sons (Pty) Ltd

PO Box 25259, Ferreirasdorp, Transvaal, South Africa

Telephone: 836 9772/3
Telegrams: Raletrux
Telex: 43 0250

Chairman: W R Hudson
Managing Director: R H Wardrop

Products: Main-line freight cars, narrow-gauge mine and estate cars; electric locomotives for mines.

Hudswell Clarke
Hudswell Clarke & Co Ltd

125 Jack Lane, Leeds LS10 1BT, England

Telephone: 0532 432261
Telegrams: Hunslt, Leeds
Telex: 55237

Chairman: P J O Alcock
Joint Managing Directors: K Alcock
G D Gawthorpe

Products: Industrial, shunting and mine locomotives; track-laying equipment.

100 hp fully flameproof double-end drive mining locomotive

Hunslet
The Hunslet Engine Company Ltd

Hunslet Engine Works, Leeds LS10 1BT, England

Telephone: 0532 432261
Telegrams: Hunslt, Leeds
Telex: 55237

Chairman: P J O Alcock
Joint Managing Directors: K Alcock
G D Gawthorpe
Sales Manager: D H Townsley

Products: Diesel-mechanical, diesel-hydraulic, diesel-electric and steam locomotives; fully flameproof surface and underground mine diesel locomotives; electric trolley and battery locomotives; flameproof diesel power packs and standard flameproof components; final drive and reverse gearboxes; diesel exhaust gas conditioners; track maintenance equipment.

Constitution: The Hunslet Engine Company has built locomotives since 1864, introduced diesel shunting locomotives in 1927 and pioneered the first flameproof diesel locomotive for coal mine working in 1939. The Hunslet Engine Company incorporates Kerr Stuart & Co, The Avonside Engine Company, Manning Wardle & Co, Kitson & Co, and The Hunslet Group includes the associate companies Hudswell Clarke & Co Ltd, Greenbat (Engineering) Ltd and Andrew Barclay Sons & Co Ltd.

53-tonne 525 hp Hunslet locomotive in Nairobi marshalling yard, Kenya Railways

28 hp 4-tonne fully flameproof mining locomotives arranged to operate in tandem

25-ton 240 hp locomotive protected for use in armament depots

36-tonne 400 hp dock shunter for West Africa

450 hp flashproof locomotive for refinery use

Standard 18-tonne estate locomotive supplied to sugar plantations in the East Indies and Caribbean

Hunslet Taylor
Hunslet Taylor Consolidated

PO Box 178, Germiston 1400, Transvaal, South Africa

Telephone: 27 11 825 1212
Telegrams: Hunsletco, Germiston
Telex: 8 0899

Chairman: P J T Herbert
Managing Director: P G E Fitch

Products: Shunting locomotives for surface operations, from 10 to 80 tonnes; underground locomotives from 2½ to 15 tonnes.

Hyundai
Hyundai Rolling Stock Co Ltd

Head office: 2-1, Shinmun-Ro, 2GA, Jongro-ku, Seoul, Republic of Korea
Postal address: KPO Box 1677, Seoul

Telephone: 725 7591/5
Telex: 23720

Works: 621 Deokjeong-Dong, Changwon, Kyungnam
Telephone: (1551) 82-1341/50
Telex: 3744

Chairman: Ju Yung Chung
President: Moon Doh Chung
Executive Vice President: Yun Jae Song
Executive Director: Chong Young Lee
Managing Director: Kyung Wook Kim

Hyundai emu on Seoul Metro Line 2

Hyundai 3000 hp diesel-electric locomotive for KNR under manufacture at Changwon workshop

Products: Electric locomotives, diesel-electric locomotives, diesel-hydraulic locomotives, industrial/mining vehicles, emu/railcars, dmu/railcars, railbuses, metro cars, trams/LRVs, coaches, general freight wagons, special freight wagons.

Affiliated companies

Hyundai Engineering & Construction Co, Ltd
178 Sejong-Ro, Chongro-Ku, Seoul
Telephone: 720 5211/20
Telex: 23111/5

Products: Design and construction of highways, railways and metro tunnels, etc.

Hyundai Engineering Co, Ltd
230-5, Apkujeong-Dong, Kangnam-Ku, Seoul
Telephone: 566 0171/5
Telex: 23583

Products: Design of high-speed railway and underground systems.

Hyundai Engine Manufacturing Co, Ltd
1-5, Chonha-Dong, Ulsan, Kyongnam
Telephone: 5 4141/9
Telex: 3815, 3501

Products: Engines for industrial use.

Hyundai Electrical Engineering Co, Ltd
460, Chonha-Dong, Ulsan, Kyongnam

Telephone: 5-4111/20
Telex: 3752

Products: Transformers, generators, motors and circuit breakers.

Since 1980 Hyundai has delivered to Korean National Railroad (KNR) 34 3000 hp diesel-electric locomotives, also 42 electric railcars to KNR and Seoul Metropolitan Government (SMG). The latter included 24 units for the 1980 inauguration of the initial 14.3 km of the Seoul Metro's circular Line 2. During 1983 Hyundai was to deliver to SMG a further 102 units for the completion of the Line 2 project, due in December, under a contract worth US$ 90 million. The order comprises 50 each of Type Mc1 and Mc2 motor cars and two trailers. These cars feature chopper control of motors and rubber chevron-spring bogies.

Constitution: Hyundai Rolling Stock Co, Ltd began rolling stock manufacture in mid-1970 as a Locomotive Division of Hyundai Heavy Industries Co, Ltd (HHI). HHI started to produce diesel-electric locomotives under licence from GM/EMD of the USA. Since then HHI's business volume has reached an annual turnover of more than US$2500 million with some 35 000 employees working in eight different divisions. For desirable concentration of mass transit technology under independent management Hyundai Rolling Stock Co, Ltd (HRS) was incorporated.

Emu cars on final assembly line

Bitumen tank wagons for Nigerian Railway Corporation

ICF
The Integral Coach Factory

Perambur, Madras 600 038, India

Telephone: 661091
Telegrams: Raildib, Madras
Telex: 7390

General Manager: C N Kapur
Chief Mechanical Engineer: R C Tandon

Products: Railway passenger coaches of all types: second-, first- and mixed classes, kitchen cars, dining cars, pantry cars, brake and luggage vans, air-conditioned first-class chair cars and two-tier sleepers, oscillograph car, track recording cars, double-deckers, motor coaches and trailers for electric multiple-units, diesel railcars, power cars and metro cars.

Production during 1981-82 totalled 730 cars. For the double-headed New Delhi-Bombay 'Rajdhani Express', ICF turned out 10 air-conditioned cars fitted with air-brakes. Air-conditioned two-tier sleeping cars for IR's metre gauge were also designed and produced. ICF shipped 32 brake-vans to the Nigerian Railway Corporation and had on hand orders from Bangladesh and Mozambique for nine passenger cars and 15 luggage vans respectively. ICF's earlier sales

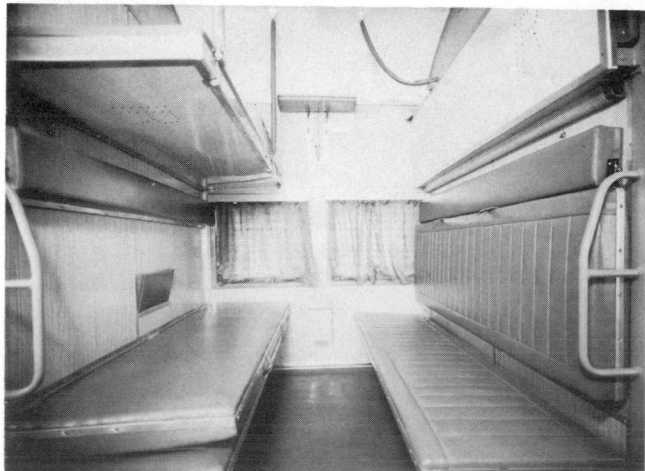

Interior of air-conditioned broad-gauge sleeping car

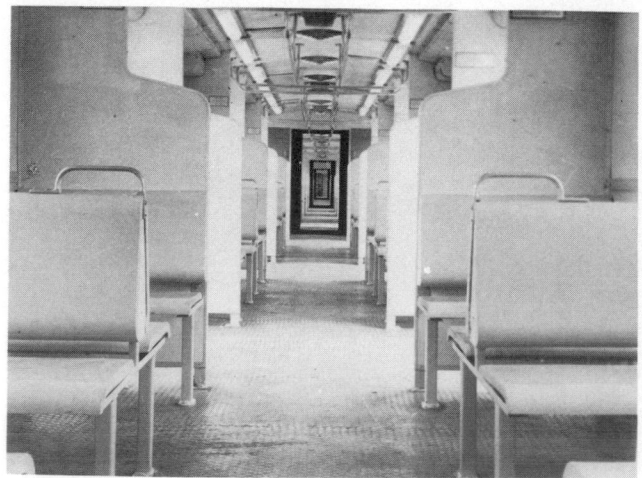

Interior of Calcutta Metro train-set

included 47 bogies to Thailand, 68 metre-gauge bogies to Burma, 244 bogies and 113 coaches of 1067 mm gauge to Taiwan, six cabooses of 1067 mm gauge to Zambia, 50 day and 10 sleeping cars of 1067 mm gauge to the Philippines, 15 third-class and two first-class cars of metre-gauge to Tanzania, 20 metre-gauge cars to Uganda and 50 metre-gauge cars to Viet-Nam.

Constitution: This is a production unit under the Ministry of Railways, Government of India, and was set up during the first Five Year Plan in collaboration with Fahrzeugwerke Altenrhein AG (FZA) of Switzerland. The collaboration agreement ended in 1961 and since then all new type of coaches have been designed and engineered entirely by ICF.

Calcutta Metro train-set

Inirail

C/Rosario Pino, 14-16, pta 15, Madrid 20, Spain

Telephone: 2797106; 2797202
Telex: 44242

Managing Director: Javier Vinader

Products: Electric, diesel-electric and diesel-hydraulic main-line locomotives; diesel-electric and diesel-hydraulic industrial and shunting locomotives; electric multiple-units; diesel-electric and diesel-hydraulic railcars and multiple-units for underground and suburban service; passenger vehicles, single- and double-deck, baggage, restaurant, etc; wagons with two axles and with bogies, closed platform, low-sided, high-sided, etc; special-purpose wagons, hopper, tank, transport of heavy loads, etc.

Constitution: Inirail was founded in 1982 to promote and co-ordinate the export sales of its three member companies: Ateinsa, Babcock & Wilcox and Maquinista, all of which are owned by Instituto Nacional de Industria.

International Car
International Car Co
Division of PACCAR

PO Box 222, Kenton, Ohio 43326, USA

Telephone: (419) 675 2381

Products: Rolling stock.

International Combustion

Clayton Works, Hatton, Derby DE6 5EB, England

Telephone: 0283 88 2382
Telegrams: Clayquip
Telex: 37581

General Manager: R A Boast

Products: Battery, trolley and diesel locomotives with electric, hydraulic or mechanical transmissions; electric- and battery-driven industrial and mining locomotives; special-purpose internal combustion engine or electric rail vehicles.

Constitution: In 1969 The Clayton Equipment Co Ltd was integrated into International Combustion Ltd and while retaining its original work site, it became absorbed into the group operation.

Italsider
Italsider SpA

Head office: Piazza Dante 7, 16121 Genoa, Italy
Works: Lovere

Telephone: 010 5999
Telegrams: Italside, Genoa
Telex: 270690

Chairman: Franco Cai
Sales Director, Export Sales: G Cattaneo

Products: Special-purpose freight wagons.

Constitution: Based on a company originally formed in 1802. Italsider was established with a new constitution in 1961.

Italtrafo
Italtrafo SpA
Member of the Finmeccanica Group

Head office: Via Nuova delle Brecce 260, Naples, Italy

Telephone: 266022; 7520633
Telegrams: Italtrafo, Naples
Telex: 71131

Works: Via Ardeatina km 21, Rome 00134

Telephone: 06 912951

Products: Electric and diesel-electric locomotives.

Jambes-Namur
Ateliers de Construction de Jambes-Namur SA

Rue du le Gare Fleurie 16, 5100 Jambes, Belgium

Telephone: 081 30 18 51
Telegrams: Jamur Jambes
Telex: 59127

Products: Industrial locomotives.

Jeffrey
Jeffrey Mining Machinery Division

PO Box 1879, Columbus, Ohio 43216, USA

Telephone: (614) 297 3123
Telegrams: Jeffrey
Telex: 245486

President: Trevor J Jones
Vice-President, Marketing: Paul L Vergamini

Products: Underground diesel, electric, battery, trolley locomotives for mining use.

Constitution: A division of Dresser Industries, Inc.

Jenbacher
Jenbacher Werke AG

6200 Jenbach, Austria

Telephone: 05244 2291-0
Telegrams: Motor Jenbach
Telex: 053756-7

Managing Director: H Wenisch
Technical Director: Dr Sollner
Sales Manager: F Franer

Products: Diesel-mechanical and diesel-hydraulic rail tractors and locomotives; passenger coaches; diesel engines; diesel compressors; diesel generator and pumping sets.

The company's range of locomotives starts with JW-engined diesel-mechanical tractors covering outputs of 6, 7.5, 11 and 15 kW and gauges of 430 to 1435 mm; it includes models with adjustable gauge and others for underground duty.

In locomotives of up to 880 kW a fluid-drive reversing gearbox simplifies application of remote radio control; locomotives of more than 440 kW are also fitted with electronic anti-slip protection.

The company's output has included 77 of its DH1500 type, a diesel-hydraulic B-B of 1100 kW, for the Austrian Federal Railway (ÖBB), and a further six of the type are in service with the Graz-Koflacher Railway (GKB). In this machine a Jenbach LM1500 engine drives through a Voith L720rU transmission via cardan shafts and Voith gearboxes. An independent Jenbach JW400 engine serves a generator for train heating. Some of the units on the ÖBB, where they form Class 2043, are equipped with electromagnetic railbrakes for pure adhesion service on the formerly rack-assisted (when steam-powered) Vordernberg-Eisenerz line.

National railways other than the ÖBB operating the company's locomotives include Soviet Railways (SZD), with 50 DH200, 50 DH400 and 37 DH600; Italian State Railways (FS), with 10 DH400 and 9 DH600; and Yugoslav Railways (JZ), with 80 DH400.

Recent passenger car construction for the ÖBB has included new couchette cars of Type Bcmoz, Eurofima-type cars (designed for 200 km/h operation) of Type Amoz and 72-seat cars of Type Bpoz for domestic services.

Constitution: The company was started in 1946 for the manufacture of diesel engines and combined units.

Type DH1500 diesel-hydraulic B-B for 1067 mm gauge Indonesian industrial plant's system; weight 52 tonnes, max speed 120 km/h

ÖBB Type 2043 diesel-hydraulic B-B on Graz-Szentgotthard (Hungary) freight at Lassnitzhöhe
(John C Baker)

Diesel-hydraulic shunter standard range

	DH100B	DH200B26	DH400B40	DH600C	DH700C54
Power output (kW)	92	132	294	440	530
No of axles	2	2	2	3	3
Gauge (mm)	1435	1435	1435	1435	1435
Weight (tonnes)	20	26	32/40	52/60	54
Starting traction (kN)	64.9	84.4	103.8/129.8	168.6/194.7	
Speed (km/h)	25	28	35	37	60
Minimum turning radius (m)	20	30	30	70	
Engine	Steyr WD 612.50	Steyr WD 615.60	Mercedes-Benz OM 404 or Cummins	Cummins VTA-1710-L1	Jenbach C240S
Gearbox model	Clark 28 000	Clark 28 000	Clark 8000	Clark 16 000	Clark 16 000

Jessop
Jessop & Co Ltd, Calcutta

63 Netaji Subhas Road, Calcutta 700 001, India

Telephone: 22 3426 49
Telegrams: Jessops, Calcutta
Telex: 021-2135; 021-7564

Works: Jessore Road, Dum Dum, Calcutta

Telephone: 57 2321

Chairman and Managing Director: P K Banerji
Director (Finance): J K Roy
Director (Commercial): V R Pappu

Products: All types of rolling stock including electric multiple-unit coaches and passenger coaches.

Constitution: Jessop and Co was founded in 1788, one of the oldest engineering firms in India. The works at Dum Dum, which cover 80 acres, comprise six separate units: wagon, coach, structural, road roller, mechanical and paper works. The works at Durgapur, built on 116 acres, manufacture heavy duty iron castings.

Jeumont-Schneider
Jeumont-Schneider SA

31-32 quai de Dion-Bouton, 92811 Puteaux Cedex, France

Telephone: (1) 776 43 23
Telex: 610 425

Chairman and Chief Executive: Christian Devin

Products: Traction equipment for electric and diesel-electric locomotives. (See also under Francorail)

Jung
Arn Jung Lokomotivfabrik GmbH

Postfach 20, 5242 Jungenthal bei Kirchen a/d Sieg, Federal Republic of Germany

Telephone: 02741 6831
Telegrams: Lokomotivfabrik, Kirchen-Sieg
Telex: 08 753 19

Products: Electric and diesel locomotives.

Typical of recent production is the RC 43 C diesel-hydraulic locomotive designed for shunting and branch-line duties. Designed as a three-axle rigid-frame locomotive, it is driven by an MTU four-stroke diesel engine and equipped with Voith hydrodynamic forward/reverse transmission. The axles are driven via cardan shafts and axle gear boxes. Axles have rubber springs and are equipped with hydraulic shock absorbers. Controls are electro-pneumatic. In service with Deutsche Bundesbahn the locomotive is frequently equipped with radio control equipment.

Type RC 43 C diesel-hydraulic locomotive

Kaeble-Gmeinder
Carl Kaeble u Gmeinder GmbH & Co

Postfach 1260, 6950 Mosbach, Baden, Federal Republic of Germany

Telephone: 06261 4041
Telegrams: Gmeinder, Mosbachbaden
Telex: 04 66111

Managing Directors: Rudolph Zornow
                       Hans Karcher
                       Friedrich Mezger
Export Sales: Friedrich Krone

Products: Diesel-electric and diesel-hydraulic locomotives up to 1200 hp; special freight wagons.

Type D36B 332 kW diesel locomotives for Norwegian State Railways (NSB)

Kalmar
Kalmar Verkstads AB

PO Box 943, 391 29 Kalmar, Sweden

Telephone: 46 480 15070
Telegrams: Kvab, Kalmar
Telex: 43029

Chairman: Sven Arnerius
Managing Director: Ingemar Strömblad

Products: Diesel-electric locomotives, diesel-hydraulic shunting locomotives, diesel-hydraulic railcars, passenger coaches, freight wagons, special wagons (eg for installation and maintenance of overhead wiring).

Prominent among recent sales have been: 100 passenger coaches for East African Railways, Kenya and Tanzania; 160 open freight wagons and 25 tank wagons for Zambia Railways; 200 first- and second-class passenger saloon cars (with an option for a further 50), 30 railcars and 18 diesel-electric locomotives for Swedish State Railways (SJ).

Development in progress includes design of a 200 km/h high-speed train (in collaboration with ASEA) for SJ, manufacture of diesel-hydraulic shunting locomotives and diesel-hydraulic railcars for SJ and also of bogies for Hyundai Heavy Industries.

Interior of Type S1 conference coach for SJ, equipped with video, slide and overhead projectors and screen

Constitution: Kalmar Verkstad was founded in 1902 and is Swedish State Railways' (SJ) major supplier of diesel locomotives, railcars and passenger cars. Kalmar Verkstad is a subsidiary of the Kalmar Kockum Group, which belongs to Swedish State Company Ltd.

Licensing agreements: Kalmar Verkstad has agreements with: ASEA, Sweden; Fiat Ferroviara Savigliano SpA, Italy; General Motors Electromotive Division, USA; and Hyundai Heavy Industries, Republic of Korea.

SJ Type T44 1650 hp diesel-electric locomotive for heavy shunting and freight haulage geared for 105-140 km/h max speeds

Interior of Type SCB second-class car for Tanzania Railways

Type S1 conference coach for SJ

Kalmar diesel locomotives

Swedish State Railways (SJ) class	Wheel arrangement	Transmission	Rated power (kW)	Max speed km/h	Total weight tonnes	No in service	Year first built	Builders		
								Mechanical parts	Engine & type	Transmission
Di3	Co-Co	Elec	1300	105	98	10	1965	Nohab/Kalmar Verkstad	GM 16-567C	GM-ASEA
M61	Co-Co	Elec	1435	105	108.6	20	1963	Nohab/Kalmar Verkstad	GM 16-567D1	GM
My	A1A-A1A	Elec	1435	133	104	15	1964	Nohab/Kalmar Verkstad	GM 16-567D1	GM
Mx	A1A-A1A	Elec	1050	133	89	45	1960	Nohab/Kalmar Verkstad	GM 16-567B	GM
Mz	Co-Co	Elec	2430	143	120	26	1967	Nohab/Kalmar Verkstad	GM 16-645E3	A/S Trige
Mz	Co-Co	Elec	2870	165	126	20	1972	Nohab/Kalmar Verkstad	GM 16-645E3	GM
Mz	Co-Co	Elec	2870	165	123	15	1977	Nohab/Kalmar Verkstad	GM 16-645E3	GM
T43	Bo-Bo	Elec	1050	95	72	50	1961	Nohab/Kalmar Verkstad	GM 12-567C	GM
T44	Bo-Bo	Elec	1230	105	76	90	1968	Nohab/Kalmar Verkstad	GM 12-645E	GM
T46	Co-Co	Elec	1230	90	150	4	1973	Nohab/Kalmar Verkstad	GM 12-645E	GM
Tb	Bo-Bo	Elec	1230	105	80	10	1969	Nohab/Kalmar Verkstad	GM 12-645E	GM
Z65	B	Hyd	265	60	28	105	1962	Kalmar Verkstad	Rolls Royce C8TFL Mk IV	Twin Disc and Deutsche Getr Gesells
Z66	B	Hyd	265	70	32	30	1971	Kalmar Verkstad	KHD F12M 716	Voith and Gmeinder

Kalmar diesel railcars

Swedish State Railways (SJ) class	Transmission	Rated power (kW) per motor	Max speed km/h	Weight tonnes per car	Total seating capacity	Length per car mm	No in service	Year first built	Builders		
									Mechanical parts	Engine & type	Transmission
Y1	Hyd	295	130	45	68	24 400	30	1980	Kalmar Verkstad/Fiat	Fiat 8217 12	Fiat SRM

Kawasaki

Kawasaki Heavy Industries Ltd, Rolling Stock Group

Head office: World Trade Centre Building, 4-1 Hamamatsu-cho 2-chome, Minato-ku, Tokyo, Japan

Telephone: 02867 3 0022
Telegrams: Kawasaki Heavy, Tokyo
Telex: 22672, 26888, (domestic) 242-4371

Works: 1/18 Wadayama-Dori 2-chome, Hyogo-ku, Kobe
Telephone: 078 671 5021

2857-2, Naka Okamoto, Kawachi-cho, Kawachi-Gun, Tochigi Pref
Telephone: (03) 435-2589

Chairman: Zenji Umeda
President: Kenko Hasegawa
Executive Vice Presidents: Renzo Nihei
Yutaki Onishi
Director (Rolling Stock): Masahiko Ishizawa

Products: Electric, diesel-electric, diesel-hydraulic locomotives; electric railcars; diesel railcars; freight cars; passenger coaches; containers.

The company has been one of five manufacturers entrusted with construction of 432 cars forming the new Series 200 train-sets for the 25 kV 50 Hz Tohoku and Joetsu Shinkansen of Japanese National Railways (JNR) which were opened in 1982. To cater for the long gradients on the Joetsu line, which traverses Honshu Island's central mountain range, the Series 200 sets have bodies of aluminium alloy, not the steel of earlier Shinkansen rolling stock, and more powerful traction motors with a continuous rating of 230 kW as against 185 kW in preceding sets; since the new lines are similarly limited to 210 km/h top speed, however, a 29:63 gear ratio has been retained. Traction motor voltage supply is thyristor-controlled and choppers govern the dynamic braking. The DT201 bogie, which has air secondary suspension, features additional protection against snow and ice, which will be a greater operating hazard in the north of the country where the new lines run. Enhanced safeguards against wintry conditions motivate many other innovations, such as the deep bodyside skirting around underfloor equipment. The bogie skirting, however, is also devised to reduce noise, which recent Japanese legislation strictly limits, and this has been the focus of other design effort, particularly with the pantographs. A 12-car set, formed of six electrically self-contained two-car units, each with its own pantograph, seats 52 'green' and 833 standard-class passengers, and also includes a buffet. Maximum axleload is 17 tonnes.

Other recent sales to JNR have included the 1.5 kV dc chopper-controlled Series 203 emu. It is fabricated in unpainted light alloy from large hollow-formed sections. Based on the JNR Series 201, the 203 was designed for the opening of through service between the JNR Johban and Tokyo Corporation Chiyoda Lines. The first 10-car set was delivered in August 1982. The route is severely graded in many places, so high acceleration and deceleration rates were specified. The weight of the car was also reduced substantially in order to reduce the thermal load of the main circuit equipments such as the main motor. All four axles in a motor car are powered with 150 kW motors and motor car weights are either 34.9 or 35.4 tonnes, with 54 seats. Maximum speed is 100 km/h. Each car is 20 metres long and trailers weigh 24 to 26.5 tonnes, with 48 or 54 seats.

In July 1981 the 1.5 kV dc Route 1 metro of the Fukuoka Municipal Transportation Bureau was partially opened to traffic with eight six-car emus manufactured by The Kinki Sharyo Co, Ltd. For the full opening, scheduled for March 1983, an order for seven six-car emus was placed with KHI and all the cars were delivered by autumn 1982. The cars are made of stainless steel. For direct connection with JNR and the Fukuoka Municipal metro, they are equipped with ATC for the subway and for manual ATS (automatic train stop device) on the JNR line.

SEPTA light rail vehicle

Series 203 emu for JNR

Emu for Fukuoka Municipal Transportation Bureau

Rubber-tyred emu for north-south line of Sapporo Municipal Transportation Bureau

Fukuoka Municipal Transportation Bureau emu cars

Car type	Motored axles per motor car	Rated output (kW) per motor	Max speed km/h	Weight tonnes per car (M-motor T-trailer)	Total seating capacity	Length per car mm	Rate of acceleration m/s²
TC				34	48	20 000	
M	4	150	90	40	54	19 500	0.917 = 3.3 km/h/s
M'	4	150		41	54	19 500	
T'C				34	48	20 000	

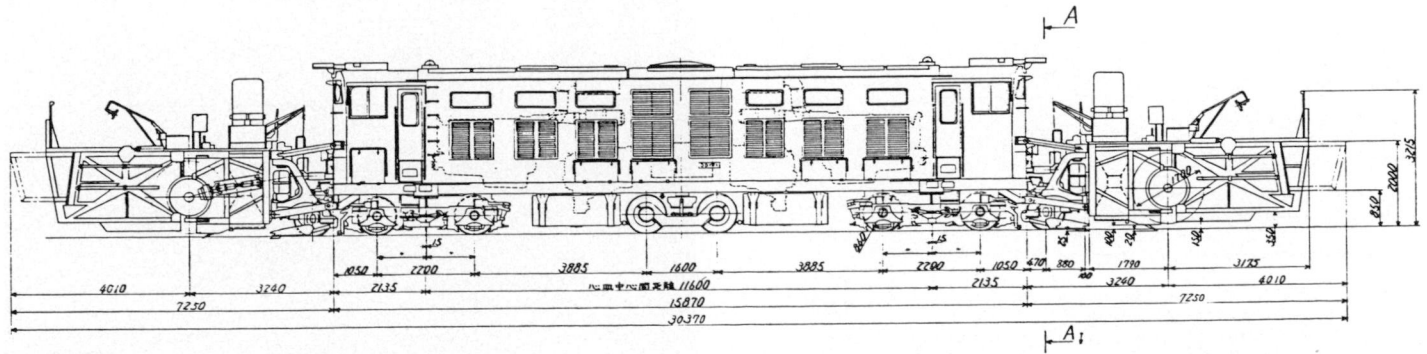
General arrangement of Type DD17 snowplough for JNR

The Series 6000 emu for Keihan Electric Railways is a new all light alloy commuter design employing large-sized hollow-formed sections. KHI received an order for 77 cars to form seven-car trains and delivery was scheduled to start in February and end in August 1983. The first five sets are arranged for 600-volt or 1.5 kV dc operation, the remainder for 1.5 kV dc. Car length is 18.2 metres.

Keihan Electric Railways Series 6000 emu

Car type	Motor cars per unit	Motored axles per motor car	Rated output (kW) per motor	Max speed km/h	Weight tonnes per car (M-motor T-trailer)
MC1	1	4	130 (at 600 V)	120	M 32.5
MC2	1	4	155 (at 1.5 kV)		M 32.5
M1	1	4			M 32
M2	1	4			M 32
T1					T 22
T2					T 22
T					T 24

Bogie of rubber-tyred Sapporo Subway east-west line emu

The company has obtained a repeat order for two four-car 1.5 kV dc emus for the Indonesian State Railways' (PJKA) Jakarta suburban system. Maximum speed is 100 km/h. The sets were delivered in February 1983.

Indonesian State Railways (PJKA) emu

Car type	Cars per unit	Motored axles per motor car	Weight tonnes per car (M-motor T-trailer)	Total seating capacity	Length per car mm (M-motor T-trailer)
TC	2		32	82	20 000
M1	1	4 × 120 kW	32	92	20 000
M2	1	4 × 120 kW	39	92	20 000

ATO- and ATC-equipped emu of Kobe New Transit System, Japan

The Ina line of Saitama New Transit Co Ltd is a medium-scale transit system managed by Saitama New Transit Co, Ltd and financed by JNR, Saitama Prefecture, Ohmiya City, Ageo City and Ina Town. It was started to improve transport in the eastern part of Ageo City, Ina Town and its surroundings to exploit the elevated infrastructure of the Tohoku-Joetsu Shinkansen line, and to promote regional development. It was to be opened for traffic in the autumn of 1983. In a joint enterprise with Niigata Engineering Co Ltd, KHI is manufacturing the bodies of 40 cars for the line. The basic system is the same as that of the new urban transit system ('New Tram') in Osaka Nanko Port Town, ie a four-wheel, rubber-tyred electric car with a side guide system. The 8 metre-long cars are unmanned; each has a 100 kW motor, weighs 10.5 to 10.8 tonnes and seats 36 to 40.

The company's Type DD17 diesel-powered rotary snowplough for Japanese National Railways is double-ended, to overcome the modern dearth of turntables. It can perform snow-clearance in either direction. Two 1100 hp engines are mounted, one for traction, the other for snow ploughing according to the direction of running. When clearing, a 6 metre-wide, 800 mm-high bank of snow of 0.3 specific gravity can be removed at a speed of 10 km/h. The unit can serve as an ordinary diesel locomotive by detaching the snowplough.

Constitution: Kawasaki Heavy Industries Ltd was formed in 1969 by the merger of Kawasaki Rolling Stock Manufacturing Co, Kawasaki Aircraft Co and Kawasaki Dockyard Co Ltd. In 1972 Kisha Seizo Kaisha Ltd was taken over and merged into Kawasaki Heavy Industries Ltd.

Emu for Indonesian State Railways (PJKA)

Kinki Sharyo
The Kinki Sharyo Co Ltd
Kinki Rolling Stock Manufacturing Co Ltd

Head office and Tokuan factory: 966-1 Inada, Higashi Osaka City, Osaka 577, Japan

Telephone: 06 745 1231
Telegrams: Kinsha Fuse
Telex: 5278911
Fax: 06 745 5135 (GIII)

Tokyo office: 527 Nippon Bldg, Ohtemachi, Chiyoda-ku, Tokyo 100

Telephone: 03 270 3431
Telex: 222 3105
Fax: 03 245 0238 (GIII)

President: Toshio Muramatsu
Managing Directors: Hiroshi Ishiguro
          Seihei Katayama
Export Sales Director: Hideaki Sakai

Products: Electric and diesel railcars; refrigerator cars; passenger and freight cars; industrial wagons and equipment.

In 1981, the company entered into a licensing agreement with SIG, Switzerland, which allows Kinki to produce articulated light railway vehicles to SIG's proven design.

All-steel emu for Fukuoka Municipal Transportation Bureau

Major purchasers of Kinki products include such domestic clients as Japanese National Railways (JNR), Kinki Nippon Railway Co, Ltd, Tokyo Rapid Transit Authority, Tokyo Metropolitan Government Transport Authority, Osaka, Fukuoka and Kyoto Municipal Transportation Bureaus, as well as customers in such countries as the Republic of Korea, Taiwan, Thailand, Hong Kong, Philippines, Burma, Egypt, Nigeria, Zambia, Mexico, Bangladesh, Indonesia, Australia, New Zealand, Argentina, Brazil, Peru and USSR.

Representative products include Shinkansen electric cars for JNR, double-deck express electric cars for Kinki Nippon Railway Co, Ltd, and the chopper-control cars for Teito Rapid Transit Authority, Fukuoka and Kyoto Municipal Transportation Bureaus. The company manufactures aluminium and stainless steel as well as steel cars.

Typical of recent commuter emu products are the all-steel sets for the Fukuoka Municipal Transportation Bureau, the aluminium alloy sets for the Kyoto Municipal Transportation Bureau and the 8000 series of aluminium alloy sets for the Teito Rapid Transit Authority.

More than 800 LRVs have been supplied to authorities in Egypt, including 190 tramcars for the Cairo Transport Authority and 30 for the Alexandria Passenger Transport Authority.

Kinki Sharyo LRVs

	Cairo	Alexandria
Gauge (mm)	1000	1435
Line current (V dc)	600	600
Tare weight (tonnes)	21.5	18.7
Passenger capacity		
Total	163	137
Seated	44	36
Length overall (mm)	15 800	12 900
Width overall (mm)	2500	2300
Height to top of roof (mm)	3340	3220
Bogie centre distance (mm)	8400	6500
Wheelbase (mm)	1900	1850
Wheel diameter (mm)	660	660
1 h rating output (kW) per motor	52	52
Motored axles per motor car	4	4
Max speed (km/h)	64	50

Tramcar for Cairo Transport Authority, Egypt

Aluminium alloy emu for Kyoto Municipal Transportation Bureau

Tramcar for Alexandria Passenger Transport Authority, Egypt

Alexandria tramcar interior

Interior of Fukuoka emu

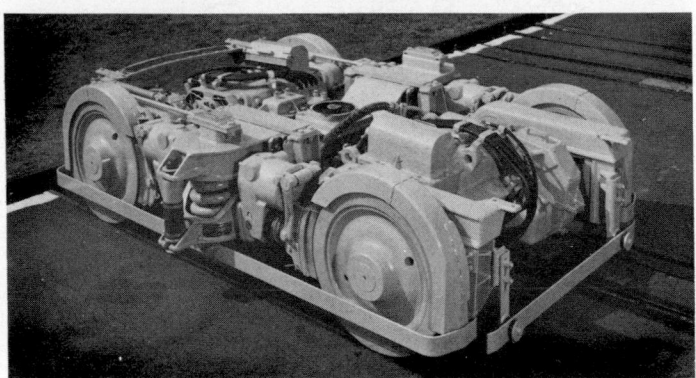
Alexandria tramcar bogie

Kinki Sharyo commuter emus

	Fukuoka		Kyoto		Teito	
Gauge (mm)	1067		1435		1067	
Line current (V dc)	1500		1500		1500	
	(Power car)	(Trailer car)			(Power car)	(Trailer car)
Tare weight (tonnes)	34	40	36		26.3	35.7
Passenger capacity			(Power car)	(Trailer car)		
Total	136	144	150	170	136	144
Seated	48	54	50	58	48	54
Length overall (mm)	20 000		20 000		20 000	
Width overall (mm)	2840		2780		2830	
Height to top of roof (mm)	4090		4040		3920	
Bogie centre distance (mm)	14 000		14 100		13 800	
Wheelbase (mm)	2100		2100		2200	
Wheel diameter (mm)	860		860		860	
1 h rating output (kW) per motor	150		130		160	
Motored axles per motor car	4		4		4	
Max speed (km/h)	90		75		100	

Kolmex

Mokotowska 49, 00-542 Warsaw, Poland

Telephone: 28 22 91
Telegrams: Kolmex, Warsaw
Telex: 813270; 813714

Managing Director: Ryszard Szymański
Sales Directors: Aleksander Gudzowaty
Krzysztof Szpilewski

Products: Electric and diesel locomotives; electric train-sets; passenger coaches; freight wagons.

Constitution: Kolmex acts as sole exporter of railway motive power and passenger and freight stock manufactured in Poland, and purchaser of imported equipment. Its members are Cegielski, Pafawag, Fablok, Konstal, Zastal and Swidnica. Since 1947 export production has totalled 2200 locomotives and other traction units, 9250 passenger coaches and emus, 177 600 freight wagons and 15 700 containers. Kolmex has exported 205 000 units of various types to 44 countries.

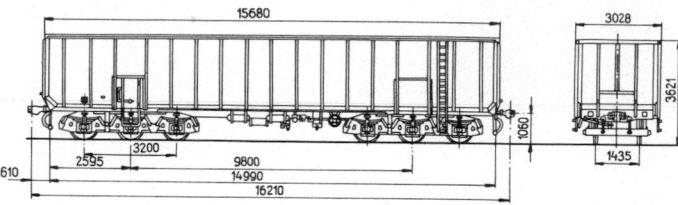

General arrangement of Type 601W 12-wheeled coal wagon, tare 30.5 tonnes, load capacity 89.5 tonnes/100 m³, max speed 100 km/h

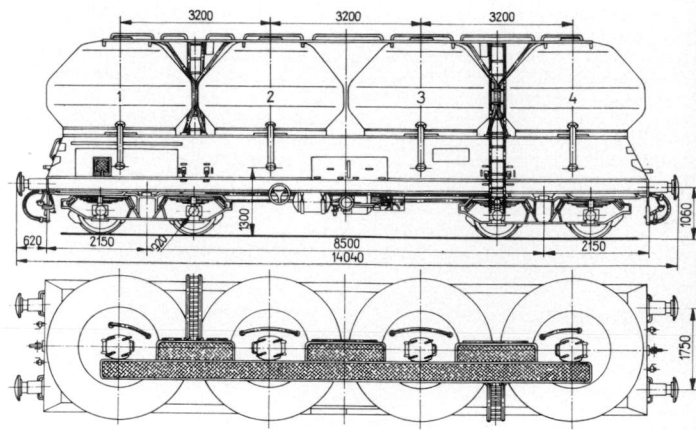

Type 408S air-discharge cement wagon, tare 24 tonnes, load capacity 56 tonnes/50 m³, max speed 100 km/h

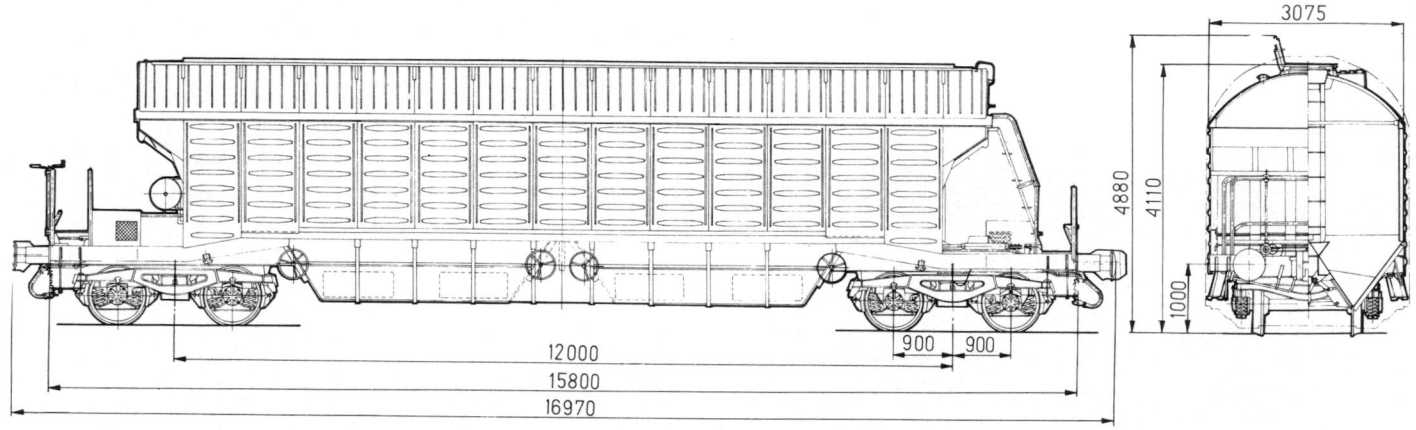

Type 420Va self-discharging grain hopper, tare weight 24 tonnes, load capacity 56 tonnes/90 m³, max speed 100 km/h

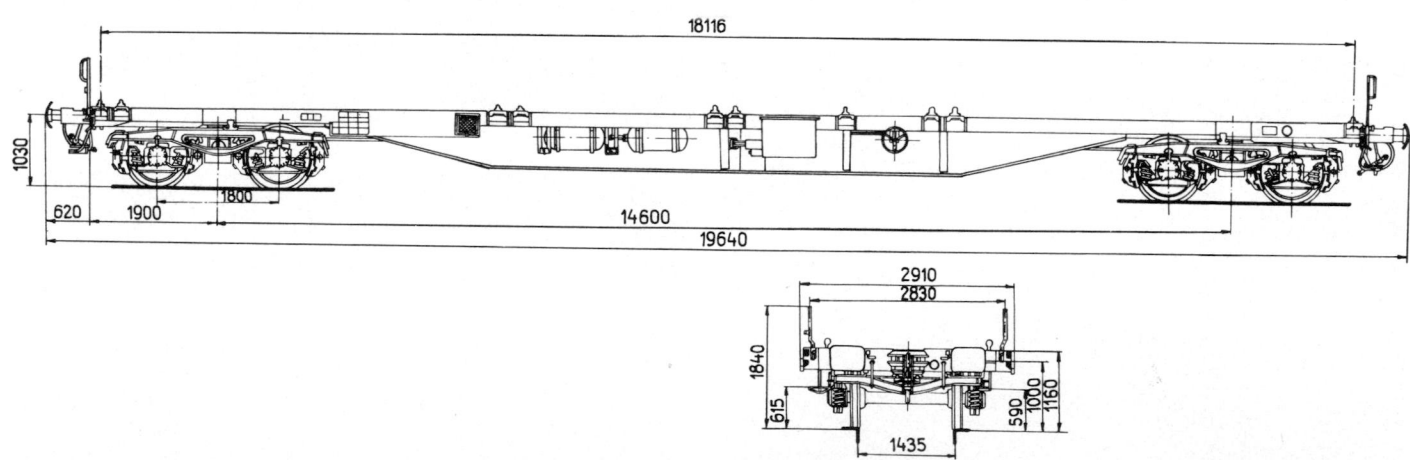

Type 413Z container wagon, with adjustable mandrels to accommodate varying container-type mixes, including Sealand 35 ft, tare 19 tonnes, load capacity 61 tonnes, max speed 120 km/h

Type 123A passenger car

Type 201E 3040 kW 3 kV dc Co-Co electric in Polish State Railways (PKP) service as Class ET22

Type 3We three-car emu in PKP service

Konstal
Steel Construction Works Konstal

ul Metalowcow 7, 41-501 Chorzow, Poland

Export sales: Kolmex, 49 Mokotowska, 00-542 Warsaw

Telephone: 41 10 51
Telegrams: Konstal, Chorzow
Telex: 033451

Products: Electric and storage battery mine locomotives and freight wagons.

Ldag-05/M flameproof mining locomotive

Lea BM-12/T flameproof mining locomotive

Korea Shipbuilding & Engineering
Korea Shipbuilding & Engineering Corporation

Head office: 1-1, 1-Ka Jongro, Jongro-Ku, Seoul, Republic of Korea
CPO Box 1520, Seoul

Telephone: 744 5577
Telex: 23669; 23415

Busan shipyard: 29, 5-Ka, Bongnae-Dong, Yongdo-Ku, Busan
PO Box 74, Busan

Telephone: 49 4161/9
Telex: 3330

Chairman: Ryun Namkoong
President: Ho Namkoong
Executive Director: Sung Hwan Park
Sales Manager: Bong Lin Choi

Products: Diesel railcars, electric railcars, passenger cars, freight cars, special-purpose rolling stock, cast-steel bogies, couplers.
The company's recent export production has included 50 passenger cars for the Malayan Railway Administration, among them air-conditioned day and night cars and buffet cars, and 581 freight cars of various types for the same authority, as well as ride-control bogies and wheelsets. Other major wagon contracts have been completed for the railways of Saudi Arabia, Sudan and Gabon.

Kraljevo
Kraljevo Car Factory

Kraljevo, Yugoslavia

Telephone: (036) 21-455
Telegrams: Vagoni
Telex: 17652

Products: Passenger coaches and freight wagons.

Krauss-Maffei
Krauss-Maffei Aktiengesellschaft

Krauss-Maffei Strasse 2, 8000 Munich 50, Federal Republic of Germany

Telephone: 089 88991
Telegrams: Kraussmaffei, Münchenallach
Telex: 05 23 163-91

Board of Directors: Dr rer pol Hans-Heinz Griesmeier
Karl Bayer
Dr Ing Joachim Huwendiek
Dipl Kfm Willi Klein-Gunnewyk
Dipl Wirt Robert Jasper
Managing Director, Transportation Division: Stefan Hedrich

Products: Diesel and electric locomotives; tracked high speed systems with contact-free suspension and guidance.
In conjunction with BBC, suppliers of the electrical equipment, the company has lately developed a three-axle diesel-electric shunting locomotive with three-phase power transmission, Type ME 05, the layout of which is easily adaptable to differing operational requirements through use of a modular construction technique. It is available either with a centre cab or with a cab at each end, and is offered with makes of engine presenting a choice of output from 500 to 800 kW. Other options include: air-operated shoe brakes or disc brakes in conjunction with a rheostatic brake; disc braking without rheostatic brake; and rubber-plate or steel-spring primary suspension. Maximum axle-loading is 25 tonnes. All locomotives are fitted with a microprocessor-controlled non-skid device that acts on the air brake, and with the Krauss-Maffei diagnostically-programmed electronic vehicle control system, which is adaptable to any known make of remote radio control apparatus. The intended engines are from the MTU high-speed series, but other makes can be substituted.

On tests over a section of the Hohenzollern State Railways where 13 km are graded at an average of 1.8 per cent, but the culminating 4 km are almost continuously 2.8 per cent and characterised by curvature down to 250 metres radius, the ME 05 recorded a starting tractive effort of 200 kN on an electric power of only 55 kW. Two of these locomotives in double-cab format acquired by Voest-Alpine AG steelworks in Linz, Austria, are arranged for normal operation by remote radio control; they can, however, be driven from the shunter's platform outside each end-cab by means of a manipulator with cable plug-in to connections in either cab. Another ME 05 customer, the Peine Salzgitter Steelworks in the German Federal Republic, which purchased three units in the centre-cab arrangement, has procured a further three. Since the ME 05's debut in 1980 Krauss-Maffei claims to have won all orders for locomotives of its general type put out to tender by West German and Austrian steel plants. An ME 05 has also been tested by the German Federal Railway (DB) as a possible successor to its V260 and V290 shunting types.

ME 05 centre-cab 0-6-0 version
Gauge: 1435 mm
Length over buffers: 10 m
Width: 3 m
Highest roof top edge: 4.06 m
Height of running board above top of rail: 1.26 m
Total wheelbase: 4 m
    alternatively: 3.8/4.2 m
Wheel diameter, new: 1000 mm
    worn: 920 mm
Total weight, max: 75 tonnes
Axle load, max: 25 tonnes
Engine rating: 500 kW
Max speed: 60 km/h
Minimum curve radius: 50 m
Minimum vertical radius: 250 m
Fuel supply: 2100 litres
Sand supply: 300/450 litres
Main air reservoir capacity: 800 litres
Brake compressor supply at 10 bar: 1800 litres/minute
    The company is redesigning its Type M500/700C diesel-hydraulic shunter as the MH 05.

In its latest batch of low-profile diesel-hydraulic B-Bs for Spanish National Railways (RENFE), the company has further increased power rating to 4000 hp without addition to locomotive weight. Created for Talgo train haulage, the first 10 locomotives of this type, delivered in 1963-64, were designed for 140 km/h maximum speed and had a rating of 2400 hp. In the second series of five, delivered in 1968-69 and arranged for 180 km/h, output was lifted to 3000 hp but axle-loading was simultaneously lowered by 20 per cent. The latest series of eight units, RENFE Class 354, is powered by two MTU 16V 396TDB engines driving through Voith L520rz UZ2 transmissions, has a maximum speed of 180 km/h and a rated output of 4036 hp, but a service weight of only 80 tonnes. The increased power fits the third series for other passenger duties as well as Talgo haulage. An availability factor of 98 per cent and a failure rate of only 1 per 1.55 million km is claimed for the first two series.

RENFE Class 354 diesel-hydraulic locomotive
Axle arrangement: B-B
Gauge: 1668 mm
Length over buffers: 19.92 m
Width: 3.04 m
Height: 3.45 m
Bogie wheelbase: 3.2 m
Distance between bogie centres: 11 m
Wheel diameter (new): 1.15 m
Service weight: 80 tonnes
Axle load: 20 tonnes
Max speed: 180 km/h
Fuel capacity: 4000 litres
Sand capacity: 500 kg
Minimum curve radius: 80 m
Diesel power rating under conditions in Spain, at 1900 rpm: 3010 kW/4036 hp
Transmission power input: 2794 kW/3800 hp

Another recent product for RENFE is the Class 250 4940 kW (6625 hp) mixed traffic electric 3 kV dc Co-Co, with electrical equipment by Brown Boveri of Zurich. This 120-tonne type, five of which have been assembled by Krauss-Maffei, the remainder in Spain, has monomotor bogies with gearing for 160 km/h maximum speed in passenger traffic, 100 km/h in freight haulage.

RENFE Type 250 mixed traffic locomotive
Wheel arrangement: Co-Co
Service weight: 120 tonnes
Axle load: 20 tonnes
Total length over buffers: 20 m
Width over side walls: 3.13 m
Height of body: 3.835 m
Distance between pivots: 10.2 m
Axle base of bogies: 3.6 m
Wheel diameter: 1.25 m
Max speed,
    passenger traffic: 160 km/h
    gear ratio: 1 : 2286
    mixed traffic: 100 km/h
    gear ratio: 1 : 3660
Tractive effort,
    passenger traffic,
    starting: 256 kN
    continuous at 80 km/h: 197 kN
    max brake effort: 168 kN
    mixed traffic,
    starting: 410 kN
    continuous at 50 km/h: 316 kN
    max brake effort: 270 kN

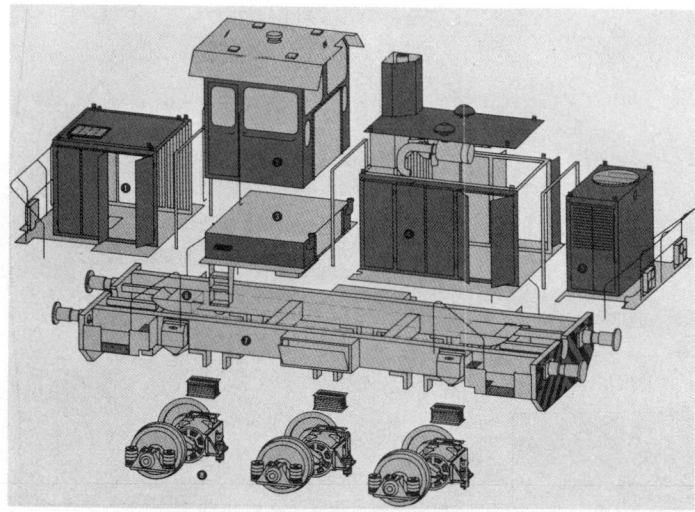

Modular design of K-M three-phase diesel-electric shunter in centre-cab ME 05 format (**1**) power electrics/electronics module (**2**) driving cab (**3**) fuel reservoir (**4**) diesel engine-generator module (**5**) cooling plant module (engine cooler, central fan and compressor) (**6**) central air channel (**7**) frame (**8**) wheel-sets with traction motors

Centre-cab Type ME 05

Double-cab, radio-controlled Type ME 05 in service with Voest-Alpine, Austria

Third series Class 354 low-profile diesel-hydraulic B-B for RENFE

Minimum curve radius,
   track: 250 m
   shops and sheds: 100 m
Lateral displacement of central wheel-set in bogie: ±20 mm
Mechanical power transmission: Alcatel with electro-pneumatic change-over of 2 speed stages.
Axle drive: BBC rubber joint cardan drive
Wheel flange greasing type: Sècheron, with electronic rail-dependent pulsing
Spray nozzles at axles 1 and 6: 2 nozzles each
Anti-skid device type: Krauss-Maffei K-Micro, one pulse generator at axles 2 and 5 each
Power rating, continuous: 4600 kW
   1 h: 4940 kW
Traction motor control: Conventional, with electro-pneumatic contactors for resistors and field suppressors, motors series-connected, or series-paralleled, Bridge transition. Automatic start with adjustable motor current up to pre-set final stage (economic stages only)
Traction motors: BBC 6 EDO 8146
Continuous rating: 2 × 1150 kW
Rated voltage: 3000/2 V
Permanent current at n = 806 rpm: 810 A
Pneumatic brakes: Automatic, graduated compressed air brake for locomotive and air-braked rolling stock, automatic vacuum brake for vacuum-braked rolling stock, direct air brake for locomotive

   As a member of the Transrapid Maglev Train consortium, Krauss-Maffei has been responsible for creation of aluminium bodies and Maglev bogie frames of the 54.2 metre-long, 192-seat two-car prototype train-set; and the rail equip-

Model of 400 km/h Transrapid maglev train to start trials on Emsland test track in 1983

ment including high-speed switches of the experimental guideway at the Emsland test centre, together with the rail-laying train. Test running, intended to demonstrate Maglev potential for speeds up to 400 km/h, was due to begin in the spring of 1983.

Constitution: The present firm of Krauss-Maffei was created by the merger in 1931 of two locomotive builders, J A Maffei AG, founded in 1837, and Krauss & Co KG, founded in 1866. In 1935-37 a factory, replacing the former two plants, was erected at Allach, a suburb of Munich.

Three-phase, all-purpose Class 120 5600 kW electric locomotive of German Federal Railway (DB); series production not anticipated before 1984

Krupp
Fried Krupp GmbH
A member of Krupp Industrie- und Stahlbau

Helenenstrasse 149, 4300 Essen 1, Federal Republic of Germany

Telephone: 0201 31901
Telegrams: Krupp, Essen
Telex: 08 57 9331

Chairman: Dr Ing Gerd Weber
General Manager of Products: Werner Gorlitz

Export Sales Manager: Dieter Hedtstuck

Products: Electric locomotives, diesel-hydraulic locomotives, multi-axle multi-purpose heavy-load carriers up to 1000-tonne capacity, ladle wagons for transporting liquid iron up to 500 tonnes, railway cranes, special rail vehicles to individual specifications.
   Recent output has included Type U20C 2150 bhp diesel-electric locomotives for Zambia, Type U15C 1720 bhp locomotives for Zaire and U22C 2150 bhp locomotives for Botswana, all built under licence from General Electric, USA. A 36-axle Schnabel car with a carrying capacity of 807 tonnes, the largest tracked vehicle in the world, was supplied to the USA.

DD 950 diesel-electric locomotive for Burma Railways Corporation

Type U20C 2150 bhp diesel-electric for Zambia

Krupp Brüninghaus
Krupp Brüninghaus GmbH

PO Box 3240, 5840 Schwerte 3, Westhofen/Westfalen, Federal Republic of Germany

Telephone: 02304 6891
Telegrams: Brüninghaus, Westhofenwestf
Telex: 8 229 615

Products: Tank and special purpose wagons.

Kuibyshev
Kuibyshev Diesel Locomotive Works

Kolomensk, USSR

Products: Diesel locomotives.

LEW
VEB Lokomotivbau-Elektrotechnische Werke "Hans Beimler"

Head office: 1422 Hennigsdorf, German Democratic Republic

Export sales: AHB Schienenfahrzeuge Export-Import

Telephone: 50
Telegrams: Elektrolok
Telex: 158 531

Products: Electric, diesel-hydraulic and diesel-electric locomotives; special electric locomotives; multiple-unit trains.

Recent products include the prototype Type 212 B-B 15 kV 16⅔ Hz electric locomotive, on extended tests in 1983, which has been designated the Deutsche Reichsbahn's (DR) standard express passenger class for the second half of the 1980s. In that role it will succeed the Type 242, of which the DR currently deploys 300. The thyristor-controlled Type 212 is a 3720 kW machine weighing 74 tonnes, with a length of 16.64 metres and a starting tractive effort of 277 kN. It is geared in its initial version for a maximum speed of 140 km/h, but a freight variant, the Class 243, geared for a maximum of 125 km/h is forecast.

The high-voltage power control embodies a 31-step multiple-contact switch and a thyristor regulator with optoelectronic transmission elements. The controlling and regulating circuits, a complex information electronics unit, have been designed on the basis of highly integrated circuits.

Series 270 multiple-unit train-set for East Berlin elevated S-Bahn

Type V100.5 diesel-hydraulic locomotive as drive unit of a ditch-cleaning unit of the German State Railway (DR)

Type BR 270 emu with dc chopper regulator

LEW electric locomotives

Class	Wheel arrangement	Line voltage	Rated ouput (kW) continuous one-hour	Max speed km/h	Weight tonnes	No in service and on order	Year first built	Builders Mechanical parts	Builders Electrical equipment
BR 212/243	Bo-Bo	15 kV 16⅔ Hz	3720	140/120	82.5	2	1982	LEW	LEW
EL 20 + 2 motor dump wagons	Bo-Bo + Bo-Bo + Bo-Bo	10 kV 50 Hz	3 × 1840	50	3 × 122	4	1983	LEW	LEW
EL 21	Bo-Bo-Bo	1.5 kV	2100	65	160	95	1981	LEW	LEW
EL 16/03	B	112 V*	17	6	12	8	1982	LEW	LEW

*Battery voltage

LEW electric multiple-units

Class	Cars per unit	Line voltage	Motor cars per unit	Motored axles per motor car	Rated output (kW) per motor	Max speed km/h	Weight tonnes per car (M-motor T-trailer)	Total seating capacity	Length per car mm (M-motor T-trailer)	No in service	Rate of acceleration m/s²	Year first built	Builders Mechanical parts	Builders Electrical equipment
BR 270	4	750 V dc	2	4	150	90	M 33.5 T 23.5	208	M 18 150 T 18 050	2	0.7	1980	LEW	LEW
G III	4	750 V dc	4	4	120	70	M 22.5 T 21.1	126	M1 14 650 M2 14 650	—	0.8	1984	LEW	LEW

A new product for industrial users is the Type 4 EL 20, an assembly of three motorised Bo-Bo vehicles of which only one is a control cab unit; the other two are dumper wagons each with a load capacity of 55 tonnes. The 4 EL 20 is essentially an electric vehicle, which can be arranged for either overhead or conductor-rail current pick-up, but for work in excavation areas without traction current supply it can operate as a diesel-electric powered by an 810 kW diesel engine. All power equipment is concentrated in the control unit. Each of the three motorised Bo-Bo units has a 1840 kW rating on electric power, so that the set can cope with a trailing load of up to 1800 tonnes on gradients as steep as 1 in 25 (with diesel-electric power the limiting grade on such tonnage is 1 in 100). The 4 EL 20 is designed for work in temperatures ranging from −50 to +40°C.

The range of industrial locomotives made by Kombinat VEB LEW Hennigsdorf includes the electric EL 21, which has been developed for open-cast mine duty; 95 of the type, which was introduced in 1981, were to be in service in the USSR by mid-1983. The EL21 is an articulated Bo-Bo-Bo suited to operate at ambient temperatures as low as −50 C and for employment on gradients as steep as 4 per cent. Its force-ventilated, series-wound, nose-suspended motors can be arranged either in series, with two motors each in three parallel groups, or all in parallel to achieve a maximum economy in operation. Control of tractive force, electric brake power and speed is by a contactor control system and with force-ventilated starting and braking resistors.

Since mid-1980, two emus of the BR 270 series, each consisting of two motor cars and two trailers, have been on trial on the third-rail Berlin S-Bahn. The BR270 is of aluminium construction with built-in dc chopper regulator, which achieves starting with minimum power losses and regenerative braking that results in power consumption savings of up to 30 per cent. Speed control is stepless with variable starting effort. Other equipment includes an electronically-controlled anti-slip device.

Kombinat VEB LEW Hennigsdorf is supplying 25 Type DTW emus for the third-rail Athens-Piraeus Railway, based on the designs manufactured since 1978 for the Berlin U-Bahn. The car bodies are made of aluminium and the bogies, of lightweight steel construction, each have a longitudinally-mounted traction motor, so that two axles are driven by one motor. Power and braking control is electronic. Starting is effected by series and parallel connection of the traction motors and via shunting and starting resistors. The starting resistors act simultaneously as braking resistors for the electric brake. Equipment includes an air-conditioning system in the driver's cab, pressure ventilation of the passenger compartments and a two-way communication installation.

The Hennigsdorf works has so far manufactured more than 1000 diesel-hydraulic centre-cab locomotives of Type V 100 for DR, the Czechoslovak State Railways (CSD), and for industrial use in the German Democratic Republic, Czechoslovakia and overseas. The latest version, the V 100.4, is designed chiefly for heavy shunting, but can also be employed in medium-heavy freight train service. It is powered by a high-speed, water-cooled, 12-cylinder engine with exhaust-gas boosting, a three-converter hydraulic transmission, cardan shaft drive of all four wheel-sets, and a rating of 735 kW. Maximum speed is 65 km/h.

The V 100.5 has been developed to power a ditch-cleaning unit (GRE) developed and constructed in co-operation with CSD and DR, but it can be employed for normal traction tasks. The ditch-cleaning unit can excavate, clean up, or renew railway ditches; plane slopes; remove ballast; and excavate completely the bed of adjacent track. The V 100.5 can apply an output of 300 kW to this work and at the same time achieve a 1-7 km/h rate of progress. When not in use the ditch-cleaning unit can be hauled at a maximum speed of 100 km/h.

Type EL 21 dc industrial locomotive

Type G III emu for Athens-Piraeus Railway

Type BR 212/243 main-line electric locomotive

Remote-controlled battery-driven Type EL 16/03 towing vehicle

Linke-Hofmann-Busch
Linke-Hofmann-Busch Waggon-Fahrzeug-Maschinen GmbH

Postfach 411160, 3320 Salzgitter 41, Federal Republic of Germany

Telephone: 214033
Telegrams: Linkebusch, Salzgitter 41
Telex: 954452

Open saloon passenger coach type Bpmz for Deutsche Bundesbahn (DB)

Technical Director: Wolfgang von Waldstätten
Commercial Director: Jürgen Isermeyer
Chief Sales Director: Siegfried Albrecht
Export Sales Director: Armin Marwede

Products: Passenger and freight cars; electric and diesel railcars and train-sets; long-haul, suburban and underground passenger cars; tramcars and light rail vehicles.

Constitution: Established in 1839 at Breslau under the name of Carbuilding Workshops of Gottfried Linke the company amalgamated with Gebruder Hofmann & Co in 1912 to form Linke-Hofmann Werke AG, Breslau. In 1928 the Waggon & Maschinenfabrik AG was formed. Busch joined the company to form Linke-Hofmann-Busch. After the Second World War the company's works at Breslau had to be abandoned, but in 1949 L-H-B resumed its activities at Salzgitter-Watenstedt, near Brunswick.

Brunswick tramcar

High-capacity bogie van with three-section sliding walls and load protection partitions

Diesel railcars for Bangladesh Railways

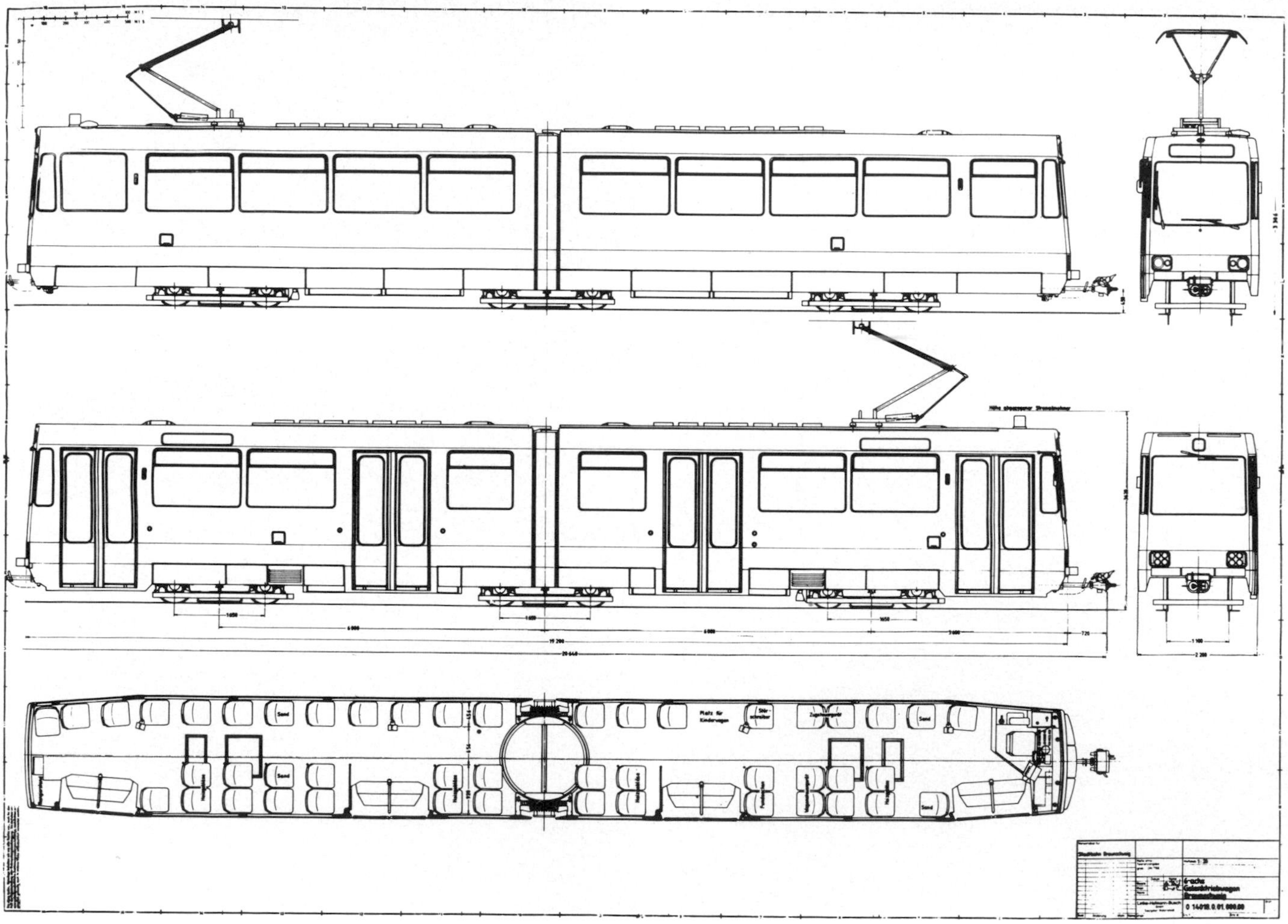

Layout of tramcars for Brunswick

LKM
Lenin Kohászati Művek
Lenin Metallurgical Works

3540 Miskolc-Diósgyör, Hungary

Telephone: 51 909
Telex: 62326

Products: Locomotives; passenger carriages; wagons; wheel discs, tyres and axles.

Locotracteurs
Société Française de Locotracteurs

40 boulevard Henri Sellier, 92150 Suresnes, France

Telephone: (1) 506 15 74
Telex: 614720

Products: Shunting locomotives.

Macosa
Material y Construcciones, SA

Head office: Plaza de la Independencia 8, Madrid 1, Spain

Telephone: 2 22 47 87
Telegrams: Material, Madrid
Telex: 2 22 47 87

Works: Herreros 2, Barcelona
Telephone: 307 05 00; Telex: 52286
San Vicente 273, Valencia
Telephone: 377 39 00; Telex: 62452
Marqués de Mudela 10, Alcazar de San Juan
Telephone: 54 1124

President: Joaquin Reig
Executive Vice President: Juan Ignacio Muñiz
Commercial Managing Director: Ildefonso Carrascosa
Commercial Director: Andrés Soler
Works Director: Francisco Rosello
Export Manager: Ramón Trénor
Financial Director: Eduardo Caballer

Products: Electric, diesel-electric and diesel-hydraulic locomotives; diesel railcars and dmus; emus and electric railcars; subway cars; passenger and freight cars.

Constitution: This company was formed in 1947 by the merger of Material para Ferrocarriles y Construcciones, SA of Barcelona and Construcciones Devis, SA of Valencia.

RENFE Class 444 inter-city emu driving trailer, air-conditioned

RENFE Class 592 air-conditioned three-car diesel-hydraulic mu for suburban and medium-distance service, built under MAN licence

RENFE Series BB9200 88-seat air-conditioned second-class cars, with reversible seats, for locomotive-hauled inter-city service at up to 160 km/h *(G F Allen)*

RENFE Class 333 3300 hp, 120-tonne diesel-electric Co-Co built under General Motors licence *(G F Allen)*

Macosa diesel locomotives

Class	Wheel arrangement	Transmission	Rated power (kW) gross	Max speed km/h	Total weight tonnes	No in service	Year first built	Builders		
								Mechanical parts	Engine & type	Transmission
GT26 CU/AC	Co-Co	Elec	2238	88.3	122.5	30	1978	Macosa	GM 16-645 E3	General Motors
SD40-2	Co-Co	Elec	2462	105	180	36	1979	Macosa	GM 16-645 E3	General Motors
J26 CW/AC	Co-Co	Elec	1641	120	109	54	1980	Macosa	GM 16-645 E	General Motors
G18 U	Bo-Bo	Elec	821	97	61	4	1981	Macosa	GM 8-645 E	General Motors
J16 CW/AC	Co Co	Elec	1455	120	104.5	20	In production	Macosa	GM 16-567	General Motors

Macosa electric locomotives

Class	Wheel arrangement	Line voltage	Rated output (kW) continuous/ one hour	Max speed km/h	Weight tonnes	No in service	Year first built	Builders	
								Mechanical parts	Electrical equipment
RENFE s/269	B-B	3 kV dc	3100/3240	160	88	11	1981	Macosa-Mitsubishi	Westinghouse SA, Mitsubishi
RENFE s/251	B-B-B	3 kV dc	4650/4860	160	132	10	1982	Macosa-Mitsubishi	Westinghouse SA, Mitsubishi
RENFE s/269	B-B	3 kV dc	3100/3240	160	88	38	In production	Macosa-Mitsubishi	Westinghouse SA, Mitsubishi

Macosa electric railcars or multiple-units

RENFE Class	Cars per unit	Line voltage	Motor cars per unit	Motored axles per motor car	Rated output (kW) per motor	Max speed km/h	Weight tonnes per car (M-motor T-trailer)	Total seating capacity	Length per car mm (M-motor T-trailer)	No in service	Rate of acceleration m/s2	Year first built	Builders Mechanical parts	Electrical equipment
RENFE 445	2	3 kV dc	2	4	240	100	M 56	152	24 600	1	0.79	1983	Macosa CAF MTM	GEE MTM Westinghouse SA
RENFE 440	3	3 kV dc	1	4	290	140	M 61 T 37 T 42	260	M 26 205 T 26 177 T 26 205	162	—	1972	Macosa	Westinghouse SA GEE MELCO
RENFE 444	3	3 kV dc	1	4	290	140	M 64 T 39 T 48	212	M 26 400 T 26 200 T 26 295	14	—	1980	Macosa	Westinghouse SA MELCO GEE
FGC111/181	3	1.2 kV dc	2	4	276	90	M 32 T 21	176	M 20 225 T 19 800	20	1.2	1983	Macosa	MTM AA
FGC211/281	3	1.5 kV dc	2	4	276	90	M 30 T 20	148	M 18 125 T 17 700	5	1.2	1983	Macosa	MTM AA

Macosa diesel railcars or multiple-units

Class	Cars per unit	Motor cars per unit	Motored axles per motor car	Transmission	Rated power (kW) per motor	Max speed km/h	Weight tonnes per car (M-motor T-trailer)	Total seating capacity	Length per car mm (M-motor T-trailer)	No in service	Year first built	Builders Mechanical parts	Engine & type	Transmission
RENFE 592	3	2	2	Hydr	169	120	M 46 T 39	228	T 23 000 M 22 620	70	1981	Macosa	MAN	Voith
712 ZTO	3	1	2	Hydr	214	120	M 29.5 T 21.5	145	M 17 200 T 17 200	20	1975	Macosa	MAN	Voith
712/714 ZTP	2	1	2	Hydr	214	120	M 38 T 29.5	144	M 21 566 T 21 566	35	1981	Macosa MAN Djuro Djakovic	MAN	Voith
ENAFER	1	1	2	Hydr	228	80	M 34.5	120	M 18 250 T 18 200	6	1984	Macosa	MAN	Voith

Mafersa
Material Sociedade Anônima

Av Raimundo Pereira de Magalhães 230, CEP 05092, São Paulo, SP, Brazil

Telephone: (011) 260-4591
Telegrams: Mafersa
Telex: (011) 23862

Chairman: José Carlos do Couto Vianna
Directors: Alvaro César Café
Marcos Ferraz Miranda
Adir Antônio Jardim Leão
José de Oliveira Naves
Seijio Ogusku

Products: Stainless steel passenger cars for metro and suburban traffic and long-distance services; passenger cars of carbon steel for suburban traffic and long-distance services; light rail vehicles; all-purpose freight cars; containers; bus chassis; underframes for railway cars and steel welded trucks; casting and forging wheels for railway and crane bridges; forged railway axles; ingots and casting steel.

Constitution: Mafersa, an authentic Brazilian company, is one of the largest industrial railway equipment complexes in Latin America with three factories in Brazil (two in the state of São Paulo and one in the state of Minas Gerais). Annual production capacity is 300 stainless steel railway passenger cars; 1200 freight cars; 120 LRVs; 140 000 forging wheels; 40 000 casting wheels; 12 000 forged railway axles; 6000 containers; 600 bus chassis; 600 steel welded bogies; and 600 underframes for railway cars.

São Paulo Metro: north-south line train-sets in service on left, new units for east-west line on right

Three-chamber hopper car for RFFSA by Mafersa

Mafersa electric multiple-units

Type	Cars per unit	Line voltage	Motor cars per unit	Motored axles per motor car	Rated output (hp) per motor	Max speed km/h	Weight tonnes per car (M-motor T-trailer)	Total seating capacity per train-set	Length per train-set mm	Cars in service	Rate of acceleration m/s2	Year first built	Builders Mechanical parts	Electrical equipment
São Paulo Metro	6	750 V dc	6	4	170	100	34	2000	21 120	306	1.12	1972	Budd Mafersa Wabco Fresinbra	Welco Villares
Rio de Janeiro Metro	6	750 V dc	6	4	190	100	40.5	2000	21 500	100	1.12	1977	Budd Mafersa Wabco Fresinbra	Welco Villares
Suburban (RFRSA)	4	3 kV dc	2	4	388	90	M 58 T A2	1300	22 100	120	0.8	1981	Mafersa Tokyu Car	Hitachi Toshiba
São Paulo Metro L/O	6	750 V dc	6	4	190	100	36	2000	21 235	6	1.12	1982	Mafersa Fresinbra Villares	Welco Villares

MaK
Krupp MaK Maschinenbau GmbH

Postfach 9009, 2300 Kiel 17, Federal Republic of Germany

Telephone: 0431 3811
Telegrams: MaK, Kiel
Telex: 02 99877/78

Directors: Dipl-Kfm H Hartung
H-O Brockmeier
Dr jur G Holtmeier
Prof Dr-Ing H-R Lembcke
Dr-Ing U Schaller

Products: Diesel-hydraulic locomotives from 230 kW up to highest power range; diesel-electric locomotives up to 1200 kW; diesel railcars for all track gauges; diesel engines for rail traction.

Constitution: MaK has continued the development of the products of the former Deutsche Werke Kiel AG (DWK) which started designing internal combustion engine railcars in 1920, and has constructed diesel locomotives since 1925.

1000 kW (1360 hp) Type G 1202 BB standard diesel-hydraulic locomotive with radio control and Voith forward-reverse turbo transmission

Lightweight Type VT 627 diesel-hydraulic railcar for German Federal Railway (DB)

1200 kW MaK Type DE 1002 diesel-electric

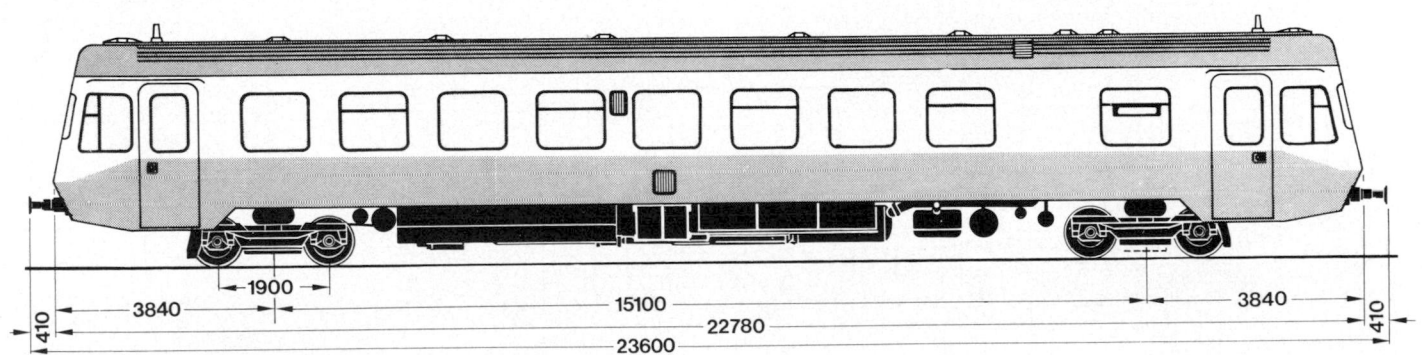

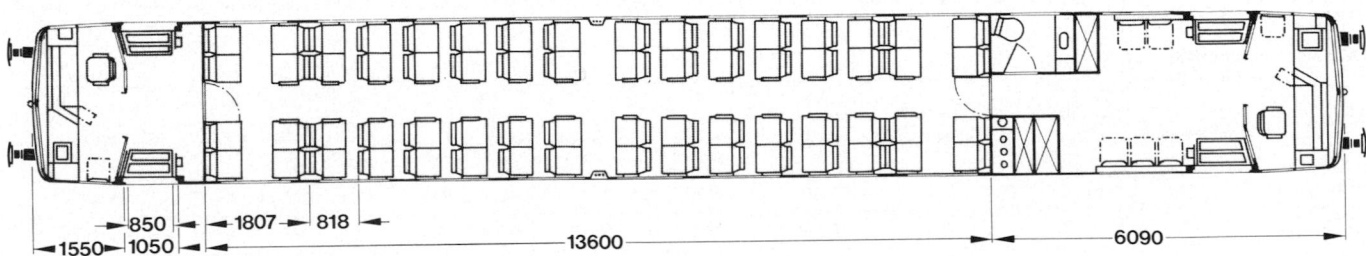

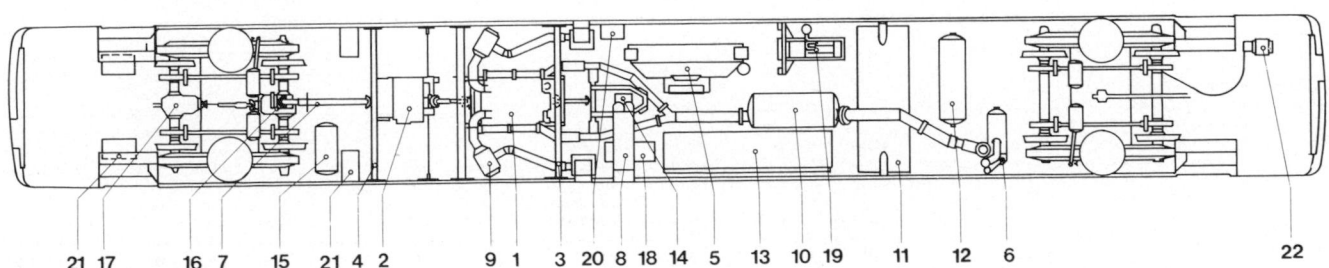

Layout of Type VT 627 railcar **(1)** diesel engine **(2)** hydraulic transmission **(3)** engine suspension **(4)** transmission suspension **(5)** cooling apparatus **(6)** water heating apparatus **(7)** cardan shaft **(8)** dynamo cooler **(9)** combustion air filter **(10)** sound absorber **(11)** fuel tank **(12)** air reservoir **(13)** battery **(14)** dynamo **(15)** air suspension reservoir **(16)** final drive gearbox **(17)** final drive **(18)** control cabinet **(19)** compressor **(20)** flange lubricator control

MaK Type G 1203 diesel-hydraulic locomotive with Voith Type L4r4 transmission

MaK Type G 1204 diesel-hydraulic locomotive with Voith Type L5r4 transmission

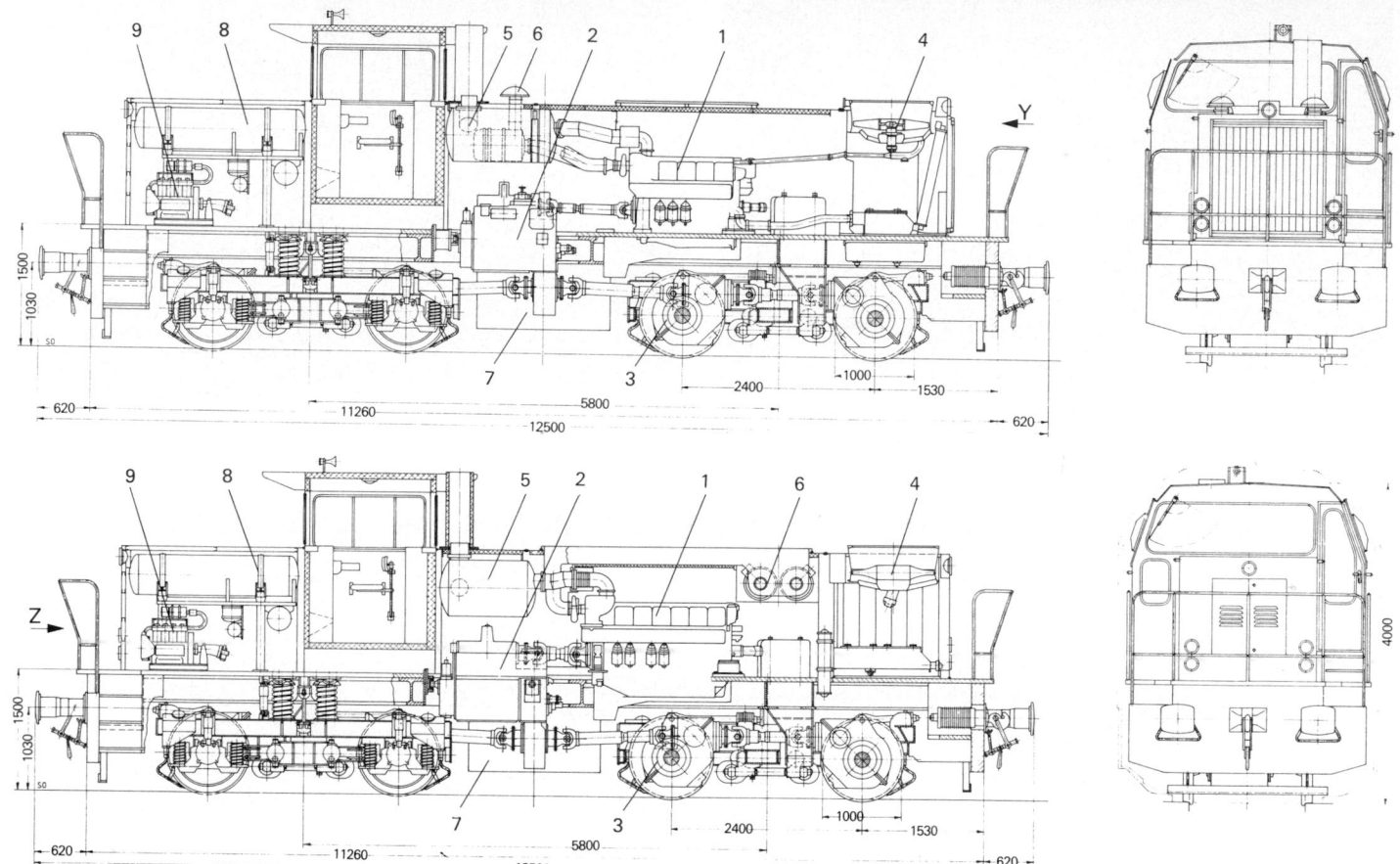

Layouts of Types G 1203 (top) and G 1204 diesel-hydraulic locomotives **(1)** diesel engine **(2)** hydraulic gear unit **(3)** wheel-set gear unit **(4)** cooling system **(5)** exhaust silencer **(6)** air intake **(7)** fuel tank **(8)** main air tank **(9)** compressor

MaK diesel locomotives

Class	Wheel arrangement	Transmission	Rated power (kW)	Max speed kmlh*	Total weight tonnes*	No in service	Year first built	Builders		
								Mechanical parts	Engine & type	Transmission
G 763	C	Hydr	560	32; 40	60-66	31	1977	MaK	MTU 6V 396 TC 13	Voith L3r4
G 1203	B-B	Hydr	745	33; 45; 70	72-88	6	1980	MaK	MTU 8V 396 TC 13	Voith L4r4
G 1204	B-B	Hydr	1120	42; 60; 80	72-88	15	1978	MaK	MTU 12V 396 TC 13	Voith L5r4
DE 501	Co	Elec (3-phase)	500	45	60-66	20	1981	MaK	MTU 6V 331 TC 12	BBC
DE 1002	Bo-Bo	Elec (3-phase)	1120	90	72-88	4	1982	MaK	MTU 12V 396 TC 13	BBC

*available alternatives

MaK diesel railcars

Class	Cars per unit	Motor cars per unit	Motored axles per motor car	Trans-mission	Rated power (kWl per motor	Max speed kmlh	Weight tonnes per car	Total seating capacity	Length per car mm (M-motor T-trailer)	No in service	Year first built	Builders		
												Mechanical parts	Engine & type	Transmission
VT 627	1	1	2	Hydr	287	120	38.7	69	23 600	5	1981	MaK	Daimler-Benz OM 424	Voith T 320
VT 628 VS 928	2	1	2	Hydr	357	120	64.1	149	M 22 575 T 22 575	3	1981	Duewag	Daimler-Benz OM 424 A	Voith T 320

MaK Type DE 501 with three-phase electric transmission

MaK Type G 763 diesel-hydraulic shunting locomotive

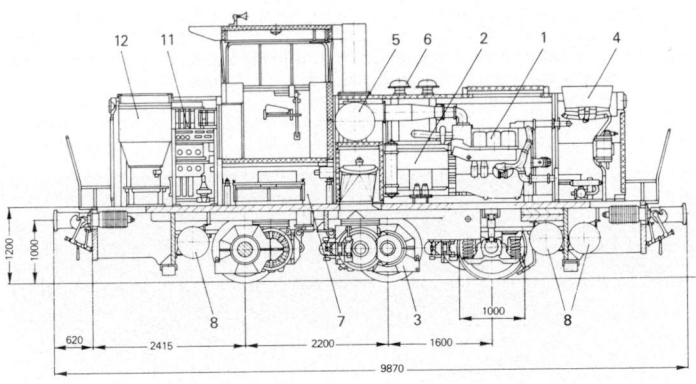

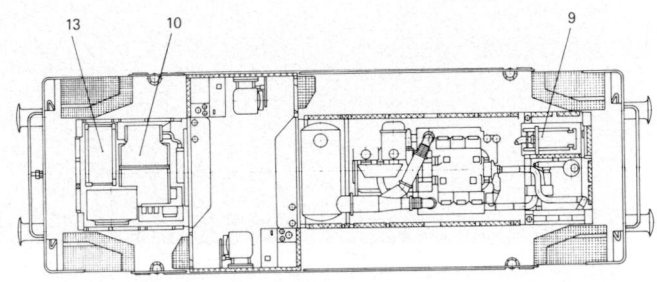

Layout of three-phase Type DE 501 diesel-electric (**1**) diesel engine (**2**) generator (**3**) traction motor and gear unit (**4**) cooling system (**5**) exhaust silencer (**6**) air intake (**7**) fuel tank (**8**) main air tank (**9**) compressor (**10**) inverter (**11**) electrical equipment (**12**) braking resistor (**13**) air brake equipment

MAN
Maschinenfabrik Augsburg-Nurnberg AG
Mechanical and Structural Engineering Division

Head office: Katzwangerstrasse 101, 8500 Nuremberg, Federal Republic of Germany
Sales office: Postfach 440 100, 8500 Nuremberg 44

Telephone: 0911 18-0
Telegrams: Manwerk, Nurnberg
Telex: 0622291

Chairman: Gerhard Neipp
Directors: Wilhelm Noller
Heinz Rädeke
Heinz Hennig

Products: Light and heavy diesel railcars and multiple-unit diesel stock; electric railcars and multiple-unit electric stock for ac/dc or ac three-phase supply; underground railway stock; urban railway stock; suspended monorails; passenger stock, luggage and mail vans; freight cars, high-capacity well wagons and bogie trucks for all applications, especially air suspension type.

Recent sales have included prototype trains and car body shells for Rio suburban services, mobile sub-stations for the German Federal Railway, and various underground and light railway vehicles.

Stainless steel-bodied emu for Rio de Janeiro suburban service

Maquinista, La
La Maquinista Terrestre y Marítima SA

General offices and works: Calle Fernando Junoy 2-64, Barcelona 30, Spain

Telephone: 345 5700
Telegrams: Maquinista
Telex: 54539

President: D Manuel Rodriguez López
Director General: D Adolfo Ramiro Fernandez

Type DH-300 diesel-hydraulic shunting locomotive with Voith transmission and Pegaso Type 9156 engine of 310 hp

FEVE 1600 hp diesel-electric locomotive by La Maquinista on Arija-Bilbao container train
(*John C Baker*)

Products: Electric and diesel locomotives, electric and diesel train-sets and railcars, train-sets for underground networks, shunting locomotives, bogies and wagons; diesel engines, complete steam turbogenerators and steam boilers for conventional power stations, industrial steam boilers, hydraulic turbines, cranes and stacker and reclaimer machines.

Recent production for railways has included: 35 Class 250 electric railway locomotives for Spanish National Railways (RENFE); 14 1600 hp diesel-electric locomotives and 14 560 hp diesel-electric train-sets for Ferrocarriles de Via Estrecha (FEVE); 25 power-cars of series 1000 for FC Metropolitano de Barcelona; 25 750 hp electric train-sets for Ferrocarriles de la Generalitat de Catalunya (FGC); and 442 type Y-21 bogies for RENFE.

Constitution: Since 1855 La Maquinista has specialised in production of railway equipment. Largest shareholder is the Instituto Nacional de Industria (INI).

1600 hp diesel-electric locomotive for FEVE, Spain, and 300 hp diesel-hydraulic shunting locomotive for General Motors plant in Figueruelas, Spain, under construction

Aluminium body of 750 hp emu for FGC, Spain

Marine Industries
Marine Industrie Limitée
Railway Car Division

Head office: 1010 Sherbrooke Street West, Suite 910, Montreal, Quebec H3A 2R7, Canada

Main works: Tracy (Sorel), Quebec J3P 5P5

Telephone: (514) 743 3351
Telegrams: Marindus, Quebec
Telex: 055 61081

Products: Coal, ore, covered hopper, gondola and flat (plain and bulkhead) freight cars.

Martin & King
Martin & King Pty Ltd

Somerton Road, Campbellfield, Victoria, Australia

Telephone: 305 4160
Telegrams: Marking, Melbourne

Products: Electric and diesel railcars; electric multiple-units; passenger coaches; freight wagons.

Constitution: An associate company of Clyde Industries Ltd.

MBB
Messerschmitt-Bolkow-Blohm GmbH
Helicopter and Transport Systems Division

Industriestrasse 4, 8850 Donauworth, Federal Republic of Germany

Telephone: 0906 711
Telegrams: Embebe, Donauworth
Telex: 51843

Technical Director: Dieter von Hummel
Commercial Director: Dieter Matthies

Products: Rail vehicles in lightweight construction for underground and rapid transit commuter services, main-line passenger coaches for short-haul and long-haul services, sleeping cars, dining cars, saloon cars, diesel and electrically powered train-sets, rail service cars, overhead line inspection and maintenance cars, track recording and dynamometer vehicles, ultrasonic inspection vehicles.

The company's recent orders have included 103 two-car sets for the 750-volt dc, third-rail Munich U-Bahn, of which six are prototypes with three-phase traction motors and a number of other novel features. These six units are being submitted to two years' evaluation before commitment to series production. To secure the light weight desirable to accommodate special electrical equipment, which has been evolved jointly by Siemens and BBC, the bodies of the six units are formed of aluminium extruded profiles which are welded automatically, a method in which MBB specialises.

MBB has developed the world's first dmu constructed in aluminium for Yugoslav Railways (JZ). By comparison with equivalent train-sets of conventional construction these lightweight vehicles will achieve considerable energy consumption savings. Designed for the special conditions of short-haul service, the cars have wide door openings and spacious entrance vestibules. Driver's cabs display a functional design and layout conforming to the latest ergonomic criteria. The underfloor diesel engine drives both axles of one bogie at the tight-coupled end of the motor car, transmission is through a fully automatic hydraulic transmission.

The company is developing innovative designs for the ICE high-speed inter-city programme. Bodies built of aluminium extrusions and adaptable to various interior configurations of seating and accommodation class are being studied in conjunction with a bogie employing fibre composite materials in construction. This latter, in association with light metal extrusions, is forecast to reduce bogie weight to 4.8-5.3 tonnes, according to type of wheel-set. Known as

Luxury tourist train sleeping-car with 12 two-berth compartments, 24.5 m long over buffers, on Egyptian State Railways

Prototype two-car 750 V dc third-rail emu for Munich U-Bahn

the HLD, the bogie basically comprises two side frames of specific flexural stiffness which are connected by cross bearers possessing torsional flexibility. Due to the torsional elasticity of the framework it is possible to employ a fairly hard primary spring, thereby divorcing flexural coach body vibrations from any pitching movement of the bogie; ride comfort and insulation from vibration are obtained through soft secondary springing. Obliquely-arranged air springs, an elastically-linked push-pull rod, lateral and vertical dampers and a roll stabiliser connect coach body and bogie. Progressive springs and end stops control lateral movement.

The company plans evolution of this bogie with both rigid wheel-sets and with the creep-controlled wheel-sets which it unveiled in 1981; the development is sponsored by the Federal Ministry of Research and Technology. In the creep-controlled model, two fixed, hollow axle shafts are connected by a creep coupling, which achieves a controlled torque transmission from one wheel of a set to the other, thereby enhancing high-speed stability and mitigating rail/wheel wear. The hollow axle holds the power supply wires to the creep coupling, which is of magnetic powder type to obtain a smooth, controlled transfer of torque between the wheels. Using creep-controlled wheel-sets it will be possible to substitute active suspension components for lateral and vertical dampers, thus enhancing the guidance imparted by the bogie to the body. The HLD will have linear eddy-current and disc brakes, which will be under both normal control and also that of a computer monitoring the bogie's behaviour in running.

A specialist British company, Willibald Grammer, has developed for the ICE prototypes a new type of passenger seat which features a folding head-rest cushion; backrest adjustment within a 10 to 42 degree range; personal tables that can be fully retracted within the armrest when not in use or swung outward to facilitate passenger movement; footrests that are adjustable both sideways and lengthwise; and armrests incorporating controls for individual

MBB creep-controlled wheel-set

Seat developed by Willibald Grammer for ICE programme

HLD fibre-composite high-speed bogie

Full-size mock-up of ICE car section

Dot matrix train itinerary information display in ICE mock-up

Armrest controls of ICE seat

lighting, radio, train information and other facilities. The passenger information system employs a dot matrix vacuum fluorescent display system for its potential to display a wide range of data in compact screens that are easily integrated into thin coverings and partitions.

MBB leads the consortium, Konsortium Magnetbahn Transrapid, undertaking construction of the 21 km-long Maglev test track at Emsland where trial running with a full-size, two-section 192-seat Transrapid 06 vehicle at speeds up to 300 km/h was scheduled to start in August 1983. The trials will be run for the Federal Ministry of Research and Technology by Magnetbahnversuchs und Planungsgesellschaft, an organisation involving the German Federal Railway

and Lufthansa. With Krauss-Maffei and Thyssen-Henschel MBB has formed a company, Transrapid International, to promote and market West German Maglev technology world-wide; this concern has already conducted feasibility studies in various inter-city corridors, including Montreal-Ottawa and Los Angeles-Las Vegas in North America, Paris-Frankfurt in Europe, Riyadh-Jeddah in Saudi Arabia, Melbourne-Sydney in Australia and Seoul-Pusan in South Korea.

Constitution: Formerly trading under the name of WMD (Waggon- und Maschinenbau Donauwörth).

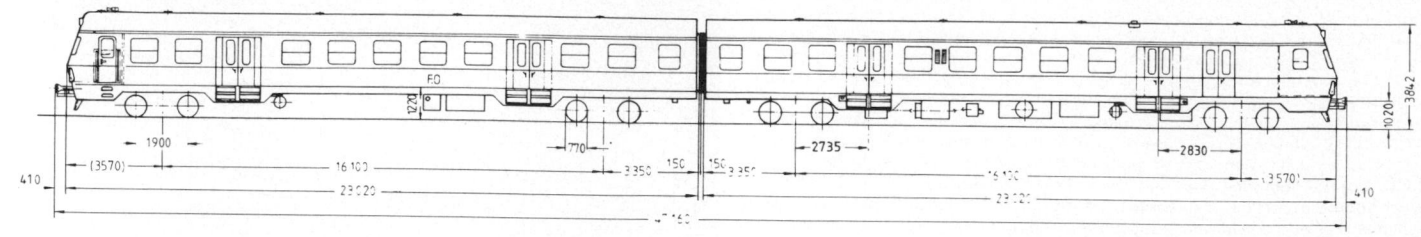

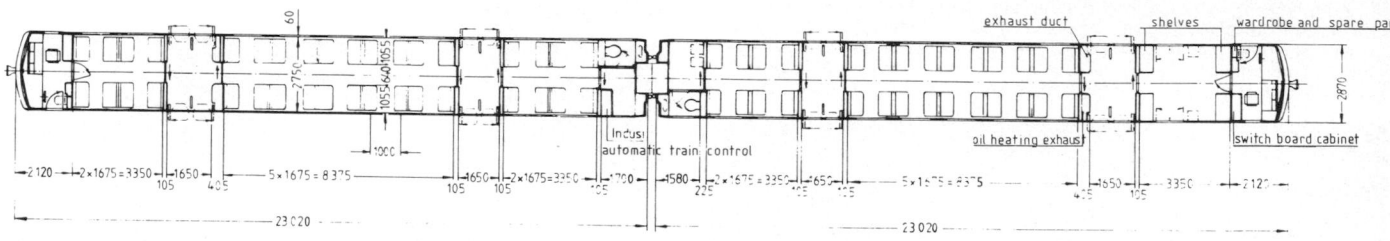

General arrangement of aluminium-bodied dmu for Yugoslav Railways (JZ)

MBB aluminium-bodied diesel multiple-units

Class	Cars per unit	Motor cars per unit	Motored axles per motor car	Transmission	Rated power (kW) per motor	Max speed km/h	Weight tonnes per car (M-motor T-trailer)	Total seating capacity	Length per car mm (M-motor T-trailer)	No in service	Year first built	Builders Mechanical parts	Engine & type	Transmission
JZ 713/715	2	1	2	Hydr	367	120	M 31.2 T 25	128	M 23 580 T 23 580	5	1983	MBB	Daimler-Benz OM 424A	Voith
JZ 711	2	2	2	Hydr	265	120	43.2	96	23 580	10	1969	MBB	Daimler-Benz	EMG

MBB electric railcars or multiple-units

Class	Cars per unit	Line voltage	Motor cars per unit	Motored axles per motor car	Rated output (kW) per motor	Max speed km/h	Weight tonnes per car	Total seating capacity	Length per car mm	No in service	Rate of acceleration m/s²	Year first built	Builders Mechanical parts	Electrical equipment
ET 420	3	15 kV	3	4	200	120	44.4 40.8 44.4	194	23 300 20 800	390	0.95	1969	MBB, LHB, Duewag WU, MAN	AEG, BBC, Siemens
ET 472	3	1.2 kV	3	4	100	100	40 34 40	196	23 165 19 490	63	0.95	1974	MBB, LHB	BBC
A2	2	750 V	2	4	180	80	25.8	98	18 575	194	1.52	1967	MBB, MAN Rathgeber	AEG, BBC
B1	2	750 V	2	4	185/50 Hz	80	29.6 28.7	98	18 775	6	1.50	1981	MBB	Siemens
ET 403	4	15 kV	4	4	240	200	60/59	183	27 450 27 160	3	0.95	1973	MBB, LHB	AEG, BBC, Siemens

MecanoExportImport

10 Mihail Eminescu Street, Bucharest, Romania

Telephone: 12 46 00
Telegrams: Mecanex, Bucharest
Telex: 10 269

Products: Electric, diesel-electric, diesel-hydraulic locomotives and railcars; passenger coaches; freight wagons.

Constitution: The Romanian enterprise specialising in foreign trade.

MecanoExportImport LDE diesel-electric Co-Co built by Electroputere

MecanoExportImport diesel locomotives

Class	Wheel arrangement	Transmission	Rated power (kW)	Max speed km/h	Total weight tonnes	No in service	Year first built	Builders		
								Mechanical parts	Engine & type	Transmission
LDE 150	Co-Co	ac/dc	1100	100	72	5	1978	23 August	MTU 12V 652	BBC
LDE 110	Bo-Bo	ac/dc	740	100	64	1	1981	23 August	23 August M 820 SR	Electroputere
LDE 3000 HP	Co-Co	ac/dc	2180/1680	160	120 ± 2%	22	1979	Electroputere, ICM Caransebes	ICM Resita 12 R 251 ELO	Electroputere
LDE 4000 HP	Co-Co	ac/dc	2900/2250	145	123	10	1982	Electroputere, ICM Caransebes	ICM Resita 16 R 251 ELO	Electroputere

Metro-Cammell

Metro-Cammell Ltd
Subsidiary of Metropolitan Cammell Ltd

PO Box 248, Leigh Road, Washwood Heath, Birmingham B8 2YJ, England

Telephone: 021-327 4777
Telegrams: Metro, Birmingham
Telex: 337601

Export sales: BRE-Metro Ltd, 14 Melbury Terrace, Marylebone, London NW1 6JU

Chairman: A H Sansome
Director and General Manager: D B Whitehouse
Director and Chief Engineer: F J Bonneres
Production Director: G E Canham
Financial Controller/Secretary: A V Tipper
Sales Manager: W J Wright

Products: Rapid transit cars for surface, sub-surface and underground routes; design and construction of cars for pre-metro and full metro and suburban rapid transit systems.

In October 1982 the Hong Kong Mass Transit Railway Corporation ordered a batch of 18 power cars with chopper control in addition to the 128 cars already in hand for the Island Line extension, bringing the total number of cars ordered for the MTRC system from Metro-Cammell to 576. With the 183 cars being supplied to the Kowloon-Canton Railway (KCR), the value of rolling stock orders won by Metro-Cammell for Hong Kong now exceeds £300 million.

Metro-Cammell is producing 90 London Transport underground cars to follow 450 surface line cars supplied for the District line.

In response to an enquiry from the West Midlands Passenger Transport Executive (WMPTE), which from 1987 faces life-expiry of the 151 dmus that British Rail operates within its area under contract, Metro-Cammell has drafted a design of a lightweight aluminium-bodied three-car dmu which could be powered by a single 350 hp engine. Existing BR dmus have a pair of 180 hp engines. The superior performance obtainable from a drive to both axles of one bogie together with improved availability and the higher seating capacity of modern light-alloy bodywork, might make feasible a 25 per cent reduction in WMPTE dmu fleet size. A single engine would also cut maintenance costs. In 1983 a British Rail order was placed for two prototype Class 151 three-car dmus.

Constitution: In the latter part of 1966 Metropolitan-Cammell absorbed the railway rolling stock business of Cravens of Sheffield. In 1969 Vickers Ltd relinquished their 50 per cent shareholding and a new company was formed for railway matters under the style of Metro-Cammell Ltd.

Type D78 emu for London Transport surface lines

Kowloon-Canton Railway emu

Metro-Cammell electric multiple-units

Type*	Cars per unit	Line voltage	Motor cars per unit	Motored axles per motor car	Continuous rated output (kW) per motor	Max speed km/h	Weight tonnes per car (M-motor T-trailer)	Total seating capacity	Length per car mm (M-motor T-trailer)	No in service	Rate of acceleration m/s²	Year first built	Builders	
													Mechanical parts	Electrical equipment
MTRC														
A	3	1.5 kV dc	2	4	91	90	M 38.4	48	M 22 850	132	1.3	1978	Metro-Cammell	GEC
B				4			M 37.4	each	M 22 000	83		1981		
C				4			M 38.8	car	M 22 000	215		1978		
D				—			T 28		T 22 000	22		1982		
KCR														
6B	3	25 kV ac	1	—	245	120	T 34	84	T 23 770	16	0.6	1981	Metro-Cammell	GEC
5				4			M 51.5	88	M 23 530	16				
6				—			T 32.2	84	T 23 770	16				
4				—			T 32.9	54	T 23 770	—				
D78 single-ended unit	6	600 V dc	4	4	50	72	DM 27.7 NDM 26.7	280	DM 18 372 NDM 18 119	59 6-car trains	1.0	1978	Metro-Cammell	GEC
double-ended unit	3		2	4			TC 18.3	136	TC 18 119					
D83 motor car trailer car	3	600 V dc	2	4		72		144 per 3-car unit	M 17 726 T 17 676				Metro-Cammell	GEC and Brush
T&W twin-body articulated unit	1	1.5 kV dc	1	4	180	80	39.4	84	27 800	88	1.0	1978	Metro-Cammell	GEC

*MTRC: Mass Transit Railway Corporation, Hong Kong
KCR: Kowloon-Canton Railway
D78: London Transport
D83: London Transport
T&W: Tyne and Wear PTE

Hong Kong MTRC emu

Articulated LRV set for Tyne & Wear Metro

Mexican National Railcar
Constructora Nacional de Carros de Ferrocarril SA

San Lorenzo 925, 5° Piso, Col de Valle, Mexico 12 DF

Telephone: 30700

Works: Cd Sahagún, Hidalgo

Telephone: 585 05 42

Products: Electric railcars, passenger cars, freight cars.

Meyer
Josef Meyer AG

4310 Rheinfelden, Switzerland

Telephone: 061 88 12 41
Telegrams: Josefmeyer, Rheinfelden
Telex: 64894

Products: Freight wagons.

MIN
Masinska Industrija Nis

Sumadijcka 1, Nis, Yugoslavia

Telephone: 45563, 45853, 44353, 41480
Telegrams: MIN, Nis
Telex: 16187, 16114

Products: Diesel-hydraulic locomotives of 1650 hp; diesel-mechanical, diesel mining and industrial and mining battery locomotives; petrol railcars; electric multiple-units; diesel multiple-units; freight wagons.

Miskin Crni
Vaso Miskin Crni

Industrija Transportnih Sredstava, 1 Masina, Sarajevo, Yugoslavia

Telephone: 41222/41234/41343
Telegrams: Miskin Crni, Sarajevo
Telex: 41119

Products: Freight wagons; passenger coaches.

Constitution: Vaso Miskin Crni was founded in 1890 and is ranked among the oldest manufacturers of railway vehicles in Yugoslavia.

Mitsubishi Electric
Mitsubishi Electric Corporation

Mitsubishi Denki Bldg, 2-3, Marunouchi 2-chome, Chiyoda-ku, Tokyo 100, Japan

Telephone: 03 218 2111
Telegrams: Melco, Tokyo
Telex: 24532

President: Nihachiro Katayama
Managing Director, International Operations Group: Shinichi Yufu
Manager, Transportation Systems Department, Itami Works: Shigeichi Yagi

Products: Complete electric locomotives; power propulsion equipment (traction motors, main drive gears, traction control gears, main transformers, rectifiers, main alternators, VVVF inverters); auxiliary electrical equipment (converters, inverters, motor-alternators); automatic train control equipment; air brake equipment for multiple-unit trains, light rail vehicles, diesel-electric locomotives, rubber-tyred vehicles on segregated tracks; monorails and electric buses.
Recent sales have included:
30 Series 251 B-B-B chopper-controlled locomotives; 169 Series 269, 279, 289 B-B locomotives; and four Series 269 B-B chopper-controlled locomotives for Spanish National Railways (RENFE) rated output 3100 kW at 3 kV dc, maximum speed 160 km/h, weight 88 tonnes;
Traction and auxiliary electrical equipment for 216 suburban double-deck emus, 48 inter-urban double-deck emus, 56 diesel-electric locomotives and 64 electric locomotives for NSW SRA of Australia;
64 emus for Argentine Railways;
1341 chopper-controlled emus for Mexico Metro;
126 sets of 65 kVA, 1.5 kV dc/415-volt ac brushless motor alternators for Victorian Railways of Australia;

TRTA Hanzomon line 10-car 1.5 kV dc emu

Osaka Municipal Transportation Bureau 750 V dc third-rail emu

5984 traction motors, 850 main transformers, 300 silicon rectifiers, 404 tap-changers and 150 ATC equipments for Shinkansen train-sets of Japanese National Railways (JNR);
110 electric locomotives for JNR (since 1970);
200 chopper-controllers for Teito Rapid Transit Authority (TRTA), Tokyo, and other Japanese municipal transportation authorities.

Latest products include:
3 kV dc, 4650 kW, 132-ton B-B-B chopper-controlled locomotives with continuous field control;
3 kV dc, 3100 kW, 88-ton B-B chopper-controlled locomotives;
Traction motors and separate excitation controller for regenerative brake to equip 1.5 kV dc, 2700 kW, 120-ton Co-Co electric locomotives;
1500 kVA ac main alternator, 205 kW traction motors and control gears for 2000 hp Co-Co diesel-electric locomotives;
140 kW continuous traction motors and control gears with separately excited regenerative brake for 1.5 kV dc emus;
750-volt dc third rail eight-car emu with eight 128 kW traction motors, regenerative braking, and two-phase chopper control, with natural cooling by boiling and condensing heat transfer (freon cooling), chopping frequency 400 Hz, maximum speed 80 km/h, for Osaka Municipal Transportation Bureau (similar electrical equipment has been produced for Mexico City emus);
750-volt dc emu including four-quadrant chopper with shunt-wound traction motor, armature chopper and reversible field chopper, freon cooling and microprocessor control;
1.5 kV dc emu featuring 130 kW traction motor, two-phase chopper control provided with freon cooling, and micro-computerised monitoring system, for Kyoto MTB;
1.5 kV dc 10-car emu, including six power cars, gauge 1067 mm, with 150 kW one-hour rating traction motors incorporating WN gear coupling, two-phase AVF chopper control, regenerative braking, freon cooling, chopping frequency 660 Hz, micro-computerised dynamic testing system, maximum speed 100 km/h, for TRTA Hanzomon line;
A 600-volt ac, 60 Hz three-phase, rubber-tyred guideway bus system, in which the vehicles feature four 90 kW dc motors per set of two motor cars and one

Tokyo Metropolitan Government Transportation Bureau chopper-controlled 1.5 kV dc emu

trailer with thyristor control, regenerative braking and computerised fully automatic operation, for Kobe Port Lines;
1.5 kV dc four-car emu, including two power cars, with eight 160 kW traction motors, separate excitation by two-phase field chopper control, regenerative/rheostatic braking, freon cooling, chopping frequency 482 Hz, maximum speed 110 km/h, for Kinki Nippon Railways;
750-volt dc emu equipped with two 160 kW three-phase traction motors driven by a VVVF inverter, with gate turn-off thyristors (GTO), freon cooling and microprocessor control;
750-volt dc light rail vehicle embodying a 120 kW three-phase traction motor driven by VVVF inverter with freon cooling and microprocessor control for Kumamoto Municipal Transportation Bureau.

Constitution: A member of the Mitsubishi Group.

Sapporo Municipal Transportation Bureau's 1.5 kV dc third-rail rubber-tyred cars

RENFE Series 269 chopper-controlled locomotive

Moës
Moteurs Moes, SA

62 rue de Huy, 4370 Waremme, Belgium

Telephone: 019 32 23 52
Telegrams: Motormoes
Telex: 41568

Chairman: M Wisse
Managing Director: G M G Verschoor
Sales Director: J Antoine

Products: Narrow-gauge diesel-hydraulic, diesel-mechanical, diesel-mining locomotives.

More Wear
More Wear Industries (Pvt) Ltd

PO Box 2199, Plymouth Road, Harare, Zimbabwe

Telephone: 67802
Telex: 41102

Products: Passenger and freight cars.

Morrison-Knudsen
Morrison-Knudsen Company Inc

PO Box 7808, Boise, Idaho 83729, USA

Telephone: (208) 345 5000
Telex: 368439

Vice-President and General Manager, Railroad Division: J G Fearon

Products: Remanufactured locomotives; locomotive wreck repairs; locomotive repowering; specialised locomotives; head-end power installations; push-pull and self-propelled passenger car, commuter car, subway car rehabilitation and modernisation; specialised car manufacturing.

Morrison-Knudsen, or M-K, maintains one of the largest non-railroad-owned locomotive remanufacturing facilities in the USA in a specially-equipped 43-acre complex at Boise, Idaho. Services include complete engine rebuild, complete rewiring, electrical cabinet update and modification, bogie rebuilding, cab

Model TE50-4S 1500 hp diesel-electric Bo-Bo powered by Sulzer engine

and hood fabrication, fuel tank fabrication, repainting, load testing, wheel true-ing, air brake rebuild and frame fabrication. The main shop can house as many as 16 locomotives simultaneously.

Following the 1978 introduction of its TE70-4S diesel-electric PZ locomotive with a Swiss-made Sulzer 3240 hp, 12 ASV 25/30 engine, M-K's innovative design of Behr cooling system, and Brown Boveri turbocharger, M-K produced the TE50-4S (tractive effort 50 000 lb, four motored axles, Sulzer engine). The TE50-4S, termed 'The Fuel Saver', has achieved more than 10 per cent fuel saving compared with other new locomotives of comparable horsepower.

The TE83-6S utilises a 16-cylinder 4800 hp Sulzer engine derated to 3600 hp in a retro-fitted SD45. The first TE83-6S entered service with the Union Pacific Railroad during 1980. Tests indicate a five per cent fuel saving, and a significant reduction of maintenance costs is anticipated from the application of the 'million-mile' cast frame engine in the TE83-6S.

Rehabilitated CTC push-pull commuter cars for Massachusetts Bay Transportation Authority

Moss
George Moss Pty Ltd

PO Box 136, 461-465 Scarborough Beach Road, Osborne Park, Mount Osborne, Western Australia 6016, Australia

Telephone: 4468844
Telegrams: Gemco, Perth
Telex: 92645

Products: Industrial locomotives and mineral wagons.

Mouty
Etablissements Mouty-Bonehill

La Sentinelle (Nord), France

Telephone: 27 45 03 86
Telex: 110815
       110742

Products: Freight wagons.

Heavy load wagon with 28 axles

MTE
Société MTE

Head office: 32 quai de Dion Bouton, 92806 Puteaux, France

Telephone: 33 (1) 776 41 62
Telex: 610 425

Works: Le Creusot, Jeumont, La Plaine St Denis, Champagne-sur-Seine, Lyons

Chairman: J Lerebours-Pigeonnière
Managing Director: H Jullien

Products: Engineering, designing and manufacture of electric, diesel-electric and diesel-hydraulic locomotives and railcars; shunting locomotives; multiple-units; bogies and electrical equipment for high-speed train-sets and for urban and suburban rolling stock, incorporating the products of the traction divisions of Jeumont-Schneider and Creusot-Loire.

Constitution: MTE was established in 1941 as a joint subsidiary of Jeumont-Schneider and Creusot-Loire in order to determine and implement traction policy, commercial strategy, design and overall technical surveys of powered rolling stock. In addition to handling over a third of French electric traction requirements, MTE is a major export company in its own right or participating with Traction-Export or the 50 c/s Group. A member of the Francorail Group.

3600 hp diesel-electric Co-Co for Iraqi Republican Railways (IRR)

Z 7300 class inter-regional electric train-set for French Railways

Mytischy
Mytischy Railway Car Works

Mytischy, USSR

Products: Passenger coaches; subway cars.

Constitution: Member of Energomachexport.

National Steel Car
National Steel Car Ltd

Head office and works: PO Box 450, Hamilton, Ontario L8N 3J4, Canada

Telephone: (416) 544 3311
Telex: 061 8255

Sales office: Suite 1011, 1155 Dorchester Boulevard West, Montreal, Quebec H3B 2J2

Telephone: (514) 866 7461
Telex: 05 24488

President and Chief Executive Officer: R W Cooke (Hamilton)
Vice President, Engineering: J A Aitken (Hamilton)
General Purchasing Agent: L Cheyne (Hamilton)
Vice President, Sales: J W Nelham (Montreal)
Secretary-Treasurer and Comptroller: M G Nichols (Hamilton)
Vice President and Works Manager: R M Lovell (Hamilton)

Products: Freight cars of all types; industrial and speciality cars and car parts.

Constitution: National Steel Car Ltd has been building railway cars since 1919 and is a wholly-owned subsidiary of Dofasco Inc, Hamilton, Ontario.

100-ton steel rotary dump 'bathtub' gondola car for CP Rail

100-ton 4550 ft³ steel covered hopper car for grain transport for Government of Canada

250-ton depressed centre flat car for Canadian General Electric

400-ton depressed centre flat car for Calgary Power Ltd

Niesky
VEB Waggonbau Niesky

18-20 Strasse der Befreiung, 892 Niesky, German Democratic Republic

Telephone: 40
Telex: 02585

Products: Open and covered goods wagons, flat wagons with and without stanchions, double-deck auto-carrier wagons, special-purpose brown coal wagons for the iron and steel industry, bogies.

Recent output has included 80 four-axle, Type Fad self-discharging wagons for conveyance of clinker and 700 Type Eas phosphate wagons, all for the metre-gauge Tunisian Railways (SNCFT); 210 four-axle flat wagons of Type Laags for Transwaggon of Switzerland; 55 four-axle flat wagons of Type Rmms for Greece; and 200 two-axle Type Ks flat wagons and 544 four-axle Type Eas open wagons for Syrian Railways.

The Type Fad four-axle clinker wagon for the metre gauge is specifically designed to deal with a grain size of 0 to 15 mm and a density of approximately 1.5 tonnes/m³; it can be used for other moisture-resistant bulk commodities as well as clinker. The body has a saddle-shaped floor to assist self-discharge, which is through four doors on each side that are operable from platforms at

Type Eas open wagon for Syrian Railways

each end of the vehicle. Tare weight is 19.5 tonnes and load capacity 30.5 cubic metres or 44.5 tonnes.

The Type Laags is a semi-permanently short-coupled pair of two-axle flat wagons, designed for adaptability to either 1435 or 1524 mm gauge, which can be supplied with the necessary fitments for ISO container transport. Its tare weight is only 25 tonnes, yet it offers a loading area of 25.74 × 3.1 metres; load weight potential is 55 tonnes. Total length of the unit over buffers is 27 metres and it is designed to operate at up to 100 km/h.

Recent products include a wagon designed to simplify the transition from conventional transport to containerisation in banana plantations, a four-axle vehicle of 914 mm gauge that is a combination of orthodox banana van and container wagon. Experience acquired with traditional four-axled banana wagons, supplied to Central America since 1970/71, has been exploited. The wagon can be run at site with car body on for conventional transport of bananas, bundles or goods, or with car body removed, to serve as a container wagon for cooling or 40 foot standard containers. The removed car bodies can be stacked to form self-supporting storage units. Car bodies or 40 foot containers are automatically locked on the substructure without any manipulation. The body has the same load and weight capacity as vehicles already existing to take up 1000 pasteboard boxes of bananas.

Overseas shipment of the vehicles is made in sections and subassemblies. By comparison with the shipment of welded car bodies, this offers considerable reduction in volume. Assembly of the wagons is effected in the customer's country with local labour and equipment. The design of the subassemblies and of the wagons enables the user to assemble the vehicles cheaply with unskilled labour.

Type of bogie: two-axled, welded narrow-gauge
Track gauge: 914 mm
Wheel diameter: 610 mm
Type of brake: parking brake
Dead weight/weight of removable car body structure: 14/5.65 tonnes
Max total weight of 40 ft container: 30.48 tonnes

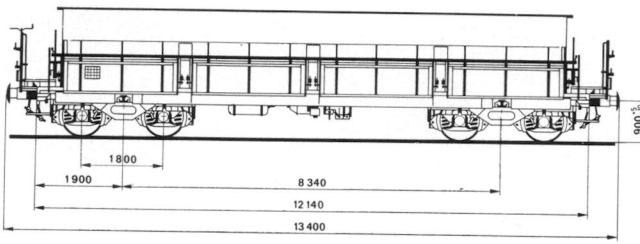

Type Fad four-axle self-discharge clinker wagon

Useful load: 21.8 tonnes
Max permissible speed: 80 km/h

Constitution: The plant took up repair of passenger, post and baggage cars in 1946, but since 1950 has specialised in freight wagon construction, a sector in which it currently offers more than 80 different types. A member of Vereinigter Schienenfahrzeugbau der DDR eV.

Exports: Schienenfahrzeuge Export-Import Volkseigener Aussenhandelsbetrieb der DDR, Otztaler Strasse 17, 1100 East Berlin

Auto-carrier with capacity for up to 14 private cars

Type Fad four-axle self-discharge clinker wagon for SNCFT, Tunisia

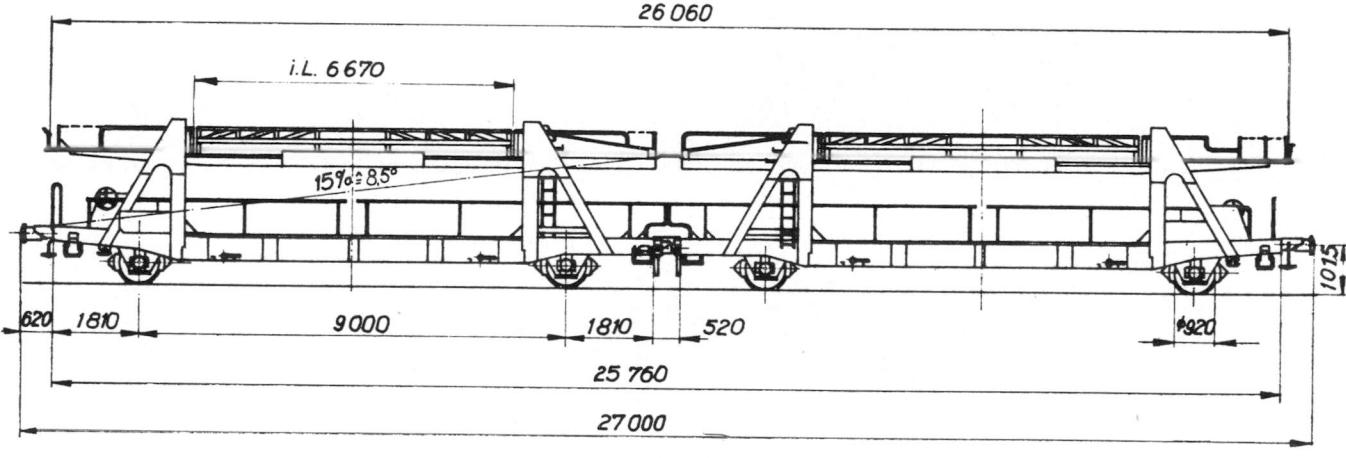

14-car capacity auto-carrier

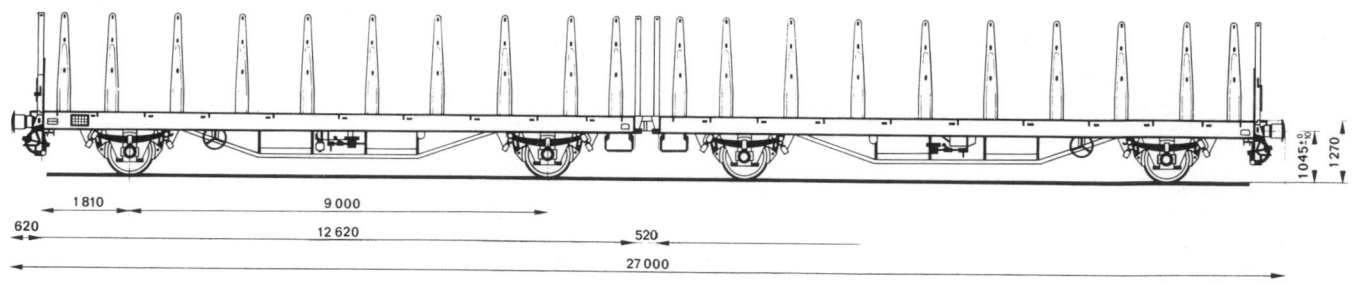

Type Laags flat wagon fitted with stanchions

Niigata
Niigata Engineering Co Ltd

4-1 Kasumigaseki 1-chome, Chiyoda-ku, Tokyo 100, Japan

Telephone: 03 504 2111
Telegrams: Nite, Tokyo
Telex: 222 7111

Chairman: Hideo Washio
Managing Director: Mitsuaki Ishiyama
Chief Sales Director: Toshio Nakamura

Products: Electric and diesel railcars; diesel-hydraulic locomotives; passenger cars; rotary snow plough.

Recent products include the Type S-500 snow plough specially designed for the Chicago Transit Authority. It has two rotary ploughs and four rotating brooms for live-rail clearance to remove snow at 1500 tons/hour. Powered by a 456 hp diesel engine, with maximum travelling speed 40 km/h, it is usable as a shunting locomotive.

Constitution: Niigata has been engaged in the manufacture of rolling stock for more than 80 years. It began production in 1896, just one year after its foundation, when the company launched its first passenger, freight and mail cars.

Type S-500 snow plough for Chicago Transit Authority

Niigata diesel locomotives

Class	Wheel arrangement	Transmission	Rated power (kW)	Max speed km/h	Total weight tonnes	No in service	Year first built	Builders Mechanical parts	Engine & type	Transmission
75 DGC	B-B	Hyd	448	25	75	6	1980	Niigata	Niigata DMF31 SBI	Niigata Converter
55 DGC	B-B	Hyd	373	27.2	55	12	1980	Niigata	Niigata DMF31 SB	Niigata Converter
40 DGC	B-B	Hyd	336	28	40	1	1977	Niigata	Cummins KT-1150-L	Niigata Converter
60 DGC	B-B	Hyd	336	25	60	1	1979	Niigata	Cummins KT-1150-L	Niigata Converter
50 DGC	B-B	Hyd	298	30.5	50	3	1972	Niigata	Niigata DMF31 SC	Niigata Converter
35 DGC	B-B	Hyd	250	31.2	35	1	1981	Niigata	Cummins NT-855-L	Niigata Converter
56 DGC	B-B	Hyd	2×448	50.5	56	5	1978	Niigata	Niigata DMF31 SBI	Niigata Converter
25 BGE	B	Hyd	134	25	25	8	1972	Niigata	Niigata DMH17C	

Niigata diesel railcars

Class	Cars per unit	Motor cars per unit	Motored axles per motor car	Transmission	Rated power (kW) per motor	Max speed km/h	Weight tonnes per car	Total seating capacity	Length per car m	No in service	Year first built	Builders Mechanical parts	Engine & type	Transmission
KIHA 40	1	1	1	Hyd torque converter	164	95	36.4	66	21.3	219	1977	Niigata	Niigata DMF15HSA	Niigata Converter DW 10
KIHA 183 limited express	7 or 10	7 or 10	1	Hyd torque converter	164	100	46.0	40	21.3	14	1979	Niigata	Niigata DMF15HSA	Niigata Converter DW 10
KIHA 184 limited express	7 or 10	7 or 10	1	Hyd torque converter	164	100	44.2	52	21.3	6	1979	Niigata	Niigata DMF15HSA	Niigata Converter DW 9A
KIHA 182 limited express	7 or 10	7 or 10	1	Hyd torque converter	328	100	42.7	68	21.3	32	1979	Niigata	Niigata DMF30HSI	Niigata Converter DW 9A
KIRO 182 limited express		1		Hyd torque converter	328	100	44.7	32	21.3	6	1979	Niigata	Niigata DMF30HSI	Niigata Converter DW 9A
KIHA 37	1	1	1	Hyd torque converter	157	95	30.8	66	20	2	1981	Niigata	Niigata DMF13S	Niigata Converter DF115A

Niigata electric railcars

Class	Cars per unit	Line voltage	Motor cars per unit	Motored axles per motor car	Rated output (kW) per car	Max speed km/h	Weight tonnes per car	Total seating capacity	Length per car m	No in service	Year first built	Builders Mechanical parts	Electrical equipment
1000 1200 1300	3	1.5 kV dc	8	4	400	90	37	66	20	3	1976	Niigata	Toyo Electric
6000	2	1.5 kV dc	8	4	400	90	37	58	20	2	1981	Niigata	Toyo Electric
250	1	1.5 kV dc	4	4	400	90	36	52	20	2	1981	Niigata	Toyo Electric

Nippon Sharyo

Nippon Sharyo Seizo Kaisha Ltd
Japan Rolling Stock Manufacturing Co Ltd

Head office: 1-1 Sanbonmatsu-cho, Atsuta-ku, Nagoya, Japan

Telephone: 882 3311
Telegrams: Nishiya, Nagoya
Telex: 447 3411

Works: Toyokawa, Nagoya, Narumi, Kinuura, Ohye and Ohtone

President: Shunichi Amano

Senior Vice President: Osamu Shinohara
Chief of Export Division: K Nishimura (Tokyo office)
K Yamaguchi (head office)

Products: Electrical and diesel locomotives and railcars; passenger coaches; freight cars of all types including tank cars; containers; tractors and trailers; steel castings; construction machinery; electrical equipment; steel-structure bridges, chemical plant and vessels.

Constitution: The founding of this company in 1896 marked the start of railway rolling stock building in Japan. It manufactures all types of motive power and rolling stock and obtains a major share of the home market as well as overseas railways in South-east Asia, Middle East, Africa, America and Australasia.

1435 mm gauge subway electric car with all-aluminium car-body for Nagoya Municipal Traffic Bureau

High-performance power bogie of bolsterless type for electric railcar

Inter-urban 1·5 kV dc railcar for Chicago South Shore & South Bend Railroad

Electric tramcar for Kumamoto Municipal Traffic Bureau, driven by first VVVF system in Japan

Series 200 Shinkansen train-set for Japanese National Railways (JNR)

VONA (Vehicle Of New Age) system for new town transportation near Tokyo

Novocherkassk
The Novocherkassk Electric Locomotive Works

V/O Energomachexport, 35 Mosfilmovskaya ul, Moscow 117330, USSR

Telex: 7565

Products: Electric locomotives and railcars.

O & K
Orenstein & Koppel AG

Head office: Karl-Funke-Strasse 30, 4600 Dortmund 1, Federal Republic of Germany

Telephone: 0231 1760-1
Telegrams: Orenkop, Dortmund
Telex: 0822 222

Main works: West Berlin, Dortmund, Ennigerloh, Hattingen, Lübeck
UK: O&K Escalators Ltd, Rylstone Street, Keighley, West Yorkshire BD21 4YA, England

Directors,
  Product Development/Production: Dipl-Ing Hans Dietrich von Bernuth
  Personnel: Walter Borchel
  Development, Heavy Plant and Machinery: Prof Dr-Ing Wolfgang Lubrich
  Marketing, Heavy Plant and Machinery: Dr Robert Mann
  Marketing, Series Machinery: Dr Günter Neuvians
  Finance: Karl Heinz Siepe

Principal subsidiary: O&K Orenstein & Koppel Ltd, Watford, Northampton NN6 7XN, England

Products: Goods wagons, escalators, autowalks, bi-modal excavators (rail and road).
  In 1983 the company was engaged on an order from the German Federal Railway (DB) for 500 bogie container wagons.

OMECA
OMECA SpA

Works: Reggio Calabria, Italy

Products: Passenger coaches of all types, freight wagons, railcars, containers, locomotives.

Constitution: The OMECA plant is jointly owned by Fiat Ferroviaria Savigliano and EFIM.

OMS
Officina Meccanica della Stanga

Corso Stati Uniti 3, 35100 Padua, Italy

Telephone: 76 04 88
Telegrams: OMS, Padova
Telex: 430218

Chairman: Dino Marchiorello
Vice-Chairman: Aldo Iaia
Managing Director: Ugo Soloni

Products: Diesel-electric locomotives, electric and diesel railcars and multiple-unit train-sets; passenger cars; freight wagons.
Recent products include vehicles of light alloy construction, the Type Le 724 driving trailer for Italian State Railways (FS); and a centre power car for the Line I stock of the Milan metro.

Milan metro centre motor-coach
Gauge: 1435 mm
Length between coupling planes: 17.54 m
Outer width: 2.85 m
Height of empty body: 3.511 m
Length between bogie centres: 11.1 m
Bogie wheelbase: 2.3 m
Seats: 40
Standing: 188
Tare: 28.5 tonnes
Total power: 400 kW
Line voltage: 750 V dc
Starting acceleration: 1.3 m/s²
Max speed: 80 km/h

Milan metro power car

The car features: a load-bearing structure entirely formed of light alloy; laminated plastic interior panelling; swing-slide doors with electro-pneumatic control; longitudinally-mounted seats with padded cushions and backs; fluorescent lighting; public address; Scharfenberg automatic couplers; electro-pneumatic, electrodynamic and electromagnetic rail brakes.

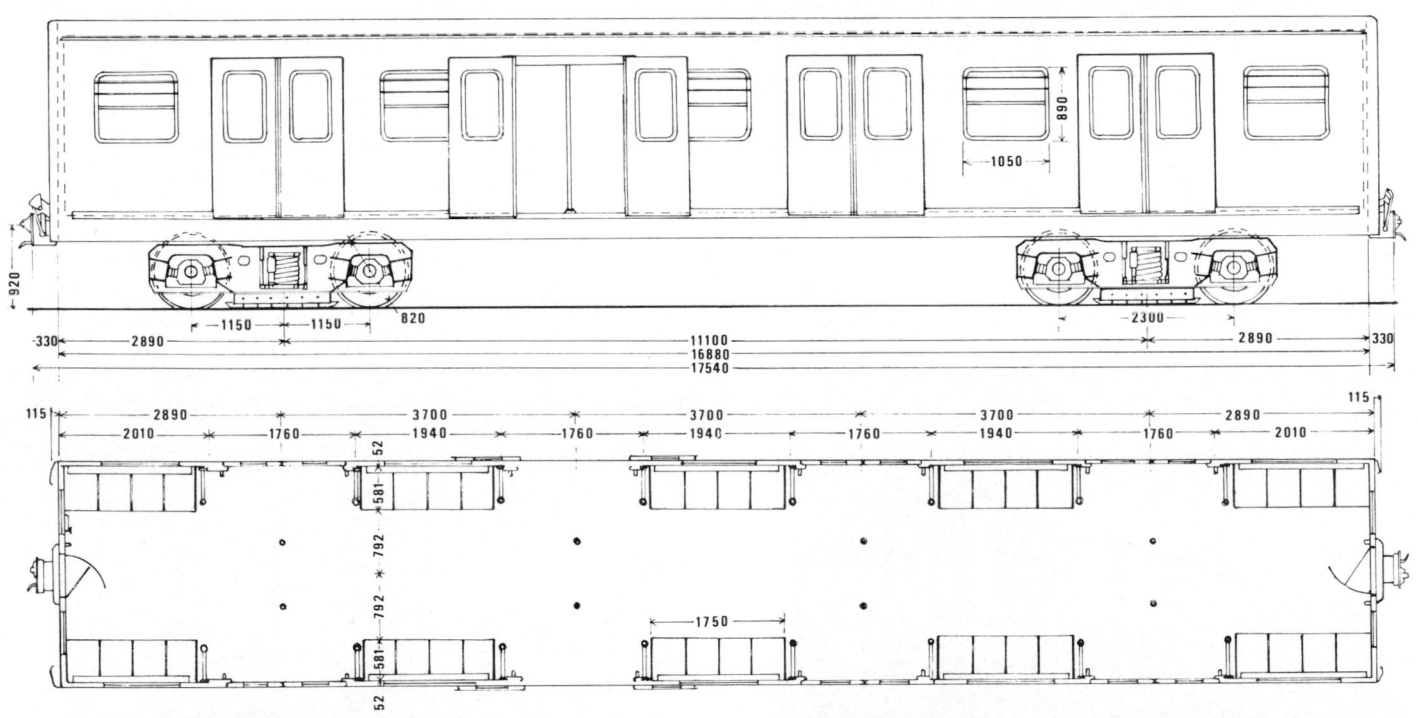

General arrangement of Milan metro power car

LRV for Azienda Trasporti Municipali ATM of Milan

Electric railcar for Ferrovie del Gargano, Italy

Type Le 724 driving trailer

Overall length between buffer and coupler: 24.78 m
Width of body: 2.78 m
Height of empty body: 3.716 m
Length between bogie centres: 17.5 m
Bogie wheelbase: 2.56 m
Seats: 72
Baggage compartment area: 8 m²
Tare in running order: 31 tonnes
Max speed: 140 km/h
The car features: a load-bearing structure entirely formed of light alloy extrusions; double doors sliding on the outside; laminated plastic interior panelling; smooth rubber floor in the compartments, and spot rubber floor in the vestibules; forced air heating; fluorescent lighting; Scharfenberg automatic coupler at the cab end; compressed-air brake with anti-skid device.

FS Type Le 724 driving trailer

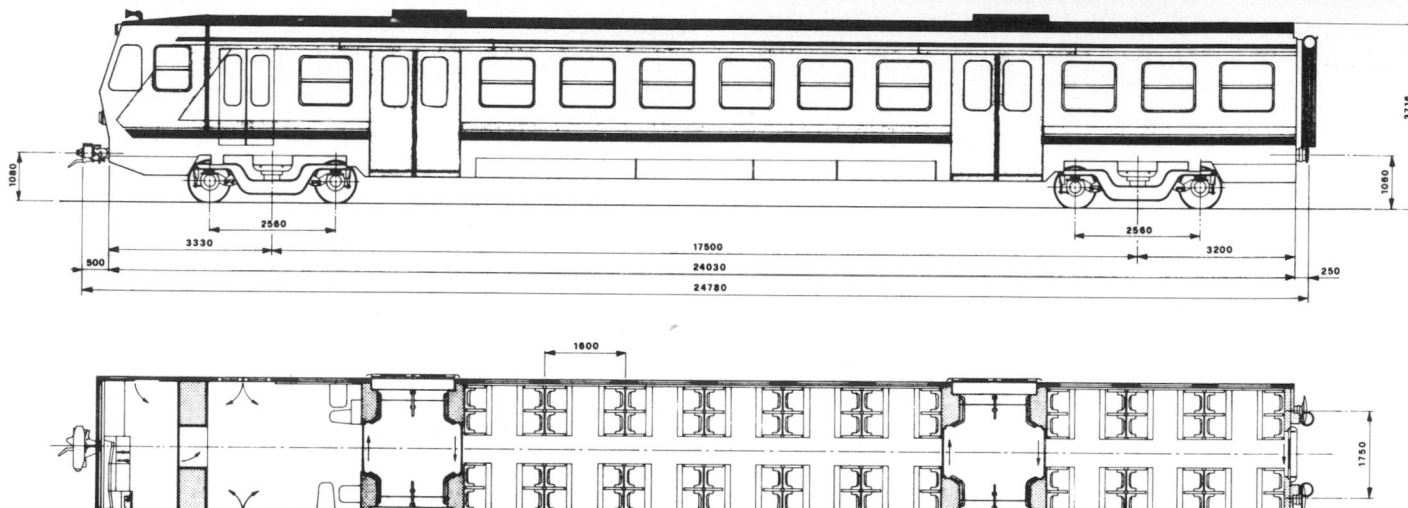

General arrangement of Type Le 724 driving trailer

Ortner
Ortner Freight Car Co

PO Box 640, 6040 Fidelity Drive, Milford, Ohio 45150, USA

Telephone: (513) 248 0300

President: Robert C Ortner
Director of Sales: A J Hurt Jr

Products: Freight cars and components. The total of the company's Rapid Discharge cars now in service is 12 000.

1500 ft³, 100-tonne covered hopper car for high-density Illmenite ore

100-tonne capacity longwood-log car

Orval
Ateliers de Matériel Ferroviaire d'Orval

53 avenue Paul-Doumer, 75016 Paris, France

Telephone: 870 82 50
Telegrams: Orvaltor, Paris
Telex: 620645

Works: Saint-Amand-Montrond 18

Telephone: 96 07 39
Telex: 760428

President: Jacques Marret
General Manager: Jacques Lafin
Commercial Manager: Philippe Gautier

Products: Freight wagons.

Constitution: Founded in 1945, the company designs and builds wagons for the transport and ease of loading and unloading of heavy products, powders and liquids, for the oil, chemical, food, forestry, steel and other industries; hopper and covered hopper cars, tank cars, open cars, flat cars, tippers, special cars. The company holds the licence for the Spitzer system of air discharge of powdered products.

Otis

Otis Elevator Company, Transportation Technology Division
A subsidiary of United Technologies

PO Box 7293, Denver, Colorado 80207, USA

Telephone: (303) 343 8780
Telex: 45 966

General Manager: L L Saunders
Manager, Marketing and Sales: R H Donlon

Products: Automated transit systems.

The Otis Network Transit is a system in the light guideway class, developed specifically to fit into highly congested sites and move people and cargo between and within buildings, horizontally and vertically, in a compatible, space-efficient manner. The space-saving feature is achieved by using vehicles equipped with Hovair air film pad suspension and electromagnetic (linear induction motor) propulsion and braking systems. This gives the vehicles an essentially frictionless omni-directional capability, with ease of steering and switching and permits direct lateral movement for compact off-line passenger loading, lane transfers, or transfer on to an elevator for vertical transport to a different elevation within buildings or complexes. All of these features are currently used in the Otis Network Transit system linking two hospital complexes at the Duke University Medical Center in Durham, North Carolina, USA. Service can be provided for on-line or off-line loading, on a scheduled or demand (call-button) activated basis in system configurations including shuttles, loops, collapsed loops (with end switchbacks), and networks. Exclusive trough-shaped guideways of about 9 feet overall width are employed, using standard steel or concrete construction. Stations can be customised to match needs, from simple platforms to elevator-type lobbies. Vehicle capacities ranging from 20 to about 80 passengers are available with optional seating/standing mix. Practical line capacities for single-vehicle operation can reach 13 000 passengers per hour per direction, depending on vehicle size and whether on-line or off-line stations are used. Trains can be used to increase capacities. Maximum line speeds up to 64 km/h are possible. Maintenance savings result from minimum maintenance space requirements and little or no propulsion/brake service requirements (no moving parts). Otis maintenance service is readily available in all US cities. Safety standards comply with modern rail and elevator requirements. All-weather operation is enhanced by non-traction propulsion and braking.

The Otis Shuttle Transit is a fully-automated, light guideway transit system developed to move people and cargo from point-to-point over relatively short distances (typically from 500 feet to about one mile). The system is designed specifically to provide true 'horizontal elevator' service for low cost. This is accomplished by using standard Otis elevator machine drives and cable equipment with a range of vehicle sizes from 20 to 120 passengers. The vehicles can be operated singly or as trains, in simple shuttles or synchronised push-pull arrangements, over exclusive guideways employing standard construction methods utilising either steel or concrete sections.

The Otis Hovair air film pad suspension system is used as a baseline with steel wheel/rail or rubber tyre suspension systems offered as options for special applications. Side-rail or centre-slot guidance is available using three basic drive configuration options.

Stations can be customised to match needs, from simple platforms to elevator-type lobbies. Two to five stations can be served by a single shuttle with connection to other shuttle lines via transfer points. A wide range of passenger capacities is available using standard equipment closely matched to the specific need to minimise cost. For example, serving two stations separated by 1000 feet, a peak-hour capacity range of from less than 500 to more than 11 000 passengers per hour per direction can be delivered using a single-lane guideway. Scheduled or demand (call-button) service is offered. Station dwell time is adjustable. Low vehicle weight per passenger space and very low unit pressure will allow the system to be overlaid on existing structures (eg building roofs) in many cases. Curves and gradients can be negotiated to connect dispersed buildings. Energy savings of the order of 30 per cent (including regeneration) can be achieved over other systems having similar capacities but using different propulsion/suspension systems.

Automatically-operated Network Transit vehicle at Duke University Medical Centre, USA

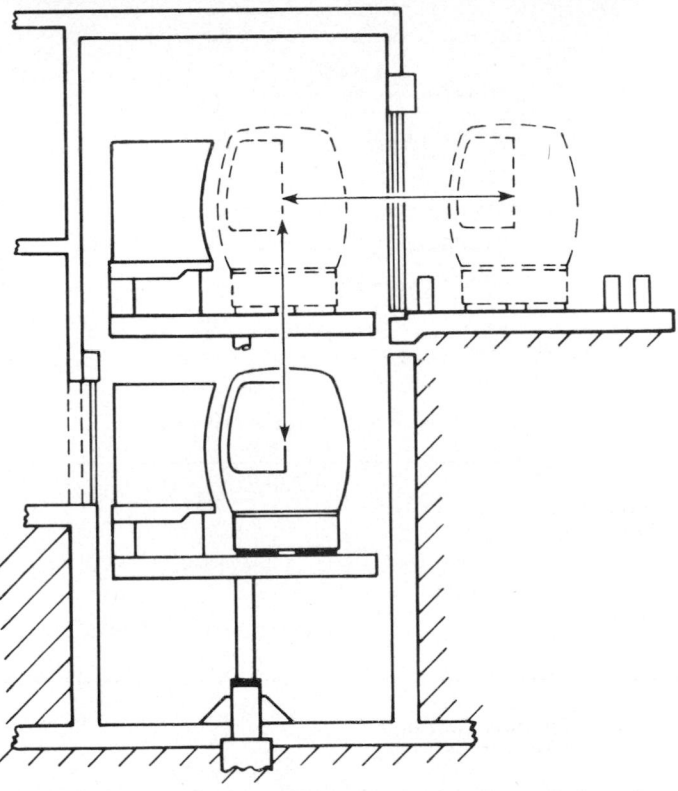

Network Transit methods of lateral/vertical transfer; compact lateral docking mechanism fits under loading platform floor or on elevator platform

Shuttle Transit 100-passenger vehicle at Denver

Pacific Car and Foundry Company
A division of Paccar

Head office and works: 1400 North 4th Street, Renton, Washington 98055, USA

Telephone: (206) 251 7700
Telex: 32-8942

General Manager: W A Robbins
Marketing Manager, Railroad Products: A G Bohorfoush Jr

Products: Freight cars.

Covered hopper with payload capacity 4750 ft³ and load limit 201 000 lb

Double-hopper ballast car, 13.36 m long over couplers

Rotary dump gondola, 16.18 m long over couplers, tare weight 57 000 lb, load limit 206 000 lb, payload capacity 4000 ft³ with levelled fill

Heavily insulated RBL refrigerator car with 508 mm travel sliding sill underframe, interior 18.57 × 3.02 m, capacity 100 short tons

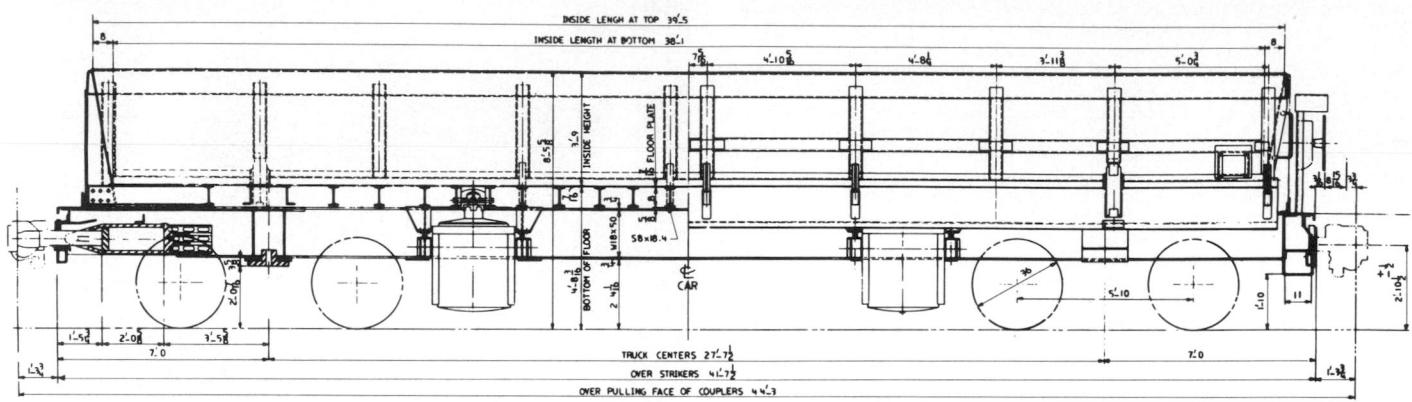

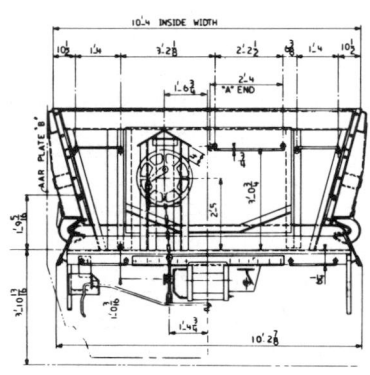

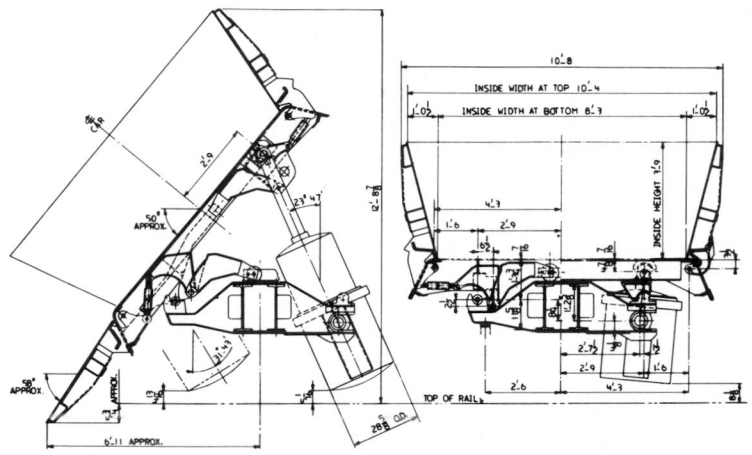

Air-side dump car, tare weight 76 000 lb, capacity 50 yds³/187 000 lb

Pafawag
PFW Pafawag

Panstwowa Fabryka Wagonow Pafawag, ul Robotnicza 12, 53-609 Wroclaw, Poland

Telephone: 340 61
Telex: 034431

Export sales: Kolmex, 49 Mokotowska, 00-542 Warsaw

Products: Electric locomotives, electric multiple-units, passenger and service cars, bogies.

Pakistan Railway Carriage
Pakistan Railway Carriage Factory

PO Box 286, Rawalpindi, Islamabad, Pakistan

Telephone: 67250, 67256, 67260
Telegrams: Carfac, Rawalpindi

Works: Sector 1-11, Khayaban-e-Sir Syed, Islamabad

Chairman: A Kalam
Managing Director: Z I Puri
Sales Director: M Marouf

Products: Passenger coaches.

PEC
The Projects & Equipment Corporation of India Ltd
A Government of India Enterprise

Hansalaya, 15 Barakhamba Road, New Delhi 110 001, India

Telegrams: Pecoind
Telex: 31-2156; 3429

Chairman: Vikram Prakash
Executive Directors: Anand Krishna
  C L Subramaniam

Products: Diesel-electric, diesel-hydraulic, electric, industrial and mining locomotives; electric multiple-units; passenger coaches of any type and design for various gauges; freight wagons of all types to suit any gauge; signalling and telecommunication equipment; spares for locomotives, coaches and wagons for export.

Over 350 coaches manufactured in India are currently operating in Taiwan, Zambia, Philippines, Burma, Bangladesh, Sri Lanka, Tanzania, Uganda and Viet-Nam.

PEC has also exported over 7300 wagons to various countries such as Uganda, Tanzania, Zambia, Hungary, Sri Lanka, Burma, Bangladesh, South Korea, Malaysia and Viet-Nam. 15 diesel-electric locomotives have been exported to Tanzania. Orders for 14 diesel-electric locomotives to IDA-financed projects of NTPC were in hand in 1982.

Constitution: PEC was formed in 1971 as a corporation under the Indian Ministry of Commerce to handle and boost the export of railway equipment and engineering goods. The Indian wagon industry, with companies such as Burn Standard Co Ltd, Braithwaite & Co Ltd, Texmaco Ltd, Cimmco Ltd and Jessop & Co Ltd, has a combined manufacturing capacity of 25 000 wagons per annum and is a regular supplier to the Indian Railways.

The Indian coach-building industry comprises the Integral Coach Factory, Madras (an Indian Railway unit) BEML, Bangalore (a unit under the Ministry of Defence) and Jessop & Co Ltd with a combined annual capacity of approximately 1500 units. These companies too regularly supply Indian Railways.

Locomotives are manufactured in Indian Railway units such as Diesel Locomotive Works, Varanasi, Chittaranjan Locomotive Works, Asansol and in the private sector by Venkateswara Transmission, Hyderabad, and Suri & Nayyar, Bangalore, for the smaller hp ranges.

Pecchioli
Costruzioni Elettromechaniche Ferroviarie Fiorentine di Ezio Pecchioli

Via Renato Bruschi 156, Sesto Fiorentino, Florence, Italy

Telephone: 4491241
Telegrams: Coelferf, Sesto Fiorentino

Products: Refrigerated wagons.

Perry
Perry Engineering Division
Johns Perry Industries Pty Ltd

Railway Terrace, Mile End South, South Australia 5031, Australia

Postal address: Box 1838, GPO Adelaide, South Australia 5001

Telephone: 352 1777
Telegrams: Sperry, Adelaide
Telex: 82493

General Manager: R M King

Products: Railway rolling stock.

Constitution: In 1966 Perry Engineering Co Ltd merged with Johns and Waygood Holdings Ltd of Melbourne to form the Johns-Perry Group and became part of an Australia-wide structural, mechanical and electrical engineering business.

69 000-litre tank car

Pidner
Pidner SA

Rua Buenos Aires 68, 36° Andar, Rio de Janeiro, Brazil

Telephone: 266 8908

Products: Passenger and freight cars.

Plymouth
Plymouth Locomotive Works Inc
A Banner Industries Inc Co

607 Bell Street, Plymouth, Ohio 44865, USA

Export sales: Banner International, Inc

448 E Tiffin Street, PO Box 269, Willard, Ohio 44890, USA

Telephone: (419) 935 6781
Telex: 241551

President: Miles W Christian
Sales Director: Beecher Caudill
Export Sales: M Fate Christian

Products: Diesel-hydraulic locomotives for heavy-duty hauling and switching ranging from 3 to 45 tons with approvals for operation in gaseous mines under Schedule 31 of Mining Safety and Health Administration (MSHA).

Plymouth Model CR-8 50-ton diesel-hydraulic locomotive

Plymouth Model MDT 45-ton diesel-hydraulic locomotive

Plymouth Model HMD 8-ton diesel-hydrostatic mining locomotive

Plymouth Model CR-8XT 120-ton diesel-hydraulic locomotive

Plymouth diesel locomotives

Industrial

	H	D	J/JW	M/W	CR-8	CR-8XT
Weight (tonnes)	4-8	10-15	15-25	30-45	45-65	70-120
Power (hp)	60-100	125-200	150-250	300-450	600-1000	600-1200
Haulage capacity (tonnes)	200	375	625	1125	1625	3000
Wheel arrangement	0-4-0	0-4-0	0-4-0 (J)	0-4-0 (M)	Bo-Bo	Bo-Bo
			0-6-0 (JW)	0-6-0 (W)		

Engines: Caterpillar, Cummins, Detroit Diesel or Deutz

Mining

	TMDR	HMD	DMD	JMD	MMD
Weight (tonnes)	4-6	4-8	10-16	15-25	25-45
Power (hp)	50-90	60-100	125-225	150-250	300-400
Haulage capacity (tonnes)	150	200	375	625	1125
Wheel arrangement	0-4-0	0-4-0	0-4-0	0-4-0	0-4-0

Engines: Caterpillar and Deutz with MSHA Schedule 24 and 31 approved

Portec Inc

300 Windsor Drive, Oak Brook, Illinois 60521, USA

Telephone: (312) 920 4600

Chairman: Thomas J Guendel
President: David H Abbott
Senior Vice President, Railroad Group: Stephen A Kovach
Senior Vice President, Commercial and Government Relations:
L L White Jr

Products: Railcars, railcar tie-down systems, track maintenance equipment and components, leasing.

Divisions
Portec Lease Corporation
300 Windsor Drive, Oak Brook, Illinois 60521

Products: Leasing and financing of Portec-manufactured rail cars, track maintenance machinery, and construction equipment products.

Railcar Division
1800 Century Boulevard NE, Suite 680, Atlanta, Georgia 30345

Telephone: (404) 329 0400

Products: Freight cars, new, modification, repair; railcar automobile shipping racks.

Recent developments include a new protective door-end for enclosed tri-level auto-carriers, or auto-racks, which has been designated RAVE (for Rack Anti-Vandalism Enclosure). The door is made up of hinged vertical slats, each weigh-ing 27.22 kg (60 lb) and easily replaceable in the event of damage. The doors are hung from a deck track by heavy-duty Litton trolleys at each upper hinge point; at the bottom they are guided by a beam only, so that straightening in the event of distortion is simple. The RAVE doors are easy to open, simple to lock, need no periodic maintenance and can be individually removed or replaced without need of a workshop visit.

RAVE end-door for enclosed tri-level auto-rack produced by Portec

100-ton car for coil steel

Bulkhead flat car for NdeM, Mexico

Portec-built 100-ton 50 yd² air-operated side-dump car

Portec-built 100-ton, 2000 ft³ capacity ballast car

100-ton, 2000 ft³ capacity copper concentrate car with automated discharge mechanism produced by Portec

Powell Duffryn
Powell Duffryn Wagon Company Limited

Head office: Cambrian House, Maindy, Cardiff CF4 3XD, Wales

Telephone: 0222 42051
Telegrams: Wagons, Cardiff
Telex: 497233

Main works: Cambrian Works, Maindy, Cardiff CF4 3XD

Managing Director: R E Morgan
Technical Director: R G Hughes
Financial Director: T D B Rosser

Principal subsidiary: Powell Duffryn Tools Ltd

Products: Railway rolling stock.

Pragoinvest
Czechoslovak locomotive export group

Ceskomoravská 23, 18056 Prague 9, Czechoslovakia

Works: CKD, Prague

Products: Diesel-electric locomotives.
   Recent orders have included 97 Type DES3100 Co-Co diesel-electric locomotives for Iraqi Republican Railways (IRRO) and 25 Type LDE 1500 diesel locomotives for Syrian Railways.
   The T669.1 was specifically designed to Soviet Railways (SZD) requirements as a heavy shunter and over 4000 have been acquired by SZD, but it is also used in Czechoslovakia, Poland, Albania, India and Iraq. The SZD classifies it as the Type CME3. The T448.0 has been redeveloped as the Type 446.2, with increased top speed of 90 km/h and lower axleload of 16 tonnes for Czechoslovak State Railways (CSD), which operates over 200.

Type T478.4 diesel for CSD

Type DES diesel-electric Co-Co of Iraqi Republican Railways

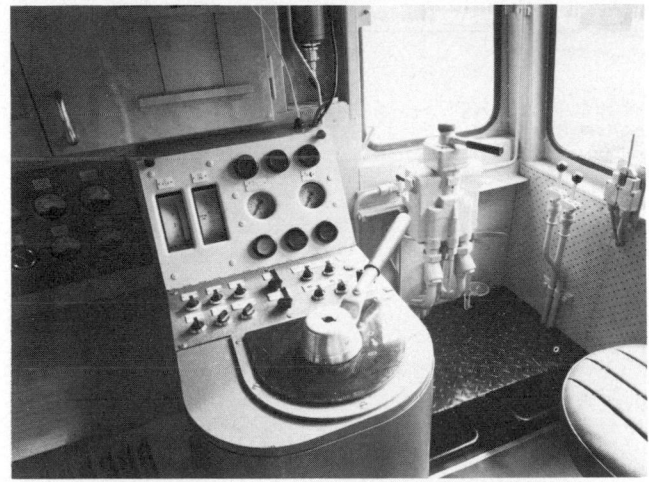
Cab interior of Type DES diesel-electric Co-Co for IRRO of Iraq

Type CME3 diesel for Soviet Railways (SZD)

Type T466.2 diesel for Czechoslovak Railways (CSD)

Pragoinvest diesel-electric locomotives

Type	CME3 (SZD)	T448.0 (CSD)	T466.2 (CSD)	T478.4 (CSD)
Wheel arrangement	Co-Co	Bo-Bo	Bo-Bo	Bo-Bo
Gauge	1520 mm	1435 mm	1435 mm	1435 mm
Length over buffers/coupler	17.22 m	13.58 m	13.58 m	16.54 m
Body width	3.08 m	3.06 m	3.06 m	3.07 m
Total wheelbase	12.6 m	9.1 m	9.1 m	11.4 m
Bogie wheelbase	4 m	2.4 m	2.4 m	2.4 m
Wheel diameter	1.05 m	1 m	1 m	1 m
Minimum curve radius	80 m	80 m	80 m	100 m
Weight in working order	123 tonnes	72 tonnes	64 tonnes	73 tonnes
Max service speed	95 km/h	70 km/h	90 km/h	100 km/h
Continuous tractive effort/km/h	226 kN/11.4 km/h	131 kN/18 km/h	121 kN/19 km/h	120 kN/30 km/h
Engine	CKD K6S 310DR	CKD K6S 230DR	CKD K6S 230DR	CKD K12V 230DR
Rating/rpm	990 kW/750	883 kW/1250	883 kW/1250	1460 kW/1100

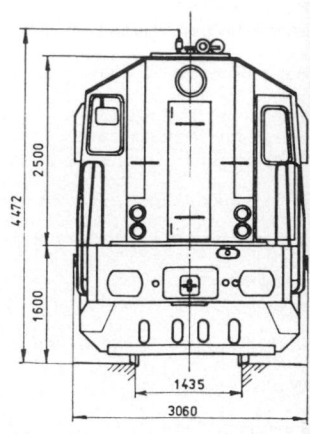

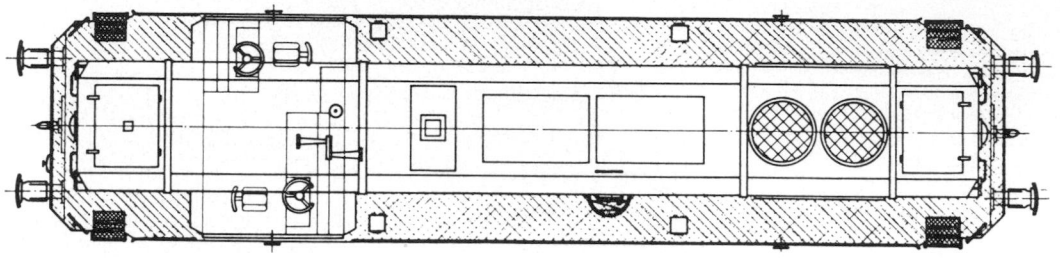

Layout of Type T466.2 locomotive

Prati-Vazquez Iglesias
Prati-Vazquez Iglesias SA

B Rivadavia 4402, 1822 Valentin Alsina, Prov Buenos Aires, Argentina

Telephone: 241 4101/4186
Telex: 122586

Products: Freight wagons for bulk commodities and piggyback.

Price
A & G Price Ltd

Private Bag, Thames, New Zealand

Telephone: 86060
Telegrams: Priceco, Thames
Telex: 2655

Managing Director: R S O'Hagan
Resident Manager: J W Wiseman

Products: Diesel-hydraulic, diesel-mechanical and battery locomotives; freight wagons.

Constitution: This company stems from a foundry and workshop set up at Onehunga near Auckland in 1868 by two brothers, Alfred and George Price.

Procor
Procor Ltd, Rail Car Division

2001 Speers Road, Oakville, Ontario L6J 5E1, Canada

Telephone: (416) 827 4111
Telex: 06 98 2241

Chairman: S H Bonser
President and Chief Executive Officer: Kenneth Jagger

Vice President, Sales: Gordon C Mills
Group Controller: Kenneth T Robins

Products: Freight wagons.

Constitution: Procor's Rail Car Division designs and manufactures tank cars and freight cars for a great variety of products, for lease to shippers in Canada and the United Kingdom. Procor operates and maintains the largest fleet of railway freight cars (over 16 500) in Canada.

Procor (UK) Limited

Horbury, Wakefield, West Yorkshire WF4 5QH, England

Telephone: 0924 271881
Telex: 556457

Managing Director: F J Swindell
Financial Controller: N Casson
Sales Manager: B T McDonnell

Products: Railway freight rolling stock.

Constitution: Procor (UK) Ltd, a member of the Marmon Group of companies, designs, builds, sells, hires, leases, repairs and maintains all types of railway freight rolling stock. With a fleet of over 3000 wagons, Procor is the largest wagon hiring company in the United Kingdom and has customers in the petroleum, chemical, food, steel, motor and construction industries.

90 tonnes glw bogie tank wagon for liquefied petroleum gas, in service with Shell (UK) Oil

102 tonnes glw wagon for steel scrap

46 tonnes glw curtain-sided van for palletised goods and general merchandise

51 tonnes glw 'Pressure-flow' pressure discharge wagon, delivered to Rugby Portland Cement Co for bulk cement movement

51 tonnes glw aggregate hopper wagon

24·21 m Procar 80-car transporter unit, longest four-axle bogie freight vehicle operating on British Rail

Pullman Standard

Division of Pullman Transportation Co (PTC)

200 South Michigan Avenue, Chicago, Illinois 60604, USA

Telephone: (312) 322 7336

President: Jack R Kruizenga
Vice President, Marketing: Gerald F Lahey
Vice President, Fleet Operations: Mitchell R Gillenwater
Vice President, Sales: Alan G Eades

Products: Freight cars.

Constitution: In 1979 Pullman announced its withdrawal from the railroad passenger car business, devoting its business to freight cars and parts. Pullman Incorporated was purchased by Wheelabrator-Frye Inc, which established Pullman Transportation Co in 1981 and owns half that company. PTC owns all rail car manufacturing assets of W-F's Pullman Standard Division and has rights to participate in other Pullman Inc businesses, which include Trailmobile Inc. Through its wholly-owned subsidiary, Pullman Leasing Co, Wheelabrator-Frye Inc operates a base fleet of more than 23 000 specialised freight cars, which are managed under contract by PTC. (See also Addenda).

Pu Zhen
Pu Zhen Rolling Stock Works

Nanjing, Kiangsu, People's Republic of China

Products: Passenger coaches; roller bearings; axle boxes; brake cylinders.
   Recent products include an air-conditioned restaurant car, with 25.5-metre long body of welded all-steel integral construction without centre sill. Designed for operation at up to 160 km/h, the vehicle rides on bogies with side frames and bolsters of cast steel, Type 209P, in which the central suspension system is of outer swing-hangar type with rocking spring plank. The kitchen equipment, which includes gas range, refrigerator and rice-cooker, is manufactured entirely in stainless steel.

Constitution: Originally a locomotive repair yard, now a passenger coach repair and manufacturing works.

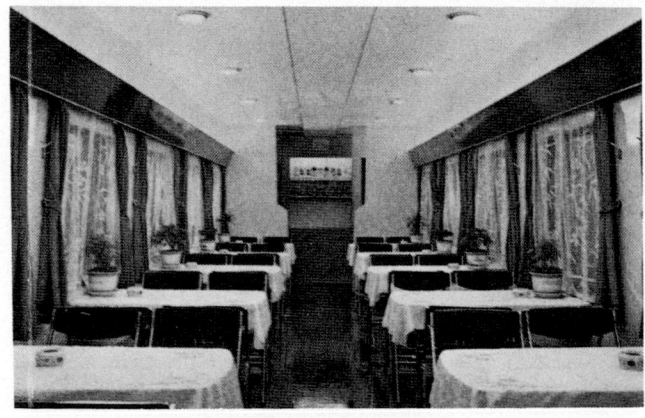

Interior of air-conditioned restaurant car

Qiqihar Car Plant
Qiqihar Railway Car Plant

Qiqihar, Heilungkiang, People's Republic of China

Products: Freight wagons including a Type D30 370-tonne flat wagon for transport of complete machines and heavy equipment.
  Recent products have included:
Type P61 covered wagon: gauge 1435 mm, tare weight 24 tonnes, load capacity 120 m³ and 60 tonnes, cast steel bogies can be fitted with roller bearings;
Type C62A high-sided open wagon: gauge 1435 mm, tare weight 21.7 tonnes, load capacity 71.6 m³ and 60 tonnes;
Type K18 coal wagon: gauge 1435 mm; tare weight 26 tonnes, load capacity 64.5 m³ and 60 tonnes, air-operated discharge doors;
Four-bogie heavy load wagon: gauge 1435 mm, tare weight 48.6 tonnes, load capacity 120 tonnes, depressed loading area 7.4 × 2.4 m, floor height above rail level 990 mm, minimum curve radius 150 m;
40-tonne high-sided wagon for Sri Lanka Railways: gauge 1678 mm, tare weight 17.5 tonnes, load capacity 40 tonnes;
50-tonne low-sided wagon for Tanzania-Zambia Railway (Tazara): gauge 1067 mm, tare weight 17.3 tonnes, load capacity 50 tonnes, floor area 33 m², all-steel welded construction, dual air- and vacuum brakes;

Four-bogie heavy load wagon

40-tonne high-sided wagon for Sri Lanka Railways

Bogies include Type 8 for use on 60-tonne wagons, and Type TZ designed for Tazara and principally used on 50-tonne wagons.

Type K18 coal wagon

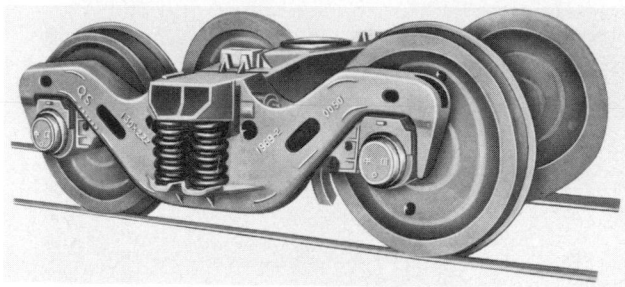

Type TZ bogie designed for Tazara 50-tonne wagons

Type 8 bogie for 60-tonne wagons

50-tonne low-sided wagon for Tanzania-Zambia Railway (Tazara)

Railway Mine & Plantation Equipment Limited

Royal London House, 22/25 Finsbury Square, London EC2P 2AS, England

Telephone: 01-606 7000
Telegrams: Minplan, London EC2
Telex: 888240

Director: J A Lee
Secretary: R T Wilshire

Products: Locomotives, rolling stock, freight bogies, permanent way materials, re-railing equipment, inspection railcars, breakdown cranes and all light railway equipment for mines and plantations.

Ramon Mugica
Herederos de Ramon Mugica SA

Barrio de Ventas s/n, PO Box 14, Irún, Spain

Telephone: (43) 62 97 00
Telegrams: Herem
Telex: 36 195

Chairman: Juan O Ohlsson
Director: José R Jusué
Sub Directors: Luis Múgica
                Iñigo Saldaña

Products: Special wagons to customer's requirements: tank cars, hopper cars, bulk powder cars, gondola wagons, tank containers.

Tank wagon for liquid asphalt

Vinyl chloride tank containers, tare 5.8 tonnes, payload capacity 19.6 tonnes/24 500 litres, 9.125 × 2.438 × 2.438 m over frame

Container wagon

Anhydrous ammonia tank wagon, 33.7 tonnes tare, payload capacity 46.3 tonnes/89 m³

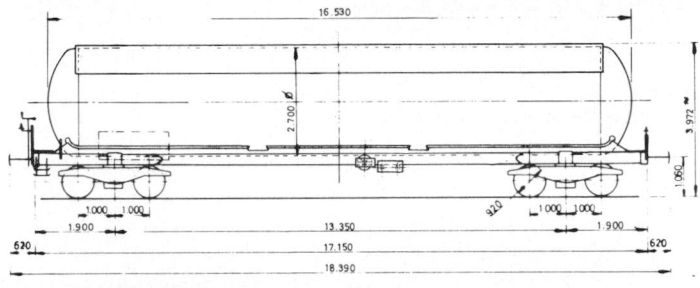

General arrangement of anhydrous ammonia tank wagon on Type Y21Cse bogies

Tank wagon with stainless steel vessel for chemical products

Tank wagon for caustic soda

Ranzi-Legnano
Ranzi-Legnano SpA

Viale Cadorna 34-40, Legnano, Italy

Telephone: 548754
Telegrams: Ranzi Legnano

Products: Diesel-mechanical and diesel-hydraulic locomotives.

Rastatt
Waggonfabrik Rastatt GmbH

Wekstrasse 2, 7550 Rastatt, Federal Republic of Germany

Telephone: 07222 33051
Telegrams: Waggonfabrik
Telex: 07 86 620

Products: Passenger and freight cars including tank and container-carrying wagons.

Reggiane
Officine Meccaniche Italiano SpA

27 Via Vasco Agosti, Reggio Emilia, Italy

Telephone: 0522 41341/41741/46041
Telegrams: Reggiane
Telex: 530665

Chairman: Prof Ing Pasquale Gerardi
Managing Director: Dr Ivan Bonora

Administrative Manager: Rag Franco Caselli
Commercial Director: Ing Ivo Braglia

Products: Electric, diesel-electric, diesel-hydraulic and diesel-mechanical locomotives; railcars; passenger, pilot, dining, sleeping, saloon cars; freight wagons; rolling stock components.

Constitution: Founded in 1904 to build rolling stock and, a few years later, steam locomotives. After being largely destroyed during 1943 the works were rebuilt and re-equipped.

Remafer
Société de Construction et de Réparation de Matériel Ferroviaire

Head office: 3 rue Christophe Colomb, 75008 Paris, France

Telephone: (1) 723 76 51
Telex: 290471

Works: 15 rue d'Alger, 51100 Rheims, France

Telephone: (26) 07 96 68
Telex: 830645

Products: Special-purpose, small and medium series of freight wagons, including cement tank wagons with fluidised and pulsed-air discharge; automatic-discharge coal wagons; and heavy-load 20-axle wagons. The company also engages in engineering studies and has lately conducted a feasibility study of local rail maintenance workshops and wagon manufacture for Communauté des Etats de l'Afrique de l'Ouest (CEAO).

Resco
Resco Ltd
PO Box 1874, London Road, Bulawayo, Zimbabwe

Telephone: 67861
Telegrams: Tensile, Belmont
Telex: 3171

Products: Steam and diesel locomotive refurbishing, electric traction assembly, freight wagons.

Resita
MecanoExportImport supplier

1 Golului Street, 1700 Resita, Romania

Telephone: 964 17111
Telex: 74215

Products: Diesel engine and locomotive components.

Ries
Adolf Ries Maschinenenbau GmbH

Schnabel-Henning Strasse 30, PO Box 2240, 7520 Bruchsal 1, Federal Republic of Germany

Telephone: 07251 15031
Telex: 07 822204

Products: Road/rail tractors.

Riga
Riga Carriage Building Works

Riga, USSR

Products: Motive power and rolling stock.

Constitution: Member of Energomachexport.

Röchling-Burbach
Röchling-Burbach Stahl-und-Waggonbau GmbH

Saarbrücken 5, Federal Republic of Germany

Telephone: 0681 770 91
Telegrams: Waggonfabrik, Saarbrucken
Telex: 4 421 466

Products: Freight cars including tank wagons.

Rosario
Industrias Metalurgicas Rosario SA

Calle 37 No 1005, 2000 Rosario, Argentina

Telephone: 33 163

Products: Passenger and freight cars.

Ruhrthaler
Ruhrthaler Maschinenfabrik, Schwarz & Dyckerhoff KG

Postfach 01 12 60, Scheffelstrasse 14-28, 4330 Mulheim/Ruhr, Federal Republic of Germany

Telephone: 0208 44131
Telegrams: Ruhrtaloko, Mulheimruhr
Telex: 0856710

Products: Diesel-hydraulic, diesel-mechanical locomotives for narrow gauge; suspended monorail.

Saalasti Oy

Arinatie 4, 00370 Helsinki 37, Finland

Telephone: 90-557 775
Telex: 124694

Chairman: Eng Tapio Saalasti

Products: Diesel shunting locomotives; road/rail shunting tractor; permanent way train crane tractors; shunting couplings; snow ploughs.

In the patented control of OTSO locomotives, start-up, speed control, change of direction and braking are operated from a single control wheel. When the driver's grip releases the handwheel or the drive lever of the radio control apparatus, the brakes are applied, the locomotive stops and the engine idles. OTSO locomotives have hydrodynamic transmission.

Some OTSO locomotive models can be supplied for metre gauge operation.

Saalasti Oy shunting locomotives

	OTSO 2	OTSO 3	OTSO 4	OTSO 5	NALLE*
Weight (tonnes)	20-25	36	40	44,46	10
Power (hp (kW))	200 (150)	300 (220)	400 (295)	560 (410)	120 (88)
Drawbar pull (kN)	70	105	125	140	250
Speed (km/h)	20	25	25	25	25
Overall length (mm)	6000	7600	7600	7600	6100
Overall height (mm)	3750	3850	3850	3850	2900
Max width (mm)	3100	3100	3100	3100	2480
Wheelbase (mm)	2500	3100	3100	3100	3450
Wheel diameter (mm)	800	960	960	960	450/1400
Transmission	hydrodynamic				

* Bi-modal rail/road tractor

Accessories available: OTSO coupling, OTSO R coupling, VAPITI coupling, brush, pointed and side ploughs, radio control, equipment for paired running

Snowplough by Saalasti Oy

110 hp diesel road/rail Little Bear shunter

Type OTSO 4 diesel shunter

Nalle road/rail tractor, as supplied to Finnish State Railways (VR)

Work train crane tractor by Saalasti Oy

Santa Matilde
Cia Industrial Santa Matilde

Export sales and head office: Rua Buenos Aires, 100-7°, CEP 20070, Rio de Janeiro, Brazil

Telephone: (021) 252 6090
Telegrams: Manganato
Telex: 021 21042

Products: Emus; passenger coaches; freight wagons; containers.

Constitution: Companhia Industrial Santa Matilde, founded in 1916, operates from two plants with 3500 employees. The Três Rios works (55 000 m²) produces emus. Conselheiro Lafaiete (33 000 m²) produces passenger coaches, freight wagons, containers and brake equipment. Annual capacity is 2400 freight wagons, 300 passenger coaches and 60 four-car emu sets.

Ore wagon built at Conselheiro Lafaiete plant for Vale do Rio Doce (CVRD) mines

Cement wagon

Scandia
Scandia-Randers A/S

Udbyhøjvej 66, PO Box 200, 8900 Randers, Denmark

Telephone: 06 42 53 00
Telegrams: Scandia, Randers
Telex: 65145

Products: Passenger and freight cars; electric railcars; railbuses.

Recent products include two prototype train-sets designed as a basis for a third generation of Danish State Railways (DSB) Lyntog (Lightning) inter-city equipment. Each set consists of five permanently coupled cars, a length dictated by Great Belt train ferry deck capacity, and is arranged for push-pull operation to avoid conveyance of locomotives on the ferry crossings, particularly with DSB's trunk route electrification in view. The trains will be propelled on to ferries and hauled off.

The Type Bfs driving trailer is a second-class open car with no external entrances, accessible only from the adjoining car, and seats 74 in 2 + 2 bays around tables. It includes two toilets. There is a Bfs at each end of the set. Accommodation in a single Type Bfm second-class trailer is similar, but this has

a single external entrance. The Type Afm trailer is a first-class, 10-compartment vehicle seating 60, with a single entrance and a toilet.

The remaining car is a Type Cfm service car, which has entrances at each end. Occupying half its body, the service area includes a buffet-bar and a train staff compartment from which train public address announcements are made. Adjoining the service area are three so-called 'flexible' compartments with folding lateral partition walls, which can be withdrawn to create a two- or three-compartment-size conference room furnished with tables and loose chairs; normal three-a-side seating is replaced when this accommodation is used as individual compartments. The Cfm car also includes a compartment for disabled passengers with room for a wheelchair. The entrance at this end of the vehicle has two retractable service lifts of up to 300 kg capacity for wheelchair loading, and the toilet is equipped for use by the disabled.

The fully air-conditioned train-set has air-operated doors, centrally lockable, and entrances with movable steps to suit varying DSB platform heights. Toilets are vacuum-operated, served in each installation by a polyurethane-insulated collection tank of 750 litres' capacity that is heated under thermostatic control. Wash basin water is drained to the track except when the train is stationary; then it is collected in a small container which is automatically flushed as train speed reaches 20 km/h. An automatic device locks toilets out of use in the event of vacuum toilet failure, saturation of the sewage collection tank or lack of water.

The set is equipped with track-to-train radio, enabling announcements from train ferry offices or other outside sources to be broadcast over the cars' pa, and at other times the relay of Danish radio programmes; each seat headrest is equipped with an individual tuner/amplifier and volume control. A main clock in the service car repeats to seven receiver clocks in other cars; each clock also features a train speed display.

The steel-bodied cars are built to the full extent of the DSB loading-gauge, which exceeds the UIC parameters, and have a maximum waist width of 3.01 metres. To maximise sound absorption, coach floors rest on rubber fitments and are not directly connected to the underframe. Two types of bogie are being evaluated, one the Schindler-Schlieren Type 76II employing large double coil springs, the other a development of an air-suspension type already in DSB service.

The company has also drafted preliminary designs for the double-deck push-pull sets which Danish State Railways plan to introduce to the Helsingör-Copenhagen-Roskilde commuter routes after electrification in 1986.

Lyntog Type Bfm second-class car interior

Prototype Lyntog train-set for Danish State Railways (DSB)

Schienenfahrzeuge Export-Import

Ötztaler Strasse 17, 1080 East Berlin, German Democratic Republic

Telephone: 2240
Telegrams: Maschexport, Berlin
Telex: 112461

Products: Locomotives; freight wagons; passenger coaches.

Constitution: The exporter of motive power and rolling stock built in the German Democratic Republic. The name was changed from Maschinen-Export in 1979.

Schindler
Schindler Carriage & Wagon Co Ltd

4133 Pratteln, near Basle, Switzerland

Telephone: 061 84 91 11
Telegrams: Schindlerwagon, Pratteln
Telex: 968010

Managing Director: P Piffaretti
Technical Director and Director of Works: H Knecht
Sales Manager: R Meury

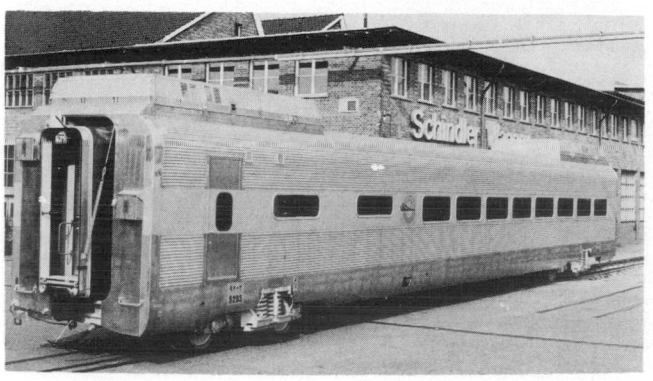

Passenger car for Saudi Arabia

Products: Electric and diesel railcars for all track gauges; passenger and freight cars.

Interior of first-class passenger coach for Saudi Arabia

LRVs for Neuchâtel Public Transport (TN) 600 V dc narrow-gauge system

Three-car emu for 15 kV 16⅔ Hz ac Bern-Lötschberg-Simplon Railway (BLS)

Schlieren
Swiss Car and Elevator Manufacturing Corp Ltd

8952 Schlieren, Switzerland

Telephone: 01 730 70 11
Telegrams: Schlieco, Schlieren
Telex: 52961

Delegate of Board of Directors: Fritz Keller
Director, Rolling Stock: Pierre Matthey
Director, Works: Helmut Agustoni

Products: Passenger coaches, motor coaches and driving trailers in all-welded steel lightweight and light alloy design; RIC couchette coaches; car transport vehicles; motor luggage cars; wagon bogies for freightliner trains, motor and trailer bogies for all types of rolling stock; streetcars, articulated twin streetcars; lifting jacks for rail and road vehicles as well as for big containers.

Constitution: The company was formed in 1899 for the manufacture of rolling stock, and an elevator department was started in 1917.

Interior of SBB's couchette coach

RIC-UIC passenger coach, series Bcm Z1 type (couchette coach) for Swiss Federal Railways

Schöma
Christoph Schöttler Maschinenfabrik GmbH

Postfach 1509, 2840 Diepholz 1, Federal Republic of Germany

Telephone: 05441 2047/2048
Telegrams: Schöma, Diepholz
Telex: 09 41217

Manager: Ing Fritz Schöttler
Sales Manager: Ing L Niermeyer

Products: Shunting, narrow gauge and mining locomotives with hydro-dynamic, hydrostatic or mechanical transmission; gang trolleys; trailers and diesel railcars.

The company has extended its product range to locomotives of 45 tonnes weight and 350 kW output. Recent sales have included 13 diesel-hydraulic underground locomotives of 24 tonnes and 185 hp for Arge Walgaustollen in Vorarlberg, Austria; eight three-axle diesel-hydraulic locomotives of 18 tonnes and 240 hp for an Egyptian sugar factory and a further order for five 24-tonne 250 hp diesel-hydraulic underground locomotives for Mass Transit Railway Corporation, Hong Kong, making a total order of 18 for construction of the Hong Kong MTR.

250 hp, 24-tonne diesel-hydraulic locomotive for construction of Hong Kong metro

SEMAF
Société Générale Egyptienne de Matériel des Chemins de Fer

Ein Helwan, Cairo, Egypt

Telephone: 782358; 782177
Telegrams: SEMAF, Ein Helwan
Telex: 92364

Chairman: Eng T El-Maghraby

Technical Director: Eng H El-Bariksy
Commercial Manager: M Habib

Products: Passenger cars, post and baggage cars, perishables and parcels vans, hospital coaches, railcar/trailers, trams and metro cars, freight wagons of all types.
Recent production has included 10 tramcars for Alexandria, 18 metro cars for Cairo, 120 passenger cars for Egyptian National Railways and 1400 freight wagons of various types for ENR Iron Steel & Phosphate Co.

Severin
Severin Car Works

Str Dunarii 3, Drobeta-Turnu Severin, Romania

Telephone: 978 12414
Telex: 42233

Products: Passenger and freight cars.

SFL
Société Française de Locotracteurs

40 boulevard Henri Sellier, 92150 Suresnes, France

Telephone: (1) 506 15 74
Telex: 614720

Products: Diesel-electric, diesel-hydraulic and electric shunting locomotives of 150 to 1500 bhp at weights up to about 100 tonnes for standard, broad and narrow gauge.
The group's latest products include a heavy-duty unit of 1000 hp conceived primarily for steel industry use, designed for adaptability to a variety of engines and transmissions, and for equipment as desired with dynamic braking, creep

control and for remote operation. A dominant item in the group's recent production has been the construction for French Railways (SNCF) of 285 Type Y8000 diesel-hydraulic shunters; these are two-axle machines with a 300 hp Poyaud engine, Voith L24sU2 transmission, cardan shaft drive and a weight of 36 tonnes. Other shunter orders have been processed for Algeria, Senegal, Madagascar and Tunisia. The group's output is characterised by modular design for standardisation of parts and sub-assemblies and similarly by use of printed circuit electronic modules to minimise electro-mechanical switchgear. Extras such as constant speed or creep control and automatic wheel-slip safeguards are available throughout the group's range.

Constitution: The Société Française de Locotracteurs, created in 1980, pools the technological experience, research, design and manufacturing of five well-known French rolling stock companies: Ets Fauvet-Girel, Alsthom-Atlantique, Société MTE, De Dietrich, Carel Fouché.

1000 bhp diesel-electric shunting locomotive

Type Y8000 300 bhp diesel-hydraulic shunting locomotive for French Railways (SNCF)

SGI
Società Gestioni Industriali SpA

48 Via Adriano Cecchetti, 62012 Civitanova Marche, Italy

Telephone: (0733) 72 918/770 555
Telegrams: Rotabili, Civitanova Marche
Telex: 560 896

Managers: Dott Giuseppe Manni (administration and sales)
Dott Ing Giorgio Caputo (technical and production)

Products: Freight cars of all types, pressure tank cars for compressed gas and acids; refrigerator cars; special tanks for motor vehicles.

Constitution: In 1957 SGI took over the business of Costruzioni Meccaniche A Cecchetti, which had been wound up previously, having been operating since 1892.

S-G-P
Simmering-Graz-Pauker AG

Head office: Mariahilfer Strasse 32, 1071 Vienna, Austria

Telephone: 02 22/93 05 21
Telegrams: Esgepe, Vienna
Telex: 32574/01 32767

Products: Electric locomotives, diesel locomotives, rack locomotives, shunting locomotives; electric railcars, diesel railcars, rack railcars; passenger coaches, service coaches, ambulance cars, wagons, special goods wagons, low platform wagons; tramways, underground railway stock and suburban trains.
The company's range includes two types of low-platform piggyback wagons with small-wheeled, four-axle bogies and movable headstocks allowing roll-on/roll-off loading over end ramps. Details are as follows:

Type E

Track gauge	1435 mm
Tread circle diameter	355 mm
Trough length	13 000 mm
Length over couplings	13 540 mm
Max width of wagon	3120 mm
Max speed	120 km/h
Tare weight	15.4 tonnes
Total payload capacity	32 tonnes
Max load over one bogie	22 tonnes

Type L

Track gauge	1435 mm
Tread circle diameter	355 mm
Trough length	18 000 mm
Length over couplings	18 540 mm
Max width of wagon	3080 mm
Max speed	120 km/h
Tare weight	18 tonnes
Total payload capacity	38 tonnes
Max load over one bogie	21 tonnes

Constitution: Simmering-Graz-Pauker AG comprises three works: two in Vienna and one in Graz. Sole shareholder is the Republic of Austria.

S-G-P low platform wagon for highway trucks, trailers and semi-trailers

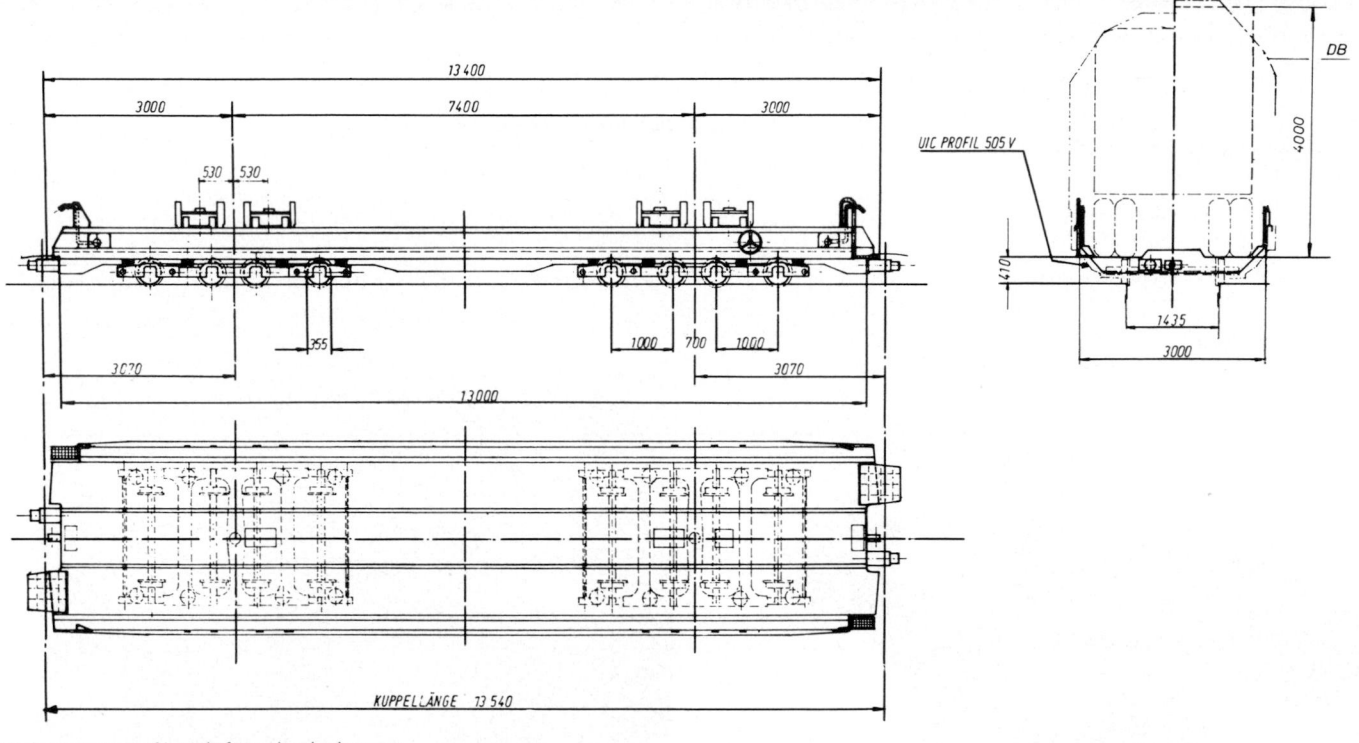

General arrangement of low-platform piggyback wagon

Siam SA
Division Electromecanica

Derqui 1868, San Justo, Buenos Aires, Argentina

Telephone: 651 0020/9
Telegrams: Siam BAires
Telex: 24181

Products: Electrical equipment for diesel and electric locomotives.

Siemens
Siemens Aktiengesellschaft
Power Engineering Group, Railway Department

Werner-von-Siemens-Strasse 50, Postfach 32 40, 8520 Erlangen 2, Federal Republic of Germany

Telephone: (09131) 71
Telegrams: Siemens, Erlangen
Telex: 6 29871

Director of Transportation Department: Eberhard Kill
Director of Rolling Stock Department: Gerhard Scholtis

Products: Electric and diesel-electric vehicles and associated electrical equipment for main-line, inter-urban, urban rapid transit, underground, narrow-gauge, industrial and mine railways, and also for trolleybus systems; power transmission and overhead contact wires including accessories and fittings, traction power supply equipment; electrical equipment for railway stations and workshops.

Recent contracts have included electrical equipment for two batches of Class 111 electric locomotives, each of nine units, for delivery to German Federal Railway (DB) in 1983-84.

Class 7E thyristor-controlled locomotive for South African Railways, with electrical equipment by the 50 c/s Group

Class 111 Bo-Bo of German Federal Railway (DB) heading 'Austria Express' (Amsterdam-Klagenfurt) over Austrian Federal (ÖBB) track at Kolbnitz *(John C Baker)*

SIG
Schweizerische Industrie-Gesellschaft
Swiss Industrial Company

8212 Neuhausen Rhine Falls, Switzerland

Telephone: 053/8 61 11
Telegrams: SIG, Neuhausenamrheinfall
Telex: 7 68 02

Chairman of the Board: Fritz Halm
Managing Director: Wolfgang Gähwyler

Director: Peter Gsell

Products: High-speed air-sprung and other types of power and trailer bogies for all kinds of rail rolling stock; specific designs of draught-free, dust- and waterproof inter-car gangway crossovers for urban, suburban, inter-urban and long-distance rolling stock.
Battery and trolley locomotives for mining, tunnelling and surface applications, including flameproof locomotives for operation in gaseous mines.

Constitution: Founded in 1853 for the manufacture of railway rolling stock.

Latest design of SIG high-speed bogie for operation at up to 200 km/h

15-20-tonne narrow-gauge electric tunnelling and mining locomotive with integral solid state control

Simplex
Simplex Mechanical Handling Ltd
Subsidiary of Wemyss & Wenham Ltd

Simplex Works, Elstow Road, Bedford, Bedfordshire MK42 9LB, England

Telephone: 0234 56422
Telegrams: Simplex, Bedford
Telex: 82254

Chairman: A M J Wemyss
Managing Director: R A Wenham

Products: Narrow-gauge diesel-mechanical and diesel-hydraulic locomotives: G Series 2¼-3 tons, 40S Series 2½-4½ tons, 60S Series 4-6 tons, U Series 5-10 tons, T Series 9-12½ tons.

Type T hydro-kinetic locomotive powered by Dorman 6 DA engine

Type 60 SD locomotive powered by Deutz F 4L 912 air-cooled diesel engine

Skoda
Skoda, Plzen

Namesti Ceskych Bratri 8, 31600 Plzen, Czechoslovakia

Telephone: 211
Telegrams: Skoda, Plzen
Telex: 154221

Export sales: Skodaexport, Vaclavske 56, Prague

Telephone: 240851
Telegrams: Skodaexport, Prague
Telex: 122413

Products: Electric locomotives.

Type 63E 4080 kW express locomotive for Soviet Railways (SZD)

Type 68E 3020 kW mixed traffic locomotive for Bulgarian State Railways (BDZ)

Type 62E 4920 kW Bo-Bo for Soviet Railways (SZD)

Type 78E1 760 kW Bo-Bo for Czechoslovak State Railways (ČSD)

Type 58E 4800 kW Bo-Bo+Bo-Bo for Czechoslovak State Railways (ČSD)

Type 66E 8000 kW Bo-Bo+Bo-Bo for Soviet Railways (SZD)

Skoda electric locomotives in production

Class*	Wheel arrangement	Line voltage	Rated output (kW) continuous/ one-hour	Max speed km/h	Weight tonnes	No in service	Year first built	Builders Mechanical parts	Electrical equipment
62E/CS4 (SZD)	Co-Co	25 kV, 50 Hz ac	4920/5100	160	126	520	1971	Skoda	Skoda
66E/CS200 50E/CS6 (SZD)	Bo-Bo + Bo-Bo	3 kV	8000/8400	200 160	156 162	40	1976	Skoda	Skoda
58E/E479.1 (ČSD)	Bo-Bo + Bo-Bo	3 kV	4800/5000	100	165	50	1980	Skoda	Skoda
78E/E458.1 (ČSD)	Bo-Bo	3 kV	760/900	80	72	35	1981	Skoda	Skoda

*SZD: Soviet Railways
 ČSD: Czechoslovak State Railways

SLM
Schweizerische Lokomotiv-und Maschinenfabrik
Swiss Locomotive and Machine Works

8401 Winterthur, Switzerland

Telephone: 052 85 41 41
Telegrams: Locomotive, Winterthur
Telex: 896 131

President, Board of Management: Rudolph Schmid
General Manager: K Vogel
Commercial Department, Deputy Vice President: Dr M Knüsli
Technical Department, Assistant Vice President: E Künzler
Works Department, Assistant Vice President: O Heiniger
Sales Department, Assistant Vice President: W Grutter

Products: Electric and thermal main-line and shunting vehicles for adhesion railways; electric and diesel traction units for rack railways, including traction units for combined rack and adhesion operation; special-purpose rail vehicles; industrial gears; gears for special vehicles.

Recent production has included six diesel rack and adhesion locomotives for the Indonesian State Railways, whose 1067 mm gauge system in West Sumatra features rack sections with maximum gradients of 7·2 per cent between Padang, Padang-Pangjang and Solok. Parts of the line, which is chiefly occupied with coal movement, are fitted with the Riggenbach rack rail of Swiss origin. SLM has been the overall contractor for the order. The resultant Type HGm4/6 locomotive weighs 55 tonnes and has an MTU engine rated at 905 kW (1230 hp) with a Voith hydrostatic drive and BBC electrical equipment. Its maximum speed in adhesion working is 60 km/h, on the rack 20 km/h.

Type Ee 6/6 II electric shunting locomotive for Swiss Federal Railways with BBC Brown Boveri electrical equipment

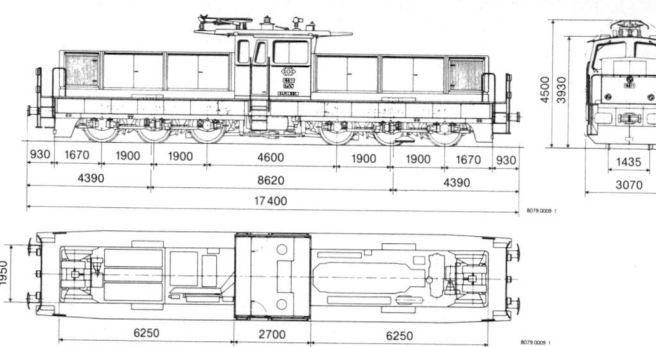

General arrangement of SBB Type Ee 6/6II

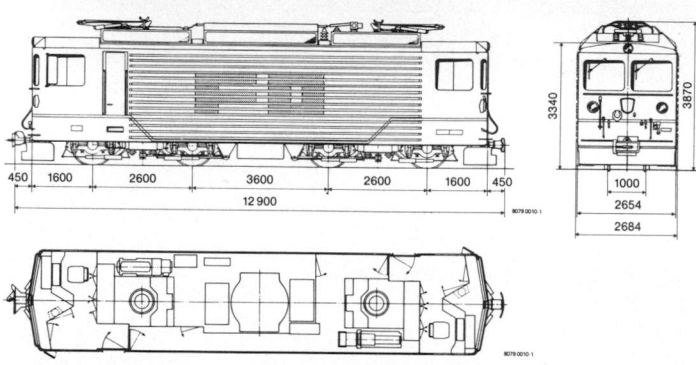

General arrangement of Furka-Oberalp Type GE 4/4III Bo-Bo

Furka-Oberalp Type Deh 4/4II rack-and-adhesion baggage power car, able to haul 4-5 cars up FOB's maximum 17.9% gradients

Furka-Oberalp Type Ge 4/4III thyristor-controlled locomotive for new Furka Tunnel car-carrying shuttle trains, able to start 350 tonnes on 3% gradient and ascend 1.8% at 80 km/h

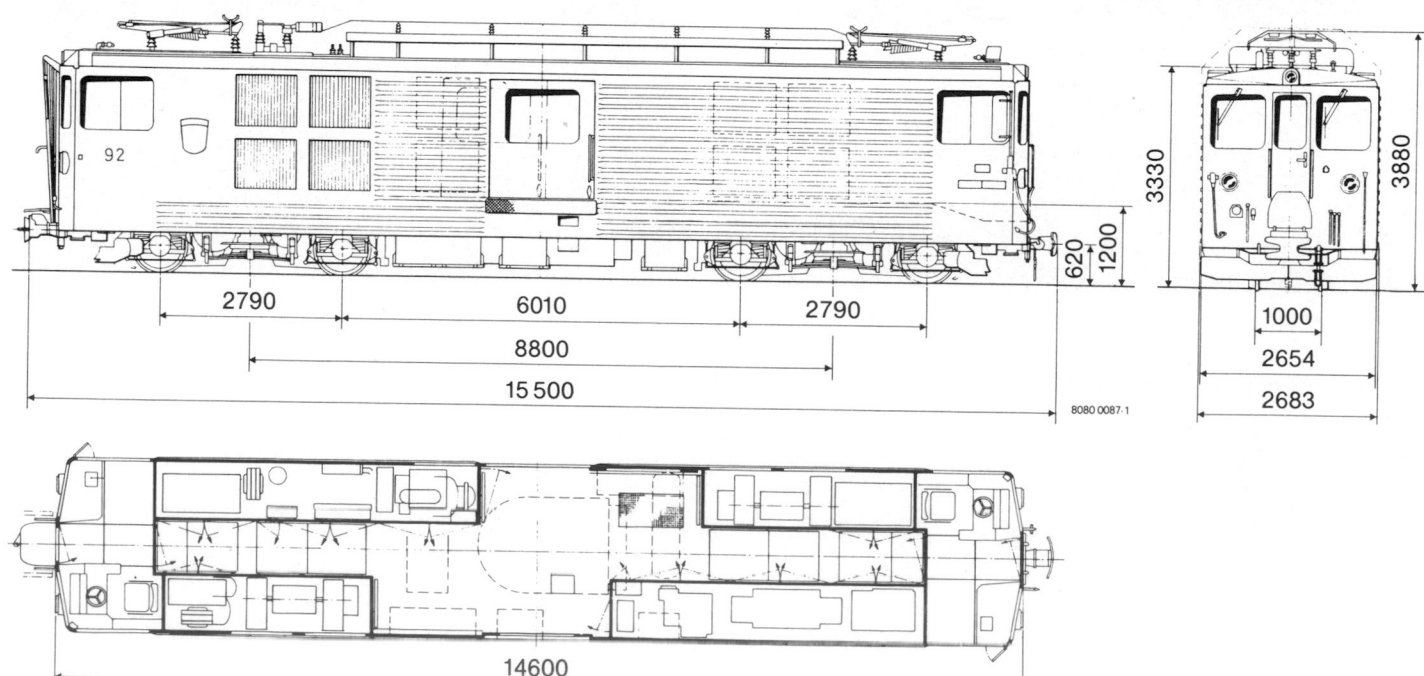

General arrangement of Furka-Oberalp Type Deh 4/4II, with lightweight steel body

Type HGm4/6 rack and adhesion diesel locomotive for Indonesian State Railways

Type Bhe 4/8 800 kW train-set with all bogies motored on one axle for rack-assisted Monte Generoso Railway, Switzerland

SLM electric locomotives

Class	Wheel arrangement	Gauge mm	Line voltage	Rated output (kW) continuous/ one-hour	Tractive effort continuous/ one-hour (kN)	at speed (km/h)	Max speed km/h	Weight tonnes	Transmission ratio	No in service	Year first built	Builders	
												Mechanical parts	Electrical equipment
SBB Ee 6/6II	Co-Co	1435	15 kV	730/860	353/305	0.10/10.2	85	106	1:7.69	10	1980	SLM	BBC Brown Boveri
Furka-Oberalp Deh 4/4II	Bo-Bo	1000	11 kV	936/1032	101.2/117.7	31.4/29.9	60	51	—	6	1980	SLM	BBC Brown Boveri
Furka-Oberalp Ge 4/4II	Bo-Bo	1000	11 kV	1520/1700	101.5/113.8	53/52	90	50	17:87	2	1980	SLM	BBC Brown Boveri

SNAV
Société Nouvelle des Ateliers Vénissieux

40 boulevard Henri Sellier, 92150 Suresnes, France

Telephone: 506 15 74
Telegrams: Fauvgir
Telex: 611 486

President: J Dambrine
Assistant General Managers: Jacques Martin
Georges Reille
Commercial Director: Joachim Lagall

Products: Railway wagons; ISO containers.

SNIA
Divisione Ingegneria

18 via Montebello, 20121 Milan, Italy

Telephone: (02) 63321
Telex: 320 503

Products: Electric locomotives; suburban train-sets; passenger coaches; freight wagons; refrigerator wagons; containers.

Socimi
Società Costruzioni Industriali Milano SpA

Head office: via S Calimero 3, 20122 Milan, Italy

Telephone: 02 5465251/5
Telex: 310331

Works: 20082 Binasco (Milan) Telephone: 02 9055605/6/7/8
07100 Sassari Telephone: 079 235056
20010 Arluno (Milan) Telephone: 02 9017666/9017803

Chairman: Dr Eng Alessandro Marzocco
Managing Director: Dr Eng Pierino Sacchi
Marketing Director: Dr Eng Corrado Lamdolina

Products: Electric train-sets for suburban railways and transit systems, diesel locomotives, passenger coaches, sleeping cars, trams, freight wagons to UIC and AAR specifications, motor and trailer bogies.

Type 214 130 hp diesel-hydraulic shunter for Italian State Railways (FS)

Commuter coach for Ferrovie Nord Milano (FNM)

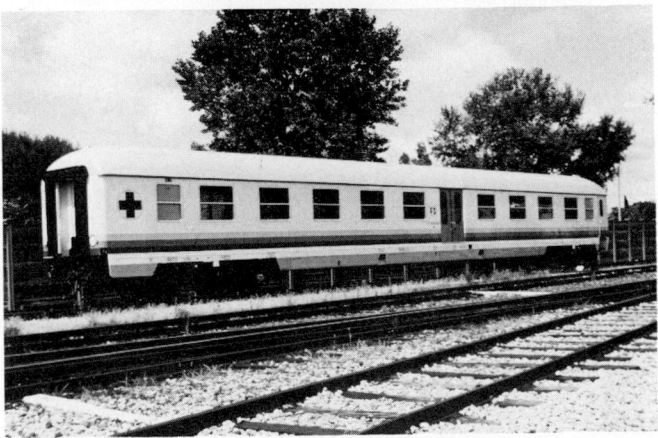

Ambulance car for pilgrimage traffic of Italian State Railways (FS)

SOFER
SOFER—Officine Ferroviarie, SpA

Via Miliscola 33, Pozzuoli (Naples), Italy

Telephone: 867 25 22 (PBX)
Telegrams: SOFER, Pozzuoli
Telex: 710048

Chairman: Dr Ing Giuseppe Capuano
General Manager: Dr Ing Giovanni Alfano

Products: Electric, diesel-electric and diesel-hydraulic locomotives; electric and diesel train-sets; diesel and electric railcars; trailers; passenger coaches of all types and classes; luggage and mail vans; motor and carrying bogies for articulated electric train-sets.

Italian State Railways (FS) Class E656 3 kV dc Bo-Bo-Bo under construction

Soferval
Société Soferval

49 avenue George V, 75008 Paris, France

Telephone: 723 56 24
Telex: 290 060

Products: Aluminium-bodied metro cars.

Constitution: Soferval was created in September 1980 to take over all activities of Franco-Belge, which had gone into receivership. Participants in Soferval were ANF-Industrie, De Dietrich, CIMT-Lorraine, Arbel, Traction CEM-Oerlikon and Alsthom-Atlantique.

Early in 1982, at the Government's instigation in pursuit of its plans to restructure the French railway supply industry, Soferval was taken over entirely by Alsthom-Atlantique. Soferval production continued with the order for rapid transit cars for MARTA (Atlanta), USA, completion of which has been assured by Alsthom-Atlantique, and on 280 Paris Interconnection cars for SNCF/RATP and 50 Type MF77 Paris Metro cars for RATP.

Soma
Soma Equipamentos Industrias SA

Head office: Parque Industrial Mariano Ferraz, Avenida Soma 700, Sumaré, São Paulo, Brazil

Telephone: (0192) 73 1000
Telex: 019 1923

São Paulo office: Avenida Brigadeiro Faria Lima, 1709, 7° Andar, Conjumto 7A, São Paulo

Telephone: 210 2218; 212 5311
Telegrams: Somafer
Telex: (011) 23692

Products: Battery locomotives; freight cars; tank cars; refrigerator cars; ore cars; ingot cars; hopper cars; car building, repairing, maintenance and leasing.

Recent products include a 14-tonne, flameproofed mining locomotive, manufactured under licence from Arn Jung Lokomotivfabrik of Kirchen, Federal Republic of Germany, with an output of 49.2 kW.

Constitution: The company was founded in 1929 and was the first company in South America to manufacture freight cars. It has specialised in the development of refrigerator cars and tank cars which are leased to various transport concerns.

Flameproof mining locomotive by Soma

Sorefame
Sociedades Reunidas de Fabricações Metálicas, SARL

Head office: Rua Vice-Almirante Azevedo Coutinho, PO Box 5, 2701 Amadora, Portugal

Telephone: 97 60 51
Telegrams: Sorefame, Amadora
Telex: 12 608/16 101

Works: Amadora

Chairman: Carlos Montez Melancia
Rolling Stock Division Manager: M Andrade Gomes

Products: Diesel and electric locomotives, diesel and electric multiple-unit train-sets, diesel and electric railcars, passenger cars.

The company's recent products include an order of 30 diesel-electric locomotives of C-C wheel arrangement for Portuguese Railways (CP). Built under licence from Alsthom-Atlantique, the design features an SACM AGO-240 V12 DSHR engine with a 3000 hp rating at 1350 rpm, coupled to an Alsthom-Atlantique ac generator. Overall length of the locomotive is 19.08 metres, width 3 metres and maximum height 4.2 metres. At 33 per cent adhesion the locomotive exerts a starting tractive effort of 40 tonnes and has a maximum speed of 120 km/h. Of the 30-unit order, 13 are equipped with rheostatic as well as air braking; the remainder are fitted with vacuum and air braking.

Among recent rolling stock contracts is one valued at over US$ 18 million from the Benguela Railway for 52 passenger cars and six vans, all in stainless steel; delivery is to begin in 1985 at a rate of four cars a month.

3000 hp diesel-electric C-C for Portuguese Railways (CP)

Constitution: The company was established in 1943, and has supplied rolling stock for Portugal, Africa, North America and Brazil as well as hydro-mechanical equipment for dams, electro-mechanical equipment for hydro-electric and thermal power stations (classical and nuclear) and equipment for the chemical and petroleum industries.

Sorefame electric railcars or multiple-units

Class	Cars per unit	Line voltage	Motor cars per unit	Motored axles per motor car	Rated output (kW) per motor	Max speed km/h	Weight tonnes per car (M-motor T-trailer)	Total seating capacity	Length per car mm	No in service	Rate of acceleration m/s²	Year first built	Builders Mechanical parts	Builders Electrical equipment
2101	3	25 kV	1	4	260	120	M 61 / T 33	60 / 96	22 620 / 22 820	24	0.64	1972	Sorefame	AEG-BB Oerlikon Siemens
2151	3	25 kV	1	4	260	120	M 61 / T 33	60 / 96	22 620 / 22 820	18	0.64	1976	Sorefame	AEG-BB Oerlikon Siemens
2201	3	25 kV	1	4	260	120	M 61 / T 33	60 / 96	22 620 / 22 820	15	0.64	1983	Sorefame	AEG-BB Oerlikon Siemens
BM 204 AC$_1$ 204 AC$_2$ 204 BD 204	4	1.5 kV dc	1	4	96	90	M 49 / T$_1$ 28 / T$_2$ 28 / T$_3$ 27	64 / 63 / 63 / 68	19 000 / 19 000 / 19 000 / 19 000	6	0.35-0.5	1970	Sorefame	GEC
M 215 C$_1$ 215 C$_2$ 215 Cl 215	4	1.5 kV dc	1	4	96	90	M 49 / T$_1$ 28 / T$_2$ 28 / T$_3$ 27	64 / 63 / 63 / 68	19 000 / 19 000 / 19 000 / 19 000	8	0.35-0.5	1977	Sorefame	GEC
M 199 C$_1$ 119 C$_2$ 119	3	1.5 kV dc	1	4	96	90	M 49 / T 28	64 / 63	19 000 / 19 000	6	0.35-0.5	1977	Sorefame	GEC
9500	3	3 kV dc	1	4	259	90	M 46 / T 32 / T 27	180	M 19 550 / T 19 200	50	1.1	1979	Consortium (Sorefame, Mafersa, ACEC, Villares)	Electrocarril
M 100	2	750 V dc	2	4	217	72	31	80	16 000	28	1.1	1983	Sorefame Alsthom-Atlantique (MTE for bogies)	Siemens

Sorefame diesel railcars or multiple-units

Class	Cars per unit	Motor cars per unit	Motored axles per motor car	Trans-mission	Rated power (kW) per motor	Max speed km/h	Weight tonnes per car (M-motor)	Total seating capacity	Length per car mm	No in service	Year first built	Builders Mechanical parts	Builders Engine & type	Builders Transmission
600	2	2	2	Mech	386	120	M 55 / M 51	175	25 880	20	1978	Sorefame EMG	Creusot-Loire Saurer SDHR 1	Voith Type T420

Sorefame diesel locomotives

Class	Wheel arrangement	Transmission	Rated power (kW)	Max speed km/h	Total weight tonnes	No in service	Year first built	Builders Mechanical parts	Builders Engine & type	Builders Transmission
CC-3000	Co-Co	Elec	2425	120	120	30	1980-81	Sorefame Alsthom-Atlantique	SACM AGO V12 DSHR	Alsthom-Atlantique

Soulé
Soulé-Fer et Froid

PO Box 1, 65200 Bagnères-de-Bigorre, France

Telephone: (62) 95 07 31
Telegrams: Soulé-Bagnères de Bigorre
Telex: 530 179

Chairman: André de Boysson
Sales Director: Dominique Outters
Technical Manager: Guy Thomas
General Secretary: Frederic De St Sernin

Second-class day coach for Gabon State Railways (OCTRA)

Soulé Type Y500 bogie

Soulé Type Y600 bogie

Products: Diesel railcars and trailers; passenger cars; insulated and mechanically refrigerated wagons; postal vans.

The company has developed a range of diesel-electric railcars, in a design adaptable to 1000, 1067 or 1435 mm gauge, which is specially conceived to suit operation in equatorial and tropical territory. The vehicle is offered with a single bogie powered with two motors, with each bogie powered by two motors, or with a single motor on each bogie, so that total output can range from 592 to 937 hp for a tare weight ranging from 44 to 54.5 tonnes. Body length is 23.1 metres. A railcar with 937 hp output can sustain a maximum speed of 110 km/h on straight and level track with a trailing load of 186 tonnes, within which total seating accommodation in railcar and trailers of approximately 700 is possible. The design allows for equipment with air conditioning as an optional extra.

Similarly developed for tropical areas, the company's range of passenger cars offers interior day, restaurant, sleeping berth and couchette layouts within a standard 22.32-metre body-shell of semi-stainless steel, at tare weights ranging from 28 to 35.5 tonnes. The company also offers passenger cars of 17.5- or 20-metre lengths, at tare weights ranging from 19 to 23 tonnes.

The car bogies are also manufactured by Soulé. Two types are available, the Y500 for a maximum axleload of 10 tonnes, and the Y600 for a maximum of 13 tonnes.

Constitution: Founded in 1862.

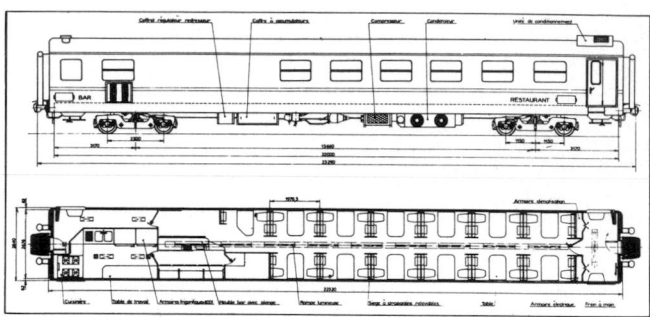

Restaurant car layout in standard 22.32 m body-shell

Diesel-electric railcar and train on Benin-Niger Railway (OCBN)

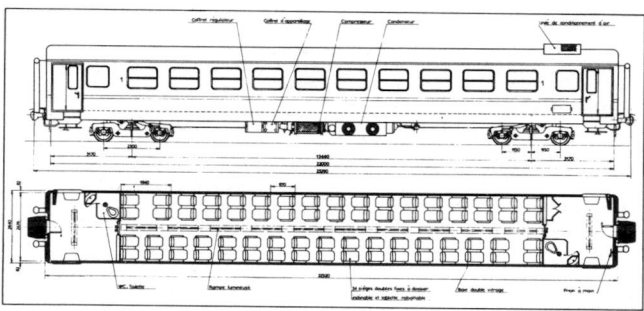

First-class car layout in standard 22.32 m body-shell

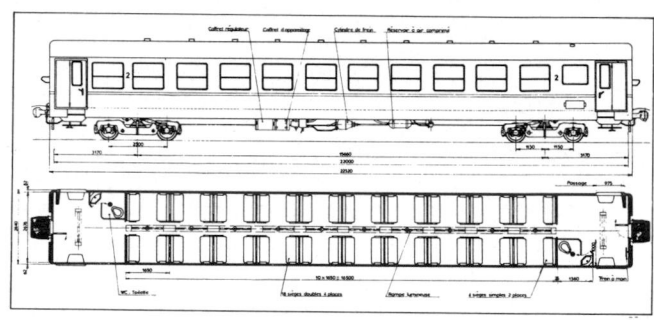

Second-class car layout in standard 22.32 m body-shell

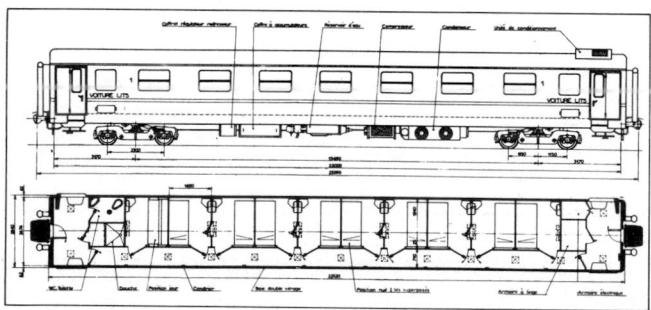

Sleeping-car layout in standard 22.32 m body-shell

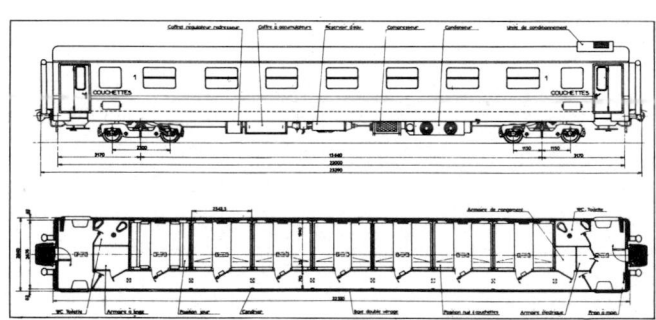

Couchette car layout in standard 22.32 m body-shell

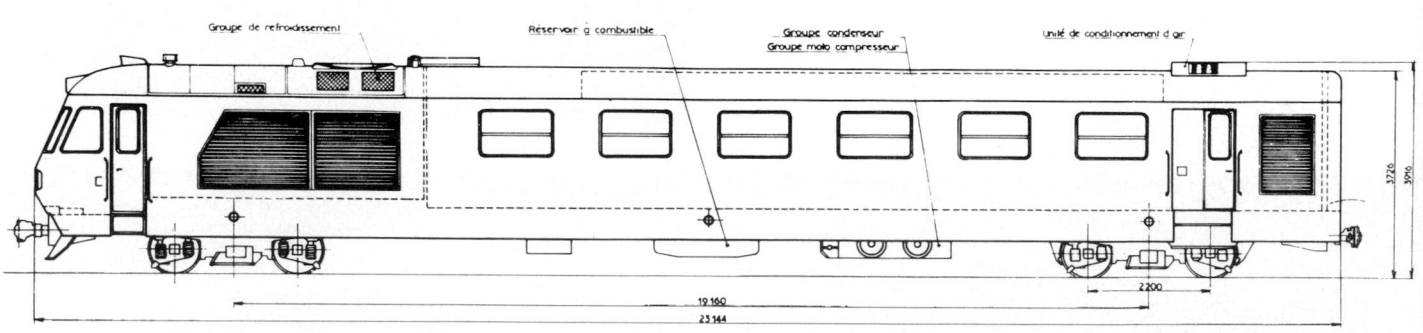

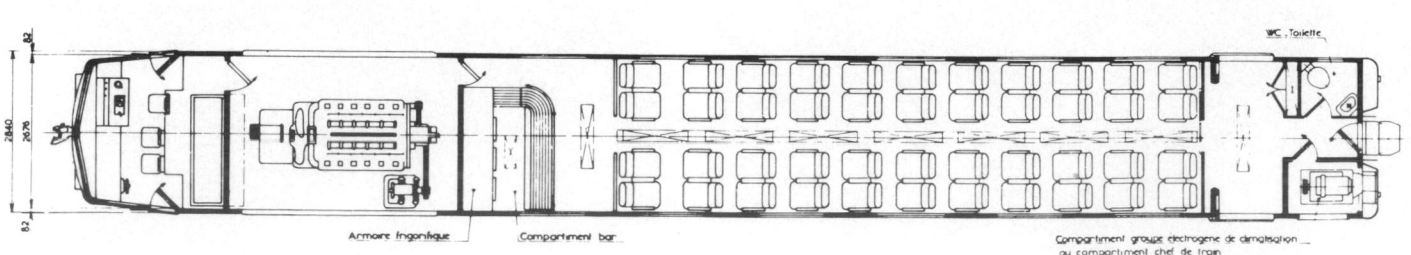

Layout of Soulé diesel railcar

Soulé single diesel railcars

Motored axles per car	Transmission	Rated power (kW) per motor	Max speed km/h	Weight tonnes	Total seating capacity	Length per car m	No in service	Year first built	Builders		
									Mechanical parts	Engine & type	Transmission
2	Elec	400	90	43	30-50	22.5	30	1965	Alsthom	SACM	Alsthom
2	Elec	400	90	39	30-50	17.5	5	1967	Alsthom	Poyaud	Alsthom
4	Elec	620	110	52	30-50	22.5	8	1969	CEM	Poyaud	CEM
2	Elec	700	110	52	30-50	22.5	2	1973	Alsthom	SACM	Alsthom
2	Elec	700	110	54	30-50	23.5	7	1976	Alsthom	SACM	Alsthom
4	Elec	700	110	56	30-50	23.5	2	1977	CEM	SACM	CEM
2	Elec	700	110	52	30-50	18	2	1982	Alsthom	SACM	Alsthom

Southern Iron
Southern Iron & Equipment Manufacturing Operations

PO Box 48500, 5000 Old Peachtree Road, Doraville, Georgia 30362, USA

Telephone: (404) 448 1800

President, Railcar Division: C Richard Barney

Vice President, Sales: Jack Foster
Director, Manufacturing: W R Walker

Products: Freight cars, freight car leasing.

Constitution: Southern Iron was founded in 1889 and is now a division of Evans Transportation Co, a wholly-owned subsidiary of Evans Products Co.

Stag
Stag Ltd

7304 Maienfeld, Switzerland

Telephone: 085 9 19 02
Telex: 7 42 69

Products: Tank wagons for the transport of dry flowable materials with pneumatic discharge.

Four-axle cement wagon in service in Thailand

Standard
The Standard Railway Wagon Co Ltd
A Mercantile Credit Co

Head office and main works: Green Lane, Heywood, Lancashire OL10 1NB, England

Telephone: 0706 64135/9
Telegrams: Wagons, Heywood
Telex: 63327

Other works: Roland Road, Reddish, Stockport, Cheshire

Chairman: P R Pollard
Managing Director: L T Reddy
Commercial Manager: P E Etherington

Products: Freight cars of all types.

Subsidiary: Railease Ltd (provides finance facilities, leasing and hiring).

Constitution: The L & Y Works at Heywood have been building railway wagons for over a century.

Bogie oil tank wagon for Bangladesh Railway

88-tonne glw pressure-discharge cement wagon

Steel Industries
K T Steel Industries Pvt, Ltd

KT Building, Broach Street, Bombay 400 026, India

Telephone: 36 35 03
Telegrams: Metticorail, Bombay
Telex: 011 2649

Chairman: T K Gupta
Chief Sales Director: N K Gupta
Export Sales Director: S R Gupta

Products: Rolling stock. In addition to supplying wagons for the home market,

Steel Industries has built mineral wagons for Iranian State Railways and supplied wagon spares to the Sri Lanka Government Railway.

Insulated milk tanker with 40 000-litre stainless-steel tank capacity

Steele
Steele & Co Ltd

25 Dalziel Street, Hamilton, Lanarkshire ML3 9AU, Scotland

Telephone: 0698 283765
Telegrams: Mountings, Hamilton
Telex: 77454

Associated company: SA Ateliers de Construction de Jambes-Namur, Belgium

Directors: E G Steele
D A Steele
M S Steele
J G Steele

Products: Locopulsor shunting machines; wagon spares.

Constitution: E G Steele & Co is a rolling stock contractor, hirer, repairer, and supplier of wagon spares. It also supplies purpose-built wagons for internal works traffic, and is the British Commonwealth supplier of the Locopulsor shunting machines.

Strojexport
(Czechoslovak foreign trade corporation for the export and import of machines and machinery equipment)

PO Box 662, Václavské n 56, Prague 1, Czechoslovakia

Telephone: 2131
Telegrams: Strojexport, Prague
Telex: 121671

Products: Strojexport handles all transactions for the export of passenger and freight rolling stock built by Czechoslovak Wagon Works.

Strömberg
Oy Strömberg Ab

PO Box 118, 00101 Helsinki 10, Finland

Telephone: 358 0 5641
Telegrams: Dynamo, Helsinki
Telex: 125386

Chairman: Mika Tiivola
Managing Director: Antti Potila
Chief Sales Director: Lars-Erik Hukkinen
Export Sales Director, Electric Drives: Vesa Kivinen

Manager, Electric Traction Systems: Veikko Hyvärinen
Sales Manager, Electric Traction Systems: Keijo Karhä

Products: Electric drives, especially traction drives for trains, undergrounds, locomotives, trams and trolleybuses.
Recent deliveries have included ac traction drives for 10 articulated trolleybuses by Adolph Saurer AG and E Frech & Hoch for the Winterthur municipal traffic authority, Switzerland; and for 33 articulated tramcars for the Rotterdam systems, for which the main contractors were Duewag of West Germany and Alpha Engineering of the Netherlands.
The company has been selected to participate in a demonstration programme of advanced metro car drives together with Garrett Corporation, with which Strömberg has a co-operation and licensing agreement.

Strømmens
A/S Strømmens Vaerksted

PO Box 83, 2011 Strommen, Norway

Telephone: (02) 717301
Telegrams: Verkstedet, Strømmen
Telex: 71 551

Managing Director: P Hauan

Technical Director: H S Svendsen

Products: Electric train-sets; diesel railcars; passenger and freight cars of all types; tramcars and subway cars; containers.

Constitution: The company was established in 1873 for the manufacture of railway rolling stock and is now the only car builder in Norway. It took over the rolling stock building activities of A/S SKABO in 1960 and A/S HÖKA in 1968. In 1979 the company became a subsidiary of NEBB, the Norwegian member of the Brown Boveri Group.

Swidnca
Wagony-Swidnca Factory

ul 35, Swidnca 58-100, Poland

Telephone: 29 83/29 89
Telex: 034222

Export sales: Kolmex, 49 Mokotowska, 00-542 Warsaw

Products: Tank wagons, flat wagons, self-discharging wagons and containers.

Tafesa
Construccion y Reparacion de Material Ferroviario

Carretera de Villaverde a Vallecas 16, Madrid 21, Spain

Telephone: 798 0454 58/62/66; 7978 300; 7978 304
Telex: 42283

General Manager: M A Simon Langarica

Products: All types of freight rolling stock, special containers, bogies and brake shoes.
Recent output has included 1000 covered wagons for Transfesa and 300 wagons for SEMAT. New developments include a dual-purpose container-carrying and piggyback wagon, and an air-discharge cement wagon.

Talbot
Waggonfabrik Talbot

Postfach 1410, Jülicherstrasse 213-237, 5100 Aachen, Federal Republic of Germany

Telephone: 0241 18210
Telegrams: Talbot, Aachen
Telex: 08 32 845

Products: Electric and diesel railcars; passenger carriages; open and covered goods wagons.
In addition to conventional stock, Talbot develops, designs and builds goods wagons with special features, such as: high-capacity wagons; sliding wall wagons with or without movable partitions and wagons with swivelling or rolling roof; self-discharging wagons for transport of bulk materials, eg saddle-bottomed wagons, wagons with rotary slide valves and bottom self-dischargers (for the transport of bulk material sensitive to moisture these wagons can be

Type Sdkms 'pocket' wagon for transport of craneable semi-trailers, containers and swop bodies

Type Fals saddle-bottomed wagon with Talbot crankshaft locking gear for bulk transport

equipped with a swivelling roof); intermodal wagons for transport of road vehicles, swop or demountable bodies and containers, such as low-level 'Rolling Highway' wagons, 'pocket' wagons and cushioned container carriers; special wagons for steel mills and mines, such as wagons with or without telescopic hoods for transport of coils, wagons for transport of plates, wagons for transport of glass panes, garbage vans, mail and luggage vans, service wagons for

building, ballasting and maintenance of tracks; containers and swop or demountable bodies with folding side walls.

Constitution: This is the oldest West German railway rolling stock manufacturer, founded in 1838.

Type Sgjkmms bogie wagon with long-travel hydraulic cushion for transport of containers and swop bodies

Type Saadkms 'Rolling Highway' wagon with four-axle bogies, for transport of lorries and trailers, semi-trailers and tractor units, swop bodies and containers

Type Saadkms wagon with retractable headstock for Ro-Ro loading of road tractor-and-trailer rigs

Type Sps flat wagon with stanchions and special securing devices, for lengthy goods, eg tubes, timbers

Type Habis sliding-wall wagon

Type Tagds hopper wagon with swivelling roof for bilateral controlled self-discharge by gravity of bulk traffics sensitive to moisture, eg grain

---

Talgo
Patentes Talgo SA

Montalbán 14, Madrid-14, Spain

Telephone: (91) 222 28 44, 222 74 50
Telegrams: Talgo
Telex: 22184

Products: Lightweight, low centre-of-gravity high-speed passenger equipment employing a patent Talgo system of vehicle suspension and wheel guidance to permit higher curving speed without passenger discomfort or undue wear of track. Each vehicle (except end-cars of a train-set) is carried on a single pair of half-axles with independent wheels. At present the equipment is used exclusively by Spanish National Railways (RENFE). The latest Talgo designs include equipment with automatically adjustable axles for easy through running between Spain and France, and equipment with pendular suspension introduced to revenue service in 1980 (see also under Spanish National Railways).

TCO
Traction CEM-Oerlikon

Head office: 37 rue du Rocher, 75008 Paris, France

Telephone: 522 9840
Telex: 650663

Works: Ornans 25290, Lyon-Villeurbanne 69267

General Manager: C Alleman
Sales Manager: A Thinières
Technical Manager: J P Jouas

Products: Electric and diesel-electric train-sets (railcars and trailers); diesel-electric locomotives of 300 to 1600 hp; metro rolling stock including pneumatic-tyred cars; rapid transit motor cars; traction motors and alternators; static converters for two, three or four-system line inputs up to 450 kW; choppers, main transformers and auxiliaries; high-voltage contactors, electronic control.

The company has supplied the electrical equipment for the 150 four-car Type MI79 emus specially designed for the Paris Interconnection services of French National Railways (SNCF) and Régie Autonome des Transports Parisiens (RATP). For these train-sets CEM-Oerlikon has supplied traction motors and all electrical equipment to suit the dual-voltage 25 kV 50 Hz ac and 1.5 kV dc overhead current systems with which the trains work. A unit has two power cars beneath which each axle is powered to produce a continuous total output of 2792 kW per set, with a maximum speed of 160 km/h; rate of acceleration is 0.85 m/s² and braking is rheostatic or, under 1.5 kV dc catenary, regenerative, combined with air. The thyristor-controlled motor employed, self-ventilated with solvent-free Class H insulation, weighs 2000 kg, has a one-hour rating of 349 kW and operates on 1.5 kV at a continuous 500 amps.

TCO is supplying the electric traction and control equipment, including chopper, traction motor and static converters for auxiliary power supply, for SNCF double-deck emus, the design of which has been developed jointly by ANF, CIMT and TCO. The first series, of which delivery began in 1982, comprises 132 1.5 kV power cars of Type Z2N; these will be followed by 100 dual-voltage 1.5 kV dc/25 kV 50 Hz power cars of Type ZR2N.

There is maximum standardisation in the equipments of both types. Thus in both the traction motors have identical chopper control arrangement; one 300 Hz fixed-frequency chopper with variable conduction time, starting current 850 amps; and one variable-frequency excitation chopper of 350 amps maximum which provides separate excitation of each bogie's two motors on braking (regenerative braking is available on both voltages). Except for roof-mounted apparatus, which includes the automatic voltage changeover sensor and control, and transformer-rectifier assembly in the dual-voltage model, bodywork differences between the two types are minimal, and wiring is greatly simplified. A 30 per cent saving in the electrical equipment's bulk and weight is claimed. The motors, of Type 4FH03262, series-connected on each bogie and suspended from the bogie frame, have the following characteristics: 750 volts, 540 amps,

French Railways Type Z2N double-deck power car, equipped by TCO

375 kW shaft horsepower, 1230 rpm. Thus each power car has a total output of 1500 kW. The static converter has a power of 80 kW and outputs of 220 volts 50 Hz, 880 volts 50 Hz and 72 volts dc. The company reports interest in the double-deck power car equipment from railways in Africa and in both North and South America.

The company has also provided traction motors and all electric traction and control equipment, including traction motor choppers, static converters for auxiliary power supply, and protection, monitoring and control devices, for the fully automated, unmanned two-power-car trains of the new Lille Metro (VAL).

Type MI79 four-car emu for SNCF-RATP Paris Interconnection service

---

Thomas Hill

Thomas Hill (Rotherham) Ltd
Subsidiary of Rolls-Royce Motors Ltd

Vanguard Works, Hooton Road, Kilnhurst, Rotherham, Yorkshire S62 5TD, England

Telephone: 0709 582571
Telegrams: Engine, Rotherham
Telex: 54421

Chairman: S S L Marshall
Managing Director: T W Hill
Marketing Director: J N Capes
Financial and Commercial Director: S B Leyland
Directors: D A Harper
           C A Simpson
           J Moore

Products: The 'Vanguard' locomotive range comprises diesel-hydraulic and diesel-electric locomotives in rigid frame and bogie configurations up to 125 tonnes and 1800 hp. Optional features include: noise-reduced cab (maximum 84 dBA at full power at the driving position); flameproofing (generally to OCMA MEC 1 recommendations, and incorporating full electrical equipment to BS5501 and certified by BASEEFA); mu operation; and radio control.

The 'Vanguard' underground personnel carriers are battery-electric manriders for use in gaseous mines. UPCs are manufactured in six-seat single units or 24-30 articulated units, on rail gauges of 600 to 914 mm.

Recent contracts have included diesel-hydraulic locomotives for defence and petrochemical establishments in the UK and abroad. In addition, 1982 saw the conclusion of a licence agreement with the Varlen Locomotive Corporation, USA, to permit Varlen to manufacture certain 'Vanguard' diesel-hydraulic and diesel-electric models for the North American market.

Constitution: Thomas Hill entered the rail traction market in 1947 marketing the 'Sentinel' locomotive range. Vanguard Works was opened in 1959, since when the company has manufactured locomotives under the 'Vanguard' trade mark. Rolls-Royce secured a controlling interest in the company in 1963, and from 1970/71 transferred production of both the 'Sentinel' and 'Yorkshire' locomotive ranges to Thomas Hill. An extension to the workshop facility was opened in 1978, significantly increasing the manufacturing capacity and improving production facilities.

Thomas Hill (Rotherham) Ltd became a subsidiary of Vickers plc with the amalgamation of Rolls-Royce Motors Ltd and Vickers during 1980.

Vanguard UPC battery electric underground personnel carrier certified for use in coal and other mines

Vanguard 60-tonne, 650 bhp diesel-hydraulic, shaft-drive locomotive

Vanguard 60/70-tonne flameproof locomotive

Thrall
Thrall Car Manufacturing Co

PO Box 218, Chicago Heights, Illinois 60411, USA

Telephone: (312) 757 5900

President: C J Duchossois
Executive Vice President: J A Thrall
Vice President, Sales: W J Somerville
Vice President, Finance: S D Christianson

Products: Freight cars.
Thrall Car has recently delivered the prototype of its lightweight, high-performance articulated flatcar to Trailer Train Co for a programme of static, dynamic and service tests. Designated ARC-5, for 'Articulated Rail Car 5-unit', the piggyback car was engineered by Thrall Car and its Whitehead & Kales Division to meet the rigorous specifications set for Trailer Train's next generation of intermodal equipment. Primary design objectives were greater trailer handling capacity than existing equipment and lighter weight.

With an average weight per individual unit of 24 300 lb, the car is able to carry 40-, 45- and 48-foot trailers, as well as 50-foot trailers with minor modifications. ARC-5 is claimed to be lighter in weight than any other competing single-purpose design capable of carrying a 50-foot trailer. Major structural elements of the 259-foot, five-platform car, including centre sill, crossbearers, end sills, bolsters and side-bearing arms, are of high strength steel. The platform which supports the trailer tyres is of extruded aluminium beams bolted to the car body. These platforms, 31 inches wide by 23 feet long, are located on each side of the centre sill. Each end of the unit is conventionally equipped with couplers and draftgears and bogie-mounted; the three intermediate units are linked by articulated connectors which semi-permanently join the units over a common bogie.

To reduce excess weight, any item weighing more than 20 lb was controlled throughout the design and manufacturing process, including bought-in components. New components and materials were used in uncoupling rods, the brake system and bogies.

As well as being able to carry 40- and 48-foot trailers with nose-mounted refrigerator units, the ARC-5 can accommodate eastern and western US bogie locations, bogie widths of 8 feet 6 inches, and king-pin settings of 36 and 42 inches. With minor equipment additions and easy adjustment of the trailer hitches, a 50-foot dry van may also be carried on each ARC-5 platform. Terminal efficiency is also gained by having the trailers face in the same direction. A dual level of protection for the trailer lading is provided by high-capacity hydraulic draftgears and cushioned trailer hitches. A specially designed air brake system is forecast to reduce brake shoe wear and prolong wheel life.

The ARC-5 is derived from the ARC-3 intermodal car conceived by Whitehead & Kales in 1975 and built as a prototype in 1981, which has recently passed all the AAR requirements for full interchange cars.

Constitution: Wholly-owned subsidiary of the Duchossois/Thrall Group.

Thrall centre beam car

ARC-5 articulated flatcar

Thyssen Henschel
Thyssen Industrie AG, Henschel

Henschelplatz 1, 3500 Kassel 2, Federal Republic of Germany

Telephone: 0561 8011
Telegrams: Henschel, Kassel
Telex: 099793

President: Hans U Wolf
General Manager (Locomotives): Manfred Kunis
Chief Engineer: Siegfried Kademann

Products: Locomotives for main-line and shunting service covering a wide power range and designed for all gauges and axle loads; diesel locomotives with hydraulic and electric (ac/dc and ac/ac) transmission; electric locomotives for all current systems; dual-power locomotives; Henschel Flexi-Float bogies; diesel engines from 200 to 600 and from 1000 to 2200 kW; axle drives for locomotives and rapid transit vehicles; spring-suspended gear wheels for railbound vehicles; research and development of new rail transport technologies such as Maglev vehicles.

The Thyssen Group is heavily involved in rail transport, both as supplier and user of railroad equipment. The product mix extends from the smallest component part to complete transport systems, while the Group also has one of Europe's largest industrial railway systems, operated by Eisenbahn und Häfen, and many Thyssen plants have a railway department operating their own locomotives. Locomotive research, development, design and production are concentrated at the Thyssen Henschel plant at Kassel. Thyssen Henschel has a very wide locomotive programme and has been active in all lines.

Diesel-hydraulic locomotives range in power from 236 kW (320 hp) upwards. Two- and three-axle standard locomotives are in service in all major industries. Four-axle bogie locomotives have recently been shipped to the Ivory Coast (Class BB150) and to Uganda (Class 73), while in 1983 orders on hand were from Indonesia (Class BB303 and Class BB306).

In 1983 main-line diesel-electric locomotives employing GM power and transmission equipment, were in production for Egypt (Class 3000), Iraq (Class DEM2500), Mali (Class CC1680) and Senegal (Class CC1700).

Diesel-electric locomotives with GM engines and BBC three-phase power transmission were under production for Denmark (Class ME). Three-axle shunting locomotives of 500 kW (680 hp) have been added to this locomotive line.

Class Di4 diesel-electric for NSB

Class ME diesel-electric for DSB

A repeat order from RAG (the West German Coal Board) was received for Class E1200 electric locomotives with BBC three-phase power transmission. Thyssen Henschel was also selected to design and build the mechanical portion for the Class EA3000 three-phase electric locmotives for Danish State Railways' 25 kV ac electrification. The German Federal Railway (DB) placed an order for additional electric locomotives of its standard Class E111.

Thyssen Henschel, together with BBC, plays an active part in the rail/wheel research programme sponsored by the Federal Ministry for Research and Technology. A major contribution to date has been the UmAn (Umkoppelbare Antriebsmasse) experimental locomotive. At low speeds the traction motors rest in the bogie frames; at higher speeds the mass of the integrated traction motor/power transmission/disc brake block is linked in transverse direction by pneumatic cylinders to the body. This bogie concept has already been successfully tested in a modified DE 2500 in trial runs up to 250 km/h.

High-speed trials carried out in 1965 confirmed the desirability of new locomotive drive systems which would utilise friction values more effectively. Thyssen Henschel and BBC therefore developed the DE 2500 locomotive series with three-phase current power transmission. Two locomotives went into trial service with the German Federal Railway (DB) and the third was used for further trials and for the testing of components for the E120 three-phase locomotive of the DB as well as for trials on Netherlands Railways (NS).

The most important feature of the new bogie is the combining of drive and brake systems to form one unit which can be borne by either car body or bogie frame according to running conditions. Thus the unsprung and primarily sprung wheel-set and bogie masses, which determine the running characteristics, can be minimised during high-speed travel on tangent track and on lines with large-radius curves by coupling the drive/brake unit to the car body. During low-speed travel on lines with sharp curves and in the vicinity of the station, where the dynamic running requirements are not so high but ease of curve negotiation is called for, the drive/brake unit is transferred to the bogie frame in such a way that it can follow its deflection angle. On this principle the unsprung wheel-set mass and primarily sprung bogie mass have been successfully limited to the minimum achievable for present-day rail vehicles with present technology. The critical maximum travelling speed has been increased to over 400 km/h without additional stabilising measures.

The four-axle diesel-electric Henschel BBC UmAn locomotive has been designed as a multi-purpose locomotive for light and medium-load fast passenger and goods train service and for heavy-load passenger service. It is intended for service on main and secondary lines built to carry a wheel-set load of 21 tonnes.

Track gauge: 1435 mm
Max speed for test purposes: 250 km/h
Max in-service speed: 160 km/h
Length overall: 19 800 mm
Wheelbase overall: 13 400 mm
Bogie centre distance: 10 400 mm
Bogie wheelbase: 3000 mm
Width overall: 3070 mm
Height overall: 4250 mm
Wheel diameter: 1000 mm
Wheel arrangement: Bo-Bo
Service weight with full supplies: 84 tonnes
Axleload with full supplies: 21 tonnes
Power: 2750 hp
Starting tractive effort: 173 kN
Diesel motor: Henschel 12 V 2423 Aa

Main generator: BBC WO 630 a 8 spec
Traction motor: BBC QDX 335 N4AC

The ICE inter-city experimental high-speed train is a further joint venture in which Thyssen Henschel is designing and constructing main components of the power cars. Since on experimental runs speeds of 350 km/h are envisaged and 300 km/h is proposed for the demonstration phase, the UmAn principle of flexibly-mounted drive units in the bogies with direct transversal coupling to the body at high speeds will be employed.

Constitution: Henschel started manufacturing locomotives in 1848 and more than 32 000 locomotives have been supplied to railways around the world.

Class CC1880 diesel-electric Co-Co for Mali

Class DEM2500 diesel-electric Co-Co for Iraq

Thyssen-Henschel diesel locomotives

Class	Wheel arrangement	Transmission	Rated power (kW)	Max speed km/h	Total weight tonnes	No in service (in production)	Year first built	Builders Mechanical parts	Engine & type	Transmission
DHG 300B	B	Hydr	236	19	40	24 (2)	1973	Thyssen Henschel	KHD	Voith
DHG 700C	C	Hydr	486	37	60	73 (9)	1972	Thyssen Henschel	MTU 6V396TC12	Voith
DE 500C	C	Elec ac-ac	486	50	60	(5)	1983	Thyssen Henschel	MTU 6V396TC12	BBC ac-ac
BB 150	B-B	Hydr	552	65	52	14	1979	Thyssen Henschel	Thyssen Henschel 12V 1516Aa	Voith
BB 306	B-B	Hydr	630	75	40	(22)	1984	Thyssen Henschel	MTU 8V396TC12	Voith
BB 303	B-B	Hydr	846	90	44	42 (15)	1970	Thyssen Henschel	MTU 12V396TC12	Voith
73U	B-B	Hydr	883	80	48	20	1981	Thyssen Henschel	MTU 12V396TC12	Voith
CC 1680	Co-Co	Elec dc/dc	1231	90	84	(2)	1983	Thyssen Henschel	EMD/GM 12-645E	EMD/GM
CC 1700	Co-Co	Elec dc/dc	1231	70	84	(3)	1983	Thyssen Henschel	EMD/GM 12-645E	EMD/GM
3000	Co-Co	Elec ac/dc	1846	120; 140	122	201 (10)	1976	Thyssen Henschel	EMD/GM 12-645E3	EMD/GM
DE 2500	Co-Co	Elec ac/dc	1846	120	111	(82)	1983	Thyssen Henschel	EMD/GM 12-645E3B	EMD/GM
ME 1500	Co-Co	Elec ac/ac	2462	175	112	19 (18)	1981	Thyssen Henschel	EMD/GM 16-645E3B	EMD/GM BBC

Thyssen-Henschel electric locomotives

Class	Wheel arrangement	Line voltage	Rated output (kW) continuous one-hour	Max speed km/h	Weight tonnes	No in service (in production)	Year first built	Builders Mechanical parts	Electrical equipment
111	Bo-Bo	15 kV 16⅔ Hz	3700	140	84	71 (10)	1975	Thyssen Henschel	BBC Siemens
EL17	Bo-Bo	15 kV 16⅔ Hz	3000	140	64	6	1981	Thyssen Henschel	BBC
E1200	Bo-Bo	15 kV 16⅔ Hz	1200	60	88	6 (5)	1976	Thyssen Henschel	BBC
EA3000	Bo-Bo	25 kV 50 Hz	4000	175	80	(2)	1984	Thyssen Henschel	BBC

Class BB303 diesel-hydraulic B-B for Indonesia

Class 73U diesel-hydraulic B-B for Uganda

Class BB150 diesel-hydraulic B-B for Ivory Coast

Experimental UmAn three-phase diesel-electric locomotive

Class E1200 15 kV three-phase electric Bo-Bo for West German Coal Board (RAG)

Components of UmAn power bogie

TIBB
Tecnomasio Italiano Brown Boveri
Transport Division

Piazzale Lodi 3, 20110 Milan, Italy

Telephone: (02) 57971
Telegrams: Tecnomasio, Milan
Telex: 310153

Products: Electric, diesel-electric and battery locomotives and electric bogie locomotives.

The company developed the full chopper control for the experimental Italian State Railways (FS) electric locomotive No E444.005 of 1976, which embodied the first application of solid-state technology to high-power electronic drives for 3 kV dc systems. A series of 90 locomotives now in production for FS, all B-B-Bs, are to a design evolved from this 1976 prototype work: 15 are Class E632 for passenger work, arranged for a maximum speed of 160 km/h, and 75 are Class E633, geared for a top speed of 130 km/h. Construction is being shared by TIBB and Fiat, and TIBB has supplied the full chopper electrical equipment for the first

FS Class D145 three-phase diesel-electric locomotive

five locomotives, which have been operational since 1979. An FS order for 100 to 150 more of the type is forecast.

The 102-tonne locomotive has a single, fully-suspended motor on each bogie, but is not articulated like earlier FS B-B-B types; the body, with a welded steel frame, is one-piece, with freedom of movement in the centre bogie. Electromechanical shoe or disc-braking is combined with an automatic skid device, supplemented by rheostatic braking. The electrical equipment comprises: modular traction equipment on three motors, each fed by its own three-column chopper (the columns are to be reduced to two as production progresses); choppers operating at fixed frequency steps with automatic checking of their precision; protection against over-voltage and excess current with electronic primer; provision for automatic attainment of the speed required with control of acceleration and absorbed current; motors' separate excitation with static feeder, regulated to obtain a series-indirect effect and automatic drop-out of the fields (the latter are interconnected in series, to ensure stability of the motor operation and prevent slipping); rheostatic braking; static converter for three-phase ac feed of the auxiliary services.

FS Class E632 and E633 B-B-B locomotives

Classes E632 and E633

Distance between buffers	17.8 m	
Max height	4.31 m	
Weight in running order	102 tonnes	
Wheel arrangement	B-B-B	
Distance between bogie pivots	10.5 m	
Bogie wheelbase	2.15 m	
Wheel diameter	1.04 m	
Traction motors	3 × T850	
Absorbed unitary power	1700 kW	
Power absorbed by locomotive		
in one-hour service	5100 kW	
	E632	**E633**
Gear ratio	33/64	27/64
Max speed	160 km/h	130 km/h
One hour speed (full field)	92 km/h	75 km/h
Continuous speed (full field)	95 km/h	77.8 km/h
Tractive effort on starting	227 kN	278 kN
in one-hour service	185 kN	227 kN
in continuous service	159 kN	193 kN

In 1982 TIBB was also manufacturing 20 mixed traffic Class D145 diesel-electric locomotives for FS. The main feature of this centre-cab design is its employment of three-phase traction technology. Each two-axle bogie is fitted with two asynchronous, nose-suspended and force-ventilated motors and the power transmission is by a synchronous, six-pole generator with three-phase exciter. The main exciting current is rectified by means of rotating diodes without sliprings. One side of each motor shaft is connected to the pinion of the reduction gear, which has a 15/79 ratio. The 12-cylinder, four-stroke engine has a 1140 hp rating at 1800 rpm, which achieves a starting tractive effort of 25 tonnes; maximum speed is 100 km/h. The 70-tonne locomotive is 14.2 metres long, with a distance of 8.3 metres between the pivots of bogies that are each of 2.5 metres wheelbase.

Constitution: TIBB has been in existence since 1903. In 1919 the Vadore Ligure factory was taken over by Tecnomasio Italiano Brown Boveri. Mechanical components and electrical equipment for rolling stock are still manufactured at Vadore Ligure while electronic equipment is produced at the Vittuone factory. Over 700 electric locomotives have been built for Italian State Railways (FS).

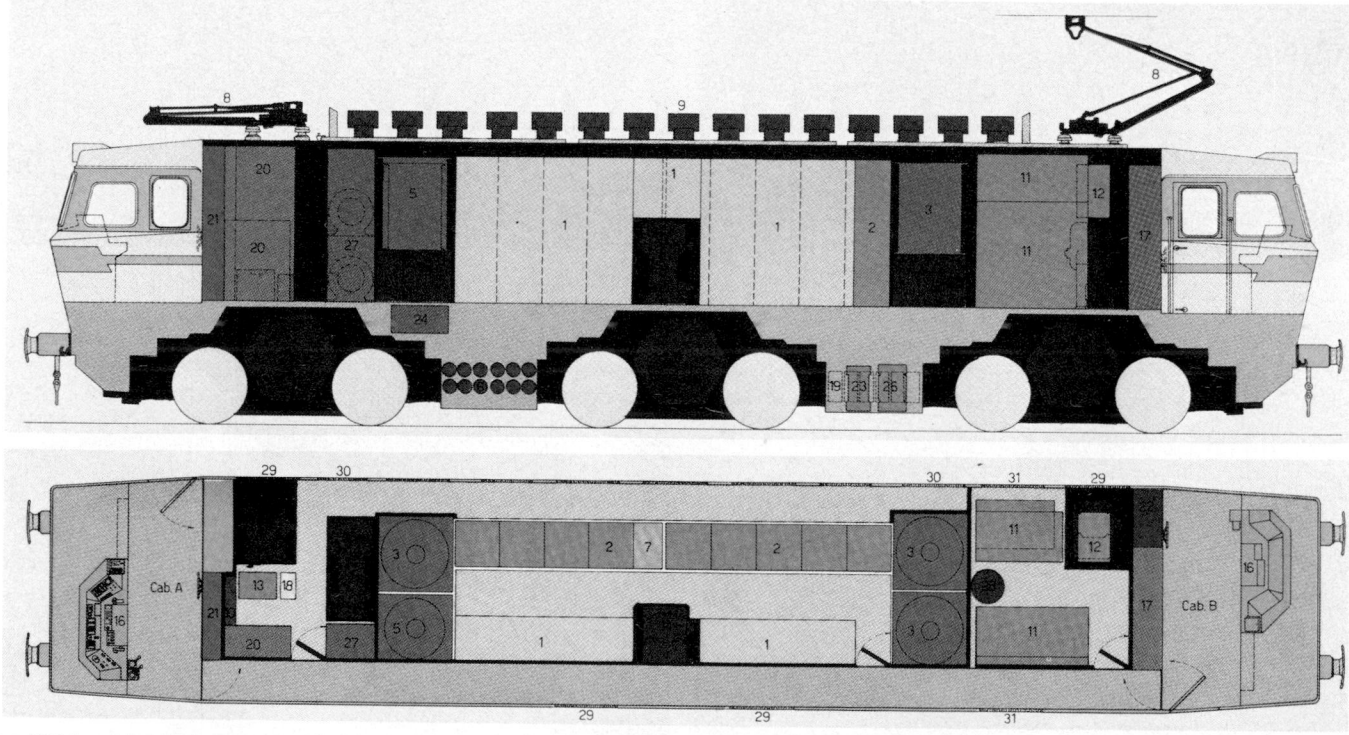

Class E632 locomotive. (1) hv switchgear (2) main chopper units (3) smoothing reactors (4) traction motors (5) line filter reactor (6) line filter capacitors (7) chopper for motor excitation (8) single-arm pantograph (9) brake resistor (10) auxiliary switchgear (11) convertor for auxiliaries (12) control electronics power supply (13) battery charge transformer (14) traction motor ventilators (15) motor-driven compressors (16) control desks (17) control electronics cubicles (18) battery rectifier (19) accumulator (20) control switches (21) relay cubicle (22) auxiliary convertor control cubicle (23) auxiliary convertor reactor (24) line filter auxiliary reactor (25) chopper and reactor cooling fans (26) excitation chopper transformer (27) pneumatic equipment (28) auxiliary convertor fan (29) traction motor air filters (30) power chopper unit air filters (31) auxiliary convertor air filters

Diesel locomotives

Class	Wheel arrangement	Transmission	Rated power (kW)	Max speed km/h	Total weight tonnes	No in service or on order	Year first built	Builders		
								Mechanical parts	Engine & type	Transmission
DE 54	Bo-Bo	Elec dc/dc	400	75	46	5	1971	TIBB	2 × Fiat 828 I	TIBB
D 145.2000 (FS)	Bo-Bo	Elec ac/dc/ac	840	100	70	20	1983	TIBB	1 × IFID365512V	TIBB

Diesel railcars

Railway	Cars per unit	Motor cars per unit	Motored axles per motor car	Transmission	Rated power (kW) per motor	Max speed km/h	Weight tonnes per car	Total seating capacity	Length per car mm	No in service	Year first built	Builders		
												Mechanical parts	Engine & type	Transmission
Circumetnea	1	1	4	Elec	60	75	32	55	17	8	1974	OM Stanga	Fiat 221	TIBB

Electric locomotives

Class (All FS)	Wheel arrangement	Line voltage	Rated output (kW) continuous	Max speed km/h	Weight tonnes	No in service	Year first built	Builders Mechanical parts	Electrical equipment
E 656	Bo-Bo-Bo	3 kV dc	4680	150	120	38	1973	TIBB	TIBB
E 444.005 (chopper)	Bo-Bo	3 kV dc	5050	200	84	1	1975	TIBB	TIBB
E 633 (chopper)	B-B-B	3 kV dc	4700	130	102	24	1979	TIBB	TIBB
E 632 (chopper)	B-B-B	3 kV dc	4700	160	102	1	1980	TIBB	TIBB

Electric railcars or multiple-units

Railway class	Cars per unit	Line voltage	Motor cars per unit	Motored axles per motor car	Rated output (kW) per motor	Max speed km/h	Weight tonnes per car (M-motor T-trailer)	Total seating capacity	Length per car mm (M-motor T-trailer)	No in service	Rate of acceleration m/s²	Year first built	Builders Mechanical parts	Electrical equipment
FS ALe 804	4	3 kV dc	2	4	220	140	M 53 T 29	280	M 26 T 24	6	1.0	1979	Breda CF	TIBB in GAI*
Garganica	1	3 kV dc	1	4	180	110	M 52	80	23	6	1.0	1980	OM Stanga	TIBB
Benevento/Cancello	1	3 kV dc	1	4	180	110	M 52	80	23	1	1.0	1980	OM Stanga	TIBB
Bari Nord	1	3 kV dc	1	4	180	110	M 52	80	23	3	1.0	1980	Casaralta	TIBB
Umbro/Aretine	1	3 kV dc	1	4	180	110	M 52	80	23	2	1.0	1980	OM Stanga	TIBB

*GAI is a consortium of several Italian rolling stock manufacturers

Tokyu
Tokyu Car Corporation

Head office: 1 Kamariya-cho, Kanazawa-ku, Yokohama, Japan
Sales and Export Department: 7, 5-cho, Yaesu, Chuo-ku, Tokyo

Telephone: 272 8091/3
Telegrams: Tokyucarcorp Tok
Telex: 0222 2020

Chairman: Toshiji Yoshitsugu
President: Ihaho Takahashi
Executive Vice-President: Ichiro Kato

Export Manager: Kenichiro Tanimoto

Products: Electric and diesel railcars; stainless-steel cars with bogie, passenger cars with bogie, bogies of various types, marine and railway containers of several types.

Constitution: This company was formed in 1948, its predecessors being the Yokohama Plant of the Tokyo Electric Express Railway Co. It built the first stainless-steel train-set in Japan following technical agreement with the Budd Company of USA in 1960. Merging Teikoku Car & Manufacturing Co of Osaka into its organisation in 1968, the company is now the largest Japanese supplier of rolling stock to home and overseas railways.

Stainless-steel car for Shizuoka Railway

Aluminium alloy car for Tokyo Metro

Tomlinson
Tomlinson Steel Ltd

PO Box P1227, Perth, Western Australia 6001, Australia

General Manager: A K R Tucker
General Sales Manager: E K Howells

Controller: P Wright

Products: Freight rolling stock.

Constitution: The company was founded in Perth, Western Australia in 1892 as Tomlinson Bros and was formed into a public company in 1951 with its present name. In April 1981 the company became a subsidiary of the Clyde Group.

Toshiba
Toshiba Corporation
Transport Equipment Export Department IOPG

1-6 Uchisaiwai-cho 1-chome, Chiyoda-ku, Tokyo, Japan

Telephone: 501 5411
Telegrams: Toshiba, Tokyo
Telex: 2 2587

President: Shoichi Saba
Senior Manager, Railway Projects: Shoji Torii
Senior Manager, Transport Equipment Export Department: Hiroaki Shimotsuya

Products: Electric, diesel-electric and diesel-hydraulic locomotives; electric and diesel railcars; trolleybuses; electric traction equipment; coach air-conditioner; industrial rolling stock.
Railway equipment has been supplied to Algeria, Argentina, Australia, Brazil, Chile, Egypt, India, South Korea, Morocco, New Zealand, Philippines, South

20 kV ac B-2-B electric locomotive of 1900 kW rating with thyristor control for Japanese National Railways

Africa, Thailand, Zaire and Zambia, as well as to Japanese National Railways (JNR) and Japanese private railways.

Important deliveries since 1981 include superconductive magnets and GTO inverters for the magnetically-levitated vehicle under development by JNR; traction equipment for Tohoku and Joetsu Shinkansen of JNR; 15 LRVs for Heliopolis Company for Housing & Development; 30 LRVs for Alexandria Passenger Transport Authority; 300 trolleybuses with chopper controllers for Mexico City and Guadalajara; 24 920 hp diesel-electric locomotives for New Zealand Railways Corporation; more than 30 GTO inverters of 60 to 170 kVA for auxiliary power supply for six railways in Japan; and monitoring devices for drivers or conductors for JNR and private railways in Japan.

Major orders in hand include 156 25 kV ac emu coaches for the Roca Line of Argentine Railways with separately-excited GTO chopper controllers; and 50 3 kV dc 3090 kW 126-tonne Co-Co electric locomotives with freon cooling chopper controllers processed by micro-computers for South African Transport Services.

Recent developments include a GTO thyristor device using 4.5 kV 2400A elements, series GTO chopper controllers for emus, passenger car air-conditioners with capacity control by VVVF inverters; and an induction motor driving system consisting of two 160 kW motors and a VVVF inverter.

Constitution: Established in 1875, the company's range of products now covers almost everything electrical and electronic from power stations to electronic computers.

JNR Series 200 train-set for Tohoku and Joetsu Shinkansen opened in 1982

920 hp diesel-electric locomotive for New Zealand Railways Corporation for shunting and branch line use

Series 201 emu for Japanese National Railways with chopper control and regenerative braking

Toshiba electric locomotives

Railway and class	Wheel arrangement	Line voltage	Rated output (kW)	Max speed km/h	Weight tonnes	Gauge mm	Use	Notes
Indian WAG2	Bo-Bo	25 kV 50 Hz	2400 continuous	80	85.2	1676	Freight	Silicon diode rectifiers
Japanese National ED72	B-2-B	20 kV 60 Hz	1900 one-hour	100	87	1067	Passenger/freight	HT arcless tapchanger and silicon diode rectifier system
Japanese National ED77	B-2-B	20 kV 50 Hz	1900 one-hour	100	75	1067	Passenger/freight	Thyristor rectifier
Japanese National EF71	Bo-Bo-Bo	20 kV 50 Hz	2700 one-hour	100	96	1067	Passenger/freight	Thyristor rectifier with regenerative brake
New Zealand Govt Ea	Bo-Bo	1.5 kV dc	960 one-hour	72	54	1067	Passenger/freight	
Japanese National EF58	2-Co-Co-2	1.5 kV dc	1900 one-hour	100	115	1067	Passenger/freight	
Japanese National EF63	Bo-Bo-Bo	1.5 kV dc	2550 one-hour	100	108	1067	Passenger	
Japanese National EF65	Bo-Bo-Bo	1.5 kV dc	2550 one-hour	115	96	1067	Passenger	

Toshiba electric multiple-units

Railway and class	Gauge mm	Cars per unit	Line voltage	Motored axles per motor car	Rated output (kW) per motor	Max speed km/h	Total passenger capacity (S seats only N nominal total)	Unit formation (M-motor T-trailer)	Notes
Japanese National 711	1067	3	20 kV 50 Hz	4	150	110	S 216	1M2T	Mixed bridge thyristor rectifier system
Korean National/Seoul MG	1435	6	20 kV 60 Hz/ 1.5 kV dc	4	120	110	N 936	4M2T	Silicon diode rectifier system
Hankyu Corp 2200	1435	8	1.5 kV dc	4	135	110	N 1180	4M4T	Thyristor chopper control with regenerative brake
Hanshin Electric 7601	1435	4	1.5 kV dc	4	110	110	N 580	2M2T	Thyristor chopper control system

Toyo

Toyo Denki Seizo KK

Toyo Electric Manufacturing Co Ltd

Yaesu Mitsui Building, No 7-2 Yaesu, 5-chome, Chuo-ku, Tokyo 104, Japan

Telephone: 03 271 6374
Telegrams: Yohden, Tokyo
Telex: 3822 392

President: Atsushi Doi

Products: Electric locomotives; diesel-electric locomotives; traction motors and electric machinery and apparatus for railway vehicles.

Constitution: Established in 1918, this company produces traction motors and control equipment for home and export. It was responsible for the axle drive with cardan shaft and steel blade coupling which is used as standard equipment by the Japanese National Railways and by many of the private railways in Japan.

Trackmobile
Division of MPB Europa BV

Osloweg 59, PO Box 5016, 9700 GA Groningen, Netherlands

Telephone: 050-185066
Telex: 77205

Products: Trackmobile Railcarmovers; these are bi-modal locomotives for private siding owners, offered with tractive efforts ranging from 4.25 to 22.68 tonnes, which have easily interchangeable rail and road running gear. Higher-powered models employ GM diesel engines of 112-130 hp with torque-converter/three-speed forward and reverse transmission, and have power steering in the rail mode. Front and rear couplers have hydraulic lift cylinders to transfer weight from attached rail vehicles to increase the Railcarmover's tractive effort. The Type 4500TM is claimed to have the power to move up to 45 100-ton rail vehicles. In the road mode, it has positive two-wheel front drive provided by a two-motor hydrostatic drive system which is independent of the six-speed rail axle transmission system. Radio control is among the optional extras.

Model 4500TM Railcarmover in road and rail modes

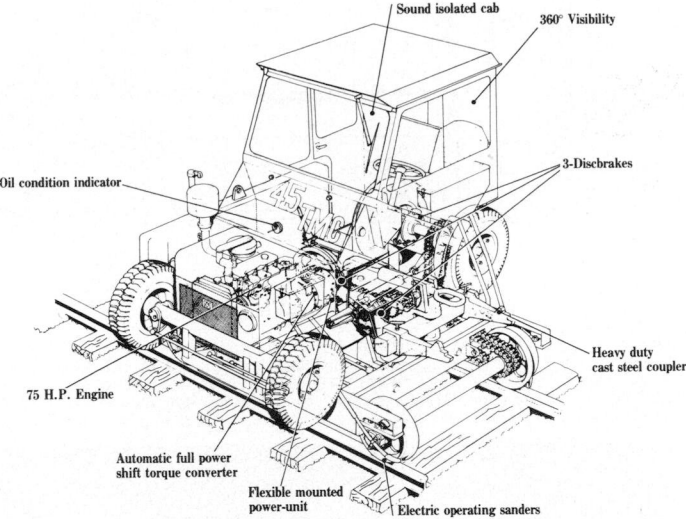

Heavy-duty Type 45TMC Trackmobile, with Perkins engine and Voith automatic single-stage torque converter/mechanical transmission

Traction—Export
Société Française d'Exportation de Matériel de Traction

3 avenue Victor Hugo, 75116 Paris, France

Telephone: 500 90 01
Telegrams: Tractionex
Telex: 270105

Products: Electric locomotives, diesel-electric locomotives, diesel-hydraulic locomotives, railcars, motor coaches and trailers for city underground and suburban rapid transit systems.

Constitution: Traction-Export is a subsidiary organisation of Alsthom and MTE, created to develop the export of rail traction equipment manufactured by Alsthom, Brissonneau, Creusot-Loire, and Jeumont-Schneider.

Transportmaschinen Export-Import
Volkseigener Aussenhandelsbetrieb der Deutschen Demokratischen Republik

Taubenstrasse 11/13, 108 East Berlin, German Democratic Republic

Telephone: 22050
Telegrams: Transmasch
Telex: 11 26 89

Constitution: Transportmaschinen Export-Import is a member of Vereinigter Schienenfahrzeugbau der DDR eV (Union of Rolling Stock Manufacturers of the German Democratic Republic) and is the sole exporter for the products of locomotive and coach and wagon factories.

Turnu-Severin
MecanoExportImport supplier

3 B-dul Dunării, 1500 Drobeta Turnu Severin, Romania

Telephone: 978 12078
Telex: 42233

Products: Passenger cars, freight wagons and tank cars for petroleum products and liquid gas under pressure.

Constitution: Member of the Wagons Manufacture Enterprises Group.

Union Carriage
Union Carriage & Wagon Co (Pty) Ltd

Marievale Road, Vorsterkroon, Nigel 1490, Transvaal, South Africa

Telephone: 739 2411
Telegrams: Unicarwag
Telex: 4 21000

Chairman: G Clark
Managing Director: J M Clarke
Commercial Manager: H F Claus
Technical Manager: B Fitton
Manufacturing Manager: J H Simmons
Chief Manufacturing Engineer: M G Shaw
Works Manager: A L du Toit

Products: Electric and diesel locomotives and passenger coaches.
   Since 1959 the company has manufactured over 4000 passenger cars for South African Transport Services. In 1982, besides engagement in large locomotive construction orders (see table below) it was active with further orders for main-line open saloons and for 17 33-tonne cars for SATS' new high-speed, push-pull inter-city project.
   The company manufactures diesel locomotives with hydraulic and electric transmissions for shunting and branch-line operations in a standard range of mass and power configurations of up to 80 tonnes and 1100 kW. Designs incorporate multiple-unit control, slow speed/high speed control, deadman or vigilance system, anti-slip slagtipping devices, dual train brakes etc.

Constitution: General Mining and Finance Corp, Anglo-American Corp and Comeng Holdings are the principal shareholders of this company. Less than 25 per cent in value of all the contracts received is spent overseas, mostly on electric traction equipment which is not obtainable from South African sources. Formed in 1957 to supply South African Railways with passenger coaches, Union Carriage has expanded its business to supply the export market and to become a major manufacturer of main-line and shunting electric locomotives.

'Ajax' type 245 kW, 40-tonne diesel-hydraulic 0-6-0 shunter

Equipment layout of Class 7E Co-Co (G 1) main rectifier cubicle with field excitation rectifier (G 2) main rectifier cubicle with auxiliary rectifier (E 2) earthing switch key box (E 37) oil cooler (L 30) auxiliary smoothing choke (M 21) oil pump (M 28) suction fans (M 33) exhauster (M 34) main compressor (M 36) traction motor blowers (M 37) oil cooler blower (M 38) braking resistor blowers (N 1) electronic control cubicle (R 4) braking resistors with permanent shunts (T 3) main transformer (1) main switchgear, bogie 1 (2) main switchgear, bogie 2 (3) auxiliary compressor and transformer damping/battery charging equipment (4) auxiliary switchgear (5) control relays (6) control and protection relays (7) inertial filters (8) air equipment frame (9) vigilance equipment frame

SATS Class 7E 25 kV 50 Hz ac electric Co-Co for Richards Bay coal line

SATS Class 9E 50 kV ac 50 Hz Co-Co for Sishen-Saldanha Bay ore line

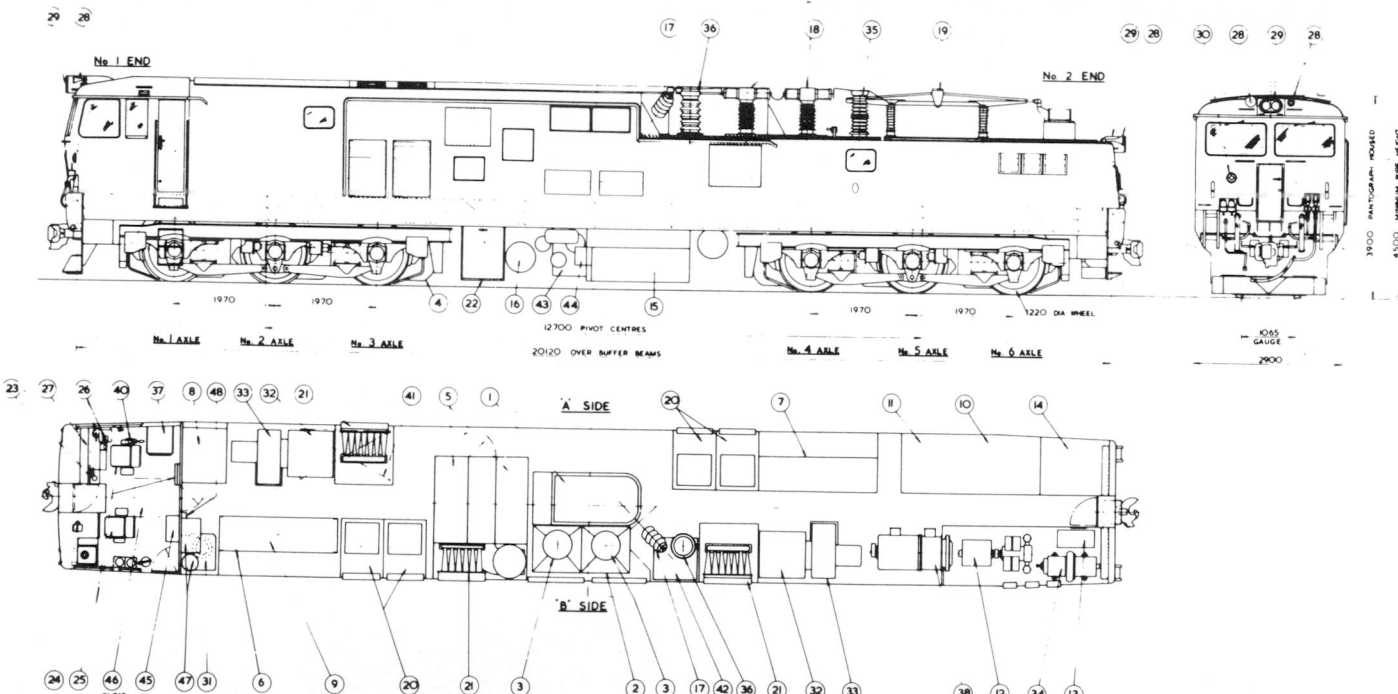

Layout of Class 9E Co-Co (1) transformer (2) transformer radiator (3) fan (4) traction motor (5) thyristor/diode rectifier (6) high-voltage equipment frame no 1 end (7) high-voltage equipment frame no 2 end (8) low-voltage equipment frame (9) electronics cubicle (above high-voltage frame) (10) power factor correction equipment (11) auxiliary control and battery charger (12) air compressor, main (13) air compressor, auxiliary (14) brake equipment (15) battery (16) air reservoirs, main (17) input bushing (18) vacuum circuit-breaker (19) pantograph (20) rheostatic brake units (21) inertia air filters (22) container for motor scooter (23) master controller (24) handbrake (25) seats (26) brake valves (27) instrument panel (28) horn (29) headlight (30) tail-light (31) toilet (32) choke (33) traction motor blower (34) exhauster (35) potential divider (36) lightning arrestor (37) refrigerator (38) motor alternator set (40) vacuum/air emergency valve (41) power supplies, etc (above no 1 TM blower) (42) MA set choke (43) condensing unit (air-conditioning) (44) battery-isolating switch (45) fixed cupboard (46) air-conditioning unit (in cab ceiling) (47) water heater and water tank (48) washbasin

SATS suburban emu power car

SATS first-class main-line passenger car

Union Carriage & Wagon electric locomotives

South African Transport Services class	Wheel arrangement	Line voltage	Traction power (kW)	Max speed km/h	Weight tonnes	No in service	Year first built	Builders Mechanical parts (Body)	Electrical equipment
5E1 6E1	Bo-Bo	3 kV	2400	80	89	555 (5E1) 960 (6E1)	1963 (5E1) 1970 (6E1)	UCW	GEC
7E 7E2	Co-Co	25 kV	3100 7E: tractive effort, starting 450 kN one-hour 325 kN at 34 km/h continuous 300 kN at 35 km/h at max speed 72 kN max braking 210 kN, 29 km/h	100	126	100 (7E) 25 (7E2)	1978	UCW	50 c/s Group
8E	Bo-Bo	3 kV	680	75	83	Manufacturing stage (107 in contract)	1982	UCW	Siemens BBC
9E 9E1	Co-Co	50 kV	3700 9E: tractive effort, max 493·9 kN continuous 383 kN	90	168	25 (9E) 4 (9E1)	1978	UCW	GEC
10E	Co-Co	3 kV	3100	90	123	Design stage (50 in contract)	—	UCW	Mitsui-Toshiba
12E	Co-Co	3 kV	2400	160	87	Manufacturing stage (5 in contract)	1982	UCW	GEC

Union Carriage & Wagon electric multiple-units

Class	Cars per unit	Line voltage	Motor cars per unit	Motored axles per motor car	Rated output (kW) per motor	Max speed km/h	Weight tonnes per car (M-motor T-trailer)	Total seating capacity	Length per car mm	No in service	Rate of acceleration m/s²	Year first built	Builders Mechanical parts	Electrical equipment
SATS suburban	8	3 kV	2	4	225	96	M 63 T 31	472 (2150 including standing capacity)	18 500	Up to 500 8-car sets	0.455	1961	Union Carriage & Wagon (Pty) Ltd	GEC

Union Tank

Union Tank Car Co
A member of the Marmon Group of companies

111 West Jackson Boulevard, Chicago, Illinois 60604, USA

Telephone: (312) 431 3111

Products: Steel, stainless-steel, and aluminium tank cars carrying liquids, compressed gases, and granular solids.

UTDC

Urban Transportation Development Corporation Ltd

2 St Clair Avenue West, Toronto, Ontario M4V 1L7, Canada

Telephone: (416) 961 9569
Telegrams: Urbantrans Tor
Telex: 0622805

Main Works: Transit Development Centre, Station A, Box 160, Kingston, Ontario K7M 6RL

President: K W Foley
Vice President, Production Application: E F Ries
Vice President, Business Development: R M Renfrew
Vice President, Manufacturing and Operations: D J Follett

Subsidiaries: Metro Canada Ltd
UTDC Services
VentureTrans Manufacturing Inc
UTDC R & D Ltd
UTDC (USA) Inc

Products: Intermediate capacity urban transit systems, Canadian Light Rail Vehicle, transit consultancy, advisory, training and support services.

The company's first Advanced Light Rapid Transit System (ALRT) was scheduled to begin test operation in the summer of 1983 and to open for public service in 1986. This runs 21.4 km from the centre of Vancouver to the suburb of New Westminster. It employs linear motor-powered, light alloy-bodied cars of 12.7 metres length and weighing 13 tonnes with fully automatic operation on the Seltrac system, whereby trains are controlled on a moving block basis at headways of a minimum one minute. A 7.1 km Intermediate Capacity Transit System (ICTS), the Scarborough Rapid Transit, was to begin commercial service in Toronto in 1984. The company is also providing a 5.2 km Central Automated Transit System (CATS) in the form of a single-track loop around the business centre of Detroit, USA, and has been engaged in consultancy and advisory projects in San Francisco, Boston (USA), Cairo and London.

Valmet

Valmet Oy, Railway Division

PO Box 387, 33101 Tampere 10, Finland

Telephone: 358 31 653322
Telegrams: Valmet, Helsinki
Telex: 22112

President: Matti Kankaanpää
General Manager, Railway Division: Esko Määttänen

Products: Diesel-hydraulic locomotives; electric multiple-unit trains; rapid transit cars; articulated tramcars; coaches for special purposes.

Recent sales have included:
Finnish State Railways (VR): all-aluminium 620 kW electric two-car train-sets (motor coach and driving trailer), seats 200, max speed 120 km/h; 1400 hp Bo-Bo diesel-hydraulic general-purpose locomotives; 355 hp diesel-hydraulic shunting locomotives;
Rapid Transit Office of the City of Helsinki: all-aluminium 1000 kW rapid transit two-car units, seats 134, max speed 90 km/h;
Helsinki City Transport: 2 × 130 kW articulated tramcars, seats 41, max speed 90 km/h;
Finnish and Swedish industry: 545 and 970 hp diesel-hydraulic shunting locomotives.

Two-axle diesel-hydraulic shunting locomotives can be supplied with engine ratings from 250 to 450 hp and alternative transmissions, gauge 1000-1676 mm, weight 20-40 tons and max speed up to 75 km/h.

Two-axle diesel-hydraulic shunting locomotive

Vers
Vers SA

Principe 27, Apartado 902, Madrid, Spain

Products: Freight wagons.

Vickers Canada
Vickers Canada Inc

5000 Notre Dame Street East, Montreal, Quebec H1V 2B4, Canada

Products: Rapid transit cars, commuter trains, double-deck coaches, car bodies, fabricated shells and parts.

Constitution: Vickers' growing involvement in public transport began with the supply of the first 369 passenger cars for Montreal's Metro. Since then the company has built double-deck commuter trains for CP Rail, supplied stainless-steel car shells for the New Haven Railroad commuter system, and self-propelled, high-speed commuter cars for the Delaware River Port Authority, Philadelphia, USA.

Montreal Metro cars

Double-deck gallery cars for CP Rail

Villares
Equipamentos Villares SA

Av Senador Vergueiro No 2000, São Bernardo do Campo 09700, SP, Brazil

Telephone: (011) 443 5500
Telex: (011) 4068

Managing Director: Sergio A Martins
Engineering Director: Olivio M S Avila
Research and Development Director: Edson Saboya
Sales Directors: Elihu Luz
F B Tosta
Controlling Director: Gregório Torkomian
Manufacturing Director, Plant I: Paulo A Mode
Manufacturing Director, Plant II: J Cassio Daltrini
Supply Director: A P Bonotto

Products: Diesel locomotives under EMD licence; electric locomotives under GEC licence; transfer cars for steel mills under Fuji Car licence; and bogies for multiple-unit train-sets under Budd Co licence.
Recent production has included 52 Type GT-22 CUM-1 diesel-electric locomotives for Brazilian Federal Railways (RFFSA); also six Type GT-26 CU-2 diesel-electric locomotives for CVRD. In 1982 Villares received orders for 10 Type SD40-2 1600 mm-gauge, 3000/3300 hp, 180-tonne diesel-electric locomotives for the CVRD Carajás Project and 35 25 kV 60 Hz locomotives for the Ferrovia do Aço Project (the Steel Railway of Brazil), manufactured under agreement with GEC Traction Ltd. The SD40-2s were to be delivered in 1984-85.

The company has developed a range of 200 to 600 bhp shunting locomotives and is branching into manufacture of rail cranes.

Diesel-electric Co-Co for RFFSA

Villares diesel locomotives

Type	Wheel arrangement	Transmission	Rated power (kW)	Max speed km/h	Total weight tonnes	No in service	Year first built	Builders		
								Mechanical parts	Engine & type	Transmission
GT-22 CUM-1	Co-Co	Elec	1846	105	108	52	1981	Villares	EMD 12-645E3B	Villares
GT-26 CU-2	Co-Co	Elec	2237	96	138	6	1981	Villares	EMD 16-645E3B	Villares
SD40-2	Co-Co	Elec	2684	105	180	10 (on order)	1983	Villares	EMD 16-645E3C	Villares

Villares electric locomotives

Wheel arrangement	Line voltage	Rated output (kW)	Max speed km/h	Weight tonnes	No on order	Delivery year	Builders	
							Mechanical parts	Electrical equipment
Co-Co	25 kV 60 Hz	3500	100	180	35	1985	Villares	GEC

Voroshilovgrad
Voroshilovgrad Diesel Locomotive Works

Voroshilovgrad, USSR

Products: Diesel locomotives.

Constitution: Member of Energomachexport.

Waggon Union
Waggon Union GmbH

PO Box 2240, 5902 Netphen 2, Federal Republic of Germany

Telephone: 0271 702 1
Telegrams: Waggonunion, Siegen
Telex: 08 72843

General Manager: Dipl-Ing Hans-Richard Hippenstiel

Products: Freight cars of all types, covered, open, mineral, tank, refrigerated, and for transport of road vehicles and containers; electric and diesel-powered railcars, railbuses, and multiple-unit train-sets; passenger cars, tramways, underground trains; double-deck buses and fabricated bogies for freight cars and passenger coaches.

Recent developments include a Type Laadkmmss 605 low-loader for the piggyback movement of road freight trailers. It is mounted on special two-axle bogies with 600/560 mm diameter wheels of a type evolved from the design created for the low-floor Type Saas-z 706 wagon of the German Federal Railway (DB); in principle its arrangement treats each pair of axles in similar fashion to a single wheel-set. Length of the vehicle over couplers is 15.2 metres and the platform area available for vehicle loading is 13.98 × 2.53 metres. Between the bogies the recessed body contains two sets of hinged tracks, so that a road trailer's main wheels can be lowered to a height of 410 mm above rail level, no matter at which end of the rail vehicle it is loaded. Headstocks with their buffers and drawgear are hinged so that road trailers can be roll-on/roll-off loaded and discharged. With a tare weight of 14 tonnes, the wagon is designed for a load capacity of 56 tonnes and a maximum operational speed of 120 km/h.

A similar type of bogie is fitted to the Type Sgjkmmss 698 container wagon, which is equipped with a central shock absorber. It has a loading area length of 14.6 metres and has a maximum load capacity of 47.5 tonnes.

Bogie hopper wagon, tare weight 22.5 tonnes, load capacity 57.5 tonnes, for grain and powder minerals

Type Laadkmmss 605 transporter for piggybacking of road trailers

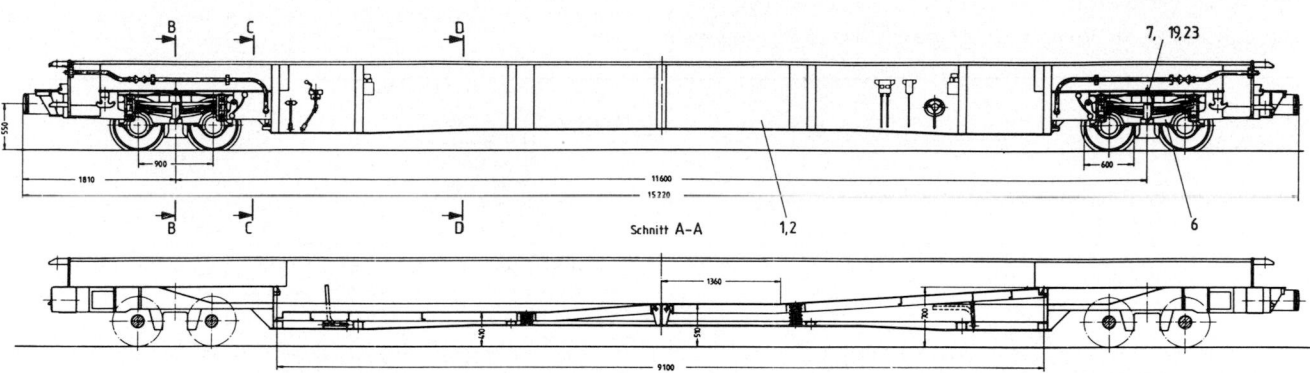

Type Laadkmmss 605 transporter layout

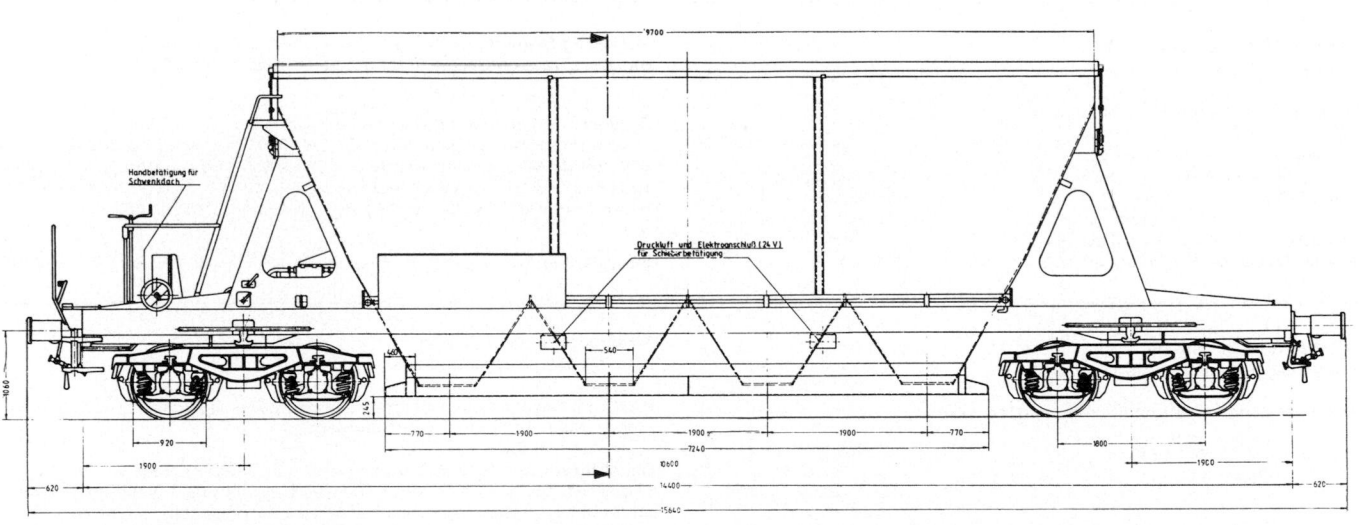

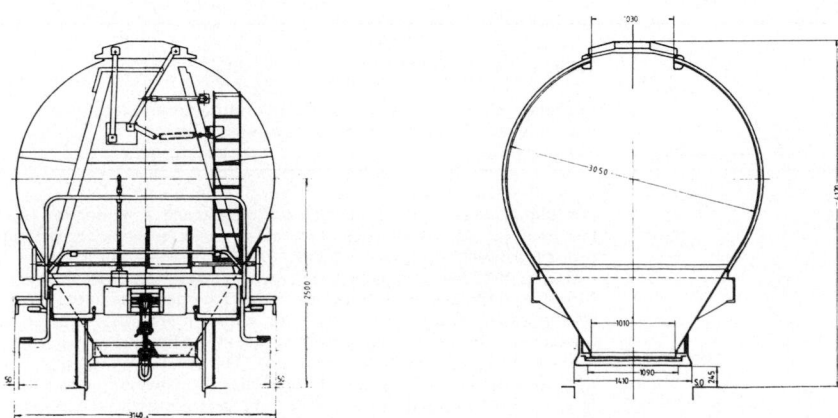

Grain and powder minerals bogie hopper wagon with dust-proof self-discharge mechanism

Constitution: This company was formed in 1971 as a result of the merger between SEAG Waggonbau (of Rheinstahl Transporttechnik) and DWM Deutsche Waggon- und Maschinenfabrik GmbH. Plants are sited at Siegen and West Berlin. Passenger coaches, type ET420 electric trains, underground trains, articulated tramcars and double-deck buses for urban traffic are built in West Berlin; tank wagons, articulated wagons for the automobile industry, ore wagons and bogie well wagons are among the major products manufactured in the Siegen works.

Type Sgjkmmss 698 container wagon

Wakamatsu Sharyo
Wakamatsu Sharyo Co Ltd

1 Kitaminato machi, 6-chome, Wakamatsu-ku, Kitakyushu 808, Japan

Telephone: 093 761 2331

Products: Freight wagons, specialised steelworks vehicles.

Walkers
Walkers Ltd

A member of the Evans Deakin Industries Group

Bowen Street, Maryborough, Queensland 4650, Australia

Telephone: 61 71 21 2321
Telegrams: Itolzak
Telex: 49718

General Manager: J R Swan
Secretary: M F Dittmann

Products: Diesel-hydraulic locomotives from 500 to 1200 hp with axleloads as low as 10 tonnes (over 150 have been supplied to various Australasian railways); passenger and freight rolling stock, emu urban cars.

In 1977, in conjunction with ASEA Australia Pty Ltd, the company obtained the contract for the first 13 three-car sets of the Brisbane suburban stainless steel emu fleet. For this project a separate modern workshop and assembly facility was erected adjacent to the main works at Maryborough. In 1979 the initial contract was extended to 72 cars and early in 1981 an additional contract for 108 cars was obtained against strong competition. This latter contract, the largest single contract obtained by the company to date, was valued at almost A$ 70 million.

Constitution: The company was started at Ballarat, Victoria, in 1864 by John Walker as The Union Foundry, to build mining machinery for the newly-opened goldfields, and the works at Maryborough were opened on the present site in 1868.

Wegmann
Wegmann & Co

Head office: August-Bode-Strasse 1, 3500 Kassel, Federal Republic of Germany

Telephone: 105 1
Telegrams: Wegmann, Kassel
Telex: 99 859

Works: Kassel-Rothenditmold (rolling stock construction)
Kassel-Bettenhausen (fittings, frames and castings)

Directors: Dr E Bode
Dr F Bode
Dr M Bode
Dr W Zimni
J Bode
W Bode

Products: Motor and trailer bogies for railway passenger cars; subway cars etc; electrically and pneumatically-operated doors for buses and railway passenger cars.

Constitution: The company was established in 1882 and has specialised in bogie design and construction.

Westinghouse SA
Formerly CENEMESA

Gran Via 10, Madrid 14, Spain

Telephone: 2 31 72 00
Telegrams: Wesma
Telex: 22430

President: D Santiago Foncillas Casaus
General Manager: S P Simpson

Marketing Manager: J C Fink
Director, Traction Group: D Angel de Nicolás Diaz de Garayo

Products: Electric locomotives, electric railcars.
Recent orders have included 65 Series 5000 emus with chopper control for the 600-volt dc Madrid Metro with 4 × 210 kW rating; and for Spanish National Railways' (RENFE) 3 kV dc electric lines, 110 B-B locomotives with chopper control rated at 4650 kW and 60 two-car emus rated at 1160 kW.

Constitution: Member of the Westinghouse Electric group of companies.

Whitehead & Kales
Whitehead & Kales International, Inc

58 Haltiner Street, Detroit, Michigan 48218, USA

Telephone: (313) 849 1200
Telex: 23 0732

Chairman: Paul A Johnston

President: James E Norris
Vice-President: William J Somerville

Products: Freight cars of all types; car components and underframes; shipping racks; containers; and special dunnage.

Constitution: Whitehead & Kales Co was founded in 1897, and employs 1000 people at its plant in Detroit. Railroad equipment, including freight cars, automobile rail shipping racks, underframes and car components, are produced at River Rouge.

Whiting
Whiting Corporation

Harvey, Illinois 60426, USA

Telephone: (312) 468 9400

Products: Shunters; speciality railcars; domestic and foreign auto and truck bi- and tri-level railcars and superstructures.

Wickham
D Wickham & Co Ltd

Crane Mead, Ware, Hertfordshire SG12 9QA, England

Telephone: 0920 2491/7
Telegrams: Wickham, Ware
Telex: 81340

Chairman and Managing Director: James Cooper
Sales Director: J E Atkinson
Chief Designer: K J F Bishop

Products: Diesel railcars and railbuses; gang trolleys; inspection cars; overhead line maintenance and inspection cars; crane trolleys; small trailers; self-propelled special-purpose vehicles; vehicle washing equipment.

During 1982 the company built two of a new type of rail service vehicle for Nigerian Railways, the Type BT75. It has been developed to provide a reasonably-priced, self-propelled unit with a mechanical hoist at one end for breakdown and repair work: for instance, the lifting of one end of a wagon to replace an axle damaged by a hot box. The vehicle is adaptable to a range of uses and can carry 4 tonnes of materials. The travelling hoist runs out on its beam to 1 metre beyond the end of the chassis, making the loading of the low, flat deck simple. The cabin has seating for up to ten persons including the driver, whose raised seat is reversible between two sets of controls. Two screw jacks are mounted on the hoist end of the chassis for stabilising the vehicle during lifting operations of up to 7.5 tonnes. The diesel engine is powerful enough for the car to haul a trailing load of 10 tonnes, and full four-gear performance up to 80 km/h is available in both directions.

Among the normal production of Wickham standard types during the year have been a number of the latest version of the Type 27 inspection trolleys for Zambia and Malaysia, with either enclosed or semi-open bodies. The most notable feature of the current cardan shaft-drive model compared with the earlier chain-driven model is the longer wheelbase, which gives greatly improved riding characteristics. Comfortable upholstered seating and car-type controls ensure relaxed driving conditions and a powerful petrol or diesel engine with four-speed gearbox and reversing box gives the trolley a good performance in either direction.

Constitution: D Wickham & Co, which was incorporated as a private limited company in 1912, has been building railway vehicles since 1922. The company pioneered the use of roller bearing axle boxes, welded steel frames, underslung springs and all steel bodies, using solid drawn square steel tubing to eliminate the conventional underframe and produce cars with a high power/weight ratio for operating under arduous mountain conditions. The company specialises in track maintenance and inspection vehicles and offers a wide range of equipment for this purpose.

Wickham Type BT75 service vehicle

Wickham Type 27 enclosed and semi-enclosed trolleys

Windhoff
Rheiner Maschinenfabrik Windhoff AG

Head office: Hovstrasse 10, Postfach 1160, 4440 Rheine, Federal Republic of Germany
Works: Rheine (rolling stock)
Rheine-Neuenkirchen (heat exchangers)
West Berlin (heat exchangers)

President: Dr Bernd Windhoff
Managers: Heinz Lörfing
Ewald Elling
Herbert Buchsch

Products: Standard types of shunting vehicle; Windhoff Tele-Trac with tractive forces up to 25 000 daN, diesel or electro-hydraulically driven, control of shunting and coupling operations by radio or by interlinking with the loading programme; shunting equipment for railway connections and sidings; turntables and traversers of all kinds for track vehicles; axle and bogie lifts for vehicle maintenance; multi-purpose track maintenance machines with extensive attachments; rail crane trucks; crib ballast removers; light trailers for track motor cars; overhead line inspection cars.

The Windhoff FU 80 is equipped with an hydraulic working platform, a workshop for all operational requirements, a spacious crew room and a driver's stand in each travelling direction. The vehicle is driven by a 10-cylinder air-cooled

Overhead line inspection car

diesel engine and has a maximum speed of 80 km/h. Shift transmission is normal, but for stop-and-go operations on site an hydrostatic drive is provided. The tractive power permits the coupling of additional loads that may be required on site, while at the same time the pneumatic braking system is designed for coping with any such loads.

Yale & Towne
Yale & Towne Inc
A subsidiary of Eaton Yale & Towne Inc

Trojan Division, Batavia, Illinois, USA

Products: Pneumatic tyred switching tractors; materials handling equipment; earth moving equipment.

Zastal
ZZPM Zastal Zelona Gora

Zaodrzanskie Zaklady Przemyslu Metalowego Zastal, ul Towarowa 10, 65-114 Zielona Gora, Poland

Telephone: 4411
Telegrams: Zastal, Zielona gora
Telex: 043201

Export sales: Kolmex, 49 Mokotowska, 00-542 Warsaw

Products: Covered wagons and dump cars for 1520 mm gauge operation (USSR exports), four- and six-axle high-sided coal wagons for 1435 mm gauge.

Constitution: The Zastal works is one of Europe's biggest freight car builders with an annual production of around 8000 wagons. Biggest buyers are Polish State Railways (PKP) and Soviet Railways (SZD).

Six-axle 904 V dump wagon for bulk density materials

Self-discharge 420 V wagon for granular foodstuffs

Zhuzou Rolling Stock Works

Zhuzou, Hunan, People's Republic of China

Products: Electric locomotives, traction motors and other electrical apparatus.
A typical product is the Type 'Shaoshan-1' 25 kV, 50 Hz ac Co-Co electric locomotive, weight 138 tonnes, with a continuous rating of 3780 kW and a maximum speed of 90 km/h. A 'Shaoshan-3' prototype built in 1980 is a 138-tonne locomotive with a top speed of 100 km/h and a 4800 kW rating.

Constitution: Built in 1936, the works was rebuilt and extended in 1949 and began to produce and overhaul steam locomotives, passenger coaches and goods wagons. In 1959, it produced its first main-line mixed traffic electric locomotive of Type Shaoshan-1. In 1964 it began to manufacture traction motors for both electric and diesel-electric locomotives. Overhaul of steam locomotives, passenger coaches and goods wagons ceased in 1980 and since then the works has engaged in mass production of high-power semi-conductor electric locomotives, traction motors for both electric and diesel-electric locomotives, traction transformers and many kinds of electrical apparatus. It has become the first electric locomotive works of China National Railway Technical Equipment Corporation.

'Shaoshan-3' 4800 kW 25 kV ac 50 Hz Co-Co

Zweiweg-Fahrzeug
Zweiweg-Fahrzeug GmbH & Co Vertriebs KG

Innlände 18, 8200 Rosenheim, Federal Republic of Germany

Telephone: 08031/15031
Telex: 525 731

Director: Adolf Low

Products: Track-guidance rollers which convert a road vehicle into a rail vehicle. Besides its use in creating a shunting unit (the resultant tractive power equals about that of a 20-ton locomotive) the device ZW 82S also permits use of the Daimler-Benz Unimog on rails as a working unit with various supplementary equipment.
A Zweiweg Unimog model ZW 82S provided with a steam-jet can be employed for points cleaning, for example; another unit equipped with a loading crane (and at the same time as a shunting unit) can haul up to 25 laden wagons. For winter operation a rotary snow plough or a drum-type snow plough can be fitted, permitting effective snow removal on rails as well as on the road.
Two special units are available for the construction and maintenance of catenary: a Zweiweg Unimog with hydraulic lifting platform and the Zweiweg road-railer with working platform which was initially constructed for the Netherlands Railways. The Zweiweg Unimog vehicles are also available for broad-gauge lines.
The Trenkle all-purpose vehicle Model A-52S equipped with guidance device ZW-52S is available for demonstrations on narrow gauge lines.
Fitted with Type ZW MB 3 track-guidance rollers, the Zweiweg-Mercedes Benz Transporter Type 308 has been passed by German Federal Railway (DB) for rail operation at up to 70 km/h and is adaptable to a variety of uses, from personnel transport to weed-killing, firefighting and, fitted with an overhead platform, catenary maintenance.
The Loctrac 150S has been approved by the German Federal Railway for up to 1200 tonnes wagonloads after extensive evaluating trials. This heavy-duty shunting unit is based on the Daimler-Benz MB Trac 1500 with an engine output of 110 kW and a total gross weight of 14 tonnes. On rails it is a shunting unit with 1200 tonnes capacity, and on the road, a traction unit for 120 tonnes payload.

Zweiweg Spezial tower vehicle Model ZW 82S for rapid transit, underground railways and tramway systems

Zweiweg-Unimog 1000 with Type ZW 82S track-guidance rollers and rail wagon continuous brake system supplied by three air reservoirs

Loctrac ZW 150S heavy-duty shunting unit

Zweiweg Unimog U 1100 L equipped as re-railing aid for German Federal Railway (DB)

Independently controlled track guiding devices allow quick on- and off-tracking with audio-visual indicators for safe operation. The air receivers of the railway wagon air braking system are automatically maintained at the correct working pressure by a pressure control compensator. The articulated buffer system allows negotiation of particularly tight curves and is easily demountable to facilitate the fitting of, for instance, a snow plough, a road sweeper, a crane or other implements depending on individual requirements.

A heavy duty three-axle Zweiweg unit based on a Unimog U 1200 traction head, 6 × 6 (six-wheel drive) for 6 tonnes payload is also available, equipped with a 20-tonne capacity HIAB crane.

Zweiweg-Mercedes Benz Transporter Type 308 in DB use

DIESEL ENGINES
FOR RAIL TRACTION

ABC

Anglo Belgian Corporation NV
43 Wiedauwkaai, Ghent, Belgium

Formed in 1912, to take over the SA des Anciens Ateliers Onghena which had been building gas engines since 1904, the company manufactures four-stroke diesel engines for marine, industrial and rail traction services.

DXS and DXC Series

Type: 6 and 8 cylinder vertical in-line, 4-cycle turbo-charged and charge air cooled (DXC), water cooled.
Cylinders: Bore 242 mm. Stroke 320 mm. Swept volume 14.72 litres per cylinder. Compression ratio 12.05:1. Cast iron wet type cylinder liners with two rubber seal rings. Cast iron cylinder heads secured by studs.
Pistons: Aluminium alloy with four compression rings (first ring chrome-plated) and one oil control ring with expander. Fully floating gudgeon pin.
Connecting rods: Heat treated alloy steel drop forged H section. Steel bearing shells lined with copper lead. Phosphor bronze bushes.
Crankshaft: Forged alloy steel crankshaft with copper lead lined steel bearing shells.
Crankcase: Cast iron.
Valve gear: One inlet and one exhaust silichrome steel overhead valve per cylinder. Valve seat insert in cylinder head. Gear-driven camshaft located inside the cylinder block.
Fuel injection: Direct injectors with one pump per cylinder.
Supercharger: Exhaust gas turbo-blower.
Lubrication: Forced feed with one lubricating and one scavenging gear pump.

Cooling system: Panel radiator with one centrifugal pump.
Starting: Electric or compressed air.

Model		DXS	DXC		6DZC
Turbo-charged		Yes	Yes	Yes	Yes
No of cylinders		6	6	8	6
Continuous rating	hp	650	900	1200	1803
	(kW)	(478)	(662)	(883)	(1326)
Max engine speed	rpm	750	750	750	1000
Bmep continuous	lb/in²	125	174	174	236
	(bar)	(8.8)	(12.22)	(12.22)	(16.6)
Bmep max 10% overload	lb/in²	138	191	191	260
	(bar)	(9.68)	(13.44)	(13.44)	(18.26)
Weight	lb	16 984	17 336	23 003	20 460
(dry without flywheel)	(kg)	(7720)	(7880)	(10 456)	(9300)
Length	in	129	129	158	158
	(mm)	(3270)	(3270)	(4025)	(4025)
Width	in	55	55	55	57
	(mm)	(1400)	(1400)	(1400)	(1450)
Height	in	64	64	64	72
	(mm)	(1620)	(1620)	(1620)	(1830)
Consumption fuel	lb/hp/h	0.349	0.343	0.343	0.348
	(g/kW/h)	(215)	(211)	(211)	(214)
Lube oil		0.5% fuel consumption			0.6% fuel consumption

Rated output: DIN specification

Alco Power Inc

100 Orchard Street, Auburn, New York 13021, USA

Although it has ceased manufacturing diesel-electric locomotives, Alco continues to manufacture diesel engines for both stationary and marine applications and for locomotives, and through licensees in various parts of the world including Canada, Argentina, Australia, India and Romania. It also continues to supply renewal parts and rebuilding components on a world-wide basis.

Alco was the first manufacturer in the USA to introduce turbo-supercharging for a diesel engine. The 12 and 16 cylinder V-type 244 model was introduced in the 1940s. First rated at 1580 hp at 1000 rpm, it was developed to give 1760 hp at the same speed. The V16 model gave 2360 hp. The 251 series with the same bore and stroke supersedes these. The engine design is approved by international regulating bodies ABS, Lloyds, GL, DNV, BV for stationary and marine service.

251 Series

Type: 6 cylinder in-line, 8, 12, 16 and 18 cylinder Vee, 4-cycle high pressure turbo-charged with charge air cooling.
Cylinders: Bore 9 in (228 mm). Stroke 10½ in (267 mm). Swept volume 668 in³ per cylinder. Compression ratio 11.5 : 1. Cast iron water cooled heat treated cylinder liners, chrome plated on inner surface. Cast iron-nickel alloy cylinder heads.
Pistons: Forged aluminium body with steel cap, embodying ring grooves, bolted on. Pistons cooled by pressure-circulated oil; piston pins are full-floating type.
Connecting rods: Drop-forged steel in an H beam cross-section. Piston-pin end has pressed steel-backed bronze bushing. Crank-pin bearing is grooveless in the load-carrying area.
Crankshaft: Alloy-steel forging, precision machined and heat-treated for hardness. Fully counter-balanced. Rifle-drilled oil passages through crankshafts.
Crankcase: Fabricated steel.
Valve gear: Air and exhaust valves are of wear-resistant alloy and are completely interchangeable. Cast iron valve guides are replaceable, and cylinder-head wear is reduced by use of replaceable stellite valve-seat inserts in the head. Two camshafts, one for each bank, inside engine block gear driven from crankshaft.
Fuel injection: Designed for flat fuel-consumption curves. System is high-pressure, with fuel supplied to cylinders by individual single-acting plunger pumps.
Turbo-charger: High pressure ratio exhaust gas driven turbo-charger. Alco-designed and built with replaceable blades on the turbine wheel. Water-cooled charge air cooler.
Fuel: ASTM specification 2-D. Other fuels can be used (heavy oils, natural gas, crudes, etc) with suitable standard modifications to fuel injection equipment and governing apparatus.
Lubrication: Forced feed with one gear driven pump.
Cooling system: Varies with type, locomotive or other installation. One Alco pump, gear driven from engine.
Starting: Motored main generator, or air.
Mounting: 4-point.

Alco 251 series engine

251 series specifications

No of cylinders		6 in line	8V	12V	16V	18V
Turbo-charged		Yes	Yes	Yes	Yes	Yes
Continuous rating	bhp	1500	1700	3000	3900	4500
Engine speed	rpm	1100	1000	1100	1100	1100
Bmep max	lb/in²	269	252	269	263	270
	(kg/cm²)	(18.9)	(17.7)	(18.9)	(18.5)	(19)
Engine weight (dry)	lb	24 700	26 400	32 300	42 500	49 000
	(kg)	(11 200)	(12 000)	(14 700)	(19 300)	(22 200)

Locomotive ratings

		6F	8V-F	12V-F	16V-F	18V-G
Turbocharger		Yes	Yes	Yes	Yes	Yes
Continuous rating		1500	1700	3000	3900	4500
Engine speed	rpm	1100	1000	1100	1100	1100
Bmep	lb/in²	269	252	269	263	270
	(kg/cm²)	18.9	17.7	18.9	18.5	19
Engine weight	lb	22 500	25 700	33 000	42 000	49 200
	(kg)	10 206	11 658	14 969	19 051	22 317
Length	ft in	12 10	11 7	15	17 9	20 7
	(mm)	3912	3531	4572	5410	6274
Width	ft in	4 8	5 1	5 1	5 1	5 1
	(mm)	1422	1549	1549	1549	1549
Height	ft in	7 5	8 5	9 1	9 1	9 5
	(mm)	2261	2565	2769	2769	2870

Shallow base ratings @ 90°F; 28.25"Hg 1500'—19 620 BTU/# D2 fuel (Ref DEMA)

Alsthom-Atlantique

Groupe Diesel SEMT-Pielstick
2 quai de Seine, 93203 St Denis, France

Telephone: 820 61 91
Telex: 620 333

SEMT-Pielstick PA4-185 Series

Type: 6 cylinder in-line horizontal; 6 and 8 cylinders in-line vertical; 6, 8, 12, 16 and 18 cylinders Vee (90°), 4-cycle, water cooled.
Cylinders: Bore 185 mm. Stroke 210 mm. Swept volume 5.65 litres per cylinder. Wet liners, individual cast iron cylinder heads. Central pre-combustion chamber fitted with pintle type injectors.
Pistons: Cast iron pistons cooled by pressure lubricating oil fed through connecting rod and piston pin into an annular chamber level with top compression ring.

Connecting rods: Identical for both banks of cylinders and arranged side by side on crankpins. Thin wall steel backed, copper, lead lined bearings for big end.
Crankshaft: Steel alloy with induction hardened journals. Balance weights bolted to circular webs. Power can be taken off from either end of engine.
Crankcase: Tunnel type frame unit, with integral timing gear case, enclosed by the sump.
Valve gear: 2 inlet and 2 exhaust valves with pressed-in valve inserts. Valves operated through roller-type followers by a single camshaft between cylinder banks.
Fuel injection: Pintle-type injectors fitted to pre-combustion chambers. Monobloc injection pump located inside Vee, controlled by hydraulic governor.
Superchargers: Exhaust gas turbo-chargers, one for 6 and 8 cylinder engines, one or two for 12 cylinders and two for 16 and 18 cylinders, between cylinder banks. Air coolers arranged on timing gear side.
Lubrication: Pressure feed throughout with pumps in sump below oil level.
Cooling: Water pumps fitted on timing gear end of frame.
Starting: Either electrically or by compressed air.

SEMT-Pielstick PA6-280 Series

Type: 6, 8 and 9 cylinders in line, 12, 14, 16, 18 and 20 cylinders Vee, supercharged, water cooled.

Cylinders: Bore 280 mm. Stroke 290 mm. Swept volume 17.85 litres per cylinder. Wet liners directly mounted in the crankcase, without cooling jackets. Individual cast iron cylinder heads. Single combustion chamber. Direct injection.

Pistons: Pistons made of light alloy, with inserted head, cooled by lubricating oil circulating in an annular chamber; oil is delivered by the connecting rod to the piston pin.

Connecting rods: Identical for both cylinder banks, arranged side by side on the crankpins. Notched connecting rod big end, bevel cut. Screwed cap. Cupro-lead shell on thin steel backing for the big end, babbitted steel bushing for the small end.

Crankshaft: Made of alloy steel, high frequency treated. Power can be taken off on either end of the shaft.

Crankcase: One piece, of Mechanite special, iron cast with crankshaft underslung bearings. Inlet air box integrated on top.

Valves: Two inlet valves and two exhaust valves per cylinder head, with inserted seats. Valves operated through rocking levers and cam followers from two camshafts (one per cylinder bank), housed in the crankcase, outside the Vee.

Fuel injection: Direct injection by means of injectors of the multi-hole type. Individual injecting pump housed in the crankcase, directly controlled by the camshafts. Injection controlled by hydraulic speed governor.

Turbo-chargers: Two per engine, driven by a turbine on the exhaust gas, and housed in the centre line of the engine above each end of the crankcase.

Air cooler at supercharger outlets, housed above the middle of the crankcase, and crossed by a special water line.

Lubrication: Two pumps of the gear type, driven by a timing gear train sunk into the sump.

Cooling: Two water pumps of the centrifugal type, driven by the timing train, one for jacket and cylinder head line, the other for air-cooler and lube-oil line.

Starting: Compressed air.

360-hour UIC test

The 18-cylinder 18PA6V-280 engine has officially run its 360-hour UIC locomotive test in accordance with ORE regulations.

SEMT-Pielstick PA4-200 Series

Type: 8, 12, 16 and 18 cylinders Vee (90°) 4 cycles, water cooled.
3 models:
DI: Direct injection
VG: Variable geometry pre-combustion chamber
VG, DS VG + 2: Stage turbo-charging

Cylinders: Bore 200 mm. Stroke 210 mm. Swept volume 6.6 litres per cylinder. Wet liners, individual cast iron cylinder heads.

Pistons: Cast iron pistons cooled by pressure lubricating oil fed through connecting rod and piston pin into an annular chamber level with top compression ring.

Connecting rods: Identical for both banks of cylinders and arranged side by side on crankpins. Thin wall steel backed, copper lead lined bearings for big end.

Crankshaft: Steel alloy with induction hardened journals. Balance weights bolted to circular webs. Power can be taken off from either end of engine.

Crankcase: Tunnel type frame unit, with integral timing gear case, is enclosed by the sump.

Valve gear: Two inlet and two exhaust valves with pressed-in valve inserts. Valves operated through roller-type followers by single camshaft between cylinder banks.

Fuel injection: Monobloc injection pump inside the Vee, controlled by hydraulic governor.
DI: Direct system, spray type injectors
VG: Variable geometry pre-combustion
VG, DS: Chamber

Superchargers: Exhaust gas turbo-chargers, one for 8 cylinder engine, two for 12, 16 and 18 cylinders, between cylinder banks. Air coolers arranged on timing gear side.

Lubrication: Pressure feed throughout with pumps in sump below oil level.

Cooling: Water pumps fitted on timing gear end of frame.

Starting: Either electrically or by compressed air.

The firm has lately secured a contract from Hitachi to supply 17 SEMT-Pielstick 12PA4-200 VG diesel engines rated at 2400 hp to equip diesel-electric railway locomotives for use in Malaya. This order is a follow-up to a Hitachi order currently being filled for 10 engines of the same type to equip railway locomotives for use in Pakistan.

SEMT-Pielstick 18PA6V-280 engine, UIC rating 1200 hp at 1050 rpm

SEMT-Pielstick 18PA4V-200 engine, UIC rating 3150 hp at 1500 rpm

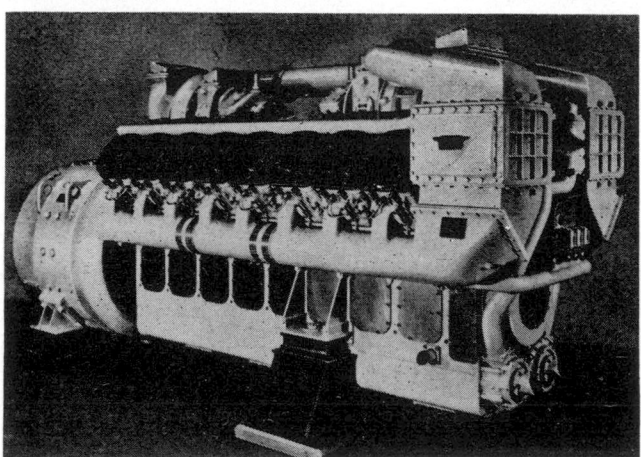

SEMT-Pielstick 16PA4V-185 engine, UIC rating 2400 hp at 1500 rpm

SEMT-Pielstick 12PA4-200 VG engine as supplied to Hitachi

| | In-Line | | | | | Vee | | |
	6 PA6L	8PA6L	9PA6L	12PA6V	14PA6V	16PA6V	18PA6V	20PA6V
No of cylinders	6	8	9	12	14	16	18	20
Supercharged	Yes	Yes	Yes	Yes	Yes	Yes	Yes	Yes
Charge air cooled	Yes	Yes	Yes	Yes	Yes	Yes	Yes	Yes
Power rating (UIC) (hp)	2400	3200	3600	4800	5600	6400	7200	8000
Engine speed	1050	1050	1050	1050	1050	1050	1050	1050
Piston speed (ft/min)	1015	1015	1015	1015	1015	1015	1015	1015
Bmep	2030	2030	2030	2030	2030	2030	2030	2030
Weight (dry) (kg)	11 200	14 400	16 000	18 800	21 500	24 100	26 200	28 500
Length (mm)	3860	4700	5120	3675	4135	4595	5055	5515
Width (mm)	1425	1425	1425	1780	1780	1780	1780	1780
Height (mm)	2630	2670	2670	2480	2480	2480	2480	2480

	PA4-200 VG				PA4-200 VG DS			
No of cylinders	8	12	16	18	8	12	16	18
Turbo-charged	Yes	Yes	Yes	Yes	Yes	Yes	Yes	Yes
Charge air cooled	Yes	Yes	Yes	Yes	Yes	Yes	Yes	Yes
Power rating (hp)	1540	2310	3080	3465	1920	2880	3840	4320
Bmep	17.3	17.3	17.3	17.3	23	23	23	23
Weight (dry) (kg)	4500	6200	7900	8800	5300	7200	9300	10 200
Length (mm)	2090	2530	3130	3430	1878	2975	3078	3378
Width (mm)	1580	1450	1700	1700	1450	1450	1850	1850
Height (mm)	1865	1800	1865	1865	2226	2285	2225	2225

		6PA4H 185	6PA4L 185	8PA4L 185	6PA4V 185	8PA4V 185	12PA4V 185	16PA4V 185	18PA4V 185	8PV4V 200	PA4 200 DI 12PA4V 200	16PA4V 200	18PA4V 200
No of cylinders		6 horiz	6 line	8 line	6 Vee	8 Vee	12 Vee	16 Vee	18 Vee	8	12	16	18
Turbo-charged		Yes	Yes	Yes	Yes	Yes	Yes	Yes	Yes	Yes	Yes	Yes	Yes
Charge air cooled		Yes	Yes	Yes	Yes	Yes	Yes	Yes	Yes	Yes	Yes	Yes	Yes
Power rating (UIC)	hp	1000	1000	1335	1000	1335	2000	2670	3000	1400	2100	2800	3150
	rpm				1500						1500		
Piston speed	ft/min				1968						1968		
	(m/s)				(10.5)						(10.5)		
Bmep	lb/in²				227						227		
	(kg/cm²)				(16)						(16)		
Weight (dry)	lb	7500	7500	9700	7100	8530	12 390	15 700	17 700	9500	13 200	17 000	19 000
	(kg)	(3400)	(3400)	(4400)	(3220)	(3870)	(5620)	(7120)	(7970)	(4300)	(6000)	(7720)	(8620)
Length	in	117.3	120.2	143.8	63.8	75.8	99.4	123.1	134.9	75.8	99.4	123.1	134.9
	(mm)	(2980)	(3054)	(3654)	(1626)	(1926)	(2526)	(3126)	(3426)	(1926)	(2526)	(3126)	(3426)
Width	in	68.9	33.9	33.9	57.1	57.1	57.1	57.1	67	62	57.1	66.9	66.9
	(mm)	(1750)	(860)	(860)	(1450)	(1450)	(1450)	(1450)	(1702)	(1575)	(1450)	(1700)	(1700)
Height	in	33.5	65.4	65.4	73.3	73.3	75.6	73.3	73.3	73.4	75.6	73.4	73.6
	(mm)	(850)	(1660)	(1660)	(1863)	(1863)	(1921)	(1863)	(1863)	(1865)	(1920)	(1865)	(1920)

Beijing
Beijing "Feb 7th" Locomotive Works
Member of China National Machinery and Export Corporation

Erhlikou, Hsichiao, Beijing, China

Telegrams: Machimpex, Beijing
Telex: 22328; 22242

The main diesel engine produced at China's "Feb 7th" works is the type 12240, having passed GB 1105-74 testing for diesel locomotives: 100-hour typing test (rated power at 1100 rpm, 2700 hp; hourly overload 3000 hp); 500-hour endurance and reliability test (rated power 2700 hp; hourly overload 3000 hp); and 100-hour intensification test (rated power 3000 hp; hourly overload 3300 hp).

Type 12240 diesel engine
Type: 12 cylinders, 4-stroke, single acting, Vee 45 degree.
Cylinders: Bore 240 mm. Stroke, main cylinder 260 mm, auxiliary cylinder 273.51 mm. Compression ratio 12.5:1.
Direction of rotation: Clockwise (viewed from main power take-off end).
Fuel injection: Solid direct.
Weight, dry: 14 600 kg.

Type 12240 engine

	Diesel engine standard design		Intensified design	
hp	2700	3000	2700	3000
rpm	1100	1100	1100	1100
Fuel consumption (g/hp/h)	153.4	156.9	149.5	153
Max combustion pressure (kgf/cm²)	120	124	113.2	130.25
Temp at turbine entrance (°C)	540	563	545	605
Exhaust gas index (Bosch)	1	1.6	0.95	1.45
Pressure of intake gas (kgf/cm²)	2.25	2.46	2.265	2.712
Temp of intake gas (°C)	62	66	58	66.5
Mean effective pressure (kgf/cm²)	15.65	17.4	15.65	19.13
Co-efficient of mechanical load (m²/min²)	75.5	75.5	75.5	75.5
Co-efficient of thermal load (hp/cm²)	0.477	0.53	0.477	0.58
Co-efficient of intensification (kg/cm². m/s)	149.1	166	149.1	183

Type 12240 diesel engine for Beijing type diesel locomotive

British Leyland
Leyland Vehicles Ltd, Leyland Power Systems
Bolton Road, Chorley, Lancashire PR7 3EL, England

Products: Flat form railcar engines, 170 to 240 bhp models, 4.5 kg per bhp four stroke.

Caterpillar
Caterpillar Tractor Co
Engine Division, 100 NE Adams St, Peoria, Illinois 61629, USA

Caterpillar Overseas SA
118 rue du Rhône, 1211 Geneva 3, Switzerland

Caterpillar builds a range of diesel engines with outputs from 85 to 1600 hp. These engines are designed for a wide range of industrial and railway applications.

Specification for all models
Cylinders: Removable wet type cylinder liners of hardened cast iron. Alloy cast iron cylinder heads with water directors and removable precombustion chambers.
Pistons: Aluminium alloy with cast-in-iron ring band, stainless steel heat plug, and chrome-faced rings.
Connecting rods: Forged of Boron steel and shot peened.
Crankshaft: Total hardened crankshaft, superfinished and dynamically balanced.
Crankcase: Strongly reinforced, one-piece alloy cast iron with large inspection plates.

Fuel injection: Gear-type transfer pumps, replaceable full-flow filter elements, individual fuel injection pumps and injection valves. Designed and built by Caterpillar. Series 3500 employ unit-type injectors by Caterpillar.

Fuel: No 2 fuel oil (ASTM Specifications D396-48T). Premium quality diesel fuel can be used, but it is not required.

Lubrication: Full pressure system. Includes gear-type pump, efficient filter elements and water-cooled oil cooler.

Cooling system: Built-in, centrifugal-type circulating pump. Thermostatic water temperature control.

Starting: Air, electric.

Caterpillar Model 3516 16-cylinder Vee engine

		D399	D398	D379	3512	3516	3508	3412	3408	3406	3306	3304
Bore & stroke	in	6.25 × 8	6.25 × 8	6.25 × 8	6.7 × 7.5	6.7 × 7.5	6.7 × 7.5	5.4 × 6	5.4 × 6	5.4 × 6.5	4.75 × 6	4.75 × 6
	(mm)	(159 × 203)	(159 × 203)	(159 × 203)	(170 × 190)	(170 × 190)	(170 × 190)	(137 × 152)	(137 × 152)	(137 × 165)	(121 × 152)	(121 × 152)
No of cylinders		V-16	V-12	V-8	V-12	V-16	V-8	V-12	V-8	1-6	1-6	1-4
Turbo-charged		Yes	Yes	Yes	Yes	Yes	Yes	Yes	Yes	Yes	Yes	Yes
Aftercooled		Yes	Yes	Yes	Yes	Yes	Yes	Yes	Yes	Yes	Yes	No
Locomotive rating	bhp*	1300	975	650	1140	1600	800	750	475	375	270	165
	rpm	1300	1300	1300	1500	1800	1500	2100	2100	2100	2200	2200
Weight (dry)	lb	14 650	12 040	9100	12 600	17 100	10 500	4720	3365	2960	2160	1655
	(kg)	(6660)	(5475)	(4140)	(5715)	(7763)	(4763)	(2141)	(1526)	(1340)	(980)	(750)
Length	in	131.9	109.8	81.7	106.2	132.5	85	78.5	62.6	65.4	62	50.3
	(mm)	(3350)	(2788)	(2075)	(2699)	(3366)	(2159)	(1995)	(1590)	(1660)	(1575)	(1280)
Width	in	61.4	61.4	61.4	67	73.9	67	60.4	48.5	35.5	30.8	32.3
	(mm)	(1560)	(1560)	(1560)	(1703)	(1878)	(1703)	(1535)	(1230)	(902)	(785)	(320)
Height	in	75.1	75.1	75.1	67.7	67.1	67.7	68.2	54.2	52.6	46.1	39.4
	(mm)	(1910)	(1910)	(1910)	(1720)	(1703)	(1720)	(1730)	(1376)	(1335)	(1170)	(1110)

* Consult factory for applicable ratings dependent on service.

Cockerill

Cockerill Mechanical Industries
Diesel Engine Department
(formerly Cockerill Sambre Mechanical Construction Division)
A subsidiary of Cockerill Sambre SA

4100 Seraing, Belgium

Telephone: 3241 36 60 00
Telex: 41225

Launched in 1965, the present 240CO series is now in its third generation. Developing 1170 to 3120 kW (1590-4240 hp) at 1000 rpm, it is being used world-wide for rail traction, marine propulsion and power generation.

A recent contract provides for delivery of 18 8TR240CO engines to power 84-tonne diesel-electric Co-Co locomotives of a new design for Viet-Nam.

Constitution: The present company is the result of the merger in 1981 of SA Cockerill and SA Hainaut-Sambre. Cockerill Sambre is the sixth largest European steel concern and employs more than 60 000 people. The group includes 150 subsidiaries located all over the world. Its Mechanical Construction Division has traditionally specialised in machinery for power generation and transportation.

The first Cockerill diesel engine was built in 1913 with assistance from its inventor Rudolf Diesel.

Series 240CO
Type: 6 and 8 cylinders in-line, 12 and 16 cylinders in Vee, 4 cycle water cooled.
Cylinders: Bore 9½ in (241.3 mm). Stroke 12 in (304.8 mm). Swept volume 13.92 litres per cylinder. Cast iron wet cylinder liners, separate cast iron cylinder heads, direct injection combustion chambers.
Pistons: Oil-cooled pistons made of aluminium alloy.
Connecting rods: Drop forged.
Crankshaft: Cro-Mo steel induction hardened pins and journals.
Crankcase: One-piece nodular cast iron cylinder block.
Valve gear: Two inlet and two exhaust valves per cylinder.
Fuel injection: Mechanical pumps and nozzles.
Lubrication: One pressure pump.
Cooling system: One centrifugal water pump.

		240CO Series			
		6TR	8TR	V12TR	V16TR
No of cylinders		6	8	12	16
Turbo-charged		Yes	Yes	Yes	Yes
Charge air cooled		Yes	Yes	Yes	Yes
Weight (dry)	lb	18 722	24 230	34 580	45 815
	kg	(8500)	(11 000)	(15 700)	(20 800)
Length	in	129.92	156.93	171.77	232.28
	(mm)	(3300)	(3986)	(4363)	(5900)
Width	in	47.64	48.03	86.62	84.25
	(mm)	(1210)	(1220)	(2200)	(2140)
Height	in	104.73	104.73	93.11	105.08
	(mm)	(2660)	(2660)	(2365)	(2669)
Speed		1000 rpm			
Continuous power*	hp	1590	2120	3180	4240
	(kW)	(1170)	(1560)	(2340)	(3120)
Bmep	lb/in²	243	243	243	243
	(kg/cm²)	(17.2)	(17.2)	(17.2)	(17.2)
Piston speed	ft/min	1999	1999	1999	1999
	(m/s)	(10.16)	(10.16)	(10.16)	(10.16)
Fuel consumption	lb/hp/h	0.336	0.338	0.332	0.322
	(g/hp/h)	(150.5)	(151.5)	(148.5)	(144)

*To UIC 623-1

Shunting locomotive powered by 6TR240CO diesel, nominal output 1500 hp at 1000 rpm

8TR240CO diesel for rail traction, output 2120 hp at 1000 rpm

V16TR240CO for rail traction, output 4240 hp at 1000 rpm

Cummins
Cummins Engine Co, Inc
Box 3005, Columbus, Indiana 47201, USA

Telephone: (812) 372 7211
Telegrams: Cumdiex, Columbus
Telex: 217 411

Cummins Engine Co manufactures a range of diesel engines from 175 to 1200 hp for a wide variety of applications. Experience in industrial and railway installations covers more than 40 years. Over 5600 sales and service outlets are located throughout the world. Cummins design features are listed for its KTA-3067-L engine.

Aftercooler: Large-capacity aftercooler results in cooler, denser intake air for more efficient combustion and reduced internal stresses for longer life. Aftercooler is located in engine coolant system eliminating need for special plumbing.
Bearings: Replaceable, precision type, steel-backed inserts. Nine main bearings, 6½ in (165 mm) diameter. Connecting rod bearings 4¼ in (108 mm) diameter.
Camshaft: Dual camshafts precisely control valve and injector timing. Lobes are induction-hardened for long life. Eighteen replaceable precision type bearings 3 in (76 mm) diameter.
Camshaft followers: Induction-hardened, roller-type for long cam and follower life.
Connecting rods: Drop-forged, H-beam 11²/₅ in (290 mm) centre-to-centre length. Rifle-drilled for pressure lubrication of piston pin. Rod is tapered on piston pin end to reduce unit pressures.
Cooling system: Gear-driven centrifugal water pump. Large-volume water passages provide even flow of coolant around cylinder liners, valves, and injectors. Four modulating by-pass thermostats regulate coolant temperature. Spin-on corrosion resistors check rust and corrosion, control acidity, and remove impurities.
Crankshaft: High-tensile strength steel forging with induction hardened fillets. Fully counterweighted and spin-balanced.
Cylinder block: Alloy cast iron with removable wet liners. Cross-bolt support to main bearing cap provides extra strength and stability.
Cylinder heads: Alloy cast iron. Each head serves one cylinder. Valve seats are replaceable corrosion-resistant inserts. Valve guides and crosshead guides are replaceable inserts.
Cylinder liners: Replaceable wet liners dissipate heat faster than dry liners and are easily replaced without reboring the block.

Fuel system: Cummins exclusive low pressure PT system with wear compensating pump and integral dual flyball governor. Camshaft-actuated fuel injectors give accurate metering and timing. Spin-on fuel filters.
Gear train: Timing gears and accessory drive gears are induction-hardened helical gears driven from crankshaft and located at front of block.
Lubrication: Large-capacity gear pump provides pressure lubrication to all bearings and oil supply for piston cooling. All pressure lines are internal drilled passages in block and heads. Oil cooler, full-flow filters, and by-pass filters maintain oil condition and maximise oil and engine life.
Pistons: Aluminium alloy, cam-ground and barrel-shaped to compensate for thermal expansion assures precise fit at operating temperatures. CeCorr grooved-skirt finish provides superior lubrication. Oil cooled for rapid heat dissipation. Two compression and one oil ring.
Piston pins: Full floating, tubular steel retained by snap rings. 2²/₅ in (61 mm) diameter.
Turbo-charger: Two AiResearch exhaust gas-driven turbochargers mounted at top of engine. Turbocharging provides more power, improved fuel economy, altitude compensation, and lower smoke and noise levels.
Valves: Dual 2¹/₅ in (56 mm) diameter poppet type intake and exhaust valves. Wear resistant face on exhaust valves.

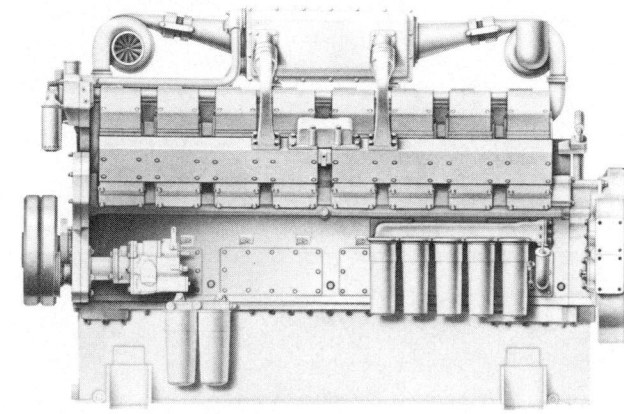

Cummins KTA-3067-L engine

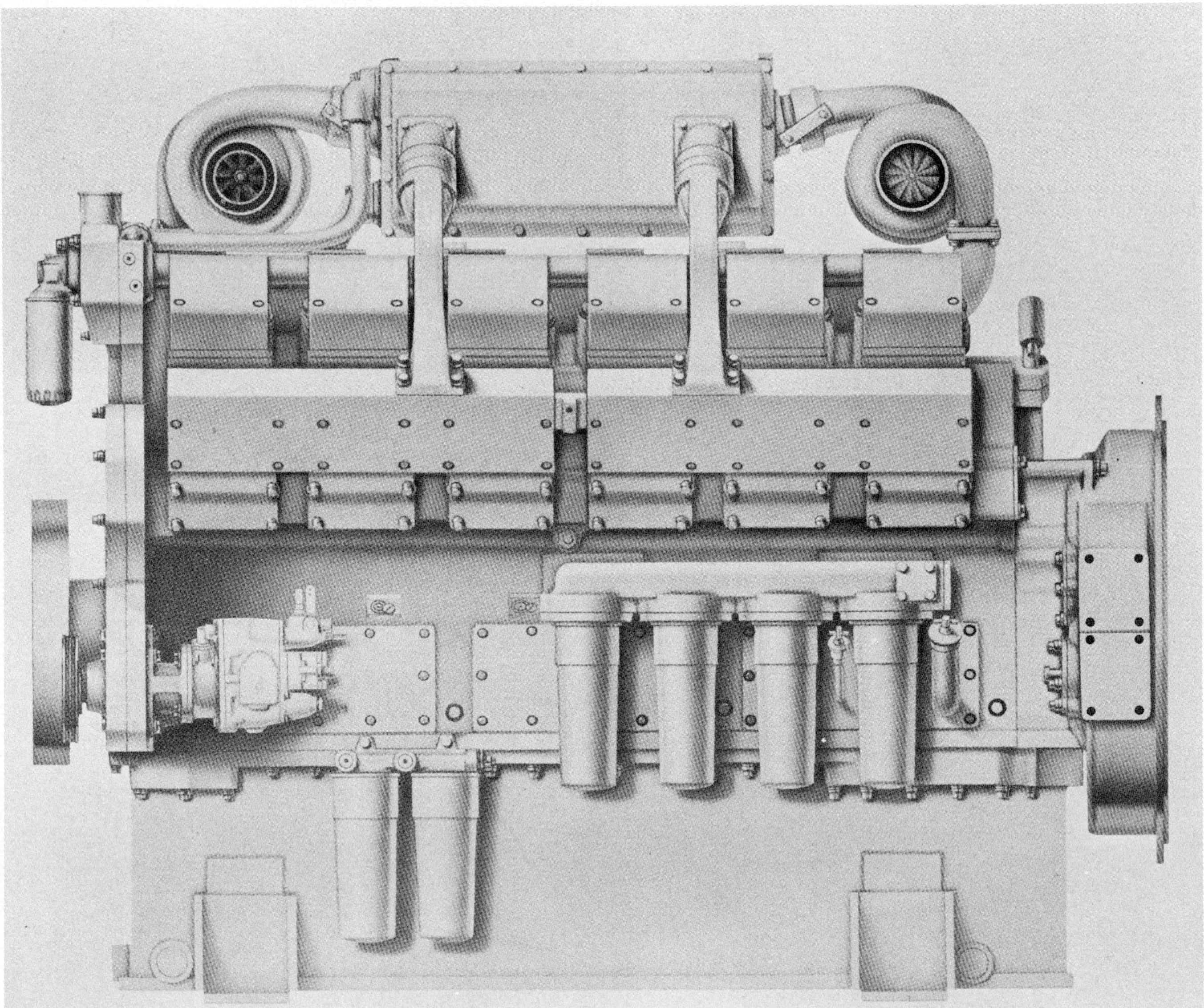

Cummins KTA-2300-L engine

Engine	Intermittent traction rating BS 2953: 1958 hp at rpm		Continuous traction rating UIC and BS 2953: 1958 hp at rpm		Displacement cubic inches (litres)	Bore and stroke inches (mm)	Number of cylinders	Aspiration	Net weight lb (kg)
Locomotive engines									
N-855-L3	235	2100	200	1900	855	5½ × 6	6	N	2590
			210	2100	(14)	(140 × 152)			(1175)
NT-855-L4	335	2100	275	1900	855	,,	6	T	2625
			285	2100	(14)				(1191)
NTA-855-L3	400	2100	335	1900	855	,,	6	T/A	2750
			340	2100	(14)				(1247)
VTA-1710-L1	700	2100	560	1900	1710	,,	12	T/A	5780
			595	2100	(28)				(2621)
VTA-1710-L2	800	2100	640	1900	1710	,,	12	T/A	5780
			680	2100	(28)				(2621)
KT-1150-L	450	2100	370	1900	1150	6¼ × 6¼	6	T	3450
			380	2100	(18.8)	(159 × 159)			(1565)
KTA-1150-L	600	2100	490	1900	1150	,,	6	T/A	3500
			510	2100	(18.8)				(1588)
KT-2300-L	900	2100	725	1900	2300	,,	12	T	7750
			765	2100	(37.6)				(3315)
*KTA-2300-L	1200	2100	975	1900	2300	,,	12	T/A	9250
			1020	2100	(37.6)				(4200)
*KTA-3067-L	1600	2100	1290	1400	3067	,,	16	T/A	12 000
			1360	2100	(50.3)				(5455)
Railcar engines									
N-855-R2	235	2100	210	2100	855	5½ × 6	6	N	2600
					(14)	(140 × 152)			(1185)
NT-855-R4	335	2100	285	2100	855	,,	6	T	2700
					(14)				(1200)
NTA-855-R	430	2100	340	2100	855	,,	6	T/A	2800
					(14)				(1255)

*Certified to BS 2953: 1958 BSI Certificate No 36791 (KTA-2300-L); Certificate No 50015 (KTA-3067-1)

Dalian

Dalian Locomotive and Rolling Stock Works
Member of China National Machinery Import and Export Corporation
Dalian, Liaoning, People's Republic of China

Telegrams: Dallocwks, Dalian China

Products: Diesel-generator sets for 'Dong Feng' type diesel locomotives. Main specifications of the Model 16240Z engine produced for the 'Dong Feng 7' are:
Bore: 240 mm
Stroke: 275 mm
Total displacement: 199 litres
Compression ratio: 125:1
Rated speed: 1100 rpm
Lowest idle speed: 500 rpm
Continuous power rating: 3600 hp
Mean effective pressure: 14.8 kgf/cm²
Max firing pressure: <120 kgf/cm²
Specific fuel consumption: 155+5 g/hp/h
Specific oil consumption: <1.5 g/hp/h
Exhaust gas temperature: <620°C

Diesel-generator set for Type 'Dong Feng 7' diesel locomotive

Deutz

Klockner-Humboldt-Deutz AG
Postfach 800509, 5000 Cologne-Deutz, Federal Republic of Germany

The Deutz Engine Works is the oldest internal combustion engine factory in the world. Started in 1864 as N A Otto & Co, it soon became Gasmotorenfabrik Deutz AG. The first engine working on the OTTO or four-stroke cycle, invented by N A Otto, was built in 1876.

Deutz diesel engines range from 3 to 9856 hp (2-7250 kW) for industrial, marine, rail, traction and automotive applications. They are all four-stroke, air-cooled (3-525 hp) or water-cooled (113-9856 hp). For rail traction series B/FL 413F, BAM 816 and PA6V 280 are used.

Series B/FL 413F
Type: 6, 8, 10 and 12 cylinder Vee 4-stroke, air-cooled, direct injection or 2-stage combustion.
Cylinders: Bore 125 mm. Stroke 130 mm. Swept volume 1.59 litres per cylinder. Compression ratio 18 : 1 (naturally aspirated), 16.5 : 1 (turbo-charged).

Series BAM 816
Type: 6 and 8 cylinder in-line, 12 and 16 cylinder Vee, 4-stroke, water-cooled, two-stage combustion system.
Cylinders: Bore 142 mm. Stroke 160 mm. Swept volume 2.53 litres per cylinder. Compression ratio 16:1.

Deutz F12L 413F 12-cylinder air-cooled engine

Deutz BA16M 816 16-cylinder water-cooled engine

Series B/FL 413F		F6L	F8L	BF8L	F10L	BF10L	F12L	BF12L	BF12L*
No of cylinders		6V	8V	8V	10V	10V	12V	12V	12V
Turbo-charged				Yes		Yes		Yes	Yes
Output (UIC)	kW	123	165	210	206	262	246	315	349
	hp	167	225	286	280	356	335	428	475
Engine speed	rpm	2500	2500	2500	2500	2500	2500	2500	2500
Length	in	41¼	47¹¹/₁₆	49⅝	55⁹/₁₆	56⁵/₁₆	62	61¹⁵/₁₆	62¼
	(mm)	(1047)	(1211)	(1260)	(1412)	(1430)	(1575)	(1573)	(1582)
Width	in	40⅞	40⅞	42³/₁₆	40⅞	44	40⅞	46¹⁵/₁₆	47¹/₁₆
	(mm)	(1038)	(1038)	(1072)	(1038)	(1118)	(1038)	(1192)	(1196)
Height	in	33⅞	33⅞	40⁹/₁₆	36⅞	41⁵/₁₆	37⅝	41⁵/₁₆	48¹⁵/₁₆
	(mm)	(860)	(860)	(1030)	(937)	(1050)	(956)	(1050)	(1243)
Weight	lb	1450	1825	2025	2180	2510	2465	2750	2860
	(kg)	(660)	(830)	(920)	(990)	(1140)	(1120)	(1250)	(1300)

*Charge air cooled

Series BAM 816		BA6M LLK U	BA6M LLK W	BA8M LLK U	BA8M LLK W	BA12M LLK U	BA12M LLK W	BA16M LLK U	BA16M LLK W
No of cylinders		6	6	8	8	12	12	16	16
Turbo-charged		Yes	Yes	Yes	Yes	Yes	Yes	Yes	Yes
Charge air cooled		Yes	Yes	Yes	Yes	Yes	Yes	Yes	Yes
Output (UIC)	kW	303	342	404	456	607	684	809	912
	hp	412	465	549	620	826	930	1100	1240
Engine speed	rpm	1800	1800	1800	1800	1800	1800	1800	1800
Length	in	72		84⅞		76¹³/₁₆		97⅛	
	(mm)	(1829)		(2156)		(1951)		(2467)	
Width	in	38¾		37½		64		64	
	(mm)	(984)		(952)		(1626)		(1626)	
Height	in	56¹¹/₁₆		58		52¹⁵/₁₆		52¹⁵/₁₆	
	(mm)	(1440)		(1473)		(1345)		(1345)	
Weight	lb	3540		4520		6395		7980	
	(kg)	(1605)		(2050)		(2900)		(3620)	

Series PA6V 280		12PA6V	14PA6V	16PA6V	18PA6V
No of cylinders		12V	14V	16V	18V
Turbo-charged		Yes	Yes	Yes	Yes
Charge air cooled		Yes	Yes	Yes	Yes
Output (UIC)	kW	3530	4120	4710	5295
	hp	4800	5600	6400	7200
Engine speed	rpm	1050	1050	1050	1050
Length	in	144¾	162¾	181	199
	(mm)	(3675)	(4135)	(4595)	(5055)
Width	in	70¹/₁₆	70¹/₁₆	70¹/₁₆	70¹/₁₆
	(mm)	(1780)	(1780)	(1780)	(1780)
Height	in	97⅝	97⅝	97⅝	97⅝
	(mm)	(2480)	(2480)	(2480)	(2480)
Weight	lb	41 360	47 300	53 020	57 640
	(kg)	(18 800)	(21 500)	(24 100)	(26 200)

Energomachexport

Deguninskaja Str, 1, Korp 4, 127486 Moscow, USSR

Principal specifications of diesel locomotive engines

Series		D49				D50			D70				M		1D
Type		4-stroke Vee				4-stroke In-line			4-stroke Vee				4-stroke Vee		4-stroke Vee
Bore	in	10.24				12.5			9.45				7.09		5.9
	(mm)	(260)				(318)			(240)				(180)		(150)
Stroke	in	10.24				13			10.63				7.88/8.26		7.09/7.35
	(mm)	(260)				(330)			(270)				(200/208.8)		(180/186.7)
Model		4D49	12D49	D49-V16	D49-F	D50	D50M	11D1M	8D70	12D70	D70	D70F	M753	M756	1D12
No of cylinders		6	12	16	16	6	6	6	8	12	16	16	12	12	12
Output	hp	1200	2000	3000	4000	1000	1000	1200	1200	2000	3000	4000	750	1000	400
Engine speed	rpm	1000	1000	1000	1000	740	740	750	1000	1000	1000	1000	1400	1500	1600
Piston speed	ft/min	1713	1713	1713	1713	1604	1604	1624	1772	1772	1772	1772	1837/1929	2087/2205	1890
	(m/s)	(8.7)	(8.7)	(8.7)	(8.7)	(8.15)	(8.15)	(8.25)	(9)	(9)	(9)	(9)	(9.3/9.8)	(10.6/11.2)	(9.6)
Bmep	lb/in²	188	156	174	232	110	110	131	196	175	196	262	105	131	82.5
	(kg/cm²)	(13.2)	(11)	(12.2)	(16.3)	(7.7)	(7.7)	(9.2)	(13.8)	(12.3)	(13.8)	(18.4)	(7.4)	(9.2)	(5.8)
Weight	lb	14 300	24 200	30 900	30 900	39 700			24 700	31 300	37 500	37 500	35 300	39 700	41 900
	(kg)	(6500)	(11 000)	(14 000)	(14 000)	(18 000)			(11 200)	(14 200)	(17 000)	(17 000)	(16 000)	(18 000)	(19 000)
Length	in	96	142	170	170	205			157	181	217	220	89.4	95.3	61.4
	(mm)	(2400)	(3600)	(4300)	(4300)	(5200)			(4000)	(4600)	(5500)	(5600)	(2270)	(2420)	(1560)
Width	in	55	63	63	63	59			63	63	63	63	42.7	44.1	33.7
	(mm)	(1400)	(1600)	(1600)	(1600)	(1500)			(1600)	(1600)	(1600)	(1600)	(1085)	(1120)	(856)
Height	in	90	102	110	110	98			110	114	118	118	47.3	58.3	42.3
	(mm)	(2300)	(2600)	(2800)	(2800)	(2500)			(2800)	(2900)	(3000)	(3000)	(1200)	(1480)	(1075)

Series		D100				D40	D45
Type		2-stroke, opposed piston				2-stroke Vee	2-stroke Vee
Bore	in	8.15				9.06	9.06
	(mm)	(207)				(230)	(230)
Stroke	in	10				11.8/11.98	11.8/11.98
	(mm)	(254)				(300/304.3)	(300/304.3)
Model		6D100	2D100	10D100	9D100-F	1D40	11D45
No of cylinders		8	10	10	12	12	16
Output	hp	2000	2000	3000	4000	2000	3000
Engine speed	rpm	850	850	850	900	750	750
Piston speed	ft/min	1417	1417	1417	1496	1476	1476
	(m/s)	(7.2)	(7.2)	(7.2)	(7.6)	(7.5)	(7.5)
Bmep	lb/in²	111	88	132	108	115	129
	(kg/cm²)	(7.8)	(6.2)	(9.3)	(7.6)	(8.1)	(9.1)
Weight	lb	34 200	42 750	46 300	50 700	23 100	30 400
	(kg)	(15 500)	(19 400)	(21 000)	(23 000)	(10 500)	(13 800)
Length	in	238.3	240.7	243.3	260.6	145.7	158.3
	(mm)	(6052)	(6115)	(6180)	(6620)	(3700)	(4020)
Width	in	66.5	56.7	68.1	59.1	69.7	66.9
	(mm)	(1690)	(1440)	(1730)	(1500)	(1770)	(1700)
Height	in	118.6	127.6	126.4	124.0	95.3	97.2
	(mm)	(3013)	(3240)	(3210)	(3150)	(2421)	(2470)

Engine model	2-5E49	1A-5E49	3-5E49R2	14E40	2-6E49	0E-1L	3A-6E49	211E-2	1E12-400	W1E6-250TRJQ3	RA3-L204A
No of strokes	4	4	4	2	4	4	4	4	4	4	2
Rated power (hp)	4000	3000	2800 (2600)	2000 (1690)	1450	1200 (1030)	1200	750	400	250	120
Cylinder arrangement	Vee-type	Vee-type	Vee-type	Vee-type	Vee-type	In-line	Vee-type	In-line	Vee-type	In-line	In-line
No of cylinders	16	16	16	12	8	6	8	6	12	6	4
Diameter of cylinder (mm)	260	260	260	230	260	318	260	210	150	150	108
Piston stroke (mm)	260	260	260	300/ 304.3	260	330	260	210	180	180	127
Rated speed (rpm)	1000	1000	1000	750	1000	750	1000	1400	1600	1500	2000
Specific fuel consumption, g/bhp/h	157+5%	151+5%	158+5%	160+5%	150+5%	165+5% (174+5%)	150+5%	155+5%	170	160+5%	190
Locomotives on which engine is used	TZ129	TZ109	RZ114	L62	RZL6Q	RZL2	RDL6A RDL8	RDL4A RDL4	RDL23B RW72	RDJ2	RW6A

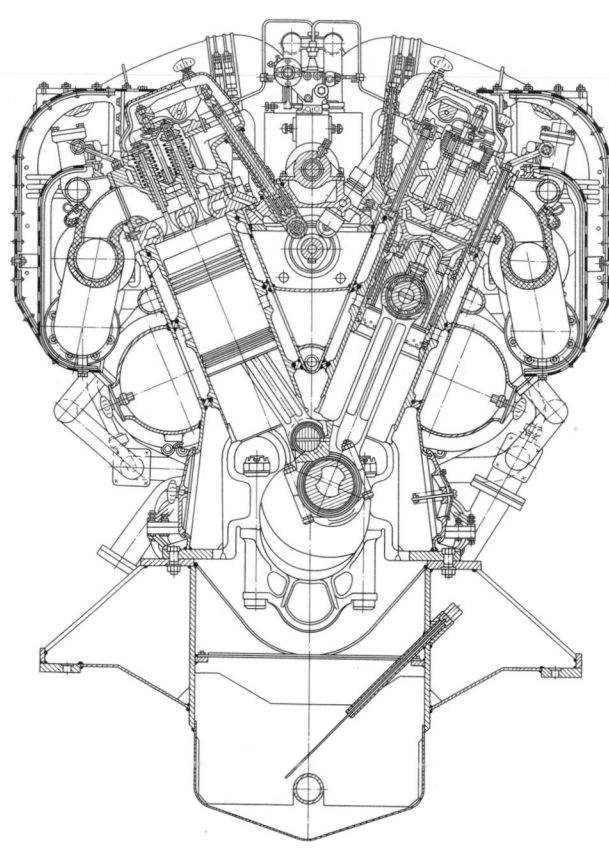

Cross-section of Model 14E40 diesel engine

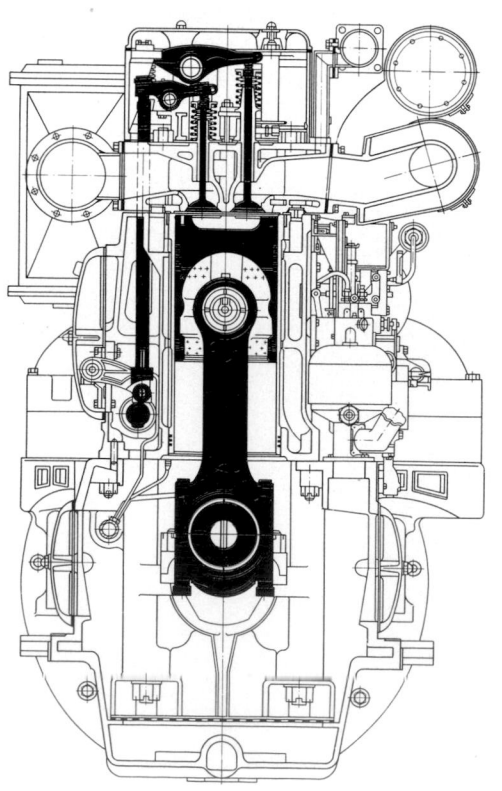

Cross-section of Model OE-1L diesel engine

Model D49 16-cylinder Vee engine, turbo-charged and charge air cooled, built by Kolomna Diesel Works

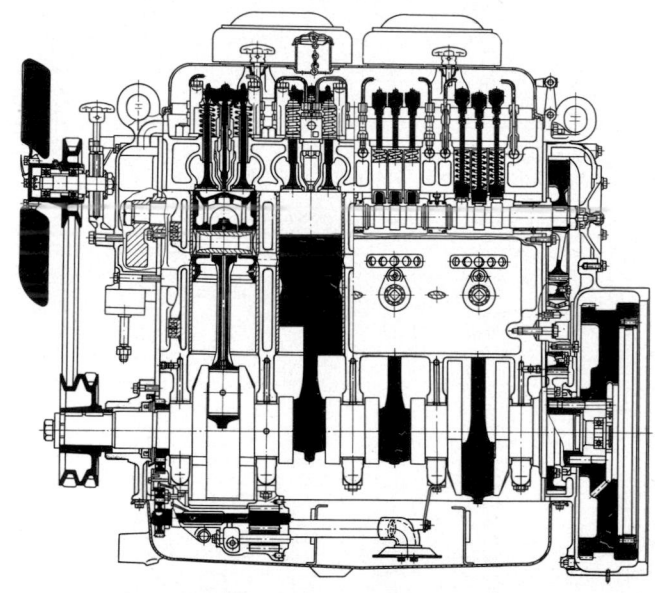

Longitudinal section of Model RA3-L204A diesel engine

Model 1E12-400 diesel engine

Fiat Concord

Fiat Concord SAIC

Cerrito 740, 1309 Buenos Aires, Argentina

Telephone: 35 3044
Telex: 012 11141

Products: Diesel engines.

Ganz-Mávag

PO Box 136, Konyves Kálmán korut 76, Budapest, Hungary

Ganz-Mávag Works build various diesel engines, mainly for their own makes of locomotive and railcar. Two typical products are:

SEMT-Pielstick 12PA4V-185 VG made under licence from Alsthom-Atlantique, France

Type: 12 cylinders in Vee, 4 stroke with variable geometry combustion chamber, turbocharged and intercooled.

Cylinders: Bore 185 mm, stroke 210 mm, swept volume 5.65 litres per cylinder. Individual cylinder heads and separate cast-iron water jackets with wet liners. Nodular graphite iron pistons with internal oil cooling.

Connecting rods: Side-by-side type.

Crankcase: Tunnel type, with integral oil sump of arc-welded steel castings and steel plates.

Fuel injection: Conventional type injection pump and pintle type injectors.

Ganz-Mávag 12VFE 17/24 12-cylinder Vee

Valve gear: Single camshaft in the Vee, with push-rods and rockers.

Output: Nominal power rating 1472 kW/2000 hp at 1500 rpm.

Dry weight: About 6700 kg complete with all accessories.

PA4 engine range also comprises 6, 8, 16 and 18 cylinder models.

Type 12 VFE 17/24-T

Type: 12 cylinders in Vee, 4 stroke with pre-chamber, turbo-charged and inter-cooled.

Cylinders: Bore 170 mm, stroke 240 mm, swept volume 5.45 litres per cylinder. Individual cylinder heads, wet liners and light metal oil cooled pistons.

Connecting rods: Fork-and-blade type.

Crankcase: Light alloy casting with separate oil sump.

Fuel injection: Jendrassik type spring injection pump and semi-open injectors.

Valve gears: Single camshaft in the Vee, with push-rods and rockers.

Output: Nominal power rating 736 kW/1000 hp at 1250 rpm.

Dry weight: About 5000 kg complete with accessories.

17/24 range also comprises 6 and 8 cylinder models.

Ganz-Mávag-Pielstick 12 PA4V-185 engine

Gardner

L Gardner & Sons Ltd

A member of Hawker Siddeley plc

Barton Hall Engine Works, Patricroft, Eccles, Manchester M30 7WA, England

Founded by the Gardner brothers in 1898 as a general engineering works on the present site, employing 80 men, the works today covers nearly 20 times the original area and has 1600 employees. In 1901 a limited company, L Gardner & Sons Ltd, was formed, and this is now part of Hawker Siddeley plc. Hot air engines and horizontal gas engines were built at first and development of the compression ignition engine followed.

Production comprises automotive, rail traction, marine and industrial engines. For rail traction the main types are L3B, 8LXB, and 6LXB from 180 to 260 hp. Gardner-powered railcars and locomotives are in service in countries throughout the world.

6LXB (vertical) and 6HLXB (horizontal)

Type: 6 and 8 cylinder, 4-cycle, vertical in-line, water cooled.

Cylinders: Bore 120.6 mm (4¾ in). Stroke 152.4 mm (6 in). Swept volume 1.7 litres per cylinder. Compression ratio 14 : 1. High tensile cast iron cylinder blocks with dry type renewable liners. Detachable cast iron cylinder heads in two 3-bore units, secured with HT studs and nuts with indented steel (corrojoint) cylinder head packing.

Pistons: Medium silicon aluminium alloy with combustion chamber in crown. 2 compression rings and one oil control ring, fully floating hollow gudgeon pin.

Connecting rods: Chrome molybdenum steel H section stampings machined all over. Pre-finished steel shell bearings lined with copper lead overlay plated for big-ends and bronze bushes for small ends.

Crankshaft: Solid one-piece chrome molybdenum steel die stamping with hollow main and crankpin journals. Pre-finished steel shell main bearings lined with copper lead overlay plated.

Crankcase: Aluminium alloy with separate detachable cast iron single cylinder block fitted with renewable dry liners.

Valve gear: One exhaust and one inlet alloy steel overhead valve per cylinder. Press fit renewable stellite-faced valve seats. Camshaft in crankcase driven by triplex bush roller chain.

Fuel injection: Multi-hole non-adjustable Gardner injectors with twin CAV type BPF (3 Ram) pumps.

Fuel: High-speed diesel fuel oil.

Lubrication: Pressure feed throughout with one gear-type pump. Additional pump and oil cooling radiator as required.

Cooling: Gardner centrifugal type pump with spherical carbon gland. Gardner multi-tube radiator and fan or proprietary make.

Starting: 24 V CAV or Simms axial motor.

8L3B

Type: 8 cylinder, 4-cycle, vertical in-line, water cooled.

Cylinders: Bore 140 mm (5½ in). Stroke 197 mm (7¾ in). Swept volume 3 litres per cylinder. Compression ratio 12 : 1. Detachable cast iron wet liners with renewable dry type liners. Detachable individual cast iron cylinder heads secured with studs and nuts. Metal to metal joint with no packing.

Gardner 6HLXB 6-cylinder horizontal diesel engine

Gardner 6LXCT engine

Pistons: Low expansion medium silicon aluminium alloy with combustion chamber in crown. Two compression rings and one oil control ring, fully floating hollow gudgeon pin.

Connecting rods: Chrome molybdenum steel stampings machined all over. Pre-finished steel shell bearings lined with copper lead overlay plated for big ends and bronze bushes for small ends.

Crankshaft: Solid one-piece chrome molybdenum steel die stamping with hollow main and crankpin journals. Pre-finished steel shell main bearings lined with copper lead overlay plated.

Crankcase: Upper and lower half type cast iron crankcase with detachable cast iron cylinder blocks.

Valve gear: One exhaust and one inlet alloy steel overhead valves per cylinder. Press-fit renewable hardened alloy iron valve seats. Camshaft in crankcase driven by triplex bush roller chain.

Fuel injection: Multi-hole non-adjustable Gardner injectors with CAV type BPF pumps.

Fuel: High-speed diesel oil fuel.

Lubrication: Pressure feed throughout with one gear-type pump. Additional pump and oil cooling radiator as required.

Cooling: Gardner centrifugal type pump with spherical carbon gland. Gardner multi-tube radiator and fan, or proprietary make.

Starting: 24 or 32 V electric starter.

Mounting: 6 point.

Gardner 8L3B 8-cylinder diesel engine

8LXC

Type: Naturally aspirated 8 cylinder, vertical in-line, direct injection diesel.

Cylinders: Bore 120.65 mm (4¾ in). Stroke 152.4 mm (6 in). Displacement 13.93 litres (851 in³). Specific fuel consumption 0.337 lb/bhp/h at 1920 rpm.

Pistons: Medium silicon aluminium alloy; combustion chamber is hemispherical, formed in the piston crown; pressure rings chromium plated; U-section, hardened and tempered cast iron oil scraper ring; fully floating gudgeon pin with aluminium retaining pads.

Connecting rods: Machined and polished chromium molybdenum steel; each rod is rifle drilled from end to end and has special alloy small end bearings; pre-finished copper/lead overlay plated big end shells.

Crankshaft: 10 bearing, dynamically-balanced chromium molybdenum steel, with hollow bored crank pins and main journals.

Fuel injection: CAV BPF mounted on Gardner cambox/governor assembly.

Fuel: High-speed diesel fuel oil.

Cooling: Circulation by a gear driven pump to the base of the cylinders, then through the cylinder heads via synthetic rubber joint rings.

Gardner 8LXC 8-cylinder diesel engine

6LXCT

Introduced in early 1981 to the truck industry, this turbo-charged diesel engine rated at 230 bhp develops over 660 lb ft torque. The 6LXCT was launched to meet the present trend for higher power ratings without the loss of payload or higher fuel consumption brought about by the use of 8-cylinder engines.

Type: Turbo-charged 6 cylinder, vertical in-line, direct injection.

Cylinders: Bore 120.65 mm (4¾ in). Stroke 152.4 mm (6 in). Displacement 10.45 litres (638 in³). Specific fuel consumption 199 g/kW/h (0.328 lb/bhp/h) at 1900 rpm; 193 g/kW/h (0.318 lb/bhp/h) at 1400 rpm.

Pistons: Medium silicon aluminium alloy; combustion chamber is hemispherical, formed in piston crown; chromium-plated pressure rings; U-section, hardened and tempered cast iron oil scraper ring; fully floating gudgeon pin with aluminium retaining pads.

Connecting rods: Machined and polished chromium molybdenum steel; each rod is rifle-drilled end-to-end and has special copper alloy small end bearings; pre-finished copper/lead overlay-plated big end shells.

Crankshaft: 8-bearing, dynamically-balanced chromium molybdenum steel, with hollow-bored crankpins and main journals.

Fuel injection: CAV BPF mounted on Gardner cambox/governor assembly.

Cooling: Circulation by a gear-driven pump to the base of the cylinders, thence through cylinder heads via synthetic rubber joint rings.

Gardner 8LXCT engine

6HLXCT

The most recent addition to the Gardner range of turbo-charged diesel engines has been developed specifically for the railway industry. Horizontally mounted, the 6HLXCT combines the advantages of a turbo-charged engine with quality and reliability within a small package.

Type: Turbo-charged, 6 cylinder, horizontal in-line, direct injection.

Cylinders: Bore 120.65 mm (4¾ in). Stroke 152.4 mm (6 in). Displacement 10.45 litres (638 in³). Specific fuel consumption 193 g/kW/h (0.318 lb/bhp/h).

Pistons: Aluminium alloy with top ring groove insert; combustion chamber is hemispherical, formed in the piston crown; pressure rings chromium-plated; U-section, hardened and tempered cast iron oil scraper ring; 46 mm (1 in) gudgeon pin with aluminium retaining pads.

Connecting rods: Machined and polished chromium molybdenum steel: each rod is rifle-drilled end-to-end and has special copper alloy small end bearings; pre-finished copper/lead overlay plated big end shells.

Crankshaft: 8-bearing, dynamically-balanced chromium molybdenum steel, with hollow bored crankpins and main journals.

Fuel injection: CAV BPF mounted on Gardner cambox.

Cooling: Circulation by gear-driven pump to base of cylinders, thence via synthetic rubber joint rings independent of main gasket.

8LXCT

This 8-cylinder turbocharged engine delivers 300 bhp at 1900 rpm. With a capacity of 13.93 litres and maximum torque of 1200 Nm at 1400 rpm it offers the highest power rating within the Gardner range.

Type: Turbo-charged 8 cylinder, vertical in-line, direct injection.

Cylinders: Bore 120.65 mm (4¾ in). Stroke 152.4 mm (6 in). Displacement 13.93 litres (851 in³). Specific fuel consumption better than 0.333 lb/bhp/h at 1900 rpm.

Gardner 6HLXCT engine

Pistons: Medium silicon aluminium alloy; hemispherical combustion chamber formed in piston crown; chromium-plated pressure rings; U-section, hardened and tempered cast iron oil scraper ring; fully floating gudgeon pin with aluminium retaining pads.
Connecting rods: Machined and polished chromium molybdenum steel; each rod rifle-drilled end-to-end with special copper alloy small end bearing; prefinished copper/lead overlay plated big end shells.
Crankshaft: 10-bearing, dynamically-balanced chromium molybdenum steel, with hollow bored crankpins and main journals.
Fuel injection: CAV BPF mounted in Gardner cambox/governor assembly.
Cooling: Circulation by gear-driven pump to base of cylinders, thence through cylinder heads via synthetic rubber joint rings independent of solid-steel main gasket.

Model		8 L3B	6LXB	6HLXB	8LXB	8LXC
No of cylinders		8	6	6	8	8
Max bhp		260	180	180	240	265
Engine speed	rpm	1300	1850	1850	1850	1920
Weight approx	lb	5523	1560	1707	2045	2459
	(kg)	(2505)	(707.6)	(774.3)	(927.6)	(111.5)
Length	in	97¾	55	55	64	64
	(mm)	(2483)	(1397)	(1397)	(1626)	(1626)
Width	in	34½	26¼	55	27	28½
	(mm)	(807)	(667)	(1397)	(686)	(727)
Height	in	50¾	45¼	26	50	50
	(mm)	(1276)	(1149)	(660)	(1270)	(1270)

GE

General Electric Co
Transportation Systems Business Operations
2910 East Lake Road, Erie, Pennsylvania 16531, USA

Series FDL (8, 12 and 16 cylinder 45° Vee)
Type: 4 cycle turbo-charged with water-cooled charge air cooler.
Cylinders: Bore 9 in (229 mm). Stroke 10½ in (267 mm). Swept volume 668 in³ per cylinder. Individual unitised cast cylinder with renewable liner and head. Compression ratio 12.7:1.
Pistons: Current-production engines use 2-piece pistons. The steel crown, contoured on the top to form the combustion chamber and on the bottom to form cooling-oil passages, is bolted to an aluminium-alloy skirt.
Crankcase: Main frame of high strength cast iron.
Valve gear: Roller type cam followers, push rods and rockers, 4 valves per cylinder. Gear-driven sectionalised camshaft on each side of engine.
Fuel injection: Individual injectors and fuel pumps.
Turbo-charger: One, exhaust driven (no gear drive to crankshaft).
Lubrication: Forced full flow filtered oil to all bearings and pistons, gear type engine driven pump.
Cooling system: Forced circulation water cooling of cylinders, turbo-charger, and intercoolers. The water passages are external of the crankcase and main frame.

General Electric 3940 hp (UIC) 16-cylinder Vee engine

Current engine specifications

Model	7FDL8	7FDL12	7FDL16
No of cylinders	8	12	16
Output (UIC) standard	1970	3233	3940
Stroke cycle	4	4	4
Cylinder arrangement	45° Vee	45° Vee	45° Vee
Bore	9 in (228.6 mm)	9 in (228.6 mm)	9 in (228.6 mm)
Stroke	10½ in (266.7 mm)	10½ in (266.7 mm)	10½ in (266.7 mm)
Compression ratio	12:7-1	12:7-1	12:7-1
Idle speed	385 rpm	385 rpm	385 rpm
Full-rated speed	1050 rpm	1050 rpm	1050 rpm
Firing order	1R-1L-2R-2L-4R-4L-3R-3L	1R-1L-5R-5L-3R-3L-6R 6L-2R-2L-4R-4L	1R-1L-3R-3L-7R-7L-4R-4L 8R-8L-6R-6L-2R-2L-5R-5L
Turbo-charger	Single	Single	Single
Engine dimensions			
Height (excluding stack)	86¼ in (2191 mm)	90⅛ in (2289 mm)*	90⅛ in (2289 mm)
Length (overall)	128½ in (3264 mm)	159½ in (4051 mm)	193 in (4902 mm)
Width (overall)	68¼ in (1734 mm)	68⅜ in (1740 mm)	68⅜ in (1740 mm)
Weight (dry)	27 000 lb (12 200 kg)	35 000 lb (15 900 kg)	43 500 lb (19 700 kg)

*Note: Domestic (USA) type engines only. The export model has a lower water header (86¼ in, 2191 mm)

GEC Diesels
GEC Diesels Ltd
Vulcan Works, Newton-le-Willows, Merseyside WA12 8RU, England

GEC Diesels Ltd is the parent company of Ruston Diesels Ltd, Paxman Diesels Ltd and Dorman Diesels Ltd.

Engine range	Company	Location
Dorman	Dorman Diesels Ltd	Tixall Road, Stafford
English Electric	Ruston Diesels Ltd	Newton-le-Willows, Merseyside
Paxman	Paxman Diesels Ltd	Colchester, Essex
Alco	Alco Power Inc	Auburn, New York 13021, USA

DORMAN ENGINES
Special features claimed for the Dorman series of diesel engines are their wide speed range, compact and robust design, excellent power to weight ratio, economical fuel consumption, standardisation and parts interchangeability.

DA Series: 4 and 6 cylinders in-line, air cooled
L Series: 6 cylinders in-line, water cooled
Q Series: 6 cylinders in-line, 8 cylinders Vee form, water cooled
S Series: 12 cylinders Vee form, water cooled

	Bore	Stroke
DA Series:	105 mm	120 mm
L Series:	127 mm	130 mm
Q Series:	159 mm	165 mm
S Series:	159 mm	190 mm

Connecting rods: Alloy steel H section stampings.
Crankshafts: Dynamically balanced, hardened steel.
Bearings: Steel backed line with reticular tin.
Crankcase: Rigid cast iron structure. Monobloc in the case of water-cooled engines and with separate barrels in the case of air-cooled units.
Cylinder heads: Water-cooled engines: high grade iron castings. Air-cooled engines: die cast light alloy.
Pistons: Aluminium alloy with toroidal combustion chamber.
Starting: Air, electric or hydraulic.

Dorman 12ST diesel engine

Model	DA Series		
	4DA	6DA	6DAT
No of cylinders	4	6	6
Turbo-charged	No	No	Yes
Charge air cooled	No	No	No
bhp continuous	68	103	123
Engine speed rpm	2500	2500	2200

Model	Q Series						
	6QT	6QTCA	6QTCW	8Q	8QT	8QTCA	8QTCW
No of cylinders	6	6	6	8	8	8	8
Turbo-charged	No	Yes	Yes	No	Yes	Yes	Yes
Charge air cooled	No	Air to air	Air to water	No	No	Air to air	Air to water
bhp continuous	382	432	432	318	490	575	575
Engine speed rpm	1800	1800	1800	1800	1800	1800	1800

Model	L Series			
	6LE	6LET	6LETCA	6LETCW
No of cylinders	6	6	6	6
Turbo-charged	No	Yes	Yes	Yes
Charge air cooled	No	No	Air to air	Air to water
bhp continuous	186	221	275	275
Engine speed rpm	2200	1800	1800	1800

Model	S Series		
	12ST	12STCA	12STCW
No of cylinders	12	12	12
Turbo-charged	Yes	Yes	Yes
Charge air cooled	No	Air to air	Air to water
bhp continuous	720	870	899
Engine speed rpm	1500	1500	1500

RUSTON DIESEL ENGINES

Ruston RK series

The RKC engine provides a maximum output of 313 hp (233 kW) per cylinder at 1000 rpm. The engine is manufactured in 6-cylinder in-line and Vee 8-, 12- and 16-cylinder forms (Vee angle 45). The engine covers a power band up to 5000 hp (3730 kW) at 1000 rpm under ISO standard reference conditions. The RKC medium-speed engine with cylinder dimensions of 254 mm (10 in) bore and 305 mm (12 in) stroke throughout the range offers long periods between overhauls with a high degree of interchangeability of components.

Type: 4-stroke water cooled, turbo-charged/charge air-cooled.

Pistons: Single-piece construction each with a cast-in cooling passage behind the top ring. Cooling oil is transferred from the connecting rod through a slipper arrangement. The ring pack includes a chrome-faced top ring, taper-faced second and third rings and a conformable oil control ring.

Connecting rods: Alloy steel forging with a shank of I section and integral bearing housing.

Crankshaft: One-piece forged in alloy steel. Separate balance weights are fitted to the crankwebs to achieve optimum oil films in the main bearings.

Crankcase: Cast-iron construction housing both cylinder liners and camshafts.

Valve gear: Two inlet and two exhaust valves in each cylinder head seated on renewable wear resisting inserts. The camshaft is chain driven from the crankshaft on in-line engines but for Vee engines a spur gear drive is used.

Fuel injection: Individual pumps and injectors for each cylinder.

Turbo-charger: Normally Napier turbo-chargers are specified but other makes can be supplied.

Lubrication: Wet sump lubrication with an engine-driven oil pump. System includes full flow filtration, thermostat and oil cooler.

Cooling: Jacket cooling system thermostatically-controlled using an engine-driven water pump.

Starting: Electric starting from the locomotive battery, either by starting windings in the driven machine or by starter motors mounted on the engine.

Engine type	Speed rpm	No of cylinders	Standard power brakepower		Approx dimensions Length		Width		Height		Approx weight of engine with flywheel	
			hp	kW	mm	in	mm	in	mm	in	kg	lb
6RKC	850	6	1630	1215	4648	183	1397	55	2235	88	12 109	26 670
	900	6	1690	1260	4648	183	1397	55	2235	88	12 109	26 670
	1000	6	1740	1300	4648	183	1397	55	2235	88	12 109	26 670
8RKC	850	8	2170	1620	4343	171	1702	67	2337	92	14 213	31 340
	900	8	2280	1700	4343	171	1702	67	2337	92	14 213	31 340
	1000	8	2320	1730	4343	171	1702	67	2337	92	14 213	31 340
12RKC	850	12	3260	2430	5207	205	1829	72	2235	88	19 293	42 540
	900	12	3380	2520	5207	205	1829	72	2235	88	19 293	42 540
	1000	12	3480	2600	5207	205	1829	72	2235	88	19 293	42 540
16RKC	850	16	4340	3240	6325	249	1803	71	2311	91	23 864	52 620
	900	16	4560	3400	6325	249	1803	71	2311	91	23 864	52 620
	1000	16	4640	3460	6325	249	1803	71	2311	91	23 864	52 620

The powers shown are available for traction duty in accordance with UIC Test Conditions: air intake temperature 20°C; charge air cooler water temperature not exceeding 45°C; altitude 300 m (1000 ft).

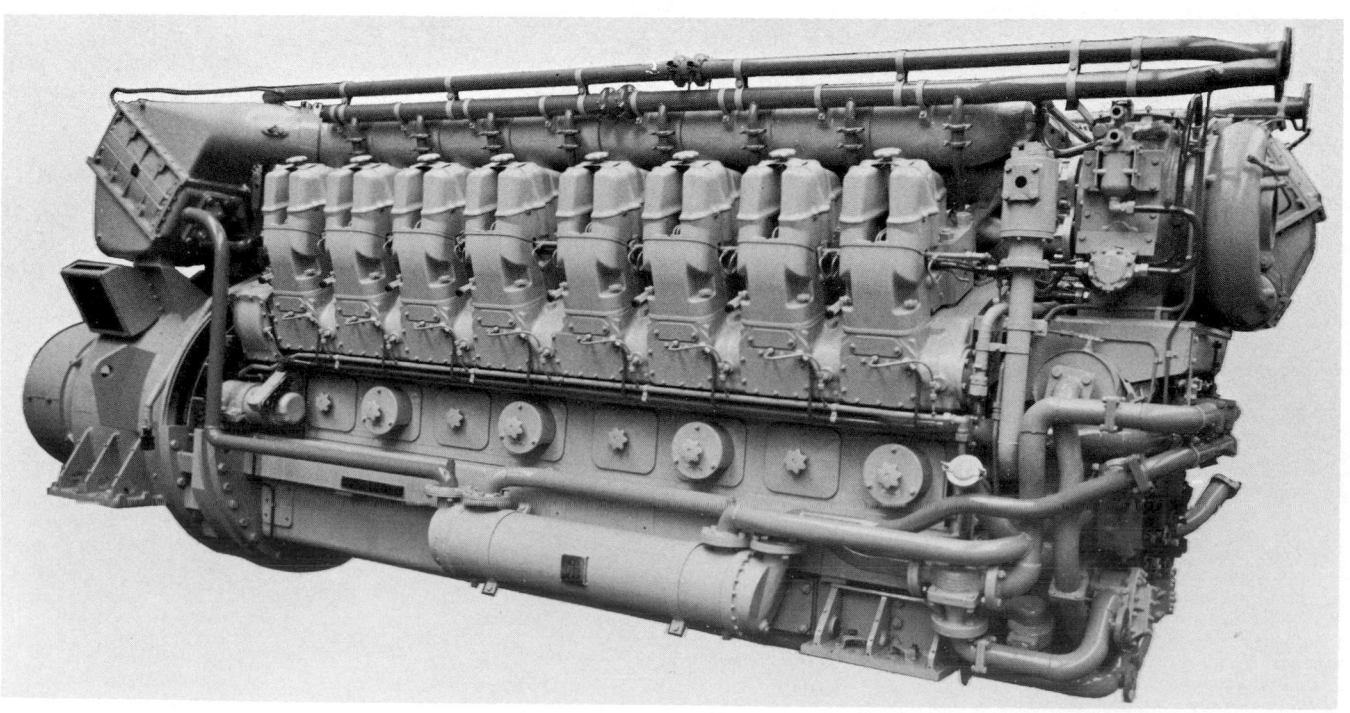

16 RKC engine, as fitted in British Rail Class 56 locomotive

PAXMAN ENGINES

First introduced into railway traction in 1930, the Paxman engines in the present range are of compact design while providing maximum accessibility for maintenance. They combine high power-to-weight ratio with the rugged construction necessary for reliable traction service. British Rail's fleet of High Speed Trains (HSTs) is powered by Paxman. Each train-set has two Valenta 12CL engines, over 200 of which have now been supplied. As at November 1981 the Valenta type had amassed over 3 million running hours. Recent orders have included similar units for the XPT train-sets for New South Wales, Australia.

Valenta 12-cylinder engine as used in British Rail High Speed Trains

12-cylinder Ventura engine, available in turbo-charged/intercooled versions, 1350/500 bhp at 1500 rpm

Engine type	Turbo charged or turbo charged/ inter-cooled	No of cylinders	Cont traction rating kW brake (bhp)	Engine speed rpm	Bmep bar (lbf/in²)	Piston speed m/s (ft/min)	Full load fuel con-sumption g/bhp/h (lb/bhp/h)	Bore mm (in)	Stroke mm (in)	Displace-ment litres (in³)	Com-pression ratio	Approx dimensions mm (in) Length	Width	Height	Crank-case centre line height	Approx dry weight kg (lb)
*6RPHCL	TC/I	6	280 (375)	1500	7.6 (110)	9.84 (1937)	192 (0.424)	178 (7)	197 (7.75)	29.3 (1790)	15.5 : 1	1638 (64.5)	1245 (49)	1753 (69)	490 (19.25)	2469 (5445)
*8RPHXL	TC	8	303 (406)	1500	6.2 (90)	9.84 (1937)	189 (0.417)	178 (7)	197 (7.75)	39 (2386)	15.5 : 1	1880 (74)	1245 (49)	1575 (62)	490 (19.25)	3016 (6650)
*8RPHCL	TC/I	8	373 (500)	1500	7.6 (110)	9.84 (1937)	192 (0.424)	178 (7)	197 (7.75)	39 (2386)	15.5 : 1	1880 (74)	1245 (49)	1755 (69)	490 (19.25)	3061 (6750)
12YHXL	TC	12	671 (900)	1500	9.2 (133)	9.84 (1937)	170 (0.374)	178 (7)	197 (7.75)	58.7 (3580)	13.0 : 1	2540 (100)	1588 (62.5)	1905 (75)	686 (27)	4898 (10 800)
12YHCL	TC/I	12	783 (1050)	1500	10.7 (155)	9.84 (1937)	170 (0.374)	178 (7)	197 (7.75)	58.7 (3580)	13.0 : 1	2540 (100)	1588 (62.5)	1955 (77)	686 (27)	5034 (11 100)
Ventura 6CL	TC/I	6	560 (750)	1500	11.4 (165)	10.8 (2125)	170 (0.375)	197 (7.75)	210 (8.5)	39.4 (2405)	13.0 : 1	1600 (63)	1420 (56)	1780 (70)	535 (21)	3320 (7320)
Ventura 8CL	TC/I	8	746 (1000)	1500	11.4 (165)	10.8 (2125)	165 (0.363)	197 (7.75)	210 (8.5)	52.6 (3207)	13.0 : 1	1700 (67)	1335 (52.5)	2110 (83)	585 (23)	3855 (8500)
Ventura 12CL	TC/I	12	1119 (1500)	1500	11.4 (165)	10.8 (2125)	165 (0.363)	197 (7.75)	210 (8.5)	78.9 (4811)	13.0 : 1	2060 (81)	1335 (52.5)	2010 (79)	585 (23)	5111 (11 270)
Ventura 16CL	TC/I	16	1492 (2000)	1500	11.4 (165)	10.8 (2125)	166 (0.365)	197 (7.75)	210 (8.5)	105.1 (6415)	13.0 : 1	2670 (105)	1335 (52.5)	2060 (81)	585 (23)	6789 (14 970)
Valenta 6CL	TC/I	6	839 (1125)	1500	17 (247)	10.8 (2125)	170 (0.376)	197 (7.75)	210 (8.5)	39.4 (2405)	13.0 : 1	2673 (105.25)	1073 (42.25)	1804 (71)	635 (25)	4730 (10 430)
Valenta 8CL	TC/I	8	1119 (1500)	1500	17 (247)	10.8 (2125)	170 (0.376)	197 (7.75)	210 (8.5)	52.6 (3207)	13.0 : 1	1936 (76.25)	1460 (57.5)	2350 (92.5)	740 (29)	5057 (11 150)
Valenta 12CL	TC/I	12	1679 (2250)	1500	17 (247)	10.8 (2125)	165 (0.363)	197 (7.75)	210 (8.5)	78.9 (4811)	13.0 : 1	2458 (96.75)	1460 (57.5)	2305 (90.75)	740 (29)	6735 (14 850)
Valenta 16CL	TC/I	16	2238 (3000)	1500	17 (247)	10.8 (2125)	173 (0.382)	197 (7.75)	210 (8.5)	105.1 (6415)	13.0 : 1	2980 (117.5)	1460 (57.5)	2350 (92.5)	740 (29)	9010 (19 870)
Valenta 18CL	TC/I	18	2522 (3380)	1500	17 (247)	10.8 (2125)	166 (0.366)	197 (7.75)	210 (8.5)	118.3 (7217)	13.0 : 1	3207 (126.25)	1460 (57.5)	2260 (89)	740 (29)	9873 (21 770)

Engine ratings: Continuous traction rating corrected for altitude of 150 m (500 ft), air temperature of 30°C (85°F) and (C engines and Valenta) water temperature to intercooler 45°C (113°F).
*Engines marked with an asterisk can be offered with an intermittent rating 10 per cent higher for shunting duty.

Dimensions: These are for engines with standard equipment.
Engine weights: These include fuel and lubricating oil filters, oil cooler (Ventura and Valenta), damper and sump, but exclude flywheel, air filters, and mounting. Those for 8, 12 and 16 YJ include fabricated housing.

General Motors Corporation

Electro-Motive Division
La Grange, Illinois 60625, USA

The Electro-Motive Division of General Motors first developed the Model 567 diesel engine in 1938 when it began locomotive manufacture at La Grange, Illinois, USA.

To provide increased horsepower and greater efficiency, the Model 645 engine was introduced in mid-1965. The major change in the Model 645 over the 567 was the increase in cylinder liner bore from 216 mm (8½ in) to 230 mm (9¹/₁ in), the stroke remaining at 254 mm (10 in).

The turbo-charged 645E3B engine introduced in 1979 and the turbo-charged 645F3 engine introduced in 1981 are a result of the search for increased product reliability, performance, and fuel economy. With increased horsepower and fuel economy these engines will be able to haul more tonnage at the same speed or the same tonnage at a higher speed than their predecessors.

Model		645E Roots blown			645E3B Turbo		645F3 Turbo	
No of cylinders		8	12	16	12	16	12	16
Traction rating	(hp)	1000	1500	2000	2250	3000	2600	3500
Engine rpm		900	900	900	900	900	950	950
Max bmep	lb/in²	94	94	94	141	141	154	154
	(kg/cm²)	(6.61)	(6.61)	(6.61)	(9.91)	(9.91)	(10.83)	(10.83)
Max piston speed	ft/min	1500	1500	1500	1500	1500	1583	1583
	(m/s)	(7.63)	(7.63)	(7.63)	(7.63)	(7.63)	(8.04)	(8.04)
Weight (dry)	lb	18 700	25 000	33 400	28 300	36 400	28 500	36 800
	(kg)	(8480)	(11 340)	(15 150)	(12 840)	(16 520)	(12 930)	(16 690)
Length	in	142	176	215	174	215	174	215
	(mm)	(3607)	(4470)	(5461)	(4420)	(5461)	(4420)	(5461)
Width	in	63	65	63	69	67	69	67
	(mm)	(1600)	(1651)	(1600)	(1753)	(1702)	(1753)	(1702)
Height	in	89	89	89	101	101	98	101
	(mm)	(2260)	(2260)	(2260)	(2565)	(2565)	(2489)	(2565)

GM Model 16-645E

GM Model 16-645F3

GMT

Grandi Motori Trieste SpA
Fiat-Ansaldo-CRDA
PO Box 497, 34100 Trieste, Italy

Telephone: 040 8991
Telegrams: Grandimotori, Trieste
Telex: 46274; 46275

Grandi Motori Trieste builds diesel engines for railway traction, marine and industrial applications. For rail traction its locomotive engine range includes series A210 and B230 from 612 to 3700 kW.

Series A210
Type: 4-stroke, turbo-charged, with charge air cooling.
Cylinders: Bore 210 mm. Stroke 230 mm.

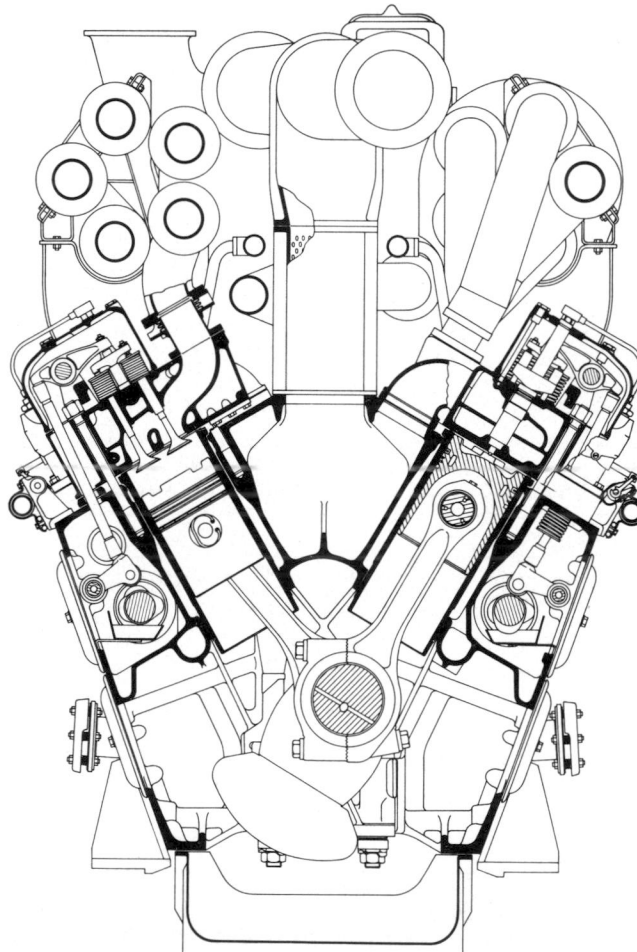

Cross-section of B230 V form

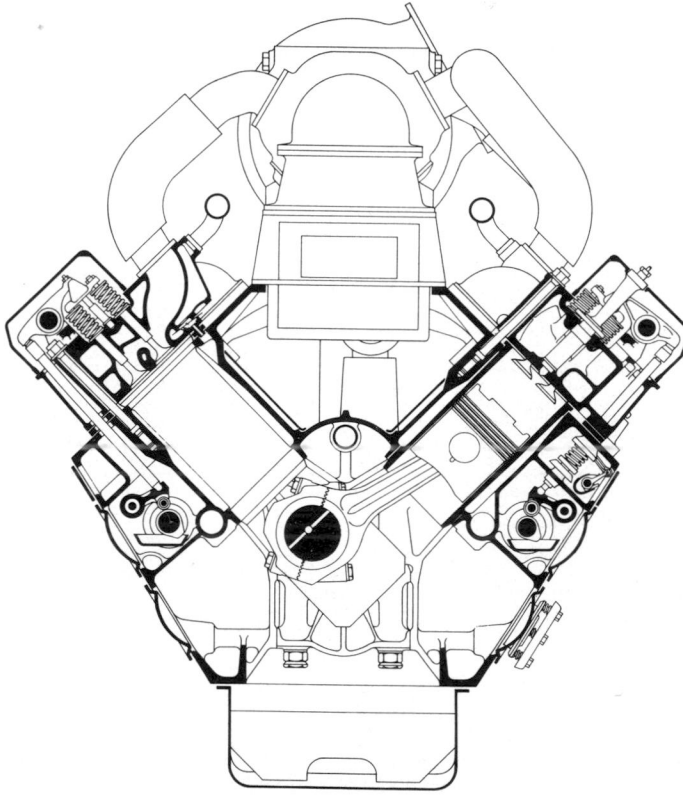

Cross-section of Type A210 engine

GMT 4-stroke diesel engine type B230.20, turbo-charged with aftercooling; 5000 bhp at 1200 rpm

12-cylinder version of Type A210 engine

The company has recently delivered 20 A210 engines to the Italian State Railways (FS) for the latter's Class D445 locomotives and in 1983 was engaged on a further order for 95 12-cylinder engines of the same type.

A210 engine

Version	Cylinder	Output kW (UIC)	Weight kg	Length mm	Width mm	Height mm
A 210.4	4 V	612	4400	1700	1770	1570
A 210.6	6 V	918	5500	2000	1770	1570
A 210.8	8 V	1224	7000	2250	1820	1930
A 210.12	12 V	1836	9500	2835	1820	2020
A 210.16	16 V	2448	11 800	3415	1820	1980
A 210.20	20 V	3060	14 600	4050	1820	2020

Length: at crankshaft   *Width:* overall   *Height:* from underside of feet

Fuel consumption: 215 g/kW/h

Series B230

Type: 4-stroke, turbo-charged, with charge air cooling.
Cylinders: Bore 230 mm. Stroke 270 mm.

The other main characteristics, common to the two types of engine are as follows:
Cylinder liners: Wet type removable liners of special cast iron.
Cylinder heads: One per cylinder, in alloyed cast iron; each has two inlet and two exhaust valves and the fuel injector in the centre.
Pistons: Aluminium alloy, oil cooled. They have three compression rings and one oil scraper ring.

Crankshaft: Highly alloyed forged steel. The surface of the pins is hardened by electric induction process. Thin-walled three metal bearings.
Frame: Cast iron.
Valve gear: One or two camshaft for in-line and Vee engines respectively driven at flywheel side. The two inlet and two exhaust valves are driven by rollers/push rods/rocker arms through a transverse piece.
Turbo-charging: Achieved by means of exhaust gas turbo-blowers operating with pulse systems. The air is then cooled in suitable coolers.
Fuel injection pumps: Of plunger type with a spiral groove. The fuel injection is controlled by rotating the plunger by means of a transversal rack.
Fuel: Gas oil.
Lubrication: Force fed by directly-driven gear pump.
Cooling: Fresh water fed by two centrifugal pumps, one for the engine, one for the oil and air cooling system.

B230 engine

Version	Cylinder	Output kW (UIC)	Weight kg	Length mm	Width mm	Height mm
B 230.4	4 L	740	5700	2290	1200	1960
B 230.6	6 L	1110	7900	2960	1200	1960
B 230.8	8 V	1480	10 300	2670	1720	2170
B 230.10	10 V	1850	12 400	3080	1720	2200
B 230.12	12 V	2220	14 300	3490	1720	2200
B 230.16	16 V	2960	18 300	4310	1720	2250
B 230.18	18 V	3330	21 900	4720	1720	2250
B 230.20	20 V	3700	24 000	5130	1720	2380

Isotta Fraschini SpA

Via Milano 7, Saronno 21047, Italy

Telephone: 02 960 3251/2/3
Telex: 332403

Isotta Fraschini builds diesel engines for rail and road traction, marine and industrial applications. For rail traction the locomotive engine range includes: series ID 19 from 450 to 680 hp, series ID 38 from 200 to 330 hp and series ID 36 from 300 to 1900 hp.

ID 19 series
12 cylinders horizontally opposed, 4-stroke, direct injection, water cooled.

ID 38/6 V series diesel engine for railway traction from 200-330 bhp at 2700 rpm

Cylinders: Bore 145 mm. Stroke 180 mm. Swept volume 35.67 litres. The output is based on UIC specification.

ID 38 series
6 cylinders, 90° Vee, 4-stroke, direct injection, water cooled.
Cylinders: Bore 128 mm. Stroke 126 mm. Swept volume 1.62 litres per cylinder. The output is based on UIC specifications.

ID 36 series
6, 8, 12 and 16 cylinders, 90° Vee, 4-stroke, direct injection, water cooled.
Cylinders: Bore 170 mm. Stroke 170 mm. Swept volume 3.858 litres per cylinder. The output is based on UIC specifications. Engine speed maximum 1800 rpm. Engine type ID 36/8 V can be supplied with cylinders opposed for railcar applications.

Isotta Fraschini Type ID 36 SS 16V engine

		ID38 series			ID36 series					
Model		N6V	SS6V	N6V	SSCV	N8V	SS8V	N12V	SS12V	N16V	SS16V
No of cylinders		6	6	6	6	8	8	12	12	16	16
Turbo-charged		—	Yes	—	Yes	—	Yes	—	Yes	—	Yes
Charge air cooled		—	Yes	—	Yes	—	Yes	—	Yes	—	Yes
bhp (UIC)		200	330	300	640	400	850	600	1285	800	1710
Engine speed	rpm	2700	2700	1650	1650	1650	1650	1650	1650	1650	1650
Weight (dry)	lb	1655	1766	3780	4000	5115	5335	7115	7445	—	9277
	(kg)	(750)	(800)	(1700)	(1800)	(2300)	(2400)	(3200)	(3350)		(4200)
Length max	in	39.37	42.91	—	53.15	—	63	—	88.55	—	118.11
	(mm)	(1000)	(1090)		(1350)		(1600)		(2250)		(3000)
Width max	in	35.43	35.43	—	47.24	—	47.24	—	47.24	—	51.18
	(mm)	(900)	(900)		(1200)		(1200)		(1200)		(1300)
Height max	in	37	37	—	51.57	—	49.60	—	58.26	—	70.86
	(mm)	(940)	(940)		(1310)		(1260)		(1480)		(1800)
Fuel consumption All models				Normally aspirated and turbo-charged = 170 g/hp/h Turbo-charged and intercooled =165 g/hp/h							

N = Naturally aspirated, SS = Turbo-charged and intercooled.

L & M Radiator, Inc

1414 East 37th Street, Hibbing, Minnesota 55746, USA

Telephone: (218) 263 8993
Telex: 29-4448

President: Alex Chisholm
Vice President: Richard Braun
Secretary/General Manager: Galen Erickson

Principal subsidiaries
L & M Radiator, Inc, El Paso, Texas
L & M Radiator, Ltd, Winnipeg, Manitoba, Canada
L y M de Mexico
L & M Radiator Pty Ltd, Australia; and South Africa

Products: Radiators and radiator cores.

JW

Jenbacher Werke AG
6200 Jenbach, Austria

Formed in 1946, this company builds diesel locomotives and diesel engines for industrial and marine purposes up to 3000 hp.

LM Series

Type: 6, 8 and 12 cylinder 90° Vee, 2-stroke, water cooled, direct injection.
Cylinders: Bore 240 mm. Stroke 250 mm. Swept volume 11.3 litres per cylinder. Cast iron with centrifugally-cast wet cylinder liners. Individual cylinder heads.
Pistons: Light alloy, oil cooled. Four compression rings, and two oil control rings.
Connecting rods: Separate side by side drop-forged with steel-backed lead-bronze big end bearings, and fixed gudgeon pin.

Crankshaft: Drop-forged, carried in steel-backed lead-bronze main bearings.
Fuel injector: Gear-driven from flywheel end of crankshaft.
Scavenge blower: Centrifugal type driven from flywheel end of crankshaft.
Lubrication: Gear pump.
Starting: Electric or compressed air.

Model		LM750	LM1000	LM1500
No of cylinders		6	8	12
Output	kW	551	735	1100
Speed	rpm	1000	1000	1000
Weight (dry)	kg	7400	8900	11 800
Length	mm	2400	2800	3600
Width	mm	1720	1720	1760
Height	mm	2150	2150	2150
Fuel consumption	g/kWh	238	238	234

Jenbacher LM1500 12-cylinder engine, output 1500 hp at 1000 rpm

MaK

Krupp MaK Maschinenbau GmbH Kiel
PO Box 9009, 2300 Kiel 17, Federal Republic of Germany

Before the Second World War Deutsche Werke Kiel produced diesel locomotives and railcars. MaK was formed after the war to continue this programme, concentrating engine production on the slow-running type M 300.

The M 282 rail traction engine is a result of continuous search for product improvement, and retains the best features of the previous designs, the M 300 and M 301. It is of compact and modern design, a medium-speed unit with high performance and extended overhaul periods.

Series M 282

Type: 6 and 8 cylinders in-line, 12 cylinder Vee, 4-stroke cycle, water cooled.
Combustion method: All M 282 series engines have direct injection.
Cylinders: Bore 240 mm. Stroke 280 mm. Swept volume 12.66 litres per cylinder. Compression ratio 12.2:1. Removable wet-type cast iron liners; individual cast iron cylinder heads bolted to cylinder block.
Pistons: A depression in the crown of the piston in conjunction with the cylinder head forms the combustion chamber. The material used for the piston is a heat-resisting light-metal alloy with the best heat conducting quality; alternatively, a divided piston with steel head can be supplied. Four self-tightening elastic piston rings are fitted on the piston. One oil control ring is arranged above the gudgeon pin.
Connecting rods: Drop forged steel.
Crankshaft: Solid forged steel.
Constructional features: Closed engine housing with hanging bearings and underhung sump. Main and big-end bearings of the bronze-lined steel shell type, with lead-tin bearing surface. The bearings can be exchanged without removing the crankshaft.
Valve gear: Each cylinder head carries two inlet and two exhaust valves. Gear train-driven camshaft in cylinder block.
Fuel injection: Bosch injectors with individual Bosch pumps.

Supercharger: Exhaust gas turbo-blower, Brown Boveri.
Starting: Electric or compressed air.
Mounting: Elastic suspension by metal bonded rubber elements.

MaK model 12 M 282 12-cylinder engine

Model		6 M 282 E	6 M 282	6 M 282	6 M 282	8 M 282	8 M 282	12 M 282	12 M 282	12 M 282
No of cylinders		6	6	6	6	8	8	12	12	12
Turbo-charger BBC		RR 180	RR 212	RR 212	RR 212	VTR 251	VTR 251	2 × RR 212	2 × RR 212	2 × RR 212
Charge air-cooled		single circuit	branched single circuit			branched single circuit		branched single circuit		
Continuous power	kW	735	1000	1100	1176	1470	1620	2000	2200	2350
Speed	rpm	1000	1000	1000	1000	1000	1000	1000	1000	1000
Max bmep	bar	11.7	15.8	17.4	18.96	17.4	18.9	15.8	17.4	18.9
Max piston speed	m/s	9.35	9.35	9.35	9.35	9.35	9.35	9.35	9.35	9.35
Bore	mm	240	240	240	240	240	240	240	240	240
Stroke	mm	280	280	280	280	280	280	280	280	280
Weight, dry	tonnes	7.8	7.8	7.8	7.8	9.4	9.4	12.0	12.0	12.0
Length	mm	2876	2934	2934	2934	3530	3530	2831	2831	2831
Width	mm	1400	1510	1510	1510	1510	1510	1650	1650	1650
Height	mm	2000	2000	2000	2000	2230	2230	2380	2380	2380
Fuel consumption	g/kW/h	210	205	208	205	205	208	202	205	204
Lube oil consumption	g/kW/h	2	2	2	2	2	2	2	2	2

MAN

Maschinenfabrik Augsburg-Nurnberg AG
Katzwangerstrasse 101, 8500 Nuremberg, Federal Republic of Germany

Telephone: (0911) 18 0
Telex: 622291

The world's first diesel engine was built at Augsburg between 1893 and 1897 by Maschinenfabrik Augsburg AG, established in 1840. Shortly afterwards a merger with Maschinenbau AG, Nürnberg, produced MAN.

The range of diesel engines produced by the Nuremberg division includes a number of underfloor engines for railway applications. The engines incorporate

MAN's M or HM system of combustion which provides controlled diesel combustion for low engine stress levels and low noise level. Direct injection confers efficient fuel utilisation and fuel economies. High unit ratings and good power weight ratios permit installation in a minimum of space.

MAN underfloor engines
Model D2866 LUE model
Type: 6-cylinder horizontal, 4-stroke, water-cooled, direct injection, turbocharged with water/air charge air cooling.
Cylinders: 128 mm bore, 155 mm stroke, 11.96 litres swept volume.
Compression ratio: 17:1.
Output: UIC rating 235 kW (320 hp) at 2100 rpm.
Torque (max): 1070 Nm at 1400 rpm.

Mitsubishi
Mitsubishi Heavy Industries Ltd

Head office: 5-1, Marunouchi 2-chome, Chiyoda-ku, Tokyo, Japan

Works: 3000 Tana, Sagamihara-City, Kanagawa Prefecture, Japan

Products: 54 to 1400 bhp engines for locomotives (1000 to 3600 rpm).

Möes
Moteurs Moes SA
62 rue de Huy, 4370 Waremme, Belgium

Products: Diesel-electric generator sets up to 1000 kVA.

Motoren-Werke
Motoren-Werke Mannheim AG
PO Box 1563, Carl-Benz Strasse, Mannheim, Federal Republic of Germany

Telephone: 3841
Telegrams: Alterbenz, Mannheim
Telex: 04 62 341

Products: Four-stroke engines of 460-1800 kW, 1500-2200 rpm, for locomotives and railcars.

Morrison-Knudsen/Sulzer
Morrison-Knudsen Company, Inc/Sulzer
Two Morrison-Knudsen Plaza, PO Box 7808, Boise, Idaho 83729, USA

Telephone: (208) 345 5000
Telex: 368439

Vice-President and General Manager, Railroad Division: Joseph G Fearon

Morrison-Knudsen has an exclusive agreement with Sulzer Bros to market the Sulzer rail traction engine to locomotive users in North America.

Sulzer Type 12ASV 25/30 engine with 3240 hp rating

		Sulzer 6ASL 25/30	Sulzer 12ASV 25/30	Sulzer 16ASV 25/30
Type		4 stroke, in line	4 stroke, V type	4 stroke, V type
Cylinders		6	12	16
Bore	(in)	9.84	9.84	9.84
	(mm)	250	250	250
Stroke	(in)	11.81	11.81	11.81
	(mm)	300	300	300
Swept volume per cylinder	(in³)	898.6	898.6	898.6
	(cm³)	14 726	14 726	14 726
Compression ratio		12.7 : 1	12.7 : 1	12.7 : 1
Rated power	(hp)	1660	3240	4320
Rated speed	(rpm)	900-1000	1000-900	1000-900
Mean effective pressure	(psi)	256	235	235
	(kp/cm²)	17.98	16.5	16.5
Mean piston speed	(ft/s)	29.5	32.8	29.5
	(m/s)	9	10	9
Nozzle pressure	(psi)	3555	3555	3555
	(kp/cm²)	250	250	250
Turbo-charger		Brown Boveri VTR251	Brown Boveri VTR321	2 × Brown Boveri VTR321
Governor		Woodward PGE	Woodward PGE	Woodward PGE

Performance data for barometer reading 28.5 inches Hg and air temperature 15.6°C (60°F).

MTU
Motoren- und Turbinen-Union Friedrichshafen GmbH
Postfach 2040, 7790 Friedrichshafen 1, Federal Republic of Germany

Telephone: 07541 207 1
Telegrams: Motorunion
Telex: 0734 280

The manufacturing programme of MTU Friedrichshafen for rail traction application includes diesel engines in the power range of 525 to 4100 kW.
  MTU Friedrichshafen diesel engines are equally suitable for diesel-hydraulic or diesel-electric drive.

MTU model 12V 396

Ruhrkohle AG locomotive powered by MTU 8 V 331 TC engine

Mixed traffic locomotive of ENFE de Bolivia re-engined with two MTU 8 V 396 TC engines

Rail traction applications

Engine	Speed	ISO 3046/1 (UIC rated power)	
	rpm	kW	hp
6 V 331 TC 12	2200	525	715
8 V 331 TC 12	2200	700	950
12 V 331 TC 12	2200	1050	1430
6 V 396 TC 12	1800	525	715
8 V 396 TC 12	1800	700	950
12 V 396 TC 12	1800	1050	1430
6 V 396 TC 13	1900	590	800
8 V 396 TC 13	1900	785	1065
12 V 396 TC 13	1900	1180	1600
16 V 396 TC 13	1900	1570	2135
12 V 652 TB 11	1500	1350	1840
16 V 652 TB 11	1500	1800	2450
12 V 956 TB 12	1500	2460	3350
16 V 956 TB 12	1500	3280	4460
20 V 956 TB 12	1500	4100	5580
12 V 1163 TB 12	1200	2460	3350
16 V 1163 TB 12	1200	3280	4460
20 V 1163 TB 12	1200	4100	5580

Train electric power supply applications

Engine	Speed	ISO 3046/1 (UIC rated power)	
	rpm	kW	hp
6 V 331 TC 12	2200	460	625
8 V 331 TC 12	2200	610	830
12 V 331 TC 12	2200	920	1250
6 V 396 TC 12	1500	415	565
	1800	460	625
8 V 396 TC 12	1500	550	750
	1800	610	830
12 V 396 TC 12	1500	830	1130
	1800	920	1250
6 V 396 TC 13	1500	450	610
	1800	515	700
8 V 396 TC 13	1500	600	815
	1800	690	940
12 V 396 TC 13	1500	900	1220
	1800	1030	1400
16 V 396 TC 13	1500	1200	1630
	1800	1380	1875

Niigata

Niigata Engineering Co Ltd
4-1 Kasumigaseki 1, Chiyoda-ku, Tokyo, Japan

Founded in 1895, one of Japan's leading engineering manufacturers, Niigata builds diesel engines for marine and industrial use up to 20 000 hp and for rail traction up to 2000 hp.

DMP81Z

Type: 16-cylinder Vee, water cooled, 4-stroke, turbo-charged and charge air cooled.
Cylinders: Bore 180 mm. Stroke 200 mm. Swept volume 5.09 litres per cylinder.

DMF31ZN

Type: 6-cylinder vertical in-line, water cooled, 4-stroke turbo-charged and charge air cooled.
Cylinders: Bore 180 mm. Stroke 200 mm. Swept volume 5.09 litres per cylinder.
General specifications for both models
Cylinders: Monobloc cast iron cylinder block and crankcase, removable cast iron liners with integral water jacket. Cast iron cylinder heads secured by studs.
Pistons: Oil-cooled two-piece pistons with three compression rings and two oil control rings; fully floating gudgeon pins.
Connecting rods: Nickel chrome steel drop-forged.
Crankshaft: Alloy steel forging, copper-lead lined steel shell bearing (DMF31ZN), roller bearing (DMP81Z).
Valve: Two inlet and two exhaust steel valves per cylinder.

Fuel injection: Bosch type injectors and Bosch type pump.
Turbo-charger: Niigata-Napier type turbo-blower. Two for DMP81Z, one for DMF31ZN.
Lubrication: Forced feed.
Starting: Electric starter.

Model		DMP81Z	DMF31ZN
Turbo-charged		Yes	Yes
Charge air cooled		Yes	Yes
No of cylinders		16V	6
Power rating (max)	hp	2000	700
Engine speed	rpm	1500	1500
Bmep (max)	lb/in²	209	167.5
	(kg/cm²)	(14.73)	(13.74)
Piston speed	ft/min	1970	1970
	(m/s)	(10)	(10)
Weight (dry)	lb	19 600	7280
	(kg)	(8900)	(3300)
Length	in	170	129
	(mm)	(4322)	(3280)
Width	in	74	51.6
	(mm)	(1880)	(1310)
Height	in	78	70.7
	(mm)	(1978)	(1795)
Fuel consumption	lb/hp/h	0.370	0.375
	(g/hp/h)	(168)	(170)

DMP81Z 16-cylinder engine

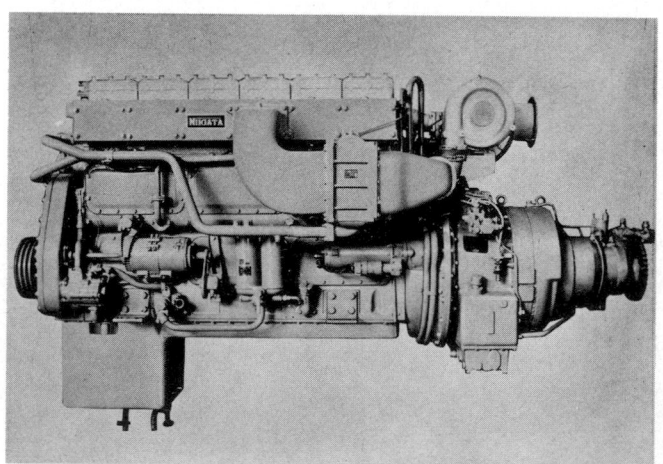

DMF31ZN 6-cylinder engine

OM

OM SpA
Head office: Piazza San Ambrogio 6, Milan, Italy
Works: Via Fiume 25, Brescia

Saurer-designed four-stroke vertical, Vee and horizontal engines for locomotives and railcars.

Rating: 150 to 1100 bhp at 1500 rpm.

Perkins Engines

Perkins Engines Group Ltd
Peterborough, Cambridgeshire PE1 5NA, England

Telephone: 0733 67474
Telegrams: Perkoil, Peterborough
Telex: 32501

Perkins Engines was founded in 1932 and manufactures high-performance diesel engines for all applications from 30 to 255 bhp. It has made major advances in diesel engine design, and has established a high reputation for the quality and reliability of its engines. Perkins engines are the most widely-used make of multi-cylinder engines for varied type of equipment in all parts of the world.

Engine	Turbo-charged	No of cylinders	Bore in (mm)	Stroke in (mm)	Swept volume in³ (litres)	Com-pression ratio	Continuous rating to BS 5514 : 1977 bhp (kW)	eng speed rpm	Max intermittent rating to BS AU 141a : 1971 bhp (Nm)	eng speed rpm	Max gross torque lbf ft (kglf)	Engine speed rpm	Length in (mm)	Width in (mm)	Height in (mm)	Bare engine dry weight lb (kg)
D3.152	No	3	3.6 (91.4)	5 (127)	152.7 (2.5)	18.5:1	39 (29)	2250	49 (36.5)	2500	118 (160)	1400	24 (610)	20.7 (526)	31.1 (791)	410 (186)
3.1522	No	3	3.6 (91.4)	5 (127)	152.7 (2.5)	18.5:1			44.5 (33.5)	2500	118 (160)	1400	24.28 (616)	18.6 (472)	31.43 (798)	600 (272)
4.108	No	4	3.125 (79.4)	3.5 (88.9)	107.4 (1.76)	22:1	38 (28)	3000	45 (33.5)	3000	83 (113)	2300	23.2 (590)	19.1 (485)	25.7 (653)	330 (145)
4.135	No	4	3.5 (88.9)	3.51 (89)	135 (2.209)	21:1			64 (47.5)	4000	101 (137)	2200	26 (660)	23.1 (586)	24.3 (616)	530 (240)
4.154	No	4	3.5 (88.9)	4 (101.6)	154 (2.522)	21:1	51.5 (38.5)	3000	61 (45.5)	3000	117 (158)	2000	27 (686)	22.2 (563)	26.5 (672)	540 (245)
4.165	No	4	3.622 (92)	4 (101.6)	164.9 (2.7)	21:1			70 (52)	3600	113 (153)	2300	25.8 (655)	25.7 (653)	32.7 (830)	445 (202)
4.182	No	4	3.74 (95)	4.13 (105)	181.6 (2.977)	21:1	66 (49)	3000	78 (58)	3000	146 (198)	1800	26.4 (670)	21 (532)	27 (684)	553 (251)
D4.203	No	4	3.6 (91.4)	5 (127)	203.6 (3.34)	17.4:1			65 (48.5)	2300	169 (229)	1350	28.2 (715)	19.4 (493)	29.4 (746)	474 (215)
4.2032	No	4	3.6 (91.4)	5 (127)	203.6 (3.34)	19:1			60 (44.8)	2600	156 (211)	1500	28.2 (717)	19.4 (493)	29.4 (746)	516 (234)
4.236	No	4	3.875 (98.4)	5 (127)	235.9 (3.86)	16:1	64 (48)	2250	82 (61)	2800	189 (256)	1450	28.3 (721)	20.7 (526)	32.1 (816)	575 (261)
T4.236	Yes	4	3.875 (98.4)	5 (127)	235.9 (3.86)	16:1	68.5 (51)	1500	100 (74.5)	2600	245 (332)	1450	28.3 (721)	22.3 (566)	32.1 (816)	609 (276)
4.2482	No	4	3.975 (101)	5 (127)	248 (4.067)	18:1			80.5 (60)	2600	205 (278)	1400	28.8 (732)	20.7 (526)	30.7 (779)	565 (257)
4.248	No	4	3.975 (101)	5 (127)	248.2 (4.07)	16:1			84 (63)	2500	194 (263)	1400	28.8 (732)	20.4 (519)	28.4 (722)	575 (261)
6.3544	No	6	6.875 (98.4)	5 (127)	353.8 (5.8)	16:1	94.5 (70.5)	2250	128 (95.5)	2800	280 (380)	1500	36.9 (937)	24.4 (620)	31 (787)	960 (435)
T6.3544	Yes	6	3.875 (98.4)	5 (127)	353.8 (5.8)	16:1	100 (74.5)	1500	150 (112)	2600	307 (498)	1500	36.8 (935)	28.4 (720)	31 (787)	981 (445)
T6.3544	Yes	6	3.875 (98.4)	5 (127)	353.8 (5.8)	16:1			159 (119)	2600	370 (502)	1600	37 (940)	28.62 (727)	31 (787)	981 (445)
V8.540	No	8	4.25 (108)	4.75 (120.7)	539.1 (8.83)	16.5:1	140 (104)	2250	180 (134)	2600	410 (556)	1700	37.3 (948)	33.8 (858)	35.5 (902)	1340 (608)
TV8.540	Yes	8	4.25 (108)	4.75 (120.7)	539.1 (8.83)	15:1	168 (125)		235 (175)	2600	571 (774)	1700	42.6 (1081)	32.6 (828)	38.6 (981)	1460 (662)
V8.640	No	8	4.63 (117.6)	4.75 (120.7)	639.8 (10.48)	16.2:1	165 (123)	1800	215 (160)	2600	485 (658)	1650	37.5 (952)	36.3 (921)	42.4 (1078)	1625 (737)
TV8.640	Yes	8	4.63 (117.6)	4.75 (120.7)	639.8 (10.48)	15:1	197 (147)	1800	255 (190)	2600	602 (816)	1700	45.1 (1144)	33.2 (844)	39 (991)	1680 (762)

3-cylinder Perkins 3.1522 diesel engine with Squish Lip combustion system for minimum exhaust emissions

D4.203 4-cylinder Perkins diesel engine

Perkins 4.2032 diesel engine with Squish Lip combustion system

Perkins turbocharged 4-cylinder T4.236 industrial diesel engine

Rolls-Royce

Rolls-Royce Motors Ltd
Diesel Division, Shrewsbury, Salop SY1 4DP, England

Telephone: 0743 52262
Telegrams: Roycar, Shrewsbury
Telex: 35171/2

Rolls-Royce manufactures a range of rationalised high-speed diesel engines for rail traction available as vertical or Vee types. The engines are also used in automotive, earth moving, generating, industrial and marine applications.

In rail traction applications complete installations (engines, transmissions and controls) tailored to customers' requirements are supplied and the company deals directly with railway builders and operators in all countries.

Rolls-Royce diesel engines for rail traction can be classified under two headings:

C Range

Comprising 4-stroke, direct injection, normally aspirated, or turbo-charged, vertical, in-line engines with outputs varying from 100 to 400 bhp. For all normally aspirated turbo-charged engines, the engine has two cylinder heads, each covering half the total number of cylinders and having one inlet and one exhaust valve per cylinder.
Type: In-line, 4-stroke, water-cooled direct injection.
Bore: 130.175 mm (5⅛ in) all models.
Stroke: 152.4 mm (6 in) all models.
Capacity: 6 cylinder 12.13 litres (742.64 in³); 8 cylinder 16.2 litres (990.19 in³).
Compression ratio: Normally aspirated 16 : 1. Turbo-charged 14 : 1.
Mean piston speed: 9.14 m/s (1800 ft/min) at 1800 rpm.
Crankcase and cylinders: Monobloc integral construction in close grained cast iron with brass push fit core plugs and differentially hardened wet-type cylinder liners.
Crankshaft: Forged chrome molybdenum steel, nitride hardened, dynamically balanced with 7 or 9 main bearings.
Connecting rods: Forged chrome molybdenum steel, drilled for lubrication to gudgeon pins and cross-drilled for cylinder lubrication.
Bearings: Pre-finished lead-bronze steel-backed shell-type; lead indium bearing surfaces.
Pistons: Tin plated aluminium alloy with straight-sided toroidal cavity combustion chambers. Molybdenum inlayed top compression rings carried in Ni-resist inserts. Spring-backed conformable type oil control rings. Fully floating nickel-chrome case-hardened gudgeon pins.
Valve gear: Overhead; in nickel chrome steel with stellited stem-tips and valve seats. Valve rockers are drilled for lubrication, and are operated by pushrods and chilled cast iron tappets.
Camshaft: Forged chrome-molybdenum steel, nitride hardened, 7 or 9 lead-bronze bearings.
Lubrication: Pressure feed to all bearings, wheelcase gears, rocker arms and compressor when engine-mounted. Engine-mounted oil-coolant heat exchanger.
Fuel injection: Jerk-type pump with hydraulic or mechanical governor. Multi-hole injectors and engine-mounted filters.
Cooling: Gear-driven circulating pump; thermostat control and heat exchanger for lubricating oil. Engine or radiator-mounted multi-belt driven fans for vertical engines. Shaft, hydrostatic or electric driven fans for horizontal engines.
Starting: Axial-type electric starter motor.
Mounting: 4-point; engine front and fly-wheel housing.

Output: Fly-wheel and fly-wheel housing to suit hydraulic, electric or mechanical transmission.

Max bmep	Continuous traction rating to BS 2953 : 1958 lb/in² (kg/cm²)	Intermittent traction rating to BS 2953 : 1958 lb/in² (kg/cm²)	Maximum rating for yard shunting locomotives lb/in² (kg/cm²)
Normally aspirated	101 (7.1)	106 (7.45)	112 (7.87)
Turbo-charged	140 (9.8)	156 (10.97)	164 (11.53)

D Range

Comprising 90° Vee-type, 4-stroke, direct injection, normally aspirated or turbo-charged, with or without charge air cooling, 8-cylinder engines with outputs ranging from 423 to 750 bhp.
Type: 8-cylinder, 90° Vee, 4-stroke, liquid-cooled.
Combustion system: Direct injection with toroidal cavity pistons.
Bore: 168.275 mm (6.625 in).
Stroke: 184.150 mm (7.25 in).
Capacity (swept volume): 32.776 litres (2000 in³).
Maximum governed rpm: 1800.
Mean piston speed: 11.11 m/s (2174 ft/min) at 1800 rpm.
Compression ratio: Naturally aspirated 15.5 : 1. Turbo-charged 13.5 : 1.
Rotation: Anti-clockwise viewed on flywheel.
Hydraulic transmission equipment: Three-stage hydrokinetic torque converter of Lysholm-Smith type, manufactured by Rolls-Royce under licence from Twin Disc Clutch Co. The operating fluid is diesel fuel oil or other approved fluids, cooled by a shell and tube heat exchanger in the engine coolant circuit. Various designs are available to suit all Rolls-Royce engines and rail traction applications.
Reversing gearboxes
(a) Rolls-Royce type CG 100, air-operated, coupled direct to torque converter ratio 1 : 1.
(b) Rolls-Royce type CGF 310, axle-mounted final drive, air-operated, ratios from 2 : 1 to 4.44 : 1.

Rolls-Royce DV8T 90° Vee type 8-cylinder engine

Model designation	bhp rating (BS 2953) intermittent rating B	Max governed speed rpm	Engine form*	A B	Stroke	No of cylinders	Valves per cylinder	Cylinder bore in (mm)	Piston stroke in (mm)	Full-load bmep lb/in² (kg/cm²)	Piston speed max rpm ft/min (m/s)	Full-load fuel consumption lb/bhp/h (g/bhp/h)	Starting system†	Complete engine weight (dry) lb (kg)	Overall length in (mm)	Overall width in (mm)	Overall height in (mm)
C6NFL	179	1800	V	—	4	6	2	5.125 (130.175)	6 (152.4)	106 (7.455)	1800 (9.14)	0.379 (172)	E	2499 (1133)	57.07 (1449)	29.12 (740)	41.3 (1039)
C6TFL	262	1800	V	A	4	6	2	5.125 (130.175)	6 (152.4)	155.2 (10.91)	1800 (9.14)	0.360 (163.3)	E	2613 (1185)	61.43 (1560)	33.8 (858)	50.97 (1295)
C8NFL	239	1800	V	—	4	8	2	5.125 (130.175)	6 (152.4)	106.2 (7.466)	1800 (9.14)	0.390 (177)	E	3079 (1396)	70.74 (1797)	31 (787)	41.3 (1039)
C8TFL	350	1800	V	A	4	8	2	5.125 (130.175)	6 (152.4)	155.5 (10.93)	1800 (9.14)	0.370 (168)	E	3242 (1470)	70.74 (1797)	33.3 (836)	49.3 (1252)
DV8N	445	1800	90° Vee	—	4	8	4	6.625 (186.275)	7.25 (184.15)	97.92 (6.884)	2174 (11.11)	0.381 (173)	E	7700 (3493)	70.95 (1802)	60.35 (1533)	63.2 (1605)
DV8T	534	1800	90° Vee	A	4	8	4	6.625 (168.275)	7.25 (184.15)	117.5 (8.261)	2174 (11.11)	0.410 (186)	E	7860 (3565)	75.9 (1927)	60.35 (1533)	67.55 (1716)
DV8TCE	618	1800	90° Vee	A & B	4	8	4	6.625 (168.275)	7.25 (184.15)	136 (9.562)	2174 (11.1)	0.380 (172.4)	E	8060 (1656)	75.9 (1927)	60.35 (1533)	67.55 (1716)
DV8—TCA	707	1800	90° Vee	A & B	4	8	4	6.625 (168.275)	7.25 (184.15)	155.6 (10.94)	2174 (11.11)	0.384 (174.2)	E	8060 (1656)	75.9 (1927)	60.35 (1533)	67.55 (1716)

*Engine form: V Vertical
90° Vee configuration
A Pressure charged
B Charge cooled

†E Electrical

SACM
SACM Diesel Division

Main works and sales office
Société Alsacienne de Constructions Mécaniques de Mulhouse
1 rue de la Fonderie, 68054 Mulhouse Cedex, France

Telephone: (89) 46 01 08
Telex: 881 699

Subsidiary companies
Société Grossol
Sales office: 157 avenue Charles de Gaulle, BP 138, 92203 Neuilly-sur-Seine Cedex

Telephone: (1) 747 51 00
Telex: 620207

Société Surgérienne de Construction Mécaniques
8 avenue de la Gare, BP 13, 17700 Surgères

Telephone: (46) 07 02 10
Telex: 790831

Société Budi
Engineering Division

The series 135 and 150 (former Poyaud engines) are manufactured by Société Surgérienne de Constructions Mécaniques. The series 175, 195 and 240 engines are manufactured by Societe Alsacienne de Constructions Mécaniques de Mulhouse. Distribution is jointly handled by the sales offices of SACM and Grossol.

SACM Type 150 RSR2 V12 engine

SACM Type 135 BSR2 engine

SACM Type 175 BSR1 V12 engine

SACM Type 240 ESR1 V12 engine

135 mm bore engines

		4LNS 4LCNS	4LS1 4LCS1	4LS2 4LCS2	6LNS 6LCNS	6LS1 6LCS1	6LS25 6LCS25	V8NS	V8S1	V8S25	V12NS	V12S1	V12S25
Former designation													
New designation		4L 135BNS1	4L 135BSD1	4L 135BSR1	6L 135BNS1	6L 135BSR1	6L 135BSR2	8V 135BNS1	8V 135BSD1	8V 135BSR2	12V 135BNS1	12V 135BSD1	12V 135BSR2
No of cylinders		4	4	4	6	6	6	8V	8V	8V	12V	12V	12V
Turbo-charged		—	Yes	Yes	—	Yes	Yes	—	Yes	Yes	—	Yes	Yes
Charge air cooled		—	—	Yes	—	—	Yes	—	—	Yes	—	—	Yes
Output (UIC)	kW	90	115	160	130	175	246	175	235	325	260	350	480
	(bhp)	(120)	(155)	(215)	(177)	(238)	(325)	(240)	(320)	(440)	(365)	(475)	(650)
Engine speed	rpm	2500	2500	2500	2500	2500	2500	2500	2500	2500	2500	2500	2500
Mean piston speed	m/s	10.16	10.16	10.16	10.16	10.16	10.16	10.16	10.16	10.16	10.16	10.16	10.16
	(ft/min)	(2140)	(2140)	(2140)	(2140)	(2140)	(2140)	(2140)	(2140)	(2140)	(2140)	(2140)	(2140)
bmep	bar	5.9	8	10	5.9	8	10.6	5.9	8	10.6	5.9	8	10.6
Weight dry	kg	760	760	760	970	995	1060	1190	1220	1300	1650	1690	1800
	(lb)	(1675)	(1675)	(1675)	(2140)	(2195)	(2335)	(2625)	(2690)	(2866)	(3640)	(3725)	(3900)
Length	mm	1060*	1060*	1060*	1460*	1460*	1460*	1279	1351	1351	1767	1866	1866
	(in)	(41.7)	(41.7)	(41.7)	(57.5)	(57.5)	(57.5)	(50.4)	(53.2)	(53.2)	(69.8)	(73.5)	(73.5)
Width	mm	710	710	710	710*	810*	810*	1098	1181	1181	1038	1174	1174
	(in)	(28)	(28)	(28)	(28)	(31.9)	(31.9)	(43.3)	(46.5)	(46.5)	(40.9)	(46.2)	(46.2)
Height	mm	965	(965)	(965)	1085*	1158*	1166*	935	935	935	935	935	1084
	(in)	(38)	(38)	(38)	(42.7)	(45.8)	(45.9)	(36.8)	(36.8)	(36.8)	(36.8)	(36.8)	(42.7)

* Dimensions for vertical engines

150 mm bore engines

		A6150 & C6150	A6150S & C6150S	A6150Sr & C6150Sr	A6150SrH & C6150SrH	6L85	A12150	A12150S	A12150Sr	A12150ZSrH	150AN 12V85
Former designation											
New designation		6L 150RNS1	6L 150RSD1	6L 150RSR1	6L 150RSR2	6L 150TSR2	12V 150RNS1	12V 150RSD1	12V 150RSR1	12V 150RSR3	12V 150TSR3
No of cylinders		6	6	6	6	6	12	12	12	12	12
Turbo-charged		—	Yes	Yes	Yes	Yes	—	Yes	Yes	Yes	Yes
Charge air cooled		—	—	Yes	Yes	Yes	—	—	Yes	Yes	Yes
Continuous rating (UIC)	kW	175	245	275	330	440	355	485	550	670	890
	(bhp)	(240)	(330)	(375)	(450)	(600)	(480)	(660)	(750)	(900)	(1200)
Engine speed	rpm	1800	1800	1800	1800	1800	1800	1800	1800	1800	1800
Mean piston speed	m/s	10.8	10.8	10.8	10.8	10.8	10.8	10.8	10.8	10.8	10.8
	(ft/min)	(2117)	(2117)	(2117)	(2117)	(2117)	(2117)	(2117)	(2117)	(2117)	(2117)
bmep	bar	5.1	6.4	7.7	9.4	10.8	5.1	6.4	7.7	9.4	10.8
Weight (dry)	kg	1900	2100	2350	2450	2600	4000	4200	4300	4400	4650
	(lb)	(4185)	(4625)	(5175)	(5400)	(5725)	(8810)	(9250)	(9470)	(9690)	(10 240)
Length	mm	1600*	2350*	2350*	2350*	2350*	2200	2400	2630	2630	2630
	(in)	(65.4)	(92.5)	(92.5)	(92.5)	(92.5)	(56.6)	(94.5)	(103)	(103)	(103)
Width	mm	1450*	1480*	1480*	1480*	1480*	1087	1087	1087	1110	1110
	(in)	(57.1)	(58.3)	(58.3)	(58.3)	(58.3)	(43)	(43)	(43)	(43.7)	(43.7)
Height	mm	850*	850*	850*	850*	850*	1390	1710	1710	1710	1710
	(in)	(33.5)	(33.5)	(33.5)	(33.5)	(33.5)	(54.7)	(67.3)	(67.3)	(67.3)	(67.3)

*Dimensions for horizontal engines.

175 mm bore engines

		175 V12A	175 V12ASHR	175 V12BZSHR	175 V12RVR	175 V16BSHR	175 V16BZSHR	175 V16RVR
Former designation								
New designation		12V 175ANS1	12V 175ASR1	12V 175BSR2	12V 175RVR1	16V 175BSR1	16V 175BSR2	16V 175RVR1
No of cylinders		12	12	12	12	16	16	16
Turbo-charged		No	Yes	Yes	Yes	Yes	Yes	Yes
Charge air cooled		No	Yes	Yes	Yes	Yes	Yes	Yes
Continuous rating (UIC)	kW	440	700	885	1030	1030	1175	1320
	(bhp)	(600)	(950)	(1200)	(1400)	(1400)	(1600)	(1800)
Engine speed	rpm	1500	1500	1500	1500	1500	1500	1500
Mean piston speed	m/s	9	9	9	9	9	9	9
	(ft/min)	(1772)	(1772)	(1772)	(1772)	(1772)	(1772)	(1772)
bmep	bar	6.5	10.4	13.2	15.3	11.5	13.2	14.7
Weight (dry)	kg	3900	4500	4800	4900	6100	6200	6400
	(lb)	(8600)	(9940)	(10 600)	(10 800)	(13 450)	(13 670)	(14 100)
Length	mm	1941	2220	2220	2220	2590	2590	2590
	(in)	(75)	(87.5)	(87.5)	(87.5)	(102)	(102)	(102)
Width	mm	1280	1330	1330	1330	1330	1330	1330
	(in)	(50.4)	(52.3)	(52.3)	(52.3)	(52.3)	(52.3)	(52.3)
Height	mm	1486	1900	1900	1900	1750	1750	1750
	(in)	(58.5)	(74)	(74)	(74)	(69)	(69)	(69)
Fuel consumption	g/kW/h	218	214	210	214	210	210	214
	(lb/hp/h)	(0.353)	(0.346)	(0.340)	(0.346)	(0.340)	(0.340)	(0.346)

95 and 240 mm bore engines

		195 V12CSHR	195 V12RVR	195 V16CSHR	195 V16RVR	195 V20CSHR	240 V12DSHR	240 V12RVR	240 V16ESHR	240 V16RVR	240 V20RVR
Former designation											
New designation		12V 195CSR1	12V 195RVR1	16V 195CSR1	16V 195RVR1	20V 195CSR1	12V 240DSR1	12V 240RVR1	16V 240ESR1	16V 240RVR1	20V 240RVR
No of cylinders		12	12	16	16	20	12	12	16	16	20
Continuous rating (UIC)	kW	1320	1470	1900	2020	2200	2420	3000	3230	4000	5000
	(bhp)	(1800)	(2000)	(2580)	(2750)	(3000)	(3300)	(4080)	(4400)	(5450)	(6800)
Engine speed	rpm	1500	1500	1500	1500	1500	1350	1350	1350	1350	1350
bmep	bar	15.9	17.7	17.1	18.2	15.9	17.8	22	17.8	22	19.4
Mean piston speed	m/s	9	9	9	9	9	9.9	9.9	9.9	9.9	9.9
Weight (dry)	kg	5000	5700	7000	7800	8500	12 000	13 000	16 500	17 000	22 000
	(lb)	(11 010)	(12 560)	(13 420)	(17 180)	(18 720)	(26 430)	(28 630)	(36 350)	(37 450)	(48 450)
Length	mm	2500	2700	4100	4100	4600	3480	3580	4190	4450	5588
	(in)	(98.5)	(106)	(161)	(161)	(181)	(137)	(141)	(165)	(175)	(220)
Width	mm	1460	1460	1460	1460	1460	1752	1803	1752	1803	1803
	(in)	(57.5)	(57.5)	(57.5)	(57.5)	(57.5)	(69)	(71)	(69)	(71)	(71)
Height	mm	1961	1961	1961	1961	2020	2610	2610	2490	2490	2610
	(in)	(77.2)	(77.2)	(77.2)	(77.2)	(79.5)	(103)	(103)	(98)	(98)	(103)
Fuel consumption	g/kW/h	205	215	205	215	205	205	215	205	215	215
	lb/hp/h	(0.332)	(0.348)	(0.332)	(0.348)	(0.332)	(0.332)	(0.348)	(0.332)	(0.348)	(0.348)

Scania

Saab-Scania AB, Scania Division
151 87 Södertälje, Sweden

Telephone: 0755 81000
Telegrams: Scania, Södertälje
Telex: 13479

The company, which produced its first internal combustion engine in 1897 and its first diesel engine in 1936, specialises in high-speed engines.

New developments and improvements were introduced to the Scania series in 1981. By modifying the engines and introducing a completely new series of injection equipment, higher outputs were attained, as well as a reduction in fuel consumption and a considerable decrease in smoke emission. In addition, the introduction of charge-air cooling widened the output range.

Scania's industrial engine programme now comprises engines with outputs ranging from 58 to 367 kW. The programme is in part a preparedness for future demands for reduced emission levels in industrial engines. Here charge-air cooling is a distinct advantage in optimising the engines to meet more stringent regulations without loss of fuel economy.

The new engines are especially adapted for operation with high average output utilisation, and the fact that the user does not always have the opportunity to run-in the engine has been taken into consideration. To reduce the danger of piston ringstick in extremely heavy operation, a Keystone-ring is fitted as upper compression ring on the piston. Increased top land clearance provides for low lubrication oil consumption, down to 0.3 g/kWh.

Generating set engines have been specially adapted for the generator speeds of 1500 and 1800 rpm. The new injection pump and single-speed Bosch RQ governor provides faster and more precise governing of engine speed. With this governor the requirements for Class A1 (high requirements of governing accuracy) in ISO 3046 are fulfilled and governing is made possible down to a lower speed droop. The new governor is also particularly well suited for governing in parallel operation of multi-engine installations.

Locomotives and railway equipment form part of the extensive product programme manufactured by Valmet Oy in Finland. The 250 B is a shunting locomotive built by Valmet and powered by a Scania DS14 with a rated output in this configuration of 283 kW (385 bhp) at 2100 rpm. A Clark power-shift transmission is used to optimise traction (a full 13.2 tonnes coupling traction) and obtain a top speed of 75 km/h. A combination of the long 4.5-metre axle distance and pivoted, full suspension axles with ballast between the axles gives a smooth and comfortable ride. The low noise emission level of the DS14 engine, with a silenced engine compartment, ensures that the sound level in the driver's cab is as low as 66 dBA. Two 250 Bs are already operational in Sweden.

Other makes of equipment employing Scania engines include the OTSO locomotives manufactured by Saalasti Engineering in Finland. The OTSO 2R is powered by a Scania DS11 with an output of 217 kW (295 hp); its operating weight is 30 tonnes and tractive effort 90 kN. The locomotive is radio-controlled. The bigger OTSO 3 HSJ has a Scania DS14 rated at 243 kW (330 hp); its operating weight is 38 tonnes and tractive effort 107 kN. Maximum speed of both models is 25 km/h.

The type LH shunting locomotive by Moteurs Moes SA, Belgium is equipped with a Scania DN8 engine rated at 99 kW (135 hp) and has a tractive effort of 40 kN and a maximum speed of 15 km/h.

Plasser & Theurer of Linz, Austria has used Scania engines in its track maintenance equipment for many years and recently received an order from the Brazilian Federal Railways (RFFSA) for 64 units each powered by a Scania DS11 engine.

Types D8, DS8, D11, DS11

6 cylinder in-line, 4-stroke, water cooled.
Cylinders: Bore and stroke. D8 and DS8 115 × 125 mm (4.53 × 4.92 in). D11 and DS11 127 × 145 mm (5 × 5.71 in). Wet type centrifugal cast iron cylinder liners, the outer surfaces directly flushed by cooling water. Alloy cast iron cylinder heads, each covering two cylinders (D8 and DS8), or three cylinders (D11, DS11).

Type DS14

8 cylinder Vee, 4-stroke, water cooled.
Cylinders: Bore and stroke 127 × 140 mm (5 × 5.51 in). Alloyed cast iron cylinder heads, one for each cylinder.
Pistons: Light alloy. For the top compression ring there is a cast-iron insert to reduce wear of the ring groove to a minimum. Compression rings and oil control ring of alloy cast iron. Top compression ring chromium-plated. Case-hardened chrome nickel steel fully floating gudgeon pins.
Connecting rods: Heat-treated special alloy steel H section stampings with steel backed indium-coated thin-wall type big end bearings, and bronze bushes.
Crankshaft: Alloy steel one-piece stamping, statically and dynamically balanced, carried in steel-backed indium-coated thin-wall type bearings. Individual bearings can be exchanged without dismounting crankshaft.
Crankcase: Cylinder block and crankcase integrally cast of cast iron alloy. The main bearing caps are steel forgings.

Scania DSI11 with charge-air cooling

Scania DSI14 with charge-air cooling

Scania DSI8 with charge-air cooling

Valmet Type 250B shunter with Scania DS14 engine

OTSO 2R locomotive with Scania DS11 engine

Valve gear: One inlet and one exhaust valve per cylinder, of stellite-faced heat-resisting steel with chromium-plated stems. Heat-resistant alloy replaceable valve seats. Hardened steel forging camshaft.

Fuel injection: Multi-hole type injectors with special cold starting device. Helical gear driven injection pump.

Turbo-charger: Exhaust gas turbo-charger.

Fuel: Diesel fuel.

Lubrication: Forced feed to all bearings and gear trains with intermittent oil supply to the valve rocker mechanism. One gear-type pump.

Cooling: One centrifugal type water pump driven from the crankshaft through Vee-belts (DS14 through gear chain). Thermostatic control for low temperature operation.

Starter: Electric.

Single-speed industrial engines for generating sets etc

Model		Prime duty* 50 Hz	Prime duty* 60 Hz	Stand-by duty** 50 Hz	Stand-by duty** 50 Hz	Stand-by duty** 60 Hz
DN8	kW	73	86	—	—	—
	(hp)	(99)	(117)	—	—	—
DS8	kW	101	119	110	—	130
	(hp)	(137)	(162)	(150)	—	(177)
DSI8	kW	107	128	123	—	147
	(hp)	(145)	(174)	(167)	—	(200)
DN11	kW	106	123	—	—	—
	(hp)	(144)	(167)	—	—	—
DS11	kW	181	213	205	241	235
	(hp)	(246)	(290)	(279)	(328)	(320)
DSI11	kW	190	226	222	273	263
	(hp)	(259)	(307)	(302)	(371)	(358)
DS14	kW	223	256	261	319	298
	(hp)	(303)	(348)	(355)	(434)	(405)
DSI14	kW	238	274	277	—	314
	(hp)	(324)	(373)	(377)	—	(427)
Engine speed	rpm	1500	1800	1500	2100	1800

Power test codes:

*ISO 3046, DIN 6270 A (overload capability 10%, 1h/6h)

**ISO 3046, DIN 6270 A (overload capability 10% intended for transient load peaks)

Moteurs Moes Type LH shunter with Scania DN8 engine

Industrial engines

Model		DN8	DS8	DSI8	DN11	DS11*	DSI11	DS14	DSI14
No of cylinders		6	6	6	6	6	6	V8	V8
Cylinder volume, cm³		7800	7800	7800	11 000	11 000	11 000	14 200	14 200
(in³)		(475)	(475)	(475)	(673)	(673)	(673)	(866)	(866)
Intermittent output kW		123	163	178	158	233	250	303	322
(hp)/rpm ISO 3046		(167)/2400	(221)/2400	(242)/2400	(215)/2200	(317)/2100	(340)/2100	(412)/2100	(438)/2100
Max torque intermittent Nm		530	735	830	775	1255	1330	1570	1695
(kpm) lbf ft/rpm		(54)/1500	(74)/1400	(85)/1600	(79)/1200	(128)/1300	(136)/1500	(160)/1300	(173)/1200
Specific fuel consumption									
g/kWh (g/hp/h)/1500 rpm		228 (168)	212 (156)	208 (153)	220 (162)	208 (153)	208 (153)	206 (152)	203 (149)
lb/kWh (lb/hp/h)/1500 rpm		0.5 (0.37)	0.47 (0.34)	0.46 (0.33)	0.49 (0.36)	0.46 (0.33)	0.46 (0.33)	0.45 (0.33)	0.44 (0.32)
Weight (dry) kg		740	760	780	905	930	950	1160	1180
(lb)		(1631)	(1676)	(1719)	(1995)	(2050)	(2094)	(2557)	(2601)

*Also available in 269 and 295 hp versions for restricted use only

SEMT

Société d'Etudes de Machines Thermiques

2 quai de Seine, 93203 St Denis, France

The Société d'Etudes de Machines Thermiques (SEMT), formed in 1947 to develop diesel engines, is a subsidiary company of Alsthom-Atlantique. It has successfully designed and developed diesel engines in the high-speed range.

The SEMT-Pielstick PA series of engines is used for rail traction, generating plants, drilling and pumping sets, and for submarine and fast ship propulsion. More than 4200 PA engines are in service around the world, manufactured by SEMT licensees.

The PA series includes the following models:

PA4-185 developing 167 hp per cylinder at 1500 rpm

PA4-200 developing 192, 250 hp per cylinder at 1500 rpm

PA5-255 developing 300 hp per cylinder at 1000 rpm

PA6-280 developing 400 hp per cylinder at 1000 rpm

SGP

Simmering-Graz-Pauker AG

Mariahilferstrasse 32, Vienna 1071, Austria

Main design features of all SGP diesel engines are minimum fuel consumption, extreme environment protection, high safety of operation and low maintenance costs. They are water-cooled, turbo-charged, four-stroke 8 or 12 Vee cylinder engines with intercooling of the charged air; fuel charging is either through pre-combustion chamber or by individual direct injection. The rating ranges from 600 to 2200 hp.

Crankcase: Spheroidal graphite cast iron crankcase with integrated air-scoop.

Cylinders: Cylinder liners are of pearlitis centrifugal cast. Cylinder heads are water-cooled, made of high alloy cast-iron with four valves and Rotocaps.

Crankshaft: Dynamically balanced chromium-molybdenum crankshaft.

Connecting rod: Drop-forged chromium-molybdenum steel, running in bearings of thin-walled ternary aluminium alloy.

Pistons: Comprising a forged light metal bottom and a high tensile steel top, bolted together by eight necked-down bolts; three compression rings and one oil ring for each piston.

Lubrication: By gear pump.

Fuel delivery: Direct injection with individual injection pumps.

Starter: Electric motor or by compressed air.

Turbo-charger: By BBC or KKK.

SGP diesel engines for rail traction

Model		S108c	S208c	T8c	T108c	T12c	T112c
Type		4-stroke Vee pre-combustion chamber	4-stroke Vee pre-combustion chamber	4-stroke Vee pre-combustion chamber	4-stroke Vee direct injection	4-stroke Vee pre-combustion chamber	4-stroke Vee direct injection
Bore	mm	160	160	190	190	190	190
Stroke	mm	190	190	220	220	220	220
No of cylinders		8	8	8	8	12	12
Turbo-charged		Yes	Yes	Yes	Yes	Yes	Yes
Charge air cooled		Yes	Yes	Yes	Yes	Yes	Yes
Output (UIC)	kW	440	510	800	990	1100	1620
	(hp)	(600)	(700)	(1100)	(1350)	(1500)	(2200)
Engine speed	rpm	1500	1500	1500	1500	1500	1500
Max piston speed	ft/min	1868	1868	2162	2162	2162	2162
	(m/s)	(9.5)	(9.5)	(11)	(11)	(11)	(11)
Bmep	lb/in²	167	196	187	230	170	250
	(kg/cm²)	(11.8)	(13.8)	(13.2)	(16.2)	(12)	(17.6)
Weight (dry)	lb	7270	7270	11 000	13 000	15 200	17 100
	(kg)	(3300)	(3300)	(5000)	(5900)	(6900)	(7750)
Length	in	93	86	88	93	131	119
	(mm)	(2360)	(2175)	(2244)	(2360)	(3325)	(3019)
Width	in	57	57	61	62	56	62
	(mm)	(1450)	(1450)	(1545)	(1580)	(1425)	(1580)
Height	in	71	61	80	69	83	69
	(mm)	(1817)	(1560)	(2035)	(1735)	(2115)	(1763)

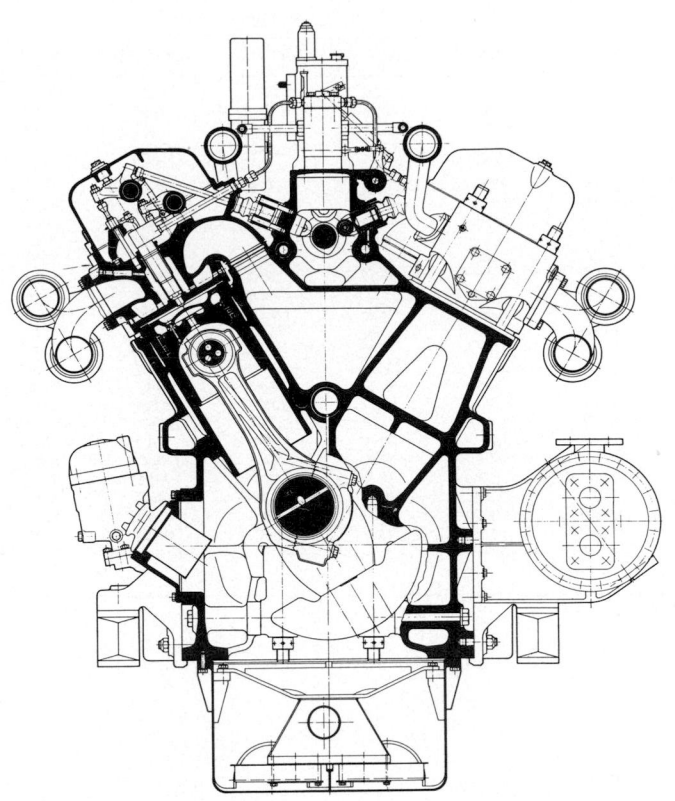

Cross-section of T112c diesel engine

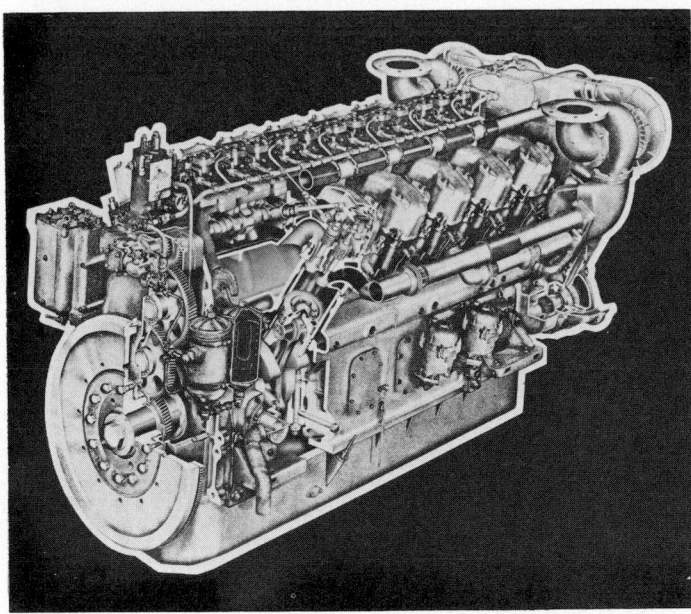

SGP Type T112c engine

Shinko

Shinko Engineering Co Ltd
1682 Motoima-cho, Ogaki 503, Japan

Telephone: 0584 89 3121
Telex: 4793 624

This is a subsidiary of Kobe Steel Co Ltd. Manufacture of high-speed diesel engines for rail traction began in 1950 and the present range is from 140 to 2000 hp. It also builds hydraulic torque converters capable of up to 1600 hp.

Vertical in-line water-cooled 4-cycle

DMF 13C	6-cylinder normally aspirated
DMH 17C	8-cylinder normally aspirated
DMH 17S	8-cylinder turbo-charged
DMH 17SB	8-cylinder turbo-charged
DMF 31SB	6-cylinder turbo-charged
DMF 31SI	6-cylinder turbo-charged and charge air cooled

DMF 31ZB	6-cylinder turbo-charged and charge air cooled
DMH 41S	8-cylinder turbo-charged
DMH 41Z	8-cylinder turbo-charged and charge air cooled
DMH 41ZB	8-cylinder turbo-charged and charge air cooled

Horizontal in-line water-cooled 4-cycle

DMH 17H	8-cylinder normally aspirated
DMH 17HS	8-cylinder turbo-charged
DMF 15HS	8-cylinder turbo-charged
DML 30HS	12-cylinder turbo-charged opposed cylinder

Vee-type water-cooled 4-cycle

DML 61S	12-cylinder turbo-charged
DMH 61Z	12-cylinder turbo-charged and charge air cooled
DML 61ZA	12-cylinder turbo-charged and charge air cooled
DML 61ZB	12-cylinder turbo-charged and charge air cooled
DMP 81Z	16-cylinder turbo-charged and charge air cooled

		Vertical in-line								
Model		DMF13C	DMH17C	DMF31SB	DMF31Z	DMF31S1	DMF31ZB	DMH41S	DMH41Z	DMH41ZB
Bore	in	5.12	5.12	7.09	7.09	7.09	7.09	7.09	7.09	7.09
	(mm)	(130)	(130)	(180)	(180)	(180)	(180)	(180)	(180)	(180)
Stroke	in	6.3	6.3	7.87	7.87	7.87	7.87	7.87	7.87	7.87
	(mm)	(160)	(160)	(200)	(200)	(200)	(200)	(200)	(200)	(200)
No of cylinders		6	8	6	6	6	6	8	8	8
Displacement	in³	777	1036	1864	1864	1864	1864	2483	2483	2483
	(litres)	(12.74)	(16.98)	(30.55)	(30.55)	(30.55)	(30.55)	(40.7)	(40.7)	(40.7)
Turbo-charged		—	—	Yes	Yes	Yes	Yes	Yes	Yes	Yes
Charge air cooled		—	—	—	Yes	Yes	Yes	—	Yes	Yes
Power rating continuous	hp	140	180	500	550	600	750	700	800	1000
Engine speed	rpm	1500	1500	1500	1500	1500	1500	1500	1500	1500
Bmep	lb/in²	93.7	90.5	139.8	153.6	167.8	209	146.5	167.8	209
	(kg/cm²)	(6.59)	(6.36)	(9.83)	(10.8)	(11.8)	(14.7)	(10.3)	(11.8)	(14.7)
Piston speed	ft/min	1576	1576	1970	1970	1970	1970	1970	1970	1970
	(m/s)	(8)	(8)	(10)	(10)	(10)	(10)	(10)	(10)	(10)
Weight (dry)	lb	2430	3090	6830	7055	7276	7716	9921	9987	10 031
	(kg)	(1100)	(1400)	(3100)	(3200)	(3300)	(3500)	(4500)	(4500)	(4550)
Length	in	65.4	79.2	105.2	105.4	109.1	105	126.6	126.6	126.6
	(mm)	(1661)	(2011)	(2672)	(2677)	(2772.6)	(2667)	(3210)	(3217)	(3216)
Width	in	44.5	44.5	37.8	49.9	51.2	49.9	42	41.9	41.9
	(mm)	(1131)	(1131)	(961)	(1269)	(1300)	(1268)	(1066.5)	(1066)	(1066)
Height	in	38.9	38.9	78.6	66.7	66.7	66.7	71	70.9	70.9
	(mm)	(987)	(987)	(1995)	(1695)	(1695)	(1695)	(1803.5)	(1803)	(1803)
Fuel consumption	lb/hp/h	0.419	0.419	0.397	0.397	0.386	0.386	0.397	0.397	0.386
	(g/hp/h)	(190)	(190)	(180)	(180)	(175)	(175)	(180)	(180)	(175)

Model		Horizontal					Vee-type			
		DMH17H	DMH17HS	DMF15HS	DML30HS	DML61S	DML61Z	DML61ZA	DML61ZB	DMP81Z
Bore	in	5.12	5.12	5.5	5.5	7.09	7.09	7.09	7.09	7.09
	(mm)	(130)	(130)	(140)	(140)	(180)	(180)	(180)	(180)	(180)
Stroke	in	6.3	6.3	6.3	6.3	7.87	7.87	7.87	7.87	7.87
	(mm)	(160)	(160)	(160)	(160)	(200)	(200)	(200)	(200)	(200)
No of cylinders		8	8	6	12	12	12	12	12	16
Displacement	in³	1036	1036	901	1803	3728	3728	3728	3728	4970
	(litres)	(16.98)	(16.98)	(14.78)	(29.56)	(61.1)	(61.1)	(61.1)	(61.1)	(81.5)
Turbo-charged		—	Yes	Yes	Yes	Yes	Yes	Yes	Yes	Yes
Charge air cooled		—	—	—	—	—	Yes	Yes	Yes	Yes
Power rating continuous	hp	180	250	250	500	1000	1100	1250	1500	2000
Engine speed	rpm	1500	1500	1600	1600	1500	1500	1500	1550	1500
Bmep	lb/in²	90.5	125.6	135.1	135.1	139.8	153.6	174.9	203.3	209
	(kg/cm²)	(6.36)	(8.83)	(9.5)	(9.5)	(9.83)	(10.8)	(12.3)	(14.3)	(14.7)
Piston speed	ft/min	1576	1576	1674.5	1674.5	1970	1970	1970	2035	1970
	(m/s)	(8)	(8)	(8.5)	(8.5)	(10)	(10)	(10)	(10.33)	(10)
Weight (dry)	lb	2420	2420	3968	7495	12 130	12 240	12 346	14 330	19 842
	(kg)	(1550)	(1550)	(1800)	(3400)	(5500)	(5550)	(5600)	(6500)	(9000)
Length	in	93.2	105.9	64.8	97.5	108.1	108.1	108.9	108.9	141
	(mm)	(2392)	(2691)	(2149.5)	(2477)	(2746)	(2746)	(2768)	(2768)	(3582)
Width	in	53.7	48.2	61.4	76.5	65	72.4	72.4	74	74
	(mm)	(1363)	(1225)	(1561)	(1944)	(1652)	(1840)	(1840)	(1880)	(1880)
Height	in	29.6	29.5	28.2	37.6	36.9	36.9	72.2	72.2	72.6
	(mm)	(753)	(750)	(716)	(955)	(936)	(936)	(1833)	(1833)	(1844)
Fuel consumption	lb/hp/h	0.419	0.408	0.397	0.386	0.397	0.397	0.386	0.395	0.395
	(g/hp/h)	(190)	(185)	(180)	(180)	(180)	(180)	(175)	(170)	(170)

Villares

Equipamentos Villares SA
Av Senador Verguiero 2000, 09700 São Bernardo do Campo SP, Brazil

Telephone: 443 5500
Telegrams: Eivilares
Telex: 443 5500

Products: Diesel engines.

TRANSMISSION SYSTEMS

ACEC
Ateliers de Constructions Électriques de Charleroi SA

PO Box 4, 6000 Charleroi, Belgium

Telephone: 3271 44 2276
Telex: 51 227

Products: Electric transmissions for diesel-electric locomotives and railcars.

Alsthom
Société Générale de Constructions Electriques et Mécaniques Alsthom

38 avenue Kléber, 75784 Paris, France

Telephone: 727 77 79
Telex: 27672

Works: Belfort and Tarbes

Telephone (Belfort): (84) 28 12 31
(Tarbes): (62) 93 02 97

Products: Complete electrical transmissions. The actual production power range with main dc generators is up to 2800 hp and with alternators up to 5000 hp.

ASEA AB
Transport Division

732 83 Vasteras, Sweden

Telephone: 46 21 100000
Telegrams: ASEA, Vasteras
Telex: 40720

Products: Complete electrical transmission systems including traction motors, gearboxes and flexible couplings for electric ac and dc locomotives, suburban and high-speed trains, mine and industrial locomotives.

Transmission unit for heavy duty with suspended traction motor, gearbox and coupling

Brissonneau & Lotz
Brissonneau & Lotz Chaudronnerie, SA

38 avenue Kléber, 75784 Paris, France

Products: Electric transmissions with main generators of up to 2400 hp.

BBC Brown Boveri
BBC Brown, Boveri & Co Ltd and Group Companies

Corporate marketing office: Postfach 58, 5401 Baden, Switzerland

Telephone: 056 75 11 11
Telex: 558214

Group companies: See under Locomotives and rolling stock

Products: Complete electrical transmissions and turbochargers for diesel engines.

Brush
Brush Electrical Machines Ltd
Traction Division
A Hawker Siddeley company

PO Box 18, Loughborough, Leicestershire LE11 1HJ, England

Telephone: 0509 63131
Telegrams: Brush, Loughborough
Telex: 341091

Products: Electric transmission systems of up to 6000 hp.

Canadian General Electric
Canadian General Electric Co Ltd

25 King Street W, PO Box 417, Commerce Court North, Toronto, Ontario M5L 1J2, Canada

Works: 107 Park Street North, Peterborough, Ontario K9J 7B5

Telephone: (705) 742 7711
Telex: 06-962826

Associated company: General Electric Co Ltd, USA

Products: Diesel-electric ac/dc and dc/dc traction systems, 600 to 4000 hp per single unit; automated rapid transit propulsion system controls.

Elektro-Mechanik
Elektro-Mechanik GmbH

596 Olpe, Postfach 40, Wendenerhutte, Federal Republic of Germany

Telephone: 02762 1631
Telex: 0876 616

Products: Hydraulic and hydro-mechanical transmissions 150/600 hp (AEG-EMG system), cardan shaft axle drives.

Ercole Marelli Group
Ercole Marelli Elettromeccanica Generale SpA

Viale Edison 50, 20099 Sesto San Giovanni, Milan, Italy

Telephone: (02) 2494
Telegrams: Marelgen Sesto S Giovanni
Telex: 31 0043; 320575

General Manager: Ing Umberto Lugo
Traction Division: Ing Mario Pastorelli

Products: Main electric equipment for all types of electric traction and auxiliary equipment; power supply and automation systems.

Fiat
Fiat Ferroviaria Savigliano SpA

Piazza Galateri 4, 12038 Savigliano (Cuneo), Italy

Telephone: 0172 33911
Telex: 220315

Products: Hydro-mechanical, hydraulic and mechanical transmissions of up to 500 hp axle drives.

Fuji Electric
Fuji Electric Co Ltd

New Yurakucho Building, 12-1 Yurakucho 1-chome, Chiyoda-ku, Tokyo 100, Japan

Telephone: 211 7111
Telegrams: Denkifuji, Tokyo
Telex: 22331

Chairman: Fukushige Shishido
President: Hideo Abe
Executive Vice President: Teruhisa Shimizu
Senior Executive Managing Directors: Takahiko Okuzumi
Takeshi Nakao

Products: Complete electric transmissions for locomotives and multiple-units.

Ganz-Mávag
Ganz-Mávag

PO Box 136, Konyves Kálmán krt 76, Budapest VIII, Hungary

Telephone: 137 020

Products: Hydraulic transmissions 250 to 1450 kW; in conjunction with co-operating company, electric transmissions of 400 to 2200 kW per unit. Transmission types include:
Type H122-11: Traction power 1045 kW, nominal input speed 1500 min^{-1}, output speed 210 min^{-1}, number of converters 2, weight 4050 kg;
Type H182-11: Traction power 550 kW, nominal input speed 1250 min^{-1}, output speed 1892 min^{-1}, number of converters 2, weight 3300 kg.

Ganz Type H122-11 transmission as fitted to Type DHM12 diesel-hydraulic locomotive for Bangladesh

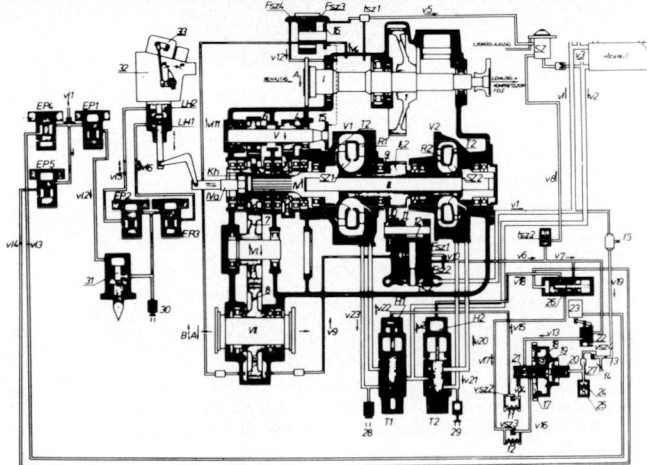

Ganz Type H122-11 transmission

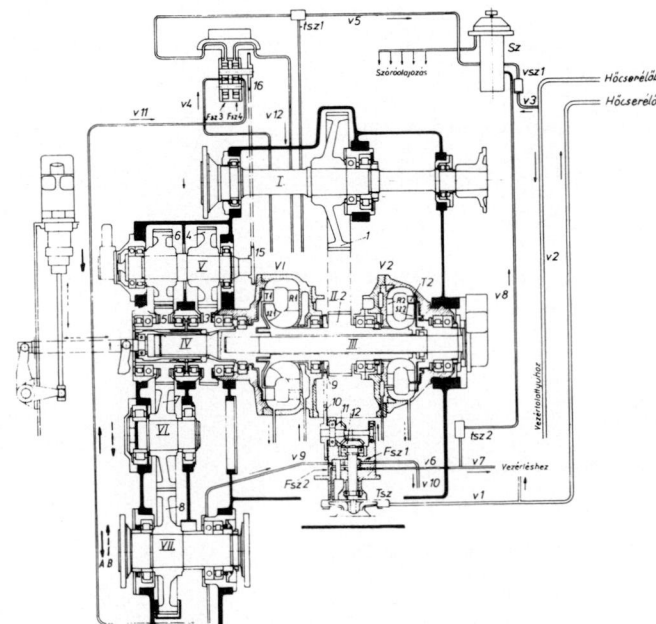

Ganz Type H182-11 transmission

GE
General Electric Co (USA)

570 Lexington Avenue, New York, New York 10022, USA

Telephone: (212) 750 3515

Works: 2901 East Lake Road, Erie, Pennsylvania 16531

Telephone: (814) 875 2234

Products: Complete electric transmissions.

GEC Traction
GEC Traction Ltd

Trafford Park, Manchester M17 1PR, England

Telephone: 061-872 2431
Telegrams: Assocelect, Manchester
Telex: 667152

Products: Electric propulsion equipment for ac and dc electric locomotives and multiple-units as well as for diesel-electric and battery vehicles and suitable for all rail gauges above 914 mm, for axle loads up to 30 tonnes, and speeds of more than 200 km/h; new and replacement gears and pinions, straight spur or helical, single or double reduction, parallel or right-angle drives.

General Electric (Brazil)
General Electric do Brasil SA

Estrada Campinas-Monte Mor km 103-13, 100 Campinas, SP, Brazil

Telephone: 41 1944
Telex: (019) 1168; (019) 1112

Associated company: General Electric Co (USA)

Products: Electrical transmissions for 1000 to 2400 hp axle-hung motors.

GM
General Motors Corporation
Detroit Diesel Allison Division

13400 West Outer Drive, Detroit, Michigan 48228, USA

Telephone: (313) 592 5000

Works: Detroit Diesel Allison Division GMC, PO Box 894, Indianapolis, Indiana 46206

Telephone: (317) 242 5000

Products: Hydraulic Torqmatic transmissions of 80 to 1000 hp.

Gotha
Getriebewerk Gotha

Karl-Liebknecht-Strasse 26, 5800 Gotha, Federal Republic of Germany

Products: Axle drives for diesel-powered vehicles.

Hidromecanica
MecanoExportImport supplier

Hidromecanica Works, 78 Boulevard Lenin, 2200 Brasov, Romania

Telephone: 921 34082
Telex: 61279

Products: Hydraulic transmissions.

Hitachi
Hitachi Ltd

6-2, Otemachi 2-chome, Chiyoda-ku, Tokyo 100, Japan

Telephone: (03) 270 2111
Telex: 22395; 22432; 24491; 26375

Products: Complete control equipment, electric transmissions and hydraulic transmissions.

Hunslet
Hunslet Precision Engineering Ltd

Hunslet Engine Works, Leeds LS10 1BT, England

Telephone: 0532 32261
Telegrams: Hunslt, Leeds
Telex: 55237

Products: Main transmission gears, forward and reverse and final drives; axle drive units for diesel-mechanical; mechanical change-speed, hydraulic and hydro-mechanical transmissions of up to 1000 hp; gearing for electrical transmissions; gears and gearboxes.

Hurth
Carl Hurth Maschinen-und Zahnradfabrik

Holzstrasse 19, 8000 Munich 5, Federal Republic of Germany

Telephone: (089) 23 70 21
Telex: 5216021

Products: Jackshaft gears; hollow shaft and bevel gear axle drive units; cardanic axle couplings; mechanical change-speed gears: alternate-speed and reverse-reduction gears of up to 500-600 hp.

Isotta
Isotta Fraschini

Via Milano 7, Saronno 21047 (VA), Italy

Products: Hydraulic and mechanical transmissions for locomotives and railcars. Axle drives for electric and diesel-powered vehicles.

Kaeble-Gmeinder
Carl Kaeble u Gmeinder GmbH & Co

PO Box 1260, 6950 Mosbach/Baden, Federal Republic of Germany

Telephone: 06261 4041
Telex: 04 66111

Products: Mechanical gears; axle drives; alternate-speed and reduction gears for hydraulic transmissions with jackshaft, cardan shaft and chain drives.

Laycock
Laycock Engineering Ltd

Archer Road, Millhouses, Sheffield 8, England

Telephone: 0742 368221
Telex: 54255

Products: Layrub flexible shafts and couplings.
The Layrub coupling is a universal coupling without working parts in the accepted sense. All relative movement is accommodated by the controlled internal displacement of compressed cylindrical rubber blocks having specially shaped end profiles. The bore of the block is reinforced by a high tensile steel screen, bonded into the rubber during vulcanisation. This screened bore provides an elastic grip on the inner 'pin' (sleeve), yet is capable of being removed when required.
The proportions of the standard resilient block are such that for the same load the deflection of the sleeve in an axial direction is about five or six times the deflection normal to the axis of the sleeve. Axial movement is readily accommodated by the Layrub blocks and so it is possible to dispense with a sliding spline. Steel sleeves are pressed into the screen of the block for attachment to the driving flange, the whole assembly being clamped by bolt and nut. The sleeve bolts are subject to tensile stress only, location and any shear being taken by the large diameter spigot of the sleeve.
Capabilities claimed for this cushioned drive are that it: absorbs shock and controls vibration; caters for large degree of axial and angular misalignment; simplifies close coupling in confined spaces; needs no servicing or lubrication; caters for operating speeds up to 10 000 rpm; transmits maximum power without power loss; is fully electrically insulated; by virtue of a spigotted drive gives extra safety; and operates in dirt, dust, sand and grit.

MaK
Krupp MaK Maschinenbau GmbH

PO Box 9009, 2300 Kiel 17, Federal Republic of Germany

Telephone: 0431 3811
Telex: 0299877/78

Products: Axle drives.

Montmirail
Ateliers de Montmirail

10 avenue de Friedland, 75008 Paris, France

Telephone: 561 14 30
Telex: 660 955

Works: Montmirail (Marne)

Telephone: 26 42 21 90

Parent company: Cie de Chemins de Fer Départementaux

Products: Asynchro mechanical change-speed transmission with cardan-shaft drive, from 200 to 3000 hp.

MPM
Meccanica Padana Monteverde SpA

Viale dell' Industria 48, 35100 Padua, Italy

Telephone: 049 773900
Telegrams: Ingranaggi, Padua
Telex: 430320

Chairman: David Monteverde
Sales Director: Vittorio Rasera
Managing Director: Vicenzo de Stefani

Products: Traction gears, special gearboxes, special axle drive units. MPM is staffed and equipped to design and manufacture complete transmission for rail vehicles with case-hardened ground and profile correction for long life and smooth running.

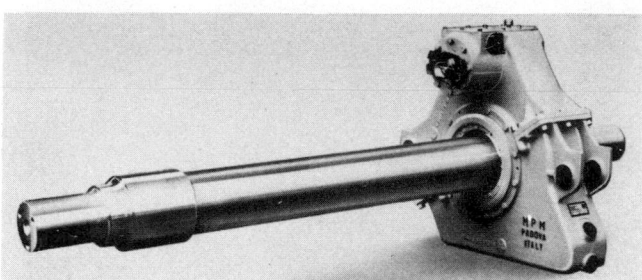

MPM axle drive unit

MPM drive unit

MTE
Société MTE

32 quai de Dion Bouton, 92806 Puteaux, France

Telephone: (33-1) 776 41 62
Telex: 610425

Works: Société Creusot-Loire, Le Creusot (S & L); Jeumont Schneider—Usines de Jeumont (Nord), La Plaine Saint Denis (Seine); Champagne-sur-Seine (S & M), Lyon (Rhone)

Products: Full range of electric transmissions.

Niigata
Niigata Converter Co Ltd

Nambu Building, 27-9 Sendagaya 5-chome, Shibuya-ku, Tokyo 151, Japan

Telephone: 03 354 7111
Telex: 2323105

Products: Nico transmissions; hydraulic torque converters.

OM
OM SpA

Piazza San Ambrogio 6, Milan, Italy

Telephone: 898351

Works: Via Pompeo Leoni 18, Milan

Telephone: 53 14 61

Products: Reverse reduction gears; OM/SRM hydraulic and hydro-mechanical transmissions built under licence; axle drives.

SCG
Self-Changing Gears Ltd

Lythalls Lane, Coventry, West Midlands CV6 6FY, England

Telephone: 0203 88881
Telegrams: Selfchange, Coventry
Telex: 31644

Managing Director: P T Warry
Sales and Marketing Director: J S Vandore
Rail Sales Executive: P J Cross

Products: Automatic transmission systems for passenger trains; and heavy transmission systems for shunting locomotive applications.

The Class 140 lightweight passenger train-sets under development by British Rail (BR) use an SCG system which was designed for these units. A fluid coupling is mounted on the engine and drives an RRE5 bi-directional automatic gearbox via a propshaft. Another propshaft leads from the output of the transmission to the RF42 final drive unit, which is axle-mounted. The gearbox incorporates electronic control to give the optimum shift quality and to maximise the operating efficiency of the whole driveline.

The BRE/Leyland Railbus is fitted with a derivative of the transmission system used in British Rail diesel multiple-unit trains. Again a fluid coupling is employed, because of its superior efficiency when compared with a torque converter. The R14 four-speed gearbox has been updated to include fully automatic control, using a system which is similar to that used in the Class 140; the RF28 final drive unit incorporates the reversing mechanism to give bi-directional running.

The Railbus installation is probably the simplest way of providing an automatic transmission system for a passenger train, while retaining high mechanical efficiency, whereas the Class 140 system derives the benefits of the latest technology for more sophisticated applications. Both transmission systems are available for sale in other applications.

The company also offers heavy duty reverse and reduction units covering diesel shunting locomotives in the 100 to 650 hp range. These are based on the RF11 unit, which is offered as standard equipment in Thomas Hill locomotives in the UK and other manufacturers overseas. SCG can also supply torque converters to match with the final drive range to provide a complete transmission package.

In addition to its standard range, SCG also operates as a design and development company to create solutions to clients' transmission requirements. SCG transmissions are licence-built in seven countries, usually where there are local content requirements for vehicle production.

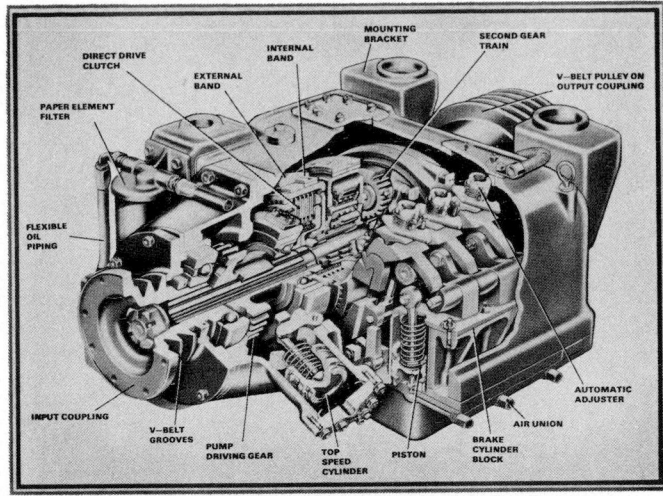

SCG Type R14 and RF28 transmission

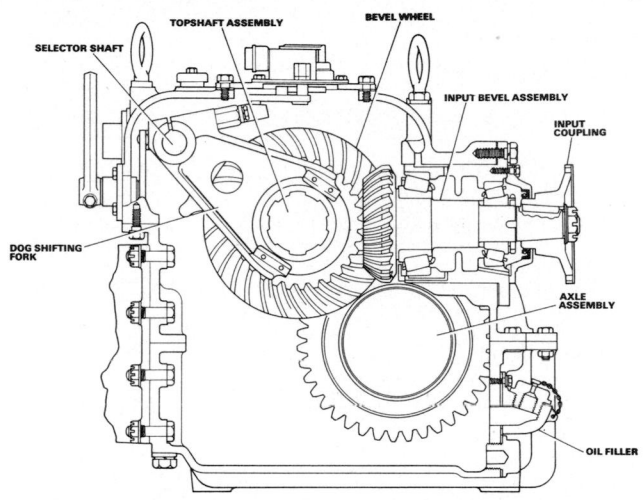

RF28 final drive unit

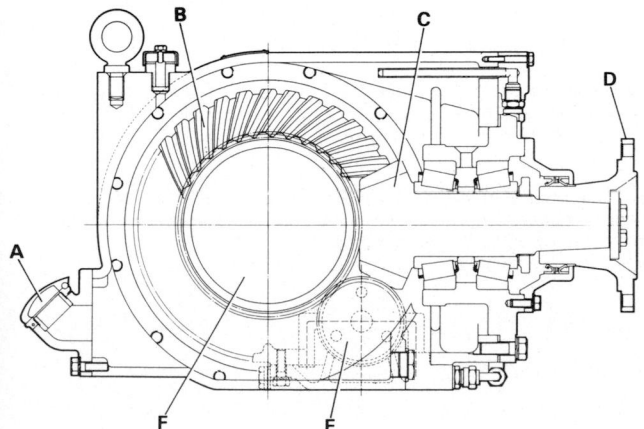

RF42 final drive unit **(A)** oil filter **(B)** bevel wheel **(C)** bevel pinion **(D)** input coupling **(E)** oil pump **(F)** axle shaft

SCG Type RRE5 bi-directional transmission

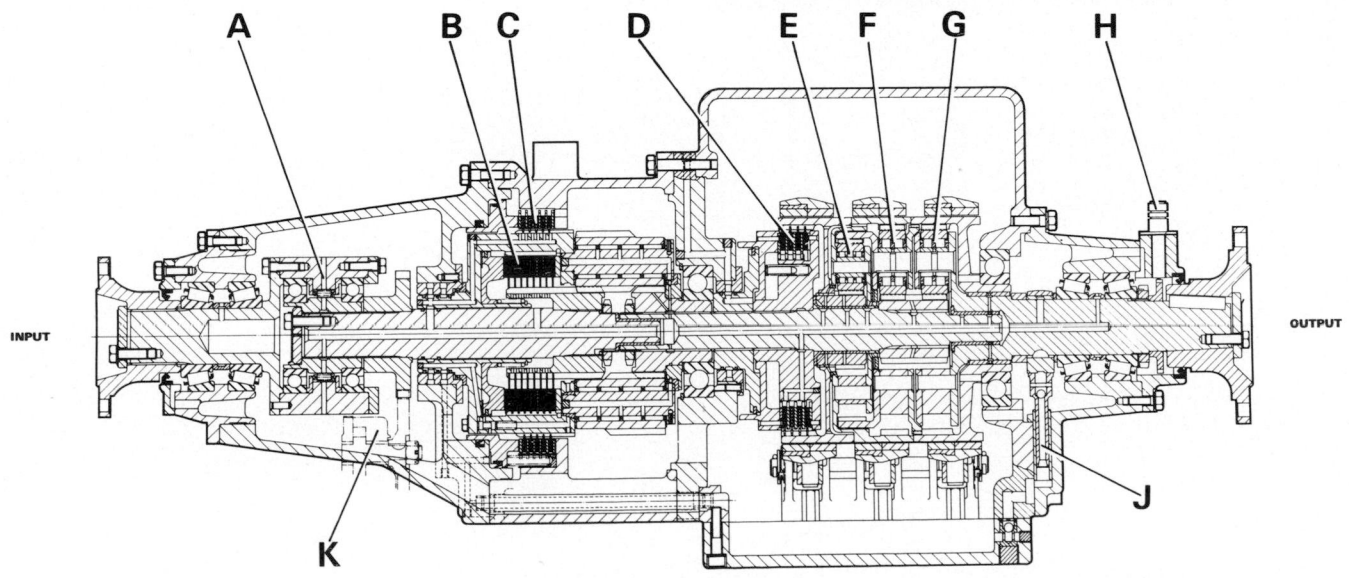

Type RRE5 bi-directional gearbox **(A)** freewheel unit **(B)** forward clutch **(C)** reverse clutch **(D)** top speed clutch **(E)** third speed gear train **(F)** second speed gear train **(G)** first speed gear train **(H)** transducer **(J and K)** oil pumps

Secmafer
Secmafer SA

Chemin des Meuniers Buchelay, 78203 Mantes, France

Telephone: 092 40 00
Telex: 600815

Products: Axle drives; hydrostatic transmissions for up to 8000 hp.

Shinko
Shinko Engineering Co Ltd

1682 Motoima-cho, Ogaki 503, Japan

Telephone: 0584 89 3121
Telex: 4793 624

Products: Cardan shaft drive hydro-mechanical transmissions of up to 1600 hp; Shinko torque converters.

Siemens
Siemens Aktiengesellschaft

Werner-von-Siemens-Strasse 50, 8520 Erlangen 2, Federal Republic of Germany

Telephone: 09131 71
Telex: 629871

Products: Electrical equipment for main-line and shunting locomotives.

SRM
SRM Hydromekanik AB

Skattegardsvagen 120, PO Box 16, 162 11 Stockholm-Vallingby 1, Sweden

Telephone: (08) 38 02 30
Telegrams: Hydessarem
Telex: 17412

Managing Director: Karl G Ahlèn
Chief Engineer: Per-Olof Bergstrom

Products: SRM hydraulic transmission of 30 to 2000 hp.

Licensees: Fiat SpA (Italy), Zahnraderfabrik Renk AG (Federal Republic of Germany), and CKD Praha (Czechoslovakia).

Strömungsmaschinen
VEB Stromungsmaschinen

83 Pirma Sonnenstein, Postschliebfach 64, Dresden, German Democratic Republic

Works: Otto-Buchwitz-Strasse 96, 806 Dresden

Products: Hydraulic couplings; hydraulic and hydrodynamic transmissions, flow converters.

Thyssen-Henschel
TGW Thyssen Getriebe- und Kupplungswerke GmbH

Sudstrasse 111, 4690 Herne 1, Federal Republic of Germany

Telephone: (2323) 497-1
Telex: 8229868

Products: Monomotor traction gears; axle drives with rubber pad couplings or hollow shaft type rubber pad couplings (inside positioned); FWH-Duewag-Axle drive; Simotrac twin-axle longitudinal drive unit.

Twin Disc
Twin Disc Incorporated

1328 Racine Street, Racine, Wisconsin 53403, USA

Telephone: (414) 634 1981
Telex: 264432

Associated companies: Twin Disc International SA, Chaussee de Namur 54, 1400 Nivelles, Belgium
Telephone: 067 2249 41
Telex: 57 414

British Twin Disc Ltd, Knight Road, Rochester, Kent ME2 2AT, England
Telephone: 0634 77855
Telex: 96182

Twin Disc (Pacific) Pty Ltd, Union Road, PO Box 126, Lavington, New South Wales 2641, Australia
Telephone: (060) 25 2577
Telex: 56923

Twin Disc (South Africa) Ltd, PO Box 75140, 2047 Gardenview, Transvaal, Johannesburg, South Africa
Telephone: 616 5018

Twin Disc (Far East) Ltd, PO Box 155, Jurong Town Post Office, 40 Lokyang Way, Jurong, Singapore 9161
Telephone: 2618909
Telex: 24284

Twin Disc Transmissoes Ltda, Rua Carlos, Seidl, 585 Caju, Cep 20 931, Rio de Janeiro, Brazil
Telephone: 264 6513
Telex: 212 3329/264 6513

Affiliated company: Niigata Converter Co Ltd, Nambu Building 27-9, Sendagaya 5-chome, Shibuya-ku, Tokyo 151, Japan
Telephone: 354 7111
Telex: 2323105

Products: Universal joints; gas turbine starting drives; power take-offs; mechanical, hydraulic and pneumatic clutches; control systems; hydraulic torque converters, power-shift transmissions.

Voith
Voith Getriebe KG

Heidenheim/Brenz, Federal Republic of Germany

Telephone: 3291
Telex: 7 14888

Products: Fluid couplings; axle drives; cooling units; hydrodynamic brakes; hydrostatic equipment; mechanical gearboxes; Voith hydraulic transmissions (turbo transmissions); torque converters; DIWA and DIWA-matic hydromechanical transmissions.

BRAKES AND DRAWGEAR

Abex
Abex Corporation (Railroad Products Group)

65 Ramapo Valley Road, Mahwah, New Jersey 07430, USA

Telephone: (201) 529 3450
Telegrams: Abexcorpor, New York
Telex: 642415

President: Raymond A Frick
General Manager, World Trade: Timothy F P Hely
530 Fifth Avenue, New York, New York 10036
Telephone: (212) 560 3200
Telex: 126605

European sales office: Karl W Kever, Manager
Augustinergasse 2, 5100 Aachen, Federal Republic of Germany
Telephone: 33003
Telex: 832849

European works: Frendo-Sud SpA, 83100 Avellino, Italy
Telephone: (825) 626808/626811

Products: Metal and composition brake shoes, disc brake pads.

AiResearch
AiResearch Manufacturing Co of California

2525 West 190th Street, Torrance, California 90509, USA

Telephone: (213) 323 9500

Products: Brake equipment.

Ajax
Ajax Consolidated Co

4615 West 20th Street, Chicago, Illinois 60650, USA

Telephone: (312) 656 0550

Products: Standard AAR Group B and Intermediate Power AAR Group L hand brakes; electro-mechanical water coolers and refrigeration units; ice-activated water coolers. Applications are for railway freight wagons, locomotives and crew equipment.

Ajax water cooler and refrigerator, specifically developed for arduous railroad service

Amsted
Amsted Industries International
A division of Amsted Industries

3700 Prudential Plaza, Chicago, Illinois 60601, USA

Telephone: (312) 645 1746
Telex: 254187

Amsted Industries International handles all business, licensing and sales of American Steel Foundries (ASF) and Griffin Wheel Company, which are divisions of Amsted Industries.

ASF
American Steel Foundries
A division of Amsted Industries

1005 Prudential Plaza, Chicago, Illinois 60601, USA

Telephone: (312) 645 1746
Telex: 254187

Products: Automatic couplers and yokes. ASF designs the Alliance coupler system. This knuckle-style coupler system covers a range of styles suitable for applications from small mine cars to the largest freight cars and passenger cars. Alliance couplers can include provision for rotary dumping, interlocking and slack control. A full range of accessories such as yokes, drawbars and transition systems is included. One recent development is the Ultra Capacity Alliance Coupler, which although able to couple freely with other knuckle-style couplers has a capacity far in excess of the standard couplers. Another recent development is ASF's Articulated Connector, which provides a proven means to fully exploit the articulated car or train principle.

All inquiries should be directed to Amsted Industries International (see above).

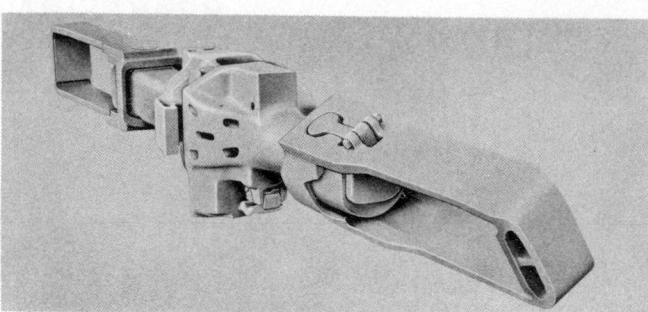

Alliance Ultra Capacity rotary coupler and yoke for rotary dumping without uncoupling freight cars

Avon
Avon Industrial Polymers Ltd

Bradford-on-Avon, Wiltshire BA15 1AA, England

Telephone: 02216 3911
Telegrams: Industrial, Bradford-on-Avon
Telex: 44856

Sales Manager: D A Washbrook
Sales Executive: J W Brockbank
Design Manager: M J Hinds

Products: Draftgear, drawgear, buffers, air-brake hose, rubber suspension systems and air springs.

Azbest

Ploce, Yugoslavia

Products: Composition brake linings built under licence from Jurid Werke of the Federal Republic of Germany.

BBC-Sécheron
BBC-Sécheron SA

14 avenue de Sécheron, 1202 Geneva 21, Switzerland

Telephone: 022 32 67 50
Telegrams: Electricité, Genève
Telex: 22130

Products: Automatic couplers, which are of three main parts:
The mechanical coupler, comprising: coupler head, designed to prevent the ingress of foreign matter into the interlocking mechanism, and serving as a support for the electrical and pneumatic couplers; draw and buffer gear, consisting of ring-spring elements or rubber elements; and supporting and centring device which maintains the uncoupled coupler in the vehicle axis even in the event of high centrifugal forces (choice of cross-beam suspension or swivelling arm is determined mainly by the horizontal pivoting angle of the coupler); and collapse features to protect the couplers and the vehicle underframe in the event of an accident or bumping at too high a speed.
The pneumatic coupler, comprising controlled valves or self-sealing check valves, which are located generally in the vertical axis under the coupler head, and automatically link one or more air lines.
The electrical coupler, comprising contact box and drive, which is resiliently fixed to the mechanical coupler head.
The low contact resistance of the strip-type plug contacts, which are self-cleaning when inserted, ensures safe transmission of electronic signals as heavy currents when several contacts are connected in parallel.
When two vehicles to be coupled approach each other at low speed the coupler heads are centred, slide together and automatically interlock at the trough of their front faces. The centring system ensures coupling security even on sharp curves or gradients. In the last phase of the coupling process, the interlocking mechanism simultaneously opens the controlled air valves which connect the vehicles' air lines (self-sealing check valves open independently of the interlocking mechanism) and the pneumatic valve controlling the drive of the electric couplers. Pushed by their drive, the electric couplers move forward and join together. The perfect centring and alignment of the contact boxes, facilitated by their elastic mounting on the mechanical coupler head, as well as the elastic fixing and the individual centring of the electric contacts, guarantee correct connection, free from wear. For vehicles not provided with compressed air, the pneumatic drive can be replaced by an electric motor.
When coupled and interlocked, the couplers form a practically rigid unit. The constant force exerted on the contact boxes by their drive, as well as their elastic suspension, prevents any relative movement between contacts. The forces are transmitted to the vehicle's underframe by a ball anchorage.
Uncoupling is either manual, by drawing the unlocking lever; or by remote control of an air cylinder from a driving cab.
The short coupler is uncoupled only when a vehicle has to be repaired and overhauled. It includes: a mechanical coupler comprising a coupler head, a centring device and, depending on the service conditions, draw and buffer gear and collapse features; a pneumatic coupler for connecting one or more air lines;

plug contacts of the standard and/or heavy-current type integrated in the mechanical coupler head for the connection of control and/or power circuits. Short couplers are locked by screws. Rubber gaskets effectively protect the plug contacts and the pneumatic coupler against humidity and dirt.

High reliability and safe operation is claimed even under the most severe climatic conditions, combined with very low maintenance and operating costs, because of: easy accessibility to the few parts exposed to wear; coupler head design that prevents ingress of foreign matter into the interlocking mechanism; the narrow strip contact surface of the couplers, which on coupling causes ice to be broken and snow or other foreign matter to be forced out through holes in the coupler head; collapse features which are easily accessible and can be replaced without having to remove the coupler; the electrical coupler's high insulation level; plug contacts which can be replaced from outside without having to open the contact box or disconnect the cables; no plug contact wear; protection of plug contacts against water and ingress of foreign matter by a triple gasket barrier; the strip-type plug contacts used (large number of contact points and self-cleaning on connection), which guarantee a low, constant contact resistance; and firm connection of electrical couplers even when the air pressure completely vanishes after prolonged immobilisation.

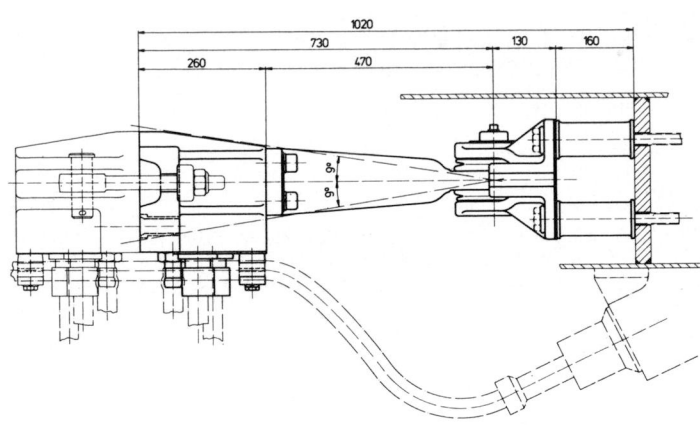

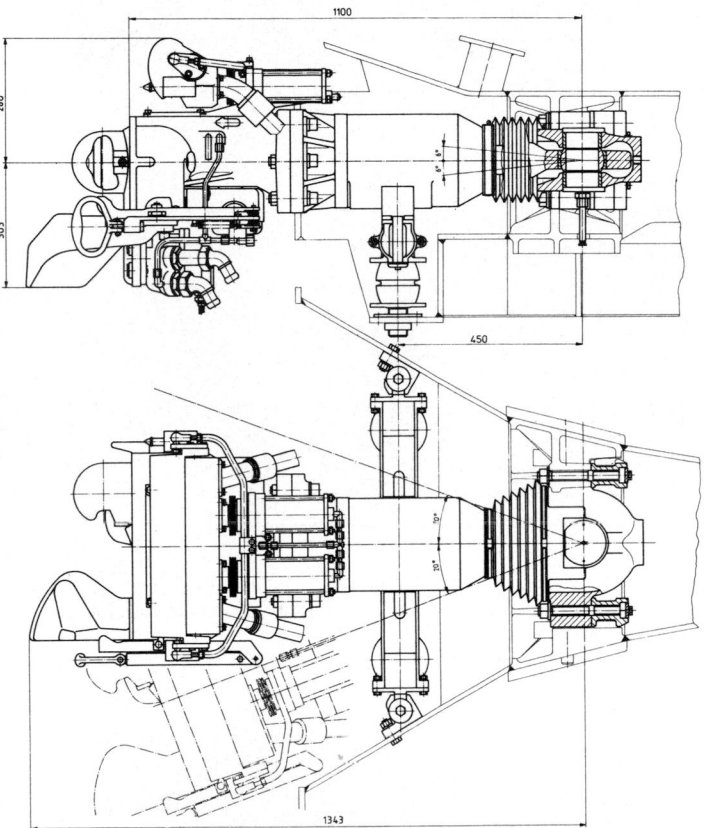

Arrangement of automatic central buffer for suburban and standard-gauge railways

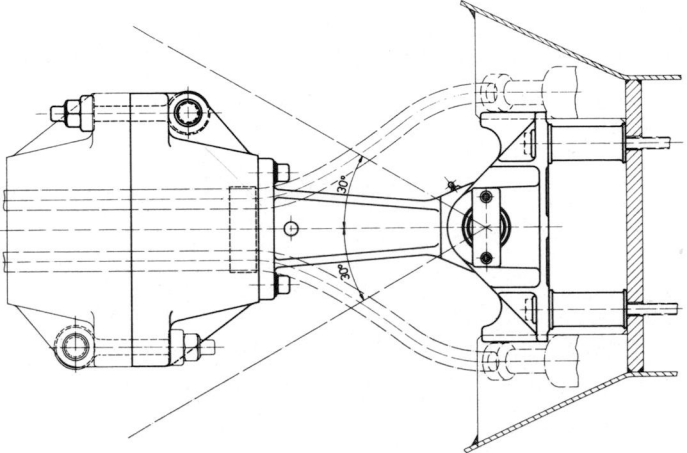

Arrangement of short coupler for secondary and underground railways

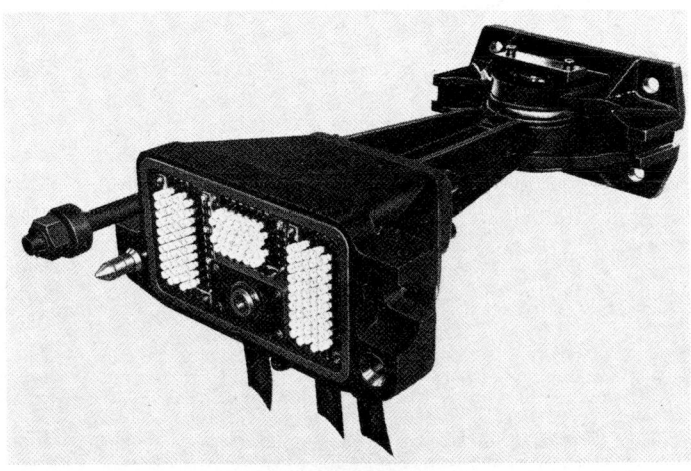

Short coupler for secondary and underground railways

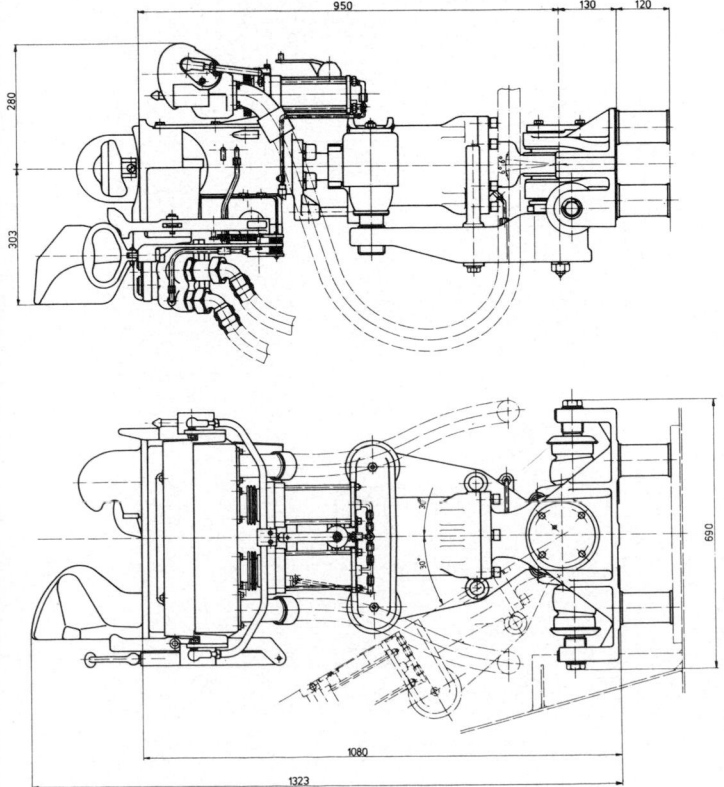

Arrangement of automatic central buffer for secondary and underground railways

Automatic central buffer coupler for suburban and standard-gauge railways

Bharat
Bharat Brakes and Valves Ltd
A Government of India undertaking

22 Gobra Road, Calcutta 700 014, India

Telephone: 44 1754
Telegrams: Cylvac, Calcutta
Telex: 021-2545

Products: Vacuum brake equipment; rotary-type high vacuum exhausters (28 in Hg), air-cooled; air brake valves and reservoirs; vertical turbine pumps.

Blair
Geo Blair & Co Ltd

Pottery Lane, Forth, Newcastle upon Tyne, England

Telephone: 610711/6
Telex: 53464

Chairman: I L Blair

Products: Extensive range of steel castings and assemblies for railway rolling stock including automatic couplers.

Bradken
Bradken Consolidated Ltd

22 O'Riordan Street, Alexandria, Sydney, New South Wales, Australia

Products: Friction draftgear.

Bremsenwerk
VEB Berliner Bremsenwerk
Member of Vereinigter Schienenfahrzeugbau der DDR eV

Hirschberger Strasse 4, 1134 East Berlin, German Democratic Republic

Telephone: 55740
Telex: 0112408

Products: Pneumatic braking equipment for rail vehicles and tramcars, brake cylinders, hydraulic shock absorbers, control valves.

Exports: Schienenfahrzeuge Export-Import Volkseigener Aussenhandelsbetrieb der DDR, Oztaler Strasse 17, 1100 East Berlin

BSI
Bergische Stahl-Industrie
A member of Thyssen Giesserei AG

Papenberger Strasse 38, PO Box 10 07 40, 5630 Remscheid 2, Federal Republic of Germany

Telephone: 02191 3641
Telex: 8513858

Products: Railway brake systems and equipment: disc brakes with high reliability, low wear, and improved thermal capacity; a large range of different brake discs meeting all demands with cooling by self-ventilation for fitting to axles and wheels; incomplete brake discs as spare parts; BSI and SAB tread brakes, brake indicator devices; UIC and special pneumatic and electro-pneumatic brake control systems of Oerlikon type; BSI electro-magnetic track brakes; automatic centre-buffer couplers of the COMPACT type and semi-permanent couplers for commuter trains, subway, rapid transit and tramway vehicles; automatic shunting couplers for UIC drawgear equipment; special steel and iron castings for the railway industry.

Recent important sales include: automatic and semi-permanent couplers for MTRC Hong Kong, Manila metro, RFFSA Rio de Janeiro and Belo Horizonte (Brazil), São Paulo and Rio de Janeiro metros, SNCV Belgium, commuter trains of Danish National Railways (DSB); disc brakes and actuator devices for Kowloon-Canton Railway, nearly all European national railways, São Paulo metro (together with Suecobras Rio de Janeiro), Amtrak and various rapid transit authorities in USA, Swiss regional railways. ONCF Morocco; special brake equipment for heavy-load steel industry vehicles as well as for advanced high-speed trains of French National Railways (SNCF), British Rail and German Federal Railway (DB).

The essential assemblies of a COMPACT coupler, that is the coupler head with air and electricity connections, the drawbar, possibly with an overload protection (shock release) feature and spring systems, and the draftgear, are offered in variable configurations to suit the individual users. The coupler head comes in two sizes and is made of cast steel in a variety of tensile strengths. It is thus consistent with any demands in terms of resistance to tensile and compressive forces. The electric coupling can be arranged on top, underneath or at the side, and the compressed air connection on top or at the bottom of the coupler head.

The drawbar and draftgear form a self-contained unit, depending upon the type of equipment. If the drawbar and draftgear are used with pre-stressed rubber elements, they may be complemented with a vertical adjustment system and overload protection feature with a shock release member. The draftgear consists simply of an articulated or joint bearing to follow the horizontal and vertical motions between vehicles if the drawbar is joined direct with a spring system. The spring systems connected with the drawbar can be made of frictional steel springs, metal-rubber springs or hydro-mechanical components at the user's option. Such an arrangement can also be provided with a compressive overload protection feature.

In these combinations of draftgears, spring systems and drawbars, the overall unit will follow all motions and take up all tensile and compressive stresses between the vehicles. A re-adjusting or resetting device retains the idle coupler in its rest position. The coupler can be operated manually, pneumatically or electrically. The main assemblies in a COMPACT coupler are detachably interlocked and each may also be used in other coupler brands.

All types within this coupler system have low-wear and reduced-maintenance design features.

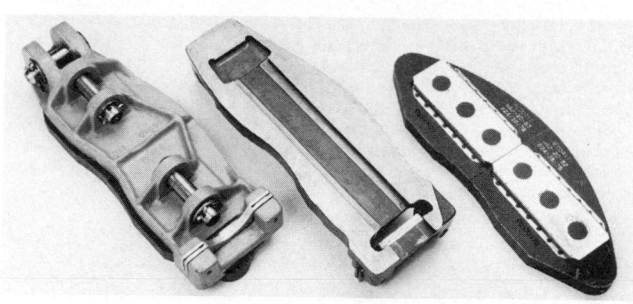

Brake pad with linings for safe and speedy replacement

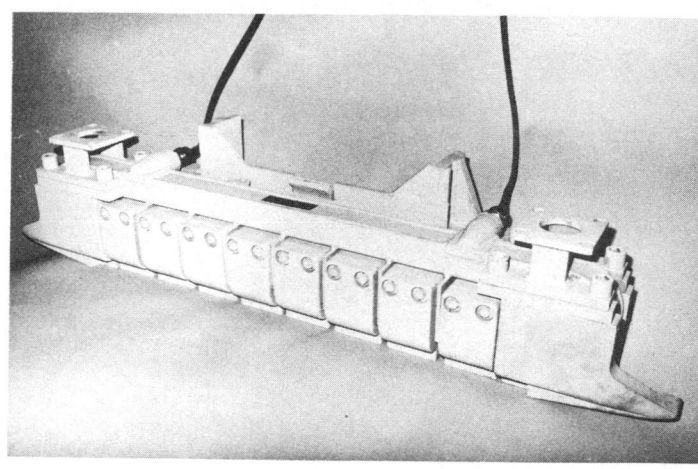

BSI track brake for high-speed vehicles

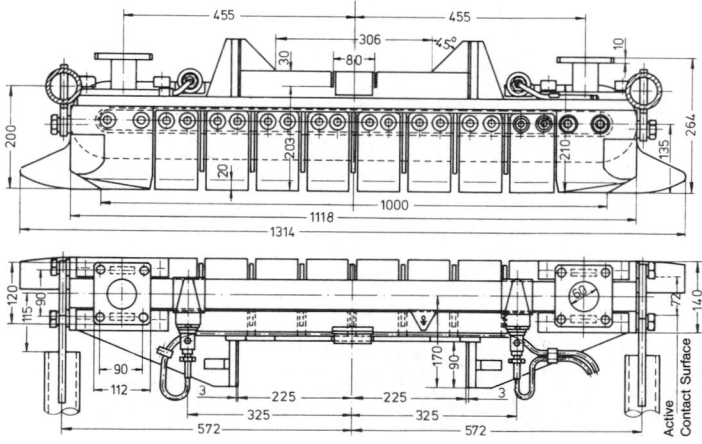

BSI electro-magnetic high-suspended Model 91.009 rail brake, adhesive force 84 kN, operating voltage 24 V, operating current 43 A

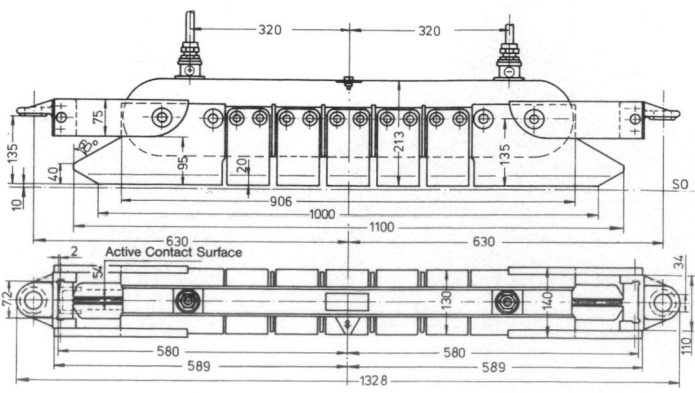

BSI electro-magnetic low-suspended Model 92.006 rail brake, adhesive force 54 kN, operating voltage 24 V, operating current 32.6 A

Automatic COMPACT coupler for all-electric LRV

BSI-COMPACT coupler of Rio de Janeiro emu with automatic electric and pneumatic connections

BSI automatic shunting coupler for UIC draftgear

Semi-permanent coupler with cable boxes for power and control currents for Mass Transit Railway Corporation, Hong Kong

BSI disc-brake application to German Federal Railway (DB) Type 403 high-speed emu in 'Lufthansa Express' charter service

Heavy-duty BSI-COMPACT coupler of new design for MTRC Hong Kong

BSI axle-mounted disc brake in heavy-duty steel industry ladle wagon bogie

Ultra-lightweight BSI-COMPACT coupler for Lille VAL metro

Complete BSI-COMPACT coupler developed for Netherlands Railways (NS) LRV

Buckeye
Buckeye Steel Castings Co

2211 Parsons Avenue, Columbus, Ohio 43207, USA

Telephone: (614) 444 2121
Telex: 810 482 1757

President: W C Buffington
Vice-President, Sales: J B Sparma
Vice-President, Sales Engineering: W D Reuter
Director, Product Engineering and Mass Transit: J R Downes

Products: Automatic couplers, draft yokes, centre plates, sill centre braces, draft sill ends.

Buffalo Brake Beam
Buffalo Brake Beam Co

400 Ingham Avenue, Lackawanna, Buffalo, New York 14218, USA

Chairman: Lester A Crone
Executive Vice-President: Richard Adams
Vice-President, Sales: R E Vey

Products: Railcar brake beams, side frame wear plates, brake rod connectors, railcar steel ladders, sill steps, bottom rod guards, coupler shank wear plates, coupler carrier wear plates and brake shoe keys.

Agent: Canada-Davanac Industries Ltd, 155 Montpellier Boulevard, Montreal, Quebec H4N 2G3, Canada

Telephone: (716) 823 4200

Buhlmann
Buhlmann SA

Rue des Coteaux 249, 1030 Brussels, Belgium

Telephone: 02 216 20 30
Telex: 61 134

Products: Pneumatic, electro-pneumatic and electro-magnetic brake equipment; electronic wheel slip and wheel slide detectors; automatic couplers.

Cardwell Westinghouse
Cardwell Westinghouse Company

332 South Michigan Avenue, Chicago, Illinois 60604, USA

Telephone: (312) 427 5051
Telegrams: Cardwell
Telex: 25 4210

President: D S Campbell
Vice President, Marketing: J L Duffy
  Mechanical Operations: V S Danielson
  Administration and Control: W C Davis
  Technical Sales and International Operations: W D Wallace

Products: Friction, rubber-friction and hydraulic-friction draftgear; hand brakes; automatic slack adjusters.

Licence agreements
Argentina: Siam di Tella Ltd, Division Electrodomestica, Tucman 633, Buenos Aires
Australia: Vickers Hadwa Division, 123 Railway Parade, Bassendean, Western Australia 6054
Bradken Consolidated Ltd, 22 O'Riordan Street, Alexandria, Sydney, New South Wales
Belgium: Acieries de Haine-Saint-Pierre & Lesquin, 7160 Haine Saint Pierre
Brazil: Cobrasma SA, PO Box 8225-ZP-1, São Paulo
Portugal: Engenharia e Comercio LDA, Rua da Alegria, 61 R/C, Lisbon 2
South Africa: Sturrock (South Africa) Ltd, 91 Commissioner Street, PO Box 2863, Johannesburg

Cardwell Westinghouse friction draftgear Mk 50

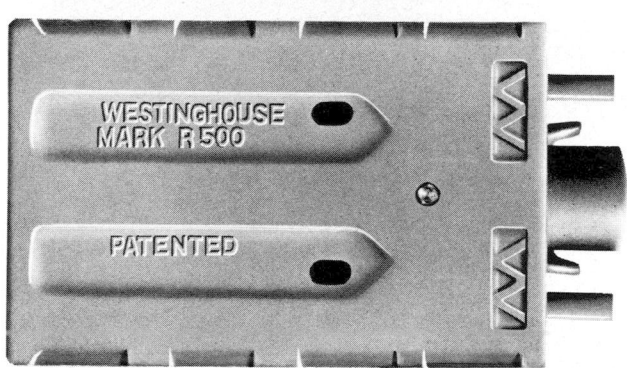

Cardwell Westinghouse rubber-friction draftgear Mk R-500

Carrier Khéops
Carrier Khéops SA

12 villa d'Este, Tour Atlas, 75643 Paris Cedex 13, France

Telephone: 583 90 01
Telex: 200 800

Managing Director: M Delauney
Export Sales Director: M Courtaigne
Sales Director: M Derenemesnil

Products: Plugs and sockets for coach coupling and equipment connection.

Cimmco International
Division of Central India Machinery Manufacturing Co Ltd

ECE House, 28-A Kasturba Gandhi Narg, New Delhi 110 001, India

Telephone: 44381-5
Telegrams: Cimwag
Telex: 31 3618

Products: Vacuum brake equipment and components, Alliance couplers, AAR standard-type Alliance couplers, MCA couplers, screw couplings.

Cobra Brake Shoes
Railroad Friction Products Corporation

Wilmerding, Pennsylvania 15148, USA

Telephone: (412) 273 1106

Chairman: R A Gilmour
Managing Director: J C Janke
Chief Sales Director: E W Kojsza

Products: Composition brake shoes and disc pads.

Agents: Cobra Friction Products Ltd, Hamilton, Ontario L8N 3T5, Canada

Cobrasma Sumaré SA
Cobrasma SA

Rua da Estacao, 523 Osasco, São Paulo, CP969, Brazil

Telephone: 801 8000
Telex: 011 33330

Works: Via Anhanguera Km 1045, Distrito de Hortolandia, CP151 Municipio de Sumaré, São Paulo, CEP 13170

Telephone: (0192) 65 1711
Telex: 019 1926

Products: Brake equipment and friction draftgear.

Cobreq
Cia Brasileira de Equipamentos

Praia do Flamengo, 200-9° andar, Caixa Postal 422, Rio de Janeiro, Brazil

Telephone: 285 2233
Telegrams: Calderon
Telex: 021 21632

Director-President: Engr Nelson Molina
Industrial Director: Engr Ali El Hage
Export Sales Director: Engr Rodolfo Luiz Darigo

Products: Non-metallic composition brake shoes and brake pads for railroad vehicles.

Commonwealth Engineering
Commonwealth Engineering (NSW) Pty Ltd

11 Berry Street, Granville, New South Wales 2142, Australia

Telephone: (02) 637 0166
Telegrams: Comeng, Sydney
Telex: 25283

Products: Miner RF170, RF185, RF361, RF444 and SL 76 draftgear; Miner hand-brakes.

Comsteel
Commonwealth Steel Co Ltd

PO Box 14, Maud Street, Waratah, New South Wales 2298, Australia

Telephone: 61 49 68 0411
Telegrams: Comsteel, Waratah
Telex: 28115

Products: Automatic couplers and drawgear.

Conbrako
Conbrako (Pty) Ltd

PO Box 14010, 167 Tedstone Road, Wadeville 1422, Transvaal, South Africa

Telephone: 34 3431
Telegrams: Conbrako
Telex: 8 4721

Products: Vacuum brakes; hand brakes; brake regulators; drawgear; shock absorbers.

Davanac
Davanac Industries Ltd

155 Montpellier Boulevard, Montreal, Quebec H4N 2G3, Canada

Products: Brake beams under licence to Buffalo Brake Beam Co, USA.

Davies and Metcalfe
Davies and Metcalfe (Equipment) Ltd

Injector Works, Romiley, Nr Stockport, Cheshire SK6 3AE, England

Telephone: 061-430 4272/5
Telegrams: Exhaust, Romiley
Telex: 668801

Chairman: Richard Metcalfe
Sales Director: E Mulryan

Products: Air brakes; electro-pneumatic braking; overspeed protection equipment; automatic couplers; two-stage air compressors; disc brakes; wheel slip detection and correction equipment.
   The company offers a range of products developed for rapid transit systems, including:
Type EBC/5 electro-pneumatic brake system, supplied with a variable (analogue) or stepped (digital) control;
Two-stage air compressors, with flange-mounted ac or dc electric motors and an integral intercooler with forced air cooling to ensure effective performance;
Metcalfe-BSI-COMPACT coupler, fully automatic with wide coupling capacity in all planes to carry up to 140 electrical connections and two through pneumatic circuits (this device also provides buffing and draftgear functions);
Spring parking brake, a spring-applied, air-released mechanism controlled from any of the driving positions;
Metcalfe-BSI disc brake sets, fully ventilated patented construction (both axle and wheel mounted sets, with actuators and release indicator systems).

Subsidiaries: Davies & Metcalfe Engineering Ltd, 22 George Street, Granville, New South Wales 2142, Australia

Davis Brake Beam
Davis Brake Beam Co

Johnstown, Pennsylvania, USA

Telephone: (814) 535 1595

Products: Solid-truss brake beams and bogie-mounted braking system manufactured under the trade-name, Truc-Pac.
   By providing simultaneous control of piston stroke and lever angularity, the Truc-Pac system is claimed to overcome deficiencies inherent in most of the compact bogie braking systems that have eliminated body-mounted rigging. These are that, without piston stroke control, the piston stroke tends to lengthen to compensate for wheel or shoe wear; or that with reliance solely on stroke control, there may be an increase in lever angularity. In both cases a reduction of braking force ensues.

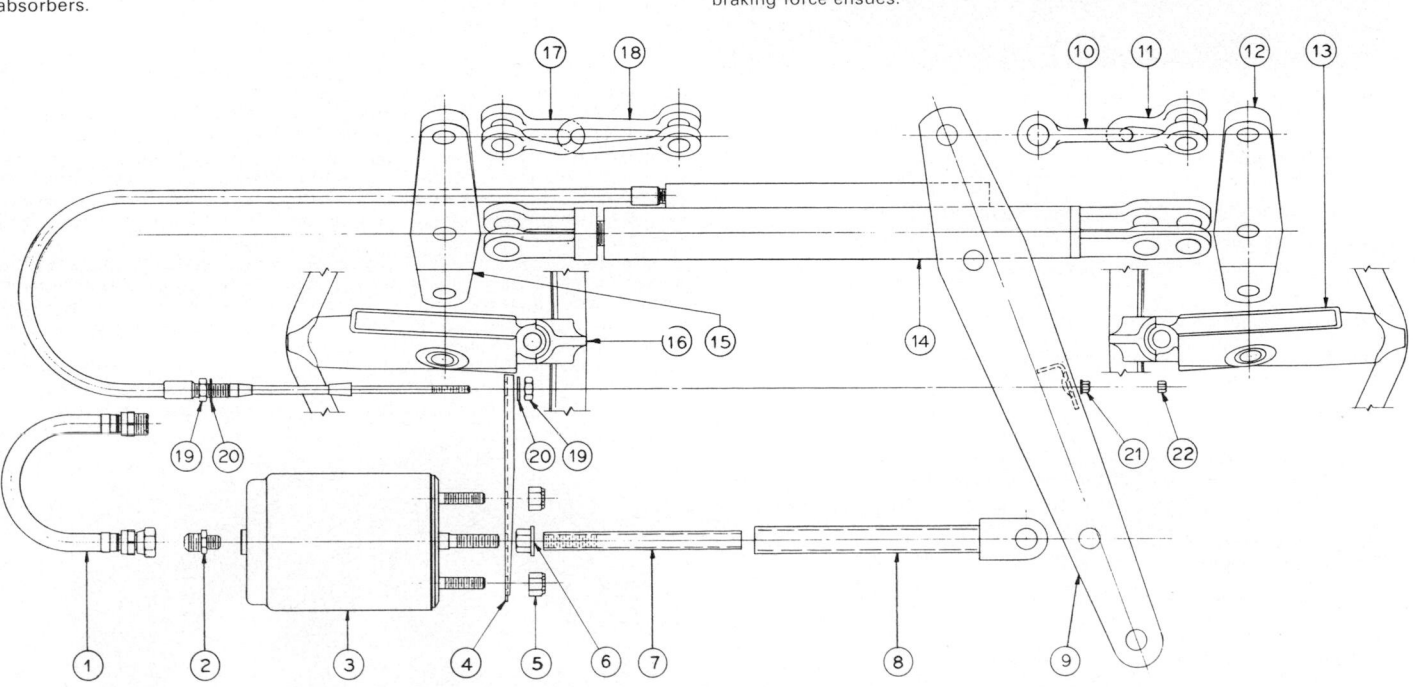

Davis Truc-Pac bogie brake (1) air hose assembly (2) male reducer (3) rotochamber (4) mounting plate (5) nylon lock nut (6) flange nut (7) push rod guide (8) push rod assembly (9) bolster lever assembly (10) clevis, straight (11) clevis, twisted (12) truck lever (13) brake beam, right hand (14) slack adjuster with cable (15) truck lever (16) brake beam, left hand (17 and 18) clevis, twisted (19) jam nut, 2 (20) lock washer, 2 (21) flange nut (22) nylon lock nut

Dimetal
Dimetal SA

Km 18 800, Antigua Carretera de Madrid, Barcelona, Torrejon de Ardoz, Madrid, Spain

Telephone: 675 11 00
Telegrams: Wabco, Madrid
Telex: 22332

President: Erique Zamacola Millet
General Manager: Jesús Ruano Alvarez
Railway Products Manager: Antonio Gonzales del Peral

Products: Brake equipment built under licences from Westinghouse Air Brake of the USA, Westinghouse Brake & Signal; door equipment of Faiveley, France.

Dresser
Dresser Industries Inc
Transportation Equipment Division

2 Main Street, Depew, New York 14043, USA

Telephone: (716) 683 6000

President: M J Franklin
Director of Marketing: W F Greenwood

Products: Automatic couplers, yokes, bogies, rotary couplers, centre castings and drawgear.

The Rotary Head coupler is a new design in unit train couplers in which all rotary motion which occurs outside the car in the coupler head, takes place on massive bearing surfaces within the coupler head itself, so that the coupler shank will not wear and tear on the draft rigging nor bind during rotation. The Rotary Head coupler operates similarly to and couples with AAR Standard 'E', 'F' and 'H' couplers. It has the AAR Standard 'F' interlocking contour and is dimensionally identical and interchangeable with the AAR Standard F70 coupler.

Dresser Rotary Head coupler

Ellcon-National
Ellcon-National Inc

30 King Road, PO Box 307, Totowa, New Jersey 07512, USA

Telephone: (201) 256 7110
Telex: 130154

Chairman: Emil P Konda
Chief Sales Director: Ryan M Caulfield

Products: Geared hand brakes, automatic double-acting slack adjusters, empty/load devices.

Licensees
Canada: Beclawat Ltd, 1128 Berlier Street, Laval, Quebec
Mexico: Dinamica SA, Avenida Madero 40, Mexico 1 DF
South Africa: Conbrako Ltd, Tedstone Road, Wadeville, Transvaal

Energomachexport
V/O Energomachexport

Deguninskaja Str 1, Korp 4, 127486 Moscow, USSR

Telephone: 1472177
Telegrams: Energoexport, Moscow
Telex: 411926

Products: Matrosov system automatic pneumatic brakes; drawgear including the type SA-3 automatic central buffer couplings.

Equip Rail
Equip Rail

12 rue Bixio, 75007 Paris, France

Telephone: (1) 556 1353
Telex: 200576

Products: Brake equipment.

Fabrika Vagona Kraljevo

Postanski FAH 90, Kraljevo, Yugoslavia

Products: Draftgear; buffers under licence from Miner; brake equipment; automatic couplers.

FNV
Fabrica Nacional de Vagoes SA

Avenida Maria Coelho Aguiar 215, 05804 Sao Paulo, Brazil

Telephone: 011 545 3588/5089
Telegrams: Fabriva, Sao Paulo
Telex: 01121901

Products: Draftgear and couplers.

Forges de Fresnes

80 rue Pasteur, 59970 Fresnes sur Escaut, France

Telephone: (27) 47 42 22

Products: Weldless brake triangles for bogie and wagons; drop forging parts.

Forja
Forja Argentina SA

Reconquista 661, 6th floor, Buenos Aires, Argentina

Telephone: 37 9833

Works: Calle 1 No 171, Barrio Talleres E, Cordoba

Products: Screw and chain couplings.

FreightMaster
A Halliburton Company

8600 Will Rogers Boulevard, Fort Worth, Texas 76140, USA

Telephone: (817) 293 4220
Telex: 75 8284

President: J G Stephenson
Sales Director: P D Howard
Manager, Engineering: R N Hodges

Products: End-of-car cushioning units; electronic training simulators, locomotive speedometer and recording systems.

The latest generation of FreightMaster's end-of-car hydraulic cushioning devices incorporates a train-action control system in addition to the equipment's proven protection of car and cargo for overspeed impacts. With over 125 000 car sets in use, FreightMaster's Type M series is the most widely-used equipment of its type in the world. The cushioning equipment may be used on box cars of all weights and types, tri-level rack cars, and all other cars that carry damage-sensitive cargos.

FreightMaster's Train Dynamics Analyzer is widely used by railroads as a fuel conservation aid. The computerised simulator has helped develop better train handling methods that contribute to lower fuel consumption. Utilising actual track profiles, a railroad can simulate a train formation with actual car weights, lengths, locomotive power and locations, then test-run the train to ascertain maximum efficiency. Railroads using the TDA for fuel conservation, in addition to driver-training programmes, have commented on the accuracy of the system's simulations. Fuel savings up to 30 per cent have been achieved.

FreightMaster Type M cushioning units

FreightMaster Train Dynamics Analyzer

Fresinbra
Fresinbra Industrial SA

Praia do Flamengo 200-9 , PO Box 422, 20 000 Rio de Janeiro, Brazil

Telephone: 021 233 2122
Telex: 021 21632

Works: Rua Lauriano Fernandes Jr 10, São Paulo

Telephone: 011 260 3122
Telex: 011 21263

Products: Pneumatic brake equipment for freight cars, commuter cars, locomotives and subways, door-operating systems, railway signalling apparatus.

Girling
Lucas Girling Ltd
Member of Lucas Industries Ltd
(see under Lucas Girling Ltd)

Graham-White
Graham-White Sales Corp

1209 Colorado Street, Salem, Virginia 24153, USA

Telephone: (703) 387 5620

President: Harvey F Bredlow
Vice President: Timothy A Kelly
Directors: Jack Thompson
Stewart Bruce

Products: Pneumatic and electro-pneumatic devices for locomotives including air brake system filters and dryers; railroad sanding systems.

Gresham & Craven
Gresham and Craven Ltd

PO Box 74, Chippenham, Wiltshire SN15 1JD, England

Telephone: 0249 654141
Telegrams: Brake, Chippenham
Telex: 449411/12

Sales Director: S J Pursey

Products: Complete vacuum brake equipments for locomotives, carriages, wagons and breakdown cranes; rotary exhausters; static and portable vacuum brake test sets; pneumatic fittings for the control of engines, gearboxes, hopper doors and dump cylinders.

Greysham
Greysham (International) Pvt Ltd

4-B Vandhna, 11 Tolstoy Marg, New Delhi 110 001, India

Telephone: 223816, 225914, 43518
Telegrams: Greyshamco
Telex: 031 3872

Managing Director: Govind Singh

Products: Complete vacuum brake equipment including vacuum cylinders 'E' and 'F' types, D A valves, couplings, release valves, rubber hoses, reservoirs and piping system; air brake equipments for wagons and coaches, manufactured under licence from Davies & Metcalfe, UK.

Griffin
Griffin Wheel Co
A division of Amsted Industries

200 West Monroe, Chicago, Illinois 60606, USA

Telephone: (312) 346 3300

Products: The company has developed and manufactures in the USA and Canada lead and asbestos-free Anchor high-friction composition brake shoes for all railroad applications.
All enquiries should be directed to Amsted Industries International (qv).

Jay Sree
Jay Sree Supply Agency

14-2 Old China Bazaar Street, Calcutta 1, India

Works: 118 Garfa Main Road, Calcutta 75

Telephone: 72 2045; 72 4323; 262390

Products: Couplers, relays, contactors, locomotive headlights, marker lights, cab lights for diesel and electric locomotives.

Jurid
Jurid Werke GmbH

Postfach 1249, 2057 Reinbek/Hamburg, Federal Republic of Germany

Telephone: 72711
Telegrams: Juridag, Hamburg
Telex: 0217834

Chairman: Dr Schroiff
Managing Director: Hr Glanz
Sales Director: Dr Ehlers

Products: Composition brake blocks; disc brake linings; friction plates. Main product line is plastic friction linings for block disc brakes made of one piece for friction sizes up to 300 cm² and in two pieces for friction area sizes over 300 cm².

Licensees: Azbest Ploce, Yugoslavia

Klöckner-Becorit
Klockner-Becorit Coalequip (Pty) Ltd

PO Box 4018, 179 Voortrekker Road, Factoria, Krugersdorp Luipaardsvlei 1743, South Africa

Telephone: (011) 664 8100
Telex: 4 20575 (offices)
4 21283 (stores)

Chairman: H K Davies
Chief Executive: K K Wehner
Executive Director: L Vercueil
Directors: P P W Beckmann
C H Brigish
G Clark
S P Ellis
R F Lansdown

Products: Miner handbrakes, Miner drawgear, New York Air Brake systems, Domange-Jarret industrial shock absorbers, Sloan slack adjusters.

Knorr-Bremse
Knorr-Bremse GmbH

Moosacher Strasse 80, 8000 Munich 40, Federal Republic of Germany

Telephone: (089) 35051
Telex: 0524228

Managing Directors: Joachim Vielmetter
Dr Alexander Bodey
Rudi Gorr
Heinz-Hermann Thiele
Product Division Director: Gerhard Kubath

Products: Single and two-pipe brake systems; direct and graduated-release air brakes; air brakes convertible for direct/graduated release; electro-pneumatic brake systems complying with UIC rules for main-line vehicles; electro-pneumatic brake systems with analogue or digital control for suburban trains, underground trains and tramcars; compressed air brake systems for blending with dynamic braking; vacuum brakes, vacuum-controlled air brakes, pneumatically-controlled vacuum brakes; load-controlled brake systems; disc brakes cpl, with brake calipers; high-power brakes; electromagnetic rail brakes; eddy-current brakes; spring-loaded brakes; air supply equipment; air dryer units; driver's brake valves and driver's brake valve systems; direct and graduated-release distributor valves; mechanically-controlled anti-skid systems; electronically-controlled anti-skid and anti-spin systems; mechanically or pneumatically-operated emergency brake equipment; 'empty-load' change-over devices; slack adjusters; brake cylinders, also with incorporated slack adjuster; block brake units; electric and pneumatic equipment for automatic train operation (ATO); pneumatic and vacuum equipment for automatic train control (ATC); deadman and vigilance devices; control equipment for air suspension systems; pneumatically-controlled unloading, tipping and associated ancillary equipment; pneumatic and electro-pneumatic door closing equipment; pneumatic and electro-pneumatic engine and transmission controls; monitoring equipment for brake operation; indicating devices for pad wear; brake testing equipment and remote-controlled terminal testing equipment; vebeo fittings; and automatic centre buffer couplers.

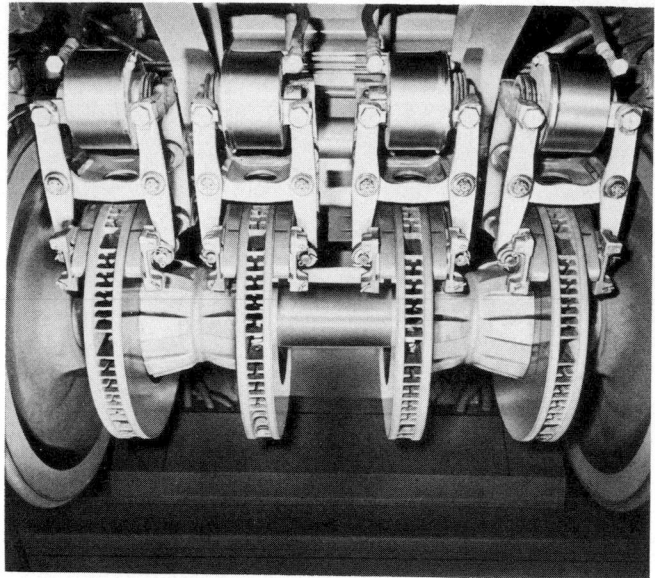

Double axle-mounted brake disc on French Railways 260 km/h TGV train-set

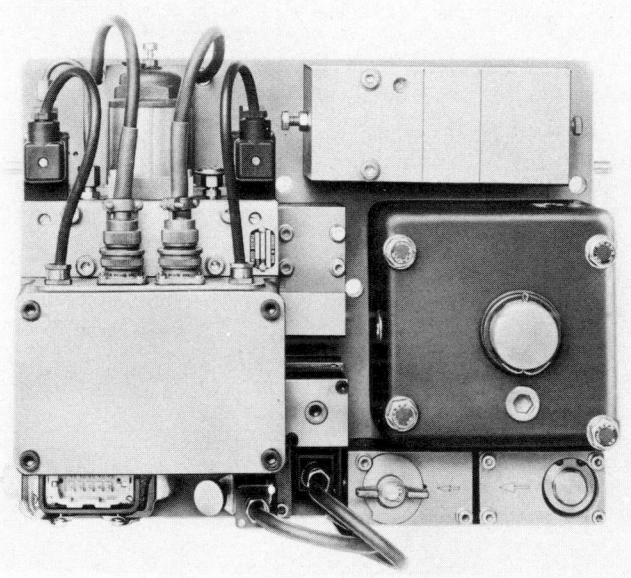

Knorr Type Kbr XII analogue brake control system, giving infinitely variable control under electronic signal processing

Type LP9950 air compressor, force-ventilated, operable at up to 2000 rpm to supply approx 800 litres/minute

Dual-chamber Type LT350 air-dryer unit, suited for high deliveries at compressor duty cycle of up to 100%

Kolmex
Foreign Trade Enterprise

PO Box 236, Mokotowska 49, 00-542 Warsaw 1, Poland

Telephone: 28 22 91; 29 92 41
Telegrams: Kolmex, Warszawa
Telex: 813270; 813714

Products: Brake equipment and components.

LDA
Engenharia e Comercio LDA

Rua da Alegria, 61 R/C, Lisbon 2, Portugal

Products: Brake equipment and friction draftgear.

Litton
Litton Connectors

95 High Street, Slough, Buckinghamshire SL1 1DH, England

Telephone: 0753 77788
Telex: 84 7548

Products: Litton LMB connectors.

Lloyd
F H Lloyd & Co Ltd
ABC Coupler Division
A subsidiary of F H Lloyd Holdings plc

James Bridge Steel Works, PO Box 5, Wednesbury, West Midlands WS10 9SD, England

Telephone: 021-520 3121
Telex: 339502

Chairman: L Robertson
Managing Director: D A Silcox

Products: Automatic couplers; semi-rigid bar couplers; draftgear; side buffers; carbon and alloy steel castings for the railway industry.

Lucas Girling
Lucas Girling Ltd
Member of Lucas Industries Ltd

Railway Product Group, Kings Road, Tyseley, Birmingham B11 2AH, England

Telephone: 021-706 3371
Telex: 338631

Works: Thermal Road, Bromborough, Cheshire
Kings Road, Tyseley, Birmingham

Products Group General Manager: P L Quinn
Sales and Service Manager: E A Leason
Export Sales: M D Evans

Products: Wheel-mounted disc brakes; transmission disc brakes; axle-mounted disc brakes; wheel slide prevention equipment.

The company's most recent order for disc brake equipment covers the supply of 248 bogie sets for Córas Iompair Éireann (CIE) main-line coaches for use on the principal inter-city routes in Ireland. The installation incorporates wheel-mounted discs and is similar to that used on British Rail Mark III coaches, of which over 1000 are in service in HST and locomotive-hauled vehicles. This order is additional to one for 160 motor and trailer bogie sets of wheel-mounted disc brakes for the Dublin suburban system.

The newly-developed, deep-vaned, wheel-mounted discs form part of the installation in two new contracts with British Rail: 96 bogie sets for Class 317 emu trailer cars and 872 bogie sets for motor and trailer cars on Class 510 emu stock. A 'spannerless' brake pad retention device for simplified maintenance is included on these vehicles. For freight operation the latest British Rail build of 460 46-tonne high capacity coal wagons (HDA) is equipped with a one wheel-mounted disc per axle empty-load brake for 96.6 km/h operation. The fittings for 250 46-tonne covered vans (VGA) incorporate two wheel-mounted discs per axle.

Recent design work has included disc brake installations for European Y25 type bogies with 813 and 920 mm diameter wheels, offering both axle- and wheel-mounted discs. These compact systems, which include the air cylinder and slack adjuster within the bogie, also incorporate a bogie-mounted parking brake. In other overseas markets further orders have been obtained for the New South Wales State Rail Authority XPT trains and for Western Australian Government Railway diesel railcars.

New developments include a range of high duty axle-mounted discs which have been introduced into the European market on suburban, suburban double-deck and inter-city stock. This disc can be supplied in monobloc or split form, the latter enabling replacement in service without wheel removal, while retaining the original mounting hub.

A new brake testing facility was commissioned in 1982 in the form of a computer-controlled dynamometer, claimed to be the most advanced in Europe. With an inertia range of 200-7900 kg/m² and a maximum speed of 200 rpm, it can reproduce the most demanding braking duties, such as with the heaviest axle load freight vehicles, rapid transit and high speed inter-city stock. The control system can simulate the effects of gradients, vehicle rolling resistance, blended supplementary braking, drag braking, and air flow on the brake at air speeds of up to 300 km/h.

Agents
Australia: Westinghouse Brake & Signal Co Ltd, 27-29 George Street, Concord West, New South Wales 2138

Denmark: Axel Ketner, 23 Frabriksparken, 2600 Glostrup

Finland: Oy Elektro Diesel Ab, Vanha Kaarelante 28, 01610 Vanta 61

Portugal: Conde Barao, Avenida 24 de Julho 62-64, Largo do Conde Barao, Lisbon

Lucas Girling disc brake caliper for LRV applications

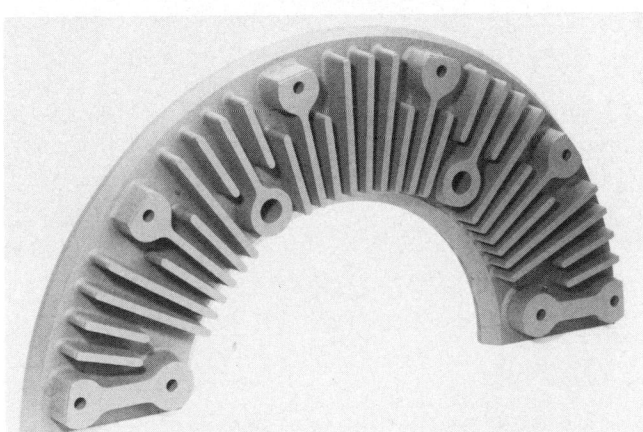
Rear view of split disc for high-speed, frequent stopping service applications on British Rail emu vehicles

Brake for either wheel- or axle-mounted disc application to both two-axle and bogie freight wagons

Disc brake trailer bogie for British Rail electric multiple-unit

Lucas Girling BDA freight brake

Lucas Girling axle-mounted 610-640 mm diameter disc brake

Maclean Fogg
Maclean Fogg Co
Railway Division

1000 Allanson Road, Mundelein, Illinois 60060, USA

Telephone: (312) 566 0010
Telex: 25-4470

President: Barry L MacLean
Vice President: S J Murphy

Products: Hand brakes, load securement systems, track bolts and fasteners.

Macosa
Material y Construcciones, SA

Plaza de la Independencia 8, Madrid 1, Spain

Telephone: 2 22 47 87
Telegrams: Material, Madrid
Telex: 22168

Products: Draftgear; buffers.

MecanoExportImport

'23 August' Works, 73428 Bucharest, Romania

Telephone: 28 30 10; 28 20 10
Telex: 10 344

Products: Brakes built under licence from Knorr-Bremse; drawgear equipment for locomotives and rolling stock.

Miner
Miner Enterprises Inc
International Division

PO Box 471, 1200 East State Street, Geneva, Illinois 60134, USA

Telephone: (312) 232 3000
Telegrams: Miner, Geneva
Telex: 720442; 190186

President: G A Withall
Vice President J R Fuenzalida
Director of Technical Services: M L McGuigan

Products: Draftgear; buffers; snubbers; hand brakes; discharge systems for bulk commodities; thermoplastic compression springs.

Foreign licensees
Argentina: Aceros Especiales SAlyc, Sarmiento 767, Buenos Aires
Australia: Commonwealth Engineering (NSW) Pty Ltd, PO Box No 29, Granville, New South Wales 2142
Belgium: Usines Emile Henricot, 1490 Court-Saint-Etienne
Brazil: FNV Veiculos e Equipamentos SA, Av Maria Coelho Aguiar, Bloco A-8 Andar, São Paulo, SP
France: Usines et Acieries de Sambre et Meuse, Tour Aurore, 92080 Paris-Défense Cedex 5
India: Burn Standard Co Ltd, 10-C Hungerford Street, PO Box No 191, Calcutta 700 017
Italy: Fiat, Divisione Ferroviaria, Corso Ferrucci, 122 Turin
Mexico: Miner y Mendez de Mexico SA, Avenida Coyoacan No 912, Mexico 12, DF
South Africa: Klockner-Becorit Coalequip (Pty) Ltd, PO Box 4018 and 4060, Luipaardsvlei 1743
Spain: Material y Construcciones SA, Herreros, 2 (PN), Barcelona 19
Switzerland: Georg Fischer Limited, 8201 Schaffhausen
United Kingdom: George Blair & Company Limited, Newcastle Alloy Steel Works, Forth, Newcastle upon Tyne NE1 3RE, England
Gloucester Railway Carriage & Wagon Co Ltd, Bristol Road, Gloucester GL1 5RS, England
J N Blair, Riverside, Market Harborough, Leicestershire LE16 7PY, England
Yugoslavia: Fabrika Vagona Kraljevo, Postanski FAH 90, Kraljevo

Foreign sales agents
Argentina: D G Cormick SRL, Casilla de Correo 5260, Buenos Aires
Chile: Peoro T Orellana M and Guillermo Campana T, Los Profetas 3629, Nunda-Santiago
Colombia: Quinteros Limitada, Apartado Aereo 4308, Bogota
Egypt: Intercontal, PO Box 33, El Mohandeseen, Cairo
Iran: Gulf Technical Consultants AG, Park Avenue, 27th Street No 7, Tehran
Mexico: Mexican Railway Appliance Company, Avenida Coyoacan No 912, Col de Valle, 03100 Mexico, DF
Pakistan: Wilcox & Islam Ltd, Spencers Building, PO Box 174, 18 Empress Road, Lahore
Peru: Restesa SRL, Casilla 804, Lima
Spain: Tecnicom, Ayala 120, Madrid 6
Thailand: Anglo-Thai Engineering Ltd, GPO Box 18, Bangkok
Turkey: Industrial Equipment and Supply Company, Nenehatun Caddesi No 124, Cankaya, Ankara

Miner y Mendez
Miner y Mendez de Mexico SA

Avenida Coyoacan 912, Mexico DF 03100, Mexico

Telephone: 559 1019/1339/1558
Telegrams: Zednem
Telex: 017 72 503

Products: Miner RF-444 and A-22-XL draftgears under licence from Miner Enterprises Incorporated; journal lubricators under licence from Miller Lubricator Company, USA.

Mitsubishi
Mitsubishi Heavy Industries Ltd

5-1 Marunouchi 2-chome, Chiyoda-ku, Tokyo 100, Japan

Telephone: 03 212 3111
Telegrams: Hishiju, Tokyo
Telex: 22443

Products: Air brakes.

NABCO
The Nippon Air Brake Co Ltd

Sannomiya Building, Nishikan 1-12, Goko-dori 7-chome, Chuo-ku, Kobe 651, Japan

Telephone: 078 251 8101
Telegrams: Nabco, Kobe
Telex: 5622-143

Tokyo office: Kokusai Hamamatsucho Bldg, 9-18, Kaigan 1-chome, Minato-ku, Tokyo 105

Telephone: (03) 437 1267
Telegrams: Nabco Intdiv
Telex: 242 2855

Works: Kobe, Seishin, Konan, Yokosuka, Tokyo

Chairman: Kenshiro Saito
Managing Director: Yuji Takahashi

Products: Various air brake systems; NABCO shoe automatic slack adjusters; door operating equipment; windscreen wiper motors.

NABCO brake systems are operating on over 35 000 emu cars of various Japanese authorities and on the Shinkansen train-sets of Japanese National Railways. NABCO has also equipped the automated, rubber-tyre peoplemover systems of Osaka and Kobe, Japan.

Newag
Newag GmbH & Co

PO Box 101201, 4100 Duisburg 1, Federal Republic of Germany

Telephone: 203 33 40 61
Telex: 0855526

Products: Composition brake shoes, shoe carriers, disc brake pads.

New York Air Brake
New York Air Brake Co
Member of the General Signal group

Starbuck Avenue, Watertown, New York 13601, USA

Telephone: (315) 782 7000

President: P Owen Willaman
Vice President, Marketing: James C Pontious
Vice President, Railroad Sales: Charles E Hart
Manager, Passenger Equipment Market: Thomas M Engle
General Manager, Engineering: Bruce W Shute

Products: Brake systems for all types of rail vehicles including freight wagons, locomotives, transit and passenger stock. Freight systems are of the ABDW type; other systems are pneumatic, electro-pneumatic, hydro-pneumatic or pure hydraulic designs. Transit products include ac or dc rotary screw-unitised (RSU) compressor and a complete line of cab-type single T-handle master controller (MC) propulsion and brake control devices.

Oerlikon Brakes
Werkzeugmaschinenfabrik Oerlikon-Buehrle Ltd

Birchstrasse 155, 8050 Zurich, Switzerland

Telephone: 01 316 22 11
Telegrams: Outil, Zurich
Telex: 822031

Products: Air brakes for automatic and manual systems, electronic anti-wheel slip equipment, electro-pneumatic controls.

Oerlikon Brakes, a department of Werkzeugmaschinenfabrik Oerlikon Buhrle Ltd, produces complete control systems for automatic and direct air brakes as well as electro-pneumatic systems. The UIC-approved Oerlikon systems have been employed in many countries since the 1940s. Current products include:

The Type FVE 700 driver's brake valve, designed for use in railcar trains for control of the Oerlikon UTB electro-pneumatic and automatic air brake. Both systems are actuated in the same control sector of the operating lever;

The UTB universal railcar distributor valve, which can be controlled either by a seven-step electrical binary code or by the brake pipe of the automatic brake pipe;

The Oerlikon multi-functional electronic system, covering automatic EP-control, anti-skid, anti-wheel slip, speed-activated switches for track brake, door-operating, pressure step, etc and odometer;

Oerlikon brake panels containing complete pneumatic, electro-pneumatic and electronic devices for the brake control of train-sets, locomotives and coaches;

The Oerlikon EBO-1, a kit-principle system for passenger coaches and goods wagons which can be used to activate automatic air brake, automatic load-proportional braking with or without R/RIC changeover, automatic empty/load braking, two-step R brake or electro-pneumatic brake.

Oerlikon UTB universal railcar distributor valve

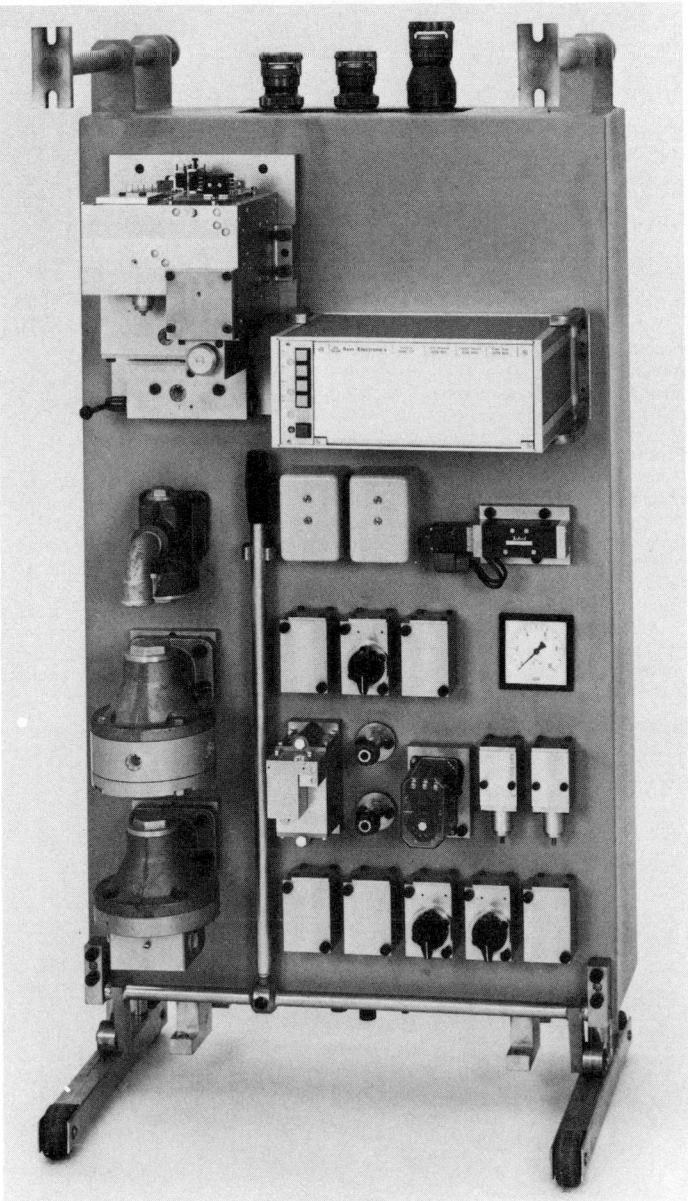

Type FVE driver's brake valve

Oerlikon brake panel

Oerlikon multi-functional electronic system

Oerlikon EBO-1 apparatus

Ohio Brass
Ohio Brass Co
A subsidiary of Harvey Hubbell Inc

380 North Main Street, Mansfield, Ohio 44902, USA

Telephone: (419) 522 7111
Telegrams: Electric
Telex: 987414

President: William R Cress
International Manager: Alex J Karcic
New Business Development (Transit): A Philip Pastouna
Marketing Manager (Transit): M F Gowing

Products: Automatic coupler systems.
   The Form 79 LRV coupler features an energy-absorption mechanism and a mechanical coupler that is self-supporting. It also shares many of the innovative design features of O-B coupler systems for rapid transit cars, including automatic and remote mechanical coupling and uncoupling; ample vertical and lateral gathering and positive alignment; freedom from relative movement at coupler faces; mechanical strength to withstand more than normal operating conditions; emergency release mechanism; and automatic coupling of air lines.
   Ohio Brass has been connected with coupler design and manufacturing since its first automatic coupler was patented in 1907. Designed to individual property specifications, O-B's automatic fabricated coupler systems are available for heavy rail, rapid transit and light rail applications.

Form 79 LRV coupler

Oleo
Oleo Pneumatics Ltd (UK)
Oleo International Holdings Ltd (Overseas)

Walcote, Blackdown, Leamington Spa, Warwickshire CV32 6QX, England

Telephone: 0926 21116/8
Telex: 311458

Products: Self-contained and casing-type hydraulic buffers for railway vehicles of all kinds, including the latest UIC standards, especially freight wagons.

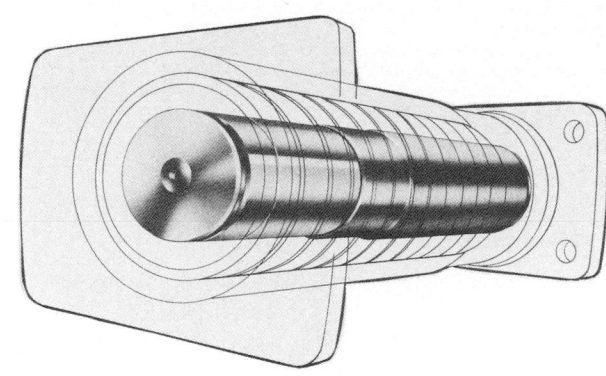

Type 3RCA hydraulic capsule unit to fit inside Ringfeder friction springs housed in casings covering 80-tonne wagon impacts at up to 15 km/h

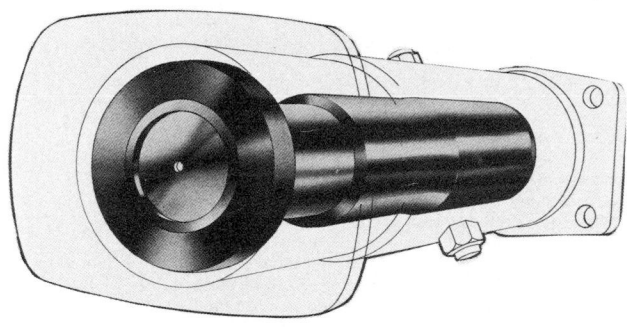

Type 5SC 'Super Buffer' capsule unit to meet UIC Code 526 or Category C for wagon buffers

Paulstra

61 rue Marius Aufan, 92305 Levallois-Perret, France

Telephone: 757 31 14
Telex: 620 898

Products: Buffers; shock absorbers for UIC automatic couplings; primary and secondary suspension springs, bushes and oil seals.

Phoenix
Phoenix AG

PO Box 90 11 40, 2100 Hamburg 90, Federal Republic of Germany

Telephone: 040 76 67 1
Telegrams: Phoenixag
Telex: 02 17571

Products: Vacuum brake hose, air spring bellows.

Purdy
Purdy Co

2400 West 95th Street, Chicago, Illinois 60642, USA

Telephone: (312) 239 4200

Products: Brake equipment.

Réservoir, Le
La Société le Réservoir

Rue Jean Henri Fabre, 03103 Montlucon, France

Telephone: 05 39 74

Products: Brake reservoirs and cylinders.

Reunert & Lenz
Reunert & Lenz Ltd

PO Box 92, Johannesburg 2000, South Africa

Telephone: 011 836 1351
Telegrams: Rockdrill
Telex: 8 7426

Departmental Director: F B Lucas
Manager: I M Dooley

Products: Brake regulators; disc brakes; parking brake equipment; load brake equipment; weighing valves; rail and wheel flange lubricators.

Ringfeder
Ringfeder GmbH

Duisburger Strasse 145, Postfach 486, 4150 Krefeld-Uerdingen, Federal Republic of Germany

Telephone: 4491
Telegrams: Ringfeder
Telex: 0853846

Products: Side buffers, draw and buffing gear for automatic central coupling, drawgear.

SAB Brake Regulator
SAB Brake Regulator Co Ltd

Howden Way, Aycliffe Industrial Estate, Darlington, Co Durham DL5 6HR, England

Telephone: 0325 312666
Telex: 58416

Products: Brake regulators, continuous and two-stage load devices for disc or tread brakes, brake cylinder slack adjuster units, resilient wheels.

SAB Broms
SAB Broms SA

Walenweg 73, 3072 Nossegem, Belgium

Products: SAB brake equipment.

SAB NIFE AB

Instrumentgatan 15, PO Box 515, 261 24 Landskrona, Sweden

Telephone: 0418 16280
Telegrams: SAB NIFE, Landskrona
Telex: 72416

Chairman: Nils Lennart Nilsson
Managing Director: H Björn Olsson
Marketing Directors: Hans Turém
　　　　　　　　　　　　Torbjörn Höglind

Products: Double-acting, rapid working brake regulators for automatic brake slack adjustment; tread brake and disc brake units; hydraulic and spring-applied parking brake equipment with mechanical, quick release device; load brake equipment for automatic adjustment of braking force; weighing valves; alkaline nickel cadmium batteries; power supply systems incapable of interruption.

The company offers a new electro-hydraulic brake system primarily designed for light rail vehicles. It is a friction brake system utilising electronic signal handling and hydraulic power transmission to operate spring-loaded disc brake calipers and provides fast, precise and stepless braking force regulation for up to four individually controlled bogies. The system consists of an electronic brake controller, a hydraulic power unit, plus control valve blocks and disc brake calipers. The electronic brake controller, the hydraulic power system and the control valve blocks are mounted in the car body.

Advantages claimed for the system are that: weight and size is reduced when compared to a conventional pneumatic brake system consisting of air cylinders, compressor, air dryer, coolers and reservoirs; the compact disc brake caliper, with an integrated automatic true slack adjuster, reduces the space requirements in the bogie; the electronic controller facilitates a flexible interaction with the propulsion system; the brake response times are short, which is necessary for good anti-skid properties; the brake is applied automatically in case of cable or contact failures; and total power consumption and noise level are low.

Each bogie is individually controlled by continuous commands to each control valve. The controller is capable of handling load brake signals. The brake system instantaneously responds to skid signals, and the electronic surveillance system continuously indicates the brake condition.

Contracts have recently been concluded for supply of brake units for 44 commuter motor cars for Chicago South Shore & South Bend Railroad and for 60 heavy rail vehicles for Cleveland, USA, valued at about SKr 9 million; also for supply of the electro-hydraulic brake system for six prototype tram cars for Genoa, Italy.

Electro-hydraulic brake system's disc brake calipers

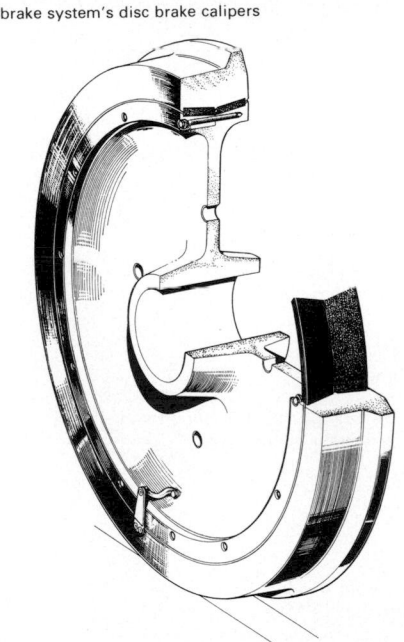

SAB low-noise V-wheel with built-in rubber rings

SAB compact Type BFC block brake unit with force amplification mechanism and automatic slack adjustment

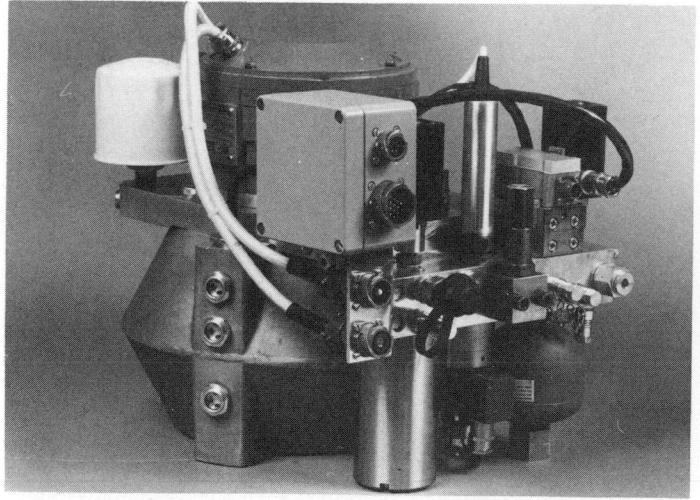

SAB NIFE electro-hydraulic brake system's hydraulic power unit

Trailer bogie disc brake supplied to Ferrovie Nord Milano (FNM)

Automatic coupler produced for Rome Metro

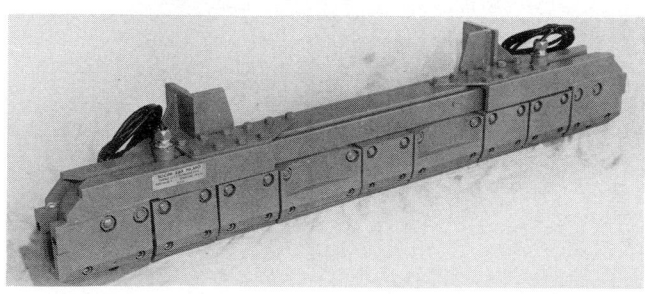

Electro-magnetic track brake

Sambre et Meuse
Usines et Acieries de Sambre et Meuse

Tour Aurore, 92080 Paris-Défense Cedex 5, France

Telephone: 778 61 62
Telex: 620 162

Chairman: Pierre Boissier
Sales Director: Gilbert Labadie

Products: Drawgear; disc brakes; shoe insert holders; couplers including UIC type, and Miner RF4-29 drawgear built under licence.

Scharfenberg
Scharfenbergkupplung GmbH

PO Box 411160, 3320 Salzgitter, Federal Republic of Germany

Telex: 954430

Products: Automatic multi-function couplers.

SKF Argentina
Compania SKF Argentina SA

Postal address: Casilla de Correo 197, 1000 Buenos Aires, Argentina
Head office: Perù 545, 1068 Buenos Aires

Telephone: 33 3061/8
Telegrams: Roulement
Telex: 9203

Chairman: Kees Kroes
Managing Director: Raúl Horacio Gaspar
Chief Sales Director: Héctor Montanini

Products: Ball and rolling bearings, axle boxes and mounting tools.

Socimi
Società Costruzioni Industriali Milano SpA

Via S Calimero 3, 20122 Milan, Italy

Telephone: 02 5465 251/5
Telex: 310331

Main works
Via E Fermi n 25, 20082 Binasco (Milan)
Telephone: (02) 9055605/6/7/8
Via Donatori del Sangue n 100, 20010 Arluno (Milan)
Telephone: (02) 9017666/9017803
Viale Porto Torres, Reg Zentu Figghi, 07100 Sassari
Telephone: (079) 235056

Chairman: Dr Eng Alessandro Marzocco
Managing Director: Dr Eng Pierino Sacchi
Marketing Director: Dr Eng Corrado Landolina

Products: Disc brakes under BSI licence, electro-magnetic track brakes, automatic couplers.

Stabeg
Stabeg Apparatengesellschaft GmbH

Reinlgasse 5-9, 1140 Vienna, Austria

Telephone: 92 23 57
Telex: 01 2466

Products: Complete air brake equipment for locos, coaches, freight wagons; air springs; drawgear; buffer and drawgear; side buffers.

Stone
Stone India Ltd

16 Taratalla Road, Calcutta 700 088, India

Telephone: 77 3077
Telegrams: Stoneco
Telex: 021 7249

Chief Executive: V K Parashar

Products: Air brakes, slack adjusters, train lighting, pantographs, superheaters. The company currently has contracts from Indian Railways and Viet-Nam State Railways grossing over US $10 million.

Combined brake and slack adjuster for emu

3 kW train-lighting alternator with flat belt pulley

Sturrock
Sturrock (South Africa) Ltd

91 Commissioner Street, PO Box 2863, Johannesburg, South Africa

Products: Friction and rubber draftgear; brake automatic slack adjusters; friction snubbers; hand brake units.

Suecobras
Suecobras Industria e Comercio Ltda

Rua Cachambi 713, 20780 Rio de Janeiro, Brazil

Managing Director: Lennart Sjostedt
Sales Manager: Eduardo Jose Gomes Gonçalves

Products: Brake regulators; disc brakes; parking brake equipment; load brake equipment; weighing valves; axleboxes.

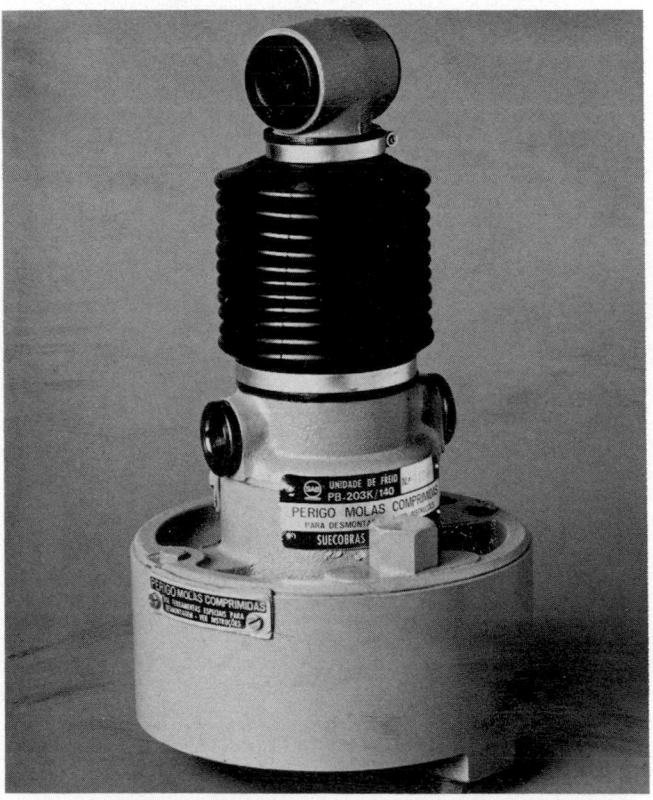

SAB Type PB brake unit for metro and main-line passenger cars with disc brakes

SAB Type RK2 automatic slack adjuster for locomotive applications

Sumitomo
Sumitomo Metal Industries Ltd

New Sumitomo Building, 1-3-2 Marunouchi, Chiyoda-ku, Tokyo 100, Japan

Telephone: 03 282 6111
Telex: 22865

Products: Couplers; draftgear and steel castings for the railway industry.

TBL
TBL Limited
A Cape Industries Co

814 Bath Road, Bristol BS4 5LH, England

Telephone: 0272 715181
Telex: 44665

Managing Director: B Weaving
Director and Product Manager, TBL Railway Friction Materials: D Brunskill

Products: Composition brake blocks for freight and passenger operations; disc brake pads; friction materials for dmu automatic transmissions.
 The company is a major supplier of composition-friction materials to British Rail and London Transport, with other applications around the world.
 Recent developments include: non-asbestos brake blocks for high-speed applications; non-asbestos disc brake pads for suburban and inter-city use; high-friction and low-friction braking materials; and non-toxic brake blocks for underground use.
 Created around a non-asbestos matrix, the brake block product range has been launched to provide a family of friction materials with different co-efficients of friction particularly for the intensive operating conditions of mass transit and emu systems. They can be used at speeds up to 170 km/h without wheel damage. Since their introduction in 1975 TBL 800 series composition blocks, originally designed for braking from speeds up to 200 km/h, have passed many British Rail tests, and are now approved for freight operations with 25-tonne axleloads braking from speeds up to 100 km/h. Tread brakes of composite materials are claimed to have twice the life expectancy of cast iron.

Licensees: Rane Brake Linings Ltd, Plot No 30 Ambattur Industrial Estate, PB No 3, Madras 600 058, India

Thomé
Thome-Industries

2 rue Alfred-de-Vigny, 75008 Paris, France

Telephone: 227 98 85
Telex: 640 105

Sales Manager: Jean Gouthiere

Products: Steel castings for railways including buffing equipment.

Tito
Oal Metalski Zavod Tito

Postfach 545, Skopje, Yugoslavia

Products: Brake regulators; disc brakes; parking brake equipment; load brake equipment; weighing valves.

Tokyu Car
Tokyu Car Corporation

1 Kamariya-cho, Kanazawa-ku, Yokohama 236, Japan

Telephone: 045 701 5151
Telex: 3822 392

Products: Disc brakes.

Universal
Universal Railway Devices Co

332 South Michigan Avenue, Chicago, Illinois 60604, USA

Telephone: (312) 427 7775

Products: Automatic slack adjusters.

Uzinexportimport

Calea Victoriei 133, Bucharest, Romania

Products: Brake regulators; disc brakes; parking brake equipment; load brake equipment; weighing valves.

Valeo
Va Leo

64 avenue de la Grande Armée, 75017 Paris, France

Telephone: 574 96 96
Telex: 280 844

Products: Automotive components.

Valtionrautatiet

Rautatiehallitus, PO Box 488, 00101 Helsinki 10, Finland

Products: Brake regulators; brake discs; distributor valves. These items are manufactured under licence exclusively for the use of VR.

Voest-Alpine
Voest-Alpine AG

Floragasse 7, 1040 Vienna, Austria

Telephone: (0222) 6547
Telegrams: Voest Alpine, Vienna
Telex: 134282

Products: Draftgear; buffers; snubbers; hand brakes; automatic couplers.

WABCO
Westinghouse Air Brake Division, American Standard Inc

Wilmerding, Pennsylvania 15148, USA

Telephone: (412) 273 1000
Telegrams: Westinghouse, Wilmerding
Telex: 866467

Vice President and General Manager: R A Gilmour
Vice President, Marketing: R W Coiner
Vice President, Sales: G E Carothers
Manager, International Marketing: D M Hart

Products: Freight wagon air-brake control equipment including control valve (type ABDW), brake cylinder, retaining valve, combined dirt collector and cut-out cock reservoir and angle cocks, Cobra high friction composition brake shoe, bogie-mounted WABCOPAC brake assembly; locomotive brake equipment including air brake control equipment with engineer's brake valve, control valve, relay valves, safety control valves and brake cylinders; air compressors; mass transit car brake equipment including control equipment, both pneumatic and electro-pneumatic; bogie-mounted brake equipment, and various transit car devices including automatic couplers, air compressor units and air spring levelling valves.

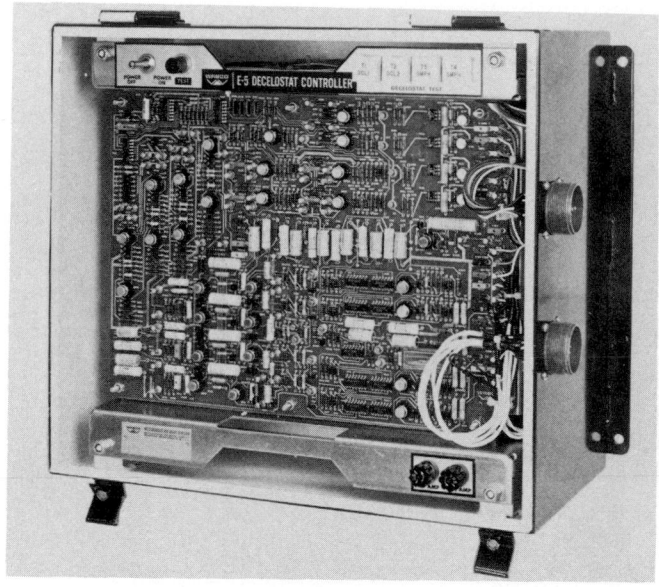

WABCO 'E' Decelostat controller to monitor and correct wheel slip, operating in conjunction with axle-mounted magnetic speed sensors

WABCO reciprocating-type locomotive air compressor driven directly by diesel engine, with intercooler between two compression stages

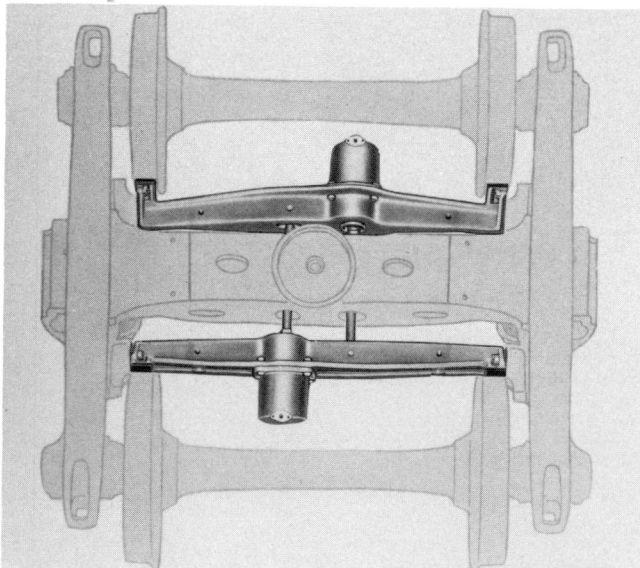

WABCOPAC brake assembly combining brake cylinder and brake beam functions

WABCO D-4, 2-stage, 2-cylinder, single acting, air-cooled compressor

WABCO 30-CDW piloting-type, console-mounted brake valve for compact cab installation

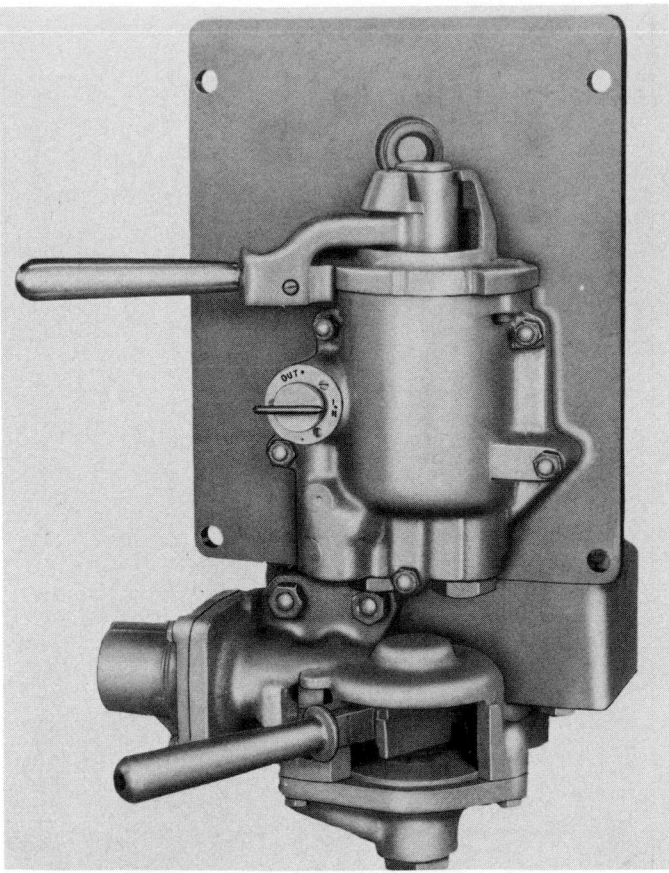

26-C self-lapping automatic brake valve arranged with pipe bracket for automatic and independent operation

Walton
Walton Products Inc

868 Sussex Boulevard, Broomall, Pennsylvania 19008, USA

Telephone: (215) 544 8410
Telex: 813 765

Chairman: G Gobrecht
Secretary: D Murphy
Contract Administration and Sales: R Rohrer

Products: Automatic couplers, including mechanical coupler assemblies, and electro-pneumatic system, designed and manufactured by Walton Electric Coupler Inc. Diaphragms, toilets, body-end doors, etc, manufactured by Walton Products Inc.

Westinghouse Brakes
Westinghouse Brakes Ltd
A subsidiary of Westinghouse Brake and Signal Co Ltd

PO Box 74, New Road, Chippenham, Wiltshire SN15 1HY, England

Telephone: 0249 65141
Telegrams: Westinghouse, Chippenham
Telex: 449411/2

Chairman: R A Willford
Managing Director: J R C Boulding
Finance Director: S R Crook
Director: E J Harris
Marketing Director: E J Widdowson

Products: Electro-pneumatic brakes for suburban and rapid transit trains; UIC-approved graduable release automatic air brakes for locomotives, carriages and wagons; AAR-approved direct release automatic air freight brakes; dual air and vacuum brakes; spring-applied brakes; parking brakes; wheelslide correction equipment; automatic warning systems; automatic train operating equipment; disc brakes and friction materials; air compressors; air dryers; air flow measuring equipment; vigilance and deadman's systems; uncouplers; air suspension equipment; brake equipment test racks and portable test trolleys.

Electro-pneumatic brakes include the Westcode EP brake with digital control, in which the electrical control circuits usually comprise three or more train wires that are connected throughout a train, and energised and de-energised by means of switches to apply and release the brake on all vehicles simultaneously. This form of control permits the brake to be graduated on and off in steps and may be used when the brake is to be operated from either a separate driver's brake controller or a combined braking and traction controller.

The Westcode system has been adapted in a variety of ways since it first entered service on Toronto metro cars in 1961. The most common arrangement control is by means of three train wires that are connected to a '7-step' relay valve included in a brake unit mounted on each vehicle in the train. With three

wires, seven different combinations of energisation are possible; the wires are energised and de-energised in a coded sequence so that each relay valve produces seven equal steps of braking pressure.

Each brake unit incorporates a pneumatic variable load feature which automatically regulates the braking pressure to compensate for load changes; thus the braking effort for any particular step of braking is always consistently proportional to the total weight of the vehicle. Blending of the air brake with the dynamic (regenerative or rheostatic) brake on motor cars is included, and features such as jerk limitation and snow brake may be added.

The train wires may be either energised to apply the brake or energised to release. Systems that operate in the energise-to-apply mode, and some that are controlled in the opposite sense and so are inherently 'fail safe', incorporate an automatic air brake or emergency air brake in addition to the electro-pneumatic brake to provide for braking in an emergency or if a train breaks in two.

Alternatively, the electro-pneumatic brake may have analogue control. In this the electrical control is usually by a wire connected throughout a train to form a continuous loop to which a variable current (or voltage) is applied via a potentiometer to operate the brake. This arrangement affords stepless control of the brake and is normally adopted when the traction equipment requires the same type of control and the two systems are to be operated from a combined braking and traction controller.

The control circuits are arranged so that for a certain value of current (or voltage) carried by the looped wire neither braking nor traction is called for; reduction of current below this value causes braking and an increase above it calls for power. The variable electrical signal is applied to an electro-pneumatic converter included in a brake unit mounted on each vehicle in the train, and this valve provides a braking pressure output which is inversely proportional to the current applied to it. Additional train wires and associated equipment are normally used to provide for braking in an emergency or if a train breaks in two; alternatively an automatic or emergency air brake may be incorporated to perform the latter function.

Analogue EP brake systems incorporate continuous blending of the air brake with the dynamic brake, and such features as jerk limitation, snow brake and speed taper, by the inclusion of electronic equipment between the variable signal circuit and each brake unit to modulate the current that is applied to the EP converter.

Electronic equipment for the modulation of analogue electrical brake control signals, the conversion of analogue and digital control signals, and the continuous blending of dynamic and air brakes, may be incorporated in electro-pneumatic brake systems.

Driver's controllers for use with electro-pneumatic brakes range from small brake controllers containing only a few cam-operated switches, through combined controllers affording control of braking and traction by means of a single handle, to complete driver's desks specially designed to blend with the interior of the cab and containing traction controls and other apparatus as well as brake control equipment.

Graduable release automatic air brakes include the UIC-approved type P4a series distributors, with variable load feature if required. Control of the pressure in the automatic brake pipe, to which a distributor on each vehicle in the train is connected, may be pneumatic by a self-lapping driver's brake valve, or electropneumatic by a small driver's brake controller and an associated control unit. The latter system is adaptable for control by manual push-buttons or automatic electrical circuits.

Direct release automatic air freight brakes include the AAR-approved Z1AW control valve, which is compatible and interchangeable with AB, ABD and ABDW control valves, using the same standard pipe bracket, and the Z1A control valve, for use when an accelerated application feature is not required.

Dual air and vacuum brakes are fitted on locomotives for use by railways that decide to change over from the vacuum brake to the automatic air brake and require locomotives that are capable of operating trains fitted with either type of brake during the period of transition. Other locomotive equipments include: vacuum-controlled straight air brakes; automatic and straight air brakes; and straight air brakes with emergency feature.

In pneumatically-controlled spring-applied brakes, spring brake units installed on the vehicles of a train apply the brake by exerting a force from a compressed spring when the air pressure in a spring brake pipe is reduced, and relax this force to release the brake when the pressure in the pipe is restored. Each spring brake unit includes an automatic slack adjuster which maintains at an approximately constant value the extension of the spring from which the braking force is derived.

Parking brakes may be of the air-released spring-applied type. Alternatively, electro-pneumatic or electro-hydraulic parking brakes may be provided in which pneumatic or hydraulic pressure is exerted to apply the brake initially, and is then relaxed to leave the brake locked on mechanically by a nut and clutch mechanism in each actuator. The brake is released by re-exerting the pressure to disengage the clutch.

A wide range of air brake cyclinders, wheel brake units and tread brake units suitable for disc brakes or tread brakes is available. Most are complete with an automatic slack adjuster. Cylinders and units are frequently designed specially to suit the layout of the bogie and may incorporate parking brake actuators when required.

Wheel spin and slide detection and correction equipment includes electronic control units, frequency generators, blowdown devices and associated valves. The equipment is normally arranged so that if a condition of incipient wheel sliding develops while the brake is applied (that is, if the deceleration of an axle begins to exceed the deceleration of the vehicle itself), a blowdown valve is opened to vent the air brake cylinders associated with the axle to allow it to regain speed. Alternatively, if the acceleration of an axle begins to exceed a pre-determined level while tractive power is being applied, the control unit may be arranged either to reduce the tractive power or to arrest it at its existing level. Circuits for connection to dynamic brake equipment and for the operation of a speedometer may also be included in the control unit.

Westinghouse air compressors range from machines suitable for mechanical drive through a pulley or coupling, to lightweight motor-driven compressors which are available separately or as part of a compact outfit complete with such items as a suction strainer, anti-freezer, intercooler, safety valve, automatic drain valve, aftercooler, air dryer, filter, silencer, mounting frame with flexible suspension units, and flexible delivery pipe. Compressors are air-cooled; motors may be totally enclosed, screen-protected or pipe-ventilated, depending upon operating conditions. All machines are robustly constructed to traction standards.

In the Westinghouse air dryer, two drying elements or 'towers', comprising pressure vessels packed with an adsorptive desiccant, are used, and are interconnected by changeover valves so that, alternately, one is used to dry the air delivered by the compressor while the other is being regenerated by a purge of dry air. The dryer is installed between the aftercooler and the brake system, and its capacity is related to the climatic conditions anticipated in service so that it is capable of removing sufficient moisture from the air to lower its dew point below the lowest ambient temperature likely to be encountered. When this is achieved, water is no longer precipitated in the system, and the problems associated with it are largely eradicated.

Air flow measuring equipment for use on locomotives to haul air-braked trains comprises an air flow measuring valve for fitment between the main air storage reservoirs and the driver's brake valve; and an indicator for mounting in the instrument panel on the driver's desk. The indicator is connected to the valve and has a scale which is directly proportional to the mass air flow through the driver's brake valve into the brake pipe; thus it provides an indication of the level of brake pipe leakage.

Apparatus specially designed and calibrated for the testing of brake equipment may be supplied, ranging from compact electronic test sets and portable test trolleys to comprehensive racks capable of testing a variety of pneumatic and electro-pneumatic valves.

Technical consultancy services are available covering all aspects of the design and engineering of brake and door equipment for railway vehicles. In addition, in conjunction with Westinghouse Signals Limited, similar services are available concerning complete train operating installations comprising all necessary control room, trackside and vehicle-mounted equipment. Service exchange facilities are available for selected brake equipment assemblies, and the equipment servicing workshop at Chippenham is able to undertake the repair of most items. Similar services are provided by associated and subsidiary companies in other countries.

Subsidiaries
Australia: Westinghouse Brake & Signal Co (Aust) Pty Ltd, PO Box 120, PO Concord West, New South Wales 2138
Canada: Westcode Ltd, 3688 Nashua Drive, Unit 'F', Mississauga, Ontario L4V 1M5
USA: Westcode Incorporated, 90 Great Valley Parkway, Great Valley Corporate Center, Frazer, Pennsylvania 19355

Associated company
South Africa: Westinghouse Bellambie (Pty) Ltd, PO Box 453, Johannesburg 2000

Driver's control desk for London Transport D78 stock

Westcode digital EP brake unit with cover removed

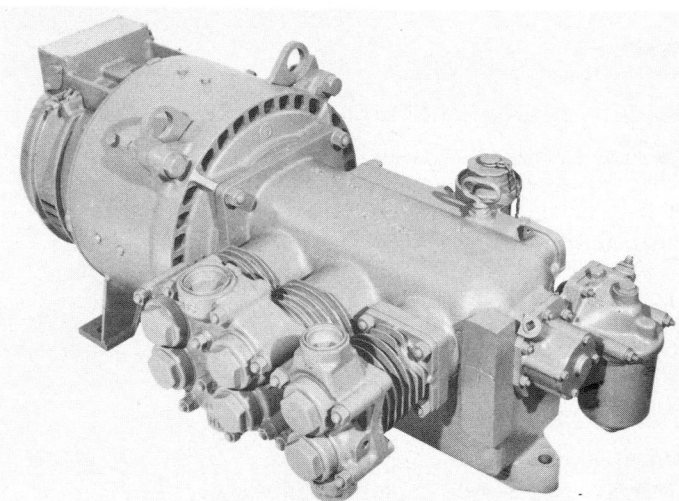

Westinghouse Type 3HC series motor-driven air compressor

Wilde
Wilde, SAICI

Monte 521, Buenos Aires, Argentina

Products: Draftgear; buffers; snubbers; hand brakes built under Miner licence.

BOGIES AND SUSPENSION SYSTEMS, WHEELS AND AXLES

Abex
Abex Corporation
Railroad Products Group

65 Valley Road, Mahwah, New Jersey 07430, USA

Telephone: (201) 529 3450
Telex: 642415

General Manager, world trade: Timothy F P Hely
530 Fifth Avenue, New York, New York 10036

Telephone: (212) 560 3200
Telex: 126605

Products: Cast steel wheels, mounted wheelsets.

Adirondack
Adirondack Steel Casting Co Inc

Watervliet, New York 12189, USA

Products: One-piece, cast steel bogies.

Ammendorf
VEB Waggonbau Ammendorf
Member of Maschinen-export

Ammendorf, German Democratic Republic

Telephone: 22050
Telex: 11 26 89

Products: Bogies (including the type KWS-ZNII) fitted to long-distance coaches for Soviet Railways; primary and secondary suspension systems, wheels, wheel-sets.

ANF-Industrie
Société ANF Frangeco

Tour Aurore, place de Reflets, 92080 Paris-Défense Cedex 5, France

Telephone: 778 62 62
Telex: 610 817

Products: Power and trailer bogies of all types.

Arad
Arad Car and Coach Bogie Works
MecanoExportImport Supplier

41-43 avenue Aurel Vlaicu, 2900 Arad, Romania

Telephone: 966 37020
Telegrams: Vagoane, Arad
Telex: 76256

Products: Bogies of Types Y22 Cs H and Minden-Deutz; axles and solid wheels.

Constitution: A member of the Wagon Manufacture Enterprises Group.

ASEA AB
Transport Division

721 83 Västeras, Sweden

Telephone: 46 21 100000
Telex: 40720

Products: Bogies incorporating rubber primary suspension for all types of railway vehicles.

The ASEA bogie with this feature, which also incorporates radial steering of the wheel-sets in curves, is in full commercial operation in commuter trains. The variant developed for passenger coaches was applied to a protracted series of comparative trials by Swedish State Railways (SJ) in 1982. Measurements confirmed the preceding calculations and proved that the average reduction of the track forces is about 40 per cent; and that the wear on wheels and rail is reduced by approximately 75 per cent in both types of service.

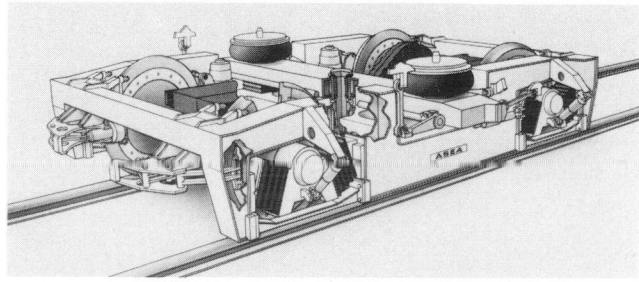

Bogie for Swedish State Railways' (SJ) Class X10 emu, with primary rubber suspension offering radial steering characteristics, and pneumatic secondary suspension

ASEA passenger car bogie with radial steering characteristics

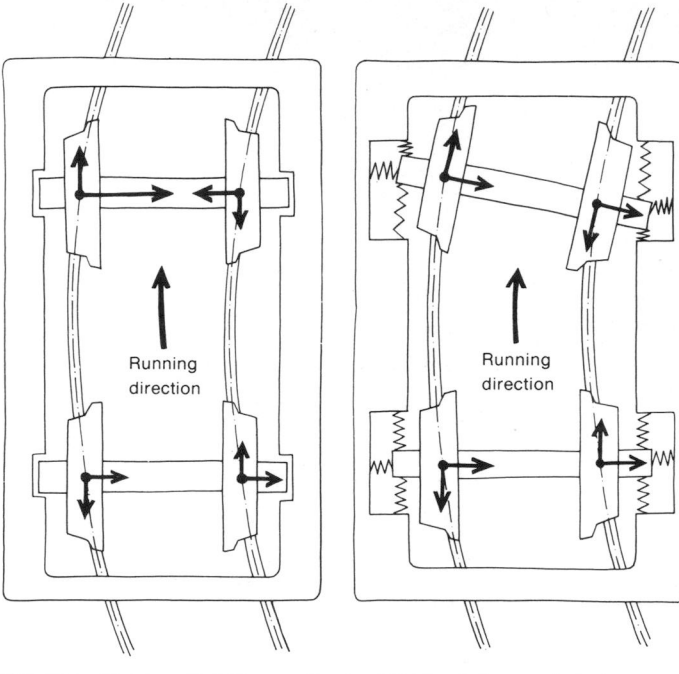

Comparison of bogies with (left) conventional and (right) radially-steered wheel-sets

ASF
American Steel Foundries
A division of Amsted Industries

3600 Prudential Plaza, Chicago, Illinois 60601, USA

Products: Ride control bogies. The ASF ride control bogie snubbing system is a built-in design that maintains constant control of spring action. The ASF side frames and bolsters exceed AAR strength requirements and can be furnished either as grade B or grade C steel castings. The pressure between the friction shoes and the side frame friction plates provides the necessary loadings to exercise optimum control. This pressure is generated by the ride control springs which force the friction shoes up the inclined ledges and outwardly against the friction plates. These ride control springs are compressed during assembly, and this amount of compression is not changed by varying bolster loads or truck spring movements, thus maintaining damping and alignment control at the light car condition. ASF is also a major producer of coil load bearing springs for all railway applications. A recent development is the Super Service Ride Control Truck which offers improved longevity and high speed stability.

Exports: All inquiries for supply outside the USA should be addressed to Amsted Industries International (qv).

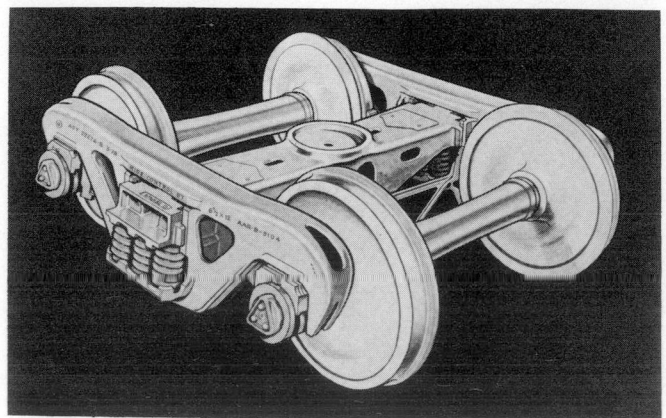

ASF ride control bogie

Avon
Avon Industrial Polymers Ltd

Bradford-on-Avon, Wiltshire BA15 1AA, England

Telephone: 02216 3911
Telex: 44856

Sales Manager: D A Washbrook
Sales Executive: J W Brockbank
Design Manager: M J Hinds

Products: Suspension systems, including air springs, chevrons and primary/secondary suspension bondings; sealing sections; air brake and steam heating hoses; gangway diaphragms; drawgear packs/buffing springs and rail pads.

Beall
Beall Manufacturing Company

112 North Shamrock, PO Box 70, East Alton, Illinois 62024, USA

Telephone: (618) 259 8154

President: W W Selby
Sales Manager: J Fairbanks
Engineering Manager: J Mager

Products: Elliptic leaf springs for locomotives and cabooses.

Bethlehem
Bethlehem Steel Corporation

Bethlehem, Pennsylvania 18016, USA

Products: Axles to AAR standards including mounted sets with or without roller bearings.

Bradken
Bradken Consolidated Ltd

22 O'Riordan Street, Alexandria, Sydney, New South Wales, Australia

Telephone: 02 699 3000
Telegrams: Bradken
Telex: 21512

Chief Executive Officer: B Meekings
Manager, Export: D Watson
Manager, Transport: I R Hunter

Products: Passenger and freight bogies, wheels, couplers.

Braine-le Comte
Usines de Braine-le Comte SA

Rue des Frères Dulait, 7490 Braine-le Comte, Belgium

Telephone: 067 553107
Telegrams: Usines, Braine-le Comte
Telex: 57458

Director and Manager: Jacques Preud'homme

Products: Wagons; bogies; three-axle bogies.

BREL
British Rail Engineering Ltd

Railway Technical Centre, London Road, Derby DE2 8UP, England

Telephone: 0332 49211
Telex: 37367

Products: BREL manufactures a complete range of bogies suitable for high-speed train-sets, diesel and electric locomotives, rapid transit and suburban railcars, and all types of freight vehicle. BREL's bogie designs are backed by the resources of the Railway Technical Centre, Derby which includes British Rail Research, the pioneers of steering axle technology, which was the most significant advance in bogie design of the 1970s. This technology has application on any railway system, but provides dramatic improvements in wheel flange and rail life where railway routes are tortuous and axleloads are high. BREL has fully patented bogie designs available for cross-braced freight bogies based on the steering axle technology for axleloads up to 25 tonnes, and also offers a rapid transit cross-braced (self-steering) bogie.

BREL's cross-braced freight bogie

BREL rapid transit cross-braced bogie

Buckeye
Buckeye Steel Castings
A Worthington Industries company

2211 Parsons Avenue, Columbus, Ohio 43207, USA

Telephone: (614) 444 2121

President: W C Buffington
Vice President, Sales: J B Sparma
Vice President, Sales Engineering: W D Reuter
Director, Product Engineering and Mass Transit: J R Downes

Products: Cast steel four-wheel bogie side frames, bogie bolsters, wagon couplers, draft yokes, centre plates, sill centre braces, draft sill ends, six-wheel bogies, span bolsters, and other castings for railroad wagons. Undercarriages for railroad passenger cars and mass transit rail vehicles. Buckeye Steel Castings is a major supplier to railroads, railcar builders, and railcar repair shops.
In addition, Buckeye manufactures steel castings and cast weldments, both machined and unmachined, for heavy industrial and earthmoving equipment, and armour steel castings for military vehicles.

Radial-axle passenger bogies by Buckeye to GSI designs

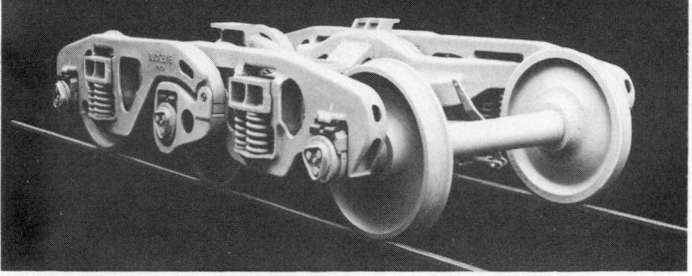
Six-wheel equalised load bogie for wagons of 150 tons or greater capacity

Mass transit car on Buckeye-GSI bogies

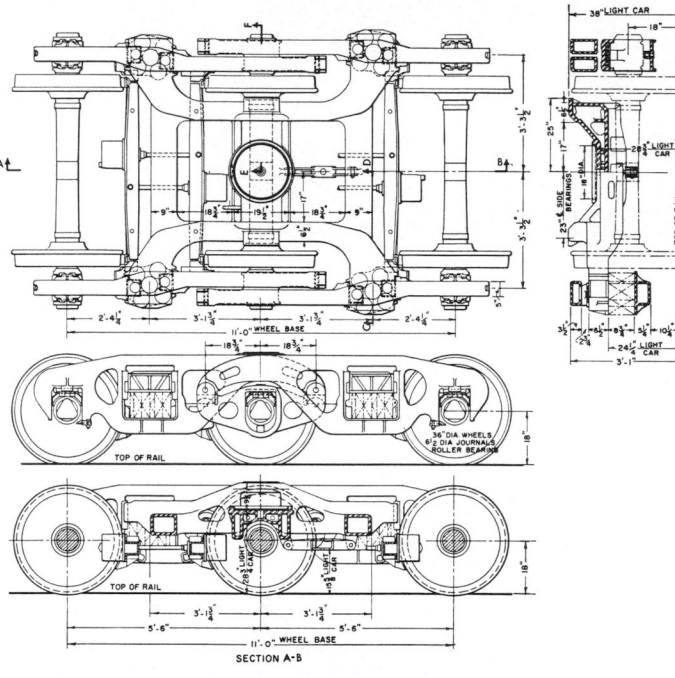

General arrangement of Buckeye six-wheel elasto-cushion bogie, embodying Barber S-2 stabilising with standard Barber friction wedges, wear plates and friction springs

Schnabel type heavy load transporter on double six- and ten-wheel bogies, load capacity 600 tons

Canadian Steel Wheel
Canadian Steel Wheel Division
Member of Hawker Siddeley Canada Inc

1900 Dickson Street, Montreal, Quebec H1N 2H9, Canada

Telephone: (514) 255 3605
Telex: 05 828603

Products: Wrought carbon steel wheels.

Cardwell Westinghouse
An American Standard Company

332 South Michigan Avenue, Chicago, Illinois 60604, USA

Products: AAR standard and alternate standard coil springs.

Cimmco International
A Division of Central Indian Machinery Manufacturing Co Ltd

ECE House, 28-A Kasturba Gandhi Marg, New Delhi 110 001, India

Telephone: 44381-5
Telegrams: Cimwag
Telex: 31 3618

Products: Cast steel bogies.

CL
CL Rail Trucks Inc

1225 Nineteenth Street NW, Washington DC 20036, USA

Telephone: (202) 887 0352
Telex: 892607, 440380

Products: Powered and trailer bogies for many railroad and rapid transit applications, including inter-city passenger cars, commuter cars, rail diesel cars, passenger and freight locomotives, rapid transit cars and light rail vehicles.

Constitution: US subsidiary of Creusot-Loire.

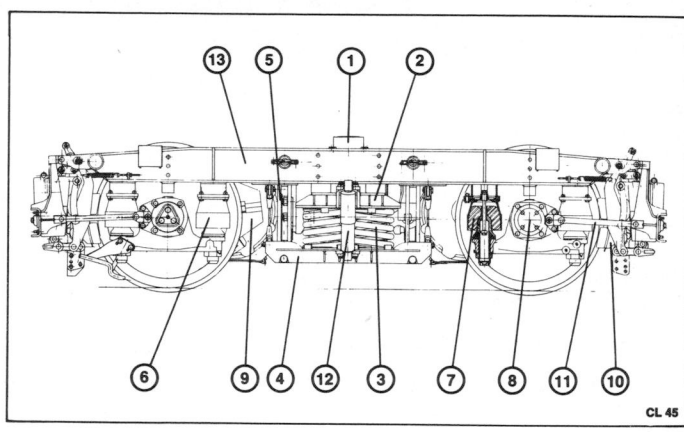

CL45 fabricated steel, 7 ft 10 in wheelbase motor bogie for commuter diesel-electric and hauled cars, for use with 2 nose-suspended motors driving through axle gearbox (1) side bearing (2) bolster (3) double-coil secondary suspension (4) spring plank (5) swing link (6) primary suspension (7) cross-section of primary suspension rubber springs (8) journal box (9) traction motor and gear case (10) tread brake (11) brake reaction lever (12) vertical hydraulic shock absorber (13) fabricated truck frame

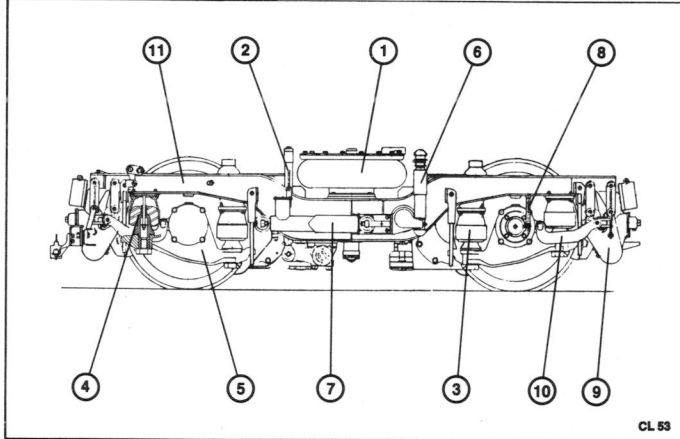

CL53 fabricated steel, 7 ft 10 in wheelbase motor bogie for commuter emu cars, for use with 2 nose-suspended motors (1) secondary suspension (rolling diaphragm air bag) (2) pneumatic levelling valve (3) primary suspension (4) section of primary suspension (5) journal box (6) vertical shock absorber (7) horizontal shock absorber (8) ground strap (9) tread brake unit (10) tread brake reaction lever (11) fabricated steel frame

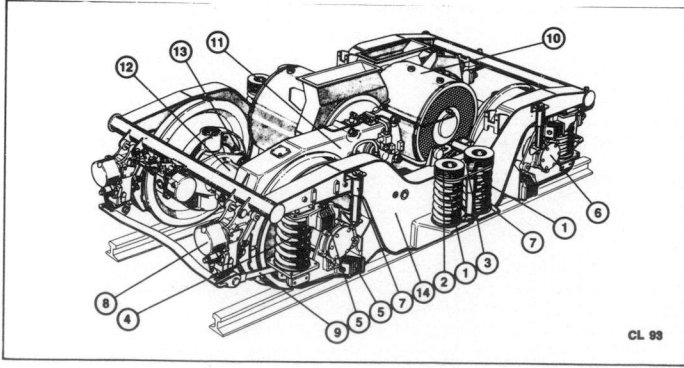

CL93 electric locomotive bogie of 9 ft wheelbase, fabricated in lightweight steel, with three-phase motors for speeds up to 240 km/h (1) secondary suspension parallel steel springs (2) metal-rubber sandwich block (3) steel connecting plate (4) primary suspension coil springs (5) primary suspension chevron blocks (6) journal box (7) full complement of shock absorbers (yaw damper, lateral shock absorber not visible) (8) double-shoe tread brake unit (9) brake shoe connecting rod (10) three-phase traction motors (11) double-reduction gear and case (12) hollow cardan shaft transmission (13) flexible drive coupling (14) fabricated steel frame

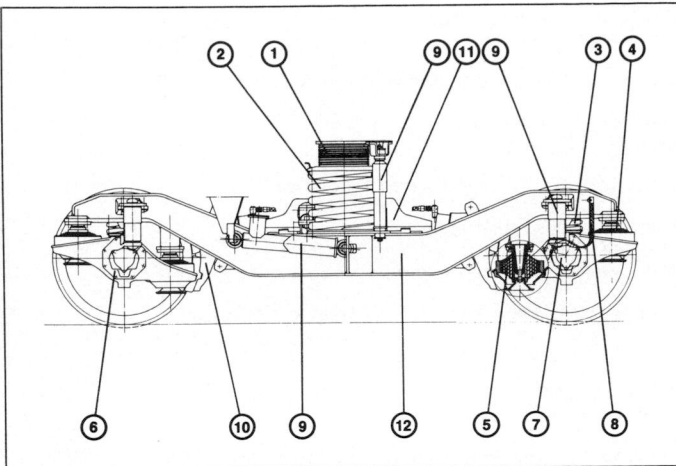

CL fabricated steel bogie for inter-city and commuter cars, adapted from French Railways' (SNCF) TGV high-speed trailer bogie, acquired by Amtrak for its Amfleet cars (1) metal-rubber sandwich block (2) secondary suspension steel coil springs (3) primary suspension steel coil springs (4) primary suspension metal-rubber axle guidance spring (5) cross-section of axle guidance spring (6) journal box (7) tapered roller bearings (8) ground strap (9) full complement of shock absorbers (10) double-shoe tread brake unit (11) bogie retention mechanism (12) fabricated steel bogie frame

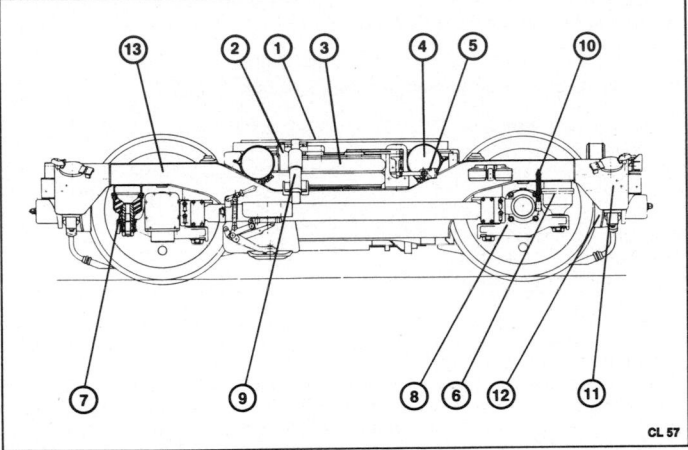

CL57 fabricated steel, 7 ft 3 in wheelbase motor bogie for rapid transit cars, adaptable to mono- or two-motor power (1) centre ring and car body interface (2) bolster (3) pneumatic secondary suspension (4) air reservoir (5) levelling valve (6) primary suspension (7) section of primary suspension (8) journal box (9) vertical shock absorber (lateral not visible) (10) ground strap (11) track sander and box (12) tread brake unit (disc brake not visible) (13) fabricated steel frame

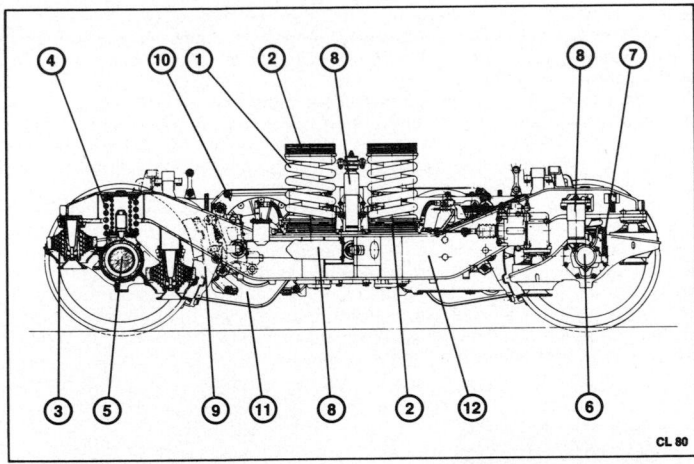

CL80 fabricated steel, 9 ft 10 in wheelbase power bogie designed for French TGV train-sets, with sliding double cardan-shaft drive from body-suspended motors (1) secondary suspension steel coil springs (2) metal-rubber spring blocks (3) primary suspension rubber-metal axle guidance springs (4) primary suspension concentric steel coil springs (5) journal boxes (6) tapered roller bearings (7) ground strap (8) full complement of shock absorbers (9) double-shoe tread brake unit (10) electric traction motors (11) transmission (12) fabricated steel frame

Cometna
Companhia Metalurgica Nacional Sarl

Rua Academica das Ciencias 5, Lisbon 2, Portugal

Telephone: 32 00 11
Telegrams: Fredalves
Telex: 12819

Railway Equipment Department

Apartado 2 (Enxarrapais), 2950 Palmela

Telephone: 235 01 60/70
Telegrams: Cometna
Telex: 17160

Chairman: Mario Caldeira
Managing Director: Florindo Ramos
Sales Manager: Julio Carlos Gaspar
Plant Manager: Alec Kelly

Products: Freight car bogies (approved by AAR); air and vacuum brake cylinders and fittings; roller bearing adapters and housings; automatic couplers; monobloc cast wheels; friction draftgear; buffers; and track material, such as complete turnouts, switches and cast manganese frogs.

Comsteel
Commonwealth Steel Company Limited

PO Box 14, Maud Street, Waratah, New South Wales 2298, Australia

Telephone: 61 49 68 0411
Telegrams: Comsteel
Telex: 28115

General Manager: G A Burrell
Marketing Manager: B Abbott

Principal subsidiary: Commonwealth Steel (Moorooka) Proprietary Limited, Newman Road, Moorooka

Products: Rolled steel wheels and tyres; axles; assembled sets; bogies and other railway castings. The company is a major supplier to all Australian rail systems and to export markets, especially India.

The company has recently completed a second-stage re-tooling programme to upgrade production of railway wheels with the commissioning of one of the world's most modern wheel machining systems at the Waratah plant of Comsteel's Mill and Engineering Products Division. The standards being progressively demanded, particularly for high-speed train operation, require wheels manufactured to close tolerances, inherently well-balanced with good surface finish and with minimum weight. The CNC equipment installed by Comsteel replaces manually-operated machines no longer adequate by modern standards. The machining capacity of the plant has also been increased to meet forecast future demands. The system includes four individual machines: three CNC-controlled Hegenscheidt vertical borers; and Stark oil injection hole drilling and tapping machines.

The overall wheel machining system is divided into two independent yet integrated stages which produce wheels to meet the differing requirements of a particular customer's order. Material handling equipment (feed conveyors, swarf removal, stackers and manipulators) has been integrated with independent machining operations, all of which are automatically operated. In addition, new wheel inspection, painting and handling facilities and a new wheel assembly shop have been commissioned.

One of Comsteel's CNC wheel machining and handling systems

Dorbyl
Dorbyl Railway Products (Pty) Ltd
A subsidiary of Dorbyl Ltd

PO Box 229, Boksburg 1460, South Africa

Telephone: 52 8276
Telegrams: Dorlonsa
Telex: 8 8024

Products: Various types of bogies under licence, including the Scheffel High Stability bogie.

Where axle loads are low the HS bogie augments rail and wheel life over 20 times; with 26-ton axle load life is increased 10 times before reprofiling of wheels. As there is no flange wear, wheels can be profiled three or four times before the same amount of metal has been removed as in one reprofiling of a wheel subject to flange wear. HS bogies are used exclusively on the South African Transport Services ore line between Sishen and the harbour at Saldanha Bay. Well over 150 million gross tons had been carried on this line by trains of 25 tons axle loading, but in 1983 the track was still in excellent condition, flange wear on wheels was negligible and wheel treads were generally lasting for more than 450 000 km between reprofilings. At that distance reprofiling was usually required only to restore wheel treads and not flanges. By 1983 SATS had covered 1.4 million km with HS bogies beneath high-speed wagons of low axle loading without any appreciable flange wear and only minimal tread wear on the wheels. It has been found that on certain applications the standard bogie is only able to travel 30 000 to 50 000 km between profilings, with most of the wear on the flange, thus causing extensive damage to the rail.

Dresser
Transportation Equipment Division, Dresser Industries, Inc

2 Main Street, Depew, New York 14043, USA

Telephone: (716) 683 6000
Telex: 91 277

President: M J Franklin
Marketing Director: W F Greenwood

Products: Bogies and bogie components; caboose cushioning and cushion underframe components including Hydra-cushion underframe equipment; couplers; yokes; draftgear and railroad steel castings.

Conventional bogie equipped with Dresser DR-1 steering assembly

Dunlop
Dunlop Polymer Engineering Division

PO Box 98, Evington Valley Road, Leicester, Leicestershire LE5 5LY, England

Telephone: 0533 730281
Telegrams: Polyeng, Leicester
Telex: 34397

Products: Rubber-bonded-to-metal springs for primary and secondary suspension systems; anti-vibration mountings; flexible bearings.

Energomachexport
V/O Energomachexport

Deguninskaja Str 1, Korp 4, 127486 Moscow, USSR

Telephone: 487 31 82
Telegrams: Energoexport, Moscow
Telex: 411 926

Products: Full range of bogies; primary and secondary suspension units; wheels; wheel-sets.

Fiat
Fiat Ferroviaria Savigliano SpA

Piazza Galateri 4, 12038 Savigliano (Cuneo), Italy

Telephone: (0172) 33911
Telex: 210234

Products: Bogies and components.

FNV
Veiculos Equipamentos SA

Avenida Maria Coelho Aguiar 215, 05804 São Paulo, Brazil

Telephone: 011 545 3546/5089
Telegrams: Fabriva, São Paulo
Telex: 01121901

Products: Barber stabilised bogies, cast steel wheels and components.

Forja
Forja Argentina SA

Reconquista 661, 6th floor, Buenos Aires, Argentina

Telephone: 37 9833
Telex: 122573

Works: Calle 1 171, Barrio Talleres 3, Cordoba

Chairman: Carlos Alberto Benavides
Managing Director: Jorge Norberto Vilaclara
Sales Director: Jorge Anselmo Garcia

Products: Wheels and wheel-sets; tyres and axles.

FreightMaster
A Halliburton Co

8600 Will Rogers Boulevard, Fort Worth, Texas 76140, USA

Telephone: (817) 293 4220

President: O E Seay

Products: Hydraulic cushioning units; electronic training simulators.

Gloucester
Gloucester Railway Carriage & Wagon Co Ltd
Subsidiary of Babcock International plc

Bristol Road, Gloucester, Gloucestershire GL1 5RS, England

Telephone: 0452 25104/5
Telegrams: Railcar, Gloucester
Telex: 437173

Chairman: E A Madenski
Managing Director: J S P Phillips
Sales Director: R A Clark
Engineering Director: R S Morris

Products: Freight bogies (primary sprung rigid frame, cast steel bogies with Metalastik rubber or helical steel spring suspension), suspension systems (including floating axles for two-axle wagons) and Miner doorgear.

The company's cast steel bogie with Metalastik rubber suspension is of springplankless type in three-piece form, but without sliding bolster guides; the connection between the bolster and the sideframe is made positively yet resiliently through inclined rubber chevron springs acting in combined shear and compression. The spring elements act as the main suspension in shear and compression and also maintain the relative positions of the moving parts of the bogie without metal wearing contacts, to a degree determined by the design of the spring and not by a 'slop' allowance.

This controlled flexibility allows for wheel drop on undulating track with an inherent restoring force in all flexures. The spring units are symmetrically angled in the frame so that the required characteristics can be obtained in all planes.

Careful design of the sideframe uses the induced reactions of these springs to relieve stresses at the centre of the frame. This allows reduced casting section and weight at this point.

Another feature of the design is that the sideframe weight for any given axleload is less than that of a conventional cast steel bogie; moreover, sideframes and springs do not have to be 'threaded' on to the bolster ends. This bogie is currently operating satisfactorily in 22 countries, and has been manufactured under licence in the USA and Canada.

The Gloucester floating axle suspension for two-axle wagons has been developed to combine efficient running at high speeds with low maintenance costs. It is designed not only for new vehicles but also for existing vehicles; on the latter, relatively simple and economic conversion from laminated to coil spring suspension can be carried out using existing wheel-sets complete with roller bearing axleboxes. When used for new vehicles, the unit will accept a modern cartridge roller bearing and will accommodate the variety of solebar heights at present planned for modern vehicles.

Gloucester two-axle pedestal suspension unit, available in versions up to 25-ton axleloads

The design aim has been to provide fairly low natural frequencies in both the vertical and lateral planes, together with reliable load sensitive friction damping characteristics. The suspension unit incorporates a bearing adapter fitted over the roller bearing unit, on which two inclined rubber pads are mounted. The saddle casting is supported by these pads and houses the suspension spring nests.

The bearing adapter (available in versions to accept modern cartridge or existing roller bearing axleboxes) positively locates the axlebox and is carried within the saddle. This has a spring platform incorporating a nest of coil springs each side of the axlebox to provide a two- or three-rate suspension characteristic.

The pedestal frame consists of the horn guides, which house the friction damper assembly, and the spring top platform. The damper unit selected has operated successfully on the Gloucester Primary Suspension range of bogies (GPS 20 and GPS 25). The friction damping is achieved by fitting an inverted pot over one spring nest per unit. This pot has inclined faces on its sides which locate against inclined guides on the pedestal, thus transferring a percentage of the vertical load into horizontal load. This load, via a damping pad, creates a frictional damping force proportional to the load carried by the wagon.

GPS 25 bogie with clasp brakes

Gloucester rubber-sprung bogie, as supplied to 1067 mm gauge Tazara Railways

Gresham & Craven
Gresham & Craven Ltd

PO Box 74, Chippenham, Wiltshire SN15 1JD, England

Telephone: 0249 654141
Telegrams: Brake, Chippenham
Telex: 449411/12

Sales Director: S J Pursey

Products: Air suspension equipment.

Griffin
Griffin Wheel Co
A division of Amsted Industries

200 West Monroe Street, Chicago, Illinois 60606, USA

Products: Steel wheels using the unique controlled-pressure pouring system into graphite moulds. These wheels are approved for all locomotive, passenger and freight applications. Griffin is the largest North American manufacturer of steel railroad wheels and is further expanding its production facilities. Griffin Pressure poured steel wheels are also manufactured under licence in many countries. The company has additionally developed and manufactures Anchor high-friction composition brake shoes.

All inquiries should be directed to Amsted Industries International (qv).

Hansens
Hansens Gummi & Packungs-Werke GmbH & Co

411 Hildesheimer Strasse, Postfach 830120, 3000 Hanover 89, Federal Republic of Germany

Telephone: 05 11 87 20 91
Telegrams: Gummihansen, Hanover-Wülfel
Telex: 9 22841

Chairman: Jürgen Hansen

Products: Rubber hoses and shock absorbers for all types of rolling stock and motive power.

In addition to standard products, the company manufactures a large number of industrial items for special purposes and processes most of the principal rubber types, both natural and synthetic, such as Perbunan (acrylic nitrile butadiene rubber), EP-rubber (ethylene propylene dien rubber), Hypalon (chlorosulphonic polyethylene), Buna (styrene butadiene rubber), Neoprene (polychlor butadiene), Butyl (isobutylene/isoprene), Viton/Fluorel (fluorine rubber), and Norsorex (polynorbornene rubber). Its range of compounds meets a wide variety of requirements as to hardness, colouring, chemical resistance and physical strength of the finished product.

Henricot
Usines Emile Henricot SA

1490 Court-St-Étienne, Belgium

Telephone: 010 61 22 05
Telex: 59071

President: Patrick Depuydt
General Manager: Marcel Claisse
Product Manager: Rudi Mertens

Products: Railway parts in cast steel; freight wagon bogies (parts and complete sets); automatic couplers and draft gears; buffing and traction devices; axleboxes; brake beams; centre plates; and miscellaneous parts in cast steel.

HDA Forgings
HDA Forgings Ltd
A Hawker Siddeley Company

Windsor Road, Redditch, Worcestershire B97 6EF, England

Telephone: 0527 64211
Telegrams: Alloys, Redditch
Telex: 337773

Products: Hand and die forged components in aluminium alloys for various railway uses.

Holland
Holland Co, Freight Equipment Division

1470 North Farnsworth Avenue, Aurora, Illinois 60505, USA

Telephone: (312) 851 8200
Telegrams: Aurora, Illinois

President: R F Murphy
Sales Director: John D Hoffmaster

Products: Hydraulic and friction snubbers; plastic wear plates; uncoupling levers.

Ilsenburg
VEB Radsatzfabrik Ilsenburg
Member of VEB Kombinat Schienenfahrzeugbau and of Vereinigter Schienenfahrzeugbau der DDR eV

Schmiedestrasse 16/17, 3705 Ilsenburg, German Democratic Republic

Telephone: 261
Telex: 088434

Products: Wheel-sets for railcars, passenger cars and freight wagons.

Exports: Schienenfahrzeuge Export-Import Volkseigener Aussenhandelsbetrieb der DDR, Otztaler Strasse 17, 1100 East Berlin

Italsider
Italsider SpA

Via Corsica 4, 16128 Genoa, Italy

Telephone: 010 5999
Telex: 270690

Products: Tyres, wheels and wheel-sets.

Koni
Koni BV

Langeweg 1, PO Box 1014, 3260AA Oud-Beijerland, Netherlands

Telephone: 01860 2500
Telegrams: Koni, Oudbeijerland
Telex: 21181

Chairman and Managing Director: P M F M Cals
Vice-President and Marketing Director: M de Koning
Chief Sales Director: G E Seckel

Products: Primary and secondary dampers; shock absorber testing equipment. In addition to the normal range of vertical and horizontal dampers Koni has developed the yaw damper which is designed to control small amplitude sinusoidal rotational movements and enable vehicles to operate at higher speeds. Recent trials of the damper on an articulated two-flatcar unit operated by Trailer Train, USA, showed that the vehicle's maximum speed could be raised from 96 to 153 km/h without incurring wheel-set oscillation.

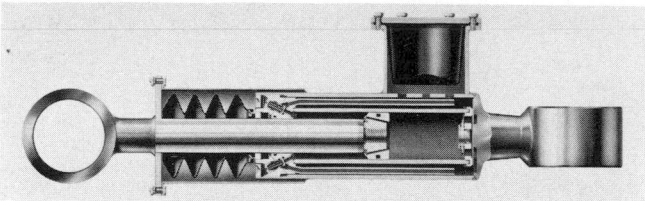

Koni adjustable damper as fitted to SNCF 260 km/h TGV train-sets

Langen & Sondermann
Langen & Sondermann GmbH & Co KG

Bergkampstrasse 57, 4670 Lunen, Federal Republic of Germany

Telephone: 0 23 06
Telegrams: LuS
Telex: 8229726

Director: Jurgen Kohl

Products: Parabolic, leaf, helical and conical springs for locomotives, passenger cars and freight wagons. Suppliers to numerous European railways.

LEW
VEB Lokomotivbau-Elektrotechnische Werke Hans Beimler

1422 Hennigsdorf, German Democratic Republic

Telephone: 50
Telegrams: Elektrolok, Hennigsdorf
Telex: 158 531

Products: Power and trailer bogies for passenger stock and locomotives. Among latest developments by LEW is a Series 277 powered bogie for use with electric multiple-units. With slight modifications the same bogie can be used for non-powered applications.

LKM
Lenin Kohászati Muvek

Lenin Metallurgical Works, 3540 Miskolc-Diósgyor, Hungary

Telephone: 51-909
Telex: 62326, 62242

Products: Wheel discs, tyres and axles for locomotives, passenger coaches and freight wagons.

Lord
Lord Corporation
Industrial Products Division

1635 West 12th Street, PO Box 10039, Erie, Pennsylvania 16514, USA

Telephone: (814) 456 8511
Telex: 914438

Products: Engineered elastomeric products for the control of vibration, shock and noise, including traction motor nose supports; Dynaflex flexible couplings; bolster mounts; roller bearing adapter mounts (LC Pads); draftgear pads; primary suspension springs (V Springs); and auxiliary equipment mounts.

Lord nose supports for axle-mounted traction motors, permitting controlled relative motion between motor and bogie frame

Dynaflex flexible couplings for drive transmission to generators and compressors to isolate torsional shock, and accommodate angular, parallel and in-line misalignment

Bolster mounts to accommodate lateral movement of locomotive bolsters more economically than conventional mechanical links

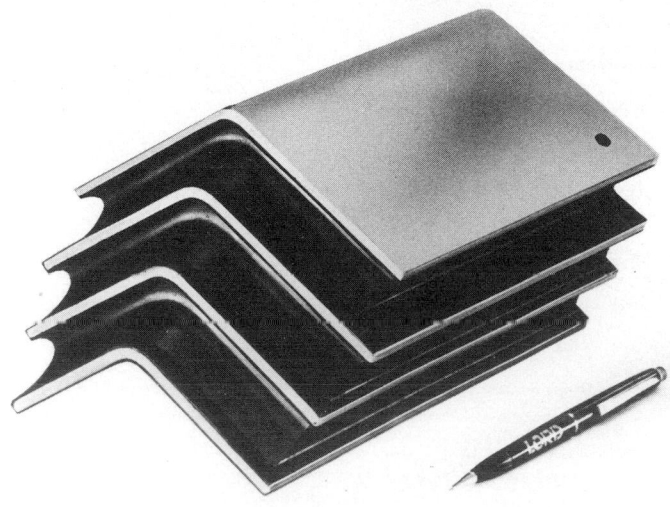

Lord primary suspension springs for rapid transit cars giving lighter bogie design

Centre pivot bearings for installation between transit car body and bogie centre plate, permitting torsional articulation, eliminating wear, and reducing high-frequency vibration

Macosa
Material y Construcciones, SA

Plaza de la Independencia 8, Madrid 1, Spain

Telephone: 2 22 47 87
Telegrams: Material, Madrid
Telex: 22168

Products: Bogies and springs.

Mafersa
Mafersa SA

Ave Raimundo Pereira de Magalhaes 320, CEP 05092, São Paulo, SP, Brazil

Telephone: 260 4591
Telegrams: Mafersa, São Paulo

Products: Wheel casting and forging; axle forging.

MAN
Maschinenfabrik Augsburg-Nurnberg AG
Railway Division

Katzwanger Strasse 101, 8500 Nuremberg 1, Federal Republic of Germany

Telephone: 0911 18-0
Telegrams: Manwerk, Nurnberg
Telex: 0622291

Products: Bogies and air suspension equipment.

Nikex
Nikex Hungarian Trading Co for products of Heavy Industry

Head office: Meszaros utca 48-54, 1016 Budapest, Hungary

Telephone: 850 935, 851 538, 851 539
Telegrams: Nikexport, Budapest
Telex: 224971

Main works
Lenin Metallurgical Works, 3540 Miskolc
Diósgyor Machine Factory, 3544 Miskolc

General Manager: J Merath
General Manager (Deputy): H Szucs
Sales Director: Z P Szädväry
Export Sales: Mrs Szára

Products: Tyres, helical springs and tyred wheel-sets.

Paulstra
Societe Paulstra

61 rue Marius Aufan, PO Box 164, 92305 Levallois-Perret, France

Telephone: 757 31 14
Telex: 620 898

Products: Rubber/elastomer suspension systems.

Paxton & Vierling
Paxton & Vierling Steel Co

PO Box 1085, Omaha, Nebraska 68101, USA

Telephone: (712) 347 5500

President: Edward F Owen
Executive Vice President: Robert E Owen
Vice President, Sales: John R Dobson

Principal subsidiaries
Northern Plains Steel Co, Fargo, North Dakota
Missouri Valley Steel Co, Sioux City, Iowa
Central Plains Steel Co, Wichita, Kansas

Products: Steel bridges; underframes; wear plates; stabilisers; and miscellaneous car parts (steel). Recent developments include a hydraulic stabiliser to eliminate bogie hunting.

Penn
Penn Machine Company

Head office: 905 Porter Building, Pittsburgh, Pennsylvania 15219, USA

Telephone: (412) 261 2561
Telex: TWX 510-698-1191

Main works: 106 Station Street, Johnstown, Pennsylvania 15905

Telephone: (814) 288 1547

Vice President, Sales: E L Van Sickel
Manager, Industrial and Transit Sales: H K Wiegand

Products: Resilient wheels; axles; pinions; and gears. Recent sales have included resilient wheels for Toronto and Philadelphia LRVs; and axles and gears for General Electric locomotives.

Phoenix
Phoenix AG

Hannoversche Strasse 88, 2100 Hamburg 90, Federal Republic of Germany

Telephone: 040 76 67 1
Telex: 02 17571

Products: Rubber/metal axle springs; pneumatic air bellows.

Pioneer
Pioneer Spring Company

23 George Street, Homebush, New South Wales 2140, Australia

Telephone: 73 1361
Telegrams: Piospring, Homebush
Telex: 22154

Chairman: K H Storey
Managing Director: P C Murray
Sales Manager: F Hemming
Export Manager: W Stephens

Products: Springs for railway suspension units.

Ringrollers
Ringrollers of South Africa (Pty) Ltd

11 Pienaar Street, Selection Park Industrial Sites, Springs, South Africa

Telephone: 56 0741
Telex: 4 21390

Chairman and Managing Director: D L Lee
General Manager: M P Kriel

Principal subsidiary: Transvaal Pipe Industries (Pty) Ltd

Products: Railway tyres; forged wheels.

Rockwell
Rockwell International, Automotive Operations
Off-Highway Projects & Supply Division

2135 West Maple Road, Troy, Michigan 48084, USA

Vice President and General Manager: William F Rebone
Sales Manager: Robert T McCloskey

Products: Complete bogies and components for locomotives.

Ruhfus
August Ruhfus GmbH Federn-Hydraulik

Budericher Strasse 7, PO Box 980, 4040 Neuss, Federal Republic of Germany

Telephone: 02101 26116
Telegrams: Ruhfus, Neuss
Telex: 08 517807

Managing Director: Ulrich Ruhfus

Products: Leaf, buffer and helical springs.

R W Mac
R W Mac Co

525 Craig Avenue, Crete, Illinois 60417, USA

Telephone: (312) 672 6376

Principal officers: R W MacDonnell
O A Shander

Products: Car-safe bogie bolster supports for 50 to 90-tonne wagons.

SAB
SAB NIFE AB

Instrumentgatan 15, PO Box 515, 261 24 Landskrona, Sweden

Telephone: 0418 16280
Telegrams: SAB NIFE, Landskrona
Telex: 72416

Products: Resilient and low-noise wheels.

Sambre et Meuse
Usines et Acieries de Sambre et Meuse

Tour Aurore, 92080 Paris-Défense Cedex 5, France

Telephone: 778 61 62
Telex: 620 162

Managing Director: Pierre Boissier
Sales Director: Gilbert Labadie

Products: Design, testing and manufacturing of bogies for all gauges, including the UIC Y25 type and its derivatives; wheels and wheel-sets. The Sambre et Meuse design of sprung bolster is made to AAR, British Rail and Crown Agents specifications.

Scullin
Scullin Steel Co

6700 Manchester Avenue, St Louis, Missouri 63139, USA

Telephone: (314) 645 0400

Products: Castings for freight wagon bogies.

SIG
Schweizerische Industrie-Gesellschaft
Swiss Industrial Company

8212 Neuhausen Rhine Falls, Switzerland

Telephone: 053 8 61 11
Telegrams: SIG, Neuhausenamrheinfall
Telex: 7 68 02

Products: Bogies for all kind of rail vehicles.

Silentbloc
Silentbloc Ltd
Subsidiary of BTR Ltd

Manor Royal, Crawley, West Sussex, England

Telephone: 0293 27733
Telex: 87177

Director/General Manager: J Anderson
Technical Director: G Sarosi
Financial Director: G Rogers

Products: Primary suspension units; damper end mountings; engine mountings; Alsthom links; resilient couplings; and numerous rubber-to-metal components.
Recent sales have included rolling rubber ring primary suspension units for British Rail's Class 317 and 510 emu power cars; and an initial batch of rolling rubber ring units for British Rail's Class 58 freight diesel locomotives.
The rolling rubber ring primary suspension unit is an axleguide in which the rubber ring replaces the lubricated bearing, allowing vertical movement between axlebox and bogie frame; it is maintenance-free during the life of the ring.
A new range of universal anti-vibration mountings is claimed to provide exceptional vibration absorption over a wide load and deflection range. Designated Flexistrip, the non-magnetic non-corrosive mountings are supplied in standard 250 mm strips which can be mounted in groups or cut to the desired length. Stiffness characteristics are thus infinitely variable, which obtains considerable versatility of application. Flexistrip comprises a rubber-to-metal sandwich of two aluminium extrusions bonded to natural rubber in one of three hardnesses specified according to application. 'Tee' slots running the full length of both aluminium strips allow unrestricted choice of positioning for fixing bolts and nuts. The type of fastener and fixing bolt length is also unrestricted. Ease of assembly and disassembly is another major feature of the new design. Two basic designs are available: solid ('strip' form); and hollow ('ring' form), each in three sizes.

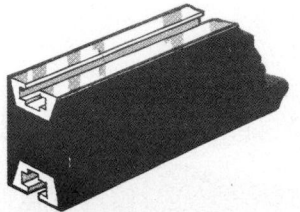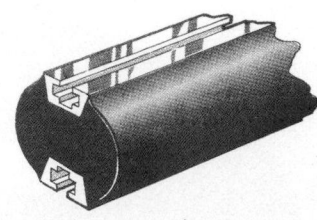

Silentbloc Flexistrip mountings

Socimi
Società Costruzioni Industriali Milano SpA

Via S Calimero 3, 20122 Milan, Italy

Telephone: 02 54 65 251/5
Telex: 310331

Main works
Via E Fermi n 25, 20082 Binasco (Milan)
Telephone: (02) 9055605/6/7/8
Via Donatori del Sangue n 100, 20010 Arluno (Milan)
Telephone: (02) 9017666/9017803
Viale Porto Torres, Reg Zentu Figghi, 07100 Sassari
Telephone: (079) 235056

Chairman: Dr Eng Alessandro Marzocco
Managing Director: Dr Eng Pierino Sacchi
Marketing Director: Dr Eng Corrado Landolina

Products: Bogies.

Trailer bogie for Ferrovie Nord Milano (FNM) vehicle

AAR-approved freight wagon bogie for 70-100-tonne glw vehicles

Monomotor bogie for Milan metro emu car

Soferval
Société Soferval

49 avenue George V, 75008 Paris, France

Telephone: 723 55 24
Telegrams: Locomoram, Paris
Telex: 290 060

Products: Standard and special bogies for passenger coaches and freight wagons.

Constitution: Absorbed by Alsthom-Atlantique in 1982.

Standard
Standard Car Truck Co

845 Busse Highway, Park Ridge, Illinois 60068, USA

Telephone: (312) 692 6050
Telegrams: Cartrucks
Telex: 27 0451

Chairman: Robert S Russell
President: William W Sellers
Manager, Sales: Edwin F Kindig
Manager, Operations: Robert P Geyer

Products: Barber stabilised bogies. The Barber load-sensitive variable damping system includes a friction shoe (iron-alloy casting with large bearing areas), hardened steel wear plate bolted and/or welded to the sideframe column, and preloaded spring which provides actuating support for the friction casting as well as C-PEP steel and elastomer centre plate extension pads; the latter effectively enlarge the centre-plate bearing surface to ensure stability.

The company also produces the Accutrak mileage indicator for railroad and transit cars.

Stucki
A Stucki Company

2600 Neville Road, Pittsburgh, Pennsylvania 15225, USA

Telephone: (412) 771 7300

President: W S Hansen
Executive Vice President: W B Thomas
Vice President, Research and Engineering: Donald Wiebe

Products: Hydraulic truck stabilisers, HS-7 and HS-7-100, designed to control harmonic rocking and vertical bounce in 50, 70 and 100-ton freight cars; single and double roller steel bogie side bearings, resilient constant contact side bearings, body side bearing wear plates and wedges for 50, 70 and 100-ton freight cars.

Stucki hydraulic stabiliser, Model HS-7, mounted in spring group of conventional freight car bogie

Sumitomo
Sumitomo Metal Industries Ltd

New Sumitomo Building, 1-3-2 Marunouchi, Chiyoda-ku, Tokyo 100, Japan

Telephone: 03 282 6111
Telex: 22865

General Manager, Sales: F Saito
Manager, Export Section: H Nakata

Products: Bogies, suspension systems, wheels and wheel-sets.

TIBB
Tecnomasio Italiano Brown Boveri
Transport Division

Piazzale Lodi 3, 20137 Milan, Italy

Telephone: (02) 5797.1
Telegrams: Tecnomasio, Milano
Telex: 310153

Products: Single and double-motor bogies for locomotives, motor-coaches, undergrounds and trams of standard and metre gauges; trailer bogies.

Union Spring
Union Spring and Manufacturing Co

New Kensington, Pennsylvania 15068, USA

Telephone: (412) 337 4571

Products: Suspension systems including Everlast springs, spring plates, under-cushion springs, journal box lids, wear plates and pedestal liners.

Unity
Unity Railway Supply Co, Inc

805 Golf Lane, Bensenville, Illinois 60106, USA

Telephone: (312) 595 4562

President: H R O'Connor
Vice President: John E Resch
Secretary-Treasurer: Robert Holden

Products: No-sway locomotive stabilisers; wheels; axles; roller bearing units.

Valdunes
Compagnie Française des Aciers Spéciaux

Immeuble Ile-de-France, 4 place de la Pyramide, 92070 Paris-La-Défense Cedex 33, France

Telephone: (1) 767 10 20
Telex: 614623

Chairman: R H Levy
Chief Sales Director: J Cambuzat

Products: Wrought solid wheels; straight axles; mounted wheel-sets.

Motored axles for French Railways high-speed TGV train-sets

Trailer wheel-sets with disc brakes for French Railways TGV train-sets

Vanguard
Vanguard Corp

PO Box 525, Highland Park, Illinois 60035, USA

Telephone: (312) 432 2425

Products: Trioid side bearings: model 173 for all types of freight wagon; model 190 for cabooses; model 1002-1 replacement for existing single solid steel roller; model 1002-2 replacement for double solid steel rollers on 90-, 100- and 125-tonne wagons.

Wickham
D Wickham & Co Ltd

Crane Mead, Ware, Hertfordshire SG12 9QA, England

Telephone: 0920 2491-7
Telegrams: Wickham, Ware
Telex: 81340

Products: Design and construction of bogies using radius arm located axlebox suspension for railcars and coaches of all gauges, and manufacture of other conventional types to specification.

Woodhead
Whitelee Engineers
A division of Jonas Woodhead Ltd

37 Adeline Street, Manchester M4 4FX, England

Telephone: 061-832 7881

Chairman: T S Richardson

Products: Laminated springs for locomotives, wagons, mine cars and commercial and public service road vehicles; rolled eye and solid forged main plates; solid and welded type buckles; conventional, featherlite and minimum leaf parabolic tapers; telescopic shock absorbers; coil springs; brake drums; shackle pins; and turned round parts.

Yusoki Kogyo
Yusoki Kogyo KK

102 Kamihamacho, Handa, Aichi 475, Japan

Telephone: 0569 21 3311
Telex: 4563 605

Products: Passenger coach and freight wagon bogies.

Zittau
VEB Federnwerk Zittau
Member of VEB Kombinat Schienenfahrzeugbau, and of Vereinigter Schienenfahrzeugbau der DDR eV

Äussere Weberstrasse 86b, 8800 Zittau, German Democratic Republic

Telephone: 2457
Telex: 0284231

Products: Leaf, circular and helical springs for rail vehicles.

Exports: Schienenfahrzeuge Export-Import Volkseigener Aussenhandelsbetrieb der DDR, Otztaler Strasse 17, 1100 East Berlin

BEARING MANUFACTURERS

Abex
Abex Corporation
Railroad Products Group

65 Ramapo Valley Road, Mahwah, New Jersey 07430, USA

Telephone: (201) 529 3450
Telex: 642415

Products: Standard steeple back bearings; alternate flat back bearings; roller bearing adapters, to AAR standards.

American Koyo
Division of Koyo Corporation of USA

29570 Clemens Road, PO Box 45028, Westlake, Ohio 44145, USA

Telephone: (216) 835 1000

General Manager: Masakazu Ueno
Manager, Sales and Marketing: Massi Takeda
Chief Engineer: Robert Erdmann

Products: ABU type journal roller bearings.

Brenco
Brenco Inc

PO Box 389, Petersburg, Virginia 23803, USA

Telephone: (804) 732 0202
Telex: 828300

President: G F Copeland
Vice-President and Secretary: Jacob M Feichtner
Vice-President, Sales: Louis E Nelsen Jr

Products: Tapered roller bearings, railroad and industrial.

Comet
Comet Industries Inc

4800 Deramus Avenue, Kansas City, Missouri 64120, USA

Telephone: (816) 483 3757

Products: Roller bearings.

FAG
FAG Kugelfischer Georg Schafer & Co

PO Box 1260, 8720 Schweinfurt, Federal Republic of Germany

Telephone: (09721) 911
Telegrams: FAG, Schweinfurt
Telex: 06 73 45-21

Products: Axleboxes (cast steel, ductile iron, light metal); journal roller bearings and package units (AAR standard and metric); gearbox bearings; traction motor bearings and complete suspension units.
The company has manufacturing plants in Austria, Brazil, Canada, West Germany, Portugal, Switzerland and the USA.

FAG
FAG Bearings Corporation

Stamford, Connecticut 06904, USA

Products: Journal roller bearings.

Garrett
Garrett Railroad Car and Equipment Inc

PO Box 2208, Newcastle, Pennsylvania 16102, USA

Telephone: (412) 658 9061

Products: Roller bearings.

Illinois
Illinois Railway Equipment Company

303 East Wacker Drive, Chicago, Illinois 60601, USA

Telephone: (312) 427 0661

Products: Economy journal centring guides; Mobil insert-type journal stops.

Koyo Seiko
Koyo Seiko Co Ltd

9-2 Sueyoshibashi, 3-chome, Minami-ku, Osaka 542, Japan

Telephone: 06 271 8451
Telegrams: Koyobrg, Osaka
Telex: 63040

Managing Director: Eizo Imura
Chief Sales Director: Yoshitaka Ikeda

Products: Axlebox, grease-sealed journal bearings (ABU type); roller bearings, ball bearings, needle roller bearings, pillow blocks.

Kugelfischer
See FAG Kugelfischer Georg Schafer & Co

Magnus/Farley Metals Inc

PO Box 934, Toledo, Ohio 43694, USA

Telephone: (419) 248 5618

President: S S Coleman

Products: Solid journal bearings; roller bearing adapters; motor support bearings; lubricator pads.

Multi-Service Supply
Multi-Service Supply Inc
Subsidiary of the Buncher Co

1080 Third Street, PO Box 149, North Versailles, Pennsylvania 15137, USA

Telephone: (412) 824 3630

Products: Roller bearings.

Nachi-Fujikoshi
Nachi-Fujikoshi Corporation

World Trade Centre Building, 4-1 Hamamatsucho 2-chome, Minato-ku, Tokyo 105, Japan

Telephone: 03 435 5111
Telegrams: Nachi, Tokyo
Telex: 24327; 26877

Products: Ball bearings, roller bearings, linear ball bearings.
Over 48 000 Nachi journal bearings of various types have been supplied for the Shinkansen high-speed emus of Japanese National Railways.

Nippon Seiko
Nippon Seiko KK

Head office: Yusen Building 3-2, Marunouchi 2-chome, Chiyoda-ku, Tokyo 100, Japan

Telephone: 03 284 1611
Telex: 02228328

International Division: Osaka Building 1-1, Kyobashi 1-chome, Chuo-ku, Tokyo 104

Telephone: 03 278 5885
Telegrams: Nskbearing, Tokyo
Telex: 02224280

President: M Hasegawa
General Manager, International Division: J Nagai

Products: Axleboxes, tapered roller bearings and package units for rolling stock, ball bearings, cylindrical and spherical roller bearings.

NTN Toyo
NTN Toyo Bearing Co Ltd

3-17-chome, Kyomachibori, Nishi-ku, Osaka, Japan

Telephone: 06 443 5001
Telegrams: Toyobear, Osaka

Tokyo office: 17-22, 7 Nishigoranda, Shinagawa-ku, Tokyo

Telephone: 03 494 5861
Telegrams: Toyobear, Tokyo

Products: Journal roller bearings.

Railko
Railko Ltd
A BBA Group Company

Loudwater, High Wycombe, Buckinghamshire HP10 9QU, England

Telephone: 062 85 24901
Telex: 848406

Products: Plastics bearings, including the Railko centre pivot liner developed to replace greased metal on UIC Y25C type bogies.
   Recently added to the Railko range of non-metallic bearing materials are Railko NF21 and NF22 non-asbestos reinforced thermosetting materials, particularly suitable for railway bogie non-lubricated applications.

RHP
RHP Industrial Bearings
RHP Bearings Limited

PO Box 18, Newark, Nottinghamshire NG24 2JF, England

Telephone: 0636 705123
Telex: 377652

Engineering Director: E Godson
Sales Director: I W Galloway
Manufacturing Director: H R G Nelson

Products: Ball and roller bearings and bearing units for traction motors, transmissions and suspensions.

SKF
Aktiebolaget SKF

415 50 Gothenburg, Sweden

Telephone: 031 37 10 00
Telex: 2350

Group Chief Executive: Lennart Johansson
Group directors
   Deputy Managing Director, Marketing: Bengt Kihlberg
   Deputy Managing Director, Finance and Information Systems: Jan Essunger
   Product Engineering and Research: Ingemar Fernlund
   Manufacturing Engineering: Bertil Ström
Division directors
   Deputy Managing Director, European Bearing Division: Mauritz Sahlin
   Director, Overseas Bearing Division: Göran Bergkvist

Products: Roller bearings.

Stassfurt
VEB Achslagerwerk Stassfurt
Member of VEB Kombinat Schienenfahrzeugbau and of Vereinigter Schienenfahrzeugbau der DDR, eV

An der Liethe 5, 3250 Stassfurt, German Democratic Republic

Telephone: 2282
Telex: 088826

Products: Roller bearings for locomotives, passenger cars and freight wagons.

Exports: Schienenfahrzeuge Export-Import Volkseigener Aussenhandelsbetrieb der DDR, Otztaler Strasse 17, 1100 East Berlin

Stucki
A Stucki Company

2600 Neville Road, Pittsburgh, Pennsylvania 15225, USA

Telephone: (412) 771 7300

Products: Roller and resilient side bearings; hydraulic bogie stabilisers.

Stucki resilient side bearings, Model 688-BR for 100-ton cars and Model 656-CR for 50 and 70-ton cars

Timken
The Timken Co

Canton, Ohio 44706, USA (US sales)
British Timken, Duston, Northampton NN5 6UL, England

Telephone (UK): 0604 52311

Managing Director, British Timken: D Ashton
Managing Director, Timken Europe: E R Knapp
Director, Marketing, British Timken: A S Paterson
Secretary/Chief Accountant: P J Scott

Subsidiaries: Manufacturing plants in Australia, Brazil, Canada, France, South Africa, United Kingdom and the USA.

Products: Tapered roller bearings.

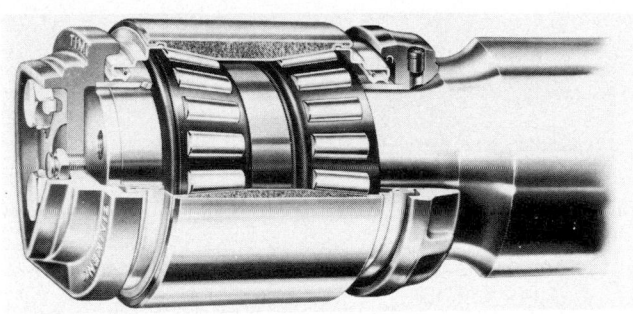

Timken AP (all-purpose) bearing

Unity
Unity Railway Supply Co, Inc

805 Golf Lane, Bensenville, Illinois 60106, USA

Telephone: (312) 595 4562

Products: Journal package including: no-sway side-bearing stabiliser; journal box rear seal; journal stop for use in rib or non-rib types; easy-ply lid seal.

Vandervell
Vandervell Products Ltd

Norden Road, Maidenhead, Berkshire, England

Telephone: 0628 23456
Telex: 847006

Chairman and Managing Director: N E Ratcliffe
Sales Director: D N Pink

Products: Plain axle bearings for rolling stock based on automotive practice. Two series: S is a replacement for brasses; R is a sleeve bearing for use as a superior bearing to roller bearings, and also as an alternative means of improving old rolling stock currently using brasses. Many advantages over rollers, particularly in prolonging the life of axles by use of u/s shafts and u/s pre-sized bushes.

PASSENGER COACH EQUIPMENT

Adams & Westlake
Adams and Westlake Co

1025 North Michigan Street, Elkhart, Indiana 46514, USA

Telephone: (219) 264 1141
Telegrams: Adlake
Telex: 25-8458

Chairman: R L Champlin
Executive Vice-President and General Manager: L F Ott
General Sales Manager: A D Rohl

Products: Windows, luggage racks and car hardware.

Air Industrie
Subsidiary of the Saint-Gobain-Pont-à-Mousson Group

75783 Paris Cedex 16, France

Products: Air-conditioning equipment.

Airscrew Howden
Airscrew Howden Limited

Weybridge, Surrey, England

Telephone: 0932 45511
Telex: 929515

Chairman: A B R Cheek
Managing Director: M C Beal
Chief Sales Director: J D Stewart

Products: Railcar air-conditioning fans, ceiling-mounted ventilator fans, main engine cooler groups, braking resistor cooling fans, electronics cooling fans, mixed flow fans, small brushless dc fans.

Typical direct-drive configuration of Airscrew Howden Mixflo fan as installed in British Rail Class 317 emus

Alna Koki
Alna Koki Co Ltd

4-5 Higashinaniwa-cho 1-chome, Amagasaki 660, Japan

Telephone: 06 401 7281
Telegrams: Alna, Amagasaki
Telex: 524 2782

Products: Aluminium window sashes and doors for electric railcars and passenger coaches.

Bayham Ltd

Daneshill West, Basingstoke, Hampshire RG24 0PG, England

Telephone: 0256 64911
Telegrams: Bayomatic, Basingstoke
Telex: 858318

Managing and Export Sales Director: W Y E George
Home Sales Director: E A Salter
Production Director: R C Laule

Subsidiary company: The Ranger Instrument Co Ltd

Products: R & G direct and remote-reading fuel and coolant tank gauges and switches for locomotives, restaurant car and sleeper drinking water; chemical effluent tank gauges for British Rail's APT.

Recent contracts have included the supply of coolant gauge switches for German Federal Railway's dmus of Type 627/628; fuel and coolant switches for Romanian Railways; and main fuel tank gauges for British Rail's HSTs and drinking water tank gauges for BR Mk III sleeping cars.

Among recent developments are R & G Minisend combination remote-reading gauges, including two-level switches, for railcar radiator water header tanks for Chausson SA, France. These sets provide drivers' panel indication of coolant level with an alarm switch for low level and engine shutdown circuit switch for total loss condition. The tank unit incorporating transmitter and the two switches is designed to fit into the shallow header tank and is rated up to 120°C at 2 bar. The float mechanism incorporates a self-cleaning magnetic drive, ensuring no leakage. The company's radiator header tank gauges are now fitted to over 1000 Class 260 and 290 diesel shunters of the German Federal Railway (DB).

Bayham radiator header tank gauge fitted to DB Class 260 diesel shunter

BBC
BBC Brown Boveri & Co Ltd and Group Companies

For companies in Federal Republic of Germany, Norway and Switzerland see under Locomotives and rolling stock

Products: Electrical equipment, complete systems for passenger comfort with power supply, lighting, heating, air-conditioning.

Beckett, Laycock & Watkinson
Beckett, Laycock & Watkinson Ltd

Acton Lane, London NW10, England

Telephone: 01-965 5403
Telegrams: Beclawat, London
Telex: 261770

Chairman and Managing Director: L W Robins
Chief Sales Director: D E W Albous

Products: Beclawat windows, door systems and route indicators.

Belz
August Belz Apparatebau GmbH

Postfach 12 25, 7990 Friedrichshafen 1, Federal Republic of Germany

Assistant General Manager: Willi Gottner
Export Manager: Manfred Carl

Products: Sapor solid and cream soap dispensers; towel cabinets; waste paper towel bins; solid and cream soap.

The company's Standard model of solid soap dispenser, manufactured in die-cast aluminium alloy to withstand vandalism, has been supplied to most European railways for washroom/toilet installation.

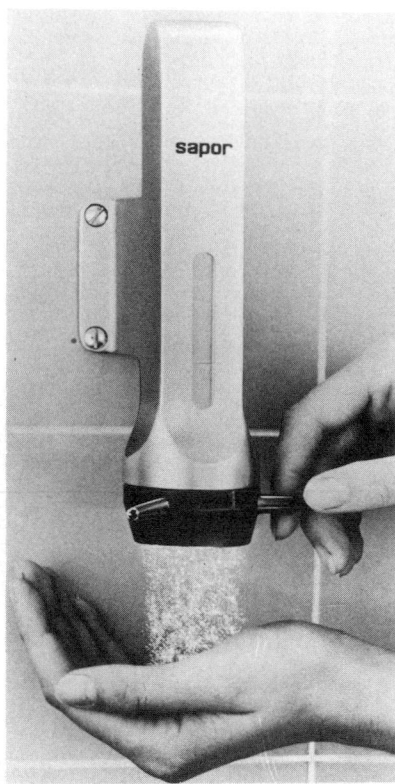

Standard Sapor soap dispenser in die-cast aluminium

Central Engineering
Central Engineering Works

Gandhi Park, Malkajgiri, Secunderabad 500 047, India

Telephone: 78328/9
Telegrams: Gangway

Principal Proprietor, Technical and Financial: G Ramjiwan Rao

Central Engineering vestibule arrangement

Products: Design, modification and manufacture of gangways, flexible gangways and vestibule bellows; and arrangement of footplate for metre-gauge and broad-gauge passenger coaches. The company specialises in maximum possible utilisation of locally available material, weight and cost reduction and ease of maintenance by the user without loss of performance.

Cimmco
Cimmco International

ECE House, 28-A Kasturba Gandhi Marg, New Delhi 110 001, India

Telephone: 44381-5
Telegrams: Cimwag
Telex: 31 3618

Products: Underframes for passenger cars and components.

Clemançon
Société Clemançon

23 rue Lamartine, 75009 Paris, France

Products: Heating and regulation equipment; lighting systems.

Conbrako
Conbrako (Pty) Ltd

PO Box 14010, 167 Tedstone Road, Wadeville 1422, Transvaal, South Africa

Telephone: 34 34 31
Telegrams: Conbrako
Telex: 84721

Products: Sliding doors; electro-pneumatic door mechanisms; coach windows.

Deans and Lightalloys
Deans & Lightalloys Ltd

PO Box 8, Grovehill, Beverley, North Humberside HU17 0JL, England

Telephone: 0482 868111

Managing Director: L A Jarvis
Directors: F Cawood
　　　　　C S Dunwoodie
　　　　　J S Thornton
　　　　　J P Jarvis

Products: Doors, seats, windows, general fittings and internal assemblies including complete sliding doors and pneumatically-operated equipment.

Electrolux-Wascator
Electrolux-Wascator AB
Environmental Systems

105 45 Stockholm, Sweden

Telephone: 08 738 60 00
Telex: 11600

Division Manager: Ragnar Zetterström

Products: Vacuum toilet and sewage systems.
　　Components of the Electrolux vacuum toilet system comprise the toilet bowl, pipework, collecting tank, vacuum set with odour-eliminating filter and control equipment. Air is extracted by the vacuum pump from the tank and thus from the piping, the vacuum being maintained by a valve in the rear of the closet bowl. This valve is opened by pressing the flushing button, whereupon air rushes into the system carrying with it the soil and the small volume of flushing water.
　　The closet bowl is of china with a sturdy seat and cover of wood finished in enamelled glass-fibre reinforced plastic. Bowls are available in both floor and wall-mounted versions, and in stainless steel for special applications. The flushing mechanism is located in an enclosure at the rear of the toilet or, in the case of the wall-hung model, behind the wall. The mechanical equipment is arranged externally in an under-chassis compartment, heated to ensure functioning at temperatures around −40°C. A carbon filter absorbs any noxious odours, thus permitting use of the toilet during stops at stations and in railway workshops. The collecting tank may be either at atmospheric pressure or under vacuum. An advantage of the former type is that it can be more readily adapted to the design of the railway vehicle. Either type of tank may be located arbitrarily relative to the toilet. The tank is emptied by connecting a sludge suction unit to the speed coupling on the tank.
　　The control equipment may be incorporated in the motor compartment under the chassis or inside the car. The control functions comprise vacuum and level control devices and an externally placed warning lamp for full tank, associated with automatic locking of the toilet doors.

Faiveley external sliding door on French Railways (SNCF) double-deck commuter car

Faiveley sliding plug-in door with folding step fitted to French Railways (SNCF) TGV train-set

Faiveley electric door operating mechanism

Electrolux vacuum toilet installation in Fiat-built Swedish State Railways Type Y1 diesel railcar (1) vacuum toilet (2) toilet operating mechanism (3) sewage line, pvc (4) collecting tank (5) vacuum pump and filter compartment (6) control equipment (7) speed coupling for discharge

Ellcon-National
Ellcon-National Inc

30 King Road, Totowa, New Jersey 07512, USA

Telephone: (201) 256 7110
Telex: 130154

Chairman: Emil P Kondera
Vice-President, Engineering: R M Caulfield
Vice-President, Special Projects: R A Nitsch
General Manager: J A Testa

Products: Hand brakes, window sashes, impact-resistant glass, stanchions, grab handles, windscreens, luggage racks, locomotive slack adjusters, slack adjusters, pellet gates.

Ercole Marelli
Ercole Marelli Elettromeccanica Generale SpA

Viale Edison 50, 20099 Sesto S Giovanni, Milan, Italy

Telephone: (02) 2494
Telegrams: Marelgen, Sesto S Giovanni
Telex: 310043; 320575

Products: Air-conditioning systems and equipment.

Faiveley
Faiveley SA

93 rue du Docteur Bauer, BP 151, 93404 Saint-Ouen (Cedex), France

Telephone: 264 12 60
Telex: 290653

Products: Manually-operated doors; electro-pneumatic doors and door gear; electric and electro-pneumatic door control fittings; electric and electronic control fittings for heating equipment; miscellaneous electronic equipment.

With a background of 50 years' experience in automatic door operating systems, the company co-operates with car-builders by assuming the entire responsibility for the design, development and production of all components of a door equipment; several alternative models are on offer for each subassembly. The company aims to assist the vehicle builder by minimising the interface to obtain rapid installation on the car body; and, assuming the entire responsibility for the correct operation of the automatic door equipment, guarantees the highest level of reliability and trouble-free maintenance and secures the highest degree of safety and comfort. Faiveley offers the widest range possible for rail passenger vehicles, from simple hinged doors for toilets to electrically-operated sliding plug-in doors, via pneumatic sliding doors for mass transit systems. It has executed 300 000 door equipment installations in 20 countries spread over five continents.

Findlay
Findlay, Irvine Ltd

Bog Road, Penicuik, Midlothian, Scotland

Telephone: 0968 72111
Telex: 727502

Chairman: James S Findlay

Products: Heating thermostats and switches.

Graham White
Graham White Sales Corp

1209 Colorado Street, Salem, Virginia 24153, USA

Telephone: (703) 387 5620

President: Harvey F Bredlow
Vice President: Timothy A Kelly
Directors: Jack Thompson
　　　　　　Stewart Bruce

Products: Distributors for heated hi-impact windshields in the USA, which are manufactured by the Sierracin/Sylmar Corporation in Sylmar, California. Also ventilators; windshield wings; mirror and windshield wing combinations; locomotive cab awnings; bell ringers; air filters; air dryers; air gauges; air gauge and pressure switch test device; test fittings; sand traps; sand shut-offs; pneumatic air timers; electric timers; check valves; directional check valves; control valves; drain valves; relay valves; operating valves; solenoid valves; locomotive water dump valves and air dryer systems.

Graviner
Graviner Ltd

Poyle Road, Colnbrook, Slough, Berkshire SL3 0HB, England

Telephone: 02812 3245
Telegrams: Crashfires, Slough
Telex: 848124

Managing Director: J A Hope
Financial Controller: N J Coleman
Technical Director: Dr R L Farquhar
Director, Land and Sea Systems: I E A Barclay
Marketing Manager, Vehicles: A R Smith

Products: Design, development and production of fire, smoke and explosion detection and suppression systems; repair and refurbishing of products.

Graviner equipment includes a wide range of detectors, each designed to react to a specific fire or overheat condition: in the case of overheat/fire, a localised or point detector (high speed re-setting switch, HSRS), a continuous pyrotechnic detector (Pyrocord) or continuous electrical detector (Firewire); in the case of flame, optical detectors (ultra-violet or infra-red); and smoke detectors. The detectors are linked to a control panel in the locomotive cab or any appropriate staff compartment in the train. The control panel can be designed to give warning lights, audible alarms, and information on the position of the fire, or overheat condition, to enable manual operation of extinguishers, and/or to automatically activate the appropriate extinguisher system. The control unit stabilises the power fed to the system, and can also provide continuous system monitoring.

Recent developments include a smoke detection and coach alarm system for sleeping cars; and an auto/manual fixed fire extinguisher valve.

The advanced smoke detectors used in British Rail's Mk III sleeping cars are of the latest ionisation/chamber type which detects smoke in the early stages of combustion from the change of impedance in the chamber. Detectors are fitted in each berth, the attendant's compartment, the end vestibules, each toilet and in the inlet and outlet ducts of the air-conditioning module.

All detectors in each car are supervised by an electronic central control unit which monitors their outputs continuously for smoke and also for serviceability of the system. In the event of a smoke indication or a fault, audible and visual warnings are given. There is a warning horn in each sleeping berth, each vestibule and all attendant's compartments. Red smoke warning lights are built into each detector unit and are also located on the bulkhead outside each berth and on the panel of the control unit. To differentiate between smoke and fault alarms, the horn sounds a continuous high-pitched note for smoke and an intermittent note for an equipment fault. The visual alarm for a fault signal is an amber indicator lamp.

Each control unit is housed in a glass-fronted cabinet in the vestibule of the sleeping car. A remote indicator panel is mounted in the attendant's compartment and in addition to providing a visual check that the system is operational also incorporates controls which allow the horns in the car to be muted, silenced or sounded manually.

The control units are also interlinked to provide an integrated detection system for the whole train. In the event of smoke being detected, or a fault, the appropriate alarm note is sounded in the attendants' cabins along the train and also in the vestibules. Alarm warning lights on the control panels identify the source and nature of the alarm. If the source is in the sleeping area, the berth responsible is indicated by the warning light on the corridor bulkhead. Inside the berth the warning light on the detector unit is illuminated and the warning horn sounds.

The system is also connected to illuminated displays in each vestibule. A red arrow lights up pointing away from the source of an alarm, as a guide to passengers evacuating the train.

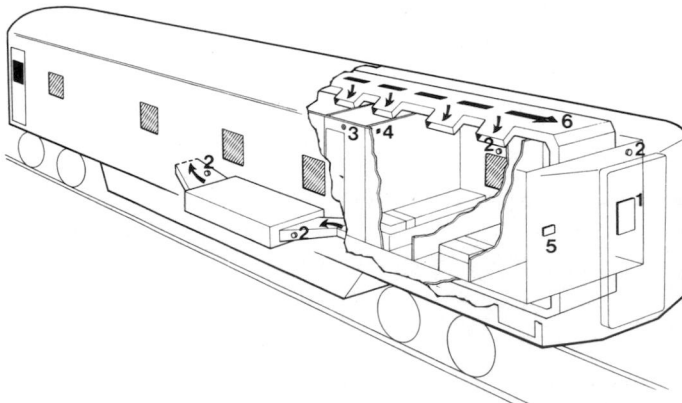

Typical Graviner sleeping car protection and alarm system (**1**) control units (**2**) smoke detectors (**3**) corridor warning lights (**4**) horn (**5**) flashing arrows (**6**) air-conditioning duct

Henshall
W Henshall & Sons

Abbot Close, Oyster Lane, Byfleet, Surrey KT14 7JT, England

Telephone: 09323 51011
Telex: 928460

Chairman: R MacDonald-Hall
Executive Director: J C Smith
Sales Director: C MacDonald-Hall
Managing Director: G J Mattingley
Technical Director: V J Chennell
Company Secretary and Financial Director: L R Mercer

Products: Catering equipment for rolling stock; ticket office equipment; Micro-aire cookers. Recent sales have included a new range of catering equipment, principally of stainless steel welded construction, for the High Speed Trains of British Rail and supply of ticket office equipment to the same organisation.

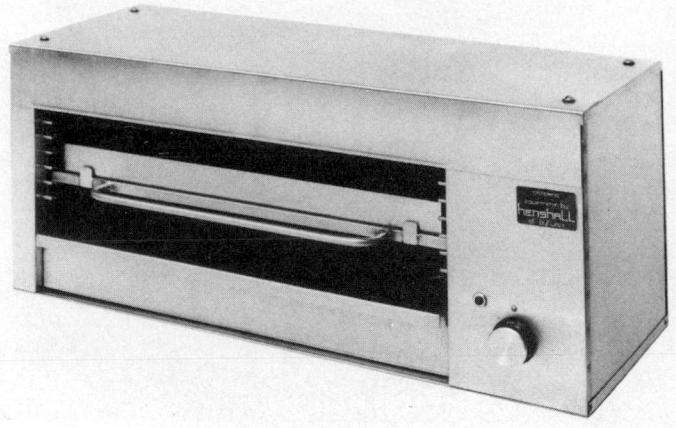

Henshall grill for British Rail (BR) HST train-sets, 686 × 307 × 303 mm

Henshall four-place boiling plate for BR HST train-sets, 700 × 600 × 385 mm

Hitachi
Hitachi Ltd

Nippon Building, 6-2, 2-chome Otemachi, Chiyoda-ku, Tokyo 100, Japan

Telephone: 03 270 2111
Telegrams: Hitach, Tokyo
Telex: 22395, 22432, 24491

Products: Air-conditioning equipment.

Hüttmann
Richard Huttmann GmbH & Co KG

3575 Kirchhaim Bez Kassel, Federal Republic of Germany

Telephone: 06422 3013/3014
Telegrams: Huttmann, Kirchhaim
Telex: 04 821 817

Products: 24-volt dc special aero fans for roof and wall mounting.

IFE
IFE Gesellschaft mbH

Patertal 20, 3340 Waidhofen/Ybbs, Austria

Telephone: 0043/7442/2545

President: Dr W Berz
Sales Director: Dr H Leihs
Managing Director: Dr H Prinz

Subsidiaries: France, West Germany, Italy, Spain, Switzerland, UK, USA

Products: Automatic door equipment with drives and electronic controls; plug-in doors for metro and long-distance coaches; micro-processors for door control.

Recent contracts have included supply of 1500 plug-in doors to the metros of Paris and Vienna; 2500 for emus of the Austrian Federal Railway (OBB); and a total of 1500 for long-distance coaches of railways in Sweden, Norway and Denmark (SJ, NSB, DSB).

IFE plug-in door fitted to Danish State Railways (DSB) Lyntog car

Insulation Equipments
Insulation Equipments Ltd

Salop Road, Oswestry, Shropshire SY11 2RR, England

Telephone: 0691 2351
Telex: 35424

Managing Director: A J Cunningham
Sales and Marketing Director: T J Calnon

Products: High-performance decorative panels and components for safety-critical environments.

The company specialises in the design and supply of prefabricated decorative linings, lightweight panel systems and bonded structures for vehicles and associated public buildings. Panels are supplied for new build, for refurbishment and prefabricated for international KD assembly. Full export sales and service facilities are available, together with ability to meet existing and anticipated international safety standards, particularly smoke emission and fire resistance (USA UMTA 'Guidelines', UK Building Regulations Class O, France M1 etc) and operators' reliability, maintainability, safety and human factor requirements under varied operating conditions. Consultancy services are available on panel design and installation techniques. Registered trade names: Melaminium and Melasteel.

Recent contracts have included provision of fire-resistant Melaminium and Melasteel lining panels for British Rail Mk III sleeping cars and multiple-unit refurbishing; London Transport D78 stock and underground station linings; Hong Kong Metro; Kowloon Canton Railway; Washington Metro; Atlanta Subway; Lisbon Metro; and Brussels Metro.

The latest developments of the company include: Melasteel decorative fire barrier panels and Melaminium decorative fire-resistant extrusion/panel systems for BR sleeping cars and other projects; Melaminium/honeycomb core self-supporting bonded structures for lightweight doors, partitions, ceilings, floors etc; and the introduction of 1.5-metre width sheet-size products in addition to 1.22-metre width, also extension of facilities to produce larger multi-formed panels to meet developing advanced design requirements.

Kismotor És-Gepgyar

Fehervari ut 44 (RB), Budapest XI, Hungary

Telephone: 452-150
Telex: 4 384

Products: Door and window gear.

Klein
Etablissements Georges Klein

36 rue Boussingault, 75013 Paris, France

Telephone: 589 58 96
Telegrams: Geoklein, Paris
Telex: 270 507

Products: Hera-type window balancing and operating devices; all types of aluminium window and automatic access controls.

Kuckuck
Kuckuck Bau Stromungstechnischer Apparate

An der Weide 39/40, Postfach 103 931, 2800 Bremen, Federal Republic of Germany

Telephone: 0421 321303
Telex: 02 44479

Products: Exhaust fans for rail vehicles and buses.

Luwa
Luwa Geratetechnik GmbH

PO Box 3609, 6000 Frankfurt am Main 1, Federal Republic of Germany

Telephone: 0611 4035 229
Telegrams: Luwa
Telex: 04-11775

Managing Director: M Freudenberg
Director, Railway Air-Conditioning: H Spannagel

Products: Air-conditioning, air-heating systems and air ventilation of all kinds.

Recent customers for the company's products include (number of equipment sets in brackets): German Federal Railway (525); German Sleeping Car Company (191); Tourist Union International (33); Airport Dusseldorf (3); Eurofima (66); International Sleeping Car Company (40); French National Railways (312); Italian State Railways (refrigerating plants) (194); Danish State Railways (33); Swedish State Railways (8); Finnish State Railways (33); Belgian National Railways (5); Iraqi Republican Railways (83); Syrian Railways (7); Tunisian National Railways (2); Iranian State Railways (483); Amtrak, USA (48); Brazil (60); Australia (26).

Roof air-conditioner, incorporating evaporators, heating battery with overheat protection and high-capacity fans with integrally-screwed filter boxes

Type KSE 9/100 combined compressor-condenser unit with overheat-proof motor embodying thermo-protection element

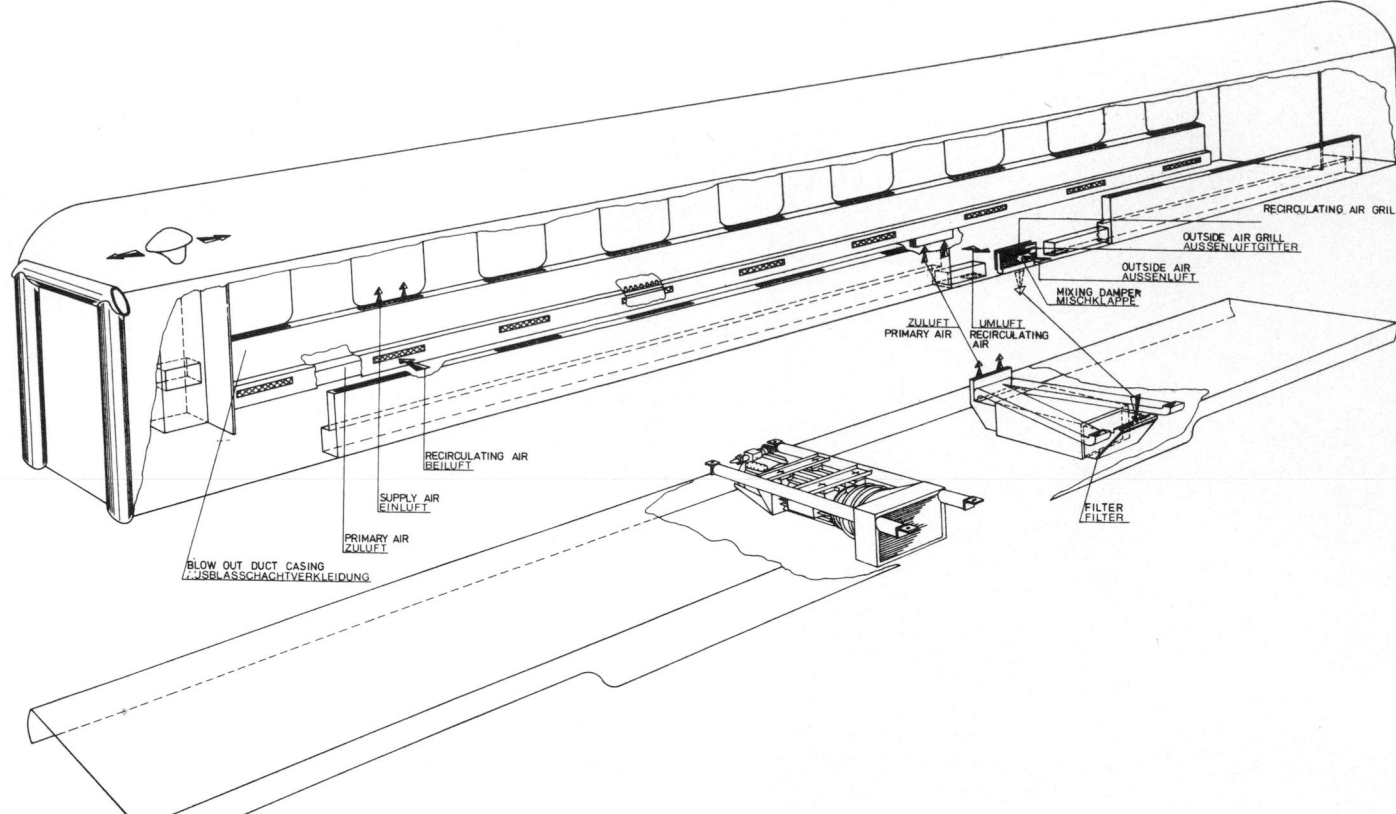

Layout of Jettair single-duct air-conditioning system

Condenser unit with refrigerant receiver and filter dryer, featuring hinged fans for easier coil cleaning

Macosa
Material y Construcçiones SA

Plaza de la Independencia 8, Madrid 1, Spain

Telephone: 222 47 87
Telegrams: Material, Madrid
Telex: 22168

Products: Sliding and plug doors, vertical sliding windows for passenger cars.

Mealstream
Mealstream (UK) Ltd
A Henshall Group Company

Manufacturing and Service Division: Fleming Way, Crawley, West Sussex, England

Telephone: 0293 546161
Telegrams: Melstam
Telex: 928460

Chairman: R MacDonald-Hall
Director: L R Mercer
Sales Manager: J Richardson

Products: Micro-aire ovens, microwave ovens, coffee-pot warmers supplied to British Rail for use in the catering vehicles of High Speed Trains and APT inter-city trains.

Middleton
Middleton Sheet Metal Co Ltd

Spring Vale Works, Middleton, Manchester M24 2HS, England

Telephone: 061-643 2462
Telegrams: Leyped, Middleton

Chairman and Chief Executive: F Pedley
Managing Director: J D Pedley
Director and Company Secretary: I Warrington

Principal subsidiaries
Middleton Welders Ltd
Aircraft Tanks Ltd
Cooper Webb Jones & Co (1967) Ltd

Products: Glycol reservoirs and louvred windows

Monogram Industries
Monogram Industries Inc
Sanitation Group

4030 Freeman Blvd, Redondo Beach, California 90278, USA

Telephone: (213) 973 0656
Telegrams: Monomatic RNDO
Telex: 69-1243

Products: On-board waste handling and sewage treatment systems; self-contained retention toilet equipment. Systems marketed world-wide include: Model 12952-001 chemical recirculating system used on French National Railways' (SNCF) RTG/TGV train-sets; Model 28000 on-board waste handling system designed for Amtrak, USA; Model 20000-001/002 centralised waste treatment system designed for Amtrak and also installed in new bi-level passenger coaches manufactured by Pullman Standard; Models 55000-002 and 15000-001 self-contained flushing toilets installed as standard production units by Amtrak, Canadian National, Swedish State Railways (SJ), Swiss Federal Railways (SBB), Finnish Railways (VR), Norwegian State Railways (NSB).

The company has recently produced two new designs of hydro-pneumatically-operated, recirculating, flushing toilet which have been adopted as standard equipment on the Amfleet II cars of Amtrak.

European office: Monogram Industries Inc, PO Box 49, 8470 De Panne, Belgium

Telephone: 058 41 38 72
Telex: 81883

Nippon Air Brake
The Nippon Air Brake Co Ltd

Sannomiya Building, Nishikan 1-12, Goko-dori 7-chome, Chuo-ku, Kobe 651, Japan

Telephone: 078 251 8101
Telex: 5622 143

Products: Door operating equipment; windshield wiper engine equipment.

Type DP-30Z door operating mechanism

Type DP-45DS door operating mechanism

Phoenix
Phoenix AG

PO Box 90 11 40, 2100 Hamburg 90, Federal Republic of Germany

Telephone: (040) 76 67 1
Telegrams: Phoenix ag
Telex: 02 17571

Products: Rubber sealing profiles for windows and doors; rubber floor coverings; air spring bellows.

Pintsch Bamag
Pintsch Bamag Antriebs- und Verkehrstechnik GmbH

Postfach 10 04 20, 4220 Dinslaken, Federal Republic of Germany

Telephone: 021 34 602-1
Telegrams: Pintsch Bamag, Dinslaken
Telex: 8551938

Products: Power supply plants, inverters for train lighting, light fittings, switchgear, electronic door controls and air-conditioning equipment.

Recent developments include a new system for the control and supervision of folding, hinged and sliding coach doors which features fault diagnosis and is adaptable to all types of car. Its salient features are: fully electronic, short-circuit-proof control with microcomputer; centralised arrangement of all functional groups in a 19-inch modular framework; closure, locking and control of all doors of a coach; identification of faults during operation and memorisation of them; indication of operational condition by means of a three-digit luminescent diode; on interrogation, indication of all faults registered in a three-second

rhythm; memorisation of up to 98 faults and irregularities in the operational procedure; routine checking of the overall system.

Advantages for the car designer include: uniform modular groups for all coach types; instantaneous adaptation to modified service conditions by simple re-programming; increased service reliability through minimisation of components; greater economy due to reduced storekeeping, simpler maintenance and low-cost repair.

PLC Peters
PLC Peters Ltd

Pasadena Close, Hayes, Middlesex UB3 3NS, England

Telephone: 01-573 6172
Telex: 934542

Chairman: Denys Randolph
Managing Director: Alan Tanner
Financial Director: Keith A Mines
Rail Division Manager: Clive Dadley

Products: Doors and door operating equipment for all types of railway operations; flushing chemical toilets; ancillary rail products. Also manufacturers of bus and coach equipment.

Recent contracts have included supply of doors and associated equipment to the Hong Kong Mass Transit Railway, Kowloon-Canton Railway, Stockholm Metro, French Railways, British Rail and London Transport; chemical toilets and servicing panels to Kowloon-Canton Railway and Victorian Railways (VicRail); automatic platform doors for the Lille Metro; and numerous orders from British PTEs and overseas operators.

Recent technical developments include a range of high-strength lightweight door leaves designed for urban trains, trams and LRVs; of bonded sandwich construction, they have cores of balsa or honeycomb. Another new product is a flushing chemical toilet, self-contained, with no discharge and simple periodic emptying and recharging procedures.

The PLC Automatic Platform Door System, designed for the Lille Metro (VAL), is a completely automatic system offering complete passenger safety and protection of an air-conditioned station environment on a railway where both trains and stations are unmanned. Positioned at the edge of the platform, the six double-leaf doors, which are normally closed, ensure the safety of passengers waiting for the train. When the train stops at the station the doors of the train line up with the platform doors and both sets of doors open simultaneously under central computer control. To allow some tolerance in the positioning of the train, the platform doors are made 300 mm wider than the train doors. After a pre-determined time interval, normally between 10 and 20 seconds, the platform doors and train doors close simultaneously. Interlock switches on both sets of doors prove that the doors are closed and locked before the train can start again.

PLC Peters door installation at Lille Metro (VAL) station

Research Products/Blankenship Corporation

2639 Andjon Drive, Dallas, Texas 75220, USA

Telephone: (214) 358 4238
Telegrams: 2639 Tx 75220
Telex: 730161

Managing Director: E Bayne Blankenship

Products: Electric incinerating toilet for diesel locomotives.

Sable
Sable Sièges Industrielles

47 rue du Pré-Saint-Gervais, 93500 Pantin, France

Telephone: 843 54 55

Products: Passenger car seating of all types for French and overseas main-line and metro systems, including equipment for French Railways TGV, Corail cars and RATP Paris Interconnexion and MI79 commuter train-sets; pneumatic driver seats for locomotive cabs; special seat studies.

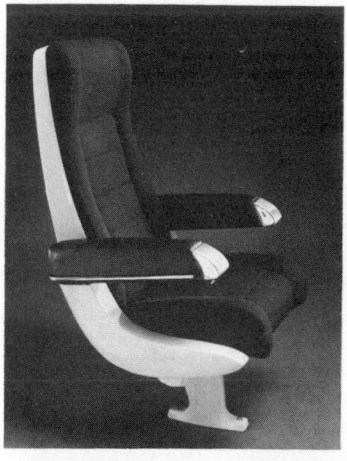

Seating by Sable

Seating by Sable

Safety Electrical Equipment
Safety Electrical Equipment Corporation

PO Box 798, Wallingford, Connecticut 06492, USA

Products: Member company of Stone International, UK, marketing the same product range.

Schaltbau

Hohenwaldeckstrasse 1, 8000 Munich 90, Federal Republic of Germany

Telephone: (098) 62 32 1
Telex: 05 23 156

Products: Heating, control and lighting equipment for passenger coaches.

SIAM
SIAM SA
Electrodomestic Division

Cnel Molinedo 1600, 1870 Avellaneda, Buenos Aires, Argentina

Telephone: 208 5421, 392 6011
Telegrams: SIAM Baires
Telex: 24181

Director: Eng Gabriel Distèfano
Commercial Manager: Alfredo Canale

Products: Absorption refrigerators and cooling units, gas/electric-operated; electric refrigerators and air-conditioners.

Socimi
Società Costruzioni Industriali Milano SpA

Head office: Via S Calimero 3, 20122 Milan, Italy

Telephone: (02) 54 65 251/5
Telex: 310331

Main works
Via E Fermi n 25, 20082 Binasco (Milan)
Telephone: (02) 9055605/6/7/8
Via Donatori del Sangue n 100, 20010 Arluno (Milan)
Telephone: (02) 9017666, 9017803

Viale Porto Torres, Reg Zentu Figghi, 07100 Sassari
Telephone: (079) 235056

Chairman: Dr Eng A Marzocco
Managing Director: Dr Eng P Sacchi
Export Sales: Dr Eng C Landolina

Products: Automatic doors.

Socimi automatic door systems on Milan metro car

Sofanor

94 rue Valériani, 59920 Quierrechain, France

Products: All types of passenger coach equipment.

Stone
Stone International Ltd

PO Box 5, Gatwick Road, Crawley, West Sussex RH10 2RN, England

Telephone: 0293 27711
Telex: 877481

Chairman: B Jenks
Marketing Director: R A Scott

Products: Air conditioning; pressure ventilation; train lighting equipment; alternators; water equipment.

Stuart Turner
Stuart Turner Ltd

Henley-on-Thames, Oxon RG9 2AD, England

Products: Pressurised water system for passenger coaches.

Tebel
Tebel Pneumatik
A member of the Alfa-Laval Group

Zwettestraat 32, Post Box 515, 8901 BH Leeuwarden, Netherlands

Telephone: 058 131323
Telex: 46045

Managing Director: A Vennis
Unit Manager: A M J Kok

Products: Air-operated swing-plug and sliding doors; windscreen wiper systems; pantograph control units; complete control units for pneumatic and electro-pneumatic systems.

Temperature
Temperature Ltd

Newport Road, Sandown, Isle of Wight, England

Telephone: 0983 402221
Telegrams: Temtur G
Telex: 86288

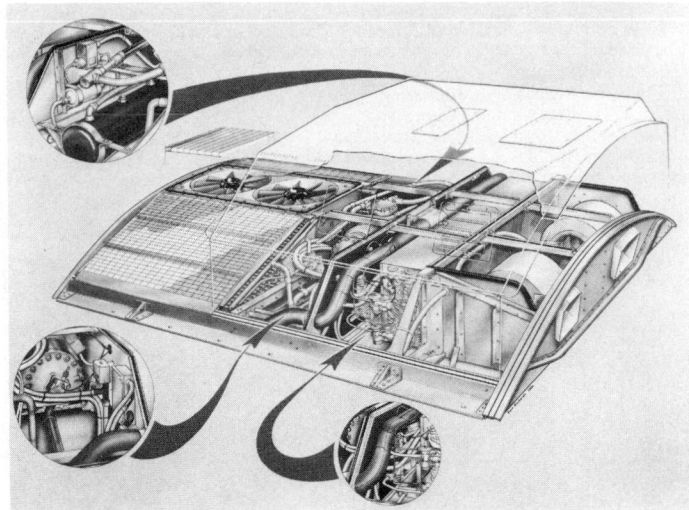

Air-conditioning unit supplied to Kowloon-Canton Railway

Products: Unit air-conditioning for all passenger stock and locomotives; heating and ventilation units for multiple-unit stock; refrigeration units for kitchen and dining cars.

Recent production has included air-conditioning units with a nominal cooling capacity of 18 kW and 6 kW of heating for British Rail's Mk III sleeping cars. These units are assembled within a rigid steel framework and mounted within the sleeping car skirt. They work in conjunction with air terminal units in each berth, where controls enable the occupants to select individual temperatures between 15 and 21°C. The air conditioners supply 2700 m³/h of conditioned air which passes through a carbon filter and sound attenuator into the main distribution ductwork of the coach. To achieve fine control of the temperature of the air off the evaporator at a constant 12°C, despite ambient variations and changes in the coach loading, the company has developed a simple but effective mechanical control system which compares favourably with the most sophisticated electronic control systems.

Toshiba
Toshiba Corporation
Transport Equipment Export Department IOPG

1-6 Uchisaiwaicho 1-chome, Chiyoda-ku, Tokyo 100, Japan

Telephone: 03 501 5411
Telegrams: Toshiba, Tokyo
Telex: 22587

Products: Air-conditioning equipment; exhaust fans; orbit fans; heaters; refrigerators; water coolers; beer coolers; lighting equipment; alternators; static GTO inverters.

About 72 000 air-conditioning units have been delivered to a number of railways, including Japanese National Railways, rapid transit systems in Tokyo, Osaka, Kobe, Nagoya, Fukuoka and Seoul, New South Wales State Rail Authority, Philippine National Railways, New Zealand Government Railways, Chilean State Railways, Korean National Railroad, Chinese People's Republic Railways and Soviet Union Railways.

Typical air-conditioners with hermetic compressors include:
RPU-1500: 4500 kcal/h, 10 m³/minute, 2 refrigerating cycles, 2.1 kW, 1240 × 930 × 400 mm, 120 kg; RPU-2200J: 8000-8500 kcal/h, 3.7 kW, 21 m³/minute, 1 cycle, 1720 × 1100 × 370 mm, 180 kg; RPU-3000J: 10 500 kcal/h, 27 m³/minute, 2 cycles, 4.6 kW, 2034 × 1100 × 346 mm, 225 kg; RPU-6000: 2000 kcal/h, 50 m³/minute, 2 cycles, 7.5 kW, 1930 × 1880 × 295 mm, 430 kg; RPU-11 000: 42 000 kcal/h, 120 m³/minute, 2 cycles, 20.6 kW, 3660 × 2000 × 5300 mm, 760 kg; split type 25 000 kcal/h unit: 25 000 kcal/h, 2 cycles, compressor condenser unit 2380 × 1180 × 630 mm, 470 kg; evaporator blower unit 920 × 1850 × 500 mm, 230 kg.

Overseas offices
North America: Houston, New York, San Francisco, Vancouver
Latin America: Bogota, Buenos Aires, Caracas, Mexico City, Rio de Janeiro, São Paulo
Europe: Athens, West Berlin, London, Vienna
Africa: Cairo, Johannesburg
Middle East: Baghdad, Dubai, Jidda, Kuwait, Tehran
South-east Asia: Bangkok, Beijing, Hong Kong, Jakarta, Manila, Taipei
Australasia: Sydney, Wellington

Toyo Denki
Toyo Denki Seizo KK

Yaesu Mitsui Building No 7-2, Yaesu 2-chome, Chuo-ku, Tokyo, Japan

Telephone: (271) 6374
Telegrams: Yohden, Tokyo
Telex: (0) 222 4666/7

Products: Door operating equipment.

Triplex
Triplex Safety Glass Co Ltd
Aircraft & Special Products Division

Eckersall Road, Kings Norton, Birmingham B38 8SR, England

Telephone: 021-458 2031
Telex: 338097

Managing Director: J W E Helliwell
Director and General Manager, Aircraft & Special Products Division: Dr R D King

Products: Design and manufacture of heated/unheated, curved/flat, framed/unframed impact-resistant transparencies for railroad and transit industries.

Among the company's latest developments are multi-laminate glass/plastic windscreen assemblies for locomotives, incorporating high impact-resistant performance, integral electrical de-icing system and fully bonded aluminium alloy frames. British Rail's APT power cars are among units which have been so equipped.

Triplex framed windscreen assembly on British Rail APT

Triplex windscreen assemblies on British Rail Class 58 freight locomotive

Triplex framed windscreen assemblies on Italian State Railways Class E633 locomotive, built by Fiat Ferroviaria Savigliano

Vapor
Vapor Corporation
Transportation Systems

6420 West Howard Street, Chicago, Illinois 60648, USA

Products: Passenger car heating and temperature controls; automatic door operating systems; dc relays; electronic speed indicators and recorders; slow-speed controls; and other locomotive accessories.

VEB
VEB Fahrzeugausrüstung Berlin
A member of VEB Kombinat Schienenfahrzeugbau and of Vereinigter Schienenfahrzeugbau der DDR eV

Andreasstrasse 71/73, 1017 East Berlin, German Democratic Republic

Telephone: 2700921
Telex: 112295

Products: Ac and dc generators; rectifiers; single and multi-voltage heating systems; single and multi-voltage transformers; control systems; oil-heating apparatus.

Exports: Schienenfahrzeuge Export-Import Volkseigener Aussenhandelsbetrieb der DDR, Otztaler Strasse 17, 1100 East Berlin

Westinghouse
Westinghouse Brakes Ltd
A subsidiary of Westinghouse Brake & Signal Co Ltd
A member of the Hawker Siddeley Group

PO Box 74, Chippenham, Wiltshire SN15 1HY, England

Telephone: 0249 654141
Telegrams: Westinghouse, Chippenham
Telex: 449411/12

Chairman: R A Willford
Managing Director: J R C Boulding
Finance Director: S R Crook
Director: E J Harris
Marketing Director: E J Widdowson

Subsidiaries
Westinghouse Brake and Signal Co (Australia) Pty Ltd
PO Box 120, PO Concord West, New South Wales 2138, Australia
Westcode Ltd
3688 Nashua Drive, Unit 'F', Mississauga, Ontario L4V 1M5, Canada
Westcode Incorporated
90 Great Valley Parkway, Great Valley Corporate Centre, Frazer, Pennsylvania 19355, USA

Associated company
Westinghouse Bellambie (Pty) Ltd
PO Box 453, Johannesburg 2000, South Africa

Products: Rail door equipment comprising electric and electro-pneumatic door operators suitable for mounting within the vehicle structure at cantrail, waist or floor levels; electric and electro-pneumatic door control systems inclusive of various interlocking features; lightweight door leaves profiled to match the vehicle bodyside; station platform edge door screens, with electro-pneumatic operated sliding doors arranged to align with the train doors and to open and close automatically.

The company supplies door equipments to rail systems world-wide including London Transport underground and surface lines, British Railways, Glasgow Underground, Tyne and Wear Metro, New Zealand Government Railways, Calcutta Metro, Seoul Subway, Southeastern Pennsylvania Transit Authority, Long Island Rail Road and Massachusetts Bay Transportation Authority.

Westinghouse bi-parting sliding plug doors fitted to Tyne and Wear Metro car

Westinghouse floor-mounted electro-pneumatic door operator as fitted to London Transport surface stock cars

Wispeco Widney
Wispeco Widney (Pty) Limited

Head office: PO Box 39094, Bramley 2018, South Africa

Telephone: (011) 786 2800
Telex: 4-24998

Main works: 35 12th Road, Kew, Johannesburg, South Africa

Chairman: S Savage
General Manager: E Rousset

Principal associate company: Faiveley (South Africa)

Products: Windows (all types), sliding hopper and double-glazed; door operating gear; doors (all types) for locomotives and passenger (suburban and mainline) rolling stock; locks and general carriage fittings.

Westinghouse waist-level-mounted electric door operator as supplied for USA

Young Windows
Young Windows Ltd

Claydon Works, Millbank Road, Wishaw ML2 0JD, Scotland

Telephone: 06983 72557
Telegrams: Windows, Wishaw
Telex: 779150

Managing Director: S H Magnus

Products: Constant balance half-drop windows; fixed windows and full drop windows.

Licensing agreements: The company has agreements with Macosa (Spain) and Sorefame (Portugal).

Young Type T41 windows installed in Norwegian State Railways (NSB) Type 69 emu passenger saloon

Yusoki Kogyo
Yusoki Kogyo KK

102 Kamihamacho, Handa, Aichi 475, Japan

Telephone: 0569 21 3311
Telex: 4563 605

Products: Door panels.

SIGNALLING, CONTROL AND TELECOMMUNICATIONS EQUIPMENT

ACEC
Ateliers de Constructions Electriques de Charleroi SA

PO Box 4, 6000 Charleroi, Belgium

Telephone: 3271 442276
Telegrams: Ventacec, Charleroi
Telex: 051 227

Products: Signal boxes; automatic block system equipment; complete level crossing equipment with operation and control of lifting barriers; centralised traffic control (CTC); automation of marshalling yards; continuous or point speed control of trains or metros; automatic braking, repeating of signals in the driver's cab.

ACI
ACI Systems Corporation

31 Dartmouth Street, Westwood, Maryland 02090, USA

Telephone: (617) 329 1980
Telex: 710 348 7593

Products: Track circuit equipment and accessories; marshalling yard equipment.

AEG-Telefunken
AEG-Telefunken Nachrichten-und Verkehrstechnik AG

Hohenzollerndamm 150, 1000 West Berlin 33, Federal Republic of Germany

Telephone: (030) 828-1
Telegrams: Elektronbahnen, Berlin
Telex: 1 85 498

Products: Signalling equipment; automatic block systems; mobile radio equipment; centralised computer-controlled traffic control; continuous automatic train control; electronic axle counters; train detection devices; process computer-controlled information display, marshalling yard equipment, control panels and desks, point machines; telecommunications, radio-telephone and data equipment.

On the German Federal Railway (DB), AEG-Telefunken equipment providing speech and data communication between trains and ground control centres constitutes the biggest non-public radio network in the world. Total cost has been DM 450 million. Austrian Federal Railways (ÖBB) and Yugoslav Railways (JZ) have adopted the AEG-Telefunken system; and so, in a modified version, has British Rail.

In this system main lines are subdivided into separate train monitoring areas, which on average are about 100 km long. The frequencies are allocated in such a way that no interference occurs at any of the borders between the various monitoring areas, not even at major railway junctions. This frequency allocation plan could be used as the future basis for an internationally adopted train radio system with frontier radio traffic.

The train radio system uses duplex communication in the 460 MHz frequency band (UIC frequency plan), with channel spacing of 25 kHz. Frequently recurring items of information for driver and control centre are transmitted as data telegrams and automatically acknowledged in both directions. Radio channel occupation is minimised by the high transmission rate of 600 bauds.

Individual items of information concerning faults and irregularities are reported as normal calls using handsets; in this case, the request or instruction to call is transmitted in code. Each traction vehicle can be addressed selectively through a maximum number of six digits. In an emergency, however, the control centre can circumvent the selective call and address all traction vehicles together in its particular monitoring area.

Radio coverage is guaranteed by a chain of wayside radio stations which are all connected in parallel to the control centre through a four-wire modulation line. Substantial benefits are gained by positioning the wayside radio stations in such a way that they guarantee continuous transition from one radio coverage area to the next.

The train radio system developed for British Rail is a voice and data radio communication system with selective calling and position code transmission, using a computer-controlled train radio control centre. Microprocessors in the traction vehicle equipment, and serial data transmission between the control units and locomotive set, make this system the most modern and advanced of its kind. The radio communication and data transmission procedures are based on the West German train radio system, but with these additional capabilities: manual or automatic (transponder principle) transmission of a four-digit position code using a second correlated data telegram; identification of any traction vehicle that sends an emergency call; reduced number of wires in the cable that connect the control units to the central equipment; use of a parallel processor with a video display in the control centre.

Operation as a whole is controlled by a dual processor system in the control centre, and by a microprocessor in the traction vehicle.

For railways with little traffic and average train speeds, AEG-Telefunken has developed a uhf/vhf train dispatching system that features exclusive use of vhf block radio to link both traction vehicles and wayside stations to the control centre. The backbone of the entire network is formed by a trackside uhf connection with a carrier frequency facility for a maximum of 72 telephone channels. One channel triggers the vhf wayside radio stations in each section while the other carrier frequency channels provide telephone and telex communication between the control centres of successive sections and other important operating points.

The vhf network in each section covers a track length of up to 150 km and comprises wayside radio stations at geographically good locations, as well as equipment for wayside stations and traction vehicles. These installations are called selectively from the control centre.

The system is engineered to the specific requirements of railway working by selective call, emergency call and subscriber disabling facilities. Simplex operation is used for radio communication. The receivers in the mobile and fixed stations work on a diversity principle so as to dispense with frequency changing within any one section.

All the wayside stations and traction vehicles employ a code call to address the control centre, where calls are stored and displayed. Further system features include a collective call enabling the control centre to address all wayside stations, as well as direct subscriber-to-subscriber communication through the control centre.

Remote control of more than one diesel shunter is possible with AEG-Telefunken portable transmitter

RZU system for production of operational graphic display by AEF 80-20 processor sifting train movement data transmitted by microcomputers at signal, point and track circuit locations

DATENFUNK-TERMINAL system developed in conjunction with German Federal Railway (DB) for direct two-way communication between portable data station and central data processing complex

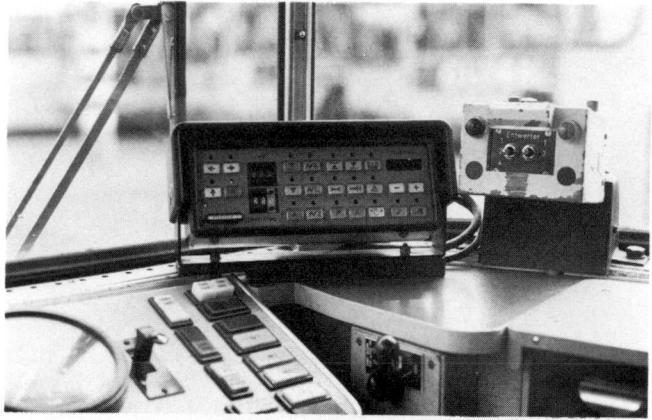

TELETRANS computer-aided traffic control system for local public transport operation combining radio-telephonic communication with data processing and storage, as fitted in Würzburg tram

Amsterdam Metro control centre equipped for fully automated operation at a cost of DM 40 million by AEG-Telefunken

AEG-Telefunken vdu displays in Ruhrkohle AG mining and port rail network traffic control centre

Algemene Sein Industrie
Algemene Sein Industrie BV
GRS—Standard Electric

Head office: Croeselaan 28, 3521 CB Utrecht, Netherlands

Telephone: (030) 94 26 46
Telegrams: Genrasig, Utrecht
Telex: 47455

Parent companies: General Railway Signal Co, Rochester, New York, USA
Nederlandsche Standard Electric Mij BV, The Hague

Manager: P J A van Dyk

Products: Power and block signalling apparatus; electrical indicating and train describer equipment; track circuit apparatus and accessories; level crossing barriers and warning signals; automatic train control and train stops; centralised traffic and remote control systems (including radio control of locomotives); marshalling yard equipment and retarders; computerised traffic control systems, etc.

Alkmaar
Nederlandse Machinefabriek Alkmaar

PO Box 50, 1800 AB Alkmaar, Netherlands

Telephone: 072 127070
Telegrams: Nemal
Telex: 57213

Director: A G J Lucassen

Products: Level crossing protection; flashing light installations; light signals; electric point machines; electric point detectors; electric point blocks.

Alsthom-Atlantique
Société Générale de Constructions Electriques et Mécaniques Alsthom
Signalling Department

Transport Division, Signalling Department, 25 rue des Bateliers, 93403 Saint-Ouen, France

Telephone: 257 12 34
Telegrams: Alsthomsig
Telex: 290.317

Managing Director: Francis Hornvilleur
Sales Director: S Dryll

Products: Point machines ac and dc; luminous signals; all types of track circuit, particularly jointless track circuits for railways and metros; manual block system; automatic block system (single- or double-track) wireless type; electric level crossing equipments with half-barriers (two or four) and signals; electric signalling systems for all stations (individual or route type); entrance-exit type with or without presetting; remote control for signalling installations; electric parking mechanism.

Ansaldo
Ansaldo Trasporti SpA

Head office: Via Nuova delle Brecce 260, 80147 Naples, Italy

Telephone: 081 7810111
Telex: 710131

Signalling Department: Via N Lorenzi 8, 16152 Genoa

Telephone: 010 41051
Telex: 270098

Chairman: Gio Batta Clavarino
Managing Director: Davide Panzeri
Commercial Director: Vincenzo Magri
Technical Director: Carlo Rizzi

Products: Power signalling apparatus; geographic relay interlocking; automatic block system; electronic track circuit and continuous cab signalling equipment; microcomputer-based automatic train operation apparatus; remote control equipments; CTC; train describer and automatic line supervision systems; level crossing automation; traffic control systems for industrial railways.

All-relay interlocking for Rome Metro's Ottaviano station by Ansaldo

Relay panel of automatic block installation at Pompei station, Italy

Connection cables for automatic block from field and Ansaldo 'Staticode' apparatus for supply, transmission, reception and decoding of track circuit currents at Pompei

Antenna Specialists
Antenna Specialists Co

Head office: 12435 Euclid Avenue, Cleveland, Ohio 44106, USA

Telephone: (216) 791 7878
Telex: 98 0732

Products: Two-way communications systems; personal security devices.

AS&I
American Sign & Indicator Corporation

PO Box 2727, 2310 Fancher Way, Spokane, Washington 99220, USA

Telephone: (509) 535 4101
TWX: 510-773-1839

Marketing Manager: John R Hebner

Products: Information display systems.
 The Mark 411 controller and Unex display combine is an advanced passenger information system which can be used for travel information or internal and external communications. The 411 keyboard controller uses a simplified command system, which enables the operator to control and monitor the entire system, creating new messages and directing them to any board in the system. This allows easy, one-time alterations should need arise. Schedules which are continually repeated can be stored, and messages can be copied, amended, erased or made to roll up. At any time the operator can inspect and edit the file. In addition, the multi-lingual system is capable of displaying several different languages simultaneously. Basic information in any language is fed into the system, where it is stored for recall and display at any time. The display's backlighting makes the face easily readable in indoor light. The ability to display messages in reverse for impact, and the addition of colour sleeves for highlighting, add to the system's versatility.
 Custom-designed for each installation, the easily expandable, modular construction enables the system to be utilised in any area, in any capacity. The entire display, which includes the drive electronics and illumination, is enclosed in an aluminium cabinet for easy installation. These modular cabinets are entirely self-supporting and can be stacked either vertically or horizontally to the required configuration.
 The company's Smart Sign is a light emitting diode (led) message display system, and is the latest addition to its electronic information systems. It is available in formats to meet the needs of any size facility, and can be expanded as needed to display different messages simultaneously on up to 96 different signs by giving instructions to one master unit. The Smart Sign has 12 display modes. Instructions are received and messages fed in through the touch keyboard. Edit functions and display options are activated by various key combinations. A mini-cassette is available for building up a library of messages, and a graphic wand enables the use of creative designs, special effects and stylistic lettering. The unit features 768 high intensity, bright red leds arranged in an 8 × 96 matrix. Tinted Plexiglas covers the led matrix for maximum readability.
 The company's recent contracts have included a Unex installation at British Rail's Manchester Piccadilly station.

Smart Sign light emitting diode message display

Autophon
Sales Management and International Sales Division

Steinstrasse 21, 8036 Zurich, Switzerland

Telephone: 01 35 85 35
Telex: 53838

Products: The company markets four basic radio communication systems: the Suba, designed for branch-line operations; the Palyma, adopted by French National Railways (SNCF), for main lines requiring practically total radio coverage; the Safra, developed for main lines with high traffic density; radio communication for shunting operations. In addition, Autophon supplies the Informatic display system for station platforms.

Bayly Engineering
Bayly Engineering Ltd

167 Hunt Street, Ajax, Ontario L1S 1P6, Canada

Products: 12 channel open wire carrier system (J Carrier); 12 channel open wire carrier system (CCITT); open wire line terminal T3-O; stackable, single channel carrier type 640; wayside radio control type 5260; party line signalling systems; remote radio control type 7772; radio telephone interface, BRT-500; in-band remote control type 5025/5026; radio transfer panel type 7710; DTMF test set TTS-01.

BBC-Sécheron
BBC-Sécheron AG
A member of the Brown Boveri Group

Postfach 40, 1211 Geneva 21, Switzerland

Telephone: (022) 32 67 50
Telex: 22 130

Products: Linear transmission of information between track and train and vice-versa; radio remote control of shunting locomotives; automatic monitoring and braking control of traction vehicles; speed control to set reference value; automatic fixed-point braking; stored running programme; radio telephone systems.

The company's recent developments include an automatic device enabling accurate braking of metro and rapid transit cars in stations, guaranteeing stops within a margin of ±0.3 metre with rolling stock of modern design. The device ensures not only accuracy but guarantees short braking time. In addition, due to its integral deceleration control system, the device reduces slide risks, as well as rolling stock wear. It can be adapted to existing vehicles. The device comprises two permanent track magnets located close to the reference stop point, eg at 130 and 30 metres where station engagement speed is 52 km/h. The second track magnet at 30 metres synchronises the computer and thus eliminates measuring errors due to sliding. The illustration shows the operating principle. When the magnet sensor CB passes over the first track magnet B, the distance counter CE starts and integrates the pulses generated by a magnetic sensor. The distance measurement operates a function generator GF, which elaborates the speed reference V_0. The function thus generated must be a parabola, so that the deceleration is constant. This parabola, determined by the braking rate of the vehicles, corresponds to a given deceleration (for instance 0.9 m/s²). It can easily be varied if the braking rate is changed later on. The pulses of the magnetic sensor drive an electronic tachometer T, the output of which gives the actual speed V. The latter is compared with the set value V_0 supplied by the function generator GF and generates a logic signal which influences the vehicle braking system.

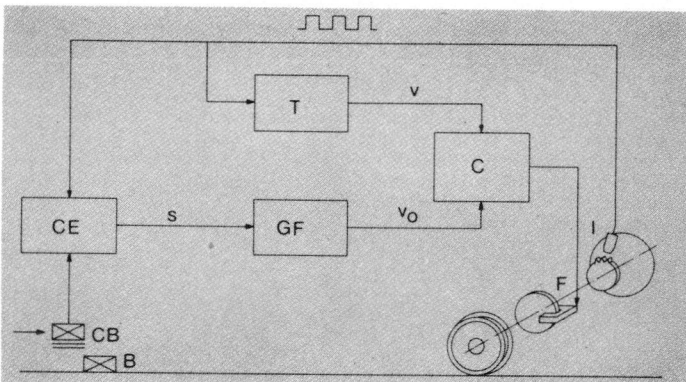

BBC-Sécheron automatic fixed point braking device for metro and rapid transit trains (**S**) distance travelled (**V**) actual speed (**V₀**) calculated set speed (**B**) track magnet (**C**) comparator (**CB**) magnet sensor (**CE**) distance counter (**F**) disc brake (**GF**) function generator (**I**) pulse counter (magnetic sensor) (**T**) electronic tachometer

BG Checo
BG Checo International Limited

110 Cremazie Blvd, West Montreal, Quebec H2P 1H6, Canada

Telephone: (514) 382 3030
Telex: 05-827615

Main works, Transtec Division: 5845 Couture Blvd, Montreal, Quebec H1P 1A8

Telephone: (514) 324 7900
Telegrams: Checo Mfg
Telex: 05-828680

President, Chief Executive Officer: F H Ernst
Executive Vice-President, Chief Operating Officer: J Corej
Vice-President, Electrical and Electronic Systems: P M Bradley
General Manager, Marketing, Electrical and Electronic Systems: W Seline
Director, Transtec Division: R Serfaty
Marketing Manager, Signalling and Train Control, Transtec Division: P Moscovici

Products: For railway signalling: survey engineering, case wiring, field installation, turnkey systems, automatic train control, wayside signalling and crossing protection systems.

Recent major contracts include the supply of automatic train control using Jeumont-Schneider technology for the Montreal Metro (Montreal Transit Bureau).

Recent products include the ACSA system, a speech synthesizer-based system for automatic in-car station announcements. ACSA-1 can provide the following information to the passengers: approaching station announcement; special station announcement; special door-opening announcements; special prerecorded on-board announcements; interchangeable message with a local interest; electronic chime for door opening and closing. The presence of the train is detected at a predetermined distance from the station, dependent on the length of the message. When the train is present, a message is transmitted to the train, which receives it and retransmits it to the passengers. The message received by the train is amplified. ACSA-1 can be equipped with a new sound system including noise sensors for improved sound quality. The equipment for message storage, selection and transmission is installed wayside in the station; the car has only a simple receiving and amplifying equipment. Power input for the station equipment is 110-220 volts ac or optionally 12-24 volts dc; the on-train equipment is adaptable to any voltage.

BICC
BICC Ltd
Formerly British Insulated Callender's Cables

21 Bloomsbury Street, London WC1B 3QN, England

Telephone: 01-637 1300
Telegrams: Bicalbest, London
Telex: 6 28811

Chairman: Sir Raymond Pennock
Executive Deputy Chairman: H G De Ville
Executive Directors: J Banks
          D H Booth
          D I Hinton
          D A Holland
          H L Jefferies
          M F Julien
          Dr D R Stewart

Products: Communication cables of all types.

British Relay Electronics
British Relay Electronics Ltd

41 Streatham High Road, London SW16 1EP, England

Telephone: 01-677 2511
Telex: 8811268

Products: Closed-circuit television systems.

Budavox
Budavox Telecommunication Foreign Trading Co Ltd

Tanács korut 3/a, POB 267, 1392 Budapest, Hungary

Telephone: 215-910
Telegrams: Budavox, Budapest
Telex: 22-5077

Managing Director: Dr László Gárdos
Directors: József Bankó
          Dr Tamas Németh

Products: Telecommunications equipment such as dispatcher-type electronic centralised telephone exchanges, data teleprocessing equipment, vhf radiotelephones etc.

Canadian General Electric
Canadian General Electric Co Ltd

Head office: PO Box 417, Commerce Court North, Toronto, Ontario M5L W2, Canada

Works: 107 Park Street North, Peterborough, Ontario K9J 7B5

International Sales Office: 1900 Eglinton Avenue East, Scarborough, Ontario M1L 2M1

Products: Automatic train control and train stops.

Carrier-Kheops
Carrier-Kheops SA

12 villa d'Este, Tour Atlas, 75643 Paris Cedex 13, France

Telephone: 583 90 61
Telex: 200 800

Managing Director: M Delaunay
Export Sales Director: M Courtaigne
Sales Director: C Derenemesnil

Products: Plugs and sockets for signalling equipment; on-train public address systems.

CGE
Compagnie Générale d'Electricité

Companies within the CGE Group covering telecommunication and data processing: CIT-Alcatel, Telic-Alcatel, GST-Alcatel, Sintra-Alcatel, CGA-Alcatel, Transac-Alcatel, EVR-Alcatel, SMH-Alcatel, SATAS, GSI-Alcatel, Locatel, SESA

54 rue La Boétie, 75382 Paris Cedex 08, France

Telephone: 563 1414
Telegrams: Electricite, Paris 8
Telex: 280.953

Products: Telecommunications equipment and systems.

Two CGE companies, CIT-Alcatel and Les Cables de Lyon, provided the telecommunications system for French Railways' Paris-Lyons TGV, in which a 442 km-long main cable handles all remote-control, signal, monitoring and alarm functions as well as track-to-train communication and all operational telephone and data-processing circuits.

Cimmco
Cimmco International

ECE House, 28-A Kasturba Gandhi Marg, New Delhi 110 001, India

Telephone: 44381-5
Telegrams: Cimwag
Telex: 31 3618

Products: Mechanical signalling equipment.

CIT-Alcatel
Compagnie Industrielle des Telecommunications

33 rue Emeriau, 75725 Paris Cedex 15, France

Telephone: 577 10 10
Telex: 250 927

Chairman: Ambroise Roux
Managing Director: Georges Pebereau

Products: Electronics and telecommunications equipment and systems.

Civel Construção
Civel Construção Industria Viacáo e Engenharia SA

Rua de Lapa 180, 11° e 12° Andares, Rio de Janeiro 20000, Brazil

Products: Wireless networks; transmission and distribution lines; installation of fixed and movable stations.

Clyde Engineering
Clyde Engineering Co Pty Ltd
A member of Clyde Industries Group

Factory Street, Granville, PO Box 73, New South Wales, Australia

Telephone: 682-2111
Telegrams: Clydeengco
Telex: 21647

Products: Railway signal equipment (under licence from GRS International, Rochester, New York, USA).

Cobrasma Sumaré
Cobrasma Sumare SA

Rua da Estação 523, Osasco, PO Box 969, CEP 06000 São Paulo, Brazil

Telephone: 011 801 8000
Telex: 011 33330

Products: All kinds of signalling apparatus.

Control Chief
Control Chief Corporation

PO Box 141, Bradford, Pennsylvania 16701, USA

Telephone: (814) 362 6811

President: C L Shields, Jr
Vice President, Sales: A Clark

Products: Radio remote control of overhead travelling cranes, front end loaders and switching locomotives; data telemetry links and anti-collision for overhead cranes.

CSEE
Compagnie de Signaux et d'Entreprises Electriques

Head office: 17 place Etienne Pernet, 75738 Paris Cedex 15, France

Telephone: 33 (1) 533 7444
Telex: 203926

Works: 15 avenue Archon Despérouses, 63201 Riom
ZI de Périgueux Boulazac, 24000 Périgueux
2 avenue Descartes, 92350 Le Plessis Robinson

Research Centre: Zone d'activités de Courtabeuf, avenue des Tropiques, 91400 Orsay

Associated companies: SAT, 41 rue Cantagrel, 75013 Paris
SAGEM, 6 avenue d'Iéna, 75016 Paris

Products: Mechanical and power signalling; electronic remote control and centralised traffic control systems; automatic block control; jointless track circuits; cab-signalling equipment; level crossing barriers and warning signals; automatic train stops and train control; marshalling yard equipment; hot box detectors; electronic treadles; safety relays.

The company's recent activity has included provision of signalling equipment for French Railways' Paris-Lyons LGV and, for RATP, signalling and central control installations for the Austerlitz-Porte d'Auteil and Vincennes-Neuilly lines of the Paris Metro, together with a prototype automatic driving system employing microprocessors. The company has also been active on the metros of Mexico City, Santiago, and Caracas, and on the national systems of Egypt, Cameroon, Morocco, Uganda, Tunisia, Algeria, Gabon and Argentina.

CSEE cab-signalling installation in French Railways TGV train-set

PRS console and route display (TCO) at Chatelet-les-Halles station on Paris RER Line B

Daido
Daido Signal Co, Ltd

Head office: No 20-2, 2-chome, Nakaikegami, Ohta-ku, Tokyo, Japan

Trading department: Shimomura Building, 3-3-10, Kyobashi, Chuo-ku, Tokyo 104, Japan

Telephone: 272 3101
Telegrams: Dissignalsk, Tokyo
Telex: 222 4586

President: Hiroshi Daikoji

Products: Route relay interlocking equipment, electronic interlocking equipment, electric signals, electric point machines, signal relays, track circuit equipment, presence detectors and treadles, automatic block signal equipment, tokenless block signal equipment, highway crossing signals and barriers, automatic train control equipment, automatic train stop equipment, CTC equipment, train describer, remote control systems, centralised monitoring systems and programmed route centre equipment.

Dimetronic
Dimetronic SA

Sierra Morena 28-34, Pol Industrial San Fernando, Torrejón de Ardoz, Madrid, Spain

Telephone: 675 42 12
Telex: 46638

Products: Electric signalling and interlockings; automatic train protection (ATP); automatic train operation (ATO); automatic train control (ATC); computer remote control systems; cab signalling; level crossing protection; automatic fare collection.

DML
DML Engineering Pty Ltd

PO Box 1076, 7 West Street, North Sydney, New South Wales 2060, Australia

Telephone: 92 0677
Telex: 27090

Products: Power signalling equipment including signal heads, posts and related equipment; ground frame releasing switches; equipment cupboards; relay racks; track circuit equipment; point machines; complete contract service covering design, supply, installation and commissioning of power signalling systems, CTC systems, yard signalling and industrial railway systems.

Among recent contracts is one with the State Rail Authority of New South Wales to provide power signalling and a CTC system over the 620 km of line between Maitland and Casino, encompassing 50 crossing loops. The route concerned is the NSW North Coast line, a single track from Maitland, near Newcastle, to the South Brisbane terminal in Queensland. The central office is situated at Broadmeadow near Newcastle. Facilities include:
track indication diagram with manual input keyboards to allow manual route setting;
computerised train describer system with through route-setting facilities. Signalmen can obtain system overview and detail loop diagrams on colour vdu displays together with train describer information and stored train data;
computerised automatic route-setting;
communication panels covering signal post phone circuits, maintenance circuits, omnibus circuits and other trunk circuits. A combining facility allows each operator to switch multiple circuits from all sources into a conference mode.

The controls and indications from each loop are transmitted to and from the central office by L M Ericsson telemetry equipment of Type JZA711. The basic data link for communications and signalling information is a composite communication cable consisting of a single 4.4 mm coaxial tube and eight vf pairs, buried in a one-metre deep trench for 570 km. A short section to Casino is covered by an existing pole route. The system is designed to be compatible with proposed electrification at 25 kV 50 Hz. An Ericsson transmission system Type ZAX120T, will provide 120 vf channels to cater for the communications requirements.

The system telemetry is grouped into four sections. There are alternative transmission paths over cable, microwave links and the cable transmission system so that telemetry transmission can be maintained even with several transmission link failures. As an ultimate backup each loop is equipped with a standby diesel alternator set and emergency control panel, to enable signals to be locally controlled when necessary. The system was to be completely commissioned during 1983.

Dowty
Dowty Electronics Ltd
Communications Division

419 Bridport Road, Greenford, Middlesex UB6 8UA, England

Telephone: 01-578 0081
Telex: 934512

Products: Ultra-link, a voice and data transmission system for use between power signalboxes and moving trains; this is a highly secure duplex radio system which allows instantaneous contact between signalmen and either individual trains or all trains in an area. British Rail has ordered an 'Ultra-link' system for its St Pancras power signalbox. Other products include on-train intercom and passenger address systems. The company's latest product is an on-train control and monitoring system which can control the power unit from a driving trailer, operate doors, etc, and carry out safety and maintenance monitoring.

Drallim Telecommunications
Drallim Telecommunications Ltd

Brett Drive, Bexhill-on-Sea, East Sussex TN40 2JR, England

Telephone: 0424 221144
Telegrams: Drallimind, Bexhill
Telex: 95285

Group Chairman: A W Millard
Group Managing Director: A Sedgwick
Director and General Manager: R Bedford
Marketing Manager: T Knott

Products: Pressurisation equipment for telephone cables and waveguides; microprocessor telephone network alarm monitoring systems for pressurised cables and security alarm systems.

DSI
Dansk Signal Industri A/S

Stamholmen 175, Avedore Holme, 2650 Hvidovre, Denmark

Managing Director: A Wiuff

Products: Relay interlockings; automatic block systems; level crossing signals and lifting gates.

Two new types of gate console have been recently introduced by DSI. Type JEGD 601, a further development of Type JEGD 50, provides locking of the gate mechanism in both end positions. Type JEGD 602 is similar, but has a declutching device for automatic down movement of the barrier in case of power failure.

The Type JEGD gate console has very few moving parts; consequently maintenance is reduced to a minimum. Normal operation will require only one annual inspection. All working parts are safeguarded against malfunction, corrosion and heavy wear, and all important joints are secured by spring washers and locking rings. The gate mechanism is protected by a glassfibre-reinforced polyester hood which will resist heavy blows and kicks. After loosening four fastening screws the hood can be removed to give access to all parts for inspection. The barrier is a light structure of wood or metal tubing which is destroyed by collision without damage to the gate mechanism. The link construction employed gives a smooth and steady barrier movement, and due to the reduction in speed when approaching the end positions, harmful vibrations are avoided.

The Type JEGD 601 prohibits movement of the barrier by external forces in 'up' and 'down' positions. In case of power failure the gate mechanism can be operated manually by a special spanner. Type JEGD 602 is not locked mechanically in its end positions; in case of power failure a maintenance circuit will declutch the gate mechanism and a flat spring will bring the barrier into horizontal position. The gate mechanism incorporates a friction clutch which offers protection against mechanical damage in case of attempts to obstruct the barrier movement by applying force greater than the pre-set value.

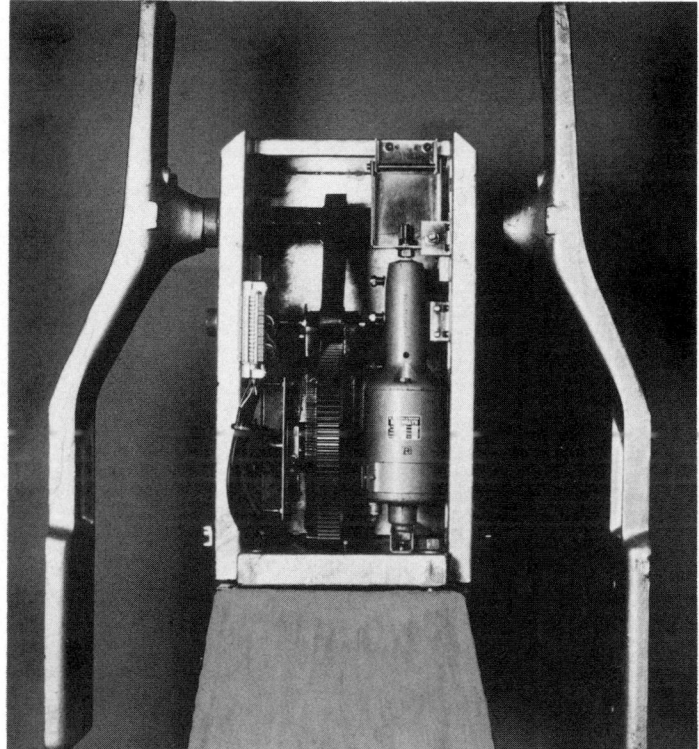

Type JEGD gate console by DSI

EFSA
EFSA

PO Box 107, avenue de Chailly 1, 1012 Lausanne, Switzerland

Telephone: (021) 32 33 53
Telex: 26278

Products: Axle counters, automatic warning systems.

Electroimpex
Electroimpex Hungarian Foreign Trading Co

PO Box 296, 1392 Budapest 5, Hungary

Telephone: 361 328 300/129 430
Telegrams: Elektro, Budapest

Products: Signalling equipment, CTC, train describers, level crossing apparatus.

Electro Pneumatic
Electro Pneumatic Corp

Corporate office and plant: PO Box 5966, 3016 Kansas Avenue, Riverside, California 92517, USA

Telephone: (800) 854 4752 (outside California)
(714) 784 0410 (inside California)

Sales, applications and field service: PO Box 1200, 204 W Kansas, Independence, Missouri 64051

Telephone: (800) 821 8510 (outside Missouri)
(816) 836 1777 (inside Missouri)

President and Chief Executive: R E Risely
Vice President and General Manager: E G Acrey

Products: Electro code bi-directional dc coded track system; electro cab 60 or 200 Hz solid state cab signal control system; highway crossing monitor, solid state Vital Timer; EPIC audio frequency track circuits; ac/dc converters for track and line applications; ac-dc track circuit for improved rusty rail shunting; solid state Stepper system for new and maintenance applications and additional electronic automatic block signalling and related apparatus.

The company's equipment is sold to and used by 32 Class I railroads in the USA. Its recent developments include Electro Code Model IIIC, developed from earlier versions of Electro Code. The all-solid state dc coded track system offers six-aspect signal control, track circuit occupancy and block indication codes; accelerated traffic reversal code is also available. It is coded at each end to control block signals without need of line circuits; fail-safe electronic circuits generate codes, transmit and receive track currents and detect codes. The system is fully bi-directional.

Electro Cab Models IIA and IIAS are wayside electronics developed from an earlier version of Electro Cab. These systems will impress coded 60 or 100 Hz energy into track circuits for detection and decoding on board locomotives where cab signals are used.

The Mini Code system is a six-control, six-indication system used between a control office and one field station; it requires dc code line.

The Electro Stepper system utilises office (OES-1) apparatus and up to 64 field station apparatus (1002) to typically transmit eight controls to and receive back 11 indications from each station; it requires a dc code line.

Electro Code IIIC dc track circuit system

Vital Timer to control electronically vital time delays in railroad signal circuits

Automatic SC-20 line battery charger

Envoys
Envoys (India) Private Ltd

A 21/23 Naraina Industrial Area, Phase-II, New Delhi 110 028, India

Telephone: 560496
Telegrams: Livewire

Products: Time-delay relays for interlockings and point motors; fail-safe flasher relays; earth leakage detectors.

Erico
Erico Products Inc

34600 Solon Road, Solon, Ohio 44139, USA

Telephone: (216) 248 0100

Vice President: R G Smith
General Manager: W E Pritts
Marketing Manager: A Weisel

Products: Power and signal bonds and track circuit connections; copper-based exothermic welding (Cadweld process).

Subsidiary companies
Brazil: Ericodo Brasil Com E Ind Ltda, Avienda Santa Marina, Nd 588-LAPA, São Paulo SP
Telephone: 263-5929/6097/7734 Telex: (011) 22410
United Kingdom: Erico Europa (GB) Ltd, 59/61 Milford Road, Reading, Berkshire
Telephone: 734 582154 Telex: 848565
Netherlands: Erico Europa BV, Jules Vernweg 75, 5015 BG Tilburg
Telephone: 013-320045 Telex: 52182
Mexico: Mexerico SA, Recursos Hidraulicos 1, Tlalnepantla Estado de Mexico
Telephone: 905 398 0033 Telex: 172644
Canada: Erico Inc, 46 Ingram Drive, Toronto, Ontario M6M 2L6
Telephone: (416) 249 3363 Telex: 06969656
France: Erico France, SARL, rue Benoit Fourneyron, PO Box 31, Zone Industrielle Sud, 42160 Andrezieux-Boutheon
Telephone: (33 77) 365656 Telex: 370074
Hong Kong: Cadweld (Asia) Ltd, 1407B Watson's Estate, North Point
Telephone: (852 5) 662611, 5-662612 Telex: 61677

Ericsson
Telefonaktiebolaget LM Ericsson

Telefonplan, 126 25 Stockholm, Sweden

Telephone: 08 719 00 00
Telegrams: Telefonbolaget, Stockholm
Telex: 174 40

Products: Design, manufacture, marketing and installation of all kinds of telecommunications systems and products including telephone telex and data communication systems, intercom systems, transmission equipment, radio communications equipment, cables, fibre optics and wires.

Signalling Systems Department

Telephone: 468 190000
Telex: 10442

Chief of Department: R Rinnan

Products: Relay and computer-based interlockings; automatic train control (ATC); automatic and tokenless block systems; level crossing protection; centralised traffic control (CTC); train describers; automatic route-setting based on computer technique; internal train control and marshalling yard equipment.

Associated companies: Member of the Ericsson group, with representatives in most countries.

F & G
Felten & Guilleaume Energietechnik GmbH

Schanzenstrasse 24, Postfach 80 50 01, 5000 Cologne 80, Federal Republic of Germany

Telephone: 0221 676-1
Telegrams: Fugenergie, Koln
Telex: 887 787-0

Products: Low and high voltage cables up to 400 kV; flexible cables; cable accessories; trolley wires; overhead transmission lines; high voltage switchboards up to 36 kV; installation of all kinds of cable systems and electrical distribution equipment.

Ferranti
Ferranti plc

Bridge House, Park Road, Gatley, Cheadle, Cheshire SK8 6HZ, England

Telephone: 061-428 3644
Telex: 666326

Products: Information displays and telecommunications equipment, computer systems.
  Recent contracts have included orders ensuing from a requirement to design and develop a communications system for London Transport. Eight systems have been installed at the northern end of the Piccadilly Line as an essential part of LTE's new computer-based signalling system. The Ferranti communication system is based on Argus 700F computer-based nodal systems interlinked by signal cables, which make use of existing underground cabling forming a double-ring configuration, running at a line speed of 9600 baud. Each nodal system connects to the local signal controller and provides for information to be transferred on to and off the ring system serially at a line speed of 1200 baud, interleaving traffic with locally generated information and removing information destined for the local controller. Other LT contracts include provision of computer-based systems to control the distribution of electrical supplies on the Central and Northern Lines.
  British Rail is installing a GTD 1000E 200-line private automatic branch exchange (PABX) in its new Westbury power signalbox. The GTD 1000E is one of a family of digital stored program controlled (SPC) PABXs, designed to serve as a private telephone exchange switching both voice and data and which can cater for up to 12 000 extensions. The system incorporates pulse code modulation (PCM) switching and state-of-the-art solid state technology. Nearly 10 000 GTD series systems have now been installed throughout the world.

Ferranti GTD 1000E digital private automatic branch exchange (PABX)

Field & Grant
Field & Grant Ltd
A member of the Adwest Group

Building 39, Pensnett Trading Estate, Kingswinfold, West Midlands DY6 7PN, England

Telephone: 0384 270171
Telegrams: Controls, Brihill
Telex: 338359

Chairman: F V Waller
Managing Director: E Jones
Chief Sales Director: B R Whiting
Production and Technical Director: K Tromans

Products: Miniature plug-in relays and plug boards to British Rail specification; shelf relays; circuit controllers; key token equipment; colour-light signals; shunt and subsidiary signals; stencil route indicators; Toton indicators.

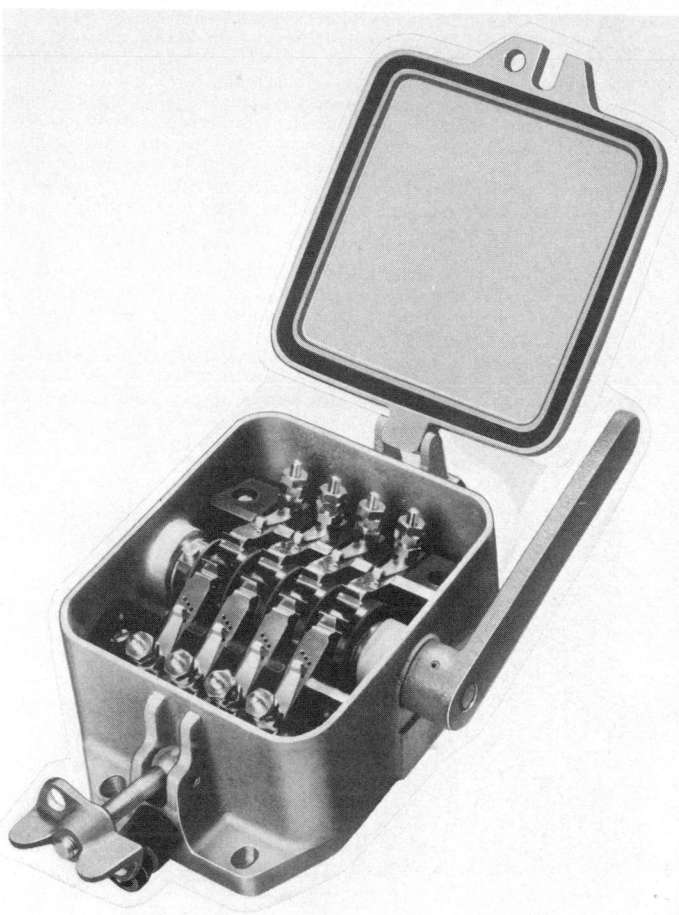

Microjust circuit controller, general-purpose low voltage unit available with two, four or six independent circuits, in aluminium casing

FreightMaster
A Halliburton Company

8600 Will Rogers Boulevard, Fort Worth, Texas 76140, USA

Telephone: (817) 293 4220
Telex: 75 8284

President: J G Stephenson
Sales Director: P D Howard
Manager, Engineering: R N Hodges

Products: Locomotive speedometer and recording system.
  The FreightMaster SDA meter system is a completely solid-state system providing locomotive crews with real-time information for better train handling; its recording capability gives managers useful operational data. Proper use of the acceleration display also helps reduce fuel consumption. Speed is displayed digitally in 0.1 mph increments. Moving forward or in reverse, it is a continuously accurate reading without 'jerkiness' or 'skipping'. Both English and metric versions are available.
  Distance is displayed by a distance counter that signals by light and buzzer when the train has travelled a measured distance. Useful on sidings, through slow orders, over hilly terrain, and in poor visibility, the reading also expedites the adjustment of throttle, dynamic and air brakes as the train passes measured distances or known landmarks. Acceleration and deceleration, displayed in mph/minute or metric units, help the engineer to detect slight grades and also to hold acceleration within safe limits and minimise drawbar forces when starting.
  The system is designed to provide reliable solid-state recordings that eliminate magnetic tape problems. Paper print-outs can be made easily from the solid-state recordings to provide location, start, stop, distance, average and maximum speed information. Thus chart-type plot of train events keyed to speed, location and time is available.

FreightMaster SDA speedometer and recorder

Frenos Calefaccion y Senales
Sociedad Española de Frenos, Calefaccion y Senales

Nicolás Fúster 2, Pinto, Madrid, Spain

Telephone: 91 6910054
Telegrams: Frenos
Telex: 46399

General Director: Nicolás Fúster
Factory Director: Agustin Lagartos

Products: Vacuum equipments; heating systems; and air brake equipments. The company has recently equipped coaches and wagons for RENFE and coaches for Madrid Metro and Barcelona.

Fresinbra
Fresinbra Industrial SA

Head office: Praia do Flamengo 200-9°, 20000 Rio de Janeiro, Brazil

Telephone: (021) 285 2233
Telegrams: Freindus

Works: Rua Lauriano Fernandes Jr 10, São Paulo, Brazil

Telephone: (011) 260 3122

Products: Railway signalling (ranging from optic signals to CTC and cab signal systems) and braking systems, under licence of Westinghouse Air Brake Co; electro-pneumatic door operating mechanism; air compressors.

Fujitsu
Fujitsu Limited

6-1, Marunouchi 2-chome, Chiyoda-ku, Tokyo, Japan

Telephone: 216 3211
Telegrams: Fujitsulimited, Tokyo
Telex: 22 833

Chairman: Taiyu Kobayashi
President: Takuma Yamamoto

Works: Kawasaki, Suzaka, Oyama, Nagano, Akashi, Minamitama, Aizu and Iwate

Related companies: Fuji Electric Co, Ltd

Products: Telephone exchange, carrier transmission and radio communication equipment; telegraph and data communication equipment; computers and data processing systems; semi-conductors and electronic components.

Futurit
Futurit Werk AG

Brambillagasse 11, 1110 Vienna, Austria

Telex: 13 3876

Products: Fibre-optics-based signalling and data systems.

GEC-General Signal
GEC-General Signal Limited

Elstree Way, Borehamwood, Hertfordshire WD6 1RX, England

Telephone: 01-953 2030
Telegrams: Railsigko, Borehamwood
Telex: 22777

Managing Director: T P Cunningham
Technical Director: J Waller
Sales Manager: W S Morton

Products: Power signalling equipment (including route relay interlocking, geographical circuitry and electro-mechanical point machines); electrical control systems; track circuit equipment and accessories; level crossing protection equipment; automatic train control; information and train describing systems; centralised traffic and remote control systems for rapid transit and personalised transit systems. As a part of turnkey projects undertakes responsibility for telecommunications systems including cab-to-control radio (free radiation, leaky feeder and/or carrier wave), special secure telephone systems, CCTV, long-line PA, clock-systems etc.
   Current contracts at the end of 1982 included:
Southern Region, British Rail (BR): Resignalling of Victoria section of London-Brighton line; and Victoria train information system;
London Midland Region, BR: Euston-Rugby train information system;
Eastern Region, BR: Anglia resignalling scheme, Cambridge and Colchester sections, together with train information systems and automatic train reporting system, Liverpool Street to Shenfield;
West Midlands County Council: As member of People Mover Group, provision of control and communication system for the advanced Maglev passenger transit shuttle, using active magnetic levitation for vehicle support and guidance, for transit line between the new air terminal at Birmingham Airport and the Birmingham International station and National Exhibition Centre;
RFFSA Brazil: Resignalling of São Paulo branch line from Pombal to Pinheirinho, including integrated CTC in association with a local installation contractor; also under sub-contract to GEC Transportation Projects Limited, supply of signalling system for Ferrovia do Aço from Jaceaba to Saudade, a new railway under construction.
   Recent technical developments include:
Microprocessor-based train describer using distributed processing techniques. Each function of a train describer is embodied in a separate micro-computer. Any number of these units can be joined together in a set of interconnected rings to provide train describers of varying power and complexity;
Remote control systems and panel processors built up from a family of electronic units which can be put together in different ways. The panel processor is a microprocessor-controlled system for driving panel indications, eliminating many non-vital relays;
Automatic train control. A coded continuous automatic train control system, which ensures driver obedience to lineside signal aspects and associated maximum permitted speeds, both of which are shown on cab displays and result in automatic application of the locomotive brakes where necessary. This system can be superimposed on both single or double rail-jointed track circuits and also jointless track circuits, in electrified or non-electrified areas.

GEC Information Systems
GEC Information Systems Ltd
A management company of the General Electric Company plc of England

PO Box 53, Coventry CV3 1HJ, England

Telephone: 0203 452152
Telex: 31361

Managing Director: Dr N W Horne
Technical and Marketing Director: C W H Ellis

Products: Specialists in the design, development and manufacture of integrated voice and data networks for the electronic office. Flexible and comprehensive integrated information systems conforming to international standards such as Teletex and X25 can be provided for the wide range of communications requirements of both small and large organisations. Systems are based on a wide range of products including voice and data digital switching systems (PABXs), telephones and terminals, computers, viewdata systems and terminals, word processors and local area networks (LANs).

GEC Projects
GEC Projects Rail Signal Division
A division of GEC Australia Ltd

373 Horsley Road, Milperra, New South Wales 2214, Australia

Telephone: (02) 772 0333
Telex: 20807

Products: Complete signalling systems, including CTC; power and mechanical equipment, track circuits, train describers, platform displays, level crossing equipment.

GEC Telecommunications
GEC Telecommunications Ltd
A management company of the General Electric Company plc of England

PO Box 53, Coventry CV3 1HJ, England

Telephone: 0203 452152
Telegrams: Springjack, Coventry
Telex: 31361

Managing Director: R G Reynolds
Deputy Managing Director: J M Price

Products: A comprehensive range of digital and analogue multiplex equipment together with associated optical fibre cable, coaxial cable and microwave-radio systems, all tailored to railway communication systems requirements; private telephone exchanges; telephone instruments.

Current overseas contracts include communications systems for Zimbabwe National Railways, and for the Ferrovia do Aco (Steel Railway) in Brazil. For both these contracts GEC is co-ordinating the design, supply and installation of the communications scheme. In the UK various contracts are in hand for the four Regions of British Rail covering 4 MHz fdm coaxial-line systems with multiplex equipment, 12-circuit carrier-on-cable systems, and 30-channel pcm systems. A new type of 30-channel pcm equipment is currently being manufactured for the Brighton multiple-aspect signalling scheme.

Current developments are concerned with increased complexity of railway operations, brought about by a concentration on high-density routes operating at a short headway, which demands reliable communication systems to maintain close supervision and control over long distances.

Two developments offer particular advantages: digital transmission systems, which have a significantly enhanced speech and data carrying capacity and can interface directly with digital exchanges; and optical fibre transmission systems, which are free from the effects of electrical induction from power lines, railway lines and lightning surges. Until recently optical fibre cables have had to contain copper conductors for power feeding and for supervisory circuits. Advances in the development of monomode fibre have made it possible to extend the spacing of the repeaters sufficiently to allow them, in most cases, to be housed at stations where a local power supply can be obtained. Since supervisory circuits can be carried on an inband system, the need for copper cables in optical fibre systems can be completely eliminated.

Installing GEC 4 MHz fdm coaxial line equipment at Peterborough station, British Rail

Glenayre
Glenayre Electronics Ltd

1551 Columbia Street, North Vancouver, British Columbia V7J 1A3, Canada

Telephone: (604) 980 6041
Telex: 04 352520

President: E K Deering
Manager, Transportation Systems: R J Pomeroy
Senior Vice-President: J W Chisholm

Principal subsidiary: Glenayre Electronics Inc, 12 Pacific Highway, Blaine, Washington 98230, USA

Products: Dc/dc converters for train-mounted radio and electronic equipment; radio-based data collection and monitoring systems; control heads for train

on-board mobile radio; DIGITRAC electronic train location system; RAILOCATOR electronic automatic identification of rolling stock, which employs vehicle-mounted transponders and track-based interrogator coil units and controllers; DIGITAIR, radio-based system, which monitors brake pipe pressure and other conditions at the rear of the train and provides a digital display of such data in the locomotive cab; and computerised train Location, Identification and Control (LIC) system.

The Location, Identification and Control (LIC) system is a distributed-intelligence system for tracking and controlling train movements from a central dispatch office, recently supplied to the British Columbia Railway. Digital processing equipment is used on board the locomotive and at the dispatch office. Central dispatch polls all trains and obtains complete operating data, which is used to generate an information display for the dispatcher. Train movement instructions from the dispatcher appear on a plain-language display in the locomotive cab. The train equipment provides: positive train location using DIGITRAC transponders; plain-language display in the locomotive; speed and location display in the cab; overspeed protection; built-in self-testing for safety and reliability; and high-speed communication by digital radio. The communications subsystem includes: a wayside-to-dispatcher trunk; complete radio coverage using selected trunk drop repeaters; and high-speed secure communications transactions. The central dispatch equipment features: a continuous polling cycle for train data collection; automatic selection of the radio site for train communications; automatic odometer calibration; automatic detection of damaged or missing transponders; video display of track diagram, track usage and train locations; computerised train sheets; supplementary information displays; and provision for connection to a larger host computer or computer network.

GRS
General Railway Signal Company

PO Box 600, Rochester, New York 14692, USA

Telephone: (716) 436 2020
Telegrams: Genrasig, Rochester, NY
Telex: 978317

President of GRS Company: G E Collins

Affiliates and associates
GEC-General Signal Ltd, Borehamwood, Hertfordshire, England
Algemene Sein Industrie BV, Utrecht, Netherlands
GRS Trading Corporation, Rochester, New York, USA
Representatives and licensees throughout the world

Products: Centralised traffic control; route-type interlockings; automatic block signalling; level crossing warning signals and gates; overlay track circuits; hot journal detection systems; automatic gravity marshalling yard systems; automatic train control; train stops and rapid transit control systems.

Among recent products is a new electronic, radio-powered automatic car identification (ACI) system, which is claimed to identify freight and mass transit cars moving at speeds up to 210 km/h (130 mph) with nearly 100 per cent accuracy. Its elements are a microprocessor-based interrogator, a transponder and a printer, computer or other logging device. In operation, the interrogator is mounted between the rails and sends a low-power RF signal to a transponder mounted on a moving car, which returns its coded identification signal to the interrogator for decoding and transmission to the logging device.

Also new is Trakode II, an advanced technology track circuit and signal control system for absolute permissive block and CTC territories, which eliminates wayside signal control lines and track relays. The microprocessor-based Trakode II provides increased capacity and performance through the use of six operating codes, reduces installation and operating costs, requires less rack space and provides solid-state electronic reliability. It is compatible with existing Trakode systems and can be installed easily without changing the present system design concepts. It controls wayside signals in both directions on single track and provides approach indications. Signal information and control instructions are transmitted through the rails by a slow-pulsed, dc coding format that recognises pulse-polarity and pulse-polarity sequence. The system's vital logic is relatively insensitive to variations in pulse width and spacing, in contrast to conventional time code format systems. Trakode II handles track circuit lengths of at least 16 000 feet at 10 ohms/1000 feet ballast, with longer circuits possible where circuits have higher ballast resistance. The system's case, 12 × 20 × 9 inches, can be rack- or shelf-mounted.

Among other recent products is Datatrain IV, a high-performance, microprocessor-based coding system that uses the latest technology to provide maximum flexibility and high security for systems with small-to-medium numbers of controls and indications. The system can operate over any transmission medium, including open lines, leased telephone lines, microwave, and fibre optic systems. Data rates of 50 to 1200 bits/second can be employed between the office module and several field modules. All circuitry is contained on plug-in printed circuit boards for ease of maintenance.

The Datatrain IV office module employs an 8-bit microprocessor. System functions may be selected by printed circuit board mounted switches. The module, 19 × 8¾ × 12 inches, is designed for rack mounting. All boards are accessible from the front, with input/output connectors in the rear of the chassis. Interfaces are provided for connection to processor-based office logic, such as GRS micro Traffic Master, Traffic Master II, or the GRS Genralogic 1 microprocessor. Interface to traditional relay logic circuits is optionally available.

The Datatrain IV field module consists of two printed circuit boards, which include an integrated circuit, wide temperature modem, as well as all code system logic and interfaces. The equipment is mounted in a 3½ × 19 × 16 inch rack-mounted module. The basic system handles up to 24 controls and 32 indications. Locations requiring more controls and indications can be accommodated by additional Datatrain IV modules.

GRS Type D1 and G1 colour-light signal units are moulded of rugged structural foam polycarbonate that makes them lightweight and impact- and weather-resistant. Modular in construction, the signal units can be stacked in the familiar two, three or four arrangement of the typical Type D signal. Multiple-aspects for the Type G1 signal are obtained by assembling two or three units in a triangular arrangement. The new signals are the latest in a growing line of GRS polycarbonate signals and also feature GRS optical designs in either glass or polycarbonate lenses. The Types D1 and G1 units have an integral sighting device moulded into the housing, which together with their light weight, permits easy installation. They may also replace earlier Types D and G signals because they mount on the same bracket assemblies and use the same lens accessories.

The new GRS colour-light signal Lamp Exchanger senses failure of the primary lamp in a colour-light signal unit and automatically replaces the lamp with a secondary lamp. Standard lamps are used. The focal position of the secondary lamp meets the requirements of the colour-light signal lens's system. The secondary lamp has the same lifetime rating as the primary lamp. The system, apt for both new and existing signal units, is compatible with ac or dc operation and with lamp wattages to 25 watts. The unit performs in the standard AAR environmental conditions. Transition time for lamp exchange is less than one second.

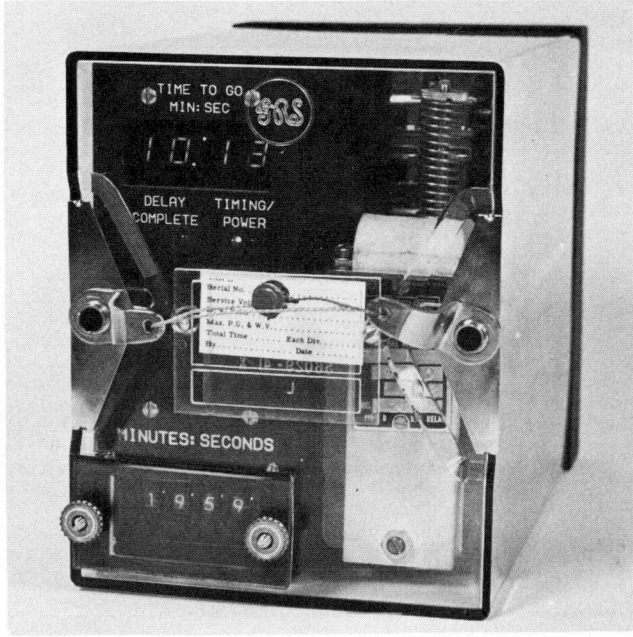

GRS Microchon Timer relay, microprocessor-based vital function timer, with integral vital relay structure electronically energised at a set time interval

GTE Lenkurt
GTE Lenkurt Inc

Dept C134, 1105 County Road, San Carlos, California 94070, USA

Telephone: (415) 595 3000
Telegrams: 910 376 4396
Telex: 348425

President: Donald O Kiser
Vice President: John A Stockford

Products: Type 9334A fibre-optic transmission system, which can be arranged by selecting appropriate plug-in modules to transmit and receive 96, 672, 1344 or 2016 pcm channels; type 914A pcm subscriber multiplex system with a variable line concentration ratio of 4:1 to 1:1 that can place up to 96 subscriber telephone lines on a single 24-channel pcm transmission line. Type 79F1 600-channel 2 GHz microwave radio system with choice of 0.25, 5 or 10-watt output power, programmable digital afc and built-in test and meter facilities; type 70F3 96-channel light-route 2 GHz microwave radio system with noise performance of 25 dBrncO or better and receiver noise figure of only 6.5 dB; type 46A3 radio multiplex system up to 2700 channels, with standard configurations including directly formed supergroup (DFSG) and direct-to-line (DTL) channel equipment; complete line of data transmission equipment.

GTE Lenkurt Type 914A pcm subscriber multiplex system

Harmon
A Division of SAB Harmon Industries Inc

R2, Box 152, Grain Valley, Missouri 64029, USA

Telephone: (816) 249 3112
Telex: 42 6398

Chief Engineer: F H Ballinger
Vice-President, Sales and Marketing: R G Clawson
International Sales Manager: B Gedda

Products: Power signalling; track circuit equipment; CTC; radio communications equipment; level crossing equipment.

Harris
Harris Corporation

Controls Division

PO Box 430, Melbourne, Florida 32901, USA

Telephone: (305) 242 4121

Chairman: Joseph A Boyd
President: John T Hartley Jr

Products: Locotrol remote control train equipment for diesel-electric locomotives. A new version of Locotrol is under development which is microprocessor-based, and which will be applicable also to electric locomotives. PROBE (programmable recording on-board evaluation) systems have recently been introduced; this is a computerised system of locomotive maintenance and train operations analysis.

RF Communications Division

1680 University Avenue, Rochester, New York 14610, USA

Telephone: (716) 244 5830
Telegrams: RF Com, Rochester NY
Telex: 978464

Vice President and General Manager: Guy Numann
Vice President, Marketing: Bruce Fennie
Vice President, International Marketing: Joe Howard
Director, National Marketing: William Cole
Vice President, Manufacturing: Robert Sturgeon
Vice President, Engineering: Joseph Hine
Director, Purchasing: Peter De Rooy

Products: Hf, vhf, uhf communications equipment and turnkey systems.

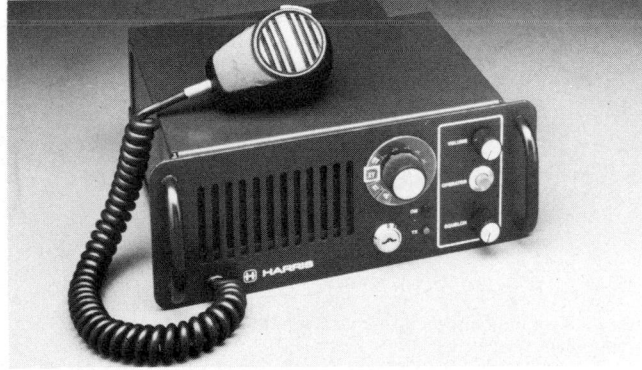

Harris Type RF-1525 vhf two-way mobile radio, 25 W, 132-174 MHz, 1-12 channels

Hasler
Hasler AG

Belperstrasse 23, 3000 Berne 14, Switzerland

Telephone: 4131 65 21 11
Telex: 32413

Group companies
Hasler Ltd, Berne
Hasler Installations Ltd, Berne
Hasler Signal Ltd, Berne
Autelca Ltd, Gümligen-Berne
Favag SA, Neuchâtel

Products: Equipment and systems for road and rail vehicles including tachographs, tachometers, remote tachometers, remaining distance recorders, electronic speed and distance measuring and recording systems for locomotives and suburban transport, electronic anti-skid systems, axlebox mileage counters.

Equipment and systems for stations and bus/tram stops including Autelca ticket vending, printing and cancelling systems, Autelca coin checking, measuring and storage systems with or without self-refilling change-return facilities, Favag precision, crystal-controlled time distribution systems, Favag public address systems for passenger announcements and service instructions, Hasler fully automatic fee-collecting systems for garages and car parks.

Communications equipment and systems for commercial and administrative applications including private branch exchanges, radio-paging systems, telex switching centres, teleprinters for automatic telex networks and for private networks, transmission systems and power supply systems, Autelca coinbox telephones.

Hasler Teloc-2000 electronic speed and distance recorder for traction units

Swiss Federal Railways (SBB) signal centre control room at Olten, showing DOMINO panoramic indication panel and control desks for keyboard-coded operation

Hitachi
Hitachi Ltd
Railway Equipment Division

Nippon Building 6-2, 2-chome, Ohtemachi, Chiyoda-ku, Tokyo 100, Japan

Telephone: (03) 270 2111
Telegrams: Hitachy, Tokyo
Telex: 22395; 22432

Products: Signalling and automatic train control equipment.

HWD
Henry Williams Limited

Dodsworth Street, Darlington, Co Durham DL1 2NJ, England

Telephone: 0325 62722
Telegrams: Williams, Darlington
Telex: 58421

Managing Director: O M Williams
Electrical Division Manager: R A Thompson
Sales Manager: L E Allen

Products: Mechanical and electronic signalling equipment; level crossing protection systems; DOMINO miniaturised control panels and mimic diagrams under licence from Integra Ltd of Zurich; Silec electro-mechanical rail treadles.

IAL
IAL Data Communications Division

Aeradio House, Hayes Road, Southall, Middlesex UB2 5NJ, England

Telephone: 01-843 2411
Telex: 24114

Products: Data communication systems, computer, security and location systems, wagon control systems.

Integra
Integra Ltd Zurich

Head office: Industriestrasse 42, 8304 Wallisellen, Switzerland
Works: Wallisellen, Vevey and Wil

Telephone: 830 16 11; 832 32 32
Telegrams: Integra, Wallisellen
Telex: 56022

President: Ing Jürg G Oehler

Products: Consulting, engineering, manufacture and installation of railway signalling and interlocking systems, centralised traffic control (CTC), electronic train describers (ATO), block equipment, last vehicle detection, automatic train control (ATC), electric switch machines and level crossing protection.
Systems offered include: DOMINO all-relay signalling schemes incorporating a packaged geographical circuit technique; RAB all-relay block systems with manual control (tokenless block) or automatic control with track circuiting, axle counting or check-out device; automatic level crossing protection with flashing lights and half-barriers; centralised traffic control (CTC) with automatic crossing loops and remote supervision of line; automatic train control, intermittent type multi-aspect ATC with or without speed control; the approach warning device (AWD) system as a simplified form of ATC; and an electronic train describer system for display of train numbers and for automatic train routing and computer-based subsystems, eg keyboard operation.

Interelec
Interelec

53 rue du Commandant Rolland, 93350 Le Bourget, France

Telephone: 838 92 06
Telex: 210 190

Chairman: Marcel Mas
General Manager: Georges Kayanakis
Marketing and Sales Manager: Jean-Michel Bouet

Principal subsidiary: IMCA, Mercaderes 37, Mexico 19 DF

Products: Electronic signalling and telecommunications, automatic control (ATP-ATO) and safety systems; fail-safe track-to-train/train-to-track transmission systems; train identification systems.
The company's recent and current contracts include metro ATC installations for 90-second headways on 12 of the Paris RATP lines, on seven lines in Mexico, and on both lines of Mexico City, Caracas, Santiago (Chile) and Rio de Janeiro respectively; and for 60-second headways on the VAL system of Lille.
Recent developments have been new ATP systems for two minute-headway operation on the metros of Lyons and Lagos. The company is also participating in the studies of ATC for the SNCF/RATP Interconnexion line of Paris.

Italtel
Società Italiana Telecommunicazioni SpA

12 Piazzale Zavattari, 20149 Milan, Italy

Telephone: 02 43881

Products: Telecommunications networks.

ITT Austria
ITT Austria GmbH

Scheydgasse 41, 1210 Vienna, Austria

Telephone: 13 222 38 00 0
Telex: 07 4579

Products: Geographic interlocking systems; automatic block; electro-hydraulic point machines; level crossing and remote control equipment.

ITT Business Systems
Data Systems Division

Works: Crowhurst Road, Hollingbury, Brighton, East Sussex BN1 8AN, England

Telephone: 0273 507111
Telegrams: Teleprinta Telex Brighton
Telex: 87 169

Chief Executive: J Ford
Marketing Director: P Benstead
Export Sales: C Buckton

Products: Remote control systems.

Jeumont-Schneider
Jeumont-Schneider SA
Division Appareillage Traction Signalisation

BP No 51, 93212 La Plaine St-Denis Cedex, France

Telephone: 33-1 820 63 73
Telegrams: Apparjeumont Paris
Telex: 620 387

Chairman: C Devin
Managing Director: Y Paris
International Sales Director: P Ricaud
Division Manager: Michel Ollict

Products: Automatic block, tokenless block, all-relay interlockings, safety relays, point machines, electronic track circuits, fail-safe data transmission axle-counter, point detectors, electromechanical and electric operation of all safety and signalling equipment, automatic train operation, CTC and remote control, telemetry systems, passenger information systems, train describer and train reporting systems.

Krauss-Maffei
Krauss-Maffei Aktiengesellschaft

Krauss-Maffei-Strasse 2, 8000 Munich 50, Federal Republic of Germany

Telephone: 089 8899551
Telegrams: Kraussmaffei, Munchenallach
Telex: 05-23 163

Products: Two-way radio specially developed for hump locomotives at Deutsche Bundesbahn's Mannheim yard.

Krone
Krone (UK) Technique Ltd

Runnings Road, Kingsditch Trading Estate, Cheltenham GL51 9NQ, England

Telephone: 0242 584900
Telex: 43350

Products: Passenger information systems, computerised or manually controlled; lineside and exchange telecommunications cabinets.

Krupp
Krupp Industrie- und Stahlbau

4100 Duisburg-Rheinhausen, Federal Republic of Germany

Products: Rail car identification systems and radio communications. Krupp offers a transmitter/receiver capable of 16 function commands for radio remote control of shunting locomotives.

Kyosan
Kyosan Electric Manufacturing Co Ltd

Head office: 4-2 Marunouchi, 3-chome, Chiyoda-ku, Tokyo, Japan

Telephone: (03) 214 8131
Telegrams: Signalkyosan, Tokyo
Telex: (222) 3178

Works: Tsurumi Factory, 29, 2-chome, Heiancho, Tsurumi-ku, Yokohama City
Osaka Factory, 12-8, Nagao kagu machi, 2 chome, Hirakata-shi, Osaka

Products: Total traffic control equipment; train describers; programmed train control equipment; relay interlocking equipment; automatic block signalling equipment; tokenless block instruments; power switch machines and relays; cab signal and cab alarm equipment; automatic train control equipment; marshalling yard computerised control equipment; car retarders; automatic route setting; highway crossing signal and crossing gates; automatic control device for diesel engine starter; ac and dc automatic voltage regulators; silicon and selenium rectifiers; power supply switching devices.

Larry McGee
Larry McGee Co

4937 Fullerton Avenue, Chicago, Illinois 60639, USA

Telephone: (312) 237 7000

President: Henry A Raczmarek
Secretary: Raymond B Woods

Products: Loudspeaker and telephone communicating systems for yards, shops, freight stations, dispatcher offices, way stations, terminals; radio control systems.

LMT
Le Materiel Telephonique

46/47 quai Alphonse Le Gallo, 92103 Boulogne-Billancourt (Hauts-de-Seine), France

Telephone: 604 81 00
Telegrams: Microphon, Paris
Telex: 20.972

Products: Electro-mechanical and electronic telephone circuit switching equipment.

Midwest
Midwest Electronic Industries, Inc

4945 W Belmont Avenue, Chicago, Illinois 60641, USA

Telephone: (312) 685 3500

Vice President, General Manager: R F Anderson
Manager, Operations: H D Vicinus
Sales Manager: C L Madonia
Director, Engineering: J E Chapman

Products: On-board communications system; public address and intercom systems. Recent contracts have included pa/ic systems for vehicles supplied to the following US rapid transit operators (main contractors in brackets): New Jersey Department of Transportation (Bombardier), Washington Metropolitan Area Transit Authority (Breda), NICTD (Sumitomo), Broad Street Subway (Nisso Iwa America), Portland Tri-Met (Bombardier) and Greater Cleveland RTA (Tokyu Car).

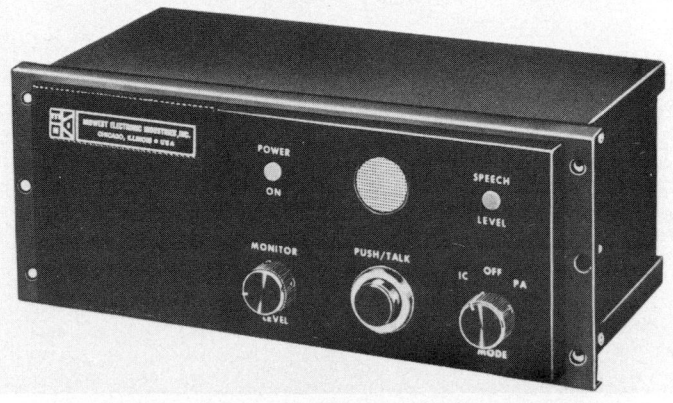

Midwest Model 330 communications control unit for locomotives or mu cars with built-in monitoring speaker, microphone, mode selector and speech-level indicator

Midwest conductor's microphone station for rapid transit cars with long-life neon lamp as visual indicator

ML Engineering
ML Engineering (Plymouth) Ltd

Estover Close, Plymouth, Devon PL6 7PU, England

Telephone: 0752 702541/702525
Telex: 45383; 45662

Chairman: J G Mobbs
Directors: G D Miller
         F G Rayers

Products: Power signalling apparatus; jointless track circuits; vital and non-vital data transmission; radio block signalling.

Modern Industries
Modern Industries Inc

101 Outer Loop, PO Box 14287, Louisville, Kentucky 40214, USA

Telephone: (502) 361 1113

Products: Power signalling, level crossing equipment; CTC; marshalling yard equipment.

Motorola
Motorola Inc
Communications Group

1301 East Algonquin Road, Schaumburg, Illinois 60196, USA

Telephone: (312) 576 7851

UK works: Armstrong Road, Daneshill East, Basingstoke, Hampshire RG24 9NN, England

Telephone: 0256 58211
Telex: 858823

Director, Manufacturing: John Dalby
Director, Distribution: Al Tingey

Products: Railway communications equipment including the Micor two-way radio now used by more than 95 US railroads and the recently introduced RSX-410 series Syntor Railroad fm two-way radio.

NEC
National Electric Control Co

1730 Elmhurst Road, Elk Grove Village, Illinois 60007, USA

Products: Wire and cable for signal, communication and locomotive use; grade level crossing gates; battery chargers for signal and communication use; cable assemblies for use with computer peripherals.

Neumann
Neumann Elektronik GmbH & Co KG

Muelheim a d Ruhr, Federal Republic of Germany

UK office: Lea Industrial Estate, 151 Lower Luton Road, Harpenden, Hertfordshire AL5 5EQ, England

Telephone: 058 27 67011
Telex: 826638

Director: D Neumann (West Germany)
Project Manager: A C Dench (UK)
Sales Manager: C C Rowlands (UK)

Products: Public address and intercom equipment, loudspeaker systems for passenger trains; multiplex remote control systems for station announcements, emergency call, control of clocks, ticket machines, etc; weatherproof and vandalproof loudspeakers and call stations; explosion-proof systems.

Nippon Signal
Nippon Signal Co Ltd

Head office: 3-1 Marunouchi, 3-chome, Chiyoda-ku, Tokyo, Japan

Telephone: (03) 212 8371
Telegrams: Signal, Tokyo
Telex: 222 2178

Works: Yono Factory, 13 1-chome, Kamikizaki, Urawa City
Utsunomiya Factory, 2-11 Hiraide Kougyo Danchi, Utsunomiya City

President: H Takeuchi
Chairman: T Hayashi
Managing Director, General Sales: T Oki
Foreign Trade Director: K Matsushima

Associated companies: Nisshin Industrial Co Ltd
Nisshin Electrical Installation Co Ltd
Nisshin Electronics Service Co Ltd

Products: Centralised traffic control (CTC); relay interlocking; automatic block signalling; level crossing signals and automatic gates; overlay track circuits; automatic train control (ATS, ATC); automatic train protection (ATP); remote control equipment (Rc); programmed route control equipment (PRC); automatic announcing system; inductive type wireless remote control equipment; electrical, electro-pneumatic point machines; various kinds of traffic control equipment; various kinds of relays for signalling; integrated traffic control system by computer (ITC), combining automated route-setting, train recording, train announcing and information display, and operational adjustment of train working.

Nokia
Nokia Engineering

PO Box 419, 00101 Helsinki 10, Finland

Telephone: 358 0 6161
Telex: 124276

Products: Telecommunications and radio equipment, level crossing equipment.

Omera
Subsidiary of TRT

49 rue Ferdinand-Berthoud, 95101 Argenteuil, France

Telephone: (3) 947 09 42
Telex: 696797

Products: Driver's alertness control equipment VACMA; automatic train approach announcer; end of train detector; time delay units NS1; remote control equipment for power substations; train indexing with automatic itinerary control.

Orlians
Orlians & Co, NV

Populierendreef 35, 2800 Mechelen, Belgium

Telephone: (015) 21 85 85
Telex: 25587

Products: Warning signals for crossing gates; signal lanterns for electric railways.

Philips
Philips Telecommunicatie Industrie BV

PO Box 32, 1200 JD Hilversum, Netherlands

Telephone: 035 899111
Telegrams: Signal, Hilversum
Telex: 43712

Managing Director: D C Geest

Products: Telecommunications (carrier, telephone and telegraph), exchanges, data systems, vehicle and train identification systems, traffic control systems.

Other products in the Philips Group

Intercommunication and public address systems	NV Philips
Fire alarm and electric clock systems	Gloeilampenfabriken, Eindhoven
Interlocking signalling systems, automatic block systems, CTC systems, wagon and train identification systems	TRT, Paris
Telemetering equipment	MBLE, Brussels

Pintsch Bamag
Pintsch Bamag Antriebs- und Verkehrstechnik GmbH

Postfach 10 04 20, 4220 Dinslaken, Federal Republic of Germany

Telephone: 0 21 34 602-1
Telegrams: Pintschbamag, Dinslaken
Telex: 8551938

Directors: Dieter Böhm
Gerhard Kummer

Products: Electrical and electronic power supply, lighting, heating and air-conditioning equipment for rail vehicles; level crossing protection equipment (hand-operated or rail-actuated) with flashlights and luminous signals, with barrier guarding and radar obstacle detection; train approach indicator for gang warning; fibre-optic luminous signal indicators; electric gas-operated infra-red and oil-fuelled circulation, compact-type point heating equipment; solid-state snow detectors; train pre-heating equipment; test sets for electrical installations on rail vehicles.

Pirelli General
Pirelli General plc

PO Box 4, Southampton, Hampshire SO9 7AE, England

Telephone: 0703 20381
Telegrams: Pigekaybel Ston
Telex: 47522

Managing Director: O F Raimondo
Divisional Manager, Power Cables: G C Turrinelli
Divisional Manager, General Cables: B L Levy
Divisional Manager, Telecom Cables: F H Penton
Buying Manager: T J Murray Cox
Chief Engineer: F R Bennett

Products: Power and telecommunications cables. Pirelli General makes a wide range of power cables, from track feeder cables to high voltage cables for track power supplies. The company has introduced low-smoke and low-toxicity reduced propagation cables for power signalling and communication purposes. The new cables, named 'Low-Smoke', were specifically designed for railway subway systems and were developed in close collaboration with London Transport. LT has been supplied with optical fibre communication cables sheathed with 'Low-Smoke' material for in-tunnel use, and with X-Flam 15 for use above ground.
Telecommunication cables for railway use include specially screened designs for use with 25 kV ac overhead systems, long distance coaxial cables and optical fibre cables.

Plessey
Plessey Controls Ltd

Sopers Lane, Poole, Dorset BH17 7ER, England

Telephone: 0202 675161
Telex: 41272

Products: Track-to-train communication for in-cab displays and automatic control systems; train-to-track communication for train location, positive train identification and wagon identification; computer-based on-train data transmission system for status monitoring, recording and evaluation; centralised control of passenger information systems; signal post and special telephone systems for use on main suburban and metro lines.

Pulse
Pulse Electronics Inc

5706 Frederick Avenue, Rockville, Maryland 20852, USA

Telephone: (301) 881 1612
Telex: TZB3840

President: Emilio A Fernandez
Vice-President: Angel P Bezos

Products: Research, development and design of electronic equipment for the railway and transit industry including, but not limited to, speed indicating and locomotive event recording equipment. Pulse Electronics has also developed an engineman alertness device, Train Sentry, which issues an automatic train stop if the engineer is disabled in any way and unable to respond. The company is supplying equipment to most major railroads in the US as well as to those of Canada, Mexico and South Africa.

The solid-state Pulse Locomotive Data Recorder, which works off existing sensing points in a locomotive, uses a closed-loop magnetic tape cartridge of computer-grade material, but of similar physical dimensions to a standard 8-track audio cartridge. Old data is continuously self-erased when recording, and the instrument will record continuously for up to 48 hours. Depending on model, it will produce a range of event data from speed, distance, elapsed time and traction motor current to such items as brake pipe reductions and reverser movement. Playback equipment supplied by the company includes a portable unit and a playback-duplicator unit for interfacing with the microprocessor-based Data Pack Scanner, which will generate reports for mechanical and operating departments.

The Pulse speedometer embodies a calibrator so that it can be set for a different wheel within 2 minutes; it is also compatible with most electrical axle drives.

Ripper
Ripper Systems
Division of Dowty Electronics Ltd

281-283 Bedford Road, Kempston, Bedfordshire MK42 8QB, England

Telephone: 0234 854080
Telegrams: Ripper, Bedford
Telex: 825072

Directors: K A Homewood
    M J Hyslop
    R A Ripper

Products: Data, control, monitoring and voice communication systems for mobile and static railway applications. The company designs and builds to customers' specific requirements or can offer a standard range of equipment, for main-line, rapid transit surface and underground rail services. Typical products are: driver-to-guard telephone links; conductor-to-passenger public address systems; driver-to-control speech and data systems; synthesized voice broadcasting and emergency alarm units; remote engine control systems.

Robot
Robot Industries Inc

7041 Orchard Street, Dearborn, Michigan 48126, USA

Telephone: (313) 846 2623

Chairman: F J O'Such
President: K Krake

Products: Power signalling apparatus; level crossing gates; barriers and warning signals; centralised traffic control and remote control systems.

Safetran
Safetran Systems Corporation

Head office: 7721 National Turnpike, Louisville, Kentucky 40214, USA

Telephone: (502) 361 1691

Works: Railroad Accessories Co, Division of Safetran Systems Corporation, 7721 National Turnpike, Louisville, Kentucky 40214; 4650 Main Street, NE, Minneapolis, Minnesota 55421; Marquardt Industrial Products Co, 9271 Arrow Highway, Cucamonga, California 91730

Products: Power signalling apparatus; track equipment and accessories; level crossing gates and warning equipment; centralised traffic control equipment; mobile radio access system; centralised dispatcher radio control system; dispatcher call decoder; communications control console; yard paging systems; intercoms; speakers.

SASIB
SASIB SpA
Division of CIR SpA

Via di Corticella 87/89, 40128 Bologna, Italy

Telephone: (051) 36 04 01
Telegrams: Sasib, Bologna
Telex: 510020

General Manager: Giancarlo Vaccari
Sales Manager: Antonio Altobelli

Products: Route control electrical interlocking systems, pushbutton- or keyboard-controlled; steady and coded current automatic block; automatically-controlled level crossing protections; continuous and intermittent cab signalling and speed control; centralised traffic control (CTC); automatic car classification systems; train describer systems; train-to-wayside communication systems (TWC); electromechanical and electronic equipment for signalling installations, such as electric switch machines, dc and ac safety relays, impedance bonds, level crossing gate mechanisms and control panels with mosaic type illuminated diagrams etc.

In recent years the company has executed major contracts for Italian State Railways (FS) that include resignalling of the Milan-Venice and Bologna-Prato main lines with push-button route-setting interlockings, four-code reversible automatic block, continuous cab signalling and automatic control of level crossing gates through audio-frequency track circuits. Similar work has lately been in progress on the FS routes between Bologna and Ancona, Rome and Viterbo, and at Ciampino and Colleferro, in the case of Rome-Viterbo with the addition of CTC and axle-counter-equipped automatic block. At Milan Central SASIB is installing a push-button route-setting interlocking with keyboard control of the whole station area; similar installations are under way at Mestre and Milan Smistamento, while CTC is being provided between Avellino and Rochetta. Abroad, the company has a contract from Hellenic Railways to cover the Trithorea-Domokos line with route-setting push-button electrical interlockings, automatic block with last-vehicle detection and STC.

In the rapid transit field, SASIB has installed on Rome Metro Line A an automatic train protection (ATP) system comprising interlockings, four-code automatic block, speed control and means to safeguard door opening within platform limits; also an automatic train supervision (ATS) system consisting of computerised data transmission, train description and train graph systems with a digital train-to-wayside (TWS) communication system.

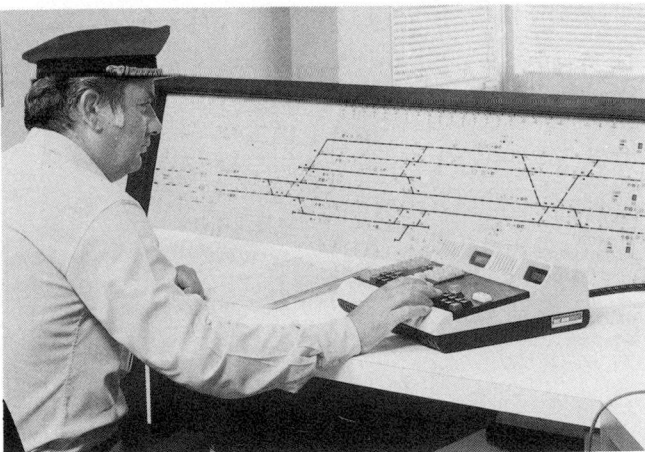

Alpha-numerical keyboard control for signalling installations by SASIB on Italian State Railways

Fibre-optic multi-aspect signal with no moving parts by SASIB

Saxby

40 rue de l'Orillon, 75011 Paris, France

Telephone: 357 65 30
Telegrams: Saxby SA, Paris
Telex: 220554

General Manager: Jacques Rey
Director, Signalling and Automation Department: André Oriol
Export Manager: Roger Barassin
Assistant Export Manager: Dominique Bastien

Products: Route relay interlocking; automatic block systems; centralised traffic control; automatic level crossing barriers; marshalling yard equipment and retarders; passenger information systems.

The company has supplied the hardware and software for the train describer and ATC system of French Railways' Paris-Lyons TGV.

Route relay interlocking panel with computerised train describers by Saxby at Sartrouville, French Railways

Scheidt
Scheidt & Bachmann GmbH

132 Breite Strasse, 4050 Mönchengladbach 2, Federal Republic of Germany

Telephone: Rheydt 4531
Telex: 0852818

Products: Power signalling apparatus; level crossing gates; barriers and warning signals; mechanical signalling equipment and accessories; automatic train control equipment and train-stops; centralised traffic control and remote control systems; automatic ticket machines.

SEL
Standard Elektrik Lorenz AG

Head office: Hellmuth-Hirth-Strasse 42, 7000 Stuttgart-Zuffenhausen, Federal Republic of Germany

Telephone: (0711) 8211
Telegrams: Stanlor, Stuttgart
Telex: 72 526-0

Works: 22 locations in Federal Republic of Germany

Associated companies: SEL has 27 associate companies outside West Germany (the name of the majority incorporating the word Standard) and utilises its association with the International Telephone and Telegraph Corporation (ITT) in providing local manufacture in many parts of the world.

Operating room of central interlocking system installed at Stuttgart Hauptbahnhof by SEL

Chief Officers: Dr H Lohr
Dr R Mecklinger
Dr G Ziechnaus

Products: Geographic relay interlocking system; computer controlled traffic control systems and continuous train control systems; electronic axle counters; automatic humping control; control panels and desks; relays; signalling equipment; switch machines; train detection devices; centralised traffic control; automatic block equipment, automatic train control; train describers and indicating systems, mobile radio equipment, cables; etc.

Control centre of Stuttgart S-Bahn network, incorporating computerised processing of data from outlying interlockings to provide forward projections and a real-time picture of train movements

SEL Canada
SEL Canada
A Division of ITT Industries of Canada Ltd

5075 Yonge Street, 8th Floor, Willowdale, Ontario M2N 6C6, Canada

Telephone: (416) 223 8611
Telex: 06-986112

General Manager: Karl U Dobler
Manager of Engineering: Walter Friesen
Sales Manager: Stuart Allen

Products: Automatic train control. SEL Canada has supplied the SELTRAC moving block train control system to Vancouver for its Advanced Light Rail Transit System, to the Toronto Transit Commission for the Scarborough Intermediate Capacity Transit System and to the Detroit downtown people mover project.

Servo
Servo Corporation of America

111 New South Road, Hicksville, New York 11802, USA

Telephone: (516) 938 9700
Telegrams: Servogram
Telex: 510 221 1872

Vice President, International Sales: W E Zwingers
Vice President, Transportation Division: W W Weeden

Products: Automatic train inspection stations, including hot box and hot wheel detectors, load profile detectors and grade crossing control systems. Recent developments include SERVOTRIM, SERVOTALK, SERVOPRINT, SERVOPROBE and SERVOSCAN.

SERVOTRIM (Servo Train Inspection Monitor) employs a memory-based data processing unit. Combined with Servo's infra-red scanners, wheel-sensing transducers, train perimeter detectors, dragging equipment sensors, hot wheel detectors and other trackside detectors, SERVOTRIM is an integrated system employing solid state digital data storage. Previously hot box detectors essentially made decisions in real time, whereas SERVOTRIM analyses train data which has been stored in digital memory. This permits the data from one journal, for example, to be compared against many factors, some of which become known only after the entire train has been scanned. With the inherent power of memory-based circuits, SERVOTRIM combines real time and post-train analysis to obtain speed and accuracy. The analysis performed by SERVOTRIM is completed within approximately one second after train passage.

SERVOTALK automatically provides immediate reports of a train passing an inspection site. Three output modes are provided: audio to drive a radio transmitter for messages to the train's crew; phone line for transmission to dispatcher's office or data centres; and ASCII code to drive a digital printer for permanent hard-copy record, for which SERVOPRINT is available. All inputs are dedicated contacts. When a train is present, direction and axle count functions are supplied by the hot box detector (HBD), as are hot box alarms. For other detectors, conditioning circuitry is supplied as required for interfacing.

SERVOTALK is a play-back only device, employing a solid state voice synthesizer. This electronic vocabulary provides a high degree of flexibility not available with a pre-recorded magnetic drum, thus allowing customised applications. The system includes many built-in switch-programmable features which can be changed by the flip of an internal switch, such as mile marker, axle count or car count, count from front or rear of train, rail 1 or 2, left or right, alarm tone duration, and the number of radio message repetitions. This switch-programmable feature allows future message changes or site relocations.

SERVOPRINT utilises a digital linear dot array printer (ASCII code) featuring a fixed thermal head. It is designed for maximum reliability and dependability; the only moving part is the paper-drive mechanism. The printer uses 5-inch heat-sensitive paper, with a paper supply that, for normal usage, will allow a full month of recording without a paper change. Printing speed is two lines per second. The unit is equipped with an audible tone alarm and a flashing red light.

SERVOPROBE train inspection verifier is designed to provide the train crew with a simple, reliable means to count cars and make bearing/wheel temperature measurements. It combines an axle or car counter and a pyrometer temperature probe in one instrument designed for left or right-handed operators. The unit is activated by extending the probe. Counting is performed by the operator as he walks the train, or as the train is slowly rolled by. When the count of the overheated bearing or wheel is reached, the probe tip is pressed firmly against one of the bolts on a roller bearing end cap assembly, or against the end of the journal on a plain bearing assembly or to the rim surface of the wheel. The 'temperature' push button is depressed and the reading is displayed on the lcd, with the reading retained even after the probe tip is removed from the surface.

SERVOSCAN HBD integrity test unit (ITU) is a new accessory system designed to be compatible with all existing SERVOSCAN HBD systems. It is used to quantitatively establish whether or not the HBD system is functioning properly. For example, the ITU can check the signal flow path from infra-red input through to alarm circuit output. The infra-red input is generated by an 'integrity heater' affixed to the inside surface of the scanner aperture blades. During a test cycle, each scanner 'sees' the radiation from the heater when the aperture blade is commanded to move into the field of view of the sensor. The processed heat signals must then initiate operation of the alarm system in order to obtain a 'system operational' indication. The test status can then be indicated on a recorder, trackside display board, talker, or any other commonly-used display device, in the field or in the dispatcher's office.

SICE
Sociedad Iberica de Construcciones Electricas

Head office: Zurbano 14, Madrid, Spain

Works: Poligono Industrial de Coslado, Madrid

Telephone: 672 15 12
Telex: 45030

Chairman: Juan Ignacio Trillo
Managing Director: Ismael Olea
Sales Director: Mateo Avellan

Products: Mechanical, power and block signalling apparatus; electrical indicating and train describing equipment; track circuit equipment; level crossing barriers and warning signals; automatic train control and train stops; centralised traffic control and remote control systems.

Siemens
Siemens AG
Railway Signalling Division

Ackerstrasse 22, 3300 Braunschweig, Federal Republic of Germany

Telephone: (0531) 706 1
Telegrams: Stellwerk, Braunschweig
Telex: 952 495

Chairman, Supervisory Board: Bernhard Plettner
Chairman, Management Board: Karlheinz Kaske
General Manager of Railway Signalling Division: Hans Kopp
Chief Sales Manager: Joachim Rempka

Products: Power signalling (all-relay interlocking); geographical circuitry (Spoorplan) interlockings; block systems; ac and dc track circuits; jointless AF track circuits; axle counters; electric point machines; colour-light signals; level crossing protection systems with lifting barriers and warning signals; centralised traffic control (CTC); computerised traffic and operational control; train describer systems; automatic vehicle identification for control and supervisory purposes; automatic train control (ATC), continuous automatic train control (CATC) for long-distance and rapid transit systems; marshalling yard automation equipment, retarders and retarder control.

By means of the geographical-type Siemens modular interlocking system MIS 801, interlockings of varying sizes, layouts and signalling requirements can be built up. To each route, signal and set of points is assigned a particular relay unit and these units are interconnected according to the track layout. For switching purposes, the K50 relay is used which, together with a new circuitry concept, guarantees the safety and reliability of the interlocking system. New design and manufacturing principles and new materials have created an improved package. Two or three-row relay units of the 19-inch format are mounted on racks above which are area grids supporting the interconnecting cables.

A feature of the Siemens electric point machine S 90 with internal locking is above-average efficiency which enables larger control distances to be covered and conductor cross sections to be lower than those of previous designs. Available in a trailable and non-trailable version, it is specially suited for modern point layouts with higher throwing resistance. The trailable version provides a smooth points movement independent of vehicle speed. A cast iron housing accommodates the motor; the rotating ball spindle drive, with clutch to limit transmission force; retention clutch with locking gear; throw bars, lock bar, detection slides and the switch contact system. A wide selection of driving motors for dc and ac (single-phase or three-phase) voltages is available.

The microcomputer system MES 80 has been developed by Siemens especially for use under difficult environmental conditions, such as on railways. It is insensitive to vibration, air contamination and aggressive steam, and operates safely in the temperature range of -40 to $+85°C$.

The microcomputer system SIMIS specially combines the functional units of the MES 80 with fail-safe operating hardware, so that whatever the error, a switch-off prevents further commands which might damage or prejudice the process control. With the SIMIS system, fail-safe data processing is possible in operations which require supreme safety, such as control and supervisory operations in railway signalling or in energy supply systems.

The Siemens microcomputer-controlled automatic train describer system displays six-digit train numbers on seven-segment gas-discharge displays. The displays have a low heat generation, are sturdy and can be easily inserted in the track diagrams.

The Siemens ZUB 100 automatic train control system features an intermittent transmission of wayside data to the train and a continuous monitoring of performance. Signal aspects and locations of speed reduction are transmitted by inductive coupling of transmitting and receiving coils. Using this data together with the relevant vehicle data, eg brake characteristics, the on-board microprocessor continuously calculates the maximum permissible speed, which is displayed to the driver and also is used for supervision of train performance. Excess of the maximum permissible speed leads to an automatic brake application. When the train passes a stop signal, it is automatically halted by the emergency brake. Dual transmission with data and supervisory circuits ascertain the necessary transmission safety. The design of the on-board microcomputer allows a highly flexible adaptation to be made to existing signal and operation systems.

Hofmannstrasse 51, 8000 Munich 70, Federal Republic of Germany

Telephone: 089 722 1
Telex: 5288 0

Products: Telecommunications equipment.

Siemens MIS 801 modular interlocking relay units

Modules of Siemens SIMIS microcomputer

Siemens Type S90 electric point machine with cover removed

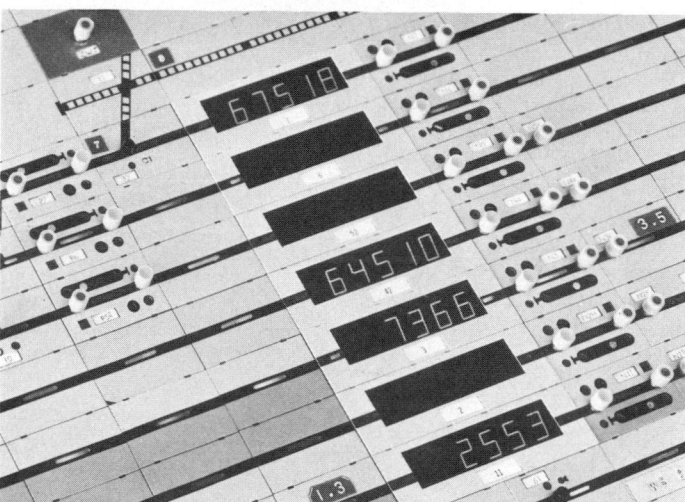

Six-digit signalling panel displays of Siemens microcomputer-controlled train describer system

Transmitting and receiving coils of Siemens ZUB100 train control system

Silec
Société Industrielle de Liaisons Electriques

69 rue Ampère, 75017 Paris, France

Telephone: 267 20 60
Telex: 280748

Chairman: C Barberot
Managing Director: J P Malaquin
Sales Director: J Fiaud

Products: Electro-mechanical treadles, safety relays, track-to-train transmission systems, on-board signal repetition devices, dead-man's handle, solid-state talking units, processing units.

The Cautor Series 69 electro-mechanical treadle will sense the passage of a train or a single vehicle travelling at speeds up to 260 km/h (the Cautor Series 82 serves for speeds up to 160 km/h) and can be used to control all functions affected by the passage of the train on the track, eg level crossing gates and lights, signals, lighting of signals and stations on the approach of the train, control of points in marshalling, and axle counting. The principle of operation is that, inside a cast iron housing, a torsion bar in high-tensile stainless steel absorbs the energy produced by the shock of the wheel on the arm and controls the reversal of electric contacts. The spring-activated return of the arm is delayed by a hydraulic damper. This ensures an adequate period of closure of the contacts whatever the time-constant of the circuits controlled, and prevents unnecessary hammering by all wheels of a passing train. Timing of the damper is adjustable continuously from 0 to 13 seconds by turning a screw. Installation is by means of a cushioned, flexible supporting iron fitting which grips the shoe of the rail. Working temperature is from −30 to +70°C, working life over 500 000 operations.

The Silec Forfex treadle has two actuating arms each of which operates its own independent contacts by means of a spring-loaded escapement mechanism. The first arm to be operated inhibits the switching action of the other arm, making the device direction sensitive.

The ground-mounted Silec frequency beacon effects transmission from the ground of simple or coded information intended to attract attention to a fixed operational feature, such as repetition of wayside signal, automatic stop, speed restriction, electronic selection of platform or step height, pantograph switching, radio channel switching, or any information helpful to driving or speed control. The essential feature of the beacon is a powerful permanent magnet with which is associated a loop. This loop is activated by an amplifier controlled by an information code generator. The code generator combines one or more of three fundamental frequencies, 15.36, 19.2 and 25.6 kHz, with the magnetic field transmission of the permanent magnet which provides for the transmission of up to 14 different codes. Transmission is ensured within a speed range of 0 to 280 km/h. Length of line between beacon and transmitter unit can be up to 1500 metres of twin telephone cable and working temperature is −30 to +70°C.

Signals from beacons are detected by the Silec information sensor. In this a local magnetic field saturates a bobbin whose poles are submitted to the influence of the magnetic field of the beacon in passing. When the magnetic field of the beacon magnet is in the right direction, that of the sensor is opposed. This leads to de-saturation of the bobbin, which is connected in the reaction circuit of a low-frequency oscillator. Under these conditions the oscillator cuts out. Thus the presence of the beacon magnetic field cancels the signal in the active region of the beacon. In the same way, an aerial connected to the sensor receives frequency signals transmitted at times by the beacon. After amplification and decoding of these signals in a processing unit they are fed to the train-borne automatic devices for control of emergency braking, activation of the speed indicator unit, control of sound warning signals etc. The transmission is ensured within a speed range of 0 to 280 km/h and the instrument is insensitive to interference from choppers.

Silec Cautor Series 69 electro-mechanical detector

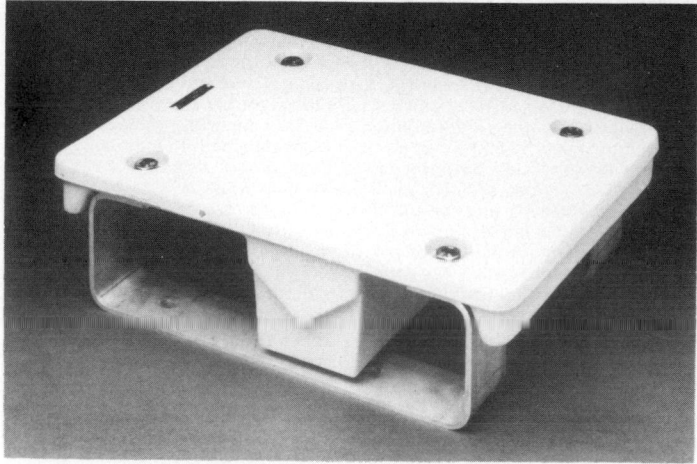

Silec frequency beacon for installation between or outside rails

Silec information sensor for vehicle mounting on bogie or below body

On-train microprocessor unit employed in SRT's L10000 ATC system

Sisembra
Sisembra Enghenaria SA

Rua Visconde Silva 38, Botofago 20000, Rio de Janeiro, Brazil

Telephone: 010 5521
Telex: 2867022

Products: Signalling equipment.

Socader
Société de Construction d'Appareils de Voie de Dietrich et Rodange

2 rue de Léningrad, 75008 Paris, France

Telephone: 293 56 10
Telex: 641217

Products: Mechanical switch locking devices; switch position command and control devices; rail insulation equipment; electrical signalling systems.

Solari
Solari & C Udine SpA

Via Gino Pieri 29, Udine, Italy

Telephone: 0432 43241
Telegrams: Solariudine
Telex: 450155

General Manager: Ing Andrea Oddi
Director, Marketing and Contracts: J W N Medlam
Director, Sales Systems: E Tosolino

Subsidiary company: Solari America Inc, 600 Madison Avenue, New York, New York 10022, USA

Products: Passenger and staff information display systems; master and slave clocks; automatic announcement systems.
   Recent contracts have covered the complete re-equipment of Florence and Salerno stations in Italy under a contract worth L900 million, and a new system for Sofia station, Bulgaria, at a contract price of US$ 200 000. The continuing Fr 54 million turnkey contract with French Railways (SNCF) for new information systems at 40 stations was to provide extensions at Nantes and Marseilles and new systems for Clermont Ferrand and Perpignan in 1983. Discussions were taking place for the provision of information systems on the Amtrak Northeast Corridor route, USA
   Latest developments include the 90 Series of central and distributed controllers for split-flap and subsidiary displays. These controllers use the most advanced microprocessor technology to improve reliability, increase the rate of change of displayed information and reduce cable installation.

SRT
Standard Radio & Telefon AB
A Swedish Company of ITT

Box 501, 162 15 Vallingby, Sweden

Telephone: 8 739 40 00
Telex: 178 50

President: P O Lindholm
Marketing Director: P O Svensson
Marketing Manager: F Nordlander

Subsidiaries: Local manufacture in many parts of the world through SRT's association with ITT.

Products: Automatic train speed supervision equipment. Supplied to Swedish and Danish State Railways, the company's L10000 ATC system provides a high-capacity data link between track and vehicles. Information from track is supplied by transponders laid between the rails. An on-board computer system processes information from track and train and displays relevant information to the driver.

STC
Standard Telephones and Cables plc

STC House, 190 Strand, London WC2R 1DU, England

Telephone: 01-836 8055
Telegrams: Relay, London WC2
Telex: 22385

Related companies: The company has business, marketing, research and trading agreements with the International Telephone and Telegraph Corporation (ITT) and its associated companies world-wide

Chairman and Chief Executive: Sir Kenneth Corfield
Marketing Director: R T Soper

Products: Coaxial line and optical cable systems, pulse code modulation equipment and frequency division multiplex equipment for railway communication networks; telephone exchanges and instruments, office intercom systems, telephone instruments, remote control and telemetry systems; teleprinters and message switching systems for teleprinter network, data terminal and modems; control and communication cables.

STC Business Systems
STC Business Systems

Hollingbury, Brighton, East Sussex BN1 8AN, England

Telephone: 0273 507111
Telex: 87169

Director, Business Systems: P R Breen
Director, Sales and Services: P J Benstead
General Sales Manager: R McLeod
Manager, Export Sales: A Tabor

Products: Comprehensive range of voice data and text communications systems and products.

Constitution: STC Business Systems is the business communications arm of Standard Telephones and Cables plc.

Telephone Cables
Telephone Cables Limited

Chequers Lane, Dagenham, Essex RM9 6QA, England

Telephone: 01-592 6611
Telegrams: Drycore, Dagenham
Telex: 896216

Chairman: O S Johnson
Managing Director: J W Baker
Commercial Director: M J Spoor
General Sales Manager: A Circus

Products: Cables for telecommunications systems.

Telkor
Telkor (Pty) Ltd

7th Floor, 192 Hendrik Verwoerd Drive, Randburg 2194, Transvaal, South Africa

Telephone: 787 9740
Telegrams: Sudamat Jhb
Telex: 4 22171

Chairman: Ian Mackenzie
Directors: Cyrus Potgeiter
              Hugh Lund
              George Anderson
              Peter Westwood

Products: Power signalling apparatus, track circuit equipment and accessories, automatic train routeing, CTC and computer-based systems. Telkor has four operating divisions: Railway Signalling; Digital Systems; Dowty Projects; and Communications. The Dowty Projects Division has a R30-million contract from South African Transport Services to supply and install the patented Dowty automatic speed control system at the Bapsfontein marshalling yards near Johannesburg.

Thomson-CSF

23 rue de Courcelles, 75362 Paris Cedex 08, France

Telephone: 563 12 12
Telex: 204 780

President: Jean-Pierre Bouyssonnie

Products: Telecommunications; optical fibre communications; audio-visual communications; rail traffic control systems; current transducers and multipliers; transformers; power semiconductors.

Toshiba
Toshiba Corporation
Transport Equipment Export Department IOPG

Offices: 1-6 Uchisaiwaicho, 1-chome, Chiyoda-ku, Tokyo, Japan

Telephone: 501 5411
Telegrams: Toshiba, Tokyo
Telex: 22587

Works: Fuchu Works, 1, Toshiba-machi, Fuchu-shi, Tokyo

Products: Automatic train control equipment; automatic train stop equipment; electrical indicating and train describing equipment; centralised traffic control and remote control systems; marshalling yard equipment, including retarders, etc.

Transcontrol
Transcontrol Corporation
A member of the Siemens Group

Head office: 75 Marcus Drive, Melville, New York 11747, USA

Telephone: (516) 249 6000
Telex: 645117

President and Chief Executive Officer: Rudolf Gottesbueren
Vice President, Engineering: Gerry Erno
Vice President, Operations: Edward Riddett

Products: Systems: centralised traffic control; wayside and car-borne signalling; interlocking consolidation; classification yard automation; manual yard control; highway crossing warning.
Apparatus: control machines; vital signal relays built to AAA standards; time element relays; overload relays; transformers; inverters; rectifiers; solid-state switch operating units.

TRT
Télécommunications Radioélectriques et Téléphoniques

88 rue Brillat-Savarin, 75640 Paris Cedex 13, France

Telephone: 581 11 12
Telex: 25 828

Products: Electronic railway signalling and telecommunications equipment.
TRT and its subsidiaries OMERA and SFTP have been active participants in French Railways' TGV programme with these systems:
A high-performance ground-train radio system which achieves a continuous exchange of information between the central control station and the trains, as well as between the trains themselves. The links cover the entire length of the Paris-Lyons line by means of 40 or so transceivers along the route.
An automatic train announcement system (SAAT) backed by computer, which monitors all train movements in real time. Each station can converse with the SAAT and introduce its own data regarding the local situation for optimum traffic management.
An automatic driver alertness system (VACMA), which both triggers the emergency brake and radio transmission of the fact to central control if the driver has become incapacitated and unable to respond normally.

TRW
TRW Inc

One Space Park, Building R4/2128, Redondo Beach, California 90278, USA

Products: Train control system; automatic train control equipment; central traffic control equipment.

Union Switch & Signal
Union Switch & Signal Division
American Standard Inc

Swissvale, Pittsburgh, Pennsylvania 15218, USA

Telephone: (412) 273 4000
Telex: 86 6448

Vice-President and General Manager: M H Sluis
Vice-President, International Operations: C F Wert
Vice-President, International Sales: L A Damasio

Products: Electronic car or train detection and identification; automatic train control; mechanical, power, and block signalling and switching; highway crossing barriers and warning signals; automatic train stops; centralised traffic control; track circuit apparatus; classification yard equipment and retarders; computerised dispatching systems for control, indication and information etc.

Branch offices: Chicago, Montreal, New York, San Francisco, Philadelphia, St Louis, St Paul, Omaha, Pittsburgh

European facility: WABCO-Westinghouse SpA, Volvera 50, Piossasco (Torino) 10045, Italy
Irish Signal Division, Upper Rock Road, Tralee, County Kerry, Ireland

Vaughan
Vaughan Systems and Programming Ltd

The Maltings, Hoe Lane, Ware, Hertfordshire SG12 9LR, England

Telephone: 0920 2282
Telex: 81516

Director, Software: A N St Johnston
Director, Engineering: G W Monk
Director, Systems: A St Johnston
Director, Production: M T C Morley
Director, Marketing: R E Beadle

Products: Train describer equipment; passenger information systems; train reporting systems. Recent contracts for British Rail have included an automatic train reporting system (ATR) for Crewe.
Vaughan installed its first train describer equipment 'package' in the existing London Midland Region Wolverhampton signalbox, to replace an existing relay/CRT describer. This was the first installation of Vaughan's software/hardware TD package, which meets the requirements of the British Rail 800 specification. A second TD package was to be installed in the new Chester power signal box. The hardware is a fully-dualled automatic changeover configuration of the well-established Vaughan 4M microprocessor system, which is modular and is thus expandable on site after installation. The software is database-controlled (parameter-steered) and enables the package to be tailored to a particular track configuration without program change. Similarly, the railway can make changes at any time by updating the database interactively on a vdu using an off-line machine. Both systems use the new Vaughan 7 × 5 led displays in the main panel; fringe signalboxes use vdus and have the capability of reading track circuit and other digital input information; all transmissions are fully checked. The regulator's vdu has access to maps covering the main panel berths and the fringe box maps. Facilities for display, printing and transmission of automatic train reports are also part of the package, as are extensive test facilities for main panel displays and fringe box systems.
The Vaughan TD is termed a 'package' because the same design of hardware and software may be applied to a wide range of track configurations. It is achieved by the combination of modular hardware from the 4M range, and a database (parameter-steered or table-driven) software package. This enables the particular configuration of the network comprising for example, berths, track circuits and fringe boxes to be set up in engineering terms, and then be converted to a computer database by a system generation process. The database in the computer memory then determines the particular functions carried out by the standard software package. The flexibility of these hardware and software techniques also allows a system to be altered or expanded after installation with a minimum of disruption to operational use. The Vaughan TD package caters for configurations of up to 200 berths with 512 track circuits. Packages can be linked to form larger systems, either within one location or distributed over several signal boxes.

Vaughan mimic panel installation at Wolverhampton

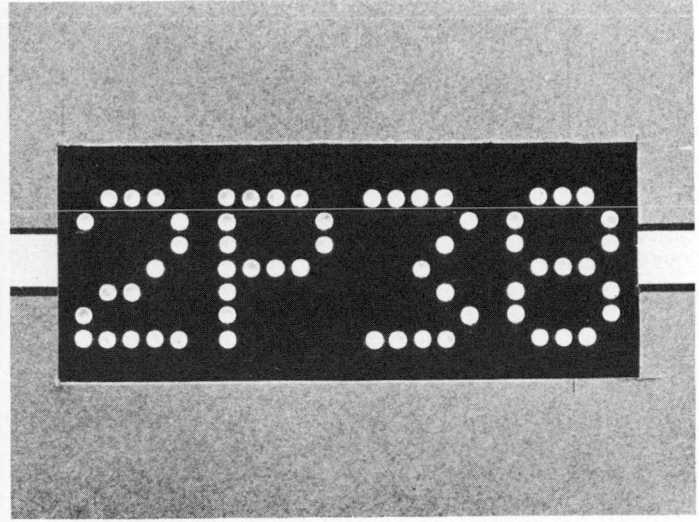

Typical Vaughan 7 × 5 dot led train description display

Western-Cullen-Hayes Model 10 crossing gate design with signs, bells, number-of-track sign, flashing lights (one-way or two-way), 'stop on red signal' sign, wooden or fibreglass gate arm with adapters to fit other manufacturers' signals

Vaughan fringe signalbox vdu and ocu set-up keyboard

WABCO-Westinghouse

207 boulevard du Souverain, 1160 Brussels, Belgium

Telephone: 73 60 53

Vice-President and Group Executive: Richard W Foxen

Products: Automatic train control; block signalling; level crossing barriers and warning signals; automatic train stops; remote control systems; centralised traffic control; train describers; track circuit apparatus; cab signalling system of both intermittent and continuous type; two-way railway radio; marshalling yard equipment and retarders, etc.

Western-Cullen-Hayes Inc

2700 West 36th Place, Chicago, Illinois 60636, USA

Telephone: (312) 254 9600
Telegrams: Wesrailsup
Telex: 25 3206

President: R L McDaniel
Sales Director: J P Schaefer

Products: Track circuiting equipment and accessories; level crossing barriers and warning lights; marshalling yard equipment; including retarders, etc.

Westinghouse
Westinghouse Brake and Signal Co Ltd
A Hawker Siddeley Company

Head office: 3 John Street, London WC1N 2ER, England

Main works
Westinghouse Signals
PO Box 79, Foundry Lane, Chippenham, Wiltshire SN15 1JD
Telephone: 0249 654141
Telegrams: Westinghouse, Chippenham
Telex: 44618

Westinghouse Brakes
PO Box 74, New Road, Chippenham, Wiltshire SN15 1HY
Telephone: 0249 654141
Telegrams: Westinghouse, Chippenham
Telex: 449411/2

Westcode Systems
PO Box 41, The Hawthorns, Langley Road, Chippenham, Wiltshire SN15 1JJ
Telephone: 0249 654141
Telex: 449411/12

Westcode Semiconductors
PO Box 57, Langley Road, Chippenham, Wiltshire SN15 1JL

Westinghouse Davenset Rectifiers
PO Box 52, Langley Road, Chippenham, Wiltshire SN15 1HX
Telephone: 0249 654141
Telex: 449124

Westinghouse Foundry
PO Box 63, Foundry Lane, Chippenham, Wiltshire SN15 1EH
Telephone: 0249 654141
Telex: 449411/12

Managing Director: R A Willford
Directors: E J Harris
    A S Hardyman
    D A Stack
    J R C Boulding
    D J Norton
    R Ward
    C Piyall
Secretary: B M K Moore

Products: Signalling equipment; remote control systems; air, electro-pneumatic and vacuum brake equipment, level crossing protection, marshalling yard equipment, traction rectifiers; computer-based train description; automatic train operation; automatic fare collection; railway door equipment; electricity power control supervision systems.

Westinghouse Signals markets a comprehensive range of products for world-wide railway signalling systems. It offers a design capability, aided by the use of computers to enhance the quality, for any signalling scheme. Control panels are designed to suit customer needs and range from large mosaic desks or diagrams, capable of being changed with the minimum of disruption to day-to-day working, to small monitoring panels for maintenance purposes.

A range of signals, the 2000 series, designed to meet British Rail specifications, is available. Main two-, three- and four-aspect, junction indicators, shunt subsidiary, stencil and banner signals plus special designs are all part of the product range. Standard electrically and electro-hydraulically operated point machines, together with their ground connections, can be supplied for various voltage inputs and ac immune.

The Style 'Q' relay forms the basis of relay production for interlocking and track circuit applications. Designed to BR specifications, about 70 different types are available. Over a million of these relays have been produced for the world's railways. In addition special relays are available for applications such as track circuits, timing and use in ac immunity areas. Relay room furniture is designed using standard components to meet the individual requirements of a signalling scheme.

Train detection track circuit equipment is available for ac and dc traction territories, for block jointless applications, for use with automatic train control and in special situations.

Apparatus cases, built to BR specifications, are available in several forms to house the lineside signalling equipment using a modular interior design to facilitate installation. Many special designs are supplied to meet a variety of conditions such as metro tunnel installations.

Remote control equipment capable of operating via standard telecommunication cables is available to provide remote control and indications to the control centre. Time (TDM) and frequency (FDM) division multiplex equipment in single or duplicate mode can be supplied.

The major clients supplied by Westinghouse Signals are British Rail and London Transport in the UK, but recent overseas railway customers include Madrid Metro, Hong Kong Mass Transit Authority, Queensland Railways, New South Wales PTC, Korean National Railways, Kowloon-Canton Railway and Bangladesh Railway. Significant contracts lately in hand have featured train describers for Brighton and the Kowloon-Canton Railway, train describers and automatic train reporting systems for Leeds, York, Brisbane, and the Korean National Railways, and signalling installations for Tyne and Wear, Salisbury, Brighton, Gascoine Wood (National Coal Board), South Shields/Pelaw, East Coast main line, and Belfast in the UK and in Bangladesh, Hong Kong, etc overseas. Automatic train control equipment is being supplied for Line 9 of the Madrid Metro on a contract valued at £1 million and a contract of similar value has been received from London Transport for equipment for a positive train identification system. Work is in hand on a £4 million contract for Zimbabwe which includes signalling, train describers and remote control of power substations for an extensive CTC system.

Notable development work includes a microprocessor-based replacement for relay interlockings, being carried out in conjunction with British Rail; a modular form of jointless track circuit for world-wide application and a fail-safe frequency multiplex data transmission system for use over fibre-optic cables and aimed at the South African market. Computer-aided design and testing is currently used in the design of signalling diagram panels, providing train running simulations, and printed circuit board testing.

Subsidiary companies
UK: Gresham & Craven Ltd
Douglas (Sales & Service) Ltd
Partridge Wilson Ltd
Australia: Westinghouse Brake & Signal Co (Australia) Pty Ltd, Victoria (signalling and rectifiers)
Westinghouse Brake & Signal Co (Australia) Pty Ltd, New South Wales (railway brakes)
Westinghouse Brake & Signal Co (Australia) Pty Ltd, New South Wales (road brakes)
Westinghouse Brake & Signal Co (Australia) Pty Ltd, Queensland (track and engineering)
ROC Hydraulics, New South Wales (hydraulics)
Canada: Westcode Ltd, Mississauga, Ontario
Italy: Secowest Italia, Turin
New Zealand: McKenzie & Holland (NZ) Ltd, Wellington
South Africa: Westinghouse Bellambie (Pty) Ltd, Johannesburg
Spain: Dimetronic SA, Madrid
USA: Westcode Inc, Frazer, Pennsylvania 19355
Powertech Inc, 0-02 Fair Lawn Avenue, New Jersey
Westcode Semiconductors Inc, New Jersey

Associated company
UK: Westinghouse Cubic Ltd

Westinghouse-Bellambie
Westinghouse-Bellambie (Pty) Ltd

Head office: 112 Clarke Street North, Alrode 1450, Alberton, Johannesburg, South Africa
Postal address: PO Box 453, Johannesburg 2000

Telephone: 864 2150
Telegrams: Bellambie, Johannesburg
Telex: 420147

Chairman: S A Boyazoglu
Managing Director: H T Jenkins

Products: General railway signalling equipment and systems design, remote control, centralised traffic control, telecontrol schemes, mechanical hydraulic lifting equipment, rail and road braking equipment.

Associated company: Westinghouse Brake & Signal Co Ltd, Chippenham, Wiltshire, England

WSF
Westinghouse Saxby Farmer Ltd

Head office: 17 Convent Road, Entally, Calcutta 14, India

Telephone: 24-7161
Telegrams: Interlock, Calcutta
Telex: 2348

Works: Above and 24 Canal South Road, Calcutta 15

Managing Director: N Ghose

Products: Mechanical and electrical signalling equipment; point layouts and mechanism; relays; point and signal machines; ball and tablet token instruments; reversers; electric control panels and illuminated diagrams; colour light signals and route indicators; wagon retarders; hump yard equipment; vacuum and air brake equipment for wagons, coaches, locomotives, compressors and slack adjusters; pneumatic, hydraulic and combined road brake equipment; electronic equipment for road traffic signals and control.

Westinghouse Saxby Farmer Ltd is a joint enterprise of Westinghouse Brake & Signal Co Ltd of London, England, and the State Government of West Bengal, India.

ELECTRIFICATION EQUIPMENT

ACEC
Ateliers de Construction Electriques de Charleroi

BP4, 6000 Charleroi, Belgium

Telephone: 3271 442276
Telegrams: Transportation Division, Charleroi
Telex: 51227

Products: Railway electrification equipment.

AEG-Telefunken
AEG-Telefunken Nachrichten- und Verkehrstechnik AG Geschaftsbereich Bahnen

Hohenzollerndamm 150, 1000 West Berlin 33, Federal Republic of Germany

Telephone: (030) 828-1
Telegrams: Elektronbahnen, Berlin
Telex: 1 85 498

Products: Complete railway electrification equipment and systems; engineering and project management; traction power supply, including substations and remote control equipment; catenary equipment for overhead line or third-rail operation; electrical equipment for locomotives and railcars or multiple-units for main-line and branch-line service, mining and industrial locomotives; electrical equipment for rapid transit trains, urban and underground railways, tramways and trolleybuses; traction auxiliaries and special equipment (train lighting and heating).

Allied Insulators
A I Insulators High Tension Products
A Division of A I Industrial Products plc

PO Box 17, Milton, Stoke-on-Trent, Staffordshire, England

Telephone: 0782 534321
Telegrams: Bullers, Milton, Stoke
Telex: 36495

Managing Director: H Turner
Works Director: R Dean
Sales Director: R G Shenton
Technical Director: B G Ecclestone

Associated manufacturing division: Bullers Engineering

Products: Insulator assemblies for feeder transmission, tracked overhead transmission, third-rail systems, pantograph support and switching apparatus. Malleable castings, steel forgings and other metal components of overhead transmission.

Alsthom-Atlantique
Société Générale de Constructions Electriques & Mécaniques

38 avenue Kléber, 75016 Paris, France

Telephone: 727 77 79
Telegrams: Alsthom, Paris
Telex: 27672

Products: Generators, alternators and traction motors.

Ansaldo
Ansaldo Trasporti SpA

Head office: Via Nuova delle Brecce 260, 80147 Naples, Italy

Telephone: 081 7810111
Telex: 710131

Products: Main traction and auxiliary electric equipment for locomotives, railcars and light vehicles; high-speed circuit breakers; traction motors; transformers; rectifiers; static convertors for ac and dc substations; design, supply and erection of feeding lines and substations; centralised control of electrification networks.

AP
AP Precision Hydraulics
A division of Automotive Products plc

PO Box 1, Shaw Road, Speke, Liverpool L24 9JY, England

Telephone: 051-486 2121
Telegrams: Autoducts, Liverpool
Telex: 629394

Director and General Manager: W Brewer

Products: Gas/hydraulic cable tensioning unit for maintenance of constant tension in catenary systems on electrified railways. Purchasers include the railways of Britain, Netherlands, Norway, Australia.

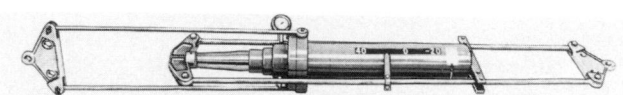

AP Constant Tensioning Unit ('Cable Tensioner'), to maintain constant predetermined tension in overhead cables, effective from −40 to +90°C

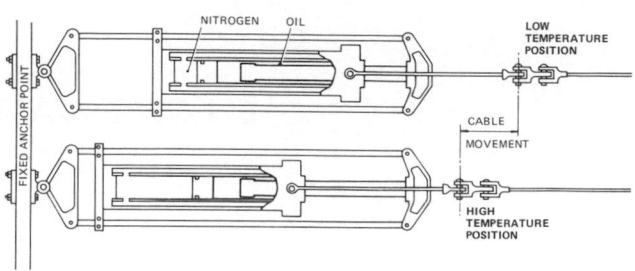

AP 'Cable Tensioner' claimed to be 38% more effective than weight and pulley systems

ASEA
ASEA AB
Transport Division

721 83 Vàsteras, Sweden

Telephone: 46 21 100000
Telex: 40720

Products: Complete substations for ac and dc systems as well as static convertors for low frequency systems; catenary systems and complete turnkey projects for electrification of railways.

Static frequency convertor from three-phase 50 Hz to single-phase 16 Hz; rating 2×15 MVA

Balfour Beatty
Balfour Beatty Power Construction Ltd
Traction and General Division

PO Box 12, Acornfield Road, Kirkby, Liverpool L33 7UG, England

Telephone: 051-548 5000
Telegrams: Bicalcon, Kirkby
Telex: 627249

Chairman: C G Moss
Managing Director: A Pearson
Commercial and Sales Director: G B Suthers

Products: Engineering studies, design, supply and installation of complete overhead equipment for railway electrification.

BBC Brown Boveri
BBC Brown, Boveri & Co Ltd

Postfach 58, 5401 Baden, Switzerland

Telephone: 056 75 11 11
Telegrams: Brownbover, Baden
Telex: 558214

Group companies: See under Locomotives and rolling stock

Products: Systems and equipment for voltage and frequency conversion from public power supply to ac or dc railway power supply; engineering, manufacture, supply and installation of complete power generating stations, complete substations, phase conversion installations, rectifiers, switchgear, transformers; engineering and supply of catenary systems.

BBC-Sécheron
BBC-Sécheron Ltd
Member of the Brown Boveri Group

14 avenue de Sécheron, 1202 Geneva 21, Switzerland

Telephone: 022 32 67 50
Telex: 22130

Chairman: H-P Schulthess
Managing Director: C Rossier
Chief Sales Director: A Reymond

Products: Transformers for railway electrification, dc traction substations. Rectifiers and circuit breakers, line protection devices for dc traction networks.

BICC
BICC Ltd
Formerly British Insulated Callender's Cables

PO Box 5, 21 Bloomsbury Street, London WC1B 3QN, England

Telephone: 01-637 1300
Telegrams: BICC G Station Codes BICCG or BIGHO
Telex: 23463; 28624

Chairman: Sir Raymond Pennock
Executive Deputy Chairman: H G DeVille
Executive Directors: J Banks
　　　　　　　　　D H Booth
　　　　　　　　　D I S Hinton
　　　　　　　　　D A Holland
　　　　　　　　　H L Jefferies
　　　　　　　　　M F Julien
　　　　　　　　　Dr D R Stewart (Australian)

Products: Electric cables of all types and their associated accessories; civil, mechanical and electrical engineering.

Brecknell, Willis
Brecknell, Willis & Co Ltd

Chard, Somerset TA20 2DE, England

Telephone: 04606 4941
Telegrams: Progress, Chard
Telex: 46518

Chairman: Lord Tanlaw
Managing Director: K B McQueen
Chief Sales Director: L F Durrans
Technical Director: A E W Hobbs

Products: Range of overhead line fittings, pantographs, third-rail shoe gear and complete current collector systems. The company also offers a consultancy service for current collection requirements as well as a complete range of battery electric vehicles. The company has pioneered Brecktrack, a safety covered conductor rail system together with new design of the single arm Highreach pantograph for electrically-propelled rapid transit vehicles. Among its latest products is the BR/Brecknell Willis high-speed pantograph for train speeds of 250 km/h with a three-metre reach.

Amtrak Type AEM-7 electric locomotive fitted with Brecknell-Willis high-speed pantograph

Brissonneau & Lotz
Brissonneau & Lotz Chaudronnerie SA

38 avenue Kléber, 75784 Paris, France

Products: Traction and generator motors.

Brush
Brush Electrical Machines Co Ltd

Falcon Works, Loughborough, Leicestershire LE11 1HJ, England

Telephone: 0509 63131
Telegrams: Brush, Loughborough Telex
Telex: 341091

Products: Complete electrical propulsion systems and traction motors.

CEM-Oerlikon

37 rue du Rocher, 75008 Paris, France

Telephone: 522 85 90/74 61
Telex: 650663

Products: Subway electric and electronic equipment.

CGE
Compagnie Generale d'Electricite

54 rue de la Boëtie, 75382 Paris Cedex 08, France

Telephone: 563 14 14
Telegrams: Electricité, Paris 8
Telex: 280953

The companies within the CGE Group covering electrical contracting are: CGEE Alsthom; Comsip Entreprise; and Controle Bailey

Products: Electrical and electronic equipment and construction.
　The Group has been concerned with numerous metro constructions in France and abroad, including those of Lyons, Marseilles, Montreal, Santiago, São Paulo, Mexico City, Rio de Janeiro, Caracas, Lisbon and Cairo.

Contransimex
Contransimex

PO Box 2006, 38 Dinicu Golescu Boulevard, Bucharest, Romania

Telephone: 180042
Telegrams: Ctrix, Bucharest
Telex: 11 606

Products: Complete electrifications.

Day & Zimmerman
Day & Zimmerman Inc

1818 Market Street, Philadelphia, Pennsylvania 19103, USA

Telephone: (215) 299 8000
Telegrams: Dayzim
Telex: 845192

Products: Complete main-line and rapid transit electrifications.

Dearmedelec
Dearmedelec SAIC

Juramento 4182/86, 1430 Buenos Aires, Argentina

Telephone: 52-6766/3409/7036

Products: Static exciting systems, traction motor transition systems, battery charge regulator.

Delta
Delta Enfield Cables Ltd

Millmarsh Lane, Brimsdown, Enfield, Middlesex, England

Telephone: 01-804 2468
Telex: 261749

Products: Accessories, power cables, rubber cables, plastic cables and specialised equipment.

Electrack
Electrack Inc

1925 K Street NW, Washington DC 20006, USA

Parent companies: General Cable (USA), Balfour Beatty Group of BICC Ltd (UK)

Products: Power supply for signalling for railway electrification projects; engineering and project management of catenary systems.

Electric Rails
Electric Rails Ltd

PO Box 123, 00191 Helsinki 18, Finland

Telephone: 8 06131
Telex: 124276

Products: Design, supply and installation of overhead equipment, supply installation of power lines.

Elektrim
Foreign Trade Company for Electrical Equipment, Poland

PO Box 638, Chalubinskiego 8, Warsaw, Poland

Telephone: 30 10 00
Telex: 814 351

Products: Electrifications, substations, overhead line equipment, dc switchgear, high-speed circuit breakers.

Elreco
Elreco Energy Products Ltd

PO Box 14178, 1988 Central Avenue, Cincinnati, Ohio 45214, USA

Telephone: (513) 621 5059
Telegrams: Elreco Cor Tln
Telex: 214539

Products: Catenary supports, rail bonds.

Ercole Marelli
Ercole Marelli Elettromeccanica Generale SpA

Viale Edison 50, 20099 Sesto San Giovanni, Milan, Italy

Telephone: (02) 2494
Telegrams: Marelgen, Sesto S Giovanni
Telex: 310043; 320575

Chairman: Luigi Nocivelli
Managing Director: Umberto di Capua

Products: Main traction and auxiliary electric equipment for locomotives, railcars and light vehicles; power supply and automation systems.

EVR
Electronique des Véhicules et des Réseaux

11 rue de la Nouvelle, 93301 Aubervillers, France

Telephone: 833 23 45
Telex: 680075

Products: Statodyne equipment.

Faiveley
Faiveley SA
Département Transport

93 rue du Docteur Bauer, 93404 Saint Ouen, France

Telephone: (1) 264 12 60
Telex: 290653

Products: Pantographs and collector shoes. The company's range of single-arm pantographs includes: the LV unit, for installation on dc or ac locomotives and power cars; and the LVT unit, for tramways and light rail vehicles. A Faiveley double-stage pantograph was mounted on the TGV unit with which French Railways secured a new world rail speed record of 380 km/h in February 1981.

Faiveley double-stage pantograph on French Railways TGV train-set

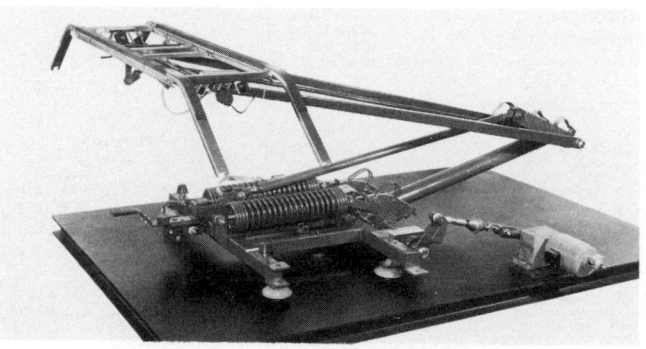

Faiveley Type LV2600 pantograph with electric control

Fuji Electric
Fuji Electric Co Ltd

New Yurakucho Building 12-1, Yurakucho 1-chome, Chiyoda-ku, Tokyo 100, Japan

Telephone: 03 211-7111
Telex: 22331, 26374

Products: Traction motor with chopper control, static convertor, brushless motor generating set, pantograph for Shinkansen (250 km/h); power supply equipment: remote supervisory control equipment with computer, freon cooling silicon rectifier, SF6 gas circuit breakers and mini high-speed circuit breakers; moulded transformer; total control systems including electric power management, station office apparatus control, data management and disaster prevention management.

GEC
GEC Rectifiers Ltd

PO Box 27, Stafford, Staffordshire ST17 4LN, England

Telephone: 0785 51222
Telex: 36203

Director and General Manager: P W Muecke

Products: Rectifiers for dc power supply, power electronics, instrumentation and control; power conditioning units for traction vehicles.

GEC Transportation Projects
GEC Transportation Projects Limited

45 Victoria Street, St Albans, Hertfordshire AL1 3UG, England

Telephone: 0727 33181
Telex: 298782

Products: Main contract for the supply, installation and project management of composite electric railway systems. (See also under Consultancies.)

General di Electricità

Via Bergognone 34, Milan, Italy

Telephone: 4242
Telegrams: Cogenel, Milan
Telex: 31092

Products: Electric transmissions.

General Electric Co (USA)

570 Lexington Avenue, New York, New York 10022, USA

Telephone: (212) 750 3515
Telegrams: Ingeco, New York

Products: Locomotives, substation equipment and automation.

Groupement 50 Hz
50 c/s Group

Löwenstrasse 29, PO Box 433, 8021 Zurich 1, Switzerland

Telephone: (01) 221 1744
Telegrams: Coordinat, Zurich
Telex: 813 954

Products: Traction rolling stock and stationary equipment for all aspects of railway electrification including planning, design, technical co-ordination and installation.
Electrifications completely furnished by the Group have included: the Lisbon-Oporto line of Portuguese Railways (CP); the lines of Korean National Railroad (KNR) from Jung to Ang, Tae to Baeg, and Yeong to Dong; and the Linea Bananera of Ferrocarriles de Costa Rica (FECOSA).

Constitution: The Group comprises ACEC of Belgium, Alsthom-Atlantique and Société MTE of France, AEG-Telefunken of France and the Federal Republic of Germany, Siemens AG of the Federal Republic of Germany and BBC Brown Boveri & Co Ltd of Switzerland.

Hitachi Cable
Hitachi Cable, Ltd

Head office: Chiyoda Building, 2-1-2 Marunouchi, Chiyoda-ku, Tokyo 100, Japan

Telephone: (03) 216 1611
Telegrams: Hitachicable, Tokyo
Telex: 222-2771

Main works: 5-1, Hitaka-Machi, Hitachi-City, Ibaraki-Pref 319-14

President: Tokugoro Mizukami
Executive Vice President: Mizo Aoki
Director and General Manager, Overseas Division: Yoshiro Sadayuki

Subsidiary companies
Hitachi Cable Philippines Inc, Manila, Philippines
Hitachi Cable (S) Pte Ltd, Singapore
Hitachi Cable America Inc, New York, USA

Products: Supply and installation of: trolley wires; AAC, ACSR, ACSR/AS; HV low-impedance coaxial feeders for ac electrification, EHV oil-filled cables; leaky coaxial cables for train radio communications, electro-magnetic induction-proof signal/communication cables, optical fibre cables; rubber pads, buffers and vibration isolators.
    Among recent contracts have been the supply and installation supervision of 16 km of leaky coaxial cable for Helsinki Metro; and of 22 km of leaky coaxial cable for Melbourne Underground Loop Authority.

Fibre-optic link for TV transmission, from left: TV monitor, analogue link receiver and remote control transmitter, fibre-optic cable, analogue link transmitter and remote control receiver, TV camera

MTE
Société MTE

32 quai de Dion Bouton, 92806 Puteaux, France

Telephone: 776 41 62
Telex: 610425

Products: Conventional control apparatus, generators, alternators, traction motors, transformers and rectifiers.

Ohio Brass
Ohio Brass Co
A subsidiary of Harvey Hubbell Inc

380 North Main Street, Mansfield, Ohio 44902, USA

Telephone: (419) 522 7111
Telegrams: Electric
Telex: 987414

President: William R Cress
International Manager: Alex J Karcic
New Business Development, Transit: A Philip Pastouna
Marketing Manager, Transit: M F Gowing

Products: Power distribution systems, car equipment, third-rail current collectors and porcelain insulators, Hi*Lite polymer insulators and power conversion equipment.
    The Ohio Brass Dynaglide contact-rail current collector weighs only 35 lb yet has the structural strength for high-speed service; it is generally attached directly to the bogie frame.
    Ohio Brass has signed a joint venture agreement to supply approximately $3 million of overhead hardware to Seoul Metropolitan Subway Corporation. Other partners in the venture are International Engineering Company, Inc, responsible for system engineering, training and construction support; and Alcoa, supplier for an aluminium T-bar system, compression fittings and equipment. The joint venture is subcontracted to Westinghouse Electric, holder of the total traction power supply contract from Seoul Metro. Equipment to be supplied by Ohio Brass includes cantilevers, section insulators, balance weight assemblies, jumpers, hangers, insulators and surge arresters, for two north-south routes, Lines 3 and 4, totalling 54 km. Above-ground catenary will be

weight-tensioned and supported by hinged cantilever attached to along-track support poles; underground contact wire will be supported by the aluminium T-bar suspended from tunnel ceiling insulators. Equipment is being designed to allow for outdoor temperatures ranging from −20 to +40°C.

Ohio Brass Dynaglide contact-rail current collector

Pirelli
Pirelli Construction and Co Ltd

Leigh Road, Eastleigh, Hampshire SO5 5YE, England

Telephone: 0703 612261
Telex: 477525
Telephone: (Fax Group 3) 0703 642662

Products: Railway overhead electrification equipment and specialised installation plant, design, provision and erection. Provision and installation of all types of power signalling and communication cables.

SAE
Società Anonima Elettrificazione SpA

Head office: Via Fara 26, 20124 Milan, Italy

Telephone: 02 67591
Telegrams: Saemilan
Telex: 310188

Main works: Lecco (CO)

Senior Manager, Construction Works: U Cocchi
Project Manager, Railways Department: C Bellani
Commercial Manager: S Storelli

Subsidiary: SIM SpA Società Italiana Montaggi, Mexico City, Mexico

Products: Masts, structures and fittings for railway electrification and construction of overhead contact lines of any voltage in both dc and ac systems.
    Recent contracts have included one valued at about US $70 million for Mexico's Irapuato line. The company has also been engaged in the design of overhead contact lines for railways in Africa, Australia and India and subsequent manufacture of structures and fittings.

SAE (India)
SAE (India) Limited

Head office: 29-30, Community Commercial Centre, Basant Lok, Vasant Vihar, New Delhi 110 057, India

Telephone: 675011, 675425, 675427
Telegrams: Saelines, New Delhi
Telex: 31-3876

Main works: Deori, PO Panagar, District Jabalpur (MP)

Director and General Manager: Gino Pace
Assistant to Director and General Manager: M Dutta

Products: Design, supply and erection of 25 kV ac 50 Hz overhead equipment, substation, switching stations and booster transformer stations for railway electrification. The company has equipped 4700 km of Indian Railways track for both 3 kV and 25 kV traction.

Siemens
Siemens Aktiengesellschaft

Werner-von-Siemens Strasse 50, 8520 Erlangen 2, Federal Republic of Germany

Telephone: 09131 71
Telex: 6 29871

Products: Railway electrification equipment.

Socimi
Società Costruzioni Industriali Milano SpA

Head office: Via San Calimero 3, 20122 Milan, Italy
Telephone: (02) 5465251/5
Telex: 310331

Main works
Via E Fermi 25, 20082 Binasco (Milan)
Telephone: (02) 9055605/6/7/8
Via Donatori del Sangue 100, 20010 Arluno (Milan)
Telephone: (02) 9017666, 9017803
Viale Porto Torres, Reg Zentu Figghi, 07100 Sassari
Telephone: (079) 235056

Chairman: Alessandro Marzocco
Managing Director: Pierino Sacchi
Export Sales and Marketing: Corrado Lardolina

Products: Pantographs.

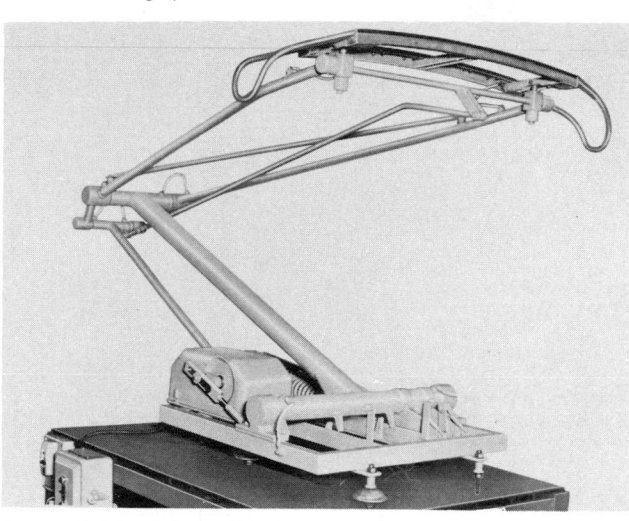

Asymmetrical pantograph by Socimi

Strojexport

PO Box 662 886, Václavské n 56, Prague 1, Czechoslovakia

Telephone: 245 041
Telegrams: Strojexport, Praha

Products: Railway electrification equipment.

TIBB
Tecnomasio Italiano Brown Boveri SpA

Piazzale Lodi 3, 20137 Milan, Italy

Telephone: (02) 5797 1
Telegrams: Tecnomasio, Milan
Telex: 310153

Products: Chopper and inverter equipment; traction motors; static and rotary converters for auxiliary services; dc and ac generators; single arm pantographs and electromagnetic rail brakes.

Toshiba
Toshiba Corporation
Transport Equipment Export Department IOPG

1-6 Uchisaiwaicho 1-chome, Chiyoda-ku, Tokyo 100, Japan

Telephone: 03 501 5411
Telegrams: Toshiba, Tokyo
Telex: 22587

Products: Dc and ac railway substation equipment; supervisory control systems; transformers; rectifiers; circuit breakers; arresters. Recent contracts have included Japanese National Railways' new Tohoku Shinkansen, completed in 1982, and the electrification of the Roca Line of Argentine Railways. For Kinki Nippon Railways, a centralised and automatic control system for 27 substations was completed in 1982.

Toyo Denki
Toyo Denki Seizo KK

Yaesu Mitsui Building, 7-2 Yaesu 2-chome, Chuo-ku, Tokyo, Japan

Telephone: 271 6374
Telegrams: Yohden, Tokyo
Telex: 222 4666/7

Products: Electric locomotives, control equipment, pantographs.

Wickham
D Wickham & Co Ltd

Crane Mead, Ware, Hertfordshire SG12 9QA, England

Telephone: 0920 2491/7
Telegrams: Wickham, Ware
Telex: 81340

Products: Overhead line inspection cars.

PERMANENT WAY EQUIPMENT

Abetong-Sabema
A-Betong AB, Sabema Material AB

PO Box 24, 351 03 Växjö, Sweden

Telephone: 470-10010
Telex: 52145

Main works: Vislanda

Divisional Manager: Knut Wickberg
Manager, Sleeper Division: Stefan Westberg

Subsidiary: Swedish Rail System SRS, Solna

Products: Concrete sleepers for main-line and turnouts in main-lines, sidings etc; sleepers for crane tracks; grade crossings; technical services in design of sleepers and manufacture.
Some 150 000 main-line sleepers per year are made for Swedish State Railways (SJ) at Vislanda, as well as sleepers for turnouts, prefabricated crane tracks and concrete elements for level crossing systems. The present plant became operational in 1977 when the B 10 prestressed reinforced monolithic sleeper came into production. It is designed for 20-ton axleloads at 200 km/h.
The company's latest contract in the sphere of planning and building plants covers a concrete sleeper factory for Malaysia with a planned annual output of 100 000, and another in Thailand with a planned annual output of 200 000.
The company has recently designed for the Hamersley Iron Ore Railway of Western Australia concrete sleepers for heavy duty switches to suit traffic specifications of 37 tonnes maximum and 30 tonnes nominal axleloads at up to 80 km/h, and annual gross train tonnages of 65 million.

Abex
Abex Corporation
Railroad Products Group

65 Valley Road, Mahwah, New Jersey 07430, USA

Telephone: (201) 529 3450
Telex: 642415

Products: Railway switches, crossings, railway track, lubricators, frogs, snow blowers, switch machines, switch stands, turnouts, spike drivers.

Abtus
Abtus Co

PO Box AS 35, Ascot, Berkshire SL5 7LB, England

Telephone: 0990 24312

Products: Power and manual bond drilling machines, track aligners, measured packing equipment.

Aebi
Robert Aebi AG

Uraniastrasse 31-33, 8023 Zürich, Switzerland

Telephone: 01 211 09 70
Telegrams: Aebi, Zürich
Telex: 813 795

Products: Rotary snow ploughs.

Al Welders
Al Welders Ltd

Academy Street, Inverness IV1 1LZ, Scotland

Telephone: 0463 39381
Telegrams: Alwelds Invss'
Telex: 75271

Chief Executive: B C Hilton
Sales Director: H L Abbott

Products: Alternative designs of rail welding machines to handle either continuous welded rail or combined programmes of continuous welded rail, switches and crossings. These machines are supplied with either ac or dc welding systems and incorporate special features for de-twist and aligning the rail ends prior to commencement of the welding operation in order to meet the tolerances and specifications demanded by major railway organisations which are designing their track systems for operating at speeds of up to 250 km/h. The machines incorporate control and post-heating systems to enable the welding of wear-resistant steels to be carried out. In addition to the design and manufacture of rail welding and ancillary machines, Al supplies complete rail welding depot installations including rail handling and cranage systems.

A & K
A & K Railroad Materials Inc

PO Box 30076, Salt Lake City, Utah 84130, USA

Telephone: (801) 974 5484
Telex: 389 406

President: K W Schumacher
Executive Vice President: M H Kulmer

Products: Complete switches, frogs, anchors, bolts, spikes, lockwashers, gauge rods, sleepers, hand track tools.

Aldon
The Aldon Co

3410 Sunset Avenue, Waukegan, Illinois 60087, USA

Telephone: (312) 623 8800

Products: Lightweight straddle-type rerailers; track levellers; track gauges; track jacks; safety derailers; rail benders.

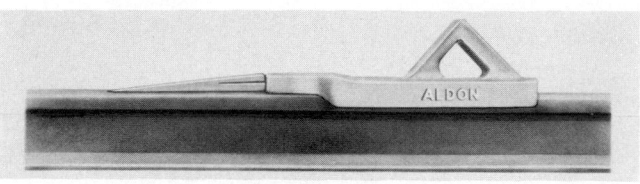

Aldon S-80 rail skid to bring heavy modern freight cars to a sliding stop

Aldon Permanent PL Rerailer, adaptable to standard, broad or narrow gauge, for instant rerailing of cars in either direction

Aluminothermique
L'Aluminothermique

15/17 rue de Chabrol, 75480 Paris Cedex 10, France

Products: Rail welding equipment. The company specialises in the Boutet processes of aluminothermic welding.

American Railroad Curvelining Corporation

137 Hollywood Avenue, Douglaston, Long Island, New York 11363, USA

Telephone: (212) 224 1135
Telegrams: Rayville, Newyork
Telex: (510) 221 1820

President: R A Fichter

Subsidiaries: Bondarc Division
                 Marine Division

Products: Track geometry analysis; curve lining computers; roll ordinators; Trakchek; Trakanalyzer.

Arneke
Heinrich Arneke & Co

Seelze, Hanover, Federal Republic of Germany

Telephone: 51 37 818

Products: Sleeper placing machines and track laying equipment.

Artimsa
Artimsa SAIC

25 de Mayo, 12th Floor, 1002 Buenos Aires, Argentina

Telephone: 31 3054/56

Products: Rail fastenings, fishplates, creep anchors.

Atlantic Track
Atlantic Track and Turnout Co

270 Broad Street, Bloomfield, New Jersey 07003, USA

Telephone: (201) 748 5885
Telex: 138049

Chairman: G L Morrow
Chief Sales Director: R H Dreesen
Export Sales Director: W F Oster

Products: New or used rail track accessories and switch material.

Atlas Copco
Atlas Copco (Great Britain) Ltd

PO Box 79, Swallowdale Lane, Hemel Hempstead, Hertfordshire HP2 7HA, England

Telephone: 0442 61201
Telegrams: Atlascopco

Products: Self-contained power tamper/drill and pneumatic equipment, pumps, tampers.

Atlas Hydraulic Loaders Ltd

Wharfedale Road, Euroway Estate, Bradford, West Yorkshire BD4 6SE, England

Telephone: 0274 686827
Telex: 51404

Directors: G Weyhausen
H Trottnow
Marketing Manager: R Smyth
Sales Manager: C Flintham

Products: Road/rail excavators.
Atlas road/rail excavators have been on permanent-way work for the world's railroads since the mid 1960s. AB 1302 DK and AB 1602 DK wheeled excavators are the most frequently selected models for rail use, since these short-deck versions keep clear of the loading gauge of adjacent tracks during many of the operations they are called upon to perform. Alternatively, their excavator super-structures can be mounted on other rail vehicles or operated as stationary units. The German Federal Railway specification for these Atlas excavators uses four large-section tyres running on the sleeper heads outside the rails, so that the tyres cannot be damaged. The excavator's normal steering lock angle is suffi-cient to drive it away from the rail track without effort, or cross points. An additional dozer and support blade gives the excavators extra load capacity, particularly along the line of the chassis.

Atlas AB 1602 DK excavator

Bain
William Bain & Co

PO Box 132, Boksburg, Transvaal, South Africa

Telephone: 892 2920
Telex: 82134

Products: Rail, points, crossings, track components.

Balteau-Sonatest Ltd

Dickens Road, Old Wolverton, Milton Keynes, Buckinghamshire MK12 5QQ, England

Telephone: 0908 316345
Telex: 826131

Managing Director: F Sansom

Products: Ultrasonic flaw detectors, wall thickness meters and industrial X-ray equipment for examination of welds, components, pressure vessels, etc.

Bance
R Bance & Co Ltd

Cockcrow Hill House, St Mary's Road, Surbiton, Surrey KT6 5HE, England

Telephone: 01-398 7141
Telex: 928280

Products: Tapered rail joint shims for maintaining jointed track; portable impact wrenches; track spanners; ballast forks; slewing bars; chisels; fishbolts and nuts; screwspikes; rail clips; shunting equipment including radio-controlled shunters.

Bance portable impact wrench

Barclay
Andrew Barclay, Sons & Co Ltd

Caledonia Works, Kilmarnock, Ayrshire KA1 2QD, Scotland

Telephone: 0563 23573/4/5/6
Telegrams: Barclayson, Kilmarnock
Telex: 778497

Chairman: C R C Fryers
Managing Director: S E H Kewney

Products: Rack track components, including sleepers, pre-assembled straight and curved sections, continuous and non-continuous (turntable) turnouts.

Beilhack
Martin Beilhack GmbH

Postfach 160, 8200 Rosenheim 2, Federal Republic of Germany

Telephone: 4033
Telex: 05 25840

Products: Light, demountable ploughs with clearing width of 3.15 metres; heavy, special snow ploughs, model PB600 with adjustable clearing width of 3 to 6 metres; demountable snow blowers with approximately 2.5 tonnes per hour clearing capacity; snow blowers with adjustable clearing head, clearing width of 3 to 6 metres; self-propelled and pushed special snow removal machines, reversible for clearing operations in both directions, with a clearing capacity of up to approximately 14 tonnes per hour.

Bethlehem Steel
Bethlehem Steel Corporation

701 East Third Street, Bethlehem, Pennsylvania 18016, USA

Telephone: (215) 694 2424

Products: Rail, fabricated trackwork, baseplates, joint bars.

BOC
BOC Limited

Great West House, Great West Road, Brentford, Middlesex TW8 9DQ, England

Telephone: 01-560 5166
Telex: 24981

Products: Hand and machine gas cutting equipment, gas and electric welding equipment.

Recent products include a portable rail cutting machine manufactured by D & M Consultants of 60 Maze Green Road, Bishop's Stortford, Hertfordshire under licence from BOC Ltd. It is marketed world-wide by D & M Consultants. Fired by oxy-acetylene, the machine clips onto the rail. The operator cuts completely through simply and rapidly by rotating a crank handle. This gives an absolutely square cut, so that worn sections can be replaced by new rail and re-welded without introducing lateral stress. Acetylene gives a fast, continuous, high-quality precision cut, which is important for subsequent re-welding. Previously, rails have been cut using a hand-held blow-pipe, but this tends to give an uneven surface and often the cut is not straight across. The new machine will handle all types of rail and will accommodate different wear conditions.

BOC portable rail-cutting machine

Bohlins
AB Erik Bohlin

Gärdsvägen 2, 171 52 Solna, Sweden

Telephone: 08/830880
Telegrams: Bohal
Telex: 10655

President: Lars Bohlin
Vice President: Hans Bohlin

Products: Stationary and mobile rail lubricators.

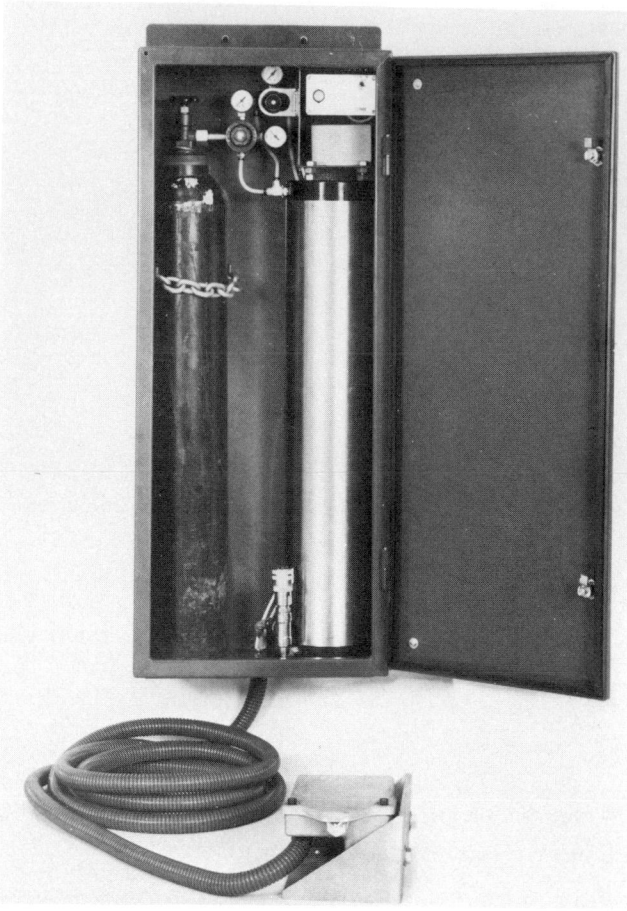

Bohlins RLB 2000 rail lubricator for 24 000 single shots set at a grease volume of 0.5 cm³; higher-capacity model available for more trains or a number of greasing points

British Steel Cumbria

Moss Bay, Workington, Cumbria, England

Telephone: 0900 4321

General Manager, BS Cumbria Track Products: J Brian Clay
Commercial Manager, Track: Stuart Askew

Products: Rail, sleepers and associated track products for railways world-wide, capable of meeting any western world rail section demand to very high physical and wear-resistant property requirements. The company's recent contracts have covered new and rehabilitated lines in Iraq, Saudi Arabia, New Zealand, Canada, USA, Brazil and Hong Kong.

The company has developed a wear-resistant rail to area specifications but with these properties (from a 1 per cent chrome alloy base):
Brinell hardness (typical) 360, guaranteed minimum 340;
Yield, typical 106 000 lb/in², guaranteed minimum 100 000 lb/in²;
Tensile, typical 169 000 lb/in².
It is designed for application to heavy-haul railroads in Australia, USA, Canada, South America etc, with severe curves, reverse curves, superelevation and gradient difficulties to achieve longer life under increasingly harsh operating conditions and axleloads of up to 35 tons.

The company has the capability to produce rail up to 120 ft unit length for economy of welding into continuous 'stringers'.

Broken Hill
Broken Hill Proprietary Co Ltd

140 William Street, Melbourne 3000, Victoria, Australia

Telephone: 600701
Telegrams: Hematite, Melbourne
Telex: 30408

Products: Rail, fishplates, sleeper plates, steel sleepers.

BTR
BTR Limited

Silvertown House, Vincent Square, London SW1P 2PL, England

Telephone: 01-834 3848
Telex: 22524

Main works
Lesteel
PO Box 4261, Luipaardsvlei 1743, South Africa

Rubber & Allied Products (Pvt) Ltd
PO Box 8034, Belmont, Bulawayo, Zimbabwe

BTREC Inc
1581 Stone Ridge Road, Stone Mountain, Georgia 30083, USA

BTR Rail Fasteners (Australia) Pty Ltd
PO Box 72, Bentley, Western Australia 6102, Australia

Fist do Brasil
Caixa Postal 049, Barueri, São Paulo, CEP 06400, Brazil

Products: FIST-BTR and B-TREC elastic rail fasteners for concrete sleepers.

Canron
Canron Inc Tamper Division

171 Eastern Avenue, Toronto, Ontario M5A 1H7, Canada

Telephone: 363 8801
Telex: 06 23289

Products: Automatic track levelling, tamping and lining machines; ballast cleaners and regulators; rail grinding and sleeper boring/placing machines; spike drivers and extractors; drilling machines; inspection cars; track laying equipment; track recording analysis equipment; track recording trolleys.

Cemafer
Cemafer Gleisbaumaschinen und Gerate GmbH

Ihringer Landstrasse 3, Postfach 1327, 7814 Breisach, Federal Republic of Germany

Telephone: 07667 585
Telex: 7722524

Products: Power wrenches, coach-screwing machines, rail drills, rail saws, sleeper drills, sleeper adzing and drilling machines, rail grinding equipment, rail benders, light tampers, inspection trolleys, trailers, portal cranes, hand tools, electric generators (portable), gauges, jacks, rail cutting machines, rail stripping machines, sleeper boring machines, sleeper placing machines, spanners, spike drivers and extractors, track laying equipment, wrenches.

Centro-Maskin
Centro-Maskin Göteborg AB

Head office: Box 47303, 402 55 Gothenburg, Sweden

Telephone: 46 31 460400
Telex: 20977

Main works: Dagjamningsgatan 1, Gothenburg

President: Anders Ilstam
Technical Director: Christer Gustafsson
Sales Manager: Christer Akesson

Subsidiary: Centro-Metalcut Inc
PO Box 5046, Rockford, Illinois 61125, USA

Products: Carbide-tipped saws; carbide-tipped drill units; grinders for reconditioning of rail. Suppliers to Canadian National and Belgian National Railways.

Centro-Metalcut machine for single-operation precision rail sawing and boring of up to 0.005 in accuracy enabling one operator to deal with a rail in 35 s

CF&I Steel
CF&I Steel Corporation
A subsidiary of Crane Co

PO Box 1830, Pueblo, Colorado 81002, USA

Telephone: (303) 561 6000
Telex: 45 2446

President: F J Yaklich
General Manager, Railroad Sales: F O Johnson

Products: Rails, sleeper plates, rail anchors and track spikes.

Chemetron
Chemetron Corporation, Railway Products Division

111 East Wacker Drive, Chicago, Illinois 60601, USA

Telephone: (312) 565 5000
Telegrams: Chemrail
Telex: 25-4383

President: C H Brandstrom
Vice President: P J Cunningham

Products: Contract welding of continuous rail of 25 to 82 foot (7.62-25 metre) lengths into quarter-mile lengths; rail welding units; rail trains; rail handling equipment; thermite welding kits (ORGOTHERM) and rail anchors.

Coles Cranes
Coles Cranes Ltd

Sales: Harefield, Uxbridge, Middlesex UB9 6QG, England

Telephone: 089 582 3777
Telex: 21619

Chairman: W A de Vigier
Managing Director: A D Steel
Home Sales Director: V J Canham
Export Sales Director: P Allison
Engineering and Marketing Director: P K Steel
Manufacturing Director: R J Buckland
Parts, Service and Purchasing Director: D H Fenner

Products: Diesel-electric, diesel-hydraulic, mobile truck-mounted, tower cranes, rough and all-terrain mobile cranes (lifting capacities from 6 to 250 tonnes).

Cooper & Turner
(Glynwed Screws and Fastenings Ltd)

Templeborough Works, Sheffield Road, Sheffield S9 1RS, England

Telephone: 0742 449011
Telex: 54607

Marketing Manager: R M Saxton
Managing Director: P C Beardsley

Products: Fish bolts, track bolts, screw spikes, crossing bolts, frog bolts.

Costain
Costain Concrete Co Ltd

Rye House, Hoddesdon, Hertfordshire EN11 0EW, England

Telephone: 0992 463037
Telex: 894396

Managing Director: David B Scott
Technical Director: John Buekett

Products: Prestressed concrete sleepers.

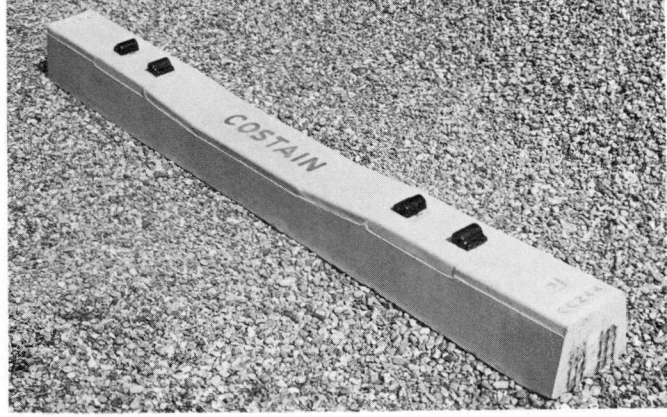

Costain prestressed concrete sleeper

Daido
Daido Steel Co Ltd

Kogin Bldg 11-18, Nishiki 1-chome, Naka-ku, Nagoya, Japan

Telephone: (052) 201-5111
Telex: 442-2243

Main works: Daido Bldg 7-13, Nishishinbashi, 1-chome, Minato-ku, Tokyo

Telephone: (03) 501-5261

Products: High manganese cast steel frogs and crossings. Recent developments include a movable-nose frog for slab track.

Dehe
Société des Entreprises A Dehe et Cie

40 quai de l'Ecluse, 78290 Croissy-sur-Seine, France

Products: Track construction and maintenance equipment.

Delachaux
C Delachaux SA

119 avenue Louis-Roche, 92231 Gennevilliers, France

Telephone: 790 61 20
Telex: 620 118

Products: Aluminothermique rail welding equipment.

Desquenne et Girail
Société Desquenne et Girail

26 rue Lalo, 75016 Paris, France

Products: Track maintenance equipment.

D'Huart
Jean D'Huart et Cie

3 rue d'Industrie, 57110 Yutz, France

Telephone: 8 256 34 81
Telex: 860006

Products: Rail, steel and timber sleepers, fishplates, other track components.

Donelli
Donelli, SpA

Via Romana 69, 42028 Poviglio, Reggio Emilia, Italy

Telephone: (0522) 689046
Telegrams: Donelli, Poviglio
Telex: 530320

Products: Ballast regulators, hydraulic cranes, jacks, sleeper placing machines, track aligners, track laying equipment, track lining machines.

Donelli offers gantry equipment as part of a complete package of track relaying machinery: gantries, rail threaders, sleeper positioners, hydraulic track lifters and slewers. The two motorised gantries combine with a lifting beam to form a 36-metre track panel lifter and sleeper laying unit. Straddling the track on which it is working, the equipment is capable of renewing 300 metres per hour. Auxiliary rails used for operation of the unit are later turned onto the new sleepers to provide the final track rail. The gantries are hydraulically operated.

The rail-threader and sleeper positioner works in conjunction with the gantry. It automatically spaces and aligns sleepers as it threads on the new rail. The unit is diesel powered and all operations are hydraulic. With outputs of up to 2000 metres per hour, the supplier claims big savings in time and manpower.

For lifting the track during new construction and relaying, Donelli markets a hydraulic track lifter and slewer which jacks the track out of the ballast. Hydraulic rail clamps grip the rail while the lifting jacks are extended onto the ballast. After lifting the machine and track, jack cylinders are tilted to displace or slew the track laterally.

Dow Mac
Dow Mac Concrete

Head office and works: Tallington, Stamford, Lincolnshire, England
Telephone: 0778 342301

Works: Eaglescliffe, Cleveland
Telephone: 0642 781811

Quedgeley, Gloucestershire
Telephone: 0452 720428

London office: 110/112 The Strand, London WC2
Telephone: 01-836 8918

Chairman: W P N Graham
Managing Director: A S Darroch
Marketing Director: N D Wiggins

Products: Dow Mac prestressed concrete sleepers; building and civil engineering components.

Durabon
Durabon Concrete Company
A Division of Dura (Pty) Ltd

Head office: PO Box 38041, Booysens 2016, Transvaal, South Africa

Telephone: 011-8352131
Telegrams: Sonsleep
Telex: 8-8327

Main works: 71 Johnson Road, Pretoriusstad, Nigel 1490, South Africa

Chairman: N B Crowngold
Managing Director: H J A Lagaay
Production Director: W Frehr

Products: Prestressed concrete railway sleepers.

Edgar Allen
Edgar Allen Engineering Limited

PO Box 42, Shepcote Lane, Sheffield S9 1QW, England

Telephone: 0742 446621
Telegrams: Alleneng, Sheffield
Telex: 547111

Products: Design and manufacture of railway switches and crossings for railways, mass transit systems, tramways, docks and harbours and steelworks; manganese steel wearing parts for locomotive and axlebox manufacturers and railway maintenance workshops.

The company is a major supplier to British Rail of manganese steel switches and crossings. Its recent business has included a contract from T W Ward for supply to Iraqi Republican Railways of cast manganese crossings; it is also supplying tramway switches and crossings to Cairo Transport Authority and Alexandria Passenger Transport.

Elektro-Thermit
Elektro-Thermit GmbH

Postfach 10 10 43, 4300 Essen 1, Federal Republic of Germany

Telephone: 0201 1731
Telegrams: Elektrothermit
Telex: 0857 1715

Managing Directors: Dr Hans Guntermann
Johann Hugo Wirtz

Products: Thermit rail welding equipment and materials, rail de-stressers, rail grinding machines, glued insulated rail joints.

Energomachexport
V/O Energomachexport
(Export company for all Soviet-built railway products)

Deguninskaja Str 1, Korp 4, 127486 Moscow, USSR

Telephone: 147 21 77
Telegrams: Moscow Energoexport
Telex: 411926

Products: Ballast cleaning machines; tamper-leveller-liner machines; track-laying cranes and gantries; snow ploughs; snow clearing and removal equipment; rail welding equipment; portable powered machines for tamping, rail cutting-drilling-grinding and spike driving-pulling; electronic and ultrasonic fault finding equipment; inspection cars; gang and maintenance railcars and trailers.

Ernest Holmes
Ernest Holmes Division (Dover Corporation)
Railroad Crane Department

2502 East 43rd Street, Chattanooga, Tennessee 37407, USA

Telephone: (domestic sales) (615) 867 2142
(export sales) (201) 842 5542

President: Don W Humphreys
Vice President: Walter Lock
Export Manager: Donald H Baldwin

Products: 100-ton railroad wrecker crane, road/rail type.

ESAB
ESAB AB

Box 8004, 402 77 Gothenburg, Sweden

Telephone: (0) 31-50 90 00
Telex: 2326

Products: Flash-welding machines. The ESAB Resistance Welding Department, at Laxa in central Sweden, has recently received an order from Indian Railways for the supply of two such machines for joining rails. ESAB has been supplying automatic flash welding machines since 1962 to customers such as the Norwegian State Railways. Each unit being supplied to India is provided with two sets of four hydraulic clamps, one set for each of the two rails to be joined. Each set of clamps has a combined maximum clamping force of 196 tonnes, while the upset force is 79 tonnes. The machines have an electro-hydraulic servo system with electronic controls developed by ESAB. The rated power of the welding transformers, at a duty cycle of 50 per cent, is 2×350 kVA. The transformers are specially designed to give a favourable distribution of current through the rails, thus ensuring rapid and uniform heat penetration. The supply of current and heat can also be vertically controlled, which is particularly valuable when welding unsymmetrical workpieces such as rails. The supply voltage is 380/440 volts, 50/60 Hz, and the weight is approximately 23 tonnes.

EWEM
Everts & van der Weyden Exploitatie Maatschappij EWEM BV

PO Box 85578, Nassauplein 25, The Hague, Netherlands

Telephone: 70-469670
Telex: 31485

Managing Director: A A G van Hees

Associated company: Unit-DE Inc, Chicago, Illinois 60606, USA (licence-holder for DE Clip)

Products: DE elastic railfastener and Unit-DE system, which includes springclip and sleeper plate or shoulder cast in concrete sleeper.

The system, which exerts a clamping force of 4400 lb per rail, compensates for the heavy vertical, lateral and longitudinal thermal and dynamic stresses caused by modern, high tonnage traffic. It does not disturb the relationship between plate and sleeper. Rail changes are made by removing the clip, taking out the old rail, putting in new rail and replacing the clip. Gauge is held firmly and spike killing is eliminated. The Unit-DE Springclip develops practically no metal fatigue and is reusable. It can be used on both wood and concrete sleepers. With wood sleepers a special rolled steel base plate or cast iron clip holder is used, depending on the type of traffic. Reinforced or prestressed concrete sleepers use cast-in clip holders.

Major users of the DE fastener are the Netherlands Railways (NS), which has 3600 km of track equipped with DE clips and has an annual requirement for 2 to 2.5 million clips, mainly for UIC 54 rails. Other users include the municipal tramway lines of The Hague and Rotterdam; the Liberian American Mining Company (Lamco), Liberia; Rheinische Braunkohle Köln; Krupp Eisenwerke and Krupp Weichenbau; Klöckner Werke Osnabrück and Klöckner-Weichenbau; Thyssen Edelstahl Krefeld and Thyssen Weichenbau; Norwegian State Railways (NSB); Surinam Railways; Compania de Vale de Rio Doce (Brazil); AT&SF, USA; National Railways of Colombia (FNC); and Madrid Metropolitan Railway.

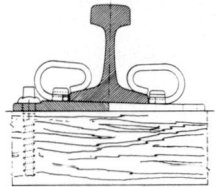 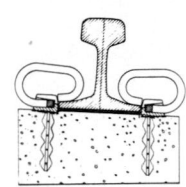 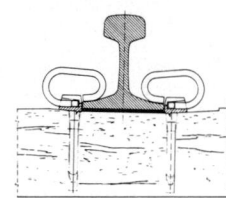

Unit-DE Springclip in use with (from left) wooden sleeper and rolled steel baseplate, concrete sleeper; hardwood sleeper with malleable cast iron clip holder

Fairfield-Mabey
Fairfield-Mabey Limited

Chepstow, Gwent NP6 5YL, Wales

Telephone: 02912 3801
Telex: 497019

Chairman: B G Mabey
Deputy Chairman and Chief Executive: J V P C Russell
Deputy Chief Executive: J Evans
Commercial Manager: D J Davies

Products: Temporary and permanent bridging. The company has developed a modular bridge available for through bridgework of any span up to 60 metres and for underbridges of up to 22.5 metres span.

Fairmont
Fairmont Railway Motors
A division of Harsco Corporation

Head office: Fairmont, Minnesota 56031, USA

Works: Fairmont, Minnesota 56031 and 6230 NW Drive, Mississauga, Ontario, Canada

Telephone: (507) 235 3361
Telegrams: Fairmotor
Telex: 910 565-2122

Export Manager: K J Nelson

Products: Inspection cars; section and gang cars; hy-rail equipment for road or rail movement; motor car engines; push cars and trailers; wheels, axles and bearings; derrick cars; ballast maintenance cars; weed control equipment; track liners; tie sprayers, tie and rail renewal equipment and rail grinding systems.

The W119-B tie inserter inserts, levels and squares new sleepers tight under the rail at the rate of three sleepers/minute. No respotting or additional handling of the units are required, says the supplier. All functions, including the inserting force of 4020 kg, are hydraulically powered and electronically controlled with very little operator effort. A three-section telescoping boom provides a reach of 4.25 metres from track centre-line, with a lift of 450 kg when fully extended. The machine will handle both timber and concrete sleepers.

Famatex
Famatex SRL

Aviendia San Martin 7910, San Martin, BA, Argentina

Telephone: 755 0352

Products: Inspection cars, light and heavy gangers' trollies.

Ferotrack
Ferotrack Engineering Ltd

332 Kilburn High Road, London NW6 2QN, England

Telephone: 01-624 0103
Telex: 8812198

Products: Electric pad point and crossing heaters.

Ferrostaal
Ferrostaal AG

PO Box 10 12 65, Hohenzollernstrasse 24, 4300 Essen, Federal Republic of Germany

Telephone: 0201 20141
Telegrams: Ferrostaal, Essen
Telex: 0857100

Directors: Dr Hans Singer
Wilhelm Haverkamp
Wilhelm Lüttenberg
Dr Klaus von Menges
Gerhard Thulmann
Hans-Ulrich Gruber

Products: Rails, baseplates, rail fastening material, wooden, concrete and steel sleepers, turnouts and crossings.

Findlay, Irvine
Findlay, Irvine Ltd

Bog Road, Penicuik, Midlothian, Scotland

Telephone: 0968 72111
Telex: 727502

Chairman: James S Findlay
Managing Director: John A Irvine
Sales Manager: J S S Macdonald

Products: Points heating controller; thermostats. The Icelert Model 162 points heating controller is suitable for controlling electric or gas points heating and a special temperature and moisture probe assembly has been designed for this particular application. It controls on a temperature and moisture detection basis and only when the temperature set point (usually 1°C) is reached and moisture is detected at the probes will a relay be activated. This gives a better degree of control than the normal thermostat working on a temperature basis only. The heated moisture probe with its snow arrester is normally fixed to a 3-inch diameter vertical pole beside the track. The temperature sensor can either be sited on this pole or clamped to the rail itself. Simple spring clamps are available for easy fixing to the rail. The temperature level at which the instrument is set to bring on heat in wet conditions is usually 3°C, to prevent the accumulation of wet snow. A Setback control can be used to prevent the rails becoming very cold even when dry, and therefore slow to raise to above freezing point. Another control knob is provided to enable the selection of a second operating point at a number of degrees below the normal operating level. The heaters will be switched on when the ambient temperature falls to this level and moisture and snow is not detected.

Foster
L B Foster Co

Foster Building, 415 Holiday Drive, Pittsburgh, Pennsylvania 15220, USA

Telephone: (412) 928 3400

President: Warren K Kearns

Products: Rail and track accessories, frog and switch material crossings, railroad ties, steel mine ties and track tools.

Framafer
Société Française de Construction de Matériel Ferroviaire

90 rue de la Gare, 57801 Bening-les-Saint-Avold, France

Telephone: (8) 704 54 54
Telex: 860243

Products: Automatic track levelling, tamping and lining machines, ballast cleaners and ballast regulators.

Francon
A Division of Canfarge Ltd

Head office: 3701 Jarry St East, Montreal, Quebec H1Z 2G2, Canada

Telephone: 722 2511
Telex: 05-829567

Main works: 8300 Pie IX Blvd, Montreal, Quebec H1Z 3T6

Vice President: Jean C Paolucci
Sales Manager: Jacques Barette

Products: Prestressed concrete sleepers.

FSSA
Ferrovias y Siderurgia SA

Cedaceros 4, Madrid 14, Spain

Telephone: 231 97 52/39 49
Telegrams: Ferrovias

President: Carlos Roeb Urqeheuer
General Manager: Luis Rios Sidro

Products: Railway track materials, turnouts, expanding joints, single and double slips, turntables, points and crossings.

Geismar
Société des Anciens Etablissements L Geismar

113 bis avenue Charles de Gaulle, 92200 Neuilly sur Seine, France

Telephone: (1) 747 55 00
Telegrams: Fermar, Neuilly
Telex: 620700

Works: 5 rue d'Altkirch, 68006 Colmar
Telephone: (89) 41 48 83
Telex: 880953

Products: Rail saws; rail drills; coachscrewing machines; fishbolt fastening machines; rail profile grinding machines; rail grinding machines; sleeper drilling machines; chamfering machines; sleeper adzing machines; lightweight ballast tampers; illumination plants; track warning devices; hydraulic rail benders; hydraulic rail joint straighteners; rail lubricators; trolleys (1 to 200 tons); inspection trolleys; rail loaders; rail pullers; rail changers; sleeper loading machines; tamping and slewing jacks; complete range of hand tools; self-propelled tracklaying gantries; thermit weld shears; hydraulic rail tensors; heavy-duty sleeper changing machine; spike drivers and pullers; combination track gauge and level; in-plant sleeper adzing-drilling-sawing machine; track-slewing and lining machines; electronic train warning device for gangs working on the track; electronic train loading gauge control device, etc.

Geismar markets a comprehensive range of track relaying equipment, which includes hydraulic portal cranes with hoisting capacities of 16, 24 and 30 tons. These machines lay or relay track at a rate of about 1000 feet (300 metres)/hour. A recent addition to Geismar equipment is a self-propelled hydraulic rail threader designed to move rail lengths to and from the track position. The machine is able to remove old rails before threading new rails into fixing and welding. Operation is by one man and all lifting and transferring movements are made hydraulically.

Other products include: rail and sleeper positioner; ballast regulators; ballast compactors; light and heavy duty traction rail cars; rail heaters (4, 8 and 16 burners); turnkey installations (machining and reclaiming of sleepers, rail welding and reclamation plants).

Gemco
George Moss Pty Ltd

461-5 Scarborough Reach Road, Osborne Park, PO Box 136, Mount Hawthorn, Western Australia, Australia

Telephone: 44 688 44
Telegrams: Gemco, Perth
Telex: 92645

Products: Hydraulic controlled track machines for sleeper extraction and replacement, track lifting, levelling, ballast scarifying, sleeper boring, spike pulling and bolt renewal. Also Australian agents for Geismar rail maintenance machines.

Genstar Costain

Head office: 1000-1520, 4 Street SW, Calgary, Alberta T2R 1H5, Canada

Telephone: (403) 264 1590
Telex: 03-821669

Main works: 12707 170 Street, Edmonton, Alberta T5L 4J6

Vice President and General Manager: John G White

Subsidiaries: Genstar Costain Tie Co Ltd, Canada
Genstar Costain Tie Co Inc, USA

Products: Prestressed concrete sleepers. Genstar Costain designs and manufactures other sleepers for specific applications. Recent contracts include one for 1.5 million concrete sleepers for Canadian National, value $60 million (second contract).

Grant Lyon Eagre
Grant Lyon Eagre Ltd

Scotter Road, Scunthorpe, South Humberside DN15 8EF, England

Telephone: 0724 862131
Telex: 527215

Managing Director: D W Schafer
Directors: J W Woodford
A Jefferson
R H L Phillips

Products: Design and installation of track work; switches and crossings, cast iron baseplates, blocks, collector shoes.

Grinaker Precast
Grinaker Precast (Pty) Ltd

PO Box 365, Brakpan 1540, South Africa

Telephone: 011 813 2340
Telex: 4 20243

Chairman: O W Grinaker
Managing Director: E J Sadie
Director, Sleeper Division: J C Havinga

Products: Prestressed concrete sleepers.

GTG
Greenside Hydraulics Ltd

Greenside Works, Chapeltown, Sheffield S30 4RY, England

Telephone: 0742 468971
Telex: 54118

Chairman: J W Thompson
Directors: Guy Lees Thompson
Margaret Thompson

Products: Rail tensors for tensioning continuous welded rail; rail support arms and rollers; rail welding jigs; track lifting machines; rail joint straightening machines; rail manipulators; rail lifting bars; lightweight trolleys; rail curving machines.

Henry Boot
Henry Boot Railway Engineering Ltd

Dronfield, Sheffield S18 6XZ, England

Telephone: 0246 414615
Telex: 547945

Chairman: A Duncan
Managing Director: D M Ingham
Manager, Construction: V Robertson
Manager, Manufacturing: J M Stevenson
Marketing and Sales Manager: J Newby

Products: Railway switches and crossings; lever boxes, sliding buffer stops and ancillary equipment; construction and maintenance of railway track.

Holland
Holland Co (Railweld Division)

1020 Washington Avenue, Chicago Hts, Illinois 60411, USA

Telephone: (312) 756 0650
Telex: 910 239 2302

President: Rene Hunziker
Export Sales Manager: Jonathan Margules
General Sales Manager: Bob Walsh

Products: Rail welding equipment and contract services for electric flash-butt welding.
Holland's MobileWelder, which welds on or off track, is a self-propelled plant which aligns, welds and shears in one programmed operation and makes electric flash-butt welding feasible in virtually any area accessible by track or highway. It features a specially designed heavy-duty industrial truck chassis with a compact, electric flash-butt welding head. The welding unit is suspended from a hydraulically powered retractable boom. Power for the welding machine is furnished by an on-board diesel-generator set. The MobileWelder accepts both rubber-tyred highway wheels and flanged wheels for running on track. The built-in hydraulic jacks facilitate wheel changing. An optional turntable can be used to straddle the track at a road crossing and reverse the machine's direction so that work can progress either way. In its rail mode the MobileWelder can weld rails set on the tie ends, in centre track; or weld the rails it is running on. For construction work on an open site it is not necessary to mount the rail wheels in order to weld strings of conventional length. The K-355A flash-butt welding machine welds all rail profiles between 85 and 155 lb. The welder clamps the loose rail ends with angle-bar accuracy.

Holland MobileWelder

Hunslet
The Hunslet Engine Company Ltd

Hunslet Engine Works, Leeds LS10 1BT, England

Telephone: 0532 432261
Telegrams: Hunslt, Leeds
Telex: 55237

Products: Self-propelled six-foot and shoulder ballast cleaning machines; rail mounted drainage trenchers.

International Track Systems
International Track Systems Inc and Railroad Rubber Products

PO Box 857, 620 West 32nd Street, Ashtabula, Ohio 44004, USA

Telephone: (216) 992 9206/993 8076

Managing Director: H L Reiter
Sales Director: B F Baker

Products: Rubber products for railway track such as butyl rubber shock barriers for use between the base of rails and steel tie plates and between the plates and sleepers.

Irvine
J E Irvine & Co Ltd

Knoll Road, Camberley, Surrey, England

Telephone: 0276 5069/21419

Products: Sleeper-placing machines and tracklaying equipments including wagon-mounted cranes for rail handling (in association with Heinrich Arneke & Co, Hanover).

Italsider
Italsider SpA

Via Corsica 4, Genoa, Italy

Telephone: 010 5999
Telegrams: Italsider, Genoa
Telex: 270690

Products: Permanent way equipment including baseplates, fishplates, clips, switches and crossings.

Jackson Jordan
Jackson Jordan Inc
O F Jordan Division

General sales office: 1699 East Woodfield Road, Schaumberg, Illinois 60195, USA

Telephone: (312) 843 3995

Works: Ludington, Michigan and Baxter Springs, Kansas

Chairman: J O'Laughlin
President: D J Donahue
Executive Vice-President: J H Bush
Sales Manager: M K Flaherty

Products: Complete line of tie tampers, automatic with or without liners (curve and tangent one unit); non-automatic switch tampers; surfacing light beam fits all manufacturers' tampers; hand tampers; Jackson/Jordan spreader-ditcher/snow plough.

Jakem
Jakem Timbers Ltd

Vistec House, 185 London Road, Croydon, Surrey CR0 2RJ, England

Telephone: 01-681 1271
Telegrams: Jakem, Croydon
Telex: 946195

Directors: D A Kitching
R A Wilson
Sales Executive: V J Mallinckrodt
Marketing Executive: R A Helyar

Products: Sleepers and bridge timbers.

Jambes-Namur
Jambes-Namur, SA des Ateliers de Construction

5100 Jambes, Belgium

Telephone: 081 30 18 51
Telegrams: Jamur, Jambes
Telex: 59127

General Manager: Jean Ma
Director, Assistant General Management: Louis Warolus
Assistant Director: Willy Jourdain
Head, Sales Department: Paul de Groote
Head, Fabrication Department: Pol Gueret
Head, Erection Department: Henri Latour
Head, Mechanical Department: Jean Magonette
Head, Research Steel Constructions: Jean Rulmont

Products: Bridges of all kinds; vibrators for testing of sleepers and rail fixing devices; vibrators for ballast car unloading; gantry cranes; mechanical handling equipment.

JW
James Walker & Co Ltd

Lion Works, Woking, Surrey GU22 8AP, England

Telephone: 048 62 5951
Telex: 859221

Director: Ing W Verbeek
Technical Manager: L B Goulding
Manager: H M Kenyon
Product Engineer: D W Aves

Products: Resilient track support materials for all types of permanent way construction; the resilient cork-elastomer materials are made without grooves or profiles with low to high stiffness characteristics to suit all types of track support construction. Rail seat pads for timber, concrete and steel sleepers on ballasted track for heavy-haul, main-line passenger and light rail applications. Resilient baseplate pads, inertia block support pads and materials for unconventional track support systems for metros in acoustically-sensitive areas in non-ballasted track construction. Rail seat pads for concrete sleepers and rail continuous support material for British Rail/McGregor PACT slab track, both developed in conjunction with British Rail's Technical Centre, Derby. Additional products include specialised adhesives for glueing in clip shoulders to concrete sleepers, prolonging life of timber sleepers and track levelling applications.

Kango
Kango Wolf Power Tools Ltd

Hanger Lane, London W5 1DS, England

Telephone: 01-998 2911
Telex: 937021

Chairman: G J Chibbett
Marketing Director: P D J Jolliffe
Export Sales Europe: R H Latham

Products: Lightweight Kango electric ballast tampers and generators; Wolf electric tools.

Kershaw
The Kershaw Companies, Inc

PO Box 9238, 2205 West Fairview Avenue, Montgomery, Alabama 36108, USA

Telephone: (205) 263 5581
Telex: 59-3416

Managing Director, International Operations: Peter H Deckert

Products: Complete range of self-propelled machines for mechanised track, switch and yard maintenance: ballast regulator and ballast broom—snow switch cleaner—brush cutter attachment; track patrol with attachments; brush type kribber; track broom; yard cleaner; dual tie saw and end remover; tie bed scarifier and tie inserter; tie end remover; tie injector; tie, bridge and bundle cranes; crawler adzer; snow switch cleaner; track and switch liner; clear way brush cutter and snow blower; super jack all; Railroader trailer; undercutter and ballast cleaner; portable set off.

Klöckner-Werke
Klöckner-Werke AG

Georgsmarienwerke, Postfach 2780, 4500 Osnabrück, Federal Republic of Germany

Telephone: 0541-3221
Telex: 09-4742

Works Director: Günter Büker
Sales Director: Hans-Heinrich Niebaum

Products: Flat-bottom rail; fishplates; special slewing fishplates; fishplates for insulated joints; inserts for insulated fishplates; tongue rails; full-web rails; guard rails; flangeway sections; conductor rails; heavy crane rails; Herkules rails and components; grooved rails; thick-web rails; ribbed soleplates; points; crossings; complete track system of flat-bottom or grooved rails; points for permanent railway without ballast bed; points with movable frogs; paving points and track of the special 'Herkules' profile; hard-surfacing of switch rails; scarfed joints; stop block devices; bonded insulated rail joints for the German Federal Railway (DB), tramways and underground railways, secondary lines and local railways, foreign state and private railways, owners of private sidings and all industrial railways; powered and idle wheel-sets; wheel-sets of light construction; wheel-sets for heavy loads; wheel-sets for gauge changes; sound-proofed wheel-sets; rubber-suspended wheel-sets; bond-shrunk wheel-sets; axles; hollow axles; solid wheels; wheel centres; tyres, and crane wheels.

Kloos Kinderdijk
Kloos Kinderdijk BV

PO Box 3, 2960 AA Kinderdijk, Netherlands

Telex: 29382

Products: Switches, crossings, turnouts and frogs.

Koehring
Koehring GmbH—Bomag Division

Postfach 180, 5407 Boppard/Rhein, Federal Republic of Germany

Telephone: 06742 2051
Telegrams: Bomag, Boppard
Telex: 04 263 16

Products: Tamping compactors, reversing vibratory plate compactors, trench compactors, double vibratory rollers, single drum vibratory rollers, double vibratory slope compactors, tandem vibratory rollers, towed vibratory rollers, sheepsfoot rollers, pneumatic-tyred rollers, soil stabilisers, refuse compactors.

Krautkrämer
Krautkrämer GmbH

Luxemburger Strasse 449, 5000 Cologne-Klettenberg, Federal Republic of Germany

Telephone: 44 60 61
Telegrams: Impulsschall, Köln

Products: Stationary rail testing installations, rail testers, rail test cars.

Lamp
Lamp Manufacturing & Railway Supplies Ltd

1 Curtis Road, Dorking, Surrey RH4 1XB, England

Telephone: 0306 88 4411
Telegrams: Lampists, Dorking
Telex: 896691

Chairman: R F Porter
Managing Director: F A Barnes
Senior Production Engineer: A Bale
Chief Sales Engineer: D Farrington

Subsidiary company: Planwell Engineering Ltd, Curtis Road, Dorking, Surrey RH4 1XB

Products: Oil and electric lamps for a variety of railway applications; switch heaters, including the Planlite 5000 designed to allow mechanical tamping machines to operate without the need to remove the switch heater from the points; terminal blocks, fuseholders and lightning arresters. Lamp has yearly contracts for its products and spare parts with British Rail.

Lamp has recently developed an electric stop block lamp, a battery-operated tail lamp and an electric speed indicator lamp for temporary use. The speed indicator lamp is a successor to the Adlake 33 oil lamp. The lamp uses standard 15½ sp screens (white on black or black on white) and, in use with British Rail, is illuminated by two 6.5-volt 150-amp lamps. In the differential situation two of the new 33 E/D lamps are mounted one on top of the other on the battery box. The lower lamp becomes the slave of the upper lamp and should the upper lamp fail the lower lamp is automatically extinguished.

Loram
Loram Maintenance of Way, Inc

3900 Arrowhead Drive, Hamel, Minnesota 55340, USA

Telephone: (612) 478 6014
Telex: 29 0391

Manager, Marketing: G A Farris

Products: Autotrack, single-track ploughs, double-track ploughs, ballast sleds, winch carts, multi-purpose machines (undercutters), autosleds, self-propelled 24-, 36-, 72- and 88-stone rail grinders, shoulder ballast cleaners, sleeper inserters, sleeper extractors, rail corrugation analysers, undertrack fabric applicators.

Recent contracts include one of three years with the Mount Newman Mining Co Pty Ltd of Western Australia for rail grinding services, using a Loram 44-stone model.

Loram 88-stone rail grinder, with three individually-monitored 20 hp grinding modules per grinding carriage

Loram self-propelled Model 1015 tie (sleeper) inserter powered by Detroit 87 hp diesel; track speed 34 km/h, tie insertion cycle, one per 12 s

Matema
Matema Materiali Meccanici SpA

Via Ardeatina Km 21, 00040 S Palomba, Rome, Italy

Telephone: 919112
Telegrams: Matistal, Pomezia
Telex: 68150

Chairman: R Blomqwist
Managing Director: R Naggar
Chief Sales Director: F Vittori
Export Sales Director: G Uccelli

Products: Track recording trolleys; automatic track levelling, tamping and lining machines; ballast cleaners; ballast regulators; heavy and light gang cars; sleeper boring machines; rail power saws; wrenches and drills; continuous-rail welding machines and grinding machines; electric generators (portable); gauges; handfacing equipment; jacks; screwing machines; sleeper placing machines; spike drivers and extractors; track laying equipment.

Matériel de Voie
Le Matériel de Voie SA

3 rue Paul Baudry, 75383 Paris Cedex 08, France

Telephone: 359 97 31
Telex: 650 248

Products: Rails, fishplates, sleepers, baseplates, grooved rail.

Matisa
Matériel Industriel SA

Head office: Matisa Matériel Industriel SA, Case Postale, 1001 Lausanne, Switzerland

Works: Renens and Crissier (Lausanne), Santa Palomba (Rome)

Products: Automatic tamper-leveller-liners; universal switch tamper-leveller-liners; medium tamper-leveller-liners; light tampers; ballast cleaners; ballast regulators; and hopper wagons; ballast compactors; track recording trolleys; rail cars and coaches; track measuring and analysing equipment; curve calculators; track renewal train; power wrenches; rail saws and rail drills; sleeper drills; and gang trolleys.

Latest equipment

B 200
Tamper-leveller-liners

Modular design providing a choice of six models:
single workhead for tamping in open track;
double workheads for tamping in open track;
single workhead for tamping in open track with check rail where obstacles are present.
Each type can be fitted with:
3 axles: front axle and rear bogie, 3-point suspension UIC standard
4 axles: 2 railway type bogies with primary steel coil spring suspension, anti-yaw dampeners. 3-point suspension, UIC standard.

B 133
Universal Tamper-leveller-liner
'Regelfahrzeug' train formation for switches and plain track
80 km/h self-propelled
100 km/h in train formation
Production speed on plain track: 500 m/h
Complete treatment of:
simple switch: 20 minutes
double switch: 30 minutes
cross-over: 40 minutes
cross-over/junction: 60 minutes

B 85
Tamper-leveller-liner
Model M with double workhead: 1000 m/h
Model N with single workhead: 600 m/h

LCR 04
Tamper-liner
For all gauges from 700 mm, restricted structure gauges, special adaptations for mine railways, steelworks, urban and metro lines.

BL 09
Light Ballast Tamper
Single head and double head.
Single or double head, motorised, for gradients up to 60 per mille, for loop lines, sidings, etc.

C 411S
Ballast Cleaner
Very high output, for worksites where advance is extra rapid
Production: 800 m³/h

C 311
Universal Ballast Cleaner
With lifting and track holding device, for difficult, sinuous, uneven tracks of restricted gauge with various fixed obstacles.
Production: 350 m³/h

12 CB 8
Ballast Cleaner
High output, proven reliability
Production: 450 m³/h

R 7 D + WB 1
Ballast Regulator with Ballast Hopper
For all transfers
Working speed: from 2 to 20 km/h in either direction
Travel speed: 80 km/h

R 770
Ballast Regulator
For all transfers from 2 to 20 km/h in either direction
Travel speed: 70 km/h

Matisa R 770 standard ballast regulator

R 780
Ballast Regulator with incorporated hopper and ballast transfer conveyor
For operation from 2 to 20 km/h in either direction
Travel speed: 80 km/h

Matisa R 780 heavy and high-performance ballast regulator

D 912
Crib and Shoulder Compactors
Production speed: 900 m/h
Optional equipment: ploughs and brush for finishing in one pass

MPV 7
Track Recording Trolley
With Matisa analyser AV 523 for numerical values of the 18 parameters
Recording speed: 35 km/h

M 462
Track Recording Railcar
With Matisa analyser AV 523 for numerical values of the 18 parameters
Recording speed: 100 km/h

MA 461
Track Recording Coach
With Matisa analyser AV 523 for numerical value of 7/8 parameters.
Recording speed: 160 km/h
Coach layout including a recording compartment, a conference room, a two-berth sleeping compartment, kitchen and toilets, as well as small workshop with generator for independent power supply of the coach and its equipment.

P 811S

Track Renewal Train
For all types of rails and sleepers and gauges from 1000 to 1675 mm.
Length: 44.6 m
Operating personnel: 4
Production speeds: 600 m/h
Worksite start up time: 12 minutes
Worksite clearance time: 10 minutes
Track travel speed: up to 80 km/h

P 811PV

New Track Laying Train
A modern design of high-speed track laying train for new track construction. For all types of rails and sleepers and all track gauges from 1000 to 1675 mm.
Length: 44.6 m
Operating personnel: 3
Production speeds: 600 m/h
Track travel speed: up to 80 km/h

Matix-Industries
Société Matix Industries

59 rue Saint-Lazare, 75009 Paris, France

Telephone: 280 65 55
Telegrams: Matixind, Paris
Telex: 650672

Products: Track maintenance machinery including inspection cars.

McGregor
McGregor Paving Ltd

Turnoaks Lane, Birdholme, Chesterfield, Derbyshire S40 2HB, England

Telephone: 0246 76971
Telegrams: McGregors, Chesterfield
Telex: 547467

Directors: J M Brown
K A Cochrane

Products: In collaboration with British Rail's Research and Development Division, Robert McGregor developed PACT—the Paved Concrete Track system. PACT was developed as an alternative to classical track of steel rails, sleepers and ballast to reduce expenditure involved in maintenance. The system consists essentially of continuously welded rails laid on a continuously reinforced concrete slab, designed to ensure that the track geometry remains within tolerance over long periods, with negligible maintenance. Resilient rail fastenings locate the rails on the slab and resilient pads are interposed between the rail foot and slab surface.

Several versions of PACT have been constructed, both in Britain and overseas.

An essential feature of PACT is the provision of custom-made slip form pavers, which can be used to construct the concrete track bed on a single width right-of-way. Associated with the pavers is machinery which dispenses and places the slab reinforcement, and carries the concrete into the paver, ensuring a continuous process of slab construction.

Installation of PACT track

Miner
Miner y Mendez de Mexico SA de CV

Av Coyoacan 912, Mexico City, DF 03100, Mexico

Telephone: 559 1019/1339/1558
Telegrams: Zednem
Telex: 017 72 503

Products: Track assemblies and maintenance equipment.

Mitsukawa
Mitsukawa Metal Works Co Ltd

21 Harima-cho-nijima, Kako-district, Hyogo Pref, Japan

Telephone: 0794 35 2288

Products: Rail fastenings, steel sleepers and forged crossings.

Modern Track Machinery
Modern Track Machinery Canada Ltd

2455 Cawthra Road, Unit 22, Mississauga, Ontario L5A 3P1, Canada

Telephone: (416) 270 7925
Telegrams: Momack
Telex: 06-960140

President: C Geismar
Vice President: J R Inglis

Products: Railway track maintenance machines and tools with after-sales service.

Products include the Track Raider car, equipped with a Volkswagen engine of either 49 or 68 hp, a four-speed syncromesh gearbox, and four-wheel hydraulic braking, weight 795 kg, which can transport up to eight men.

Monier
Monier Limited

Head office: The Monier Building, 6-8 Thomas Street, PO Box 295, Chatswood, New South Wales 2067, Australia

Telephone: (612) 411 9611
Telegrams: Monier, Sydney
Telex: 26673

Chairman: E S Owens
Managing Director: M A Besley
Group General Manager: R S H Duncan
Operations Manager, Sleepers and Contracting: N D Knowles

Associated companies
Flex-Lox Industries
3065 Kilgard Road, Abbotsford, British Columbia V2S 5Z5, Canada
Telephone: (604) 853 0054
Telex: 04 363547

P T Monier Indonesia
J1 R S Fatmawati No 72/12, Cipete, Block A, Kebayoran Baru, Jakarta Selatan, Indonesia
Telephone: 71 4625, 71 4914, 71 6142
Telegrams: Monierindo, Jakarta
Telex: 47262

Nippon Monier KK
7th Floor, Nisshoki Building, 41 Kamiyama-cho, Kita-ku, Osaka Shi, Japan
Telephone: 06 315 6551
Telex: 5772648

CI Holdings
86 Jalan Ampang, Kuala Lumpur, Malaysia

Monier Tile (NZ) Limited
17 Laureston Avenue, Papatoetoe, New Zealand
Telex: 2553

Monier (PNG) Limited
PO Box 328, Port Moresby, Papua New Guinea
Telephone: 25 3344
Telex: 22175

CPAC — Monier
1516 Pracharat 1 Road, Bangkok, Thailand
Telephone: 585 0111
Telex: 2251

Monier Company
1091 N Batavia Street, Orange, California 92667, USA
Telephone: (714) 538 8822
Telex: 910-593-1630

Products: Concrete sleepers; plant and equipment for manufacture of prestressed concrete sleepers.

Monier has developed an efficient and economical method of producing prestressed concrete sleepers adaptable to a wide range of plant capacity requirements. The system is available for licence.

Other products manufactured by Monier include pre-cast level crossings, box culverts, concrete pipes, prestressed concrete piles and bridge girders, spun concrete transmission and lirhting poles and many other products used in engineering and building construction industries.

Recent contracts have included a A$10 million order for concrete sleepers for reconstruction of the line from Muswellbrook to Newcastle, New South Wales. The contract, from the State Rail Authority of New South Wales, involves the supply of 215 000 sleepers and is part of a A$70 million reconstruction of 126 km of track to handle the increasing freight load into Newcastle.

Track with Monier concrete sleepers

Morrison-Knudsen
Morrison-Knudsen Co Inc
Railroad Division

Park Center, 500 East Baybrook Court, PO Box 7808, Boise, Idaho 83729, USA

Telephone: (208) 345 5000
Telex: 368439

Products: Track construction.

NCM
Nederlandse Constructiebedrijven en Machinefabrieken NV

Schieweg 2, PO Box 10, Delft, Netherlands

Telephone: 15 569244
Telegrams: Necem, Delft
Telex: 31031

Products: Rails and accessories, switches, crossings and turntables, track-mobiles.

NEI
NEI Cranes Ltd

Smith House, Rodley, Leeds LS13 1HN, England

Telephone: 0532 579001
Telegrams: Cranes Rodley
Telex: 55159

Products: Heavy diesel breakdown cranes, turntables, track laying machines, hydraulic railway equipment.

Nippon Kido Kogyo
Nippon Kido Kogyo Co Ltd

21-1 Nishi Shinjuku 1-chome, Shinjuku-ku, Tokyo, Japan

Telephone: 03 343 8321
Telex: 222 28 11

Products: Pre-cast concrete slab track, concrete sleepers, rail fastenings, insulated joints.

Nippon Kokan
Nippon Kokan KK

1-2, 1-chome, Marunouchi, Chiyoda-ku, Tokyo, Japan

Telephone: (03) 212-7111
Telegrams: Kokannk, Tokyo; Kokan Jukoo, Tokyo; Kokanship, Tokyo
Telex: 222-2811; 222-2816

Chairman: Hisao Makita
President: Minoru Kanao

Products: Rails to meet all internationally recognised specifications including AREA, ASTM, UIC, BS and JIS.
The company has developed two types of premium rails employing a new manufacturing process for high strength steel. The tensile strength of the steel is more than 120 kg/mm² and Brinell hardness is 340-405. One type is the New Head Hardened (NHH), with high wear-resistant and anti-shelling properties; high weldability; defect-free stable quality; and a deep and uniformly hardened steel zone. The other type is Alloy Head Hardened. This has similar features to the NHH, with the addition of improvement of the heat-affected zone after welding.
The steel is produced mainly by a continuous casting machine including a vacuum degassing process, which results in very clean steel with low non-metallic inclusions and very low sulphur and hydrogen content.

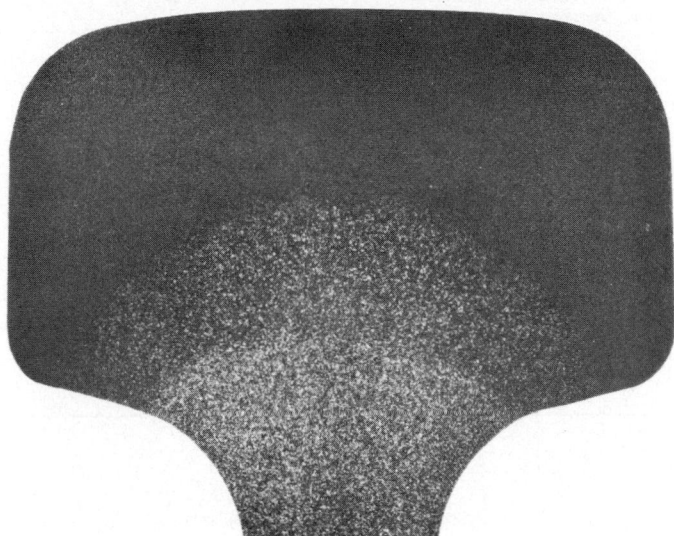

Macroscopic structure of NHH rails

Omark
Omark Trak-Lok Railway Fasteners
A Division of Omark Industries

2091 Springdale Road, Unit 9, Cherry Hill, New Jersey 08003, USA

Telephone: (609) 424 1718
Telex: 834605

President: William Langman
Manager: Angelo M D'Attoma

Principal subsidiary: Omark Australia Ltd
Waddikee Road, Lonsdale, South Australia, Australia

Telegrams: Sportco, Adelaide, South Australia
Telex: 82800

Products: Trak-Lok railway fastening system; Trak-Lok steel sleepers.

Orton
Orton McCullough Crane Company

Oakbrook Executive Plaza, 1211 West 22nd Street, Oakbrook, Illinois 60521, USA

Telephone: (312) 654 1695
Telegrams: Orcrane

Products: Cranes and heavy lifting gear.

Pandrol
Pandrol Ltd

9 Holborn, London EC1N 2NE, England

Telephone: 01-242 5252
Telegrams: Pandrol, London
Telex: 21474

Managing Director: B Clough
Sales Director: J Beal-Preston

Products: Pandrol rail fastenings, lockspikes and elastic rail spikes, pandriver rail fastening machines.

Permali
Permali Gloucester Ltd
Bristol Road, Gloucester GL1 5SU, England

Telephone: 0452 28282
Telex: 43293

Product: Glued rail joints.

Persöner
Persöner Sparteknik AB

Box 1512, 271 00 Ystad, Sweden

Telephone: 0411 13800
Telex: 33235

Managing Director: Torsten Ek
Export Manager: Bertil Olsson

Products: Construction and maintenance of track, manufacture of switches and crossings, point locks, braking buffer stops and auxiliary equipment; rails; wood, concrete and steel sleepers; baseplates; signalling systems.

Persöner point lock

Pettibone Ohio
Pettibone Ohio Corporation
A subsidiary of Pettibone Corporation

6917 Bessemer Avenue SE, Cleveland, Ohio 44127, USA

Telephone: (216) 641 4000

President: J Porter
Vice President and General Manager: T M Cavender

Products: Points, switches, crossings, track parts, materials handling equipment.

Phoenix
Phoenix AG

PO Box 90 11 40, Hannoversche Strasse 88, 2100 Hamburg 90 Harburg, Federal Republic of Germany

Telephone: (040) 76 67 303
Telex: 02 17 611

Products: The company has developed an effective and economical noise and vibration damper for U- and S-Bahn track laid in the vicinity of surface building foundations. Called CentriCon, it is adaptable both to classically ballasted track foundations or to solid-slab track bases. It consists of six self-centring sheet-rubber spring elements and two sheet-rubber fasteners. Height is only 70 mm. Centricon is available in a range of material strengths and is thus adaptable to a variety of axle-loadings without involving alteration of basic track parameters.

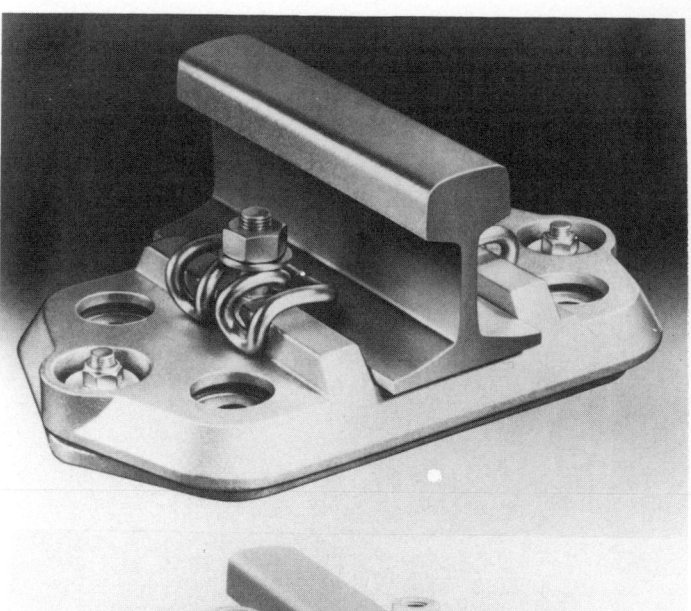

Phoenix CentriCon noise-reduction system

Pintsch Bamag
Pintsch Bamag Antriebs- und Verkehrstechnik GmbH

Postfach 10 04 20, 4220 Dinslaken, Federal Republic of Germany

Telephone: 213 46 02/1
Telex: 0855 1938

Products: Automatic propane-fuelled infra-red point heating equipment and solid state snow detectors.

Plasser
Plasser & Theurer

Head office: Johannesgasse 3, 1010 Vienna, Austria

Telephone: 52 66 01
Telegrams: Bahnbau, Vienna
Telex: 132117

Main works: Pummererstrasse 5, 4020 Linz

Products: Automatic track tamping, levelling and lining machines; universal points and crossing tamping machines; ballast consolidating machines; ballast regulators; ballast cleaning machines; track (re) laying machines; gantry cranes; rail rectification machines; track recording cars; railway motor vehicles; railway cranes and lightweight equipment for track maintenance.
The Plasser & Theurer 08 Series of tamping machines covers a range for the most varied conditions and demands.
Outstanding features of the 08-275 points and crossing tamping machines are the lateral moveable tamping heads, the sidewards tiltable tamping tools and the operator's cabin which is situated immediately in front of the working units.
The ballast regulators SSP 103 and SSP 100 have an x-shaped centre plough which enlarges their working capability.
The dynamic track stabiliser DGS applies lateral vibration and horizontal pressure to the track, thus stabilising it immediately after the tamping operation.
The RM 76 U is the first undercutter cleaner which, as well as dealing with plain track, can also undercut and clean switches and crossings.
The assembly line principle was applied to track relaying by Plasser & Theurer in 1968 with the development of the track relaying train SUZ 2000. Today the series SUZ J and SUM-SMD (high speed track laying and relaying machines in modular design) are manufactured, and can be adapted for any railway conditions.
Various types of panel laying cranes and gantry cranes are included in the sales programme.

Plasser & Theurer 08 series

	08-16	08-32	Track tamping machines				S & C tamping machines		
			08-16 DN	08-32 DN	08-16 SP	08-32 SP	08-275	08-275 DN	08-275 SP
Weight (tonnes)	42	44	40	42	30	32	43	41	31
Front axle load, each (tonnes)	10	10	18	18	15	15.5	10	18	15
Rear axle load, each (tonnes)	11	12	11	12	15	16.5	11.5	11.5	16
Engine output	165 kW (225 hp) at 2000 rpm	206 kW (280 hp) at 2000 rpm	165 kW (225 hp) at 2000 rpm	206 kW (280 hp) at 2000 rpm	165 kW (225 hp) at 2500 rpm	206 kW (280 hp) at 2500 rpm	206 kW (280 hp) at 2000 rpm	206 kW (280 hp) at 2000 rpm	165 kW (225 hp) at 2500 rpm
Speed under own power	80 km/h		80 km/h		65 km/h		80 km/h	80 km/h	80 km/h
Length over buffers (mm)	18 710		18 710		15 440		18 710	18 710	15 440
Height above rail top (mm)	3285		3285		3300		3300	3300	3300
Width (mm)	3050		3050		3050		3130	3130	3050
Distance between bogie pivots (mm)	11 000		—		—		11 000	—	—
Distance bogie pivot-front axle (mm)	—		11 000		—		—	11 000	—
Wheelbase (mm)	—		—		9500		—	—	9500
on bogies (mm)	1500		1500		—		1500	1500	—
Wheel diameter (mm)	710		710		710		710	710	710
Gauge	Standard: 1435 mm, other gauges possible								

The self-propelled track recording and analysing car EM 80 works with electronic track measuring systems which have proven their reliability under the most severe conditions.

The EM series offers different sizes of track measuring and recording cars for the most varied working conditions.

With the K 355 A PT, flash butt welding, previously restricted to stationary practice, has been made mobile and can now be carried out on track.

The rail rectification machine SBM 200 reprofiles in situ side- and headworn rails. The GWM 220 is a rail grinding machine for plain track, switches and crossings.

To suit the demands of customers a wide range of special machines for track maintenance and track works is supplied, including all kinds of motor vehicles and one- or twin-jib heavy railway cranes as well as lightweight track maintenance equipment.

Unomatic 08-16 SP tamping machine

Plassermatic 08-275 S & C tamping machine

RM76 UHR ballast-cleaning machine for plain track or switches

Duomatic 08-32 tamping machine

SUM 1000 I high-speed track relaying machine

Plastica
Plastica Kunststoffwerk GmbH

Ambrosius-Brand Strasse 20, Postfach 2165, 5828 Ennepetal 1, Federal Republic of Germany

Telephone: 02333 7821/92
Telegrams: Plastica Ennepetal
Telex: 0823 382

Managing Director: Dr Hucke

Products: Resilient rail fastenings and insulating elements.

Pluto
Société d'Exploitation des Poutres de Levage Universelles et Travelleuses Oleopneumatiques

BP 63, 78000 Les Mureaux, France

Telephone: 097 881 34 42

Products: Track laying and replacement wagon.

Portec Inc
Railway Products Division

300 Windsor Drive, Oak Brook, Illinois 60521, USA

Telephone: (312) 920 4600

Chairman and Chief Executive, Portec Inc: Thomas J Guendel
President and Chief Operating Officer, Portec Inc: D H Abbott
Senior Vice President and Railroad Group Executive: S A Kovach
General Manager, Railway Products Division: W K Knight
General Manager, RMC Division: R D Jackson

Products: Standard, compromise, and insulated rail joints; rail joint insulation; rail anchors; direct fixation fastening systems; rail and flange lubricators; weld-mate safety strap; Curv Bloc anti-rail tipping device; sleeper anti-splitting devices; sleeper wear plates; testing services.

RMC Division

PO Box 1888, Pittsburgh, Pennsylvania 15230

Telephone: (412) 782 6000

Products: Railroad ballast cleaning and tamping machines; tie removal, track laying; spot car repair systems; spike-driving machines; jet sand/snowblowers; and other maintenance-of-way equipment.

RMC Division Zapper with gauger combines track gauging system with Zapper hydraulic spike driver

Portec RMC Division Brushcutter for cutting in a swathe up to 5.5 m from track centre line

RMC Division Ichabod 20-ton hydraulic crane telescoping boom handling 40 000 lb working load at 10 ft radius, 5525 lb at 40 ft radius

Portec RMC Division Jet Snow Blower for transit systems featuring bevel top for use in confined tunnels

Portec RMC Division Hurricane Jet Snow Blower

RMC Division Anchormaster for setting and applying 12-16 rail anchors per minute

RMC Division motor car

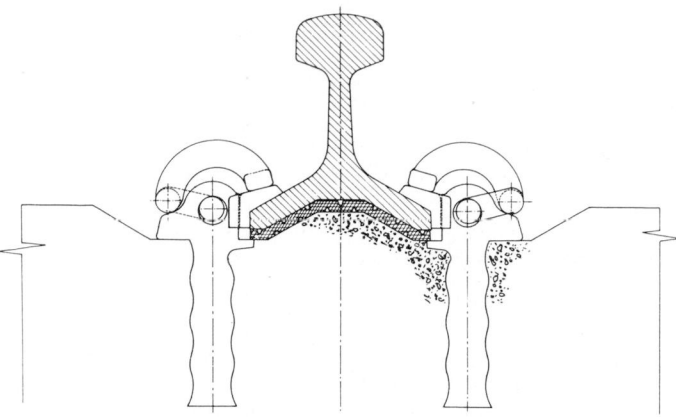
Pouget's Type Y rail with Pandrol fastenings

RMC Division Tie Knock-Out (TKO) machine

Pouget Type VT-3 portable tamping set

Portec (UK)
Portec (UK) Ltd

Vauxhall Industrial Estate, Ruabon, Wrexham, Clwyd LL14 6UY, Wales

Telephone: 0978 820820
Telegrams: Tracman, Wrexham
Telex: 61369

Managing Director: Derek J Joy
Sales and Marketing Manager: Jonathan Walker

Products: Rail and flange lubricators; switch slide chair lubricators; insulated rail joints; adhesion fluid applicators; rail anchors; wagon retarders; two-way rail benders; air lifting equipment; and track maintenance machines.

Pouget
Pouget, Etablissements SA

190 bis avenue de Stalingrad, 93240 Stains, France

Telephone: 826 62 12
Telegrams: Motovoipouget Stains
Telex: 630574

Products: Tracklaying gantries; coach screwing machines; sleeper drills; rail saws; rail drills; portable vibrating tampers; rail grinding machines; rail loaders; sleeper adzing and drilling machines; jacks; hand tools; light ballast cleaner; rail cutting machines with disc; ballast regulator; Type 'Y' rail for heavy load, high-speed track; concrete sleepers; fastenings.

Recent products include the RL-10 portable ballast regulator machine, which can be used for a variety of purposes, such as cleaning of stations and approaches on secondary lines, on new tracklaying sites after ballasting, during maintenance and following re-ballasting, etc. It is derailable by four men, and performance from 200 to 300 metres per hour is possible, according to the amount of cleaning work.

A new generation of portable tampers, the VT-3 portable ballast tamping set, with a larger eccentric mass and an improved vibration-damping system, ensures a very superior tamping performance and reduces fatigue for the operators; the handles can be adjusted to suit the operator's height. In addition, handling and safety are greatly improved through reduced weight and a dual cut-out device.

Pouget Type RL-10 portable ballast regulator machine

Premsa
Industrio e Comercio Premsa SA

Av Nossa Senhora do O 565, 02715 São Paulo, Brazil

Telephone: 266 8188

Products: Rail, points, crossings, track components.

PS Concrete
PS Concrete Co, Ltd

Head office: 4-1, 3-chome Marunouchi, Chiyoda-ku, Tokyo, Japan

Telephone: 03 216 1981
Telegrams: PS Concrete, Tokyo
Telex: 2224691

Main works
Nanao
59 Hobu, Yatashin-machi, Nanao-shi, Ishikawa-ken
Kamonomiya
370, Nakashinden, Odawara-shi, Kanagawa-ken
Zenibako
206, 3-chome Zenibako, Otaru-shi, Hokkaido
Mizushima
6, 2-chome Kaigandoori, Mizushima, Kurashiki-shi, Okayama-ken
Itami
1, aza Tanokuchi, Aramaki, Itami-shi, Hyoogo-ken

Minakuchi
6236, Ooaza Minakuchi, Minakuchi-cho, Koogagun, Shiga-ken

Kurume
1200, Shirakuchi Araki-cho, Kurume-shi, Fukuoka-ken

Kitagami
426 14 Chiwari, Aza Murasakino, Iitoyo-cho, Kitagami-shi, Iwate-ken

Jinmachi
1-62, 2-chome, Jinmachi Nishi, Higashine-shi, Yamagata-ken

Chairman: Masaji Uemura
President: Marekata Kondo
Senior Managing Director, Technical: Kazutoyo Ishida
  Accounting: Kaname Kobayashi
  Business Development: Kiyotachi Mouri
  General Affairs: Haruo Fukagawa

Subsidiaries: Japan Consultant Co, Ltd
  Hatano Seisakusho Co, Ltd

Products: Prestressed concrete sleepers; concrete track slabs; construction of prestressed concrete railway bridges.

Racine
Racine Railroad Products Inc

PO Box 4003, 1524 Frederick Street, Racine, Wisconsin 53404, USA

Telephone: (414) 637 9681

Chairman and Chief Executive Officer: G W Christiansen, Sr
Vice-Chairman and Treasurer: Robert C Schrimpf
President: George W Christiansen, Jr
Service Engineer: R L Turner

Products: Portable rail saws; drills and cut-off machines; rail clip applicators and adjusters; electronic gaugers; vibrators; re-gauge adzer; rail profile grinder; spike hole filling material and applicators.

Rails Co
The Rails Company

101 Newark Way, Maplewood, New Jersey 07040, USA

Telephone: (201) 763 4320
Telex: 138 206

President: G N Burwell
Export Sales Director: E A Judge

Products: Rail anchors, switch point locks, switch heaters (propane and natural gas), snow detectors.

The Hot Air Blower (HAB) point heater system, which is particularly effective in extreme conditions, is part of the company's line of heaters, including propane and natural gas heaters. The system has been operated using fuel oil, natural gas and propane and is now offered in totally electric form.

An improved electric HAB switch heater is now available. Designated the HAB-HP-2000 Electric, it features new high-velocity heat distribution nozzles that provide increased effectiveness in protecting switch parts from freezing. As in previous HAB electric switch heaters, a high pressure blower forces air around the combustion chamber and through the duct work, assuring even transfer and distribution of heat. The new high-velocity nozzles permit air to pass through more slowly, so that it is heated more and then ejected under higher pressure which dislodges snow further down the track. All the heat energy is distributed to the snow between point and stock rail and relatively little is used for heating the rail and tie plates. Warm air can be directed to the tie spaces as well. The positive action of the forced air system and the high capacity blower that delivers up to 1200 cubic feet per minute of hot air minimise losses due to cold air movement over the rail. This operating efficiency permits reductions in kW requirements or added effectiveness for the same kW output. The HAB-HP-2000 measures 24¾ × 28⅜ inches at the base. Its 2 hp motor runs at 3450 rpm on 240 volts ac, but it can also be supplied at 480 and 600 volts, three-phase ac. The heating element is adjustable to provide a selection ranging from 6.5 to 52 kW for three-phase power systems.

Rails Company also offers HAB switch heaters utilising oil, natural gas or propane as well as Type RTS propane gas, Type LP low-pressure natural gas and Type TH tubular electric switch heaters.

At the start of a snow or ice storm the Snow Detector automatically activates snow melting equipment, and may transmit a signal to maintenance men. As soon as the storm is over, the Snow Detector turns heaters off.

Rails Co Hot Air Blower (HAB) point heater

Ralph McKay
Ralph McKay Limited

36-46 Hampstead Road, Maidstone, Victoria, Australia

Telephone: 317 8961
Telegrams: Agridisc
Telex: 31538

Main works: Maidstone, Victoria
           Port Wakefield Road, Gepps Cross, South Australia

Chairman: L J Yeo
Chief Executive: W McGuire

Subsidiary: Ralph McKay (Canada) Limited

Products: McKay 'Safelok' elastic rail fastening system; rail anchors; dog spikes; wear plates. Safelok track sections have recently been completed or are under construction for the Australian National Railway's Adelaide Hills and Trans-Australia lines, the Hamersley Iron Railway, Quebec North Shore & Labrador Railway, the USRA's FAST track at Pueblo, Colorado, Netherlands Railway, Canadian Pacific and Canadian National Railways.

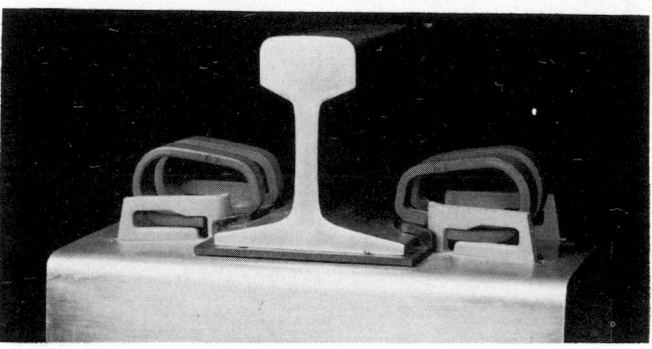

Model of Safelok elastic fastening system

Safelok track installation on Hamersley Iron Railway, Pilbara region

Raychem
Raychem Corp

300 Constitution Drive, Menlo Park, California 94025, USA

Telephone: (415) 361 3333
Telex: 34 8316

Chairman and Chief Executive: Paul M Cook
Chief Operations Officer: Robert M Malperin

Products: Halogen-free wire and cable; switch point heaters; space heaters; high voltage and medium voltage joints and terminations.

Remafer
Société de Construction et de Réparation de Matériel Ferroviaire

3 rue Christophe Colomb, 75008 Paris, France

Telephone: 723 76 51
Telex: 290471

Products: Recent products include the DAD 981 self-propelled maintenance unit. The Y27 EL bogies incorporating two self-drive axles obtain speeds of up to 60 km/h. Alternatively, using a neutral drive mode, a DAD 981 may be incorporated in a maintenance train. An hydraulic-powered arm with a suitable cutting head may be rotated horizontally through 360 degrees, and there is a 150-degree vertical pivoting facility. Both locomotion and movement of the arm are controlled from one cab. Provision has also been made for remote control using an 8-metre control cable unit. The arm is equipped with a 1.8-metre cutting head and an area of up to 10 metres from the track can be effectively processed. Working speeds are dependent on the vegetation density, etc; for example, a very short cutting or pruning operation would require a 6 km/h speed.

Special fail-safe security features are incorporated in the specification. These devices lock the controls to regulated parameters or 'stops'; hence the fully hydraulic systems cannot foul overhead power lines or other fixed structures. Transmission lines may remain live during maintenance. Accidental fouling of adjoining tracks is also precluded.

Currently the units are used by SNCF, gauge UIC; however, other international gauge specifications are feasible, including a combined mechanical chemical treatment design. This later variant cuts and sprays the vegetation to control growth.

Remafer Type DAD 981 self-propelled maintenance unit, weight 46.2 tonnes

Rexnord
Railway Equipment Division

Export sales head office: 3073 South Chase Avenue, Milwaukee, Wisconsin 53201, USA

Licensee: Noyes Bros Pty Ltd, Frederick Street, St Leonard's, New South Wales, Australia

Products: Trackliners, switchliners, self-propelled adzers, rail drills, surf-rail grinders, heavy duty rail grinders, utility grinders, spike hammers, hydraulic spike pullers, spike straighteners, tie drills, self-propelled spike pullers, hydraulic power jacks, dun-rite gauging machines, hydra-spikers, line indicators, E-Z lifts, tie spacers, rail gang spikers, X-level indicators, track-inspectors, one-man scarifier inserters and tie removers.

New machines for sleeper renewal include the Woodchuck, which will kick out the sleeper plate and remove the high wood from a plate-worn or rail-worn sleeper, allowing the sleeper to be removed in one piece without disturbing the track line or surface. The high wood that has been removed is automatically dumped into a bin placed for that purpose in the forward section of the machine. With the exception of travelling and locating, the action of the machine can be completely automatic. In test and demonstration, the Woodchuck has been able to remove high wood and kick off the sleeper plate at the rate of up to eight sleepers per minute.

The Tie Puller has been designed as a compatible machine for removing one-piece sleepers at the rate of up to eight per minute. Jaws, which are located on a telescoping boom, are moved into a position on either side of the sleeper to be removed. These jaws will slide under the rail on either side of the old sleeper, entering almost 300 mm into the centre section, to give sufficient surface on which to grasp the old sleeper before it is removed. The operator then has the control to squeeze the tie and, initially, start its removal. Once the sleeper has broken loose, the operator places the controls on automatic; the boom will then remove the sleeper, dropping it clear of the work area and then relocate itself, preparatory for the next removal.

The Nordberg Model CHP hydraulic spike puller has been upgraded with several new features. There are push-button controls, a powered transverse carriage and a removable lower case to the puller apparatus. A powered propulsion model will also be available.

The new Nordberg Super B multi-purpose automatic spiker has a feed that will accept used and reconditioned spikes and a single-trigger controller; its optional equipment includes a variable gauger, fixed gauger, jib boom and winch, nippers and spike straightener. Powered by a 76 hp, 2250 rpm engine it has a travel speed of up to 48 km/h. Also new is the Nordberg variable gauger, which reads from the inside of the ball, not the web.

Rexnord Woodchuck

Nordberg Super B automatic spiking machine

Readout dial on variable gauger

Rexnord Tie Puller for one-piece sleeper removal

Richardson & Cruddas
Richardson & Cruddas (1972) Limited

P Box No 4503, Sir J J Road, Bombay 400 008, India

Telephone: 866832 39
Telegrams: Ironworks, Bombay
Telex: 011-3662

Chairman and Managing Director: P P Sharangpani

Products: Manufacture of railway points and crossings; pressed steel turnout sleepers; steel track; sleepers; slide chairs, etc; fabrication of overhead structures for railway electrification.

Robel
Robel GmbH & Co

Thalkirchnerstrasse 210, 8000 Munich 75, Federal Republic of Germany

Telephone: 7233011
Telegrams: Robelco, Munich
Telex: 05-23012

Products: Powered ganger's trolleys with hydraulic tipping platform and crane, trailers, stationary and mobile machines for processing sleepers and rails, equipment for loading and unloading long-welded rails, rail drilling machines, rail saws, power wrenches, rail grinders, hydraulic rail benders, ratchet track jacks and spanners, gauges, portal cranes etc.

Recent products include the Robel power wrench 30.82 for all track bolting jobs. It is equipped with: two-speed gear; reverse gear; spur gear (for maximum force); metal cone clutch; and hydraulic torque adjuster uninfluenced by clutch wear. The torque may be adjusted exactly by hydraulic servo actuation; the amount of wear is adjusted automatically. The hand lever is vertically adjustable. A short-time increase of torque can be obtained through a cut-off lever without changing basic adjustment. Chassis has roller bearings.

Robel's latest design of a hydraulic four-spindle power wrench, the 07.14, is a depot tool suitable for tightening and loosening four sleeper screws or hook bolt nuts simultaneously or for boring four pegs. It is equipped with an infinitely variable hydrostatic drive and consists of a support frame, three-phase ac drive motor, hydraulic multiple pumps and a corresponding hydraulic system as well as two double screw aggregates. The screw and drill spindles can be adjusted to the required distance to the rail centre and inclined correspondingly. As each screw motor is individually driven by its own hydro pump, speed and torque of each screwing spindle can be controlled separately via a torque meter. All wrench heads are equipped with hydraulically-controlled grippers which lift up the spring rings and clamping plates simultaneously during loosening of hook bolt nuts. The removed parts are ejected into receptacles on the inner sides of the supports.

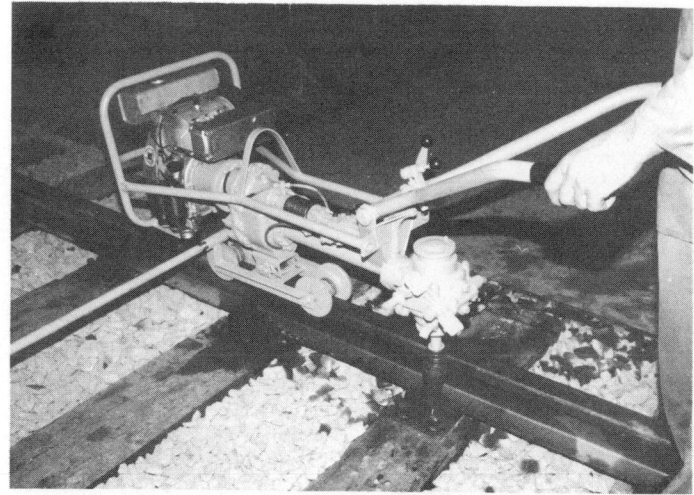

Robel Type 30.82 power wrench

Robel Type 43.32 rail threader with freely adjustable wheel-sets for smooth travel while adjusting rail gauge during relaying

Robel Type 07.14 power wrench in depot use

Robel permanent way maintenance wagon Type 54.17 with telescopic crane

Robel Type 10.35 fishplate-hole rail drill, for use on switches and both grooved and plain rail

Motor-generator for Type 62.04 tamper, trolley-mounted for rail movement

Robel electric tamper Type 62.04

Robel Type 13.80 rail cutter, petrol-engined, with electronic ignition, high-speed governor and centrifugal clutch, capable of up to five cuts per easily interchangeable cutting disc

Type RR-2/200 fitted with hydraulic mechanism by which a Rolba snowplough can be turned without a turntable

Rothe Erde-Schmiedag
Rothe Erde-Schmiedag AG

Tremoniastrasse 5-11, 4600 Dortmund 1, Federal Republic of Germany

Telephone: (0231) 186 07
Telegrams: Rotheerde Dtd TW 245
Telex: 822245

Chairman: H Krause
Technical Director: H Hofmann
Commercial Director: Dr J Remmerbach

Products: Permanent way fixing materials for all types of timber; ribbed sole plates for track and switches; clip plates; coach screws; hook bolts; elastic fastenings.

RS
Roger P Sonneville

Tour Maine-Montparnasse, BP 133, 33 avenue du Maine, 75755 Paris Cedex 15, France

Telephone: 538 73 20
Telex: 260 881

Products: Steel and reinforced two-block sleepers, elastic insulated fastenings.

Rolba
Rolba AG

Zurcherstrasse 51, 8620 Wetzikon, Switzerland

Products: Rotary snow ploughs from 10 to 1000 hp.

The Rolba RR-300-D-S high-performance rotary snowplough employs a single Cummins six-cylinder turbo-charged diesel engine for propulsion of the purpose-built carrier vehicle as well as to drive the cutter assembly. Fully hydrostatic transmission guarantees adjustment to the clearing of any kind of snow. The variable axial piston pump as well as the two variable axial piston motors allow maximum use of propulsion power, with infinitely variable speeds for forward and reverse motion. The rotary plough head can clear snow up to a height of approximately 2.5 metres in one run, the casting distances varying from approximately 6 to 28 metres depending on the gear selected. The rotary head can be hydraulically lifted and lowered by approximately 300 mm. A powered hydraulic device which raises the complete unit 30 mm above rail level enables it to be turned through 180 degrees under one operator's control without a turntable.

RTW
Evans/Railway Track-Work Company
Affiliate of Evans Product Co Transportation Systems & Industrial Group

2381 Philmont Avenue, Bethayres, Pennsylvania 19006, USA

Telephone: (215) 947 7100

Vice-President and General Manager: R A Jean
Vice-President, Sales: Edward T Stuhl

Rolba Type RR-3000 high-performance rotary snowplough

Evans/RTW Model 111-A Track Mule

Products: Tie handlers; cross grinders; rail drills; track skeletonisers; anchor cribbers; vibrators; track cranes.

Equipped with hydraulic operating and control systems, including rail-handling clamps that lock to the rails for added safety, the Evans/RTW Model 3580 Utility Crane permits the operator to accurately position an 11.89-metre (39-foot) rail without assistance. The new unit, featuring a heavy-duty steel frame and boom of welded high-tensile steel plate, has a one-ton lift capacity at its maximum extension of 7.92 metres (26 ft) and a maximum lift of 1450 kg (3200 lb) at 5.5 metres (18ft). Diesel powered, it operates at on-track speeds of 32 km/h (20 mph) and is also available in an optional model for speeds up to 56 km/h (35 mph). For easier manoeuvrability, the single-seat deck rotates 360 degrees and can cycle continuously in either direction. Attachments include a sleeper bucket for lifting and transporting five sleepers at a time, a concrete sleeper handler head, and a magnetic head for roadbed cleaning and pick-up of spikes, joint bars, and other steel pieces.

With lift capacity to 11 300 kg (25 000 lb), travel speed to 56 km/h (35 mph) and telescoping boom reach to 10.67 metres (35 ft) horizontal and 10.36 metres (34 ft) vertical, the Evans/RTW Model 111-A Track Mule is both heavy-duty and versatile. Designed for lifting and manoeuvring in repair or maintenance operations, the Model 111-A performs a variety of functions such as rail threading, material or crew transport and light yard switching. An enclosed and heated operator's cab provides good visibility on all four sides; the blind spot behind the operator is covered by television camera. All functions are controlled by three levers and two foot pedals. Engine is a GMC GV-71 diesel of 238 hp at 2100 rpm. Automatic couplers for haulage and locomotive air brakes are fitted.

Evans/RTW Model 3580 utility crane

Sateba
Sateba International SA

262 boulevard St-Germain, 75007 Paris, France

Telephone: (1) 705 71 18
Telex: 200808

Managing Director: Claude Cazenave
Director: Denis Vallet

Products: Vagneux-type two-block and monobloc concrete sleepers; sleeper design; factory design and installation, supply of machinery, personnel training and technical assistance.

Scania
Saab-Scania AB, Scania Division
151 87 Södertälje, Sweden

Telephone: (46) 755 810 00
Telex: 10200

Products: Scania has recently gained a SKr17.5 million contract to supply 17 motor maintenance trolleys to Swedish State Railways (SJ). They are based on components from the new Scania T112 truck models. The first generation of Scania motor trolleys were based on the Scania L111 chassis and a total of 51 motor trolleys was supplied to the Swedish State Railways in 1979-82. The new vehicles are designated Motortralla 112. In winter the vehicles, equipped with front and side plough blades and track-clearing units, are used for snow clearance. The extended cab can accommodate six people, including the driver. Equipment also includes a two-way communications radio and a 6-tonne-metre loading crane. Overall weight is 21 tonnes and top speed about 80 km/h. The trolley is equipped with a turntable device and the entire vehicle can be quickly turned on the track. Export sales are handled exclusively by Swedish Rail System AB SRS.

Scania T112 motor maintenance trolley

Schlatter
Schlatter AG HA

Bandstrasse, 8952 Schlieren, Switzerland

Telephone: 01 730 0951
Telegrams: Elektropunkt Schlieren
Telex: 53054

Products: Dc-railwelder Type GAAS with inbuilt upset-removing device; portable railwelder Type AAS 50.

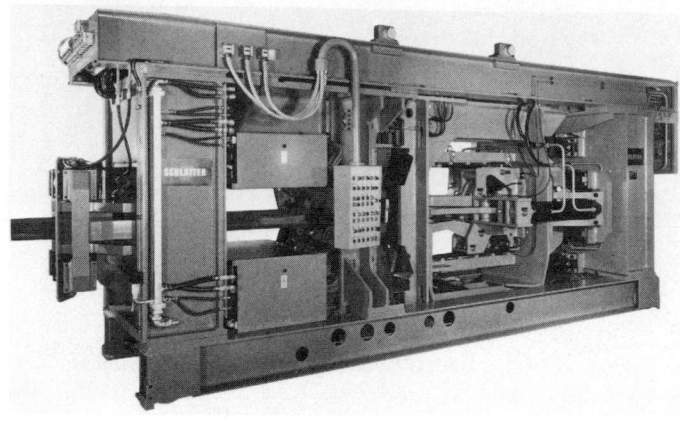

Type GAAS 80 automatic railwelder

Schramm
Schramm Inc

800 East Virginia Avenue, West Chester, Pennsylvania 19380, USA

Telephone: (215) 696 2500
Telex: 83 5455

Products: Pneumatractors; portable compressors; industrial compressors; Rotadrills; air tools. The HT300B Pneumatractor can be fitted with four flanged wheels to permit its use in track maintenance and construction; its 300 cubic feet/minute compressor can power heavy-duty drills, torque wrenches, spike drivers and tampers.

Schramm HT300B Pneumatractor in rail use

SECEMM
Société d'Etudes et de Constructions Electriques, Mécaniques et Métallurgiques

15/17 rue Chabrol, 75480 Paris Cedex 10, France

Products: Track maintenance and inspection equipment, including rail grinding units of several types, lateral deburring machines, rail heaters, rail de-scaling machines, electrode ovens, and rail butt-end cutters.

SECEMM Type TL80 road/rail tractor

Secmafer
Secmafer SA

Chemin des Meuniers, Buchelay, 78203 Nantes, France

Telephone: 092 40 00
Telex: 600815

Managing Director: Jean-Jacques Boyer

Products: Complete track relaying trains for mechanised track maintenance and construction; fully automatic relaying gantries; ballast regulators; track assembly and lining machines; fully automatic ballast cleaning and levelling machines; shunting locomotives, etc.

Secmafer markets beam and gantry systems for mechanised track maintenance and rehabilitation, consisting of two mobile gantries connected by a longitudinal beam. Power is supplied by 80 hp diesel engines. The gantries are telescopic, allowing work to be carried out beneath overhead wires and in confined areas such as tunnels. The machines can position new track (prefabricated panels or single ties) at a rate of 350 metres per hour.

In 1975 Secmafer built a new type of gantry/beam system which, sold to Iran and Scandinavia, increases track relaying speeds to 600 metres per hour. The 216 M10 gantries and 401 BR beam form a monobloc assembly about 18 metres long. As in previous models, they simultaneously dismantle two old track panels of 18 to 24 metres in length, and on a second pass relay the corresponding number of new sleepers.

Main differences between the new and old models is that motive power consisting of two diesel-air engines rated at 250 hp each, is installed on the beam instead of the gantry. This, says the maker, leaves two solid but streamlined gantries with all wheels driven, achieving increased adherence to the running rails and a firm guarantee against derailment.

SEI
Société de Construction et d'Embranchements Industriels

80 rue Taitbout, 75009 Paris, France

Telephone: 874 66 83
Telex: 660515

Main works: Soissons, La Cote-Saint-André (Isère), Toulouse

President and Director General: Gérard Coffin
Director General: Jacques Darre

Subsidiaries
SMEI
Société Meridionale des Embranchements Industriels
110 boulevard de l'Embouchure, 31200 Toulouse
Telephone: (61) 47 57 41
SLEI
Société Lyonnaise des Embranchements Industriels
70 rue Parmentier, 69007 Lyons
Telephone: (78) 72 45 08
Telex: 380532
JB-VFC
Jardin & Billiard-Voies Ferrées-Canalisations
6 rue Desire-Ruggieri, 75018 Paris
Telephone: 257 14 18
Telex: 640538
Sogafer
Société Gabonaise Ferroviaire
BP 3978, Libreville, Gabon
Telephone: (19 241) 72 35 60
ETF
Société Européenne de Travaux Ferroviaires
4D Chaussée de Lille, 7790 Warneton, Belgium

Products: The SEI Group is the official manufacturer and supplier for both the SNCF and the RATP in France. Abroad, it supplies points and crossings to a large number of national railway companies. SEI produces a complete range of specialised equipment including standard SNCF turnouts and diamond crossings, specially designed for high-speed main tracks. It also builds points and crossings which are adapted to private sidings and which take into account both the layout of the line and the intensity of its traffic. The points consist of flexible switch-rails of different lengths. The common crossings and diamond crossings are constructed either with assembled rails or with cast steel.

The SEI Group also manufactures all the necessary permanent way equipment for turnouts (points operating mechanisms, switch-rails locking devices, etc), and for the standard track (rails, sleepers, fastening systems, buffer stops, scotch blocks, insulating fishplates, stuck insulating joints, mixed rail sections made up of different rail sections welded together using the Aluminotherm process). The Group's Soissons plant is specially equipped to harden its rails thermically which gives a surface resistance to the rails of above 120 kg/mm².

The SEI wide-grooved rail is offered in two different profiles. The SEI 70 G type is especially suitable for heavy traffic; French National Railways (SNCF) uses this type of rail for its own installations of embedded tracks. The SEI 60 G type is lighter and lower but has the same moment of inertia as the French 46 kg standard flat-bottom rail.

The wide-grooved rail ensures a very good watertight contact at ground level, and protects the infrastructure, thus appreciably reducing maintenance costs. Depending on the type of the ground grooved-rail, points and crossings are laid on either wooden sleepers and ballast, longitudinal concrete sleepers or reinforced concrete slabs.

SIG
Schweizerische Industrie-Gesellschaft
Swiss Industrial Company

8212 Neuhausen Rhine Falls, Switzerland

Telephone: 053 8 61 11
Telegrams: SIG, Neuhausenamrheinfall
Telex: 76 551; 76 802

Chairman: Fritz Halm
Managing Director: Wolfgang Gähwyler
Director, Coach Factory: Peter Gsell
Head, Track Maintenance Machinery and Vice-director: Ulrich Pistor

Subsidiaries: SIG Maskin, Oslo
SIG Maskin, Stockholm

Products: Track maintenance machinery, including the SIG 120 C light tamper for plain track, points and crossings; the SIG 130 L tamper-leveller-liner for plain track; and the SIG 130 B tamper-leveller-liner for plain track, points and crossings. A licence for tamper manufacture has been granted to Kershaw Manufacturing Co Inc, Alabama, USA.

SIG 130 L tamper-leveller-liner for plain track

SOCADER
Société de Constructions d'Appareils de Voie de Dietrich et Rodange

2 rue de Leningrad, 75008 Paris, France

Telephone: 293 56 10
Telex: 641217

Products: SOCADER's annual production capacity amounts to 3000 standardised track points and crossings. The production range includes: diverging, symmetrical or flexured turnouts; tandem turnouts, diverging or symmetrical; diamond crossings; diamond crossings with single slip; diamond crossings with double slip; simple or scissors cross-overs; turnouts for interlaced track. SOCADER also produces and markets: switches and frogs; expansion joints for long-welded rails or bridges; insulated joints; derailer; buffer stop; switch drive; and mechanical safety equipment (switch locking devices and controllers, side-chair-lockings). SOCADER has manufactured railway points and crossings for the major railroad systems in France and, on differing gauges, throughout the world. It also deals in points and crossings especially studied and produced for metros (steel or rubber-tyred) and tramways, for steel factories to support continuous traffic of special wagons with axleloads of 50 to 60 tons; roadways (especially harbours, factories and workshops); and the track of handling and lifting machines (cranes, gantry-crane, travelling cranes, etc).

Sola
Ing Guido Scheyer

Postfach 36, 6840 Gotzis, Austria

Products: Track measuring equipment.

Sollinger Hütte
Sollinger Hutte GmbH

3418 Uslar Han, Federal Republic of Germany

Telephone: 05571 2021
Telegrams: Sollinger Hütte
Telex: 0965716

Products: Track liners, ballast regulators, inspection cars and trolleys.

Speno
Speno International SA

22-24 parc Chateau-Banquet, 1211 Geneva, Switzerland

Telephone: 022 32 84 07
Telex: 23921

Products: In-track rail rectification and reprofiling units; wave formation recording car.

Sperry
Sperry Rail Service
Division of Automation Industries Inc, a unit of Penn Central Corporation (NYSE)

Head office: Shelter Rock Road, Danbury, Connecticut 06810, USA

Telephone: (203) 748 9243
Telegrams: Sperry Pro
Telex: 710/456 6372

President: W J Gallagher
Managing Director: P B Simpson
Vice-President: K E Ault

Australian office: Automation Sperry Ltd, Rydalmere, New South Wales, Australia

Sperry owns and operates a fleet of 26 induction-ultrasonic cars and three all-ultrasonic cars.

Spie Batignolles
Société Spie Batignolles (Service Voies Ferrées)

6-8 rue du Quatre Septembre, 92130 Issy-les-Moulineux, France

Products: Track construction and maintenance equipment.

SRS
Swedish Rail System AB SRS

Framnäsbacken 18, PO Box 1031, 171 21 Solna, Sweden

Telephone: 8 830 660
Telegrams: Railsystem, Stockholm
Telex: 104 06

Managing Director: Ingvar Svensson

Products: Concrete sleepers; Hambo rail fastenings; machines developed for the mechanical mounting of sleepers and fastenings; gantry cranes; rail threaders; hydraulic track lifters; switch exchanger; Stormobil hi-rail vehicles; Clicomatic rail lubricators.

The SRS Clicomatic rail lubricator consists of a steel cabinet and a grease gun housing connected by a grease hose. All components are mounted in the cabinet, except the grease gun with nozzle, solenoid valve, and the vibratory sensor, which are installed in the grease gun housing. The Clicomatic is driven by compressed nitrogen gas and controlled by an electronic control unit, powered by a standard 9-volt battery. Gas pressure is reduced by a regulator applying a constant pressure on the grease in the container right through the grease hose to the grease gun. Passing trains create vibrations in the track which are monitored by the vibratory sensor in the grease gun housing. A signal then activates the electronic control unit, which opens the solenoid valve at preset intervals, activating the grease gun. The grease is then ejected through a four hole nozzle, hitting the rail flange with four drops. The intervals between the impulses can be preset for different times. This means that while the sensor is registering vibrations either one or several grease shots can be released during a train passage, depending on the preset intervals. This allows optimal lubrication fully adapted to various local conditions, such as train speeds, axle loads, length of trains etc. Swedish State Railways (SJ) has 1800 units in use and reports considerable resultant reduction in wear on wheel flanges and rail heads.

The SRS Stormobil is in daily use on SJ as a rail/road catenary inspector for overhead work. SJ will have 41 SRS Stormobils operational at the end of 1984. The Stormobil's lift chassis is provided with a hydraulically-operated wheel carriage which supports and guides the front end, at the same time locking the front axle. A driving bogie which pivots through ±100 degrees is mounted at the rear. The rear of this bogie has hydraulic vertical adjustment. The bogie incorporates a drive unit which powers all four wheels. Both front and rear arrangements are spring-suspended. The drive unit in the bogie is fed from an external power source connected to the power take-off on the vehicle gearbox. The drive can be controlled from the cab for forward/reverse speeds of 0-70 km/h and from the working platform for forward/reverse speeds of 0-5 km/h. Gear changing takes place in the planetary gearbox on the bogie. All travelling wheels are provided with brakes which can be operated both from the cab and working platform.

The design has recently been modified in the following respects: the front end rail wheel assembly has been moved in front of the front road axle; total weight of vehicle is now 11 tonnes; the working speed controlled from the platform is 7.25 km/h in both directions; there is no limitation on platform slewing radius in superelevated curves up to 10 degrees; the clearance height from rails to bottom of working platform is 8 metres, giving a working height of about 9.5 metres; the load capacity on the platform is now 350 kg; and fully equipped, the SRS Stormobil can load additionally 2250 kg.

SRS also markets the new Scania MTR112 motor trolley (see also under Scania).

Scania MTR112 trolley equipped for snow clearance

SRS Clicomatic high-capacity, low-maintenance rail lubricator, widely used on Swedish State Railways (SJ)

SRS Stormobil road/rail vehicle, with hydraulic, pneumatic and other tools, manoeuvring on to its rail wheels

SRS switch exchanger, for speedy replacement of prefabricated point and track panels

Products: Railroad rails; sleeper plates. A major supplier of rails to Canadian National Railways.

Sydney Steel manufactures rails to all major national and international specifications, including AREA, ASTM, BSS, CNR, CPR, ISO and UIC. Sydney rails are produced in carbon, high silicon, and premium alloy grades. Sections range from 70 to 136 lb/yd (37 to 70 kg/m) and lengths are supplied up to 82 feet (25 metres). According to the specifications required, rails may be either control cooled to ensure diffusion of hydrogen from the steel or produced from vacuum degassed steel. All rail ends are milled. When specified, the top end rail surface is end-hardened to reduce wear at rail joints. Standard rail length is 78 feet, although rails 39 to 82 feet (12 to 25 metres) are produced.

Szarka
Szarka Enterprises, Inc

PO Box 2027, Livonia, Michigan 48151, USA

Telephone: (313) 427 5535

President: Paul J Szarka
Vice-President: L B Szarka

Products: FAB-RA-CAST rail/road grade crossing surface. Special features include: pre-fabricated metal end ramps, prevent damage usually associated with 'dragging' equipment, and restrict expansion/contraction throughout the limits of the crossing; a poured-in-place rubber-resin flange-way filler encapsulates the crossing against penetration by ice, snow, rain, dirt and debris, aids drainage at the crossing location, makes the crossing safe for small-wheeled vehicular, as well as pedestrian traffic, and eliminates damage to vulnerable products such as glassware, electronic parts, etc, by creating smooth passage; boiled linseed oil and mineral spirits treatment, plus broom finish surface prevents skidding, hydroplaning, eliminates spalling or scaling, and provides resistancy to salts, the elements, as well as car drippings; the product is removable, interchangeable and relocatable without loss of materials; immediate delivery for tangent and curved crossings.

All crossings are unconditionally guaranteed and installed under manufacturer's supervision.

The company's proprietary SEI rubber-resin flange-way filler material is offered for use in all types of open flange-ways at crossings, and/or adjacent highway expansion joints. Cryogenically-processed rubber and moisture cured polyurethane are provided complete with installation instructions. The filler contours precisely to any configuration within two hours, and has a unique recovery capability when depressed by rail or vehicular traffic.

SRS ballast wagon with movable spreader

Stedef
Société d'Études Ferroviaires

320 bureaux de la Colline, 92213 Saint-Cloud Cedex, France

Telephone: (1) 602 56 00
Telex: 200 888

General Manager: J H Lemoussu

Products: Track materials and equipment including elastic fastenings.

Fortax resilient clip (with tie plate) by Stedef for continuous welded rail on timber sleepers

Nabla RNTC spring fastener by Stedef for concrete sleepers, twin- or monobloc, as used on French Railways' high-speed LGV

Sydney Steel
Sydney Steel Corporation

PO Box 1450, Sydney, Nova Scotia B1P 6K5, Canada

Telephone: (902) 564 5471
Telegrams: Systco
Telex: 019-35197

Chairman: M H Cochrane
Acting President: E A Boutilier

FAB-RA-CAST crossing installation

Close-up of FAB-RA-CAST surface

Tamper
Division of Canron Corp

2401 Edmund Road, West Columbia, South Carolina 29169, USA

Telephone: (803) 794 9160
Telex: 573423

Products: Tamper manufactures a complete range of railway track maintenance of way equipment including ballast cleaning and dressing machines, bolting machines, brush cutters and attachments, track lubricators, frog and switch point grinders, track gauges, mobile generator sets, inspection and recording cars, spike drivers, spike pullers, production tampers, switch tampers, spot tampers, tie inserters and removers, track levelling and lining equipment, rail saws, rail drills, rail bolting machines, rail change-out units, track renewal units, snow blowers and a complete contracting service.

Templeton
Templeton, Kenly and Co

2525 Gardner Road, Broadview, Illinois 60153, USA

Telephone: (312) 865 1500
Telegrams: Temkenco, Broadview, Illinois
Telex: 6871027

President: H G Fromm
Senior Vice President, Marketing: J K Clements
Vice President, International: L Bruggeman

Products: Mechanical trip/track jacks, hydraulic rail puller and expanders, hydraulic rerailing system.

Tetsudo-Kiki
Tetsudo-Kiki Co Ltd
Yaeso, 1-5-5 Chuo-ku, Tokyo, Japan

Telephone: 03 271 5341

Products: Points and crossings, expansion and glued insulated joints.

Thermit Welding
Thermit Welding (GB) Ltd

Ferry Lane, Rainham, Essex RM13 9DP, England

Telephone: 76 22 626
Telex: 291380

Directors: D H Guntermann
M Geiger
F Baldrey
B Spencer

Products: Portable rail welding equipment; welding consumables; insulated rail joints.

Thomas Robinson
Thomas Robinson & Son Ltd

Railway Works, Fishwick Street, Rochdale, England

Telephone: 0706 47811
Telex: 635321

Chairman: D W Povey
Managing Director: I Davis
Director and Chief Executive: C Heap

Subsidiaries
Northern Woodworking Machinery Co Ltd, Halifax, Yorkshire
S S Stott Ltd, Haslingden, Rossendale, Lancashire
Thomas Robinson & Son Pty Ltd, Revesby, New South Wales, Australia

Products: Sleeper inciser; sleeper adzing and boring, chair/sleeper screwing machines.

Thosti-BBRV
Thosti Bauaktiengesellschaft and Bureau BBR Ltd

Thosti Bauaktiengesellschaft
Postfach 10 25 47, 8900 Augsburg 1, Federal Republic of Germany
Bureau BBR Ltd
Riesbachstrasse 57, 8034 Zurich, Switzerland

Telephone: 01 252 19 10
Telegrams: Bureaubbr, Zurich
Telex: 53521

Products: Prestressed concrete sleepers, over 3 million of which have been delivered to the German Federal Railway (DB) since 1954. More than 7 million of the Thosti-BBRV type have now been manufactured also in Italy, South Africa, Malawi, Turkey, Costa Rica, New Zealand and India at the rate of a million a year.

Thos W Ward
Thos W Ward (Railway Engineers) Ltd

Midland Foundry, Osmaston Street, Sandiacre, Nottingham NG10 5AN, England

Telephone: 0602 390125

Chairman: W M Tomlinson
Managing Director: J J Hancock
Directors: P B Dodson
E W Marwood
E E Caseldine
B Waterhouse

Products: Switches and crossings in all rail weights and associated fittings.

Thyssen
Thyssen AG vorm August-Thyssen Hutte

Kaiser-Wilhelm Strasse 100, Postfach 1100 67, 4100 Duisburg 11, Federal Republic of Germany

Telephone: (203) 52-1
Telex: 85543

Products: Permanent way material: heavy rails, including highly wear-resistant THS 11 special grade; light rails; fishplates for light and heavy rails; light and heavy sleepers; guide rails.

Thyssen Engineering
Thyssen Engineering GmbH

Werk Dortmund, Körnebachstrasse 1, Postfach 269/270, 4600 Dortmund 1, Federal Republic of Germany

Telephone: (231) 527761
Telex: 822186

Products: Bridge construction: trough and deck bridges of the plain girder, truss and bascule type; switches and crossings according to West German and foreign standards (including German Federal Railway) of rails S 41, S 49, S 54, UIC 54, UIC 60 and foreign standard sections of strengths from 680 to 1080 N/mm²; curve points and small curve points for radii of up to 100 metres; tramway switches; point devices with inner stock rail bracing and brace point locks of the latest design; cross frogs of welded and high-strength friction grip block construction; cross frogs of monobloc type, of special alloys (among other things, with 12 to 14% manganese content); cross frogs with resilient-mobile ends; scarfed joints; drag shoe ejectors; small curve switches; loose sets of steel or wooden sleepers with fasteners; transition rails; insulated rail joints according to the latest regulations; rail surface hardening, austenitic and pearlitic, for tensile strengths from 1180 to 1570 N/mm²; structural steel buildings; elevated structures for off-station track area, station platform roofs, halls.

Tipco
Tickins Industrial Products Ltd

1 Coventry Road, Bramalea, Ontario L6T 4B1, Canada

Telephone: (416) 791 9811
Telex: 06-97799

President: J J Tickins

Products: Track bits; track bit sharpening; point protectors.

Tokyo Keiki
Tokyo Keiki Co, Ltd

Head office: Nishi-Gotanda 1-chome 31, Shinagawa-Ku, Tokyo, Japan

Telephone: 03 490 0821
Telegrams: Tokyokeikitgo
Telex: 246 6193

Works: Minami-Kamata 2-chome 16, Ohta-Ku, Tokyo

Interior of Tokyo Keiki ultrasonic rail flaw detector car for Japanese National Railways (JNR) Shinkansen high-speed lines

Director and General Manager, Industrial Division: Norimi Abe

Products: Ultrasonic flaw detector, Model UM and SM series and accessories; portable rail detector, Model PRD II; and ultrasonic thickness meter, Model UTM 100. The company has also supplied an ultrasonic rail flaw detector car for the Tohoku Shinkansen of Japanese National Railways (JNR), in addition to two already in use on the Shinkansen between Tokyo, Osaka and Hakata.

Tokyo Keiki Type UM-721R ultrasonic flaw detector, equipped to store data for subsequent analysis, part of the automatic wheel and axle inspection and cleaning lines in 26 JNR depots

Tokyo Keiki Type PRD-II portable rail flaw detector

Toyo Kizai
Toyo Kizai Co Ltd

Head office: PO 100, 6-7, Marunouchi 3, Chiyoda-ku, Tokyo, Japan

Telephone: 03 214 6871

Main works: PO 254, 10-12, Amanuma, Hiratsukashi, Kanagawa Pref

President: Kenji Ishizuka
Director, Export Department: Shuichi Okumura

Products: Rail fastenings such as sleeper tie-plates, spring clips, bolts, nuts, spikes and sleeper pads.
The company's new Type U resilient spring clip for timber sleepers has unique shape and mounting method for which patents have been applied. High resistance to canting of rails is claimed. This clip has dispensed with fine adjustment of screw spike tightening torque which is needed to provide a given rail fastening torque in conventional types of fastenings, a smaller number of component parts and is therefore easy to handle.

Toyo Kizai Type U resilient spring clip for timber sleepers

Toyo Kizai double elastic fastener for wooden sleepers

Toyo Kizai double elastic fastener for prestressed concrete sleepers

TPI
Transit Products, Inc

PO Box 87459, College Park, Georgia 30337, USA

Telephone: (404) 996 6900
Telex: 80-4294

Works: 1864 Sullivan Road, College Park, Georgia 30337

President: H M Mize Jr
Operations Manager: L E McAffee
Manager, Products: W R Harper Jr
Assistant Manager, Products: P J Curley

Principal subsidiary: TPI Construction Services

Products: Direct fixation rail fasteners; special trackwork; composite and co-extruded conductor rail; insulator chairs for conductor rail; concrete and wood sleepers; resilient rail fasteners for heavy haulage; catenary equipment test laboratory for track components.
Recent products include a new resilient fastener for heavy rail using the company's patented spring clip; a radical development allows installation by a fully mechanised rail gang.
Recent contracts have included supply to NFTA (Buffalo, New York), special trackwork fasteners; MARTA (Atlanta, Georgia), special trackwork fasteners; WMATA (Washington), timber sleepers; NYCTA (New York) special trackwork fasteners; and New Orleans Public Belt Railway, concrete sleepers.

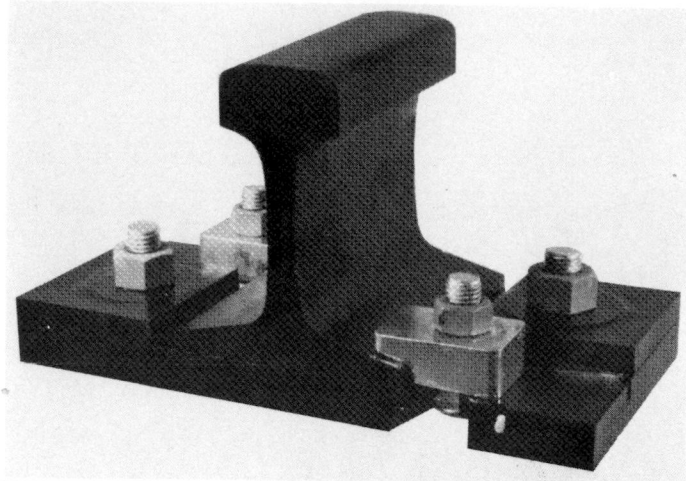

TPI Type H-10 fastener

TPI Type H-10 fastener modified for use with Pandrol spring clip

Adjustable TPI Type H17 fastener for heavy-haul railroads

Trackmaster
Trackmaster (Pty) Limited

Head office: 4 Davey Road, Industria North, PO Box 80017, 1701 Ridgeview, South Africa

Telephone: (011) 27 5171
Telegrams: Mecantrak, Maraisburg
Telex: 4-25876

Main works: 4 Davy Road, Industria North

Chairman: F J Douwes
Directors: N C Segal
P B Morgan
J F Pretorius

Products: Railway track construction and maintenance machinery and equipment including rail saws/friction cutter, drills, grinders, creep adjusters, changers, destressing device, transporters/trolleys, loaders, benders, sleeper drills; powered rail cars and trucks, track gauges and various hand tools including spanners, jacks, slewing bars etc.

TREC
Tempered Railway Equipment Co
Subsidiary of the Tempered Spring Co Ltd

PO Box 20, Park Works, Foley Street, Sheffield S4 7YU, England

Telephone: 0742 20031
Telex: 54103

Products: Elastic rail fastenings, including BTREC system and CS-Springlock for concrete sleepers, KTG for K-type baseplates and KT for switches and crossings.

Unit Rail Anchor
Unit Rail Anchor Company

Suite 2336, 2 North Riverside Plaza, Chicago, Illinois 60606, USA

Telephone: (312) 454 1813
Telex: 28-3407

President: Richard A Pinto

Products: Rail anchors; spring washers; MH rail and wheel flange lubrication system; spring clips.

Vöest-Alpine
Vöest-Alpine AG

Floragasse 7, 1040 Vienna, Austria

Telephone: (0222) 6547
Telex: 34282

Products: Rails, switches, fishplates, soleplates, steel and plastic sleepers.

Von Roll
Von Roll Ltd
Machinery and Handling Systems Division

PO Box 2701, 3001 Berne, Switzerland

Director: Dr Eckehard Hanert
Vice Director: Kuno Schnider

Products: Rail fastenings, points, crossings; racks and rack turnouts for cogwheel railways; turnouts; turntables and transfer tables.

Vossloh-Werke
Vossloh-Werke GmbH

Postfach 1860, 5980 Werdohl 1, Federal Republic of Germany

Telephone: 02392 521
Telegrams: Vosslohwerke
Telex: 08 26 444

Products: Resilient rail fastenings including: Tension Clamp Skl 1 on concrete sleepers with lateral angled guide plates; Tension Clamp Skl 3 on timber sleepers with ribbed plates.

Western-Cullen-Hayes
Western-Cullen-Hayes Inc

2700 West 36th Place, Chicago, Illinois 60632, USA

Telephone: (312) 254 9600
Telegrams: Wesrailsup, Chicago
Telex: 253206

Vice President: R L McDaniel
Sales Director: J P Schaefer

Products: 'Burro' locomotive cranes, rail tongs and threaders, panel track lifters; multiple rail lifters, derails, track liners, rail benders, power drills, hand drills; 'Western' (formerly Buda) hydraulic, journal and mechanical jacks, 100 models from 3 to 100 tons capacity; bumping posts, derails, vehicle warning lights.
Western-Cullen-Hayes is a consolidation of the Western Railroad Supply Co, the Cullen-Friestedt Co and the Hayes Track Appliance Co.

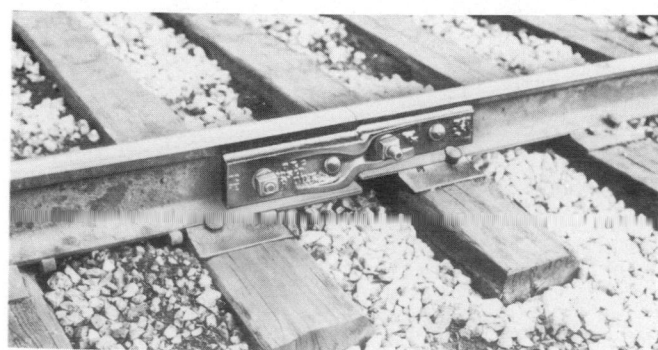

Western-Cullen-Hayes compromise rail joint

Western-Cullen-Hayes switch point guard in manganese steel, preventing derailment on worn points

Windhoff
Rheiner Maschinenfabrik Windhoff AG

Hovestrasse 10, Postfach 1160, 4440 Rheine, Federal Republic of Germany

President: Dr Bernd Windhoff
Managers: Heinz Lörfing
Ewald Elling
Herbert Bucksch

Products: Overhead line inspection and maintenance cars, multi-purpose track maintenance machines with extensive attachments programme, rail crane trucks, crib ballast removers, light track motor trailers.

Windhoff Type VG80 track maintenance car as supplied to Egyptian Railways

Wheeling-Pittsburgh
Wheeling-Pittsburgh Steel Corporation

Head office: 4 Gateway Center, PO Box 118, Pittsburgh, Pennsylvania 15230, USA

Telephone: (412) 288 3600
TWX: 710 664 4820

Main works: Steubenville, Yorkville, Martins Ferry and Canfield, Ohio; Benwood, Beech Bottom and Follansbee, West Virginia; Monessen and Allenport, Pennsylvania

Board Chairman and President: Dennis J Carney
Executive Vice President: Thomas D Moore

Subsidiary: Wheeling Corrugating Company

Products: Carbon and alloy rails and sleeper plates; rails are currently produced in 115, 132 and 136 lb sizes, but other standard sizes are being added.

Wickham
D Wickham & Company Ltd

Crane Mead, Ware, Hertfordshire SG12 9QA, England

Telephone: 0920 2491-7
Telegrams: Wickham, Ware
Telex: 81340

Products: A range of self-propelled railway track and overhead line inspection cars, crane cars, maintenance gang trolleys, and other special-purpose vehicles; also hand and push cars and track tools.

Yamato Kogyo
Yamato Kogyo Co Ltd

380 Kibi, Otsu-ku, Himeji, Hirohata PO Box 8, Japan

Telephone: 0792 73 1061

Products: Rails, points, joints and track components.

Zwicky
Zwicky Engineering Limited
Sky Hi Division
A member of EIS Group plc

Molly Millars Lane, Wokingham, Berkshire RG11 2RY, England

Telephone: 0734 793636
Telegrams: C F Taylor, Wokingham
Telex: 848852

Directors: R F D Reed
P F Drewitt
J J Hobbs
B H Wormsley
Sales Manager: F E Bing

Products: Track and wagon hydraulic jacks; jack test rigs; rail benders; rail hole broach units (hand or power operated); air-draulic power packs; glueing machines.

AUTOMATIC FARE SYSTEMS

AEG-Telefunken
AEG-Telefunken Nachrichten- und Verkehrstechnik AG Geschäftsbereich Bahnen

Hohenzollerndamm 150, 1000 West Berlin 33, Federal Republic of Germany

Telephone: (030) 828-1
Telegrams: Elektronbahnen, Berlin
Telex: 1 85 498

Products: Ticket machines; ticket cancellers; ticket vending machines; data recording ticket machines; automatic multiple service ticket machines.

Almex
AB Almex

Sankt Goransgatan 160B, Stockholm, Sweden

Postal address: Box 30105, 104 25 Stockholm

Telephone: 468 54 02 20
Telegrams: Mexal, Stockholm
Telex: 10646

Chairman: Arne Blomgren
Managing Director: Richard Björk

Products: Systems and machinery for fare collection and ticket issuing.

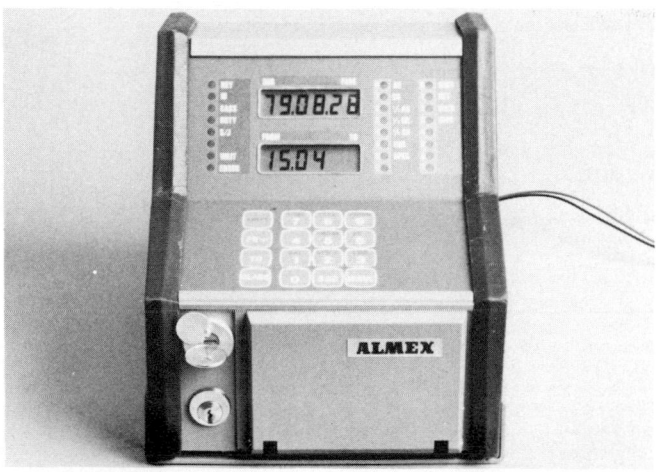

Almex prototype Series II electronic ticket machine terminal unit

Almex Model M ticket canceller

Almex prototype Series II electronic ticket machine printer

Almex PDR data-recording ticket-issue machine as used by Austrian Federal Railway (ÖBB) and FEPASA, Brazil

ARC
Automatic Revenue Controls Ltd

Home Park Estate, Station Road, Kings Langley, Hertfordshire WD4 8LZ, England

Telephone: 09277 66110
Telex: 924617

Chairman: F D Penny
Managing Director: P R Ellwood
Operations Director: J Lincoln
Director: W H Fryer
Director and Company Secretary: I A D Mann

Subsidiary: Automatic Revenue Controls Inc, Maryland, USA

Products: Automatic fare collection systems, including ticket issuing machines, passenger control barriers, magnetic ticket systems, coin and token-operated systems and computerised audit control. The company has developed a microprocessor-controlled magnetic ticket barrier system.

A recent example of ARC's automatic fare collection systems is that supplied to the Glasgow Underground, which is based on a flat fare. Entry to stations is by means of magnetically-encoded tickets, which are processed by automatic barriers, where they are striped and magnetically cancelled, except in the case of season tickets. Exit barriers are uncontrolled. To suit Glasgow's integration of travel on buses, trains and Underground there is a special 'transcard' which is also processed by the automatic barriers, and which enables passengers to interchange between all three modes.

The ticket barriers designed and manufactured by ARC consist of a stainless steel structure mounted on a plinth in which are housed three modular major sub-assemblies: turnstile mechanism; ticket reader/transporter; and the electronics unit. A special feature of the barriers and in particular the ticket reader/transporter, is ease of access for maintenance and clearance of any possible ticket jams, etc.

The ticket itself is Edmondson size, 60 × 30 × 0.27 mm. It is coated on one side with a magnetic oxide and the data is recorded on a longitudinal track along the centre of the ticket using a phase encoding technique. When the ticket is presented to an entry barrier it covers a throat photocell and in response the processor starts the motor and transports the ticket across the magnetic heads which read the ticket data.

The heart of the barrier, controlling all its functions, is a microcomputer with its programme stored in ROM memory. Having read the data from the ticket, the processor performs certain checks to establish the validity of the ticket and either accepts or rejects it accordingly. In the former case the ticket is cancelled magnetically, using a second magnetic write head, and a coloured ink stripe is applied to the ticket along its length to visually invalidate it. The ticket is then returned, a sign is illuminated instructing the passenger to proceed and the turnstile is released, giving access to the station and trains. In the event the ticket is invalid it is returned unaltered to the passenger, who is instructed by appropriate signs to report to the station booking office. The use of the microcomputer enables a high degree of flexibility in the system: future changes to the fare structure, ticket encoding etc can be easily accomplished by replacing the programme memory.

The microcomputers in each automatic barrier also communicate with the station booking office panels. The communication is a serial asynchronous channel using a 20 mA current loop. The barrier transmits to the booking office details of all transactions by ticket type and receives from the booking office time and date information, which it uses to check the validity of tickets. It also receives commands which dictate the mode of operation, eg 'entry only', 'exit only', 'emergency mode', 'out of service', 'free/power off'. In all cases the processor illuminates the corresponding signs on the barrier and controls the direction of release of the turnstile.

The remote booking office panel, also designed and manufactured by ARC, is under microcomputer control. As well as sending time and date information, which it derives from a crystal-controlled clock, and other various commands to the barriers and ticket machines as dictated by the station staff, it receives transaction data from a number of barriers and totalises the transactions by ticket type, displaying the accumulated totals to the booking office staff. Remote printers or other computer-compatible storage devices can also be interfaced to the booking office control panels to give more comprehensive transaction and audit data.

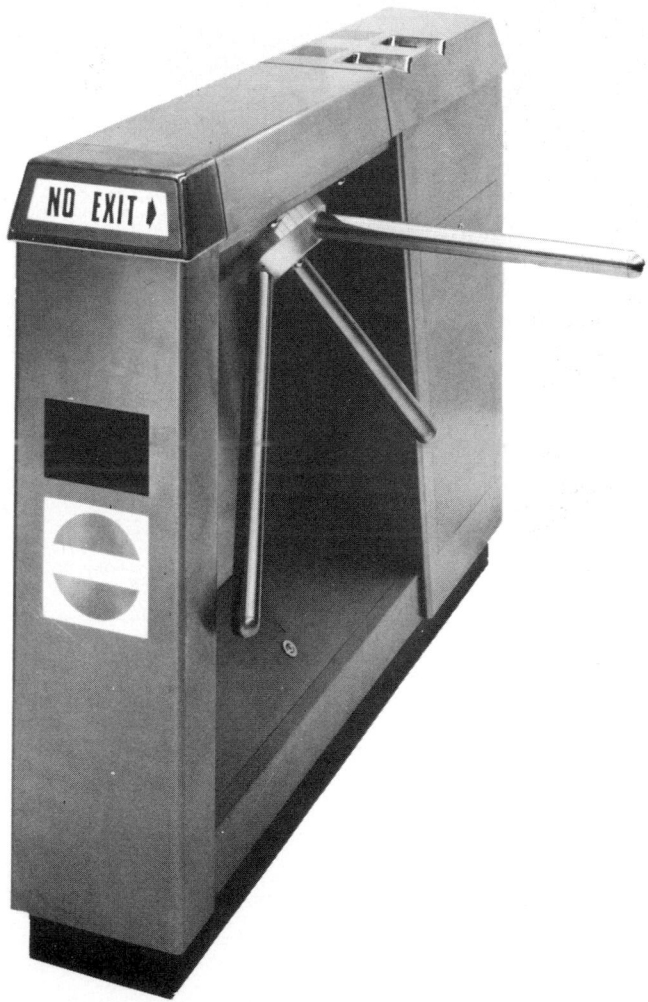

ARC ticket barrier for Glasgow Underground

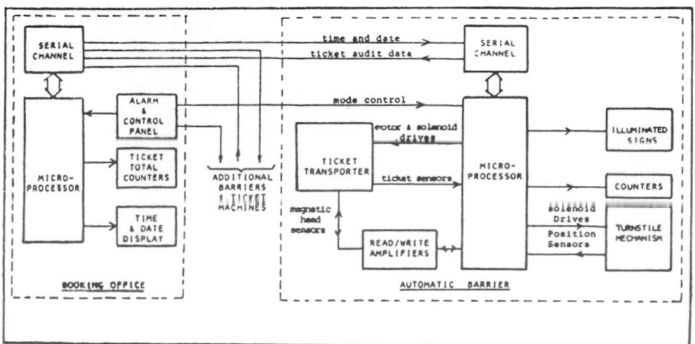

Layout of barrier and booking-office processors in ARC's Glasgow Underground installation

Automatic Systems
Automatic Systems SA

Boulevard de l'Europe 9, 1301 Wavre, Belgium

Telephone: 010 41 37 09
Telex: 59089

General Manager: Michel Coenraets
Export Manager: Albert Milican
Market Development Manager: Richard Boon

Products: Full range of gates, turnstiles and special electro-mechanical barriers, card readers, ticket dispensers.

Camp
Camp

8 rue de Torcy, 75018 Paris, France

Telephone: 201 46 27
Telex: 240166

Products: Automatic fare collection equipment.

CGA Alcatel
Compagnie Générale d'Automatisme

Head office: 12 rue de la Baume, 75008 Paris, France

Works: Le Plessis-Pâté, 91220 Bretigny-sur-Orge

Telephone: (6) 084 95 40
Telex: 691262

Subsidiaries: Société Camp (France)
Alta Technology Inc (USA)
Sogima (Italy)
CGA GmbH (Federal Republic of Germany)
CGA de Venezuela (Venezuela)

Products: Automatic fare collection equipment; stand-alone microprocessor-based equipment for issue of and controlling magnetically encoded tickets; automatic gates with reversible ticket transport; automatic vending machines; ticket office machines; data collection equipment.

CGA Alcatel has lately been awarded the contract for a trial afc system, comprising both ticket transport readers and 'wipe-thru' readers for monthly tickets, by Toronto Transit Commission.

Other recent major contracts have covered:
Caracas Metro
Value of contract: Fr 120 million; no of stations 36; no of lines 2; total traffic 1.5 million/day (estimated); fare structure, zonal (1 to 8); ticket types: magnetic (single, multiple, monthly, 5 types of reduction, staff passes)
Equipment: 138 entrance gates; 138 exit gates and 152 reversible gates; 300 automatic ticket issuing machines; 73 booking office machines; 4 central ticket manufacturing machines; 4 central computers (station level microcomputer); 93 change-giving machines.
System type: stand-alone logic
Gates (passage-way): turnstiles
Gates (reader): 4 slots reversible linear reader
Automatic ticket issuing machine: multi-fare machine for one ticket type (single ride), coder and needle printer
Booking office machine: coder and needle printer driven by a stand-alone electronic with microprocessor, console comprising a keyboard and display screen
Central system: station level microcomputer for data acquisition
Central ticket manufacturing machine: printing and coding machine; ticket issued in ticket magazine for hand selling.

Baltimore Metro
Value of contract: Fr 50 million; no of stations 9 + 3; no of lines 1; total traffic 100 000/day; fare structure, zonal and transfer; ticket types: magnetic and pass for metro and bus compatible transfers
Equipment: 115 entrance and exit gates; 50 automatic ticket issuing machines; 15 booking office machines; 2 central ticket manufacturing machines; 2 central computers.
System type: stand-alone logic
Gates (passage-way): turnstiles
Gates (reader): four slots reader (reversible entry/exit gate)
Automatic ticket issuing machine: change-giving recycling type
Booking office machine: booth registration and control panel together with station controller
Central system: on-line computer connected via MODEM and station controller to individual afc equipment
Central ticket manufacturing machine: with automatic ticket dispenser loader.

Hong Kong Mass Transit Railway Corporation, Island Line
Value of contract: Fr 70 million; no of stations 25 + 12; no of lines 3 (Modified Initial System, Tsuen Wan Extension, Island Line); total traffic 1.5 million/day; fare structure, zonal; ticket types: one-way, multi-ride, stored value
Equipment: 137 entrance gates; 225 exit gates (reversible); 320 automatic ticket issuing machines (free issued); 36 booking office machines; 16 encoder-sorters; 1 station computer
System type: recirculated credit card-size tickets
Gates (passage-way): turnstile
Gates (reader): reversible ticket transport (linear, with 4 slots)

Booking office machine: ticket transport for frontal insertion of tickets, stand-alone operation; passenger display unit

Central system: station level microcomputer (PDP 11-23) for data storage on floppy and Winchester diskettes

Encoder-sorter: sorting and encoding machine from exit gate ticket containers to automatic issuing machines' magazines

The company's Data 128 vending machine can issue up to 6144 types of tickets and automatically select one of two types of support media: light cardboard for short-term and plastic for long-term use. Data 128 hardware supplied to French Railways (SNCF) comprises: a 'destination' panel consisting of 16 rows and 8 columns, ie 128 destinations in alphabetical order; a 'ticket' list so that the following can be selected: one-way, return, weekly pass, monthly pass, etc; a 'class' list so that the following can be selected: 1st class, 2nd class, full price, half price; a display screen for messages; a cancellation button; a single coin slot; and change-giving function. As an option, a bank note tray or a credit card slot can be added to the machine.

Seven types of coins are accepted. The machine sorts and counts the coins before transferring them to bags specially designed to be taken directly to the bank. Storage of up to 1500 coins of each type is provided.

CGA Alcatel reversible control gate to process tickets in either direction

CGA Alcatel semi-automatic booking office ticket issue machine for both cardboard Edmondson-format short-trip and pvc long-season tickets

Control Systems
Control Systems Ltd

The Island, Uxbridge, Middlesex UB8 2UT, England

Telephone: 0895 51255
Telex: 22225

Chairman: F D Penny
Managing Director: G Porritt
Divisional Director, Transport Systems: B A Marks
Export Sales and Marketing Manager: C A Bulley
Export Sales Manager: J B C de Jager

Products: Electrically-controlled ticket issuing systems assembled from standard modules in configurations designed for individual requirements.

Crouzet
Crouzet Transports

25 rue Jules Védrines, 26027 Valence, France

Telephone: (75) 42 91 44
Telex: 34 5802

Products: Automatic fare collection systems.

Crouzet ticket machines on Tyne and Wear transit system

Cubic Western
Cubic Western Data
A member of the Cubic Corporation

5650 Kearny Mesa Road, San Diego, California 92111-1380, USA

Telephone: (714) 268 3100
Telegrams: Cubic
Telex: 68 31138

Chairman: Raymond L de Kozan
General Manager: Marlyn L Hicks

Products: Automatic fare collection equipment including entry and exit only barriers, reversible barriers, ticket vendors, change makers, addfare machines (excess fares), ticket analysers, sorter/encoders, coin sorter/counters, control/monitor units, central audit units; credit card-operated self-service ticket vendors.

The company's major afc installations include the Washington Metro of WMATA, the intermodal Metro and bus system of Atlanta (MARTA), San Francisco (BART), Philadelphia (PATCO) and the Chicago commuter network of the Illinois Central Gulf RR in the USA; the Hong Kong Mass Transit Railway; and the Sydney Eastern Suburbs system of the Public Transit Commission of New South Wales.

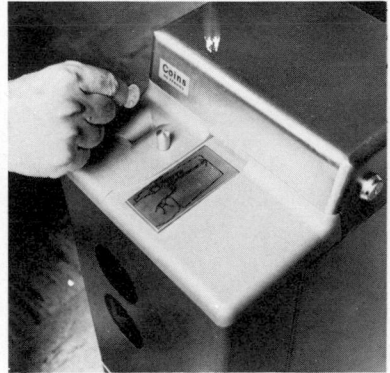 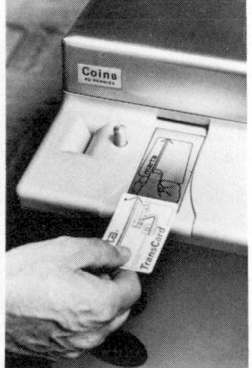

Cubic Western Data turnstile gates in Atlanta to accept coins or MARTA tokens (left), or prepurchase tickets including monthly passes (right)

A recent $4.3 million contract for automatic computerised fare collection equipment has been gained from the Metropolitan Dade County Transportation Administration (Miami), Florida. It covers production and installation of microprocessor-controlled faregates in all 20 of the system's stations. The equipment is to accept fares from passengers in coins and plastic magnetic strip, multi-ride monthly tickets. The fare collection equipment provides for passengers transferring from the overground metro system to the administration's downtown people circular system, as well as for bus-to-metro transport. Transfer will be with plastic or paper credit-card size magnetic-strip tickets. Initial installation of equipment was set for November 1983 for opening in December 1983. Final installation of all remaining equipment would be made by November 1984 in time for complete opening of the system in December 1984.

The company's new Type FD010 electronic ticket machine has these capabilities: provision and issue of valued and cancelled tickets; calculation of duty for the operator; statistics (transfer on to discettes or magnetic tapes); remote control system of ticket cancelling; possibility of connection of a change-giver; systematic control operation; identity control of operation module; control memory which recalls all transactions of the previous four weeks linked with the identity of the operator; all variables (tariffs and summer season) filed in the operation module.

Operational characteristics: microprocessor control; alphanumerical printed work; alphanumerical readings; autonomous time and date system with leap-year calendar and reserve power; 6 K-byte memory in operation module; 4 K-byte control memory in ticket printer; interface for cancelling of tickets; IBIS interface; data security; operating voltage 18-30 V; steady current approx 0.4 A; peak current approx 1.5 A; weight 6.5 kg; height 160 mm; width 200 mm; depth 320 mm.

Cubic Western Data exit gates, with Addfare machine for excess fares registered

Elgeba ticket vending machines on Amsterdam Metro

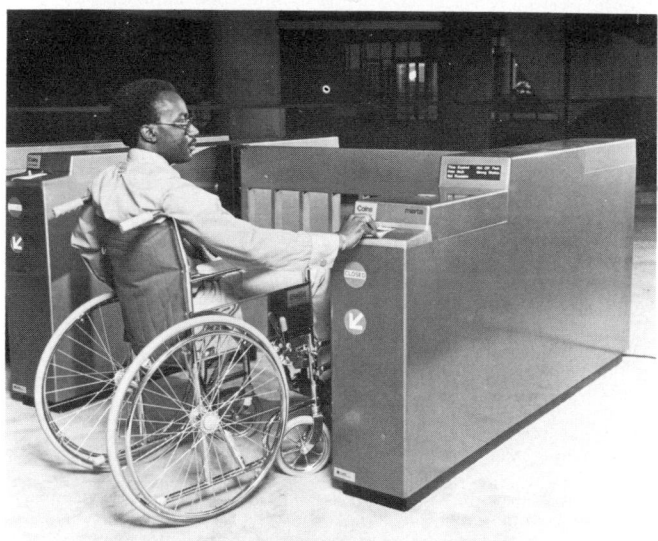

Cubic Western Data turnstile for handicapped on MARTA

Elgeba microprocessor-controlled ticket canceller as used by over 90 European transport authorities

Electronique Serge Dassault

55 quai Carnot, 92214 Saint-Cloud, France

Telephone: 602 50 00
Telegrams: Electrodassault
Telex: 250787

Products: Automatic fare collection systems.

Elgeba
Elgeba Gerätebau GmbH

Postfach 6028, Eudenbacher Strasse 10-12, 5340 Bad Honnef 6, Federal Republic of Germany

Telephone: 80048
Telex: 885 223

General Director: Werner Roch

Products: Ticket cancelling, vending and issuing machines. The company's recent contracts have covered urban transport in Cologne, Düsseldorf and Munich, and in Amsterdam and The Hague.

Elgeba Type FD 010 electronic ticket machine

GEC Traffic Automation
GEC Traffic Automation Ltd

Elstree Way, Borehamwood, Hertfordshire WD6 1RX, England

Telephone: 01-953 2030
Telex: 22777

Products: Automatic fare collection systems.

Hasler
Hasler AG

Belperstrasse 23, 3000 Berne 14, Switzerland

Telephone: 31 652111
Telex: 32413

Products: Autelca ticket-vending, printing and cancelling systems, Autelca coin-checking, measuring and storage systems with or without self-refilling change-return facilities; Hasler fully automatic fee-collecting systems for garages and car parks.

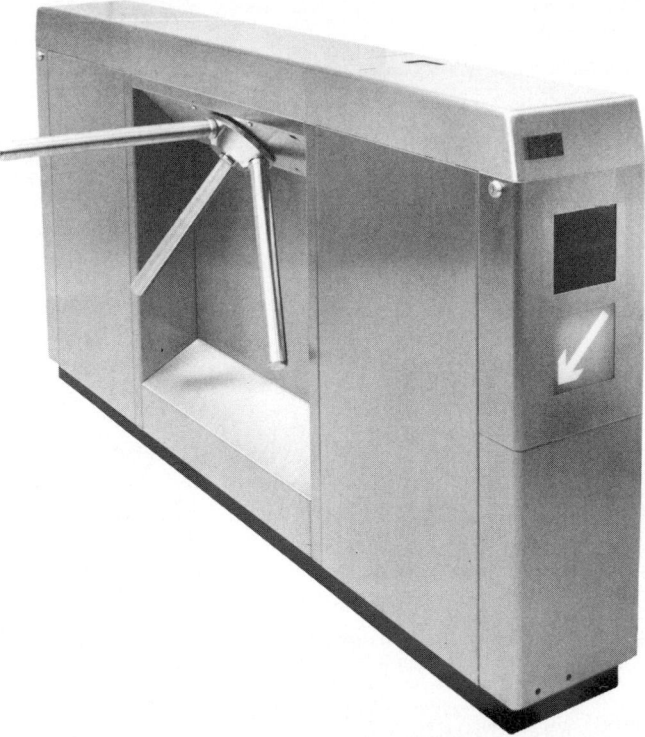

Entry/exit turnstile for Madrid Metro

Autelca ticket-vending machine

Hawker Siddeley Revenue Controls
Hawker Siddeley Revenue Controls Ltd

177 Nutfield Road, Merstham, Surrey RH1 3HH, England

Telephone: 07374 4021
Telex: 946678

Products: Automatic fare collection systems.
   Turnstiles recently installed by the Madrid Metro are an example of the company's equipment range. Capable of controlling entry and exit, but currently used for entry only, the unit features a ticket transport mechanism for checking the validity of an Edmondson-sized magnetically encoded ticket, modifying the code as required for the validity of singles, returns or multi-ride tickets and printing, with an impact matrix printer, details of the remaining validity or number of rides. The unit can also process both Edmondson and credit card size tickets through the same transporter.
   An interim ticket issuing system (INTIS) is used by British Rail for issuing tickets from booking offices. Using matrix printers under microprocessor control for printing, and both a printed tally roll and magnetic tape for audit the machine functions on its own, or as part of a complete revenue collection system.
   An example of the passenger operated machines that can be configured from the standard modules is the multi-fare machine that can issue up to 12 different types of tickets to 351 destinations from blank stock. Each ticket is individually printed and magnetically encoded. Payment for the ticket can be by note or coins, with full re-circulating change facilities. Full facilities for the collection and recording of audit, statistics and operation diagnostics are contained within the machine and are available for on-line transmission.

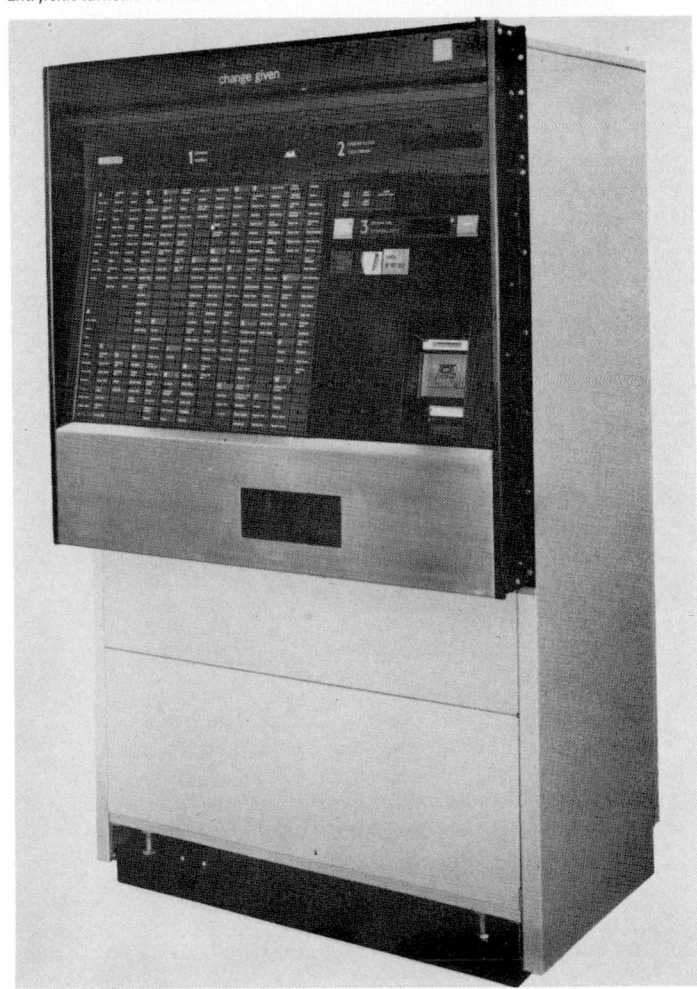

HSRC multi-fare machine

Laakmann
H Laakmann KG Kartonfabrik

Bonsfelderstrasse 1-4, 5620 Velbert-11-Langenberg, Federal Republic of Germany

Telephone: (0) 2127 3016
Telegrams: Laakmann, Langenbergrheinland
Telex: 08516863

Chairman: H W Laakmann
Managing Directors: H J Schwering
                        Dr W R Roloff
Chief Sales Director: E Junkersfeld
Export Sales: R Mollenkott

Products: Railway tickets and ticket reels for automatic vending machines.

Landis & Gyr
Landis & Gyr Ltd

Victoria Road, North Acton, London W3 6XS, England

Telephone: 01-992 5311
Telex: 21486

Chairman: G Straub
Managing Director: G E Robertson
Sales Manager: P A Arnold

Products: Bank note acceptors, escrow and storage system, coin verifier, recirculatory change systems, etc; subscriber telephone equipment.

Nippon Signal
Nippon Signal Co Ltd

Head office: 3-1, Marunouchi 3-chome, Chiyoda-ku, Tokyo, Japan

Telephone: (03) 212 8371
Telegrams: Signal, Tokyo
Telex: 222 2178

Works: Yono Factory, 13-8, Kamikizaki 1-chome, Urawa City
Utsunomiya Factory, 11-2, Hiraide Kougyo Danchi, Utsunomiya City

Associated companies: Nisshin Industrial Co, Ltd
Nisshin Electrical Installation Co, Ltd
Nisshin Electronics Service Co, Ltd

President: H Takeuchi
Chairman: T Hayashi
Managing Director, General Sales: H Shinohara
Director, Foreign Trade: K Matsushima

Products: Automatic fare collection equipments such as bill changer, ticket vending machine, gate controller, passenger gate, automatic fare adjusting machine, ticket issuing machine for station staff, data processing machine.

Omron
Omron Tateisi Electronics Co

Head office: 10, Tsuchido-cho, Hanazono, Ukyo-ku, Kyoto, Japan

Telephone: (075) 463 1161
Telegrams: Omronelco, Kyoto
Telex: 5422889

Information Control Systems HQ, Fare Collection Systems Division: 4-10 Toranomon, 3-chome, Minato-ku, Tokyo 105

Telephone: 03 436 7127
Telex: 2424087

Products: Automatic fare collection system including money changers, coin/bill-operated ticket vendors (also with transfer ticket readers), ticket checking and collecting gates, ticket issuing machines, automatic fare adjuster, season ticket issuing machines.

SASIB
SASIB SpA
Division of CIR SpA

PO Box 311, via di Corticella 87/89, 40128 Bologna, Italy

Telephone: (051) 360401/358561
Telegrams: SASIB, Bologna
Telex: 510020

Products: The microprocessor-controlled SB4 operates a completely automated service for ticket offices. Revision of fares can be accomplished by actuating a key-operated switch without interrupting the ticket sale. The SB4 ticket issuing and accounting machine also provides an accounting and statistical control. The company also produces the OB5, a compact modular ticket cancelling machine with a wide range of uses, which can be manually or remotely controlled.

Scheidt & Bachmann
Scheidt & Bachmann GmbH

132 Breitestrasse, Postfach 580, 4050 Mönchengladbach 2, Federal Republic of Germany

Telephone: (02) 166 4531
Telex: 0852818

Products: Automatic fare collection and ticket vending machines.

Thorn EMI
Thorn EMI Electronics Limited, Wells Division

Wookey Hole Road, Wells, Somerset BA5 1AA, England

Telephone: 0749 72081
Telex: 44254

General Manager: A P Mayhead
Commercial Manager: W S Denman

Products: Ticket-issuing equipments and systems; automatic revenue collection systems and equipments; passenger control barriers; ticket preparation equipments; management control systems; data capture and retrieval systems and equipments; total system studies. The company has developed and supplied to British Rail clerk-operated (booking office) ticket machines, portable ticket machines and passenger-operated ticket vendors.

Toshiba
Toshiba Corporation
Automation Systems Group: Electronic Systems Department IOEP

1-6, Uchisaiwai-cho, 1-chome, Chiyoda-ku, Tokyo 100, Japan

Telephone: 03 501 5411
Telegrams: Toshiba, Tokyo
Telex: 22587

Overseas offices
North America: Houston, New York, San Francisco, Toronto, Tustin (California), Vancouver
Latin America: Bogota, Buenos Aires, Caracas, Mexico City, Rio de Janeiro, São Paulo
Europe: Athens, West Berlin, London, Vienna
Africa: Cairo, Johannesburg
Middle East: Baghdad, Dubai, Jidda, Kuwait, Tehran
South-east Asia: Bangkok, Beijing, Hong Kong, Jakarta, Manila, Taipei
Australasia: Sydney, Wellington

Products: Automatic fare collection systems.
Customers include: Japanese National Railways, Teito Rapid Transit Authority, Sapporo Municipal Transportation Bureau, Tokyu Corporation, Osaka Municipal Transportation Bureau, Kinki Nippon Railway, Odakyu Electric Railway, Seibu Railway, Tobu Railway, Nagoya Municipal Transportation Bureau, Hankyu Corporation, Nankai Electric Railway, Keihin Express Electric Railway, Keihin Electric Railway, Hanshin Electric Railway, Nagoya Railroad, Transportation Bureau Tokyo Metropolitan Government, Kobe Rapid Transit Railway, Keisei Electric Railway, Kobe Municipal Transportation Bureau, Nishi Nippon Railroad, Kyoto Municipal Transportation Bureau, Fukuoka Municipal Transportation Bureau, Japan Travel Bureau and Kobe new Transit Railway.

Products include: Season ticket renewal machine, which is operated by a passenger by inserting the old season ticket to duplicate the original and destination station and depressing a button to specify the duration of validity; the fare is calculated and displayed automatically and upon insertion of exact money by coins and/or bank notes, the new season ticket is issued. Outline dimensions 750 × 1300 × 1800 mm; weight approx 600 kg; ticket issued, plastic (57.5 × 80 mm); currencies accepted, coins (up to 3 denominations), notes (up to 3 denominations); issuing speed approx 10 s after completion of operations by passenger; power consumption less than 2500 VA, 50 Hz.

Ticket vending machine, including change dispenser. The fare button is a variable fare display type. Upon a fares revision a change of fare indication on the fare button can be effected easily by replacing software. A thermal-dot print system is employed and a microcomputer is used for the processing unit; thus printing can be completely controlled with the software. A bill-processing unit can also be installed and sales data can be recorded. Weight approx 350 kg; processing capacity within 3 s of depressing the fare button; 30 × 57.5 mm tickets cut from paper roll capable of producing 5000 tickets; currencies accepted, coins (up to 3 denominations), notes (1 denomination); power consumption 500 to 700 VA.

Multi-function booking office machine, which issues season tickets and single journey, return or tour ticket including express or limited express charge. With on-line data transmission, the single journey or return ticket can be issued with seat booking. The attendant depresses buttons to specify the original station, destination station, intermediate station, duration of validity and discount rate. For season ticket issue the attendant has also to insert an application form, filled in by the patron to transcribe the patron's signature on to the season ticket. Configuration consists of control units, destination select switch board, function keyboard, fare display, magnetic disc drive, magnetic tape cassette unit, and cash drawer in main cabinet and ticket printing unit in separate cabinet. Weight main cabinet approx 210 kg, ticket printing unit approx 90 kg; tickets issued: plastic season ticket (57.5 × 85 mm), paper ticket (57.5 × 85 mm) for single or return ticket and those with express or limited express charge, paper tour ticket (57.5 × 120 mm); thermal transfer ticket printing for large and small characters, route maps and symbols for student or child indication; up to 512 stations can be specified by individual buttons and up to 1440 by booklet-type keyboard; power consumption less than 2000 VA, 50 Hz.

Automatic flap-door-type gate, available in three models: entry, exit, and reversible. The equipment is provided with a four-flap door, human detector, and ticket pooling mechanism; processing capacity is up to 60 passengers/minute. A belt transport system minimises ticket jamming. A microcomputer is built into each unit, giving a positive check on every passenger: modifications in routes or fares can be covered by revised software. Weight approx 350 kg (one set consists of two stanchions); ticket processed: single ticket including fare-adjusting ticket (30 × 57.5 mm) and season ticket (57.5 × 85 mm); ticket inserting direction: single ticket, four positions (ends and sides) on the face and back respectively, eight positions in all; season ticket, two positions (on the face and back respectively), four positions in all; power consumption 600 to 700 VA.

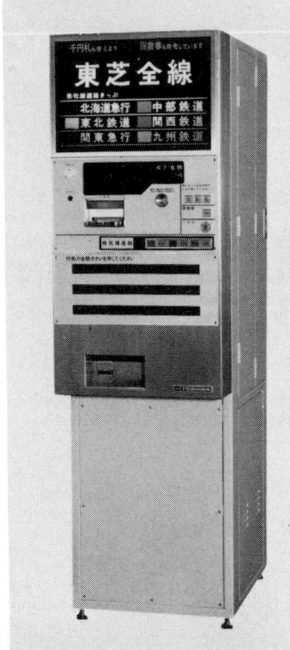

Toshiba automatic season ticket renewal (left) and ticket vending machines

Toshiba season ticket-issuing machine

Toyo Denki
Toyo Denki Seizo KK

7-2 Yaesu 2-chome, Chuo-ku, Tokyo 104, Japan

Telephone: (271) 6374
Telegrams: Yohden, Tokyo
Telex: (0) 222-4666/7

Products: Season ticket issuing machine, automatic ticket gate equipment.

Triumph-Adler
Triumph-Adler Vertriebs-GmbH

Furtherstrasse 212, 8500 Nuremberg, Federal Republic of Germany

Products: Automatic fare collection systems.

Xamax
Xamax AG

Birchstrasse 210, 8050 Zurich, Switzerland

Telephone: 01/311 65 65
Telex: 56328

Principal Directors: Dr C Hobi
H Haug

Products: Ticket vending machines incorporating advanced microprocessor control, diagnosis of errors with display, quick, unlimited change of rates, electronic single-coin monitor, automatic print-out of accounting and statistical data, stamping of desired data on tickets, multi-issue potential, paper reserve for approximately 15 000 tickets and a self-filling cash-box, contents 6 litres. Recent clients have included Calgary, Canada, and the Athens Metro, Greece.

Toshiba automatic gate

YARD AND TERMINAL EQUIPMENT

Abex
Abex Corporation
Railroad Products Group

65 Valley Road, Mahwah, New Jersey 07430, USA

Telephone: (201) 529 3450
Telex: 642415

Products: Yard control systems.

ACEC
Ateliers de Constructions Electriques de Charleroi SA

PO Box 4, 6000 Charleroi, Belgium

Telephone: 3271 442276
Telegrams: Ventacec, Charleroi
Telex: 051 227

Products: Yard control systems.

AEG-Telefunken
AEG-Telefunken Nachrichten- und Verkehrstechnik AG Geschäftsbereich Bahnen

Hohenzollerndamm 150, 1000 West Berlin 33, Federal Republic of Germany

Telephone: (030) 828-1
Telegrams: Elektronbahnen, Berlin
Telex: 1 85 498

Products: Marshalling yard equipment; automatic humping control; control panels and desks; point machines.

AEG-Telefunken supplies up-to-date equipment and systems covering train splitting and combining, running distance or target braking, rail brake control and transport equipment controls and the remote control of marshalling locomotives, for marshalling yards, both new and to be extended.

Aldon
The Aldon Company

3410 Sunset Avenue, Waukegan, Illinois 60087, USA

Telephone: (312) 623 8800/1

Products: Wheel blocks, wheel chocks, warning signs, portable friction rail skids, car stops, bumping posts, electric and pneumatic car shakers, winch-type car pullers, electric car haulers, power car movers, portable grip-pull car movers, car door wrenches and pullers, automatic bulk car gate openers and retarders.

Allen
Allen Cranes (Northampton) Ltd

Salthouse Road, Brackmills Industrial Estate, Northampton NN5 7DT, England

Telephone: 0604 65211
Telex: 311264

Products: Goliath-type rail-mounted container cranes. Capacity up to 40 tonnes for road to rail transfer operations. Electric overhead travelling container cranes associated with refuse, disposal compaction stations.

Allis-Chalmers

Industrial Truck Division, 21800 South Cicero Avenue, Matteson, Illinois 60443, USA

Telephone: (312) 747 5151

Acting General Manager: Russell E Story
Marketing Manager: E A Wehr
General Sales Manager: John S Pink Jr
International Marketing Manager: Fred G Owen

Products: Heavy duty sideloaders and front loading forklift trucks.

Amhoist
American Hoist and Derrick Co

63 South Robert Street, St Paul, Minnesota 55107, USA

Telephone: (612) 228 4321

Products: Yard mobile wagon cranes; rail-mounted cranes (diesel-electric and diesel-hydraulic); lattice boom cranes (crawler and truck-mounted).

Ansaldo
Ansaldo Trasporti SpA

Head office and works: Via Nuova delle Brecce 260, 80147 Naples, Italy

Telephone: 081 7810111
Telex: 710131

Offices: Via Bergognone 34, 20144 Milan

Telephone: 02 42441
Telex: 332192; 314337

Via N Lorenzi 8, 16152 Genoa

Telephone: 010 41051
Telex: 270098

Chairman: Gio Batta Clavarino
Managing Director: Davide Panzeri
Commercial Director: Vincenzo Magri
Technical Director: Carlo Rizzi

Products: Yard control equipment and yard layout design; power signalling apparatus; geographic relay interlocking; remote control equipment; level crossing automation.

ASEA
ASEA AB
Transport Division

721 83 Västerås, Sweden

Telephone: 46 21 100000
Telex: 40720

Products: Together with the Swedish State Railways (SJ), ASEA has developed a hydraulic retarder with self-regulating braking power for use in railway marshalling yards. The spiral-type retarder consists essentially of a steel cylinder bolted to the rail. As each wagon wheel passes the retarder it runs on a spiral cam, which under hydraulic resistance forces the cylinder to rotate one revolution, thus braking the wheel. Each time the cylinder rotates it starts an internal hydraulic pump, which yields an oil flow proportional to the wheel speed. At the pre-set value the oil flow is shut off and is not released again until the oil pressure corresponds to a braking force of 10 kNm. The wagons will therefore be braked smoothly and precisely. Retarders working according to this principle do not require any measuring device or computer control. A recent order has been obtained for 1560 retarders from Bulgaria for the Sofia yard, to add to installations already achieved in yards as follows:

Country	Location	No of retarders
Canada	Vancouver	12
Denmark	Copenhagen	425
German	Dresden	850
Democratic Republic	Halle	280
	Seddin (Potsdam)	135
Italy	Milan	500
Sweden	Helsingborg	725
	Gothenburg	1200
	Malmö	750
	Sundsvall	350
Switzerland	Basle	21

French Railways (SNCF) has taken delivery of a modified ASEA automatic wagon haulage system for use in the Villeneuve Saint Georges depot for TGV train servicing. Regrinding of TGV wheels on a special pit lathe developed by the French company Sculfort requires accurate positioning by an external device, since the trains' traction power supply is disconnected. The ASEA system consists of two coupling carriages running on special rails located inside the normal track, one in front of and the other behind the lathe. A 4000 kg capstan moves the carriages at a maximum speed of 1 m/s and positions a wheel axle over the lathe with an accuracy of ±20 mm. The lathe operator is able to control each coupling carriage independently from a control panel. A special safety interlocking system prevents both carriage systems from being operated simultaneously. SNCF has ordered a similar haulage system for the TGV depot at Montrouge in the Paris area, and the Paris Transport Authority (RATP) has ordered a system of the same type for its Massy depot.

ASEA automatic wagon haulage system in use at SNCF Villeneuve St Georges TGV depot

ASEA hydraulic retarders in Helsingborg yard, Sweden

Babcock & Wilcox
Babcock & Wilcox Española

Alda de Recalde 27, Bilbao 9, Spain

Telephone: 415700
Telex: 33776

Products: Container handling cranes with 50 tonnes lift capacity above the spreader.

BBC Brown Boveri
BBC Brown, Boveri & Company Ltd

Postfach 85, 5401 Baden, Switzerland

Telephone: 056 75 11 11
Telegrams: Brownbover, Badenschweiz

Products: Radio remote control of shunting locomotives.

BP—Battioni & Pagani
BP—Battioni & Pagani SpA

Località Croce, 43058 Sorbolo (Parma), Italy

Telephone: 0521/798229-798220
Telex: 530081

Products: A complete range of side-loaders, including container handling machines up to 55 tons capacity and heavy machines fitted with telescopic top spreaders and special top clamps for intermodal transport movements; a range of heavy-duty fork-lift trucks of 4 to 38 tons capacity including machines fitted with spreader attachments for container handling.

Heavy-duty fork-lift truck by BP-Battioni & Pagani

Caillard Levage
Caillard Levage

BP 1368, 76065 Le Havre Cedex, France

Telephone: (35) 25 81 31
Telex: 190616

Director: P Renard

Products: Gantry cranes, container cranes of 25 tonnes capacity, bulk unloaders, bulk cranes, general cargo hook cranes, rail breakdown cranes, floating cranes.

Clyde
Clyde Engineering Co Pty Ltd

Factory Street, Granville, PO Box 73, New South Wales 2142, Australia

Telephone: 682 2111
Telex: 21647

Products: Yard control equipment, including retarders.

Coles
Coles Cranes Ltd

Harefield, Uxbridge, Middlesex UB9 6QG, England

Telephone: 089 582 3777
Telex: 21619

Products: Coles mobile port tower and mobile port cranes equipped with appropriate spreaders for handling freight containers in ports, rail yards and inland container terminals (lifting capacities from 6 to 250 tonnes).

Conrad-Stork
Conrad-Stork Kraanbouw BV
Member of Grootint

Waaderweg 80, PO Box 1551, 2003 BP Haarlem, Netherlands

Telephone: 023 319170
Telex: 41048

President: F L M Spit
Director, Sales: Th Ter Pelle
Director, Engineering: M C de Weerd

Products: Ship-shore container cranes, bridge-type container stacking cranes, railway gantry cranes for containers, and multi-purpose cranes.

Costamasnaga
Costamasnaga SpA

Viale 4 Novembre, Costamasnaga (Como), Italy

Telephone: 855 192
Telex: 380184

Products: Container handling cranes for rail and sea terminals.

Coventry Climax
Coventry Climax Ltd

Sandy Lane, Coventry CV1 4DX, England

Telephone: 0203 555355
Telex: 312414

Managing Director and Chief Executive: G Simpson
Director of Finance and Planning: G Trippas
Sales and Marketing Director: B Childs
Director of Purchasing: R Sadler
Engineering Director: A E Woolner
Production and Personnel Director: D Griffiths
UK Sales Director: A D R Sproul
Parts and Service Director: D Minchella
Company Secretary: W S Collins

Products: Fork-lift trucks and side loaders.

Coventry Climax Type EA2.0 electric fork-lift with 2000 kg lifting capacity at 500 mm load centre

Coventry Climax Type DA2.5 diesel-powered, pneumatic-tyred fork-lift with 'clean' version of Perkins 4.203 engine

Cowans Sheldon
NEI Cranes Ltd

Head office: NEI Cranes Ltd, Smith House, PO Box BR5, Town Street, Rodley, Leeds LS13 2TG, England

Main works: PO Box 9, St Nicholas Works, Carlisle, Cumbria CA1 2PA

Telephone: 0228 24196
Telegrams: Cowans, Carlisle
Telex: 64136

Director and General Manager: S M Baker

Products: Railway breakdown cranes; diesel-mechanical, diesel-electric and diesel-hydraulic breakdown cranes; GP rail cranes; twin-jib tracklaying cranes; maintenance/gang trolleys; rail loaders/unloaders; single line track panel laying gantries and cranes; container transfer vehicle; side-mounted rail loading cranes; traversers; turntables; and railway workshop overhead cranes.

Cowans Sheldon 12-tonne GP crane for British Rail

Coventry Climax Type R2.0 moving mast reach truck to full metric specification, with 2 tonnes basic lift capacity at 600 mm

Cowans Sheldon 60-tonne breakdown crane for Tanzanian Railways

Coventry Climax Type CS3.0 side-loader with 3 tonnes basic lifting capacity at 600 mm load centre, power hydrostatic steering and four-wheel brakes

Cowans Sheldon twin-jib tracklaying crane for British Rail

Dickertmann
Gebr Dickertmann Hebezeugfabrik AG

PO Box 2109, Hakenort 47, 4800 Bielefeld 1, Federal Republic of Germany

Telephone: 0521 323021
Telex: 09 32 750

Products: Gedi shunting winch type 289; screw jacks type 370 for lifting locomotives, wagons and other heavy loads; lifting equipment for complete trains.

Dimetal
Dimetal SA

San Fernando de Henares, Apartado Correos 14.485, Madrid 5, Spain

Telephone: 675 1100

Railway Products Manager: Antonio González del Peral

Products: Yard control signalling equipment.

Diversey Wyandotte
Diversey Wyandotte Corp

1532 Biddle Avenue, Wyandotte, Michigan 48192, USA

Telephone: (313) 281 0930

Products: General maintenance and overhaul cleaning compounds; degreasers; rust removers; paint strippers; locomotive and car-washing products.

Dowty Group plc
Dowty Hydraulic Units Ltd

Arle Court, Cheltenham, Gloucestershire, England

Telephone: 0242 21411
Telegrams: Dowty Group, Cheltenham
Telex: 43176

Products: Hydraulic retarders and pneumatic boosters for continuous speed control of freight cars. The Dowty speed control system, developed and perfected over 20 years, is based on retarding units. These units, which have pre-set sensitivity, are bolted to the inside of the rails at intervals along the track. The hydraulic retarders are completely self-contained and need no exterior power supply. Where gradients are insufficient the retarder can be combined with a pneumatic booster unit to accelerate freight cars moving below the control speed. Dowty's continuous speed control systems are operating in a wide variety of conditions in marshalling yards in the United Kingdom, Federal Republic of Germany, Switzerland, Hungary, Finland, Norway, USA, Canada, Japan, India, Australia and South Africa. 42 000 Dowty high-capacity retarders and 18 000 booster retarders will be installed in the 64-track Sentrarand yard, South Africa.

Dowty high-capacity hydraulic retarders in Atchison, Topeka and Santa Fe Railway's Flynn marshalling yard at Oklahoma City

Dowty retarders in Sentrarand yard, South Africa

Durbin-Durco
Durbin Durco Inc

1435 Woodson Road, St Louis, Missouri 63132, USA

Telephone: (314) 993 4750
TWX: 910763-0798

Products: Tie down hooks and hook assemblies; hoists; compression units; corner protectors; shock absorbers; winch and ratchet load binders; wire rope fittings.

Ericsson
Telefonaktiebolaget L M Ericsson

PO Box 42015, 126 25 Stockholm, Sweden

Telephone: 08 1900 90
Telegrams: Ellemsignal
Telex: 10442

Products: Yard communications and signalling control equipment.

Ernest Holmes
Ernest Holmes Division (Dover Corporation)

2505 East 43rd Street, Chattanooga, Tennessee 37407, USA

Telephone: domestic sales: (615) 867 2142
export sales: (201) 842 5542
Telex: 132246

President: Don W Humphreys
Vice President: Walter Lock
Export Manager: Donald H Baldwin

Products: Automotive towing and recovery cranes (breakdown cranes).

Fergusson
Alex C Fergusson Company

Spring Mill Drive, Frazer, Pennsylvania 19355, USA

Telephone: (215) 647 3300

Products: Cleaners, sanitisers and lubricants.

Godwin Warren
Godwin Warren Engineering Ltd

7-9 Emery Road, Brislington, Bristol BS4 5PW, England

Telephone: 0272 778399
Telegrams: Goodwill, Bristol
Telex: 449375

Chairman: D J Simpson
Managing Director: A D Parsons
Marketing Director: A G D Soames
Financial Director: J G Jeffrey
Technical Director: G S Murdie
Production Director: A J Sanders

Subsidiary company: Godwin Warren Engineering Inc, USA (see below)

Products: Friction buffers, retarders and wheel stops; level crossing barrier systems; automatic wagon locators. The automatic wagon locator is designed to secure wagons or tankers during loading and discharge; it is normally custom-manufactured to specific order. Fold-out wheel stops and retarding buffers are employed to provide added protection for the system, especially where complicated rail movements are involved.

Friction buffers and retarders as supplied to British Rail (BR)

Godwin Warren Engineering
Godwin Warren Engineering Inc

Suite 100, 3320 Holcomb Bridge Road, Norcross, Georgia 30092, USA

Telephone: (404) 449 3446
Telex: 543061

Chairman: D J Simpson
Managing Director: A D Parsons
Finance Director: J G Jeffrey
Production Director: A J Sanders
Product Engineering Director: M T Strange
Director and Vice President: G S Murdie

Products: Frictionally controlled buffer stops, mine car arresters and level crossing barrier systems.

Grove
Grove Cranes Ltd

Between Towns Road, Cowley, Oxford, England

Telephone: 0865 776271
Telex: 837 463

Products: National Crane, truck or wagon mountable, with marine lifting system pedestal-mounted; rough terrain cranes; industrial cranes.

Industrial 36 National Crane model, 6.8 mT capacity, in railway mountable version

National 800 series crane, chassis-mounted for test purposes only

GRS
General Railway Signal Co

PO Box 600, Rochester, New York 14692, USA

Telephone: (716) 436 2020
Telegrams: Genrasig, Rochester, New York
Telex: 978317

President: G E Collins

Products: Yard control systems.
  Class-Matic Mark II systems expedite car handling in large yards, and integrate swift, safe car marshalling with efficient computerised management information systems. Class-Matic uses dual-process control computers (on-line and backup) and GRS interfaces to commercially available peripherals.
  GRS ground equipment for the system includes: Type E160 heavy-duty electric car retarders, Type F5 weight-responsive hydraulic retarders for tangent tracks, Type F4 hydraulic skating retarders, Model 6 high-speed trailable electric switch machines, dragging equipment detectors, radar speed detectors, and colour-light hump and trim signals.

Speed Frate is a GRS equipment package especially developed for smaller yards. It provides substantial benefits in car handling speed, damage control, work simplification, and in customer satisfaction. With the Speed Frate system, a small yard can marshall four to five cars a minute, with one man handling all car speed control and routing. Equipment cost and earth moving too are of modest proportions—for example, less than a 2.1-metre hump is ample for up to 18 tracks. GRS ground equipment for the system includes: Type F4 weight-responsive hydraulic car retarders; Speed-Frater high-speed electric point machines; control panel and colour-light signals.
  The Distributed Computer System (DCS) consists of an array of minicomputers, each with its appropriate group of modular interface units. It is the most recently developed Class-Matic II configuration and has very substantial advantages in efficiency as well as in economy. The DCS system 'distributes' the yard functions of process control and management information among several minicomputer/interface module groups: for example, one for automatic retarder control, one for automatic car routing, and one for management information reports. A unique, modular GRS system, it permits building-block engineering of a process and information system. DCS can be precision-matched to the needs of a specific yard, and economically expanded or altered later according to needs.

Haacon
Josef Haamann Hebe- und Transporttechnik

PO Box 11 40, 6982 Freudenberg, Federal Republic of Germany

Telephone: 9375 571
Telex: 689224

Products: Stationary container lifting systems; jacks and winches.

Hauhinco
Hauhinco Maschinenfabrik G Hausherr Jochums GmbH & Co KG

Zweigertstrasse 28/30, PO Box 10 16 61, 4300 Essen 1, Federal Republic of Germany

Telephone: 0201 771071
Telegrams: Hauhinco, Essen
Telex: 857 834

Products: Wagon shunting equipment for classification and sorting tracks at marshalling yards and industrial sites; railway weighing systems.
  The latest addition to the company's automatic systems is a device that overcomes the operating handicaps of static wagon weighing equipment. The Hauhinco in-movement weigher, the Fahrtwäger, weighs wagons by the axle or bogie with the accuracy of static weighers while they are in motion during marshalling. A special filtering process has been developed jointly with Industrie-Automation, Heidelberg, and the Kaiserslautern University, with support from the state of Nordrhein-Westphalia, to eliminate from the weighing results by complex algorithm any distortions arising from the wagon's movement; this requires the use of sophisticated microprocessors to be economically viable. The Fahrtwäger closes the one major gap in a fully automated shunting process.

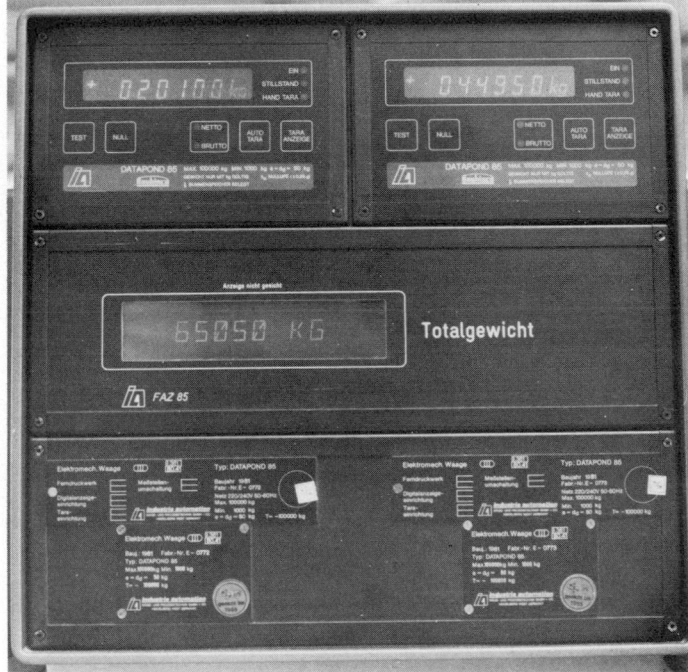

Hauhinco Fahrtwäger digital display

Hauhinco Fahrtwäger track installation

Hungarian Crane
Hungarian Shipyards and Crane Factory

Vaci ut 202, Budapest XIII, Hungary

Telephone: 496 370
Telex: 22 5047

Products: Container gantry cranes.

Hymid
Hymid Graemross Ltd

Rosebery Road, Anstey, Leicester LE7 7EJ, England

Telephone: 0533 364248
Telex: 36183

Managing Director: R L Clarke
Directors: R Beswick
           K G Andrews

Products: Equipment for wagon handling including wagon controllers, Hydra-brakes, automatic wheel and buffer stops; squeezer retarders; hydraulic systems and power packs.

Hymid wagon controllers

Hyster
Hyster Europe Ltd

PO Box 54, Berk House, Basing View, Basingstoke, Hampshire RG21 2HQ, England

Telephone: 0256 61171
Telex: 0256 858384

Managing Director: William H Flemming
Marketing Director: David Evans
General Sales Manager: Graham Lovatt

Products: Lift trucks for handling loads from 1 to 37 tonnes, including 20, 30 and 40 foot ISO containers.

2 tonnes load capacity Hyster H4 OXL diesel-engined lift truck with single-speed powershift transmission

IHI
Ishikawajima-Harima Heavy Industries Co Ltd

New Ohtemachi Building, 2-chome 2-1 Ohtemachi, Chiyoda-ku, Tokyo 100, Japan

Telephone: 03 244 6496
Telegrams: IHICO, Tokyo
Telex: 22232

Products: Standard dockside container crane; multi-purpose dockside container crane (IHI's Universe); elevated track system for container terminals.

Model of IHI elevated track system for container terminals

Integra
Integra Ltd Zurich

Industriestrasse 42, 8304 Wallisellen, Switzerland

Telephone: 830 16 11
Telegrams: Integra, Wallisellen
Telex: 56022

Products: DOMINO unit construction panels for marshalling yard control systems; alpha-numerical keyboard control.

Jambes-Namur
Ateliers de Construction de Jambes-Namur SA

5100 Jambes, Belgium

Telephone: 30 18 51
Telegrams: Jamur-Jambes
Telex: 59127

Managing Director: Ma Jean
Chief of sales: André Riquette

Products: 'Locopulseur Pulso' shunting machine; transporters; elevators; trucks. The Locopulseur Pulso shunting machine is a single-wheel vehicle capable of moving freight cars weighing 160 to 200 tons on straight level track. It can also move cars in curves, split a line of cars and handle a car on a turntable.

Jones
Jones Cranes Limited
Member of The 600 Group Ltd

PO Box 13, Letchworth, Hertfordshire SG6 1LU, England

Telephone: 04626 2360
Telegrams: Jones, Letchworth
Telex: 82112

Managing Director: J R Wheatley
Sales Director: F Richmond
Technical Director: G Innes
Financial Director: K E Peers
Works Director: T M Mountford

Products: Mobile, crawler-tracked and truck-mounted cranes with lifting capacities up to 45 tons.

Jones IF15 mobile crane, for handling 15 tonnes at full extent of 9.64 m jib and manoeuvring in confined locations

Cummins diesel-powered Jones 971T truck crane to lift 45 tonnes at 3.7 m radius and capable of fast travel on both tarred and laterite roads

Kone
Kone Corporation Crane Division

PO Box 6, 05801 Hyvinkää, Finland

Telephone: 271
Telegrams: Kone
Telex: 15-122 or 15-175

President: Pekka Herlin
Executive Vice President: Gerhard Wendt
Director, Crane Division: Heikki Harjuvaara
Director, Marketing: Carl-Johan Numelin

Products: Container handling dockside cranes, multi-purpose cranes, railway terminal gantry cranes, cargo and container handling gantry cranes, container storage cranes, overhead travelling cranes for containers and other loads.

Kone type CT4 40 tonnes container crane loading for Swedish State Railways (SJ)

Kyosan
Kyosan Electric Manufacturing Co Ltd

4-2 Marunouchi, 3-chome, Chiyoda-ku, Tokyo, Japan

Telephone: (03) 214 8131

Products: Yard control equipment.

Letourneau
Marathon Letourneau Company
Subsidiary of Marathon Manufacturing Company, Longview Division. Marathon Manufacturing is a wholly-owned subsidiary of Penn-Central Corporation

PO Box 2307, Longview, Texas 75606, USA

Telephone: (214) 753 4411
Telex: 730 371

President: Paul Glaske
Vice President, Sales: Ron Glass
Vice President, Marketing: Stuart Roberts

Products: Gantry cranes and the 'Letro Porter' handling equipment for containers and piggyback trailers.

Liebherr
Liebherr Container Cranes Ltd

Head office: Killarney, Co Kerry, Ireland

Telephone: 064 31511
Telex: 26946

UK sales office: Liebherr Great Britain Ltd, Travellers Lane, Welham Green, Hatfield, Hertfordshire, England

Telephone: 65381
Telex: 261271

Directors: K Noelke
R Geiler
P Bickel
Secretary: H Brunner

Products: Liebherr Container Cranes Ltd manufactures and sells rail-mounted container handling cranes for ship-to-shore terminals, railway and trucking terminals and storage yards. Sizes, speeds and safe working loads to meet all international tenders and specific customers' requirements.

Mitsubishi
Mitsubishi Heavy Industries Ltd

5-1 Marunouchi, 2-chome, Chiyoda-ku, Tokyo, Japan

Telephone: 03 212 3111
Telex: 22282

Products: Straddle carrier and gantry cranes.

Modern Industries
Modern Industries Inc

101 Outer Loop, PO Box 14287, Louisville, Kentucky 40214, USA

Products: Yard control equipment.

NEI
NEI Cranes Ltd

Smith House, Rodley, Leeds LS13 1HN, England

Telephone: 0532 579001
Telegrams: Cranes, Rodley
Telex: 55159

Products: Container transporter cranes, Goliath transporter cranes, all types of bridge crane and other cranes.

Nelcon
Nelcon BV

Doklaan 22, PO Box 5303, 3008 AH Rotterdam, Netherlands

Telephone: 10 281222
Telex: 28003

Director, Sales: T E M Kocken

Products: Ship-to-shore cranes; bridge-type container stacking cranes; rail/road transfer container cranes; multi-purpose cranes; straddle carriers; mobile cranes; self-propelled railway cranes up to 25 tons capacity for normal rail gauge.

Recent deliveries have included two container ship-to-shore cranes in Felixstowe and a rail/road transfer container crane at Europe Container Terminus, Rotterdam. Further container ship-to-shore cranes have been ordered by Um Qasr, Iraq (two), Yanbu, Saudi Arabia (three), Gothenburg, Sweden (one), Aruba (one) and Curaçao (one).

Nelcon container transfer gantry

Nippon Signal
Nippon Signal Co Ltd

Head office: 3-1 Marunouchi, 3-chome, Chiyoda-ku, Tokyo, Japan

Telephone: (03) 212 8371
Telegrams: Signal, Tokyo
Telex: 222 2178

Works: Yono Factory, 13-8, Kamikizaki 1-chome, Urawa City
Utsunomiya Factory, 11-2, Hiraide Kougyo Danchi, Utsunomiya City

Associated companies: Nisshin Industrial Co, Ltd
Nisshin Electrical Installation Co, Ltd
Nisshin Electronics Service Co Ltd

President: H Takeuchi
Chairman: T Hayashi
Managing Director, General Sales: T Oki
Director, Foreign Trade: K Matsushima

Products: Automatic freight car control system for marshalling yards, automatic self-gravity car-retarder equipment and various indication control boards for passengers.

Noord-Nederlandsche
Noord-Nederlandsche Machinefabriek BV

St Vitusstraat 81, PO Box 171, Winschoten, Netherlands

Telephone: 05970 15225
Telex: 53096

Products: Road/rail range of Trackmobile shunting units.

Paceco
Paceco Inc
Subsidiary of Fruehauf Corp

PO Box 3400, Gulfport, Mississippi 39503, USA

Telephone: (601) 896 1010
Telex: 58 9924

President: John F Martin
Vice President, Operations: Harry E Greenwood
Vice President, Administration: Adam J Consolatti
Assistant to President, Engineering: Charles H Zweifel
Vice President, Marketing: Lester C Stephens

Products: Rubber-tyred and rail-mounted Transtainers for handling loads up to 50 tons; Universal lifting spreaders; Shiptainer cranes; Portainer pierside handling crane.

Peiner
Peiner Maschinen-und Schraubenwerke AG

PO Box 1649, 3150 Peine, Federal Republic of Germany

Telephone: 05171 501
Telegrams: Peinerag Peiner
Telex: 09 26 62

Products: Container cranes; container stacking cranes (either rail-mounted or rubber-tyred); straddle carriers; spreaders; harbour cranes for handling general cargo and bulk material; shipyard cranes; tower cranes; grabs; scaffolding equipment; towers and masts for radio installations; industrial fasteners.

Peiner ship-to-shore container crane

Peiner rubber-tyred container stacking crane

Peiner three-high straddle carriers

Penetone
Penetone Corporation

74 Hudson Avenue, Tenafly, New Jersey 07670, USA

Telephone: (201) 567 3000

Products: Rolling stock cleaners and equipment.

Ross and White
The Ross and White Company

50 West Dundee Road, Wheeling, Illinois 60090, USA

Telephone: (312) 537 0060

President: C P Ross
Vice President: R W Burrill
Vice President, Sales: T W Skweres

Products: Railway sand handling equipment including cleaning, drying, storage and delivery of sand to locomotives; Buck Cyclone Cleaners for rail passenger coach interiors incorporating high-pressure, high volume hand guns; brush scrubbing systems for passenger coach exteriors; pressure washing equipment for locomotives.

Saalasti
Saalasti Oy

Arinatie 4, 00370 Helsinki 37, Finland

Telephone: 90 557 775
Telex: 124 694

Products: Diesel shunting locomotives; road/rail shunting tractors; rail repair locomotives; shunting couplings; snow ploughs.
   The Saalasti Oy bi-modal Little Bear shunter is a rear-wheel driven tractor whose rear road wheels have been removed and replaced with flanged steel wheels provided with rubber spring action. The hubs of these flanged wheels are provided with drums for the drive of traction wheels with pneumatic tyres. The rear pneumatic wheels for driving off rail over terrain are mounted to the rear chassis of the tractor by articulated joints. They are lowered hydraulically by a valve controlled from the cabin. The front end is provided with small flanged wheels, also lowered from the cabin, for driving on rails.
Weight: 10 tonnes
Transmission: Hydrodynamic
Engine: 88 kW/2400 rpm
Tractive effort, μ = 0.3: 2500 kp
Haulage capacity: 500 tons
Speed on rails: 25 km/h
   on pneumatic wheels: 12 km/h
Length: 6100 mm
Height: 2900 mm
Width: 2480 mm
Brakes: Hydraulic drum brakes and mechanical parking brake. Train brake if necessary
Accessories: Pushing plate for moving snow and cleaning railway yards
Optional accessories: Brush machine, snow blower, plough pushing plate.
   The company's OTSO brush plough fitment enables snow clearance to be continuous during shunting operations. With the brush plough in the lower position the track is cleared nearly to the sleepers. The rail brushes clean the rails from inside. Over local obstacles such as a level crossing it is not necessary to lift the plough. Switches may be approached normally with the plough lowered. Before the plough reaches the switch tongue, airblowing can be started by use of a cab pedal and continued until the switch tongue is passed.

Saalasti Oy 'Little Bear' road-rail shunting tractor

Saalasti Oy 'OTSO' shunting coupling

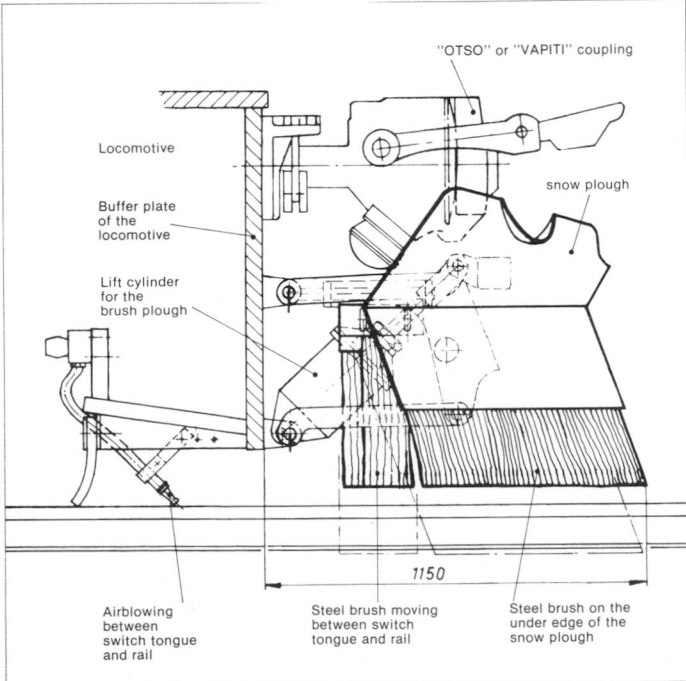

Saalasti Oy brush snowplough attachment

Saalasti Oy 'Vapiti' shunting coupling

Safetran
Safetran Systems Corporation

7721 National Turnpike, Louisville, Kentucky 40214, USA

Telephone: (502) 361 1691

Products: Marshalling yard communication systems.

Saxby

40 rue de l'Orillon, 75011 Paris, France

Telephone: 357 65 30
Telex: 220554

Products: Route relay interlocking, automatic block systems, centralised traffic control, automatic level crossing barriers, marshalling yard equipments and retarders, passenger information systems.

SEL
Standard Elektrik Lorenz AG

Hellmuth-Hirth-Strasse 42, 7000 Stuttgart-Zuffenhausen, Federal Republic of Germany

Telephone: 0711 8211
Telex: 72 526-0

Products: Mobile radio equipment; automatic humping control; yard control equipment.

Siemens
Siemens Aktiengesellschaft

PO Box 433, Ackerstrasse 22, 3300 Braunschweig, Federal Republic of Germany

Telephone: 706-1
Telex: 9 52 858

Products: Yard control equipment and retarders.
The microcomputerised MICOR control system is of modular design, high reliability and easy handling, and guarantees a high rate of throughput in the distribution area and a target-accurate slowing-down in the allocation tracks.

MICOR modular frame for control of two retarders

Smith Bros & Webb
Smith Bros & Webb Ltd

Britannia Works, Arden Forest, Industrial Estate, Alcester, Warwickshire, England

Telephone: 0789 763222
Telex: 338212

Chairman: O D Smith
Managing Director: K J W Woolley
Technical and Production Manager: M Clayton
Sales Manager: S B Miles
Commercial Manager: J G Ziegler
Contracts Manager: M W Patterson
Export Sales Manager: R Myatt

Products: Britannia fully-automatic train washing system. Operators which have selected Britannia equipment include British Rail (over 40 systems) for its Inter-City and HST operations; the Tyne and Wear PTE; the Piraeus Metro in Greece; the Lisbon Metro system; and the Western Australian Government.
The company has wide experience in designing rail washing systems for unusual geographic locations, to meet extremes of temperatures, arid and wet climates and in situations where space constraints have been extremely limiting. SB&W's own trained engineers are available to supervise installations anywhere in the world.
The Britannia washing system is controlled by track switches and incorporates easily replaceable brush sections contoured to carriage profile. Long life 'X' section polypropylene filaments are a feature of its construction and help to reduce operating and maintenance costs. Splash cowls are fitted to enclose the sides and rear of brushing units. Automatic frost protection facilities can be incorporated. All metal components are shot-blasted before painting. The washing cycle is activated by track switches, and the brush units, water pumps and chemical pumps are operated in sequence by contactors and timers on the main control panel. The latter is located in a control room, housing main pumps and connected by service ducts to the brush and spray stations. Plant switch-off may be by timers or additional track switches. An electrical interlocking facility guarantees non-operation of the plant by trains moving in the reverse direction.

British Rail HST passing through typical Britannia train washing system; note roof brush in operation

Tyne & Wear Metro units undergoing Britannia four-stage washing cycle

Steele
E G Steele & Co Ltd

25 Dalziel Street, Hamilton, Lanarkshire ML3 9AU, Scotland

Telephone: 0698 283765
Telegrams: Mountings, Hamilton
Telex: 77454

Associated company: SA Ateliers de Construction de Jambes-Namur, Belgium

Directors: E G Steele
J G Steele
D A Steele
M S Steele

Products: Locopulsor shunting machines; wagon mountings.

Stothert & Pitt
Stothert & Pitt plc

PO Box 25, Bath, Avon BA2 3DJ, England

Telephone: 0225 314400
Telegrams: Stothert, Bath
Telex: 44311

Group Managing Director: Allan Cheetham
Managing Director, Crane Division: T E R Torrance
Sales Director: J D Gittins
Commercial Director: D Moss

Products: Telescopic spreader beams, twin lift spreader beams, automatic or manual fixed length spreader beams; bridge cranes for container marshalling and for loading on road/rail transport; quayside transporter cranes for loading container vessels; jib cranes for container handling.

Strachan & Henshaw

PO Box 103, Ashton Works, Ashton Vale Road, Bristol BS99 7TJ, England

Telephone: 0272 664677
Telex: 44170

Products: Wagon tipplers, positioners, traversers and holding devices for handling random wagons or unit trains at marshalling yards, transhipment terminals and industrial sites; wagon haulage and propulsion systems; stackers and reclaimers for terminal stockyards; rail wagon loading installations; special purpose mechanical handling equipment.

Systems are individually designed to meet specific plant requirements, with all wagon movements, whether of random wagons, rakes, or complete coupled trains, precisely controlled and integrated with loading and unloading plant operations. With all movements thus integrated, speeds and timings are optimised to minimise loads on machinery and risk to personnel. With appropriate use of interlocks and automatic sequence control, a complete installation for unloading a unit train of over 10 000 tonnes in under two hours can be operated by one person from a remote panel.

As top-unloading wagons can show valuable operating economies compared with bottom-dump hopper wagons, demand for tippler installations for new terminal developments is very active and Strachan & Henshaw is currently supplying new high-throughput plants to terminal operators in USA, Canada, Mexico, South Africa, Australia and the People's Republic of China. Strachan & Henshaw wagon marshalling systems also provide useful economies and improve plant efficiency at installations of all sizes and levels of complexity, including where the rate of working is less intensive and movements irregular.

Among the more recent wagon tippler projects undertaken are several contrasting installations in North America. Coal exported from western Canada via the new shipping terminal at Ridley Island will be transported overland by unit trains of rotary-coupler wagons expected to gross around 10 000 tonnes. These will be discharged in a tandem rotary tippler designed to work at up to 75 wagons per hour.

In the USA a unit train installation at Irvington generating station, Tucson, Arizona, is on a site which dictates a 0.75 per cent uphill grade on either side of the unloading station, with just enough room to site the tippler on a level base. Two matched positioners work in unison to index trains through the single-barrel tippler, one positioner a wagon length behind the other; one holds the train on the grade while the other runs back two wagon lengths ready for the next forward movement. Strategically-located axle stops provide added protection against unwanted movements and help relieve end coupling loads on the wagon in the tippler. The system is designed to unload up to 36 wagons per hour.

At the Massey coal terminal, Newport News, Virginia, coal is delivered in trains of conventional open wagons of varying size and fitted with non-rotary couplings. Trains are assembled in random order. Wagons are therefore uncoupled in pairs for unloading in the tandem tippler, which is of Strachan & Henshaw Crescent design to permit use of a charger running on a parallel track to draw the wagons forward by means of a side arm engaging the lead coupler of each pair. This also ejects emptied wagons from the tippler while preventing re-engagement of the couplings with those on the full wagons.

Two installations similar to that at Massey but each with two tandem Crescent tipplers positioned in parallel, are due to enter service in 1984 at new coal transhipment facilities at the ports of Qinhuangdao and Shijiusuo in the People's Republic of China.

Chain-driven S & H wagon-positioner serving elevated iron tippler in Guinea, system including traverser and ram-type pusher to clear empty wagons from traverser

First S & H twin-barrel tippler at Richards Bay Coal Terminal

Takraf
VVB Takraf

701 Leipzig, German Democratic Republic

Telephone: 7 92 20
Telex: 051577

Products: Container transporters and stackers; side-loading inter transport transfer devices; railway wrecking and general-purpose cranes.

Telkor
Telkor (Pty) Ltd

PO Box 50836, Randburg 2125, Transvaal, South Africa

Telephone: 787 9740
Telegrams: Sudamat Jhb
Telex: 4 22171

Chairman: I Mackenzie
Managing Director: Cyrus Potgieter
Directors: George Chancel
Robert Brodie
Peter Westwood

Products: Yard control equipment including retarders.

Thyssen
Thyssen Umformtechnik/Bergbautechnik

Werk Wanheim, Ehinger Strasse 80, Postfach 28114, 4100 Duisburg 28, Federal Republic of Germany

Telephone: (203) 732-1
Telex: 855 861

Products: Marshalling yard retarders and wagon-moving equipment. The company has equipped with retarders more than 60 shunting yards of the German Federal Railway (DB), of West German industry and of railway companies abroad. The Hamburg-Maschen shunting yard alone incorporates as many as 136 Thyssen retarders.

Toshiba
Toshiba Corporation
Transport Equipment Export Department IOPG

1-6 Uchisaiwai-cho 1-chome, Chiyoda-ku, Tokyo, Japan

Products: Yard control equipment including retarders.

Transcontrol Corporation
A subsidiary of Siemens

6 Manhassett Avenue, Port Washington, New York 11050, USA

Telephone: (516) 883 6900

Chairman: M Zeiler
Managing Director: John M Pelikan
Chief Sales Director: Gerald Erno
Export Sales Director: Edward Riddett

Products: Yard control systems.

Tysol
Tysol Products Inc

919 N Michigan Avenue, Chicago, Illinois 60611, USA

Telephone: (312) 642 4823

President: Edward M Johnson
Purchasing Agent: Alan S Johnson

Products: Rolling stock cleaning equipment.

Unilok
Unilokomotive Ltd
International Division

Mervue Industrial Estate, Galway, Ireland

Telephone: (091) 7035/7034/63098/68370
Telegrams: Locomotive
Telex: 28375, 28941

Production and international sales were taken over from the Hugo Aeckerle Co of Hamburg in 1976 and all sales and production are now controlled from Ireland.

Products: Unilok road/rail switching locomotives for industrial and railway siding work: D Series type for normal shunting duties and E Series model for rough terrain, tractive effort ranging from 5000 to 12 500 kg. Many patented features including hydraulic weight transfer system. Built for all gauges and all coupler systems, and in rail service world-wide.

Union Switch
Union Switch & Signal Division
American Standard Inc

Swissvale, Pennsylvania 15218, USA

Telephone: (412) 273 4000
Telex: 86 6448

Products: Yard control systems and retarders.

Valmet
Valmet Oy
Materials Handling Division

Tampere Works, PO Box 387, 331 01 Tampere 10, Finland

Telephone: 358 31 653 322
Telex: 22140

General Manager: P Heikkilä
Export Manager: J Heinämäki

Products: Container stacking carriers, up to three-high stacking of 2.89 metres high containers; mobile gantry cranes of 22 to 30 tons lifting capacity; fork-lift trucks of 12 to 40 tons capacity; industrial straddle carriers of 13 to 60 tons capacity; special equipment for ro-ro ships, etc; RTD 4014 reach stacker for four-high container handling at the first row and three high at the second row.

Vickers Aquamatic
A Vickers company

Gomersal Works, Gomersal, Cleckheaton, West Yorkshire BD19 4LQ, England

Telephone: 0274 873422
Telegrams: Vickerseng, Cleckheaton
Telex: 51347

Chairman: J R Wareing
Managing Director: C Shield
Product Manager: J F Wood
Sales Manager: P Newton

Vickers Aquamatic train washer at British Rail's Clacton emu depot

Vickers Aquamatic bogie washer at London Transport's Acton works

Products: Design, manufacture and installation of drive-through washing and brushing systems for railcars, ranging from the simplest detergent/water wash-up to fully automatic installations for daily detergent washing and periodic acid removal of oxides and staining; supporting control systems, water storage, effluent treatment and water re-cycling systems; railway workshop cleaning plant including bogie washing installations.

Vickers Aquamatic has recently supplied a combined regular washing and acid cleaning plant to British Rail, Chingford, for emu trains and has earlier installed similar machines at British Rail, Clacton and Southend. London Transport use machines at its Stonebridge Park, Hainault and Ruislip depots. Washing and acidic units are operating in Hong Kong at MTRC and KCR and also at Caracas Metro (phosphoric-foam), which has recently ordered a second machine. Another current order is a machine for daily washing for Seoul Metro.

Vickers Aquamatic bogie washers are installed at the British Rail, Derby and Glasgow depots, and at London Transport, Acton and one has been ordered for the Seoul Metro.

Vickers Aquamatic train washer at Kowloon-Canton Railway depot, Hong Kong

Vollert
Hermann Vollert KG Maschinenfabrik

7102 Weinsberg/Wurtt, Federal Republic of Germany

Telephone: 0728 736
Telex: 07 28 736

Products: Shunting mules of various types; wagon transfer tables; radio-controlled diesel, battery or electric robot locomotives of varying sizes and power including models capable of moving 3000-tonne trains; remotely-controlled functions include disengagement of couplings and infinitely variable mule speed for accurate wagon spotting at discharge points, etc.

Vollert robot shunter

Vollert robot shunter servicing refuse-processing power plant

Wabco Westinghouse

207 boulevard de Souverain, 1160 Brussels, Belgium

Telephone: 73 60 53

Products: Two-way radio equipment; yard control systems and retarders.

Warrington Tractors

Winwick Road, Warrington, Cheshire, England

Telephone: 0925 36122
Telex: 517297

Managing Director: D A Banks
Sales Manager: J Hillman

Products: Mersey rubber-tyred shunting tractor, 80 to 180 hp.

6-cylinder, 120 hp four-wheel drive Mersey tractor for British Steel Corporation, with automatic tow coupler; haulage capacity 160 tons

120 hp Mersey tractor for British Nuclear Fuels Ltd with front shunting blade and rear 1½-ton fork-lift attachment

Western-Cullen-Hayes Inc
Western-Cullen Division

2700 West 36th Place, Chicago, Illinois 60632, USA

Telephone: (312) 254 9600
Telegrams: Wesrailsup
Telex: 25 3206

Vice-President: R L McDaniel
Sales Director: J D Schaefer

Products: Yard control equipment including retarders.

Westinghouse
Westinghouse Brake and Signal Co Ltd

Chippenham, Wiltshire, England

Telephone: 0249 4141
Telex: 44941

Products: Yard control equipment.

Whiting
Whiting Corporation

15700 Lathrop Avenue, Harvey, Illinois 60426, USA

Telephone: (312) 468 9400
Telex: 2 53274

Managing Director: H K Waters
Chief Sales and Export Sales Director: D E Lins

Products: Yard control systems; jacks; Hydrabrake car speed retarder; train washing systems; Trackmobile wagon movers; transfer table with remote car movers; rip jacks; interior hopper and tank car washers.

Windhoff
Rheiner Maschinenfabrik Windhoff AG

Hovestrasse 10, Postfach 1160, 4440 Rheine, Federal Republic of Germany

President: Dr Bernd Windhoff
Managers: Heinz Lörfing
        Ewald Elling
        Herbert Bucksch

Products: Tele-Trac shunting vehicle with tractive forces up to 40 000 daN, diesel or electro-hydraulically driven, control of shunting course and coupling operations by radio or by interlinking with loading programme; marshalling yard equipment; turntables and traversers; screw jacks for lifting locomotives, wagons and other heavy loads; lifting equipment for complete trains.

Windhoff Tele-Trac shunter at automatic coal-loading installation

Zagro
Zagro Bahn und Baumaschinen GmbH

Muhlstrasse 13, 6927 Bad Rappenau-Grombach, Federal Republic of Germany

Telephone: 07266 458
Telegrams: Zagro
Telex: 782381

Products: Yard shunting system incorporating special rail-mounted chassis powered by an unmodified fork-lift truck.

Zone Controls
Zone Controls Ltd

Building 39, Pensnett Trading Estate, Brierley Hill, West Midlands DY6 7PN, England

Telephone: 0384 270171/2/3
Telegrams: Controls Brihill
Telex: 338359

Chairman: F V Walter
Managing Director: E Jones
Export Sales Director: B R Whiting

Products: Railway signalling equipment.

WORKSHOP EQUIPMENT

Aabacas
Aabacas Engineering Co Ltd

Kelvin Road, Wallasey, Merseyside L44 7DN, England

Telephone: 051 638 5932
Telegrams: Aabacas, Wallasey

Managing Director: G K Clayton
Works Director: M J Yates
Sales Director: R G Howe
Chief Designer: J W Storer

Products: Electric wire rope hoists up to 20 tons swl capacity; single and double girder overhead electric travelling cranes (standard and custom-built designs, capacities up to 30 tons and spans up to 25 metres); overhead cranes; Goliath and Semi-Goliath cranes; jibs; gantries.

Aabacas offers a fully metricated standard range of portal building cranes which are based on double girder construction, warren-braced on the top section with an eight-wheel in-running crab with hoist supported within the girders. The best possible side hook approaches are assured and a hook height is kept at approximately gantry rail level, with the crane girders a minimum of 300 mm above the hook position, to secure substantial overhead clearance for stacked workpieces etc, and obtain high side walls beneath the gantry. An addition to the Aabacas range is a fully metricated arrangement of single girder underhung electric travelling cranes.

The company has recently installed two radio control cranes at British Rail workshops, Baileyfield, Portobello, Edinburgh. These were 2-tonnes swl, 22 120 mm span double-girder overhead cranes with push-button floor control and alternative radio control of each crane separately or of two cranes in tandem. Radio control was based on the Telemotive system, but the company is also pursuing remote control by an infra-red system.

Aabacas two-off 5-tonnes swl 25.5 m span double girder Class II duty cranes with two-speed operation on all motions

AEG-Telefunken
AEG-Telefunken Nachrichten- und Verkehrstechnik AG Geschäftsbereich Bahnen

Hohenzollerndamm 150, 1000 West Berlin 33, Federal Republic of Germany

Telephone: (030) 828-1
Telegrams: Elektronbahnen, Berlin
Telex: 1 85 498

Products: Electric equipment for electric motors; generator and control equipment repair shops.

Alzmetall
Machine Tool Factory and Foundry Friedrich & Co

Postfach 1169, 8226 Altenmarkt/Alz, Federal Republic of Germany

Telephone: 08621 881
Telex: 5 63124

Products: Drilling machines, boring mills.

Atlas
Atlas Engineering Company

84 Lillie Road, London SW6 1TN, England

Telephone: 01-385 9323
Telegrams: Fabricants, London SW6
Telex: 8951847

Chairman: H J Kemp
Sales Director: P J Hines

Products: Mobile railway lifting jack (up to 35 tons capacity); wheel profile trueing machines; crank axle turning machines; jacks; screwing machines; underfloor wheel trueing machines; double wheel lathes; hydraulic wheel presses.

Bahco Ventilation
Bahco Ventilation Ltd

Bahco House, Beaumont Road, Banbury, Oxon OX16 7TB, England

Telephone: 0295 57461
Telex: 837657

Managing Director: K D Green
Technical Director: G W Reynolds
Sales Manager: R E Aston
Supplies and Services Manager: C C Weaver

Products: Workshop heating, ventilation and air-conditioning systems.

CAM Industries
CAM Industries Inc
Peerless Tool Division

215 Philadelphia Street, PO Box 227, Hanover, Pennsylvania 17331, USA

Telephone: (717) 637 5988
Telegrams: Cam
Telex: 840470

President: Charles A McGough

Products: Specialists in dc electric motor equipment for manufacturing and repair workshops; workshop equipment for electric traction motor and generator repair shops; planning service for creation of electrical equipment servicing departments in traction workshops. Clients include the railways of Kenya, India, Bangladesh, Pakistan and the mass transit systems of Hong Kong, Seoul, Munich and Philadelphia.

Type DJ universal armature machine with traction motor armature in armature support steadies with bearing cartridge and drive assembly, set up for commutator trueing with armature in standard bearing

Peerless Type MGU universal armature extractor for generators, alternators, and traction motors (with adaptor plate for traction motors on dolly)

Type CW automatic continuous tig welding machine with EMD-67 traction motor armature supported between centres

Type MDU automatic mica undercutting machine with generator armature in unit and dust collector in operation

Heavy-duty portal-type wheel lathe for reprofiling of wheel-sets, Type 165

Cimmco
Cimmco International

ECE House, 28-A Kasturba Gandhi Marg, New Delhi 110 001, India

Telephone: 44381-5
Telegrams: Cimwag
Telex: 31 3618

Products: Machinery and equipment for manufacture and maintenance of rolling stock.

Dickertmann
Gebr Dickertmann Hebezeugfabrik AG

PO Box 2109, Hakenort 47, 4800 Bielefeld, Federal Republic of Germany

Telephone: 0521 323021
Telex: 09 32 750

Products: Spindle lifting jacks, underfloor elevators, bogie lifting platforms, various types of hoist.

Farrel Rochester
Farrel Rochester Division

565 Blossom Road, Rochester, New York 14610, USA

Telephone: (716) 288 4600
Telex: 978-453

Vice President, Metal Working: A W Sampson
Director, Railroad Equipment: W J Hegedus

Products: Complete line of wheel and axle maintenance equipment such as axle lathes, wheel borers, wheel lathes, mounting and demounting presses: one machine or complete shop with company's handling equipment for auto-shop operation on turnkey basis.

The company has lately supplied a full axle machining production line from forging to finished axle with wheel boring and automated mounting line to Indian Railways.

A recent technical development is the Farrel Wheel-Matic, a fully automated, computer-controlled wheel lathe for turning worn wheels. The machine is supplied with its own probe station to determine exactly the amount of metal to remove from each wheel to restore the profiles.

Hegenscheidt
W Hegenscheidt

514 Erkelenz/Brd, Postfach 2109, 4800 Bielefeld 1, Federal Republic of Germany

Telephone: 02431 6011

Products: Planning, production and supply of complete plants with integrated conveying systems for maintenance of railway wheel-sets; special single machines for cleaning, crack detection, inspection and profile turning of wheel-sets as well as for machining of axles; plant for machining of single wheel blanks including automatic loading and transport equipment; special machines for turning of wheel hub bores and tyres.

Type 10E CNC-controlled underfloor wheel lathe for reprofiling of wheel-sets in situ

Probat
Probat-Werke

4240 Emmerich/Rhein, Federal Republic of Germany

Telephone: 25 61
Telegrams: Probat, Emmerich
Telex: 8 125 154

Products: Spring testing machines for coil, leaf and torsion springs; hardness testers; tensile, compression and bending test systems; microprocessor control equipment for testing machines.

Subsidiary: Tarno Grocki, Tarnotest Prufsysteme GmbH
Resser Strasse 94, Postfach 1220, 4240 Emmerich 1, Federal Republic of Germany
Telephone: 02822 70060; Telex 08125154

Vickers
Vickers plc Design and Projects Division

Wessex House, Market Street, Eastleigh, Hampshire SO5 4FD, England

Telephone: 0703 619722
Telex: 477313

Managing Director: C V Chester-Browne
Engineering Director: R F C Butler
Director, Industrial Projects: A R Feely
Manager, Railway Projects: R R Vye
General Manager, Metal Industries: N V Lewis

Products: Selection, supply and setting to work of all equipment needed to overhaul, maintain, repair and clean rail vehicles and their components for metro, main-line and suburban railway systems; provision of design and consulting services for workshop layouts and special-purpose equipment design; design and supply of diagnostic test equipment for rail vehicles; supply of trackwork and other allied equipment.

Major contracts have included the design, supply and setting to work of workshop equipment for the Hong Kong Mass Transit Railway and the Kowloon-Canton Railway. With the completion of the Propatria workshop for the Caracas Metro the Division is now starting work on the Las Adjuntas workshop for the second line. Work is also under way for the supply of workshop and track maintenance equipment for lines 3 and 4 of the Seoul Metro.

Vickers Aquamatic train wash supplied by Vickers Design & Projects to Caracas Metro

Wagner
Gustav Wagner Maschinenfabrik

Postfach 113, 7410 Reutlingen, Federal Republic of Germany

Telephone: 07121 2081
Telex: 0729846

Products: Rail sawing and drilling machines.

Windhoff
Rheiner Maschinenfabrik Windhoff AG

Hovestrasse 10, Postfach 1160, 4440 Rheine, Federal Republic of Germany

President: Dr Bernd Windhoff
Managers: Heinz Lörfing
Ewald Elling
Herbert Bucksch

Products: Spindle lifting jacks; hydraulic wheel-set and bogie lifts.

Lifting jacks by Windhoff

Yvac
Yvac Company Inc

Suite 1713, 1 World Trade Center, New York, New York 10048, USA

Telephone: (212) 432 0192
Telegrams: Yvaccomp

Products: Designers and builders of railroad shop facilities.

CONTAINERS AND INTERMODAL EQUIPMENT

Note: For intermodal wagons see also under Locomotives and rolling stock and Private freight car leasing companies

Ackerman/Fruehauf Corp & Co

Ludwig-Richter-Strasse 1-9, 5600 Wuppertal-Vohwinkel, Federal Republic of Germany

Telephone: 0202 7392 0
Telex: 8591 754

General Manager: Willi Back
Sales Director: Utz Eisenrigler
Export Sales Director: Ewald Wirthmann

Products: Containers for the transport of standard European railway pallets; part of a demountable swap-body system known as Eurotainer.

With the support of the Federal Republic of Germany's Ministry of Technology the company has developed a flexible combination of motor trailer and one-, two- or three-axle platform chassis, the GLZ Kombi-Lastzug (Tandem Semi-Trailer), for simple and economical road transfer of Eurotainer swap-bodies. Four arrangements are possible, allowing for movement of two 7.15-metre swap-bodies with a total laden weight of 28 tonnes, a single 7.15-metre swap-body of either 14 or 20 tonnes glw, or a 12.3-metre swap-body with a glw of 25 tonnes.

GLZ Kombi-Lastzug with single-axle platform trailer and single 7.15 m swap-body

GLZ Kombi-Lastzug with double-axle trailer for 7.15 m swap-body with 20 tonnes glw

Adamson Containers Ltd

A division of Acrow

Station Road, Reddish, Stockport, Cheshire, England

Telephone: 061-432 0211
Telex: 668174

Deputy Managing Director: J B Corcoran
General Sales Manager: R A Walker

Products: All-steel, all-welded freight containers constructed to ISO standards and conforming to UIC regulations; security units; steel pallets; accommodation units.

Recent orders include a Sea Containers Ltd contract for 2200 containers, worth nearly US $7 million in total, and one from Flexivan Inc for 600 containers worth over US $1.5 million.

Agents and licensing agreement: The company has a licensing agreement with Equimental, Portugal.

20 ft ventilated container by Adamson

20 ft curtain-side container by Adamson

AGA
AGA Tankcontainer GmbH

Lichtenberger Strasse 24, 7100 Heilbronn, Federal Republic of Germany

Telephone: 07131 10981

Products: ISO tank containers; container repairs and cleaning services; container components.

Blatchford
Ralph Blatchford & Co

West Road, Midsomer Norton, Bath, Avon BA3 2AB, England

Telephone: 0761 412281

Products: The Linercrane, developed for Freightliners Ltd in conjunction with that company and British Rail's Technical Centre. Self-propelled by a Rolls-Royce C6 220P 190 hp engine, the 22.5 metre-long, 66-tonne Linercrane is a container transfer vehicle mounted on Gloucester RC&W GP525 bogies. It can deal with the majority of ISO container types up to 40 feet long, top-lifting boxes and corner-lifting flats. Hydraulic legs are extended for support when container transfers are being made. The two transverse container lifting gantries can be folded flat on the vehicle's central platform, within loading gauge, for inter-terminal movement, which can be at up to 120 km/h when the Linercrane is hauled by other traction. Within yards the Linercrane can also move about under its own power at up to 25 km/h carrying a container of up to 30 tonnes glw on its platform. The prototype Linercrane is designed for operation on standard gauge with 3.4 to 4.25 metre track centres, but versions for different track parameters are planned.

BN
Constructions Ferroviaires et Métalliques 'BN' SA
BN Spoorwegmateriel en Metaalconstructies NV

8200 Brugge 2, Belgium

Telephone: 050 330721-51
Telex: 811.22

Products: General and special containers.

Braidesi
Costruzioni Meccaniche Braidesi SpA

Via XXIV Maggio 10, 12042 Cuneo, Italy

Telephone: 43611
Telex: 21366

Products: Open and tilt-type steel dry freight containers.

Bremer
Bremer Waggonbau

Pfalzburger Strasse 251, PO Box 110 109, 2800 Bremen, Federal Republic of Germany

Telephone: 0421 454011

Products: Dry freight and insulated ISO containers.

BSL
Bignier Schmid-Laurent

25 quai Marcel Boyer, BP 205, 94203 Ivry sur Seine, France

Telephone: (1) 671 85 00
Telex: 270615

Products: 20, 30 and 40 feet stainless-steel tank containers supplied for all the major leasing companies, operating and shipping lines.

Budd
The Budd Company

Trailer Division Headquarters, Downington, Pennsylvania 19335, USA

Telephone: (215) 458 5301

Products: Aluminium, plastic/plywood, refrigerated and insulated trailers and containers.

Butterfield
W P Butterfield Engineers Ltd

PO Box 38, Shipley, West Yorkshire BD17 7HA, England

Telephone: 0274 52244
Telegrams: Tanks, Shipley
Telex: 51583

Chairman: M J Bradford
Managing Director: R J Brook
Chief Sales Director: C O Farmer

Products: 20 × 8 × 8 feet module size, ISO tank containers for carriage of bulk liquids and gases.

Comet
Comet Trailer Corporation

3808 North Sullivan Road, Spokane, Washington 99216, USA

Telephone: (509) 924 4800
Telegrams: Spokane WA
Telex: 32-6358

President: Steve Owens
Vice President, Manufacturing: Curtley Kidwell
Vice President, Engineering: Gerald Sill
Sales and Marketing: Fred A Yates

Products: Dry freight and refrigerated containers supplied to Alaska Railroad.

Containertechnik
Containertechnik Hamburg GmbH & Co

Heilwigstrasse 75, 2000 Hamburg 20, Federal Republic of Germany

Telephone: 4 60 20 31
Telex: 213571

Products: 20- and 40-foot end-door, side-door, open-top, half-height, bulk, flats, ventilated and tank containers.

Crane Fruehauf
Crane Fruehauf Ltd

Export sales: Toftwood, Dereham, Norfolk, England

Telephone: 0362 5353
Telex: 97251

Managing Director: Philip Croft
Container Sales Director: Barry J Fiske

Products: Dry freight, insulated and refrigerated containers; Tilt-tainers, container tanks, hopper container tanks to ISO, TIR, Lloyds, ABS and UIC standards.

Davis
W H Davis & Sons Ltd

Langwith Junction, Mansfield, Nottingham NG20 9RZ, England

Telephone: 0623 74 2621
Telex: 37657

Chairman: W H T Davis
Directors: C W Davis
　　　　　　D Sharpe
Secretary: J Cowling
Sales Manager, Rolling Stock: M S Burge
　Containers: D G Bradley
　Trailers: M E Price

Products: Multistack 20-, 30- and 40-foot dry freight containers.

Dorsey
Dorsey Trailers Inc

1409 Hickman Street, Elba, Alabama 36323, USA

Telephone: (205) 897 5711
Telegrams: Elba, Alabama 36323
Telex: 810 744 3110

President: G L Collier
Vice-President, Sales: Joe B DeVane

Products: Piggyback trailers, vans, chassis.

Eimar
Constructora de Equipos Industriales y Marinos, SA

Poligono Industrial de Malpica, Calles A-D, Zaragoza, Spain

Telephone: 299350
Telex: 58163

Products: ISO steel dry freight containers.

FFG
Fördertechnische Forschungsgesellschaft mbH

PO Box 1226, Mühlendamm 1, 2000 Hamburg-Schenefeld, Federal Republic of Germany

Telephone: (040) 83 03 22 01

Products: Self-propelled, rail-mounted ULS (Umschlagfahrzeug Lässig-Schwannhäusser) container transfer vehicle, part of the 'Freight Traffic and Transport Chains' intermodal programme involving 18 companies, financially sponsored by the Federal Ministry for Research and Technology, which is being co-ordinated by TUEV Rhineland (Technical Surveillance Association of the Rhine Region). Main features of the project in addition to the ULS are a computer guidance system for rail-to-rail transhipment points and an automatic container locking gear for container wagons.

The ULS is fitted with extending gantries which can be retracted within the loading gauge for rail movement, but which in the operating position enable it to transfer containers from its own platform to a road vehicle or vice versa, from itself to ground or vice versa, or from ground to ground across itself. The ULS, in addition to its own carrying capacity of two 20-foot ISO containers, can haul up to two container-laden wagons, making it apt for rail feeder service of small private or experimental terminals from a main container terminal. In 1983 the German Federal Railway (DB) was to begin regular service with three ULS to connect terminals at Schweinfurt, Bamberg, Hof, Coburg and Kulmbach with the main container network of its subsidiary Transfracht.

ULS self-propelled container-handling and transfer vehicle

Finsam
Finsam A/S

PO Box 3064, Elinesberg, Oslo 2, Norway

Telephone: 02 441860
Telex: 18050

Products: Containers and refrigerating systems.

Fruehauf
Fruehauf Division

10900 Harper Avenue, Detroit, Michigan 48232, USA

Telephone: (313) 267 1000
Telex: 23 5351

Division President: George F Malley
Vice President and General Sales Manager: Charles P Jacoby
Vice President, New Trailers: Quinn Thomas
  Engineering: Adrian F Hulverson
  Operations: Joseph P Silk

Products: All sizes and types of dry freight, insulated and refrigerated tank, platform and open top trailers and containers.

Fruehauf France

2 avenue de L'Aunette, 91130 Ris-Orangis, France

Telephone: (6) 943 30 00
Telex: 691 381

Chairman: J Gaschard
International Sales Director: Bruno Chabert
Container and Intermodal Sales Manager: Jean Richard

Products: Dry cargo and refrigerated ISO containers in steel and grp plywood; dry and refrigerated vans; TIR tilt platform trailers for intermodal movements; TIR tilt cargo and refrigerated swop-bodies or inland containers (UIC Class II and III).

Graaff
Graaff Kommanditgesellschaft

Postfach 160-180, 3210 Elze 1, Federal Republic of Germany

Telephone: 05068 180
Telex: 0927 168

Products: Dry freight, insulated, refrigerated, top loading and tank containers.

Gränges Graver
SA Gränges Graver NV

Molenweg 107, 2660 Willebroek, Belgium

Telephone: (031) 86 71 11
Telex: 31 293

Products: 20-, 30- and 40-foot aluminium tilt containers for transporting dry chemicals.

Hansa
Hansa Waggonbau GmbH

Pfalzburger Strasse 251, Postfach 110 109, 2800 Bremen 11, Federal Republic of Germany

Telephone: 45 40 11
Telex: 0244423

Products: Dry freight plastics/plywood ISO containers.

Hungarian Shipyards
Hungarian Shipyards and Crane Factory

Vaci ut 202, Budapest XIII, Hungary

Telephone: 200-800
Telex: 22-5047

Products: 20-foot all-steel containers and 20-foot tank containers built to ISO, UIC and TIR standards; production is approved by the Hungarian State Railways (MAV).

Kolmex
Foreign Trade Enterprise

PO Box 236, Mokotowska 49, 00-542 Warsaw 1, Poland

Telephone: 28 22 91; 29 92 41
Telegrams: Kolmex, Warszawa
Telex: 813270; 813714

Products: 20- and 40-foot freight containers.

McArdle
Thomas McArdle Ltd

Industrial Estate, Coe's Road, Dundalk, Louth, Ireland

Telephone: 042 35533
Telex: 24572

Products: Full range of containers to ISO standards and conforming to UIC requirements.

Mitsubishi
Mitsubishi Heavy Industries Ltd

5-1 Marunouchi 2-chome, Chiyoda-ku, Tokyo, Japan

Telephone: 03 213 3111
Telex: 22443

Products: Aluminium and plywood dry freight and refrigerated containers.

Morteo Soprefin
Morteo Soprefin SpA

Corso Andrea Podesta 8, 16128 Genoa, Italy

Telephone: (10) 53891
Telex: 270570

Directors: Armando Colombo
         Giacomo Cocino

Products: Freight, standard, non-standard, refrigerated and general purpose containers; flats; one-way or light containers (non-ISO); accommodation units.

40 ft standard container by Morteo Soprefin

20 ft open container by Morteo Soprefin

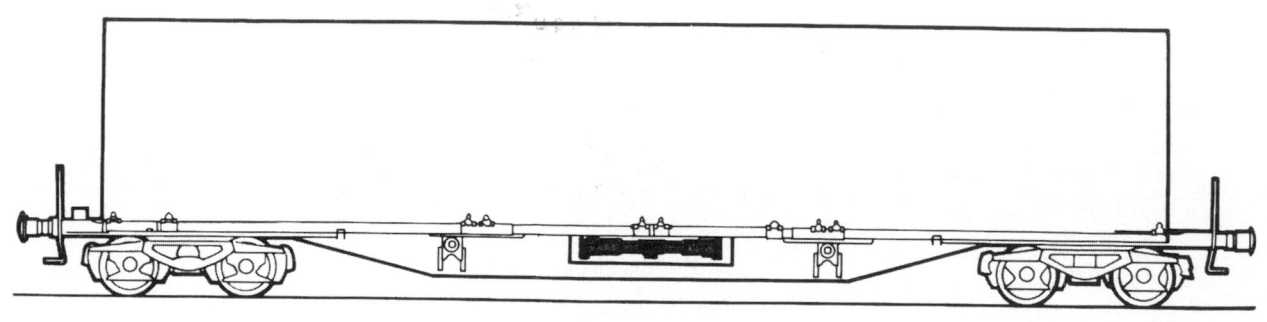

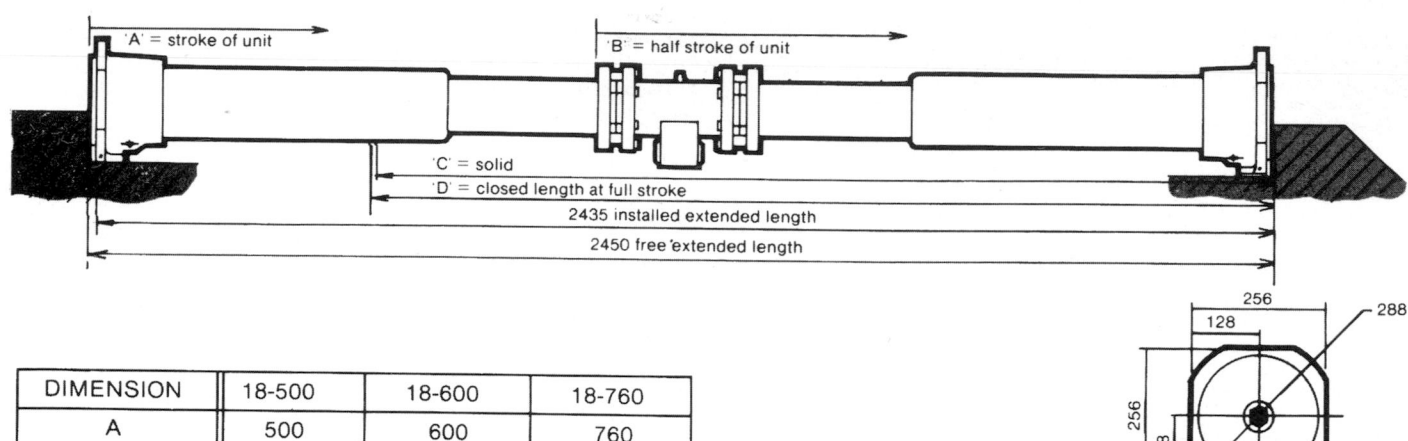

'A' = stroke of unit

'B' = half stroke of unit

'C' = solid

'D' = closed length at full stroke

2435 installed extended length

2450 free 'extended length

256
128
288
256
128
230

DIMENSION	18-500	18-600	18-760
A	500	600	760
B	250	300	380
C	1830	1830	1660
D	1935	1835	1675

Oleo Type 18 container wagon shock absorber

Oleo
Oleo Pneumatics Ltd

Blackdown, Leamington Spa, Warwickshire, England

Telephone: 0926 21116
Telex: 31148

Products: The long-stroke (up to 760 mm) Type 18 container protection shock absorber, developed for container-carrying wagons of the moving platform or sliding-sill type. Widely used in Europe and Scandinavia, the Oleo SA unit is available with various strokes and fits the standard (UIC 529 OR) pocket. Decelerations are controlled within 2 g (19.6 m/s²) under impact.

Pacton
Pacton BV

PO Box 50, Strangeweg 1, Ommen, Netherlands

Telephone: 05 291 15 0 0
Telex: 42199

Products: Dry freight, tank and special-purpose containers.

Portec
Portec Shipping Systems Division

300 Windsor Drive, Oak Brook, Illinois 60521, USA

Telephone: (312) 920 4600

Products: Rail car tie-down systems and intermodal and freight car components; tie down systems and components; intermodal components (fixed and retractable twist locks, container pedestals, bridge plates, special fabricated hitch struts); freight car components (centre plates, vibrator castings, handholds, anchor channels); other equipment (special tie-down systems for flat bed trailers and chassis, fixed and retractable twist lock assemblies, large and small fabrications of all types).

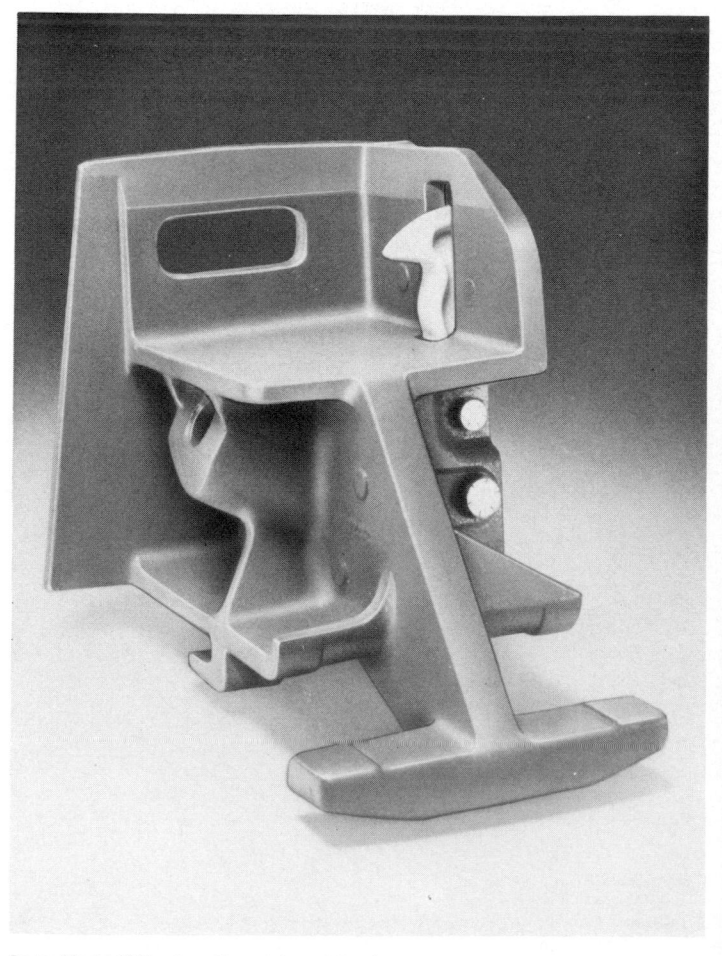

Portec Model 2200 automatic container pedestal

Ray Smith
Ray Smith Demountables Ltd

Botolph Bridge, Oundle Road, Peterborough PE2 9QP, England

Telephone: 0733 63936
Telex: 32267

Products: Container handling equipment, including the Klaus Kranmobil 32.
The KM32 is a totally self-contained unit based on a specially constructed semi-trailer chassis, and suitable for operation with most 32-ton gvw tractor units. Independent petrol or diesel engines to the operator's choice can be fitted to provide power for the hydraulic system. One operator alone mans the Klaus Kranmobil and carries out all container-handling operations with the aid of a portable console. There are two stabilisers per side and independent control of each enables positioning to avoid obstructions such as railway lines, buffers, bollards etc. Separate operation of the two lifting davits for elevation and transfer through more than 180 degrees is also possible from the console. The machine will transfer containers from rail to road vehicles or vice versa, from ground to vehicles, or from vehicles to stacking area. It will double stack containers and as it is extendable and complete with telescopic spreader it will handle standard 20-, 30- and 40-foot containers. Slings are available for bottom lift if necessary for flat bed types and other containers where bottom-lift facilities are needed. For travel on a public highway, stabilisers, lifting davits, etc fold into overall dimensions of 2.5 metres wide and 4 metres high. Overall length for travelling condition is approximately 15.5 metres.

Steadman side-lift container handler

Klaus Kranmobil KM32 sideloader transferring 20 ISO tank from rail to road vehicle, fitted with Ray Smith 'Ten-Plus' demountable body platform, which has retractable ISO twist locks

SNAV
Société Nouvelle des Ateliers de Vénissieux

40 boulevard Henri-Sellier, BP 144, 92154 Suresnes Cedex, France

Telephone: (1) 506 15 74
Telex: 611 486

Products: Steel, aluminium, plywood containers to ISO, UIC and TIR standards.

South African Transport Services

Paul Kruger Building, Private Bag X47, Johannesburg 2000, South Africa

Telephone: 713 2100
Telegrams: SAR, Johannesburg
Telex: 2-24205; 2-24087

Director General: Dr E L Grové

Products: ISO type 3- and 6-metre containers for dry and liquid freight for own use only.

Steadman
Steadman Containers Ltd

150 Glidden Road, Brampton, Ontario L6W 3L2, Canada

Telephone: (416) 457 9700
Telex: 06-97536

President: Dion P McGuire
Vice President, Finance and Administration: Michael Robertson
Vice President, Manufacturing and Operations: Ralph Wade

Products: Containers, container handling equipment.

Strick
Strick Corporation

225 Lincoln Highway, Fairless Hills, Pennsylvania 19030, USA

Telephone: (215) 949 3600
Telex: 84-3412

Chairman: Sol Katz
President: Joseph Bertsch
Chief Sales Director: Joseph Puchino
Export Sales Director: Frank Katz

Products: Full range of dry freight containers, van trailers and skeletal chassis together with insulated and refrigerated units.

US piggyback trailer by Strick

Thyssen
Thyssen Industrie AG

Postfach 11 00 67, 4100 Duisburg 11, Federal Republic of Germany

Telephone: (0203) 52-1
Telex: 8 55 401; 8 55 483

Main works
Thyssen Umformtechnik/Bergbautechnik
Werk Langschede, Ardeyer Strasse 100, Postfach 20, 5758 Frondenberg

Telephone: (2378) 82-1
Telex: 827758

Werk Hausach
Mannesmannplatz, Postfach 1180, 7613 Hausach

Telephone: (7831) 77-1
Telex: 7 525718

Products: Pallets, steel containers, refrigerated containers, plywood containers, storage containers.

Tokyu
Tokyu Car Corporation

Container Sales, Yaesu-Mitsui Building, 7-5 chome, Yaesu, Chuo-ku, Tokyo, Japan

Telephone: 272 7061
Telex: 0222 2020

Products: Steel and grp/plywood dry freight and refrigerated containers.

Trailor
Trailor SA

5 Route No 10, Coignières, BP49, 78311 Maurepas Cédex, France

Telephone: 050 61 26
Telex: 698896

Products: Dry containers and trailers.

Unikon
Fabryka Urzadzen Wagonowych Unikon

70-893 Szczecin, Poland

Telephone: 61271
Telex: 042221

Products: Containers.

Four-shell WEW Likwitainer 'R' containers

WEW
Westerwälder Eisenwerk Gerhard GmbH

5241 Weitefeld/Sieg, Federal Republic of Germany

Telephone: 02743 1071
Telex: 875323; 8763537

Managing Director: Helmut Gerhard
Managing Director, Production: Gustav Adolf Lichtenhäler
Sales Manager: Rainer Seibert

Products: Tank containers for the transport of hazardous and non-hazardous liquids, granular bulk solids and gases.

The company's latest product is the 'WEW Multitank', a 20 000-foot platform-compatible intermediate size tank container for carriage of liquids, gases, and dry bulk. Capacities range from 3000 to over 9000 litres. The 'WEW Multitanks' bridge the gap between light 'pallet' type portable tanks and drums (2000 litres or less) and ISO tank containers. The newly developed uniform corner fittings permit handling, lashing, interlocking, stacking, and storing in any position; and they are easily moved by existing standard fork-lift trucks, cranes, lorries, and flat bed trailers without need for heavy container handling gear. At the same time they can easily be fed into the ISO system by means of standard 20-foot platform based containers. 'WEW Multitanks' are designed to all leading codes and regulations for the intermodal carriage of hazardous liquids, gases, and dry bulk.

Size	Dimensions	Rating (to)
1	2.2 × 2.2 × 2.4 m	10
3/4	2.2 × 2.2 × 1.8 m	8
1/2	2.2 × 2.2 × 1.2 m	6
3/8	2.2 × 1.1 × 1.8 m	4
1/4	2.2 × 1.1 × 1.2 m	3

Other containers offered by the company include:

Four-shell WEW-Likwitainer R design, the largest 20 ft IMO Type 2 tank container available, for low hazard and non-hazardous liquids and pressurised dry bulk; test pressure 2.65 bar; stainless 304; capacity 27.7 m³; approved for all modes world-wide; heated, insulated;

WEW Beam Type IMO 2 20 ft tank container for low hazard and non-hazardous liquids; test pressure 2.65 bar; stainless 316; capacity 23 m³; approved for all modes; bolted frame/tank connection; heated, insulated;

WEW swap tank, the IMO 1 Special, for highly corrosive liquids; test pressure 4.0 bar; rubber-lined; capacity 11 m³; for road, rail, piggyback, and ro/ro traffic; ISO bottom structure suited for grappler-arm handling; top discharge;

Full-frame 20 ft IMO 1 Special tank, for all flammable and many multiple hazard liquids; test pressure 6 bar; stainless 316; capacity 20 m³; alternate top and bottom discharge; increased rating 30 tons.

WEW Beam Type IMO 2 tank containers

WEW Type IMO 1 Special swap-body containers

WEW Multitank LMO 1 unit, 2.4 × 2.2 × 2.2 m, capacity 7500 litres, 10 tons rating

WEW full-frame IMO 1 Special containers

York
York Trailer Co Ltd

Northallerton, North Yorkshire DL7 8UE, England

Telephone: 0609 3155
Telex: 58600

Managing Director: S Beckett
Chief Sales Director: J A Keirle
Export Sales Director: J F Davies

Products: Kangaroo TIR and other commercial trailers.

York-built Kangaroo trailer being loaded by gantry crane

PRIVATE FREIGHT CAR LEASING COMPANIES

EUROPE

Armita

Apollolaan 109, Amsterdam, Netherlands

Telephone: 736117
Telex: 12147

Vehicles: Tank cars 840, open wagons 132

Bodegas Regias

Av F Rodriguez Pandiella, 2 Leon, Spain

Telephone: 22 0985

Vehicles: Wine tank wagons

British Railway Traffic & Electric Co Ltd

Horbury, Wakefield, West Yorkshire WF4 5QH, England

Telephone: 0924 271881
Telex: 556457

Vehicles: 3500

Convoy

Diepenbrockstrasse 5, 1077 VX Amsterdam, Netherlands

Telephone: 723443, 72933
Telex: 12147

Vehicles: 352 tank wagons

Fert & Cie

PO Box 877, 2 rue Fendt, 1211 Geneva 1, Switzerland

Telephone: 022 34 8800
Telex: 22 139

Vehicles: 270 wine tank wagons

Invatra
Industrial de Vagones y Transportes SA

Poligone Industrial Alces, Alcazar de San Juan, Cuidad Real, Spain

Telephone: 511113

Vehicles: 58 tank wagons

Liga de Propietarios de Vagones de España

Juan Alvarez Mendizábal, 30-4° Centro, Madrid-8, Spain

Telephone: 2 47 82 86

President: Miguel Salis, General Director of Transfesa

The association comprises 53 of the more important private owners of railway wagons in Spain.

Metransa
Manipulaciones Especiales y Transportes SA

Telephone: 467 2700
Telex: 42081

Vehicles: 158 tank wagons

Procor (UK) Limited

Horbury, Wakefield, West Yorkshire WF4 5QH, England

Telephone: 0924 271881
Telex: 556457

Managing Director: F J Swindell
Financial Controller: N Casson
Sales Manager: B T McDonnell

Products: Railway freight rolling stock.

Constitution: Procor (UK) Ltd, a member of the Marmon Group of Companies, designs, builds, sells, hires, leases, repairs and maintains all types of railway freight rolling stock. With a fleet of over 3000 wagons, Procor is the largest wagon hiring company in the United Kingdom and has customers in the petroleum, chemical, food, steel, motor and construction industries.

Railease Ltd

Green Lane, Heywood, Lancashire, England

Telephone: 0706 64135
Telex: 63327

Vehicles: 395

Savesa SA

Oquendo 4, 4° A, San Sebastian, Spain

Vehicles: 200 bogie tank wagons

SEWAR
Société Exploitation de Wagons Reservoirs

43 rue de Provence, 75009 Paris, France

Telephone: 874 5508
Telex: 280564

Vehicles: 1650 wagons for foodstuffs transport

SGTL
Société Générale de Transport de Liquides

43 rue de Provence, 75009 Paris, France

Telephone: 874 5508
Telex: 280564

Vehicles: 200 tank wagons

SGW
Société de Gerance de Wagons Grande Capacite

7 rue de Bucharest, 75362 Paris Cedex 08, France

Telephone: 293 38 00
Telex: 658597

Vehicles: 13 000 high-capacity open wagons

Steele
E G Steele & Co Ltd

25 Dalziel Street, Hamilton, Lanarkshire ML3 9AU, Scotland

Telephone: 0698 283765
Telex: 77454

Vehicles: 121

STS
Storage and Transport System Ltd

Railway House, 31-34 Railway Street, Chelmsford, Essex CM1 1NJ, England

Telephone: 0245 350222
Telex: 995915

Chairman: J R M Rocke
Managing Director: R M Barclay
Directors: C Courau
J de Bruyn
J F Weerts
J Mouleart

Principal subsidiaries: STS (Wagon Sales) Ltd
Marcroft Engineering Ltd
Coalville, Leicester LE6 4DT
Radstock, Bath BA3 3QU
The Docks, Burry Port, Dyfed, South Wales SA16 0LT

STS wagon for liquid carbon dioxide transport

Products: Hiring, leasing, and sale of all types of wagon; modifications and repairs carried out by Marcroft Engineering.

Recent developments include a 51-tonne cement wagon for Blue Circle Industries, offering single-point gravity discharge or bilateral pressure discharge using the STS Powderjet fluidisation system. This system offers very clean discharge, with typical residues of 100 to 150 kg, and low maintenance costs on its STS Powderjet fluidisation system; it can discharge the payload of 37.4 tonnes in about 25 to 30 minutes.

The STS two-axle 51-tonne wagons for Class A petroleum products feature a 1 per cent-slope drainage channel in the base of the tank; this ensures complete tank drainage and enables frequent changes in the grade of product carried to be made without need of steam cleaning.

A batch of 80-tonne cereal wagons was to be delivered early in 1983.

STS 51-tonne glw two-axle cement wagon with STS Powderjet fluidisation system

Tiger Railcar Ltd

Fifth Floor, Alliance House, 12 Caxton Street, London SW1H 0QS, England

Telephone: 01-222 7692
Telex: 916201

Managing Director: R W Bull
Director, Nacco SA, President, Tiger Europe: D MacNaughton

Principal subsidiary: Tiger European Financial Services Ltd
173/176 Sloane Street, London SW3

Products: Full service leasing of all types of rail cars; contract haulage of rail freight in UK and Continental Europe.

Recent additions to the company's fleet include hopper cars for the conveyance of china and ball clay, manufactured in 1982 by Fauvet Girel and used in contract haulage of approximately 200 000 tonnes annually in UK distribution. A novel feature of these cars is their discharge characteristic in sticky substances, such as ball clay, and their rotating roof which facilitates movement of the cars within the BRW5 loading gauge with the roof open.

China clay hopper built by Fauvet Girel

Tiger Railiner for palletised goods with Tautliner side walls

Traffic Services
Traffic Services Ltd

Clarendon House, 11/12 Clifford Street, London W1X 2HD, England

Telephone: 01-629 8434
Telex: 25252

Chairman and Managing Director: J M B Gotch
Operations Director: Miss V A Steele
Finance Director and Company Secretary: G R Thomson
Director (Divisional Chairman): P D T Roberts

Products: International rail freight transport in privately-owned bulk wagons; international freight forwarding; movement of bulk liquid chemicals, liquefied gases, bulk wine and whisky, bulk solids including especially china clay and grain in Polybulk hopper wagons; also transport of packed materials, bagged cargo and cased wines.

In the UK the company manages rail movement in privately-owned bulk rail wagons; here its principal acitivity is grain distribution under the trade name 'Grainflow', which was launched in 1980 and developed in conjunction with British Rail. Under this scheme the company operates some 60 hopper wagons of 92 metre³ capacity, each capable of loading 58 tonnes of grain. Customers include most of the country's major grain companies.

The company also acts as agent for Ermefer SA, Geneva, handling all bulk movements of wine and whisky to and from the UK in the Ermefer fleet of over 100 stainless steel bulk tank wagons, each with 60 tonnes' capacity. It has several other major contracts covering trainload movement between the UK and Continental Europe.

Polybulk wagon for bulk solids

Ermefer tank wagon for bulk wine movement

Tramesa
Transportes Mixtos Especiales SA

Oquendo 5, 4° B, Spain

Telephone: 943 424208/428568

Vehicles: 146 chemical tank wagons

Vagones Frigorificos SA

Marques de Valdeiglesias 8, Madrid 4, Spain

Telephone: 231 71 04
Telex: 44081

Vehicles: 97 refrigerated cars; 151 hopper wagons

VTG

VTG Vereinigte Tanklager und Transportmittel GmbH
Member of the Preussag Group

Neue Rabenstrasse 21, Postfach 30 55 40, 2000 Hamburg 36, Federal Republic of Germany

Telephone: (40) 44 19 11
Telex: 2 17008-0

Chairman: Dr Horst Matthies
Managers: Roelf Janssen
Dr Klaus-Jürgen Juhnke
Heinrich Sikora

Principal subsidiaries: VTG (UK) Limited London, VTG Wien, VTG Basel, ALGECO SA France, SA ALGECO Belgique

Products: Renting of rail tank wagons and special wagons for the transport of liquid, gaseous and powdered products of the petroleum and the chemical industry; and of large-capacity rail wagons and coil wagons for freight transport between UK and the Continent; door-to-door transport services with tank containers for all kinds of liquids.

A recent addition to the VTG fleet is a pressurised-gas tank wagon with 22 tonnes axleloading and a capacity of 107 metres³. It has been developed for use mainly in block trains. VTG began building petroleum tank wagons of 22 tonnes axleload in 1979 and by 1982 had 12 block trains of such vehicles, totalling 240 wagons, in service, with a load capacity of 1400 tonnes per train.

To achieve increased payload, the new pressurised-gas wagon was also designed with the higher axleload; its maximum capacity is 54.7 tonnes. The wagon is optimally designed for the transport of heavy gases such as butane, butadiene and ammonia on routes where 22-tonne axleloads are permitted, but it is equally economical for the carriage of light gases such as propane, propene and their mixtures on routes which allow no more than 20 tonne axleloads, as in international traffic. It has been developed from the 95 metre³ pressurised-gas tank wagon, but has a 12 per cent greater capacity. For service in block trains it can be equipped on request with quick-acting couplers. In spite of its large capacity, it can be filled on a normal 14-metre weighbridge. Like all VTG's special freight wagons, it is licensed internationally for all routes. When empty it can be run at up to 120 km/h.

Phosphoric acid tank with internal rubber lining, 38 m³ capacity

VTG pressurised-gas tank wagon for 22 tonnes axleload with 107 m³ capacity

VTG petroleum tank wagons for 22 tonnes axleload with 95 m³ capacity, largest of their kind in Europe

VTG (UK)

VTG (UK) Limited
A subsidiary of VTG Vereinigte Tanklager und Transportmittel GmbH

Carrier House, Warwick Row, London SW1E 5ER, England

Telephone: 01-828 2257/8
Telex: 916592

Directors
R Baumgarten (VTG, Hamburg)
M Miehe (ALGECO SA, Paris)

Products: Lessor of railway vehicles to oil and petroleum companies in the UK and Western Europe.

NORTH AMERICA

American Refrigerator Transit Co

1102 Mopac Building, 210 N 13th Street, St Louis, Missouri 63103, USA

Telephone: (314) 622 2716

President: R J Dunne Jr

Vehicles: 2185

Bi-Modal Corporation
Subsidiary of North American Car Co

200 Railroad Avenue, PO Box 767, Greenwich, Connecticut 06836-0767, USA

Telephone: (203) 629 4692
Telex: 1282825

President: Robert S Reebie

Vehicles: 250 RoadRailers

(See also under Locomotives and rolling stock)

CGTX Inc

Suite 1600, 1600 Dorchester Blvd West, Montreal, Quebec H3H 1P9, Canada

Telephone: (514) 931 7343
Telex: 05 267562

Chairman: A W McKenzie
President and Chief Executive Officer: R D Cole

Products: Lessors of railway rolling stock in Canada: tank cars and freight cars.

Vehicles: 7113

Chicago Freight Car Leasing Co
Chicago Freight Car Leasing Co

205 W Touhy Avenue, Park Ridge, Illinois 60068, USA

Products: New and rebuilt freight wagons of all types; leasing services.

Vehicles: 3800

Evans Railcar Leasing Co
A subsidiary of Evans Products Co

2550 Golf Road, Rolling Meadows, Illinois 60008, USA

Telephone: (312) 640 7000
Telex: 206411

Vehicles: 7598

FGE-Fruit Growers Express Co

1625 K Street NW, Suite 700, Washington DC 20006, USA

Telephone: (202) 659 2945
Telex: 89 2670

Main works: 16 Roth Street, Alexandria, Virginia 22314

President: C N Taylor
Vice-President, Marketing and Sales: J E Chapman
Vice-President, Production: W K Levenson
Vice-President, Service Operations: D A Watts
Vice-President, Finance: R C Braun

Products: New freight cars of all designs; new cabooses; specialises in insulator and refrigerator cars; 140-ton capacity flat cars.

Vehicles: 10 745

GATX
General American Transportation Corp

120 South Riverside Plaza, Chicago, Illinois 60606, USA

Telephone: (312) 621 6200
Telex: 25-3623/4502

Main works: PO Box 128, Masury, Ohio 44438

President: James M Goff
Senior Vice President, Operations: George C Yates
Vice President, Sales: Robert E Lynch

Products: Tank wagons, special-purpose freight cars, railcar leasing, repair, maintenance and fleet management services.
GATX operates the world's largest independent railcar fleet, numbering more than 57 000 cars. The GATX tank car fleet includes the TankTrain system, a series of tank cars interconnected with flexible hoses that allow the entire string to be loaded and unloaded from one connection. Major advantages of TankTrain include lower facility capital costs, reduced loading and unloading times, less manpower, and safer handling for the crew, commodity and environment. An individual string of two to 22 TankTrain cars can be loaded at a rate of 3000 gallons (11 355 litres)/minute. TankTrain cars are available in a wide range of sizes for virtually any non-pressure liquid commodity. In January 1982 GATX began to offer prototype cars for handling molten sulphur. These 100-ton (90.7-tonne) cars have a 12 950-gallon (49 000-litre) nominal capacity and are available for loading in two- to nine-car strings. They are coiled and insulated with separate steam lines for fittings. As with other GATX TankTrain vehicles, the molten sulphur cars feature a vapour recovery system that collects vapours from all cars at a single point for proper disposal.
The GATX Airslide car is a covered hopper car for transporting finely divided commodities such as flour, sugar, starch and cement. Fabric in the bottom of each hopper trench allows the lading, when aerated through a built-in air chamber, to flow easily from the car. The most recent GATX 4566 cubic foot (129.2 cubic metre) Airslide car allows shippers to take advantage of incentive freight rates by carrying larger loads.

Vehicles: 62 617

4566 ft³ Airslide car to transport flour to bakeries in New York State

Flexible hose linking TankTrain cars

Itel Rail
A subsidiary of Itel Corporation

Head office: Itel Corporation
55 Francisco Street, San Francisco, California 94133, USA

Telephone: (415) 955 9546
Telex: 34234

Works: Itel Rail
Two Embarcadero Center, San Francisco, California 94111

Chairman, Chief Executive Officer and President, Itel Corporation: James H Maloon
Senior Vice President, Finance and Administration, and Chief Financial Officer, Itel Corporation: William P Twomey
Vice President, Government Affairs, Itel Corporation: Carl V Lyon
President, Itel Rail: Edward M O'Dea

Products: Primarily per diem operating leases of general purpose boxcars to Class II and Class III ("short line") US railroads. Most leases are for 15 years and provide for payments of rentals solely from a portion of car rentals received by the lessee railroad for the period the leased equipment is on the tracks of other railroads. As of December 1981, Itel Rail's fleet numbered 18 520 units, consisting of 13 530 general purpose boxcars, 1540 flatcars, 3070 piggyback trailers, 200 gondolas and 180 special-purpose hopper cars.

Three-car TankTrain unit being loaded for shipment in Alaska

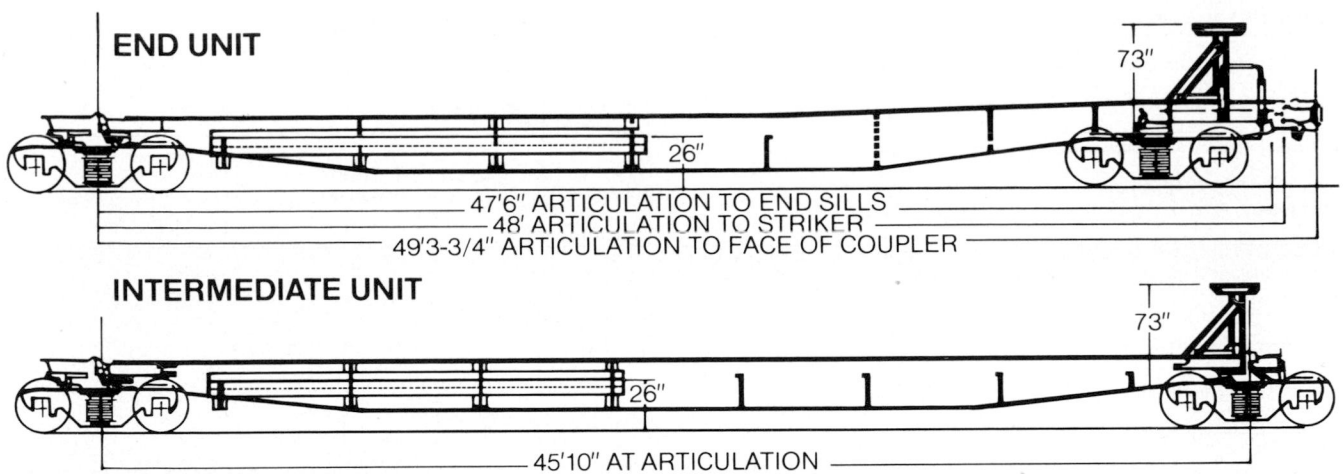

END UNIT

73"

26"

47'6" ARTICULATION TO END SILLS
48' ARTICULATION TO STRIKER
49'3-3/4" ARTICULATION TO FACE OF COUPLER

INTERMEDIATE UNIT

73"

26"

45'10" AT ARTICULATION

IMPACK car general arrangement

In 1981 Itel Rail began marketing a new lightweight, trailer-carrying railcar known as IMPACK. Designed for operation in intermodal railroad service, the IMPACK car consists of individual units connected by a simplified coupling system. The IMPACK car is 35 per cent lighter than the standard flat car of similar trailer capacity which results in significant fuel savings. The units which make up one IMPACK car are each capable of carrying either a 40-, 45- or 48-foot trailer. Any number of the units may be semi-permanently coupled by articulated pin-type connectors; the end units are equipped with conventional railcar couplers to allow connection to other rolling stock or locomotives. The first IMPACK cars in Burlington Northern service have a platform height 660 mm (26 inches) above rail level for low centre of gravity and low clearance profile. Load capacity per unit is 65 000 lb. IMPACK cars are also in service with Southern Pacific and under test by Trailer Train.

Vehicles: 18 520

IMPACK cars in test service with Trailer Train

Morrison-Knudsen
Morrison-Knudsen Company, Inc

One Morrison-Knudsen Plaza, PO Box 7808, Boise, Idaho 83729, USA

Telephone: (208) 345 5000
Telegrams: Emkayan
Telex: 368439

President and Chief Executive Officer: W H McMurren
Executive Vice President, Industrial/Mining: E M Armstrong
Group Vice President, Manufacturing Specialities: L D Stoddard
Vice President and General Manager, Railroad Division: J G Fearon

Principal subsidiaries
International Engineering Company, Inc
The H K Ferguson Company
National Steel and Shipbuilding Company
Northern Construction Company, Ltd

Products: Vehicles for engineering construction world-wide.

Morrison-Knudsen 70-ton ballast car

North American Car Corporation
A Tiger International company

33 W Monroe Street, Chicago, Illinois 60603, USA

Telephone: (312) 853 5000

President: J H Ozanne
Vice-President and General Manager: R N Tidball
Vice-President, Sales: G D Birmingham

Vehicles: 62 000. The company also offers management services.

Pacific Fruit Express Co

100 Valley Drive, Brisbane, California 94005, USA

Telephone: (415) 541 1021

Vice-President and General Manager: T D Ellen

Vehicles: 5169

PLM Inc

50 California Street, San Francisco, California 94111, USA

Telephone: (415) 989 1860

Vehicles: 1800, including coal, covered hoppers and tank cars

Procor Ltd

2001 Speers Road, Oakville, Ontario L6J 5E1, Canada

Telephone: (416) 827 4111

Vehicles: 15 000

Pullman Leasing Co

200 South Michigan Avenue, Chicago, Illinois 60604, USA

Telephone: (312) 322 7070

President: J R Kruizenga
Vice-President and General Manager: G F Lahey
Vice-President, Sales: A G Eades

Vehicles: 24 635

Railbox Co

101 North Wacker Drive, Chicago, Illinois 60606, USA

Telephone: (312) 853 3223

President: C D Buford

Vehicles: 24 956

Railgon Co

101 North Wacker Drive, Chicago, Illinois 60606, USA

Telephone: (312) 853 3223

President: C D Buford

Vehicles: 4000

Railroad Resources Inc

2211 E Highland Avenue, Suite 115, Phoenix, Arizona 85016, USA

Telephone: (602) 954 9410

Main works: 3211 S 43rd Avenue, Phoenix, Arizona 85005

President: Charles R Newman
Vice President: Brian K Alexander

Products: Speciality car and locomotive sales and leasing; speciality cars include ballast/aggregate cars and air/side dump cars,

Richmond Leasing Co

1700 West Loop South, Suite 1500, Houston, Texas 77027, USA

Telephone: (713) 877 8040

Chairman: W D Harbin

Vehicles: 7000

Trailer Train
Trailer Train Company

101 North Wacker Drive, Chicago, Illinois 60606, USA

Telephone: (312) 853 3223

President: R C Burton Jr
Vice-President, Equipment: E T Hartley
Vice-President, Finance: N V Reichert

Products: The company acquires, finances and maintains for US railroads pools of flatcars including 49 571 intermodal, 26 564 for carrying automobiles and 14 029 special-purpose flatcars. Its capital stock is owned by 27 operating railroads, the trustee of the estate of one former railroad and three non-railroad companies. It has two wholly-owned subsidiaries; Railbox Company operates 24 956 boxcars and Railgon Company 4000 general-service gondola cars. Trailer Train is currently active in the development of new lightweight intermodal cars.

Vehicles: 90 763

Trinity Industries Leasing Co

PO Box 10587, Dallas, Texas 75207, USA

Telephone: (214) 631 4420
Telex: 73 0250

Executive Vice-President: R G Brown
General Sales Manager: W R Marley

Vehicles: 4572

Union Tank
Union Tank Car Co
A member of the Marmon Group of companies

111 West Jackson Boulevard, Chicago, Illinois 60604, USA

Telephone: (312) 431 3111

Products: Steel, stainless-steel, and aluminium tank cars carrying liquids, compressed gases, and granular solids.

Vehicles: 43 000

United Equipment Leasing Associates

2550 Golf Road, East Tower, Rolling Meadows, Illinois 60008, USA

Telephone: (312) 640 7000

Vehicles: 1906

US Rail Services Inc

1744 North Greenville Avenue, Richardson, Texas 75081, USA

Telephone: (214) 234 2295

Chairman and President: M M Christy
Vice-President and General Manager: D A Summers
Vice-President, Sales: R M Dwyer

Vehicles: 3372

INTERNATIONAL
RAILWAY ASSOCIATIONS AND AGENCIES

INTERNATIONAL

International Union of Railways (UIC)
Union Internationale des Chemins de Fer

14 rue Jean-Rey, 75015 Paris, France

Telephone: 273 01 20
Telex: 270835

President: M S Houška (Czechoslovak State Railways)
Secretary General: M J Bouley
Chief Executive Officers: M K Ebeling
M V Canyn

The UIC was founded in 1922. The object is the standardisation and improvement of railway equipment and operating methods, in particular international traffic. All principal European railways are members and also a considerable number of non-European countries; total membership is 85, of which 43 railways are European, 17 African, 16 Asian, six American and three Australian. The UIC has a number of specialist agencies: the Office for Research and Experiments (ORE) for the pooling of technical research; the Documentation Bureau, for the exchange of information between railways (publishes ten times a year *A Selection of International Railway Documentation* in English, French, German and Spanish, jointly with the International Railway Congress Association); the Statistics Bureau, which publishes *Annual Summary of Monthly Statistics*; the Railway Film Bureau, enabling information to be exchanged in this field; and the Central Clearing House in Brussels, which is responsible for settling accounts between railways.

Office de Recherches et d'Essais—ORE
Oudenoord 60, 3513 EV Utrecht, Netherlands
Telephone: 314646

Bureau Central de Compensation—BCC
49A ave Fonsny, Section 31, 1060 Brussels, Belgium

Bureau International du Film du Chemin de Fer—BFC
88 rue Saint-Lazare, 75009 Paris, France

Bureau de Documentation—BD
Bureau de Statistiques—BS
14 rue Jean-Rey, 75015 Paris, France

International Railway Congress Association (IRCA)
Association Internationale du Congrès des Chemins de Fer

85 rue de France, 1070 Brussels, Belgium

Telephone: (02) 522 62 83

Management Committee
President: E Flachet, Director General, Belgian National Railways
Vice-Presidents: P Gentil, Director-General, French Railways; J Palmer, Deputy Secretary, Transport Industries, Department of Transport
Secretary General: L Verberckt, Ingénieur en Chef, Belgian National Railways

Established in 1885 the IRCA exists to promote the development of railway transport by all possible means. It holds periodic congresses and general or specialised meetings, supplying information on specific problems to members and publishing technical reviews.
The Association bulletins are published in English, French, German, Russian and Spanish.

International Union of Public Transport (UITP)

19 avenue de l'Uruguay, 1050 Brussels, Belgium

Telephone: 673 33 25; 673 04 66
Telex: 63916

President: Dr Ing F Pampel, Hamburg
Vice-Presidents: I Bäckström, Stockholm
C Henrard, Brussels
I S Irwin, Edinburgh
K Klopotov, Moscow
A Marzotto, Rome
C Quin, Paris
D T Scannell, New York
General Secretary: Andre J Jacobs

This association established in 1885 pools information and experience of urban and interurban public transport undertakings, operating buses, tramways, trolleybuses, metropolitan and light railways for joint study and research and promotes the technical and economic development of the industry.
Publications include the reports of congresses, technical papers, and a periodic review and a bibliographical card index. They are published in English, French and German.

Central Office for International Railway Transport (OCTI)
Thunplatz, 3006 Berne, Switzerland

Telephone: (031) 43 17 62
Telegrams: OCTI, Berne
Telex: 33 268

Chairman of Administrative Committee: Fritz Anliker
Director-General: Peter Trachsel

The OCTI is a permanent inter-governmental secretariat set up to facilitate and ensure the application of the international convention concerning the carriage of goods by rail (CIM) including the international regulations concerning the carriage of dangerous goods by rail (RID), the haulage of private owners' wagons (RIP), the carriage of containers (RICo) and the carriage of express parcels (RIEx); and the international convention concerning the carriage of passengers and luggage by rail (CIV) and the additional convention to CIV relating to the liability of the railway for death of and personal injuries to passengers.
The conventions CIM/CIV form a uniform legal basis for international railway transport and for such shipping lines and road services as are defined in these conventions. The uniform law created by the conventions is based on the following principles:
it applies to all consignments of goods dispatched under a through consignment note for transport over the territory of at least two of the contracting states;
the railways have an obligation to carry;
charges must be calculated according to tariffs legally in force and duly published; these tariffs apply to all users on the same conditions;
the railway undertakings participating in an international transport venture form a community, responsible collectively for the execution of the contract of carriage.
The 33 states contracted to adhere to the CIM/CIV conventions are: Algeria, Austria, Belgium, Bulgaria, Czechoslovakia, Denmark, Finland, France, German Democratic Republic, Federal Republic of Germany, Greece, Hungary, Iran, Iraq, Ireland, Italy, Lebanon, Liechtenstein, Luxembourg, Morocco, Netherlands, Norway, Poland, Portugal, Romania, Spain, Sweden, Switzerland, Syria, Tunisia, Turkey, United Kingdom and Yugoslavia.
The conventions govern the following:
CIM: about 250 000 km of railway lines, 2500 km of road services and 15 000 km of shipping lines;
CIV: about 210 000 km of railway lines, 12 000 km of road services and 15 000 km of shipping lines.
CIM has been applied to the traffic between its contracting states since 1893 and CIV since 1928. Being revised at regular intervals, the conventions are kept up-to-date and adapted to the new requirements of international trade. The conventions now in force were adopted by the 7th Revision Conference in 1970 and have been effective as from January 1975. From the 8th Revision Conference the Convention on International Carriage by Rail (COTIF) of May 1980 emerged with a new structure. The body of the text of COTIF contains the constitutional provision while the uniform transport law is found in two appendices, the uniform rules concerning the contract for international carriage of passengers and luggage by rail (CIV) (Appendix A) and the uniform rules concerning the contract for international carriage of goods by rail (CIM) (Appendix B). COTIF has been signed by all the member states of CIM/CIV and should come into force in 1985.
OCTI edits a bi-monthly bulletin containing the information necessary for the application of the conventions, as well as studies, judgements and important information for the interpretation, application and development of railway transport law.

Intercontainer
Company for International Transport by Transcontainers
Société Internationale pour le Transport par Transcontainers

Margarethenstrasse 38, 4008 Basle, Switzerland

Telephone: 22 25 25
Telegrams: Transcofer, Basle
Telex: 62 298

Chairman: Mauro Ferretti
General Manager: G Fléchon
Manager, Operating Department: R Bouvry
 Finance and General Affairs: C Loffel
 Commercial Service: P Schmelter
 Technical Service: G Sempio
 Marketing Services: G L E M Koopman
 Organisation and Data Processing Department: L Février

The national railway administrations of the following European countries participate in Intercontainer:
Austria, Belgium, Bulgaria, Czechoslovakia, Denmark, Finland, France, German Democratic Republic, Federal Republic of Germany, Greece, Hungary, Ireland, Italy, Luxembourg, Netherlands, Norway, Poland, Portugal, Spain, Sweden, Switzerland, United Kingdom, Yugoslavia and (through a co-operation agreement) Romania and Turkey.

Scope of operations
As common commercial agency of its member railways, Intercontainer's task is to market international container transportation by grouping consignments to form large, regular traffic flows. Individual railways can then reduce their unit costs, which in turn results in keener prices for Intercontainer. The price advantage is passed on by Intercontainer to its customers in proportion to the scale and regularity of their traffic. Intercontainer is represented in each country, either by the relevant railway itself or through a firm appointed by it.

Services

The transportation services provided by Intercontainer fall into three categories:

1. Movement of containers individually, or in small groups by TEEM (Trans-Europ-Express Merchandises) and TEC (Transports Européens Combinés) services.
2. Specialised container trains: TECE services.
3. Company trains for individual customers.

Individual container movements

The facilities provided are extremely diverse. All specialised container terminals, of which over 500 are already operational throughout the European rail network, can be served. While the majority of freight stations and private sidings throughout Europe are open to Intercontainer consignments, preference is given to development of the flows between the natural centres of concentration.

Within the catchment area of each terminal, Intercontainer can usually provide a range of road collection and delivery services, either with vehicles of its local representative or of the national railway concerned. Customers, too, have direct access to the terminals with their own road vehicles.

To obtain the best possible transit times, individual container consignments and small groups are normally carried on the widely developed network of TEEM and TEC trains.

Specialised container trains (TECE)

These services operate along routes with a regular large scale volume of traffic and form a basic network of special container trains, connecting the most important industrial centres in Europe.

They offer the following advantages: rapid, regular and reliable transit, by direct terminal-terminal container trains; no shunting, the transit time being considerably reduced; often no formalities at frontiers; customs clearance at the terminals; movement between well-equipped terminals where INTERCONTAINER road services are available, when required; competitive rates.

Services between the Federal Republic of Germany and Greece started in 1982 and others, for example between West Germany and Scandinavia, were planned for 1983.

Services are shown in the accompanying table.

Company trains

In addition, trains for single customers operate regularly on different routes under similar conditions to TECE trains and at particularly favourable rates. For special traffic of sufficient volume, extra trains can be arranged on demand.

Terminals

Intercontainer does not operate its own terminals; these are operated by railways or private companies, and over 500 are in operation.

Intercontainer 80 ft articulated flat wagon, one of a fleet of 100

Containers and wagons

Intercontainer transports all ISO standard containers (20, 30, 40 feet); in addition containers diverging slightly from the norms, such as European inland containers, swap or demountable bodies and demountable 35 foot maritime containers are also carried.

Intercontainer does not own any containers at the moment, but some of its representatives also have containers available, under interchange agreements for international traffic.

Intercontainer owns 1903 specialised 60 foot (18.5 m) wagons, 410 specialised 40 foot wagons and 100 specialised 80 foot wagons, all built for its own use.

Several hundred 60 and 40 foot wagons, the latter of a completely new type, are under construction.

Trans-Europ-Container-Express (TECE)

Route in both directions	Trains per week	Terminals served	Transit time in hours
Amsterdam/Rotterdam—Basle—Milan	5	Amsterdam/Rotterdam* Basle SBB Milan Rogoredo Milan Smistamento Rho	36
Zeebrugge/Antwerp—Basle (only north-south)	5	Zeebrugge/Antwerp* Basle SBB	17
Antwerp—Turin/Novara/Milan	5	Antwerp* Turin Dora Novara Milan Rogoredo Milan Smistamento	36

Route in both directions	Trains per week	Terminals served	Transit time in hours
Dunkirk—Turin/Milan	5	Dunkirk (Port) Novara Turin Dora Rho Milan Rogoredo Milan Smistamento Melzo	36
Amsterdam/Rotterdam—Antwerp/Zeebrugge	10	Amsterdam/Rotterdam* Antwerp*/Zeebrugge	4
Paris—Turin/Novara/Milan	5	Paris la Chapelle Turin Dora Novara Milan Rogoredo Milan Smistamento	24
Rotterdam—Le Havre	5	Rotterdam* Le Havre (Port)	20
Hamburg—Copenhagen	5	Hamburg Waltershof Copenhagen Hodsbanegard Copenhagen Frijhavn	18
Hamburg—Århus	5	Hamburg Waltershof Århus	12
Gothenburg—Oslo	5	Gothenburg Skandiahamnen Oslo*	12
Antwerp/Bressoux—Milan	4	Antwerp* Bressoux Luino Rho Milan Rogoredo Melzo	40
Zeebrugge—Milan	6	Zeebrugge Novara Rho Milan Rogoredo Milan Smistamento Melzo	36
Neu Ulm—Salonika/Athens	1	Hamburg Wilhelmsburg Frankfurt a M Ost Cologne Eifeltor Dusseldorf Bilk Mannheim Rbf Neu Ulm Salzburg Thessaloniki Volos Aghii Anargyri (Athens)	54

*Several terminals in port area

Rolling stock

Series Lgs 40 ft

This two axle, 11·5-tonne tare wagon has a useful length of 12 620 mm with an overall length of 13 860 mm and is capable of accepting a maximum container length of 40 ft or swap-bodies of Groups 1, 2, 3 and 4. The load platform is 1175 mm above rail with 920 mm diameter wheels and a wheelbase of 9000 mm. Average maximum load varies between 20·5 and 28·5 tonnes depending upon the category of the line.

Series Sgs 60 ft

This four axle, 18-tonne tare wagon has a useful length of 18 400 mm with an overall length of 19 640 mm and is capable of accepting a maximum container length of 60 ft. Certain wagons are equipped for the carriage of 35 ft units and others for the carriage of swap-bodies (two of Group 1 and/or two or one of Group 4). The load platform is 1170 mm above rail with 920 mm diameter wheels; distance between bogie pivots is 14 600 mm and the minimum curve radius acceptable is 75 metres. Average maximum load varies between 46 and 62 tonnes depending upon the category of the line.

Series Sggos 80 ft

This six axle, 26-tonne tare triple bogie wagon has twin useful lengths of 12 930 mm with an overall length of 27 000 mm; it is capable of accepting a maximum container length of 80 ft. The load platform is 1170 mm above rail with 920 mm diameter wheels; the distance between bogie pivots is 10 700 mm and the minimum curve radius acceptable is 75 metres. Average maximum load varies between 64 and 88 tonnes depending upon the category of the line. Each half wagon may only carry up to half the authorised load and, in addition, the total weight of the loads on the two inner 20 ft positions must not exceed 40 tonnes on Category C lines and 33 tonnes on Category B lines.

Rates and charges

Among the factors upon which quotations depend are: traffic volume, routes involved, whether loaded or empty, loaded weight and regularity of consignments. Rates are independent of the nature of the goods and are usually quoted per container and a one-year rates stability is normally maintained.

Traffic

In 1981 INTERCONTAINER carried 783 755 20 ft equivalent units.
This traffic was made up as follows:

Maritime traffic	60%
Direct traffic (Continent/UK)	5%
Between Continental stations	32%
Far East via USSR	3%

The intercontinental market

Movements of containers between ports and their hinterlands, and from one port to another, make up this sector of Intercontainer's markets, and constitute 60 per cent of all containers carried. Since 1968 the growth rate has been spectacular due to the growth of container line shipping.

Containerisation extends to a major part of the liner trade on routes between Europe and the rest of the world. Extension to the trades with South America, India, East and West Africa and more of South-east Asia will inevitably be pursued, giving further opportunities; the long term evolution of this sector will clearly be influenced both by the progress of world trade and by efforts of the major lines to rationalise their services around the European continent.

For some years, a not inconsiderable proportion of traffic moving between Europe and the Far East (Japan, South Korea, Hong Kong, Singapore, the Philippines) has been carried in containers on rail services through the Soviet Union to the port of Nakhodka. The volume of consignments using this route has progressed rapidly from year to year until, in 1981, about 19 000 containers were carried under Intercontainer alone.

A further increase seems inevitable, especially with the improvement in the quality of services offered over this route, but it is expected to slow down and level out on a more or less steady balance with traffic using the direct sea route.

The European market

The European market still has considerable potential. It has not been possible to attack this market more than superficially, chiefly because of the priority which had to be given to the intercontinental market, where containerisation was a fait accompli and rail had to make its presence felt without delay.

Because the major competitor for European traffic is road transport and containerisation cannot be taken for granted, it is necessary to 'sell' the concept of the container. This is a much more complex and difficult task than selling rail services for deep-sea container traffic. It also implies that the railways demonstrate their confidence in containerisation and willingness to promote it by taking concrete measures, both commercially and technically.

As far as Intercontainer is concerned, the European market represents the best chance rail containerisation has for the future.

Representatives

Austria
Generaldirektion der Oesterreichischen Bundesbahnen (OeBB)
Verkaufsdirektion, Abteilung IV/5, Gauermanngasse 4, 1010 Vienna
Telephone: (222) 5650 ext 5329
Telex: 112104

Belgium
NV Interferry (ITF)
Zomerweg 26, 2030 Antwerp
Telephone: (31) 41 69 50
Telex: 32529

Bulgaria
Bulgarische Staatseisenbahnen (BDZ)
Generaldirektion ul Iwan Wazow 3, Sofia
Telephone: 843 43 34, 843 44 34
Telex: 22423

Czechoslovakia
ČSKD-Intrans
Krisikova 2, 18686 Prague 8
Telephone: 21 24 ext 5533
Telex: 121738

Denmark
Danske Statsbaner (DSB)
Generaldirektoratet Godssalgskontoret, Kalvebod Brygge 32, 1560 Copenhagen V
Telephone: 14 04 00 ext 3437
Telex: 27054

Finland
Valtionrautatiet (VR)
Rautatiehallitus, Vilhonkatu 13, 00101 Helsinki 10
Telephone: (90) 71 77 11
Telex: 1230151

France
Compagnie Nouvelle de Conteneurs (CNC)
BP No 55, 20 rue Hector Malot, 75560 Paris Cédex 12
Telephone: (1) 346 1205
Telex: 220500

Germany, Democratic Republic (DR)
VEB Deutrans-Transcontainer (DDR-Cont)
Frankfurter Allee 212, 1130 East Berlin
Telephone: (2) 559 43 48
Telex: 113096

Germany, Federal Republic (DB)
Transfracht Deutsche Transportgesellschaft mbH
Gutleutstrasse 160/164, 6000 Frankfurt (Main)
Telephone: (611) 23890
Telex: 41 45 45

Greece
Organisme des Chemins de Fer Helléniques SA(CH)
Direction Commerciale
Section Intercontainer, 1-3 rue Karolou, Athens 107
Telephone: (21) 524 4828
Telex: 215 187

Hungary
Mavtrans-MÁV Szàllitmanyozasi Iroda
Deak Fernc-ùtca 23, 1378 Budapest V
Telephone: 172569
Telex: 225 343

Ireland
Còras Iompair Éireann (CIE)
Office of the Commercial Manager
Transport House, Bachelor's Walk, Dublin 1
Telephone: 741851
Telex: 5695

Italy
Istituto Nazionale Transporti (INT)
Via Savoia 19, 00198 Rome
Telephone: (6) 86 18 51
Telex: 680 504

Luxembourg
Luxfreight
Place de la Gare 9, Luxembourg
Telephone: (352) 4 99 01
Telex: 2288

Netherlands
Holland Rail Container BV
(NV Nederlandse Spoorwegen)
Dienst van Commerciele Zaken
Postbus 2025, 3500 HA Utrecht
Telephone: (30) 35 30 42
Telex: 70 131

Norway
Norges Statsbaner (NSB)
Hovedadministrasjonen, Salgsavdelingen, Storgaten 33, Oslo 1
Telephone: (2) 20 95 50 ext 2147
Telex: 11168

Poland
Przedsiebiorstwo Spedycji Krajowej Zarzad (PSK)
ul Ordona 2a, 01-237 Warsaw
Telephone: 36 69 23
Telex: 813 670

Portugal
Companhia dos Caminhos de Ferro Portugueses (CP)
Servicio comercial de Mercadorias Internacional Contentores, Largo dos Caminhos de Ferro, 1100 Lisbon 2
Telephone: (19) 86 41 81
Telex: 12382

Romania
Chemins de Fer Roumains
Direction Mouvement et Commercial, Bureau Trafic Combiné, Boulevard Dinicu Golescu 38, Bucharest
Telephone: 1718 80
Telex: 11553

Spain
RENFE
Direccion Comercial, Mercancias, Traficos Intermodales, Paseo del Rey 32, Madrid 8
Telephone: (1) 247 97 52
Telex: 27632

Sweden
Statens Jarnvagar (SJ)-Centralforvaltningen
Kommersiella avdelningen, Klarabergsviadukten 49, 105 50 Stockholm C
Telephone: 762 43 16
Telex: 19410

Switzerland
Chemins de Fer Fédéraux Suisses (CFF/SBB/FFS)
Service Commercial, Trafic Marchandises, Mittelstrasse 43, 3030 Berne
Telephone: (31) 60 22 45
Telex: 32500

Turkey
Turkiye Cumhuriyeti Devlet Demiryollari
Hareket Dairesi Baskanligi, Ankara
Telephone: (41) 241220
Telex: 42571

United Kingdom
(Harwich Terminal)
British Rail
European Traffic Office, 163-203 Eversholt Street, London NW1 1BG
Telephone: 01-387 9400 ext 2548
Telex: 269 295

(Freightliner Terminals)
Freightliners Limited
43 Cardington Street, London NW1 2LR
Telephone: 01-388 0611
Telex: 24743

(Felixstowe)
Cory Brothers
Powell Duffryn House, Dock Estate, Felixstowe, Suffolk IP11 8RP
Telephone: 039 42 78822
Telex: 98434

Yugoslavia
Zajednica Jugoslovenskih Zeleznica (JZ)
Zastupnistvo Intercontainera, Nemanjina 6/II, 11000 Belgrade
Telephone: 682525
Telex: 11166

Interfrigo
(International railway-owned company for refrigerated transport)

General management: Wettsteinplatz 1, PO Box 341, 4005 Basle, Switzerland
Registered office: 85 rue de France, Brussels, Belgium

Telephone: 26 33 33
Telegrams: Interfroid Basle
Telex: 62 231; 63 372

Board of Directors
Chairman, Deputy General Manager, French National Railways: J Dupuy
Vice-Chairman, Operations Manager, Netherlands Railways: D C Hasselman
General Manager, Swiss Federal Railways: K Wellinger
Director-General, Italian State Railways: G de Chiara
Members
  Director, Sales and Production, Danish State Railways: R Jensen
  Chief Freight Manager, British Railways Board: H C Sanderson
  Director, German Federal Railway: H Wiedermann
  Manager of General Management, Belgian State Railways: R Squilbin
Secretary
  Chief Legal Adviser to Belgian State Railways: Mr Bière
Auditors
  Chief Financial Inspector, Belgian State Railways: A Duchêne
  Director, Italian State Railways: G Scanri
  Financial Department, Swiss Federal Railways: Mr Hauser
  Financial Department, French National Railways: Mr Soret
General Management
  General Manager: W Gritz
  Administrative and Financial Manager: M Barca
  Technical Manager: P Cresti
  Commercial Manager: H Nygaard
  Operating Manager: G Schick
  General Studies Manager: P Bombois
  Data Processing Manager: J-L Gatez

In 1981 the total number of ton-km of traffic was 3911 million. Average load per wagon was 13.9 tons compared with 13.5 in the preceding year.

	Ton-km loaded (million)	Percentage change in relation to preceding year	Index (1978 = 100)
1978	3950	− 8.5	100
1979	4020	+ 1.8	101.8
1980	3885	− 3.4	98.4
1981	3911	+0.7	99

The company's total rolling stock decreased from 7152 units at the end of 1980 to 6974 units at the end of 1981.

Type of stock	In service end-1980
1. **Refrigerator wagons**	
GC (Continental loading gauge)	1555
GC (British loading gauge)	1321
TGC	3677
SC	101
Total	6653
2. **Insulated wagons**	
GC (Continental loading gauge)	38
GC (British loading gauge)	9
TGC	5
SC	21
Total	73
3. **Liquid nitrogen wagons**	
GC (Continental loading guage)	1
GC (British loading gauge)	5
Total	6
4. **Mechanically refrigerated wagons**	
2-axle	176
Bogie	50
Total	226
5. **Mechanically refrigerated containers**	
40-foot	4
Total	4
6. **Crew dormitory cars**	12
Grand total	6974

The insulated, refrigerator and mechanically refrigerated wagons hired by Interfrigo in international traffic decreased from 17 317 units at the end of 1980 to 16 523 units at the end of 1981.

Financial
The profit and loss account for 1981 showed a profit of BFr 4 097 402 plus BFr 120 626 carried forward from the preceding year.

Interfrigo representatives
Austria
Oesterreichische Bundesbahnen (OeBB)
Verkaufsdirektion, Abt IV/3, Gauermanngasse 4, 1010 Vienna
Telephone: (222) 5650/5324
Telex: 112104

Belgium
NV Interferry
Zomerweg 26, 2030 Antwerp
Telephone: 541 69 50
Telex: 32529

Bulgaria
UEE-"BDZ"-Eisenbahnkühltransporte Interfrigo-Zentralbüro
Gavril Genov-Strasse 1, Sofia
Telephone: 87 82 02
Telex: 22423

Czechoslovakia
"CSKD Intrans"/Oddĕleni Interfrigo
Karlin Křižikova 2, 18686 Prague 8
Telephone: 2124 ext 4953
Telex: 121 486

Denmark
Danske Statsbaner (DSB)
Kalvebod Brygge 32, 1560 Copenhagen V
Telephone: (01) 140400
Telex: 27054

Finland
Valtionrautatiet (VR)
Rautatiehallitus, PB 488, 00101 Helsinki 10
Telephone: 90 717 711
Telex: 12-301151

France
Stef
93 boulevard Malesherbes, 75008 Paris
Telephone: 563 0522
Telex: 280969

Germany, Democratic Republic
Deutsche Reichsbahn—Ministerium fur Verkehrswesen
Interfrigo-Büro, Voss-Strasse 33, 1086 Berlin 8
Telephone: 4931 891
Telex: 112250

Germany, Federal Republic
Operating representation
Deutsche Bundesbahn
Zentrale Transportleitung—Abteilung VW
Kaiserstrasse 3, 6500 Mainz 1
Telephone: (06131) 15 58 47/15 58 25
Telex: 4187732

Commercial representation
Transthermos GmbH
Parkstrasse 123, Postfach 100929, 2800 Bremen 1
Telephone: (0421) 340 21
Telex: 244457; 245518

Greece
Hellenic Railways Organisation Ltd
Karolou Street 1/3, Athens 107
Telephone: 524 78 38
Telex: 215187

Hungary
Magyar Allamvasutak (MAV), Vezérigazgatósága 8B,
Interfrigo-Vezérkepviselet, Népkoztársaság Utja 73, 1940 Budapest VI
Telephone: 428-575; 220-660/183
Telex: 224342

Iran
Iranian State Railways (RAI)
49 West Takhte Jamshid Avenue, Tehran
Telephone: 525121-28
Telex: 213103

Ireland
Córas Iompair Éireann (CIE)
Office of the Commercial Manager, Transport House, Bachelor's Walk, Dublin 1
Telephone: 741851
Telex: 5695

Italy
Ferrovie Italiane dello Stato
Direzione Generale (for transports in refrigerator wagons)
Piazza della Croce Rossa, 00161 Rome
Servizio Movimento
Telephone: 8490/2136
Telex: 610089
Servizio Commerciale e del Traffico
Telephone: 8490/2329
Telex: 610089

Istituto Nazionale Trasporti
(for transports in mechanically refrigerated wagons and containers)
Via Savoia 19, 00198 Rome
Telephone: 861 851
Telex: 68504

Luxembourg
Chemins de Fer Luxembourgeois
Service commercial
9 place de la Gare, Luxembourg
Telephone: 49901
Telex: 2288

Netherlands

NV Nederlandse Spoorwegen (NS)
Dienst van Commerciele Zaken, Cz 119
Katreinetoren, 3500 HA Utrecht
Telephone: (030) 35 45 52
Telex: 70131

Norway

Norges Statsbaner (NSB)
Hovedadministrasjonen, Storgaten 33, Oslo 1
Telephone: 20 95 50
Telex: 11168

Portugal

Companhia dos Caminhos de Ferro Portugueses (CP)
Departamento Comercial
Largo dos Caminhos de Ferro, 1100 Lisbon
Telephone: 86 41 81; 86 61 01/8
Telex: 12382

Romania

Caile Ferate Romane (CFR)
Service Interfrigo
Bulevardul Dinicu Golescu 38, Bucharest 7
Telephone: 17 20 60
Telex: 11553

Spain

Transfesa
Bravo Murillo No 38-2', Apartado 3225, Madrid (3)
Telephone: 448 89 00
Telex: 27745; 22632

Sweden

Statens Jarnvagar (SJ)
Godstransport avdelningen, 105 50 Stockholm
Telephone: 8 762 2000
Telex: 19410

Switzerland

Frigosuisse
National representation
Schweizerische Bundesbahnen
Kommerzieller Dienst Guterverkehr
Mittelstrasse 43, 3000 Berne
Telephone: (031) 60 25 48
Telex: 691212

Betriebsabteilung-Sektion 6
Schwarztorstrasse 57, 3000 Berne
Telephone: (031) 60 39 71
Telex: 69121 4

Bahnhofkuhlhaus AG
Munchensteinerstrasse 93, Postfach 111, 4002 Basle
Telephone: (061) 50 44 11
Telex: 62271

Société de Gares Frigorifiques et Ports Francs de Genève
rue Blavignac 5, Case postale 88, 1227 Carouge
Telephone: (022) 43 87 60
Telex: 28177

Marco Celoria SA
Fabrique de glace, 6830 Chiasso
Telephone: (091) 44 26 02

Turkey

Turkiye Cumhuriyeti Devlet Demiryollari (TCDD)
Hareket Dairesi Baskanligi, Ankara
Telephone: 24 12 20 ext 205
Telex: 42571

United Kingdom

General commercial representation
Freight Director
British Railways Board
163 Eversholt Street, London NW1 1BG
Telephone: 01-387 9400 ext 3496/4435
Telex: 269295

Yugoslavia

Zajednica Jugoslovenskih Zeleznica (JZ)
Zastupnistvo Interfriga i Intercontainera (1-4)
Nemanjina 6/11, 11000 Belgrade
Telephone: 682-525
Telex: 11166

International Association of Rolling Stock Builders
Association Internationale des Constructeurs de Matériel Roulant (AICMR)

12 rue Bixio, 75007 Paris, France

Telephone: 705 36 62
Telegrams: Interwagon, Paris

President: O J Bronchart
Delegate General: J L Burckhardt (Swiss)

AICMR was founded in 1934 and represents rolling stock builders in Western Europe at international level. The object of the association is to defend the collective interests of its members, and rail transport in general, with regard to international organisations. Its main activity consists of gathering and circulating information among its members with a view to promoting railways.

International Container Bureau (BIC)
Bureau International des Containers

38 cours Albert 1, 75008 Paris, France

Telephone: 225 82 24
Telex: 643 142

General Secretary: P Fournier

Established in 1933 under the auspices of the International Chamber of Commerce as a non-profit making association, Bureau International des Containers is the only non-governmental organisation linking all groups interested in containerisation and multi-modal transport: carriers, manufacturers, operators, lessors, shippers, forwarders, etc. It is backed up by international organisations such as FIATA, FIDI, IATA, ICS, IRU, UIC and national container and multi-modal organisations. Its objectives are: to contribute to the expansion of containerisation and multi-modal transport; to facilitate professional discussions on all subjects connected with containers and multi-modal transport; and to gather specialised documentation for the benefit of its members.

International Federation of Railway Advertising Companies

British Transport Advertising Ltd, 77 Newman Street, London W1A 1DX, England

Telephone: 01-636 7722
Telex: 299583

Chairman: C Picard
France Rail Publicité, 58 avenue de la Grande Armée, 75840 Paris, France
Secretary: D M Hatchell
British Transport Advertising Ltd

International Organisation for Standardization (ISO)
Organisation internationale de normalisation

Case postale 56, 1 rue de Varembé, 1211 Geneva 20, Switzerland

Telephone: 34 12 40
Telegrams: Isorganiz
Telex: 23887

President: D C Kothari (India)
Vice-President: Jan Ollner (Sweden)
Treasurer: Gérard Fatio
Secretary General: Olle Sturen

International Sleeping Car Company (CIWLT)
Cie Internationale des Wagons-lits et du Tourisme

40 rue de l'Arcade, 75381 Paris Cedex 08, France

Telephone: 268 24 00
Telegrams: Wagolits, Paris
Telex: 643 241

Chief Executive, Member of the Board: Jacques-Bernard Dupont
Deputy Chief Executive: François Boyaux
Finance Director: André Frandeboeuf
Personnel Director: Jean-Pierre Mayet
Legal Director: Jean-Pierre Martinaud
Director, Railway Services Division: Wilhelm Scheiff
Director, Travel Division: Hervé Gourio
Director, Hotels Division: Jacques Bellin
Director, Computer Services: Jean-Pierre Greiveldinger
Director, Representative of the General Management (Brussels): Jacques de Meeus d'Argenteuil

Since 1971, most CIWLT sleeping cars and dining cars have been taken over, so far as upkeep and renewal are concerned, by the railways which operate them. CIWLT staffs, caters and maintains the sleeping and dining cars on behalf of the various railways.

International Rail Transport Committee (CIT)

Managing Railway: General Management of the Swiss Federal Railways, Legal Division, Mittelstrasse 43, 3030 Berne, Switzerland

Telephone: 60 25 65; 60 27 94

President and Chairman: Roger Desponds
Secretary: Eric Bertherin

CIT's purpose is to improve the international law for rail transport, which is based on the so-called Conventions of Berne for the Carriage of Passengers and Luggage (CIV) and the Carriage of Goods (CIM), as well as to regulate uniformly other matters connected with international transport law. Founded in 1902, CIT has at present roughly 300 members among transport undertakings from the countries who apply the Berne Conventions, ie all European countries (except Albania, Iceland and USSR), Turkey, Syria, Iraq, Iran and the Maghreb countries. For over 50 years Swiss Federal Railways (SBB) has been the Managing Railway of the association.

The international conventions CIM and CIV govern the relations between the parties to a contract of carriage, but they cannot be applied without the existence of uniform regulations for implementation, which it is CIT's main task to work out and publish. CIT has to distinguish between regulations which are as binding for the user as tariffs and which, in some countries, require the approval of the supervisory authorities, and those which either regulate the relations between the transport undertakings or which contain common instructions for various railway services. In addition, CIT represents the railways at the conferences for the revision of the CIV and CIM conventions, and at other meetings for the discussion of problems concerned with the international transport law.

Any railway, shipping or road transport company can become a member of CIT, provided it is subjected to either or both the CIV and CIM and has accepted the appropriate additional uniform regulations.

CIT co-ordinates its activities with those of the International Union of Railways (UIC) which, as parent organisation, is responsible for ensuring the uniformity and improvement of railways' operating and business conditions. CIT is always in contact with the Central Office for International Railway Transport (OCTI), the inter-governmental organisation for the management of the conventions of Berne, and the international federations of railway users, in particular with FIATA.

International Union of Private Railway Wagon Owners' Associations (UIP)
Union Internationale d'Associations de Proprietaires de Wagons Particuliers

General Secretary, Via Carzo 12, Case Postale 142, 6902 Lugano-Paradiso, Switzerland

Telephone: (091) 54 16 21/54 52 14
Telex: 73 774

Secretary General: Walter Suter

International Union of Railway Medical Services (UIMC)

85 rue de France, 1070 Brussels, Belgium

Telephone: 02/523 80 80 ext 2503/2504

President: Dr R Wirth
Treasurer: D N Nordvik SNCB

UIMC's objective is promotion of the progress of medicine in its application to all matters connected with railway operating. The methods chiefly employed are the organisation of periodical scientific conferences, publication of a review and the development, with the object of obtaining information and furthering scientific knowledge, of contacts between the doctors of the different railway networks.

Organisation for the Collaboration of Railways (OSShD)

Hoza 63/67, Warsaw, Poland

Telephone: 216154
Telegrams: Komtrans

Executive Committee Chairman: Stefan Batkowski
Secretary: F Kotora

Established in 1956, the Organisation's purpose is to develop rail traffic and exchange information between its 13 Socialist country members, Albania, Bulgaria, People's Republic of China, Cuba, Czechoslovakia, German Democratic Republic, Hungary, Korean People's Democratic Republic, Mongolian People's Republic, Poland, Romania, USSR and Viet-Nam.

CONTINENTS

Latin American Railway Association

Avda Córdoba 883, 6° piso, 1054 Buenos Aires, Argentina

Telephone: 311 9463; 32 5151

General Secretary: Emiliano A S Flouret
Administrative Secretary: Felipe Muniain
International Transport Department: Alberto Paolini
Accounting Department: Dr Juan A Molina
General Co-ordinator of ALAF Magazine: Dr Jorge Gutracht
Training and Technical Assistance: Ing Angel Ceci
Economic Adviser: Ing Ignacio Echevarria
Technical Adviser: Ing Justo Baliño
President of the Information Systems: Ing Francisco Gorostiza
Standards Department: Atilio Sanguinetti

The Association was founded at a meeting of Latin-American railway representatives in Argentina in 1964. Principal objectives are the creation of transcontinental routes; settling of traffic interchange problems; development and integration of Latin-American railways; elimination of frontier and customs difficulties; the exchange of technical information and the sale, loan or exchange of railway material between members; co-ordination of railway industries in Latin America and the creation of a code of standards for Latin-American built railway equipment and the formation of a Latin-American Railway Bank.

Pan American Railway Congress Association (ACPF)

Av 9 de Julio 1925, Piso 13, Ofic 1301, 1332 Buenos Aires, Argentina

Telephone: 38 4625/8911
Telegrams: Panriel
Telex: 0122507

President: Div Gral Eng Juan Carlos de Marchi
1st Vice-President: Emilio Calderon Puig (Representative of the National Commission of Mexico)
2nd Vice-President: Representative of the National Commission of the host country of the next Congress
General Secretary: Eng Cayetano Marletta Rainieri
Treasurer: Casimiro C Vallejos
Special Adviser: Atilio Molteni

The Association, founded in 1907, is a technical consultant body of the Organisation of American States and its members are both the governments and the railroads of the American continents. Its intention is to promote the development of rail transport and in this connection periodically holds congresses in different cities of the continents. In 1975 the XIII Panamerican Railway Congress was held in Caracas (Venezuela); in 1978 the XIV Congress in Lima (Peru) and in 1981 in Mexico; on these occasions the delegates signed the declarations that take on the names of these capital cities. These referred to, respectively: the oil energy crisis; social accounting (or accounting sincerity) and the methodology for applying the latter in the different countries. In each country there is a National Commission whose members are appointed from Government and railways.

Union of African Railways (UAR)

Avenue Tombalbaye 869, PO Box 687, Kinshasa, Zaire

Telephone: 23861
Telex: 21258

President: Tom Mmari (General Manager, Tanzania Railways)
Vice-Presidents: Representatives from
Tunisia Railways for North Africa
Kenya Railways for East Africa
Congo Railways for Central Africa
Benin-Niger Railways for West Africa
Malawi Railways for Southern Africa
Secretary-General: Adama Diagne
Director of Economic Studies and Planning: M Gaili Khalifa
Director of Technical Studies: J M Sahouegnon

The constituent conference of the UAR took place in Addis Ababa in 1972 under the aegis of the United Nations Economic Commission for Africa (ECA) with the financial co-operation of the German Development Foundation.

The 27 railway administrations in UAR membership are those of Algeria, Angola, Benin-Niger, Cameroon, Congo, Egypt, Ethiopia-Jibuti, Gabon, Ghana, Guinea, Ivory Coast-Upper Volta, Kenya, Libya, Malawi, Mali, Morocco, Mozambique, Nigeria, Senegal, Sudan, Swaziland, Tanzania, Tanzania-Zambia (TAZARA), Tunisia, Zaire and Zambia.

During 1982/83 the Union celebrated its 10th anniversary, held several seminars and committee meetings, and made studies and recommendations on standardisation and normalisation.

EUROPEAN

Association of European Railway Component Manufacturers (AFEDEF)
Association des Fabricants Européens d'Equipements Ferroviaires

12 rue Bixio, 75007 Paris, France

Telephone: 705 36 62
Telegrams: Interwagon, Paris

President: J P Ballerin (France)
Delegate General: J L Burckhardt (Swiss)

AFEDEF was founded in 1979 and represents associations of railway component manufacturers in Western Europe. The object of the association is to defend the collective interests of its members, and rail transport in general, with regard to international organisations. The main activity is assembly and circulation of information among members with a view to promoting railways.

European Company for the Financing of Railroad Rolling Stock (EUROFIMA)

Rittergasse 20, 4001 Basle, Switzerland

Telephone: 22 33 40

General Manager (CEO): Heinz Weber

European Conference of Ministers of Transport (ECMT)

19 rue de Franqueville, 75775 Paris Cedex 16, France

Telephone: 524-82 00
Telegrams: Ministrans, Paris
Telex: 611040

Council of Ministers
Chairman: J C Viana Baptista, Minister of Transport and Communications, Portugal
Vice-Chairmen: Mrs Y Koppernaes, Minister of Transport and Communications, Norway
V Balzamo, Minister of Transport, Italy
Committee of Deputies
Chairman: A C Aires, General Director of Land Transport, Portugal
Secretary-General: Georges Billet

European Diesel and Electric Locomotive Manufacturers' Association
Constructeurs Européens de Locomotives Thermiques et Electriques (CELTE)

12 rue Bixio, Paris 75007, France

Telephone: 705 36 62
Telegrams: Interwagon, Paris

President: Eric Kocher (Federal Republic of Germany)
Delegate General: J L Burckhardt (Swiss)

CELTE was founded in 1953 and represents locomotive and internal combustion engine manufacturers in Western Europe. The object of the association is to defend the collective interests of its members and rail transport in general, with regard to international organisations. Its main activity is the assembly and circulation of information among its members with a view to promoting railways.

European Freight Timetable Conference

Czechoslovak State Railways, Na Prikopě 33, 110 05 Prague, Czechoslovakia

Telephone: 2122/3029
Telegrams: Domini Praha CEM/EGK
Telex: 121096

President: Ing Ladislav Stros
Secretary: Josef Basta

European Passenger Train Timetable Conference
Conférence Européenne des Horaires des Trains de Voyageurs (CEH)

c/o Direction Générale des Chemins de Fer Fédéraux Suisses, Hochschulstrasse 6, 3030 Berne, Switzerland

Telephone: (031) 60 11 11
Telex: 32500

President: K Wellinger, General Manager, Swiss Federal Railways

European Wagon Pool (Europ Agreement)
Communauté d'Exploitation des Wagons Europ (Convention Europ)

Société Nationale des Chemins de Fer Belges, Leuvense weg 21 rue de Louvain, 1000 Brussels, Belgium

Telephone: (02) 513 18 70
Telex: 24607

Organisme Repartiteur Central du Pool-TEN

20 rue de Rome, 75008 Paris, France

Telephone: 285 92 47
Telex: 097

Chief of Organisation: H Kunze

In 1971 the railways of France (SNCF), Federal Republic of Germany (DB), Switzerland (SBB), Italy (FS), Belgium (SNCB), Netherlands (NS), Austria (OBB), Denmark (DSB) and Luxembourg (CFL) formed a consortium to lease and assume full maintenance and marketing responsibility for all existing sleeping-cars operated on international circuits by both CIWLT and DSG, the dining-car and sleeping-car company of the Federal Republic of Germany. The Pool also took over responsibility for renewals. It operates the cars under the acronym of TEN, for 'Trans Euro Nacht/Nuit/Notte/Night'.

TEE
Trans-Europ-Express

Netherlands Railways, Moreelsepark 1, 3500 HA Utrecht, Netherlands

The Managing Administration of the TEE-Group, with offices at the headquarters of the Netherlands Railways in Utrecht, is charged with co-ordinating the TEE activities of the member administrations, and with studying the possibilities of improving existing services and developing others. Motive power units and rolling stock are individually owned and operated by the various railway administrations in the Group. However all trains carry the 'TEE' emblem and have to satisfy certain minimum specifications as to speed and comfort.

For accountancy purposes, because each country has its own currency, the money basis adopted is the UIC franc. The tariff applicable to TEE trains consists of the first class fare in force in each of the countries in which they operate, plus a supplement in proportion to the distance.

As more Western European railways have re-cast their internal timetables on an intensified regular-interval pattern offering similar standards of speed and convenience to both second- and first-class passengers, the international TEE network has steadily contracted. Many TEE services have been replaced by dual-class international 'Inter-City' trains to a specification promulgated by the UIC.

TEE services, October 1982

Name of train	Route	Distance		Booked time		Inter-mediate stops	Average end-to-end speed	
		miles	km	h	min		mph	km/h
Adriatico	Milan-Bari	540	869	9	25	14	57	92
Ambrosiano	Milan-Rome	393	632	6	13	2	63	102
Aquitaine	Paris Austerlitz-Bordeaux	361	581	4	05	3	88	142
Brabant	Paris Nord-Brussels Midi	194	312	2	27	—	79	127
Le Capitole	Paris Austerlitz-Toulouse	443	713	5	59	4	74	119
Etendard	Paris Austerlitz-Bordeaux	361	581	4	03	3	89	143
Etoile du Nord	Paris Nord-Amsterdam	344	554	5	04	6	67	109
Faidherbe	Paris Nord-Tourcoing	168	271	2	23	3	71	114
Gayant	Paris Nord-Tourcoing	168	271	2	26	4	69	111
Gottardo	Milan-Zurich	171	276	4	01	3	43	69
Ile de France	Paris Nord-Amsterdam	344	554	5	11	6	67	108
Jules Verne	Paris Montparnasse-Nantes	246	396	3	17	1	75	121
Klober	Paris Est-Strasbourg	313	504	3	55	1	80	129
Mediolanum	Munich-Milan	370	595	7	04	7	52	84
Memling	Paris Nord-Brussels Midi	194	312	2	28	—	78	126
Oiseau Bleu	Brussels Nord-Paris Nord	198	318	2	42	3	73	118
Rheingold	Basle-Amsterdam	482	776	7	35	14	64	102
Rubens	Paris Nord-Brussels Midi	194	312	2	26	—	79	128
Settebello	Milan-Rome	393	632	5	55	2	66	106
Stanislas	Paris Est-Strasbourg	313	504	3	52	1	81	130
Vesuvio	Milan-Naples Mergellina	524	843	8	15	3	64	102
Watteau	Paris Nord-Tourcoing	168	271	2	22	3	71	115

Union of European Railway Industries
Union des Industries Ferroviaires Européennes (UNIFE)

12 rue Bixio, 75007 Paris, France

Telephone: 705 36 62
Telegrams: Interwagon, Paris

President: Eric Kocher (Federal Republic of Germany)
Delegate General: J L Burckhardt (Swiss)

UNIFE was founded in 1975 by AICMR and CELTE as an umbrella organisation of all associations of builders connected with railways. The object of the association is to defend the collective interests of its members, and rail transport in general, with regard to international organisations. Its main activity is the assembly and circulation of information among its members with a view to promoting railways.

United Nations Economic Commission for Europe

Palais des Nations, 1211 Geneva 10, Switzerland

Telephone: 34 60 11

Executive Secretary: J Stanovnik
Deputy Executive Secretary: Y P Chestnoy
Director Transport Division: J Duquesne

Established in 1947 to advise and help with the reconstruction of Europe. It has three main working parties for rail, road and inland water transport.

In the rail transport field it deals with customs, frontier formalities for passengers and goods; the exchange of transport equipment; the introduction of automatic coupling; the unification and standardisation of rolling stock; the adoption of a standard type of electro-pneumatic brake measures for achieving high speed in rail transport; problems related to noise in railway operations; method of reducing railway energy consumption; and computers in railway operations.

NATIONAL

ARGENTINA

Chamber of Railway Industries
Cámara de Industriales Ferroviarios

Alsina 1607, Buenos Aires

Telephone: 40 5063 5571 4967

President: Eng E G Nottage
Secretary: J C Bietti

AUSTRALIA

Railways of Australia Committee

6th Floor, Embank House, 325 Collins Street, Melbourne 3000

Telephone: 61 2545
Telex: 31109

Executive Director: N J Gazzard

An association of Australia's five government-owned railway systems: Australian National Railways, Queensland Railways, State Rail Authority of New South Wales, VicRail and Westrail. The Railways of Australia Committee evolved from the Australian and New Zealand Railways Conference Secretariat in 1975, and is responsible for: promotion, examination and co-ordination of inter-system operations and activities; execution of inter-system policy decisions and directions of Commissioners; servicing inter-system requirements of freight clients and prospects; analysis and control of freight consists, wagons and RACE containers (Railways of Australia Container Express); promotion of Railways of Australia in overseas passenger markets; national public relations activities; and promotion of Railways of Australia as an integrated network.

ARRDO
Australian Railway Research & Development Organisation

576-8 Lonsdale Street, Melbourne 3000

Telephone: 609 7900
Telex: 37484

Executive Director: Dr P R Grimwood

AUSTRIA

Federation of Private Railways
Fachverband der Schienenbahnen

Bauernmarkt 13, 1010 Vienna

Telephone: 63 94 51, 63 98 92

Directors: Dr W Pycha
　　　　　　Dipl Ing I Stern

Manager: Dr V Schlaegelbauer

The Federation associates 22 railways, 10 tramway and bus operators and 21 private wagon owners.

Federation of Cable Railways
Fachverband der Seilbahnen

Bauernmarkt 13, 1010 Vienna

Telephone: 63 94 51, 63 98 92

President: Dr Gunther Schoffel
Manager: Dr Viktor Schlagelbauer

CANADA

Canadian Transport Commission
(Railway Transport Committee)

Les Terrasses de la Chaudière, Ottawa, Ontario K1A 0N9

Telephone: (819) 997 7046

Chairman: John Magee
Commissioners: M D Armstrong, J-L Bourret, J G Drainville, J M McDonough, R J Orange, A-M Trahan, J F Walter, B R Wolfe
Executive Director Railway Transport Committee: J Heads
Director Safety & Services: J H Green
Director Standards & Development: R L Gray
Director Rail Economic Analysis: M C Tosh

Railway Association of Canada

1117 Ste Catherine Street West, Montreal, Quebec H3B 1H9

General Manager: J M Beaupré

The Association, which unites all Canadian railways operating a minimum 80 km of route, aims to foster the interests and efficiency of all Canadian railways and to represent them on matters of common interest, jointly or severally, in dealings with the Government of Canada, the Railway Transport Committee of the Canadian Transport Commission and other public bodies.

Canadian Freight Association

Eastern Lines
1162 St Antoine Street, Montreal, Quebec H3C 1B5
Telephone: (514) 861 8331
Telex: 055 60744

Chairman: P J Lavallee

Western Lines
Room 1100, 215 Garry Street, Winnipeg, Manitoba R3C 3PE

Chairman: K W Juvonen

Canadian Institute of Guided Transport

Queens University, Kingston, Ontario K7L 3N6

Telephone: (613) 547 5777

Executive Director: Prof C E Law

The Institute was founded jointly by the Ministry of Transport, Canadian National Railways, CP Rail and Queens University in 1970 to establish a centre for research and interest in the improvement of Canadian guided ground transport systems, and to facilitate co-ordination within the Canadian transport industry. VIA Rail Canada Inc and the Urban Transportation Development Corporation of Ontario (UTDC) have recently been added to the sponsors of the Institute.

Canadian Railway & Transit Manufacturers Association

1 Yonge Street, Suite 1400, Toronto, Ontario M5E 1J9

Telephone: (416) 363 7261

President: C W Smith
Vice-President: G C Mills
Manager: Alex C Dick

Canadian Urban Transit Association

234 Eglinton Avenue East, Suite 301, Toronto, Ontario M4P 1K5

President: Lloyd G Berney
Executive Director: A Cormier

DENMARK

Institution of Railway Signal Engineers
Telfon-og Sikringsteknisk Forening

40 Sølvgade, Copenhagen K

Chairman: U Hass Andersen

FRANCE

Railway Industries Association
Fédération des Industries Ferroviaires

12 rue Bixio, 75007 Paris

Telephone: 705 36 62

GERMANY, FEDERAL REPUBLIC

German Sleeping & Dining Car Company (DSG)
Deutsche Schlafwagen und Speisewagen Gesellschaft mbH

18-22 Guiollettstrasse, 6000 Frankfurt (Main)

Telephone: 0611 71 64-1
Telegrams: Speisewagen ffm
Telex: 04 11 918

Chairman: Franz Eichinger
Directors: Heinz Streichardt
　　　　　　Dr Hans J Gerhards

The limited liability company is a wholly-owned subsidiary of the German Federal Railway (DB), charged with provision of all train catering, sleeping-car and couchette car services on the DB, and also with the operation of certain station restaurant, buffet and other services in premises leased from the DB. The station restaurant activity, which in three cases includes adjacent hotel operation, is in each case entrusted to an independent subsidiary of DSG. The company also operates the catering services on the Puttgarden-Rødby (Denmark) train ferries through a subsidiary. It has two workshops for the maintenance of its rail vehicles, at Munich-Neuabing and Hamburg-Langenfelde.

In 1982 the company was operating 177 restaurant cars, 46 Quick-Pick self-service cafeteria cars, 7 snack-bar cars, 182 sleeping and 219 couchette cars, together with 458 Minibars (train snack trolleys). With these, in the summer of 1982, it was covering 220 trains daily with catering cars, 360 with Minibars, 100 with sleeping and 164 with couchette cars.

Vehicle of TUI Ferien-Express stock built by Waggon Union, with interior design by DSG, for rail-based package tour operation by Touristik Union International

Couchette compartment of TUI Ferien-Express

German Locomotive Industry Association
Verband der Deutschen Lokomotivindustrie

Lyonerstrasse 16, 6000 Frankfurt (Main) 71

Telephone: 0611 6666 741

President: Hans U Wolf
Director: G Morsey-Picard

Railway Rolling Stock Industry Association
Verband der Waggonindustrie eV

Lindenstrasse 30, 6000 Frankfurt (Main)

Telephone: 0611 727244

Chairman: Dr Ing Christian Stiefel
Director: Ivo Wolz

Rolled Steel Association Permanent Way Group
Walzstahl Vereinigung Fachgruppe Oberbau

Kasernstrasse 36, 4000 Dusseldorf

Telephone: 0211 829 314
Telex: 858 18116

Secretary: H-H Brasak

Switch and Crossing Manufacturers Association
Fachverband Weichenbau

Markischer Ring 55, 5800 Hagen

Director: K-H Meier

Private Railways Association of German Federal Republic
Bundesverband Deutscher Eisenbahnen (BDE)

Volksgartenstrasse 54a, 5000 Cologne

Telephone: 31 50 75/76/77/78

Chairman: H Elliger
Executive Director: M Montada

An association of 280 operators covering 170 public and private port and industrial railways together with bus, cable railway and ski-lift administrations.

The railways are categorised as Nichtbundeseigene Eisenbahnen (NE). However, those offering public service are up to 89 per cent publicly-owned, with over 60 per cent of their capital in the hands of the towns and districts they serve, 18 per cent owned by the Land (province) in which they operate and 5 per cent by the Federal Government. Of these over 40 provide passenger services covering approximately 1000 km, in some cases electrified, and record some 500 million passenger-km a year. The public-service NE overall record over 80 million tonnes and 1000 million tonne-km of freight a year. As much as 25 per cent of all railborne freight in West Germany completes some of its transit over NE systems.

ITALY

College of Italian Railway Engineers
Collegio Ingegneri Ferroviari Italiani

Via G Giolitti 34, 00185 Rome

Telephone: 462129

President: Dr Ing L Misiti
Secretary: Dr Ing M Perilli

JAPAN

Japan Railway Construction Corporation (JRCC)

Sanno Grand Building 14-2, Nagatacho 2-Chome, Chiyoda-ku, Tokyo

Telephone: 581 6581
Telegrams: Tetsudokodan-Tokyo

President: Iwao Nisugi
Vice-President: Kimimasa Akitomi

The Corporation undertakes the greater part of new railway construction in Japan with Government finance. When built, the railways are transferred or leased to Japanese National Railways (JNR) or the appropriate private railway administration.

Japan Railway Electrification Association Inc

JTB Building, 1-6-4 Marunouchi, Chiyoda-ku, Tokyo

Telephone: 211 3895/6

President: M Otobe
Director: Hirofumi Hosojima

Japan Private Railways Association

Kotsukosha Building, 1-6-4 Marunouchi, Chiyoda-ku, Tokyo

Telephone: 211 1401

President: S Hirata

Japan Railway Engineers Association

5-18 Otemachi 2-chome, Chiyoda-ku, Tokyo 100

Chairman: Dr-Eng S Seki
Executive General Manager: G Nishio

Japan Rolling Stock Exporters Association

Tekko Building, 8-2 Marunouchi 1-chome, Chiyoda-ku, Tokyo

Telephone: 201 3145

President: K Yotsumoto
Senior Managing Director: T Koizumi

Japan Society of Mechanical Engineers

Sanshin Hokusei Building, 4-9 Yoyogi 2-chome, Shibua-ku, Tokyo

Secretary: S Mutoh

SPAIN

Transfesa
Transportes Ferroviarios Especiales

Bravo Murillo 38-2, Madrid 3

Telephone: 4 48 89 00

President: José Fernandez Lopez
Executive Director: E Fernandez Fernandez
Managing Director: C Gancedo-Rodriguez Carazo

The company promotes freight transport between Spain and other countries in its privately-owned ventilated and refrigerated wagons fitted with inter-changeable axles to negotiate the break of gauge.

UNITED KINGDOM

Crown Agents for Oversea Governments and Administrations

4 Millbank, London SW1P 3JD

Telephone: 01-222 7730
Telegrams: Crown, London SW1
Telex: 916205

Senior Crown Agent and Chairman: S A W Eburne
Crown Agent and Deputy Chairman: P W Bulfield
Crown Agents: A C Frood
      Sir Peter Gadsden
      K J Johnson
      Sir Gordon Mackay
      D Probert
      D Williams
      W M H Williams
Board of Management
Managing Director and Chairman: A C Frood
Financial and Administration Controller: A H N Molesworth
Director of Buying Services: W Bowyer
Director, Africa: D V Moule
Director, Middle East and Caribbean: J C Rowley
Director, Asia and Pacific: P F Berry
Director of Financial Services: H Dale
Director of Engineering: B M W Bennell
Director of Personnel: R H Wilkinson
Director, Technical Services: A J D Simpson
Divisional Director, Transport: K F Douglas
Head of Railway Department: R H Boxall

Representative offices
Bahrain: Room 404, 4th Floor, Manama Centre, Manama, State of Bahrain
Telephone: 254672
Telegrams: Crown, Bahrain
Telex: 8307
Barbados: PO Box 82, Barclays Bank Building, Roebuck Street, Bridgetown
Telephone: 60458
Telegrams: Crownagent Barbados
Telex: 2311
Kenya: PO Box 47246, IPS Building, Kimathi Street, Nairobi
Telephone: 25524; 26917; 335783
Telegrams: Millbank, Nairobi
Telex: 22536
Malaysia: 7th Floor, Angkasa Raya Building, 123 Jalan Ampang, Kuala Lumpur 0404
Telephone: 483915 and 483927
Telegrams: Crogen, Kualalumpur
Telex: 30924
Nigeria: 2 Mundubawa Avenue, PO Box 978, Kano
Telegrams: Crownagent, Kano
Western House, 8/10 Broad Street, PO Box 583, Lagos
Telephone: 630476 and 635889
Telegrams: Crownagents, Lagos
Telex: 21416
Papua New Guinea: PO Box 5790, Boroko
Telephone: 259777
Telegrams: Crownag, Port Moresby
Telex: 22370a/b
Singapore: Suite 706, Cathay Building, Mount Sophia, Singapore 0922
Telephone: 3368266
Telegrams: Millbank, Singapore
Telex: 22171
Tanzania: PO Box 4190, Dar es Salaam
Telephone: 25650 and 29244
Telex: 41218
Thailand: 3rd Floor, Siam Tanakarn Building, 133 SO1 Asoke/Sukumvit 21, GPO Box 1866, Bangkok
Telephone: 392-1904
Telex: 82136
Uganda: c/o British High Commission, PO Box 7070, Kampala
Telephone: 57059
Telex: 61202
USA: 3100 Massachusetts Avenue NW, Washington DC 20008
Telephone: (202) 462 1340
Telegrams: Crown, Washington
Telex: 64642
Zimbabwe: Barclays Bank Building, 2nd Floor, 66-68 Manica Road, PO Box 4200, Harare
Telephone: 708602
Telex: 4169

Supplies and inspection offices
Bangladesh: c/o Hotel Continental, PO Box 504, Dhaka
Telephone: 252912-9
Telegrams: Crown, Dhaka
Telex: 642408
Hong Kong: Room 314, Hyatt Regency, Hong Kong, 67 Nathan Road, Kowloon
Telephone: 683528
Telegrams: Crownagent, Hongkong
Telex: 73127
India: Kada Building, 2nd Floor, 22 Richmond Road, Bangalore 560 025
Telephone: 55141; 579167
Telegrams: Crown, Bangalore
Telex: 845-454
Japan: 6th Floor, Shin Fuyo Building, 2-26, Isobedori, 4-Chome, Fukiai-ku, Kobe 651
Telephone: (078) 232 3083/3084
Telegrams: Agents Crown Kobe
Telex: 5622-872
Singapore: Crown Agents Services Ltd, 609 Cathay Building, Mount Sophia, Singapore 0922
Telephone: 3368266
Telegrams: Millbank, Singapore
Telex: 22171

The regional offices in Singapore, Malaysia and the USA also deal with purchasing. There are also inspection offices in the industrial regions of the UK and in the Federal Republic of Germany and Singapore.

Association of British Railway Carriage & Wagon Manufacturers

7 Ludgate Broadway, London EC4V 6DX

Chairman: L T Reddy
Secretaries: Peat, Marwick, Mitchell & Co

Association of Consulting Engineers

Alliance House, 12 Caxton Street, Westminster, London SW1H OQL

Telephone: 01-222 6557
Telex: 268312

Chairman: W K E Jones
Secretary: Major-General P J M Pellereau
Deputy Secretary: Cdr G D Palmer

Association of Minor Railway Companies

Offices of Midland Railway Centre, Butterley Station, Ripley, Derbyshire DE5 3TL

Telephone: 0773 47674

Chairman: A G W Garraway (Festiniog Rly)
Vice-Chairman: D Ferreira (Ravenglass & Eskdale Rly)
Secretary: E Hett (Midland Railway Trust)

Member companies
Bala Lake Railway
Bluebell Railway Co
Bowes Railway
Brecon Mountain Railway
Dart Valley Railway
Derwent Valley Railway Co
Fairbourne Railway Ltd
Felixstowe Dock & Railway Co
Festiniog Railway Co
Great Central Railway
Gwili Railway Co
Isle of Man Railways
Isle of Wight Railway Co Ltd
Keighley & Worth Valley Railway Co
The Kent & East Sussex Railway
Lakeside & Haverthwaite Railway Co Ltd
Leighton Buzzard Narrow Gauge Railway Soc Ltd
Lincolnshire Coast Light Railway
Llanberis Lake Railway Co
Middleton Railway Trust Ltd
Midland Railway Trust
Nene Valley Railway
North Norfolk Railway Co Ltd
North Yorkshire Moors Railway
Ravenglass & Eskdale Railway Co
Romney Hythe & Dymchurch Light Railway Co Ltd
Severn Valley Railway Co Ltd
Sittingbourne & Kemsley Light Railway Co
Snailbeach District Railways
Snowdon Mountain Railway Ltd
Steamtown Railway Museum Ltd
Stocksbridge Railway Co Ltd
Strathspey Railway Co Ltd
Talyllyn Railway Co
Trafford Park Co
Welsh Highland Light Railway (1964) Limited
Welshpool & Llanfair Light Railway Preservation Co Ltd
West Somerset Railway Co Ltd
Winchester & Alton Railway Co Ltd
Yorkshire Dales Railway

Associate members
Foxfield Light Railway
Market Bosworth Light Railway
National Railway Museum
Pleasurerail
Railway Preservation Society of Ireland
Swanage Railway Co

Association of Private Railway-Wagon Owners Ltd

18 Great Marlborough St, London W1V 2NJ

Telephone: 01-439 8733/4/5

Chairman: R M Barclay (STS Ltd)
Secretary: M S Burge (W H Davis & Sons Ltd)
Treasurer: J M B Gotch (Traffic Services Ltd)

The Association has 24 member companies owning approximately 7500 wagons.

Chartered Institute of Transport

80 Portland Place, London W1N 4DP

Telephone: 01-636 9952

President: L S Payne
Director General: Brig D N Locke
Secretary: L F Aldridge

Council of Engineering Institutions

2 Little Smith Street, London SW1P 3DL

Telephone: 01-222 3912

Secretary: D B Wood

Diesel Engineers and Users Association

18 London Street, London EC3R 7JR

Telephone: 01-481 2393

Secretary: J W Nairn

Federation of Civil Engineering Contractors

Cowdray House, 6 Portugal Street, London WC2A 2HH

Telephone: 01-404 4020
Telex: 8955101

Institution of British Engineers

Regency House, 3 Marlborough Place, Brighton, East Sussex BN1 1UB

Telephone: 0273 601399

Secretary: Dorothy Henry

Institution of Civil Engineers

Great George Street, London SW1P 3AA

Telephone: 01-222 7722
Telegrams: Institution London SW1

President: J V Bartlett
Secretary: J C McKenzie

Institution of Electrical Engineers

Savoy Place, London WC2R 0BL

Telephone: 01-240 1871
Telex: 261176

Secretary: H H W Losty

Institution of Mechanical Engineers Railway Division

1 Birdcage Walk, London SW1H 6JJ

Telephone: 01-222 7899
Telex: 917944

Chairman: I D Gardiner
Executive Officer: A T H Tayler

Institution of Railway Signal Engineers

Telephone: 01-262 3232 ext 5734

Hon General Secretary: R L Weedon, 21 Avalon Rd, Earley, Reading, Berkshire

Permanent Way Institution

27 Lea Wood Road, Fleet, Hampshire GU13 8AN

Telephone: 02514 3643

Hon General Secretary: L J Harris

Private Wagon Federation

7 Ludgate Broadway, London EC4V 6DX

Telephone: 01-248 1541
Telex: 8812908

Chairman: F J Swindell
Secretaries: Peat, Marwick, Mitchell & Co

Railway Industry Association of Great Britain

9 Catherine Place, London SW1E 6DX

Telephone: 01-834 1426

Director: G R Curry

Wagon Repairing Association

7 Ludgate Broadway, London EC4V 6DX

Telephone: 01-248 1541
Telex: 8812908

Chairman: R E Morgan
Secretaries: Peat, Marwick, Mitchell & Co

UNITED STATES OF AMERICA

American Association of Railroad Superintendents

18154 Harwood Ave, Homewood, Illinois 60430

Telephone: (312) 799 4650

President: J F McGinley
Secretary: P A Weissmann

American Public Transit Association (APTA)

1225 Connecticut Avenue NW, Washington DC 20036

Telephone: (202) 828 2800

Chairman: Joseph Alexander
President: James H Graebner
Executive Vice President: Jack R Gilstrap
Secretary-Treasurer: Harvel Williams

APTA is the organisation which represents transit operators in the USA and Canada, including all systems operating rail facilities. In addition to more than 300 operating members, APTA also has more than 300 associate members including contractors, consultants, manufacturers and suppliers.

American Railroad Truck Lines Association

1684 Highland Parkway, St Paul, Minnesota 55116

Telephone: (612) 699 9125

President: A B Cable (Asst General Manager, Frisco Transport Co)
Secretary: K G Heimbach

American Railway Car Institute

303 East Wacker Drive, Suite 732, Chicago, Illinois 60601

Telephone: (312) 861 0714

Chairman: J C Felten (Evans Products Co)
President, Secretary and Treasurer: E T Ahnquist
Vice Chairman: J T Egbert (Greenville Steel Car)
Vice President: J E Carroll, Jr (FMC Corporation)

American Railway Development Association

131 West Lafayette Blvd, Detroit, Michigan 48226

President: D A Cox
Secretary: A E Callewaert

American Railway Engineering Association

2000 L Street NW, Washington DC 20036

Telephone: (202) 835 9336

President: R E Haacke
Executive Director: L T Cerny

American Short Line Railroad Association

2000 Massachusetts Ave NW, Washington DC 20036

Telephone: (202) 785 2250

President and Treasurer: P H Croft
Vice-President and General Counsel: Thomas C Dorsey
Traffic Department
  Vice President: K G Ozburn (Atlanta)
  Vice President: W F Gralewski (Chicago)
  Vice President: J S Dow (Washington)
Regional Vice-Presidents
  Pittsburgh, Pennsylvania: R R Firestone
  Modesto, California: G O Ellison
  Moultrie, Georgia: W L Pippin
  East Camden, Arkansas: D Ghent
  Cicero, Illinois: M C Kirby

American Society of Mechanical Engineers Rail Transportation Division

Chairman: Harry M Jones, Chief Engineer, Railroad Division, The Timken Company, 1835 Dueber Avenue SW, Canton, Ohio 44706
Secretary-Treasurer: B J Eck, Director, Production Engineer, Griffin Wheel Company, 200 W Monroe Street, Chicago, Illinois 60606

Association of American Railroads

American Railroads Building, 1920 L St NW, Washington DC 20036

Telephone: (202) 835 9100

Chicago office: 59 East Van Buren St, Chicago, Illinois 60605
Telephone: (312) 939 0770
New Jersey office: Gateway 1, Suite 2610, 7-45 Raymond Plaza West, Newark, New Jersey 07102
Telephone: (201) 623 0703
Research Center: 3140 South Federal St, Chicago, Illinois 60616
Telephone: (312) 567 3575
Transportation Test Center: PO Box 11130, Pueblo, Colorado 81001
Telephone: (303) 545 5660

President and Chief Executive Officer: William H Dempsey
Executive Vice-President: Richard E Briggs
Vice President, Assistant to President: John E Murray
Vice President and General Counsel: J Thomas Tidd
General Solicitor: Hollis G Duensing
Vice Presidents
  Information and Public Affairs: Daniel L Lang
  Legislative Department: William H Darden
  Economics and Finance Department: Harvey A Levine
  Railinc: Henry W Meetze
  Research and Test Department: William J Harris, Jr
  Operations and Maintenance Department: A William Johnston
Secretary and Treasurer: David B Barefoot
Controller: J C Sattery
Executive Director, Intermodal Policy Studies Group: L Leland Lane

Founded in 1934, the AAR is the central co-ordinating and research agency of the railroad industry. Its activities cover railroad operation and maintenance, statistics, medical problems, co-operative advertising, rates, communications, signals, car exchange rules, safety, police and security matters, as well as industry-wide problems in the data processing field.

Association of Railroad Advertising Managers

President: J J Stallmann (Assistant Vice President, Director of Advertising, Pullman Standard)
Executive Secretary: J D Singer

Association of Railroad Editors

American Railroads Building 405, Washington DC 20036

President: Diane S Curry, Brotherhood of Railway and Airline Clerks, Three Research Place, Rockville, Maryland 20850
First Vice-President: Robert E Lee, Union Switch and Signal Division, American Standard Company, 1789 South Braddock Avenue, Pittsburgh, Pennsylvania 15218
Second Vice-President: Chris Stevens, The Chessie System, Terminal Tower-Box 6419, Cleveland, Ohio 44101
Secretary-Treasurer: J Ronald Shumate, Association of American Railroads, 1920 L Street NW, Room 405, Washington DC 20036

Membership: 80 organisations in the USA, Canada, Mexico.
124 individual members.

Locomotive Maintenance Officers' Association

3144 Brereton Ct, Huntington, West Virginia 25705

Telephone: (304) 523 7276

President: R G Clevenger
Secretary: J J T Koerner

National Mediation Board

1425 K St NW, Suite 910, Washington DC 20572

Chairman: Robert J Brown
Member: Robert O Harris
Executive Secretary: Rowland K Quinn, Jr
Staff Mediation Director: E B Meredith
General Counsel: Ronald M Etters
Hearing Officer: David H Cohen

National Railroad Adjustment Board

220 South State St, Chicago, Illinois 60604

Chairman: D A Hampton

The National Railroad Construction and Maintenance Association Inc

9331 Waymond Avenue, Highland, Indiana 46322

Telephone: (219) 924 1709

President: Myrtle Sawyer Hammock
1st Vice President: E Don Matson
2nd Vice President: J M (Bud) McGrath
Executive Director: larry shields
Secretary: Ronald M Brown

This national trade association unites contractors specialising in the engineering and construction of railroads (passenger and freight), excavation of tunnels, erection of railroad bridges, placement of signals, switches and crossings; rehabilitation, removal, relocation of rails, and maintenance of ways. The present membership consists of 62 contractors in 23 states, Canada and the Federal Republic of Germany, and 66 associate members (suppliers).

National Railroad Intermodal Association

2 N Charles, Baltimore, Maryland 21201

President: A B Smith (Director, Intermodal Sales, Conrail)
Secretary: B A Bentz

National Railway Labor Conference

Suite 500, 1901 L Street NW, Washington DC 20036

Telephone: (202) 862 7200

Chairman: C I Hopkins, Jr

National Transportation Safety Board

800 Independence Avenue SW, Washington DC 20594

Chairman: James B King
Members: Elwood T Driver
Patricia A Goldman
G H Patrick Bursley
F H McAdams
General Counsel: John M Stuhldreher
Managing Director: James Shepard

Railcar Repair Association

Berwind Railway Service, PO Box 249, Hollidaysburg, Pennsylvania 16648

President: J M Monroe

Railroad Personnel Association

American Railroads Building, Washington DC 20036

Telephone: (202) 835 9151

President: A J Graham Jr
Secretary: Neil D Mann

Railroad Public Relations Association

1920 L Street NW, Washington DC 20036

Telephone: (202) 835 9561

President: Edwin E Edel
Secretary: Diane S Liebman

Railroad Retirement Board

844 Rush Street, Chicago, Illinois 60611

Telephone: (312) 751 4500

Chairman: William P Adams
Members: Earl Oliver
C J Chamberlain
Chief Executive Officer: James T Brown

Railway Engineering-Maintenance Suppliers Association Inc (REMSA)

5600 Marina Drive, Holmes Beach, Florida 33510

Telephone: (813) 778 4121

President: W J Gallagher (Sperry Rail Service)
Secretary: R L McDaniel (Burro Crane Inc)
Executive Secretary: L D McGuan

REMSA co-operates with meetings and conventions of American Railway Engineering Association, Engineering Division of Association of American Railroads, Roadmasters and Maintenance of Way, and American Railway Bridge & Building Associations. It also holds indoor and outdoor exhibitions of railway engineering and maintenance of way equipment and products.

Railway Progress Institute

700 Fairfax St N, Alexandria, Virginia 22314

Telephone: (703) 836 2332

President: R A Matthews
Chairman: R B Wyland
Vice-Chairman: W S Hansen
Treasurer: R F Griffin

Railway Supply Association Inc

332 S Michigan Ave, Suite 1457, Chicago, Illinois 60604

Telephone: (312) 939 4478

President: L Dale Gaeth (Griffin Wheel Company)
Vice President: W W Sellers (Standard Car Truck Co)
Executive Secretary: W J Burrows (Railway Supply Association, Inc)

The Association provides a permanent organisation of railroad suppliers to co-operate with the railroads by holding periodic educational meetings and exhibitions for railroad fraternities and organisations, with the aim of improving the efficiency, safety, maintenance and operation of railroads based upon latest research and development.

Railway Systems Suppliers, Inc

Suite 234, 400 Penn Center Blvd, Pittsburgh, Pennsylvania 15235

Telephone: (412) 823 2190

Chairman and President: James R Higginbottom
Executive Vice President: Vincent D Burget
Executive Director, Secretary and Treasurer: John W Hansen

A trade association representing suppliers to the communication and signal segment of the rail transport industry. Its primary function is to sponsor a trade exhibit for its member companies in conjunction with the annual meeting of the Association of American Railroads Communication and Signal Division.

Roadmasters and Maintenance of Way Association of America

Cary Building, 18154 Harwood Ave, Homewood, Illinois 60430

Telephone: (312) 799 4650

President: R V Hernandez
Secretary: P A Weissmann

CONSULTANCY SERVICES

American Transit Corporation
A subsidiary of Chromalloy American Corporation

120 South Central Ave, St Louis, Missouri 63105, USA

Telephone: (314) 726 9200

Vice-President: Paul J Ballard

Capabilities
Professional transit-management; maintenance/operations analysis; consulting and planning services. ATC currently manages 22 transit systems at 19 locations in 15 US states.

Ammann & Whitney

Two World Trade Center, Suite 1700, New York, New York 10048, USA

Telephone: (212) 524 7228

Partner: Allen M Custen

Capabilities
Engineering of new rail facilities; inspection and rehabilitation of existing rail facilities.

Projects
Reconstruction of trackage, one swing bridge, eleven fixed bridges and Providence Union station for the Northeast Corridor Improvement Project (three projects, $50 million); inspection and analysis of 112 km (70 miles) of elevated mass transit structures for the New York City Transit Authority; programme to study noise and vibration problems on elevated mass transit systems in the USA for the Department of Transportation; inspection, analysis and contract documents for the rehabilitation of Boston's subway tunnels totalling 24 km (15 miles) for the MBTA; detailed analysis and programme development of rail transit alternatives in the Queens-Midtown corridor in New York City for the New York City DOT; construction management for signal enclosures, relay room and signal tower for the New York City Transit Authority; design of Lindbergh Central station, including control building and parking lots, for MARTA, Atlanta, Georgia.

Angus McDonald & Associates Inc

2150 Shattuck Avenue, Berkeley, California 94704, USA

Telephone: (415) 548 5831

President: Angus N McDonald

Projects
Financial planning for California Transportation Commission ($200 000); economics and finance project BART impact programme ($190 000) for Metropolitan Transportation Authority (MTC), Berkeley, California.

Arthur Andersen & Co

1666 K St NW, Washington DC 20006, USA

Telephone: (202) 862 3100

Partners: Jack L Mann

William T Van Lieshout, Spear Street Tower, Suite 3500, One Market Plaza, San Francisco, California 94105

Telephone: (415) 546 8200

David R Kaye, 1 Surrey Street, London WC2R 2PS, England

Projects
Management information systems planning, design and installation for variety of transit and railroad clients in the USA and UK; performance audits of transit operations for regional and state oversight agencies.

W S Atkins & Partners

Woodcote Grove, Ashley Road, Epsom, Surrey KT18 5BW, England

Telephone: 03727 26140
Telegrams: Kinsopar Epsom
Telex: 266701

Principal officers
Director, Transportation Engineering Division: F J Parker
R C Collins
R D Burke

Capabilities
WS Atkins & Partners has experience in railway projects in many parts of the world. In addition to its own engineering staff, it can draw on the planning and management specialists of the rest of the WS Atkins Group. Capabilities include feasibility studies, traffic forecasts, cost estimates, detailed design of trackwork, civil and structural engineering, architectural design, signalling/communications and systems engineering and supervision of construction. Studies devoted to the socio-economic aspects of a project, route assessment, environmental impact analysis, rationalisation of services, operating methods, future strategy, inventories of facilities and asset valuations are also undertaken.

Projects
WS Atkins & Partners has completed many commissions related to railway projects, including:

Design of main-line railways in Saudi Arabia.
Suburban modal interchanges in Melbourne, Australia.
Land use and traffic forecasts in UK.
Container terminal feasibility in Australia.
Multi-modal facilities in Tasmania.
Route selection and environmental impact analyses for Channel Tunnel rail link in UK.
Signal and telecommunication, services maintenance rationalisation for British Rail.
Suburban rail service feasibility in Venezuela.
Railway workshop modernisation in New South Wales.
Valuation of entire steelworks railway system in Sweden.
Studies and designs for rail systems and main-line links in Algeria, Morocco, UK and Venezuela for power generation, coal and steel industries.
Feasibility study and outline design for suburban railway in Mexico.

WS Atkins & Partners is a substantial contributor to the British Metro Consultants Group which is acting as general consultant for the Baghdad Metro project. The consultant's duties include architecture, station design, engineering, management consultancy and training services covering the whole project. Stage 1 consists of 32 km of underground running lines and 38 stations, together with depots and workshops.

Another current commission covers the feasibility study, detailed design and supervision of construction for a container-handling railway at the Jeddah Islamic Seaport. This project involves railway layout and container handling facilities at the port, a new inland customs clearance depot with railway layout, the main-line rail link between the port and depot with signalling and telecommunications systems, and the provision of power supplies, motive power and rolling stock.

Rail yards at SNS steelworks, El Hadjar, Algeria

Michael Baker Jr Inc

4301 Dutch Ridge Rd, Beaver, Pennsylvania 15009, USA

Telephone: (412) 495 7711

Principal: Edgar C Richardson

Capabilities
Rail transit planning and design.

Projects
East Busway ($65 million) for Port Authority of Allegheny County (PAT); Section EHB of Northeast Corridor Improvement Project; and terminal bulk storage facility near Pittsburgh for Chessie System.

R L Banks & Associates Inc

900 17th St NW, Washington DC 20006, USA

Telephone: (202) 296 6700

President: Robert L Banks

Capabilities
Economic analysis, urban transport planning, policy development, cost accounting.

Projects
Recent and current projects include: planning for construction of a 19.3 km rail connection to a 3.2 GW electric generating plant being built by the Intermountain Power Agency in Utah; examining the feasibility of expanding rail commuter service between Havre de Grace and Washington for the Maryland State Railroad Administration; projecting economic prospects of western railroads for the US Department of Justice; analysing economic impacts of private car ownership for the Association of American Railroads; assisting the Grand Trunk Western Railroad in the acquisition of former lines of the Chicago, Milwaukee, St Paul & Pacific Railroad; assisting the Coal Exporters Association with rail freight rate negotiations; advising the Port Authority of New York & New Jersey with respect to the pending sale of the Consolidated Rail Corporation; analysing rail cost and service issues for the New York Department of Transportation; assisting Big Stone Partners, a consortium of electric power companies, with freight rate negotiations; planning rail transport to serve the White Pine Power Project in Nevada; assisting the Louisville River Port Authority in contract negotiations for rail access; providing traffic management services for the Monongahela Railway; assisting the Southern Pacific Transportation Company in trackage rights negotiations.

Barton-Aschman Associates Inc

820 Davis St, Evanston, Illinois 60201, USA

Telephone: (312) 491 1000

Senior Vice-President: Michael A Powills, Jr

Projects
Metropolitan area rail transportation and economic development study in Dubuque, Iowa for the East Central Intergovernmental Association ($95 000); economic analysis of branch lines and secondary main lines in South Dakota for the South Dakota Department of Transportation ($42 000); feasibility study of using vintage railroad equipment for intra-park transport within Indiana Dunes National Lakeshore for the US National Park Service ($38 000); alternatives analysis and draft environmental impact statement for a new rapid transit line in Chicago's Stevenon/Archer Avenue corridor for the City of Chicago ($80 000); light rail alternatives analyses in Dallas, St Louis and Orange County, California; demand analysis for rapid transit systems in the West Park Corridor, Houston, the Wilshire Boulevard Corridor, Los Angeles and in Queens Borough, New York City.

BVC-Berlin
Berliner Verkehrs-Consulting GmbH

Bayreuther Strasse 4, PO Box 30 39 44, 1000 West Berlin, Federal Republic of Germany

Telephone: (030) 211 50 81

Managing Directors: Anton Mauerer
Rudolf Janousch

Capabilities
Planning, design and execution of rail transit systems; management, operation, maintenance and repair.

Bechtel Incorporated
Hydro & Community Facilities Division

50 Beale Street, San Francisco, California 94119, USA

Telephone: (415) 768 6945
Telegrams: Wateka- SF, Ca
Telex (international): 470195
(domestic): 34783

Associated companies
Bechtel Power Corporation (same address)

Capabilities
Started in 1898, Bechtel's headquarters are located in San Francisco, California, with world-wide regional offices. The staff totals nearly 30 000 permanent employees, over half of whom are graduate engineers and technical personnel.

Rail projects are the responsibility of Bechtel's Hydro and Community Facilities Division, with its headquarters in San Francisco. The Rail Projects Department in this division is staffed with railway specialists, planners, engineers, and project managers covering all principal railroad disciplines. Bechtel performs railway services in terms of techno-economic feasibility studies, master planning, preliminary and final engineering, procurement services, construction engineering, and construction, or a combination of these. When called upon to handle complete packages Bechtel also offers assistance in securing required financing.

Recent projects

Assignment	Completion date
Delaware & Hudson restructuring study: economic/engineering study	1981
Delaware & Hudson alternatives and short term action plan: economic/engineering study	1982
Study of organisational requirements for the proposed national programme of rail electrification	1981
Analysis of the Union Pacific/Missouri Pacific/Western Pacific and the Norfolk and Western/Southern Railroad mergers: economic/engineering study	1981
Las Vegas/Los Angeles high speed/super speed ground transportation: engineering services for feasibility study	1982
Northeast Corridor Improvement Project: for high-speed rail service Boston to Washington (750 km). Technical support for all phases	1983
Somerset Railroad: environmental analysis, preliminary and final design, procurement and construction management for a coal hauling railroad	1984

Blauvelt Engineering Co

1 Park Ave, New York, New York 10016, USA

Telephone: (212) 481 1600

Partner: Francis M Fuerst

Capabilities
Rail transit facilities design; construction and operating inspection.

Projects
Vienna Line ($40 million) for Washington Metropolitan Area Transit Authority (WMATA); Oakland station, South Line ($12.5 million) for Metropolitan Atlanta Rapid Transit Authority (MARTA).

Bogen Jenal Engineers PC

983 Willis Avenue, Albertson, New York 11507, USA

Telephone: (516) 747 4220

President: Samuel A Bogen
Vice-President: Joseph R Jenal

Projects
Final M/E design for Washington Metro sections.

Bogen, Johnston, Lau & Jenal PC
A Minority Business Enterprise

983 Willis Avenue, Albertson, New York 11507, USA

Telephone: (516) 747 4220, (212) 895 3358

President: Wallace O Johnston
Vice-President: Samuel A Bogen

Projects
Design of following work on the Northeast Corridor (Washington to Boston) Improvement Project for Federal Railroad Administration: Connecticut River Bridge, movable bridge control house, power, bridge controls, utilities ($6 million); Portal Bridge, movable bridge power and bridge controls ($7.5 million); track improvements, Bush River, Maryland to Perryville, Maryland ($10 million); interim signals, Washington DC to Hudson, New Jersey ($5 million); signal system renovation, Massachusetts Bay Transportation Authority ($2.5 million); mechanical and electrical final design, Delavan station, Buffalo ($11 million).

Bolt Beranek and Newman Inc

50 Moulton Street, Cambridge, Massachusetts 02138, USA

Telephone: (617) 491 1850

Sales Transportation Manager: Carl E Hanson

Projects
Vehicle noise control consulting engineering for New York City Transit Authority (NYCTA); environmental analysis and preliminary engineering on the Boston southwest corridor for Massachusetts Bay Transportation Authority (MBTA). Additional projects: noise and vibration assessment and control for Amtrak, Northeast Corridor Improvement Project; locomotive quieting project for US Department of Transportation; wheel/rail noise research for US Department of Transportation.

Booker Associates

10905 Fort Washington Road, Suite 306, Fort Washington, Maryland 2022, USA

Telephone: (301) 292 9440

Vice-President/Manager: Robert D Baldwin

Capabilities
Traffic planning; light rail design; maintenance facilities.

CAM Industries International

215 Philadelphia St, PO Box 227, Hanover, Pennsylvania 17331, USA

Telephone: (717) 637 5988
Telex: 840-470

Capabilities
Planning and equipping of railway electric shops, including methods development in traction motor and generator-repair and maintenance, equipment specification, machine commissioning and operator training.

Projects
The company has active projects with Nigerian Railways, Zambia Railway, Indonesian Railways, Korean National Railroad, Saudi Railways, and Atchison Topeka & Santa Fe, Southern Pacific and Family Lines systems in the USA.

CANAC Consultants Ltd

International consulting subsidiary of Canadian National Railways

PO Box 8100, Montreal, Quebec H3C 3N4, Canada

Telephone: (514) 877 4816/3500
Telegrams: Condiv, Montreal
Telex: 055 60753

President: W H Bailey

Capabilities
Provides comprehensive management (administration, planning, information systems, costing, project control), engineering, procurement, training and other consulting services in relation to the design, construction, operation, direct management and maintenance of new or existing surface transport facilities including railway, highway, water and intermodal transport networks as well as hotels and telecommunications. Specialises in direct or consultative management of any aspect of existing railway operations or design and construction of new rail lines (including signalling and telecommunications) and railway facilities. Since 1971 CANAC has undertaken over 300 projects in some 45 countries on every continent.

Projects
Two of CANAC's early contracts in Africa are still in progress. In Guinea CANAC is providing expertise for Halco (Mining) Inc, Compagnie des Bauxites de Guinée and l'Office d'Aménagement de Boké in all areas of management and operations on the Chemin de Fer de Boké. In Zambia specialists provide technical assistance in the area of motive power maintenance, as well as design of training modules in the areas of telecommunications operations and computer systems analysis, in a programme sponsored by the World Bank.

Elsewhere in Africa, the Régie des Chemins de Fer Abidjan-Niger has contracted CANAC for technical assistance in locomotive maintenance and repair, while the Société Nationale des Chemins de Fer Zairois has sent officers to Canada to undergo training. In Tanzania, under a Canadian International Development Agency-financed project, CANAC specialists are responsible for training Tanzanian nationals in locomotive maintenance and repair procedures at the Railway's Morogoro workshop.

In South America, CANAC consultants are in Brazil providing advisory services to MONASA Consultoria e Projetos Ltda in track-laying in the construction of a 900 km extension to the Carajas Railway.

In Asia, consultants from CANAC started work on the design of the Bang Sue container freight station complex in 1982 for the State Railway of Thailand, a World Bank-sponsored project. In Bangladesh specialists are involved in the rehabilitation and quality control of locomotives for the Bangladesh Railway Corporation.

In Canada, CANAC's Canalog Division has signed contracts with VIA Rail Inc. The major contract with VIA is for the design of maintenance facilities in Halifax, Montreal, Toronto, Winnipeg, Edmonton and Vancouver. In Western Canada, CANAC experts are involved in the electrification of 120 km of a new spur line for British Columbia Railway. CANAC, in association with Canadian Pacific Consulting Services Limited and Swederail Consulting, is in the process of preparing the detailed design of the catenary system, the traction power system and is assisting BCR in other areas.

Rail-welding by alumino thermite-technique on CANAC project in Guinea

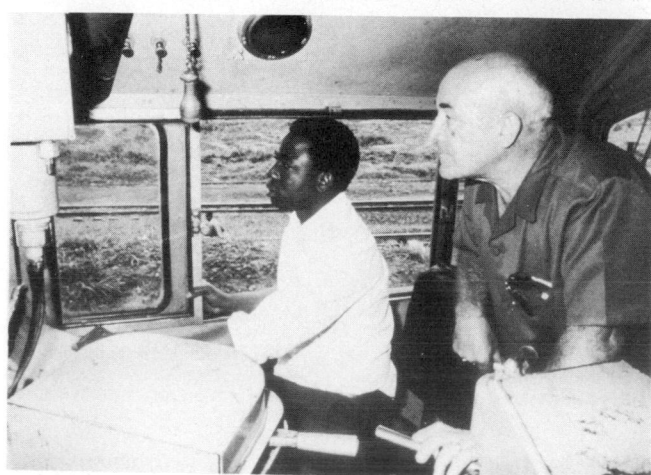

CANAC technical assistance on Zambia Railway

Canadian Pacific Consulting Services Ltd

740 Rue Notre Dame Ouest, Bureau 760, Montreal, Quebec H3C 3X6, Canada

Telephone: (514) 395 7002
Telex: 055-60147

Subsidiary: Servicos de Constructoria Pacifico Canadaiense SA, Apartado 248, Centro Colon, SA Jose, Costa Rica

Branch office: Canadian Pacific Consulting Services Ltd, 105 Hagley Building, Concord Plaza, 3411 Silverweed Road, Wilmington, Delaware 19810, USA

Telephone: (302) 478 3181

Parent company: Canadian Pacific Limited

Chairman of the Board: J A McDonald
President: G T Fisher
Executive Vice-President: J Denis Bélisle
Vice-President: R H Ballantyne
Comptroller: A Kostanuik

Capabilities
Canadian Pacific Consulting Services is the international consulting arm of Canadian Pacific. As an active member of the Canadian Pacific group, CPCS is able to call upon the professional, technical and latest methods of interfacing rail, truck and ship traffic, and the ability to provide cost-benefit studies using computer-oriented financial analysis programmes for any given present and foreseeable traffic requirements places it in a unique position to optimise any conceivable transport investment. Through its affiliation with the Canadian Pacific group, CPCS is able to call upon the professional, technical and operating personnel of any of the group's member companies to meet specific engineering, research, economic, marketing or supervisory requirements of individual projects anywhere in the world.

Projects
Railway clients served by Canadian Pacific Consulting Services Ltd have included the following:
Turkish State Railways; Korean National Railroad; Tunisian National Railways; Congo-Ocean Railway; Egyptian Railways; Mozambique Railways; Honduran National Railways; Venezuelan National Railways; Rede Ferroviaria Federal SA of Brazil; Malayan State Railways; Bangladesh Railway; Indonesian State Railways; Western Australian Government Railways; Quebec North Shore and Labrador Railway; British Columbia Railway; Togo Railway; Ghana Railway; East African Railways Corp; State Railway of Thailand; Mt Newman Railway (Australia); Hamersley Iron Ore Railway (Australia); Quebec Cartier Mining Railway (Canada); Peruvian National Railways; Sri Lanka Railway; Nicaraguan Pacific Railway; Cameroon National Railways; South African Railways; Panama Railroad; Jamaican Railway Corporation; La Société Nationale des Transports Ferroviaires of Algeria; Caminhos de Ferro Portuguese; White Pass and Yukon Railway; Costa Rican National Railways.

Can Deub Fleissig and Associates

11 Hill Street, Newark, New Jersey 07102, USA

Telephone: (201) 643 3919

Vice-President: Burton R Cohen

Projects
Environmental impact statement ($975 000) for New Jersey Department of Transportation (DOT).

Capital Consultants

5508 Wilson Lane, Bethesda, Maryland 20014, USA

Telephone: (301) 656 1180

Principal Partner: Edwin L Mueller

Projects
Automated transit guideway survey (under $10 000).

C-E Maguire Inc

31 Canal Street, Providence, Rhode Island 02903, USA

Telephone: (401) 272 6000

Executive Vice-President: Vincent M Cangiano

Projects
Red Line extension tunnel design ($110 million) for Massachusetts Bay Transportation Authority (MBTA); Section E2 tunnel design ($38 million) for Washington Metropolitan Area Transit Authority (WMATA); Orange Line transport study ($40 million) for MBTA; Northeast Corridor rail improvement, New Haven to Guilford ($22 million) for Federal Rail Administration; five-year improvement rail and drainage study (5.2 miles of rail) for ER Dupont de Nemours & Co Inc; Catskill Mountain Railroad study for conversion to steam tourist operation.

Century Engineering Inc

32 West Road, Towson, Maryland 21204, USA

Telephone: (301) 823 8070

Vice-President: Robert G James

Projects
Glebe Road station section design ($31 million) for Washington Metropolitan Area Transit Authority (WMATA).
Baltimore North Corridor Transportation alternative study.

Chase, Rosen & Wallace Inc

901 North Washington Street, Alexandria, Virginia 22134, USA

Telephone: (703) 836 7120

Vice-President: Stanley B Rosen

Projects
Mass transit improvement studies (bus and rail): NJ Transit, NY-MTA, Union County (NJ), services for elderly and handicapped (UMTA), Camden County (NJ); transit telephone information projects; electric trolleybus feasibility projects (UMTA).

Cities Corporation

102 Mount Auburn Street, Cambridge, Massachusetts 02138, USA

Telephone: (617) 491 8007

Director of Transit Mapping: Barbara Petersen

Projects
System map design projects for Rhode Island Public Transit Authority (RIPTA) and Metro Regional Transit Authority, Akron, Ohio.

Clough Associates

24 Aviation Road, Computer Park, Albany, New York 12205, USA

Telephone: (518) 458 7795

Partner: William A Harbour

Capabilities
Light and heavy rail rapid transit design and operation; automatic fare systems; complete project management.

Cole Sherman & Associates Limited

2025 Sheppard Avenue, East Willowdale, Ontario M2J 1W3, Canada

Telephone: (416) 491 4503
Telegrams: CSAlnc, Tor
Telex: 06 966647

President: R J Cole
Vice-Presidents: T J Sherman
                D E W Wicks

Capabilities
Cole, Sherman & Associates Ltd, was founded in 1954 and is a wholly-owned Canadian company operating under the guidance of its principals and partners. With offices in Toronto, Hamilton, London and Calgary, the company has been providing engineering services to railway clients including Canadian Pacific Ltd, Canadian National Railways, VIA Rail, GO Transit, and Ontario Northland Railway. Assignments have included track layout and geometric Improvements to accommodate high-speed inter-city travel, the development of signalling systems, the design of various types of grade separations, and the redevelopment of complex rail corridors. Other completed projects include diesel locomotive repair shops; light and heavy freight car repair facilities; component rebuild shops; passenger coach shops and high-speed and standard servicing facilities. These projects have been undertaken both as separate entities within operating yards and as components of an overall assignment for a total yard, including inspection, servicing and maintenance buildings, together with feed, release and storage track and the associated operational studies.

Projects
Complete design and construction management services for the Toronto Area Transit Operating Authority's maintenance and servicing facilities for GO Transit passenger trains.
Complete engineering design and site supervision of the diesel repair shop and all associated site service in Toronto for Canadian Pacific Ltd, together with complete engineering design and site supervision for the spot car repair shop, freight car repair shop, freight terminal and mechanised terminal.
Complete design and engineering services and resident field supervision for Ontario Northland Railway's maintenance and repair facilities in North Bay, Ontario.

Complete engineering design for Canadian National Railway's maintenance building in Concord, Ontario.
Pre-design systems study to determine VIA Rail's maintenance facility requirements for its complete rolling stock fleet.
Structural consultants and engineering team leaders for a rapid transit planning study for the Urban Transportation Development Corporation.
Complete systems study and programme development for Canadian Pacific's Angus locomotive repair shop operations in Angus, Ontario.
Assistance to the Toronto Transit Commission in the design of a 6.75 km (4.2-mile) elevated light rail transit system.

Terence J Collins Associates, Inc

Woodfield Lake Office Court, 953 North Plum Grove Road, Suite B, Schaumburg, Illinois 60195, USA

Telephone: (312) 843 7300

President: Terry Collins

Projects
Concept development and preparation of the performance specification for a consolidated radio communications and train supervision system for the Chicago Transit Authority. This system covers the entire CTA rapid transit system, above and below ground, and introduces communications capability for emergency services' agencies (police and fire) when in the subway. The system also includes integration of bus and rail supervisory functions. The company was involved in all phases of the project including bid evaluations, system construction and implementation, and system acceptance activities. Contract value $14 million.

Analysis of system parameters for preparation of a performance specification for a system-wide transit information system (TIS) for the Southwest Ohio Regional Transit Authority of Cincinnati, Ohio. System features included automatic passenger counter (APC) information collection and processing, vehicle location, interfaces to computer run cutting systems (RUCUS), long-range computerised management information systems (MIS) and UMTA Section 15 reporting. Contract value $2 million.

Joint participation with Barton-Aschman Associates in a proposal to contract for the modernisation, extension and operation of Subterraneos de Buenos Aires (SBA). Contract value may exceed $1000 million.

Provision of practical operating experience in support of Lester B Knight and Associates and Louis T Klauder and Associates for the start-up operation of the San Diego Trolley, Inc. Unique aspects include joint right-of-way with an operating freight railway, and barrier-free, self-service fare collection. Responsibility included development of rule book and standard operating procedures for employees, and of selected training materials. Contract value $86 million.

Preparation of training materials for maintenance and transport employees for repair, trouble-shooting and operation of a computer-based radio/data communications system for the Detroit Department of Transportation, Southeastern Michigan Transportation Authority. Activities included review of existing programmes/materials, development of new materials (including media/mode selection) and administering of the developed programmes. Contract value $30 000.

Provided operations experience assistance to the Lea, Elliott, McGean/De Leuw Cather joint venture in the multi-modal analysis for the Dallas Area Rapid Transit Board. This analysis covered conventional rail transit mode, a linear induction motor (LIM)-based mode and monorail. Properties across the world were surveyed, and where the technology lacked actual application/experience, the analysis team worked to identify areas requiring further investigation. All aspects of each mode, such as reliability analysis and likely vendors, were evaluated.

Project management of a radio/data communication system for the Municipality of Metropolitan Seattle (Metro). This system is to meet Metro's communications needs through 1990 for a fleet of nearly 2400 buses (100 per cent greater than the 1982 fleet), over 1000 vans, and some 300 supervisory/support vehicles. The system includes novel control arrangements, necessitated by Seattle's rugged topography. Integration with existing and planned Metro data systems, including system-wide AVL/AVM functions was also required. Involvement began with development of a 'prime data base' covering Seattle's existing system and projected needs, continued with performance specification development, includes bid reviews, and will culminate in supervision of system acceptance activities. Contract value $7 million.

Assisting Daniel, Mann, Johnson and Mendenhall in the revitalisation project on the New York City Transit Authority. This ambitious undertaking offers the consultant team a wide range of opportunities, in areas such as station modernisation, rehabilitation of fixed plant facilities, and specialised operations assistance, including inter-car safety barriers. Contract value $5700 million.

Responsibility for conducting acceptance testing of the data facility supporting Detroit Department of Transportation's radio/data communications system. Involvement began with review of the vendor-submitted computer statement of work and acceptance test plan, and culminated in the issue of a report on system acceptance recommendations. Contract value $2.4 million.

Conducting investigations into automated telephone information systems (TIS) for the Municipality of Metropolitan Seattle (Metro). Seattle's system-wide implementation of a TIS system would be the most ambitious undertaking of its kind in North America. Preliminary investigations into existing technologies and comparisons with Metro's requirements have been made. Possible system configurations (down to user access details) have been developed along with system cost estimates. Contract value $2.5 million (estimated).

Preparation of a performance specification for a radio/data communications system for the Dallas Transit System. This includes the total re-equipping of all DTS buses, management, and support vehicles to operate in the 800 MHz frequency range. The system design is readily-expandable to accommodate regional service/communications needs, and adaptable to automated data interfaces with other systems such as automatic passenger counter (APC) and automatic vehicle location (AVL). The system is to be fully operational by August 1984, with all installation work complete substantially before that deadline. Contract value $3.5 million.

Comsul Ltd

417 Montgomery Street, San Francisco, California 94104, USA

Telephone: (415) 989 6700

President: Peter B Valentine
Vice-President and Chief Executive Officer: Colin W Halford

Projects
Providing engineering services in the planning, design, testing and review of the combined communications network for San Francisco Municipal Railway.

Connell Metcalf & Eddy

1320 S Dixie Highway, PO Box 34 1939, Coral Gables, Florida 33134, USA

Telephone: (305) 665 9241

President: Thomas S Rooney

Capabilities
Design of rapid transit stations; design of line sections; design of maintenance facilities.

CRS Group Inc

1100 Milam Building, Suite 500, Houston, Texas 77002, USA

Telephone: (713) 658 9511

Member companies: Caudill Rowlett Scott Inc
CRS Group Engineers Inc
CM Constructors/Managers Inc
Intergroup Development Inc

President: Charles B Thomson

Projects
Engineering consultants for Washington Metropolitan Area Transit Authority (WMATA) and Metropolitan Area Rapid Transit Authority (MARTA); claims consultant for Bay Area Rapid Transit District, San Francisco (BART); engineering consultant for the Chessie System; construction manager for Denver Regional Transit District (RTD) Transit Mall; bridge designer for Burlington Northern Railroad, Chicago & Eastern Illinois Railroad, Chicago & Northwestern Railroad, Gulf, Mobile & Ohio Railroad, Illinois Central Gulf Railroad, Peoria & Pekin Union Railroad, Saint Louis-San Francisco Railroad and Norfolk & Western Railroad; marshalling yard designer for Louisville-Nashville Railroad; bridge designer for Southern Railroad Company.

The company has provided comprehensive engineering services for the Weyerhauser Company's new short line, the Golden Triangle Railroad, to its pulp and paper mill at Columbus, Mississippi; and for relocation of a Burlington Northern line to facilitate construction of the Tennessee-Tombigbee Waterway.

Custom Engineering Inc

2805 S Tejon, Englewood, Colorado 80110, USA

Telephone: (303) 781 7585

Vice-President and General Manager: Carlos A de Moraes

Capabilities
Systems engineering and assessment; planning and economics; light rail transit systems design and operation.

Dalton-Dalton-Newport Inc

3605 Warrensville Center Road, Cleveland, Ohio 44122, USA

Telephone: (216) 283 4000

Vice-President: Frederick J Richardson

Projects
Northeast Corridor high-speed passenger programme design sections (three); high-speed rail passenger study, Ohio Rail Transportation Authority; classification yard, Ames, Iowa, Chicago and North Western Railroad.

Daniel, Mann, Johnson, & Mendenhall

3250 Wilshire Blvd, Los Angeles, California 90010, USA
(other offices world-wide)

Telephone: (213) 381 3663

Vice-President/Transportation: Gerald W Seelman

Projects
Rehabilitation of New York City Transit facilities for New York City Transit Authority ($7000 million).
Ways and structures for Los Angeles metro rail system, Southern California Rapid Transit District ($1200 million).
Design of Vancouver, British Columbia, advanced light rail transit system ($350 million).
Design of Baltimore rapid transit system for Maryland Mass Transit Administration ($850 million).
Operation and management of national bus system for Saudi Public Transport Company.
Design of Houston regional rail and bus mass transit programme for Metropolitan Transit Authority of Harris County ($1000 million).

Day & Zimmerman Inc

1818 Market Street, Philadelphia, Pennsylvania 19103, USA

Telephone: (215) 299 8461
Telegrams: Dayzim
Telex: 845192

Senior Vice-President: Frederick D Brown

Projects
Design of system-wide elements for Niagara Frontier Transportation Authority's light rail transit system ($439 million).
Electrification design, 12th Street station design and construction management for South-Eastern Pennsylvania Transportation Authority's (SEPTA) centre-city commuter rail tunnel ($300 million).
Design and construction management of modernisation of electrification for Connecticut Department of Transportation's New Haven commuter rail line ($5 million).
Programme monitoring and review for Federal Railroad Administration's Northeast Corridor Improvement Project.
Development and implementation of project control systems for Niagara Frontier Transportation Authority, South-Eastern Pennsylvania Transportation Authoririty, Baltimore Region Rapid Transit System and the Urban Transportation Development Corporation.

Deconsult
Deutsche Eisenbahn Consulting GmbH

Postfach 700 467, 6000 Frankfurt (Main) 70, Federal Republic of Germany

Telephone: (0611) 6319-1
Telegrams: Deconsult, Frankfurtmain
Telex: 4 14 516

Supervisory Board: E Schneider
P Koch
K Peiffer
W Vaerst
General Managers: F W Moller
G F Scheller
Management, Railway and Mass Rapid Transit Projects: K L Haucke
Management, Traffic Technology: G Pintag
Commercial Administration Manager: D Christofzik
Personnel Manager: M Senne
Civil Engineering Manager: E-D Wendt
Electrical and Mechanical Engineering Manager: K Großmann
Traffic and Transport Manager: D Lehnert
Transportation Economy Manager: P Hohn

Capabilities
Deconsult, an international consulting enterprise, carries out planning and consultancy work in the transport sector all over the world. The main accents in such activities are placed upon national and municipal railway networks. The firm was founded in 1966 by the Federal German Railways and the Deutsche Bank AG, which are the only shareholders.

At present, Deconsult employs about 200 engineers and economists. As Deconsult operates a staff exchange scheme with the German Federal Railway, both the home office staff and the expert teams working abroad can be quickly supplemented to meet current requirements.

Associated offices: Deconsult has offices in:
Abidjan, Ivory Coast; Algiers, Algeria; Baghdad, Iraq; Bangkok, Thailand; Chittagong, Bangladesh; Damascus, Syria; Lisbon, Portugal; Kinshasa and Lubumbashi, Zaire; Ma'an, Jordan; Mandalay, Burma; Rio de Janeiro, Brazil; Taipei, Taiwan; Tabora, Tanzania; Cairo, Egypt; Nairobi, Kenya; Ougadoujou, Upper Volta.

Projects
Deconsult has executed or is at present executing projects in the following countries:
Algeria, Argentina, Bangladesh, Benin, Brazil, Botswana, Burma, Cameroon, Costa Rica, Egypt, West Germany, Ghana, Greece, Guinea, India, Indonesia, Iran, Iraq, Ivory Coast, Jordan, Kenya, South Korea, Liberia, Luxembourg, Malaysia, Mali, Pakistan, Paraguay, Peru, Portugal, Saudi Arabia, Sudan, Switzerland, Taiwan, Tanzania, Thailand, Togo, USSR, USA, Upper Volta, Venezuela, Viet-Nam, Yugoslavia, Zaire and Zimbabwe.

Projects (civil engineering)

Country	Client	Description of project	Completion
Algeria	Société Nationale des Transports Ferroviaires	Detailed engineering for rehabilitation and new construction of lines	1985
Egypt	Egyptian Railways	Detailed engineering and site supervision for rehabilitation of permanent way	1984
Germany, Federal Republic	German Federal Railway (DB)	High speed railway line Hanover-Wurzburg, computer controlled supervision of construction	1984
		Supervision "Westliche Riedbahn"	1984
Iraq	Iraqi Republic Railway	Railway line Kirkuk-Baiji-Haditha, feasibility study, preliminary and final design, elaboration of tender documents, supervision of works	1986
Taiwan	Engineering Office of Taipei Underground Project (TRUPO)	Preliminary and final design tendering and site supervision for underground system construction in Taipei City	1986

Projects (electrical and mechanical)

Country	Client	Description of project	Completion
Bangladesh	German Society for Technical Co-operation	Rehabilitation of passenger coaches of the Bangladesh Railway	1984
Burma	German Society for Technical Co-operation	Training of workshop personnel	1984
Brazil	Enefer, Consultoria	Technical assistance for RFFSA-electrification project of the lines Rio-Belo Horizonte-São Paulo	1981
Tanzania	Tanzania Railway Corporation	Technical assistance for maintenance of diesel locomotives	1984
Zaire	German Society for Technical Co-operation	Management and technical assistance for maintenance services with SNCZ	1983

Projects (signalling, telecommunications)

Country	Client	Description of project	Completion
Germany, Federal Republic	Gesellschaft fur Reaktorsicherheit	Comparative study of security systems of German Federal Railway and nuclear power plants	1982
Kenya	Kenya Railways	Detailed engineering and supervision of telecommunications project	1984

Transport studies

Country	Client	Description of project	Completion
Portugal	Metropolitano de Lisboa	Study of implementation railbound traffic within the 'Corredor de Lourdes'	1982
Tunisia	DEG, West Germany	Transport connections between West European countries and Tunisia	1981

Miscellaneous projects

Country	Client	Description of project	Completion
Burma	GTZ	Training workshop	1984
Germany, Federal Republic		State of the art of rail/wheel technology	1984
Zaire	Office des Routes	4 ferry boats with load capacity of 120 and 35 tons	1982
	ONATRA	Supervision of works for urban railway system	1985

Impression of Deconsult design for Ponte Pequena metro station, São Paulo, Brazil

Deconsult electrification project in Taiwan

Signal panel operators under Deconsult training in Indonesia

Delcan

5008 86th Street, Suite 100, Edmonton, Alberta T6E 5S2, Canada

Telephone: (403) 468 6757

Vice-President, Business Development, Prairie Region: R Wayne Bowes

1217 Centre Street North, Calgary, Alberta T2E 2R3

Telephone: (403) 276 9861

Vice-President, Operations, Prairie Region: Dave A Vallis

Capabilities
Light rail transit planning and engineering; transit maintenance facilities engineering.

De Leuw, Cather & Company (DCCO)

1211 Connecticut Avenue NW, Washington DC 20036, USA

Telephone: (202) 828 3800
TWX: 7108220061

Offices: Chicago, Anchorage, Buffalo, Denver, East Hartford, New York City, Pasadena, San Francisco and District of Columbia. Various overseas offices including Abu Dhabi, Kuwait, Lima, Bangkok and Singapore

Associate companies: De Leuw, Cather International Limited
De Leuw, Cather & Company of New York, Inc
De Leuw, Cather & Company of Michigan
De Leuw, Cather & Company of Virginia
De Leuw, Cather Professional Corporation
James A Caywood Professional Corporation

President: J A Caywood
Senior Vice-Presidents
   Deputy Manager, Central/West Region: L D Hazzard
   Manager, International Region: V P Lamb
   Manager, Eastern Region: R S O'Neil
   Manager, Central/West Region: G M Randich
Vice-President: T Langford
Treasurer/Financial Manager: C J Blase
Vice-Presidents
   Manager, Engineering Management Services: C L Alvarez
   Deputy Manager, International Region: D S Gedney
   Corporate Business Development: M R Sproles
   Quality Assurance: L A Dondanville
   Corporate Services: D W Harig
Controller and Assistant Treasurer: L Alvarez
Secretary: D K Jorgensen
Manager, Business Development Services: E A Fairhead

Capabilities

Services undertaken by DCCO include: feasibility studies, preliminary and final design, site development, surveys, soils investigations, specifications and cost estimates, contract documents, construction supervision, construction management.

Projects

DCCO, in a joint venture with The Ralph M Parsons Company, is currently responsible for the management of the Northeast Corridor Improvement Project. This Federal Railroad Administration programme to rehabilitate the 744 km (456-mile) rail line and facilities between Washington DC and Boston will allow Amtrak passenger services to operate at speeds up to 193 km/h (120 mph)

Main line relocations, extension, consolidations and improvements: Major projects have been completed in California, Georgia, Illinois, Indiana, Iowa, Massachusetts, Michigan, Minnesota, Nebraska, Nevada, New Jersey, Pennsylvania, Texas, and Wisconsin as well as Canada, Indonesia, and Turkey.

Railroad grade separations and related studies: Assignments involving a variety of disciplines have been completed in 15 US states, Australia, and Jordan.

Railroad appraisals, inventories and operational studies: Engineering and economic analyses; revenue studies; operational studies; valuation appraisals; and condition reports for major railroad facilities in the United States, Canada, Philippines, Jamaica, Venezuela, Chile, Turkey, Saudi Arabia and China; feasibility studies for Bosphorus Railway Tunnel.

Railroad signalling and communications: Projects have included automatic interlocking circuits; remote control interlocking; electrification; design of signal and communication systems or modifications to existing facilities; and automatic crossing protection.

Yards, shops, and terminal facilities: Modernisation of existing facilities or construction of new facilities in 13 states, Thailand, and Venezuela. Design of Norfolk and Western Landers intermodal facility.

Tracklaying in Northeast Corridor Improvement Project, jointly managed by DCCO

Symbolically gold-painted, the millionth new concrete sleeper in the Northeast Corridor Improvement Project installed near Perryville, Maryland, in December 1982

DKS Associates

405 14th Street, Suite 610, Oakland, California 94612, USA

Telephone: (415) 763 2061

Principal: William H Dietrich

Capabilities

Urban transport planning; light rail transit system design.

C H Dobbie and Partners

Francis House, Francis Street, London SW1P 1DQ, England

Telephone: 01-834 2923
Telex: 917220

Projects

Station buildings including Birmingham International station serving National Exhibition Centre; Harecastle tunnel and line diversions; sidings; carriage washing plants; wagon repair shops, overhead electrification foundations for Kowloon-Canton Railway, Hong Kong; maintenance shop at Sha Tin, Hong Kong; signal boxes, computer centre and telephone exchanges, over 400 bridges for British Rail; survey and design for new railways in Guinea and Liberia.

Dubin, Dubin and Moutoussamy

221 North La Salle Street, Suite 2300, Chicago, Illinois 60601, USA

Telephone: (312) 641 0700

Architect: Arthur D Dubin

Projects

Modernisation of Loyola station ($2.8 million), Granville station ($1.3 million) and Davis station ($500 000) for Chicago Transit Authority (CTA).

New stations and ancillary facilities with 3.26 km of tunnel, track and platform work ($55 million) in association with Harza Engineering Co: Zoological Park station, Cleveland Park station, Van Ness station, (1) chiller plant, (3) transformer substations, for Washington Metropolitan Area Transit Authority (WMATA); new station, 12th Street (Roosevelt Road) on the Illinois Central Gulf Railroad for the Regional Transportation Authority (RTA), Chicago, a project including new gate-station house, pedestrian bridge, platforms, warming houses, elevators, track relocation, extension of 12th Street (Roosevelt Road) over tracks, all to serve as a gateway to the Chicago World's Fair of 1992 (cost to be determined).

Artist's impression of Davis Street station improvement for Chicago Transit Authority by Dubin, Dubin and Moutoussamy

Thomas K Dyer Inc

1762 Massachusetts Avenue, Lexington, Massachusetts 02173, USA

Telephone: (617) 862 2075

President: T K Dyer
Executive Vice-President: W K Hale

Capabilities

Civil engineering design; bridge and structural design; signalling and communication design; trackwork; feasibility studies.

Projects

Track improvement project involving rehabilitation of tracks, signals and tractive power on several transit lines ($34 million) on the Massachusetts Bay Transportation Authority (MBTA).

Rehabilitation of signal system and train control on four-track main line, Jamaica to Penn Station, New York ($50 million).

Dynatrend Inc

21 Cabot Road, Woburn, Massachusetts 01801, USA

Telephone: (617) 935 3960

Director, Program Development: Rudolph G DiLuzio

Capabilities
Light rail, rapid rail, and commuter rail technologies. Track structures safety analysis.

Projects
Rail-related analysis for the US Department of Transportation Systems Center, Cambridge, Massachusetts to provide analytical services in support of studies related to track structures and development of performance standards directed toward the improvement of railway safety. Value approximately $1 million.

Ground transport support services for the US Department of Transportation, Transportation Systems Center, to provide engineering analytical, and planning support services for ground transport systems. Value approximately $950 000.

Rail modernisation planning for the Urban Mass Transportation Administration to identify the methods currently used by the US rapid rail industry for planning capital project improvements and develop analytical techniques which may be applied to the project planning and selection process. Value approximately $100 000.

Edwards and Kelcey
Edwards and Kelcey Inc
Edwards and Kelsey Engineers, Inc

Central office: 70 South Orange Avenue, Livingston, New Jersey 07039, USA

Telephone: (201) 994 4520
Telex: 138807

Regional offices
286 Congress Street, Boston, Massachusetts 02210
Telephone: (617) 542 4576

4930 West 77th Street, Minneapolis, Minnesota 55435
Telephone: (612) 835 6411

53 Park Place, New York, New York 10007
Telephone: (212) 619 5300

325 Chestnut Street, Philadelphia, Pennsylvania 19106
Telephone: (215) 922 5413

Washington Building, Suite 434, 15th Street and New York Avenue NW, Washington DC 20005
Telephone: (202) 638 0010

120 South Riverside Plaza, Chicago, Illinois 60606
Telephone: (312) 876 0784

16510 Northchase Street, Suite 110, Houston, Texas 77060
Telephone: (713) 447 1776

Subsidiary: Wyer, Dick & Co
70 South Orange Avenue, Livingston, New Jersey 07039
Telephone: (201) 994 3494

120 South Riverside Plaza, Chicago, Illinois 60606
Telephone: (312) 876 0784

16510 Northchase Street, Suite 110, Houston, Texas 77060
Telephone: (713) 447 1776

Capabilities
Rail planning and design; vehicle and maintenance facilities; rail transit and commuter operations and facilities.

Projects
Planning, environmental studies, evaluations, operations, management, design and construction management for railways, terminals, tunnels and bridges.

Electrack Inc

6525 Belcrest Road, Hyattsville, Maryland 20872, USA

Telephone: (301) 779 6868

Vice President: Kenneth W Addison

Capabilities
Rail electrification cost and technical feasibility studies; traction power, substation, catenary and structures design; construction; management.

Projects
Northeast Corridor Improvement Project: design and management of substations and catenary improvements for 240 km/h (150 mph) operation from Washington DC to Boston, Massachusetts, for Federal Railroad Administration, value $25 million.

Missouri-Kansas-Texas Railroad: design, engineering and programme management of electrification of 520 route-km (325 route miles), value $7.7 million.

Rehabilitation design for railroad bridge on Interstate Highway I-97 for State of Maryland, value $188 000.

Power augmentation study, specifications and procurement assistance for Southeastern Pennsylvania Transportation Authority (SEPTA), value $48 900.

Design and specifications for repair of frequency converter, for SEPTA, value $85 600.

Elrail
Elrail Consultants Pty Ltd

67 St Pauls Terrace, Brisbane, Queensland 4000, Australia

Telephone: 07 229 4950
Telex: 42238

Capabilities
Consultant engineers.

Ensco Inc

2560 Huntington Avenue, Alexandria, Virginia 22303, USA

Telephone: (703) 960 8500

Chief Scientist: Ta-Lun Yang

Capabilities
Track geometry and rail flaw inspection; dynamic test and evaluation of vehicles; diagnostic test and analysis of track and vehicle problems; catenary/pantograph test and inspection.

Envirodyne Engineers Inc

222 West Adams Street, Chicago, Illinois 60606, USA

Telephone: (312) 263 0114

Senior Vice President: Marshall Suloway
Vice Presidents: Charles F May
Edward D Ripple

Projects
Design for rail transit car storage yard and maintenance facility in Chicago ($43 million); rehabilitation design for rail stations on the New Jersey Transit system ($8 million); study of St Louis Gateway railyard consolidations ($400 million); new station design for Miami-Dade County system ($6 million).

W A Fairhurst & Partners

Cragside House, Heaton Road, Newcastle upon Tyne NE6 1SN, England

Telephone: 0632 657112
Telex: 53440

Projects
Fairhurst has been responsible to the Tyne and Wear Passenger Transport Executive for the following projects which are part of the Tyne and Wear Metro: 350-metre long steel truss bridge across the Tyne between Newcastle and Gateshead; installation of overhead line equipment throughout the 56 km length of Metro, including design of all structural elements, procurement of components and supervision of installation; design of the depot for all equipment installed in the Metro; inspection of 40 existing bridges that cross or carry the Metro together with design and contract supervision where necessary.

Fairhurst were engineers and project managers for construction of a rail spur and sidings integrated with the stockyard and loading areas of the new £26 million steel fabricating plant of Cleveland Bridge & Engineering Co Ltd at Darlington, England.

Fleming Corp

400 Olive Street, St Louis, Missouri 63102, USA

Telephone: (314) 241 9550

President: Charles Fleming

Capabilities
Station design and transport planning.

Fluor Australia Pty Limited

616 St Kilda Road, Melbourne, Victoria 3004, Australia

Telephone: (61 3) 520 444
Telex: 30062

Associated companies
Fluor Engineers, Fluor Constructors, Fluor Mining & Metals, Fluor Ocean Services, Fluor Power Services, Fluor Drilling Services, Fluor Oil and Gas, Daniel International Corporation, Civil Mechanical Maintenance Pty Limited, Pilbara Industries Pty Ltd.

Managing Director: J C Melbourne
Manager, Railway Division: N W Prince

Capabilities
Feasibility and operational studies; financial planning; engineering; procurement; construction and project management for railway or integrated multi-discipline projects. Capabilities cover general and heavy haul trackwork, earthworks, structures, electrification, rail grinding, flaw detection, track geometry measurement.

Associated companies offer railway construction and maintenance services.

Projects

Upgrading and maintenance (including rail profile grinding and track renewal with concrete sleepers) using Matisa P811: Hamersley Iron Railway from Paraburdoo to Dampier, Western Australia.

Design and construction management: rail extension Elura, New South Wales for EZ Industries Limited.

Construction management: rail extension and upgrading for Newlands coal project, Queensland, for MIM Holding Limited.

Ford, Bacon & Davis

2 Broadway, New York, New York 10004, USA

Telephone: (212) 344 3200

Manager: C N Peterman

Projects

Appraisal of property belonging to Chicago, Rock Island and Pacific Railroad; assisting the Federal Railroad Administration with review and approval of certificates for improvements of acquired railroads; development of a manual on panic control for the New York City Transit Authority.

Foster Engineering, Inc

847 Howard Street, San Francisco, California 94103, USA

Telephone: (415) 543 1193

President: H A Foster

Projects

Design, management, construction administration for various rail transit projects for Bay Area Rapid Transit District (BART), City of San Francisco Municipal Railway, and Niagara Frontier Transportation Authority, Buffalo, New York.

Freeman Fox & Partners

25 Victoria Street (South Block), Westminster, London SW1H 0EX, England

Telephone: 01-222 8050
Telegrams: Traction, London SW1
Telex: 916018

Partners: J T Edwards
W T F Austin
B P Wex
W C Brown
M F Parsons
D A Meyers
D R Wolstenholme
C W Brown

Consultants: Sir Ralph Freeman
O A Kerensky
C D Crosthwaite
Anthony Bull
J C A Roseveare

Transportation Engineer: G W Wallwork
Railway Engineer: A J S Blanchfield

Associated companies (in respect of railway work)

Freeman Fox & Partners (Far East), 42-46 Gloucester Road, Hong Kong

Telephone: 5-272127
Telex: 73868

Partners: J T Edwards
B P Wex
D A Meyers
J Webb
R A Chaning Pearce

Freeman Fox International Ltd, 42-46 Gloucester Road, Hong Kong

Telephone: 5-272127
Telex: 73868

Directors: J T Edwards
B P Wex
M F Parsons
D R Wolstenholme
J F Webb
W K Chan
R A Chaning Pearce
D G Morton
R L Taylor

Halcrow Fox & Associates (see below)

Directors: F A Sharman
J O Tresidder
D S Kennedy
B K Hartshorne
T M Ridley
J T Edwards
A N Muir Wood
D A Meyers

Capabilities

Freeman Fox & Partners was founded in 1857 by Sir Charles Fox who, with his two sons, quickly established an international consultancy primarily concerned with railway work in the UK, including the Great Central and Liverpool Overhead Railways, and the Charing Cross to Hampstead and Highgate sections of London Transport's Northern Line, and overseas, including North and South America and especially Southern Africa. The association with South African, Rhodesian (Zimbabwean) and Benguela railways has continued until recent times.

Although the firm's activities have diversified into other fields such as long-span bridges, highways, power stations (hydro and thermal) it has remained involved in railways. Since 1964 regional and urban planning studies have been made by the firm's transport section, now Halcrow Fox & Associates. Freeman Fox & Partners was the principal consultant for the Hong Kong Mass Transit Railway (on which work is continuing) and is also a principal member firm of the British Metro Consultants Group for the Baghdad Metro and the lead firm for British Mass Transit Consultants for the Taipei Metro (see below). The firm is also part of a team engaged on a light railway study for Valencia, Venezuela.

Projects

Principal railway projects currently in hand or undertaken since 1972 are:
Baghdad Metro: Freeman Fox & Partners is a principal member of the British Metro Consultants Group (a consortium of British consultants) retained by the Baghdad Rapid Transit Authority for planning and supervision of design and construction of the Baghdad Metro. The Group's work covers all civil engineering, architecture, electrical and mechanical engineering, and it will advise on training programmes and implementation procedures. The first stage comprises two lines totalling 32 km with 38 stations, depots and workshops. Operational trials are planned for 1985. The Group's appointment extends until 1989 by which time the whole of Stage 1 is due to be in operation.
Taipei Metro: Freeman Fox & Partners is the leading firm in British Mass Transit Consultants (BMTC) retained by the Ministry of Communications in Taiwan. BMTC is completing a detailed and comprehensive study of the technical, economic and financial feasibility of the proposed system and is determining the priority line. By 2000 the system is intended to consist of four lines with a railway bypass line for freight.
Hong Kong Mass Transit Railway: The firm's work on this system began in 1966 with the Hong Kong Transport Study and continued uninterrupted through the planning and construction stages of the Initial System (Kong Kaw and Kwung Tong lines) and the Tsuen Wan extension completed in 1982. Currently the firm is working on the elevated section including station design of the Island Line that is to connect with the Kong Kaw line at Admiralty station.

Gannett Fleming

PO Box 1963, Harrisburg, Pennsylvania 17105, USA

Telephone: (717) 763 7211

Chief, Mass Transit: Robert J Dietz

Capabilities

Transport systems analysis and planning; feasibility studies and preliminary designs for light rail, rapid rail and commuter rail; design of maintenance facilities; comprehensive construction management.

Projects

Final design and construction services for Lindenwold line (PATCO) expansion programme ($35 million), Buffalo, New York; Light Rail Rapid Transit System ($60 million), and rail maintenance facilities ($12 and $10 million) for Chicago Transit Authority, Chicago, Illinois, and Southeastern Pennsylvania Transportation Authority, Philadelphia, Pennsylvania; Detroit regional transit alternatives analysis ($1.6 million) for Southeastern Michigan Transportation Authority (SEMTA); feasibility and preliminary engineering for DPM systems ($90 and $80 million) for Georgia Department of Transportation (DOT) and SEMTA; economic and transportation feasibility study ($125 000) for the City of Norfolk, Virginia; Phase 1 preliminary engineering and design ($1 million) for the Miami Downtown People Mover for the Metropolitan Dade County, Florida; construction management for re-electrification and rehabilitation of the Erie-Lackawanna Railroad ($220 million) for the New Jersey DOT.

GEC Transportation Projects Ltd

45 Victoria Street, St Albans, Hertfordshire AL1 3UG, England

Telephone: 0727 33181
Telex: 298782

Managing Director: Harry Kline
Projects Director: Eric Dalgleish
Marketing Director: Jim Cohen
Technical Director: Eric Riches
Commercial Director: Brian Snow
Financial Director: Colin Drewett

Capabilities

Main contractors, project managers and system engineers for composite mainline, suburban, metro and mass transit railway systems.

Projects

Projects in hand under the company's design and management totalling some 2350 track-km:

Iranian State Railways: During 1975 a protocol agreement signed on behalf of the Governments of the United Kingdom and Iran affirmed that contracts for the electrical and mechanical work necessary for a high-speed railway would be negotiated with GEC-TPL for approximately 1000 km of main line between Tehran and Tabriz. GEC-TPL was closely involved in the preliminary design in conjunction with British Rail which, through its subsidiary Transmark, received the preliminary design contract under the protocol.

Federal Railways of Brazil (RFFSA), Steel Railway: GEC-TPL signed a contract in November 1976 as main contractor for the provision of electrification, telecommunications, signalling and locomotive equipment operating at 25 kV ac for the Federal Railways of Brazil. As well as system design responsibility, the contract includes the supply of equipment and services for the rail links between the iron ore centre of Belo Horizonte and the major steel complex at Volta Redonda, a distance of some 400 route-km, and the port of Sepetiba near Rio de Janeiro. When completed, the new rail link will carry quadruple-headed trains of up to 15 000 tons at speeds of up to 60 km/h. It is expected to transport 50 million tons of iron ore each year initially and later 100 million tons from Belo Horizonte and Jeceaba to Volta Redonda. The route will also provide limited passenger services.

National Railways of Zimbabwe: In 1981 GEC-TPL was awarded a contract by the National Railways of Zimbabwe to provide project management services for its first 25 kV ac major railway electrification project, the 300 route-km (350 track-km) between Harare and Gweru, which is its most heavily used freight and passenger line. The services include planning and co-ordination, technical studies and financial management. GEC companies are supplying substations and telecommunications equipment.

Ministry of Communications and Transport, Mexico: GEC-TPL was awarded a contract in 1981, in conjunction with a leading Mexican company, for project management services on behalf of the Ministry to supervise the engineering co-ordination and integration, planning and programming, and installation of equipment for Mexico's first 25 kV ac main-line electrification project. This comprises 250 route-km (500 track-km) between Mexico City and Queretaro, with suppliers from Italy, USA and Japan appointed by the client.

Seoul Metropolitan Subway Corporation: In April 1982 GEC-TPL was awarded a major contract for Lines 3 and 4 of the Seoul Metro covering some 57 route-km (129 track-km) to be electrified at 1.5 kV dc. GEC-TPL is responsible as main contractor for the supply of rolling stock (402 cars), yards and workshops equipment, track maintenance equipment and track materials, and also as managing contractor for total management and system engineering services for the integration of all the principal mechanical and electrical equipment on Lines 3 and 4. GEC Traction is supplying the main electrical equipment and control systems for the cars with Daewoo Heavy Industries of South Korea building and assembling the cars. The total combined length of the lines involves 35 passenger stations and two car yards, with the supply of the fixed systems from the USA. Project completion is scheduled for the end of 1984.

Empresa Brasileira do Transportes Urbanos (EBTU), Recife Metropolitan trains: In April 1982 GEC-TPL, in conjunction with a Brazilian consortium, signed a contract for the design and supply of equipment for the Recife Metropolitan Suburban Railway, to be electrified at 3 kV dc over a route length of 23 km (47 track-km). This includes responsibility for the design and supply of the fixed systems including substations, overhead catenary, telecommunications and signalling systems, while under a separate contract GEC Traction is supplying propulsion equipment to a Brazilian coach builder.

West Midlands County Council, Birmingham Airport UK (Maglev): GEC-TPL is acting as project managers and system engineers for a project to build the first revenue-earning magnetic levitation peoplemover system at Birmingham Airport. This project will provide an efficient and low operating-cost passenger link between the airport terminal, main-line railway station and the National Exhibition Centre at Birmingham.

Gellman Research Associates Inc

100 West Avenue, Jenkintown, Pennsylvania 19046, USA

Telephone: (215) 884 7500

President: Aaron J Gellman
Vice-President: Joseph J Schmidt
Associates: W Bruce Allen
Joseph E Phillips

Capabilities

Financial planning; rate negotiations; economics of railroad loss and damage indemnification; asset valuation analysis; preparation and presentation of expert testimony; rehabilitation and acquisition financing; asset disposition; forecasting; traffic analysis and costing; reorganisation economics; car ownership decision problems; revenue division analysis.

Projects

Recent GRA rail projects have included:

Financial analysis and rail regulation studies in connection with the Northeast rail crisis; analysis of USRA's Preliminary System Plan (PSP) and Final System Plan (FSP); analysis of PSP and FSP projections of inflation rates, traffic levels, and car utilisation; consultation in connection with the Regional Rail Reorganization Act of 1973 (3R Act) and the Railroad Revitalization and Regulatory Reform Act of 1976 (4R Act); planning and developing of rail service for a major new coal mine; valuation of a railcar fleet for the National Railway Utilization Corporation; preparation of a major feasibility study on selling loss and damage indemnification as a separate and distinct rail service; preparation of a case study of the Norfolk & Western-Wabash-Nickel Plate merger; estimation of the competitive advantage to be realised by prospective acquirers of the Detroit, Toledo & Ironton Railroad; preparation and presentation of testimony on behalf of the trustees of the Erie Lackawanna and Lehigh Valley Railroads; evaluation of Milwaukee Road restructure plan for Interstate Commerce Commission; studies of passenger/commuter operations for New Jersey Department of Transportation; analysis of shipper benefits from Automatic Car Identification

systems; feasibility study of Philadelphia-Pittsburgh corridor TOFC service for Pennsylvania Department of Commerce; for the Interstate Commerce Commission, estimated transit time efficiencies of run-through train service against regular multi-carrier interchange routes between similar points; analysis of relative costs and revenues of interchange traffic at a particular gateway; analysis in detail of the economic and traffic characteristics of the New England railroads for four alternative corporate alignments; estimation of cost savings and traffic statistics that would result from construction of a new rail freight tunnel under the Hudson river.

Gibbs & Hill Inc

11 Penn Plaza, New York, New York 10001, USA

Telephone: (212) 760 4725
Telegrams: Gibbshill, New York
Telex: 127636; 234475

Branch and subsidiary offices

Gibbs & Hill Inc, 8420 West Dodge Road, Omaha, Nebraska 68114
Telephone: (402) 391 0330 Telex: 9106220294

Gibbs & Hill Inc, 226 West Brokaw Road, San Jose, California 95110
Telephone: (408) 280 7091

Gibbs & Hill Inc, 5501 LBJ Freeway, Dallas, Texas 75240
Telephone: (214) 934 6600

Gibbs & Hill Inc, 1250 19th Street NW, Washington DC 20036
Telephone: (202) 785 1901

Gibbs & Hill Española, SA, Magallanes, 3 Planta 9, Madrid 15, Spain
Telephone: 447 2800 Telegrams: Gandhesa, Madrid

GIBSIN Engineers Limited, 710 Chia-hsi, Second Building, 96 Chung Shan North Road, Section 2, Taipei, Taiwan
Telephone: 531-4250 Telegrams: Gibsin, Taipei, Taiwan
Telex: 785 26350

Parent company

Dravo Corporation, One Oliver Plaza, Pittsburgh, Pennsylvania

Chairman of the Board: Alexander Matiuk
President and Chief Executive Officer: Roy H Gordon
Senior Vice Presidents: Frank Hutchinson
K L Scheppele
Vice Presidents
 Power: H R Rock
 Power: F W Gettler
 Planning and Development, Domestic and International: Marvin S Blair
 Consulting Engineering: P P DeRienzo
 Transportation and Transmission Division: F L Gilman
 Arch/Urban Development Division: R W Yokom
 Manager (Dallas): S J Weston
 Manager (San Jose): Peter Cartwright
Managing Director (Madrid): R Safier
Vice President (Far East): S M Loo
Senior Vice President, Corporate Operations: R Breach
Vice President, Finance: N G Fornella

Capabilities

Gibbs & Hill was founded in 1911 to provide engineering and design services for the then new field of railway electrification. The company has designed the electrification systems for over 70 per cent of all ac rail systems in the United States. Following incorporation in 1923, the firm began diversifying into a number of related fields, including power engineering, now the major source of company business.

In 1965, Gibbs & Hill became a wholly owned subsidiary of Dravo Corporation, expanding the capabilities of both companies.

Overall, the company has a staff of more than 3300 professional and support personnel, providing a variety of vital services.

The Transportation and Transmission Division operates as an integrated group with a permanent technical staff of over 100, together with all necessary supporting personnel. Assignments in the transport field have comprised: engineering and economic feasibility reports; system planning studies; alternative transportation mode studies (bus, rail, private car); preliminary design and cost estimates; environmental impact studies and reports; preparation of project loan applications; site and right-of-way investigations; comprehensive investigations and appraisals of available hardware and rolling stock. Additionally, actual detailed engineering and design services have been furnished for: railroad and rapid transit electrification, including traction power supply and transmission facilities, substations, and overhead catenary or third-rail distribution systems; signalling and train control; communications; automation; operations analysis and computer simulation; shops, yards and terminals; waste treatment and disposal facilities; steam generation; and all ancillary and supporting facilities.

Projects

Texas Utilities Services, Inc, Dallas, Texas: Engineering and design services for a complete 25 kV, 60 Hz catenary-type distribution system including several configurations of wood and steel supporting structures, together with all necessary catenary arrangements, insulator assemblies and hardware. This system has been developed for the electrification of two lignite haulage railroads in eastern Texas.

Port Authority of Allegheny County, Pittsburgh, Pennsylvania: General architectural and engineering services for design of all facilities required for implementation of the Authority's Transportation Implementation Programme, Stage I—Light Rail Transit System: system description; overall system requirements; passenger vehicles; right-of-way and support structures; switches and transfer mechanisms; platforms and stations; maintenance, storage, and shop and yard areas; control system; communications system; traction power and distribution system; maintenance provisions.

Gibbs & Hill's participation will be principally with respect to system definition, electrification, traction power, signals and train control, communications, and value capture analysis. Work performed in joint venture with Parsons, Brinckerhoff, Quade & Douglas.

New Jersey Department of Transportation, Trenton, New Jersey: A major project comprising the comprehensive physical rehabilitation and electrification of the New York and Long Branch Railroad between South Amboy and Red Bank, a distance of about 15 miles (24 km), Gibbs & Hill's portion of the work includes the design of all electrification facilities, as well as all signals, communications and controls. The work is being done under subcontract to Edwards & Kelcey.

Engineering and design services for a major modernisation and rehabilitation programme of the Erie-Lackawanna Railway, an important link in the New York suburban area commuter network. The project includes the following assignments: conversion of the existing 3 kV dc traction power system to 25 kV 60 Hz; rehabilitation and reconstruction, where necessary, of 58 route miles (92.8 km) of overhead catenary system; extension of electrification system from Dover to Netcong, a distance of 10 route miles (16 km); modifications to signal and communication systems to ensure compatibility with the ac traction power system; modification of existing heavy repair shops to accommodate new self-propelled rolling stock; provision of substantial additions to car storage facilities; siting and architectural design of three new passenger stations; all necessary related modifications to existing facilities, auxiliary apparatus and systems.

Maryland Mass Transit Administration, Baltimore, Maryland: Engineering services as electric utility rate consultant to the Administration in connection with the Baltimore Subway Project. Gibbs & Hill is performing research, analysing and preparing data and presentation materials for a power rate schedule to be used by the Administration in its negotiations with the local utility company.

Metropolitan Transportation Authority, New York: Engineering services for studies, design and supervision of construction in connection with the $200 million plus rehabilitation programme of the Long Island Rail Road which has the highest density commuter traffic of any railroad in the world. The plan involves extension of the electrification system, purchase of new rolling stock, design of 60 new traction-power substations, new central supervisory control system, increase of wayside electric traction system to permit train operation at speeds of up to 100 mph (160 km/h), improved track alignment, and potential connections with New York City's rapid transit systems. New electrification facilities, including substations, will be required for 46.2 additional track miles (74.4 km). This work performed by Parsons, Brinckerhoff-Gibbs & Hill, with Gibbs & Hill responsible for all electrical engineering.

Washington Metropolitan Area Transit Authority (WMATA), Washington DC: Engineering and design of automatic computerised train control, signal, and communications system for the fully automated transit system of Washington DC.

Conrail, Philadelphia, Pennsylvania: Engineering services to evaluate the technical and economic feasibility of providing electrified freight service from Pittsburgh (Conway) to the Eastern markets between Alexandria, Virginia (Potomac Yard) and Newark, New Jersey, and to estimate the improvements which can be achieved by improving the existing signalling and communication system are being studied. The study is especially complex in that it entails the evaluation of both presently electrified and non-electrified rail lines totalling more than 615 route miles. Both commercial frequency and 11 kV 25 Hz systems require study. A complete operations analysis is being performed to arrive at representative train consists and schedules for all route segments. Optimum diesel and electric locomotive sizes are developed along with fleet size, fleet management and dispatching policy, power change points and maintenance shop locations. Energy requirements for both modes are defined. Track lines, sidings, yards, spurs, etc, were evaluated to assess adequacy for future traffic projections. Maintenance costs for each mode of operation are detailed.

Greiner Engineering Sciences Inc

Principal offices: PO Box 23646, Tampa, Florida 33623, USA

Telephone: (813) 879 1711

Senior Vice-President: N William Bryan

One Village Square, Baltimore, Maryland 21210

Telephone: (301) 323 8100

Vice-President: Charles B Mudd

Projects
North Shore Rapid Transit studies and design ($100 million) for Massachusetts Bay Transportation Authority—Phase 1; environmental analysis for North Shore Rapid Transit improvements ($250 million)—Phase II; Northeast Corridor railroad line study and design, including Niantic River Bridge, for Federal Railroad Administration ($5 million); subconsultant on two additional line sections of the Northeast Corridor railroad system; design of a 3-mile elevated line section for the Dade County Rapid Transit System; design and construction inspection for a 2160-metre-long line section of the Washington Metro; design, environmental studies and construction inspection for the award-winning Florida East Coast Railway movable-span bridge over New River in Ft Lauderdale.

Gutteridge Haskins & Davey Pty Ltd

Principal offices: 20 Young Street, Sydney, Neutral Bay, New South Wales 2089, Australia

Telephone: (02) 9082399
Telex: 25648

97 Franklin Street, Melbourne, Victoria 3000

Telephone: (03) 665 0222
Telex: 33262

87 Wickham Terrace, Brisbane, Queensland 4000

Telephone: (07) 2217955
Telex: 41276

Projects: See below.

Halcrow Fox and Associates

97-99 Borough High Street, London SE1 1LX, England

Telephone: 01-403 2933

Managing Director: J O Tresidder

Capabilities
Feasibility studies; metro and LRT planning.

Hamburg-Consult
Gesellschaft für Verkehrsberatung und Verfahrenstechniken mbH

Steinstrasse 20, 2000 Hamburg 1, Federal Republic of Germany

Telephone: (040) 32104 2131
Telegrams: Hochbahn hc
Telex: 02-162 277

Parent company: Hamburger Hochbahn Aktiengesellschaft (Hamburg Public Transport Company)

Managing Directors: Josef Hoffstadt
Fritz Pampel
Martin Runkel
Peter Kirchhoff (Deputy)
Vice Directors: Peter Lenke
Arnold Mies

Gutteridge Haskins & Davey projects

Project	Client	Value	Description
New Elaroo Cane Tramway	Proserpine Co-operative Sugar Milling Association	$6 million	Feasibility study for route selection, design standards, costing and full project management for 30 km of sugar cane tramway; project includes 2 major and 6 minor bridges
Abbot Point coal export terminal	MIMETS Development Pty Ltd	Stage 1: $57 million	Design of onshore facilities including 15 km rail spur, balloon loop and unloading station
Queensland main line electrification	Queensland Railways	$183 million	Gladstone—Blackwater, Blackwater—Emerald (680 km), project management; Brisbane—Gladstone (660 km), civil, track and structures concept design
Antiene—Drayton spur	The Shell Co of Australia Ltd Thiess Bros Pty Ltd Electricity Commission of NSW	$9 million	Feasibility study, survey, detail design and supervision of 9.5 km spur line and balloon loop serving Drayton open-cut coal mine; project includes major overpass over New England Highway
Mount Thorley Junction—BBC Colliery	Wambo Mining Corporation Pty Ltd United Mining Pty Ltd Buchanan Borehole Collieries Pty Ltd	Report	Transport and environmental study of proposed 23 km common user rail spur with 2 or 3 balloon loops; project includes major crossing of Hunter River near Singleton
Dartbrook Mine transportation study	Bellambi Coal Company Pty Ltd	Report	Detailed pre-feasibility study of coal transport options for proposed Upper Hunter open-cut mine. Detail design of 3 km balloon loop
Electrification of Illawarra Railway, NSW	State Rail Authority, NSW	$100 million	Project management and design of 53 km of double track main-line electrification
Ravensworth Colliery railway works	Elcom Collieries Pty Ltd	$2 million	Project management of coal loading facility and 3 km balloon loop; including design
Bridge over North Coast Railway at Rossglen, NSW	Department of Main Roads, NSW	$302 000	Design of concrete underpass at a difficult skew under Pacific Highway, NSW; replaces timber structure
Railway bridge over Parkes Street, Parramatta, NSW	State Rail Authority, NSW	$170 000	Design of overpass, part of quadruplication of Main Western Line

Capabilities

Hamburg-Consult is a subsidiary of the public transport company, the Hamburger Hochbahn, and works in close connection with the management of the parent company as well as other affiliated local railroad companies.

Activities comprise consultancy services and advice in all fields of public short-distance transport systems: electric suburban railways, underground railways (RTS), modern light railways and streetcars, unconventional public transport (such as automated cabin taxis and monorails), bus and ferry services.

Projects

Helsinki Metro (1970-83): Preparation of basic technical and economic principles for rolling stock and operations: investigations into rolling stock/route layout systems up to and including the draft timetable using an analogue data processing unit: basic planning principles for operational layouts, tracks and stations as well as workshops and sidings; management techniques for operations and operating control, models for decentralised and centralised operating control and for automatic operations; technical components of the automation system, continuous train-running control equipment, passenger information, passenger handling and ticket machines; results of automatic trial operations; suggestions for draft tender specifications; recommendations for track current supply and live rail feed control; expert opinion on trial driving car, preparation of tender specifications for purchasing rolling stock in series production. Planning of the subway workshop; expert opinion on a test motor train unit; functional and economical proving of the capacity of the track configuration of two stations.

Other rapid transit studies: Radiotelephone system for West Berlin in conjunction with AEG-Telefunken; planning Dusseldorf U-Bahn; optimum routing for Munich tunnel sections; construction advice on Vienna and Baghdad metros; wheel rail investigations for Lisbon metro; fire investigations on the rubber-tyred Montreal metro; transit system reliability study for Denver, Colorado, USA; several investigations of rail transit operation without personnel; automatic train operation by data processing techniques; development of the failure monitoring system BEFUND to detect and evaluate vehicle defects and to store failure data (the system is controlled by a microprocessor and data from this unit are transmitted to an operational central control); investigations of an integrated transport system rail transit-taxi (INTAX); investigations of subway vehicles with small profile and of different sizes; checking signalling project for the Bielefeld municipal railway; feasibility study for small profile train in Karlsruhe; specification for an international tender on subway vehicles for Athens metro; investigation of means to benefit from co-efficient of adhesion with dc and three-phase current propulsion; studies of reliability and maintenance of modern metro vehicles.

Delon Hampton & Associates

6001 Montrose Road, Rockville, Maryland 20852, USA

Telephone: (301) 984 8833

President: Delon Hampton

Projects

Design of catenary support structures for a 274 km (170-mile) section of the Northeast Corridor Improvement Project (NECIP); sub-consultant for design of Section E-7a of the Washington Metropolitan Area Transit Authority's heavy rail transit system; prime consultant for design of Amtrak's Ivy City yard and shop; joint venture designing the F3 section of the Washington Metro; construction inspection for two sections of the O'Hare Airport rail transit extension for the Chicago Transit Authority.

Harbridge House, Inc

11 Arlington Street, Boston, Massachusetts 02116, USA

Telephone: (617) 267 6410

Chairman: Charles D Baker
President: George J Rabstejnek

Subsidiary: Development Science Services, Inc

Offices: Boston, New York, Washington DC, Chicago, Northbrook, London, Frankfurt am Main

Capabilities

Management consulting, education, and research; specialising in transport, financial services, and economic analysis.

Projects

Recent projects have included:
Boston & Maine Railroad study: For the Massachusetts Port Authority, and in co-operation with the Massachusetts Bay Transit Authority, the Commonwealth of Massachusetts Office of Transportation and Construction, and the New England Regional Commission, Harbridge House developed and analysed alternative viability plans for the Boston & Maine Railroad. Topics covered were: provision for substantial commuter traffic; the financial feasibility of the freight system; a physical freight-flow model; a right-of-way valuation; methods for improving the efficiency of operations; and pertinent labour-management questions.
New England regional rail study: Subsequent to the Boston & Maine rail study, Harbridge House was selected by the New England Regional Commission (NERC) to conduct a comprehensive study of all the New England railroads. The study was designed to: identify, define, and assess the socio-economic and

environmental importance of various levels of rail service to the New England region; evaluate the economic viability of the various New England railroads and major segments thereof; analyse various possible alternative physical and institutional configurations of the New England rail system; and provide an analytic methodology which will be available to public decision-makers on a continuing basis. Basic research incorporated data findings on revenue, freight flow and capacity, and configuration of the New England rail system.
Wisconsin State rail plan: For the Wisconsin Department of Transportation, Harbridge House has engaged in a large-scale effort to develop and implement a comprehensive rail plan. The plan covers both freight and passenger (intercity and commuter) services. Harbridge House collected and analysed data in various categories, including costs and revenues of existing services, developed demand forecasts, performed economic and operational analysis, identified alternatives to existing rail operations, and determined the relative costs and benefits of these alternatives.
Amtrak planning and consulting: For Amtrak, Harbridge House has provided business planning assistance, focusing on the national climate and competitive environment facing the client. Planning objectives included: defining the role of Amtrak within the US transport system as a whole; evaluating its performance to date; defining its objectives, and strategies for achieving them; and anticipating potential opportunities and risks, and planning appropriate responses.
Study of rail passenger service: For the US Railway Association (USRA), Harbridge House conducted a study of rail passenger service in the north-east and mid-west regions of the United States. The research effort for this study included:
A survey of existing rail passenger service in terms of scope (routes, stops, frequency, and passenger traffic) and quality (condition of track and facilities, and passenger satisfaction);
Identification of potential additional passenger rail services. This has involved review of Amtrak and Department of Transportation plans, ICC hearings on rail service, and plans of state and local transportation planning bodies, including evaluation of demand forecasting methodologies;
Identification of passenger rail services which would be considered by USRA in its plan to restructure rail service in the regions;
Identification of potential interfaces between desirable levels of passenger service and the overall rail system in the regions.
Northeast Corridor project study: For the Office of Policy and Planning of the US Department of Transportation, Harbridge House conducted an evaluation of passenger demand forecasts for the proposed Northeast Corridor (NEC) improved high-speed rail (IHSR) system;
Study of high-speed rail impact on other transport modes: For the US Department of Transportation, Transportation Systems Center, Harbridge House analysed selected impacts of high-speed passenger rail service (HSRS) legislation on alternative transport modes (specifically, auto, air, and bus in the Northeast Corridor.
Training programme in joint labour-management problem solving: For the US Federal Mediation and Conciliation Service, Harbridge House developed and conducted a two-day training programme designed to help labour-management committees in the railroad industry to develop the key skills necessary for resolving problems of common interest and concern. The programme is based on recently developed techniques for problem analysis, negotiation, and conflict resolution.
BN senior management needs assessment: For Burlington Northern, Inc (BNI), Harbridge House interviewed 50 senior level and mid-level BNI executives to assess the development needs of the company's senior managers in relation to changing expectations for their performance. The interviews served to identify the changing strategic directions of the company and managers' reactions to those changes, emerging success profiles for senior managers of the future (including accountabilities, skills, and activities), and educational/developmental needs. As a result of the needs analysis, Harbridge House provided recommendations for specific developmental activities and developed detailed curricula for educational programmes for two levels of management.
Study of market demand for rail freight facility: For New York State Urban Development Corporation and the New York City Office of Economic Development, Harbridge House conducted a study of the market demand for a rail freight facility at a 60th Street yard. The primary focus of the study was to assess the potential demand for intermodal (TOFC/COFC) rail services at 60th Street. This involved the identification of intercity traffic flow throughout the New York City metropolitan area as well as a geographic and modal breakdown of traffic. It also involved the conduct of direct interviews with and mail surveys of shippers for the purpose of identifying the shipping activities and practices of firms in areas likely to use a 60th Street facility. Based on the survey/interview findings, forecasts of future intercity traffic demand and future TOFC/COFC traffic volumes were developed as alternative scenarios. An assessment of the design and operating considerations for a 60th Street TOFC site was also included, as well as an evaluation of the economic impact and key marketing considerations.
Transcontinental freight shipment analysis: For a Washington DC law firm and in support of the cross-examination of expert witnesses appearing on behalf of the proposed Missouri Pacific-Union Pacific merger, Harbridge House prepared analyses of impacts of the economic and strategic position of transcontinental markets in selected key materials, notably coal and trona (soda ash).

Harza Engineering Company

150 South Wacker Drive, Chicago, Illinois 60606, USA

Telephone: (312) 855 7000

Vice-President: Ramon S La Russo

Projects

Buffalo, New York: Amherst station on the Buffalo light rail transit system for Niagara Frontier Transportation Authority.
Washington DC: Section A-6 Rockville route, two miles rock tunnels and three stations ($100 million) for WMATA metro.
Buffalo LRT system: construction cost $9 million.

Station on Shady Grove route A-6 of Washington Metro, designed by Harza

Harza design for Amherst station of Buffalo LRT system

Hawker Siddeley Rail Projects Ltd

Bishop Meadow Road, Loughborough, Leicestershire LE11 0RF, England

Telephone: 0509 36201
Telex: 341925

Chairman: T W B Sallitt
Deputy Chairman: E J Harris
Managing Director: G S W Calder
Marketing Director: D R Speirs

Capabilities
Hawker Siddeley Rail Projects co-ordinates all the railway activities of the Hawker Siddeley group and markets and manages turnkey railway projects. The group includes such companies as Brush Electrical Machines, Brush Transformers, Hawker Siddeley Canada and Westinghouse Brake & Signal. The rail project company is controlled by directors of the various constituent railway-orientated companies. Services extend from advice and assistance in the preparation and presentation of a preliminary study, co-ordination of several contracts with individual Hawker Siddeley companies within a single contract, to management of complete turnkey railway projects, including provision of financial arrangements. Hawker Siddeley companies have experience of urban transport projects in London, Toronto, Hong Kong, New York and Boston.

The Henderson Busby Partnership

Cusick House, Church Street, Ware, Hertfordshire SG12 9EF, England

Telephone: 0920 3988
Telex: 817298

Directors: Andrew B Henderson
Robert H Busby
T H Rosbotham
C W H Hay
J T Smith
Divisional Directors: M K Czechowski
J H H Williams
B M Green
M G Howard
R Arnott
B H North
Consultants: D S Binnie
C F Carlton
D M S Fairweather
G A Hughes
J G Jackson
Dr D Maltby
D McClure-Fisher
Prof H P White
G A Wilmot
J F H Tyler
B J Parkinson

Capabilities
Henderson Busby, a completely independent firm of consulting engineers and economists, provides a complete range of services in connection with the management, operation, maintenance and engineering of railway systems. Founded in 1862, the firm has been involved in railway and other transport projects in 72 countries around the world. These include transport studies, economic investment and cost-benefit studies, feasibility studies, operating and management investigations, design services, construction supervision, planning, co-ordination and advisory services and inspection services.

Projects
The firm is undertaking a number of major railway projects in Iraq with a total capital value of well over £1000 million. One is the study, design and supervision of construction of a major new 250 km/h railway from Baghdad via Kut to Um Qasr. The feasibility study, which covered both the economic and engineering aspects, has been completed. The work involved an evaluation of alternative routes between Baghdad and Um Qasr with two main options along the Tigris and Euphrates valleys respectively. The design parameters were based on a high-speed railway (200-250 km/h) and axleloads of 20 to 24 tonnes. A full socio-economic study was carried out which took into account the regional development through which the railway would pass. The report evaluated the technical problems, which involved construction through difficult terrain, as well as a full economic study based on a cost benefit analysis. The traction and rolling stock requirements were considered in depth and the design allowed for intensive services and double-tracking within the confines of the urban areas. The scheme also involves multi-span bridges over the Tigris and Euphrates rivers as well as the Gharraf Canal.

In addition, the firm has been appointed as consultants to undertake similar work for a railway extension to Fao and from Mosul to Zakho, in both cases to the same high-speed standards. Henderson Busby has also been appointed to carry out the consultancy work associated with the second Basra station.

Henderson Busby was appointed as consultant by the Iraqi Republic Railways Organisation (IRRO) to carry out the project management and inspection of 175 locomotives and 4500 wagons for which IRRO has placed orders with builders in Poland, France, West Germany, Yugoslavia and Czechoslovakia.

The detailed design of a 200 km/h Jubail-Dammam main line railroad in Saudi Arabia has recently been completed by Henderson Busby. The capital value of the works will be over £800 million. The firm is responsible for the railway engineering, operating and economic and financial work being done as part of the feasibility study and engineering design. The firm surveyed the route, identified alternative alignments, forecast potential traffic, recommended outline operating procedures and estimated construction costs. Detailed design of the permanent way, stations, goods yards, workshops, signalling and telecommunications systems have been prepared in addition to detailed economic and financial assessments and a staff training scheme.

Henderson Busby is a member of the British Metro Consultants Group which was appointed as General Consultants to the Baghdad Rapid Transit Authority for the Baghdad Metro Project. BMCG is preparing the preliminary design of Phase I of the system and is responsible for the implementation of the detailed design works and construction contracts. Phase I, due to be completed by 1990, will comprise two lines with 36 stations with a total route length of 32 km. The Metro will serve the four corners of the urban area with a conventional underground rapid transit service operating six-car trains. The two lines interconnect at a central station located in the central business district of Baghdad.

In England, Henderson Busby is consultant to West Midlands County Council for Maglev, the magnetically-levitated peoplemover system between Birmingham Exhibition Centre and Birmingham Airport.

Henderson Busby acts as permanent advisor to Benguela Railway on all engineering and operational matters. It is responsible for preparing all technical specifications, drawings etc, for purchase of all equipment and has advised on locomotive and rolling stock design and purchases and on a new railway alignment 137 km long and monitored its construction.

Since 1885 Henderson Busby has been retained as consultants to the Antofagasta (Chile) & Bolivia Railway and continues to provide advice on all aspects of the railway's operation and inspects all their engineering purchases. Periodical visits are made to inspect the railway and to advise on future technical policy. For legal purposes a valuation of all assets has been made.

The company has completed phase one of a coal transport study for Mozambique. It is planned to extract 10 million tonnes of coal from the fields around Moatize in the inland province of Tete for export through the port of Beira, which is sited on an estuary and suffers from siltation and subsequent draught limitations which impose tidal delay to most ships. The existing route and methods of operation have been studied with a view to increasing the current axleload limit from 16 to 20 tons on the 1067 mm gauge. The route length between Moatize and Beira is 550 km and the line crosses the Zambesi river approximately midway between Moatize and Beira. Alternative routes have been studied with a particular view of utilising the excellent natural deep water port of Nacala. Phase 2, yet to be undertaken, will concentrate in detail on the recommended route.

Henderson Busby has carried out an initial review of the telecommunications network of the National Railways of Zimbabwe. A comparison of the costs of installing either a micro-wave or a cable system as the backbone of the telecommunications network has been made.

The company is reviewing the choice of vehicles and their associated systems for the London Docklands light transit system. During this review the firm will make an engineering reconnaissance of the route, determine the range of feasible costs, establish the essential characteristics required and identify suitable types of vehicles before preparing its recommendations.

Henningson, Durham and Richardson Inc

8404 Indian Hills Drive, Omaha, Nebraska 68114, USA

Telephone: (402) 399 1000

Executive Vice-President: Robert A Rohling

Capabilities
Rail rapid transit (line and station designs); terminal and transfer facilities design; light rail and peoplemover design; railroad structures design and inspection; railroad trackwork design and inspection; and construction administration services.

Projects
Plans and specifications for 2.6 km of line and one station ($25 million), for Metropolitan Atlanta Rapid Transit Authority (MARTA); plans and specifications, 4 km of line, and four stations ($30 million) for Washington Metropolitan Area Transit Authority (WMATA); plans and specification for 2.66 km of line, including a major aerial guideway for Dade County Rapid Transit System; selection by the Chicago & North Western and Union Pacific Railroads to be Engineer-of-Record and provide construction administration services for the upgrading and new construction associated with 160 km of spur connector in eastern Wyoming.

IBI Group

156 Front Street West, Toronto, Ontario M5J 2L6, Canada

Telephone: (416) 596 1930

Managing Director: N A Irwin

Projects
LRT systems design including stations, yards and shops, Calgary, Canada; automatic vehicle monitoring systems for the Toronto surface bus system and GO Transit commuter rail system, Toronto, Canada; automatic fare collection systems for GO Transit, Toronto, and Calgary LRT; railway relocation studies; commodity movement system studies.

Iffland Kavanagh Waterbury PC

1501 Broadway, New York, New York 10036, USA

Telephone: (212) 944 2000

President: Jerome S B Iffland

Capabilities
Rail transit station, line section (tunnelling, cut-and-cover, sunken tube, at grade, elevated) and maintenance facilities design; construction management.

Projects
Rosecroft Route Section F3 for Washington Metropolitan Area Transit Authority, Washington DC: Final design of four major construction contracts consisting of 4085 feet each of double shield-driven soft earth tunnel and one station (Navy Yard station) and cross-over box involving 1000 feet of cut-and-cover construction. Estimated construction cost $135 million.
Rehabilitation of Marcy Avenue station for New York City Transit Authority: Resident engineering and construction inspection services for the rehabilitation and modernisation of an elevated rapid transit station including additions of stairs between street and platform levels, replacement of platforms with precast concrete panels, replacement of canopies, expansion of fare areas, etc. Estimated construction cost $6 million.
Renovation and modernisation of three-rail transit car barns for New York City Transit Authority: Complete A/E services for the preparation of final contract documents. Estimated construction cost $9 million.

IIT Research Institute

10 W 35th Street, Chicago, Illinois 60616, USA

Telephone: (312) 567 4009

Research Director: Milton Pikarsky

Capabilities
Rail technology.

Institution of Public Administration

1717 Massachusetts Ave NW, Washington DC 20036, USA

Telephone: (202) 667 6551

Director Transport-Technology: Sumner Myers

Projects
Technical assistance to service and method demonstration programme ($184 000); study of alternative means of financing mass transportation systems ($135 000) for Urban Mass Transportation Administration (UMTA).

International Engineering
International Engineering Co Ltd

180 Howard Street, San Francisco, California 94105, USA

Telephone: (415) 442 7300
Telex: 470040 (ITT)
       278362 (RCA)
       34376 (WUD)
       677058 (WUI)

Capabilities
Railway design and electrification engineering.

JARTS
Japan Railway Technical Service

No 3 Marunouchi-Nomura Building, 2-1-2 Otemachi, Chiyoda-ku, Tokyo, Japan

Telephone: (03) 241 6731
Telegrams: Railwaytechs, Tokyo
Telex: 25254

Capabilities
JARTS was set up to co-operate with overseas countries in the development of main-line, suburban and transit railways, operating under the guidance of Japan's Ministry of Transport and in co-operation with Japanese National Railways. Fields of activity include: studies, surveys and projects relating to land transportation (railway, subway, monorail), construction of new lines, modernisation and improvement of railway track, electrification, dieselisation, modernisation of rolling stock, automatic train control and centralised traffic control, seat reservation systems, marshalling yard automation.

Projects
Recent projects have included:
Argentina: Consulting services for the electrification of the Roca line of the Argentine Railways (1973-74, 1975).
Australia: Technical study of the modernisation of railways for the State Rail Authority of New South Wales (1978).
Bolivia: Feasibility study for the rehabilitation programme of the east and west lines of the Bolivian National Railways (1979-80). Preparation of the basic design and the tender document for constructing a detour of the section between Taperas and Robore of the east line (1980-81).
Brazil: Advice to Amazônia Mineração SA on constructing the Carajás ore railway line (1974), and preliminary study for the design of ore wagons (1979); preliminary survey for the railway improvement programme of Belo Horizonte and adjacent areas, for Rêde Ferroviária Federal SA (1979-80); consulting services for the study of the conceptual design of the control centre to be established at Juiz de Fora, for Rêde Ferroviária Federal SA, in conjunction with Enefer Consultoria, Projetos, Ltda (1980); technical co-operation services to Rêde Ferroviária Federal SA for the establishment of standards and criteria for track maintenance (1980-81).
Cameroon: Technical co-operation to the Cameroon National Railways Authority for the improvement of railway track (1979).
Chile: Preliminary survey for the modernisation of the Chilean State Railways (1980).
China: Advice to the Ministries of Railways and Transport on the construction of railway lines to transport coal and facilities at coal shipping ports (1980-81).
Egypt: Feasibility study of the electrification of the Cairo-Alexandria line, and review of the rolling stock specifications, for the Egyptian Railways (1978-79).
Indonesia: Preliminary study for JABOTABEK railway development projects of the Indonesian State Railways (1978-79); study for the development of railway transport in the metropolitan area of Jakarta (JABOTABEK), for the Indonesian Government (1980-81).
Iran: Consulting services for the Tehran-Mashhad rapid electric railway project, for the Iranian Government (1976-77).
Mexico: Preliminary feasibility study for the construction of Mexico City suburban railways (1977); study for the ac electrification project of the trunk lines of the Mexican National Railways (1980-81).
New Zealand: Study for the electrification project of the North Island main trunk of the New Zealand Railways (1976-77, 1977-78).
Nigeria: Technical co-operation with the Nigerian Railway Corporation for the maintenance of rolling stock (1978).
Paraguay: Study of the electrification and modernisation project of Ferrocarril Presidente Carlos Antonio López (1974, 1980).
Philippines: Consulting services for the improvement of the maintenance and repair system of diesel railcars of the Philippine National Railways, for the Government of Philippines (1979-80).
Senegal: Study for the construction of an ore line between Dakar and Koudékourou (Faleme) (1977).
Sri Lanka: Study for the modernisation and rehabilitation of the Sri Lanka Government Railways (1980-81).
USA: Consulting services for the Northeast Corridor Improvement Project between Boston and Washington, for the Federal Railroad Administration, DOT, in conjunction with De Leuw, Cather/Parsons (1977-79); study of the high-speed rail test track plan, for the Joint House/Senate Committee of the State of Ohio (1979); review of specifications of rolling stock and bid evaluation, for the International Bank for Reconstruction and Development (1979); consulting services for the Ohio High-speed Intercity Rail Passenger Plan, for the Ohio Rail Transportation Authority, in conjunction with Dalton Dalton Newport Inc (1979-80); consulting services for the preliminary design of the passive tilt system of Amcoach, for the Federal Railroad Administration, DOT (1980-81).
Venezuela: Technical co-operation with the Caracas Metro concerning the propulsion system of vehicles for the projected new line (1977).

Bernard Johnson Inc

5050 Westheimer Road, Houston, Texas 77056, USA

Telephone: (713) 622 1400

Vice President: John M Zimmer

Capabilities
Transit systems planning and engineering; railcar and locomotive maintenance facilities; trackwork, yards and bridges.

Raymond Kaiser Engineers Inc

A subsidiary of Raymond International Inc

PO Box 23210, Oakland, California 94623, USA

Telephone: (415) 271 4355

Vice-President, Transportation: Zoltan A Stacho

Projects

Design and systems construction management, 22.5 km (13.5-mile) Baltimore Region Rapid Transit project ($980 million) in joint venture, for Maryland Mass Transit Administration;

Design, 32 km (20-mile) rapid transit system ($982 million), in joint venture, for Metropolitan Dade County, Florida;

Final design and construction consultation, 7.8 km (4.7-mile) transit, railway and highway. Boston Southwest Corridor, ($720 million) in joint venture, for Massachusetts Bay Transportation Authority; programme management, design, corridor planning ($1000 million) in joint venture, Regional Transit Program, Houston;

Sub-systems general engineering consultant ($2000 million) Metro Rail Subway Starter Line, Los Angeles.

KAMPSAX International A/S

Dagmarhus, Raadhuspladsen, 1553 Copenhagen V, Denmark

Telephone: (01) 14 14 90
Telegrams: Kampsax, Copenhagen
Telex: 15508

Subsidiary and associate companies

KAMPSAX (Nigeria) Ltd, PO Box 5810, Lagos, Nigeria

Geoplan A/S, Dagmarhus, 1553 Copenhagen V (aerial photography and mapping)

Geodan, Gribskovvej 2, 2100 Copenhagen Ø (soils survey, geotechnical engineering)

Geodata A/S, Dagmarhus, 1553 Copenhagen V (computer services)

Parent company

KAMPSAX A/S, Dagmarhus, 1553 Copenhagen V

Managing Directors: Mogens Kierulff
Niels Brockenhuus-Schack
Erik Norsk
Svend Østrup
Chief Railway Engineer: A Carlsen
Chief Engineer, in charge of overseas acquisition: Ulf Blach

Capabilities

Founded in 1917 as a general Danish civil engineering firm, the firm entered the international market as consulting engineers in 1927. In Denmark, the firm provides complete engineering services including construction.

As consultants, the company has the capacity and experience to undertake a wide range of projects. Transport and communications have been the most important KAMPSAX activities, with major projects covering all modes of transport. One of the earliest tasks was the consulting services related to the Trans-Iranian Railway, a major international engineering undertaking between the World Wars.

The company undertakes design and supervision, and covers planning, maintenance, and training activities as well. In recent years KAMPSAX has performed preliminary investigations, preparation of country-wide and regional long-term transport development and investment programmes, and project feasibility studies, and has provided technical assistance for improvement of maintenance, and for administration and management of public sector transport agencies.

Projects

In 1972 the firm conducted a pre-feasibility study for a new railway in Iran between the port of Bandar Abbas and Kerman and Bafq on the existing railway, as well as for a line between Kerman and Zahedan. In 1974, KAMPSAX was awarded a contract for final studies, complete design, and construction supervision of the 900 km Bandar Abbas—Kerman/Bafq electrified double-track railway. Rising from the coast to 2500 metres above sea level, it crosses very difficult terrain. Completed in mid-1977, the modern railway design covered a total of 26 km of bridges, 17 km of tunnels, 60 000 metres² of station buildings and 800 staff dwellings.

The firm was entrusted with the preparation of a new complete design manual dealing with the principles of electrification of new and existing lines, and signalling and telecommunications systems in order to achieve uniformity in the entire network.

KAMPSAX was engaged by the Iranian Government to draw up technical specifications and establish a procurement programme for electric locomotives for the entire 6000 km rail network in Iran.

In 1979 the firm was entrusted with the study and design of a single-track 143 km line joining Chachoengsao on the existing State Railway of Thailand to Port Sattahip on the Gulf of Thailand. KAMPSAX is supervising the railway's construction.

In 1982 the Danish and Swedish International Development Agencies assigned to KAMPSAX, in a joint venture with Swederail, a study of the railway rolling stock in nine countries of Southern Africa: Angola, Botswana, Lesotho, Malawi, Mozambique, Swaziland, Tanzania, Zambia and Zimbabwe. The objective is to assess possible transport collaboration between these states and to determine future rolling stock needs.

A T Kearney Inc

222 S Riverside Plaza, Chicago, Illinois 60606, USA

Telephone: (312) 648 0111

Vice-President Transportation: John Throckmorton

Capabilities

Kearney's rail practice began in 1945 with studies for several Midwestern railroads. This early work consisted of developing data and recommendations to improve operations, maintenance, purchasing and stores, traffic cost analysis, organisation and staffing, management development and training of personnel, abandonment studies and a wide range of railroad policy decisions. Since 1955, Kearney's consulting services to the railroad industry have expanded rapidly. Kearney has worked for over 20 client railroads, and a similar number of clients in industries peripheral to the rail industry. In addition, Kearney has worked for a number of federal and state agencies in the rail area such as the Federal Railroad Administration, the Interstate Commerce Commission, and the United States Railway Association; and also for the Association of American Railroads.

Kearney has also been retained to aid many railroads in the management of their trucking operations and intermodal yards, analysis of corporate strategy, implementation of marketing and cost-based pricing strategies, development of management information systems, improvement of rail terminal operations, and studies of facilities consolidation. Kearney's railroad engagements have also encompassed many other phases of management and innovation, such as programmes to benefit from the unit train concept; development of standard cost systems, rates and divisions, economic analysis, tariff qualifications, administrative and clerical controls, profit and productivity improvement studies; development of new freight-handling techniques, facility and equipment improvements; development of specifications for freight cars, yard modernisation, freight car utilisation, container handling systems, work measurement and labour standards, cost reduction studies of yards and maintenance shops; and selection and training of personnel for new innovative activities, such as industrial engineering and marketing. Such engagements often require the use of simulation and systems design techniques coupled with industrial engineering expertise.

Kearney has acquired or developed several computerised models which have a variety of applications:

Train performance calculator (TPC), used to perform unit train analysis, development of network/railcar operations, and many other applications including the evaluation of train operations;

Line capacity analysis model (LCAM), used to quantify line capacity impacts from the addition of passenger and commuter trains to freight operations and proposed signalling improvements involving CTC with or without the addition of passing sidings;

Dynamic yard model, used to simulate rail hump yard operations so that overall impacts of productivity improvements or changes in train blocking and scheduling could be determined. This model is also extremely useful for yard design projects;

Intermodal terminal performance model, a computer simulation model of a rail intermodal terminal which utilises mechanical loading equipment. The output of the model is a variety of operating statistics and cost for a user-specified environment. Flexibility in the choice of schedules, equipment and design is available to the user. The model is structured so that fluctuations in operation and utilisation rates, as measured by the simulation, are major influences on intermodal terminal costs.

Intermodal line haul cost model, developed to cost the movement of the intermodal consists between origin and destination. The model includes the following cost elements which can be directly impacted through technology: equipment ownership costs, train crew costs, fuel costs, and maintenance of way costs. The model can be used for costing train consists containing several car types and loading specifications.

Projects

Assignments covered by Kearney deal with: railroad corporate strategy; marketing and pricing strategies; unit train economic feasibility; simulation and systems design; truckline subsidiary analysis; terminal operations; intermodal terminal operations; intermodal planning and operations; industrial engineering and methods; railroad research and technology; facilities consolidation; forecasting; productivity improvement; railcar leasing strategy; railroad service assessment; cost analysis; government rail research; and regulatory policy analysis.

Clients have included:

Railroads: Burlington Northern; Canadian National; Canadian Pacific; Chessie System; Chicago and North Western; Denver and Rio Grande Western; Detroit Toledo and Ironton; Grand Trunk Western; Illinois Central Gulf; Kansas City Southern; Missouri Pacific; Norfolk and Western; St Louis-San Francisco; Southern; Southern Pacific; Union Pacific; Western Pacific

Railroad suppliers and car leasing companies: AFC Industries; General American Car; North American Car; Pullman, Inc; Union Tank Car Company

Governmental agencies and organisations: Amtrak; California Department of Transportation; Central Illinois Public Service Commission; Federal Railroad Administration; Interstate Commerce Commission; United States Railway Association

Kennedy & Donkin

Westbrook Mills, Godalming, Surrey GU7 2AZ, England

Telephone: 04868 25900
Telegrams: Kinematic, Godalming
Telex: 859373

Partner in charge of transport work: J Alexander Kennedy
Chief Engineer, Transportation: A R Cotton

Associates: Kennedy and Donkin International, Hong Kong

Capabilities

Kennedy and Donkin, founded in 1889, is an independent partnership providing engineering services in electrical and mechanical engineering. A member of the Association of Consulting Engineers, the firm has a current staff of just under 750, of whom 350 are professionally qualified. Activities cover generation, transmission, distribution and utilisation of electric power, passenger and freight transport systems. The firm's Transportation Department is staffed by engineers with wide experience of transport organisations and of industry.

Services to railway administrations and transport authorities cover organisation, motive power, rolling stock, power supply control and distribution, system safety and movement control, telecommunications, track, environmental control, escalators, fare collection and other related electrical and mechanical equipment.

Projects

Mass transit railways

Hong Kong Mass Transit Railway: In association with Freeman Fox and Partners as main consultants, Kennedy and Donkin International participated in all stages of study, design, specification, supervision of construction and commissioning. From an initial start in 1966, approval for the first stage of construction in 1974, contract placing in July 1976 to the completion of the Initial System (15.6 km) within programme and budget in February 1980, Kennedy and Donkin International played an integral part in the design team. This involvement was continued with the planning and construction of the extension to Tsuen Wan (11 km), brought into service early in 1982, and with the further extension along the north side of Hong Kong Island (12.4 km), scheduled for completion in 1985-86.
Istanbul Metro: In 1978 the firm provided assistance on rolling stock, power supply and train control systems for a feasibility study undertaken by Freeman Fox and Partners and Botek SA of a proposed 12 km line in Istanbul.
United Kingdom: In 1979 the firm completed for a client a study of control equipment for battery-operated vehicles.
Venezuela: In 1981 an Anglo-Venezuelan consortium consisting of Kennedy and Donkin International, Freeman Fox and Partners, Martin and Voorhees and led by the Venezuelan firms Occoidesa, VBL and INCICA was appointed by the City of Valencia as consulting engineers for studies and design of a light railway system. Equipment for the first 10 km stage of the system will be supplied and installed by a European consortium. The remainder of the consulting work concerns the preliminary design of the system, which will involve up to 50 km of track and at least three lines.
Taiwan: In 1981 British Mass Transit Consultants (of which Kennedy and Donkin is a member) was retained by the Taiwan Ministry of Communications to provide consultancy services for the Taipei mass rapid transit system. A detailed and comprehensive study of the technical, economic and financial feasibility of the system has been submitted and preliminary designs are complete.
Iraq: In 1981 the British Metro Consultants Group (of which Kennedy and Donkin is a member) was awarded a contract to design, implement and put into service the first stage of the Baghdad Metro. The group has completed the outline designs, specifications and tender documents and will be responsible for the review of the contractors' detailed designs, factory inspection of manufactured items and the monitoring of the installation work.
London Dockland Public Transport Project: Between November 1982 and February 1983 Kennedy and Donkin was associated with the Henderson Busby Partnership in undertaking a review of the strategic plans prepared by the London Docklands Development Corporation and making recommendations in respect of the preferred type of vehicle system for this project.

Main-line and freight railways

Jeddah Islamic Seaport, Saudi Arabia: Kennedy and Donkin is providing specialist services to Saudi Consulting House and W S Atkins Group on locomotives, rolling stock, workshops, train control and operation on this project, which is to design a dedicated railway system to link a new inland customs clearance depot with Jeddah Islamic Seaport, a distance of some 15 km.
Rede Ferroviaria Federal SA electrification: In collaboration with Brazilian consulting engineering firm, Hidroservice, Kennedy and Donkin was responsible to RFFSA in 1975 for determining all the technical parameters associated with the proposed electrification of the main-line railway between Rio de Janiero and São Paulo (Barra Mansa—Manoel Feio). This included technical specifications for locomotives, power supply and overhead wire system components. The project was of special interest since the suburban sections at both ends of the main line are already electrified at 3 kV dc and compatibility of these systems with the eventual main-line electrification parameters was one of the principal considerations.

Kennedy and Donkin was appointed in 1976 to assist the principal consultants to RFFSA in the up-grading of the dc power supplies to the railway in the São Paulo area.
Tasmania, railway rehabilitation (signalling): In response to the request from Maunsell & Partners, Perth, in 1973, Kennedy and Donkin prepared a report with recommendations on the rehabilitation of signalling for the Tasmanian Government Railways.
Taiwan Railway electrification: Financed by the International Bank for Reconstruction and Development (IBRD), Kennedy and Donkin carried out in 1971 an economic feasibility study for the Taiwan Railway Administration of the electrification of the trunk lines of the Taiwan Railways at 25 kV. Various development programmes and associated traffic forecasts for the succeeding 20 years were prepared based on the alternative use of electric and diesel traction on the trunk lines in order to determine the programme most beneficial to the Taiwan economy. In this study, Kennedy and Donkin led the team and was assisted by China Engineering Consultants, Freeman Fox and Partners and Freeman Fox Associates.

In 1975 the firm was appointed as expert advisers to the Taiwan Telecommunications Authority to report upon the likely interference to be experienced within its telecommunication circuits as a result of the electrification of the main trunk line on the island at 24 kV 60 Hz ac and to propose suitable remedial action.
East African Railways, railway study: Kennedy and Donkin (Africa) was appointed in 1972 by East Africa Railways in association with transport planners Freeman Fox and Associates and economists Cooper Brothers and Co, to study and make recommendations to the Railway and the three Governments concerned on the future operation of passenger services over the whole system and of the freight and passenger services on some branch lines. This study provided information on the effect of closing or of curtailing passenger traffic on certain branch lines found to be uneconomic and devised procedures for recovering costs of such lines required to remain open for social or communication purposes.

Lester B Knight & Associates Inc

549 W Randolph Street, Chicago, Illinois 60606, USA

Telephone: (312) 346 2100

Vice Presidents: Benjamin F Svoboda
Dominick J Gatlo

Capabilities

Transport and environmental studies; railroads and rapid transit systems planning and design.

Kuttner, Collins Group
(with affiliated offices)

Head office: 61 Lavender Street, Milsons Point, New South Wales 2061, Australia
Telephone: 929 7411
Telegrams (all offices): Calculus
Telex: 24432
276 The Avenue, Parkville, Victoria 3052
Telephone: 387 2622
366 Queen Street, Brisbane, Queensland 4000
Telephone: 229 3322
PO Box 230, Canberra, Australian Capital Territory 2608
Telephone: 49 1055
26 Broome Street, Nedlands, Western Australia 6009
Telephone: 386 6572
62 Cavanagh Street, Darwin, Northern Territory 5790
Telephone: 81 7744
PO Box 783, Bandar Seri Begawan, Brunei
Telephone: 3370
175B Goldhill Shopping Centre, Thomson/Newton Road, Singapore 11
Telephone: 25 22611
20A, Jln SS/2/61, Petaling Jaya, Selangor, Malaysia
Telephone: 762111
KC-Romaho, PO Box 4483, Jakarta, Indonesia
Telephone: 815712

Principals: W L Kuttner, G A Collins
Additional Directors (Victoria): M J Smyth
J G Flather
J Colquhoun
Associate Directors: P R Brown, A Weiss

Capabilities

Railway works constitute a specialised sub-division within the general scope of the firm's civil engineering practice.

Projects

1981: Evaluating proposals for electrification of coal network, New South Wales, covering 100 km of track and associated handling facilities.
1981-82: Civil and structural engineering design and project management of the A$72 million Port Waratah coal handling and shiploading facility, including pollution control systems, for ships up to 120 000 tons dwt. A wide range of civil engineering works included railway trackwork some 30 km in length, including 110 leads.
Coal transportation study for the Public Transport Commission of New South Wales: The firm's contribution consisted of the design, preparation of preliminary layouts and estimate of cost for the provision of crossing and refuge loops in 75 different locations throughout the State. Most locations required two to four alternative layouts and estimates to allow for varying standard train lengths. Close and continuing liaison was maintained with the Railways Division of the PTC. The work included inspecting each location and assessing the condition of trackwork, the drainage and earthworks required, and the general practicality of each proposal. The estimated cost of the work, allowing for the longest train in each location, is A$53 million.

The firm has been responsible for the civil engineering and trackwork component of a joint feasibility study for the Government of Malaysia for reconstruction of the marshalling yards at Kuala Lumpur, the construction of some 45 km of new suburban track, 4 km of elevated rapid transit city track and the construction of new warehousing facilities at the marshalling yards. The work is in the design stage.

Laramore, Douglass and Popham

332 South Michigan Ave, Suite 940, Chicago, Illinois 60604, USA

Telephone: (312) 427 8486

Vice-President: Robert H Steinberger

Projects

Power supply and substation improvements ($60 million) for Massachusetts Bay Transportation Authority (MBTA); power supply and catenary system ($25 million) for Dept of Public Property, City of Philadelphia, Airport High Speed Line (AHSL); substation modernisation ($7 million) for Northern Indiana Commuter Transportation District (NICTD); dc distribution for O'Hara extension project ($6 million), City of Chicago.

J W Leas and Associates Inc

910 Potts Lane, Bryn Mawr, Pennsylvania 19010, USA

Telephone: (215) 525 1952

President: J Wesley Leas

Capabilities
Fare collection system studies, fare structure analyses, fare collection equipment specifications and revenue control procedures for rapid and mass transit operations.

Projects
Fare collection system studies for light rail system of SEMTA, Detroit and for buses of MTA, Baltimore and NFTA, Buffalo; fare structure analyses for NJT, Newark and MTDB, San Diego; fare collection equipment specifications for heavy rail systems of MRT, Singapore, MTA, Baltimore, MTA, Miami and TTC, Toronto, for light rail systems of NFTA, Buffalo and for revenue control procedures of SCCTA, San Jose.

Light Rail Transit Association

1007 Roland Heights Avenue, Baltimore, Maryland 21211, USA

Telephone: (301) 467 9256

Designer: Jack L O'Donnell (Telephone: (301) 744 5984)

Capabilities
Design of light rail transit systems.

Lochner Inc

20 N Wacker Drive, Chicago, Illinois 60606, USA

Telephone: (312) 372 7346

President: Harry W Lochner Jr

Capabilities
Rail and transit planning and design.

London Transport International Services Limited
A wholly-owned subsidiary of London Transport Executive

55 Broadway, Westminster, London SW1H 0BD, England

Telephone: 01-222 5600 extensions 3684/6/7
Telegrams: Passengers, London
Telex: 8812227
Facsimile: 01 22 1142

Managing Director: Vacant (Deputy: D H Coombs)
Secretary: D G Keep
Consultancy Managers, Americas and UK: D H Coombs
  Europe, Africa and Middle East: D T Coughtrie
  Far East and Australasia: L W Rowe

Capabilities
Formulation and evaluation of public transport policies and plans; technical advice on rail transit design and construction; operational advice and guidance for rail and bus systems; transit marketing and passenger information services. Staff are seconded directly from their posts in London Transport to advise clients or supplied from a specialist pool of permanent consultants.

Projects
Baghdad: London Transport International is associated with a British group of consultants who are responsible for the design and supervision of construction of the new Baghdad Metro. London Transport International is ensuring that the railway will conform to modern operating principles. Detailed advice is being given on matters such as timetabling, training of staff, station layouts and fares systems, and also on the architectural design of stations.
Caracas: A team of senior London Transport advisers is resident in Caracas to assist the CA Metro de Caracas in establishing its new Metro. Advice has been given on the operational aspects of the construction and equipping of the Metro; technical, operational and maintenance standards, procedures and methods; training of staff; and financial matters such as revenue control and tariff systems.
Dublin: Assistance covering rolling stock and signalling design has been provided to CIE in connection with the electrification of the Dublin Suburban railway.
Glasgow: Advice and assistance was given to the Strathclyde Passenger Transport Executive on the commissioning of the Glasgow Subway. The work involved a wide range of activities including programming and progressing of works; design and safety aspects of signalling equipment and standards for its installation; training courses and standing instructions for engineering staff, rules and regulations; commissioning of rolling stock; signal maintenance and electrical engineering matters.
Greece: London Transport International is providing general mechanical and electrical engineering advice in connection with the manufacture of 75 new cars for the Athens—Piraeus Railway Company.

Hong Kong: London Transport International has been associated with the Hong Kong Mass Transit Railway project since the planning days and has formed part of a consortium led by Freeman Fox and Partners which has served as adviser to the Hong Kong Government and the Mass Transit Railway Corporation. Apart from general operating and planning advice, London Transport International has undertaken training for Mass Transit Railway staff and was also responsible for technical inspection work in respect of electrical equipment, rolling stock, signalling equipment and lifts and escalators being manufactured in the United Kingdom and in the Federal Republic of Germany. London Transport International has also provided expertise for the Mass Transit Railway Corporation by seconding serving London Transport staff to work in Hong Kong during the commissioning of the new railway. Advice has lately been given on signal and rolling stock maintenance.
India: London Transport International has been involved in training several members of staff from both Indian Railways and the Calcutta Metro. Courses have been run in London on matters such as railway planning, operating, and maintenance.
Manchester: London Transport International has provided mechanical engineering design and operations input to a feasibility study of a possible LRT system covering the Greater Manchester area.
New York: London Transport International is assisting the General Consultant with advice on aspects of New York City Transit Authority's Capital Revitalization Program. London Transport International is providing a substantial team of consultants drawn from varied mechanical and civil engineering and operations backgrounds to assist in the modernisation of the Authority's two major train overhaul and repair shops and rehabilitation of its thirteen car barns.
Singapore: In 1979-80 work was carried out on a preliminary engineering design study for the planning of a proposed rapid transit railway system for Singapore. In 1982 London Transport International returned to Singapore as part of a team of consultants to participate in the MRT system design and project staging study. This involved the evaluation of the phase III system and the updating of previous last estimates made for the MRT. The determination of the 1990 operational network was also carried out taking into account integration with a comprehensive bus network.
Taipei: London Transport International participated in a feasibility study of a rapid transit network for Taipei and for the preparation of preliminary engineering design documents for the priority line. London Transport International is mainly concerned with operational planning aspects for the proposed system. Advice on automatic fare collection and organisation structure was also given for a new rapid transit authority.
Tyneside: A team of London Transport International advisers has assisted the Tyne and Wear Passenger Transport Executive on a variety of matters connected with the opening of the Newcastle Metro system. Rolling stock engineers have recently advised on fault-finding techniques and maintenance staff training, while other advice is being given in the field of signalling and communications.
USA: In 1980-81 work was carried out with a firm of American consultants on ground-borne noise and vibration caused by railway rolling stock in tunnels.

London Transport International advised the Rio de Janeiro Metro on staff training

Louis T Klauder and Associates

2000 Philadelphia National Bank Building, Philadelphia, Pennsylvania 19107, USA

Telephone: (215) 563 2570
Telegrams: LTKlauder PHA
Telex: 83-4783

Partners: Louis T Klauder, Sr
    John R Vollmar
    J Richard Tomlinson
    David H Cushwa
    Louis T Klauder, Jr
    Albert N Ferrari
    John W Irvin
Associates: Henry T Raudenbush
    Rush D Touton, Jr
    Robert B Watson
    John J Wilkins
    Paul S Earley
    Richard F Sullivan
    V Terry Hawthorne
    William A Mullen

Capabilities

Louis T Klauder and Associates, consulting engineers, offers a wide variety of engineering, managerial and planning services designed specifically for the transport field. Based in Philadelphia, Pennsylvania, since its founding in 1921, the firm has provided professional and technical assistance to numerous clients throughout the United States and Canada, as well as in Australia, Brazil, Japan, New Zealand and Spain.

Projects

Latest assignments undertaken by Louis T Klauder since 1978 include assistance of the following electric rolling stock purchases:

Year	No of cars	Car type	Owner
1978	312	Commuter	Metropolitan Transportation Authority of the State of New York (for Metro North and LIRR service)
1979	44	Commuter	Northern Indiana Commuter Transportation District
	94	Rapid transit	Washington Metropolitan Area Transportation Authority
1981	200	Rapid transit	Washington Metropolitan Area Transportation Authority
	26	Light rail	Tri County Metropolitan Transportation District of Oregon
	50	Light rail	Port Authority Transit, (Pittsburgh, Pennsylvania)
1982	55	Light rail	Massachusetts Bay Transportation Authority
	30	Light rail	Santa Clara County Transit District
	28	Light rail	Sacramento Transit Development Agency
	54	Commuter	Metropolitan Transportation Authority of the State of New York (for New Haven Line service)

Engineering review, inspection and acceptance services provided for purchase of non-electric commuter cars during 1981-82 include:

Year	No of cars	Type	Owner
1981	117	Push-pull	New Jersey Transit

The firm has also assisted in the purchases of 776 locomotive-hauled passenger cars, 75 multiple-unit electric cars and two three-unit articulated gas-turbine trains for inter-city passenger services since 1965.

Maunsell Consultants

6 Claremont Street, South Yarra, Victoria 3141, Australia

Telephone: 240 0541
Telegrams: Mauncivil, Melbourne
Telex: 31067

Managing Partner: J B Laurie
Partners: L M Ramage
D J Lee
P G Sands
P H F Andrew
G N Fernie
D M A Hook
J W Downer
J G Clayton
J A Leslie
P H N Norman
B Richmond
H B James
P H Gray
R A Cochrane
E V Jenkins
D J Macleod

Associated companies
G Maunsell & Partners
London, England
Contact:
Managing Director: D J Lee
Yeoman House, 63 Croydon Road, Penge, London SE20 7TP
Also offices in Birmingham, Swansea, Manchester and Witham
Telephone: 01-778 6060
Telegrams: Mauncivil, London SE20
Telex: 946171

Maunsell & Partners Pty Ltd
Melbourne, Australia
Contact:
Managing Director: J B Laurie
6 Claremont Street, South Yarra, Victoria 3141
Also offices in Perth, Sydney, Canberra, Hobart, Brisbane and Adelaide
Telephone: 240 0541
Telegrams: Mauncivil, Melbourne
Telex: 31067

Maunsell Consultants Asia
Kowloon, Hong Kong
Contact:
Managing Partner: J W Downer
1 Kowloon Park Drive, Kowloon, Hong Kong
Telephone: 3-695251
Telegrams: Mauncivil, Hong Kong
Telex: 44458

Maunsell Consultants Ltd
Baghdad, Iraq
Contact:
Resident Partner: S I Al-Kubaisi
PO Box 615, Baghdad
Telephone: 5517422
Telegrams: PL 615 Baghdad
Telex: 2542

Sindhu Maunsell Consultants
Bangkok, Thailand
Contact:
Resident Partner: Sindhu Pulsirivong
Chongkolnee Building, 56 Suriwong Road, Bangkok
Telephone: 233-7950
Telex: 81157

Maunsell Consultants PNG
Port Moresby, Papua New Guinea
Contact:
Resident Partner: D R Wallace
Mogoru Moto, Champion Parade, Port Moresby
Telephone: 212955
Telex: 22126

Chan Chee Wah Maunsell & Partners
Singapore
Contact:
Managing Partner: Chan Chee Wah
15-04 Bukit Timah Shopping Centre, 170 Upper Bukit Timah Road, Singapore 2158
Telephone: 4694188
Telegrams: Mauncivil, Singapore
Telex: 24297

Maunsell SARL
Paris, France
Contact:
Resident Director: D R H Maher
73 Rue Laugier, Paris 75017
Telephone: 380 86 04
Telex: 290626

Capabilities

The firm of G Maunsell & Partners was established in London to provide civil engineering consultancy services both in the British Isles and overseas. A branch office was established in Melbourne and this later became the head office of a separate Australian firm named Maunsell & Partners, which was incorporated as a proprietary company in 1970 and practices under the name Maunsell and Partners Pty Ltd.

Following a reorganisation of the activities of the firms designed to improve world-wide operations, the international partnership of Maunsell Consultants was formed. This international partnership comprises the partners of G Maunsell & Partners and the directors of Maunsell & Partners Pty Ltd, and normally undertakes assignments in all parts of the world other than the British Isles and Australia, which are served by the appropriate constituent firms. The remaining organisation operates chiefly in the countries in which they are located.

The group is operating in many parts of the world and is registered with bodies concerned with world-wide developments, such as the International Bank for Reconstruction and Development, the United Nations Industrial Development Organisation, the Asian Development Bank, etc.

Some of the range of services offered are:

Engineering: The group can provide co-ordinated planning and control of a project from its inception to final completion. Particular aspects of this work are:
Feasibility studies and report estimates.
Detailed design, preparation of working drawings, contract documents, etc.
Evaluation of tenders and placing of contracts.
Supervision of construction and certification of interim and final payments to contractors.
Full contract management services, with computer back-up for major multi-discipline engineering contracts.
Land survey: A comprehensive and fully experienced land survey section, employing the latest techniques and equipment, is available to undertake work anywhere in the world. Electronic equipment is available to facilitate accurate linear measurement over any terrain.
Ground exploration: The group employs qualified personnel fully experienced in soil mechanics, foundation engineering and geology and it arranges and supervises contracts for ground exploration.
Transport studies: A traffic engineering department was established in 1963 and is able to undertake transport studies of all kinds together with the associated economic and cost benefit analyses, route location, traffic management and studies of environmental effects.
Town and regional planning: One of the individual consultants in the group is a past president of the Town Planning Institute and additionally, there are strong links with architects, landscape architects, building quantity surveyors and others so that the group is able to handle assignments involving town or regional planning.
Environmental and health engineering: The Health Engineering section designs and supervises the construction and installation of water supply systems, sewage treatment plants and solid waste disposal facilities. The group has been particularly active in the field of solid waste disposal and undertakes comprehensive studies which cover economic appraisal and management aspects. The group is well equipped to advise on liquid waste disposal problems. Expansion of the Group's activities in the fields of irrigation and major water supply schemes has been recently accomplished.

The organisation is active in the field of environmental engineering and carries out surveys to evaluate and appraise pollution of all forms including noise and gaseous emissions.

Economic studies: When the scope of the work so demands, the group associates with various specialist firms or individuals who are experts in the field of economics.

Computing: Comprehensive computer facilities are available for the solution of problems in engineering design, traffic engineering, and land and marine surveying while specialised programmes for use with the foregoing have been developed by the group's engineers and applied mathematicians.

Projects since 1977

Completion	Project	Country	Client	Value US$ million (when built)
in hand	Design of quad-ruplication of 2.5 route km of heavily trafficked suburban system	Australia	State Railway Authority of New South Wales	6.05
in hand	Mass Transit Railway Island Line: 5 underground stations, shafts and ground level works	Hong Kong	Mass Transit Railway Corporation Hong Kong	285
in hand	Mass Transit Railway Tsuen Wan Extension: 4 underground stations and 400 m tunnel	Hong Kong	Mass Transit Railway Corporation Hong Kong	90
1978	Mass Transit Railway: 2 underground stations and 1100 m tunnel	Hong Kong	Paul Y Construction Ltd	55
1977	Mount Newman Railway: 31 km new route and duplication of 65 km railway and sidings	Australia	Mount Newman Mining Company	50

Lai Wan station of Hong Kong Mass Transit Railway during construction

Modjeski & Masters

PO Box 2345, Harrisburg, Pennsylvania 17105, USA

Telephone: (717) 761 1891

Partner: R E Felsburg

Capabilities
Rail structures; rail layout and design.

Projects
Project JBA: Northeast Corridor Improvement Project, bridge replacement and bridge rehabilitation, for De Leuw Cather/Parsons;
Tennessee-Tombigbee Waterway, Columbus bridge, inspection of construction, for Illinois Central Gulf Railroad;
Sterling, Illinois grade separation and track relocation, Chicago & Northwestern Transportation Company, for Illinois Department of Transportation;
22 bridges, rehabilitation design and inspection of construction for the Norfolk and Western Railway;
Alton, Illinois bridge replacement design on the Burlington Northern Railroad, for the Corps of Engineers;
Lake Pontchartrain, Louisiana bridge replacement design for the Norfolk Southern Railroad;
Galveston, Texas bridge rehabilitation plans and emergency services on the Berwick Bay, Louisiana bridge for the Southern Pacific Transportation Company;
Hackensack, New Jersey, Conrail system, bridge inspection for the Port Authority of New York and New Jersey;
Peoria, Illinois bridge, inspection of construction for the Peoria and Pekin Union Railway Company;
Huey Long Bridge inspection/rehabilitation plans, at New Orleans, Louisiana for the New Orleans Public Belt Railroad.

Morrison-Knudsen Company, Inc

Two Morrison-Knudsen Plaza, PO Box 7808, Boise, Idaho 83729, USA

Telephone: (208) 345 5000
Telex: 368439

Vice President and General Manager, Railroad Division: J G Fearon

Subsidiary: International Engineering Company, Inc (IECO)
180 Howard Street, San Francisco, California 94104

Capabilities
Morrison-Knudsen ranks as one of the largest and most widely experienced railroad engineering and construction operations in the world. Design/engineering work for the railroad industry is performed by Morrison-Knudsen's Railroad Division and International Engineering Company, Inc (IECO), Morrison-Knudsen's San Francisco-based subsidiary. Morrison-Knudsen Company, Inc has been engaged in the design of various heavy civil engineering projects, including railroads and their associated facilities since 1915. Comprehensive programmes for increasing the safety, speed and economy of railroad services have evolved from extensive studies and economic evaluations determining the size, capacity, location and disposition of various elements making up a railroad system.

In the design of railroads and maintenance facilities, M-K's staff is experienced in field reconnaissance, site and route surveys, preparation of economic studies, quantity and cost estimates, yard trackage layouts and facilities design. A partial inventory of M-K's railroad engineering accomplishments totals well over 22 000 km of overland railways.

Projects
Some of the more recent railroad engineering projects undertaken by Morrison-Knudsen's subsidiaries and divisions are:

Railway West Surinam: Morrison-Knudsen recently completed a 70 km pioneering railroad in the Republic of Surinam for the transport of bauxite from mine to port. The construction programme, over approximately 3½ years, included the clearing of a 72 km corridor through jungle, excavation of 6.3 million cubic metres of earth and rock, supply of track, tracklaying and ballasting of the standard gauge rail. Other work included the erection of bridges and installation of 4.3 km of culvert, construction of a 12-metre-wide service road, and erection of 14 permanent dwellings, engineering offices, a riverside shiploading quay and rail maintenance shop.

NACC railcar repair and maintenance facility, Douglas, Wyoming: Morrison-Knudsen designed and completed the construction of a railcar repair and maintenance facility at Douglas, Wyoming for the North American Car Corporation. The facility was designed to maintain a fleet of 5000 hoppers a year on a single-shift basis. Major features of the shop include four lead tracks (12.2 km of new track), air-cushion turntables for wheel transfer, two 20-ton bridge cranes, propane-fired generating sets for production of all electricity required on-site and storage capacity for 200 cars.

Erie-Lackawana and New York Long Branch Railroad electrification: IECO is providing full construction management services for rehabilitating the existing track and conversion of the catenary system and substations from 3 kV dc capacity to 25 kV ac along the 107 km of route.

Northeast Corridor electrification design: IECO is participating with other engineering firms in the upgrading of the 272 km electrical system and the track structure from Washington DC to Trenton, New Jersey, to facilitate train speeds of up to 192 km/h. The project also calls for the realignment of curves and of high-speed crossovers, and the upgrading of the system from its present 11 kV level to 25 kV. IECO is providing design, engineering and construction expertise for several other electrification projects and feasibility studies in the United States and overseas.

MBTA subway system 'Redline Extension', Cambridge, Massachusetts: Under joint venture contract, Morrison-Knudsen is expanding the Massachusetts Bay Transportation Authority's subway system by extending two parallel tunnels a total of 5 km and adding four sub-surface stations in the Boston Metropolitan area.

Union Pacific Railroad diesel running repair facilities: Morrison-Knudsen designed and constructed a diesel running repair facility at North Platte, Nebraska for the Union Pacific Railroad. The UP facility is the largest and most modern running repair facility in the USA, capable of maintaining a fleet of over 600 locomotives. Scheduled repair and inspections are completed on over 400 locomotives per month by handling 40 locomotives simultaneously inside the shop building. The facility requires a total staff of over 300 for round-the-clock operations. An adjacent washing facility is capable of washing 200 locomotives per day in temperatures ranging from −7 to 43°C.

Locomotive repair shop, Tubarao, Brazil: M-K/IECO completed engineering designs for a locomotive repair shop complex at Tubarao, Espirito Santo, Brazil for Companhia Vale Do Rio Doce. This complex was designed to maintain a fleet of 200 locomotives with provisions in the facility for expansion to a fleet of 300 locomotives. Fuelling, sanding and washing facilities were provided in the design. IECO also prepared the engineering design for an earlier maintenance shop at Tubarao, as part of an overall terminal complex for CVRD.

Muni Metro rail centre, San Francisco, California: This facility was designed by IECO for the maintenance, storage and terminal facilities of a new fleet of 110 standard LRVs acquired by the San Francisco Municipal Railway. Washing and sanding facilities were provided in the design.

Study for rolling stock maintenance, RFFSA, Brazil: This project involved managing a study team to review, update, and, as necessary, supplement the design of the maintenance shop plans as these items related to the system-wide 'Five Year Plan of Action and Investment' of Rede Ferroviaria Federal SA (RFFSA), Brazil.

RMC railcar maintenance facility, Alliance, Nebraska: Morrison-Knudsen designed and has completed the construction of a railcar preventive maintenance facility at Alliance, Nebraska for Railcar Maintenance Company. This is capable of handling 3000 unit-train coal cars per year on a double-shift basis. Ancillaries include a bogie shop and a semi-automated wheel shop for reconditioning wheel/axle assemblies. A primary feature of this shop is a car-body rotator, designed and manufactured by M-K, which is designed to lift the car body from the trucks, rotate it 90 degrees, lower it on to two transfer carts and move it to either side of the main shop track. This provides easier access for repair of centreplates and underframe structure. Upon completion of the necessary repairs, the process is reversed. The car body is returned to the upright position, lowered on to reconditioned bogies and moved to the next station.

Itel Corporation railcar maintenance facility, Pueblo, Colorado: Preliminary engineering was performed for Itel Corporation. Included was the development of conceptual design and construction and operating cost estimates for a railcar maintenance facility near Pueblo, Colorado. The facility was designed to serve a 2000-car fleet initially with future expansion to 5000 cars. The proposed facility ultimately includes a main shop building with four through tracks for inspection and preventive maintenance and two tracks for heavy repair. Support facilities include a shop for reconditioning and repairing railcar bogies, and automated wheel/axle shop, a bearing reconditioning facility, a paint shop and supporting yard tracks and storage areas. In addition to capital and operating cost estimates, an operating plan was developed, which included equipment and manpower requirements.

Commuter car assembly plant, Erie, Pennsylvania: Another facility for the railway industry was a 32 500 metre² commuter car assembly plant constructed by Morrison-Knudsen near Erie, Pennsylvania, for the General Electric Company. The first production from the plant of high-speed rapid transit cars was delivered to agencies of New York and Connecticut for use on the New Haven Line.

Great Salt Lake Causeway: Morrison-Knudsen has completed the design and construction of the Great Salt Lake Causeway in Utah. It rises from a dredged foundation trench, from 54 to 182 metres in width, to a maximum height of 30 metres. Over 41 million metres³ of fill material was handled in three-and-a-half years of earthmoving. The causeway, which replaced an old wooden trestle, was completed nine months ahead of schedule.

Australian port-to-mine railroads: The construction of pioneer port-to-mine railroads to transport iron ore from deposits in the outback of Western Australia to the coast along the Indian Ocean was completed in 1973. A total of 1124 km of track was constructed for the four roads using continuous-welded rail. Tracklaying operations included a day in which 7 km of track were laid, spiked and anchored in 11 hours 40 minutes, and a month in which 80 km of track were completed.

Black Mesa and Lake Powell Railroad: The world's first 50 kV electrified railway was designed, built and equipped by Morrison-Knudsen/IECO, under a turnkey programme. It is a 124 km automated coal transport route in northern Arizona. Train loading and unloading are all automatically regulated by an extensive 'Rail-safe' automation system which stops the train in the event of any malfunction in the train or control system.

Operations and maintenance: Morrison-Knudsen is also experienced in railroad operations. The Wabash Valley Railroad Company, a subsidiary of Morrison-Knudsen, formerly operated short-line railroads in Kansas and Illinois, which M-K has renovated and reconstructed to FRA Class I standards. M-K has operated and maintained other railroads in the USA and overseas. These include Vermont Northern Railroad in Vermont and the Black Mesa-Lake Powell Railroad in Arizona; the Hamersley Iron Railroad, the Mount Newman Railroad and the Robe River Railroad, all in Australia; the Quebec North Shore and Labrador Railroad in Canada; the Orinoco Railroad in Venezuela; the Southern Peru Copper Railroad in Peru; and the Burlington Northern Railroad at Libby, Montana. Work with these and other railroads has included maintenance of trackage, signal systems, rolling stock and locomotive remanufacturing, and a comprehensive programme of personnel training.

Procurement: Morrison-Knudsen also offers a capable and experienced organisation for the procurement of railroad materials, equipment, supplies, subcontracting and the appropriate expediting services to complement the procurement. This service is the responsibility of M-K's Railroad Division and supported by the Procurement Department.

Manufacturing and remanufacturing: For these activities see the Locomotives and rolling stock section.

M-K Railroad Equipment Leasing Company: M-K Leasing Company, a wholly-owned subsidiary, specialises in short-term operating leases of both motive power and rolling stock. The fleet consists of 130 ballast cars equipped with M-K patented ballast doors and locomotives ranging from 600 to 3000 hp.

Consulting services: Morrison-Knudsen has considerable experience in the development of comprehensive transport analysis, where its services cover a wide range of modes, commodities and objectives. Morrison-Knudsen has conducted comprehensive analysis of railroad operations, pricing and services, developed rail costing and financial control systems, evaluated alternative rail and competitive modal type investments, examined carrier traffic and revenue patterns, developed comprehensive long-term forecasts, projections and operating plans, constructed extensive railroad reorganisation programmes, developed variable cost studies, investigated freight rates and divisions thereof, conducted alternative rail route evaluations, and developed the necessary information for clients to make intelligent and well-informed decisions about the feasibility of mergers and acquisitions.

Mott, Hay & Anderson

20/26 Wellesley Road, Croydon, Surrey CR9 2UL, England

Telephone: 01-686 5041
Telegrams: Lydonist, Croydon
Telex: 917241

Associated and subsidiary companies

Mott, Hay and Anderson International Limited, Consulting Engineers, Croydon
Mott, Hay & Anderson Electrical & Mechanical Services, Croydon
Mott, Hay & Anderson Structural & Industrial Consultants, Croydon
Mott, Hay, Preece Cardew, Railway and Rapid Transit Consultants, Croydon
Heap Digby & Associates, 44 Wallington Square, Wallington, Surrey SM6 8RY
Telephone: 01-647 1025
Telex: 261597
Parsons Brown and Newton, Abford House, 15 Wilton Road, London SW1V 1LT
Telephone: 01-828 9203
Telex: 919000
John Connell-Mott, Hay & Anderson, 60 Albert Road, South Melbourne, Victoria 3205, Australia
Telephone: 699 5533
Telex: 32071
Girec SA, 430 avenue Louise, BP 5, 1050 Brussels, Belgium
Telephone: 640 3320
Telex: 22647
Linjasuunnittelu Oy, Sentnerikuja 3, Helsinki 40, Finland
Telephone: 5625511
Telex: 122845
Mott, Hay & Anderson Far East and Mott, Hay & Anderson Hong Kong Ltd, 2401 Sun Hung Kai Centre, 30 Harbour Road, Wanchai, Hong Kong
Telephone: 5-757105
Telex: 63892
MRT Consulting Engineers (Nigeria) Ltd, 13 Ekiti Street, Bodija Estate, PMB 5594, Ibadan, Nigeria
Telex: 31447
Mott, Hay & Anderson Asia Pte and Mott, Hay & Anderson Overseas, 1702 17th Floor, International Plaza, Anson Road, Singapore 0207
Telephone: 2201833
Telex: 27163
Transit and Tunnel Consultants Inc, Suite 811, The Rand Building, 14 Lafayette Square, Buffalo, New York 14203, USA
Telephone: (716) 853 7800
Telex: 91593

Directors

J V Bartlett
C D Brown
S G Tough
B L Bubbers
E M T Powell
J A Turnbull
R Beresford
J M Whitefield
E A Cruddas
A A Cairncross
K W Torpey
T J Thirlwall
R A Vickers
R Hodges
J E D Lord
D E Palmer
E H Norie
P J Clayson
A Newton
J D T Kirk

Capabilities

Founded in 1902 the Mott, Hay & Anderson group operates throughout the world as engineering and project management consultants. Since 1970 it has operated in over 60 countries and a number of permanent links have been established with consulting engineering practices in other countries.

The group is linked by a degree of common ownership. Each member of the group is independent and controlled by its own board of directors.

The group deploys a staff of about 1000 professional and technical personnel. Its capabilities cover:

Engineering (civil, structural, electrical and mechanical): Surveys and investigations; feasibility studies and cost estimates; planning studies; design and preparation of contract documents; tender evaluation; supervision of construction, installation and site management.

Geotechnical services: Comprehensive service including soil and rock mechanics studies, ground engineering design, specification and management of land and marine site investigations.

Transport studies: Transport engineering, including traffic studies and management, cost-benefit analyses, route location, transport co-ordination.

Project management: Co-ordination and control of all work from conception of a scheme to completion.

Computing services: Comprehensive computing services for engineering research and design, including provision of specialised programmes and development of new applications and systems.

Inspection services: Inspection of materials, plant and equipment during manufacture, supervision of specialist processes and sampling and testing of construction materials.

Recent projects

Project	Completed	Approx construction cost	Details
Tehran-Tabriz Railway, Iran	1980	£810 million (civil works)	Design of civil works for 630 km high speed twin-track electrified railway replacing single-track diesel-operated railway
Medellin rapid transit, Colombia	1980	£280 million	Study and preliminary design of 25 km mass rapid transit system including 19 stations
Athens-Thessaloniki Railway, Greece	1980	£500 million (civil works)	Feasibility study and design of civil works for modernisation and extension of 600 km railway link and associated branch lines
Jubilee Line, Stages 2 & 3, London Underground, UK	1980	—	Preliminary survey and studies for proposed 12 km extension of Stage 1
VicRail suburban train maintenance, Australia	1981	—	Study of maintenance facilities and requirements
Adelaide Metropolitan Area Railway Communications, Australia	1981	—	Specialist assistance with study of railway signalling and communications requirements
'Euroroute', UK/France	1981	£6000 million	Preliminary study for new viaduct/submerged tube tunnel for rail and road
Tripoli-Misurata railway and Tripoli Central station, Libya	1981	£235 million	Study and design of station complex and 200 km main-line railway
Gibraltar Straits Link, Spain/Morocco	1982	£1000 million	Feasibility study of tunnel link of approximately 39 km length, to feature roll-on, roll-off train traffic
Las Adjuntas railway depot, Caracas, Venezuela	1982	£30 million	Study, design assistance and project management for stabling and maintenance facility for 85 trains
Melbourne underground rail loop, Australia	—	£195 million	Design and supervision of civil works and overall project management
Antwerp Metro, Belgium	—	£9 million	Design and supervision of construction of new extensions
Brussels Metro, Belgium	—	£10.3 million	Design and supervision of new sections
Dublin Suburban Railway, Ireland	—	£50 million	Design and supervision for electrification of 45 km line, Howth to Bray; study and preliminary design of 12 km electrified line from Tallaght to Heuston
Tyne & Wear Metro, UK	—	£250 million	Design and supervision of civil works, electrical and mechanical building services and ventilation systems; overall project management
Buffalo Light Rail Rapid Transit system, USA	—	£75 million	Design and construction management of 5.6 km underground section of light rail rapid transit, including 5 stations
Caracas Metro, Lines 1 and 2, Venezuela	—	£1000 million	Design, site supervision and advice on new rail rapid transit system
Charleroi Metro, Belgium	—	£3 million	Design of 1.5 km section, comprising tunnels, viaducts and 3 stations
Singapore Mass Transit Railway	—	—	Phase III study and preliminary design for 45 km system, followed by comprehensive traffic study in 2 stages up to system design and project staging for new mass rapid transit
Maputo-Chicualacuala and Beira-Machipanda Railway, Mozambique	—	£10 million	Rehabilitation studies covering track, maintenance, operations and telecommunications aspects
Vancouver Rapid Transit, Canada	—	£300 million (entire project)	Subway and ventilation design assistance
Caracas Suburban Railway, Venezuela	—	—	Design of two new lines, workshops and stations serving Caracas and its principal airport and seaport
Bilbao Metro, Spain	—	—	Preliminary studies for new system
Los Angeles Metro, USA	—	£500 million (entire project)	Advice, during preliminary design stage, on alignment, tunnelling methods, station location and layout etc
Greater Manchester Light Rail Transit System, UK	—	—	Feasibility study of transit system using British Rail routes and city centre routes

Tyne and Wear Metro

Mott, Hay & Anderson has been entrusted by the Tyne & Wear Passenger Transport Executive with the design and supervision of construction of the tunnels and stations in the central areas of Newcastle and Gateshead which comprise the underground core of the system. The 4.75-metre diameter running tunnels in Newcastle pass through glacial drift consisting mostly of boulder clay and were shield-driven using boom type tunnelling machines. According to ground conditions the tunnels are lined with bolted precast concrete or cast iron segments. The 7-metre diameter station tunnel enlargements and crossovers up to 10-metre diameter utilise high strength modular cast iron linings. Low-pressure compressed air was used to limit the undesirable effects of waterbearing and/or weak strata.

In order to stabilise the honeycomb of old coal workings along the Gateshead route a preliminary contract to explore and fill the cavities was let. The arched section tunnels, 5 metres wide and 6.9 metres high, were supported initially with steel ribs prior to construction of an in-situ concrete lining. At the portals short lengths of the tunnel were built in in-situ concrete using a cut-and-cover technique.

There are seven stations within the underground portion of the system, some presenting complex problems of construction. The technique of excavation beneath a preconstructed roof slab supported by piles was employed to minimise disruption at some locations. Main electrical and mechanical services for the underground stations, including lifts and escalators, were designed by the firm's associated Mechanical and Electrical Group.

Construction of the metro started in October 1974 and the work has been programmed for the 55 km system to become operational in phases, reaching completion in 1983.

The firm is also fulfilling a project management role which includes co-ordination, programming and cost monitoring of all project elements through commissioning to operation. Estimated construction cost (1980) is £250 million.

Tripoli—Misurata railway

In 1978, Mott, Hay and Anderson was appointed by the National Consulting Bureau to plan and design a new 200 km railway between Tripoli and Misurata. Traffic surveys were carried out and passenger and freight traffic forecasts prepared. Investigations were undertaken to identify industries where potential rail traffic could justify branch lines. Economic analyses were carried out to compare transport costs by rail with alternative transport costs by road. Operating studies were undertaken to evolve an operating strategy and train service plans were prepared. Motive power studies identified the characteristics and number of locomotives, whilst rolling stock studies identified the types and number of coaching stock and freight wagons. Signalling and telecommunications studies reviewed the alternatives for train control and communications and made recommendations for the optimum system. The civil engineering planning studies identified alternative route corridors after completing geotechnical, hydrological development planning, and topographical studies.

Preliminary designs for freight yards, bridges, culverts, viaducts, drainage and measures to combat wind blown sand were prepared. Maintenance studies for locomotives, rolling stock, permanent way, structures, signalling, telecommunications, mechanical and electrical equipment and road vehicles were undertaken and the organisation, equipment buildings and staff identified.

On approval of the planning and engineering studies the firm prepared detailed designs and contract documents for the complete project. The contract documentation was prepared in both the Arabic and English languages.

Estimated construction cost is £220 million.

Dublin Suburban Railway electrification

In 1977, Mott, Hay & Anderson International Ltd was appointed consulting engineers to Córas Iompair Éireann for the Dublin Suburban Railway electrification project between Howth and Bray, a distance of approximately 45 km; the project forms the first phase of a proposed metro system for Dublin. The firm's brief has been extensive from initial recommendation on the choice of transport system to the design and supervision of construction/installation of the power systems and equipment with further responsibilities for the rolling stock design and for interfacing and compatibility between the various engineering disciplines.

A 1500-volt dc overhead line system is being provided, fed by five substations each with dual feed to the Electricity Supply Boards' 38 kV grid. The overhead line is a lightweight, automatically-tensioned, pre-sagged contact system. The substations have twin transformers and rectifiers rated to enable a service to be maintained in the event of incapability of an individual unit. Traction supplies are controlled and monitored by a computer-based telemetry system installed in the control centre at Connolly. From information displayed on visual display monitors, a single operator can control the power supplies from a desk mounted keyboard.

The rolling stock consists of emus with a motored car and a trailing car. They are being designed to be suitable for running in future bored tunnels of the proposed underground section. Features include chopper controls, regenerative braking, passenger-operated doors with driver override, driver and passenger radio communication with control centre. The emus are all equipped with an automatic train control system which has to be compatible with the new signalling system being installed for the diesel trains which will still be operating over part of the line. Of particular interest is a fail-safe frequency detector which is being developed to ensure that frequencies generated by the chopper control are within a selected band width so as not to interfere with the signalling system.

The electrified system and rolling stock used on the Howth-Bray line will enable Córas Iompair Éireann to operate a six-car emu service generally at four-minute headways with three-minute headways in the central area. The new service is due to commence in 1983.

Estimated cost of the project is £60 million.

As an additional brief, Mott, Hay & Anderson in association with John B Barry & Partners has also been commissioned to undertake the design of a new rapid transit railway line from Tallaght to Dublin, forming the second phase of a new metro system for Dublin. Estimated cost of this project is £60 million.

Caracas Metro, Line 2 and Las Adjuntas depot

Mott, Hay & Anderson International Ltd has undertaken the preliminary design and route selection for Line 2 of the Caracas Metro between Silencio in the city and Caricuao, a centre of population with around 200 000 inhabitants. The line will generally follow the valley of the river Guaire and the corridor served has a total population of 600 000. Of the 26 km total length of the line, approximately 8 km will be elevated, 6 km in tunnel and 12 km in shallow cutting or on the surface. The scheme includes 13 stations, of which eight will be underground. The stations at Caricuao are designed as elevated structures. Following the route selection study the firm was engaged to carry out the final alignment and detailed design of the southern 22 km of the line, which includes nine stations.

As part of Line 2, a rolling stock maintenance depot is required. This is to be located at the out-of-town end of the line at Las Adjuntas. A terminal station for passengers and a 1.5 km test track are included in the project. The depot will provide storage for 40 train-sets, workshops for both light and heavy maintenance, workshops for permanent way, a control tower, offices and the usual staff services. A train washing facility and a turntable are included in the complicated track layout and a system of internal roads links various parts of the depot.

After formulating the master plan for the depot and obtaining the approval of the client, the track geometry data was put on to a specially developed computer programme and the layout drawings plotted on to survey drawings of the area using a CADMAC plotter. The computer programme can be used to plot a drawing of any location at any scale and was also used to provide setting-out information to the contractor installing trackwork. Provision of specialist detailed design advice as well as project management formed part of the firm's brief. The work was commissioned by various consulting engineers for CA Metro de Caracas, and the estimated construction cost is £450 million.

Maputo-Chicualacuala and Beira-Machipanda railway rehabilitation study

Mott, Hay & Anderson International Ltd in association with Maxwell Stamp Associates, has been commissioned by the UK Overseas Development Administration to carry out rehabilitation studies on railway systems in Mozambique. The studies are being carried out under British technical co-operation arrangements. The brief involves a study of two lines from the port of Maputo to the Zimbabwe/Mozambique border at Chicualacuala and from Beira port to Machipanda, also on the Zimbabwe/Mozambique border. The lines have a combined length of approximately 850 km. The study examines the existing operating arrangements, signalling, telecommunications, permanent way and motive power (steam and diesel), in addition to rolling stock, power supplies, workshops and other maintenance facilities.

Economic studies undertaken have forecast future traffic levels over each of the lines and a future train service pattern has been developed.

Improvements to infrastructure, equipment and maintenance procedures, which will enable the future train service to be achieved, have been identified and costs and benefits allocated. A preliminary cost/benefit study has been carried out on each of the improvement options and they have been ranked in order of priority for allocation of the available aid funds.

Implementation studies are currently in progress for the Limpopo and Beira-Machipanda Railway Lines.

Estimated capital cost for the rehabilitation works is £10 million.

Bored tunnel section of Caracas Metro Line 1, for which Mott Hay & Anderson acted as adviser to Consorcio Grid APM and other Venezuelan consultants

Unloading a Howth-Bray Suburban electrification emu car at Dublin

Plaza Venezuela station, Caracas Metro Line 1, nearing completion

Peter Muller-Munk Associates
Division of Wilbur Smith & Associates

Room 717, Four Gateway Center, Pittsburgh, Pennsylvania 15222, USA

Telephone: (412) 261 5161

Director: Paul R Wiedmann

Projects
Advanced concept train (ACT-1) for AiResearch/Urban Mass Transit Administration (UMTA);
Australian Urban Passenger Train (AUPT) for Ministry of Transport, Australia;
Station signage system for Greater Cleveland Regional Transit Authority.

The MVA Consultancy
Transportation Planning and Management Consultants

112 Strand, London WC2R 0AA, England

Telephone: 01-836 9381
Telegrams: Martinvor, London WC2
Telex: 298648

Directors: Martin Richards (Managing Director)
Alan Powell
Simon Coventry
Brian Large
Hugh Neffendorf
Mick Roberts

Capabilities
The consultancy, formerly known as Martin and Voorhees Associates, is a British company of transport, planning and management consultants which has been commissioned for more than 90 projects either exclusively or partially concerned with railways. These cover a wide range including rail investment, planning, operating and marketing. The company undertakes a comprehensive range of projects concerned with the planning of transport systems covering urban, regional, national, corridor and rural areas. These are concerned with the short-term issues of marketing, operation and management as well as the longer-term issues of investment policy. The consultancy was originally formed in 1968 as a subsidiary of AMV Inc, with whom it still continues to have an association.

Clients for rail and rail-related studies in United Kingdom have included: British Rail; Northern Ireland Railways; London Transport; Greater Manchester Passenger Transport Executive; West Midlands Passenger Transport Executive; Mid and South Glamorgan County Councils; South Yorkshire County Council; Tyne and Wear County Council; West Midlands County Council; West Yorkshire County Council; London Borough of Hackney; Highlands and Islands Development Board; Peak Park Planning Board; Redditch Development Corporation; Transport and Road Research Laboratory.

International clients include: International Union of Railways (UIC); Córas Iompair Éireann (CIE), Ireland; Public Works Department, Hong Kong; Mass Transit Corporation, Hong Kong; Ministry of Transport, Netherlands; Urbanisticki Zavod Grada Beograda, Yugoslavia; Pakistan Government; Ministry of Communications, Libya; Ministry of Transport, Victoria, Australia; EYSER (Madrid) for Commission for Planning, Valencia Region, Spain; National Railroad Passenger Corporation (Amtrak), USA; Valencia Metro Authority, Venezuela.

The consultancy undertakes railway projects at many different levels including strategic studies (investment, operating and marketing), transport planning and co-ordination, and studies concerned with short-term issues in respect of facilities such as catering and reservations or pricing and promotion.

Projects
Investment studies
In Glasgow, the consultancy is completing a study of the impact of re-opening the city's underground system, following an £80 million modernisation programme. Considering all types of travel patterns, the study has adopted a cost-benefit approach to assessment of the overall effects of the investment, and has

considered the impact of service changes on journeys for individual trip purposes, social impacts, changes in land use, and development and property values.

In the West Midlands the consultancy is advising the County Council and the Passenger Transport Executive on a study to investigate the effects of linking the rail services to Stourbridge in the west and to Dorridge to the east via a reinstated link across Birmingham city centre. Following extensive data collection the consultancy will be providing detailed advice on the development of disaggregate modelling techniques.

The Ministry of Transport in the Netherlands has commissioned the consultancy to develop a model for forecasting long-distance travel demand. This is an integral part of the Ministry's evaluation of the proposed new railway line between Lelystad and Groningen, the Zuiderzee Line.

Local rail or area studies
The consultancy has undertaken a number of planning studies concerned with optimisation or rationalisation of urban railway networks.

In a follow-up study commissioned by the London Borough of Hackney, the consultancy is evaluating the implications of British Rail's plans to re-route the North London Line, between Dalston and the City, and assessing the feasibility, costs and movements implications of alternative proposals put forward by the borough. This study is drawing on the findings of a preliminary study commissioned by the borough which evaluated a number of alternative plans for the route using a cost-benefit approach, assigning passengers to alternative modes on the basis of time and fares, and calculating the resource time and capital and operating costs of the options analysed.

Rail rapid transit studies
In Venezuela, the consultancy has begun a network and operations design study for the proposed Valencia Metro system. The study will include engineering requirements, operating patterns, demand forecasting, the effects on competing modes, and the traffic management measures demanded by the new system.

National City Management Company

9720 Town Park Drive, Suite 109, Houston, Texas 77036, USA

Telephone: (713) 772 1272

President/General Manager: Stan Gates Jr

Projects
Management contracts with West Palm Beach, Florida; Shreveport, Louisiana; Colorado Springs, Colorado; Spokane Transit System, Spokane, Washington.

PAR International

200 Madison Avenue, Morristown, New Jersey 07960, USA

Telephone: (201) 267 8900

President: Louis C Ripa

Projects
State airport system plan report for New Jersey Department of Transportation (DOT); transportation centre (multi-modal) ($60 million) for Essex County, New Jersey.

Parsons Brinckerhoff CENTEC Inc
Parsons Brinckerhoff CENTEC International Inc

8200 Greenboro Drive, Suite 1000, McLean, Virginia 22102, USA

Telephone: (703) 442 7740
Telex: 89 9493

President: R K Pattison
Senior Vice-President: R A Symons

Projects
Consultant in joint venture with others for preliminary and final location and design of 850 km line in Morocco;
Consultant for study of rehabilitation and upgrading of the Sudan Railway's system;
Advisors to Government of Colombia for the design of a coal haul railroad;
Consultant for the design of the track signal and bridge rehabilitation programme for the Massachusetts Bay Transportation Authority;
Design of track work for Niagara Frontier Transportation Authority, Buffalo, New York light rail rapid transit system;
Railroad design for the US Corps of Engineers.

Ralph M Parsons Company

100 West Walnut, Pasadena, California 91124, USA

Telephone: (213) 440 2000

Vice-President: Forrest C Six

Projects
US Department of Transportation: Programme management of the $2500 million Northeast Corridor Improvement Project to upgrade 456 miles (734 km) of rail line between Boston and Washington DC. Project has included rehabilitation of track, electrification, bridges, stations, signalling, communications and introduction of automated track laying system (TLS) for first-time installation of concrete sleepers in United States.

Maryland Department of Transportation: Construction management of the $790 million Baltimore Region Rapid Transit System, consisting of underground and elevated rails, stations and auxiliary support systems. (Additional rail project information is listed under De Leuw, Cather & Company, which is a wholly-owned subsidiary of The Parsons Corporation.)

Peat, Marwick, Mitchell & Co

1025 Connecticut Ave NW, Washington DC 20036, USA

Telephone: (202) 223 9525

Principals: D M Hill, C Macdorman

Projects
Alternatives analysis restudy for Metropolitan Washington Council;
Alternatives analysis study for Southeastern Michigan Transportation Authority (SEMTA).

Peregrine and Partners

PO Box 3, Royston, Hertfordshire SG8 7BU, England

Telephone: 0763 42384
Telex: 817178

US associates: H K Friedland and Associates, PO Box 893, Solana Beach, California 92075, USA
Telephone: (714) 481 9339

Gianotti Associates, 380 Station Road, Bellport, New York 11713
Telephone: (516) 286 9492

Capabilities
Established in 1950, the firm has an international practice in mechanical engineering design, manufacture and commissioning of prototypes and working machinery for governments, universities, consulting firms and major industry; invention; arbitration.

Pickering-Wooten-Smith-Weiss Inc

821 S Barksdale, Memphis, Tennessee 38114, USA

Telephone: (901) 726 0810

Vice-President: Don P Smith

Projects
Preliminary plans and feasibility studies for Highland Street/Southern Railway, City of Memphis.

Wm S Pollard Consulting Inc

1395 Madison Avenue, Memphis, Tennessee 38104, USA

Telephone: (901) 726 6300

President: William S Pollard

Projects
Environmental impact assessment, Wilmington Outer Loop (approximately $167 000) for North Carolina Department of Transportation (DOT).

Rail India Technical & Economic Services Ltd (RITES)

27 Barakhamba Road, New Delhi House, New Delhi 110 001, India

Telephone: 44261
Telegrams: Ritesrail, New Delhi
Telex: 031-4143, 031-3996

Chairman: P N Kaul
Managing Director: R Parthasarathy
Director, Technical: J Sharan
Director, Finance: G C Sharma
General Manager, Projects: A N Shukla

Rail India Technical and Economic Services Ltd is an organisation formed under the Ministry of Railways, Government of India, to meet the needs of professional consultancy service in all facets of railway technology. The company has over 500 experts in various fields for transport consultancy and management. RITES also maintains an active computerised roster of over 3000 experts in various disciplines from which specialists can be drawn from Indian Railways and other organisations, depending upon requirements.

Capabilities
Techno-economic feasibility studies and project appraisals; investment planning and cost analysis; engineering surveys; transport studies and traffic surveys; detailed design, engineering and documentation for new line construction, doubling, gauge conversion and railway electrification projects; system design and specifications for electric power supply, signalling and telecommunications; advice on tender invitation, evaluation of bids and award of contracts; contract administration; construction supervision and contract management; organisation structuring, staffing studies and manpower planning; work studies and inventory control; management information systems; planning rolling stock requirements, advice on selection and design of

rolling stock; planning facilities for maintenance and repair of rolling stock; planning railway production units; workshop and rolling stock maintenance management; line capacity studies, transport optimisation studies and operation research; merry-go-round systems for bulk transport; design of training facilities and training of personnel; quality assurance, inspection and testing.

Projects

	Client	Project description
Algeria	National Society of Rail Transport (SNTF)	Survey of new line from Aintouta to M'Sila
Ghana	Ministry of Transport and Communications	Technical services for maintenance of rolling stock and training of personnel
India	Bihar State Government (PWD)	Detailed survey and engineering of high level road bridges across River Kosi and River Gango
	Assam State Government (PWD)	Techno-economic feasibility cum detailed investigation for bridge across River Brahmaputra
	UP State Electricity Board	Anpara Super Thermal Power Station merry-go-round system
	National Aluminium Co Ltd	Turnkey consultancy services for rail transport system
	National Thermal Power Corporation	Turnkey consultancy for rapid coal transport system
Iraq	State Railway Organisation	Design and general engineering services
	New Railway Implementation Authority	Provision of integrated technical and economic services; studies for new railway direct lines for cement movement
Jordan	Aqaba Railway Corporation	Technical and professional services for maintenance and operation
Mozambique	Direccão Nacional dos Portos e Caminhos de Ferro (DNPCF)	Technical services for strengthening management of railways
Philippines	Philippines National Railway	Consultancy for improvement and rehabilitation of railways
Tanzania	Tanzanian Railway Corporation	Training of personnel
Tanzania & Zambia	Commonwealth Secretariat	Consultancy, salary review, Tazara
Zambia	Zambia Railway Board	Management support for implementation of World Bank project; productivity study of Kabwe workshop
Zimbabwe	National Railway of Zimbabwe	Technical services for railway operation and management

Railway Systems Design Inc

105 Hagley Building, Concord Plaza, 3411 Silverside Road, Wilmington, Delaware 19810, USA

Capabilities
Railway signalling and communications systems.

Real Estate Research Corp

1101 17th St NW, Washington DC 20036, USA

Telephone: (202) 223 4500

Vice-President: C H Broley

Projects
People movers for US Department of Transportation.

Rendel Palmer & Tritton

61 Southwark Street, London SE1 1SA, England

Telephone: 01-928 8999
Telegrams: Rendels, London SE1
Telex: 919553

Associate companies
RPT Economic Studies Group
61 Southwark Street, London SE1 1SA
Telephone: 01-928 4222. Telex: 266664
Bush & Rennie Associates
Bush & Rennie International Ltd
53 Bishopric, Horsham, Sussex
Telephone: 0403 50694. Telex: 877542
Rendel Scott Furphy
390 St Kilda Road, Melbourne, Australia
Planave SA
Rua Costa Ferreira 106, Rio de Janeiro, Brazil
PT Indulexco
Jalan Abdul Muis 42, Jakarta Pusat, Indonesia

Partners: P A Cox
J C Munro
R Downham
P J Clark
L W Hinch
D W Hookway
E T Haws
P J A Corfield
J A Sweetapple
B J Dixon-Smith
Consultants: J L Koffman
D M S Fairweather

Projects
Railway consultancy projects completed since 1970 or at present under way include:

Northern Ireland Railways: Redevelopment of York Road terminal and workshops, Belfast; new freight yard at Adelaide, Belfast; reconstruction of Belfast Central railway and new Central station; review of motive power and rolling stock.

British Rail: Channel Tunnel rail link, preliminary plans for 27 km of route; design of 23 bridges and erection schemes for Eastern Region; reports and preliminary design of 11 bridges.

Australia: Investigation and report on Burragorong-Scarborough railway (60 km); Goldsworthy-Kennedy Gap railway, design of 96 km of new line; Mount Newman Mining Co, reporting and advising on locomotives and track maintenance problems; feasibility study for a 70 km railway in Western Australia; investigation and report on a railway from German Creek to the Queensland coast (220 km).

Malaysia: Investigation, report and outline relocation plan for Port Dickson railway.

Jordan: Survey, design and construction of El Hasa-Manzil extension (25 km); preparation of tender documents and reports on tenders for locomotives, rolling stock, workshop and track maintenance equipment and extensions to signalling system; transport study for carriage by road and rail of imports and exports; feasibility study for railway extension from Aqaba to Wadi 2; review of previous studies and new rail route to phosphate deposits at Shadiya.

Sudan: Comparative study of road and rail transport for agricultural products.

Brazil: General transport studies, including railways, for all major Brazilian ports and for Amazonas and San Salvador regions.

Kenya: Survey and design of the Kerio Valley Railway (315 km) including 5 km of tunnel in association with East African Engineering Consultants, Kenya.

Iraq: Member of the British Metro Consultants Group for Baghdad.

Indonesia: Rail utilisation study for Surabaya Port; railway feeder line study for Java; national transport demand study.

Kenneth R Roberts & Associates Inc

10560 Main Street, Suite 515, Fairfax, Virginia 22030, USA

Telephone: (703) 591 6008

President: Kenneth R Roberts

Capabilities
Microcomputer-based software and hardware systems for: vehicle and driver scheduling; equipment maintenance; transportation planning; 'dial-a-ride'; parts inventory; transit information; passenger counting; schedule development; payroll accounting.

Projects
Recent projects include equipment for 'dial-a-ride' systems in Akron, Ohio, Syracuse, New York and Mount Pleasant, Michigan.

Rummel, Klepper & Kahl

1035 North Calvert Street, Baltimore, Maryland 21202, USA

Telephone: (301) 685 3105

Partner: A L Deen Jr

Projects
Shady Grove extension of Rockville route, 4.3 km ($35 million) for Washington Metropolitan Area Transit Authority (WMATA); Phase I Section B of the Baltimore Region Rapid Transit System, 10 km ($53 million) for Mass Transit Administration of Maryland (MTA).

S & A Systems Inc

8035 East Thornton Freeway, Dallas, Texas 75228, USA

Telephone: (214) 328 4649

President: J G Srygley

Capabilities
Rail transit-related computer studies; maintenance systems; scheduling.

Projects
Control system simulation for Metropolitan Atlanta Rapid Transit Authority (MARTA).

STV Engineers

11 Robinson Street, Pottstown, Pennsylvania 19464, USA

Telephone: (215) 326 4600
Telex: 84-6430

Chairman: R L Holland

Key rail staff: C E Defendorf
F G Fisher
D M Servedio
I P Yatzkan
P E Craig
J T Pesuit, Jr
R S Frees
B H Clark, Jr

Capabilities
Transport planning; system and facility design; rolling stock engineering; operations and maintenance analysis.

Projects
Northeast Corridor high-speed rail passenger service improvement study (construction cost $4000 million) for Federal Railroad Administration (FRA).
Railroad track maintenance inspection programme in northeastern and midwestern USA (construction cost $160 million) for US Railway Association (USRA).
Freight car and locomotive rehabilitation programme loan application analysis (construction cost $60 million) for FRA.
New York Dock Railway waterfront modernisation project (construction cost $30 million) for New York State Department of Transportation and FRA.
Commuter rail rolling stock upgrade study and engineering (construction cost $26 million) for Massachusetts Bay Transportation Authority.
Philadelphia Center city commuter rail connection sections (construction cost $360 million) for City of Philadelphia.
Evaluation of train signal/control system equipment and technology (engineering fee $550 000) for FRA.
Northeast regional railroad inventory (engineering fee $750 000) for USRA.
Storage yard and maintenance facilities modernisation and expansion study (engineering fee $250 000) for New York City Transit Authority.
Twin Cities light rail feasibility study (engineering fee $150 000) for the Metropolitan Council, St Paul, Michigan.
In-plant inspection of rolling stock, LaGrange, Illinois (engineering fee $27 164) for Massachusetts Bay Transportation Authority.
Morris Park and Richmond Hill shop and yard improvements for Long Island Rail Road, New York.
Hightower Road and Oakland City elevated mass transit rail line sections and stations for Metropolitan Atlanta Rapid Transit Authority, Atlanta, Georgia.
Grand Central Station subway station rehabilitation for New York City Transit Authority.
Final design for West Side storage yard for Metropolitan Transportation Authority, New York.

Schimpeler Corradino Associates

1429 South Third Street, Louisville, Kentucky 40208, USA

Telephone: (502) 636 3555

Principal: Joseph C Corradino

Projects
Rapid transit implementation for Metropolitan Dade County Transit Agency, Miami; transit alternatives analysis in Houston, Texas; Dallas, Texas; and Detroit, Michigan; environmental impact assessment guidelines for US Department of Transportation, Urban Mass Transportation Administration.

Seelye Stevenson Value & Knecht Engineers & Planners

99 Park Avenue, New York, New York 10016, USA

Telephone: (212) 687 4000

Capabilities
Track and fixed facilities design; passenger stations and terminal design; rolling stock rehabilitation and procurements.

Sheridan Associates

575 Lexington Ave, New York, New York 10022, USA

Telephone: (212) 750 6960

President: James J Sheridan

Projects
ACT-1 vehicle design for General Electric Corp.

Simpson and Curtin
Division of Booz, Allen & Hamilton, Inc

400 Market Street, Philadelphia, Pennsylvania 19106, USA

Telephone: (215) 627 5450

President: Michael G Ferreri

Projects
Commuter rail contract management study for the Massachusetts Bay Transportation Authority;
Organisation and management development assistance to the Long Island Rail Road;
Car maintenance management assistance to the Long Island Rail Road;
Performance audit of the Bay Area Rapid Transit District;
Organisation and management study for the Chicago Transit Authority;
Management and organisation study for the Louisiana Department of Transportation;
Management and organisation study for the West Yorkshire County Council.

Frank C Smith & Associates

8585 Stemmons Freeway, Dallas, Texas 75247, USA

Telephone: (214) 630 4716

Principal: Frank C Smith

Projects
System availability studies in support of UMTA programme for Urban Mass Transportation Administration (UMTA).

Smith & Howard Associates Inc

1735 Eye Street NW, Suite 704, Washington DC 20026, USA

Telephone: (202) 223 5133

President: Irving P Smith

Capabilities
The firm serves as Washington representative to transit systems and transit equipment suppliers. In addition, technical studies are performed with specialisation and regulatory studies as well as studies pertaining to marketing.

Wilbur Smith and Associates

155 Whitney Avenue, New Haven, Connecticut 06507, USA

Telephone: (203) 865 2191

Chairman: Wilbur S Smith

Projects
Florida rail plan and intermodal transportation study for Florida Department of Transportation: state-wide assessment of rail lines and rail-truck transfer points.
New Jersey railroad users assistance project for State of New Jersey: assist rail users in negotiations with Conrail.
Pinellas County, Florida SCL railroad corridor freight analysis for Florida Department of Transportation: rail freight corridor feasibility study.
Montana State rail plan update for State of Montana: state-wide evaluation of Montana railroad system.
Railroad element Mississippi multi-modal transportation plan for State of Mississippi: state-wide evaluation of rail lines and railroad services.
Railroad element, Iowa Blue Ribbon task force on transportation: examination of state policies and funding relative to all modes of transport.
Hampton and Branchville railroad evaluation study for the H&B Railroad: assessment of the value of this short-line railroad.
Singapore mass rapid transit system for provisional Mass Rapid Transit Authority: co-ordinating design consultants with DCI for new rapid transit system.

Sodeteg-TAI

Route de la Minière, 78530 Buc, France

Telephone: 956 8060

Commercial Manager, Transportation Division: Narcisse Louis

Capabilities
Study and construction of transport systems; metro train control, power control and communications; light rail transit systems; marshalling yard automation.

Sofrerail
Société Française d'Etudes et de Réalisations Ferroviaires

3 avenue Hoche, 75008 Paris, France

Telephone: (755) 97 08
Telegrams: Sofrerail, Paris
Telex: 280084

President: Marcel Tessier
Managing Director: Bernard Broca
Technical Director: Hubert Autruffe
Commercial Director: Dominique Boblet
Deputy Technical Director: Jean-Bernard Bergouignan

Capabilities
Sofrerail is a private company, founded in 1957, the first of its kind to supply consultancy services for all fields of railway activity.

Overall studies involve: reorganisation of rail networks, preparation of investment plans, construction of new lines and electrification projects. Special studies cover very diverse sectors: analysis of transport costs, tariff reform, containerisation, maintenance of rolling stock, modern track maintenance, signalling and telecommunications systems and adaptation to traffic and town planning projects. Technical assistance is carried out by teams of specialists and technicians for the application, down to working level, of the resulting recommendations.

Sofrerail is backed up by the important knowledge and know-how potential of high-level engineers, economists and managers, as well as technicians of the French National Railways (SNCF).

Sofrerail has carried out numerous railway and transport studies in more than 80 countries on behalf of governments, international agencies and railway administrations.

Projects
Algeria: Technical assistance for preliminary diagnosis of tunnels; preparation of documents to issue call for bids; scrutiny of the offers and preparation of the contracts; checking of studies for rehabilitation of the tunnels (1979-83).
Argentina: Technical assistance with traffic, permanent way, railway master plan (1980-83).
Botswana-Swaziland: Setting up of a regional railway training scheme (1982-84).
Congo, People's Republic: Training and improvement of managerial staff of the rolling stock and drivers' departments (1983-84).
Gabon: Supervision and control of the construction of the Transgabonese Railway first phase, Owendo-Booué (1979-83); extension of the assignment to the second phase, Booué-Franceville (1983-88).
Indonesia: Improvement of the mining line from Bukit Asam coal mine to the sea: detailed studies, preparation of documents for call for bids, supervision of the works (1982-87); detailed study and design of a transport network for Phase II of the North Sumatra oil palm project, in association with BCEOM (1981-83).
Iraq: Study of the Baghdad loop line and railway complex (1979-82); study of the Baghdad-Mosul line with a branch line to Baquba and Khaniqin (1980-83); preliminary design of Kirkuk-Suleymaniya line (1981-82); design of the new Suleiman Beg-Khaniquin line (1981-82); design of Mosul station (1981-82).
Jamaica: Technical assistance for the rehabilitation of the Jamaica Railway Corporation (JRC) (1978-80); scrutiny of a call for bids for the purchase of diesel-electric locomotives, spare parts and tools for maintenance (1981); technical assistance to JRC in the fields of track maintenance, locomotive rehabilitation and rolling stock maintenance (1981-84).
Jordan: Participation in studies of the economic feasibility of developing the Shidiyah rock phosphate deposit: railway infrastructure and operation (1982-83).
Libya: Study of rolling stock: definition of specifications (1981-83); study of setting-up and organising the administration of the Libyan Arab Railways (structures, personnel, regulations, buildings) (1981-83).
Morocco: Detailed design and study of a new standard-gauge line from Marrakesh to Agadir and Laayoun; preparation of the documents to call for bids (1977-83).
Nepal: Feasibility study of the construction of an electrified railway network: traffic forecasts, definition of the lines to cope with the needs, economic results for the community (1982-83).
Nigeria: Scrutiny of bids made for the construction of the new lines from Port Harcourt to Makurdi and Oturkpo to Ajaokuta (1979); supervision of the engineering works for the Port Harcourt to Makurdi and Oturkpo-Ajaokuta lines (1981-84); study of the equipment necessary (signalling, telecommunications, rolling stock, workshops, energy supplies).
Senegal: Participation in studies for MIFERSO concerning railway and port facilities for handling iron ore from La Faleme (1981-83).
Sudan: Revision of the methods used to compute transport costs; adaptation of tariffs; study of road competition, mainly on the Port Sudan-Khartoum axis.
Uganda: Technical assistance in rehabilitating the network (1980-84).

Sofretu
Société Française d'Etudes et de Réalisations de Transports Urbains

12/14 rue Jules César, 75012 Paris, France

Telephone: (31-1) 346 11 26
Telegrams: Sofretu, Paris
Telex: 210120

Chairman and General Manager: M Ernst

Capabilities
As a subsidiary of RATP (the Paris transport authority), Sofretu has at its disposal all the experience and the know-how of the engineers and technicians of the parent company, It is exclusively concerned with urban transport engineering: buses, trolleybuses, trams and subways. Its expertise embraces administrative, technical and financial analyses of existing situations; general traffic studies; transport plans; preliminary project and detailed design; drafting of technical specifications; drafting of invitation to tender files; assistance during tender selection; in-situ and in-plant fabrication checks; start-up assistance; and personnel training

Projects
Analyses and general studies: Lille, Marseilles, Nantes, Ankara, Athens, Bogota, Casablanca, Curitiba, Dakar, Kinshasa, Kuwait, Cairo, Recife, Santiago de Chile, São Paulo, Singapore, Tehran

Preliminary project and detailed design: Lille, Lyons, Marseilles, Nantes, Toulouse, Abidjan, Athens, Bogota, Curitiba, Cairo, Montreal, Santiago de Chile, Tehran

Technical specifications, bids of tender, construction follow-up: Lille, Lyons, Marseilles, Nantes, Abuja, Algiers, Atlanta, Caracas, Cairo, Mexico, Montreal, Rio de Janeiro, Santiago de Chile, São Paulo, Tehran, Tunis

Personnel training: Lyons, Marseilles, Abidjan, Caracas, Cairo, Montreal, Rio de Janeiro, Santiago de Chile, Tehran

Steer, Davies & Gleave

68 Upper Richmond Road, London SW15 2RP, England

Telephone: 01-874 6583

Director: James K Steer

Capabilities
Marketing, market research; metro and light rail investment appraisal.

Sundberg-Ferar Inc

1548 American Center, Southfield, Michigan 48034, USA

Telephone: (313) 356 8600

President: Richard A Heck

Projects
Bay Area Rapid Transit District (BART): follow-up on new 'C' car production; control centre design; Washington Metropolitan Area Transit Authority (WMATA); follow-up vehicle designs.

Sverdrup Corporation

801 North Eleventh, St Louis, Missouri 63101, USA

Telephone: (314) 436 7600

Vice-President: Gordon R Pennington

Projects
Cut-and-cover tunnel and two stations ($200 million), part of the Boston Red Line extension, for Massachusetts Bay Transportation Authority;
Frankford Elevated Railway reconstruction ($300 million), involving 11 stations, three bridges, trackwork, and communication facilities, for the City of Philadelphia;
Modernisation of 10 rapid transit stations ($30 million) in Manhattan, Brooklyn and Queens, for New York City Transit Authority;
Upper Harlem Line improvements ($30 million), including new high-level platforms, new overhead pedestrian crossings, and more than 47 km (29 miles) of power-carrying rail, for Metropolitan Transportation Authority of New York;
Five-year capital improvement programme ($150 million), for Long Island Rail Road facilities in New York; also new 8 km (5-mile) electrified main line ($19 million);
Environmental and engineering study for 100 km (62-mile) coal-haul line in Utah for the Denver & Rio Grande Western Railroad;
Locomotive service complex ($3 million) in Fort Worth, Texas, for the Missouri Pacific Railroad;
Subway rehabilitation project ($20 million) in Newark, involving 11 stations, for New Jersey Transit Corporation;
Lead consultant for bridges and tunnels on the 730 km (456-mile), $2500 million Northeast Corridor Improvement Project between Washington DC and Boston, Massachusetts;
Relocation and consolidation of East St Louis rail yard, used by 17 railroad companies, for the Illinois Department of Transportation;
Railroad rehabilitation studies for the US Railway Association.

Relocation and consolidation of East St Louis yard, Illinois

Swederail Consulting AB

105 50 Stockholm, Sweden

Telephone: 46 87 62 37 80
Telegrams: Statsbanan, Stockholm
Telex: 19410

President: Per-Erik Olson

Swederail Consulting is a subsidary of the Swedish State Railways, SJ, and two major Swedish consultancies, Scandiaconsult and VIAK. It is independent of any industrial, construction or banking interest.

Projects

Feasibility study and preliminary engineering for rehabilitation and electrification of railways in Southern Mozambique and Swaziland; the study covers a railway network of almost 1000 km of prime economic strategic importance for transport of merchandise of various kinds from major countries in Eastern Africa to the Indian Ocean.

Feasibility study design and final construction of electrification of Tumbler Ridge coal line of British Columbia Railways in Western Canada; the project includes studies and design of 50 kV 60 Hz electrification in an area of very severe climate conditions. The railway is designed for heavy hauls.

Syscon Corporation

1054 31st St NW, Washington DC 20007, USA

Telephone: (202) 342 4000

Senior Programme Engineer: William V Garvey

Projects

Analysis and specification for automated telephone transit information system ($80 000) for Washington Metropolitan Area Transit Authority (WMATA); Designed/implemented automated information dissemination system ($95 000) for Southeastern Pennsylvania Transit Authority (SEPTA).

TAMS Engineers
Tippetts-Abbett-McCarthy-Stratton

The TAMS Building, 655 Third Avenue, New York, New York 10017, USA

Telephone: (212) 867 1777
Telegrams: Tamseng New York
Telex: ITT 422188, RCA 223055, WU 125674

Partners: John Lowe, III
Wilson V Binger
Raymond J Hodge
Austin E Brant, Jr
John E Bardes
Robert F Heins
Dana E Low
Eugene O'Brien
Donald R Peirce
Patrick J McAward, Jr
Philip Perdichizzi

Capabilities

Tippetts-Abbett-McCarthy-Stratton (TAMS), founded in 1942, offers international services in engineering, architecture and planning. The firm's project work, carried out in more than 70 countries, has included ports, highways, railroads, bridges, airports, dams, agricultural and regional development, economic and feasibility studies, and urban planning. Besides its New York headquarters, TAMS maintains 23 branch offices world-wide and throughout the United States.

TAMS has more than 30 years' experience in the planning, design and inspection of railroad facilities, having been involved in the engineering of more than 4000 km of railroads throughout the world. Projects range from planning new lines through jungle or desert to rapid transit systems in US cities. Services provided by TAMS include location and alignment, trackwork, bridges, tunnels and marshalling yards. The firm has also provided track location and development studies at Wilmington, Delaware; Philadelphia, Pennsylvania; Providence, Rhode Island; and other locations. Rapid transit facilities have been planned and designed for Boston, New York, Baltimore, Washington DC and Atlanta, Georgia.

Services provided overseas have included rail transport feasibility studies for Congo, Upper Volta, Turkey, Republic of Korea and Burma, among others. In West Africa, the 455-mile Transgabon Railroad is being built through rain forest, savannah and swampland to facilitate the transport of vital resources (iron ore, manganese, wood). The TAMS-engineered COMILOG ore-transport system in Congo and Gabon, comprising 300 km of railroad and 80 km of tramway, has been operating successfully for more than 20 years. The Mt Newman Iron Ore Project, Australia, built a new 420 km railroad between Mt Newman and Port Hedland. In Canada, a 320 km railroad was built to connect the Quebec Cartier Mining Company's iron ore mine at Lac Jeannine with Port Cartier on the north shore of the St Lawrence River.

Projects

Recent projects have included:

Transgabon Railroad: TAMS, in association with the firms of BCEOM and Sofrerail and Electroconsult of Italy, was retained by OCTRA, the Transgabon Railroad Authority, to provide engineering services in connection with the design review and supervision of construction of the Transgabon Railroad. Services include the review of designs prepared by the contractors and supervision of the construction of all works below the ballast level from Libreville to Franceville, totalling approximately 730 km of railroad.

Mount Newman Railroad, Western Australia: TAMS provided architectural and engineering services to the Mount Newman Iron Ore Corporation for an iron ore project in Western Australia, including the design of a 451 km main-line railroad from the mine property to a port 1287 km north of Perth. Services included planning and route location studies; preparation of final plans, specifications, and cost estimates; layout for the ore processing and loading areas; design for railroad yards and maintenance and repair shops; communications and signal systems; technical procurement assistance in connection with rolling stock and maintenance equipment; and planning of the project infrastructure and staff housing.

COMILOG Railroad, Congo: TAMS conducted a field reconnaissance, engineering and economic feasibility study for a manganese ore transport system in Congo and Gabon for the Compagnie Minière de L'Ogooue (COMILOG). The project involved 298 km of railroad and 80 km of tramway from Dolisie, ore storage and handling facilities at the mine area, transfer stations, and port and harbour facilities at Pointe Noire. TAMS provided detailed designs, contract documents, and specifications for the construction of these facilities and assistance for the procurement of rolling stock, rails, ties, accessories and steel for the various structures.

Long Island Rail Road Midtown Terminal, New York: TAMS performed technical studies and preliminary designs for the proposed East Midtown Terminal of the Long Island Rail Road, to be located in the vicinity of 48th Street and Third Avenue. The extension of the Long Island Rail Road will enter Manhattan from Queens through the lower level of the 63rd Street tunnel, which is currently under construction. The study included the approach section from 63rd Street to the terminal, and the storage section, which will extend from the terminal to 42nd Street, all beneath Third Avenue. The terminal is planned as a three-level subterranean structure with connections to all existing and planned transport facilities in the immediate area.

Vine Street station, Atlanta, Georgia: TAMS provided final designs to the Metropolitan Atlanta Rapid Transit District for section DW-31 of Atlanta's subway system. This section in central Atlanta includes the Vine Street station and design of 1128 metres of aerial and subway structures.

Metro subway, Washington DC: TAMS provided final design and technical inspection of construction services for the 760-metre-long Section A-2 of the Washington Metro. The engineering involved design of 670 metres of twin-bore earth and mixed-face tunnel, a section of cut-and-cover construction, one fan shaft, and the underpinning of two major buildings. The firm is also engineering the 2.3 km-long Section F-003 of the Metro. Its services, in association with other consultants, have included all engineering and architectural design for a centre-platform air-conditioned station, station ancillary areas, three vent shafts, two fan shafts, the underpinning of eleven structures in the Washington DC Navy Yard, soil stabilisation of four major sewers, underpinning of the South Capitol Street Underpass, and 1.9 km of twin-bore earth tunnel.

Long Island Rail Road facilities, Pennsylvania Station, New York City: Rehabilitation and expansion work is being performed for the Long Island Rail Road, and the estimated construction cost is $420 million.

New York City Transit Authority: An expansion of the Jamaica Yards and Shops is being carried out at an estimated construction cost of $23 million.

Consolidated Edison of New York: TAMS recently completed a study for the rail transport of coal from mines in the eastern coal states to Consolidated Edison's generating plant in New York City.

Transit and Tunnel Consultants Inc

14 Lafayette Square, Suite 811, Rand Building, Buffalo, New York 14203, USA

Telephone: (716) 853 7800

President: Richard W Wilson

Capabilities

Transit and Tunnel Consultants, Inc was formed in 1972 to bring together a broad range of disciplines related to transit and tunnel technology. Founders of the firm, Hatch Associates Ltd of Toronto, and Mott, Hay and Anderson International Ltd of London, both affiliates of Transit and Tunnel Consultants, Inc, have played major roles on numerous large transit projects. Activities cover: feasibility studies: examining the viability of the project as a whole, alternative methods of fulfilling requirements, basic concepts and standards, costs entailed and benefits to be derived; surveys and preliminary designs; detailed designs, drawings and specifications, and bid documents; preparation, awarding, financial control, and final settlement of contracts; project management; construction management

The firm's wide experience in tunnelling includes design and construction management in all types of ground from water-bearing silts and sands to rock. Under difficult tunnelling conditions, techniques such as compressed air, ground treatment and freezing have been employed. The ground conditions, together with the type and location (urban or rural) of the facility, form the major constraints on design. T & TC and its affiliates have carried out projects in both soft ground and rock involving full-face and part-face excavators, tunnelling shields, and conventional drill-and-blast methods. Tunnel linings have been developed to suit the specific requirements of the project and have ranged from segmental linings in cast iron, steel and precast concrete to cast-in-place concrete.

On many projects, both planning requirements and construction costs result in the selection of cut-and-cover methods rather than a tunnelled solution. T & TC is highly experienced in the design of cut-and-cover structures in both rock and soft ground, employing the full range of available techniques for ground support.

Projects

Design and construction management of Buffalo light rail rapid transit 5.6 km twin rock tunnel including five stations ($160 million) for Niagara Frontier Transportation Authority.

Transmark
Transportation Systems and Market Research Limited

45 Seymour Street, London W1H 5AE, England

Telephone: 01-723 3411
Telegrams: Transmark London W1
Telex: 8953218

Parent company: British Railways Board, Rail House, Euston Square, London NW1 2DZ

Chairman: J G Urquhart
Managing Director: K V Smith
Deputy Managing Director: D L Bartlett
Directors: M E Beesley
        D Fowler
        J E Todd
        A H Wickens
        R J Withers
        Roy W Wright

Capabilities
Transmark is a company linked to the British Railways Board, formed in 1969 to undertake transport consultancy, give technical advice and carry out market research throughout the world.

Consultants have extensive experience of working on British Rail, and have also acquired wide transport knowledge as a result of completing projects in every continent. They thus combine a sound theoretical background with wide practical experience. Some 2000 senior managers and specialist engineers from British Rail can also be called upon to augment Transmark's permanent staff with their own particular managerial or technical expertise which ranges from civil engineering and computers to planning and marketing. Indeed, Transmark has the backing of all the resources of the British Railways Board, including the latter's world-renowned Railway Technical Centre as well as associated companies, which have such diverse interests as shipping, containers, hovercraft, hotels, catering, rolling stock construction, property development and advertising.

A wide variety of projects has been undertaken in more than 65 countries, ranging from short visits by a single railway specialist to major studies covering all railway disciplines and technical assistance programmes. Clients include national and state governments, international lending agencies, national and privately-owned railways and many industrial and commercial organisations.

Projects in 1982

Country	Client	Description
Australia	New South Wales Commonwealth Engineering (Comeng) Comeng/State Rail Authority State Rail Authority	High Speed Train licence agreement Inspection of equipment for XPT HST workshop training Operating advice and direction on efficient implementation of resignalling schemes at Strathfield Electrification and associated works on the Illawarra line: assistance with design and construction supervision Strategic movement of export coal from northern coalfields to the port of Newcastle
	Queensland Queensland Railways	Brisbane suburban electrification design contract Queensland main-line electrification design contract
	Victoria VicRail	Jolimont rail yard property development review Operating studies Review of carriage maintenance facilities Provision of high level management assistance Passenger route service improvements
Austria	Shell Coal International	Line capacity study for coal traffic Trieste—Austria
Bangladesh	Overseas Development Administration	Maintenance assistance at Saidhpur and Pahartali railway workshops Training Institute for Bangladesh Railways
Brazil	GEC	Electrification of the Belo Horizonte Railway: technical consultancy and staff training
	Ptel/Electra (Rio de Janeiro)	Amza electrification, overhead equipment consultancy
	EPC	Technical advice on track expansion joints
Canada	VIARail	Advice on permissible speeds in the Halifax region Demand forecasting study
	Alberta Government	High speed passenger rail link between Calgary and Edmonton (demand forecasting study)
Denmark	Danish State Railways	Assistance with testing new train-sets
Egypt	Egyptian National Railways	Rolling stock maintenance, long-term assistance Organisation study Technical assistance Apprentice training Cairo Metro, contract administration
Gabon	Trans-Gabon Railway (OCTRA)	Study of special steels Techno-economic evaluation of Pandrol-Nabla track fastenings
Hong Kong	Hong Kong Government (Secretary for the Environment)	Kowloon-Canton Railway (KCR) modernisation and electrification, implementation phase KCR stations consultancy, design of new and remodelled stations Kowloon Tong interchange station, detailed design

Country	Client	Description
	Westinghouse Brake and Signal Company	KCR, signalling design KCR, circuit checking
	Mass Transit Railway Corporation	Training in non-destructive testing
	Kowloon-Canton Railway Corporation	Traffic forecasts
India	British Council (for Indian Railways)	Provision of lecturers at railway staff college in Baroda
Iraq	Ministry of Transport and Communications	Baghdad Metro, general consultancy
	New Railways Implementation Authority (NRIA)	Design of Baghdad-Basra railway doubling (543 km) Metre gauge study, Baghdad-Erbil via Kirkuk
	NRIA/Iraqi Republic Railway Organisation	Training centre consultancy requirements
	George Wimpey	Baghdad—Basra via Kut, advice on signalling and communications contractors
Ireland	Córas Iompair Éireann	Training of signal linemen
Ivory Coast	World Bank	Assistance in appraisal mission of RAN railway
Korea, Republic	Hawker Siddeley Rail Projects	Busan subway, assistance with offer
Libya	Libyan Department of Road Transport and Railways	Evaluation of construction tenders Ras Jedir—Tripoli Assessment of French consultancy reports concerning locomotive and rolling stock design specification and procurement and a management study
New Zealand	New Zealand Railways	North Island main-line electrification technical consultancy and advice on project management and maintenance organisation
Nigeria	Nigerian Railway Corporation	Training of railway officers
Pakistan	Pakistan Railways (funded by World Bank)	Feasibility study for main-line electrification, Khanewal-Karachi
Saudi Arabia	Saudi Arabian Government	Western Region railway study
	Rio Tinto Zinc	Az Zabirah bauxite railway
South Africa	South African Transport Services	Implementation and sale of CROWS, CAMP and CEPS computer programmes
Sudan	Overseas Development Administration	Provision of livestock transport adviser Design of road/rail cattle transhipment facilities
Tanzania	Tanzania Railway Corporation (funded by Kuwait Fund for Economic Development)	Feasibility study for the expansion of the Tabora Railway training college
Uganda	Bertlin and Partners (for Overseas Development Administration)	Study of requirements for containerisation in Uganda
UK	Northern Ireland Railways	Centralised traffic control design Aid with EEC regulations Modernisation of all NIR's level crossings
USA	Federal Railroad Administration	Task order consultancy agreement
	Federal Railroad Administration/ Michigan Department of Transportation	Detroit-Chicago high speed rail privatisation study
	Port Authority of New York (PATH)	Provision of representative for engineering advisory board to consider refurbishment of tunnel under the Hudson River
	Union Switch and Signal Company (WABCO) in conjunction with CIE	Extension of existing rail clamp lock licence agreement to incorporate AAR requirements
	American Steel Foundries (Amsted)	Bogie licence agreement
Zimbabwe	GEC	Training of Zimbabwe railway engineers
	Zimbabwe Railways	Comprehensive training of Zimbabwe graduate engineers in UK
General	World Bank/Overseas Development Administration	Developing countries' railway track standards study

Total: 91 projects in 29 countries/states

Transpo Group Inc

23-148th Avenue SE, Bellevue, Washington 98007, USA

Principal: Daniel I Riley

Projects
Transit, transport and traffic engineering/planning consultants.

Transportation Development Associates Inc

316 Second Ave South, Seattle, Washington 98104, USA

Telephone: (206) 682 4750

President: William R Eager

1155 Sherman Street, Denver, Colorado 80203, USA

Telephone: (303) 839 1346

Vice President: David D Leahy

Projects
Transit projects in the western United States and Canada;
Industrial market research (transit) for North America;
Transport for resorts in Colorado, Washington, Alaska;
Transport requirements of energy development in western Colorado;
Parking and traffic analyses for hospitals, hotels and other developments.

Transurb Consult SC

2-4 rue des Colonies, 1000 Brussels, Belgium
Telephone: (02) 511 25 72; 511 94 72; 512 04 61; 512 97 81

President: J Groothaert
General Manager: Pierre M de Smet

Transurb Consult was formed in 1972 to bring together for world-wide deployment the various aspects of Belgian transport technology. Its capital is equally apportioned between Belgian Railways (SNCB), Luxembourg Railways (CFL), the Brussels Public Transport Company (STIB) and Belgian consultants experienced in mass transport. Transurb Consult's experience derives from its members' operation of over 4000 km of national railway, mainly electrified, with more than 2000 locomotives and transport units; of an urban public transport network comprising 35 km of metro, with 49 stations, 62 km of LRT and 261 km of bus lines; and from its consulting departments.

Capabilities
The main skills of Transurb Consult are in the following areas: passenger traffic (urban, suburban, inter-city and international) and goods (collection, forwarding and delivery); railway, underground, tram, trolleybus, bus and all inter-modal transport catering for transport of goods or passengers from door to door, mine to plant or supplier to user (rail-road, rail-shipping, etc); all town planning involved in the improvement of transport. Its main services are: expert report or preliminary study; feasibility study; detailed engineering study; terms of references; supervision and commissioning; co-operation and staff training and technical assistance for start-up of revenue service.

Since 1972 Transurb Consult has acted in Algeria, Argentina, Bangladesh, Brazil, Cameroon, Canada, Central African Republic, Chile, Congo, Gabon, Greece, Guinea, Hong Kong, Iran, Iraq, Ivory Coast, Jordan, Lebanon, Mali, Mauritania, Netherlands, Niger, Philippines, Senegal, Spain, Sudan, Thailand, Togo, Tunisia, Upper Volta, Zaire.

Recent overseas contracts

Country	Client	Year	Project
Gabon	Transgabonese Railways Office (OCTRA)	1982	Complete construction of a main rolling stock maintenance depot: design, study and supply of equipment, steelwork and cladding; construction drawings for civil engineering and services distribution; transport of equipment and materials to the site; civil engineering and building construction work; erection of steelwork, cladding and assembly of equipment and machine tools; commissioning
	Société des Transports des Villes SOTRAVIL	1982	Feasibility study for implementation of a bus transport system in Port Gentil and Franceville
Guinea	Office National du Chemin de Fer de Guinée (ONCFG)	1982	Feasibility for rehabilitation of the railway between Konakry and Kankan (660 km)
Ivory Coast	Régie Abidjan-Niger (RAN)	1982	Professional training for analysis of oils for engines and cooling water Preliminary study with a view to improvement of operation
Malaysia	Malayan Railway Administration (KTM)	1982	Modernisation of the training centre for railway personnel at Sentul (study of the training function)
Tunisia	City of Sfax	1982	Feasibility study for the implementation of a light rail transit system
Zaire	Société Nationale des Chemins de Fer Zairois (SNCZ)	1982	Staff training for rolling stock department, track department, signalling and management
EEC	EEC	1981	Computer study dealing with examination of the commercial function and its contribution to the determination of the transport supply of various railways for national and international passenger and freight traffic
Malaysia	Belgian Agency for cooperation and development	1981	Appraisal of electrification between Butterworth and Singapore (850 km) and double-tracking over 70 km
Thailand	Thailand State Railway	1981	Expert report on improvement of signalling and telecommunications
Togo	Ministry of Transportation	1981	Assistance in management and railway programming
Zaire	Office National des Transports (ONATRA)	1981	Management study dealing with the reorganisation of the Bureau's accounting system Complete engineering study for the Matadi-Kinshasa railway line (365 km) covering: stationary and electric power supply plants; determination of rolling stock specifications; study of energy supply (SNEL network) and its distribution (catenaries, substations); study of signalling, telecommunications and remote controls; equipment of vehicle maintenance shops, etc
	SNCZ	1981	Detailed engineering study for the improvement of the Kamina-Ilebo railway line by realignment of the section between Kamina and Molu-Molu (133 km)
Algeria	SNTF	1980	Preliminary study of future signalling systems
Bangladesh	Bangladesh Railway Board	1980	Feasibility study of a central maintenance for 400 main-line and shunting locomotives; detailed construction studies; supervision of the construction and installation of equipment; acceptance of works; maintenance staff training
Brazil	Cobrasma	1980	Economic and technical feasibility study for a light rail transit system in Salvador de Bahia: analysis of demand; determination of present network with future projection; choice of priority line; operating programme
Chile	Universidad Catolica de Santiago	1980	Preliminary economic and social study of metro or railway penetration alternatives at Santiago (19 km) dealing with: operation; rolling stock; equipment; signalling; depot workshop; fares; cost estimate for project's construction.
Congo	Agence Transcongolaise des Communications	1980	Assistance in supervision of civil engineering works on realignment of Bilanga-Loubomo section (150 km)
Iraq	Sybetra	1980	Advisory services for study and laying of the connecting track and of railway installations of Alkaïm industrial complex
Philippines	Ministry of Transport and Communications	1980 -84	Complete engineering assignments for construction of light rail transit system in Manila within the scope of a turnkey project: 14 km of double-track viaduct line, 22 elevated stations, 64 vehicles with a capacity per unit of 374 passengers; signalling equipment; one workshop, one depot; administrative and socially-oriented facility buildings; staff training; commissioning of the system
Tunisia	SNCFT	1980	Report on heat engines of type DK electric diesel locomotives
Algeria	SNTF	1979 1980	Study of reorganisation of the accounting and financial system comprising: analytical accounting; general accounting; examination of financial functions; and management control, IBRD project
International	UIC	1979	Master plan for short-term development of EEC railway network
Ivory Coast	RAN	1979 1981	Technical assistance in reorganisation of the vehicle maintenance shops
Jordan	Jordan Railways	1979	Preliminary study of a rail link with the Hedjaz railway line for direct passenger transport between the Amman (Zarqa and Jiza) suburbs and the business centre
Zaire	SNCZ	1979 1980	Management study dealing with the elaboration of cost prices per category of traffic
Hong Kong	Mass Transit Railway Corporation	1978 -79	Feasibility study and preliminary design for installation of light rail transit system to serve Island Corridor; Phase I main study: track; expropriations; depots; energy supply; simulation by computer; study and choice of layouts; analysis of possibilities for conversion to subway system Phase II main study as detailed preliminary design and specifications for: operation; rolling stock; signalling; electric power supply; depots; and fares policy

Transurb Inc

85 Saint Catherine St West, Montreal, Quebec, Canada H2X 3P4

Telephone: (514) 871 9555

President: B E Novak

Capabilities
Comprehensive mass transit studies; rail-based transit studies and design; planning and design of ancillary services.

Trevor Crocker & Partners

Drive House, 323/339 London Road, Mitcham, Surrey CR4 4BE, England

Telephone: 01-640 1981
Telex: 942153

Capabilities
Trevor Crocker & Partners carries out feasibility and economic studies for new railway facilities, transport and traffic studies, route location studies, bridges, railways, workshops and ancillary facilities, preparation of specifications and tender documents, supervision of construction.

Projects
Australia
  Tom Price-Paraburdoo Railway
  Hamersley Railway

Iraq
  Baghdad-Erbil-Mosul high-speed railway
  Assessment of alternative sleeper designs

UK
  Feasibility studies for British Rail on reconstruction of Liverpool Street station
  Reconstruction of London Bridge station
  Gatwick Airport station
  Railway workshops
  15 rail over motorway bridges
  Bridgeworks for London-Bedford electrification
  40 underline and overline bridges
  Bridgeworks for Preston-Blackpool electrification
  British Rail Eastern Region: design of bridgeworks
  National Coal Board: design and supervision of construction of trackwork, bridgework, loading and weighing facilities for major colliery surface works

Tudor Engineering Co

149 New Montgomery Street, San Francisco, California 94105, USA

Telephone: (415) 982 8338

President: Louis W Riggs

Projects
Rapid transit system ($2500 million) for MARTA, Atlanta;
Rapid transit system planning for Metro de Caracas, Venezuela ($1000 million).

Urban Engineers Inc

19th St and Delancey Place, Philadelphia, Pennsylvania 19103, USA

Telephone: (215) 546 3222

Vice-President: K Yervant Terzian

Projects
Airport high speed rail line ($70 million) and city centre commuter rail connection ($320 million) for the City of Philadelphia.
General consultant to Southeastern Pennsylvania Transportation Authority (SEPTA).

Bridge work design for Philadelphia airport link

Urbitran Associates

15 Park Row, Suite 2610, New York, New York 10038, USA

Telephone: (212) 267 6310

President: Robert B Lee
Executive Vice-President: Michael Horodniceanu

Projects
Evaluation of automated guideway transit alternative analyses ($105 000) for UMTA;
Subcontract: Detroit DPM Phase 1 preliminary engineering and environmental impact analysis ($26 000);
Application of transportation system safety methodology for rail rapid transit and rail facilities ($25 000);
Seoul monorail study for the development of an automated guideway system connecting Seoul with the 1988 Olympic site ($20 000);
Subcontract: scheduling, station utilisation and commuter service improvements for the New York State MTA's Conrail north lines ($30 000);
Subcontract: evaluation of passenger circulation element, ie stairs, escalators, platforms, turnstiles, etc, for eight NYC Transit Authority stations as part of a system-wide improvement programme ($35 000)
Economic feasibility studies for New Jersey railroad stations at Trenton and Metropark as part of the Northwest Rail Corridor Improvement Project ($40 000).

URS Company Inc

370 Seventh Avenue, New York, New York 10001, USA

Telephone: (212) 736 4444

President: Irwin Rosenstein

Projects
Glenmont Section for WMATA; Mondawin station for Baltimore.

Past projects undertaken include:

Client	Project	Length (ft)	Special features	Estimated cost ($)
MBTA	Haymarket Square, Charlestown	600	Sunken tube line	4.6 million
NYCTA	Utica Avenue Subway, Section 1	2791	A typical transition	23 million
NYCTA	Utica Avenue Subway, Section 2	4630	2 stations	58.3 million
NYCTA	Utica Avenue Subway, Section 3	2410	Cut & cover line	20.4 million
NYCTA	Utica Avenue Subway, Section 4	2420	Cut & cover line	20.2 million
NYCTA	Utica Avenue Subway, Section 5	2685	1 station	39.2 million
NYCTA	Utica Avenue Subway, Section 6	2515	1 station	33.6 million
NYCTA	Utica Avenue Subway, Section 7	2370	Cut & cover line	18.6 million
NYCTA	Utica Avenue Subway, Section 8	2515	1 terminal station	35.4 million
NYCTA	Utica Avenue Subway, Section 9	1853	Maintenance & storage yard	25.1 million
WMATA	New Carrollton Route, Section D4a	4372	Earth tunnels	23 million
WMATA	New Carrollton Route, Section D4b	1065	1 station & cut & cover line	18.5 million
WMATA	New Carrollton Route, Section D4c	698	1 station	11 million
WMATA	L'Enfant-Pentagon Route, Section L1	3263	Sunken tube & cut & cover line	37 million
WMATA	Glenmont Route, Section B11 (4 contracts)	10 500	7700 ft twin rock tunnels, 2000 ft cut and cover box section, 800 ft Glenmont Station & 1800-car parking garage	85 million
MARTA-PBTB	Proctor Creek Branch, Section DP 23	5625	Cut & cover and at grade line and station	15.2 million
Baltimore Rapid Transit	Mondawmin Station—Section NW-06	645	Deep cut & cover	13.4 million

VTN Consolidated Inc

PO Box C-19529, 2301 Campus Drive, Irvine, California 92713, USA

Telephone: (714) 833 2450

Direction Transportation: Robert Evans

Wallace, Roberts and Todd

1737 Chestnut Street, Philadelphia, Pennsylvania 19103, USA

Telephone: (215) 564 2611

Partner: David A Wallace

Projects
Baltimore Metro Phase II transportation plan;
System-wide environmental impact and route selection studies ($2.3 million) for the Washington Metropolitan Area Transit Authority.

Harry Weese & Associates

600 Fifth St NW, Washington DC 20001, USA

Telephone: (202) 637 1761

Vice-President: Robert J Karn

Projects
Washington Rapid Rail Transit System: general architectural consultant for 100-mile (160 km), 86-station system;
Metropolitan Dade County aerial transit system: general architectural consultant for 21-mile (33 km) 20-station system;
Buffalo, New York, Light Rail Transit system: general architectural consultant for 6.4-mile (10 km), 14-station system;
Penn Central station study: general architectural consultant in Harrisburg, Pennsylvania.

RAILWAY SYSTEMS

AFGHANISTAN

In May 1982 the first railway tracks appeared in Afghanistan with completion, after three years' work by Afghan and Soviet labour, of an 816 metres-long combined rail and road bridge over the Abu Darja river, the border with the USSR, and the projection over it of a rail link from the Buehara-Tashkent line of Soviet Railways (SZD) near Termez to Hairaton in Afghanistan. This penetration was to be continued into Afghanistan, beginning with a 200 km line to Pali-Khumri, some 160 km north of Kabul.

Before the Soviet incursion into Afghanistan the then government had endorsed plans drafted by the French consultants Sofrerail for a rail system of 1815 km connecting Kabul with Kandahar and Herat; with Pakistan Railways at Chaman; and with Iranian State Railways at Islam Quala and Tarakun.

ALBANIA

Albanian State Railways (HëS)
Hekurudhaeä Shqiperisë

Drejitoria e Hekurudhave, Tirana

Minister of Transport: Luan Babameto

Gauge: 1435 mm
Route length: 400 km

Railway construction has been made difficult by the predominantly mountainous terrain, with 70 per cent of the territory at elevations of more than 328 metres (1000 feet). The remainder of the country consists of a lowland on the Adriatic coast through which the main Fier-Progozhine-Lac line runs. Tirana, the capital and principal city, forms the railhead on the Vorë-Tirana section.

Transport development
All means of transport are state-owned with highways the main carriers of passengers and freight.

The first lines built in Albania were the 168 km, 600 mm and 336 km, 700 mm gauge military lines constructed by the Austrian army engineers in the final stage of the First World War. These were, however, completely destroyed by the retreating Austrian troops in 1918. It was a 12 km industrial railway of 950 mm gauge, built around 1930 by an Italian firm exploiting the asphalt mines of Selenicë and Mavrovë near the port of Vlorë (Valona), which formed the country's first lasting railway.

During the Italian occupation of Albania the first plans for a public railway from Durrës to Tirana were drawn up and some minor construction work carried out. But full construction was not completed until after the Second World War when the new Communist Party government of Albania undertook a vast industrialisation programme, calling for extensive railway building. The first section of Albanian Railways from Durrës to Peqin (41 km) was opened in 1946 and this line was extended 30 km to Elbasan in 1950. In the meantime, another line from Durrës to Tirana, 38 km long, was completed in 1949. Building then continued at a much slower pace. In 1964 a 29 km spur from Vorë on the Tirana line to the superphosphate fertiliser plant at Laç was opened for traffic and one year later an industrial spur line east of Elbasan was completed.

A 54 km line from Rogozhinë on the Elbasan branch to a second fertiliser factory at Fier was completed in 1969.

There is a short length of narrow-gauge industrial line which is not operated by the Albanian State Railways. This 950 mm gauge runs from Vlorë, on the Adriatic, 8 km to the bitumen mine at Selenicë with a 4 km branch to Mavrove.

Traffic
Railway freight traffic is mainly bulk transport with nickel and chrome ore, asphalt, wood, coal and cement being the main commodities. Recent traffic figures have not been made available.

Civil engineering
In April 1979 an agreement was signed between Albania and Yugoslavia, under which a standard-gauge line was to be built connecting a new Albanian railhead at Shkoder with Yugoslav Railways' recently completed Belgrade—Bar line at Titograd. This will be Albania's first rail link with a foreign railway. The line will carry chromite and nickel ore mined in Albania into East Europe while Yugoslav raw materials and finished goods are expected to flow south into the terminal at Tirana. Construction from Lac to Albania began in November 1979 and by November 1981 had reached the new railhead at Shkoder. A new agreement to continue construction for 75 km from Titograd to Tirana was signed in April 1982. Completion was expected in 1984. A 40 km projection of the Durrës-Fier line to the Adriatic port of Vlorë began in August 1982.

Most lines are laid with rails weighing 43 kg/m imported from Czechoslovakia. Maximum axle load is 21 tonnes.

Locomotives and rolling stock
Albania has no railway industry, therefore all equipment, especially rolling stock and motive power, must be imported. A first batch of steam locomotives came from Chrzanow works in Poland, whose engines were similar to PKP's Tkt-48 class standard general-purpose superheated 1D1 (2-8-2) tank type. Some second-hand engines seem to have found their way from Poland to Albania too. In 1958, Albanian Railways bought their first two diesel-mechanical class BN 150 shunting locomotives from CKD Praha, followed by two more of the same type and two 750 hp Bo-Bo diesel-electric road locomotives of CSD's T 435.0 class in the next year. Two other T 435.0 went to Albania in 1961 and three of the same class in 1962. Four more diesel-electrics of the slightly heavier T 458.1 class were delivered in 1967.

Passenger cars are mostly two-axled from the railways of the German Democratic Republic, Hungary and Czechoslovakia, but an increasing number of bogie coaches are being put into service. Chinese-built passenger coaches are running on lines served by the railway's original second-hand rolling stock until 1975.

Freight cars generally are old 15-tonne two-axle types; more recently purchased stock includes modern bogie cars with a capacity of 45 tonnes, built in Czechoslovakia, Hungary, and China. Recent purchases include a contract for 55 covered wagons placed with Masinska Industrija Nis of Yugoslavia in 1980; an order for 50 more was delivered in 1982. Albania's first two domestically-built freight wagons (60 tonne capacity each) left the railway works at Durrës in mid-1980.

ALGERIA

Ministry of Transport

Algiers

Minister: Salah Goudjil
Secretary-General: A Salah-Bey
Director, Infrastructure and Rail Transport: A Zahi

Algerian National Railways (SNTF)
Société Nationale des Transports Ferroviaires

21-23 boulevard Mohamed V, Algiers

Telephone: 61 1510
Telegrams: Cefafer, Algiers
Telex: 52 455

Director General: Amar Bousbaa
Commercial Director: Bouifrou Tahar
Operating Director: Rachid Rabhi
Director of Technical/Economic Studies and Planning: Budin Karim
Director of Personnel and General Administration: Ahmed Merouani
Director of Rolling Stock: Mustapha Arris
Director of Purchasing: Ali Touri
Director of Fixed Equipment: Abdenour Hadji
Director of Finances: Ali Tain

Gauges: 1435 mm; 1055 mm; 1000 mm
Route length: 2632 km; 1258 km; 256 km
Electrification: 256 km at 3 kV dc

Transport development
In 1972 Algeria's nationally-owned railways had 4074 route-km of which 319 km were electrified. Rationalisation measures cut this to 3890 km by the end of 1980, but new lines planned or underway will substantially increase existing route length by the end of the 1980s.

The network at present consists primarily of two standard-gauge coastal lines running east and west from Algiers: about 550 km westward to the railhead at Oujda (where a connection is made with Moroccan Railways—ONCFM), and about 370 km eastwards to a connection with the 520 km north-south line at Od Rahmoun. In addition to standard-gauge spur lines, a 300 km (partly electrified) 1435 mm gauge line runs parallel with the Tunisian border (providing international connecting services at Souk-Ahras with Tunisian National Railways—SNCFT) from the port of Annaba to Djebel Onk. Major narrow-gauge lines run from Mohammadia (on the Algiers-Oujda line) to Kenadsa and Blida to Djelfa.

From 1976 two organisations replaced the former Société Nationale des Chemins de Fer: the Société Nationale des Transports Ferroviaires (SNTF) in charge of day-to-day operations and the Société Nationale d'Etudes et de Réalisation de l'Infrastructure Ferroviaire in charge of track renewals and new works planning.

Since Algeria gained independence in 1962, the economic importance of the railways has gradually increased in accordance with the country's industrialisation programme. In the 1960s Algeria followed the general African continental trend, dedicating most of its infrastructure investment to roads and until 1974 denying the Algerian Railways (SNTF) any cash for track renewal. The Government now regards SNTF as the chief national carrier of raw materials and of the country's booming industrial output. It is seen both as a key to easing the rising traffic problems in the areas of the four main cities, Algiers, Annaba, Constantine and Oran, and also as a vital tool in regional development strategy, above all in the High Plateau.

After 1975 SNTF's traffic jumped from 6·3 million to 10·8 million tonnes of freight in 1981, and from 10·2 million to 30·4 million passenger journeys (2070 passenger-km); freight tonne-km reached 2687 million in 1981, with freight transported grossing 10·6 million tonnes. The 1981-85 National Development Plan envisages continued growth at 8 per cent per annum, so that by 1985 SNTF's freight could be three times the volume of a decade earlier and passenger movement four times greater.

The biggest problem facing SNTF is lack of capacity; none of its lines were built to handle present traffic demand. The eastern half of the network is already saturated with iron ore, coke and steel traffic; the problems will grow even bigger when the new blast furnace at El Hadjar steelworks (commissioned in March 1980) works up to a full capacity of 3·6 million tonnes/year. Adding to SNTF's capacity problems are coke imports through Annaba, shipments of phosphates annually from Djebel Onk, and movements of industrial bulk materials needed to fuel the continuing expansion of industry.

Under the country's 1980-84 economic plan the Government is committed to a heavy investment in SNTF to fit rail transport for the demands both of new industry and of the agricultural development now accorded considerable priority. Importance is also attached to enlargement both of long-haul and suburban rail passenger capacity, in view of traffic growth which is averaging more than 3 per cent a year consistently. In 1981, of a total of DA 22 500 million budgeted for national transport investment, DA 16 600 million was earmarked for the SNTF.

Since 1979 the Algerian government and the SNTF administration have engaged consultancy teams from Austria, Belgium, Italy and India to aid SNTF improvements. Also undertaking consultancy work for SNTF during 1979-81 was Deutsche Eisenbahn Consult (Deconsult), which was carrying out a survey on restructuring all railway lines and services in the heavily-congested Algiers commuter area by 2000.

Capacity enlargement
Priority, naturally, is recovery of track neglect on the existing system up to 1975. Teams armed with

modern mechanised equipment have been established in each of the Oran, Boufarick, Constantine and Annaba areas to pursue rolling programmes of renewal with heavy-duty rail, continuously welded to the maximum extent track configuration allows; and civil engineering structures are being strengthened to accept vehicles of up to 20 tonnes individual axleloading throughout SNTF's standard-gauge network.

Besides lengthening existing passing loops on single-track routes to permit operation of trains up to 1200 metres long instead of the previous 800 metres maximum, and also laying in additional loops, SNTF has launched some large-scale projects to double-track single lines which are quite inadequate for latter-day industrial development. The first such undertaking was formally set in motion by President Chadli Bendjedid in February 1980 between Ramdane-Djamel, 67 km north of Constantine, and El-Gourzi, 38 km south of Constantine. This vital link between Algiers and the fast-developing petrochemical port of Skikda as well as Annaba, was previously double-track only for 18 km between Constantine and El-Khroub, was handicapped by gradients as steep as 1 in 50 and curves sharper than 200 metres radius in its negotiation of the Constantine mountains, and with an axleload limit of 18 tonnes could carry only 9000 tonnes of freight a day. Under a scheme estimated to cost DA 2200 million which is being managed by COGEFAR and Italconsult of Italy, the line is being doubled throughout the 64·8 km from Ramdane-Djamel to Constantine and the 20·6 km south from El-Gourzi to El Khroub, along with substantial realignments. The task involves laying 233 km of new track, constructing 34 bridges, including the 650 metre-long Beni-Brahim viaduct, and boring three tunnels aggregating 4206 metres in length. In many places the line has been completely rebuilt to iron out curves and avoid treacherous ground. In conjunction with the installation of heavier UIC 54 continuously welded rail on concrete sleepers of SL Type U (1722 per km), this will raise permissible freight speed from 60 to 90 km/h and allowable wagon axleloadings from 18 to 28 tonnes. The next phase of the work will be installation of modern automatic signalling. When that is commissioned the line's train operating capacity should be doubled and a throughput of 7 million tonnes a year should be possible. Completion of this project is now anticipated at the end of 1985.

Resignalling and a complete renewal of its telecommunications network ranks high in SNTF's current modernisation activity. Among other things, the railway aims to make track-to-train radio communication a standard feature on its principal routes.

West of Constantine some double-track already exists on the littoral main line to Algiers and Oran, and the creation of more is among the projects contemplated for use of a $ 477 million loan obtained from Austria for infrastructure modernisation in July 1981. The credit is for drawing over a period of 15-20 years. A 16-company Austrian group including Simmering-Graz-Pauker, Jenbacher Werke, Plasser & Theurer and Voest-Alpine, is one of the largest concerns collaborating in SNTF modernisation.

The first double-tracking scheme to be submitted to study with these funds, employing the West German Deutsche Bundesbahn's consultancy, covers the 43.5 km from El Harrach, on the outskirts of Algiers, to Thenia. An Austrian group led by Universale Hoch- und Tiefbau gained an S 3800 million contract to execute this in 1982. A further S 157 million contract provided for reconstruction planning of 350 km of trunk routes from Thenia eastward to Setif, and between Skikda and Annaba.

The Indian Railway Construction Company (IRCON) gained a Rs 350 million turnkey contract to construct 23 km of 1055 mm-gauge railway near Saida, between Mohammadia and Kenadsa, to serve a cement works.

New railways

The El Hadjar steel complex gets its ore in a daily flow of 1500-tonne trains from mines at Ouenza and Bou Khedra, about 190 km south of Annaba (whence the imported coal for its coking plant is also ferried by unit train). The ore line was electrified at 3 kV dc before the Second World War and most of the ore trains, plus trains of phosphates from the mines at Djebel Onk further south, are powered by 32 2700 hp electric locomotives procured from the East German builders LEW in the early 1970s. The section from Souk-Ahras to Annaba now carries over 3 million tonnes of ore and approaching 1 5 million tonnes of phosphates a year. As the rail input and output at El Hadjar grows, SNTF is concerned to avoid choking the approaches to Annaba and the rail area in the port itself. That prompted the first steps toward construction of Algeria's biggest long-term

rail construction project, a second east-west transversal line deep inland, the so-called High Plateau route from the area of the phosphate deposits in the east to Sidi Bel Abbes, south of Oran. The total distance involved is over 1000 km.

At the end of 1978 Italconsult was contracted to study the section from Tebessa to Ain M'Lila as a start to the enterprise. Completion of this would have had the immediate operational value of separating phosphate traffic for the west from the freight flows to Annaba. Soon afterwards, however, a newly-formed Planning Ministry decided that more use must be made of local skills and resources, and that foreign consultancy was preferably obtained from politically non-aligned countries. In 1980 a series of agreements with India led to a contract with RITES, the Indian Railways consultancy, for provision of technical, management assistance and staff training services in the period up to 1985. A joint Algerian-Indian study group was formed to plan a different first section of the High Plateau route, the 140 km from Ain-Touta, on the line south from Constantine to Biskra, to M'Sila, where a new aluminium plant was in urgent need of rail service. A 60 km line from M'Sila to the existing east-west transversal at Bordj Bou Arreridj was also committed to study. In June 1982 President Chadli Bendjedid inaugurated the works between Ain-Touta and M'Sila, which are expected to be complete in mid-1985.

In 1982, however, French companies were granted a contract to build the line from Tebessa to Ain M'Lila, on the main line from Algiers to Constantine, and also to construct a new 130 km railway from Ramdane Djamel to the new port of Jijel-Djendjen, west of Skikda. These two contracts together involved 370 km of route and were valued at some Fr 14 000 million. At the same time SNTF was discussing with the Chinese a contract to build a line across the heart of the Sahara looping southward from Touggourt, in the south-east, through Ouargla then north-west via Ghardaia and Laghouat to Ain Ouessara, on the projected High Plateau route.

The most impressive project among SNTF's drafts awaits a decision whether to develop the ore deposits in the far south-west of Algeria, considering that the sources in the north-east are estimated to satisfy the demands of El-Hadjar for only 30 years. Following preliminary appraisals by the Ministry of Industry and Energy and by SNTF, engineering study of a new 1450 km standard-gauge railway to ferry ore to Mohammadia, on the Oran-Algiers main line, has got as far as committal to engineering study by Canadian Pacific Consulting Services. Starting at Gara Djebilet, the railway would strike a new path to the vicinity of Bechar, north of which it would supersede a historic narrow-gauge line to Air Sefra. The new railway would not be electrified, because of Algeria's ready resources of oil. The prospectus envisages operation of 180-wagon trains grossing well over 10 000 tonnes behind four diesel locomotives.

In the Oran area the freight depot at Sid-El-Bekkai is being reconstructed, and at Constantine, besides a rebuilding of the main station and introduction of new local passenger services, a new marshalling yard is planned at Ain M'Lila.

Algiers Urban Railway

Passenger and freight traffic growth has seriously outstripped capacity in the four principal cities and ports, above all in Algiers. The main Algiers Maritime station is a terminus, hemmed between the port and the cliffs which the city surmounts so that it cannot be enlarged.

SNTF's aim by the 1990s is to convert the terminus into a branch leaving a new cross-city suburban line at Place Emir Abdel Kader. The cross-city line will be created by driving a line underground westward beneath the densely populated Casbah to Bab el Oued. The tunnelling will be a delicate job, though, because of the high water table in the area. New stations will be built on the extension. This suburban SNTF extension will parallel and be integrated with Line 1 of the Algiers metro.

At the same time SNTF intends to divert traffic from the centre of Algiers by creating a rail-road passenger interchange at Dar el Beida, in a thriving development area to the south, with a branch to the adjacent Houari Boumedienne airport. The works planned at Dar el Beida, which is to become Algiers' main passenger station, will also open up a route for east-west freight traffic via the existing transversal that will give it a through run avoiding the centre of Algiers between Thenia and Blida. Inter-city trains on the Oran-Constantine axis will transfer Algiers passengers to and from local trains at Dar el Beida. Further relief for Algiers Maritime station will be obtained by constructing a new station in the city's downtown business area at Tafourah. A new chord line will enable through running between Tafourah and Blida via Dar el Beida, and new lines are also to connect Tafourah and Dar el Beida with residential development north-east of the city around Ain Charb. SNTF plans to accompany these developments by redeveloping installations in the port area and shifting the centre of freight handling and train marshalling from Agha to a new yard and depot further east at Rouiba, near Dar el Beida. Completion of the entire Algiers network development is not expected before the year 2000.

Traction and rolling stock

SNTF is spending heavily to continue the well-advanced expansion and modernisation of its traction and rolling stock. In 1981, SNTF announced a fresh contract with the Algerian builders SN Metal for 1505 new freight wagons, including 150 for phosphates, 300 tank vehicles, 400 flats and 400 vans; and a C$35 million order was placed with General Motors of Canada for 25 more GT26CW diesel locomotives. In June 1982 the Government announced that SN Metal was to deliver 3400 wagons in the period up to 1986. In total SNTF's purchasing programme under its 1981-85 Development Plan features 40 new main-line locomotives, 100 new shunting locomotives, some 1900 freight wagons and 450 new passenger cars. At the end of 1982, following purchase of 60 second-hand coaches from the German Federal Railway, a Fr 2500 million order was placed with Francorail for 400 new first- and second-class cars.

Some freight trains are operated with the Locotrol system in which a slave locomotive in the middle of the train is controlled by radio from the lead locomotive. The system is being used primarily to increase

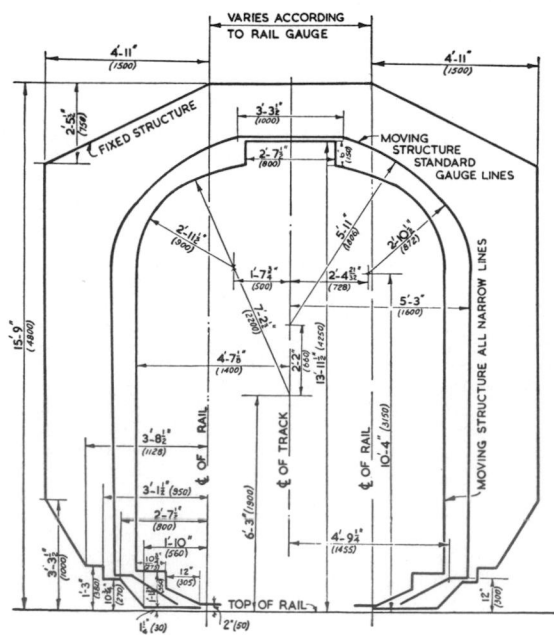

the length and carrying capacity of unit phosphate trains.

On 1435 mm gauge SNTF operates 32 electric and 176 diesel locomotives, 33 diesel railcars and 35 locotractors. Coaching stock totals 483 cars and freight stock 11 868 vehicles. Narrow-gauge traction comprises 42 diesel locomotives, two diesel railcars and six locotractors; narrow-gauge coaching stock totals 33 vehicles and freight stock 2426 wagons.

The 42 narrow-gauge locomotives are capable of change of bogie for 1435 mm-gauge operation, as are more than 2400 freight wagons.

Electrification

Algeria has only one electrified line running 256 km (single-track) between Tébessa and Annaba at 3000 volts dc. No new electrification is planned for 1981-86, thanks to cheap home-produced oil.

Signalling

Electrically-operated mechanical signals are gradually being replaced by colour-light signal displays throughout the system, while on new lines and upgraded tracks automatic signalling is being installed. During 1981 signalling and telecommunications were being modernised on the 253 km Thenia-Setif line, and the 117 km Skikda-Annaba single-track east-west trunk line sections.

Diesel locomotives

Class	Wheel arrange-ment	Trans-mission	Rated power hp	Tractive effort Max kg	Continuous at kg	kmh	Max speed kmh	Wheel dia mm	Axle load tonnes	Total weight tonnes	Length mm	No built	Year first built	Builders Mechanical parts	Engine	Transmission
Standard gauge																
040DA	A1A-A1A	Elec	1520	24 700	19 414	16·9	96	1066	21·3	124·6	17 700	15	1946	Baldwin	Baldwin	Westinghouse
040DB	A1A-A1A	Elec	1520	25 200	14 060	23·3	130	1066	21·3	124·6	17 700	25	1947	Baldwin	Baldwin	Westinghouse
040DC	A1A-A1A	Elec	1014	22 800	14 700	15·2	85	1066	17·4	103·1	16 175	20	1948	Baldwin	Baldwin	Westinghouse
040DD	A1A-A1A	Elec	1520	21 400	17 000	20·0	120	1016	19·5	110·7	16 896	5	1950	Alco	Alco	GE
040DG	A1A-A1A	Elec	1622	21 500			120	1016	19·8	113·8	17 050	5	1951	Alco	Alco	GE
060DB	Co-Co	Elec	1315	16 800	12 600	15·0	120	950	14·5	87·0	17 200	10	1956	Schneider	Baldwin	Schneider
060DC	Co-Co	Elec	1840	30 000	15 500		120	1050	18·9	113·4	19 814	37	1957	Alsthom	SACM	Alsthom
060DD	Co-Co	Elec	3300		26 020	26·6	124	1016	20·0	120·0	20 745	29	1971	GM	GM	GM
—	Co-Co	Elec	3000	—	30 490	—	120	—	19·8	119	31	19	1980	GM	GM	GM
—	Bo-Bo	Elec	1100/1000	—	15 240	13·8	96	1016	—	65·2	11 580	70	—	GM	GM	GM
40EA	B	Mech	40				12	900	5·3	10·6	5610	3	1955	Moyse	Renault	
80DA	B	Mech	80				17	950	10·4	20·8	6770	23	1955	Moyse	Renault	
150DEA	B	Elec	150				25	950	15·9	31·8	6770	5	1952	Moyse	Ricardo	
150DEB	B	Elec	150				60	1050	16·9	33·8	8900	8	1956	Decauville	Poyaud	Oerlikon
200DA	C	Mech	200				29	1016	11·0	32·5	7930	14	1948	Hunslet	Gardner	
200DB	B	Mech	200				29	1050	16·0	32·0	8180	5	1955	Billard	Willème	
200DC	B	Mech	200				29	1050	16·0	32·0	8170	1	1957	Billard	Willème	
400DA	B	Hydr	400				55	1050	17·3	34·6	9360	16	1956	ANF	Saurer	Voith
400DB	B	Hydr	400				55	1050	18·4	36·7	9360	8	1960	Billard	Saurer	Voith
400DC	B	Hydr	400				50	1050	17·3	34·6	9360	4	1962	De Dietrich	Saurer	Voith
600DA	D	Hydr	600				60	1100	15·4	61·4	10 920	10	1971	LEW	LEW	LEW
600DB	D	Hydr	600				60	1100	15·4	61·4	10 920	10	1972	LEW	LEW	LEW
1055 mm gauge																
060YDA	Co-Co	Elec	960		14 800	20·0	85	914	12·0	72·0	18 550	10	1953	De Dietrich	Sulzer	Oerlikon
060YDB	Bo-Bo-Bo	Elec	920	16 000	9200	18·0	80	920	10·0	59·0	13 360	10	1958	Alsthom	SACM	Alsthom
060YDC	Bo-Bo-Bo	Elec	935	18 500	10 000	19·0	80	920	12·0	72·0	14 396	6	1961	Alsthom	SACM	Alsthom
Y80DA	B	Mech	80				17	950	10·1	20·2	7060	2	1959	Moyse	Berliet	
Y150DA	C	Hydr	150		6160	4·8	22	860	9·9	29·6	7340	10	1951	LLD	Willème	
Y200DA	B	Mech	200				29	1050	12·0	24·0	8070	1	1957	Billard	Willème	
1000 mm gauge																
XZZDN	Bo-Bo	Elec	600				90	860	9·6	38·4	16 200	5	1938	De Dietrich	Saurer	Oerlikon
X200DA	B	Mech	200				29	1050	12·0	24·0	8290	4	1957	Billard	Willème	

Electric locomotives

Class	Wheel arrange-ment	Line current	Rated power hp	Tractive effort Continuous at kg	kmh	Max speed kmh	Wheel dia mm	Total weight tonnes	Length mm	No built	First built	Builders Mechanical parts	Electrical equipment
6BE	Co-Co	3 kV dc	3120	22 500	37·5	80	1250	134·1	18 922	8	1958	Alsthom	Alsthom
6CE	Co-Co	3 kV dc	2700	24 600	30·0	80	1350	130·0	18 640	32	1972	LEW	Skoda

ANGOLA

Ministry of Transport & Communications

PO Box 1250-C, Luanda

Telephone: 70061; 73270
Telex: 3108

Minister of Transport: Fernando Faustino Muteka

Caminhos de Ferro de Angola

PO Box 1250-C, Luanda

Telephone: 70061; 73270
Telegrams: Supervia
Telex: 3108

Director: A de S E Silva
Deputy Technical Director: R M da C Junior

Gauge: 1067 mm; 600 mm
Route length (four railways combined): 2798 km; 154 km

Transport development

Portuguese colonialists developed an extensive transport and communications network until Angola became independent in 1975, since when civil war has seriously disrupted both highway and rail services. In 1972, when fighting broke out between rival liberation movements, there were 72 323 km of highways and 3049 of railways. Four previously independent railways are now amalgamated in a national system, the Caminhos de Ferro de Angola, but because of internal political problems the four railways have so far been unable to integrate operation fully or handle international traffic consistently. The Angolan Government announced in 1981 that three new railway lines totalling 1130 km were under consideration: (1) a 640 km line linking the Benguela and Luanda Railways; (2) a 240 km link between the Benguela and Moçâmedes Railways; (3) a 250 km branch from Mbanza (Congo) to a new port at Soya on the River Zaire. Also foreseen is extension of the first line 500 km to link up with the Zaire National Railways and extension of the second line by about 270 km to link up with the railway in Namibia.

Traction and rolling stock

The four railways combined operate 120 steam and 114 diesel locomotives, 25 railcars, 243 passenger cars and 4011 freight cars. An order for 52 passenger and six baggage cars was placed with Sorefame in 1983, when 12 diesel locomotives were to be delivered by General Electric of Brazil. Orders for 259 freight wagons were out to tender.

Moçâmedes Railway
Caminho de Ferro de Moçâmedes

Caixa Postal 130, Sá de Bandeira, Moçâmedes

General Manager: L de M G Cipriano

Gauge: 1067 mm
Route length: 899 km

The Caminho de Ferro de Moçâmedes consists of a 858 km line running from Moçâmedes on the west coast to Menongue in the interior via Lubango, Matala and Entrocamento; spur lines connect at Lubango (running 150 km south-east to Chibia) and Dongo (running 109 km south to Cassinga). Ore branch lines from Cassinga North (16 km) and Cassinga South (94 km) carried 6 million tonnes of ore annually to Moçâmedes when lines were operating normally. A programme of track rehabilitation has now been drafted.

Luanda Railway
Porto e Caminhos de Ferro de Luanda

PO Box 1250-C, Luanda

Telephone: 70061; 73270

Director: J M Ferreira do Nascimento

Gauge: 1067 mm; 600 mm

Route length: 505 km; 31 km

Founded in 1886 the Luanda State Railway runs 496 km from the port of Luanda east to Malange, serving an iron, cotton and sizal producing region.

Caminho de Ferro do Amboim

Puerto Amboim

General Manager: A V Ferreira

Gauge: 600 mm
Route length: 123 km

Founded in 1922 the railway operates a single line between the port of Amboim and the coffee growing region at Gabela. A priority is replacement of steam with diesel traction and a new telecommunications system is to be installed.

Benguela Railway
Caminho de Ferro de Benguela

PO Box 32, Lobito

Telegrams: Lobitanga, Lobito
Telex: 18253

President: Dr L Supico Pinto
Vice President: Eng F M Falcão
Director-General: Eng F F de M de Sampaio
Deputy Director-General: C Silinge

Gauge: 1067 mm
Route length: 1415 km

The Benguela Railway should be a major traffic route to the sea for Zambian and Zaire copper, but the connection from the port of Lobito across Angola to the Zaire border at Dilolo, where it is connected with Zaire National Railways, has been disrupted by guerrilla action since 1975.

During 1980 the Organization of Petroleum Exporting Countries increased the amount of rehabilitation aid available for the Benguela Railway with a $ 3 million loan to help finance purchase of 630 freight wagons, 12 main-line and six shunting locomotives, a tamping machine, spare parts, workshop and technical assistance. The 12 main-line diesel-electric locomotives were to be delivered by General Electric of Brazil in 1983. Sorefame has an order for 52 passenger cars and six luggage vans, and early in 1983 bids to build 259 new freight cars were being sifted. New maintenance workshops have been established at Huambo. In conjunction with track work and telecommunications rehabilitation it is hoped that these measures will restore the level of transit traffic to 90 000 tonnes a month.

Investment plans 1983 (US $ 000)

Locomotives	
6 diesel-electric shunters	3312
Loco-hauled passenger cars (58)	18 136
Freight wagons (900)	34 762
Freight car rebuilding	5770
Civil engineering	15 000
Communications	4665
Computerised management systems	1650
Workshops	3650
Total	86 945

Caminho de Ferro de Benguela

Benguela Railway diesel locomotives

Loco number	Wheel arrangement	Transmission	Rated power hp	Tractive effort Max lb (kg)	Continuous at lb (kg)	mph (km/h)	Max speed mph (km/h)	Wheel diameter in (mm)	Total weight tonnes	Length ft in (mm)	No built	Year first built	Builders Mechanical parts	Engine & type
D1-D4	C	Hydraulic	425	24 000 (10 890)	9000 (4080)	12 (19)	17 (27)	40 (1016)	40	28' 5½'' (8680)	4	1960	North British	Paxman 8RPHXL
580-81	C	Hydraulic	425	24 000 (10 890)	9000 (4080)	12 (19)	17 (27)	40 (1016)	41	28' 5½'' (8680)	2	1972	Andrew Barclay	Paxman 8RPHXL
D101-D122	Co-Co	Electric	2150	59 520 (27 000)	50 400 (22 800)	12 (19)	64 (103)	36 (914)	90	55' 00'' (16 764)	22	1972	General Electric	General Electric

ARGENTINA

Secretariat of Transport & Public Works
Secretariat de Estado de Transport y Obras Publicas

25 de Mayo 459, 1002 Buenos Aires

Telephone: 32 6311

Secretary: Gaston Cossettini

Under Secretary for Transport: Ezequiel Ogueta

The Secretariat controls all forms of public and privately-owned transport in Argentina. Railways are governed by Argentine Railways (FA).

Argentine Railways (FA)
Ferrocarriles Argentinos

Avenida Ramos, Mejia 1402, 1104 Buenos Aires

President: Gaston Cossettini
Executive Vice-President: Nestor Fernandez
Director and Chief Executive, Operating: D A Fernandez
Chief Executive, Finance: Carlos F Martin
Director of Economic Studies: Horacio M Allemand
Director, Finance: J Olego
Mechanical Director: Jorge A Bilotti
Director, Way and Works: J Sala
Director, Planning: A A Nova
Director, Transport: D L B Chiappori
Commercial Director: D A Guidice
Supplies Director: Col Sica
Director, Data Processing: D J Almeida
Chief of Public Relations: Mayor (RE) D Jorge A V Mastropietro
Regional Managers
FC Gen Roca: J Legnazzi
FC Gen Belgrano: J Pozo
FC Gen Urquiza: Angel S Butti
FC Gen San Martin: C Pettinaroli
FC Gen Mitre: E Giles
FC DF Sarmiento: L Chiappori
Buenos Aires Metropolitan: D N Cinat

Gauge. 1000 mm; 1435 mm; 1676 mm
Route length: 35 476 km
Electrification: 116 km at 550 and 800 V dc

Divisions	Gauge
Roca	1676 mm
	750 mm
Mitre	1676 mm
San Martin	1676 mm
Sarmiento	1676 mm
Urquiza	1435 mm
Belgrano	1000 mm

The military administration which took over control of FA in April 1976 passed the railway back to a civil administration in April 1979.

Infrastructure rehabilitation
Following the decision to rehabilitate FA to serve as the trunk-haul backbone of the country's transport system, recuperation of neglected infrastructure maintenance has been a first priority. Much of the work has been entrusted to private contractors, leaving FA's own civil engineers to concentrate on day-to-day maintenance, but to step up its own capability FA has been acquiring mechanised track maintenance equipment from Matisa, Plasser & Theurer and Jackson; with these FA aimed to cover 1700 km in 1982 and 2000 km in 1983. At the start of the 1980s some two-thirds of the rail in use was over 40 years old, but FA's recent purchases have included 43 000 tonnes of new rail from Iscor, South Africa, and Somisa, Argentina, together with over 2 million tonnes of timber sleepers from local suppliers. Following previous renewals in the Buenos Aires Metropolitan Division, tenders were being sought in 1982 for complete renovation of the line from Retiro to Boulogne-sur-Mer at a cost of almost Pesos 85 000 million.

Concurrent improvement of signalling and communications has been treated with similar urgency. Recent CTC extensions have completed coverage of the Retiro-Villa Rosa metropolitan line in an installation of Wabco equipment by Desaci of Argentina, and the Mitre line's Retiro terminal in Buenos Aires, where daily operating capacity has thereby been increased from 600 to 1000 trains; in the latter instance Desaci has installed Siemens equipment.

In August 1982 a through route between FA and Uruguayan State Railways was forged for the first time. The medium was a combined rail and road thoroughfare over the new Salto Grande dam.

Electrification
The long-delayed electrification of the Roca line serving Buenos Aires suburbs began in December 1981. The main contracts were secured by a Japanese consortium led by Marubeni Corporation and including Toshiba, Mitsubishi Electric and Hitachi; local companies involved are Fabricaciones Militares, SIAM and Fiat Materfer for some rolling stock items, and Desaci, Techint, Ecofisa, Sade and Impresit-Sideco for the civil engineering and installation works; the track is being renewed integrally with the electrification.

The first stage of the electrification, which is at 25 kV 50 Hz, will run from Plaza Constitución to Glew y Ezeiza; the second will cover the Plaza Constitución-La Plata and Elisa lines, a total of 83 km. Inauguration date for the first stage is set for 1985, employing twin-sets of three-car emus, of which an initial order of 52 is planned, most to be constructed in Japan but six to be built by local industry. A passenger throughput of 18 000 per hour is envisaged, which will be an 80 per cent improvement on the capacity of the Roca line's existing diesel-powered push-pull trains; this advance will be facilitated by resignalling for three-minute headways on the Roca line. The sec-

ond stage of the scheme was to be put in hand in 1983, with Marubeni again the contractor.

FA has drafted a 15-year 25 kV ac electrification plan costed at the equivalent of US$ 2100 million to cover approximately 3500 km of main and suburban lines radiating from Buenos Aires, to be executed in three phases: 1983-86; 1987-90; and 1991-97. The main lines involved are those to Bahia Blanca, Cordoba, Mendoz and Mar del Plata. The suburban routes are those to Gonzales Catan Pilar and Villa Rosa, also those to Jose L Suarez and Moreno, which would be converted from their present dc, in addition to the Roca lines already being wired.

Diesel traction
Steam traction was eliminated in 1980 (in 1965 FA operated 3177 steam locomotives and still had 1025 active in 1975) and FA has recently acquired its first new main-line diesel locomotives since 1972. Between 1979 and 1981 it purchased 80 diesel-electric Co-Co locomotives from General Motors, comprising 1650 hp units for its 1676 mm gauge network and 2475 hp units for the 1435 mm system. FA is now rationalising its previously diverse fleet and concentrating on units of either General Motors, General Electric or Alco/Bombardier manufacture, to eliminate difficulties in spares procurement. Since 1979 FA has also taken delivery of 127 304 hp diesel-hydraulic locotractors of Cockerill design, of which 30 were built in Belgium, the remainder locally by AFNE under licence. At the end of 1982 FA was operating 1196 diesel-electric and eight electric main-line locomotives, 669 emu cars, 262 diesel railcars, 2247 passenger cars and 43 190 freight cars.

Productivity
Since 1965 extensive closures of lightly-trafficked rural lines have cut FA's route-km from almost 68 500 to 35 476 at the close of 1982. No further network contraction is now planned. At the same time staff has been substantially reduced, more particularly since 1975; the current total is approximately 95 000, compared with 172 500 in 1965.

Traffic
Rehabilitation progress and energetic marketing by the reorganised FA administration have stemmed a declining freight tonnage trend, but in face of unrestricted road competition and the global recession FA is a long way off course for the objective of 35 million tonnes a year set for the 1980s under the modernisation plan of 1977. The 1981 figure was 16·3 million tonnes and a gross of between 17 and 19 million was anticipated in 1982, or almost 15 per cent more than in 1978. Replenishment of FA's wagon fleet has included numerous special-purpose designs for such commodities as grain and petroleum products, plus container flats and a stock of bi-level auto-carriers. To expand its capability in this respect, however, FA is encouraging private wagon ownership.

FA also aims to contract with private enterprise for management and marketing of rail container services in the Buenos Aires-Tucumán and Buenos

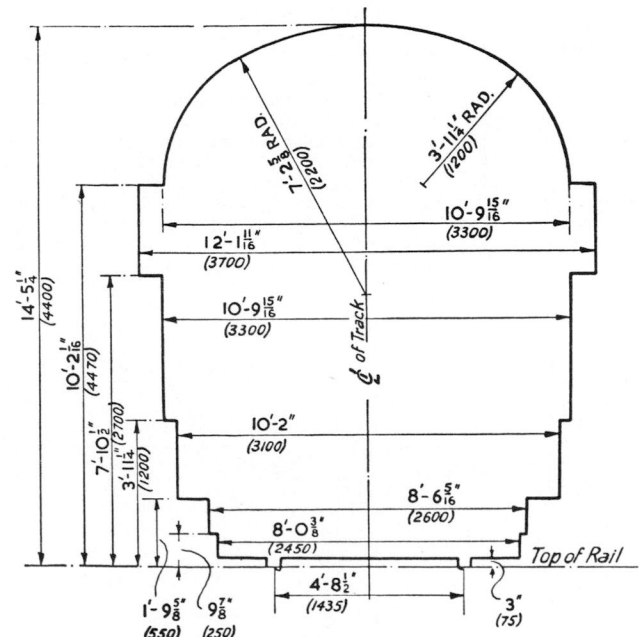

Northwest Region—standard gauge

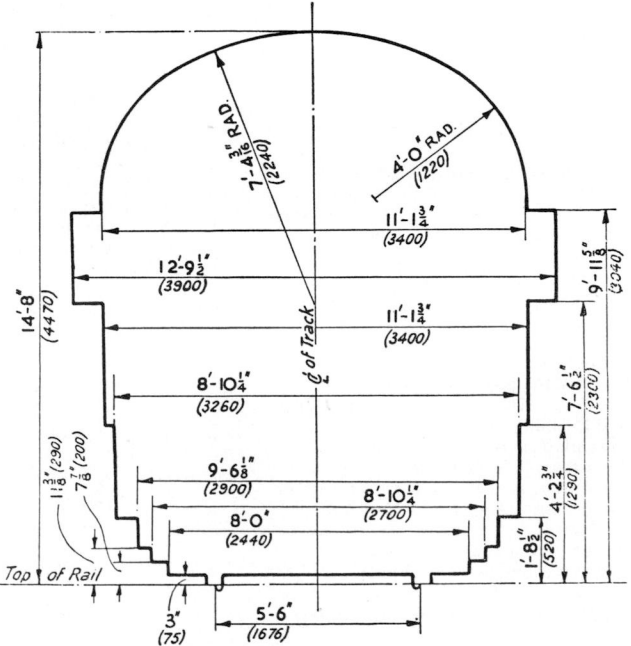

Central and Southwest Regions—1676 mm gauge

Aires-Cordoba corridors. This is a freight sector in which growth has been significant, though as yet FA has only six container transhipment terminals. In 1982 FA inaugurated piggyback services for movement of cattle-carrying road trailers, 20 to a train, over the 500 km from Catrilo and General Pico to Buenos Aires.

In another privatisation move, the passenger services on 87 branch lines were offered to private enterprise in 1982. The infrastructure would remain a charge of FA, which would also retain responsibility for the lines' freight services.

Drastic curtailment of route-km has naturally checked growth of passenger journeys and the trend has been intensified by withdrawal of lightly-loaded trains elsewhere. Infiltration of new or refurbished cars in main-line services and an aggressive marketing policy deploying cheap fares did not prevent a fresh recession of traffic in 1981, when passenger-km declined from 12 700 million to 11 400 million and passenger journeys from 393·7 million to 349 million. However, all sleeping-cars are now air-conditioned and cinema cars are offered on day trains in the Buenos Aires-Rosario, Buenos Aires-Tucuman and Buenos Aires-Mendoza cor-

ridors to compensate for lack of speed. The best non-stop train from Rosario to the capital, for instance, takes 4 hours 7 minutes over the 314 km, while 5 hours is the best on offer for the 400 km run from the capital to Mar del Plata. These routes are top of the FA list for conversion to a quality inter-city operation through infrastructure renewal and increased frequency. Maximum speeds of 120-130 km/h are the objective on key broad-gauge main

lines; that would cut at least one and a half hours from the throughout Rosario-Mar del Plata transit time.

Following an agreement reached between FA and the Cordoba Municipality in 1981, local consultancy firms have been commissioned to design a 23 km regional metro system for Cordoba. Existing alignments are to be adapted. Electrification has not yet been decided.

Fiat diesel railcar

Diesel-electric locomotives

Type	Wheel arrangement	Transmission	One-hour rating hp	Continuous tractive effort kg	Max speed km/h	Weight tonnes	Length m	First built	Builders		
									Mechanical parts	Engine	Transmission
Alco RSO 16	Co-Co	Alternator	3500	18 235	120	108	16	1958	Alco	Alco	GE
GE U12C	Co-Co	Electric	2600	19 780	97	80	14·08	1959	GE	CB	GE
GE U18C	Co-Co	Electric	3400	17 917	124	93	15·85	1960	GE	CB	GE
GE U13C	Co-Co	Electric	2540	21 500	97	80	14·13	1962	GE	GE	GE
Alco RSD-30	Co-Co	Electric	2525	19 340	100	80	15·35	1963	Alco	Alco	GE
G 22 CU	Co-Co	Electric				85·7	15·5	1972		GM	
GT 22 CU	Co-Co	Electric				100·3	17·37	1972		GM	
Transfer Fiat	Co-Co	Electric				55·1	13·22	1966		Fiat	

AUSTRALIA

Department of Transport

Civic Permanent Centre, Allara Street, PO Box 367, Canberra City, ACT 2601

Telephone: 47 3333
Telegrams: Transport
Telex: 6221

Minister: R J Hunt
Secretary: C C Halton
Chairman, Australian National Railway Commission: L E Marks

Australian National Railways

Norwich Centre, 55 King William Road, North Adelaide, South Australia 5006

Telephone: 2674300
Telegrams: AUSrail, Adelaide
Telex: 88445

Chairman: L E Marks
General Manager: Dr D G Williams
Assistant General Manager, Engineering and Planning: M L Nayda
Administration: T M Williams
Tasmania: A F Maddock
Operations and Marketing: M E Gigney
Finance and Supply: N B Walkern
Chief Planner: D R Green
Operations Manager: J W Charter
Marketing Manager: J C Stewart
Sales Manager: J D Harris
Chief Mechanical Engineer: J M Dudley
Chief Civil Engineer: D P Smith
Signals/Communications Engineer: D J Both
Administration Manager: W E May

Industrial Relations Manager: R B Bury
Personnel Manager: C Perry
Transport Co-ordinator: M H Ind
Manager, Research and Development: C Schaumloffel
Manager, Passenger Services: R L Fry
Manager, LCL Business: Vacant
Public Relations Manager: N F Travers
Accounting Controller: W Gallagher
Corporate Finance Manager: R G Fullgrabe
Stores Controller: J S Dawson
Manager, Computer Information Service: Vacant

Gauges: 1435 mm; 1067 mm; 1600 mm
Route length: 2609 km; 2683 km; 2395 km

Constitution
AN is responsible for the management and operation of railways owned by the Commonwealth Government and provides a key link in the chain of inter-system rail transport operating round Australia. It is a statutory authority under the Australian National Railways Act operating as a commercially-oriented business enterprise on behalf of the people of Australia.

Operating offices
Adelaide, South Australia; Port Augusta, South Australia; Launceston, Tasmania.

Commercial offices
Sydney, New South Wales; Melbourne, Victoria; Perth, Western Australia.

AN comprises:
Mainland
Trans-Australian Railway (1435 mm) from Port Pirie (South Australia) to Kalgoorlie (Western Australia), 1782 km;

Port Augusta-Whyalla branch (1435 mm), 75 km;

Central Australia Railway (1435 mm), Sirling North-Marree, 350 km, and Marree-Alice Springs (1067 mm), 869 km;

North Australian Railway, Northern Territory (1067 mm), Larrimah, 502 km (not operating);

Australian Capital Territory Railway (1435 mm), Canberra-Queanbeyan (New South Wales Government System), 8 km;

Tarcoola (South Australia) on Trans-Australian Railway-Alice Springs (1435 mm), 831 km, completed 1980 to allow closure of flood-prone Marree-Alice Springs line.

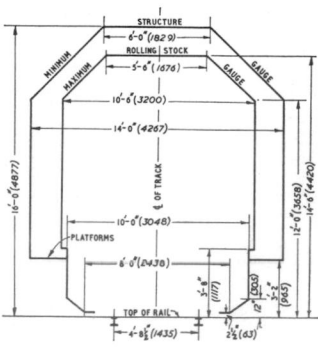

AN 1435 mm gauge (former Commonwealth Railways)

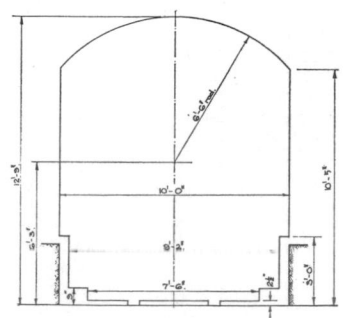

AN 1067 mm gauge lines in Tasmanian Region (former Tasmanian Government Railways)

Tasmanian Region: (formerly Tasmanian Government Railways).
Length and gauge: 851 km, 1067 mm

Track length totals

Tasmania, narrow gauge: 851 km
Mainland, narrow gauge: 963 km
   standard gauge: 3440 km
   broad gauge: 2395 km
   Total: 7649 km

Freight traffic

Tonnage (million)	1978	1979	1980
Tasmania	1·850	2·141	2·324
Mainland	8·773	10·562	10·021
Total	10·623	12·703	12·345

Tonne-km (million)			
Tasmania	284·5	383·1	420
Mainland	4744·9	5235	5331
Total	5029·4	5618·2	5751

Computerised wagon control

Australian National is developing a computerised wagon control system which will improve the efficiency of freight movement and rolling stock utilisation both within AN's system and throughout Australia's railways; give staff and customers current information on the location, origin, destination, load, consignee and sender of any vehicle; and provide operating and maintenance sections with accurate information on any aspect of wagon utilisation. The system is based on New Zealand Railway's traffic monitoring system and some of the successful features of the State Rail Authority of New South Wales and VicRail systems.

Intermodal services

AN operates regular container services between Adelaide and Darwin, Alice Springs and Tennant Creek while piggyback is operated over both the Trans-Australian Railway and the Central Australia Railway by semi-trailers and pantechnicons.

The Railways of Australia Container Express (RACE) operates containerised freight by high-speed block trains throughout Australia. RACE operates between Sydney and Brisbane, Sydney and Melbourne.

Piggyback transport of loaded road vehicles on the Central Australia and Trans-Australian lines has shown outstanding growth since 1979.

Piggyback transport

	Central Australia Railway	Trans- Australian Railway	Total
Tonnes (000)			
1979-80	20·5	98·0	118·5
1980-81	116·7	123·1	239·8
Variation	+469·3%	+25·6%	+102·4%
Revenue (A$ million)			
1979-80	0·424	1·927	2·351
1980-81	2·621	2·826	5·447
Variation	+518·2%	+46·7%	+131·7%

Track utilisation

	1978/79	1979/80	1980/81
Locomotive km (000)	20 490	21 093	21 229
Railcar km (000)	1599	1489	1484
Gross tonnes km hauled (million)	14 392·5	15 066·4	14 512·9

Civil engineering
Alice Springs-Darwin Railway

In February 1981 the Commonwealth Government authorised the survey, design and preliminary planning of a standard-gauge railway link between Alice Springs and Darwin and in January 1983 the then Prime Minister Malcolm Fraser approved construction of the 1504 km line for completion in 1988-89. It will be funded with A$500 million of Federal finance. The route from Alice Springs will be across the Macdonell Range and in close proximity to the Stuart highway to Birdum, from where it will generally follow the alignment of the abandoned 1067 mm-gauge Northern Australian Railway to Darwin, though substantial deviations from the path of the old line will be made in places to allow for more generous curvature and grading. By the start of 1983 surveying of the whole route was well advanced and the alignment of the first 220 km northward from Alice Springs had been settled. Construction was expected to begin in 1984.

The completed line is likely to run at least two weekly passenger trains, for which the title 'Maluka' has been selected, in addition to the existing Alice Springs-Port Pirie 'Ghan'. Rolling stock may feature

some components of the New South Wales State Rail Authority 160 km/h XPT equipment, which ANR has indicated interest in testing over the transcontinental Nullarboor Plain route with later Alice Springs-Port Darwin application in mind.

Meanwhile the transcontinental 'Indian-Pacific' luxury train service has been curtailed to two trips each way weekly. Its operation has been losing A$1·5 million a year and in 1979-81 the service had suffered from keenly price-competitive bus competition and a considerable number of cancellations through labour disputes and endeavours by the railways involved to negotiate staff reductions. AN and New South Wales SRA were considering introduction of a through Sydney-Alice Springs passenger service in 1983.

Finances

	1978/79	1979/80 (A$ 000)	1980/81
Revenue			
Goods	103 186	126 056	143 356
Livestock	4923	5458	6849
Passenger	12 038	12 748	15 249
Parcels and mails	1915	1769	2420
Other	9767	11 940	13 479
Total revenue	131 829	157 971	181 353
Expenditure			
Operation of services	75 920	87 775	99 343
Maintenance of services	74 189	79 744	86 596
Administrative and general	14 030	14 315	19 842
Depreciation and obsolescence	13 757	13 464	14 301
Interest	4112	4233	4221
Insurance	4153	4606	3001
Long service leave	5170	5036	5459
Superannuation	13 407	13 626	11 280
Total expenditure	204 738	222 799	244 043

Note: Commonwealth subsidy to meet an operating loss of A$ 62.69 million in 1980/81 was A$ 56 million.

Locomotives and rolling stock

	Broad gauge 1600 mm	Standard gauge 1435 mm	Narrow gauge 1067 mm	Total
Locomotives	101	102	113	316
Railcars & trailers	21	3	—	24
Passenger cars*	69	156	18	243
Brake, power & relay vans*	117	96	73	286
Freight stock	4682	3277	2798	10 757
Service stock	315	617	431	1363
Total	5305	4251	3433	12 989

*Includes vehicles jointly operated with other railway systems.

Class 900 diesel in Australian National green and gold livery on grain hopper haulage in South Australia

Loading of road transport of ANR's Northern Region operational centre of Port Augusta for piggyback rail transport across the Trans-Australian Railway to Western Australia

Adelaide to Crystal Brook standardisation

A formal agreement between the Commonwealth and South Australian Governments providing for a standard-gauge line connection between Adelaide and Crystal Brook was ratified in September 1980. The agreement also incorporated provision for extension of the standard gauge to Outer Harbour.

The work has been planned in three stages. Stage One involved all work between Crystal Brook and Islington, and branch lines to Gillman Yard, Outer Harbour and Dry Creek to Pooraka. This has been completed at a cost of A$60 million and was inaugurated in December 1982 by Adelaide's first despatch of a 1435 mm-gauge train. It has opened up Adelaide's Outer Harbour and the city's northern metropolitan area to access by 1435 mm-gauge freight trains.

The project's cost has been curbed by achieving gauge conversion through the expedient of moving one rail inward wherever possible. In Stage One this was feasible over 170 km, but in addition 43 km of new 1435 mm-gauge track was laid, also 80 km of mixed gauge (with 250 sets of mixed-gauge pointwork) and 25 km of other line. New facilities provided at Adelaide include a Dry Creek 1435 mm-gauge marshalling yard, Islington freight terminal and an automated bogie exchange facility, employing a radio-controlled Teletrac vehicle mover, at Dry Creek to cater for through traffic from Melbourne to Perth or Alice Springs.

Stage Two involved the remainder of the project and includes a new standard-gauge track from Islington to Mile End, major alterations to the Mile End freight yard and connections to the Inner Harbour area of the port. This was scheduled for completion in May 1983, at a cost of A$10 million.

Stage Three, to be finished early in 1984 at a cost of A$22 million, covers installation of main-line CTC and creation of a new interstate passenger terminal near Mile End yard to handle all AN passenger operation in the city.

Loxton Freight Centre

Designs have been commissioned for construction of a new regional freight centre at Loxton to serve the Riverland area of South Australia.

Passenger traffic

The number of passenger journeys on major long-distance services has been:

	1978/79	1979/80	1980/81
Overland (Adelaide-Melbourne)	180 000	178 200	179 800
Indian Pacific and Trans-Australian (Port Pirie-Kalgoorlie section)	77 000	67 400	67 300
Ghan (Port Pirie-Alice Springs)	8600	11 400	18 600

Patronage of South Australian country passenger services continued to decline steadily, the number of single journeys in recent years being:

1978/79	295 200
1979/80	253 500
1980/81	228 000

Planned investment 1982/83 (A$ 000)

Locomotives	6000
Freight cars	698
Civil engineering and machinery	33 012
Signalling and communications	9441
Yards and terminals	556
Workshops	1475
Computers	825
Total	52 007

Diesel locomotives

Class	Region	Introduced	Power (kW)	Type	Gauge (mm)
500	Central/North	1964/69	373	D/E	1600 1435
600	North	1965/70	1340	D/E	1435
700	Central/North	1971/72	1490	D/E	1600 1435
800	Central	1956/57	490	D/E	1600
830	Central/North/Tasmania	1959/70	670	D/E	1600 1435 1067
900	Central	1951/53	1190	D/E	1600
930	Central	1955/67	1190	D/E	1600
AL	North	1976/77	2240	D/E	1435
CL	North	1970/72	2240	D/E	1435
DE	North	1948	260	D/E	1435
DR	North	1964	112	D/H	1435
GM1	North	1951/52	1120	D/E	1435
GM12	North	1955/67	1300	D/E	1435
NB	North	1957	105	D/H	1067
NC	North	1966	186	D/H	1067
NJ	North	1971	1120	D/E	1067
NSU	North	1954/56	635	D/E	1067
NT	North	1965/68	970	D/E	1067
U	Tasmania	1958/60	76	D/M	1067
V	Tasmania	1948/64	152	D/M	1067
VA	Tasmania	1948	114	D/M	1067
W	Tasmania	1959	250	D/H	1067
X	Tasmania	1950/52	450	D/E	1067
XA	Tasmania	1951/52	450	D/E	1067
Y	Tasmania	1961/71	595	D/E	1067
Z	Tasmania	1972/73	1340	D/E	1067
ZA	Tasmania	1973/76	1750	D/E	1067

Class GM1 diesel on Trans-Australian line

Track

Standard rail: Flat bottom throughout, weighing 53, 46·8, 39·7, 31·2, 29·8, 24·8, 29·8 to 20·3 kg/m
Joints: Fishplates, bolts and welding
Rail fastening: Dog spikes, elastic rail spikes, with or without plates
Cross ties (sleepers): Impregnated hardwood 8 ft × 9 in × 4½ in (2438 × 228 × 114 mm), 4 ft 8½ in (1435 mm) gauge; 6 ft × 8 in × 4½ in (1828 × 203 × 114 mm), 3 ft 6 in (1066 mm) gauge; CR.2 prestressed concrete on Tarcoola-Alice Springs line
Spacing: 1600 to 690 per km
Filling: Crushed stone and gravel ballast
Minimum curve radius: 4·4°
Max gradient: 1·25%

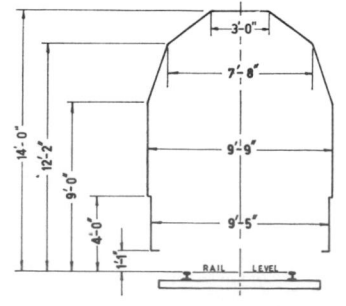
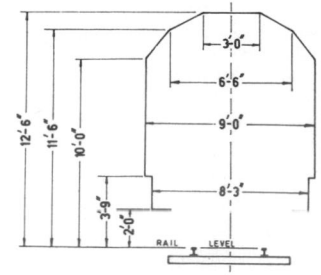

AN loading gauge for former South Australian Railways **(left)** 1600 and 1435 mm lines and **(right)** 1067 mm line

State Railway Authority/SRA (New South Wales)

Transport House, 11-31 York Street, Sydney, New South Wales 2000

Telephone: 219 8888
Telex: 25702

Chairman: Alex Carmichael
Chief Executive: David Hill
Deputy Chief Executive: Ron Christie
Deputy Chief Executive (Industrial Relations): Pat Johnson
Managing Director, Urban Transit Authority: Eric Lyndon
Employee Representative (elected): Jack Lennon
Labor Council Representative: Len Darnely
Secretary: Roger Ford
Director of Finance: Len Corkill
Deputy Chief Operations Manager: Geoff Callingham
Chief Engineering Manager: Ken Hickson
Chief Development Manager: Rob Schwarzer
Chief Mechanical Engineer: Eric Watts
Chief Civil Engineer: Doug Neil
Chief Electrical Engineer: Lo Salmon
Chief Signals and Communications Engineer: John Rees
Executive Engineer: Bill Newton
Capital Works Engineer: John Brew
Stores and Supply Manager: Gerry Cranny

Trading and Catering Manager: Max Braithwaite
Locomotives Manager: Frank Godfrey
Traffic Manager: Kevin Gill
Manager General Freight: Robert O'Loughlin
Commercial Manager: Alan Young
General Manager Workshops: Ken Heard

Gauge: 1435 mm
Route length: 9876 km
Electrification: 488·4 km at 1·5 V dc overhead

Transport development

The railways of New South Wales are controlled by the state which also operates bus services.

Under major reorganisation of public transport services, the former Public Transport Commission has been replaced by two new bodies: the State Rail Authority (SRA) and the Urban Transit Authority. SRA now operates all rail passenger and freight services in New South Wales and UTA handles bus and ferry services in Sydney, Wollongong and Newcastle.

Freight traffic

In 1982 SRA's coal export capacity through Newcastle was lifted by 2 million tonnes annually through the institution of regular working with 42-wagon trains grossing some 4200 tonnes each; in fact, rail capacity now outstrips mine loading capacity, but improvements in the latter are in hand. SRA is committed to an expenditure of A$245 million on new locomotives and wagons to cope with increased coal exports, which are forecast by 1985

to raise annual coal tonnage to 42 million, more than twice the 1979/80 figure. In addition, extra investment is being made in track and in loop lines. At Saxonvale, a new 5 km branch line and balloon loop off the Mount Thorley line was almost complete in 1982. At Mount Thorley, the SRA is negotiating a 16 km extension complete with balloon loops. At Drayton a new spur line and balloon loop was scheduled for completion in October 1982. To service the Hunter Valley Number One mine development, a new loading bin was being built. Major stockpiles and overland conveyors are associated with the project. In 1985, about 6 million tonnes are likely to be handled here. At Ulan, a new line and balloon loops are being built at a cost of A$62 million. In the Hunter region, which is the State's major coal-producing area, the SRA has a staff of 4000.

Following an outlay of A$93 million on new freight wagons since 1975 the Authority intends to invest a further A$220 million before 1985 on 1000 coal hopper, 550 container-carrying, 540 open, 250 ore and 660 other types of freight wagon.

Intermodal services

Two maritime container terminals, served by rail, are located at Sydney. The Balmain or White Bay Terminal which, owned by the Maritime Services Board, is operated under lease by Seatainer Terminals Ltd, and the Glebe Island Terminal also owned by the Maritime Service Board, is operated as a 'common user' terminal under lease by a consortium—Glebe Island Terminals Pty Ltd. Each is also served by road.

At Newcastle, container ships call at No 1 Throsby Wharf and No 4 Western Basin Wharf, each of which is serviced by rail.

Container consolidation depots in Sydney are at Chullora and Leightonfield, 18 km and 24 km respectively from the Balmain/Glebe Island Terminals. These depots are served by captive container trains 24 hours, seven days a week.

Further rail-served container complexes are located at Homebush and Yennora 26 km and 29 km from Balmain/Glebe Island respectively, specialising mainly in containerisation of export wool.

Passenger traffic

Major event of the 1980s has been the debut of the XPT, the Comeng-built version of British Rail's HST 200 km/h push-pull inter-city train-set. The first unit to be commissioned established a new Australian rail speed record of 183 km/h between Albury and Wagga Wagga on 6 September 1981. The initial order for 10 power cars and 20 trailers to form four sets, with two power cars spare, was soon raised by four power cars and 16 trailers to create an additional two train-sets. Instead of the originally proposed five trailers, each set now includes six, partly to secure extra train-crew accommodation.

Main differences between XPT and the British HST lie in the employment of stainless steel, using stressed skin constructional techniques, for the bodies and underframes, which are mounted on modified versions of the BR BT-10 air-suspension, bolster-swing link bogies; rating of the Paxman Valenta engine at 2000 hp; gearing of the power cars for higher tractive effort and maximum speed of 160 km/h to suit Australian conditions; and a redesigned power car, of shorter length than that of the HST and with a one-piece driving cab module moulded from laminated fibreglass, to reduce power car weight to 71 tonnes.

The first commercial XPT service was introduced between Sydney and Orange (extended to Dobbo on alternate days), superseding the locomotive-hauled 'Central West Express'. The second followed in May 1982 between Sydney and Kempsey (504 km), the third in place of the 'Riverina' between Sydney and Albury (643 km) in August. With availability of the extra vehicles and creation of six two-power car- and six-trailer sets, with two power cars spare, further XPT routes from Sydney to Canberra and Tenterfield were to be inaugurated in the autumn of 1983. Time savings with the XPT are substantial: Sydney-Kempsey (504 km) in 6 hours 42 minutes as against a previous best of 8 hours 28 minutes; and Sydney-Orange (321 km) in 4 hours 44 minutes against a previous best of 5 hours 7 minutes. The increase in seating capacity following the XPTs' introduction has permitted progressive withdrawal of existing stock for refurbishing, notably the air-conditioned Class 900 diesel train-sets, which besides interior remodelling with improved seating are being fitted with more powerful engines and mounted on new bogies, to become Class SP2.

In the autumn of 1982 SRA and VicRail were discussing introduction of a Sydney-Melbourne XPT service which would cover the 961 km between the two cities in 10 hours, as against 12 hours 35 minutes by present services. This would be an

Unit coal hopper train hauled by three Class 442 2150 hp diesel-electric locomotives

Air-conditioned double-deck interurban emu

extension of the 'Riverina' Sydney-Albury XPT working, which in the summer of 1982 was recording 55 per cent more passenger-journeys than its 1981 predecessor.

In October 1982 a demonstration through train was run between Sydney and Alice Springs. A regular service was thereafter being negotiated by the railways involved.

The major influence on the 1981/82 financial year passenger journey growth of almost 8 million was increased travel on the Sydney metropolitan area's double-deck emus. Also notable was the 76 per cent increase recorded in the first month of the Gosford-Wyong electrification extension, a further stage in the overall Sydney-Newcastle scheme which was completed in the spring of 1982 at a cost of A$28 million.

Traffic

	1980/81	1981/82
Total freight tonnage (million)	40·281	40·406
Total freight tonne-km (million)	10 521·2	10 709·7
Average net freight train load (tonnes)	863	899
Total passenger journeys (million)	212·9	220·8

Finance

Revenue (A$ million)	
Passengers and baggage	168·131
Freight, parcels and mail	451·373
Trading and catering	22·908
Rents	10·582
Other	10·222
Government supplement	387·409
Total	1050·625

Expenditure (A$ million)	
Staff/personnel expenses	688·752
Materials and services	361·873
Total	1050·625

Finance

The State's worst drought of the century coupled with the world-wide recession had by the autumn of 1982 reduced SRA revenue by A$ 80 million and threatened to leave the system with a 1982/83 deficit of more than A$500 million, well in excess of the A$448 million support foreseen in the State Government's budget. As a result SRA launched cost-cutting measures, including a recruitment freeze; weekend yard closures; manning reductions at smaller stations, and in sleeping and dining cars; and storage of surplus traction and freight rolling stock. The planned capital expenditure of A$308 million for the financial year 1982/83 was not affected.

Investment

The State Government allocated A$308 million for SRA capital investment in its 1982/83 budget. A major item is continuing construction of double-deck emu cars. Recent deliveries of these vehicles from A Goninan & Co have included the first 10 air-conditioned vehicles (the bulk of the fleet has fan-assisted ventilation); another innovation is public address, which is being retro-fitted to existing cars. Under the 1982/83 provisions 50 more double-deck suburban electric cars were to come into service at the rate of almost one a week, at a cost of A$50 million. They would bring the total number of double-deck cars in use to 721, or two-thirds of the metropolitan fleet. The Blue Mountains and Central Coast lines would receive 20 air-conditioned double-deck interurban cars, at a cost of A$20 million, to swell the interurban fleet to 86. A further 80 interurban cars will be ordered later to serve the Newcastle and Wollongong areas when electrification is completed in 1986.

The success of the XPT services led to provision of A$15 million for four power cars and 16 trailers for the projected Northern Tablelands and Canberra XPTs. Class 900 diesel train-sets were to be refurbished as Class SP2.

A total of 150 new locomotives are on order, and nearly 50 would be delivered during the year. The orders include 90 new Class 81 diesel locomotives.

The number of coal wagons was to be doubled at a cost of A$40 million. More than A$30 million would be spent on track strengthening and rebuilding to cater for heavier coal trains. Concrete sleepers would be used on a major scale for the first time in

Aluminium-bodied 76-ton grain hopper

Stainless steel 100-ton coal hopper

XPT train-set

New South Wales. Maintenance of wheat lines which are used mainly for the movement of the year's crop would cost another A$21 million. The Government agreed that this work should proceed despite reduced production as a result of the drought.

Expenditure on electrification from Wyong to Newcastle would amount to A$23·5 million with completion due in 1984. Electrification works for Waterfall to Wollongong and Port Kembla would involve another A$25 million. Because of earlier uncertainty in Federal-State funding arrangements, the project may not be completed until 1986. A new station would be built south of Campbelltown and electrification would extend to that point.

The rebuilding of signalling and communications would cost another A$30 million and the replacement programme involving work on 50 bridges a further A$7 million.

In the metropolitan area work would proceed at a cost of A$7 million on the quadruplication of the line between Granville and Westmead; duplication between Gymea and Caringbah; and extra track facilities north of Hornsby. In addition, 100 railway stations would be upgraded and refurbished. Another A$1 million was to be spent on expanding facilities at country freight centres. NSW SRA was also allocated A$6·4 million for main-line upgrading by the Federal Government.

Traction and rolling stock

The SRA is constantly upgrading its passenger and freight vehicle and locomotive fleets. Deliveries were completed during 1981 of 30 Class 80 diesel-electric and 10 Class 85 electric locomotives which at 2700 kW (3600 hp) are the most powerful locomotives of any type ever built in Australia. Orders were then placed for 50 more electric locomotives valued at A$90 million, and with Clyde Engineering for 80 more diesel-electric locomotives worth A$130 million. A new locomotive maintenance facility has been established at Lithgow and servicing facilities for XPT trains, the latter at a total cost of A$12 million.

In the autumn of 1982 NSW SRA took delivery from Clyde Industries Ltd of the first of 80 Class 81 3000 hp diesel-electric locomotives, procured chiefly for freight haulage. The inaugural batch was put to coal haulage between Ulan/Newdell and Newcastle. Two of the new type in multiple will be able to haul 42-wagon coal trains of 4200 tonnes gross which previously required triple-heading; a pair of Class 81s will also be able to lift the gross weight of wheat trains from the previous maximum of 1800 to 3000 tonnes. The locomotives are finished in a new exterior livery of red, yellow and orange which is being standardised in the country operations of NSW SRA and has been applied to the network's refurbished country service passenger cars.

At the close of 1982 SRA was operating 49 electric and 538 diesel locomotives, 45 diesel train-sets (including XPTs), 38 diesel railcars and 13 trailers, 695 emu cars, 640 passenger cars and 11 559 freight wagons.

Electrification

Electrification to Wollongong and Port Kembla is due for completion by 1985 at an estimated cost of A$ 181·5 million. Electrification of the 171 km from Campbelltown to Goulburn is expected to follow. The Gosford-Newcastle electrification was operational as far as Wyong in 1982 and, depending on finance, should be finished by mid-1984 at a likely cost of A$ 132 million. It may be followed by wiring from Newcastle to Muswellbrook.

Signalling and telecommunications

A total expenditure of A$ 75 million on signalling and telecommunications is envisaged in the period up to 1986. Already new computer-aided signalling centres have been commissioned in the inner Sydney area and at Strathfield, and more are to come in the busy metropolitan area of 469 route-km, which deals with over 600 000 suburban passengers daily. The 610 km North Coast line is being brought under CTC, governed from a single office at Broadmeadow, Newcastle, and similar installations are being provided on the southern main line to Albury and between Aberdeen and Werris Creek.

Civil engineering

Since 1976 over 1000 km of track has been renewed, in many places with heavier rail and concrete sleepers. On the key coal routes the objective now is strength for 25-tonne axleloads. Suburban tracks have been quadrupled between Seven Hills and St Marys (15 km) and similar action is to be taken between Granville and Westmead, along with doubling of the single line between Gymea and Caringbah. Many obsolete timber bridges are being replaced.

Track

Rail
Type to AS1085
30 kg/m: 2900 km approx
35 kg/m: 700 km approx
40 kg/m: 1400 km approx
46 kg/m: 1200 km approx
53 kg/m: 3600 km approx
60 kg/m: (proposed)

Cross ties (sleepers)

Type	Thickness	In plain track and curves
Hardwood	115 mm	1660/km
Concrete	165 mm	1660/km
Steel	9 mm	1660/km

Fastenings

Dog spikes and lock spikes:	in timber sleepers
Resilient fasteners:	in some timber sleepers
Resilient fasteners:	in concrete and steel sleepers

Minimum curvature
Branch lines: 100 m (90 m very seldom)
Main lines: 240 m (110 m very seldom)
Max gradient
Branch lines: 4%
Main lines: 3% (2·5% more frequent)
Max axleload: 25 tonnes
Max gradient, compensated
Main lines: 3·3% = 1 in 30 (electric traction on City Railway). 1·5% = 1 in 66 elsewhere
Branch lines: 4·4% = 1 in 25 and 3·3% = 1 in 30
Max gradient, uncompensated
Main lines: 2·5% = 1 in 40, but there is a 30·5 km electrified length of 1 in 30 to 1 in 33 on the Blue Mountains
Branch lines: 3·3% = 1 in 30 and 2·5% = 1 in 40
Longest continuous uniform gradient: Werris Creek to Binnaway Branch, 13 km of 1% grade, 75% curved with radii varying from 282 to 1207 m (6·2° to 1·45°) with average of 503 m (3·5°). Compensated grade, single track, no tunnels
Worst combination of curvature and gradient: On Batlow Line: radius of 90 m (19·3° curve) on 4% (1 in 25) compensated grade
Max altitude: 377 m on main Northern Line, 645 km from Sydney

Passenger rolling stock under order or delivered 1980-82

Class	Type	No ordered	Supplier	Ordered	Delivered
XF, XBH, XBR	Trailer cars for XPT	20	Comeng	1979	1981-82
XF, XBH, XBR	Trailer cars for XPT	15	Comeng	1982	—
DIM, DIT	Double-deck interurban motor and trailer	46	Comeng	1980	1981-82 (34)
DIM, DIT	Double-deck interurban motor and trailer	80	Comeng	1982	—
	Double-deck force-ventilated suburban motor and trailer	92	A Goninan	1980	1981-82 (66)
	Double-deck force-ventilated suburban motor and trailer	100	A Goninan	1982	—

Freight rolling stock under order or delivered 1980-82

Class	Type	No ordered	Supplier	Ordered	Delivered
NQAY	Container flat	100	Electric Power Transmission	1980	1981
NPRY	Cement tank	25	Comeng	1980	1981-82
NLDF	Covered van	40	Mittagong Engineering	1981	1982
NHTF	Coal hopper	150	Comeng	1981	1982
NHFF	Coal hopper	600	Electric Power Transmission	1982	1982 (24)

Motive power under order or delivered 1980-82

Class	Type	Wheel arrangement	Power (kW)	Max speed (km/h)	No ordered	Supplier	Ordered	Delivered
80	Diesel-electric locomotive	Co-Co	1650	130	20	Comeng	1980	1981-82 (18)
81	Diesel-electric locomotive	Co-Co	2237	115	80	Clyde Eng	1980	1982 (5)
XP	Diesel-electric XPT power car	Bo-Bo	1500	160	10	Comeng	1979	1981-82 (10)
86	Electric locomotive	Co-Co	2700	115	50	Comeng	1981	—
XP	Diesel-electric XPT power car	Bo-Bo	1500	160	5	Comeng	1982	—

Diesel locomotives

Class	Wheel arrangement	Transmission	Rated power (kW)	Max speed km/h	Total weight tonnes	No in service	Year first built	Builders Mechanical parts	Engine & type	Transmission
42	Co-Co	Elec	1192	113	122	5	1955	Clyde Eng	EMD 16-567C	EMD
421	Co-Co	Elec	1341	113	110	10	1965	Clyde Eng	EMD 16-567C	EMD
422	Co-Co	Elec	1492	124	110	20	1969	Clyde Eng	EMD 16-645E	EMD
44	Co-Co	Elec	1341	121	108	54	1957	A E Goodwin	Alco 12-251B	GE/AEI
44	Co-Co	Elec	1341	129	112	37	1965	A E Goodwin	Alco 12-251C	AEI
442	Co-Co	Elec	1492	120	115	34	1971	A E Goodwin	Alco 12-251C	GE/AEI
442	Co-Co	Elec	1492	120	115	6	1973	A E Goodwin	Alco 12-251C	Mitsubishi
45	Co-Co	Elec	1341	120	112	39	1962	A E Goodwin	Alco 12-251C	GE/AEI
47	Co-Co	Elec	745	113	85	18	1972	A Goninan	Caterpillar D399	Hitachi
48	Co-Co	Elec	708	120	75	165	1959	A E Goodwin	Alco 6-251B	GE/AEI
49	Co-Co	Elec	652	124	81	18	1960	Clyde Eng	EMD 8-567C	EMD
70	C	Hyd	410	72	49	10	1960	Comeng	Caterpillar D397	Voith
73	B-B	Hyd	484	64	50	50	1970	Walkers	Caterpillar D379	Voith
80	Co-Co	Elec	1492	130	121	48	1978	Comeng	Alco 12-251CE	Mitsubishi
81	Co-Co	Elec	2237	115	129	5	1982	Clyde Eng	EMD 16-645E3B	EMD
x100	B	Hyd	69	24	18	2	1962	NSWGR	Bedford 300	Allison
x200	B	Hyd	216	51	30	18	1963	NSWGR	Cummins NHRS-6-B1	Allison

Electric locomotives

Class	Wheel arrangement	Line voltage	Rated output (kW) continuous/one-hour	Max speed km/h	Weight tonnes	No in service	Year first built	Builders Mechanical parts	Electrical equipment
46	Co-Co	1·5 kV dc	2533/2816	115	114	39	1956	Beyer Peacock	Metropolitan Vickers
85	Co-Co	1·5 kV dc	2700/2880	130	123	10	1979	Comeng	Mitsubishi

Electric multiple-units (1·5 kV dc)
Single-deck suburban

Class	Cars per unit	Trailer cars per unit	Control trailer cars per unit	Motor cars per unit	Motors per car	Rated output per motor kW	Max speed km/h	Tare weight tonnes	Seating capacity per car	Length over coupling faces mm	Cars in service	Acceleration	Year first built	Builders Mechanical parts	Electrical equipment
Motor car 4 1923	2*	—	2	2	205	—	51	71	19 399	31	NA	1925	Leeds Forge	Metropolitan Vickers
Motor car 4 1927	2*	—	2	2	205	—	50·4	71	19 399	50	NA	1928	Govt Dockyard	Metropolitan Vickers
Trailer car 4 1927	2	—	2*	—	—	—	35·5	79	19 399	148	—	1928	Govt Dockyard	—
Motor car 4 1927	2*	—	2	2	205	—	50·4	76	19 399	66	NA	1928	Clyde Engineering	Metropolitan Vickers
Motor car 4 1927	2*	—	2	4	120	115	50·4	76	19 399	48	NA	1928	Clyde Engineering	Metropolitan Vickers & AEI
Motor car 4 1940	2*	—	2	2	205	—	50·2	64	19 757	15	NA	1941	Tullochs	Metropolitan Vickers
Motor car 4 1940	2*	—	2	4	120	115	50·2	64	19 757	8	NA	1941	Tullochs	Metropolitan Vickers & AEI
Trailer car 4 1940	2	—	2*	—	—	—	34	72	19 755	10	—	1941	Tullochs	—
Trailer car 4 1950	2	—	2*	—	—	—	34	72	19 755	75	—	1954	Tullochs	—
Motor car 4 1950	2*	—	2	4	120	115	50·8	56	19 757	46	NA	1954	Tullochs	Metropolitan Vickers & AEI
Motor car 4 1955	2*	—	2	4	123	115	52·5	59	19 856	36	NA	1954	Comeng	Metropolitan Vickers
Trailer car 4 1955	2	—	2*	—	—	115	33·7	70	19 856	40	—	1955	Comeng	—

* These cars do not belong to the class concerned

Double-deck suburban

Class	Cars per unit	Trailer cars per unit	Control trailer cars per unit	Motor cars per unit	Motors per car	Rated output per motor kW	Max speed kmlh	Tare weight tonnes	Seating capacity per car	Length over coupling faces mm	Cars in service	Acceleration	Year first built	Builders Mechanical parts	Electrical equipment
Trailer car T7801-T4920	4	2	—	2*	—	—	—	32·5	132	20 218	120	—	1964	Tullochs	—
Motor car C3805-C3857	4	2*	—	2	4	135	115	45·4	112	20 218	53	0·8	1971	Comeng	Mitsubishi
Motor car C3858-C3911	4 2	2* —	— 1*	2 1	4	135	115	45	112	20 219	54	0·8	1973	Comeng	Mitsubishi
Control trailer D4011-D4020	2	—	1	1*	—	—	—	33·8	126	20 219	10	—	1973	Comeng	—
Trailer car T4921-T4962	4	2	—	2*	—	—	—	33·6	130	20 219	42	—	1973	Comeng	—
Motor car C3912-C3986	4 2	2* —	— 1*	2 1	4	135	115	45·4	112	20 219	75	0·8	1976	Comeng	Mitsubishi
Control trailer D4021-D4070	2	—	1	1*	—	—	—	33·8	114	20 219	50	—	1976	Comeng	—
Trailer car T4963-T4987	4	2	—	2*	—	—	—	33·6	130	20 219	25	—	1976	Comeng	—
Motor car C3001-C3080	4	2*	—	2	4	135	115	45	113	20 216	80	0·8	1978	A Goninan	Mitsubishi
Trailer car T4101-T4170	4	2	—	2*	—	—	—	33·6	130	20 217	70	—	1978	A Goninan	—
Motor car T3741-T3765	2	—	1*	1	4	135	115	45	112	20 219	25	0·8	1978	Comeng	Mitsubishi
Control trailer D4071-D4095	2	—	1	1*	—	—	—	33·8	114	20 219	25	—	1978	Comeng	Mitsubishi
Air-cond motor car C3501-C3504 & 3550	2	—	1*	1	4	135	115	46·9	108	20 385	5	0·8	1981	A Goninan	Mitsubishi
Air-cond cont trailer D4096-D4099 & 4216	2	—	1	1*	—	—	—	41·2	108	20 385	5	—	1981	A Goninan	Mitsubishi
Forced ventilated motor car C3505-C3549	4	2*	—	2	4	135	115	46·9	106	20 385	45	0·8	1981	A Goninan	Mitsubishi
Forced ventilated trailer car T4171-T4215	4	2	—	2*	—	—	—	41·2	118	20 385	45	—	1981	A Goninan	Mitsubishi

*These cars do not belong to the class concerned

Double-deck inter-urban

Class	Cars per unit	Trailer cars per unit	Control trailer cars per unit	Motor cars per unit	Motors per car	Rated output per motor kW	Max speed kmlh	Tare weight tonnes	Seating capacity per car	Length over coupling faces mm	Cars in service	Acceleration	Year first built	Builders Mechanical parts	Electrical equipment
Trailer car	4	2	—	2	—	—	130	40	92	23 965	8	—	Converted from motor car by NSW SRA in 1982		
Trailer DDC9001-DDC9004	4	2	—	2*	—	—	130	40	96	23 965	4	—	Converted from control trailer by NSW SRA in 1981		
Trailer car DTF9011-DTF9012	4	2	—	2*	—	—	130	40	100	23 825	2	—	1969	Comeng	
Trailer car DTF9021-9022	4	2	—	2*	—	—	130	40	100	23 825	2	—	1969	Comeng	
Motor car DCM8021-DCM8036	2	—	1*	1	4	140	130	59	88	23 968	16	0·65	1977	Comeng	Mitsubishi
Control trailer DCT9031-DCT9044	2	—	1	1*	—	—	130	39	94	23 968	14	—	1977	Comeng	Mitsubishi
Motor car DIM8037-DIM8068	4	2*	—	2	4	140	130	59	96	23 968	37†	0·65	1980	Comeng	Mitsubishi
Trailer car DIT8191-DIT9114	4	2	—	2*	—	—	130	39	112	23 828	14†	—	1980	Comeng	Mitsubishi

*These cars do not belong to the class concerned
†At completion of contract

Single-deck inter-urban

Class	Cars per unit	Trailer cars per unit	Control trailer cars per unit	Motor cars per unit	Motors per car	Rated output per motor kW	Max speed kmlh	Tare weight tonnes	Seating capacity per car	Length over coupling faces mm	Cars in service	Acceleration	Year first built	Builders Mechanical parts	Electrical equipment
Motor car CF5001-CF5040	4	2*	—	2	4	123	115	50	52	20 574	40	—	1958	Comeng	Metro-Vickers
Trailer car TF6001-TF6020 ETB6021-ETB6040	4	2	—	2*	—	—	—	30	64	20 574	40	—	1958	Comeng	Metro-Vickers

*These cars do not belong to the class concerned

Queensland Government Railways

Railway Centre, 305 Edward St, Brisbane, Queensland 4000

Telephone: 225 0211
Telex: 41514

Minister of Transport: D F Lane
Deputy Commissioner and Secretary: R T Sheehy
Assistant Commissioner, Electrification: D V Mendoza
Director, Planning and Development: G L Boyd
Commercial and Marketing Manager: W D Gill
Superintendent of Transport: D G Collins
Chief Engineer: H N Walker
Signals and Communications Engineer: D E Evans
Chief Mechanical Engineer and Workshops Superintendent: J F Jeffcoat
Rolling Stock Engineer: G Skippen
Design and Construction Engineer: H Graham
Chief Accountant: K J Hodda
General Manager, Brisbane: C V Walton
  Toowoomba: K E Neil
  Rockhampton: T K Keating
  Townsville: W L Fraser

Gauge: 1435 mm; 1067 mm
Route length: 111 km; 9858 km
Electrification: 113 km at 25 kV 50 Hz ac

Transport development

Queensland Railways are the second longest in route-km in the British Commonwealth and are state-owned, serving the whole of the north-east part of Australia. Apart from the 1435 mm inter-state line connecting Brisbane with Sydney via the coast all QR lines are 1067 mm gauge.

Traffic

The aggregate tonnage of goods and livestock carried during the 1981/82 financial year showed an increase of 2·156 million tonnes when compared with the results of the previous year. Total revenue from these commodites increased from $383·7 million in 1980/81 to $481·2 million. Increases were recorded in railings of coal, minerals, sawn timber, grain, primary produce including fruit and sugarcane, general merchandise, and container traffic.

Passenger traffic showed increases in both suburban and country areas, with the most significant increases again being recorded in the Brisbane suburban electrification area; overall passenger numbers totalled 34·24 million as compared with 31·87 for 1980/81.

Coal traffic, which at present contributes 25 million tonnes to QR's annual volume, is forecast to reach 60 million tonnes by 1985 and 90 million tonnes by 1990. To cope with the rapidly rising flows to the shipping terminals at Gladstone and Hay Point QR has installed more than 800 km of new line since 1965 and reconstructed a great deal of existing route.

Freight traffic

	1978/79	1979/80	1980/81	1981/82
Freight train-km (million)	24·468	24·386	23·020	24·198
Freight revenue earnings (A$ million)	284·7	324·2	383·7	481·2
Freight tonnage (million)	36·541	38·440	41·504	43·659
Freight tonne-km (million)	10 925	11 465	11 982	13 079
Average haul per tonne (km)	295·59	294·67	285·57	297·94

Passenger traffic

		1979/80	1980/81	1981/82
Passenger train-km	Country	4 086 890	4 096 778	4 259 819
	Suburban	4 116 233	4 164 919	4 237 690
Passenger revenue (A$)	Country	7 497 957	8 514 319	10 297 997
	Suburban	8 478 714	10 080 270	12 648 731
Passenger journeys	Country	1 476 084	1 543 557	1 644 599
	Suburban	28 006 135	30 329 707	32 592 362

Diesel locomotives

Class	Wheel arrange-ment	Trans-mission	Rated power hp	Tractive effort Max lb (kg)	Tractive effort Continuous at lb (kg)	Tractive effort mph (km/h)	Max speed mph (km/h)	Wheel dia in (mm)	Total weight tons	Length ft in (mm)	No built	Year first built	Builders Mechanical parts	Builders Engine & type	Builders Transmission
1150	Co-Co	Elec	1100	59 200 (26 850)	31 000 (14 100)	10·5 (16·9)	50 (80)	36 (914)	89	56' 0⅞" (17 091)	13	1952	General Electric (USA) and Australian Electrical Industries	Cooper Bessemer (USA) FVL-12T	General Electric (USA) and Australian Electrical Industries
1170	A-1-A+ A-1-A	,,	640	26 880 (12 200)	19 750 (8960)	9·6 (15·4)	,,	,,	60	41' 6" (12 649)	12	1956	Walkers (Aust)	Cooper Bessemer (USA) FWA-6T	Australian Electrical Industries
1200	Co-Co	,,	1280	60 000 (27 200)	30 500 (13 850)	12·7 (20·4)	,,	37·5 (952)	90	54' 10⅜" (16 722)	10	1953	Vulcan Foundry (UK)	English Electric (UK) 12-SVT	English Electric (UK)
1250 (Locos 1250-54)	Co-Co	,,	1440	,,	41 500 (18 800)	10·3 (16·6)	,,	,,	85·7	52' 11" (16 129)	5	1959	English Electric (Aust)	,,	,,
1250 (Locos 1255-66)	Co-Co	,,	1440	,,	,,	,,	,,	,,	87·3	,,	12	1960	,,	,,	English Electric (Aust and UK)
1270 (1270-81)	Co-Co	,,	1440	,,	,,	,,	,,	,,	90	,,	16	1964	,,	,,	,,
(1282-99)	,,	,,	,,	,,	41 500 (18 825)	10·3 (16·6)	,,	,,	,,	,,	14	1966	,,	,,	,,
1300	Co-Co	,,	1795	,,	48 500 (22 000)	11·1 (17·6)	,,	,,	88	51' 5" (15 672)	45	1967/ 71	English Electric (Aust)	English Electric 12-CSVT	English Electric
1400	A-1-A+ A-1-A	,,	1310	36 288 (16 400)	28 000 (12 700)	14·7 (23·7)	,,	Drivers 40 (1016) Idlers 30 (762)	76 (Fab bogie) 78·8 (CS bogie)	47' 10⅜" (14 590)	13	1955	Clyde Eng (Aust)	General Motors EMD (USA) 12-567C	General Motors EMD (USA)
1450	Co-Co	,,	1310	54 432 (24 700)	42 000 (19 050)	9·5 (15·3)	,,	40 (1016)	90	52' 8⅜" (16 062)	10	1957	,,	,,	,,
1460 (1460-1501)	Co-Co	,,	1310	,,	50 820 (23 050)	7·5 (12·1)	,,	,,	,,	53' 1⅜" (16 189)	42	1964	Commonwealth Eng (under sub-contract to Clyde Eng)	,,	General Motors EMD (USA) & Clyde Eng (Aust)
(1502 on)	,,	,,	1500	,,	,,	8·8 (14·1)	,,	,,	,,	,,	29	1967	,,	General Motors 12-645 E	,,
	Co-Co	,,	1500	60 480 (27 430)	50 820 (23 050)	8·8 (14·1)	,,	,,	90	52' 7¼" (16 034)			,,	,,	,,
1550 2400 2450 2470	Co-Co	,,	1500	60 480 (27 433)	50 820 (23 050)	8·7 (13·9)	,,	40 (1016)	90	59' 2¼" (18 040)	86	1972	Commonwealth Eng (under sub-contract to Clyde Eng)	General Motors EMD (USA) 12-645 E	General Motors EMD & Clyde Eng (Aust)
1600	Co-Co	,,	838	41 500 (18 800)	30 000 (13 600)	7·8 (12·6)	,,	37·5 (952)	61·5	44' 2" (13 462)	18	1963	English Electric (Aust)	English Electric (UK) 6-CSRKT	English Electric (Aust and UK)
1620	,,	,,	838	,,	,,	,,	,,	,,	62·5	45' 5" (13 843)	28 6	1967	,,	,,	,,
1700	Co-Co	,,	875	39 650 (18 000)	33 600 (15 250)	7·1 (11·4)	,,	,,	59	43' 10" (13 360)	12	1963	Commonwealth Eng (under sub-contract to Clyde Eng)	General Motors EMD (USA) 8-567CR	General Motors EMD (USA) Clyde Eng (Aust)

Class	Axle arrange- ment	Trans- mission	Rated power hp	Max lb (kg)	Tractive effort Continuous at lb (kg)	mph (km/h)	Max speed mph (km/h)	Wheel dia in (mm)	Total weight tons	Length ft in (mm)	No built	Year first built	Builders Mechanical parts	Engine & type	Transmission
1720	Co-Co	,,	1000	,,	,,	8·4 (13·5)	,,	,,	62·5	43' 11⅜" (13 395)	56	1966	,,	General Motors EMD (USA) 8-645E	Clyde Eng (Aust)
2100 2130 2150 2170 2141	Co-Co	,,	2000	64 500 (29 256)	50 820 (23 050)	11·5 (18·5)	,,	40 (1016)	96	59' 2¼" (18 040)	68 1970/ 72	1970/	,,	General Motors EMD (USA) 16-645E	General Motors EMD (USA) Clyde Eng (Aust)
2350 2370	Co-Co	,,	2350	64 500 (29 256)	50 400 (22 860)	14·5 (23·2)	37·5 (952·5)	40	90	56' 2" (17 120)	16	1975	English Electric (Aust)	English Electric 12 CSVT Mk III	English Electric
GL26C-2	Co-Co	,,	3000	—	30 490	—		40 (1016)	93·5	64' (19 510)	48	1980	Clyde Eng	General Motors EMD (USA) 16-645E3	General Motors EMD (USA) Clyde Eng
Dh	B-B	Hyd	465	25 000 (11 350)	18 000 (8150)	6 (9·7)	,,	36 (914)	40	36' 5" (11 100)	73	1968 1970	Walkers Ltd (Aust)	Caterpillar D355 Series E	Voith L42 or U2 (West Germany)

Note: 1250 Class locomotives numbered 1250 to 1254 have been upgraded from original 1290 hp to 1440 hp.

Diesel railcars

Class	Wheel arrange- ment	Trans- mission	Rated power hp	Max speed km/h (mph)	Wheel dia mm (in)	Total weight tonnes (tons)	Length mm (ft in)	No built	Year first built	Builders Mechanical parts	Engine & type	Transmission
1800	2 axle power bogie 2 axle STD bogie	Epicyclic 4 speed gearbox	153	72 (45)	762 (30)	26·77 (26·35)	14 890 (48' 10¼")	12 power 12 trailer	1952	Drewry Car Co Ltd	Gardner CL3 vert	Wilson- Drewry type SE4
1900	2 axle bogie	2 off epicyclic 4 speed gearbox	2 × 125	80 (50)	838 (33)	40·64 (40)	17 577 (57' 8")	2 passenger luggage	1956	Commonwealth Engineering under licence to Budd Car Co	AEC 9.6 litre horizontal	Self Changing Gears Ltd Type R14
2000	2 axle bogie	Epicyclic 4 speed gearbox	150	80 (50)	838 (33)	25·40 (25)	17 297 (56' 9")	21 passenger 17 passenger luggage 4 passenger trailer	1956	Commonwealth Engineering	AEC 11.38 12.5 litre horizontal	Self Changing Gears Ltd Type R14

Electric railcars

Class	Wheel arrange- ment	Line current	Rated output kW	Tractive effort (full field) Max kg	Continuous at kg	km/h	Max speed km/h	Wheel dia- meter mm	Weight tonnes	Length mm	No built	Year first built	Builders Mechanical parts	Electrical equipment
1979 emu	2 axle bogie	25 kV 50 Hz single phase	1080 (8 driving axles per set)	14 276	8668	50	100	840	Tare DM 40·74 M 42·22 DT 34·54	23 050	27 3-car sets in service at 30.6.82	1979	Walkers Ltd	ASEA

Finances

Total revenue for 1981/82 reached a level of A$520·26 million, an increase of A$103·5 million over 1980/81. Principal increases were recorded in the following categories:

	(A$)
Coal	57 913 280
Other minerals	9 381 966
Wheat	4 646 286
Other grains	6 535 162
General merchandise	12 155 092
Container traffic	2 607 706
Passengers	4 352 139

Working expenses were $588 million, which were $101·9 million or 20·96 per cent more than the previous year. Wage increases accounted for A$44·5 million, and fuel cost rises for A$6·7 million, due not only to price increases but also an increased consumption of 5·46 million litres. Increases in tonnages hauled during the year, including export coal from newly developed mines, brought about the increased usage.

The net deficit for 1981/82 after allowing for revenue and interest charges was A$157 million, compared with A$142·7 million in 1980/81. Earnings per train-km increased to 1591·24 cents, from 1332·38 in the previous year. However, working expenses (exclusive of other revenue charges) increased from 1554 to 1798·6 cents per train-km. Working expenses exceeded earnings by 207·32 cents per km.

Planned investment 1982/83 (A$000)

Diesel main-line locomotives (44)	59 600
Electric main-line locomotives (13)	24 800
Electric multiple-units (13)	29 007
Passenger cars (7)	4400
Freight cars (961)	41 400
Containers	2300
New track construction (250 km)	170 000
Other track improvements	69 000
Bridges and buildings	22 600
Electrification	7500
Signalling and communications	11 100
Yards and terminals	10 000
Workshops	3665
Miscellaneous	3030
Total	466 597

Locomotives

The fleet of locomotives in service at mid-1982 totalled 573, an increase of 14 compared with the previous year. Contracts were let for 53 more locomotives for coal traffic and tenders invited for a further 13 units. QR has used the Locotrol system since 1974; with its aid 100-wagon, 5300-tonne coal trains are operated on the Blackwater-Gladstone coal line, employing five 2500 hp traction units.

Wagons

Wagon stocks at the end of the financial year totalled 24 120, an increase of 368 over the preceding year. Of these, 5505 were engaged in bulk coal and mineral traffic. Contracts have been negotiated for the construction of 1406 large coal wagons. Deliveries from the order for 122 bulk sugar wagons have progressed, and a contract was let for construction of 30 flat-top wagons for the transport of concrete sleepers, which are to be used on heavy haulage lines in central Queensland.

Passenger vehicles

The number of cars in service in mid-1982 was 868. New deliveries were offset by the withdrawal of obsolete stock, with some selected units being converted to wagons and vans. An order for five first-class and five economy class cars was completed, and the cars are in operation on 'Sunlander' trains. Deliveries of 10 single sleeping berth compartment roomette cars were expected during 1982/83.

Electrification

Brisbane suburban system: The 25 kV 50 Hz electrification between Ipswich and Ferny Grove and between Kingston and Shorncliffe, comprising 102 route-km, had been completed by August 1982. Construction is progressing on the 38 route-km between Petrie and the newly extended Lota line to Thorneside. Further extensions are planned from Kingston to Beenleigh, Petrie to Caboolture and Petrie to Kippa-Ring. Including the Merivale Bridge A$215 million has been spent to date and the estimated cost to complete the programme is A$45 million.

The Brisbane suburban electrification is estimated to save 12 megalitres of diesel locomotive fuel per annum and release 24 diesel-electric locomotives and four railcars for other services. Transfer of passengers from road to rail is expected to result in savings of 10 megalitres of motor fuel per annum.

Main-line electrification: Queensland has completed feasibility studies of electrification between Blackwater Mines and Gladstone Ports, Brisbane and Rockhampton and Brisbane and Toowoomba. Further preliminary evaluations have been made of electrification of the Goonyella Railway and Newlands-Collinsville-Abbot Point, each of which indicated viability.

The detailed design of Emerald to Gladstone Ports and the preliminary design of Gladstone to Brisbane was completed in January 1982. Construction planning provides for initial electrification of the main line between Blackwater and Gladstone with the subsequent progressive connection of all the Blackwater area mines. Subsequently the implementation plan provides for electrification of all the export coal hauls to Hay Point and Abbot Point terminals with the eventual electrification of the main North Coast Line from Brisbane.

The initial implementation programme from Emerald and Blackwater Mines to Gladstone is estimated to cost A$183 million (at end-1981 values).

New lines

The following projects, valued in total at over A$500 million, have been authorised and in several cases commenced:

Construction of the Newlands to Abbot Point coal line, which incorporates the upgrading of 78 km of existing track from Collinsville to Merinda, construction of an 81 km branch line to Newlands Mine and a 17 km railway connecting the new port of Abbot Point to the existing North Coast Line. Contracts for these projects were let in 1982.

The Curragh Project, which involves construction of a 17 km branch line from Curragh Mine to the Central Line near Blackwater, 20 km of duplication on the Central Line and 19 km of duplication on the North Coast Line, for the export of coal through the port of Golding at Gladstone. Contracts for these developments were let in 1982.

The Laleham Project, incorporating the duplication of 6 km of track on the Central Line, 9 km of track on the North Coast Line and construction of two passing loops (approximately 2 km long) on the Central Line. This project will allow the haulage of an increased quantity of coal to Gladstone from an existing mine in the Blackwater area.

Construction of a 40 km railway from the German Creek coal mine to the Gregory branch line to allow haulage of German Creek coal to Gladstone. Construction was completed early in 1982 and train operation from the mine began in March. Construction of the German Creek to Norwich Park railway (23 km) and the Oaky Creek spur line (6 km), for the haulage of coal from the German Creek and Oaky Creek mines to the new port of Dalrymple Bay adjacent to the existing Hay Point export facility, were to be finished in mid-1983.

The Riverside Project and Blair Athol Projects, which will also allow coal to be hauled to the new port of Dalrymple Bay from these two new mines. Riverside requires the construction of a 10 km spur line to connect it to the existing Goonyella Railway, and Blair Athol the construction of a 110 km branch to connect it to the same system. The Blair Athol branch will have three passing loops 2¼ km long. Contracts for these projects were let in 1982.

The four projects to export coal through Dalrymple Bay incorporate a 142 km section of the existing Goonyella Railway in their haul route. This section, from Coppabella to Dalrymple Bay, is to be progressively duplicated by the end of 1984, with the construction of 125 km of new track between existing passing loops and station yards. These projects will embody QR's first large-scale use of concrete sleepers.

The Boundary Hill Spur Line (6 km), which deviates from the existing Moura Short Line between Graham and Earlsfield. It will enable the haulage of coal from Boundary Hill for the Gladstone Power House. Construction work was to be completed in January 1982.

The major track upgrading project from Townsville to Mount Isa continued and complete track relaying from Duchess to Mount Isa was completed; construction costs were A$1·78 million. Further progress on track upgrading from Caboolture to Gladstone was recorded in 1981/82, with realignments and relaying accompanying the CTC programme.

Construction of a 60 km line from Beenleigh to Gold Coast has been submitted to feasibility study. QR has been allocated A$5·9 million from Federal funds for main-line upgrading projects.

Signalling

Single-line working by staff-and-ticket or electric staff is being replaced by CTC. Major coal routes have been CTC-operated since 1975. To improve train movements on other busy lines CTC installation is being expanded as part of a A$25 million programme. Installation of CTC over 700 km between Brisbane and the Central Queensland coal mines (via Gladstone, Rockhampton and Blackwater) was completed in 1982. Computer-aided CTC is being installed over 122 km of the North Coast Line between Caboolture and Gympie in conjunction with the Brisbane electrification area resignalling; suppliers are Westinghouse Brake & Signal Co and DML Engineering Ltd. Commissioning was to begin in September 1982.

A continuing programme for the modernisation of signalling systems throughout the State has been undertaken in recent years. The Brisbane metropolitan area consisting of 11 km of quadruplication, 10 km of triplication, 118 km of duplication and 34 km of single line will have been completely resignalled and entirely operated from a central signalling complex at Mayne by the end of 1983. A 27 metres-long signalling diagram console of the entrance-exit push-button type has been installed, which in addition to the normal indications incorporates the displays of a computer-based train describer system.

The remainder of the state railways are mainly single line, of which 1040 km is operated under train order regulations, 6207 km by a staff-and-ticket system, 1118 km by an electric train staff system, 1282 km by various centralised traffic control systems, and 149 km is duplicated line operated by automatic colour light signals or block telegraph signalling.

At the end of 1982 658 km of the CTC-signalled lines were operated from computer-based control centres. The diagrams have light-emitting diode (led) displays, keyboards are used to interface with the computer and visual display units are provided to display train running information. Present planning is for all CTC systems to be upgraded to this standard as additions or significant alterations are undertaken.

Communications in the electrified Brisbane suburban area employ immunised 0·9 mm metallic pair PEUT cables as the bearers for 30-channel pcm systems. These systems are used for both trunk and local traffic. Local traffic uses sectionalised physical pairs, on the same cable, carrier-hauled to central locations via the pcm systems.

Outside the suburban area open wire construction predominates with 3- and 12-channel systems providing the links between major centres.

In association with a number of major coal export projects, microwave radio systems were to be provided for improved reliability purposes on the

Unit coal train hauled by three Class 2100 diesels in central Queensland

Brisbane suburban electrification emu

Townsville-Bowen-Collinsville and the Mackay-Coppabella sections towards the end of 1983.

The majority of teleprinter traffic is routed through a computer-based message switching system employing a small minicomputer which was commissioned in 1975.

Radio is used extensively, with a uhf system on suburban electric stock providing continuous driver-to-control communications, vhf for driver-to-guard communication in country areas, a variety of uhf yard systems for shunting applications in major marshalling yards, and vhf and uhf car-to-base systems.

Track
Standard rail: Flat bottom 60, 53, 47, 41, 40, 31 and 30 kg/m, purchased in lengths of 12·2 or 13·75 m. Minor branch lines, 20 kg. Heavy-haul routes, 60 and 53 kg/m. Normal main-line standard, 47 kg/m
Joints: 6- and 4-hole angle and bar fishplates
Cross ties (sleepers): Mostly unimpregnated local hardwood timber 2150 × 230 × 115 mm, or 150 mm thick on heavy haul lines. Purchase of treated sleepers has now commenced, as well as concrete sleepers for new heavy-haul lines and a small number of steel sleepers for branch lines. Extended use of concrete sleepers being considered due to increasing shortage of timber
Spacing: 1640 per km generally on main lines (steel and concrete sleepers, 1460 per km)
Rail fastening: Normal standard 16 mm-square dogspike, with 19 mm dogspikes used in 150 mm-thick timber sleepers on heavy-haul tracks. Elastic rail spikes now discontinued. Indirect fastenings used with concrete and steel sleepers or timber sleepers in curves on new heavy-haul lines
Ballast: Mainly crushed rock in new work, but river gravel used on many branch lines
Max curvature: Generally 17·3° = radius of 100 m, with a few curves down to 21·8° = 80 m
Max gradient: 3% = 1 in 33 uncompensated, but generally not exceeding 2% (1 in 50)
Longest continuous gradient: Between Brisbane and Gympie, ruling grade 1 in 75 with 2 sections (one 3·2 km long) of 1 in 50
Max altitude: 925 m near Cairns

Max permitted speed
Freight and heavy-haul unit trains: 60 km/h
Passenger: 80 km/h max for locomotive-hauled passenger trains and express freight trains, 100 km/h electric stock in Brisbane suburban area
Max axleload: 16·3 tonnes diesel locomotive; 19·8 tonnes on some mineral wagons
Bridge loading: All bridges on important lines can carry loading equivalent to Coopers E25-E30. Many equivalent to Coopers E35 and most new construction to this standard. Heavy-haul mineral lines have bridges built to carry Coopers E50 loading
Welded rail: Rails purchased in short lengths flashbutt welded at depot into 61 and 110 m lengths. Long rails welded up to 244 m on unplated track, and 440 m on plated track. On heavy-haul lines rails welded continuously. Site welding is generally by thermite process and 2500 welds recently carried out by mobile flashbutt welding machine. Total length of track with welded rail now approximately 4200 km. Standard method of laying is by mechanised gang using a Pettibone speed swing crane

South Australia State Transport Authority

PO Box 2351, North Terrace, Adelaide, South Australia 5001

Telephone: 218 2200
Telex: 88535

Chairman: J D Rump
General Manager: J V Brown
Management Services Manager: D F Callow
Finance Manager: A L Porter
Personnel Manager: C Williamson
Chief Traffic Manager: R J Heath
Chief Engineer: C R Stewien
Development Manager: R N Johns

Gauge: 1600 mm
Length: 131 route-km (including rights exercised over 26 km of Australian National Railways tracks)

Since the 1978 transfer of the country railway system of the State to the Australian National Railways, the Authority controls only the metropolitan railway system of Adelaide. This is used by freight services to and from the country system as well as by suburban rail services, which are integrated with the bus and tram services also run by the Authority in the city.

The Authority operates two diesel locomotives, four steam locomotives (for promotional purposes only), 121 diesel railcars, 42 trailers and 33 special-purpose passenger cars. Comeng Aresco Pty Ltd

Noarlunga Centre rail-bus interchange station

Adelaide railcar depot nearing completion in March 1983

completed an order for 12 power cars and 18 trailers in 1981.

Traffic
Passenger journeys increased on all modes from 77·5 million (rail 13·815 million) in 1980/81 to 79·74 million (rail 14·698 million) in the 1981/82 financial year.

Engineering
Reconstruction of the Adelaide railcar depot was due for completion in April 1983 at a cost of A$10·25 million and design work has commenced on the resignalling of the whole of the Adelaide metropolitan rail system at an estimated cost of A$25 million.

Class 2000/2100 and 300/860/40 diesel train-sets at Adelaide

Diesel train-set comprising two Class 300 power cars and a Class 860 trailer

Class 830 Goodwin-Alco diesel locomotive

Prototype refurbished railcar 2301 and trailer 2501

Diesel railcars or multiple-units

Class	Cars per unit	Motor cars per unit	Motored axles per motor car	Transmission	Rated power (kW) per motor	Max speed km/h	Weight tonnes per car	Total seating capacity	Length per car mm	No in service	Year first built	Builders		
												Mechanical parts	Engine & type	Transmission
300 motor (driving)	2×300 1×860	2	2	Hydraulic torque converter/ direct drive	163·4 170·8 156·7	95	40·7 42·7 41·9	91 91 89	20 015	41 20 12	1955 1959 1968	South Aust Railway Workshops, Islington	GM 6-71 Rolls-Royce C65 FLH GM 6-71	Twin Disc
860 trailer (non-driving)	1×860 with 2×300	2×300	—	—	—	95	30·2	56	16 980	24	1955	South Aust Railway Workshops, Islington	—	—
400 motor (driving)	Single car	1	2	Hydraulic torque converter/ direct drive	163·4 156·7	95	42·6	80 78	20 015	20 17	1959 1968	South Aust Railway Workshops, Islington	GM 6-71 GM 6-71	Twin Disc
2000 motor (driving)	1 with either 1 or 2× 2100	1	4	Hydraulic torque converter/ 2-stage Voith turbo T420r	373	110	68	64	25 500	12	1980	Comeng Aresco	MAN D3650 HM7U 4-stroke Flat 12	Voith
2100 trailer (driving)	1 or 2× 2100 with 1×2000	—	—	—		110	42	106	25 500	18	1980	Comeng Aresco	—	—

Diesel locomotives

Class	Wheel arrangement	Transmission	Rated power (kW)	Max speed km/h	Total weight tonnes	No in service	Year first built	Builders		
								Mechanical parts	Engine & type	Traction motor
830	Co-Co	Elec	727 max 671 traction	110	71·4	2	1959	AE Goodwin Ltd	Alco Diesel Series 251 6 cyl	General Electric 761

The Emu Bay Railway Co Ltd
A member of the EZ Industries Ltd Group

Wilson Street, Burnie, Tasmania 7320

Telephone: 004 31 2822
Telegrams: Emubay
Telex: 58521

Chairman: Sir Edward Cohen
Manager: A G Norton

Gauge: 1067 mm
Route length: 133 km (143 track-km)

Traction and rolling stock
The company operates 13 diesel locomotives, two passenger cars and 123 vacuum-braked freight wagons.

Track
Rails are 31 and 41 kg/m, permitting a 14·5 tonnes maximum axleload. Maximum gradient is 1 in 40 and minimum curvature 100 metres.

Victorian Railways (VicRail)

67 Spencer Street, Melbourne, Victoria 3000

Telephone: 6 1001
Telegrams: Railways, Melbourne
Telex: 33801

Victorian Railways Board
Chairman: A S Reiher
Members: R W Ellis
L M Perrott
F R G Strickland
N G Wilson
R H Hodges
General Manager: R J Gallacher
Assistant General Manager (Technical): J K Brodie
Assistant General Manager (Operations and Marketing): J Hearsch
Assistant General Manager (Finance and Administration): B G Smethurst
Secretary for Railways: I J Reiher
Acting Director of Operations: R T Barden
Acting Chief Operations Manager: F Blencowe
Chief Transportation Manager: P Helbig
Chief Freight Manager: J S Bell
Chief Marketing Manager: M W B Ronald
Chief Mechanical Engineer: G Swift
Chief Workshops Manager: F R Uhe
Chief Civil Engineer: J J Emmins
Chief Electrical Engineer: W R Wilkins
Chief Internal Auditor: P J Stow
Comptroller of Accounts: J K McGowan
Comptroller of Stores: T J Way
Director of Personnel: R A Jennison
Acting Group Manager, Suburban Planning: A M Hurse
Acting Group Manager, Country Passenger Services: D Watson
Acting Director of Planning: J N Lade
Director, Management Controls: J H Thompson
Solicitor for Railways: C Berry
Manager, Trading and Catering Services: G Watts

Finance Manager: I D Dunkerley
Manager, Public Relations: M N Alexander

Gauge: 1600 mm; 1435 mm
Route length: 5434 km; 332 km
Electrification: 717 km at 1·5 kV dc

Transport development
VicRail is responsible for the provision, maintenance and operation of the network of rail lines that serve the State of Victoria. More than 6000 km of track serve the country areas, suburban network and the link between Victoria, the eastern states capitals of Sydney and Brisbane and the capitals to the west, Adelaide and Perth. The country and inter-state lines are operated by diesel-electric locomotives except for one 1·5 kV dc electrified line in the south-east totalling 417 route-km.

In addition there is an electrified suburban network serving metropolitan Melbourne with over 300 route-km and nearly 200 stations. Suburban rolling stock is made up of more than 140 six- or seven-car trains.

A recent addition to this network, commissioned in 1981, is an underground loop serving the central business district of Melbourne which is fully integrated with the suburban network.

In 1982 the State Government announced its intention to disband the State's eight existing transport authorities, including VicRail, and replace them from July 1983 with four new authorities: a Metropolitan Transit Authority for urban and suburban train, tram and bus services; a State Transport Authority for all non-metropolitan public transport; a road safety and licensing authority; and a road construction authority. VicRail Chairman Alan Reiher was appointed Director-General of Transport in this new structure, to take responsibility for planning, policy development and budgeting for all transport authorities.

Also in 1982, as a corollary to its policy of deregulating road transport, the State Government annulled VicRail's common carrier obligations.

Freight services
VR has been steadily rationalising freight services and in mid-1979 opened a network of 35 regional freight centres served from Melbourne by fast overnight freight trains. Highway trucks deliver and collect freight from the centres privately under contract. Freight is palletised or otherwise used as much as possible.

Grain comprises around 25 per cent of annual tonnage and freight revenue, as VR is one of the few Australian railways which lacks large bulk coal or mineral traffic. Other important freights include industrial raw materials and finished goods railed over the inter-state trunk routes linking Melbourne with Sydney and Adelaide. Moving in trainloads over relatively long hauls, this traffic represents 46 per cent of VR's annual freight totalling around 3400 million tonne-km. It is subject to fierce road competition, but the repeal of VicRail's common carrier duty now makes possible a more flexible and selective response. New marketing drives have been mounted for intermodal traffic, for long-term contracts in inter-state steel and cement flows, and in new market areas such as rice and aggregates.

Intermodal services
The railway operates four special container services: Melbourne-Sydney (nightly), Melbourne-Brisbane (daily), Melbourne-Adelaide (nightly), Melbourne-Perth (every five days).

Passenger services
The biggest of VR's passenger movements takes place in Melbourne over a major suburban commuter network (nearly all electrified at 1500 volts dc) where the railway handles more than 350 000 passengers a day over an average journey of 16 km.

The suburban services are being re-equipped with Comeng-built stainless-steel bodied six-car emus under an A$108·5 million order covering 50 sets of 200 power cars and 100 trailers, but performance of the initial units delivered raised doubts about agreement to completion of the contract unless reliability were improved. As a result of some progress in this respect the State Government agreed in October 1982 to an order for 45 more train-sets (270 cars) worth at least A$180 million. Rate of production was also to be doubled from 10 to 20 sets a year, to complete replacement of the 27 surviving so-called 'Red Rattler' train-sets, now 65 years old.

By the end of 1983 VicRail expected to have re-equipped all its country routes with 54 new stainless steel-bodied, air-conditioned Type N cars, built in VicRail's Newport workshops. At the same time VicRail aimed to have eliminated all remaining station refreshment stops on its country services with the application throughout the network of a modular catering service purveying food and drink pre-prepared and packaged for modular distribution at a central Melbourne catering plant. To execute the service 18 new buffet cars have been built and 10 existing cars rebuilt to match with microwave ovens and modular storage. On-train meals are served in disposable packs for consumption at seats.

In February 1983 the State's Transport Minister announced intention to acquire three sets of New South Wales SRA's XPT high-speed equipment, for use on the 'Spirit of Progress' and 'Intercapital Daylight Express' services, with half the cost borne by the Federal Government. To exploit the XPT's speed potential, the 307 km Albury-Melbourne Spencer Street line would be upgraded at a cost of A$45 million. However, a VicRail team was simultaneously studying Talgo operation in Spain.

Motive power and rolling stock
Electric locomotives 30; diesel-electric locomotives 257; diesel railcars 13; diesel trailers 8; emus 148 comprising 572 power cars and 475 trailers; passenger coaches 318; freight wagons 12 178; containers 216.

Electric railcar units under order or delivered 1980-82/83

Delivery in fiscal year	Stainless steel power units (M car)
1979/80	30
1980/81	53 (contract completed)

Supplier: Martin and King, Melbourne
Power: 450 kW continuous (all axles powered)
Max speed: 115 km/h

Delivery in fiscal year	Stainless steel power units (M car)	Trailer units (T car)
1981/82	32	16
June-November 1982	24	12

Supplier: Commonwealth Engineering (VicRail) Pty Ltd
Power: 496 kW continuous (all axles powered)
Max speed: 115 km/h

Passenger train cars under order or delivered 1980-82/83

Delivery in fiscal year	No of units	Builder
1981/82	24	VicRail
1982/83 (to November 1982)	9	VicRail

Freight rolling stock under order
25 Type VQDW bogie flat container wagons to be constructed in 1983. Builder: VicRail.

Martin & King Pty Ltd is to refurbish 13 Class T diesel locomotives.

Investment plans 1982

	(A$000)
Diesel main-line locomotive refurbishing	1265
Locomotive-hauled passenger cars (42)	15 940
Self-propelled cars (7)	3160
Freight wagons	6625
Containers	640
Other intermodal	932
Track improvements	19 065
Track maintenance machines	3560
Bridges and buildings	15 174
Signalling and telecommunications	6313
Yards and terminals	9733
Workshops	900
Total	83 307

Civil engineering
Up to 1990 VR plans to improve track standards between Melbourne, Albury and Serviceton (about 750 km) by replacing the existing 94 lb/yd rail with new 60 kg/m section. Concrete sleepers will also be installed.

Traffic

	1978/79	1979/80	1980/81	1981/82
Freight tonnage (million)	11·19	13·45	12·72	11·62
Freight tonne-km (million)	3100	3888	3704	3427
Average net train load (tonnes)	326·81	369·44	360·36	368·27
Average wagon load (tonnes)	20·35	22·75	22·92	24·02
Passenger-km (million)	2076·5	1933	NA	NA
Passenger journeys (total) (million)	93·89	88·91	NA	NA

Finances
Revenues

	1978/79	1979/80	1980/81	1981/82
			(A$ million)	
Passengers and baggage	57·3	62·7	74·9	96·3
Freight and mail	104	135·4	155·8	147·8
Miscellaneous			25·5	16·1

Expenses

Staff charges	263·5	282·8	315·1	332·1
Materials and services	84·3	109·8	132·8	164·2
Depreciation	0·4	0·4	0·4	12·9
Financial charges	23·5	27·9	31·1	37·1

Freight rolling stock under order or delivered 1980-82/83

Delivery in fiscal year	Class	Type	No of units	Builder
1979/80	VHGY	bogie wheat hopper	30	VicRail
1979/80	VQFX	bogie container wagon	75	VicRail
1979/80	VQCX	bogie container wagon	75	VicRail
1980/81	(nil construction)			
1981/82	VPCX	bogie bulk cement wagon	50	VicRail
1981/82	VHEY	bogie briquette hopper	7	VicRail
1982/83	VHEY	bogie briquette hopper	28	VicRail
(to November)	VHHY	bogie grain hopper	15	VicRail

Museum station, the first of VicRail's three new underground stations operational in 1981

VicRail air-conditioned emu by Comeng

Track
Standard rail: Flat-bottomed 47, 53 and 60 kg/m rail rolled in 13·72 m lengths
Cross ties (sleepers)
Timber: Non-treated Australian hardwoods (Red Gum, Ironbark, Box Stringbark and Messmate)
Dimensions: 1600 mm gauge 2·705 m × 250 × 125 mm; 1435 mm gauge 2·59 m × 250 × 125 mm
Spacing: 685 mm centres
Concrete: Prestressed concrete with cast-iron shoulders to take Pandrol rail clips
Dimensions: 2·67 m × 275 × 145 mm at midspan (208 mm deep at ends). Rail seat canted at 1 in 20
Spacing: 670 mm centres

Fastenings
Timber: Most track fastened with dogspikes. Sleeper plates used on all tracks except 60 lb/yd branch lines, double shouldered and canted at 1 in 20. 'Fair' deep bow one-piece rail anchors used instead of pads. Approx 150 km of track relaid in 60 kg/m rail on rolled double-shoulder sleeper plates with Pandrol clips and 3 lock spikes per rail foot
Concrete: Pandrol rail clips, rail pads and insulators used on 53 and 60 kg/m rail laid on concrete sleepers
Ballast: Generally broken stone, usually volcanic basalt, but granite, rhyodicite and diabase also

used. For rail lengths up to 55 m, 250 mm bearing depth with 300 mm shoulder width. For long or continuously welded rail, 300 mm deep with 405 mm shoulder width

Max gradient
Main line: 2·08% = 1 in 48
Branch line: 3·33% = 1 in 30
Trackwork design standards: Curves of less than 2400 m radius transitioned. Main-line curves for 100 km/h traffic to be 830 m radius minimum, while for 50 km/h main-line traffic minimum radius should be 400 m
Suburban electrified lines to have 250 m minimum radius; minimum radius of sidings to be 150 m; minimum radius through platforms 600 m
Max altitude: 591·3 m near Wallace, Melbourne-Serviceton line
Welded rail: Standard 13·72 m rail lengths welded into 27·5-82 m lengths at the central flashbutt welding depot, Spotswood. Once laid, rails thermit-welded into 328 m lengths or continuously welded rail. Stress control measures taken during field welding to ensure the continuously welded rail is in an unstressed condition within the temperature range of 33-38°C
Max axleload: 22·36 tonnes on C class diesel-electric locomotives

Major repair work in progress
Spot ballast cleaning, based on priorities; sleeper renewal at 6/10 years according to line classification; surfacing, associated with sleeper cycle; independent surfacing between the major sleeper and surface cycles; replacement of 47 kg at 100 MGT rails with 60 kg rails and upgrading 60 lb lines with the released material; continuous welding of track from 270 ft lengths; bridge upgrading with Armco pipes.

Electrification
Completion of the Werrible scheme was programmed for the end of 1983.

New construction
The Ringwood-Bayswater track doubling was finished in 1983 and that between Ringwood and Croydon was due for completion at the end of 1983.

Signalling and telecommunications
Urgent priority has been given to installation of CTC on the Ararat-Serviceton section (251 km) of the Melbourne-Adelaide freight line. Track-to-train radio is to be provided on all traction units by the end of 1984.

Diesel locomotives

Class	Wheel arrangement	Transmission	Rated power kW	Max kN	Tractive effort Continuous at kN	kmlh	Max speed kmlh	Wheel dia mm	Total weight tonnes	Length mm	No built	Year first built	Builders Mechanical parts	Engine & type	Transmission
B	Co-Co	Elec	1193	267	178	17·7	133	1016	114	18 542	26	1952	Clyde-GM	GM 16-567B	GM
C	Co-Co	Elec	2460	330	289	23·4	133	1016	135	20 177	10	1977	Clyde-GM	GM 16-645E3	GM
F	C	Elec	260	148	49	12	32	1232	51	8915	7	1951	Eng Elec	Eng Elec 6KT	EE
H	Bo-Bo	Elec	820	199	150	14·2	100	1016	82	13 386	5	1968	Clyde-GM	GM 8-645E	GM
S	Co-Co	Elec	1342	285	239	15·3	133	1016	116	18 567	16	1957	Clyde-GM	GM 16-567C	GM
T	Bo-Bo	Elec	708	169	125	15·3	100	1016	70	14 554	28	1955	Clyde-GM	GM 8-567C	GM
			708	169	150	12·1	100	1016	70	13 386	52	1959	Clyde-GM	GM 8-567CR	GM
			820	169	150	12·1	100	1016	70	13 386	14	1966	Clyde-GM	GM 8-645E	GM
W	C	Hyd	485	120	—	—	32	1232	49	9169	16	1959	Tulloch	Mercedes-Benz MB 820B	Krupp
X	Co-Co	Elec	1343	285	239	15·3	133	1016	114	18 364	6	1966	Clyde-GM	GM 16-567E	GM
			1640	285	239	17	133	1016	116	18 364	18	1970	Clyde-GM	GM 16-645E	GM
Y	Bo-Bo	Elec	485	159	78	16	65	1067	65	13 284	50	1963	Clyde-GM	GM 6-567C	GM
			559	159	78	16	65	1067	65	13 284	25	1968	Clyde-GM	GM 6-645E	GM

Electric locomotives

Class	Wheel arrangement	Line current	Rated output kW	Max kN	Tractive effort (full field) Continuous at kN	kmlh	Max speed kmlh	Weight tonnes	Length mm	No in service	Year built	Builders Mechanical parts	Electrical equipment
E	Bo-Bo	1500	460	108	63	25	65	56	11 786	5	1928	VicRail	VicRail
L	Co-Co	1500	1790	209	112	48	120	99	17 983	25	1952	Eng Elec	Eng Elec

Diesel railcars

Class	Transmission	Rated power kW	Max kN	Tractive effort Continuous at kN	kmlh	Max speed kmlh	Total weight tonnes	Length mm	No built	First built	Builders Mechanical parts	Engine	Transmission
DRC	Hyd	400	—	—	—	113	63	24 105	4	1971	Tulloch Cummins Voith	Two Cummins NTA 855R	Voith T113R
DERM	Hyd	205	—	—	—	97	47	17 180	10	1930	GM	Twin GM 6-71	GM transfer gearbox 1.48:1

Western Australian Government Railways (Westrail)

Westrail Centre, West Parade, East Perth, Western Australia

Telephone: 326 2811
Telex: 92879

Commissioner: W I McCullough
Assistant Commissioner: A E Williams
Chief Traffic Manager: T A Swan
Chief Civil Engineer: M J Abbott
Secretary for Railways: W T Tobin
Chief Mechanical Engineer: W T Adamson
Marketing Director: B M Sutherland
Director, Management Services Bureau: D G Stevenson

Class L 2386 2162 kW Co-Co diesel-electric main-line locomotive

Chief Accountant: C H Menagh
Signal and Communications Engineer: R Davern

Gauge: 1067 mm; 1435 mm; dual gauge
Route length: 4396 km; 1229 km; 148 km

Transport development

Railways play an important role in the development of Western Australia, contributing to the success of the state's mining ventures and agricultural shipments to the coast for export. The Western Australian Government operates all railways running through the state with the exception of the Trans-Australian line between Kalgoorlie and the South Australian border and four iron ore railways in the northern region.

New lines

Under consideration at the start of 1983 was a plan for a new 1870 km railway from Perth via Eneabba and Meekatharra to the Pilbara ore region. It would connect with the Hamersley Iron Ore line to Dampier and also with the railway from Mount Newman to Port Hedland, on the north coast. A second proposal under study envisages a new coal line from Collie to the port of Bunbury via Donnybrook.

Freight traffic

A total of 20 million tonnes of freight was hauled by Westrail during the 1981/82 fiscal year, a decrease of some 0·27 million tonnes on the previous year's figures. Despite increases in freight charges and a significant reduction in staff numbers, fuel and labour cost rises were again the major factors in the increase of expenditure and led to a deficit of A$ 35·3 million. The State Government's new land freight transport policy, under which Westrail has been progressively forced to compete for traffic on commercial bases, has had a considerable impact on the railway's business.

Westrail's major haulage in 1980/81 was 5·75 million tonnes of bauxite from Alcoa's mines at Jarrahdale to the company's refinery at Kwinana. Grain traffic recovered from the effects of severe drought in the previous year and reached 3·64 million tonnes. Iron ore railed from Koolyanobbing to the Australian Iron and Steel Pty Ltd blast furnace at Kwinana, a distance of 500 km, declined by 0·73 million to 0·91 million tonnes.

Alumina, a regular contributor to Westrail's annual haulage, totalled 2·07 million tonnes. Coal haulage amounted to 1·52 million tonnes, a decrease of 110 000 tonnes on the previous year. This was caused by reduced demand from some private users as well as from the State Energy Commission's power stations at Bunbury, Kwinana and Metropolitan areas. Demand for mineral sands haulage totalled 0·96 million tonnes, including that road hauled between Capel and Bunbury. General rail freight to and from other states was just below 1 million tonnes. Woodchips hauled in the southwest of the State between Manjimup and Bunbury reversed its previous upward trend, dropping by 232 000 to 500 000 tonnes.

Freight tonne-km (million)

1979	1980	1981	1982
4178·8	4730·6	4488·6	4398

Freight tonnage (million)

1979	1980	1981	1982
19·2	21·3	20·27	19·78

Intermodal services

Westrail operates a comprehensive network of road freight services in conjunction with its rail programme. In 1980/81 just over 2·58 million km were run by Westrail trucks to areas not served by rail or as ancillary to existing train services. Piggyback freight is a developing business.

Following deregulation of parcels and merchandise freight within the State, Westrail has formed a joint intermodal company, Total Western Transport Pty Ltd, with a road haulier, Mayne Nickless.

Motive power and rolling stock

Ten new air-conditioned railcars for suburban services have entered service, replacing obsolete units with high maintenance costs. The 68-seater, air-conditioned cars, designed and built by A Goninan to a semi-monocoque format of stainless steel panels, have reinforced glass fibre body ends. Five are power cars, each with two Cummins six-cylinder, 208 kW flat engines driving through Voith hydraulic transmissions. The trailers embody a GM 110 kW diesel-generator set for auxiliary service power. The air-suspension bogies are disc-braked. Use of railbuses for some Perth suburban services is under study.

Delivery began early in 1982 of 13 new 1640 kW DB class narrow-gauge locomotives, introduction of

which would ensure the progressive phasing-out of older locomotives in service for more than 25 years. The new locomotives are built by Clyde Engineering. A wagon-building programme to cater for baux-

ite, alumina, grain and caustic soda among other products added 92 vehicles to stock in 1981/82; this included 35 wagons for copper-zinc concentrates and three petroleum tankers.

Class RA diesel and unit alumina train loading at Alcoa refinery, Pinjarra

Container transfer in Westrail's Kewdale terminal

Bauxite discharge on the move from special-purpose hoppers at Kwinana

Civil engineering

Rehabilitation of the railway between Kwinana and Koolyanobbing, which started in 1977, is on schedule. In addition to this contract work, renewal of timber sleepers and replacement of gravel ballast with crushed rock on the standard-gauge line between Kalgoorlie and Leonora has been completed; a total of 140 km on this route has been re-railed with 47 kg/m continuous welded rail. Upgrading of the 134 km between Mundijong and Picton has been put in hand. In 1982 Westrail was allocated A$1 million for main-line upgrading from Federal Government funds.

The narrow-gauge railway to the Alcoa alumina refinery at Wagerup has been substantially completed. The 9 km spur line to the Worsley alumina refinery site has been finished.

Track

Standard rail: Flat-bottom in 13·72 and 27·4 m lengths, weighing 46·6, 40·61 and 60 kg/m; and older material of varying weights
Joints: Fishplates; but in relaying the lengths are flashbutt-welded to 274 and 109·5 m, then thermit-welded into 439 m lengths or into continuous rail
Rail fastenings
Concrete sleepers: Fist BTR fastenings or Pandrol fastenings
Timber sleepers: Dogspikes or Pandrol fastenings
Cross ties (sleepers)
Concrete: Standard gauge: 2·6 m × 300 × 205 mm
Dual gauge: 2·6 m × 300 × 210 mm; 2·6 m × 300 × 190 mm
Timber (local hardwood jarrah, Wandoo etc)
  Standard and dual gauge: 2·5 m × 225 × 150 mm; 2·5 m × 225 × 130 mm
  Narrow gauge: 2·1 m × 225 × 130 mm; 2·1 m × 225 × 115 mm
Spacing: Standard gauge: concrete 1493/km, timber 1640/km
Narrow gauge: 1310/km
Ballast: 38 mm crushed rock ballast on main lines. Iron stone gravel on minor branch lines
Curves, minimum radius
Main lines: 242 m = 7·25° curve
Branch lines: 141 m = 12·5° curve
Max gradient: 1 in 40 = 2·5%
Max altitude: 500 m Wallaroo
Axleloading: 1067 mm gauge main lines 19 tonnes, branch lines 11 tonnes
1435 mm gauge main lines 24 tonnes, branch lines 16 tonnes

Electrification

A recent Westrail study on electrification demonstrated the economic viability of electrifying the line between Kwinana and Bunbury and its associated branch lines immediately, followed by the Kwinana-Kalgoorlie line later in the 1980s.

Signalling and communications

The first stage of centralised traffic control between Picton and Coolup was commissioned in October 1981. In the control centre Westrail is using micro-computers for the first time. The system checks that an operator's commands are valid and that there are no constraints on transmitting the information to the field equipment through telemetry links.

Passenger traffic

	1978	1979	1980	1981
Passenger-km,				
rail (million)	97·3	98·3	94	93·8
road (million)	36·8	44·4	48·8	54·2
Passengers carried,				
rail	230 737	233 688	233 193	229 410
road	159 418	168 584	184 526	198 427

Finances

	1978	1979	1980	1981
Income (A$ million)	150·6	156	175·7	182·4
Expenses (A$ million)	166·6	180	203·8	219·6

1435 mm-gauge 'Prospector' railcar train between Perth and Kalgoorlie

Class RA diesel and woodchip train

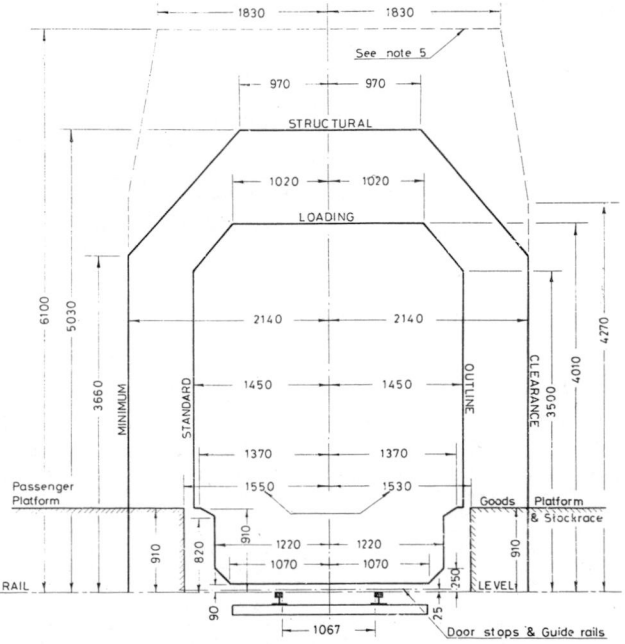

Westrail's 1067 mm loading and structural gauge

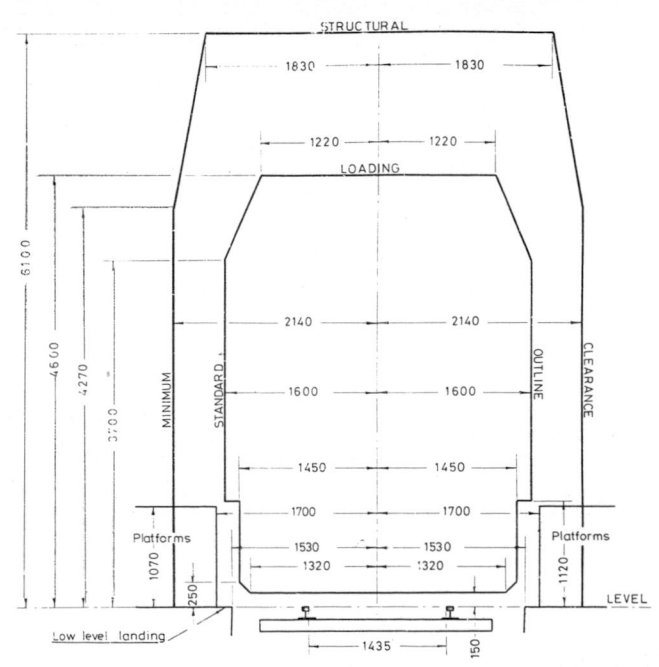

Westrail's 1435 mm loading and structural gauge

Main-line diesel locomotives

Gauge mm	Class	Wheel arrangement	Trans-mission	Rated power kW	Max kN	Tractive effort Continuous at		Max speed km/h	Wheel dia mm	Total weight tonnes	Length mm	No built	First built	Builders Mechanical parts	Engine	Transmission
						kN	km/h									
1067	A	Co-Co	Elec	1063/977	240	226	12	100	1016	89·16	15 036	12	1960	Clyde Eng Co	EMD 12-567C	EMD D25-D29
,,	AA	,,	,,	1230/1120	240	226	14	100	1016	90·51	15 036	5	1967	Clyde Eng Co	EMD 12-645E	EMD D25-D29
,,	AB	,,	,,	1230/1120	240	226	14	100	1016	96	15 494	6	1969	Clyde Eng Co	EMD 12-645E	EMD D32-D29
,,	C	,,	,,	1145/1035	240	200	14·5	96	1016	90·42	15 088	3	1962	English Electric	English Electric 12 SVT	EE 822 6C-548
,,	D	,,	,,	1640/1490	310	245·3	18	90	1016	107·85	17 044	5	1971	Clyde Eng Co	EMD 16-645E	EMD D32-D29
,,	DA	,,	,,	1640/1490	310	245·3	18	90	1016	96·72	17 044	7	1972	Clyde Eng Co	EMD 16-645E	EMD D32-D29
,,	DB	,,	,,	1660	—	244·5	17·7	90	1016	108	18 000	13	1982	Clyde Eng Co	EMD 16-645E	EMD D32-D29
,,	F	A1A-A1A	,,	560/510	163·7	99·6	15·3	80	952	64·92	12 800	7	1958	English Electric	English Electric 6 SRKT	EE 827/4C-525
,,	G	Co-Co	,,	768/708	240	191·2	9·5	90	952	76·2	12 496	2	1963	,,	English Electric 8 SVT	EE 819/7E-548
,,	N	Co-Co	,,	1940/1790	371	241	21	105	952	103·46	17 000	11	1977	Comm Eng Co	Alco type	5GTA11B4-761 AS
,,	R	,,	,,	1454/1338	275	226·9	17·5	96	952	94·05	15 240	5	1968	,,	English Electric 12 CSVT	EE 822/16J-548
,,	RA	,,	,,	1454/1342	298	226·9	17·5	96	952	96	16 306	10	1969	,,	,,	EE 822/16J-548
,,	X, XA, XB	2-DO-2	,,	824/779	124·5	53·3	39	88	800	79	14 630	48	1954	Metro-Vickers	Crossley HST V8	MV TG 4203-136

Shunting diesel locomotives

Gauge mm	Class	Wheel arrangement	Trans-mission	Rated power kW	Max kN	Tractive effort Continuous at		Max speed km/h	Wheel dia mm	Total weight tonnes	Length mm	No built	First built	Builders Mechanical parts	Engine	Transmission
						kN	km/h									
1067	B	0-6-0	Hyd	396/353	102·3	80	10	42	1016	38·96	7785	10	1962	Comm Eng Co	Cummins VT-12-B	Twin Disc-Wiseman
,,	E	0-6-0	,,	186	80	—	—	40	915	26·42	5588	1	1957	Comm Eng Co	Rolls Royce C6SFL	Twin Disc-DF 11 500
,,	M	B-B	,,	522/484	—	109	9·6	53	1016	49·66	10 961	2	1972	Walkers Ltd	Cummins VTA 1710-L	Voith L4r4U2-G
,,	MA	B-B	,,	522/484	—	109	9·6	53	1016	44·8	10 955	3	1973	Walkers Ltd	Caterpillar D379B	Voith L4r4U2-G
,,	T	0-6-0	Elec	492/447	111·2	69	18·6	65	1016	37·35	7569	5	1967	Tulloch	Cummins VT-12-825	Brush TG 78-43 TM 68-46
,,	TA	0-6-0	,,	492/447	111·2	69	18·6	65	1016	38·10	7569	10	1970	Tulloch	Cummins VTA-1710-L	Brush TG-43 TM 68-46
,,	Y	Bo-Bo	,,	306/280	102·3	40	18·5	72	915	38·80	10 020	18	1953	British Thompson Houston	Paxman 12 RPHI	RTB 8944-B.T.H. 124 PV
,,	Z	0-6-0	Mech	106/96	37·8	—	—	28	800	15·14	5752	3	1953	Drewry Car Co	Gardner 8 LW	Wilson Epicyclic
1435	K	Co-Co	Elec	1454/1388	298	189	19	130	1016	114·3	16 764	9	1966	English Electric	English Electric 12 CSVT	EE 822/16J-538
*1435	KA	Co-Co	Elec	1454/1342	293	226·9	17·5	96	952	99	16 306	3	1969	English Electric	English Electric 12 CSVT	EE 822/16J 548
,,	L	,,	,,	2386/2162	337·2	311·4	21	135	1016	134·00	19 355	25	1967	Clyde Eng Co	EMD 16-645E3	EMD AR1O-D77
,,	H	Bo-Bo	,,	708/641	240	167·7	10	100	1016	72·38	12 952	5	1965	English Electric	English Electric 6 CSRKT	EE 819/8F-538
1435	J	Bo-Bo	Elec	485/447	159·2	117·8	11·2	100	1016	66·64	13 004	5	1966	Clyde Eng Co	EMD 6-567C	EMD D25-D29

*Locomotive converted from 1067 mm gauge class RA unit in 1974.

Diesel railcars

Gauge mm	Class	Wheel arrangement	Trans-mission	Rated power kW	Max kN	Tractive effort Continuous at		Max speed km/h	Wheel dia mm	Total weight tonnes	Length mm	No built	First built	Builders Mechanical parts	Engine	Transmission
						kN	km/h									
1067	ADG	1A-A1	Hyd	112				80	800	30·99	19 050	18	1954	Cravens	AEC A 219	Voith DIWA 501
1067	ADX	1A-A1	Mech	112				80	800	33·53	19 050	10	1960	Westrail	AEC A 220	BUT B 14
1067	ADH	1A-A1	Hyd	112				80	800	30·99	19 050	4	1963	Cravens	AEC A 219	Voith DIWA 501
1067	ADK	1A-A1	,,	195				85	800	33·28	20 254	10	1968	Comm Eng Co	Cummins NHHTO-6-B1	Voith DIWA 501
1435	WCA	1A-A1	,,	283				144	940	68·22	27 076	5	1972	Comm Eng Co	MAN D 3650 HM6U	Voith T113R

Western Australian ore railways

Goldsworthy Railway

PO Box 84, Port Hedland, Western Australia 6721

Telephone: (091) 721122

Gauge: 1435 mm
Route length: 179 km

Superintendent: J Fitzgerald
Assistant Superintendent: A Cane

Traffic
In 1981/82 tonnage declined from 6·48 to 5·91 million as a result of reduced world demand for ore, but the average haul rose because of a higher degree of working from a mine close to the railhead as opposed to one nearer the shipment port.

Rolling stock: 8 diesel locomotives, 262 wagons.

Track
Rail: 50·4 kg/m (PS)
Cross ties (sleepers): Jarrah (timber)
Thickness: 127 mm
Spacing: 1687/km
Fastenings: Cut-spikes
Minimum curvature radius: 3°
Max gradient: 1·04%
Max axleload: 24 tonnes

Diesel locomotives

Class	Wheel arrangement	Transmission	Rated power (kW)	Max speed km/h	Total weight tonnes	No in service	Year first built	Builders Mechanical parts	Engine & type	Transmission
H	Bo-Bo	Elec	708	128	70	2	1965	English Elec	English Elec	English Elec
K	Co-Co	Elec	1452	128	108	6	1966	English Elec	English Elec	English Elec

Hamersley Iron Ore Railways

PO Box 283, Dampier, Western Australia 6713

Telephone: 850233
Telex: 99043

Manager: I J Williams

Gauge: 1435 mm
Route length: 400 km

Traffic
Ore tonnage in 1981 totalled 29·2 million.

Rolling stock: 47 diesel locomotives, 2442 ore wagons, 3 passenger cars. In 1982 the railway took delivery from Clyde Engineering of the first of five GM-EMD Type SD50 diesel-electric Co-Cos, the first of this model to serve in Australia, as replacements for Alco Type C628s. Six Alco C636 units have been rebuilt.

Mount Newman Railroad

Nelson Point, Port Hedland, Western Australia 6721

Telephone: (091) 73 8888
Telex: 99271

Railroad Manager: W D Wallwork

Gauge: 1435 mm
Route length: 426 km

Transport development
The railway is owned by Mt Newman Mining Co Pty Ltd, which manages the Mt Newman Iron Ore Project on behalf of members of the Mt Newman Joint Venture and which is a wholly-owned subsidiary of The Broken Hill Proprietary Co Ltd. Mining operations were inaugurated in January 1969, since when over 325 million tonnes of ore have been shipped to Australian and foreign steelworks. The railway, which runs from Mt Newman to Port Hedland, on the north coast, allows 32·5-tonnes maximum axleloadings, one of the highest figures in the world.

The single-track route has 14 passing loops approximately 3 km long and two loops each of 2 km. In 1982 it was carrying 69 trains a week, each of 144 cars grossing some 18 000 tonnes fully loaded and hauled by a trio of 2680 kW diesel locomotives. Maximum speed of a fully loaded train is generally 65 km/h, but coasting at up to 75 km/h is permitted over some sections. The sophisticated facilities at the Mt Newman railhead allow a train to be fully loaded in only 70 minutes, so that a train-set can be turned, loaded and re-manned within 114 minutes. Each return journey over the 426 km route from Port Hedland to Mt Newman and back is scheduled in 19½ hours; ore dumping at the port takes 2 hours and 3 hours are allowed at Port Hedland for locomotive servicing.

Traffic
The recession has reduced tonnages and the company is planning accordingly.

	1981	1982
Total freight tonnage (million)	31·79	26·7*
Total freight tonne-km (million)	13 542	11 374*
Average net trainload (tonnes)	13 600	13 600
Average wagon load (tonnes)	99	99

*Forecast

To reduce costs the company is studying the feasibility of operating longer trains. The possibilities are either formations of up to 180 cars' length with use of banking locomotives or trains of as many as 240 cars interspersed with slave locomotives fitted for remote Locotrol control from the head-end units.

Traction and rolling stock
The company operates 53 diesel locomotives, 2077 ore cars, 19 tank cars, 30 ballast cars, 10 flatcars and one passenger car. A prototype 'loco logger' has been developed to monitor performance of engines (in 16 parameters) and other components while a locomotive is in use on the track, as a diagnostic aid to maintenance. Experiments are being conducted with South Africa's Scheffel cross-braced bogie, but the company is also examining the possibility of eliminating wagon bogies in favour of four independently suspended axles to reduce tare weight.

Signalling
The railway is operated by CTC, supplemented by track-to-train radio, from a control centre at Port Hedland. Interlockings can function automatically in the event of any failure in the CTC telemetry.

Track
In 1982 installation of 49 000 steel sleepers was completed out of a prospective total of 190 000. Following initial experiments with Japanese-manufactured head-hardened rail, all future rerailing will be executed with it; its high cost is forecast to be more than offset by longer life in curves and by reduced calls for wheel replacement. Research continues into wheel/rail interface problems in conjunction with the Melbourne Research Laboratories of The Broken Hill Pty Co.

Rail: 66 and 68 kg/m cwr (standard carbon on tangent and head-hardened on curves and some tangents)
Cross ties (sleepers): Timber, 150 mm thick; steel, 120 mm thick
Spacing: Timber 1875/km; steel 1515/km
Fastenings: Dogspike, Pandrol Traklok (steel sleepers)
Minimum curvature radius: 527 m
Max gradient: 1·5%
Max axleload: 32·5 tonnes (nominal)

Diesel locomotives

Class	Wheel arrangement	Transmission	Rated power (kW)	Max speed km/h	Total weight tonnes	No in service	Year first built	Builders Mechanical parts	Engine & type	Transmission
Alco C636	Co-Co	Elec	2680	112	190	16	1966	Goodwin	Alco 2515	GE
Alco M636	Co-Co	Elec	2680	112	190	37	1971	Goodwin/Comeng	Alco 2515	GE

Robe River Railroad

PO Box 21, Wickham, Western Australia 6720

Telephone: 87 1001
Telex: 99058

Railroad Superintendent: B J Kenny

Gauge: 1435 mm
Route length: 187 km

Rolling stock: 16 diesel locomotives, 761 wagons. For the 1982 opening of its 17 km extension to a new Eastern Deepdale yard, the company acquired a further Alco C636 locomotive, together with 40 more 100-tonne ore wagons, the latter from Tomlinson Steel.

AUSTRIA

Ministry of Transport

Elisabethstrasse 9, 1010 Vienna

Minister: Dr Karl Lausecker
Heads of Division: Dr K Halbmayer
        Herbert Wild

Austrian Federal Railways (ÖBB)
Österreichische Bundesbahnen

Elisabethstrasse 9, 1010 Vienna

Telephone: 56500
Telegrams: Genbandion
Telex: 3103

President: Dkfm Dr Alfred Weiser
Vice-President: Karl Novak
Managing Director: Dr Wolfgang Pycha
Deputy Managing Director: Dr Otto Seidelmann
Executive Directors: Dr Friedrich Herzog
  Dipl Ing Dr Roman Jaworski
Chief of Finance and Accounts: Dr H Mittenecker
Staff Office, Data Processing and Cybernetics:
Seilerstätte 1, 1010 Vienna
   Manager: Dipl Ing Rudolf Waitzer
Staff Office, Finance and Accounts: Hegelgasse 7,
1010 Vienna
   Manager: Dr H Pregant
Administrative Director: Dr M Posch
Personnel Director: Dr Herbert Schartl
Financial Director: Dipl Ing Johann Mlinek
Operating Director: Dr Josef Pucher
Sales Directorate: Gauermanngasse 2-4, 1010
Vienna
   Sales Director: Dr Karl Zach
Engineering Directorate: Langauergasse 1, 1150
Vienna
   Chief Engineer: Dipl Ing Viktor Köttner
Construction Directorate: Elisabethstrasse 18, 1010
Vienna
   Director, Construction Engineering: Dipl Ing
   Franz Pröll
Purchasing Directorate: Operngasse 24, 1010
Vienna
   Purchasing Director: Dr L Raeth
Electrical Engineering Directorate: Daffingerstrasse
4, 1030 Vienna
   Chief Electrical Engineer: Dipl Ing Gunther
   Winkler

Gauge: 1435 mm; 1000 mm; 760 mm
Route length: 5331 km; 426 km
Electrification
   1435 mm: 2941 km at 15 kV 16⅔ Hz ac
   760 mm: 91 km at 6·5 kV 25 Hz ac

Transport development

By far the greatest part of the Austrian rail system is
operated by Austrian Federal Railways, including all
the main lines. At the head of ÖBB affairs is an

Class 1044 Bo-Bo locomotive at Jenbach with through train from Munich to Italy via the Brenner *(John C Baker)*

Class 4010 emu on Bregenz-Vienna inter-city service at Lambach *(John C Baker)*

Class 4020 emu on Kufstein-Innsbruck local service at Jenbach *(John C Baker)*

18-member Administrative Council and a four-man directorate for day-to-day management. The council, which has a three-year term, comprises 12 members appointed by the Government. The directorate has a five-year mandate from the Government.

Investment in the ÖBB's commercial activity has long been separated from that assigned to socially necessary ÖBB local operations in the Government's annual budgeting. In late 1982, in a move to put ÖBB's accounting as a whole into better balance, the Government proposed legislation to create full State financial responsibility for all non-commercial ÖBB services. It was also suggested that major rail investment projects, such as the projected new high-speed exit from Vienna to the west, should be treated as separate enterprises for funding purposes.

Results	1981	1982*
	(million)	
Total passenger journeys	170·11	170·2
Total passenger-km	7042·8	7320
Total freight tonnes (excluding parcels)	50·27	50·04
Total freight tonne-km (excluding parcels)	10 318·43	10 102·62
* Provisional figures		

Revenue (S million)	1980	1981
Total passenger revenue	3383·89	4071·96
State compensation revenue, passenger	2393·1	2709·4
Freight revenue	8796·01	9186·33
State compensation revenue, freight	711·7	857·75
Other income	4184·4	4808·5
Expenditure (S million)	23 443·05	25 541·9

Provisional figures for 1982 show income totalling S 22 640 million against expenditure of S 28 140 million, by comparison with 1981 a rise of 0·2 per cent in the former against one of 4·9 per cent in the latter.

Freight traffic

The maintenance of an almost unchanged total tonnage level in 1982 masked differences in the different categories of freight. Inland traffic was down by 0·6 per cent, but in the international sector, though imports and exports fell slightly, transit traffic rose 2·3 per cent. During 1982 improvements in freight working included an increase in the number of overnight trains interconnecting domestic centres to 35, and the offer of guaranteed transits over 86 itineraries; reduction of time allowances for wagon transfers between connecting trains in yards; reduction of frontier allowances; and curtailment of the limits on weekend working in marshalling yards. A new central department for promotion of intermodal traffic was established at headquarters and the number of intermodal terminals raised to 12.

The ÖBB is making a particular bid for piggyback traffic. In late 1982 orders were placed with Jenbacher-Werke for 350 low-loading wagons with 300 mm-diameter wheels to the Talbot (German Federal Republic) pattern, which the Austrian firm will build under Talbot licence. ÖBB is keen to establish a European pool of such vehicles. It aims to establish piggyback services from Vienna to Switzerland via the Arlberg Tunnel, where in 1982 work had begun to create clearances for piggybacking for road vehicles of up to 3·7 metres in height, as the Swiss Federal Railway has done in the Gotthard Route tunnels; the eventual aim is to make room for road vehicles of up to 3·92 metres height through the Arlberg Tunnel. The 3·7-metre clearance requires attention to only 80 metres of the bore, but 3·92 metres will demand enlargement over 2·55 km of the tunnel's length. ÖBB also envisages piggyback services to France and possibly to Spain.

In 1983 deliveries were being completed of 350 bogie container-carrying wagons fitted with shock absorbers. Designed for 120 km/h maximum speed, the wagons have an 18·4 × 2·75 metres loading platform, weigh 23 tonnes and have a payload capacity of 57 tonnes. A further 350 bogie container wagons, not shock absorber-fitted, were being delivered between 1982 and 1985.

Passenger traffic

In the summer of 1982 the regular-interval pattern of service considerably extended under the brand-name 'Austrotakt'. ÖBB introduced its first regular-interval scheme with Vienna-Salzburg operation every two hours in 1975, following with similar changes between Vienna and Graz in 1976 (intensified to hourly in 1978), Vienna and Villach in 1978, and Vienna and Bruck an der Mur (hourly) in 1981. In

Class 2043 diesel-hydraulic B-B at Matrei on Lienz-Innsbruck 'Korridorzug' *(John C Baker)*

Type BRmpz car with 29-seat restaurant and 12-seat second-class saloon

Class 1099 electric locomotive and 760 mm-gauge 'Mariazeller' refurbished vehicles, including buffet car, at Mariazell *(John C Baker)*

the 1982 timetable an hourly pattern was inaugurated between Vienna, Linz and Salzburg and, following the completion of the single-line Rosenheim curve that obviates reversal of through trains in the Salzburg-Kufstein corridor in West Germany, a two-hourly operation between Vienna and Innsbruck (with a general transit time acceleration of 21 minutes as a result of the Rosenheim curve benefit). Other changes included a measure of fixed-interval timetabling, with substantial acceleration, in services between Austrian and Swiss centres, such as Vienna-Basle and Klagenfurt-Basle/Zurich. The new timetable involved the addition of 25 extra long-distance services daily.

Significant increases in passenger-journeys on main routes were recorded during the summer of 1982 as a result of the expanded 'Austrotakt' timetable. The 19 trains daily between Vienna and Salzburg showed a rise of 9·4 per cent, the 20 between Salzburg and Vienna one of 13·8 per cent, while the seven between Innsbruck and Salzburg via the new Rosenheim curve added 22·7 per cent, those in the reverse direction 11·2 per cent. Also successful was an expansion of car-carrying facilities on principal passenger trains. In July and August the Vienna-Innsbruck 'Transalpin' was carrying an average of 25 vehicles, its counterpart in the reverse direction 15. To match this development ÖBB began in November 1982 to take delivery from Jenbacher-Werke of 25 more bogie double-deck car-carriers of Type DDm, capable of maximum express train speed, which would raise the total stock of such vehicles to 35.

To provide for this expansion ÖBB has been steadily modernising its locomotive-hauled passenger car fleet. By the end of 1983 it will have taken full delivery of a special building programme, valued at S3500 million, of 600 cars. The orders have included 450 cars of basically Eurofima pattern, or UIC Type Z, for international use, among them 15 Type Dmsz baggage cars and 15 Type Amz first-class compartment cars delivered in 1982 by Simmering-Graz-Pauker.

For ÖBB's next generation of inland service cars a final design was selected from three prototypes produced by Simmering-Graz-Pauker and 190 were due for delivery by the end of 1983. The new Type Bmpz 80-seater second-class saloon, fitted with remotely-controlled plug doors and designed for 160 km/h operation, has been built for compatibility with ÖBB's existing fleet of 800 so-called 'Schlieren' cars for internal services, but is longer in body, at 26·4 metres. Other variants of the basic design delivered in 1982 included 15 Type BDmpsz, 36 tonnes tare, with 40 second-class seats and a large baggage compartment of 4·3 tonnes payload capacity; 10 Type BRmpz, 40 tonnes tare, with a 29-seat restaurant, a telephone kiosk and a 12-seat second-class saloon capable of conversion into additional restaurant accommodation; and 40 Type Ampz, 36 tonnes tare, with a 54-seat first-class saloon.

Traffic 1982

	(million)	% change with 1981
Passenger journeys	170·2	+0·1
Passenger-km	7320	+3·9
Freight tonnes	50	−0·6
Freight tonne-km	10 103	−2·1

Vienna Schnellbahn
From May 1982 the Vienna S-Bahn network was further extended with inauguration of a 15-minute interval service between Meidling and Liesing, and between Florisdorf and Leopoldau. Civil and signal engineering works for this cost S1130 million.

In view of its expanding and intensified services the S-Bahn is being equipped with a computer-based traffic control system embodying automatic station announcements derived from the train-describer apparatus, due to be fully commissioned by the summer of 1983, and with a network-wide track-to-train radio communication system; the latter cannot be installed until 1984-86 because of financial constraints.

Narrow gauge modernisation
The ÖBB owns Austria's only electrified narrow-gauge passenger railway, the 760 mm-gauge Mariazellerbahn running 85 km from St Pölten to Mariazell. It was in fact the country's first electrified railway, since it was wired at 6·5 kV 25 Hz ac in 1911. In 1982 the ÖBB was undertaking track works to raise its permissible speeds and refurbishing the line's passenger stock with new seating, public address and, externally, the standard ÖBB crimson and ivory livery. An innovation was the conversion of a former dual-class car into a buffet-car with 12 seats at four tables, to run in the daily 'Mariazeller' express between St Pölten and Mariazell.

Reconstructed station buildings at Kufstein

ASEA-built Class 1043 Bo-Bo with Tauern route freight at Kolbnitz *(John C Baker)*

Class 2067 diesel-hydraulic shunter at Lambach *(John C Baker)*

Electrification

At the start of 1980 50.5 per cent of ÖBB's route-km was electrified at 15 kV 16⅔ Hz. A further 10-year programme of electrification was then announced, valued (in 1980 money terms) at S4300 million. The first four schemes, covering 145 km, were:

Tulln-St Pölten (completed 1981);
Absdorf-Hippersdorf-Krems (completed in September 1982);
Leopoldau-Wolkersdorf-Mistelbach (to be completed 1983);
Krems-Herzogenburg (to be completed 1985).

Further projects, with estimated completion dates, were to be:

Absdorf-Hippersdorf-Sigmundherberg (1984);
Heiligenstadt-Penzing (1986);
Attnang-Puchheim-Ried-Schärding (1987);
Steindorf bei Strasswalchen-Brauna (1989);
Sigmundsherberg-Gmünd (commencing 1986-88);
Graz Ostbahnhof-Fehring (commencing 1986-88);
Lendorf-Lienz (commencing 1986-88).

Traction and rolling stock

In the first half of 1983 ÖBB took delivery from Simmering-Graz-Pauker of its first new electric shunting locomotives since 1956. The five new units, Class 1063, are centre-cab Bo-Bos with three-phase commutatorless traction motors with a 80 km/h maximum speed and a 1500 kW rating, capable of 24 tonnes tractive effort. First assignments of the locomotives were to marshalling yard work at Hall in Tyrol, Graz and Vienna.

At the end of 1982 ÖBB withdrew the last 1435 mm-gauge steam locomotive on its active inventory, the 2-8-2 tank No 93.1326. There remain on ÖBB books 11 metre-gauge and 13 760 mm-gauge steam locomotives, while no fewer than 20 1435 mm-gauge Class 52 2-10-0s survive in private ownership, most of them in working order.

At the end of 1982 ÖBB was operating 695 electric and 500 diesel locomotives, 172 emu cars, 84 diesel railcars, 3661 passenger cars, 819 baggage and postal vans and 35 937 freight wagons. During 1982 orders were placed for 250 Type Gabs, 400 Type Fcs and 200 Type Sgjs freight wagons.

Infrastructure

Major item in the 1982 civil engineering programme was continued work on construction of new automated, concentration marshalling yards at Vienna and Villach.

Further double-tracking of the mountain trunk routes was completed; 40 per cent of the Tauern route between Schwarzach-St Veit and Spittal-am-Millstättersee is now double-tracked. The main line between Villach and Arnoldstein is being doubled in association with the new marshalling yard project at Villach.

Investment

The ÖBB's principal investment projects have been accorded high value in the Government's work creation programmes, the second of which assigned the railway S5500 million. As a result ÖBB would have investment funds totalling S34 000 million available over the years 1982-84, 50 per cent more than in the previous three years. Purchases in 1983 were to include a further 173 passenger cars.

The Government had set total investment in the ÖBB for 1983 at S10 200 million, an increase on 1982 of S1190 million.

In pursuit of its long-term aim to raise maximum passenger train speeds where alignments are favourable, the OBB has been preparing 15·3 km of its Nordbahn between Stillfried and Hohenau for test operation at 200 km/h. The main aim is to develop design standards for a proposed new 46 km high-speed exit from Vienna through the Wienerwald to St Pölten. This is now regarded as the first priority in new line construction. Prospects of a new Brenner base tunnel route have receded into the very distant future; European Economic Community aggrement to contribute to its cost is regarded as a prerequisite of further study. The ÖBB favours a 60 km tunnel from Innsbruck through to Bolzano, but the Italians fear a project of such grandeur would never be amortised financially and argue for a 24 km tunnel between Matrei and Vipiteno only. For the forseeable future, however, the Italians are likely to regard improvement of rail connections with their own ports as the first call on their available funds, so far as improvement of export/import freight facilities is concerned.

Class 1063 Bo-Bo with three-phase motors for heavy yard shunting

New marshalling yard at Wolfurt

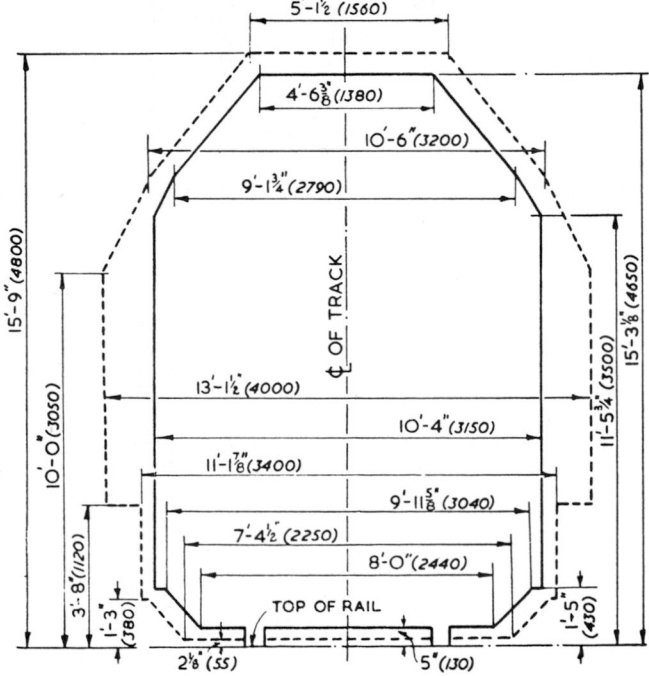
ÖBB structure and clearance gauge

Track
Experiments are being conducted on the Südbahn at St Egyden with the Soviet form of concrete track foundation framework.

Standard rail
Standard gauge: 53·81, 49·43, 44·35 kg/m
Narrow gauge: 26·15 kg/m

Length
Standard gauge: 30 and 60 m
Narrow gauge: 20 m

Cross ties (sleepers)
Standard gauge: impregnated wood 2600 × 260 × 160 mm
also steel and concrete
Narrow gauge: impregnated wood 1600 × 200 × 130 mm

Cross ties spacing
Standard gauge: 600-700 mm (1540 per km)
Narrow gauge: 810 mm (1235 per km)

Rail fastening
Standard gauge: resilient fastening, ribbed slabs, clips and bolts, keyed plates and bolts, Pandrol (spring U-bolt) and Macbeth (spring grip spike)
Narrow gauge: base plates and spikes

Filling
Standard gauge: broken stone ballast
Narrow gauge: broken stone ballast

Thickness under sleepers
Standard gauge: 200-300 mm
Narrow gauge: 150 mm

Minimum or sharpest curvature
Standard gauge: 9.7 = minimum radius of 180 m
Narrow gauge: 29.1 = minimum radius of 60 m

Max gradient compensated
Standard gauge: 1 in 22 (4.6%)
Narrow gauge: 1 in 40 (2.5%)

Max gradient uncompensated
Standard gauge: 7.4%

New central signalbox at Vienna Matzleinsdorf

Max combination of gradient and curvature
Standard gauge: 1:46 with 125 m curve radius
Narrow gauge: 1:40 with 100 m radius
Gauge width with max curvature
Standard gauge: 20 mm
Narrow gauge: 20 mm
Max super elevation
Standard gauge: 160 mm
Narrow gauge: 60 mm

Max axleload
Standard gauge: 20 tonnes
Narrow gauge: 12 tonnes

Max permitted speeds
Passenger trains, standard gauge: 140 km/h
 narrow gauge: 50 km/h
Freight trains, standard gauge: 120 km/h
 narrow gauge: 40 km/h

Electric locomotives

Class	Wheel arrange-ment	Line current	Rated output hp	Tractive effort (full field) Max lb (kg)	Continuous lb (kg)	at mph (km/h)	Max speed mph (km/h)	Wheel dia in (mm)	Weight tonnes	Length ft in (mm)	No built	Year built	Builders Mechanical parts	Electrical equipment
1010	Co-Co	15 kV. 1/16⅔	5400	57 300 (26 000)	26 500 (12 000)	62 (99)	81 (130)	51⅛ (1300)	110	58' 7" (17 860)	20	1955	SGP	ABES
1110	Co-Co	15 kV. 1/16⅔	5400	61 700 (28 000)	30 900 (14 000)	53 (85)	68 (110)	51⅛ (1300)	110	58' 7" (17 860)	30	1956	SGP	ABES
1020	Co-Co	15 kV. 1/16⅔	4350	65 300 (29 600)	33 000 (15 000)	44 (71)	56 (90)	49¼ (1250)	120	61' 0" (18 600)	47	1941	Krauss/Lofag	AEG/ÖSSW
1040	Bo-Bo	15 kV. 1/16⅔	3200	44 000 (20 000)	22 500 (10 200)	44 (71)	50 (80)	53⅛ (1350)	80	42' 5" (12 920)	16	1950	Lofag	ABES
1041	Bo-Bo	15 kV. 1/16⅔	3200	57 300 (20 600)	22 500 (10 200)	44 (71)	50 (80)	53⅛ (1350)	83	50' 3" (15 320)	25	1952	SGP	ABES
1042	Bo-Bo	15 kV. 1/16⅔	4770	46 296 (21 000)	26 455 (12 000)	57 (91)	80 (130)	49¼ (1250)	84	53' 2" (16 220)	58	1963	SGP	BES
1042-500	Bo-Bo	15 kV. 1/16⅔	5360	46 296 (21 000)	24 900 (11 300)	63 (102)	93 (150)	49¼ (1250)	84	53' 2" (16 220)	176	1967	SGP	BES
1043	Bo-Bo	15 kV. 1/16⅔	4830	66 100 (30 000)	37 000 (16 800)	48 (78)	84 (135)	49⅛ (1260)	77.4 ‡	51' 1½" (15 580)	10	1971/72	ASEA	ASEA
1044	Bo-Bo	15 kV. 1/16⅔	5400	70 600 (32 024)	47 400 (21 500)	55 (88)	99 (160)	51⅛ (1300)	83	52' 6" (16 000)	2	1974	SGP	BES
1141	Bo-Bo	15 kV. 1/16⅔	3400	48 500 (22 000)	20 000 (9040)	53 (85)	68 (110)	51⅛ (1300)	80	46' 9½" (14 260)	30	1955	SGP	ABES
1046	Bo-Bo	15 kV. 1/16⅔	2200	26 500 (12 000)	11 350 (5150)	58·7 (94·5)	78 (125)	41 (1040)	67	53' 7" (16 330)	25	1956	Lofag	ABES
1062	D	15 kV. 1/16⅔	870	41 900 (19 000)	11 900 (5400)	30 (49)	31 (50)	44⅞ (1140)	68	35' 6" (10 820)	12	1955	Lofag	ABES
1018	1-D-1	15 kV. 1/16⅔	4400	42 900 (19 450)	24 900 (11 300)	65 (105)	80 (130)	63 (1600)	110	55' 6" (16 920)	8	1939	Lofag	AEG; Siemens
1161	D	15 kV. 1/16⅔	980	30 900 (14 000)	12 300 (5570)	22 (36)	25 (40)	44⅞ (1140)	56	34' 5½" (10 500)	21	1928	Lofag	AEG
1245	Bo-Bo	15 kV. 1/16⅔	2400	45 750 (20 750)	22 900 (10 400)	36 (58)	50 (80)	53 (1350)	82	42' 8" (12 920)	38	1934	Lofag	ABES
1670	1A-B-A1	15 kV. 1/16⅔	3100	40 800 (18 500)	22 500 (10 200)	47 (75)	62 (100)	53 (1350)	107	47' 5½" (14 460)	26	1928	Lofag/Krauss	Siemens

‡Nos 1043-01, 02, 03 (1971) = 77 tonnes
 No 1043-04 (1972) = 82 tonnes

Diesel locomotives

Class	Wheel arrangement	Transmission	Rated power hp	Tractive effort Max lb (kg)	Continuous at lb (kg)	mph (km/h)	Max speed mph (km/h)	Wheel dia in (mm)	Total weight tons	Length ft in (mm)	No built	Year first built	Builders Mechanical parts	Engine & type	Transmission
2020	B-B	Hyd	2200	52 150 (23 640)	37 300 (16 950)	12·5 (20)	68 (110)	39⅜ (1000)	75.4	59' 10" (18 240)	1	1960	SGP	2×SGP T 12b	Voith
2043	B-B	Hyd	1500	45 182 (20 500)	30 636 (13 900)	30·5 (19)	62 (100)	37⅜ (950)	67·2 / 67·7	48' 5" (14 760) / 51' 8½" (15 760)	76	1964	Jenbach	JW 1500	Voith
2045	Bo-Bo	Elec	1000	34 200 (15 500)	13 450 (6100)	20·6 (33·2)	56 (90)	39⅜ (1000)	71	48' 6¾" (14 800)	18	1952	SGP	2×SGP S 12a	ELIN/ÖBBW
2050	Bo-Bo	Elec	1520	40 100 (18 200)	32 700 (14 850)	13·1 (21·1)	62 (100)	41 (1040)	75·5	58' 2½" (17 740)	18	1958	Henschel	GM 12-567C	GM
2060	B	Hyd	196	22 500/11 300 (10 200/5130)	15 200/7700 (6900/3500)	2·2/4·3 (3·5/6·9)	19/37 (30/60)	37 (940)	27·4	22' 0" (6700)	100	1954	Jenbach	Jenbach JW200	Voith
2062	B	Hyd	390	27 000/18 400 (12 270/8350)	17 600/12 000 (8000/5450)	4·7/7 (7·6/11·2)	25/37 (40/60)	37 (940)	32	26' 3" (8000)	45 / 20	1958 1965	Jenbach	JW 400	Voith
2067	C	Hyd	600	33 070 (15 000)	26 500 (12 000)	4·3 (7)	40 (65)	44⅞ (1140)	49·1	33' 11" (10 340)	63	1959/64	SGP	SGP S 12a	Voith
2095	B-B	Hyd	600	21 200 (9600)	16 700 (7600)	7·5 (12·0)	37 (60)	35½ (900)	32	34' 1½" (40 400)	10 / 5	1961 1962	SGP	SGP S 12a	Voith
2143	B-B	Hyd	1500	42 757 (19 400)	29 754 (13 500)	11 (18)	62 (100)	37⅜ (950)	65.4	51' 6" (15 760)	33	1965	SGP	T12c	Voith

Graz-Köflach Railway
Graz-Köflacher Eisenbahn- und Bergbau-Gesellschaft (GKB)

Grazbachgasse 39, 8010 Graz

Director: Ing Heribert Rabitsch

Gauge: 1435 mm
Total route-km: 92·5
Total track-km: 160·2

Route structure
The railway, which since the Second World War has been a subsidiary of the Alpin-Montan group though it is operated as an autonomous entity, heads south from its own station at Graz to Lieboch, where it branches north-west to Köflach and south to Wies. In addition the company operates 28 bus routes in West Steiermark.

Traffic
Regular passenger service is provided chiefly by diesel railcars, but the company also maintains steam locomotives of Classes 29, 152, 56 and 50 for special charter train operation.

Rolling stock
The company operates 3 diesel-electric locomotives, 6 diesel-hydraulic line-haul locomotives, 6 diesel-hydraulic shunters, 11 diesel railcars and 21 trailers, 41 passenger cars and 464 freight wagons. Its latest railcars are articulated Type VT70 twin-units with MTU engines and Brown Boveri electric transmissions, built by Simmering-Graz-Pauker to a Linke-Hofmann-Busch design under licence.

Traffic	1979/80	1980/81	1981/82
Passenger journeys	2 600 000	2 449 800	2 690 000
Passenger-km	68 117 000	68 089 800	73 331 000
Freight tonnage	1 520 000	1 317 587	1 270 000
Freight tonne-km	45 313 000	40 761 823	39 200 000
Total passenger income (S)	70 380 000	79 457 000	85 855 000
Total freight income (S)	98 717 000	101 631 000	96 602 000
Total expenditure (S)	268 174 000	293 092 000	303 714 000

Two GKB Class 750 diesel locomotives on Graz-Köflach freight at Premstätten Tobelbad *(John C Baker)*

GKB Type VT750 diesel railcars on Wies-Eibiswald to Graz service at Premstätten-Tobelbad *(John C Baker)*

Class	Wheel arrange- ment	Trans- mission	Rated power hp	Max tractive effort kg	Wheel dia mm	Total weight tonnes	Length mm	Years built	Builders		
									Mechanical parts	Engine & type	Transmission
Diesel line-haul locomotives											
1500						64-72	12 000	1975/78	Jenbach/Henschel	Jenbach LM1500	Voith L720rU2
750						48	9500	1964/69	JAM Zeltweg	MAN and MTU	BBC dc-dc
700						60	9860	1977	MaK	MaK	Voith L4r4U2
600						48	10 660	1973	Jenbach	Jenbach JW600	Voith L26StV
390	C	Hyd	400	12 000	1150	38	9440	1955	Henschel	Jenbach JW400	Voith L37U2
360	C	Hyd	360	12 000	1100	36	9460	1940?	MBA	Jenbach JW400	Voith L37U2
Diesel railcars											
VT10						24	13 288	1953-55	Uerdingen	Büssing U10	ZF ES 75
VT50						20.2	12 750	1951-52	Uerdingen	Büssing U10	ZF ES 75
VT70						54	30 186	1980-81	SGP/LHB	Büssing DTYUE	BBC ac-dc

BANGLADESH

Bangladesh Railway Board (BRB)

Railway Building, Chittagong

Telephone: 500120 139
Telegrams: Railboard
Telex: 66200

Chairman, Railway Board and Member, Administration, Planning and Engineering: Maqbul Ahmad
Member, Mechanical and Procurement: M M Haque
Member, Operation and Commercial: Mahmud Hasan
Member, Finance: A Z M Abdul Ali
Deputy Chief Electrical Engineer: S Islam
Chief Planning Officer: M Nazmul Haque
Chief Operating Superintendent: A K M Zainul Abedin
Chief Mechanical Engineer: A M Z Mahmud
Chief Mechanical Engineer, Design, Development and Construction: R Ahmed
Chief Signal and Telecommunication Engineer: S A B M Karimushan
Chief Engineer: M S Zaman
Deputy Chief Engineers:
   (East) A K M Saiful Alam
   (West) A B M Shamsuddin Ahmed
Divisional Manager, Dhaka: A K M Amanul Islam Chowdhury
Divisional Manager, Chittagong: M M Hossain
Divisional Manager, Paksey: M Wahed Ali
Divisional Manager, Lalmonirhat: M Rahman

Gauge: 1676 mm; 1000 mm
Total route length: 973 km; 1910 km

Transport development
With few roads, Bangladesh Railway is the principal transport organisation of the country. The railway has always played a vital role in the development of the country and in the expansion of trade, commerce and industry. Most export and import traffic is still rail-borne.

Freight traffic
In 1980/81 freight traffic receded. Compared with just under 3·1 million tonnes in 1979, carryings totalled only 2·9 million. Measured in tonne-km, the drop was from 838·4 million to 765 million.

Passenger traffic
A slight rise in passenger traffic was recorded, from 89 million journeys in 1979 to 89·3 million in 1980/81, but the year's total fell substantially short of the record figure of 92 million set in 1978. Passenger-km rose to 5359 million.

Motive power and rolling stock
At the start of 1982 BRB was operating 170 steam and 240 diesel locomotives. The most recent high-power designs are by Bombardier-MLW. A number of existing locomotives have been re-engined with assistance from Bombardier. BRB also operated four single-unit diesel railcars. Steam is to be phased out by 1985.

The stock of 1682 passenger cars has lately been supplemented by 11 metre-gauge coaches built in BRB's own workshops and 62 cars from Pakistan

Railways' Islamabad works. A further 11 cars have been ordered from Projects & Equipment Corporation of India.

At the start of 1982 freight wagon stock totalled 16 717 following importation of 937 new vehicles from British Rail Engineering, Standard Railway Wagon and W H Davies, UK. In addition 250 wagons were under construction in BRB workshops.

During the 1981/82 accounting period BRB was due to receive from Japanese builders 12 broad-gauge locomotives acquired with the aid of a Saudi Arabian loan; purchase of a further 12 broad-gauge units, from Bombardier, was being financed by Canadian International Development Agency (CIDA). Forward plans covered acquisition of 311 metre-gauge and 84 broad-gauge passenger cars, of which 72 broad-gauge and 28 metre-gauge cars would be bought with Japanese financial help and 24 metre-gauge cars, to be built by Scandia-Randers, with Danish aid. Over 1500 new metre-gauge and 1500 new broad-gauge wagons were to be obtained, but to curtail imports BRB has been required by the Government to create manufacturing capacity of 750 wagons a year at its Saidpur and Pahartali workshops; the former plant is also to establish an annual output of 120 passenger cars. Equipment of wagon stock with vacuum brakes is a high priority, with the immediate objective of continuously braking at least half the vehicles in all freight trains, which average 1000 tonnes of payload on the metre-gauge and 1200 tonnes on the broad gauge.

Canadian MLU-14 diesel electric locomotive

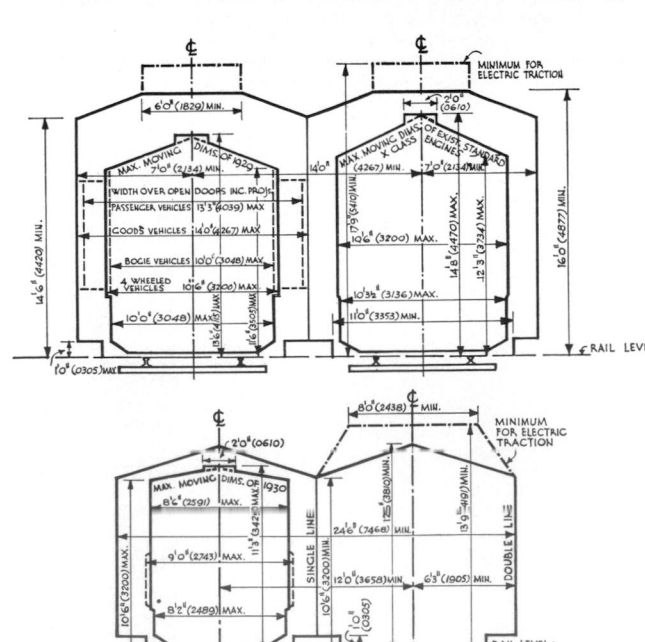

Loading and structure-design diagrams for Bangladesh Railways showing (top) for broad-gauge trucks and (bottom) for metre-gauge

Planned investment 1982/83 (Taka 000)

Diesel-hydraulic shunting locomotives (38)	352 000
Passenger cars (51)	153 000
Freight wagons (120)	60 000
Track works and machinery	190 000
Bridges and buildings	100 000
Signalling and communications	308 000
Yards and terminals	2000
Workshops	100 000
Miscellaneous	487 000
Total	1752 000

Infrastructure

BRB's second Five-Year Plan, launched in mid-1980, envisaged renewal or upgrading of 970 km of track by 1985. Upgrading comprises installation of welded 34 kg/m rail on the metre-gauge and 40 kg/m rail on the broad-gauge, together with other improvements to lift axleload limits to 12 tonnes on the metre- and 18 tonnes on the broad-gauge. The Asian Development Bank has helped to finance the work between Dhaka and Chittagong, where 170 km of the 428 km were treated in 1980 and completion was expected by the start of 1982, and CIDA the activity on three other routes. Track is being doubled between Dhaka and Chittagong, and between Faridpur and Barisal, and over the former route BRB has been studying electrification possibilities. The track improvements were forecast to cut the Dhaka-Chittagong passenger journey time from eight to five hours.

Under the second Five-Year Plan 14 major junctions were to be equipped with relay interlockings and a microwave network set up for inter-divisional communication. Three important junctions, Parbattipur, Santahar and Ishurdi, were being equipped with the L M Ericsson line-to-line route control system.

Track

Rail types and weights: 75 lb 'A', 90 lb 'A' FF BSS rails, 50 lb 'R', 60 lb 'R', 90 lb 'R' FF BSS rails, 50 NS, 50 ISR and 80 lb

Cross ties (sleepers)

Thickness: wooden sleeper BG 5 in; steel through sleeper BG ½ in; cast iron CST/9 block; wooden sleeper MG 4½ in; steel through sleeper MG 11/32 in; cast iron sleeper CST/9 (block)

Spacing: N+1, N+2, N+3, N+4, and N+5

Rail fastenings: Fishplates, fish boxes, dog spikes, bearing plates, anchor bearing plates, round spikes, steel keys and steel jaws and rail anchors of different sizes

Signal and train control installations: Relay and mechanical interlocking

Railway-owner shipping services, train and road vehicle ferries

Routes served

(i) Jagannathganj-Serajganj ghat (passenger ferry services)

(ii) Bahadurabad-Tistamukh ghat (passenger and wagon ferry services)

Vessels employed: 1 steamer, 6 tugs, 9 barges

BELGIUM

Ministry of Communications

62 rue de la Loi, 1040 Brussels

Telephone: 02 218 60 60

Minister: Herman de Croo
Chief of Cabinet: Firmin de Wolf
Secretary-General: M Poppe

Société Nationale des Chemins de Fer Belges (SNCB) Nationale Maatschappij der Belgische Spoorwegen (NMBS)

85 rue de France, 1070 Brussels

Telephone: 523 80 80; 523 62 40
Telegrams: Railbel

General Manager: E Flachet
Assistant General Managers: A Soete
    L De Smet

General Manager's Office
Chief Inspector, Assistant to Manager: J Roolant
Chief Legal Adviser: J Biere
Chief Engineers: P Dubus
    V Vanderstappen
    L Verberckt
Press and Public Relations Officer: W Van Gestel
Operating Department
Manager: M de Wulf
Chief Engineer, Assistant to Manager:
  P Fransen
  A Couvreur
Chief Engineers: R Decooman
    J Dekempeneer
    D Demonie
Equipment Department
Manager: J Neruez
Chief Engineer, Assistant to Manager: R Verboven
Chief Engineers: L Gueret
    H Laurent
    H Malengreau
    J Vandenberghen
    P Weytens
Chief Inspector: F Van Den Berghen
Permanent Way Department
Manager: L Dogniez
Chief Engineers: L Franssen
    B Dhaenens
    P de Cramer
    H Eeckels
    J Quinet
    R Vervaet
Chief Inspector: P Baecke
Financial Directorate
Manager: E Arijs
Chief Inspector, Assistant to Manager: A Duchène
Chief Inspector: M Hendrickx
Commercial Department
Manager: F De Haeck
Chief Inspectors: C Lokker
    R Boonen
    E Marnef

Personnel and Social Services Department
Assistant General Manager: L de Smet
Chief Medical Officers, Assistants to Manager: G David
    J Javaux
Chief Inspector, Assistant to Manager: A Mahu
Chief Medical Officers: G David
    J Javaux
    R Van Roy
Chief Inspectors: M Lefebure
    H van Noten
Electric Services and Signals
Manager: M Colle
Chief Engineer, Assistant to Manager: H De Sutter
Chief Engineers: P Bienfait
    A Duquesne
    A Houwen
    P Leroy
    F Lauwers
Purchases
Manager: J Carlier
Chief Engineer: O Willems
Chief Inspectors: E Ruelle
    F Moraux
Information
Manager: H Van Poucke
Chief Engineer: Y Van der Veken

Gauge: 1435 mm
Route length: 4235 km (3930 km operational)
Electrification: 1761 route-km at 3 kV dc

Constitution

All standard-gauge lines are operated by the SNCB, all metre-gauge light railways, in addition to its bus services, by the Société Nationale des Chemins de Fer Vicinaux (SNCV). A fusion of the two undertakings, with the corollary of rationalisation of competing passenger operations and better co-ordination of services, has been proposed and is supported by the trades unions, but is not favoured by the present Minister.

Finance

SNCB recorded its worst-ever financial performance in 1981 with a deficit of BFr 5870 million. With the country's general economic state simultaneously in serious disarray, the Transport Minister first ordered rescheduling of SNCB's investment programme over a longer time-scale, together with some passenger train service cuts, then required a number of rationalisation schemes and in September 1982 took emergency powers intended to reduce SNCB's support from the state by 1 per cent a year in real money terms up to 1987. This last action provoked strike action by railwaymen.

Many forms of state subvention have climbed sharply since the early 1970s. SNCB is relieved of staff pension and at-work insurance expenses; in 1971 the state covered those provisions with BFr 1771 million, but the 1981 figure was BFr 14 334 million. The state's contribution to infrastructure upkeep on the railway as a freight network climbed during the same period from BFr 1334 million to BFr 4621 million (but touched BFr 6229 million in 1980). State relief of the SNCB from some central financial charges regarded as unfairly affecting its competitive ability, standing at BFr 1771 million in 1971, was BFr 4622 million a decade later. With other grants for such items as enforced retention of unremunerative services and level-crossing maintenance included, SNCB was in 1981 drawing an aggregated BFr 48 302 million of state cash, compared with a combined passenger, freight and miscellaneous revenue of only BFr 25 792 million.

Class 27 electric locomotives at Brussels Midi *(Marcel Vleugels)*

Freight

Since 1965 SNCB's share of Belgium's total freight has slipped in tonnage from 16·7 to 13·1 per cent, in tonne-km from 31·4 to 26·2 per cent. The erosion has been chiefly in domestic traffics and imports. But SNCB has preserved almost intact its strength in solid fuel transport and inputs to heavy industry, where it claims respectively about a half and two-thirds of the global market; in the steel industry's output, about 45 per cent of which is railborne; and in international transit traffic of all kinds. In this last sector SNCB shifts almost as much tonnage as road and inland waterways combined. Most of the resilient traffics are those for which SNCB has secured a term-based contract, which provides statutory licence to escape the straitjacket of published, Government-regulated tariff scales. SNCB contract traffic climbs annually. In 1981 it accounted for 6600 million of the year's gross tonne-km.

Competition is fierce. Road transport's only restraint on rate-cutting is a set of guidelines prescribed by its own trade organisation; and although it is subject to licensing in three categories (local, up to 25 km radius, and international) there is no curb on quantity. Inland waterway transport is more circumscribed. A Government-run regulatory organisation prevents excessive transport capacity and also sets tariffs, but without any reference to those ordained for SNCB. Waterway operators' contribution to infrastructure costs, extracted as a per tonne-km navigation rights tax, is very low. Where the railway is obliged to compete on its basic, published tariff scales, therefore, its main hope is to appeal on superior service and all-weather reliability.

Approximately 90 per cent of roughly 10 million tonnes of ore imported annually through Antwerp continues inland by rail. Most of it is for the Belgian steel-producing complexes at Liège, Charleroi, Schaerbeek and La Louvière, but a fifth is destined for Luxembourg plants and French firms also take some. Unlike the coal wagon fleet, most of the ore-carrying wagons are privately-owned. In 1983 SNCB was testing five prototype Type Faals articulated six-axle ore wagons designed for 150 tonnes glw operation; the side-door hoppers were designed by SNCB in conjunction with the steel industry.

Coal traffic has had a lift from the Government's decision in the early 1980s to switch oil-fired electricity generating stations to coal (in the spring of 1979 the oil shortage's impact on Belgium was so severe that SNCB could not keep its diesel stocks at minimum subsistence level). At the start of 1982 13 power stations were taking a gross input of 2·2 million tonnes a year but the flow was expected to be 4 million tonnes by the year's end. The imported coal is mostly shipped through the big Stocatra mineral terminal at Antwerp, which has an annual throughput of over 10 million tonnes, but some is railed from Ghent. The Government authorised SNCB to acquire 500 Fads bogie hoppers for the power station feeds, but two of the plants are supplied by container, because they were some distance from the nearest railway and it was more economical to tranship from rail to road with a mobile container lift at the nearest existing railhead than to build a new branch and rail discharge terminal.

The mineral and coal traffic is predominantly siding-to-siding in unit trains generally limited to 1800 tonnes gross and 80 tonnes maximum wagon glw. SNCB aims to raise both figures, but a lift of total train weight hinges on a bigger fleet of 5000 kW locomotives, because of challenging gradients in the east of the network, and an axleload limit relaxation on track life and economic justification for more widespread renewals with heavier rail.

Proposals for a rationalisation of freight services were to be formulated in the spring of 1983. The aim was likely to be further concentration on trainload flows, with likely closure of some marshalling yards, and a further reduction in the number of centres rail-served by less-than-wagonload and parcels operations.

Further wagon orders were authorised by the Minister of Communications in the autumn of 1981. They comprised 750 tippler wagons and 200 Type Tads wagons with automatic discharge. The orders were placed with Gregg Europe 80 Constructions Ferroviaires, La Brugeoise-Nivelles and Usines de Braine-le-Comte, at a total cost of BFr 1436 million.

Intermodal

Like other mainland European railways, SNCB has found its intermodal traffic bucking the recessionary trend in almost all other freight sectors. Growth in container movement, however, had been slender compared with the sharp rise in piggyback, up to the start of 1982. SNCB has a firm grip on the ISO container movement into and out of Antwerp. Of the

Revenue (BFr million)

	1980	1981
Passengers and baggage	8776·5	9165·4
Freight		
Wagonloads	11 460·9	10 972·1
Less-than-wagonloads	3332·8	3278·3
Other income	2122·9	2015·2
Financial income	337·4	360·5
Total	26 030·5	25 791·8
State compensation in respect of social tariffs and track maintenance	20 572·9	21 908·4
Total	46 603·4	47 700·2

Expenses (BFr million)

Administration	1773·3	1906·4
Infrastructure upkeep	4746·3	5472·6
Signalling, telecommunications, electrification fixed assets	5301·1	5964·4
Traction	17 282·1	19 237·5
Terminals	15 766·5	16 994·8
Road transport, publicity, etc	693·2	763·5
Renewals	7860·0	7800·0
Insurance	290·0	230·0
Financial charges	4322·6	7260·2
Total	58 035·1	65 629·4
Less state compensation to equalise terms of competition and to cover financial charges	−10 568·1	−12 059·3
Total	47 466·9	53 570·1

Class 20 7180 hp Co-Co on train from Milan at Brussels Midi *(Yves Steenebruggen)*

Monomotor-bogie 3070 hp Class 26 electric locomotive *(Yves Steenebruggen)*

total of almost 174 000 containers passing through the port in 1981, 62 400 (compared with 70 760 in 1980) were channelled through the eight-track SNCB container terminal between the port's 6th Basin and Churchill Dock. The outstanding feature on the piggyback sector, as elsewhere in Europe, has been the rapidly increasing use of rail for transport of demountable, or 'swap' bodies. The Belgian piggyback marketing company is Transport Route Wagon (TRW). Services in French-type 'Kangarou' wagons are offered, principally to and from France, through terminals at Antwerp, Brussels, Charleroi and Liège, Ro/ro services with West German-pattern low-loaders to and from the Federal Republic of Germany, Italy and Austria through terminals at Antwerp, Brussels, Ostend and Zeebrugge. Apart from maritime terminals, SNCB serves inland container transhipment centres at Athus, Brussels, Charleroi, Liège Bressoux and Mechelen.

Intermodal subsidiary companies
Container traffic
SA Interferry
Zomerweg 26, Antwerp
Telephone: 031 41 69 50

Piggyback traffic
SA Transport Route Wagon
Rue A Vandenpeereboom, Gare de Bruxelles Ouest, 1080 Brussels
Telephone: 02 425 62 51; 428 47 77; 426 83 13

Passenger
Although the decline in passenger traffic volume was reversed in 1981, the revival was short-lived; 1982 ended with a serious fall, especially in international traffic, as a result of the recession. In response to the Government's call for savings timetables were from May 1982 shorn of some 2000 passenger workings a week, or about 8 per cent of the total. These initial casualties were almost all under-patronised early- and late-weekday or weekend trains (a few lines are now closed at weekends), but further cuts were likely.

Although the SNCB-SNCV merger is now effectively aborted, at the start of the 1982 summer timetables a pilot co-ordination scheme was introduced for evaluation on the line from Charleroi to Mariembourg, 49 km, serving an area with a catchment population of 85 000 (the city of Charleroi itself excluded). Before May diesel locomotive-hauled push-pull trains were, in this short distance, serving 16 intermediate stations. Consequently they averaged less than 48 km/h end-to-end in some cases, and that in competition with a parallel and thoroughly modernised Route Nationale 5. Yet between Charleroi and the city's suburban periphery at Walcourt, 22 km out, 19 trains plied each way every weekday, aggregating 2250 passenger journeys daily, and over the remainder of the route 13 each way, generating only 600 journeys a day between them. At the same time, SNCV was simultaneously running 38 weekday services between Charleroi and Philippeville, for an average daily load factor of 1660 passengers. In the revised service six stations have been shut and their business left to SNCV bus routes, which have in turn been redrafted to act more as rail feeders than rivals. More trains are limited-stop, achieving end-to-end transit savings of up to 15 minutes, and a more ample service has been secured without any additional resources.

In 1984 SNCB plans to introduce a completely redrafted timetable on the Netherlands Railways pattern, to take account of social and residential changes. The aim is an augmented inter-city service, in part exploiting the new Class 300 electric multiple-units, and bringing more centres within the orbit of direct service by this type of train; and complementary rationalised short-haul services. The whole will be schemed to an immaculate regular-interval pattern, and designed to eliminate changes of train for longer-haul travellers from many intermediate-size population centres, such as Leuven and St Niklaas, and to minimise interchanges or slack connections on other journeys. Although parts of the Brussels-Ostend route have been improved for 160 km/h, faster end-to-end inter-city timings are not a prime objective; SNCB cannot afford to discard 50 kg/m rails and existing sleepers for new track with 60 kg/m rail, which is regarded as essential for higher speed, until the existing permanent way is fully life-expired.

Renewal of SNCB's inter-city coach fleet with 580 Type M4 cars, due for completion in 1985, is well advanced. The full order comprises 50 first-class, 430 second-class, 65 first-class brake-composite vehicles and 35 second-class cars including snack bar and luggage compartment.

The Amsterdam-Brussels service is to be re-equipped by the summer of 1986. Netherlands Railways are to provide 59 new cars, of a type not yet

Class 51 diesel-electric Co-Co on freight near Hasselt *(Marcel Vleugels)*

Recent electrification: junction of Visé/Montzen and Liers/Liège lines at Glons

SNCB's Antwerp port container terminal

decided, and the SNCB 12 new dual-current locomotives designated Class 11 for a series of six-car push-pull trains, envisaged as operating at up to 160 km/h (100 mph); reversible operation will accelerate the trains' turnround in the dead-end terminus of Antwerp Central. The SNCB Class 23 dual-voltage locomotives at present covering this service will be re-assigned. Also planned for operation at up to 160 km/h by 1984 is the Paris-Mons-Brussels service; some level crossings on this route are being replaced by bridges in anticipation.

SNCB took delivery in 1982 of 20 new self-service cafeteria cars. They supplemented its existing catering-car fleet of four restaurant cars, two self-service cars and 12 buffet cars, employed chiefly on international workings. To supersede the 147 Type 13 side-corridor cars used in international service, SNCB planned to follow the M4 series with 40 new couchette cars and 150 RIC cars of basically Eurofima type. These would be for the Brussels to Lille, Amsterdam and Paris services.

Electrification

The state has put up a direct grant of BFr 43 000 million for electrification, or about 60 per cent of the total budgeted. The target is to raise the route-km under wires from 1746 in mid-1982 to 2450, or roughly 80 per cent of the network traversed by passenger trains. The electrification's primary objective is to relieve the congested core of the system through Brussels by creating new electrified west-to-east transversals through Flanders, from Antwerp via Aarschot, Hasselt and Montzen to Aachen in West Germany, and from Mouscron via Mons, Charleroi and Liège to Montzen and Aachen. In full the scheme will complete an electrified ring embracing the border crossings to Lille (in France), Ghent (on the main Ostend-Brussels line), Antwerp, Aachen, Liège, Charleroi and Mons.

By May 1982 the northern, Flemish transversal was under wires right through to Liège via Hasselt and Visé, a junction close to the Dutch and West German borders (an electrified connection has also been created between this route and that from Brussels to Liège, energised in the 1950s, by wiring between Aarschot and Leuven). Continuation of the electrification from Visé to Montzen, at present the main artery for the heavy freight traffic between Antwerp and the Ruhr, was tabled for 1984, but it is hoped to develop a faster route into West Germany from Visé via Maastricht, in the Netherlands, a line which is more amicably graded than that via Montzen; because of financial constraints on the Netherlands Railways this may be impossible before 1985/86. Also inaugurated in May 1982 was electrification from Denderleeuw to Zottegem.

Much other infrastructure work accompanies these main-line electrifications. Earlier phases of the Flemish transversal scheme, for instance, raised the maximum running speed between Antwerp and Lier from 90 to 120 km/h, and to 140 km/h between Lier and Aarschot. Vital to the speed increase is the elimination of level crossings, quite profuse in Belgium. Multi-aspect colour-light resignalling for reversible working on both tracks is another important concomitant, but for economy crossovers are now being spaced at 20 to 25 km instead of 15 km intervals.

In 1983 the Walloon transversal electrification was completed by wiring from La Louvière, east of Mons, via Piéton to Charleroi. Charleroi to Namur was electrified in the 1950s, Namur on to the Liège complex in the 1970s.

Despite an annual electrification progress rate of 150 to 180 km, the 1976-80 content of the 10-year plan has not been fully executed. Brussels-Tournai, for instance, will not now be completed until the second half of the 1980s. But with that exception, the central area of the SNCB will be almost entirely electrified by the mid-1980s.

Apart from the operating and energy-saving benefits of extended electrification, especially on the 2000-tonne freight trains plying between Antwerp and the Liège region, the objective of the additional transversal wiring is to segregate the principal passenger and freight flows. Between Antwerp and Liège inter-city passenger traffic on the older, direct electrified route via Leuven is now divorced from the freight, which travels via Aarschot and Hasselt. With the aid of the Aarschot-Leuven wires and some extension to come further south, freight from Antwerp to the Charleroi industrial basin will from 1984 be able to avoid Brussels without interruption of electric traction.

Further electrification in progress covers these lines, with expected completion dates: Visé-Montzen-Aix-la-Chapelle (1984); Schellebelle-Termonde-Malines (May 1983); Jurbise-Ath (1984); Tournai-Brussels, a scheme involving practically new line construction over 20 km between Enghien and Ath, to ease numerous curves, eliminate level

Results	1979	1980	1981	1982
Total train-km (million)	95·3	97	98·9	NA
Total freight tonnes (million)	74·3	71·5	70	62·7
Total freight tonne-km (million)	8600	8000	7600	6818
Average haul (tonnes)	115·5	112·6	108·1	NA
Average net train load (tonnes)	365·5	347·8	339·2	NA
Average wagon load (tonnes)	34·4	34·6	35·8	NA
Total passenger-km (million)	6954·8	6962·9	7078	6879
Total passenger journeys (million)	163	163·7	166·8	162·6

Class 300 two-car emu

Class 800 emu, seating 56 first- and 302 second-class passengers

crossings and allow a 160 km/h speed limit (1985); and La Louvière-Piéton-Charleroi (May 1983).

Following the deceleration of investment, the planned electrifications covering Namur-Dinant, Angleur-Marloie, Montzen-Welkenraedt and Herbesthal-Eupen are not now set a firm time-scale.

Locomotives

The new Class 27 electric locomotives, of which all 60 were to be delivered by the end of 1983, were being used initially on the heaviest express trains taking the Ostend-Brussels-Liège-Aix-la-Chapelle axis, hitherto worked by 1880 kW locomotives of Classes 22 and 23, which are limited to 130 km/h though most of this route is passed for 140 km/h. The Class 27 has a much higher power, 4150 kW, and is capable of 160 km/h, but is designed for mixed traffic work. Weighing 84 tonnes, with a starting tractive effort of 24 tonnes, the 18·65 metre-long Class 27 is equipped both to work in multiple and also to operate push-pull with rakes of the new M4 cars; each of its four axles is powered by a fully-suspended, chopper-controlled 1050 kW motor, and all wheels are fitted with flange-greasers to facilitate negotiation of 100 metre-radius curves. It can operate at half power under the Netherlands Railways 1·5 kV catenary. Blended air and rheostatic braking is fitted. Special attention has been paid to ergonomics in the design of the cab, which has also been shaped with particular care for aerodynamic effect. The cab is force-air ventilated, the windscreen is heated and fitments for the crew's comfort include a refrigerator and hot plate.

Further locomotives on order are 30 units of a new 3 kV Class 21, with slightly less power than the Class

Interior of Class 800 emu second-class saloon

27; 12 dual-voltage (1·5 and 3 kV) units of Class 11; and 12 units of a new dual-voltage (3 and 25 kV 50 Hz) Class 12, to be delivered in 1984-85, for through working to and from France.

In the first half of the 1970s SNCB had invested heavily in freight stock renewals, acquiring 14 000 new wagons, so that an annual wagon order rate of around 500 suffices for the current 1976-87 modernisation plan's duration. Most of the rolling stock renewal money has been allocated to 139 electric locomotives, starting with the 25 5820 kW Class 20 Co-Cos and continuing through the new Class 27 to the forthcoming Classes 21, 11 and 12; 236 emus, 140 of them the new inter-city Class 300 twin-set;

80 Eurofima cars for international service; 720 locomotive-hauled cars for internal service; and 130 bi-level commuter cars for commuter operation, though the Government has so far authorised an order for 65 only, to be constructed in Belgium.

Locomotives and rolling stock in service 1982

	Line-haul	Shunting
Locomotives		
electric	277	3
diesel-electric	457	447
diesel-hydraulic	7	—
Railcars		
electric	519	—
diesel	83	—
trailer cars, diesel	13	
Passenger coaches	2375	
Freight wagons	40 570	

At the end of 1982 electric traction covered 37 per cent and diesel 63 per cent of freight haulage. Passenger services were 20 per cent locomotive-hauled, 24 per cent diesel locomotive-hauled, 49 per cent provided by emus and 7 per cent by diesel railcars.

Civil engineering

In the overburdened Brussels area, a total investment of BFr 8100 million is underway. To relieve pressure on the underground, six-track Nord-Central-Midi crossing of the city's heart, a third track is being added to other routes in the metropolitan area, and reversible signalling extended. In 1982 the extra track was already commissioned between Brussels Nord and the airport and a new spur laid in. This allows some passenger traffic from the Liège and Leuven directions to be handled in the Quartier-Leopold station of the city, on the exit from Brussels Nord towards Namur, and to be stopped short of the critical downtown layout, besides creating room for the airport and other stopping services to be overtaken by faster workings. Installation of a third track over 17 km of the Namur route between Brussels-Schuman and Genval is programmed for completion by 1985.

In 1982 SNCB had 862 km of 120 km/h, 240 km of 130 km/h and 503 km of 140 km/h or better route. Nothing yet operates at 160 km/h in public service, but a significant distance has already been made fit for it in the course of electrification and the SNCB is building up traction and rolling stock arranged for that speed. SNCB is, however, waiting until whole routes have been upgraded to their ultimate potential and a full complement of suitable stock is in place before it redrafts timetables for the higher speed.

International routes are the priority for 160 km/h working. Parts of the Ostend-Brussels route are already in 160 km/h order. By 1985, after completion of realignments and level crossing suppressions already in progress between Brussels and Mons, and delivery of the new dual-voltage Class 12s, the Paris services should be next: then, with benefit of the other chopper-controlled dual-voltage 160 km/h type to come, Class 11, and new six-car push-pull sets formed from 11 driving and 48 non-driving trailers, the Brussels-Amsterdam route, and also Antwerp-Ghent.

Signalling and telecommunications

SNCB is to equip all traction units and put in the ground apparatus for track-to-train radio communication at a cost of BFr 300 million. In mid-1982 the equipment was on order from Pye and fitting was expected to start during 1983.

The major single item on the signalling investment list is a new route-relay centre for Brussels Midi, to oversee the entire layout on the city's southern side plus the key north-south links, a network covering about 120 route-km in total and carrying some 2000 scheduled train movements daily. Now that passenger and freight streams are or will be segregated, the latter re-routed out of the area (see above), SNCB is to equip this centre with computer programming of the operation (with a spin-off actuating station train information devices in the

control area). However SNCB does not feel the time is yet ripe to embark on computerised non-relay interlockings.

A new signalling centre has just been completed at Liège, supervising not only the 13-track Guillemins station and its daily throughput of 450 scheduled trains, but also the city's 20 km freight ring route, with just over 500 train movements a day. Others are budgeted for Antwerp, Charleroi, Ghent, Brussels Nord, Brussels Quartier Leopold and Halle.

Another innovation has been installation of a 4·2 km optical fibre link to convey telephone channels through the Brussels Junction tunnels between Nord and Midi stations; each of five 0·05 mm-diameter fibres can carry 1920 conversations.

Investment

Annual rail investment for 1983 was trimmed by 25 per cent compared with 1982. The contraction has added at least two years to the SNCB's 1981-85 Five-Year Plan electrification component, of which 249 km were achieved in 1981; a further 1082 km are covered by orders already placed. Concomitant emu orders have also been deferred.

SNCB's investment budget for 1983 was as follows:

	BFr (million)
Electric locomotives	3030
Loco-hauled passenger cars	911
Mu cars (Type AM)	3595
Freight wagons	1408
Intermodal developments	135
Major track works	3948
Track maintenance equipment	364
Bridges and buildings	2636
Electrification	3163
Signalling and telecommunications	2797
Computerised management systems	143
Yards and terminals	483
Shops and repair facilities	546
Miscellaneous	648
Total	23 817

Track

Standard rail: Flat bottom, 60 kg/m main lines, 50 kg/m secondary lines

Length: Main lines: 216 m rails welded into 1·5-2 km sections between expansion joints. Secondary lines: 27·028 m

Joints: 4-hole and 6-hole fishplates

Rail fastenings: Soleplates and screws for wood sleepers. Type RN flexible fastenings on RS concrete sleepers; rigid clips on FB concrete sleepers. Pads are inserted under the rail when concrete sleepers are used. Pandrol fastenings are used in tunnels

Cross ties (sleepers): Generally oak, 2600 × 280 × 140 mm. Sections of welded-rail track have been laid with two types of concrete sleeper: Type RS (two blocks joined by a steel bar) with Type RN flexible rail fastenings, and Type FF (two blocks and a tie) with rigid fastenings

Spacing: 1665 to 1370 per km

Filling: Broken stone or slag

Max curvature
Main line: 2·18° = radius of 800 m
Secondary line: 3·5° = radius of 500 m
Running lines: 8·75° = radius of 200 m
Sidings: 11·7° = radius of 150 m

Max gradient: 1·8% = 1 in 55½; except 2 sections of 3·5% = 1 in 28½

Max altitude: 536 m at Hockai on Pepinster-Trois Ponts line

Max permitted speed: 140 km/h on major main lines. 120 km/h on all other main lines

Max axleload: Certain locomotives have axleload of 24 tonnes. Except for certain bridges they can operate anywhere on the system, subject to speed restriction.

SNCB loading and structure gauge

Diesel locomotives

Class	Wheel arrange-ment	Trans-mission	Rated power hp	Tractive effort Max lb (kg)	Tractive effort Continuous lb (kg)	Max speed mph (km/h)	Wheel dia in (mm)	Total weight tons	Length ft in (mm)	No built	Year first built	Builders Mechanical parts	Builders Engine & type	Builders Transmission
51	Co-Co	Elec	2150	61 200 (27 750)	37 250 (16 900)	75 (120)	39¾ (1010)	117	66' 1¾" (20 160)	93	1961	Cockerill-Ougrée	Cockerill-Ougrée	ACEC-SEM
59	Bo-Bo	Elec	1750	44 000 (20 000)	37 500 (17 000)	75 (120)	44 (1118)	87	53' 1" (16 180)	55	1955	Cockerill; Baume et Marp	Cockerill (licence Baldwin)	ACEC (licence Westinghouse)
52-53	Co-Co	Elec	1720	55 000 (25 000)	35 500 (16 100)	75 (120)	39¾ (1010)	108	61' 10" (18 850)	13 19	1955	Anglo-Franco-Belge	GM (USA)	GM (USA) Smit

Diesel locomotives

Class	Wheel arrangement	Trans-mission	Rated power hp	Tractive effort Max lb (kg)	Tractive effort Continuous lb (kg)	Max speed mph (km/h)	Wheel dia in (mm)	Total weight tons	Length ft in (mm)	No built	Year first built	Builders Mechanical parts	Builders Engine & type	Builders Transmission
54	Co-Co	Elec	1900	55 000 (25 000)	27 500 (12 500)	87 (140)	,,	108	,,	8	1957	Anglo-Franco-Belge	GM (USA)	GM (USA) Smit
55	Co-Co	Elec	1950	61 200 (27 750)	38 000 (17 250)	75 (120)	,,	110	64' 2⅜'' (19 550)	42	1961	Brugeoise et Nivelles	GM (USA)	ACEC-SEM (licence GM)
60	Bo-Bo	Elec	1400	44 000 (20 000)	24 250 (11 000)	75 (120)	,,	85·4	56' 11'' (17 350)	106	1961	Cockerill-Ougrée	Cockerill (licence Baldwin)	ACEC
64	Bo-Bo	Hyd	1400	45 200 (20 500)	(P)25 350 (11 500) (F)37 500 (17 000)	(P)75 (120) (F)51 (82)	44 (1118)	82	57' 5'' (17 500)	6	1962	Ateliers Belges Réunis; ABR	Cockerill-Ougrée	Voith
62 Bogie Flexicoil	Bo-Bo	Elec	1425	47 600 (21 600)	24 250 (11 000)	75 (120)	39¾ (1010)	80	55' 1'' (16 790)	136	1961	Brugeoise et Nivelles	GM (USA)	GM (USA)
62 Bogie BN	Bo-Bo	Elec	1425	47 600 (21 600)	24 250 (11 000)	75 (120)	,,	81·6	,,	3	1961	Brugeoise et Nivelles	,,	ACEC (licence GM)
62 Bogie BN	Bo-Bo	Elec	1425	47 600 (21 600)	24 250 (11 000)	75 (120)	,,	,,	,,	35	1962	Brugeoise et Nivelles	,,	ACEC (licence GM)
75	B-B	Hyd	1460	42 978 (19 500)	(P)25 350 (11 500) (F)27 500 (17 000)	(P)75 (120) (F)51 (82)	44 (1118)	76 / 79	,, / ,,	6 / 6	1963 / 1965/6	Brugeoise et Nivelles	GMC 2-speed / Type 12-567DI	Voith
70	B-B	Hyd	950	39 700 (18 000)	(P)27 500 (12 500) (F)46 300 (21 000)	(P)50 (80) (F)31 (50)	39¾ (1010)	72	43' 9½'' (13 350)	3	1962	ABR	ACEC (licence MAN)	Voith L.217
91	B	Hyd	245	21 800 (9900)	16 000 (7250) 7500 (3400)	(1g)13 (21) (2g)28 (45)	36¼ (920)	35·4	21' 9'' (6625)	60	1961	Cockerill-Ougrée	Cockerill-Ougrée	Cockerill-Ougrée
91	B	Hyd	335	22 000 (10 000)	(S)21 560 (9800) (L)10 340 (4 700)	13 (21) 28 (45)	49⅝ (1262)	36	21' 9'' (6625)	60	1961	Cockerill Brugeoise et Nivelles ABC	GM HM	Twin-Disc + Cockerill
92	C	Hyd	350	(S)33 000 (15 000) (L)20 700 (9400)		(S)17 (28) (L)28 (45)	49⅝ (1262)	50·55	34' 1½'' (10 400)	24	1960	Brugeoise et Nivelles	SEM	Voith
84	C	Hyd	550	(S)35 300 (16 000) (L)33 000 (15 000)		(S)20 (33) (L)31 (50)	,,	55·8	34' 11¼'' (10 650) 33' 3½'' (10 150)	35 25 10	1963 1955 1959	ABR; Baume et Marpent	Anglo-Belgian Company	Voith L 37U
85	C	Hyd	550	,,		,,	,,	58·5	32' 10'' (10 000)	25	1956	Forges, Usines et Fonderies Haine St Pierre	SEM	Turbo-transmission Voith L37U Inverseur-réduct SEMt.B.122
83	C	Hyd	550	,,		,,	,,	57	35' 3¼'' (10 750)	25	1956	Cockerill-Ougrée	Cockerill-Ougrée (lic Hamilton) 695 SA	Turbo-transmission Voith L37U Invers-reduct
80	C	Hyd	650	(S)38 800 (17 600) (L)28 400 (12 900)		(1g)24 (38) (2g)49 (78)	49¼ (1250)	52·1	34' 0'' (10 360)	69	1960	Brugeoise et Nivelles; ABR	Maybach	Voith
70	Bo-Bo	Elec	700	44 000 (20 000)	34 000 (15 400)	31 (50)	42⅛ (1070)	83	39' 10¼'' (12 150)	6	1954	Baume et Marpent	Anglo-Belgian Company	ACEC (licence Westinghouse)
71	D	Hyd	750	52 900 (24 000)		31 (50)	49⅝ (1262)	90	37' 8'' (11 480)	5	1956	Baume et Marpent	SEM	Turbo-transmission Voith L217A Invers-reduct
72	D	Hyd	750	(S)48 500 (22 000) (L)43 600 (19 800)		(S)20 (33) (L)31 (50)	,,	80	39' 7½'' (12 080)	15	1956	Brugeoise et Nivelles	SEM	Voith L37Z
82	C	Hyd	650	42 978 (19 500)		37 (60)	49⅝ (1262)	57	36' 7¾'' (11 170)	75	1965/6	Brugeoise et Nivelles; Atel Belges Réunis	Anglo-Belgian Company Type DXS 6 cyl	Voith L217U
73	C	Hyd	750	47 386 (21 500)		37 (60)	49⅝ (1262)	56	36' 7¾'' (11 170)	75	1965/8		Cockerill-Ougrée Type T695A 6-cyl	Voith L217U
74	C	Hyd	750	47 386 (21 000)		37 (60)	49⅝ (1262)	59	36' 7¾'' (11 170)	10	1977	Brugeoise et Nivelles	Anglo-Belgian Company 6 DXC	Voith L217V

Electric locomotives

Class	Wheel arrangement	Line current	Rated output hp	Tractive effort (full field) Max lb (kg)	Tractive effort (full field) Continuous lb (kg)	at mph (km/h)	Max speed mph (km/h)	Wheel dia in (mm)	Weight tonnes	Length ft in (mm)	No built	Year built	Builders Mechanical parts	Builders Electrical equipment
20	Do-Do	3000 V dc	2200	44 000 (20 000)	21 000 (9800)	30 (49)	62 (100)	53⅛ (1350)	91·5	42' 3½'' (12 890)	20	1940	Baume Marpent	ACEC Charleroi SEM Ghent
20	Co-Co	3000 V dc	7180	70 100 (32 000)	52 100 (23 600)	50 (80)	100 (160)	49¼ (1250)	111	63' 11¾'' (19 500)	15	1975	Brugeoise et Nivelles	ACEC Charleroi
22	Bo-Bo dual-current	3000/ 1500 V dc	2560	44 000 (20 000)	27 600 (11 500)	32 (51)	81 (130)	49⅝ (1262)	87	59' 0¾'' (18 000)	50	1954	Brugeoise et Nivelles	ACEC Charleroi SEM Ghent

Electric locomotives

Class	Wheel arrangement	Line current	Rated output hp	Tractive effort (full field) Max lb *(kg)*	Continuous at lb *(kg)*	mph *(km/h)*	Max speed mph *(km/h)*	Wheel dia in *(mm)*	Weight tonnes	Length ft in *(mm)*	No built	Year built	Builders: Mechanical parts	Electrical equipment
23	Bo-Bo	3000 V dc	2560	44 000 *(20 000)*	27 600 *(12 000)*	32 *(51)*	81 *(130)*	,,	93·3	59′ 0¾″ *(18 000)*	82	1955	Atel Metallurgiques de Nivelles	ACEC Charleroi SEM Ghent
25	Bo-Bo	3000 V dc	2560	44 000 *(20 000)*	27 600 *(12 500)*	32 *(51)*	81 *(130)*	,,	83·9	59′ 0¾″ *(18 000)*	22	1960	Brugeoise et Nivelles	ACEC Charleroi SEM Ghent
25·5	Bo-Bo dual current	3000/ 1500 V dc	2560	44 000 *(20 000)*	21 600 *(12 500)*	32 *(51)*	81 *(130)*	49⅝ *(1262)*	83·9	59′ 0¾″ *(18 000)*	8	modified 1973	Brugeoise et Nivelles	ACEC Charleroi SEM Ghent
26	B-B Mono motor bogies	3000 V dc	3070	58 200 *(26 400)*	34 400 *(15 600)*	30·7 *(49.5)*	100 *(160)*	45¼ *(1150)*	82·4	56′ 5″ *(17 280)*	48	1963/73	Brugeoise et Nivelles	ACEC Charleroi
28	Bo-Bo	3000 V dc	2700	44 000 *(20 000)*	25 600 *(11 600)*	32 *(51)*	81 *(130)*	49⅝ *(1262)*	85	56′ 4½″ *(17 180)*	3	1949	Baume-Marpent	ACEC Charleroi SEM Ghent
15	Bo-Bo triple-current	25 kV 50 Hz 3000/ 1500 V dc	3600	38 400 *(17 400)*	22 000 *(10 000)*	56 *(91)*	93 *(150)*	49¼ *(1250)*	77·7	58′ 3″ *(17 750)*	5	1962	Brugeoise et Nivelles	ACEC Charleroi
16	Bo-Bo quadri current	25 000 V 50 Hz 15 000 V 16 Hz 3000 V dc 1500V	3780	44 000 *(20 000)*			100 *(160)*	49¼ *(1250)*	84	54′ 7¾″ *(16 650)*	8	1966	Brugeoise et Nivelles	ACEC Charleroi Siemens
18	C-C quadri current	25 000 V 50 Hz 15 000 V 16⅝ Hz 3000 V dc 1500 V dc	6050	37 300 *(17 000)*	26 500 *(12 000)*	81 *(130)*	112 *(180)*	43⅓ *(1100)*	113	72′ 5⅓″ *(22 080)*	6	1973	Brugeoise et Nivelles	Alsthom
27	Bo-Bo	3000 V dc	5650	39 900 *(18 100)*	37 385 *(16 960)*	54·8 *(88·2)*	100 *(160)*	47¾ *(1215)*	85	61′ 2¼″ *(18 650)*	60	1982/83	Brugeoise et Nivelles	ACEC Charleroi

BENIN

Ministry of Transport

Cotonou

Minister: François Dossou

Organisation Commune Benin-Niger des Chemins de Fer et des Transports (OCBN)

PO Box 16, Cotonou

Telephone: 31 33 80
Telegrams: Orcodani Cotonou
Telex: 5210

General Manager: Alidou Boukary
Deputy General Manager: Assane Arima Hari
Director of Motive Power and Rolling Stock: Antoine Tchibozo
Director of Fixed Installations: Nicholas Lawson
Director of Operations: Daniel Aisse
Director of Supplies: J Elegbe
Director of Technical Studies: M de Souza

Gauge: 1000 mm
Route length: 578 km

Transport development

OCBN operates, on behalf of Niger and Benin, a total route length of 578 km of single-track metre-gauge railway consisting of:
Northern Line: from Cotonou to Parakou via Pahou 438 km
Eastern Line: from Cotonou to Pobè 107 km
Western Line: from Pahou to Sègboroué 33 km
From Parakou freight traffic is transported by road.

A future project is the extension of the Northern Line from Parakou to Dosso, a distance of 480 km. An agreement was signed in 1976 between Niger and Benin for the construction of a rail link between Parakou and Niamey to give Niger access to the sea at Cotonou and construction began in 1978. Finance remains the major problem; cost of the 622 km route has been estimated at Fr CFA 93 000 million. With feasibility studies by Bceom-Sofrerail-Sedes finished it was hoped to start construction in 1982 for completion by 1988.

Traffic	*1979*	*1980*
	(000)	
Total passenger journeys	1665·6	1782·6
Total passenger-km	143 017·5	162 763
Total freight tonnes	349·9	344·2
Total freight tonne-km	139 883·4	142 624·2

Motive power and rolling stock

Number of locomotives in operation at the end of 1980 totalled 21 diesel-electrics, nine shunting tractors. Railcars totalled eight and other stock consisted of 45 passenger coaches and trailers and 461 freight cars.

Track

Within the limits of the OCBN budget and with aid from FAC subventions, track is being upgraded. Work in progress includes the complete renewal of track using rail weighing 30 kg/m in place of the existing 22 kg/m rail; closer sleeper spacing under 22 kg rail, 1770 sleepers per km in place of the existing 1330; and ballast renewals.

Rail used weighs 30 kg/m in 14-metre bars, thermit welded into 154-metre lengths. After laying in track the joints are thermit welded in situ from station to station. The rails are secured by clips and bolts to 'Cameroun' type metal sleepers 1750 mm long and 232 mm wide.

Container operation

Present stock consists of 20 of 8.8 cubic metres for domestic use and 8 independently owned transcontainers 35 ft × 8 ft × 8 ft 6 in for service between France and Niger via OCBN.

BOLIVIA

Ministry of Transport and Communications

Av Camacho, Edificio La Urbana, La Paz

Minister: Hernando Poppe Martinez

Bolivian National Railways
Empresa Nacional de Ferrocarriles (ENFE)

Estacion Centrale, Plaza Zalles, Casilla 428, La Paz

Telephone: 327401; 354756
Telegrams: ENFE, La Paz

General Manager: Ing Armando Murillo Cazas
Deputy General Manager: Ing Rafael Echazú Brown
Operations Manager: Ing David Dominguez Marañon
Administration Manager: Lic Valentin Quiroga Sarmiento
Deputy Manager, Way, Works and Telecommunications: Ing Ciro Uribe Saavedra
Deputy Mechanical Manager: Ing Armando Fernàndez
Planning Director: Ing Blás Monzón Chungara
Investment Director: Ing Hugo Pareja Bonifáz
Heads of Departments
- **Law:** Dr Jaime Arancibia
- **Finance:** Lic Edwin Ortiz Cortéz
- **Traffic:** Marcelino Barro
- **Traction:** Ing Carlos Terán Pool
- **Industrial Relations:** Jaime Cusicanqui
- **Diesel Maintenance:** Elias Vera

Gauge: 1000 mm
Route length: 3628 km

Transport development

Bolivia is a landlocked country and lack of communications has made virtually impossible the sort of economic development the country needs. The railways are of major importance as the principal means of access to ports on the Pacific and Atlantic Oceans via the neighbouring countries. These essential international railway connections are as follows:
with Chile to the Pacific ports of Arica and Antofagasta;
with Argentina to the Atlantic ports of Rosario and Buenos Aires;
with Brazil to the Atlantic port of Santos;
with Peru (by ship across Lake Titicaca to Puno) to the Pacific port of Matarani.

Empresa Nacional de Ferrocarriles (ENFE) consists of two separate rail systems: Andean, operating 2152 km of route; and Eastern, operating 1386 km of route. There is no connection between them as yet, but a link line is planned between Aiquile—Santa Cruz and Zudañez—Santa Cruz, and to connect with Torabuco-Sucre. In 1982 work was continuing on the Santa Cruz—Trinidadi line. The 88 km from Rio Yapacani to Rio Grande was to be completed by the end of 1982.

Connection of the Andean and Eastern networks would be the final link in a 3952 km line from Brazil's Atlantic port of Santos to Chile's Pacific port of Arica. The Aiquile-Santa Cruz section was originally planned as the so-called North Route within a preliminary engineering study made in 1976.

As part of the interconnection plan, the associated consulting firms, CONSA SRL of Bolivia, and IATASA of Argentina, have studied the technico-economic feasibility of the construction of a section between Vallegrande and Zudañez.

A feasibility study was started in November 1982 on the fourth rehabilitation phase of the Bolivian Railways, continuing the previous three phases, which have been completed, in co-operation with the Spanish consultants INECO.

Traffic

ENFE's 1979-80 purchase of 60 passenger cars from Fiat Concord, Argentina, stimulated a sharp rise of passenger traffic in 1980. The year's total of 528.9 passenger-km was almost twice the figure of a decade earlier; gains were registered on both networks. Freight traffic also increased, though not so spectacularly; export/import goods constituted 77·3 per cent of the total.

Motive power and rolling stock

	Line-haul	Shunt-ing
Locomotives in service		
diesel-electric	54	—
diesel-hydraulic	5	4
Railcars, diesel	14	—
Passenger cars		119
Freight wagons		2103

Track

Rail: 30, 32, 37, 40 kg/m
Cross ties (sleepers): Wood
Thickness: 120 mm
Spacing: in plain track: 1450/km
  in curves: 1640/km
Minimum curvature radius: 76 m
Max gradient: 30% compensated on curves
Max axleload: 15 tonnes

Traffic

	1978	1979	1980	1981
Total freight tonnage (000)	1186	1196	1300	1265·8
Total freight ton-km (million)	495	493	646	620·48
Total passenger-km (million)	397	362	528·9	482·2
Total passenger journeys (000)	1236	1212	1700	1575·8

Finances

	1978	1979	1980	1981
	(B$ million)			
Total revenues	769	851	1145	1586
Total expenditure	895.4	1018.1	1396	1530·8

General Electric-built U10B diesel-electric locomotive

Mitsubishi-built diesel-electric re-engined with MTU 12 V 956TB 2460 kW engine

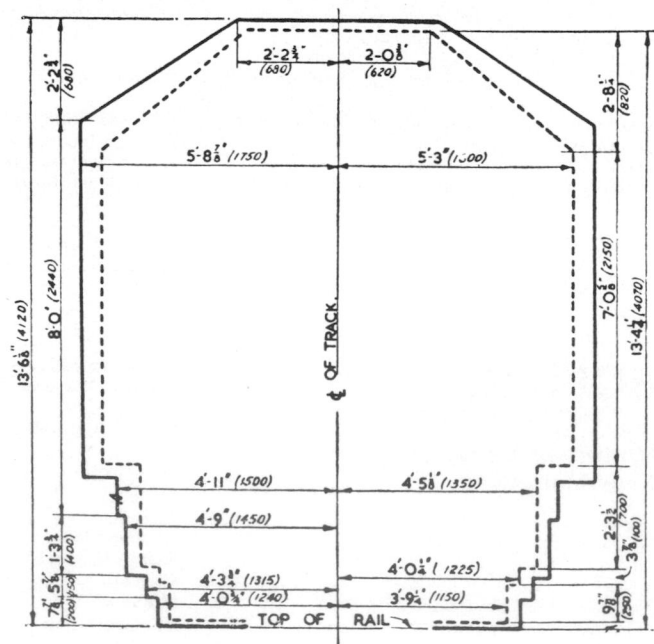

ENFE loading and structure gauge

Diesel locomotives

Class	Wheel arrangement	Transmission	Rated power kW	Tractive effort Max kg	Continuous kg	at kmlh	Max speed kmlh	Wheel dia mm	Total weight tonnes	Length mm	No in service	Year first built	Builders Mechanical parts	Engine & type	Transmission
950	Bo-Bo-Bo	Elec	1270	20 400	9200	28	70	1000	81·6	16 800	20	1968	Hitachi Mitsubishi	MAN VGV 22/30 ATL	Hitachi Mitsubishi
1000	Bo-Bo-Bo	Elec	2028	22 200	10 150	42	100	1000	84	17 800	16	1978	Hitachi Mitsubishi	MTU 12 V 956TB 11	Hitachi Mitsubishi
521	Bo-Bo	Hyd	535	5000	2700	25	70	910	45	14 000	4	1968	Hitachi	Hitachi MAN RGV 18/12 TL	Hitachi
841	Bo-Bo	Hyd	1070	—	—	—	70	910	55	—	5	1968	Hitachi Mitsubishi	MAN RGV 18/12 TL (two)	Hitachi
U 20C	Co-Co	Elec	2030	34 000	11 000	40	114	1016	88·9	17 000	8	1976	General Electric	FDL 12 GE	General Electric
U 10B	Bo-Bo	Elec	675	25 000	5500	40	103	914	49·8	13 000	9	1977	General Electric	D 398 Caterpillar	General Electric

Diesel railbuses

Cars per unit	Motor cars per unit	Motored axles per motor car	Transmission	Rated power (hp) per motor	Max speed kmlh	Weight tonnes per car (M-motor T-trailer)	Total seating capacity	Length per car mm	No in service	Year first built	Builders Mechanical parts	Engine & type	Transmission
2	1	2	Mech	240	80	M 18·5 T 14·8	44+54	13 757	10	1967	Ferrostaal	Cummins	Zahnfabrik
2	1	2	Mech	285	100	M 26 T 23·5	32+58	14 280	2	1978	Ferrostaal	Cummins	NT855R4
3	1	2	Mech	335	100	M 26 T 23·5	32+16	14 280	2	1978	Ferrostaal	Cummins	NT855R4

BOTSWANA

The country, formerly the British Protectorate of Bechuanaland, is traversed by 707 km of line managed by the National Railways of Zimbabwe. This comprises principally the NRZ route from Bulawayo, Zimbabwe, to Mafeking, South Africa, but includes the 60 km-long Selebi-Pikwe branch. The Botswana Government already owns the branch, but now plans to take over and run the entire system with its own railway management and staff. The French consultancy Sofrerail was in 1982 contracted to advise on staff training and creation of a railway organisation, with a view to execution of the takeover in 1987.

Plans have also been formulated for a Trans-Kalahari line of 1400 km length, of which 850 km would be in Botswana, to channel Botswana coal to Walvis Bay, Namibia, on the west coast, for export shipment. Progress depends on solution of the political problems enveloping Namibia.

BRAZIL

Ministry of Transport

Esplanada dos Ministérios, Bloco 9, 70 062 Brasilia DF

Rio office: Praça Mauà 10, Rio de Janeiro RJ

Minister: Cloraldino Severo

Rede Ferroviaria Federal SA (RFFSA)

Praca Procópio Ferreira 86, Rio de Janeiro

Telephone: (011) 291 2185
Telegrams: Referro
Telex: 21 927

President: Carlos Alysio Weber
Vice President: Augusto José Braga de Andrade
Director, Stores: Altredo Arold Simon
Director, Engineering: Eng Américo Maia
Director, Metropolitan Transport: Heinz Manfred Hertz
Director, Administration: Eng Paulo Marcos Mazoni Andrade
Director, Personnel: Dr Hélio Duarte do Nascimento
Director, Operations: René Fernandes Schoppa
Director, Commercial: Mauro Rolf Fernandes Knudsen

Gauge: 1600 mm; 1000 mm; 762 mm
Route length: 1817 km; 21 068 km; 202 km
Electrification: 879 km at 3 kV dc

Transport development
In addition to 13 Federal-owned lines there are several other railways in operation, some owned by autonomous Federal departments, some by State governments, and some privately. RFFSA is now administered by seven regional authorities and one commuter railway division (Rio de Janeiro). They are:

Recife Region (SR-1), serving the provinces of Maranhão, Piaui, Rio Grande do Norte, Ceará, Paraiba, Pernambuco, Alagoas, Sergipe and Northern Minas, Bahia. The region is sub-divided into two management divisions: Fortaleza (SP1-1), with head offices at Praça Castro Carreira, Fortaleza, Ceará; and Recife Division based at Av Rio Capibariba 147, Recife PE. A single operating division is based on São Luis.

Belo Horizonte Region (SR-2), serving the provinces of Minas Gerais, Goiàs, Brasilia (DF), São Paulo and Estado do Rio. Headquarters: Rua Sapucai 383, Belo Horizonte MG.

Rio de Janeiro Region (SR-3), serving the provinces of Rio de Janeiro, Minas Gerais, São Paulo and Espirito Santo. This region is divided into the Juiz de Fora, the broad gauge division (SP3-1), and the campos narrow gauge division (SP3-2), both based at Praça Cristiani Otoni, 4° andar, Rio de Janeiro.

São Paulo Region (SR-4), serving the provinces of São Paulo and Mato Grosso, which is based at Praça Alfredo Issa 48, 20° andar, São Paulo. Two divisions operate within the region: São Paulo Division (SP4-1), Praça da Luz 1, São Paulo; and Bauru Division (SP4-2), Praça Machado de Melo, Bauru, São Paulo.

Curitiba Region (SR-5), serving the provinces of Parana and Santa Catarina and based at Rua João Negrão 940, 1° andar, Curitiba PR.

Porto Alegre Region (SR-6), serving the provinces of Santa Catarina and Rio Grande do Sul with headquarters at Rua Voluntàrios da Pàtria 1358, Porto Alegre RS. An independent group of lines centred on Tubarão forms a separate operating division, based at Rua Rui Barbosa 39, Tubarão SC.

Salvador Division (SR-7), with headquarters at Praça da Inglaterra, 4° andar, Salvador BA.

Greater Rio Suburban Special Division, the special autonomous division created for Greater Rio de Janeiro, based at Praça Cristiana Otoni, 5° andar, Rio de Janeiro.

Route-km
Metre guage

Regions	Total	Length (km) electrified
SR-1 Recife	4818	—
CSP-1 São Luis	790	—
SP-1.1 Fortaleza	1415	—
SP-1.2 Recife	2613	—
SR-2 Belo Horizonte*	4321	436
SR-3 Rio de Janeiro	1472	—
SP-3.1 Juiz de Fora	—	—
CSP-3 Campos	1472	—
SR-4 São Paulo	1613	—
SP-4.1 São Paulo	—	—
SP-4.2 Bauru	1613	—
SR-5 Curitiba	3409	—
SR-6 Porto Alegre	4061	—
SP-6 Porto Alegre	3886	—
CSP-6 Tubarão	175	—
SR-7 Salvador	1914	50
DES-Greater Rio Suburban	158	—

*Includes 202 km of 760 mm gauge

1600 mm gauge

Regions	Total	Length (km) electrified
SR-2 Belo Horizonte	118	—
SR-3 Rio de Janeiro	1170	174
SP-3.1 Juiz de Fora	1170	174
SR-4 São Paulo	287	199
SP-4.1 São Paulo	287	199
DES-Greater Rio Suburban	226	175
Rede Ferroviària Federal SA	1801	548

To conserve energy the Government has given high priority to a number of new projects, partly financed by taxation of road vehicles and their fuel and lubricants. The biggest schemes, including the Steel Railway and the Soya Railway, have been designed and are being managed by Engefer, a subsidiary of RFFSA specifically created in 1975 to supervise new railway construction under the Transport Ministry's national programme.

Steel Railway
The first 319 km section of the projected 740 km line was begun in the spring of 1979 and was programmed for opening in September 1983, at a cost of over US$ 1000 million. This first stage will connect Belo Horizonte, Jeceaba and Itutinga with the big steelworks complex at Volta Redonda; the second stage will project the line into the state of São Paulo. Over 24 000 staff have been engaged on construction of the route, which follows a difficult path through mountainous terrain in Minas Gerais and Rio de Janeiro provinces. No less than 135 million cubic metres of earthworks have been incurred, together with boring of 70 tunnels grossing 50 km in length and erection of 95 bridges and viaducts with a total length of 27 km. The longest tunnel is one of 8.7 km beneath the Serra de Mantequiera, which was constructed with the New Austrian Tunnel-Driving Method (NATM); the longest viaduct is 761 metres, with 24 spans; and the highest, 81.8 metres above ground. The track is 1600 mm gauge, with minimum curve radii of 900 metres and minimum gradients of 1 per cent, and a permissible axleloading of 30 tonnes maximum. Welded 68 kg/m rail in 240-metre lengths has been laid on timber (at 1852/km spacing) or concrete monobloc (at 1667/km spacing) sleepers.

The line is being electrified at 25 kV 60 Hz and signalled by GEC Transportation Projects Ltd. It will initially employ 35 180-tonne 3500 kW Co-Co locomotives with thyristor control built locally by Equipamentos Villares SA to a GEC design and embodying electrical equipment supplied from the UK. They will be based on the GEC design for South African Railways' Sishen-Saldanha ore line. The signalling will incorporate CTC and automatic train stop (ATS) systems and telecommunications will include a microwave system. Operating capacity will be 28 daily pairs of trains loading to a maximum of 7000 tonnes northbound, permitting an eventual annual throughput of over 50 million tonnes; the initial annual total is expected to be 24 million tonnes, primarily of ore, steel products, limestone and cement. Except on the steepest gradients maximum speeds of 80 km/h and 60 km/h have been set for empty and loaded trains respectively.

It was announced in 1982 that, because of Government curbs on expenditure in the country's difficult financial position, opening of the line's first section from Volta Redonda to Bom Jardim had been deferred until late 1984. This will be initially with diesel traction. Operation of the remainder from Bom Jardim to the Belo Horizonte ore deposits would not start until the end of 1985. By the end of 1982, however, most of the civil engineering was complete.

Soya Line
Engineering studies for the initial 97 km section of new railway to provide better access to the port of Paranagua for the fast-growing soya industry in eastern Parana and southern Mato Grosso have been completed. This first stage is to run south of the existing Curitiba-Paranagua line; it would be laid to the metre gauge at first, but the track formation will allow for later substitution of 1600 mm gauge. The same applies to the proposed second stage, a 243 km new line from Guarapuava to Cascavel, beyond which point, under an agreement concluded with Paraguay in 1980, a further 400 km of new 25 kV ac electrified railway is planned via the border at Salto de Guaira to Asuncion. In 1982, however, the project was stalled by a World Bank decision to defer loan finance for it.

Coal railways
Numerous new line projects have been programmed to cover the Government's drive for better utilisation of the country's coal resources, and these are also being managed by Engefer. In addition, to facilitate the movement of coal northward, RFFSA's southern main line between Porto Alegre and São Paulo is being upgraded at a cost of Cr 800 million to lift its operating capacity from 3 to 10 million tonnes a year by 1984. In 1982 the Minister of Transport approved construction of a 50 km line to rail coal from the Leao mines in Rio Grande do Sul to the port of Conde in São Jeronimo.

Suburban passenger railways
RFFSA's long-haul passenger business is negligible, amounting to only 0.5 per cent of the national market in total, but major schemes to improve city suburban services are under way.

Rio de Janeiro: MAN is supplying 60 new four-car emus with GEC Traction power equipment; construction is shared with Santa Matilde. Signalling, telecommunications, electrification and existing train-sets are also being modernised and in 1982 a French consortium gained a Fr 900 million contract covering the supply of fixed equipment here and in São Paulo. A Japanese consortium including Mitsui and Toshiba has secured other contracts worth Cr 3900 million. Investment in the network is already over Cr 20 000 million.

Belo Horizonte: A Franco-Brazilian group headed by Francorail has a contract worth Fr 900 million to establish the first stage of a 3 kV dc electrified suburban system that will eventually total 111 km.

Porto Alegre: Under management of a new RFFSA subsidiary, Trensurb, a 42.7 km, 21-station electrified line is being established from the northern suburbs to the city centre, at a cost of Cr 862 million. A contract for 100 emu cars has been won by a Japanese consortium of Hitachi, Nippon Sharyo Seizo Kaisha and Mitsui, financed by a World Bank loan.

Salvador: In 1980-82 over Cr 5000 million was being invested in the first phase of establishing a 69 km suburban passenger network.

Recife: A 32 km, 26-station electrified network is being created, which is to include conversion to 1600 mm gauge of the Recife Central-Jaboatão line and a metre gauge freight bypass from Lacerda to Prazeres. In 1982 negotiations were completed for loans of US$232.7 million from a consortium headed by Lloyds Bank International and of US$84 million from a German Federal Republic consortium to advance this project. For this and the Belo Horizonte scheme 50 four-car emus have been ordered from Brazilian manufacturers.

Fortaleza: Signalling modernisation and some double-tracking are the centrepieces of improvements in this area, for which about Cr 1000 million has been budgeted.

In 1982 RFFSA recorded 395.9 million passenger journeys and 10 385.5 million passenger-km.

Investment
The 1982-84 investment programme of RFFSA totals Cr 627 000 million. It was fortified in 1982 by negotiation of several major loans on the international market and by the Government's approval of an emergency programme to aid the country's railway supply industry. Under the latter a first order was placed with two Brazilian firms for 400 freight wagons at the end of 1982, backed by funds from the National Social Development Bank.

Freight
Iron ore accounts for 29 per cent of the current total tonnage, coal for 11 per cent, petroleum products for 9 per cent and iron and steel products for almost 8 per cent. New wagon orders are concentrating on high-capacity vehicles for unit train working. The Government has ordered that wherever practicable freight must be moved by rail or ship. In 1982 freight totalled 69.8 million tonnes and 31 686 million tonne-km.

Operations management
A computer controlled system to monitor the use, performance and maintenance of rolling stock, Sogeop, has been established. This supplements the existing Sinop train planning system.

Traction and rolling stock
Since 1979 orders have been placed for over 300 new locomotives. They have included 120 units each from Villares and EMAQ, and 60, half broad- and half narrow-gauge, from GE-Brasil at a cost of US$ 80 million. In 1982 Bombardier was contracted to re-engine and recondition 84 diesel-electric locomotives for C$52 million.

On 1676 mm gauge RFFSA operates 473 diesel and 42 diesel locomotives, 446 emus, six dmus, two diesel railcars, 110 passenger cars and 14 101 freight wagons; on narrower gauges, 49 steam, 1092 diesel and 26 electric locomotives, 15 diesel railcars, six dmus, 18 electric railcars, 959 passenger cars and 30 040 freight wagons.
(See also Addenda)

Financial results

	1979	1980	1981	1982
		Cr million		
Revenues				
Passengers and baggage	1160	2099.5	4845.3	9898.7
Average receipt per passenger-km (Cr)	132	218	480	NA
Freight and mail	13 120.8	28 765.9	58 185.8	118 047.8
Average receipt per freight tonne-km (Cr)	460	855	1846	NA
Other revenues or compensation	32 809	74 624	218 984	425 382.6
Total	47 089.9	105 490	284 311	553 329.1
Expenditure				
Total	57 479.8	105 869	297 913.3	629 529.9

One of 120 electric railcars (3 kV dc) built mainly for commuter services around Rio de Janeiro

General Electric diesel-electric locomotive 60 tonnes, 900/810 hp

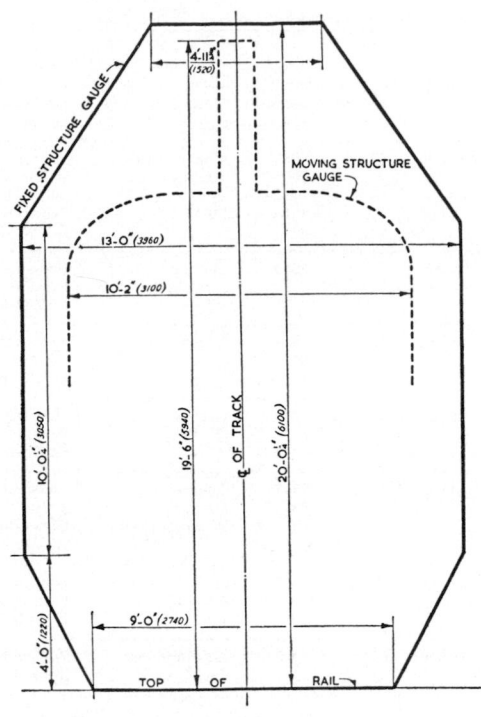

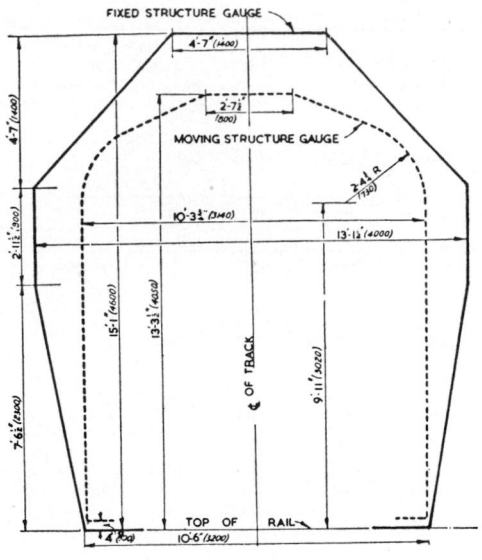

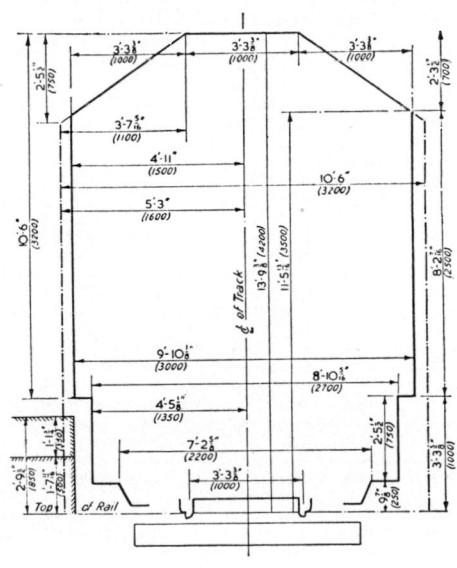

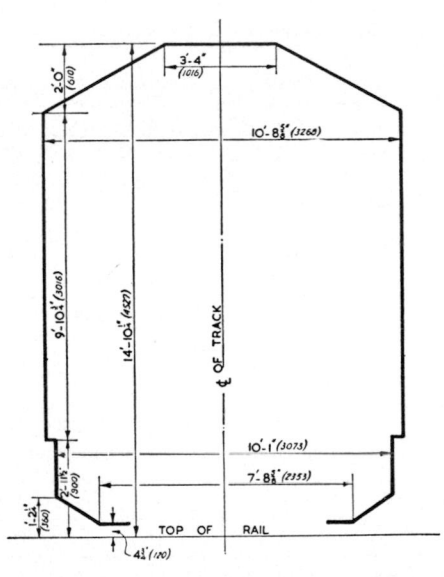

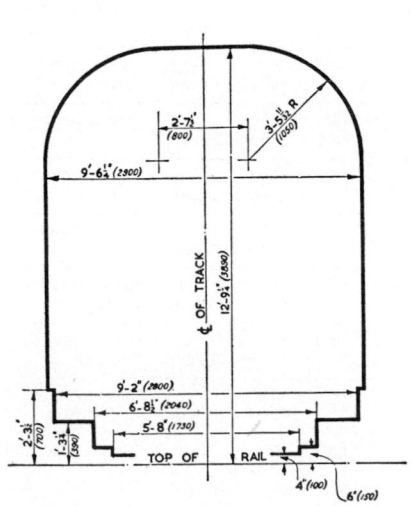

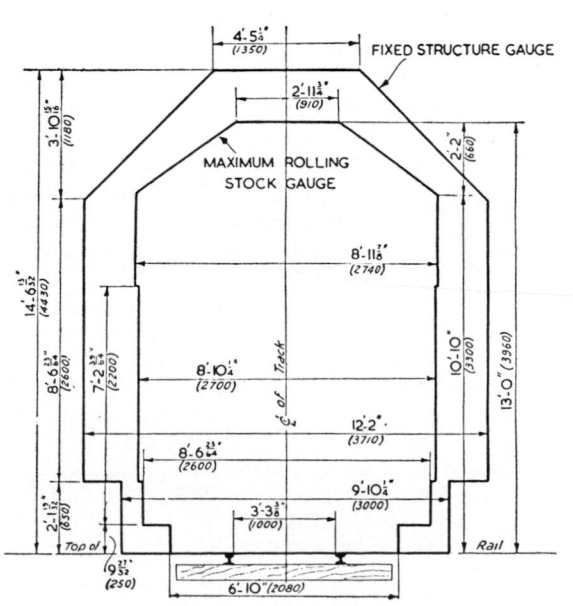

Six types of loading and structural gauge employed on Brazil's railway lines

Electric locomotives

Gauge mm	Class	Wheel arrangement	Line current	Rated output hp	Tractive effort (full field) Max kg	Continuous at kg	kmlh	Max speed kmlh	Wheel diameter mm	Weight tonnes	Length mm	No in service	First in service	Builders Mechanical parts	Electrical equipment
1000	—	B-B	3000 V	1000	9080	—	—	80	1092	50	12 040	22	1951/60	Metropolitan Vickers	Metropolitan Vickers MV188
1000	—	B-B	3000 V	1073	9000	—	—	65	1016	43	11 800	4	1954/60	IRFA	Brown Boveri GOTM 1522
1600	—	B-B	3000 V	3000	—	15 600	—	100	1257	110	16 270	7	1959	Siemens-Schuckert	Siemens Schuckert VB320/22
1600	—	B-B	3000 V	3780	38 560	—	—	45	1118	106	16 760	12	1972/80	Hitachi	Hitachi DES 100-701-762 EFFZO-HGO
1600	—	C-C	3000 V	4400	—	21 120	27·2	117	1168	123	16 857	6	1963	General Electric	General Electric GE-729
1600	—	2C+C2	3000 V	4470	—	17 000	58	117	1168*	165	23 539	8	1947/48	General Electric Westinghouse	Westinghouse 375-A General Electric GE-729-B1
1600	—	C-C	3000 V	3000	25 850	—	—	100	1219	127	20 520	16	1949/55	English Electric	English Electric EE 514A
1600	—	2C-C2	3000 V	4470	—	17 000	58	117	1168*	165	23 539	6	1948/49	Westinghouse	Westinghouse 375-A-5

*Guide wheel diameter: 914.4 mm

Diesel locomotives: metre gauge (see also Addenda)

Class	Wheel arrangement	Transmission	Rated power hp	Tractive effort Max kg	Continuous at kg	kmlh	Max speed kmlh	Wheel dia mm	Total weight tonnes	Length mm	No built	First built	Builders Mechanical parts	Engine & type	Transmission
RS-3	C-C	Elec	1750	—	20 140	18	97	1016	96	15 951	40	1953/54	Alco-GE	Alco-12.244E	GE-761-41/GE-584
RS-8	B-B	Elec	900	—	—	—	95	914·4	62·6	13 802	20	1958	Alco Products, Inc	Alco-251	GE-761/GE5GT584D3
RSD-8	C-C	Elec	900	—	—	—	95	914·4	68·1	13 802	47	1958/59	Alco Products, Inc	Alco-251 B	GE-761/GE5GT584D3
Baldwin	C-C	Elec	1750	—	17 014	20·6	72	—	102	17 678	1	1954	Baldwin-Westinghouse	Baldwin-608-A	Westinghouse 563-A/47-8Z
Whitcomb	C-C	Elec	660	—	—	—	—	—	66	—	4	1948/50	Baldwin-Westinghouse	Stell & MWM	—
MX-620	C-C	Elec	2150	—	21 120	21·3	103	914·4	96	17 634	26	1980	Emaq-Eng Emaq SA	Alco-251-CE	GE761PA14/GT581P51/GY27PF1
EE	A1A-A1A	Elec	1000	—	—	—	96·5	863·6	73·2	15 326	1	1954	English Electric	BRKT-EE	English Electric
—	B	Elec	150	6015	—	—	30	762	19·5	8275	2	1970	EFCB	Cummins-HBI-600	GE740/5GT1503W1
—	B	Elec	180	—	—	—	—	15	—	1	1976	EFL	Cummins	—
B-30/30-IGE763	B	Elec	110	4500	—	—	—	838	15	5674	2	1958	International-GE	Cummins-HRC-4-B1	GE-763A-1/GT1519-A1
U-5B	B-B	Elec	600	12 500	9200	17	64	914·4	49·9	11 402	66	1961/62	GE-General Electric	Caterpillar-D-379	GE-5-GE-761-A1/GE-5-GE761B1/GE-5GT601-B1/GE-5GAG-146B
U-5B	B-B	Elec	600	12 473	—	—	65	914·4	50	11 500	22	1961	GE-General Electric	Caterpillar-D-379	GE-5-GE-761B1/GE5GM601-B1
U-8B	B-B	Elec	900	13 625	—	—	96	914·4	54·5	11 380	60	1961	GE-General Electric	Caterpillar-VD398	GE-761 & GT-601
U-9B	B-B	Elec	990	16 600	—	—	96	914·4	66	15 144	2	1957	GE-General Electric	Cooper-Bessemer FWB-6	GE-5GE761-A1/GE-5GT599-A1
U-10B	B-B	Elec	1050	15 200	—	—	96	914·4	60	11 380	79	1971/72	GE-General Electric	Caterpillar-D398B	GE-5GE761/5GT601-B1
U-12B	B-B	Elec	1320	17 500	—	—	96	914·4	70	15 144	29	1958/59	GE-General Electric	Cooper-Bessemer FVBL-8T	GE-5GE761-A1
U-12C	C-C	Elec	1320	20 000	—	—	96	914·4	80	15 144	15	1958	GE-General Electric	Cooper-Bessemer FVBL-8T	GE-5GE761-A1/GE-5GT581
U-13B	B-B	Elec	1420	17 500	—	—	96	914·4	70	15 144	49	1963	GE-General Electric	General Electric 7-FDL-8	GE-5GE761-A3/GE-GT581-C
U-20C	C-C	Elec	2150	—	22 800	19	103	1016	108	16 947	77	1974/77	GE-General Electric	General Electric 7-FDL-12	GE-5GE761-A10/GE-5GT581-C11
U 20C	C-C	Elec	2150	—	24 670	—	103	1016	108	16 916	49	1975/77	GE-General Electric	General Electric 7-FDL-12D16	GE-5GE761-A9/GE-5GT581-C11
—	B	Elec	150	6800	—	—	32	—	23·1	5540	6	1946/47	GE-General Electric	Cummins-HBI-600	GE-733-F1/GE 1503-XL
—	C-C	Elec	660	—	10 050	—	75	838	64	11 765	9	1947/56	GE-General Electric	Cooper-Bessemer FWL-6T	GE-5GE747-B1/GE-5GT-571-B1/GE5GMG14684
—	C-C	Elec	660	—	—	17	75	838	60	11 785	3	1956	GE-General Electric	Caterpillar-D398	GE-5GE747-B1

Diesel locomotives: metre gauge (see also Addenda)

Class	Wheel arrangement	Transmission	Rated power hp	Max kg	Tractive effort Continuous at kg	km/h	Max speed km/h	Wheel dia mm	Total weight tonnes	Length mm	No built	First built	Builders Mechanical parts	Engine & type	Transmission
B-12	B-B	Elec	1125	—	—	24	97	1016	68	13 563	9	1953	General Motors Corp	GM-12-567-B	GM-D-19/ GM-D15 & 8078909
G-8	A1A-A1A	Elec	950	—	12 720	15	72	1016	71·7	14 336	2	1958	General Motors Corp	GM-8-567-C	GM-D-29/GM-D15E
G-8	B-B	Elec	950	—	12 720	15	72	1016	68·9	14 336	46	1958/60	General Motors Corp	GM-8-567-C	GM-D-29/GM-D15E
G-12	A1A-A1A	Elec	1425	—	15 180	20	100	1016	78·2	13 106	15	1957	General Motors Corp	GM-12-567C	GM-D-29/D-12F
G-12	B-B	Elec	1425	—	15 180	15	72	1016	72·4	14 336	74	1958/60	General Motors Corp	GM-12-567C	GM-D-29/D-12F AH159A1 & A7159A2
G-12	B-B	Elec	1425	—	15 180	20	100	1016	72·4	13 106	64	1958/60	General Motors Corp	GM-EMD-12.567C	GM-EMD-D-29/ EMD D-12 E
G-12	B-B	Elec	1425	—	15 180	20	100	1016	72·4	13 106	28	1958/60	General Motors Corp	GM-EMD-12.567C	GM-EMD-D-29/ EMD D-22 F
G-22U	B-B	Elec	1650	—	15 540	21·7	97	1016	73	15 493	129	1971/74	Macosa-GM-EMD	GM-645-E	GE-Maquinista D-29 Cenemesa-D-32T
G-22CU	C-C	Elec	1650	—	21 500	14	97	1016	92	15 970	24	1970/71	Macosa-GM-EMD	GM-645-E	GE-Maquinista D-29CC Cenemesa-D-32T-5553414
G-26CU	C-C	Elec	1650	—	—	—	97·2	1016	108	15 764	35	1974/75	Macosa-GM-EMD	GM-645-E	GM-D29/D-32T
GL-8	A1A-A1A	Elec	950	17 010	15 370	—	100	1016	68	13 584	3	1962	General Motors Corp	GM-8-567-C	GM3D29/GMD25-E
GL-8	B-B	Elec	950	—	14 175	—	100	1016	56·7	12 192	7	1961	General Motors Corp	GM-8-567-CR	GM-D29/ EMD-D25-E
GL-8	B-B	Elec	950	—	14 810	12	100	1016	59·3	12 344	3	1961	General Motors Corp	GM-8-567-CR	GM-D29/ GM-D-25-E
GL-8	B-B	Elec	950	17 010	15 370	—	100	1016	62	12 344	18	1960/62	General Motors Corp	GM-567-C	GM-D29/GM-D25-E

Electric multiple-units (see also Addenda)

Gauge mm	Class	Wheel arrangement	Line current	Rated output hp	Max kg	Tractive effort (full field) Continuous at kg	km/h	Max speed km/h	Wheel diameter mm	Weight tonnes	Length mm	No in service	Year first in service	Builders Mechanical	Electrical
1000	E1/9	B-B	3000 V	—	—	—	—	—	965·2	52·1	15 204	9	1962	American Car Foundry and General Electric	General Electric- GE-735A2
	E101/109	B-B	3000 V	—	—	—	—	—	965·2	55	17 800	9	1962	American Car Foundry and General Electric	General Electric- GE-735A2
1600	1/101	B-B	3000 V	700	—	—	—	—	965·2	56	20 000	61	1936	Metropolitan Vickers	Metropolitan Vickers MV155 MG-81A
	102/201	B-B	3000 V	1032	—	—	—	—	965·2	60·1	22 000	96	1954	Metropolitan Vickers	Metropolitan Vickers MV251 MG-91DY
	400	B-B	3000 V	1372	—	—	—	—	914·4	63·1	22 000	94	1964	Fábrica Nacional de Vagões Cia Brasileira Material Ferroviário S/A Cia Industrial Santa Mathilde S/A	General Electric GE-754 GMG-172A-2
	500	B-B	3000 V	1260	—	—	—	—	—	—	22 000	60	1976	Hitachi Ltd	Hitachi HS-360/CLG-361
	600	B-B	3000 V	1372	—	—	—	—	965·2	60	26 000	20	1977	Material Ferroviário S/A Mafersa	—
	A-B-C	B-B	3000 V	800	—	—	—	110	965·2	52·7	20 640	3	—	English Electric	English Electric-EE522A
	101/130	B-B	3000 V	1200	—	—	—	96·6	914·4	63·8	25 907	29	1956/57	The Budd Co	General Electric-GE-754A2
	401	B-B	3000 V	1200	—	—	—	—	914·4	61·9	25 907	30	—	Material Ferroviário S/A The Budd Co	—
	431	B-B	3000 V	1200	—	—	—	—	914·4	60	25 908	20	—	Material Ferroviário S/A The Budd Co	—
	141-146	B-B	3000 V	1200	—	—	—	96·6	914·4	83·3	25 907	6	—	Material Ferroviário S/A The Budd Co	General Electric-5GE-754A2
	Alvo-Rada	B-B	3000 V	700	—	—	—	—	914·4	56	20 000	3	—	Metropolitan Vickers	—

Diesel locomotives: 1600 mm gauge (see also Addenda)

Class	Wheel arrange- ment	Trans- mission	Rated power hp	Max kg	Tractive effort Continuous at kg	kml/h	Max speed kml/h	Wheel dia mm	Total weight tonnes	Length mm	No built	First built	Builders Mechanical parts	Engine & type	Transmission
RS-1	B-B	Elec	1650	—	19 250	17·7	104	1016	108	15 697	5	1948/ 49	Alco-GE	Alco-12-244	GE-752E1/ GT-564-C1
RS	B-B	Elec	1100	—	15 400	12·8	96	1016	109·7	16 909	26	1945	Alco-GE	Alco-539	GE-731D3/ GT-553-C3
RS	B-B	Elec	1100	22 680	—	—	96·6	1016	109·7	17 303	3	1948/ 56	Alco	Alco-539	GE-5GE731-D3/ 5GT-553-C3
RS-3	B-B	Elec	1750	—	23 835	15·2	104	1016	109	16 990	38	1946/ 52	Alco (Montreal Locomotive Works)	Alco-12.244	GE-5GE752E1
RSD-12	C-C	Elec	1950	—	36 013	9·4	104	1016	163·4	17 721	9	1962/ 63	Alco	Alco-12.251	GE-752PC4/ GT582-A2
S-1	B-B	Elec	720	—	13 230	10	96	1016	90	13 577	5	1943/ 44	Alco	Alco-539	GE-731D31/ GT522-A4
Baldwin A-608	C-C	Elec	1750	—	32 950	11·2	55	1066·8	147·5	17 678	3	1952	Baldwin Westinghouse	Baldwin-Lima Hamilton 608-A	Westinghouse 370DEZ/471BZ
—	B	Elec	150	6105	—	—	30	762	20·4	8275	3	1970	EFCB	Cummins-HB 4BI-600	GE-740/ 5GT1503W1
—	B-B	Elec	720	15 400	—	—	88	914·4	64	11 278	15	1955	General Electric	Cooper-Bessemer FWL-6T	GE-5-761A1/ 5GT-571-C3
—	B-B	Elec	720	15 400	—	—	88	914·4	80	11 278	30	1956	General Electric	Cooper-Bessemer FWL-6T	GE-5-761A1/ 5GT-571-C3
U-5B	B-B	Elec	600	—	15 422	6·2	64	914·4	51·3	11 403	19	1961	General Electric	Caterpillar D-379	GE-761-A1/GT-601
U-6B	B-B	Elec	700	—	15 200	7·9	64	914·4	57	11 073	20	1967	General Electric	Caterpillar D-379B-V8	GE-761A5/ 5GT-601-C1
U-23C	C-C	Elec	2500	—	34 686	13	120	1016	165	20 497	20	1976	General Electric	GE-7-FDL-12	GE-752E8-A/ GT-586
U-23C	C-C	Elec	2500	—	34 686	13	120	1016	175	20 497	3	1976	General Electric	GE-7-FDL-12	GE-752E8-A/ GT-586
U-23C	C-C	Elec	2500	—	38 900	11·6	112·6	1016	180	20 497	147	1972/ 76	General Electric	GE-7-FDL-12	GE-752E8-A/ GT-586
SD-18	C-C	Elec	1950	—	35 174	10·5	104	1016	163·4	18 504	41	1962/ 63	General Motors Corp	GM-16-567-D1	GM-EMD-D47E1/ EMD-D22C
SD-38	C-C	Elec	2200	—	37 235	10·6	96·8	1016	163	18 550	44	1967	General Motors Corp	GM-16-645-E	GM-EMD-D77/ EMD-D32
SD-40	C-C	Elec	3300	—	37 235	17·7	113	1016	163	18 590	3	1967	General Motors Corp	GM-16-645-E	GM-EMD-D77/ EMD-AR10-D14
SD-40-2	C-C	Elec	3300	—	—	13·7	104·5	1016	180	20 980	36	1980	General Motors Corp	GM-16-645-E-3	GM-EMD-D77/ EMD-AR-10-D14
—	B-B	Elec	1050	—	14 740	12·1	104	—	115	16 760	3	1980	Hitachi Ltd	Alco-6-251-B	

Diesel railbuses and railcars (see also Addenda)

Class	Wheel arrange- ment	Trans- mission	Rated power hp	Max kg	Tractive effort Continuous at kg	kml/h	Max speed kml/h	Wheel dia mm	Total weight tonnes	Length mm	No built	First built	Builders Mechanical parts	Engine & type	Transmission
Railbuses **Metre gauge** M	B-B	Hyd	436	—	—	—	90	838	41·1	18 745	10	1962	The Budd Co	General Motors Corp GM-6-71-MOD: 6080	Allison Div Motors-Railcars Transmission- GM-Torkmatic
M-RDC	B-B	Hyd	436	—	—	—	90	838	41·1	18 745	5	1963	The Budd Co	—	—
1600 mm gauge M	B-B	Hyd	550	—	—	—	—	863·6	54·5	25 908	1	1962	The Budd Co	General Motors Corp GM-110	—
Railcars **Metre gauge** M	B-B	Hyd	1600	—	—	—	100	838	45	18 880	12	—	Ganz-Màvag	Ganz 12VFE 17/24	HM 912-10
Minuano	B-B	Hyd	400	—	—	—	—	—	40·5	17 041	4	—	—	MAN W8V17,5/ 22A	J M Voith-L24
1600 mm gauge M	B-B	Hyd	935	—	—	—	—	838	59·3	25 880	12	1974	Ganz-Màvag	Ganz 12 VFE 17/24	

Ferrovia Paulista SA (FEPASA)

Praça Júlio Prestes 148, São Paulo

Telephone: 01 223 7211
Telex: 011 23799

President: Chafic Jacob
Assistant Director: Fábio José de Araujo
Director, Administration: Ismael Menezes Armond
  Finance: Nelson Angelo Cucchieratto
  Commercial: Dr Ignázio Gandolfo
  Operations: Inácio Mauricio Figueiredo
  Human Resources: João Carlos Casella
Technical: Antonio Angelo Brunelli

Gauge: 1600 mm; 1000 mm; mixed
Route length: 1587 km; 3418 km; 61 km

FEPASA was formed in 1970 to consolidate the operation of five railways owned by the State of São Paulo. There are three divisions: First (the former Paulista and Araraquara); Second (the former Sorocabana); Third (the former Morgiana and São Paulo—Minas).

Freight
After a slight setback in 1981, when freight tonnage turned marginally downward, 1982 was set to show resumed growth with a likely year-end total of almost 22 million tonnes. That compares with a gross of 12·13 million recorded in 1978. Further rises were recorded in average train and wagonloads, continuing the drive for greater productivity of assets.

Drastic action in 1976 rid the railway of most of its long-distance passenger and general freight traffic. Since then FEPASA has concentrated on haulage of a dozen major commodities in bulk, headed by oil (running at over 3 million tonnes a year in 1982), agricultural produce, phosphates, cement and alcohol. A continuing growth of freight tonnage to 26·8 million tonnes a year by 1987 has been budgeted. FEPASA plans to acquire 3600 additional freight wagons in the period up to 1985. Freight rolling stock now totals 13 264 wagons.

Financial results
Revenue (Cr million)

	1981/82
Passengers and baggage	2551·2
Freight, parcels and mail	28 409·8
Other income	18 588·2
Total	49 549·2

Expenditure (Cr million)

	1981/82
Staff/personnel expenses	22 746·6
Materials and services	11 381·6
Depreciation	7713·3
Financial charges	152 352·1
Total	194 193·6

Passenger
Passenger traffic regressed in 1982 in face of the recession and other national problems, but FEPASA is budgeting for dramatic growth of its suburban business as a result of the modernisation now in progress. From a total of 56 million passenger-journeys in 1982, volume in this sector is forecast to climb to 110 million a year by 1987.

Besides emus and railcars, passenger rolling stock presently totals 269 cars for long-haul traffic, which is not expected to rise.

Traction
The drive to rationalise use of diesel and electric traction, avoiding diesel haulage under wires, made further strides in 1980, when electric traction was responsible for 2878 million tonne-km, an 88 per cent improvement compared with 1978. Ten 1491 kW diesel-electric C-Cs from General Electric of Brazil have been added to stock, raising the diesel locomotive fleet to 369, of which 72 are shunters. Electric locomotives total 147, of which 130 are line-haul. FEPASA also owns four diesel railcars and 160 emus.

Electrification
FEPASA is investing substantially in improvement of its existing electrified route-length of 1156 km and in extensions. A two-stage plan has been started under financial arrangements with French, Swiss and German Federal Republic banking concerns, which together are putting up US$ 106 million, while Brazilian credit concerns are funding a further US$ 214 million.

Under the first stage the 611 route-km of metre gauge from Uberaba to Mayrink are being electrified at 3 kV dc, with completion scheduled for the

FEPASA Type 6350 3269 kW electric Co-Co locomotive at Rio Claro *(Sergio Martire)*

GE-built Type 6370 2-C + C-2 electric locomotive on FEPASA freight in Campinas *(Sergio Martire)*

Traffic

	1980/81	1981/82*
Total freight tonnage (000)	19 673·4	21 898·5
Total freight tonne-km (million)	6893·4	7355·7
Average net freight train load (tonnes)	665	698
Average freight wagon load (tonnes)	42·5	42·8
Total passenger-km (million)		
suburban	1092·7	1070·2
long-haul	1466·8	1291
Total passenger journeys (million)		
suburban	57·5	56·3
long-haul	5·9	5·2
Average length of passenger journey (km)		
suburban	19	19
long-haul	249	249

* Estimated

end of 1984. The US$320 million turnkey contract for this project was secured by a Franco-Brazilian consortium, led by Francorail-MTE and including the 50 c/s Group. It is a preliminary to electrification of the whole Uberaba-Santos export corridor, which is also being streamlined by construction of a new 77 km Mayrink-Helvetia bypass to eliminate 100 metre-radius curvature. This new line, which is being constructed on a ruling gradient of 1 per cent with 600-metre minimum radius curves, was also to open in 1984; its cost is estimated at just over Cr 24 000 million.

Modernisation of the Helvetia-Guaian line at a cost of Cr 20 000 million, with support from the National Economic Social Development Bank, was approved in 1982.

The second stage of the overall plan involves modernisation of sub-station equipment on the existing electrified network. For this stage 31 new electric locomotives will be acquired, to add to 39 ordered for the first stage. Both batches will be of the same type, the EC362 B-B based on the Alsthom-Atlantique standard-gauge Class 1600 delivered to Netherlands Railways; delivery was to begin in 1982. The chopper-controlled locomotives, with a maximum tractive effort of 300 kN and an hourly 2600 kW rating, are expected to start with haulage of 1500-tonne trains on the Uberaba-Mayrink line, but to work eventually with 3000 tonnes, which would give the new railway an annual operating capacity of 23 million tonnes.

Suburban passenger modernisation

In 1982 FEPASA was completing the first of three stages in a programme due for full completion at the end of 1985 to replace metre-gauge services on the western side of São Paulo with a high-capacity broad-gauge operation. Total cost will be Cr 67 201 million. Tracks are being renewed, stations rebuilt, the electrification modernised, and the existing CTC replaced with a new cab-signalling and speed-control form of ATC; bi-directional operation on multi-track sections has also been provided. To serve the new system a total of 150 three-car, chopper-controlled and stainless-steel bodied emus has been ordered. Two-thirds are being furnished by a Franco-Brazilian group comprising Francorail, Cobrasma, Industria Electrica Brown Boveri of Brazil, CEM-Oerlikon and Jeumont-Schneider, the remaining third, which have Budd bodies and Pioneer bogies, by a consortium of ACEC, Mafersa, Villares and Sorefame.

When all three stages of the project are complete the daily operating capacity of the system will have been lifted from 200 000 to 1·1 million passengers. Delivery of 75 six-car emus was in progress in 1982.

Track
Rail
Type: TR 37, TR 45, TR 50, TR 55, TR 57, TR 68
Weight: 37, 45, 50, 55, 57, 68 kg/m
Cross ties (sleepers)

Wood: 1000 mm gauge 2 × 0·22 × 0·16 m; 1600 mm gauge 2·8 × 0·24 × 0·17 m
Spacing: 1000 mm gauge 1600/km; 1600 mm gauge 1667/km
Rail fastenings: GEO or K; ML
Concrete block: 1000 mm gauge 0·68 ×0·29 × 0·211 m; 1600 mm gauge 0·68 × 0·29 × 0·239 m
Spacing: 1500/km
Fastenings: RN
Concrete (monoblock): (1000 mm gauge only) 2 × 0·22 × 0·21 m to 2 × 0·32 × 0·242 m
Spacing: 1500/km
Fastenings: RN
Minimum curve radius: Main lines 150 m; branches 90 m
Max gradients: Main lines 2·0%; branches 3·0%
Max axleload: 1000 mm gauge 20 tonnes; 1600 mm gauge 25 tonnes

Investment plans 1983 (Cr 000)

Electric locomotives (80, delivery 1983-86)	17 459 370
Freight rolling stock	22 314 670
Locomotive rebuilding	3480
Wagon rebuilding	124 360
New line construction	19 943 190
Track improvements	3 174 110
Electrification	30 474 820
Track maintenance machines	204 200
Bridges and buildings	470 000
Signalling and telecommunications	637 360
São Paulo suburban modernisation	12 236 350
Yards and terminals	351 650
Workshops	469 350
Miscellaneous	599 272
Total	108 462 082

Workshop modernisation plans

Location	(Cr 000)					
	1983	1984	1985	1986	1987	Total
Campinas	125 282	141 448	91 436	22 396	19 028	399 590
Facilities maintenance	90 257	101 371	75 607	6567	1515	275 317
Equipment purchases	35 025	40 077	15 829	15 829	17 513	124 273
Jundiai	20 881	17 344	14 145	3536	3452	59 358
Facilities maintenance	13 556	12 966	9935	—	—	36 457
Equipment purchases	7325	4378	4210	3536	3452	22 901
Rio Claro	128 734	138 838	67 524	106 170	57 253	498 519
Facilities maintenance	115 515	111 559	62 472	90 931	30 142	410 619
Equipment purchases	13 219	27 279	5052	15 239	27 111	87 900
Sorocaba	97 254	70 626	93 903	51 686	55 569	369 038
Facilities maintenance	55 628	25 090	42 300	10 306	10 104	143 428
Equipment purchases	41 626	45 536	51 603	41 380	45 465	225 610
Total	372 151	368 256	267 008	183 788	135 102	1326 505
Facilities maintenance	274 956	250 986	190 314	107 804	41 761	865 821
Equipment purchases	97 195	117 270	76 694	75 984	93 541	460 684

Diesel-electric locomotives

Class	Wheel arrangement	Rated power kW	Tractive effort Continuous at kg	km/h	Max speed km/h	Wheel diameter mm	Total weight tonnes	Length mm	No built	Year first built	Builders* Mechanical parts	Engine & type	Trans-mission
3100	C + C	447	9934	14	80	838	64	11 785	20	1948	GE	CB	GE
3200	B – B	894	15 422	17	138	910	71·2	14 970	22	1957	GE	CB	GE
3500	C – C	671	11 200	18	95	1050	68·1	14 232	9	1957	GE	Alco	GE
3600	B – B	652	13 370	13	100	1016	56·7	12 344	13	1961	GM	GM	GM
3600	B – B	652	15 370	13	100	1016	60·5	11 300	23	1960	GM	GM	GM
3650	B – B	976	16 300	18	100	1016	74·9	14 429	30	1957	GM	GM	GM
3700	B – B	574	12 650	14	90	1050	70	14 500	27	1969	LEW	SACM	LEW
3750	B – B	835	12 650	20	100	1050	74	14 500	16	1968	LEW	SACM	LEW
3800	C – C	1491	22 800	19	103	914	108	16 990	110	1974	GE	GE	GE
7000	B – B	1304	19 600	20	105	1016	110·6	17 120	17	1958	GM	GM	GM
7050	B – B	976	18 160	16	124	1016	80	14 589	18	1959	GM	GM	GM
7760	B – B	574	12 600	14	90	1050	74	14 500	36	1967	LEW	SACM	LEW
7800	C – C	1491	22 800	19	103	914	108	16 990	26	1977	GE	GE	GE

*GE = General Electric
GM = General Motors
LEW = LEW Hennigsdorf
SACM = Société Alsacienne de Constructions Mécaniques de Mulhouse
CB = Cooper Bessemer

Electric locomotives

Class	Wheel arrangement	Line current	Rated output kW	Tractive effort Continuous at kg	km/h	Max speed km/h	Wheel diameter mm	Weight tonnes	Length mm	No built	Year first built	Builders* Mechanical parts	Electrical equipment
2000	1 – C + C – 1	3000 V dc	1729	12 450	12	90	1118	130	18 590	25	1943	GE	GE
2050	1 – C + C – 1	3000 V dc	1729	12 750	17	90	1118	130	18 590	21	1943	West	West
2100	B – B	3000 V dc	1371	11 800	22	90	1117	72·7	13 942	30	1968	GE	GE
6100	2 – C + C – 2	3000 V dc	2846	—	—	145	—	165	—	5	1982	West	rebuilt FEPASA
6150	2 – C + C – 2	3000 V dc	2846	—	—	145	—	165	—	5	1982	West	rebuilt FEPASA
6350	C – C	3000 V dc	3269	22 800	20	134	1168	144	18 339	10	1967	GEBSA	GEBSA
6370	2 – C + C – 2	3000 V dc	2846	14 600	22	145	1168	165	23 101	22	1940	GE	GE
6410	C + C	3000 V dc	1134	13 600	9	65	1015	107	15 291	6	1927	West	West
6420	1 – C + C – 1	3000 V dc	1619	16 620	11	80	1168	133·3	18 212	1	1928	GE	GE
6450	2 – D + D – 2	3000 V dc	3470	35 000	9	110	1200	242·6	27 076	5	1951	GE	GE
6500	B – B	3000 V dc	341	6890	8·5	64	1016	55·5	12 649	9	1924	GE	GE
6510	B – B	3000 V dc	341	6890	8·5	65	1016	55·5	12 649	8	1947	GE	GE

*GE = General Electric   West = Westinghouse   GEBSA = General Electric do Brasil

Electric multiple-units

Class	Cars per unit	Line voltage dc	Motor cars per unit	Motored axles per motor car	Rated output (kW) per motor	Max speed km/h	Weight tonnes per car (M-motor T-trailer)	Total seating capacity	Length per car mm (M-motor T-trailer)	No in service	Rate of acceleration m/s²	Year first built	Builders
4000	3	3000	1	4	130	90	M 44·5 T 25·8 T₁ 25·1	270	M 17 300 T 17 300	2	—	1943	Pullman Standard Car
4100	3	3000	1	4	168	80	M 40 T 30 T₁ 30	270	M 18 300 T 18 300	30	—	1957	Kawasaki Rolling Stock Ltd
9000	3	3000	1	4	207	90	M 49·8 T 32 T₁ 29	270	M 21 000 T 24 000	98	0·7	1978	Cobrasma IE Brown Boveri MTE, TCO
9500	3	3000	1	4	259	90	M 48 T 32 T₁ 28	270	M 22 000 T 27 000	30	0·55	1978	Mafersa Villares Sorefame, ACEC

Diesel railcars

Class	Cars per unit	Motor cars per unit	Motored axles per motor car	Transmission	Rated power (kW) per motor	Max speed km/h	Weight tonnes per car	Total seating capacity	Length per car mm	No in service	Year first built	Builders
5000	1	1	2	Hydraulic	81	90	41·1	56	18 745	2	1962	Budd
5010	1	1	2	Hydraulic	81	90	42·9	48	18 745	2	1962	Budd

Companhia Vale do Rio Doce (CVRD)

Reserves of high-quality iron ore estimated at almost 16 000 million tonnes were discovered in the Serra dos Carajás, in the far north of the country, in 1967 and subsequently deposits of manganese, copper, nickel and bauxite were also revealed. The recession delayed exploitation, but engineering of an 890 km railway to transport the ore to the Atlantic port of São Luis was begun in 1978. In 1982 CVRD, the country's largest ore company, was granted a US$304 million loan from the World Bank and

obtained a further US$123 million loan from West German interests towards the cost, which is now estimated to total more than US$4500 million. A further loan of US$600 million was under negotiation with the European Economic Community. Completion of the infrastructure is forecast for 1985.

The 1600 mm-gauge railway crosses mostly flat terrain, so that maximum gradients can be restricted to 0·4 per cent for loaded and 1 per cent for empty trains, and curvature will be to a minimum 860 metres radius. It is being electrified at 50 kV 60 Hz ac, but electric traction may not be operative until 1987. There are no tunnels and the most significant engineering work is a 2·3 km viaduct over the Toca-

tins river at Maraba. Tracklaying by the Brazilian companies Rodominas and Odebrecht began in 1982.

In the summer of 1982 also the first orders were placed for rolling stock. Brazilian firms were to begin delivery in 1984 of 5278 wagons, all but 400 (for cement) of which would be ore hoppers of probably 100 tonnes glw. In 1983 an initial order was placed with Villares for ten 3300 hp diesel-electric locomotives to the GM SD-40 design, with an option for 23 more.

CVRD already operates mineral railways. Its rail investment planned for 1983 totalled Cr 9085 million.

BULGARIA

Bulgarian State Railways (BDZ)

Iwan-Wazov Str 3, Sofia

Telephone: 87 30 45/674575
Telex: 22423

Minister: Vassil Tzanov
General Manager, Railways: Stoil Ferdov
Traffic Manager: Atanas Tonev
Mechanical Engineer: Genadi Kolev
Signalling and Telecommunications Manager: I Covatshev
Infrastructure Manager: G Detcheu
Rolling Stock Manager: D Mantchev
Commercial Director: S Hhristov

Gauge: 1435 mm; 760 mm
Route length: 4045 km; 245 km
Electrification: 1650 km at 25 kV 50 Hz ac

Transport development
Rail transport has taken an increasingly important role in Bulgaria's communications network following the government's 1980 decision to freeze highway-hauled transport volumes. The increased volume of freight budgeted in the 1981-85 five-year plan is being taken by railways. Structurally, the railway network is basically complete. In recent years, only a few sections of lines have been built either to rationalise the transport system or to create transport facilities for some new industrial objectives and sources of raw materials: Dulovo-Silistra, Zlataritza-Elena, Tscherven brajag-Zlatna Panega, etc. The systematic development of the different modes of transport, including railway transport, and the rational distribution of goods between these modes is the responsibility of the national Transport Authority which combines all the modes, including road transport; this ensures a high degree of efficiency in railway transport.

Traffic
Latest estimate is that the railway will carry 101 million tonnes in 1985 (22 800 million tonne-km), compared with 17 760 million tonne-km in 1980 and 17 705 million tonnes in 1976. Passenger traffic, which was 100·5 million journeys (7035 million

Class 42 (Skoda type 46E) for express passenger trains and freight hauls

passenger-km) in 1980, is expected to rise to 106 million in 1985.

Motive power and rolling stock
Main-line diesels have been built in Romania and the Soviet Union with Hungary and the German Democratic Republic supplying shunters; eight Type V60 diesel-hydraulics were delivered by LEW Hennigsdorf in 1982. The Czechoslovak Skoda works has supplied BDZ with all its electric locomotives: 41 type 42E (Em) Bo-Bo units delivered in 1962/63, 20 type 46E1 Bo-Bo units (1965/66), 30 type 46E2 Bo-Bo units (1967), 20 type 46E3 Bo-Bo locos (1968), 20 type 46E4 units (1970), 23 type 64E1 Bo-Bo units (1971), 20 type 64E2 Bo-Bo units (1973), 13 type 64E3 Bo-Bo units (1974), 14 type 68E1 Bo-Bo units (1975).

The structure of the wagon fleet has been greatly improved by the modernisation of existing wagons and the introduction of heavy-duty and specialised goods wagons for carrying a variety of goods at speeds of 100 to 120 km/h.

The exacting demands for a better passenger ser-

vice have led to a rapid renewal of the fleet of passenger coaches and to the additional introduction of coaches offering a higher level of comfort.

Electrification
Electrification of most of the principal railway lines has now been completed, using single-phase ac with a voltage of 25 kV and 50 Hz frequency. The whole of the 633 km Sofia - Mezdra - Gorna - Orjahovitza - Dybovo - Karlovu - Sofia ring is now under wires. The aim is to electrify the whole 2400 km main-line network by 1985 so that 75 to 80 per cent of traffic will be hauled by electric traction. Main routes still awaiting complete electrification include: Ruse-Varna (212 km), Gorna-Orjahovitza-Varna (220 km), Sofia-Dragoman on the Yugoslav border.

Permanent way and installations
Installation of continuous welded rails has allowed train speeds to be increased to 100-120 km/h on some sections of line. By 1985 double-tracking should be complete on the Sofia-Gorna

Orjahovitza-Varna, Sofia-Plovdiv-Stara Zagora-Burgas and Sofia-Mezdra-Lom main lines. On key routes BDZ is aiming, after double-tracking, for speeds of 140 to 160 km/h for passenger trains and from 100 to 120 km/h for freight trains by perfecting vehicle design, permanent way and signalling techniques.

On high-density lines 60 kg/m rail is laid. Rail of 49 kg/m is used elsewhere, laid on Bulgarian prestressed concrete sleepers secured with K-type fastenings. Track is built for an axleload of 20 tonnes nation-wide and 23 tonnes on a few selected sections. About one-quarter of the main-line system has continuous welded rail and this is being extended.

As part of plans to speed delivery of freight and co-ordinate the operations of rail and road transport, loading and unloading is being concentrated at 100 to 150 terminals. This will help create conditions for full mechanisation of freight handling operations, with more efficient use of containers, pallets and packages.

Signalling
By 1980, a total of 621 km had been equipped with semi-automatic relay blocking, and 400 level crossings were fitted with automatic crossing devices.

Up to 1980, some 1000 route-km of open lines were equipped for CTC, and some 70 per cent of all locomotives were equipped for automatic train control. All stations on the principal lines are being equipped with modern relay-type signal cabins.

BDZ class 43 (Skoda type 68E) electric Bo-Bo locomotive for mixed traffic, equipped with dual controls for tandem operation

BURMA

Burma Railways Corporation

PO Box 118, Bogyoke Aung San Street, Rangoon

Telephone: 14455
Telegrams: Rheostat

Managing Director: Colonel Seng Ya
General Manager: U Aye Pe
Deputy General Manager: U Kyaw Myint
Chief Traffic Manager: U Tun Aung
Chief Mechanical and Electrical Engineer: U Saw Clyde
Chief Engineer: U Kyaw Hlaing

Gauge: 1000 mm
Route length: 3137 km

Transport development
Burma has a metre-gauge network comprising a main section and two short isolated sections of railway. The most important line connects the two principal cities, Rangoon the capital, and Mandalay 619 km to the north. Three passenger trains daily run in each direction, the fastest taking a scheduled 12 hours to cover the journey. Two classes of travel, upper and lower, are offered.

Motive power and rolling stock
Burma Railways has recently strengthened its fleet of diesel-electric locomotives with 12 1600 hp units from Alsthom-Atlantique of France. Delivery brought the number of Alsthom-built motive power units in operation by the railway to 139.

Steam locomotives	217
Diesel locomotives	139
Diesel railcars	13
Passenger coaches	1214
Freight wagons	9040

Track
Standard rail: Flat bottom BS
Main line: 75 and 60 lb (37.2 and 29.8 kg) in 39 ft lengths
Main branches: 60 lb (29.8 kg)
Other branches and sidings: 50 lb (24.9 kg)
Joints: Suspended; joint sleepers 14 in centres. Rails joined by fishplates and bolts
Welded track: 117 ft (35.7 m) lengths. Thermit welded in situ.
Cross ties (sleepers): Hardwood (Xylia Dolabriformis) and creosoted soft wood, 8 in × 4½ in × 6 ft (203 × 115 × 1829 mm)
Spacing
Main line: N + 3
Branch line: N + 2
(N = length of rail in linear yards)

Rail fastening: Dog spikes, elastic rail spikes (Elastic Rail Spike Co Ltd, London). Macbeth rail spikes (Exors of James Mills Ltd, Cheshire, England) are under experimental use
Filling (ballast): Broken stone, 2-¾ in (50.8-19.1 mm), shingle on branch lines
Thickness under sleeper: 6 in (150 mm)
Max curvature
Main line: 6° = radius of 955 ft (291 m)

Branch line: 17° = radius of 338 ft (103 mm)
Max gradient
Main line: 0.5% =1 in 200 compensated
Branch line: 4.0% = 1 in 25 compensated
Max permitted speed
Main line: 30 mph (48 km/h)
Branch line: 20 mph (32 km/h)
Max axleload: 12 tons on 75 and 60 lb rail
Bridge loading: Indian Railway Standard ML

Ordinary-class passenger car supplied by Kawasaki

Class DD 900 diesel-hydraulic locomotive, rated at 960 hp

CAMEROON

Ministry of Transport

Yaoundé, PO Box 1608

Telephone: 22 34 72

Minister: A K Ngome
Secretary General: M Meva'a M'Eboutou
Technical Adviser: R H M Awazi
General Manager, Transport: N Amadou

Regie Nationale des Chemins de Fer du Cameroun (Regifercam)

PO Box 304, Douala

Telephone: 42-60-45
Telegrams: Regifercam, Douala
Telex: 5607

President and General Manager: Adolph Moudiki
Deputy Director Generals: R Kamo
                                 H Leyrat
Administrative Manager: Mpacko Ndedi
Financial Manager: Alfred Tamfu
Engineer, Traction and Rolling Stock: Moyo Djoko
Engineer, Way and Works: A Monayong

Gauge: 1000 mm
Route length: 1168 km

The Cameroon system consists of two single-track lines: the West line running 172 km from Bonaneri to Nkongsamba operated by Regifercam and the Transcameroun line opened in 1974 between Douala-Ngaoundéré (935 km), Otele-Mbalmayo (37 km), and Mbanga-Kumba (29 km).

Motive power and rolling stock

In 1982 Regifercam operated 46 diesel-electric locomotives, 11 railcars, 32 locotractors, 107 passenger cars and 1501 freight vehicles. Delivery of a C$13·4 million order for 10 1700 kW diesel-electric locomotives from Bombardier was due to begin in mid-1983. Tenders were sought in 1983 for construction of a new locomotive depot and enlargement of workshops at Douala.

Civil engineering

Following completion of the Transcameroun line to Ngaoundéré (930 km from Douala) it was decided to re-align the Douala-Yaoundé section to match the standard of the Yaoundé-Ngaoundéré extension. The Transcameroun Railway Authority (Office du Chemin de Fer Transcamerounais) has undertaken the task, with the support of funds from Kreditanstalt für Wiederaufbau (Frankfurt/Main), the German Federal Government, Canada, European, Saudi and African Development Funds, and Fonds d'Aide et de Cooperation. The work has been phased in five stages:

(1) Douala-Edéa; re-alignment to reduce distance from 84 km to 71·25 km
(2) Edéa-Eséka; 89·2 km reduced to 81·2 km
(3) Eséka-Makak; 44·9 km reduced to 36·25 km
(4) Makak-Otélé; 30·3 km reduced to 27 km
(5) Otélé-Yaoundé; 59·4 km reduced to 48·5 km.

At the start of 1983 the work was complete but for the most difficult stretch, the 25 km from Eséka to Maloumé, which entails construction of three tunnels aggregating 3295 metres in length and five viaducts with a total length of 875 metres. Tenders were sought for construction of this final stretch in 1982. Cost is estimated at CFA Fr 34 000 million.

Signalling

A French consortium (Alsthom-Atlantique, Jeumont-Schneider, CSEE, Saxby) won a contract in 1980 to install signalling equipment, telephones and loudspeakers at Douala.

Planned investment 1982-83 (CFA Fr000)

Locomotives	414 500
Rolling stock	368 800
Track	215 000
Track machinery	200 000
Structures	125 000
Signalling and communications	220 000
Yards and terminals	995 000
Miscellaneous	545 000
Total	2953 300

CANADA

Transport Canada

Place de Ville, Ottawa, Ontario K1A ON5

Telephone: (613) 996 5861

Minister: Jean-Luc Pepin
Deputy Minister: Arthur Kroeger
Sr Assistant Deputy Minister: T J Wilkins
Asst Deputy Minister, Strategic Planning: N Mulder
Asst Deputy Minister, Co-ordination: Dr Geneviève Sainte-Marie
Administrator, Surface Transportation: R Y J Giroux
Chairman, Canadian Transport Commission: J A D Magee

Surface Administration (CSTA)

Railway Transportation Directorate
Director General: K Henderson
Freight Capacity Development: A E Pokotylo
Railway Relocation & Crossing: J H Galvin
Railway Planning: R C McElman
Railway Passenger Development: R Tittley
Director General, Transportation and Handling Grains Group Directorate: M E Farquhar

The Railway Transportation Directorate is a policy advisory group with responsibility for Federal interests in the various fields of railway activity.

The Freight Capacity Development Branch of CSTA investigates and encourages the development and implementation of improved systems and methods which will increase railway productivity and capacity. This work is carried out in conjunction with the two major railways and includes the development of joint track use between CN and CP, and the monitoring of railway services and equipment supply.

The Grain Transportation Branch is responsible for policies and programmes related to the improvement of grain handling and transport. The branch serves in a policy advisory role to the Minister of Transport and the Minister responsible for the Canadian Wheat Board.

The Railway Planning Branch develops guidelines for the role of railways in Canada and the form of appropriate federal government involvement to facilitate the administration of railway and railway-related programmes. The branch is also responsible for the department's involvement in rates and subsidies and for the co-ordination of railway legislative improvements.

The Railway Passenger Development Branch is responsible for determining the requirements of a modern and efficient rail passenger service. VIA Rail Canada Inc has been created to provide passenger services previously operated by Canadian National and Canadian Pacific.

Electrification

The Minister of Transport announced in 1982 the creation of a Commission including representatives from Canadian National, Canadian Pacific and VIA Rail as well as of his Ministry and of the National Research Council to study the possibilities for Canadian main-line electrification and propose national standards.

Grain rate settlement

Years of clamour by Canadian National and Canadian Pacific for relief from the historic Crow's Nest Pass agreements which have pegged rates for haulage of grain from the Prairies to the West Coast and to the Great Lakes ports since 1925 were answered in February 1983. The Transport Minister announced that the uneconomic rates of 15 cents a bushel would be phased out in exchange for CN and CP commitments to increase investment during the 1982-83 crop year from C$530 million to C$807 million to raise rail capacity, notably in western Canada. As an immediate offset for the two railways' combined annual loss on grain transport of at least C$300 million the Ministry agreed to pay them an interim C$313 million. Thereafter a statutory annual payment of C$652 million was proposed, in addition to the sums already put up by the Government to subsidise grain hopper wagon purchases and upkeep of Prairie branch lines. The latter, said the Minister, would reach almost C$1000 million over the ensuing three years, providing for purchase of 3840 grain hoppers as well as for more branch line rehabilitation.

The proposals were embodied in a Bill presented to Parliament in May 1983. This specified an annual payment of C$651·6 million grain transport subsidy to the railways. In return the railways were required to guarantee both investment at present levels annually, and also to fulfil preset levels of grain shipment. The Government intended that the rise of rail grain compensation should stimulate investment in big main-line-located silos which could be served by unit trains, so that branch lines and their smaller silos could be progressively eliminated.

Algoma Central Railway

PO Box 7000, Sault Ste Marie, Ontario P6A 5P5

Telephone: (705) 949 2113
Telex: 067 77254

Chairman: Henry N R Jackman
President: Leonard N Savoie
Vice-President, Rail: Stanley A Black

Gauge: 1435 mm
Route length: 518 km

Development

Incorporated in 1899, the company operated for many years chiefly as a wilderness railroad transporting iron ore and forest products out of Northern Ontario. Since 1960 it has become a diversified transport company moving cargo by water, rail and road. Its main line runs 474·7 km north from Sault Ste Marie and serves the natural resource, manufacturing and tourist industries of the Algoma region, operating a regular thrice-weekly passenger train each way and seasonal tourist trains as well as providing a freight service. The company also sails a fleet of 12 dry bulk cargo vessels, principally on the Great Lakes and the St Lawrence Seaway. It deploys a trucking fleet on routes extending from Detroit, Michigan, USA to Toronto and Montreal, and has developed commercial real estate complexes in Sault Ste Marie and Elliot Lake, in addition to the 850 000 acres it owns, inclusive of mineral and timber rights, in the Algoma region.

Traffic

	1980	1981
Total freight tonnage (million)	4·067	4·119
Total freight tonne-km gross (million)	1677·5	1659
Total passenger-km (million)	45·826	47·183
Total passenger journeys	257 787	260 541
Average length of passenger journey (km)	177·8	181·1

Finance

Revenue (C$ million)

Passengers and baggage	2·572
Freight, parcels and mail	29·041
Other income (Government subsidy, lands and forests, switching, demurrage)	4·948
Total	36·561

Expenditure (C$ million)

Staff/personnel expenses	16·468
Materials and services	12·193
Depreciation	1·916
Total	30·577

Investment

The company is increasing its traction fleet by six GP 38-2 2000 hp Bo-Bo diesel-electric locomotives ordered from General Motors of Canada. In 1981 it inaugurated a multi-year programme of main line improvement with installation of 10 miles of 115 lb rail in its Soo Subdivision.

Traction and rolling stock
The company owns 33 locomotives, comprising nine EMD 3000 hp Type SD-40, two EMD 1750 hp Type GP-9, 20 EMD 1500 hp Type GP-7 and two diesel-electric switchers. Its rolling stock consists of 52 passenger cars, which include business and restaurant cars, and 1507 freight cars.

Track
Rail type: 115 RE, 100 RA, 85 CPR, 80 ASCE

Sleepers: Wood 8 ft × 7 in × 9 in
Spacing: 1822/km
Fastenings: Splice bars
Minimum curve radius: 1°
Max curve radius: 13·5°
Max gradient: 1·7%
Max axleload: 67 000 lb

British Columbia Railway

1095 West Pender Street, Vancouver, British Columbia V6E 2N6

Telephone: (604) 683 1381
Telex: 04 352752

President and Chief Executive: M C Norris
Vice-President, Finance: J R Clarke
  Industrial Relations: P A MacDonald
  Operations and Maintenance: N A McPherson
  Administration and Secretary: G L Ritchie
  Marketing and Sales: A C Sturgeon
Chief Mechanical Officer: G L Kelly
Chief Engineer: V W Shtenko
Manager, Operations and Maintenance: A T Shannon
Chief of Transportation: I H Nichols

Gauge: 1435 mm
Route length: 1952·5 km

Development
The British Columbia Railway's main track is geographically segregated into two operating divisions; the Cariboo, and Peace River—Omineca divisions.

Within each of these lie the following subdivisions. Cariboo Division: The Squamish subdivision is the southernmost on the railway, running from Mile 0·0 at North Vancouver, to Mile 157·5 (Lillooet). It is followed by the Lillooet subdivision which runs from Mile 157·5 to Mile 312·7 (Williams Lake) and the Prince George subdivision, which extends from Mile 312·7 to Mile 462·5 (Prince George).
Peace River—Omineca Division: The Peace River portion runs from Prince George, over the Chetwynd subdivision from Mile 462·5 to Mile 659·3 (Chetwynd). The Fort St John subdivision is next, running from Mile 659·3 to Mile 816·5 (Beatton). The railway's northernmost subdivision, the Fort Nelson, follows, extending from Mile 816·5 to Mile 979·4 (Fort Nelson). It should be noted that the 21·1-mile Mackenzie Industrial Lead and the 61·1-mile Dawson Creek subdivisions are also included in the Peace River Division.

The Omineca portion begins at Odell, which lies in the Chetwynd subdivision. It is composed of the Stuart subdivision, which runs from Mile 0·0 at Odel to Mile 151·5, and the Takla subdivision, which extends from Mile 151·5 to Mile 336·0. Beyond Driftwood, which is situated at Mile 220·0, extension construction work was suspended in April 1977.

The economic significance of the British Columbia Railway can be gauged from the fact that some 20 per cent of net rail freight tons loaded in British Columbia originates on the BC Rail line. The railway services approximately 700 carload shippers in the province, including 70 planer and sawmills, six veneer and plywood plants and seven pulp mills. With railway connections at North Vancouver, Prince George and Dawson Creek, BC Rail's freight service extends to all corners of North America. The two national railways of Canada and two major US carriers form a network which links BC Rail with major points on the continent.

Established lines have undergone substantial upgrading since 1977 to make them capable of carrying the increasing tonnage generated. Major programmes have included rail re-laying, ballasting, sleeper-replacement, grade stabilisation, curve elimination and bank widening. New sidings and yards have also been constructed. A three-year upgrading of the Fort Nelson extension was completed in 1981.

The railway's principal yard facilities are at North Vancouver, Squamish, Lillooet, Williams Lake, Quesnel, Prince George, Fort St James, Mackenzie and Fort St John. Industrial Parks are situated at Williams Lake, Prince George, Mackenzie, Fort St John, Dawson Creek, Fort St James and Fort Nelson for the benefit of rail-oriented industries.

British Columbia Railway yards at North Vancouver

Snow clearance near Garibaldi, north of Vancouver

Traffic

	1980	1981
Total freight (tonnes)	7875 345	7565 720
Total freight tonne-km (million)	8281·8	7296·5
Average net freight train load (tonnes)	693·74	784·34
Total passenger journeys	73 514	74 600
Total passenger-km	314 178	308 297
Average length of passenger journey	248·9	197·1

Traffic
The railway operates a rail freight service, principally engaged in transporting British Columbia's natural resources from the central interior and northern parts of the Province. Approximately three-quarters of total traffic volume is derived from the forest industry. One major market is the eastern USA. Bulk commodities now dominate the total traffic volume.

In its eighth year of operation, the Royal Hudson steam excursion train, operated by the railway under contract with the Provincial Government, carried 56 980 passengers on 99 trips, compared with 59 388 passengers on 100 trips in the previous year. Traffic on the railway's regular passenger service in 1981 increased to 74 600 from 73 514 in 1980.

Results (C$ 000)

	1981	1982
	(C$ 000)	
Operating revenues	152 539	159 696
Operating expenses		
Operations	47 266	46 883
Road maintenance	28 582	25 759
Equipment maintenance	46 146	45 281
Depreciation	17 125	17 436
Other	14 176	15 183
Government assistance	(3812)	(8725)
	149 483	141 817
Railway operating profit	3056	17 879
Other income (expense)		
Interest expense	(54 800)	(52 303)
Application of debt servicing grant	52 591	49 985
	(2209)	(2318)
Other income	2318	3023
	109	705
Net income	3165	18 584
Opening deficit	335 855	332 690
Closing deficit	332 690	314 106

Net income in 1982, at C$18·6 million, was the highest in the company's history, despite a 4·7 per cent decline in traffic because of a slump in worldwide lumber demand.

Motive power and rolling stock

At the end of 1982, the railway utilised the following equipment:

Diesel locomotives	126
Freight cars	9811
Diesel railcars (Budd RDC)	5
Passenger cars	6

During 1980/81 the railway purchased 12 new GM-EMD SD40-2 3000 hp diesel locomotives, equipped to permit mid-train remote control operation.

Diesel locomotives

Class	hp	No of units	Manufacturer
SW10	1000	3	MLW
RS16	1600	24	MLW
RS18	1800	30	MLW
RS20	2000	8	MLW
RCL20	2000	8	MLW
RS25	2500	12	Alco
RS30	3000	29	MLW
GF30 (GM SD40-2)	3000	12	GM (Canada)

RCL	Cabless robot-control locomotive
RS	Road switcher
S	Switcher
F	Freight

Civil engineering

A decision to extend the railway 420 miles from Fort St James to Dease Lake was announced in December 1969. Construction was halted in April 1977, at which time rail-laying had been completed for 237 miles. Total contribution to the railway from the Federal Government for its portion of construction costs was C$ 80 million. The extension is now operational to Driftwood 145 miles (232 km) north of Fort St James.

The railway's 250-mile (400 km) Fort Nelson extension, completed in September 1971, was upgraded to branch-line standards through completion in October 1981 of a three-year rehabilitation programme costing approximately C$ 41·5 million. This consisted of renewing sleepers and ballast, rehabilitating existing rail, relaying 50 miles of 85 lb rail with 100 lb rail, cut and bank widening and revisions and construction of a 520-foot-long, 80-foot-high earth-fill crossing at Elleh Creek, 37 miles south of Fort Nelson, to replace a bridge destroyed by a massive landslide in June 1977. The upgrading programme has reduced derailments and maintenance-of-way costs and has resulted in increased operating efficiency.

Tumbler Ridge electrification

The development of British Columbia's north-east coalfields offers encouraging traffic prospects for the future and during 1982 work continued on construction of BC Rail's 129 km Tumbler Ridge branch line to the coalfield area. At the end of the year the grade work was three-quarters and the boring of the 9 km Table and 6 km Wolverine Tunnels roughly half complete. Three of the six major bridges were finished.

The Tumbler Ridge branch is now to be electrified at 25 kV 50 Hz ac and tenders were to be sought for the fixed installations from pre-qualifiers in 1983. First reason for the decision to electrify was that a 230 kV BC Hydro power transmission line was in place already to serve the north-east coal project and Tumbler Ridge townsite. Second, electrification would avoid C$15 million in tunnel ventilation costs in the two major tunnels. A third factor was the availability of energy conservation funding. C$5 million towards the cost of electrification was provided by the Federal government's energy conservation and renewable energy development and demonstration programme and was matched by a further C$5 million from provincial government sources.

Seven Type GF6C 6000 hp Co-Co electric locomotives have been ordered from General Motors of London, Ontario. Delivery will commence in late 1983. Costing approximately C$2·5 million per unit, they will be full-width car-body units 20·7 metres in length, fitted with EMD's HTC high-adhesion bogie and radar speed measurement devices for slip control. They will normally operate in back-to-back pairs. Transformers and converters will be supplied by ASEA. Rheostatic braking will be provided. Each

Budd diesel railcar of British Columbia Railway

Location Identification Control installation at North Vancouver

Tumbler Ridge branch construction in progress

train will consist of 98 118-tonne hopper cars equipped with rotating couplers to permit unloading without the necessity to break up trains.

Capital cost of the electrification is put at C$57 million, as against C$42·8 million for diesel operation.

The coal will move in unit trains along the branch line to Anzac and down BC Rail's main track to Prince George for interchange with the CNR for the run to the coal port at Prince Rupert. Before long total coal tonnage moving over BC Rail's line each year should far surpass total annual tonnage of all commodities now being handled by the railway. This broadening of the traffic base will reduce the railway's present heavy dependence on forest products.

The railway's new headquarters, BC Rail Centre, in North Vancouver's Lonsdale Quay Development, built at a cost of C$ 13·8 million, was due to be completed by the end of 1982. It will consolidate some 500 employees from nine separate areas in one central location.

In March 1983 BC Rail was to commission a radio-controlled, computer-assisted traffic control system known as Location Identification Control (LIC) over 251 km (156 miles) of its Squamish subdivision between North Vancouver and Lillooet. Total cost of research and development and the purchase of equipment from Glenayre Electronics Ltd was C$3·6 million.

Using an existing chain of six microwave stations, 122 track-mounted transponders laid between the rails and a computer at a despatch centre in North Vancouver, it will give reports on train positions and speeds at 5-second intervals. The railway has fitted 31 freight locomotives and five Budd diesel railcars with terminals which visually display the train speed, indicate its whereabouts to within $1/10$ mile accuracy, and show whether it has authority to proceed. Trainmen will continue to use the microwave network for voice contact with train despatchers.

The computer in North Vancouver will relay train positions to a large diagrammatic display board. The computer will glean its information about train whereabouts through the microwave chain, which it will use to conduct a continuous sweep of the subdivision, interrogating trains as to their whereabouts. The memory circuits of the equipment carried on the traction units not only record positions yielded by transponders but note odometer readings. Using a combination of the two sets of information, the computer can track the position of trains travelling between transponders to an accuracy of 160 metres.

Cabooses are being equipped with simple transmitting devices to indicate whether the vehicles have cleared switchpoints at sidings.

Artist's impression of GM-EMD GF6C 6000 hp 25 kV 50 Hz electric locomotives for Tumbler Ridge branch

Canadian National (CN Rail)

PO Box 8100, Montreal, Quebec H3C 3N4, Canada

Telephone: (514) 877 5430
Telex: 055 605 19

Chairman: J H Horner
President and Chief Executive Officer: J M LeClair
CN Rail, President and Chief Operating Officer: R E Lawless
  Vice-President, Operations: J L Cann
  Vice-President, Marketing: J H D Sturgess
  Vice-President, Finance and Planning: J Horrocks
  Chief of Transportation: J A Reoch
  Chief of Motive Power and Car Equipment: V H Mizrahi
  Chief Engineer: P R Richards

Gauge: 1435 mm; 1067 mm
Route length: 38 454 km; 1146 km

CN Rail is the largest operating division of Canadian National, a diversified transport and communications company owned by the Canadian Government. Other divisions of the company include the Grand Trunk Corporation, which connects the Canadian railway system with the industrial heartland of the United States through CN-owned railways; and CN Enterprises, which is responsible for all non-rail activities of the corporation, including CN Telecommunications, CN Trucking (transcontinental trucking subsidiaries operating across Canada), CNX (express freight), CN Hotels and Tower, CN Marine (ferry operations and coastal shipping on Canada's east coast), CN Real Estate, CN Exploration (mineral and petroleum resource development), and CANAC Consultants (international transport consulting).

CN Rail, Canada's largest railway system, serves all 10 provinces and the two northern territories and provides access to the country's rich natural resources. In the island province of Newfoundland, CN Rail's subsidiary TerraTransport operates rail, intermodal, package freight and bus services.

Results
In recent years, following an extensive corporate restructuring, and a recapitalisation which saw the conversion to equity of more than C$800 million of debt held by the Federal government, CN has moved into profit. However, hard-hit by the economic recession of 1981-82, CN Rail operations showed a net loss of nearly C$35 million in 1982.

CN unit coal train in Alberta

Results	1980	1981 (C$ 000)	1982
Revenues	2 664 373	3 074 585	2 961 504
Expenses	2 429 125	2 859 619	2 996 403
Income (loss)	235 248	214 966	(34 899)

Improvement is anticipated for 1983 and beyond, based on the likelihood that some general economic recovery would begin in 1983, and on the 1983 revision by the Canadian Government of out-of-date statutory rates for the transport of western Canadian grain destined for export (see under Transport Canada).

CN Rail's subsidiary TerraTransport lost some C$32 million in 1982. Plant rationalisation and improvements in productivity continue to receive strong emphasis and significant reduction of the deficit is expected in 1983 and subsequent years.

Freight
The volume of freight traffic carried by CN Rail, expressed in revenue ton-miles, fell by 11·7 per cent in 1982 compared with 1981, despite a 6·8 per cent increase in the handling of grain at both commercial and statutory rates. There was an increase of 1·8 million tons, or 12·4 per cent, in the volume of grain

carried at statutory rates, but because these so-called Crows Nest Pass rates amounted to only one-fifth of the operating cost, the volume rise compounded financial losses. Declines in freight movements were steepest in the fuels and chemicals, ores, minerals and metals, and automotive sectors. Overall freight revenues in 1982 were C$2290 million, down by C$189 million, or 7·6 per cent, from 1981.

Other income
Revenues from other sources also declined. The operating contract with VIA Rail Canada, the Crown Corporation responsible for rail passenger services, produced C$340·4 million, or C$2·8 million less than in the previous year. This reduction was a consequence of the cutback in late 1981 of about 20 per cent of national rail passenger services. Government payments for losses on subsidised branch lines rose to C$212·8 million, an increase of C$92·2 million over 1981, of which C$71·5 million was for losses incurred in prior years.

Economies
The severe reductions in traffic and income forced a major curtailment of expenditure and employment levels in 1982. Total employment was reduced by approximately 5500, or 10 per cent of the work force. The measures taken were effective in reducing expenses. However, the effect of inflationary pressure was nonetheless significant, due to a 12 per cent increase in the general wage scale over 1981 and a 14 per cent increase in the cost of diesel fuel. The costs of other materials and services rose by an average seven per cent.

Capital expenditure
In 1982 CN Rail made capital expenditures of C$470·2 million, of which C$174·3 million was for replacement and renewal of basic roadway, plant and property. Programmes for the installation of new replacement rail cost C$71·1 million and required 541·6 km of rail. A total of 1·4 million new wooden and concrete sleepers were installed at a cost of C$38·4 million. Track ballast enhancement programmes involved a capital expenditure of C$20·2 million.

Expenditure on rolling stock and other equipment was C$123·5 million, and covered the acquisition of 20 diesel-electric locomotives, 300 woodchip gondola cars and 100 piggyback freight cars.

Nearly C$83 million was spent in 1982 on CN Rail's plant expansion programme, aimed at increasing capacity on the western main line between Winnipeg, Manitoba, and Vancouver, British Columbia. This expansion is required to carry projected increased volumes of bulk export commodities, including grain, potash, sulphur, and petro-chemicals. In addition, C$42·2 million was spent on the British Columbia North Line, which will carry unit trains of coal from new mining developments in north-east British Columbia to Prince Rupert.

Double-tracking
For CN Rail, the key to expanding capacity in western Canada is the double-tracking of heavily-travelled sections of the railway's western main line. In 1980-82 double-tracking began in earnest, with expenditure approaching C$143 million. During 1983-87, following full resolution of the statutory grain rate problem, CN Rail plans to spend C$700 million on double-tracking in western Canada. If this expansion had been carried out in an earlier era, it might have been necessary to double-track the entire line at prohibitive cost. Though the work carried out in the 1980s will be expensive, the application of new technologies means that only critical sections need be doubled. State-of-the-art signalling and communication techniques, which take advantage of new computer technology, provide hitherto unavailable refinements in train movement control, and permit operation of the system as if it were double-tracked for its entire length. This, in turn, will confer the capacity increases needed before the end of the century.

In western Canada CN Rail's capital spending will total C$338 million in 1983. Capacity expansion from Winnipeg west on CN Rail's south line to Vancouver and its north line to Prince Rupert will cost C$192 million. A further C$122 million will be spent on rail system maintenance programmes and the balance of C$24 million will go towards the expansion of intermodal terminals and the introduction of general productivity projects. The C$192 million for capacity expansion will include terminal improvements at Winnipeg, Edmonton, Jasper, Boston Bar and North Vancouver, and signal system improvements between Kamloops and Boston Bar.

Upgrading the British Columbia north line will require C$105 million for rail, sleepers, ballast,

CN Rail unit train of Government-owned grain hoppers in Quebec

CN Rail lays approximately 350 000 concrete sleepers a year

First of 20 new diesel locomotives based on Bombardier's 3200 hp HR616 Co-Co design, with wide, tapered body and new air ducting system for improved snow protection

drainage, bridges, sidings and signalling work, as well as terminal improvements at Prince George, Smithers, Watson Island, Terrace, Endako and Ridley Island at Prince Rupert. On the south line, at a cost of C$87 million, CN Rail will bring into service a further 200 km of double track between Edmonton, Alberta and Valemount, British Columbia. Work will continue on another 35 km of double track in Alberta and British Columbia.

Following full resolution of the statutory grain rate problem, CN Rail estimates that in 1983-87 it could increase its planned capital expenditure of C$2100 million some 73 per cent by a further C$1600 million. Much of the addition would be allocated to capacity expansion programmes, and C$2600 million, about 60 per cent of the total capital expenditures, would be spent on the west.

Almost C$1100 million would be spent on the south route to Vancouver. Of that amount, C$700 million would be required for double-tracking and a further C$75 million for signal systems. Work at major terminals would take C$252 million, and C$38 million would be spent at intermediate terminals. Equipment facilities would require C$18 million.

Almost C$500 million would be spent on the north line to Prince Rupert, about half of it on upgrading the plant. Improved signal systems on the line would require expenditures of C$100 million, with siding extensions accounting for another C$45 million. Equipment facilities would take C$40 million and new buildings C$11 million.

Maintaining the existing rail infrastructure in the west would absorb C$712 million over the same five-year period and provision of a suitable equipment fleet would require C$714 million; of that, C$484 million would be spent on acquisitions, C$190 million on conversions of existing equipment and C$40 million on intermodal equipment.

Assuming full resolution of the statutory grain problem, it was estimated that between 1983 and 1987 approximately 9700 person-years of work would be created. The seasonal nature of construction activity means that the number of jobs generated in railway work would be considerably higher.

Intermodal development

CN Rail continues to seek new business opportunities and the 'Laser' piggyback service for the movement of highway trailers between Toronto and Montreal is a case in point. Based on market studies, knowledge of modern distribution techniques and productive use of existing facilities and equipment, this service, launched in late 1982, offered shippers a competitively-priced, fuel-efficient alternative to congested highway routes, and is expected to be profitable.

In 1982 TerraTransport began implementing a marketing and operational programme to shift emphasis from conventional rail cars to containers. This was to be accomplished by establishing a rail container service for general traffic to and from Newfoundland. TerraTransport has already started to convert existing boxcar traffic to containers and this process will be expanded in the near future for traffic presently moving by bulkhead flatcars, hopper cars, and tank cars. In the latter case disposable liners are used for corrosive cargo. This initiative is expected to improve the marketability of railway transport in Newfoundland and help to slow down the deficit of the company.

Computerised traffic control

In 1982 CN Rail commissioned the first stage of an advanced computer-based traffic control system developed 'in-house' by a working group from its Engineering and Transportation departments. The design permits quick and inexpensive modifications, and is claimed to offer more flexibility than currently available off-the-shelf systems. Each installation consists of a display control board which monitors trains between the various subdivisions of territory controlled; a micro-computer with access to central management information system (MIS) computers; and various communications auxiliaries.

Each section of the system is being introduced in four phases. Phase I puts the system on-line but leaves manual control entirely with dispatchers. The system remains in this mode until 'debugging' is complete. Phase II provides automatic signal clearing for both opposing and following movements. In addition, computerised meet logic, using averaged train running times for the territory controlled, will predict the locations of train meetings and, unless otherwise instructed by the controller, the computer will programme signals to execute the meets.

Phase III brings the MIS computers on stream. At present, communication between the train dispatcher and other operating personnel is generally verbal with all records being compiled manually. Phase III will see data links established between the

CN Rail's P-811 track renewal train, the only one in Canada, for laying up to 2 miles of concrete-sleepered track a day

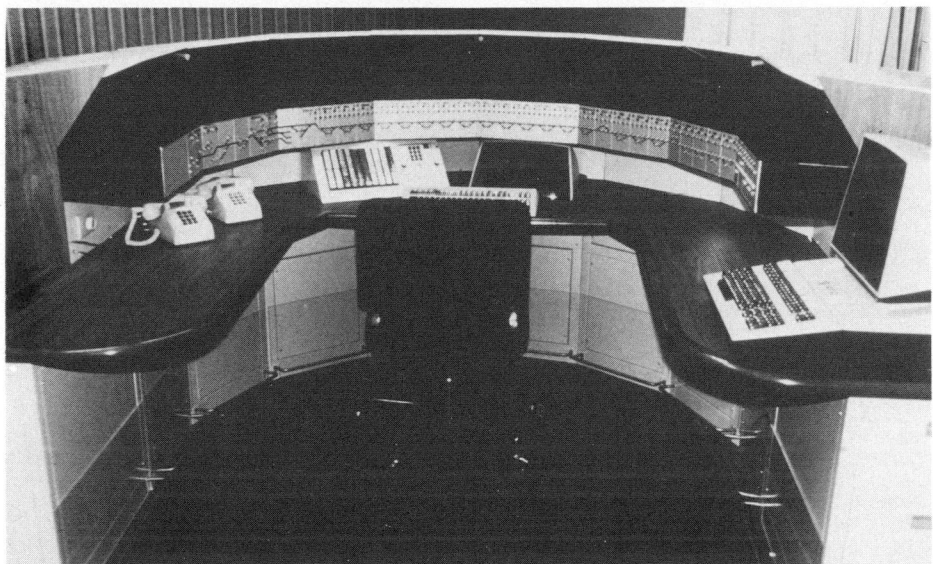

Operating console of CN Rail's new computer-based traffic control system

MIS computers and selected remote terminals, and the train dispatcher. All transmissions and data recording relating to train sheets, line-ups, train orders, clearances, dangerous and dimensional traffic, and crew consists will be made through the MIS computers. In addition, the computers will automatically generate various historical data and summaries which are now not available. A significant reduction in train dispatcher workload will be achieved, allowing controllers more time for critical operating decisions.

Phase IV refines the computerised meet logic to include train priorities, weight-to-power ratios and their impact on train movements, scheduling, temporary speed restrictions and routing. The system will be able to predict meeting points for all opposing movements, recalculate when necessary, by making adjustments as trains progress, and give the estimated times of arrival at terminating stations. This phase will also see the installation of colour-graphics video displays which will show a time/distance plot of trains under control.

A prototype system went into service in Winnipeg, Manitoba, in July 1978, on the line from Winnipeg to Atikokan, Ontario. The prototype provided the first CTC capability on that part of CN Rail's major link to Thunder Bay. The production system went on-line in Edmonton, Alberta in June 1982 at a cost of C$1·3 million. During the development and installation in Edmonton, new approaches to system programming methods, plus an increase in signals staff, achieved a four-to-five-year advance in overall system implementation time. This will permit developers to meet CN Rail's plant expansion schedules and balance workloads, and will offer even greater returns from existing MIS computer installations. The next installation was scheduled for Kamloops, British Columbia in March 1983.

Automated hump yard

A pilot project to automate train activities within a hump yard is under way at Symington Yard in Winnipeg. Robot locomotives are being computer-controlled to perform all the work necessary within the yard.

Railway Electronic Identification System (REIS)

Working with an Edmonton firm, CN Rail is developing a transponder-based-system which electronically identifies each car in a passing train.

Track

Rail, types and weights: Current sections being bought are 136 RE, 132 RE, 115 RE and 100 ARA-A. Balance is 31 different older sections 130 to 50 lb/yard

Cross ties (sleepers)

Thickness

Wood: Main lines: 7 or 6 in (180 or 150 mm)
   Branch lines: 6 in (150 mm)
Concrete (CN 60A): 8 in (200 mm) at rail seat

Spacing

Wood: Main lines: 3110 per mile (1932/km)
Concrete: 2640 per mile (1765/km)

Rail fastenings

Wood: 6 or 5½ × ⅝ in (150 or 140 × 16 mm)
Concrete: Pandrol

Welded rail

Electric pressure flash-butt welded into lengths of about 1480 ft (451 m) in central plants. After unloading at laying site rail may be electric pressure flash-butt field welded by portable plants into longer lengths before laying, or welded by aluminothermic process after laying.

(See Addenda for Montreal commuter operation)

Diesel locomotives

Class	hp	Max speed km/h	Continuous tractive effort 000 kg	Weight in working order (tonnes) On drivers	Total	Year built	No of units	Builder
Newfoundland								
GR-9b	875	96	17	111	166	1956	6	GM
GR-12a	1200	96	40	221	221	1952	3	GM
GR-12b	1200	96	40	222	222	1953	6	GM
GR-12g	1200	96	40	226	226	1956	24	GM
GR-12p	1200	96	40	227	227	1958	3	GM
GR-12x	1200	96	40	227	227	1960	9	GM
Canadian lines								
Boosters (no engines)								
MH-00a	—	64	36	259	259	1964-65	9	CN
GH-00a	—	105	49	258	258	1978	19	GM
MY-00a	—	64	36	253	253	1964-65-66	6	CN
GH00b	—	105	49	258	258	1980	4	GM
GY00a	—	105	49	258	258	1980	12	GM
Road switching								
ER-6a	600	88	23	140	140	1950	3	GE
GH-20b	2000	105	49	257	257	1972-73	14	GM
GH-20b	2000	105	49	257	257	1972-73	9	GM
GY-12d	1200	105	40	246	246	1956	2	
GR-12m	1200	105	30	159	239	1958	29	GM
*GR-12s	1200	105	30	158	238	1959	5	GM
*GR-12t	1200	105	30	160	239	1959	15	GM
*GR-12w	1200	105	30	160	239	1959	18	GM
*GR-12z	1200	105	30	159	238	1960	10	GM
GR12zc	1200	105	30	158	237	1959	5	GM
GR-12d	1200	105	40	225	225	1956	13	GM
	1200	105	40	246	246	1956	3	
GR-12f	1200	105	40	225	225	1956	21	GM
GR-12h	1200	105	40	226	226	1956-57	21	GM
GR-12k	1200	105	40	226	226	1957	15	GM
GR-121	1200	105	40	225	225	1958	16	GM
GR-12r	1200	105	40	223	223	1958	31	GM
GR-12u	1200	105	40	223	223	1959	19	GM
GR-12y	1200	105	40	222	222	1960	40	GM
GR-12e	1200	105	40	246	246	1955-56	5	GM
MR-14b	1400	105	30	160	240	1959	7	MLW
MR-14c	1400	105	30	160	240	1960	31	MLW
GRG-12n	1200	105	40	246	246	1958	4	GM
GR-12n	1200	105	40	246	246	1958-59	14	GM
MR-20a	2000	105	50	262	262	1973	28	MLW
MR-20b	2000	105	50	260	260	1974	30	MLW
MR-20c	2000	105	50	260	260	1976	20	MLW
MR-20d	2000	105	50	260	260	1981	10	MLW
MR-18e	1800	129	44	235	235	1959	28	MLW
MRE-18g	1800	148	38	255	255	1960	4	MLW
MR-18g	1800	148	38	239	239	1960	2	MLW
MR-24a	2400	120	47	260	260	1964	2	MLW
MR-24b	2400	120	47	260	260	1966	19	MLW
MR-24c	2400	120	47	260	260	1967	17	MLW
MR-18b	1800	120	47	246	246	1957	54	MLW
MR-18c	1800	120	47	246	246	1957-58	28	MLW
MR-18d	1800	120	47	247	247	1958	44	MLW
MR-18f	1800	120	44	233	233	1959	13	MLW
GR-418a	1800	105	49	257	257	1981-82	12	GM
GR-418b	1800	105	49	257	257	1982	5	GM
GR-25a	2500	105	49	257	257	1964	2	GM
GR-430a	3000	105	50	260	260	1966	9	GM
GR-430b	3000	105	50	259	259	1967	4	GM
	3000	143	50	259	259	1967	2	
GR-17p	1750	143	33	238	238	1957	7	GM
	1750	105	44	236	236	1957	23	
GR-17y	1750	105	44	235	235	1959	7	GM
GR-17n	1750	105	44	232	232	1957	20	GM
GR-17q	1750	105	44	232	232	1958	16	GM
GR-17t	1750	105	44	230	230	1958	23	GM
GR-17u	1750	105	44	229	229	1959	64	GM
GR-17z	1750	105	44	229	229	1959	13	GM
GR-17a	1750	105	44	248	248	1955	22	GM
GR-17f	1750	105	44	247	247	1955-56	38	GM
GR-17g	1750	105	44	240	240	1956	6	GM
GR-17h	1750	105	44	247	247	1956-57	35	GM
GR-17m	1750	105	44	247	247	1957	19	GM
GR-17r	1750	105	44	248	248	1957-58	8	GM
GR-17za	1750	105	48	248	248	1957	5	GM
GR-17zb	1750	105	48	248	248	1958-60	5	GM
GR-20b	2000	105	49	257	257	1972-73	38	GM
GR-20c	2000	105	49	257	257	1973-74	50	GM
Road passenger								
GPA-17a	1750	143	33	256	256	1954-55	11	GM
GPA-17b	1750	143	33	256	256	1955	1	GM
GPA-17c	1750	143	33	256	256	1957	7	GM
GPA-17d	1750	143	33	257	257	1957	10	GM
GPA-17e	1750	143	33	257	257	1958	9	GM
GPB-17a	1750	143	33	256	256	1954-55	9	GM
GPB-17b	1750	143	33	256	256	1955	1	GM
GPB-17c	1750	143	33	256	256	1957	7	GM
GPB-17d	1750	143	33	256	256	1957	10	GM
GPB-17e	1750	143	33	256	256	1958	7	GM
MPA-18c	1800	148	38	261	261	1955	2	MLW
MPA-18a	1800	148	38	259	259	1958	6	MLW
MPA-18b	1800	148	38	258	258	1959	26	MLW
MPB-18c	1800	148	38	258	258	1955	2	MLW
MPB-18a	1800	148	38	258	258	1958	7	MLW
MPB-18b	1800	148	38	258	258	1959	5	MLW

Class	hp	Max speed km/h	Continuous tractive effort 000 kg	Weight in working order (tonnes)		Year built	No of units	Builder
				On drivers	Total			
Switching								
MH-10r	1000	64	49	258	258	1959	5	MLW
MH-10r	1000	64	49	258	258	1959	4	MLW
MY-10r	1000	64	47	253	253	1959	10	MLW
GY-9d	900	64	36	253	253	1958	6	GM
GS-12a	1200	64	36	247	247	1952	10	GM
GS-12e	1200	64	36	246	246	1956	11	GM
GS-12f	1200	64	36	246	246	1957	3	GM
GS-12g	1200	64	36	246	246	1959	2	GM
GS-8a	800	64	36	232	232	1951	22	GM
GS-8b	800	64	36	232	232	1951	12	GM
GS-9a	900	64	36	229	229	1953-54	24	GM
GS-9c	900	64	36	232	232	1957	10	GM
GS-9d	900	64	36	233	233	1958	10	GM
GS-9d	900	64	36	249	249	1958	3	GM
MS-10e	1000	64	34	230	230	1954	1	MLW
MS-10g	1000	64	34	230	230	1955-56	27	MLW
MS-10h	1000	64	34	231	231	1955	2	MLW
MS-101	1000	64	34	229	229	1956-57	17	MLW
MS-10n	1000	64	34	228	228	1957	6	MLW
MS-10p	1000	64	34	232	232	1958	7	MLW
MS-10q	1000	64	36	233	233	1959	23	MLW
MS-10r	1000	64	47	246	246	1959	7	MLW
Road freight								
*MF-30a	3000	120	73	386	386	1967	2	MLW
*MF-30b	3000	120	74	388	388	1967-68	42	MLW
*MF-36a	3600	120	74	388	388	1970	12	MLW
*MF-36b	3600	120	74	388	388	1971	17	MLW
*GF-30c	3000	105	74	389	389	1967	8	GM
*GF-30d	3000	105	74	388	388	1967-68	66	GM
*GF-30e	3000	105	74	389	389	1969	50	GM
*GF-30h	3000	105	74	388	388	1969-70-71	48	GM
*GF-30k	3000	105	74	388	388	1971	50	GM
*GF-30m	3000	105	74	388	388	1971	15	GM
*GF-30n	3000	105	74	385	385	1975	20	GM
*GF-30p	3000	105	74	385	385	1975	17	GM
*GF-30q	3000	105	74	387	387	1976	15	GM
*GF-30r	3000	105	74	384	384	1978	20	GM
*GF-30s	3000	105	74	384	384	1979	10	GM
GF-30t	3000	105	74	387	387	1980	30	GM
GF-30u	3000	105	74	387	387	1980	10	GM
GF-620a	2000	105	71	372	372	1976	4	GM
GFA-17a	1750	105	44	229	229	1972-73-74	30	CN
GFB-17a	1750	105	44	230	230	1972-73	10	CN
GF-430a	3000	129	47	262	262	1974	50	GM
	3000	105	50	262	262	1974	40	
GF-430b	3000	105	50	262	262	1974	40	GM
GF-430c	3000	105	50	263	263	1975	102	GM
GF-430d	3000	105	50	261	261	1976	35	GM

*6 axle A1A A1A
Notes: GM   General Motors Diesel Ltd
       EMD   General Motors (Electro-Motive Division)
       MLW   Montreal Locomotive Works
       GE   General Electric
All units have 40 in diameter wheels, 4 axles (B-B) except as shown by * and are diesel-electric

Electric locomotives

Class	Wheel arrangement	Line current	Rated output hp	Tractive effort (full field)			Max speed mph (km/h)	Wheel dia in (mm)	Weight tonnes	Length ft in (mm)	No built	Year built	Builders	
				Max lb (kg)	Continuous lb (kg)	at mph (km/h)							Mechanical parts	Electrical equipment
Z-1-a	B+B	3000 V dc	1100	78 699 (173 500)	8436 (18 600)	36·5 (22·7)	88 (55)	1168 (46)	86	11 379 (37' 4")	6	1914	GE	GE
Z-4a	B+B	3000 V dc	1100	91 400 (201 500)	9707 (21 400)	33·6 (20·9)	88 (55)	1295 (51)	101	12 192 (40' 0")	5	1924	English Electric	EE
Z-5a	B-B	3000 V dc	1100	77 883 (171 700)	8119 (17 900)	36·3 (22·6)	96 (60)	1016 (40)	86	13 056 (42' 9⅞")	3	1950	GE	GE

Grand Trunk Corporation

The Grand Trunk Corporation is the holding company for CN's three wholly-owned US railways. For details of results and railroads see US Class I railroads section.

VIA Rail
VIA Rail Canada Ltd

1801 McGill College Avenue, Suite 1300, Montreal, Quebec

Telephone: (514) 286 2311

Chairman: Harold Renouf
President and Chief Executive: Pierre Franche
Executive Vice President: B Eldon Horsman
Vice-President, Marketing: Howard E Whiting
  Development: R Bechamp
  Operations: R J Guiney
  Human Resources: J-P Laroche
  Law and Secretary: G Fortin
  Finance and Administration: J A Hanna
Director General, Corporate Affairs: Gilles Dufault
  Public Relations: E LeBlanc

Vice-Presidents
  VIA Atlantic: A W Raftus
  VIA Quebec: J L Moisan
  VIA Ontario: R L Borden
  VIA West: H F Murray

Total track operated: 18 500 km

Originally incorporated as an independent subsidiary of Canadian National in 1977, VIA Rail Canada Inc became an autonomous Crown Corporation in April 1978. VIA is responsible for the management of all those rail passenger services previously operated by CN and CP Rail, except commuter services.

VIA's creation was a tangible response to the Canadian Government's January 1976 rail passenger policy calling for a new approach to passenger rail services in return for which the Federal Government would consider absorbing 100 per cent of the losses incurred. (Since 1967, under the terms of the National Transportation Act, the Federal Government had been paying the railways for 80 per cent of their passenger service losses.) In 1976, the last year during which CN and CP Rail were mostly responsible for passenger services, the railway companies had a joint loss of C$ 55 million on passenger services despite the subsidy programme.

VIA contracts with the Federal Government for the provision of those rail passenger services specified by the Minister of Transport. In turn, VIA contracts with railway companies for the operation of these services and with non-railway companies for the provision of incidental goods and services. Corporately, VIA's primary responsibility centres on the performance of customer services (on-board services, information, reservations, fares, baggage handling, store functions, claims handling, marketing, advertising and accounting).

During 1978, VIA purchased CN's passenger fleet for approximately C\$ 54 million and CP Rail's passenger fleet for C\$ 13 million, including motive power. The Corporation has executed a major refurbishing programme.

In March 1980, VIA introduced a computerised reservations and automated ticketing system, RESERVIA. Developed in co-operation with Air Canada, the new system is fully compatible with the airline's.

While VIA has not yet purchased the stations it requires, the Corporation has launched major studies, the purpose of which is to identify suitable sites for intermodal transport centres.

Service reduction

As the price of providing adequate funding for new equipment and a sustained level of operating subsidy for VIA inter-city corridor operation in Ontario and Quebec, Transport Minister Jean-Luc Pepin ordered a 19·5 per cent reduction in VIA services in 1981. Despite strong public opposition the cuts were executed in mid-November 1981. They included elimination of the overnight 'Atlantic Limited' between Montreal and St John, New Brunswick, of the 'Super Continental' transcontinental service via Ottawa, Saskatoon, Edmonton and Jasper to Vancouver, reduction of daily to thrice-weekly operation on six country routes and abolition of 13 daytime inter-city services. In the Montreal-Ottawa, Montreal-Toronto and Toronto-Windsor corridors, however, 'Rapido' service was expanded to 18 trains.

The Government argued that the country could not afford more than C\$ 500 million a year to operate and equip VIA, and that this would be inadequate to keep pace with the escalating upkeep costs of VIA's obsolescent, inherited equipment if the VIA network were not reduced. In exchange for the cutbacks, VIA was offered C\$ 1100 million of operating subsidies for the ensuing three years and, for the same period, a C\$ 46 million capital budget. The latter would cover purchase of 10 additional LRC trains for extension of their use to the Maritimes and the west, improvement of equipment on the residual transcontinental service, and renewal or refurbishing of VIA's fleet of 85, mostly Budd RDC railcars.

LRC introduction

VIA took delivery from Bombardier Inc of 21 LRC locomotives and 50 LRC passenger cars in 1981/82. A further 10 LRC locomotives and 50 cars, worth C\$ 100 million, were ordered for delivery in 1983, and options agreed for 20 more sets, to be delivered in 1983-84. The LRC locomotives and their automatic tilt-body cars are designed for operation at up to 200 km/h, but are presently limited to 155 km/h (temporarily reduced to 128 km/h in late 1982 while measures were taken to improve locomotive riding).

The full public service debut of LRC equipment was held back by teething troubles until June 1982, when three daily round trips between Montreal and Toronto, three between Montreal and Ottawa, two between Montreal and Quebec and one each between Ottawa and Toronto, Toronto and Windsor and Toronto and Sarnia became operative. With the delivery of the additional 10 locomotives and 50 cars in 1983 additional services between Edmonton and Calgary, Halifax and St John-Fredericton, and Montreal and the Maritimes were planned.

Statistics released by the Canadian Transport Commission in 1982 showed VIA Rail's inter-city corridor services to be incurring losses of: Montreal-Quebec, C\$9·8 million; Montreal-Ottawa, C\$13·4 million; Montreal-Toronto. C\$41·2 million; Ottawa-Toronto, C\$12·8 million; Toronto-Sarnia, C\$19·3 million; Toronto-Niagara Falls, C\$4·5 million; Toronto-Windsor, C\$22·5 million; and Montreal-Quebec (CP), C\$2·9 million. However, VIA Rail claims 15 to 20 per cent of the Montreal-Toronto and 25 per cent of the Toronto-Windsor inter-city passenger travel market. It is confident that with faster transits it can capture 30 to 40 per cent of the total Canadian inter-city market in the 300-400 km journey range. It was therefore preparing in 1983 to present to the Government a plan for rail route restructuring, allied to some new infrastructure construction, which would give its trains a segregated right-of-way between Windsor, Toronto, Ottawa, Montreal and Quebec and permit an intensified LRC service at speeds up to 200 km/h. Cost of the scheme was put at C\$2000 million. The objectives include a 3 hours 40 minutes transit between Toronto and Montreal, compared with 4½ hours at present, and 1½ hours between Montreal and Quebec, compared with 2 hours 40 minutes at present.

For more immediate improvement of the Montreal-Quebec service, VIA Rail has been considering reopening Quebec's former downtown station, Gare du Palais, in place of the suburban station at Ste Foy currently in use, reverting to an inter-city route through Montreal's Mount Royal tunnel, and building new stations at Laval and Trois Rivières.

Finance

VIA Rail was seeking in 1982 to renegotiate the terms for its use of CN and CP infrastructure and personnel. Payments in 1981, at C\$397 million, were close to the C\$400 million total of Government subsidy.

Traction and rolling stock

At the end of 1982 VIA Rail was operating 148 diesel-electric line-haul locomotives, 85 diesel railcars, seven diesel trailer cars and 940 passenger cars. The last UAC Turbotrain equipment has been withdrawn; its final revenue-earning runs were made in October 1982.

Traffic	1981
Number of passengers carried (000)	8009
Total passenger-miles (000)	1 936 226
Average revenue per revenue passenger-mile (cents)	6·845
Train-miles operated (000)	14 724
Car-miles operated (000)	100 231
Average occupancy rate (%)	52·9
Average number of passenger-miles per train-mile	136
Average number of employees	4135

Finances	1981
Revenue (C\$ million)	160 841
Average receipt per passenger-mile (cents)	9·527
Operating expenses (C\$ million)	397 217
General and administrative expenses (C\$ million)	38 334

Diesel locomotives

Class	Wheel arrangement	Transmission (rated)	Rated power hp	Tractive effort Continuous at lb	Max speed mph	Wheel dia in	Total weight 000 lb	Length ft in	No built	Year first built	Builder	Engine type
(VIA)												
MPA-27a (LRC)	4	71:32	3700	—	125	40	250	63' 8''	31	1981	B/MLW	251F
(Ex-CN)												
GPA-17a	4	58:19	1750	33 000	89	40	257	54' 8''	11	1954	GM	567-C
GPA-17b	4	58:19	1750	33 000	89	40	257	54' 8''	1	1955	GM	567-C
GPA-17c	4	58:19	1750	33 000	89	40	257	54' 8''	16	1957	GM	567-C
GPA-17d	4	58:19	1750	33 000	89	40	258	54' 8''	10	1957	GM	567-C
GPA-17e	4	58:19	1750	33 000	89	40	258	54' 8''	8	1958	GM	567-C
GPB-17a	4	58:19	1750	33 000	89	40	257	50'	9	1954	GM	567-C
GPB-17b	4	58:19	1750	33 000	89	40	257	50'	1	1954	GM	567-C
GPB-17c	4	58:19	1750	33 000	89	40	257	50'	7	1957	GM	567-C
GPB-17d	4	58:19	1750	33 000	89	40	257	50'	9	1957	GM	567-C
GPB-17e	4	58:19	1750	33 000	89	40	256	50'	7	1958	GM	567-C
MPA-18c	4	62:21	1800	38 000	92	40	260	54'	1	1955	MLW	251-B
MPA-18a	4	62:21	1800	38 000	92	40	259	54'	6	1958	MLW	251-B
MPA-18b	4	62:21	1800	38 000	92	40	259	54'	25	1959	MLW	251-B
MPB-18c	4	62:21	1800	38 000	92	40	262	53' 2''	1	1955	MLW	251-B
MPB-18a	4	62:21	1800	38 000	92	40	258	53' 2''	7	1958	MLW	251-B
MPB-18b	4	62:21	1800	38 000	92	40	258	53' 2''	5 Total (114)	1959	MLW	251-B·
(Ex-CP)												
DPA-15a	4	58:19	1500	33 000	89	40	263	54' 6''	2	1953	GM	567-B
DPA-17	4	58:19	1750	33 000	89	40	263	54' 6''	2	1953	GM	567-BC
DPA-17a	4	58:19	1750	33 000	89	40	260	54' 6''	7	1954	GM	567-C
DPA-15b	4	58:19	1500	33 000	89	40	260	54' 6''	2	1952	GM	567-B
DPA-15f	4	58:19	1500	33 000	89	40	260	54' 6''	2	1952	GM	567-B
DPA-17	4	58:19	1500	33 000	89	40	260	54' 6''	2	1952	GM	567-BC
DPA-15d	4	58:19	1500	33 000	89	40	260	54' 6''	1	1951	GM	567-BC

Diesel locomotives

Class	Wheel arrange- ment	Trans- mission (rated)	Rated power hp	Tractive effort Continuous at lb	Max speed mph	Wheel dia in	Total weight 000 lb	Length ft in	No built	Year first built	Builder	Engine type
DPA-22a	6	57:20	2250	27 000	85	40	331	70' 3''	2	1949	GM	567-B
DPB-17a	4	58:19	1750	45 000	89	40	255	54' 6''	5	1954	GM	567-C

Total (25)

CP Rail
Canadian Pacific Limited

Windsor Station, Montreal, Quebec H3C 3E4

Telephone: 395 5151
Telegrams: Canpacry

Chairman and Chief Executive Officer: F S Burbidge
President: W W Stinson
Vice-Presidents, Corporate: R T Riley
  Finance and Accounting: J P T Clough
  Law and General Counsel: D S Maxwell
  Administration and Public Affairs: I B Scott
  Personnel: J C Anderson
  Secretary: J C Ames

CP Rail
Executive Vice-President: R S Allison
Vice-Presidents
  Operation and Maintenance: J P Kelsall
  Industrial Relations: R Colosimo
  Marketing and Sales: R C Gilmore
  Purchases and Materials: J M Bentham
  Pacific Region: J D Bromley
  Prairie Region: C R Pike
  Eastern Region: D C Coleman
  Atlantic Region: G E Benoit
Assistant Vice-Presidents
  Marketing: R J Ritchie
  Sales: W J Ryan
  Intermodal Services: R A Teoli
General Managers, Pricing: J L DiFruscia
  Grain and Passenger Services: W H Somerville
  Overseas Trade: D T Sweeney
  Marketing: G R Mackie
Chief of Transportation: J H Geddis
Chief Engineer: J Fox
Chief Mechanical Officer: W Mummery

Gauge: 1435 mm
Length: 24 644 km

Canadian Pacific Limited operates a multi-faceted transport company with extensive routes and facilities in Canada and throughout the world. The company was incorporated in 1881 primarily to build and operate a transcontinental railway in

Revenues	1978	1979 (C$ million)	1980	1981
Freight	1235·376	1395·717	1544·649	1789·864
Passenger	23·55	61·788	68·08	73·844
Other railway	46·42	43·4	45·776	51·288
Coastal steamships	22·109	24·435	18·201	21·026
Government payments	100·98	93·691	96·887	134·955
	1428·435	1619·031	1773·593	2070·977

Expenses	1978	1979 (C$ million)	1980	1981
Maintenance	421·718	460·233	493·35	581·381
Traffic	27·308	29·371	33·766	37·798
Other operating	521·51	603·565	666·837	799·852
General and administrative	202·016	216·657	231·385	275·302
Depreciation	80·176	82·626	87·266	98·280
Fixed charges	22·4	21·6	20·7	27·800
Income taxes	77·362	96·242	118·694	123·396
	1352·49	1510·294	1651·998	1943·809

Canada. Today, its transport and related operations include railway, trucking and express, telecommunications, airlines and ocean shipping.

The company also holds 70·7 per cent of the total outstanding shares of Canadian Pacific Enterprises Limited, which controls and provides strategic direction to a group of resource-oriented and manufacturing companies with operations in Canada, the USA and abroad.

CP Rail operates 15 316 miles of route extending from the Maritimes to the Pacific coast and controls another 4700 miles in the USA. Its equipment includes more than 65 000 freight cars and 1300 diesel locomotives. CP Rail's network of lines stretches from coast to coast with important extensions in the USA in the states of Vermont, New York, Illinois, Wisconsin, Minnesota and North Dakota.

The railway has developed sophisticated unit train systems for moving bulk commodities such as coal and sulphur; has one of North America's most advanced automated freight classification yards at Calgary to handle rapidly-increasing freight shipments to and from the Pacific coast; provides piggyback service (the movement of highway trailers on railway flatcars) and domestic container service across the country and operates commuter pas-

senger train services in the provinces of Quebec and Ontario.

CP Rail has played a leading role in the development of container traffic in Canada. The railway is a joint owner of Brunterm Limited, a C$ 4 million container terminal at St John, New Brunswick.

Results
Net income from CP Rail in 1981 amounted to C$ 127·1 million, C$ 5·6 million more than in 1980, and total revenue to C$ 2071 million compared with C$ 1774 million in 1980. Major commodities contributing to 1981's higher revenue were petrochemical products, piggyback and containers (TOFC/COFC), and iron and steel.

Total rail expenses in 1981 were C$1944 million, up from C$ 1652 million in 1980 because of continued escalation of labour rates and material and fuel prices. Fuel prices in 1981 were some 47 per cent above those for 1980.

In 1982 Canadian railways, like those of the USA, were hit by the worst traffic downturn since the 1930s as a result of the recession. By the year's end tonnage was likely to be at least 10 per cent and perhaps as much as 15 per cent down on 1981 carryings.

CP Rail unit coal train on recently completed Notch Hill loop with maximum 1 per cent gradients

CP Rail was anticipating a slight improvement in traffic volume in 1983, mainly in export and US traffic. Gains were expected from the western natural resources sector, particularly coal, potash, forest products and petrochemicals. Very little improvement in domestic traffic was predicted, however.

Intermodal development

Believing that the most effective medium for competition in the domestic merchandise market will increasingly become the container rather than the boxcar, CP Rail has since 1978 spent over C$ 55 million on containers for internal traffic and ancillary equipment. A major feature of this development has been CP Rail's 44¼ foot-long container, a size coming within 9 inches of the standard truck trailer length but still capable of allowing two containers to be loaded on an 89-foot rail flatcar. Pioneered in box form, the bigger container has since been developed into a range including flats and temperature-controlled containers for perishables. CP Rail has also produced a 29 foot 5 inch box with re-usable plastic bag liner, which can be used for bulk commodities and, since the loaded liner is removable for discharge, recharged with fresh goods for the backhaul. These containers can be loaded three to a flatcar. One of CP Rail's motivations for moving more into containers for domestic traffic is their greater aptness for backhaul loads than boxcars.

Investment

Following the Federal Government's proposals to resolve the Crows Nest Pass grain rate problem (see under Transport Canada), CP Rail announced its intention to spend C$315 million for capital projects and an additional C$722 million on maintenance and repair work during 1983. A further C$39 million, funded by the Federal Government, would be spent to continue rehabilitation of Prairie branch lines.

These expenditures, about 75 per cent more than would have been possible from internally-generated funds, were made possible by the Federal Government's announcement of interim payments to cover railway losses from grain transport and continuation of capital cost allowances on railway investments. The C$315 million capital programme will enable the start of work on a number of new CP Rail expansion projects across Canada, as well as continuation of projects in progress or begun in 1982. Assuming parliamentary enactment of comprehensive legislation dealing with Crow grain losses, CP Rail will plan a C$3000 million capital programme in the five-year period to 1987. It will go to tender for the main tunnelling work at Rogers Pass (see below) towards the end of 1983, but only assuming adequate Crow legislation and general economic improvement.

The five-year plan encompasses the construction of additional main-line capacity valued at approximately C$760 million; purchase of diesel locomotives, freight cars and work equipment worth more than C$720 million; expenditure of C$113 million to build new repair and maintenance facilities; installation of new technology communications and traffic control systems costing C$144 million; and expansion of terminals and customer facilities at a cost of C$184 million. Western expenditures in 1983 included major rail, sleeper, ballast and bridge replacement programmes worth C$89 million. A further C$38 million will be spent to make similar improvements in the rail system serving eastern Canada.

Main items of the capital programme are:
A C$40 million four-year expansion project at Golden, British Columbia, where a new rail yard and car repair plant will be installed to service coal unit trains running between south-eastern British Columbia and Roberts Bank;
A three-year C$15 million combined locomotive and car repair facility at Moose Jaw, Saskatchewan, to service diesel locomotives and freight cars for grain, potash and lumber shipments;
A four-year C$40 million project to install CTC on the 420-mile (676 km) railway corridor between Winnipeg and Thunder Bay, Ontario;
More than C$20 million on double-tracking and grade improvement work in the Rogers Pass-Revelstoke area of the Selkirk Mountains in British Columbia to provide additional capacity to carry growing volumes of grain, coal, potash, sulphur and other commodities to tidewater for export;
Purchase of 50 new diesel-electric locomotives, 30 for main-line use, mostly in western Canada, and 20 for grain service on Prairie branch lines, from General Motors of Canada at a cost of C$70 million;
Major construction, at a cost of about C$13 million, of a C$16 million shop at Winnipeg where the expanding fleet of diesel-electric locomotives in western Canada can be repaired and maintained;

CP Rail's 44¼ ft domestic container with same cubic capacity as standard truck trailer

CP Rail unit grain train on Lethbridge Viaduct, Alberta

CP Rail's Rogers Pass project; the longer dotted line represents proposed 9-mile tunnel under Mount MacDonald, the shorter a one-mile tunnel under the Trans-Canada Highway

A C$7 million start on C$16 million worth of intermodal terminals at Edmonton, Regina and Calgary. The major intermodal expenditure will be at Edmonton;
More than C$5 million to extend radio communications between dispatchers and trains across Canada, and on a micro-wave link between Golden and Field, British Columbia;
More than C$5 million to continue installation of hot box detectors;
More than C$5 million on machines to maintain and repair track;
More than C$4 million on highway vehicles;
Other work includes modernisation of the main marshalling yard at Calgary, extension of a wheel shop at Winnipeg, and a terminal operating building at Coquitlam, British Columbia.

New Rogers Pass tunnel

In 1982, CP Rail received authority from the Canadian Transport Commission to undertake a C$ 600 million railway grade project in the Rogers Pass area of the Selkirk Mountains in British Columbia. Since 1976 CP Rail has already spent C$ 320 million in capital improvements of its roadway to increase its operating capacity.

The Rogers Pass project will include driving two tunnels with a total length of 10 miles (16 km), building 11 bridges and laying 21 miles (33 km) of new main-line track. It will reduce the westbound grade to the summit from a maximum of 2·6 per cent to a maximum of one per cent.

The new trackage is designed to eliminate the most restrictive bottleneck on CP Rail's 625-mile, 80 per cent single-track main line between Calgary and

Vancouver, which is nearing saturation with traffic. With its reduced grades, the line will allow the railway to run more and longer freight trains which will carry increasing tonnages of coal from British Columbia and Alberta, sulphur and petrochemicals from Alberta, potash from Saskatchewan, and grain from all parts of the Prairies to the Pacific coast for export to overseas buyers. An operating capacity increase of about 50 per cent is anticipated through ability to raise trainload tonnages and at the same time eliminate attachments of assistant locomotives and their occupation of track on their return to the foot of the grade.

The project is the last of four double-tracking schemes designed to increase main-line track capacity between Calgary and Vancouver. The other three projects, costing a total of C$ 46 million, are located in Notch Hill and Revelstoke in British Columbia and at Lake Louise in Alberta. The Notch Hill and Revelstoke schemes were completed in 1979

and the Lake Louise in 1981. When the Rogers Pass project is complete, heavy westbound trains will use the new one per cent-graded route and lighter eastbound trains the historic route, through the Connaught Tunnel of 1916, which threads Mount MacDonald 300 feet above the proposed alignment of the new summit tunnel.

During 1982, a total of C$22 million was spent on preparatory work for this project, including clearing the right-of-way for the new track and construction of tunnel portals.

Traction
CP Rail is in the third year of a 10-year, C$200 million programme to reshape its existing diesel force into a more powerful and flexible diesel force by the end of the 1980s. The programme involves rebuilding and modifying more than 400 locomotives at a cost of C$48 million, and acquiring up to 160 of the most efficient diesel units available at a cost of

C$162 million. The railway will also retire more than 300 of its older, first generation locomotives.

Purchases in 1982 included 30 Type SD40-2-3000 hp and 20 Type GP38-2 2000 hp diesel units from General Motors of Canada at a total cost of approximately C$50 million.

Communications
In a move to eliminate the problem of maintaining vital rail communications in the avalanche-prone area between Revelstoke and Glacier, British Columbia, CP Rail train crews and dispatchers can now transmit messages via the Anik B satellite. Anik, in a geosynchronous or stationary orbit above the earth, replaces the traditional system of pole lines, with their need of continuous upkeep and replacement, with one featuring instantaneous communications, message transmission towers and 12-foot diameter receiving dishes.

Cartier Railway
Cie de chemin de fer Cartier

Port Cartier, Quebec G5B 2H3

President: G Massobrio
Vice-President: J M R Gagnon
Comptroller: A Le Bel
General Manager: B H Boissé
General Superintendent, Transport: G Gendreau
Divisional Superintendent, Operations: H R McKay
Divisional Superintendent, Maintenance: J L Leblanc
Chief Engineer, Transport: P D Giacomin
Director of Purchases: A E Anto
Superintendent, Signalling and Communications: L R Martin
Superintendent, Technical Services: R H Tupper

Gauge: 1435 mm
Route length: 443 km

The 191-mile (307·4 km) railroad built to convey iron ore concentrate from Lac Jeannine (mine and concentrator site) to Port Cartier (harbour site) was completed in 1960. In 1972 an 86-mile (138·4 km) railroad extension was built to Mt Wright where a second concentrator was being built for another iron ore mine exploitation.

In 1975/76 a 3-mile (4·8 km) bypass was constructed to transport crude ore from Fire Lake

(which was opened to compensate for the closing of the Lac Jeannine mine) to Lac Jeannine (concentrator site). Also in 1975/76 13 additional sidings were built for these late mining developments.

The ore is worked in unit trains of 12 500 tons average weight, but varying from 90-car trains of 11 000 tons in the depth of winter to 150-car trains of 14 000 tons of ore in summer; in winter ambient temperatures can drop to –40°C. Trains are operated without cabooses, with a two-man crew of engineman and conductor, normally with two 3600 hp locomotives at the front and a third at the rear under Locotrol remote control from the front end. This format was standardised after experiments with various train-sizes up to 298 cars with six 3600 hp locomotives.

The present size best matches the cycle time of the fixed installations, which provide continuous loading and discharge at the port, the latter by a double-car Strachan & Henshaw rotary dumper which works at the rate of 3800 tons an hour. In winter the railroad normally has three 150-car Locotrol-worked trains and three others operational on the Mt Wright service, two trains of 100 cars on the Lac Jeannine service.

Computerised control has been superimposed on the CTC system, which is supplemented by centrally-controlled hot box detectors and point heaters. Radio communication with crews is employed for despatch of train orders.

The railroad has all but completed conversion of

its main-line track with continuously-welded 132 lb rail, RE control-cooled, which it has been undertaking at the rate of 30-40 miles a year. Hardwood 8 ft 6 in × 9 in × 7 in sleepers are employed.

The railway is a subsidiary of United States Steel.

Traffic
	1980/81	1981/82
Total freight tonne-km (million)	16 100	12 900
Average net freight train load (tonnes)	13 650	13 650
Average freight wagon load (tonnes)	91	91

Track
Rail: Std carbon; head hardened and % chrome 65·53 kg/m
Cross ties (sleepers)
Type: Hardwood
Thickness: 177 mm
Spacing: 1865/km
Fastenings: Cut spikes and Trak-lok clips on test section
Minimum curvature radius: 250 m
Max gradient: 1·35% against empty trains; 0·40% compensated against loaded trains
Max axleload: 31 tonnes

Motive power and rolling stock
Total fleet consists of 54 diesel-electric line-haul locomotives and 2160 freight wagons.

Diesel locomotives

Class	Wheel arrange-ment	Trans-mission	Rated power hp	Tractive effort continuous lb (kg)	Max speed mph (km/h)	Wheel dia in (mm)	Total weight tons	Length ft in (mm)	No built	Year first built	Builders Mechanical parts	Engine & type	Trans-mission
RS	Bo-Bo	Elec	1750	60 000 (27 216)	65 (104·6)	40 (1016)	130	56' 2" (17 120)	7	1960	GM (London)	GM Diesel & V-16	GM
RS	Bo-Bo	Elec	1800	64 900 (29 439)	65 (104·6)	40 (1016)	129	56' 11¾" (17 367)	7	1960	MLW (Montreal)	251- & V-12	MLW
RS	Co-Co	Elec	2400	96 530 (43 786)	65 (104·6)	40 (1016)	193	67' 1" (20 447)	6	—	Alco (New York)	251-B & V-16	Alco
RS	Co-Co	Elec	3000	103 000 (46 721)	65 (104·6)	40 (1016)	195	69' 6" (21 298)	10	1966	Alco (New York)	251-E & V-16	Alco
RS	Co-Co	Elec	3600	104 000 (47 174)	65 (104·6)	40 (1016)	186	69' 10" (21 298)	16	1970-3	MLW (Montreal)	251-F & V-16	MLW
RS	Co-Co	Elec	3600	108 000 (48 989)	65 (104·6)	40 (1016)	194·2	69' 6" (21 184)	3	1968	Alco (New York)	251- & V-16	Alco
RS	Co-Co	Elec	3600	108 000 (48 989)	65 (104·6)	40 (1016)	200	69' 10" (21 285)	5	1975	MLW (Montreal)	251-F & V-16	MLW

Ontario Northland Railway

195 Regina Street, North Bay, Ontario P1B 8L3

Telephone: (705) 472 4500
Telex: 067 76103

General Manager: P A Dyment
Assistant General Manager: D E MacDougall
Senior Operating Officer: K J Moorehead

Gauge: 1435 mm
Route length: 925 km

The railway, which is owned by the Government of Ontario, recorded 5·68 million net tonnes of freight in 1981.

Finance
Revenues
	1981 (C$)
Passengers and baggage	2 678 707
Freight, parcels and mail	38 887 053
Food services	709 801
Total	42 275 561

Expenditure
	1981 (C$)
Total	47 911 407

Motive power and rolling stock
The railway operates 24 line-haul and six switching diesel-electric locomotives, four diesel train-sets (ex-Dutch/Swiss 'TEE' train-sets used on 'Northlander' service), 20 passenger cars and 988 freight cars. Recent additions are six GM Type GP 38-2 2000 hp diesel locomotives delivered at the end of 1982.

Track
Rail: 125·77 kg/m
Cross ties (sleepers)
Wood: Thickness 180 mm
Spacing: 1886/km
Fastenings: 4 spikes per sleeper on tangent, 8 spikes
per sleeper on curves
Minimum curvature radius: 300 m
Max gradient: 1·5%
Max axleload: 29 500 kg (65 000 lb)

Former Dutch/Swiss TEE equipment forming 'Northlander'
at Toronto's Union station

Diesel locomotives

Class	Wheel arrangement	Transmission	Rated power kW	Max kg	Tractive effort continuous kg	at km/h	Max speed km/h	Wheel dia mm	Total weight tonnes	Length mm	No built	Year first built	Builders		
													Mechanical parts	Engine & type	Transmission
SD40-2	C-C	Elec	2237·1	42 676	37 727·4	17·87	104·6	1016	170·7	20 980	8	1973	GM	645E3	GM Main Gen
GP38-2	B-B	Elec	1492·5	28 803	25 151·6	16·9	104·6	1016	115·67	18 034	10	1974	GM	645E	GM Main Gen
FP7-A	B-B	Elec	1118·55	29 283	18 160	17·8	104·6	1016	117·1	16 662	22 (11 in service)	1951	GM	567BC	GM Main Gen
GP-9	B-B	Elec	1304·97	29 337	22 700	16·9	104·6	1016	117·34	17 120	6	1956	GM	567C	GM Main Gen
RS-3	B-B	Elec	1193	28 125	21 283	15·2	104·6	1016	112·5	17 068	12 (3 in service)	1951	Alco	Alco 250	Gen Electric
RS-10	B-B	Elec	1193	29 275	24 062	12·8	104·6	1016	117·1	17 373	4 (2 in service)	1956	Alco	Alco 250	Gen Electric

Quebec North Shore and Labrador Railway

PO Box 1000, Sept-Iles, Quebec G4R 4L5

Chairman: R F Anderson
President: B Mulroney
Executive Vice-President: R Geren
Senior Vice-President: J B Galligan
Senior Vice-President: W F Miller
Secretary/Treasurer: K Eldridge
Manager: G A Dolliver

Gauge: 1435 mm
Route length: 638.77 km

Construction of the 356 miles (573 km) of main track between the port of Sept-Iles and Schefferville commenced in 1950 and was completed in 1954. This construction required the operation of the largest civilian airlift in history. A branch line of 38 miles (61·2 km) between milepost 224 and Carol Lake was completed in 1960. 40 per cent of the mileage is curved track. Operation is based on working of 240-car Locotrol trains with four SD-40 locomotives and average net trainloads of 22 670 tonnes.

Traffic

	1980/81	1981/82
Total freight tonnage (million)	28 458	18 595
Total freight tonne-km (million)	14 200	9280
Average net freight train load (tonnes)	22 670	22 670
Average freight wagon load (tonnes)	96·5	96·5
Total passenger-km (million)	16·114	17·160
Total passenger journeys	49 582	52 800
Average length of passenger journey (km)	325	325

Finance (C$ million)

	1981/82
Revenue	
Total	86·741

Expenditure	1981/82
Staff/personnel expenses	29·134
Materials and services	48·828
Depreciation	14·586
Financial charges	4·323
Total	96·871

Motive power and rolling stock
The fleet at the end of 1982 consisted of 76 diesel-electric locomotives, 4575 freight wagons and 23 passenger coaches.

Track
Rail: 65·5 kg/m
Cross ties (sleepers)
Hardwood: 27·5 × 35·4 × 425·2 mm
Spacing: 2080/km
Fastenings
Standard track, 165 mm (5½ in)
Minimum curvature radius: 220 m
Max gradient: 1·32%
Max axleload: 33 tonnes

Diesel locomotives

Class	Wheel arrangement	Transmission	Rated power (hp)	Tractive effort Continuous at		Max speed	Wheel diameter	Total weight tonnes	Length ft in (mm)	No in service	Year first built	Builders		
				lb (kg)	mph (km/h)	mph (km/h)	in (mm)					Mechanical parts	Engine & type	Transmission
SD-40	C-C	Elec	3000	84 000 (38 000)	11·1 (17·86)	71 (114·26)	40 (1016)	174	65' 8" (20 015)	21	1966-71	GM	GM	GM
SD40-2	C-C	Elec	3000	84 000 (38 000)	11·1 (17·86)	71 (114·26)	40 (1016)	174	68' 10" (20 980)	44	1972	GM	GM	GM
GP-9	B-B	Elec	1750	48 000 (22 000)	11·1 (17·86)	71 (114·26)	40 (1016)	109	56' 7" (17 247)	11	1954-60	GM	GM	GM

White Pass and Yukon Route

PO Box 4070, Whitehorse, Yukon Territory Y1A 3T1

President and Executive Officer: T H King
General Manager, Railroad: M P Taylor

Gauge: 915 mm
Route length: 178 km

The White Pass & Yukon Route railway, consisting of British Columbia-Yukon Railway, British Yukon Railway, Pacific & Arctic Railway & Navigation Co, was built during 1898-1900 to transport men and

supplies to the goldfields of the Klondike. The 110·7-mile (178 km) narrow-gauge railway has operated all year round between Skagway, Alaska and Whitehorse, Yukon. Originally financed by British interests and constructed under the supervision of Canadian contractor Michael Heney, the railway, part of The White Pass & Yukon Corporation Ltd, is totally Canadian-owned.

The White Pass railway carried general freight for a declining Yukon population until 1942 when the US Army leased the railway for the duration of the Second World War to haul material for the construction of the Alaska Highway. At the end of the war new mines came into operation in the Yukon and the railway became part of the White Pass integrated

ship, train, truck and freight service. The railway underwent major upgrading in 1969.

The railway closed in October 1982 following the shutdown of its principal source of traffic, the Cyrus Anvil lead-zinc mine, and its reopening was in serious doubt. It was firmly announced that no passenger trains would run in the 1983 summer season.

Motive power and rolling stock
The White Pass has 19 line-haul and two switching diesel-electric locomotives on the fleet roster and also operates some 2-8-2 steam locomotives. Rolling stock consists of 378 freight train wagons and 30 passenger coaches.

Line-haul diesel locomotives

Class	Wheel arrangement	Trans-mission	Rated power hp	Tractive effort Max lb	Tractive effort Continuous lb	Max speed mph	Wheel diameter in	Total weight tons	No built	Year first built	Builders Mechanical parts	Builders Engine & type	Builders Transmission
90	C-C	Elec	900	50 000	24 000	40	34	85	11	1954	General Electric	Alco Power 251B	General Electric
101	C-C	Elec electric	1200	53 590	35 000	65	36	105	8	1969	MLW	Alco Power 251D	General Electric

CHILE

Ministry of Works

Morando 71, Santiago

Minister of Transport: Gen Caupolican Boisset
Chief of Land Transport Department: R A R Carvajal

Chilean State Railways (EFE)
Empresa de los Ferrocarriles del Estado de Chile

Libertador Bernardo O'Higgins Av, 924 Casilla 134D, Santiago

Telephone: 89116
Telegrams: Railacoff

Governing Council
President: José M Edwards
Vice President: Hugo Castro Rubio
Directors: General Jorge A Correa Gatica
 Victor Aquiles López Barrenechea
 Omar Quintanilla Hoffman
 Colonel Hugo Sepulveda Fuentes

Director-General: General Jorge Augusto Correa Gatica
Deputy Director-General: Ing Anibal Gajardo Prieto
Managers
 Technical: Ing Fernando Ipinza Mayer
 Finance: Ing Eduardo Pérez Echeñique
 Commercial: Sergio Sotomayer Moreno
 Traffic: Ing Roberto Darrigrandi Chadwick
 Administration and Personnel: Ernesto Valenzuela Ayala
 Development: Ing Jorge Champin Dattwyler
 Planning: T Moll A
 Way and Works: C Weippert T
 Electrification and Signalling: L Hernandez G
Chief Engineer: J Zunino N
Chief of Public Relations: A Barahona Zuleta

Gauge: 1676 mm; 1000 mm
Route length: 4257 km; 3291 km
Electrification: 1503·7 km (1676 mm gauge) and 79·6 km (1000 mm gauge) at 3 kV dc

The system consists of four networks:
Red Norte: Extends from Calera, near Valparaiso, to Iquique (main-line route length 1880 km); spur from Augusta Victoria to Socompa (181 km), linking with Argentine Railways; branch routes. Metre-gauge; diesel operation.
Red Sur: Extends from Valparaiso to Santiago and Puerto Montt (total route length 1266 km, including branch lines). 1676 mm gauge; electric operation on section Valparaiso-Los Andes-Santiago-Concepción; diesel operation and some steam freight services on section Concepción-Puerto Montt.
FC Arica: Extends from Arica to Visviri (206 km), linking with Bolivian Railways and rising from sea level to 4257 metres within 39 km with a six per cent gradient. Metre-gauge, diesel operation.
FC Transandino: Extends from Los Andes to Caracoles (71 km), linking with Argentine Railways. Metre-gauge, electric operation, part rack rail.

Rationalisation
Drastic rationalisation, including closures of 500 km of route and a severe staff reduction to 9500 compared with 28 000 in 1973, followed a Government requirement of 1978 that EFE eliminate its need of a state operating subsidy, which was terminated in 1979, along with assistance for the servicing of internal and external debts. At the same time EFE was granted commercial freedom to set its own rates and to recruit or dispense with labour. A considerable amount of work, such as rolling stock and track maintenance, has been let out to private enterprise; in the long term the Government's aim is that EFE should manage only the infrastructure and that private companies should lease running rights to operate their own rolling stock with their own staff.

Passenger traffic
Business is almost entirely concentrated on the Red

Sur. Passenger working on the metre-gauge system north of Santiago has been all but extinguished under the rationalisation, because of inability to compete effectively with strong, unregulated road competition.

Between Santiago and Valparaiso (186 km) the 1676 mm gauge trains take over three hours, but EFE is considering alternative plans for new lines of route that would reduce journey times spectacularly; rival bus services have use of a motorway. The cheaper of these projects, estimated to cost US$ 262 million and incurring 46 km of new construction, 16 km of it in tunnel under the Barriga mountains, would reduce the distance to 121 km and journey time to 65 minutes if maximum speed were 125 km/h. The deviation would be electrified at 3 kV dc, for compatibility with existing electrification, and the line would be engineered with a ruling gradient of 15 per cent and a minimum curve radius of 1500 metres. Also under consideration is a scheme for a rapid transit railway encircling Santiago.

Alameda station, Santiago, is the first to be treated under a station remodelling plan. Other recent developments include the launch of an accompanied car-carrying train service.

Freight traffic
The principal traffic is iron ore, which in 1980 accounted for 9 million of the Red Norte's aggregate 9.9 million tonnes of freight, flowing from mines in the north to the ports of Chanaral, Caldera, Huasco and Coquimbo. A number of private companies have been enlisted to co-operate with EFE in expansion of its freight business.

Electrification
At the Government's request electrification of the Laja-Temuco (190 km) and Santiago-San Antonio (120 km) sections has been studied; further action is unlikely until more traffic has been accumulated and hydro-electric power schemes have been realised. The Santiago-San Antonio line is already partly electrified.

Traction and rolling stock
EFE planned to eliminate residual steam working between Concepción and Osorno by 1983 through rehabilitation of unserviceable members of its diesel locomotive fleet of 189 units and rebuilding some units from the metre-gauge network with 1676-mm bogies. A C$2·1 million order for five new diesel locomotives and spares was placed with Bombardier of Canada in 1982. In 1981 a US$ 5 million credit was secured from Gruppo Aziendo Italiano for the acquisition from Italian companies of spares to rehabilitate 19 electric locomotives and eight emus stored as unserviceable. Other passenger stock, some of 1920s vintage, is being refurbished.

At the start of 1983 EFE owned 154 steam, 188 diesel and 104 electric locomotives, 44 emus, 13 dmus, 29 railbuses, 656 passenger cars and 5263 freight cars.

Track and signalling
Installation of long-welded rail continues as resources allow and 59 kg/m rail has been laid on some key sections. EFE is also extending electric signalling and block working in place of token operation, and plans to install CTC between Talca and Puerto Montt.

Long-distance emu by Kawasaki

Antofagasta (Chile) & Bolivia Railway

Ferrocarril de Antofagasta a Bolivia

Bolivar 255, Casillas S-T, Antofagasta

Telex: 9191

General Manager: G Menendez
Operations Manager: F Courbis
Traffic Manager: E Sotomayor
Technical Manager: H Pavez
Chief Mechanical Engineer: G Moya

Gauge: 1000 mm
Route length: 724 km

The railway operates 22 diesel locomotives, 32 railcars, 88 passenger cars and 2486 freight wagons.

Track
Rail: 75/65 lb/yd
Minimum curvature radius: 90 m
Max gradient: 3·5%
Max axleload: 15 tons

Arica—La Paz Railway (FCALP)

Ferrocarril de Arica a la Paz

Casilla 9-D, Arica

Telephone: 31101
Telex: 221067

Director-General: Jorge Correa G
General Manager: Rodrigo Navarro A
Secretary: Carlos Cousins R
Deputy Director, Operations: Armando Salgado V
Departmental Chief, Traffic: Guillermo Pizarro O
  Commercial: Andres Ediap B
  Personnel: Eugenio Avendaño L
  Finance: Jaime Calderon V
  Supplies: Juan Villarreal C

Gauge: 1000 mm
Route length: 206 km (Chile section)

For more than half a century the Arica to La Paz Railway, belonging to the Chilean State Railways, has been railing freight and passengers between Chile and Bolivia. Its origin goes back to the years following the end of the War of the Pacific (1883) and its building was provided in the Peace and Friendship Treaty subscribed by the Chilean and Bolivian governments in 1904. The Chilean government financed the construction of the complete network of the line.

Because of its difficult mountain route, FCALP reflects one of the most remarkable examples of railway engineering. In turn, it represents 'the shortest route from the Pacific to Bolivia', (its own slogan), covering 440 km between the port of Arica in Chile to the Bolivian capital city of La Paz. The difficulties arising out of its ascending layout to the Bolivian plateau and its high operational and maintenance costs are the main reasons for its low profitability.

Traffic

	1981	1982
Total freight tonnage (000)	106	50
Total freight tonne-km (000)	21·938	10·298
Average net freight train load (tonnes)	277	234
Average freight wagon load (tonnes)	21	22
Total passenger-km (000)	4·793	1·935
Total passenger journeys	401	229
Average length of passenger journey (km)	200	176

Finance (Ch$000)

Revenue	1981	1982
Passengers and baggage	7·866	3·072
Freight, parcels and mail	143·132	78·084
Other income	9·294	7·616
Total	160·292	88·772

Expenditure	1981	1982
Staff/personnel expenses	73·423	77·861
Materials and services	57·531	25·098
Depreciation	7·914	8·141
Financial charges	26·843	NA
Total	165·711	111·100*

*Less financial charges, not yet available

Track
Rail: Arica division (127·7 route-km) 27·5 kg/m
    Y division (78·5 route-km) 39·8 kg/m
Cross ties (sleepers)
Timber: Thickness 152 × 254 mm (6 × 10 in) or 152 × 203 mm (6 × 8 in)
Metal: Thickness 240 × 80 mm
Spacing: Timber (10 in) 1640/km, (8 in) 1786/km
    Metal 1200/km
Fastenings: Arica division sole plates
    Y division anchor spikes
Minimum curvature radius: 94 m
Max gradient: 6·05%
Max axleload: Arica division 25 tonnes
    Y division 35 tonnes

Motive power and rolling stock
The Arica to La Paz Railway operates seven General Electric diesel-electric locomotives. For its passenger service, FCALP operates one Schindler railcar and seven hauled cars. Freight stock consists of 290 wagons.

Diesel locomotives

Class	Wheel arrangement	Transmission	Rated power (kW)	Max speed km/h	Total weight tonnes	No in service	Year first built	Builders Mechanical parts	Builders Engine & type	Builders Transmission
Dt 13100 (GE U13-C)	Co-Co	Elec	971	95	85	5	1967	GE	GE FDL-8	GE
Dt 6000	Co-Co	Elec	442	80	64	1	1954	GE	Cooper Bessemer FWL-6T	GE
Dt 3000	Bo-Bo	Elec	199	48	40	1	1953	GE	Cummins HBI-600	GE

Diesel railcars

Cars per unit	Motor cars per unit	Motored axles per motor car	Transmission	Rated power (kW) per motor	Max speed km/h	Weight tonnes per car	Total seating capacity	Length per car mm	No in service	Year first built	Builders Mechanical parts	Builders Engine & type	Builders Transmission
1	1	2	Mech	155	75	33·6	32	14 600	1	1955	Schindler	A Saurer BXD-SL	A Saurer 8 SF

CHINA, PEOPLE'S REPUBLIC

Chinese People's Republic Railways (CPRR)

Ministry of Railways, Beijing

Minister of Railways: Chen Pu-Ru

Gauge: mainly 1435 mm
Route length: 52 000 km approx
Electrification: 1782 km at 25 kV 50 Hz ac

Transport development
A drastic reduction in the number of Government Ministries at the outset of 1982 was paralleled, simultaneously with the appointment of a new Minister of Railways, by rationalisation of the railways management as a measure to help accelerate modernisation. The 13 former Deputy-Ministerial Railway posts have been reduced to three and there

was comparable slimming at lower management levels. All specialist departments are now staffed only by specialists.

In November 1982 Vice-Premier Wan Li called for an acceleration of new railway and construction work under a fresh three-year programme. A 40 per cent rise in passenger and freight traffic was sought by 1990, and intermediate targets of 1200 million tonnes of freight and 1100 million passenger-journeys were set for 1985, compared with totals of 1048 million and 942 million respectively recorded in 1981. Railway tonne-km have already multiplied more than thirty-fold and passenger-km over seven-fold since 1949.

The Ministry of Railways at present administers 20 railway bureaus and 16 sub-bureaus throughout China, as well as most of China's 33 locomotive and rolling stock factories via the Locomotive and Rolling Stock Factories Department.

The Chinese People's Republic Railways (CPRR) consists of six major regions or routes:
Northeast Region made up of three main lines, Harbin-Suiching, Harbin-Manchouli and Harbin-Talien, together with about 60 secondary lines.
Beijing-Paotou and **Paotou-Lanchow lines** linking

Beijing with Inner Mongolia, Shansi, Hopei, Ningsia and Kansu.
Tianjin-Shanghai Railway which runs along the eastern seaboard through the North China Plain to Nanking (via the Yellow and Huai river basins) and Shanghai.
Lung-Hai and **Lanchow-Sinkiang lines** which link the Yellow Sea coast with the north-east frontier over 3600 km.
Beijing-Kwangchow running north-south through the Beijing region and five provinces.
Southwestern Region, including Paochi-Chengtu, Chengtu-Chungking, Chengtu-Kunming, Yunau-Kwangsi and Hunan-Kweichow lines.

Motive power
China's modern locomotive park was originally based on Soviet-built stock, delivered between 1956 and 1959. Among the most significant of Soviet deliveries were about 1000 second-hand FD 2-10-2 class steam units. These relatively new and powerful locomotives represented a considerable upgrading of China's fleet of ageing pre-war Consolidations, Mikados and so on. They were converted to Chinese gauge at Changchun and dubbed the

'Friendship' class. Soviet specialists also helped the Chinese to build the Heping ('Peace') steam locomotive, a more powerful 2-10-2 very similar to the Soviet LV 1-5-1 which was then just going out of production in the Soviet Union. The first prototype was assembled at Talien in 1956 and the Heping was in serial production by 1959. Some 9000 steam locomotives were still active in 1982, since vigorous expansion of diesel traction and electrification was still inadequate to match traffic demand. There was some concern over extended reliance on oil fuel. Consequently the Class QJ 2-10-2 class is over 3000 strong.

European and Japanese locomotive builders entered the Chinese railway scene after 1960. Imports of diesel locomotives from France and the Federal Republic of Germany were followed by an input from Romania in 1975, but thereafter local skills and technology were sufficiently developed for the railways to rely on domestic manufacture. At first production was based on Soviet twin-unit designs, but by 1981 the railways were running 300 of the Dong Feng DF4 type 3600 hp Co-Co units with ac/dc transmission.

To serve newly-electrified lines, Chinese builders have supplied new 138-tonne Shaoshan SS3-type electric locomotives, a development of the preceding SS1 and SS2 designs offering enhanced adhesion and equipped with single-arm pantographs. Most of the Shaoshan series have a one-hour rating of 4200 kW at 44·6 km/h (continuous rating 3780 kW at 45·9 km/h) and employ silicon rectifiers with tap-changer control of power, but the latest version is rated at 4800 kW and, though still equipped with silicon rectifiers, has thyristors to regulate motor excitation. All have a maximum speed of 95 km/h. Over 30 plants throughout the country now have traction manufacturing capacity, eight of them absorbed exclusively in electric traction.

Electrification

More important stages of the electrification plan have been completed since 1980, raising the total of 25 kV 50 Hz electrified route to 1782 km. Electric traction was inaugurated in 1980 over the 362 km Xiangfan-Ankang section of the recently constructed railway that cuts through three mountain ranges on its path to Chongqing: finished in 1980, this line was built with electrification in view. In January 1983 electrification was brought into use further south, over 117 km of the 505 km line between Chengdu and Chongqing, which the wires will reach by 1985. The catenary is also being projected from Baoji north-west to Tianshui and Lanzhou, and Baoji-Lanzhou was to become operational in 1984. The 443 km Baoji-Lanzhou line, part of the east-west Lenghai Railway transversal built in 1937, bears a heavy traffic not envisaged in its original construction parameters and consequently upgrading proceeds alongside electrification. Clearance expansion for the catenary has had to cover 90 tunnels. An encouragement to electrification in this region centring on China's first electrified main line, from Baoji to Chengdu, is the local resources of hydro-electric power.

A further recent electrification landmark was energisation of the 120 route-km of double track between Shijiazhuang, capital of Hebei province, and Yangquan, centre of a high-quality coal-mining industry. Wiring then moved on to the remaining 115 km to Taiyuan, capital of Shanxi province, on the line from Datong to Xianyang, which was finished in 1982; this route's coal throughput is expected to climb from 80 million to 112 million tonnes a year by 1985. Also being electrified is the Beijing-Datong route. Datong is a key coal-producing centre in Shanxi province; most of the local output is transported over the 379 km double-track route to feed generating stations and blast furnaces in Beijing and Tianjin, but some is also exported through the port of Qinhuangdao. Ultimately the objective is to weld together these separate electrified lines by wiring the route from Jining through Taiyuan to Xianyang and Baoji, together with the line from Beijing to Zhengzhou.

By the start of 1983 electrification was operative on at least part of five trunk routes and a further 2700 route-km of wiring was prescribed by 1990. At the outset of 1983 electrification was in progress over 1398 route-km, comprising Tianshui-Lanzhou (353 km); Beijing (Fengtai yard)-Datong (377 km); Ziyang-Chongqing (387 km); Ankang-Daxian (280 km). Work was soon to begin over the residual 290 km beyond Daxian of the new mountain route from Xiangfan and Ankang to Chongqing.

The principal electrifications scheduled to follow were between Baoji and Zhengzhou (680 km); Kunming and Guiyang (639 km); Beijing and Qinhuangdao (330 km); and Yueshan and Changye (150 km).

Rolling stock

Changes in the characteristics of rolling stock design are forecast in view of the quest for 160 km/h passenger train operation on trunk routes, and for 120 km/h merchandise and 100 km/h mineral freight train working. At present maximum speeds are 110

Henschel diesel-hydraulic locomotive for Chinese Railways

Alsthom-built 4000 hp diesel-electric locomotive

Qian Jin 2-10-2 steam locomotive

km/h (passenger) and 80 km/h (freight), but average freight train running speed is 50 km/h.

Long-term speed aims are likely to see the broadly Soviet pattern of heavy passenger car superseded by designs employing lightweight bodyshells and modular components. However, a significant rise in passenger speed will be impossible unless line capacity can be lifted by increasing the pace of the main trunk routes' predominance of slow-moving freight trains, and that predicates a massive wagon-building programme adopting roller bearings and up-to-date suspension systems, as well as designs of high-capacity vehicle equipped for automatic loading and discharge, to accelerate flows of bulk freight. Some trunk-line sections in the eastern and coastal provinces bear over 80 million gross tonnes of traffic annually and are occupied by more than 120 trains daily in each direction. Already wagons with a 50-tonnes payload capacity account for over 80 per cent of the wagon fleet.

New lines

In 1982 the route-length of the Chinese People's Republic Railways was over 52 000 km, compared with 20 000 km in 1949, but only 6000 km were double track. Roughly 1000 km of new line are being added to the system every year, partly to relieve pressure on the heavily occupied trunk routes in the east of the country, where the bulk of the network is concentrated, partly to extend railways into the western provinces which are almost without rail transport. The target is an 80 000 route-km system by the end of the century.

The most daunting project, construction of a 2200 km line from Xining, in Tsinghai province, to the Tibetan capital, Lasa, was in 1980 halted at Golmud, 835 km out. The rest of the route lies almost entirely at 4000 metres or more above sea level, up to a peak of 5000 metres at the Tangla pass, in a region where not only is the terrain permanently frozen to a depth of several metres and ambient temperature below −20°C for six months of the year, but seismic disturbance is also a chronic difficulty. These conditions have demanded exhaustive research into durable track structures before construction can continue. The thinness of the air will demand pressurised passenger car interiors and special designs of diesel locomotive with two-stage turbocharging.

China's busiest artery is the north-south route from Beijing to Guangzhou (formerly Canton), and in the country's east a recent priority has been this line's relief by the construction of links between other existing routes to its east and west so as to create two additional and parallel trunk lines from north to south. In 1982 only the Xupu-Yidu section remained to be built for completion of a western alternative from Jiaozuo southward as far as Liuzhou, in the Guanxi autonomous region. To the east a new 551 km railway from Wuhu to Giuxi was finished in 1982; this addition makes the Beijing-Shanghai line a route to Jiangxi province also. Tracklaying was complete on a 125 km line from Fuyang to Hainan, on the Xuzhou-Hefei-Wuhu route, which besides creating further north-south relief was particularly aimed to ease bulk freight flows. Also completed in 1982 was the 220 km Handan-Changzhi line across the Taihang mountains to link Hebei and Shanxi provinces; its construction involved 49 tunnels and 108 bridges.

Construction of 274 km Beijing-Qinhuangdao line

One of 293 bridges on the Beijing-Qinhuangdao line under construction

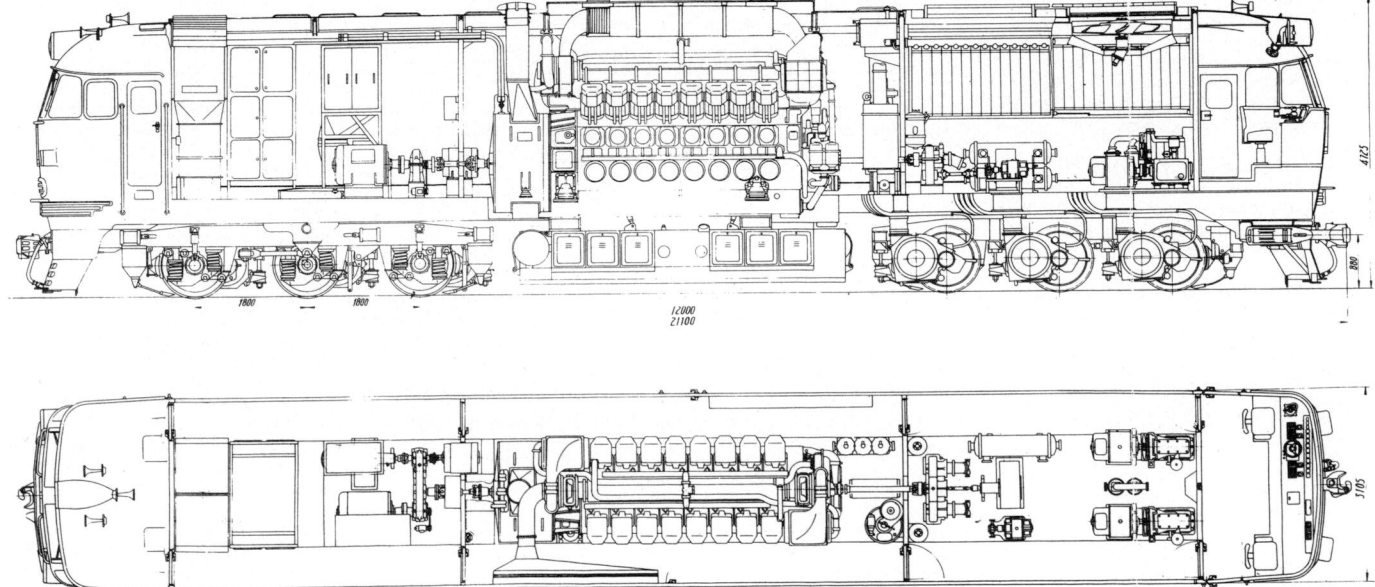

Layout of Dong Feng 4

Another urgent need is to improve rail service of existing ports and to provide it for harbours scheduled for development into major ports. To cater for export coal from the north-eastern province of Shinxu, two such railways were launched in 1982 for completion by 1986. One is a 300 km line from the Shandong coalfield focussed on Yanzhou to the port of Shijiusuo (where big maritime development is planned), the other a new 270 km line from Beijing to the country's major coal-handling port, Qinhuangdao. These are two of the three new line projects for which the aid of the Japanese International Cooperation Agency (JICA) has been enlisted; the third will run from Guangzhou to Henyang. A Japanese loan of 65 million yen was secured in 1982 to help fund the Beijing-Qinhuangdao project. JICA is also assisting in the upgrading of the heavily congested line from Beijing to Tianjin, at present the only path from the capital to Qinhuangdao, and also the route of traffic to and from Shanghai.

Under the new three-year plan announced late in 1982 new lines totalling 1700 km of single-track and 1500 km of double-track are programmed, chiefly in the north, south-west and east. Besides relief of pressure in the coastal sectors the aim is improved haulage capacity for coal, and for coal and phosphates from Yunnan and Guizhou.

Another new outlet for the Shandong coalfield was to be established by a 150 km line from the Beijing-Zhengzhou route at Xinxiang to Heze; a new deep-water port at Fangcheng was to be linked with Nanning, on the Liuzhou-Pingxiang route, by a 180 km railway; and a 275 km line was to be projected from Xinxiang via Heze to Yanzhou. In the far south Guangdong province has financially stimulated construction of the Sanshui-Yaogu section of the prospective 300 km Guangzhou-Maoming line, which by 1984 should be operative and saving Guangzhou-Zhanjiang traffic a considerable detour via Henyang; the Guangzhou-Henyang line is also to be double-tracked, however.

In the far north-east of the country a 227 km line has been opened between Fuli, on the Harbin-Shungyashan route, to Qianjin.

New stations are to be erected at Beijing (its fourth), Shenyang and Shijiazhuang, and work on one at Shanghai has begun, 2 km west of the exist-

Dong Feng 4 diesel locomotive

ing station. Seven marshalling yards are also to be built under the 1983-85 plan.

Signalling

Modernisation of signalling and traffic control is another urgent necessity. By 1981 over 1100 stations had been equipped with electrical interlocking and 36 000 km with a semi-automatic relay block system, but only 800 route-km were as yet under CTC control. Over 8000 km were provided with track-to-train radio communication. In association with double-tracking, signalling modernisation is under way between Beijing and Guangzhou, and between Tianjin and Fuzhou. A computer-aided traffic control system is the focus of forward research and planning.

Two hump marshalling yards, Fengtai West in the Beijing area and Nanxiang, in the Shanghai region, had by 1981 been fitted out with electronic aids such as speed-measuring radar, rolling wagon weight detectors and distance-to-coupling siding occupancy readers. From experience here and with

target-speed braking through hydraulic retarders at Harbin a standard automation system, backed by micro-computer data processing systems, was under development for the country's main yards.

Permanent way

Standard rails are 50 kg/m, with 43 kg/m on less busy routes. These two types account for the bulk of the system's track, but 60 kg/m has been applied to key routes radiating from Beijing since 1978. Continuously welded, with elastic fastenings, prestressed concrete sleepers and hard rock ballast, 60 kg/m rail is regarded as adequate for all foreseeable operating requirements. Sleepers are spaced 1760 per km.

Supplementing China's standard-gauge railroads is a system of lightweight, narrow-gauge lines. Information on this system is scanty, but the pattern in Honan province is revealing. In 1973 the Honan network was about 960 km in length and reached into thirty counties. The gauge is described as half that of an ordinary railroad, and is therefore probably 750 mm.

COLOMBIA

National Railways of Colombia (FNdeC)
Ferrocarriles Nacionales de Colombia

Calle 13, No 18-24 Bogotá

Telephone: 2775577
Telegrams: Ferrocarriles

President: José Fernando Isaza Delgado
Principal Members of the Board
    Beatriz Echeverry de Kurk
    Luis Carlos Sarmiento Angulo
    Rafael Pavia L
    Alvaro Vargas Garcia
    Enrique Luque Carulla
Director General: Alfonso Orduz Duarte
Deputy-Director: Fernando Tavera Bahamon
Secretary General: Rodrigo Toledo Zamora
Administrative Director: Betssy Wilches de Rodriguez
Commercial Director: Eduardo Rodriguez Ardila
Financial Director: Hebert Cabrera Martinez
Secretary-General: Rodrigo Toledo Zamora
Planning Manager: Jorge Sossa Beltran
Manager, Way and Works: José Hernan Garcia Martinez
Systems Manager: Heriberto Zarate Olarte

Gauge: 914 mm
Route length: 3403 km

Organisation

	Total route-km	Route-km in operation
Central	1354	1287
Pacifico	889	494
Santander	400	400
Magdalena	420	420
Antioquia	340	221
Total	3403	2822

Traffic

	1978	1979	1980	1981
Freight tonnes (million)	2·68	2·39	1·93	1·34
Freight tonne-km (million)	1232	1105·42	861·56	624·76
Passenger journeys (million)	2·56	2·45	2·21	1·69
Passenger-km (million)	342·23	322·40	315·21	230·36

Finance

	1978	1979	1980	1981
		(million pesos)		
Revenue	1960·78	2106·31	3133·23	2310·46
Expenditure	2823·99	3146·39	4634·53	5200·37
Government subsidy	72·53	478·34	200	249·25

Results

	1981
Total freight tonnage	1347 453
Total freight tonne-km	624 762 984
Average net freight train load (tonnes)	298
Average freight wagon load (tonnes)	30
Total passenger-km	230 362 391
Total passenger journeys	1695 761
Average length of passenger journey (km)	136

Finances

	1981
Revenue	(million pesos)
Passengers and baggage	232·325
Freight, parcels and mail	1554·893
Other income	523·243

Expenditure

	1981
	(million pesos)
Staff/personnel expenses	3439·300
Materials and services	712·520
Depreciation	104·076
Financial charges	944·477

Investment

For 1983 FNdeC was planning the following investment (million pesos):

Refurbishing of diesel locomotives	542·5
Refurbishing of freight vehicles	485·9
Track improvements	624·8
Bridges and buildings	75·8
Communications	84·6
Miscellaneous	478·4
Total	2292

In 1981 a World Bank loan of US$ 77 million was secured to support a US$ 176 million programme of infrastructure rehabilitation which the Government authorised at the end of 1982. First priority is the route from Bogota to the north coast at Santa Marta, followed by that south from Puerto Berrio to the west coast port of Buenaventura. The Government was negotiating a further World Bank loan of 5000 million pesos for investment in traction, rolling stock, track machinery, signalling and telecommunications.

A new 150 km standard-gauge line, Government-sponsored, is being built from a big open-cast coal field in the Cerrejon B area of the Guajira peninsula to a deep-water port at Bahia Portete. The field's reserves have been put at 1600 million tonnes. Electrification of the line has been under discussion, also its extension further inland to other coal deposits at La Jagua and San Jorge. The new line is envisaged as operating 100-wagon trains of 10 000 tonnes load capacity with trios of locomotives.

Other new line projects

Studies for a 200 km link between Saboya and Puerto Carare have been undertaken. The line would provide a new connection between the northern and Atlantic lines. Balanced gradient would be 2·2 per cent, minimum curve radius 150 metres. Rails would be 56 kg/m to handle coal traffic from the Checua and Lenguazaque deposits totalling about 5·5 million tonnes a year. Government approval has been obtained for this project. A route has been selected and a photo-geological study has been carried out.

The most important proposed new link is likely to be between Barbosa and Puerto Berrio, designed to replace the uneconomic service between La Dorada and Facatativa. Steep gradients and narrow curves mean that trains travelling between the coast and the Mexican border have to be split up. From preliminary investigations it seems likely that the possible variant will run from Garavito on the Bogota-Barbosa branch. It would continue through easy mountainous terrain over 90 km to Landazuri where the line would descend to the plains before reaching Carare, on the Puerto Berrio-Santa Marta line. Mountainous sections would have a maximum gradient of two per cent and the cost would be approximately $360 million. Feasibility studies were ordered in 1981.

A line between Bogota and the port of Buenaventura was started in 1913 and abandoned in 1930 when the railhead had reached midway point on the Ibague—Armenia section of the line. Now an alternative route is under consideration which would replace the entire 109·7 km Ibague—Armenia section with an 11·6 km tunnel cut-off.

Other lines under study would provide direct rail connections to the regions of the Caribbean, Barranquilla and Cartagena at an estimated cost of $660 million.

Reconditioning programme

In view of the state of tracks, owing to lack of maintenance and resources, shortage of traction and rolling stock, FNdeC has found it necessary to execute an emergency reconditioning programme to meet the increasing demand for rail transport. This programme has been started with US$8 million from the National Federation of Coffee-Growers, mainly for repairing locomotives, and will continue with a US$149 million programme financed by the World Bank and the Government until 1985. This will consist of reconditioning 511 km of track, purchasing track materials, repairing bridges, reconstructing buildings, purchasing tools for workshops and purchasing freight handling equipment. Eight locomotives will be bought, and 200 gondola cars for transport of minerals.

This emergency plan will concentrate on the Atlantic line, with its connections to Medellin, Bogotá and Bucaramanga, but will not neglect branches which, although not having at the present any great density of traffic, will be of prime importance in the future, with the development of the cement, coal and iron and steel programmes which are gradually advancing in the Cundimarca and Boyacá areas. A medium-term programme will continue the reconditioning in 1985-86. The long-term programme includes the integration of the network with the construction of the Armenia-Ibagué project and the Cartago-Medellin connection, studies of which have been partly completed; definitive design is awaited.

Special attention is being paid in modernisation to electrification and a possible change in gauge, should growth in traffic justify this.

Motive power

154 diesel-electric, six steam locomotives; 23 diesel railcars and 12 trailers.

Rolling stock

Total number of passenger train coaches, 270 (including 13 sleeping, 23 restaurant, 1 bar car and 28 luggage vans); freight wagons, 5311.

Track

Rail: 37 and 29 kg/m
Cross ties (sleepers): Wood
Thickness: 150 mm
Spacing: In plain track 1666/km
in curves: 1700/km
Minimum curvature radius: 80 m
Max gradient: 3·8%
Max speed: 62 km/h
Max axleload: 15 tonnes
Max altitude: 2900 m

Diesel locomotives

Type	Wheel arrangement	Transmission	hp	Tractive effort Max kg	Tractive effort Continuous at kg	Tractive effort Continuous at kmlh	Max speed kmlh	Wheel dia mm	Weight tons	Length mm	Year first built	No in service	Manufacturers Mechanical	Manufacturers Transmission
GE-U6	Bo-Bo	Elec	600	53 000	9810	15·9	80	914	53	10 211	1960	8	GE	GE
GE-U8	Bo-Bo	Elec	800	58 000	12 000	16	80	914	58	10 211	1961	7	GE	GE
GM GA-8	Bo-Bo	Elec	800	54 500	11 960	15·8	85	838	54·5	10 823	1964	2	GM	GM
GE U10-8	Bo-Bo	Elec	1000	60 000	12 550	16·2	80	914	60	11 171	1969/73	74	Alco-GE	GE
—	Co-Bo-Co	Elec	1200	114 300	22 900	16·8	48	833	114·7	17 323	1953	5	GE	GE
GE U12, U13	Co-Co	Elec	1400	88 000	17 500	16	80	914	88	13 903	1958	24	GE	GE
GM GR-12	Co-Co	Elec	1425	91 000	17 860	15·8	85	1016	91	14 427	1963	24	GM	GM
GE-U20C	Co-Co	Elec	2000	90 000	19 050	22	80	914	90	15 926	1964	10	GE	GE

CONGO

Ministry of Transport & Civil Aviation

Brazzaville

Minister: M Mounthault

Chemin de Fer Congo-Océan (CFCO)

PO Box 651, Pointe Noire

Telephone: 94-25-63
Telegrams: Congoocèan
Telex: 8231

General Manager (Agence Transcongolaise des Communications—ATC): François Bita
Technical General Manager (ATC): Pierre Lepetit
Director (CFCO): Medard Okoumou
Technical Director (CFCO): Roland Soudee

Gauge: 1067 mm
Route length: 510 km

Transport development

Congo is served by the Congo-Ocean Railway which extends from Pointe Noire to Brazzaville; a 285 km branch line, built by the Compagnie Minière de l'Ogooue (Comilog) connects Mont-Belo station (200 km from Pointe Noire) with M'Binda and public service over this line is now provided by the Congo-Ocean Railway.

The CFCO is a department within the Agence Transcongolaise des Communications (ATC).

Traffic

In 1981 CFCO operated 2560 passenger, 1309 mixed and 2929 freight trains. The number of passengers carried was 2337 million (compared with 1903 million in 1979) and passenger-km totalled 358 million (259 million in 1979). Freight, however, has suffered a severe recession since 1979. The 1981 totals were 1·39 million tonnes (3·58 million in 1979) and 546 million tonne-km (880 million in 1979).

Motive power and rolling stock

CFCO operates 44 diesel-electric locomotives, 21 diesel shunters, six diesel railcars, 85 passenger cars and 1829 freight wagons.

Investment

In 1982-83 substantial orders were placed with British manufacturers. British Rail Engineering (BREL) was to supply 36 saloon passenger and restaurant cars, to a design adapted for the 1067 mm gauge from British Rail's Mk III coach, and 155 freight wagons worth a total of £22·8 million; the order would involve the first production run of the cross-braced bogie developed by BR's Technical Centre. British Steel Corporation (BSC) was to supply rails and baseplates under a contract worth £3·7 million for realignment of the Brazzaville-Pointe Noire line, and 30 000 tonnes of rail for the Cerrejon coal line under a further contract worth £7 million.

COSTA RICA

Ministry of Public Works and Transport

San José

Telephone: 33 12 63
Telex: 2493

Minister: R A Monge
Director, Transport Division: R C Salazar
Director-General, Railways: M D Umana

Ferrocarriles de Costa Rica (FECOSA)

Apartado Postal No 1, Zona 3, San José

Telephone: 26 00 11
Telex: 2393

President: L D Bolanos
General Manager: J Vargas
Operations Manager: C J Volio
Projects Director: A Rodriguez
Finance Director: A Sales
Departmental Heads
Chief Transportation, Atlantic Division: I Solano
Chief Transportation, Pacific Division: M T Alvarado
Electromechanical Engineer: C Cruikshank
Maintenance of way: A Cruz

Gauge: 1067 mm
Route length: 700 km
Electrification: 128 km at 15 kV 20 Hz; 106 km at 25 kV 60 Hz

The country's two principal railways, the National Atlantic and the Pacific, were merged under the title of Ferrocarriles de Costa Rica in 1977.

Traffic

Bananas form a substantial part of the traffic on FECOSA's Atlantic route with about 710 000 tonnes (40 million crates) exported annually through the port of Limón. Following government plans to double banana output in the next few years the railway has been upgrading and electrifying the main banana rail route from Rio Frio to Limón.

Motive power

Number of electric locomotives	26
Number of diesel locomotives	50

Rolling stock

Number of passenger coaches	90
Number of freight wagons	1500

Electrification

The former Pacific Railway was electrified at 15 kV 20 Hz in 1929-30. Under the 1977 decree which created FECOSA, modernisation and electrification of the Atlantic Railway was to be put in hand. As a result, the 106 km Moin-Rio Frio main line has been completely relaid with 43 kg/m long-welded rail on concrete sleepers under the supervision of Canadian Pacific Consulting Services, new yards have been installed at both ends, bridges strengthened for 16-tonne axleloads, and electrification at 25 kV 60 Hz executed by the 50 c/s Group under the leadership of AEG-Telefunken. The Group has also supplied 12 dual-voltage 1200 kW Bo-Bo electric locomotives which are adaptable either to the new Atlantic Railway system or to the 15 kV 20 Hz system of the Pacific Railway. The latter is ultimately to be converted to 25 kV 60 Hz when its generating plant falls due for renewal. In the meantime a 58 km extension of the Pacific Railway from El Roble, near

Puntarenas, to a new cement factory at Colorado will be electrified at 15 kV 20 Hz, but the works will be designed for easy conversion to the higher voltage. President Rodrigo Carazo formally inaugurated electric operation between the Atlantic port of Moin and Río Frío in February 1982.

Integration of the Atlantic and Pacific railways is hampered by the fact that the only present connection is a steeply-graded track through the streets of San José. The intention is to form a new connection to the south of Alajuela, close to Costa Rica's International Airport where branches of the two networks are only 3 km apart.

Traction and rolling stock
Apart from the new electric locomotives mentioned above, FECOSA has recently procured 15 diesel locomotives worth US$ 6 million from General Electric and obtained three locomotives of 1067 mm gauge secondhand from Canadian National, which used them in Newfoundland. FECOSA has built two 14-tonne railbus prototypes with 200 hp Cummins engines in its own workshops. Freight wagon acquisitions have included 320 new wagons from Cobrasma.

Ferrocarril del Sur la Cra
Compania Bananera

Golfito, Puntarenas

Telephone: 75 02 63

General Manager: J F Campos
Superintendent: A G Alvaro

Gauge: 1067 mm
Route length: 231 km

Motive power and rolling stock
Diesel-electric locomotives 14; diesel railcars 16; passenger cars 18; freight wagons 641.

CUBA

Cuban National Railways (FdeC)
Ferrocarriles de Cuba

Ave Independencia y Tulipan, Havana

Minister of Transport: G Garcia Frias
Director-General, Railways: A Betancourt Perez
Director, Traffic: J Fernandez
Director, Western Division: A Montero
Director, Central Division: M Palacios
Director, East-Central Division: L de la Cruz
Director, Eastern Division: R Boffil
Director of Locomotives: E Moreda
Director, Rolling Stock: J Alfonso
Director, Finance: A Coviella
Director, Passenger Services: P Vila
Director, Freight: R Ruvira
Director, Communications: H Carcia

Gauge: 1435 mm
Route length in public service: 5196 km
Electrification: 199 km at 1·2 kV dc

Transport development
The railway accounts for most of Cuba's freight transport movements which are largely based on shipments of sugar, together with its by-products of rum and molasses, tobacco and citrus fruits. Large deposits of nickel, manganese and chrome in the south-east and substantial deposits of copper near Santiago de Cuba are expected to contribute largely to future rail loadings.

All the public service railways in the country are operated by the FdeC. The system is being progressively rationalised, uneconomic lines being closed down and replaced by road transport.

The Cuban Government invested Pesos 650 million in railway modernisation during the 1976-80 Five-Year Plan under an integrated development programme for railway, highway and maritime transport.

Bombardier Type MX 624 diesel locomotive recently supplied to Cuban National Railways

Traffic

	1980
Freight tonne-km (million)	2165
Freight tonnes carried (million)	14.1
Passenger-km (million)	1802
Passenger journeys (million)	20

Civil engineering
Despite continuing economic problems, largely brought about by the collapse of world sugar prices, reconstruction of the Havana-Santiago de Cuba line has continued. Total length of the new track being installed is 1170 km, comprising 837 km of main line, 224 km of sidings and passing loops and 109 km of feeder branch lines. Line is being laid with Soviet-supplied type P50 (51·48 kg/m) rail in 12·5 metre lengths; sidings are being laid with 44·62 kg/m rails, also from the Soviet Union. Sleepers are prestressed monobloc concrete, type Cuba 71. The project involves reconstruction of 400 bridges.

Sugar railways
The railways serving the sugar plantations and factories total 9638 km of which some 65 per cent are standard gauge. The rolling stock on the sugar industry railway is only used during the sugar cane harvest (100 days). Cuba intends to increase its sugar production to 10 million tons in the next few years and modernise the railway network simultaneously, as well as using it for the transport of other agricultural products and minerals.

Traction and rolling stock
FdeC operates 435 diesel and 12 electric locomotives, 85 diesel and 15 electric railcars, 523 passenger and baggage cars and 8217 freight cars.

CZECHOSLOVAKIA

Czechoslovak State Railways (ČSD)
Ceskoslovenské Státni Dráhy

Na příkopě 33, 110 05 Prague 1

Telephone: 2122
Telegrams: Domini, Praha
Telex: 121096

Minister of Transport: Ing V Blažek
First Vice-Minister: Ing J Lajčiak
Vice-Ministers: Ing L Blažek
Ing J Filinský
Ing S Houška
J Dykast
Department Directors
Finance: Ing Z Slezák
International: Ing J Šir
Personnel: Ing V Mácha
Movement and Traffic: Ing L Štros
Traction: Ing V Farbula
Track: Ing V Mazel

Telecommunications and Signalling: Ing I Laniček
Material: Ing J Hlaváč
Research and Development: Ing Z Holub
Electrotechnical: Ing A Ďurčansky
Technical: Ing M Glos
Public Relations: M Kozák

Gauge: 1435 mm; 1524 mm; various narrow gauges
Route length: 12 883 km; 102 km; 157 km
Electrification: 1126·4 km at 25 kV 50 Hz; 1957 km at 3 kV dc; 87 km at 1·5 kV dc; 6 km at 900 V dc

Transport development
Overall responsibility for all forms of transport throughout the country—railways, road, urban, waterways, internal airlines—is vested in the Ministry of Transport.

The ČSD system is divided into four administrative regions each of which is largely autonomous,

being responsible for traffic and for management and control of all installations and equipment in its area:

Railway	Headquarters
Eastern	Bratislava
Midland	Olomouc
North-Eastern	Prague
South-Western	Pilsen

Though only 21·7 per cent of its route-mileage is double-track, ČSD is the country's principal means of transport for heavy freight, notably the coal and lignite output of Bohemia and Moravia, imports from the USSR and the industries of Slovakia. As a result, in 1981 70 per cent of all freight tonne-km recorded in the country was by rail (ČSD's share in the 1950s was 95 per cent), but though road's share of the remainder was only 27 per cent its command of non-bulk freight gained it 80 per cent of all movement in pure tonnage terms.

Traffic

	1979	1980	1981
Total freight tonnes (million)	283·3	286·2	286·6
Total freight tonne-km (million)	65 972	66 210	66 455
Total passenger journeys (million)	411·5	415·6	404·6
Total passenger-km (million)	18 152	18 043	17 910

More than two-thirds of ČSD's freight moves over 17 per cent of its route-mileage, comprising chiefly the two east-west transversals: from Cheb, in western Bohemia near the West German border, to the USSR frontier at Cierna-nad-Tisou, in the far east of Slovakia, a distance of 1290 km; and from Cheb via Plzen, Prague, Kolin, Brno and Bratislava to the Hungarian border at Stúrovo on the Danube, a distance of 753 km. The first of these routes is 83 per cent electrified at 3 kV dc, double track throughout and signalled with automatic colour-lights. The second, which interconnects 15 per cent of the population and is a key passenger route, is 86 per cent double-tracked and 50 per cent automatically signalled; the 106 km single-track section between Cheb and Plzen, which has a daily throughput of 130 trains, has been CTC-controlled since 1967. This second route is presently electrified with two systems. From Cheb it is 25 kV ac, which since the end of 1982 has extended to cover the 118 km as far as Chrást. A 59 km gap follows to the start of Prague's 3 kV dc network, but 25 kV ac is resumed at Kutná-Hora, near Kolin, for the remainder of the route.

Increase of east-west operating capacity is a priority, because of Slovakian industrialisation and the scale of USSR traffic. Between 1948 and 1980 ČSD freight tonne-km as a whole quintupled, but it rose ninefold in Slovakia, which sees 38 per cent of total ČSD freight operation. In 1980 ČSD-SZD traffic through the big change-of-gauge transhipment terminal at Cierna-nad-Tisou aggregated 23·3 million tonnes, of which only 8 per cent comprised Czechoslovak exports.

Consequently ČSD has been compelled to upgrade formerly secondary lines and seeks to develop a third, southern transversal of 921 km from Plzen through České-Budějovice, Jihlava, Breclav, Trnava, Zvolen to Kosice. At present less than 10 per cent of this route is double track, but a further 148 km, between Leopoldov and Zvolen, is programmed for early doubling and subsequent electrification (after 1985). At the end of 1982 263 km or 28·5 per cent of the route was electrified at 25 kV ac and this was about to be raised through a catenary extension of some 85 km on the north Bratislava bypass.

Traffic

In 1981 ČSD registered 286·6 million tonnes and 66 455 million tonne-km of freight. This was only 5 per cent above 1976 figures, whereas the 1961-75 rise was 57 per cent, which indicates the bigger role now played by road transport. However, the 1981-85 National Plan's intent to save 12 million tonnes of fuel oil a year by greater resort to indigenous solid fuel as well as to nuclear energy will benefit ČSD. Average gross load of ČSD freight trains is 1200 tonnes.

ČSD-Intrans container traffic was running at a total of some 15 000 boxes and 286 million tonnes in 1981. Terminals were situated at Prague, Plzen, Brno, Bratislava, Presov and Cierna, but ČSD aimed to have some 20 terminals operative by 1985; recently opened is one at Nitra, east of Bratislava. There is a regular container unit-train service between Prague and Moscow.

Since a peak of 643 million journeys and 21 600 million passenger-km in 1961, the former figure has dropped by over a third, the latter by only 14 per cent, a contrast which reflects the simultaneous rise of private car ownership from 6 to about 45 per cent of Czechoslovak households. Journeys declined by a further 2·5 per cent in 1981. In 1981, however, the Government substituted rail service for a number of local bus routes to conserve oil, a move which coincided with ČSD's completion of a fleet of over 500 lightweight Type M-152 diesel railcars. Built by Studěnka in Moravia, powered by a Skoda 154 kW engine, seating 55 with standing room for 40, and with a maximum speed of 80 km/h, these vehicles monopolise passenger operations over more than 2250 route-km of ČSD. Inimical route characteristics and the mixed-traffic nature of ČSD's traction limit average express train transits even on the key Prague-Brno-Bratislava route to an average of 75 km/h.

Finance	1982
Revenues	*(Cr million)*
Passengers and baggage	1931
Freight, parcels and mail	17 691
Sidings	379
Wagon demurrage	1594
Other	68
Total	21 663

USSR-built Class T679.1 diesel-electric Co-Co for freight at Karlovy Vary *(Gottfried Schilke)*

ČSD Class E458.0 3 kV dc shunting Bo-Bo at Prague *(Gottfried Schilke)*

ČSD Class T478.3 diesel-electric Bo-Bo *(Yves Steenebruggen)*

Expenditure	1982 (Cr million)
Staff/personnel expenses	4644
Materials and services	3407
Depreciation	3504
Repairs and maintenance	2282
Contributions for social security, interest, etc	4655
Total	18 492

ČSD Class M-152 lightweight diesel railcar, built by Studénka

Electrification

Electric traction is now available over 23 per cent of ČSD route-mileage and hauls 62 per cent of all traffic. The north operates at 3 kV dc, the south at 25 kV ac; the only junction of the two systems at present is at Kutná-Hora, 77 km east of Prague.

The 1981-85 national plan scheduled only a 2 per cent increase in ČSD investment, to Cr65 000 million for the period, but within this the amounts assigned to electrification and signalling have been improved 81 and 141 per cent respectively. The target for 1985 is 3530 km of electrification, 38 per cent of it 25 kV ac, and for 1990 4173 km, 40 per cent 25 kV ac. There will be three ac/dc meeting-points by 1985, six by 1990.

Of the 541 km to be newly electrified by 1985, two-thirds will be at 25 kV ac. Except for 1983 completion of the southern part of the Prague-Decin link with the German Democratic Republic and the northern part of the Prerov-Breclav line, a segment of the Warsaw-Vienna main route, 3 kV dc extensions will be confined to gap-filling. In ac, the main task is in Bohemia, on the Prague-Plzen stretch of the Cheb-Stúrove transversal. Completion of a new rail-road Danube bridge at Bratislava will improve the route to Hungary and also allow the cross-town line to be transformed into a rapid transit route, the Rycholodráka, connecting the city with its new satellite town of Peteralka.

Civil engineering

A major development of 1981 was completion of a 3 km double-track, electrified and partly subterranean bypass in Prague, to eliminate reversals of through north-south traffic in the Prague Stredni area.

Track

Main lines are generally laid with 49 kg/m rail, secondary lines with 30 to 40 kg/m. However almost 10 per cent of all route-km is now relaid with 65 kg/m rail, since the lines concerned, carrying freight trains of increasing weight, are recording 60 to 80 million tonne-km of traffic a year.

Signalling

By the end of 1982 automatic block and colour-light signalling had been installed over 10 per cent of the ČSD network and at 15 per cent of its junctions and stations. Most secondary lines are worked by a tele-

Class ES 499.0 (Skoda Type 55E) dual-voltage 4000 kW locomotive

phonic despatching system with signalling at stations.

Traction and rolling stock

ČSD operates approximately 1400 electric locomotives, 220 emus, 3400 diesel locomotives, 1200 diesel railcars and 200 000 freight wagons; recent figures of hauled passenger cars are not available, but 1300 new vehicles have been acquired since 1977.

Funds have been allocated for acquisition of 190 more electric locomotives from Skoda to cover the electrification extensions now planned. Series production of 100 dual-voltage 3 kV dc/25 kV ac locomotives to the prototype ES499.1 Bo-Bo design was to begin in 1984. A dual-voltage 3 kV dc/15 kV 16⅔ Hz ac Class EX499.2 for through working into the German Democratic Republic is also forthcoming, together with a new 3 kV dc type with thyristor chopper motor control for domestic ČSD use.

Some Skoda-built electric locomotives for ČSD

Class	E499.2	ES499.0	458.0	426.0	E699.1	43E (57E)	30E	E499.0
Year of production	1978	1974	1973	1972	1960	1960	1959	1953
Wheel arrangement	Bo-Bo	Bo-Bo	Bo'-Bo'	Bo'-Bo'	Co-Co	Bo-Bo	Bo-Bo	Bo-Bo
Max speed (km/h)	120	160	80	80	90	90	120	120
Traction current system	3000 V dc	3000 V dc 25 kV, 50 Hz	25 kV, 50 Hz	3000 V dc	3000 V dc	3000 V dc	3000 V dc	3000 V dc
Gauge (mm)	1435	1435	1435	1435	1435	1435	1435	1435
Diameter of driving wheels (mm)	1250	1250	1050	1050	1250	1250	1250	1250
Distance between bogie centres (mm)	8300	8300	6300	6300	9400	8170	8170	8170
Bogie wheel base (mm)	3200	3200	2800	2800	4500	3330	3330	3330
Height with pantographs lowered (mm)	4640	4640	4625	4650	4500	4640	4640	4640
Max width (mm)	2940	2940	3000	3000	2950	3040	3040	3040
Length over buffers (mm)	16 740	16 740	14 400	14 400	18 800	17 210	17 210	15 600
Total weight (Mp)	84	87·4	72	72	120	86	84	80
Axleload (Mp)	21	21·85	18	18	20	21·5	21	20
No of traction motors	4	4	4	4	6	4	4	4
No of running notches (incl weak-field notches)	—	56	notchless control	36	51	43	43	43
Gear ratio	—	1:2·162	1:4·6	1:3·48	1:4·238	1:3·11	1:2·27	1:2·27
Continuous transformer output (kVA)	—	5450	1540	—	—	—	—	—
Motor voltage control	rheostatic	rheostatic	thyristor	rheostatic	rheostatic	rheostatic	rheostatic	rheostatic
Axle drive	—	Skoda-system	nose suspended motors	nose suspended motors	nose suspended motors	Skoda-system	Skoda-system	Sécheron system
Auxiliary drives	—	3000 V dc	220 V dc	3000 V dc	3000 V dc	3000 V dc	3000 V dc	3000 V dc
Continuous power (kW)	4000	4000	880	800	2640	2032	2032	2032
Speed (mean wheel diameter 1215 mm, full field) (km/h) rims (MP)	—	108·5	29·5	32·3	48·7	46·2	63	63
Tractive effort at driving wheel	13·1	13·1	10·9	8·8	19·6	15·7	11·4	11·4
Tractive effort at max speed (Mp)	10	10	2	2·4	7·5	7·5	7	7
Max tractive effort (Mp)	26	26	16·4	16	36	26	26	26
Continuous power of rheostatic dynamic brake (kW)	3600	3600	—	—	—	—	—	—

Diesel locomotives

Type	Wheel arrange-ment	Trans-mission	Nominal output kW	Tractive effort Max kg	Continuous at kg	kmlh	Max speed kmlh	Wheel dia mm	Total weight tonnes	Length mm	Year first built	Manufacturer Mechanical parts	Engine & type	Transmission
T466.2	Bo-Bo	Elec	883	15 000	12 000	20	90	1000	64	13 580	1977	CKD	CKD K65230DR	CKD
T478.4	Bo-Bo	Elec	1460	17 000	12 500	30	100	1000	74·4	16 500	1978	CKD	CKD KV12230DR	CKD
T679.1	Co-Co	Elec	1435	25 000	18 000	22	100	1050	116	17 550	1966	USSR	USSR 14D40	USSR

Electric multiple-units

Type	Wheel arrange-ment	Current system	Nominal output kW	Tractive effort Max kg	Continuous at kg	kmlh	Max speed kmlh	Wheel dia mm	Total weight tonnes	Length mm	Year first built	Manufacturer Mechanical parts	Electrical equipment
EM 488.0	Bo-Bo + 2′ 2′ + 2′ 2′ + 2′ 2′ + Bo-Bo	3000 V dc	2000	23 000	12 000	57	110	1000	233	122 500	1974	Vagónka Studénka	MEZ Vsetin
SM 488.0	B-B + 2′ 2′ + 2′ 2′ + 2′ 2′ + B-B	25 kV 50 Hz	1680	19 000	9000	67	110	920	239	122 500	1968	Vagónka Studénka	MEZ Vsetin

DENMARK

Ministry of Transport

Frederiksholms Kanal 27, 1216 Copenhagen K

Telephone: 01 126242
Telex: 22 275

Minister: Arne Melchior
Permanent Under-Secretary of State: J L Halck

Danish State Railways (DSB)
Danske Statsbaner

Sølvgade 40, 1349 Copenhagen K

Telephone: 01 140400
Telex: 22 275

General Manager: Ole Andresen
Directors
   Commercial and Transport: E Rolsted Jensen
   Audit and Supply: S A Jenstrup
   Finances and Planning: Allan Andersen
   Personnel: G Kragballe
   Way and Works: Ebbe Falk-Sørensen
   Mechanical Engineering: Verner Adelkvist

Gauge: 1435 mm
Route length: 2461 km
Electrification: 135 route-km at 1·5 kV dc

Transport development

DSB accounts for 97 per cent of total Danish passenger rail traffic and 99 per cent of the total freight rail traffic. The remainder is carried out by a number of smaller private railway companies. DSB's rail network is nation-wide and has about 200 manned stations.

The railway is a Government department with staff having the status of civil servants; the General Manager has the status of a State Secretary of the Transport Ministry. DSB is subject to Government control; staff redundancies are not normally permitted and staff reductions are obtained through wastage. Quantity licensing for road hauliers is in force in Denmark, affording some protection to rail. Private car ownership per head (1981 figures) is 0·267.

Traffic

DSB's passenger traffic is characterised by the fact that Denmark is divided into a number of islands and peninsulas. Moreover, the relatively short distances and the location and size of Copenhagen (population of Greater Copenhagen: 1·735 million) also influences the traffic pattern. The traffic structures east and west of Store Baelt do not have a great deal in common. On Zealand the daily commuting in the metropolitan area dominates traffic patterns with S-trains alone accounting for almost 75 per cent of DSB's total rail passenger journeys. On the other hand, local train traffic west of Store Baelt is of more modest proportions. The

Prototype Lyntog train-set

Copenhagen-Fredericia line carries principal long-distance passenger traffic while the Copenhagen-Jutland route provides express ferry connections between Kalundborg and Århus.

The geography of the country makes ferries a necessity; DSB operates ten routes with a total of 29 ferries and other vessels either alone or in conjunction with the Swedish State Railways (SJ), the Deutsche Bundesbahn (DB) and the Deutsche Reichsbahn (DR). Three of the routes are served by rail/road ferries.

Long-cherished schemes to bridge the 25·75 km waterway, which interrupts communications between Copenhagen and the east of the country, are in limbo. In 1980/81 DSB installed three big new ferries of identical design, the *Dronning Ingrid*, *Prins Joachim* and *Kronprins Frederik*, all built in local yards; terminal improvements at Korsor and Nyborg match the bigger vessels' greater carrying capacity. The trio has been designed for feasibility of later adaptation to accommodate road vehicles, but have been commissioned as exclusive passenger-and-train ferries. They are also being employed exclusively for transfer of passenger trains and freight wagons.

Each of these three latest ferries embodies on its rail deck 495 metres of track, which makes room for 18 standard European coaches of 26·4-metre length. The tracks are flanked by platforms, making it easy for passengers to detrain and make for the two upper decks during the crossing, which lasts 60 minutes. Upper-deck accommodation is designed for 2000 passengers and includes a restaurant and two cafeterias. DSB runs no restaurant cars because

25 kV ac electrification catenary erected in Zealand

of the ample time for train passengers to dine on the ship during the Store Baelt crossing. Dimensions are as follows:

Length overall	152 m
Width between fender lists	23·7 m
Height from keel to top of wheelhouse	21·6 m
Speed (at 15 000 bhp)	18·9 knots
Dead weight tonnage	4490 tons
Gross registered tonnage	10 606 tons
Passenger-carrying capacity	2000
Total track length	495 m

DSB inter-city passenger service over the Store Baelt is at fixed hourly intervals in each direction and the transhipment of the trains has been brought to a fine art. The timetable allows only 9-10 minutes for loading, no more than 15 minutes for discharge of the vehicles from the ship and continuation of the rail journey. As a result the fastest trains, the Lyntog or 'Lightning' trains, which are otherwise non-stop between Copenhagen and Odense, cover the 189 km in only 154 minutes for a creditable average of 73·7 km/h.

DSB's regional services are fixed-interval. Departures from Copenhagen for Elsinore and Roskilde are scheduled every half-hour, for Holbaek, Ringsted, Sorø, Slagelse, Kalundborg, Nykøbing and Naestved every hour. It is intended to expand the regional traffic on Zealand as and when DSB's economic framework allows.

A renewal of the regional railway traffic in Jutland and on Funen took place with the delivery of 31 new Type MR diesel railcars in 1978-79. They have been put into service on the sections Odense-Svendborg, Odense-Fredericia, Vejle-Herning-Struer, Århus-Skanderborg-Herning, Århus-Langa-Struer and Fredericia-Esbjerg.

Passenger traffic

The rapid 1978-80 growth of DSB's passenger traffic volume has now been reversed. After a more modest 3 per cent increase in journeys and one of just over 5 per cent in passenger-km during 1981, volume in mid-1982 was down 6 per cent following the first of a succession of severe Government-ordered price rises: an 18 per cent increase in April 1982 was to be followed by rises of 12 per cent in April and 6 per cent in November 1983.

Public service with two prototype five-car trainsets of a new design of push-pull 'Lyntog' equipment, powered by Class ME diesel locomotives pending electrification, was launched in 1982. Each set includes a conference room in its centre vehicle and general equipment includes a multi-channel radio point at the headrest of each passenger seat (for fuller details see Locomotives and rolling stock under Scandia-Randers). The push-pull arrangement will allow main-line locomotives to propel the 'Lyntog' trains straight on to train ferries and thus reduce waiting time at the ferry ports.

Freight traffic

In the later 1970s DSB concluded that its only hope of effective competition in the domestic freight market lay in progressive abandonment of classic wagonload handling and simultaneous concentration on unitised loading. Complete conversion to containerised handling of one form or another was envisaged by 1990. The total of public rail freight depots was to be considerably reduced to a core of comprehensively mechanised intermodal transhipment terminals, ideally open to both DSB and privately-owned road transport. Eleven specialised centres of this kind have already been established and considerable progress achieved in the development of a 20-foot container system, including special provision for palletised goods, on the lines of the West German DB's 'Haus-zu-Haus' operation. In conjunction with this method DSB hoped to market its own total distribution and warehousing packages (it deploys its own 500-strong fleet of road freight vehicles).

Dedication to total containerisation is now waning. One reason is realisation that the 1100 or so customers with their own private sidings are not prepared to dispense with traditional wagonload service. Another is the fact that international freight traffic of orthodox pattern is not contracting. DSB is, however, moving to create a domestic and international piggyback operation.

After a further tonnage regression in 1981 as a result of the recession, DSB's overall freight performance in 1982 had its first boost from the Government's decision to encourage coal-fuelling of electricity generating stations with the start in August of a 200 000 tonnes a year flow of imported coal from Esbjerg to the Herning (Jutland) power station in trains of 18 Type Fals bogie wagons. Privately owned, the hoppers are built by Scandia-Randers to a Talbot design, have a 54·5-tonnes payload capacity and power-operated discharge

Traffic

	1979	1980	1981
Total train-km (000)	46 700	48 170	—
Total freight tonnes (000)	7041	6709	6456
Total freight tonne-km (million)	1780	1705	1574
Total passenger-km (million)	2915	3803	4003
Total passenger journeys (million)	116·467	130·413	134·124

Finance (DKr million)

	1979	1980	1981
Revenue			
Passenger and baggage	1137	1351	1592
Freight, parcels and mail	862	855	756
Ferry operations			527
Catering			155
Other sources			310
Total	1999	2206	3340
Expenditure			
Staff	2178	2399	2973
Materials and services	1042	1338	1395
Depreciation	187	207	235
Financial charges	335	367	402
Total	3742	4311	5005

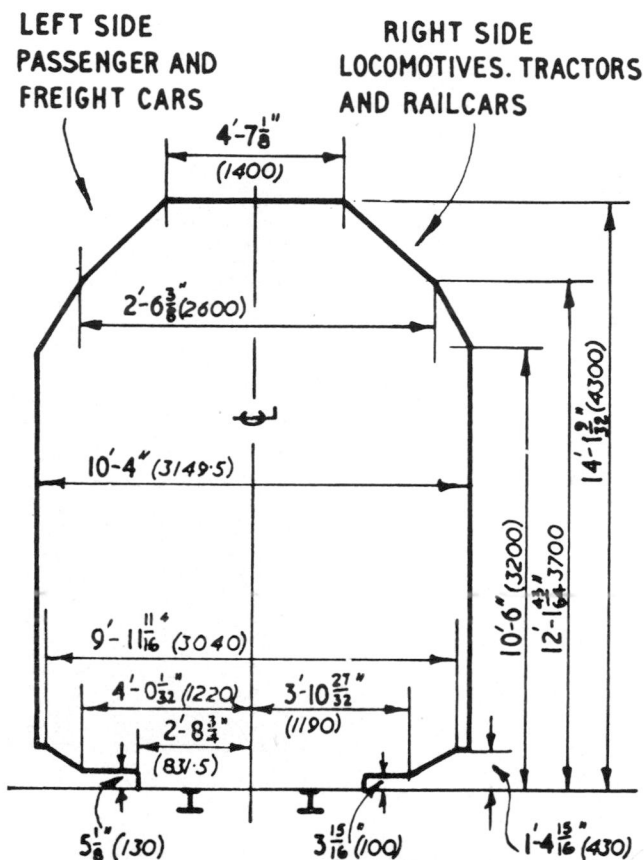

LEFT SIDE PASSENGER AND FREIGHT CARS

RIGHT SIDE LOCOMOTIVES. TRACTORS AND RAILCARS

Interior of prototype Lyntog train-set

doors. The only area of freight showing a stable rate in 1981 was again the international, running at 3·8 million tonnes for the year and including some important new clients for import/export traffic with the Federal Republic of Germany.

Motive power and rolling stock

Motive power and rolling stock operated by DSB in 1982 were: 316 line-haul diesel locomotives; 85 shunting tractors; 37 diesel railcars; 921 passenger coaches; 5977 freight wagons; 58 diesel train-sets; 208 electric train-sets for Copenhagen suburban lines. DSB also operates 586 buses.

Deliveries during 1982 were 16 diesel locomotives, 22 diesel railcar units, 100 passenger cars and 100 freight wagons. On order at the start of 1983 were 21 diesel locomotives, two three-phase ac electric locomotives, 32 diesel railcar units, 22 passenger cars and 50 freight wagons.

Electrification

Copenhagen suburban services are as yet the only electrified services in Denmark, operating on 1500 volts dc overhead supply, but following Parliamentary approval DSB has begun a 25 kV ac main-line electrification which may see half the 2000 km network energised by the mid-1990s.

On the first route from Copenhagen to Helsingør the major clearance construction works were finished during 1982 and erection of masts for the Rungsted-Helsingør section was to be completed in 1983. Trial running is due in 1984 and electric trains should be operating between Copenhagen and Helsingør by 1985. Electrification west of Copenhagen towards Korsør and Rødby will begin in 1982 although electric trains are unlikely to be operating before 1986. In the course of electrification maximum line speed will be raised to 175 km/h wherever possible; the new Class ME diesel locomotives are arranged for this limit. The two prototype locomotives so far ordered for the scheme feature three-phase ac motor technology.

Investment

DSB's 1983-88 plan envisages modernisation of a number of secondary lines, double-tracking of the Vipperød-Holbaek and quadrupling of the Tastrup-Roskilde-Køge lines, together with numerous measures to improve reliability, including installation of more point heaters, workshop and signalling improvements, and purchases of additional traction and new inter-city rolling stock. An order for prototype double-deck rolling stock for the electrified Copenhagen-Helsingør line was likely to be placed with Scandia-Randers late in 1983: the manufacturer has already prepared a design for a 26·4-metre vehicle with 135 seats. With completion of the Hundige-Køge S-Bane extension at the end of 1983, regular interval passenger service was to be launched between Roskilde, Køge and Naestved. The plan calls yet again for a Government decision on the Store Baelt bridge issue, with the alternative of approval for further improvement of the waterway's ferry facilities, which could involve concentration of the west shore terminal operations on Knudshoved: this is presently the terminal of the road transport ferry link with Halskov, whereas the train ferry terminal is at Nyborg.

Following experience in the very severe winter of 1981-82, DSB made expenditure on protective measures a priority. In two years a total of DKr25 million has been spent to equip 300 traction units with snowploughs and to purchase four 350 hp

Class MR diesel railcar set

Class ME 3420 hp diesel-electric with three-phase motors

Dronning Ingrid, one of three latest Store Baelt ferries

Interior of Class MR dmu

3900 hp Class Mz diesel-electric Co-Co

self-propelled rotary snowploughs and 19 independent prow-fronted ploughs for locomotive propulsion. A further DKr50 million has been invested to raise DSB's total of gas or electric point-heaters to 3200.

DSB planned investment in 1983 covered (DKr000):

Diesel-electric locomotives (15)	44 000
Electric locomotives (2)	31 200
Self-propelled passenger cars (48)	170 100
Hauled passenger cars (28)	35 400
Track work and maintenance machinery	106 900
Electrification and signalling	216 800
Intermodal equipment	112 100
Communications	69 700
Yards and terminals	25 000
Workshops	71 500
Miscellaneous	98 000
Total	1 416 000

Signalling

In 1981 DSB completed installation in Jutland of 14 local interlockings in which the functions are executed by micro-computer logic. Two independent programmes operating in parallel compare outputs to ensure fail-safe working of the single processor performing the interlocking functions. The operators at each station work with alpha-numerical keyboards and colour vdus showing layout status, but the installations are arranged for alternative unitary control from a single centre covering the whole 113 km of route involved. Suppliers were Dansk Signal Industri.

DSB plans to begin replacement of existing systems with computer-based equipment in 1985. Following an experimental optic fibre cable installation in the Copenhagen suburban area a further use is planned on the electrified Copenhagen-Helsingør line.

Track

Rail: Flat-bottom, 60-37 kg/m
Crossties (sleepers)
Twin-block concrete: RS, SL and S 75
Thickness: 200 mm
Creosoted beech
Thickness: 160 mm
Spacing: 1600/km

Fastenings: RS and S 75
Minimum curvature radius: 190 m
Max gradient: 1·25%
Max axleload: 20 tonnes

Ferry services

DSB is Denmark's major passenger-carrying ferry operator, serving a total of ten routes. In 1981 these maritime services recorded a total of 25·5 million passengers, a rise of 4 per cent on 1980 overall, but on the Store Baelt the growth was 7 per cent, to a gross of just over 4 million journeys. Busiest of all services, however, was the Puttgarden-Rødby which DSB shares with West Germany's DB, where the aggregate for the year was 5 million.

DSB ferry services

		km
Korsør-Nyborg	passenger and rail ferries	26
Halsskov-Knudshoved	passenger and car ferries	19
Kalundborg-Samso	passenger and car ferries	41
Bøjden-Fynshav	passenger and car ferries	14
Helsingør-Helsingborg (Sweden)	passenger, rail and car ferries	5
Copenhagen-Malmö (Sweden)	rail ferry	30
Rødby Faerge-Puttgarden (W Germany)	passenger, rail and car ferries	19
Gedser-Warnemünde (E Germany)	passenger, rail and car ferries	48
Kalundborg-Aarhus	passenger and car ferries	89
Esbjerg-Fanoe	passenger and car ferries	3·5

The services are operated by 29 DSB ferries, 1 motor boat and 4 foreign ferries.
The DSØ, a DSB subsidiary and joint venture with the Swedish State Railways (SJ) runs:

Dragör-Limhamn (Sweden)	passenger and car ferries	17
Copenhagen-Malmö (Sweden)	passenger hydrofoils and catamarans	36

Control centre of ATO-equipped Copenhagen S-Bane emu system

DSB intermodal depot with 40 tonnes-capacity transfer crane

Diesel locomotives

Class	Wheel arrangement	Transmission	Rated power (kW)	Max speed km/h	Total weight tonnes	No in service	Year first built	Builders Mechanical parts	Builders Engine & type	Builders Transmission
MZ 1401-1426	Co-Co	Elec	2426	143	120	26	1967	Nydqvist & Holm, Frichs	GM 16-645-E3	Thrige
MZ 1427-1446	Co-Co	Elec	2867	165	121-126	20	1972	Nydqvist & Holm, Frichs	GM 20-645-E3	GM
MZ 1447-1461	Co-Co	Elec	2867	165	123	15	1977	Nydqvist & Holm, Frichs	GM 20-645-E3	GM
MX 1001-1045	1A1-1A1	Elec	1047	133	89	45	1960	Nydqvist & Holm, Frichs	GM 567C, 12 cyl	Thrige
MV 1101-1159*	1A1-1A1	Elec	1250	133	99	5	1954	Nydqvist & Holm, Frichs	GM 567B, 16 cyl	GM, Thrige
MY 1101-1159*	1A1-1A1	Elec	1433	133	102	54	1954	Nydqvist & Holm, Frichs	GM 567C, 16 cyl	GM, Thrige
MT 151-167	B-B	Elec	361	90	52	17	1958	Frichs	MTU MB 12V 493 AZ 1	Titan
MH 201-203	C	Hydr	323	60	45	3	1957	Henschel	MAN-W 8V 17·5/22A	Voith
MH 301-420	C	Hydr	323	60	41	115	1960	Frichs	MAN-W 8V 17·5/22A	Voith
ME 1501-1516	Co-Co	Elec	2426	175	115	16	1981	Thyssen-Henschel, Scandia	GM 16-645-E3B	BBC
Tractor 101-116	B	Mech	123	60	28	16	1951	Ardelt-Werke	MAN-W 5V 17·5/22A	Ardelt
Tractor 117-146	B	Mech	123	60	28	29	1955	Frichs	Frichs 4185 CA	Ardelt
Tractor 251-290	B	Hydr	94	45	17	40	1966	Frichs	Leyland UE 680	Voith

*Designation depends on the engine, which is interchangeable between the types

Diesel railcars or multiple-units

Class	Cars per unit	Motor cars per unit	Motored axles per motor car	Transmission	Rated power (kW) per motor	Max speed km/h	Weight tonnes per car (M-motor T-trailer)	Total seating capacity	Length per car mm (M-motor T-trailer)	No in service	Year first built	Builders		
												Mechanical parts	Engine & type	Transmission
MR/MRD	2	2	2	Hydr	239	130	34·5	128	22 500	53	1979	Duewag/ Scandia	KHD F12L413F	Voith
MA	8	2	2	Hydr	809 (traction) 218 (auxiliary)	160	M 51 T 26-29	257	M 20 080 T 18 250-18 400	5	1963	MAN/ Wegmann/ Linke Hofmann	Maybach MD 650/1 (traction) MWM TRHS 518A (auxiliary)	Voith

Railcars

Class	Cars per unit	Motor cars per unit	Motored axles per motor car	Transmission	Rated power (kW) per motor	Max speed km/h	Weight tonnes per car (M-motor T-trailer)	Total seating capacity	Length per car mm (M-motor T-trailer)	No in service	Year first built	Builders		
												Mechanical parts	Engine & type	Transmission
MO*			2	Elec	184 (2 motors 120 per railcar)	65		37	20 930	37	1935	Frichs	Frichs 6185CA	Titan

*Withdrawal imminent

Electric multiple-units (Copenhagen suburban lines)

Class	Cars per unit	Line voltage	Motor cars per unit	Motored axles per motor car	Rated output (kW) per motor	Max speed km/h	Weight tonnes per car (M-motor T-trailer)	Total seating capacity	Length per car mm (M-motor (T-trailer)	No in service	Rate of acceleration m/s²	Year first built	Builders	
													Mechanical parts	Electrical equipment
MM/FS	2	1·5 kV dc	1	4	147	100	M 42 T 28	130	M 20 270 T 20 270	139	0·75	1968	Scandia	GEC
MM/FU/ MU/FS	4	1·5 kV dc	2	4	147	100	M 42 T 29 M 43 T 28	260	M 20 270 T 20 340 M 20 340 T 20 270	65	0·75	1975	Scandia	GEC
FC/MC/ MC/FC	4	1·5 kV dc	2	4	210, 218	120	M 46 T 34	250	M 20 100 T 20 790	4	0·90	1979	Scandia	ASEA, GEC

DOMINICAN REPUBLIC

Ministry of Public Works and Communications

Santo Domingo

State Secretary: Fernando Periche Vidal

Central Romana Railroad

Central Romana, La Romana

President: C Morales T
Vice-President and General Superintendent: R J Rivera

Gauge: 1435 mm
Route length: 375 km

The railroad operates 15 locomotives and 950 freight cars.

ECUADOR

Ministry of Public Works

Quito

Minister: Ing Edwin Ripalda Bonilla
Under-Secretary: Ing Walter Schuldt Solis
Director-General: Ing Carlos Alarcón

State Railways of Ecuador (ENFdeE)
Empresa de los Ferrocarriles del Estado

PO Box 159, Bolivar 443, Quito

Telephone: 216 180
Telegrams: Chimborazo

General Manager: Economista César Velasco Oláya
Traffic Manager: Vicente Cevallos C
Diesel Maintenance Engineer: Guillermo Montolvo R
Transport and Telecommunications Engineer: Manuel Andrade A
Motive Power Superintendent: Guido Jaramillo
Permanent Way Engineers: José Guevara G
Guido Gallo
Chief Technical Dept: Víctor Marchán A

Gauge: 1067 mm
Route length: 965 km

Transport development
Ecuador, 275 000 square km in area, is bordered by the Pacific Ocean on the west, Colombia on the north, and Peru on the south and east. There are three public service railways including the Ferrocar- ril Guayaquil-Quito, the Ferrocarril Quito-Ibarra-San Lorenzo and the Ramal Austral Sibambe-Cuenca, all state-owned, and several industrial railways. The management structure is based on regional head- quarters at Quito, Ibarra and Cuenca.

The state railway system is operated by the Empresa de los Ferrocarriles del Estado. In 1981 the Ministry of Public Works commissioned a feasibility study for remodelling this system and construction of some 1000 km of new lines.

The principal line, 452 km long, connects Guaya- quil, the main port and largest city of the country, with Quito, which lies at some 2800 metres altitude in the Sierra of the Andes. From Duran, the terminus for Guayaquil, the line runs across low lying plains for 87 km to Bucay, at the foot of the western slopes of the Andes. Over the next 79 km the line climbs 2940 metres at an average grade over the whole section of 3·7 per cent (1 in 27). The line strikes many sharp curves, and several stretches are laid on a grade of 5·5 per cent (1 in 18), including a double reversing zig-zag which was required to negotiate a particularly awkward mountain outcrop known as the Nariz del Diablo (Devil's Nose). Once the summit of this section is reached at Palmira, 3238 metres in altitude and 166 km from Duran, the line remains in the high Sierra, never falling below 2500 metres, and rising to 3609 metres at the overall summit of Urbina, 264 km from Duran.

Riobamba, 230 km from Duran, is the major intermediate station on the line, and the terminus of the daily mixed train from Duran. Between Duran and Bucay, on the coastal section, mixed trains are operated by both steam locomotives and diesels of a fleet of Spanish-built Euskalduna, Alco-type Co-Co general purpose locomotives, which have been introduced in recent years. In addition, there is a supplementary service of small passenger railcars which operate from Duran to intermediate stations on this section. Beyond Bucay freight is handled mainly by Baldwin-built 2-8-0 steam locomotives, the most recent of which date from the 1950s.

Between Riobamba and Quito there is a diesel- hauled service of freight trains, and in addition a service of modern railcars operates three times a week in each direction between Duran and Quito, taking some 12 hours over the journey.

The two remaining lines of the system link Quito with San Lorenzo, on the north-west coast of Ecuador near the Colombian border; and Sibambe, 131 km from Duran on the main line, with Cuenca, an important provincial capital in the southern part of the country. The San Lorenzo line is 373 km long and was finally completed, with the aid of French backing, in 1957. Regrettably, San Lorenzo has failed to show the promise as a thriving port that was originally expected of it. Freight services are operated on this line by diesel locomotives, with the Cuenca line's small railcars providing a passenger service. The Cuenca line is operated mainly by steam locomotives and small railcars, and is 148 km long.

Railway	Gauge	Route length km
FC Guayaquil-Quito	1067 mm	446
*FC Quito-San Lorenzo	1067 mm	373·5
FC Sibambe-Cuenca	1067 mm	145·5

*The FC Quito-San Lorenzo is operated as a separate railway.

The Guayaquil to Quito line was built in sections between 1873 and 1908, the major work on the western slopes of the Andes being carried out at the turn of the century. Originally operated by a private company with capital from the USA and United Kingdom, the railway was taken into State control in 1944. Road competition is keen, particularly between Riobamba and Quito where the line is paralleled by the Pan American Highway, and much of the equipment in operation shows signs of considerable age.

Investment 1983 (US$000)	
Locomotives (6)	7000
Freight cars (30)	1892
Track works	3328
Track maintenance machines	500
Signalling	300
Yards and terminals	200
Miscellaneous	100
	13 320

Motive power and rolling stock

Locomotives in service	
(diesel-electric)	13
(steam)	9
Railcars in service	31
Passenger coaches	50
Freight wagons	205

Electrification

During 1980 consultants from Hungary and Italy completed preliminary studies for the feasibility of electrifying the ENFE system.

EGYPT

Ministry of Transport, Communications and Shipping

Cairo

Minister: Soliman Metwalli

Egyptian Railways (ER)

Station Building, Ramses Square, Cairo

Telegrams: Railways, Cairo
Telex: 92616

Chairman: Eng Kamal Hashmat Gado
Deputy Chairmen,
  Operation and Regions: Eng A S Fayed
  Track and Structures: Eng Moustafa Kamel Hassan
  Mechanical and Electrical Engineering: Eng M Hasan El Sahn
  Transport Planning: Dr A Kader Lasheen
General Manager: A Abu Mawash

Gauge: 1435 mm
Route length: 4321 km
Electrification: 25 km at 1·5 kV dc

The railways in Egypt are mainly confined to the more fertile area of the Nile Delta, with a line following the course of the Nile southward to Shallal, just below Aswan.

The Egyptian Railways, which forms the largest system in the country, extends from the Mediterranean down the Nile Valley, serving the Nile Delta, Cairo, Alexandria, Port Said, Ismailia, Suez and connecting at Shallal, its southernmost point, with the river steamers of Sudan Railways. From El Quantara, on the Port Said-Ismailia line, a branch runs east following the coast and connects with Israel Railways.

The first section was between Alexandria and Cairo, opened to traffic in 1854. This was the first railway in Africa.

Traffic

In modern times ER has always been primarily a passenger railway, recording four to five times as many passenger-km as freight ton-km. Figures in 1982 were 486 million passenger journeys and 18 765 million passenger-km, 7·5 million tonnes of freight and 2302 million freight tonne-km. These results compare with targets of 355 million passenger journeys and 13 million tonnes of freight set in ER's 1976-80 re-equipment plan. In terms of

passenger-km, volume has more than doubled since 1970. ER has correspondingly expanded train lengths substantially, with the aid of 600 new mainline day cars and 605 new suburban cars acquired since the mid-1970s; the suburban stock has supplanted some 340 diesel railcars. Freight, on the other hand, has declined owing to indifferent performance; its main constituent is 2 million tonnes of ore a year on the Baharia-Helwan line.

Motive power

During the 1976-80 plan period 220 locomotives became obsolete. Consequently acquisition of new motive power has been one of the investment priorities and at the start of 1981, following the Transport Ministry's release of a further E£100 million for railway investment, Transport Minister Soliman Metwalli forecast purchase of a further 180 diesel locomotives. In the course of 1981 orders worth C$ 137 million in total were placed with General Motors of Canada Ltd for 143 Type G22W locomotives. Stock at the end of 1982 comprised 575 line-haul and 147 shunting diesel locomotives.

Turbotrains

Introduction of three ten-car turbotrain sets built by ANF-Industrie to public service over the 208 km between Cairo and Alexandria was scheduled for May 1983. (For details of the turbotrain design see under ANF-Industrie in the Locomotives and rolling stock section). After completion of the Alexandria-Itay Baroud bypass, which in conjunction with an existing Nile west bank line between Itay Baroud and Cairo will keep freight out of the turbotrains' path, it was intended to exploit the new equipment's 160 km/h capability to achieve Cairo-Alexandria transit times of 2 hours at the most, compared with 2 hours 35 minutes by previous services, inclusive of two intermediate stops. The ultimate objective is a 1½ hour timing, with each of the train-sets completing three round trips daily.

Initially, however, the turbotrains were confined to the existing limit of 110 km/h pending completion of the Cairo-Alexandria line's upgrading. Track reconstruction was being executed by Les Travaux du Sud-Ouest (TSO) on behalf of Egyf-Rail, a civil engineering consortium with 51 per cent Egyptian and 49 per cent French participation. The route was being relaid with welded 54 kg/m rail on concrete sleepers, and by March 1982 some 100 single-track km were finished.

Carrying up to 150 trains an hour in the Cairo and Alexandria suburban areas and 60 to 80 on the intervening main line, the route was also being re-signalled by French industry. Six control centres of the entrance-exit route relay type with associated train describers were being established at the line's main centres in conjunction with four-aspect colour-light signalling. The route is already equipped with the Siemens system of ATC.

Rolling stock

Coaching stock purchases have been given priority over freight vehicles because of the passenger fleet's lack of substantial enlargement since the early 1960s, since when rail passenger journeys per annum have trebled. At the end of 1980 the two luxury 18-car, air-conditioned overnight trains formed from 42 cars built by Messerschmitt-Bölkow-Blohm were put into service on the Cairo-Luxor-Aswan route. Running non-stop between Cairo and Luxor in either direction, each train-set comprises sleeping cars, two bar-lounges and a generator car; pre-prepared meals are served to passengers in their compartments from galleys in each sleeping car. Orders for a further 150 air-conditioned, stainless steel-bodied luxury cars for the Cairo-Aswan route were placed with Carel Fouché in 1981, for 1983 delivery, and with MBB for 40 additional generator cars. The French purchases have been facilitated by a French Government loan of E£34 million. Assets have also been lately enlarged by delivery of passenger cars constructed in Romania. At the close of 1982 rolling stock totalled 21 dmus, 52 emus, 2576 passenger cars, 17 railcars and 17 142 freight wagons.

Rolling stock purchases planned between 1982 and 1986 have a total value of E£375 million.

Signalling

At the start of 1983 negotiations were in progress with French industry for resignalling of the 370 km line from Cairo's southern periphery to Assyout, in the direction of Aswan, from a single control centre.

The Cairo-Alexandria route has been equipped with Siemens Indusi AWS in preparation for the turbotrains. Spending on signalling between 1982 and 1986 will total E£249 million. Contracts have been let for resignalling between Benha and Cairo, a route to be quadrupled between Qalyub and the capital. Following the recent CTC installation at Cairo, others are to be established at Alexandria, Assyout, Luxor, Mersa Matsuh, Tanta and Zagazig.

New lines

A 96 km line from Port Said to the Nile Delta has been completed from El Mansura to Matareyya, but the final 24 km to Port Said entails a crossing of the Manzala lake and that is unlikely to be ready before 1985. A second project will keep freight clear of the high-speed turbotrain passenger operation between Alexandria and Cairo. This is a 120 km line exclusively for freight use between Alexandria and a junction with the existing Cairo route at Itay Baroud, beyond which point operating capacity has been enlarged by track modernisation and signalling modernisation. Some 65 km of this bypass had been completed by Egyf-Rail at the end of 1982. Further west a 108 km line from Etahad to El Amiriya, west of Alexandria, was completed in February 1983.

Other new railways in hand include a 590 km line which will span the Nile and connect phosphate mines at Tartour in the western desert with a new Red Sea port at Safaga, intersecting the Cairo-Aswan route between Qena and Nag'Hammadi. The prospective annual load for this railway is 12 million tonnes. The 227 km section of this line, east of the Cairo-Aswan route, is being built for opening at the end of 1984. In 1983 construction of the western 363 km from Qena to Abu Tartour had just begun.

Also envisaged is the southward extension of the north-south railway from its present limit at El-Sadd El-Aali to the Sudanese border at Wadi Halfa. This scheme integrates with the Master Plan to interlink all the railways of the African continent.

Cairo Regional Metro

The biggest single item in ER's current infrastructure programme is the first stage of a Cairo Regional Metro scheme to relieve the capital's intolerable traffic congestion. French consultants drafted a metro scheme some years ago, but it was shelved until the Government accepted its necessity in 1978.

Cairo metro emu trailer car by ANF-Industrie, France

Lengthy negotiations secured a financial agreement with the French Government for the first E£80 million stage of a three-line, 125 km network which is now under way.

This initial phase is providing a rapid transit line from ER's main Cairo station at Ramses Square to Helwan, obtained in part by thoroughly refurbishing and electrifying an existing 24 km of line from Bab El-Louq to Helwan. Shipping to Egypt of an order for 52 three-car train-sets from ANF-Industrie and Alsthom-Atlantique was completed in 1982, and in July 1981 the Interinfa-Arab company, a Franco-Arab group, won a Fr 1000 million contract for the civil and signal engineering work, which proceeds in three stages. French participants in the consortium are headed by Alsthom-Atlantique and include CSEE and Jeumont-Schneider. The project is supervised by ER's Underground Metro Organisation.

EL SALVADOR

Ministry of Public Works

Palacio Nacional, San Salvador

Minister: Jorge Antonio Seaman S

El Salvador National Railways (FENADESAL)
Ferrocarriles Nacionales de El Salvador

CEPA: Boulevard de los Héroes, Edificio Torre Roble, San Salvador
FENADESAL: Avenida Peralta 903, San Salvador

Telephone: (CEPA) 24 11 33
(FENADESAL) 21 89 40
Telex: 20-194 Area 301

President (CEPA): Ing José Luis Andreu Ruiz
General Manager: Ing Heriberto Reyes V
General Manager, Railways (CEPA): Lic Juan Agustin Núñez B
Head of Railway Planning: Ing Héctor Romero Paz
Head of Operations (FENADESAL): Lic Carlos Arturo Flores
Chief Transportation: Ing Luis Alfredo Carballo R
Chief Traffic: Andrés Escoto
Chief Equipment: Ing Oscar Efraín Calles
Chief Maintenance of Way: Oscar Allen Villalta

Gauge: 914 mm
Route length: 602 km

Transport development
Ferrocarriles Nacionales de El Salvador (FENADESAL) was formed from two railways which were formerly the property of overseas companies: the Salvador Railway, which passed to the state in 1965 under the name of Ferrocarril de El Salvador (FES); and the International Railways of Central America (IRCA), a railway undertaking that includes the railway system and port at Cutuco, which was nationalised in 1974 under the name of Ferrocarril Nacional de El Salvador (FENASAL).

The two undertakings were merged under state control in May 1975, together with the port of Cutuco, and renamed Ferrocarriles Nacionales de El Salvador (FENADESAL). The railway is now administered by the Comision Ejecutiva Portuaria Autonoma (CEPA).

FES and FENASAL are divided into three districts: District No 1 which comprises San Salvador (the capital) to the port of Cutuco, Department of La Union (East Zone of the country), (252 km).
District No 2 which runs from San Salvador to the frontier of El Salvador with Guatemala (146 km), and a branch to Ahuachapan, in the west of the country (60 km).
District No 3 which runs from San Salvador to the port of Acajutia, on the Pacific Ocean (104 km), and includes a branch from Sitio del Nino to Santa Ana in the west (40 km).
Studies began in 1978 on the renewal and rehabilitation of the 602 km three-line system. Aimed at increasing freight and passenger capacity to meet growing demand following El Salvador's social and economic growth, the studies include a master plan for the port of Cutuco, owned and managed by FENADESAL.

Traffic
The country's political unrest had a severe impact on the railway's business in 1980, and the position deteriorated in 1981, when total freight tonne-km and passenger-km were less than half the figures of 1979.

Traffic

	1980	1981
Total freight tonnage	434 272	284 962
Total freight tonne-km	55 143 259	30 861 386
Average net freight train load (tonnes)	119	98
Average freight wagon load (tonnes)	21·5	21·5
Total passenger-km	26 985 961	14 050 388
Total passenger journeys	1 695 868	906 476
Average length of passenger journey (km)	15.9	15.5

Finance 1981 (C000)
Revenue

Passengers and baggage	414
Freight, parcels and mail	4314
Other income	1394·4
Total	6123·2

Expenditure

Staff/personnel expenses	9897·1
Materials and services	4281·4
Depreciation	457·8
Financial charges	1·6
Total	14 637·9

Investment
Expenditure planned for 1982 was costed at 3·36 million colones, of which 960 000 colones were earmarked for construction of a 5·8 km connection between the District 2 and 3 systems at Apopa.

Motive power and rolling stock

Diesel-electric locomotives (GM Type GA-8 Bo-Bo of 635 kW, weight 65 tonnes)	10
Steam locomotives	1
Passenger coaches	40
Freight wagons	550

Track
Rail: 37·2 kg/m
Sleepers: Wood 150 × 200 × 214 mm
Spacing: 1667/km
Minimum curvature radius: 80 m on main lines, 60 m elsewhere
Max gradient: 3·9%
Max axleloading: 17·5 tonnes

ETHIOPIA

Chemin de Fer Djibouti-Ethiopien (CDE)

PO Box 1051, Addis Ababa

Telephone: 47 250
Telegrams: Djibeba, Addis Ababa

Director-General: Channie Tamiru

Gauge: 1000 mm
Route length: 781 km

Transport development
Rail and highway traffic and development was severely affected by guerilla activity throughout the 1970s. There are two separate railways: the larger is the metre gauge CDE Railway running from the port of Jibuti to Addis Ababa, a route length of 781 km of which 100 km are in Jibuti; the other is the 950 mm gauge Northern Ethiopia Railway, 306 km long, running from the Red Sea port of Massawa inland to Agordat, but which has been out of action since 1978.

At the start of 1982 a major change in the railway's constitution was announced. The previous controlling company of the Jibuti-Addis Ababa Railway, Compagnie du Chemin de Fer Franco-Ethiopien de Jibuti à Addis Ababa, was replaced by a new organisation, Chemin de Fer Djibouti-Ethiopien (CDE), under joint control of the republics of Jibuti and Ethiopia, but with its headquarters remaining in Addis Ababa. The Transport Ministers of the two countries were to occupy the positions of President and Vice-President of the new company, which was remitted to consider urgently the renewal of the railway's track and its rolling stock. Late in 1982 a US$11 million loan for the purchase of passenger cars was secured from the European Economic Community.

Rolling stock

Diesel railcars	5
Trailers	13
Passenger coaches	37
Freight wagons	636

Track
Rail type: 20 kg, 25 kg, 30 kg
Sleepers: Metalbloc
Fastenings: Clips and bolts

Motive power and rolling stock*
Diesel locomotives

No of units	Type	Builder year	Engine type	Rated power hp	Transmission	Total weight tonnes	Max speed km/h
9	Bo-Bo	SLM 1950/51	SLM 6VO25	580	Elec	48	70
6	Bo-Bo	Alsthom 1955	MGO V12SHR	675	Elec	48	70
3	Bo-Bo	Alsthom 1963	MGO V12BSHR	840	Elec	50	70
2	Co-Co	Alsthom 1965	Pielstick 16PA4	1850	Elec	78	60
2	Co-Co	Alsthom 1968	Pielstick 16PA4	1850	Elec	78	90
6	C	Coferna 1955	Poyaud 6PX1	180	Hyd	26	25
4	C	Billard 1955	Poyaud 6VPX1	205	Hyd	33	30
4	Bo-Bo	Alsthom 1973		1200	Elec	52	70

*All figures shown are the latest available prior to guerilla activity starting in 1977/78.

FINLAND

Ministry of Communications

Helsinki

Telephone: 17361
Telegrams: Valtioneuvosto, Helsinki

Minister: J Wahlström
Secretary-General: R J Auvinen
Head of Railway Affairs: J Pohjola

Finnish State Railways (VR)
Valtionrautatiet

Vilhonkatu 13, 00100 Helsinki 10

Telephone: 7071
Telegrams: Valtraut, Helsinki
Telex: 12301151

Director General: Herbert Römer
Chief Director and Director of Traffic Department:
Panu Haapala
Technical Chief Director: Pertti Lattunen
Directors
  Administrative Department: Eero Jaakkola
  Economy Department: Paavo Virkkunen
  Civil Engineering and Permanent Way Department: Erkki Tattari
  Mechanical Engineering Department: Esa Piironen

Gauge: 1524 mm
Route length: 6071 km
Electrification: 1057 km at 25 kV 50 Hz ac

Transport development

The railway network was shaped for a large part in the last century, when the railways were the most important form of transport in long-distance traffic. Only a few lines have been built since the Second World War, during a period of rapid changes in the economy and the social structure of the country. In the last few decades, the railway network has been considerably improved, so that traffic with 20-ton axleloads is now generally permissible. The maximum admissible speed for passenger trains is 120 km/h and the average speed approximately 80 km/h.

With the population concentrated in large centres, the number of railway stations in the thinly populated areas has diminished. For that reason, the main purpose in improving the railway network in recent years has been to renew the present system and to complete it with new lines, creating fast connections between large population centres and improving mass transport around them.

Freight traffic

Despite deepening recession VR's freight carryings in 1982 were running only 3·7 per cent below those of 1981. Domestic carryings were almost sustaining the 1981 level and the drop was principally due to a 10 per cent decline in traffic with the USSR, as a result of structural changes in Finnish-Soviet trade. Eastern exchange traffic had been the mainspring of the 1981 tonnage record, rising 7 per cent in that year to a total of 9·2 million tonnes.

A major development in 1982 was reorganisation of the less-than-carload operation. Its main thrust was concentration of the rail involvement and transfer to road of wider-ranging collection and delivery functions.

In the intermodal sector VR has developed a swop-body technique known as the AJA System, which was at the prototype stage in 1982. The rail wagons have a deck rotatable through 35 degrees from longitudinal for ease of swop-body transfer to road vehicles, which are fitted with lift and chain devices to haul a body on to the frame.

Class Sr 1 electric passenger and freight locomotive

Sm 2 electric multiple-unit

Prototype Class Fau coal wagon

Traffic	1981	1982	% change
Freight (000 tonnes)			
Wagonload	29 335	28 253	−3·7
Part-load	513	492	−3·9
Total	29 848	28 745	−3·7
Total tonne-km (million)	8391	8000	−4·7
Passenger traffic			
Total long-distance journeys	9101	9214	+1·2
Total local journeys in Helsinki area	29 645	29 959	+1·1
Other local journeys	2270	2234	−1·6
Total journeys	41 016	41 407	−1·0

The number of rail terminals equipped with cranes capable of handling containers is 20, of which 13 have 30 to 60 tonne capacity gantries for transhipment of 40-foot containers. The frontier station of Vainikkala on the border with the USSR and the rail terminal between Finland and Sweden at Tornio are equipped with mobile gantry cranes for container handling.

VR has no purpose-built container-carrying wagons. Containers are carried on four-axled bogie wagons capable of carrying three 20-foot (6·1-metre) containers. The two-axled type of wagon can take either two 20-foot or one 40-foot (12·2-metre) container. Stock of the bogie flatcars totals 2100, of the two-axle flatcars 2400.

Passenger traffic

The number of passenger journeys reached a new record of 41·4 million, 1 per cent more than in 1981. Growth was at the same level in both long-haul and Helsinki local journeys.

The popularity of car-sleeper services has grown considerably in recent years, and in the spring of 1981 a new car-sleeper service was introduced between Helsinki and Rovaniemi. A total of 17 200 accompanied cars were conveyed in 1982, 9·5 per cent more than in 1980.

Finance

Operational objectives were redefined in an action and economy plan for the years 1983-88 drawn up during 1982. In accordance with stipulations in the 1982 state budget, the central objective is to improve results by 1991 by FMk 500 million at 1982 prices.

By the end of 1988 total revenues from wagonload traffic are to cover 40 per cent of general costs, in addition to special costs involved in this service. According to sales plans, wagonload traffic should grow an average of around 2 per cent a year from 1982 to 1988. This growth is not sufficient for traffic revenues to cover the present deficit entirely. The greatest cost savings will be obtained in railway yard work by a gradual change to one-man locomotive operation and by decreasing shunting work.

By the end of 1991 total revenues from part-load traffic must cover 20 per cent of general costs, in addition to special costs. Profitability will be improved and VR's transport share increased through developing competitive ability. Operations will be rationalised by concentration on lines where sufficiently strong direct freight flows can be arranged through the use of concentrated feeder transport. VR will abandon wagon-to-wagon transfer loading completely. Freight handling will also be reduced by utilising demountable bodies, which will also increase possibilities for competing for direct customer-to-customer deliveries.

The financial objective for passenger traffic is that in the early years of the 1990s total revenues from passenger traffic should cover 30 per cent of general costs, in addition to special costs involved in this service. Long-distance and Helsinki area traffic revenues must cover special costs by 1988 and 1986 respectively. According to sales plans, long-distance passenger traffic and traffic in the Helsinki area should grow an average of 3 per cent a year from 1981 to 1988.

In spite of the 3 per cent annual growth in passenger volume, train-km will not be increased. Staff savings will be obtained mainly through investments in computer-controlled operation and a random sampling system of ticket inspection in Helsinki area traffic.

In accordance with a programme for the development of local traffic, the structure of local services outside the Helsinki area will be changed so that the railway will concentrate mainly on worthwhile feeder services. Some unprofitable train services will be eliminated, and numerous small stations will be closed.

The local traffic development programme assumes that local passenger services will be maintained for social reasons on a broader scale than would be possible from the point of view of VR's finances, provided that VR is reimbursed for costs exceeding the revenues of such traffic. The unprofitable train services which will be eliminated by the programme (about 7 per cent of total train-km) will be replaced by other transport connections according to plans made by the Ministry of Communications.

In 1982 passenger traffic continued to grow and passenger volumes reached new record levels. Owing to traffic growth and higher tariffs, receipts from passenger services also continued to increase at a faster rate than costs incurred in the provision of this service. On the other hand, because of the decrease in the volume of freight traffic, freight receipts increased less than transport costs. Accordingly, the profitability of passenger services rose somewhat, while that of freight traffic fell, although it was still clearly better than the cost coverage attained by the passenger business.

Wagonload freight receipts showed an increase of 4 per cent compared with the previous year, amounting to over FMk 1300 million. However, costs incurred grew more than receipts, which covered 82 per cent of the cost. In 1981 the figure was 93 per cent.

Part-load freight receipts have not been sufficient in recent decades to cover the cost of this service. In 1982 the volume of part-load freight declined from

Finance (FMk million)

Revenue	1981	1982	% change
Freight traffic	1450·7	1505·4	+3·8
Passenger traffic	520·7	575·5	+10·5
Other	144·0	180·3	+25·2
Total	2115·4	2261·2	+6·9
Expenses			
Wages and salaries	1440·8	1543·3	+7·1
Social security payments	91·0	105·9	+15·2
Pensions	270·3	287·8	+6·5
Other staff payments	62·7	65·4	+4·3
Energy	250·1	264·8	+5·9
Material and other expenditure	310·5	362·5	+16·7
Total	2426·3	2629·7	+8·4
Results			
Deficit before depreciation	310·9	368·5	+18·5
Depreciation	379·6	429·9	+13·3
Deficit after depreciation	690·5	798·4	+15·6

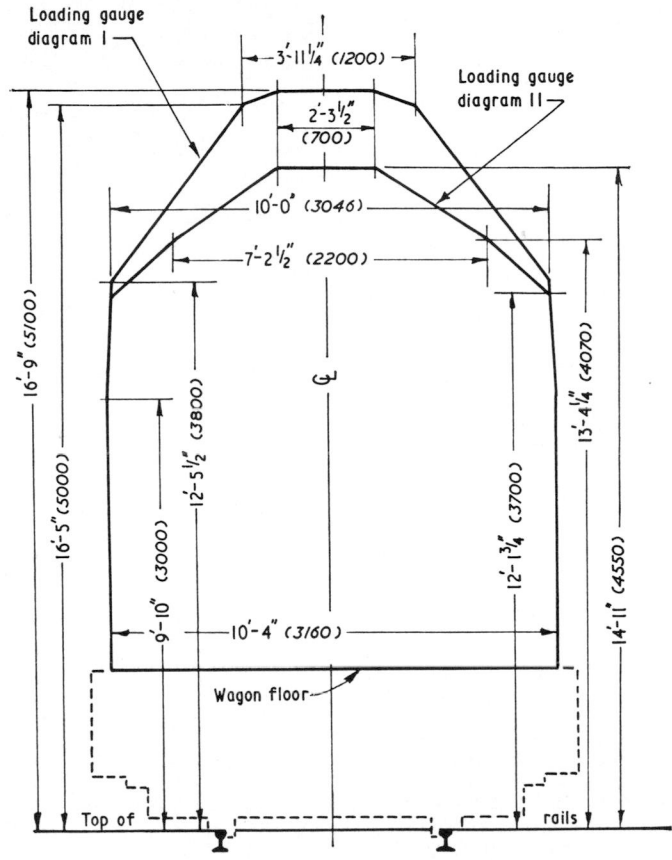

Class Sv 1 prototype electric locomotive with ac squirrel-cage motor

the level of the previous year. Since tariffs were increased twice during the year, however, receipts rose by over 18 per cent. Costs increased more slowly than receipts, so profitability increased. Part-load freight receipts covered 68 per cent of the cost of this service.

Passenger traffic receipts for 1982 showed an increase of 11 per cent over the previous year. Costs increased at a slower rate than receipts. Passenger receipts covered 64 per cent of the cost of this service. The greatest increase in profitability was shown by local traffic in the Helsinki area, due to a growth in passenger volume. Receipts covered 70 per cent of costs, compared with 67 per cent in 1981. In the long-distance passenger sector, cost coverage rose from 65 to 67 per cent. Local passenger services outside the Helsinki area continued to produce a poor coverage of costs. Receipts for the year under review managed to offset 37 per cent of costs.

VR's deficit is increased by the public obligation to maintain local passenger services outside the Helsinki area and on lesser-used lines. The new financial programme assumes that these tasks will continue to be performed in their present scope, as long as the railway receives remuneration for the additional costs incurred in providing them. Local rail traffic outside the capital can never be made profitable, and financial objectives will remain unachieved unless adequate subventions are received.

Investments

Funds budgeted for investments in 1983 (FMk 000):

Main-line electric locomotives (10)	63 500
Shunting diesel-hydraulic locomotives (6)	5400
Passenger cars (42)	47 500
Railcars (1)	8300
Freight wagons (275)	44 640
New line construction	43 100
Track improvements	109 300
Track maintenance machinery	19 600
Electrification	64 200
Bridges and buildings	62 990
Signalling and telecommunications	62 665
Computerised management systems	6000
Yards and terminals	49 000
Workshops	35 530
Miscellaneous	24 500
Total	646 225

Motive power and rolling stock

An important objective has been to obtain the capability for flexible response to immediate commercial opportunity. This has been partly achieved with existing types of wagons, partly with rebuilt wagons. A total of 245 Type Hk wagons has been rebuilt to transport sugar beet, for example. To improve the profitability of ore carrying, a new cylinder-shaped tank wagon (Type Uao) has been designed; it has an axleload of 22 tonnes. Other recent designs include a high-capacity Type Fau coal wagon and Type Ocpp timber wagon with fixed side stanchions to allow dense load stacking.

VR has also been working with domestic industry to improve its rolling stock. 1980 saw emergence of two prototype locomotives after extensive rebuilding. Running trials with an Sv 1 electric locomotive equipped with squirrel-cage motors, and with a Dr 15 diesel locomotive re-equipped with a more powerful engine and an electric transmission, continued in 1982.

At the end of 1982 VR had 266 diesel locomotives and 98 electric locomotives for main-line services, as well as 112 diesel shunting locomotives. Diesel train-sets totalled 22 and electric train-sets 100. Power units for railcars totalled 99 and trailers 59. The number of light traction units amounted to 125. Deliveries in 1982 comprised seven Class Sr 1 electric and seven Class Tve 4 shunting locomotives. Four more Type Sr1 electric locomotives were to be delivered from the USSR in 1983 and a further six in 1984. They will have rectifiers of Swedish and power semi-inductors of West German design.

Freight vehicles used in commercial traffic totalled 20 759 and passenger cars 764. Deliveries in 1982 comprised 54 passenger cars and 339 freight vehicles from VR's Pasila workshops.

During 1982 two prototypes were built of a new series of coal wagons (Fau) for unit train operation. They are equipped with a new type of bogie which has an axleload of 22 tonnes and have a side-tipping frame which allows rapid unloading. 70 Hkkg wagons were rebuilt into Hbl series wagons for transporting sawn goods. Production of this series continues.

Twelve new Type Eil and Eilf local traffic coaches were built during the year and put into trial use; they are prototypes for a series which is scheduled for production in 1984-86.

Investments (FMk million)	1981	1982	% change
Railway construction	22·5	31·7	+40·7
Lines, bridges and station tracks	199·1	193·3	−2·9
Buildings	68·5	76·9	+12·2
Control and safety equipment	40·7	47·5	+16·9
Electrification fixed installations	101·8	82·3	−19·2
Low-voltage and high-power installations	37·2	35·3	−5·1
Traction units and rolling stock	180·1	180·4	+0·2
Machinery and road vehicles	67·6	55·9	−17·4
Other investments	6·9	5·2	−23·7
Total	724·4	708·5	−2·2

Type Eil second-class car for Helsinki-Riihimäki service; 12 prototypes have been built at Pasila

Class Dr 12 diesel-electric passenger and freight locomotive

Dv 12 all purpose diesel-hydraulic locomotive

VR's new swop-body transfer system

Track

All major main lines have been upgraded, continuous-welded and electrified since 1960 or are now being electrified. Track renewal is now concentrated on major transverse arteries. In addition, replacement of light rails with heavyweight rail is well under way on a number of branch lines with frequent traffic. When investments required for track renewal can be cut down, the emphasis will shift to track maintenance.

Track renewal has focussed on lines included in the electrification plan. The most important such projects in 1982 involved the Kirkkonummi-Karjaa, Tampere-Pori, Pieksämäki-Jyväskylä and Seinäjoki-Ylivieska lines. In 1983 upgrading was to be concentrated on the Lielahti-Pori/Rauma and Karjaa-Kirkkonummi lines.

UIC rail weighing 54·45 kg/m is electric resistance-welded in workshops into 150-metre lengths; after laying at site these are thermit-welded into continuous lengths. Both wood and concrete sleepers are used, the latter being West German prestressed type. Rails are secured to wood sleepers by Hey-Back fastenings, and to concrete sleepers by Pandrol and RN. Future programmes provide for installation of continuous welded rail at a rate of about 100 km of track per year. Total distance of cwr at the end of 1982 was 3063 km.

In 1982 construction continued on the link to the seaport of Tahkoluoto and on the line between Juurikorpi and Salmenkylä. The 11 km Tahkoluoto line will run from Mäntyluoto Harbour in Pori to Tahkoluoto Harbour, and was to be finished in 1983, while the 14 km Juurikorpi-Salmenkylä line, replacing the existing section from Inkeroinen to Salmenkylä, was to be commissioned, fully electrified, in 1984.

Electrification
Work in progress

	Route-km	For completion
Kokkola-Oulu	200	1983
Pieksämäki-Iisalmi	166	1984
Juurikorpi-Hamina	18	1984
Imatra-Joensuu	192	1987
Future electrification planned		
Tampere-Pori and Peipohja-Rauma	208	1988
Tampere-Jyväskylä-Pieksämäki	233	1990

Signalling and safety equipment
At the end of 1982 VR had over 130 all-relay inter-locking boxes (suppliers: Siemens, LME, WSSB and USSR). Line radio systems were in operation over approximately 4500 route-km. VR has now decided to adopt the Ericsson ATC system which Swedish and Norwegian State Railways have installed.

At marshalling yards, radio systems comprising 222 relaying base stations and several hundred portable radios were in use. All diesel and electric locomotives were equipped with radio telephones, which could use both line radio and marshalling yard radio systems.

Ferry service
A ferry service is run between Helsinki and Lübeck/Travemünde, West Germany, but rail wagons are not carried on this route, which provides an international container service to central and southern Europe.

There is also a train ferry service between Hanko, Finland, and Travemünde, West Germany, run by Oy Railship Ab. The route was opened in February 1975 and is operated with a three-deck train ferry. For rail transport the company has a number of flat wagons and covered wagons with changeable wheel-sets (gauges 1435 mm and 1524 mm).

Diesel locomotives

Class	Wheel arrangement	Trans-mission	Rated power kW	Max lb	Tractive effort Continuous at lb	mph	Max speed mph	Wheel dia mm	Total weight tons	Length mm	No in service	First built	Builders Mechanical parts	Engine & type	Transmission
Dr 12	Co-Co	Elec	1400	28 000	12 800	30	75	1180	121·8	18 560	36	1959-63	Lokomo Oy, Valmet Oy	Tampella-MAN V8V 22/30 mAuL	Strömberg-BBC
Dr 13	Co-Co	Elec	2060	28 300	19 400	30	87	950	98·1	18 576	78	1962-66	Alsthom, Lokomo Oy, Valmet Oy under licence by Alsthom	Tampella-MGO V 16 BSHR (two engines)	Strömberg-Alsthom
Dv 12	B-B	Hyd	1000	17 000	12 600	20	78	1000	60·8	14 000	183	1964-66	Lokomo Oy, Valmet Oy	Tampella-MGO V 16 BSHR	Voith L 216 rs
Dv 12	B-B	Hyd	1000	17 000	12 000	20	78	1000	69	14 000		1974-79	Valmet Oy	Tampella-MGO V 16 BSHR	Voith L 216 rs
Dv 12	B-B	Hyd	1000	18 700	12 600	20	78	1000	65·6	14 000		1965-68, 1971-72	Lokomo Oy, Valmet Oy	Tampella-MGO V 16 BSHR	Voith L 216 rs
Dv 15	D	Hyd	620	18 800	14 300	10	47	1180	60	11 930	58	1958-61	Lokomo Oy, Valmet Oy	Tampella-MAN W8V 22/30 AmA	Voith L 217 U
Dv 16	D	Hyd	700	18 800	14 850	10	53	1270	60	11 930	28	1962-63	Lokomo Oy, Valmet Oy	Tampella-MAN W8V 22/30 AmAuL	Voith L 217 U
Dv 11	D	Hyd/ Mech	620	16 500	12 000	10	47	1180	56	11 930	2	1958-59	Lokomo Oy, Valmet Oy	Tampella-MAN W8V 22/30 AmA	Tampella-SRM D S 1,2
Dr 14	B-B	Hyd	875	24 100	21 900	5	47	1050	86	14 000	24	1969-72	Lokomo Oy	Tampella-MAN R8V 22/30 ATL	Voith L 206 rsb

Electric locomotives

Class	Wheel arrangement	Rated power kW	Max lb	Tractive effort (full field) Continuous at lb	mph	Max speed mph	Wheel dia mm	Weight tons	Length mm	No built and ordered	Builders Mechanical parts	Electrical equipment
Sr1	Bo-Bo	3100	57 400	39 700	44	87	1250	83	18 960	100	Energomachexport (Novocherkassky Works) USSR	Strömberg

FRANCE

Ministry of Transport

246 boulevard Saint-Germain, 75700 Paris Cedex 07

Telephone: 544 39 93
Telex: 250 038

Minister: Charles Fiterman
Director of Cabinet: Claude Martinand
Chief of Cabinet: Daniel Davisse
Member of Cabinet: Guy Braibant
Technical Advisers: Pierre Bégault
        Jacques Chauvineau
        Jean-Paul Jouary

French National Railways (SNCF)
Société Nationale des Chemins de Fer Français

88 rue Saint-Lazare, 75436 Paris Cedex 09

Telephone: 285 60 000
Telex: 290936

President: A Chadeau
Director General: Paul Gentil
Assistant General Managers
    Jean Dupuy
    Louis Lacoste
    Marc Pieffort
Secretary General: Paul Reverdy
Director of Communications: Yves Chenel

Directors
    General Studies and Research: Raymond Monnet
    Personnel Manager: Pierre Descoutures
    Finance: Jean Vieux-Pernon
    Budget: R Petit
    Data Processing: André Lemaire
    Transport: Roger Gérin
    Passenger Sales: Olivier Weber
    Freight Sales: Jean Luc Flinois
    Engineering (Fixed Installations): Jean Alias
Engineering Department Chiefs
    Track Design and Research: Georges Janin
    Signalling: Alain Vial
    Electrical Installations: René Delavergne
    Buildings: Gilbert Renault
    Civil Engineering: Jean-Louis Picquand
    General Studies and New Lines: Guy Verrier

LGV Atlantique: Etienne Chambron
Motive Power and Rolling Stock: Roger Forray
Department Chiefs
  Traction Equipment Maintenance: Jean Quessart
  Rolling Stock Maintenance: Paul Monsérié
  Design: Gérard Coget
  Testing: André Révillon
  Investment: Maurice Gaide
  Laboratories: Yves Devaud
  Energy: Henry Molins
  SERNAM: Didier Sautter

Gauge : 1435 mm
Route length: 34 590 km
Electrification: 5581 km at 1·5 kV dc; 4966 km at
25 kV 50 Hz ac; 115 km at 750/850 V dc (third-rail)

New status

With the expiry, at the end of 1982, of its 1937
contract with the state and shareholders, new legislation changed the SNCF from the status of a semi-
private limited company to an industrial and commercial public corporation, responsible for operating, improving and developing the national rail
network according to public service principles, in
accordance with the Transport Law of 30 December
1982. This took effect from January 1983. The new
Transport Law, based on the concept that every-
body has a right to transport and modal choice, is
the cornerstone of the Socialist government's
transport policy, which aims to meet the needs of
users while giving the best economic and social
value for money to the community as a whole,
through: realistic assessment of transport costs as
well as social costs (financial and otherwise) borne
by users and third parties; establishment of bases
for fair competition between transport operators
and modes, coupled with efforts to promote complementary development and co-operation, especially through selectivity with regard to infrastructures, and rational evolution of intermodal transport; participation of local communities in transport
policy-making and implementation within a decentralised planning framework; priority for development of public passenger transport; fair rewards for
the carrier, covering the real costs of services provided; and harmonisation of working conditions.

The Law specifies the new SNCF's assets, which
are public in character although administered exclusively by the SNCF, and defines membership of
the new Board, which consists of 18 members
including seven representatives of the State, five
members chosen for their competence and six
members elected by staff (one representing management). A subsequent decree prescribes that of
the seven State representatives, six shall be nomi-
nated by the Ministers of Transport (2), Economy
and Finance (1), Budget (1), Planning and Regional
Development (1), Industry (1). The five chosen for
their competence comprise two representatives of
users (1 passenger, 1 freight), two members
selected for their knowledge of regional and local
railway issues and one chosen for his personal
expertise in the transport field. The decree fixes the
term of office for each member at five years.

Under new public service statutes the Board has
both a policy-making and executive role, whereby 'it
shall define the SNCF's general policy, determine
the objectives of the group and implement the programme contract signed by the State and the public
corporation. It shall deliberate on all aspects of the
company's activities (finance, investments, organisation, etc). It shall be consulted on the corporation's remit, authorise the signing of the programme contract and define the corporate plan'. The
State will, however, exercise a supervisory role
through a government commissioner who sits on
the Board and holds a consultative vote. Another
decree has set up an economic and financial supervisory body, headed by a representative from the
inland revenue department, who also sits on the
Board in a consultative capacity.

Under the new Law, State financial support
henceforward covers not only operational costs as
in the past but also the development of the SNCF,
which is a new departure. The Law states that this
support is granted 'because of the essential contribution made by rail transport to the economic and
social life of the nation, its role in meeting the right
to transport and its advantages in terms of safety
and energy'. This support also takes into account
'the specific responsibilities of the enterprise in
respect of infrastructures and the aim progressively
to improve the financial situation'. Finally, the
SNCF's accounting system is required to ensure that
the 'real economic costs of the tasks it performs on
behalf of State and regional communities respectively be quantified'.

The reconstitution of the SNCF therefore represents a radical change of direction, since the Law
sanctions the concept of public service, defines new

TGV train-set passing block section marker

TGV depot, Villeneuve

TGV high-speed crossover, negotiable at 160 km/h

principles governing relations between the public
corporation and the State and introduces a democratic form of public service management with
worker representation on the Board. The SNCF has
thus become a public corporation with legal and
financial autonomy while remaining subject to business rules and practices.

TGV/LGV progress

After carrying its five millionth passenger within its
first year of operation, in September 1982, the
Paris-Lyons LGV recorded its 10 millionth passenger as early as April 1983. (The SNCF now terms
its high-speed railways *Lines à Grande Vitesse*, or
LGV, reserving the term TGV for their train-sets.)
The total number of passengers carried in the first
year was 5·563 million, of which 1·544 million travelled first class. The SNCF assessed some 2 million of
the journeys or over 5000 a day as new business. On
the Paris-Lyons axis itself the LGV figures resulted in

a doubling of pre-TGV carryings, while over the
SNCF's Sud-Est Region as a whole they contributed
to a 15 per cent increase.

Of the additional traffic 1000 to 1500 passengers a
day were reckoned to be gains from the air, 2000 to
2500 gains from the road and 1000 to 1500 newly
generated travel. Research further identified 37 per
cent of the traffic as professional and 22 per cent of
the journeys as out-and-back within the day. Average load factor of all trains for the year was 61 per
cent, in excess of SNCF forecasts for the initial
period of operation at less than the density of service and speed of transit planned following commissioning of the northern third of the LGV at the
end of September 1983.

At the end of the first year's operation 62 TGV
train-sets were operational, comprising 55 standard
first/second-class units, six all first-class units (employed on weekday business travel-peak services;
they are not used on Saturdays or Sundays) and the

first of the seven triple-voltage sets for the four daily through workings between Paris and Lausanne via Vallorbe due to begin in January 1984. Together they had amassed over 18 million km of running, with the standard sets rostered to 1336 km of running daily. Following solution of some early teething problems, the SNCF claimed performance of both vehicles and track was without technical difficulty: operation within 15 minutes of schedule was said to be 97 per cent.

Infrastructure work on the final third of the LGV Sud-Est to Lieusaint, junction with the historic Sud-Est main line 29·4 km from Paris Gare de Lyon, was due for completion in May 1983, to allow some months for test running in advance of commercial service. Total LGV Sud-Est infrastructure cost is now put at Fr 7500 million (1982 values), only 5 per cent above 1974 estimates, while the price of the initial tranche of 87 TGV sets and the further 10 ordered in 1982 is now put at Fr 4500 million (1982 values), or slightly less than 4 per cent over the 1974 budget. However, on the first year's commercial achievement of Fr 1039 million revenue against Fr 504 million operating costs, the SNCF was confident of at least the 17 per cent budgeted return on the investment, with hope of full amortisation as early as 1989, while social benefit was assessed at more than 30 per cent. In December 1982 the SNCF further raised the TGV order with Alsthom-Atlantique by 20 power cars and 70 trailers, to be delivered from mid-1984.

From May 1983 maximum speed on the Paris Sud-Est LGV was to be lifted to 270 km/h. With inauguration of the complete TGV timetable at the end of September there would be nine basic daily workings to and from Marseilles and seven to and from Montpellier, in addition to three services to and from Geneva and other workings to and from Dijon, Besançon, St Etienne and Chambéry. The standard time of 2 hours for the journey between Paris Gare de Lyon and the new Part-Dieu station in Lyons, expected to open in June 1983, would represent an average speed of 213·6 km/h (132·7 mph) for the 427·2 km distance.

At the inauguration of service to Marseilles in May 1982, SNCF announced that it planned works to allow TGV trains a top speed of 200 km/h over the existing infrastructure between Lyons and Marseilles. This would entail signalling modifications, some track realignment, installation of six additional traction current substations between Pierrelatte and Marseilles, and suppression of 38 level crossings. To avoid disruption of the line's heavy traffic, signalling for reversible working on the running lines would be installed between Pas-des-Lanciers and Marseilles, and between Avignon and Miramas; and additional running lines would be laid in, a single track between Orange and Le Pontet, and double track between Tarascon and Miramas, and L'Estaque and Marseilles.

LGV Atlantique and LGV Nord

The new administration of President Mitterand asked SNCF in 1981 to prepare preliminary plans for a second high-speed line, LGV-Atlantique. This would take the shape of a lateral Y and involve 340 km of infrastructure. Its exit from Paris Montparnasse would be largely on the surviving path of the abortive Gallardon commuter railway to Chartres; near Courtalain, south of Chartres, the LGV would fork into links with the existing Bordeaux main line near St-Pierre-des-Corps and with the existing Brest and Nantes routes near Laval and Angers respectively. Cost is put at Fr 12 000 million.

Like LGV-SE, the second LGV would be engineered for a maximum of 300 km/h and is thought likely to operate at that speed from the start. The new line would be more easily graded than the LGV-PSE, with a maximum of 1 in 67. TGV-Atlantique train-sets would embody aerodynamic outline changes by comparison with TGV-PSE sets and be built with 10 instead of eight trailers for a total seating capacity of 480 per unit. The total requirement for the LGV-Atlantique would be 95 train-sets.

At the start of 1983, with Government favour of the project publicly expressed, the scheme awaited formal declaration of public utility as the signal for action. Methods of finance were under discussion with the Government, which had made clear it would not leave the SNCF to fund the project by borrowing, as the previous Government had in the case of the LGV Sud-Est. (In 1982 the SNCF confronted an accumulated deficit of Fr 49 000 million as a result of its historically meagre capital base and the burden of heavy borrowing to meet rising interest on loans, as well as other problems of previously inadequate compensation for mandatory social rail services, heavy staff pension commitments and a State contribution to infrastructure

TGV buffet-bar

Meals at first-class TGV seats, catering by Wagons-Lits subsidiary Soprenolit

Dual-voltage No BB22283 leaving Nice with a Bayonne train of Corail stock *(John C Baker)*

costs of only 40 per cent.) The SNCF's new constitution and the country's new Transport Law provide that State involvement in rail infrastructure expense is no longer statutorily limited to support of freight operation but available for development of the railway network as a whole.

The LGV Atlantique promises more benefits than reductions in journey times from Paris (gains in brackets) to Nantes down to 2 hours 10 minutes (1 hour 10 minutes), to Rennes down to 2 hours 5 minutes (50 minutes), to Le Mans down to 1 hour (40 minutes) and to Bordeaux down to 3 hours 5 minutes (45 minutes). Its execution will, in particular, save expenditure essential to relieve the impending saturation of Paris's western and south-western rail approaches assessed at Fr 2000 million over the remainder of the 1980s and Fr 800 million in the 1990s. Provided the public utility declaration was available by the end of the 1983 summer, completion of the LGV-Atlantique for public service in 1989 was possible. It would by then be complemented by completion of the main-line electrification schemes in Brittany, but matching electrification from Poitiers to La Rochelle hinged on agreement to public subsidy of at least a third of the cost, because of the comparatively low contribution to total costs of the line's traffic.

The Federal German Government has agreed to open discussion of a possible LGV-Nord from Paris to Cologne. Studies have shown that Northern French territory alone would not generate sufficient traffic to justify investment in an LGV-Nord. The ideal remains a Paris-Brussels LGV-Nord associated with a Channel tunnel: the resultant combination of Franco-British, Anglo-Belgian and domestic French traffic would probably produce 23 million passenger journeys a year, little less than the LGV Sud-Est's prospective 25 million. A Paris-Brussels/Cologne LGV-Nord is reckoned to have a 16 million annual passenger journey potential, at which level the return on its investment would be less than that assessed for the LGV-Atlantique and only a third of the LGV Sud-Est's.

Postal TGV
The French Post Office has ordered two eight-car and one four-car TGV train-sets to substitute rail for air mail service between Paris and the south and east of France via TGV-PSE, starting in 1984. The Post Office calculates that with TGVs their operation can be performed just as capably overnight as with air, but at a sixth of the energy cost. These sets will have self-adjusting air suspension, to ensure that car floors are always level with mail terminal platforms no matter how heavily they are loaded with mail container trolleys. A 10-car unit is planned to carry a gross 75 tonnes of mail in 250 containers, five times the capacity of the aircraft it will supersede.

TGV train-set
Each TGV-PSE train-set is formed of two power cars and eight trailers, but six bogies are motored; the trailers are articulated as one unit. The power bogies are Type Y230, trailer bogies Type Y231. Thyristors regulate voltage at motor terminals, operating as a mixed bridge on 25 kV ac and as a chopper on 1·5 kV dc. Each bogie is driven by two motors, working at 1070 volts 530 amps, but capable of withstanding 1000 amps for up to seven minutes without overheating. The motors are body-mounted to limit

TGV train-set

	Dual-voltage dual-class	Dual-voltage first-class	Tri-voltage dual-class
Length over couplers (m)	200·19	200·19	200·19
Tare weight in working order (tonnes)	386	384	386
Weight available for adhesion (tonnes)	194	194	194
Continuous power rating (kW)			
At 25 kV 50 Hz	6450	6450	6450
At 1·5 kV dc	3100	3100	3100
At 15 kV 16⅔ Hz	—	—	2800
Max speed (km/h)	270	270	270
Seating capacity			
1st class	111	287	111
2nd class	275	—	275

unsprung weight and transit power mechanically through a tripod arrangement with two cardan joints. The power bogies have rheostatic braking to supplement electro-pneumatically-operated disc brakes: clasp brakes are also fitted, primarily to clean wheels, and they operate only below 200 km/h.

TGV track
Rails: UIC 60 kg/m standard section, tensile strength 800 N/mm², continuously-welded, inwards inclined at 1 in 20
Sleepers: Twin-block Type U41, weight 245 kg, 2·4 m long, at 600 mm centre spacing
Fastening: Nabla, with 9 mm pad between rail and sleeper
Ballast: 320 mm minimum depth below sleepers

TGV signalling
TGV-PSE is controlled from a centre (PAR) in the vicinity of Paris Gare de Lyon, which houses both current and train describer-aided traffic controllers in the same room. There are no active lineside signals; drivers are guided entirely by continuous cab signalling, which provides 10 aspects covering freedom to proceed at maximum line speed, warnings of reduction to 220, 160 or 80 km/h in ensuing sections, instruction to proceed within either of the speeds mentioned, and requirement to stop or proceed on sight at a maximum of 30 km/h. The signalling is linked to automatic speed-check and braking systems. Block sections, of a standard 2100-metre length, are indicated by markers serving as either absolute stopping positions (lettered) or stop-and-proceed positions. Each block is covered by a CSEE UM71 voice frequency jointless track circuit capable of 18 rates of frequency shift, which are picked up by each train-set through inductive coils, one of which is located ahead of each end axle of the unit. An additional discrete transmission system employing track-mounted cable loops and offering up to 14 frequencies supplies further information to trains,

Metrazur service, expanded with financial support from local authorities, en route from Ventimiglia to Cannes behind No BB25669 *(John C Baker)*

Type X2100 diesel railcar and trailer

for example to activate or deactivate the cab signalling on entrance to or exit from the new line. Lineside sensors linked to PAR watch for hot boxes.

TGV catenary

Masts: H-section steel at up to 63 m spacing
Wiring: Bronze carrier of 65 mm² section, tension 14 kN; stitch wire 15 m long in 35 mm² bronze cable, tension 4 kN; droppers of stranded copper cable, 5 mm diameter; contact wire of 120 mm² hard-drawn copper, tension 14 kN
Insulators: Glass supporting catenary; synthetic at sectioning points
Max depth: 1·4 m
Initial sag: 0·1 per cent of the span, to achieve level pantograph trajectory
Contact wire rise: 240 mm possible, but normal uplift is 120 mm

Finance

As a prelude to new arrangements according with the SNCF's revised status from January 1983 the Government's 1983 transport budget featured a change in its SNCF provisions. The annual infrastructure grant, deriving from the 1883 conventions under which the State assumed responsibilities for the former railway companies' fixed assets, was withdrawn, also the separate grant to compensate for SNCF operation of unremunerative lines and the *Subvention Forfaitaire d'Exploitation*, a measure formulated in the 1979 contract revision to equalise road-rail terms of freight competition. Instead the Government introduced a global grant of Fr 9144 million under the head of 'Maintenance of the Railway's Potential'. Another innovation was a capital grant of Fr 2000 million as a first step to amortisation of the SNCF's accumulated deficit of some Fr 49 000 million. In total, the Government budgeted Fr 27 311 million for the SNCF under all heads, including compensation for obligatory tariff reductions and staff pensions. This was a 17·6 per cent increase on the 1982 total.

Expenditure was a more aggravating problem in 1982 because of the Government's legislation, effective from the start of the year, which reduced the working week to 39 hours and legalised a fifth week's annual leave with pay. In anticipation, SNCF had had to recruit extra staff, raising its total from 248 600 to 253 000.

For 1982 SNCF budgeted receipts of Fr 53 200 million against expenditure of Fr 56 800 million. The percentage of receipts deriving under different heads was expected to be: freight and postal traffic, 29·2; passengers and baggage, 28·2; SERNAM, 6·4; Subvention Forfaitaire, 5·6; infrastructure grant, 10·7; State compensation for public service obligation, 4·6; compensation for conurbation services, 2·1; compensation for obligatory tariff reductions, 7·4; miscellaneous income 5·8. Wages and salaries were forecast to account for 58·3 per cent of the expenditure; other percentages were likely to be: traction energy, 3·9; goods and services, 22·2; taxes, 1·7; depreciation, 4·7; and financial charges, 9·2.

Investment

The SNCF's investment plan for 1983 provided for expenditure of Fr 9384 million and authorisation of forward commitments totalling Fr 8170 million. Of the former sum 19 per cent was allocated to the TGV/LGV, 62 per cent to the remainder of the main-line system and 19 per cent to the suburban network; of the forward commitment the respective allocations were 10·5, 73 and 16·5 per cent. A third of the non-suburban sums was earmarked for traction and rolling stock. The suburban component included the RER Line C Vallée de Montmorency-Invalides project and the extension of the Cergy line to Pontoise.

Actual expenditure in 1983 would cover (Fr million):

Locomotives and rolling stock	3655
New infrastructure	1415
Infrastructure improvements and track machinery	865
Electrification	792
Signalling and telecommunications	1385
Level crossings	321
Yards, terminals, depots and workshops	427
Miscellaneous	440

Electrification

Electrification completed in 1982 covered the following lines:

Elne—the Spanish frontier at Port-Bou (1·5 kV dc)	30 km
Lille—the Belgian frontier at Tourcoing (25 kV 50 Hz ac)	12 km
Tours—Saumur and Thouars (25 kV 50 Hz ac)	103 km
Pontoise—Gisors (25 kV 50 Hz ac)	40 km

Diesel railcar train from Nice to Cuneo at Tende *(John C Baker)*

Type Z9500 dual-voltage express emus south of Avignon

In addition to the remaining 117 km of the LGV Sud-Est, a major electrification due for completion in September 1983 was the 229 km from Saumur to Angers and Le Mans to Nantes, largely at 25 kV 50 Hz ac but including some 12 km of 1·5 kV dc links with the existing catenary at Tours and Le Mans. Accompanying elimination of 79 level crossings, realignment and resignalling for 200 km/h between Le Mans and Nantes would enable the four fastest daily Paris-Nantes (396 km) transits each way to be trimmed to less than 3 hours from September 1984. Electrification of the further 93 km to Le Croisic has been included in the 1983 budget for completion by 1986 at a cost of Fr 400 million.

Other electrifications in progress in 1983 were:
Port of Rouen left bank, 13 km at 25 kV ac, completed in January 1983;
Corbeil-La Ferté-Alais, one of the few remaining un-electrified sections of the Paris suburban network, 20 km at 1·5 kV dc, for completion in January 1984;
Miramas-Fos, 16 km at 1·5 kV dc, for completion in May 1983, the first phase of electrification of the whole coastal system linking ports and industry between Miramas and Marseilles;
Perpignan-Villefranche-Vernet-les-Bains, 47 km at 25 kV 50 Hz ac;
Dreux à Plaisir-Grignon, 49 km at 25 kV 50 Hz ac, to be finished in August 1984;
Amiens-Rouen, 121 km at 25 kV 50 Hz ac, for completion in September 1984;

Lyons to Grenoble, St André-le-Gaz-Chambéry, 172 km at 25 kV 50 Hz ac, for completion in the spring of 1985, following which Grenoble would have direct TGV service in 3 hours 20 minutes from Paris.

Further electrifications to be provided for in the SNCF's 1983 budget were: Nevers-St Germain-des-Fossés, the first step in the electrification of the Paris-Clermont-Ferrand main line; Rennes-St Brieuc; and Nantes-Le Croisic.

Paris suburban system

In December 1981 an important stage of the Paris Interconnexion scheme was reached with inauguration of the 1·78 km tunnel linking the new low-level suburban station at Paris Gare du Nord (the eastern half of which was opened in September) with the RER system at Châtelet-les-Halles.

As a first step to full Interconnexion service, the timetables of Line B North (SNCF Aulnay-Mitry-Roissy) and South (RATP Robinson-Massy-Saint-Rémy-les-Chevreuses) were integrated from January 1983. In May 1983, with the SNCF and RATP by then operating a combined fleet of 65 Type Z8100 Interconnexion emus, through running from north to south was to be launched with eight trains an hour; in February 1984, with 94 Z8100 sets available, this was to rise to 12 trains an hour; and at the end of 1984, with 111 Z8100s in use, to 20. The total of Z8100 sets on order has been lifted to 120, 51 for the SNCF and the remainder for the RATP, as a result of a fresh RATP order for 38 units.

Under the original Interconnexion programme it was planned that from 1986 services from Orry-la-Ville would be added to the underground flow by extension beyond Gare du Nord to Châtelet-les-Halles and later beyond the latter station to destinations such as Juvisy, Melun and Evry in the south-east. This through working would constitute RER Line D. However, doubts have arisen as to the feasibility of attempting to channel the east-west Line A, north-south Line B and D services at 60 second headways over the Châtelet-Gare de Lyon subterranean double-track, even with highly sophisticated moving block signalling systems; concern has been aggravated by belief that a more intensive peak-hour service will be needed on Line A. In 1983 the longer-term Interconnexion plan was under review, with construction of two additional tracks between Châtelet and Gare de Lyon one of the options under study.

A change in the method of financing Paris commuter travel from October 1982 required employers in the Paris Region to pay directly 40 per cent of the cost of their employees' *Cartes Oranges*, which cover unlimited travel within a defined area of the metropolis for a week or a month. From October 1983 the employers' share was to rise to 50 per cent. At the same time the transport premium of Fr 23 per employee levied on employers was withdrawn, but not the *Versement Transport*, a 2 per cent tax on the gross paybill of firms with more than 10 employees in inner Paris (the *Petite Couronne*) and 1·2 per cent on similarly qualified companies in the outer *Grande Couronne*. The application of the *Versement Transport* in provincial France was simultaneously revised to apply at a rate of 0·5 per cent to all towns with 50 000 or more inhabitants.

In March 1982, after five years of controversy, the extension of RER Line C to serve the Vallée de Montmorency, north of Paris, with branches to Argenteuil and Pontoise, was approved by Ministerial decision. Many environmental objections had been raised to the project, which to a considerable extent involves adapting existing but under-utilised lines. The junction with the existing Line C from Versailles RG/St Quentin-en-Yv will be in the neighbourhood of Champ de Mars. Cost of the infrastructure at 1981 values was estimated as Fr 1065 million, but the social-cost/benefit return was put at 33 per cent. The new cross-Paris route from north-west to south of the city which the project will create is claimed to benefit a catchment population of a million that is likely to generate at least 45 million journeys a year, or 10 per cent of the total Parisian suburban traffic.

Passenger traffic

In face of the recession the SNCF revised its 1982 forecasts in mid-year and the end result accorded with the modified budget. Main-line journeys rose from 265 in 1981 to 269 million, passenger-km by 2 per cent from 48 170 to 49 100 million, strongly influenced by the LGV Sud-Est's 15 per cent increase of overall traffic on the Paris-south-east France axis, but also by successful application of several market-oriented fare schemes. Growth was also registered in the suburban traffic sector, where passenger-km rose from 7500 million in 1981 to 7650 million.

Special measures taken to improve service to the public included the provision of 550 additional staff for passenger guidance at stations; appointment at the 50 principal stations of an officer specifically responsible for service to the public; enlarged budget for station maintenance and cleaning; increase of modern telephone centres for information from 65 at the end of 1982 to 101 by the end of 1983; acquisition of 10 000 self-help luggage trolleys to double the number available at stations; and further station modernisation. A list of 200 principal stations for renovation was drafted in 1978 and at the end of 1982 the programme had reached the halfway point; this activity is absorbing 4 per cent of the SNCF's annual investment budget.

Following its introduction of four dual-class 'Corail'-equipped 200 km/h services on the Paris-Bordeaux route in 1980-81 a fifth was added each way, making three 'Corail 200' and two TEE workings; and a similar operation was launched on the Paris-Toulouse route in 1982. The selected trains were the southbound morning 'Capitôle' (Sundays excepted, while on Saturdays the evening train was affected) and the evening return.

Other developments pursued in 1982 included a further all-sleeping overnight cross-country train, from Nantes to Nice via Bordeaux and including car-carriers as well as sleeping and couchette cars. A further creative tourist service with special on-train diversions, following the example of the 'Cévénol' and 'Alpazur', the 'Aubrac', was launched between Paris, Millau and Béziers, equipped with

Passenger traffic

Main-line system	1980	1981	Improvement (%)
Passenger journeys (million)	253	265	4·6
Passenger-km (million)	46 880	48 170	2·7
Gross revenue excluding State compensations (Fr million)	9273	10 865	17

Total including Paris suburban	1980	1981	1982	
Passenger journeys (million)	685	695	700·3	1·9
Passenger-km (million)	53 500	55 700	56 581	2·1

Corail cars. Total Corail car stock at the end of 1981 was 3300 after eight years of construction.

All further rural service closures were suspended in 1981 at the incoming Mitterand Government's instruction, pending further devolution to the Regions of powers to control public transport provision in their territories. At Ministerial request four stopping train services were revived in 1981-82: Clamecy-Corbigny; Ax-les-Thermes-Latour-de-Carol; Ballan-Chinon and La Ferté-Milon-Reims.

At the Government's further instigation the SNCF was in 1983 studying the case for restoring local passenger service over several more stretches of main line and branch: Sarreguemines-Béning (22 km); Sarrebourg-Rémilly (103 km); Elbeuf-Sitteville (17 km); Caen-Flers (65 km); Le Mans-La Flèche (50 km); Le Havre-Fécamp (44 km); Tarbes-Bagnère-de-Bigorre (22 km); Nimes-Alès (49 km); Toulon-Hyères (20 km); and Gretz-Longueville (50 km).

With the contraction of TEE services the SNCF is converting to second class, for standard dual-class *rapide* operation, five compartment and 11 saloon cars of its first-class 1964 stainless-steel Paris-Brussels stock, and 17 compartment and 12 saloon

cars of its 1969 'Grand Confort' cars. The principal change is a reduction of corridor or gangway width to permit four-a-side seating, of a new design by Compin, in both open and compartment vehicles. The first complete 'Grand Confort' train-set including second-class conversions was to be launched on the Paris-Toulouse 'Capitôle' service in May 1983.

The first application of bi-level cars to services outside the Paris area was due to begin in October 1983 with delivery from CIMT-Valenciennes of the first of 31 Type V02N cars (to form six train-sets with one spare car) for the busiest services of the Nord-Pas de Calais Regional network, principally those between Lille, Douai and Arras. The initial investment of Fr 85 million has been funded by the Regional authorities, to be repaid by the SNCF within 15 years. In 1983/84 the Regional authority is also putting up half the Fr 14 million cost of refurbishing or providing with car parks 14 local stations in its territory, while at least one main station will be renovated with the customary contribution of half the cost through a combination of direct urban authority grant and a temporary local ticket surcharge to amortise a loan.

Type MI79 Paris Interconnexion emu on RER

Railcar operation at Bastia station, Corsican Railways, opened 1982 *(John C Baker)*

Freight traffic

The recession occasioned a disquieting decline in 1981. Total tonnage fell 10·5 per cent from 217 million in 1980 to 194 million, and tonne-km by 7·6 per cent from 67 860 million to 62 790 million. The regression continued in 1982, though not so steeply, with a drop of 6·7 per cent to approximately 183 million tonnes and of 5 per cent to 60 554 million tonne-km, compared with the original hope of a revival to 64 500 tonne-km. The losses were again predominantly in heavy industrial freight. Agricultural traffics showed increases of up to 7 per cent, while previous levels were more or less sustained in a number of sectors, such as chemicals, paper and packaging, and motor vehicles. One consolation was that in many sectors the SNCF is now retaining a steady market share.

Additions to the wagon fleet in 1982 included a new design of cattle wagon, of which 800 have been ordered; the first of 1000 new-type flat wagons of two axles for transport of farm machinery and vehicles; an additional 500 bogie wagons with mechanically-operated, retractable canvas one-piece roof and side-walls; and new wagons for transport of wood pulp and 2-metre logs.

A new subsidiary, Sefergie, was created in 1982 to assist in the financing of private siding installations.

Plans for 1983 included introduction of a new type of wagon suited to the bulk distribution of consumer products; 1000 were to be ordered. Additional intermodal terminals were to be established at Toulouse, Valenton, Avignon and Bordeaux. In the development of local multi-function freight terminals (GMF), of which 560 are ultimately to be established covering the whole SNCF system, a trial effort would be made to secure local financial involvement in a Regional freight scheme similar to those operative in the passenger sector. A new facility, Midex, would be set up under which SNCF wagons could be assigned to a customer's exclusive use on a contractual basis.

The Fercam scheme, whereby SNCF itself hires road collection and delivery to form part of a door-to-door package inclusively priced to wagonload freight customers, maintained its annual growth of 35 per cent since 1978 and exceeded 2 million tonnes.

Additions to the range of special-purpose wagons were forecast. At the end of 1981 orders were placed for 1000 new wagons with low central floor, over 3 metres in width and with 13·5-metre length of loading area, for the transport of light road vehicles, tractors and agricultural machinery; also foreseen were new cattle wagons and an order for 1000 of a new two-axle curtain-sided wagon with 12·5 metres of load area for palletised goods.

Intermodal

The future relationship of CNC, the container traffic-marketing subsidiary, and Novatrans, the piggyback operating company, has been under study following sustained growth of the *caisse mobile*, or swap-body, element of Novatrans traffic. In the first 10 months of 1982, when Novatrans traffic as a whole climbed 15 per cent in tonnage to 2·7 million and 19 per cent in tonne-km to 2300 million, *caisse mobile* carryings soared a further 40 per cent. *Caisses mobiles* now account for 48 per cent of all Novatrans business.

Together with six other European railways and seven other intermodal traffic organisations the SNCF and Novatrans have formed a research association, Interunit, to study development of new recessed-floor wagon designs adaptable to both swap-body and road trailer conveyance: and also to appraise the possibilities of establishing a standard swap-body pool and of standardising swap-body handling systems.

Novatrans abandoned its 'Kangarou' technique of Ro/Ro piggyback loading and discharge of road trailers with special tractors at the end of 1982. The wagons are still in use, but all Novatrans terminals now tranship exclusively by top-lifting. The 'Kangarou' technique required special fitments on road trailers which are now unnecessary.

Intermodal subsidiaries
Piggyback operations
Novatrans
21 rue du Rocher 8°, Paris 75

Telephone: 387 41 79
Telex: 650625

Container operations
Compagnie Nouvelle de Cadres (CNC)
20 boulevard Diderot, Paris Cedex 12

Telephone: 345-32-20
Telegrams: Cadroferdir, Paris
Telex: 22500

Synchronous-motor 5600 kW test locomotive No BB10004

SNCF special conference/cinema car

Interior of conference/cinema car

Corsica

From January 1983 the SNCF took over the operation of Corsican Railways.

Traction and rolling stock

At the start of 1982 SNCF was conducting comparative trials with two types of three-phase electric transmission, to assess both relative performance merits and relative effect on signalling apparatus. One locomotive, No BB7003 (ex-BB15007), had been modified by Alsthom-Atlantique and Francorail with new electrical apparatus feeding two independent rectifier-inverter circuits through a smoothed dc link, with a separate inverter supplying each of four 1200 kW asynchronous squirrel-cage induction motors. The locomotive was mounted on new bogies, each fitted with two motors. The other trialist was also a modified BB15000, No BB10004 (ex-BB15055), which was converted by Jeumont-Schneider and MTE. No BB10004 is equipped with Jeumont-Schneider synchronous motors, each of which consists of a rotor forming the motor inductor and a stator serving as motor armature. Thyristors undertake the current distribution in the stator conductors. Compared with an asynchronous motor, the synchronous is simpler, needing no auxiliary electronic device to switch current between thyristor branches except at extremely low speeds; the switching is achieved by electromotive forces generated by the rotating motor. Further benefits claimed for the synchronous system are high reliability, because of the inverter simplicity; increased efficiency because there is no switching loss; reduced maintenance requirement because of the absence of a commutator; and the ease of dynamic braking.

In its revised form No BB10004 is a 5600 kW unit with a top speed of 200 km/h. Tests throughout 1982 disclosed no adverse effects of the system on signalling circuitry and have, according to the SNCF, revealed no limitations to the technique or to its application to all forms of electric traction and to diesel-electric locomotives. As to performance, No BB10004 has sustained 200 km/h with a 16-car train of Corail stock up a 0·25 per cent gradient and accelerated a 2050-tonne freight from rest to a steady 82 km/h on a 0·88 per cent incline. A constant output of 5600 kW has been proved attainable at 200 km/h, with tractive effort continuous at 100 kN. Starting tractive effort of No BB10004 with gearing set at 73:33 was 320 kN, tapering off to 280 kN at 70 km/h. Two pre-production dual-current prototypes have also been ordered for 1984 delivery; they will be obtained by conversion of two BB22000 locomotives. Performance of the synchronous motor system has already been found so satisfying that its use in TGV-Atlantique train-sets is probable.

At the start of 1983 the SNCF had an effective electric traction stock of 2475 locomotives, 68 TGV train-sets and 715 other emus. Deliveries during 1983 would include nine 5490 hp 1·5 kV dc locomotives, Nos BB7402-10, a type of which over 200 are now in service, and 30 Type Z5600 power cars for the Type Z2N Paris commuter bi-level emus. Rennes would acquire 20 new dual-voltage Class BB22200, half of them arranged for 200 km/h, the remainder for 160 km/h, to serve the expanding electrification in the Angers area. Also expected were the final 18 units of the 50 Type Z8100 Paris Interconnexion emus, 15 Type Z7300 dc emus of the latest design for regional service, destined for the Bordeaux area, and the balance of the 18 Type Z9500 dual-voltage express emu order for Marseilles. Units of the latter kind will replace ETG gas turbine mus on Lyons-Grenoble and Lyons-Annecy services in mid-1985, after completion of the Lyons-Grenoble/Chambéry electrification. TGV train-set deliveries in 1983 were to comprise 14 standard dual-voltage sets and the remaining six triple-voltage sets for the Paris-Lausanne service to be launched in January 1984.

Diesel traction at the end of 1982 comprised 2144 locomotives, 1402 locotractors and 820 railcars, in addition to which SNCF operated 53 gas turbine-powered train-sets. In this sector 1983 was expected to see withdrawal of some of the SNCF's high-power diesel prototypes, Nos BB66692, 69001-2 and CC70001. Additions to stock would include 30 Class Y8000 locotractors. Three Type X2100 440 kW, 140 km/h, 56-seater diesel railcars remained to be delivered of the order for 50 placed with ANF-Industrie in 1980; they were to be followed in 1984-86 by 53 railcars of revised design classified X2200, also to be constructed by ANF-Industrie, which was additionally commissioned to manufacture 72 matching trailers designated Class XR6000.

The other important electric traction development of 1982 was delivery of first power cars for the Paris Type Z2N bi-level emus. The first arrivals were 1·5 kV dc, for units destined eventually for Paris RER

SNCF special audio-visual conference car

Interior of SNCF audio-visual conference car

Control room of recently-completed PRS controlling 329 route-settings, with computer-based routeing programmer, at key Paris south-west suburban junction of Juvisy

Line C but to enter service first on SNCF Paris south-eastern suburban services. By the end of 1984 delivery of 132 should be complete. The first two prototypes of the dual-current version, of which 68 power cars are on order for the Vallée Montmorency-Invalides line, were due to appear in January 1984.

Each train-set will be formed of two power cars and two or three intermediate trailers, with capability for mu operation of two sets; Scharfenberg couplers are fitted at the extremities of each set. Total output of each unit's chopper-fed motors is 2800 kW for a weight of 216 (4 cars) or 257 tonnes (5 cars) in the 1·5 kV dc version, 224 or 265 tonnes respectively in the dual-voltage variant. Total length of a four-car unit is 98·76 metres, of a five-car 123·04 metres, and total seating capacity is 70 first-class and 464/480 in a four-car or 632/648 in a five-car unit according to type (dc/dual-voltage); there is room also for 63 first-class and 388/408 second-class standees in a four-car and 530/550 in a five-car unit, so that a dc five-car set has a maximum passenger capacity of 1331. Maximum speed is 140 km/h, acceleration rate 0·90 m/s² from 0 to 50 km/h and average braking deceleration the same.

Locomotive-hauled passenger stock at the end of 1982 totalled 11 076 cars, of which 8326 were of express category. Orders placed included one with ANF-Industrie and de Dietrich for 80 Type VU couchette cars, 30 of which were destined for Franco-Spanish traffic. SNCF freight stock totalled 167 200 vehicles; in addition 83 300 privately-owned vehicles were in use.

Electric locomotives: principal classes

Class	Wheel arrangement	Line current	Rated output hp	Tractive effort (full field) Max lb (kg)	Continuous lb (kg)	at mph (km/h)	Max speed mph (km/h)	Wheel dia in (mm)	Weight tonnes	Length ft in (mm)	No built (and/or on order) 1.1.83	Year built	Builders Mechanical parts	Electrical equipment
2D2-9100	2-Do-2	1500 V dc	5010	61 700 (28 000)	41 200 (18 700)	44 (70·5)	87 (140)	39⅜ (1000) 68⅞ (1750)	144	59' 4" (18 080)	35	1950	Fives-Lille	Cie Electro-Mécanique
BB-8100	Bo-Bo	1500 V dc	2850	67 000 (30 400)	36 000 (16 300)	25·8 (41·5)	65 (105)	55⅛ (1400)	92	42' 5" (12 930)	171	1949	Alsthom	Alsthom
BB-8500 (2 gear ratios)	B-B	1500 V dc	4000	44 300 (20 100) 73 850 (33 000)	28 200 (12 800) 46 700 (21 200)	51·3 (82·5) 30·6 (49·2)	93 (140) 56 (90)	43¼ (1100)	79	48' 3"-51' 1" (14 700-15 570)	146	1965	Alsthom	Alsthom
BB-7200	B-B	1500 V dc	5490	66 100* (30 000)	30 400* (13 800)	60* (97)	112* (180)	49¼ (1250)	85	57' 4¼" (17 480)	202 (+38)	1976	Francorail Alsthom	Francorail Alsthom
BB 9200 BB-9300	Bo Bo	1500 V dc	5230	58 500 (26 500)	32 600 (14 800)	58 (93)	100 (160)	49¼ (1250)	82	53' 2" (16 200)	91 40	1958 1968	MTE	MTE-CEM
BB-9400	B-B	1500 V dc	2210	60 600 (27 500)	34 800 (15 800)	31 (50)	81 (130)	40⅛ (1020)	60	47' 3" (14 400)	131	1959	Fives-Lille-Cail	MTE
CC-6500 (2 gear ratios)	C-C	1500 V dc	8000	64 700 (29 347)	60 400† (27 397)	38·5† (62)	62 (100) 137 (220)	45 (1140)	116	66' 3" (20 190)	74	1969	Alsthom MTE	Alsthom MTE
CC-7100	Co-Co	1500 V dc	4740	58 500 (26 500)	34 600 (15 700)	49·5 (79·5)	93 (150)	49¼ (1250)	107	62' 1" (18 922)	58	1952	Alsthom	Alsthom
BB-12000	Bo-Bo	25 kV 50 Hz	3350	79 400 (36 000)	41 900 (19 000)	29·5 (47·5)	75 (120)	49¼ (1250)	83	49' 10½" (15 200)	146	1954	MTE	MTE
BB-13000	Bo-Bo	25 kV 50 Hz	2900	55 100 (25 000)	26 000 (11 800)	40·5 (65)	75 (120)	49¼ (1250)	85	49' 10½" (15 200)	53	1954	MTE	MTE
BB-16000	Bo-Bo	25 kV 50 Hz	5610	69 500 (31 500)	33 500 (15 200)	53 (85)	100 (160)	49¼ (1250)	84	53' 2" (16 200)	60	1958	MTE	MTE
BB-15000	B-B	25 kV 50 Hz	5840	64 000* (29 000)	33 000 (15 000)	62* (100)	112 (180)	49¼ (1250)	88	57' 4¼" (17 480)	62	1971	Alsthom	Alsthom
BB-16500 (2 gear ratios)	B-B	25 kV 50 Hz	3500	72 700 (33 000)	24 900 (11 300) 42 300 (19 200)	51 (82) 30 (48)	93 (140) 56 (90)	43¼ (1100)	74	47' 3" (14 400)	294	1958	Alsthom	Alsthom
BB-17000 (2 gear ratios)	B-B	25 kV 50 Hz	4000	44 300 (20 100) 73 850 (33 000)	28 200 (12 800) 46 700 (21 200)	51·3 (82·5) 30·6 (49·2)	93 (140) 56 (90)	43¼ (1100)	78	48' 3"-49' (14 700-14 940)	105	1965	Alsthom	Alsthom
CC-14100	Co-Co	25 kV 50 Hz	2520	94 700 (43 000)	51 200 (23 200)	17·7 (28·5)	37 (60)	43¼ (1100)	126	62' 0" (18 890)	96	1954	Alsthom	Alsthom
BB-22200 (2-current)	B-B	25 kV 50 Hz 5380 and 1500 V dc 5490		66 100* (30 000)	30 400* (13 800)	60* (97)	112* (180)	49¼ (1250)	89	57' 4¼" (17 480)	150 (+30)	1976	Francorail Alsthom	Francorail Alsthom
BB-25100 (2-current)	Bo-Bo	25 kV 50 Hz 5610 and 1500 V dc 4620		81 600 (37 000)	39 000 (17 700)	52 (83·5)	81 (130)	49¼ (1250)	83	53' 3" (16 200)	70	1964	MTE	MTE
BB-25200 (2-current)	Bo-Bo	25 kV 50 Hz 5610 and 1500 V dc 4620		68 300 (31 000)	32 600 (14 800)	62 (99·5)	99 (160)	49¼ (1250)	83	53' 2" (16 200)	51	1964	MTE	MTE
BB-25500 (2-current) (2 gear ratios)	B-B	25 kV 50 Hz 4000 and 1500 V dc 4000		44 300 (20 100) 73 850 (33 600)	25 100 (11 400) 41 900 (19 000)	51 (82) 30 (48)	93 (140) 56 (90)	43¼ (1100)	78	53' 3"-51' 1" (14 700-15 570)	194	1964	Alsthom	Alsthom
CC-40100 (4-current) (2 gear ratios)	C-C	25 kV 50 Hz 6000 15 kV 16⅔ Hz 6000 3000 V dc 6000 1500 V dc		32 000 (14 500) 44 500 (20 200)	19 000 (8600) 27 000 (12 000)	95·4 (153·5) 68 (110)	149 (240) 99 (160)	42½ (1080)	108	72' 3¼" (22 030)	10	1964	Alsthom	Alsthom

* Some units re-geared for higher tractive effort and 100 km/h maximum
† Low gear

Diesel locomotives: principal classes

Class	Wheel arrange-ment	Trans-mission	Rated power hp	Max lb (kg)	Tractive effort Continuous at			Max speed mph (kmlh)	Wheel dia in (mm)	Total weight tons	Length ft in (mm)	No built	First built	Builders		
					lb (kg)	mph (kmlh)								Mechanical parts	Engine & type	Transmission
A1A-A1A 62000	A1A-A1A	Elec	510	32 200 (14 600)	27 800 (12 600)			60 (96)	42⅛ (1070)	110	58' 1" (17 700)	100	1946	Baldwin	Baldwin 606 HA	Westinghouse
A1A-A1A 68000 and 68500	A1A-A1A	Elec	2230	67 000 (30 400)	39 700 (18 000)	19 (30·6)		81 (130)	49¼ (1250)	106	58' 8½" (17 920)	108	1963	CAFL Fives-Lille-Cail	Sulzer 12LVA 24 or SACM-AGO V12 DSHR	CEM
CC65500	Co-Co	Elec	1620	80 700 (36 600)	47 800 (21 700)			50 (80)	47¼ (1200)	123	63' 8½" (19 420)	35	1955	CAFL	Sulzer 12LDA28	CEM
CC65000	Co-Co	Elec	1320	56 200 (25 000) 37 500 (17 000)	32 800 (14 900) 19 000 (8600)			75 (120)	41¼ (1050)	112	65' 0" (19 814)	20	1956	Alsthom CAFL	SACM MGO 12 VSHR	Alsthom
CC72000 mono-motor bogies (2 gears)	C-C	Elec	3060	19 300 (36 400) 81 600 (37 000)	30 900 (12 400) 51 800 (23 500)	34·7 (65) 21·5 (34·5)		100 (160) 53 (85)	44⅞ (1140)	114	66' 3¼" (20 190)	91	1967	Alsthom	SACM-AGO V16 ESHR	Alsthom
CC72075 mono-motor bogies (2 gears)	C-C	Elec	4000	19 300 (36 400)	11 000 (21 000)	99 (52)		99 (160) 53 (85)	44⅞ (1140)	118	66' 3¼" (20 190)	1	1973	Alsthom	SEMT-Pielstick PA6-280	Alsthom
BB63000	Bo-Bo	Elec	480 590	37 500 (17 000) 37 500 (17 000)	23 100 (10 500) 24 200 (11 000)	6 (10) 8 (13)		50 (80) 50 (80)	41¼ (1050) 41¼ (1050)	68 68	48' 2" (14 680) 48' 2" (14 680)	108 142	1953 1957	Brissonneau et Lotz Brissonneau et Lotz	Sulzer 6LDA22C Sulzer 6LDA22D	Brissonneau et Lotz Brissonneau et Lotz
BB63500	Bo-Bo	Elec	610	37 700 (17 100)	28 400 (12 900)	7·5 (12)		50 (80)	41¼ (1050)	68	48' 2" (14 680)	603	1956	Brissonneau et Lotz	SACM MGO V12 SH	Brissonneau et Lotz
BB66000	Bo-Bo	Elec	1130					75 (120)		72	48' 10½" (14 898)	315	1959	Alsthom	SACM-MGO V16 BSHR	CEM
BB66400	Bo-Bo	Elec	1130					75 (120)		68	49' 1½" (14 972)	106	1968	Alsthom	SACM-MGO V16 BSHR	CEM
BB66600	Bo-Bo	Elec	1210					75 (120)		71	48' 10½" (14 898)	11	1962	Alsthom	SEMT 12PA4	CEM
BB67000 mono-motor bogies (2 gears)	B-B	Elec	1930	45 400 (20 600) 68 300 (31 000)	26 500 (12 000) 39 700 (18 000)	26 (42) 17·4 (28)		87 (140) 56 (90)	45¼ (1150)	80	56' 1" (17 090)	192	1963	Brissonneau et Lotz MTE	SEMT-Pielstick 16PA4	MTE Oerlikon
BB67400	B-B	Elec	2070	63 934 (29 000)	31 746 (14 400)	23 (37)		87 (140)	49¼ (1250)	83	56' 1" (17 090)	232	1969	Brissoneau et Lotz MTE	SEMT-Pielstick 16PA4	MTE Oerlikon
BB71000	B-B	Mech	540	37 500 (17 000)				50 (80)	34 (860)	55	38' 10½" (11 850)	30	1965	Fives-Lille-Cail	Poyaud	Asynchro
C61000	C	Elec	380	35 250 (16 500)	18 300 (8500)			37 (60)	55⅛ (1400)	53	31' 2" (9500)	48	1950	CFMH	Sulzer 6LDA22A	CEM
Y 7100	B	Hyd	175	16 300 (7400)				34 (54)	41¼ (1050)	32	29' 4" (8940)	209	1958	Billiard Decauville	Poyaud 6PYT	Voith
Y 7400	B	Mech	175					37 (60)	41¼ (1050)	32	29' 4" (8940)	488	1963	Decauville De Dietrich	Moyse/Poyaud 6 PYT	BV Asynchro
Y 8000 (2 gears)	B	Hyd	290	13 600 (6750)	2750 (1247)	20		37 (60)	41¼ (1050)	36	33' 9" (10 140)	180 (+35 on order)	1977	Moyse Fauvet Girel	Poyaud Y12-52ONS	Voith

GABON

Gabon State Railways (OCTRA)
Office du Chemin de Fer Transgabonais

PO Box 2198, Libreville

Telephone: 244 78; 209 74
Telex: 5307

Chairman: Emmanuel Mefane
General Manager: Charles Tsibah
Deputy General Manager: Félix Kacka-Obelembia
Director of Administration: G Mozogo Ovono

Gauge: 1435 mm
Route length: 338 km

The Gabonese Government announced the decision to construct the first section of the Trans-Gabon Railway from Libreville/Owendo to Booué in 1972. Construction work started in 1974 and the first section between Owendo and N'Djolé (183 km) opened to traffic in January 1979.

The OCTRA plans originally called for construction first of the main Owendo-Booué section, and later extensions south to Franceville and north to iron ore fields at Belinga. However, the economic case for continuous construction of the Booué-Franceville line was found to be overwhelming, as there are large deposits of manganese at Moanda in the Haut-Ogooué as well as extensive reserves of timber. The present manganese output of only two million tonnes a year is transported from Moanda by a 75 km aerial ropeway across the border into the Congo at M'Binda, and thence by the Comilog and Congo-Ocean railways to Pointe-Noire for export. The Franceville extension will enable production to be expanded over 10 or 15 years to five million tonnes.

A contract for construction of the 340 km Booué-Franceville section was signed with the Eurotrag consortium in 1982. The first sleeper was formally placed by President Mitterrand of France during his visit to Gabon in January 1983. At the same time train services were inaugurated over the 162 km from N'Djolé to Booué, which was finished at the end of 1982.

The 230 km branch northwards to Belinga, where vast iron ore deposits are awaiting exploitation, will be financed by the Somifer (a consortium formed by Bethlehem Steel and several European mining companies). There seems little doubt that the branch will be built eventually, but the present world recession in the steel industry makes development of the Belinga ore fields less urgent.

Similar track standards have been devised for both sections of the Trans-Gabon. Rail will be 50 kg/m throughout, laid on 1670 wood sleepers per km in 25 cm of ballast; maximum axleload will be 23 tonnes. Steepest gradient against coast-bound trains will be 1 per cent between Franceville and Booué, and 0·5 per cent onwards to Owendo. East-bound, the maximum grade is 1·5 per cent throughout. Several major river crossings are required, and standard steel spans are being designed for these. There is only one tunnel on the line, of 280 metres at Junckville.

Traffic

When the line is completed OCTRA expects an annual traffic of 2·2 million tonnes of logs; 12 million tonnes of iron ore (eventually rising to 25 million tonnes), and five million tonnes of manganese ore.

The line will also carry about 400 000 passengers a year.

In 1980 freight traffic totalled 310 668 tonnes, compared with 59 664 in 1979.

Motive power and rolling stock

OCTRA's first 12 locomotives (six built by Alsthom-Atlantique and six by General Electric) were delivered during 1977. The Alsthom units are B-B design with a nominal (UIC) rating of 3000 hp, although under Gabon's severe climatic conditions the rating is reduced to 2800 hp. A single AGO V12 DSHR diesel engine is fitted which drives a three-phase alternator and rectifier set supplying dc to the two traction motors. Each locomotive weighs 92 tonnes and has a top speed of 85 km/h. The body is 15·8 metres long. Four more Alsthom B-Bs were due for delivery in 1983. In contrast the UM22C General Electric locomotives have a Co-Co wheel arrangement. They are rated at 2200 hp and are powered by a 7FDL12D25 series 265777 diesel engine. Weight is 108 tonnes.

In addition OCTRA operates four 450 hp Moyse locomotives and two railcars. Rolling stock totals 10 passenger cars, five railcar trailers and 352 freight

OCTRA GE Co-Co and Alsthom B-B diesel-electric locomotives

wagons (excluding service vehicles). New wagon deliveries from Brazil and Morocco were scheduled in 1983.

At the start of 1983 tenders were invited for equipment to serve the completed line to France-ville. These covered 20 main-line and 10 diesel shunting locomotives for 1984-87 delivery; and six first-class couchette cars with bar, ten second-class couchette and three restaurant cars, for 1984-86 delivery.

GERMANY (Democratic Republic)

Ministry of Transport

Vossstrasse 38, 1086 East Berlin

Telephone: 490
Telex: 11 2564

Minister and General Manager, German State Railway: O Arndt
State Secretary: Dr H Schmidt

German State Railway (DR)
Deutsche Reichsbahn

Vossstrasse 38, 1086 East Berlin

Telephone: 490
Telex: 11 2564

General Manager: O Arndt
Departmental Heads
  Traffic Operating: P G Kienast
  Mechanical and Electrical: R Wagner
  Permanent Way: L Damitz
  Motive Power and Rolling Stock: H Wesarg
  Safety Installations and Telecommunications: H Klemm
Chief Operations Officer: H Krüger

Gauge: 1435 mm; narrow gauge
Length: 14 222 route-km; 280 km
Electrification: 1928 km at 15 kV 16⅔ Hz ac

Traffic

Government policy directs the maximum possible amount of bulk transport on to the DR. At the start of the 1980s the railway was logging some 54 000 million tonne-km of freight a year, more than two-thirds of the total recorded by all forms of transport in the country, and over 24 000 million passenger-km. Road transport fell by 20 per cent in the first half of 1982. Part of the traffic was transferred to the railways and part to the waterways.

Traffic	1981	1982
Total freight tonnage (million)	315·2	322·5
Total freight tonne-km (million)	544 000	540 000
Average freight wagon load (tonnes)	20·34	20·19
Total passenger-km (million)	23 000	24 500
Total passenger journeys (million)	601	619
Average length of passenger journey (km)	38	39·5

Electrification

At the start of 1982 1788 route-km were electrified. Begun in 1954, the routes concerned were principally those from Leipzig to Magdeburg, via both Halle and Dessau, but electrification had also been

USSR built 3000 hp Type 131 diesel-electric and hopper train at Sangerhausen *(John Chalcraft)*

BR 212 3720 kW Bo-Bo prototype

installed from Leipzig to Dresden and Reichenbach; from Dresden to the frontier of Czechoslovakia, to Karl-Marx-Stadt and a junction with the Reichenbach line; and from Grossheringen to Neudietendorf.

The next major projects were to complete electrification of the routes from Leipzig and Dresden to Berlin. By the end of May 1982 the electrification of a part of the southern Berlin Ring route was completed, so that the freight trains from Dresden, Leipzig and Erfurt could reach the Seddin marshalling yard without a locomotive change. The Schönefeld-Glasower Damm section of the southern Berlin Ring, the DR's most heavily trafficked stretch, has also had a third track installed. At the end of 1982 the electrification between Saarmund and Priort had been completed and was continued from Priort in the direction of Birkenwerder, extending thus to the north side of the Berlin Ring. By the end of 1982 a total of 140 km had been electrified during the year.

In 1982 it was announced that the pace of electrification was to be stepped up for energy saving reasons. In the period 1981-85 a further 826 route-km were to be electrified, to raise electric traction's share of DR train working from 20 to more than 30 per cent and to put almost 15 per cent of the DR network under wires. The primary objective is to electrify the route from the Berlin Ring through Neustrelitz and Waren to the ports of Rostock and Warnemünde.

The Governments of the two Germanys are also considering creation of a through electrified route between their countries. The likeliest link-up would be between Brunswick and Helmstedt, where at present there is a gap of only 47·5 km between the two catenaries on the Helmstedt-Magdeburg stretch. A shorter route to Berlin would be from Hanover via Oebisfelde and Stendal, but this would involve the German Federal Republic in electrifying the 72·1 km of its system from Lehrte to Oebisfelde.

At the outset of 1981 the Transport Ministers of the German Democratic Republic and Czechoslovakia agreed to close the gap of 13 km between their two electrified networks at Schöna (DDR) and Decin (CSSR). The DR and CSD would then develop a dual-voltage 15 kV 16⅔ Hz and 3 kV dc locomotive to enable through running between East Berlin and Prague via Bad Schandau.

Traction and rolling stock

For heavy freight haulage the six-axle BR 250 electric locomotive has been developed. The first example of the fifth series appeared early in 1982 and BR 250 production was continuing in 1983. With electrification now to be pressed ahead in the plains of the north, and the demand for electric locomotives further increasing, the first prototype of a new four-axle design has been created by Kombinat VEB Lokomotivbau-Elektrotechnische Werke 'Hans Beimler' Hennigsdorf. The express passenger version, arranged for a maximum speed of 140 km/h, is the BR 212, with a more aerodynamically-styled body than previous DR designs. Its four motors are more powerful than those of the BR 250, giving it a one-hour rating of 3720 kW and a tractive effort of

BR 250 Co-Co 15 kV 16⅔ Hz electric locomotive

Two Class 110 diesel-hydraulics on Stralsund-Oranienburg train *(John Chalcraft)*

Electrification mast installation on DR is accelerated by widespread use of helicopters

DR bi-level commuter cars, built by VEB Waggonbau Görlitz, loading at Halle

248 kN. Measuring 16·64 metres over buffers, the BR 212 weighs 82·5 tonnes, with a maximum axleloading of 21 tonnes, and is equipped with rheostatic braking. The freight version is the BR 243, with maximum speed limited to 120 km/h and a tractive effort of 280 kN, and this is to be committed to mass production before the BR 212.

At the end of 1982 the DR operated 10 567 passenger cars and 149 217 freight wagons, but the latter figure was to be raised by purchase of 6800 wagons from the German Federal Railway (DB) at a cost of DM 7000-8000 each.

Intermodal development

The DR is rapidly developing container freight, which by the start of the 1980s had reached a volume of over 3·6 million tonnes and 500 000 container movements a year, including a substantial amount of international exchange with other Comecon countries and of maritime traffic through Rostock. Operation is centred on some 430 trains running weekly between 20 public terminals and seven contained within industrial premises. The traffic is mostly moved on purpose-built bogie flat wagons capable of 100 km/h running speed. Intensification of the drive to containerise was announced in 1983.

Civil engineering

DR has reduced route length from 14 298 km in 1975 to 14 222 km. The track consists of Type S49 and R65 rails, flash-butt welded in the workshops in 25-metre lengths and then thermit-welded after laying in continuous lengths. The rails are laid on 6 mm thick rubber pads or 5 mm thick wooden (poplar) pads, secured by Type K fasteners either on 160 mm thick wooden or 200 mm thick concrete sleepers.

The equipment of the DR has been further improved with rational safety and telecommunications technology by the introduction of more efficient push-button signal boxes and relay interlocking systems, modern track crossing safety installations, as well as the construction of automatic train stopping devices and an automatic block system.

Ferries

Train ferry services are at present operated to Scandinavia from special-purpose docks at Sassnitz on the traditional Kings Route and from Warnemünde to Gedser.

Following a June 1982 agreement between the Soviet and German Democratic Governments preparations are in hand for introduction of a direct train ferry link between the two countries in the autumn of 1986. The present overland rail transit via Poland takes up to three days between points chiefly benefitting from the train-ferry project, which will cut the journey times to as little as 20 hours. The service will be operated by six giant double-deck ferries each with a capacity of 130 broad-gauge wagons. They will provide three sailings every 24 hours over the 440 km passage between Klaipeda, in the USSR, and a new port under construction at Mukran, south of Sassnitz. The facilities at Mukran will permit simultaneous loading or discharge from each deck of a ferry, and will include a gauge-changing installation.

Erfurt marshalling yard control room

Primary retarders at Seddin yard

DR inter-city express headed by USSR-built diesel-electric Co-Co

Track-mounted rubber wagon brakes in DR yard reception siding

Electric locomotives

Type	BR 250	BR 211	BR 242	E 211	BR 251	EL 104	E 04	E 06
Service weight (tonnes)	120 + 5%	80 + 3%	80 + 3%	80 + 3%	120 + 5%	130 + 3%	80 + 5%	120 + 3%
Track gauge (mm)	1435	1435	1435	1435	1435	1435	1435	1435
Wheel arrangement	Co-Co	Bo-Bo	Bo-Bo	Bo-Bo	Co-Co	Co-Co	Bo-Bo	Co-Co
Length over buffers (mm)	19 600	16 260	16 260	16 106	18 640	18 640	16 320	18 700
Max width (over car body/hand rails) (mm)	2970/3090	3050	3050	3080	3065	3050	3050	3050
Height above top of rail with pantograph lowered (mm)	4650	4530	4530	4550	4585	4290	4490	4490
Distance between bogie pivots (mm)	11 200	7800	7800	7500	9800	9800	7800	10 200
Minimum curve radius (m)	140	140	140	125	140	100	140	140
Height of trolley wire (mm) max	6700	6500	6500	6440	6360	6100	6700	6700
min	4850	4950	4950	4940	4960	4500	4700	4700
Trolley voltage	15 kV +15% −20%	15 kV +15% −20%	15 kV +15% −20%	25 kV +15% −24%	25 kV +15% −20%	3000 V +20% −33%	3000 V +20% −30%	3000 V +20% −30%
Rated frequency	16²/₃ Hz	16²/₃ Hz	16²/₃ Hz	50 Hz	50 Hz	—	—	—
No of traction motors	6	4	4	4	6	6	4	6
Rated power (one-hour rating) (kW)	5400	2920	2920	3360	3660	2440	2120	3180
Tractive effort at rated power (Mp)	19·6	10·4	14·4	14·9	32	24·6	17	25
Speed at rated power (km/h)	100	98	72	80	38	32	45·5	45·5
Max service speed (km/h)	125	120	100	160	80	74	120	120
Max tractive effort on starting (Mp)	47·4	23	25·2	29·3	45·5/54	40	25	36
No of traction notches	31	28, including 14 continuous traction notches		infinitely variable	34	48/22	40	43

Diesel locomotives

Class	Wheel arrange-ment	Trans-mission	Rated power hp	Max lb (kg)	Tractive effort Continuous at lb (kg)	mph (km/h)	Max speed mph (km/h)	Wheel dia in (mm)	Total weight tons	Length ft in (mm)	No built	Year first built	Builders Mechanical parts	Builders Engine & type	Builders Transmission
106 (V 60)	D	Hyd	650	38 570 (17 500) 27 770 (12 600)	36 145 (16 400) 20 280 (9200)	7 (4·5) 14 (9)	19 (30) 38 (60)	43·2 (1100)	60	35' 8½" (10 880)		1960	VEB Lokomotiv-bau-Elektrotech-nische Werke "Hans Beimler"	12 kV D 18/21	VEB Strömungs-maschinen Pirna
107 (V 75)	B-B	Elec	750	45 400 (20 600)	22 920 (10 400)	9 (14)	38 (60)	39·3 (1000)	63	41' 2½" (12 560)		1962	CKD Praha	6 S 310 DR	
110 (V 100)	B-B	Hyd	1000	46 300 (21 000) 33 060 (15 000)	33 060 (15 000) 20 720 (9 400)	7 (11) 11 (17)	63 (100)	39·3 (1000)	64	45' 9" (13 940)		1966	VEB Lokomotiv-bau-Elektrotech-nische Werke "Hans Beimler"	12 kV D 18/21 A-II	VEB Strömungs-maschinen Pirna
118 (V 180)	B-B	Hyd	1800 2000	47 400 (21 500) 57 300 (26 000)	27 330 (12 400) 35 700 (16 200)	13 (21)	75 (120)	39·3 (1000)	78	63' 10" (19 460)		1962	VEB-Lokomotiv-bau "Karl Marx"	12 kV D 18/21 A-I 12 kV D 18/21 A-II	VEB Strömungs-maschinen Pirna; Voith
118 (V 180)	C-C	Hyd	2000	57 300 (26 000)	35 700 (16 200)	13 (21)	75 (120)	39·3 (1000)	90	63' 10" (19 460)		1966	VEB Lokomotiv-bau "Karl Marx"	12 kV D 18/21 A-II	VEB Strömungs-maschinen Pirna; Voith
120 (V 200)	Co-Co	Elec	2000	84 440 (38 300)	54 900 (24 900)	9·5 (15·1)	63 (100)	41·3 (1050)	116	57' 7" (17 550)		1966	Voroshilovgrad USSR	14 D40	Charkov Works USSR
130 (V 300)	Co-Co	Elec	3000	66 100 (30 200)	38 800 (17 600)	21·4 (34·5)	87 (140)	41·3 (1050)	120	67' 8" (20 620)		1969	Voroshilovgrad USSR	6 D49	Charkov Works USSR
131	Co-Co	Elec	3000	77 160 (35 000)	59 500 (27 000)	13·4 (21·5)	63 (100)	41·3 (1050)	122.5	67' 8" (20 620)		1973	Voroshilovgrad USSR	6 D49	Charkov Works USSR
132	Co-Co	Elec	3000	66 140 (30 000)	44 530 (20 200)	20·2 (32·5)	75 (120)	41·3 (1050)	123·6	67' 8" (20 620)		1973	Voroshilovgrad USSR	6 D49	Charkov Works USSR

GERMANY (Federal Republic)

Ministry of Transport

Kennedyallee 72, Postfach 20 0100, 5300 Bonn 2

Telephone: 3001
Telegrams: Bundesverkehrsministerium, Bonn
Telex: 885700

Minister: Werner Dollinger
Secretary of State: Alfred Bayer
Parliamentary Secretary: Dr Dieter Schülte
Railways Department Manager: Dr Beck

German Federal Railway (DB)
Deutsche Bundesbahn

Friedrich-Ebert-Anlage 43-45, 6000 Frankfurt (Main)

Telephone: (0611) 265-1
Telex: 04 414 087

Chairman of the Board: Hans Wertz
Directorate
Chairman: Dr Reiner Golke

Sales: Hemjö Klein
Personnel: Heinz Frieser
Financial: Hans-Joachim Gröben
Planning: Wilhelm Pällmann
Production: Hans Wiedemann
Technical: Peter Koch

Manager, Central Sales Organisation, Mainz: Dr jur Hans-Joachim Koenig
  Central Transport Control, Mainz: D Treutler
  Central Office, Workshops, Mainz: H Troche
Engineer-in-charge, Mechanical and Construction: Dipl-Ing H Binneweis
Federal Railway Central Office (Research and Procurement), Minden (Westphalia): Johann Peter Blank
  Munich: Theo Rahn

Gauge: 1435 mm
Route length: 28 335 km
Electrification: 11 179 km at 15 kV 16²/₃ Hz ac

Transport development
While nominally independent, DB is subject to a large degree of Government control, operating with the objective of providing optimum nation-wide transport services in accordance with commercial principles. A significant change in the character of the DB's Directorate was legislated in 1981. Its membership was increased from five (including the chairman) to eight and all but one of the previous incumbents were replaced. Moreover, each of the new directorate members, excluding the chairman, was assigned a specific area of functional responsibility: personnel; sales and subsidiaries; production; technical planning; investment and finance; economic planning. The fixed five-year term of appointment was also discarded; henceforward members could be appointed for varying terms of two to six years. Delineation of functional responsibility throughout the DB's organisation was a fundamental point of the new policy.

At centralised office level, the Central Sales Organisation (ZVL), Mainz, carries out inter-regional functions of price formation, market observation, research, sales planning and promotion. The Advertising and Publicity Office (WER), Mainz, is primarily in charge of inter-regional publicity. The Centralised Transport Control Office (ZTL) is responsible for planning, control and supervision of all transport activities. The Central Office for Modernisation and Rationalisation of Workshops (ZW), Mainz, is in charge of rolling stock repairs. Two central research and procurement offices (BZÄ) at Minden and Munich perform centralised functions in the field of purchase and technical development. The Central Office for Industrial Management and Data Processing (ZB), Frankfurt, is mainly responsible for statistics, costing and operations research. The Social Office (BSA), Frankfurt, is in charge of all social matters.

The total network of DB is sub-divided into 10 regions for which regional headquarters are responsible. These are: Essen; Frankfurt (Main); Hamburg; Hanover; Karlsruhe; Cologne; Munich; Nuremberg; Saarbrücken; and Stuttgart.

Finance

The railway's ultimate balance sheet for 1982 showed a deficit of DM 4450 million, only DM 10 million more than budgeted but some DM 406 million in excess of the 1981 figure. The worsening loss was attributed chiefly to the recession's effect on freight. Although long-haul passenger traffic including that by tourist charter train receded, the passenger business as a whole sustained the previous year's levels because of increased military, scholar and professional commuter travel; in the last category the rise, achieved despite growth of unemployment, demonstrated some disinclination to use the private car for economic reasons. Interest payments on the DB's borrowed capital have now reached a level at which the total threatens to exceed annual investment.

In its report on its 1981 results, published late in 1982, the DB Directorate reorganised its accounts to demonstrate that, on a basis of fair comparison with its competitors, it was not in deficit on its strictly commercial operations. This involved treating infrastructure as well as obligatory social train services separately, and produced a loss of DM 5100 million on the former, one of DM 700 million on the latter, and consequently a surplus of DM 1800 million on strictly commercial train operations.

Federal support for DB 1982

Compensation for social services	(DM million)
Local passenger	3392·5
Long-distance passenger	62·5
Bus services (students' traffic)	95
Retention of unremunerative lines	6·4
Saar Region reduced tariffs	35
Intermodal traffic	128·7
Total	3720·1
Compensation for obligations affecting terms of competition, eg level crossing upkeep, staff insurance	4575
Federal obligations as DB owner	
Interest payments on loans and capital	953·6
Loan amortisation	16·7
Investment grants	3304·3
Liquidity assistance	486·4
Total	4761·0
Miscellaneous	
Local public transport grants	431
Oil tax relief	180
Total	611
Total	13 667·1

Passenger services

Major changes in the framework of the DB's long-haul passenger services from May 1983 were elimination of all remaining TEEs except for the 'Rheingold' and Milan-Munich 'Mediolanum', the relaunch of the 'Rheingold' as the system's flagship train, and introduction of a new category, the *Fernexpress* (FD), aimed at the tourist market. Besides restoration of a three-car Munich section, separated from the Amsterdam-Basle train at Mannheim to take the longer, scenic route to the Bavarian capital via the Neckar valley and Heilbronn to Stuttgart, and thence via Schwäbisch-Gmünd, Aalen and Donauwörth to Munich, the 'Rheingold' included in this section a 'Club Car' with similar facilities to those of its counterpart in the 'TUI-Ferien Express': tourist services, entertainment and catering specialties. Train staff included a hostess.

Nine pairs of FD trains were introduced on other tourist itineraries from main centres such as Dortmund, Hamburg, Munich and Frankfurt to popular destinations outside the Inter-City (IC) network, such as Berchtesgaden, Constance, Vienna, Klagenfurt, Zurich and Paris. Some of them were redesignated D-trains redesignated, like the 'Donau-Kurier' and 'Wörthersee-Express.' A feature of five of these workings was service by refurbished 'Quick-Pick' self-service catering cars offering specially low-priced dishes and draught beer. All FD trains also included a children's nursery compartment.

With continuing deliveries of new air-conditioned second-class saloons all IC trains would include two of these vehicles in addition to compartment cars from the autumn of 1984. By March 1983 the DB expected to have completed installation of coin-operated telephone kiosks for passengers in 131 saloon cars employed in the IC network; with the exception of IC trains to and from France and Belgium and the 'Mediolanum' TEE, and weekend-only workings, all IC and TEE trains on the DB would then have the telephone facility.

	Result 1979	Result 1980	Result 1981	Budget 1982
Revenue		(DM million)		
Passengers, baggage and parcels	4948	5290	5805	6290
Freight	8869	9210	9216	9890
Other	2110	2161	2231	2461
Federal contribution	8083	8829	7678	9249
Total	24 010	25 490	24 930	27 890
Expenses				
Personnel	18 338	19 540	20 198	21 432
Direct operating costs	3467	3795	4084	4490
Indirect operating costs	2931	3110	3011	3465
Financial charges	2314	2329	2719	2893
Other	536	526	666	70
Total	27 586	29 300	30 678	32 350
Deficit	3576	3810	4044	4460

Three pairs of direct 'Airport-Express' trains between the Mannheim-Ludwigshafen area and Frankfurt Airport, introduced in 1978, have proved unremunerative and were abandoned in May 1983. But at the same time additional longer-distance service of Frankfurt Airport station was begun by trains including early morning ICs to Amsterdam and from Düsseldorf and their balancing late afternoon return trains, as well as by some further long-haul D and E trains. The charter 'Lufthansa-Airport-Express', employing Type 403 high-speed emus staffed by the airline, had its service contract renewed for a further year and now runs four times daily between Düsseldorf and Frankfurt Airport stations. During 1982 the service's average loading steadily increased to 8500 passengers a month; during some special events in Cologne and Frankfurt in late summer and autumn demand per trip was as high as 200 seats, necessitating the complex addition to the working units of a trailer extracted from the 403 set held in reserve at Düsseldorf. The cost of the service to Lufthansa was DM 7·5 million for the first year.

Type 403 emu in Lufthansa livery

Lufthansa service in Type 403 emu on Düsseldorf-Frankfurt Airport feeder flight

To improve Inter-City economics the DB is studying prospective bi-level and long-body single-level car designs. As a first step in the latter category, Linke-Hofmann-Busch has been commissioned to build 10 27·5-metre, 12 compartment, 72-seater compartment cars with a less expensive form of air-conditioning than that applied to the 26·4-metre second-class Inter-City saloons. Delivery is scheduled for 1984. The prototypes will differ in some equipment details.

300 km/h ICE train-set
The Ministry of Research and Technology has made a grant of DM 44 million toward the cost of building a self-propelled four-car high-speed train-set, the Inter City Experimental (ICE). The DB and the country's railway supply industry are finding the remaining DM 28 million for the project. The aim was to complete design by the end of 1983, begin construction in 1984 and have the ICE ready for trials, eventually at up to 350 km/h, by the end of 1985. The project is being led by the Munich Research office of the DB and managed by Deutsche Eisenbahn Consult of Frankfurt.

The two end power cars, each weighing 74 tonnes, will be streamlined and steel-bodied. All axles will be powered with a three-phase induction motor employing the UmAn flexible drive system with power block mass transfer (see under Thyssen-Henschel in Locomotives and rolling stock). Pantographs, housed in a roof recess, will be manufactured of lightweight insulating materials developed in space technology and therefore require no insulated mounting frame.

The aluminium-bodied intermediate trailers will weigh 39·3 or 41·4 tonnes. To permit four-a-side seating in first class without sacrifice of spaciousness (see under Messerschmitt-Bölkow-Blohm in Locomotives and rolling stock), body width will be 3·2 metres, so that the ICE will be barred from DB routes that have not been remodelled with 4-metre instead of 3·5-metre track centres. Two types of trailer bogie, one air-suspended and the other conventionally steel sprung will be used at first, but MBB's air-suspension bogie employing composite fibre components may also be tested. Braking will be eddy current as well as dynamic and disc. The length of the four-car unit will be 89·6 metres. Four more fully-equipped trailers will be inserted in the formation for passenger demonstration runs.

S-Bahnen
Completion of the Hamburg S-Bahn network was brought a step nearer in 1982 with commissioning of double track to Pinneberg and establishment of an intensive service between there and the city-centre core of the system. An addition of the new line to Harburg Rathaus was due in the autumn of 1983, followed a year later by the extension to Neugraben.

Rhein-Ruhr-Wupper S-Bahn construction between Bochum and Dortmund made progress, as did the massive conversion of Düsseldorf Hbf into a main line/S-Bahn/U-Bahn interchange; realignment of the approaches to the rebuilt station of the S-Bahn tracks from Duisburg and Düsseldorf Airport was nearing completion in 1982. The scheme has involved creation of a six-track layout between Düsseldorf and Duisburg. Four S-Bahn routes will converge on Düsseldorf Hbf, where a daily interchange of 100 000 passengers with U-Bahn routes is expected. Extension of the Bergisch Gladbach-Cologne-Chorweiler S-Bahn line to Worringen was begun.

In Rhein-Main S-Bahn territory, work was in progress on four of the seven tunnel sections involved in the third and last stage of projecting the S-Bahn through the heart of Frankfurt am Main; tracklaying and station equipment in the so-called Zeiltunnels, where S- and U-Bahn share the route, was continuing. The downtown S-Bahn service was to be extended from Hauptwache to a future U-Bahn underground interchange station at Konstablerwache in May 1983. Completion of the cross-town tunnel to the city's Sud station was programmed for 1988.

After two years' work boring of the 5·5 km Hasenberg Tunnel for the southern extension of the Stuttgart S-Bahn was completed in the autumn of 1982 with a breakthrough between the two workfaces. The tunnel should be lined ready for tracklaying in 1984 to enable its use by public service in 1985. It will convey a line from the city-centre station at Schwabstrasse to Vaihangen and thence southeastwards by a 2·4 km branch to Stuttgart-Echterdingen airport. Extension to Leinfelden should be finished in 1987.

Agreement was reached in 1981 for creation of the first stage of a Nuremberg S-Bahn, covering lines from the city's Hbf to Roth, Altdorf and Lauf, total 67

Class 151 8400 hp freight Co-Co on northbound train at Bruchsal *(John C Baker)*

Dual-voltage thyristor-controlled Class 181 Bo-Bo at Karlsruhe *(Günter Barths)*

Class 103 9970 hp Co-Co at Freiburg with Genoa-Frankfurt IC train, including 'Quick-Pick' cafeteria next to locomotive *(John C Baker)*

route-km, to be worked by Class 141 locomotive-hauled push-pulls. At the close of 1978 the infrastructure work involved had been costed at DM 746 million, of which, under the Federal GFVG statute, 60 per cent would be covered Federally; under the local 1981 agreement the rest would be shared by the Bavarian Land Government and the Nuremberg city authority. An S-Bahn core is also to be created in the heart of Cologne.

Freight traffic

A Grünnetz (Green Network) has been created to concentrate the maximum amount of intermodal traffic (KLV) into dedicated trains offering overnight transits between the majority of main centres. A similar Rotnetz (Red Network) covers high-rated merchandise wagonload traffic conveyed in overnight inter-yard through trains (Eilgüterzüge) and TEEM. The rest of the freight operation is denominated the Schwarznetz (Black Network).

Freight traffic volume in 1982 was 7·2 per cent down on 1981, but intermodal traffic managed a slight rise from 12·7 million to 12·8 million tonnes (in contrast to a 2 per cent decline in the country's road freight). The increase was predominantly in piggyback freight, where there was a growth of 7·5 per cent to 5·9 million tonnes and of 4·5 per cent to 2700 million tonne-km. Influential in this growth was the inception of more Ro/Ro 'Rollende Landstrasse' services with low-floor, small diameter-wheel wagons of SGP and Talbot manufacture. Some internal services, such as Munich-Cologne and Hamburg-Cologne, were averaging an 80 to 85 per cent load factor. The tonnage rise in all types of international piggyback operation was as much as 23 per cent, the tonne-km increase 28 per cent. In January 1983 a new overnight Rollende Landstrasse service was set up between Breda, in the Netherlands, and Mannheim. Demand for piggyback services was encouraging moves to form a private company to lease special-purpose wagons, in view of the DB's inability to enlarge its Rollende Landstrasse fleet because of the investment level freeze imposed by the Government. Container traffic, on the other hand, regressed, by 3 per cent in internal traffic and by 3·5 per cent, from 7·2 million to 6·9 million tonnes in ISO container business.

During 1982 intermodal terminal improvements were put in hand at Hannover-Linden, Karlsruhe, Cologne Eifeltor, Regensburg, Hamburg-Rothensburgort, Mannheim and Nuremberg. Other terminals to be treated in 1983 included Frankfurt Ost, Freiburg, Harburg, Ludwigsburg, Bochum-Langendreer and Hannover-Würfel. In November 1982 DB and its piggyback and container subsidiaries, Kombiverkehr KG and Transfracht GmbH, formed a consortium, DUSS, to pursue road-rail co-operation in the planning, increase and financing of intermodal terminals. The DB has also established a special intermodal office in its central sales headquarters at Mainz.

Another encouraging exception to the general 1982 trend was the throughput at ports. Bremen's ore traffic, all of which is railborne inland, rose 20 per cent to 3·9 million tonnes; and Bremerhaven's container traffic, in which the DB claims an 80 per cent share of the long-distance inland hauls, increased by 3·4 per cent. At Hamburg the year's tonnage of 2·5 million was almost 3 per cent up on 1981 and included a record total at Hamburg-Waltershof. Overall the DB claims a 36 per cent share of the port's total inward and outward tonnages, compared with road's 30 per cent.

The DB is raising the permissible maximum axleload of both two- and four-axle freight wagons from 20 to 22·5 tonnes.

Rail traffic

	1980	1981	1982
Total passenger journeys (million)	1107	1097	1100·9
Total passenger-km (million)	40 499	41 311	39 864
Total freight (million tonnes)	332·8	317·8	278·5
Total freight tonne-km (million)	62 515	60 874	56 513

Traction and rolling stock investment

In the face of diminished capital resources, increased deficit and frozen levels of State support the DB had to trim its earlier investment plans for 1983 by some DM 500 million. Even so the total budgeted, DM 4700 million, was about DM 500 million more than outgoings in 1982. Of this total DM 900 million was earmarked for the Neubau- and Ausbaustrecke programmes, compared with DM 700 million in the previous year. New traction purchases have been cut back: in 1983-85 electric locomotive deliveries will be limited to 35 Class 111, of which 10 will be assigned to the Rhein-Ruhr

Class 140 4850 hp Bo-Bo on unit coal train

Class 111 4850 hp Bo-Bo at Jenbach, Austria, with Hook of Holland-Innsbruck express *(John C Baker)*

S-Bahn/U-Bahn interchange at Frankfurt Konstablerwache, for completion 1986 with U-Bahn tracks flanking S-Bahn at lower level

S-Bahn. Commitment of the three-phase Class 120 to series production is now unlikely to result in deliveries earlier than 1986. Other traction deliveries expected in 1983 were 18 Class 472 dc three-car emus for the Hamburg S-Bahn.

Coaching stock deliveries would include 113 air-conditioned second-class saloons for long-haul traffic, to add to the 174 operational at the start of the year; and 83 cars of three different designs for the

Rhein-Ruhr S-Bahn, which operates locomotive-powered push-pulls and not emus. In all 2905 freight wagons of various types were expected: 430 Type Eaos open wagons; 285 Type Sgjkkmms container wagons; 350 Type Hbikkf-tt sliding-wall bogie vans with fixed internal partitions; 660 Type Fals hoppers for coal and iron ore; 30 six-axle Type Faals ore wagons with 100 tonnes' payload capacity; 400 Type Res flat wagons; 450 Type Sps pipe wagons;

100 Type Samms flat wagons for steel coil; and 200 Type Tadgs grain hoppers.

Total cost of deliveries expected in 1983 was approximately DM 1000 million.

Civil engineering

Progress with the DM 3700 million, 99 km Mannheim-Stuttgart 'Neubaustrecke' in 1983 hinged on completion of the statutory planning processes for further sections; but infrastructure work on the DM 11 700 million, 327 km Hanover-Würzburg 'Neubaustrecke', of which 128 route-km was agreed by the end of 1982, would be pressed forward in the area of Fulda and on the southern section of the line, where 14 tunnels and 50 bridges would be amongst the new undertakings. Expenditure on the first of these schemes in 1983 would be DM 150 million, on the second DM 585 million. Boring of the Hanover-Würzburg line's longest tunnel, the 10·748 km Landrücken 15 km south of Fulda, was begun in December 1982.

Of the 585 'Ausbaustrecke' improvements of existing lines planned, 260 have been completed and 150 were in hand in 1983. One of the major schemes progressing under this head is the installation of a third track over the 41 km between Nordheide and Rotenburg, on the Hamburg-Bremen-Münster route, at a cost of DM 200 million; this is to be finished in 1986. Other 'Ausbaustrecke' projects in hand during 1983, for which DM 220 million was budgeted under this head, were Dortmund-Braunschweig, Hamburg-Hanover, Guessen-Friedburg, Frankfurt-Mannheim and Würzburg-Nuremberg-Augsburg. Capacity enlargement of the Rhine Valley route between Karlsruhe and Basle, by addition of a second pair of 250 km/h tracks as far as Offenburg and a third track beyond, in conjunction with some realignments to permit higher speed, is a major scheme to come. The DB hopes that the legal processes concerning the scheme will be completed in time for work on the Karlsruhe-Offenburg stretch to begin in 1986.

Completion of the new Riedbahn approach to Mannheim Hbf, avoiding reversal of Frankfurt-Basle/Stuttgart trains, was expected by 1985. Other important civil engineering works to be undertaken in 1983 included construction of a new four-track S-Bahn bridge over the Rhine between Düsseldorf and Neuss and of another to carry the Main-Neckar line over the Wiesbaden line and the locomotive yard outside Frankfurt Hbf.

Electrification

The DB has raised its economic criteria for electrification. Schemes must now show a 15 per cent annual return on investment, not merely avoid worsening the railway's financial situation. This was likely to defer such further electrification projects as Basle-Singen-Lindau and Neustadt/Black Forest-Donaueschingen. However, agreement was reached with the Land Government of Baden-Württemberg in February 1983 for double-tracking of the Basle-Lindau line, at a cost of DM 44 million.

After a false start in 1980, when costs outran the funds which the DB could make available for the project, a new agreement was reached in May 1982 for electrification of the 38 km from Frankfurt via Niedernhausen (Taunus) to Limburg (Lahn). The Land Government of Hesse made a grant of DM 40 million towards the expected total cost of DM 66·5 million and the work was to begin in 1983 for completion by 1986. Also put in hand was electrification of the 76 km between Goldshöfe and Crailsheim, at a cost of DM 32 million, for completion by 1985. The Sarrebruck-Hanweiler-Bad Rilchingen electrification was extended 2 km over single track to the Franco-German border station of Sarreguemines.

A further stage in electrification of the Hamburg port layout was completed with wiring of the Hausbruch-Hohe Schaar link between the two banks of the Süderelbe. The aim of the DM 10·3 million electrification, the cost of which is 50 per cent borne by the Hamburg Free and Hansa City, which owns the port railway system of some 670 km, is to wire the access to all port yards from which trains are run direct to the main-line network, to avoid locomotive changes. Thus the 5600-tonne ore trains from Hansaport to the Peine-Salzgitter plant near Hanover, for example, can be started with their main-line traction in place.

Track

Standard rail: Type S49, weighing 49·5 kg/m, type S54, 54·5 kg/m and type S64, 64·9 kg/m. Lengths generally 30-120 m
Type of rail joints: 4- and 6-hole fishplates
Cross ties (sleepers): Wood; steel; reinforced concrete
Wood sleepers impregnated beech, fir or oak, 2600 × 260 × 160 mm

Motive power and rolling stock (units)

	1975	1979	1980	1981
Steam locomotives	256	—	—	—
Electric locomotives	2629	2688	2705	2715
Diesel locomotives	3097	3109	3088	3081
Light motor tractors	1666	1375	1265	1264
Electric railcars	1076	1514	1590	1619
Battery railcars	237	237	237	237
Diesel railcars	227	246	246	249
Rail buses	672	391	319	311
Passenger coaches	17 726	14 910	14 731	14 505
Luggage vans	1303	1054	1048	1027
Freight wagons (total)	287 365	279 416	282 412	282 318
Covered wagons	124 119	121 308	121 186	121 180
Open wagons	92 447	83 839	83 917	85 100
Flat wagons	70 799	74 269	77 309	76 038

	1975	1978	1979	1980	1981
Length of line operated (km)					
Standard gauge	28 771	28 507	28 533	28 450	28 355
Narrow gauge	25	25	25	25	25
Total	28 796	28 532	28 558	28 475	28 360
Single-track	16 572	16 295	16 290	16 210	16 092
Multiple-track	12 224	12 237	12 268	12 265	12 268
For passenger traffic only	515	539	563	568	578
For freight traffic only	4615	4965	4980	5296	5678
For passenger and freight traffic	23 666	23 028	23 015	22 611	22 106
Electrified	10 011	10 657	10 887	11 159	11 179
Number of private sidings served	NA	NA	NA	11 098	11 122
Equipped for track-to-train radio	NA	NA	NA	13 439	14 169

Roll-on/roll-off piggyback loading of 'Rollende Landstrasse' low-floor wagons

Type 420 emu on Rhein-Main S-Bahn Frankfurt Hbf-Airport-Wiesbaden service at Mainz *(John C Baker)*

Steel, 2600 mm × 9 mm weighing 86·3 kg
The latest type of RC sleeper (Spannbetonschwelle B58) weighs 235 kg, is 2400 mm long, 190 mm thick under rails, 280 mm wide at bottom and 136 mm at top
Spacing: 650-800 mm
Rail fastenings: Baseplates and bolts, clips and spring washers with thin rubber or wood (poplar) pad between rail and plate; resilient rail spikes with wood and concrete sleepers and resilient rail clips with steel sleepers
Max gradient: Main lines: 2·5% = 1 in 40
Secondary lines: 6·6% = 1 in 16·5
Max curvature
Main lines: 9·7° = minimum radius 180 m
Secondary lines: 17·5° = minimum radius 100 m
Gauge widening on curves
Radius over 300 m: 0 mm
Radius 300-200 m: 5 mm
Radius 200-150 m: 10 mm
Radius 150-120 m: 15 mm
Radius 120-100 m: 20 mm
Max superelevation: 150 mm on curves of 180 m radius and under
Rate of slope of superelevation: Generally 1: 10V (V = speed in *mph*). On occasion this may be increased to 1: 8V up to 1 in 400. On reverse curves the permissible limit is 1: 4V up to 1 in 400
Max altitude: Main line: 967 m between Klais and Mittenwald. Highest station Klais, 933 m
Secondary line: 969 m between Bärenthal and Aha on the Titisee-Seebrugg line
Max axleloading: 20 tonnes
Welded rail: Total length of track laid with welded rails (end-1974) 53 000 km

Container operations
Container operations, domestic and international, are operated on behalf of the DB by:
TRANSFRACHT GmbH
Gutleutstrasse 160-164, 6000 Frankfurt (Main)
Telephone: (611) 23 03 51
Telex: 41 45 45

Piggyback operations
Piggyback services, domestic and international, are managed and marketed by:
KOMBIVERKEHR GmbH
93 Breitenbachstrasse, 6000 Frankfurt (Main)
Telephone: 0611 79191
Telex: 0411627

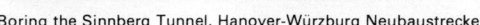

Type 628 diesel railcar set

Boring the Sinnberg Tunnel, Hanover-Würzburg Neubaustrecke

Six-axle ore wagon (type Fad 150), payload 102 tonnes

Four-axle high capacity freight wagon with sliding walls, loading capacity 195 m³, payload 25·5 tonnes

---

Altona-Kaltenkirchen-Neumünster Railway
Eisenbahngesellschaft Altona-Kaltenkirchen-Neumünster

Steinstrasse 20, 2000 Hamburg 1

Telephone: 32 10 41

General Managers: Dr Fritz Pampel
Josef Hoffstadt

Gauge: 1435 mm
Route length: 216 km

The company operates a group of local railways: Hamburg-Eldelstedt-Neumünster; Tiefstack-Glinde; Hamburg-Bergdorf-Geesthacht; Elmshorn-Barmstedt-Oldesloe; and the Alsternordbahn. In combination they record some 6 million passenger-journeys a year. Their combined operating stock comprises 14 diesel-hydraulic locomotives, 16 diesel multiple-units, 14 diesel railcars and five trailers.

Bentheim Railway
Bentheimer Eisenbahn AG

Bahnhofstrasse 24, Postfach 72, 4444 Bentheim Bad

Telephone: 05922 802

Gauge: 1435 mm
Route length: 66 km

The Bentheim Railway is the principal system, but the company also operates the Ahaus-Enscheder and Ankum-Bersenbrücker Railways. Passenger traffic totals some 4·3 million journeys a year and freight totals approximately 585 000 tonnes annually. The group operates 12 diesel-hydraulic locomotives.

Cologne-Bonn Railway
Köln-Bonner Eisenbahn AG (KBE)

Am Weidenbach 12, 5000 Cologne 1

Telephone: 0221 21 93 11
Telex: 8 882 671

Managers: Dr W Meyer
Joseph Prinz
H Schoessler
G Storck

Gauge: 1435 mm

Route length: 92 km
Electrification: 70 km at 750 V dc

In 1974 the Köln-Bonner Eisenbahnen, Kölner Verkehrsbetriebe (KVB) and Stadtwerke Bonn Verkehrsbetriebe were fused as the Stadtbahn Rhein-Sieg organisation, to integrate local tracked transport in the Cologne-Bonn region. In 1978 the systems were physically integrated to create a through 44 km light railway between the city centres of Bonn and Cologne, at a cost of DM81 million. The resultant Stadtbahn welds together the KBE main lines and the U-Bahn and tramway systems of Cologne and Bonn. In Cologne the Stadtbahn LRV train-sets

share tracks with the local tram services, to permit which the traction current systems of all the companies involved were standardised at 750 volts dc during the conversion process.

The Stadtbahn route is along the west banks of the Rhine via Wesseling. KBE also has its Vorgebirgs route via Brühl, which is its principal freight line. Freight working on the Stadtbahn route is restricted to the latter's Wesseling-Hersel section, which KBE freight for the Wesseling Rhine quays can reach by a branch from Brühl.

KBE operates one electric locomotive, 41 electric railcars, four trailers, 23 diesel locomotives and 591 freight wagons.

Cologne-Frechen Benzelraeth Railway
Köln-Frechen-Benzelräther Eisenbahn

Scheidtweilerstrasse 38, 5000 Cologne 41

Telephone: 08 881 701
Telex: 5471

Managers: Dr W Meyer
D Bollhöfer
H Schoessler
G Storck

Gauge: 1435 mm
Route length: 39 km

Electrification: 10 km at 750 V dc

The railway is operated by the Kölner Verkehrsbetriebe AG and for 10 km of its route is electrified to permit through running; it owns no electric traction units, only 14 diesel locomotives and 30 freight wagons.

East Hanover Railway
Osthannoversche Eisenbahnen AG

Biermannstrasse 33, Postfach 436, 3100 Celle

Telephone: 051 41 7041
Telex: 925 215

Director: Dr H W Wolff
Transport Manager: H H Dehning

Gauge: 1435 mm
Route length: 326 km

The company also operates the 14·8 km Buxtehude-Harsefelder, 6·4 km Steinhuder-Meer Railways and the Verkehrsbetriebe Elbe-Weser GmbH.

The railway's principal business is freight, which in 1982 amounted to 2·053 million tonnes and 118·5

million tonne-km, with maximum trainloads operated reaching 1800 tonnes. The railway is laid with 41 to 49 kg/m rail on wood or concrete sleepers and can sustain a maximum axleloading of 20 tonnes. Maximum gradient is 1 in 60 and minimum curve radius 300 metres.

The railway owns 23 diesel-hydraulic locomotives, three diesel-electric locomotives, one diesel railcar, one petrol railbus, one passenger car and 48 freight wagons.

Diesel-hydraulic locomotives

Wheel arrangement	Rated power (kW)	Max speed km/h	Total weight tonnes	No in service	Year first built	Builders		
						Mechanical parts	Engine & type	Transmission
C-C	1500	70	108	2	1964	KHD	2 × KHD/BT 12M 625	Voith
B-B	1200	80	80	2	1973	MaK	MaK/8M 282 AK	Voith
B-B	1100	70	80	1	1969	KHD	KHD/BA 12M 528	Voith
B-B	1000	60	80	2	1979	MaK	MTU/12 V 331 TC 12	Voith
B-B	850	70	68	2	1960	KHD	KHD/BT 12 M 625	Voith
D	900	66	72	4	1963	MaK	MaK/MA 301 Fak	Voith
D	750	63	68	1	1959	MaK	MaK/Ma 302CK	Voith
D	600	69	62	1	1954	MaK	MaK/Ma 301A	Voith
D	500	74	68	3	1959	MaK	MaK/MS 301D	Voith

Hohenzoller Provincial Railway
Hohenzollerische Landesbahn AG

Hofgartenstrasse 39, 7450 Hechingen

Director: Günter Zeiger

Gauge: 1435 mm
Route length: 107 km

The railway runs from Sigmaringen and Sigdorf to Eyach and Kleinengstingen. In 1981, with a turnover of DM 6·6 million, it recorded 982 283 passenger journeys and 321 939 tonnes and 24·9 million

tonne-km of freight. The company also operates bus routes aggregating 595·4 km.

Rolling stock comprises four 956 kW, one 860 kW, one 698 kW and two 176 kW diesel locomotives, seven twin-engined diesel railcars of 228-282 kW total power, four control, five intermediate trailers and four freight wagons.

Peine-Salzgitter Transport
Verkehrsbetriebe Peine-Salzgitter

Postfach 100670, 3320 Salzgitter 1

Manager: H Gasch

Gauge: 1435 mm
Route length: 173 km

This heavy industrial system comprises two systems, the 54 km Peine Railway and the 119 km Salzgitter Railway. Freight movement grosses over 35 million tonnes and 250 tonne-km a year. Rolling stock comprises 82 diesel locomotives, 1380 freight wagons and four diesel railcars.

Regental Railway
Regentalbahn AG

Bahnhofsplatz 1, Postfach 1320, 8374 Viechtach

Telephone: 09942 417/418

Manager: Willi Höppner

Gauge: 1435 mm
Route length: 63 km

The railway operates three Bavarian lines, from Lam to Kötzing, Deggendorf to Metten, and Gotteszell to

Blaibach, carrying some 200 000 passengers a year in all. In 1982 it operated four diesel locomotives, 10 diesel railcars and three trailers, five passenger cars and four freight wagons. The railcar fleet includes one of Waggon Union's new standard type for private railways (see South-West German Railways) for its Lam-Kötzing line.

South-West German Railways
Südwestdeutsche Eisenbahnen AG

Friedrichstrasse 59, 7630 Lahr/Schwarzwald

Telephone: 07821 22011-22014
Telex: 754809

Gauge: 1435 mm; 750 mm
Length: 168 km; 37 km

The group was created in 1972 and operates 12 railways and bus services covering a 5000 km network of routes in the province of Baden-Württemberg. A financial surplus has been continuously achieved on operations since the group's formation. At the start of 1982 its activity was enlarged by a takeover of the Meckesheim-Aglasterhausen line of the German Federal Railway, which the latter was proposing to close. Freight carried in 1982 totalled 510 000 tonnes.

The group is currently planning to convert its rail system to one man-train crewing backed up by radio links between drivers and a control centre.

In 1982 the Group was operating one steam locomotive (used only for special trips sponsored by private organisations over three stretches of its system), 11 diesel locomotives, 29 diesel railcars, 42 passenger cars and 102 freight cars.

In 1982 it took delivery of the first three prototypes of a new design of diesel railcar specially created for West Germany's private railways by Waggon Union of Berlin and the Bundesverband Deutscher Eisenbahnen (BDE). For economy, the new vehicle marries components of standard road bus and German Federal passenger vehicles. It is also equipped with sufficient power to haul a 400-tonne tail-load of freight on level track, and can be fitted for remote radio control to serve as an unmanned shunting unit. Each car is fitted with a 260 hp motor on each

New Waggon-Union built railcar VT124 on mixed train at Aglasterhausen *(John C Baker)*

bogie with hydraulic transmission, and has a maximum speed of 90 km/h. Seating capacity is 84 and fittings include a chemical toilet, public address, passenger-operated automatic doors, and a ticket-issuing and change-dispensing apparatus at the driving position.

The railway's maximum permissible axleloading is 20 tonnes.

Wanne-Bochum-Herne Railway
Wanne-Bochum-Herner Eisenbahn

Am Westhafen 27, 4690 Herne 2

General Manager: R Görl

Gauge: 1435 mm
Length: 14 km

This heavy industrial railway records some 7 million tonnes and 33 million tonne-km of freight a year. It is operated by 11 diesel-hydraulic locomotives and owns 386 freight wagons.

Westphalian Provincial Railway
Westfälische Landes-Eisenbahn GmbH

Beckumer Strasse 70, Postfach 2820, 4780 Lippstadt

Telephone: 029 41 78011

Director: H Elliger

Manager: J Kückmann
Operating Manager: Dr G Müller

Gauge: 1435 mm
Route length: 151 km

The lines operated are Lippstedt to Warstein and Neubeckum, Neubeckum to Westkirchen and

Münster, Soest to Brilon Stadt, and Borken to Burgsteinfurt. Passenger services were abandoned in 1975 and the railway currently carries over 1 million tonnes of freight a year, over tracks with a maximum axleloading of 20 tonnes and a minimum curve radius of 140 metres; rail weight varies from 33 to 60 kg/m. The railway owns 19 diesel locomotives and 101 freight wagons.

Wurttemberg Railway
Württembergische Eisenbahn GmbH

Königstrasse 1B, 7000 Stuttgart 1

Telephone: (0711) 295741

General Managers: Dr Karlheinz Gückler
Willi Ries
Josef Sowa

Gauge: 1435 mm; 1000 mm
Length: 114 km; 19 km

The WEG comprises the main Württembergische Eisenbahn, with seven lines aggregating 85 route-km of 1435 mm gauge and the Amstetten-Laichingen line's 19 route-km of metre gauge, and also the two lines of the Württembergische Neben-bahnen GmbH, totalling 29 route-km of 1435 mm gauge. In 1981 the combined enterprise recorded

1·877 million passenger journeys and 294 186 tonnes of freight. The company also operates 364·8 km of bus routes in its territory around Stuttgart.

The main system owns 13 diesel railcars, 17 passenger cars and one freight wagon. The Neben-bahnen operates nine diesel railcars and nine passenger cars, which include two power cars and a trailer of the new standard Waggon Union design for the country's private railways, also one diesel locomotive.

GHANA

Ministry of Transport and Communications

PO Box M38, Ministry Branch Post Office, Accra

Secretary: A H Iddrishu Mahama

Ghana Railway Corporation (GR)

PO Box 251, Takoradi

Telephone: 2181
Telegrams: Railway

General Management: In 1981 the functions were assumed by a committee including members of the RITES and CANAC consultancies.

Chairman, Management Committee: S S Nayak
Training and Manpower Planning Manager: J B Yorke
Administrative Officer: J R Holdbrooke
Personnel Manager: F A Amissah
Chief Engineer: S Oduro
Chief Mechanical Engineer: F G Asamoah
Traffic Manager: K S Boham
Senior Signalling and Telecommunications Engineer: J C Acquah
Senior Electrical Engineer: J K Ankomah
Chief Stores Superintendent: G A Sey

Gauge: 1067 mm
Route length: 953 km

Transport development
With only 3890 km of paved highways serving a population of over 8·5 million in a total area of 303 500 km², the Ghana Railway is of major national importance. The rail network consists of a main line running from Takoradi to Kumasi and Accra (595

km). From Huni Valley on the Kumasi line north of Takoradi, a spur runs about 28 km to Kotoku. Branch lines run to Sekondi, Prestea, Kade, Awaso and Tema.

A proposal to extend the railway from Awaso to Sunyani has not yet got off the ground, mainly because inflation has increased investment costs and interest charges.

Ghana's railway network has excessive curvature in several sections, and this tends to reduce line capacity. For example, between Kumasi and Takoradi there are 504 curves in a section of 270·48 km. Realignment of the permanent way on these sections is increasing minimum curve radius to 335 metres, improving train speeds and lessening the risk of derailments and damage to property.

Track renewal, some track relaying, and installation of many new switches and crossings is planned. Also included in the plan is the replacement of existing 39·7 kg/m rail by 45 kg/m rail, and a ballasting programme to provide for a depth of 15·7 cm of ballast on existing track and 23·6 cm on track which is to be relaid; this will involve laying 63 000 tonnes of ballast a year, and should result in a minimum of 15·7 cm beneath sleepers on all tracks after 12 years.

At the end of 1982 a US$42 million loan towards the cost of renovating GR's western lines was negotiated with the African Development and World Banks.

Motive power and rolling stock

Locomotives, steam	90
diesel-electric	78
diesel-hydraulic	10
Railcars, diesel	4
Passenger train coaches	182
Freight train cars	3862

In 1982 an order was placed with Brush for six diesel-electric Bo-Bos with Rolls-Royce 485 kW engines, intended for shunting and local freight trips. The order was worth £2·5 million.

Track

Standard rail, type and weight
Sekondi-Nsuta: RBS 40·2 kg/m
Nsuta-Obuasi: ARA 39·7 kg/m
Obuasi-Kumasi: RBS 39·7 kg/m
Kumasi-Tafo: BS 29·8 kg/m
Tafo-Accra: RBS 29·8 kg/m

Prestea branch: RBS 29·8 kg/m
Cen Prov Rly: BS 29·8 kg/m
Awaso branch: ASCE 37·2 kg/m
Joints: 4-hole fishplates
Cross ties (sleepers): Standard steel; and wood 127 × 254 × 1981 mm
Spacing: 1365 per km
Rail fastenings
Wood sleepers: Dog spikes, Macbeth spike anchors, elastic rail spikes. Tests are being made with Lockspikes (UK) and single shank spring spikes (West Germany)
Steel sleepers: Keys, 1 and 0 clips, ARA clips, ABK clips
Filling: Mainly crushed granite, some gravel
Max curvature
Sekondi-Kumasi 8° 40' = radius of 202 m
Kumasi-Accra 8° 40' = radius of 202 m
Cent Prov Rly 8° 40' = radius of 202 m
Prestea branch 17° = radius of 103 m
Awaso branch 6° = radius of 291 m
Max gradient: 1·25% = 1 in 80; except Prestea branch 2·5% = 1 in 40
Longest continuous gradient: 10 km with ruling grade of 1·25% and max curves of 8° 40'
Max altitude: 286 m near Kumasi
Permitted speeds
Freight trains 56 km/h

Passenger trains 64 km/h
Except Prestea branch:
Freight trains 29 km/h
Passenger trains 40 km/h
Axleloading
Sekondi-Kumasi-Accra 16 tons
Central Province Railway 12½ tons
Prestea branch 13½ tons
Awaso branch 16 tons
Gauge widening on sharpest curve: 25 mm
Superelevation on sharpest curve: 89 mm
Rate of slope of superelevation: 13 mm per rail length

Signalling
A separate project aimed at providing a centralised traffic and telecommunications system which will rely heavily on radio-telephone links is under way. The cost is estimated at Cedis 5 million. Most important features of the project are:
extension of the trunk dialling telephone system;
radio-telephone communication between control post and cab;
automatic train reporting;
centralised message centre, with telegraph/teleprinter system;
Takoradi region traffic control;
centralised traffic control feasibility studies.

GREECE

Ministry of Mercantile Marine, Transport and Communications

Xenofontos Street 13, Athens

Minister: Evangelos Yannopoulos
Secretary: A Roussopoulos
Head of Railways Department: I Karagiannis

Hellenic Railways Organisation (CH)
Organisme des Chemins de Fer Héllénique SA

1-3 Karolou Street, Athens 107

Telephone: 362 4402
Telex: 215187

Governor and Chairman: Andreas Lambrinopoulous
Directors
Personnel: E L Xenos
Operation: J Vraskos
Traction: S Sabethai
Track: G Kranidis
Organisation Design and Planning: N Karagiorgas
Supplies: G Efstathiadis
Commercial: D Sgouros
Finance: P Konstaninidis
Workshops Manager: B Papageorgiu
Regional Management
Athens: G Charamis
Thessaloniki: V Panagiotakis
Peloponnesus: A Paranikolaou

Gauge: 1435 mm; 1000 mm; 750 mm
Route length: 1597 km; 870 km; 22 km

Transport development
Greek highways total just over 35 500 km of which most are classified as provincial roads. The Hellenic Railways Organisation (CH) operates a 2479 km railway network, of which only 119 km is double-tracked, in three sections. The railway from Athens to the Peloponnese, serving Patras and southern Greece, is metre gauge but most of the older lines are standard gauge.

The network is linked to certain large ports of the country (Piraeus, Thessaloniki, Volos, Alexandroupolis, Kalamata and Patras) and with industrial complexes.

Traffic
The railway's share of the country's passenger market has been reduced to 6 per cent following a 25 per cent decline in rail travel since 1977 and no more than 10 per cent of inter-urban freight moves by rail. The decline continued in 1981, with a 3·1 per cent fall in the sum of passenger-km and freight tonne-km compared with 1980. The prime reason was a steep 14 per cent decline in freight traffic, particularly inland movement, whereas passenger traffic rose by 3·5 per cent.

The freight traffic's inadequacy is due partly to more intensive road competition as Greece's road system improves, and the road hauliers' pricing

freedom which the railway is denied, partly to CH's shortages of traction and rolling stock, and its maintenance shortcomings. Since Greece's entry into the European Economic Community in January 1981, moreover, CH has lost the exclusive right to movement of the produce of Farmers' Co-operatives, which is open to competition from private road haulage.

Results

	1981
Total passenger journeys (000)	10 387
Total passenger-km (000)	1 515 059
Total freight tonnage (000)	2995
Total freight tonne-km (000)	693 389

Finance (Dr million)

	1981
Operational revenue	5476
State support	1741
Total	7217
Operational expenditure	9977
Financial charges	464
Total	10 441
Operating deficit	3224
Expenditure on track and rolling stock	433
Expenditure on materials purchases	1180

One of four 4-car diesel-hydraulic sets supplied in 1976 by Ganz-Màvag for use on metre-gauge ex-SPEP lines *(Helmut Reichelt)*

CEH express headed by MLW-built 3550 hp type MX627 Co-Co diesel-electric *(Marcel Vleugels)*

Modernisation

The change of Government in 1981 was followed by undertakings to raise rail investment and accelerate the long-overdue modernisation of CH.

The principal project under way in 1982 was doubling of the Inoi-Tithorea (95 km) section of the Athens-Thessaloniki main line and relaying with UIC54 continuously welded rail on two-block concrete sleepers, with minimum curve radius of 2000 metres. Doubling of the 60 km Domokos-Larissa section was completed during the year and tenders were sought for installation of automatic block signalling, ultimately to be extended to the whole route (it has already been applied between Tithorea and Domokos). The total cost of Dr 8500 million has been supported by loans from the European Investment Bank (US$ 21 million) and a West German banking consortium (US$ 42 million).

Key objectives remain:
Infrastructure upgrading throughout the Athens-Thessaloniki route, including double-tracking between Larissa and Platy, except for the difficult, 65 km/h-limited mountain section between Tithorea and Domokos (122 km); this section's operation has been improved by a CTC installation obtained from Sasib of Italy;
A new Athens marshalling yard;
Private siding connection of major industries;
Creation of a container terminal at Piraeus; at present only Athens and Thessaloniki have such facilities and a weekly container train between these two centres was inaugurated in 1982.

Under the present Government, however, the scheme to convert the Peloponnese network from 1000 to 1435 mm gauge has been discarded, as have plans for additional branches in the 1435 mm-gauge system.

Electrification

Under the present Government the long-discussed electrification of the 587 km Athens-Thessaloniki-Idomeni main line seems set to go ahead, along with its upgrading, at an estimated cost of Dr 38 500 million over a 10-year period. The Government has set a target date of 1991 for completion, with the greater part of the work executed under its 1983-87 national economic plan. The project is deemed vital to Greece's trade with the rest of the EEC.

The originally-planned order of work has been changed and it will now begin over the 76 km from Thessaloniki to the Yugoslav border at Idomeni. Bids for installation of 25 kV 50 Hz and colour-light signalling throughout this section were to be submitted by mid-May 1983. The hope is that, with the benefit of route realignment where possible for 200 km/h, the Athens-Thessaloniki passenger journey time will be halved to 4 hours after completion of the whole project, including double-tracking throughout apart from the Tithorea-Domokos section.

In February 1983 a 10-year co-operation agreement was signed between Greece and the USSR which provided for Soviet assistance in the railway's modernisation and electrification projects.

Investment

Expenditure budgeted for 1983 (Dr 000):

New line construction	1500
Track improvements	450
Track maintenance equipment	50
Bridges and buildings	200
Signalling and communications	1000
Electrification	200
Yards and terminals	70
Workshops	100
Miscellaneous	120
Total	3690

Besides the main Athens-Thessaloniki line projects, work planned for 1983 included: continuation of infrastructure renovation on the Alexandroupolis-Ormenion (173 km) and Thessaloniki-Promachon (143 km) lines; further work on the connection to the planned Syria train ferry terminal at Volos; reorganisation of rolling stock maintenance workshops; purchase of new rolling stock and of a new computer for the development of data systems.

Planning for 1983-87 includes the commencement of the following development projects:
Completion of Athens-Thessaloniki axis modernisation, including double line construction for speeds of 200 km/h between Larissa and Platy (134 km), with installation of automatic signalling;
Conversion of Paleofarsalos-Kalambaka metre-gauge line (80 km) to 1435 mm;
Construction of goods station and marshalling yards for the Athens area at Thriassio Pedio;
Installation of automatic electric signalling on the Thessaloniki-Promachon (143 km) and Platy-Amynteo-Kozani-Florina (220 km) lines;
Modernisation of the Athens-Corinth-Patras line (230 km).

Expenditure on all these projects will be some Dr 90 000 million. In the years 1983-87 some Dr 40 million will be required for start-up of the projects.

Rolling stock

Diesel traction purchases have in recent years been circumspect in hope of electrification, but in 1982 CH took delivery of 10 4000 hp locomotives from MecanoExportImport, Romania. Also in 1982 CH sought tenders for 25 1435 mm-gauge and 10 metre-gauge diesel railcar units.

In 1982 CH operated 193 diesel locomotives, 110 diesel railcars, 85 railcar trailers, 468 passenger cars and 10 866 freight wagons.

Alsthom 2100 hp diesel-electric Co-Co, fitted with SEMT 16 PA 4 diesel engine

Three-car Esslingen diesel train-set built by Ferrostaal

Diesel locomotives

Class	Wheel arrangement	Transmission	Rated power (hp)	Max speed km/h	Total weight tonnes	No in service	Year first built	Builders Mechanical parts	Builders Engine & type	Builders Transmission
1000 mm gauge										
CC AD 1600 A1	Co-Co	Elec	1600	90	80	10	1967	Alsthom	Pielstick PA 4-185	
DL 537	Co-Co	Elec	1350/1200	96	80·3	12	1965	Alco	Alco 251D	
48 BB HI	B-B	Hyd	2 × 322·5	90	48	20	1967	Mitsubishi	GM 71N	Niigata
1435 mm gauge										
MX 636	Co-Co	Elec	3550	149	124	10	1974	MLW Canada	Alco 251F	
MX 627	Co-Co	Elec	2700	149	120	20	1973	MLW Canada	Alco 251F	
2000 HP	Co-Co	Elec	2000	120	108	10	1966	Siemens	Maybach MD 870	
CC AD 2100 CI	Co-Co	Elec	2100	105	89·4	26	1967	Alsthom	Pielstick PA 4-185	
DL543	Co-Co	Elec	2150/2000	120	107	7	1966	Alco	Alco 251C	
DL500C	Co-Co	Elec	1950/1800	120	107	10	1963	Alco	Alco 251B	
KM 10B	Bo-Bo	Elec	1065	109	63·5	13	1973	General Electric	Caterpillar D398B	
DL 532B	Bo-Bo	Elec	1050/950	105	64·6	10	1962	Alco	Alco 251B	
LDH 70	B-B	Hyd	700	70	48	12	1973	FAUR 23 August	Maybach-Mercedes 820 Bb	Voith
Y60	C	Hyd	650	60	51	30	1962	Krupp	Maybach GT06A	Voith

GUATEMALA

Guatemala Railways
Ferrocarriles de Guatemala (FEGUA)

9a Ave, 18-03 Zona 1, Guatemala City

Telephone: 83031-39
Telegrams: Ferrocarril
Telex: 5342

Director: Carlos Humberto Del Valle Paz
Assistant Manager: M Cordon Meraz

Gauge: 914 mm
Route length: 602·7 km

The company, which became state-owned under its present title in 1968, operates 30 diesel locomotives, 43 passenger cars and 277 wagons. Recent additions are four Type MX620 2000 hp locomotives from Bombardier.

Bandegua Railway
Cia de Desarrollo Bananero de Guatemala Ltd

Edificio La Galeria 5° Nivel, 7 Avenue 1444, Zone 9, Guatemala City

Telephone: 478-026/052/102

Manager: Mario O Mena
Division Controller: Armando Paz
Director of Engineering: Luis A Martinez V
Transportation Superintendent: Ramiro Arriaga
Mechanical Superintendent: Dionisio Badillo

Gauge: 914 mm
Route length: 148 km

The company operates 11 diesel locomotives, 17 railcars, 18 passenger cars and 106 freight wagons.

GUINEA

Chemin de Fer de la Guinée (ONCFG)

PO Box 581, Conakry

Telegrams: Ofergui

Director: Sekou Camara

Gauge: 1000 mm
Route length: 662 km

Transport development
The railway from Conakry to the River Niger joins the limits of navigability of the Upper Niger (Kouroussa) with the sea port of Conakry on the coast of Guinea. The railway was opened from Conakry as far as Kouroussa in 1910. In 1914, it was extended as far as Kankan, on the River Milo, a tributary of the Niger.

Studies have been completed and initial earthworks started on a new 1400 km Trans-Guinea line which will link new bauxite deposits at Tougue and Dabola and the agricultural region of Nimba with the port of Conakry.

The new line, to be built to metre-gauge standards, will partly replace the existing Conakry-Kouroussa railway, as much of the present track is too lightly laid and gradients are too steep to handle growing traffic. Maximum gradient at present is 15 per cent compensated and maximum axle loading 13 tonnes. Existing 20 kg/m rails are to be replaced by 30 kg/m sections.

The Trans-Guinea (as it is to be called) will in part replace the lightly-laid 600 km metre-gauge track. Its basic function is to link bauxite deposits at Tougue and Dabola and iron ore mines at Simondou as well as Nimba with Conakry, but as the main line and branches will penetrate large tracts of the country hitherto unexploited, it will also boost agricultural, forestry and industrial development.

Motive power and rolling stock
The present motive power fleet includes 30 mainline diesel locomotives and 16 diesel railcars. Rolling stock includes 20 passenger coaches and 500 freight wagons.

Industrial railways
There are three other lines in operation, all serving mineral deposits.

The CF de Fria, opened in 1960, carries the products of the bauxite mine and aluminium plant at Fria to the port of Conakry. It is of metre gauge, 143 km long single-track, laid with 46 kg/m continuous welded rail on metal sleepers. Three Alsthom 1100 hp diesel-electric locomotives hauling 50-tonne load wagons transport some 500 000 tonnes of export per year.

The CF de la Compagnie Minière de Conakry is a standard gauge line 14 km long, running between an iron ore mine on the outskirts of Conakry and the port. About 800 000 tonnes per year are carried to the port using two Alsthom 700 hp diesel-electric locomotives.

The Boke Railway is a mineral ore line, running 134 km inland from Port Kamsar on the coast of Guinea. Built by a consortium of European contractors, the line was inaugurated in 1973 and has since then been operated by CANAC Consultants on behalf of the Guinea government and the railway administration, Office d'Aménagement de Boke. CANAC was initially contracted to manage the operation of the line and to train Guinean staff for self management.

The first half of the line runs through the coastal sea plain while the upper half reaches into the foothills of the Fouta Djalon mountains. The line is standard gauge with 60 kg/m continuously welded UIC profile rail laid entirely on steel sleepers. The line has a capacity of 12 million tonnes annually with ore moving in European-built wagons hauled by US-built rolling stock. In 1975 a passenger operation was started.

HONDURAS

Honduras National Railway (FNH)
Ferrocarril Nacional de Honduras

San Pedro Sula

Telephone: 52 1266

Minister of Communications: J Azcona Del Hoyo
General Manager: E Vitanza Funez
Assistant Manager: J A Vaquero
Supply Manager: A Suazo Natute
Chief of Commercial Services: J Blas Mayen
Trainmaster: J D Rosales
Director of Operations and Maintenance: A Escobar Sandoval

Gauge: 1067 mm; 914 mm

Length: 277 km; 318 km

FNH operates 128 km of its 1067 mm-gauge system and the remainder is operated by Tela R R Co. The 914 mm system is operated by the Standard Fruit Co.

Traction and rolling stock comprises two steam and eight diesel-electric locomotives, 16 passenger cars and 530 freight cars. Provision of container handling facilities for banana traffic at San Pedro Sula and Puerto Cortes is under study.

Standard Fruit Company's Railway

50 California Street, San Francisco, California 94111, USA

Local office: La Ceiba

General Manager, La Ceiba: D Dehorenzo

Gauge: 914 mm

Length: 445·7 km

The railway is operated with 19 diesel-electric and four diesel-mechanical locomotives, 25 passenger and 751 freight cars.

Tela Railroad Company

Apartado Postal No 30, San Pedro Sula, Cortes

Telex: 5532

General Manager: K F Koch
Superintendent: G S Collart
Purchasing Manager: R Pell

Gauge: 1067 mm
Route length: 165 km

The railway is operated with 24 diesel-electric locomotives, 19 railcars, 21 passenger cars and 1357 freight wagons. Rail installed is 22·7-34 kg/m, minimum curve radius 3 degrees, maximum gradient 0·62 per cent and maximum axleloading 6·82 tonnes.

HONG KONG

Kowloon-Canton Railway (British Section KCR)

Hung Hom, Kowloon

Telephone: 3-646321
Telegrams: Hongrail
Telex: 73380

Chief Executive: D M Howes
General Manager, Railway: U L Wong
Assistant General Manager (Technical): J B Manson
Assistant General Manager (Traffic): Y H Choi
Terminals Manager: K Y Ngan
Operating Manager: T L Ma
Planning Manager: S S Choi
Railway Chief Electrical and Mechanical Engineer: B T Chiu
Rolling Stock Engineer: Y H Chang
Chief Civil Engineer: K S Chung
Permanent Way Engineer: M Elvy
Departmental Secretary: K C Cheng
Treasury Accountant: M T Shum

Gauge: 1435 mm
Route length: 33·5 km
Electrification: 33·5 km at 25 kV 50 Hz ac

The Kowloon-Canton Railway (British Section) has been in existence since 1910. Originally a unitary project of the British Chinese Corporation, the line's eventual construction in British and Chinese segments was enforced by the New Territories' cession to the UK. The 33·5 km British Section was laid in 1906-11 as single track. By the mid-1970s the line's internal passenger traffic was already in excess of 10 million journeys a year, but then a daily total of 500 000 by 1991 became the prospect with the Government's decision to ease overcrowding in Hong Kong by creating new housing and industry between Kowloon and the frontier.

The Hong Kong Government decided in 1981 to transmute KCR into a public corporation, headed by a Chief Executive.

Double-tracking and electrification

A HK$ 2000 million scheme to transform the single-track railway into a double-track commuter line also carrying freight was begun in 1975. In the course of it the track was reballasted for a maximum speed of 120 km/h. The job was simplified to some extent by the original constructors' forethought in building a formation spacious enough to take a second track in the open. The tunnels to be tackled included one of 2·4 km through Beacon Hill. Here the original single-line bore had present-day shortcomings as a result of repair after wartime sabotage, so a completely new double-track tunnel was driven through the range.

In 1977 British Rail's consultancy Transmark was called in to cost and recommend on the further modernisation needed to fit the KCR for its future role. Their advice was that the line should be electrified and re-equipped with modern colour-light signalling to allow a passenger service by multiple-unit trains running, if need be, at a headway of only 90 seconds in the inner suburban area.

Freight from China would still be hauled by diesel traction. However, partly to prepare for possible extension of Chinese electrification to the frontier the electrification would be at 25 kV ac. This, the resignalling and other works, which include three new stations, existing station reconstruction with high platforms and improved facilities, widespread installation of more substantial track on concrete sleepers, and provision of an automatic fare collection system, were finished from Kowloon to Shatin for inauguration of public emu service in May 1982. The operation was launched with remarkably few teething troubles, and availability of the emus and their punctuality exceeded 90 per cent, conducing to a passenger traffic growth of over 60 per cent. Completion of the electrification to the Chinese border at Lo Wu was anticipated in July 1983.

The electrification contract for fixed works was let to the Traction & General Division of Balfour Beatty Construction; Metro-Cammell won the contract to build and GEC Traction the order to power the air-conditioned, sliding-door train-sets; colour-light signalling with CTC was executed by Westinghouse Brake & Signal Co.

The initial order for 135 cars in three-car sets is divided between 19 inner- and 29 outer-suburban units, the former second-class only but the latter dual-class, with the toilets and baggage space. With a maximum speed of 120 km/h the units can average 64 km/h between stops.

Traffic

	1979/80	1980/81	1981/82
Total freight tonnage (million)	2010	1945·39	1797·14
Total freight tonne-km (million)	73·677	67·429	61·103
Total passenger-km (million)	419·279	432·712	371·803
Total passenger journeys (million)	18·902	18·949	16·371
Average length of passenger journey (km)	22·18	22·84	22·71

Revenues

	1978/80	1980/81	1981/82
		(HK $ million)	
Passengers and baggage	30·817	42·314	39·57
Freight, parcels and mail	30·351	36·097	38·14
Other income	3·737	3·938	6·20
Total revenues	64·905	82·349	83·92

Expenditure

	1979/80	1980/81	1981/82
		(HK $ million)	
Staff/personnel expenses	34·122	43·497	51·14
Materials and services	23·924	27·52	38·00
Depreciation	4·988	5·107	6·63
Financial charges	4·45	4·239	11·57
Total expenditure	67·484	80·363	106·42

KCR emu by Metro-Cammell with GEC Traction power equipment

KCR electrification

Three 2000 hp locomotives delivered by General Electric between 1974 and 1977

A marshalling yard at Lo Wu, consisting of seven tracks with an overall length of 3139 metres (10 300 ft), was completed at the end of 1979.

Rolling stock
The system operates 12 diesel locomotives, 96 emu cars and 102 freight wagons.

Track
Rail: UIC 54 (54 kg/m)

Cross ties (sleepers): Prestressed concrete, 203 mm thick, spaced 700 mm centre to centre

Rail fastenings: Pandrol rail clip, type PR429A with Pandrol glass reinforced nylon insulators

Minimum curvature: Main line: 300 m
Sidings: 180 m

Max gradient: 1 in 100

Max speed: 120 km/h throughout

Diesel locomotives

Class	Wheel arrange-ment	Trans-mission	Rated power kW	Max kg	Tractive effort Continuous at kg	kmlh	Max speed kmlh	Wheel dia mm	Total weight tonnes	Length mm	No built	First built	Builders
G-12	Bo-Bo	Elec	977	18 300	14 800	—	99·8	1016	72	13 564	3	1954	The Clyde Engineering Co Pty Ltd, Australia
G-12	Bo-Bo	Elec	839				99·8	1016	71	13 564	2	1954	The Clyde Engineering Co Pty Ltd, Australia
G-16	Co-Co	Elec	1343	29 980	22 900	—	99·8	1016	98	17 272	3	1961	Electro-Motive Division, General Motors Corporation, USA
G-16	Co-Co	Elec	1455	30 000	22 900	—	99·8	1016	98	17 272	1	1965	The Clyde Engineering Co Pty Ltd, Australia
G-26	Co-Co	Elec	1492	—	22 880	—	99·8	1016	98	15 764	1	1973	Electro-Motive Division, General Motors Corporation, USA
G-26	Co-Co	Elec	1641	—	22 880	—	99·8	1016	98	15 764	2	1976	Electro-Motive Division, General Motors Corporation, USA

Electric multiple-units (3-car units)

Class	Rated output kW	Tractive effort (weak field) Continuous at kN	kmlh	Max speed kmlh	Wheel diameter mm	Weight unit tonnes	Length unit mm	Year first built	Builders Mechanical parts	Electrical equipment
Emu	4 × 227	37·6	87	120	850	175	73 100	1981-82	Metro-Cammell Ltd, UK	GEC Traction

HUNGARY

Hungarian State Railways (MÁV)
Magyar Allamvasutak

Népköztársaság utja 73-75, 1940 Budapest VI

Telephone: 220-660
Telex: 224342

Director General: Zoltán Szücs
Assistant General Managers
  András Mészáros
  Sándor Urbán
  Alajos Mester
Chief of Secretariat: Jenő Toppantó
Chief of International Section: Dr László Várkonyi
Departmental Managers
  Planning and Development: Béla Maráz
  Construction and Track Maintenance: István Kummer
  Traction and Workshops: János Csárádi
  Automation and Signalling: László Fülöp
  Commercial: Erik Maizl
  Financial: Dr Péter Kisbalázs
  Traffic and Operating: I Egri

Gauge: 1524 mm; 1435 mm; 760 mm
Route length: 35 km; 7316 km; 265 km
Electrification: 1604 km at 25 kV 50 Hz ac

Class M61 diesel at Badacsony station on Lake Balaton

Transport development
Centred on Budapest, railway lines radiate to all sectors of Hungary, providing international connections with Austria, Czechoslovakia, Soviet Union, Romania and Yugoslavia.

Under its 1981-85 plan MÁV investment is limited. Available funds are being used to modernise tracks for greater axleloads; to install more safety equipment, such as telecommunications, as this enlarges the capacity of the railway and saves labour; and for a start on reconstruction of several large marshalling yards and junctions; to extend electrification and eliminate steam traction; to extend the use of computers, first at border stations; and to take a major step in freight containerisation.

Traffic
The downward trend of MÁV passenger traffic as a whole continued in 1982, notably in short-haul journeys, which have dropped by more than 100 million a year since 1972. The 1982 decline was most marked in urban areas, because of rising use of

Class V43 silicon rectifier electric locomotive, in production since 1963, with nearly 400 in service *(E Barnes)*

private cars, decentralisation of industry and general introduction of a five-day working week. Long-distance journeys, however, sustained the growth of over 7 million a year recorded since 1972 until all passenger traffic recoiled from a doubling of rail fares in September 1982.

A development from the start of the 1982-83 passenger timetables in May was through working to Vienna of a Hungarian restaurant car in the Budapest-Basle 'Wiener Walzer'; previously the car was detached at Hegyeshalom, the frontier. Train catering on MÁV is performed by Utasellato, a company created in 1948, which in 1982 was staffing 29 restaurant, 63 buffet, 32 sleeping and 27 couchette cars, and also running 478 station restaurants.

In the freight sector 1982 carryings were below budget and transit freight traffic was 7 per cent down on 1981 because of the recession. A main aim for 1983 was to stimulate container traffic growth along with creation of more container terminals; a new installation was opened at Szeged in 1983. In 1982 the volume of container traffic was 670 000 tonnes.

Electrification

Long-term electrification plans aim to have 80 per cent of tonne-km hauled by electric traction by the year 2000. 96 per cent of MÁV passenger trains are already electrically hauled. With conversion of the 104 km between Cegled and Kiskunfelyyhaza/Kiskunhalas on the Budapest-Belgrade line, a through

Traffic	1979	1980	1981
Passenger journeys (million)	293·1	282·4	269
Passenger-km (million)	13 469	13 550	13 389
Freight tonnes (million)	133 114	129 500	130 303
Freight tonne-km (million)	24 331	24 024	23 951

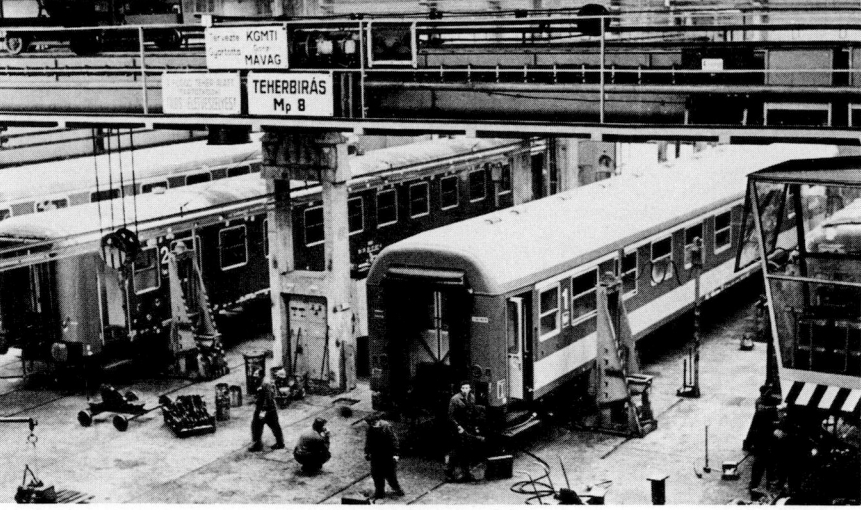

Workshop for repair and maintenance of passenger coaches

New restaurant car interior

New MÁV restaurant car from German Democratic Republic

Thyristor-controlled, 3600 kW Type V63 electric locomotive

electrified transversal between the Soviet and Yugoslav borders has become available.

A further 88 route-km were electrified in 1982, the 50th anniversary of the country's first electrification, bringing the total under wires to 1604km, or 22 per cent of the network. The main achievement was completion of the Budapest-Kelenföld-Dunajvaros scheme, begun in 1981, on the main route from the capital to Pecs in southern Hungary.

Civil engineering
Under the 1981-85 programme about 1300 km of track is to be upgraded for axleloads of more than 20 tonnes. In 1981 the MÁV finished the reconstruction of the Budapest-Debrecen-Záhony, Budapest-Miskolc-Nyiregyháza lines and of part of the Budapest-Hegyeshalom line. All new rails are 54·3 kg/m laid on prestressed concrete sleepers with a ballast depth of 50 cm. Minimum curve radius is 1200 metres and normal top speed is 140 km/h. About 60 per cent of the network had continuous welded rail at the end of 1982.

In 1982 a further 210 route-km were upgraded, so that a total of 3200 route-km or 38 per cent of the national system was fit for speeds of 100 km/h or over. A major project progressed was further work on the Budapest-Hegyeshalom line, the scheme for which includes creation of a new alignment in the area of Tatabanya; for this scheme 340 million forint were budgeted in 1982. Another important task in hand, at a cost of 250 million forint, was the renovation of Budapest Kelenföld station, outside which a new flyover was being established.

Traction and rolling stock
MÁV steam locomotive stock was reduced from 1050 to 133 by the start of 1982 and it was expected that regular steam working would end in 1983. Three types remained in 1982, the Class 424 4-8-0, the Class 324 2-6-2 and the Class 375 2-6-2 tank, working chiefly in the west and north-west of the country, notably around Györ and in the Tatra mountains near the Czechoslovak border.

Additions to stock in 1982 were 18 Class V43 2200

kW Bo-Bo electric locomotives, the type responsible for 90 per cent of MÁV's electric haulage and 53 per cent of its total tonne-km; four Type M41 1325 kW diesel-hydraulic B-B locomotives; 50 Type By passenger cars and 570 freight wagons. Cost was 1300 million forint.

In 1983 the Budapest Institute of Automobile Construction Research was commissioned to design and build a prototype lightweight railbus and trailer derived from the Ikarus 200 road bus. The pair of vehicles together would have a length of 25 metres and seat 78, with standing room for 86.

Signalling
Automatic interlocking covers about 3000 km and automatic block signalling about 1000 km. The block system with colour-light signalling and automatic train stop facilities are complemented by track-to-train transmission of information.

A further 90 route-km were equipped with automatic block in 1982 and the track-to-train radio network was extended.

Electric locomotives

Class	Wheel arrange-ment	Line current kV	Hz	Rated output kW	Tractive effort (full field) continuous kg	Max speed kmlh	Wheel dia mm	Weight tonnes	Length mm	Year first built	Builders Mechanical parts	Electrical equipment
V41	Bo-Bo	25	50 ac	1020	14 600	80	1040	73	12 290	1958	Mavag	Ganz
V42	Bo-Bo	25	50 ac	1210	15 500	80	1040	74	12 290	1960	Mavag	Ganz
V43	B-B	25	50 ac	2210	15 000	130	1180	78	15 700	1963	Mavag	Ganz
V63	Co-Co	25	50 ac	3680	24 800	160	1250	118	19 600	1975	Mavag	Ganz

Diesel locomotives

Class	Wheel arrange-ment	Trans-mission	Rated power kW	Max kg	Tractive effort Continuous at kg	kmlh	Max speed kmlh	Wheel dia mm	Total weight tonnes	Length mm	Year first built	Builders Mechanical parts	Engine & type	Transmission
M28	B	Mech	100	5490	5250	5	30	950	20	7390	1955	GVM	Ganz	GVM
M31	C	Hyd	330	15 700	9600	7	60	1232	45	9830	1958	Mavag	Ganz	Voith
M32	C	Hyd	260				60	920	36	9510	1973	Mavag	Ganz	Ganz
M40	Bo-Bo	Elec	440	24 300	13 600	13·7	100	1040	75·6	13 590	1966	Mavag	Ganz	Ganz
M41-21	B-B	Hyd	1320	19 740	12 700	20	100	1040	66	15 500	1973	Mavag	Pielstick/Ganz	Voith/Ganz
M44	Bo-Bo	Elec	440	18 600	12 030	8·3	80	1040	62	11 290	1956	Mavag	Ganz	GVM
M61	Co-Co	Elec	1430		21 000	19·2	100	1040	108	18 900	1963	Nohab	GM	GM
M62	Co-Co	Elec	1470		20 000	20	100	1050	120	17 560	1965	Lugansk	Kolomna	Charkov
M63	Co-Co	Elec	2200	40 000	21 700		130/160	1250	120	19 540	1971	Mavag	Ganz	GVM
MDa	B-B	H/M	590	9700	6600	20	100	920	41	15 520	1969	Mavag	Ganz	Ganz
M43	B-B	Hyd	330	14 000	11 000	5	60	920	48	11 460	1974	Aug 23	Aug 23	
M47	B-B	Hyd	520	15 000	11 500	5	70	920	48	11 460	1974	Aug 23	Aug 23	

Diesel railcars

Class	Wheel arrange-ment	Trans-mission	Rated power kW	Max speed kmlh	Total weight tonnes	Length mm	Year first built	Builders Mechanical parts	Engine & type	Transmission
Bz	1A	H/M	140	70	19	13 970	1977	Vagonka Studenka	Liaz Jablonec	Praha

Gyor-Sopron-Ebenfurt Railway (GySEV)
Gyor-Sopron-Ebenfurti-Vasut

Matyas Kiraly Utca 19, 9401 Sopron

General Manager: L Oroszvary

Gauge: 1435 mm
Route length: 84 km (Hungary), 82 km (Austria)

The Austrian and Hungarian components of this

international link are under separate operational management. Of the 5·5 million tonnes of freight carried by the railway in 1981, 70 per cent was international.

The railway owns 18 steam and 16 diesel locomotives, 68 passenger cars, 10 diesel railcars and 479 freight wagons.

INDIA

Indian Government Railways (IR)
Ministry of Railways (Railway Board)

Rail Bhavan, New Delhi 110 001

Telephone: 38893-41
Telegrams: Railways, New Delhi
Telex: 031 3561

Minister for Railways: A B A Ghani Khan Choudhury
Minister of State for Railways: C K Jaffer Sharief
Chairman: K T V Raghavan
Railway Board Members
    T N Ramachandran (Mech Eng)
    C K Swaminathan (Traffic)
    S Sarath (Staff)
Advisers
    Electrical Engineering: S Sarath
    Industrial Relations: T H Mahdev
    Finance: M S Gill
Directors
    Electrical Engineering: A Nandkeolyar
    Mechanical Engineering: H D Bhalla
    Finance: N K Renari
    Traffic, Commercial: K L Thapar
    Traffic, Operation: R P Singh
    Stores: A B Banerjee
    Planning: H C Johari
    Signalling and Telecommunications: K Subramanian
    Civil Engineering: T Prakash
    Statistics and Economics: M P Gupta
    Accounts: I K Rasgotra
    Workshops: M K Gamkhar
    Safety: P S Misra
    Works: G Shankar
Manufacturing Units
    Chittaranjan Locomotive Works: K Raman
    Diesel Locomotive Works: M G Verma
    Integral Coach Factory: I M Sahni
Research, Design and Standards Organisation
    Director General: L F X Freitas

Gauge: 1676 mm; 1000 mm; 762 mm; 610 and 762 mm
Route length: 31 828 km; 25 166 km; 4246 km
Electrification: 5179 km of 1676 mm gauge, mostly at 25 kV 50 Hz ac, but with some at 1·5 kV dc; 166 km of 1000 mm gauge

Transport development

Indian Railways, organised under one management as a Central Government undertaking, is the main artery of the nation's inland transport. IR is Asia's largest and the world's second largest state-owned railway system under unitary management.

The railway is made up of nine zonal systems: Central, Eastern, Northern, North Eastern, Northeast Frontier, Southern, South Central, South Eastern and Western.

Traffic

Indian Railways performs two-thirds of the country's freight movement by mechanical transport and almost 40 per cent of India's total passenger transport. The country's road systems are underdeveloped and nation-wide operating licences for road haulage are controlled by Central Government.

Traffic

	1981
Total passenger journeys (million)	3612·576
Total passenger-km (million)	208 558
Total freight tonnes (million)	195·935
Total freight tonne-km (million)	147 652·46

Since the mid-1960s road has become the country's major passenger carrier, but latterly the trend to road has been tempered by the price of oil. Air transport's share is only 4 per cent of all passenger-km. Rail passenger fares are still extremely cheap by world standards and, despite road competition, growth of passenger-km has been unchecked since the 1950s. A computer-based seat reservation system is being established in main centres.

Lack of line capacity has become an acute problem on key routes, such as parts of that between Delhi and Bombay where the annual gross is some 20 million tonnes a year. In the non-suburban sector, which accounts for about 1600 million of all passenger-km, this problem has been tackled by increasing many express and mail train loads to 18-22 cars with, in some cases, double-heading. Where the latter is practised cars have had to be

Type MG air-conditioned sleeping car for 1000 mm gauge

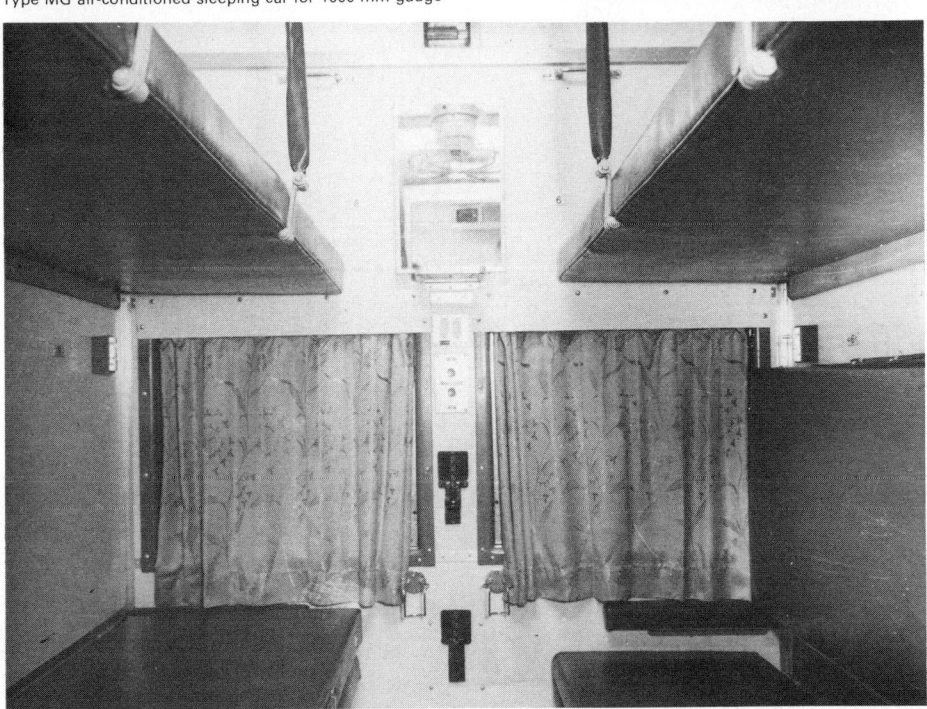
Berth of Type MG sleeping car

Air-conditioned chair car for 'Rajdhani Express'

fitted with stronger couplers. Extra power cannot always be spared from IR's limited resources, however: thus, for example, the 21-car 'Howrah Kalka Mail' from Calcutta to Delhi is headed by a single Class WAM-4 electric locomotive scheduled to run the 1440 km in 23 hours. The flagship twice-weekly 'Rajdhani Express' between Bombay and Delhi has become India's first fully air-braked, air-conditioned passenger train; it covers the 1388 km, hauled by a pair of Class WDM-2 diesels, in 16 hours 35 minutes. With introduction of new Class WAP electric locomotives featuring Flexicoil bogies and axle-hung motors the Delhi-Calcutta 'Rajdhani' is to operate at a maximum speed of 130 km/h; on the Bombay-Delhi route the limit is 120 km/h, but over most of the IR 1676 mm-gauge network speed is restricted to 110 km/h; on metre gauge the ceiling is 75 km/h.

If present trends continue it is anticipated that IR will need 14 000 replacement and additional passenger cars by 1985, but there is doubt that manufacturing capacity or funds will extend even to covering the 7500 cars that will have become life-expired by that date.

The chief measures taken to enlarge freight operating capacity (and also to enhance productivity and efficiency) are recourse to more unit train working, block train segregation of high-capacity, roller bearing-equipped wagons and pursuit of the maximum 4500-tonne trainloads feasible within existing passing loop parameters. Operation of 7500-tonne trains is in mind for some routes.

IR's freight output has suffered some decline since the later 1970s. For this a number of reasons have been adduced, internal as well as external; they include problems of keeping investment pace with the demands of the national economy for introduction of modern operating methods and equipment, particularly as IR slipped into deficit at the end of the 1970s. Operating ratio in 1981 was 96·1 per cent. However, the national Planning Commission has envisaged IR producing 237 000 million tonne-km of freight by 1985. In 1982 orders were placed for 20 000 wagons, mostly bogie hoppers, for delivery over three years at a cost of Rs 6000 million.

In 1981 the Rail Traffic Enquiry Committee reported that if IR was to fulfil its expected role for the rest of the century, it would require investment of Rs 360 000 million. The Committee concluded that the funds would need to be spent as follows:

	Rs million
Locomotives	22 499
Passenger cars	16 654·6
Electric multiple-units	18 367·8
Freight cars	50 647·6
Other rolling stock and spares	10 697·6
Electrification	78 670
New lines	16 010
Signalling	71 320·1
Workshops	16 641·4

Electrification, track doubling and resignalling on key routes are priorities to augment operating capacity. About 85 per cent of IR's total originating freight is moved on 1676 mm-gauge lines, so there is no eronomic case for a massive programme of gauge conversion, but it is being pressed where break-of-gauge transhipment is heavy, or traffic is overtaxing the narrower-gauge lines. A worsening problem is the backlog of track maintenance, estimated at 13 600 km of primary and 7500 km of secondary track by the beginning of 1983.

Electrification proceeds at the rate of some 290 km a year, with the initial aim of completing interconnection of the four chief metropolitan areas of the country, Delhi, Bombay, Calcutta and Madras.

For its 1983-84 plan IR was seeking Rs 17 750 million from the Government. The World Bank approved a loan of US$398·5 million for establishment of a diesel locomotive component works, the importation of prototype electric locomotives and of traction and rolling stock components. The World Bank is also funding consultancy and training in connection with the installation of a computer-based wagon control. In 1983 Rs 22·5 million was secured from the OPEC Fund for International Development.

Central Railway

Victoria Terminus, Bombay

Telephone: 268041

General Manager: T N Ramachandran

Gauge: 1676 mm; 1000 mm; 762 mm; 610 mm
Route length: 5632 km; 382 km; 367 km; 303 km
Electrification: 312 km at 25 kV 50 Hz ac; 303 km at 1·5 kV dc

The system was initially formed in 1951 from the Great Indian Peninsula, Dholpur State, Nizam's State and Scindia State Railways. In 1966 parts of the network were hived off to the newly-created South Central Railway zone, and Central now takes in railways throughout the greater part of Madhya Pradesh, southern Uttar Pradesh and central Maharashtra States.

Traffic
Central Railway accounts for a fifth of the aggregate of passenger-km and freight tonne-km on IR's 1676 mm lines. Traffic has soared since the start of the 1970s, fuelled by rapidly rising originating and transit flows of coal to generating plants and industry generally. Originating tonnage of 17·7 million in 1981-82 was a record for CR.

In the passenger sector the daily throughput of the 192 km Bombay commuter network has climbed from 1·4 million journeys to 2·4 million in 1981. A daily timetable of 842 trains is operated with 68 1·5 kV dc train-sets and Rs1600 million are being invested in a capacity enlargement programme to halve headways to 3 minutes and raise the daily total to 1184. Segregation of main-line trains in a new terminal between Kurla and Vikhroli is a possibility. CR was the first IR Zone to adopt bi-level passenger cars, which were introduced on the Bombay-Pune 'Sinhagad Express' in 1978. More long-haul services were switched from steam to diesel traction in 1982 and five pairs of overnight trains now feature air-conditioned sleeping cars. Through coach working between Bombay and Gorakhpur became possible with conversion of the Lucknow-Gorakhpur line to 1676 mm gauge.

Infrastructure
To increase operating capacity, a third track is being added on the difficult ghat sections of the main lines out of Bombay to Igatpuri and Pune, at the expense of substantial tunnelling; work on the Igatpuri route is complete and only a portion of the Pune route remained to finish in 1982. Construction of a new 971 km coastal line from Bombay to Mangalore is under way and the work has reached Roha, 146 km from Bombay; the first 84 km to Pen have been completed and the 20 km from Apta to Pen were opened to traffic in February 1983. In 1982 electrification of the routes between Tughlaka and Mathura (122 km) and Diva and Bassein (42 km) was in progress, and the former is to be extended from Mathura to Itarsi, where CR's biggest route-relay interlocking scheme to date has been commissioned. Electrification is also to be undertaken between Bhusaval and Nagpur. Parts of the route between Itarsi and Nagpur are being double-tracked, as are sections between Juheki and Chheoki.

Traction and rolling stock
At the start of 1982 CR was operating on the 1676 mm gauge 717 steam, 176 electric (including some dual-voltage) and 269 diesel locomotives, one railcar, 3398 passenger cars including emu vehicles, and 56 204 freight wagons. The metre-gauge lines were steam-powered by 39 locomotives and the narrow-gauge systems disposed of 58 steam locomotives, four diesel locomotives, five railcars, 194 passenger cars and 811 freight wagons.

Eastern Railway

14-16 Government Place East, Calcutta 700 001

Telephone: 23 2006-8

General Manager: C K Swaminathan

Gauge: 1676 mm; 762 mm
Route length: 4070 km; 132 km
Electrification: 1218 km at 25 kV 50 Hz ac

The Eastern Railway is among India's biggest Zonal railways, running mainly in the states of West Bengal and Bihar, and also in parts of Uttar Pradesh and Madhya Pradesh. It was formed in 1952 from the Bengal-Nagpur Railway and parts of the East Indian Railway, but in 1955 the Bengal-Nagpur was transferred to the new South Eastern Railway Zone.

Almost all passenger services are operated by a fleet of 231 electric locomotives. Over 600 emu cars are operating on the suburban system as three-car sets and more than 700 trains run daily from Calcutta's passenger terminal at Howrah and Sealdah.

Developments
Improvements are under way on the Calcutta-New Delhi line to raise speeds from a present maximum of 130 km/h to 160 km/h. Conversion of fishplated track and short welded panels into long welded and continuous welded sections is in hand, together with replacement of 90 lb/yd rail with 52 kg/m on concrete and steel sleepers with elastic fastenings.

Surveys have been completed on four projected new lines: Budge Budge to Namkhana via Diamond Harbour (100 km, broad-gauge), Gaya to Rajgir (45 km, broad-gauge), Ranchi Road to Giridih via Koderma (196 km), Mandar Hill to Baidyanathdham (55 km).

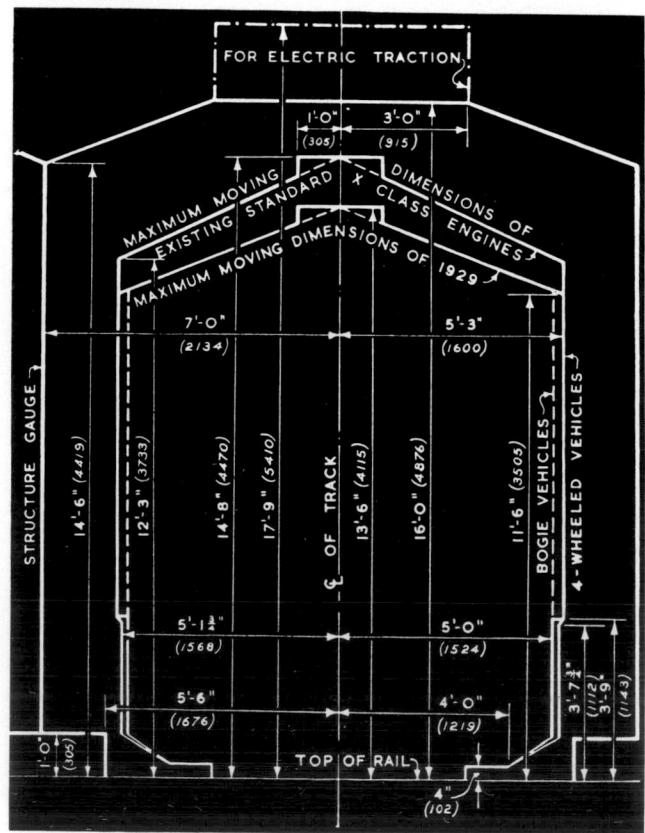

Broad gauge

Traffic

In 1980/81 passenger volume rose to 492·5 million journeys, compared with 487 million in the previous financial year; the greater part of the rise was in commuter traffic, which accounted for a total of 353 million journeys. Freight traffic was up by a million tonnes to a total of 47·7 million, of which 38 million was coal; the average daily coal wagon loadings for the year climbed to 4381.

Traction and rolling stock

At the start of 1982 the railway operated, on the broad gauge: 889 steam, 239 electric and 251 diesel locomotives, 2758 passenger cars, 647 emu cars, 64 429 freight cars; and on the narrow gauge: 19 steam locomotives, three diesel railcars, 91 passenger cars and 75 freight cars. A new emu maintenance depot was being completed at Sealdah in 1982 and another was to be built at Bendel to sup-

plement existing facilities at Narkeldanga and Howrah, where a new electric locomotive depot is planned. The main electric traction works at Kanchrapara was being modernised with the help of a World Bank loan.

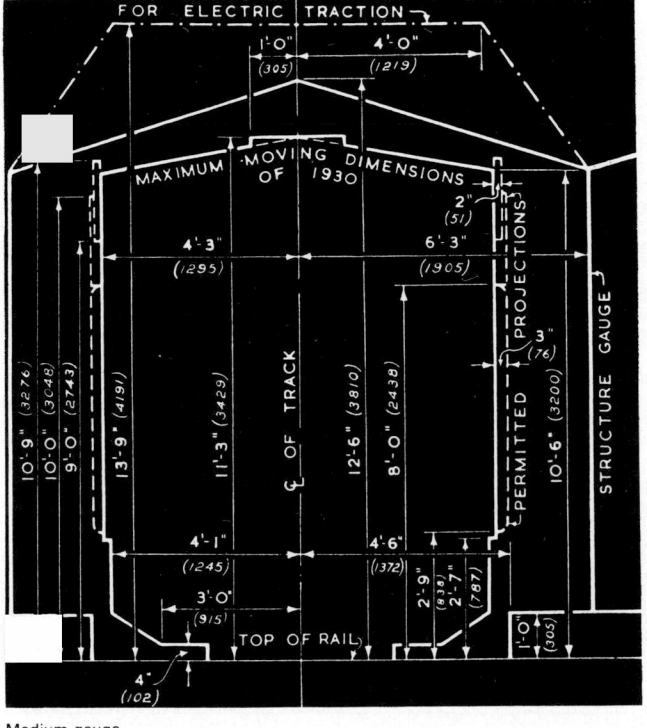

Medium gauge

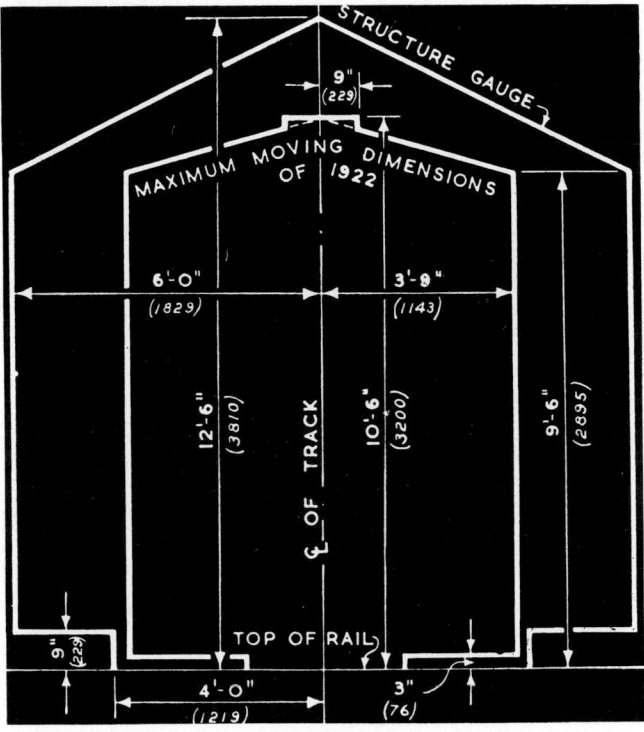

Narrow gauge

Northern Railway

Baroda House, New Delhi 1

Telephone: 387227

General Manager: R Srinivasan

Gauge: 1676 mm; 1000 mm; 762 mm
Route length: 6998 km; 3430 km; 260 km

Electrification: 572 km of 1676 mm gauge at 25 kV 50 Hz ac

The railway was created in 1952 from parts of the Eastern Punjab Railway, of the East Indian Railway, and of the Western Railway, together with the Jodhpur and Bikaner Railways. Its territory extends from Delhi through the Punjab, Haryana Delhi, Himachal Pradesh and parts of Jammu, Kashmir, Rajasthan and Uttar Pradesh States.

At the end of 1981 NR began a Rs 500 million project to extend its 1676 mm-gauge Pathankot-Jammu line further north-west to Udhampur.

At the start of 1982 the railway operated, on 1676 mm-gauge: 55 electric, 197 diesel and 1045 steam locomotives; 3025 passenger cars, 58 923 freight wagons; on the metre-gauge: 41 diesel and 321 steam locomotives, 971 passenger cars and 6629 freight wagons; and on the 762 mm-gauge: 15 diesel and 37 steam locomotives, 141 passenger cars and 286 freight cars.

North Eastern Railway

Gorakhpur, UP

General Manager: D Hariram

Gauge: 1676 mm; 1000 mm
Route length: 218 km; 4945 km

Increases of population and economic development now exert extreme pressure on the predominantly narrow-gauge network of the NER, which consists

of part of the Assam and onetime Mobay, Baroda & Central India Railways and Oudh Tirhut Railway. It covers Bihar and Uttar Pradesh from Achnera in the west to Katihar in the east. In 1981 the railway completed enlargement to 1676 mm-gauge of its key Samastipur-Barabanki route. Similar conversion of the 180 km Barauni-Katihar line was due for completion in 1982, to be followed by enlargement of the 158 km Bhatni-Varanasi line. The first of these two projects achieved conversion throughout of NER's trunk route and also connection with the newly

extended 1676 mm network of the Northeast Frontier Railway, thereby creating much improved rail access to Assam from all parts of India. The second will greatly simplify freight interchange with the Central, Eastern and Northern Railways.

At the start of 1981 NER operated 808 steam and 212 diesel locomotives, 3634 passenger cars and 28 320 freight cars. Its 1982 investment plans envisaged acquisition of 40 new diesel-electric, 40 new steam locomotives and 400 new passenger cars for its 1676 mm-gauge system.

Northeast Frontier Railway

Maligaon, Gauhati 781 011, Assam

Telephone: 88422

General Manager: K T V Raghavan

Gauge: 1676 mm; 1000 mm; 610 mm
Route length: 639 km; 2901 km; 87 km

The NFR was hived off from the North Eastern Railway in 1958. It serves the whole of Assam and North Bengal, parts of North Bihar, the states of Arunachal, Manipur, Meghalaya, Mizoram, Nagaland, Tripura, and embraces all railways north-east of the Ganges and east of Katihar. Its 610 mm-gauge component is the world-famous Darjeeling-Himalaya

Railway, still worked by 19th century steam power, which takes 7 hours for the scenic journey of 87 km from New Jaipalguri to Darjeeling.

A rise of no less than 44 per cent in originating freight tonnage during 1981/82, to a total of 3·6 million, with a concomitant lift of freight tonne-km to 3741 million, narrowed the deficit. Revenue grossed Rs 90 million against expenditure of Rs 160 million. A further improvement of traffic to 4 million tonnes and almost 4900 million tonne-km was hoped for in 1982/83.

By late 1983 NFR was due to complete an important Rs 620 million extension of its 1676 mm-gauge system over 164 km from New Bongaigaon to Gauhati, capital of Assam. Construction of the new alignment was through terrain intersected by many water courses, which entailed erection of 134 bridges of 5·27 km aggregate length; the biggest carries the new railway over the Brahmaputra river. Completion will open up through running at greatly

reduced transit times to all the country's 1676 mm-gauge main lines. At the same time other extensions to the system totalling 184 km were being executed on the metre gauge at a total cost of Rs 620 million; penetrating previously rail-isolated areas, they will be finished between 1984 and 1986. A further 10 new lines are being surveyed.

Track upgrading throughout the 1145 km metre-gauge line from Katihar to Tinsukia was due for completion in 1982. Following installation of new repair facilities at New Bongaigaon, 1676 mm-gauge passenger cars will no longer have to be transferred to the Eastern Railway for overhaul, though the move will remain necessary for 1676 mm-gauge locomotives.

At the start of 1982 NFR was operating 78 steam locomotives, 563 passenger cars and 81 freight wagons on the 1676 mm gauge, 318 steam and 103 diesel locomotives, 1892 passenger cars and 11 143 freight cars on the metre gauge.

Southern Railway

Park Town, Madras 600 003

Telephone: 39101

General Manager: C M Malik

Gauge: 1676 mm; 1000 mm; 762 mm
Length: 2007 km; 4474 km; 148 km
Electrification: 188 km of 1676 mm gauge at 25 kV

50 Hz ac; 164 km of 1000 mm gauge at 25 kV 50 Hz ac

Formed in 1951 from the previous Madras & Southern Mahratta, Mysore and South Indian railways, the Southern extends from Mangalore on the west coast and Kanya Kumari in the south to Renigunta in the north-west and Gudur in the north-east. Electrification is concentrated in the Madras suburban area and on the main line from Madras to the fringe of South Central Railway territory at Vijayawada.

A major project launched in 1982 was construction of a 327 km 1676 mm-gauge line from Karur to the south coast at Tuticorin and also to Tirunelveli, at a cost of Rs 430 million. The scheme partly involves conversion of existing metre-gauge lines between Madurai and Maniyachi (127 km).

In 1982 the railway operated on 1676 mm gauge 195 diesel and 219 diesel locomotives, 42 emus, 2448 passenger cars and 21 811 freight cars; on narrow gauge 371 steam and 20 electric locomotives, 45 emu power cars and 121 trailers, six diesel railcars, 2119 passenger cars and 7853 freight cars.

South Central Railway

Rail Nilayam Secunderabad, Andhra Pradesh

Telephone: 500 371

General Manager: S M Kaul

Gauge: 1676 mm; 1000 mm
Route length: 3165 km; 3313 km

The South Central Railway (SCR) was set up in 1966 from portions of the Southern and Central Railways and plays a major role in the industrial and agricultural development of the region. It covers the states of Andhra Pradesh and Goa, north-west Karnataka and south-west Maharashtra.

Fresh traffic growth was recorded in 1981/82. An increase of over 2 million lifted originating freight to 19·3 million tonnes and with transit freight included the year's gross was 37·6 million tonnes. Tonne-km rose from 17 048 million to 21 491 million. Equally important, as a consequence of numerous productivity measures including concentration of roller-bearing, centre-buffer wagons in unit trains, organisation of more siding-to-siding unit train workings and of heavier trainloads, the 1676 mm-gauge wagon-day average was lifted from 79·6 to 111 km and diesel locomotive utilisation improved by a third to 449 km a day. Originating passenger journeys were up some 5 per cent to 161 million and passenger-km increased from 17 048 million to 21 491 million. Operating ratio was 84·9 per cent.

Principal raw material moved is coal, which

accounted for more than 40 per cent of originating freight. Coal movements are expected to increase dramatically by 1992, when the Singareni collieries in Andhra Pradesh may be producing 24 million tonnes annually (compared with 9·5 million tonnes in 1979) and numerous new coal-fired generating plants will have come on stream. The other major bulk freight flow is iron ore from the Hospet-Bellary region to Madras for export, which the railway plans to move in 4500-tonne unit trains. Many new industries are arising in SCR territory, including steelworks, 21 cement plants and a fertiliser plant at Kakinada, which promise considerable traffic growth.

SCR has no considerable suburban traffic, relying mainly for passenger growth on improved inter-city services. Among these are the prestigious 'Andhra Pradesh Express' which runs between Secunderabad and New Delhi (1670 km) in under 24 hours and the 'Minar' express running between Secunderabad and Bombay (800 km) in about 13 hours. Of the railway's 495 daily passenger workings, 100 are in the superfast mail or express category.

Developments
Major projects due for completion in 1982 included construction of a broad-gauge line between Bibinagar on the Delhi-Hyderabad line and Nadikudi (149 km), and conversion of the metre-gauge section between Guntur and Macherla (130 km).

The railway's forward corporate plan envisages building 269 km more of new lines at a cost of Rs649 million, track doubling over 177 km at a cost of Rs420 million, conversion of 244 km of metre-gauge

route to 1676 mm gauge at a cost of Rs649 million and enlargement of several principal passenger stations.

Electrification has been completed over SCR's 295 km (Gudur-Vijayawada) section of the Madras-Gudur-Vijayawada line; its operation is shared with the Southern Railway which has electrified the 136 km southern section to Madras. Future electrification plans aim to extend the Gudur-Vijayawada wiring by 543 km, from Vijayawada to Balharshah and between Secunderabad and Kazipet. Work was launched between Gudur and Tirupati in January 1983.

Surveys have been conducted for these other major projects:
Construction of a new line between Hyderabad and Peddapalli on the Delhi route, designed to bypass Kazipet;
Construction of a new link from Nizamabad to the coalfield at Ramagundram;
Conversion of the eastern metre-gauge line from Miraj to Hospet and Londa to Vasco to broad-gauge (1016 km);
Conversion to broad-gauge of the 470 km line between Guntakal and Guntur;
Construction of a new broad-gauge line from Nandyal to Yerraguntla (125 km).

Traction and rolling stock
In 1982 the railway operated 554 steam and 229 diesel locomotives; 1362 passenger cars and 11 760 freight cars on 1676 mm gauge, 376 steam and 78 diesel locomotives, 996 passenger cars and 12 671 freight cars on metre-gauge.

South Eastern Railway

Garden Reech, Kidderpore, Calcutta 700 043

Telephone: 45 1741

General Manager: R P Singh

Gauge: 1676 mm; 762 mm
Route length: 5511 km; 1479 km
Electrification: 1421 km at 25 kV 50 Hz ac

SER was created in a 1955 partition of the Eastern Railway and comprises the lines of the former

Bengal-Nagpur Railway centred on Calcutta.

Mainstay of SER's traffic is freight generated by steel mills, coalmines and export ore with 87 per cent of the railway's earnings coming from freight traffic. Passenger traffic is increasing and by 1982 the railway expected to be carrying over 78 million suburban and 112 million long-distance passengers.

Work started in 1980 on the 180 km direct line from Banspani to Jhakapura which will provide better access to the deep water port of Paradip for export ore trains. It will avoid the lengthy detour through Kharagpur for trains carrying iron and manganese ore from the Orissa deposits.

In the passenger sector, work was under way on a broad-gauge line between Howrah and Amta in the Calcutta suburbs.

Surveys have been carried out for a number of new lines. Most important is a 190 km link from Talcher to Sambalpur. Conversion to broad-gauge is planned for narrow-gauge lines running from Gondia to Jabalpore and Nagpur to Chindwara.

At the start of 1981 SER was operating on its 1676 mm gauge 249 electric, 229 diesel and 618 steam locomotives, 36 emus, 2735 passenger cars, 56 270 freight cars; and on its 762 mm gauge 34 diesel and 102 steam locomotives, 435 passenger cars and 2077 freight cars.

Western Railway

Churchgate, Bombay 400 020

Telephone: 298016

General Manager: S Sarath

Gauge: 1676 mm; 1000 mm; 762 mm
Route length: 3085 km; 6118 km; 1135 km
Electrification: 496 km

Formed in 1951, the railway comprises the former Bombay, Baroda & Central India, Jaipur State, Gaekwar of Baroda's, Cutch State, Saurashtra and Rajasthan Railways.

The railway is IR's busiest passenger carrier and moves 10 per cent of the country's freight. Originating freight traffic in 1981/82 grossed 22·6 million tonnes. Since 1982 its passenger working has included operation of IR's first fully air-braked train, the Bombay-Delhi 'Rajdhani Express'.

The major infrastructure improvement under way in 1982 was electrification of the 1388 km Bombay-Delhi main line following its double-tracking; the latter was heading for completion in 1984. Electric operation was already possible as far as Vadodara en route to Ahmedabad. New line construction comprised principally a 1676 mm-gauge connection of 219 km between Kota, Chittogarh and Nimach,

25 kV ac/1500 V dc type WCAM1
electric locomotive

and a metre-gauge line from Bhuj to Naliya. It was expected that the 1676 mm-gauge conversion of the 567 km route from Viramgan to the ports of Okha and Porbandar would be finished by the close of 1983.

At the start of 1982 the railway was operating, on its 1676 mm gauge: 74 electric, 174 diesel and 495

steam locomotives, 211 electric power cars and 385 trailers, 2072 passenger cars and 36 299 freight cars; on the metre gauge: 155 diesel and 649 steam locomotives, five railcars, 3148 passenger cars and 21 174 freight cars; and on the 762 mm gauge: 89 steam locomotives, two railcars and seven trailers, 319 passenger cars and 1066 freight cars.

Indian Railways track
Rail, types and weight

	Type/specification
Flat bottom	
65 kg steel rails	Gost 8160 & 8161-56
Wear-resistant rails	
60 kg/m	UIC 860/0 grade 'C'
Wear-resistant rails	
52 kg/m	UIC 860/0 grade 'B'
Medium manganese	
flat bottom 52 kg/m	IRS speen T 12

Sleepers: Wooden, cast iron, concrete and steel sleepers. The standard now adopted for high-speed trunk routes is concrete or steel trough

Concrete: Monobloc, thickness at rail level 196·25 mm, length 2750 mm. With Pandrol Rail clips, thickness at rail level 210 mm, length 2750 mm. Two block concrete sleepers, thickness at rail level 215·5 mm, length 722 mm each with MS angle iron tie bar of 75 × 75 × 10 mm

Wooden
Broad gauge 2750 × 250 × 130 mm
Metre gauge 1800 × 200 × 115 mm
Narrow gauge 1500 × 180 × 115 mm

Spacing: 1540/km

Rail fastenings
Fish plates and bolts and nuts to suit rail type, viz 65 kg, 60 kg, 52 kg

Fittings for concrete sleepers:

	Drawing No
Monobloc	
Pandrol clips	PR 401
Nylon liners	RDSO/T-383
Grooved rubber pads	RDSO/T-382
Inserts	RDSO/T-381
Twin-block	
Grooved rubber pads	RDSO/T-476
Clips and clamps	IRN 202 RDSO/T-465
Liners	RDSO/T-466
Bolts and nuts	RDSO/T-477
Rubber heel pads	RDSO/T-479

Fittings for steel trough sleepers:

Spring steel loose jaws	IRS spn T12
MS keys	T 405 (m), IRS spn T8
(for high speed tracks)	
Modified loose jaws	RDSO/T-1801

Grooved rubber pads	RDSO/T-382
Pandrol clips	PR-401

Fittings for wooden sleepers:

Mild steel or cast iron bearing plates	IRS spn T7
Screw spikes, Round spikes, Dog spikes or Rail screws	IRS spn T466
Keys	BG T405 (M) & MG T413 (M)

Rail anchors (for high speed tracks)

CI bearing plates	RDSO/T-646
Screw spikes	RDSO/T-650
Pandrol clips	PR-401
Grooved rubber pads	RDSO/647

Fittings for cast iron sleepers:

Tie bars	BG T404(M), MG T433(M)

Standard method of welding: New rail is flash butt welded in workshops into 3 or 5 rail bar lengths, carried to site on specially designed wagons then alumino-thermic welded into cwr lengths after laying in position.

Electric locomotives

Class	Wheel arrange-ment	Line current	Rated output hp	Tractive effort (full field) Max kg	Continuous at kg	kmlh	Max speed kmlh	Wheel dia mm	Weight tonnes	Length mm	Year built	Builders Mechanical parts	Electrical equipment
WAM1	Bo-Bo	25 kV ac	2830	25 000	14 900	52	112·5	1140	74	15 892	1960	Group	
WAM2	Bo-Bo	25 kV ac	2790	25 242	14 500	52	112·5	1090	76·03	15 000	1961	Mitsubishi	
WAM3	Bo-Bo	25 kV ac	2790	25 242	14 500	52	112·6	1090	76	15 000	1964	Mitsubishi	
WAM4	Co-Co	25 kV ac	3640	33 840	17 600	56	120	1092	112·8	18 974	1971	CLW	Bhel & CLW
WAMB	Co-Co	25 kV ac	4000	—	—	—	100	—	120	—	1979	CLW	Bhel & CLW
WAMR	Co-Co	25 kV ac	4000	—	—	—	160	—	120	—	1979	CLW	Bhel & CLW
WAG1	B-B	25 kV ac	2900	30 000	23 700	33	80	1140	85·2	17 092	1963	Group & CLW	
WAG2	B-B	25 kV ac	3120	30 000	22 600	38	80	1140	85·2	16 882	1964	Hitachi	
WAG3	B-B	25 kV ac	3150	30 000	23 200	36·5	80	1140	87·32	17 092	1965	Group	
WAG4	B-B	25 kV ac	3150	30 000	23 200	36·5	80	1140	87·6	17 216	1967	CLW	
WCAM1	Co-Co	25 kV ac/ 1500 V dc	2640 2930	33 840 28 200	16 000 22 600	60 35	120	1092	112·8	20 950	1975	CLW	Bhel & CLW
YAM1	B-B	25 kV ac	1630	19 500	12 300	34·5	80	865	52	13 150	1965	Mitsubishi	
WCM1	Co-Co	1500 V dc	3170	31 000	17 690	48·3	120·5	1220	123·98	20 834	1955	EE Co Ltd & Vulcan Foundry	
WCM2	Co-Co	1500 V dc	2810	31 298	12 300	61·7	120·5	1092	112·8	20 066	1957	EE Co Ltd & Vulcan Foundry	
WCM3	Co-Co	1500 V dc	2460	28 200	10 220	65	120·7	1220	113	19 583	1961	Hitachi	
WCM4	Co-Co	1500 V dc	3290	31 250	18 700	47·5	120·5	1220	125	20 000	1961	Hitachi	
WCM5	Co-Co	1500 V dc	3170	31 000	17 690	48·3	120·5	1220	124	20 168	1961	CLW	
WCG2	Co-Co	1500 V dc	4200	35 600	21 900	52·5	80	1092	135	19 974	1971	CLW	Bhel & CLW

Diesel railcars

Class	Wheel arrange-ment	Trans-mission	Rated power hp	Max kg	Tractive effort Continuous at kg	kmlh	Max speed kmlh	Wheel dia mm	Total weight tonnes	Length over head stock mm	Year first built	Builders Mechanical parts	Engine & type	Transmission
1676 mm gauge WRD1	1A-1A1	Mech	400	—	—	—	110	915	47·4 (tare) 82·10 (loaded)	22 241 (buffer to buffer)	1958	Commonwealth Eng Co Ltd, Australia	Leyland EN-900H	SCG Epicylic SE4
1000 mm gauge YRD1	B'-2	Mech	—	—	—	—	88	724	28·5 (tare) 37·5 (loaded)	18 700	1956	M/s Fiat Co, Italy	Fiat 700-110/3	Fiat Fiat/Twin Disc Italy
		Hyd-Mech	225	—	—	—								
YRD2	1A-2	Hyd-Mech	180	—	—	—	88	724	30 (tare) 39 (loaded)	18 440	1956	M/s Nippon Sharyo, Japan	Shinko 1MH-17h	Shinko, Japan
YRD3	1A-2	Mech	200	—	—	—	72	724	31 (tare) 40 (loaded)	19 500	1956	ICF, India	Leyland 0.680(H)	Wilson SC 2G
YRD4	1A-2	Hyd	285	—	—	—	93	724	31 (tare) 40 (loaded)	19 500	1967	ICF, India	Kirloskar Cummins NHHR TO-6	Kirloskar Twin Disc, India

Electric railcars

Class	Wheel arrangement	Line current	Rated output hp	Tractive effort (full field) Max kg	Continuous at kg	km/h	Max speed km/h	Wheel dia mm	Weight tonnes	Length mm	Year built	Builders Mechanical parts	Electrical equipment
1500 V dc BG emus													
WCU3	Bo-Bo	1500 V dc	1200	7400	6980	52·2	104	915	160·88	85 344	1951	M/s British Thompson Houston	M/s Metro Cammell
WCU4	Bo-Bo	1500 V dc	1080	7000	5816	49·9	104	914·4	161·49	85 344	1951	M/s Metro Cammel	M/s English Electric Co
WCU5	Bo-Bo	1500 V dc	1080	7000	5816	49·9	104	914·4	170·8	82 904	1956	M/s Breda Ferroviaria Milomo, Hitachi	M/s English Electric Co
WCU6	Bo-Bo	1500 V dc	1120	7200	6465	48·15	104	914·4	177.86	82 904	1957	Hitachi	Hitachi
WCU7	Bo-Bo	1500 V dc	1120	7200	6465	48·15	104	914·4	174·9	82 904	1958/59	NSSK	NSSK
WCU8	Bo-Bo	1500 V dc	732	10 000	3846	54·5	104	952	120·9	62 178	1958/59	MAN	AEG
WCU10	Bo-Bo	1500 V dc	1096	7500	6100	49·2	104	914·4	166·2	82 904	1959	M/s Breda Ferroviaria	M/s Ansaldo Sangeorgic
WCU12	Bo-Bo	1500 V dc	840	11 000	4592	49·75	104	952	141·23	62 178	1961	Jessop	AEI
WCU13	Bo-Bo	1500 V dc	744	13 320	4200	48·6	105	952	116·11	64 722	1970 / 1960	ICF / Jessop	Bhel / Bhel
WCU14	Bo-Bo	1500 V dc	744	13 320	4200	48·6	105	952	116·11	64 722	1970 / 1960	ICF / Jessop	Bhel / Bhel
WCU15	Bo-Bo	1500 V dc	744	13 320	4200	48·6	105	952	116·11	64 722	1970 / 1960	ICF / Jessop	Bhel / Bhel
25 kV ac/dc BG													
WAU-1 SIG (conv)	Bo-Bo	3000 V dc/ 25 kV ac	848	8900	4400	50	104	952·5	117	64 312	1958/59	SIG	Sécheron
WAU-2 Jessops (conv)	Bo-Bo	3000 V dc/ 25 kV ac	840	11 600	4592	49·75	104	952	141·23	62 178	1959/60	Jessop	AEI
25 kV ac BG													
WAU-3 (Hitachi)	Bo-Bo	25 kV ac	900	12 600	4240	58·2	96	915	151·58	82 904	1966	ICF	Hitachi
WAU-4	Bo-Bo	25 kV ac	896	13 100	4900	49·5	105	952	148·3	86 243	1964	ICF	Bhel
25 kV ac MG													
YAU-1	Bo-Bo	25 kV ac	688	9000	2550	70·7	90	MC 838 TC 725	112	81 134	1966	ICF	M/s Nichoman, Japan

Diesel locomotives

Class	Wheel arrangement	Transmission	Rated power hp	Tractive effort Max kg	Continuous at kg	km/h	Max speed km/h	Wheel dia mm	Total weight tonnes	Length over head stock mm	Year first built	Builders Mechanical parts	Engine & type	Transmission
1676 mm gauge														
WDM1	Co-Co	Elec	1977	27 900	19 300	19	104	1016	112	16 777	1958	Alco, USA	Alco 251-B-12 cyl	GE, USA
WDM2	Co-Co	Elec	2636	30 450	24 600	18	120	1092	113	15 850	1962	DLW, India	DLW 251-B-16 cyl	Bhel, India
WDM3	B'-B'	Hyd / Hyd-Mech	2500	High-speed 22 000 / Low-speed 25 080	14 000 / 20 000	28 / 18·5	120	1092	76	14 800	1970	Henschel, West Germany	MD-108 oz 20 cyl	Myu, West Germany
WDM4	Co-Co	Elec	2636	28 200	20 600	24	120	1092	113	17 270	1962	GM, USA	GM567D3 16-cyl	GM, USA
WDS1	Bo-Bo	Elec	193	11 550	5000	10	56	965	46	9061	1945	GE, USA	Caterpiller D-17000-8 cyl	GE, USA
WDS2	O-C-O	Hyd	440	High-speed 9200 / Low-speed 15 420	7300 / 14 750	7·55 / 3·86	54 / 27·6	1092	51	7265	1945	Krauss-Maffei, West Germany	MAN W 8V-17-5/ 22A 8 cyl	Voith, West Germany
WDS3	O-C-O	Hyd	618	High-speed 10 400 / Low-speed 1700	7500 / 18 000	12 / 4	65	1092	57	9430	1961	MaK, West Germany	Maybach MD-435 8 cyl	MaK, West Germany

Class	Wheel arrangement	Transmission	Rated power hp	Tractive effort Max kg	Continuous kg	at kmlh	Max speed kmlh	Wheel dia mm	Total weight tonnes	Length over head stock mm	Year first built	Builders Mechanical parts	Engine & type	Transmission
WDS4	0-C-0	Hyd or Hyd-Mech	700	High-speed 11 500 Low-speed 18 000	8500 16 900	13 5·5	65 27	1092	60	9730	1969	CLW, India	MaK/CLW 6M28A(k) 6 cyl	Kirloskar, India
WDS4A	0-C-0	Hyd	660	High-speed 16 700 Low-speed 18 000	12 400 17 000	8 5	65	1092	60	9730	1968	CLW, India	MaK, West Germany 6M282A(k) 6 cyl	Voith, West Germany
WDS5	Co-Co	Elec	1065	31 500	32 300	3·2	109	1092	126	15 400	1967		Alco 251-B-6 cyl	GE, USA
1000 mm gauge YDM1	B'-B	Hyd	634	10 920	8230	12	88	864	44	10 630	1955	North British, UK	Paxman 12 rph XL	Voith, UK
YDM3	1B-B' 1	Elec	1390	14 300	10 300	24·5	80	Driving 865 Carrying 762	58	12 350	1962	GM, USA	GM 12 567c 12 cyl	GM, USA
YDM4	Co-Co	Elec	1400	18 935	19 200	15·65	96	965	72	13 818	1962	DLW, India	DLW/251-D 6 cyl	Bhel, India
YDM4A	Co-Co	Elec	1400	18 935	19 200	11·6	96	965	72	13 818	1964	MLW, Canada	MLW/251-D 6 cyl	GE, Canada
YDM5	C'-C'	Elec	1390	21 792	11 250	22·35	80	865	69	13 260	1964	GM, USA	GM 12 567c 12 cyl	GM, USA
N/ZDM1	B'-B'	Hyd	145	8790	7500	5	33	700	29	8400	1955	Arn Jung, West Germany	MWM TRHS 518 S 6 cyl	Voith, West Germany
ZDM2	B'-B'	Hyd-Mech	700	10 560	8500	12·5	50	700	32	9120	1964	MaK, West Germany	Maybach MD 435 8 cyl	MaK, West Germany
ZDM3	B'-B'	Hyd-Mech	700	10 500	9800	6·4	32	700	35	10 300	1971	CLW, India	CLW/MaK 6M 282Λ (k) 6 cyl	Kirloskar

INDONESIA

Indonesian State Railways (PJKA)
Perusahaan Jawatan Kerata Api

Jalan Geraja, 1, Bandung, Java

Telephone: 58001-6
Telegrams: Qdirutka BD
Telex: 28263

Chief Director: Ir Soedjono Karmadibrata
Corporate Secretary: Drs Hersubno
Director Personnel: Ir Soeharso
Director of Finance: Imam Rustadi, SH
Director of Operations: Ch N Latief, SH
Director, Traction Rolling Stock and Workshops: Ir Sandjojo
Director of Fixed Installations: Ir Soeparto
Chief of Planning Centre: Vacant
Chief of Research and Development Centre: Prof Ir Partosiswojo
Chief of PT Inka (Rolling stock plant): Ir Soetijanto
Chief of Education Training Centre: Asmanu, BE
Chief Auditor: Soedharmoen Pintodihardjo

Gauge: 1067 mm; 750 mm
Route length: 6380 km; 497 km
Electrification: 77 km at 1·5 kV dc

Transport development
The railway network in Indonesia is confined to the islands of Java (including Madura) with about 4900 km and Sumatra with about 2000 km of route length. The system was built up to its present size during the 70 years prior to the Second World War, at which time 40 per cent of the network was owned privately. Nationalisation took place in the 1940s and 1950s.

Organisationally, the railway is divided into six regional divisions (three in Java and three in Sumatra), and 17 departmental sub-divisions (11 in Java and six in Sumatra).

Traffic
Results in 1980/81 sustained the recovery achieved since the mid-1970s, when traffic slumped to little more than 10 per cent of the volume recorded two

Jakarta area commuter emu *(Marcel Vleugels)*

Traffic	1979/80	1980/81
Total train-km (million)	26·627	25·317
Total freight tonnage (million)	4·310	4·308
Total freight-km (million)	1001·269	973·923
Total passenger-km (million)	5894·769	6037·481
Total passenger journeys (million)	38·574	40·063

Finances Revenue (Rp million)	1979/80	1980/81
Passengers and baggage	26 802	31 822
Freight, parcels and mail	12 529	14 483
Ferry services*	1789	1967
Total	41 120	48 272

* Ferry services operate between: Merak (Java)-Panjang (Sumatra); Ujung (Surabaya Java)-Kamal (Madura); Banyuwangi (Java)-Gilimanuk (Bali).

decades earlier because of the country's concentration of investment on new roads. Since 1976 passenger journeys have doubled. Freight traffic has not been so vigorously revived and has been on a plateau since 1979, but is still almost 40 per cent above the nadir of 1976.

Electrification

The electrified system in Java covers the line between Jakarta and Bogor and some sections around the city of Jakarta. It is being expanded under the Jabotabek scheme into a regional network envisaged as catering for 20 million people by the end of the century. The first phase of the project, likely to start in 1983, is electrification of Jakarta's western loop from the city's Tanjungpriok terminus via Duri to Manggarai. After that the catenary will be projected to Bekasi, Serpong and Tanggerang.

Investment

Japan Railway Technical Service (JRTS) was engaged and has completed feasibility studies of the so-called Jabotabek project for a system of suburban lines radiating from Jakarta to Tanggerang, Bogor and Bekasi, which President Suharto has categorised as a priority project to be completed by 1990. The Government contemplates an expenditure of US $1900 million on Jabotabek by the century's end. This will cover total electrification of the network involved, provision of additional tracks where traffic is intense, transfer of some sections to elevated rights-of-way to eliminate level crossings, two new orbital lines and purchase of up to 700 new emu cars.

Canadian Pacific Consulting Services is assisting in a US$ 200 million project to upgrade the 410 km 1067 mm-gauge route in Sumatra for the unit-train movement of 2-3 million tonnes of coal a year from the Bukit Asam field to a new south coast port of Tarahan for shipment to an electricity generating station on Java. Parts of the route are also used by other bulk freight flows. Remaining 30 kg/m rail is being replaced by welded 50 kg/m rail on concrete sleepers (but 42 kg/m rail is not being immediately renewed), ballast reinforced to a depth of at least 250 mm throughout, numerous bridges strengthened, extra passing loops provided and two new branches constructed to ballast quarries. When finished, the works will lift maximum axleloadings from 13 to 18 tonnes and line speed to 60 km/h for freight and 90 km/h for passenger trains. Mechanical signalling is being retained, but traffic control by single-line token will be superseded by radio control through a new uhf/vhf radio network. Hawker Siddeley Canada is to supply 370 wagons for the unit coal trains.

Elsewhere, the port of Meneng is being rail-connected under a US$ 185 million project, for which the support of a US$ 66 million World Bank loan has been secured; the new line's main purpose will be fertiliser transport, for which 200 wagons are to be acquired to operate in unit trains.

General Electric Class CC201 diesel-electric (GE Type U18C) at Surabaya with an overnight express *(Marcel Vleugels)*

SLM-built 905 kW rack-and-adhesion locomotive

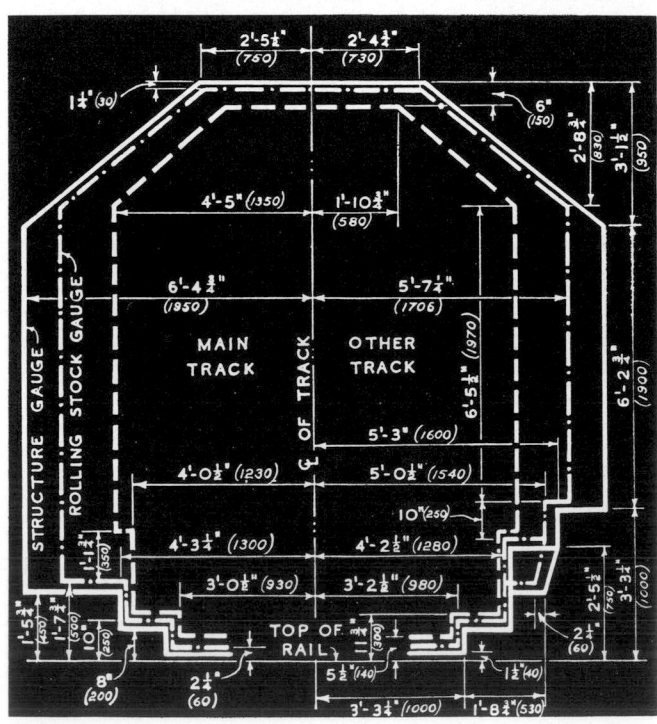

Loading gauge: main lines

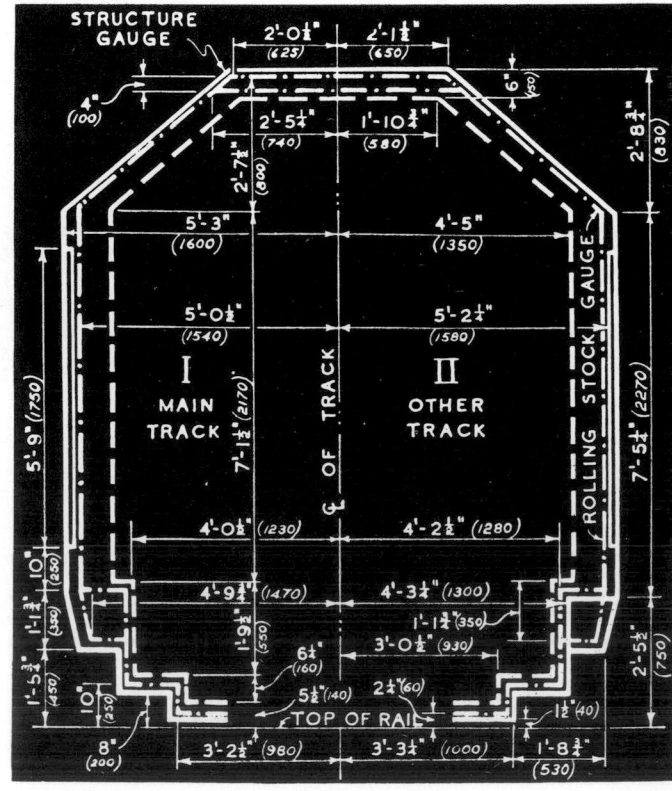

Loading gauge: secondary lines

Traction and rolling stock

A separate company, PT Industri Kereta Api (PT Inka), has been established to supervise a major programme of local freight wagon assembly, chiefly from Japanese-manufactured kits, at the Madiun workshops. The current 1979-84 investment plan envisages acquisition of 1250 extra wagons and 300 new passenger cars with which maximum speeds can be lifted from 80 to 100 km/h.

For the rack rail lines in West Sumatra six 905 kW Type HGm4/6, 55-tonne rack-and-adhesion diesel locomotives with MTU engines, Voith hydrostatic drive, and BBC electrical equipment have been acquired from SLM, Switzerland. Other traction purchases include 20 diesel railcars from Kawasaki Heavy Industries for service in Java and Sumatra, which were delivered in the summer of 1982. In 1981 tenders were sought for 215 more diesel railcars; and early in 1982 a Japanese consortium led by Sumitomo and including Kawasaki Heavy Industries, Hitachi and Nippon Sharyo Seizo Kaisha secured an initial contract for 21 cars, and also for signalling apparatus, for the first stage of the Jabotabek project. Kawasaki was also manufacturing 198 wagons for PJKA, which was seeking tenders for 200 covered fertiliser wagons for the Meneng port project. Hyundai and Daewoo are supplying 1300 coal wagons for Sumatra.

In 1982 orders worth US$60 million were placed with General Electric for 34 Type U18C 1600 kW Co-Co and 30 Type U18A1A 1600 kW A1A-A1A diesel-electric locomotives. Thyssen-Henschel secured a Dm30 million order for 15 more Type DGH 1000 diesel-hydraulic B-B locomotives to supplement 48 already operated by PJKA.

In 1984-88 PJKA intends to build 126 passenger and 1436 freight cars in its own PT Inka plant, and thereafter five emus, 10 dmus and 600 freight cars a year.

At the outset of 1982 PJKA was operating 294 steam, nine electric and 389 diesel locomotives, 40 emus, 86 diesel railcars, 1094 passenger cars and 13 515 freight wagons.

Signalling

Some 2580 route-km are now equipped with Siemens & Halske mechanical tokenless block, located at 247 centres in Java and 45 in Sumatra, and 50 additional installations were programmed for 1982-83. All-relay interlocking, already operational at Bandung and Solo, was to be provided at Cikampek, Cirebon, Yogya, Semarang and Wonokromo in 1982-83.

Track
Standard rail
1067 mm gauge: 14A 42·59 kg/m; R3 33·4 kg/m; R2 25·75 kg/m

750 mm gauge: R10 16·4 kg/m
600 mm gauge: ID 12·38 kg/m
Type of joints: Fishplates and bolts; welding also used
Cross ties (sleepers): Mainly untreated teak, 2000 × 220 × 120 mm; some metal (thickness 100 mm). Cross ties spacing: main line, 680 mm; branch line, 800 mm
Rail fastening: Base plates, spikes and screws, elastic fastenings (chiefly Pandrol)
Filling (ballast): Stone ballast, 50-70 mm
Thickness under sleeper
Main line: 8·75° = minimum radius 200 m
Branch line: 11·6° = minimum radius 150 m
Max gradient: 4%; 7% (rack sections)
Minimum curvature radius: 150 m
Max altitude: 1246 m near Garut, Java
Max axleload
Main line: 15 tons
Branch line: 8-10 tons
Max bridge loading
Main line: 8·75 tonnes/m
Branch line: 5·56 tonnes/m
Max permitted speed
Main line: Passenger trains, 100 km/h
Freight trains, 70 km/h
Branch line: Passenger trains, 59 km/h
Freight trains, 45 km/h

Diesel locomotives

Class	Wheel arrangement	Transmission	Rated power hp	Max kg	Tractive effort Continuous at kg	km/h	Max speed km/h	Wheel dia mm	Total weight tons	Length mm	No built	Year first built	Builders Engine & type	Transmission	Repowering
CC 200	Co-Co	Elec	1600	21 623	14 074		100	908	96	17 070	27	1951	12V 244E GE		Alco 12V 250 (7 locos)
CC 201	Co-Co	Elec	1950		11 825		100	952	84·8	14 133	38	1976	7 FDL 8 GE		
BB 200	A1A-A1A	Elec	875				120	1016	74·8	14 006	35	1956	B-567CR GM		
BB 201	A1A-A1A	Elec	1310	21 810		15	120	1016	78	14 026	11	1964	G12 567C GM		
BB 202	A1A-A1A	Elec	1100	21 810		12·7	100	1016	65	12 900	8	1968/ 71	GL8 645E GM		
BB 203	A1A-A1A	Elec	1500				100	904		14 133	11	1978	7 FDL 8 GE		
BB 300	B-B	Hyd	680	10 100			75	909	36	11 890	30	1956	MB 820 B		
BB 301	B-B	Hyd	1500	15 800	11 700	19	120	904	52	13 380	50	1962/ 69	MD655/12V 538TB10	L630 r U2	MB12V 652 TB11 (23 locos)
BB 302	B-B	Hyd	1100	14 520	12 500	15	80	904	44	12 810	6	1969	MB820/ 12V493TZ10	L520 r U2	
BB 303	B-B	Hyd	1150	14 100	11 500	15	90	904	42·8	12 320	42	1971/ 77/78	MB12V 493 TW10	L520 r U2	
BB 304	B-B	Hyd	1500	17 150	11 700	20	120	904	52	13 380	11	1974	MB12V 652 TB11	L720 r U2	
C 300	C	Hyd	350	9800	9250	4·5	30	904	30	8020	20	1964	MB 836 B	L 203 U	
C 301	C	Hyd	260		5750	6·5	30	877	14.5	5240	8	1969	BV 71 N60	DBG 115	
D 300	D	Hyd	340	10 200		5	50	904	34	9279	30	1956	MB 836 B	2WIL1.15	8V92GM (14 locos)
D 301	D	Hyd	340	8400		5	50	904	28	8980	80	1960	MB 836 B/2	2WIL1.15	8V92GM (22 locos) 8V71GM (7 locos) 12V71GM (6 locos) MWM TD232V12 (10 locos)

Electric locomotives

Class	Wheel arrangement	Line current	Rated output hp	Tractive effort (full field) Continuous at kg	km/h	Max speed km/h	Wheel dia mm	Weight tonnes	Length mm	No built	Year first built	Builders Mechanical parts	Electrical equipment
BBC	1AA-1AA	1500 V	1130	4200	72·5	90	1500	69·2	12 530	4	1924	BBC & Winterthur	BBC
WH	1AA-1AA	1500 V	880	5900	40	75	1350	72	15 050	6	1928		
AEG	1B-1B	1500 V	1200		70·5	90	1350	79	14 100	3	1924		

Electric railcars

Class	Wheel arrangement	Line current	Rated output hp			Max speed km/h	Wheel dia mm	Weight tonnes	Length mm	No built	Year first built	Mechanical parts	Electrical equipment
MCW5/	AA-AA	1500 V	1248			100	860	49·4	20 000	20	1976		Traction motor HS 836

Diesel railcars

Class	Wheel arrange-ment	Trans-mission	Rated power hp	Tractive effort Max kg	Tractive effort Continuous at kg	Tractive effort at kmlh	Max speed kmlh	Wheel dia mm	Total weight tons	Length mm	No built	Year first built	Builders Mechanical parts	Builders Engine & type	Builders Transmission
MBW/M MADW	D	Hyd	215	200			90	784	36	19 640	10	1964		BV-71	Diwabus U + S
MCW301	1A-2	Hyd	180		4110	10	90	774	45	20 000	12 units	1976		DMH 17H	TC-2A
MCW302	1A-2	Hyd	290		4910	10	90	774	46	20 000	26 units	1978/ 80		DMH 17HSA	TC-2S

IRAN

Ministry of Roads & Transportation

Sepahbod Gharani Avenue, Corner of Nasser Avenue, Tehran

Telephone: 899676

Minister: Dr M H Nezhadhosainian

Iranian State Railways (RAI)

Rahe-Ahan Square, Tehran

Telephone: 555120
Telegrams: Rahan

President: S M Alizadeh
Vice-Presidents
  Technical and Operating: Abdul Majid Afzal
  Finance: A Saidi
  Planning: S Afshar
  Construction: M M Khalili
Directors
  Traction: N Pourmiza
  Electrical: M H Saghatchian
  Permanent Way: R Rostami
  Communications and Signalling: A Shikh-mohammad
  Operations: Dj Hadjian
  Purchasing: Y Tahbaz
  Accounting: A Ghazvini
  Training: H R Mehrzama
  Planning: H Birdjani
  Technical Studies: M R Nabavi

Gauge: 1435 mm; 1676 mm
Route length: 4473 km; 94 km
Electrification: 145 km at 25 kV 50 Hz ac

Political upheavals and the conflict with Iraq have slowed one of the world's largest rail expansion programmes. It was to modernise and extend the country's rail network to link all major urban and industrial centres by the creation of 10 000 km of new tracks and the electrification and doubling of existing lines. Little had been achieved, however, before the revolution which deposed the Shah in 1979 and since then only one scheme has been pursued.

The first project provided for the electrification of the Bandar Shahpur-Andimeshk-Tehran line and its double-tracking, because of the projected expansion of port facilities at Bandar Shahpur.

The western tracks connecting Tehran with Turkey via Tabriz were also to be electrified and transformed from single to double track. New tracks were to be laid between Mianeh and Tabriz to shorten the Tehran-Tabriz line by 110 km. A similar project was planned for the Tehran-Isfahan-Zarand line and construction work on the 80 km stretch between Zarand and Kerman was actually completed in 1978.

The existing Tehran-Mashad line was to be doubled, realigned and electrified for operation at up to 240 km/h.

Railway experts were also working on another set of plans to extend the existing network. These provided for construction of 700 km of track to connect Bandar Abbas with Kerman and integrate the Persian Gulf port with the nation-wide network, and for a link with Pakistan by construction of 550 km of track from Kerman to the border at Zahedan. RAI's presently isolated stretch of 1676 mm-gauge railway connects Zahedan with the Pakistan frontier at Mirjaveh.

Other projects envisaged the creation of lines from Isfahan to the Soviet border, a line along the Caspian coast, an Isfahan-Shiraz-Bushehr line and Bandar Pahlavi-Qazvin, Qom-Qasr-e-Shirin (Iraq border), Andimeshk-Kermanshah-Sanandaj-Maragheh, Mashad-Zahedan-Chahbahar railways, also a Persian Gulf coastal line to connect Bandar Abbas with Bandar Shahpur.

With the completion of these projects the country's total track would be increased from 4500 to more than 14 000 km, connecting all major Iranian urban and industrial centres and linking the country's rail network to the Soviet Union, Pakistan, Afghanistan, Turkey and Iraq.

The only known progress until 1982 had been with construction of the 700 km Bafq-Sirjan-Bandar Abbas and 550 km Kerman-Zahedan lines, and with the 25 kV 50 Hz electrification over the 145 km from Tabriz to the USSR border at Djulfa, executed by Technoexport of the USSR. This was completed but long inoperative for lack of traction. In 1982, however, delivery began of eight 3600 kW locomotives based on Swedish State Railways Type Rc 4, with electrical equipment by ASEA and bodywork by SGP of Austria. Shortly afterwards RAI announced that three main projects in the expansion plan would be pressed ahead; the line from Kerman to the Strait of Harmuz port, Bandar-Abbas, for completion by 1987; the Kerman-Zahedan line, to be started in 1983; and a 110 km line from Ahwaz to Bandar Khomeini, considered vital for imports traffic.

Motive power
At the end of 1981 RAI's motive power fleet consisted of 414 diesel-electric locomotives (183 of 1500 kW power or higher) and four Turbotrains from ANF-Frangeco, France.

Standard diesel locomotives operated by RAI were provided by General Motors. 134 GM 3300 hp locomotives have been delivered, but in 1981 RAI was running a number of borrowed Soviet Railways locomotives to overcome difficulties in procuring spares for its US-built units. During 1981 RAI agreed a barter arrangement for delivery of 50 locomotives from Romania against a supply of oil.

For heavy shunting, RAI has 28 Hitachi locomotives with an output of 1050 hp, continuous tractive effort of 12·4 tonnes, Bo-Bo axle arrangement and top speed of 100 km/h.

Rolling stock
At the end of 1981 RAI had a fleet of 12 262 freight wagons, and operated 570 passenger cars.

Track
Standard rail
Main line
Type U33, 46 kg/m
Type IIA, 38·4 kg/m in 12·5 m lengths
Type III, 33·5 kg/m in 12 m lengths
Branch line
Type IV, 30·9 kg/m in 12·8 m lengths
American, 34·7 kg/m in 10 m lengths
Rail joints: 4 and 6-hole fishplates; and welding
Cross ties (sleepers): Creosote impregnated hardwood, steel and concrete. Wood 2600 × 250 × 150 mm. Steel 2400 × 300 × 70 mm. Concrete sleepers under welded rail
Spacing
Wood sleepers: 1360 per km
Steel sleepers: 1450 per km
Rail fastenings
Wood sleepers: sole plates, screws and bolts
Steel sleepers: clips and bolts
Filling: Part broken stone, and part river ballast; minimum 200 mm under sleepers
Max curvature: 7·9° = minimum radius 220 m
Longest continuous gradient: 16 km of 2·8% (1 in 36) grade between Firouzkouh and Gadouk
Max altitude: 2177 m near Nourabad station
Max axleloading: 25 tons
Max permitted speed
Freight trains: 55 km/h
Passenger trains: 80 km/h

General Motors Co-Co No 90-802

Tehran station with Hitachi Bo-Bo locomotive on station pilot duties

IRAQ

Ministry of Transport

Karrada Dakhil, Baghdad

Minister: S Ghaidan

Iraqi Republican Railways (IRR)

Central Station, Damascus Square, Baghdad

Telephone: 30011
Telex: 212272

President: T T Abdul Razzak
Directors General
  Traffic and Operations: M Mahommed Mahdi
  Administration: Khalid S Ammar
  Track: Hashim Habib Sarsam

New Railways Implementation Authority

Central Station, Damascus Square, Baghdad

Telephone: 30021

Secretary-General: Raad al Umari

Gauge: 1435 mm; 1000 mm
Route length: 1502 km; 533 km

New lines

A state of war with Iran has not deterred Iraq from pressing ahead with its grandiose plan to invest the equivalent of US$ 20 000 million, largely obtained from oil, minerals and other state industry profits, in 2700 km of new railways. The New Railways Implementation Authority (NRIA) was established in September 1980 to co-ordinate the construction activity. Its objective is to create high-capacity, standard-gauge rail links between all major cities in the country.

The first of the new projects was completed in 1981. This was a 115 km line linking the phosphate mines at Akashat in the west of the country to a fertiliser plant at Al Qaim. Consultants for this project were Sotecni of Italy and contractors, Mendes Junior.

Al Qaim, in the Euphrates valley, stands on the route of a 404 km line under construction from Baghdad via Ramadi and Haditha to the Syrian border at Husaiba, for which the contractors are also Mendes Junior. Costed at over US$ 2500 million, inclusive of necessary motive power and rolling stock, this new line was reaching completion in 1983. Its building has entailed earthworks aggregating 44 million cubic metres, 2·7 million cubic metres

of new ballast, 640 000 cubic metres of concrete, 120 000 tonnes of rail and 1·667 million concrete sleepers. Like all new lines it has been engineered for 250 km/h, partly for ease of maintenance in the immediate future, when speeds will be limited to 140 km/h for passenger and 100 km/h for freight; but a transitory period of 200 km/h and 120 km/h freight speed is envisaged later in the advance to the higher speed, particularly if it is decided to embark upon electrification. Track specifications call for UIC 60 kg/m rail fastened by Pandrol clips to prestressed concrete monobloc sleepers, with ballast depth of 350 mm. The main contractor for the Baghdad-Usaiba line's colour-light signalling and CTC is WSSB of the German Democratic Republic; the National Buildings Construction Corporation of India has the Rs 630 million contract for the line's stations and traction depots and workshops.

From Haditha on this route a 252 km transversal, built initially as single track with provision for later doubling, is under construction via Baiji to Kirkuk, which involves bridging the Euphrates, Tigris and Therthar rivers. Consultants for the scheme, which includes a new marshalling yard and passenger terminal at Kirkuk and was launched in 1982 for completion by 1986, have been Deconsult. The work is being executed by Hyundai Engineering and Namkwang Construction under project management by Deconsult and its sub-contractors, China Railway Foreign Service Corporation. The line will be CTC-controlled with the complement of track-to-train road and hot box detectors.

At present the line from Baghdad via Khanaqin to Kirkuk and Erbil is metre-gauge. This is to be replaced by a 480 km standard-gauge line from Baghdad to Mosul on a more direct route, with a branch to Khanaqin (at present dubious because of relations with Iran) and a 160 km extension beyond Mosul to Zakho on the Turkish border. Sofrerail were consultants for the preliminary study of the Baghdad-Mosul scheme, Henderson Busby for the continuation to Zakho. At the start of 1983 tender documents were in preparation.

The largest single project embraces a new 910 km double-track route south from Baghdad to the port of Um Qasr. At Kut the line will split, the primary arm making for Basra via Nasiryah, the secondary arm taking the Tigris route via Amara. This new route would be constructed with a ruling gradient of 0·5 per cent and a minimum curve radius of 5000 metres. The scheme envisages a new marshalling yard at Shuiaba. Engineering design has been undertaken by Henderson Busby and civil engineering tenders for three of the line's six sections were under consideration early in 1983. In 1982 Transmark, British Rail's consultancy, was commissioned to undertake an upgrading design study, including an electrification assessment, for the existing 543 km route between Baghdad and Basra via Diwaniya (together with similar work on the 425 km metre-gauge line from Baghdad to Kirkuk and Erbil).

A line already under construction south of Bagh-

dad is a 242 km double-track bypass to the west of the present Baghdad-Basra line, which has been conceived to increase the latter's capacity and serve new cement plants. Running from Samawa northwards to Mussayib, it is due for completion in 1984. Consultants have been Sotecni and the first 30 km were being built by IRCON of India, which also has the line's signalling and telecommunications equipment contract. Sotecni have also been the consultants for a prospective 130 km line from Karbala to Ramadi, to provide access to the north for cement plants at Karbala.

A key component of the new main-line plans is a Baghdad Belt Line of 112 km, from which the new trunk routes would spring. This scheme, involving three major river bridges and a 7·5 km tunnel, is also motivated by anxiety to separate Baghdad area passenger and freight traffic to the maximum extent. Again Sotecni are the main consultants, with Sofrerail of France as sub-consultants, and construction bids were likely to be called in 1983. Freight handling is to be concentrated on a new yard, depot and workshop complex at Yousifia, in south-west Baghdad. A new locomotive workshop is being erected near Baghdad by the Francorail consortium.

Other new line projects include a 150 km line from Salman Pak, south-east of Baghdad on the putative route of the new Baghdad-Kut line, to Khanaqin; and a 95 km branch from Basra to the port of Fao, on the Shatt al Arab waterway. The first of these, for which Sofrerail are the consultants, is likely to be low on the priority list because of the hostilities with Iran. Henderson Busby has completed a feasibility study of the second.

Agreement has been concluded between Iraq and Turkey to renew studies of a direct link between the two countries' rail systems, to avoid the present 70 km transit of Syrian territory between Kurtalan and Mosul.

Traction and rolling stock

Huge orders for locomotives and rolling stock have already been placed in connection with the network expansion programme. Placement of contracts supervised by Henderson Busby, in partnership with Guthrie and Craig, of the UK, have entrusted Francorail-MTE with an order for 72 3600 hp diesel-electric locomotives for the Baghdad-Husaiba line, Pragoinvest with one for 21 1100 hp diesel shunters, Kolmex with one for 2505 freight wagons, ANF-Industrie with one for 260 special-purpose freight wagons and Invest-Import of Yugoslavia with one for 78 passenger cars and 1960 freight vehicles. Bombardier of Canada was commissioned to supply spares worth US$ 14·5 million for the 61 2000 hp Type MXS620 diesel locomotives the company delivered in 1975-76. Total orders covered by the 1983 budget comprised 146 main-line and 161 shunting locomotives, 384 passenger cars and 6016 freight wagons.

Also in 1981 Thyssen-Henschel won an order worth DM250 million for 82 2485 hp mixed-traffic

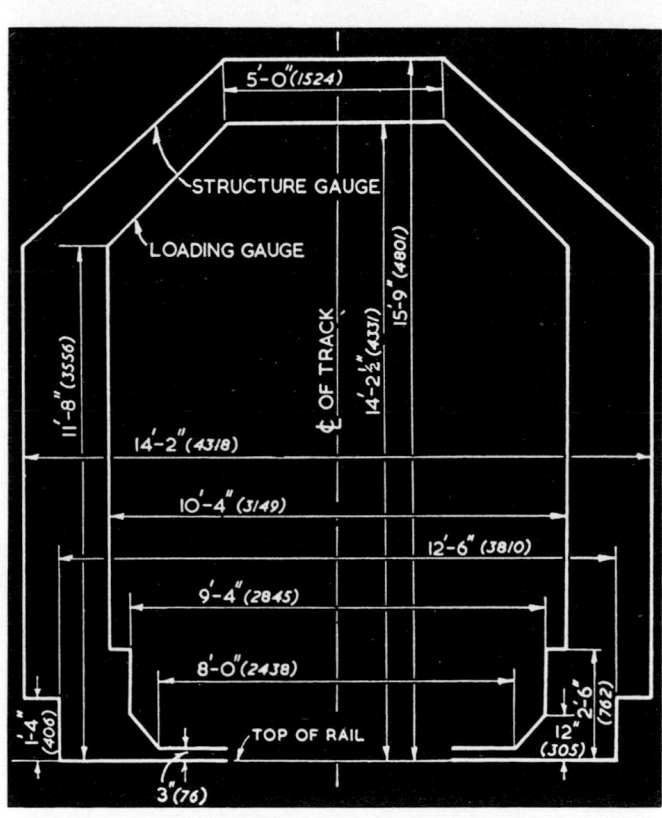

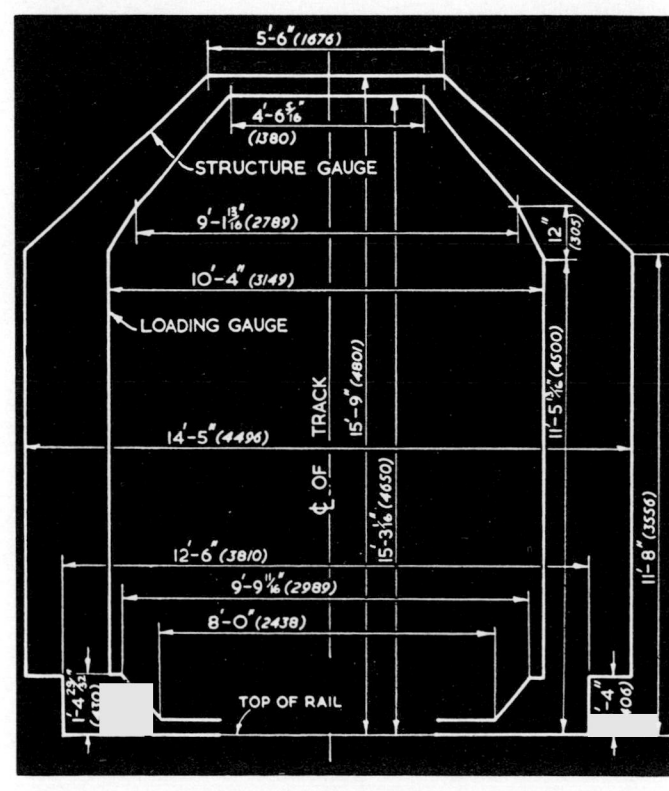

diesel-electric locomotives, to be delivered from 1983 onwards. In 1982 ANF-Industrie was contracted to supply between 1983 and 1985 a total of 236 air-conditioned passenger cars including 25 luggage-generator coaches, 70 first-class couchette cars, 10 restaurant cars, 25 sleepers, 100 second-class day cars and six special cars for VIP travellers.

In 1982 the railway was operating 259 diesel-electric locomotives, 400 passenger cars and 5931 freight wagons on 1435 mm gauge. The metre-gauge system operated 73 steam locomotives, 158 passenger cars and 2746 freight wagons.

IRELAND

Department of Transport

Kildare Street, Dublin 2

Telephone: 01 789522
Telex: 24651

Minister: Jim Mitchell
Secretary: N McMahon

Córas Iompair Éireann (CIE)
Irish Transport Company

Heuston Station, Dublin 8

Telephone: 771871
Telex: 5153

Chairman of the Board: Liam St John Devlin
Members: J F Higgins
L O'Brien
H L McKee
N Faller
S Linehan
J Keenan
M Purcell
T Flynn
R O Donovan
J W F Loughlin
T Tobin
General Manager: J F Higgins
Assistant General Managers
Marketing: C Finegan
Personnel: P Murphy
Finance: M Grace
Operations: E J O'Connor
Secretary: P G Byrne
Solicitor: M J Kenny
Purchasing Officer: D V Stephens
Mechanical Engineer (Rail): R P Grainger
Chief Civil Engineer: P O Jennings
Manager, Freight Division: D Looney
Freight Marketing Manager: W Flannery
Passenger Marketing Manager: H M Oliver
Manager, Strategic and Corporate Planning: J Markham
Staff Relations Manager: J B Hodgins
Computer Services Manager: T J Curtin
Manager, Dublin City Services: J Browne
Manager, Public Affairs: D O Máolalai
Area Managers
Dublin: E O'Connor
Cork: E B Kehoe
Galway: C MacGiolla Ri
Limerick: N Kennedy
Waterford: J A O'Connor

Gauge: 1600 mm
Route length: 1989 km

Transport development
Since 1980 the management of Córas Iompair Éireann (CIE) has been faced with the results of two investigations by independent analysts. In the first report, submitted early in 1980, Prof Christopher Foster of the London School of Economics questioned whether Irish railways had any enduring future. The country, he argued, was particularly unsuited to commercial railway operation and its use of railways was the lowest in the EEC; were the railways to be closed, he calculated that the country would be saved £135 million over a five-year period.

Meanwhile the then Government had already commissioned McKinsey International to undertake an exhaustive investigation of all CIE activity. Their 300-page report, published early in 1981, reckoned that over a span of 25 years the difference in cost to the community of preserving or closing CIE's core main-line system would be negligible: so while there was no case for expanding the rail system, there was equally none for significant closures. That apart, however, McKinsey advocated some drastic reshaping of the national transport services.

The main conclusions affecting the railways were not merely that they should be divorced from bus activity through a break-up of CIE into three new and independent companies. They should also be

Two-car emu by Linke-Hofmann-Busch for Howth-Bray electrification

Class B diesel-electric Bo-Bo and Waterford-Dublin unit container train for Bell Lines

Class B diesel-electric Bo-Bo and Drogheda-Dublin unit cement train

debarred from road freight operation, which would effectively confine them to trainload service. Such a simplified railway, said McKinsey, would have no need of CIE's separate Freight Division and could be administered by one all-purpose headquarters, the more so as CIE's present area management structure would be redundant once the road activity was hived-off. Moreover, in McKinsey's view, rail management's role should be further reduced to that of a contractor by vesting policy-making authority for levels of service and pricing in the Department of Transport, so that the putative Railways Board would be responsible only for efficient operation, containment of cost and productivity. The then Government's reception was decidedly guarded and since then other national anxieties have pre-empted political and public concern.

McKinsey's pronouncements were depressing reward for CIE's rationalising response to the consultants' findings in a 1971 study also commissioned by the Government. Three years later CIE unveiled a Development Plan to implement the McKinsey recommendations which featured a particularly sweeping reorganisation of the rail freight business, then operating largely as it had done between the wars. Those plans were nearly all implemented by 1980.

Developments on the passenger side covered the provision of a total fleet of air-conditioned rolling stock, and this with the purchase of 18 Class 071 locomotives provide more comfortable service and faster journey times between all major locations.

Aimed at containing the rising railway deficit, the plan involved modernisation of stations and depots, introduction of new equipment and handling methods and redeployment of manpower. The plan took six years to implement.

Government support pegged

In 1983 progress was put seriously at risk by CIE's inevitable inclusion in activities hit by stringent Government measures to deal with the country's worsening economic state. The Government subvention for all CIE operations in 1983 was pegged at £86 million and CIE was forbidden to continue external borrowing to close any remaining gap between income and expenditure. Cutbacks in rail as well as bus services were consequently under consideration, as well as deferment of some resignalling and station improvement work. Planned investment in all CIE operations was reduced by 25 per cent to £60 million, of which £40 million was earmarked for the Dublin suburban electrification.

Freight traffic

Less-than-wagonload freight has been reshaped into a framework of economical trunk train working between a limited number of road-served transhipment terminals. CIE adopted containerisation for this Uniload system, which operates between 40 railheads. The sundries are packed into caged pallets which are then loaded in delivery sequence into 10-foot ISO containers. Major terminals in the network, such as Dublin North Wall, which was comprehensively rebuilt for the new concept, and Cork North Esk are gantry crane-equipped for container trans-shipment; elsewhere transfer is by fork-lift. A fleet of almost 200 skeletal rail wagons, 42 feet (12·8 m) long and able to carry four containers, was procured for the reorganised system. Recently rising traffic in bagged domestic coal has been fitted into the container system, using a version of the curtain-sided container.

The running of a regular service of special-purpose vehicles for major enterprises has become a steadily larger component of CIE rail freight working since the launch of the Development Plan. One or two of these deals have involved the reopening of closed lines to cater for new industries.

Mechanisation of loading and discharge was a key objective of the 1974 Development Plan and this has helped to implant CIE firmly in the movement of fertiliser and cement from production centres to railhead distribution stores. For both traffic specialised wagons have been produced at Inchicore, in the case of cement two types, one for bagged, the other for bulk traffic.

By the close of the 1970s CIE's rail freight traffic volume was almost 50 per cent higher than in 1965, but the recession has stunted growth and tonnage is currently on a plateau of around 3·75 million tonnes a year. Nevertheless, CIE management retains its confidence that rail carryings could reach 8 million tonnes a year by early the next century if there is no impediment to its Development Plan strategy, which it is unfolding in a rolling programme of five-year plans.

Mechanised placement of cwr track for Howth-Bray electrification

Ticket-operated entry/exit gates at Pearse station on Howth-Bray electrified route

Traffic

	1979	1980	1981
Freight tonnage (000)	3800	3629	3722
Freight tonne-km (million)	629	637	691·5
Average wagon load (tonnes)	12·3	13·9	14·45
Passenger-km (million)	1112·5	1032	994·6
Passenger journeys (000)	17 886	16 654	15 358

Finances
Revenue

	1979	1980	1981
		(£000)	
Passenger	23 340	27 820	29 441
Freight	11 326	12 929	16 004
Total	34 666	40 749	45 445

Expenditure

Staff	38 847	47 281	56 735
Materials and services	27 961	34 839	38 897
Depreciation	3470	3819	4407
Financial charges	3943	4540	5625
Total	74 221	90 479	105 664

Passenger traffic

CIE also believes that it can double its main-line passenger traffic to 17 million journeys a year by 2005. Hopes are dependent on CIE's ability to continue the infrastructure improvements carried out on its main lines in the past decade, such as resignalling and installation of well-aligned track with continuous welded rail, and thereby to cut journey times between main centres still shorter. In mind, for instance, is a transit of 2 hours 20 minutes for the 265·5 km from Dublin to Cork instead of the present best of 2 hours 55 minutes, and one of 3 hours for the 264 km from Dublin to Westport, as against a current best of 3¾ hours.

Motive power and rolling stock

CIE's motive power fleet in 1982 consisted of 192 diesel locomotives. Freight wagons totalled 3564; passenger coaches 433.

Following purchase of 95 passenger cars based on British Rail's Mk II Inter-City design in 1970, CIE in 1981 placed an order with British Rail Engineering Ltd for 124 cars based on the BR Mk III design, but with automatically-closed entrance doors in aluminium. A proportion of the order is to be supplied in kits for assembly at CIE's Inchicore works. Deliveries are due to commence in late 1983. Inchicore works built 28 bogie tippler wagons for CIE in 1982.

Track

Standard rail: Flat bottom; 113, 95, 92 and 85 lb/yd. Bullhead; 90, 87 and 85 lb/yd
Cross ties (sleepers): Timber, 130 mm thickness; concrete, 210 mm thickness
Spacing: Concrete 1454/km plain track, 1555/km curved track; timber, 1313/km straight and curved track
Rail fastenings: Wood sleepers, CI chairs and baseplates; concrete sleepers, H-M & Pandrol fastenings
Minimum curvature radius
Running lines: 140 m
Sidings: 80 m
Max gradient: 1 in 40
Longest continuous gradient: 8·45 km, with 1% (1 in 100) ruling gradient
Max altitude: 192 m at Barnagh, Co Kerry
Max permitted speed: 120 km/h
Max axleloads: 16·75 tonnes for locomotives, 18·5 tonnes for wagons

Electrification

Following the recommendations of a Dublin Trans-portation Study of 1971, which advocated creation of a rapid transit rail system in the city, 36·2 route-km are being electrified at 1·5 kV dc from Bray, 23·3 km south of Dublin Connolly station, to Howth, 12·9 km to the north. On completion CIE is hopeful of Government authority for extension from Bray southward to Greystones with the addition of a branch to the new town of Tallacht, which will ultimately house 80 000. Inauguration of the Howth-Bray electrification was scheduled for September 1983. The 40 two-car emus to run the service, which are being built by Linke-Hofmann-Busch, with thyristor chopper-controlled traction equipment by GEC Traction, have air suspension and passenger-operated sliding doors and feature regenerative braking.

Except on the 5·6 km Howth Junction-Howth branch the emus will share the route with diesel locomotive-hauled trains, for which lineside colour-light signalling is being retained. The emus will also have continuous cab signalling with automatic braking control, activated by coded currents passed through the running rails, detected by coils on the emus and processed on board, plus track-to-train radio. The resignalling work has been executed by Wabco Westinghouse. All level crossings on the route will be remotely controlled from a new centre at Connolly with TV monitoring back-up.

Class AR diesel-electric Co-Co and Dublin-Cork express

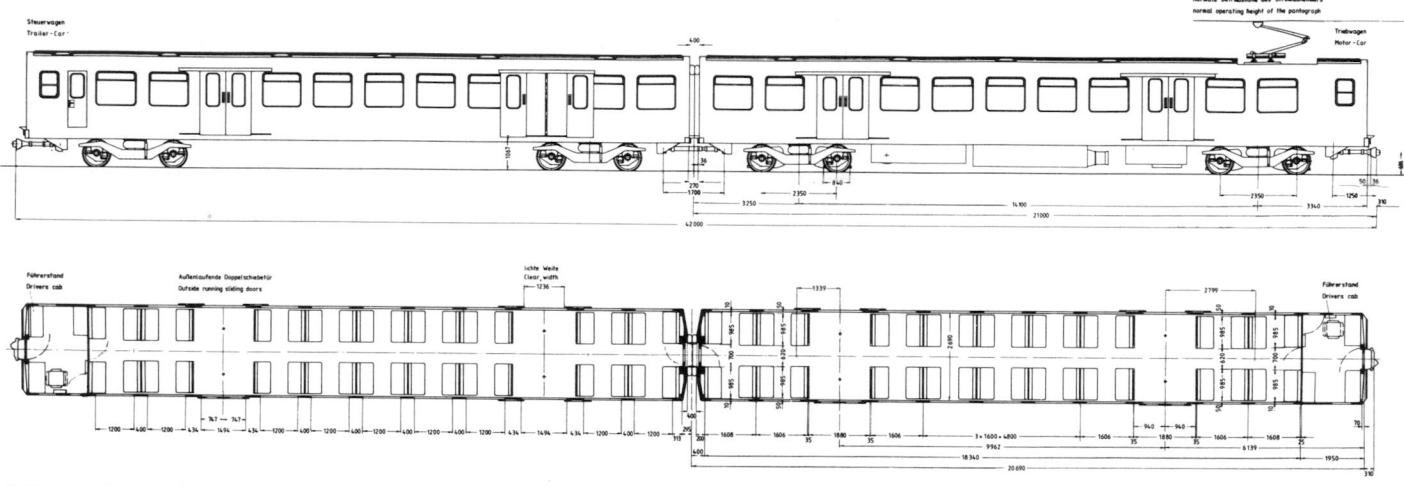

Dublin suburban emu by Linke-Hofmann-Busch

Diesel locomotives

Class	Wheel arrange-ment	Trans-mission	Rated power hp	Max lb (kg)	Tractive effort Continuous at lb (kg)	Continuous at mph (km/h)	Max speed mph (km/h)	Wheel dia in (mm)	Total weight tons (tonnes)	Length ft in (mm)	No built	First built	Builders Mechanical parts	Engine & type	Transmission
071	Co-Co	Elec	2475/ 2250	65 000 (29 484)	43 264 (19 625)	16·4 (26·39)	89 (143·2)	40 (1016)	99 (100·6)	51' 0'' (15 545)	18	1976	GM	GM12-645 E3	
AR (01)	Co-Co	Elec	1325/ 1250	54 000 (24 494)	18 000 (8165)	21·5 (34·6)	75 (120·7)	38 (965)	82 (83·3)	51' 0'' (15 545)	50	1955/ 56	Metro-Cammell	GM12-645 E	
AR (01)	Co-Co	Elec	1650/ 1500	43 300 (19 656)	22 415 (10 166)	21·5 (34·6)	75 (120·7)	38 (965)	82 (83·3)	51' 0'' (15 545)	9	1956	Metro-Cammell	GM 12-645	
B (121)	Bo-Bo	Elec	950/ 875	36 000 (16 330)	30 400 (13 789)	8 (12·9)	77 (123·9)	40 (1016)	64 (65)	39' 10'' (12 141)	15	1961	GM	GM 567 CA	
B (141)	Bo-Bo	Elec	950/ 875	36 000 (16 330)	27 500 (34 304)	9 (14·5)	77 (123·9)	40 (1016)	67 (68)	44' 0½'' (13 424)	37	1962/ 63	GM	GM 567 CR	
B (181)	Bo-Bo	Elec	1100/ 1000	37 500 (17 010)	26 400 (11 975)	11 (17·7)	89 (143·2)	40 (1016)	67 (68)	44' 0½'' (13 424)	12	1966	GM	GM B-645 E	
CR (201)	Bo-Bo	Elec	1100/ 1040	34 200 (15 513)	14 200 (6441)	22·2 (35·7)	75 (120·7)	38 (965)	61½ (62·5)	42' 0'' (12 802)	31	1957/ 58	Metro-Cammell	GM B-645 E	
CR (201)	Bo-Bo	Elec	950	29 500 (13 378)	12 250 (5556)	22·2 (35·7)	75 (120·7)	38 (965)	61½ (62·5)	42' 0'' (12 802)	2	1958	Metro-Cammell	Maybach	
E (401)	0-6-0	Hyd	400	25 300 (11 476)	—	—	—	38 (965)	42¾ (43·4)	31' 4¼'' (9 557)	27	1962/ 63	CIE	Maybach MD 650	

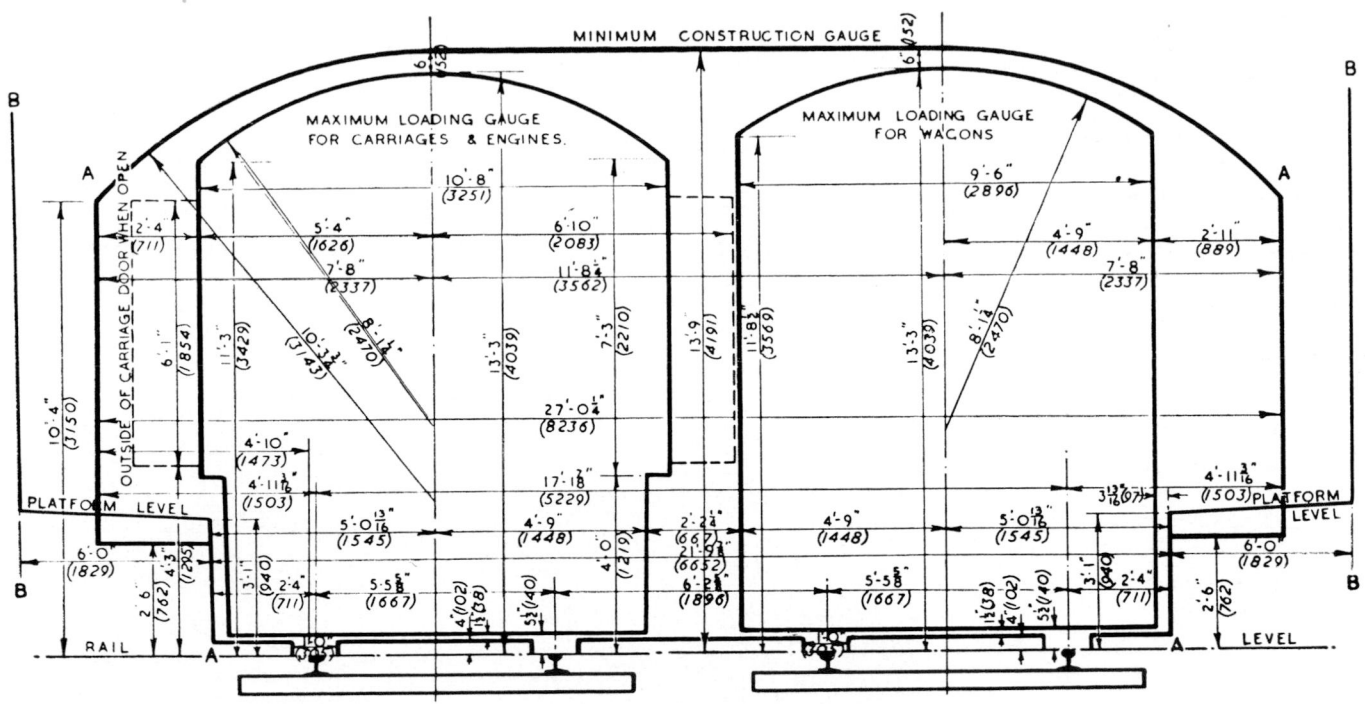

NOTE
AA Minimum distance for all works along line including signal boxes, signal posts, lamps etc.
BB Minimum distance for all station works above platform level. Level of passenger platforms only may be inside the construction gauge.

ISRAEL

Ministry of Transportation

1 Eben Gabirol, Jerusalem

Minister: Meir Amit
Director General: Ehud Shillo

Israel Railways (IR)

Central Station, PO Box 44, Haifa

Telephone: 04 641761
Telegrams: Rakevet, Haifa
Telex: 46570

General Manager: Zvi Tsafriri
Deputy General Manager: I Bar-Ilan
Deputy General Manager (Admin): L Heyman
Traffic and Commercial Manager: E Inbal
Assistant General Manager and Public Relations:
D Guy
Chief Engineer: K Slutzker
Head of Planning and Development: A Golan
Head, Supply and Stores Department: P Trichter
Chief Signalling and Telecommunications Engineer: M Lozar
Legal Adviser: H Malka
Chief Economist: I Falkov

Gauge: 1435 mm
Route length: 516 km (Sinai line: 86 km)

Transport development
Israel Railways are state-owned and operated as a separate economic enterprise by the Ministry of Transport. The Government and the Knesset (Parliament) Economic Committee determine the tariffs as part of general transport policy. Passenger services are subsidised at the rate of about 50 per cent of their cost, freight services at 12 per cent. Permanent employees are considered civil servants. They work in three shifts round the clock. The network is entirely single line.

Passenger
Only 230 route-km are operated by passenger trains, because of the strong national competition from Dan-Egged bus services, which cover a 10 000 route-km network with some 5000 vehicles. The railway's share of the national travel market, in terms of passenger-km, is less than five per cent. On the main Haifa-Tel Aviv route, however, average transit speed is 90 km/h, compared with 65 km/h by the buses. Following a slump of 40 per cent in passenger journeys between 1972 and 1979, the pres-

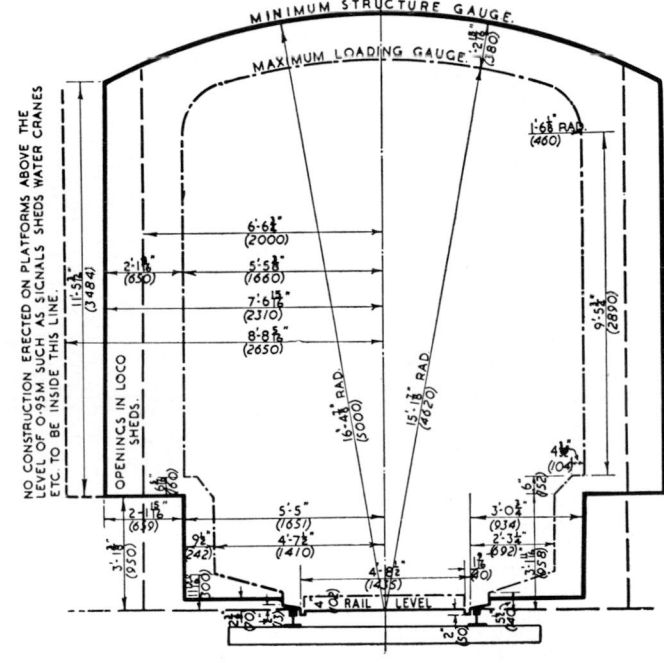

Structure and loading gauge for
1435 mm standard-gauge track

Traffic	1979/80	1980/81	1981/82
Passenger journeys (million)	2·9	3·2	3·14
Passenger/km (million)	222	246	242·16
Freight tonnage (million)	5·1	5·4	5·32
Freight tonne-km (million)	768	810	805·8

ent level is far below the 388 million recorded in 1972.

Freight
In contrast to passenger traffic, the volume of freight has almost doubled since 1972, when only 421 million tonne-km were recorded. In this sector IR's market share is 20 per cent. Roughly half the tonnage is potash from the Dead Sea and phosphates from Oron and Har Zin, which are conveyed over the Negev line to the port of Ashdod in unit trains of up to 4000 tonnes hauled by two GM Type G26 2200 hp Co-Co diesel-electrics in multiple. Container traffic has been developed from Haifa.

Investment
To relieve the overburdened Negev line and shorten the previously circuitous route of the unit mineral

trains to Ashdod via Lod, a 21 km link has been completed from Qyryat Gat, on the Negev line between Be'er-Sheva and Lod, and Ashqelon, south of Ashdod. This has shortened the unit trains' route by 80 km. The project was a necessary prelude to the long-cherished but frequently deferred construction of a 160 km line from Har Zin, reached in 1977, to the Red Sea port of Eilat, for which an annual freight volume of 2·3 million tonnes has been forecast.

A 6 km branch line has been built from a point near Pardess Hanna to the 1400 MW Hadera power station projected for the alternative use of oil or coal, both imported. Daily consumption of coal, imported via Haifa in the initial stage, later on via Eilat, is 10 000 tons. Seven coal trains run from Haifa to the station every 24 hours, mainly at night. The investment in all these facilities is estimated at IL 300 million (1978 prices), including special rolling stock.

The Ministry of Transportation has approved construction of a branch from Nahil Zin to a potash works at Sedom, on the Dead Sea.

In 1982 Israel Railways announced a public investment project costing an estimated US$666 million, covering the period until the year 2000. The Sedom-Ein to Hazeva line will be extended towards the south as far as Eilat, and there are also plans in this phase to build a station at Tzomet Remez and improve the Ashqelon to Ashdod line.

At a later stage, it is hoped to construct a new, more direct link between Tel Aviv and Jerusalem, as well as a new line to the north, linking Qiryat-Shemone and Carmiel. Finally, the coastal route (Naharya to Tel Aviv) will be electrified.

Investment

Investments totalling US$24·48 million planned for 1983 included outlays of: US$2·26 million for two main-line diesel-electric locomotives; US$14·76 million for 15 passenger cars; US$2·4 million for 102 freight wagons; and US$40·1 million on infrastructure.

Traction and rolling stock

Diesel locomotive stock comprises 41 main-line units, consisting of 27 GM Type G12 1425 hp units delivered 1952-61, five GM Type G16 1950 hp units delivered 1960-61, and nine GM Type G26 2200 hp units delivered 1971-78; and 18 diesel-hydraulic shunters, mostly of Maybach and Deutz manufacture. Coaching stock comprises 95 vehicles, including buffet cars and eight British Rail Mk II cars imported in 1977; West German-built dmu sets of 1956 have been de-motorised and are used as hauled stock. Freight stock totals 2110 vehicles.

ITALY

Ministry of Transport

Piazza della Croce Rossa, 00100 Rome

Minister: Mario Casalinuovo

Italian State Railways (FS)
Ferrovie dello Stato Italia

Piazza della Croce Rossa, 00100 Rome

Telephone: 06 855 667
Telegrams: Ferstato, Rome
Telex: 610089

Director General: Ercole Semenza
Vice-Directors-General: G de Campora
  L Misiti
  A D'Alessio
  A Bonforti
Heads of Departments
  Operations: L Chiara
  Commercial and Traffic: Mauro Ferretti
  Motive Power and Rolling Stock: Eduardo Cardini
  Electrical Installations: Renato Proia
  Maintenance and Construction: G Ruoppolo
  Administration: A Amerio
  Financial: F de Simone
  Supplies and Stores: R Maggi
  Medical: Mario Monti
  Research Institute: Giulio Giovanardi
Divisional Managers
  Ancona: Aristide Loria
  Bari: G Massaro
  Bologna: L Marino
  Cagliari: D Gagliardo
  Florence: Ferdinando Salvatore
  Genoa: S Lattore
  Milan: Federico Renzulli
  Naples: L Parisella
  Palermo: Armando Colombo
  Reggio Calabria: Antonino Bitto
  Rome: E Mori
  Turin: L Ballatore
  Trieste: R Troilo
  Venice: Quirido Castellani
  Verona: Salvatore Puccio

Gauge: 1435 mm; 950 mm (Sardinia)
Route length: 16 403 km; 71 km
Electrification: 8807 km at 3 kV dc

Transport development

Italian State Railways (FS) operates as a governmental department. Under a law passed in 1980 FS now has more autonomy and commercial freedom (previously most FS plans and activities were controlled by the Ministry of Transport). The Minister retains responsibility for broad strategy decisions only, leaving operations and planning in the hands of the railway's board and director general.

Finance
Revenue	1981
	(L million)
Passengers and baggage	2 096 324·8
Freight and postal traffic	937 257·6
Other, including compensations	1 935 899·4
Total	4 964 481·8

Expenditure
Administration	230 411·7
Operation	2 093 761·9
Traction and rolling stock	2 063 771·9
Fixed installations	1 466 379·1
Financial charges	573 928·5
Total	6 408 253·1

Class E633 3 kV dc full chopper locomotive

Type nB2 coach for short- and medium-haul regional services

Traffic

	1978	1979	1980	1981	1982
		(million)			
Total passenger journeys	390·2	385·8	381·4	395·8	396
Total passenger-km	39 200	39 700	39 600	40 100	40 277
Total freight tonnes	50·92	54·4	56·35	50·96	50
Total freight tonne-km	16 639	17 742	18 384	17 115	16 856

Integral plan

After years of uncertainty resulting from the precarious state of the national economy, the railways at last seem to be assured of funds for a substantial programme of improvements. In December 1980 an Integral Plan (*Piano Integrativo*) was approved by the Transport Commission of the Chamber Deputies and in September 1981 the necessary decree was signed by Transport Minister Balzamo of the then Government of Signor Spadolini. This budgeted for the FS a total of L 12 450 000 million over the period to 1985. It was recognised, however, that even this sum would be inadequate to execute all urgently needed works and additional funds were sought in loans; during 1981 US$ 500 million were obtained from an international consortium.

Of the total sum, L 8 800 000 million was to be spent on infrastructure improvements, the remainder on traction and rolling stock. It was also ordained that 43 per cent of the infrastructure money should be invested in the southern half of the country.

The plan envisages acquisition of 340 new dc electric locomotives (including 25 for Sardinia), 95 line-

haul diesel locomotives, 270 shunting locomotives, 1100 inter-city passenger cars, 1250 short-haul passenger cars, 30 self-service cafeteria cars, 400 couchette cars, 60 sleeping cars, 500 commuter passenger cars and 12 000 freight wagons, including substantial numbers of container and piggyback vehicles.

Under the infrastructure heading the plan put priority on improvements affecting international traffic, which, moreover, the EEC made a prerequisite for any financial assistance from Community funds. Such aid was highly desirable because the amount allocated to some of the Plan's projects fell some way short of their total cost: for the Verona-Bologna route double-tracking, for instance, L 41 000 million as against L 200 000 million; for similar widening of the Adriatic dorsal from Termoli to Vasto, L 120 000 million against L 400 000 million; and for doubling between Parma and La Spezia, L 120 000 million against L 300 000 million.

A considerable amount of four- and double-tracking is scheduled in the Integral Plan, the former chiefly to segregate urban commuter traffic, the latter in a number of cases to enlarge the capacity of some important routes, such as Genoa-Ventimiglia, Ancona-Bari-Lecce and Udine-Tarvisio. Apart from the Rome-Florence Direttissima (see below), the four-tracking schemes cover: Turin to Trofarello (9 km), on the route to Genoa, nearing completion in 1982; Milan Rogoredo to Melegnano (13 km) on the Bologna route, begun early in 1983 and expected to take five years for completion; Milan to Treviglio (26 km) on the Venice route; and Florence Prato to Sesto Fiorentino (10 km) on the Bologna route, and to Empoli on the Pisa route.

To accelerate the projects essential to raise the FS share of the national freight market, presently no higher than 15 per cent, special decentralised departments have been established in five regions to bypass the overloaded channels of procedure between Government and FS headquarters in Rome. Each special unit includes technicians as well as administrators.

International routes were the focus of immediate attention. During 1983 the tunnel construction to finish the 23·6 km double-tracking between Bussoleno and Salbertrand would complete the addition of a second track throughout the 106 km between Modane and Turin. On the Brenner route into Austria work was to start in mid-1983 on a new tunnel between Ponte Gardena and Campodazzo to facilitate an 8 km realignment of the route. With Swiss contributions in grant and loan totalling SwFr 60 million another tunnelling project was in hand through Monte Olimpino, between Chiasso and Como. The present tunnel, which will be abandoned, is in poor state; besides easing the ruling gradient of the main line from 1·8 to 0·8 per cent and raising the maximum permissible speed to 120 km/h, the replacement project will create a tunnel to Class C1 loading-gauge parameters, which will enable extension of DB-SBB 'Rollende Landstrasse' piggyback trains beyond Chiasso and into Italy for the first time. As a result of rising traffic on the recently reopened Ventimiglia-Cuneo line via Tende, the Vievola-Ventimiglia section is to be electrified. A new freight terminal, linked to the main coastal trunk road by a tunnel under the town, is to be constructed at Ventimiglia.

A feature of the Integral Plan is marshalling yard modernisation. A major new yard, Domodossola II, is being built to complement the widening of the BLS Lötschberg route through Switzerland to the Simplon Tunnel; it will absorb all wagonload traffic sorting so that the existing Domo I yard can be devoted to unit train servicing. At the same time, the approach roads from Milan and Novara on the Italian side are to be upgraded for 20-tonne axleloads, resignalled and refurbished with new substations to permit operation of heavier loads. The foundations of Domo II were finished in 1982; tracklaying was expected to take a further five years, during which the Domodossola-Gallarate and Novara-Premosello lines would be upgraded to expedite the yard's forecast throughput of 12 million freight tonnes a year. Other yards on the modernisation programme include Milan and Bologna San Donato. The first section of the new Turin-Orbassano yard, designed to become one of Europe's largest, was completed in June 1981; it will eventually have 152 km of tracks covering 1·66 million square metres and process 5000 wagons daily.

Florence-Salerno four-tracking

The last stage of the Rome-Florence Direttissima is now unlikely to be ready before 1990. At the end of 1982 the 11 km between Chiusi South and North were almost finished but their commissioning depended on completion of the 41 km between Chiusi North and Arezzo South, probably in 1984. The original line of route north of Arezzo has been discarded because of geological difficulties complicating the prospective construction of a 14·5 km tunnel. A new 44 km alignment that minimises tunnelling has been selected between Arezzo South and Figline and this is unlikely to be ready for operation before 1990. Meanwhile, the 20 km between Rovezzano and Figline has also been impeded by problems in boring the 11 km San Donato tunnel and its opening is not expected before 1985. A 29 km bypass of Florence is to leave the main route in San Donato tunnel and join the Bologna main line north of the city at Prato, serving en route a new station beneath the present station of Santa Maria Novella. The cost of the Direttissima has been seriously affected by inflation. Up to the end of 1982 the Italian Parliament had had to authorise L827 000 million for the 264 km scheme and its connections to the existing route; this sum was exclusive of the cost of the Florence bypass, which will eliminate reversal in the city of through Rome-Milan traffic, and for which funds had not yet been authorised.

An important complementary scheme nearing completion in 1983 was creation of a separate

Bi-level push-pull driving trailer

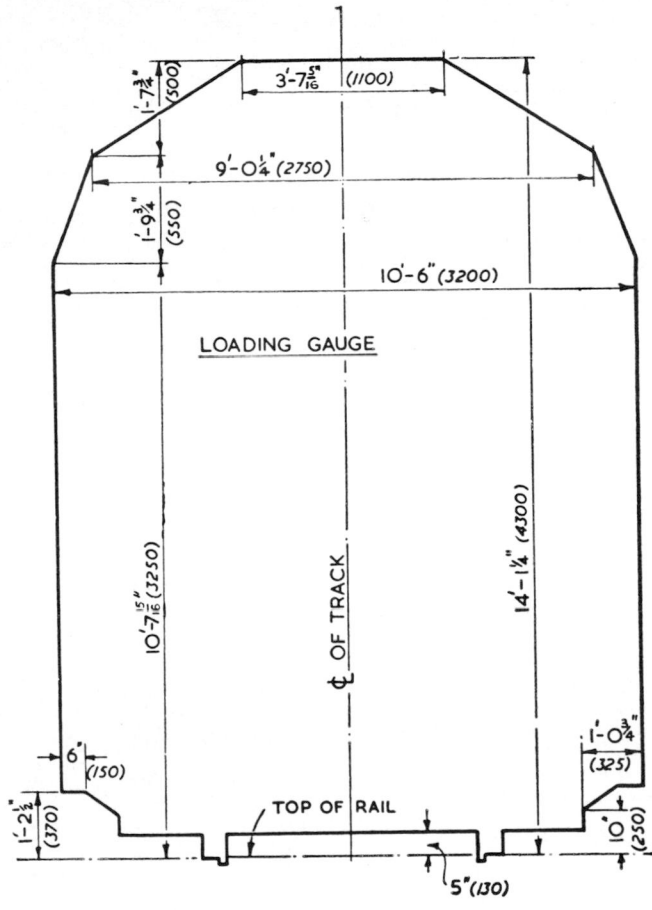

LOADING GAUGE

Minimum lateral clearance between loading gauge (above) and fixed gauge varies according to the radius of curvature eg:

		Clearance	
Radius of curve m		inside of curve mm	outside of curve mm
250		150	150
200		200	210
150		283	310
100		676	706
70		1177	1211

freight route south of Rome which bypasses the Naples area, where the scheme will permit much-needed improvement of local passenger services. The final link in this project is the L150 000 million double-tracking between Cancello and Sarno, to connect the earlier electrification of the inland Rome-Caserta-Cancello line with the new Santa Lucia Tunnel bypass in the Salerno area. Included in the scheme is a new L80 000 million marshalling yard at Caserta.

Passenger services

Despite the failure of a Milan-Turin regular-interval timetable introduced in the 1960s, because of operating problems, the principle was to be revived for a push-pull semi-fast service every two hours (except 0915-1215) between Rome and Naples in the summer of 1983. A timing of 2½ hours for the 214 km, inclusive of 11 intermediate stops, was envis-

aged. If this is successful the scheme may be extended to the Milan-Florence and Milan-Venice routes. The Rome-Naples service was to be operated with the latest Type nA, nAB and nB medium-distance coaching stock. A number of diesel and electric locomotives have been repainted to match these vehicles' livery of pearl grey with broad horizontal lining in purple and orange, which has been standardised on all recent reversible commuter equipment such as bi-level commuter cars, the new Type ALe 724 emu cars and their Le 884 trailers, and most recently some of the earlier hauled commuter stock with sunken central floors. Another recent addition to the expanding range of FS liveries is one of rose-red above the waistline and of pearl grey below, with a broad rose-red band superimposed, for FS day and couchette cars of Type UIC-X.

Passenger train punctuality improved in 1982, with only 17 per cent of all trains arriving more than

5 minutes behind time; in 1981 the figure was 64 per cent. This was attributed both to peace on the labour front and to a substantial infusion of new traction and rolling stock. Another relief was lifting of the two years-long limitation of express and 'rapido' trains to 130 and 140 km/h respectively, with only few trains of the latest stock excepted, while some 30 000 axle bearings were examined for suspected welding flaws. Operation in the Rome area was improved by turning round a number of local services at Ostiense and Tiburtina stations instead of Rome Termini.

A succession of three increases in 1982 followed by a further rise of 20 per cent in February 1983 virtually doubled previous FS fare levels.

Freight

With some 16 000 life-expired wagons withdrawn in recent years, so that practically the entire fleet is fit for at least 80 km/h operation, FS is aiming to raise annual tonne-km to more than 19 000 million by 1986. Unit train operation has been raised to 31 per cent of the total. At the same time the number of stations handling wagonload traffic has been halved to less than 1000 and a minimum distance for wagonload transits of 100 km imposed.

Intermodal traffic rose 8·5 per cent to 2·43 million tonnes in 1981 and constituted 14 per cent of all FS freight business. An internal Po Valley-southern Italy piggyback working has been added to the international services of this kind, which generated 1·56 million tonnes in 1981. Intermodal terminals have been or are being established at Milan, Padua, Verona, Leghorn, Bologna, Parma, Naples, Bari and Reggio Calabria.

Regional schemes, Milan and Turin

In May 1982 the then Prime Minister Spadolini formally launched construction of a new cross-Milan line as the first step toward creation of an integrated Milan conurbation rail and road transport system. Extending 13·2 km from Rogoredo to Certosa, on the main line to Turin, the new link's centrepiece will be a 5·9 km double-track tunnel between the city's Porta Garibaldi and Porta Vittoria stations, with five new stations below ground. Besides interconnecting the main lines to and from the south (Genoa), east (Piacenza and Treviglio, by a 3·3 km-long branch from Porta Vittoria) and north-west (Turin and Domodossola), the link will throw off a connection to the Ferrovie Nord Milano system at Bovisa, enabling integration of FNM and FS services. It will have four interchanges with the Milan metro. Operation of the tunnel line with a proportion of bi-level train-sets is planned to achieve a peak-hour capacity of 36 000 passengers/hour each way. The Milan car-sleeper terminal is to be moved to San Cristoforo station from Porto Vittoria. The new terminal will be situated in an area with good road connections to the city centre and main trunk roads.

In 1983 FS signed an agreement with the Turin city authorities aiming to establish a similar regional rail system. This equally envisages construction of a cross-city tunnel to create main through axis between Lingotto, Porta Susa, Dora and Stura (Porta Nuova terminus would remain the city's main station for long-haul trains). The scheme involves the quadrupling of 15-20 route-km, a work already

Chopper-controlled Type E633 Bo-Bo-Bo electric locomotive

Type UIC-X couchette car in new rose-and-grey livery

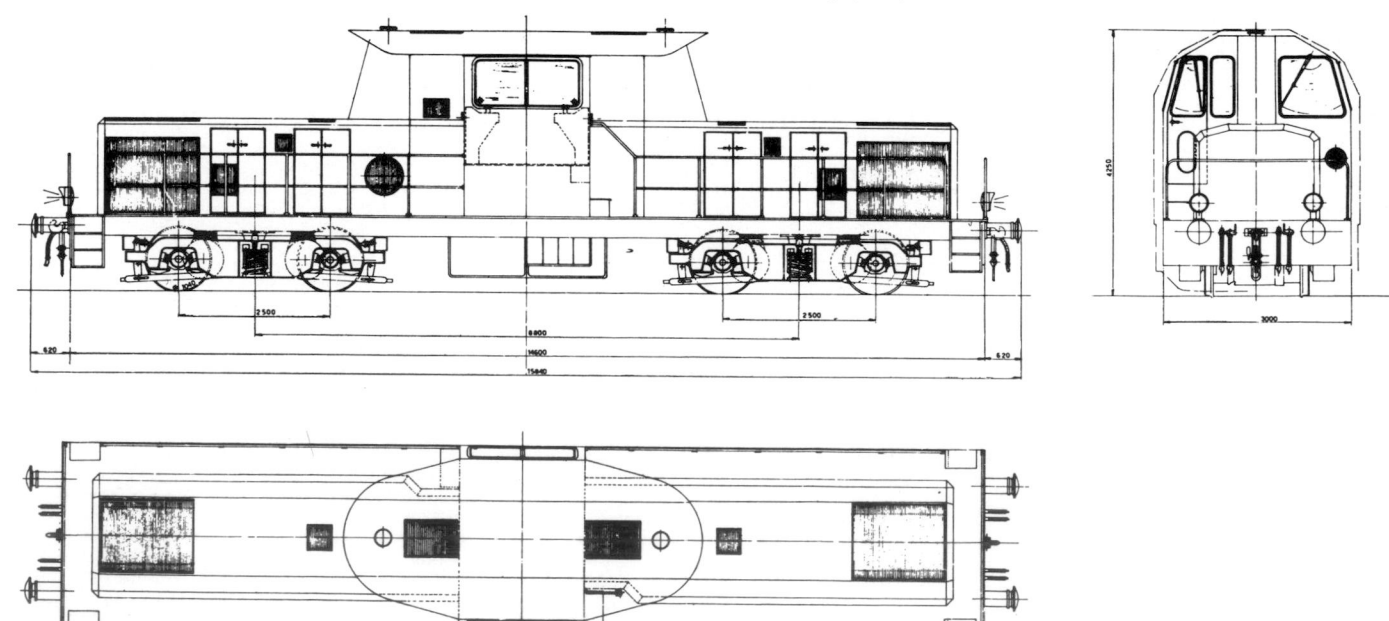

1140 hp Class D145 diesel-electric locomotive with inverter drive and three-phase motors

begun south of Porta Susa. Porta Susa would be the starting-point for a link with Caselle airport, 15 km from the city centre, over the independent Torino-Ceres Railway, which would be embraced in the proposed regional scheme and abandon its Ponte Mosca terminal. Subject to Treasury approval the FS allocated L50 000 million of Integral Plan funds to the project; the Turin authorities were to put up L94 000 million.

Airport links
The 2 km single-track branch to Pisa airport was formally opened in January 1983. Now planned is a 2 km double-track branch to Rome's Leonardo da Vinci airport at Fiumcino, to be taken from the Ponto Galeria-Fiumcino branch and built on an elevated structure. The airport emu service would terminate at Rome Ostiense because of inadequate capacity for additional traffic at Rome Termini. As far as Ponte Galeria the line from Ostiense is at present the main route for trains to Pisa and Genoa, but for the latter a new route is being created by following the existing single-track path from Trastevere to St Peters with a new double-track electrified line, which from St Peters turns west to join the Pisa main line at Maccarese. Between St Peters and Maccarese the new bypass will be joined (in its Aurelia Tunnel) by a new orbital link with the Rome-Florence main line; the latter will thread a 4·4 km tunnel, the Monte Mario, in its progress through Rome's northern suburbs.

A connection to Turin's Caselle airport, a 15 km line involving use of part of the independent Torino-Ceres Railway, is contemplated as part of a regional transport scheme. A further airport link currently under study by FS is one of 2 km from the Palermo-Trapani line in Sicily to Palermo's Punta Raisi airport.

Messina Straits Bridge
A proposal to bridge the Straits of Messina between southern Italy and Sicily has been agreed in principle by the FS.

Electrification
Ansaldo Trasporti has been appointed the main contractor for the 25 kV 50 Hz ac electrification of the Cagliari-Porto Torres and Olbia lines in Sardinia, which is being undertaken to provide an ac electrification shop window for Italian industry. Ansaldo will be responsible for the supply of vehicles, automation and signalling apparatus, power supply and central control. The project includes track doubling between Cagliari and Decimomannu, enlargement of two tunnels and upgrading for maximum speeds of 125-140 km/h south of Oristano.

Further 3 kV dc electrification proposed under the Integral Plan covers the following lines: Chiasso-Casale-Valenza; Cremona-Mantua (accompanied by CTC installation); Brescia-Olmeneta; Venice Mestre-Castelfranco Veneto-Padua; Faenza-Granarolo-Russi; Potenza-Metaponto-Taranto; Metaponto-Sibari-Cosenza (including CTC); Lamezia Terme-Catanzaro L; Reggio Calabria-Melito; Fiumertorto-Roccapalumba-Porto Empedocle; and Aragona-Caniccati-Caltanisetta-Bicocca.

Traction and rolling stock
Orders were placed in 1982 for a pair of high-power chopper-controlled electric locomotive prototypes, a 6000 kW Type E665 Co-Co for freight haulage and a Type E666 Co-Co with 160 km/h maximum speed for passenger service. Bo-Bo versions of the design are also planned: a 3500 kW Class E453 for freight and a Class E454 passenger counterpart. Designs were being drafted for a 6000 kW Class E402 Bo-Bo with 250 km/h capability.

Resources were strengthened in 1982 by delivery of 30 electric (Classes E632, E633 and E656) and 18 diesel locomotives (Class D145 and D445), the latest Type ALe 724 1120 kW emu power cars and trailers, more Type ALn dmu cars, 50 Type UIC-X long-haul passenger cars, 226 medium-distance passenger cars of the latest design, 28 Type MU and T2 sleeping cars, 12 couchette cars, 63 bi-level commuter and 98 other short-haul passenger cars. Freight stock purchases comprised 338 Type Rgs, 304 Type Gabs, 199 Type Shimins, 160 Type Sgs, 133 Type Habis and 77 intermodal wagons.

The Type E633 and Type E632 Bo-Bo-Bo units have chopper control. The E632 is geared for 160 km/h maximum speed with a starting tractive effort of 227 kN, the E633 for 130 km/h with a starting tractive effort of 278 kN. A further 122 type E633s were ordered in December 1982. In 1982 the first Type E633s were confined to the Brenner and Bologna routes from Verona, pending clearance of other routes for freedom from interference from the new type's chopper equipment. System-wide acceptance was unlikely before 1984.

Class D445 diesel locomotive

Class 444 Bo-Bo electric and Naples-Rome inter-city express

Milan Rogoredo intermodal terminal

The new medium-distance passenger stock is to a design featuring two central vestibules each with double-door entrances giving access to three saloons seating 82 in the second-class version. Internal decor makes vivid use of colours. Length over buffers is 26·4 metres, distance between centres of the Fiat bogies 19 metres, doorway width 1·2 metres, floor height above rail 1·09 metres and tare weight 35·4 tonnes. Of the initial order 60 cars were built at Naples by SOFER as push-pull driving trailers, with electrical equipment by Ansaldo, and of this series four were constructed with 'panoramic' driving cabs for push-pull operation with Type D445 diesel locomotives.

Of the material budgeted under the Integral Plan approval had been obtained by the end of 1982 for acquisition of 150 dc electric locomotives, 50 diesel locomotives, 150 locotractors, 700 long-distance, 360 medium-distance central vestibule, 800 medium-distance side-corridor, 200 couchette, 20 cafeteria, 150 bi-level, 20 low-floor commuter, 70 baggage and 120 generator cars, and 10 206 freight wagons of various types. Orders for no fewer than 8400 wagons were placed in 1982. They included 2300 flatcars for development of intermodal services; in this category FS was to take delivery in 1983 of 350 Type Saadss piggyback cars built by Costamasnaga to a Talbot design under licence. Early in 1983 orders were placed for 91 sleeping cars, to swell the stock of only 44 cars of recent build in the FS total of 216 at the start of the year. Orders were soon to be placed for a new medium-distance emu stock principally for routes in southern Italy and Sicily; they would comprise 72 Type ALe 582 motor cars (a design derived from the ALe 724), 54 Type Le 562 driving trailers and 18 Type Le 763 intermediate trailers.

Flying and burrowing inter-connections of Rome-Florence Direttissima and original Rome-Florence route at Orte North

Track
Monobloc prestressed concrete sleepers are being used almost exclusively in current track upgrading and doubling projects. Length of sleeper is 2·3

metres, but for new track where speeds may exceed 160 km/h, a new design with a length of 2·6 metres is being adopted. Ballast is crushed stone chips with a minimum depth of 35 cm below the sleeper base. In new construction a sub-ballast consisting of a granular mixture with 3 per cent cement content is being laid to a depth of 20 cm. For rail renewals, and all new lines, UIC 60 (60 kg/m) rails are being used, fastened with K-type clips. FS installs about 850 km of new track each year. Some key routes are being made fit for maximum axleloads of 25 tonnes.

Out of 20 700 track-km of running lines, principal routes account for 13 000 track-km; all are now laid with 50 or 60 kg/m rail for axleloads of 20 or 22 tonnes. For other routes 46 or 49 kg/m rail is used with the exception of 1500 track-km laid with 36 kg/m section.

Switches are being renewed at a rate of 4500 a year.

Signalling

For speeds above 150 km/h, automatic block with coded current cab repetition is being adopted. Cab repetition is integrated with automatic speed control. For speeds up to 180 km/h on the Rome—Florence Direttissima the following speeds are encoded (km/h): 250-230-200-150-100-60-30. Sasib is supplying equipment to fit 350 traction units for use of the system.

At the end of 1982 Milan Central and its approaches were to come under the control of a new electronic route-relay interlocking and signalling centre.

Train ferries

A new three-deck train ferry equipped with inter-deck lift, the *Garibaldi*, has been installed on the Civitavecchia-Golfo Aranci (Sardinia) route; it has an 80-freight wagon capacity. Two further ferries are to be ordered under the Integral Plan.

Investment

The following investments were envisaged in 1983 (L million):

Diesel locomotives (40)	
Electric locomotives (65)	
Passenger cars (250)	450 000
Multiple-unit cars (75)	
Freight cars (1500)	
New line construction	410 000
Track improvements	800 000
Track maintenance machines	105 000
Electrification	80 000
Signalling and telecommunications	133 900
Intermodal development	80 000
Yards and terminals	430 000
Bridges and buildings	115 000
Miscellaneous	162 500
	2 397 400

Electric locomotives

Class	Wheel arrangement	Line current	Rated output hp	Tractive effort (full field) Max kg	Continuous kg	at kmlh	Max speed kmlh	Wheel dia mm	Weight tonnes	Length mm	No built and/or on order	Year built	Builders Mechanical parts	Electrical equipment
E626	Bo-Bo-Bo	3000 V dc	2100	22 800 / 26 200	11 800 / 13 700	52 / 45	95	1250	93	14 950	448	1928	Savigliano; CGE; Brown Boveri; Elettromeccaniche Saronno; Breda; OM; Ansaldo; CENSA Saronno; Reggiane; Fiat	Marelli; Savigliano; CGE; Brown Boveri; Elettro-meccaniche Saronno; Breda; OM; Ansaldo; CENSA Saronno
E428	2-Bo-Bo-2	3000 V dc	2800	20 000 / 22 000	10 500 / 11 500	77 / 71	130	1880	135	19 000	241	1934	Breda; Ansaldo; Reggiane; Fiat; Brown Boveri	Breda; Ansaldo; Marelli; Brown Boveri
E424	Bo-Bo	3000 V dc	1660	19 500	9500	55	100	1250	72·4	15 500	158	1943	Breda; Savigliano; Ansaldo; Reggiane; Brown Boveri; OM	Breda; Savigliano; Ansaldo; Marelli; Brown Boveri; CGE
E444	Bo-Bo	3000 V dc	4020	23 600	12 800	105	200	1318	82	16 840	113	1967	Savigliano; Breda; Casaralta; Fiat	OCREN; Asgen; Savigliano
E636	Bo-Bo-Bo	3000 V dc	2100	22 000	11 500	52	110	1250	101	18 250	469	1940	Breda; Brown Boveri; Savigliano; OM; Reggiane; Pistoiesi	Breda; Brown Boveri; Savigliano; CGE; Ansaldo S Giorgio
E645	Bo-Bo-Bo	3000 V dc	4320	29 200	16 800	72	120	1250	112	18 290	93	1964	Breda; Brown Boveri; Savigliano; OM; Reggiane; Pistoiesi; IMAM	Breda; Brown Boveri; Savigliano; CGE; Marelli; Ansaldo S Giorgio; OCREN
E646	Bo-Bo-Bo	3000 V dc	4320	23 800	13 500	92	150	1250	110	18 250	203	1958	Breda; Brown Boveri; Savigliano; OM; Reggiane; Pistoiesi; IMAM	Breda; Brown Boveri; Savigliano; CGE; Marelli; Ansaldo S Giorgio; OCREN
E656	Bo-Bo-Bo	3000 V dc	4200	24 900	13 100	103	160	1250	120	18 290	275	1975	TIBB	TIBB
E632	Bo-Bo-Bo	3000 V dc	5805	23 150	16 215	95	160	1040	102	17 800	15	1979	Fiat; TIBB	Ansaldo; Marelli
E633	Bo-Bo-Bo	3000 V dc	5805	28 350	19 680	77·8	130	1040	102	17 800	197	1979	Fiat; TIBB	TIBB
E321	C(0-3-0)	3000 V dc	325	9000	5000	20·5	50	1318	36	9280	50	1960	FS; Verona	Bown Boveri
E321	C	3000 V dc	190	9000	5000	20·5	50	1310	36	9280	40	1961	Officine FS Verona (Transformte de loc)	TIBB
E322	C	3000 V dc	190	9000	5000	20·5	50	1310	36	9280	20	1961		
E323	C	3000 V dc	190	11 700	8400	11	65	1040	46	9240	30	1966	TIBB	TIBB
E324	C	3000 V dc	190	11 700	8400	11	65	1040	45	9240	10	1966	TIBB	TIBB

Diesel locomotives

Class	Wheel arrangement	Transmission	Rated power hp	Tractive effort Max kg	Continuous kg	at kmlh	Max speed kmlh	Wheel dia mm	Total weight tonnes	Length mm	No built and/or on order	Year first built	Builders Mechanical parts	Engine & type	Transmission
D341	Bo-Bo	Elec	1400	18 500	7850	26	110	1040	64	14 480	68	1957	Fiat	Fiat 3212.SF or Breda-Paxman 12 YLX	Brown Boveri; OCREN
D342	B-B	Hyd	1600	20 800	14 500	19	140	1040	63	14 500	20	1957	Ansaldo	2 Ansaldo-Maybach MD435	Maybach Mekydro C 32

Class	Wheel arrangement	Transmission	Rated power hp	Max kg	Tractive effort Continuous at kg	km/h	Max speed km/h	Wheel dia mm	Total weight tonnes	Length mm	No built and/or on order	Year first built	Builders Mechanical parts	Engine & type	Transmission
D343	B-B (monomotor bogies)	Elec	1500	19 000	11 000		130		59·5	13 240	75		Fiat; OM	Fiat 218 SSF or Breda-Paxman 12YJC	TIBB generator; 2 traction motors Breda-Elettromeccanica; OCREN
D443	B-B (monomotor bogies)	Elec	2000	22 000	14 000		130		69·5	14 400	50	1967	Fiat; OM	Fiat 2312 SSF or Breda-Paxman 12 YLC	ASG generator; 2 traction motors Breda-Elettromeccanica; OCREN
D235	C	Hyd	350	14 600	9000	7·4	40 Sw 55 Line	1070	39	9540	45	1961	Badoni; Jenbach; OM	Carraro; Jenbach; OM	Hydrotitan; Voith; OM
D234	C	Hyd	400	13 500	7100	9	40 Sw 60 Line	1310	36	9340	37	1961	Breda; OM	Breda; OM	OM
D225	B	Hyd	250	9800	7000	4·2	30 Sw 55 Line	900	28	8322	97	1956	Breda; Jenbach; Greco	Breda; Jenbach; Deutz	Breda; Voith
D141	Bo-Bo	Elec	700	19 000	12 000	10	80	1040	62	13 240	3	1962	TIBB; Reggiane	Fiat MB	Brown Boveri
D345	B-B	Elec	1350	19 000	11 270	25·1	130	1040	61	13 240	145	1970	Breda Pist; Sofer; Savigliano	218SSF GMT	TIBB; Marelli; Italtrofo
D445	B-B	Elec	2120	22 000	14 500	23·5	130	1040	72	14 100	95	1970	Savigliano	2112SSF GMT	Asgen
2435	C	Hyd	500	14 000	11 000	6·5	60	1040	48	9240	312	1962	Reggiane OM CNTR	MB820- Frot Gas D26N12V BRIF JW 600 CNTR	OM-SRM BRIF-Voith L24
214	B	Hyd	130	5700	4000	4	35	910	22	7158	175	1963	Badoni; Greco; Simm CNTR	8217-02,001 Fiat	BRIF-Voith L33
D145	Bo-Bo	Elec	1140	25 000			100	1040	70	15 240	10	1981	Fiat Fr Savigliano		Elettromeccanica Parizzi three-phase

Circumvesuviana Railway
Strade Ferrate Secondarie Meriodionali SpA

Corso Garibaldi 387, 80142 Naples

Telephone: 332600
Telegrams: Circumvesuviana, Napoli

President: Rocco Basilico
Director-General: Dr Ing Lucio Conalli
Finance Director: Dr Ing Ulisse Paci
Vice-Director of Finance and Traffic Manager: Dr Ing Carmine Sergio
Director of Administration: Giuseppe Errico
Director of Personnel: Dr Mario Picardi
Chief of Works and Maintenance: Dr Ing Claudio Novelli
Traction Manager: Dr Ing Michele di Matteo
Electric Installations Manager: Dr Ing Antonio Sarnataro

Gauge: 950 mm
Route length: 146 km
Electrification: 146 km at 1·5 kV dc

This busy suburban rail serves the hinterland of Naples with lines that make a circuit of Vesuvius and extend to Nola, Baiano, Sarno via both Ottaviano and Poggiomarino, and along the coast to Sorrento. The Sorrento branch, completed in 1947, is largely in tunnels, one of which is 4·8 km long with a station

Three-car Circumvesuviana emu by Sofer

inside the bore. In 1981 passenger journeys totalled 62·6 million for revenue of L 11 470 million against expenditure of L 67 570 million. The service is furnished by 85 three-car emus and the company also operates eight electric power cars, two diesel locomotives and 18 hauled passenger cars.

North Milan Railway (FNM)
Ferrovie Nord Milano

Piazzala Cadorna 14, 20123 Milan

Telephone: 864 051; 805 2046; 871 143
Telegrams: Ferrovie Nord Milano

Chairman: A Rezzonico
Vice-Chairman: G Troielli
Managing Director: Dr Ing Arnaldo Siena
General Manager: C Gaifami
Operating Manager: G Cesi
Administration Manager: O Giacominelli

Gauge: 1435 mm
Route length: 218 km
Electrification: 200 km at 3 kV dc

The railway serves the north Milan suburbs with a main route from Milan to Como and to Laveno on Lake Maggiore; the latter has a branch from Saronno to Novara. In 1982 FNM recorded 32·97 million passenger journeys and 130 000 tonnes of freight. Revenue was L 16·12 million against expenditure of L 75·73 million. Rolling stock comprises nine electric, one steam and seven diesel locomotives, 62 electric power cars, 189 emu trailers, 51 hauled passenger cars and 222 freight wagons. In 1983 FNM was investing L33 000 million; purchases were including 12 locomotives, six power cars and 12 trailers. The power cars, Type E750, are similar to the latest FS Type Ale 724, and were introduced in six-car formations including four bi-level trailers.

Track is laid with 50, 43 and 30 kg/m rails on wood and concrete sleepers. Minimum curve radius is 4 to 6 degrees, maximum gradient 3 per cent and maximum permissible axleloading 16-18 tonnes.

IVORY COAST — UPPER VOLTA

Regie des Chemins de Fer Abidjan-Niger (RAN)

PO Box 1394, Abidjan 01, Ivory Coast

Telephone: 32 02 45
Telegrams: Ferdia Abidjan
Telex: 564

BP 12, Ouagadougou, Upper Volta

Telephone: 369 03

President: Desire Boni
Director-General: Lancina Konate
Deputy Director-General: Delchan Ouedraogo
Technical Manager: Bony Aboh
Administrative Director: Ibrahima Coulibaly
Director Rolling Stock and Traction: Ousseyni Diarra
Director Track and Structures: Kla Privat
Director Studies and New Projects: N'Da Ezoa
Financial Director: Christopher Yesso
Commercial Director: Gbon Coulibaly
Transport Director: André Balma
Head of Personnel and Social Affairs Service: Abokan Patrice
Head of Supplies and Shops Service: Fofana Salifou
Head of Hotels and Tourism Service: Xavier Ouedraogo
Head of Professional Services: Dupont Robert
Head of Information Service: Aby Abagnilin
Head of Telecommunication and Signalling Service: Bazie Nabilébié
Head of Management Services: Mamadou Diaby
Head of Press and External Affairs Office: Bernard Combes

Gauge: 1000 mm
Route length: 1182 km

Transport development

Despite a good network of permanent roads the railway is a vital link with the Upper Volta, which particularly relies on it for transport of goods to and from the coast. The railway comprises a principal line which connects Abidjan, capital of Ivory Coast, with Ouagadougou, capital of Upper Volta, and two branches, one of 12 km from Abidjan to the oil port of Vridi and the other of 14 km from Azaguie to Ake-Befiat. Two additional lines are planned: San Pedro-Mout Klahoyo (325 km) and Ouagadougou-Tambao (375 km). In 1981 the Upper Volta Government sought tenders to build the long-cherished extension to the manganese fields at Tambao, beyond which the line may eventually extend to Tin Hrassan, near the Mali and Niger frontiers. Bank credits totalling FrCFA 4400 million have been secured to finance the project. The Tambao extension is embraced by a feasibility study of schemes to interconnect the railways of the six countries forming the Economic Community of West Africa (CEAO), Senegambia, Ivory Coast, Mali, Mauritania, Niger and Upper Volta, which CEAO and the African Union of Railways (UAC) were preparing to commission in 1982.

RAN is a bi-national industrial and commercial organisation with financial autonomy and with its activities governed by a convention signed in 1960 between the Republic of the Ivory Coast and the Republic of Upper Volta. The director-general comes from the Ivory Coast; the deputy director-general from Upper Volta.

Infrastructure improvements

Double-tracking of the 477 km between Abidjan and Tafiré continues. The section between Bouaké and Pétionara was due for completion at the end of 1982, to be followed by work between Pétionara and Tafiré.

Investment

The following sums were budgeted for investment over the 1981-85 period (FrCFA 000):

Shunting locomotives (4)	971 000
Locomotive-hauled passenger cars (10)	1 526 400
Railcars	258 090
Luggage vans	537 000
Intermodal equipment	115 000
Double-tracking	4 229 418
Other track improvements	2 360 000
Track maintenance machines	224 300
Station buildings	120 000
Signalling and telecommunications	1 216 425
Yards and terminals	102 000
Workshops	571 000
Other	1 382 990
Total	13 683 623

Traffic

	1978	1979	1980	1981
Freight ton-km (million)	630	543	615	616
Freight tonnage	899 000	761 000	813 772	834 321
Passenger-km (million)	1200	1172	1252	1074
Passenger journeys (million)	3·7	3·556	3·51	3·42

Finances

	1977	1979	1980
			(Fr CFA million)
Revenue	11 776	14 245	23 089
Expenses	12 035	14 064	22 955

In 1981 the Ivory Coast Government agreed to contribute FrCFA 11 500 million to RAN investment funds over the ensuing five years to help finance new locomotive and rolling stock purchases, including passenger cars as well as further infrastructure improvements. The latter would include reconstruction of six main stations, four marshalling yards and branches to the industrial areas of Vridi and Banco.

Traction and rolling stock

RAN operates 51 main-line diesel-electric locomotives, a fleet headed by 19 GM 2250 hp Co-Cos of 90·7 tonnes acquired in 1979 and supplemented by six more 2250 hp Class GT22LC units obtained from General Motors of Canada in 1981. The remainder are mostly French-built 1800 hp Bo-Bos. The 39 diesel shunters are chiefly Henschel-built, mostly obtained in 1979-80 and of 450-750 hp, but including four GM units delivered in late 1981 for Pétroci traffic. A total of 28 railcars and 13 trailers, the great majority of the former 57-tonne 950 hp vehicles by CIMT, is operated. Locomotive-hauled coaching stock numbers 174 vehicles, including 12 restaurant cars and 13 couchette cars; it features a stock of 55 air-conditioned stainless-steel-bodied cars supplied by Carel-Fouché in 1977-80. Recent acquisitions of 426 vehicles to meet rising traffic demand have built the wagon stock up to 1690 vehicles.

Signalling

21 of RAN's stations in the Ivory Coast and 11 in Upper Volta are being equipped with a system of colour-light signalling and power point operation based on French Railways NSI relay system, which RAN is standardising. Installation is by Cie Electro-Mécanique, a French subsidiary of BBC Brown Boveri.

Track

Rail: 26, 30, 33, 36, 37 kg/m
Ballast: Granite, 800-1200 litres/m, hard sandstone, 700 litres/m
Cross ties (sleepers): Metal, 1550 per km; concrete SL (Blochet), 1357 per km; concrete monobloc, 1500 per km
Minimum curvature radius: 500 m, being raised to 800 m
Ruling gradient: 10%

JAMAICA

Ministry of Public Utilities and Transport

2 St Lucia Avenue, Kingston 5

Minister: Hon P Charles
Permanent Secretary: H A Scott

Jamaica Railway Corporation (JRC)

PO Box 489, 142 Barry Street, Kingston

Telephone: 922 6621
Telegrams: Diesel Dan, Kingston

Chairman: John Allgrove
General Manager: Whilston Taylor
Chief of Operations: L L B McNally
Chief Civil Engineer: Kerrith Foster
Chief Mechanical Engineer: G Mitchell

Gauge: 1435 mm
Route length: 330 km

Transport development

The island of Jamaica is intersected by 5000 km of main roads, of which about 75 per cent are asphalted, and the railway which is centred on the principal port town of Kingston. The railway has a vital role in transport to the ports of bauxite, of which Jamaica is a major world producer.

Motive power and rolling stock

Locomotives in service
Diesel-electric: Line haul 28; shunting 3
Railcars, diesel: 6
Trailers: 3 Wickham; 14 Rolls-Royce
Passenger train coaches: 21
Freight cars: (JRC) 266; (Alcan) 113; (Alcoa) 40; (Revere) 21

In 1982 a contract worth Fr 55 million was placed with Alsthom-Atlantique for six 2000 hp Type AD 20B, 68-tonne Bo-Bo diesel-electric locomotives with alternator/dc transmissions and rheostatic braking; the locomotives will have a starting tractive effort of 20 900 kg and a maximum speed of 105 km/h. In 1982 a fresh contract for technical assistance was signed with Sofrerail.

JAPAN

Ministry of Transport

1-3, 2-chome, Kasumigaseki, Chiyoda-ku, Tokyo

Telephone: 580-3111

Minister: Takashi Hasegawa
Director-General, Railway Supervision Bureau: Y Nagamitsu
Director-General, National Railways Department: Y Tanahashi
Director-General, Private Railways Department: T Hattori

Japanese National Railways (JNR)

6-5, Marunouchi 1-chome, Chiyoda-ku, Tokyo

Board of Directors
Chairman: Fumio Takagi
Vice-Chairman: Kazumasa Mawatari
Members: Kiyoshi Kawarabayashi
Takei Tojo
Sogo Okamura
Koji Takahashi
Koichi Sakata
Koji Iwase
Tadatoshi Ino
Tetsuo Hanya
Kunitake Nawata
Misao Sugawara
Masashi Hashimoto
Kenko Misaka
Keiichi Yoshida
Teruo Yoshida
Kyoji Tsubouchi
Tetsuo Takeuchi

President: Fumio Takagi
Vice-President, Executive: Kazumasa Mawatari
Vice-President, Engineering: Koji Takahashi
Advisor Directors
  Head Office: Kenko Misaka
  Shinkansen Administration: Koichi Sakata
  Hokkaido Region: Misao Sugawara
  Osaka Region: Teruo Yoshida

Tokyo Metropolitan Sphere HQ: Tadatoshi Ino
Head Office, Staff Relations: Koji Iwase
Kyushu Region: Keiichi Yoshida
Head Office: Masashi Hashimoto
Kyoji Tsubouchi
Tetsuo Takeuchi
Tetsuo Hanya
Kunitake Nawata

Director, Public Relations Dept: Yoshiyuki Yamamoto
International Dept: Hotsumi Harada
Technical Development Dept:
Yoshihiro Kyotani
Makoto Kato
Shigeo Naganuma
Shigeo Niinomi
Michito Tanaka
Purchasing and Stores Dept: Teruhumi Akiyama
Train Operation: Shuichiro Yamanouchi
Passenger Dept: Hiroshi Suda
Freight Dept: Yosihiro Omori
Construction Dept: Hiroshi Okada
Shinkansen Construction Dept: Akira Takayama
Track and Structures Dept: Taizo Nozawa
Electrical Engineering Dept: Yoshisuke Muto
Rolling Stock and Mechanical Engineering Dept:
Yoshitake Ishii
Motor Transportation Department: Michitaro Yamaoka
Railway Technical Institute: Kainen Watanabe
Rolling Stock Design: Yoshitake Ishii
Structure Design: Hidehiko Abe

	1981
Route length (km)	21 419
Double- and multi-tracked sections	5654
	(26·4%)
Electrified sections	8435
	(39·4%)
Narrow gauge lines	
dc	4965
ac	3470
Shinkansen	
ac	1177

Electrification: 1067 mm gauge: 4965 km at 1·5 kV dc
3470 km at 20 kV 50/60 Hz ac
1435 mm gauge: 1805 km at 25 kV 60 Hz ac

Transport development

The first public railway in Japan was opened between Shimbashi (Tokyo) and Yokohama by the state in 1872. Thereafter the State Railways continued to grow as a Government Department until 1949, when the present Japanese National Railways (JNR) was established as a public corporation. With its capital wholly invested by the state, JNR is operated under the supervision of the Ministry of Transport.

A number of important matters are subject to the authorisation of the Minister:
Construction of new lines and acquisition of private railways or other transport modes;
Operation of new ferry lines or new motor transport services in connection with rail operation;
Suspension of services or line closures;
Electrification and other major projects.

Management Improvement Plan

Following passage of the Law Providing Special Measures for Promotion of JNR Rehabilitation in December 1980, the Minister of Transport in May 1980 approved a JNR Management Improvement Plan. This aimed by 1985 to save 94 900 staff as follows: 19 500 through modernisation of work methods and train service reductions; 18 600 through productivity improvements such as one-man operation; 8900 through equipment modernisation, such as CTC; 11 800 through reductions in terminal and yard staffing; 21 100 through transfer of some work to contractors; and 15 500 through closure of 77 rural and unprofitable lines. Some of the staff saving, it was hoped, would be achieved by accelerated retirement. Many stations handling less than 800 passengers daily would become unmanned, equipped with ticket-issuing machines. To reduce JNR's high capital costs, investment levels would remain unchanged throughout the period.

The overall aim of the plan, which included measures to concentrate still more on bulk transport, both of freight and passengers, on key volume routes, was to transform the loss on the trunk lines' operating account to a 490 000 million yen surplus and cut the operating loss on local lines from 350 000 million yen in 1980 to 220 000 million yen by 1985. The accelerated retirement provisions would, however, more than double pension expenses to 770 000 million yen in 1985. Nevertheless the plan envisaged an overall reduction of the annual deficit to 990 000 million by 1985.

Type 581 emu with passive body-tilting system

Type EF 66 dc electric locomotive (Ken Matsuzawa)

Dual-voltage (20 kV 50/60 Hz ac and 1500 V dc) 2550 kW Type EF 81 electric locomotive

Type ED75 electric locomotive

By the end of 1982 the Ministry of Transport had approved closure of 40 secondary lines and JNR had submitted 31 more shutdowns for approval. In sum these affected 13 per cent of JNR's route-km. The next stage of procedure, public enquiries, was due to begin in April 1983.

The plan's full implementation would reduce JNR assets as follows:

	1980	1985
Route length, km	21 322	18 420
Passenger stations		
Manned	2892	600
Unmanned	2293	3870
Total	5185	4470
Freight stations	1358	800
Yards	193	100
Rolling stock		
Locomotives	4061	3600
Passenger cars	29 219	28 000
Freight cars	99 846	92 000
Buses	2547	2400
Ferries, total		
gross tonnage	72 000	65 000

Note: All entries are for the beginning of both fiscal years except route lengths, which are as of the start of fiscal 1980 and the end of fiscal 1985.

JNR break-up ordered

In 1982 the Commission on Administrative Reform advocated the break-up of JNR into a number of smaller and separately managed units. The proposal was supported by the then Prime Minister, Zenko Suzuki, and later in the year endorsed by his successor, Yashukiro Nakasone, whose Government has made a key issue of reform of the railway system. The Diet enacted a Bill supporting the idea and setting a target date for change of July 1987. At the end of 1982 a five-man Reconstruction Management Council including the Transport Minister was appointed to organise the break-up.

Traffic

JNR's share of total national freight moved per annum has collapsed from 50 per cent in the 1950s to around 18 per cent, compared with 51 per cent for coastal shipping and 39 per cent for road haulage. JNR's share of passenger traffic was 24 per cent in 1981 compared with 15 per cent by private railways, 14 per cent by buses, 42 per cent by private motor cars and 5 per cent by air.

Freight traffic

Freight traffic again receded in 1981. Oil accounted for 13·6 per cent of the gross, followed by limestone 13·2 per cent, cement 12·5 per cent and coal 5·2 per cent. Tonnage of principal commodities declined because of reduction in total shipments by all modes and diversion to other modes of transport. Container traffic decreased by 7 per cent in tonnage and 5 per cent in ton-km compared with the previous year. In 1983 JNR was planning to launch a piggyback operation between Tokyo and centres in Kyushu, employing 30-car trains of 13·2 metre-long wagons with 350 mm diameter wheels to dip their floors to within 450 mm of rail level. The projected rail transit of 15 to 16 hours to Kokura or Kitakyushu will save 7 hours by comparison with the through-out road haul of some 1000 km.

Operating capacity reduction planned
(000)

				1980	1985
Passenger train-km/day	Shinkansen			178	230
	Conventional lines	{	Limited and ordinary expresses	414	310
		{	Other trains	845	850
Freight train-km/day				470	400
Baggage car-km/day				407	360
Ferry-km				2463	2290
Bus-km				118 000	110 000

Total freight

	Tons carried		Ton-km	
	(million)	Index	(000 million)	Index
1965	200	100	56·4	100
1976	141	70	45·5	81
1977	132	66	40·6	72
1978	133	67	40·4	72
1979	136	68	42·3	75
1980	122	61	37	66
1981	111	56	33	59

Series 200 train-set on Joetsu Shinkansen elevated structure with concrete slab track

Telephone kiosk as installed in all Shinkansen train-set buffet cars

'Green'-class saloon of Series 200 Shinkansen train-set

In face of the unchecked decline and under the intensifying political pressures for economic rationalisation, JNR announced that from February 1984 its already curtailed freight operation would be still more severely pruned. Freight depots would be halved to a total of 457, and marshalling yards reduced from 110 to 40, with the resultant redundancy of some 200 electric and 500 diesel locomotives, 55 000 wagons and 30 000 railwaymen.

Container freight

	Tons carried (000)	Ton-km (million)
1965	1906	1197
1976	11 532	9022
1977	10 017	8035
1978	10 286	8387
1979	11 487	9325
1980	9955	8197
1981	9244	7788

Passenger traffic

The total volume of domestic passenger travel in 1981 was 790 500 million passenger-km, an increase of no more than 1·1 per cent on the preceding year, which reflected stagnation of the economy and a persisting depression of expenditure on personal consumption. Broken down by mode, the year's totals of 312 000 million passenger-km for private cars, 124 100 million for private railways and 31 000 million for airlines represented rises of 2·3, 2·2 and 4·5 per cent respectively on the previous year. JNR's gross of 192 100 million passenger-km, however, was 0·5 per cent down on the preceding year. As a result, JNR's share of total passenger traffic fell to 24·3 per cent.

While ordinary passenger traffic, at 113 800 million passenger-km showed a decrease of 1·2 per cent, commuting passenger traffic at 78 300 million passenger-km displayed a decrease of only 0·4 per cent. The combined total of 192 100 million passenger-km was 99·1 per cent of the target figure of 193 800 million set by the Management Improvement Plan. The Shinkansen gross of 41 700 million passenger-km was almost equal to the 1980 total.

In the category of passenger traffic by special express and ordinary express trains operated on the 1067 mm gauge, travel by special express, probably because of upgrading from ordinary express to special express, rose by 1·3 per cent while that by ordinary express declined by 15·3 per cent. The total volume of both special express and ordinary express travel, at 40 800 million passenger-km, fell by 3·8 per cent compared with the preceding year.

In 1980 urban emu travel declined by 2 per cent, but in 1981 it was up 1·2 per cent to 56 800 million passenger-km. The slump in travel by local trains continued. In 1981 the total in this sector was 9500 million passenger-km, a fall of 5·3 per cent.

Some curtailment of passenger services on the 1067 mm-gauge network was planned in 1982 following opening of the Tohoku and Joetsu Shinkansen.

Passenger journeys (million)

	Ordinary	Commuter	Total
1965	2043	4679	6722
1976	2582	4598	7180
1977	2509	4560	7068
1978	2444	4553	6997
1979	2392	4539	6931
1980	2376	4448	6825
1981	2348	4445	6793

Finances

Financial results have shown deficits every year since 1964, despite continued efforts to restore financial stability. In 1981, a net loss of 1 085 900 million yen was registered, consisting of an 892 200 million yen general net loss and 193 700 million yen charged as specific retirement allowance net loss. The general net loss was a slight improvement of 1 per cent on the 1980 figure.

At the end of fiscal year 1981 the total of JNR's long-term, short-term and other liabilities was an accumulated 12 249 300 million yen.

Shinkansen

The first two Shinkansen carried 1800 million passengers between opening of the first in October 1964 and August 1982 without a single casualty. Passengers carried in 1981 numbered 125·6 million (a daily average of 344 000), the same as in the

Passenger-km (million)

	Shinkansen	Conventional lines		Total
		Express	Local	
1965	10 651	39 522	123 841	174 014
1976	48 147	50 815	111 778	210 740
1977	42 187	46 655	110 810	199 653
1978	41 074	44 244	110 526	195 844
1979	40 986	43 301	110 403	194 690
1980	41 790	42 407	108 947	193 143
1981	41 717	40 784	109 614	192 115

Note: Express includes both limited express and ordinary express trains.

Railway passenger traffic in Tokyo metropolitan area
(daily average 000)

	JNR	Private railways	Subways	Total
1965	8819	7041	2063	17 923
1976	10 596	9209	4875	24 680
1977	10 577	9546	5030	25 153
1978	10 577	9756	5039	25 372
1979	10 527	9822	5086	25 435
1980	10 379	10 000	5487	25 866
1981	10 424	10 163	5625	26 212

Train operation during rush hours in Tokyo metropolitan area
(as of November 1980)

Route	Line	Train consist (cars)	Load factor (%)	Headway (minutes)
A	Tokaido	15	225	3½
B	Yokosuka	15	223	5½
C	Keihin Tohoku	10	252	2½
D	Yamanote	10	233	2½
E	Joban (rapid service)	10	274	6
F	Joban (local service)	10	247	3⅓
G	Sobu (rapid service)	15	231	4
H	Sobu (local service)	10	244	2⅔
I	Chuo (rapid service)	10	258	2⅙
J	Chuo (local service)	10	185	3

Railway passenger traffic in Osaka metropolitan area
(daily average 000)

	JNR	Private railways	Subways	Total
1965	2304	5284	1021	8609
1976	2538	6320	1958	10 816
1977	2481	6403	2047	10 931
1978	2446	6445	2084	10 975
1979	2391	6287	2095	10 773
1980	2303	6069	2184	10 555
1981	2282	6042	2262	10 586

Notes: The figures for each mode of transport indicate ordinary ticket and commutation pass users combined.
Tokyo and Osaka metropolitan areas refer to an area 50 km in radius from Tokyo station and Osaka station respectively.

Series 201 thyristor chopper-controlled emu

previous year; passenger-km were 41 720 million; and the distance travelled per passenger 332 km.

Two trains are presently scheduled every hour for through operation between Tokyo and Hakata, and up to nine trains per hour between Tokyo and Shin Osaka. Because of reduced demand for the stopping Kodama services of the Tokaido and Sanyo lines, on some of which load factors have lowered to 30 to 40 per cent, some 16-car train-sets were to be reduced to 14 or 12 cars. Each car removed would save 17 million yen a year in running and maintenance costs.

Under the Law for Construction of Nationwide High-speed Railways, enacted in May 1970, construction of three Shinkansen lines, Tohoku (Tokyo—Morioka), Joetsu (Omiya—Niigata) and Narita (Tokyo—New Tokyo International Airport), was proposed.

The third and fourth Shinkansen opened in 1982. The Tohoku Shinkansen to Morioka in northern Honshu was inaugurated in June, followed by the Joetsu Shinkansen to Niigata in November. Both services had at first to start from Omiya, because environmental controversy has deferred extension of the route into central Tokyo until the mid-1980s.

JNR operates 60 trains daily on the Tohoku Shinkansen, including 27 fast trains covering the 465 km between Omiya and Morioka in 3 hours 17 minutes. On the Joetsu Shinkansen, 42 trains run daily and the fastest covers the 270 km between Omiya and Niigata in 1 hour 45 minutes. Fast trains on the Tohoku line have been named 'Yamabiko' (echo), semi-fast trains 'Aoba' (green foliage); corresponding titles selected for the Joetsu trains are 'Asahi' (rising sun) and 'Toki' (crested ibis).

Both new lines pass through heavy winter snow areas; the section between Jomokogen and Niigata on the Joetsu Shinkansen, in particular, has severe snowfalls, with depths reaching 4 metres. This has required special measures against snow. Tracks between tunnels in mountainous areas are all sheltered to protect them from avalanches. On viaducts in open country, an automatic snow melting system is installed; it detects the start of a snowfall and sprays warm water to melt the snow before it accumulates or freezes.

The area along the Tohoku Shinkansen has less snowfall than along the Joetsu, and snow accumulation is usually less than 1 metre. Trains are provided with snow ploughs to drive the snow into recess areas on the viaduct. At turnouts snow-melting devices melt the snow that falls from trains. All underfloor equipment is encased to prevent snow adhesion. Snow-air separators are also installed at the air intakes for equipment cooling and car ventilation.

Earthquake sensors are installed at substations along the new lines. When a strong earthquake occurs, sensors work to stop trains automatically. In addition, on the Tohoku Shinkansen, detectors are installed at eight places along the Pacific coast, 40 to 100 km away from the track. Warnings from these detectors are used to reduce train speeds before the arrival of shock waves from an undersea earthquake.

Eight groups of dispatchers (train, railcar, track maintenance, electric power, passenger information, and three groups responsible for signalling, communications and systems) control both new lines. The control centre is in Tokyo station, adjoining that for the Tokaido-Sanyo Shinkansen.

The Joetsu Shinkansen threads the country's central mountains and advanced tunnelling technology was used to bore long tunnels. Tunnels between Takasaki and Nagaoka account for 106 km of the section's 137 km length. The 22·23 km Daishimizu Tunnel, is currently the longest in the world and took 5¼ years to complete. To avoid level crossings almost all construction in flat country is on elevated concrete viaduct. Noise and vibration impacts are reduced by barriers and special construction techniques.

The series 200 emus for the two new Shinkansen lines are 12-car sets with 230 kW motors as opposed to the 180 kW of the first Shinkansen train-sets, because of the new lines' shorter distance between stations and longer gradients, with a ruling slope of 15/1000. Car bodies are entirely of welded aluminium alloy, with deep side skirts, one of numerous anti-snow protection devices, integrally formed into the body structure.

For the present maximum speed on the new lines is limited to the existing Shinkansen 210 km/h standard, but it is hoped that anti-noise measures have now been perfected to the extent that a lift to at least 230 km/h will be feasible before long. Legally noise levels alongside Shinkansen viaducts must now be below 75 phon and vibration less than 70 decibels. To fulfil this requirement for 24 000 dwellings alongside the Shinkansen between Tokyo and Fukuoka cost JNR 75 000 million yen.

Revenues and expenses of General Account
(000 million yen)

	1976	1977	1978	1979	1980	1981
Operating revenues	1993·1	2369	2570·2	2902·1	2963·7	3173·0
Passenger	1515·1	1869	1949·9	2155	2242·4	2403·5
Freight	277·9	307	309·5	353·9	329·6	311·4
Miscellaneous	71·4	79·7	88·8	96·8	102·5	115·4
Financial rehabilitation subsidies	114·8	158·6	221·9	296·4	289·1	342·8
Operating expenses	2915·6	3214·7	3471·4	3744·6	3964·3	4325·4
Personnel	1396·8	1530·2	1656·7	1730·3	1858·7	2007·2
Material	875·6	939	969	1060·7	1201·4	1263·9
Taxes and other public payments	21·8	23·7	25·5	27·3	29·9	32·6
Interest and bond handling expenses	316	401·9	477·7	552·5	476·4	603·0
Depreciation	305·3	319·8	342·5	373·8	397·8	418·8
Operating profit or loss	−922·5	−845·7	−901·2	−842·5	−1000·6	−1152·4
Non-operating revenues	12·1	15·6	18·6	23·9	35·9	73·1
Non-operating expenses	3·7	3·9	4·2	3·2	43·7	6·6
Net profit or loss	−914·1	−833·9	−886·7	−821·8	−1008·4	−1085·9
General net loss	—	—	−809·9	−728·2	−830	−822·1
Specific retirement allowance net loss	—	—	−76·8	−93·6	−178·4	−263·8

Note: In 1976 a Separate Account for Specified Government Loans was established, this is separate from the General Account.

Profit and loss account of trunk lines and local lines for fiscal 1981

	Trunk lines (including commuter lines in metropolitan areas)	Local lines	Buses	Total
Route-km	12 644·7	10 174·3	14 052·6	36 871·6
	(55·4%)	(44·6%)		
Traffic volume — Passenger-km (000 million)	183·0	9·5	2·5	195
	(95·1%)	(4·9%)		
Traffic volume — Ton-km (000 million)	32·7	1·3	0	34·0
	(96·3%)	(3·7%)		
Revenues (000 million yen)				
Passenger	2269·8	94·9	38·7	2403·4
Freight	293·1	17·5	0·8	311·4
Miscellaneous	110·3	4·5	0·6	115·4
Subsidies	212·5	128·2	2·1	342·8
Total	2885·7	245·1	42·2	3173·0
	(92·2%)	(7·8%)		
Expenses (000 million yen)				
Operating	2735·1	497·4	71·2	3303·7
Capital	912·0	100·3	9·4	1021·7
Total	3647·1	597·7	80·6	4325·4
	(85·9%)	(14·1%)		
Operating profit or loss (000 million yen)	−761·4	−352·6	−38·4	−1152·4
Non operating profit or loss (000 million yen)	60·9	5·3	0·3	66·5
Net profit or loss (000 million yen)	−700·5	−347·3	−38·1	−1085·9
	(64·6%)	(32%)	(3·5%)	(100%)
General net loss	−486·4	−303·6	−32·1	−822·1
Specific retirement allowance net loss	−214·1	−43·7	−6·0	−263·8

Shinkansen revenue and expenses
(000 million yen)

	1965	1976	1977	1978	1979	1980	1981
Revenue	55	546·7	615·9	652·6	698·9	728·8	788·9
Expenses	67·8	330·7	370·5	374·3	399·1	430·5	446·6
Operating ratio (%)	123	60	60	57	57	59	57

Shinkansen traffic

	1965	1976	1977	1978	1979	1980	1981
Passengers carried (000)	30 967	143 465	126 796	123 690	123 767	125 636	125 619
Passenger-km (million)	10 651	48 147	42 187	41 074	40 986	41 790	41 717
Average passengers per day (000)	85	393	347	339	338	344	344
Average distance per passenger (km)	344	336	333	332	331	333	332

Seikan Tunnel

In January 1983 the two headings of the Seikan pilot tunnel met and the opening of the main 53·85 km tunnel was set for 1986. With the likelihood that both Tohoku and Joetsu Shinkansen will run at a loss, the former at around 300 000 million yen, the latter at around 100 000 million yen a year, the prospect of a Shinkansen extension from Morioka northwards through the tunnel to Hokkaido's capital, Sapporo, has become remote. The Honshu-Hokkaido passenger service on the 1067 mm-gauge link that will now thread the tunnel will be completely uncompetitive with Tokyo-Sapporo air transits of about 6 hours and is certain to lose money. Yet Japan Railway Construction Corporation is seeking to levy from JNR an annual fee of 80 000 million yen for use of the tunnel on its completion at a likely cost of 531 000 million yen.

Traction and rolling stock

Locomotives in service

steam	5
electric	1760
diesel-electric	25
diesel-hydraulic	2046

Passenger stock

railcars, electric	11 455
railcars, diesel	4948
trailer cars, electric	6295
locomotive hauled	6070
Freight wagons	91 375
Containers for door-to-door service	6626

A new electric locomotive class is the 2850 kW chopper-controlled Class EF67 Co-Co, which has been produced to supersede elderly 1350 kW 2-Co+Co-2s on a main-line banking assignment.

New design plans include double-deck sleeping cars for the 1067 mm gauge and a lighter Shinkansen train-set.

Train-km by type of traction 1982

(daily average 000)

Passenger trains
Electric locomotives: 118·3 (8·4%)
Electric railcars: 887·0 (63%)
Diesel locomotives
and railcars: 402·5 (28·6%)

Freight trains
Electric locomotives: 311 (76·5%)
Diesel locomotives: 95·6 (23·5%)

Automatic Linear Pneumatic System

JNR has embarked on a research programme to develop a linear motor-powered, rubber-tyred train and track system known as Automatic Linear Pneumatic (ALPS), for 160 km/h short-haul operation. In mind is service of the satellite towns located at up to 80 km from Tokyo's centre. Interest in rubber tyres arises from the hopes of noise and vibration suppression which have cost JNR so dearly in, notably, Shinkansen operation.

Maglev system

JNR continued to experiment with maglev (magnetically levitated) vehicle technology on a 7 km test guideway near Miyazaki. Test vehicle ML-500 reached a record speed of 517 km/h in December 1979, bringing this series of tests with an inverted T-shaped guideway to a successful conclusion. The guideway then was modified into a U-shaped configuration, and tests were run with a new vehicle, MLU-001, as a single car and as a two-car train. In September 1982 coupled cars MLU 001-1 and 001-3 reached 262 km/h in levitated operation and for the first time were carrying three persons aboard. A third car has been added, and tests were to continue into 1983.

Electrification

Work completed in 1982 included the Tazawako line from Morioka to Omagari at 20 kV 50 Hz, to coincide with the Joetsu Shinkansen opening.

Signalling

A total of 11 422 km, or 53 per cent of all the JNR narrow-gauge lines, are installed with automatic block signals, and 6144 km (29 per cent) are under centralised traffic control (CTC). Relay interlocking systems are installed in 2366 stations, or 44·6 per cent of the total number. Lately JNR has developed a computerised interlocking and plans to install this system widely in the near future.

The Shinkansen system of continuous cab signalling and ATC has been installed on two Tokyo commuter lines, the 34·5 km Yamanoye and the 49 km Keihin-Tohoku from Omiya across Tokyo to Kamata. Extension of the system to the Negishi and Akabane lines is planned.

Tokyo control centre of Tohoku Shinkansen

Main features of first four Shinkansen

	Tokaido Tokyo- Shin Osaka	Sanyo Shin Osaka- Okayama	Okayama- Hakata	Tohoku Tokyo- Morioka	Joetsu Omiya- Niigata
Route length	515 km	161 km	393 km	496 km	270 km
Tunnels	69 km (13%)	58 km (36%)	223 km (57%)	115 km (23%)	106 km (39%)
Bridges	57 km (11%)	20 km (12%)	31 km (8%)	78 km (16%)	30 km (11%)
Fastest journey time, end-to-end	3 h 10 min	58 min	2 h 28 min	3 h 17 min	1 h 50 min
Max speed			210 km/h		
Minimum curve radius	2500 m	4000 m	4000 m	4000 m	4000 m
Max grade	20/1000	15/1000	15/1000	15/1000	15/1000
Minimum longitudinal curve radius	10 000 m	15 000 m	15 000 m	15 000 m	15 000 m
Construction gauge		Height: 7700 mm		Width: 4400 mm	
Rolling stock gauge		Height: 5450 mm		Width: 3400 mm	
Rail		60·8 kg/m			
		1500 m long-welded rails			
Track gauge		1435 mm			
Formation width	10·7 m	11·6 m	11·0 m	11·6 m	11·6 m
Distance between track centres	4·2 m	4·3 m	4·3 m	4·3 m	4·3 m
Power system	154 kV or 77 kV 2 lines	275 kV or 220 kV 2 lines		275 kV 2 lines	
Feeder system	25 kV 60 Hz ac single phase booster-transformer	25 kV 60 Hz ac single phase auto-transformer		25 kV 50 Hz ac single phase auto-transformer	
Catenary system	Composite compound	Heavy compound	Heavy compound	Heavy compound	Heavy compound
Train control		ATC (automatic train control) CTC (centralised traffic control) COMTRAC (computer-aided traffic control)			
Opening date	October 1964	March 1972	March 1975	June 1982 (Omiya-Morioka)	November 1982
Seating capacity, Hikari train				1342	
Seating capacity, Kodama train				1483	
Seating capacity, all Tohoku and Joetsu trains				885	

Electrification in progress, November 1982

Line	Section	Route-km	Line current
Echigo	Kashiwazaki-Niigata	83·8	1·5 kV dc
Yahiko	Yahiko-Higashisanjo	17·4	1·5 kV dc
Takayama	Gifu-Toyama	225·8	1·5 kV dc
Fukuchiyama	Takarazuka-Fukuchiyama	90·5	1·5 kV dc
Sanin	Kyoto-Kinosaki	159·6	1·5 kV dc
Nara	Kizu-Kyoto	34·7	1·5 kV dc
Kansai	Kizu-Nara	7·0	1·5 kV dc
Wakayama	Gojo-Wakayama	52·1	1·5 kV dc
Kisei	Wakayama-Wakayamashi	2·3	1·5 kV dc
Chikuhi	Meinohama-Nijinomatsubara	37·6	1·5 kV dc
Yobuko	Nijinomatsubara-Karatsu	5·0	1·5 kV dc
Karatsu	Karatsu-Nishi Karatsu	2·3	1·5 kV dc
Total		718·1	

Diesel locomotives

Class	Wheel arrange-ment	Trans-mission	Rated power hp	Max lb (kg)	Tractive effort Continuous at lb (kg)	mph (km/h)	Max speed mph (km/h)	Wheel dia in (mm)	Total weight tons	Length ft in (mm)	Year first built	Builders Mechanical parts	Engine & type	Transmission type
DD 51	B-2-B	Hyd	2200	39 680 (18 000)			59 (95)	33¹³/₁₆ (860)	84	59' 1" (18 000)	1962	H M K	2×1100 hp DML 61Z	DW 2A DW 2A
DD 53	B-2-B	Hyd	2200	39 680 (18 000)			59 (95)	33¹³/₁₆ (860)	81	53' 2" (16 200)	1964	K	2×1100 hp DML 6182	DW 2AR DW 2AR
DD 13	B-B	Hyd	1000	37 040 (16 800)			44 (70)	33¹³/₁₆ (860)	56	44' 7½" (13 600)	1957	K M N H	2 × 500 hp DMF 31SB	DS 12/135
DD 14	B-B	Hyd	1000	40 870 (18 540)			44 (70)	33¹³/₁₆ (860)	58	47' 0" (14 325)	1960	K	2 × 500 hp DMF 31 SBR	DS 12/135

Class	Wheel arrangement	Transmission	Rated power hp	Max lb (kg)	Tractive effort Continuous at lb (kg)	mph (km/h)	Max speed mph (km/h)	Wheel dia in (mm)	Total weight tons	Length ft in (mm)	Year first built	Builders Mechanical parts	Engine & type	Transmission type
DD 15	B-B	Hyd	1000		36 380 (16 500)		44 (70)	33¹³/₁₆ (860)	55	44' 7½" (13 600)	1961	N	2 × 500 hp DMF 31 SBR	DS 12/135
DD 16	B-B	Hyd	800		31 750 (14 400)		47 (75)	33¹³/₁₆ (860)	49	38' 10" (11 840)	1972	J N R N K	DML 61Z	DW 2A
DE 10	AAA-B	Hyd	1350		43 000 (19 500)		53 (85)	33¹³/₁₆ (860)	65	46' 5" (14 150)	1966	K N H	DML61ZA, B	DWA
DE 11	AAA-B	Hyd	1350		46 300 (21 000)		53 (85)	33¹³/₁₆ (860)	70	46' 5" (14 150)	1968	K N	DML61ZA, B	DWA
DE 15	AAA-B	Hyd	1350		43 000 (19 500)		53 (85)	33¹³/₁₆ (860)	65	46' 5" (14 150)	1967	N	DML61ZA, B	DWA
DF 50	B-B-B	Elec	1200		27 550 (12 500)	10.9 (17.5)	56 (90)	39⅜ (1000)	76	53' 10" (16 400)	1965	K N T H	MANV6V22/30mA Sulzer 8LDA25	
Shinkansen 911	B-B-B	Hyd	2200		59 500 (27 000)	100 (160)		35⅞ (910)	90	63' 8" (19 400)	1964	N	2 × 1100 hp DML61Z	DWZB
Shinkansen 912	B-B	Hyd	740		30 865 (14 000)	44 (70)		33¹³/₁₆ (860)	56	44' 7¼" (13 600)	1959	N	2 × 370 hp DMF 31S	DS 12/135

Electric locomotives

Class	Wheel arrangement	Line current	Rated output kW	Tractive effort (full field) Continuous at lb (kg)	mph (km/h)	Max speed mph (km/h)	Wheel dia in (mm)	Weight tonnes	Length ft in (mm)	Year built	Builders
ED 71	B-B	20 kV 50 Hz	1900	35 270 (16 000)	26·5 (42·4)	59 (95)	44 (1120)	67	47' 3" (14 400)	1959	M T H
ED 72	B-2-B	20 kV 60 Hz	1900	31 100 (14 100)	30·5 (49·1)	62 (100)	44 (1120)	87	57' 1" (17 400)	1961	T
ED 73	B-B	20 kV 60 Hz	1900	31 100 (14 100)	30·5 (49·1)	62 (100)	44 (1120)	67·2	47' 3" (14 400)	1962	T
ED 74	B-B	20 kV 60 Hz	1900	31 100 (14 100)	30·5 (49·1)	62 (100)	44 (1120)	67·2	46' 11" (14 300)	1962	M
ED 75	B-B	20 kV 50 Hz	1900	31 100 (14 100)	30·5 (49·1)	62 (100)	44 (1120)	67·2	60' 4½" (18 400)	1963	M H T
ED 76	B-2-B	20 kV 50 or 60 Hz	1900	31 100 (14 100)	30·5 (49·1)	62 (100)	44 (1120)	90·5	60' 4½" (18 400)	1965	H M T
ED 77	B-2-B	20 kV 50 Hz	1900	31 100 (14 100)	30·5 (49·1)	62 (100)	44 (1120)	75	51' 10" (15 800)	1965	H M T
ED 78	B-2-B	20 kV 50 Hz	1900	31 100 (14 100)	30·5 (49·1)	62 (100)	44 (1120)	81·5	58' 9" (17 900)	1968	H
EF 59	2C + C2	1500 V dc	1350	26 000 (11 800)	26 (42)	56 (90)	49¼ (1250)	106·6	65' 4¼" (19 920)	1963	JNR (R B)
EF 62	C-C	1500 V dc	2550	51 600 (23 400)	24·2 (39)	62 (100)	44 (1120)	96	59' 1" (18 000)	1962	K T To
EF 63	B-B-B	1500 V dc	2550	51 600 (23 400)	24·2 (39)	62 (100)	44 (1120)	108	59' 3" (18 050)	1962	T M K
EF 64	B-B-B	1500 V dc	2550	44 850 (20 350)	28 (45)	71 (115)	44 (1120)	96	58' 9" (17 900)	1964	T K To
EF 65	B-B-B	1500 V dc	2550	44 850 (20 350)	28 (45)	71 (115)	44 (1120)	96	54' 2" (16 500)	1964	K To T N
EF 66	B-B-B	1500 V dc	3900	43 200 (19 590)	44·9 (72·2)	75 (120)	44 (1120)	100	59' 8½" (18 200)	1968	K To
EF 67	B-B-B	1500 V dc	2850	46 630 (21 150)	30·5 (49·1)	62 (100)		99·6	55' 11½" (17 050)	1981	JNR
EF 70	B-B-B	20 kV 60 Hz	2300	42 990 (19 500)	26·1 (42)	62 (105)	44 (1120)	96	54' 11½" (16 750)	1961	H M
EF 71	B-B-B	20 kV 50 Hz	2700	46 500 (21 100)	28·6 (46·1)	62 (100)	44 (1120)	100·8	60' 8" (18 500)	1968	M T
EF 30 Dual current	B+B+B	1·5 kV dc 20 kV 60 Hz	1800	30 420 (13 800)	29 (46·7)	53 (85)	39⅜ (1000)	96	54' 4" (16 560)	1960	H M T
EF 81 Dual current	B-B-B	1·5 kV dc 20 kV 50 Hz	2550	44 050 (19 980)	28·4 (45·7)	62 (115)	44 (1120)	100·8	61' 0" (18 600)	1968	H M
EF 80 Dual current	B-B-B	1·5 kV dc 20 kV 50 Hz	1950	31 970 (14 500)	29·8 (48)	62 (105)	44 (1120)	96	57' 5" (17 500)	1962	H M

Abbreviations
M: Mitsubishi Electric Co, Mitsubishi Heavy Industries
T: Tokyo Shibaura Elec Co
H: Hitachi Mfg Co
K: Kawasaki Heavy Industries
To: Toyo Elec Co
N: Nippon Sharyo Seizo Ltd

Electric railcars

Class	Line voltage	Motored axles per motor car	Rated output (kW) per motor	Max speed kmlh	Weight tonnes per car (M-motor T-trailer)	Seating capacity per motor car	Length per car mm	No in service	Year first built	Builders Mechanical parts	Builders Electrical equipment
103	1·5 kV dc	4	110	100	M 39·7 T 28·8	54	20 000	3399	1962	N T H K Kn	H T M Fe To
105	1·5 kV dc	4	110	100	M 40·5 T 27·8	60	20 000	60	1980	T	H T M Fe To
201	1·5 kV dc	4	150	100	M 41·7 T 30·6	54	20 000	210	1979	N T H K Kn	H T M Fe To
113	1·5 kV dc	4	120	100	M 41 Ts 36·3	72	20 000	2977	1963	N T H K Kn	H T M Fe To
115	1·5 kV dc	4	120	100	M 38·7 T 28·5	76	20 000	1808	1962	N T H K Kn	H T M Fe To
117	1·5 kV dc	4	120	110	M 43·7 Tc 35·9	64	20 000	156	1979	N K Kn	H T M Fe To
415	1·5 kV dc 20 kV ac	4	100	100	M 37·9 Tc 29·6	96	20 000	217	1960	N K Kn	H T M Fe To
153	1·5 kV dc	4	100	110	M 37·3 T 27·5	84	20 000	254	1958	K Kn N	H T M Fe To
455	1·5 kV dc 20 kV ac	4	120	110	M 43·4 T 33·1	84	20 000	539	1965	N T H K Kn	H T M Fe To
711	20 kV ac	4	150	110	M 45·6 Tc 32·2	78	20 000	114	1963	H T K	H T M Fe To
183	1·5 kV dc	4	120	120	M 42·5 Ts 32·4	68	20 000	352	1972	N T K Kn	H T M Fe To
185	1·5 kV dc	4	120	110	M 43·3 T 33·6	68	20 000	178	1980	N T K H Kn	H T M Fe To
381	1·5 kV dc	4	120	120	M 36·1 Ts 35·0	76	21 300	991	1973	N H K Kn	H T M Fe To
485	1·5 kV dc 20 kV ac	4	120	120	M 39·6 Tc 40·2	72	20 500	1251	1968	H T K N	H T M Fe To
583	1·5 kV dc 20 kV ac	4	120	120	M 43·7 T 35·3	45	20 500	1860	1967	H T K N Kn	H T M Fe To
781	20 kV ac	4	150	120	M 46·2 T 42·9	64	20 500	48	1978	H K	H T M Fe To

Shinkansen train-sets (all cars powered)

Class	Cars per unit	Line voltage	Motor cars per unit	Motored axles per motor car	Rated output (kW) per motor	Max speed kmlh	Weight tonnes per car	Seating capacity per motor car	Length per car mm	Cars in service	Year first built	Builders Mechanical parts	Builders Electrical equipment
0	16	25 kV ac	16	4	185	210	56·0	100	25 000	2240	1963	N T H K R	H T M Fe To Se
200	12	25 kV ac	12	4	230	210	56·5	100	25 000	432	1980	N T H K R	H T M Fe To Se

Diesel railcars

Class	Driven axles	Transmission	Rated power (hp)	Max speed kmlh	Weight tonnes per car	Seating capacity per car	Length per car mm	No in service	Year first built	Builders Mechanical parts	Builders Engine & type	Builders Transmission
80	4	TC2A	180 × 2	100	41·2	72	21 100	262	1961	F NT	DMH17H D S NT	S NC
183	2	DW10	220	100	47·4	68 40	21 300	54	1978	F NT	DMF15HSA D S NT	S NC
28	2	TC2A	180	95	34·1	84	20 805	857	1961	F NT	DMH17A D S NT	S NC
58	4	TC2A	180 × 2	95	39·4	84	21 300	132	1961	F NT	DMH17A D S NT	S NC
40	2	DW10	220	95	37·3	66	21 300	373	1977	F NT	DMF15HSA D S NT	S NC
47	2	DW10	220	95	35·9	76	21 300	362	1976	F NT	DMF15HSA D S NT	S NC

Abbreviations
M: Mitsubishi Electric Co, Mitsubishi Heavy Industries
T: Tokyo Shibaura Elec Co
H: Hitachi Mfg Co
K: Kawasaki Heavy Industries
To: Toyo Elec Co
N: Nippon Sharyo Seizo Ltd
Kn: Kinki Nihon Sharyo
Fe: Fuji Denki
F: Fuji Juko
NT: Niigata Tekko
S: Shinko Zouki
D: Daihatsu
NC: Niigata Converter

Major private railways

Hankyu Corporation

8-8 Kakutacho, Kita-Ku, Osaka

Telephone: 06 373 5088

President: Sadao Shibatani
Vice-Presidents: Okikazu Yamaguchi
　　　　　　　　Masaharu Nagata
　　　　　　　　Kohei Kobayashi

Gauge: 1435 mm
Route length: 141.2 km
Electrification: 141·2 km at 1·5 kV dc

Traffic

	1980/81	1981/82
Total passenger-km (million)	721	733
Total passenger journeys (million)	10·368	10·670
Average length of passenger journey (km)	14·4	14·6

Finance (million yen)

Revenues	1981/82
Passengers and baggage	68 358
Other	43 563
Total	111 921

Expenditure	1981/82
Direct operating costs	100 183
Depreciation	4983
Financial charges	3150
Total	108 316

The Corporation was set up in 1907 to construct a

Hankyu emu leaving Osaka

600-volt interurban railway to develop suburban Osaka, and is now a diversified enterprise as well as a railway operator. Since converted to 1·5 kV, the railway serves nine lines with 96 stations and runs over 1000 eight-car trains daily on its Kobe line and to Kyoto, over 700 a day to Takarazuka. The exit from Osaka is six-track. Traffic is CTC-controlled from a centre in Osaka.

The railway owns 712 powered and 534 trailer cars, over two-thirds of which are air-conditioned

and of which the latest employ solid state chopper control; 112 cars have been added to stock since 1980 and 33 were ordered for 1983 delivery. Substations are solid state. An automatic train stop system is combined with speed-control cab signalling. Tracks are predominantly laid with 50 kg/m rail on both wood and prestressed concrete sleepers, spaced 1720 per km, and permitting a maximum axleload of 17·5 tonnes. Minimum curve radius is 100 metres.

Electric railcars or multiple-units

Cars per unit	Line voltage	Motor cars per unit	Motored axles per motor car	Rated output (kW) per motor	Max speed km/h	Weight tonnes per car (M-motor T-trailer)	Seating capacity per car	Length per car mm	No in service	Rate of acceleration m/s²	Year first built	Builders Mechanical parts	Electrical equipment
4, 6, 7, 8, 10	1·5 kV dc	2, 4, 4, 4, 6	4	130 140 150 170	110	M 35-38 T 25-28	145	19 000	M 712 T 534	0·72	1948-82	Sumitomo Metal Industries Nippon Air Brake Alna Koki	Toshiba Corporation Toyo Electric Mfg Co

Kei-Han Electric Railway

1-47-5 Kyobashi, Higashiku, Osaka

President: Seitaro Aoki

Gauge: 1435 mm
Route length: 90 km

Electrification: 90 km at 600 V dc

The railway operates 312 emus, 324 other power cars and 402 trailers.

Keihin Electric Express Railway

20-20, Takanawa 2-chome, Minato-Ku, Tokyo

Telephone: 03 443 5111

President: Michio Iida

Gauge: 1435 mm
Route length: 83·8 km
Electrification: 1·5 kV dc

Traffic

	1980/81	1981/82
Total passenger-km (million)	5180·7	5273·9
Total passenger journeys (million)	378·6	384·5
Average length of passenger journey (km)	13·68	13·72

Finance (million yen)

Revenues	
Passengers and baggage	37 805·6
Other income	53 187·3
Total	90 992·9

Expenditure	
Staff/personnel	25 189
Materials and services	38 940·5
Depreciation	6921·5
Financial charges	16 547·0
Total	87 598·0

The railway owns 585 electric power cars and 63 trailers. Its track is laid with 50 kg/m rails on 165 mm thick prestressed concrete sleepers with elastic fastenings, with a minimum curvature of 60 metres radius. Maximum axleloading is 13·7 tonnes.

Electric railcars or multiple-units

Class	Cars per unit	Line voltage	Motor cars per unit	Motored axles per motor car	Rated output (kW) per motor	Max speed km/h	Weight tonnes per car (M-motor T-trailer)	Total seating capacity	Length per car mm	No in service	Rate of acceleration m/s²	Year first built	Builders Mechanical parts	Electrical equipment
1000	2 4 6 8	1500 dc	2 4 6 8	4	75·9	105	M 35	108 228 348 468	18 000	356	3·5	1958	Kawasaki, Tokyu, Sumitomo etc	Mitsubishi, Toyo, Koito etc
800	3 6	1500 dc	3 6	4	100	100	M 35	140 284	18 000	99	3·5	1978	Kawasaki, Tokyu, Sumitomo etc	Mitsubishi, Toyo, Koito etc
2000	8	1500 dc	6	4	120	105	M 35 T 29	440	18 000	8	3·0	1982	Kawasaki, Tokyu, Sumitomo etc	Mitsubishi, Toyo, Koito etc

Keisei Electric Railway

10-3, 1-chome, Oshiage, Sumidaku, Tokyo

Telephone: 625 2111

President: M Sato

Gauge: 1435 mm
Route length: 82 km
Electrification: 82 km at 1·5 kV dc

The railway operates 399 emu cars.

Kinki Nippon Railway

6-chome, Uehommachi Tennojiku, Osaka

Telephone: 06 771 3331

President: Yoshinori Ueyama

Gauge: 1435 mm; 1067 mm; 762 mm
Route length: 586·7 km
Electrification: 1·5 kV (1435 mm gauge) and 750 V (narrow gauge) dc

Part of a conglomerate with wide-ranging commercial interests, like the majority of Japan's private

railways, the Kinki Nippon runs limited expresses throughout the Kinki and Tokai areas of Japan. Its main line is inter-city, connecting Osaka and Nagoya, and it also serves Nara, Kyoto and the Ise-Shima National Park.

Rolling stock includes bi-level and vista-dome passenger cars. It comprises 12 electric locomotives, 1696 emu cars and 37 freight wagons.

Nagoya Railroad
Meitetsu Corporation

2-4, 1-chome, Meiki, Nakamura-ku, Nagoya

Telephone: 571 2111

President: K Takeda

Gauge: 1067 mm
Route length: 543 km
Electrification: 543 km at 1·5 kV dc and 600 V dc

Between 1941 and 1944 the private urban railways of the Nagoya region were knitted into a coherent regional network by conversion of downtown tram tracks into an inter-system connection focussed on a new underground Shin-Nagoya station alongside the Japanese National Railways station. Since then the system has been rationalised by some closures, but new lines have been laid to cater for fresh suburban development, such as the Chita line in 1980. Besides the Nagoya Railroad, the diversified corporation also runs bus, taxi, road freight, sea ferry and air-taxi services, hotels, restaurants and travel agencies.

The Shin-Nagoya station handles over 800 trains

a day, with 25 trains hourly each way on the main route between Shin Gifu/Inuyama and Toyoake/Otagawa. Electrification was progressively standardised at 1·5 kV dc after the unification of the system, but some 600 volts dc survives on lines to the north of Gifu.

Rolling stock totals 14 electric locomotives, 791 emu cars, 12 diesel railcars (employed for a joint service over Japanese National Railway tracks between Jingumae and the Toyama region, via a connection between the two systems at Shin Unuma) and 44 freight wagons. Over half the emu fleet is of post-1955 construction, with lightweight bodies, rheostatic braking and fully suspended motors.

Nankai Electric Railway

6-12 Nanba-shinchi, Minami-ku, Osaka

President: D Kawakatsu

Gauge: 1435 mm; 1067 mm
Route length: 191 km

Electrification: 191 km at 600 V dc

The railway operates 575 emu cars and 91 freight cars. It runs from Osaka to Wakayama.

Nishi Nippon Railroad

11-17 Tenjin 1-chome, Fukuoka

Telephone: 092 761 6631

President: Hirotsugu Yoshimoto

Gauge: 1435 mm
Route length: 95·5 km
Electrification: 95·5 km at 1·5 kV dc

The railway owns 264 electric power cars, 257 trailers and seven freight wagons. Track is laid with 37, 40 and 50 kg/m rails, allowing 14·3 tonnes maximum axleloadings; minimum curvature is 130 metres.

Odakyu Electric Railway

8-3 Nishi-shinjuku 1-chome, Shinjuku-ku, Tokyo

President: S Hirota
Gauge: 1067 mm
Route length: 120·1 km
Electrification: 120·1 km at 1·5 kV dc

The railway runs from Shinjuku, Tokyo, to Gotemba and Yumoto. It owns four electric locomotives, 701 emu cars and 15 freight wagons. A 1·1 km, 600-volt dc monorail is also operated.

Seibu Railway

16-15 1-chome, Minami-Ikebukuro, Toshima-ku, Tokyo

President: Yoshiaki Tsutsumi

Gauge: 1067 mm
Route length: 178·2 km
Electrification: 178·2 km at 1·5 kV dc

Part of a multi-faceted corporation that includes hotels, housing and road transport among its businesses, the railway serves the western suburbs of Tokyo with two main routes radiating from terminals on or near Japanese National Railways' city-centre Yamanote loop, the 43·8 km Ikebukuro and 22·6 km Shinjuku lines. These lines throw off and are

in some cases interconnected in the suburbs by 10 branches. The Ikebukuro terminus deals with an average of 700 train workings daily, with departures at 1½ minute headways in the evening peak.

Traffic runs at some 555 million passenger journeys a year, of which 67 per cent are made on season tickets and generate 46 per cent of total receipts. In peak travel periods load factors average 234 per cent, calculated on the following basis: 100 per cent, nominal car seat and standing capacity fully occupied; 150 per cent, ability to read a magazine preserved; 200 per cent, space available only to read a pocket book; 250 per cent, no passenger limb movement possible; 300 per cent, extreme limits of physical tolerance. Beyond 200 per cent trains can only be further loaded with the aid of platform 'pusher' staff specifically employed for the purpose. The railway also moves some 850 000 tonnes of

freight a year, 90 per cent of it cement on the Ikebukuro line and owns 78 freight cars. The railway's operating ratio is approximately 87 per cent.

Improvements in progress include construction of a 6 km branch, partly underground, from Ikebukuro, rejoining the existing line near Nerima, and the quadrupling of the Ikebukuro route for 4·6 km from Nerima to Shakujikoen.

The fleet of 845 emu cars comprises 12 types and is formed into 216 train-sets; most numerous type is the air-conditioned 101 series, dating from 1969, which numbers 330 cars. Six 'Red Arrow' six-car units are used for a supplementary-fare service, including perambulated buffet, on the Ikebukuro line. The 10 locomotives comprise four ex-JNR Westinghouse-built units of 1922 build and four recent Mitsubishi-built Type E851 96-tonne B-B-Bs of 2250 kW.

Takamatsu Kotohira Electric Railroad

320 Sakuramachi, Takamatsu City

Gauge: 1435 mm
Route length: 60·2 km
Electrification: 60·2 km at 600V/1·5 kV dc

The railway runs 80 emu power cars, 78 trailers and two freight wagons.

Tobu Railway

1-2, 1-chome, Oshiage, Sumida-ku, Tokyo

Telephone: 623 5111

President: Kaichiro Nezu

Gauge: 1067 mm
Route length: 483·2 km
Electrification: 471 km at 1·5 kV dc

The railway's main line runs 135 km northward from Tokyo to Shimoimaichi and Nikko, with branches to Utsunomiya and Isezaki. The railway operates 36 electric locomotives, 549 emus, 809 passenger cars, three diesel cars and 567 freight cars.

Tokyu Corporation

26-20 Sakuragaika-cho, Shibuya-ku, Tokyo 150

Telephone: 463 1111
Telex: 2423395

President: Noboru Gotoh

Gauge: 1372 mm; 1067 mm
Route length: 5·1 km; 94·4 km
Electrification: 5·1 km, 1372 mm gauge at 600 V dc
　90·4 km, 1067 mm gauge at 1·5 kV dc

The railway is one of 234 companies and eight non-profit institutions within the Corporation, which was established in 1922 and now covers real estate enterprises, bus and taxi companies, department

stores, supermarkets, construction companies, road freight, railcar building, advertising agencies, construction companies, shipping, airline and air freight activity with 100 aircraft. The rail network is located in the south-west of the Tokyo metropolitan area and with an average daily record of 2 million passenger journeys is the busiest in the capital's suburban area. Average length of passenger journey is only 8·5 km.

Traffic

	1979/80	1980/81
Total train-km (million)	13·935	13·795
Total passenger journeys (million)	736·867	745·543
Total passenger-km (million)	6143·3	6350·9

Signalling

On the Tohyoko, Mekama, Ohimachi, Ikegami and Penetoshi lines a total of 81·6 route-km is equipped with a cab signalling ATC system and automatic train stop operated through the track circuiting.

Fare collection

Ticket issue and revenue data collection are automatic. Ticket issue is by both uni- and multi-functional machines which also cover season tickets, supplemented by fare adjustment machines. Gate machines check and collect.

Track

Tokyu employs 50 kg/m rail on prestressed concrete sleepers of 150-160 mm thickness, with double elastic fastenings.

Rolling stock

Tokyu operates 605 electric power cars and 195 trailers. The great majority of the vehicles has been built in the Corporation's own workshops, including its most recent additions of 45 power cars in 1979, 29 in 1980, 25 in 1981 and 34 in 1982. These were all for the 1067 mm gauge, in each case featuring four 130 kW motors and arranged for a maximum speed of 120 km/h.

Tokyo metropolitan area passenger transport
(end-March 1980)

	No of carriers	Operating km	No of passengers (million)	% of total passengers
Japanese National Railways	1	788	4108	24
Other public railways	3	210	1933	11
Private railways	15	908	3876	23
Buses	35	—	2291	14
Taxis and private limousines	—	—	906	5
Private cars	—	—	3899	23
	54	1906	17 013	100

Operations (end-March 1981)

	Tokyu	Average of 13 other largest private railways
Per operating km per day:		
Revenue (million yen)	1·311	0·553
Operating income (000 yen)	204	62
No of passengers (million)	746	453
Total track-km operated	99·5	211·6

At present, Tokyu ranks in the middle group in terms of track-km operated, but first in terms of revenue per operating km and carries the third largest number of passengers.

Finance

	Fiscal year ended March			6 months ended September	
	1979	1980	1981	1980	1981
Revenue from railway operation (million yen)	39 008	45 362	47 596	23 682	25 651
Cost of railway operation (million yen)	31 943	35 832	39 914	18 878	21 078
Operating income (million yen)	7065	9530	7682	4804	4573
Passenger journeys (million)	725	737	746	378	387

JORDAN

Ministry of Transport

PO Box 1929, Amman

Telephone: 41461
Telex: 1541

Minister: Eng Ali Al-Suheimat
Permanent Secretary: Eng Hashem Taher

Hedjaz Jordan Railway (HJR)
Aqaba Railway Corporation (ARC)

PO Box 582, Ministry of Transport, Amman

Telephone: 55413; 55414
Telex: 1236

Director-General (HJR): M R Qoseini
Director-General (ARC): Sahel Hamzeh
Deputy Director-General: M K Emad Eddeen
Departmental Heads
  Finance: A Jukhadar
  Operating and Mechanical: O Khreisheh
  Traffic: S L Nasser
  Permanent Way: M Al-Bataineh
  Engineering: M K Emad Eldein
  Stores and Supplies: M I Abu Taha

Gauge: 1050 mm
Route length: 618 km

ARC

A separate directorate for the newly-formed Aqaba Railway Corp (ARC) was set up in May 1978 and ARC began operation as a separate concern in 1979.

ARC's function is haulage of phosphates from mines at Al-Hassa to the Red Sea port of Aqaba over a 260 km network of new and reconstructed lines, which are passed for 16-tonne axleloads. Part of the route, from Al-Hassa to Hettiya, is the original Hedjaz Railway rehabilitated; the remainder is new. ARC also connects with HJR at Batn el Ghul.

In 1982 ARC was extended to serve a further phosphate mine at Wadi el Abyad, north of El Hassa and east of Menzil, the output of which raised its exclusively phosphates traffic from 1·63 to 2 million tonnes per annum. Tonnage was expected to reach 4 million tonnes by 1985. Phosphate carryings could be trebled by development of a further source at Shediya, 30 km south of Ma'an, but in the meantime ARC hopes to break into the maritime traffic of other commodities, including containerised freight, flowing between Aqaba and Amman. RITES provides technical and supervisory assistance under a contract lasting until September 1984.

A prime concern in face of this expected growth is the limitations of the existing infrastructure, with its curves of 125 metres radius and ruling gradient of 2·7 per cent, which is unbroken for 30 km between Batn el Ghul and Aqaba. This restricts train length to 30 wagons of 42 tonnes payload each and enforces double-heading. Curvature has dictated adoption of Scheffel cross-braced bogies in recent wagon deliveries, which also feature air-operated discharge doors. If the Shediya mine begins production as planned in 1988, construction of a better-aligned route to Aqaba may be unavoidable.

The block signalling between El Hassa and Umran is controlled by uhf radio, employing fail-safe frequency-division multiplex apparatus, and extension of this method to Wadi el Abyad was being planned in 1983, for execution by mid-1985. A vhf radio system, using mobile sets, connects train and station staff with the Ma'an control centre.

ARC's traction comprises 18 GE Type U20C 2150 hp, three GE Type U18C 1850 hp, eight GE Type UL7C 1750 hp diesel-electric locomotives and nine 650-850 hp diesels. Wagon stock totalled 276 at the end of 1982. Deliveries in 1983 were to include 60 wagons from Fauvet-Girel with aluminium bodies,

offering an increased payload per vehicle of 47 tonnes.

HRC

ARC's expanding traffic has been at the expense of HRC, which saw its annual freight movement collapse from 1·18 million tonnes in 1978 to 5781 tonnes by 1980, and its freight tonne-km from 311·9 million to some 450 000 over the same period. Passenger traffic, too, slumped from 96 649 journeys and 6·9 million passenger-km in 1976 to 47 578 and 6 million respectively in 1980. The only passenger trains are run twice weekly between Amman and Damascus, with coaching stock dating from the line's opening in 1901-08. HRC operates five GM 950 hp diesel-electric locomotives and seven oil-fired steam locomotives of Japanese build.

The future of HRC is heavily dependent on a positive conclusion to the long-running tri-partite discussions between Jordan, Syria and Saudi Arabia over revival of the whole Hedjaz Railway route as a modern, standard-gauge line from Damascus through Amman to Medina. Syria intends to build from Damascus to Deraa with Soviet aid, but Jordan is still considering the proposal in terms of national transport need and Saudi Arabia regards the scheme as a decidedly long-term item in its railway planning.

Meanwhile, HRC has begun upgrading its track, which has an axleload limit of 10·5 tonnes. The Menzil-El Hassa section (26 km), used by ARC phosphate trains, has been completely reconstructed on a widened formation, with ballast and bridges renewed, and long-welded S33 section rail on prestressed concrete sleepers. HRC's 1981-85 plan envisages similar work from Ma'an to Batn el Ghul and from Menzil to Amman. The upgrading provides for a maximum of 100 km/h, as opposed to the previous limit of 60 km/h.

New lines in the Amman area, one to serve the Queen Alia airport under construction south of the capital, another to the University of Jordan, 12 km from the heart of Amman, and a third to provide a commuter operation to Zarqa, to the north, have been studied by Transurb of Belgium.

KAMPUCHEA

Cambodia Railways
Chemins de Fer du Cambodge

Railway Headquarters, Phnom Penh

Telephone: 25156
Telegrams: Fercam, Phnom Penh

President and Managing Director: In Nhel
Deputy Managing Director: Seng Kim Chun
Technical Director: Bou Saman
Chief, Mechanical Engineering: Khlaut Thol
Chief, Permanent Way: Youg Sokhon
Chief, Operating: Em Thoul

Gauge: 1000 mm
Route length: 649 km

The 385 km line from Phnom Penh, the capital, to Poipet where connection is made with the State Railway of Thailand, was built in two sections in 1930-32 and 1939-40 when the entire area was known as French Indo-China. The first section, to Mongkolborey, was built and worked by the Compagnie des Chemins de Fer du Sud de l'Indochine. This was purchased in 1936 by the Chemin de Fer Non Concédés de l'Indochine. In July 1952, all lines within Kampuchea (then Cambodia) were formed into the Chemins de Fer du Cambodge.

Because of the country's recent troubles only 33 per cent of the system is in operation. The newest line on the system, between Phnom Penh and Kompong Som (264 km), opened in 1969, has been closed to traffic since 1970 owing to damage caused during hostilities. This is the country's only rail outlet to the sea, other than via Thailand to Bangkok. The Phnom Penh—Poipet line has been largely unusable since 1978, but in 1982 plans to reopen the 139 km to Battambang were announced.

Motive power
The majority of the railway's present traction requirements were at last available report met by 13 diesel-electric locomotives and a large number of steam locomotives. Backbone of the diesel-electric fleet were Alsthom-built BB 1200 hp units fitted with MGO-V12 BZSHR engines delivered in 1966/67. Due to lack of spares, however, the workshops department had been experiencing difficulties in keeping these locomotives in operation. In 1982 20 locomotives and 265 passenger cars were reported serviceable.

Permanent way and installations
A line linking Phnom Penh and Ho Chi Minh City (formerly Saigon) has been projected for a number of years but consistently cancelled owing to hostilities. The line would fill one of the missing links in the Transasian Railway Project. It was announced in mid-1978 that a new line was to be built between Samrong and Kompong Speu City following a study by Chinese engineers.

KENYA

Kenya Railways (KR)

PO Box 30121, Nairobi

Telephone: 21211
Telex: 22254

Chairman: L W Wambaa
Managing Director: D K Ngini
Directors: G F Kuchio Masbay
Dr K Otara
N K Lelei
J D Mturi
D R Kamau
J B O Omondi
Corporation Secretary: Gideon P Mbito
Chief Traffic Manager: Brown Waweru
Chief Civil Engineer: Joel Mudhune
Chief Mechanical and Electrical Engineer: Omar F Alkizim
Chief Personnel Manager: Charles Muthee
Chief Accountant: Zadock Baraza Kambogo Shimba
Chief Supplies Officer: James Karanja

Gauge: 1000 mm
Route length: 2084 km

Transport development
The break-up of the East African Railways Corporation in 1976 gave rise to the creation of three separate railway systems and the birth of Kenya Railways in 1977 with its headquarters in Nairobi. It is a state corporation run by a board of directors. The Kenya Railways operates the main line from Mombasa through Nairobi, Nakuru and Eldoret to the border of Kenya with Uganda and the branch line joining the Lake Victoria town of Kisumu to the farming centre of Nakuru. The rest are branch lines linking Nairobi to Nanyuki near Mt Kenya, Gilgil to Nyahururu, Voi to Taveta, Kisumu to Butere, Konza to Magadi and Rongai to Solai. The railway is also responsible for lakes services within Kenya.

Traffic
The former East African Railways when originally developed had no other competitive modes of transport. Today Kenya Railways is not only faced with severe road competition parallel to its routes, but also the white oil pipeline which from February 1978 carried all white petroleum products between Mombasa and Nairobi. Despite the competition, the railway remains the main transport mode for bulk goods, most of which are agricultural inputs, industrial and mining products.

Traffic

	1980	1981	1982
Total freight tonnage (000)	4287	4248	4065
Total freight tonne-km (million)	2276·6	2240·6	2097·04
Average net freight train load	567	560	573
Average freight wagon load	14·89	15·11	15·18
Total passenger-km (million)	702·88	774·22	748
Total passenger journeys (000)	2401	2356	2370
Average length of passenger journey (km)	293	329	328

Finances

	1979	1980	1981	1982
		(Sh million)		
Revenue from passengers, baggage and mail	51·884	56·123	62·715	88·046
Revenues from freight	488·695	555·033	736·929	874·7
Total revenues	575·877	611·156	879·815	962·746
Operating expenses including depreciation and other provisions	NA	828·161	879·222	1093·882

Freight tonnage receded slightly in 1981 and 1982 in face both of recession and of KR difficulties with rising staff costs and spare parts shortages, but was still ahead of the 1978 figure of 3·8 million tonnes. Passenger journeys, on the other hand, were still rising and in 1982 were 48 per cent above the 1978 total of 1·6 million.

Investment
In 1981 the World Bank approved a US$ 58 million loan with a 20 years' term to help finance a US$ 133·8 million improvement plan scheduled for execution by 1985. KR itself is financing the plan with US$ 42·7 million, the Government of Kenya with US$ 8·9 million, the African Development Bank with US$ 7·5 million and Kreditanstalt für Wiederaufbau with US$ 16·7 million. The programme covers installation of heavier rail over 108 km, relaying 73 km between Nakuru and Kisumu, and on the Kitale branch, purchase of track maintenance machinery, new hopper wagons and traction and vehicle spares, yard and terminal improvements, telecommunications improvements between Nairobi and Mombasa, expanded staff training facilities, and commissioning of technical assistance in management and planning development. A priority is development of container traffic, for which terminals are being installed at Embakasi, near Nairobi and later at Eldoret, in the Rift valley. A Mombasa-Embakasi container train service was to be launched late in 1983.

A decision was taken in 1981 to proceed with the engineering design of the first stage of the new Kerio Valley line northward from Rongai, near Nakuru, to Sigo, to cater for the fluorine mineral deposits in the Baringo uplands. Connection with the proposed Sudan Railways line from Wau to Juba on the Upper Nile is the ultimate possibility.

Surveys and financial studies were completed in 1982.

Motive power and rolling stock
Fleet numbers at the end of 1982: 229 diesel locos; 552 passenger coaches; 7757 freight wagons.

Between 1979 and 1981 six Class 93 main-line diesel-electric locomotives were received, completing an order placed on General Electric Co of USA. Seventeen Class 62 general-purpose diesel-hydraulic locomotives were received in 1979 to complete an order placed on Thyssen Henschel Rheinstahl AG of West Germany. Also acquired were 35 Class 47 shunting locomotives, the full quantity ordered from Hunslet Holdings Ltd, UK. A Canadian loan of C$2 million was secured in 1982 for purchase of spares for the 15 MLW-built Class 92 locomotives of 1971. In 1983 KR was converting 10 of these units from dc to ac transmission because of generator problems. It hopes also to re-engine some of its English Electric units.

The coaching stock will be reinforced with a further 11 cars from Kalmar Verkstad in 1983, followed in 1984 by a £23·8 million order of 74 cars, including five buffet and four restaurant cars, from British Rail Engineering. Freight stock will be increased by 95 wagons from BRE-Metro including bogie hoppers, and 24 wagons from Kalmar Verkstad.

Track
Rail: 29·76, 39·68, 47·12 kg/m
Cross ties (sleepers): Steel and timber (thickness 5 in)
Spacing: 1476/km
Fastenings: 'K' type and Pandrol
Minimum curvature radius: 106·7 m
Max gradient: 4%
Max axleload: 18 tons

Class 47 shunter delivered by Hunslet (UK) 1978-80

Class 93 diesel-electric locomotive

Diesel locomotives

Class	Wheel arrange-ment	Trans-mission	Rated power hp	Max lb (kg)	Tractive effort Continuous at lb (kg)	mph (km/h)	Max speed mph (km/h)	Wheel dia in (mm)	Total weight tons	Length ft in (mm)	No built	Year first built	Builders Mechanical parts	Engine & type	Transmission
92	1Co-Co1	Elec	2550	77 000 (35 000)	43 500 (19 730)	16·5 (26·4)	45 (72)	37½ (953)	113·64	59' 1¼" (18 015)	15	1971	MLW Ind	Alco 251F	GE Canada
93	Co-Co	Elec	2610	66 138 (30 000)	52 299 (23 700)	13·64 (22)	45 (72)	37½ (953)	98·9	60' 1¼" (18 320)	26	1978	GE (USA)	GE 7FDL12	GE (USA)
87 (90)	1Co-Co1	Elec	1840	51 600 (23 300)	44 500 (20 180)	11·7 (18·8)	45 (72)	37½ (953)	101·5 (Adhe-sive)	55' 7¼" (16 948)	10 14 20	1960 1964 1967/8	English Electric	EE 12 CSVT	EE
72	1Bo-Bo1	Elec	1240	40 000 (18 150)	32 500 (14 750)	10·7 (17·2)	45 (72)	37½ (953)	70·1	43' 9¼" (13 341)	10	1972	GEC Traction	EE 8CSVT	GEC
71 (91)	1Bo-Bo1	Elec	1240	40 000 (18 150)	32 000 (14 400)	10·5 (17·7)	45 (72)	37½ (953)	69	43' 9¼" (13 341)	10	1967	English Electric	EE 8CSVT	EE
62	B-B	Hyd	760	27 750 (12 500)	21 825 (9 900)	7·8 (12·3)	45 (72)	37½ (953)	38	37' 5" (11 404)	56	1977	Rheinstahl AG	MTU MB 12V 493 T210 (10) MTU EB 12V 396 TC11 (46)	Voith L520-U2
46 (86)	D	Hyd	606 (2×303)	32 900 (14 900)			20 (32)	39½ (1003)	48	36' 1¼" (11 007)	22	1967	Andrew Barclay	2 × Cummins	British Twin Disc CF 11500
35	C	Hyd	300	24 460 (11 100)	20 000 (9070)	3·8 (6·1)	17 (27)	39½ (1003)	36	29' 7¼" (9023)	15	1972	Andrew Barclay	Paxman 8 RPHL	Voith L320V
47	D	Hyd	525	35 060 (15 900)	23 590 (10 700)	17·5 (28)		39½ (1003)	52	31' 9½" (9680)	35	1979	Hunslet Holdings	Rolls Royce DV8TCE	Voith L2r3ZU

KOREA (Democratic People's Republic)

North Korea Railway

Pyongyang

The railway system is known to total over 4000 route-km of 1435 mm gauge. Electrification at 25 kV 50 Hz has been pursued on key routes and covers at least 500 km, but no recent information on the system or its traffic is available.

KOREA (Republic)

Ministry of Transportation

Seoul

Minister: Kyung Nole Chi
Vice-Minister: Jae Chul Lee
Permanent Secretary: Jong Ha Ju

Korean National Railroad (KNR)

168 Bongrae-dong, Jung-ku, Seoul

Administrator: Hae Joong Hwang
Deputy Administrator: Young Kwan Kim
Director General, Business Management: Young Kook Shin
  Civil Engineering Bureau: Hee Kook Kim
  Rolling Stock Bureau: Joong Min Kim
  Electrical Bureau: Yong Deuk Kim
  Finance and Accounting: Sung Yeung Hwang
  Transportation Bureau: Hyung Bae Kim
Director, Overseas Co-operation Division: Suk Ki Bang

Gauge: 1435 mm; 762 mm
Route length: 3074 km; 52 km
Electrification: 428 km at 25 kV 50 Hz ac

Transport development

The backbone of the railway system is the 444 km double-track Gyeongbu line, running between the nation's two principal cities, Pusan on the south-east coast across the Tsushima Straits from Japan and the capital city of Seoul in the north-west. Principal intermediate cities reached by this route include Taegu and Taejon. While it constitutes less than 15 per cent of total KNR route-km, the Gyeongbu line accounts for nearly half of the system's operating revenues. A second north-south route, and a revenue source second only to the Gyeongbu line, is afforded by the Chungang (Central) and Tonghaenambu lines. Diverging from the south-west from the Gyeongbu line at Taejon, the Honam line reaches into the rich agricultural plain of North and South Cholla provinces and the important south-western port of Mokpo. Branching from the Honam line at Iri is the Cholla line, which extends southward to Yosu, an important southern port and the site of a major oil refinery.

Linking these two lines across the south coast of South Korea with the Gyeongbu line near Pusan is the Kyongchon line. The Yongdong line, which links the east coast with the Chungang line at Yongju, was extended northward to the major east coast city of Kangnung. KNR's second route to the east coast was completed through the heart of the Taebaek mountain range late in 1973.

The solitary 762 mm branch, opened in 1937 from Suweon to Songdo, is to be converted to 1435 mm by 1986 and extended 8 km to the port of Inchon.

Traffic

Main road development and growth of coastal shipping have cost KNR its leading role in the nation's transport system, but rail traffic still rises. In 1982 KNR's share of the total passenger market was 25 to 27 per cent, of freight 44 to 48 per cent. A new upsurge of passenger journeys to 500 million, with 60 per cent of the total registered in the Seoul suburban area, was anticipated in 1982. Freight was expected to climb 6 per cent to 52 million tonnes, of which coal, the outstanding stimulus of freight growth, would represent 22 million tonnes, cement 10 million tonnes. Container traffic as yet accounts for only 600 000 tonnes.

Fifth five-year plan

KNR's fifth five-year plan (1982-86) envisages continuing growth of business to 798 million passenger journeys and 65·4 million tonnes of freight a year. To cope with it an investment of US$1900 million is budgeted.

Key item is construction of a new high-speed line between Seoul and Pusan, where density of passenger service already enforces segregation of most freight operation to the night hours. It is hoped to complete feasibility studies by 1986 and start construction of the first Seoul-Daejeon (150 km) section that year.

Other objectives are: double-tracking between Jecheon and Yeondang (25·3 km); upgrading of the Janghang and Jeonra lines to the ports of Janghang and Yeosu; acquisition of 276 locomotives, 464 passenger cars (in this department increase of air-conditioned stock from 28 to 78 per cent of the total, adoption of air suspension and introduction of long-haul compartment cars are planned) and 3465 freight wagons; acceleration and intensification of long-haul passenger services; introduction of com-puterised ticket issue and seat reservation; development of unit train freight working and of container transport; construction of new freight depots in principal centres, notably at Seoul, where two complexes are planned, one of 10 million tonnes a year capacity south of the city at Bugog, the other to the north-east at Seongbug; and increased mechanisation of track maintenance.

Electrification

Electrification of the 338·4 km from Seoul to Bugpyeong at 25 kV 60 Hz ac was completed between 1968 and 1975, and interconnected with the 1·5 kV dc Seoul metro, which results in employment of dual-voltage commuter emus (those owned by KNR are coloured blue, those owned by the city of Seoul are red, while the pure 1·5 kV dc emus belonging to Seoul are green). The electrified route-km carry 40 per cent of the nation's freight. Following agreement to a World Bank loan of US$ 122 million in 1983, the 64 km extension of electrification from Jecheon to Yeongju was to be put in hand.

Results (million)	1981
Total passenger journeys	441·129
Total passenger-km	21 528·49
Total freight tonnes	47·182
Total freight tonne-km	10 637

Finance (million won)	1981
Receipts from passengers and baggage	218 356·5
Receipts from freight and mail	141 732·1
Total revenue	360 088·6
Total operating costs	433 037·6

Motive power and rolling stock

The 1435 mm gauge traction in operation at the start of 1982 included 432 diesel and 90 electric locomotives, 340 emu cars and 126 diesel railcars, including two five-car long-haul units. Other passenger stock in operation totalled 2151 locomotive-hauled cars, including 28 dining and 31 sleeping cars; and the railway owned 16 565 freight cars. Orders were to be placed in 1983 for 320 bulk cement and 261 side-dump coal wagons.

Track

Main lines are mostly laid with 50 kg/m rail, but in 1981 KNR applied 60 kg/m rail to some heavily trafficked sections. Some secondary lines have 50 kg/m rail, others 37 kg/m. Sleepers are mostly wood, but more than a quarter are of locally-manufactured concrete. In 1982 only 200 km of route had long-welded rail, but a major welding programme has been launched. Maximum speed is generally 80 km/h, but 90 km/h on the Honam (Daejeon-Mogpo) and 110 km/h on the Gyeongbu (Seoul-Pusan) lines.

In 1982 762 km of route were double-tracked.

Additions were in progress on the Honam line between Iri and Sonjeongri (98 km), to be completed by 1985, and over 13 km of the Gyeongwon line in the Seoul area, between Seongbug and Euijeongbu.

Signalling

In 1982 650 km of KNR were equipped with automatic block signalling and 246 km of route were CTC-controlled. The fifth five-year plan aims to increase the latter total by 500 km. Over 550 traction units were equipped to work with KNR's automatic train-stop equipment and 603 had been fitted with track-to-train radio. With the support of the World Bank loan agreed in 1983, CTC was to be installed over the 127 km between Jecheon and Cholam, on the electrified main line.

GM-built 3000 hp diesel loco hauling limited express coaches

European 50 c/s Group locomotive on Chungang line

Diesel locomotives

Manufacturer's type (KNR class)	Wheel arrangement	Rated power hp	Max speed kmlh	Wheel diameter mm	Total weight tons	Length mm	No in service	Year first built	Builders Mechanical parts	Engine & type
SW 8 (2000)	Bo-Bo	800	105	1016	94·5	13 420	13	1957	GMC (USA)	8-567 BC
SW 1001 (2100)	Bo-Bo	1000	105	1016	87	13 610	28	1969	,,	8-645 E
G8 (3000)	Bo-Bo	875	105	1016	75	14 325	51	1959	,,	8-567 CR
Alco (3100)	Bo-Bo	950	105	914	71·5	14 650	6	1967	Alco (USA)	6-251 B
GM (3200)	Bo-Bo	875	105	—	—	—	42	1968	GMC (USA)	—
G12 (4000)	Bo Bo	1310	105	1016	78·5	14 325	15	1963	GMC (USA)	12-567 C
G12 (4100)	Bo-Bo	1310	105	1016	85	14 325	10	1966	,,	12-567 C
G22 (4200)	Bo-Bo	1310	105	1016	88	14 170	22	1967	,,	12-567 E
SD9 (5000)	Co-Co	1750	105	1016	141	18 500	29	1957	,,	16-567 C
SD18 (6000)	Co-Co	1800	105	1016	147	18 500	14	1963	,,	16-567 D
SDP28 (6100)	Co-Co	1800	105	1016	147	18 500	6	1966	,,	16-567 E
SDP38 (6200)	Co-Co	1800	105	1016	147	18 500	17	1967	,,	16-567 E
SDP38 (6300)	Co-Co	1800	105	1016	148	18 500	23	1967	,,	16-567 E
G26CW (7000)	Co-Co	2000	105	1016	99	15 765	10	1969	,,	16-645 E
GT26CW (7500)	Co-Co	3000	105	1016	132	19 650	96	1972	,,	16-645 E3
GT26CW (7100)	Co-Co	3000	120	1016	132	19 650	50	1975	,,	16-645 E3

Diesel railcars

KNR series	Wheel arrangement	Transmission	Rated power hp	Max speed kmlh	Wheel diameter mm	Total weight tons	Length mm	No built	Year built	Builders Mechanical parts	Engine & type
600	Bo-Bo	Hydraulic Converter	420	105	864	51	21 500	11	1962	Niigata (Japan)	N-855-R (Cummins USA)
,,	,,	,,	,,	,,	,,	,,	,,	32	1963	Kinki (Japan)	,,
,,	,,	,,	,,	,,	,,	,,	,,	36	1966	Kawasaki (Japan)	,,
,,	,,	,,	360	,,	,,	,,	,,	9	1963	Niigata (Japan)	DMH 17 (Japan)
700	,,	,,	420	,,	,,	,,	,,	12	1966	,,	N-855-R (Cummins)
,,	,,	,,	360	,,	,,	,,	,,	8	1966	,,	DMH 17 H (Japan)
160*	,,	,,	210	,,	711	25	14 750	6	1965	KNR	N-855-R (Cummins)
100*	,,	,,	360	,,	914	33·9	10 400	2	1969	Niigata (Japan)	DMH17C (Japan)
200†	,,	Electric	4×112	110	—	58·5	21 000	4	1979	Daewoo	Cummins KTA-1150L

*762 mm gauge †Operates in two five-car units with Type 300 and 400 trailers on long-haul services

Electric locomotives

KNR series	Wheel arrange- ment	Line current	Rated output hp	Tractive effort continuous at tons	Tractive effort continuous at kmlh	Max speed kmlh	Wheel diameter mm	Weight tons	Length mm	No built	Year first built	Builders Mechanical parts	Builders Electrical parts
8000	Bo-Bo-Bo	ac, 1ø, 25 kV (60 Hz)	5300	31.3	46	85	1250	132	20 730	90	1972	Alsthom MTE	AEG ACEC

Electric multiple-units

Class	Cars per unit	Line voltage	Motor cars per unit	Motored axles per motor car	Rated output (kW) per motor	Max speed kmlh	Weight tonnes per car (M-motor T-trailer)	Total seating capacity	Length per car m	No of cars in service	Rate of acceleration kmlhls	Year first built	Builders Mechanical parts	Builders Electrical equipment
Commuter	4	25 kV ac or 1500 V dc		4	160	110	Tc 33·3 M 42·1 M 46·1	—	20	76	—	1974	Hitachi	Hitachi
Commuter	4, 6, 8 or 10	25 kV ac or 1500 V dc	2, 4 or 6	4	120	110	Tc 34·5 M 43·5 M' 46·5	T 48 M 54 M' 54	20	212	2·5	1976	Daewoo	Daewoo & Hitachi (Japan)
Commuter	4, 6, 8 or 10	1500 V dc	4 or 6	4	150	100	MC 41·5 M1 40·5 M2 40·5	MC 48 M1 54 M2 54	20	32	3·0		Daewoo	Hitachi
Inter-city	10	25 kV ac	6	4	120	100	Tc 43·5 M 51·5 M' 51·0 Tb 40·0 Ts 37·5	561	20	20	2·0	1979	Daewoo	Daewoo & Hitachi

LAOS

Intention to build a rail connection with Viet-Nam was announced by the Government in 1982. At present Laos is the only South-east Asian country devoid of railways.

LEBANON

Chemins de Fer de l'Etat Libanais (CEL)
Transport en commun de Beyrouth et de sa Banlieue CEL/TCB

PO Box 109, Souk El-Arwan, Beirut

Telephone: 233619

Director General: Antoine Barouki
Chief of Traffic and Operation: A Ramadan
Chief of Traction and Rolling Stock: E Boutros
Chief of Track and Structures: S Aouad

Gauge: 1435 mm; 1050 mm

Route length: 331 km; 84 km

The state took over the railways in January 1961. The narrow gauge includes 32 km of ABT system rack rail, on 7 per cent gradient. A narrow-gauge railway runs from Beirut to Damascus, connecting at Rayak with a branch of the standard-gauge line which runs from Tripoli through Hous, Hama and Aleppo to the Turkish frontier and from Nusaybin to the Iraq frontier at Tel Kotchek. A standard-gauge line also runs from Nakowia to Tripoli. In 1983 the Government authorised an expenditure of £L37 million to rehabilitate the Zahrani-Tripoli coastal line.

Traffic
In 1980 CEL recorded 26 558 passenger journeys, 8·57 million passenger-km, 558 271 tonnes and 42·01 million tonne-km of freight.

Traction and rolling stock
For its 1435 mm gauge CEL owns 13 steam and four diesel-electric locomotives, two diesel-electric shunters, seven passenger cars, two baggage cars and 661 wagons. The diesel-electric locomotives are headed by 1700 hp, 96-tonne units of Polish manufacture. The 1050 mm-gauge stock comprises 19 steam locomotives, one diesel tractor, eight passenger cars, four baggage cars and 229 freight wagons.

Track
Max axleload: 16 tonnes on standard gauge lines; 13 tonnes on narrow gauge lines
Curves, minimum radius: 1435 mm gauge: 218 m; 1050 mm gauge: 100 m
Gradient, max: 2·0% uncompensated; 7·0% on rack rail section
Altitude, max: 1487 m

LIBERIA

Transport development
There are three railways in Liberia, all constructed for iron ore transports:
(1) Bong Mining Co (from Monrovia to Bong Town), a joint West German and Italian undertaking;
(2) National Iron Ore Co Ltd (from Monrovia to Mano on the Sierra Leone border), an American/Liberian organisation;
(3) Lamco JV Operating Co set up by the Liberian American-Swedish Minerals Co and Bethlehem Steel Corporation.

Bong Mining Company

PO Box 538, Monrovia

Telephone: 221 55; 210 26
Telex: 4269; 4569

General Manager: H-J Rietzsch
Technical Manager: H-G Schneider

Maintenance Mechanical Superintendent: S Abdullai
Railroad Engineer: W Bauer
Chief Workshop Engineer: B Dietsche
Locomotives and Rolling Stock: R Knaut
Trackmaster: I Woods

Gauge: 1435 mm
Length: 78 km

The company operates four diesel-electric line-haul locomotives, six diesel-hydraulic shunters, a railbus, 186 ore and 36 other freight wagons.

Lamco Railroad
Lamco JV Operating Company

Roberts International Airport

Telephone: 211 65; 218 07
Telegrams: Lamco, Monrovia
Telex: 4260; 4293

Manager, Lamco Railroad: H N Bas Koenen
Railroad Operating Superintendent: John Hart
Railroad Engineering Superintendent: Björn Ekrem

Gauge: 1435 mm
Route length: 267 km

Lamco, the Liberian American-Swedish Minerals Co, is an iron ore mining company with mines at Nimba and Tokadeh. The railroad is operational between mines at Nimba and the deep water port in Buchanan, and carries more than 250 million gross tonnes over its 30-tonne axleload route. Ruling gradients for loaded and empty trains are 0·5 and 1·7 per cent respectively. The whole line is CTC and ATC controlled. In 1983 feasibility studies for a 110 km link between the Lamco line at Grebo and the Bong line at Bong Town were initiated.

A further tonnage decline to 7·2 million tons was anticipated in 1983.

Motive power and rolling stock
At the end of 1982 motive power consisted of 26 diesel-electric locos and four ex-British Rail Type 126/1 diesel railcars. The number of ore wagons totalled 588.

Traffic

	1980/81	1981/82
Total net freight tonnage (million)	11·37	10·8
Total net freight tonne-km (million)	3288·5	2872·5
Average net freight train load (tons)	8500	8500
Average freight wagon load (tons)	94	94

Track
Rail: 65·5 kg/m
Cross ties (sleepers): Tropical hardwood 180 × 230 × 2600 mm
Spacing: 1835/km
Fastenings: Spring spike, DE and Pandrol
Minimum curvature radius: 500 m
Max gradient: Empty ore trains 1·7%; loaded ore trains 0·5%
Max axleload: 30 tons

Diesel locomotives

Class	Wheel arrangement	Transmission	Rated power (kW)	Max speed kmlh	Total weight tonnes	No in service	Year first built	Builders		
								Mechanical parts	Engine & type	Transmission
Hg-16	Co-Co	Elec	1342	105 (service limit 80)	178	14	1962	Henschel	General Motors	AEG
SD-10	Co-Co	Elec	1342	105 (service limit 80)	178	2	1980	General Motors	General Motors	—
GP 10	Bo-Bo	Elec	1342	105 (service limit 80)	120	2	1979	General Motors	General Motors	—
SW-900	Bo-Bo	Elec	671	105 (service limit 80)	120	5	1962	General Motors	General Motors	—
Ex BR Class 08	0-6-0	Elec	298	32	49	5	Design 1933 Purchased 1973	British Rail	EE 6 KT	English Electric

Diesel railcars

Class	Cars per unit	Motor cars per unit	Motored axles per motor car	Transmission	Rated power (kW) per motor	Max speed kmlh	Weight tonnes per car	Total seating capacity	Length per car mm	No in service	Year first built	Builders		
												Mechanical parts	Engine & type	Transmission
BR Class Swindon (126/1)	2	2	4	Mech	AEC 105 Leyland 135	100	39	52	20 460	4	1956 (Purchased 1972)	BR	(2) AEC 220W (2) Leyland 680	SCG

National Iron Ore Co Ltd

PO Box 548, Monrovia

General Manager: C R Tapia

Railroad Superintendent: R T Allen
Locomotive Shop Superintendent: B Lokker

Gauge: 1067 mm
Length: 145 km

The railway was opened in 1951. It operates 11 diesel locomotives, 253 ore and 28 other wagons. A US$51 million railway improvement scheme was launched in 1982 as part of a plan for increased ore output.

LIBYA

Department of Road Transport & Railways

Tripoli

General Manager: M A O Benkafu

With the dismantling of the British projection of 1435 mm gauge from Egypt to Tobruk laid in the Second World War, no railways have run in Libya since 1965. Also discarded is the 950 mm system built around Tripoli and Benghazi on the eve of the First World War.

The present Government, however, intends to build a new 1435 mm-gauge system from the Tunisian frontier to Tripoli and Misratah, then inland to Sebha, the country's third city, in the heart of a mineral-resource area. A longer-term objective is to construct a further, coastal line from Misratah to the Egyptian border via Benghazi and Tobruk.

In 1982 the Government commissioned Sofrerail to create a new railway administration, define methods of administrative and operating management, plan the administrative buildings and also programme the installation of personnel. A further contract required Sofrerail to draft traction and rolling stock specifications and the relevant tender documents. The Government aims to complete the railway from the Tunisian border to Tripoli by the end of 1986, then the section from Tripoli to Misratah, and to have the line operational as far as Sebha by the end of 1988. Misratah is the site of a major steel plant which will be fed with raw materials by unit trains from the Sebha area. Service by air-conditioned passenger trains is also planned.

LUXEMBOURG

Luxembourg Railways (CFL)
Société Nationale des Chemins de Fer Luxembourgeois

9 place de la Gare, PO Box 1803, 1018 Luxembourg

Telephone: (352) 4 99 01
Telegrams: Raillux, Luxembourg
Telex: 2288

President: Georges Thorn
General Manager: Justin Kohl
Assistant Director, Technical: Ernest Junck
Assistant Director, Administration: Romain Kugener
Operations Manager: Robert Molitor
Mechanical Manager: Charles-Leon Mayer
Fixed Plant and Signalling Manager: Robert Tonnar
Personnel Manager: Jean Meyer
Commercial Manager: Emile Kamphaus
Financial Manager: Joseph Offenheim
Internal Control Manager: Gilbert Schmit
Planning Manager: Joseph Lentz

Gauge: 1435 mm
Route length: 270 km
Electrification: 143 km at 25 kV 50 Hz ac
19 km at 3 kV dc

Traffic	1979	1980	1981
Total freight ton-km (million)	713	665	584·89
Total freight tonnage (million)	18·7	17·4	15·13
Total passenger-km (million)	285	280	252·15
Total passenger journeys (million)	NA	NA	11·633

Traffic
Traffic volume regressed further in 1982 as a result of the recession. Initial indications were that freight tonnage compared with 1981 was down 8 per cent, tonne-km 5·5 per cent, passenger journeys down 1·5 per cent and passenger-km down 4·2 per cent.

Bettembourg-Dudelange marshalling yard
In October 1982 Luxembourg Railways opened a high-capacity automated marshalling yard at Bettembourg-Dudelange. The project took six years of work from the drawing-board stage. In the 1970s CFL had no adequate marshalling yard. The few old-fashioned yards were scattered over the country and coming to the end of their service life. Detailed studies showed that it was feasible to concentrate the majority of marshalling operations in one single hump yard and Bettembourg, at the junction of the two main lines to Belgium - France - Switzerland - Italy and the mining basin and West Germany respectively, was a suitable site, both from the geographical and traffic standpoint. It also had room for extension.

A final project worked out between 1974 and 1976 was approved towards the end of 1976 by the Luxembourg Ministry of Transport. The plan provided for a marshalling capacity of 2500 wagons per day, but after an alarming downtrend in the steel industry's crude steel output, it was decided to reduce the size of the new installation to fit in with revised forecasts for the next ten years (2000 wagons maximum). The final cost amounted to LFr 1485 million. Construction began in 1978. Although the yard has a traditional configuration, the monitoring, control and shunting command systems are computerised. It will take over the operations of the Wasserbillig, Esch/Alzette Belval-Usines and Dudelange-Usines yards, and part of those normally handled at Luxembourg. The yard has a handling capacity of 2000 wagons per day and covers an area of about 50 hectares. Included is 55·918 km of track, of which 42·68 km is electrified, and 198 points and crossings are installed. CFL's first container/piggyback terminal has also been installed at Bettembourg.

Finances

	1980	1981
	(LFr million)	
Revenues	6167·4	6613·3
Expenses	6401·9	6930·8

CFL is supported by a public service grant, which amounted to LFr 1650 million in 1981.

Electrification
The decision was taken in November 1981 to electrify the only remaining diesel-operated through route, Luxembourg - Troisvièrges (- Luttich), which runs 75 km from north to south and is CFL's second busiest route.

Investment
Investments planned for 1983 (LFr 000):

Freight wagons (90)	81 114
Track construction and improvement	215 700
Electrification	23 000
Bridges and buildings	36 800
Signalling and telecommunications	92 200
Yards and terminals	2500
Miscellaneous	98 550
Total	549 864

Motive power
During 1982 CFL operated 19 electric and 59 diesel-electric locomotives, eight two-car dmus and seven emus totalling 15 cars.

Track
Rails: UIC 60, 54 and U33
Sleepers: Wood
  Thickness: 150 mm
  Spacing: 1435 mm
Rail fastenings: 'K' fastenings

Signal and train control: CFL is pursuing a plan to concentrate signalling of each route on a single centre, supported by one at Luxembourg itself.

All-relay interlocking signalboxes with illuminated diagram and push-button control cover 116 km route length. Supplied by Siemens and Integra, as follows:

	km
Luxembourg—Wasserbillig	37
Berchem—Oetrange	12
Luxembourg—Kleinbettingen	18
Bettembourg—Rodange	29
Luxembourg—Pétange	20

Hybrid installations consisting of electronic circuits and relay switching, frequency control, automatic colour-light signalling for two-way working. Supplied by: Jeumont Schneider, Siemens, Integra, as follows:

	km
Luxembourg—Wasserbillig	37
Berchem—Oetrange	12
Bettembourg—Berchem	4

Installation of AWS equipment in traction units was a major item of planned 1983 investment. Also decided is equipment of all units for track-to-train radio.

MADAGASCAR

Réseau National des Chemins de Fer Malagasy (RNCFM)

Araben'ng Fahaleovantena, BP 25, Antananarivo

Telephone: 205-21
Telex: 222-33

General Manager: Samuel Razanamipisa
Technical Manager: André Andriamampianina
Financial Manager: Robert Ramboasalama

Gauge: 1000 mm
Route length: 883.5 km

Transport development
Most of the RNCFM system, comprised of two networks, is situated in the central-eastern region of Madagascar. The northern railway consists of three lines: TCE (Antananarivo-Eastern Coast line) linking the capital of Antananarivo with Toamasina harbour (374·79 km); MLA (Moramanga-Lac Alaotra) line serving the rice-producing region of Lake Alaotra (167·4 km); TA line which links Antananarivo to the thermal springs of Antsirabe (154 km). The southern railway consists of the FCE linking Fianarantsoa to the port of Manakava (163·3 km). The railway is a state-operated industrial and commercial enterprise with financial autonomy and its own legal entity.

Because of the Republic's difficult terrain, highways are few although development plans for the 1980s place emphasis on an improved communications network.

Finances
Revenues (FMG million)

	1980	1981
Passengers and baggage	1173	1319·3
Freight, parcels and mail	2836	3048·6
Other income	374	517·7
Total	4383	4885·6

Expenditure (FMG million)

Staff personnel expenses	2752	2879·6
Materials and services	1777	2203·1
Depreciation	78	824·5
Financial charges	220	398·1
Total	5530	6305·3

Investment
Investments planned for 1983 were (FMG million):

Track improvements and machinery	2216
Bridges and buildings	264
Signalling and communications	370
Yards and terminals	161
Miscellaneous	284
Total	3295

Track
Rails: 30-36 kg/m
Sleepers: Mainly steel, spaced 1530 per km in plain track, 1630 per km in curves
Fastenings: Crapaud type
Minimum curvature radius: 50 m
Max gradient: 35%
Max axleload: 20 tonnes

Type BB 220 diesel-electric locomotive

First-class passenger car

Traffic

	1979/80	1980/81	1981/82
Total freight tonnage (000)	715·6	733·3	617·58
Total freight-km (million)	231·948	233·804	187·711
Total passenger-km (million)	303·552	273·948	245 506·8
Total passenger journeys (million)	NA	NA	3·126

Motive power and rolling stock

	Number		
Diesel locomotives	36	Trailer cars	56
Diesel railcars	13	Passenger coaches	28
		Freight wagons	1357

Diesel locomotives

Class	Wheel arrangement	Transmission	Rated power hp	Max speed km/h	Total weight tonnes	No in service	Year first built	Builders
BB 200	Bo-Bo	Elec	1050	70	56	6	1965	Alsthom/SACM
BB 220	Bo-Bo	Elec	1200	70	58	18	1973	Alsthom/SACM
BB 120	Bo-Bo	Elec	750	70	52	11	1954	Alsthom/SACM
BBBB 301	Bo+Bo−Bo+Bo	Elec	3600	70	125	1	1971	CEM/SACM
BB 400 (Shunting)	Bo-Bo	Elec	450	50	52	2	1982	Fauvet Girel

Diesel railcars

Class	Cars per unit	Motored axles per motor car	Transmission	Rated power hp per motor	Max speed km/h	Weight tonnes per car	Total seating capacity	Length per car mm	No in service	Year first built	Builders Mechanical parts	Engine & type	Transmission
ZM 510	1	1	Mech	80	80	6·6	21	13 245	2	1952	Carel Fouché	Panhard	Glaenzer
ZE 800	1	2	Elec	500	70	33	36	18 864	6	1958	De Dietrich	SACM	Alsthom
ZE 900	1	2	Elec	580	70	39	43	18 830	5	1967	Soulé	Poyaud	Alsthom
For delivery 1983	1	1		950	70		36	18 000	1	1982	Soulé		

MALAWI

Ministry of Transport and Communications

Private Bag 322, Capital City, Lilongwe 3

Telephone: 730122
Telegrams: Trancom, Lilongwe

Minister: E Bakili Muluzi
Permanent Secretary: R N L Nkomba

Malawi Railways Ltd (MR)

PO Box 5144, Limbe

Telephone: 652244
Telegrams: Marailas, Limbe
Telex: 4116

Chairman: D Z U Tembo
Directors: J Kachingwe
 N N P Thindwa
 F L Mambiya
 O T Muenifumbo
 Dr H P Bandawi
 R N L Nkomba
General Manager: N S Husemeyer
Deputy General Manager: W C Salima
Assistant General Manager (Technical Services): W W Gordon
Assistant General Manager (Operations): R G Nkana
Chief Accountant: H J Binney
Chief Civil Engineer: R F Maclean
Chief Mechanical Engineer: F J Kent
Chief Personnel Manager: V F Sinjani
Chief Traffic Manager: P T K Nyasulu
Lake Service Manager: N R Brown
Stores Superintendent: F W Ntonya
Security Superintendent: A E G Mankhambo
Management Accountant: G H Woodcock
Internal Auditor: S M Munthali
Company Secretary: T K B Phiri

Gauge: 1067 mm
Route length: 789 km

Transport development
A single-track line runs from Mchinji near the Zambian border through Lilongwe and Blantyre to the southern border with Mozambique. This line connects with the Mozambique port of Beira. In 1970 a 101 km line was opened from Nkaya to Nayuci on the eastern border with Mozambique and connects with the port of Nacala. During 1980 the 103 km extension from Lilongwe to Mchinji, the last Malawi station, 11 km from the Zambian border, was completed.

In addition to the railway the administration operates passenger and cargo services on Lake Malawi and local road collection and delivery services in Lilongwe and Blantyre.

Traffic
Since the severe fall of passenger traffic following closure of the Mozambique-Zimbabwe border in 1976 volume has recovered to the extent that record figures were recorded in 1980, but in the freight sector almost all commodities showed a slight downturn in 1981. Traffic with Zambia has increased. Freight traffic has been marked by a rising use of containers for export/import consignments through the Mozambique port of Nacala; despite difficulties, over 70 per cent of imports through Nacala, oil excluded, are now containerised.

Traffic

	1980/81	1981/82
Total freight tonnage (000)	1303	1189
Total freight tonne-km (000)	246 925	233 365
Average net freight train load (tonnes)	221·18	228·11
Average freight wagon load (tonnes)	24·86	24·55
Total passenger-km (000)	79 723	77 937
Total passenger journeys (000)	1287	1287
Average length of passenger journey (km)	62·9	60·5

Finance	1980	1981
Revenues	(MK 000)	
Passengers and baggage	939	1537
Freight, parcels and mail	9881	14 486
Other income	6999	3985
Total	17 819	20 008

Expenditure	1980	1981
	(MK 000)	
Staff/personnel expenses	5542	5465
Materials and services	8558	12 376
Depreciation	1895	2742
Financial charges	951	1495
Total	16 967	22 078

Motive power and rolling stock
The diesel fleet consists of 34 main-line diesel-electrics, 11 diesel-hydraulic main-line locomotives, eight diesel-hydraulic shunters and one diesel railcar. The rolling stock fleet consists of 858 goods wagons and 31 passenger coaches.

Despite temporary lease of some traction units to Mozambique and Zimbabwe, the main problems of availability have occurred in the wagon fleet. They were mitigated in 1982 by purchase of 83 covered and 15 tank wagons on hire from SATS since 1980, and by progressive conversion of 83 low-capacity vans to container-carrying flatcars. The Federal German Government financed a study of rolling stock need, which is expected to total 450 freight wagons and 10 passenger cars.

Investment
Investments budgeted for 1983 (MK·000):

Track improvements	2136
Track maintenance machines	80
Bridges and buildings	264
Communications	370
Yards and terminals	161
Miscellaneous	284
Total	3295

Upgrading of the route between Balaka and the southern border continued in 1982. Main workshops at Limbe were to be re-equipped with aid of finance from the Federal German Government.

Track
The 113 km link from Lilongwe to Mchinji uses BS 80 'A' flat-bottomed rail and prestressed concrete sleepers.
Standard rail: 40 and 30 kg/m. All re-railing is now with 40 kg/m
Cross ties (sleepers): Steel trough, 1750 mm long; hardwood 2000 × 127 × 254 mm; concrete 2000 × 228 mm base. Concrete sleepers, locally manufactured, will be applied to future upgrading schemes.
Spacing: Plain track 1312/km; curves 1476/km
Rail fastening: Clip and steel key, elastic spikes, Pandrol clips with concrete sleepers
Filling: Broken stone and earth
Minimum curvature radius: 15·8° = 363 m
Max gradient: 2·27% = 1 in 44
Max axleload: 15 tonnes
Max permitted speed: 56 km/h, restricted in hill section to 24 km/h
Max altitude: 1107 m

Class	Wheel arrangement	Transmission	Rated power hp	Max kg	Tractive effort Continuous at lb	mph	Max speed kmlh	Wheel dia in	Total weight tons	Length ft in	No built	Year first built	Builders Mechanical parts	Engine and type	Transmission
Diesel locomotives															
Shunter	0-6-0	Hyd	340	20 200			24	40	40·5	25' 6''	2	1962	Bagnall	RR C8-Tel-IV	Twin Disc
Shunter	0-6-0	Hyd	355	21 800			25	41	43	24' 0''	2	1967	A Barclay	Cummins NT 400	Twin Disc
Shunter	0-6-0	Hyd	388	33 800			16	43	40	25' 4''	4	1975	Hunslet (UK)	Cummins NT 400	Twin Disc
Transfer	Bo-Bo	Hyd	525	23 000			35	33	38	32' 4''	7	1969	Hunslet (SA)	Cummins VT 12	Niigata
Main-line	Bo-Bo	Hyd	492	20 350			35	34	38	34' 6''	4	1968	N Sharyo	Cummins NTA 380	Niigata
Main-line	Co-Co	Elec	1200	50 000	40 000	8	50	36	81	46' 3''	14	1963	M Cammell	Sulzer	AEI
Main-line	Co-Co	Elec	1500	72 000	60 500	10	64	36	86	57' 7''	20	1973	MLW	Alco 8-251-E	GE
Diesel railcars															
PRC	Ao-Io	Hyd	200	33 000			50	34	33		2	1952	Drewry	Leyland Re-902	V Sinclair 550

MALAYSIA

Ministry of Transport

Wisma Perdana, Tingkat 5-7, Jalan Dungun, Damansara Heights, Kuala Lumpur

Minister: Dato' Lee San Choon
Secretary-General: Dato' Ishak bin Tadin

Malayan Railway Administration (PKTM)
Pertadbiran Keretapi Tanah Melayu

PO Box 1, Kuala Lumpur

General Manager: Encik Ahmad Badri bin Mohamed Basir
Deputy General Manager: Encik Abdul Rahim bin Abdul Jalal
Chief of General Administration: Hanim binti Ali
Chief of Research and Planning: Masri bin Ahmad
Director, Finance: D Gabriel
  Civil Engineering: Loh John Kee
  Mechanical Engineering: Lee Jee Luan
  Traffic: Mohd Zin bin Yusop
  Commerce: Abdul Rahim bin Osman
  Signalling: P Satyamoorthy
  Stores Superintendent: Omar bin Abdullah
  Chief of Computer Unit: Chan Kim Beng

Gauge: 1000 mm
Route length: 1659 km

Principal route is the 787 km main line from Singapore north through the capital, Kuala Lumpur, to Butterworth, one of Malaysia's principal sea ports on the west coast of the peninsula. Short branches reach sea ports at Port Weld, Telok Anson, Port Kelang and Port Dickson. The other major route is the 528 km east-coast line running northwards from a junction with the Singapore—Butterworth main line at Gemas to Kota Baaru and Tum Pat. Both lines are linked with the State Railway of Thailand.

Freight traffic
While PKTM carried record freight tonne-km in 1979 the railway's market share of business remains only 11 per cent. Traction shortages influenced a decline in 1981, to the extent of reducing total revenue by almost 6 per cent.

	1978	1979	1980	1981
Freight tons carried (000)	4142	4188	NA	3400
Tonne-km (million)	1293	1357	1737	1123

Passenger traffic
PKTM operates a comprehensive network of passenger services over almost all its lines. In addition to ordinary train services, the system operates day and night express trains on Singapore—Kuala Lumpur and Kuala Lumpur—Butterworth routes, and a single daily express between Gemas and Tum Pat on the east coast line. In conjunction with the State Railway of Thailand, PKTM operates the tri-weekly International Express between Butterworth and Bangkok. Since 1970 long-distance travel has soared spectacularly, lifting annual passenger-km from 620 million to over 1600 million at the start of the 1980s. Passenger revenue now surpasses that of freight and volume is forecast to scale almost 3000 million journeys a year by 1990.

English Electric diesel-electric Co-Co and freight at Singapore *(Marcel Vleugels)*

PKTM diesel shunter marshalling passenger cars at Singapore *(Marcel Vleugels)*

The Ekspres Rakyat (People's Express) introduced in 1976 is PKTM's most popular express service. Operating daily between Singapore and Butterworth via Kuala Lumpur, the train is equipped with both air-conditioned and non-air-conditioned coaches offering a high standard of comfort. Completing the 787 km run in slightly more than 13 hours, the Ekspres Rakyat service has proved extremely successful; the 394 km from Singapore to Kuala Lumpur are covered in 6½ hours.

A new inter-city train service called Express KTM was started in March 1980 on the Kuala Lumpur—Butterworth and Kuala Lumpur—Singapore routes.

	1979	1980	1981
Passengers carried (000)	6243	NA	7400
Passenger-km (million)	1382	1586	1640

Investments
A loan of US$ 1·8 million has been used by Malayan Railways to finance purchase of new telecommunications and signalling equipment, as part of a US$ 80 million, five-year (1976-81) programme to modernise railways in Malaysia. During the plan period about 40 per cent of passenger coaches were replaced by 34 air-conditioned luxury class coaches and 53 economy-class (non-air-conditioned) coaches, to improve passenger services and reduce operating costs. Freight stock purchases included 341 bogie oil tank wagons, 117 latex tank wagons, 139 bulk hopper wagons, 122 palm oil tank wagons, 100 container flat wagons, 50 cattle wagons and 150 bogie underframes. About US$ 12·153 million was spent on track renewals and realignments, US$ 6·382 million on new diesel main-line locomotives,

US$ 4 million on diesel shunters, and nearly US$ 6 million on signalling and telecommunications.

Early in 1981 a five-year programme to expand passenger-km to 1649 million and freight tonne-km to 1963 million by 1985 was announced. The programme included double-tracking of the 150 km route from Seremban to Rawang and upgrading with reinforced concrete sleepers. Further new lines were planned: a 7 km link between Johore Bahru international airport and the main line to Senai; another airport link from Sungai Way, in Kuala Lumpur; and a connection between Tampoi and the port of Johore. Freight development would include the reconstruction of the main Kuala Lumpur yard at Brickfields and acquisition of container handling equipment.

Tenders were soon afterward sought for 15 main-line 2200 hp diesel locomotives with Pielstick PA4-200VG engines, a contract subsequently secured by Mitsubishi and Hitachi (value 4600 million yen) with a provision for some of the units to be assembled in Malaysia, for 10 diesel shunters and for 32 passenger cars (18 of which were to be air-conditioned). Ten more locomotives were ordered from Hitachi in 1982.

Investments budgeted under the 1981-85 plan (Ringgit 000):

Diesel-electric main-line locomotives (65)	55 000
Diesel-electric shunting locomotives (30)	13 000
Diesel-hydraulic main-line locomotives (25)	11 750
Diesel-hydraulic shunting locomotives (15)	2674
Passenger cars (350)	175 000
Freight wagons (4063)	406 300
New lines and track improvements	62 300
Track maintenance machines	6000
Bridges and buildings	16 350
Signalling and communications	7200
Yards and terminals	25 000
Miscellaneous	2690
Total	783 264

New standard-gauge trunk route

Later in 1981, however, a change of Government was followed by a decision which seems to have nullified at least some of the investment previously budgeted. Starting probably in 1986, a new 1435 mm-gauge line, double-track and electrified, is to be built from Butterworth to Kuala Lumpur and the new port at Johore, which is to be developed in preference to Singapore. Subsequently a further 1435 mm-gauge line may be laid from Kuala Lumpur to the east coast at Kuantan and thence northward to Kuala Trengganu, site of planned industrial development in association with offshore oil and gas developments. These projects have superseded some of the narrow-gauge extensions previously proposed and also curtailed the previously planned rolling stock investment. Preliminary design surveys of the Butterworth-Kuala Lumpur-Johore line were being conducted by Japanese consultants in 1982.

Signalling

Full relay interlocking is being installed at 10 stations on the Butterworth-Singapore trunk route by ML Engineering (Plymouth) Ltd, and at two locations on the Port Dickson branch. Siemens is equipping sections of the west coast line with tokenless block and colour-light signalling of stations.

Motive power and rolling stock

The fleet in 1982 comprised one steam and 135 diesel locomotives. The passenger stock totalled 361 coaches. Freight wagons totalled 5156 units. Immediate requirements are up to 50 additional passenger cars and 390 wagons, mostly container flats.

Civil engineering

All 30 kg/m rail on the east coast line is being replaced to complete an upgrading programme of all main-line track to 40 kg/m standards. The latest permanent way improvement plans call for increasing the system's maximum operating speeds from 80 km/h to 97 km/h entailing extensive realignments, and for relaying of 550 km before 1985. A new 31 km link between the main line and the new port of Pasir Gudang in Johore opposite Singapore is expected to be complete in 1984.

Track

Standard rail: Flat bottom in 40 ft (12·2 m) lengths
Main line: 80 lb/yd (39·7 kg/m)
Branch lines: 60 lb (29·8 kg/m) being changed to 80 lb/yd
Joints: 4-hole flat or angle fishplates and welding
Rail fastening: Elastic spikes
Cross ties (sleepers): Malayan secondary hardwoods impregnated with 50/50 mixture of creosote and diesel fuel oil; primary hardwoods on bridges. 10 in × 5 in × 6 ft 6 in (254 × 127 × 1981 mm). In accordance with ESCAP recommendations for Southeast Asia, all new supplies 9 in × 4½ in × 6 ft 6 in-7 ft 0 in (229 × 114 × 1981-2134 mm)
Spacing: 2 ft 6 in (762 mm)
Filling: 2½ in limestone ballast to a depth of 6 in under sleepers
Max curvature: 3° = radius of 582 m; except in hill sections with some curves of 9° = radius of 194 m and 12·25° = radius of 142 m
Ruling gradient: 1% = 1 in 100; except Taiping Pass 1·25% = 1 in 80
Longest continuous gradient: 8·2 km on Prai-Singapore main line, with 1·25% (1 in 80) grade, sharpest curve 12.25° (142 m radius) for a length of 320 m
Gauge widening on curves
Nil down to 6·5° curve = radius of 268 m
¼ in (6·4 mm): 6·5° to 9° curve = radius of 268 m to 194 m
¾ in (9·5 mm): 9° to 13° curve = radius of 194 m to 134 m
½ in (12·7 mm): below 13°
Super-elevation on sharpest curve: 89 mm
Rate of slope of super-elevation: Steepest permissible gradient 1 : 300 or 11 times max permissible speed of section in mph
Max altitude: 137 m near Taiping
Max axleload: 16 tons
Max permitted speed: Express passenger trains on Butterworth—Singapore line: 80 km/h; other trains 72 km/h; freight trains: 56 km/h
Welded rail: Rails used are 80 lb in 40 ft lengths flashbutt welded at depot into 480 ft lengths. After laying, these are sometimes Thermit-welded into 960 ft continuous lengths.

Welded rails are secured by Elastic rail spikes and Pandrol clips to wood sleepers.

MALI

Chemins de Fer du Mali (RCFM)

BP 260, Bamako

Telephone: 229 67; 229 68
Telegrams: Fermali, Bamako
Telex: 586

Director General: Noumoucounda Savané
Secretary General: Cheick Kouyate
Deputy Director-General: Mamadou Sidibe
Director of Personnel: Bakary Kouyate
Director of Supplies: Mamadou Bah
Finance: Almany Saounera
Operations: Mamadou Sidibe
Way and Works: Mamadou Bah
Commercial: Kader Diallo

Gauge: 1000 mm
Route length: 641 km

The former Dakar—Niger Railway starts at Dakar in Senegal and runs inland via Kayes to the River Niger. The present CF du Mali is that portion of the line inside its territory, the remainder being the CF du Sénégal. A new line linking Bamako, capital of Mali, with Conakry, capital of Guinea, is planned to give Mali an alternative outlet to the Atlantic with a route length of 800 km, of which 600 km will be in Guinea.

Motive power

CFM operates a total of 16 line-haul diesel locomotives, nine diesel shunters, three diesel-electric railcars, eight trailers, 20 passenger coaches and 381 freight wagons. In 1983, as a result of analyses by Deconsult and the World Bank, plans were drafted for purchase of seven line-haul and six shunting diesel locomotives, three dmus, 12 passenger cars and 200 freight cars.

Traffic

	1978	1979	1980
Total passenger journeys	590 733	655 827	630 000
national	533 810	594 401	—
international	56 923	61 426	—
Total passenger-km (000)	133 147	152 179	157 054
national	109 498	125 522	—
international	23 649	26 657	—
Total freight tonnage	341 790	311 700	306 000
national	79 960	72 010	—
international	261 830	239 690	—
Total freight tonne-km (000)	150 630	143 820	—
national	25 760	24 720	—
international	124 870	119 100	—

Diesel-electric locomotive by Alsthom-Atlantique

950 hp diesel-electric railcar delivered by Soulé in 1977

MAURITANIA

Chemins de Fer (SNIM-SEM)

PO Box 42, Nouadhibou

Telephone: 114
Telex: 459

General Manager: Baba Ould Sidi Abdallah
Director of Harbour Railway: Boughourbal Moulaye Abasse
Head of Movement and Traction: Chiaa Ould Limam
Head of Permanent Way: Sidi Haiba Ould Teiss

Gauge: 1435 mm
Route length: 689 km

The line, completed in 1963, runs from Nouadhibou (ex-Port Etienne) to Tazadit for the transport of iron ore from the mines at F'Derik (ex-Fort Gouraud).

Built and originally operated by Miferma, the line was nationalised in 1974 and is now operated by Société Nationale Industrielle et Minière (SNIM).

Traffic
Principal traffic is iron ore shipments. Passenger traffic was stopped in 1978.

	1981
Number of freight trains	531
Distance covered (km)	690 300
Freight tonnes	7476 000
Freight tonne-km (million)	4857.696

Motive power and rolling stock
Equipment listed in 1982 consisted of 32 main-line diesel-electric locomotives, 11 shunting diesel-electrics, 1417 freight wagons (81 flat wagons, 1265 ore wagons, 71 miscellaneous wagons) and eight passenger-carrying cars.

Track
Standard rail: 54 kg/m UIC
Welded joints: Practically the whole line was laid with long-welded rail. 8 × 18 m railbars were flash-butt welded at the depot into 144 m lengths, which after laying were Thermit welded into continuous rail. Longest individual length of welded rail is 80 km
Cross ties (sleepers): Type U28 steel, weight 75 kg
Spacing: 600 mm
Rail fastening: Clips and bolts to metal sleepers
Max curvature: 1·75° = minimum radius of 1000 m
Max gradient: 0·5% (1 in 200) against loaded trains
1·0% (1 in 100) against empty trains
Max altitude: 350 m
Max axleload: 25 tonnes
Max speed: Loaded trains 50 km/h; empty 60 km/h
Type of signalling: Radio control

MEXICO

Department of Transport and Communications

Avenida Universidad y Xola, Mexico 12, DF

Telephone: 519 87 28

Secretary: Rodolfo Félix Valdes
Under-Secretary: Ing Miguel Angel Barborena

Ferrocarriles Nacionales de Mexico (FNdeM)

Avenida Central 140, Col Guerrero, Mexico 3, DF

Telephone: 547 52 40; 547 90 60; 541 60 90

Chairman: Ing Rodolfo Félix Valdés
General Director: Eduardo A Cota
Assistant Manager, Administration: Lic Jorge Sánchez Curiel
 Finance: Roberto Rangel Luna
 Motive Power and Rolling Stock: Ing Eduardo Harfuch K

Freight train hauled by three 2250 hp General Electric diesel-electric locomotives assembled at Aguascalientes

Operations: Salvador Vega Mascareñas
Planning and Organisation: Ing Francisco Javier Gorostiza P
Purchases: Gaspar Hernández Tapia
Systems: Guillermo Vásquez R
Telecommunications: Ing Salvador Rosales H
Traffic: Alejandro Cochegruz Q
Way and Structures: Ing Joaquín Camacho G
General Comptroller: Adolfo González Arellano

Gauge: 1435 mm; 914 mm
Route length: 15 007 km; 427·7 km

In January 1977, Lic Jose Lopez Portillo, Constitutional President of Mexico, ordered the merger of all Mexican railway enterprises: Pacific Railway, SA de CV; Chihuahua-Pacific Railway, SA de CV; Sonora-Baja California Railway, SA de CV; Southeastern United Railways, SA de CV—with the National Railways of Mexico. The merger's completion has, however, proceeded more slowly than anticipated. The Southeastern system was not absorbed until March 1982. The rest of the systems listed were to be fully absorbed during 1983.

FNdeM extends from the northern border with the USA from the cities of Matamoros and Nuevo Laredo, Tamaulipas, from Piedras Negras and Ciudad Acuña, Coahuila and from Ciudad Juarez, Chihuahua to the southern border with Guatemala at Ciudad Hidalgo, Chiapas.

On the Gulf of Mexico, it connects with the ports of Coatzacoalcos, Veracruz, and Tampico, and also, as a result of the mergers, Campeche and Progreso. On the Pacific Ocean, it connects with the ports of Puerto Madero, Salina Cruz, and with Manzanillo; and, since the 1980 completion of a line from Coróndiro, the port of Lázaro Cárdenas.

In the interior, it connects the important cities of Mexico City, Queretaro, Leon, Aguascalientes, Zacatecas, Durango, Toreon, Chihuahua, San Luis Potosi, Saltillo, Monterrey, Ciudad Frontera (Coahuila), Morelia, Guadalajara, Colima, Pueblo, Oaxaco, Jalapa and Orizaba.

It interchanges in Coatzacoalcos with the Ferrocarriles Unidos del Sureste. In Guadalajara with the Ferrocarril del Pacifico and in Chihuahua and Ciudad Juarez with the Ferrocarril Chihuahua al Pacifico.

The railroad has 19 divisions with 117 operating districts.

Constitution of FNdeM	Track km	% total freight traffic
National Rys of Mexico	14 283	82·4
Pacific Ry	2310	11·9
Chihuahua-Pacific Railway	1515	2·8
Southeastern United Railways	1384	1·9
Sonora-Baja California Ry	523	1·0
	20 015	100

Division	Districts
Cárdenas	5
Centro	8
Golfo	4
Guadalajara	6
Jalapa	4
Mérida	6
Mexicano	3
México	9
Monclova	8
Monterrey	4
Pacifico	6
Pueblo	10
Querétaro	10
San Luis	6
Sureste VCI	8
Sureste NT	3
Sureste PA	3
Tenosigue	4
Torreón	10

Traffic

NdeM has already shaped much of its working of major commodities, principally ore and grain but also fertilisers and cement, into block trains that are not remarshalled en route. With the aim of lifting maximum trainloads to 5600 tonnes on some routes, NdeM is adopting the Locotrol system of mid-train 'slave' locomotive control. A 7200-tonne train is already being operated for grain heading south from the USA to Guadalajara, two trains of which are combined as one for part of their run.

A drastic reduction of the points at which less-than-wagonload freight is handled from over 600 to just 42 is in hand, to fit the railway for its prime role as a bulk mover. The railway is keen, though, to expand its merchandise business through piggyback (refrigerated trailers incoming from the US

MLW-built Type M424 diesel-electric Bo-Bo

MLW-built Type M424 between Las Vigas and Jalapa on Mexico City-Vera Cruz line with freight

Traffic

	1979	1980	1981	1982*
Freight tonnage (million)	54·783	55·113	57·961	41·841
Freight tonne-km (million)	NA	NA	35 583	24 168
Passenger-km (million)	3279	3057	3079	2602
Passenger journeys (million)	16·653	16·637	16·014	13·568

*Figures for first nine months.

Finances (million pesos)

Revenues	1979	1980	1981	1982*
Passengers and baggage	370	398	508·7	741
Freight and mail	8392	11 139	13 121	13 767
Other revenue		691	910	1179
Total revenues	9721	13 224	14 539	15 687

Expenses				
Staff personnel expenses	8471	11 371	15 056	15 514
Materials and services	2761	3340	4090	4479
Depreciation	674	1073	3355	4106
Financial charges	1914	2883	3705	6222
Total expenses	17 129	26 105	26 206	30 321

*Figures for first nine months.

now amount to some 15 000 a year) and containers, and is energetically promoting the construction of private sidings.

Passenger traffic

In mid-1982 NdeM's then Director-General, Luis Gomez Z, urged abandonment of unprofitable passenger services in face of the railway's rising problems in financing its increase of capacity, particularly for the transport of grain. At the same time Gomez considered there was justification for development of some key passenger routes, particularly that between San Antonio in the USA, Monterrey and Mexico City.

Investment

At constant money values annual investment in the NdeM was hoisted 60 per cent in the late 1970s, excluding capital expenditure on new railways, which are built to the account of the Department of Communications and Transport. With the aid of loans from the World Bank, US Export-Import Bank and other sources totalling US$1500 million, NdeM was budgeting investments of up to US$2000 million in 1980-82, to which the Ministry was adding US$1200 million for new or upgraded lines. These plans were, however, cut back by a national economic crisis.

Much of the investment in the 1981-85 Five-Year Plan was earmarked for locomotives, rolling stock and related equipment to a value of 50 600 million pesos. No fewer than 615 diesel-electric locomotives were to be acquired, most of them under a contract with General Electric (US) covering delivery of up to 100 units a year. In 1980 GE delivered 150 units, General Motors 31 and Bombardier-MLW 26. The forward programme envisaged receipt of 60 2250 hp, 27 2400 hp and 17 3000 hp units in 1981, 97 2250 hp, 11 2500 hp and 95 3000 hp units in 1982, 60 2250 hp units in 1983, 100 2250 hp units in 1984 and 148 2250 hp units in 1985. Most of the GE-built locomotives are being assembled at NdeM's Aguascalientes workshops.

Planned NdeM investment for 1983 was as follows (million pesos):

Diesel-electric locomotives (100)	5059·0
Freight wagons (1666)	10 578·0
Track improvements	4376·1
Track maintenance machinery	721·6
Bridges and buildings	268·9
Signalling and telecommunications	1057·0
Yards and terminals	364·8
Workshops	603·1
Miscellaneous	774·7
Total	23 803·2

New lines and line relocations

The Department of Communications and Transportation's concurrent five-year plan, costed at 35 000 million pesos in 1980, provided for five new lines:

A 323 km double-track route to replace the present A and B routes on the Mexico City-Huehuetoca-Querétaró-Irapuato axis, where freight occupation is near saturation point;

A 118 km double-track line between Monterrey and Saltillo on the Laredo-Mexico City route, with an easier alignment than the existing route's, which constricts operating capacity;

A new and direct 300 km line between Mexico City and Tampico;

A new 200 km line from Cardel to Alamo, to obtain a direct connection between Veracruz and Tampico/Altamira and avoid the long climb to the Central Plateau at present faced by freight from the south-east to the north;

New lines totalling 338 km between Guadalajara and Encarnación and between Salinas and Laguna Seca, to shorten the distance between Guadalajara and Monterrey and secure better connections between Guadalajara and the industrial complexes of the country's north-east.

Relocation projects covered the routes between Teotihuacán, Orizaba, Córdoba and Veracruz; between Mexico, Acámbaro, Uruapan and Lázaro Cárdenas; and between Córdoba and Coatzacoalcos.

New marshalling yards were to be installed at Monterrey, Guadalajara, Coatzacoalcos and Coyotepec. The last-named, 48 km north of Mexico City, was to be designed for a daily throughput of 5500 freight cars.

Economic crisis

Infrastructure improvements were, however, substantially decelerated in 1982 because of the country's economic crisis and the austerity measures prescribed by the new President, Miguel de la Madrid Hurtago, after his inauguration in December, to satisfy IMF conditions for rescheduling the country's large external debt. The new Mexico-Irapuato double-track line will now be completed to Querétaro in 1984 and to Irapuato in 1985, while the new 118 km double-track line from Monterrey to Saltillo is scheduled for completion in 1986. Construction of the new short line between Mexico and Tampico will start in 1985 and be completed after 1990; the Veracruz-Tampico line should be in service in 1988, the sections being built to shorten the distance between Guadalajara and Monterrey in 1986. The relocation projects between Teotihuacan, Orizaba, Córdoba and Veracruz should be completed in 1987, and between Córdoba and Coatzacoalcos and Acámbaro and Uruapan in 1985. Construction of the new Mexico City yard

Mexico City Buenavista station concourse

Diesel-electric locomotives: 1435 mm gauge
(July 1982)

Class	No in service	Output (hp)	Manufacturer and type		Wheel arrangement	Year built
DE-2	1	600	GE	GE-70	Bo-Bo	1962
DE-4	2	1200	Alco-MLW	RSD-39	Co-Co	1963
DE-5	2	1000	Alco	S-2	Bo-Bo	1944/51
DE-6	16	1000	Alco	RS-1	Bo-Bo	1950/60
DE-10	1	1350	EMD	F-2	Bo-Bo	1946
DE-12	2	2800	GE	U-28-C	Co-Co	1980
DE-13	1	1600	Alco	FA-2	Bo-Bo	1951
DE-14	1	1500	EMD	GP-7	Bo-Bo	1952
DE-15	150	3000	GE	C-30-7	Co-Co	1979/80/81
DE-16	4	1600	Baldwin	AS-616	Co-Co	1954/63
DE-17	22	1750	EMD	F-9, FP-9	Bo-Bo	1954/56
DE-18	71	1310	EMD	G-12	Bo-Bo	1956/57/58/60/61/63/64
DE-19	16	2500	GE	U-25-C	Co-Co	1980
DE-21	8	1750	EMD	GP-9	Bo-Bo	1956/58/59/65
DE-22	73	1800	Alco-MLW	RS-11	Bo-Bo	1957/58/63/64
DE-23	21	1800	EMD	G-16	Co-Co	1958/60
DE-24	64	1800	Alco	RSD-12	Co-Co	1958/60/61/62/64
DE-25	34	1800	EMD	GP-18	Bo-Bo	1961/62/63
DE-26	35	2400	Alco	Century 424	Bo-Bo	1964/65
DE-27	50	2500	EMD	GP-35	Bo-Bo	1964/65
DE-28	18	800	EMD	GA-8	Bo-Bo	1964/67/71
DE-29	32	2750	Alco	Century 628	Co-Co	1967/68
DE-30	9	3000	EMD	GP-40	Bo-Bo	1967
DE-31	84	3000	EMD	SD-40, SDP-40	Co-Co	1968/70/71/72
DE-32	16	3000	MLW	M-630	Co-Co	1972
DE-33	98	3000	EMD	SD-40-2	Co-Co	1972/73/74/75/80
DE-34	60	1500	EMD	SW-1504	Bo-Bo	1973
DE-35	126	3600	GE	U-36-C, C-36-7	Co-Co	1973/74/75/80
DE-36	36	1800	GE	U-18-B	Bo-Bo	1974
DE-37	131	2250	GE	U-23-B, B-23-7	Bo-Bo	1975/80/81/82
DE-38	107	2000	EMD	GP-38-2	Bo-Bo	1975/76/79
	14	2500	GE	U-25-B	Bo-Bo	1980
	53	2400	MLW	M-424	Bo-Bo	1980/81
CNW 900	6	3000	GE	U-30-GE	Co-Co	(1)
6900	7	2800	GE	U-28-B	Bo-Bo	(1)
9700	44	3000	GE	U-30-B	Bo-Bo	(1)
DH 10	4	2400	Alco	PA-4	Bo-Bo	(1)
MLW 200	4	2000	MLW	DL-420	Co-Co	(1)
DH 600	18	2750	Alco	C-628	Co-Co	(1)
DH 700	12	3000	GE	U-30-C	Co-Co	(1)
DH 800	3	3600	EMD	SD-45	Co-Co	(1)
CN 3200	10	2400	MLW	C-424	Bo-Bo	(1)
	42	3000	GE	C-30-7	Co-Co	1982
	11	2250	GE	B-23-7	Bo-Bo	1982

Diesel-electric locomotives: 914 mm gauge

Class	No in service	Output (hp)	Manufacturer and type		Wheel arrangement	Year built
FUS-80	4	800	EMD	GA-8	Bo-Bo	1960/64
FUS-100	7	900	Alco	S-6	Bo-Bo	1955/56/60
FUS-300	3	1600	Alco	RS-3	Bo-Bo	1951
FUS-400	3	1800	Alco	RS-11	Bo-Bo	1956
FUS-500	24	2000	Alco	Century 420	Bo-Bo	1966
		2000	EMD	GP-38		1971
		2000	EMD	GP-38-2		1972/75/80
		2250	GE	U-23-B		1980
		2400	MLW	M-424		1981
		2000	EMD	GP-38-2		1981/82
FUS-600	4	3000	EMD	SD-40-2	Co-Co	1973

(1) Purchased second hand. No record as to year built

(Coyotepec) should be finished in 1988, Monterrey terminal in 1986, Guadalajara terminal in 1988 and Nuevo Laredo terminal in 1986.

Electrification

The first step to the objective of electrifying the entire core of the FNdeM system, conveying 80 per cent of its traffic, is being taken on the new route from Mexico City to Querétaro. Extension beyond Querétaro to San Luis Potosi is to follow.

The Mexico City-Irapuato line is being electrified at 25 kV 60 Hz and provided with modern signalling and communication systems. It will be fed through nine substations, receiving current at 230 kV 60 Hz. Each substation will be provided with two monophasic transformers of 20 MVA capacity and outlet voltage of 27·5 kV. The catenary on the main line will be of polygonal design, allowing train speeds up to 160 km/h. The substations and equipment for sectioning the catenary will be supervised and remotely controlled from two electric dispatching centres located in Mexico City and Querétaro.

Contracts have been assigned to the suppliers of the first stage of the electrification project as follows: General Electric (USA) for the locomotives; Società Anonima Elettrificazione (Italy) for the catenary; Ansaldo, Società Generale Elettromeccanica (Italy) for the substations; WABCO-Westinghouse International Co (USA) for the signalling; Union Switch and Signal for CTC with computer-aided despatching; and Sumitomo Corp (Japan) for the communications system.

The electrification programme has also been delayed by the national economic crisis. At the end of 1982 NdeM hoped to be operational to Querétaro by the end of 1984, to Irapuato by 1986 and to San Luis Potosi by 1988.

Meanwhile the first of the 39 Type E60C 4400 kW Co-Co locomotives ordered from General Electric were completed in 1982. Cost of each 168-tonne locomotive is US$7·1 million. The parallel-connected motors are thyristor-controlled and all power control circuits are solid state. Maximum starting tractive effort is 520 kN, continuous tractive effort 365 kN and maximum speed 110 km/h. The locomotives are designed for mixed traffic employment.

Signalling

Installation of a modern telecommunications system and of electronic centralised traffic control (CTC) was put in hand in 1975 and was due for completion in 1982. From 1977 onwards areas of the system were progressively brought within the compass of a new hierarchy of high-capacity microwave links affording up to 120 speech channels, and of a vhf radio system for direct communication between control bases and train and track crews.

The microwave links have been exploited to set up a central, computer-based management data apparatus known as SCINCO and modelled on the TOPS system of the US Southern Pacific Railroad. The microwave equipment has been supplied by Nippon Electric of Japan, the vhf radio apparatus by Motorola of the USA.

Motive power and rolling stock

At the end of 1982 the National Railways of Mexico's motive power and rolling stock was as follows:

	Units
Diesel-electric locomotives	1553
Railcars (diesel)	37
Freight cars	39 058
Passenger train cars	528

NdeM was expecting to receive 20 1500 hp and 80 3000 hp locomotives in 1983, 20 1500 hp, 13 1800 hp and 74 3000 hp locomotives in 1984 and 20 1500 hp, 40 2250 hp and 23 3000 hp locomotives in 1985. Investment in new freight wagons under the Five-Year Plan (1981-85) was expected to total 13 420 vehicles at a value of 32 800 million pesos.

Track

Rail: 19·8-44·6 kg/m (3769 km); 49·8-57 kg/m (11 665·7 km)
Cross ties (sleepers): 7 in × 8 in × 8 ft
Spacing: In plain track 2000/km; in curves 2028/km
Minimum curvature radius: 14°
Max gradient: 4·17%
Max axleload: 22 tons

First of GE Type E60C 4400 kW electric Co-Cos for NdeM

MOROCCO

Ministry of Public Works and Communications

Rabat

Telephone: 268 01

Minister: Mansouri Ben Ali

Moroccan Railways (ONCFM)
Office National des Chemins de Fer du Maroc

Rue Abderrahmane Alghafiki, Agdal, Rabat

Telephone: 747-47
Telex: 31907

General Manager: Moussa Moussaoui
Chief Engineers: A Benjelloun
M Temri
D Kanouni
Heads of Departments
 Operations: Zine-El-Abidne Achour
 Motive Power and Rolling Stock: A Bouamri
 Permanent Way and Works: M El Aichaoui
 Administration: A Benali

Gauge: 1435 mm
Route length: 1779 km
Electrification: 709 km at 3 kV dc

Transport development

While an extensive network of well-surfaced highways links all principal Moroccan towns, the railway is growing in importance, particularly for mineral transports. The ONCFM system is at present largely confined to the north-western coastal region.

The railway runs about 220 km south from Tangier to the Sidi-Kacem junction with the north-west coastal line to Rabat (continuing to the present railhead at Marrakech via Sidi-el-Aidi and a spur to Oued-Zem) and east to Oujda, via Fez, to link up with Algerian Railways at the frontier. A line running due south from Oujda skirts the Morocco-Algerian frontier as far as the south-east railhead at Bou-Arfa.

GM Type G26C diesel-electric leaving Fez with passenger train for Algerian border *(Marcel Vleugels)*

The National Railway Corporation is a public industrial and commercial enterprise with its own legal entity and financial autonomy working under the administrative umbrella of the Ministry of Transport.

Gibraltar link

Although a joint Spanish-Moroccan committee has advocated that a fixed link across the Straits of Gibraltar be a bored railway tunnel, the Moroccan Government has expressed its preference for a bridge anchored to submarine works. The tunnel alternative is rejected on grounds of lack of data on the terrain beneath the Straits and the unfavourable models of the so far abortive English Channel Tunnel project and the time-scale and cost over-runs of Japan's Seikan Tunnel project.

Traffic

The 1981 passenger traffic figures were a record. Freight traffic has also risen at a steady rate of some 5 per cent annually since the mid-1970s, principally because of growing bulk hauls of grain, fertiliser, petroleum products and cement as well as phosphates, the biggest traffic. ONCFM now has the resources to move 25 million tonnes of phosphates a year.

Finances	1979	1981
Revenues	344·58	533·05
Expenses	418·13	657·12

Motive power and rolling stock

The fleet in 1982 consisted of 114 diesel locomotives, 80 electric locomotives, eight diesel railcars, 275 passenger coaches (including three sleeping and eight couchette cars) and 9429 freight wagons.

Recent deliveries have included eight GM Type G26CW-2 2000 hp Co-Cos and 13 GM Type SW1001 1100 hp Bo-Bo shunters for Roches Noires yard, Casablanca. During the year eight three-car emus based on the SNCB Type AM80 design were ordered from BN, Belgium, and in 1983 orders for 12 electric locomotives were placed with Japanese builders, supported by a Japanese loan of 468 million yen.

Electrification

Electrification of the newly doubled, 83 km line between Youssoufia and the port of Safi was to be launched in 1983. Electrification from Benguerir, on the main Rabat-Casablanca-Marrakech route, to Youssoufia was likely to be finished in 1983.

New lines

New track projects under the 1978-82 plan included: Soviet-built rail line from a new phosphate mine at Meskala to Essaouria on the Atlantic coast; A 955 km link from Marrakech to Laayoun; Doubling of the line between Benguerir and Safi; Doubling of the 90 km Casablanca—Rabat line, in progress in 1982, to permit introduction of a regular-interval passenger service, and later to be continued to Fez; Construction of a cut-off near Matmata on the Fez-Oujda line, because the original alignment is to be inundated by works in connection with the King Idris dam; A 125 km line linking Beni-Ensar with the Taourirt region; Extensive track renewals throughout the system and construction of 14 new branch lines for ONCFM customers.

The Marrakech-Laayoun project was formally inaugurated by King Hassan II in April 1981. The route crosses the Atlas Mountains between Marrakech and Agadir, a 272 km segment involving tunnels and bridgework aggregating respectively 27·1 km and 15·8 km in length. Shortly after the inaugural ceremony, ONCFM announced that it planned to extend this line a further 850 km from Laayoun southward to Boujdour, Ad Dakhla and Lagwira, across the frontier from the Nouadhibou port terminus of the Mauritania Railway.

A second plan unveiled was for an 800 km line south-westward around the Atlas range from Bouarfa to a junction with the Marrakech—Laayoun line near Taroudant, which en route would tap deposits of manganese at Imini, of cobalt at Bou Azzer, and of phosphates at Ouarzazate. A third new line proposed was one of 225 km from Guercif, on the Fez-Oujda line in the north, southward to Midelt.

Extension of the Casablanca-Khouribga line to cater for phosphates traffic from Ben Mellal has been deferred, but the double track as far as Khouribga is being upgraded. A new 125 km line from Nouasseur, south of Casablanca, to the port of Jorf Lasfar was nearing completion in 1982. Thereafter a second line to the port was to be laid from Souk-Sebt, on the Benguerir-Safi route.

Traffic

	1978	1979	1981
Total freight tonne-km (million)	3749	3409·6	3896·2
Total freight tonnage (million)	25·1	22·619	27·057
Total passenger-km (million)	840	835	1139·8
Total passenger journeys (million)	5·910	5·865	6·128

Empty ONCFM phosphates train leaving Casablanca *(Marcel Vleugels)*

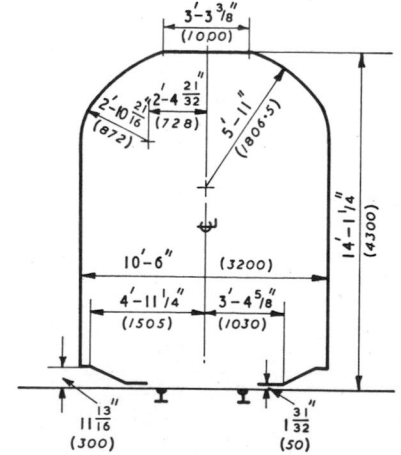

Polish-built Type E-1000 (based on PKP Type ET22) and passenger train on upgraded track at Mohammedia *(Marcel Vleugels)*

MOZAMBIQUE

Mozambique State Railways (CFM)
Caminhos de Ferro de Moçambique

PO Box 276, Maputo

Telex: 6438
Telegrams: Ferroporto, Maputo

National Director: Eng Ferreira Mendes
Deputy National Director: Dr Isaias Muhate
Director of Finance: Oscar Dinis
Commercial Director: Dr Isaac Mugama Matolo
Director, Engineering: Eng Rui Fonseca

Planning: Edmundo de Oliveira
Maputo Railway: Eng Ilidio Dinis
Beira Railway: Eng Ramiro Lopes da Silva
Nampula Railway: R P dos Santos
Inhambane Railway: J Andrade
Quelimane Railway: Francisco Laice
Human Resources: Inácio Rodrigues Junior

Gauge: 1067 mm
Route length: 3004 km

Transport development

The Mozambique Railways (CFM) is made up of five distinct systems linking the coastal ports to the hinterland. From north to south of the country these are:

CFM—Nampula

Gauge: 1067 mm
Route length: 963 km

This line runs from the port of Nacala, with a branch to Moçambique, westward to Cuamba and Lichinga. A new line has been built from Cuamba to connect at the border with Malawi Railways' new link line and afford Malawi rail access to the port of Nacala.

CFM—Beira

Gauge: 1067 mm
Route length: 950 km

From the port of Beira the line runs eastwards to connect with Zimbabwe Railways at Machipanda.

From Dondo Junction, 29 km from Beira, a line runs northward to connect with Malawi Railways with an extension from Dona Ana to Moatize.

A new line 83 km long was built from Inhamitango to Marromeu to replace the old 915 mm gauge length.

CFM—Inhambane

Gauge: 1067 mm; 750 mm
Route length: 98 km; 147 km

This consists of the isolated Xai-Xai to Mauéle line, with a branch from Manjacaze to Chicomo.

CFM—Quelimane

Gauge: 1067 mm
Route length: 160 km

Also an isolated line, running 150 km inland between the coastal town of Quelimane and Mocuba.

CFM-Maputo

Gauge: 1067 mm
Route length: 1296 km

From the port of Maputo lines run west to connect with South African Railways at Kamatipoort, north to Chicualacuala and south-westwards to connect with Swaziland Railways at Goba. A new line of 75 km is being built from Umpala, on the Goba line to Salamanga.

In the south, there are four railway lines, with the port of Maputo as railhead:

Goba line (to the Swaziland border) 64 km
Ressano Garcia line (to the
South African border) 88 km
Limpopo line (to the Zimbabwe
border, at Chicualacuala) 528 km
Xinavane line (domestic service) 93 km
Branch lines (domestic service) 71 km

The first joins up at the border of Swaziland with the Swaziland Railway, which connects the Umbovu Ridge iron-ore complex at Kadake with the port of Maputo. The second continues into the Republic of South Africa. The third line goes through Zimbabwe to Zambia, Botswana and south-east Zaire. Motor vehicles, chemicals, fertilisers and general cargo comprise the main inward traffic; copper, mineral ores, and maize are the principal outward commodities. Its electrification is under study. This line also in effect serves the Limpopo valley. The fourth line is the natural outlet for the sugar-cane produc-ing region of Xinavane and cattle and dairy products of the Gaza province.

The British Government funded a study of improved outlets for coal mined in the Moatize area, near the Zimbabwe border, which has potential output of 10 million tonnes a year. Because of port limitations at Beira, the study considered a new 700 km railway from Dona Ana to the port of Nacala; such a project would have the additional benefit of connecting the presently isolated Mocuba-Quelimane line with the rest of the system.

Traffic

	1981
Freight tonne-km (million)	1 211 800
Freight tonnage (million)	7780
Passenger-km (million)	605 810
Passenger journeys (million)	11 935

Traction and rolling stock

CFM operates 58 line-haul and 20 shunting steam locomotives, 99 diesel-electric line-haul locomotives, 38 diesel-hydraulic shunters, 25 diesel railcars, 200 passenger cars and 8000 wagons.

Since 1979 the traction fleet has been strengthened by the delivery of 32 Type DH 125 1250 hp diesel-hydraulic shunters from Romania and a further 20 Type U20C 2200 hp locomotives from General Electric do Brasil.

Investment

Reconstruction of CFM's deteriorated trunk route tracks is a top priority, in view of the demands for access to the ports of traffic to and from the country's landlocked neighbours. Loans from Canadian, French and Portuguese sources are helping to fund the US$120 million rebuilding of the line from Nacala to Cuamba with 45 kg/m rail on concrete sleepers: in 1983 Sofrerail won a contract to supervise the exercise, which is being carried out by a Franco-Portuguese consortium. A grant from the UK of US$20 million is supporting similar action on the Beira-Machipanda line, starting with the severely-graded 100 km near the Zimbabwe border, where 30 kg/m rail is to be replaced by 40 kg/m, curves eased to a minimum radius of 500 metres and ruling gradient from 1·2 to 2·4 per cent. In a subsequent phase the route is to be double-tracked for 27 km between Beira and Dondo.

In 1981 31 km between Maputo and R Garcia were rebuilt with 45 kg/m rail on prestressed concrete monobloc sleepers. Sections programmed for rehabilitation in 1982-83 were: Dondo-Moatize; Goba-Salamang; Maputo-Chicualacuala; Beira-Machipanda; and Nacala-Entrelagos.

Rail installations at Maputo

NEPAL

Ministry of Works & Transport

Babar Mahal, Katmandu

Minister: Hon K B Shahi

Nepal Government Railway (NR)

Birganj

Acting Manager: Devendra Singh
Acting Traffic Officer: Pratap Bahadur

Gauge: 760 mm
Route length: 10 km

There are only two short railways within Nepal, operating in the Terai, a fertile and level strip adjacent to the border with India. The Janakpur Railway (JR) runs from Jaynagar in Bihar State, India, across the Nepal border north and west to Janakpurdam (32 km) and on to Bizulpra (21 km).

The Nepal Government Railway (NR) runs from Raxaul in Bihar State across the Nepal border to Birganj (9 km). The line was originally built as a key link in the railway-road-ropeway transport system that supplied the mountain-locked valley of Katmandu, closed to the outside world until the early 1950s. The line, now terminating at Birganj, for-merly continued north to the base of the Siwalik Hills at Amlekhganj.

Development

The Government is now undertaking to develop Hetauda into a new industrial centre. As part of the scheme, preliminary feasibility studies have been made for the construction of a new rail line from Raxaul to Hetauda.

At the request of the Nepal Government, Indian Railways has made two studies of possible railway extensions from Raxaul to Hetauda. The first was for a metre-gauge line which would essentially follow the existing rail route. The second called for an entirely new alignment for a broad-gauge line which would pass to the east of Birganj. The first scheme, however, has been virtually abandoned due to the curvatures and grades necessary.

Janakpur Railway (JR)

Janakpur

Telephone: 157
Telegrams: Janakrail

Manager: B B Pradham
Administration Officer: J B Thapa
Traffic Officer: G P Upadhya

Assistant Engineer: D B Kharka

Gauge: 760 mm
Route length: 53 km

The Janakpur Railway (JR) was originally built as a timber line designed to open the virgin jungle to the north of Janakpurdam. As the forest has long since been cut, the railway now operates primarily to provide access in an area with few roads. Passengers are the main source of revenue with pilgrims to the temples of Janakpurdam forming the bulk of traffic. In 1981/82 the railway recorded 24 029 passenger-km.

In recent years JR officers have been upgrading track by laying new sleepers and second-hand 16 kg/m rail to replace existing 12·5 kg/m profile. Locomotives (including two Garratts) and wagons released from the Nepal Railway have been rebuilt and pressed into service. Current stock comprises 11 steam locomotives, 22 passenger cars and 72 freight wagons.

NETHERLANDS

Ministry of Transport & Public Works

Plesmanweg 1, The Hague

Telephone: 74 74 74
Telegrams: VXW, den Haag
Telex: 32562

Minister: Nelli Smit-Kroes
Secretary General: Dr P C de Man
Director-General of Transport: Dr H A de Groot

Netherlands Railways (NS)
NV Nederlandse Spoorwegen

Moreelsepark 1, 3511 EP Utrecht

Telephone: 030-359111
Telex: 47257

President and Chief Executive: L F Ploeger
Directors and Members of the Management Committee
  H M Clemens
  D C Hasselman
  J Walter
  L W Wansink
  J C W Jong
Manager, Operating: D C Hasselman
  Passenger: K Geveke
  Freight: H G R Jacobs
  Finance: J Walter
  Staff: H M Clemens
Chief Rolling Stock and Workshops Engineer: C Moolhuyzen
Chief Infrastructure Engineer: G Verheul
Chief Public Relations Officer: G Hupkes

Gauge: 1435 mm
Route length: 2956 km
Electrification: 1799 km at 1·5 kV dc

Transport development
Rail services within the Netherlands are run by NS, a limited company with shares held wholly by the state. Until 1963 NS showed an annual profit on its operations. From 1964 onwards NS passenger services have incurred a deficit which has grown year by year. Initially the railway covered its losses by borrowing, but the Government now provides compensation under the EEC Harmonisation Order 1191. Freight traffic is operated on an avoidable cost basis, but also subsidised.

Traffic
The 1982 change of coalition government from centre-left to centre-right in political shading and the return to the Transport Minister's chair of Mrs Smit-Kroes was followed by a harsher approach to the NS passenger traffic subsidy. The 1983 figure was cut by Fl 40 million to Fl 942 million and annual reductions of Fl 75 million were sought in 1984 and subsequent years. In April 1983 the Minister raised fares by more than the inflation rate and further increases were to follow.

These measures were expected to halt the growth of NS passenger traffic, which in 1982 climbed yet again from 9230 to 9380 million passenger-km, producing an 8·4 per cent rise of income to Fl 1005 million. The 1982 figure compares with only 8013 million passenger-km registered in 1977; no more than 200 million of the subsequent growth is attributed to the three new lines added to the route-km since 1977. Marketing schemes developed since 1978, including various types of family and seasonal tickets, have been influential in the achievement.

Except for domestic container business, which accounted for only 400 000 tonnes, all types of freight traffic were severely depressed in 1982. A decline of almost 14 per cent was incurred in tonnage, with a concomitant 11·6 per cent drop in revenue to Fl 267 million and a loss pushed up from Fl 67 million in 1981 to over Fl 100 million. To reduce costs NS was planning from May 1983 to shut 32 more freight depots, concentrate almost all marshalling on Kifhoek, Venlo and Amersfoort yards, and trim head office freight staff by 6 per cent; subsequent closure of 23 more wagonload freight depots was likely. The 17 per cent loss in piggyback traffic in 1981 was, however, recovered in 1982 and a new route was established between Breda and Mannheim; piggyback services mostly run from Rotterdam Nord to South Germany, Switzerland and Italy. They are managed by the Dutch marketing company, Trailstar, and now employ Talbot-built low-loading, drive-on, drive-off rail transporters. At

Type DH II diesel-hydraulic two-car unit for local non-electrified service in Groningen and Friesland provinces

Inter-City first-class car interior

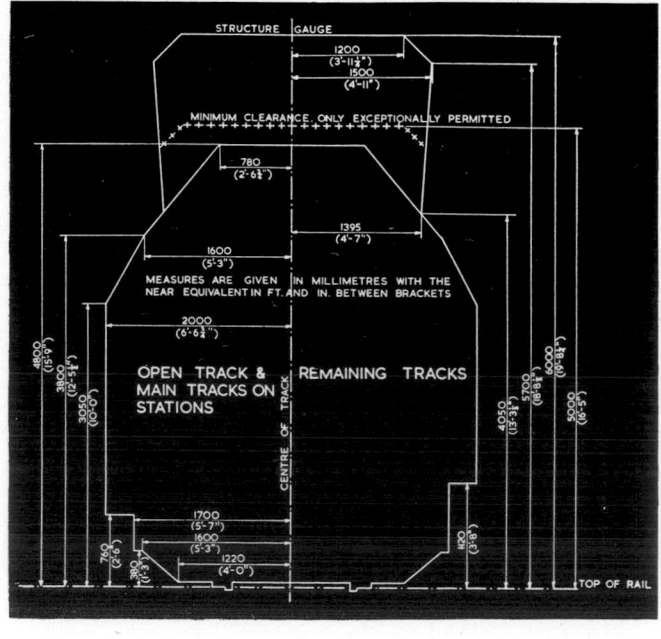

the start of 1983 new arrangements for subsidy of NS freight operations were still to be agreed.

In 1982, following consideration of three independent studies commissioned by the previous administration, the former Government agreed to underwrite the maintenance of a rail freight service, subsidised if necessary, for the next 10 years. One of these studies identified an annual traffic potential of 28·5 million tonnes by 1985, given development in rail freight method and technology. The importance of rail service to the port of Rotterdam was also stressed. A second report recommended continuation of the avoidable cost basis for NS freight accounting. The third advocated purposeful action to equalise the terms of competition (inland waterway operators are reckoned to cover only 1-2 per cent of their true infrastructure costs) and regulate national transport capacity. NS estimates put the railway's traffic potential at only 23·6 million tonnes by 1987.

A substantial proportion of the increase was expected from intermodal traffic, despite rising waterway competition, which includes use of purpose-built container barges. A subsidiary company, Holland Rail Container, has been established to develop container business, for which, in October 1982, new terminals at Leeuwarden and Heerlen were added to those already functioning at Rotterdam Nord, Amsterdam and Veendam (the last two are privately-owned). In 1982 a shuttle container train service was inaugurated between European Container Terminal (ECT) Rotterdam and Blerick, near Venlo, for traffic to and from the Federal Republic of Germany.

In 1983 the Government agreed to grant Fl44 million towards the Fl75 million cost of a new yard and connections at Maashaven West, in the Rotterdam area, together with associated expansion of Kijfhoek central yard, to cater for the 1984 opening of ECT's second container terminal at Maasvlakte. This is expected to generate 45 000 rail container loads annually by 1987, in addition to a transfer movement of 10 000 between Maasvlakte and ECT's Waalhaven terminal.

Finances (Fl million)	1980	1981
Revenues		
Passengers and baggage	845	930
Government support	930	987
Freight and mail	295	302
Other revenues	125	146
Total	2195	2365
Expenditure		
Staff/personnel	1483	1530
Materials and services	499	570
Depreciation	201	216
Financial charges	29	80
Total	2212	2396

Traffic	1979	1980	1981	1982
Total freight tonnage (million)	21·8	22·1	21·5	18·2
Total freight tonne-km (million)	3380	3470	3400	2912
Total passenger-km (million)	8514	8910	9200	9381
Total passengers carried (million)	186·5	197·1	205·1	208
Total passenger train-km (million)	93·7	96	98	NA

Hem Tunnel

In May 1983 Queen Beatrix opened the 2419 metre-long Hem Tunnel, a three-track underwater crossing of the North Sea Canal to replace the previous double-track swing bridge handicapping the busy route between Amsterdam and North Holland, which carries 10 million passengers and 4·5 million tonnes of freight a year. At its centre the tunnel floor is 23·8 metres below the canal's surface, so that the concrete-paved tracks have to dip sharply at 1 in 40; to avoid any risk of freight trains being checked in the dip a special signalling system differentiates between freight and passenger trains.

Sloterdijk and Schiphol line extension

The Hem Tunnel is the centrepiece of a transformation of the NS layout to the north and west of Amsterdam which will continue during the 1980s. More earthworks of an abortive 1930s Amsterdam orbital railway project (already part-used for the Schiphol-RAI extension) are being adapted to project a connection from the Schiphol Airport line around the west of the city to Sloterdijk and thence to Amsterdam Central, with which the Airport

Hem Tunnel under construction

Amsterdam-Brussels push-pull near Dordrecht *(John C Baker)*

Refurbished Class 1100 Bo-Bo, with new cab front, on The Hague-Venlo train of Inter-City cars near Dordrecht *(John C Baker)*

should have direct rail service by 1986. An LRT line is to be laid alongside the standard-gauge NS route to serve local traffic.

At Sloterdijk a new three-level station is being built, with the relocated Amsterdam Central-Haarlem route at the base, road interchange facilities in the centre, and the new link from Schiphol Airport at the top level. Direct connection between the Schiphol line and the Hem Tunnel route to North Holland is planned at a later date. NS hopes the new Sloterdijk facilities will relieve pressure on Amsterdam Central, where enlargement of operating capacity is circumscribed environmentally, though passenger handling facilities are to be comprehensively reconstructed by 1985.

Flevoland line

Opening of the new electrified main line from the Amsterdam-Amersfoort route at Weesp as far as Almere is programmed for 1987, to Lelystad by 1988. Total cost of the project is now put at Fl1612 million; as a new line its capital cost is met on *à fonds perdu* basis by the Government, which similarly treats expansions of operating capacity on the existing network judged essential in the national interest. Weesp station is being rebuilt and enlarged as a future interchange between Flevoland-Schiphol-The Hague and Amersfoort-Amsterdam Inter-City services; that role depends, however, on further use of the 1930s orbital earthworks to create a link between Amsterdam RAI and the Utrecht line, and of a further spur to the Amersfoort line at Diemen. Also possible in the future is extension of the Flevoland line, engineered for 160 km/h, to Groningen.

Utrecht LRV

January 1984 is the planned inauguration date of the 17·5 km LRV line which the NS is constructing from Utrecht Central station to Bieuwegein and IJsselstein. The line will be operated by 27 LRVs built by SIG.

Investment plans 1982-87

Governments up to 1982 had all accepted NS projections of passenger traffic rising from 9200 million to 10 500 million passenger-km by 1987 and the NS case that the increase cannot be accommodated without greater investment to enlarge capacity at key operational bottlenecks, and to accelerate overdue equipment renewals.

Over the period to 1987 NS had been broadly authorised by the administration which resigned in 1982 to invest annually Fl1300 million a year on rolling stock and Fl1300 million on infrastructure, while the Government would invest Fl1250-1300 million a year on new lines and essential capacity enlargements, but the new Government's attitude had only been revealed on one major item up to the end of 1982.

Bottlenecks: 14 have been identified as needing enlargement. The previous centre-left Government had agreed to finance work on eight; the remainder would be covered by the NS. Among the most important are:

Layout enlargement at Utrecht, first phase cost (with two to follow): Fl150 million;

Four-tracking between Leiden and The Hague, cost: Fl130 million;

Flyover at Boxtel, cost: Fl150 million;

Double-tracking of Westervoort canal bridge, cost: Fl118·5 million;

Replacement of double-track swing with four-track fixed bridge at Gouda, cost: Fl130 million;

Replacement of swing with fixed bridge at Leiden, cost: Fl185 million;

Flyover at Roosendaal, cost: Fl140 million.

Works in progress in 1982, with forecast completion dates in brackets, included double-tracking between Zaandam and Hoorn via Purmerend (1986) and new river bridges at Deventer (1983), Nijmegen (1985) and Culemborg (1983).

One of the new Transport Minister's earliest pronouncements concerned the biggest and costliest project under the bottleneck head, replacement of the double-track Nieuwe Maas lifting bridge between Rotterdam and Dordrecht. She rejected her predecessor's approval in principle of a 3 km four-track tunnel and advocated the less costly (by about Fl130 million) alternative of a bridge. However, the NS has been allowed to seek new ways of financing a tunnel.

Electrification: Lines under consideration for fresh electrification at 1·5 kV are: Zwolle-Emmen (favoured politically, but not by NS); Kerkrade-Heerlen; Maastricht-Eijsden (to connect with SNCB electrification on the route to Liège); Nijmegen-Venlo-Roermond; and Dordrecht-Geldermalsen-Arnhem.

Stations: To serve new residential development sites have been earmarked for 32 new stations.

Alsthom-built 5630 hp Class 1100 Bo-Bo on freight haulage test at Best *(John C Baker)*

Unit ore train from Rotterdam Maasvlakte hauled by four Class 2200 diesels *(Marcel Vleugels)*

Investment planned for 1983 covered (Fl000):	
Locomotives (including 5 Class 1600 electric)	37 000
Multiple-units (189 cars)	183 000
Other passenger cars	45 000
Freight wagons	13 000
Intermodal equipment	4000
New lines	193 000
Other infrastructure work	70 000
Track maintenance equipment	6000
Signalling and communications	147 000
Yards and terminals	56 000
Miscellaneous	222 000
Total	976 000

Traction and rolling stock

At the end of 1982 the order for 226 new locomotive-hauled Inter-City cars from Talbot was almost complete. The order for 58 Alsthom-Atlantique Class 1600 electric locomotives was completed in May 1983, and would be followed by 40 more Type ICIII Inter-City emus in 1984/85.

Also to be delivered in 1984/85 are 75 double-deck cars, to be built by Talbot to a new NS specification, which are needed primarily to mitigate acute capacity problems in the Amsterdam-North Holland route, where commuter growth has been very marked. Further purchases will cover 59 cars of new design (18 second-class, 10 first-class, 10 dual-class, two second-class with kitchen intermediate trailers and 11 second-class driving trailers) for push-pull operation on the Benelux service, 15 three-car Type SGMIII ('Sprinter') emus and 45 trailers to expand existing SGMII 'Sprinter' sets to three cars. Delivery of the Benelux equipment will begin in 1986.

For non-electrified lines 19 single-unit DHI and 31 twin-unit DHII railcars have been obtained, from Waggonfabrik Uerdingen. Based on DB's VT627 design, the NS cars are powered by Cummins 280 hp engines.

At the beginning of 1982 NS operated 218 electric and 127 diesel-electric locomotives, 573 emu sets, 92 dmu sets, 22 diesel railcars, 33 electric postal railcars, 402 passenger cars and 14 523 freight wagons.

Signalling

The investment plan envisages a substantial increase of route-km signalled for reversible working, primarily to simplify track maintenance under traffic. By 1986 The Hague, Haarlem, Utrecht, Amersfoort and Amsterdam are to be equipped with central route-relay interlocking signalboxes and automatic train describer apparatus, and NS's first computerised interlocking was to be installed at Hilversum in 1983. The ultimate objective is to control the entire network from about 20 signalling centres.

In November 1982 NS decided to extend track-to-train radio to its whole system and traction units over the ensuing five years. The system to be adopted will be compatible with that of the German Federal Railway.

Civil engineering

The economics of fitting the Groningen-The Hague route for 160 km/h are being studied.

Track

Standard rail, weights
Main lines: 46·9 and 63 kg/m
Branch lines: 38 and 46 kg/m
Standard rail, lengths
Main lines: 24 and 30 m
Branch lines: 15 and 18 m
Rail joints: 4-hole fishplates and bolts; some welding
Cross ties (sleepers): Hard and soft wood, 250 × 150 × 2600 mm
Cross ties spacing
Main lines: 1666 per km
Branch lines: 133? per km
Rail fastenings: Coach screws (on hard wood), coach screws and soleplates (on soft wood), ribbed soleplates and bolts, ribbed soleplates and curved stirrups of spring steel. Elastic fastening with curved stirrups for both wood and concrete sleepers, the clips fitting into a cast iron housing having two pins glued into concrete sleeper or pressed into wood. Cast iron chairs and bolts. Pads under rails are grooved rubber 4 mm thick or wooden wearing plates 4 mm thick.

Experimental sections laid with 'Zig-zag' concrete block and steel tube track construction.

Filling: Gravel or broken stone, 10-80 mm
Minimum thickness under sleeper: 200 mm
Max curvature: 5·8° = minimum radius 300 m
Max gradient, compensated: 2% = 1 in 50 (on Sittard-Hertzogenrath line)
uncompensated: 1·43% = 1 in 70 (on Sittard-Hertzogenrath line)
Longest continuous gradient: 8·85 km of 1 in 300 grade with three curves of 1500 m radius
Worst combination of gradient and curvature: 1 in 175 (0·57%) gradient with curves of 300 m radius
Gauge widening on sharpest curve: 7 mm
Super elevation on sharpest curve: 120 mm on track in gravel. 150 mm on track in broken stone
Rate of slope of super elevation
Speed higher than V 105 km/h: 1 in 8V
Speed 105 km/h or less: 1 in 1100 with minimum of 1 in 600
Altitude, max: 181·7 m on Simpelveld-West German frontier section
Max axleloading: 21 tons
Max permitted speed
  Passenger trains: 140 km/h
  Freight trains: 60 km/h
  Fast freight trains: 90 km/h

Type IC III Inter-City emu at Utrecht *(D Ward)*

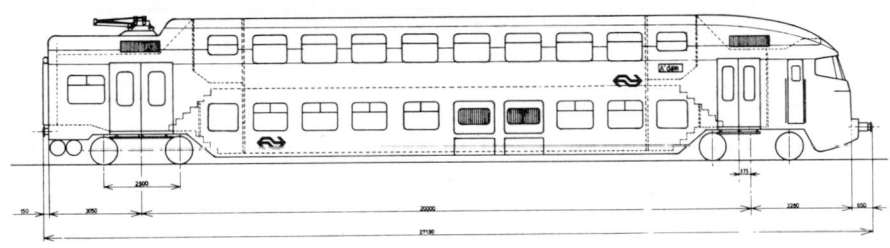

Layout of NS bi-level driving trailer

Diesel locomotives

Class	Wheel arrangement	Transmission	Rated power hp	Max lb (kg)	Tractive effort Continuous at lb (kg)	mph (km/h)	Max speed mph (km/h)	Wheel dia in (mm)	Total weight tons	Length ft in (mm)	No built	Year first built	Builders Mechanical parts	Engine & type	Transmission
2400 2500	Bo-Bo	Elec	850	36 400 (16 500)	12 830 (8090)	12 (20)	50 (80)	39⅜ (1000)	60	41' 1" (12 520)	129	1954	Alsthom	SACM, V 12 SHR	Alsthom
2200 2300	Bo-Bo	Elec	900	40 800 (18 500)	27 000 (12 250)	8·7 (14)	62 (100)	37⅜ (950)	74	45' 11½" (14 010)	150	1955	Allan Schneider	Stork, Schneider (lic Superior) 40 C-LX-8	Heemaf Westinghouse
511-545 601-665	C	Elec	400	32 100 (14 600)	14 436 (6550)	6 (10)	19 (30)	48⅜ (1230)	47	29' 9" (9070)	35	1949	English Electric	EEC, 6 KT	EEC
200-300	Bo	Elec	72				60 (98)	39⅜ (1000)	21	23' 7½" (7220)	148	1934-1951	Schneider-Werkspoor	Stork, Hengelo	Heemaf: ETI; Hengelo or Slikkerveer

Electric locomotives and railcars

Class	Wheel arrangement	Line current	Rated output hp	Tractive effort (full field) Max lb (kg)	Continuous lb (kg)	at mph (km/h)	Max speed mph (km/h)	Wheel dia in (mm)	Weight tonnes	Length ft in (mm)	No built (incl on order)	Year first built	Builders Mechanical parts	Electrical equipment
1500	Co-Co	1500 V dc OH	3220	45 000 (20 400)	20 000 (9100)	44·2 (78)	84 (135)	43 (1092)	69	59' 0'' (17 983)	6	1954	BR	
1300	Co-Co	1500 V dc OH	3870	51 000 (23 100)	28 600 (13 000)	31 (50)	84 (135)	49¼ (1250)	111	62' 2'' (18 950)	15	1952	Alsthom	Alsthom
1200	Co-Co	1500 V dc OH	3000	43 500 (19 700)	22 400 (10 200)	31 (50)	84 (135)	43¼ (1100)	108	59' 4'' (18 080)	25	1951	Werkspoor-Baldwin	Heemaf-Westinghouse
1100	Bo-Bo	1500 V dc OH	2580	34 200 (15 500)	14 300 (6500)	31 (50)	84 (135)	49¼ (1250)	80	42' 7½'' (12 980)	58	1950	Alsthom	Alsthom
3001/3035 (MP)	Bo-Bo	1500 V dc OH					87 (140)	37²/s (950)	52	86' 4'' (26 400)	35	1965	Werkspoor	Werkspoor
1600	Bo-Bo	1500 V dc OH	5630				100 (160)	49¼ (1250)	85	57' 9'' (17 640)	58	1981	Alsthom-Atlantique	Jeumont-Schneider
EL2	(2-Bo)+ (Bo-2)	1500 V dc OH					86 (140)	37²/s (950)	85	170' 3'' (52 140)	244	1966/76	Werkspoor Talbot	Heemaf/Smit
ELD4	(2-2)+ (Bo-Bo)+ (Bo-Bo)	1500 V dc OH					86 (140)	37²/s (950)	168	331' 7'' (101 240)	30	1964/65	Werkspoor	Heemaf/Smit
SGM II	Bo-Bo Bo-Bo	1500 V dc OH	1720				80 (125)	37²/s (950)	106	171' 3'' (52 200)	75	1975/80	Talbot SIG	Oerlikon Holec
ICIII	Bo-Bo (2-2)+ (2-2)	1500 V dc OH	1675				1675 (160)	37²/s (950)	114	264' 5'' (80 600)	87	1977	Talbot Wegmann	Heemaf/Smit TCO

NEW ZEALAND

Railways Department

Minister's Office, Parliament Buildings, Wellington C1

Minister: George Gair

New Zealand Railways Corporation (NZR)

Bunny Street, Wellington

Telephone: 725 599

Railways Corporation Board
Chairman: Lyndsay Papps
Directors: Sir Allan Wright
        Peter Egan
        Joseph Auton
        Charles Hercus
        Arnot McConnell
        Robert Lorimer
General Manager: T M Hayward
Deputy General Manager, Personnel: H G Purdy
Assistant General Manager, Engineering and Development: M R H Henare
Assistant General Manager, Finance and Administration: A E McQueen
Chief Mechanical Engineer: J T Hudson
Chief Civil Engineer: W I Jones
Chief Traffic Manager: A R Thomson
Director, Finance and Accounts Branch: K D McGavin
Director, Stores Branch: J E Burley
Director, Road Services Branch: G C Watt
Director of Planning (Electrification and Shipping): E J Knox
Commercial Manager: A E McInnes
Director, Land Division: L S Harding
Publicity and Advertising Manager: I G Holland

Gauge: 1067 mm
Route length: 4418 km

Railways development
New Zealand Railways was established as a corporation independent of Government control in April 1982. The Corporation now has full responsibility for the operation of over 4400 km of railways linking almost all the main centres of population in New Zealand, together with passenger and freight services over more than 10 000 route-km of highway, and a rail and road vehicle and passenger ferry service across Cook Strait. Over 20 000 people are employed by the Corporation.

Dx locomotive with mixed freight train

Class Dc locomotive, rebuilt by Clyde Engineering, on East Coast trunk line container train

Traffic

Rail freight for the year ending March 1982 increased by 1·1 per cent to 11 520 million tonnes. The average length of haul for the year increased to 283 km, and the increase in traffic resulted in a 3·6 per cent increase in net tonne-km, to 3265 million. Passenger journeys totalled 14·339 million, a 3·8 per cent decrease on the previous year. The Government is inclined to replace almost all NZR passenger services by road transport and has resisted restitution of the Wellington-Auckland sleeper train, withdrawn in 1979.

Finances (NZ$ million)

	1980	1981	1982
Revenue	349·126	420·461	507·347
Expenditure	404·931	471·498	563·977

Motive power and rolling stock

Number of locomotives in service at the end of 1982:

Steam	2
Diesel-electric	328
Electric	11
Diesel-mechanical and diesel-hydraulic	180

Passenger stock in service: three Rm 'Silver Fern' and two PW S&E railcars, 168 electric multiple-units, 269 carriages and 307 vans.

Freight wagons

A total of 463 new goods wagons were placed in service during the year. These comprised 200 PK, 90 UK, 20 UKA, 10 US and 3 USA class bogie flat-top wagons for the transport of containers and other freight; 60 USL bogie flat-top wagons for the transport of logs; and 80 ZA class bogie box wagons. In addition, a number of other wagons were modified to handle specialised freight.

New wagons authorised for construction at the end of March 1982 totalled 466, comprising 84 NK four-wheel container wagons; 118 PK and 34 UBM bogie flat-top, 130 USL bogie log wagons, and 100 ZA class bogie box wagons.

Motive power

During 1981/82 a programme to rebuild all bogies for DX locomotives was initiated as a forerunner to the full overhaul of these locomotives, which is to begin in 1982/83; two are being fitted with a number of new features to improve their performance in service. The rebuilding and modernising of DA and DB class locomotives under contract with the Clyde Engineering Company in South Australia has continued with the close involvement of New Zealand Railways personnel. By March 1982 78 of the 90 locomotives shipped to Australia had been returned rebuilt and were in service. The programme to fully overhaul 10 DG class locomotives for use as 'slaves'

New commuter emus by Ganz-Màvag in service on Paekakariki and Hutt Valley routes from Wellington

Class Da locomotive rebuilt as Class Dc by Clyde Engineering Company with close involvement of NZR personnel

Class Da locomotive and container train leaves Kaimai tunnel

to the rebuilt DG class continued and four units were completed by mid-1982. All DSC class shunting locomotives originally built in New Zealand have now been re-engined and treated to other improvements; 52 have been fitted with Cummins and 18 with Rolls-Royce engines.

By mid-1982 Toshiba Corporation had completed and delivered 12 of the 18 DSG class high-powered shunting locomotives for work in major yards; the first six were working in the Wellington area, the second six in the Christchurch area.

Containers
To supplement NZR's box-wagon fleet, 200 6-metre GSX and 200 3-metre GSX containers were delivered by Daewoo, Republic of Korea. The smaller containers hold 10 000 kg of freight, either in bulk or as small-lot individual consignments, while the larger, with a 16 070 kg loading capacity, are intended primarily for palletised loading.

Passenger stock
The final batch of 15 two-car Hungarian emus arrived after the end of the financial year, completing the total of 44 two-car units received from Ganz-Mávag of Budapest. The first 30 units entered service in the Wellington area during the year and fitting-out, tests and commissioning continued on the remaining 14 units. Debarred from investing in new longer-haul passenger stock, NZR is refurbishing cars of 1940s vintage with new running gear, underframes and interior furnishing.

Electrification
Approval was given in December 1981 for the calling of tenders for the electrification of the North Island main trunk railway line between Palmerston North and Hamilton. The six-year electrification project will cost an estimated NZ$188 million, which includes over NZ$20 million within the railway's normal works investment programme for the replacement of signals and communications equipment and associated work. Tenders have been called internationally and locally for contracts covering locomotives, traction, overhead and power supplies, signals and communications, earthworks and tunnelling. In 1983 a 15-company Japanese group led by Sumitomo and Toshiba, and including Mitsubishi, Hitachi, Nippon Signal and Nippon Electric, announced intention to bid for the fixed works and the supply of 24 locomotives.

Earthworks were begun on the Marton-Palmerston North section and five tunnels broached. Electrification will be introduced by commissioning separate sections of track, with completion of the Taumarunui-Hamilton section expected in early 1988.

Progress on the extension of suburban electrification from Paekakariki to Paraparaumu proceeded speedily. The NZ$1·9 million electrification project was expected to be complete in early 1983.

Civil engineering
Construction work on the Mangaweka-Utiku deviation was completed and following the official opening in November 1981 a further major bottleneck on the North Island main trunk railway was eliminated.

The old section with its steep grades, sharp curves and high maintenance tunnels subsequently closed. The NZ$16·5 million deviation runs from south of Mangaweka township to rejoin the main line near Utiku. Three major bridges are a feature of the new deviation: the South Rangitikei (315 metres long, 80 metres high); the Kawhatau (160 metres long, 75 metres high); and the North Rangitikei (160 metres long, 80 metres high).

The Swanson deviation was also opened during the year, improving rail access to the north and enabling larger and heavier trains to run north of Auckland. The NZ$960 000 deviation swings left from Swanson and follows a 1 in 60 grade across the major culvert over Swanson stream.

NZ$7 million was spent during the year maintaining and upgrading the Christchurch-Picton line in the South Island. Much of the work consisted of realigning tracks and 'weather-proofing' the line, which entailed cutting back steep faces that bordered the line at some places. A better than 99 per cent reliability rate was achieved in 1981/82, following the upgrading of the line.

Computerised wagon control
NZR's Traffic Monitoring System (TMS) was established nation-wide in December 1980 and has performed reliably. Two significant new programming developments for the TMS computer system were begun in 1981. The first involves the processing of TMS archived movements to permit analysis and searching of historical wagon movements. This will require the use of NZR's Finance and Account Branch's computer for storage and analysis of the wagon movement information. Up to two years of wagon movement information will be kept for on-line enquiries.

The second development, started in 1982, will see the matching of wagon loadouts to waybill records. A pilot scheme is underway at Kinleith and Palmerston North. When finally implemented, the system will allow accurate and comprehensive audits of the charging for wagon loads to be carried out much more easily and quickly.

During 1981 Cabinet approval was obtained for the purchase of new computing equipment for the second stage of TMS, which will allow more information to be obtained from the scheme. Tenders were called in October and were being evaluated at the year's end.

A move to market TMS overseas has been the formation of DATARAIL, a joint venture between NZR and PROGENI, a New Zealand computer company. DATARAIL will provide railway and computer consultants to install TMS on any overseas rail network.

44-tonne capacity NZR coal hopper wagon

South Rangitikei viaduct on Mangaweka-Utiku deviation on North Island main trunk line

Traffic Monitoring System (TMS) operators with latest NZR development in computerised wagon-movement control

Investment

Investments planned for 1983 covered (NZ$000):

Electric locomotives (2)	900
Diesel locomotives, new (12) and rebuilt (12)	6020
Electric multiple-units	12 980
Freight wagons (189) and containers (46)	8883
Track work	1850
Track maintenance equipment	1890
Bridges and buildings	6780
Electrification	5020
Signalling	2450
Yards and terminals	4380
Workshops	8763
Miscellaneous	6630
Total	66 546

Track

Rail

Main line: 50 kg/m; 91 lb/yd; 85 lb/yd

Provincial lines: 91 lb/yd; 85 lb/yd; 75 lb/yd; 70 lb/yd

Branch lines: 70 lb/yd; 55 lb/yd

Longest length continuous welded rail: 8·5 km (through Kaimai tunnel)

Relaid in new rail: 105 km

Welding method: Flash butt in depot, Thermit in field. New rails flash butt welded in depots into 76·8 m lengths and transported to site for laying. Short rail in track may be Thermit welded into similar lengths. Continuous welded rail is formed on straight track by Thermit process with lapped expansion joints at extremities and epoxy glued joints

Cross ties (sleepers)

  NZ Pinus radiata (all lines)

  Concrete (main lines only)

Cross tie spacing

Main line: Timber 650 mm

Fastenings

Main lines: Timber: Pandrol spring fastenings on bedplates with rubber pads; clips, screw spikes, spring washers on double-shoed bedplates. Spring clips and screw spikes without bedplates

Concrete: Pandrol spring fastenings with rubber or plastic pads and nylon insulators

Branch lines: Timber: Elastic spikes, screws and dog spikes cascaded from higher-ranking lines

Laying method: Concrete: By NZR designed and built sleeper-laying machine

Timber: Laid manually either in face or by spotting

Dimensions

Concrete: 254 × 190 × 2134 mm

Timber: 200 × 150 × 2134 mm

Wellington-Auckland express freight of Class Zp covered wagons and containers headed by 2750 hp Class Dx locomotive

'Southerner' daylight express between Christchurch and Invercargill

Diesel locomotives

Class	Wheel arrange- ment	Trans- mission	Rated power gross kW	Rated power net kW	Tractive effort continuous at kN	Tractive effort continuous at kmlh	Weight tonnes	Max axle load tonnes	Year into service	Builders Mechanical parts	Builders Engine & type	Total North Island	Total South Island	Use
Da	A1A-A1A	Elec	1065	980	140	21·2	79	14·7	1955-67	GM	12-567C	65		GP
Db	A1A-A1A	Elec	710	655	100	20·1	68·5	11.7	1965-66	GM	8-567CR	9		Branch
Dbr												8		
Dc	A1A-A1A	Elec	1230	1020	140	21·2	82·75	15	1977	GM	12-64E	75		GP
Df	Co-Co	Elec	1230	1020	194	16·5	86·6	14·4	1979	GM	12-645E	16	14	GP
Dg	A1A-A1A	Elec	560	475	90	16·3	70	11·9	1955-56	EE	6 SRKT		26	Freight
Di	Co-Co	Elec	755	640	132	14·5	63	10·5	1966	EE	6 CSRKT		5	Freight
Dj	Bo-Bo-Bo	Elec	780	585	128	16·9	65	10·9	1968-69	Mitsubishi	CAT D398		62	GP
Dx	Co-Co	Elec	2050	1940	207	27·4	97·5	16·3	1975-77	GE	7 FDL-12	48		GP
De	Bo-Bo	Elec	490	410	56	24·8	52	13	1952-53	EE	6 SKRT	10	5	Shunting
Dh	Bo-Bo	Elec	678	570	150	20	54	13·5	1978	GE	CAT D398 B	6		Shunting
Dsc	Bo-Bo	Elec	2×155	2×150	46	13·7	41	10·3	1959-67	AEI/NZR	RR C6TFL Cummins NT855	45	25	Shunting
Ds	C (0-6-0)	Mech	152				24·6	8·9	1949-54	Drewry	Gardner 8L3	2	4	Shunting
Dsa	C (0-6-0)	Mech	152				30	10·2	1953	Drewry	Gardner 8L3	10	2	Shunting
Dsa	C (0-6-0)	Hyd	235				30·5	10·2	1956-57	Bagnall	CAT D343T	10		Shunting
Dsa	C (0-6-0)	Mech	235				31·3	10·9	1954-58	Hunslet	CAT D343T		12	Shunting
Dsa	C (0-6-0)	Hyd	235				30·5	10·2	1967	Mitsubishi	CAT D343T		12	Shunting
Dsb	C (0-6-0)	Hyd	280				38·1	12·7	1967	Mitsubishi	CAT D343T		3	Shunting
Dsb	C (0-6-0)	Hyd	263				37·4	12·7	1954-55	Drewry	CAT D343T	17	5	Shunting

Railcar

Rm	Elec	750	660	39	55	111	14·2	1973	KHI Toshiba	CAT D398	3	

Electric locomotives

Eo	Bo-Bo	960		101	33	55	13·7	1968	Toshiba		5	Freight
Ew	Bo-Bo-Bo	1345		104	44·5	76	12·7	1951-52	EE		6	Suburban passenger

Electric multiple-units

DM/D	450		38	42·6	42·4	10·7	1936-47	EE		40/70	Suburban passenger
EM/ET	400			72·1	12·9	1982	Ganz-Mávag		30/30	Suburban passenger

NICARAGUA

Nicaragua Railway
Ferrocarril de Nicaragua

Apartado Postal No 5, Managua

Telephone: 22160; 22802; 22803
Telex: 1239

General Director: R Espinosa
Operations Manager: Roger Moreno G
Head of Engineering: M Ramos
  Maintenance and Equipment: R Zamora
  Permanent Way: Ing H Gutierrez

Gauge: 1067 mm
Route length: 344 km

The railway, running from Corinto to Granada with branches to Rio Granda and Puerto Sanonio, operates nine diesel locomotives, four railcars and 195 freight wagons. Track is laid with 20, 25 and 30 kg/m rails, maximum permissible axleloading is 13·5 tonnes, minimum curve radius 157 metres and maximum gradient 2·5 per cent.

NIGERIA

Ministry of Transport and Aviation

Abeo Kuta

Minister: Dr U Dikko

Nigerian Railway Corporation (NRC)

PMB 1037, Ebute Metta, Lagos

Telephone: 44302
Telegrams: Railways, Lagos

Chairman: Col J T Useni
Administrator: Dr P E Japka
Assistant General Managers: A O Adewoyin
                        S O Omotoso
Chief Civil Engineer: A F A Babutunde
Chief Mechanical and Electrical Engineer: J N Ileoyonsi
Chief Signal Engineer: S L O Ojekwe
Stores Controller: A L Ayonrinde

Gauge: 1067 mm
Route length: 3523 km

Transport development
Nigeria has the most extensive highway and railway networks in West Africa. The Federal Government has responsibility for 30 000 km of primary and secondary highways as well as NRC.

The former Nigerian Government Railways was converted to a statutory corporation by Act of Parliament in 1955. The board of NRC now comprises a chairman and eight members responsible for determining the policy of the Corporation subject to approval by the Federal Commissioner for Transport. Day-to-day administration is under the supervision and control of the Administrator (General Manager) who is also chief executive of NRC.

The entire network is, apart from the Departments based at Lagos headquarters, divided into five districts.

Traffic
There has been a continuous fall in freight traffic haulage for the past few years. In 1973/74 NRC handled 1·7 million tonnes (1307 million tonne-km) falling to 335 000 tonnes (274 million tonne-km) in 1977/78. During 1978/79 a rise in traffic was detected, and by 1983 the railway expects to be hauling about 550 000 tonnes a year.

Passenger traffic has also revived following a continuing reduction in journeys recorded between 1973 and 1978 when traffic fell to an all-time low of 2·2 million journeys and 383 million passenger-km. By 1982/83 NRC hoped to record 5·5 million journeys a year.

Motive power and rolling stock
In 1982 NRC owned 133 steam locomotives, 144 main-line diesel locomotives, 39 diesel shunters, 655 passenger cars and 6729 freight wagons.

Standard-gauge project
In 1981 the Government engaged Sofrerail to undertake a detailed engineering study of the first planned stage of a new standard-gauge system; a 463 km line from Port Harcourt to Makurdi; and a 217 km line from Oturkpo to the new steelworks at Ajaokuta being built by the USSR. The Port Harcourt-Makurdi line was to be engineered for 160 km/h, with UIC60 rails on concrete sleepers, maximum gradient 1 per cent and minimum curve radius 1200 metres.

Early in 1982 the first three of the six segments into which the construction has been divided were under contract: Umuahia-Enugu to Dumez of France; Utonkon-Makurdi to Partisanski of Yugoslavia; and Oturkpo-Ayangba on the Ajaokuta line to a Swiss/Chinese consortium including, on the Swiss side, Electrowatt and Noga. Later in the year, however, the US$2500 million scheme had to be postponed indefinitely. Because of the receding world demand for oil and its declining price, it proved impossible to finance two of the six contracts, besides which the country had to curb imports. The future of the branch to the Ajaokuta steelworks, already begun, and of the plant itself, was uncertain.

Investment
During 1981 a contract for 516 tank wagons was placed with Daewoo Heavy Industries and Hyundai Rolling Stock of South Korea; the wagons were to be mounted on Gloucester RCW Co Ltd rubber-sprung bogies manufactured under licence in South Korea.

Track
Rail: BS60R 29·8 kg/m; BS70A 34·7 kg/m; BS80R, 80A 39·7 kg/m
Cross ties (sleepers): Steel, 130 × 7·5 mm
Fastenings: Pandrol: K Type

Signalling
Signalling is mechanical, with single/double wire operation at 220 locations, but one main junction is equipped with route relay interlocking by Westinghouse Brake & Signal Co. In 1983 this company gained a N5·5 million contract to install colour-light signalling, power-operated, over 576 km of NRC main lines.

NORWAY

Ministry of Communications

Møllergt 1-3, Oslo

Telephone: 11 90 90
Telegrams: Samferdselsdepartment

Minister: Inger Koppernäs
Under-Secretary of State: S Pettersen
Secretary-General: Erik Ribbu

Norwegian State Railways (NSB)
Norges Statsbaner

Storgaten 33, Oslo

Telephone: 20 95 50
Telex: 11 168

Central Administration
  Chairman of the Board: Thorleif Løken
  General Manager: Robert F Nordén
  Public Relations: Reidar Skaug Høymork
Administration and Finance
  Chief Director: Tore Lindholt

Director, Administration: B Egeland-Eriksen
Director, Personnel: Odd Wessel Larsen
Director, Purchase and Stores: Oddvar Bø
Director, Finance: Helge Skudal

Operation and Commerce
  Chief Director: Knut Skuland
  Director, Operations: Yngre Pedersen
  Director, Commerce: Kjell Fålun

Engineering
  Chief Director: Karsten Krogsaeter
  Director, Rolling Stock: Per Bøyum
  Director, Electrification: Kjell Moi
  Director, Way and Works: H Hartmark

Gauge: 1435 mm
Route length: 4241 km

Traffic

Fierce fare increases enforced by the Transport Minister and aggregating 45 per cent over a 12-month period halted the growth which had achieved recorded journey and passenger-km totals in 1980 and 1981. In the first half of 1982 journeys were down 3 per cent and passenger-km 6·1 per cent.

The major 1982 passenger development was the launch between Oslo and Trondheim of the accelerated 'Dovesprinten' service employing three-phase Type El 17 electric locomotives and B7 passenger cars. The previous schedule of around 7 hours for the 553 km distance was cut to 6 hours 35-37 minutes, though initially the operation was troubled by teething problems with the three-phase locomotives.

The Type B7 low-slung-body passenger cars are by Strømmens Vaerkstad A/S. A bodyshell formed of extruded aluminium profiles manufactured by Alusuisse helps keep tare weight down to 36 tonnes. Centre of gravity of the vehicle, 26·1 metres long overall, is low enough to keep maximum height to 3·85 metres above rail top; cross-sectional profile allows for possible tilting at up to 8 degrees on curves. Bogies are by Wegmann, with secondary air suspension, disc and clasp brakes (the latter for tread-cleaning) and provision for ultimate fitment of hydraulic tilting gear. First-class vehicles only are air-conditioned.

Freight traffic continued to recede in the first half of 1982, with another serious fall of 14·8 per cent in the Ofoten line ore tonnage succeeding a decline of 20 per cent in 1981. International freight tonnage alone managed an increase, reversing a downturn of 1981.

Finances

	1981 (NKr million)
Revenue	2171
Expenses	2848
Financial charges	182
Deficit	859

Investment

Unlike other forms of Norwegian transport NSB again had its investment budget cut back in 1983 to a figure that trailed the rate of inflation. The ceiling was fixed at NKr 826·4 million, NKr 250 million less than NSB had sought and only 2·7 per cent above what was spent in 1982. The main casualty would be the rate of progress with the new Oslo Central station project. Planned expenditure for 1983 was announced as (NKr 000):

Electric locomotives	23 600
Passenger cars	223 200
Freight wagons (80)	37 200
Track works	282 300
Track maintenance machinery	20 000
Bridges and buildings	12 500
Signalling and communications	68 000
Electrification	42 400
Yards and terminals	49 500
Miscellaneous	27 300
	787 200

NSB has pressed for authority to invest NKr 8500 million up to 1989, claiming that otherwise its rising backlog of maintenance and renewals will enforce contraction of railway operations as well as continue to impair the railway's competitive ability. The fruits of such investment would improve revenue and eventually reduce the amount of Government subsidy; the higher rate of expenditure would not be necessary after 1989. The Government, for its part, was in 1982 preparing a paper on the railway's future.

Traffic

	1980	1981	1982*
Freight tonnage (million)	30·668	25·866	12·021
Freight tonne-km (million)	3014	2825	1386
Passenger journeys (million)	37·95	38·92	19·3
Passenger-km (million)	2393·5	2424·5	1124

* First six months only

Infrastructure

The heaviest capital expenditure on permanent way recently has involved the Nordland line where a continuous section of 325 km from Jørstad to Mo i Rana has been renewed with heavier rails, concrete sleepers and crushed stone ballast. Improvement work has also been carried out on the Rauma and Røros lines.

NSB has entered a period in which its catenary systems require replacement. Catenary renewal has already been carried out on the Oslo-Lillestrøm and Brakerøya-Kongsberg sections and on the Ofoten line.

Extension of CTC has continued on the Oslo-Bergen line. Installation of Ericsson ATC started in 1981 and was in use on the whole section from Lillestrøm to Otta early in 1982. A track-to-train radio system compatible with that of the Swedish State Railways is to be adopted, to facilitate inter-railway traction operation.

Class El 17 electric locomotive and B7 cars forming Oslo-Trondheim 'Dovesprinten'

Interior of Type B7 low-profile passenger car

Class El 16 electric locomotive

Class Di 4 diesel-electric Co-Co locomotive by Henschel

The first phase of the building of Oslo Central station was completed in 1981. This phase included the administrative and operations building, the main concourse and ramps to the platforms. Efforts have otherwise been concentrated on the building of platforms and work in connection with the tunnel giving access to the new suburban traffic platforms for the Østfold line.

North Norway Line

Feasibility studies for the construction of a line from Fauske to Narvik, and Tromsø, to connect these ports directly with the rest of the NSB network, were completed in 1981, but the subsequent change of Government made further action on the controversial project improbable. The proposed route is 476 km long and much of the 183 km from Fauske to Narvik would have to be tunnelled through the mountains enclosing a succession of fjords in its path. As a result the Fauske-Narvik section would take 10 years to build, and the projection on to Tromsø a further six years. A branch would be constructed from Bjerkvik to Harstad, on the island of Hinnøya. Total infrastructure cost has been estimated at NKr4400 million and that of electrification throughout at a further NKr1100 million.

Traction and rolling stock

Following considerable problems encountered with the six Class El 17 three-phase electric locomotives obtained in 1980, NSB reverted to the ASEA-built thyristor-controlled Class El 16 for its 1982 order for seven electric locomotives. NSB needs a minimum of five new electric locomotives a year, and in view of the constraints on its capital investment resources it has been considering the possibility of financing some of its purchases through loans.

In 1983 NSB was taking delivery of the first of a new Class 6950 series of 25 two-car emus for the Oslo area, built by Strømmens Vaerkstad A/S. Changes by comparison with earlier units include air suspension, doubled heating and ventilation capacity, and moulded plastic seating structures.

In 1982 NSB placed a NKr 140 million order with Uerdingen for 15 Type BM 92 two-car diesel-electric units for its longer non-electrified routes, such as Hamar-Trondheim and Trondheim-Bodø. Each unit will be equipped with a pair of 357 kW motors and asynchronous electric transmissions similar to that of NSB's Di 4 diesel and El 17 electric locomotives.

At the start of 1982 NSB's motive power park consisted of 170 electric locomotives, 93 diesel locomotives, 132 electric motor coaches, 45 diesel railcars and 153 locotractors. Rolling stock included 792 passenger coaches and 8518 freight wagons.

Track

Rail: S 54 kg/m, S 49 kg/m, 41 kg/m
Cross ties (sleepers): Concrete; wood
Thickness: 170 mm; 140 mm
Spacing: 650 mm; 600 and 650 mm
Rail fastenings: On main lines the principal fastenings to wood sleepers are Hey-Back and Deenik. Pandrol fastenings have been adopted as standard fastenings on concrete sleepers. On the Bergen-Tunestveit line, and in long tunnels where UIC54 and S64 rails are used, the fastening is elastic double-shaft railspikes on hardwood sleepers without baseplates.
On branch lines the fastenings consist mainly of dog spikes, wedge plates and Hey-Back.
Pads under rails: With Hey-Back fastenings a thin, 1·25 mm rubber pad is inserted between rail and baseplate.
With Pandrol fastenings a 5 mm thick plastic pad is inserted between rail and concrete sleeper.
As a general rule pads are not used under rails except with Hey-Back fastenings.

Electric locomotives

Class	Wheel arrangement	Line current	Rated output hp	Tractive effort (full field) Max lb (kg)	Continuous at lb (kg)	Continuous at mph (km/h)	Max speed mph (km/h)	Wheel dia in (mm)	Weight tonnes	Length ft in (mm)	No built (on order)	Year built	Builders: Mechanical parts	Builders: Electrical equipment
El 8	1-Do-1	15 kV 16⅔ Hz	2830	35 700 *(16 200)*	19 000 *(8650)*	52 *(83)*	68 *(110)*	43⅞ *(1110)*	83	45′ 3¼″ *(13 800)*	16	1940-49	Thunes	Norsk Electrisk; Brown Boveri
El 9	Bo-Bo	15 kV 16⅔ Hz	970	22 700 *(10 300)*	13 700 *(6200)*	22 *(36)*	37 *(60)*	39⅜ *(1000)*	48	33′ 5½″ *(10 200)*	3	1947	Thunes	Norsk Electrisk; Brown Boveri
El 10	C	15 kV 16⅔ Hz	700	23 400 *(10 600)*	11 700 *(5300)*	17 *(27)*	28 *(45)*	43¼ *(1100)*	47	31′ 6″ *(9600)*	17	1949-52	ASJ	ASEA
El 11	Bo-Bo	15 kV 16⅔ Hz	2280	35 280 *(14 300)*	17 640 *(7800)*	44 *(71)*	62 *(100)*	40⅜ *(1025)*	62	47′ 5″ *(14 450)*	40	1951-64	Thunes	Norsk Electrisk; Brown Boveri
El 12	1-D+D-1	15 kV 16⅔ Hz	6520	99 200 *(45 000)*	8157 *(3700)*	31 *(60)*	47 *(75)*	53⅛ *(1350)*	180	82′ 4″ *(26 490)*	4	1954-57	Motala	ASEA
El 13	Bo-Bo	15 kV 16⅔ Hz	3600	41 900 *(19 000)*	28 700 *(13 000)*	43 *(69)*	62 *(100)*	53⅛ *(1350)*	72	49′ 2½″ *(15 000)*	37	1957-66	Thunes	Norsk Electrisk; Brown Boveri
El 14	Co-Co	15 kV 16⅔ Hz	6900	77 200 *(35 000)*	47 619 *(21 700)*	41 *(76)*	75 *(120)*	50 *(1270)*	105	58′ 5″ *(17 740)*	31	1968-73	Thunes	Norsk Electrisk; Brown Boveri
El 15	2 (Co-Co)	15 kV 16⅔ Hz	14 700	171 600 *(78 000)*	111 480 *(53 400)*	44 *(71)*	75 *(120)*	49¼ *(1250)*	132	130′ 4″ *(19 900 +19 900)*	6	1967	Thunes	ASEA-Per Kure
El 16	Bo-Bo	15 kV 16⅔ Hz	6040	72 311 *(32 800)*	45 194 *(20 500)*	48 *(78)*	87 *(140)*	51 *(1300)*	80	50′ 11″ *(15 520)*	6 (7)	1977-78/83	Strømmens	ASEA
El 17	Bo-Bo	15 kV 16⅔ Hz	4080	52 911 *(24 000)*			93 *(150)*	43¼ *(1100)*	64	53′ 6″ *(16 300)*	6	1981	Henschel	BBC Mannheim

Diesel locomotives

Class	Wheel arrangement	Transmission	Rated power hp	Tractive effort Max lb (kg)	Continuous at lb (kg)	Continuous at mph (km/h)	Max speed mph (km/h)	Wheel dia in (mm)	Total weight tons	Length ft in (mm)	No built	First built	Builders: Mechanical parts	Builders: Engine & type	Builders: Transmission
Di 2	C	Hyd	575 600	30 600 *(13 900)*	26 500 *(12 000)*	3·7 *(6)*	50 *(80)*	49¼ *(1250)*	45	32′ 10″ *(10 000)*	6 48	1954 1958	MaK Thunes	MaK MS301A BMV-LT6	Voith
Di 3a	Co-Co	Elec	1775	48 500 *(23 000)*	37 900 *(17 200)*	14 *(23)*	65 *(105)*	40 *(1016)*	102	61′ 0″ *(18 590)*	32	1954-69	Nohab	GM 16-567C	GM-ASEA
Di 3b	A1A	Elec	1775	37 478 *(17 000)*	30 864 *(14 000)*	11 *(26)*	81 *(143)*	40 *(1016)*	104	62′ 0″ *(18 900)*	3	1959	Nohab	GM 16-567C	GM-ASEA
Di 4	Co-Co	Elec	3300	39 365 *(56 000)*			87 *(140)*	43¼ *(1100)*	113.6	68′ 3″ *(20 803)*	5	1981	Henschel	GM 16-645E313	GM-BBC

PAKISTAN

Ministry of Railways

Islamabad

Telephone: 20977
Telex: 5714

Minister: Lt Gen S Qadir
Secretary: A Kalam
Director, Traffic: S S M Jafri
Director, Civil Engineering: J J D'Mello

Pakistan Railway (PR)

Shara-E-Sheikh Abdul Hameed Bin Badees, Lahore

Telephone: PABX Junction lines 60671
Telegrams: Railboard
Telex: Lahore 672/Karachi Port 3852

Chairman, Railway Board: Abdul Kalam
General Manager: Amanullah Zafar
Deputy General Manager: Jafar Wafa
Board Members
Mechanical Engineer: Z I Puri
Traffic: M Y Khan
Finance: Kh Shafqat Ali
Chief Operating Superintendent: G M Khan
Chief Commercial Manager: Kh M Arshad
Chief Controller of Stores: M I Hassan
Chief Controller of Purchase: Aslam Hussain
Chief Personnel Officer: A H Mahmood
Chief Electrical Engineer: Saeed Hassan Shah
Chief Engineer, Way and Works: F Ahmad
Chief Mechanical Engineer: A R Qureshi
Chief Engineer, Surveys and Construction: M Y Arif
Chief Officer (Research): S Mahmood
Chief Signal and Telecommunications Engineer: Z D Babar
Chief Officer (Organisation and Research): M A Yousuf
Chief Officer (Traffic): H I Hussan
Financial Adviser and Chief Accounts Officer: A Ahmed

Gauge: 1676 mm; 1000 mm; 762 mm
Route length: 7758 km; 446 km; 611 km
Electrification: 290 km of 1676 mm gauge at 25 kV 50
Hz ac

Transport development

The PR system comprises the whole of the North-Western system of the former British India rail network with the exception of lines in the south-western Punjab. The main routes connect Karachi with Hyderabad, Multan, Lahore, Rawalpindi, Peshawar, Quetta and Zahidan.

A five-year Rs 6773 million development plan was announced in December 1977 for the period 1978-82. Major items of expenditure included: purchase of 133 diesel-electric locomotives; rebuilding of 60 locos and 25 diesel railcars; construction of 750 passenger coaches; and extension of the Lahore—Khanewal electrification to Samasatta (117 km). New concrete sleeper plants were to be set up to reduce dependence on imported timber and four of these, at Khanewal, Kotri, Shahinabad and Kohat, were completed in 1981 at a cost of Rs 212 million.

Another essential project was provision of modern telecommunications to replace the existing open-line network. The core of the system would be a microwave link between Karachi and Rawalpindi, with branches to Quetta, Multan and Lahore. Outlying areas would be served by uhf links, while vhf radio would be provided at about 200 base stations and in 500 locomotives, giving voice communication between controllers and moving trains. Automatic block signalling was to be installed between Hyderabad and Lodhran and tokenless block between Lodhran and Wazirabad. Total cost was put at Rs 372 million. This project was begun in 1981 with World Bank assistance and was ready for commissioning in March 1983.

Traffic	1978/79	1979/80
Freight tonnes (million)	NA	11·9
Freight tonne-km (million)	9370	8598
Passenger-km (million)	16 500	17 308

Part of a further World Bank loan of US$50 million secured in 1982 was to be employed to develop container handling facilities at Lahore Dry Port.

Motive power and rolling stock

At the start of 1981 PR disposed of 404 steam locomotives, 468 diesel-electric locomotives, 29 electric locomotives, 57 diesel railcars and 116 trailers, 2641 passenger cars and 34 846 wagons on its broad-gauge system. The metre-gauge network possessed 36 steam locomotives, 140 passenger cars and 999 wagons; and the narrow-gauge system 41 steam locomotives, 158 passenger cars and 561 freight wagons.

With over 80 per cent of the steam locomotive fleet life-expired and 25 per cent of the diesel locomotives due for renewal, rehabilitation of the traction fleet is a high priority. The greater part of the latest World Bank loan is allocated to improvement of maintenance facilities.

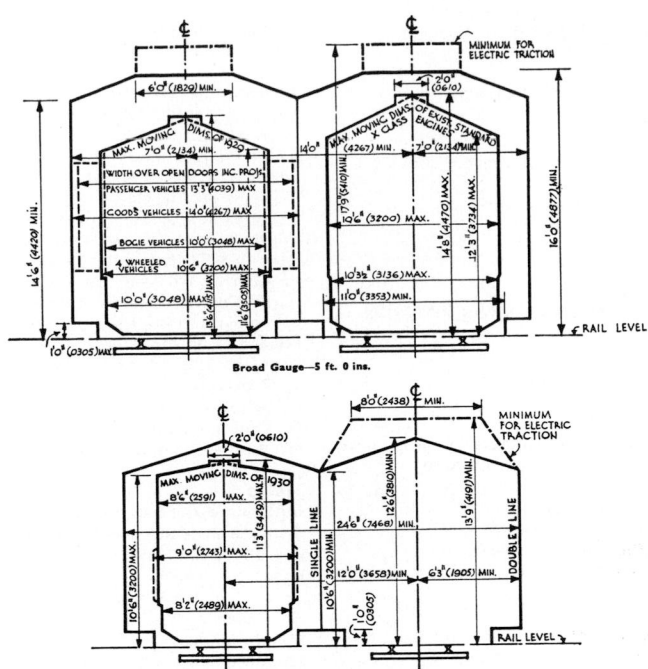
Broad Gauge—5 ft. 0 ins.

Metre Gauge—3 ft. 3⅜ in.

With the assistance of the Canadian International Development Agency, 51 Alco 1400-1600 hp locomotives constructed in 1950-56 have been remanufactured under Bombardier supervision in PR workshops with new Type 12-251 2000 hp engines and in 1982 Bombardier was granted a further contract for similar treatment of 42 more locomotives. Earlier, in December 1980, with finance equivalent to US$45 million from the Overseas Economic Corporation of Japan, an arrangement was reached with the Marubeni Corporation of Japan for Hitachi to establish diesel locomotive manufacturing capacity in Pakistan at Sihala, near Rawalpindi. Included in the deal was supply of 30 fully-assembled new locomotives and eight more in kit form for local assembly.

Investments

Capital investment planned by PR mid-1983 to mid-1984 was as follows (Rs million):

Diesel locomotives (18)	220
Passenger cars (114)	168·43
Freight wagons (125)	26·56
Rolling stock improvements	815
Workshops	40
Infrastructure works	361·89
Electrification	29
Yards	25·29
Signalling and communications	49·93
Miscellaneous	229·77
	———
Total	1950·87

With the aid of a US$385 million World Bank Loan PR was to invest a total of Rs 4685 million in 1982-84.

Electrification

PR's first electrification project was completed in 1970 when the 286 route-km Lahore-Khanewal line was electrified at 25 kV 50 Hz. Feasibility studies have been entrusted to Transmark for extension from Khanewal to Karachi, and to Electroconsult of Italy for electrification from Sibi to Quetta (130 km).

Rapid transit

The Federal Communications Ministry has proposed a double-track rapid transit system as the solution to Karachi's transport problems. Called the Integrated Mass Rapid Transit System, the underground line will link Mereweather Tower with North Karachi via Saddar, Liaquatabad and North Nazimabad, the route with the highest traffic density. It will also be linked with the Karachi Circular Railway which will be improved and extended to North Karachi. According to the Ministry study, the population of Karachi (4·5 million in 1978) will increase to 6·9 million by 1985 and 12·6 million by 2000. Peak hour traffic is expected to rise to between 30 000 and 40 000 an hour each way, on the route of the proposed rapid transit railway alone, by 1985. The annual recurring losses resulting from the lack of such a system are estimated at Rs 86 million in 1985. The study recommended against increasing the number of buses in the city on the grounds that this would aggravate air pollution and result in more accidents.

PANAMA

Chiriqui National Railroad
Ferrocarril Nacional de Chiriqui

David City, Chiriqui

President and General Manager: J A Segovia F

Gauge: 914 mm
Length: 169 km

The railway operates five diesel locomotives, five railcars, 15 passenger cars and 40 freight cars.

Panama Railroad
Ferrocarril de Panama

PO Box 2023, Balboa

President: Dr A Royo

Gauge: 1524 mm
Length: 76 km

Managed by the Ports Authority (Autoridad Portuaria Nacional), the railway owns six diesel locomotives, 24 passenger cars and 312 wagons.

United Brands Company Railway

Chiriqui Land Company, Division de Armuelles, Apartado 6-2637/8, Estafeta El Dorado, Panama City

Manager, Technical Services: Thomas F Quinn, Jr

Gauge: 914 mm
Length: 30 km

The railway operates 11 locomotives, 10 railcars, 10 passenger cars and 375 freight wagons. Track is formed of 70 kg/m rails; minimum curve radius is 3·2 degrees and maximum gradient 2·5 per cent.

PARAGUAY

Ministry of Public Works and Communications

2° Piso-Gral, Diaz y Albirdi, Asunción

Minister: Gen J A Cáceres

Ferrocarril Presidente Carlos Antonio Lopez

Mejico 145, CC 453 Asunción

President: A Gomez O
Chairman of the Board of Directors: Ricardo Garay
Director: Arq Miguel Angel Barrios Arce
Manager: Dr Modesto Ali
Chief Accountant: M Miranda
Director of Planning: Dr W Netto
Chief of the Traffic Dept: D Dalla F
Chief of the Workshop and Traction Dept: Genaro León
Chief Engineer: P Rojas
Chief of Maintenance of Way: C Royg F
Purchasing Agent: L Gonzales de Valdez
General Secretary: R Ayala
Chief of the Personnel Dept: J Ferreira C

Gauge: 1435 mm
Route length: 441 km

Transport development
Paraguay has four separate railways, only one being a passenger carrier, the FC Presidente Carlos Antonio Lopez, the others being industrial lines in western Paraguay and the Chaco.

The FC Presidente CA Lopez, Government owned and operated, is the longest in the country, extending from Asunción south-east to Encarnación and Pacú-Cua (375 km) with a branch from San Salvador to Abai 65 km long. At Encarnación two wood-burning paddle-steamer train ferries, British-built in 1911-15, cross the River Alto Parana to connect at Posadas with the Argentine Railways (FC General Urquiza). The Asunción-Buenos Aires journey of 1477 km takes 38 hours.

The present name was adopted when the former FC Central was acquired by the Paraguayan Government at the end of 1961.

Traffic
Both passenger and freight traffic have been steadily rising since the mid-1970s. The railway's market share of freight movement in Paraguay is 10 per cent.

	1979	1980
Freight tonnes	172 680	191 724
Freight tonne-km (million)	NA	34·4
Passenger journeys	223 695	287 318
Passenger-km (million)	NA	22·4

New lines
New links are a possibility with the Argentine Railways (FA), via a road-rail bridge planned over the River Parana which would open up a link with FA's Urquiza line; and with Brazil's new Soya line from Guaira to Asunción, which would afford the Paraguayan system access to the Brazilian port of Paranagua. New construction of 360 km would be involved in Paraguay, to make connection with the existing system at Villarica, 130 km from Asunción, on the line to Encarnación, and of 400 km in Brazil. The connection is planned in metre gauge, which would entail conversion of the Asunción-Villarica section to mixed gauge.

Motive power and rolling stock
In 1982 the railway operated 21 British-built (Yorkshire Engine Co, 1953) wood-burning steam locomotives, 19 passenger cars and 147 freight wagons.

Investment
With hydro-electric power due to come on stream from the Itaipú dam scheme in 1983-88, 25 kV ac electrification, track reconstruction and resignalling of the 72 km route from Asunción to Pagaguari awaits Government approval.

In 1982 FCPCAL was budgeting to spend 150 million guaranis, two-thirds of the sum on track works. Pending an electrification decision, the main priority is to relay the 140 km section from Villaria to General Artigas.

PERU

Ministry of Transport and Communications

Avenida 28 de Julio, Lima

Telephone: 319206, 245088
Telex: 25511

Minister: Carlos Pestano Zevalos
Secretary: Maria E S de Ortigas
Director of Railways: Col G Fernandez Davila

ENAFER-Peru
Empresa Nacional de Ferrocarriles del Peru

Apartado 1378, Ancash 207, Lima

Telephone: 28-9440
Telex: 25068

Chairman: A Dall 'Orto
General Manager: R Linan
Technical Manager: G C Tolezzi
Admin Manager: H Del Carpio
Technical Adviser: C I Mercer
Technical Adviser, Operations: V Foulkes
Chief of Purchasing: A Celis
Chief of Projects: D San Roman
Chief of Planning, Research and Development: A Estrada
Assistant Manager, Personnel: G Sendon
Assistant Manager, Finance: A Guterriez

Transport development
ENAFER-Perú was formed in 1972 with the nationalisation of The Peruvian Corporation railways, a private company which ran most of Peru's railways and the Lake Titicaca services. The system now comprises the Central and Southern Railways with headquarters in Lima and Arequipa respectively.

Investment
An overdue rehabilitation plan was begun following political changes in Peru in mid-1980 and provision of a Government loan worth US$ 60 million. Orders were placed with General Motors Canada for five 3000 hp diesel-electric locomotives, with MecanoExportImport of Romania for 22 passenger cars, with Cobrasma of Brazil for 392 freight wagons, with Bombardier-MLW of Canada for traction components, including eight locomotive bodies, engines and transmissions, and with Domtar of Canada for 240 000 sleepers. Further orders

Type DL538 diesel locomotive by Bombardier-MLW

were placed in 1981/82 covering 100 freight vans from BRE-Metro Ltd and 100 other wagons from British Rail Engineering Ltd (BREL); 470 more covered vans from a consortium including Ciá Industrial Sta Matilde of Brazil; 16 more passenger cars from Romania; and 6500 tonnes of rails and other permanent way equipment from Austrian suppliers. BREL was also commissioned to supply 200 of its cross-braced bogies, and negotiations were in hand covering supply of 200 further bogies and 200 more wagons from this source.

In another 1980 arrangement the Henderson Busby Partnership was commissioned to study electrification of the Central Railway, with financial aid from the British Overseas Project Fund.

In an eight-year programme, ENAFER hopes also to electrify sections of the Southern Railway between Cuzco and Machu Picchu, and to undertake the planned extensions from Tambo del Sol to Pucallpa in the north, and from Puno to Desaguadero in the south, the latter to supersede the Lake Titicaca ferry link with Bolivia.

Investment
In 1983 ENAFER was planning to spend as follows (US$000):

Diesel-electric	
locomotives (18)	32 300
Passenger cars (139)	55 200
Railcars (8)	10 600
Freight wagons (663)	41 400
Track and track equipment	42 500
Communications	20 000
Workshops	48 000
	250 000

Tenders were sought in 1982 for the supply of 11 2450 kW diesel locomotives for the Central and Southern Railways.

Traffic

	1980
Freight tonnes	2·212 million
Passenger journeys	4 million

Diesel locomotives

Class	Wheel arrangement	Transmission	Rated power hp	Max lb (kg)	Continuous at lb (kg)	mph (km/h)	Max speed mph (km/h)	Wheel dia in (mm)	Total weight tonnes	Length ft in (mm)	No built	Year first built	Mechanical parts	Engine & type	Transmission
DL 531	Co-Co	Elec	675		(18 000)			40	71·6	(14 198)	1	1958	Alco	6 cyl 251 B	
DL 532	Bo-Bo	Elec	950		(14 736)	(14·5)	(80)	40	69·4	(14 390)	5	1974	MLW	6 cyl 251 B	
DL 535A	Co-Co	Elec	1200		(23 760)	(8·1)	(80)	40	69·7	(15 420)	2	1967	Alco	6 cyl 251 B	
DL 535B	Co-Co	Elec	1200		(23 760)	(8·1)	(80)	40	81·4	(15 410)	14	1963	Alco	6 cyl 251 B	
DL 538	Co-Co	Elec	1200		(22 068)	(8·1)	(80)	40	81·0	(15 410)	5	1974	MLW	6 cyl 251 D	
DL 500	Co-Co	Elec	1340		(20 863)	(19·5)	(100)	40	63·7	(17 958)	6	1956	Alco	12 cyl 251 B	
DL 543	Co-Co	Elec	1800		(23 818)	(19·2)	(100)	40	110	(17 794)	11	1962	Alco	12 cyl 251 B	
DL 560	Co-Co	Elec	2400		(32 600)	(14·8)	(105)	43	110	(17 272)	14	1964	Alco	16 cyl 251 B	
DL 560	Co-Co	Elec	2400		(32 600)	(14·8)	(105)	43	110	(17 120)	15	1974	MLW	16 cyl 251 E	
GR-12	Co-Co	Elec	1310	212 000 (96 300)	53 400 (24 220)	7 (12)	65 (105)	40 (1016)	67·4	47' 4" (14 427)	5	1964	General Motors	GM 12-567C	General Motors
GA-8	Bo-Bo	Elec	800	127 000 (57 700)	22 450 (10 185)	6·6 (10·6)	45 (72)	33 (838)	73·1	32' 6" (9754)	3	1964	General Motors	GM 8-567C	General Motors
G22CW	Co-Co	Elec	1500	197 100 (89 480)	62 000 (28 200)	7·2 (11·5)	62 (100)	40 (1016)	89·5	46' 6" (14 173)	1	1976	General Motors	GM 12-645E	General Motors
G18W	Bo-Bo	Elec	1000	143 800 (65 228)	35 674 (16 200)	8 (13)	71 (114)	40 (1016)	65·2	38' 0" (11 582)	1	1976	General Motors	GM 8-645E	General Motors
GT26CW-2	Co-Co	Elec	3000	—	67 141 (30 490)	—	62 (100)	40 (1016)	119	—	7	1982	General Motors	GM 16-645E3	General Motors

Central Railway
ENAFER—Ferrocarril del Centro
Ferrocarril del Centro del Perú

Ancash 201, Lima

Manager: A Soto H
Operations: P O'Brien
Mechanical: J Wright
Engineering: W Medina

Gauge: 1435 mm; 914 mm
Route length: 378 km; 129 km

The standard gauge main line runs from Callao to Huancayo where it connects with the 914 mm-gauge line to Huancavelica. There are 66 tunnels with aggregate length of 8·9 km, 59 bridges and nine zig-zags (reversing stations) on the standard gauge section and 38 tunnels on the narrow gauge line.

The main line climbs from sea level to its highest point of 4782 metres in the Galera Tunnel in 171 km from Callao on an average gradient of 1 in 25 (4 per cent). The highest point on the system is 4829 metres at a siding at La Cima on the Ticlio-Morococha branch. This makes it the highest standard gauge line in the world. The steepest gradients occur in the first 222 km from Callao, at sea level, to Oroya at 3726 metres above sea level. Track renewal was begun in 1981.

Rolling stock
Three oil-burning steam, 32 diesel-electric, one diesel-mechanical locomotives. 1117 freight cars, 32 passenger cars, 10 railcars.

Southern Railway
ENAFER—Ferrocarril del Sur
Ferrocarril del Sur

Casilla 194, Arequipa

Manager: A Rivera
Traffic: D Yupanqui
Mechanical: D Russell
Operations: E Vizcarra
Chief Engineer: R Ricketts
Stores: G Paz

Gauge: 1435 mm; 914 mm
Route length: 924 km; 171 km

The standard gauge main line runs from Mollendo to Juliaca, 476 km, where the line divides, to Puno, 47 km, for connection with the Lake Titicaca steamer service to Bolivia; and to Cuzco, 338 km, where it connects with the 914 mm-gauge line to Quillabamba.

The main line climbs from sea level to its highest point at Crucero Alto, 4477 metres, in 359 km from Mollendo on an average gradient of 1 in 33 (3 per cent).

The steamer service on Lake Titicaca at 3818 metres is the highest in the world.

Rolling stock
48 diesel-electric, three diesel-mechanical and five oil-burning steam locomotives, 925 freight cars, 108 passenger cars, 23 railcars.

Steamship service
Lake Titicaca 204 km from Puno, Peru to Guaqui, Bolivia.

Ships include one train ferry, three passenger-freight vessels, one dredger and two launches.

Tacna-Arica Railway
(Administered by Southern Railway)

A Aldarracin 484, Tacna

Gauge: 1435 mm
Route length: 62 km

Rolling stock
Two steam locomotives, 42 freight cars, one passenger car, nine railcars.

Track
Standard rail
  80 lb/yd (39·7 kg/m) BS(R)
  75 lb/yd (37·2 kg/m) BSS
  75 lb/yd (37·2 kg/m) ASCE
  70 lb/yd (34·7 kg/m) ASCE
  70 lb/yd (34·7 kg/m) Livesey
Lengths: 24, 30, 33, 39 and 46 ft
Joints: 4-hole angle fishplates and bolts
Cross ties (sleepers): Peruvian hardwood, 8 in × 6 in × 8 ft (1435 mm track), 8 in × 6 in × 6 ft (914 mm track)
Made-up sleepers consisting of 2 blocks of reinforced concrete joined by a piece of used rail have been used in sidings and on straight stretches of main line
Spacing
  Main line: 1600-1700 per km
  Branch line: 1365-1700 per km
Rail fastenings
Soleplates and ⅞ in coachscrews
Soleplates and ⅝ in dogspikes

ML DI 560 at Desamparados station, Lima

Pandrol fastenings are being fitted where new 80 lb/yd rail is being laid
Filling: 2-4 in broken stone ballast; 6 in under tie on main lines and 3 in on branch lines.
Max curvature: 17·5° = minimum radius 100 m
Max gradient: 4·7% (Central Railway); 4% (Southern Railway)
Worst combination of curve and grade: 156 m curve on 4·22% (1 in 23·7) grade for 235 m
Gauge widening on sharpest curve: ½ in (12·7 mm)
Super-elevation on sharpest curve: 4 in (101·6 mm) speed limited
Rate of slope of super-elevation: 1 in 360
Max altitude: 4829 m on Central Railway at La Cima

siding on Ticlio-Morococha Branch, 173 km from Callao. On main line 4782 m inside Galera Tunnel, 172 km from Callao
Max axleloading
  Central Railway: 1435 mm, 18 tonnes; 914 mm, 14 tonnes
  Southern Railway: 1435 mm, 17 tonnes; 914 mm, 14 tonnes
Bridge loading: Coopers E-40
Max permitted speed
  Standard gauge:
  80 km/h on level and low gradient section
  50 km/h on high gradient sections
  Narrow gauge: 60 km/h

Empresa Minera del Centro del Peru
(Division Ferrocarriles)

PO Box 2412, Augusto N Wiese No 891, Lima 1

Telephone: 275210
Telex: 63839

Executive President: F Remy
General Manager, Operations: Ing A Zuzunaga
Manager, General Services: Ing H Paz
Superintendent of Railways: Ing C Kocerha
Chief Operations Officer: V Zúñiga

Chief Mechanical Officer: Ing R Benites
Chief Engineer, Way and Structures: Ing C Ortiz
Accountant of Railways: J Carrillo

Gauge: 1435 mm
Route length: 212·2 km

Motive power and rolling stock
The fleet in 1982 consisted of: two steam shunting locomotives; eight line-haul diesel-electric locomotives; four petrol railcars; 13 passenger coaches; 689 freight wagons.

Traffic	1978	1979	1980
Total freight tonne-km (million)	117·7	122·9	126·9
Freight tonnage (million)	1·05	1·115	1·092
Passenger-km (million)	39·31	40·72	43·689
Passenger journeys	518 516	540 139	578 604

PHILIPPINES

Philippine National Railways (PNR)

943 Claro M Recto Avenue, Manila

Telephone: 210011

Chairman: Vacant
Vice-Chairman and General Manager: Juan N de Castro
Members: Alfredo Pio de Roda, Jr
    Aber P Canlas
    Victor Nituda
    Antonio M Locsin
    Juan C Tuvera
    Eulogio de Guzman
    Rodolfo Ante
Assistant General Managers
  Administration: Manuel M Palafox
  Railway Operations: Engr Cesar Casipit
  Engineering: Engr Ramon Mariano
  Acting Staff Director: Engr Cesar Poblete
  Planning and Acting PEG Director: Engr Jose Nuguid
  CSE and Special Projects: Engr Simeon dela Cruz
  Energy Conservation: C V Poblete
  Acting Special Assistant, Office of the General Manager: Rodolfo Alejandro
    Roberto Castañeda
    Julian Tongson
Corporation Auditor: E Gozar
Corporation Secretary: Mariano Abad
Chief, Executive Department: Salvacion M Bundoc
Personnel Manager: L Datiles
Chief, Corporate Legal Officer: Rodolfo G Flores
Chief, Accounting Department: Lina Bartolome
Chief Construction Engineer: Justo Bonuel
Chief, Engineering Department: Miguel Añonuevo
Mechanical Superintendent: Prospero Yap
Medical Director: Epitacio Alcantara
Purchasing Agent: Federico Nadurata
Real Estate Manager: Ricardo Agbunag
Manager, Motor Service: Cesar Diaz
Marketing Manager: Cipriano Dizon
Treasurer: Julita Vida
Internal Auditor: Francisco Aure
Manager, Commuter Service Management Body: Ramon Jimenez
Chief, Civil Security Office: Mauro Dar
Chief, Planning, Research and Statistic Office: Eleuterio Galvante
Chief, Data Centre: Romulo Magtira

Transport development
The PNR rail system operates passenger and freight services in Luzon Island from Camilag, 14 km from the port of Legaspi in the south, to the northern railhead at San Fernando, via Manila.

Rehabilitation
A major project for the total rehabilitation of Philippine National Railways 460 km Main Line South, from Manila to Camilag (the remaining 14 km to Legaspi has been closed since landslip damage in 1976), got under way in May 1979 following the granting of the US$ 24 million loan from the Asian Development Bank. The work has involved spreading 367 000 cubic metres of new ballast and 383 000 cubic metres of earthworks and laying 604 800 new sleepers. New and recovered 37 kg/m rails were being welded in 60-metre lengths. Completion of the project in 1983 would be followed by a cut from 16 to 9 hours of passenger train timings over the 378 km between Manila and Naga. A new route under construction from Camilag to Legaspi was also to be finished in 1983.

Following completion of work on its Main Line South, PNR hopes to refurbish similarly the 226 km

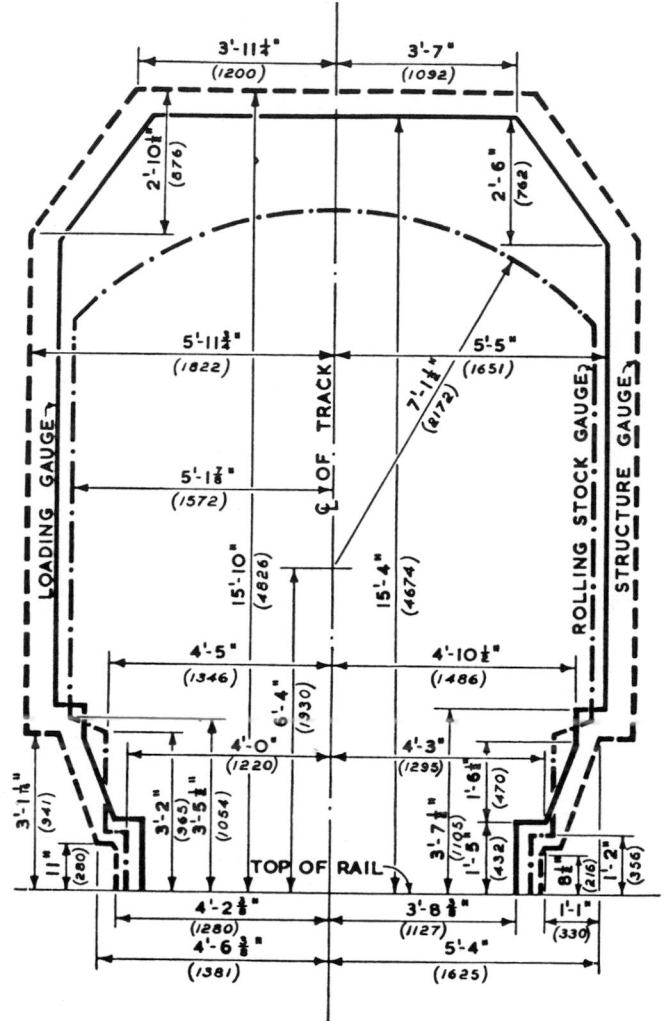

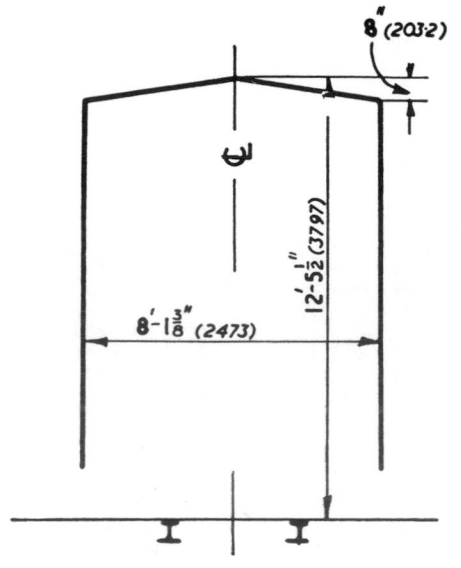

Main Line North from Manila to San Fernando and to resuscitate its 92 km Cabanatuan branch at a cost of 547 million pesos. Doubts voiced by the Government about the whole future of railways in the Philippines unless there was substantial and comparatively speedy evidence of a return on the money invested in Main Line South appear to have been set at rest.

Because inadequate investment has never fully recovered Second World War damage, deteriorating infrastructure and equipment have cost PNR a steady loss of main-line freight and passenger traffic; even the diesel multiple-unit commuter service established in the Manila area in the 1970s now logs only 60 per cent of the passenger journeys recorded in 1977. That should improve with construction of a new maintenance depot at Manila capable of housing 200 dmu cars. PNR is also inhibited from seeking new bulk freight flows because of the capital expense involved in restoring lifted tracks to the vicinity of several new heavy industrial plants. In 1983, however, rehabilitation of the 60 km line from the port of Batanga to Calamba, to convey 880 000 tonnes of coal a year to eight cement works, became a possibility with Canadian aid.

Locomotives and rolling stock
PNR operates 120 diesel locomotives, 220 diesel railcars, 308 passenger cars and 1457 freight cars.

Investments
Investment planned for 1983 covered (pesos 000):
Traction and rolling stock

overhaul	47 500
Camilag-Legaspi deviation	7000
Track works	34 000
Signalling and communications	4000
Miscellaneous	20 000
	112 500

Track
Standard rail
Main line: 65 lb/yd (32·2 kg/m) in 30 and 33 ft lengths
75 lb/yd (37·2 kg/m) in 33 ft lengths
Branch lines: 65 lb/yd (32·2 kg/m) in 30 ft lengths
54 lb/yd (26·8 kg/m) in 30 ft lengths
45 lb/yd (22·3 kg/m) in 23 ft lengths
Rail joints: Angle bars with slots for spikes

Cross ties (sleepers)
Main line: 'Molave' wood, 5 in × 8 in × 7 ft (127 × 203 × 2133 mm), spaced at 22 in (558 mm)
Branch line: 'Molave' wood, 5 in × 8 in × 7 ft (127 × 203 × 2133 mm), spaced at 24 in (610 mm)
Bridge ties: 'Yacal' wood, 8 in × 8 in × 8 ft (203 × 203 × 2438 mm), spaced at 16 in (406 mm)
A limited number of steel ties are also used
Rail fastenings: Track spikes; bolts with square nuts; 'Hipower' nutlock washer; elastic rail spikes
Filling: Volcanic slag; river gravel with 15% sand; some crushed rock
Max curvature
Main line: 9·2° = minimum radius 190 m
Branch line: 11½° = minimum radius 150 m
Max gradient: Compensated, 2·6% = 1 in 38½
Uncompensated, 1·2% = 1 in 83
Max axleload: 29·5 tonnes
Max permitted speed: 60 km/h
Signalling: In the Manila terminal area 13·6 km of double track line with semaphore signals are controlled from interlocked cabins. On single track lines elsewhere trains operated on English 'Staff' system or by telegraph or telephone communication from station to station.

Motive power

Type (road no)	900 type	1000 type	2000 type	1500 type	2500 type	3000 type	4000 type
Wheel (or axle) arrangement	C-C	C-C	C-C	B-B-B	B-B	B-B	B-B
Max speed (km/h)	130	95	95	95	95	95	50
Dimensions							
Width (mm)	2717	2821	2821	2749	2749	2743	2921
Height (mm)	3732	3683	3683	3372	3687	3687	3687
Weight (tonnes)	81·6	82·6	87	61·4	54·4	54·4	47·1
Builders	General Electric	General Electric	General Electric	Alsthom	General Electric	General Electric	General Electric
Tractive effort (kg)	24 495	16 965	16 965	17 235	11 975	14 605	74 840

POLAND

Ministry of Transport

ul Chalubińskiego 4, 00-928 Warsaw

Telephone: 24 43 00

Minister of Transport: Janus Kamiński
Under-Secretaries of State: J Glowacki, Cz Gościłowicz, K Jacukowicz, A Markowski, J Raczkowski
Office of the Minister: K Trzciński
Director, Press Service: K Pierzyński
  International Co-operation: L Skolasiński (Telex: 813614)
  Economic Department: F Daszczuk
  Financial Department: Cz Gierałtowski
  Chief of Investments: E Kopciński
  Press Service: S Poźniak

Polish State Railways (PKP)
Polskie Koleje Państwowe

ul Chalubińskiego 4, 00-928 Warsaw

Telephone: 24 43 00
Telegrams: Polfer, Warsaw
Telex: 813898

Commercial Director: L Malinowski
Traffic Director: M Raczkiewicz
Traction Director: J Skoniecki
Rolling Stock Director: A Graniewski

Director, Maintenance: A Golaszowski
Director, Signalling and Telecommunications: Z Mościcki

Gauge: 1435 mm; 785 and 600 mm
Route length: 24 360 km; 2812 km
Electrification: 7370 km at 3 kV dc; 40 km at 600 V dc

Transport development
Shortage of capacity has been PKP's major problem ever since independence in 1918. During the 1970s traffic demand increased more rapidly than the capacity of the railways; PKP entered the 1980s with the biggest traffic volume in Europe (excepting the Soviet Union) plus one of the most intensively-used

British-designed EU07 electric locomotive, also operated in twin-unit freight version as ET41 *(John Chalcraft)*

3000 hp Class SP-47 locomotive delivered in 1977/78 by Cegielski

EW-58n emu which first entered service in 1976

railway systems anywhere in the world. Projects in the 1981-85 plan called for increasing the rate of electrification from the 300 km a year achieved during the 1970s to 500 km annually, track doubling over 1200 km, new line construction, and purchase of 50 000 freight wagons, 750 electrics, 500 diesels and 350 train-sets. Progress, however, has naturally been affected by the political and economic problems of the country since 1981.

During 1982 there were several changes in the administration of Polish railway affairs. At the start of the year PKP was given responsibility for rolling stock repair plants and others constructing railway material which were previously in the charge of the Ministry of Transport. Later in the year the posts of Transport Minister and PKP Director General were separated and more direct responsibility transferred to PKP by the dissolution of all the Ministry's regional directorates. At the same time it was revealed that, allowing for the devaluation of the zloty during the period, PKP's working deficit had almost tripled between 1976 and 1980. PKP was among industries guaranteed access to foreign exchange for priority requirements in 1983.

The country's political problems had their repercussions in a drastic 16.7 per cent reduction of PKP's freight traffic in 1981, from which there was hardly any recovery in 1982, despite a sharp resurgence in coal movement. The troubles also aggravated PKP's chronic problems of track maintenance and rolling stock availability, while inability to obtain foreign exchange for purchase of spares grounded about a third of the SP45 and SU46 diesel locomotive classes, compelling recourse to a 2.6 per cent increase in use of steam for both passenger and freight trains on non-electrified lines. Commissioning in 1983 of a new repair shop at Gniewczyna, in south-east Poland, would, it was hoped, ease the problems of wagon shortage, which have been exacerbated by lack of capacity to handle more than a third of the repair requirement. New production has lately been at a rate meeting only 15 per cent of the annual wagon shortfall through unserviceable vehicle withdrawals. In 1981 and 1982 PKP's share of the country's total freight movement nevertheless rose from 29.3 to 33 per cent, while road's slipped from 66.5 to 61.4 per cent, because of fuel shortage.

The passenger operation was also affected by a 10 per cent decline in rolling stock availability and over 7 per cent of scheduled trains had to be withdrawn in 1981, yet passenger volume rose because of national petrol shortages. Express train fares and monthly season ticket rates were doubled at the start of 1983.

In normal times some of PKP's densest lines were carrying 14 million tonnes/km a year. This resulted in severe track wear. In order to overcome the problem the railway planned during the 1980-85 period to create separate but parallel lines on each route, particularly on the overworked links between Silesia and the Baltic.

Motive power and rolling stock

In 1982 32.2 per cent of PKP's total motive power fleet consisted of electric locomotives, 44.2 per cent were diesel and 23.6 per cent steam. In 1982 electric traction was responsible for 64.3 per cent of all tonne-km, diesel for 29.2 per cent and steam for 6.5 per cent. It was originally planned to phase out steam traction by 1984, but in order to reduce oil imports PKP decided to prolong the operation of steam locomotives.

New purchases during the 1980-85 plan were to include two new types of electric locomotives for passenger traffic (a Bo-Bo unit of 3200 kW with individual drive on each bogie and top speed of 140 km/h; a Co-Co model of 4800 kW designed for 160 km/h operation) and a batch of three-car emus providing 164 seats and room for 400 standing passengers.

In 1982 PKP was operating 1109 steam, 1522 electric, and 2527 diesel locomotives, 950 emu power cars and 1750 emu trailers, 93 diesel railcars and an undisclosed number of trailers, 6226 passenger cars and 168 801 freight wagons.

Material on order or delivered during the year stood in 1982 at: 70 Class ET22, 21 Class ET21 and three Class E42 electric locomotives; 15 Class ST44 diesel locomotives; 50 Class EN57 emus and five Class EN57 control trailers; 301 passenger cars and 1513 freight wagons.

Electrification

In 1981 223 route-km were electrified, including the Herby Nowe-Wieluń-Kępno (102 km), Zgierz-Kutno (57 km) and Tłuszcz-Łochów (21 km) lines, together with some sections in Silesia and the Szczecin and Lublin regions. By the end of 1981 7091 route-km were under catenary, 29.1 per cent of all 1435 mm-gauge lines.

Traffic

	1980	1981	1982
Total freight tonnage (million)	482.062	401.519	391.1
Total freight tonne-km (million)	134 737	109 835	110 804
Average net freight train load (tonnes)	735	722	720*
Average freight wagon load (tonnes)	33.3	33.24	33.6*
Total passenger-km (million)	46 324.5	48 238	49 266
Total passenger journeys (million)	1100.5	1113.6	1108.3
Average length of passenger journey (km)	42.3	43.5	45*
* Provisional figures			

PKP Class ET42 twin-unit electric freight locomotive, built in USSR and based on Soviet domestic dc designs

Class ET21 electric Co-Co by Pafawag

Class ET22 electric Co-Co by Pafawag

Class E9 94 emu of 1970 for 600 V dc suburban line near Warsaw, built by Pafawag

In 1982 319 route-km were electrified, including Wrocław-Scinawa-Wróblin Glogowski (a section of the main Wrocław-Zielona Góra-Szczecin artery), and the Lochów-Malkinia section (29 km) of the Warsaw-Białystok main artery, the Tiuszcz-Wyszków section (21 km) of the Tiuszcz-Ostroleka route, some sections in Silesia with a total length of about 100 km, and some sections in the Szczecin and Skarzysko regions. The entire 180 km Warsaw-Białystok line should be under wires by 1984. By the end of 1982 7410 km were electrified, 30·4 per cent of the total network. In subsequent years a steady step-up of electrification pace is planned to 400-500 km yearly so as to achieve a network of about 9000 km in 1985 and over 11 000 km in 1990.

Permanent way

In 1970-80 over 1200 km of new lines were built, including a main line connecting Silesia with Warsaw between Zawiercie and Grodzisk Mazowiecki and the 'Iron-Sulphur Line' from Hrubieszów to Katowice steelworks. On main trunk routes UIC 60 rail is being laid and on other primary lines S49 rail. With wooden sleepers up to 250 mm ballast depth is prescribed, with concrete sleepers up to 300 mm.

At the beginning of 1980 18 per cent of all lines had 60 kg/m rails, 70 per cent 49 kg/m and 12 per cent 42 kg/m. By the end of 1985 the percentages will be 30 heavy, 65 medium and 5 lightweight rail. By 1985 about 9000 km will have concrete sleepers and eventually they will be installed on 63 per cent of PKP track.

Rail welding is being carried out at the rate of 2000 km a year and by 1985 15 000 route-km will be of continuous welded rail.

Track

Rail, type and weight: S60 60·34 kg/m; S49 49·43 kg/m; S42 42·48 kg/m
Cross ties (sleepers)
Wooden: Types: IB, IIB, IIO thickness 150 mm; IIIB, IIIO, IVO thickness 140 mm
Concrete: Types: BL-3 thickness 210 mm; INBK-3 thickness 202 mm; INBK-4 thickness 180 mm;

INBK-7 thickness 190 mm; INBK-8 thickness 183 mm; PBS-1 thickness 180 mm
Spacing
Traditional track: 1566, 1600, 1720, 1733/km
Cwr: 1680 and 1700/km

Minimum curvature radius (m)

	Lowland	Foothills	Mountains
Newly constructed lines			
Trunk	2000	1500	800
Primary	1500	1000	600
Secondary	800	500	400
Local	500	300	300
Modernised lines			
Trunk	1500	1200	600
Primary	1200	600	400
Secondary	600	400	300
Local	400	250	200

Max gradient
Main trunk and primary: 6%
Secondary: 10%
Local: 20%
Max axleload: 20 tonnes

Class ET40 electric dc Bo-Bo + Bo-Bo built by Skoda

Diesel locomotives

Class	Wheel arrangement	Transmission	Rated power (kW)	Max speed km/h	Total weight tonnes	Year first built	Builders Mechanical parts	Engine & type	Transmission
SM 40/41	Bo-Bo	Elec	441	80	61·7	1958	Ganz-Mávag	Ganz XVI IV 170/240	Ganz
SM 03	B	Mech	111	45	24	1959	Fablok	Nowotko	"Zastal" Zielona-Góra
SM 30	Bo-Bo	Elec	257	58	36	1959	Fablok	Nowotko DVSa-350	Dolmel
SM 42	Bo-Bo	Elec	588	90	72	1963	Fablok	HCP 8 VCD22T	Dolmel
SP 42	Bo-Bo	Elec	588	90	70	1966	Fablok	HCP 8 VCD22T	Dolmel
ST 43	Co-Co	Elec	1544	100	116	1965	Ep Craiova	Sulzer 12 LDA 28	BBC
ST 44	Co-Co	Elec	1471	100	116	1966	WFBL-Voroshilovgrad	Kolomna 14D20	Charkow
SP 45	Co-Co	Elec	1287	100	96	1967	HCP	HCP Fiat 2112SFF	Dolmel
SU 46	Co-Co	Elec	1650	120	102	1974	HCP	HCP Fiat 2112SSF	Dolmel
SM 31	Co-Co	Elec	882	80	120	1976	Fablok	HCP	Dolmel
SM 48	Bo-Bo	Elec	882	100	116	1976	PZM-Lugansk	PDG-YM	Charkow
SP 47	Co-Co	Elec	2200	140	114	1978	HCP	HCP Fiat 2116SSF	Dolmel

Electric multiple-units

Class	Cars per unit	Line voltage dc	Motor cars per unit	Motored axles per motor car	Rated output (kW) per motor	Max speed km/h	Weight tonnes per car (M-motor T-trailer)	Total seating capacity	Length per car mm (M-motor T-trailer)	Rate of acceleration m/s²	Year first built	Builders Mechanical parts	Electrical equipment
EW 54	3	3000	1	4	120	110	M 55 T 33	approx 200	M+T approx 20 500	approx 0·4	1948	ASJ-Kockum	ASEA
EW 55	3	3000	1	4	145	110	M 57 T 33	220	M 20 500 T 20 600	0·5	1959	Pafawag	Dolmel
EN 57	3	3000	1	4	145	110	M 57 T 34	212	M 21 570 T 20 700	0·5	1961	Pafawag	Dolmel
EW 58	3	3000	2	4	206	120	total 146	212	M 21 300 T 20 940	0·75-1·00	1975	Pafawag	Dolmel
EN 94	2	600	2	2	56·5	80	total 40	80	total 26 800	0·3	1969	Pafawag	Dolmel

Electric locomotives

Class	Wheel arrangement	Line voltage dc	Rated output (kW) continuous/one hour	Max speed km/h	Weight tonnes	Year first built	Builders Mechanical parts	Electrical equipment
ET 21	Co-Co	3000	1860/2400	100	112	1957	Pafawag	Dolmel
EU 05	Bo-Bo	3000	2032/2344	125	82·5	1960	Skoda	Skoda
EU 06/07	Bo-Bo	3000	2000/2080	125	80	1963	Pafawag	Dolmel
ET 22	Co-Co	3000	3000/3120	125	120	1971	Pafawag	Dolmel
EP 05	Bo-Bo	3000	2032/2344	140/160	80	1973	Skoda	Skoda
EP 08	Bo-Bo	3000	2080/3000	140	80	1973	Pafawag	Dolmel
ET 40	Bo-Bo+Bo-Bo	3000	4080/4680	100	164	1976	Skoda	Skoda
ET 41	Bo-Bo+Bo-Bo	3000	4000/4160	125	167	1978	HCP	Dolmel
ET 42	Bo-Bo+Bo-Bo	3000	4480/4840	100	164	1978	Novocherkassk	Novocherkassk

PORTUGAL

Ministry of Transport and Communications

Rua da Prata 8, 1100 Lisbon Codex

Telex: 12251

Portuguese Railways (CP)
Companhia de Ferro Portugueses

Calçada do Duque 20, 1294 Lisbon

Telephone: 36 31 81
Telex: 12382

Board of Directors
Chairman: Dr António José Barros de Queiroz Martins
Members: Dr Jorge Magalhães Saraiva
Dr Francisco Trindade Calha
Eng Francisco António Carapinha
Dr Albano Figueiredo e Sousa

Administration Main Officers
Public Relations and Press: Dr Américo Ramalho
Administration Secretary: Dr Luis Beato

Operations
Director: Ing Vítor Biscaia
Assistant Director: Ing F Oliveira Santos
Commercial Department: Ing Álvaro Campelo
Fixed Installations Department: Ing F Oliveira Santos
Northern Region: Ing Fernando Ávila
Central Region: Ing Jorge Vilaverde
Cascais Line: Ing Assis Barbosa
Sintra Line: Vilaça e Moura

Financial Director: Dr Tavares Fernandas

Personnel Director: Dr António Farinha Marques

Purchasing and Supplying Division
Manager: Camarate de Campos
Assistant Manager: Abilio Lopes

Gauge: 1668 mm; 1000 mm
Route length: 2858 km; 758 km
Electrification: 1668 mm gauge, 406 km at 25 kV 50 Hz ac; 26 km at 1·5 kV dc

Following the 1974 revolution and full nationalisation in April 1975 of a railway system that until then was largely a private enterprise, CP was promised in 1976 a Government-backed investment on a large scale to overtake the serious previous neglect of track, traction and rolling stock. Proclaiming a policy of transport integration, the new regime also undertook to redefine CP's role and assure it of adequate financial compensation for transport the railway was expected to provide as a social service, for example, carriage of commuters at cheap rates.

As the 1970s progressed, unfortunately, national economic difficulty and political uncertainty prevented the full honouring of these commitments. CP found itself forced to borrow heavily to cover essential equipment purchases and infrastructure work it had put in hand as agreed, but which the Government could not now fund to the extent promised; and compensation for social services was not forthcoming to the degree anticipated.

Finances

	1978	1979	1980	1981
		(Contos* million)		
Revenues				
Passengers and baggage	2·826	3·497	4·406	5·988
Freight and mail	0·921	1·100	1·426	1·781
Total	10·598	11·434	12·899	18·115
Expenditure				
Staff/personnel	5·196	5·945	7·176	9·040
Materials and services	1·678	1·925	2·833	3·361
Depreciation	0·382	0·453	0·514	0·628
Financial charges	2·286	2·658	3·186	3·947
Total	10·241	11·794	14·478	17·979

*Conto = 1000 escudos

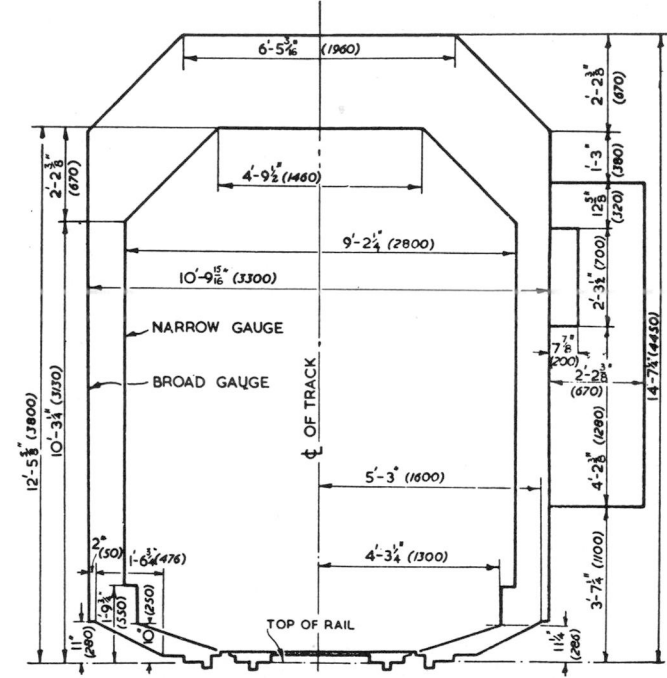

Commuter emu operating in Oporto area

At the end of 1982, when CP's accumulated debts stood at Esc 23 500 million in contrast to traffic revenues of less than Esc 10 million a year, the Government clamped new financial curbs on the railway's expenditure and ordered a cessation of staff recruitment.

Traffic	1980	1981
Passenger journeys (million)	224·2	213·38
Passenger-km (million)	6076·9	5855·7
Freight tonnes (million)	3·736	3·672
Freight tonne-km (million)	1000·57	1002·75

Passenger

A powerful motivation to give CP a higher ranking in the country's investment priorities is the extraordinary growth of rail passenger travel since the oil crisis. Measured in passenger journeys, volume rose from 104·5 million to 117·3 million between 1970 and 1973, but then soared to almost 225 million in 1980, though it has subsequently dipped slightly.

A good deal of the upsurge has been in commuter travel around Lisbon and Oporto, sparked by Government-inspired fare schemes to encourage more use of the railway. That has created capacity problems on CP's core main line between Lisbon and Oporto which demand urgent resolution by addition of a third or even two extra tracks from Lisbon to the north, possibly as far as Entroncamento, from Lisbon to Cacem on the route to Sintra, and from Oporto south to Aveiro. CP also wants to extend electrification in the Oporto commuter area.

However, CP has also registered a substantial increase of long-haul passenger traffic as a result of improving service quality and frequency. On the key Lisbon-Oporto artery, electrified at 25 kV 50 Hz ac, the day's principal all first-class trains, which include a lounge car, can now make a top speed of 140 km/h in places. As a result they cover the 337 km between the two cities in three hours, inclusive of one stop en route.

For further improvement of long-haul services Sorefame is building 123 air-conditioned cars to the French Railways' 'Corail' pattern, but with bodies of stainless steel, a Sorefame speciality.

Freight

Though CP has managed a slight year-on-year growth of freight tonnage since the oil crisis and has significantly improved the economics of its freight working through acquisition of higher-capacity wagons and development of more trainload operation, its scope has been limited by the scarcity of industrial rail connections. Until the 1960s national economic planning was obsessed with road transport. As a result rail connection was ignored when most post-war steel, cement, pulp and paper plants, and oil refineries were erected.

With the encouragement of CP's improving freight service quality, industries have lately been persuaded to lay in rail connections to their plants at their own expense at the rate of about 20 a year. Some have also been coaxed into investing in their own.

Now bigger, state-sponsored projects are in mind to make more of Portugal's bulk freight accessible to CP unit train operation. Although the late 1970s scheme to build a new and separate 37 km access line to the port, refinery and industrial complex of Sines, south of Lisbon, was curtailed partly through financial stringency (but much more modest than expected development at Sines itself has since justified the retrenchment), CP is hopeful of support for construction of new approach lines to the ore fields in the north-east of the country.

At present the mines of Moncorvo are served only by the narrow, metre-gauge tracks with which CP serves the whole mountainous territory north of the main line eastward from Oporto to the frontier at Barca d'Alva, except for the littoral area traversed by broad-gauge lines northward to Vigo in Spain. The Miranda mines are only some 10 km from the Oporto-Barca d'Alva broad-gauge main line at Pocinho, but are not rail-connected.

To set up a unit-train feed from these ore fields to the industries of Oporto and Sines, CP wants to lay a broad-gauge rail access to both; and also, so as to keep the flow for Sines and the south of the country clear of Oporto, to install a new railway over the 60 km from Pocinho to the Beira-Alta main line from Spain to central Portugal. Achievement of these aims, CP calculates, would all but double its freight tonnage.

Intermodal freight development is also on the agenda, and in 1982 CP launched its first piggyback operation, an overnight service between Lisbon and Oporto. The aim is to set up a joint exercise with the nationalised road haulage industry, though state control has not excluded the small independents from this business.

Investment

First proposed in the 1960s, replacement of the centenarian Maria-Pia rail bridge over the River Douro at Oporto has lately been given the go-ahead by the Government. The elegant Maria-Pia bridge, 354 metres long, which leaps the river on a span arching 61 metres above the water, was designed by Gustave Eiffel, and built in 1876-77. It is the only rail link between the CP system north of the Douro and the rest of the country. If it is blocked, rail traffic between north and south has to detour as far east as Spain, via Barca d'Alva, RENFE's Salamanca line and back into Portugal at Fuentes de Onoro.

Type 2600 2880 kW electric locomotive

Metre-gauge Alsthom-built 715 hp diesel-electric Bo-Bo of 1976

Alsthom railcar built for CP

Canadian-built diesel delivered by MLW in 1979

The Maria-Pia bridge is beset by numerous restrictions. It is only single-line and though latter-day reinforcement has raised its historic axleload limit of 12 tonnes to 19·5 tonnes, which accommodates modern locomotives, the new ceiling is not high enough to tolerate the glw potential of today's high-capacity freight wagons. The biggest wagons can only be allowed over the bridge if their load is less than maximum. Moreover, all train speed over the ancient metal structure is limited to 20 km/h, double-heading of trains with two locomotives is prohibited and train-lengths too have to be restricted, to avoid all risk of the metalwork buckling.

Overruling opposition from the city of Oporto, the Government has now approved construction of a new double-track rail bridge 350 metres upstream from the Eiffel structure. The Maria-Pia bridge, however, will be preserved, despite the steadily rising cost of its upkeep; since its centenary in 1977 it has been designated a national monument. The first calls for construction tenders of the new bridge were issued in November 1982. It was hoped to start work late in 1983 and finish by the end of 1986.

The project's estimated cost of Esc 4000 million includes provision for 2·1 km of double-track approach lines from Vila Nova de Gaia (on the south side) and Campanhã (on the north); a 250-metre tunnel under Serra do Pilar; resignalling of the whole Oporto rail complex; a new marshalling yard, probably at São Mamede de Infesta, and new workshops at Araùjo. The bridge itself will feature a central span of some 300 metres' length rising 65 metres above the waterway.

CP will still remain severed on its key north-south route by the Tagus at Lisbon, as at present the first rail bridge over the river is some 56 km upstream from the capital at Setil and served only by a single-line route. Consequently CP has two Lisbon passenger terminals, Santa Apolonia north of the river and Barreiro on the south bank.

CP wants a new double-track rail bridge north of the city, possibly in the Alverca area, which could be allied to construction of a new main Lisbon through station near Rego. That would be sited conveniently close to the international airport at Portela. Meantime, CP ships maintain a link for passengers between the two present Lisbon termini.

Investments planned for 1983 were as follows (Esc million):

Electric locomotives and railcars	1104
New lines and track renewal	1122
Bridges and buildings	1024
Electrification	43
Signalling and telecommunications	417
Workshops	132
Miscellaneous, including rolling stock modernisation	1308
	5150

Traction and rolling stock

In 1982 CP placed orders with Sorefame for a further 43 day and 22 couchette cars of new stainless-steel bodied Corail type, bringing the total in production to 123. Further orders covered 14 two-car diesel sets for the Lousa line and 17 narrow-gauge two-car diesel sets for the Povoa do Varzim line.

At the start of 1983 CP's broad-gauge stock comprised 188 diesel and 46 electric locomotives, 97 three-car emus, 32 three-car and 20 two-car dmus, 38 diesel railcars and 69 trailers, 456 passenger cars and 5086 freight wagons. The narrow-gauge stock consisted of 21 steam and 17 diesel locomotives, eight four-car and 22 two-car dmus, 11 diesel railcars, 29 trailers, 37 passenger cars and 434 freight wagons.

Track

Standard rail
Broad gauge: 30-55 kg/m in 8-18 m lengths
Narrow gauge: 20-36 kg/m in 8 and 12 m lengths

Cross ties (sleepers)
Broad gauge: 260 × 130 × 2600 mm, spacing 605 mm
Narrow gauge: 230 × 120 × 1800 mm, spacing 820-850 mm
Rail fastening: Screw spikes or bolts. 'RN' flexible fastenings used with welded rail

Filling: Broken stone gravel or earth
Max curvature
Broad gauge: 5.9° = minimum radius 300 m
Narrow gauge: 29° = minimum radius 60 m
Max gradient
Broad gauge: 1·8% = 1 in 55½
Narrow gauge: 2·5% = 1 in 40
Longest continuous gradient
Broad gauge: 8·3 km of 1·4% grade with curves varying from 590 to 1501 m in radius
Narrow gauge: 7·2 km of 2·5% grade with curves varying from 75 to 500 m in radius
Max altitude
Broad gauge: 812·7 m
Narrow gauge: 849·7 m
Max axleloading
Broad gauge: 19·5 tonnes
Narrow gauge: 11 tonnes
Max permitted speed
Broad gauge: 100 km/h
Narrow gauge: 80 km/h

Welded rail: Thermit process is used. Rail used weighs 54, 50, 45, 40 kg/m in 18 and 24 m lengths. The length of continuous welded rail is usually 840 m but occasionally 960 m. Rails are secured to sleepers by RN flexible clips.

Interior of Lisbon-Oporto inter-city lounge car

Diesel railcars

Series	Wheel arrangement	Trans-mission	Rated power hp	Tractive effort Max kg	Continuous at kg	kmlh	Max speed kmlh	Wheel dia mm	Total weight tonnes	Length mm	No built	Year first built	Builders Mechanical parts	Engine & type	Transmission
9101/103 (NG)	B-B	Hyd	240	4100	—	—	70	700	22	15 500	3	1949	Nohab	Scania Vabis	Lisholm-Smith
9301/310 (NG)	Bo-Bo	Elec	320	9000	—	—	70	820	37	19 510	8	1954	Allan	AEC	Smith
9601/622 (NG)	BO 2' + 2' 2'	Elec	383	4500	2850	36	90	880	64·36	38 550	22	1976	Alsthom	SFAC	Alsthom
0051/056 (BG)	(1A) (A1)	Hyd	240	3750	—	—	80	700	26	15 560	3	1947	Nohab	Scania Vabis	Lisholm-Smith
0101/115 (BG)	(1A) (A1)	Hyd	252	2500	—	—	100	700	33·3	22 490	12	1948	Nohab	Saab-Scania	Voith
0301/325 (BG)	Bo-Bo	Elec	360	—	—	—	100	920	51·5	23 630	24	1954	Allan	SSCM	Smith
0501/506 (BG)	B' 2'	Mech	384	—	—	—	120	910	56·5	27 780	6	1953	Fiat	Fiat	Fiat
0401/419 (BG)	(1A) (A1) + 2' 2'	Hyd	560	6200	—	—	110	850	94·1	51 960	19	1965	Sorefame	Rolls-Royce	Rolls-Royce
0601/0640 (BG)	2' B' + B' 2'	Hyd	775	11 400	7600	22	120	920	110	53 480	20	1979	Sorefame	SFAC	Voith
0751/0766 (BG)	AA + 11	Mech	277	2900	—	—	90	900	32	27 500	16	1968	Waggon-fabrik	Pegaso	Pegaso-Z1
9701-40 (NG)	2B + B2 + 2B + B2	Mech	720	—	—	—	60	750	92	—	10	—	Fiat (acquired from Yugoslav Railways)		

Electric railcars

Class	Wheel arrangement	Line current	Rated output (hp)	Tractive effort Max kg	Continuous at kg	kmlh	Max speed kmlh	Wheel dia mm	Weight tonnes	Length mm	No built	Year first built	Builders Mechanical parts	Electrical equipment
2001/2025	Bo'Bo'+2'2' +2'2'	25 kV 50 Hz	1469	11 700	6000	40	90	1000-850*	117	71 060	24	1956	Sorefame	Siemens-AEG-Oerlikon
2051/2074-2082/2090	Bo'Bo'+2'2' +2'2'	25 kV 50 Hz	1469	11 700	6000	40	90	1000-850*	123·6	71 060	33	1956	Sorefame	Siemens-AEG-Oerlikon
2101/2124	2'2'+Bo'Bo' +2'2'	25 kV 50 Hz	1716	11 700	6240	64	120	1000-850*	132·8	71 060	24	1970	Sorefame	Siemens-AEG-Oerlikon
2151/2168	2'2'+Bo'Bo' +2'2'	25 kV 50 Hz	1716	11 700	6240	64	120	1000-850	132·8	71 060	18	1977	Sorefame	Siemens-AEG-Oerlikon

*Electric trailer cars

Diesel locomotives

Class	Wheel arrangement	Transmission	Rated power hp	Max kg	Tractive effort Continuous at kg	kmlh	Max speed kmlh	Wheel dia mm	Total weight tonnes	Length mm	No built	Year first built	Builders Mechanical parts	Engine & type	Transmission
9001/003	Bo-Bo	Elec	572	11 500	11 000	15	70	950	46	11 174	3	1959	Alsthom	SACM MGO	Alsthom
9004/006	Bo-Bo	Elec	590	11 500	9000	17·5	70	950	46	11 174	3	1959	Alsthom	SACM	Alsthom
9021/031	Bo-Bo	Elec	715	11 500	10 600	21·5	70	950	46.65	11 360	11	1976	Alsthom	SACM	Alsthom
1001/1006	C	Mech	160	7600	—	—	41·5	991	30·4	7815	6	1948	Drewry	Gardner	Sinclair
1021/1025	B	Elec	425	9720	9720	12	65	1050	36	9090	5	1968	Moyse	Deutz	Moyse
1051/1068	B	Elec	120	7000	7000	4	38	1050	28·3	7280	13	1955	Moyse	Moyse	Moyse
1101/1112	Bo-Bo	Elec	255	10 000	4258	10	56	965	41·2	10 210	11	1946	GE	Caterpillar	GE
1151/1186	C	Hyd	250	11 400	—	—	58	1090	42	8517	36	1966	Sorefame	Rolls-Royce	Rolls-Royce
1201/1225	Bo-Bo	Elec	600	16 000	12 200	13	80	1100	64·7	14 680	25	1961	Sorefame	SACM	Brissoneau & Lotz
1301/1312	A1A-A1A	Elec	1020	15 900	11 140	27	120	1016	95·4	17 060	12	1952	Whitcomb	Superior	Westinghouse
1401/1467	Bo-Bo	Elec	1025	16 100	14 200	19	105	950	64·4	12 720	65	1967	Sorefame	EE	EE
1501/1521	A1A-A1A	Elec	1730	—	2100	21	120	1016	111	16 988	17	1948	Alco	Alco	GE
1551/1570	Co-Co	Elec	1700	24 300	19 300	22·5	120	1016	89·7	17 905	20	1973	MLW	MLW/Alco	Canadian-GE
1801/1810	Co-Co	Elec	2050	26 000	17 750	31	140	1100	110·3	18 680	10	1968	EE	EE	EE
1961/1973	Co-Co	Elec	2251	45 000	28 200	18·75	120	1016	121	19 895	13	1979	MLW	MLW	Canadian-GE
1901/13	Co-Co	Elec	3000	39 600	25 600	23·2	100	1100	120	19 100	13	1981	Soretame	SACM	Alsthom
1931/47							120			18 800	17				

Electric locomotives

Class	Wheel arrangement	Line current	Continuous rating kW	One hour output kW	Max lb	Tractive effort Continuous at lb	mph	Wheel diameter mm	Weight tonnes	Length mm	No built	Builders Mechanical parts	Electrical equipment
2551-2570	Bo-Bo	25 kV ac 50 Hz	2044	2176	44 600	26 700	39	1300	70·5	15 380	20	Sorefame	50 c/s Group
2601-2612	B-B	25 kV ac 50 Hz	2880	2930	71 500* 46 800	42 000* 26 200	34 55	1140	78	17 480	12	Alsthom	50 c/s Group

*Low gear (monomotor bogie)

ROMANIA

Romanian State Railways (CFR)
Caile Ferate Romane

Bdf Dinicu Golescu 38, Bucharest 7

Telephone: 18 40 20; 17 20 60; 17 18 80

Minister of Transport and Telecommunications: V Bulucea

Commercial and Operating Director: C Rosu
Motive Power and Rolling Stock Director: I Balanescu
Technical Director: Gh Turbut
Way and Works Director: C Ruianu
Personnel Director: I Lepadat
Financial Director: N Dracea
Organisation and Audit Director: P Mateescu
Planning Director: A Manescu
Locomotive and Rolling Stock Engineer: G H Tanase
International Co-operation: Gh Balasolou
Stores: M Balanescu

Gauge: 1435 mm; 610 and 762 mm
Route length: 10 515 km; 568 km
Electrification: 2046 km at 25 kV 50 Hz ac

Transport development
Following a government decision to place increasing emphasis on rail communications, freight volume hauled by CFR grew at an annual rate of 4·4 per cent during the 1975-80 period. A smaller rate of increase in tonne-km recorded is anticipated during the 1980-85 period due to a trend towards shorter hauls designed to reduce consumption of fuel and energy. Passenger traffic fell in the late 1970s following an increase in private automobile ownership.

Traffic

	1980
Freight tonnage (million)	282
Freight tonne-km (million)	79 755
Passenger journeys (million)	320*
Passenger-km (million)	NA

*About half CFR's passenger journeys is in the form of commuter traffic and about 30 per cent in long-distance traffic.

1981-85 Development Plan

In July 1981 the World Bank approved a loan of US $125 million to Romania's Investment Bank, of which US$94 million was assigned to Romanian State Railways (CFR). Together with provision of US$186·7 million from CFR's internal funds and a further contribution from Romanian Government funds, this ensured advance with CFR's 1981-85 Development Plan.

Motive power and rolling stock

Both diesel-hydraulic locomotives (450, 750 and 1250 hp) and diesel-electric locomotives (2100, 3000 and 4000 hp versions with engines built under Sulzer, Alco and Maybach licences) are operated by the railway. Two types of electric locomotives are used on the single-phase 25 kV 50 Hz lines: a 5100 kW Co-Co built under an ASEA licence (240 are operating on CFR lines); and a 3400 kW Bo-Bo. Orders are being placed for 330 new freight wagons under the 1981-85 plan.

Despite intensive commuter operation in the Bucharest, Brasov and Constanţa conurbations, CFR has hitherto employed no emus. Since 1979, however, it has been testing a five-car prototype, in which the second and fourth vehicles are power cars, that has been produced entirely by domestic

industry: Grivitsa of Bucharest, Electroputere, and the factories of Craiova and Reşiţa. A production order for 24 sets was placed in 1982.

Electrification

Two electric main lines at present connect CFR with international traffic: Bucharest — Constanţa and Bucharest — Craiova — Timisoara — Arad — Curtici. They allow electric operation from Curtici on the Hungarian western border to Constanţa on the Black Sea coast. The other main electrified routes run north from Bucharest to Ploesti, Brasov, Dej, Buzau, Adjud and Bacau.

Three lines were in course of electrification in 1982: Galati—Faurei and Bacau—Pascani (on the main Bucharest—Suceava line to the USSR border and Moscow) in the east of the country; and the formidable Transylvanian Alpine route of 229 km between Brasov and Teius, of which 129 km as far as Sighisorara had been wired by the spring of 1982. During 1982 electrification of the 27 km Ciulnita—Calarsi line has begun. The area around Deva, in western Transylvania, was to be a focus of electrification work in 1983, covering the 55 km from Dej to Cluj in the north, a step towards creating a north-south route between the Ukraine and Bulgaria that avoids Bucharest; continuation of the Transylvanian Alpine scheme beyond Sighisorara to Teius (170 km); and wiring from Simeria, near Deva, to Hunedoara (15 km).

The 1981-85 plan covers electrification of a further 470 route-km.

More new electrified branches are being built. Early in 1983 construction of the 30 km Stoeneasa link through the Zaranduli mountains connecting Brad with Deva, in the west, was nearing comple-

tion; this would open up a new route from Deva to Arad and relieve the 140 km main line along the Muresul valley, which was nevertheless to be double-tracked. Work had begun on a new 30 km branch connecting Tirgu Neamt with Pascani, on the main route from Bucharest to Suceava and Lvov. A new route between Bucharest and Transylvania via Sibiu is being created by construction of a 50 km link between Ramnicu Vilcea and Pitesti.

Civil engineering

Under the 1981-85 plan, line capacity is to be increased by doubling 125 km of single track covering three main-line segments. Doubling has been given priority following intense industrialisation throughout Romania.

New track construction will permit axle loading to be raised from 16-18 tonnes to 20·5 tonnes and enable a maximum running speed of 160 km/h. 60 and 65 kg/m rail is now being installed on type T16 and T17 concrete sleepers. Ballast depth is 30 cm and minimum curve radius 500 metres.

Welded rails have been laid on 70 per cent of trunk and main lines and about 700 km were to be welded annually during the 1980s.

A new bridge is to be erected over the Danube at Cernavoda, some 150 km from Bucharest on the main line to Constanţa, where a new 32-track marshalling yard was completed in 1981; the latter is to be automated.

Signalling

Automatic block covers 3650 km. About 120 km per annum is due to be equipped with automatic block. CTC is not widespread. ATS covers the entire 1435 mm-gauge network.

SAUDI ARABIA

Saudi Government Railroad Organisation

PO Box 92, Dhahran

Telephone: 22 042
Telegrams: Saudirail, Dammam
Telex: 601050

President: Faysal M Al-Shehail
Vice-President: Abdul Mohsin Bashawri
Assistant Presidents
  Administration and Personnel: Fahad Zamil Al-Hazmi
  Transportation: Mohammed A Bubshait
  Engineering: Ahmed Saeed Afandi
  Finance: Burham Hamdi
Directors
  Planning and Budget: Assad Salim Shatara
  Operations: Salah Saleh Al-Ahmedi
  Motive Power and Equipment: Abdul Latif Ali
  Permanent Way: Abdullah S Al-Wabil
  Telecommunications: Mohammed A Sayegh
  Finance: Abdulla G Oreini
  Accounts: Saud A Al-Tobayyeb
  Purchasing: Yousef H Dardas
  Stores: Shamsan Ahmed Naimi
  Technical Adviser: Saud I Al-Gehairan

Gauge: 1435 mm
Route length: 578 km

Transport development

The railway from the port of Dammam to the oil-fields at Alqaiq and on to Riyadh via Hofuf has been operating since 1951. There is a daily train service to and from Riyadh and the route is radio-controlled. In the 1960s and early 1970s the rail system was neglected, but since the late 1970s SGRO has been recognised as essential to relieve overpressed air and road facilities, and considerable investment has been undertaken to fit the railway for its complementary role in bulk movement.

1981-85 Investment Plan

For the period 1981-85 the Government almost doubled its previous funding for SGRO to SR5000 million. As a result, in its third Five-Year Plan covering this term, SGRO put in hand rehabilitation of its existing system, works to raise the Dammam-Riyadh route's operating capacity to 5 million tonnes of freight by 1985, traction and rolling stock purchases, establishment of adequate workshops, and measures for effective staff training.

Principal infrastructure project is the transformation of the Dammam-Riyadh main line. The 140 km of the existing route from Dammam to Hofuf are

Traffic

	1978/79	1979/80	1980/81
Total freight tonne-km (000)	396 871	NA	458 400
Total freight tonnage (000)	1403	1453	1294
Total passenger-km (million)	85·927	89	87·514
Total passengers carried	264 007	275 446	267 017

Revenues	1978/79	1979/80	1980/81
		(Saudi Riyals 000)	
Passengers and baggage	3603	3682	3333
Freight and mail	13 333	16 113	13 901
Total revenues	16 933	19 795	17 234

Expenditure	1978/79	1979/80	1980/81
Staff/personnel	63 720	85 714	99 568
Materials and services	14 364	57 369	67 772
Depreciation	17 760		45 171
Financial charges	31 981	30 496	212 511
Total expenditure	127 825	173 579	425 022

being double-tracked and re-aligned for 150 km/h maximum speed, with continuously-welded UIC 60 rail on concrete sleepers, the latter manufactured in a plant established locally at Hofuf. Contractor for this US$114·5 million segment of the job is Archirodon Construction (Overseas) Co SA of Greece. Completion was expected in September 1983.

Beyond Hofuf a new and direct double-track route of 308 km is being built and engineered for 150 km/h, with continuously-welded UIC 60 rail on concrete monobloc sleepers set in a 300 mm-deep bed of ballast; maximum gradient will be 1 per cent and maximum permissible axleloading 28 tonnes. Completion date for the whole project is 1984.

Construction from Hofuf to Khurays, valued at US$104 million, has been entrusted to Railway Construction Pakistan (Railcop), the remainder, valued at US$139 million, to a consortium of Saudi companies and Archirodon. The Hofuf-Riyadh project is scheduled for completion by mid-1985. New stations are being built at Riyadh, Dammam and Hofuf and a locomotive depot at Dammam. Traffic will be controlled by route relay interlocking, tokenless block, with level crossing automatic barriers worked by soft-lead batteries recharged by solar power.

The completed new route will be 100 km shorter than the old. That, combined with higher permissible speed (the present limit is 110 km/h) and new signalling and traffic control systems (for which tenders were called in 1983), should enable Dammam-Riyadh passenger transit times to be cut by as much as 3 hours to 3¾ hours end-to-end and also achieve a substantial reduction in the current freight transit times of 10 hours. At present there is no signalling or block working on the Dammam-Riyadh route; traffic is controlled entirely by vhf

radio communication between locomotive drivers and a central control at Dammam.

The next major project is to be construction of a 100 km line from Dammam to the Jubail steel manufacturing complex. A design has been completed by Atkins Henderson consultants and in 1982 the Government assigned 1000 million Riyals to the scheme. Also planned is expansion of the freight terminal at Riyadh, already successfully developed for container transhipment under the management of Kanoo Terminal Services, a joint Saudi-Dutch organisation.

For its fourth Five-Year Plan to start in mid-1985 SGRO is conducting preliminary studies covering possible electrification, at 25 kV ac, starting with an 18 km link between Jeddah container terminal and port; urban transit schemes for Riyadh, including an airport link and the Dammam-Al-Khobar-Dhahran conurbation; and new lines in the country's major population and commercial corridors: Riyadh-Jeddah-Mecca-Medina, with a branch to the Yanbu industrial complex; Dammam-Jubail-Kuwait; Medina-Jordan-Damascus; and along the Gulf coast to Qatar and the United Arab Emirates.

Traction and rolling stock

First traction orders under the third Five-Year Plan were for six 3000 hp C-C diesel-electrics from Francorail of France, six SDL50-2 3000 hp Co-Co diesel-electrics and five 1000 hp Bo-Bo diesel-electrics from GM. The existing fleet is largely GM, including three GT22CW 2000 hp units, six SDL38-2 2000 hp units and seven FP7 or FP9 1500 hp units. Freight wagon orders placed in 1982 covered 263 (including 13 bi-level car-carriers) from Daewoo of South Korea, 50 flats from CAF in Spain, 40 from Cobrasma of Brazil, 185 from firms in Taiwan and 40 from Belgian builders. Orders for 40 more passenger cars were expected in 1983.

Cream of the coaching stock are 18 stainless-steel, air-conditioned cars delivered by Schindler-Schlieren in 1979. A further 40 passenger cars are to be acquired. All SGRO wagons are bogie, with AAR-E automatic couplers and Westinghouse air brakes.

Number of diesel-electric locomotives (January 1982): 18 line-haul; 19 shunting.
Number of passenger coaches: 58. Number of freight wagons: 1515.

Track
All main-line track renewals are now being undertaken with continuously-welded UIC 60 kg/m rail on prestressed concrete sleepers with elastic fastenings. All ASCE 80 lb/yd is being replaced.

Rail types and weights: UIC 54, UIC 60, AREA 100 lb and AREA 115 lb
Cross ties (sleepers): Wooden 2600 × 250 × 150 mm
Spacing: 1666 per km
Rail fastenings: Base plate and spikes and elastic spikes

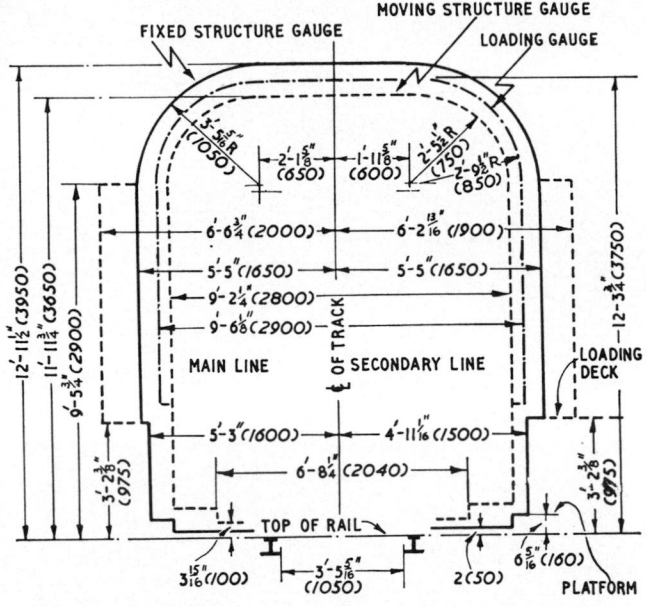

Reconstructed Hedjaz Railway

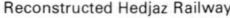

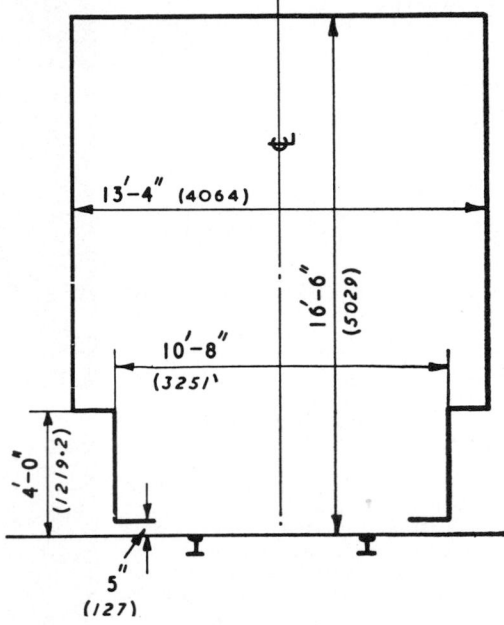

Saudi Government Railway

SENEGAMBIA

Ministry of Public Works, Town Planning, Housing and Transport

Administrative Building, Dakar

Minister: Mamadu Diop

Regie des Chemins de Fer du Sénégal (RCFS)

PO Box 175, Cité Ballabey, Thies

Telephone: 51 10 13
Telex: 789

President: O S Thiaw
General Manager: O Diene
Deputy General Manager: L Venault
Heads of Departments
  Commercial: Momar Gueye
  Operations: Mademba Sy
  Finance: H Vinches
  Motive Power and Rolling Stock: Babacar Ndao
  Way and Works: C Toure
  Stores: Guy Queyroux

Gauge: 1000 mm
Route length: 1033 km

Transport development
As one of West Africa's most industrialised countries, Senegal (which was united with Gambia as Senegambia in 1982) has a well-developed highway system. The railway system consists of two basic main lines running from Dakar to St Louis and Linguère in the north-east and the border with Mali in the east. The system was originally part of the Federal West African Railway Authority (AOF) before transfer to the Mali Federation in 1960. The disintegration of the Mali Federation caused the division of the former Dakar—Niger system into two networks. The present RCFS system is a legal entity with financial autonomy. The principal line extends 1286 km from Dakar in Senegal to Koulikoro, the terminus of the railway in Mali.

The RCFS consists of the following lines:

	km
Dakar to Kidiri	643
Dioubel-Touba branch	47
Guinguinéo-Koalack branch	21
Thiès to St Louis du Sénégal	193
Louga to Linguère	129
	1033

Motive power and rolling stock
Diesel locomotives: 29 main-line and 26 shunters
Railcars: 11
Passenger coaches: 104
Wagons: 983

Investment
In 1981 a subsidiary of the railway, Industries Chimiques du Sénégal, obtained a US $19·3 million loan towards the total US $23·4 million cost of rail-serving the country's principal fertiliser plant. RCFS subsequently sought tenders for the supply of three new main-line locomotives, 30 hopper wagons, 40 acid tank wagons, 230 tonnes of rail and 5500 steel sleepers for the project.

A FrCFA 15 500 million rehabilitation plan was launched in 1982. Its first fruits were delivery at the end of the year of two 500 hp diesel shunters from Fauvet-Girel and 12 coaches from Spanish builders, the latter for employment on Dakar-Mali trains. Further orders were placed with Spanish constructors for three 1600 hp Bo-Bo locomotives and 172 freight wagons, with an additional three 1600 hp units, five more 500 hp shunters and 60 more wagons to be ordered shortly.

As to infrastructure, the main east-west line is to have track strengthened over the 193 km from Kaffrine to Tambacounda, and completely relaid over the 121 km thence to the Mali border at Kidira. The Industries Chimiques du Sénégal railway is to be connected to the Taiba branch.

SOUTH AFRICA

Ministry of Transport Affairs

Sanlam Centre, Pretoria

Telephone: 217555

Minister: The Hon H S J Schoeman
Administrative Secretary to the Ministry of Transport Affairs: J M Muller
Private Secretary to the Ministry of Transport Affairs: S J van Blommestein
Commissioners: A S D Erasmus
    P L S Aucamp
    J T Albertyn

Department of Transport

Forum Building, Struben Street, Pretoria

South African Transport Services (SATS)

Paul Kruger Building, Wolmarans Street, Johannesburg 2001

Telephone: 713 2100
Telex: 4-2087; 4-24205

Director General: Dr E L Grové
Deputy General Managers: H J L du Toit
    H A Loots

Assistant General Managers
  Technical: J C de Waal
  Manpower: J G Benadé
  Planning: H S F Hagen
  Staff: Dr A T Moolman
  Harbours: P H de Bruin
  Commercial: B J Groenewald
  Management Science: J C B Irving
  Passenger Services and Road Transport: B J Lessing
  Finance: G M Holz
  Operating: G D van der Veer
  Airways: F J Swarts
Chief Mechanical Engineer (Pretoria): P A Marais
Chief Civil Engineer (Johannesburg): R D Hill
Chief Engineer (Signals and Telecommunications) (Johannesburg): C G Badenhorst
Chief Electrical Engineer (Johannesburg): J B Quail

System Managers
  Johannesburg: A S le Roux
  Cape Town: E W Kirsten
  Durban: W J Mitchell
  Pretoria: D Fourie
  Port Elizabeth: G D Engelbrecht
  East London: A J Jonker
  Windhoek: M F Myburgh
  Bloemfontein: R H Belcher
  Saldanha: P C Lombard
  Kimberley: E Kruger

Gauge: 1065 mm; 610 mm
Route length: 22 876 km; 705 km
Electrification: 5522 km at 3 kV dc
    861 km at 50 kV ac
    743 km at 25 kV ac
    2 km at dual 3 kV dc/25 kV ac

Transport development
The South African Transport Services rail network is divided into ten systems, each under a manager.

Freight
A further slight freight tonnage increase in 1981/82 was chiefly sustained by the continuing rise in the volume of coal exports, which climbed by almost 2·4 million tons to a total of 30·6 million tons, of which 27·7 million tons were railed to Richards Bay. The weekly number of trains ferrying coal from the Transvaal fields to Richards Bay varied between 68 and 78, each comprising 88 air-braked CCR wagons weighing 80 tons laden. Three 88-wagon trains formed of the new CCL-5 wagons with a payload capacity of 83 tons were also commissioned. The total of trains includes three double formations grossing 176 wagons and hauled by eight locomotives. The total rise in coal traffic over the year was 2·2 million tons, or 4·5 per cent, to a gross of 60 million tons. Iron and manganese ore export tonnages were up 1·6 million (12·3 per cent) and 7000 tons respectively on 1981 figures.

Container traffic rose by a further 8·9 per cent over the year to a gross of 2·46 million tons. Up to four air-braked container trains, each consisting of 50 wagons, were being operated daily in both directions between City Deep (Johannesburg) and Durban at the end of the year. Air-braked container trains consisting of 40 to 50 wagons were also being run daily, Mondays to Fridays, in both directions between City Deep and Port Elizabeth, and between City Deep and Cape Town; the City Deep-Port Elizabeth trains additionally convey containers for Kroonstad, Welkom, Virginia, Bloemfontein and East London, with the containers for East London carried by ordinary goods trains between Bloemfontein and East London. Containers for Klerksdorp, De Aar and Namibia are conveyed on the City Deep-Cape Town trains; those for Namibia travel on from De Aar on ordinary goods trains.

At the Bayhead (Durban) container terminal 137 022 containers were handled during the year, an increase of 25 401 compared with 111 621 containers the previous year. The new administrative building was completed and brought into use during the year. The Belcon container terminal at Bellville was commissioned in June 1982. It was envisaged that the container facilities at Capital Park, Pretoria, would be completed during 1984.

Rising demand for passenger travel was unchecked and its significance, coupled with the equally unrelenting escalation of passenger service deficits, led to the creation in May 1980 of a separate passenger administrative department under a newly-created Assistant General Manager (Passenger Services and Road Transport). The passenger business loss has soared from R44·3 million in 1962/63 to R485 million, and if unchecked threatens to breach R2000 million by 1990. Debate continued on the extent to which the railways should be relieved of the financial burden for maintaining socially necessary services; so far the relief extends only to payment of interest on capital invested in passenger services, which in 1980/81 amounted to R241 million.

Long-distance passenger journeys in 1981/82 were 2·48 per cent more than in the previous year, suburban up 3·89 per cent. To alleviate the overcrowding of suburban trains, the number of coaches on most workings was increased to 14. On the Natal system all the platforms between Rossburgh and Pinetown, with the exception of Malvern and Sarnia, have been lengthened to accommodate the longer train-sets, but extensions in the residential areas of the Cape Peninsula were still in the initial stage in 1982.

Following its 1978 trials of a Class 6E locomotive and passenger car fitted with the Scheffel cross-anchor, or High Stability (HS), bogie at up to 244 km/h, the railway is to test-market a prototype 200 km/h train on certain medium-distance routes.

Class 7E1 locomotives and Ermelo-Richards Bay coal train

Class 6E1 electric locomotive

Class 9E1 electric locomotive

Given a favourable response, Johannesburg—Durban is the likely route for a first, firm public service.

Traffic

	1980/81	1981/82
Total freight tonnage (million)	184·533	188·181
Total freight tonne-km (million)	99 173·025	103 885·957
Average net freight train load (tonnes)	710	735
Total passenger-km (million)		
Main lines	7268·7	7369
Suburban	12 931·9	13 632·8
Total passenger journeys (million)	725·428	752·997
Average length of passenger journey (km)		
Main lines	164	162
Suburban	19	19

Electrification

To minimise reliance on imported oil, SATS has embarked on an electrification programme embracing some 4309 track-km, with the aim of having 80 per cent of the system's tonne-km electrically-powered by the mid-1980s. In so doing, it has also switched from 3 kV dc to 25 kV 50 Hz ac for future extensions, even where, as between Beaufort West and De Aar, schemes connect with existing 3 kV dc sections. This follows SAR's highly successful initiation of high-voltage ac electrification on its Transvaal-Richards Bay coal line in the 1970s.

Electrification projects comprising 2247·66 route-km and 4309·41 track-km were in hand or authorised at the end of 1982. The 3 kV dc projects comprised Pretoria North-Pyramid; Houtheuwel-Potchefstroom (doubling); Union-Vooruitsig (doubling); Sentrarand marshalling yard and its approaches.

The major 25 kV ac projects in progress, with their estimated cost in 1982 money values and projected completion dates, are:

	(R million)
Beaufort West—De Aar, 432 track-km (1983)	53·21
Pyramid—Pietersburg, 416 track-km (1983)	75·22
Port Elizabeth—De Aar, 778 track-km (1984)	100·07
East London—Springfontein, 707 track-km (1985)	92·86
Bloemfontein—Noupoort, 378 track-km (1985)	42·99

The Pyramid South-Thabazimbi and Pendoring-Atlanta sections were energised at 25 kV ac during the year. Satisfactory progress was made with the electrification work at Sentrarand and it is expected that it will be completed on schedule. Other new electrification projects currently undertaken are also on schedule.

A contract for the electrification of the De Aar-Port Elizabeth line was entered into during the year at a cost of R20·362 million for overhead track equipment and R7·8 million for the 25 substations. The initial cost of this 25 kV ac electrification is approximately R47 000 per single track-km, compared with R75 000 per single track-km for dc electrification.

Four years of service of electric working between Ermelo and Richards Bay have proved the wisdom of electrifying at 25 kV ac and in extending this form of electrification to other lines. The gross traffic handled on the Ermelo-Richards Bay line during 1981/82 was 21·4 Giga ton-km for goods and 0·057 G-ton-km for passengers, for which 484·6 Gwh of energy was consumed. The specific energy consumption for the year was 22·62 Wh/ton-km compared to an average of 30·7 Wh/ton-km for the country as a whole.

Greater reliability of locomotives, substation and overhead equipment on ac systems is also evident; the average of occurrences causing power disruption of the coal line were respectively 6·5 per 1000 STK/month on the ac sections of the line, 9·3 on the dc.

Traction and rolling stock

At the start of 1983 the railway was operating 1647 steam, 2056 electric and 1549 diesel locomotives, 6081 locomotive-hauled passenger cars, 1375 motor and 3486 trailer emu cars and 187 139 freight cars.

Class 25NC 4-8-4 steam locomotive No 3450, built by Henschel in 1953, has been experimentally modified as Class 26 to embody the practice developed by the Argentinian engineer, L D Porta (after whom

Financial results (railways only) (R 000)

Expenditure	1980/81	1981/82
Administrative and general charges	134 487	175 882
Maintenance of permanent way and works	473 848	612 384
Maintenance of rolling stock	379 273	469 444
Motive power operating expenses	553 385	691 835
Traffic and vehicle running expenses	600 886	765 272
Cartage service	61 932	77 926
Depreciation	344 172	203 589
Higher replacement costs	—	272 836
Interest on funds	3161	10 596
Financing costs	513 846	557 667
Miscellaneous	79 193	93 287
Catering and bedding services	27 272	33 874
Publicity and advertising	379	494
Grain elevators	3817	5465
Pre-cooling services	19 908	23 619
Road transport services	106 186	136 550
Tourist service	32 248	42 019
	3333 993	4172 739

Revenue	1980/81	1981/82
Passengers	437 475	530 576
Parcels	63 086	79 045
Mail	13 095	17 148
Goods	1939 819	2299 247
Coal	366 130	450 602
Livestock	13 068	14 292
Rents and storage	28 197	34 808
Miscellaneous	156 728	186 469
Interest received	94 972	121 647
Miscellaneous receipts	33 970	49 945
Catering and bedding services	23 499	30 617
Publicity and advertising	982	1222
Grain elevators	4963	8568
Pre-cooling services	19 852	23 549
Road transport services	103 510	131 388
Loss carried to appropriation account	1379	150 228
	3333 993	4172 739

Durban port container terminal

High-capacity air-braked coal wagon for Richards Bay coal line

No 3450 has been named), from the theories of André Chapelon for higher thermal efficiency. Painted bright red, and thus known popularly as the 'Red Devil', No 3450's main alterations are: the replacement of a conventional firegate by a firebox in which the coal is gasified, somewhat as in a coke oven, to minimise combustion losses; a specially contrived twin-chimney exhaust and draughting system to match; increased superheating to achieve a maximum steam temperature of some 450°; and the passage of 15 per cent of the exhaust steam through a heat exchanger mounted on top of the smokebox. In average conditions No 3450 is expected to show economies of 10 and 12·5 per cent respectively in coal and water consumption by comparison with orthodox locomotives of its type. Conversion of 87 of the 89 Class 25C condensing locomotives to non-condensing Class 25NC has been completed; of the remaining two, one is being preserved, the other kept active for promotional purposes.

A total of 390 new standard-gauge coaches comprising 50 emu motor coaches, 108 emu trailers, 28 first-class, 119 first- and second-class composite and 85 third-class main-line saloons, was commissioned in 1981/82. At the close of the year 1828 new coaching vehicles of various types, as well as 17 coaches for high-speed inter-city passenger services and two new-generation stainless steel electric train-sets consisting of 12 coaches each, were on order, or authorised for acquisition.

Provision was made in the capital budget for the year ending March 1983 for acquisition of 190 emu trailers and 147 emu motor coaches.

A total of 3864 new vehicles of various types, of which 822 were built by the Mechanical Department and 3042 by local industry, was placed in service during the year. Altogether 5323 goods vehicles and four cranes were scrapped. The number of goods vehicles on order, or authorised, and still to be placed in service totalled 12 559, including 20 steam-heating vehicles and three diesel-hydraulic breakdown cranes.

Provision was made in the capital budget for the year ending March 1983 for acquisition of 500 AYLJ ballast wagons, 3000 BLJ high-sided open wagons, 800 FSLJ covered wagons, 750 OLJ fruit wagons, 150 LALJ mechanical refrigerator wagons, 200 QZLJ explosives wagons, 1200 SHLJ container wagons, 100 SFLJ flat wagons, 200 XBLJ cement tank wagons and 50 XSLJ sulphuric acid tank wagons. It was also decided to convert 200 type B and DZ wagons to type NPSLJ wagons for the conveyance of rails instead of purchasing new wagons.

Although the number of standard-gauge merchandise-carrying vehicles in service decreased from 174 292 to 172 638, the total merchandise-carrying capacity increased from 6 296 495 to 6 415 247 tons and the average carrying capacity per vehicle from 36·13 to 37·16 tons. So as to utilise fully the intended upgrading of the most important main lines, all new wagons acquired for the bulk of the network will be designed with 80 tons glw but with 104 tons glw on the coal line. The programme to raise the carrying capacity of certain types of wagons in the existing fleet is continuing.

Civil engineering

Construction of the new Sentrarand marshalling yard continued and the supply for it of 41 978 retarder and 18 100 booster/retarder units by Dowty was arranged. The first module of the yard was put into operation in November 1982.

At the close of the year new line construction in progress included:

Kensington-Bellville	12·9 km
Table Bay Harbour-Kensington:	
Chempet line electrified	
double-track link	8 km
Chempet-Atlantis single line	32 km

During 1981/82 investments in new works on open lines and in the improvement and extension of existing facilities amounted to R889·8 million, representing an increase of R307 million compared with the previous year. This figure does not include the construction of new lines, new harbour works, the acquisition of rolling stock, road transport vehicles, aircraft or the construction of pipelines.

The estimated total investments under the main categories of the 1981/82 programme of new works on existing lines amounted to R5574·4 million, the amounts actually authorised prior to April 1981 to R4753·3 million, and the investments sanctioned during 1981/82 to R606 million, while the anticipated cost of the schemes under consideration or awaiting approval at March 1982 amounted to R214·7 million.

A R63 million scheme, programmed for completion by 1984, has begun to eliminate the handicaps of sharp curvature and a 1 in 40 gradient confronting

Modified Class 26 4-8-4 *L D Porta*, known as the 'Red Devil'

First module of Sentrarand marshalling yard

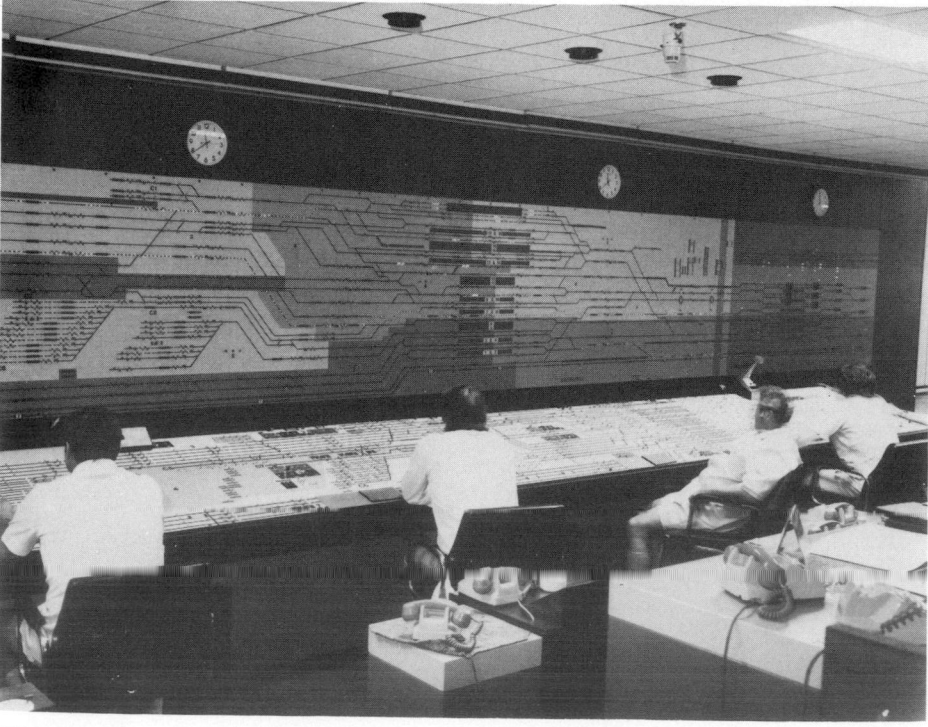

CTC control room

northbound traffic in the Hex River Pass, on the Johannesburg—Cape Town route, which necessitate load reduction over the affected section. The major item in the scheme is a new 13·5 km tunnel, the longest in South Africa, for which contracts were let in August 1980; two other tunnels, one of 1·09 km, the other of 1·21 km length, will also be necessary. The main tunnel will have an 800 metre-long crossing loop at its midpoint. The new route will ease the ruling gradient to 1 in 66 and sharpest curvature from 200 to 600 metres.

At present SATS has 47 high-capacity on-track tampers, consisting of 27 Electromatics and 20 Plassers, all on long-term hire contracts. In addition there are 31 medium-capacity machines owned by SATS, but these are gradually being replaced by contract machines. There are 13 ballast-cleaning machines in use on contract as well as 10 ballast regulators and one track stabiliser, also all on contract.

A six-year contract has been entered into with E C Lenning for the hire of two 48-stone rail-grinding trains. A 24-stone machine has been in use since 1979 on contract from Speno through E C Lenning.

A corrugation recording car has been adopted by E C Lenning using basic Speno equipment to measure rail corrugations at ±40 km/h. The car produces an analogue strip chart printout together with a digitised tape, which is processed on a shore-based computer, to give a digital printout every 50 metres, and to classify the defects in four degrees of severity.

Track defect analysis is measured by one EM 80 recording car owned by SATS, fitted with an on-board computer rebuilt to the latest standards. This unit will shortly be joined by three Plasser EM 80s on hire contract; they have been specially built to enable recordings to be done with a measuring axleload variable between 15 and 26 tonnes.

The world's first on-track flash-butt rail welder built outside the USSR is now in operation at Bethal. This uses a welding head built by Matix of France and fitted to a self-propelled rail vehicle, developed to their own design by E C Lenning. This unit has the shear built into the head and the head can be used to post-heat the rails to provide controlled cooling of the weld.

SATS has in addition 174 light tampers for renewals work and 6500 petrol-driven hand tamping machines. There are also a large number of small self-powered track tools, such as rail saws, drills, grinding machines etc, totalling some 7500 self-powered units.

Infrastructure investment plan 1982-83

	(R million)
Construction of new lines	105·375
New works on open lines	277·983
Relaying, strengthening	82·136
Regrading and deviations	11·93
Improvements, buildings etc	177·518
Electrification	28·506
Telecommunications	21·64

Signalling and telecommunications

Microprocessors are being applied to a widening range of operations. They have been incorporated in the mini-CTC system installed between De Aar and Touws River, in which eight centres each control approximately 70 route-km. In these centres train descriptions are reproduced on vdus and the operators can store routes; the new system also controls a time/distance graph plotter. All functions at the new Sentrarand yard will be controlled by distributed microprocessor systems, and here and at the new Durban traffic control an automatic train-routing system based on microprocessors is being provided.

The whole Durban suburban train service is CTC-controlled from the new Durban centre, which has been arranged to allow simultaneous arrival and departure of trains from every platform in the new Durban station. This permits a theoretical headway of 72 seconds between 12-car trains, and allows trains to be scheduled at 3-minute intervals for a 2-minute stop in the station.

Electric suburban stock

The fleet in 1982 consisted of 1220 motor coaches and 3131 trailer cars of Type 5M2/5M2A; and 88 motor coaches and 222 trailer cars of Type 4M1/4M2.

Coaches per train-set: 8, 11 or 14
Motor coaches per train-set: 2, 3 or 4
Motored axles per motor coach: 4

Class 7E 25 kV ac locomotive employed on Richards Bay coal line

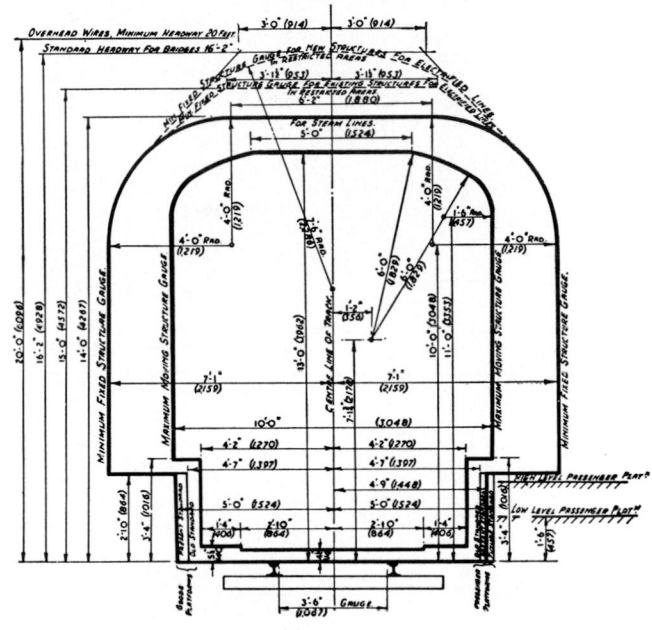

CTC installations

Year	Location	Route-km	Main contractor
	Kamfersdam—Postmasburg	205	S&H
	Bloemfontein—Springfontein	139	S&H
	Houtheuwel—Klerksdorp	131	S&H
	Volksrust—Newcastle	57	S&H
	Union—Volksrust	228	WBS
	Queenstown—Burgersdorp	154	WBS
	Cradock—Noupoort	152	WBS
	Wellington—Touwsrivier	184	Telkor
	Sishen—Saldanha	880	Telkor
	Vryheid—Richards Bay	197	S&H
	Piet Retief—Vryheid	160	S&H
	Piet Retief—Ermelo	114	WBS
	Ermelo—Broodsnyersplaas	80	WBS
	Ogies—Broodsnyersplaas	53	SATS
	Broodsnyersplaas—Wonderfontein	65	SATS
	Brits—Pretoria North	41	Telkor
	Witbank—Eerste Fabrieke	96	Telkor
	Ogies—Witbank	27	SATS
	Witbank—Waterval Boven	143	Telkor
	Waterval Boven—Nelspruit	102	WBS
	Nelspruit—Lebombo	113	SATS
	Kaapmuiden—Hoedspruit	168	GEC
	Whites—Welkom	24	GEC
	Montclair Area	34	S&H
	Klerksdorp—Veertienstrome	230	S&H
1980/81	Wintersnest—Mabopane	20	Telkor
1980/81	Newcastle—Wig	15	GEC
1980/81	Touwsrivier—De Aar Matjiesfontein—Jan de Boers	44	SATS
1980/81	Broodsnyersplaas—Wonderfontein Gelukplaas—Wonderfontein	57	SATS
1980/81	Nyanga—Strandfontein	13	SATS
1981/82	Vooruitsig—Clavis	14	WBS
	Touwsrivier—De Aar Jan de Boers—Prince Albert Road	154	SATS
		4094	

S&H	Siemens and Halske
WBS	Westinghouse Brake and Signal Company
GEC	General Electric Company
SATS	South African Transport Services

Rated output of motors
Type 5M2/5M2A
One-hour: 1450 V, 230 A, 945 rpm: 302 kW full field
  1450 V, 255 A, 1075 rpm: 340 kW weak field
Continuous: 1450 V, 165 A, 1047 rpm: 220 kW full field
  1450 V, 180 A, 1212 rpm: 242 kW weak field

Type 4M1/4M2
One-hour: 1450 V, 170 A, 1040 rpm: 227·5 kW full field
  1450 V, 175 A, 1245 rpm: 235 kW weak field
Continuous: 1450 V, 150 A, 1070 rpm: 200 kW full field
  1450 V, 160 A, 1285 rpm: 208 kW weak field
Max speed: 97 km/h

	5M2/5M2A	4M1/4M2
Weight of motor coach		
(tons)	69	67
trailer (tons)	35	33
Average seating capacity		
motor coach	46	64
trailer	75	108
Length (m)	18·38	18·3
Acceleration		
(normally loaded		
level tangent track)	0·44 m/s	0·44 m/s
Year first built	1958	1954
Builders: Mechanical	Union Carriage and Wagon Co	Metro-Cammell
Electrical	General Electric Co	General Electric/ Metro-Vickers

Steam locomotives

Class	Type	Stock at 31/3/82	Year into service
1065 mm gauge			
Steam tank locomotives			
H-2	4-8-2	1	1903
Garratt articulated			
GEA	4-8-2+2-8-4	6	1946-47
GMA	4-8-2+2-8-4	24	1954-56
GMAM	4-8-2+2-8-4	84	1953-58
GO	4-8-2+2-8-4	25	1954
Steam tender locomotives			
12-R	4-8-2	70	1912-22
12-A	4-8-2	23	1912-22
12-AR	4-8-2	44	1912-22
14-R	4-8-2	84	1913-15
14-CRB	4-8-2	50	1919-22
14-CRM	4-8-2	12	1918-22
15-A	4-8-2	2	1914-25
15-AR	4-8-2	115	1914-25
15-BR	4-8-2	1	1920
15-CA	4-8-2	79	1926-30
15-F	4-8-2	250	1938-49
19	4-8-2	1	1928
19-A	4-8-2	3	1929
19-C	4-8-2	1	1935
19-D	4-8-2	230	1937-49
23	4-8-2	106	1931-39
24	2-8-4	98	1949-50
25-C	4-8-4	2	1953-55
25-NC	4-8-4	50	1953-54
25-NC*	4-8-4	87	1953-55
Miscellaneous locomotives			
S	0-8-0	1	1929
S-1	0-8-0	37	1947-54
S-2	0-8-0	100	1952-53
610 mm gauge			
NC-15	2-8-2	21	1911-53
Garratt	Various	40	1928-68
	Total	1647	

* Converted from Class 25-C

Motive power under order for delivery 1982-87

Electric locomotives (dc)

Class and type	Wheel arrange-ment	Max speed km/h	Main con-tractor	Expected deliveries					
				1982	1983	1983/84	1984/85	1985/86	1986/87
6E1 (Series 9)	Bo-Bo	113	UC&W	36	—	—	—	—	—
6E1 (Series 10)	Bo-Bo	113	UC&W	3	10	34	8	—	—
6E1 (Series 11)	Bo-Bo	113	UC&W	—	—	—	33	12	—
8E	Bo-Bo	75	BBC/ Siemens	—	2	40	44	14	—
10E (Series 1)	Co-Co	90	Mitsui	—	—	—	5	40	5
12E (high-speed)	Bo-Bo	150	UC&W	5	—	—	—	—	—

Electric locomotives (ac)

Class and type	Wheel arrange-ment	Max speed km/h	Main con-tractor	Expected deliveries				
				1982	1983	1983/84	1984/85	1985/86
7E2 (Series 1)	Co-Co	88	50 c/s Group	24	—	—	—	—
7E2 (Series 2)	Co-Co	88	50 c/s Group	—	—	40	—	—
7E3	Co-Co	88	Nissho Iwai	—	—	42	18	—
9E* (Series 2)	Co-Co	90	GEC Traction	4	2	—	—	—
11E	Co-Co	90	General Motors SA	—	—	—	19	11

*50 kV ac

Diesel-electric locomotives

Class and type	Wheel arrange-ment	Max speed km/h	Main con-tractor	Expected deliveries		
				1982	1983	1983/84
36-200 (Series 2) (shunting)	Bo-Bo	90	General Motors SA	18	—	33
37-000	Co-Co	100	General Motors SA	36	—	—

Electric motor coaches

Class and type	Wheel arrangement	Tractive effort kN	Max speed km/h	No ordered	Year ordered	Main contractor	Expected deliveries			
							1982	1983	1983/84	1984/85
5M2A (Series 14)	Bo-Bo	59	100	203	1981	UC&W	58	26	78	41
6M prototype	Bo-Bo module of 2 motor coaches and 1 trailer coach	201 per set	110	1 train-set consisting of 4 modules	1982	Hitachi	—	—	1 train-set	—
7M prototype	Bo-Bo module of 2 motor coaches and 2 trailer coaches	216 per module	±100 still to be finalised with contractor	1 train-set consisting of 3 modules	1982	Consortium AEG/BBC/ Siemens	—	—	—	1 train-set

Diesel-electric locomotives

Class	Wheel arrange-ment	Rated power kW	Max axle load kg	Tractive effort continuous kN	Tractive effort continuous km/h	Max speed km/h	Wheel dia mm	Total mass tonnes	Length mm	No built	Year first built	Builders Mechanical parts	Builders Engine and type	Builders Transmission
31	Bo-Bo	985/ 895	18 900	145	18	90	915	74	15 150	45	1958	GE	Cooper Bessemer	General Electric
												GE	1 4-stroke V-8 turbocharged and aftercooled C-B type FVBL-8	4 dc 4 pole axle-hung 5E type 5GE 761 A4
32-000	Co-Co	1475/ 1340	10 160/ 12 700	146	27	100	762/ 915	93	16 866	115	1959	GE	Cooper Bessemer	General Electric
												GE	1 4-stroke V-12 turbo-charged and aftercooled C-B type FVBL-12	6 dc 4 pole axle-hung GE type 5GE 76 A3
32-200	Co-Co	1475/ 1340	10 160/ 12 700	146	27	100	767/ 915	93	16 866	10	1966	GE	General Electric	
												GE	1 4-stroke V-12 turbo-charged and aftercooled GE type 7FDL-12	6 dc 4 pole axle-hung GE type 5 GE 761A9
33-000	Co-Co	1605/ 1490	15 749	178	24	100	915	91	16 866	65	1965	GE	General Electric	
												GE	1 4-stroke V-12 turbo-charged and aftercooled GE type 7FDL-12	6 dc 4 pole axle-hung GE type 761 A6
33-200	Co-Co	1640/ 1490	15 749	178	24	100	915	91	17 474	20	1966		EMD General Motors	
												EMD	1 2-stroke V16 roots blown EMD type 16-645-E	6 dc 4 pole axle-hung EMD type D 29CC-7
33-400	Co-Co	1605/ 1490	15 749	178	24	100	915	91	16 866	115	1968		General Electric	
												GE	1 4-stroke turbo-charged and aftercooled GE type 7 FDL-12	6 dc 4 pole axle-hung GE type 5 GE 761 A 6
34-000	Co-Co	2050/ 1940	18 850	218	26	100	915	111	17 982	125	1971		General Electric	
												GE	1 4-stroke V-12 turbo-charged and aftercooled GE type 7 FDL-12	6 dc 4 pole axle-hung GE type 5 GE 761 A 13
34-200	Co-Co	2145/ 1940	18 850	218	26	100	1016	111	19 242	50	1971		EMD General Motors	
												EMD	1 2-stroke V-16 turbo-charged and aftercooled EMD type 16-645 E 3	6 dc 4 pole axle-hung EMD type 29B
34-400	Co-Co	2050/ 1940	18 850	218	26	100	915	111	17 928	139	1973		South African GE-DC Locomotive Group South Africa	
												GE	1 4-stroke V-12 turbo-charged and aftercooled GE type 7 FDL-12	6 dc 4 pole axle-hung GE type 5 GE 761 A 13
34-600	Co-Co	2145/ 1940	18 850	218	26	100	1016	111	19 202	100	1974		General Motors South African (Pty) Ltd	
												GM SA	1 2-stroke V-16 turbo-charged and aftercooled EMD type 16-645-E3	6 dc 4 pole axle-hung EMD type D 29B
34-800	Co-Co	2140/ 1940	18 850	218	26	100	1016	111	19 202	58	1978		General Motors South African (Pty) Ltd	
												GM SA	1 2-stroke V-16 turbo-charged and aftercooled EMD type 16-645 E3	6 dc 4 pole axle-hung EMD type 29B
34-900	Co-Co	2050/ 1940	18 850	218	26	100	915	111	17 982	1	1979		South African GE—DC Locomotive Group	
												GE	1 4-stroke V-12 turbo-charged and aftercooled GE type 7 FDL-12	6 dc 4 pole axle-hung GE type 5 GE 761 A13
35-000	Co-Co	1230/ 1160	13 720	161	21	100	915	82	15 152	70	1972		General Electric	
												GE	1 4-stroke V-8 turbo-charged and aftercooled GE type 7 FDL-8	6 dc 4 pole axle-hung GE type 5GE 764-C

Diesel-electric locomotives

Class	Wheel arrange-ment	Rated power kW	Max axle load kg	Tractive effort continuous kN	km/h	Max speed km/h	Wheel dia mm	Total mass tonnes	Length mm	No built	Year first built	Builders Mechanical parts	Engine and type	Transmission
35-200	Co-Co	1195/1065	13 720	161	19	100	915	82	16 485	150	1974		EMD General Motors—25 General Motors South African (Pty) Ltd—125	
												EMD & GM SA	1 2-stroke V-8 turbo-charged and aftercooled EMD type 8-645E3	6 dc 4 pole axle-hung EMD type D 29CCBT
35-400	Co-Co	1230/1160	13 720	161	21	100	915	82	15 152	100	1976		South African GE— DC Locomotive Group South Africa	
												GE	1 4-stroke V-8 turbo-charged and aftercooled GE type 7FDL-8	6 dc 4 pole GE type 5GE 764-C1
35-600	Co-Co	1195/1065	13 720	161	19	100	915	82	16 485	100	1976		General Motors South African (Pty) Ltd	
												GM SA	1 2-stroke V-8 turbo-charged and aftercooled EMD type 8-645 E3	6 dc 4 pole axle-hung EMD type D29 CCBT
36-000	Bo-Bo	875/800	18 500	141	14	100	915	72	15 151	124	1975		South African GE— DC Locomotive Group South Africa	
												GE	1 4-stroke V-8 turbo-charged and aftercooled GE type 7 FDL-8	4 dc 4 pole axle-hung GE type 5 GE 764-C1
36-200	Bo-Bo	875/800	18 500	141	14	90	1016	72	14 150	50	1980		General Motors South African (Pty) Ltd	
												GM SA	1 2-stroke V-8 roots blown EMD type 8-645E	6 dc 4 pole axle-hung Type D29B
37-000	Co-Co	2340/2170	21 000	245	26	100	1016	125	19 202	62	1981		General Motors South African (Pty) Ltd	
												GM SA	1 2-stroke V-16 turbo-charged and aftercooled EMD type 16-645E 3B	6 dc 4 pole axle-hung EMD type D31
91-000	Bo-Bo	52/480	12 000	86	15	50	838	44	10 580	20	1973	GE	Caterpillar	General Electric
												GE	1 4-stroke V-8 turbo-charged and aftercooled CAT type D 379	4 dc 4 pole GE type 5GE 778 A1 gear case axle-mounted

Electric locomotives

Class	Wheel arrange-ment	Line current kV	Rated output (one-hour/ continuous) kW	Max load kg	Tractive effort (full field) Continuous kN	at km/h	Max speed km/h	Wheel dia mm	Total mass kg	Length mm	No built	Year first built	Builders Mechanical parts	Electrical equipment
Es	Bo-Bo	3	896	17 018	73	19	40	1219	68 075	13 310	24	1936	SAR—4, Werkspoor Holland—10, Metro Vickers—10	
														4-Metro Vickers 182R traction motors
1E 1ES	Bo-Bo	3	896	17 018	73	39	70	1219	68 075	13 310	39 38	1936	Metro Vickers	
														4-Metro Vickers 182R traction motors
3E	Co-Co	3	2016/1704	18 796	119	51	100	1219	113 797	17 199	28	1948	Metro Vickers	
														6-Metro Vickers 187 traction motors
4E	Co-Co	3	2262/1878	13 209/21 845	141	46	100	762/1295	157 488	21 844	40	1952	North British	
														6-GEC WT 580 traction motors
5E	Bo-Bo	3	1508/1300	21 591	104	44	100	1219	86 364	15 494	180	1955	English Electric	
														4-EE 529 traction motors
5E1	Bo-Bo	3	1940/1456	21 591	122	43	100	1219	86 364	15 494	690	1959	Metro Vickers—135 Union Carriage and Wagon Co Ltd—555	
														4-MV 281 or 4-AEI 281 AZX or 4-AEI 281 AX or 4-AEI 281 X traction motors
6E	Bo-Bo	3	2492/2252	22 226	193	41	110	1219	88 904	15 494	80	1970	Union Carriage and Wagon Co Ltd	
														4-AEI 283 AZ traction motors
6E1	Bo-Bo	3	2492/2252	22 226	193	41	110	1219	88 904	15 494	917	1969	Union Carriage and Wagon Co Ltd	
														4-AEI 283 AZ traction motors
EXP/AC	Bo-Bo	25	2492/2252	22 226	190	41	110	1219	85 500	15 494	1	1975	Union Carriage and Wagon Co Ltd 50 c/s Group	
													Union Carriage and Wagon Co Ltd	4-AEI 283 AZ traction motors

Electric locomotives

Class	Wheel arrange-ment	Line current kV	Rated output (one-hour/ continuous) kW	Max load kg	Tractive effort (full field) Continuous kN	at km/h	Max speed km/h	Wheel dia mm	Total mass kg	Length mm	No built	Year first built	Builders Mechanical parts	Electrical equipment
7E	Co-Co	25	3240/ 3000	21 000	300	35	100	1220	123 500	18 465	118	1978	50 c/s Group (Siemens Ltd)	
													Union Carriage and Wagon Co Ltd	6-MG 680 traction motors
7E1	Co-Co	25	NA/ 3000	21 000	300	35	100	1220	123 115	18 430	100	1979	Nissho Iwai	
													Dorman Long	6-Hitachi HS-1054-GR traction motors
9E	Co-Co	50	4068/ 3780	28 000	388	34.5	90	1220	166 300	21 132	31	1979 (ex-ISCOR 1978)	GEC Engineering (Pty) Ltd	
													Union Carriage and Wagon Co Ltd	GEC Traction 6-GEC G415AZ traction motors

SPAIN

Ministry of Transport & Communications

Paseo de la Castellana, Nuevos Ministerrios, Madrid 3

Minister: L Gámir Casares
General Director of Land Transport: Juan Antonio Guitart y de Gregorio

Spanish National Railways (RENFE)
Rede Nacional de los Ferrocarriles Españoles

Final Pio XII s/n Charmartin, Madrid 16

Telephone: 733 62 00
Telex: 23420

President: Ramon Boixados Male
Vice-President: Pelayo Martinez-Regidor
Director General: E M Carreño
Commercial Director, Passenger: J Pérez Palencia
Commercial Director, Freight: J D Perucho
Director of Operations: Juan Luis Rùiz Nuñez
Director, Transport: J Moreno de Mesa
Director, Investment: J Escalano Paul
Director, Rolling Stock: J R Fernandez
Director, Personnel: M Corsini Freese
Director of Way and Works: J C Barron Benavente
Director of Planning: A Dionis Soler
Director of Finances: A Pena Sanchez

Gauge: 1676 mm; 1000 mm
Route length: 13 553 km; 19 km
Electrification: 1676 mm gauge: 6185 km at 1·5 and 3 kV dc; 46 km at 6 kV 25 Hz
1000 mm gauge: 19 km at 1·5 kV dc

Transport development
Most of the country is served by broad-gauge lines with other gauges mainly confined to the northern coastal routes, although there are also several narrow-gauge railways operating branch-line services down the west and east coasts.

Twelve-year plan
In July 1981 a special Ministerial commission completed consideration and approval of a 12-year plan, envisaging an annual investment of Pta 100 000 million, to raise the competitive efficiency of RENFE and reduce its deficit. The plan will be 95 per cent Government financed. Its main features, aimed to raise annual passenger-km to 39 400 million, were:
Passenger
Reorganisation of the long-haul passenger service to reduce the emphasis on radial departures and create 95 new services between regional centres bypassing Madrid;
Reduction of daytime inter-city transit times by 40 per cent and establishment of a 98 km/h minimum commercial speed through upgrading of key routes over 350 km in length for 160 km/h maximum speed and curtailment of station stops;
Establishment of minimum 80 km/h average speed for locomotive-hauled or railcar trains making inter-city transits of 350 km or more;
An increase from 22 to 51 per cent of the berth proportion in overnight trains on runs of over 350 km, chiefly by greater use of couchettes;

Talgo Pendular train-set

Talgo Pendular first-class saloon

Traffic

	1979	1980	1981	1982
Freight tonne-km (million)	10 592	10 887	10 603	10 503
Freight tonnage million)	35·8	36·5	35·13	32·59
Passenger-km (million)	12 671	13 527	14 261	14 703
Passenger journeys (million)	157	167	176	181·4

Trebling of daytime service frequencies in main inter-city corridors and substantial increases elsewhere;
Establishment of 50 km/h minimum end-to-end speed in local services and increase of peak-hour frequency to 10 minutes; for this new train-sets would be needed;
Construction of 307 km of new conurbation commuter routes;
Standardisation of air-conditioning.
Freight
Drive for more unit train operation, raising its proportion of all traffic from 25 to 62 per cent;

Increased availability of special-purpose wagons, especially for petrochemicals, and a concomitant drive for more private wagon ownership and private sidings;
Creation of a new company, ATIMER, to promote and develop intermodal traffic, especially in containers; an annual potential of 6 million tonnes of additional traffic was foreseen through development of door-to-door container operation, for which 39 new transhipment rail terminals would be created within five years at a cost of Pta 2200 million, and 2000 container flat wagons bought at a cost of Pta 6000 million.

Infrastructure
Double-tracking to be extended from 16 to 37 per cent of total route-length;
Electrification to be extended within three years from 5473 to 8060 km (36 to 57 per cent of the network);
A further 1039 of RENFE's 6931 open level crossings to be protected.
Rolling stock
A total of 1351 electric locomotives, 170 diesel shunters, 2427 passenger cars, 24 000 freight wagons and 12 000 containers to be purchased.

The most important infrastructure schemes projected for 1982-84 under the Plan were: the start of a new 90 km line from Brazatortas, on the Ciudad Real-Badajoz route, to Cordoba, to create a more direct route to the south-west; double-tracking of the existing line via Despenaperros; realignment of the Bilbao-Miranda de Ebro and Oviedo-León routes in the Orduna and Pajares passes; and the completion of double-tracking on the Zaragoza-Madrid and Castellon-Tarragona routes. In sum, completion of these works by 1985 would add an estimated 11 per cent to operating capacity and improve rolling stock utilisation by 10 per cent. The Brazatortas line would save 100 km of distance between Madrid and major centres in the south-west, reducing Madrid-Cordoba journey time to less than 3 hours.

Other major new lines embodied in the General Plan are betwern Irun and Alsasua; Velayos, north of Avila, and Villalba; and Manzanares to Ciudad Real. Double-tracking is to be extended throughout the Madrid-Ciudad Real-Cadiz, Valencia-Tarragona, León-Vigo and Madrid-Leride-Barcelona routes. Immediate candidates for electrification are the sections between: La Encina and Alicante; Linares and Huenejar (north of Almeria); and La Coruna and El Ferrol. Numerous extensions, double-trackings and electrifications are planned in the Madrid, Barcelona and Valencia suburban areas.

Finances

The Government made available in 1982 the full RENFE subvention planned within the total of Pta 322 000 million budgeted for the 1982-84 period (20 per cent of the Plan total), but by the end of the year there was fear that if the recession persisted the time-scale of the 12-year General Railway Plan would be prejudiced by the economy's inability to spare sufficient finance. The Plan is being funded out of the national budget and is hence vulnerable to the general state of the economy.

At the start of 1982 RENFE loan indebtedness stood at Pta 124 870 million. During 1982 further loans were obtained of Pta 10 000 million, US$80 million, Euro $100 million, DM100 million (from Dusseldorf banking interests) and DM750 million (from Japanese sources).

Revenue	1980	1981
	(Pta million)	
Passenger	28 800	33 139
Freight	34 128	36 010
Mail	4474	4594
Other	10 392	20 961
Total	77 794	94 704
Expenses		
Staff	83 206	96 252
Energy	7970	12 433
Materials	30 526	43 445
Amortisation	11 350	13 164
Interest	9173	9267
Total	142 225	174 561
Deficit	64 431	79 857

Traffic

The upward trend in passenger journeys was maintained in 1982, with a fresh rise of 3·1 per cent. Within this figure long-distance travel was up 2·9 per cent, other journeys up 3·6 per cent. In the long-haul sector overnight travel declined on several routes because of the age of the equipment employed and uncompetitive speed, but this was more than offset by rising patronage of day trains re-equipped with the 9000 series cars or the increasing stock of Talgo (Pendular) train-sets. Overall, Talgo equipment performed 8 per cent more train-km than in 1981 and Pendular sets were introduced to additional day services, such as Madrid Chamartin-Gijon via Pajares and Madrid Atocha-Cadiz/Huelva. In 1983 Talgo Pendular sleeper sets were to make their debut on domestic routes, notably Madrid-Barcelona. The Fiat 'Basculante' tilt-body prototype emu returned to commercial service in 1982 between Madrid Atocha and Jaen. With employment of the new Class 444 emus on other inter-city services, such as Madrid-Valencia, the older TER and TAF sets

Class 444 inter-city emu

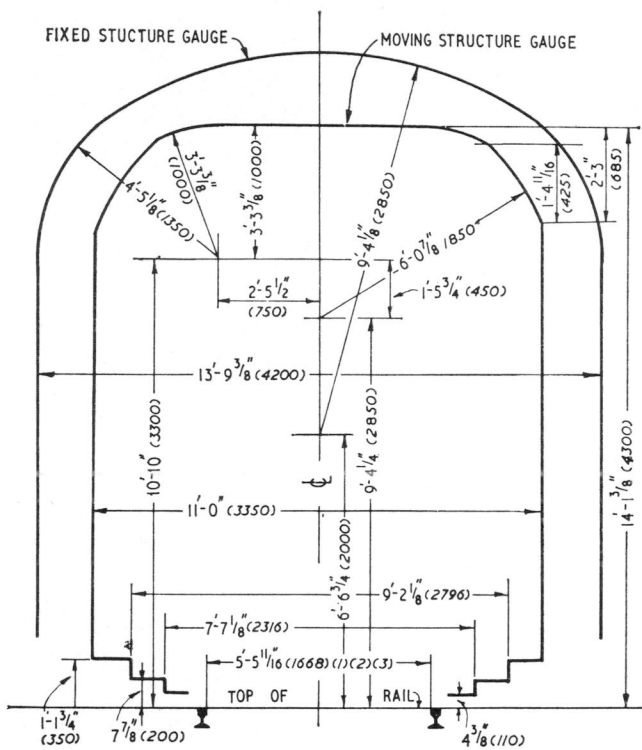

FIXED STUCTURE GAUGE — MOVING STRUCTURE GAUGE

Passenger-km 1979-82

	1979	1980	1981	1982	Variation (%)
			(million)		1981-82
Long-distance	7623	8287	8897	9151	+2·9
Express trains	5660	5940	6332	6593	+4·1
Talgo	796	938	1024	1106	+8
TER and TAF	810	808	729	637	−12·6
Emus	357	601	812	815	+0·4
Local and regional	5048	5240	5364	5552	+3·6
Total	12 671	13 527	14 261	14 703	+3·1

were increasingly relegated to less important services.

Apart from containers and parcels despatched by passenger train or special parcels train, freight lost volume in 1982. Worst affected traffic was petroleum products, where considerable tonnage was surrendered to pipelines. Container traffic rose 21·9 per cent in tonne-km to 1287·8 million for the year, which saw the opening of new TECO terminals at Tarragona, Puertollano, Huelva, Vigo (for refrigerated container traffic) and, in a joint exercise with FEVE, at Santander.

A significant private siding development of 1982 was completion of a connection with General Motors' car factory at Figuerelas, Zaragoza. Since 1978 120 new private sidings have been installed; a total of 1500 is an objective of the General Railway Plan.

Talgo

The latest model of Talgo coaching stock, the Talgo Pendular, has a passive body-tilting system designed to permit curve negotiation at a 20 per cent higher speed than the normal limit without discomfort to passengers. The range includes sleeping-car sets with wheel-sets adjustable to gauge-change for a through Paris—Madrid and Paris—Barcelona overnight service. Initial RENFE orders for Pendular vehicles cover 132 day and 56 sleeping cars.

The Talgo body-tilting system employs no sensors, electronic detectors or hydraulic systems, but relies on a natural pendular action in reaction to centrifugal force. At 13·14 metres over couplers the 2·83 metres-wide Pendular cars are slightly longer than previous Talgo models. They employ the patent Talgo automatic guidance system of their half-axles with independent wheels, and the Talgo air suspension, with disc brakes, and are designed for 180 km/h maximum speed. The bodies, monocoque structures of soundproofed aluminium extrusions, are air-conditioned. The sleeper sets include a 30-seater restaurant, a 16-seater cafeteria-bar and a mix of cars with either six compartments for single- or double-berth accommodation, or five tourist-class compartments offering up to four berths each, also a baggage-generator car. Although designed for 190 km/h, Talgo Pendular equipment is currently limited to 140 km/h (160 km/h on French Railways).

Electrification

The 19 km of electrification completed in 1982 covered extra tracks installed in doubling. At the end of the year 3 kV dc electrification was started on the mineral line in the south from Almeria to Heuneja Dolar and the mines of Marquesado, where it is planned to operate heavy mineral trains with the latest Type 250 locomotives hauling and propelling. Renewal of catenary was launched on a number of routes, including Madrid Atocha-Linares and Miranda de Ebro to Irun and Bilbao. The 76 km line from Miranda de Ebro to Alsasua has been converted from 1·5 kV to 3 kV dc.

Capacity enlargement

Major event of 1982 was the completion of the 27 km double-track, electrified Barcelona loop after seven years' work which included 7 km of tunnelling. Laid with 54 kg/m rail on concrete sleepers, with a ruling gradient of 0·15 per cent and minimum curve radius of 1000 metres, the new line diverts traffic bound for France from the city's busy centre. The loop joins the Madrid line at San Vicente de Calders and is now taken by most long-distance trains from Barcelona to the centre and south of the country, leaving local traffic to follow the coastal line.

The double-tracking of the Andalusian main line from Madrid to Cordoba was taken a further 42 km, between Manzanares and Santa Cruz de Mudela. Other double-tracking was in progress between León and La Robla (24 km), on the north-western main line from León to Gijón, between Villaboma and Nubledo (11 km), to benefit Asturian mineral traffic; between Valencia and Castellon; and between El Higueron and Almodovar (19 km), on the Madrid Atocha-Seville route. The León-La Robla widening was originally planned as the prelude to construction of a new 47 km double-track route through the Pajares pass, including a 23 km tunnel, at a cost of Pta 40 000 million, so as to eliminate the fierce gradients of the historic route. That scheme has now been discarded on the grounds of cost. With availability of the 4650 kW Class 251 electric locomotives on this route RENFE is to rest content with improving the existing infrastructure. At the approach to Miranda de Ebro a new 4 km alignment is being constructed on the Bilbao route to eliminate several urban level crossings and prepare for the forthcoming creation of a new station in the city.

During 1982 156 km of other main-line track was renewed and the number of level crossings further reduced to 959 protected, 550 with half-barriers and 6812 unprotected; in 1974 the totals were respectively 2271, nil and 8099.

Traction and rolling stock

At the start of 1983 RENFE operated 15 Talgo diesel locomotives, 378 other line-haul diesel locomotives, 363 diesel shunters, 477 electric locomotives, 1505 locomotive-hauled passenger cars, 227 sleeping cars, 244 postal cars, 2303 emu and dmu vehicles (including railbuses) and 31 604 wagons (10 495 privately-owned wagons were also in use).

Traction delivered in 1982 comprised 10 Class 250, 13 Class 251 and one Class 269 electric locomotive, one Class 440 emu, 35 Class 592 and 30 Class 593 dmus; and for RENFE's solitary narrow-gauge line, Cercedilla to Navacerrada, three two-car Class 442 emus. Krauss-Maffei completed the first of the eight Series III low-profile diesel-hydraulic B-Bs for Talgo haulage; in this latest batch total power output of the two Maybach engines has been raised to 4000 hp, without increase of the 80 tonnes' service weight, fitting the units for other heavy-duty passenger work as well as Talgo duty. Completion of the orders for 40 Class 250 and 30 Class 251 was expected in 1983, together with further deliveries of the Class 440 suburban emu. Delivery began in 1983 of 110 Class 269-200 3100 kW electric locomotives of the Mitsubishi pattern introduced with a series of 21 units in 1980-81. The new batch was ordered in 1982 from a consortium including CAF, Macosa, Ateinsa, Westinghouse and General Electric of Spain.

The Class 250 4600 kW C-C electric locomotives, of which the first five were built by Krauss-Maffei-BBC while the remainder are being assembled in Spain, has monomotor bogies with individual cardan-shaft drive to each axle to fit it for use on fast

Class 269 electric locomotive and train of Series 9000 cars

Series 9000 second-class saloon interior

Freight 1980-82

	1980	1981	1982
Tonnage		(000)	
Wagonload	30 216·3	29 245·2	26 847·3
Containers	1482·7	1578·1	1901·8
Less-than-carload	416·0	382·4	362·2
Parcels	147·0	144·7	148·2
Internal service	3426·8	2938·6	2534·7
Mail	840·4	844·2	799·3
Total	36 529·2	35 133·2	32 593·5
Tonne-km		(million)	
Wagonload	8663·8	8370·7	8119·3
Containers	931·0	1056·1	1287·8
Less-than-carload	257·9	237·1	224·6
Parcels	64·6	63·6	65·1
Internal service	609·7	513·5	465·7
Mail	360·3	361·9	341·3
Total	10 887·3	10 602·9	10 503·8

passenger trains at a maximum of 160 km/h or on freight trains at a maximum of 100 km/h. The last five locomotives of the series are to be equipped with BBC chopper control. The class is fitted with dual vacuum and air braking to cover the RENFE transition from one system to the other.

The Class 251 4650 kW B-B-B is a chopper-controlled derivative of the Class 269 B-B built under

Mitsubishi licence by CAF, WESA and MELCO. Like the 269, the 251 has monomotor bogies affording alternative gearings for 100 km/h and 160 km/h maxima. Its weight is 129 tonnes. Equipped with rheostatic and two-stage air braking, the 251s were first assigned to the steeply graded Pajares pass route between León and Gijón, in the Cantabrian mountains.

The three-car emus of the MAN-Macosa Series 592 and of the Fiat-CAF Series 593 are built in Spain. The order for Series 592 totals 70, for Series 593, 62. The two designs are very similar, each comprising two power cars and trailer with Scharfenberg couplers and with a set total of 228 seats. Bodies are air-conditioned, with air-operated plug doors. Series 592 is mounted on MAN bogies with helicoidal primary and air secondary suspension, and Knorr-operated disc brakes, and each power car is fitted with two 290 hp MAN-Büssing engines with Voith transmission. Scharfenberg couplers are fitted at the extremities of each unit, plug doors are air-operated and the cars are air-conditioned; seats, standard with those of the new 9000 type locomotive-hauled cars and of the Type 444 emus, are reversible. Up to three sets can be driven in multiple.

The fleet of 210 railbuses will be reduced following completion of the Class 592 and 593 dmu deliveries. Only the 38 units of Type M-Rc are being refurbished for extended service, in western Spain and in Galicia.

Coaching stock deliveries in 1982 comprised 50 more 9000 series inter-city cars and the first cafeteria cars using the same body-shell, 65 Talgo Pendular and 14 Talgo III cars, including a kitchen-bar car. The Talgo III deliveries raised the total stock of this type to 87 first-class, 113 second-class, 24 second-class train-end, 23 kitchen-bar and 23 brake-end cars, plus 15 independent head-end power cars for use on Talgo III trains hauled by Japanese-built electric locomotives. The 50 Corail cars hired from French Railways in December 1980 were returned in late 1982.

Orders have been placed with CAF for 137 cars with interchangeable bogies (Y32 for 1435 mm, GC-1 for 1668 mm) to be employed on international services. Over 80 per cent of locomotive-hauled cars were air-braked by the end of 1982.

The Class 9000 inter-city car is of open-saloon layout, air-conditioned and arranged for 76 first- or 88 second-class seats within a length of 25·62 metres over couplers. Two types of disc-braked bogie have been employed in the initial series, a broad-gauge version of the Fiat F80SL, and a Spanish design, the CAF GC-1, drived from the SNCF Type Y32 and the Eurofima bogie. The cars are designed to operate at up to 160 km/h.

Between 1982 and 1984 RENFE envisaged the following purchases: 123 electric locomotives (100 to cover increased traffic); 106 dmus (60 to cover extra traffic); 40 emus (30 to cover additional traffic); 377 passenger cars (150 to cope with extra traffic) and 1000 wagons.

Macosa was in 1983 completing a prototype chopper-controlled emu, the CDT1, conceived as a RENFE standard design for suburban traffic.

Series 592 dmu by Macosa

Series 592 dmu interior

Signalling

By the end of 1982 the distance controlled by automatic block and CTC had been increased to 5402 km; the major task then in hand was installation of CTC over the 146 km between Miranda de Ebro and Castejon de Ebro. ATC was operative over 833 km and the sections scheduled to acquire this equipment in 1983 were Torralba—Casetas (172 km), on the Barcelona—Madrid route; and Castejon—Logrono—Miranda (146 km), on the Zaragoza—Bilbao route.

AEG-Telefunken is to supply track-to-train radio equipment for 3850 route-km and 1065 traction units. The first route to benefit will be Madrid—Barcelona.

Track
Standard rail
Main lines: 54·4 kg/m for all relaying. 45 kg/m and UIC 54·1 kg/m in 12 and 18 m lengths
45 kg/m rail being replaced

Branch lines: 42·5 kg/m in 12·4 m lengths
28·3-40·5 kg/m rail being replaced
Rail joints: Suspended; 4- or 6-hole fishplates and welding
Sleepers
Wooden: Mainly creosoted oak, pine, and sometimes beech. 2600 × 240 × 140 mm for ordinary track. For points, crossings etc, 3, 3·5, 4 and 4·5 m of same width and thickness (centre crossing sleeper being 4500 × 300 × 140 mm), and for expansion joints 2600 × 350 × 140 mm. Special sleepers of up to 6·2 m used for diagonals on double track
Reinforced concrete sleepers: Type RS for 54 and 45 kg rail with a thickness of 220 mm. Made in Torrejón, Venta de Baños and Alcázar de San Juan
Spacing for 45 kg rail: 20 for 12 m lengths: 640 mm spacing for inner sleepers
30 for 18 m lengths: 620 mm
Rail fastenings: Screw spikes on wood sleepers and elastic clamps on reinforced concrete sleepers. Elas-

tic fastenings for wood sleepers also being tested
Filling: Crushed limestone or quartz ore: 40-80 mm
300 mm under sleepers on main lines
200 mm under sleepers on secondary lines
Max curvature: Generally 5·85° = min rad of 300 m except 7·6° = min rad of 230 m on Ripoll-Puigcerdá line and 8·75° = min rad of 200 m on Cordoba-Almorchón line
Max gradient: 4·1% = 1 in 24½ on Ripoll-Puigcerdá line
Longest continuous gradient: 8·27 km of 2% (1 in 50) grade, with 5·85° curves (300 m radius) on 4·84 km
Max altitude: 1494 m on Ripoll-Puigcerdá line
Max axleload: 22 tons
Max permitted speed
Talgo Pendular trains: 180 km/h
Talgo trains: 140 km/h
Diesel train-sets (TAF): 110 km/h
Other trains: 100 km/h

Diesel locomotives (line-haul)

Class	Wheel arrange-ment	Trans-mission	Rated power hp	Max kg	Tractive effort Continuous at		Max speed kmlh	Wheel dia mm	Total weight tonnes	Length mm	No built	Year first built	Builders Mechanical parts	Engine & type	Transmission
					kg	kmlh									
313	Co-Co	Elec	1370	18 480	19 300	14	120	1016	83·9	16 237	50	1965	Euskalduna Alco	Alco Products 251-D	General Electric GEE
314	Co-Co	Elec	1445	18 450	18 625	16·4	120	1067	86	15 526	1	1967	Macosa	General Motors 567-C	General Motors
316	Co-Co	Elec	2180	24 090	18 200	21·7	120	1016	110	17 872	16	1955	Alco	Alco 251-C-3	General Eléctrica
318	Co-Co	Elec	1980	24 090	18 200	21·7	120	1016	110	17 872	24	1958	Alco	Alco 251-B	General Electric
319	Co-Co	Elec	1977	23 100	18 450	21·6	120	1067	103	18 472	103	1965	EMD General Motors Macosa	EMD General Motors 567-C	EMD General Motors

Diesel locomotives (line-haul)

Class	Wheel arrange-ment	Trans-mission	Rated power kW	Tractive effort Max kg	Continuous at kg	km/h	Max speed km/h	Wheel dia mm	Total weight tonnes	Length mm	No in service	Year first built	Builders Mechanical parts	Engine & type	Transmission
321	Co-Co	Elec	2180	24 640	19 325	22·5	120	1016	111	18 567	80	1967 1970	Alco, CAF, Naval Euskalduna	Alco	General Electric GEE
333	Co-Co	Elec	3345	31 710	28 100	23·5	151	1067	120	20 700	93	1974	Macosa	General Motors 645 E 3	General Motors
340	B-B	Hyd	2 × 2000	25 500	17 093	30	130	1016	88	19 750	32	1966	Krauss-Maffei Babcock & Wilcox	Maybach-Mercedes MD 870/1	Maybach-Mercedes
350	Bo-Bo	Elec	898	18 480	NA	NA	140	840	66	11 989	4	1950	ACF	Maybach MD650	Mekydro
352	B-B	Hyd	2 × 1200	22 100	16 400	20·5	140	950	76·3	17 450	10	1964	Krauss-Maffei Babcock & Wilcox	Maybach-Mercedes MD 650/18	Maybach-Mercedes
353	B-B	Hyd	2 × 1500	25 500	19 000	20	180	1150	88	19 000	5	1969	Krauss-Maffei	Maybach-Mercedes MD6552	Maybach-Mercedes
354	B-B	Hyd	2 × 2000	—	—	—	180	1150	88	19 000	8	1982	Krauss-Maffei	Maybach-Mercedes MD6552	Maybach-Mercedes

Note: Classes 350, 352 and 353 are 'Talgo' locomotives

Electric locomotives

Class	Wheel arrange-ment	Line current	Rated output hp	Tractive effort (full field) Max kg	Continuous at kg	km/h	Max speed km/h	Wheel dia mm	Weight tonnes	Length mm	No built and on order	Year built	Builders Mechanical parts	Electrical equipment
250	C-C	3000 V	6170	NA	20 090 32 220	80 50	160 100	1250	120	20 090	40	1981	Krauss-Maffei	BBC
251	B-B-B	3000 V	6235	NA	NA	NA	160 100	NA	132	NA	30	1981	Mitsubishi-CAF	Westinghouse
269	B-B	3000 V	4155	34 200	16 620 26 820	66·3 40·3	140/80	1250	88	17 270	108	1973	Mitsubishi-CAF	Cenemesa (Westinghouse)
269-200/ 500/600	B-B	3000 V dc	4155	34 200	14 580 23 555	75·2 45·7	160/90	1250	88	17 270	157	1973/81	CAF	Westinghouse
274	Co-Co	1500 V	2210*	27 720	17 700		90	1300	99	17 026	24	1944	Devis	Sècheron
276/ 286	Co-Co	3000 V dc	3000	33 600	16 500	49·5	110	1250	120	18 932	136		Alsthom-Macosa CAF-MTM Euskalduna Babcock & Wilcox	Alsthom-Sice, GEE-Oerlikon Exp Ind Westinghouse
277	Co-Co	3000 V dc	3000	31 300	13 850	58	110	1220	120	20 657	75		Vulcan-Foundry	English Electric
278	Bo-Bo-Bo	3000 V dc	3000	31 710	16 800	48	110	1118	120	20 193	29		Wesa-SE Construc Naval	Westinghouse
279/289	B-B	1500/ 3000 V	3670	31 200	14 000/ 22 500	69/ 43	130/ 80	1250 (1120)	80	17 270	56		Mitsubishi-CAF	Mitsubishi-Cenemesa
280	B-B	1500/ 3000 V	3000	22 400	12 100/ 20 700		120/ 70	1250	80	17 600	4		Alsthom	Alsthom
281	Bo-Bo	3000 V dc	NA	20 950			65	1400	74·8	11 912	7	1929	CAF	CAF
282	Bo-Bo	1500 V dc	1120	18 900	12 200		70	1270	67·5	12 600	5	1932	Babcock & Wilcox	General Electric

*One-hour rating

Catalanes Railways (FGC)
Ferrocarriles de Generalitat de Catalunya

Plaza Cataluña 1, Barcelona 2

Telephone: 302 48 16

Director: E Roig
Manager: A Chimenos

Gauge: 1435 mm; 1000 mm
Length: 50 km; 143 km
Electrification: 1435 mm, 50 km at 1·2 kV dc
1000 mm, 58 km at 1·5 kV dc

The Regional Government has been studying the feasibility of laying a new 1435 mm-gauge line from Barcelona to the French frontier at Puigcerda. It has lately budgeted Pta 22 380 million for infrastructure improvements in the Barcelona area and for purchase of 25 new Alsthom-type emus. Delivery of eight new locomotive-hauled and 16 self-propelled cars was anticipated in 1983.

In 1982 FGC was operating 10 diesel locomotives, 14 electric and 14 diesel railcars, 24 passenger cars and 422 wagons on metre gauge, 56 electric power cars and 28 passenger cars on 1435 mm gauge.

FGC Barcelona—Terrassa emu near Les Planes *(John C Baker)*

Spanish Narrow-Gauge Railways (FEVE)
Ferrocarriles Españoles de Via Estrecha

General Rodrigo 6, Madrid 3

Telephone: 2 33 70 00

Chairman: F-J S Martinez de Azagra
Vice-Chairman: A F-O y Aguilera
General Manager: J Fanlo
Financial Manager: J-B Camacho del Castillo
Equipment Manager: P G-H Gonzalez

Electrification: 196·5 km at 1·5 kV and 600V dc (1·5 kV is being standardised)

Transport development
FEVE is a public company under the Ministry of Transport, Tourism and Communications. It was set up in 1965 and operates the majority of public Spanish narrow-gauge railways, with the principal exception of those locally administered by the provincial administrations of Catalonia and of the Basque country.

In recent years some FEVE lines have been transferred to other management:

Bilbao—San Sebastian	108·5 km
Amorebieta—Bermeo	29·1 km
San Sebastian—Hendaye	20·9 km

(transferred to the Basque General Council in May 1979)

Bilbao suburban railways	43·7 km

(transferred to the Basque General Council in December 1978)

Barcelona—Manresa and branches	135·9 km
Barcelona—Sabadell and Tarrasa	41 km

(transferred to the Catalan Government in November 1978)

Plaza de España to Carabanchel suburban railway	9·6 km

(transferred to the Madrid City Authority in November 1978, although at present operated by Compañia del Metropolitano Madrileño).

Traffic
1981 was marked by a substantial increase in freight traffic, which is principally of coal, minerals and containers.

Passenger journeys	35·5 million
Passenger-km	491·6 million
Total freight tonnes	5 million
Total freight tonne-km	174·9 million

New container handling facilities are to be installed and some of the existing facilities are to be extended at Ferrol, San Ciprián, La Maruca, Navia, Santander, Luchana and Ariz.

Demand was expected to rise by 1985 to 42·5 million passenger journeys, by 1990 to 54·5 million, together with 117 million tonnes of freight.

Finance (1981)

Income (Pta million)	1769
Expenditure (Pta million)	6326

Investment
Outstanding improvement and expansion projects under way are:
Conversion of the Langre railway between Gijón and Pola de Laviana, the third oldest in Spain, and its branch lines, to metre-gauge;
Conversion of the suburban railway system in Valencia into an underground system, due for completion of its first phase in 1985.
Many bridges and tunnels have been strengthened, many track-km renewed, and many level crossings automated or otherwise modernised.

Traction and rolling stock
In 1982 FEVE operated 97 diesel and 11 electric locomotives, 110 diesel railcars, 80 emus, 57 passenger cars, 29 baggage cars and 3233 freight cars. Material on order included 14 1600 hp diesel-electric locomotives manufactured under licence from Alsthom by Maquinista Terrestre y Maritima de Barcelona; 14 diesel-electric trains also manufactured by Maquinista Terrestre y Maritima de Barcelona under licence from Brown Boveri (electrical equipment), and Linke-Hofmann-Busch (mechanical parts); and 10 electric trains manufactured by Babcock and Wilcox in Bilbao under licence from AEG and General Electric of Spain (electrical equipment) and Ganz-Mávag of Hungary (mechanical parts). Further substantial emu and dmu orders were to be placed in 1983.

In 1982 the wagon fleet was reinforced with 200 46 tonnes-capacity flat wagons from Macosa and Ateinsa. In 1983 delivery began of 400 41-tonnes-

FEVE electric locomotives near Deba with Bilbao—San Sebastian train (John C Baker)

FEVE emu approaches San Sebastian from Rentaria (John C Baker)

Northern Zone

	Gauge (mm)	Route length (km)
Ferrol—Gijón	1000	320·8
San Esteban de Pravia—Oviedo	1000	103·8
Oviedo—Santander	1000	223·4
Santander—Bilbao	1000	144·2
León—Bilbao	1000	326·6
Gijón—Laviana*	1440	54·8

* In course of conversion to 1000 mm.

South-eastern Zone

	Gauge (mm)	Route length (km)
Valencia Railways	1000	114·6
Alicante—Denia	1000	92·6
Cartagena—Los Nietos	1000	19·7
Mallorca Railways	1000	29

capacity coal wagons with automatic couplers and power-assisted discharge doors to an Arbel design, built by CAF.

Electrification and signalling
Heavily trafficked lines which are either not electrified or which employ obsolescent 600 volts dc equipment are being electrified at 1500 volts dc. This has necessitated the construction of various new substations or the modification of existing substations. Some of these sections are being supplied with CTC. The electrified sections within the FEVE network are: Gijón — Avilés — Pravia; Lierganes —

Orejo — Santander — Puente San Miguel; and Cabezón de la Sal and Valencia Railways (all lines).

Track
Rail: 45 kg/m and 54 kg/m
Max axleload: 15 tonnes
Sleeper spacing: 1500 per km
Minimum radius of curvature: Main line 100 m
Average radius of curvature: 250 m
Max gradient: 36%, between Cartagena and Los Nietos
Longest tunnel: 4 km, La Florida, between Gijón and Pola de Laviana

SRI LANKA

Ministry of Transport

1st Floor, Galle Face Secretariat, Colombo 1

Minister: K B Ratnayake

Sri Lanka Government Railways (SLGR)

PO Box No 355, Colombo 10

Telephone: 21281

General Manager: G P S Weerasuriya
General Manager (Administration): K D D Pathiratne
General Manager, Technical: D C Lelwela
Transportation Superintendents
  Operating: R B Dissanayake
  Motive Power: J N I Karunaratne
  Administrative: T D de S W Jayasundera
Commercial Superintendent: K Gunasekera
Deputy Chief Engineer, Track and Bridges: S Panchacharevel
Deputy Chief Engineer, Construction: W K B Weragama
Signal Engineer: U C N Fernando
Chief Mechanical Engineer: T Gunasekra
Stores Superintendent: D R Jayasinghe
Chief Accountant: W C Perera

Gauge: 1435 mm; 750 mm
Route length: 1453 km; 59 km

Transport development
SLGR is based at Colombo, from where lines radiate north along the coast to Illarankulam, south to Matara and east to the Central Highlands. From the Central Highlands the main line runs to Talaimannar, where a ferry provides links with India's Southern Railway. Branch lines run to Trincomalee and Betticalo, ports on the Bay of Bengal. A narrow-gauge railway runs from Colombo inland to Ratnapura.

Traffic is currently around 5·8 million passenger-km and 390 million passenger-km a year. The system operated at a loss of Rs236 million in 1981.

Traffic
A development of 1982 was the launch of inter-city express passenger services between Colombo and Kandy (to a 2½ hour schedule for the 115 km) and Colombo and Galle. In the freight sector, the railway has launched a unit container train service for movement of export tea from plantations to port.

Motive power and rolling stock
In 1982 SLGR operated 106 diesel-electric, 103 diesel-hydraulic and nine diesel-mechanical locomotives; 84 steam locomotives; 69 diesel-hydraulic railcars; 1231 passenger cars; and 3988 freight cars. SLGR was taking delivery of 16 1000 hp diesel-electric Bo-Bos of 66 tonnes each built by Brush Electrical Machines Ltd with General Motors 645E engines; also of 200 steel-bodied passenger cars built on reconditioned underframes and bogies and of 190 new steel-bodied passenger cars, the latter from MecanoExportImport of Romania. Hyundai Rolling Stock Co Ltd of South Korea was supplying 58 tank wagons and 100 other new freight cars.

Civil engineering
A capacity enlargement scheme has been launched over the 14·5 km between Colombo Fort and Ragama. A third 1676 mm-gauge track is being installed, and at the same time a 7 km branch is being built from Kelaniya to an oil refinery near Sapuraskande.

Signalling
Work has begun on installation of a centralised traffic control system based on Colombo; in 1983 CTC territory was expected to reach as far as Polghawela, 73 km from the capital, on the line to the north-west. Double-line tracks operated by CTC are signalled with automatic block signals with a minimum headway of three minutes at an average speed of 48 km/h. BBC Brown Boveri has been commissioned to prepare a telecommunications modernisation plan.

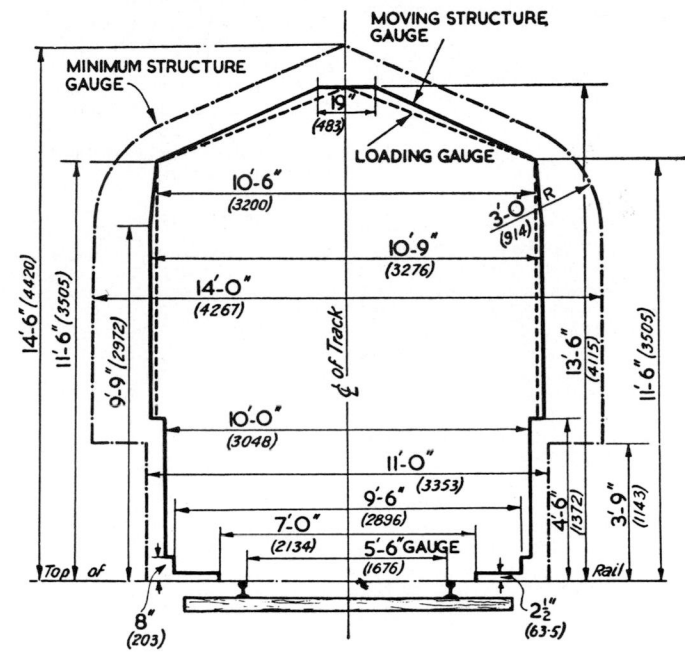

Diesel locomotives

Class	Wheel arrangement	Transmission	Rated power hp	Max lb (kg)	Continuous at lb (kg)	mph (km/h)	Max speed mph (km/h)	Wheel dia in	Total weight tons	Length ft in (mm)	No built	Year first built	Mechanical parts	Engine & type	Transmission
M1	A1A-A1A	Elec	1000	33 700 (15 300)	24 600 (11 160)	11·7 (18.8)	55	43	88	50' 9'' (15 469)	25	1953	Brush	Mirrlees JS12VT	Brush
M2	A1A-A1A	Elec	1425	35 840 (16 250)			55	40	79	46' 9'' (14 250)	10	1954	GM	GM 567C	GM
M2C	A1A-A1A	Elec	1425	44 240 (20 070)			55	40	79	43' 0'' (13 106)	2	1961	GM	GM	GM
G2	Bo-Bo	Elec	625	35 000 (15 875)	15 000 (6800)		20	43	54	37' 9'' (11 506)	8	1951	North British Loco Co	Paxman 12RPHXL	GEC
S2	Bo-Bo	Hyd	789				56	43	55	55' 0'' (16 764)	15	1959		Maybach MD 435	Maybach Mekydro K104U
S3 S4	Bo-Bo	Hyd	880				56	36	47	55' 0¾'' (16 780)	30	1959		MAN L12V 18/21	Maybach Mekydro K104U
N1	1-C-1	Hyd	492	20 150 (9040)			30	36	41	28' 0¾'' (8550)	5	1953		Deutz T8 M233	Krupp
P1	C (0-6-0)	Jack shaft & coupling rod drive	132	9000 (4080)			19·5	33	20	20' 2¾'' (6165)	4	1950	Hunslet	Ruston Hornsby	Hunslet Patent
T1	Bo	Elec	180				34	37	61' 0'' (18 593)	24	1947		English Electric Type 6H	English Electric
Y	C (0-6-0)	Hyd	550	29 900 (13 562)	1900 (5700)	6·0 (20)	26 (42)				28	1967	Hunslet	Rolls-Royce DV8T	Twin Disc CF 12800
W1		Hyd					50 (80)						Henschel		
W2		Hyd					50 (80)						VEB		

SUDAN

Ministry of Transport & Communications

Khartoum

Minister: Khalid Hassan Abbas

Sudan Railways (SRC)

PO Box 43, Atbara

Chairman: Ali Ameer Taha
General Manager: S Mohamed el Tayeb
Deputy General Managers
  Mohamed El Hassan Osman
  M Ahmed el Tayeb
Director of Civil Engineering: Abdelsalam el J Salih el Awad
Director of Traffic: Abdel Ghafour Tewfig
Director of Mechanical and Electrical Engineering: Ismail Ahmed Mahmoud

Gauge: 1067 mm
Route length: 4786 km

Transport development

The single-track railway used to be the main transport mode in Sudan, carrying nearly 75 per cent of the nation's passenger and freight traffic. But whereas in 1971 its share of a national total of 3693 million freight tonne-km was 2683 milion, by 1980 the railway was recording only 1908 million out of a total of 5818 million. Main reasons were the halving of cotton production (with concomitant diversion of a high tonnage of ground nuts, previously railed for export, to conversion into domestic cooking oil), development of well-surfaced roads between Port Sudan and Khartoum, and the railway's serious shortcomings.

SRC has been rigidly shackled by the Government to uncommercial rates dating from its years of transport monopoly for its staple freight traffic, so that in 1982 it was running at a deficit of S£24 million. The acute shortage of foreign currency has prevented purchase of spares, fuel and particularly lubricating oil, as well as deferring badly needed capital expenditure. Consequently in 1982 only half the stock of locomotives and passenger cars was seviceable, and on the trend of that year as much as two-thirds of the wagon fleet was likely to be un-usable by the end of 1983. In 1978-81 only 500 km of track were relaid.

By virtue of its location and extent, Sudan Railways forms an important part of the master plan for linking the African railway systems. The extension of the railway line from Nyala, the terminus of the western extension, to Geneina, near the border of Chad, would provide a future link with the railways of West Africa. The extension of the line from Dein, on the western extension, to Hofrat Elnahas, near the border of the Central African Republic would achieve the same purpose. Finally, by extending the railway line from Wau to Juba and then to Nimuli, near the border of Uganda, a link would be made with the railways of East Africa.

Motive power and rolling stock

In 1982 the railway owned about 30 serviceable steam locomotives and 272 diesel locomotives (though fewer than 150 were serviceable), nine diesel railcars, 5321 passenger cars and 6127 freight cars.

In 1982 delivery was completed of 20 2500 hp and 10 1650 hp diesel locomotives by Thyssen Henschel with GM engines and transmissions. Ten of the Class 1700 locomotives were purchased for the Livestock and Meat Marketing Corporation by the World Bank in 1981 and are supposedly assigned to LMMC block cattle trains.

Track

Standard rail: Flat bottom, 50 lb/yd (24·7 kg/m) in lengths of 30 ft (9·14 m); and 75 lb/yd (37·2 kg/m) in lengths of 36 ft (10·97 m); joined by fishplates and bolts. 90 lb BS rail for relaying Khartoum-Port Sudan line
Cross ties (sleepers): Steel; and wood impregnated under pressure in mixture of creosote and oil (½ and ½), 9 in × 5 in × 6 ft 6 in. Concrete used in a few cases as an experiment
Spacing: 1275/km under 36 ft long 75 lb rail, 1311/km under 30 ft long 50 lb rail (12 per rail)
Rail fastenings: 50 and 75 lb rails: screw spikes and elastic spikes
90 lb rail: clips and screw spikes. Pandrol fastenings in service under test
Steel sleepers: steel keys being replaced by clips with bolts and nuts

Filling: Generally earth, but some stretches of quarry spoil and ballast
Max curvature: (main line) 4·5° except few at 5·0°
Max gradient: 0·66% (1 in 150), except on section in Red Sea Hills between Summit and Port Sudan 1% (1 in 100). Gradient compensation for curves 0·04% per 1° curvature
Longest continuous gradient: Overall gradient from Port Sudan to Summit (129 km), 0·7%, with continuous 3·75 km of 0·98%. Only short level sections, including 3 stations, in whole 129 km
Worst combination of gradient and curvature: 1% grade with 4½° curve-radius of 388 m
Gauge widening on curves: ¼ in (6·4 mm) on curves of 4° and over
Super-elevation on sharpest curve: 3 in (76 mm) max
Rate of slope of super-elevation
¹/₆ in (4.2 mm) per rail length for curves under 3° = radius of 1910 ft (582 m)
⅓ in (8.4 mm) per rail length for curves of 3° and over
Max axleloading
75 lb track: 16½ tons
50 lb track: 12½ tons
Max bridge loading: 17 units BS
Max speed
50 lb track: 50 km/h
75 lb track: 60 km/h
Max altitude: 918·5 m at Summit station on Port Sudan line

Diesel locomotives

Series	Transmission	Wheel arrangement	Horsepower	No built	Builder	Year first built
100	Hyd	B	340	6	RSH	1962
400	Elec	C	300	3	English Electric/ Hawthorn Leslie	1936
403	Elec	C	350	5	English Electric/ Dick Kerr	1951
450	Hyd	D	350	4	Henschel	1958
460	Hyd	C	500	2	Henschel	1962-64
600	Hyd	C	650	30	Kawasaki	1968
700	Hyd	C	500	20	Henschel	1976
1000	Elec	Co-Co	1850	65	EE/Vulcan	1960-69
1200	Elec	Co-Co	1850	15	Cockerill	1961
1400	Elec	A1A-A1A	1500	2	Hitachi	1964
1500	Elec	A1A-A1A	1500	20	Hitachi	1969
1600	Hyd	B-B	1500	1	Henschel	1965
1601	Elec	Co-Co	1650	10	Henschel	1981
1700	Elec	Co-Co	1650	20	General Electric U15C	1975-81
1800	Elec	Co-Co	2300	20	General Electric U22C	1975
1900	Elec	Co-Co	2500	20	Henschel/ General Motors	1975
1950	Elec	Co-Co	2400	10	General Motors JT22LC-2	1981

SWAZILAND

Ministry of Works, Power & Communications

PO Box 58, Mbabane

Telephone: 422321

Minister: V G Leibrant
Permanent Secretary: G Mabila

Swaziland Railway (SR)

Swaziland Railway Building, Johnston Street, PO Box 475, Mbabane

Telephone: 42486
Telex: 2053

Chairman: J S Murphy
Chief Executive Officer: H D L Slabbert
Financial Director: D E Greenslade
Operating Manager: G S Coates
Chief Civil Engineer: H L Moffatt
Chief Mechanical Engineer: K Mathur

Gauge: 1067 mm
Route length: 455 km

Transport development

Swaziland's railway was completed in 1964. It is a corporate body established under the Swaziland Proclamation of 1962 and managed by a Railway Board appointed by the Minister of Works, Power and Communications. The main route is from Ka Dake to Goba (310 km), with lines from Phuzumoya to Lavumisa/Golela (92 km) and Mpaka to Komati Poort (55 km).

Traffic

	1980/81	1981/82
Freight tonnage (million)	1·233	1·211
Freight tonne-km (million)	143·2	137·8

Finances

	1980/81	1981/82
	(Emalangeni million)	
Revenue	7·163	9·130
Expenses	8·594	10·039

Motive power and rolling stock

Twelve Type 14R steam locomotives leased from South African Transport Services, two diesel locomotives and 854 freight wagons.

Civil engineering

In February 1981 Swaziland's parliament approved construction of a 120 km link from Mpaka to Komati

Poort in the eastern Transvaal; 55 km will be in Swaziland and 61 km in South Africa. The line will provide a through north-south line across Swaziland using the Mpaka-Phuzumoya section of the Ka Dake-Mlawula line and the 95 km Phuzumoya-Golela southern link to South African Transport Services. Traffic expected for the line includes minerals and ores from eastern Transvaal. Phosphoric acid, fruit and timber will also be carried. Tenders for construction of the Swaziland section were being sought in late 1982. Also under discussion is the upgrading of the east-west line crossing the

Mozambique border at Lomanhasha, for access to the port of Maputo.

Track	Ka Dake-Goba	Phuzumoya-Golela
Rail	40 kg/m	48 kg/m
	(sidings 30 kg/m)	
Sleepers	hardwood	concrete
Thickness	127 mm	200 mm
Spacing	814 mm	700 mm
Fastenings	soleplates and coachscrews	first BBR
Welded rail	126 km	92 km

SWEDEN

Ministry of Transport & Communications

Vasagatan 8-10, 103 33 Stockholm

Telephone: 8763 1000
Telex: 17328

Minister: Curt Boström
Under-Secretary: Monica Sundström
Secretary-General: Barbo Fischerström

Swedish State Railways (SJ)
Statens Järnvägar

105 50 Stockholm C

Telephone: 46 87622000
Telegrams: Statsbanan, Stockholm
Telex: 19410

General Manager: Bengt Furbäck
Chief Officers
Freight: E Sundén
Passenger: B Hammarberg
Train Operations: Y Gelotte
Economics and Corporate Planning: P Jönsson
Personnel: T Persson
Finance and Purchasing: M Högberg
Fixed Installations: P G Andersson
Rolling Stock: B Marklund
Information and PR: H Rosengren

Gauge: 1435 mm; 891 mm
Route length: 11 424 km; 326 km
Electrification: 7094 km at 15 kV 16⅔ Hz ac

Transport development
In per capita terms, Sweden has the largest railway length in Europe (1·5 km of track per 1000 inhabitants) in spite of numerous branch line closures during the 1970s.

Policy control of the Swedish State Railways (SJ) is exercised by a Board consisting of eight members under the chairmanship of the Director General. Seven members are appointed by the Government. The heads of the nine departments and the Director General constitute the Directorate (consultative function).

Government policy
In 1982-83 Government and railway management undertook a fundamental reappraisal of SJ's financing, administrative structure and services. The main reasons were the recession's traumatic impact on a railway which previously relied on bulk raw material

hauls in its freight sector (its 1983/84 Lappland ore traffic forecasts, for instance, were for only 11 million tonnes as against 30 million tonnes a few years before) and a dwindling return from SJ's adventurous across-the-board passenger fare cuts of 1979.

Over much of Sweden the rail service is tenable only as a state-funded social service. The country is Europe's fourth largest in land area, yet its population of just over 8 million is less than Greater London's, and 90 per cent of the people live below the Gothenburg-Sundsvall diagonal. The majority of SJ's 11 700 km network which carries a meagre 8 per cent of its total traffic is frankly treated as a social service. Here SJ operates on a contractual basis to levels prescribed by the Government, which by law covers the deficit, amounting to SKr 864 million in the 1981/82 financial year. Over the rest of the system SJ is obliged to operate commercially and viably, apart from a government compensation for statutory fare concessions to special passenger categories such as students and pensioners.

SJ's self-sufficiency extends to funding a higher proportion of its investment from its own resources than any other Western European national railway except British Rail. And as well as providing for depreciation on replacement costs, it has to pay an annual interest of 13 per cent on the substantial state capital in the rail system. By 1982 it was financially incapable of fulfilling either obligation.

The consultant firm McKinsey was called in and reported to the Transport Minister in June 1982. In one respect the report disappointed railwaymen by skating over the difficult ground of realistic attribution of costs between commercial and social sector balance sheets where SJ's two kinds of service share use of assets. At least 30 per cent of SJ's total costs are considered to be shared.

Even after its key recommendations had been carried out, McKinsey could see no future hope of SJ's commercial sector meeting its full solvency obligations. As a result, the Government proposed a financial reconstruction of SJ. A Bill laid before the Riksdag in 1983 advocated cutting state capital in SJ by a third, or about SKr 1000 million; the transfer of ten more unprofitable routes aggregating 938 km from the commercial to the social sector, which

Class Rc5 490 hp electric locomotive

Class T44 diesel-electric locomotive built by Nohab

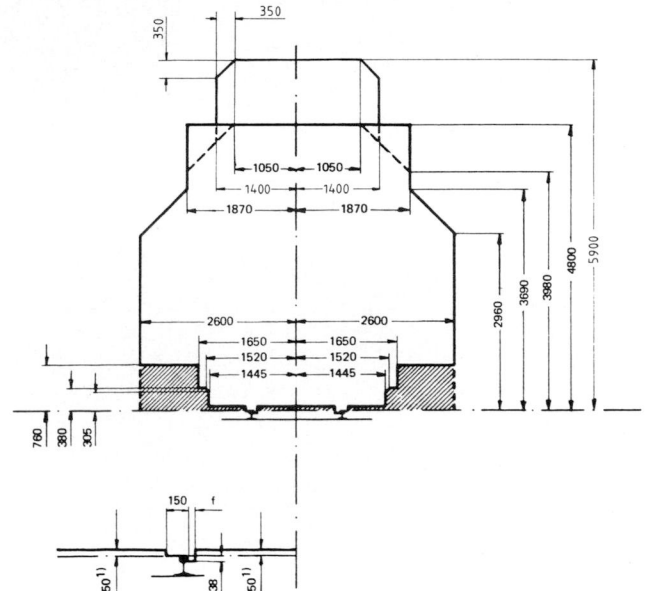

would reduce SJ's commercial sector to only 37 per cent of total route-km; and state assumption of decision-making and total or at least partial responsibility for future major investment in SJ's infrastructure. A complete state takeover of the rail infrastructure was considered but rejected.

The forecast effect of these suggestions on SJ's 1983/84 budget, was: first, state support of SKr 1463 million instead of SKr 995 million for social sector operations; second, a reduction of interest and depreciation provisions by some SKr 450 million in total. Thus instead of a prospective deficit of some SKr 470 million SJ could look forward to breaking even after meeting financial charges if the proposals are implemented.

The first of McKinsey's major criticisms was that in both passenger and freight business the rail effort was short on saleable quality and lacked marketing thrust. The latter was answered in February 1983 by a comprehensive SJ management reorganisation. In each of the railway's eight administrative regions (Malmö, Gothenburg, Norrköping, Stockholm, Örebro, Gävle, Sundsvall and Lulea), operating and sales functions were reshaped as unitary marketing departments, each under a marketing chief with direct responsibility to SJ's general manager.

Freight

Freight is the sector in which SJ has accepted the major challenge in a 1981 agreement with the then Government to work for viability within two years, in exchange for a guaranteed real growth of investment funds over the ensuing five years. Until the 1980s SJ's freight results have been heavily dependent on ore movement from the deposits in the north of the country. It has accounted for around 40 per cent of all hauled tonnage, so that the worldwide slump in steel production was the prime factor in a slide of SJ's gross freight tonnage from 57·6 million to 45·1 million tonnes and of its total freight tonne-km from 16 600 million to just over 14 400 million between financial years 1979/80 and 1981/82.

A determined drive for high-rated merchandise freight has been mounted to make SJ less sensitive to heavy industrial fluctuations and has already chalked up some marked successes. The Swedish Parliament has supported SJ's bid for intermodal traffic in particular by voting finance for a discounted rate for consistent intermodal customers. In 1981 a special tariff was on offer to clients despatching more than 110 containers or road semi-trailers a year on out-and-back transits between SJ terminals. In 1982 SJ was operating 37 container terminals, of which 16 were equipped with 30-tonne gantry cranes, the remainder with sideloaders or fork-lifts of 10-25 tonnes' capacity. SJ itself has a stock of some 600 20-foot containers, 600 7·15-metre demountable bodies and 160 platform containers for clients' use.

In the late 1970s SJ added piggybacking of road freight trailers to its intermodal techniques, employing top-lift loading of pouched-frame wagons. Besides domestic services between Stockholm and both Oslo and Gothenburg it co-operates with Norwegian State Railways (NSB) in the operation of through trains between Oslo and both Gothenburg and Stockholm which offer assured overnight transits.

SJ's biggest challenge in the freight sector is adjusting to fundamental changes in the Swedish economy. Industry is moving into more developed production, for example, to local output of paper instead of just pulp for its manufacture, so that its freight is of smaller volume but demands more sophisticated transport. SJ therefore needs urgently to build up a fleet of special-purpose wagons. Its present wagon fleet is mostly of conventional open and box types, too big and poorly

utilised. By 1987 SJ aims to invest in 6000 new freight wagons from its own resources. But it hopes to encourage more customer investment in private wagon ownership as the rail product develops.

The largely pulp, paper and timber industry flow to north-west Europe is seen as a ripe market for the railways. Short-sea shipping, SJ's chief competitor, has a problem of ageing vessels; and road haul has become expensive. SJ would like to change the latter to an intermodal exercise, especially in view of a major McKinsey recommendation that the railway strive for more intermodal business.

SJ's four existing train ferry routes do not match up to the north-west Europe market specification. That from Trelleborg to Sassnitz, in the German Democratic Republic, recently re-equipped with an 800-passenger ferry embodying 700 metres of track on its rail deck, lacks spare capacity. The remaining options are via the Helsingborg-Helsingör or Malmö-Copenhagen routes into Denmark. However the ferry link span on the first of these routes cannot accept loaded piggyback flatcars, a technique which SJ holds to be a key to deeper market penetration; and thereafter the rail route into West Germany is either an uncompetitively lengthy one via Flensburg, or via the Rødby-Puttgarden train ferries, which have track room only for a string of five wagons. With a potential 5 million tonnes of West German traffic to be won in the Sundsvall region alone, SJ must plan for full trainload operation throughout to be competitive. Hence the economic studies were almost completed in early 1983 for the launch of a new high-capacity train ferry operation between Trelleborg and Travemünde. SJ would

Class Y1 diesel-hydraulic railcar, used primarily on non-commercial SJ network

Stockholm-Gothenburg 'City Express' conference saloon

265 hp Class V5 diesel-hydraulic locomotive by Henschel

Wagon class H bis

open the Trelleborg-Travemünde service with a chartered road ferry offering a deck capable, after conversion, of housing at least 400 metres and perhaps up to 600 metres of rail tracks. The objective is a regular piggyback train operation to and from the Ruhr's Neuss railhead, where connection would be made with piggyback trains to and from south Germany, Basle and perhaps France as well.

SJ has been preparing for a major role in coal movement, since Sweden anticipates importation of some 6 million tonnes a year by the end of the 1980s. The difficulty here will be to persuade customers to invest in railhead discharge equipment that will maximise the economy of trainload working with modern high-capacity wagons. SJ recognises that it will have to develop hopper wagon designs equipped to safeguard their loads from icing up in the depth of winter; electric heating of the wagon bodysides is the likely method.

Finances
To finance the cheap passenger fare scheme, Sweden's Parliament voted to assume part of the fixed costs of the rail network. Thus for the fiscal year 1981/82 the railway was relieved of capital costs amounting to SKr 264 million (comprising SKr 180 million in depreciation and SKr 84 million in financial charges).

Passenger traffic
A restructure of the passenger service was begun in 1983 following reappraisals of the 1979 cheap fare scheme's results. These showed that the slight first-class market gains of 1980 had not been held, whereas the domestic airlines were steadily increasing traffic; and that the upward trend in second-class rail travel had also been halted. The long-haul service would therefore be reshaped in three categories: a premium-fare, first class-only, limited-stop 'City Express' operation in peak business hours on a few key routes radiating from Stockholm where the railway was reasonably speed-competitive with air, supplemented by a comparable night service on one or two others that were speed-handicapped, such as Stockholm-Sundsvall; a regular-interval dual-class express service probably modelled on the German Federal IC operation; and market-oriented cheap-fare trains, run principally at week-ends, to maximise potential in the 'bargain-hunting' travel market.

The first fruit of the new policy was the February 1983 inception of a Stockholm-Gothenburg 'City-Express', twice each way daily, non-stop on one working and one-stop on the others, covering the 456 km in 4 hours 5-10 minutes. Train-sets of 1960s-vintage first-class cars, including armchair saloons, were refurbished for the service, which additionally offered fully audio-visually equipped conference rooms, telephone service, diner catering styled by a prominent Stockholm restaurateur and hostess service.

SJ operates passenger traffic by train partly on its own account (mainly long-distance) and partly under contract to regional authorities (especially commuter services around Stockholm, Gothenburg and Malmö). In 1981/82 SJ's own traffic amounted to 22·6 million journeys (−3 per cent) and 5430 million passenger-km (−4 per cent); while services operated under contract totalled 54 million journeys (−1 per cent) and 1180 million passenger-km (−0 per cent). Compared with 1980/81 the number of passengers in long-distance trains dipped by 2 per cent; first-class decreased by 7 per cent.

Traction and rolling stock
In 1981 SJ received Government approval to obtain three prototype six-car train-sets with an automatic body-tilting system. Although these T200 train-sets will not be able to exploit their 200 km/h top speed on more than a third of SJ's trunk route mileage, their higher curving speed without passenger discomfort is expected to secure journey time savings between Stockholm and Malmö of 1½ hours and between Stockholm and Gothenburg or Sundsvall of an hour. The three prototypes will be tested for two years between Stockholm and Gothenburg, a journey on which they are forecast to average 150 km/h throughout, before production orders are placed. The first route to be taken over by the high-speed trains would be Stockholm-Gothenburg, not until 1990 at the earliest, followed by Stockholm-Malmö, Stockholm-Sundsvall and Gothenburg-Malmö. Several tenders for the prototype train-sets were being evaluated early in 1983. SJ envisages a unit with a total power output of about 3000 kW, with motors under simple thyristor control, with the second and fifth cars in each set motored; a maximum car weight of 60 tonnes and axleloading of 15 tonnes has been specified.

At the end of 1982 SJ was taking delivery of 40 ASEA-built, thyristor-controlled Class Rc5 electric

Class X10 emu in violet and blue livery for southern Sweden operation

Class X10 emu interior

Traffic	1979/80	1980/81	1981/82	1982/83
Freight tonnage (million)	57·6	49·4	45·1	40·3
Tonne-km (million)	16 580	15 030	14 425	13 545
Passenger-km (million)	6632	6824	6610	6392
Passenger journeys (million)	73·8	78·1	76·6	75·1

Bo-Bos, 18 Class T44 1670 hp diesel-electrics and 34 Type X10 emus, 25 for the Stockholm commuter area and nine for south Sweden. Internally revised, the X10 design was envisaged as a probable replacement for the now outdated X5, X8 and X9 emus on longer-haul workings in the Malmö and Gothenburg areas, though for a number of duties the respective merits of mu and push-pull operation are being debated. No decision had yet been taken on the diesel railcar type to replace a number of units reaching life-expiry.

A Volvo hydrostatic transmission has been under test in two Type Z65 diesel shunters and also in a Type Y1 diesel railcar.

Renewal of the freight wagon fleet has a major claim on SJ's enlarged investment resources. In 1982 stocks included over 800 flat wagons specially fitted with a long-stroke (760 mm) shock absorber for container conveyance and more were being procured. By mid-1982 SJ was deploying over 4000 of its Type Hbis standard sliding-door covered van; taring 15 tonnes, an Hbis has a payload capacity of 25 tonnes, and a proportion of the stock is fitted internally with movable transverse partitions so that palletised goods can be loaded in two layers.

SJ is also refining its steel-carrying equipment. Deliveries in 1982 included 151 new four-axle wagons for conveyance of slabs, billets and blooms, each with a payload capacity of 67·5 tonnes.

At the start of 1982 SJ operated:

	Line-haul	Shunting
Electric locomotives	626	116
Diesel-electric locomotives	152	—
Diesel-hydraulic locomotives	23	379
Electric railcars		35
Diesel railcars		216
Electric trailer cars		35
Diesel trailer cars		20
Electric multiple-units		127
Diesel multiple-units		5
Passenger train coaches		1630
Freight train cars		42 730

Investment
Several extensive infrastructure projects are under investigation. In the Stockholm region a new pair of tracks is planned from Älvsjö to Flemingsberg

(8 km) in the south, and from Karlberg to Ulriksdal (6 km) in the north, to cope with rising commuter traffic managed by SL, the Greater Stockholm public transport company. Cost is estimated at SKr 640 million. An almost complete reconstruction of the track system at Stockholm Central is also needed; this and a rebuilding of Hagalunds yard (the maintenance and service station in Stockholm) will cost about SKr 260 million. Neither project can be financed from SJ's resources and execution depends on political decision and subvention.

In a second phase there is need of a further 28 km of new double-track southwards to Flemingsberg. This new line would either follow a new route via Grödinge to Järna or alternatively the existing alignment to Södertälje; the former would allow easier curvature. This scheme would cost SKr 1000 million.

In the northern part of the country work has already started on the first 14 km of double-track between Ånge and Bräcke (30 km). This project is budgeted at SKr 150 million and will be completed in 1986.

Traffic on the Gothenburg-Malmö line has reached the limit of single-track capacity. Economical and technical feasibility studies for double-tracking and realignment to secure higher passenger speed would be completed in early 1983.

At Helsingborg studies have been undertaken with a view to expanding the ferry berths and concentrating operation at one new station, to replace the present two. A fixed link with Denmark via a tunnel between Helsingborg and Helsingör is still under consideration, but the Swedish and Danish governments have not agreed it.

Signalling
By the start of 1983 automatic train control (ATC) was operative over 1500 km of route and by the end of 1984 all remaining major lines would be equipped with the system. Extension of CTC continues at a rate of about 40 km per year.

Another urgent problem is the great number of level crossings, totalling nearly 23 000, though only 6000 are on lines in SJ's commercial sector. Great efforts are made to reduce the number drastically and about 500 were to be closed in 1983, either through construction of new roads or through supersession by bridges. Smaller crossings can generally be closed by an agreement with the owner.

Civil engineering
In 1982 about 230 km of track was renewed and the total length of continuously welded tracks was about 5000 km at the end of the year. All renewal is now with SJ50 rails (50 kg/m) and concrete sleepers. Two systems of fastenings are used, Pandrol and a Swedish type, Hambo. The Hey-Back system with wooden sleepers is almost abandoned due to cost. Some secondary line has been renewed with reconditioned SJ43 rails and wooden sleepers with spikes. In sidings and on industrial lines lighter rail sections are used, but they are in decline. No further track is being built with these rail sections.

Normal sleeper spacing on SJ main tracks is 650 mm, sufficient for a 20-tonne axleload. The spacing is 600 mm on curves with a radius below 1000 metres and 550 mm if the radius is less than 500 metres. An even smaller sleeper spacing of 500 mm is used on the heaviest loaded freight line in the north, where the axleload is 25 tonnes and the annual gross tonnage is up to 50 million.

Track
Standard rail: Type SJ 50, 50 kg/m
Cross ties (sleepers)
Concrete
Type B10: 320 × 222 × 2500 mm
Type S3: 320 × 220 × 2500 mm
Wooden
Type 1: 240 × 165 × 2600 mm
Type 2: 220 × 155 × 2600 mm
Rail fastenings: Wooden sleepers: Hey-Back
Type B10: Concrete sleepers, Hambo
Type S3: Pandrol
Sleeper spacing
Main lines: 650 mm; 1538 per km
Secondary lines: 750 mm; 133 per km
Spacing reduced to 500 mm on Kiruna-Riksgränsen ore line

Ferries
The Swedish State Railways is linked to the continental railway network by four ferry routes: Helsingborg-Helsingör (DSB), Malmö-Copenhagen (DSB), Trelleborg-Sassnitz (DR) and Ystad-Swinoujscie (PKP). Two of these are freight only, the Copenhagen and the Swinoujscie crossings. Swedish ferries operate the Copenhagen (one ferry) and Sassnitz routes (two or three ferries). On the Trelleborg-Sassnitz route a new 800-passenger

Revenues (SKr million)	1979/80	1980/81	1981/82
Passengers and baggage			
(excluding bus and local ferry)	1467	1647	1909
Average receipt per passenger-km (SKr)	0·221	0·241	0·289
Freight (excluding mail)	2639	2799	2910
Average receipt per freight ton-km (SKr)	0·159	0·186	0·202
Compensation for operating unprofitable lines	720	788	864
Bus traffic	411	520	653
Miscellaneous receipts	485	487	516
Total	5722	6241	6852
Expenses (SKr million)			
Staff and personnel	3923	4200	4524
Materials and services	1531	1649	1839
Depreciation*	498	829	935
Financial charges*‡	162	177	229
Total	5952	6678	7527
Deficit for the year		437	445

* After deduction for relief of capital costs
‡ Interest on state capital not shown

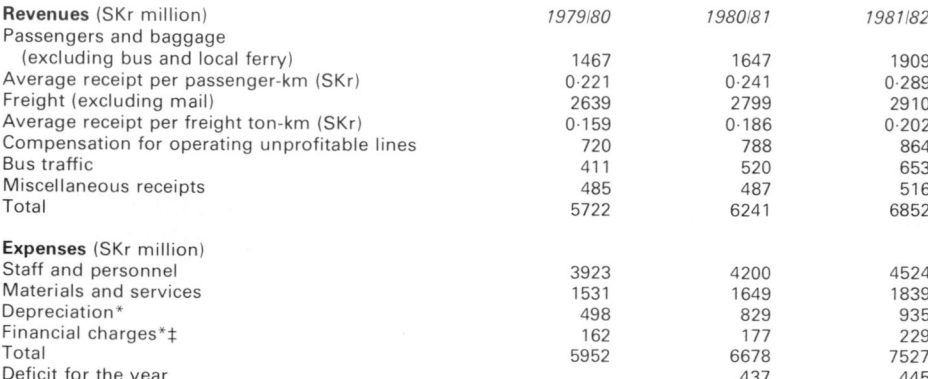

Stockholm Aarsta intermodal terminal

Alpha-numerical operator's console and vdus in Gothenburg computer-based interlocking centre

ferry entered service in 1982, with a length of 170 metres, width 23 metres and track capacity 700 metres.

Buses
SJ operates 1550 buses over 22 000 km. In 1982 the bus fleet recorded 90 million bus-km.

Electric railcars

Class	Wheel arrangement	Line current	Rated output hp	Max kg	Tractive effort (full field) Continuous at kg	kmlh	Max speed kmlh	Wheel dia mm	Weight tonnes	Length mm	No built (on order)	Year first built	Builders Mechanical parts	Electrical equipment
X1	Bo-Bo + 2'2'	15 kV 16⅔ Hz	1500	10 500	6300	71·3	120	920	79	49 550	104	1967	KVAB, ASJ Lp	ASEA
X5	2-Bo + 2'2' + Bo-2	15 kV 16⅔ Hz	1360	7900	3800	90·9	135	900	136	72 200	6	1948	Kockum, ASJ Lp	ASEA
X6	2'2' + Bo-Bo + 2' 2'	15 kV 16⅔ Hz	1500	12 200	5900	66·6	100	966	145	73 720	3	1960	Kockum, ASJ Ar	ASEA
X7	2-Bo	15 kV 16⅔ Hz	600	5900	2600	60·7	90	800	47	22 650	26	1949	ASJ Lp	ASEA
X8	2-Bo + 2'2' + 2'2' + Bo-2	15 kV 16⅔ Hz	1360	7900	3800	90·9	135	900	167	87 610	2	1947	ASEA	ASEA
X9	1A-A1	15 kV 16⅔ Hz	230	1800	850	74·5	115	676	26/21	17 500	46	1960	HC (Hilding Carlsson)	ASEA
X10	Bo-B + 2'2'	15 kV 16⅔ Hz	1550	10 600	5200	90	140	920	100	49 868	7 (18)	1982	Hägglunds	ASEA
X16	B-2	15 kV 16⅔ Hz	230	1850	900	72·2	110	676	21	17 550	18	1955	ASJ Ar	ASEA
X17	B-2								21	17 550	12	1955	ASJ Ar	ASEA

Electric locomotives

Class	Wheel arrangement	Line current	Rated output hp	Max lb (kg)	Tractive effort (full field) Continuous at lb (kg)	mph (kmlh)	Max speed mph (kmlh)	Wheel dia in (mm)	Weight tonnes	Length ft in (mm)	No built (on order)	Year first built	Builders Mechanical parts	Electrical equipment
Da	1-C-1	15 kV 16⅔ Hz	2500	45 200 (20 500)	21 200 (9600)	43·2 (69·5)	62 (100)	60¼ (1530)	75	42' 8'' (13 000)	93	1952	Nohab; ASJ; Motala	ASEA
Du	1-C-1	15 kV 16⅔ Hz	2500	34 600 (15 700)	21 100 (9600)	43·2 (69·5)	62 (100)	60¼ (1530)	80·4	42' 8'' (13 000)	237	1925	Nohab; ASJ; Motala	ASEA
Dm	1-D+D-1	15 kV 16⅔ Hz	5600 / 6500	137 000 (62 000) / 137 000 (62 000)	63 500 (28 800) / 63 500 (28 800)	32·4 (51·8) / 37 (59)	47 (75) / 47 (75)	60¼ (1530) / 60¼ (1530)	180-186.4 / 190	82' 3¾'' (25 100)	19	1953 1971	Nohab; ASJ; Motala	ASEA
Dm3	1-D+D+ D-1	15 kV 16⅔ Hz	8400	205 000 (93 000)	96 000 (43 500)	32·4 (51·8)	47 (75)	60¼ (1530)	258.4	115' 8'' (32 250)	3	1960	Nohab; ASJ; Motala	ASEA
Dm3	1-D+D+ D-1	15 kV 16⅔ Hz	9750	205 000 (93 000)	96 000 (43 500)	37 (59)	47 (75)	60¼ (1530)	273.2	115' 8'' (35 250)	15*	1967	Nohab; ASJ; Motala	ASEA
F	1-Do-1	15 kV 16⅔ Hz	3500	44 500 (20 200)	20 000 (9100)	58·7 (94·5)	84 (135)	60¼ (1530)	102	49' 11¾'' (15 230)	24	1942	Nohab; ASJ; Motala	ASEA
Hg	Bo-Bo	15 kV 16⅔ Hz	1760	40 200 (18 300)	18 500 (8400)	34·1 (54·9)	50 (80)	43¼ (1100)	64·8	41' 0'' (12 500)	55	1942	Nohab; ASJ; Motala	ASEA
Ma	Co-Co	15 kV 16⅔ Hz	4500	82 500 (37 400)	36 800 (16 700)	44·4 (71·5)	63 (100)	51⅛ (1300)	105	55' 1½'' (16 800)	32	1953	Nohab; ASJ; Motala	ASEA
Ra	Bo-Bo	15 kV 16⅔ Hz	3600	43 200 (19 600)	20 000 (9100)	65·5 (104·5)	93 (150)	51⅛ (1300)	64	49' 6½'' (15 100)	10	1955	Nohab; ASJ; Motala	ASEA
Rc1	Bo-Bo	15 kV 16⅔ Hz	4900	61 700 (28 000)	34 600 (15 700)	49 (78·8)	84 (135)	51⅛ (1300)	80	50' 9'' (15 470)	20	1967	Nohab; ASJ; Motala	ASEA
Rc2	Bo-Bo	15 kV 16⅔ Hz	4900	61 700 (28 000)	34 600 (15 700)	49 (78·8)	84 (135)	51⅛ (1300)	77	50' 11'' (15 520)	100	1969	Nohab; ASJ; Motala	ASEA
Rc3	Bo-Bo	15 kV 16⅔ Hz	4900	52 900 (24 000)	31 900 (14 500)	57 (91·8)	100 (160)	51⅛ (1300)	77	50' 11'' (15 520)	10	1970	Nohab; ASJ; Motala	ASEA
Rc4	Bo-Bo	15 kV 16⅔ Hz	4900	61 700 (28 000)	34 600 (15 700)	48·5 (78)	84 (135)	51⅛ (1300)	78	50' 9'' (15 470)	121	1975-81	Nohab; KVAB	ASEA
Rc5	Bo-Bo	15 kV 16⅔ Hz	4900	61 700 (28 000)	34 600 (15 700)	48·5 (78)	84 (135)	51⅛ (1300)	78	50' 11'' (15 520)	4 (36)	1982	Hägglunds	ASEA
Rm	Bo-Bo	15 kV 16⅔ Hz		65 000 (31 400)	50 600 (23 000)	34·2 (55)	63 (100)	49¼ (1250)	92	50' 11'' (15 570)	6	1977	Nohab	ASEA
Ub	C	15 kV 16⅔ Hz	700	29 800 (13 500)	16 700 (7600)	15·5 (25)	28 (45)	43¼ (1100)	47·4	31' 6'' (9600)	90	1930	Nohab; Motala	ASEA
Uc	C	15 kV 16⅔ Hz	700	29 800 (13 500)	16 700 (7600)	15·5 (25)	28 (45)	43¼ (1100)	49·2	31' 6'' (9600)	1	1933	Nohab	ASEA
Ud	C	15 kV 16⅔ Hz	840	28 600 (13 000)	15 200 (6900)	20 (32)	37 (60)	43¼ (1100)	50·4	31' 6'' (9600)	25	1955	Nohab; ASJ; Motala	ASEA

Notes: Class Du, rebuilt from Dg, Dk and Ds
Class Rc, thyristor control
* Rebuilt from Class Dm to Dm3

Diesel railcars

Class	Wheel arrangement	Trans- mission	Rated power hp	Max kg	Tractive effort Continuous at kg	kmlh	Max speed kmlh	Wheel dia mm	Total weight tonnes	Length mm	No built	Year first built	Builders Mechanical parts	Engine & type	Transmission
Y1/YF1	1A-A1	Hyd	400	6900	—	—	130	920	45	24 400	100	1979-81	Fiat	Fiat 8217.12	Fiat SRM
Y3	Bo-Bo	Hyd	1240	12 600	—	—	140	920	64	19 620	6	1966	LHB	KHD BF12M716	Voith and Gmeinder
Y6-Y8	B-2	Mech & Hyd	200	2050	—	—	115	670	19	17 550	272	1953	Hägglund ASJ Linköping KVAB Elcsiöverken	Scania Vabis D815	Vulcan Sinclair, Wilson

Diesel locomotives

Class	Wheel arrangement	Transmission	Rated power hp	Max lb (kg)	Tractive effort Continuous at lb (kg)	mph (km/h)	Max speed mph (km/h)	Wheel dia max (mm)	Axle load tonnes	Total weight tonnes	Length ft in (mm)	No built (on order)	Year first built	Builders Mechanical parts	Engine & type	Transmission
T21	D	Hyd	800	41 200 (18 700)	26 500 (12 000)	7·5 (12)	50 (80)	49⅜ (1255)	14·2	57	37' 1" (11 300)	51 3	1955 1956	MaK ASJ	MaK MA 301A	Voith and MaK
T42	Bo-Bo	Elec	1445	47 600 (21 600)	25 300 (11 500)	14·3 (23)	62 (100)	40 (1015)	18	72	47' 3" (14 400)	1	1954	GM	GM 12-567C	GM
T43	Bo-Bo	Elec	1445	47 600 (21 600)	28 200 (12 800)	14·3 (23)	59 (95)	40 (1015)	18	72	46' 8¾" (14 240)	50	1961	Nohab	GM 12-567 D1	ASEA (GM licence)
T44	Bo-Bo	Elec	1670	48 600 (22 100)	36 000 (16 500)	11 (17)	56 (90)	40½ (1030)	19	76	50' 6¼" (15 400)	90 (18)	1968	Nohab	GM 12-645E	GM
Tb snow-plough	Bo-Bo	Elec	1670	48 600 (22 100)	36 000 (16 500)	11 (17)	59 (95)	40½ (1030)	18	72	50' 6½" (15 400)	10	1969	Nohab	GM 12-645E	GM
Tc snow-plough	B	Hyd	625	19 400 (8800)	13 700 (6200)	8 (13)	56 (90)	38¾ (985)	16	32	46' 8¾" (14 200)	20	1969	Nohab	KHD BF 12M 716	Voith and Gmeinder
Tp	1-C-1	Hyd	750	23 800 (10 800)	18 700 (8500)	7·5 (12)	40 (65)	43¼ (1100)	10	46	35' 1¼" (10 700)	10	1954	MaK	MaK MA 301A	Voith and MaK
V4	C	Hyd	265	34 800 (15 800)	30 400 (13 800)	3·1 (5)	43 (70)	38¾ (985)	16	48	33' 9½" (10 300)	10	1972	Henschel	Deutz BF12M717	Voith and Gmeinder
V5	C	Hyd	265	34 800 (15 800)	30 400 (13 800)	3·1 (5)	43 (70)	38¾ (985)	16	48	34' 11" (10 640)	40	1975	Henschel	Deutz BF12M717	Voith and Gmeinder
Z4p	B	Hyd	160	10 300 (4700)			25 (40)	30 (760)	7	14	21' 0" (6400)	25 14	1950 1956	Kalmar Verkstads	Scania Vabis D812	Atlas Diesel and Kalmar Verkstads
Z43	B	Hyd	160	14 500 (6600)			34 (55)	38⅛ (970)	10	20	28' 10½" (8800)	52 64	1951 1958	Kockums Mek Kalmar Verkstads	Scania Vabis D812	Atlas Diesel and Kalmar Verkstads
Z64	B	Hyd	240	20 500 (9300)			33 (53)	33½ (850)	14	28	24' 2¼" (7370)	35	1953	Klöckner Humboldt Deutz	Deutz T4M 625	Voith and KHD
Z65	B	Hyd	295	20 500 (9300)			37 (60)	38¾ (985)	14	28	30' 3¾" (9240)	102	1962	Kalmar Verkstads	Rolls-Royce C8TFL MK IV	Twin Disc and Deutsche Getriebe Gesellschaft
Z66	B	Hyd	295	21 160 (9600)			43 (70)	38¾ (985)	16	32	33' 9½" (10 300)	30	1971	Kalmar Verkstads	KHD F12 M 716	Voith and Gmeinder
Z67	B	Hyd	381	18 900 (8600)			43 (70)	38¾ (985)	15	30	30' 6" (9300)	3 28	1978 1981	Gmeinder Hägglunds	Cummins KT-1150-L	Voith and Gmeinder

Note: Class Tp, Z4p 891 mm gauge
Class Z67 rebuilt from Z61, Z62 and Z63 locomotives

TGOJ Railways
Gränges TGOJ

Eskilstuna

Telephone: 016 13785
Telex: 46081

Chairman: M Värmon
General Manager: R Johanson

Gauge: 1435 mm
Length: 300 km
Electrification: 300 km at 15 kV 16⅔ Hz ac

The railway, which operates in central Sweden, owns 32 electric locomotives, 13 emus, six diesel locomotives and 2043 freight wagons. Its main route is entirely under CTC control.

Nordmark Klarälvens Railways
Nordmark Klarälvens Järnvägar

Hagfors

Telephone: 0563 11000

Chairman: S Gyll

Managing Director: R Kihlberg
Motive Power Superintendent: L Carell

Gauge: 891 mm; mixed 891/1435 mm
Length: 100 km; 10 km
Electrification: 110 km at 16 kV 16⅔ Hz ac

The railway, which operates in west central Sweden

between Hagfors, Munkfors and Karlstad, operates six ASJ/ASEA 900 hp, 35·2-tonne electric and four 180 hp diesel-hydraulic shunters, all 891 mm gauge, together with 458 freight wagons. Track employs 24·8-43 kg/m rail, minimum curve radius is 250 metres, maximum gradient 1·45 per cent, and maximum axleloading 12 tonnes (20 tonnes on 1435 mm gauge).

SWITZERLAND

Ministry of Transport, Communications & Power

Berne

Minister: W Ritschard

Swiss Federal Railways
Schweizerische Bundesbahnen (SBB)
Chemins de Fer Fédéraux Suisses (CFF)
Ferrovie Federali Svizzere (FFS)

Hochschulstrasse 6, 3030 Berne

Telephone: 60 11 11
Telegrams: Fervojo, Berne
Telex: 32500

Railways Board of Administration
Chairman: Carlos Grosjean
Members
Werner Meier
Franco Robbiani
Karl Bolfing
Jean Babel
Pierre Arnold
Hans Munz
Max Rüegg
Alfred E Sarasin
Jakob Stucki
Jean-Pascal Delamuraz
Paul Biderbost
Bernardo Lardi
Kurt Schweizer
Arthur Schmid
Secretary: Dr Arnold Schärer
President and Manager of Financial and Staff Dept:
Ing Roger Desponds
Departmental Managers
 Traffic Department: Hans Eisenring

Technical Department: Dr Werner Latscha
Heads of Divisions
 Secretariat: Dr Arnold Schärer
 Organisation and Planning: Hans Walter
 Financial: Heinz Diemant
 Personnel: Karl Hartmann
 Medical: Dr Rudolf Gränicher
 Legal: Dr Eric Bertherin
 Passenger Traffic: Samuel Ed Berthoud
 Freight Traffic: Vacant
 Traffic Control: Jean-P Berthouzoz
 Stores (at Basle): René Auberson
 Operating: Max Rietmann
 Traction and Workshops: Ing Jacques Bonny
 Electric Power Stations: Jörg Stöcklin

Gauge: 1435 mm; 1000 mm
Route length: 2860 km; 74 km
Electrification: 1435 mm gauge, 2834 km at 15 kV 16⅔ Hz ac
 1000 mm gauge, 74 km at 15 kV 16⅔ Hz ac

New contract with Government

In 1981 the SBB's contract of service with the Federal Government was revised on a temporary basis, to operate from 1982 to 1986 pending full implementation of the Conception Globale Suisse des Transports (CGST) advocated by a Government-appointed special commission in 1978. The CGST proposals were unlikely to complete Federal parliament and Cantonal government consideration and be ready for *submission to national referendum before late 1983.

The main points of the temporary agreement were:

Increase of Federal compensation for SBB's regional passenger services to SwFr 460 million a year, virtually covering the current loss on these operations;

Freedom for SBB to rationalise and up-price its country-wide small consignment freight service, to cut the loss thereon to SwFr 50 million at most by 1986;

Promise of legislation to grant SBB full commercial freedom in all freight and passenger sectors not covered by social obligations, following which SBB would be expected to cover direct costs of its wagonload and trainload freight working (the shortfall in 1981 was about 18 per cent);

Government to assume responsibility for investment to increase operating capacity and improve capability of SBB.

Finance

Provisional accounts for 1982 showed a deficit of SwFr 498 million, SwFr 196 million more than budgeted and SwFr 230 million worse than in 1981. The continent-wide recession was held principally culpable. In the passenger sector the effects were reduced by the May 1982 introduction of the system-wide Taktfahrplan (regular-interval timetable) and its increased train-km, so that business volume was held roughly at 1981 levels, whereas in the mid-1970s recession it diminished. But with international traffic particularly hard-hit passenger receipts were SwFr 46 million or 4·4 per cent below budget, despite a March 1982 fares increase. Freight revenue was off target by SwFr 130 million, or 10·6 per cent, though up on 1981 revenue.

On the other hand, an unexpectedly high rate of inflation added SwFr 40 million to budgeted expenses. However, compensations, which were based on the new 1981 contract with the Federal Government, were as budgeted: SwFr 460 million in support of regional passenger services, SwFr 150 million in support of parcels service (SwFr 25 million less than in 1981); SwFr 10 million towards piggyback freight development (which ceases after 1986); and SwFr 143 million from capital restructuring.

A report on SBB's managerial performance commissioned from the Zurich consultants Hayek Engineering AG, in the preparation of which SBB staff collaborated, has claimed that SBB can cut its costs by SwFr 90-140 million a year. Recommendations included greater exercise of market pricing, especially in the freight sector; exploitation of railway-owned property through creation of a property management subsidiary; and a restructure of top management to devolve more responsibility to individual managers in key areas such as marketing, operations and investment. Staff savings amounting to between 1000 and 1500 posts were identified.

In an early response to the report SBB announced in April 1983 that measures had already been taken to modify investment decision-making procedures; reduce operating staff; cut rolling stock requirements through more push-pull working, more intensive rostering of passenger cars and revised maintenance schemes; mechanise more track maintenance; and raise workshops productivity. On the marketing front, discounted tariffs were being offered to new freight customers throughout the summer of 1983.

Freight

Freight traffic held its 1981 levels during the first half of 1982 but in the second was severely eroded by the recession and also the strength of the Swiss franc, which cut back exports and imports. Most severely hit was transit traffic, constituting about a quarter of SBB's total tonnage, which fell back 14·3 per cent over the year as a whole compared with 1981. Domestic freight traffic fell by 4·3 per cent. As a result freight train-km were to be reduced by 19 500, or 3·7 per cent, in the 1983/84 schedules. ISO container freight was slightly down in 1982, as was the rate of piggyback growth, but the latter was nevertheless in total 8·2 per cent up on 1981 carryings, rising from 54 570 to 58 972 road vehicles (almost 47 000 travelled with their drivers). Altogether, the 1982 freight movement in all categories was 3·5 million tonnes or 8 per cent down

Mk IV air-conditioned Intercity car in new dark green and pearl livery, with logo on red background

Mk IV car first-class interior

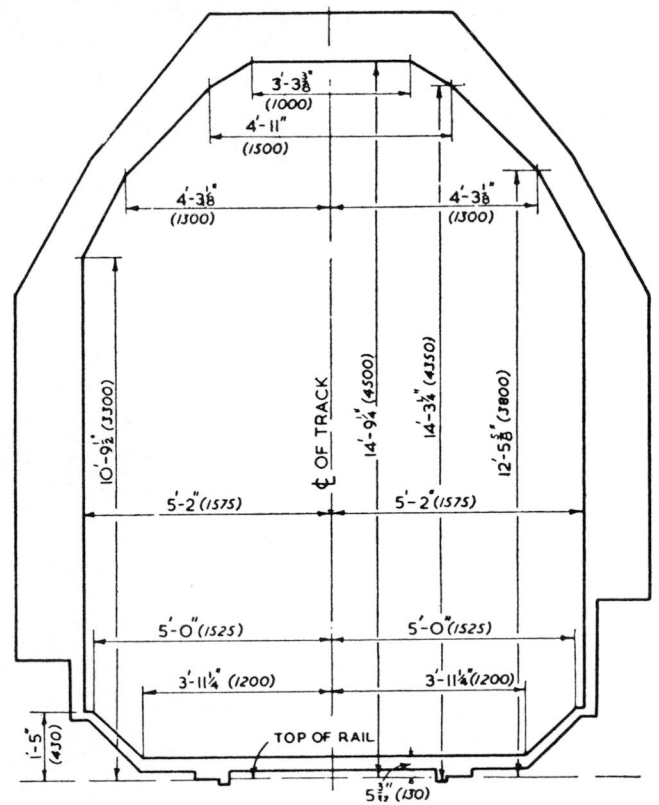

on budget, at a total of 41·9 million tonnes, 7·5 per cent less than in 1981. Tonne-km were 8·9 per cent down at 6501 million. Receipts were correspondingly off target by SwFr 130 million, or 10·6 per cent, though up on 1981 revenue.

Transit traffic accounts for 27·7 per cent of SBB's total freight tonnage and is dominated by iron and steel in various forms, including scrap, but ISO containers are second in the transit volume table. Two-thirds of SBB's annual 2·3 million tonnes of ISO container freight are on international transit, principally to and from Italy, and the container volume is now almost matched by that of piggyback. Of the latter, 90 per cent is transit traffic.

Growth of piggyback has been stimulated by the programme of enlarging the Gotthard route tunnels, which has achieved clearance for virtually all standard European road lorry-and-trailer rigs conveyed on Ro-Ro train-sets of Talbot small-wheeled, four-axle bogie low-loaders. The line can accept road vehicles with a box height of 3·7 metres above ground level. In 1982 the route carried eight piggyback trains each way daily, but SBB aims eventually to provide a shuttle of seven piggyback services each way daily between Basle and Lugano Vedeggio, in addition to 12 daily international transit services to and from Italian terminals. After the Italian State Railways' completion of the new Monte Olimpino tunnel deviation south of Chiasso it is hoped to extend the Freiburg im Breisgau to Lugano service to Milan Greco. Though piggyback covers its direct operating costs, its revenue fell short of total costs by SwFr 9·7 million in 1981 and since 1982 has had to shoulder an annual charge of SwFr 3·3 million in respect of the tunnel enlargements.

Taktfahrplan

In May 1982 SBB introduced its national regular-interval timetable, the Taktfahrplan, which established patterned passenger services interconnecting with each other on all routes at fixed intervals, with supplementary workings at the peak hours. Thus at Zurich Intercity and fast trains from and to all routes make smart connections with each other in a fixed sequence repeated between 19 minutes to and 13 minutes past each hour of the day, and at the same time are fed by and feed into patterned local services.

The timetable is basically arranged on a one-hour cycle, in which each route has an Intercity train calling only at principal centres, a fast train serving principal stations and medium-sized towns, and a regional stopping train catering for local traffic and also feeding the first two types of train. On some less busy routes the cycle is two-hourly; some lines are covered only by stopping trains, the Intercity trains are confined to the trunk routes, and on a few Intercity and fast trains alternate in each hourly cycle. At Basle the Taktfahrplan interlaces with the German Federal Railway (DB) fixed-interval Intercity service.

To implement the Taktfahrplan the daily operation was stepped up from 175 000 to 212 000 train-km, a rise of 20 per cent, establishing an average of 99 trains (including freight) per route-km, an intensity second in Europe only to that of the Netherlands Railways.

Overall, passenger journeys in 1982 were 0·6 per cent down on 1981, at 217 million, and passenger-km 1·3 per cent down at 8968 million.

New lines

At Sargans a new 4 km chord line was completed in 1983; it will save reversal of trains running between Zurich and Buchs, many of which are international to and from Austria via the Arlberg route. A new station has been built at Sargans and a second track laid from the chord's junction with the existing single-line route at Trübbach to Weite. A new Integra signalbox has been installed at Sargans.

Other double-tracking in progress in 1983, with completion dates bracketed, covered the following sections: Yverdon to Grandson, including an underpass at Pecos, on the Jura foothills line (1983); Uster to Wallisellen (substantially financed by the Canton of Zurich, for commuter service improvement), on the Glattal line (1984); and Niederglatt to Glattbrug, to complete double-tracking from Zurich to Eglisau on the Schaffhausen line (1985). The Käferberg line, which increases trackage between Zurich and Oerlikon from two to four, was commissioned in May 1982.

Following the successful performance of the Zurich Airport link, opened in June 1980, Geneva's international airport is to be rail-connected by a loop in a project costed in 1980 at SwFr 189 million; of that SwFr 64 million will be Federally funded and the Canton of Geneva will contribute SwFr 12 million. The Geneva link will follow the Lyons route out of the city's main Cornavin station to Chatelaine, then diverge on 2·5 km of new line serving a station beneath the airport terminal, which would become the Geneva terminus of trains from the Simplon route and Berne. Completion is expected in 1987.

Zurich RER

In a November 1981 referendum the Canton of Zurich public approved by a considerable majority creation of the so-called Zurich RER. The Canton itself has voted credits of SwFr 523 million towards

Traffic	1978	1979	1980	1981
Total train-km (million)	94·221	95·050	96·287	96·061
% of train-km by diesel	0·5	0·3	0·2	0·5
by electric	99·5	99·7	99·8	99·5
Total freight tonnage (million)	38·896	43·979	46·270	45·261
Average haul (km)	155·9	158·2	159·6	157·7
Average net train load	216	216	253	249
Average wagon load (tonnes)	14·2	14·9	15·3	15·5
Total passenger-km (million)	8·094	8·294	9·179	9·100
Total passengers carried (million)	203·443	205·602	216·302	218·243
Passengers carried 1st class (million)	15·724	15·868	17·186	17·446
2nd class (million)	187·719	189·734	199·116	200·797
Average length of passenger journey (km)	39·8	40·3	42·4	41·7

Revenues	1978	1979	1980	1981
Passengers and baggage (SwFr million)	833·1	868·2	942·5	966·6
Average receipt per passenger-km (SwFr)	0·103	0·101	0·099	0·104
Freight and mail (SwFr million)	974·3	1034·6	1128·9	1106·2
Average receipt per freight tonne-km (SwFr)	0·153	0·149	0·153	0·155
Total (SwFr million)	2400·8	2473·4	2675·5	2696·4

Expenditure				
Staff/personnel (SwFr million)	1868·6	1880·4	1972·7	2107·8
Materials and services (SwFr million)	483·5	504·1	556·6	573·6
Depreciation (SwFr million)	344·9	384·6	403·6	426·9
Financial charges (SwFr million)	326·4	328·7	336·1	348·5
Total (SwFr million)	3023·4	3097·8	3269·0	3456·8

Intercity train at Zurich Airport station

Type Re6/6 Bo-Bo-Bo with Cerbère-Hamburg 'Hispania' of German Federal Railway (DB) cars *(John C Baker)*

the infrastructure, leaving the SBB to bear SwFr 130 million in recognition of the scheme's side-benefit for other SBB traffics; rolling stock costs of SwFr 585 million will also be covered by the SBB. Construction is expected to begin in 1983 and be completed in 1990. The scheme provides for a new cross-Zurich line from Langstrasse in the west, diving underground at Zurich Hbf, passing beneath the Limmat and Sihl rivers, then veering north-east at Stadelhofen and running via Dübendorf to Dietlikon. It will unite existing Zurich suburban lines to create an integrated urban network.

Construction was formally inaugurated in April 1983. At the end of 1982 the SBB and Zurich authorities agreed that the RER should be operated with bi-level train-sets, of which prototypes would be ordered in 1984 for delivery in 1986 or 1987 and probable test on the Zurich-Uster-Rapperswil line. A set would comprise three trailers, each 27 metres long, offering a total seating capacity of 70 first- and 300 second-class, flanked by two 2500 kW RDe 4/4, 15-metre power cars each with a single end cab. Total tare weight of a set would be 210 tonnes, its maximum speed 125 km/h.

In February 1983 a further local referendum approved additional underground construction in the city. The privately-owned Sihltal-Zurich-Uetliberg Railway (SZU) is to be extended 1 km, partly in immersed tunnel on the Sihl riverbed, from its present Selnau terminus to a new underground station, on the south side of Zurich Hbf.

High-speed transversal

In the spring of 1983 the Federal Parliament was debating a report on measures to implement the CGST, which deferred new transalpine schemes but supported progress with the 200 km/h national rail transversals advocated in the 1978 CGST, from Lausanne via Berne to St Gallen, and from Basle via Olten to Chiasso. The plans embrace in all 235 km of route, but envisage realigning 45 km of existing route for the higher speed. Of the remaining new construction, 65 km would be in tunnel, chiefly between Basle and Olten. Total cost of the new infrastructure has been put at SwFr 4000 million. The results of the scheme would be journey times of only 39 minutes between Berne and Lausanne, 48 minutes between Berne and Zurich, and 2 hours 4 minutes from Zurich to Geneva (no new infrastructure is foreseen between Lausanne and Geneva, where maximum speed would remain 140 km/h). Consultations with Cantonal governments on bases for launching the project were in progress.

The SBB has already begun preliminary engineering study of some proposed sections of the high-speed routes. One of the most advanced envisages a 10 km cutoff on the Berne-Zurich route, from the junction with the Lötschberg route at Berne-Löchligut through a 6 km tunnel beneath the Grauholz hills, to a point near Hindelbank. This deviation would bypass the curves and congestion around Zollikofen. Meanwhile, use of Talgo equipment on the existing route is under consideration.

Traction and rolling stock

In 1981 the SBB operated 734 standard-gauge and two metre-gauge line-haul electric locomotives, 169 electric shunting locomotives, two diesel-electric line-haul and 107 shunting locomotives; six combined electric/diesel-electric shunters and 430 locotractors. Passenger stock included 175 standard-gauge and 16 metre-gauge electric railcars and 3714 hauled cars. Freight wagons totalled 31 236.

Traction deliveries in 1981-83 comprised further units of a new order for 45 Class Re 4/4 II electric locomotives and in 1982 trials began with the four Re 4/4 IV prototypes, SBB's first locomotives with thyristor control. Compared with the Re 4/4 II, the Re 4/4 IV is designed to raise the maximum express passenger train load on the non-Alpine main lines from 660 to 700 tonnes, and the single-headed maximum load for such trains or fast freights up the 2·6 per cent grades of the Gotthard route from 460 to 650 tonnes. It has a one-hour rating of 4960 kW, compared with an Re 4/4 II's 4560 kW, and its maximum speed is raised from 140 to 160 km/h. The mechanical parts are by SLM, the electrical equipment by BBC Brown Boveri. Series production of the Re 4/4IV has been deferred because of the downturn in Gotthard freight traffic and shortage of investment resources, given the need to finance construction of a new RBDde 4/4- and -BT emu series. On the other hand, orders for a further 27 Class Re 4/4 II have been placed for 1984-85 delivery.

Orders have been placed for four prototypes of a new power car and driving trailer set. The Type RBDe 4/4 power car is to employ continuous control of tractive effort with four-stage converters and commutation chokes, will have regenerative braking and be arranged for 140 km/h top speed instead

Type Re 4/4 III 6320 hp Bo-Bos leave Aarau line with southbound Gotthard route freight at Rotkreuz *(John C Baker)*

Class Re 4/4 IV thyristor-controlled locomotive No 10102 at Brig with Geneva-Milan train of FS cars *(John C Baker)*

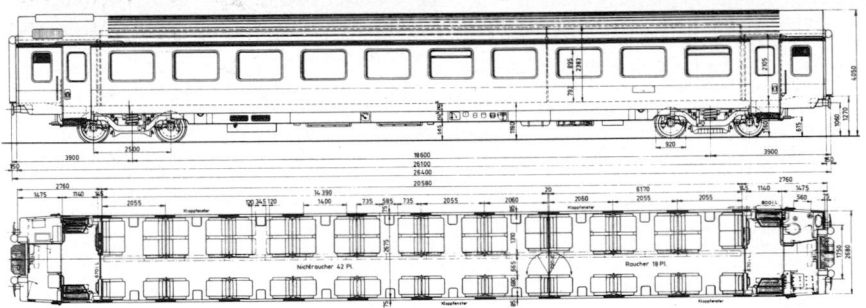

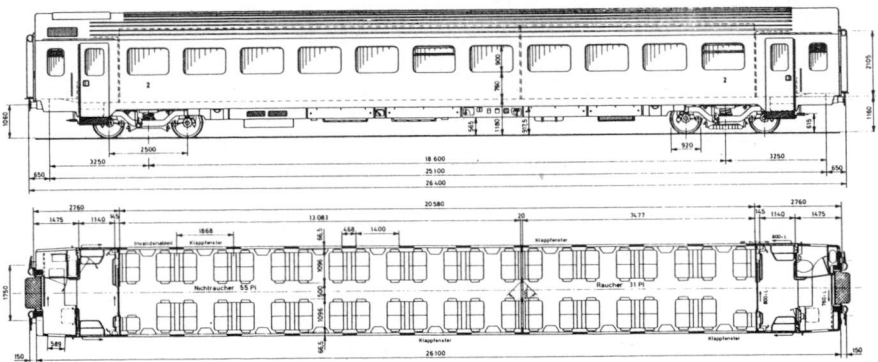

(Top) Mk IV first-class, 60 seats **(bottom)** Mk IV second class, 86 seats

of the 125 km/h limit hitherto normal on SBB rail-cars; it will seat 56 and tare 68 tonnes. The trailer will seat 72 and weigh 37 tonnes. The new units will be capable of running either as a two₂car set, as a push-pull unit with additional trailers inserted, or two of the power cars can be used to enclose a number of trailers for a high-density operation. The new design will thus be adaptable to a wide range of services.

Deliveries have begun of the 120 second-class cars of the new air-conditioned Mk IV design intended for standardisation on Intercity services. With saloon layouts, the new cars are built to the general European 26·4-metre body length and tare 43 tonnes. In April 1983 it was decided to order a further 30 first-class and 70 second-class cars (to bring the total stock in delivery or to come to 110 first-class, 190 second-class) and four 52-seat dining cars. A further 21 dining cars are likely to be sought for 1986-87 delivery.

Signalling
With the aid of a Federal grant of SwFr 5 million, installation of track-to-train radio is to be accelerated. Preliminary discussions have been held with the postal authorities on introduction of train telephone facilities.

The use of automated devices is being extended as the number of unstaffed stations increases. On the Gotthard line at Claro recent installations automatically report to Biasca detection of hot boxes, binding brakes, security of loads and any load shifting that infringes clearances. A further device, installed between Gümlingen and Rubigen, automatically detects and reports discrepancies in an individual freight wagon's wheel-loadings as a result of faulty loading. Wider application of these devices hinges on an assessment of their cost-saving through damage prevention in relation to their purchase prices.

The SBB is experimenting with fibre-optic cable communication between Lucerne and Zug.

Brunig line
The metre-gauge Brunig line, from Lucerne via Meiringen (reverse) to Interlaken, is a vital link between central Switzerland and the Bernese Oberland. Its route crosses the Brunig pass at a summit of 1002 metres, which is approached from the Meiringen side by a gradient of 12 per cent and on the northern side, where the ascent is more gradual, on stretches of 10-11 per cent. This necessitates sections of Riggenbach rack totalling 9·28 km. A daily timetable of 34 passenger trains in summer, 31 in winter, is operated the whole length of the route, but the total is 74 between Lucerne and its suburbs of Hergiswil.

The present Brunig traction fleet comprises two Type HGe 4/4 1600 kW Bo-Bo locomotives built in 1954 and 16 Type Deh 4/6 930 kW six-axle motor luggage vans built in 1941-42. All are limited to 50 km/h, which is now a handicap on the easily-graded sections either side of the Brunig pass, as is a single motor luggage-van's limitation to a 60-tonne load on the rack sections. Before ordering the 17 new traction units required to renew the traction fleet, SBB has ordered four prototype Bo-Bos based on a general specification agreed with the BVZ, LSE and FO Railways. These thyristor-controlled Type HGe 4/4 II will be built by SLM with Brown Boveri electrical equipment, will have regenerative braking and, unlike the existing motor luggage-vans (in which the central two axles are exclusively for rack

Brunig line train leaves Lucerne past new Brunig traction depot, opened 1982

New signal centre at Olten

engagement), will have their motored axles equipped with retractable rack engagement gear. Each axle will be powered by a 483 kW motor; maximum tractive effort with adhesion will be 230 kN, with rack engaged 280 kN; and maximum speed with adhesion will be 100 km/h, on rack 30 km/h uphill and 25 km/h downhill. Delivery will be in the winter of 1985-86.

Diesel locomotives

Class	Wheel arrange-ment	Trans-mission	Rated power hp	Max lb (kg)	Tractive effort Continuous at lb (kg)	Tractive effort at mph (km/h)	Max speed mph (km/h)	Wheel dia in (mm)	Total weight tons	Length ft in (mm)	No built	Year first built	Builders Mechanical parts	Builders Engine & type	Builders Transmission
Bm 4/4 II (18451-52)	Bo-Bo	Elec	830	22 000 (10 000)	9700 (4400)	31·4 (50.6)	68 (110)	41 (1040)	65	48' 10¾" (14 900)	2	1939	SLM	Sulzer	Brown Boveri
Bm 4/4 (18401-26)	Bo-Bo	Elec	842	48 500 (22 000)	28 700 (13 000)	10·9 (17·5)	47 (75)	41 (1040)	72	41' 6" (12 650)	26	1960-65	SLM	SLM	Sécheron
(18427-46)	Bo-Bo	Elec	842	48 500 (22 000)	28 700 (13 000)	10·9 (17·5)	47 (75)	41 (1040)	72	43' 1¾" (13 150)	20	1968-70	SLM	SLM	Sécheron
Bm 6/6 (18501-14)	Co-Co	Elec	1300	75 000 (34 000)	41 900 (19 000)	11·5 (18·5)	46 (75)	41 (1040)	106	55' 9½" (17 000)	4 10	1954-55 1960-61	SLM	Sulzer	Brown Boveri Sécheron
Em 3/3 (18801-06)	C	Elec	440	26 500 (12 000)	15 400 (7000)	10·5 (17)	40 (65)	41 (1040)	50.5	32' 7¾" (9950)	6	1959-60	SLM	SLM	Sécheron
(18807-41)		Elec	440	27 800 (12 600)	15 400 (7000)		40 (65)	41 (1040)	50·5	32' 10½" (10 020)	35	1963-64	SLM	SLM	Brown Boveri Sécheron
Am 6/6 (18521-26)	Co-Co	Elec	1950	18 181 (40 000)	18 181 (40 000)	8·25 (13.2)	53 (85)	49 (1260)	111	57' 1" (17 400)	6	1976	Thyssen-Industrie AG Henschel	Chantiers de l'Atlantique	Brown Boveri

Electric locomotives

Class	Wheel arrange-ment	Line current	Rated output hp	Tractive effort (full field) Max lb (kg)	Continuous lb (kg)	at mph (km/h)	Max speed mph (km/h)	Wheel dia in (mm)	Weight tonnes	Length ft in (mm)	No built	Year built	Builders Mechanical parts	Electrical equipment
Ae 6/6 (11401-02)	Co-Co	15 kV 16⅔ Hz	6000	80 160 (40 000)	48 400 (22 000)	46 (74)	78 (125)	49⅝ (1260)	124	60' 4½" (18 400)	2	1952-53	SLM	Brown Boveri/ Oerlikon
(11403-50)			6000	80 160 (40 000)	48 400 (22 000)	46 (74)	78 (125)	49⅝ (1260)	120	60' 4½" (18 400)	48	1955-60	SLM	Brown Boveri/ Oerlikon
(11451-11520)			6000	80 160 (40 000)	48 400 (22 000)	46 (74)	78 (125)	49⅝ (1260)	120	60' 4½" (18 400)	70	1962-66	SLM	Brown Boveri/ Oerlikon
Ae 8/14 (11801)	1A-A1A-A1+ 1A-A1A-A1	15 kV 16⅔ Hz	7000	110 000 (50 000)	57 300 (26 000)	40 (65)	62 (100)	63⅜ (1610)	240	111' 7" (34 000)	1	1931	SLM	Brown Boveri historical locomotive
Be 4/6 (12303-12)	1B-B1	15 kV 16⅔ Hz	1760	39 700 (18 000)	20 300 (9200)	32 (52)	47 (75)	60¼ (1530)	107	54' 4" (16 260)	30	1920	SLM	Brown Boveri
(12313-42)			2040	39 700 (18 000)	23 400 (10 600)	32 (52)	47 (75)	60¼ (1530)	110	54' 4" (16 260)	30	1921-23		
(12320 = historical locomotive, other scrapped)														
Re 4/4 I (10001-26)	Bo-Bo	15 kV 16⅔ Hz	2480	31 000 (14 000)	17 800 (8100)	51·5 (83)	78 (125)	41 (1040)	57	48' 2¾" (14 700)	26	1946-48	SLM	Brown-Boveri; Oerlikon; Sécheron
(10027-50)			2520	31 000 (14 000)	18 000 (8200)	51·5 (83)	78 (125)	41 (1040)	58	48' 10¾" (14 900)	24	1950-51		
Re 4/4 II (11101-106)	Bo-Bo		6320	57 300 (26 000)	37 500 (17 000)	62 (100)	87 (140)	49⅝ (1260)	80	48' 6¾" (14 800)	6	1964	SLM	Brown Boveri; Oerlikon; Sécheron
(11107-155)	Bo-Bo	15 kV 16⅔ Hz	6320	57 300 (26 000)	37 500 (17 000)	62 (100)	87 (140)	49⅝ (1260)	80	48' 10¾" (14 900)	49	1967-68	SLM	Brown Boveri; Oerlikon; Sécheron
(11156-304)	Bo-Bo		6320	57 300 (26 000)	37 500 (17 000)	62 (100)	87 (140)	49⅝ (1260)	80	50' 6¾" (15 410)	149	1969-74	SLM	Brown Boveri; Oerlikon; Sécheron
(11305-349, 11371-97)	Bo-Bo										45	1981-85	SLM	Brown Boveri
Re 4/4 III (11351-11370)	Bo-Bo		6320	62 830 (28 500)	44 310 (20 100)	53 (85)	78 (125)	49⅝ (1260)	80	50' 6¾" (15 410)	20	1971	SLM	Brown Boveri; Oerlikon; Sécheron
Re 4/4 IV (10101-04)	Bo-Bo	15 kV 16⅔ Hz	6745	67 440 (30 590)	47 210 (21 415)	53 (85)	100 (160)	49⅝ (1260)	80	51' 10" (15 800)	4	1982	SLM	Brown Boveri
Re 6/6 (11601-689)	Bo-Bo-Bo	15 kV 16⅔ Hz	10 600	88 600 (40 200)			87 (140)	49⅝ (1260)	120	63' 4½" (19 310)	89	1972-80	SLM	Brown Boveri; Sécheron
Ae 3/5 (10201-26)	1-Co-1	15 kV 16⅔ Hz	1800	31 000 (14 000)	17 000 (7700)	39 (63)	56 (90)	63⅜ (1610)	81	40' 5" (12 320)	24	1922-25	SLM	Sécheron
Ae 3/6 III (10261-271)	2-Co-1	15 kV 16⅔ Hz	1800	31 000 (14 000)	17 000 (7700)	39 (63)	56 (90)	63⅜ (1610)	89	45' 1¾" (13 760)	11	1925-26	SLM	Sécheron
(10264 = historical locomotive, other scrapped)														
Ae 3/6 II (10401-20)	2-C-1	15 kV 16⅔ Hz	2000	33 000 (15 000)	18 300 (8300)	40 (65)	62 (100)	63⅜ (1610)	99	46' 5" (14 150)	20	1924	SLM	Oerlikon
(10421-60)			2000	33 000 (15 000)	18 300 (8300)	40 (65)	62 (100)	63⅜ (1610)	97	46' 5" (14 150)	40	1925-26		
(10439 = historical locomotive, other scrapped)														
Ae 3/6 I (10601-36)	2-Co-1	15 kV 16⅔ Hz	1920	31 000 (14 000)	18 500 (8400)	38·5 (62)	62 (100)	63⅜ (1610)	92	48' 5" (14 760)	36	1921-25	SLM	Brown Boveri
(10637-86)			2100	33 000 (15 000)	19 400 (8800)	40 (65)	68 (110)	63⅜ (1610)	95	48' 5" (14 760)	50	1925-27		
(10687-712)			2100	33 000 (15 000)	19 400 (8800)	40 (65)	68 (110)	63⅜ (1610)	94	48' 5" (14 760)	26	1927-28	SLM	Oerlikon
(10713-14)			2100	33 000 (15 000)	19 400 (8800)	40 (65)	68 (110)	63⅜ (1610)	95	48' 5" (14 760)	2	1929	SLM	Sécheron
Ae 4/6 (10801-12)	1A+Bo+A1	15 kV 16⅔ Hz	5540	49 000 (22 200)	38 800 (17 600)	53 (85)	78 (125)	53⅛ (1350)	105	56' 7" (17 250)	12	1941-45 rebuilt 1961-63	SLM	Brown Boveri; Oerlikon; Sécheron
Ae 4/7 (10901-72)	2-Do-1	15 kV 16⅔ Hz	3120	44 000 (20 000)	28 700 (13 000)	40 (65)	62 (100)	63⅜ (1610)	118	54' 11½" (16 750)	72	1927-31	SLM	Brown Boveri (53); Oerlikon (52); Sécheron (22)
(10973-002)			3120	44 000 (20 000)	28 700 (13 000)	40 (65)	62 (100)	63⅜ (1610)	123	56' 1¼" (17 100)	30	1931-34		
(11003-27)			3120	44 000 (20 000)	28 700 (13 000)	40 (65)	62 (100)	63⅜ (1610)	118	54' 11½" (16 750)	25	1931-34		
Be 4/7 (12501-06)	(1-Bo-1)- (Bo-1)	15 kV 16⅔ Hz	2400	44 000 (20 000)	25 600 (11 600)	35 (56)	50 (80)	63⅜ (1610)	111	53' 5¾" (16 300)	6	1922	SLM	Sécheron
(12504 = historical locomotive, other scrapped)														
Be 6/8 II (13251-59, 61, 63-65)	1C-C1	15 kV 16⅔ Hz	3640	66 000 (30 000)	48 000 (21 800)	28 (45)	47 (75)	53⅛ (1350)	126	63' 9¾" (19 450)	13	1920-21 (1942-47)	SLM	Oerlikon
(13253 = historical locomotive, Ce 6/8 II 14253, all others withdrawn)														
Ce 6/8 II (14266-85)	1C-C1	15 kV 16⅔ Hz	2240	57 300 (26 000)	37 000 (16 800)	22 (36)	40 (65)	53⅛ (1350)	128	63' 9¾" (19 450)	20	1920-22	SLM	Oerlikon
De 6/6 (15301-03)	C+C	15 kV 16⅔ Hz	1170	39 700 (18 000)	25 400 (11 500)	17 (27.5)	31 (50)	41 (1040)	73	45' 11" (14 000)	3	1926	SLM	Brown Boveri
Ee 3/4 (16301-02)	1-C	15 kV 16⅔ Hz	585	19 900 (9000)	12 800 (5800)	17 (27.5)	25 (40)	41 (1040)	49	32' 2" (9800)	2	1923	SLM	Brown Boveri
Ee 3/3 (16311-26)	C	15 kV 16⅔ Hz	585	19 900 (9000)	12 800 (5800)	17 (27·5)	25 (40)	41 (1040)	45	29' 6¼" (9000)	16	1928		
(16331-50)			585	19 900 (9000)	12 800 (5800)	17 (27·5)	25 (40)	41 (1040)	45	29' 10½" (9100)	20	1930-31	SLM	Brown Boveri
(16351-76)			585	19 900 (9000)	12 800 (5800)	17 (27·5)	25 (40)	41 (1040)	11	31' 10" (9700)	26	1932-42		
(16381-414)			680	22 000 (10 000)	14 330 (6200)	18·4 (29.6)	31 (50)	41 (1040)	39	31' 2" (9500)	34	1944-47		
(16421-24)			680	26 500 (12 000)	15 400 (7000)	16·5 (26·5)	28 (45)	41 (1040)	45	31' 2" (9500)	4	1951	SLM	Brown Boveri Oerlikon; Sécheron
(16425-30)											6	1956		
(16431-36)			680	26 500 (12 000)	15 400 (7000)	16·5 (26·5)	28 (45)	41 (1040)	45	31' 2" (9500)	6	1961		
(16437-40)											4	1962		
(16441-60)			680	26 500 (12 000)	15 400 (7000)	16·5 (26·5)	28 (45)	41 (1040)	44	31' 2" (9500)	20	1966	SLM	Brown Boveri; Oerlikon; Sécheron

Electric locomotives

Class	Wheel arrangement	Line current	Rated output hp	Tractive effort (full field) Max lb (kg)	Continuous at lb (kg)	mph (km/h)	Max speed mph (km/h)	Wheel dia in (mm)	Weight tonnes	Length ft in (mm)	No built	Year built	Builders Mechanical parts	Electrical equipment
Ee 3/3 II (16501-02) (16503-04)	C	2-current	685	29 800 (13 500)	15 400 (7000)	16·5 (26·5)	28 (45)	41 (1040)	46	31′ 2″ (9500)	2	1957	SLM	Brown Boveri
			730	28 700 (13 000)	15 650 (7100)	16·8 (27)	28 (45)	41 (1040)	46	31′ 2″ (9500)	2	1957	SLM	Oerlikon
(16505-06) (16511-19)			685	29 800 (13 500)	15 400 (7000)	16·5 (26·5)	28 (45)	41 (1040)	46	31′ 2″ (9500)	11	1958 1962-63	SLM	Sécheron
Ee 3/3 IV (16551-60)	C	4-current	529	26 500 (12 000)	13 250 (6000)	14·8 (23·8)	37 (60)	41 (1040)	48	32′ 8″ (10 020)	10	1962-63	SLM	Sécheron
Ee 6/6 (16801-02)	C+C	15 kV 16⅔ Hz	1370	53 000 (24 000)	30 900 (14 000)	16·5 (26·5)	28 (45)	41 (1040)	90	48′ 8¾″ (14 850)	2	1952	SLM	Brown Boveri; Sécheron
Eem 6/6 (17001-06)	C+C	15 kV 16⅔ Hz and diesel	1045 533	53 000 (24 000) 53 000 (24 000)	26 500 (12 000) 26 500 (12 000)	14·8 (23·8) 7·5 (12)	40 (65)	41 (1040)	104	58′ 7″ (17 850)	5	1970-71	SLM	Sécheron
Ee 6/6 II (16811-20)	Co-Co	15 kV 16⅔ Hz	1000	76 430 (34 670)	76 430 (34 670)	6 (10)	52 (85)	52 (1260)	104	58′ 6″ (17 400)	10	1980	SLM	Brown Boveri

Note— Series Ae 4/7. Nos 10939-51 and 11009/17 weight 120 tonnes
Series Ee 3/3 II operate on 15 kV 16⅔ Hz and 25 kV 50 Hz
Series Ee 3/3 IV operate on 15 kV 16⅔ Hz and 25 kV 50 Hz and on 1500 V and 3000 V dc

Berne-Lötschberg-Simplon Railway (BLS)

11 rue de Genève, 3001 Berne

Telephone: (031) 221182
Telegrams: Feralpi

Manager: Dr F Anliker
Assistant Manager: Dipl Ing O Käppeli
Secretary: E Michel
Commercial Manager: H Eggen
Traffic Manager: W Zürcher
Traction and Workshops Manager: Dipl Ing K Müri
Chief Engineer, Construction: Dipl Ing F Kilchenmann

Gauge: 1435 mm
Route length: 115 km (BLS only); 130 km (other Group railways)
Electrification: 115 km at 15 kV 16⅔ Hz ac

Development

Upon completion of the BLS main line from Frutigen through the Lötschberg Tunnel to Brig in 1913, a number of minor railways in the area, known as the 'Berne Decree Railways' and worked under special guarantees from the Canton of Berne, were incorporated in the Lötschberg system, though each retained separate financial and operating identity. As a result of this, subsequent amalgamations and other accessions to the Group, it now embraces the Spiez - Erlenbach - Zweisimmen Railway (SEZ), Gürbetal - Berne - Schwarzenburg Railway (GBS) and Berne - Neuchâtel Railway (BN). Rolling stock of these four companies and the BLS is pooled, but its use is recorded and each company correspondingly remunerated. The group also owns 18 Lake Thun and Brienz ships and the Interlaken bus company, Auto AG.

The BLS system covers the main lines from Thun to Spiez and Interlaken, and from Spiez via the Lötschberg Tunnel to a junction with the Swiss Federal Railways at Brig. The Lötschberg route is one of Europe's most vital international rail links. BLS also owns the link through the Grenchenberg tunnel between Lengnau and Moutier (MLB), which forms part of the shortest route between Geneva and Basle.

Financial results

Revenue (SwFr million)	1980	1981
Passengers	62 861	63 927
Freight, parcels and mail	45 163	42 261
Other	44 824	52 345
Total	152 848	158 733

Expenditure (SwFr million)	1980	1981
Staff expenses	92 480	98 207
Materials and services	42 637	40 230
Depreciation	16 928	17 081
Financial charges	3147	3112
Total	155 192	158 630

Traction and rolling stock

At the start of 1983 BLS (including the BN, SEZ and GBS) operated 54 electric locomotives, 23 diesel

Traffic (BLS only)	1979	1980	1981
Total passenger journeys (000)	7651·9	8052·9	8182
Total passenger-km (million)	191	201	203·7
Total freight tonnes (million)	NA	4·99	4·69
Total freight tonne-km (million)	253·9	262·3	233·3

New Kander Viaduct near Frutigen, with original viaduct behind

New push-pull stock

shunters, 30 electric railcars, 175 passenger cars and 397 freight wagons.

In 1982 delivery was completed of 10 new push-pull train-sets ordered for the additional services run from May 1982 in the national regular-interval timetable. Six Class Re 4/4 locomotives have also been delivered to cater for the extra traffic created by the double-tracking of the Lötschberg route. Two buffet cars for the through Basle-Interlaken/Brig train-sets have been purchased from the Bodensee-Toggenburg Railway.

In 1983 orders were placed with Altenrhein and SIG for six three-car and two two-car emus.

Civil engineering

The BLS is engaged on a 10-year programme to complete the double-tracking of the Lötschberg main line. In 1976 the Swiss Parliament voted credits of SwFr 620 million for the project, but the first tranche of funds was not made available until May 1978 and the railway began the job with its own resources in 1977. In 1982, with double track operative from Frutigen to Blausee and from Lalden to Brig, the route's proportion of double track had been raised to 59·7 km or 71 per cent. Work was then concentrated on the sections from Felsenburg to Kandersteg in the north, and Hohtenn to Ausserberg in the south, also on the new workshops and traction depot at Spiez.

The Lötschberg Tunnel was built with double track, but although the rest of the route was constructed in anticipation of doubling the extra width of infrastructure has so deteriorated that much of its earthworks and bridge foundations have had to be replaced. A total of 19 new bridges and viaducts have been needed, including a second, 265-metre Kander Viaduct near Frutigen, and a new 85-metre single-span bridge over the Rhône at Brig; the latter and additional approach spans to be added to the Bietschtal Viaduct are or will be all-steel, the rest of concrete. Two new single-track tunnels have been required for the second track, one of 1·6 km at Hondrich, the other of 1·5 km at Mittalgraben, in the Lonza gorge; the existing tunnels were not completely finished off for double-track when built and from these some 150 000 cubic metres of rock have had to be excavated without prejudice to the line's heavy traffic, averaging 110 trains daily. In all, 20 tunnels with an aggregate length of 10·2 km have to be enlarged. To step up the traction current supply for the line's doubled operating capacity, the BLS is being connected with the Swiss Federal Railway's 15 kV system at each end of the route.

Frutigen station has been rebuilt and that at Spiez is to be both reconstructed and enlarged, together with track doubling on the Interlaken line as far as Faulensee. The doubled Lötschberg route is being signalled for reversible working throughout. When stations are closed it will be remotely controlled from three centres, at Spiez, Kandersteg and Goppenstein.

Twin-unit Type Ae 8/8 locomotive and international express near Kandersteg

Type Re 4/4 locomotive and regional train on Bietschtal bridge

Type Re 4/4 locomotive and air-conditioned BLS train-set on Luogelkinviaduct, Lotschberg southern slope

Electric locomotives and railcars

Owner	Type	Running no	Total	Built	Max speed km/h	Wheel diameter mm	Weight tonnes	Length m	Motors No	Motors one-hour rating hp	Builders
Locomotives											
BLS	Re 4/4	161-165	5	1964-67 }				} 15·1			
BLS	Re 4/4	166-173	8	1970 }							
BLS	Re 4/4	174-176 }									
SEZ	Re 4/4	177 }	7	1972-73 }	140	1250	80	15·47	4	6780	SLM, BBC
GBS	Re 4/4	178 }									
BN	Re 4/4	179-180 }									
BLS	Re 4/4	181-189	9	1974-75							
BLS	Re 4/4	190-195	6	1982-83							
BLS	Ae 4/4	251-252	2 }	1944-55	125	1250	80	15·6	4	4000	SLM, BBC
BLS	Ae 4/4	257-258	2 }								
BLS	Ae 6/8	202-208	7	1926-43	100	1350	120	20·26	12	6000	Breda/SLM, SAAS
BLS	Ae 8/8	271-275	5	1959-66	125	1250	160	30·23	8	8800	SLM, BBC
BLS	Ce 4/4	308	1	1920 (54)							
GBS	Ce 4/4	311, 313	2	1920 (55-56) }	65	1250	64	12·34	2	1000	SLM, BBC
BN	Ce 4/4	315-316	2	1924 (56) }							
BLS	Ee 3/3	401	1	1943	40	1040	38	9·2	1	615	SLM, SAAS
Railcars											
BN	Be 4/4	761-762	2	1953	120	1040	68	23·7	4	2000	SIG, SAAS
GBS	Be 4/4	763	1	1956							
BLS	De 4/5	796	1	1929 (43)	90	1040	58	20·9	4	1600	SLM, SIG, SAAS
BN	Be 2/4	722	1	1935	90	820	16	19.4	2	300	SIG, MFO
SEZ	ABDe 2/8	701	1 }	1935 (46, 73)	100	920	26	42·1	2	400	SLM, SAAS
GBS	ABDe 2/8	703	1 }								
SEZ	ABDe 2/8	702	1 }	1938 (46, 73/74)	110	920	26	42·1	2	480	SLM, SAAS
GBS	ABDe 2/8	704	1 }								
SEZ	ABDe 4/8	741	1 }								
GBS	ABDe 4/8	742	1 }	1945-46	110	920	55	46·8	4	960	SIG, SAAS
BN	ABDe 4/8	743	1 }								
BLS	ABDe 4/8	746-748	3	1954-55 (70-73) }	125	1100	60	47·46	4	1600	SIG, BBC, SAAS, BLS
BLS	ABDe 4/8	749-750	2	1957 (68, 69) }				47·3			
BLS	ABDe 4/8	751									
SEZ	ABDe 4/8	752	5	1964	125	1100	62	47·8	4	1600	SIG, BBC, SAAS, BLS
GBS	ABDe 4/8	753									
BN	ABDe 4/8	754-755									
BLS	ABDZe 4/6	731	1 }	1938 (75/76)	110	920	56	41·5	4	960	SIG, SAAS
BN	ABDZe 4/6	736-737	2 }								
GBS	BDZe 2/6	711	1	1938 (73/74)	80	920	26	30	2	480	SIG, SAAS, BLS
BLS	RBDe 4/4	721-722 }									
SEZ	RBDe 4/4	723-724 }	10	1982	125	940	68	25	4	2200	SIG, SWS, BBC
GBS	RBDe 4/4	725-729 }									
BN	RBDe 4/4	730 }									

Bernese Oberland Railways (BOB)
Berner Oberland-Bahnen, Wengernalp-Bahn (WAB) and Jungfraubahn (JB)

3800 Interlaken

Telephone: 036 22 52 52

Director: Dr Roland Hirni

The Group comprises the following railways:
Berner Oberland-Bahnen. Operates 24 route-km of metre-gauge from Interlaken Ost to Lauterbrunnen and Grindelwald, electrified at 1·5 kV dc. Sections of route employ Riggenbach rack to cope with maximum gradients of 1 in 11. A steam locomotive, privately owned, is operated on special excursions.

The railway also operates the 7·3 km, 800 mm-gauge, Riggenbach rack Schynigge Platte mountain railway (SPB) starting from Wilderswil, which is electrified at 1·5 kV dc, and the Bergbahn Lauterbrunnen (BLM). The BLM comprises a cable funicular from Lauterbrunnen to Grütschalp and a metre-gauge line along the rim of the Lauterbrunnen valley's western wall from Grütschalp to Mürren.
Wengernalp-Bahn (WAB). An 800 mm-gauge line, running from Grindelwald and Lauterbrunnen to Kleine Scheidegg, 2060 metres above sea level and immediately below the Jungfrau mountain chain. It is electrified at 1·5 kV dc, and employs Riggenbach rack throughout.

BOB railways

Railway	BOB	SPB	WAB	JB	BLM
Route-length (km)	23·6	7·3	19·2	9·3	5·7
Max gradient (%)	12	25	25	25	60
Minimum curve radius (m)	90	60	60	100	40
Steam locomotives	—	1	—	—	—
Electric locomotives	5	11	8	5	—
Electric railcars	10	—	24	10	4
Diesel tractors	1	—	—	—	—
Passenger cars	45	26	40	20	2
Baggage cars	15	—	—	—	—
Freight wagons	31	6	55	15	4
Service vehicles	3	2	11	3	2

WAB trains cross near Wengernalp

JB trains cross at mouth of the tunnel into the Jungfrau range

Jungfraubahn (JB). This metre-gauge line, starting from Kleine Scheidegg, tunnels through the Jungfrau range to attain the highest altitude of any European railway at Jungfraujoch, 3405 metres above sea level on the ridge between the Jungfrau and Mönch mountains. It employs the Strub rack system and is electrified at 1100 volts 50 Hz three-phase ac.

The Group also operates two other rope-worked funiculars, the Harderbahn at Interlaken and the Allmendhubel at Mürren.

BOB train on the Grindelwald line

Bodensee-Toggenburg Railway (BT)
Bodensee-Toggenburg-Bahn

Bahnhofplatz 1a, 9001 St Gallen

Telephone: (071) 23 19 12

General Manager: Walter Dietz

Gauge: 1435 mm
Route length: 65·9 km
Electrification: 65·9 km at 15 kV 16⅔ Hz ac

The BT is a concessionary undertaking, with just over 40 per cent of its capital owned by the Federation, 34·5 per cent by the Cantons of St Gallen, Thurgau and Appenzell, and 21·7 per cent by local communities in these Cantons.

Single-track throughout, the BT is an important cross-country operator. Starting from the Swiss Federal station at Romanshorn on Bodensee (Lake Constance), it rejoins Swiss Federal tracks for the passage of St Gallen; then, resuming on its own track, the BT line runs to Wattwil and there branches to its terminus at Nesslau. From Wattwil, however, BT operates over Swiss Federal lines to the junction with the South Eastern Railway (Südost-bahn) at Rapperswil, whereby it runs a through Romanshorn St Gallen - Lucerne service jointly with the other two railways. Ruling gradient on the BT-owned route is 2·4 per cent.

Type RABDe 4/12 push-pull set

Traffic	1980	1981
Total freight tonnage	616 137	660 136
Total freight tonne-km (000)	7420	7297
Average net freight train load (tonnes)	99·6	110·1
Total passenger-km (000)	69 931	69 694
Total passenger journeys (000)	4734	4788
Average length of passenger journey (km)	14·77	14·56

Finance	1981
Revenues (SwFr 000)	
Passengers and baggage	9578·6
Freight, parcels and mail	4752·9
Other income	3130
Compensation	1541·3
Total	19 002·8
Expenditure (SwFr 000)	
Staff/personnel expenses	13 871
Materials and services	5368
Depreciation	3706·2
Financial charges	5·9
Total	22 951·9

Investment
The railway has embarked on a major traction and rolling stock renewal programme. For the start of the national regular-interval timetable (Taktfahrplan) in May 1982, wherein BT's train-km was increased by 15 per cent, six new three-car Type RABDe 4/12 push-pull train-sets were ordered. Builders were Fahrzeugwerke Altenrhein, power bogies were specially developed by SIG and electrical equipment was by Brown Boveri. Bodywork is an

Park-and-ride facility at Herisau, junction with Appenzeller Railway

integral structure of all-welded lightweight steel. The 80-tonne power car's bogies have all axles powered for a total one-hour rating of 1700 kW, which is adequate for subsequent insertion of a third trailer if required; power secondary suspension combines steel coil and rubber, but the trailer bogies have load-sensitive secondary air suspension. Apparatus not needing frequent attention, such as the main transformer, is underfloor-mounted; high voltage gear and dynamic brake resistances are roof-mounted. Trailer weights are 45 to 46 tonnes.

In 1983 BT was also to order eight new 3000 kW Bo-Bo locomotives to replace its six 50 year-old Type Be 4/4 and provide for traffic increases. Delivery would be in 1985-86; builders would be SLM, with electrical equipment by Brown Boveri. Maximum speed would be 110-125 km/h, weight 72 tonnes and estimated price per unit SwFr 4·75 million.

Traction and rolling stock
BT operates six line-haul electric, one shunting electric, eight diesel shunting and one steam locomotive (for special use only), 14 emu power and 26 emu trailer cars (forming 12 train-sets), 34 other passenger cars and 48 internal service wagons.

Signalling
The entire BT route-mileage is signalled by Integra Domino panels at stations.

Track
Rail: 46 and 36 kg/m*

Cross ties (sleepers): Wood, thickness 150 mm
Steel, thickness 11 mm
Spacing: 1166
Fastenings: K and Ae (screw)
Minimum curvature radius: 183 m

Max gradient: 2·4%
Max axleload: 20 tonnes

*All 36 kg/m rail was to be replaced by 46 kg/m in 1983-84

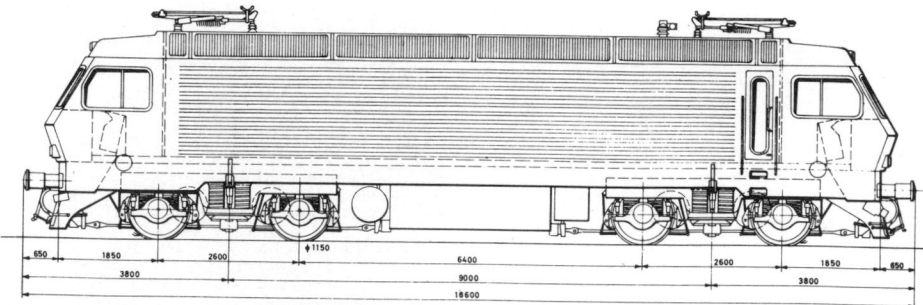

Outline of new BT 3200 kW Bo-Bo to be ordered in 1983

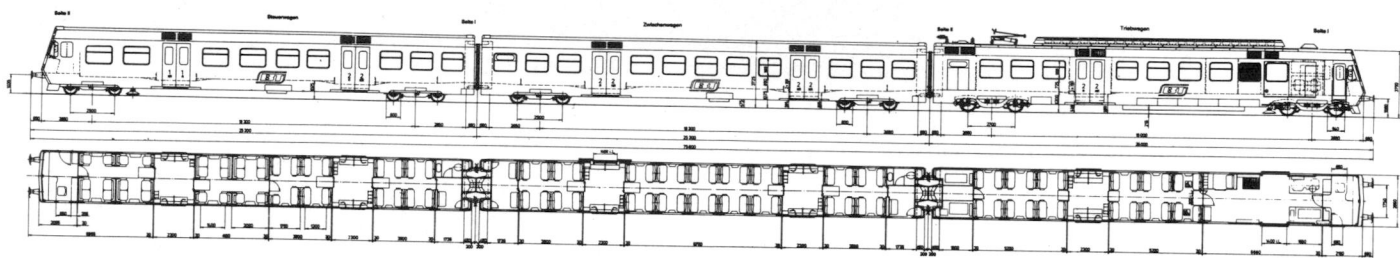

Type RABDe 4/12 layout

Electric locomotives

Class	Wheel arrangement	Line voltage	Rated output (kW) continuous/one-hour	Max speed km/h	Weight tonnes	No in service	Year first built	Builders Mechanical parts	Electrical equipment
Line-haul	Bo-Bo	15 kV 16⅔ Hz	1180	80	66	6	1931	SLM	SAAS
Shunting	B	15 kV 16⅔ Hz	238	65	28	1	1966	SLM	MFO

Electric railcars or multiple-units

Class	Cars per unit	Line voltage	Motor cars per unit	Motored axles per car	Rated output (kW) per motor	Max speed km/h	Weight tonnes per car (M-motor T-trailer)	Total seating capacity	Length per car m (M-motor T-trailer)	No in service	Year first built	Builders Mechanical parts	Electrical equipment
Emu	3	15 kV 16⅔ Hz	1	4	425	125	M 71 T 36/35	183	M 25 T 25·3	6	1982	FZA/SIG	BBC
Emu (semi-permanent)	4	15 kV 16⅔ Hz	1	4	526	110	M 73 T 32/30	247	M 23·7 T 24·03	4	1960	SIG	BBC
Emu	2	15 kV 16⅔ Hz	1	2	295	90	M 59 T 29	114	M 23·7 T 24·1	1	1932 (modernised 1965)	SIG	SAAS
Emu	2	15 kV 16⅔ Hz	1	2	295	90	M 58 T 30	114	M 22·85 T 23·98	1	1932 (modernised 1965)	SIG	SAAS
Railcar	1	15 kV 16⅔ Hz	1	3	295	80	M 68	46	M 22	1	1938 (modernised 1981)	SIG	SAAS
Railcar	1	15 kV 16⅔ Hz	1	2	295	80	M 62	56	M 22·53	1	1952	SLM/SWP/BT	SAAS

Brig-Visp-Zermatt Railway (BVZ)
Brig-Visp-Zermatt Bahn

Nordstrasse 9, 3900 Brig, Valais

Telephone: 028 23 13 33
Telex: 69 5171

Manager: R Perren
Permanent Way: O Häberli
Electrical Engineer: K Hächler
Traction: H Tribolet
Finance: A Zurbriggen

Gauge: 1000 mm
Route length: 43·4 km
Electrification: 43·4 km at 11 kV 16⅔ Hz ac

The BVZ is part adhesion, part Abt rack (over four sections of its ascent from Visp to Zermatt, where the ruling gradient is 12·5 per cent). It was the first Swiss railway to equip its whole route with CTC; this is controlled from a centre at Brig, with which all BVZ traction units are in radio communication through transmitter-receivers.

Single-line throughout, with passing loops, the BVZ records over 2 million passenger journeys annually and moves about 50 000 tonnes of freight. Its busiest section is the final 8 km from Täsch to Zermatt; the former is the limit of motor transport to Zermatt, which is still kept inaccessible to road vehicles. Over this section the basic service of 11 Brig-Zermatt trains each way daily is supplemented by a push-pull shuttle, for which SIG in 1975 built six

train-sets. Each is powered by a 48·7-tonne, 1485 hp Bo-Bo locomotive with SAAS thyristor control and SLM bogies. Trailers are of all-welded light alloy, weighing 11·8 to 13 tonnes according to class of seating; driving trailers tare 13·8 tonnes. To enable 2000 passengers an hour to be moved each way between Täsch and Zermatt in peak seasons, this section is provided with an automatically-controlled passing loop at Kalten Boden.

In 1982 BVZ was engaged on a comprehensive rebuilding of Zermatt station. To safeguard winter operation it is being reconstructed under cover, with new offices including buffet-restaurant, three passenger tracks (one pitted), a freight depot and an oil terminal. The other major project active in 1983 was construction of a new rolling stock depot at Brig.

BVZ operates six electric, three diesel-electric and one steam locomotive, one diesel tractor, five two-car emus, four motor luggage vans, six driving trailers, 52 hauled passenger cars, three baggage and mail cars, and 83 freight wagons.

BVZ also controls the metre-gauge, Abt rack Gornergrat Railway from Zermatt to the Gorner Glacier.

Tasch-Zermatt push-pull shuttle train at Zermatt

Emmental-Burgdorf-Thun Railway (EBT)
Emmental-Burgdorf-Thun Bahn

Bucherstrasse 1, 3400 Burgdorf 1

Telephone: (034) 22 3151
Telex: 69 12 32

Director: Dr Charles Kellerhals
Vice-Director: R Burkhard
Technical Manager: W Ramseyer
Operations Manager: H Bleuler
Commercial Manager: J P Hubmann
Financial Manager: R Rohn

Gauge: 1435 mm
Route length: 71 km
Electrification: 71 km at 15 kV 16⅔ Hz ac

The EBT Group of railways connects the north and south of the Canton of Berne, and also reaches out to the hinterland of Lucerne. It comprises the following railways, which are under common management: Solothurn - Moutier (SMB); Solothurn - Burgdorf - Hasle - Ruegsau - Konolfingen - Thun, and Hasle - Ruegsau - Langnau (EBT); and Ramsei - Sumiswald and Langenthal - Huttwil - Wolhusen (VHB). There are eight interchange stations with the Swiss Federal Railway (SBB).

Type De 4/4 Bo-Bo locomotive re-using power equipment of withdrawn railcars

Emmental-Burgdorf-Thun-Bahn (EBT)

Gauge: 1435 mm
Length: 71·2 km and 5 km of common route with SBB
Electrification: 76·2 km at 15 kV 16⅔ Hz ac

Traffic	1980/81	1981/82
Total freight tonnage	1 987 366	2 041 035
Total freight tonne-km (000)	28 182	27 695
Total passenger-km (000)	47 825	48 609
Total passenger journeys (000)	4377	4483

Finance	
Revenues (SwFr)	*1981*
Passengers and baggage	5 806 502
Freight, parcels and mail	14 313 560
Other income	7 507 336
Total	27 627 398

Expenditure (SwFr)	*1981*
Staff/personnel expenses	23 232 795
Materials and services	7 912 580
Depreciation and financial charges	2 944 833
Total	34 090 208

Solothurn-Münster-Bahn (SMB)

Gauge: 1435 mm
Length: 21·5 km and 1·5 km of common route with SBB
Electrification: 23 km at 15 kV 16⅔ Hz ac

New Oberburg station

Traffic	1980/81	1981/82
Total freight tonnage	158 155	148 309
Total freight tonne-km (000)	3392	3188
Total passenger-km (000)	6050	5945
Total passenger journeys (000)	584	574

Finance	
Revenues (SwFr)	*1981*
Passengers and baggage	734 041
Freight, parcels and mail	1 220 557
Other income	646 649
Total	2 601 247

Expenditure (SwFr)	1981
Staff/personnel expenses	1 732 420
Materials and services	2 046 823
Depreciation and financial charges	476 568
Total	4 255 811

Vereinigte Huttwil-Bahnen (VHB)

Gauge: 1435 mm
Length: 63·1 km and 0·9 km of common route with SBB
Electrification: 64 km at 15 kV 16⅔ Hz ac

Traffic	1980/81	1981/82
Total freight tonnage	523 769	497 337
Total freight tonne-km (000)	13 387	13 481
Total passenger-km (000)	19 266	18 842
Total passenger journeys (000)	1857	1825

Finance

Revenues (SwFr)	1981
Passengers and baggage	2 264 764
Freight, parcels and mail	5 316 156
Other income	1 848 147
Total	9 429 067

Expenditure (SwFr)	1981
Staff/personnel expenses	7 713 932
Materials and services	5 363 494
Depreciation and financial charges	1 281 684
Total	14 359 110

Traction and rolling stock

At the start of 1983 the Group was operating 16 electric locomotives, three steam locomotives, 25 power cars, 16 driving trailers, 27 locotractors, and 68 passenger and baggage cars.

Recent acquisitions have included two Re 4/4 III locomotives of the Swiss Federal type, three BDe 4/4 II power cars with driving trailers, and eight two-car units comprising RBDe 4/4 power car and Bt trailer. But a substantial proportion of the traction and rolling stock is obsolescent and a problem in face of the intensified service the EBT now runs under the national Taktfahrplan. Equally important are adequate resources for the system's heavy freight traffic. Four new 1600 hp De 4/4 Bo-Bo power units have recently been created economically, at a cost of SwFr 800 000 each, by re-using the motors and electrical equipment of 30-year-old BDe 2/4 railcars with new bodies and bogies; the conversion was executed in conjunction with the SWS works of Schlieren. Three more Re 4/4 III locomotives have been ordered under a 1982-86 investment programme of SwFr 133 million and were to be delivered in 1983. Under the same programme 13 new RBDe 4/4 II power cars with associated driving trailers and other passenger cars have been ordered for 1984-85 delivery.

Civil engineering

EBT plans to double its single-track route between Berthoud and Oberburg. A longer-term aim, for the benefit of its freight traffic, is to achieve connection of its Berthoud-Emmenmatt line with the BLS. A new station was opened at Oberburg in 1982.

Signalling

CTC was commissioned between Huttwil and Lotzwil in 1982.

Furka-Oberalp Railway (FO)
Furka-Oberalp Bahn

Postfach 97, 3900 Brig, Valais

Telephone: 028 23 66 66
Telex: 38 215

Director: S Zehnder

Gauge: 1000 mm
Route length: 100·4 km
Electrification: 100·4 km at 11 kV 16⅔ Hz ac

The FO is the important central link in a metre-gauge route, formed by a trio of railways, from Zermatt on the Canton Valais to St Moritz and Chur in the Canton Grisons, the itinerary of the famous 'Glacier Express'. The FO section extends from Brig, junction with the Brig-Visp-Zermatt, to Disentis, junction with the Rhaetian. The FO employs the Abt rack system over 22·2 km to negotiate a maximum gradient of 11 per cent.

Traffic	1980	1981
Total passenger journeys (million)	1·538	1·819
Total passenger-km (million)	25·01	29·14
Total freight and mail tonnes	40 112	36 463
Total freight and mail tonne-km (million)	1·016	0·755

Financial results	1980	1981
Revenues (SwFr million)		
Passengers	8·074	11·157
Freight	1·743	1·565
Compensation and subvention	2·409	2·449
Total	12·226	15·171

Expenses (SwFr million)	1980	1981
Staff	11·422	12·904
Materials and services	4·634	4·935
Renewals and construction	2·563	3·818
Depreciation	2·228	2·237
Financial charges	0·036	0·002
Total	20·850	23·896

Furka Base Tunnel

In June 1982 the new Furka Base Tunnel was formally opened. In 1971 the Federal Government decided that year-round communication with the military redoubt in the mountains around Andermatt was essential and approved the boring of the tunnel to bypass the exposed FO section from Oberwald to Realp, which is mostly between 2000 and 3000 metres above sea level and has always had to be closed to traffic annually between October and April.

The 17·38 km tunnel was begun in 1973. The project was budgeted originally at SwFr 74 million in 1970, but the final cost, including that of works at the

Type Deh 4/4 emerges from Furka Tunnel with Brig-Göschenen train (*John C Baker*)

stations on each side of the tunnel, reached SwFr 224·69 million at 1972 price levels, or SwFr 318·5 million at 1983 money values as a result of inflation and unforeseen geological problems which protracted the work and also enforced a deviation from the original planned course. Two crossing loops have been installed in the tunnel, which is otherwise single-track. With the tunnel's completion adhesion working is possible throughout from Oberwald to Andermatt, cutting 30 minutes from journey times between these two points. Oberwald station has been considerably enlarged to serve as the terminus of a new accompanied car-carrying shuttle service to and from Andermatt. The 'Glacier Express' now becomes an all-year-round service. By February 1983 road traffic through the tunnel was averaging over 300 vehicles a day.

Traction and rolling stock

In 1979-80 stocks were enlarged to provide for intensified service following the Furka Base Tunnel's opening. For push-pull services SLM supplied four Type Deh 4/4 power-baggage cars and 20 new trailers and six driving trailers, also built by SIG, were added to the fleet. For two new tunnel car-carrier train-sets 12 roofed car-carrier wagons, five Ro/Ro wagons and two driving trailers were procured, also two SLM-built, Brown Boveri-powered Type Ge 4/4 III Bo-Bo locomotives to a design derived from the Rhaetian thyristor-controlled Type Ge 4/4 II. Weighing 49·5 tonnes and with a one-hour rating of 2280 hp, the Ge 4/4 III can work 350-tonne trains through the tunnel at a maximum speed of 90 km/h.

In 1982 the FO was operating two diesel-electric, eight electric locomotives, 14 electric power cars, 72 passenger cars, four baggage cars, 17 car-carriers and 64 freight wagons. All locomotives are equipped for radio communication with control centres at Brig and Andermatt.

Montreux-Oberland Bernois Railway (MOB)
Chemin de Fer Montreux-Oberland Bernois

Rue du Lac 36, 1815 Clarens

Telephone: 021 61 55 22
Telex: 453 129

Managing Director: E Styger
Marketing Manager: P Sangy
Traffic Manager: R Kaller
Way and Works Manager: M Sandoz
Traction and Workshops Manager: W Borer

The MOB Group comprises three railways:

Montreux-Oberland Bernois

Gauge: 1000 mm
Route length: 75·3 km
Electrification: 75·3 km at 860 V dc

The main line runs from Montreux via Gstaad to Zweisimmen. Its climb away from the Lake of Geneva to Les Avants and the 2·4 km Col de Jaman tunnel, with stretches of 7·3 per cent gradient, is the steepest line in Switzerland worked by adhesion. The summit is 1105 metres above sea level.

From Zweisimmen a branch runs to Lenk. In 1978-79 this branch, abandoned to freight-only operation since 1975 because of deterioration and indecision over possible reconstruction as a standard-gauge extension of the BLS Spiez-Zweisimmen line, was rehabilitated with 36 kg/m rail and automatic block signalling. The work, two-thirds financed by the Federal and Berne Cantonal Governments, also included construction of a new alignment out of Zweisimmen bypassing four level crossings. The restored branch was made fit for 110 km/h by suitably geared traction units.

Traffic

In 1979 MOB introduced Western Europe's first air-conditioned narrow-gauge rolling stock. New dome-roofed bodies were mounted on existing underframes to form a 'Panoramic Express', which since May 1982 has been extended to run twice daily from Montreux via Zweisimmen to Lenk and back (a bar-car is featured on two of the workings). The demand for the service prompted construction of a second four-car set, introduced on a Zweisimmen-Montreux return service in May 1982 and two further panoramic cars were completed in 1983, bringing the stock to 10, to meet demand. To take over 'Panoramic Express' haulage from the present modernised motor coaches, and for planned unit freight train developments, MOB has ordered four 1000 kW Type GDe 4/4 Bo-Bo locomotives of 52 tonnes weight for delivery in 1983.

Between 1979 and 1981 MOB increased its passenger traffic by 21·2 per cent, while in 1980 and 1981 its freight tonnage almost doubled as a result of new cement and gravel market penetration. Under the national Taktfahrplan train services were augmented by 10 per cent and reorganised in three categories: *accélérés*, connecting with Simplon and Lötschberg main-line trains; direct (eight trains); and express (four trains).

Traffic	1980	1981
Total passenger-km (million)	36·5	38·5
Total freight tonnes	30 000	53 600
Total freight tonne-km	626 000	1 201 800

Finance (SwFr million)		
Revenues	1980	1981
Passengers and baggage	7·5	8·05
Freight, parcels and mail	1·1	1·16
Other (including compensations)	2·6	2·9
Total	11·2	12·11

Expenditure	1980	1981
Staff	11·2	12·57
Materials and services	3·7	4·01
Financial charges	0·4	0·54
Depreciation, etc	2·0	2·1
Infrastructure renewals	—	1·36
Total	17·3	20·58

Investment

Major investments in hand have been construction of a new Moosbach Tunnel, 400 metres long, at a cost of SwFr 9·7 million, and extension of automatic

'Panoramic Express' hauled by two baggage-power cars at Montreux *(John C Baker)*

'Panoramic Express' second-class saloon

Type ABDe 4/8 441 kW electric railcar of 1978 build and two-trailer train on Lenk branch

block signalling to the entire length of all three systems in the network, which would be completed at the end of 1983.

Track
The railway uses 36 kg/m rail fixed to steel sleepers, spaced 1660/km, by Swiss Federal Railways Type A fasteners. Minimum curve radius is 56/80 metres, maximum gradient 7·3 per cent and maximum axleloading 13 tonnes.

Traction and rolling stock
The MOB operates six electric and three diesel locomotives, 19 electric railcars, six two-car emus, 39 passenger cars and 140 freight wagons.

Montreux-Glion Railway

Gauge: 800 mm
Route length: 2·73 km

Glion-Rocher-de-Naye Railway

Gauge: 800 mm
Route length: 7·6 km

These two railways, both employing the Abt rack system to cope with ruling gradients, respectively, of 13 and 22 per cent, are a continuous system. But the Montreux-Glion is basically a Montreux suburban railway, the Rocher-de-Naye its tourist continuation to a spectacular mountain viewpoint above Lake Geneva.

Electric locomotives

Class	Wheel arrangement	Line voltage	Rated output (kW) continuous one-hour	Max speed km/h	Weight tonnes	No in service	Year first built	Builders Mechanical parts	Electrical equipment
DZe 6/6	Bo-Bo-Bo	860 dc	950	55	63	2	1931	SIG Neuhausen	BBC Baden
GDe 4/4	Bo-Bo	860 dc	1000	100	50	4	1983	SLM Winterthur	BBC Baden

Diesel locomotives

Class	Wheel arrangement	Transmission	Rated power (kW)	Max speed km/h	Total weight tonnes	No in service	Year first built	Builders Mechanical parts	Engine & type	Transmission
Gm 4/4	Bo-Bo	Elec	530	80	44	2	1976	Moyse	Poyaud	Moyse Leroy-Sommer
Tm 2/2	B-B	Hyd	85	33	15	1	1953	Klöckner-Humboldt-Deutz	Deutz	Voith-Turbo

Electric railcars or multiple-units

Class	Cars per unit	Line voltage	Motor cars per unit	Motored axles per motor car	Rated output (kW) per motor	Max speed km/h	Weight tonnes per car (M-motor T-trailer)	Total seating capacity	Length per car mm	No in service	Rate of acceleration m/s²	Year first built	Builders Mechanical parts	Electrical equipment
BDe 4/4	1	860 dc	1	4	72	50	29	16	14 210	3	0·3	1905	SIG	Alioth
Xe 4/4	1	860 dc	1	4	72	50	29	—	14 210	1	0·3	1906	SIG	Alioth
BDe 4/4	1	860 dc	1	4	95	50	33	12	14 500	2	0·5	1912	SIG	Alioth
BDe 4/4	1	860 dc	1	4	110	50	36	14	15 500	2	0·5	1924	SIG	BBC
BDe 4/4	1	860 dc	1	4	116	75	36	36	16 520	4	0·6	1944	SIG	BBC
ABDe 4/8	2	860 dc	1	4	116	75	M 36 T 18	98	33 100	2	0·6	1944-74 1944-81	SIG/MOB	BBC/MOB
ABDe 8/8	2	860 dc	2	8	110	70	60	86	33 500	4	0·7	1968	SIG	SAAS
Be 4/4	1	860 dc	1	4	77	40	30	64	17 500	1	0·5	1973	ACMV/MOB	BBC/MOB
Be 4/4	1	860 dc	2	4	44	60	29	56	16 560	2	0·4	1975-81	SWS	SAAS
ABDe 4/8	2	860 dc	1	4	116	80	49·5	97	33 620	4	0·7	1976-79	SIG	SAAS

Rhaetian Railway (RhB)
Rhätische Bahn

7002 Chur

Director: Dr J Hatz
Chief Engineer: W Altermatt
Chief Mechanical Engineer: F Skvor

Gauge: 1000 mm
Route length: 375 km
Electrification: 248 km at 11 kV 16⅔ Hz ac
   28 km at 2 kV dc
   61 km at 1 kV dc

The Rhaetian Railway is a vital means of communication in the mountainous east of Switzerland, where the Grisons has been termed the 'Canton of 150 Valleys'. Serving the Engadine, the valley of Poschiavo, the Davos area, Arosa and the Grisons Oberland, the railway connects the Canton with the Swiss Federal Railway system in Chur and Landquart, with the Furka-Oberalp Railway in Disentis/Muster, and with the Italian State Railways in Tirano.

The core of the Rhaetian network is electrified at 11 kV 16⅔ Hz. But the Bernina Railway of 61 km from St Moritz to Tirano was electrified at its construction in 1908-10 at 1 kV dc and retains that system. The Bernina is the only Swiss transalpine line that avoids tunnelling, attaining a summit of 2257

RhB three-car push-pull train-set with 1000 hp power car, built by FZA Altenrhein for 11 kV network

metres above sea level at Alp Grüm; for 27 km or 44 per cent of its total distance it is graded at 7 per cent but works entirely by adhesion. The Chur-Arosa

Railway of 28 route-km, which the Rhaetian absorbed in 1943, is electrified at 2 kV dc; on this line the ruling gradient is 6 per cent.

The Rhaetian system as a whole has 118 tunnels and avalanche shelters aggregating 39 km in length and 498 bridges and viaducts totalling 12 km in length. Its longest tunnel is the 6 km Albula.

Traffic

The RhB records over 7 million passenger journeys and 600 000 tonnes of freight a year. Income includes Cantonal subventions and compensations, and in accordance with the Federal law of 1957 concerning socially necessary private railways, 85 per cent of the final deficit is borne by the Federal Government.

Traction and rolling stock

The RhB operates 60 electric locomotives, 40 electric railcars, 300 passenger cars (including five restaurant cars), and 1295 freight wagons (including refrigerated vans and vans with sliding walls for palletised traffic).

A further 13 Type Ge 4/4 II 1700 kW locomotives of the type introduced in 1973, with thyristor control, are on order from SLM, with Brown Boveri electrical equipment. Also on order in 1983 were 10 new passenger cars and 23 freight wagons. The passenger vehicles are of a new Type EW III design by Altenrhein, claimed to be 30 per cent cheaper than previous Swiss narrow-gauge models through adoption of a plug-in method of construction with aluminium sections. Weighing 21-22·5 tonnes and 16·45 m long, each car is mounted on SWP 74 bogies with flexicoil suspension. The cars were to be used on a new Chur-Tirano (Italy) summer train named the 'Bernina Express'.

Development

In March 1982 the RhB presented the Cantonal Government with plans for a 21·5 km cut-off from Klosters to Lavin, on the line from Samedan to Scuol-Tarasp, which would halve present journey times between Landquart and the Lower Engadine, at the extreme east of the RhB system, via the Albula line. The scheme would involve a long tunnel under the Silvretta mountain group, which would take nine years to complete and would be constructed with two internal passing loops. It would be bored with clearances ample enough for conveyance of standard-gauge freight wagons on metre-gauge transporters, and its traffic would feature a regular shuttle of car-carrying trains similar to those which the RhB already operates elsewhere on its system.

In 1982 RhB announced a SwFr 130 million investment plan, 85 per cent Federally funded and 15 per cent financed by the Grisons Canton, covering new rolling stock, track, signalling, depot and workshop improvements.

RhB Type Ge 4/4 2300 hp electric Bo-Bo for 11 kV network

Bernina line train at Lake Bianco Pass summit

Solothurn-Zollikofen-Berne Railway (SZB)
Solothurn-Zollikofen-Bern Bahn

Berne-Worb Railways (VBW)
Vereinigte Bern-Worb Bahnen

Bahnhofhochhaus, Postfach 119, 3048 Worblaufen

Telephone: 58 58 11

Manager: P Scheidegger

Gauge: 1000 mm; mixed 1435 and 1000 mm
Route length: SZB: 34·5 km; 3·5 km
  VBW: 21 km; 4 km
Electrification: SZB: 38 km at 1·25 kV dc
  VBW: 2·3 km at 600 V dc
    8·9 km at 800 V dc
    13·8 km at 1·25 kV dc

These two Berne suburban railways are jointly managed. Part of VBW is electrified at 800 volts dc, the system of the Berne city tramway network with which both railways were connected before the 1960s. Then the SZB's original surface route into Berne was superseded by a new segregated double-track route from Worblaufen which finally tunnelled 1·2 km to a new four-platform terminus beneath the reconstructed Berne main station. The VBW was then mostly re-electrified at 1·25 kV and its route modified to funnel its trains into the new Berne subterranean terminus.

Type Be 4/8 emu of SZB on double track between Worblaufen and Zollikofen; mixed gauge on right-hand side allows movement of 1435 mm-gauge freight wagons

For this development SIG created a new design of emu, with Brown Boveri traction equipment, which has since served as the basic pattern for several other Swiss private railways. The two-car unit comprises a 400 hp, 47·5-tonne, welded steel-bodied power car with all axles powered, Type Be 4/8, and a welded aluminium alloy-bodied trailer, with seating for 136 and standing room for 84. The set has blended dynamic and electro-pneumatic disc braking for normal applications, and electro-magnetic track brakes for emergencies.

Traffic

	1981 SZB	1981 VBW
Total freight tonnage	194 343	91 315
Total freight tonne-km	1 448 449	447 094
Total passenger-km	82 042 405	39 008 972
Total passenger journeys	8 069 310*	5 335 370†
Average length of passenger journey (km)	10·2	7·31

* 3% increase over 1980
† 1·6% increase over 1980

Finance (SwFr)

Revenues

	VBW	SZB
Passengers and baggage	5 399 020	9 462 340
Freight, parcels and mail	571 165	1 369 727
Other income	990 764	2 593 414
Grants	640 255	1 575 888
Total	7 601 204	15 001 369

Expenditure

	VBW	SZB
Staff/personnel	5 283 603	12 607 083
Materials and services	3 857 827	5 964 834
Depreciation	1 299 728	2 641 608
Financial charges	4417	—
Total	10 445 575	21 213 525

Traction and rolling stock

The SZB operates three electric and two diesel locomotives, eight electric power cars, 16 trailers, 12 two-car emus, and six passenger cars. The VBW operates three electric locomotives, eight electric power cars, seven trailers, nine two-car emus and seven passenger cars. All SZB train-sets are being equipped with bars for the sale of both travel tickets to passengers boarding at unstaffed halts, and also of light refreshments. The two systems share 68 freight wagons.

Track

Rail: VST 36 36 kg/m
Cross ties (sleepers): Wood (80%) 150 × 250 mm
Spacing: 1667/km
Fastenings: Type K with elastic spikes (SKL)
Minimum curvature radius: 100 m
Max gradient: 4·5%
Max axleload: 20 tonnes

Type ABt mixed-class driving trailer delivered to SZB in 1981, built and equipped by FFA, SWA and BBC

VBW train on Muri line

Electric traction units

Class	Line voltage	Motored axles per motor car	Rated output (kW) per motor	Max speed km/h	Weight tonnes per car	Total seating capacity	Length per car mm	Year first built	Builders Mechanical parts	Builders Electrical equipment
SZB										
BDe 4/4										
No 1	1·25 kV dc	4	512	75	36	36	1849	1916	SWS	MFO
No 3	1·25 kV dc	4	512	75	36	36	1818	1929	SWS	MFO
No 4-6	1·25 kV dc	4	512	75	35	40	1910	1950	SWS	MFO
No 21-23	1·25 kV dc	4	512	75	37	48	1910	1955	SWS	MFO
Be 4/8										
48-59‡	1·25 kV dc	4	314	75	49	128	4000	1974/78	SIG	BBC
De 4/4 locos										
No 101-102	1·25 kV dc	4	256	50	34	—	1280	1961/65	SZB	MFO
103	1·25 kV dc	4	548	40	40	—	1368	1975	SZB	BBC/AEG†
Geu 4/4 locos†										
No 121	1·25 kV dc	4	132	45	23	—	1153	1912	SIG	MFO/Deutz
No 122	1·25 kV dc	4	256	50	38	—	1400	1916	SWS	MFO/Deutz
VBW										
BDe 4/4										
No 35	800 dc	4	240	65	28	40	1579	1930	SIG	MFO
No 36	800 dc	4	368	65	27	40	1552	1913	SIG	MFO
No 37	800 dc	4	218	60	25	40	1552	1913	SIG	MFO
No 38	800 dc	4	218	60	24	40	1525	1913	SIG	MFO

Electric traction units

Class	Line voltage	Motored axles per motor car	Rated output (kW) per motor	Max speed kmlh	Weight tonnes per car	Total seating capacity	Length per car mm	Year first built	Builders Mechanical parts	Builders Electrical equipment
VBW Be 4/4 71	800 dc	4	294	65	26	40	1636	1925	SIG	SAAS
72-73	800 dc	4	294	65	27	40	1622	1948	SWS	BBC
74	800 dc	4	240	65	28	40	1672	1961	SWS	MFO
Be 4/8 41-47 60-61‡	1·25 kV dc	4	314	75	49	128	4000	1974/78	SIG	BBC
De 4/4 locos 105	1·25 kV dc	4	412	50	32	—	1070	1924	SIG	MFO
Ge 4/4 locos 111-112	800 V/1·25 kV	4	471	35	34	—	965	1927	AEG	AEG

* With additional diesel generating group
† Rebuilt by SBB/VBW
‡ Two-car units, one car motored

South Eastern Railway
Südostbahn

8820 Wädenswil

Telephone: (01) 780 31 57

Director: E A Gross

Gauge: 1435 mm
Route length: 46·85 km

Electrification: 46·85 km at 15 kV 16⅔ Hz ac

The South Eastern Railway, together with the Swiss Federal and the Bodensee-Toggenburg, jointly operates an important cross-country inter-city passenger service from Romanshorn and St Gallen to Lucerne, using the tracks of all three railways. The South Eastern segment of the route runs from Rapperswil to the Swiss Federal station at Pfäffikon, and from there to the Swiss Federal at Arth-Goldau. Branches serve Wädenswil and Einsiedeln.

Traffic	1981
Total freight tonnage	128 177
Total freight tonne-km	1 380 423
Average freight wagon load (tonnes)	14·5
Total passenger-km	40 209 580
Total passenger journeys	3 122 919
Average length of passenger journey (km)	12·9

Finance Revenues (SwFr)	1981
Passengers and baggage	6 145 372
Freight, parcels and mail	3 167 786
Other income	1 375 786
Total	10 688 944

Expenditure (SwFr)	1981
Staff/personnel expenses	8 788 935
Materials and services	7 590 232
Depreciation	1 791 322
Financial charges	75 342
Total	18 245 831

Traction and rolling stock
The railway operates four electric locomotives, 12 electric power cars, 37 passenger cars and 20 freight wagons.

Track
Rail: SBB.- profile type I, 48·85 kg/m
Cross ties (sleepers): SBB standard
Spacing: 1666/km
Fastenings: Verlegeart K on wood and steel sleepers, A on steel sleepers, B on concrete sleepers
Minimum curvature radius: 143 m
Max gradient: 5%
Max axleload: 20 tonnes

South Eastern Railway push-pull train-set of power car and two trailers

Electric railcars

Class	Cars per unit	Line voltage	Motor cars per unit	Motored axles per motor car	Rated output (kW) per motor/ one-hour	Max speed kmlh	Weight tonnes per car	Length per car m	No in service	Year first built	Builders Mechanical parts	Builders Electrical equipment
ABe 4/4	1	15 kV 16⅔ Hz	1	4	706	80	46·5	19·6	6	1939	SIG/SLM/SWS	BBC/MFO/SAAS
De 4/4	1	15 kV 16⅔ Hz	1	4	955	90	47	15·8	2	1939	SLM/SWS	BBC/MFO/SAAS
BDe 4/4	1	15 kV 16⅔ Hz	1	4	2060	110	72	23·7	8	1959	SIG	BBC

Electric locomotives

Class	Wheel arrangement	Line voltage	Rated output (kW) one-hour	Max speed kmlh	Weight tonnes	No in service	Year first built	Builders Mechanical parts	Builders Electrical equipment
Re 4/4 III	Bo-Bo	15 kV 16⅔ Hz	4700	120	80	1	1967	SLM	BBC/MFO
Te	B	15 kV 16⅔ Hz	252	60	28	1	1943	SLM	SAAS

SYRIA

Ministry of Transport

Damascus

Minister: Nouharrah Tayyara

Chemins de Fer Syriens (CFS)

BP 182, Aleppo

Telephone: 13900; 13901
Telex: 31009

President and Director General: Ing N Kassouha
Deputy Director General: Ing M Saboumi
Directors
Technical Development: Naoufal Kassouha
Rolling Stock and Traction: Ing M Kattash
Movement and Traffic: Mikhayel Jerjos
Fixed Installations: Dr-Ing Adnan Elias
Judicial Affairs: M S Halwani
Financial Affairs: Omar Sultan
Stores and Purchasing: Adib Meymeh
Medical: Dr Sabet Issa
Planning and Statistics: Ing Laurent Khayat
Signalling and Telecommunications: Ing H A'Raj

Gauge: 1435 mm
Route length: 1533 km

All standard gauge lines in Syria are operated by the Chemins de Fer Syriens, and comprise the lines from the Lebanese border via Homs and Aleppo to the Turkish border and in the north-east, the connecting line between the Turkish and Iraqi borders. A line runs from the oilfields of Kamechli to the port of Latakia (750 km). The final section of the Homs-Palmyra line was opened to phosphates traffic (destined for the port of Tartus) in 1980.

The extension of the railway from Homs southwards to Damascus (194 km) was opened to freight traffic in March 1983. Laid with 50 kg/m rail, it has been engineered for a maximum speed of 120 km/h. The scheme heavily involved Soviet engineers, and earlier in 1981 a fresh Soviet loan was secured to enable a start on further lines from Deir Ezzor to

Traffic	1980	1981	1982
Freight tonne-km (million)	577	713	708
Freight tonnage (000)	2400	NA	NA
Passenger-km (million)	333	424	390
Passenger journeys (000)	1300	NA	NA

First-class air-conditioned car by VEB Bautzen, German Democratic Republic

Abou-Kamal (150 km) and from Tartus to Latakia (80 km). The first of these will link up with Iraq's new Baghdad-Husaiba line. At the start of 1983 engineering design of the Tartus-Latakia line was complete and construction was to begin during the year. To follow this project priority is now placed on a new 203 km line from Palmyra to Deir Ezzor.

Traction and rolling stock

In 1982 the railway was operating 77 diesel locomotives, 10 shunters, 10 diesel railcars, 110 passenger cars, 38 baggage vans and 2585 freight wagons. It had begun to take delivery of 80 Type 1145 2800 hp diesel-electric locomotives from the USSR, 20 shunters from Czechoslovak industry, 1400 freight wagons from firms in the German Democratic Republic and 49 passenger cars from MecanoExportImport of Romania. For the opening of the Homs-Damascus line orders were placed with VEB Bautzen and Görlitz for 358 new passenger cars including sleeping and restaurant cars and 100 air-conditioned first-class cars; deliveries were proceeding in 1982-83.

Interior of new first-class car by VEB Bautzen

Chemin de Fer du Hedjaz

BP 134, Damascus

Director General: Mohamed el Bizem
Deputy Director General: Rasmi Mahrousse
Manager, Traffic Department: Fouad Arabi
Manager, Accounts Department: Dib Habbouche

Gauge: 1050 mm
Route length: 307 km

In addition to its own 240 km route length, the CF du Hedjaz also operates the 67 km narrow-gauge Damascus-Zerghaya line on behalf of the Syrian Government.

The Hedjaz Railway originally extended 1303 km from Damascus to Medina to carry pilgrims to the Holy Cities of Mecca and Medina. During the 1914-18 war the southern portion was severely damaged and the 844 km section from Maan in Jordan to Medina in Saudi Arabia was left derelict. In 1977 Syria, Jordan and Saudi Arabia formally agreed to commission from Dorsch Consult of West Germany a feasibility study for a replacement standard-gauge line using 60 kg/m rail, re-routed where necessary to improve alignment for high passenger speed, and designed to acceptable standards for operation of 25-tonne axleload freight wagons.

In 1981 Syria accepted the West German consultants' report and advised the Saudis and Jordanians that it was going ahead with the 114 km of the route from Damascus to Deraa, near the Jordanian border. With the Homs-Palmyra line finished in September 1980, the Damascus-Deraa extension was allocated the required funds in Syria's 1980-85 National Plan. Neither Jordan nor Saudi Arabia took complementary action. The Saudi Government's reaction was that though it still regarded resurrection of the Hedjaz Railway throughout as a worthwhile long-term objective, it would not make a commitment to execute its part of the scheme without more exhaustive research.

In November 1982 an agreement was signed between the Syrian Ministry of Planning and the Soviet Administration of Economic Affairs with Foreign Countries to cover construction of the new Hedjaz Railway in Syria under the loan agreement signed in May 1981. The new Syrian Hedjaz section is expected to come into operation in 1986.

TAIWAN

Ministry of Communications

Taipei

Minister: Ci Lien

Taiwan Railway Administration (TRA)

2 Yen-Ping North Road, Section 1, Taipei

Telephone: 5511131
Telex: 21837

Managing Director: P Tong
Deputy Managing Directors
 C H Tu
 Y L Po
 Y C Loh

Chief Engineering: S F Chen
Chief Secretary: K M Lee
Superintendents
 Transportation Department: S C Chang
 Civil Engineering Department: C P Chang
 Mechanical Engineering Department: C L King
 Electrical Engineering: S M Chen
 Purchase and Stores Department: I C Chen
 Planning Department: C W Meng
 Hualien Office: H S Wan
 General Affairs Department: H Chiang
 Accounting Department: Y S Hsiang
Chief, Finance Control Office: H Chiang
Chief, Personnel Office: L L Ma
Chief, Electronic Data Processing Office: S Huang

Gauge: 1067 mm
Route length: 1091 km
Electrification: 495 km at 25 kV 60 Hz ac

Transport development

The Taiwan Railway is the principal artery of transport on the island of Taiwan. It consists of three lines: the West Line with its branches; the East Line;

and the new 81·6 km North Link Line from Nanshenghu to Tienpu. Completed in 1979 after six years' work at a cost of NT$7300 million, 39 per cent Government-funded, this 1067 mm-gauge project ended the isolation of the 762 mm-gauge East Coast line. Conversion of the latter to 1067 mm has since been achieved.

The West Line, a double-tracked railway system, 1067 mm in gauge, stretches from north to south along the West Plain area of the island, linking the two big seaports of Keelung and Kaohsiung with the intermediate cities of Taipei, Hsinchu, Tai-chung, Chang-hua, Chia-i and Tai-nan. In the middle section of the system there are two routes from Chu-nan to Chang-hua: the Coast Line and the Mountain Line, 91·4 km in length, through the cities of Miao-li, Feng-yuan, and Tai-chung.

Along a narrow valley area of the east coast the single-tracked 762 mm-gauge East Line from Hualien to Taitung (170 km) has now been converted to 1067 mm and through Taitung-Taipei service was inaugurated in July 1982. Almost an hour has been cut from passenger train times between Hualien and Taitung, and the through trains between Taipei and Taitung take 5½ hours for the 377 km. The scheme was also a further step in completion of an unbroken island ring route.

Traffic
Economic depression and competition from other modes halted traffic growth in 1981, but Government-approved tariff increases induced more passengers to take premium-fare trains and boosted revenue. The railway's chief freight commodities are cement, limestone, grain, fertilisers, coal and coke.

Finance (NT $000)

Revenue	1980	1981
Passenger	4069 119	6018 463
Freight	1297 471	1938 679
Other	2172 888	2507 065
Total	7539 478	10 464 207

Expenses		
Running expenses	1695 682	2246 279
Station expenses	1133 726	1432 636
Maintenance of way and structures	1077 083	1123 914
Maintenance of electrical equipment	420 338	412 355
Maintenance of vehicles	2136 794	2300 217
Other operating expenses	1992 693	2328 357
General and administrative expenses	519 606	618 854
Total	8975 922	10 462 612

Operating profit or loss	(1436 444)	1595
Non-operating income	2453 896	2079 498
Non-operating charges	2737 402	2764 760
Non-operating deficit	(283 506)	(685 262)
Loss	(1719 950)	(683 667)

Motive power and rolling stock
In 1981 the railway took delivery of five electric locomotives by General Electric and 200 air-conditioned passenger cars from the local supplier, Tong Eng Iron Works Ltd. Total stock comprised:

Steam locomotives	43
Electric locomotives	100
Diesel-electric locomotives	169
Diesel railcars	71
Diesel trailer cars	10
Emus	20
Passenger coaches	1600
Freight cars	7646

Renewals ordered for 1982 comprised acquisition of five high-power diesel-electric locomotives, 30

Traffic

	1978	1979	1980	1981
Total freight ton-km (million)	2495	2516	2588	2393
Total freight tonnage (million)	16·3	16·7	18	16·9
Total passenger-km (million)	7949	7275	7919	7946·9
Total passengers carried (million)	122·2	107·8	139	130·7

air-conditioned diesel railcars and 88 coal wagons, and the remodelling of 12 narrow-gauge diesel locomotives, 50 passenger cars with air-conditioning and 80 freight cars. Four self-steering bogies were obtained from South Africa for trial.

Civil engineering
Construction of the 98 km South Coast link from Taitung to Fang-Liao proceeds, entailing 33 tunnels of 37 km aggregate length and 40 bridges with a total length of 5 km, but is now unlikely to be finished before the end of 1988. The project is absorbing 41 per cent of TRA's planned NT $49 200 million investment in the 1983-89 period. Completion of the North Link has overtaxed the single line through I-Lan to Hualien, on the north-east coast, and this is being doubled, realigned in places and equipped with automatic block and new telecommunications to lift its operating capacity from 90 to 230 trains daily; 16 km of double track already existed and conversion of the remaining 79 km is programmed for completion by June 1984.

Taipei underground link
The trunk railway in Taipei is to be put underground to eliminate the traffic congestion caused by level crossings on Chunghua Road and to establish a transport centre in the Taipei station area as a foundation for a future mass transit system in the Taipei Metropolitan Area. The project involves a new line

starting from west of Sungchiang Road to the east of Wanhua station, including Taipei main station, with a total length of 4·05 km of which 3·4 km will be in tunnel. Deutsche Eisenbahn Consulting GmbH has been selected as general consultant for the project, which was to be launched in the 1983/84 financial year.

The stations involved will be Nankang, Sunshan, Huashan and Wanhua. A new car maintenance yard will be established in Panchiao. Taipei main station will become a four-level through station, instead of a terminal, and its capacity will be considerably expanded. A bypass line will eventually be constructed for freight traffic in order to maximise the rail capacity in the city for commuter traffic. The project is expected to last eight years and cost over US$30 million.

Signalling

Absolute block system	1981
Single-track (no of sectors)	86
Double-track (no of sectors)	1
Double-track automatic block signalling (km)	87·2
Single-track automatic block signalling (km)	80·5
Centralised traffic control system (CTC) (km)	466·1
Interlocking plant	
Relay	37
Electric	19

Tze Chiang express, formed of emu built by British Rail Engineering with GEC Traction electrical equipment

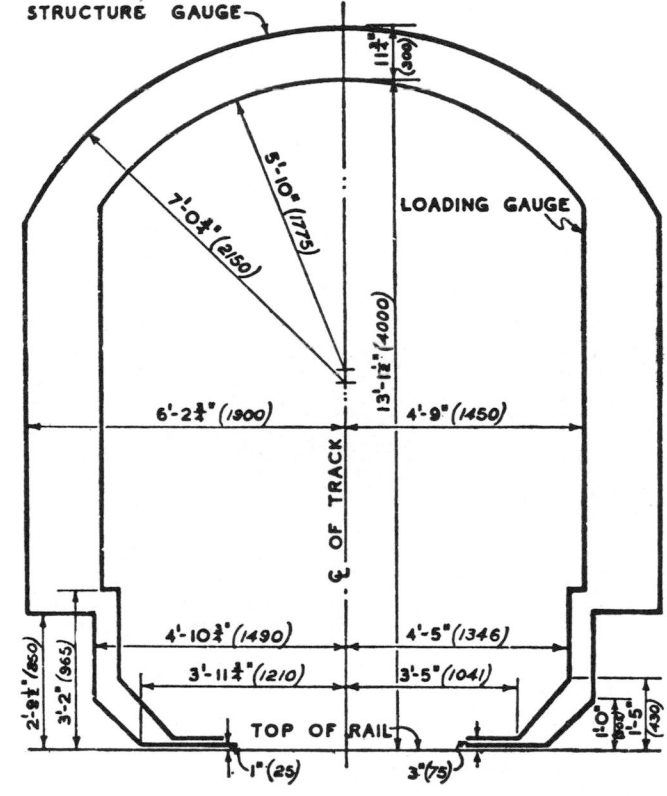

Diesel locomotives

Class	Wheel arrangement	Transmission	Rated power hp	Max kg	Tractive effort Continuous at kg	kmlh	Max speed kmlh	Wheel dia mm	Total weight tonnes	Length mm	Year first built	Builders
R	A1A	Elec	1650		15 180	19·2	100	1016	78	14 266	1960	EMD, GM
S	Bo-Bo	Elec	950		12 860	14	75	838	54	11 230	1966	EMD, GM
G-22CU	Co-Co	Elec	1500		22 970	—	100	1016	84·4	—	1981	EMD, GM

Electric locomotives

Class	Wheel arrangement	Line current kV	Rated output hp	Tractive effort (full field) Continuous kg	Max speed kmlh	Wheel dia mm	Weight tonnes	Length mm	Year built	Builders
E100	Bo-Bo	25	2752	18 500	110	1220	72	14 050	1977	GEC, UK
E200	Co-Co	25	3758	20 100	110	914	96	16 459	1977	GE, USA

Electric railcars

Class	Wheel arrangement	Line current kV	Rated output hp	Tractive effort (full field) Continuous kg	Max speed km/h	Wheel dia mm	Weight tonnes	Length mm	Year built	Builders
EM	Bo-Bo	25	1711	6180	120	860	55	20 350	1978	GEC, UK

TANZANIA

Tanzania Railways Corporation (TRC)

PO Box 468, Dar es Salaam

Telephone: 26241
Telex: 41308

General Manager: Tom A K Mmari
Assistant General Manager, Operations: E N Makoi
Assistant General Manager, Services: O R Kitenge
Chief Traffic Manager: K S Mtwangi
Chief Mechanical Engineer: H Sakwari
Chief Civil Engineer: P J Kyesi
Chief of Manpower: A M Semaya
Chief Supplies Manager: H H Mnubi
Chief of Management Services: F J Mohamed

Gauge: 1000 mm
Length: 2600 track-km

One of 50 passenger coaches on order for 35 sleeping and 10 restaurant cars built by BREL and supplied by BRE-Metro Ltd for service from Dar es Salaam to Tabora, Kigoma and Mowanza

Following the formal break-up of the East African Railways Corporation in 1977, Tanzania set up the independent Tanzanian Railways Corporation to operate the former EAR lines wholly within Tanzania. In the succeeding years severance has posed TR numerous problems.

In 1982 consultants completed a study sponsored by the Canadian International Development Agency (CIDA) and advocated both reorganisation measures and an investment equivalent to US$740 million over the next 20 years. Priorities were laid on staff training, improvement of communications and signalling, rolling stock purchases, and reballasting of track. Until these items had been covered, complete relaying of the main line to Kigoma should be suspended, since a higher level of traffic was needed to tax the strength of the existing rails, and plans for a new 540 km line from Arusha to Musoma on Lake Victoria deferred.

The consultants concluded that the existing wagon fleet was adequate to raise freight traffic by 50 per cent over five years if it was more efficiently controlled. For passenger traffic already running at 2 million journeys a year and forecast to reach 10 million by the late 1990s, however, traction and coaching stock were insufficient. A management training centre must be established, and training also set up for efficient use of the diesel locomotive overhaul depot at Morogoro, a crucial need since the loss of access to major overhaul facilities in Kenya. A maintenance depot has been established at Tabora.

CIDA has followed earlier financial aid for rolling stock and infrastructure improvements with a sum of TSh 514 million chiefly for projects between Dar es Salaam and Morogoro, including a telecommunications system. Other aid for TRC's five-year rehabilitation scheme has been secured from Denmark and the European Economic Community.

A freight wagon assembly plant is being set up at Puga, west of Dar es Salaam, by the Tanzanian National Development Corporation (NDC). It will be run jointly by the NDC and Kalmar Verkstad of Sweden.

Kagera River Basin scheme

The Kagera River Basin Organisation, sponsored by the United Nations Organisation, and representing Burundi, Rwanda, Uganda and Tanzania, has commissioned survey and design studies for a 2000 km system of lines to afford Burundi and Rwanda access to the ports of Dar es Salaam and Mombasa. For Tanzania this proposes a new 400 km railway from Arusha, present terminal of the TRC line north-westward from Tanga, to Musoma on the eastern shore of Lake Victoria.

Traction and rolling stock

In 1982 TR was operating 64 steam and 120 diesel locomotives, 291 passenger and baggage cars and 3065 freight wagons. Kalmar Verkstad delivered 20 new passenger cars in 1982 and 35 cement wagons with Gloucester Carriage & Wagon rubber-sprung bogies were ordered from Scandia-Randers. Bids were sought for supply of five shunting locomotives, 30 container and 45 ballast wagons.

Track

TR employs 80A 39·8 kg/m, 60A 30·54 kg/m and GH5C 27·85 kg/m rails permitting a maximum axleload of 13·7 tonnes for locomotives and 14·2 tonnes for freight wagons. Minimum curve radius is 107 metres and maximum gradient 2·2 per cent.

Investment plans 1983 (TSh million)

Main-line diesel locomotives (12)	24·2
Diesel shunters (18)	5·6
Passenger cars (20)	7
Freight cars (30)	6
Track work and equipment	13
Signalling and communications	17
Other	4·2
Total	77

Tanzania-Zambia Railway Authority (TAZARA)

PO Box 2834, Dar es Salaam

Telephone: 64191
Telex: 41059

General Manager: Maj-Gen C J Nyirenda
Deputy General Manager: A G I Shayo
Chief Mechanical Engineer: M S Shankaya
Chief Civil Engineer: H S Mawona
Traffic Manager: D Mwape
Personnel Manager: F J Kateya
Supplies Manager: I Z Mutakyahwa
Finance Manager: J M Nyakyoma
Regional Manager, Zambia: J Kasono
Regional Manager, Tanzania: R S Seme

Gauge: 1067 mm
Route length: 1860 km (891 km in Zambia, 969 km in Tanzania)

The Tanzania-Zambia Railway (TAZARA) was constructed following an agreement signed in September 1967 between the Governments of Tanzania and Zambia, and of the People's Republic of China. Under the agreement, China provided finance and technical services for a rail link of approximately 1860 km from Dar es Salaam in Tanzania to Kapiri Mposhi in Zambia, together with equipment, two workshops and other auxiliary facilities, at an estimated cost of TSh 2 866 200 million. The loan repayment was to commence in 1983 and to be spread over 30 years, with each country responsible for 50 per cent. Because of their economic problems, however, both countries were in 1983 seeking to renegotiate the repayment terms.

Construction began officially in 1970 and tracklaying was completed in 1975. The line has 147 stations of which 93 were opened at the initial stage of operations. Trial running of freight and passenger services began in 1975 and the hand-over of the railway and full transportation operations commenced in 1976.

The Tanzania-Zambia Railway is designed with a gauge that permits through goods traffic operations with contiguous railways in Central Africa, in particular Zambia Railways. Its performance, however, has been handicapped by serious problems of traction, rolling stock and track maintenance, of inadequate funds, and the international political strains of the continent. Whereas the railway's designed capacity is 5 million tonnes of freight a year, it has yet to register more than 1·5 million tonnes. Unsatisfactory port facilities at Dar es Salaam have driven Zambia to desert the TAZARA for other routes and ports.

However in March 1983 the Southern African Development Coordination Conference agreed to finance a rehabilitation programme and to consider extensions of the line to make it an outlet to the sea for more countries, including Zaire.

The Council of Ministers consisting of three Ministers each from Zambia and Tanzania is the organ established by the two Governments to exercise overall control on the railway. All the railway assets are vested in TAZARA, a corporate body whose principal organ is the Board of Directors consisting of five members each appointed by the two Governments. For operational purposes, the whole railway is divided into two regions for Tanzania and Zambia, with respective regional headquarters at Dar es Salaam and Mpika.

Motive power and rolling stock

At the beginning of 1982 TAZARA owned and operated 102 Type DFH2 main-line diesel-hydraulic locomotives of Chinese manufacture, 100 passenger coaches and 2100 freight wagons.

With financial aid from the German Federal Government, orders were placed in 1981 with Krupp for 14 2360 kW diesel-electric locomotives, of which deliveries were proceeding in 1983; they were destined for the steeply graded Mlimba-Chazi section of the route; 11 more were likely to be sought. From MTU 16 engines were ordered to re-motor existing diesel-hydraulic locomotives, which would be finished in 1983; to improve availability of the DFH2s, spares worth TSh 50 million were ordered from Chinese suppliers. An early product of the traction rehabilitation was increase of the Dar es Salaam-Kapiri Mosha (Zambia) passenger service from two to three trains weekly.

Track
Rail: 45 kg/m
Sleepers: Prestressed concrete
Spacing: 1520/km
Minimum curvature: Mainly 300 m, in some places even 250 and 200 m
Max gradient: 1 in 50, but ruling gradient 1 in 100
Max altitude: 1789·43 m, Uyole near Mbeya
Max axleload: 20 tonnes

Chinese-built diesel-hydraulic locomotive under inspection in TAZARA's locomotive sheds near Dar es Salaam
(National Council for US-China)

THAILAND

Ministry of Communications

5 Rajdammern Avenue, Bangkok 1

Minister: A Sirigaya
Under Secretary of State: M L Jeongjan Kambhu

State Railway of Thailand (RSR)

Yodse, Bangkok 10500

Telephone: 2230341

Board of Commissioners
Chairman: Gen Tienchai Sirisumpan
Members: Manus Corvanich
  Pol Lt Gen Prakob Weeraphan
  Dr Sunthorn Satirathai
  Pol Maj Gen Chatchai Upapong
  Maj Gen Vichit Vichitsonggram
  Bodi Chunnananda
  Banyong Saralamba
Management
General Manager: Banyong Saralamba
Deputy General Managers
  Operating: Smer Sakhakorn
  Development and Planning: Prachoom Annavadhana
  Administrative: Hiran Radeesri
  Railway Advisor: Dhawat Sangpradab
Chief of Department attached to the General Manager: Prasith Singhapundu
Chief Mechanical Engineer: Somsak Prabhavasit
Deputy Chief Mechanical Engineers
  Workshops: Chalor Siricharoen
  Motive Power: Sombongse Charubhumi
  Chief Civil Engineer: Chamras Ukachoke
Deputy Chief Civil Engineers
  Permanent Way: Choomsin Duabbhasuta
  Modernisation: Thawee Dhamaraksa
Traffic Manager: Amorn Charoenbhantaraks
Deputy Traffic Managers
  Operation: Akom Suthiwan
  Service: Boonroeng Phonglumchiag
Comptroller: Amporn Larnlua
Deputy Comptroller: Pramote Chutima
Personnel Manager: Chawarn Boonyawat
Marketing Manager: Chird Boonyaratavej
Deputy Marketing Manager: Thasanai Chantarangkul
Stores Superintendent: Preecha Swasdiburi
Chief, Development Co-ordinating Bureau: Sriyudh Sirivedhin
Superintendent, Railway Training Centre: Somchai Chulacharitta
Chief, Legal Bureau: Chaveng Varavit
Chief, Medical Bureau: Kasam Isarangkura na Ayudhya
Chief, Signalling and Telecommunications Bureau: Thaworn Hongskul

Gauge: 1000 mm
Route length: 3735 km

Transport development
RSR is playing a vital role in the nation's economic and industrial development following a decision by the Government during the 1970s to invest heavily in railway projects. The US$1400 million which the Government has allocated RSR for investment in its 1982-86 plan is twice the amount offered under the 1977-81 plan. The aim is that by 1986 RSR shall double its freight tonne-km from 2656 million in 1981 to 5700 million, and raise annual passenger journeys from 78·9 million to 117 million. Early in 1983 a 2600 million Baht loan was being negotiated with the World Bank towards double-tracking and rolling stock elements of the 1982-86 plan, which has been costed overall at 7900 million Baht.

Traffic
Passenger and freight tariffs have been kept at a low level by the Government, but in 1981 the World Bank made loans conditional on substantial increases. In June freight rates were hoisted as much as 73 per cent, which set back volume growth in that sector, but the 35 per cent lift of passenger fares had no effect on business because the increase was so tempered to third-class passengers that rail travel remained 20 per cent cheaper than use of buses. Between 1970 and 1981 RSR's passenger-km climbed from 5600 million to 9483 million, but there was a slight recession in 1982. Increase of maximum speed to 80 km/h as a result of a continuous programme of track strengthening since the mid-1950s makes the long-haul trains competitive with road public transport in speed; in this sector revenue has risen 20 per cent since the fare increases, but overall the rate rises have been insufficient to offset sharply climbing fuel and labour costs.

Finances	(million Baht)
Revenues	*1979/80*
Passengers and baggage	1280
Freight and mail	812
Total	2313
Expenses	
Staff/personnel	1223
Materials and services	1117
Depreciation	168
Financial charges	75
Total	2585

Motive power and rolling stock
In 1982 RSR was operating eight steam, 170 diesel-electric and 56 diesel-hydraulic locomotives, 40 shunters, 62 diesel railcars and 64 trailers, 1111 passenger cars and 8843 freight wagons.

Much of the increased investment funds will be assigned to traction and rolling stock purchases to cope with the prospective growth of traffic. In May 1982 orders were placed with Alsthom-Atlantique for nine more of RSR's principal main-line type, the 2250 hp diesel-electric Co-Co with Pielstick PA4 engine, following the additional 30 of the type acquired in 1981 from German Federal Republic builders with a loan from that country. To be delivered by May 1983, these locomotives are for use on the Sattahip port extension and container trains serving a new terminal at Bang Sue, Bangkok. MTU is supplying Series 396 V12 1070 hp, 1500 rpm

Traffic	*1978/79*	*1979/80*	*1980/81*	*1981/82*
Total freight tonnage (million)	6·2	6·2	5·92	5·52
Total freight tonne-km (million)	NA	2900	2600·5	2421
Total passenger-km (000 million)	6·8	8·9	9·48	9·23
Total passenger journeys (million)	64·1	74·3	78·8	80·3

engines to re-power 27 Henschel locomotives acquired in 1963. RSR was further expected to seek 50 2400 hp mixed traffic, six 1200 hp, and 16 shunting locomotives.

Twenty two-car dmus have been ordered for delivery by October 1983, 13 as replacements for existing stock, seven for Sattahip port line passenger service. Built by Mitsui of Japan, the sets' power cars have DBSFRG 100 engines and Niigata hydraulic transmission. Orders for 24 additional sets were expected.

The passenger car fleet is likely to be enlarged by 624 new cars under the 1982-86 plan; of these about a quarter would be assembled at RSR's Makkasan workshops, Bangkok. New wagon orders are expected to total some 1500. Conversion from vacuum to air braking is planned, and the 1982-86 investment programme allocates 234 million Baht to the changeover.

In 1983 Daewoo of South Korea had 238 freight wagons under construction for the Sattahip line, comprising 158 bogie covered (BCG), 60 bogie container flat (BCF) and 20 bogie full van (BFV) vehicles. Complete delivery was due by August 1983.

Electrification
Electrification of the line from Bangkok to Chiang Mai was committed to study by Sofrerail in 1975 and with aid from the German Federal Republic has lately been reconsidered by West German consultants. This would be associated with realignments on the 250 km mountain sector between Sila At and Chiang Mai to ease the ruling gradient from 2·5 to 1 per cent.

Investment plans 1983	(US$000)
Diesel-electric main-line locomotives (35)	29 751
Diesel-hydraulic main-line (5) and shunting (10) locomotives	6692
Passenger cars and dmus	13 505
Freight wagons (238)	9001
New lines	38 909
Track improvements and machinery	9036
Bridges and buildings	2122
Signalling	268
Yards and terminals	765
Workshops	2568
Other	11 977
Total	124 594

Civil engineering
The new 134 km line from Sattahip port to Chachoengsao, east of Bangkok, should be finished in 1983. It has been engineered for 20-tonne axleloads and 100 km/h maximum speed, will be operated by tokenless block between station interlockings associated with power-operated points, and will run passenger as well as freight trains. The latter will include unit mineral and container trains, the latter plying to and from new Bangkok terminals. A 40 km extension beyond Sattahip to industrial development at Rayong is possible.

A number of other new lines are proposed, among them: Suphan Buri to Mae Sod via Tak, a segment of the Trans-Asian Railway concept conceived to link Asian and European rail systems, which could eventually connect RSR with the Union of Burma Railways; a 60 km branch from the Bangkok-Chiang Mai main line at Phitsanlok to the new Larn Krabue oilfield; Suphan Buri to Lop Buri, to establish a link between northern and southern lines other than via Bangkok; an extension of the southern line's Khiri-Rattanikhom branch to the coast at Phuket; and Khuan Niang, also in the south, to a planned new deep-water port at Songkhla. Alternative routes to Songkhla were submitted to consultants for study in 1983. Parts of the northern and north-eastern lines are being double-tracked; Deconsult has been commissioned to report on improving the 230 km line from Uttaradit to Chiang Mai.

Large-scale works are under study in the Bangkok area. One project is the elevation of some 11 km of the approach lines from Bang Sue and Makkasan to Hua Lampong terminus, to obviate the present alignment's frequent intersection by level crossings. Another is the extension of the Maeklong line to a connection with the main RSR network, which at the Bangkok end would entail a new, elevated 5 km connection between the city's Hua Lampong and Wongwien termini. At its western end the Maeklong line would be plugged into the Southern main line near Pak Tho. This scheme, involving some 25 km of new route construction, almost half of it elevated or on bridges, is being evaluated as an alternative to doubling the Southern line so as to enlarge the latter's operating capacity. Meanwhile, in connection with the Sattahip port traffic a new marshalling yard, container and central freight terminal are being constructed in the Bang Sue area, north of the city, at Paholyothin. Sattahip port will be fully operational in 1984.

A great deal of track renewal since 1955 has raised the maximum axleload to 13·5 tonnes, which will be capable of further increase to 15 tonnes on main lines when a bridge renewal programme is complete. Since 1969 RSR has changed from 35 kg/m to 40 kg/m rail for main lines with an annual throughput in excess of 5 million tonnes gross.

Signalling

Current plans provide for equipment of 201 stations with electric interlocking and installation of automatic block colour-light signalling between 78 points on the north, north-eastern and southern lines. An automatic train stop system is to be installed between 435 stations and 230 traction units fitted to work with it.

Sleepers

Type	Untreated hardwood	Creosote-treated softwood	2-block concrete (RS-type)
Thickness (mm)	150	124-150	200
Spacing per km	1430-1540	1430-1540	1540

Workshops

The RSR's workshops comprise: Makkasan, the central plant in Bangkok; and regional workshops comprising Uttaradit in the north, Nakhon Ratchasima in the north-east and Thung Song in the south. To increase workshop capacity and efficiency the 1982-86 investment programme allocates 89·844 million Baht for the procurement of machine tools and the expansion of working area and office at Makkasan, and 67·934 million Baht for the improvement of three regional workshops.

Rail

Type	Weight (kg/m)	% of track length
BS 50 R	24·8	4·32
BS 60 R & 60 ASCE	29·77	7·37
BS 70 R	34·76 }	62·77
BS 70 A & 70 ASCE	34·84 }	
BS 80 A	39·8	20·86
Others	37, 37·5, 42·5	4·68

Minimum curvature radius: 180 m
Max gradient: 2·6%
Max altitude: 574·9 m
Max axleload: 13·75 tonnes

Diesel locomotives

Class	Wheel arrangement	Transmission	Rated power hp	Max tractive effort at wheel rim kg @ % Adhesion Weight	Minimum continuous tractive effort kg @ kmlh	Max speed kmlh	Wheel dia mm	Service weight tons	Length mm	No on book	Year introduced	Builders Mechanical parts	Builders Engine & type	Builders Transmission
Sulzer	Bo-Bo	Elec	735	10 000 @ 21·5%	4600 @ 27·5	65	914	46·5	12 100	3	1947	Sulzer Bros, Switzerland	Sulzer 6LDA 25	Oerlikon Switzerland
Davenport	Bo-Bo	Elec	500	14 770 @ 30%	5700 @ 16	82	914	48·12	9893·2	30	1952	Davenport, USA	Caterpillar D.397	Westinghouse, USA
Davenport	Co-Co	Elec	1000	24 000 @ 30%	11 370 @ 16	92	914	80	16 954·4	15	1955	Davenport, USA	Caterpillar D.397	Westinghouse, USA
Hitachi	Co-Co	Elec	1040	21 600 @ 30%	13 140 @ 12·76	70	914	72	14 300	20	1958	Hitachi, Japan	MAN, W 8 V 22/ 30 m AUL	Hitachi, Japan
GE	Co-Co	Elec	1320	22 500 @ 30%	17 963 @ 13	103	914	75	16 288	50	1965	General Electric, USA	Cummins, VT 12-825 B1, VTA-1710-L	General Electric, USA
Alsthom	Co-Co	Elec	2400	24 800 @ 30%	20 600 @ 21	95	914	82·5	16 258	52	1975	Alsthom, France, Krupp and Henschel, West Germany	SEMT Pielstick, 16PA 4V.185	Alsthom, France
AHK	Co-Co	Elec	2400	24 800 @ 30%	20 600 @ 21	100	914	82·5	16 258	30	1980	Alsthom, Krupp, Henschel	SEMT Pielstick 16PA4 185VG	Alsthom, France
Alsthom	Co-Co	Elec	2250	26 000	20 600	100	914	80·8	15 000	9	1983	Alsthom	SEMT Pielstick 16 PA4	Alsthom, France
Krauss-Maffei	C	Hyd	440	12 000 @ 33·33%	7450 @ 7·55	27	1106	36	8350	5	1955	Krauss-Maffei, West Germany	MAN, W 8 V 17.5/ 22A	Voith, West Germany
Hunslet	C	Hyd	1240	19 100 @ 33%	2430 @ 12·1	19·5	1106	30	7658	5	1964	Hunslet, England	Gardner, 8L 3B	Voith, West Germany
Henschel	B-B	Hyd	1200	17 160 @ 33%	14 900 @ 11	90	914	52	12 800	27	1964	Henschel, West Germany	Maybach, MB.12V 493 TY 10	Voith, West Germany
Krupp	B-B	Hyd	1500	18 150 @ 33%	15 250 @ 14·5	90	914	55	12 800	29	1969	Krupp, West Germany	Maybach, MB.12V 652 TB 10	Voith, West Germany

Diesel railcars

Class	Wheel arrangement	Transmission	Rated power hp	Max tractive effort at wheel rim kg @ % Adhesion Weight	Minimum continuous tractive effort kg @ kmlh	Max speed kmlh	Wheel dia mm	Service weight tons	Length mm	No on book	Year introduced	Builders Mechanical parts	Builders Engine & type	Builders Transmission
Teikoku	1-4 wheel bogie driving trailer	Hyd-mech	300	—	—	60	851	Power 25·9 Trailer (1) 16 (2) 17·5	17 000	6	1961	Teikokucar, Japan	Cummins NHHRBS-600	Niigata, Japan
Niigata	2-4 wheel bogie driving trailer	Hyd-mech	320	4460		85	851	Power Type A 31 Type B 31 Trailer 33·75	20 800	3	1962	Niigata, Japan	Cummins NHHRS-6-B	Niigata, Japan

Diesel railcars

Class	Wheel arrangement	Transmission	Rated power hp	Max tractive effort at wheel rim kg @ % Adhesion Weight	Minimum continuous tractive effort kg @ kmlh	Max speed kmlh	Wheel dia mm	Service weight tons	Length mm	No on book	Year introduced	Builders Mechanical parts	Builders Engine & type	Builders Transmission
Tokyu	2-4 wheel bogie driving trailer	Hyd-mech	440	4560	2260 @ 25	85	851	Power Type A 36·8 Type B 37 Trailer 26·9	20 800	7	1965	Tokyu, Japan	Cummins NHH-220-B-1	Niigata, Japan
Hitachi	2-4 wheel bogie driving trailer	Hyd-mech	440	4560	2310 @ 27	85	851	Power Type A 37·5 Type B 37·3 Trailer 27·5	20 800	10	1967	Hitachi, Japan	Cummins NHH-220-B-1	Niigata, Japan
Hitachi	2-4 wheel bogie driving trailer	Hyd-mech	440	4380	2340 @ 25	90	851	Power Type A 38·5 Type B 38·3 Trailer 28·6	20 800	28	1971	Nippon Sharyo & Hitachi, Japan	Cummins NHH-220-B-1	Niigata, Japan
Tokyu (stainless)	2-4 wheel bogie driving trailer	Hyd-mech	220	5400	2175 @ 30	70	851	Power Type A 33·6 Type B 32·2 Trailer 27·8	20 800	4	1971	Tokyu, Japan	Cummins NHH-220-B-1	Niigata, Japan

TUNISIA

Tunisian National Railways (SNCFT)
Société Nationale des Chemins de Fer Tunisiens

67 avenue Farhat Hached, Tunis

Telephone: 242 188
Telex: 719

President/Director General: Hédi Zeghal
Assistant Director General: Chedamsi Mohamed
Traction and Rolling Stock Manager: Mékki Cheour
Development Manager: Mokhtar Mehri
Financial Director: Bellil Ahmed
Chief of Rolling Stock: M Chaouch
Permanent Way and Works Director: Abdelmajid Bazarbacha
Stores Manager: H Dahmouni
Commercial Manager: Abdelmajid Hassaine

Gauge: 1435 mm; 1000-1050 mm
Route length: 479 km; 1534 km

Since the end of the 1970s SNCFT has undergone a major change in its affairs stemming largely from a 1979 agreement by the Government to cover the cost of new infrastructure and to service the debts of loans for infrastructure payments.

Finance (000 dinars)	1981
Traffic receipts	29 787
Miscellaneous revenue and compensations	14 297
Total	44 084
Expenditure	51 211

Traffic	1979	1980	1981
Total freight ton-km (million)	1478	1710·8	1707·1
Total freight tonnage (million)	7·6	8·342	8·264
Total passenger-km (million)	737	862·06	1010·65
Total passengers (million)	25	28·004	30·683

Motive power and rolling stock
At the start of 1982 SNCFT operated on 1000-1050 mm gauge 90 diesel locomotives, 28 diesel railcars, 69 railcar trailers, 82 passenger cars and 4795 freight cars. The stock of the 1435 mm-gauge lines comprised 24 diesel locomotives, 18 diesel railcars, 25 trailers, eight passenger cars and 973 freight wagons. Following its 1980 acquisition of 20 three-car diesel-hydraulic train-sets from Ganz-Mávag for express services, the railway took 1981 delivery of 10 suburban four-car diesel train-sets from the same builder. A 1983 order for six electric train-sets for the new Sousse-Monastir line and for 100 passenger cars was also obtained by Ganz-Mávag; soon afterwards tenders were called for a further 33 passenger cars. Between 1979 and 1981 SNCFT enjoyed a 20 per cent rise in passenger journeys.

Delivery was to begin in 1983 of a C$26 million locomotive order from Bombardier comprising nine Type MXS 620 1770 kW units for metre gauge and 13 Type MXS 624 1620 kW units for 1435 mm gauge. An order for 20 diesel-hydraulic locomotives has been placed with Ganz-Mávag.

Civil engineering
The new 129 km Gafsa-Gabes phosphate line was opened by the Prime Minister in May 1983. Phosphates, a traffic concentrated in the Gafsa-Sfax-Gabes area, account for half the railway's total tonnage, and in recent years 700 special-purpose

wagons have been acquired from builders in the German Democratic Republic for its conveyance.

Considerable improvements have been executed and are planned at the approaches to Tunis. A new main station was inaugurated in 1980, segregating metre- and standard-gauge traffic, and completion of a chord on the outskirts has opened direct access to the freight yards and eliminated the reversal of standard-gauge freight trains in the passenger station. Double-tracking of the standard gauge from Tunis to Djeedeida is on the agenda, as is doubling of the metre gauge from Tunis southward to Sousse; the Kuwait Fund for Arab Development has put up 39 million dinars for the installation of a third track on this route as far as Bordj Cedria. Elsewhere a 17 km deviation is being built between Sidi Saad and Hadjeb El Aioun.

New lines are also planned to give rail connections to Kairouan and Sidi Bou Zid, and between Jendouba and Le Kef, and Gafsa and Magen bel Abbes.

Electrification
Electrification of the 25 km between Sousse and Monastir has been entrusted to Ansaldo Trasporti at a cost of 15 million dinars.

Investment
A five-year development plan issued by the Government late in 1982 provides for construction of a

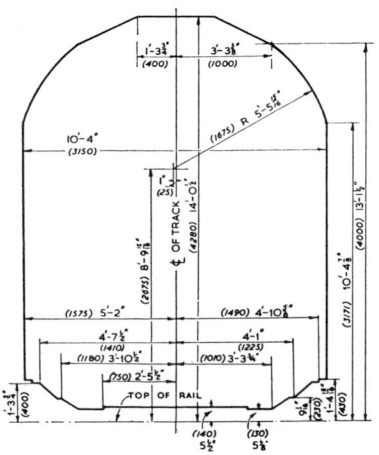

Standard gauge
All vehicles

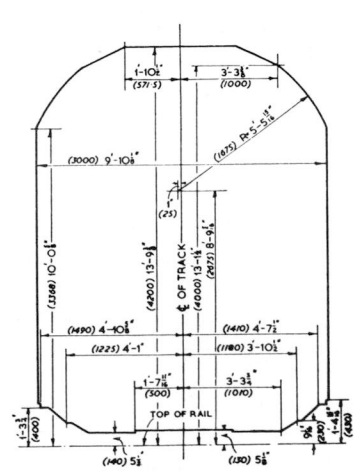

Metre gauge
Locomotives and passenger cars

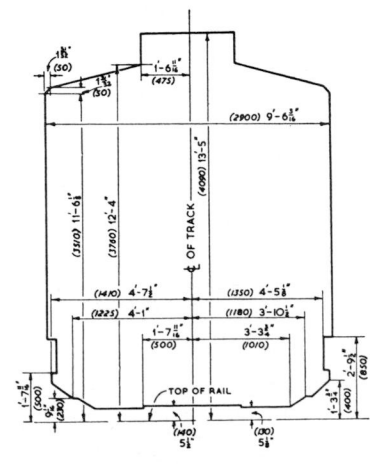

Metre gauge
Freight cars

70 km line from Gabes to Médenine, completion of double-tracking from Tunis to Sousse and purchase of 78 locomotives, 143 passenger cars and 1200 freight cars. In 1983 SNCFT was budgeting the following capital expenditure (million dinars):

Passenger cars (133)	19
Intermodal equipment	1·2
New lines	26·8
Track work and machinery	26·18
Bridges and buildings	5·299
Signalling and communications	14·335
Yards and terminals	14·285
Workshops	8·955
Electrification	1·6
Total	117·654

Track
Standard rail
Standard gauge: Flat bottom, 36-46 kg/m in lengths of 12-18 m
Metre gauge: Flat bottom, 25-36 kg/m in lengths of 7·8-12 m
Welded joints: Thermit welding of rail joints
Cross ties (sleepers): Oak impregnated with creosote; metal; concrete RS type
Standard gauge: 120 × 220 × 2600 mm
Metre gauge: 120 × 220 × 2000 mm
Spacing: 1500/km
Rail fastenings: Wood sleepers: spikes
Metal sleepers: clips and bolts
Concrete sleepers: special resilient fittings
Filling: Broken stone
Max curvature
Standard gauge: 7° = minimum radius 250 m
Metre gauge: 11·6° = minimum radius 150 m

New Tunis-Ville station, with Ganz-Màvag 4-car suburban dmu *(Marcel Vleugels)*

Max gradient: 2% = 1 in 50
Gradients

	Standard gauge	Metre gauge
Level	29%	22%
Up to 0·5%	37%	26%
0·5 to 1%	20%	26%
1 to 2·5%	14%	26%

Max altitude: 952 m on line Haidra to Kasserine
Max speed
Standard gauge
Railcars: 100 km/h
Diesel trains: 70 km/h
Max axleload
Standard gauge: 21 tonnes
Metre gauge: 18 tonnes

TURKEY

Ministry of Communications

Ankara

Minister: Prof Dr Mustafa A Aysan
Director-General of Land Transport: Necati Aydemir

Turkish State Railways (TCDD)
Türkiye Cumhuriyeti Devlet Demiryollari

Genel Müdürlügü, Ankara

Telephone: 11 35 30
Telex: 42571

President and Director General: Ender Çetinkaya
Assistant Director General: Halil Aydoğdu
Members of the Board of Management
  Halil Aydoğdu
  Ahmet Kabakçi
  Mustafa Kivrikoglu
  Niyazi Sahin
  Necdet Kalfa
Deputy Directors General
  Hasim Saltik
  Mete Kiziloğlu
  Ferhat Alp
Permanent Way: Mustafa Aksun
Traction: Erdoğan Dinçer
Commercial: Ali Ihsan Kunday
Financial: Ismail Gültekin
Operations: Hikmet Basiplikgi
Personnel: Ahmet Gülleroğlu
Fixed Installations: Oktay Bilkay
Construction: K Bayhan
Research and Planning: Azmi Körükçü
Ports: Cumhur Yener
Administration: Ibrahim H Erisen

Gauge: 1435 mm
Route length: 8193 km
Electrification: 204 km at 25 kV 50 Hz ac

Master Transport Plan
In September 1982, as promised, the Government endorsed a master transport plan which greatly increased planned investment in TCDD up to 1990. The total budgeted for the period is 711 000 million Turkish lira. In addition, considerable funds have been separately allocated to the Ministry of Public Works for construction of a number of new lines.

Traffic	1977	1979	1980	1981	1982
Freight tonne/km (million)	7633	5769	5167	4719	6325
Freight tonnes (million)	16·4	NA	11 781	11 592	NA
Passenger-km (million)	5087	6799	6011	6105	5656
Passenger journeys (million)	112·6	NA	113·9	123	119

Finances	1980	1981	1982*
Revenue		(TL million)	
Passengers	2577·0	3355	5353
Freight and mail	11 917·0	19 354	26 548
Other	7162·7	7720	8786
Subsidies	19 099·5	22 316	27 094
Ports	NA	6054	10 775
Total	40 756·2	58 799	78 556
Expenditure			
Staff	27 619·4	30 971	37 772
Materials	7734·3	22 503	31 872
Depreciation	1176·3	1514	2062
Financial charges	11 511·0	6079	6120
Total	48 042	61 067	77 826

* Provisional estimate

Infrastructure improvements
In 1982 the Government released US $15 million to allow resumption of work on the 259 km electrified, double-track Arifye-Sincan cut-off, which will shorten the route between Istanbul (Haydarpasa) and Ankara by 100 km, besides enlarging the operating capacity of the present single-track main line between the country's two biggest cities. The work had been suspended in February 1981 for lack of funds.

The original intention to design the cut-off for very high speed has been dropped to save money, but TCDD still hopes that on completion the shortened route will offer Ankara-Istanbul transit times of 5 hours or less, compared with a fastest journey of 7½ hours at present. The cut-off will not be finished until 1995.

The second priority is to realign, double-track, resignal and electrify the 577 km iron ore route from the Divrigi mines in east central Turkey southwards to the ports of Adana and Iskerendun, also the site of a steelworks. A Saudi loan is financing this project and half its requirement of 80 3000 to 3600 kW locomotives. The objective is to double the line's present carrying capacity of 6 million tonnes a year. It is planned to complete electrification by 1987, the three sections of double-tracking aggregating 320 km by 1993, and resignalling and installation of CTC throughout by 1988.

Other new lines included in the Master Plan are a 25 km branch from Menemen to the Aliaga oil refinery, in the west near Izmir; an 80 km cut-off between Toprakkala and Köprüagzi, north of Iskenderun, to bypass the steep gradients through Fevzipasa; another cut-off, of 40 km, between Ulas and Bedirli in central Turkey, to avoid the detour through Sivas and Kalin; and a new link of 140 km with Iraq to obviate transit traffic's present need to pass through Syria. This last was agreed in Iraqi-Turkish discussions in November 1982 and the consultants Henderson Busby have the design commission. Yet to be decided in 1982 was whether the new connection to Zakho in Syria would be projected from Kurtulan or Nusaybin on TCDD.

The Government has commissioned a feasibility study for an 8 km double-track tunnel under the Bosphorus between Yenikapi, in Istanbul, and Haydarpasa. It has been completed by Botek and the US consultancies, De Leuw Cather and Sverdrup & Parcel. Besides main-line traffic the tunnel would carry a suburban service connecting with the first line of the proposed Istanbul metro, between Topkapi and Levent on the European side of the Bosphorus. The Government has allocated 806 000 million lira for fulfilment of this and other urban rail transport schemes.

Electrification
At present electrification is concentrated in the Istanbul and Ankara areas. In addition to the Divrigi-Iskenderun/Adana route, lines now to be electrified (prospective completion dates in brackets) are: Halkali-Edirne-Kapikule, on the Bulgarian border,

290 km (1986); Arifye-Eskişehir, in eastern Turkey, 182 km (1988); and Karabük-Zonguldak, on the Black Sea coast in a mining and steelworks area, 124 km (1988). Also on the programme are expansion of the Ankara and Izmir suburban systems.

Investment
TCDD's investment budget for 1983 covered (TL million):

Electric locomotives	600
Diesel locomotives	3350
Passenger cars (30) and mu cars (12)	1900
Freight cars (1100)	5500
Intermodal development	7·5
New lines	1691
Track maintenance and machinery	5559·5
Bridges and buildings	1827·5
Electrification	1466
Signalling and communications	1934·5
Yards and terminals	858·5
Workshops	870
Others	13 915·5
	39 480

Signalling
Major extensions are planned of CTC, at present installed only between Haydarpasa and Ankara. At the start of 1982 bids were sought for full coverage of the 577 km Iskenderun-Divrigi line.

Traction and rolling stock
To match expanding electrification TCDD has considered rebuilding a number of its French-pattern 2400 hp diesel-electric Co-Cos as straight 4200 hp electric units. At the same time, to overcome its shortfall of line-haul diesel locomotives (the reason for persistence with steam) TCDD agreed in 1982 to lease 15 refurbished Class 211 diesel-hydraulic locomotives from the German Federal Railway (DB).

The Master Plan provides for the following acquisitions in the 1983-93 period: 358 main-line and 160 shunting diesel locomotives; 120 electric locomotives; 69 emus; 530 passenger cars; and 21 300 freight wagons. Local manufacturing capacity at the Eskişehir (ELMS), Sidemas and Advas works is to be expanded. The objective is an annual manufacturing output at ELMS of 60 main-line and 15 shunting diesel locomotives, 20 electric locomotives and 75 diesel engines; at Sidemas of 1800 wagons in 1986, rising to 3000 by 1991; and at Advas of 100 passenger cars. It is hoped to complete the first home-built electric locomotive in 1984. Steam should be

2400 hp Co-Co main-line diesel-electric locomotive powered by Pielstick 16 PA4-185 engine, supplied by TCDD's Eskişehir plant, near Sivar *(Marcel Vleugels)*

eliminated from scheduled service in 1985, but 200 locomotives will be retained as a reserve.

Locomotives in service (1982)
Steam	529
Electric	18
Diesel	470
Diesel railcars	19
Emus	61
Dmus	14

In addition the railway operates 1053 passenger coaches and 20 215 freight wagons.

Civil engineering
At present TCDD's maximum speed is 120 km/h, and that attainable only by the front-rank passenger train on parts of the Hydarpasa-Ankara route. TCDD aims during the 1980s to ease main-line curves to a minimum 900 metres radius with 160 km/h top speed as the target. Other objectives under the Master Plan are renewal of 4234 km of track and achievement of fully mechanised track maintenance. In June 1982 TCDD contracted with Matisa for the supply of 77 machines of various types.

Track
Rails: 49·05 kg/m
Sleepers: Steel, wooden, concrete
Spacing: 600-750/km
Fastenings: DB, KHN
Minimum curvature radius: 250 m
Max gradient: 2%
Max axleload: 20 tonnes

Diesel locomotives

Class	Wheel arrangement	Transmission	Rated power hp	Tractive effort Max lb (kg)	Continuous at lb (kg)	mph (km/h)	Max speed mph (km/h)	Wheel dia in (mm)	Total weight tons	Length ft in (mm)	No in service	Year first built	Builders Mechanical parts	Engine & type	Transmission
U18C	Co-Co	Elec	1980	60 900 (27 620)	51 000 (23 134)	18 (29)	60 (97)	38 (965)	102	56' 6'' (17 220)	4	1957	GE (USA)	Cooper-Bessemer FV-12	GE
ML2700	C-C	Hyd	2700	73 400 (33 300)	65 150 (29 550)	10·5 (17)	62 (100)	39⅜ (1000)	111	64' 6½'' (19 670)	2	1961	Krauss-Maffei	Maybach MD655	Voith
DN	C	Hyd	360	18 200 (8250) 29 300 (13 300)	2650 (1200) 5950 (2700)	2·5 (4)	31 (50) 25 (40)	43¼ (1100)	40·5	30' 4¼'' (9250)	38	1953	MaK	MaK MS-304	Voith
DH 44100	D	Hyd	800	24 900 (11 300) 40 560 (18 400)	4000 (1800) 7300 (3300)	3·7 (6)	50 (80) 30 (48)	49¼ (1250)	58	37' 1'' (11 300)	6	1953-54	MaK	MaK MA-301 A	Voith
DH6500	C	Hyd	650	29 000 (13 150) 35 500 (16 100)	4400 (2000) 8800 (4000)	5 (8)	37 (60) 18 (30)	49¼ (1250)	48·8	34' 5¾'' (10 510)	13	1960	Krupp-Eslingen	Maybach GTO 6 A	Voith
DH4101	C	Hyd	400	15 750 (7150) 30 650 (13 900)	1870 (850) 4630 (2100)	5 (8) 2·5 (4)	37 (60) 18 (30)	37⅜ (950)	42	30' 5¼'' (9280)	1	1960	Jenbach	Jenbach Werke JW 400	Voith
DH6001	C	Hyd	600	24 800 (11 250) 35 000 (15 900)	3850 (1750) 7780 (3500)	5 (8) 2·5 (4)	37 (60) 18 (30)	97⅜ (950)	48	30' 8'' (9350)	1	1959	Jenbach	Jenbach Werke JW 600	Voith
21500 (U20C)	Co-Co	Elec	2150	82 700 (37 500)	76 100 (34 500)	10 (16)	71 (114)	40 (1016)	111	56' 6'' (17 220)	15	1965	GE (USA)	GE FDL12	GE
DE 24000	Co-Co	Elec	2400	86 650 (39 300)	46 300 (21 000)	14·6 (24·2)	75 (120)	43¼ (1100)	112.8	62' 6'' (19 040)	213	1970	SMTE-ELMS	Pielstick 16PA4-185	Alsthom
DE 18000	Bo-Bo	Elec	1800	57 760 (26 200)	30 850 (14 000)	44·5 (27·8)	50 (80)	43¼ (1100)	80	54' 0'' (16 440)	17	1970	SMTE-ELMS	Pielstick 12PA4-185	Alsthom
DH 3600	C	Hyd	360	18 210 (8260) 29 300 (13 300)	2650 (1200) 5950 (2700)	2·5 (4)	15·5 (25) 31 (50)	43¼ (1100)	40·5	30' 4¼'' (9250)	19	1971	ELMS	ELMS 360	Voith
DE 1800	A1A-A1A	Elec	1800	46 300 (21 000)	29 200 (13 244)	18 (30)		97	54' 0'' (16 440)	20	1978	ELMS	Pielstick 12 PA4-185	Jeumont-Schneider

Electric locomotives

Class	Wheel arrangement	Line current	Rated output hp	Tractive effort (full field) Max lb (kg)	Continuous lb (kg)	at mph (km/h)	Max speed mph (km/h)	Wheel dia in (mm)	Weight tonnes	Length ft in (mm)	No in service	Year built	Builders Mechanical parts	Electrical equipment
4001-4003	Bo-Bo	25 kV 50 Hz	2200	41 900 (19 000)	23 150 (10 500)	39 (62·5)	56 (90)	51⅛ (1300)	77·5	52' 11⅜" (16 138)	3	1955	MTE	Alsthom-Jeumont-SW
40001-40015	B-B	25 kV 50 Hz	4000	69 500 (31 500)	47 130 (21 350)	30·6 (49)	81 (130)	43¼ (1100)	77	49' 3" (15 010)	15	1971	MTE	Groupement 50 Hz

Electric railcars

Class	Wheel arrangement	Line current	Rated output hp	Tractive effort (full field) Max lb (kg)	Continuous lb (kg)	at mph (km/h)	Max speed mph (km/h)	Wheel dia in (mm)	Weight tonnes	Length ft in (mm)	No built	Year built	Builders Mechanical parts	Electrical equipment
80001-80030	BO²+2'2'+2'2'+BO'²	25 kV 50 Hz	1380	26 900 (12 200)	21 600 (9800)	30 (48)	56 (90)	43¼ (1100)	158	288' 9" (88 000)	30	1955	MTE	Alsthom
14001-14030	2B'O'+2'2'+2'2'	25 kV 50 Hz	1400	41 300 (18 721)	13 600 (6171)	38 (61·3)	74 (119)	43¼ (1100)	118	216' 6" (66 000)	30	1979	MTE	Groupement 50 Hz

UGANDA

Uganda Railways Corporation (URC)

PO Box 7150, Nasser Road, Kampala

Telephone: 32419; 54961; 50851; 58059
Telex: 61111

Acting Managing Director: J K Nduru
Chief Special Assistant: E J Mulondo
Chief Mechanical Engineer: S Kwesiga
Chief Traffic Manager: C Karamagi
Chief Supplies Officer: A Wafakale-Mwambu
Planning and Development Officer: J Muhumuza
Acting Chief Accountant: Alfred Kiiza

Gauge: 1000 mm
Route length: 1268 km

Development

Uganda Railways Corporation (URC) was created after the 1977 dissolution of East African Railways. Since then it has suffered seriously from political dissension between its former partner countries in EAR, from the civil war in its own country and resultant damage, and from a decline in the performance of Ugandan industry and agriculture.

URC started rehabilitation under a National Recovery Programme in 1980, commencing a signalling modernisation, financed by French aid, with station interlockings and tokenless block, the construction of an engineering workshop at Nalukolongo (nearing completion in 1982) with the involvement of Henschel Export of the Federal Republic of Germany, new rolling stock orders, and construction of new Lake Victoria wagon ferries, the first of which would be commissioned in 1983.

Alsthom-Atlantique supplied 14 2000 hp Co-Co diesel-electric locomotives of the manufacturer's Type AD20C, powered by a SEMT-Pielstick 12PA4185VG engine. To suit URC's present track, these units have a maximum axleload of only 12·5 tonnes. Also obtained were 20 1200 hp diesel-hydraulic locomotives from Thyssen Henschel, earlier suppliers of 10 other diesel-hydraulics and six diesel shunters. A fleet of 84 new passenger coaches was ordered from VEB Waggonbau Görlitz in the German Democratic Republic and 143 40-tonnes capacity wagons from Indian builders. The 84 passenger cars include 10 couchette vehicles and some restaurant cars. Following initial deliveries URC was able in 1982 to start a daily passenger train service from Kampala to Gulu and Pakwach.

Survey and design of a new railway has been put in hand by the Kagera River Basin Organisation, a United Nations-sponsored body formed by Uganda, Rwanda, Burundi and Tanzania to develop the Kagera River area and open up access to the Dar es Salaam and Mombasa ports for Rwanda and Burundi. So far as URC is concerned, the project envisages a branch from the Kampala-Kasese line at Bihanga to Gisenye in Rwanda. This, in conjunction with planned construction in Rwanda and Burundi, would establish a north-south link between URC and the Tanzania Railways Corporation Dar es Salaam-Kigoma line at Iringa.

Alsthom-Atlantique Type AD20C diesel-electric Co-Co for URC

Passenger cars for URC by VEB Waggonbau Görlitz

In 1982 the railway recorded 2·3 million passenger journeys and hauled 297·6 million tonnes of freight. Traffic has picked up with a recovery of national industry and agriculture and consequently URC was planning to order some 40 new passenger cars and 800 freight wagons. Its present stock comprises 60 diesel-electric locomotives, 60 passenger cars, four restaurant cars and 400 freight wagons. Relaying and realignment of the Kampala-Port Bell-Namanve line was expected to begin in 1983.

As a member of the African Central Corridor transport system, Uganda is benefitting from the provision of European Economic Community funds for improvement of wagon ferry terminals and port facilities on Lake Victoria at Jinja, Port Bell, Mwanza, Musoma and Bukoba.

Interior of new 80-seater economy class saloon

UNION OF SOVIET SOCIALIST REPUBLICS

Soviet Union Railways (SZD)

Ministry of Communications, Novo Basmannaya 2, Moscow 107174

Administration
Minister for Railway Transport: Nikolai Siemenovich Konarev
Deputy Ministers: V S Kolpakov
　　　　　　　　Alexander Golovaty
Department for International Communications: Anatoli Porfireyvich Korotky

Gauge: 1520 mm; 600-1435 mm
Route length: 143 300 km; 2606 km
Electrification: 19 300 km at 25 or 2 × 25 kV 50 Hz ac, 26 400 km at 3 kV dc

Transport development
The general management of railways and underground (metro) rail transport throughout the whole of the Soviet Union is vested in the Ministry of Railway Transport, which has its headquarters in Moscow. The Ministry has several directories (departments), including the main operating department in charge of corresponding branches of railway industry (traction, freight, passenger, locomotive economy, electrification and energy economy, track, signalling and communications, industrial railway transport and metro/underground railways, as well as main departments of material-technical supplies, capital construction, plants for the repair of rolling stock and production of spare parts, and others).

Traffic	1975	1980	1981	1982
Total freight tonne-km (million)	3 236 500	3 439 900	3 503 200	3 464 500
Total freight tonnes (million)	3621·1	3728·2	3762·5	3725
Total passenger-km (million)	312 500	332 100	344 600	347 900
Total passenger journeys (million)	3470·5	3558·7	3576·4	3578·8

The whole railway network is divided into 32 railways each of which has an administrative structure similar to that of the Ministry.

The 32 railways are as follows:

Azerbaidhanian	Alma-Atinsk
Baikal-Amur	White Russian (Byelorussian)
East Siberian	Gorkovsk
Far Eastern	Donetsk
Trans-Baikal	West Kazakhstan
West Siberian	Trans-Caucasian
Krasnoyarsk	Kemerovsk
Kuibyshev	Lvovsk
Moldavian	Moscow
Odessa	Okytabraskaya
Baltic	Volga
Dniepr	Sverdlovsk
Northern	North Caucasian
Central Asian	Tselinn
South Eastern	South Western
Southern	South Ural

Traffic
Passenger volume growth has decelerated since 1975 as private car ownership increased, low-priced and heavily subsidised air networks expanded, bus operations spread, and new metros help to stunt the rise of SZD's suburban rail travel. Even so, passenger-km have risen by 10 per cent since 1975, passenger journeys slightly less, reflecting the greater proportion of increase in long-distance rail travel. In 1982 SZD accounted for 45 per cent of all passenger traffic in the country; and in the height of summer runs 19 000 long-haul and 17 000 local trains a day.

Between 1975 and 1980 freight traffic climbed no less than 200 000 million tonne-km, with the most rapid rise seen in unit train movement. SZD has 66 per cent of the total freight movement in the USSR. One of the most spectacular areas of growth is intermodal (reflected in considerable construction of suitable wagons), with container traffic rising from 26·3 million tonnes to over 40 million by 1980. Then only 7·6 million tonnes was moving in large containers, but a much higher proportion of these, chiefly 20-tonne, is envisaged in the 72-75 million tonnes objective for 1985. At present, however, only 100 of the 1300 container-handling points are equipped to tranship ISO containers. Under the 11th Five-Year Plan, 350 container terminals are to be modernised and 65 new ones created.

Freight traffic declined slightly in 1982 to 3725 million tonnes and 3 456 000 million tonne-km, chiefly because of a downturn in oil, timber, cement and fertiliser traffics. Passenger volume, however, rose 1 per cent.

1981-85 Plan
The 1981-85, 11th Five-Year Plan raises the resources for SZD investment by 29 per cent compared with the previous 1976-80 Five-Year Plan. The aim of the 11th Plan is to raise freight movement by 14·6 per cent in terms of tonne-km and rail passenger-km by 10·8 per cent compared with performance under the Ninth Five-Year Plan. This implies a figure of 3 950 000 million freight tonne-km a year by 1985, or over 485 million more than the total recorded in 1982. A priority is to improve the rail connections between the Far East, Siberia, the north, the Urals and the country's European centres.

2TE116 6000 hp main-line diesel locomotive

TEP70 4000 hp passenger diesel locomotive

The 11th Five-Year Plan calls for construction of 3580 km of new railway, track-doubling over 5000 km, 6400 km of electrification and installation of CTC and block signalling over 15 000 km.

Major projects to be pursued included the rebuilding of the routes from Surgut to Urengoi and Yagelnoye and in mid-Siberia, which serves the Kuznetsk coalfield. With the growth of oil and gas production in West Siberia, construction of railways in Central Asia and Kazachstan has become a priority. Also needed are means to transport agricultural produce and coal from Akibastuz. Rail links in the Urals, the Volga region, the north-west and in the central area of European Russia need modernising, with the provision of increased operating capacity in the south of the territory last-mentioned.

The current Plan also provides for the reconstruction or renovation of 250 stations and the introduction of a new ticket-issuing and control system, known as Express 2, in the passenger sector. The latter will employ a third-generation computer apparatus.

In 1982 the railways moved 3725 million tonnes of freight, where volume was down by comparison with 1981, and 3578·8 million passengers: that is, over 10 million tonnes of freight and about 10 million passengers were transported daily. Over 80 per cent of total freight consisted of coal and coke, petroleum products, non-ferrous metals, mineral construction materials, fertilisers, timber, and grain. The structure of passenger traffic was 10·5 per cent long-distance and 89·5 per cent commuter in journeys, 72 per cent long-distance and 28 per cent commuter in terms of passenger-km.

New lines

In the course of the 1976-80 Five-Year Plan new line construction aggregated 3200 km. Some 3900 km of double-tracking was completed and over 15 000 km were equipped with automatic block and CTC.

Centrepiece of new construction was work on the 3145 km Baikal-Amur Magistral (BAM). In late 1982 there remained a gap of some 500 km to be built between the eastern and western sections of the project. The line should be ready for opening throughout by 1986. It is being built in fearsome geological and climatic conditions, in territory where temperatures range from −60°C in winter to 40°C in summer; almost half the route is in the permafrost area. The worst problems have been encountered in boring the 15 km Severomuyskiy tunnel, begun in 1978, through critical difficulties with underground rivers and quicksands. The tunnel is not being abandoned, but a 30 km bypass has been laid around it to avoid deferment in the opening of this BAM section. In all the project at completion will have entailed 200 million cubic metres of earthworks, 357 million cubic metres of earth-shifting, 123 major bridges and eight tunnels totalling 30 km in length. In full operation, the BAM is expected to move some 35 million tonnes of bulk freight annually from east to west in unit trains of up to 9000 tonnes weight. (Elsewhere, 10 000-tonne freights are already run between Rybnolė and Pérovo.) A further new transversal route of 4800 km length from central Russia to the BAM at Lake Baikal is now planned.

The so-called 'Little BAM' is already operational, running 402 km from the BAM proper at Tynda through the permafrost and across the Aldan, Amga and Lena rivers to Berkatit. A 750 km northward extension via Tommok to the important town of Yakutsk, at present rail-less, has been surveyed. This extension will tap important deposits of apatite at Seligdor, iron ore at Tayezhny and coal in South Yakutia.

In 1982 a new line was opened between Riga and Tallinn, the Latvian and Estonian capitals, reducing the rail distance between the cities from 441 to 350 km.

Another project completed in 1982 was a 770 km railway from Surgut to the Siberian natural gas fields at Novyy Urengoi. A 60 km bypass of Ufa was also commissioned, and in the far south a 100 km, mountain-piercing line between Idzhevan and Razdan forging a new connection between Tbilisi and Yerevan; it includes six tunnels aggregating 16 km and seven high viaducts, and attains a summit of more than 1800 metres.

In all 1259 km of new route were commissioned in 1981-82, and over 1800 km of double- or triple-tracking was accomplished.

Amongst new projects at the design stage was a 180 km electrified line, involving the boring of a 17 km tunnel, from Tbilisi to Ordzhonikidza, the Aragvi valley and the Caucasus, which would reduce the rail journey from Tbilisi to Moscow by no less than 950 km. Also contemplated are a 200 km line across the Karakum desert in Turkestan between Rybnow and Saja; and a further relief of the overloaded Moscow-Kuibyshev-Ufa line by construction of 300 km of alternative route between Progromnoje and Pugatshevsk.

Electrification

SZD employs three electrification systems: 1·5 kV dc for suburban railways; 3 kV dc and 25 kV 50 Hz elsewhere. The 3 kV dc system is still being extended where traffic volume is not considered to warrant ac. In planning electrification of the Baikal-Amur line SZD decided that to solve power supply problems on a route of such long and severe gradients without expensive recourse to reinforced catenary and contact wires, and extra substations, the solution was to employ a 2×25 kV system. This has now been adopted for other difficult and intensively-used routes, such as Orsha to Minsk and Brest.

A number of very long routes are already electrified throughout. One is the 3903 km line from the Finnish border at Luzhaika through Moscow, Kharkov, Rostov-on-Don, Tbilisi and Yerevan to Zod. Another is the 7025 km route from Orsha in the west through Moscow, Kuibyshev and Novosibirsk to Karymskaya in the east.

During 1981-82 more than 1900 km of lines was electrified. By 1983 the total length of electrified route in use had reached 45 700 km (31·9 per cent of total route-mileage), including 19 300 km of lines at 25 kV ac or 2×25 kV ac. The 1981-85 Plan prescribed electrification of over 6000 km, so that the proportion of electric traction in haulage would be increased to 60 per cent by the termination of the Plan. The first railways to be electrified would be located east of Lake Baikal and in the Soviet Far East (Karymskaya-Bira), the Kazan and Vagai lines, and sections connecting Karaganda and Mointy, Orsha and Brest, Tselinnograd and Koktchetav-Peski Tsleinnyie-Utyak. As a result, an electrified trunk route would be formed between Brest and Khabarovsk; a second electrified outlet would be created from the Kuznetsk coal basin and Ekibastuz to the Urals; and a third electrified line would operate between the European centre and the Urals.

In 1982 the share of electric traction in freight haulage reached 57·8 per cent. Average annual tonnage of freight traffic on each electrified line in 1982 was nearly 44 million tonnes, as against 15 million tonnes on lines served by diesel traction, and 24·3 million tonnes throughout the network. Soviet electrified railways, which form less than 4 per cent of the world's total, carry more than 25 per cent of the world's aggregate rail traffic.

Main items of the recent electrification programme have included the 226 km section from Karanganda to Mointy in Khazakstan, which was finished in 1982, the 226 km stretch from Bira to Arkhara and the line from Orsa to Baranovici. The two latter were 2×25 kV ac schemes. The Bira-Arkhara scheme in eastern Siberia, also completed in 1982, converted a further stretch of the Trans-Siberian route from Moscow to Vladivostok. The Orsa-Baranovici, besides embracing the Byelorussian capital Minsk in the SZD's electrification network, constituted a further extension of catenary on the Moscow-Brest trunk route; the Orsa-Borisov section of this scheme, which achieved electrification from Moscow to Minsk, was finished in November 1981. Electrification of this last throughout was part of the 6400 km of further electrification which SZD planned to achieve between 1981 and 1985. By mid-decade end-to-end electrification of the 9000 km trunk route from Brest to Chabarowsk should also be finished.

SZD Type ER200 prototype 200 km/h electric train-set

VL80T electric locomotive

TEP75 6000 hp passenger diesel locomotive

By the end of 1982 a further 500 km or more of electrification was ready for use. With commissioning of 124 km between Vologda and Cherepovets, catenary was reaching further towards Leningrad on a second route from Moscow, the Northern Railway. The first 105 km of catenary on the route north from Tselinnograd to Koktchetav, in Khazakstan, was energised; a further 150 km electrification of the Turkestan-Tashkent route in the far south of Khazakstan took the wires close to this line's junction with the lateral route from Samarkand to Leninabad, in Tadzhikstan; and in the mid-Urals electrification of the Moscow-Kazan-Sverdlovsk route, the Gorki Railway, was pressed 190 km further west from Sverdlovsk, between Krasnoufimsk and Yanaul.

Traction

The Tenth Five-Year Plan demanded the addition to SZD stock of 3000 electric locomotives, 8000 mainline and 2500 shunting diesel locomotives, 15 000 passenger cars and 390 000 freight cars. The Plan envisages the proportion of all tonne-km worked by electric traction rising from 55 to 62 per cent during the Plan's currency.

At present the basic freight haulier on ac electrified lines is the eight-axle twin-unit Type VL80, first introduced in 1971 and subsequently developed in different sub-types, such as the VL80R with thyristor control and regenerative braking, and latest (1980) VL80S. The versions chiefly in use are the 6520 kW VL80S and VL80T, both twin-units, but the VL80S also appears in a three-unit variant with a one-hour rating of 9780 kW to fit it for unit trains of up to 10 000 tonnes from the east. For future needs SZD has created the eight-axle, twin-unit Type VL84, of which two prototypes have been evaluated since 1979.

The VL84 has been built to the permissible limits of SZD's 25 tonnes axleload limit; it scales 200 tonnes and with more powerful traction motors than the VL80 has a one-hour rating of 7600 kW. To take account of the aim for faster freight working, the VL84 is designed for a top speed of 120 km/h, as against the 110 km/h of the VL80 and is fitted with automatic speed control. The prototypes have rheostatic braking, with resistances capable of absorbing 6800 kW, but models for the long slopes of the Baikal-Amur line will have regenerative braking. With the Baikal-Amur line in mind, SZD has conducted tests with freight trains of 2 km length between Siberia and Moscow.

For freight haulage on dc lines the standard VL10 Bo-Bo twin-unit has been superseded by the 200-ton VL10U, with a one-hour rating of 5360 kW, which is also produced in a four-unit, 10 700 kW version for 10 000-tonne freight haulage that is classified VL11. The VL10U design has been further modified with additional transformer and rectifier as a dual-voltage unit, the VL82M, but SZD does not yet have the justification to extend the limited number of this type to mass production.

Two new high-power models are currently being designed, each twin-units with 12 axles and weighing 300 tonnes. The ac unit is the VL85, with fully-suspended traction motors, a one-hour tractive effort of 72 tonnes at 54 km/h, and a one-hour rating of 11 000 kW. Its mechanically-similar dc counterpart is the VL15, with a one-hour rating of 9000 kW. Both will be arranged for a maximum speed of 120 km/h.

Passenger electric locomotives are supplied by Czechoslovak industry. For the ac system the ChS4T Co-Co, introduced in 1973, was still in production in 1982. For its dc lines SZD needs a machine with higher tractive effort in the low and medium-speed range than the CS200 8400 kW Bo-Bo twin-unit, which was designed with the proposed increase of maximum speed on the Moscow-Leningrad line to 200 km/h in mind. This, the intended successor to the CS2 Co-Co, has not been manufactured in large quantities. For ability to deal with heavier trains SZD in 1982 unveiled the 8400 kW Bo-Bo twin-unit Type CS200, geared for a maximum speed of 160 km/h. Developments of this design planned are a CS7, with all traction motors series-connected for heavy haulage at medium speed, and a mechanically-similar CS8 for the ac network.

Still in production in 1982 as SZD's heavy freight diesel was the 12-axle, twin-unit Type 2TE10V or 2T310M with a pair of 3000 hp engines, a design which also exists in a 9000 hp three-unit variant, the 3TE10M. These locomotives have two-stroke engines and dc generator transmission. The twin-unit Type 2TE116, also a 6000 hp locomotive, has four-stroke engines and alternator/rectifier transmission. For passenger haulage the standard diesel-electric classes, also still in production, are the single-unit, 3000 hp Type TEP60 and its twin-unit 6000 hp variant, the 2TEP60. The latest shunting

Freight headed by Class VL8 electric locomotive

Parallel humping in a marshalling yard

types are the 1200 hp TEM2a diesel and the 1350 hp ChME3 electric.

Higher-power diesel prototypes are now being evaluated. For freight, the twin-unit Co-Co Type 2TE121 has a pair of four-stroke 4000 hp engines and fully-suspended traction motors; it is capable of hauling 8000 tonnes on the level. For passenger traffic a Co-Co with a single 4000 hp, 16-cylinder four-stroke engine and alternator transmission, the TEP70, has been manufactured in limited quantity; this 129-tonne unit, which also has fully-suspended traction motors, is arranged for 160 km/h top speed. It is now to be superseded by the much more potent Type TEP75, of which two prototypes have entered service. This embodies a single 24-cylinder engine of 6000 hp.

For freight haulage on the Baikal-Amur line SZD is pursuing a four-unit, 550-tonne design, the 4TE130. This will incorporate a 3000 hp engine in each unit.

The concentration on new express electric locomotive designs suggests disinclination to pursue development of high-speed self-propelled train-sets, at least in the immediate future. Since 1977 SZD has been evaluating a 200 km/h 11 500 kW Type ER200 14-car unit developed at Riga alongside a Czechoslovak set comprising a Skoda-built 8400 kW Type 66E and 14 cars. The former has been in public service between Moscow and Leningrad, but the route's track and operating conditions have limited the scope to exploit its top speed.

Official statistics do not reveal numbers of locomotives in use or produced, but for 1982 show that electric locomotives totalling 3·7 million hp output and diesel locomotives totalling 3·6 million hp were manufactured.

Rolling stock

The SZD wagon fleet is now predominantly bogie, with an average vehicle payload of 63·5 tonnes, and roughly 50 per cent equipped with roller bearings; automatic couplings are standard. Standardisation of roller bearings will be a feature of the 11th Five-Year Plan; they are now applied to all new construction. New vehicles are designed for a maximum speed of 120 km/h, but at present maximum operating speeds for freight trains remain 90 km/h for full loads, 100 km/h for empties.

In recent years the proportion of special-purpose wagons in new construction has been considerably increased, to 30 per cent of the total; it includes auto-carriers. Use of four-bogie, eight-axle wagons with 120-125 tonnes glw capability has so far been limited to a few routes and production accordingly restricted, but it is now rising; with such wagons average train weight can be lifted by more than a third without increase of train length.

According to official statistics, 58 600 new wagons were produced by USSR plants in 1982, in addition to imports from other Comecon countries; Romania's Arad plant, for instance supplied 3000 of a 20 000-vehicle order for grain wagons, of which a further 7500 were to be built in 1983, the remainder in 1984.

The 1981-85 Plan provided for construction of 390 000 freight cars and over 15 000 passenger coaches. It is expected that 17 new types of freight cars will be launched into mass production. The most important types include: a utility flat car, 19·6 metres long, capable of carrying heavy and large-size cargoes; a utility all-metal boxcar with internal space of 140-150 cubic metres; an eight-axle utility gondola car without doors, dimensions of 1-T type; a flat car to carry large-capacity containers provided with an improved shock-absorber system; and 'sandwich' wall-type refrigerator cars employing an aluminium alloy, low-alloy steel and polyurethane foam technique.

The passenger car fleet now contains more compartment stock and air-conditioned sleeping and dining cars. New all-metal coaches are designed for speeds up to 160 km/h; they are provided with forced ventilation and electric heating.

Track

During the course of the 1981-85 Plan the installation of R75 75 kg/m and R65 65 kg/m rail was to be extended by 30 500 km. There is increasing recourse to asbestos ballast, which because of extremely low moisture content is much less vulnerable to freezing during winter transport or installation; in addition, it is claimed to pack more rapidly than gravel or broken stone, achieving full density after five trains' passage, and to offer more resilience.

SZD is looking for a 25 per cent increase in rail life by 1985 and is therefore increasing its research in and output of heat-treated rails. A surface hardness of 450 Brinells is the objective. Extension of continuous welded rail installations from 48 000 route-km at the end of 1980 to 80 000 by 1985 is another goal. Heavy investment in mechanised equipment is envisaged.

Track strengthening concentrates on installation of new rail types, including thermally-treated rails, continuous welded rail (cwr), concrete sleepers, heavy and sloping crossovers and switches, and extensive application of ballast of broken stone and asbestos. The bulk of rail used is the R65 65 kg/m type, but 75 kg/m is used on sections where traffic is the heaviest. The total length of main tracks laid with R65 rails amounts to about 50 per cent of the whole; thermally-treated rails have been installed over 36 per cent of main tracks and cwr over 26 per cent. All major main lines use improved ballast of broken stone, graded gravel and asbestos, which is now in place over 85 per cent of their length. Asbestos ballast is already used on more than 20 000 km.

Between 1981 and 1985, Soviet Railways were to be supplied with 11 million tonnes of new rails, 25 per cent more than under the Tenth Five-Year Plan; 80 per cent would be thermally-hardened. By the termination of the current Five-Year Plan, the total length of cwr will have reached 80 000 km. Major overhauls of track will increase at least 28 per cent. More than half will be on lines carrying very heavy traffic in the Urals, Siberia and Soviet Far East. Nearly twice as much metal as under the Tenth Five-Year Plan is allocated to replacement of old bridge spans.

During 1981-85 Soviet Railways was to receive over 120 tracklaying cranes and nearly 300 levelling, tamping and profiling machines, the same number of snow-removing machines, much other machinery and equipment. Efficient use of all these machines and mechanisms will make it possible by 1985 to raise the level of mechanisation in major overhauls to 87 per cent, in medium repairs to 76 per cent, in repairs involving removal of track to 68 per cent, and in regular track maintenance to 40 per cent.

Rails: Standard types: R 75, R65, R50 (74·4, 64·6 and 51·5 kg/m respectively)

Sleepers
Wooden: saturated with oil antiseptics, length 2750 mm (for extra heavyweight traffic, 2850 mm), thickness 150-180 mm

Ferro-concrete sleepers: S-56-2 and S-56-3, prestressed, length 2700 mm, height 193 mm at under-rail section, 135 mm at mean section

Spacing
On straight sections: 1840/km
On curves: 2000/km

Signalling

At the start of 1983 over 5000 km were equipped with automatic block and CTC or power signal centres. The Plan prescribes some 15 500 km of fresh installation. SZD is intending to develop continuous cab signalling on some sections. Also planned is a big improvement of telecommunications capacity, with provision of 60-channel high-frequency systems in additional areas and 120-channel coaxial cable systems at a number of main centres.

Marshalling yard control centre

Tracklaying train

Yards and terminals

In 1981-82 much work was carried out to develop major marshalling yards. More than 500 km of track was laid in classification, receiving and departure yards and 3200 sets of points were incorporated in electric centralised control systems.

20 marshalling yards are using computerised and automated systems. That number is to rise by five under the current Plan and a further 40 hump yards are to be mechanised. In all, SZD has about 100 major yards. In general, the Plan provides for heavy investment in cybernetics in all forms of management and traffic control.

In the automated marshalling yards humps are equipped with complex systems: automatic centralised hump release controls (GATs-KR), also providing registration of the actual release programme from the humps and the entry of wagons into each track of the marshalling yard; automatic controls regulating the rolling speed of rakes from the humps (ARS); and automatic assignment of release speeds depending on the coupling length (AZSR).

These systems are functionally connected to each other. Of further significance are automatic hump locomotive signalling devices (ALS) which respond to the specific working conditions of locomotives approaching humps and during division of the trains. For spaced and accurate braking of wagon 'cuts' on marshalling yard humps use is made of

pneumatically-operated retarders of the following types:

Pincer-weight: KV-72
Pincer-pressure-lifting: KNP-5-73 which has the following characteristics:
Braking power 1·25 m of suppressing energy weight
Time lag of braking action 0·6 s
Time to release brakes 1·0 s.

The KV-72 and KNP-5-73 retarders are for the exit tracks from the most heavily-used humps. Special single-rail hydraulic weight retarders of Type TsNII-3V are used for humps where processing is automatically controlled, for exit tracks from lower-capacity humps and for profiled shunting tracks. Up to four linked retarders of this type are fitted in one braking position.

Marshalling yards are equipped with a pneumatic mail system for the despatch of transportation documents from the arrival yard to the central technical office (TsTK) and from there to the despatch yard. An advance train information communications system supplies details of the composition of incoming trains.

All information regarding trains, preparation of marshalling sheets, numerical calculation of carriages accumulated on the tracks of marshalling yards and the formulation of practical lists of trains to be formed is carried out by EVM (computers).

Electric locomotives

Class	Wheel arrangement	Line current	Rated output one-hour kW	Tractive effort (full field) Max lb (kg)	Continuous at lb (kg)	mph (km/h)	Max speed mph (km/h)	Wheel dia in (mm)	Weight tonnes	Length ft in (mm)	Year first built	Builders Mechanical parts	Electrical equipment
VL 8	Bo+Bo+ Bo+Bo	3 kV dc	4200	77 800 (35 300)	66 800 (30 300)	27·5 (44·3)	62 (100)	47¼ (1200)	184	90' 3½'' (27 520)	1955	Novocherkassk Works	Novocherkassk Works
VL 10	2×Bo-Bo-	3 kV dc	5200	88 000 (40 000)	72 750 (33 000)	32·3 (52)	62 (100)	49¼ (1250)	184	99' 10½'' (30 440)	1961	Tiflis Works	Tiflis Works
VL 60	Co-Co	25 kV 50 Hz	4140	70 100 (31 800)	58 000 (26 300)	34·2 (55·1)	62 (100)	49¼ (1250)	138	68' 3'' (20 800)	1957	Novocherkassk Works	Novocherkassk Works
VL 60K	Co-Co	25 kV 50 Hz	4650	70 500 (32 000)	58 200 (26 400)	34·5 (55·6)	62 (100)	49¼ (1250)	138	68' 3'' (20 800)	1962	Novocherkassk Works	Novocherkassk Works
VL 80K VL 80T	2×Bo-Bo	25 kV 50 Hz	6520	99 400 (45 100)	90 200 (40 900)	33·3 (53·6)	68 (110)	49¼ (1250)	184	107' 9'' (32·840)	1963 1967	Novocherkassk Works	Novocherkassk Works
VL 80S	3×Bo-Bo	25 kV 50 Hz	10 780	149 100 (67 650)	135 300 (63 350)	33·3 (53·6)	68 (110)	49¼ (1250)	288	161' 7'' (49 260)	1980	Novocherkassk Works	Novocherkassk Works
VL 80R	2×Bo-Bo	25 kV 50 Hz	6520	99 400 (45 100)	90 200 (40 900)	33·3 (53·6)	68 (110)	49¼ (1250)	192	107' 9'' (32 840)	1967	Novocherkassk Works	Novocherkassk Works
VL 82M dual-current	2×Bo-Bo	25 kV and 3 kV dc	6040	93 476 (42 400)	88 185 (40 000)	31·7 (51·6)	68 (110)	49½ (1250)	192	107' 9'' (32 840)	1972	Novocherkassk Works	Novocherkassk Works
VL 84	2×Bo-Bo	25 kV 50 Hz	7600	—	—	—	75 (120)	—	200	—	1979	Novocherkassk Works	Novocherkassk Works
CS2T	Co-Co	3 kV dc	4620	41 888 (19 000)	35 274 (16 000)	199 (320)	99 (160)	49¼ (1250)	126	61' 1'' (18 920)	1972	Skoda Works, Czechoslovakia	Skoda Works, Czechoslovakia
CS4T	Co-Co	25 kV 50 Hz	5200	38 360 (17 400)	37 038 (16 800)	67 (107)	112 (180)	49¼ (1250)	126	65' 7'' (19 880)	1973	Skoda Works, Czechoslovakia	Skoda Works, Czechoslovakia
CS200	2×Bo-Bo	3 kV dc	8400	101 400 (45 995)	45 900 (20 820)	138 (86)	125 (200)	49¼ (1250)	157	108' 6½'' (33 080)	1975	Skoda Works, Czechoslovakia	Skoda Works, Czechoslovakia

Diesel locomotives

Class	Wheel arrangement	Trans-mission	Rated power hp	Tractive effort Max lb (kg)	Continuous at lb (kg)	mph (km/h)	Max speed mph (km/h)	Wheel dia in (mm)	Total weight tonnes	Length ft in (mm)	Year first built	Builders Mechanical parts	Engine & type	Transmission
TE-3	2×Co-Co	Elec	4000	128 000 (58 200)	95 200 (43 200)	12·4 (20)	62 (100)	41⅜ (1050)	252	111' 4'' (33 940)	1953	Voroshilovgrad	2 × 2D 100	Elektrotyazh-masch
TE-7	2×Co-Co	Elec	4000	73 800 (33 500)	34 000 (15 400)	34·8 (56)	87 (140)	41⅜ (1050)	252	111' 4'' (33 940)	1957	Transmasch Works	2 × 2D 100	Elektrotyazh-masch
TE-10	Co-Co	Elec	3000	92 600 (42 000)	59 500 (27 000)	14·3 (23)	62 (100)	41⅜ (1050)	129	61' 1'' (18 610)	1958	Transmasch Works	10 D 100	Elektrotyazh-masch
2TE-10V†	2×Co-Co	Elec	6000	185 200 (84 000)	11 596 (52 600)	15·5 (25)	62 (100)	41⅜ (1050)	276	122' 2'' (37 220)	1960		2 × 10 D 100	Elektrotyazh-masch
2TE-10L	2×Co-Co	Elec	6000	185 200 (84 000)	114 600 (52 000)	14·9 (24)	62 (100)	41⅜ (1050)	258·6	111' 4'' (33 940)	1961	Voroshilovgrad	10 D 100	CKD Prague
TEP-10	Co-Co	Elec	3000	66 350 (30 100)	38 100 (17 300)	22·4 (36)	87 (140)	41⅜ (1050)	129	61' 1'' (18 610)	1960	Transmasch Works	10 D 100	Elektrotyazh-masch
TEP-60	Co-Co	Elec	3000	55 750 (25 300)	27 500 (12 500)	31·1 (50)	100 (160)	41⅜ (1050)	129	63' 2'' (19 250)	1960	Kolomna Works	D 45 A	Elektrotyazh-masch
TEM-1	Co-Co	Elec	1000	79 400 (36 000)	44 000 (20 000)	5·6 (9)	56 (90)	41⅜ (1050)	123	55' 8'' (16 970)	1959	Bryansk Works	2 D 50	Elektrotyazh-masch
TEM-2	Co-Co	Elec	1200	79 400 (36 000)	46 300 (21 000)	8·7 (14)	62 (100)	41⅜ (1050)	120	55' 8'' (16 970)	1960	Bryansk Works	PD-IM	Elektrotyazh-masch
VME-1	Bo-Bo	Elec	600	39 700 (18 000)	20 300 (9300)	7·1 (11·5)	50 (80)	41⅜ (1050)	69	42' 2'' (12 850)	1958	Ganz-Mávag	XVIIV 170/240	Ganz-Mávag
ChME-2	Bo-Bo	Elec	750	48 500 (22 000)	22 900 (10 400)	8·7 (14)	43 (70)	41⅜ (1050)	64	40' 10½'' (12 460)	1959	CKD Prague	6S310-DE	CKD Prague
ChME-3	Co-Co	Elec	1350	81 350 (36 900)	50 700 (23 000)	7·1 (11·4)	59 (95)	41⅜ (1050)	123	56' 9'' (17 000)	1964	CKD Prague	K6S310 DK	CKD Prague
TG 16	2×B-B	Hyd	3280	99 200 (45 000)	83 800 (38 000)	12·4 (20)	53 (85)	41⅜ (1050)	136	101' 4½'' (30 900)	1966	Lyudinovsk Works	M 756AC	
TG-102	2×B-B	Hyd	4000	119 300 (54 100)	72 000 (39 400)	12·2 (19·5)	75 (120)	41⅜ (1050)	160	96' 8'' (29 460)	1960	Leningrad Works	4 × M 756A	
TGM-1	C	Hyd	400	30 800 (14 000)	24 700 (11 200) 12 350 (5600)	3·1 (5) 6·2 (10)	19 (30) 37 (60)	41⅜ (1050)	48	32' 8½'' (9970)	1956	Murom Works	ID12-400	Murom Works
TGM-3	B-B	Hyd*	750	49 470 (22 440)	43 000 (19 500) 19 850 (9000)	4·3 (7) 9·3 (15)	19 (30) 37 (60)	41⅜ (1050)	68	41' 4'' (12 600)	1958	Lyudinovsk Works	M 753B	Lyudinovsk Works
TGM-6	B-B	Hyd	1200	52 470 (23 800)	30 860 (14 000)	9·3 (15)	25 (40) 50 (80)	41⅜ (1050)	80	46' 11'' (14 300)				

Diesel locomotives

Class	Wheel arrangement	Transmission	Rated power hp	Max lb (kg)	Tractive effort Continuous at lb (kg)	mph (km/h)	Max speed mph (km/h)	Wheel dia in (mm)	Total weight tonnes	Length ft in (mm)	Year first built	Builders Mechanical parts	Engine & type	Transmission
TGM-10	C/C	Hyd	1200	79 400 (36 000)	67 000 (30 400) 33 500 (15 200)	42 (6·8) 8·4 (13·6)	25 (40) 50 (80)	41⅜ (1050)	121	55' 8" (16 970)	1961	Bryansk Works	PD-2	Kaluga Works
2TE116	2×Co-Co	Elec	6000	—	114 600 (52 000)	14·6 (23·5)	75 (120)	41⅜ (1050)	2 × 138	111' 4" (33 398)	1971	Voroshilovgrad	5D49 (2D70)	Elektrotyazhmasch
M62	Co-Co	Elec	2000	—	44 092 (20 000)	12·4 (20)	62 (100)	41⅜ (1050)	116·5	57' 7" (17 550)	1965	Voroshilovgrad	14D40	Elektrotyazhmasch
TEP75	Co-Co	Elec	6000	—	39 683 (18 000)	43·5 (70)	100 (160)	48 (1220)	138	71' 2½" (21 700)	1976	Kolomensk Works	I/D40	Elektrotyazhmasch
TEP70	Co-Co	Elec	4000	—	37 478 (17 000)	31·1 (50)	100 (160)	48 (1220)	126	67' 2" (20 470)	1973	Kolomensk Works	5D49	Elektrotyazhmasch
TEM7	Do-Do	Elec	2000	55 400 (59 400)	32 000 (35 000)	10·3 (11·7)	62 (100)	41⅜ (1050)	180	70' 5½" (21 500)	1976	Lyudinovsk Works	2D49	Elektrotyazhmasch
2TE121	2×Co-Co	Elec	8000	—	132 277 (60 000)	—	62 (100)	—	300	—	1980	—	—	—
4TE130	4×Co-Co	Elec	12 000	—	229 281 (104 000)	—	62 (100)	—	276	—	—	—	—	—

* Class TGM-3 has fluid-mechanical transmission.
† Also produced in three-unit 3 × Co-Co form as 3TE10M.

UNITED ARAB EMIRATES

Plans have been formulated for a high-speed rail link between Abu Dhabi and its international airport.

UNITED KINGDOM

Department of Transport

2 Marsham Street, London SW1P 3EB

Telephone: 01-212 3434

Secretary of State, Transport: Tom King
Parliamentary Secretaries: David Mitchell
Lynda Chalker

Railways
Under-Secretary: J Palmer
Assistant Secretaries: J A Page, A T Baker, H Pryce
Railway Inspectorate
Chief Inspecting Officer: C F Rose
Inspecting Officers: P M Oliver, A G B King, C B Holden, A G Townsend Rose
Assistant Inspecting Officers: A Cooksey, D A Sawer
Senior Railway Employment Inspector: J H Seager

British Rail
British Railways Board

Euston Road, PO Box 100, London NW1 2DZ

Telephone: 01-262 3232

Members of the Board
Chairman: Sir Peter Parker
Vice Chairman and Chief Executive (Railways): R B Reid
Vice Chairman: Derek Fowler
Members: *Lord Caldecote
*Ian Campbell
*Simon Jenkins
*Sir Robert Lawrence
*Prudence Leith
*H R MacLeod
Geoffrey Myers
*Michael Posner
James G Urquhart
*Part-time members

Business Sector Directors
Freight: H C Sanderson
Parcels: M Connolly
Inter-City: C Bleasdale
Provincial Services: J K Welsby
London and South-east: D D Kirby

British Rail Regions
General Managers
Eastern Region: F Paterson
London Midland Region: Malcolm Southgate
Scottish Region: George Mackie
Southern Region: D D Kirby
Western Region: W P Bradshaw

Director, Operations: M Holmes
Civil Engineering: M Purbrick
Mechanical and Electrical Engineering: M Casey
Signal and Telecommunications Engineering: W Whitehouse

Gauge: 1435 mm
Length: 17 226 km
Electrification: 1909 km at 25 kV 50 Hz ac
1791 km at 750 V dc third-rail
27 km at 1·5 kV dc overhead

Transport development
The British Rail Group consists of the operational railway business, and subsidiary activities (Sealink operating ferry services, British Rail Engineering Ltd running manufacturing and repair facilities, Freightliners Ltd handling container trains, British Transport Hotels Ltd, Travellers Fare handling station and train catering, British Rail Property Board, British Transport Advertising responsible for commercial advertising on properties and vehicles owned by several nationalised undertakings, British Rail Investments Ltd and the Transmark railway consultancy company).

During 1981 BR developed a system of business sector management for each of its five main activities: freight; parcels; Inter-City passenger; London and South-east; and provincial services. Directors were appointed for each of these businesses, responsible to the Chief Executive (Railways) for the performance of their sectors. The aim was to bring together the traditional geographical management, with all its strengths, and the individual business management approach already well established in the subsidiary businesses. More accountability by directors for their prime-user assets and business results was expected to sharpen the incentives to reduce costs and improve efficiency.

Financial objectives are set for each rail sector and subsidiary businesses covering a period of three to five years. Specific constraints, known as External Financing Limits (EFL) are imposed by the Government on the funds which can be obtained by BR from Government sources (including grants and loans) within a single financial year.

Serpell Report
A report on the finances of British Railways (compiled by a four-member committee chaired by Sir David Serpell, a former BR Board member) was published in March 1983. It consisted more precisely of two reports, since one Committee member, Alfred Goldstein, had been unable to agree with his colleagues, was not a signatory to the report proper, and had compiled his own minority report.

The decision to set up this Committee originated in a request from British Railways Board to the Government for an independent enquiry into railway finances, the hope being thereby to convince Government of the urgent need for a railway investment policy and for establishment of a more realistic contract to cover BR's Public Service Obligation (maintenance of socially necessary passenger services). The 1974 Transport Act prescribed continuation of a broadly unchanged network size and level of passenger services but in real money terms the PSO grant for the purpose has been reducing from year to year. The Board also hoped the enquiry would produce guidelines on objectives and financing which would serve to define a rail network of appropriate size, structure and quality. In response to this request, the Government set up the Serpell Committee in May 1982. Its terms of reference were 'to examine the finances of the railway and associated operations, in the light of all relevant considerations, and to report on options for alternative policies and their related objectives, designed to secure improved financial results in an efficiently run railway in Great Britain over the next twenty years'.

The resultant report came under scathing criticism in most quarters for its inadequate research and ill-judged use of computer models. Its view of BR's future was wholly negative, finding expression in a number of different options examined in the light of how they would affect the amount of state aid required. The most radical option would result in the network being cut from 16 700 to 2600 route-km in length, a move claimed to produce a profit of £34 million a year. It made no comparisons with situations in other countries; also, it was compiled with the aid of a consultancy said to have little experience of railway matters. In considering either investment or disinvestment in passenger services, the Report took neither quality factors nor their effect on revenue into account. It failed to consider the case for investment in business development, concentrating instead on cost-cutting.

In brief, the Report found that the BR Board was wrong to suggest that more financial support was needed to maintain present network size; and that a smaller network generally needed less subsidy, so that by cutting the size of the railway drastically, far less state aid would be needed, and such a network might even become economically viable.

The conclusions, were based on several invalid assumptions. For instance, it was claimed that despite closure of certain centres on passenger lines of route, the remaining parts of the line concerned would continue to produce 80 per cent of the revenue they had earned previously. Then, even if the origin or destination of a freight service were deleted, the per-mile revenue on remaining sections of line was assumed to be fully retained. BR estimate that the Report's harshest option, involving the maximum network cuts, far from producing a £34 million profit per annum, would actually result in an annual loss of at least £100 million.

Other conclusions rejected by the BR Board included the suggestion that BR should lower maintenance, renewal and operating standards, and the statement that, for the present network size, there were no significant arrears of track renewal and maintenance. Items in the Report regarded by BR as 'unreliable' include an overstatement of the potential for further cost reductions, and a failure to take account of the negative effect of proposed cost-cutting on customers and hence on revenue.

Labour disputes

The first half of 1982 was disfigured by bouts of serious industrial action as the trades unions bitterly resisted introduction of fresh productivity measures, with severe consequences for both traffic and finance. By the end of the year, however, management had secured agreement to flexible staff rostering in place of a rigid eight-hour day; to one-man operation of emus on the newly-electrified St Pancras/Moorgate-Bedford London outer suburban system, the first on BR to be equipped with track-to-train radio; to trial one-man operation of fully air-braked freight trains; and to a common entry grade of trainman, combining the roles of guard and assistant driver in the line of promotion to driver.

A vexed issue remaining was the BR Board's intention to close two of British Rail Engineering Ltd's 12 workshops, Shildon and Horwich, because of a substantially reduced workload through BR's more productive use of greatly reduced traction and rolling stock resources. A fresh threat to BREL's capacity was posed by the Serpell Report, the conclusions of which included a suggestion that BR could more economically purchase its traction from major overseas manufacturers with mass production capability.

In 1981-82 the BR workforce was reduced by a further 16 652 posts (10 per cent) and that of BREL by 5469 (15 per cent). More than half the saving agreed with the Government of 38 300 staff between 1981 and the end of 1986 was thus achieved already.

After correction for the distortions caused by the labour strikes, BR claimed that during 1982 labour productivity had improved by 8 per cent, passenger train loads by 5 per cent and freight train loads by 1 per cent. Track and signalling unit costs were reduced by 2 per cent, those of administration by 5 per cent and those of operating by 4 per cent.

Freight traffic

A new company style management for Railfreight, with improved financial monitoring and cost control, a sharper focus on marketing and sales, and improved management of major customer accounts, helped the business to limit the effects of strike action and the recession. Through vigorous reshaping of its products and by winning new business, Railfreight achieved an operating surplus, after ancillaries but before interest, of £9.9 million. Weak markets in the steel and construction sectors also reduced traffic available, but by the end of 1982 Railfreight's marketing share in its main business sectors had returned to the levels achieved before the rail strikes. More customers applied for grants given under Section 8 of the 1974 Railways Act supporting the movement of freight by rail on environmental grounds. In October 1982 the maximum grant towards the cost of facilities was raised from 50 to 60 per cent. Fourteen new grants awarded in 1982, totalling £2 million, were expected to bring another 500 000 tonnes of rail traffic annually.

Marketing successes during the year included further growth of 'Grainflow' services for bulk movement of cereals in privately-owned hopper wagons; new petroleum flows switched from barge and coastal shipping to rail; and a second scheme for taking refuse by rail in containers from Greater Manchester to disposal sites.

The progressive build up of Speedlink overnight scheduled services for traffic in wagonload quantities continued with the number of daily trunk services rising from 72 to 85, and carryings up by over

Class 56 3250 hp Co-Co and Merry-Go-Round train of automatic-discharge coal hoppers at Blyth power station, near Newcastle

Class 40 2000 hp 1Co-Co1 diesel and Speedlink freight from Glasgow Mossend to Harwich Parkeston Quay in East Anglia (John C Baker)

20 per cent at 4.3 million tonnes. In the final quarter of 1982 alone, Speedlink turnover rose 13 per cent over the same period in 1981, as a result of new business won to rail and the transfer of existing traffic from traditional wagonload services. In addition to more Grainflow traffic, Speedlink sales successes included movements of paper, bottled drinks, agricultural lime, fertilisers, cars, industrial chemicals and bricks. Orders were placed for 250 new sliding-door high capacity Railfreight vans with a payload of 29 tonnes, roof height access for forklift equipment and 75 cubic metres capacity.

Against intense competition, the parcels business lost ground due to the rail strikes. Improvements in customer service led to early signs of a recovery, with receipts totalling £92 million for the year and an operating surplus, before interest, of £8 million.

The labour strikes caused a 5 per cent drop in the gross revenue of Freightliners Ltd, compared with 1981 and against a forecast of continued growth. Customer confidence suffered, and competitors seized the opportunity to move in on the company's markets. Nevertheless business levels recovered towards the year end and were better than expected in the deep sea, Irish and European sectors, enabl-

ing the operating loss to be contained at £4.4 million. Freightliner assumed full responsibility in 1983 for marketing container traffic to and from Europe and for chartering container shipping services between Harwich and Zeebrugge. A second Freightliner terminal was to open in 1983 at Felixstowe; built by the Felixstowe Dock and Railway Company with the aid of the biggest ever grant made under Section 8 of the 1974 Railways Act, the new terminal will more than double the annual capacity for container movements through Felixstowe.

Carryings (million tonnes)

	1979	1980	1981	1982
Coal and coke	93	94	95	88.4
Iron and steel	25	13	18	14.3
Oil and chemicals	21	18	16	14.6
Building and construction	19	19	16	16.1
Freightliner	8	7	7	6.5
Other traffics	3	2	2	2
Total	169	153	154	141.9

Passenger traffic

Under the Transport Act 1974 BR receives an annual Public Service Obligation grant (PSO) with which it is required to sustain the same level and quality of service as existed in 1974, and at the same time cover total costs out of fare revenue and PSO grant combined. In 1975 BR was further required to work within a level of PSO grant that would be unchanged in terms of real money values from year to year. Subsequently, however, the real money value of the PSO grant was steadily reduced; it fell by 17 per cent between 1975 and 1979. The BR Board estimated that the 1982 grant was some £80 million less than the amount needed to execute the maintenance and renewals essential to fulfil the obligations of the 1974 Act. In addition BR received £73 million from the conurbation Passenger Transport Executives (PTEs) in Strathclyde (Greater Glasgow), Greater Manchester, Merseyside, West Midlands, Tyne & Wear, South Yorkshire and West Yorkshire where local train services are run to patterns and at fare levels specified by the PTEs as suits their overall, multi-modal public transport policy.

In 1981 the Government set an objective of full Inter-City passenger service self-sufficiency by 1985 as the price of Government endorsement for further main-line electrification. This requirement was recognised in the business sector management development mentioned earlier. Though the Inter-City network was not modified for public marketing and promotion, administratively it was reduced to the hard core of key trunk routes radiating from London and the main north-east to south-west cross-country trunk route. In Scotland, for example, all main-line services except those to England over the East and West Coast routes are now administratively in the 'Provincial Services' sector management group.

Attainment of Inter-City sector self-sufficiency has been made more difficult by the Government's total deregulation of road coach operation under its 1980 Transport Act, following which a large number of cheaply-priced trunk road services were set up in direct competition with rail.

Although 1982 receipts at £933 million were down less than 10 per cent on 1981, the rail strikes cost the passenger business an estimated £150 million in lost revenue. It faced the additional problems of lower levels of traffic due to the recession and keen competition from long-distance coaches. Passenger journeys at 630 million were down 12 per cent, and passenger miles at 17 000 million were down by 11 per cent. There was no general increase in fares in 1982 and this, together with marketing initiatives, led to a recovery of traffic levels towards the end of the year. By the end of 1982 Inter-City volume was back to 1981 levels, and net revenue was improving.

Inter-City 125 services were introduced between Sheffield, Nottingham, Derby and London St Pancras with minimum investment by redeployment of the diesel HST fleet. Passenger carryings increased immediately. Delivery of the last two sets on order brought the total of Inter-City 125 trains in service to 95, covering 45 per cent of Inter-City train mileage.

The sleeper market was revitalised with the delivery of the first of 210 Mk III air-conditioned trains. Introduced first between London, Edinburgh and Aberdeen, the new sleepers then took up service between London, Glasgow and Inverness. To test the market for long-distance overnight rail travel at competitive prices, a new 'Nightrider' concept was introduced between London, Edinburgh and Aberdeen, offering first-class air-conditioned travel and an all-night buffet service at cheap fares. 'Nightrider' soon achieved an average load factor of 73 per cent.

With business levels down, costs were trimmed by slimming services to match demand and by scrapping some 700 older passenger coaches.

London and South-east revenue at £447 million was 8 per cent down on 1981 due to the strikes, which encouraged some commuters to find alternative ways of getting to and from work. Most of these customers returned to rail but rising unemployment also reduced levels of commuting. Work continued on a £120 million project to resignal and improve track layouts on the London Victoria-Brighton main line and delivery of new trains was completed for the Bedford-St Pancras/Moorgate route, although lack of agreement on the rate of pay for drivers in one-man operation delayed the start of electric services until late 1983. To improve conditions on routes from London Liverpool Street and to the Kent coast, 358 emu coaches were refurbished. The selective slimming of services enabled 231 older coaches to be withdrawn, with significant savings in operating costs.

Agreement was reached with the Greater London Council on electrification of the line to North Woolwich as part of a package of improvements designed to encourage redevelopment of London's

New bulk grain hoppers for use in Speedlink service between Diss, Norfolk, and Muir of Ord, Scotland *(John C Baker)*

Class 47 Co-Co and Freightliner for Felixstowe port *(John C Baker)*

Class 317 25 kV ac emu for London St Pancras/Moorgate-Bedford service

Docklands. A new station was opened at Milton Keynes, built with the help of Milton Keynes Development Corporation, to serve both Inter-City and London-bound traffic.

Passenger journeys (000)

	1980	1981	1982
Full-fare	201 509	184 429	159 000
Reduced-fare	227 521	211 534	202 900
Season ticket	331 162	322 525	268 200
Total	760 192	718 488	630 100

Passenger-km (million)

	1980	1981	1982
Full-fare	10 780	10 459	8528
Reduced-fare	12 389	11 746	11 907
Season ticket	8528	8528	6919
	31 697	30 733	27 354

Passenger receipts (£ million)

	1981	1982
Ordinary: full fares	419·2	358·0
reduced fares	347·7	335·4
Total ordinary	766·9	693·4
Season tickets	255·9	230·7
Total	1022·8	924·1

Freight and parcels receipts (£ million)

	1981	1982
Coal and coke	274·1	270·5
Iron and steel	65·0	51·9
Other	138·6	134·8
Freightliner, haulage receipts	26·0	21·0
Parcels	119·4	92·2
Total	623·1	570·4

Freight and parcels traffic (tonnes million)

	1981	1982
Coal and coke	95·2	88·4
Iron and steel	18·2	14·3
Other	33·8	32·7
Freightliner, haulage (estimated)	7·0	6·5
Parcels (estimated)	0·9	0·7
Total	155·1	142·6
Total net tonne miles (estimated) (million)	10 877	9867

Railway operating account (£ million)

	1981	1982
Gross revenue		
Passenger		
Fares and charges	1022·8	924·1
Contract payments	810·2	887·2
	1833·0	1811·3
Freight	503·7	478·2
Parcels and Post Office mails	119·4	92·2
Miscellaneous	18·9	18·6
Total	2475·0	2400·3
Expenditure		
Train services	1055·7	1046·2
Terminals	263·8	254·5
Miscellaneous traffic expenses	50·4	54·3
Track and signalling	602·9	620·3
General expenses	423·9	460·3
Provision for replacement of passenger assets	80·3	87·6
Total	2477·0	2523·2
Railways net (loss)	(2·0)	(122·9)
Net income		
Operational property (letting)	28·0	28·7
Commercial advertising	4·6	4·7
Station catering	1·4	(0·8)
Train catering	(6·8)	(7·0)
	27·2	25·6
Operating surplus/(loss)	25·2	(97·3)

Group profit and loss account (£ million)

	1981		1982	
	Rail businesses	Non-rail businesses	Rail businesses	Non-rail businesses
Turnover				
Business income	1858·0	230·5	1675·2	254·1
Government contract payments	810·2		887·2	
Total	2668·2	230·5	2562·4	254·1
Operating surplus/(loss)				
Railways	25·2		(97·3)	
Freightliner	0·1		(4·4)	
Rail workshops	0·2		(1·5)	
Non-operational property		9·0		11·1
Sealink UK Ltd		(0·7)		2·7
British Transport Hotels Ltd		(2·4)		(1·6)
Total operating surplus/(loss)	25·5	5·9	(103·2)	12·2
Share of net (loss) of associated companies				(1·9)
Other income	11·4	0·4	11·1	0·2
	36·9	6·3	(92·1)	10·5
Corporate expenses	4·9		5·7	
Surplus/(loss) before interest	32·0	6·3	(97·8)	10·5
Interest				
Interest on capital debt to Secretary of State	50·2		52·0	
Other interest and other financing charges	20·2	7·7	29·0	6·7
Intra-group interest paid/(received)	(2·8)	2·8	(2·6)	2·6
Surplus/(loss) after interest	(35·6)	(4·2)	(176·2)	1·2
Taxation paid/(recovered)	0·1	(0·1)		
	(35·7)	(4·1)	(176·2)	1·2
Exchange gain		0·1		
Surplus/(loss) before extraordinary items	(35·7)	(4·0)	(176·2)	1·2
Extraordinary items	6·9	18·3	8·1	10·7
Surplus/(loss) after extraordinary items	(28·8)	14·3	(168·1)	11·9
Less amounts transferred to reserves	7·8	14·9	8·1	9·3
	(36·6)	(0·6)	(176·2)	2·6
Group (loss) after transfers to reserves	(37·2)		(173·6)	

Analysis of rail operating costs

	1980		1981		1982	
	£ million	%	£ million	%	£ million	%
Staff expenses	1398	58	1578	60	1593·3	59
Materials, supplies and services	716	30	728	28	751·2	28
Fuel and power	170	7	195	7	185·6	7
Depreciation and amortisation	117	5	136	5	151	6
	2401		2637		2681·1	

Estimated results 1982

(£ million)

	Inter-City	London and South-east	Provincial (including PTEs)	Total
Income	350	447	136	933
Direct expenses				
Train services	225	279	207	711
Terminals	46	96	60	202
Miscellaneous	9	11	5	25
	280	386	272	938
Contribution	70	61	(136)	(5)
Indirect expenses				
Infrastructure	122	194	212	528
Administration and general	106	149	124	379
Replacement charge	34	33	21	88
	262	376	357	995
	(192)	(315)	(493)	(1000)
Other income	(3)	6	4	7
Interest	17	28	6	51
Net result (before PSO payments)	(212)	(337)	(495)	(1044)
Payment by PTEs				73
Payment by Central Government				817
Unsupported (loss)				(154)

Investment

In 1981 the British Railways Board issued a Rail Policy statement setting out a case for increased investment and a forecast of the deterioration that was inevitable if the stringent cash limits imposed on BR were not eased, or alternatively if the mandate set BR in the 1974 Transport Act were not revised. A main problem was that the heavy investment in the wake of the 1955 Modernisation Plan and the greatly reduced levels since the 1970s were creating a mounting obsolescence in signalling, track renewals and particularly traction; almost 10 per cent of the BR dmu and emu fleet was between 20 and 30 years old.

The BR statement forecast that if there was no change in the real value of permitted investment over the ensuing 10 years, the shortfall of new assets would have the following consequences:

Track mileage withdrawn from traffic as unfit for use: 3000, rising rapidly
Mileage carrying temporary speed restrictions (356 at end of 1982): 800
Annual failure rate of mechanical signalling: 10%, rising
Resultant annual duration of train delays: 8500 h, rising
Availability of locomotives: 50%
Availability of emus: 70%
Availability of dmus: 60%
Availability of loco-hauled coaches: 75%.

The decisions necessary to halt these trends, stressed the BRB, must be taken in 1981; but they were not. In its 1981-85 Corporate Plan (subsequently affected by Government decisions to hold the EFL level for three years and also by the serious labour disputes of 1982) BR had hoped to average £414 million of investment annually between 1981 and 1990, comprising £306 million under its Government ceiling at the time; £72 million to recover the backlog of asset renewals; and £36 million for main-line electrification. In its Rail Policy statement it proposed an annual average of £567 million, the chief extra items comprising £92 million for the London and South-east, mainly commuter network; £10 million for improved airport link services; and £51 million for the single-line Channel Tunnel scheme agreed with French Railways.

In sharp contrast, the costs of 1982's labour disputes had to be sharply reflected in the year's capital spending. To keep within the Government's cash limit constraints (EFL), investment was limited to £161 million, compared with the Government's permitted ceiling of £269 million. This was the lowest outlay in BR history.

Asset reductions 1982

Marshalling yards	−15	(20%)
Locomotives and traction units	−99	(3%)
Locomotive-hauled coaches	−602	(12%)
Locomotive-hauled non-passenger vehicles	−568	(20%)
Freight vehicles	−17 711	(17%)

Investment planned 1983 (£000)

Main-line diesel locomotives (24)	18 900
Locomotive-hauled passenger cars (90)	17 500
Advanced Passenger Train (APT)	1900
Mu cars (175 electric, 22 diesel)	50 700
Freight wagons	1000
Track improvements	2300
Track maintenance machines	6100
Electrification	10 300
Bridges and buildings	10 200
Signalling and telecommunications	87 500
Yards and terminals	20 900
Workshops	10 400
Other	33 100
	270 800

Traction and rolling stock

At the end of 1982 BR was operating 2798 diesel locomotives, 266 electric locomotives, six APT power and 30 APT trailer cars, 197 HST power and 709 HST trailer cars, 4617 locomotive-hauled passenger cars, 2962 dmu and 7247 emu cars and 87 955 freight wagons.

Class 210 four-car demu

Class 210 demu interior

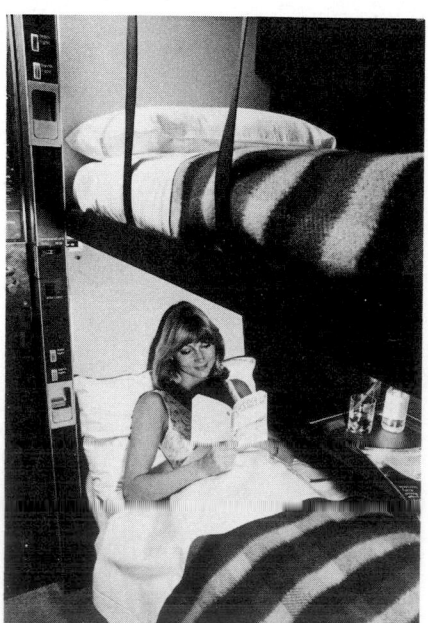
Mk III sleeping-car berth

Air-conditioned Mk III sleeping-car

An APT-P set was briefly introduced to public service between Euston and Glasgow in December 1981, but soon withdrawn for further private development following failures partly attributable to unprecedentedly severe winter weather but also affecting reliable performance of the automatic body-tilting apparatus and other equipment. A prototype 200 km/h, 9000 hp Class 89 Co-Co electric locomotive has been ordered, but it was stressed that this was not diminution of faith in the APT concept, only recognition that the favourable alignment of some routes scheduled for electrification would not fully exploit the higher curving speed of more costly APT technology. However, since service speeds above 200 km/h are now foreseen as impracticable on several counts in the immediate future, the concept was in 1983 being revised before seeking authority for series production of 20 trainsets. The new version, designated APT-U, will be a push-pull of up to 10 trailers with locomotives at each end, each drawing power through its own pantograph. The trailers alone will incorporate body-tilting, but will not be articulated and will be disc-instead of hydrokinetically-braked. Four 25 kV ac HST power cars have been ordered as prototype traction.

The first Class 58 3300 hp heavy freight diesel-electric locomotive prototype, designed to have many components in common with a putative Class 88 heavy freight 25 kV electric Co-Co and also to be suitable for export markets, emerged in 1982 (see under BREL in Locomotives and rolling stock for further details).

A total of 200 new emu vehicles was added to stock in 1982, comprising chiefly Class 317 25 kV ac sets for the London Midland Region's new St Pancras—Bedford service. At the end of the year the first of 74 Class 455 one-class, four-car emus for the Southern Region's third-rail dc suburban system was completed.

Dmu replacements still awaited decisions on investment, on electrification and on the relative merits in specific operating and commercial situations of new dmu designs and the several railbus versions derived from the LEV prototype. The latter comprise BR's Class 140 twin-unit, with strengthened body, power doors, toilet and Class 210 demu cab; the single-unit R3, broadly retaining the simplicity of the LEV; and a twin-unit version of the R3, classified 141 by BR. Production cost of the Class 141 has been put at £300 000, compared with £965 000 for a bogie Class 210 three-car demu.

Class 210 demu prototypes have been produced in a three- or four-car format, the three-car as a suburban unit with 203 second-class seats, the four-car for longer hauls with 22 first-, 232 second-class seats and lavatory facilities. Of the two prototype sets, the three-car has a MTU 12V 396 TC12 195 kW, 1500 rpm engine, the four-car a GEC 6RP200 rated at 839 kW at 1500 rpm. A 650-amp, 1200-volt, three-phase ac alternator transmission is associated with four axle-hung motors similar to those of Class 317 emus, each rated at 190 kW at 1630 rpm, in a single power car. This achieves a maximum tractive effort of 92 kN per power car.

Orders were, however, placed for 20 Class 141 sets for delivery in 1983-84. The prototype Class 210 demus' projected construction cost on a production basis has proved too expensive for a quantity build. Consequently an intermediate-range underfloor-engined dmu is being developed. Orders were placed in 1983 for four three-car sets, to be delivered by the end of 1984. The vehicle interiors will be similar to that of the latest emus and the Class 210, but the sets will have a lower installed power-to-weight ratio giving significantly lower manufacturing costs yet a performance about 10 per cent better than existing sets for a similar fuel consumption. Maintenance costs and reliability are forecast to be significantly better. Two designs will be built to a common commercial specification by British Rail Engineering Ltd and Metro-Cammell. Derivations of these units, together with the four-wheel lightweight vehicles of Class 141, are expected to form the basis of all future replacement dmus.

Orders were also placed in 1983 for 28 Mk IIIb passenger cars with APT-type seating for the West Coast main line; and for 32 HST trailers with a high-density 76-seat second-class layout, to reinforce HST units on the East Coast main line.

Electrification

A joint British Rail/Department of Transport study published in 1982 a report concluding that there was a strong financial case for electrifying 52 per cent of the network as quickly as possible. This would cover 9250 route-km and bring 83 per cent of all passenger and 68 per cent of all freight train mileage under electric haulage.

The return, it was stated, would be greater if the task could be completed within 20 rather than 30 years; the additional net investment incurred (at

Changes in assets and activities	1963	1982
Total track mileage	47 543	25 690
Total passenger route-mileage	12 915	8930
Railway and workshops staff (including Freightliners Ltd subsidiary)	476 545	194 592
Passenger stations	4306	2369
Freight depots	5165	339
Freight marshalling yards	602	59
Total locomotives (including steam in 1963)	11 304	3016
Total multiple-unit cars, electric and diesel	11 129	11 135
Total hauled passenger, mail, parcel cars	20 469	6696
Total freight vehicles	862 640	71 452
Loaded passenger-train miles (million)	233·433	185·2
Loaded freight train-miles (million)	91·601	27
Total passenger journeys (million)	921·514	630·1
Total passenger-miles (estimated) (million)	19 575	17 000
Net freight ton-miles (million)	16 537	9867

New Milton Keynes station, a joint BR-Milton Keynes Development Corporation project

Class 58 3300 hp diesel-electric Co-Co for freight haulage

1976 prices) would be £576 million, since the £723 million fixed equipment costs would be offset by a £147 million saving in renewal of diesel with electric traction rather than like for like. The conclusions were based on exhaustive analysis of annual performance, traction deployment and maintenance, and three varied traffic forecasts, reviewed in each case at six different levels and speeds of electrification. The Government responded with a broad commitment to a 10-year rolling programme of electrification, but then required further submis-

sions from BR on a route-by-route basis with updated financial justification on revised criteria.

At the start of 1983, therefore, with completion of the 86 route-km Moorgate/St Pancras—Bedford scheme in the London area in mid-1982, the only further major electrifications approved were: extension of the East Anglian 25 kV 50 Hz from Colchester to Harwich and Norwich; and Paisley to Ayr and Ardrossan for the Strathclyde Passenger Transport Executive, in this case with financial aid from the Scottish Office of the Government and the

European Economic Community. In April 1982 the BRB resubmitted the case for electrification of the East Coast main line from Hitchin to Leeds and Newcastle, having reappraised it to meet the Government's new criteria, but it was rejected; a further revised submission was made in the spring of 1983.

Civil engineering
Track renewals in 1982 totalled 668 km, but because of the constraints on expenditure this figure was 314 km less than the calculated requirement. With this fresh deficit the back-log of renewal work rose to 1450 km.

Signalling
Almost 18 000 track-km have been equipped with continuous colour-light signalling, following an increase of 286 track-km in 1982. There are just over 500 automated level crossings, a further 72 level crossings having been automated during 1981/82; in addition some 170 level crossings are remotely supervised by closed circuit television.

The National Signalling Plan envisages that the majority of Inter-City, commuter and important freight routes will ultimately be controlled from about 75 major signalling centres. So far nearly 50 centres have been established, with the remainder of the system controlled from about 2100 manual signal boxes. Four new schemes costing a total of £40 million were announced in 1983 for Leicester, Chichester, Dundee and East Anglia.

The automatic warning system (AWS) now covers 8050 route-km. The installation of hot axle box detectors has continued and these are installed at 166 locations.

A National Telecommunication Plan provides extension-to-extension dialling between approximately 200 railway telephone exchanges. Only a few geographical areas remain unconnected to the system and development is now giving way to renewal, as some earlier parts of the system are 25 years old. Plans are now being drawn up for the long-term renewal of the network using electronic exchangers, digital transmission and optical fibre trunk cables. The network carries the equivalent of £75 000 worth of telephone calls each working day and provides the base system for many data systems.

A National Radio Plan aims to provide two-way radio contact between lineside and traffic staff and a control base. It will have 32 control centres and about 250 static transmitting points. Schemes have been completed covering the whole of the West Coast main line from London to Glasgow, London Liverpool Street to Bishop's Stortford and Clacton and London Fenchurch Street to Southend. Schemes to provide signalbox-to-train communication are almost complete on the GN (London) inner suburban lines and between Bedford and St Pancras, London.

Development work is proceeding on two pilot schemes for radio signalling. This will replace conventional signal boxes and block sections with a central dispatching system whereby 'tokens' of authority to traverse a given section of line will be indicated electronically in the cab of suitably fitted traction units by means of radio signals. Track simplification and line singling together with automatic operation of level crossings will eliminate most, if not all, block posts; the remaining passing loops will be controlled either by radio or fitted with self-setting trailable points. The first lines to be so equipped will be those between Dingwall and Kyle of Lochalsh and Ipswich-Lowestoft.

Electric locomotives

Control room of new West Hampstead power signal box, covering 70 route-miles from London St Pancras/Moorgate to Irchester, north of Bedford

Prototype Class 140 two-car diesel unit

A contract for a solid state interlocking system at Leamington Spa, using micro-processors, has been signed with two private sector manufacturers; a similar pilot scheme for automatic route setting on the busy Southern Region network at Haywards Heath, Sussex, has been brought forward to 1983.

Track
A prototype 'Stoneblower' pneumatic ballast injection machine gives a higher standard of track maintenance than the ordinary tamping machine and also works faster, thus reducing the overall time when engineers need possession of the track. Arrangements are being made for the machine to be developed and marketed by a leading manufacturer.

Also nearing completion is a novel structure gauging vehicle which will improve the accuracy of costing new rolling stock design and electrification schemes. The vehicle will record at speed the co-ordinates of all lineside structures in a format suitable for transfer to a central data base.

A 23 km diversion of the East Coast main line away from the area of the new Selby coalfield was to be opened in October 1983. It would be available for operation at 200 km/h by mid-1984.

Rail: FB54 (113A)
Cross ties (sleepers): Prestressed concrete, thickness 203 mm
Spacing: 1540/km in lines with speeds 160 km/h and over; 1430/km other lines; 1650/km on curves sharper than 800 m radius on high speeds/tonnage routes; 1540/km on curves sharper than 800 m on lower speeds/tonnage routes
Fastenings: Pandrol clip
Minimum curvature radius: 400 m
Max gradient: 1:35
Max axleload: 25 tons

Class	Wheel arrangement	Supply voltage	Rated output hp	Tractive effort Max lb at % adhesion		Continuous at lb	mph	Max speed mph	Wheel dia mm	Total weight tonnes	Length m	No in service	Year first built	Builders Mechanical parts	Electrical equipment
73/0*	Bo	Third rail 660/750 V dc	Third rail dc 1600 Diesel 600	42 000 34 100	25 20·3	9600 16 100	55·5 10	80	1013	76·3	16·3	6	1962	BR/EE	EE
73/1*	Bo-Bo	Third rail 660/750 V dc	Third rail dc 1600 Diesel 600	40 000 36 000	24 21·4	7800 13 600	68 11·5	90	1013	76·8	16·3	41	1965	BR/EE	
81	Bo-Bo	25 kV ac	3300	50 000	28·6	17 000	71	100	1216	79·4	17·2	22	1959	BRCW	AEI
85	Bo-Bo	25 kV ac	3300	50 000	27·5	17 000	71	100	1216	82·5	17·2	40	1960	BR	AEI
86/0	Bo-Bo	25 kV ac	3600	68 000	31·8	20 000	67	100	1140	86·8	17·2	20	1965	BR/EE	AEI
86/1	Bo-Bo	25 kV ac	4000	58 000	30·3	21 300	87	100	1150	86·8	17·2	3	1965	BR/EE	AEI
86/2	Bo-Bo	25 kV ac	4000	46 500	24·8	19 200	77·5	100	1152	86·2	17·2	58	1965	BR/EE	AEI
86/3	Bo-Bo	25 kV ac	3600	58 000	31·8	20 000	67	100	1150	82·8	17·2	19	1965	BR/EE	AEI
87/0	Bo-Bo	25 kV ac	4000	58 000	31·6	21 300	87	100	1150	83·3	17·2	35	1973	BR/EE	AEI
87/1	Bo-Bo	25 kV ac	5000	58 000	33·2	21 600	84	100	1150	79·1	17·2	1	1975	BR/EE	AEI

* Electro-diesel

Diesel locomotives

Class	Wheel arrangement	Transmission	Rated power hp	Max lb at	% adhesion	Continuous lb	at mph	Wheel dia mm	Total weight tonnes	Length mm	No in service	Year first built	Mechanical parts	Engine & type	Transmission
03	0-6-0	Mech	204	15 300	22.6	15 300	3.75	1088	30.7	7904	42	1958	BR	Gardner 8L3	Vulcan Sinclair Type 23
08	0-6-0	Elec	350	35 000	31.9	11 100	8.8	1368	50.4	8892	704	1952	BR	EE 6KT	2 EE traction motors
09	0-6-0	Elec	350	25 000	22.5	8700	11.6	1368	50.4	8892	26	1959	BR	EE 6KT	2 EE traction motors
13	0-6-0-0-6-0	Elec	(Twin-350) Total 700	70 000	26	32 000	3.75	1368	121.9	18 265	2	1962	BR	EE 6KT	4 EE traction motors
20	Bo-Bo	Elec	1000	42 000	26	25 000	11	1088	73.5	14 221	215	1957	E	EE 8SVT	4 EE traction motors
25/1	Bo-Bo	Elec	1250	45 000	27	20 800	17.1	1124	74.9	15 352	28	1961	BR	Sulzer 6LDA28/B	4 AEI traction motors
25/2	Bo-Bo	Elec	1250	45 000	27.5	20 800	17.1	1124	74.2	15 352	100	1963	BR	Sulzer 6LDA28/B	4 AEI traction motors
25/3	Bo-Bo	Elec	1250	45 000	28.7	20 800	17.1	1124	71.8	15 352	57	1966	BR	Sulzer 6LDA28/B	4 AEI traction motors
26/0	Bo-Bo	Elec	1160	42 000	25.4	30 000	11.25	1088	75/79.1	15 428	14	1958	BRCW	Sulzer 6LDA28	4 Crompton Parkinson T/Ms
26/1	Bo-Bo	Elec	1160	42 000	23	30 000	11.25	1088	74.5	15 428	25	1958	BRCW	Sulzer 6LDA28	4 Crompton Parkinson T/Ms
27/0	Bo-Bo	Elec	1250	40 000	24	25 000	14	1088	74.5/72.3/77.4	15 428	39	1961	BRCW	Sulzer 6LDA28B	4 GEC traction motors
27/1	Bo-Bo	Elec	1250	40 000	23.5	25 000	14	1088	77.3/76.7	15 428	9	1962	BRCW	Sulzer 6LDA28B	4 GEC traction motors
27/2	Bo-Bo	Elec	1250	40 000	23.6	25 000	14	1088	72.9	15 428	8	1962	BRCW	Sulzer 6LDA28B	4 GEC traction motors
31/1	A1A-A1A	Elec	1470	42 800	25.4	22 250	19.7	1088/1000/1088	111	15 428	213	1958	Brush	EE 12SV	4 Brush traction motors
31/4	A1A-A1A	Elec	1470	35 900	20.8	18 700	23.5	1088/1000/1088	112.6	15 428	24	1959	Brush	EE 12SV	4 Brush traction motors
33/0	Bo-Bo	Elec	1550	45 000	26.3	26 000	17.5	1088	77.7	15 428	63	1960	BRCW	Sulzer 8LDA28	4 Crompton Parkinson T/Ms
33/1	Bo-Bo	Elec	1550	45 000	26	26 000	17.5	1088	78.5	15 428	19	1960	BRCW	Sulzer 8LDA28	4 Crompton Parkinson T/Ms
33/2	Bo-Bo	Elec	1550	45 000	26	26 000	17.5	1088	77.5	15 428	12	1962	BRCW	Sulzer 8LDA28	4 Crompton Parkinson T/Ms
37	Co-Co	Elec	1750	55 500	23.5	35 000	13.6	1088	102.2/107.7	18 696	308	1960	EE	EE 12CSVT	6 EE traction motors
40	1Co-Co1	Elec	2000	52 000	21.1	30 900	18.8	1124	130.7/130.2	21 123	95	1958	EE	EE 16SVT	6 EE traction motors
45/0	1Co-Co1	Elec	2500	55 000	21.1	30 000	25	1124	136.8/137.5	20 644	59	1960	BR	Sulzer 12LDA28A	6 Crompton Parkinson T/Ms
45/1	1Co-Co1	Elec	2500	55 000	22.5	30 000	25	1124	134.9	20 644	50	1960	BR	Sulzer 12LDA28A	6 Crompton Parkinson T/Ms
46	1Co-Co1	Elec	2500	55 000	21.8	31 600	23.3	1124	140.5	20 644	32	1961	Brush/BR	Sulzer 12LDA28B	6 Brush traction motors
47/0	Co-Co	Elec	2580	62 000	23.3	30 000	26	1124	120.6/108.6	19 328	241	1963	Brush/BR	Sulzer 12LDA28C	6 Brush traction motors
47/3	Co-Co	Elec	2580	62 000	24.7	30 000	26	1124	113.7	19 326	81	1963	Brush/BR	Sulzer 12 LDA28C	6 Brush traction motors
47/4	Co-Co	Elec	2580	55 000	20.6	30 000	26	1124	120.4/125.1	19 320	172	1963	Brush/BR	Sulzer 12LDA28C	6 Brush traction motors
47/7	Co-Co	Elec	2580	55 000	20.6	30 000	26	1124	122.5	19 328	12	1979	BR	Sulzer 12LDA28C	6 Brush traction motors
47/9	Co-Co	Elec	3300	57 325	22	32 600	32.3	1124	113.7	20 848	1	1979	BR	Ruston	6 Brush traction motors
50	Co-Co	Elec	2700	48 500	18.8	33 000	23.5	1088	116.9	20 824	50	1967	EE	EE 16SVT	6 EE traction motors
56	Co-Co	Elec	3250	60 700	22	53 950	43.2	1143	125.2	19 355	111	1976	BR/Brush	GEC Diesels 16KT3CT	6 Brush traction motors
58	Co-Co	Elec	3300	—	—	42 580	17.7	1120	130	19 130	1	1982	BR	Ruston RK3ACT	6 Brush TM 73-62 motors

Diesel-electric multiple-units

Class	Formation	Engine/ alternator or generator	No & rated hp of traction motors	Max speed mph	Weight tonnes	Length m	Power cars	Driving trailers	Trailer cars	Year introduced	Mechanical	Electrical
201	DMBS+TS+TS +TF+TS+DMBS	EE 500 hp/ EE (Gen'r) 4SRKT	2 × 250 + 2 × 250	75	DMBS 55 / TS 29.5 / TF 30.5	18.4 / 18.4 / 18.4	8		16	1957	BR Eastleigh	EE
202	DMBS+TS+TS +TF+TS+DMBS	EE 500 hp/ EE (Gen'r) 4SRKT	2 × 250 + 2 × 250	75	DMBS 56 / TS 30.5 / TF 31.5	20.3 / 20.3 / 20.3	22		44	1957	BR Eastleigh	EE
203	DMBS+TS+TB +TF+TS+DMBS	EE 500 hp/ EE (Gen'r) 4SRKT	2 × 250 + 2 × 250	75 / 75	DMBS 56 / TS 30.5 / TF 31.5 / TB 34.5	20.3 / 20.3 / 20.3 / 20.4	9		15	1958	BR Eastleigh	EE

Diesel-electric multiple-units

Class	Formation	Engine/ alternator or generator	No & rated hp of traction motors	Max speed mph	Weight tonnes		Length m	No in service Power cars	Driving trailers	Trailer cars	Year intro- duced	Manufacturer Mechanical	Electrical
204	DMBS+DTC	EE 600 hp/ EE (Gen'r) 4SRKT	2 × 250	75	DMBS DTC	57 32·5	20·3 20·3	4	4		1958	BR Eastleigh	EE
205	DMBS+TS+DTC	EE 600 hp/ EE (Gen'r) 4SRKT	2 × 250	75	DMBS TS DTC	57 30·5 32·5/34·5	20·3 20·3 20·3	29	29	29	1957	BR Eastleigh	EE
206	DMBS+TS+DTS	EE 600 hp/ EE (Gen'r) 4SRKT	2 × 250	75	DMBS TS DTS	55 29·5 30	18·4 18·4 20·4	6	5	6	1965	BR Eastleigh (units reformed from classes 201 & 416)	EE
207	DMBS+TC+DTS	EE 600 hp/ EE (Gen'r) 4 SRKT	2 × 250	75	DMBS TC DTS	57 31·5 31·5	20·3 20·3 20·3	19	19	19	1962	BR Eastleigh	EE
210	DMBS +TC+TS+DTS DMS+TS+DTS	GEC 1125 hp (Alt'r) MTU 1225 hp (Alt'r)	4 × 255 4 × 255	75	DMS DTS TC TS		19·83 19·92	1	1	2	1982	BREL Derby	Brush GEC
253	DMB+2TF+TRUB/ TRSB +4TS+DMB	Paxman 2250 hp/ Brush (Alt'r)	4 × 460 + 4 × 460	125	DMB TF TRUB TRSB TS	70 33 35 35 34	17·8 23 23 23 23	102		346	1976	BREL Crewe & Derby	Brush
254	DMB+2TF+TRSB +TRUK+4TS+DMB or DMB+2TF+TRUB +5TS+DMB	Paxman 2250 hp/ Brush (Alt'r) Paxman 2250 hp/ Brush (Alt'r)	4 × 460 + 4 × 460 4 × 460 + 4 × 460	125 125	DMB TF TRSB TRUK TRUB TS	70 33 35 37 35 34	17·8 23 23 23 23 23	95		363	1978	BREL Crewe & Derby	Brush

Electric multiple-units (ac and ac/dc)

Class	Formation	Supply voltage	No and rated hp of traction motors	Max speed mph	Bogies	Brake system	Control system	Weight tonnes		Length m	Type	No in service	Region	Year intro- duced	Builders Mechanical	Electrical
302	DTS+TC+ MBS+BDTS	25 kV/ 6·25 kV	4 × 192	75	Double bolster	EP	Tap changing contactors	MBS DTS BDTS TC	55 32·5 36·5 30·5/31·5	20·3 20·3 20·3 20·3	Non gangway	112	ER (GE & LTS)	1958	BR	GEC (EE)
303	BDTS+MBS+ DTS	25 kV/ 6·25 kV	4 × 207	75	Double bolster	EP	Tap changing camshaft	MBS DTS BDTS	56 34·5 38	20·3 20·3 20·3	Non gangway Sliding doors	86	ScR (Glasgow)	1960	Pressed Steel	GEC (AEI)
304	DTS+TC+ MBS+BDTS	25 kV	4 × 207	75	Double bolster	EP	Tap changing camshaft	MBS BDTS DTBS TC	54·5 36/37 32/32·5 31·5/32·5	20·3 20·5 20·5 20·3	Non gangway	44	LMR	1960	BR	GEC (AEI)
305/1	DTS+MBS+ BDTS	25 kV/ 6·25 kV	4 × 157	75	Double bolster	EP	Tap changing camshaft	MBS DTS BDTS	55 31·5 35	20·3 20·3 20·3	Non gangway	52	ER (GE)	1959	BR	GEC
305/2	DTS+TC+ BDTS	25 kV/ 6·25 kV	4 × 200	75	Double bolster	EP	Tap changing camshaft	MBS DTS BDTS TC	55 32·5 36·5 30·5/31·5	20·3 20·3 20·3 20·3	Non gangway	18	ER (GE)	1960	BR	GEC
307	BDTS-R+MS +TC+DTS	25 kV/ 6·25 kV	4 × 174	75	Single bolster	EP	Resistance contactors	MS DTS DTBS TC	47·5 31·5 31 30·5/31·5	20·3 20·3 20·3 20·3	Non gangway	32	ER (GE)	1956	BR	GEC (EE)
308/1	DTS+TC+ MBS+BDTS	25 kV/ 6·25 kV	4 × 200	75	Double bolster	EP	Tap changing contactors	MBS DTS BDTS TC	55 33 36·5 31·5	20·3 20·3 20·3 20·3	Non gangway	33	ER (GE)	1961	BR	GEC (EE)
308/2	DTS+TC+ MLV+BDTS	25 kV/ 6·25 kV	4 × 192	75	Double bolster	EP	Tap changing contactors	DTS BDTS TC MLV	33 36·5 31·5 52	20·3 20·3 20·3 20·3	Non gangway	5	ER (LTS)	1961	BR	GEC (EE)
308/3	DTS+MBS+ BDTS	25 kV/ 6·25 kV	4 × 200	75	Double bolster	EP	Tap changing contactors	MBS DTS BDTS	55 31·5 35	20·3 20·3 20·3	Non gangway	3	ER (GE)	1961	BR	GEC (EE)
308/4	DTS+TC+ MBS+BDTS	25 kV/ 6·25 kV	4 × 192	75	Double bolster	EP	Tap changing contactors	MBS DTS BDTS TC	52·5 33 36·5 31·5	20·3 20·3 20·3 20·3	Non gangway (converted 308/2)	4	EE (LTS)	1973	BR	GEC (EE)
309/1	DMBS+BDTS	25 kV/ 6·25 kV	4 × 282	100	Common- wealth	EP	Tap changing contactors and camshaft	DMBS BDTS	60 40	20·3 20·3	Gangwayed throughout	4	ER	1962	BR	GEC
309/2	DTC+TB+ MBS+BDTC	25 kV/ 6·25 kV	4 × 282	100	Common- wealth	EP	Tap changing contactors and camshaft	MBS DTC BDTC TC	57 36·5 40 36·5/34	20·3 20·3 20·3 20·3	Gangwayed throughout	8	ER (GE)	1962	BR	GEC
309/3	DTC+TS+ MBS+BDTC	25 kV/ 6·25 kV	4 × 282	100	Common- wealth	EP	Tap changing contactors and camshaft	MBS DTC BDTC TS	57 37·5 40 35	20·3 20·3 20·3 20·3	Gangwayed throughout	7	ER (GE)	1962	BR	GEC

Electric multiple-units (ac and ac/dc)

Class	Formation	Supply voltage	No and rated hp of traction motors	Max speed mph	Bogies	Brake system	Control system	Weight tonnes		Length m	Type	No in service	Region	Year introduced	Builders Mechanical	Electrical
309/4	BDTS+TC+ TS+DMBS	25 kV/ 6·25 kV	4 × 282	100	Common-wealth	EP	Tap changing contactors and camshaft	DMBS 60 BDTS 40 TS 34·5 TC 35·5		20·3 20·3 20·3 20·3	Gangwayed throughout (converted 309/1)	4	ER (GE)	1973	BR	GEC
310	RDTS+MBS+ TS+DTC	25 kV	4 × 270	75	BR Schlieren	EP	Tap changing contactors	MBS 57 BDTS 34·5/37·5 BDTC 34·5 TS 31·5		20·3 20·3 20·3 20·3	Partially gangwayed	49	LMR	1966	BR	GEC (EE)
311	BDTS+MBS DTS	25 kV/ 6·25 kV	4 × 222	75	Double bolster	EP	Tap changing camshaft	MBS 58 DTS 34·5 BDTS 37·5		20·3 20·3 20·3	Non gangway Sliding doors	19	ScR (Glasgow)	1967	Craven	GEC (AE)
312/0	BDTS+MBS+ TS+DTC	25 kV	4 × 270	90	BP 14 Motor BT 8 Trailer	EP	Tap changing contactors	MBS 56 DTC 33 BDTS 35 TS 30·5		20·3 20·3 20·3 20·3	Gangwayed between vehicles	26	ER (GN)	1976	BREL	GEC
312/1	BDTS+MBS+ TS+DTC	25 kV/ 6·25 kV	4 × 270	90	BP 14 Motor BT 8 Trailer	EP	Tap changing contactors	MBS 55·5 DTC 33 BDTS 35 TS 30·5		20·3 20·3 20·3 20·3	Gangwayed between vehicles	19	ER (GE)	1975	BREL	GEC
312/2	RDTS+MBS+ TS+DTC	25 kV	4 × 270	75	BP 14 Motor BT 8 Trailer	EP	Tap changing contactors	MBS 55·5 DTC 33 BDTS 35 TS 30·5		20·3 20·3 20·3 20·3	Gangwayed between vehicles	4	LMR	1975	BREL	GEC
313	DMS+TS+ DMS	25 kV/ 750V dc	4 × 110 + 4 × 110	75	Bx1	West-code	Resistance camshaft	DMS 35 BDMS 36·5 TS 30·5		20·3 22·2 20·3	Gangwayed between vehicles Sliding doors	64	ER	1976	BREL	GEC/ Brush
314	DMS+TS+ DMS	25 kV	4 × 110 + 4 × 110	75	Bx1	West-code	Thyristor	DMS 36 TS 31		20·3 20·2	Gangwayed between vehicles Sliding doors	16	ScR (Glasgow)	1979	BREL	GEC/ Brush
315	DMS+TS+ TS+DMS	25 kV	4 × 110 + 4 × 110	75	Bx1	West-code	Thyristor	DMS 36 TS 31		20·3 20·2	Gangwayed between vehicles Sliding doors	61	ER (GE)	1980	BREL	GEC/ Brush
317	DTS+MS+ TS+DTS(B)	25 kV/ 6.25 kV	4 × 332	90	MS BP20C+ BP20D (one of each) DTS DT13A+ DT136 TS BT13 DTSB BT13A+ BT136 (one of each)	EP	Thyristor	DTS(A) 30 MS 50 TC 28 DTS(A) 29		20·13 20·18 20·18 20·18	Gangwayed	45	LMR	1982	BREL	GEC
370 (APT)	DTS+TS+ TS+TRSB+ TF+TBF+M (normal train formation is 2 sets in multiple)	25 kV	4 × 1000	125	BP17/ 17A Motor BP 18/19 BT 11/ 11a BT 12/ 12a Trailer	Hydro-kinetic	Thyristor	DTS 35 TS 21 TRSB 24 TF 24 TBF 33 M 67		21·4 21 21 21 21·4 18·4	Gangwayed throughout	6	LM & ScR	1979	BREL	ASEA

Electric multiple-units (dc)

Class	Formation	Supply voltage	No & rated hp of traction motors	Max speed mph	Bogies	Brake system	Control system	Weight tonnes		Length m	Type	No in service	Region	Year introduced	Builders Mechanical	Electrical
405	DMBS TS TS DMBS	750 V dc Third rail	2×250 + 2×250	75	Single bolster	Auto air	Resistance contactors	DMBS 43/42 TS 27/28		19·3 19·3	Non gangway	33	SR	1946	SR	EE
410/1	DMBS TC TB DMBS	750 V dc Third rail	2×250 + 2×250	90	Common-wealth TB Single bolster Others	EP	Resistance contactors	DMBS 41 TC 31·5 TB 35·5		20·3 20·3 20·4	Gangwayed throughout	1	SR	1956	BR	EE
410/2	DMBS TC TB DMBS	750 V dc Third rail	2×250 + 2×250	90	Single bolster Motor Commonwealth and/or Single bolster Trailer	EP	Resistance camshaft	DMBS 41 TC 31·5 TB 35·5		20·3 20·3 20·4	Gangwayed	8	SR	1959	BR	EE
411/1	DMBS TC TS DMBS	750 V dc Third rail	2×250 + 2×250	90	Single bolster	EP	Resistance contactors	DMBS 41 TC 31·5 TS 31·5		20·3 20·3 20·3	Gangwayed throughout	1	SR	1956	BR	EE

Electric multiple-units (dc)

Class	Formation	Supply voltage	No & rated hp of traction motors	Max speed mph	Bogies	Brake system	Control system	Weight tonnes		Length m	Type	No in service	Region	Year introduced	Builders Mechanical	Electrical
411/2	DMBS TC TS DMBS	750 V dc Third rail	2×250 + 2×250	90	Single bolster Motor Commonwealth or Single bolster Trailer	EP	Resistance camshaft	DMBS TC TS	41 31·5 31·5	20·3 20·3 20·3	Gangwayed throughout	30	SR	1958	BR	EE
411/3	DMS TBC TS DMS	750 V dc Third rail	2×250 + 2×250	90	Single bolster Motor Commonwealth Trailer	EP	Resistance camshaft	DMS TBC TS	41·5 35·5 31·5	20·3 20·3 20·3	Gangwayed throughout (refurbished 411-2)	89	SR	1978	BR	EE
413/2	DTC DMBS DMBS DTC	750 V dc Third rail	2×250 + 2×250	90	Single bolster	EP	Resistance contactors	DMBS DTC	42 32	20 20·4	Non gangway	13	SR	1951	BR	EE
413/3	DTC DMBS DMBS DTC	750 V dc Third rail	2×250 + 2×250	90	Single bolster	EP	Resistance contactors	DMBS DTC	42 32	20 20·4	Non gangway	11	SR	1957	BR	EE
414/2	DMBS DTC	750 V dc Third rail	2×250 + 2×250	90	Single bolster	EP	Resistance contactors	DMBS DTC	42 32·5	20 20·4	Non gangway	2	SR	1957	BR	EE
414/3	DMBS DTC	750 V dc Third rail	2×250	90	Single bolster Motor Commonwealth and Single bolster Trailer	EP	Resistance camshaft	DMBS DTC	42/41 32·5	20 20·4	Non gangway	169	SR	1957	BR	EE
415/1	DMBS TS TS DMBS	750 V dc Third rail	2×250 + 2×250	75	Single bolster	EP	Resistance contactors	DMS TS	40/42 28/27	19·3/ 20 19·3	Non gangway	194	SR	1951	BR	EE
415/2	DMBS TS TS DMBS	750 V dc Third rail	2×250 + 2×250	75	Single bolster	EP	Resistance camshaft	DMS TS	42/41 28/27/ 29·5	20 19·3/ 20·4	Non gangway	70	SR	1957	BR	EE
415/4	DMBS TS TS DMBS	750 V dc Third rail	2×250 + 2×250	90	Single bolster	EP	Resistance contactors	DMBS TS	40 28	19·3 19·3	Non gangway	16	SR	1951	BR	EE
416/1	DMBS DTS	750 V dc Third rail	2×250	75	Single bolster	EP	Resistance contactors	DMBS DTS	40 30	19·3 19·3	Non gangway	34	SR	1957	BR	EE
416/2	DMBS DTS	750 V dc Third rail	2×250	75	Single bolster	EP	Resistance contactors	DMS DTS	40·5/40/ 42 32·5/30	20 20·4	Non gangway	88	SR	1951	BR	EE
418	DMBS DTS	750 V dc Third rail	2×250	90	Single bolster	EP	Resistance contactors	DMBS DTS	40 30	19·3 19·3	Non gangway	21	SR	1974	BR	EE
418/2	DMBS DTS	750 V dc Third rail	2×250	90	Single bolster	EP	Resistance camshaft	DMBS DTS	42 32	20 20·4	Non gangway (converted 414/3)	2	SR	1957	BR	EE
419	DMLV	750 V dc Third rail	2×250	90	Single bolster	EP	Resistance camshaft	DMLV	47·7	20·3	Non gangway	10	SR	1965	BR	EE
420/1	DTC MBS TB DTC	750 V dc Third rail	4×250	90	Single bolster Motor B5 Trailer	EP	Resistance camshaft	MBS DTC TBS	49 36/35 35	20·3 20·3 20·3	Gangwayed throughout	18	SR	1965	BR	EE
420/2	DTC MBS TB DTC	750 V dc Third rail	4×250	90	Mark 6 Motor B5 Trailer	EP	Resistance camshaft	MBS DTC TBS	49 36/35 35	20·3 20·3 20·3	Gangwayed throughout	10	SR	1970	BR	EE
421/1	DTC MBS TS DTC	750 V dc Third rail	4×250	90	Single bolster Motor B5 Trailer	EP	Resistance camshaft	MBS DTC TS	49 36/35 31·5	20·3 20·3 20·3	Gangwayed throughout	35	SR	1964	BR	EE
421/2	DTC MBS TS DTC	750 V dc Third rail	4×250	90	Mark 6 Motor B5 Trailer	EP	Resistance camshaft	MBS DTC TS	49 36/35 31·5	20·3 20·3 20·3	Gangwayed throughout	101	SR	1970	BR	EE
423/0	DTC MBS TS DTC	750 V dc Third rail	4×250	90	Mark 6 Motor B5 Trailer	EP	Resistance camshaft	MBS DTC TS	49 32·5/35 31·5	20·3 20·3 20·3	Gangwayed throughout	181	SR	1967	BR	EE
423/1	DTC MBS TS DTC	750 V dc Third rail	4×250	90	Mark 6 Motor B5 Trailer	EP	Resistance camshaft	MBS DTC TS	49 32·5/35 31·5	20·3 20·3 20·3	Gangwayed throughout (converted 423)	12	SR (Gatwick)	1963	BR	EE
430	DMBS TB TRBF DMBS	750 V dc Third rail	4×365 + 4×365	90	Mark 6 Motor B5 Trailer	EP	Resistance camshaft	DMBS TB TRBF	51·5 35 35·5	20·3 20·3 20·3	Gangwayed throughout	15	SR	1966	BR	EE

Electric multiple-units (dc)

Class	Formation	Supply voltage	No & rated hp of traction motors	Max speed mph	Bogies	Brake system	Control system	Weight tonnes		Length m	Type	No in service	Region	Year introduced	Builders Mechanical	Electrical
455	DTS MS TS DTS	750 V dc Third rail	4×205	75	BT13 BP27 BT13	EP	Resistance camshaft	DTS MS TS	29 36 28	19·3 19·3 19·3	Gangwayed throughout	—	SR	1983	BR	
485	Variable	650	2×240	45	LTE Type Z Motor LTE Type V Trailer	EP	Resistance contactors	DMS DTS TS	32/39 17 18	16·2 15·8 15·7	Ex-LTE Sliding doors	6	SR (Isle of Wight)	1967	LT	CP
486	DMS TS DTS	650	2×240	45	LTE Type Z Motor LTE Type V Trailer	EP	Resistance contactors	DMBS DTS TS	32/29 17 18	16·2 15·8 15·7	Ex-LTE Sliding doors	5	SR (Isle of Wight)	1967	LT	CP
487	Variable	660	2×190	35	Single bolster rubber springs	Auto air	Resistance contactors	DMBS TS	29 20	15 15	Non gangway Sliding doors	28	SR (Waterloo & City)	1940	EE	EE
491	DTS TBS TF DTS	750	Non powered Normally worked with Class 430	90	B5	EP		DTS TF TBS	32·5 33·5 35·5	20·3 20·3 20·3	Gangwayed throughout Non powered	34	SR	1966	BR	
501	DMBS TS DTS	630	4×185	75	Single bolster	EP	Resistance contactors	DMBS DTBS TS	48 30·5 29·5	18·5 18·5 18·5	Non gangway	40	LMR (Watford)	1957	BR	GEC
503	DMBS TC DTS	650	4×135	75	Single bolster	EP	Resistance contactors	DMBS DTS TS	36·5 22·5 21·5	18·5 18 17·8	Non gangway Sliding doors	42	LMR (Wirral)	1956 1938	BRCW EE	Met Camm MV
504	DMBS DTS	1200 V dc Guarded third rail, side contact	2×141	75	Double bolster	EP	Resistance contactors	DMBS DTS	50 30	20·4 20	Non gangway	21	LMR (Bury)	1959	BR	EE
506	DMBS TS DTS	1500 V dc overhead	4×185	75	Single bolster	EP	Resistance contactors	DMBS TS DTS	52 27 28	19·2 17·4 17·6	Non gangway Sliding doors	24	LMR (Glossop)	1959	BRCW/ Met Camm	EE
507	DMS TS DMS	750 V dc Third rail	8×110	75	B×1	West-code	Resistance camshaft	DMBS TS DMS	36 31 36	20·3 20·2 20·3	Gangwayed between vehicles Sliding doors	33	LMR (Southport)	1979	BREL	GEC
508	DMS TS TS DMS	750 V dc Third rail	8×110	75	B×1	West-code	Resistance camshaft	DMS TS BDMS	36 31 36	20·3 20·3 20·3	Gangwayed between vehicles Sliding doors	41	SR/LMR	1980	BREL	GEC

Northern Ireland Railways Co Ltd (NIR)

Central Station, East Bridge Street, Belfast BT1 3PB

Telephone: 0232 35282
Telex: 747 953

Chairman: Sir Myles Humphreys
Chief Executive: Roy Beattie

Gauge: 1600 mm

Route length: 328 km

Development Plan
NIR is seeking Government approval for a 10-year, £90 million development plan which includes CTC installation, automation of level crossings, construction of a cross-Belfast link between the city's York Road and Central stations, and rolling stock renewals. Immediate proposals cover purchase from British Rail Engineering of nine three-car dmus based on the latest BR design.

Traction and rolling stock
The railway operates five diesel-electric and three diesel-hydraulic locomotives, 29 diesel-electric power cars and 44 trailers, 25 passenger cars and 20 freight wagons.

Track
Rail: 50, 54 and 56 kg/m
Minimum curvature radius: 184 m
Max gradient: 1·6%
Max axleload: 18 tonnes

UNITED STATES OF AMERICA

Department of Transportation

400 7th Street SW, Washington DC 20590

Secretary: Elizabeth Dole
Deputy Secretary: D M Trent
Assistant Secretary for Policy and International Affairs: J T Connor
Assistant Secretary for Governmental Affairs: L L Verstandig
Assistant Secretary for Administration: R L Fairman

Director of Public Affairs, Office of Secretary: Linda Gosden
Administrator of Federal Aviation Administration: J Lynn Helms
Administrator of Federal Highway Administration: R A Barnhart
Administrator of Urban Mass Transportation: A E Teele Jr

Federal Railroad Administration

400 7th Street SW, Washington DC 20590

Telephone: (202) 426 4000

Eastern office: 434 Walnut Street, Rm 1020, Philadelphia, Pennsylvania 19106
Telephone: (215) 597 0750
Southern office: 1720 Peachtree Road NW, Atlanta, Georgia 30309
Telephone: (404) 881 2718

Southwestern office: 819 Taylor Street, Rm 11A23, Fort Worth, Texas 76102
Telephone: (817) 334 3601
Western office: Two Embarcadero Center, Suite 630, San Francisco, California 94111
Telephone: (415) 556 6411

Administrator: Vacant
Deputy Administrator: T A Till
Chief Counsel: J H Mason
Associate Administrator for Administration: W W Wilson

Associate Administrator, Office of Safety: J W Walsh
General Manager, Alaska RR: F H Jones
Acting Associate Administrator for Research and Development: D L Spanton
Public Affairs Officer: J R Winston
Associate Administrator, Federal Assistance: W E Loftus
Associate Administrator for Intercity Programmes: L S Thompson
Acting Assistant Administrator for Policy: J C Rooney

Interstate Commerce Commission

12th & Constitution Ave NW, Washington DC 20423

Telephone: (202) 275 7414

Chairman: R H Taylor Jr
Vice-Chairman: R E Gillam Jr
Commissioners: F Andre
H Gradison
J L Simmons
M Sterrett

Secretary: Agatha L Mergenovich
Managing Director: W R Johnson
General Counsel: J H Broadley

Urban Mass Transportation Administration (UMTA)

Department of Transportation, 400 7th Street SW, Washington DC 20590

Telephone: (202) 426 4043

Administrator: Arthur E Teele, Jr
Deputy Administrator: Charles A Gargano
Executive Director: Raymond J Sander
Executive Secretariat: Karen Abbott

UMTA is the Federal agency responsible for providing financial assistance to American cities to improve mass transportation. Approximately 80 per cent of all transit capital improvements made in the United States are financed with Federal funds from the agency, which also provides assistance in planning, research and development and operation of public transport systems.

Late in 1982 Congress and the President passed the Surface Transportation Act of 1982 which, from an increased petrol tax, allocated $1100 million a year to a newly-created transit account in the Highway Trust Fund up to 1987. It also lifted UMTA transit funding from $2650 million in 1982 to $3650 million in 1983, rising to $4150 million in 1986. Other provisions included $240 million for the Washington DC Metro and $75 million for several commuter rail schemes in 1983. Almost immediately, however, the Administration counteracted these measures by proposing a drastic 1984 reduction in transit operating assistance, through a cut of UMTA's appropriation for that financial year by $776 million to $1974 million, in addition to which $150 million was trimmed from the budgeted petrol tax proceeds on grounds of downward-revised revenue projections.

In 1983 the Reagan Administration withdrew its opposition to funding new transit system starts.

National Railroad Passenger Corporation (Amtrak)

400 N Capitol Street NW, Washington DC 20001

Telephone: (202) 383 3000

President and Chairman of the Board: W Graham Claytor
Executive assistant: Beverly Balanda
Chief Operating Officer, Group Vice President, Operations and Maintenance: Thomas P Hackney, Jr
Operations and Maintenance, Vice President: Frank D Abate
Vice President and Chief Engineer: D F Sullivan
President, Washington Terminal Co: Robert A Herman
Marketing and Business Development, Group Vice President: William S Norman
Vice President, Sales: James Callery
Vice President, Transportation Marketing: Robert E Gall
Vice President, Corporate Planning: Timothy P Gardner
Finance and Administration, Group Vice President: D R Brazier
Vice President, Finance and Treasurer: C W Hayward
Vice President, Labor Relations: George F Daniels
Vice President, Computer Services: George E Gautney
Vice President, Personnel: John N Stulak
Passenger Services and Communications, Group Vice President: M L Clark Tyler
Vice President, Passenger Services: Eugene N Eden
Vice President, Government Affairs: James H English
Vice President, Corporate Communications: Vacant
Assistant Vice President, Corporate Development: A Welters
Vice President and General Counsel: Paul F Mickey, Jr
Corporate Secretary: Sandra Spence

Amtrak was created when the Rail Passenger Service Act was enacted in October 1970 and services began in May 1971. During its first ten years Amtrak created the first nation-wide rail passenger service in the USA with services (save the Denver, Colorado to Salt Lake City, Utah route of the Denver & Rio Grande Western Railroad) under one management.

Except in the Boston-New York-Washington Northeast Corridor, Amtrak's rail passenger service is totally dependent upon the condition of track and related facilities that are owned, designed, maintained and operated by the private freight-hauling railroads. The design of track and lack of new passenger car technology in the USA limit Amtrak's ability to improve train frequency.

Oakland-Bakersfield 403(b) service, 'San Joaquin'

Class AEM-7 electric locomotive and train of Amfleet II cars

Member railroads

The 13 railroads that signed contracts with Amtrak and immediately began operating Amtrak service were: The Santa Fe; Burlington Northern; Baltimore & Ohio-Chesapeake & Ohio (now Chessie System); Milwaukee Road; Louisville & Nashville and Seaboard Coast Line (now Seaboard System); Missouri Pacific; Penn Central (now part of Conrail); Richmond, Fredericksburg & Potomac; Southern Pacific; Union Pacific; Gulf, Mobile & Ohio and Illinois Central (now the Illinois Central Gulf). Because of route expansions, Amtrak later signed contracts with the Boston & Maine; Central of Vermont; Canadian National; Grand Trunk Western; Norfolk & Western; and Delaware & Hudson.

Three railroads—the Denver & Rio Grande Western, the Rock Island, and the Southern—were offered contracts by the Amtrak Incorporators in 1971, but they chose not to operate under the Amtrak system. After January 1975, these companies were free to petition appropriate regulatory bodies to discontinue service. Denver & Rio Grande Western maintained its passenger operation until 1983. Then, with freight profits reduced by recession, and with its 'Rio Grande Zephyr' losing heavily and operating increasingly aged equipment, DRGW agreed to this train's replacement in April by a re-routed Amtrak 'San Francisco Zephyr', for which the historic name of 'California Zephyr' was revived. During 1979-80 the Rock Island ceased all operations and the Southern Railway agreed to transfer the operation of its last remaining passenger service, 'The Southern Crescent' (running between Washington and New Orleans via Atlanta), to Amtrak.

Services

In January 1979, under the Carter Administration, the Secretary of Transportation recommended a plan to 'streamline the national network' of rail passenger service. A 43 per cent reduction of the Amtrak network to 2525 route-km was advocated. Congress refused to trim by more than 17 per cent, which was effected with the discontinuation of five long-haul routes and the addition of one long-haul service. In October 1981, Amtrak was directed by Congress to further tighten the route structure by discontinuing several non cost-effective services to meet new funding constraints ordered by the Reagan Administration.

The Amtrak legislation also provides for states or regional agencies to obtain service not included in the Basic System. Under this Clause 403(b) provision the local jurisdiction must at present assume 50 per cent of the solely related losses of operating the service, plus capital expenses for equipment, facilities or track repair, but the Reagan Administration seeks to raise the proportion to 100 per cent.

Finance
The Reagan Administration has attempted in all its budgets to reduce substantially the amount of Federal funding for Amtrak under both operating and capital expenditure heads. For fiscal year 1982 it proposed $613 million, as against a total of $993 million provisionally assigned by the outgoing Carter Administration. Congress, however, was not agreeable and a sum of $788 million was eventually agreed, as a result of which less than 10 per cent of the network's route-mileage had to be sacrificed. For fiscal year 1983 the Reagan Administration was proposing a $600 million Amtrak support, with only $16 million allocated to capital projects, whereas under the latter head Amtrak was requesting a minimum of $134 million, for purchase of 70 Amfleet II sleeping-cars and catering cars, more locomotives to supersede life-expired FL9 diesels and also for infrastructure improvements.

The compromise figure eventually agreed by the Administration was $700 million, $88 million less than the figure voted by the House of Representatives and $35 million below the Senate's proposal. It was forecast that the budget would leave only $50 million for capital improvements. In April 1983, however, Congress voted Amtrak a further $80 million for job-creating investment.

For financial year 1984 Amtrak was seeking $807 million, including $155 million for capital improvements. The request assumed continuation of all 403(b) services, for which the Reagan Administration seeks elimination of all Federal responsibility. The Administration, in contrast, was planning a $676 million allocation for Amtrak and a switch of 100 per cent financial responsibility to State administration for retention of 403(b) services.

Although passenger-km declined 12·7 per cent in 1982, to 19·04 million journeys, total revenue rose from $506 million in 1981 to $557·8 million. Ticket sales of $426 million were supplemented by sales of surplus vehicles, real estate transactions and use of the Beech Grove workshops, Indianapolis, for overhaul and assembly of urban transit vehicles for other operators and companies. The target set by Congress of 50 per cent coverage of costs from revenue was met three years ahead of schedule; the actual ratio was 50·1 per cent, against 42 per cent in 1981. Expenditure was $103 million below budget. Loss for the year was $555 million, as against $720 million in 1981.

With labour-related expenses approaching 60 per cent of the total annual operating budget, the company embarked upon a series of workforce reduction efforts reaching both management and agreement-covered personnel. These actions were combined with numerous cost containment programmes and deferral of many discretionary expenses.

Washington Terminal Company
Amtrak owns the Washington Terminal Company (WTC), which operates the train facility and trackage adjacent to the Federally-owned Union station in Washington DC. A $50 million capital project for a Northeast Corridor maintenance base is planned for the site. In 1983 Amtrak and the Department of Transportation agreed a $70 million scheme to restore the original Washington Union station to passenger use; it has been derelict, superseded by a temporary station nearby, since the early 1970s.

Traffic	1980	1981
Total train-miles (million)	29·613	30·84
Total passenger journeys (million)	21·219	20·61
Total passenger-miles (million)	4582·2	4761·7

Labour agreements
An important cost-saving achievement of 1982 was a series of new agreements with the labour unions in the Northeast Corridor, where from the start of 1983 all on-train personnel became Amtrak employees. An hourly wage rate superseded the traditional mileage basis for pay, and new flexibility of labour deployment was secured through the merger of several staff grades into two classifications, conductor and assistant conductor. Also

Results (years ending 30 September) ($ million)

	1980	1981
Revenues		
Operating revenue	428·682	496·469
Federal and state operating payments	658·086	712·065
Amortisation of capital payments	21·707	—
Total operating revenues	1108·475	1208·534
Operating expenses		
Train operations	306·031	345·743
Maintenance of equipment	328·253	339·819
Maintenance of way	70·498	80·085
On-board services	115·141	123·161
Stations	66·410	75·782
Marketing and reservations	66·795	87·303
General support	58·124	95·274
Taxes and insurance	31·368	30·542
Depreciation and amortisation	60·158	74·810
Total operating expenses	1102·778	1252·519
General and administrative expense	19·167	24·333
Interest expense, net of capitalised interest for 1981 and 1980 of $4·851 million and $7·536 million respectively	31·302	59·792
	1153·247	1336·644

Refurbished Metroliner emus have been switched to New York and Philadelphia to Harrisburg services

Bi-level Superliner cars in Chicago-Seattle 'Empire Builder' service

Superliner diner, upper floor

agreed with the Brotherhood of Locomotive Engineers were changes in work rules and a gradual transition to longer hours.

Auto-train revival

Amtrak was in 1983 making preparations to revive a passenger-and-auto-carrying overnight service between Lorton, Virginia, and Sanford, Florida, using the ground facilities and auto-carrying vehicles of the former Auto Train company which went into liquidation in September 1980 and ceased operation of the service in May 1981.

Traction and rolling stock

Construction of two prototype sleeping-cars and one dining car as a basis for a new generation of single-level vehicles was approved in 1983. Although it was expected that the vista-dome cars taken over at Amtrak's foundation would gradually disappear following the introduction of new bi-level Superliner cars, Amtrak's Beech Grove workshops were in 1983 fitting seven ex-Northern Pacific Budd-built vehicles of this type for head-end electric auxiliaries power and refurbishing their interiors; the first of the reconditioned cars was added to the Chicago-Washington 'Capitol Limited' in March 1983. This scheme was part of a $27·4 million scheme to add 43 more cars to the 530 inherited vehicles already fitted with head-end power and known as the 'Heritage Fleet'; the new additions would include 23 sleepers and 10 dining cars, six of the latter former Santa Fe Hi-Level stock.

At the end of 1982 Amtrak was operating 62 electric locomotives, 220 diesel-electric locomotives, 14 Turboliner power cars, 109 emu cars, 14 diesel railcars and 1390 locomotive-hauled cars, including 169 mail/baggage cars.

Northeast Corridor

Six segments covered by regional commuter authorities apart, Amtrak has owned the 557 km Boston-New York-Washington Northeast Corridor route since 1976, including six of its stations: Baltimore, Wilmington, Philadelphia (30th Street), Newark, New York Penn Station and Providence. An Improvement Project (NECIP) is nearing completion. It has been lately budgeted at $2500 million, but the Reagan Administration's 1984 budget proposals aim to terminate Federal funding that year at a total of $2190 million.

The route's original Metroliner emus have been transferred to the New York/Philadelphia-Harrisburg service and replaced by locomotive-hauled trains of new 60-seat, leg-rest coaches on all Metroliner service.

With most of the NECIP work completed the Federal Railroad Administration authorised a maximum speed of 193 km/h on some sections between New York and Washington, chiefly in Maryland, while 160 km/h has become possible north of New York. As a result, in October 1982 two daily Metroliner services were introduced each way on 3 hour 55 minute schedules between Boston and New York, inclusive of three intermediate stops, the fastest timings since use of the UAC Turbotrains on the route and a 45-minute improvement on subsequent schedules. Besides full dining car service, a perambulating trolley service of drinks and free snacks was offered on these services. Following completion of point and crossing work south of New York in mid-1983, restoration of a 2½-hour New York-Washington schedule was likely.

Commuter rail service is operated on the Northeast Corridor by the following agencies:
Maryland Department of Transportation: Baltimore-Washington rail service;
Southeastern Pennsylvania Transportation Authority (SEPTA): Wilmington-Philadelphia service and, in conjunction with New Jersey Department of Transportation, Trenton-Philadelphia service;
New Jersey Department of Transportation: commuter rail between Trenton and New York Penn Station;
Metropolitan Transportation Authority: Long Island Rail Road service, sharing Penn Station and the East River Tunnel;
Metropolitan Transportation Authority and Connecticut Department of Transportation: West End commuter service utilising the New Haven to New Rochelle segment of the corridor on its route to Grand Central Station in New York City;
Massachusetts Bay Transit Authority: commuter rail service on the Attleboro to Boston segment of the corridor.

Rail freight service on the Northeast Corridor, all operated by Conrail, currently consists almost entirely of delivery and pick-up on industrial sidings and some through trains operating non-stop between major yards.

Superliner economy bedroom

Superliner family bedroom, extending full car-width

Class E60CP electric locomotive and 'Crescent' equipped with Heritage Fleet cars in Northeast Corridor

Electrification

At present 554·6 route-km and 1720·1 track-km of the Amtrak Northeast Corridor system are electrified at 12·5 kV ac 25 Hz. Extension to a further 24·5 route-km between New York City and New Rochelle, New York, is at the design stage.

Emerging corridors

At a Congressional request, Amtrak and the US Department of Transportation examined during 1980-81 an emerging rail corridors plan which contemplated the development of faster and more frequent rail passenger services in 24 selected intercity corridors ranging in length from 105 to 673 km. This plan visualised increases in train frequency and higher speeds of up to 127 km/h. Both of these goals depended upon the ability of Amtrak to obtain funding from the Government for enough new cars to support increased frequency and to work out a track improvement programme with the privately-owned freight-hauling railroads. Annual capital cost of setting up the specified service in all 24 corridors was estimated at $1171 to 1542 million.

Type	Wheel arrangement	Output hp	Max speed mph	Weight lb	Length ft in	Height ft in	Width ft in	No in service	Year built	Builders
Diesel locomotives										
F40PH	B-B	3000	103	259 000	56' 2"	15' 5"	10' 7"	30	1976	GM
F40PH	B-B	3000	103	262 000	56' 2"	15' 5"	10' 7"	64	1977/78	GM
F40PH.	B-B	3000	110	262 000	56' 2"	15' 5"	10' 7"	97	1979/81	GM
SDP40F	C-C	3000	103	396 000	72' 4"	15' 3"	10' 3"	8	1974	GM
P30CH	C-C	3000	103	386 000	72' 4"	15' 4"	10' 8"	11	1975	GE
E8A	A1A-A1A	2400	98	337 000	70' 3"	14' 10"	10' 8"	5	1949/53	GM
FL9	B-A1A	1750	89	290 000	58' 8"	14' 8"	10' 6"	6	1957	GM
Electric locomotives										
E60CP	C-C	6000	120	387 000	71' 3"	14' 7"	10' 5"	6	1974	GE
E60CP	C-C	6000	120	366 000	71' 3"	14' 7"	10' 5"	26	1974	GE
AEM-7	B-B	5800	125	201 500	51' 2"	14' 8"	10' 5"	47	1979/82	GM

US high-speed railway projects

Moves to develop new high-speed inter-city services in the USA intensified in 1982. The only major setback was that in the November elections Ohio voted decisively, 2·4 million to 710 000, against a sales tax to develop an 845 km network in that state, whereupon the seven-year-old Ohio Transportation Authority was abolished and its staff and functions transferred to the state Department of Transport.

The front-runner was American High Speed Rail Corporation (AHSR), spearheaded by Amtrak's ex-President Alan Boyd as Chairman and ex-Vice President Lawrence Gilson as President. Following finance of initial studies to the extent of $5 million by the 83-year-old Japanese former industrialist, Ryoichi Sasakawa, who also secured pledges of $800 million in Japanese investment, AHSR was confident of starting construction of a Shinkansen-type 182 km line from San Diego to Los Angeles with an extension to Los Angeles international airport in 1984. Management of the project has been entrusted to the Fluor Corporation, with First Boston Corporation as financial advisers.

During 1982 AHSR instigated passage of a California state law to exempt the project from environmental review and authorising issue of $1250 million in tax-exempt state revenue bonds to help finance the $2060 million scheme. By the start of 1983, however, a Californian movement to block acceptance of Japanese Shinkansen technology without full evaluation of other systems, and also to require submission of the scheme to environmental impact studies, was gathering considerable strength.

In Texas, the Texas Railroad Transportation Company was in 1983 seeking to purchase from Burlington Northern a half-share of the ex-Rock Island, 340 km Houston-Dallas line and to use its infrastructure for a French LGV-type system. The Pennsylvania High Speed Rail Passenger Commission was about to appoint engineering consultants to conduct a feasibility study, partly state and partly Federally funded, for a 565 km high-speed line between Philadelphia and Pittsburgh.

A notable recruit in 1983 to TGV-US, the organisation spearheaded by Alsthom to market French technology, was Federal Railroad Administrator Robert W Blanchette, who left the FRA to head the company. British interests were reported to be seeking a partnership with Budd, General Motors and Bechtel, taking the view that success depended on US manufacture. Budd, however, was also promoting Thyssen-Henschel maglev technology and, following a study of the 370 km Los Angeles-Las Vegas route undertaken with joint Federal, state and local funding, hoped to have a maglev system operating between the two cities at speeds of up to 400 km/h by 1991.

The Alaska Railroad
US Department of Transportation
Federal Railroad Administration

PO Box No 7-2111, Anchorage, Alaska 99510

Telephone: (907) 265 2667
Telex: 25-378

General Manager: Frank H Jones
Assistant General Manager: Arnold T Polanchek
Superintendent of Transportation (Acting): Jack A Hepworth
Chief Engineer: Francis C Weeks
Manager, Marketing and Sales: John T Gray
Chief Counsel: David M Roderick
Manager, Budget and Accounting: Ronald M Risch
Chief of Security: Marcie G Trump
Manager, Operating Rules: Kenneth H Greene
Manager, Safety: John K Nielson
Chief of Administration: James B Blasingame
Chief Mechanical Officer: Michael J Sudol
Manager, Planning: William F Coghill
Manager, Personnel: Donald A Harvey
Manager, Supply and Procurement: Peggy R Thomas
Manager, Data Processing: James E Pinkston
Manager, Industrial Development Real Estate: Merle W Akers
Manager, Transportation and Customer Service: Robert W Davison

Route length: 846 km

Development
The Alaska Railroad runs a single-track main line of 756 km from the ports of Seward on the Gulf of Alaska, and Whittier, on Prince William Sound, northward through Anchorage and McKinley National Park to Fairbanks, and eastward to Eielson, with branches serving Eielson Air Force Base, Fairbanks International Airport, Palmer and the Suntrana coalfield.

Legislation to transfer the Alaska Railroad from Federal to State ownership was enacted by the US Congress in 1983 and the Federal Budget for 1983 ended Federal funding of the railroad. The transfer of responsibility, unlikely to be fully effected until 1984, will allow the State the opportunity to determine the role it wants the railroad to play in serving Alaska's future transport needs. The State of Alaska passed a bill in 1982 creating an Alaska Railroad Transfer Advisory Committee to study the Alaska Railroad in detail and provide recommendations to the Alaska Legislature in 1983 for long-term operation and management of the railroad under State ownership.

During the mid-1970s, construction of the trans-Alaska pipeline brought heavy traffic to The Alaska Railroad. Profits derived from that period of service have been invested in upgrading equipment, track and roadbed. Completion of the pipeline was followed by a severe drop in traffic and decline into deficit, which at one time provoked talk of discontinuing passenger service. In the 1980s, however, traffics have fully recovered.

Record year
Total revenues in the 1982 financial year were $58·8 million, up 33·9 per cent from $43·9 million in 1981, and surpassing the previous 1976 peak during construction of the trans-Alaska oil pipeline by 12 per cent. The increase in revenues outpaced the increase in expenses. As a result, the earned surplus, or net profit after depreciation, reached a new record of $9·6 million, up almost 200 per cent from $3·3 million in 1981. Freight revenues rose 40·9 per cent, passenger revenues increased 31·5 per cent and other revenues were up 4·5 per cent.

All-time traffic records were secured in both freight and passenger operations. Total freight tonnage was 4 502 916, compared to 3 366 061 in 1981, a 33·9 per cent increase, and a record 69 506 carloads of freight were handled, up 35·5 per cent on 1981. Gains in gross ton-miles were 22·4 per cent and in revenue train miles 13·8 per cent.

The railroad carried 175 116 passengers, topping the previous best of 162 107 in 1953 by 8 per cent. Total passenger miles were 15 068 658, compared to 13 626 675 in 1981, an increase of 10·6 per cent. A revenue/cost ratio of 79 per cent was achieved for passenger operation, a 16 per cent improvement over 1981.

Underlining the significance of the railroad's gains in 1982 was the productivity of its employees. The average number of permanent employees declined 3·3 per cent over the previous year despite a substantial increase in freight movements. Employee productivity in terms of revenue per employee jumped from $67 085 to $84 968 for an overall gain of 27 per cent. The Federal Railroad Administration recognised the railroad's success in 1982 with an award plaque honouring the managers and all employees of the Alaska Railroad. The upward trend was expected to continue in 1983.

A contract has been signed with the State of Alaska to transport grain for export. The State has purchased 20 covered hopper grain cars and leased 2·7 acres of railroad land at Seward where an $8·5 million grain terminal is under construction. The first export of Alaskan grain from the Big Delta region in interior Alaska via the railroad was scheduled for autumn 1983.

Alaska Railroad freight train powered by 3000 hp locomotives on Whittier-Anchorage service

The first volume shipments of coal from Alaska to a Pacific coast country, deferred from 1982 because of world market conditions, were about to begin. A test shipment of 28 000 tonnes which moved by rail from Healy left Anchorage in December 1980 for Seoul, Republic of Korea. Following the announcement in April 1981 that the test shipment results were acceptable, the railroad participated in numerous meetings culminating in signed agreements and contracts during 1981 that provided for the export of a minimum of 220 000 tons in 1982, a minimum of 550 000 tons in 1983 and at least 880 000 tons in 1984 and beyond. The export coal moves via the Alaska Railroad from the mine site near Healy 584 km to the port of Seward. The railroad port facilities are used and 14·7 acres of adjacent railroad land has been leased to construct a multi-million dollar port-side facility for coal unloading, stockpiling, and transloading. At Healy a rapid-loading tipple with automatic computerised controls has been installed; it permits loading of trains in motion.

Other business developments include yard changes utilising piggypackers at Anchorage and Fairbanks to more efficiently and cost-effectively handle piggyback (TOFC) rail movements.

Freight traffic

Increased spending both for home construction, highway and public works projects as well as private business structures in Anchorage accounted for the 53 per cent jump in sand and gravel tonnage. The continued escalation in southbound petroleum products from the Fairbanks refinery to provide fuel for the Anchorage international airport, plus the first export of rail-hauled refined petroleum to the Continental United States, contributed to the growth in petroleum movements. The large-scale rail movement of iron and steel products from Seward to Fairbanks destined for the North Slope oil fields was a major reason for the 44 per cent increase in manufactures and miscellaneous products.

Passenger traffic

Major increases in passenger ridership occurred on special trains and on the Anchorage-Denali-Fairbanks trains. The increases were due primarily to the marketing application of contract-type techniques similar to those used in the freight sector. These involved closer relationships with national tour operators, tour wholesalers, and travel agents. Special trains were actively promoted.

Traffic

	1980/81	1981/82
Total freight tonnage (000)	3362·1	4502·9
Total freight tonne-km (000)	654 863	770 711
Average freight wagon load (tons)	65·5	64·8
Total passenger-km (000)	21 925·3	24 245·5
Total passenger journeys	161 068	175 116
Average length of passenger journey (km)	136·1	138·5

Finance
Revenues ($000)

Passengers and baggage	2627
Freight, parcels and mail	48 023
Other operating	4795
Non-operating	3352
Total	58 797

Expenditure ($000)

Staff/personnel expenses	33 221
Materials and services	12 303
Depreciation	3712
Total	49 236

The major achievements in 1981 and 1982 were financial. The total revenues in 1981 were an increase of almost 52 per cent over 1980 and exceeded only in the oil pipeline construction year of 1976. In contrast, expenses were held to a 17 per cent gain. This resulted in an earned surplus or net profit after depreciation of $3·3 million compared to a net loss in 1980 of $5·8 million.

These positive operating and financial results assume greater significance because they were achieved with the lowest employment level in the history of the railroad.

Civil engineering

The largest construction and major maintenance effort since the earthquake repair work in 1964 and 1965 was achieved in 1982. This increased level of roadbed and maintenance included replacing more sleepers, relaying new rail, and using an improved grade of crushed ballast.

100-ton capacity open-top hopper car purchased 1982

Freight traffic (000 tonnes)	1980	1981	1982
Sand and gravel	396·2	1796·8	2753·8
Coal	590·2	653·0	653·6
Petroleum, oil, lubricants	251·7	379·1	439·4
Manufactures and miscellaneous	292·1	311·9	449·9
TOFC/COFC (piggyback)	92·4	112·5	122·4
Forest products	108·8	100·7	77·0
Agricultural products	9·9	8·1	6·8
Total	1741·3	3362·1	4502·9
Total freight tonne-km (million)	436·039	654·863	770·711

Investment

Capital and major maintenance programme expenditures

			($ million)			
	1978	1979	1980	1981	1982	Total
Buildings	0·1	0·1	0·2	1·8	1·5	3·7
Roadbed, track & other facilities	2·8	2·2	3·3	4·5	4·3	17·1
Equipment	0·3	0·7	1·8	6·2*	6·6	15·6
Other projects	0·4	6·4†	0·2	0·9	0·3	8·2
Total	3·6	9·4	5·5	13·4	12·7	44·6
Funded by						
Appropriations	3·0	9·3	5·0	12·6	6·2	36·1
Railroad earnings	0·6	0·1	0·5	0·8	6·5	8·5

*$4·24 million for rehabilitation of 10 passenger cars
†$6·3 million for Seward and Whittier dock facilities

Diesel locomotives

Class	Output hp	Weight (tons)	Built/ rebuilt	No of units	Builder
GP-40-2, road	3000	132	1975	6	EMD
GP-40-2, road	3000	132	1976	5	EMD
GP-40-2, road	3000	132	1978	4	EMD
GP-40-2, (rebuilt GP-35)	3000	132	1964/80	1	EMD
GP-35, road	2500	132	1964	3	EMD
E-8, passenger	2400	158	1956/74	2	EMD
GP-7, road	1600	128	1951/77	10	EMD
FP-7, passenger	1500	128	1951	13	EMD
RS-3, switcher	1600	115	1953	12	Alco
RS-1, switcher	1600	115	1953	5	EMD
300 hp switcher	300	45	1944	4	GE
Total				65	

Signalling and communications

A microwave radio telecommunications system is being progressively extended from Seward to Fairbanks. It features use of solar-powered microwave repeaters in remote locations.

Motive power and rolling stock

The railroad has acquired one HEP (head-end-power) unit and refurbished ten ARR passenger cars at a cost of $4·2 million. The refurbishing included conversion from steam to electric power for heat and air conditioning, renewed wiring, increased seating, new upholstering, and interior and exterior painting. The upgraded ten-car train was placed in daily service between Anchorage and Fairbanks during the summer tourist season of 1982.

Increased capability to handle bulk petroleum was achieved with the arrival of two eight-car Tank-Trains leased by North Pole Refinery. Each Tank-Train transports 200 000 gallons. Loading or unloading of the entire TankTrain can be accomplished from one tank car, thereby greatly reducing the loading and unloading time.

In service with the Alaska Railroad are 34 line-haul and 31 switching diesel-electric locomotives; 52 passenger cars (including seven dome chair cars); and 1808 freight cars.

Traction and rolling stock acquisition 1981-82

1981: 2 EMD 2400 hp E-8 locomotives purchased from Amtrak;
25 quad hopper 100-ton capacity open top cars purchased;
8 SP-TOFC 89 ft flats leased;
10 TOFC 89 ft flats purchased (built 1963)

1982: 52 quad hopper 100-ton capacity open top cars purchased;
1 HEP power car purchased (rebuilt 1982);
24 TTAX 89 ft flats leased

Track

Rail: 115 lb/yd RE—Standard Carbon (57·16 kg/m)
Cross ties (sleepers): Treated fir and hardwood, 2045 × 203 × 178 mm
Spacing: 2019/km
Fastenings: 4 or 6 hole angle bars, steel spikes
Minimum curvature radius: 14·5%
Max gradient: 3%
Max axleload: 28·576 kg

Class I railroads

The following main section lists Class I railroads, which by Interstate Commerce Commission definition remain systems with a gross revenue of $50 million or more. The second section lists the more important companies in the Class II and III category. At the close of 1982 35 railroads qualified as Class I, but if account is taken of the mergers affecting a number of them, the total of Class I systems or conglomerate systems is reduced.

Class I systems

Railroad	Corporate owner
Alabama Great Southern	Southern
Atchison, Topeka & Santa Fe	—
Baltimore & Ohio	CSX
Bessemer & Lake Erie	US Steel
Boston & Maine	(purchase by Guilford Transportation Industries pending)
Burlington Northern	
Central of Georgia	Southern
Chesapeake & Ohio	CSX
Chicago & North Western	
Chicago, Milwaukee, St Paul & Pacific	(purchase by Grand Trunk Corporation pending)
Cincinnati, New Orleans & Texas Pacific	Southern
Consolidated Rail (Conrail)	
Delaware & Hudson	(purchase by Guilford Transportation Industries pending)
Denver & Rio Grande Western	
Detroit, Toledo & Ironton	Grand Trunk Western
Duluth, Missabe & Iron Range	US Steel
Elgin, Joliet & Eastern	US Steel
Florida East Coast	
Grank Trunk Western	Grand Trunk Corporation
Illinois Central Gulf	—
Kansas City Southern	
Long Island	
Louisiana & Arkansas	KCS
Missouri-Kansas-Texas	
Missouri Pacific	Union Pacific
National Railroad Passenger Corporation (Amtrak)	—
Norfolk & Western	NS
Pittsburgh & Lake Erie	—
St Louis Southwestern	Southern Pacific Transportation Corporation
Seaboard System	CSX
Soo Line	
Southern Pacific	Southern Pacific Transportation Corporation
Southern	NS
Union Pacific	
Western Maryland	CSX

Atchison, Topeka and Santa Fe Railway Company

80 East Jackson Boulevard, Chicago, Illinois 60604

Telephone: (312) 427 4900

Chairman and Chief Executive Officer: John J Schmidt
Executive Department
President and Chief Executive, Chicago: L Cena
Executive Vice-President: D G Ruegg
Executive Vice-President, Chicago: W J Swartz
Vice-President, Purchases and Materials, Topeka: C C Glover
  Law: G Svolos
  Information Systems: W L Paul
  Real Estate and Industrial Development: J R Scott
  Accounting: W J Taylor
  Personnel and Labour Relations: F L Elterman
  Public Relations: W C Burk
  Executive Representative, San Francisco: R E Welk
    Washington DC: F N Grossman
Operating Department
Vice-President: J R Fitzgerald
Chief Mechanical Officer: T D Mason
Assistant Chief Mechanical Officers:
  K A Wolfe
  L L Luthey

Unit coal train loading at York Canyon, New Mexico, for circuit run to Kaiser steel mill, Fontana, California

Los Angeles-Chicago unit TOFC train of 'Ten-Pack' sets near Victorville, California; in 1982 five 10-car 'Ten-Pack' trains were operational

Assistant General Manager, Mechanical Department, Topeka: R H Berry
   Amarillo: V G Nail
   Los Angeles: R T Dennisen
Superintendent of Safety, System: R D Shaver
Director, Technical Research and Development, Topeka: C R Kaelin
General Superintendent of Transportation: D G McInnes
General Manager
   Topeka, Eastern Lines: R L Banion
   Amarillo, Western Lines: D P Valentine
   Los Angeles, Coast Lines: Q W Torpin
Chief Engineer, System: W S Autrey
Assistant Chief Engineer: H G Webb
Assistant General Manager, Engineering, Topeka: C L Holman
   Amarillo: E C Honath
   Los Angeles: W W Toliver

Finance Department
Vice-President and Treasurer: Frank Bregar

Traffic Department
Senior Vice-President: F J Wright
Vice-President: T J Fitgerald
Assistant Vice-President, Pricing: J A Grygiel

Gauge: 1435 mm
Length: 19 374 km

Santa Fe Industries Inc became the parent company of The Atchison, Topeka and Santa Fe Railway Company and its subsidiaries in 1968. Through its subsidiaries, Santa Fe is currently involved in transportation, natural resources, real estate, construction and forest products.

Lines and territories

Santa Fe operates 19 374 route-km extending from Chicago to the Gulf of Mexico and the Pacific Coast. In July 1979, Santa Fe reached an agreement to purchase from the Pennsylvania Company the remaining 50 stock interest in the Toledo, Peoria and Western Railroad, a 484 km system known as The Peoria Road previously owned jointly by Santa Fe and the Pennsylvania Company.

Early in 1983 Norfolk Southern announced that it owned 5·1 per cent of Sante Fe stock. This prompted speculation that moves were afoot to effect the first transcontinental merger.

Performance 1981

Steady growth in pre-tax contribution from rail operations, which had quadrupled in the previous four years, was interrupted in 1981 by the nation's recession. However, productivity was improved in several areas. In addition, after excluding a dramatic growth of coal traffic, a small increase in market share of inter-city rail traffic was registered. Despite problems, the pre-tax contribution of $110·4 million was the third highest in the railroad's history. With deteriorating economic conditions, however, pre-tax contribution in the first half of 1982, at $25·3 million, was less than half the outturn at the same stage of 1981.

TOFC unit train headed by EMD GP35 locomotives in Cajon Pass

Computer-controlled classification yard at Barstow, California

Prototype 'Fuel Foiler' containers loaded on 'Ten-Pack' train-set

Motive power distribution bureau, Chicago

Carloadings were down 5 per cent and reductions occurred in virtually every type of traffic except piggyback, which was up about 11 per cent and coal, which became volume leader with a 26 per cent increase. The biggest disappointment was grain, traditionally the railroad's largest traffic segment, where the decrease of 16 per cent resulted primarily from declining exports.

Coal traffic growth should continue. Southwestern coal has become an increasingly viable alternative for use in manufacturing, processing and electrical generating industries as oil and natural gas have increased in cost. At year-end the railroad was employing as many as 59 sets of equipment to provide unit coal train service for 19 separate movements. Total coal shipments reached a record 26·8 million tons, accounting for 23 per cent of the total freight tonnage. In 1971 coal accounted for only 5 per cent. Santa Fe expects to be handling about 31 million tons annually by 1985. Nearly all coal shipments have been for domestic consumption, but coal from Santa Fe territory is beginning to penetrate the Far Eastern market.

Another source of future growth is coal from the San Juan Basin in north-west New Mexico, which has several thousand million tons of virtually untapped coal reserves. In March 1981 the Interstate Commerce Commission granted Santa Fe authority to construct the proposed Star Lake Railroad, which will extend northward from the main line about 40 miles east of Gallup, New Mexico. Work on the initial segment was expected to begin in mid-1982, with first shipments anticipated for early 1984 from the Lee Ranch mine, to be operated by Santa Fe Mining, Inc.

The 11 per cent increase in piggyback traffic resulted from growing acceptance of the railroad's marketing programmes, especially for shipment of perishables, a widened recognition by trucking companies of the advantages to them from using economical rail service for the line haul, and deregulation. Piggyback shipments of perishables showed a dramatic increase of 135 per cent, reaching over 28 000 trailerloads. At year-end over 4000 shipper-owned trailers were dedicated to this Santa Fe service, and that number continued to grow. About 40 000 trailerloads of perishables were expected in 1982. Also rising was the conclusion of contracts with trucking firms to handle the line-haul portion of their business.

However, since piggyback traffic was freed from regulation by the Interstate Commerce Commission in March 1981, freedom of rail carriers to publish rates and tailor service based on demand has resulted in severe competition between them, as well as between the rail and trucking industries. To keep expenses in line with necessarily lower unit prices the railroad improved productivity in two important ways. As recently as 1979, Santa Fe's percentage of empty trailer backhauls was 61 per cent, due primarily to the fact that the great majority of piggyback business had been westbound. The dramatic response to efforts to attract perishable traffic, plus some new marketing arrangements worked out with trucking companies, resulted in the empty backhaul ratio being reduced to 22 per cent in 1981.

Productivity improvements
Gross ton miles produced per man-hour worked was improved from 2471 in 1980 to 2546 in 1981.

Several steps were taken during the year that should result in continuing productivity improvements.

An agreement was reached which will eventually result in reduction of one employee on each train and yard crew. This reduction is being implemented on an attrition basis, with savings being shared with those remaining employees who were in train service when the agreement was reached. In a second move, 45 small stations were replaced by 19 regional freight offices, which have direct access to a central computer and thus can provide prompt billing services as well as accurate information relating to car movements, location, supply and other data. In 1982 150 additional stations were to be superseded by 53 regional freight offices.

Progress continued in implementation of the PLUS computer system, which incorporates the best features of the existing management programmes and those employed by other railroads. PLUS will help line managers make operating decisions relating to train operations and improve the timely flow of data to the central computer system.

Capital expenditures
Capital expenditures in 1981 of $280·3 million were down $36·5 million from 1980, and included the acquisition of 432 new freight cars and 83 new locomotives. Another 706 freight cars and 123 locomotives were remanufactured in company shops. 227 miles of new and 120 miles of reconditioned welded rail and 1·7 million new sleepers were installed.

The programme for 1982, subject to traffic volumes, anticipated capital expenditures of $271 million. Major items included 55 new locomotives and 75 freight cars, plus the remanufacturing of 125 locomotives and 868 cars. Planned renewal programmes anticipated laying 132 miles of new and 232 miles of reconditioned welded rail and the insertion of 1·8 million new sleepers.

Rail traffic (000 million revenue ton-miles)	1980	1981	% change
Merchandise	11·8	13·0	10·2
Coal	7·6	9·5	25·0
Grain	10·9	9·3	(14·7)
Food products	9·4	8·9	(5·3)
Chemicals	9·5	8·7	(8·4)
Non-metallic minerals	4·2	3·9	(7·1)
Metal products	3·0	3·3	10·0
Petroleum products	3·1	3·1	
Farm products	2·5	2·9	16·0
Paper products	2·5	2·4	(4·0)
Building materials	2·0	1·8	(10·0)
Forest products	1·8	1·5	(16·7)
Vehicles and parts	1·4	1·4	
All other	3·7	5·5	48·6
Total	73·4	75·2	2·5

Road chassis for 'Fuel Foiler' container

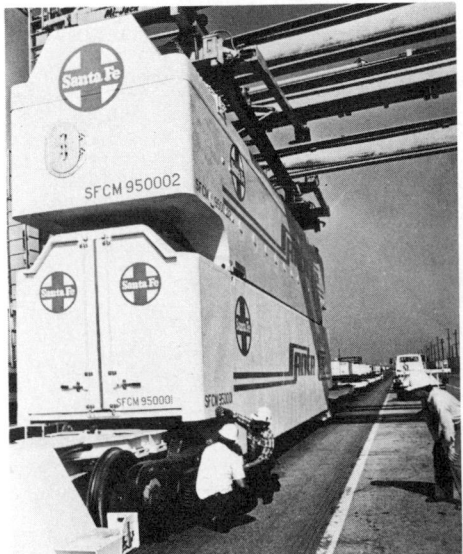

Double-stacking of prototype 'Fuel Foiler' containers

Standard fork-lift truck enters a 'Fuel Foiler' container

Investment

Capital spending in 1983 was set at $121 million. Major items would be the remanufacture of 125 locomotives, modification of over 900 intermodal cars to carry 45 foot road trailers, pursuit of bridge replacements and purchase of computers and related equipment.

Outlook

A study released during 1981 by an independent research firm predicted that railroad revenue ton-miles would increase 35 per cent from 1980 to 1990. This optimistic outlook is consistent with internal studies which anticipate a dramatic growth in business and industry throughout Sante Fe territory.

'Fuel Foiler' container

A new type of freight container has been developed with the aims of improved equipment utilisation and fuel efficiency. The 45-foot long prototypes have an aerodynamic exterior shaped approximately like an 'A' and are designed to be stacked two-high aboard Sante Fe's 'Fuel Foilers'. The two 'legs' of the container straddle the 'Fuel Foiler's' centre sill and ride just above the rails, giving a low centre of gravity. The container can accommodate up to 55 tons of bulk commodities or palletised packaged goods, and could easily be modified to handle liquids. Its versatility would enable its use for shipment of grain or coal to the Far East and manufactured goods on the return, for example. It is fitted with a trough hatch at the top for loading bulk materials, and gates at the bottom of each leg for speedy unloading. A grated deck inside allows bulk materials to flow through easily, and yet provides a level support for package goods. Standard fork-lift trucks can be driven inside. Sante Fe has also developed a special chassis to road-transport the container.

The new container has good aerodynamic characteristics: when loaded aboard the 'Fuel Foiler' railcars there is a minimum void between containers, which greatly reduces the wind drag experienced from the open space between conventional containers. The containers can be stacked six-high aboard ship or in staging areas. When in rail service they would be stacked two-high when empty or loaded with light materials, but would not be double-stacked with bulk materials. Three containers have been built of fibreglass and three of aluminium. They are being made available to customers for loading with a variety of products to accumulate experience in actual service. Sante Fe will decide whether to build more or licence others to build them after testing determines both their practicality and acceptance by shippers.

Length: 45 ft
Width: 8 ft
Height: 10 ft 3 in
  double stack above top/rail: 19 ft 6¾ in
Volume: 2400 ft³
Tare weight: 10 000 lb
Load limit: 109 500 lb
Loaded container on 10-pack 'Fuel Foiler' car tare weight, end unit: 28 000 lb
  interior unit: 20 800 lb
Bogies (7 × 12 in axle): 125 tons
Capacity of single axle: 78 750 lb
  single unit (platform): 157 500 lb
Curve limitations,
  horizontal: 30°
  vertical: 2½°
Wheel loading, interior unit: 923 lb/in dia
  end unit: 647 lb/in dia
  (vs 1036 lb/in on 125-ton hopper car)
  (vs 913 lb/in on 100-ton hopper car)
Ratio of lading to car and container: 3·3
  (vs 3·2 for 100-ton hopper car)

Traffic

	1978	1979	1980	1981
Route miles operated	12 230	12 209	12 161	12 041
Revenue freight				
Carloads handled (000)	1650	1765	1826	1733
Tons of revenue freight (million)	97·6	109	119·1	117·2
Revenue ton-miles (million)	66 200	72 700	73 400	75 200
Revenue tons per train	1532	1674	1636	1703
Freight revenue ($ million)	1491	1837	2185	2318
Average freight revenue per ton-mile ($)	2·25	2·52	2·94	3·04
Average revenue per ton ($)	15·28	16·77	18·09	19·54
Average haul per ton (miles/km)	678/1041	666/1071	616/991	642/1033
Average revenue per car ($)	904	1036	1181	1322
Average train speed (km/h)	46·7	45	30	29·6
Freight train performance				
Gross ton-miles (cars and contents) (million)	148 400	159 900	160 000	159 500
Freight train hours (000)	1476	1552	1550	1491
Freight train-km (million)	69·3	69·4	71·8	70·7
Freight train car-miles/km				
Loaded (million)	1366/2197	1441/2318	1422/2275	1401/969

Finance

Operating revenues ($ million)

	1978	1979	1980	1981
Freight	1491·3	1836·8	2184·8	2318·1
Other	39·5	44·8	49·0	52·7
Total	1530·8	1881·6	2233·8	2370·8
Operating expenses				
Way and structures	265·7	314·7	356·4	389·6
Equipment	330·8	409·1	470·3	533·4
Transportation	643·9	831·2	992·4	1099·9
General and administrative	150·8	160·4	180·6	192·6
Total	1391·2	1715·4	1999·7	2215·5
Operating income	139·6	166·2	234·1	155·3
Other income—net	23·1	31·2	29·1	36·7
Interest expense	36·2	39·5	50·2	64·2
Income before taxes	126·5	157·9	213·0	127·8
Net income	93·6	128·5	162·9	112·3

Motive power and rolling stock

Locomotives

	1978	1979	1980	1981
Diesel units	1748	1870	1940	1991
Average hp per unit	2378	2403	2456	2475
Total hp (000)	4156	4470	4745	4912
Average age (years)	8·7	7·8	7	6·3
Freight train wagons				
Box	23 189	24 114	24 042	23 566
Gondola	8776	8692	8423	7848
Hopper (open top)	6028	5994	6088	5796
Hopper (covered)	16 794	17 620	18 239	18 419
Tank	1238	1120	1063	1102
Refrigerator	5542	4484	4356	3286
Autorack	1379	1375	1164	938
Flat (general and special)	2710	2663	2536	2426
Flat (TOFC)	2061	2070	2309	2452
Total	67 717	68 132	68 220	65 883
Average capacity per freight train car (tons)	75·39	78·71	77·37	78·46
Average age (years)	13	12·9	13	13·3

Diesel locomotives (end-1981)

Class	No in class	Builders	Type	hp	Year built
1215	29	EMD	SSB1200	1200	1973-79
1300	3	Alco	CRSD20	2050	1975-76
1310	20	EMD	GP7	1500	1973-80
1450	1	EMD	SW900	900	1957
1460	1	EMD	SWBLW	1500	1970
2000	28	EMD	GP7	1500	1973-77
2050	193	EMD	GP7	1500	1973-80
2244	56	EMD	GP9	1750	1978-80
2417	220	EMD	CF7	1500	1970-78
2700	14	EMD	GP30	2250	1962/63/76
2800	30	EMD	GP35	2500	1964/65/70
3000	74	EMD	GP20	2000	1976-80
3200	57	EMD	GP30	2250	1962/63/76
3300	115	EMD	GP35	2500	1964/65/70
3500	59	EMD	GP38	2000	1970
3600*	17	EMD	GP39-2	2300	1974
3617	52	EMD	GP39-2	2300	1975
3669	14	EMD	GP39-2	2300	1977
3683	13	EMD	GP39-2	2300	1979
3696	10	EMD	GP39-2	2300	1980
3800	10	EMD	GP40X	3500	1978
3810	30	EMD	GP50	3500	1980
4000*	20	EMD	SD39	2300	1969
4600	79	EMD	SD26	2625	1971-78
5000	19	EMD	SD40	3000	1966
5020	37	EMD	SD40-2	3000	1977
5058	13	EMD	SD40-2	3000	1979
5071	54	EMD	SD40-2	3000	1979
5125	45	EMD	SD40-2	3000	1980

Diesel locomotives (end-1981)

Class	No in class	Builders	Type	hp	Year built
5170	23	EMD	SD40-2	3000	1981
5200	14	EMD	SD40-2	3000	1978
5300	4	EMD	SD45	3600	1980
5304	27	EMD	SD45	3600	1979
5426	4	EMD	SD45	3500	1980
5430	7	EMD	SD45	3600	1981
5490	4	EMD	SD45	3600	1980
5500	42	EMD	SD45	3600	1966
5590*	24	EMD	SD45	3600	1969
5625	77	EMD	SD45-2	3600	1972-73
5705*	9	EMD	SD45-2	3600	1974
5900	32	EMD	F45	3600	1968-70
5940	3	EMD	FP45	3600	1967
5950	3	EMD	F45	3600	1968/70
5990	3	EMD	FP45	3600	1967
6300	49	GE	U23B	2250	1970-71
6350	14	GE	B23-7	2250	1978
6364	26	GE	B23-7	2250	1979
6390	15	GE	B23-7	2250	1980
7484	16	GE	B36-7	3600	1980
7500*	20	GE	U23C	2250	1969
8010	54	GE	C30-7	3000	1977-78
8064	35	GE	C30-7	3000	1979
8099	24	GE	C30-7	3000	1980
8123	30	GE	C30-7	3000	1981
8500*	25	GE	U33C	3300	1969
8700	40	GE	U36C	3600	1972-73
8736	27	GE	U36C	3600	1974
8770	30	GE	U36C	3600	1974-75

* Lessee owner

Boston and Maine Corporation

Iron Horse Park, North Billerica, Massachusetts 01862

Telephone: (617) 663 9300

Trustees: R W Meserve, B H Lacy
President and Chief Executive Officer: A G Dustin
Vice-President: W J Rennicke
Vice-President and General Counsellor: J J Nee
Vice-President and General Manager, Transportation: S B Culliford
Vice-President, Marketing and Sales: M V Smith
Vice-President, Personnel, Labour Relations: B E Rice
Assistant Vice-President, Information Services: M M Sutin
General Attorney/Claims: J E O'Keefe
Accounting
Vice-President, Finance: P W Carr
Comptroller: T J Reilly
Vice-President, Equipment: W J Grabske
Vice-President Engineering: V R Terrill
Chief Engineer, Structures: C D Pierce
Director of Purchasing and Stores: R V Muehike
Chief Engineer, Communications and Signals: T Trovato
Chief Engineer, Construction and Design: V V Mudholkar

Gauge: 1435 mm

Length: 2532·6 km

Lines and territories
The principal lines of the Boston & Maine run north and west from Boston through the states of Maine, New Hampshire, Vermont, Massachusetts, and in eastern New York State where it makes connections at Albany and Schenectady with other lines.

Essentially a freight operating railway, the company is under contract with the Massachusetts Bay Transportation Authority (MBTA) to continue passenger service within a 32 km radius of Boston, with some reimbursement of excess expenses by the Authority.

Finance and ownership
In April 1982 the Interstate Commerce Commission approved the offer to purchase the Boston & Maine by Guilford Transportation Industries (GTI). GTI is owned by Timothy Mellon, who seeks to form a new consolidated rail system in the north-eastern USA. GTI acquired Maine Central in 1981 and in mid-1982 the ICC approved its further bid to take possession of the Delaware & Hudson. GTI was to purchase all 3 million shares of B&M common stock for $24·25 million and distribute 2600 redeemable preference shares, worth $26 million, to the US Government, subject to approval by the B&M bankruptcy court. B&M has been in the hand of trustees since the beginning of 1971, but a steady process of subsequent reorganisation, coupled with the proceeds of commuter line sales to MBTA, held promise that the company would break even by the early 1980s.

Creditors were due to vote on a reorganisation plan in March 1983, acceptance of which would remove the last barrier to completion of GTI purchase.

Traffic
About 85 per cent of B&M's freight tonnage is received from connecting lines and two-thirds of it terminates on the system. Forest products from northern New England or Canada predominate. Since bankruptcy the railroad has substantially contracted its network.

Following full integration of the GTI network and B & M's purchase of discarded Conrail tracks in Connecticut and acquisition of trackage rights to New York and New Haven, B & M envisaged expansion of its new fast, short intermodal train concept into markets between Montreal and New York, and between northern New England and Buffalo, Toronto, New York and Philadelphia. This followed the 1982 launch, in conjunction with Central Vermont, of an overnight 'Rocket' TOFC service between Boston and Montreal. The two railroads secured union agreement to operation of the 'Rockets' with a two-man crew and no caboose up to a maximum load of 15 cars. A similar operation, the 'East Wind', was mounted between Bangor, Maine and New Haven.

Locomotives and rolling stock
B&M's rolling stock and motive power fleet stands at 114 line-haul and 48 switching diesel-electric locomotives; 3226 freight cars; and 51 diesel-electric railcars operated for owners MBTA.

Burlington Northern (BN)

176 East Fifth Street, St Paul, Minnesota 55101

Telephone: (612) 298 2121

Chairman and Chief Executive Officer: Richard C Grayson
President and Chief Operating Officer: Walter A Drexel
Executive Vice-President, Operations: William F Thompson
Senior Vice-President, Maintenance and Transportation: Earl J Currie
Vice-President, Transportation: Thomas C Whitacre
  Maintenance and Engineering: George W Thompson
  Operations Services: Bill C Davidson
Vice-President and General Manager,
  Twin Cities Region: Charles J Bryan
  Chicago Region: Wayne A Hatton
  Denver Region: Wayne L Arntzen
  Springfield Region: Roy L Buchanan
  Billings Region: William A Thompson
  Fort Worth Region: James H Brown
  Seattle-Portland Region: William W Francis

Senior Vice-President, Marketing and Sales: Darius W Gaskins
Vice-President, Marketing and Pricing: Richard M Gleason
  Sales and Service: William H Egan
  Industrial Development and Property Management: Joseph R Galassi
Senior Vice-President, Coal and Taconite: John H Hertog
Vice-President, Coal and Taconite Equipment and Service: Thomas R Hackney
  Coal and Taconite Pricing: Otis W Cobb
Senior Vice-President, Administration and Planning: Robert F Garland
Vice-President, Strategic Planning: Michael M Donahue
  Labor Relations: Al E Egbers
  Accounting: Charles C Roberts
  Information Resource: George R Clinkenbeard
  Human Resources: Fran J Coyne
Vice-President, Purchasing and Material: John Tierney
  Public Affairs: Lawrence H Kaufman
  Law: Donald E Engle

Gauge: 1435 mm
Length: 46 982 km

Lines and territories
Burlington Northern was formed in March 1970, by merger of Chicago, Burlington & Quincy Railroad, Great Northern Railway, Northern Pacific Railway and Spokane, Portland and Seattle Railway. The territory it served covered 19 states and two Canadian provinces and reached from the Great Lakes and the Ohio river to California and the seaports of the Pacific Northwest. In addition, BN owned the Colorado and Southern Railway Co, and the Fort Worth and Denver Railway Co (now fully absorbed), which extended its territory via Denver to the Gulf of Mexico at Houston and Galveston, Texas.

The merger of the St Louis-San Francisco Railway Co (the Frisco) into Burlington Northern became effective in November 1980. The BN-Frisco merger created a 29 200-mile rail system, stretching from Washington and Oregon through the timber and mining regions of the Northern Tier States and the farming areas of the Midwest and as far south as Pensacola, Florida. The combined companies now operate in 25 states and two Canadian provinces with a work force of more than 46 000. The Frisco has been integrated into BN's system and is not controlled separately, as has been the case in certain other recent railroad mergers. Its 4500-mile territory has become BN's sixth operating region with headquarters in Springfield, Missouri, and divisional offices in Springfield, Memphis and Tulsa. The others on BN are at Chicago, Minneapolis, Denver, Billings, Seattle-Portland and Fort Worth.

BN Railroad is a subsidiary of the holding company Burlington Northern Inc. In addition to rail service, the holding company's activities include sale of timber and logs, manufacture of forestry products, industrial development and property management, oil and gas exploitation, coal and Taconite ore mining.

Traffic

Historically, BN's railroad has derived about three-quarters of its gross freight revenue from three commodities: coal, grain and forest products. Although BN's coal traffic has increased steadily since 1970, grain and forest products traffic has been subject to cyclical downturns in demand. Coal and grain movements were primarily responsible for a 3 per cent decrease in railroad traffic volume during 1982 to an estimated 156 911 million revenue ton-miles. In 1981, coal traffic volume rose 12 per cent to 92 400 million revenue ton-miles, or 53 per cent of all revenue ton-miles generated by the railroad during the year. Coal revenues in 1981 rose 29 per cent to $1200 million or 29 per cent of total gross freight revenues. New records for a month's coal traffic were set in August 1982, when originating tonnage scaled 10·9 million, 1061 trains were loaded, unit train carloadings reached 111 101 and the daily average of unit train dispatches was 34, with a peak on one day of 46.

A new 127-mile extension of line between Gillette and Orin, Wyoming, was placed in operation in November 1979 to serve the coal mining region of eastern Wyoming. The resulting improvement in unit train productivity enabled BN to handle all of its customers' coal needs as scheduled in 1982 with capacity to spare. During 1982, the railroad originated 117 million tons of coal, compared with 112 million tons in 1981 and 100 million tons in 1980. The total 1982 BN coal movement was 124 million tons, the highest in BN history.

Since 1976, Burlington Northern has invested $1100 million to increase its capacity to haul coal. Major improvements include the Gillette-Orin line and a new locomotive and car service and repair complex at Alliance, Nebraska. Coal-hauling equipment investments since 1976 total more than $600 million. In addition, the company has made other substantial investments to increase train-handling capacity over key segments of its railroad. Capital improvements include installation of heavier weight rail and new signalling systems.

Capital spending allocated to coal transportation represents approximately 50 per cent of total funds invested in the railroad since 1976. The company's ability to secure an adequate return on its railroad investment depends, to a large extent, on its success in hauling increasing amounts of coal and on its ability to maintain coal freight rates at levels that will cover costs, keep pace with inflation and provide additional funds for reinvestment.

GE Type B30-7A 3000 hp cabless locomotive

GE Type SL144 switching locomotive

10 000-ton unit coal train negotiating the Horseshoe curve, Nebraska, part of a $13·6 million double-tracking and curve realignment project finished in 1982

BN Railroad in 1982 moved approximately 920 million bushels of grain, down 4 per cent from the 959 million bushels it hauled in 1981. The decline in traffic volume was due to depressed commodity prices, a slump in the grain exports and the increased efficiency with which grain is moved to market.

To improve freight car utilisation, the railroad began in December 1978 to experiment with single origin-single destination grain service. Unit train rates on corn were introduced in August 1980, followed by the inauguration of unit train rates on wheat four months later. By the end of 1982, BN had loaded more than 5000 grain unit trains. Burlington Northern is the nation's largest grain hauler, commanding approximately 20 per cent of the national rail market share of grain traffic.

Intermodal

In February 1983 Road-Rail Transportation Co, Inc, and BN announced that they were negotiating establishment of RoadRailer service between Chicago and Houston. The service would operate up to six days a week between five Road-Rail terminals in BN's Chicago-to-Houston corridor. Proposed to start in the third quarter of 1983, the service would be called the South-West Xpress. Final agreement was contingent on approval by the Department of Justice, labour negotiations, preparation of South-West Xpress terminals, and determination of service schedules.

Under the proposed agreement, BN would provide locomotives and train crews to move Road-Railers in dedicated trains between South-West Xpress terminals in Chicago, Kansas City, Tulsa, Dallas-Fort Worth, and Houston. The South-West Xpress also would extend its service to areas beyond the terminals via highway. Road-Rail, a subsidiary of The Bi-Modal Corp, would own and operate the terminals, and market and sell South-West Xpress service.

Burlington Northern provides direct TOFC/COFC service from the Great Lakes to the Pacific Northwest, from the Canadian Border to the Gulf Coast. TOFC/COFC service is provided through the use of the following owned or leased equipment: 5175 semi-trailers and 293 railroad flats designed for TOFC/COFC service. Towns with ramp facilities include:

Alabama: Birmingham; Mobile.
Arkansas: Fayetteville; Fort Smith; Osceola; Rogers.
Colorado: Akron; Boulder; Colorado Springs; Denver; Fort Collins; Golden; Greeley; Longmont; Loveland; Pueblo; Trinidad; Windsor.
Florida: Pensacola.
Idaho: Lewiston.
Illinois: Aurora; Centralia; Chicago; Galesburg; Moline; Peoria; Quincy; Rochelle; Rockford.
Iowa: Burlington; Creston; Des Moines; Dubuque; Ft Madison; Keokuk; Ottumwa; Sioux City.
Kansas: Wichita.
Kentucky: Paducah.
Minnesota: Cloquet; Crookston; Duluth; Minneapolis; St Cloud; St Paul; Thief River Falls; Warroad; Winona.
Mississippi: Amory; Tupelo.
Missouri: Cape Girardeau; Carthage; Crystal City; Hannibal; Joplin; Kansas City; Lamar; Neosho; St Louis; Springfield; West Plains; West Quincy.
Montana: Billings; Bozeman; Butte; Glendive; Great Falls; Havre; Helena; Livingston; Miles City; Missoula; Shelby; Whitefish.
Nebraska: Alliance; Columbus; Fremont; Grand Island; Hastings; Lincoln; McCook; Omaha; Scottsbluff; Seward.
North Dakota: Devils Lake; Dickinson; Fargo; Grand Forks; Jamestown; Mandan; Minot.
Oklahoma: Ada; Enid; Lawton; Miami; Muskogee; Oklahoma City; Tulsa.
Oregon: Albany; Eugene; Klamath Falls; Portland; Salem.
South Dakota: Sioux Falls.
Tennessee: Memphis.
Texas: Abilene; Amarillo; Corsicana; Dallas; Fort Worth; Galveston; Houston; Irving; Lubbock; Paris; Plainview; Sherman; Teague; Wichita Falls.
Washington: Aberdeen; Bellingham; Everett; Longview; Pasco; Seattle; Spokane; Tacoma; Wenatchee; Yakima.
Wisconsin: La Crosse; Prairie du Chien; Superior.
Wyoming: Casper; Cheyenne; Gillette; Newcastle; Wheatland.
British Columbia: Vancouver.
Manitoba: Winnipeg.

Finance

Rail operating expenses during 1982 decreased 3 per cent to $3630 million. Diesel fuel expense for the year fell 20 per cent to $500 million, due to the

Traffic	1980	1981	1982*
Total freight train-km (million)	92	101·3	85·92
Total freight tonnage (million)	226·7	256·7	228·9
Average haul (km)	1043	1096	1105
Average net trainload (tons)	2724	2786	2936
Average wagon load (tons)	68	68·3	70
* estimate			

Finance ($ million)	1979	1980	1981	1982*
Rail operating revenues	2635·8	3253·9	4088·0	3806·5
Rail pre-tax income	41	165·3	303	115
Rail revenues				
Passengers and baggage	27	36·5	24	28
Freight and miscellaneous	2608·7	3216·4	3752·8	3448·9
Rail operating expenses				
Way and structures	551·5	635·1	774·0	778·1
Equipment	591·6	685·7	826·4	805·5
Transportation	1161·9	1421·1	1790·9	1706·7
General and administrative	207	233·9	338·6	339·8
* estimate				

Three EMD SD40-2 locomotives heading freight over the newly completed Sioux City Bridge in 1981

Clearance-measurer, mounted on Hy-Rail truck, fitted with 110 flexible feelers

decline in business. Fuel expense for the year comprised about 14 per cent of total operating expenses. Way and structures expense increased 5 per cent to $778·1 million during 1982. Equipment expense in 1982 declined 2 per cent to $805·5 million, reflecting a business downturn, equipment in storage, and efforts to properly size the car and locomotive fleets.

Railroad capital spending during 1982 totalled about $393 million, including outlays of $110 million in new equipment, and $271 million in roadway improvements. Total rail capital spending during 1982 was $351·7 million.

Signalling

In 1982, new CTC was installed over 106·9 miles. Some 259 miles of existing CTC was acquired from former Milwaukee Road trackage, and at year's end another 106·8 miles was brought in from the Fort Worth & Denver Railway. Total CTC coverage by January 1983 was 7765 miles.

Civil engineering

During 1982, a total of 1134 track miles of new and secondhand rail was laid. By January 1983 BN had 10 036 miles of continuously welded rail. In 1982 nearly 3·5 million sleepers were inserted, and 10 134 miles of track was surfaced with 3·5 million cubic yards of ballast.

Investment

BN's capital spending budget for 1983 of $465·7 million, 18 per cent more than in 1982, was the largest announced for the US railroad industry. Its main item was construction of a new classification yard at Galesburg, Illinois, to replace an existing two-hump facility, for a total cost of $80 million. The new six-group, 46-track yard, embodying state-of-the-art electronic control systems, will have a classification capability of 3000 cars a day and will be designed with scope for subsequent addition of two more yard groups. Also included is a new traction maintenance and servicing facility, and an intermodal hub centre. BN is concentrating more of its TOFC/COFC traffic generally on hub centres.

Apart from new traction (see below), other items in the plan were installation of over 300 miles of CTC, relaying of some 1000 miles of track and surfacing of 10 000 miles more, expansion of a bridge renewal programme and a series of intermodal, yard and terminal improvements. Acquisition of new intermodal car equipment was also forecast.

Traction and rolling stock

Locomotive stock at the end of 1982 totalled 2829 line-haul and 376 switching units. BN also operated 141 commuter passenger cars and 91 209 freight cars.

BN was one of the few railroads to announce new traction orders early in 1983. Main item, valued at $50 million, was 67 cabless 3100 hp Type B30-7A, to supplement the 53 of this type delivered in 1982, from General Electric. In 1983 BN was also to place in service the first three General Electric Type B30-8s embodying microprocessor technology. GE was also commissioned to undertake an intensive two-year research and development programme aimed at evolution of a locomotive capable of using processed coal to power an internal combustion engine. BN has further entered into a partnership with Chessie System, Babcock & Wilcox/McDermott International and American Coal Enterprises (ACE) of Akron, Ohio, to study the feasibility of constructing a prototype of the ACE 3000 design of coal-powered reciprocating steam locomotive.

Hydraulic dumper unloads woodchips at a paper company's hopper in Everett, Washington

Diesel units delivered 1980-82

Year	Quantity	Builder	Model	hp	Max speed (mph)	Wheel arrangement	Max weight (lb)
1980	5	EMD	GP38-2	2000	66	B-B	267 000
	195	EMD	SD40-2	3000	66	C-C	415 000
	80	GE	C30-7	3000	70	C-C	413 000
	10	EMD	GP50	3500	66	B-B	275 000
1981	40	EMD	GP39-2	2300	66	B-B	261 000
	15	GE	C30-7	3000	70	C-C	413 000
1982	53	GE	B30-7A	3000	70	B-B	266 000

Diesel-electric locomotives

Class	Wheel arrangement	Rated power hp	lb	Tractive effort continuous at mph	Max speed mph	Wheel diameter in	Total weight tons	Length ft in	No owned	Year acquired	Builder
SW-10	B-B	1000	31 200	10	50	40	125	44' 8''	55	1966-72	EMD
SW-1	B-B	600	24 000	10	50	40	100	44' 5''	11	1940-50	EMD
SW-900	B-B	900	28 000	10	50	40	116	43' 7½''	1	1957	EMD
SW-7	B-B	1200	35 600	10	50	40	125	44' 5''	40	1949-50	EMD
SW-9	B-B	1200	35 600	10	50	40	125	44' 5''	29	1950-53	EMD
SW-12	B-B	1200	35 600	10	50	40	125	44' 6''	95	1938-65	EMD
SW-15	B-B	1500	45 000	12	65	40	130	44' 8''	71	1967, 1973	EMD
NW-2	B-B	1000	31 200	10	50	40	125	44' 5''	70	1939-49	EMD
NW-12	B-B	1200	31 200	10	50	40	125	44' 5''	4	1975-76	EMD
GP-5	B-B	1350	31 250	15	65	40	121	56' 2''	16	1958-59	EMD
GP-7	B-B	1500	41 000	11	65	40	125	55' 11''	51	1951-53	EMD
MP-15	B-B	1500	45 000	9·3	65	40	131	47' 8''	5	1975	Alco
GP-15-1	B-B	1500	47 000	10	65	40	129	54' 11''	25	1977	Alco
GP-9	B-B	1750	44 000	12	65	40	125	56' 2''	261	1954-59	EMD
GP-10	B-B	1800	44 000	14	65	40	128	55' 11''	26	1974-76	EMD
GP-18	B-B	1800	44 000	12	65	40	124	56' 2''	7	1960	EMD
GP-20	B-B	2000	45 000	14	65	40	128	56' 2''	59	1960-61	EMD
GP-38	B-B	2000	55 000	10·7	65	40	131	59' 2''	35	1970	EMD
GP-39-2	B-B	2300	58 200	8·5	65	40	131	59' 2''	40	1981	EMD
GP-38-2	B-B	2000	55 000	10·7	65	40	131	59' 2''	152	1972-74	EMD
GP-30	B-B	2250	51 000	12	65	40	130	56' 2''	46	1962-63	EMD
GP-35	B-B	2500	51 200	12	65	40	131	56' 2''	75	1963-65	EMD
GP-40	B-B	3000	48 000	13	77	40	150	59' 2''	37	1966-68	EMD
GP-40-2	B-B	3000	54 500	11·3	65	40	131	59' 2''	25	1979	EMD
GP-50	B-B	3500	62 000	9·7	70	40	138	59' 2''	10	1980	EMD
U23C	C-C	2250	82 000	7·5	70	40	185	67' 3''	9	1969	GE
U28B	B-B	2800	51 000	13·5	77	40	137	60' 2''	9	1966-67	GE
			40 000	17·5	79						
B-30-7A	B-B	3000	64 600	8·4	70	40	135	61' 2''	53	1982	GE
U30B	B-B	3000	51 500	13	79	40	136	60' 2''	44	1966-68	GE
U30C	C-C	3000	90 500	8·4	70	40	206	67' 3''	179	1968-75	GE
			74 000	11·4	70	40	194				
C-30-7	C-C	3000	90 500	8·4	70	40	208	67' 3''	242	1976-80	GE
			82 000	8·4	70						
U33C	C-C	3300	76 500	9·2	70	40	195	67' 3''	64	1968-71	GE
			75 000	12·7	79						
SD-7	C-C	1500	67 000	6	65	40	150	60' 8½''	78	1952-53	EMD
SD-9	C-C	1750	67 500	8	65	40	162	60' 8''	128	1954-58	EMD
SD-38-2	C-C	2000	81 000	6·8	65	40	196	68' 10''	4	1979	EMD
SD-40	C-C	3000	74 500	9	77	40	191	65' 9½''	43	1966-71	EMD
SD-40-2	C-C	3000	71 000	13·2	65	40	193	68' 10''	835	1980	EMD
			90 474	8·5	65	40	208				
			74 500	9	77	40	193				
SD-45	C-C	3600	74 200	9	77	40	193	65' 9½''	217	1966-71	EMD
			71 000	13·2	77	40	193				
			82 300	8·5	65	40	196				
F-45	C-C	3600	71 000	13·2	77	40	193	67' 5½''	46	1969-71	EMD
			74 200	9	77	40	193				

CSX Corporation

PO Box C-32222, Richmond, Virginia 23261

Telephone: (804) 355 2899

Chairman and Chief Executive Officer: Hays T Watkins
President: A Paul Funkhouser

In November 1980 Chessie System Inc merged with Seaboard Coast Line Industries to form the CSX Corporation. While maintaining their separate identities, managements and operations, the Corporation's constituents, Chessie System Railroads, Seaboard System Railroad (a revised title) and the Richmond, Fredericksburg and Potomac Railroad, have been co-ordinated into a single system serving 22 states, the District of Columbia, and a Canadian province. With 43 450 km of track, it has become the longest rail system in the nation. Under the new CSX Corporation the carriers continue to publish separate annual financial and statistical reports. Railroad activity generates 93 per cent of the Corporation's revenue.

For details of railroads under the control of this holding company, see under the railroads named.

Traffic

The world-wide economic weakness was reflected in the traffic and transport revenue figures for 1982. General commodity traffic was down 17 per cent from 1981. The only bright spot was intermodal traffic, which was up 7 per cent over 1981, but because of competitive pressures had lower than normal profit margins.

Coal traffic, which had shown significant growth since 1980 and remained strong until the third quarter of 1982, slumped dramatically by year-end. However, total coal tonnage for 1982 did reach 224 million tons, which was only 8 per cent below 1981's all-time record of nearly 245 million tons and only 2 per cent below the 229 million tons handled in 1980, the previous record. Most of the decline was in domestic tonnage, clearly reflecting the low level of production in the industrial sector. Export tonnage, at some 35·2 million tons, was down slightly from 1981's record 36·5 million tons.

Merger-related benefits realised in 1982 totalled $24 million, bringing the total benefit thus far realised from consolidations and efficiencies implemented as a result of the 1980 Chessie-Seaboard merger to $81 million, some $10 million above the amount planned for this period in 1980.

Most of the 1982 merger-related benefits came from operating improvements. Improved car utilisation, for example, continued to be achieved through integrated management of the Seaboard and Chessie car fleets. Attention also was given to increasing locomotive utilisation by operating trains over shorter, joint routes and consolidating yard and terminal operations. Another merger benefit emphasised in 1982 was the exchange of competitive pricing information between Chessie and Seaboard for use in volume purchases.

The steady growth of intermodal traffic, up 7 per cent to 782 000 loads, was read as a strong signal of the change under way in inter-city transport. In the mid-1970s Chessie provided hardly any piggyback services, having determined dedicated piggyback services did not offer an adequate return, given the then prevailing regulatory environment. Chessie continued to offer piggyback service, but, until 1977, when a limited schedule of special trains commenced operations, it was provided within regular train service and came to Chessie through third parties. In effect, Chessie was wholesaling the cost-effective, long-haul segment of the piggyback move. Passage of the Staggers Act and the ICC's decision to exempt piggyback traffic from regulation eliminated the time-consuming rate approval process of the Interstate Commerce Commission for piggyback moves.

This allowed Chessie to intensify its penetration of the piggyback market with the Chessie Motor Express (CMX), launched in early 1981 as a marketing experiment. With this Chessie took a direct, retail approach, retaining control of prices and service levels and offering a complete, door-to-door, road-rail-road service and pricing package, all on one bill of lading, to shippers and receivers.

Entering the piggyback market in early 1981 with less than 100 customers, CMX quickly expanded, handling more than 62 800 truck loads for more than 775 active customers in 1982, which was in excess of a 200 per cent growth rate over 1981. CMX's total revenue has also grown, reaching $15 million in 1982, four times 1981's $3·5 million.

Through the early 1950s Seaboard operated a crack passenger train, the 'Orange Blossom Special,' from north-eastern cities to Florida. In 1982 the name was revived for a fleet of TOFC freight trains which carry produce from Florida to north-eastern markets and mark an aggressive campaign to recapture a major share of a $200 million market; this was lost in the 1960s when, driven by regulatory constraints and service complexities, packers and buyers alike opted for the more flexible, door-to-door service of road services.

The opportunity for CSX partner Seaboard to return to the market arose when both piggyback and perishables traffic were deregulated by the Staggers Act. With the end-to-end merger of Seaboard and Chessie in 1980, moreover, the reach of Seaboard's service had been dramatically extended directly into the north-east markets. The new 'Orange Blossom Special' is a fully-integrated road-rail road transport service which has been sold through one-on-one sales calls and a co-ordinated sales promotion and advertising campaign. With the co-operation of two key unions, the Brotherhood of Locomotive Engineers and the United Transportation Union (UTU), Seaboard operates the train making only two, instead of five, crew changes. Also, in addition to the engineer, the train operates with a reduced crew of a conductor and only one trainman in accordance with crew consist agreements negotiated between Seaboard and the UTU.

The 'Orange Blossom Special' moves over the highway to Seaboard's Taft yard in Orlando. There, a special train is formed each day which operates via Seaboard to Richmond and CSX's Richmond, Fredericksburg and Potomac Railroad to Washington DC. Chessie continues the operation to Wilmington, Delaware, from where the trailers are again on the road, delivered by CMX throughout the north-east, often within 24 hours of the train's departure from Orlando.

New services added during 1982 included two all-piggyback trains on Seaboard and Chessie's extension of its door-to-door, road-rail-road freight service between Toledo/Detroit and East Coast/south-west points, also between Cleveland, Pittsburgh, Akron, Youngstown, Buffalo and the West Coast markets. The new piggyback trains accelerate service provided by Seaboard through its Cincinnati and Atlanta terminals to customers in the New Orleans area and points in Florida. Chessie significantly improved service between Chicago and southern points during the year, reducing transit time on some traffic as much as 36 hours, by consolidating terminal operations into one yard, greatly reducing terminal handling. Also, countering route closings and surcharges placed on paper and paper products, and to develop additional business, Chessie and Seaboard in 1982 opened a paper distribution centre in Philadelphia. In its first full year of operation, it generated $4·5 million in revenue.

Seaboard and Chessie also completed a number of mergers, acquisitions, consolidations and reorganisations during the year, to improve service, reduce costs and streamline administrative and operating departments.

Reorganisation

At the end of 1982 the merger of the Louisville & Nashville and Seaboard Coast Line railroads was completed, creating the Seaboard System Railroad. The name previously used to describe the rail network, The Family Lines Rail System, was discontinued. Coinciding with that merger, the Clinchfield, the Georgia and the West Point Route were placed under the new Seaboard banner. The merger pro-

'Orange Blossom Special' Orlando, Florida-Wilmington, Delaware TOFC perishables train in Seaboard territory

duces external and internal benefits, offering customers the convenience of dealing with just one railroad for shipments across the 13-state, 16 000-mile Seaboard system; and significant cost savings by eliminating duplicate internal operations.

Chessie reorganised its commercial function, establishing five customer-oriented regional service centres at the major operating hubs of Baltimore, Pittsburgh, Cincinnati, Chicago and Detroit. This change closely matched Seaboard's organisational structure, which eased co-ordination of customer needs between the two CSX rail units.

At Seaboard, the reorganisation and consolidation of its operating department in Jacksonville was completed and three operating divisions were merged into other divisions. Chessie also consolidated its operating department into eastern and western regions.

Contract successes

Using provisions of the Staggers Act, Chessie and Seaboard took a number of commercial initiatives in 1982 to establish both short and long-term contracts, cancel unprofitable joint rates and close inefficient routes. In total, the two rail units entered into 290 contracts in 1982. Generally, they provided volume-based rate reductions to shippers while establishing service and equipment performance standards and assuring the rail units of additional revenue. An innovative contract which combined price, service and equipment incentives was concluded with one car manufacturer; as a result, Chessie secured new business worth over $50 million annually.

In 1982 Seaboard signed a number of major coal transport contracts with shippers in the south and south-east. The bulk of Seaboard's coal originates in eastern Kentucky. To expedite these movements, Seaboard has completed major track work to increase capacity on the main lines that serve the coal fields, including double-tracking and improved switching and signalling. Work began in 1982 and continued in 1983 on the extension of sidings to enable an increase in the length of unit coal trains from 72 to 90 cars. This would improve Seaboard's productivity and equipment utilisation, provide a more attractive rate structure for coal shippers and increase Seaboard's revenue.

As a result of 1982's activity, Seaboard and Chessie now have 338 contracts in effect. Ranging in term from one to 20 years, they account for about $1000 million in freight revenue annually and have a total value over their terms of about $5000 million.

Chessie and Seaboard in 1982 also made extensive use of the Staggers Act provisions which allow railroads to close inefficient and costly routes to through traffic which can be handled over other, more efficient routes providing long-haul advantages or productivity improvements.

Distribution service

Seaboard and Chessie expanded their bulk intermodal distribution service (BIDS). New terminals were opened by Chessie in Philadelphia and Charleston, West Virginia; Seaboard added new facilities at Tampa, New Orleans and Charlotte, bringing to 29 the number of BIDS terminals operated by the two CSX units.

BIDS offers two major benefits. First, manufacturers of bulk commodities significantly cut their distribution costs and increase their delivery flexibility by combining long-haul movement of their product by rail to centrally-located distribution points with the short-haul, local delivery by truck directly from the rail car. Second, at some BIDS terminals, other value-added services are available, such as packaging, drumming, warehousing and fixed silo/tank storage of bulk commodities.

Rock Island takeover

Chessie consummated a 50-year lease for an 89-mile segment of the former Chicago, Rock Island & Pacific Railroad in 1982, extending its service area to an important industrial section of north central and north-western Illinois. Chessie began serving a portion of the line in 1980, soon after the Rock Island's bankruptcy. At that point, business levels were minimal, and service could not be improved due to the physical condition of the line. A $2 million track rehabilitation effort launched in 1981 and completed in 1982 solved the service problem and volume, as predicted, has grown to the point that the line now generates about 31 000 carloads and approximately $30 million a year in revenue.

Co-operating with Westmac Corporation, a major grain shipper on its Michigan Division, Chessie inaugurated a new load-in-motion concept for the loading of unit grain trains which significantly cuts loading time, increases equipment utilisation and speeds service. The new service resulted in Chessie gaining about 1100 carloads of grain traffic and $1.2 million in revenue.

Investment

Chessie System railroad capital spending for 1983 was provisionally set at $63.6 million. Major components would be: signalling and communications ($25.4 million); yard and terminal improvements ($20 million); track work ($16 million); and new freight cars ($2.2 million). Important single items planned were a CTC installation at Huntingdon, Virginia and a new hopper car repair plant at Newport News, Virginia.

Finance

Transport revenue was $4600 million in 1982, a decrease of $505 million, 10 per cent, as compared to 1981, but $57 million or 1 per cent, above 1980. The decline, despite freight rate increases aggregating about 24 per cent over the 1980-82 period, reflected the depressed nature of the key industrial sectors of the economy which have traditionally provided the majority of the rail traffic hauled by the company's rail units. The only traffic group which showed improvement over 1981 was intermodal, which was up 7 per cent in volume, but down 5 per cent in revenue due to intense competition and over-capacity in both the rail and trucking industries.

Coal traffic is the largest volume commodity handled by the CSX rail units as well as their largest revenue producer and a major contributor to profits. Compared to 1981 when the company's rail units set new coal-handling records on virtually a weekly basis, 1982 tonnage was down 8 per cent, at 224 million tons. Coal revenues were $1700 million, or 37 per cent of total transport revenue. Coal traffic was expected to remain sluggish through early 1983 after which renewed growth was expected from the increasing number of domestic utility power units being built to burn coal, those being converted from oil to coal, and increased industrial demand as the domestic and world economies recovered.

By year-end, domestic utilities had completed the conversion of 13 units within the domestic coal marketing areas served by the CSX rail units. Also, domestic utilities had 48 coal-fired units in various stages of planning and development which could use CSX-originated coal. Further, two export facility expansions were completed, a new export facility was in operation and two were in advanced stages of construction at the end of 1982. All three of the new export facilities are served exclusively by CSX's rail units.

Auto-related traffic continued a four-year decline,

mirroring a further reduction in total auto sales and domestic auto production in 1982; shipments of phosphates and fertilisers were off for the third year running, reflecting world-wide economic and financial weakness as well as the perilous economic condition of the American farmer and the impact of high interest rates on agri-business; chemicals were also down, illustrating the chemical industry's close ties to the automotive, fertiliser, paper and home construction industries. Paper product shipments were down as well, due to general economic conditions and depressed export demand. Metals shipments also declined, principally as a result of the depressed nature of the domestic steel industry which was operating at about 47 per cent of capacity during 1982, the lowest level since 1938.

CSX's rail units were able to significantly reduce operating expenses by $500 million in 1982 in spite of inflation's impact on material and labour costs, which approximated $266 million. This was accomplished through a combination of work force reductions and cost-control programmes, in part reflecting a 17 per cent year-to-year decline in traffic. While these efforts did not offset the massive revenue losses, they were substantial.

Work force reductions were largely accomplished through attrition early in the year, but quickly involved permanent and temporary lay-offs as the year progressed. By year-end, the rail units had reduced employment 17 per cent, with plans in place to make further reductions in early 1983.

Cost-control programmes during the year included selective reductions of locomotive and equipment repair and maintenance activities, reduction in planned track maintenance programmes and cutbacks in many other areas of operations. Further reductions were possible due to lower demand for freight cars and locomotives and freight services, as a result of economic conditions, and additional merger-related co-ordinations.

Essential equipment and track maintenance programmes, however, were completed during the year as planned. A total of 3.8 million sleepers and 757

miles of rail were installed, 11 214 miles of track surfaced and 760 locomotives and 10 652 freight cars repaired and returned to service. The company also constructed 685 new hopper cars at its Raceland car-building facility.

Also affecting the operating expense levels of the rail units in 1982 were new labour contracts, all but one of which was successfully negotiated by the industry without a work stoppage. The single exception was the contract with the Brotherhood of Locomotive Engineers (BLE). Negotiations with the BLE progressed through mid-year, but reached an impasse in September which resulted in a four-day work stoppage despite fulfillment of the exhaustive procedures of the Railway Labor Act. The strike was resolved by an Act of Congress.

Overall, the newly negotiated labour contracts resulted in an increase in year-end 1982 average wage rates of 8 per cent above 1981. For 1983, it was projected that such rates would increase 7.2 per cent above 1982. The contracts also include important provisions which should result in improved productivity in railroad operating crafts in future years. Significant among these measures was the agreement with the United Transportation Union which provides for an arbitration process that eventually should lead to elimination of cabooses on most freight trains.

The total cost of materials and supplies was essentially even with 1981 due to reduced fuel usage, resulting from service curtailments; reductions in maintenance activities; and the favourable impact of the rail units' volume purchases. Further, the price of diesel fuel, reflecting the generally declining price of energy throughout the year, declined from $1.01 per gallon in January 1982 to $0.93 by year-end, an 8 per cent drop from 1981 price levels.

Reflecting the depressed economy, the company's rail units had 1359 locomotives and 50 330 freight cars stored at the end of 1982. The reduced demand for this equipment resulted in a revision in the estimated service lives of this equipment.

Principal revenue-producing commodities ($ million)

	1980	1981	1982
Automotive	268.2	296.2	255.5
Chemicals	372.2	416.2	367.1
Construction materials	292.0	308.6	252.3
Food	172.0	187.1	151.4
General commodities	265.6	294.3	213.1
Grain	285.8	282.2	266.0
Intermodal	247.4	242.0	230.5
Metals	303.6	360.7	206.9
Paper	426.8	487.5	454.9
Phosphates and fertilisers	314.8	337.7	280.7
Coal	1357.3	1638.3	1667.9
Total	4305.7	4850.8	4346.3

Operating ratios (%)	1978	1979	1980	1981	1982
General and administrative	8.0	7.3	7.9	7.8	8.2
Way and structures	16.3	16.9	17.3	17.9	19.4
Equipment	24.7	22.9	21.6	21.8	22.9
Transport	43.9	44.1	43.9	42.7	44.5
Total	92.9	91.2	90.7	90.2	95.0

	1978	1979	1980	1981	1982
Revenue ($ million)	3472.5	4027.0	4497.0	5059.0	4554.0
Expenses ($ million)					
General and administrative	277.5	294.8	352.6	395.9	375.6
Way and structures	566.1	680.3	777.5	902.6	881.2
Equipment	860.1	922.9	972.8	1104.7	1044.3
Transportation	1523.7	1774.3	1975.6	2158.3	2027.2
Total	3227.4	3672.3	4078.5	4561.5	4328.3
Operating income ($ million)	245.1	354.7	418.5	497.5	225.7

Chessie System Railroads
(Affiliated Chesapeake and Ohio Railway, Baltimore and Ohio Railroad, and Western Maryland Railway)

Terminal Tower, Cleveland, Ohio 44101

Telephone: (216) 623 2402

Chairman of Board: Hays T Watkins
Vice-Chairman of Board: A Paul Funkhouser
President and Chief Executive: John T Collinson
Executive Vice-President, Administration: Norman G Halpern
Operations: Richard G Rayburn

Senior Vice-President, Law: R W Donnem
Sales: James B McCahey Jr
Commercial: John S Lanahan
Finance: P R Goodwin
A R Carpenter
Vice-President, Coal Traffic: Jerry E Gobrecht
Casualty Prevention: William F Howes Jr
Labour Relations: D S Garda
Marketing Services: Jerome D Krasenstein
Engineering and Maintenance: K C Morriss
Transportation: F W Yocum Jr
R C McGowan
W L Ollerhead

Lines and territories
The Chesapeake and Ohio Railway Company is a wholly-owned subsidiary of CSX Corporation. C & O's principal subsidiaries are The Baltimore and Ohio Railroad Company (B & O), 99 per cent owned by C & O, and Western Maryland Railway Company (WM), 94.6 per cent owned by C & O and B & O, and the Chicago South Shore and South Bend Railroad (South Shore), 94.4 per cent owned by C & O. C & O, B & O, WM, and South Shore together constitute one of the major rail systems in the United States. This affiliated group has adopted the appellation Chessie System Railroads.

Chessie railroads constitute the nation's largest coal hauling system and are major transporters of merchandise freight.

C & O's principal lines extend from the coal fields of southern West Virginia, eastern Kentucky and southern Ohio eastward to Newport News, Virginia and Washington, DC, westward to Louisville, Cincinnati and Chicago and northward through Columbus and Toledo to Detroit. Another principal line extends from Chicago eastward through Grand Rapids and Detroit, to Buffalo. Owned mileage in Canada and trackage rights between St Thomas, Ontario, and Buffalo form a connecting line from the east through Detroit to Chicago and through Detroit to the eastern shore of Lake Michigan.

B & O operates an extensive rail system in 11 states and the District of Columbia. Principal lines extend from Philadelphia, through Baltimore and Washington to Cumberland, Maryland, and from Cumberland by separate routes to Chicago and St Louis. A third important line extends from Cincinnati to Toledo.

WM's principal lines extend from Baltimore north-west to Connellsville, Pennsylvania and south-west into West Virginia where they connect with the B & O at Cherry Run. WM also has a line extending from Hagerstown, Maryland, to Shippensburg, Pennsylvania. The WM was to lose its separate identity in April 1983.

South Shore operates an electric interurban railroad from Chicago to South Bend, Indiana, and has diesel locomotive-hauled freight operations serving Hammond, East Chicago, Gary, Michigan City and South Bend, Indiana, and the Burns Harbor, Indiana, industrial complex.

Traffic

Chessie's railroads operate under uniform policies and are managed as an integrated system. Operations are characterised by a relatively high proportion of terminal switching to support merchandise traffic in the heavily industrialised north-east. Schedule and blocking policy is designed to minimise the car handling required in yards and to provide the best dock-to-dock service.

The commodity moving in largest volume for the company is bituminous coal. Coal originated on company lines comes principally from West Virginia and eastern Kentucky, and also from Pennsylvania, Ohio, Illinois, and Maryland. The company moves most of such coal north to the industrial Midwest and the Great Lakes region, east to the Chesapeake Bay region for shipment to domestic and foreign ports, and west to the Ohio River for loading on barges. Based on management estimates derived from reports of the US Geographical Survey, coal fields served by the company contain about 18 600 million tons of coal reserves. The company serves over 400 mine outlets and handles coal for export to foreign markets through coal-dumping facilities located at Newport News, Virginia, and Baltimore, Maryland.

Traction and rolling stock

At the close of 1982 the Chessie System railroads operated in total 2054 diesel locomotives, six Budd diesel railcars (one RDC-1, three RDC-2, two RDC-4), eight passenger cars and 110 708 freight cars.

Freight cars delivered 1980-1982/83

C&O	1590
B&O	432
WM	500
Total	2522

Track

Rail: 122 CB
Cross ties (sleepers): Hardwood, thickness 7 × 9 in
Spacing: 1875/km
Fastenings: Snap on woodings-unit
Max gradient: 2%
Max axleload: 32 tons

Traffic

	1976	1977	1978	1979	1980
Revenue ton-miles (million)	53 896	52 073	51 514	54 643	54 937
Freight train-miles (000)	23 947	23 861	23 539	25 175	24 480
Average revenue tons per carload	61·4	62·9	62·6	64·6	67·7
Average revenue tons per train	2251	2182	2188	2178	2244
Revenue ton-miles per man/h	647	630	617	631	669
Carloads originating on line (000)	1981	1966	1902	1972	1930
% ratio of railway operating expenses to railway operating revenues	89·7	91·7	93·5	90·9	90·2

Finance

	1978	1979	1980
Railway operating revenues ($ million)			
Merchandise	915·4	1008·4	995·5
Coal, coke and iron ore	583·1	722·2	921·5
Other freight and passenger	109·7	128·9	119·0
Total	1608·3	1859·5	2036·0
Railway operating expenses ($ million)			
Way and structures	277·097	315·014	366·717
Equipment	388·164	414·458	423·700
Transportation	711·770	825·330	880·451
General and administrative	127·388	135·668	166·317
Total	1504·419	1690·470	1837·185
Earnings for railway operations	103·889	169·092	198·815
Other income — net	37·782	60·734	62·983

Trainload of motor vehicles in fully-enclosed secured rack wagons

Northbound haul of 190 empty coal hoppers at Prince, West Virginia, behind a B-30-7, a GP40 and a GP40-2 *(P J Howard)*

Diesel locomotives ordered or delivered 1980-1982/83

								Builders	
Class	Wheel arrangement	Transmission	Rated power hp	Max speed mph	Total weight tons	No	Year built	Mechanical parts	Engine & type
GP15-T	Bo-Bo	Elec	1500	65	122	25	1981	EMD	8-645E3C
GP40-2	Bo-Bo	Elec	3000	65	138·75	50	1980	EMD	16-645E3
GP40-2	Bo-Bo	Elec	3000	65	138·75	26	1981	EMD	16-645E3
B30-7	Bo-Bo	Elec	3000	70	138·75	14	1980	GE	7 FD L16
B30-7	Bo-Bo	Elec	3000	70	138·75	20	1981	GE	7 FD L16

The Chesapeake and Ohio Railway Company (C & O)

| Route miles | 4680 (7820 km) |
| Total miles of track operated | 9571 (15 412 km) |

Freight wagons: 58 722

Locomotives (January 1983)
Multi-purpose

Builder	Class	hp	Total
EMD	GP15-T	1500	25
GE	U23-B	2250	30
EMD	GP30	2250	42
GE	U30-C	3000	13

Builder	Class	hp	Total
EMD	GP35	2500	39
EMD	GP40	3000	50
EMD	GP38	2000	60
EMD	GP39	2300	20
EMD	GP40-2	3000	93
EMD	GP-7	1500	127
EMD	GP-9	1750	190
EMD	SD-18	1800	19
EMD	SD-35	2500	9
EMD	SD-40	3000	63
GE	U30-B	3000	35
GE	B30-7	3000	64
			881

Switcher

Builder	Class	hp	Total
EMD	NW-2	1000	28
EMD	SW-9	1200	9
EMD	SW-7	1200	18
EMD	SW-9	1200	20
EMD	SW-1	600	1
			76

Total all C&O units: 957

Baltimore and Ohio Railroad Company (B & O)

| Route miles | 5113 (8227 km) |
| Total miles of track operated | 9806 (15 791 km) |

Freight wagons: 44 896

Locomotives (January 1983)
Multi-purpose

Builder	Class	hp	Total
EMD	GP40-2	3000	217
EMD	SD-7	1500	5
EMD	SD-9	1750	10

Builder	Class	hp	Total
EMD	GP35	2500	40
EMD	GP40	3000	160
EMD	GP38	2000	70
EMD	GP-7	1500	28
EMD	GP-9	1750	252
EMD	GP30	2250	69
EMD	SD-35	2500	15
EMD	SD-40	3000	8
EMD	SD-40-2	3000	20
EMD	SD-20-2	2000	5
			899

Switcher

Builder	Class	hp	Total
EMD	NW-2	1000	51
EMD	SW-9	1200	16
EMD	SW-1	600	9
EMD	SW-900	900	25
EMD	TR-3	1000	4
EMD	SW-12	1200	7
EMD	TR-4	1200	3
			115

Total all B&O units: 1014

Western Maryland Railway Company (WM)

| Route miles | 1174 (1889 km) |
| Total miles of track operated | 1972 (3176 km) |

Freight wagons: 7090

Locomotives (January 1983)
Freight

Builder	Class	hp	Total
EMD	BL-2	1500	1
			1

Multi-purpose

Builder	Class	hp	Total
EMD	GP35	2500	5
EMD	GP40	3000	5
EMD	GP40-2	3000	34
EMD	GP-7	1500	4
EMD	GP-9	1750	41
EMD	SD-35	2500	5
EMD	SD-40	3000	12
Total			106

Trailer units

WM	Slug	2
Total		2

Total all Western Maryland units: 109

Chicago, Milwaukee, St Paul and Pacific Railroad Company
(The Milwaukee Road)

516 West Jackson Boulevard, Chicago, Illinois 60606

Telephone: (312) 648 3000

Trustee: Richard B Ogilvie'
President and Chief Executive Officer: Worthington L Smith
Law Department: Robert H Wheeler, Counsel for the Trustee
Vice President, Reorganisation: Thomas F Power
   Marketing: Peter C White
   Administration: Lawrence W Harrington
   Property Management: James T McGuire
Operations
Vice President, Operations: Paul F Cruikshank
Assistant Vice President, General Manager: William F Plattenberger
   Mechanical: Robert F Nadrowski
   Chief Engineer: Nathan E Smith

Lines and territories

Until early 1980 the Milwaukee Road operated approximately 9800 route-miles (15 780 route-km) in 16 states. At the beginning of March 1980, with the approval of its reorganisation court, the railway placed in effect an embargo, or cessation of train operations, on approximately 6000 route-miles (9650 route-km), and since then has been operating, with some exception, only those lines which are generally considered as representing the ultimately reorganised system. All lines west of Miles City (in eastern Montana) were embargoed, as was considerable mileage in the states of South Dakota and Iowa, and lesser sections of line elsewhere.

Lines presently operated, comprising approximately 3000 route-miles (4800 route-km), extend principally from Louisville, Kentucky, on the east, through Chicago, Milwaukee, and St Paul-Minneapolis to Duluth, Minnesota. There are important projections from this route to Green Bay, Wisconsin, and Wausau, Wisconsin. Milwaukee's Chicago-Kansas City route has become significantly important, and grain-gathering lines in northern Iowa and southern Minnesota are expected to be included in the scope of the ultimately reorganised railway.

A line between Ortonville, Minnesota (at the South Dakota border) and Miles City, Montana, approximately 500 miles (800 km), and two branches extending from it, were abandoned in 1982 and the segment between Terry, Montana, and Ortonville, Maryland, sold to the South Dakota Railroad Authority.

The routes embargoed during March 1980 were subsequently approved for abandonment. A revised plan of reorganisation was submitted to the Court and to the Interstate Commerce Commission in September 1981. It envisages the size of the reorganised railroad as approximately 2900 route-miles (4667 route-km). In August 1982 Grand Trunk Corporation firmed up a bid to acquire the reorganised system.

The smaller Milwaukee Road serves 74 per cent of the customers of its previous 9800-mile system, and when operations and acquisitions by other railways, and state rail authorities, are considered, about 90 per cent of the patrons of the total Milwaukee system will continue to receive rail service.

Between 1977 and 1981 approximately $95 million was spent, over and above funds used for maintenance in the normal course of business, to rehabilitate the track of the smaller-size railway. This, combined with continuing locomotive and car rehabilitation programmes, has greatly improved the Milwaukee's standards of service. These projects were funded through the Railroad Revitalization and Regulatory Reform Act of 1976, State and shipper programmes, and internally.

The railroad has two principal subsidiaries: Milwaukee Motor Transportation Company, and Milwaukee Land Company. Milwaukee Motor provides COFC/TOFC services at 12 locations for the railroad, and operates over-the-road trucks under common carrier rights. Milwaukee Land Company is a property development, timber producing, and land sales company.

Finance

In 1981, consolidated operating revenues were $404·359 million and operating expenses and costs were $486·753 million. Figures for the previous year were respectively $389·957 million and $455·446 million. Preliminary figures for 1982 showed a loss of $21·6 million on the year's working.

In December 1977, Milwaukee Road filed a voluntary petition for reorganisation under Section 77 of the Federal Bankruptcy Act. Subsequently, the court appointed a trustee of the properties of the Milwaukee Road to operate the railroad, including its subsidiaries, and to develop a plan of financial reorganisation.

In the first quarter of 1983 Milwaukee Road reported its first operating profit since 1977, a net of $3·4 million on revenues of $87 million.

Grand Trunk takeover

Grand Trunk Corporation has made an agreed bid to acquire the Milwaukee Road. Following Milwaukee's 1983 filing of an amended reorganisation plan for a 5200-mile system, approval of the Milwaukee's reorganisation court and of the ICC to the takeover was expected in 1984.

Freight traffic

During 1981, food products were the prime commodities for which the Milwaukee Road provided transport, accounting for 17·6 per cent of the railroad's total revenue. Other groups included: farm products 14·2 per cent, coal 13·1 per cent, pulp and paper products 10·7 per cent, transport equipment 8·1 per cent, chemicals 8·2 per cent, primary metal products 5·2 per cent, waste and scrap 4 per cent.

COFC/TOFC

The Milwaukee Road has piggyback ramps at 12 locations. Container handling facilities are at Chicago (Franklin Park), Illinois; Green Bay, Wisconsin; Kansas City, Missouri; Minneapolis-St Paul, Minnesota; and Milwaukee, Wisconsin.

Effective from the beginning of February 1982, the Milwaukee integrated its rail COFC/TOFC functions and all elements of the Milwaukee Motor Transportation Company into a single unit which will seek out profitable sales opportunities, form intermodal price/service packages to address markets, and then promote these programmes and conduct inter-railroad negotiations. Since 1978, when its Sprint COFC/TOFC dedicated trains (three each way most days) entered service and subsequently won a major share of intermodal traffic in the Chicago—St Paul/Minneapolis corridor, Milwaukee Road has become known for innovation in rail/highway intermodal transport.

Passenger traffic

Chicago area commuter services were transferred

to the Regional Transportation Authority in October 1982. Amtrak inter-city passenger trains operate over the Milwaukee Road between Chicago, Milwaukee and St Paul.

Motive power and rolling stock

As of January 1982 the railroad operated 439 EMD diesel-electric locomotives, and had 160 stored and available for disposal following the system's reduction in size. The freight car fleet totalled 14 973. For unit coal train operation between southern Indiana and Lake Michigan 210 hoppers have been leased from Portec Inc.

Locomotives retained for future use comprised the following line-haul units:

Type	Units
FP45	2
F40C*	15
SD45	5
SD40-2	89
GP9	52
GP38-2	16
SD9	1
SD7	3
SD10†	21
SDL39**	10
GP20‡	51
GP40	72

Yard switchers

MP15AC	64
SW1200	37
SW9	1
Total	439

* Leased from North West Suburban Mass Transit, and from Nortran for Chicago commuter service
† Former SD7/SD9 upgraded
**Exclusive model, owned only by Milwaukee
‡ Former GP9, upgraded

Civil engineering

During 1982 the 111-mile Austin-Jackson, Minnesota grain-gathering line and the Wisconsin Valley line were rehabilitated, the former at a cost of $22·5 million, part-financed by the Federal Rail Service Continuation Programme ($9·2 million), local shippers' organisations ($2·7 million) and Minnesota DOT ($5·6 million). The shippers would be completely repaid, the DOT to the extent of $2·9 million. Former Rock Island track in south-eastern Iowa, which from November 1982 became part of the Milwaukee's Chicago-Kansas City main route, was improved.

Signalling

Automatic block is operative over 1491 route-miles (2400 route-km) of the system, chiefly between Chicago and Clinton, Iowa, and Chicago and Ortonville, Montana. CTC controls 677 route-miles (1090 route-km).

Investment

Capital spending plans for 1983 included an outlay of $28·7 million on track improvements, and of $2·4 million for CTC installation.

Chicago and North Western Transportation Company

One North Western Center, Chicago, Illinois 60606

Telephone: (312) 559 7000

President and Executive Officer: James R Wolfe
Senior Vice-President, Finance: John M Butler
  Planning and Public Affairs: J W Conlon
  Law: L T Duerinck
  Systems and Materials: R D Leach
  Administration: R W Russell
  Traffic: Raymond E Degnan
  Operations: James A Zito
Vice-President, Engineering: James A Barnes
  Transportation: Edward A Burkhardt
  Rates and Divisions: A M Handwerker
  Marketing: D A Christensen
  Personnel: R L Wilson
  Labour Relations: R W Schmiege
  Sales: E E Harney
  Equipment Management: R A Jahnke
Assistant Vice-President Motive Power: J D O'Neill

Gauge: 1435 mm
Length: 10 835·8 km

The North Western was incorporated in Delaware in March 1970, under the name North Western Employees Transportation Corporation. Its present name was adopted in May 1972. The company has been engaged in business since 1972 when the employees purchased the transportation assets and assumed the transportation obligations of the former Chicago and North Western Railway Company and certain of its subsidiaries.

The company is engaged primarily in hauling freight traffic in the Midwest. It operates in the eleven states of Illinois, Wisconsin, Michigan, Iowa, Minnesota, Nebraska, South Dakota, North Dakota, Missouri, Kansas and Wyoming. Besides its primary freight activity, in the Chicago metropolitan area the company also provides suburban passenger service.

The most significant events in Midwestern railroading in 1980 were cessation of operations by the Rock Island Railroad and substantial withdrawal from service by the Milwaukee Road. Beginning in April C & NW began operating portions of both of these railroads without government subsidy.

In May, North Western executed an interim compensation agreement with the Trustee of the Rock Island to operate approximately 800 miles (1300 km) of Rock Island lines, including the main line between St Paul-Minneapolis and Kansas City and grain-gathering branch lines in north-western Iowa. North Western was also operating approximately 150 miles (240 km) of Milwaukee Road track, principally grain feeder lines in Iowa, and completed a purchase agreement with the Milwaukee Road's Trustee for a 7-mile (11·25 km) stretch in north-west Iowa between Marathon and Albert City. A bidding struggle between C & NW and Soo Line for full purchase of the St Paul-Minneapolis-Kansas City trackage of 720 miles seemed won by C & NW in 1983 with an offer of $93 million; but Soo Line unexpectedly counter-bid $100 million in the spring of the year. C & NW has continued its efforts to rid itself of its own excess branch lines. The total relinquished since 1968 is 3500 miles (5630 km).

Financial results

	1978	1979	1980
Operating revenues ($ million)			
Freight	583·388	669·472	844·636
Suburban passenger	39·108	42·345	53·909
Other	29·116	35·48	37·127
Total	651·612	747·297	935·672
Operating expenses ($ million)			
Transportation	296·584	350·937	426·636
Way and structures	90·667	113·558	134·368
Equipment	156·396	195·506	222·757
Depreciation	22·551	24·359	25·721
General and administrative	50·359	51·278	62·139
Total	616·557	735·638	871·621

Wyoming Coal Project

To prepare for greater participation in western coal movements, C & NW launched its Wyoming Coal Project some years ago. In October 1980 an ICC Administrative Law Judge issued an initial decision granting the application of the company and its wholly-owned subsidiary, Western Railroad Properties, Inc (WRPI) for authority to construct a 56-mile (90 km) connector line from the company's present line in east central Wyoming to a connection with the Union Pacific Railroad at Joyce, Nebraska. The decision also approved the terms of ownership and operation of the C & NW-Burlington Northern (BN) jointly-owned Gillette line extending north into the coal fields from Orin and Shawnee, Wyoming, the construction of which was completed by BN in November 1979.

For some years C & NW sought to obtain around two-thirds of the estimated $460 million cost of the project in Federal Railroad Administration loans. This was strongly opposed by Burlington Northern (BN) as inequitable treatment of a competitor. After various legal processes and negotiations in the course of 1980-81, agreement was reached on the major issues; resolution of others was expected in time for construction to begin in late 1982. The key factor was an undertaking by a group of banks to lend up to $414 million to finance construction. C & NW was to find $25 million and Union Pacific Corporation the remainder of the money.

Besides the 56 miles of new track, the project involves rehabilitation of 45 miles (72 km) of existing track to complete the link between Union Pacific at Joyce, Nebraska, and the 103-mile (166 km) Gillette line at the entrance to the Powder River basin. The Gillette line was undertaken as a joint BN/C & NW exercise, but BN completed it alone because C & NW could not raise its share of the funding. In 1982 the Interstate Commerce Commission ruled that C & NW should pay BN $76·194 million for the right to operate over the Powder Basin line, based on a complex formula. No user fees would be charged. BN disapproved the compromise and was to appeal against the decision in the courts.

Freight traffic

Intermodal traffic rose 22 per cent in 1982, but otherwise traffic was so depressed by the recession that in the first nine months of the year a loss of $13·2 million was incurred, compared with a profit of $41 million in the same period of 1981. A 10 per cent reduction of staff was planned in 1983, but there was a return to profit in the year's first quarter.

Investment

In recent years C & NW has embarked on the largest capital expenditure and long-term lease programmes in its history. Future planned investment includes $50 million to equip the east-west main line with CTC, $75 million to build a modern classification yard in central Iowa, and another $40 million to complete double-tracking the west end of the main line.

Traction and rolling stock

C & NW operates 1027 and 59 switching diesel locomotives, 18 passenger cars and 34 924 freight cars.

GP50 diesel locomotives
purchased from EMD in 1980

Conrail
Consolidated Rail Corporation

Six Penn Center Plaza, Philadelphia, Pennsylvania 19104

Telephone: (215) 977 4000

Chairman and Chief Executive Officer: L Stanley Crane
President and Chief Operating Officer: Stuart M Reed
Executive Vice President, Finance and Administration: Robert H Platt
Senior Vice President, Marketing and Sales: James A Hagen
    Operations: Richard B Hasselman
    Law: John W Rowe
Vice President, Treasurer: H William Brown
    Law: Bruce B Wilson
    Public Affairs: Richard W Garbett
    Sales: Alfred A Michaud
    Government Affairs and Washington Counsel: William B Newman
    Information Systems: Michael D Sims
    Marketing: Charles N Marshall
    Resource Development: Richard C Sullivan
    Transportation: Donald A Swanson
    Labour Relations: Robert E Swert
    Controller: Robert V Wadden
    Materials and Purchasing: Jeremy T Whatmough
Assistant Vice President and Chief Mechanical Officer: Joseph S Fadale
Secretary: Allen D Schimmel

Gauge: 1435 mm
Length: 23 948 km

Conrail was created as a private, profit-making corporation by an Act of Congress and began operations in April 1976. It was conveyed most of the rail properties of the Central of New Jersey, Erie Lackawanna, Lehigh and Hudson River, Lehigh Valley, Penn-Central and Reading lines. Conrail is primarily a freight railroad and its purpose is to create a viable, private-sector rail freight system in the north-east and Midwest, providing efficient and essential rail service to its customers.

At the beginning of 1983, Conrail operated over 14 884 route-miles (23 953 route-km) in 15 states (Connecticut, Delaware, Indiana, Illinois, Kentucky, Maryland, Massachusetts, Michigan, Missouri, New Jersey, New York, Ohio, Pennsylvania, Virginia, West Virginia), the District of Columbia and two provinces of Canada (Ontario and Quebec).

By early spring 1983, Conrail had met one of its two major goals, to provide freight customers with reliable service as good as that of any other US railroad. It had also made significant progress toward financial self-sufficiency and entry into the private sector (the US Department of Transportation currently held most of Conrail's outstanding common stock).

In progressing toward the second goal, in 1983 Conrail faced two profitability tests as mandated by the Northeast Rail Service Act of 1981 (NERSA). In June 1983, the United States Railway Association (USRA) Board of Directors was to determine if Conrail could become profitable; in November 1983, the USRA Board was to determine if Conrail actually was profitable between June and October. Conrail management had expressed confidence that with even a minimal national economic recovery, the railroad would be able to pass the profitability tests in 1983. The next step in the Federally-designed process would be Conrail's transfer to the private sector, in a manner yet to be determined by the US Department of Transportation (DOT). Goldman Sachs, an investment banking firm, was engaged by the DOT to assist in this process.

In mid-1983 a consortium of labour unions announced its readiness to bid $2000 million for Conrail. Chase Manhattan Bank agreed to put up $500 million in cash to secure the purchase. At the same time Conrail passed the first profitability test prescribed by NERSA, which ensured that it would not automatically be sold off piecemeal.

Conrail has five operating regions with 17 divisions within those regions:
Eastern Region, Philadelphia, Pennsylvania: New Jersey division, Elizabeth, New Jersey; Philadelphia division, Philadelphia, Pennsylvania; Harrisburg division, Harrisburg, Pennsylvania;
Northeastern Region, New Haven, Connecticut: New England division, Springfield, Massachusetts; Mohawk-Hudson division, Utica, New York; Buffalo division, De Pew, New York;
Central Region, Pittsburgh, Pennsylvania: Allegheny division, Altoona, Pennsylvania; Pittsburgh division, Pittsburgh, Pennsylvania; Youngstown division, Youngstown, Ohio;

Southern Region, Indianapolis, Indiana: Columbus division, Columbus, Ohio; Southwest division, Indianapolis, Indiana;
Western Region, Detroit, Michigan: Cleveland division, Cleveland, Ohio; Toledo division, Toledo, Ohio; Chicago division, Chicago, Illinois; Canada division, St Thomas, Ontario; Detroit division, Detroit, Michigan; Michigan division, Jackson, Michigan.

Freight traffic

Conrail transported approximately 177 million tons of freight in 1982. The key commodities involved were: coal, coke and ore (73·1 million tons); iron and steel (16·6 million tons); farm and food products; chemicals and allied products (14·4 million tons); and automotive products (6·2 million tons). Total revenue-earning net ton-mileage was 69 000 million. Conrail operates 36 piggyback terminals.

Each day an average of 34 (including four mail) Conrail TOFC TrailVan trains in dedicated point-to-point service operate between the North Atlantic ports and the Midwest. Of these, 13 directly connect the three Conrail terminals at Portside, South Kearny, and North Bergen in New Jersey with other areas on the Conrail system.

Conrail also has 15 Flexi-Flo terminals throughout the north-east and Midwest. Flexi-Flo is a liquid and dry bulk commodity rail-truck transfer system. After a 22 per cent growth in 1981, a further 15 per cent increase in Flexi-Flo business was recorded in 1982.

Conrail's back-haul programme of truck-competitive discount rates for shippers who can fill boxcars which would otherwise return empty to their owner railroads in the west and south also created an increase of nearly 65 per cent in freight business in 1981, again despite an overall decrease in carloadings of freight.

Major classification yards are located at Conway (Pittsburgh); Enola (Harrisburg); Selkirk (Albany); Buckeye (Columbus); Elkhart (Indiana); Frontier (Buffalo); Big Four (Indianapolis); De Witt (Syracuse); Allentown (Pennsylvania); Stanley (Toledo); and Oak Island (Newark, New Jersey).

Conrail runs an average of 566 through and 242 local freight trains daily.

Financial recovery

In its first five years of operation, Conrail focused on the enormous task of restoring reliable rail freight service mainly through a massive rehabilitation and upgrading of the deteriorated physical system it inherited. Nearly $3300 million was invested by the Federal government in Conrail up to June 1981. Since then Conrail has not required Federal funding for operations or rehabilitation, and does not anticipate the need for such funds in the future. During 1982, Conrail and its subsidiaries obtained private sector financing of $45 million for equipment and plant improvements, bringing the cumulative private sector financing to 1040 million from April 1976, to the end of 1982.

From 1976 to 1980, Conrail reported some $1500 million in losses, including a $243·7 million loss in 1980, while it completed the accelerated upgrading of the deteriorated rail properties inherited from its bankrupt predecessors. In 1981, Conrail reported its first net income ($39·2 million) on a basis using depreciation accounting for track structure. The income was the result of major initiatives in three areas: significant employee wage increase concessions, major operating cost reductions, and innovative and agressive marketing and sales programmes.

By continuing initiatives begun in 1981 and by utilising provisions of NERSA, Conrail in 1982 overcame a 20·5 per cent decline in carloadings of freight traffic handled to report a net income of $174·2 million. This included $91 million resulting from the sales of tax benefits under Federal 'safe harbour' leasing regulations, and $44·1 million from settlements of accounts with various passenger agencies for which Conrail had operated rail services until the end of 1982. A net income of $200 million was forecast for 1983.

Conrail was able to make substantial cost reductions in 1981-82 in several specific areas, the foremost being through employee wage increase concessions in May 1981. This action helped spur Congress to enact NERSA in August 1981, which allowed Conrail to make necessary workforce reductions: substituting one-time severance payments funded by the Federal government for long-term wage or job guarantees for several categories of unneeded employees; launching a substantial programme to eliminate several thousand miles of excess rail lines; and transferring commuter service obligations to designated regional and local agencies in the north-east.

The agreement by Conrail's union workforce on wage increase concessions, which Conrail estimated would total approximately $300 million between 1981 and 1984, was implemented by deferring the first 12 per cent in wage increases negotiated nationally in the new three-year contract between management and rail labour. Conrail's non-union employees made proportionate wage sacrifices.

As part of its overall reduction of excess plant, in 1982 Conrail completed the first phase of a branch line rationalisation programme authorised under NERSA. The company eliminated approximately 2600 route-miles of line. While the programme reduced Conrail's route system by about 15 per cent, actual revenue losses were less than 1 per cent. The process led to the creation of nine new short-line railroads, which took over operations of about 139 miles of the affected lines; in addition, four existing short-line railroads assumed service on another 218 miles of line. The second phase of the NERSA-expedited branch line abandonment programme began for Conrail in autumn 1982 with the filing of 'Notices of Insufficient Revenue' on 39 line segments, covering 152·6 miles. This phase of the expedited branch line abandonment programme was to be in effect until November 1983.

In January 1983, as mandated by NERSA, Conrail transferred its commuter rail service operating obligations to local authorities in the New York, northern New Jersey, Connecticut, Maryland and Philadelphia metropolitan areas.

In 1982 agreement was reached with Canadian National and Canadian Pacific for disposal to them of Conrail's 999-year lease of 274 miles of the Canada Southern, including the main line between Niagara Falls and Windsor, Ontario, and also of the Niagara River Bridge and the Detroit River Tunnel. However, the sale was contested by Cantunn Inc, a Detroit-based company anxious to buy the Detroit-Niagara Falls and Detroit River Tunnel line for a TOFC link-up with the GTI network.

Another major force in Conrail's financial turnaround has been the marketing actions taken as a result of the Staggers Rail Act of 1980. In 1982 Conrail negotiated more than 180 transport contracts, guaranteeing the railroad annual revenue estimated at $300 million while assuring customers of stable freight car supplies and transport prices as well as service guarantees in many instances. Conrail also reduced prices on the rail transport of commodities such as coal, steel, and fluxing stone while offering a wide variety of customised service packages.

In 1981 Conrail began revising and restructuring complex and unwieldy tariffs. The first such revision (grain) converted more than 4000 pages of tariffs, supplements, routing guides and other indexes into a slim, 70-page tariff.

Conrail has continued its profit-oriented approach to marketing by requesting the Interstate Commerce Commission (ICC) to deregulate boxcar traffic and to cancel joint rates with other railroads where expensive and unnecessary interchange could be eliminated. The ICC announced in March 1983 that it had voted to exempt railroad boxcar traffic from regulation. To ensure that each carload of freight pays its own way, Conrail imposed surcharges on certain unprofitable traffic movements, and instituted proportional rates in place of unsatisfactory joint rates with other railroads.

Traction and rolling stock

At the start of 1983 Conrail operated 3472 locomotives, 104 643 freight cars and 2000 cabooses, but a great deal of equipment was in store, including 30 per cent of the locomotive fleet. Nevertheless, orders were placed for late 1983 delivery with EMD for 40 3500 hp SD50 locomotives, value $48 million, and with General Electric for 60 3700 hp Bo-Bos, value $66 million, because of these modern types' superior fuel efficiency.

Track

A massive programme of track work since 1976 has installed about 5000 miles of continuous welded rail, which by the end of 1982 was continuous throughout the water-level route between New York and Chicago, apart from an 11-mile section to be covered in 1983. Compared with slow orders totalling 8000 miles throughout the network in 1976, at the end of 1982 incidence had been reduced to 200 miles on Conrail's core main-line mileage of 6400, and 2600 miles elsewhere. Installation of cwr proceeds at a rate of 450 miles a year, using 132 lb rail as standard, under programmes which in 1983 were expected to absorb $625 million in maintenance, $100 million in capital improvements funded by Conrail and $115-125 million in others funded by Government agencies.

Delaware & Hudson Railway Company

D & H Railway Building, 40 Beaver Street, Albany, New York 12207

Telephone: (518) 462 7600

President and Chief Executive: C R McKenna
Vice-President, Sales and Marketing: T E O'Brien
Vice-President, Finance: D D Muir

General Manager: J R Williams
General Superintendant, Transportation: C P Belke
Chief Mechanical Officer: C G MacDermot
Chief Engineer: T P Schmidt

Gauge: 1435 mm
Length: 2734 km

In 1982 the Interstate Commerce Commission approved Guilford Transportation Industries' (GTI) takeover of control of the railroad for $500 000, despite opposition from six railroads including Canadian National, Canadian Pacific and Conrail. Also approved was re-scheduling of D & H's $60 million debt to the Federal Government. Completion of the GTI purchase was, however, dependent on defeat of litigation against GTI's acquisition of the Boston & Maine. The D & H, which operates 136 locomotives and 4764 freight cars, forms part of the GTI three-railroad scheme for single-line service between main New England centres and connections with the south and Midwest.

The Denver and Rio Grande Western Railroad Company

PO Box 5482, 1 Park Central, 1515 Arapahoe Street, Denver, Colorado 80217

Telephone: (303) 629 5533

Chairman of the Board, President and Chief Executive Officer: W J Holtman
Vice-President, Traffic: J D Key
  Fuel Traffic: H E Cash
  Finance: H W Bushacher
  Sales: J J Martin
  Market Development: C D Brainard
Vice-President and General Counsel: S R Freeman
General Manager, Operating: A H Nance
Purchasing Agent: S A Silverman
Chief Mechanical Officer: J E Clancy
Chief Engineer: E H Waring
Chief Transportation Officer: L R Parsons
Signal Engineer: F A Dunham

Gauge: 1435 mm
Length: 2948 km

The Denver and Rio Grande Western Railroad Company was founded in 1873. The Rio Grande Railroad operates from Denver and Pueblo, Colorado, on the east, to Salt Lake City and Ogden, Utah, on the west. It also owns the 90-mile, 914 mm-gauge Silverton railway. D & RGW was the last Class I railroad to operate its own long-distance passenger service, the thrice-weekly Denver—Salt Lake City 'Rio Grande Zephyr', independently of Amtrak, but agreed a takeover by Amtrak from April 1983. Six 'Zephyr' cars were sold to Amtrak.

Rio Grande Industries, Inc (Denver) was established in 1969 as a holding company to control Denver and Rio Grande Western Railroad, and to permit diversification. Although the railroad continues to be its most important activity, diversification has been made into real estate development (Leavell Development Co, Denver, Colorado); people-moving systems (Arrow Development Co), though this concern was sold off in 1980; information industries (Computer Sharing Services); and trucking (Rio Grande Motor Way).

Traffic

Revenues from coal shipments of $138·6 million represented 48 per cent of total freight revenue in 1982, maintaining the rise in proportion of the previous ten years. Non-coal traffic decreased $42 million, or 22 per cent. Commodities showing the largest declines included food products, lumber, barytes, and iron and steel products. Virtually all commodities suffered from the recession, which affected steel production, construction activity and coal usage by utilities receiving coal from Colorado and Utah mines. Coal shipments were further adversely affected by reduced export demands after the first quarter of 1982. Coal revenue was thus 0·4 per cent down on its 1981 record figure. However the cumulative increase over 1977 revenue from coal stood at almost 220 per cent. In the first quarter of 1983 coal revenues were running 15 per cent below comparable 1982 levels.

Revenues from intermodal traffic increased by 4·6 per cent. Trailer-on-flat car (TOFC) revenues reached more than $23·5 million and import/export traffic moving in containers continued to be a strong market, with over 10 000 containerloads handled in transcontinental mini-landbridge service for a major steamship line.

Intermodal services increased further with the conversion of several commodities from movement by rail boxcar to TOFC and highway trucks. Canned goods and wines from West Coast origins, in particular, moved in trailers, as buyers purchased truckload rather than carload quantities. This shift to intermodal freight movement of many commodities was expected to continue.

Finance

For the first time since 1970, the Rio Grande Railroad recorded a decline in operating revenue in 1982.

D&RGW unit coal train headed by five SD40 diesels

Total revenues at year-end were $292·5 million, a decrease of $42·5 million, and 12·7 per cent under the $335 million reported for 1981. Much of the decline was attributed to reduced freight volumes, which were primarily the result of the slow-down in production experienced by industries nation-wide. However, while ton-miles of freight decreased 15 per cent, increases in freight rates brought the average revenue per ton mile up 2 per cent to 2·91 cents.

Passenger revenues increased from $1·6 to $2·2 million, or 37·5 per cent, due to higher passenger fares and an increase in patronage. Despite these improved revenues, passenger service continued to show substantial deficits and was terminated in April 1983.

Operating income for the year was $23·3 million, a decrease of 52 per cent from the record earnings of $48·6 million reported in 1981. This large decline was directly related to the drop in freight volume, but this also contributed to a decrease in operating expenses of $17·2 million, or 6 per cent, to $269·2 million. Track maintenance decreased $5·3 million, or 9 per cent, while equipment maintenance decreased $6·3 million, or 11 per cent.

Considered as a percentage of revenues, roadway maintenance increased from 17·2 to 17·9 per cent and equipment maintenance from 16·5 to 16·7 per cent. During the year, the cost of locomotive fuel decreased from $59 million to $46·5 million, a 21 per cent decline, and the average cost per gallon decreased from $1·04 to 96 cents, an 8 per cent decline. As a percentage of revenues, fuel decreased from 17·6 to 15·9 per cent.

As a percentage of revenues, wages and benefits increased from 37·9 per cent in 1981 to 46·3 per cent in 1982. Average employment decreased 8 per cent, but average wage rates were up 13 per cent.

Rail merger case

In December 1982, consolidation of Union Pacific, Missouri Pacific and Western Pacific Railroads became effective. The Rio Grande Railroad opposed this consolidation and at the end of 1982 was appealing the Interstate Commerce Commission's decision to permit the consolidation, based on the grounds that it is anti-competitive. It was claimed that while the consolidated companies can now serve a larger territory, smaller railroad lines, such as the Rio Grande, have lost some of their 'friendly' connections.

At the same time that the consolidation became effective, Rio Grande was granted trackage rights over the Missouri Pacific line between Pueblo, Colorado and Kansas City, Missouri. If the consolidation were allowed to stand, Rio Grande would have to generate substantial new revenues on the trackage rights to offset the loss of net revenues which the consolidation would cause.

Investment

Although originally budgeted at over $50 million, actual capital expenditures in 1982 were limited to $37 million due to lower traffic levels. Major expenditures were for the purpose of expanding track capacity and expediting train operations. Specific projects included the construction and extension of sidings, the start of the installation of a new ventilation system in the Moffat Tunnel, modernisation of the wheel shop in Denver, and various communication and signal improvements.

Expenditures for new rail decreased as 18½ track-miles of new rail and 259 000 new sleepers were installed in 1982, compared to 66 miles of rail and 354 000 sleepers in 1981.

The general decline in freight volume caused freight cars and locomotives to be in surplus supply during the year. The company's only major equipment purchase totalled $12·7 million for 350 new 100-ton capacity coal cars to service the continued demand projected for coal loading. In addition, six new 100-ton bulkhead flat cars, 20 TOFC/COFC cars and 50 flat-bottom gondolas were obtained under short-term leases.

Outlook for 1983

The easing of inflation, gains in productivity and the

opportunities presented by obtaining trackage rights to Kansas City, were expected to create conditions for sustainable earnings growth, although first quarter income was 5 per cent down on 1982. Marketing efforts to increase the traffic being interchanged at Ogden, Utah with the Southern Pacific Railroad would receive particular emphasis.

In the east, there have been encouraging indications that marketing combinations with other carriers can be helpful to the Rio Grande.

Locomotives and rolling stock

The fleet of diesel-electric locomotives at January 1983 was 282. D & RGW also operates five steam locomotives on the narrow-gauge Silverton system. Total freight car fleet was 10 947.

Diesel locomotives

Class	Wheel arrangement	Rated power hp	Starting traction effort lb	Total weight tons	Length ft in	Built	No in service	Builders	Engine & type	Gen/alt type
SW1200	B-B	1200	61 000	123	44' 5"	1965	10	EMD	12-567C	D25C
SW1000	B-B	1000	60 000	123	44' 8"	1966-68	10	EMD	8-645E	D25C
GP30	B-B	2250	62 000	129/130	56' 2"	1962	25	EMD	16-567D3	D22DT
GP35	B-B	2500	62 000	130	56' 2"	1964-65	22	EMD	16-567D3A	D32
GP40	B-B	3000	65 000	138	59' 2"	1966-71	42	EMD	16-645E3	AR10
GP40-2	B-B	3000	65 000	139	59' 2"	1972-74	35	EMD	16-645E3	AR10
GP7	B-B	1500	60 000	122	55' 11"	1952	1	EMD	16-567B	D12B
SD7	C-C	1500	89 000	184	60' 8½"	1953	5	EMD	16-567B	D12C
SD9	C-C	1750	89 000	184	60' 8½"	1957	10	EMD	16-567C	D12C
SD45	C-C	3600	93 000	195	65' 9½"	1967-68	26	EMD	20-645E3	AR10
SD40T-2	C-C	3000	92 000	194	70' 8"	1974-78	57	EMD	16-645E3	AR10
SD40T-2	C-C	3000	92 000	194	70' 8"	1980	16	EMD	16-645E3B	AR10
F9B	B-B	1750	59 000	124	50'	1955	2	EMD	16-567C	D12
F9A	B-B	1750	60 000	124	50' 8"	1955	1	EMD	16-567C	D12
GP9	B-B	1750	60 000	123	56' 2"	1955-56	20	EMD	16-567C	D12B

The Family Lines Rail System

(See Seaboard System)

Florida East Coast Railway Company

1 Malaga Street, St Augustine, Florida 32084

Telephone: (904) 829 3421

President: W L Thornton
Executive Vice-President, Operations: R W Wyckhoff
Vice-President, Traffic: J E Corbett
  Real Estate: W E Durham Jr
  Industrial Development: R J Barreto

Secretary: C F Zellers Jr
General Manager, Transportation: M E Deputy
General Mechanical Superintendent: S D Smith
Chief Engineer, Maintenance of Way: R W Fondren
Superintendent, Signalling and Communications: H E Webb

Gauge: 1435 mm
Length: 859 km

The core of the Florida East Coast system is its trunk route from Jacksonville to Miami. The railroad is notable for its determined acceptance of a confrontation over labour work-rules which struck it in 1963. As a result, uniquely among Class I US railroads, it is not bound by such constraints as the 100-mile working day for train crews, distinctions between road and yard crews, fixed numbers of train crew or separate seniority dates for different tasks. This has enabled FEC to surpass by a considerable margin the traction and rolling stock productivity norm of other railroads in its territory, even though it is a terminal system, with no bridge traffic, between interchanges with other railroads.

The company operates 62 line-haul, four switching diesel locomotives and 2546 freight cars.

Grand Trunk Corporation (GTC)

Grand Trunk Corporation is a holding company formed in 1971 to embrace the three Canadian railroads operating within the USA: Grand Trunk Western (GTW); Duluth, Winnipeg & Pacific (DWP); and Central Vermont (CV). DWP and CV are Class II railroads. Since then, GTW has expanded considerably, first by acquisition of redundant Conrail trackage in the Saginaw Bay City-Midland, Michigan, region, then in 1980 by taking control of the 478-mile Detroit, Toledo & Ironton (DTI), now a wholly-owned subsidiary of GTW and in 1981 of the 59-mile Detroit & Toledo Shore Line. The expanded GTW is now known as the Grand Trunk Rail System.

In late 1981 Grand Trunk Corporation and Milwaukee Road announced that they were discussing

a possible integration of the two systems, after the latter had been reorganised into the 2900 route-mile network adumbrated by its trustee following bankruptcy. Such a merger would form a continuous rail system around the foot of Lake Michigan, open up through routes from Chicago to Kansas City, St Paul/Minneapolis and Duluth, improve average freight-haul distances and diminish GTW's dependence on the automobile industry, which generates a third of its revenues. GTC's bid for acquisition of the Milwaukee Road was made publicly firm in May 1982. It was hoped, with ICC approval, to make the purchase effective by the start of 1985. In advance of the merger's fulfilment, reorganisation of train working, backed by a joint marketing offensive, achieved two-day reductions in transits between the Canadian border and Kansas City, Louisville, Minneapolis/St Paul and Chicago.

GTC experienced a loss of C$54·5 million in 1982, compared to a profit of C$40·5 million in 1981. The loss was caused largely by the recession, which severely affected the US Midwest, including GTC's automotive traffic base, and by provision for the impairment in value of the Central Vermont (see below). Traffic levels were further depressed by competitive pressures within the transportation industry. Pricing freedom allowed by deregulation led both railroads and motor carriers to reduce rates selectively, in order to capture lucrative, long-term contract traffic from other carriers. While GTC lines lost some traffic through this process, traffic gains were also obtained although at lower revenue levels. In response to the downturn in business in 1982, GTC reduced manpower by 10·3 per cent, made substantial reductions in capital programmes and cut back some train operations.

Grand Trunk Rail System

Grand Trunk Western Railroad Co

131 West Lafayette Boulevard, Detroit, Michigan 48226

Telephone: (313) 962 2260

President: J H Burdakin Sr
Senior Vice-President, Marketing: W H Cramer Jr
  Finance and Administration: P E Tatro
Vice-President, Operations: G L Maas
  Personnel and Labour Relations: R Guregian
  General Counsel: E C Opperthauser
Chief Engineer: J M Letro
Chief Mechanical Officer: R G Lipmyer

Executive Assistant and Corporate Secretary: E G Fontaine

Gauge: 1435 mm
Length: 2734 km

The railway operates 269 diesel locomotives and 13 645 freight cars.

Illinois Central Gulf Railroad
(An IC Industries Company)

Two Illinois Center, 233 N Michigan Avenue, Chicago, Illinois 60601

Telephone: (312) 565 1600

President and Chief Executive Officer: Vacant
Senior Vice President, Operations: James E Martin
Vice President: G C Stuckey
Vice President and Chief Mechanical Officer: Paul F Deady
Senior Vice President and Chief Financial Officer: G E Konker
Senior Vice President, Marketing: Harry J Bruce
Vice President, Materials Management: John H Moss
Vice President and Chief Engineer: John W Lager
Vice President and Chief Transportation Officer: Ivan B Hall
Secretary: John B Goodrich
Vice President, Communications and Computer Services: James C Taylor
Vice President, Market Development: Richard P Bessette
Vice President, Sales: Richard L Rushing
Vice President, Pricing: Gerald F Mohan
Director, Corporate Relations: Robert W O'Brien
Senior Vice President, Human Resources and Special Projects: Martin W Fingerhut
Senior Vice President, Law: Percy W Johnston
Vice President, Energy Management and Operations Administration: Chris W Damiano
Vice President, Car Management: Douglas D Hagestad
Vice President, Real Estate: Rixon A Irvine
Vice President and Comptroller: Don R Montgomery
Vice President, Coal: Robert P Neubauer
Vice President, Automotive/Intermodal: W G Bumpus
Assistant Vice President, Treasurer: Sandor A Loevy
General Manager, Safety/Technical Training: Nick J Andrews

Gauge: 1435 mm
Length: 12 162 km
Electrification: 64·5 km of 1·5 kV dc (Chicago commuter area)

IC Railroad Activities include IC Industries' major transport subsidiary, the Illinois Central Gulf Railroad (ICG), its subsidiaries, and railroad real estate. The Illinois Central Gulf operates in 12 states in the heartland of America and runs from the Great Lakes to the Gulf of Mexico, providing rail connection between some 2000 communities, including Chicago, St Louis, Memphis, New Orleans, Birmingham, Louisville, Omaha, Kansas City, Montgomery and Mobile. In 1981 IC Industries announced, however, that one of its new long-term corporate goals was to merge or sell ICG Railroad when terms and timing were most advantageous for its shareholders.

The ICG system includes 1·5 kV dc in the Chicago suburban area, over which it operates a fleet of 165 bi-level emu cars owned by the Chicago South Suburban Mass Transit District.

Since 1972 ICG has trimmed its network from 15 540 to 12 162 route-km, a reduction of 22 per cent. The ultimate objective is a system of approximately 11 260 route-km.

Unit coal train from southern Illinois mines to Chicago, headed by GP11 diesel units

TOFC loading at ICG's Chicago intermodal exchange terminal

Traffic
ICG is the major railroad in Illinois and northern Iowa. Through intensive marketing efforts and innovations, ICG has established itself as an integral part of the nation's grain distribution system by providing year-round service to the agricultural sector. ICG maintains a strong advantage over other rail carriers as it provides a direct access to the Gulf of Mexico. Unit grain trains provide grain shippers rates that are truck- and barge-competitive.

Approximately 90 per cent of ICG coal traffic now moves in train load or unit train shipments; of this total, 70 per cent is moved in non-ICG equipment under reduced rates, thereby minimising ICG capital and equipment requirements. Coal is, and is expected to continue to be, a major contributor to ICG's growth. ICG is strategically positioned in the extensive Illinois Basin coal fields, encompassing Illinois, Indiana, and western Kentucky, and containing an estimated 115 000 million tons of recoverable coal reserves. In this sector ICG has entered into the longest term contract ever to be signed by a US railroad and shipper. The 20-year tariff contract calls for the transport of 26 million tons of Illinois coal to a new power generating station at Marom, Indiana.

A new prospect for ICG is the development of foreign markets for coal from ICG-served mines. ICG has worked with overseas utilities and other coal users to bring to their attention the merits of using Illinois Basin coal and has co-operated with US coal companies to establish delivered BTU costs via the port of New Orleans that are competitive with coal now moving through eastern seaboard ports.

Further recognition of the European market potential for Illinois Basin coal came in late 1981 with announcement by Hunt International Coal & Trading Corporation of a $100 million coal transhipment facility to be constructed on the Mississippi River at Granada, Louisiana, between New Orleans and Baton Rouge. The ICG would provide sole rail service to the Granada export coal terminal, which will be capable of handling 100-car unit trains with an unloading loop track and related coal-handling facilities. The terminal will accommodate 60 000-ton colliers initially and 150 000-ton vessels when Mississippi River dredging is completed. The terminal was scheduled for operation in 1983 and would receive coal from Alabama, Appalachian and other Midwestern coal fields, in addition to the Illinois Basin.

ICG forecast that 1 million tons of export coal would be handled by 1983 at the existing Ryan-Walsh facility near New Orleans, through which the ICG's 1981 export coal tonnage was moved. This was expected to represent 3·5 per cent of ICG's total coal tonnage in 1983. Export coal is forecast to grow significantly in 1984 when the Granada export terminal is fully operational. Total export coal movements were anticipated to grow dramatically and to account for $70 million, or approximately 24 per cent of coal revenues, by 1986.

At the southern end of the railroad, chemical complexes produce a significant contribution to ICG's revenue mix. Louisiana, ranked first in chemical industry growth, represents a major portion of ICG's loadings. ICG is one of the largest US rail carriers of chemicals. The 90-mile stretch between Baton Rouge and New Orleans is particularly rich in such natural resources as lime, salt, sulphur, crude oil, and natural gas. Although constituting only 3 per cent of total ICG trackage, it generates over 12 per cent of tonnage and 20 per cent of freight revenue.

One of the nation's heaviest paper mill concentrations is in the ICG-served states of Alabama, Mississippi, Louisiana and Tennessee. Since ICG is the major railroad in Mississippi, the growing wood and paper products industries of that state have benefitted from ICG innovations for moving both raw materials and finished products.

Automobiles and automobile parts are also an important commodity group for ICG as it moves the products of steel mills, automakers and northern factories for domestic and foreign markets. Enclosed tri-level cars and special boxcars move new autos and auto parts to their destinations.

Deregulation benefits

One of the most important provisions of deregulation is the ability of railroads to enter into contracts with shippers. By the end of 1981, ICG had entered into, or was actively negotiating, 41 contracts representing about $118 million in annual gross freight revenues. Among them were:

ICG's second joint-line, five-year agreement with Borden Chemical Company and the Chicago & North Western Railroad to move methanol from Geismar, Louisiana, to Sheboygan, Wisconsin;

A three-year contract with Air Products & Chemicals Inc, to move more than 40 000 tons of vinyl chloride from Baton Rouge and Geismar, Louisiana, to Calvert, Kentucky;

A contract with Freeman United Coal Mining Company to move 140 000 tons of Illinois Basin coal to New Orleans for shipment to Spain;

A multi-million dollar, 17-month unit grain train contract with Cargill covering shipments of export grain from Illinois and Iowa points to Gulf of Mexico ports;

A five-year pact with Ford Motor Company to transport vehicles and tractors from points in Michigan, Ohio and Ontario to the south and south-west, worth nearly $7 million each year.

Intermodal traffic

Truck-rail-truck is one example of ICG's innovations. ICG developed special pallets and a shrink-wrap process which save money and time in the movement of steel from the Chicago area to St Louis, Kansas City and Iowa.

ICG has one of the most efficient and versatile intermodal operations in the country, and operates four piggyback trains daily between Chicago and New Orleans on high-speed schedules. An experimental RoadRailer service between Louisville and Memphis was terminated in October 1982 on grounds of inadequate traffic.

In order to provide better road-to-rail TOFC operations, ICG has implemented 12 Hub Centers, truck/rail facilities which provide co-ordinated highway/rail access to customers within a 300-mile radius within 21 states. This concept capitalises on main-line rail service, improves load balance, and increases equipment utilisation. Another intermodal development, Plan V less-than-truckload (LTL), allows ICG to compete with motor carriers in door-to-door service.

ICG has worked to improve its schedules through co-ordinated service with other railroads. Transit time is cut and equipment utilisation is improved through such non-yard connections as The Link, Delta Cannonball, the Cotton Belt Connection, the Chicago Connection and others.

Contribution to freight revenue in 1982

	(%)
Chemicals	17
Paper products	16
Grain	10
Grain mill products	12
Coal	12
Bulk commodities	9
Automotive	6
Piggyback (TOFC)	5
Metals	5
Lumber	4
Other	4

Investment

Capital investment in ICG plant, property and equipment in 1981 amounted to $293 million, including the purchase value of leased assets. ICG installed 1·5 million new sleepers, 278 miles of continuous welded rail and 21 124 carloads of ballast. In addition, 4541 miles of track were surfaced. $296

Traffic

	1980	1981	1982*
Total freight tonnage (000)	98 238	94 507	61 541
Total freight ton-miles (million)	31 991	29 236	17 832
Average net train load (revenue ton-miles)	1687	1671	1653
Average wagon load (tons)	65·08	66·5	67·7

* First nine months only

Chicago Commuter Division

	1980/81	1981/82
Total passenger-miles (million)	282·46	242·85
Total passenger journeys (million)	15·494	11·721
Average length of passenger journey (miles)	21	20·4

Results

	Six months ended 30 June ($ million)		
	1980	1981	1982
Sales and revenues	495·9	535·9	493
Pre-tax income (loss)	27·3	36·9	(1·5)
Total employees	20 932	18 609	16 415

Motive power rolling stock under order or delivered (1980-1982/83)

No of units	Wheel arrangement	Type	Power (hp)	Year built
28	Bo-Bo	SW-14	1300	1980
24	Bo-Bo	GP-11	1850	1980
15	Co-Co	SD-20	2000	1980
1	Bo-Bo	GP-35	2500	1980
1	Bo-Bo	GP-40	3000	1980
51	Bo-Bo	SW-14	1300	1981
3	Bo-Bo	GP-11	1850	1981
2	Bo-Bo	GP-26	2600	1981
9	Bo-Bo	'Slugs'*	—	1981
11	Bo-Bo	SW-14	1300	1982
17	Co-Co	SD-20	2000	1982
1	Co-Co	SD-40-2	3000	1982

*Auxiliary units

Freight rolling stock under order or delivered (1980-1982/83)

1980

Quantity	Car type	Supplier
200	70-ton pulpwood	ICGRR
300	100-ton covered hopper	Pullman Standard
50	100-ton airslide covered hopper	General-AM

1981

Quantity	Car type	Supplier
500	100-ton covered hopper	Pullman Standard
100	100-ton gondola	ICGRR
175	100-ton bulkhead flat	Portec

1982

Quantity	Car type	Supplier
175	100-ton bulkhead flat	Portec

million was budgeted for ICG capital investment in 1982, largely in the physical plant.

One of the most important efficiency indicators resulting from these improvements has been substantial increases in locomotive and freight car utilisation. In 1981 locomotive availability reached a new high of 91 per cent; average daily locomotive failures dropped 23 per cent and the improved roadbed resulted in fewer minor running repairs. The improved roadbed also permitted more uniform operating speeds and improved train handling, resulting in reduced fuel consumption. Over the 1977-81 period ICG achieved a 7 per cent reduction in gallons of diesel fuel consumed per thousand gross ton-miles.

Line closures

In 1981 service was terminated on 761 miles of uneconomic branch lines, bringing total line terminations to 1700 miles, or 18 per cent of system mileage, since 1977. At year end the ICG had favourable rulings from the Interstate Commerce Commission for termination of service on 115 miles, applications pending on 150 miles and a 1982 programme to eliminate a further 232 miles. Implementation of these pending actions would reduce the ICG system to about 7000 miles, 27 per cent less than the ICG was required to operate in 1976.

Traffic density has been improved 19 per cent from 6·7 million gross ton-miles per route-mile in 1976 to 8·0 in 1981. System density remained constant in 1981 even with a 7 per cent decline in car and trailer loads. Coal movements were down only 4 per cent despite a 72-day coal miners' strike in the ICG's service area.

Finance

IC Railroad Activities reported a pre-tax income in 1981 of $82 million on $1070 million revenues. This was 46 per cent above the company's previous record achieved in 1980.

Signalling

ICG has CTC operating over 992 route-miles, automatic block over 2485 route-miles and automatic train stop over 339 route-miles. Automatic train control employing coded rail currents is now operative between Champaign and Centralia, Illinois, and between Waterloo and Fort Dodge, Iowa; the apparatus was supplied by Union Switch and Signal Company.

Locomotives and rolling stock

At the end of 1982 ICG was operating 944 line-haul diesel locomotives and 155 switching locomotives. Wagon stock totalled 39 207. Its Commuter Division operated two diesel locomotives, two diesel railcars, 165 emus, two dmus and six passenger cars. ICG has its own locomotive remanufacturing plant at Paducah, Kentucky, the third largest US locomotive manufacturing facility, and its own freight car building and rehabilitation shop at Centralia, Illinois.

Diesel-electric locomotives

Class	Wheel arrangement	Rated power hp	Tractive effort Continuous at lb	mph	Max speed mph	Wheel diameter in	Total weight tons	Length ft in	No in service 1.1.82	First built	Builders	Engine & type
SW-1	Bo-Bo	600	24 000	7·5	45	40	98	44′ 5″	2	1946	EMD	6-567
SW-8	Bo-Bo	800	32 000	7·7	45	40	115	44′ 5″	3	1952	EMD	8-567
SW-900	Bo-Bo	900	36 000	7·1	45	40	114	44′ 5″	4	1957	EMD	8-567

Diesel-electric locomotives

Class	Wheel arrangement	Rated power hp	Tractive effort Continuous at lb	mph	Max speed mph	Wheel diameter in	Total weight tons	Length ft in	No in service 1.1.82	First built	Builders	Engine & type
SW-1R	Bo-Bo	1000	28 000	11	45	40	108	44' 5''	1	1946	EMD	8-567
SW-7	Bo-Bo	1200	31 000	12	45	40	124	44' 5''	2	1950	EMD	12-567
SW-7R	Bo-Bo	1200	31 000	12	45	40	124	44' 5''	1	1950	EMD	12-567
SW-9	Bo-Bo	1200	31 000	12	45	40	124	44' 5''	4	1951	EMD	12-567
SW-9R	Bo-Bo	1200	31 000	12	45	40	124	44' 5''	1	1951	EMD	12-567
SW-13/SW-13B	Bo-Bo	1300	28 000	11	45	40	125	44' 5''	15	1939	EMD	12-567
SW-14	Bo-Bo	1300	31 000	12	45	40	125	44' 5''	112	1950	EMD	12-567
SD-28	Co-Co	1800	46 000	12	65	40	167	60' 8''	2	1965	EMD	12-567D1
GP-9/18/28	Bo-Bo	1750/1800	40 000/44 600	11/12	65	40	124/123	56' 2''	86	1950/1964	EMD	16-567/16-567C
GP-8/10/11	Bo-Bo	1600/1850	40 000/44 600	11/12	65	40	123/133	56' 2''	500	1950/1954	EMD	16-567 (completely remanufactured by ICG)
GP-38, 38A, 38-D	Bo-Bo	2000	46 715	12·8	76	40	131/133	59' 2''	53	1970	EMD	16-645E
GP-38-2	Bo-Bo	2000	46 000	10·9	65	40	129	56' 2''	55	1962	EMD	16-567D3
GP-30	Bo-Bo	2250	52 000	11·8	71	40	129	56' 2''	28	1964	EMD	16-567D3A
GP-35	Bo-Bo	2500	52 000	12	71	40	131	59' 2''	46	1966	EMD	T/C 16-645E3
GP-40	Bo-Bo	3000	54 600	11	65	40	139	59' 2''	37	1969	EMD	T/C 16-645E3
GP-40A	Bo-Bo	3000	46 700	13	76	40	136	60' 2''	17	1967	GE	T/C 16 cyl Type FDL-16
U-33-C	Co-Co	3300	90 600	10·5	71	40	193/209	65' 9''	9	1969	EMD	T/C 16-645E3
SD 40/40A	Co-Co	3000	82 100	11·1	65	40	208	68' 10''	46	1973	EMD	T/C 16-645E3
SD 40-2	Co-Co	3000	78 000	11·1	65	40	184/189	60' 8''	14	1959	EMD	T/C 16-645E8
SD 20	Co-Co	2000	48 000	12·8	65	40	198	65' 9''	42	1966	EMD	T/C 20-645E3
SD 45	Co-Co	3600	82 100	11·3	65	40	131	56' 2''	1	1962	EMD	16-567D3A
GP-26	Bo-Bo	2250	52 000	11·8	71	40	124	44' 5''	2	1951		Booster unit 'Slug'
SD 28	Co-Co	1850							2	1965	EMD	16-567D1

Kansas City Southern Lines
(The Kansas City Southern and Louisiana & Arkansas Railway Companies)

114 West 11th Street, Kansas City, Missouri 64105

Telephone: (816) 556 0303

Chairman of the Board and Chief Executive Officer: Thomas S Carter
President: vacant
Vice-President, Marketing: M F McClain
 Pricing: L J Tamisiea

Personnel: J L Deveney
Law: R E Zimmerman
Secretary: A P Mauro
Vice-President and Comptroller: T A Giltner
Vice-President, Operations: J E Gregg
Assistant Vice-President, Mechanical: J B Rogers
 Maintenance of Way: A W Reid
Superintendent of Locomotives: D R Johnson

Gauge: 1435 mm
Length: 1199·5 km

Kansas City Southern Lines is a member of the Kansas City Southern Industries group of companies. In addition to road and rail transport, KCSI owns television and radio stations, a plant manufacturing specialised industrial vehicles, coal mines and financial service companies.

The Louisiana & Arkansas Railway is controlled by KCSI but is separately operated. The main line runs direct from Kansas City to the Gulf ports of New Orleans, Louisiana and Port Arthur, Texas. A line runs west from Shreveport to Dallas.

Traction and rolling stock (including Louisiana & Arkansas equipment) comprises 280 diesel locomotives and 7677 freight cars.

Louisiana & Arkansas Railway Company

114 West Eleventh Street, Kansas City, Missouri 64105

Telephone: (816) 556 0303

Chairman, President and Chief Executive: T S Carter
Senior Vice-President: M F McClain
Senior Vice-President, Law: R E Zimmerman
Vice-President: L H Rowland
 Sales: H W Davis
 Traffic: L J Tamisieia

Comptroller: T A Giltner
Operations: J E Gregg

Gauge: 1435 mm
Length: 1200 km

Long Island Rail Road Company

93-02 Sutphin Boulevard, Jamaica Station, Jamaica, New York 11435

Telephone: (212) 526 0900

President: R H H Wilson
Vice-President, Operations: L A Baggerly
 Finance and Administration: T P Moore
 Planning and Systems: F S Sanda
 Personnel Management: J F De Santo
General Counsel and Secretary: Thomas M Taranto
Chief Transportation Officer: C W Powers
Chief Engineer: Charles H Gaut
Chief Mechanical Officer: James W Yaeger
Director, Operations and Service Planning: Donald O Eisele
Director, Public Affairs: Alexandra Zetlin

Gauge: 1435 mm
Length: 199 km
Electrification: 103 km at 700 V dc

LIRR is the third oldest railroad in the world still operating under its original name. It is the busiest railroad in the USA, providing the nation's most concentrated rail service to one of its fastest growing areas. LIRR records over 80 million passenger journeys annually and carries over 1·5 million tons of freight. Revenue in 1981 totalled $204 million against expenditure of $429 million.

The LIRR is a wholly-owned subsidiary of the Metropolitan Transportation Authority, an agency of the State of New York, whose members constitute the railroad's Board of Directors.

Rolling stock
The railroad operates 67 line-haul and eight switcher diesel locomotives. The stock of 1018 passenger vehicles includes 764 class M-1 multiple-unit passenger cars, covering service on its inner suburban electrified lines in New York City, Nassau and Suffolk counties. Service to other points on the system is provided by diesel locomotive-hauled trains. In 1983 LIRR, which has embarked on a five-year capital improvement programme, was expected to begin electrification of 20 further miles of main line between Hicksville and Ronkonkoma, also 5 miles of the Port Jefferson branch between Huntington and Northport, at a total estimated cost of $146·5 million.

The majority of diesel services are push-pull, with an EMD diesel locomotive at the east end and a power unit shell (traction motors removed) with engineer controls at the west end. The 152 coaches assigned to push-pull service were converted during 1971-80 from electric multiple-units. LIRR will receive a share of the 1778 cars ordered under the Metropolitan Transportation Authority's five-year $6500 million programme announced in December 1981.

Missouri-Kansas-Texas Railroad Company

701 Commerce Street, Dallas, Texas 75202

Telephone: (214) 651 6700

Chairman of the Board and Chief Executive Officer: Reginald N Whitman
President and Chief Operating Officer: Harold L Gastler
Executive Vice President, Financial: Karl R Ziebarth
Vice President, Executive Representative: Billy R Bishop
   Administration: William H Zeidel
   Real Estate and Industrial Development: Harold O Brandt

Finance Department
Executive Vice President, Financial: Karl R Ziebarth
Vice President, Accounting: William L Dorcy
Assistant Vice President, Comptroller: H Rudy Williams
   Systems: Dennis L Bailey
Treasurer: Richard E McCormick
Corporate Secretary: Jordan T Bass

Operating Department
Vice President, Operation: Thomas G Todd
General Manager: M L Janovec
Assistant Vice President, Mechanical: Martin F Rister
   Maintenance of Way and Structures: P E Jacquinot
General Superintendent Transportation: O Chris Putsche
Superintendent Transportation: Donald D Doyle
Chief Engineer: Richard N Wagnon

Piggyback and Highway Services
(Coordinated and Katy Transportation Companies)
Assistant Vice President and General Manager: G Brian Bleakney

Traffic Department
Vice President, Traffic: Harry T Dimmerman
Assistant Vice President, Traffic: George J Elking
   Traffic: Jerry M Sheridan
Manager TOFC Sales: J Eddie Warren

Marketing Department
Vice President, Marketing: Thomas F Steiniger

Gauge: 1435 mm
Length: 4489 km

Lines and territory

The Missouri-Kansas-Texas Railroad, familiarly known as the 'Katy', operates from Kansas City and St Louis in the north, to Oklahoma City, Tulsa and Altus in western Oklahoma, and south through Dallas and Fort Worth to San Antonio and Galveston in Texas.

Principal traffic is in the movement south to port of wheat, lumber, steel products, coal, crushed stone, automobiles and trucks.

Historically, the M-K-T's greatest weakness has been its heavy dependence on its northern connections for merchandise and grain traffic moving to shippers at competitive on-line points. Such traffic is inherently subject to diversion, and consequently M-K-T was seriously affected by the Burlington Northern/Frisco merger in 1980 and the Union Pacific/Missouri Pacific consolidation in 1982. However, as a condition of approval of the UP/MP transaction, the ICC granted M-K-T trackage rights from Kansas City north to Atchison, Lincoln, Omaha, and Council Bluffs, and west to Topeka to offset some of the anti-competitive effects of the consolidation. Permanent agreements governing the costs and terms of these trackage rights have been entered into with the Union Pacific, and as a consequence the M-K-T withdrew certain defensive legal actions. The market access which these trackage rights provide was expected to partially offset the certain losses as a result of the Union Pacific diverting carloads previously moved over the M-K-T to its new subsidiary, the Missouri Pacific.

Of equal importance, the M-K-T and its wholly-owned subsidiary, the Oklahoma, Kansas & Texas Railroad (OKT), were able to enter into satisfactory agreements for the acquisition of some 650 miles of line previously owned by the estate of the bankrupt Rock Island for $55 million. Financing was provided by Federal and state government sources. OKT was established in mid-1980 to operate the Rock Island trackage temporarily. These operations were ended at the close of 1981, then resumed on a permanent basis after the purchase in November 1982. This acquisition provided the M-K-T with access to

Northbound M-K-T train (headed by units leased from Conrail) passes under a Southern Pacific overpass at Houston, Texas
(Bruce Blalock)

Finance

Finance	1979	1980	1981	1982
		($000)		
Operating revenues	168 791	240 167	307 665	231 047
Expenses				
Operating	125 159	168 304	216 092	161 898
Depreciation and amortisation	10 763	10 890	10 979	10 674
Railway taxes	12 196	15 029	19 234	15 304
Equipment and joint facility rentals, net of related rental income	14 635	35 951	49 937	29 732
Total expenses	162 753	230 174	296 242	217 608
Operating income	6038	9993	16 847	13 439
Other expenses, net	7411	7926	2793	
Income before income taxes	(1373)	8630	2067	4600

Traffic (including OKT)

	1980	1981	1982
Average miles of road operated*	2982	2963	2790
Freight train-miles (000)	3 390 639	3 827 575	2 872 767
Gross ton-miles (000)	16 127 297	17 318 058	12 733 742
Revenue ton-miles (000)	8 581 495	9 436 705	6 803 272
Freight revenue ($ million)	225·408	290·124	218·510
Average revenue per ton-mile (cents)	2·62	3·07	3·21
Source of revenue (%)			
Freight	94·2	93·5	94·2
Other services (no passenger/mail service)	5·8	6·5	5·8

*Includes mileage operated at year's end by OKT: 1980, 815 miles; 1981, 788 miles; 1982, 650 miles.

originating grain, stone, and petroleum coke traffic and has already begun to make a contribution to M-K-T's traffic base.

Traffic for the first four months of 1983 was modestly above the same period of 1982, reflecting both losses as a result of mergers and gains from the northern extensions and the OKT, as well as the slow upturn in the national economy. However, revenue per car was lagging sharply behind the comparable period of 1982.

M-K-T's thin financial resources were strained to their utmost in 1982 by the need to close out heavy capital expenditure commitments made in prior years and to repay substantial sums borrowed for equipment acquisition and track rehabilitation over the previous decade. Capital expenditures were $52·2 million in 1982, considerably above the $33·8 million of 1981, including $40 million of the purchase price of the OKT booked as a capital item. Consequently, working capital and cash were reduced over the year. This was exacerbated by the strike of one of the operating unions in September, which seriously disrupted cash flow and reduced receivables.

Traffic

Freight volume on the M-K-T alone for 1982 was 297 267 carloads, a 15·8 per cent decrease compared to the 347 414 cars handled in 1981. This percentage was in line with the industry aggregate of 14·2 per cent. The decline was mainly due to the shutdown of the M-K-T's subsidiary, OKT, in December 1981, but other factors contributing were the continuing recession and the impact of the BN/Frisco merger, as well as the consummation of the UP/MP consolidation in November. Revenue net

ton-miles in 1982 were 6·693 million, a decrease of 20·3 per cent from 1981.

The lack of export movements of grain, along with the mergers and the shutdown of the OKT, resulted in M-K-T showing a 41 per cent decrease in grain carloadings compared with 1981. Most other commodities were down in comparison to 1981, particularly those items related to the steel, drilling and construction industries.

With the national reduction in all shipments, a surplus of transport equipment was created in all modes. These factors led to wholesale reduction in transport rates. M-K-T's freight revenue (excluding the OKT) in 1982 decreased some 14·2 per cent from 1981's record, and revenue per car rose only $14·50 over 1981, a mere 2 per cent increase.

Even though the coal market demand fell off substantially during 1982, M-K-T coal loadings for the year 1982 were down by only 5 per cent, compared with the record set in 1981, and reflected a 47 per cent increase over 1980 coal loading.

Chemical traffic was up 5 per cent, which compared quite favourably to the decline of 18 per cent experienced by all western railroads. The increase was mainly attributable to increases in piggyback (TOFC) handling of cleaning compounds as well as contract activity in connection with traffic moving from one to the Gulf Coast area.

Crushed stone decreased by 19 per cent below the 1981 figures, primarily due to a sharp decline in construction starts on homes, shopping malls, parking lots and road work. M-K-T signed numerous contracts on crushed stone which were expected to improve volume for 1983, as should the substantial increase in highway construction and repair. The same factors also caused a decline in M-K-T lumber traffic of 12 per cent, compared with a decline for all western railroads of 25 per cent.

One bright spot in 1982 was TOFC traffic, which increased by 38 per cent in volume and 39 per cent in revenue, or by $5·5 million. The US rail industry as a whole showed only a 10 per cent increase. This increase was caused by customers reducing inventories and switching from box car to TOFC and truck. A large part of the increase reflected traffic tendered by consolidators. Another favourable comparison was shown in automobile traffic, where a small gain was shown. Improvements were planned for M-K-T's ramps at St Louis, Kansas City, and Dallas, which should ensure continued growth in TOFC traffic, in spite of the severe competition created by the various mergers and changes in Federal regulations permitting heavier, wider, and longer trucks to be used nation-wide.

Operations and maintenance
In contrast to 1981, when the M-K-T faced the challenge and opportunity of handling the heaviest volume in its history, the year 1982 began and continued in a declining economy with declining traffic. Such an environment presented a very different challenge: continuing competitive service while reducing expenses to offset declining revenues. Train miles were decreased 15 per cent and yard engine hours 21 per cent compared to 1981. The average daily employment for the year was reduced by 15 per cent compared to 1981, with reduction of 22 per cent in the latter part of the year.

Materials and supply costs, including fuel, stabilised to some extent in 1982, with fuel costs actually declining in late 1982. Wage rates and supplements, however, were approximately 12 per cent above the 1981 cost. The overall result, though transport expenses decreased 11 per cent, was an increase in the ratio of transport costs to revenue from 36·6 per cent to 38 per cent on the pre-1978 basis of railroad accounting, due mostly to declining revenue.

Track
During 1982, 254 837 sleepers were inserted; 3908 cars of ballast were applied; 1426 miles of track were surfaced and smoothed; and 15·9 miles of new welded rail and 35·6 miles of relay welded rail were placed in service. These physical units were, however, below the record 1981 pace, so that the track maintenance ratio fell from 19 to 14.9 per cent of revenue.

Internally generated funds were used to perform major rehabilitation projects covering 21·3 miles between Dallas and Waxahachie, Texas, and 14·1 miles between Burg and Navy, Oklahoma. In addition to these projects, 20 miles of secondhand 112 lb rail was purchased, welded and installed between Walker, Missouri and the Missouri-Kansas state line, funded in part by an FRA grant administered by the State of Missouri.

In addition, two major projects were completed: a new permanent rail welding plant in Denison, Texas, and a new weigh-in-motion track scale in Parsons, Kansas.

During 1983, the M-K-T planned to continue the long-term sleeper and ballast programme on its main line, as well as upgrading of certain track sections by installation of both new and relayer welded rail. Continued upgrading of the Sedalia Subdivision in conjunction with the State of Missouri was

M-K-T services at Wichita Falls, Texas *(Dr Theron Baber)*

Diesel-electric locomotives

Builder	Class	No of units	hp
EMD	Freight F-3	1	1750
EMD	Road switch GP-40	60	3000
EMD	Road switch GP-38	4	2000
EMD	Road switch SD40-2	37	3000
EMD	Road switch GP-38-2	18	2000
EMD	Road switch GP-7	33	1500
EMD	Switch SW-9, SW-1000 and SW-1200	18	1200
EMD	Switch SW-1500	6	1500
EMD	Switch (Slug)	1	—
GE	Road switch U23B	11	2250
Baldwin	Switch (repowered)	6	1500
Alco	Road switch RS-3	6	1500
EMD	Switch MP-15AC	4	1500
EMD	Slug (Road)	1	—

also scheduled. Rehabilitation of the OKT main line would begin in 1983.

Capital expenditure
The largest single outlay in 1982 on the M-K-T's own books was $15 million for the permanent rail freight easement between Dallas and Fort Worth, purchased from the Rock Island estate. Heavier rail and associated improvements cost $6·2 million, and additions to the computer system cost $1·6 million. The largest equipment item was the purchase of locomotives previously leased, and new capitalised leases covering other units, totalling $2·5 million. Retirements largely reflect the expiration of capitalised leases; these expired and were not renewed on 1521 cars, including 532 box cars, during 1982.

Electrification
At the end of 1981 the company's investigation of electrification feasibility over its 521 km main line

from Fort Worth to Houston was taken to the stage of appointing a prime engineering consultant, Electrack, a subsidiary of the British company, BICC. Electrack's preliminary engineering study was finished in 1982. Early calculations were that the electrification fixed works would cost less than $100 million, but that other expenditure would total some $200 million, mostly for installation of immunised CTC and telecommunications. Some 20 to 24 electric locomotives would be required.

Signalling
At the start of 1983 46 route-miles of the system were controlled by CTC and 713 route-miles by automatic block. An additional 16·5 miles of CTC was installed during 1982.

Locomotives and rolling stock
At the start of 1983 M-K-T operated 163 line-haul and 40 switching diesel-electric locomotives and 5464 freight cars.

Missouri Pacific Railroad

210 N 13th St, St Louis, Missouri 63103

Telephone: (314) 622 2232
Telex: 44 7105

Executive Department (St Louis)
Chairman: J C Kenefick
President: R G Flannery
Executive Vice-President, Law and Finance: C B Schaefer
  Marketing and Sales: W P Barrett
Senior Vice-President, Law: M M Hennelly
  Marketing and Sales: G A Craig
  Operations: R K Davidson
Vice-President, Executive Department: J E Angst
  Operations: K D Hestes
  Transportation: C E Dettmann
  Administration: D L Manion
  Information and Control Systems: G S Sines
  Staff: J G German

Gauge: 1435 mm
Length: 18 197 km

EMD 3500 hp GP-50 locomotives, used initially in pairs on Chicago-Houston and Chicago-Fort Worth TOFC trains

Missouri Pacific (MoPac) is among the largest United States corporations, with revenues approaching $2000 million annually, and serves 12 mid-western, south-western and southern states. The states served include about one-third of the land area of the continental United States and roughly one-fifth of its population. The rail lines extend west from the Mississippi River to the foothills of the Rockies; south and south-west from Chicago, St Louis and Omaha to the Gulf of Mexico and the US-Mexico border.

MoPac connects with virtually all US railroads at such points as: Chicago; St Louis; Kansas City; Pueblo, Colorado; Memphis, New Orleans and the Texas cities of Sweetwater and El Paso. Sometimes called the 'North American Rail Link', Missouri Pacific connects directly with the railroads of Mexico at Laredo, El Paso and Brownsville, Texas and feeds traffic to Canada through its rail connections at Kansas City and Chicago. It serves 12 Gulf Coast ports extending from New Orleans to Brownsville.

MoPac is divided into four operating districts: Western, with headquarters at Kansas City; Eastern, with headquarters at North Little Rock; Texas, with headquarters in Dallas; Southern, with headquarters at Houston.

In December 1982 the Missouri Pacific Railroad became a sister line of the Union Pacific Railroad following the merger of Missouri Pacific Corporation into the Union Pacific Corporation. Missouri Pacific retains its separate identity and its headquarters at St Louis. Missouri Pacific and Union Pacific now offer single-line service to shippers in 4500 communities in 21 states.

Traffic

The railroad is the USA's largest carrier of chemical products. Other principal commodity markets are grain products, autos and parts, coal, metals, foods,

Missouri Pacific tri-level auto-rack train

Upgrading of newly-purchased Conrail trackage

Dallas-bound TOFC train on the Mississippi River, south of St Louis

MoPac unit coal train operation

aggregates, paper and petroleum products. In 1982 coal carryings rose 18 per cent to a gross of 37·4 million tons.

MoPac operates three major automated and computer-controlled classification yards, at Fort Worth, Kansas City and North Little Rock. A fourth automated yard at East St Louis, Illinois, on the Alton & Southern Railway, is operated jointly with the St Louis-Southwestern.

Freight car operations are scheduled and monitored through a computerised all-line system known as transportation control system (TCS). The central computers are located in St Louis and are linked to some 350 terminals. The latter include some 60 customer service centres at key locations.

Service between Chicago and St Louis was upgraded in 1982 with the purchase from Conrail of 70·6 miles of route, which was modernised with the installation of 75 000 sleepers and welded rail.

	1980	1981
Revenue tons (million)	127·6	119
Revenue tonne-km (million)	92 764	90 691
Average net train load (tons)	3967·7	4062·7
Average wagon load (tons)	56·7	57·7

Finance ($ 000)	1980	1981
Revenues	1 755 671	1 979 928
Expenditure	1 632 283	1 831 605

Preliminary figures for 1982 showed a net income for that year of $149 million.

Investment

MoPac planned in 1983 to install a further 137 miles of CTC and 550 miles of microwave communications. Intermodal terminals at Dallas, Memphis and St Louis would be enlarged and 106 miles of cwr laid. A new intermodal terminal serving the Dallas area was opened at Mesquite, Texas, in 1982.

By 1983, a microwave network was to extend from St Louis to Kansas City and from Kansas City to Fort Worth, Houston, and New Orleans.

A major item of 1982 was an outlay of $40 million on a new locomotive heavy repair shop at North Little Rock, one of the first steps in a planned $118 million 1982-86 programme of capital improvements to the railroad's traction and car repair, maintenance and servicing facilities. The North Little Rock facility will have locomotive remanufacturing capability. Completion was scheduled for November 1983.

Locomotives and rolling stock
Number of diesel-electric locomotives in service 1983: 1602
Number of freight wagons 1983: 49 240

Track
Rail: Steel, 68 kg/m
Cross ties (sleepers): Wooden, thickness 178 mm
Spacing: Main line 2017/km
Fastenings: Spike
Max curvature radius: 20°
Max gradient: 2·9%
Max axleload: 35·2 tonnes

Motive power under order or delivered 1980-82/83

Year	Model	Wheel arrangement	Supplier	Power (hp)	Max speed (mph)	No of units
1980	GP38-2	B-B	EMD-GMC	2000	65	132
	SD40-2	C-C	EMD-GMC	3000	65	30
	GP50	B-B	EMD-GMC	3500	65	10
	B23-7	B-B	GE	2250	65	20
	SL-1	B-B	MoPac	None	55	9
					Total	201
1981	GP15-1	B-B	EMD-GMC	1500	65	20
	GP38-2	B-B	EMD-GMC	2000	65	45
	GP50	B-B	EMD-GMC	3500	65	20
	B23-7	B-B	GE	2250	65	15
	B30-7A	B-B	GE	3000	65	30
	SL-1	B-B	MoPac	None	55	9
					Total	139
1982	MP15DC	B-B	EMD-GMC	1500	65	37
	GP15-1	B-B	EMD-GMC	1500	65	80
	B30-7A	B-B	GE	3000	70	25
	SL-1	B-B	MoPac	None	55	1
					Total	143

No locomotives on order for 1983.

Freight rolling stock under order or delivered 1980-82/83

Year	No of units	Description	Builder
1980	1000	100 ton, 4600 ft³ covered hopper	ACF
	500	100 ton, 3700 ft³ open hopper	Bethlehem Steel
	200	100 ton, 7000 ft³ wood chip open hopper	Greenville
	47	100 ton, 60 ft box car	Pacific Car
	150	Cabooses	MoPac RR
	120	Bi-level auto racks	Whitehead & Kales
	13	Bi-level auto racks	Whitehead & Kales
	309	100 ton, 65 ft gondola	Greenville
	6	100 ton, 52 ft gondola	Evans
	32	100 ton, 60 ft box car	ACF
1981	300	100 ton, 3700 ft³ open hopper	Union Pacific
	100	100 ton, 52 ft coil steel cars	Thrall
	500	100 ton, 52 ft gondola	Greenville
	500	100 ton, 2980 ft³ covered hopper	ACF
	50	100 ton, 50 yd³ air dump cars	Difco
	184	100 ton, 4750 ft³ covered hopper	North American and Thrall
	180	Tri-level auto racks	Paragon
	180	Tri-level auto racks	Portec
	123	Bi-level auto racks	Whitehead & Kales
	98	Tri-level auto racks	Whitehead & Kales
	86	Cabooses	MoPac RR
1982	150	100 ton 62 ft insulated box cars	Pacific Car
	50	100 ton 4566 ft³ airslide covered hopper	General American
	13	Cabooses	MoPac RR
	50	100 ton, 50 yd³ air dump cars	Difco
	139	Tri-level auto racks	Portec
	400	70 ton, 50 ft box cars	Pullman Standard

No freight rolling stock on order for 1983.

MoPac transportation control system (TCS) terminal

MoPac is the largest US rail haulier of petrochemical products, in terms both of carloadings and revenue

Diesel locomotives

Class	Wheel arrangement	Transmission	Rated power (kW)	Max speed kmlh	Total weight tonnes*	No in service	Year first built	Builders		
								Mechanical parts	Engine & type	Transmission
Switch										
SL-1	B-B	Elec	(Slug)	88·5	117	23	1978	EMD	—	EMD
SW-9	B-B	Elec	895·2	88·5	112	29	1951	EMD	EMD 12-567	EMD
SW-12	B-B	Elec	895·2	88·5	112	139	1954	EMD	EMD 12-567	EMD
SW-15	B-B	Elec	1119	88·5	121	4	1972	EMD	EMD 12-645	EMD
MP-15	B-B	Elec	1119	104·6	121	62	1974	EMD	EMD 12-645	EMD
Road switch										
GP-15-1	B-B	Elec	1119	104·6	119	190	1976	EMD	EMD 12-645	EMD
GP-18	B-B	Elec	1342·8	104·6	115	117	1960	EMD	EMD 16-567	EMD
GP-28	B-B	Elec	1492	104·6	119	2	1964	EMD	EMD 16-645	EMD
GP-35M	B-B	Elec	1492	104·6	117	18	1964	EMD	EMD 16-645	EMD
GP-38	B-B	Elec	1492	104·6	120	6	1966	EMD	EMD 16-645	EMD
GP-38-2	B-B	Elec	1492	104·6	121	326	1972	EMD	EMD 16-645	EMD
U23-B	B-B	Elec	1678·5	104·6	122	38	1973	GE	GE FDL-12	GE
B23-7	B-B	Elec	1678·5	104·6	121	85	1978	GE	GE FDL-12	GE
GP-35	B-B	Elec	1865	104·6	117	47	1964	EMD	EMD 16-567	EMD
B30-7A	B-B	Elec	2238	112·7	117	55	1981	GE	GE FDL-12	GE
GP-50	B-B	Elec	2611	104·6	124	30	1980	EMD	EMD 16-645	EMD
SD-40	C-C	Elec	2238	104·6	177	90	1967	EMD	EMD 16-645	EMD
SD-40-2	C-C	Elec	2238	104·6	178	232	1973	EMD	EMD 16-645	EMD
SD-40-2C	C-C	Elec	2238	104·6	189	74	1976	EMD	EMD 16-645	EMD
U30-C	C-C	Elec	2238	104·6	179	35	1968	GE	GE FDL-16	GE

* 2204·6 lb/tonne

Norfolk Southern Corporation

PO Box 3609, One Commercial Plaza, Norfolk, Virginia 23510

Telephone: (804) 629 2600

Chairman and Chief Executive: Robert B Claytor
President and Chief Operating Officer: Harold H Hall
Executive Vice-President, Administration: J L Jones
   Marketing: Arnold B McKinnon
   Law: John S Shannon
   Finance: John R Turbyfill
Vice-President, Coal and Ore: William B Bales
   Public Affairs: Edward T Breathitt
   Material Management: R Alan Brogan
   Industrial Development: Robert S Geer
   Sales: Samuel D Guy
   Accounting: Jean Jones
   Management Information Services: John L Jones
   Treasurer: Thomas H Kerwin
   Taxation: Daniel L Kiley
   Marketing Services: Edward G Kreyling
   Pricing: John R McMichael
   Public Relations: W F Geeslin
   Corporate Development: D Henry Watts
   Personnel: Joseph R Neikirk

In March 1982 the ICC approved formation of the Norfolk Southern Corporation (NS). NS is a holding company with headquarters at Norfolk, Virginia, established to co-ordinate the merger of Norfolk & Western and Southern Railways, which was largely motivated by the 1980 creation of CSX (qv). As in CSX, both railroad members of NS continue to maintain their headquarters, Norfolk & Western in Roanoke, Virginia and Southern in Washington, and operate autonomously.

However, several terminal operations have already been consolidated and a number of new through routes and through locomotive and crew workings created for an estimated saving of $20 million a year in operating costs. After the merger became operational in June 1982, an $18·5 million expenditure was launched to upgrade 66 miles between Muncie and Fort Wayne, Indiana for 60 mph operation and to open up through working between Chicago and the mid-south via Cincinnati, was completed. This development was backed by a new $8·6 million intermodal terminal at Landers Yard, Chicago, which NW put in hand in 1982. Also to be rationalised were manufacturing and repair facilities.

Unit coal train in West Virginia

The merger is an end-to-end consolidation, unifying the NW, which stretches from Norfolk, Virginia, west to Kansas City, Missouri, and north into the key markets of Chicago, Detroit and Cleveland, with the Southern, which blankets the south-east, from New Orleans, Louisiana, Mobile, Alabama, and Palatka, Florida, north to Cincinnati, Ohio, and Washington DC; and from East St Louis, Illinois, and Memphis, Tennessee, eastward to the Atlantic ports of Norfolk, Virginia, Morehead City, North Carolina, Charleston, South Carolina, Savannah and Brunswick, Georgia, and Jacksonville, Florida. The railroads connect at 17 common points, with major connections at East St Louis; Cincinnati; Bristol, Altavista, Danville, Lynchburg, Norfolk and Norton, all in Virginia; and Winston-Salem and Durham, North Carolina.

A principal benefit is the establishment of five new major routes: the Altavista Gateway route, the Lynchburg-Knoxville Cutoff route, the Mid-South Corridor route, the Kansas City Gateway route and the Shenandoah Corridor route. Single-system service from Southern Railway points in the south-east is now offered by shorter, more efficient routes to the north via the Hagerstown, Maryland, gateway, to the Midwest via the Altavista, Bristol, Lynchburg and Cincinnati gateways, and to the west via the St Louis and Kansas City gateways. NW points in the Midwest such as Chicago, Detroit and Cleveland similarly obtain single-system service to Southern Railway points in the south such as Atlanta, Birmingham, New Orleans and Memphis.

Though NS ranks fifth among Class I railroads in trackage, number of locomotives and employees, and in operating revenue, and fourth in annual revenue ton-mileage, it is the most profitable, generating over a third of the total net income of all Class I railroads. In 1982 its profit was $411 million.

It was announced early in 1983 that Norfolk Southern's purchases of Santa Fe Industries stock had reached 5 per cent of the total issued. This prompted speculation that association to form a transcontinental route might be in mind. Such an affiliation had in fact been discussed by the two companies' chairmen in mid-1982, but NS stated that its stock acquisitions were merely considered advisable investment.

Traffic

Coal, which generates 51 per cent of NW revenues and 19 per cent of Southern's, was down 2 per cent on 1981 carryings to 126·3 million tons in 1982. A further recession was expected in 1983.

Investment

NS was planning capital expenditures of $180·1 million in 1983. Of this total $146·9 million was allocated to infrastructure improvements, including installation of 400 miles of cwr. A new connection would be installed between NW and Southern systems at Hurt, Virginia. No new locomotive purchases were included and few freight cars.

Norfolk and Western Railway Company

8 North Jefferson Street, Roanoke, Virginia 24042

Telephone: (703) 981 4000

President: Richard F Dunlap
Vice-President, Operations: H L Scott Jr
Vice-President and Comptroller: T C Hostutter
General Manager, Transportation: Leon Atkinson, Jr
  Motive Power and Equipment: R R McDaniel
Chief Engineer: G R Janosko
Assistant Chief Engineer, Signals and Communications: C A Hoeser

Gauge: 1435 mm
Length: 12 824 km

The Norfolk and Western operates from Norfolk, Virginia and Buffalo, New York, in the east, through 14 states and one province of Canada, to St Louis, Kansas City and Omaha, Nebraska, in the west. It serves the rich coal fields of West Virginia, southern Ohio and eastern Kentucky, as well as the industrial centres of Cleveland, Pittsburgh, Chicago, Detroit, Columbus and Cincinnati. Non-railroading subsidiaries include mining, docks and hotels. The railroad generates 99 per cent of the company's revenue.

Three of NW's major non-railroad subsidiaries, Pocahontas Land Corporation, Pocahontas Kentucky Corporation, and Pocahontas Development Corporation, engage in the acquisition and subsequent leasing of coal, oil, gas and timberlands in four states. Other non-railroad subsidiaries engage in land resource transactions, operation of a hotel and leasing or other disposition of rail property and equipment. During 1981 NW completed the previously announced acquisition of the operating assets of Illinois Terminal Railroad, a small carrier operating in the St Louis area and in southern Illinois. The ITRR's operations have been integrated into NW's system.

Traffic

The company created a coal traffic record during 1981, when it originated 23·8 million tons in the third period, the best quarter in NW history. The railroad also posted the best single month's loadings, 9 million tons in October. Coal handled at the Norfolk transloading facilities also set records, with 10·2 million tons in the fourth quarter, and 3·7 million tons in October. 23 December was the busiest single day in the history of NW's coal piers, when 159 808 tons were transloaded.

Under freedom granted in the Staggers Rail Act of 1980, NW in 1981 began negotiating transport contracts covering export coal shipments, and now more than half of its export shipments are covered by such agreements. These contracts closely coordinate shipments of coal with vessel arrivals.

Motive power and rolling stock

At the end of 1982 NW owned 1206 line-haul and 111 switcher diesel locomotives, 85 895 freight cars, and 23 passenger cars.

Traffic	1979	1980	1981
Total freight train-miles (million)	17·7	16·0	14·9
Total net tonnage (million)	146·8	141·6	142·5
Total ton-mileage (million)	48 440	48 698	49 191
Average haul (miles)	335·04	342	341·8
Average net train load (tons)	2778·81	3027·6	3275·8

	1979	1980	1981
		($ million)	
Railway operating revenues			
Coal, coke and iron ore	663·730	805·635	961·104
Merchandise	714·386	698·840	758·155
Total freight	1378·116	1504·475	1719·259
Passenger	1·160	1·123	1·227
All other transportation	30·047	25·045	30·633
Incidental and joint facility	21·571	28·891	34·788
Total	1430·894	1559·534	1785·907
Railway operating expenses			
Way and structures	212·365	245·073	291·967
Equipment	261·433	284·902	292·266
Transportation	545·503	570·396	629·024
General and administrative	104·223	114·542	128·668
Total	1123·524	1214·913	1341·925
Net revenue	307·370	344·621	443·982

Fully-enclosed tri-level rack cars provide protection for automobiles

General Electric Type C36-7 locomotive

Southern Railway Company

PO Box 1808, 920 15th Street NW, Washington DC 20013

Telephone: (202) 383 4000

President: E B Burwell
Vice-Presidents
 Transportation: P R Rudder
 Engineering: W W Simpson
General Manager, Intermodal Transport Services: R A Wharton
 Transportation: A L Adams

Gauge: 1435 mm
Length: 16 412 km

The Southern Railway System, comprising the Southern Railway and its subsidiaries, operates in 13 states east of the Mississippi River, principally south of the Potomac and Ohio Rivers. The numerous subsidiaries include the Alabama Great Southern; Cincinnati, New Orleans and Texas Pacific; and Central of Georgia Railroads. A new acquisition in January 1982 was the Kentucky & Indiana Terminal Railroad.

Norfolk Southern Corporation
In March 1982 the Interstate Commerce Commission approved the merger of Norfolk & Western and Southern under the aegis of a non-railroad holding company, Norfolk Southern Corporation, or NS (qv). The merger became operational in June 1982. Each railroad retained its own headquarters and a considerable measure of autonomy, but some route rationalisation was undertaken, also immediate unification of sales forces.

Locomotives and cars
Total Southern System locomotive fleet at the start of 1982 consisted of 1499 diesel-electric locomotives (including equipment under capital leases). Freight cars owned totalled 75 359; leased 1303.

Locomotives in service

Type	Number
SW1	5
SW7	33
SW8	1
SW9	10
NW2	32
TR2	5
SW1500	47
MP15DC	46
FP7	4
Booster	25
GP7	58
GP9	20
GP18	24
GP30	113
GP35	72
GP38	114
GP38AC	56
GP38-2	257
GP39-X	6
GP40-X	3
GP50	90
SD7	1
SD9	2
SD35	107
SD40	29
SD40-2	127
SD45	68
U23B	69
B23-7	54
B36-7	6
U30C	5
U33C	10
Total	1499

Computer-aided traffic control
Following completion in 1980 of its computerised freight data processing system, TIPS, which links 246 terminals and mini-computers in yards and depots throughout the system to a central computer at Atlanta, Southern is proceeding with extension of its computer-assisted train dispatching system. The first installation of the latter, in 1980, was at the north end of the Alabama Division between Birmingham and Sheffield, a coal train route with a normal daily throughput of 30 to 40 trains. In 1981 the system was being applied to the Birmingham-Atlanta and Cincinnati-Chattanooga lines; completion of the former, expected in 1983 at a cost of $24 million, would have CTC operative throughout the 950 miles from Washington to Birmingham.

In Southern's computer-aided dispatching system, the operator's station includes four colour

Traffic	1978	1979	1980	1981
Revenue freight (million tons)	149·7	160·8	160·9	152·4
Revenue ton-miles (million)	51 283	54 622	54 554	53 157

	1980	1981
		($ million)
Railway operating revenues		
Freight	1597·451	1751·074
Demurrage	21·607	20·907
Other	18·654	18·688
	1637·712	1790·669
Interest income	30·665	48·356
Gain on sale of property	11·597	10·063
Other income	15·950	25·069
Total income	1695·924	1874·157
Railway operating expenses		
Way and structures		
Rent for lease of road	5·091	5·329
Other way and structure expense	276·941	276·674
Total	282·032	282·003
Equipment		
Time/mileage equipment rent	(6·566)	(14·050)
Other equipment rent	56·913	73·750
Other equipment expense	244·458	274·139
Total	294·805	333·839
Transportation	616·407	670·095
General and administrative		
State and local taxes (operating)	34·973	39·074
Other general and administrative	117·310	126·189
Total	152·283	165·263
Total operating expenses	1345·527	1451·200
Miscellaneous deductions	11·695	8·852
Interest expense	74·821	83·229
Total expenses	1432·043	1543·281
Income before income taxes	263·881	330·876

Computer-aided dispatcher's position

Southern freight in northern Alabama

cathode ray tubes, radio communications equipment, a command keyboard, and a data input keyboard. Two mini-computers operate the system and two printers create permanent records. Two of the CRT displays show track layout and train locations, including train numbers and directions, and how all switches are lined. One colour scope is used to display the dispatcher's train sheet; this can be updated regularly by entering new information on the data keyboard.

The fourth colour tube displays the projected meeting and passing of trains on the controlled line over the next several hours. This is called the 'meet-pass plan' and is constantly being updated as new information becomes available. Taking into account train length, track conditions, priorities and a number of other factors, the computer sets a pattern of train movement. The dispatcher can accept it, or enter changes and have the plan re-computed. The system also lays the groundwork for some other improvements, including automatic payroll records and a better grasp of locomotive and car availability.

Pittsburgh & Lake Erie Railroad Co

Commerce Court, 4 Station Square, Pittsburgh, Pennsylvania 15219

Telephone: (412) 261 3201

Chairman: E H Neese
President and Chief Executive Officer: R E Thompson
Executive Vice-President: G E Neuenschwander
Vice President, Finance and Treasurer: H P Nesbitt
Executive Vice-President, Development: B B Smyth
General Manager, Operations and Planning: C R Holley
Chief Mechanical Officer: H C Christie
Chief Engineer: R F Butter
Superintendent, Signals and Communications: R E Ross
Director, Purchases and Materials: T M Durko

Gauge: 1435 mm
Length: 459·6 km

The P&LE was part of the New York Central from 1889. NYC, originally a 50 per cent owner, acquired more stock after 1965, so that its successor, Penn Central, eventually owned over 90 per cent of the company. When Penn Central collapsed, P&LE fought for and secured an amendment to the Rail Reorganisation Act of 1973 that precluded the inclusion of solvent railroads in Conrail, which preserved P&LE's autonomy. In February 1979, with the aid of external finance, the sale of P&LE from Penn Central to a new Pittsburgh & Lake Erie Company based in Pittsburgh was achieved.

P&LE is heavily dependent on the steel industry, the raw materials and products of which account for three-quarters of its annual loadings. Its other principal traffic is steam coal. In sum, it moves more than 20 million tons of freight a year. More than half its stock of freight cars has been bought new or refurbished since 1970.

P&LE, with CSX and Conrail, shares equally the ownership of the 146-mile (235 km) Monongahela Railway. Other subsidiaries are the Montour, Youngstown & Southern and Pittsburgh, Chartiers & Youghiogheny Railroads.

Traffic	1980/81	1981/82
Total freight tonnage (million)	19·537	12·5
Total freight tonne-miles (million)	2263	1677
Average net freight train load (tons)	NA	5083
Total passenger-miles (million)	2·214	2·072
Total passenger journeys	99 438	93 000
Average length of passenger journey (miles)	22	22

Finance ($ million)	1981	1982
Revenues	82·641	47·276
Expenditure	72·647	60·553

Track
Rail: 65·48 kg/m
Cross ties (sleepers): Wooden, thickness 7 in
Spacing: 2019/km
Fastenings: Splice bars
Minimum curvature radius: 0° 20'
Max gradient: 1·19%

Locomotives and rolling stock
P&LE operates 33 line-haul and 65 switching diesel locomotives and 16 907 freight cars.

Diesel locomotives

Class	Wheel arrangement	Transmission	Rated power (hp)	Max speed km/h	Total weight tonnes	No in service	Year first built	Builders Mechanical parts	Builders Engine & type	Builders Transmission
U28-B	B-B	Elec	2800	112	136·5	21	1966	GE	GE-7FDL16	GE
GP38-2	B-B	Elec	2000	105	137·75	6	1977	EMD	EMD 645-E	EMD
GP38-2	B-B	Elec	2000	105	130	4	1977	EMD	EMD 645-E	EMD
GP-7	B-B	Elec	1500	88	123·4	2	1953	EMD	EMD 16-567 B	EMD
SW 1500	B-B	Elec	1500	105	128·7	40	1971	EMD	EMD 645-E	EMD
MP-15	B-B	Elec	1500	105	128·7	25	1975	EMD	EMD 645-E	EMD

Seaboard System Railroad

500 Water Street, Jacksonville, Florida 32202

President and Chief Executive Officer: Richard D Sanborn
Executive Vice-President, Operations: R D Spence
Executive Vice-President, Sales and Marketing: Welborn E Alexander Jr
Executive Vice-President, Law, Public Affairs: Philip M Lanier
Senior Vice-President and Chief Financial Officer: Alexander J Mandl
Vice-President, Management Information Services: Jack M Cooper
  Sales: James D Bozard
  Marketing: James W Hoeland
  Transportation: K C Dufford
  Engineering and Maintenance: A C Jones Jr
  Purchases: C R Millichip
  Industrial Development: J R LeGrand
  Phosphates and Chemicals: A M Daniel
  Coal: J E Nall

Gauge: 1435 mm
Length: 24 809 km

The Family Lines System was formed in 1968 through the merger of the Seaboard Air Line Railroad and the Atlantic Coast Line Railroad. SCL owned the Louisville and Nashville Railroad (into which the Monon was merged in July 1971), and leased, equally with L & N, the Clinchfield and Georgia Railroads. Combination of the SCL and L & N, with their subsidiary rail carriers, created a system of some 16 000 miles (25 750 km), serving 13 states. L & N continued to operate as a separate company.

Seaboard System's new logo

In November 1980 Family Lines merged with Chessie System Railroads to form a 27 000 route-mile (43 452 km) railroad in 22 states and a Canadian province under a holding company, CSX Corporation, based in Richmond, Virginia, which also has a controlling interest in the Richmond, Fredericksburg & Potomac Railroad. From the start of 1983 Family Lines was reconstituted as the Seaboard System Railroad. Also merged in the Seaboard System were Family Lines members the Georgia, Atlanta & West Point, Western Railway of Alabama and Clinchfield systems. The Clinchfield therefore disappeared from the individual Class I railroad list.

Seaboard System constitutes the major railway system in Florida and the coastal states to the north of Florida, ie Georgia, South and North Carolina, as well as Virginia, Alabama, Tennessee, Kentucky, Indiana and Illinois (Chicago).

Investment

Plans for 1983 included construction of two new intermodal terminals: a second facility in the Atlanta area, the system's main source of TOFC traffic, and one in Chicago near the Belt Railway's Clearing Yard, the latter at an estimated cost of $10.9 million.

Also envisaged was a $13.5 million locomotive-servicing facility, capable of dealing with 600 units a month, at Waycross, Georgia, and purchase of 25 3000 hp locomotives.

Expenses 1982 ($ million)
Seaboard Coast Line Railroad

Way and structures	217.6
Locomotives	81.9
Freight cars	204.9
Other equipment	23.2
Transportation	553.3
Administration	96.0
Total	1176.9

Seaboard Coast Line Railroad	1979	1980	1981	1982
Freight revenue ($ million)	1015.6	1179.7	1279.7	1153.5
Tons of revenue freight (million)	165.9	173.5	163.2	143.6
Revenue ton-miles (million)	36 060	37 636	36 335	31 501

Louisville and Nashville Railroad	1979	1980	1981	1982
Freight revenue ($ million)	945.9	1037.3	1244.0	1084.8
Tons of revenue freight (million)	133.9	131.5	136.0	113.9
Revenue ton-miles (million)	38 778	38 836	40 402	33 810

Locomotives and rolling stock

At the end of 1982 the System owned or leased 2477 diesel locomotives and 117 673 freight wagons.

Louisville and Nashville Railroad

Way and structures	196.1
Locomotives	86.6
Freight cars	167.4
Other equipment	24
Transportation	500.1
General and administration	80.9
Total	1056.1

Soo Line Railroad

Soo Line Building, PO Box 530, Minneapolis, Minnesota 55440

Telephone: (612) 332 1261

Executive
President: Thomas M Beckley
Executive Vice-President: Charles H Clay
Vice-President and General Counsel: Byron O Olsen
Vice-President, Traffic: Ray H Smith
Vice-President, Accounting: Richard L Murlowski

Operations and Maintenance
Executive Vice-President: Dennis M Cavanaugh
Assistant Vice-President, Administration: Lloyd L Wasnick

Transportation Department
General Superintendent: Clifford C Leary
Director of Transportation Operations: David H Nelson
Director of Transportation Administration: Larry A Anderson
Director of Transportation Equipment: Donna J Anderson

Mechanical Department
Chief Mechanical Officer: George N Barker

Engineering Department
Chief Engineer: Warren B Peterson
Assistant Chief Engineer, Bridge and Structures: Donald I Kjellman
Public Contracts Engineer: James H Tone

Traffic	1979	1980	1981
Route length (miles)	4512	4445	4433
Freight handled (carloads)	441 000	404 000	363 000
Revenue freight handled (million tons)	26.754	25.122	23.262

Financial results	1979	1980	1981
		($ million)	
Railway revenues	290.511	314.265	329.659
Railway expenses	246.268	264.004	278.714
Railway operating income	44.243	50.261	50.945
Interest income	5.697	7.457	10.545
Other income (net)	2.548	3.237	4.921
Fixed charges	7.907	10.405	10.850
Contingent interest	1.213	1.205	1.063
Income before income taxes	43.368	49.345	54.498

Soo Line has temporarily shelved 1982 plans to create a holding company in order to facilitate diversification and new capital-raising.

During 1982 the Soo Line acquired the 82-mile Minneapolis, Northfield & Southern Railroad.

Traffic
Grain production in Soo's territory set a new record in 1981, but Soo Line suffered a volume decrease of 17 per cent. Soo moved a greater volume of grain from country elevators, including the highest single month's total in its history in August, but the movement from terminal elevators to eastern mills or for export fell substantially.

Chemical group volume was down 9 per cent. Unit train movements of potash, in which the Soo has a major participation, increased in 1982, however.

Container traffic represents over 70 per cent of Soo's intermodal business. Soo participates extensively in the movement of import and export container traffic, with the preponderance of the moves taking place through its connections with Canadian railroads serving St Lawrence Seaway ports. In December 1981 Soo opened a new inter-modal facility in Minneapolis to handle the growing volume of container and piggyback traffic in and out of the Twin Cities. The new $750 000 facility has storage capacity for more than 1000 containers or trailers.

Locomotives and rolling stock
In 1983 Soo Line was planning to purchase one 3000 hp and two 2000 hp locomotives to replace units destroyed in accidents. In 1982 Soo Line was operating 214 line-haul and 33 switcher diesel locomotives and 12 500 freight cars.

Southern Pacific Company

Southern Pacific Building, One Market Plaza, San Francisco, California 94105

Chairman and Chief Executive Officer: D K McNear
President, Southern Pacific Co: R D Krebs
Executive Vice-President, Planning and Finance: R J McLean
  Corporate Relations: L E Hoyt
Vice-President, Operations: Vacant
  Traffic: Vacant
  Transportation: W J Lacy
  Maintenance: D M Mohan
  Pricing and Market Planning: R A Sharp
Vice-President: J A Sage
Vice-President and Controller: E L Johnson
Vice-President, Purchasing: D K Rose
Vice-President, Public Relations: L M Phelps
Vice-President, Government Relations: R W Taggart
Vice-President and General Counsel: H A Waterman
Vice-President, Sales: J E Neal
Assistant Vice-President and Treasurer: B G McPhee
Secretary: A G Richards
Chief Mechanical Officer: R Byrne
Assistant Vice-President, Maintenance of Way and Engineering: H B Berkshire

Gauge: 1435 mm
Length: 17 638 km

Lines and territory
The Southern Pacific Company (SP) is the chief railroad constituent of the Southern Pacific Transportation Company conglomerate. Southern Pacific operates in the west, south-west and Midwest and is one of the largest railroads in the USA. SP's lines run from San Francisco north to Portland, Oregon, east to Ogden, Utah, and south to Los Angeles. From Los Angeles the SP line runs east, roughly parallel to the Mexican border, through Phoenix and El Paso, where it connects to a line northeast to Tucumcari in New Mexico, and on to Kansas City with connections to Chicago. East from El Paso the SP line, known as the Sunset Route, continues to Galveston, New Orleans and to Fort Worth and Dallas, which are also important traffic feed points.

The Northwestern Pacific Railroad Company is operated as part of the overall Southern Pacific organisation. St Louis Southwestern Railway Company (Cotton Belt), a subsidiary of the Southern Pacific Transportation Company, acquired in 1980 the bankrupt Rock Island Railroad's line between Santa Rosa, New Mexico, and St Louis, Missouri for $57 million. This acquisition reduced the company's route for movement of transcontinental traffic through the St Louis gateway by approximately 400 miles (640 km). The company then undertook a $97 million rehabilitation of the line from Tucumcari, New Mexico, to Topeka, Kansas, to restore the tracks for 60 mph (96 km/h) operation. In 1982 SP was seeking to increase its purchases of ex-Rock Island line to 1140 miles by acquisition of a further 152 miles in Kansas, Arkansas and New Mexico.

In 1983 SP reorganised its network into three regions: Northern, covering central California and northward to Oregon, eastward to Utah; Eastern, the St Louis Southwestern Railway (Cotton Belt) and some lines in Texas; and Southern, which also takes in the ex-Rock Island lines acquired. Abandonment of the northern half of the Northwestern Pacific Railroad subsidiary was being sought in 1983 as a result of a $10 million loss in 1982 which was compounded by winter storm damage that would cost $3 million to repair.

SP's trucking subsidiary provides common carrier services throughout the USA. Southern Pacific Pipe Lines Inc distributes refined petroleum products over 2480 miles (4000 km) of pipeline in Oregon, Nevada, Central and Northern California, and along the south-western border of the USA from California to Texas.

Diversification
Southern Pacific Company has pursued a policy of diversification for many years. In addition to holdings in other railways, it owns a trucking company and an international freight forwarder; the latter handles containerised freight shipments at the many ports it serves and is active as an air freight forwarder. The company's pipelines distribute petroleum products in California, Nevada and Arizona from sources in Texas and California. SP also owns land (over 3 million acres), extensive mineral and oil rights, timberlands and real estate including terminal buildings, and the company plans to intensify development of its non-railway real estate.

SP is active in leasing through a wholly-owned subsidiary, Bankers Leasing Corporation, and operates a 275-mile (443 km) coal slurry pipeline to bring coal from Arizona to a steam-powered electric plant in Nevada.

In 1982, however, SP sold its Southern Pacific Communications and Satellite Companies to GTE Corporation.

Financial results

Operating income for Southern Pacific rail lines in 1981 was $84 million, compared to $93·3 million for the year before. The regression was severe during the year's fourth quarter, when the railroads reported operating income of only $16·8 million, as against $41·7 million in the same period in 1980. Railroad carloadings were down 3 per cent from 1980 overall, but down 11 per cent in the fourth quarter compared to the same period the year before.

In 1982 SP's net income dropped 27 per cent to $125 million on revenues down 5 per cent to $5900 million.

	1980	1981
	($ million)	
Operating revenues	2859·666	3272·378
Net income	155·946**	167·671*

 * Includes $12 million gain on sale of federal income tax benefits and $6·2 million gain on exchange of common stock for debentures.
** Includes $10·8 million gain on sale of securities.

Passenger traffic

Amtrak operates all inter-city passenger services in Southern Pacific territory, but SP maintains commuter services between San Francisco and San Jose, California, under an agreement with the State of California.

Locomotives and roling stock

Railroad equipment owned or leased at the end of 1982 consisted of 2384 diesel locomotives, 54 565

SP's Los Angeles intermodal transportation centre

SP's Double-Stacker COFC articulated car

Southern Pacific's TOFC/COFC terminal at Oakland, California

SP classification yard at Roseville, California

freight cars, 92 passenger train cars, 2046 company service units and cabooses.

Intermodal traffic

Intermodal traffic climbed 42 per cent in the first nine months of 1982. To cover its rising TOFC traffic SP ordered conversion of 450 old open-type car transporters into piggyback flats at a cost of $6 million.

Many containers are moved in expedited and dedicated piggyback trains, others in transcontinental manifest trains. SP's container terminals are located at Oakland, San Francisco and Los Angeles, California; Houston, Dallas and Barbours Cut, Texas; New Orleans and Lake Charles, Louisiana; St Louis, Missouri; and Memphis, Tennessee. Rail services connect with all American and foreign flag ocean carriers calling at Pacific coast and Gulf ports and SP is involved with other rail carriers in band bridge movements between the US Pacific and Atlantic coasts, as well as to Gulf points for destination delivery or further ship movement to Europe.

A new intermodal terminal is being built at Roseville, near Sacramento in north central California, and the Brooklyn yard at Portland modernised. Itel is to supply SP with 200 of its new Impack TOFC cars.

Investment

SP tabled a capital budget of some $100 million for 1983. Major items were $6 million for the first phase of a $13 million intermodal terminal project at Long Beach, California and $12·6 million for rehabilitation of the ex-Rock Island Armourdale yard at Kansas City. A three-year programme of CTC installation and capacity enlargement in the Houston area would be started and a locomotive servicing facility developed at San Antonio. About 250 miles of track would be relaid. Significant equipment expenditure would be confined to remanufacture of 24 locomotives at a cost of $19 million.

The former Rock Island Armourdale yard at Kansas City was in 1983 being rehabilitated at a cost of $12·6 million, with the aid of $5 million in Federal Government guaranteed loans. This project com-

plements the $105 million improvements already effected on the former Rock Island Tucumcari, New Mexico-Kansas City line, culminating in the 1982 installation of CTC over the formerly double-track, automatic-block 83 miles between Topeka and Herington.

TRACS yard computer system

A new on-line track assignment computer system developed by SRI International and known as TRACS has been installed for evaluation at SP's West Colton yard. Working in real time, TRACS reduces yard work by assigning cars being humped to classification tracks that will minimise additional switching or rehumping when cars are removed from the pullout end of the yard. Operating from a matrix that matches incoming cars with outward trains, TRACS projects the accumulation of cars for each classification block and ensures that, when designated classification tracks are full, additional blocks of cars assigned to them are reallocated in a way that keeps related blocks as close to each other as possible.

St Louis Southwestern Railway Co

243 North Lindbergh Road, St Louis, Missouri 63141

Telephone: (314) 991 9100

Chairman: D K McNear
President: R D Krebs
Executive Vice-President: L E Hoyt
Assistant Vice-President, Sales: D H Skelton
  Controller: E L Johnson
  Operations: W J Lacy

Maintenance of Way and Engineering: H B Berkshire
General Managers: W C Hoenig
                   R D Bredenberg
Chief Mechanical Officer: R Byrne

Gauge: 1435 mm
Length: 3939 km

The railway operates in Illinois, Arkansas, Missouri, Tennessee, Louisiana, Texas, Kansas, Oklahoma

and New Mexico. Familiarly known as the Cotton Belt system, since 1932 it has been under the control of the Southern Pacific and 98 per cent of its capital stock is now owned by the Southern Pacific Transportation Company. Under the corporate umbrella of this organisation the two Class I railroads together constitute one of the main rail links between the Middle West and the Pacific coast.

The St Louis Southwestern has a fleet of 256 linehaul and 53 switcher diesel locomotives and 18 961 freight cars.

Union Pacific Corporation

345 Park Avenue, New York, New York 10154

Telephone: (212) 826 8200

Chairman, Board of Directors, and Chief Executive Officer: James H Evans
President and Chief Operating Officer: William S Cook
Vice-Chairman: J R Meyer
Chairman of the Executive Committee: E T Gerry
Senior Vice-President, Finance: William F Surette
  Law: William J McDonald
  Planning and External Affairs: Charles L Eaton
Vice-President, Corporate Relations: Richard W Anthony
  Washington Affairs: E P Kopp
  Strategic Planning: R S Davis
  Employee Relations: John P Halan
  Taxes: John R Mendenhall
Vice-President and Controller: J W Otto
Vice-President and Treasurer: Harry B Shuttleworth
Secretary: Charles N Olsen

In 1969 a new holding company was formed, the

Union Pacific Corporation. The Union Pacific Railroad Company is now a corporate subsidiary of the Corporation.

In 1971 the basic business activities of the parent Corporation were realigned into operating groups:

Transportation
Union Pacific Railroad Company, 1416 Dodge Street, Omaha, Nebraska 68179

Oil and gas
Champlin Petroleum Company, 5301 Camp Bowie Blvd, Fort Worth, Texas 76107

Land
Upland Industries Corporation, 110 North Fourteenth St, Omaha, Nebraska 68102

Coal and other minerals
Rocky Mountain Energy Company, 4704 Harlan Street, Denver, Colorado 80212

Pacific Rail System merger
In September 1980 formal applications were filed with the Interstate Commerce Commission seeking a merger of Union Pacific and Missouri Pacific, and acquisition of Western Pacific by Union Pacific. Late

in 1982 the Interstate Commerce Commission approved consolidation of the three railroads in Pacific Rail Systems Inc (PRSI). Conditions imposed included grants of trackage rights to Southern Pacific (Kansas-St Louis), Denver & Rio Grande Western (Pueblo-Kansas City) and Missouri-Kansas-Texas (Kansas City-Omaha/Council Bluffs, Lincoln and Topeka), but several other claims for trackage rights were rejected. At the end of the year the US Supreme Court rejected appeals against the ICC ruling from Santa Fe, Kansas City Southern, Denver & Rio Grande Western and Southern Pacific, the last-mentioned challenging the legality of the merger in principle under the Pacific Railroad Acts. The merger thereupon became operative, though Southern Pacific intended to continue court actions.

PRSI, a wholly-owned subsidiary of Union Pacific Corporation, was formed as a holding/management company to own and control the three railroad properties. The three maintain their separate corporate identities, but Western Pacific has become a subsidiary of UP Railroad and is operated as one of the latter's districts. The traffic departments of all three railroads, moreover, have been merged for development and marketing of the combined network as a unitary system, with a common operating, service and pricing policy.

Union Pacific Railroad Company

1416 Dodge Street, Omaha, Nebraska 68179

Telephone: (402) 271 3258
Telex: 484491; 484501

President: John C Kenefick
Vice-President, Operation: J R Davis
  Traffic: Walter P Barrett
  Executive Department: C Howard Burnett
Controller: John P Deasey
Vice-President, Finance and Administration: T B Graves Jr
  Labour Relations: P A Jordan
  Management Information Services and Communications: J L Jorgensen
  Law: C B Schaefer
Chief Mechanical Officer: J F McDonough
Chief Engineer: R M Brown
General Signal Engineer: E A Krause

Gauge: 1435 mm
Length: 14 635 km

Lines and territories
The Union Pacific operates in 13 states. The system extends from Council Bluffs, Iowa and Kansas City, Missouri in the east, to the Pacific Coast ports including Portland, Oregon; Vancouver; Longview,

Trailer Train Co 4-Runner on UP trial

Tacoma and Seattle, Washington; Los Angeles Harbor and Long Beach, California.

The Union Pacific has a reciprocal arrangement with 32 other railroads to avoid breaking up trains and switching at intermediate points.

Traffic

Carloadings and revenue ton-miles were down 6 and 5 per cent respectively in 1981, reflecting a significant fall-off in traffic during the last quarter. Nevertheless, largely through a highly effective cost control programme and productivity gains, the railroad was able to improve its profitability. Employment levels were reduced, and with less equipment in use savings also were achieved by cutting back some equipment and roadway programmes. Operating efficiencies softened the impact of a 13 per cent increase in fuel prices, from 87 cents a gallon in December 1980, to 98 cents in December 1981. The fuel consumption rate per gross thousand ton-miles, which had been reduced 16 per cent from 1972 to 1980, improved another 4 per cent in 1981, lowering expenses by $12·8 million. For the fifth consecutive year, the railroad reduced the time the average car spends in yards by as much as 10 per cent at some of its terminals. It also raised the average number of cars and the weight of each train without sacrificing average train speed.

As a result of these and other cost-control programmes, UP reduced its operating ratio from 80·9 to 80·3. Its average haul of 717 miles continued to lead the industry in 1981, but was slightly below 1980's record of 727 miles due to fewer long-haul shipments of corn, lumber and autos. Prices for shipments on a revenue ton-mile basis improved 10 per cent over 1980 and helped to offset inflation's impact on operating costs.

The railroad's consumer-related traffic categories, such as autos, lumber, general merchandise and farm products, were sharply affected by the recession. On the basis of revenue ton-miles, motor vehicles and parts were down 19 per cent from a depressed 1980 level; farm and forest products also fell 19 per cent; and food products were off 12 per cent.

In contrast, UP's strong coal traffic continued a vigorous growth pattern that began in the mid-1970s. Total coal tonnage increased 16 per cent from 28 million tons in 1980 to 32·6 million tons in 1981. Export coal shipments to the West Coast bound for Japan, South Korea and Taiwan were particularly strong, rising from 1·2 million to 4·9 million tons.

The key Union Pacific coal route for export shipments is the 784-mile main line from Salt Lake City to the ports of Long Beach and Los Angeles. Since 1976, total traffic on this line, which traverses some of the most rugged country in the United States, ranging from the Rockies to the Mojave Desert, has increased from 10 to 25 trains a day.

UP is well ahead with a major programme to expand and streamline the Salt Lake City-Los Angeles corridor. Some of the projects include an $8 million line-straightening programme at Crestline, Utah; 16 new sidings or siding extensions in Utah, Nevada and California; several bridge improvements; and the $9 million classification yard at

Three SD40-2 units and UP intermodal freight near Caliente, Nevada

Snow-clearance between Ashton and Tetonia, Idaho

Unit coal train loading on loop at Hanna, Wyoming

Yermo, in southern California, which opened in September 1981. Yermo, the third UP classification yard to come on line since 1978 and the sixth in the entire system, has markedly improved traffic flow as far east as North Platte, Nebraska. But its primary role is to speed traffic from the West Coast to the Utah gateways, by relieving pressure on the East Los Angeles and Las Vegas yards.

UP is supporting development of coal facilities at major ports it serves on the West Coast. Union Pacific Corporation also is participating in a $4 million engineering and environmental programme for a proposed deep-water coal terminal on its property at the port of Long Beach. The Long Beach terminal could add 15 million tons of coal-shipping capacity from the West Coast by the mid-1980s.

During 1981, the railroad invested $86·9 million for roadway improvements, which would not only serve the anticipated rise in export coal, but also position Union Pacific to handle higher levels of traffic throughout the system as business improved.

In December 1981, Union Pacific Corporation and Chicago and North Western Transportation Company received commitments from a group of banks to finance a project which would allow the C&NW to originate coal in the Powder River Basin of eastern Wyoming and interchange that coal over a 56-mile link to Union Pacific in north-western Nebraska. The project is scheduled to become operational by 1984 and is expected to increase UP's coal traffic by 25 million tons annually within five years of completion.

Normally one of the strongest performers in Union Pacific's diversified commodity mix, grain traffic, which had nearly doubled to 17 million tons from 1975 to 1980, declined 21 per cent to 14 million tons in 1981. An unexpectedly sharp downturn in grain prices reduced shipments in the last half of the year.

Intermodal

Despite the sluggish national economy, Union Pacific Railroad's volume of intermodal traffic grew about 8 per cent during 1981 and a further 28 per cent in 1982. Among UP's 1981 developments in this sector was a trial of Trailer Train Co's fuel-saving '4-Runner' TOFC unit between Los Angeles and Chicago. It is designed to carry the longer 45-foot trailers which are already the US industry standard for motor carriers. UP is to operate 100 of these sets over a five-year period and preliminary indications are that a train of 25 4-Runner sets loaded with 100 TOFC trailers could save up to 9200 gallons of diesel fuel on two round trips between Chicago and Los Angeles.

4-Runner specification

Length: 58·22 m (191 ft)
Weight: Approx 19·5 tons per trailer
Capacity: 4 trailers up to 45 ft long
Type of trailers: 2 × 44 ft intermediate decks to carry standard 45 ft dry vans with 36 in kingpin spacing; 2 × 47 ft end decks to carry 45 ft refrigerated trailers with nose-mounted refrigeration units with 36 or 42 in kingpin spacing
Clearance: 4·93 m (16 ft 2 in) for 4·11 m (13 ft 6 in) trailer
Wheelbase: 10·06 m (33 ft)
Gross load per car: 162·6 tonnes (358 400 lb)
Height of tare platform above rails: 800 mm (31½ in)
Distance between 45 ft trailers: 254 mm (10 in)
Brakes: Composition shoe type

The 4-Runner has been designed to meet all AAR interchange and FRA safety standards. It is used only between lift-on and lift-off intermodal terminals; its non-retractable trailer hitches will not permit circus-style loading and unloading. It has a skeletonised deck consisting of a centre sill and end sills, a platform beneath the trailer's tyres and a grating platform surrounding the trailer hitch. Each deck has all required safety appliances.

Each deck is carried on two self-steering single-axle wheel-sets. Wheels are 28 inches in diameter, several inches smaller than the wheels on most conventional rail equipment, to achieve reduced wind resistance and lower overall height.

The 4-Runner is interchangeable with other types of cars. The interconnecting drawbars between its four vehicles may be disconnected with standard railroad maintenance equipment. The 4-Runner unit might be expanded from four vehicles to 10 if that seemed desirable. It is not as yet designed to handle containers, since its sponsors see demand centred mainly on intermodal cars which will road handle trailers, but a COFC 4-Runner could be built.

Another important 1981 development, made possible by the Staggers Act's deregulation provisions, solved some of the problems of imbalance in transcontinental COFC traffic. Under agreements

Relocation at Crestline summit, with replaced horseshoe curve on the right

Traffic

	1979	1980	1981
Railroad system (track miles)			
Main line	5028	5028	5028
Branch line	4478	4429	4259
Yards, sidings and other main line	6415	6430	6521
Total	15 921	15 887	15 808
Track miles of continuous-welded rail (at year-end)	2676	2887	3106
Track miles under CTC (at year-end)	3123	3297	3329
Freight operations			
Operating ratio	81·4	80·9	80·3
Revenue ton-miles (million)	74 049	79 210	74 893
Revenue carloads (000)	1829	1755	1648
Revenue tons carried (million)	104·2	109·0	104·4
Average haul (miles)	711	727	717
Average price of diesel fuel (per gallon)	$0·56	$0·83	$0·97
Maintenance operations			
Track miles of rail replaced			
New	345	346	314
Used	213	149	129
Track miles reballasted	1848	2325	2375
Sleepers replaced (000)	801	748	811

During each of the three calendar years, approximately 90 per cent of the railroad's main line consisted of 133 lb/yd rail. In addition, approximately 70 per cent of the main line road had a traffic density of at least 20 million tons per mile and approximately 60 per cent had a Federal maximum speed limit of 80 mph.

Commodities

% of total	1979 tons	1979 Freight revenue	1980 tons	1980 Freight revenue	1981 tons	1981 Freight revenue
Coal	22·8	10·6	25·7	12·2	31·3	15·9
Farm products	16·1	14·0	18·4	17·5	15·5	14·2
Other mineral products	16·2	6·9	15·7	6·8	15·3	7·3
Soda ash and chemicals	12·0	13·2	11·1	13·1	11·0	13·7
Food products	10·1	12·7	9·6	12·8	8·5	12·0
Forest products	9·3	11·6	7·8	9·9	6·7	9·0
Freight, all kinds	4·0	11·9	3·2	9·9	3·5	10·1
Motor vehicles and parts	1·7	7·4	1·3	6·3	1·1	6·3
Other	7·8	11·7	7·2	11·5	7·1	11·5
	100%	100%	100%	100%	100%	100%
Total (million)	104·2	$1725	109·0	$1986	104·4	$2088

reached between American President Lines (APL), Union Pacific, Chicago & North Western Transportation Company (C&NW), and Transway International Corporation, a New York-based holding company that owns a number of major domestic freight forwarding companies, APL, a trans-Pacific carrier accounting for a heavy eastbound flow of intermodal import cargo from the Far East to the Midwest and North Atlantic regions, provides its containers after discharge to Transway International subsidiaries that generate domestic rail shipments predominantly in the opposite direction. Trailers or

containers which the railroads would otherwise have hauled empty, eastbound for Transway and westbound for APL, are instead filled in both directions. The railroads, in exchange for large commitments of filled containers made possible by this balanced cargo programme, agreed to enter into contractual arrangements to ensure consistency of service and equipment utilisation. The APL/Transway agreements, the largest single shipping contracts in UP's history, were expected to generate $100 million a year in traffic flow. One train leaves Los Angeles and Seattle each week, reaching New

York City's key terminal in South Kearny, New Jersey, by the fourth day.

Union Pacific serves directly two of APL's principal West Coast ports, Los Angeles and Seattle, and a third, Oakland, by interline connections. All major intermodal terminals on UP can handle both TOFC and COFC traffic. Besides Omaha the ramps are located at Cheyenne, Los Angeles, Portland, Seattle, Salt Lake City, Denver and Kansas City. UP continues to give intermodal trains special treatment at Bailey Yard in North Platte, Nebraska. UP runs all intermodal traffic in dedicated trains. Union Pacific derives about 12 per cent of its freight revenue from intermodal traffic, but foresees the proportion rising to 25 per cent by 1986.

Finance

Union Pacific Railroad Company's net income increased in 1981, although traffic levels in all major commodities, except coal, and trailer and container shipments, were down on the previous year. Net income rose 1 per cent to $167·1 million from record earnings of $165·1 million in 1980. Revenues were up 5 per cent, from $2100 million in 1980 to $2200 million in 1981.

Total expenses were $2000 million, up 5 per cent over the $1900 million spent in 1980. Diesel fuel costs rose 6 per cent, from $289·2 million to $305·3 million. Other major expenses were salaries and benefits, up $58 million or 7 per cent. Federal income taxes rose $24·5 million or 43 per cent, primarily as a result of a lower investment tax credit.

Results continued to deteriorate in 1982, over the first three-quarters of which revenues were $1404·7 million against $1643·8 for the same period of 1981, whereas expenses were reduced only from $1408·7 million to $1254·8 million. In September 1982 car-loadings were running 18 per cent below 1981 levels.

Over 1982 as a whole UP Railroad generated $105 million of Union Pacific Corporation's total net income for the year of $327 million (down 20 per cent on 1981) from total revenues of $5900 million, which was 8 per cent less than in 1981.

Investment

Although track maintenance programmes were reduced in 1981, they remained high in relation to traffic levels. Total roadway maintenance of $288·5 million included the installation of 811 000 sleepers, relaying of 305 miles of main line with new rail, and the reballasting and resurfacing of 2375 miles of track. Union Pacific is the only major US railroad with section gangs who inspect each mile of the main line at least once a week. The railroad added 248 miles of continuous-welded rail in 1981, bringing its total to 3106 miles or 52 per cent of the railroad's main line.

With an average of about 500 locomotives in storage during the last two quarters, equipment maintenance costs were pared $37 million from the 1981 budget. Lower traffic levels also affected 1981 capital expended on equipment, which was $47·5 million, down 84 per cent from 1980. During the year, UP purchased 41 freight cars and constructed 1135, nearly all of which were hopper cars for coal and grain shipments. No new locomotives were acquired due to large additions to the fleet in 1979-80 and the current slowdown in traffic.

UP's 1982 capital budget of $163 million was 21 per cent higher than 1981 capital expenditures of $134 million. Nearly 80 per cent of the outlays, or $128 million, was invested in a record roadway programme, up nearly 50 per cent over 1981 expenditures. The programme included $33 million for roadway improvement projects in the Salt Lake City-Los Angeles/Long Beach corridor.

During 1982 two major line relocations were completed. One at Meacham, Oregon, eliminated several restrictive curves at a cost of $4·6 million. The other, at Crestline, Nevada not only eliminated several restrictive curves, but shortened the main line by approximately 0·8 mile. This project, costing $8 million, featured the railroad's first use of concrete sleepers; 3170 were installed in conjunction with cwr. A $6 million project to install CTC between Provo and Lynndyl, Utah was completed early in 1983. At Nampa, Idaho a $2 million locomotive repair shop was constructed.

New equipment purchases in UP's $71·8 million capital spending plans for 1983 were confined to 168 auto-racks, but 15 switching locomotives would be rebuilt. Of the total, $55·4 million was assigned to infrastructure work.

It was anticipated that 100 miles of main-line rail would be replaced along with 65 miles of curve rail, and that 60 miles of branch lines would be relaid with second-hand rail. The total cost of this work would be over $40 million.

Concrete sleeper installation in Crestline summit realignment

Expenditures ($ million)	1979	1980	1981
Capital			
Equipment	217·6	288·4	47·5
Road, structures and other	87·4	96·7	86·9
	305·0	385·1	134·4
Maintenance			
Track repair and replacement	133·1	144·9	143·0
Equipment repair and other	341·6	388·3	411·1
	474·7	533·2	554·1

Diesel locomotives

Series	Builders	Model	hp	No
Line-haul freight				
1-50	EMD	SD-45	3600	43
60-64	EMD	SD-45-M	3600	6
99	EMD	SD-24-M	3000	1
103, 121	EMD	GP-7	1500	2
131-341	EMD	GP-9	1750	44
307-344	EMD	GP-9M	2000	3
400-446	EMD	SD-24	2400	10
474-494	EMD	GP-20	2000	3
600-650	EMD	GP-40	3000	51
700-735	FMD	GP-30	2250	26
700B-739B	EMD	GP-30	2250	28
740-763	EMD	GP-35	2500	20
800-875	EMD	GP-30	2250	62
2000-2059	EMD	GP-38-2	2000	60
2400-2539	GE	C-30-7	3000	140
2810-2959	GE	U-30-C	3000	148
3000-3122	EMD	SD-40	3000	121
3123-3808	EMD	SD-40-2	3000	684
6900-6946	EMD	DD-40-X	6600	45
9000-9005	EMD	GP-40-X	3500	6
Total				1503
Line-haul passenger-freight				
1400-1409	EMD	SDP-35	2500	10
Road switchers				
1871-1877	EMD	TR-5	1200	1
1870B-1877B	EMD	TR-5	1200	1
Total				2
Yard switchers				
1007-1095	EMD	NW-2	1000	21
1200-1242	EMD	SW-10	1200	43
1800-1841	EMD	SW-7 & 9	1200	20
Total				84
Total locomotives				1599
S1-S8 electric trailers				7

Track

Rail: 133 AREA, 66·2 kg/m

Cross ties (sleepers): Wooden, thickness 7 in

Spacing: 2019/km

Fastenings: $\frac{5}{8} \times \frac{5}{8} \times 6\frac{1}{4}$ in cut track spikes

Max curvature radius: 12° (except 16° in 2 terminal areas)

Max gradient: Main line 2·33%, branch line 4%

Max axleload: 65 750 lb (unrestricted operation), 78 750 lb (with 40 mph speed restriction on main line and primary branch track)

Powder River Basin Project

The Chicago & North Western (C&NW) and Union Pacific Corporation obtained commitments from a group of banks to finance construction of the Wyoming Powder River Basin Coal Transportation Project (see under C&NW) The project consists of three principal rail segments to be operated by C&NW. The first is a 103-mile (166 km) line from Shawnee,

Wyoming on C&NW's east-west line north to Coal Creek Junction, Wyoming, which is to be owned jointly with the Burlington Northern Railroad pursuant to an Interstate Commerce Commission order. This joint line has already been completed and is being operated by BN. The second segment involves the complete rebuilding of 45 miles (72 km) of existing C&NW east-west line between Shawnee and Crandall, Wyoming. The third segment is construction of 56 miles (90 km) of new railroad from Crandall to Joyce, Nebraska to connect with an existing Union Pacific Railroad line. These latter two segments will be owned by a trust for a newly created Union Pacific Corporation subsidiary and leased to a C&NW subsidiary.

Locomotives and rolling stock

At the end of 1982 Union Pacific owned 1599 diesel-electric locomotives, and operated 61 065 freight cars owned and leased.

United States Steel Corporation

The US Steel Corporation owns all the common stock of three Class I railroads.

Following its costly purchase of Marathon Oil, US Steel announced in 1982 that it was open to purchase offers for its three Class I and some other railroads. Because of the steel industry's recession the Bessemer & Lake Erie was working on a one-shift-daily basis in mid-1982; it was recording 42·6 per cent fewer car-loadings than in 1981, while Duluth, Missabe & Iron Range was 40 per cent down.

Bessemer and Lake Erie Railroad Company

PO Box 68, Monroeville, Pennsylvania 15146

Telephone: (412) 829 6600

President: D H Hoffman
Vice-President, Finance: V W Kraetsch
  Operations: F A Fitzpatrick
  Marketing: T J Siegel
General Manager, Operating: M R Seipler

General Superintendent, Equipment: W D McNeilly
Chief Engineer: M Rougas

204·9 route miles (328 km); 64 locomotives; 9555 freight cars

Duluth, Missabe and Iron Range Railway Company

Missabe Building, Duluth, Minnesota 55802

Telephone: (218) 723 2115

President: D H Hoffman
Vice-President, Finance: V W Kraetsch
  Operations: F A Fitzpatrick
General Manager: C O Ferner
General Superintendent: M G Alderink
Chief Engineer: G Liljeblad

441 route miles (709 km); 66 locomotives; 7007 freight cars

This railway connects the Mesabi Range iron ore deposits with the ports of Duluth and Two Harbors on Lake Superior, from where the ore is shipped to the steel centres throughout the Midwest.

Elgin, Joliet and Eastern Railway

PO Box 880, Maple Road, Joliet, Illinois 60434

Telephone: (412) 566 6420

President: D H Hoffman
Vice-President, Operating: F A Fitzpatrick
General Manager: J F Madden
General Superintendent: H J Brehm
Chief Engineer: R F Beck

199·8 route miles (320·2 km); 100 locomotives; 10 220 freight cars

Western Pacific Railroad Company

526 Mission Street, San Francisco, California 94105

Telephone: (415) 982 2100

President: R C Marquis
Vice-President, Law: W G Treanor
  Operations: C G Yund
  Marketing: R G Meldahl
  Marketing Services: P Richard McElheney
  Market Development and Pricing: M W Watson

  Finance: Richard W Stumbo, Jr
  Intermodal: T R Brown
  Industrial Development: C J J Gray
Chief Engineer: J T Smith
Chief Mechanical Officers: R E Shideler
                           J S Miller

Gauge: 1435 mm
Length: 2390 km

Lines and territories
Western Pacific is a wholly owned subsidiary of Western Pacific Industries Inc. It operates in the western portion of the USA, providing freight service from the San Francisco Bay area through California and Nevada to Salt Lake City, Utah. The railroad also provides service north and south between the Bay area and the Oregon line.

An application for acquisition of the railroad by Union Pacific and its absorption in the Pacific Rail System (qv) was filed with the ICC in September 1980.

Locomotives and rolling stock
WP operates 134 line-haul and 10 switching diesel locomotives and 5612 freight cars.

Other US railroads

Note: * = Class II Railroad, with revenues in the $10-50 million range

Aberdeen & Rockfish Railroad Co

PO Box 917, Aberdeen, North Carolina 28315

Telephone: (919) 944 2341

President: R Veasey

47 route miles (75·6 km); 3 locomotives; 224 freight cars

Aliquippa and Southern Railroad Co

PO Box 280, Aliquippa, Pennsylvania 15001

Telephone: (412) 378 6011

General Superintendent: R B Shafer

49·7 route miles (80 km); 19 locomotives; 1195 freight cars

Ann Arbor Railroad System

Operated by Michigan Interstate Railway Company*

PO Box 619, Owosso, Michigan 48867

Telephone: (517) 723 7823

Chairman, President: V M Malanaphy
Vice-President and General Manager: A J Hogg

393 route miles (632·5 km); 16 locomotives; 701 freight cars

The Apache Railway Company

PO Box E, Snowflake, Arizona 85937

Telephone: (602) 536 4697

President and Chief Executive: H C Davenport
Chief Mechanical Officer: C J Hazard

45 route miles (72·4 km); 10 locomotives; 545 freight cars

Apalachicola Northern Railroad Co

PO Box 50, Port St Joe, Florida 32456

Telephone: (904) 227 1131

President: J C Belin
Executive Vice-President: B R Gibson

96 route miles (154·5 km); 11 locomotives; 261 freight cars

Ashley, Drew and Northern Railway Company

PO Box 757, Crossett, Arkansas 71635

Telephone: (501) 567 8631

President: S R Tedder
Vice-President, Operations: P H Schueth

41 route miles (66·1 km); 6 locomotives; 2076 freight wagons

Atlanta and St Andrews Bay Railway Company

PO Box 729, 514 E Main St, Dothan, Alabama 36302

Telephone: (205) 792 0975

Chairman and President: A V Hooks
Chief Engineer and General Superintendent: D R Davis
Chief Mechanical Officer: T L Edwards

89 route miles (143·2 km); 13 locomotives; 828 freight cars

Bangor and Aroostook Railroad Company

Northern Maine Junction Park, RR2, Bangor, Maine 04401

Telephone: (207) 848 5711

Chairman of the Board: Frederick C Dumaine
Chairman of the Executive Committee and Chief Executive Officer: Joseph B Ely II
President: W E Travis

Vice-President, Operations: L W Littlefield
  General Counsel: W M Houston
  Marketing: H L Cousins, Jr
  Finance: O H Bridgham
  Traffic: H G Goodness
Assistant Vice-President, Operating Transportation: R P Groves
Manager, Highway Division: S F Corey
Chief Mechanical Officer: H W Hanson
Chief Engineer: V J Welch

Gauge: 1435 mm
Length: 746·1 km

Traffic	1980/81	1981/82
Total freight tonnage	3 626 515	2 977 172*
Total freight tonne-km (000)	774 260	686 750
* Estimate		

Finance		
Revenues ($)		1981/82
Freight, parcels and mail		25 892 448
Other		13 732 793
Total		39 625 241

Expenditure ($)	1981/82
Staff/personnel expenses	19 950 605
Materials and services	16 296 713
Depreciation	1 790 022
Financial charges	536 497
Total	38 573 837

Motive power and rolling stock under order or delivered 1981-82
233 70-ton EOC box cars, built by Berwick Forge & Fabricating

Track
Rail: 115 RE 57·05 kg/m, 112 RE 55·56 kg/m, 100 ARA 49·61 kg/m, 80 ARA 39·74 kg/m
Cross ties (sleepers): Treated hardwood, thickness 152·4 mm

Spacing: 1772/km
Fastenings: 178 × 304·8 mm Dbl sh 1:40 cant
Minimum curvature radius: 10°
Max gradient: 1·25%
Max axleload: 62 750 lb unrestricted, 65 250 lb with restrictions

Traction and rolling stock
33 locomotives; 3595 freight cars

Diesel locomotives

Class	Wheel arrangement	Transmission	Rated power (kW)	Max speed km/h	Total weight tonnes	No in service	Year first built	Builders Mechanical parts	Engine & type	Transmission
SW-9	Bo-Bo	Elec	895	105	122	3	1951	EMD	EMD 12-cyl 567B	EMD
F-3	Bo-Bo	Elec	1119	105	120	2	1947	EMD	EMD 16-cyl 567BC	EMD
BL-2	Bo-Bo	Elec	1119	105	123	1	1949	EMD	EMD 16-cyl 567BC	EMD
GP-7	Bo-Bo	Elec	1119	105	123	15	1950	EMD	EMD 16-cyl 567BC	EMD
GP-9	Bo-Bo	Elec	1305	105	125	4	1954	EMD	EMD 16-cyl 567C	EMD
GP-38	Bo-Bo	Elec	1491	105	130	8	1966	EMD	EMD 16-cyl 645E	EMD

Belfast and Moosehead Lake Railroad

11 Water St, Belfast, Maine 04915

Telephone: (207) 338 2330

President: H C Hutchings
General Manager: C D Leavell

33 route miles (53.1 km); 4 locomotives; 3 freight cars

Belt Railway Company of Chicago

6900 South Central Ave, Chicago, Illinois 60638

Telephone: (312) 496 4000
Telex: 254357

President and General Manager: R E Dowdy

Vice-President and Controller: R G Rubino
General Superintendent, Operating: J Overbey
Chief of Motive Power and Purchasing Agent: K H Smith
Superintendent, Car Department: J D Mowery
Chief Engineer: W G Taylor

The Belt Line intersects and connects all Chicago trunk lines for interchange of traffic. Its Clearing Yard has a working capacity of 12 600 cars and the ability to hump four trains simultaneously during classification.
The principal functions of the Belt Railway are location and switching service for over 325 industries; and classification and interchange of freight cars for its twelve owners and for other non-owner roads. In connection with this classification the Belt provides blocked train service for the benefit of many of its owners in connection with their run-through train operations.

27 route miles (43·5 km); 48 diesel-electric locomotives

Birmingham Southern Railroad Co

PO Box 579, Fairfield, Alabama 35064

Telephone: (205) 783 2821

President: M R Seipler
General Manager: J W Read

91 route miles (146·4 km); 21 locomotives; 796 freight cars

Black Mesa & Lake Powell Railroad

Salt River Project, PO Box 1980, Phoenix, Arizona 85001

Superintendent: G Kester

78 route miles (126 km), electrified at 50 kV 60 Hz; 6 electric, 1 diesel locomotive; 123 hopper wagons

Butte, Anaconda and Pacific Railway Company

Box 1421, 300 West Commercial Ave, Anaconda, Montana 59711

Telephone: (406) 563 7121

President: J W Greene
Vice-President: G W Parker
Superintendent of Transportation: G J Allen

Gauge: 1435 mm
Length: 191·5 route-km

Traffic	1980	1981
Total freight tonnage	1 798 345	714 067

Finance		
Revenues ($)		1981
Freight, parcels and mail		6 990 496
Investment		4 165 265
Interest		543 118
Total		11 698 879

Expenditure ($)		1981
Staff/personnel		3 095 611
Materials and services		1 061 190
Depreciation		171 935
Total		4 328 736

Track
Rail: AREA 57·07 kg/m
Cross ties (sleepers): Fir, thickness 177·8 mm
Spacing: 4792/km
Fastenings: Fish plate head free joints
Minimum curvature radius: 10°
Max gradient: 4·01%
Max axleload: 34 tonnes

Traction and rolling stock
8 locomotives; 427 freight cars

Diesel locomotives

Class	Wheel arrangement	Transmission	Rated power (hp)	Max speed (mph)	Total weight tonnes	No in service	Year first built	Builders Mechanical parts	Engine & type
GP-7	Bo-Bo	Elec	1500	88	120	2	1952	EMD	General Motors 16-5678
GP-9	Bo-Bo	Elec	1750	88	124	4	1957	EMD	General Motors 16-5676
GP-38-2	Bo-Bo	Elec	2000	105	125	2	1977	EMD	General Motors 16-8-8

California Western Railroad

PO Box 907, Foot of Laurel St, Fort Bragg, California 95437

Telephone: (707) 964 6371

President: W B Kyle
General Manager: H A Foltz

40 route miles (64·4 km); 4 diesel, 2 steam locomotives; 10 passenger train coaches

Camas Prairie Railroad Co

13th & Main Streets, PO Box 1166, Lewiston, Idaho 83501

Telephone: (208) 743 1821

President: M E Merrett

256·7 route miles (413·6 km)

The Camas Prairie Railroad is solely an operating company for the Union Pacific and Burlington Northern railroads.

Cambria & Indiana Railroad Co

1275 Daly Ave, Bethlehem, Pennsylvania 18015

Telephone: (215) 694 5971

President: T H Semmel
General Manager: R N Young

62 route miles (100 km); 18 diesel locomotives; 956 wagons

Cedar Rapids and Iowa City Railway Co

PO Box 351, Cedar Rapids, Iowa 52406

Telephone: (319) 398 4448

President: D Arnold
General Superintendent: A C Courtney

53 route miles (85 km); 8 locomotives; 59 freight cars

Central of Georgia Railroad Co

99 Spring Street, Atlanta, Georgia 30303

Chairman: H H Hall
President: R E Franklin
Vice-President, Operating: W W Simpson
Assistant Vice-President, Mechanical: J G Moore
  Maintenance of Way: H L Rose

2207 route miles (3551.8 km); 117 line-haul and 33 switching locomotives; 4160 freight cars

Central Vermont Railway

2 Federal Street, St Albans, Vermont 05478

Telephone: (802) 527 7518

President: J H Burdakin
Vice-President: W H Cramer
General Manager: P C Larson
Mechanical Officer: R M Harmon
Chief Engineer: T J Fawcett
Superintendent of Transportation: R L Rixon
Marketing Manager: D A Caster
Director of Purchasing: R M Garner
Corporate Secretary: E G Fontaine

Gauge: 1435 mm
Length: 606.5 km

The railway operates 23 diesel locomotives (all leased) and 1209 freight vehicles.
  The competitive pattern of rail traffic in New England changed drastically with the Interstate Commerce Commission's approval of Guilford Transportation Industries' purchase of the Boston & Maine, Maine Central and Delaware & Hudson Railroads. These ownership changes, coupled with effects of deregulatory pricing, seriously reduced the Central Vermont's ability to compete on a profitable basis in the future. Realising this change could likely be permanent, Canadian National instructed GTC to seek a buyer for the line in 1982, but this was rescinded in 1983.

Chicago and Illinois Midland Railway Co*

PO Box 139, Springfield, Illinois 62705

Telephone: (217) 522 1323

President: B L Thomas
Executive Vice-President and General Manager: William G Harvey
Vice-President and Assistant Treasurer: K A Jesiolowski
Superintendent: A S Alstott
Chief Mechanical Officer: W M Baginski
Chief Engineer: R E Pearson

Gauge: 1435 mm
Length: 194.7 km

Traffic	1980	1981
Total freight tonnage	8 030 107	7 313 723

Finance ($)		1981
Total revenues		19 174 485
Total expenditure		14 205 321

Track
Rail: 132 lb/yd
Minimum curvature radius: 10°
Max gradient: 1.64%
Max axleload: 66 000 lb

Traction and rolling stock
20 locomotives; 1212 freight cars

Chicago South Shore and South Bend Railroad (Electric)*

Carroll Avenue, Michigan City, Indiana 46360

Telephone: (219) 874 4221

President and General Manager: A W Dudley
Director Freight Sales and Services: E F Woods
Superintendent of Transportation: R D Shipley
Chief Engineer: C F Mulrenan

76 route miles (122 km), electrified at 1.5 kV dc; 10 diesel locomotives; 50 electric passenger cars; 27 freight cars. In 1982 passenger revenues totalled $4.8 million, subsidies $4.6 million, freight $8.9 million and earnings $3.1 million.

Colorado & Wyoming Railway Co*

PO Box 316, Pueblo, Colorado 81002

President: F J Villa
General Superintendent: G A Martin
Traffic Manager: G R Stelert

110.7 route-miles (178 km); 6 line-haul and 12 switching locomotives; 939 freight cars

Columbus and Greenville Railway Co

PO Box 6000, 201 19th Street North, Columbus, Mississippi 39701

Telephone: (601) 328 6331

Chairman, President and Chief Executive: S Y Wilhite
Vice-President, Traffic and Marketing: B Wharry
Vice-President and General Manager: R E Ross
Vice-President and Chief Engineer: J M Strickland
Chief Mechanical Officer: T R Swift

168 route miles (270.4 km); 19 locomotives; 1160 freight cars

The Corinth and Counce Railroad Co

Highway 57, PO Box 128, Counce, Tennessee 38326

Telephone: (901) 689 3145

President: C W Byrd

26 route miles (41.8 km); 4 diesel-electric locomotives; 556 freight cars
Connects at Corinth, Mississippi with ICG and SR.

Detroit & Mackinac Railway

Tawas City, Michigan 48763

Telephone: (517) 362 3461

President: C A Pinkerton III

405 route miles (652 km); 12 locomotives; 1422 freight cars

Escanaba and Lake Superior Railroad

PO Box 158, Wells, Michigan 49894

Telephone: (906) 786 0693

Chairman: W W Larkin
President: J C Larkin
Secretary: A K Larkin

204.6 route miles (329 km); 5 locomotives; 74 freight cars

Galveston Wharves

PO Box 328, 123 25th Street, Galveston, Texas 77553

Telephone: (713) 765 9321

Chairman, Board of Trustees: L G Farmer
Executive Director: C S Devoy

44 route miles (70.8 km); 5 locomotives; 200 freight cars

Great Western Railway Co

Loveland Depot, PO Box 537, Loveland, Colorado 80537

Telephone: (303) 667 6883

President: I L Bielenberg
Executive Vice-President and General Manager: Byron F Andrews

58 route miles (93.3 km); 3 EMD SW-1 and 1 EMD SW-9 diesel-electric locomotives; 145 freight cars

Green Bay and Western Railroad Co*

PO Box 2507, Green Bay, Wisconsin 54306

Telephone: (414) 497 0411

President: C J Hockaday
Vice-President, Executive: S P Selby
  Traffic: V J Maloney

254 route miles (409 km); 19 locomotives; 2076 freight cars

Green Mountain Railroad Corp

PO Box 468, Bellows Falls, Vermont 05101

Telephone: (802) 463 9531

President, Chief Executive and General Manager: G E Davis
Chief Operating Officer: R W Adams
Vice-President and Chief Mechanical Officer: J M Hebda
Vice-President and Chief Engineering Officer: R Ashcroft

50 route miles (80.4 km); 5 locomotives; 503 freight cars; 2 passenger coaches

Houston Belt & Terminal Railway Co

202 Union Station Building, Houston, Texas 77002

Telephone: (713) 546 3100

President and General Manager: H W Ritter

53 route miles (85.3 km); 23 locomotives

Indiana Harbor Belt Railroad Co

Union Station, Chicago, Illinois 60606

Telephone: (312) 768 9170

President: R B Hasselmann
General Manager: A B Cravens

114 route miles (183.5 km); 107 locomotives; 33 freight cars

Lake Erie, Franklin and Clarion Railroad

PO Box 430, East Wood St, Clarion, Pennsylvania 16214

Telephone: (814) 226 9684

President and Chairman of the Board: J F Miller
Executive Vice-President: J L Hartle

15 route miles (24.1 km); 6 locomotives; 1123 freight cars

Lake Superior & Ishpeming Railroad Co*

105 East Washington Street, Marquette, Michigan 49855

Telephone: (906) 228 7979

President and Chief Executive: J J Scullion
General Manager: G D Bantle
Chief Engineer: T O Stokkhe

55 route miles (88.5 km); 19 diesel locomotives; 2709 freight cars

Lamoille Valley Railroad Co

RFD 21, Stafford Ave, Morrisville, Vermont 05661

Telephone: (802) 888 4255

President: R L Gensburg
General Manager: E A Lewis

99 route miles (159·3 km); 3 Alco 1600 hp Bo-Bo locomotives; 50 freight cars

Laurinburg and Southern Railroad Co

PO Box 546, Laurinburg, North Carolina 28352

Telephone: (919) 276 0786

President: Murphy Evans
Vice-President and General Manager: W S Jones

28 route miles (45·1 km); 9 locomotives; 344 freight cars

Louisiana Midland Railway Co

PO Box 110, Jena, Louisiana 73142

Telephone: (318) 992 4860

President: C E Burroughs

77 route miles (123 km); 3 diesel locomotives; 1018 freight cars

Maine Central Railroad Company

242 St John St, Portland, Maine 04102

Telephone: (207) 773 4711

Chairman: Timothy Mellon
Vice-Chairman: John F Gerity
President: David A Fink
Vice-President, Sales and Marketing: George H Ellis
General Manager, Operations: Anselm Tupper
General Superintendent: David A Snyder
Chief Mechanical Officer: Stewart P Park Jr
Chief Engineer: James O Born
Accounting and Finance Department
Comptroller: John Michaels
Treasurer: Stanley W Watson

Gauge: 1435 mm
Length: 1213 km

The Maine Central Railroad Company is a freight-only railroad which operates in Maine, New Hampshire, Vermont and New Brunswick. Maine Central serves all of the large population centres and with two exceptions the industrial centres of the State of Maine.

The Portland Terminal Company, a wholly owned subsidiary, operates railroad facilities in Portland, South Portland and Westbrook. Under a joint contract it provides exclusive terminal services for Boston and Maine Corporation and Maine Central Railroad Company. It also provides for traffic to and from the Grand Trunk Railway (Canadian National) at Portland.

In 1980 Maine Central was acquired by United States Filter Corporation. In 1982 the ICC approved purchase of the railroad by Guilford Transportation Industries Inc for $20 million. GTI was creating a 4050-mile network in New England by acquiring also the Delaware & Hudson and Boston & Maine Railroads.

Results

Consolidated net earnings of $4·434 million for 1981 showed a substantial improvement of 81·5 per cent over 1980. Traffic volume as measured by net ton-miles slipped fractionally below 1980, declining by 0·7 per cent. Several freight rate increases were authorised by the Interstate Commerce Commission, totalling 8·4 per cent. Due to competitive considerations, the entire increase was not taken on some commodities.

The Maine pulp and paper industry continued an aggressive programme of plant expansion and modernisation; two new projects were started during the year.

Maine Central began moving coal to the Martin Marietta cement plant in Thomaston at the end of 1980. In 1981 nearly 50 000 tons had been handled in the first significant coal movement for Maine Central in several years. The railroad expected to handle

Quadruple-heading of Maine Central freight service

about 75 000 tons of coal to Thomaston in 1982. Maine Central is working with several major industries in Maine which are either evaluating or initiating coal conversion.

Net ton-miles remained reasonably stable in 1981, declining less than 1 per cent compared to 1980 in spite of the economic impact of a deepening national recession. Improved efficiency throughout the system resulted in a 2 per cent decline in train miles.

Traction and rolling stock

In 1981 Maine Central acquired 200 new 77-ton capacity all steel boxcars equipped with 10-foot sliding doors. One new caboose was purchased in the

continuing programme to upgrade the fleet. Three secondhand 2500 hp and one secondhand 1750 hp locomotive were placed in service.

Number of locomotives in service (January 1983): 56 line-haul units; 11 switchers. Freight train wagons: 4333.

Track

Rail: AREA, ARA-A, and ASCE sections, 37-58 kg/m
Cross-ties (sleepers): Hardwood, thickness 150-180 mm
Spacing: 1860/km
Fastenings: 16 × 152 mm spike
Max gradient: 2·2%
Max axleload: 29·82 tonnes

Traffic	1978	1979	1980	1981
Revenue tons (million)	8·134	8·202	7·798	7·455
Revenue ton-miles (million)	919·8	929	894	887·9

Financial results	1978	1979	1980	1981
		($ million)		
Railway operating revenues	50·782	56·858	64·870	69·903
Other income	1·287	1·147	1·090	3·164
Total income	52·070	58·006	65·960	73·067
Railway operating expenses	47·617	52·893	60·986	65·880
Interest	2·206	2·065	1·924	1·780
Miscellaneous expenses	0·530	0·160	0·171	0·169
Total expenses	50·354	55·118	63·082	67·829
Earnings before income taxes	1·716	2·888	2·878	5·238

Diesel locomotives

Class	Wheel arrangement	Transmission	Rated power (kW)	Max speed kmlh	Total weight tonnes	No in service	Year first built	Builders Mechanical parts	Builders Engine & type	Builders Transmission
U-25B	Bo-Bo	Elec	1864	112	132	9	1965	GE	GE	GE
U-18B	Bo-Bo	Elec	1342	112	125	10	1975	GE	GE	GE
GP-38	Bo-Bo	Elec	1491	104	128·5	13	1966	EMD	EMD	EMD
GP-9	Bo-Bo	Elec	1304	104	130	1	1963	EMD	EMD	EMD
GP-7R	Bo-Bo	Elec	1118	104	124	23	1950	EMD	EMD	EMD
SW-7	Bo-Bo	Elec	894	104	124	3	1950	EMD	EMD	EMD
SW-9	Bo-Bo·	Elec	894	104	124	2	1951	EMD	EMD	EMD
RS-11	Bo-Bo	Elec	1342	104	123	2	1956	Alco	Alco	GE
S-3	Bo-Bo	Elec	492	96	98	1	1953	Alco	Alco	GE
S-1	Bo-Bo	Elec	492	96	99	3	1949	Alco	Alco	GE

Maryland & Delaware Railroad Co

106 Railroad Avenue, Federalsburg, Maryland 21632

Telephone: (301) 754 5735

President: J A Hannold

148 route miles (236 km); 4 diesel locomotives; 135 freight cars

Maryland and Pennsylvania Railroad Co

A subsidiary of Emons Industries Inc

490 East Market St, York, Pennsylvania 17403

Telephone: (717) 848 2877

Chairman of the Board: R Grossman
President: J W Marino
Vice-President and General Manager: J Douglas Kostishack

64 route miles (106·8 km); 6 locomotives; 1728 freight cars

The Maryland and Pennsylvania is among the oldest continuously operating US railroads, having been originally chartered as the Maryland Central in 1867. It serves as a switching point, 50 miles north-west of Baltimore, where it connects with the Chessie System and Conrail.

McCloud River Railroad Company

PO Box A, McCloud, California 96057

Telephone: (916) 964 2141

President: W J Herndon

96 route miles (154 km); 4 locomotives; 247 freight cars

Michigan Northern Railway Co

PO Box 359, 110 W North Street, Cadillac, Michigan 49601

Telephone: (616) 775 0193

President: E A Andrus

432 route miles (695 km); 7 diesel locomotives; 42 freight cars; 2 passenger cars

Monongahela Railway Company*

P&LE Terminal Building, Pittsburgh, Pennsylvania 15219

Telephone: (412) 261 3201

President: H G Allyn, Jr
Superintendent: D E Gratz
Chief Engineer: R F Butter

146 route miles (235 km); 11 locomotives; 10 freight cars

Nevada Northern Railway Co

PO Box 476, East Ely, Nevada 89315

Telephone: (702) 289 4791

President: R R Leveille

148 route miles (238 km); 3 locomotives; 75 freight cars

New York, Susquehanna and Western Railroad Corporation

1 Railroad Avenue, Cooperstown, New York 13326

Telephone: (607) 547 2555

President: W G Rich

Member of Delaware Otsego System, which also includes the: Cooperstown and Charlotte Valley Railway; Central New York; Fonda, Johnston & Gloversville; and Lackawaxen & Stourbridge Railroads

61 route miles (98 km); 8 locomotives; 202 freight cars

North Louisiana & Gulf Railroad Co

PO Drawer 550, Hodge, Louisiana 71247

Telephone: (318) 259 3336

Chairman and President: E R Manning

40 route miles (64 km); 5 diesel locomotives; 994 freight cars

Octoraro Railway Inc

PO Box 146, Kennett Square, Pennsylvania 19348

Telephone: (215) 444 0238

President and General Manager: M Bennett

68 route miles in service (109 km); 4 diesel-electric locomotives; 142 freight cars

Oregon & Northwestern Railroad Co

PO Box 557, Hines, Oregon 97738

Telephone: (503) 573 2091

President: E Hines

51 route miles (82 km); 4 locomotives; 439 freight cars

Oregon, California & Eastern Railway Co

PO Box 1088, Klamath Falls, Oregon 97601

Telephone: (503) 882 5596

President: J P Tessier

66 route miles (105 km); 11 diesel locomotives; 150 freight wagons

Patapsco & Back Rivers Railroad

1275 Daly Avenue, Bethlehem, Pennsylvania 18175

Telephone: (215) 694 5971

President: T H Semmel

106 route miles (170 km); 32 diesel locomotives; 279 freight cars

Pittsburg and Shawmut Railroad

One Glade Park, RD3, Kittaning, Pennsylvania 16201

Vice-President, Traffic: J Reale
General Manager, Operations: G B Pettengill

96 route miles (154·5 km); 12 locomotives; 1296 freight cars

Providence and Worcester Railroad Co*

PO Box 1490, 1 Depot Square, Woonsocket, Rhode Island 02940-9205

Telephone: (401) 765 2000

President: O R Harrold
Vice-Presidents: R D Finizia
              A E Kaulbach
General Manager: R P Chrzanowski
Chief Mechanical Officer: I M Filler

360 route miles (576 km); 12 locomotives; 1070 freight cars

Richmond, Fredericksburg and Potomac Railroad Co*

PO Box 11281, 2134 West Laburnum Avenue, Richmond, Virginia 23227

Telephone: (804) 257 3200

President: J J Newbauer
Vice-President, Executive Department: R L Beadles
Comptroller: F A Crovo, Jr
Chief Engineer: James C Hobbs
Chief Mechanical Officer: W E Durham
General Traffic Officer: J W Moore
General Superintendent, Transportation: J D Doswell

113·8 route miles (183 km); 41 diesel locomotives; 1619 freight cars

The RF & P is an important 'bridge' from Washington DC in the north to Richmond, Virginia in the south. At Washington it connects to the B & O and Penn Central (now part of Conrail), and at Richmond to the Seaboard Coast Line. Part of CSX Corporation (qv).

Roscoe, Snyder & Pacific Railway Co

PO Box 68, Roscoe, Texas 79545

Telephone: (915) 766 3394

Chairman of the Board: R B Mize
President: C Holt

32 route miles (51·5 km); 2 locomotives; 685 freight cars

Sacramento Northern Railway

1025 19th Street, Sacramento, California 95814

Telephone: (916) 442 0819

President: R C Marquis

146·9 route miles (236·4 km); 3 diesel locomotives; 99 freight cars

San Francisco Belt Railroad

Suite 221, World Trade Center, San Francisco, California 94111

Telephone: (415) 956 3874

President: W B Kyle
Vice-President: L T Cecil
Superintendent: S L Leal

58 route miles (98·3 km); 3 locomotives

Operated by Port Railroads Inc.

Santa Maria Valley Railroad Company

PO Box 340, Santa Maria, California 93456

Telephone: (805) 922 7941

President: Marian Hancock Barry
Vice-President and Manager: S J Sword

18 route miles (29 km); 8 locomotives

Seattle & North Coast Railroad

2150 North 107th Street, Seattle, Washington 98133

Telephone: (206) 367 3155
Telex: 910 444 4065

President: A G Allen
Executive Vice-President: L E Bunting
Vice-President, Finance and Secretary: H Kimmerle Culver

Gauge: 1435 mm
Length: 81 km

Traffic	1980/81	1981/82
Total freight tonnage	101 101	141 505
Total freight tonne-km	1 248 000	1 747 000

The company has begun loading intermodal containers direct to take advantage of further domestic and foreign (Far East) markets and traffic patterns. The railroad is also testing the passenger market with charters and excusions between Port Angeles and Port Townsend (50 miles) along its 'Olympic Peninsula Route'.

Track
Since taking over the railroad in early 1980 from the Milwaukee Road, the company has launched a major track rehabilitation, replacing 65 lb and 75 lb rail with new 100 lb and 115 lb rail to accommodate the heavier loads its shippers want to send.

Traction and rolling stock
6 EMD diesel locomotives, consisting of 3 1500 hp F7s, 2 1200 hp SW1200s and a 600 hp SW1; 335 freight cars; 2 passenger cars

Sierra Railroad Company

13645 Tuolumu Road, Sonora, California 95370

Telephone: (209) 532 3685

President: J L Foster
General Manager: P B Rundle

50 route miles (80·5 km); 3 diesel locomotives; 2 freight cars

South Buffalo Railway Co

2558 Hamburg Turnpike, Lackawanna, New York 14218

Telephone: (716) 821 1000

President: T H Semmel
Vice-President, Operations: H J Umberger

93 route miles (148 km); 29 diesel locomotives; 200 freight cars

Spencerville & Elgin Railroad Co

PO Box 7, Spencerville, Ohio 45887

Telephone: (419) 647 4373

President and Chief Executive: D L Meeker

169 route miles (271 km); 6 diesel locomotives; 3150 freight cars

Spokane International Railroad Co*

1416 Dodge Street, Omaha, Nebraska 68179

Chairman and Chief Executive: J H Evans
President: J C Kenefick
Vice-President, Operations: J R Davis
   Traffic: W P Barrett
Chief Engineer: R M Brown

150 route miles (240 km); 85 freight cars

Stockton Terminal & Eastern Railroad

1330 North Broadway Avenue, Stockton, California 95205

Telephone: (209) 466 7001

President and General Manager: L Hardaway Jr

16 route miles (25·7 km); 5 diesel locomotives; 200 freight cars

Terminal Railroad Association of St Louis

906 Olive Street, St Louis, Missouri 63101

Telephone: (314) 342 4200

President: L J King
Vice-President and General Manager: C R Hurt

300 track-miles (482·7 km); 63 diesel locomotives

Texas Mexican Railway Co*

PO Box 419, Laredo, Texas 78042-0419

Telephone: (512) 722 6411
Telex: 76 34 11

Chairman of the Board and Chief Executive Officer: A R Ramos
President and Chief Operating Officer: C H Darnell Jr
Vice President, Operations and Chief Mechanical Officer: H A Martinez
   Finance and Comptroller: Z Solis

Gauge: 1435 mm
Length: 253 km

Traffic	1981
Total freight tonnage	3 166 246
Average net freight train load (tons)	4337
Finance ($ 000)	1981
Revenues	
Freight, parcels and mail	25 600
Interest	1306
Other	532
Total	27 438
Expenditure	
Staff/personnel	7855
Materials and services	8457
Depreciation	2998
Financial charges	204
Taxes, current	2454
deferred	1083
Total	23 051

Track
Rail: 90 lb RA (43·74 kg/m); 100 lb RE (49·6 kg/m); 110 lb RE (54·56 kg/m); 115 lb RE (57·05 kg/m); 136 lb RE (67·46 kg/m)
Cross ties (sleepers): Wooden, thickness 7 in
Spacing: 1988/km
Fastenings: ⅝ × 6 in track spikes
Max curvature radius: 6°
Max gradient: 0·75%
Max axleload: 65·75 tons

Traction and rolling stock
16 diesel locomotives; 1121 freight cars

Diesel locomotives

Wheel arrangement	Transmission	Rated power (kW)	Max speed km/h	Total weight tonnes	No in service	Year first built	Builders Mechanical parts	Builders Engine & type
B-B	Elec	1118·6	91·73	133·1	2	1950	EMD	567
B-B	Elec	1305	91·73	133·1	1	1958	EMD	567-C
B-B	Elec	1342·3	91·73	133·1	3	1963	EMD	567-D
B-B	Elec	1491·4	91·73	134·2	10	1966	EMD	645

Texas & Northern Railway Co*

PO Box 38565, Dallas, Texas 75238-0565

Telephone: (214) 340 6603

President and Chairman: W H Jamieson
Executive Vice-President: M N Benton
Vice-President, Operations: G E Pitts
   Purchases: E Sellars
   Finance: R A Tracy

7·6 route miles (12·2 km); 17 locomotives; 653 freight cars

Texas, Oklahoma & Eastern Railroad

421 E Stilwell, Dequeen, Arkansas 71832

Telephone: (501) 534 3582

President: L E Endicott

40 route miles (64 km); 9 diesel locomotives; 1332 freight cars

Toledo, Peoria & Western Railroad Co*

2000 East Washington Street, East Peoria, Illinois 61611

Telephone: (309) 694 8400

President: R E McMillan

472 route miles (759·4 km); 29 diesel locomotives; 382 freight cars

Transkentucky Transportation Railroad Inc

199 East Main Street, Lexington, Kentucky 40507

President and General Manager: C F Powell
Superintendent, Operations: Robert A Adams

50 route miles (80 km); 8 locomotives; 50 freight cars

Tuscola & Saginaw Bay Railway

538 E Huron Street, Vassar, Mississippi 48768

President: C J Lapp
Vice-President, Operations: P J de Wolf

220 route miles (354 km); 5 diesel locomotives; 170 freight cars

Union Railroad Co

PO Box 68, Monroeville, Pennsylvania 15146

Telephone: (412) 829 6600

President: D H Hoffman

31 route miles (49 km); 115 diesel locomotives; 1754 freight cars

Upper Merion and Plymouth Railroad Co

PO Box 404, Conshohocken, Pennsylvania 19428

Telephone: (215) 275 2066

President and General Manager: J N Ball

15 route miles (24·1 km); 3 locomotives; 1609 freight cars

Vermont Railway Inc

267 Battery Street, Burlington, Vermont 05401

Telephone: (802) 658 2550

President: J R Pennington
Vice-President, Operations: C H Bischoff

131·5 route miles (211·6 km); 6 diesel locomotives; 1200 freight cars

Washington Terminal Co

Union Station, Washington DC 20002

Telephone: (202) 289 2381

President: R A Herman

33 track miles (53 km); 8 diesel locomotives

West Virginia Northern Railroad Inc

PO Box 458, Kingswood, West Virginia 26537

Telephone: (304) 329 1050

Chairman: R Grossman
President: J Marino
Vice-President, Operations: J D Kostishack

A subsidiary of Emons Industries Inc, serving coal-mining companies and interchanging with the Chessie System.

17 route miles (27·4 km); 3 diesel locomotives

Winchester & Western Railroad Co

PO Box 264, Winchester, Virginia 22601

Telephone: (703) 662 2600

President: W L Woods
Manager: W P Light

18 route miles (28·9 km); 5 diesel locomotives; 325 freight cars

Yakima Valley Transportation Co

104½ West Yakima Avenue, Yakima, Washington 98902

President: M E Merritt

21 route miles (33·8 km); 2 electric locomotives

Transit systems and authorities

In certain conurbation areas regional authorities operate longer-distance commuter services with their own equipment over trackage acquired from railroads, or have the services operated by railroads under contract. These operations are distinct from the metro and light rail activities covered in the Rapid Transit section.

California Department of Transportation (Caltrans)

1120 North Street, PO Box 1499, Sacramento, California 96807

Telephone: (916) 322 5480

Director: John J Kozak

Caltrans funds the Peninsula commuter operation over Southern Pacific tracks between San Francisco and San Jose, which takes in the so-called 'Silicon Valley'. In 1982 it sought bids for 42 new stainless-steel, bi-level cars for the operation.

Massachusetts Bay Transportation Authority (MBTA)

50 High Street, Boston, Massachusetts 02110

Telephone: (617) 722 5000

Route length: 574 km

MBTA operates 43 diesel locomotives and 243 passenger cars over 796 km of ex-Penn Central and Boston & Maine trackage bought in the 1970s. The stock includes 95 elderly ex-B&M Budd RDC railcars, 32 of which have been refurbished internally and modified as non-powered trailers by Morrison-Knudsen. MBTA seeks a $37 million UMTA grant to treat the rest of the fleet. The traction stock includes new EMD F40 locomotives.

Metropolitan Transportation Authority (MTA)

347 Madison Avenue, New York, New York 10017

Telephone: (212) 878 7000

Chairman: R Ravitch

MTA's sphere of operations in the New York area includes the Long Island Rail Road (qv). A sub-sidiary, Metro-North Commuter Rail Division, was created to take over Conrail commuter services in MTA territory from the start of 1983, following Conrail's relief from commuter passenger operation under the Northeast Rail Service Act of 1982.

New Jersey Transit

180 Boyden Avenue, Maplewood, New Jersey 07040

Telephone: (201) 761 8300

President: J C Premo
General Manager: G Heinle

From the start of 1983 former Conrail commuter passenger operations over ex-Erie, Lackawanna, Jersey Central, Pennsylvania and New York & Long Branch lines in New Jersey were added to those already managed for the New Jersey Department of Transportation.

Northeast Illinois Railroad Corp (NIRC)

300 North State Street, Chicago, Illinois 60610

Chairman: Lewis W Hill
Vice-President: J E Cole
Chief Operations Officer: J A Pochron
Chief Mechanical Officer: R C Runyon
Chief Engineering Officer: V L Stoner

Gauge: 1435 mm
Length: 205·3 km

NIRC is the commuter railroad operating arm of the Chicago Regional Transportation Authority (RTA). The RTA, which since 1979 has operated without direct state subsidy, covers the Chicago area services operated on tracks of the Chicago & North Western, Illinois Central Gulf, Milwaukee Road (since October 1982) and Rock Island companies; purchase of the Rock Island trackage was completed in December 1982. Burlington Northern still retains control of its commuter service between Chicago and Aurora, however, because the tracks are shared with BN freight. Following fare increases that doubled rates within a year, passenger journey volume has receded about 25 per cent since 1980.

To replace its inherited EMD Type E locomotives on the C&NW lines, the RTA in 1982 ordered 24 EMD Type F40PH-2 3000 hp units from EMD. NIRC operates 41 line-haul and three switching diesel locomotives and 217 passenger cars, including bi-levels.

Port Authority of Allegheny County

Beaver and Island Avenue, Pittsburgh, Pennsylvania 15233

Chairman: James A Romanelli
Executive Director: James R Maloney

The Port Authority operates two weekday commuter trains along a 29·3 km right-of-way from downtown Pittsburgh to the borough of Versailles.

PAT has recently completed a $9·4 million revitalisation of this commuter rail operation, which included the purchase of two rebuilt diesel locomotives, the rehabilitation of ten passenger coaches, the construction of three 'park-n-ride' lots and a new McKeesport Transportation Center; the new centre provides a major interchange for bus and rail commuters.

South Eastern Michigan Transportation Authority (SEMTA)

13th Floor, 660 Woodward Avenue, Detroit, Michigan 48226

Telephone: (313) 256 8600

Director of Operations: R Shrauner
Commuter Rail Manager: J R Wolfe

SEMTA operates over 42·3 km of route with five diesel locomotives and 23 passenger cars.

Southeastern Pennsylvania Transportation Authority (SEPTA)
Regional High Speed Division

Edison Building, 130 South 9th Street, Philadelphia, Pennsylvania 19107

Telephone: (215) 574 7300

Chairman: L Gould
General Manager: D L Gunn

SEPTA operates over 1599 track-km, of which it owns 367 km, with 359 emu cars, three locomotives and four diesel railcars. From the start of 1983 it assumed former Conrail commuter passenger operations over ex-Reading and Pennsylvania Railroad routes in its territory.

URUGUAY

State Railways Administration (AFE)
Administración de Ferrocarriles del Estado

Casilla de Correo 419, Calle La Paz 1095, Montevideo

Telephone: 8 95 51; 8 58 66

President: Col E R Mila
Vice-President: Col L·H Melgar
Director: L A Garcia Troise
Secretary General: Carlos Baldomir
General Manager: Ing M Esteva Sureda
Assistant General Manager: Ing J C Barozzi
Manager, Operations: Ing J Camano
Manager, Traction: Eng H C Chapuis
Manager, Way and Works: R J Paolillo
Chief Signalling and Communications: Ing Francisco Puppo
Chief Supply Manager: I Beltrami

Gauge: 1435 mm
Route length: 3004 km

New rail links with Argentina have been the major features of recent development. The plan includes development of the littoral line and continued extension of the central line northwards from km 329. A new 27 km section between Mercedes and Ombucito was completed in 1979, providing a cut-off for the existing Chamberlain-Durazno link with Argentina. A new 2·8 km line over the Salto Grande dam to a link with the General Urquiza Division of Argentine Railways was opened in August 1982, following which a through Salto-Concordia (Argentina) passenger service was inaugurated.

Traffic
The effect of the new Salto Grande link with Argentine Railways on traffic was reduced by the recession and limited availability of equipment, which combined to cause a severe downturn of both passenger and freight volume in 1981 and 1982.

One of 15 diesel train-sets built for AFE during 1977/78 by Ganz-Mávag

Traffic	1979	1980	1981	1982
Total freight tonnage (million)	1·406	1·369	1·2	1
Total freight tonne-km (million)	N/A	N/A	221	180
Total passenger-km (million)	454·8	417·5	339	274
Total passenger journeys (million)	N/A	N/A	3·3	3·2

Modernisation
In 1983 AFE was seeking World Bank aid for a 1984-89 modernisation plan to include new traction and rolling stock, workshop rehabilitation, improved signalling and telecommunications and track reconstruction. Meanwhile, following an agreement with Voest-Alpine of Austria for supplies of track materials, which ensured supply of 5000 tonnes of 50 kg/m rail and other items in 1983, track upgrading has continued. A considerable length of new cwr has already been installed between Colon and Las Piedras, and between Sudriers and Verdum.

New lines
AFE now hopes to undertake the long planned extension of the Florida-Tupambae line beyond km 329. In 1982 the Ministry of Transport invited tenders for construction of 18 km of new line, including a bridge over the River Negro at Piccada de las Piedras, to cater for the region south-east of Tacuarembo.

Investment
Planned capital spending in 1983 covered (US$ 000):

Locomotives (12 line-haul, 5 shunting)	11 600
Freight wagons (20)	1200
New line building	15 986
Track improvements and equipment	20 011
Signalling and communications	2148
Other	6324
Total	57 269

Motive power and rolling stock
Resources were strengthened in 1981 by 14 diesel railbuses and 16 trailers obtained second-hand from the German Federal Railway (DB), arrival of which released locomotives for freight haulage.

Steam locomotives	10
Diesel railcars	26
Diesel multiple-units	16
Diesel railbuses and trailers	30
Passenger coaches	83
Freight cars	2759

Diesel locomotives

Class	Wheel arrangement	Transmission	Rated power hp	Max kg	Tractive effort Continuous at kg	kmlh	Max speed kmlh	Wheel dia mm	Total weight tonnes	Length mm	Year first built	Builders Mechanical parts	Engine & type	Transmission
GE	C-C	Elec	1500	25 500	21 100	15	95	1041	102	16 986	1952	Gardner-Denver Westinghouse	Alco 250 and 244	G Electric
Alsthom	B-B	Elec	825	16 000	9800	16	90	1000	56	13 496	1963	Alsthom	MGO 12 VASH	Alsthom
Ganz-Mávag	B-B	Hyd-Mech	925	8200	5500	20	100	920	48	16 330	1977	Ganz-Mávag	GM 12 VFE 17/24	GM HM 912
Alco 1600	A-1A	Elec	1600		17 650	20	120	1016	108					
Alco/GE 1500	C-C	Elec	1475		25 000	20	100	1016	102					
Alsthom 800	B-B	Elec	800		9800	20	90	1016	56					

VENEZUELA

Venezuela State Railways (Ferrocar)
Instituto Autónomo, Administración de Ferrocarriles del Estado

ave Principal los Ruices, Edif Stemo Pisos 1, 2, 3, Apartado 146, Caracas 1071

Telephone: 41 61 41

Chairman and General Manager: Manuel Vásquez Moya
Vice-President: Igor José Colmenares Guevara
Comptroller: F Alvarez M
Planning Manager: Pedro José Briceño
Legal Adviser: M Hernandez
Public Relations and Chief of Personnel Office: Alirio Capella Heredia
Manager, Operations: Freddy Castejón
 Development: Jesús Ramón Carrera
 Freight: Adaulfo Giménez
 Administration and Finance: Oscar A Aguilar
Superintendent: Domingo Javier

Gauge: 1435 mm
Route length: 173 km

Transport development
Progress with the plan to reverse the closures of the 1950s and create a 3700 km rail system by 1990 is considerably slower than anticipated. So far only the 173 km line from Puerto Cabello to Barquisameto is operational. The extension of this line southward from Yaritagua, just short of Barquisameto, to Acarigua and Barinas, was still in progress in 1982, when the scheme was enlarged by the draft of a link between this route and El Vigia, La Fria and San Cristobal, south of Lake Maracaibo. The projection from Moron, on the existing route, to Yaracal and Riecito, was in progress only over the first 45 km to Tucacas. Of the total budgeted 1982 investment of 722 million Bolivars, 615·5 million was earmarked for new line construction.

Still only a paper draft was the east-west transversal from Barcelona through Caracas to Valencia, or its alternative route from Anacao to Valencia and Acarigua. The same applied to the 335 km eastern trunk route from Guanta, on the coast, southward

through Anacao to Ciudad Guayana on the Orinoco River.

Following the 1981 reorganisation of the railway under a new title, Ferrocar, and Director-General, a revised master scheme was produced. This laid priority on construction of the line from Guanta to the south, and its projection as far as Matanzas in Bolivia. At the same time an existing railway running 179 km for the conveyance of ore from Ciudad Piar, in the south-east, to Puerto Ordaz would be upgraded and connected to the new railway by a bridge of some 2 km over the Orinoco.

Another new priority is a 120 km/h rapid transit line of 32 km from Caracas to the Caribbean port of La Guaira, to be electrified at 1·5 kV dc and adhesion-worked despite the difference of 1000 metres in altitude between Caracas and the coastline, and the mountain range between. Construction has been entrusted to a West German group comprising MAN, Deutsche Eisenbahn Consulting, Siemens, Ferrostaal and AEG-Telefunken, which will supply 31 three-car emus (by MAN), signalling, track, traction current supply apparatus and a maintenance depot. Completion has been set for 1984.

New coal line

In September 1982 the Government authorised immediate construction of a 100 km line to ferry coal from a mine at Guasare, in the north-west of the country, to a power station and planned steelworks at Sur Maracaibo, on the western shore of Lake Maracaibo. Engineering design of the project is entrusted to MKI International-Cosa, an organisation including Morrison-Knudsen and a Venezuelan company. Planned throughput is 5 million tonnes a year for the power station and 1·2 million tonnes for the steel plant. The line, scheduled for opening in 1985, is likely to be electrified at 50 kV ac and will work with 60-wagon unit trains hauled by a pair of locomotives.

Signalling

The single-track Puerto Cabello-Barquisameto line is CTC-controlled with WABCO equipment.

Track

Rail employed is 100 lb/yd ASCE on wood or Dywidag concrete sleepers spaced 1670 per km. Minimum curve radius is 700 metres, maximum permitted axleload 31·75 tonnes, and maximum speed is 70 km/h.

Motive power and rolling stock

Ferrocar operates eight diesel locomotives of 1750-2000 hp, three 400 hp diesel shunters, two diesel-mechanical railcars, 33 passenger cars and 284 freight wagons. In 1982 the railway planned to acquire four more main-line and two shunting locomotives.

Traffic	1981
Total freight tonnage	121 894
Total freight tonne-km	13 511 244
Total passenger-km	9 715 637

Finances	
Revenues (Bolivars)	1981
Passengers and baggage	301 777
Freight and mail	2 541 242
Total	2 843 019

Expenditure (Bolivars)	
Staff/personnel	9 808 013
Materials and services	1 072 667
Depreciation	2 993 852
Total	13 874 532

Ferrocar 290 hp diesel-mechanical railcar

Intermodal train at Puerto Cabello

VIET-NAM

Viet-Nam Railways (DSVN)
Duong Sat Viet Nam

180 Nam Bo Street, Hanoi

Telephone: 54998; 58281

Director-General and Vice-Minister, Railways: Trau Lu

Vice-Directors-General
  Administration: Trau Mau
  Rolling Stock: Dau Cao Hy
  Civil Engineering: Nguyen Tri
  Traffic: Nguyen Van Truy
  General Services: Pham Van Giap
  Development: Nguyen Van Tu

Gauge: 1435 mm; 1000 mm; mixed gauge
Route length: 170 km; 2200 km; 230 km

The railway is administered in three Divisions: Northern, based on Hanoi; Central, based on Donang; and Southern, based on Ho Chi Minh City.

The last metre of track on the 1730 km trans-Viet-Nam railway, linking Hanoi with Ho Chi Minh City (formerly Saigon) was laid in December 1976.

The railway operates 106 steam and 88 diesel locomotives, 600 passenger cars and 3500 freight cars. Passenger volume is around 50 million journeys a year; freight aggregates over 9 million tonnes. In 1982 orders were placed with India's Projects and Equipment Corporation for 15 1350 hp, 251D-engined diesel-electric Co-Co locomotives, similar to Indian Railway's Type YDM4; and with Belgian industry for 16 1760 hp, 84-tonne diesel-electric Co-Cos.

YUGOSLAVIA

Yugoslav Railways (JZ)
Zajednica Jugoslovenske Zeleznice
(Community of Yugoslav Railways)

Nemanjina 6, Belgrade 11000

Telephone: 685 722
Telex: 12495

General Manager: Nikola Filipovic
Administration and Safety: S Hodak
Planning and Development: S Vukovic
Commercial and Personnel: Ratko Tatalović
Technical: N Lemez
Operating: R Milaku
Traction and Rolling Stock: Jovan Pejovic
Works and Modernisation: V Gligorov
Financial: D Fogel
Regional Managers
  Belgrade: Z Nastic
  Sarajevo: V Smajlovic
  Zagreb: T Novacic
  Skopje: Risto Petrovski

  Ljubljana: Dipl Ing Joze Slokar
  Novi Sad: Tima Ilin
  Pristina: Beca Zenon
  Titograd: Milivoje Lausevic

Gauge: 1435 mm
Route length: 9393 km
Electrification: 2585 km at 25 kV 50 Hz
  755 km at 3 kV dc

Priority concern to develop the country's road system in the years preceding the 1973 oil crisis has eroded JZ's share of national transport, particularly in passenger travel. In 1982 JZ recorded 110·7 million passenger journeys compared with 236 million in 1964; and though freight tonne-km has risen, from some 22 000 million in 1976 to 26 165 million in 1982, JZ's percentage of the national market in that period slipped from 52·1 to 49·2.

Since the oil crisis, however, investment in JZ has been increased and measures taken to equalise terms of competition for freight and encourage intermodal system development. In 1980, for instance, a road transport fuel tax was decreed to contribute funds for rail re-equipment, and in 1982 the country's republics were presented with a programme to establish a national complex of well-equipped railheads as distribution centres to be fed by unit trains, and from which road delivery vehicles would radiate. Containerisation would be fostered by an investment of 2000 million dinars on transhipment terminals at the sea ports of Bar, Koper, Ploce and Rijeka, and at the river ports of Senta, Ljubljana, Belgrade and Zagreb.

International transit traffic represents 10 per cent of JZ's total freight movement. Fuelled by increasing use of Yugoslav ports for Comecon traffic to the USSR, by produce from Greece for north-west Europe, and by mineral flows to Austria, Federal Republic of Germany and Czechoslovakia, this element is expected to grow substantially—one reason for the willingness of such agencies as the World Bank and European Investment Bank to help finance electrification and other infrastructure improvements on the main east-west arterial routes of JZ.

At the end of 1982 the Government gave JZ a high ranking in the list of industries for priority development in face of enforced economies elsewhere in the national economy. Industry was urged to make more use of the railway to relieve pressure on roads. As a means for JZ development, a loan worth US$62 million was secured from the European Investment

Bank and 3000 million dinars was made available to JZ for purchase of rolling stock from Yugoslav manufacturers.

Traffic

Although the 1982 traffic volume plan was not fulfilled, JZ managed a significant increase of passenger journeys and passenger-km and also a rise of freight tonne-km, though total tonnage was down by comparison with 1981. The freight figures reflected a remarkable 27 per cent rise of 575 000 tonnes in transit traffic, with the greater part of it coming from Federal German-Bulgarian trade via the Jesenice-Gevgelija main line; this was up no less than 80 per cent, or 220 000 tonnes, to 500 000 tonnes. Port traffic rose 12 per cent. In recent years domestic freight traffic has been eroded by rising coal consumption close to sources, transfer of almost half JZ's oil movement to pipelines, more recourse to local supplies of construction materials and reduction of agricultural products to processed items before despatch.

	1981	1982
Total passenger journeys (million)	104·9	110·7
Total passenger-km (million)	10 510	11 265
Total freight tonnes (million)	85·9	85·7
Total freight tonne-km (million)	25 720	26 165

Finance

The loss on the 1982 working was 3487 million dinars, despite an increase of state and provincial compensations to a total of 16 900 million dinars. The deficit was twice the 1981 figure. To rectify the trend the Government authorised a 17 per cent increase of passenger and freight tariffs at the end of 1982.

Electrification

At the end of 1981 2979 route-km were electrified. Recent electrification has been at 25 kV 50 Hz, but in the far west of the country a few routes retain the 3 kV dc of early electrification. In the latter area JZ plans to convert the existing Zagreb-Rijeka route to 25 kV 50 Hz ac, even though it has hopes of replacing this severely speed-restricted but intensively-used line with a new high-speed link before the end of the century.

With completion of some vital trunk route schemes in the west of the country at the start of the 1980s, the electrification component of the 1981-85 Five-Year Plan lays emphasis on the eastern half of the country. It envisages 1279 route-km of additional electrification, to raise the percentage of the network under wires to 45 per cent and the proportion of electrically-hauled trains from 62 to 70 per cent.

A major achievement of recent electrification has been the secondary main line of 220 km from Sunja to Doboj. In 1980 a 55 km stretch of this scheme was finished, its signalling and telecommunications installations included, in 100 days by the contractor, Energoinvest of Sarajevo. Also wired recently were the 110 km between Botovo and Dugo Selo, further to the north-west.

It is hoped to energise the Skopje-Gevgelija section of the key transversal in 1986 and at that date to have the route electrified throughout from Sezana in the north-west to the Greek border; by then the section from Zagreb to Rijeka and Sezana will have been converted from 3 kV dc to obtain continuous working at 25 kV ac. Completion in 1986-87 of electrification over the mountainous 281 km from Bosanski Novi via Knin to Split will extend the availability of electric traction to all the country's chief ports.

In the longer term, JZ aims to electrify the 386 km Macedonian transversal from Lapovo to Skopje and its 75 km Kraljevo-Pozega offshoot; the 134 km line between Subotica, near the Hungarian border, and Vinkovici, on the Belgrade-Zagreb route; also several Bosnian branches, including the 79 km between Tuzla and Brčko. To be electrified too is the 84 km line from Belgrade Dunav to Vrsac.

New lines

Restraint of Government expenditure precludes immediate progress with new routes, except for the 24·5 km link to be built from Titograd, on the Belgrade-Bar line, to·meet at the frontier with the Albanian line being erected beyond Shkoder. This will be commissioned in 1985. Also making slow progress for financial reasons is the massive reformation of the Belgrade network, begun in 1976, which aims to supersede the dead-end central station and its inconvenient approach from Zagreb with a new one served by a through route tunnelled beneath the city. Construction of the new eastern approach began in 1980. This is in the form of a north-south line from Pont de Pancevo, on the Danube, to Topcider, from which, at National Library, lines will branch north-west via a new city through station and a bridge over the Sava to a junction with the present exit to Zagreb at Belgrade Nova. Completion of the whole scheme is unlikely before 1990. The western Belgrade bypass from Batajnica, on the Zagreb route, to Ostroznice and Makis yard, completed in 1976, is to be double-tracked by 1985. Other double-tracking planned is on the main west-to-east route for 50 km from Stalac to Nis, between Zagreb and Sesvete. After 1985 JZ hopes to lay a new 240 km/h railway from the Austrian frontier at Jesenice to Ljubljana, and one from Zagreb to Rijeka.

Signalling

CTC centres are to be established at Belgrade, Ljubljana, Novi Sad and Skopje. The installations will include track-to-train radio communication. Over 980 route-km are programmed for signalling and telecommunications re-equipment under the current Five-Year Plan.

Investment

Investment in 1982 totalled 10 100 million dinars, 30 per cent less than in 1981 in real money terms. Under the 1981-85 Plan, which projects 65 000 million dinars spending in total, JZ is to acquire 102 electric and 111 diesel locomotives, 107 mu sets, 671 passenger cars and more than 13 000 freight wagons. Another main objective is to raise maximum permissible speed on the Jesenice-Gevgelija transversal and its branch between Bis and the Bulgarian border from 100 to 160 km/h. A large proportion of JZ investment is funded from the proceeds of road vehicle fuel taxation.

Traction and rolling stock

At the start of 1983 JZ owned 259 steam, 441 electric and 771 diesel locomotives, 86 emus, 307 dmus comprising 675 engines, 2324 passenger cars and 47 199 freight wagons. The aim is now to eliminate steam through the current Five-Year Plan's electrification and subsequent re-assignment of diesel traction; the remaining steam power is largely concentrated around Vojvodina in the north and Kosovo in the south-east.

At the end of 1981 JZ took into service the first prototype of a new thyristor-controlled ac electric locomotive design developed jointly by its own engineers and those of Rade Koncar, Zagreb. The thyristor-controlled Type 442 is a Bo-Bo with a continuous rating of 4400 kW, intended for mixed traffic use; deliveries from a series order are unlikely before 1984. During 1982 JZ requested tenders for the supply of a number of 25 kV 50 Hz air-conditioned, three-car emus, each to include a buffet car, with a maximum speed of 120 km/h.

JZ's latest diesel locomotive purchases are 30 2450 hp diesel-electric Co-Cos of 100 tonnes weight, built locally by Djuro Djakovic under GM-EMD licence. In 1982 an order was placed with Messerschmitt-Bolkow-Blohm (MBB) for 27 two-car dmus. MBB supplied JZ with 10 dmus in 1969-70, since re-engined, but the new sets will have aluminium bodywork as opposed to the lightweight steel of the earlier models. The new sets are for service in Slovenia and will be delivered in 1985. Five will be for inter-city work, and will include a small kitchen for service to the unit's total of 92 rotating armchair seats with folding tables. The remainder will be for short-haul work, seating 108 and with standing room for 64. The single power unit in each set will have a 367 kW motor and hydraulic transmission; up to four sets will be capable of multiple-unit working. Some of the order is to be assembled locally by Boris Kidric.

New passenger car orders are to include 58 vehicles of the UIC Type Z pattern. They will be built locally by Gosà at its Palanka works.

Wagon procurement is running at a high level. A total of 860 four-axle and 920 two-axle wagons were added to stock in 1981; and deliveries of 2400 more were programmed in 1982.

JZ emu by Ganz-Màvag

Diesel locomotives

Class	Wheel arrangement	Trans-mission	Rated power hp	Tractive effort Max kg	Continuous at kg	km/h	Max speed km/h	Wheel dia mm	Axle load tons	Total weight tons	Length mm	No built	Year first built	Builders Mechanical parts	Engine	Transmission
644	Bo-Bo	Elec	600	16 650	12 030	8·5	80	1040	15·4	61·7	12 290	80	1960	Måvag	Ganz	Ganz
642	Bo-Bo	Elec	825	16 000	10 950	14·5	80	1100	16·8	67·2	14 740	104	1961	Dj Djakovic	MGO/Dj Dj	Br&L/RK
643	Bo-Bo	Elec	925	16 800	10 800	16·5	80	1100	16·8	67·2	14 740	22	1967	Br&L/Dj Dj	MGO/Dj Dj	Br&L
644	A1A-A1A	Elec	1650		26 400		100	1016	14·9	96	14 173		1975	Macosa	GM	GM
661	Co-Co	Elec	1950	21 200			120	1016	18	108	17 272	218	1960	GM	GM	GM
662	Co-Co	Elec	1650	22 000	10 600	28·4	120	1100	16	96	17 740	17	1965	Dj Djakovic	MGO/Dj Dj	RK/Sever
663	Co-Co	Elec	3300		30 490		124	1016	19·8	118	19 520	14	1972	GM	GM	GM
664	Co-Co	Elec	2200		26 290		124	1016	16·3	108	15 764	58	1972	GM	GM	GM
665	Co-Co	Elec	2750				127			127		20	1972	MLW	MLW/Alco	GE
731	C	Hyd	400	12 500	3600	17	60	950	14	42	10 500	44	1958	Jenbach/Dj Dj	Jenbach	Voith
732	C	Hyd	600	13 100	6000	17	80	950	14·5	43·5	10 500	77	1969	Dj Djakovic	Jenbach	Voith
733	C	Hyd	600	15 800	5000	18	60	1250	16	48	10 180	37	1968	Dj Djakovic	MGO/Dj Dj	Voith
740	B-B	Hyd	600	10 900	3100	33	50	850	8	32	11 600	40	1968	Dj Djakovic	MGO/Dj Dj	Voith
741	B-B	Hyd	1500	21 300	17 750	14	120	920	16	64	14 000	3	1966	MIN	Maybach	Maybach
742	B-B	Hyd	1650	19 200	16 800	12	120	1000	17	68	14 400	60	1972	MIN	Pielstick	CKD-SRM
743	B-B	Hyd	1600				120	950	16	65	15 340	1	1975	Dj Djakovic	MGO/Dj Dj	Voith
761	C-C	Hyd	1950	24 000			120	950	16·5	97·8	20 270	3	1957	Krauss-Maffei	Maybach	Maybach

740: 760 mm gauge. RK: Rade Koncar Zagreb. Br&L: Brissonneau & Lotz

Electric locomotives

Class	Wheel arrangement	Line current kV type	Rated power hp	Tractive effort Max kg	Continuous at kg	km/h	Max speed km/h	Wheel dia mm	Total weight tonnes	Length mm	No built	Year first built	Builders Mechanical parts	Electrical equipment
341	Bo-Bo	3 dc	2130	19 000	13 800	53	95	1250	78	16 024	1	1954	Alsthom	Alsthom
342	Bo-Bo	3 dc	3060		14 700		120	1250	76	15 800	40	1968	Asgen	OMFP
362	Bo-Bo-Bo	3 dc	4550	33 000	26 400	45	120	1250	110	18 400	40	1960	Asgen	OMFP
363	Co-Co	3 dc	3750	25 000	15 400	63	125	1100	114	20 190	40	1976	Alsthom	Alsthom
441	Bo-Bo	25 50Hz ac	5550	28 000	17 700	65	120	1250	78	15 470	190	1967	SGP/RK	Traction Union
461	Co-Co	50 50Hz ac	6840	42 000	26 500	69·5	120	1250	126	19 800	45	1972	Electroputere	Electroputere

ZAÏRE

National Office of Transport & Communications (ONATRA)

BP 1 228, Kinshasa 1

Telephone: 22 109; 24 736

State Commissioner: M K Wakatana
General Director: K M Mbumba
Director, Road, Rail and Air: Mukondolo Ngoyi Tshibambe

Société Nationale des Chemins de Fer Zairois (SNCZ)

PO Box 297, Lubumbashi

Telephone: 92 393

Director General: G Gunst
Director, Administration: K N Tambu
Director, Traffic: Robert Baudour
Operating Manager: F Strumane
Commercial Manager: S Mukendi

Gauge: 1067 mm; 1000 mm; 615 mm; 800 mm
Route length: 4884 km; 126 km; 136 km; 1023 km
Electrification: 858 km of 1067 mm gauge at 25 kV 50 Hz

Transport development

SNCZ was created in 1974 by the merger of five former railways: La Compagnie des Chemins de Fer Kinshasa — Dilolo — Lubumbashi (KDL); Les Chemins de Fer des Grands Lacs (CFL); Matadi — Kinshasa (CFMK); Mayumbe (CFM); and Chemins de Fer Vicinaux Zaïrois (CVZ). SNCZ is state owned.

The former KDL railway serves the important mining centres of the Shaba — Lubumbashi, Likasi, Kolwezi and Mososhi — and other important mining and industrial areas such as the manganese mine at Kisenge, cement works at Lubudi, collieries at Luena, diamond mines at Mbuji-Mayi, etc. Expanding agricultural and forest product industries have developed along the line of its route. It connects at Ilebo (ex-Port Francqui) with the ONATRA inland waterway services; and at Kabongo with the CF des Grands Lacs (CFL). Parts of the ex-KDL line in the mining region are electrified at 25 kV 50 Hz. All SNCZ lines are single track.

Internationally, KDL has connections at Dilolo with the CF du Benguela (CFB) in Angola to the Atlantic port of Lobito; and at Sakania with Zambia Railways and, further on, Zimbabwe Railways, CF du Moçambique, and South African Transport Services.

Since 1980 ONATRA has had a ten-year lease of two routes in the east, the 366 km of 1067 mm gauge between Kinshasa and the port of Matadi, and the 136 km of 615 mm gauge between Boma and Tshela. At Matadi the railway is to be projected via a new road-and-rail bridge over the Zaïre river, already erected, to the deep-water port of Banana, down river from Boma. The Matadi line, with the route via Zambia to South Africa, are the principal rail routes for the country's exports.

At present SNCZ is seriously handicapped by the state of its track, which enforces a speed limit of 45 km/h, and the poor availability of traction and rolling stock because of lack of spares; the latter has reduced traction in use to little more than 50 per cent of the total and necessitated expensive lease of South African freight vehicles for movements to that country.

However, with the aid of a loan from Belgium, 175 wagons were in 1982 on order from Belgian manufacturers, and it was hoped to procure 100 ore hoppers for the electrified lines. With the backing of loans from other sources, 250 km of rail and track maintenance equipment were also ordered from Belgium, and nine shunting locomotives from Nisho-Awai, Japan.

Electrification

At the end of 1980 Deutsche Eisenbahn Consulting completed a World Bank-financed study and advocated an extension of 25 kV 50 Hz ac electrification to the 365 km Matadi-Kinshasa 1067 mm-gauge railway; in 1982 assistance was sought from Belgium to finance the scheme, which was forecast to cost over Z200 million. It would exploit hydro-electric power from plants on the Zaïre river at Inga and Zouga. The consultants proposed use of 2600 kW six-axle locomotives capable of working 1000-tonne trains. Meanwhile, with the aid of a US $10 million loan from the Arab Bank for Economic Development in Africa, the National Transport Office has begun relaying the line. The electrification has been embodied in ONATRA's purchasing plans up to 1984.

Traction and rolling stock

As part of its 1979-81 modernisation plan, executed with aid of credits from the International Development Association, SNCZ placed an order with Krupp in 1981 for eight 1700 hp diesel-electric Co-Cos. A total of 75 obsolete German Federal Railway passenger cars were bought, at DM 80 000 each, for use on Kinshasa commuter services.

Locomotives in service 1982:

	Line	Shunting
Electric	56	—
Diesel	85	63

Diesel railcars: 17
Passenger coaches: 444
Freight wagons: 5267

Track
Standard rail: Vignole 59 and 80·6 lb/yd (29·3 and 40 kg/m) in lengths of 10 and 12 m

Joints: Fishplates and bolts
Cross ties (sleepers): Steel T.2243 (MI) weighing 51 kg each, under 37 and 40 kg rail. T.3376C weighing 42 kg each, under 29·3 kg rail. RS type prestressed concrete sleepers and T.3401A wooden sleepers under long welded rail
Spacing: 1500 per km
Rail fastening: By lugs or clips and bolts to steel sleepers. RN flexible fastenings to concrete sleepers
Filling: Broken stone

Max curvature: 8·75° = radius 200 m
Max gradient: 1·25% (1 in 80) except between Tenke and Bukama 2% (1 in 50)
Max altitude: 1614 m at Dilongo-Yulu near Tenke on Bukama line
Max permitted speed
Electrified lines: 52 km/h
All other lines: 45 km/h
Max axleload: 15 tons nominal; 20 tons in special cases

Diesel locomotives

Class	Wheel arrange-ment	Trans-mission	Rated power hp	Tractive effort			Max speed mph (km/h)	Wheel dia in (mm)	Total weight tons	Length ft in (mm)	No built	Year first built	Builders		
				Max lb (kg)	Continuous at lb (kg)	mph (km/h)							Mechanical parts	Engine & type	Transmission
1300	Co-Co	Elec	1650	48 000* (21 750) 57 750† (26 190)	55 500 (25 200)	6·8 (11)	37 (60)	36 (914)	87·3	46' 4½'' (14 134)	38	1971-72	GE (USA)	GE FDL8	GE 76/A10
1260	Co-Co	Elec	1500	33 000* (15 000) 39 700† (18 000)	29 750 (13 400)	13·6 (21·8)	45 (72)	42 (1067)	80	51' 6'' (15 700)	12	1969-70	Hitachi	MAN V22/30ATL	
1200	B-B	Hyd	550	24 800* (11 250) 29 800† (13 500)	22 300 (10 120)	4 (6·4)	20·5 (33)	36·6 (880)	45	37' 9'' (11 500)	25	1968	Hitachi	Cummins VT-1710L	Twin-Disc
1160	B (0-4-0)	Hyd	320	19 800 (8970)	16 500 (7500)	3.1 (5)	19 (30)	33 (840)	30	17' 1¾'' (5225)	13	1965	Cockerill	Cummins NHRS-6	Twin-Disc
1530/40	B-B	Hyd	1310	28 700 (13 000)			44 (70)	37·6 (950)	52	38' 6'' (11 722)	8	1967	Krupp	MTU 12V 538 TB 10	Voith
60	0-6-0	Hyd	250	7425 (3375)				30·6 (774)	13·5	—	2	1955	Tubize	Cummins NTA	Twin-Disc
70	0-4-0	Hyd	335	8800 (4000)				30·6 (774)	16	—	7	1958	Cockerill	Cummins NTA	Voith
80	B-B	Hyd	510	17 600 (8000)				30·6 (774)	32	—	12	1969	Nippon Sharyo	Cummins VT 1710 L	Niigata
1050	B-B	Hyd	515	22 000 (10 000)				37·6 (953)	40	—	8	1973	Henschel	Henschel 12 V 1516 A	Voith
1010	1-D	Hyd	800	29 700 (13 500)				50 (1270)	58	—	2	1959	FUF/HSP	MTU MD 440	Voith
20	C	Hyd	185	8800 (4000)				30·6 (774)	16	33' 0'' (10 000)	4	1958	Moes	Leyland 0680	Twin-Disc

* 25% adhesion.   † 30% adhesion, using sand.

Electric locomotives

Class	Wheel arrange-ment	Line current	Rated output hp	Tractive effort (full field)			Max speed mph (km/h)	Wheel dia in (mm)	Weight tonnes	Length ft in (mm)	No built	Year built	Builders	
				Max lb (kg)	Continuous at lb (kg)	mph (km/h)							Mechanical parts	Electrical equipment
2200	Bo-Bo	25 kV 50 Hz ac	2200	41 900 (19 000)	28 200 (12 800)	28·3 (45·5)	40 (65)	51⅛ (1300)	76	50' 1'' (15 260)	9	1956	Brugeoise et Nivelles	ACEC
2300	Bo-Bo	,,	2040	48 500 (22 000)	36 800 (16 700)	19·5 (31·5)	40 (65)	43⅜ (1100)	75	53' 4'' (16 260)	11	1958	Brugeoise et Nivelles	ACEC
2400	Bo-Bo	,,	2000	39 700 (18 000)	26 500 (12 000)	28 (45)	43 (70)	40 (1016)	60	44' 8¾'' (13 630)	2 9	1960 1964	Brugeoise et Nivelles	ACEC
2600	Bo-Bo-Bo	,,	3250	69 300 (31 500)	50 550 (22 980)	23 (37)	43 (70)	40 (1016)	93	56' 0'' (17 069)	20	1974	Hitachi	ACEC
200	Bo-Bo	,,	640	46 300 (21 000)	17 200 (7800)	13·7 (22)	28 (45)	36 (914)	62	45' 9½'' (13 960)	5	1970	Hitachi	ACEC

ZAMBIA

Ministry of Power, Transport & Communications

Block 33, Fairly Road, Lusaka

Telephone: 213211

Minister: H Mwale
Permanent Secretary: E S S Nebwe

Zambia Railways (ZR)

PO Box 80935, Kabwe

Telephone: 222201-7
Telex: 81230

Railway Board
Chairman: P J Chisanga
Members
  Senior Chief Mushili
  Ngenda Imutowana
  A B Munyama
  Maj-Gen Charles Nyirenda
  F S Kazunga
  E S S Nebwe
Zimco Representatives: Financial Director
  Executive Assistant (Transport)
Management
General Manager: B M Monze
Assistant General Manager, Operations and Technical: B Chewe
  Administration: C C Ndymba
Industrial Participation and Public Relations Manager: A S Lubinda
Marketing Manager: P C Nkonkomalimbe
Personnel Manager: F C Mulenga

Financial Controller: C Sengebwila
Supplies Manager: F C Ngulube
Data Processing Manager: V Gupta
Passenger Manager: F B Munkasu
Chief Civil Engineer: F M C Sinzala
Chief Mechanical Engineer: M Shankaya
Chief Signal and Telecommunications Engineer: K Nogrove
Chief of Transportation: D Mwape

Gauge: 1067 mm
Route length: 1204 km

Transport development
Formerly part of Rhodesia Railways, Zambia Railways was segregated as an autonomous system in 1976. It comprises the old RR system north of the Victoria Falls Bridge, to which was added in 1970 the 164 km Zambesi Sawmills Railway from Livingstone to Mulobezi. Since its independence, ZR has been

handicapped by the political crises in the region and the problems of some neighbouring railways, which have clouded definition of the landlocked country's rail routes to the sea ports with uncertainty. Rail outlets are of critical importance to Zambia's copper industry, which generates 90 per cent of its exports. The Tazara Railway's operating difficulties have restricted the potential of its route to Dar es Salaam, originally envisaged as Zambia's primary export rail route, and with the Benguela Railway to Lobito affected by the unrest to the west, the Victoria Falls route has lately been moving almost twice as much traffic as the Tazara. Assignment of copper traffic to the Tazara or Victoria Falls routes is decided by the Government.

In 1981 the Government moved to end unfettered competition between road and rail, influenced by concern to limit high-priced oil imports and highway wear and tear. ZR was brought within the orbit of Zimco, a holding company for all state-owned enterprises and which already embodies the country's two road haulage companies.

Rehabilitation

In 1980 Zambia secured international loans totalling US$120 million towards a rehabilitation programme for ZR costed at US$184·9 million. Sources involved included the World Bank and its associate, the International Development Association, the African Development Bank, the EEC, Japan, OPEC, the West German Kreditanstalt fur Wiederaufbau and the Swedish International Development Authority.

In the sphere of physical re-equipment, the programme covered renewal of 112 km of track between Sibanyati and Mookamunga, extension and improvement of crossing loops, CTC and telecommunications renewal, purchase of traction and freight stock, and improvement of maintenance facilities. In addition, technical help and an electrification study were budgeted. In 1982 the Aydin Corporation, USA, won a US$8·6 million contract to supply a microwave communications system. At the time of the study ZR freight traffic amounted to some 5 million tonnes a year, but a 50 per cent increase was foreseen by 1990 as the result of a major agricultural development programme and new industrialisation, especially in fertiliser and petro-chemical production. Passenger traffic amounts to about 1·5 million journeys a year.

Electrification

In 1981 Deconsult was commissioned to undertake a feasibility study of electrification of the 421 km route between Kabwe and Nkana-Kitwe at 25 kV ac 50 Hz.

New lines and track

In 1981 Indian Railway Construction Co was commissioned to build a 20 km link between Chipata in Zambia and Mchinji in Malawi and to begin in 1982. The agreement also provided for training of Zambian railwaymen in India. The Government has budgeted US$ 4·5 million towards the new line's construction costs.

The focus of track renewal is a stretch of line where 40 kg/m rail has prevailed rather than the 45 kg/m which predominates on most other ZR main lines; in the relaying, 54 kg/m rail is being employed. ZR is establishing its own concrete sleeper plant at Kafue to speed installation of continuous welded rail track. A major problem still to be solved is the state of the 13-span Kafue River bridge, which imposes a 5 km/h limit on all traffic and also limits loading gauge clearances.

Finance was arranged in 1982 for study of a 700 km line between Chingola, Chilabomwe and Luacano in Angola; and tenders were sought for construction of a 30 km line from Chipata to Mchinji in Malawi.

Traction and rolling stock

At the start of 1982 ZR was operating 101 diesel-electric locomotives, 17 diesel railcars, 85 passenger cars and 3831 freight wagons. Recent deliveries have included completion of an order for 10 diesel-electric locomotives built to a General

Hitachi railcar at Monze *(Robin Cooper)*

Electric design by Krupp. Freight stock has been considerably strengthened with the import of 400 wagons from Japan, 300 from Sweden, 235 from Zimbabwe and 50 from Belgium.

Signalling and telecommunications

CTC on the 848 km Kitwe-Livingstone line, one of the first such installations in Africa, which has deteriorated through inadequate maintenance, is being renewed with all-electronic apparatus, operating from a centre at Kabwe, by Siemens AG, at a cost of US$15·8 million. Microwave channels are being leased from the national Post Corporation for the use of new data-processing equipment and also to establish a track-to-train radio communications system; Japan Electric Consulting Co is advising on this project.

Investment

In 1983 ZR was planning the following investments (Kwacha 000):

Freight wagons (100)	3000
Track work and machinery	16 000
Bridges and buildings	3000
Signalling and telecommunications	20 000
Other	10 000
Total	52 000

ZIMBABWE

Ministry of Transport

Causeway, Harare

Telephone: 700693

Minister: Farai Masango

National Railways of Zimbabwe (NRZ)

Metcalfe Square, PO Box 596, Bulawayo

Telephone: 72211
Telex: 3173

Chairman, Railway Board: J M Magowan
Deputy Chairman: R J Hedley
Members
  R G Pascoe
  A C Thompson
  L C Vambe
  N Lea-Cox
Secretary: P J Murray
General Manager: N Lea-Cox
Deputy General Manager: J R Avery
Assistant General Manager, Services: J E Bolton
  Traffic: A J K Chiwara
  Manpower: L D Msimbe
  Engineering and Supplies: D A M Cook
Chief Mechanical Engineer: I W Clark
Chief Civil Engineer: H Anderson
Personnel Managers: E L Burrowes
                        I Magwenzi

Chief Accountant: F L Kenny
Chief Electrical Engineer: W L Gillman
Chief Signal Engineer: R S Sawyer
Chief Commercial Manager: R E Bull
Chief Planning Officer: A G Keefe
Chief Traffic Manager: A J Mackenzie
Supplies Manager: J A Hartley

Gauge: 1067 mm
Route length: 3394 km

Triple-headed DE6 locomotives hauling NRZ liner (unit freight) train

Electrification: 335 km at 25 kV 50 Hz ac

Transport development

Despite an adequate highway network, rail services are Zimbabwe's major form of transport with lines linking with Mozambique, South Africa, Botswana and Zambia. During 1978 the border between Zambia and Zimbabwe was reopened at Victoria Falls and since that year the railway has been responsible for operating services through Botswana.

Electrification

At the end of 1980 contracts were signed for the 25 kV 50 Hz ac electrification and resignalling of the 325 km route between Harare and Dabuka. Provision of overhead wiring, following the latest British Rail sagged-simple design with steel-cored aluminium catenary and hard-drawn copper contact wire, has been undertaken by Balfour Beatty Power Construction Ltd, substation and other control equipment by GEC Switchgear Ltd; CTC resignalling is being executed by Westinghouse Brake & Signal, and a microwave and mobile train radio communications system by GEC Telecommunications Ltd. The project was to be completed in 1983. The order for 30 thyristor-controlled 2300 kW Co-Co locomotives, with an option for 10 more, was secured by the 50 c/s Group of Europe. The electrification costs are being covered by a British Government loan. The bodywork and final assembly of the locomotives is being undertaken in the Zeco workshops at Bulawayo. Mechanical parts and bogies are supplied by Simmering-Graz-Pauker. Project leader is BBC, which is supplying the electrical equipment.

At the end of 1982 finance had yet to be settled for the second electrification scheme from Dabuka to the Mozambique border at Chiculacuala. A third scheme will cover the 464 km from Bulawayo to Victoria Falls, to integrate with Zambia's electrification plan.

Traction and rolling stock

At the start of 1983 NRZ was operating 123 steam, 330 diesel locomotives, 390 passenger cars and 12 759 freight cars. A substantial number of diesel locomotives were out of use, however; classes chiefly affected were DE4, DE5 (entirely immobilised in October 1982 for lack of spares), DE8 (under consideration for conversion to straight electric traction) and DE9.

To overcome its critical motive power non-availability problem, NRZ has accelerated the refurbishing of 87 of its Garratt steam locomotives. The shortage of skilled diesel maintenance staff was tackled by a contract with RITES of India for short-term hire of artisans pending fulfilment of NRZ's training programmes.

To help cover the enforced return of borrowed locomotives to SATS in 1981, NRZ hired nine units from Mozambique and four from Zambia. In 1982 NRZ took delivery of 60 2250 hp Type GT22LC diesel-electrics from General Motors (USA), classified DE10A by NRZ.

Track

Under a six-year, Z$87 million programme, 54 kg/m rail is to become the main line standard by 1987 and relaying is up to schedule. Elsewhere relaying with 45 kg/m rail on concrete sleepers is also progressing.

Investment

For 1983/84 NRZ was budgeting the following capital expenditure (Z$000):

Electric locomotives (30)	37 911·6
Diesel locomotives (61*)	48 000
Passenger cars (6)	1200
Freight wagons (85)	2300·5
Intermodal development	5543·2
Track improvements	22 691·4
Bridges and buildings	8016·7
Track machinery	320
Electrification	21 248·5
Signalling and communications	15 553
Yards and terminals	2660·9
Workshops	1358·9
Other	1350
	166 154·7

* Delivered 1982
Capital expenditure for the 1982-87 period has been budgeted in total at Z$332·5 million.

Traffic	1979/80	1980/81
Revenue-earning tonnes (000)	12 687	13 153
Gross tonne-km (million)	14 167	13 541
Total passenger journeys (000)	991	1580

Revenue ($ million)	1979/80	1980/81
Freight	121·35	143·41
Passenger	5·51	8·50
Miscellaneous	1·68	2·44
Total	128·54	154·35

Expenditure ($ million)	1979/80	1980/81
Locomotives	51·35	53·14
Rolling stock	16·14	13·77
Tracks and signalling	12·61	16·26
Renewal of group assets	2·02	8·52
Operating buildings and equipment	3·73	4·40
Terminals and train operating	26·31	32·17
Freight handling	2·03	2·99
Passenger facilities	2·26	2·85
Total	116·45	134·1

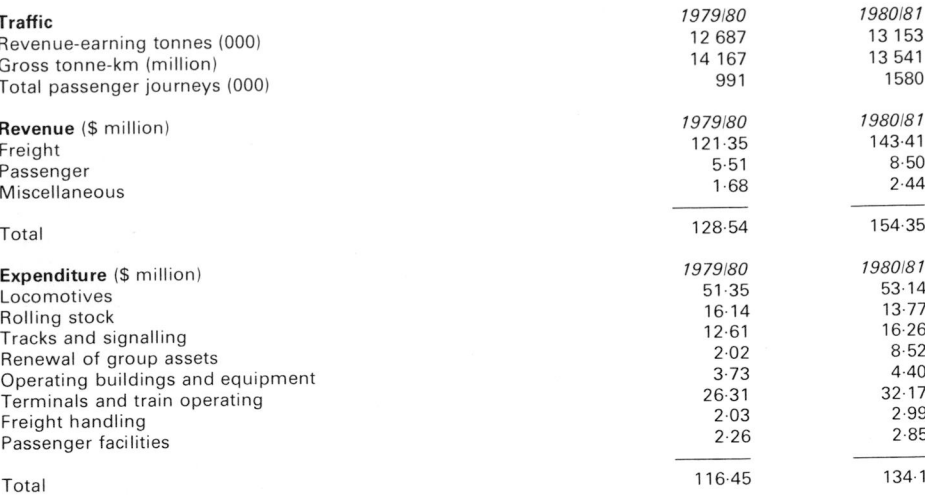

Overhead wiring near Que Que

Dabuka container terminal

Laying panels of concrete sleepers

16A class Garratt No 625 after refurbishment in 1979

Principal diesel locomotives

Class	Wheel arrange-ment	Trans-mission	Rated power hp	Max lb (kg)	Tractive effort Continuous at		Max speed mph (km/h)	Wheel dia in (mm)	Total weight tons	Length ft in (mm)	Year first built	Builders		
					lb (kg)	mph (km/h)						Mechanical parts	Engine & type	Transmission
DE2	1 Co-Co 1	Elec	1710	60 500 (27 440)	36 000 (16 330)	13.6 (22)	55 (88)	Driven 37½ (952) Carrier 28½ (724)	113	56' 0" (17 069)	1955	English Electric	English Electric 16 SVT	English Electric
DE3	1 Co-Co 1	Elec	1850	59 000 (26 760)	40 000 (18 140)	13 (20·9)	66 (106)	Driven 37½ (952) Carrier 28½ (724)	110	51' 1" (15 570)	1962	English Electric	English Electric 12 CSVT	English Electric
DE4	Co-Co	Elec	1730	50 000 (22 680)	37 500 (17 010)	13·5 (21·9)	60 (96)	40 (1016)	92	51' 1" (15 570)	1963	Brush Electric	GEC Type 8RKCT	Brush Electric
DE6	Co-Co	Elec	2090	—	47 300 (21 450)	12 (19·3)	72 (116)	36 (514)	89	52' 0" (15 850)	1966	GE (USA)	GE FDL-12	GE
DE10A	Co-Co	Elec	2250	—	44 195 (20 047)	—	72 (116)	40 (1016)	84·5	57' 0" (17 370)	1981	GM (USA)	GM (12-645E3)	GM

RAPID TRANSIT AND UNDERGROUND RAILWAYS

ARGENTINA		**HONG KONG**		**SPAIN**	
Buenos Aires	690	Hong Kong	700	Barcelona	685
				Bilbao	688
AUSTRALIA		**HUNGARY**		Madrid	707
Adelaide	682	Budapest	690	Seville	725
Melbourne	709				
		INDIA		**SWEDEN**	
AUSTRIA		Calcutta	691	Gothenburg	697
Vienna	730	Madras	707	Stockholm	726
BELGIUM		**INDONESIA**		**SWITZERLAND**	
Antwerp	682	Jakarta	701	Neuchâtel	713
Brussels	689				
Charleroi	692	**IRAN**		**TAIWAN**	
Liège	703	Tehran	727	Taipei	726
BRAZIL		**IRAQ**		**THAILAND**	
Belo Horizonte	687	Baghdad	684	Bangkok	685
Porto Alegre	720				
Recife	720	**ISRAEL**		**TUNISIA**	
Rio de Janeiro	721	Haifa	698	Tunis	729
São Paulo	723				
		ITALY		**TURKEY**	
BULGARIA		Genoa	696	Ankara	682
Sofia	725	Milan	711	Istanbul	701
		Naples	713		
CANADA		Rome	721	**USSR**	
Calgary	692	Turin	729	Alma Ata	682
Edmonton	695			Baku	684
Montreal	711	**IVORY COAST**		Chelyabinsk	693
Toronto	728	Abidjan	682	Dnepropetrovsk	694
Vancouver	729			Erevan	695
		JAPAN		Gorki	697
CHILE		Fukuoka	696	Kharkov	701
Santiago	723	Hiroshima	700	Kiev	702
		Kobe	702	Kuibyshev	702
CHINA, PEOPLE'S REPUBLIC		Kyoto	702	Leningrad	703
Beijing	686	Nagoya	713	Lvov	706
Tianjin	727	Osaka	716	Minsk	711
		Sapporo	724	Moscow	712
COLOMBIA		Tokyo	727	Novosibirsk	716
Bogota	688	Yokohama	731	Omsk	716
Medellin	709			Riga	720
		KOREA, REPUBLIC		Sverdlovsk	726
CUBA		Pusan	720	Tashkent	726
Havana	699	Seoul	725	Tbilisi	726
CZECHOSLOVAKIA		**MEXICO**		**UK**	
Bratislava	689	Guadalajara	698	Glasgow	697
Prague	720	Mexico City	710	London	705
				Newcastle upon Tyne	714
EGYPT		**NETHERLANDS**			
Cairo	691	Amsterdam	682	**USA**	
		The Hague	698	Atlanta	683
FINLAND		Rotterdam	721	Baltimore	685
Helsinki	699	Utrecht	729	Boston	688
				Buffalo	691
FRANCE				Chicago	693
Lille	704	**NIGERIA**		Cleveland	693
Lyons	707	Lagos	703	Dallas	694
Marseilles	708			Denver	694
Nantes	713	**NORWAY**		Detroit	694
Paris	718	Oslo	717	Honolulu	701
Toulouse	729			Houston	701
		PAKISTAN		Los Angeles	706
GERMANY, DEMOCRATIC REPUBLIC		Karachi	701	Miami	710
Berlin (East)	687			Newark	713
		PERU		New York	714
GERMANY, FEDERAL REPUBLIC		Lima	705	New York—New Jersey	715
Berlin (West)	687			New York (Staten Island)	716
Bochum	688	**PHILIPPINES**		Philadelphia	719
Cologne	694	Manila	708	Pittsburgh	719
Dortmund	695			Portland	720
Duisburg	695	**POLAND**		Sacramento	722
Dusseldorf	695	Lodz	705	San Diego	722
Essen	696	Warsaw	730	San Francisco	722
Frankfurt am Main	696			San Juan	723
Hamburg	698	**PORTUGAL**		Washington	730
Hanover	699	Lisbon	705		
Munich	712			**VENEZUELA**	
Nuremberg	716	**ROMANIA**		Caracas	692
Rhine-Ruhr	720	Bucharest	690	Valencia	729
Wuppertal	731				
		SINGAPORE		**YUGOSLAVIA**	
GREECE		Singapore	725	Belgrade	686
Athens	683				

Abidjan
Ministère des Travaux Publics et des Transports

Abidjan, Ivory Coast

Type of system: Planned metro

General: Studies of a north-south 19 km, metre-gauge metro were carried out in 1978. It would run partly underground.

Adelaide
State Transport Authority

PO Box 2351, Adelaide, South Australia 5001, Australia

General Manager: J V Brown
Traffic Manager: R J Heath
Chief Engineer: C R Stewien

Type of system: Metropolitan heavy rail, non-electrified

All metropolitan, rail, tram and bus passenger services are under unitary control.

Gauge: 1600 mm
Route length: 141 km
(in tunnel): 1·8 km

Number of lines in operation: 4
Number of stations: 105
Average distance between stations: 1·2 km
Gradient (max): 1 in 45
Curvature (minimum): 200 m
Speed (design max): 110 km/h
(average commercial): 40 km/h
Rail type: 47 kg/m
Tunnel type: Hand-excavated and brick or concrete-lined

Rolling stock
Number of cars: 120 motored (diesel-hydraulic), 42 trailers
Main supplier: South Australian Railway Workshops, Classes 300, 400, 860; Comeng, Classes 2000, 2100
Year of introduction: Classes 300, 400, 860 1955-70; Classes 2000, 2100 1980-81

Car dimensions

	300, 400	860	2000, 2100
Length	20·015 m	16·98 m	25·5 m

(Classes 860 and 2100 are trailers)
Capacity, seated/crush: Class 300, 90/140; Class 400, 80/140; Class 860, 56/110; Class 2000, 64/140; Class 2100, 160/190
Tare and loaded weight: Class 300, 400, 42/51 tonnes; Class 860, 56/110 tonnes; Class 2000, 64/140 tonnes; Class 2100, 106/190 tonnes
Doors: Sliding single leaf, 910 mm wide
Motors per car: 2, except Class 2000, 4
Motor rating: Class 300, 156·7, 163·4 or 170·8 kW; Class 400, 156·7 or 163·4 kW; Class 2000, 373 kW
Max design speed: 120 km/h

Traffic
Max line capacity (one-way): 3 minute headway
Frequency of train services: 30 minutes off-peak, 20 minutes peak
Passenger journeys: (1982) 14·7 million

Alma-Ata

Alma-Ata, USSR

A 9 km line to link the main rail station with the city centre and its south-western suburbs is in course of design.

Amsterdam
Gemeentevervoerbedrijf Amsterdam (GVBA)

Stadhouderskade 1, Amsterdam, Netherlands
Telephone: 020 160 128
Telex: 16091

Managing Director: J M Ossewaarde
Director, Metro: L F Dammers

Type of system: Full metro

Gauge: 1432 mm
Route length: 18 km
(in tunnel): 3·5 km
(elevated): 14·5 km
Number of stations: 20
(in tunnel): 5
(elevated): 15
Average distance between stations
(in tunnel): 800-900 m
(elevated): 1100-1300 m
Tunnel type: In order to keep out ground water, sections of the underground portions were built by the pneumatic caisson method, which involved building pre-fabricated rectangular tunnel segments on the surface and sinking them into their final positions (with the tunnel roof 4·5 metres below surface level). Some 250 metres were

achieved by cut-and-cover construction. The outer stretches of the initial line were all built on viaduct or embankment. The tunnels, 4·1 metres high above rail level and 8·3 metres wide, carry two tracks.
Gradient (max): 3·2%
Curvature (max): 300 m
Speed (design max): 70 km/h
(average commercial): 35 km/h
Rail type: 49 kg/m (S49) on wood sleepers, ballasted
Electrification type: 750 V dc, third rail

Rolling stock: Two-car units, permanently coupled, built by Linke-Hofmann-Busch, each on four motored bogies, built by MAN, with electrical equipment by Siemens.

Car type	MI.1	MI.2
Number of units: 44		
Car dimensions (length)	18·27 m	18·67 m
(width)	3·01 m	3·01 m
(height)	3·54 m	3·54 m

Passenger capacity: per twin-set:
98 seated
200 standing
Power per unit: 4 × 195 kW at 33·5 km/h

Rating	180 kWH	—
Brakes	Rheostatic	
Weight (tare)	27	27

Trains are one-man operated with units multipled up to a maximum of four

Traffic
Trains/track/hour: 12 (Bijlmer-South)
16 (Bijlmer-East)
Train capacity (max): usual 600 (2 units); peak 900 (3 units)
Total passengers/track/hour: 25 200
Train headways: Peak hour, on main line 3¾ minutes, on two extensions 7½ minutes and 10 minutes; off-peak, 5 minutes on main line
Number of passengers: (1981) 94 000/day
Signalling: Automatic block system: signals, cables etc by ASI Utrecht; control panel, computers etc by AEG, West Berlin
Fare structure: Zonal fares, integrated with suburban trains and regional buses (local area only)

System development
Originally planned as a 78 km network, the Amsterdam metro's further extension has been blocked by vigorous opposition to further intrusion on the city's fabric. Late in 1980 the line from East and South Bijlmer finally reached Amsterdam Central station, but following extension to two more city-centre stations, due for completion in 1982, no further development was planned. Curtailment of the original network plan has caused a serious revenue shortfall in relation to operating expenses.

Ankara
TC Ankara Belediye Baskanligi

Planlama Mudurlugu, Ankara, Turkey

The city has set up a transit authority which planned a full metro, but the scheme has not been endorsed by the Turkish Government. The original plans were for an 11·4 km, 18-station double-track metro system with 9·2 km underground. Track was to be standard gauge (1435 mm), current collection by third rail at 750 volts dc. Now it seems likely that the metro plan will be shelved in favour of a light rail system. A first 3·5 km section of the latter has been put in hand.

Antwerp
Maatschappij voor het Intercommunaal Vervoer te Antwerpen (MIVA)

Grote Hondstraat 58, 2000 Antwerp, Belgium

Telephone: 218 4111

Managing Director: A Blondè
Operating Manager: J du Mon
Rolling Stock Manager: G Vandenbril
Fixed Installations Manager: M Verdonck

Type of system: Pre-metro, light rail

Gauge: 1000 mm
Route length: Pre-metro 5·1 km; light rail 79·8 km
(in tunnel): 5·1 km (pre-metro)
Light rail route length on private right-of-way: 34·8 km (in city 10·1 km, in suburbs 24·7 km)
Number of lines: 2 pre-metro, 8 conventional
Number of stations: Pre-metro 5 (all in tunnel)
Average distance between stations: 530 m
Rail weight and type: 61·7 kg/m grooved; 50 kg/m flat-bottomed (vignole)

Diamant station

Track type: Normally sleepers on ballast; some sections rails directly on concrete with resilient pads
Tunnel type: Bored double-track and cut-and-cover; future work shield tunnelling, single-track
Electrification type: 600 V dc, overhead

Rolling stock
Number of cars: 166 PCC cars, all motored and one-man operated
Main supplier: NV Spoorwegmaterieel en Metaalconstructies, Bruges (formerly La Brugeoise et Nivelles); and ACEC, Charleroi
Car dimensions: Length 14·017 m, width 2·2 m, height 3·081 m
Capacity: 100 (crush) with 31 seated
Tare and loaded weights: 16·2/24·7 tonnes; tare weight of car with Scharfenberg couplers, 17 tonnes

Traffic
Total passenger journeys: (1982) including those on 63·9 km of conventional tramways, 37·3 million

System development
The city decided in the late 1960s to start pre-metro conversion of the city-centre sections of its light rail system. The first 1·3 km double-track tunnel section was opened in March 1975.

Tunnelling of a connection between the first pre-metro line at Schijnpoort with the second at Carnot was completed in 1982. In 1983 work was proceeding on a 2·8 km extension of Line 2 from Carnot westward to interchanges with Line 1 at Opera, and on the continuation of Line 1 northward via an interchange at Astrid towards Schijnpoort. During the year it was hoped to start tunnelling under the River Schelde for an extension from

Control centre at Opera station

Groenplaats, western terminal of the first axis, for 1·5 km to the expanding suburb of Linkeroever. Other extensions aggregating 5·6 km are in mind to establish a pre-metro network of 21 stations by 1988. However, rate of progress is uncertain because of Belgium's economic problems and government reluctance to commit investment funds in advance.

Athens
Athens/Piraeus Electric Railways Co Ltd (ISAP)

67 Athinas St, Athens, Greece

Telephone: 32 48 311
Telex: 21 9998
Telegrams: HSAP, Athens

Managing Director: M Th Passas

Type of system: Rapid transit

Gauge: 1435 mm
Route length: 25·84 km
(in tunnel): 3 km
(elevated): 0·76 km
Number of lines: 1
Number of stations: 21
(in tunnel): 3
(elevated): 1
Average distance between stations: 1·36 km
Track type: Flat-bottomed rail laid on timber sleepers and ballast
Tunnel type: Cut-and-cover
Electrification type: 600 V dc, third rail
Signalling: Electric automatic block

Traffic
Max line capacity (one way): 9300 passengers per hour

Train headways: 3½ minutes (peak)
Capacity per car
(seated): 166 (old types), 222 (new types)
(standing): 439, 472
Passenger journeys: (1981) 83 million

Car type		
(year introduced)	1925	1952-58-68
Number of units:	61	74
Car dimensions		
(length)	13·8 m	17·8 m
(width)	2·7 m	2·86 m
(height)	3·66 m	3·6 m
Passenger capacity per car		
(total)	120	180
(seated)	36	56
Motors per car	4	4
Train composition		
(minimum)	2	2
(max)	5	4
Brakes	air	regenerative and air
Body material	wood	steel
Motor rating	95 kW	120 kW

Power per train (minimum): 4 kW/tonne
(max): 8·5 kW/tonne
Acceleration (max): 0·7 m/s²

Deceleration (normal service): 0·6 m/s²
(emergency): 1·1 m/s²
Max design speed: 80 km/h
Bogies: MAN with two motors per motor car
Distance between bogie pivots: 10·9 m
Weight (empty in tonnes):
Motor cars: 37·2 metallic, 31·54 wooden
Trailers: 25·8 metallic, 17 wooden
In the summer of 1982 delivery began of 25 two-car sets, in which all cars are powered with 120 kW motors, from LEW Hennigsdorf of the German Democratic Republic
Cars on order: 15 five-car train-sets (3 motor cars, 2 trailers), also suitable for operation on proposed Athens Metro, on order from MAN/Siemens with motors rated at 145 kW and electronically controlled by choppers. Electric brake designed as combined regenerative and dynamic brake. Delivery due 1983-84

System development
Following studies funded by the Ministry of Transport and Communications two new routes are planned: one of 18·7 km from Egaleo 2 in the south-west to Gerakas in the north-east; another of 9·5 km from Daphni in the south-east to Sepolia. Construction has, however, been deferred. The two would intersect at Syntagma. Nine new 1800 kVA substations were due for commissioning in 1983 and tenders were invited for CTC installation in 1982.

Atlanta
Metropolitan Atlanta Rapid Transit Authority (MARTA)

Suite 2200, 401 West Peachtree St NE, Atlanta, Georgia 30365, USA

Telephone: (404) 586 5050

Board Chairman: C C Long
Board Vice-Chairman: M S Murray
General Manager: K M Gregor
AGM Transit Operations: W C Nix
   Transit System Development: L D Ballou
   Planning and Public Affairs: Morris J Dillard
   Finance and Administration: P Kesserich

Type of system: Full metro, integrated with bus feeder services

Gauge: 1435 mm
Number of lines: 2
Number of stations: 17
Total route length: 21·9 km
Rail weight and type: 119RE (52·12 kg/m)
Track type: Continuously-welded rail with Pandrol clips on concrete sleepers. Elastomer springing under track in residential areas to reduce vibration.

MARTA elevated section

Screens on surface and elevated sections to reduce noise

Axleload: 13·8 tonnes
Minimum curve radius: 230 m
Max gradient: 3%
Electrification type: 750 V dc, third rail
Signalling and control: General Railway Signal automatic train protection, automatic train operation and automatic line supervision

Rolling stock
Number of cars: 120
Supplier: Franco-Belge (now Soferval)
Car dimensions: Length 23 m, width 3·2 m, height 3·6 m
Capacity: 68 seats in cars with single driver's cab; 62 in cars with cab at each end; standing room for 140
Tare weight: 37 tonnes
Max speed: 114 km/h
Cars on order: 30 two-car sets, value $35 million, from C Itoh and Hitachi to be delivered in 1984, with an option for 70 more. Traction equipment for the first 30 units being supplied by Garrett, USA

Traffic
Passenger journeys: (1982) 53·9 million
Revenue control equipment: Cubic Western Data faregates

System development
The rail system is planned as a north-to-south, east-to-west cross of two lines aggregating (with branches) 56·6 km in route-length, intersecting in downtown Atlanta's business district at Five Points. A third of the ultimate 40-station system is to be elevated and 16 km underground.

With a Federal UMTA grant and local funding through a sales tax, an 18·6 km central section of the east-west line was completed by stages in 1979. In view of inflating costs and delays occasioned by environmental impact studies, litigation and real estate negotiation, to which have been added uncertainties about future Federal funding under the Reagan Administration, initial hopes of treating the network construction as one continuous project have been modified into a five-phase plan. In 1982 the north-south line was extended from North Avenue to Arts Center and work proceeded on projection 9·8 km northward to Brookhaven and 4·2 km southward from West End to Lakewood, for 1984 completion.

The residue of Phase B and Phase C will complete the north-south line from Doraville throughout to Atlanta airport. This is regarded as a high priority (it could be achieved by 1985 following the release of considerable funds for system extensions in the Federal 1983 budget) not only because of the airport traffic's importance, but because the northern line will penetrate the city's most affluent suburbs. Phase D will complete the east-west line, and Phase E will add three branches.

Peachtree Center station, carved out of solid rock

MARTA operations control centre

Baghdad
Baghdad Rapid Transit Authority

Baghdad, Iraq

Secretary-General: J Al Saadi

Type of system: Planned metro

Gauge: 1435 mm

Number of lines: 2
Number of stations: 37
Route length: 32 km
Electrification type: 1·5 kV dc, overhead
Tunnel type: 60% bored, remainder cut-and-cover

Rolling stock
The metro will employ 83 three-car train-sets, with a top speed of 80 km/h and acceleration of 1 m/s². They will be air-conditioned and seat 84 passengers in each car with room for 84 standees.

System development
The British Metro Consultants Group of 10 companies has been appointed to create the first stage of the Baghdad metro. Line 1 is to run from Aadhamiya to Al-Thawra, Line 2 from Masbah via Aqaba bin-Nasir Square to Mansour, with interchange in the central area at Khalani Street. Construction was to begin in 1983, aiming for operational trials in 1986 and revenue operation in 1987.

Following Phase 1, extensions totalling 11 km are planned in Phase 2, and the addition of a third line to establish a regional system in Phase 3.

Baku
Baku Metropolitan

Ulitsa Inglaba 17, Baku 37063, USSR

Chief Executive: Igor Abasovich Khankishiev
Chief Engineer: Chingiz Mamedovich Rufullaev

Type of system: Full metro

Gauge: 1524 mm
Route length: 19·6 km
Number of lines: 2
Number of stations: 12
Average distance between stations: 1·8 km
Speed (design max): 75 km/h
  (average commercial): 42 km/h
Rail type: 50 kg/m
Minimum curve radius: 300 m
Max gradient: 4%

Electrification type: 825 V, third rail

Rolling stock
Car type (year introduced): 1960
Number of cars: 108 (all motored)
Car dimensions (length): 18·8 m
  (width): 2·7 m
Passenger capacity (per car):
  (total): 170
  (seated): 44
Weight: 32 tonnes
Motors per car: 4
Motor rating: 66 kW
Train composition (minimum): 5
  (max): 5
Brakes: Regenerative and electromagnetic
Body material: Steel

Traffic
Trains/track/hour: 20
Train capacity (passengers): 850

Total passengers/track/hour (peak): 17 000
Train headways: 3 minutes
Passenger journeys (weekday): 172 000
  (annually): 40·8 million
Signalling: Automatic train stop. Radio-telephone communication between trains and the central command post

System development
In late 1967 the first 10·1 km section of line was opened, with seven stations, four of which lie at deep level and are served by high speed escalators. This line connects three main districts, the western administrative, the eastern residential and the central industrial.

The system was enlarged during the 1970s. Now under construction are extensions totalling 6·7 km, with four stations. Under study are further extensions totalling 11·8 km, with seven stations. The metro serves a city population of 1·5 million.

Baltimore
Maryland Mass Transit Administration

109 East Redwood Street, Baltimore, Maryland 21202, USA

Telephone: (301) 383 3434

Administrator: D A Wagner
Project Manager, Rapid Transit Development: R J Murray

Type of system: Full metro under construction

Gauge: 1435 mm
Route length: Section A, 12·8 km
(in tunnel): 7·2 km
Number of stations: Section A, 9
(in tunnel): Section A, 6
Average distance between stations: 2 km
Gradient (max): 1 in 25
Curve radius (max): 186 m (main line)
Speed (design max): 112 km/h
(average commercial): 43 km/h
Rail type: 57 kg/m RE continuous welded
Tunnel type: Horseshoe in rock (44%), shield-driven in soft earth (56%).

The Lexington Market tunnels were chosen for a demonstration project involving the use of precast concrete tunnel liners for the first time in a US rapid transit tunnel below the water table. Baltimore's other earth tunnels used steel liners. UMTA funded 100 per cent of the test programmes, and the cost differential, up to $700 000, between the use of concrete tunnel liners and conventional steel liners.
Electrification type: 700 V dc, third rail
Signalling: Automatic train control (WABCO Union Switch & Signal AF-400 system), from operations control centre, will direct trains from start to stop, regulate speeds at six levels from 19·2 to 112 km/h, space trains and route them through switches and crossovers

Rolling stock
Number of units: 72 cars, all motored, in twin units
Car dimensions
Length: 30 m
Width: 3 m
Height 3·5 m
Number of doors per side: 3 sets biparting doors each side
Number of passengers per car (total): 166
(seated): 76
Motors per car: 4
Motor rating: 130 kW
Acceleration (max): 3·0 mph/s
Deceleration (normal service): 2·1 mph/s
(emergency): 3·2 mph/s
Max design speed: 112 km/h
Bogies: Budd Co Pioneer
Brakes: Tread air brakes—WABCO
Weight: 38 tonnes

Rogers Avenue station

The Budd-built cars have been purchased in a joint venture with Miami. Bought under the Buy America provision of the Surface Transportation Act, the Baltimore-Miami vehicle was designed with general specifications in an effort to produce a car that would be standardised in the industry. Cars are of stainless steel, and designed to operate as married pairs. Microprocessor control for both propulsion and ATO is a feature of the Westinghouse regenerative chopper equipment. Trains will be composed of a minimum of two cars and a maximum of six. Baltimore also has an option to buy 28 additional cars for the planned Section B extension of the system.

Traffic
Max number of trains per hour (one way): 30
(one way-planned): 15
Train headways (planned): 4 minutes (peak hours), 10 minutes (other)
Max train capacity (seated): 444
(standing): 1200

System development
Section A of the Baltimore Region Rapid Transit System, a distance of 12·8 km, was scheduled for opening in mid-1983. Cost of construction is calculated at $797 million, including purchase of 72 cars, funded 80 per cent by Federal UMTA grant and 20 per cent by the State of Maryland (but, in the latter case, only after a bitter struggle by highway-oriented opposition in the Maryland Assembly in 1976).

The double-track Section A extends from the Charles Center station in the retail-business district of Baltimore City to the Baltimore City-Baltimore County line at Reisterstown Plaza. It includes nine stations (six subway and three elevated) 7·2 km in subway, less than 1·5 km on the ground, and 4 km of elevated structure.

Section B, a 9·6 km extension of the Section A line from Reisterstown Plaza to Owings Mills, within the median strip of the new Northwest Expressway, was approved by the Maryland Assembly in 1980, and begun in 1981; completion is likely in 1986-87, at a cost of $190 million, financed chiefly by interstate highway transfer funds. Under Phase II planning by the Maryland Department of Transportation, several other corridors are being evaluated for future expansion.

A computer-equipped operations centre at Lexington Market station will hold information on train performance and scheduling, but it will be up to dispatchers to handle irregularities. This system has the capability for upgrading to full computerised control if desired in the future.

Automatic fare collection, using encoded cards and equipment by Alta/CGA, is planned in the Baltimore system. Fares are expected to be compatible with MTA bus fares.

It is expected that approximately 83 000 persons will use Section A daily.

Bangkok
Expressway and Rapid Transit Authority of Thailand

Phaholyothin Road, Bangkok 9, Thailand

Telephone: 5795176
Telegrams: ETA, Bangkok

General Manager: C Burapharat
Project Director: V Ratanaphol

Type of system: Planned metro

Gauge: 1435 mm
Route length: 59 km approx
Track length: 117·7 km
(in tunnel): 1·155 km

Number of stations: 59
(in tunnel): 1
Average distance between stations: 900 m
Max length of station platforms: 120 m
Max speed: 80 km/h
Electrification type (planned): 1·5 kV dc, third rail

Rolling stock
Car type: 2-car unit
Number of units: 2
Car dimensions: Length 18 m, width 2·9 m, height 3·5 m
Total floor area: 47·85 m²/car
Number of doors per side: 3 per car
Door width: 1·3 m
Number of passengers per car: 189-216
(seated): 42-48

System development
The Expressway and Rapid Transit Authority of Thailand, formed in 1975, has proposed a three-line initial mass transit rail system for Bangkok for projected opening by 1986. The lines include: Pra Kanong-Bangsue (23 km); Wong Wiang Yai-Lard Phrao (20 km); Dao Khanong-Makkasan (16 km).

By early 1982 the Government had put up US$40 million for system design, land purchase and construction of two river bridges. The system will be almost entirely elevated because of difficult soil conditions. The Government is offering international consortia 30-year contracts to build and operate a system expected to record 22 million passenger-km a year by 1990, but none of the seven pre-qualifying bidders were prepared to accept the financial risk of recouping their investment from operation.

Barcelona
FC Metropolitano de Barcelona SA (SPM)

PO Box 831, Ronda de San Pablo 41, Barcelona 15, Spain

Telephone: (93) 241 00 07

Director General, Barcelona Municipal Transport (Metro and buses): Juan Molina Vivas

Director of Metro: Fernando Coello Goyri
Commercial and Marketing Director, Barcelona Municipal Transport: Jesus Zandueta Vera

Type of system: Full metro

The whole system is underground, except the Mercado-Sta Eulalia section of Line I and a section in Buxeres station.

Gauge: 1674 mm (Line I only); 1435 mm
Route length: 51·4 km with 50·2 km in tunnel
Projected new lines (in construction or projected): 72·8 km
Number of lines: 5 (I, III, III-B, IV, V) all double-track
Number of stations: 74
(in tunnel): 71
Average distance between stations: Line I, 620 m; Line III, 660 m; Line III-B, 640 m; Line IV, 760 m; Line V, 780 m

Rail weight and type: 54 kg/m UIC 54
Track type: New lines, sleepers on concrete; other lines, sleepers on ballast
Electrification type: Line I, 1·5 kV dc; others, 1·2 kV dc
Current collection: Line I, steel third rail; Lines III and V, catenary; Lines III-B and IV, aluminium third rail

Rolling stock
Number of cars: 426
Main suppliers: Macosa, MAN

Type 1100 cars have been built by Macosa and MAN. The MAN cars are of welded, lightweight steel construction. Each set can seat 72 passengers with a normal maximum load of 328 and crush load of 528. Barcelona Metro was expected to call tenders at the beginning of 1982 for construction of another 26 units.

Traffic
Train headways: Peak hours, $3^2/_5$ minutes; off-peak, $4^3/_5$ minutes
Passenger journeys: (1981) 590 060
Changing social patterns in the city are blamed for the decline in use of the metro
Signalling: Automatic block, with ac track circuits, and colour-light signals. CTC on Line IV. Automatic control system in preparation

Further extensions planned: In 1982 Line IV was extended at each end by a total of 5·82 km. Extensions of Line V at each end, by 3·5 km from La Paz to Ventura, and by 1·2 km from San Indefonso to Cornella Centro, were nearing completion

Pueblo Seco station on Line III

Further extensions under construction

Line	Route	km	Stations	Scheduled completion
III	Lesseps—Montbau	3·4	4	1983
V	La Paz—Marques de Montroig	3·4	4	1983
I	Torras y Bages—Santa Colona	2	3	1983
I	La Torrassa—Hospitalet Catalones	2·2	4	1984
II	Pueblo Seco—Sagrade Familia	4·2	4	1984

At the end of 1982 a total of 21 km was under construction.

Recent rolling stock

Series	Year introduced	Motors	Gauge (mm)	Weight (kg) Motor	Trailers	length (mm)	Capacity Seated	Standing	Current	Power
1000	1970-74	100	1435	29 900	—	16 500	36	200	1200 V catenary	$4 \times 136 = 544$ hp
1100	1974-79	108	1435	29 900	—	16 500	36	200	1200 V conductor	$4 \times 136 = 544$ hp

Ferrocarriles de Generalitat de Catalunya (FGC)

1 Plaza de Cataluna, Barcelona, Spain

Telephone: 302 48 16

President: Jose Ma Juncadella Bures
General Manager: Conde de Servia

Type of system: Full metro

Gauge: 1435 mm
Route length: 9 km
(in tunnel): 4·4 km
Number of lines: 2 (radial)
Number of stations: 12
Average distance between stations: 0·79 km

Rail type: Flat-bottomed
Gradient (max): 4%
Curvature (max): 150 m
Speed (design max): 60 km/h
(average commercial): 30 km/h
Electrification type: 1·3 kV, overhead

Rolling stock
Car type (year introduced): 1959
Number of units: 72 (all motor cars)
Car dimensions (length): 19 m
(width): 2·70 m
Passenger capacity (per car):
(total): 116
(seated): 56
Motors per car: 4
Ratings: 92 kWh

Train composition (minimum): 1
(max): 2

Traffic
Trains/hour/track: 24
Train capacity (passenger): 232
Total passengers/track/hour (peak): 5570
Train headways: $2\frac{1}{2}$ minutes
Passenger journeys annually: 26·5 million

System development
This line was originally wholly on the surface, and steam-operated. It has since been electrified, and its intown section (under the Calle de Balmes) has been rebuilt in tunnel. At Sarria it connects with the surface system which has the same gauge, running on to Tarrasa and Sabadell.

Beijing
Metropolitan Railway Department

Beijing Municipal Council City Administration Building, Beijing, People's Republic of China

Type of system: Full metro

Gauge: 1435 mm
Route length: 23·6 km, all in tunnel
Number of lines: 1
Number of stations: 17
Average distance between stations: 1·4 km
Track type: Concrete slab
Tunnel type: Cut-and-cover, 4·1 m wide, 4·35 m high
Electrification type: 750 V dc, third rail

Minimum curve radius: 250 m
Max gradient: 2·4%
Signalling: Relay interlocking, automatic block, centralised traffic control, cab signalling, automatic train stop. Metro operated from one control room with electronic facilities for monitoring and controlling all turnouts and signals

Rolling stock
Main suppliers: Changchun Rolling Stock Plant (Jilin province) and Xiangtan Electrical Machinery Plant (Hunan province)
Types: 3 in BJ (Beijing) series
Max speed: 80 km/h
Capacity: 60 seats per car, 126 standing. Cars operated in four-car sets, each with total capacity of 744

Traffic
Train headways: Peak hours, 5 minutes; off-peak, 10 minutes
Number of passengers daily: 120 000

System development
A 53 km system is planned, to be built in three phases. the first phase projected a route from Beijing main-line station to Apple Farm station. Construction started in 1965 and was completed in 1969.
  The second phase neared completion in 1981. It comprises a 16 km line from the eastern terminal, Beijing's main railway station, which loops north, west and south to rejoin the main line at Fuxingmen station. Due to open in 1982, it has 12 stations and links with a six-station section of main line to form a circle. The third phase plans a 13 km cut-and-cover line from Xizhimen station on the new loop to the Summer Palace, with nine intermediate stations.

Belgrade
Architecture and Town Planning Department, Energoproject Division

Boulevard Lenina 12, Novi Beograd 11000, Yugoslavia

Telephone: 450168
Telegrams: Energo Beograd
Telex: 12184

Type of system: Planned metro

Construction began in 1978 on a projected five-line 68 km metro for completion by the year 2000. An initial project, totalling 14·2 km, with 11·8 km underground, is in hand.
  A plan for development of urban transport services adopted by Belgrade City Council includes provision for the construction of 22·5 km of new surface tramway lines and 1·5 km of underground tramway. The new lines will be designed to act as a permanent urban transport solution for some passenger flows, or as feeders to the planned metro system. Some lines will run to new residential areas. Length of the tramway network by 1985 should be 115·4 km. The whole of the network will be gradually improved to modern light rail standards. Three existing Yugoslav Railways (JZ) lines will also be integrated into the city's urban/suburban network of public transport after completion of the city's new central, through station and its approaches.

Belo Horizonte
Brazilian Federal Railways (RFFSA),
Belo Horizonte Region

Rua Sapucai 383, Belo Horizonte, Minas Gerais, Brazil

Telephone: 222 7293
Telex: 0311088

Type of system: Planned rapid transit

A French-Brazilian consortium, led by Francorail, was awarded a contract in 1981 to create a suburban railway network in Brazil's third largest city. The scheme involves construction of a new 1600 mm-gauge double track, electrified at 3 kV dc, over the 38 km from Belo Horizonte south to Betim, and will probably continue electrification north of the city to

Horto and General Carreiro. The city's suburban network of 111 km is expected to be carrying 400 000 passengers a day by 1985.

Rolling stock of similar character to that provided by the same builders for FEPASA will be supplied by TCO (France) in collaboration with Cobrasma and IEBB (Brazil). Other companies involved include Jeumont-Schneider and SIGLA (signalling), Sodeteg-TAI, Spie Batignolles, Kreisa and CGEE/Alsthom.

Berlin (East)
VE Kombinat Berliner Verkehrs-Betriebe (VEB)

Rosa-Luxemburg Str 2, 102 Berlin, German Democratic Republic

Telephone: (02) 51 03 11

Type of system: Full metro

Gauge: 1435 mm
Route length: 16 km
(in tunnel:) 12·4 km
Number of lines: 2
Line A, Pankow-Thalmannplatz, small profile, 7·49 km, including 5·32 km in tunnel
Line E, Alexanderplatz-Friedrichfeld, large profile, 7·095 km, entirely in tunnel
Number of stations (total): 22
Average distance between stations: 730 m
Gradient (max): 4%
Curvature (max): 74 m
Speed (design max): 50 km/h
(average commercial): 25 km/h
Electrification type: 750 V, third rail

Traffic
Trains/track/hour: 30
Train capacity (passengers): 1200
Total passengers/track/hour (peak): 36 000
Train headways: 2 minutes
Passenger journeys annually: 61 million

Rolling stock

Car type	A1	A2	E3
Number of units	165[1]	89[2]	52[3]
Car dimensions			
(length)	12·1 m	12·4 m	18 m
(width)	2·3 m	2·3 m	2·6 m
(height)	3·2 m	3·2 m	3·4 m
Passenger capacity per car			
(total)	129	122	163
(seated)	27	26 motor cars	38
		34 trailers	
Motors per car	4	4	4
Rating	60 kWh	60 kWh	60 kWh
Train composition			
(minimum)	4	4	4
(max)	8	8	8

[1]   92 motor cars; 73 trailers small profile
[2]   45 motor cars; 44 trailers small profile
[3]   26 motor cars; 26 trailers large profile

Acceleration (max): 1·15 m/s²
Deceleration (emergency): 1·2 m/s²
Brakes: Electro-pneumatic

LEW lightweight train

Berlin (West)
Berliner Verkehrs-Betriebe (BVG)

Potsdamer Str 188, 1000 Berlin 30, Federal Republic of Germany

Telephone: (0311) 2561
Telex: 183 329
Telegrams: Bevauge, Berlin West

Commercial Manager: Willi Diedrich
Operating Manager: Joachim Piefke
Engineering Manager: Hans-Erhard von Knobloch

Type of system: Full metro

Gauge: 1435 mm
Route length: 100·8 km
(in tunnel): 86·3 km
(elevated): 6·2 km
Number of lines: 9, all double track
Number of stations served: 111, including 16 interchange stations
(in tunnel): 77
Average station spacing: 770 m
Rail weight and type: S 41, 41 kg/m
Track type: Conventional sleepers on ballast
Max gradient: 1 in 25 (4%)
Minimum curve radius: 74 m on running lines; 50 m on sidings
Tunnel type: There are two sizes of tunnel: 'large-profile' on the former North-South Company lines (now lines 6, 7, 8, 9 and E), and 'small-profile' on the former Elevated and Underground Company lines (now lines 1, 2, 3, 4, and 5). All are double-track rectangular tunnels, with and without centre supports; the large-profile tunnels are 6·9 m wide and 3·6 m high from rail level, while the small-profile tunnels are 6·24 m wide and 3·4 m high. Construction was mostly by cut-and-cover method, the tunnels being generally just below surface level. Tunnel linings are of concrete.
Electrification type: 780 V dc, third rail
One-man operation: All trains
Signalling: Electromagnetic, Siemens
Automatic control: In May 1981 automatic train operation using the Seltrac ATO system was inau-

Type A3 small-profile train-set of 1960 design

gurated on Line 4. Trains start automatically and are operated at all stages over the line by the computer-based system. An inductive loop cable embedded in the track transmits instructions to the train. Two-way communication is independent of wheel/rail contact. Minicomputers at the control centre make it possible for despatchers to control operations over the line. Each train carries a microprocessor to intercept commands and transmit vehicle data back to control. Seltrac also transmits information to display units on trains, giving next station and destination.

Rolling stock
Number of cars: 656 large profile, 360 small profile, all motored

Main suppliers: Waggon Union, electrical equipment by AEG/Siemens
Car dimensions: Small-profile lines, 12·53 m long (two-car set with Scharfenberg couplers, 25·66 m), 2·3 m wide; large-profile lines, 15·5 m long, 2·65 m wide
Most recent large-profile car stock: F (FS = control car, FK = converter or compressor cars)
Car dimensions: Overall length 16·05 m, width 2·65 m
Number of seats: 38
Capacity: Crush, 197 passengers
Tare weight: 1973-77 deliveries, FS/FK 18·68/19·62 tonnes; 1979 deliveries, FS/FK 19·1/19·05 tonnes
Permitted gross weight: 1973-77 deliveries, FS/FK 31·48/32·42 tonnes; 1979 deliveries, FS/FK 31·84/31·79 tonnes

Construction: Bodies frame-built light metal, bogies light-weight steel
Max speed: 70 km/h
Control: Automatic cam control mechanism
Braking system: Electric brake operated as separately excited resistance brake to standstill, thyristor-controlled
Doors: Electropneumatic door closing installation. Doors remain closed until train stops.
   Trains are equipped with a 24 V radio and 24 V radio telephone, plus a 110 V PA system

Traffic
Train headways: Peak hours, 2½ minutes; off-peak, 5 minutes; evenings, 10 minutes
Passenger journeys: (1981) 362 million
Max number of cars per train: Large-profile lines 6; small-profile 8
Max line density: approx 41 000 passengers per hour (Line 7)
Average scheduled speed (including stops)
Large-profile lines 33·5 km/h
Small-profile lines 28·8 km/h

System development
The BVG authority operates bus services in the western sector of Berlin in addition to its U-Bahn. There has been progressive building of new lines and extensions to existing lines in Berlin's western sector since the Second World War. A further 5·3 km extension to Spandau is due to open in 1984; additional rolling stock is to be ordered for this event.

Type F large-profile stock of 1973-75

Bilbao
Bilbao Metropolitan

Bilbao, Spain

Type of system: Metro under construction

Construction work started in April 1978. The first section, running 6 km from Moyua to Basauri, is due to open in 1983. The second section will run 5·9 km between Santurce and Baracaldo and the third for 6·3 km from Moyua to Baracaldo. The infrastructure is being created in part from Spanish National Railways (RENFE) 1668 mm-gauge 3 kV dc and local 1·5 kV dc metre-gauge lines. The ultimate size of the network was uncertain at the end of 1982.

Bochum
Bochum-Gelsenkirchener Strassenbahnen AG (Bogestra)

Postfach 10 22 69, 4630 Bochum 1, Federal Republic of Germany

Telephone: 693936
Telex: 08 25 870

Type of system: Pre U-Bahn

Gauge: 1000 mm; 1435 mm (north-south line)
Route length: 5·6 km, all in tunnel
Number of lines: 3

Number of stations: 7
Average distance between stations: 550 m
Tunnel type: Built by New Austrian Tunnel Construction Method
Electrification type: 600 V dc, overhead

Rolling stock
Type M (articulated)
Car dimensions: Length 20·44 m, width 2·3 m, height 3·306 m
Average and crush capacity: 101/166 (36 seats)
Motors per car: 2
Motor rating: 150 kW
Floor height: 880 mm
Tare and loaded weight: 28·8/38·65 tonnes
Max speed: 80 km/h

Type B (north-south line)
Car dimensions: Length 28 m, width 2·65 m, height 3·365 m
Capacity: 72 seated, 112 standing
Motors per car: 2
Motor rating: 235 kW
Floor height: 1 m
Tare weight: 39 tonnes
Max speed: 80 km/h

System development
The first 3·3 km (metre-gauge) of a planned 43 km pre U-Bahn network was completed in 1981 on an east-west axis, running via Bochum Hbf. A 6·7 km stretch of a 1435 mm-gauge north-south line is under way for completion in 1988-89.

Bogota
Secretaria de Obras Publicas Alcaldia de la Ciudad Distrito Especiale de Bogota

Bogota, Colombia

Type of system: Planned metro

Feasibility studies have been completed for a proposed 92 km metro and the first 21 km line is to run north-south through the city centre. Bids for its construction were to be called for in 1983, with the aim of launching work in 1984.

Boston
Massachusetts Bay Transportation Authority (MBTA)

50 High St, Boston, Massachusetts 02110, USA

Telephone: (617) 722 5000
Telex: 617 722 3304

Chairman: J F Carlin
General Manager: James O'Leary
Director of Operations: J J White
Chief Engineer: Ralph L Duval

Type of system: Full metro (3 lines); light rail (1 line)

Gauge: 1435 mm
Route length: 111·526 km, including:
   Orange Line (full metro) 17·464 km
   Blue Line (full metro) 9·469 km
   Red Line (full metro) 37·389 km
   Green Line (light rail) 47·201 km
(in tunnel): 28·72 km (Orange Line 2·955 km; Blue Line 3·378 km; Red Line 13·888 km; Green Line 8·498 km)
(at surface level): 73·316 km (Orange Line 7·135 km;

Blue Line 6·091 km; Red Line 23·501 km; Green Line 36·587 km)
(elevated): 9·489 km (Orange Line 7·373 km; Green Line 2·115 km)
Number of stations: 85
(in tunnel): 28
(elevated): 6
Distance between stations
Orange Line, longest 2·527 km, shortest 324 m
Blue Line, longest 1·708 km, shortest 842 m
Red Line, longest 3·175 km, shortest 351 m
Green Line, longest 2·378 km, shortest 364 m
Rail weight and type: 38·556 kg/m (ASCE); 45·36 kg/m (ARA-B); 68·04 kg/m (RE)
Track type: Combination of conventional sleepers on ballast, wooden sleepers on steel and concrete sleepers with resilient pads. All rail renovations, line extensions and reconstruction will be with continuous welding and resilient pads
Tunnel type
Orange Line, cut-and-cover and caisson
Blue Line, single bored and cut-and-cover
Green Line, cut-and-cover
Red Line, cut-and-cover and single bored (Red Line extension single bored)
Gradient (max): 5%

Curvature (max): 122 m
Speed (design speed): 80 km/h
   (average commercial): 31 km/h
Electrification type: All 600 V dc. Collection: Red Line, third rail; high speed section of Red Line, catenary; Orange Line, third rail; Blue Line, third rail and catenary; Green Line, catenary
Signalling: Blue Line, automatic block (GRS and Wabco); Orange Line, automatic block (Wabco); Red Line, automatic train operation (GRS) and automatic block (Wabco); Green Line, automatic block (Wabco)
Automatic control: Red Line has automatic speed control on approx 69% of its present km. Station stops and starts under control of driver

Rolling stock: 658 cars
Heavy Rail
Type of car: 1400
Year of introduction: 1962
Dimensions: Length 21·18 m, height 3·784 m, width 3·155 m
Number of motored cars: 88
Average and crush capacity: 54/308
Tare and loaded weight: 32·672/52·231 tonnes

Doors: Sliding outside doors, width 1·27 m, height 1·905 m
Main supplier: Pullman Standard

Type of car: 1500 Silverbird (single car)
Year of introduction: 1968
Dimensions: Length 21·18 m, height 3·86 m, width 3·086 m
Number of motored cars: 24
Average and crush capacity: 60/228
Tare and loaded weight: 29·239/43·718 tonnes
Doors: Inside sliding doors, width 1·219 m, height 1·905 m
Main supplier: Pullman Standard

Type of car: 1600 Silver Bird
Year of introduction: 1968
Dimensions: Length 21·18 m, height 3·86 m, width 3·086 m
Number of motored cars: 52
Average and crush capacity: 64/239
Tare and loaded weight: 28/43·176 tonnes
Doors: Inside sliding doors, width 1·219 m, height 1·905 m
Main supplier: Pullman Standard

Type of car: 1100
Year of introduction: 1956-57
Dimensions: Length 16·764 m, height 3·65 m, width 2·882 m
Number of motored cars: 92
Average and crush capacity: 46/224
Tare and loaded weight: 26·589/40·814 tonnes
Doors: Outside sliding doors, width 1·27 m, height 1·905 m
Main supplier: Pullman Standard

Type of car: No 12 Orange Line (new cars referred to as 'Orange Blossoms')
Year of introduction: 1981
Dimensions: Length 19·812 m, height 3·65 m, width 2·819 m
Number of motored cars: 36
Average and crush capacity: 58/220
Tare and loaded weight: 30·086/44·057 tonnes
Doors: Inside sliding doors, width 1·219 m, height 1·905 m
Number of cars on order: 84
Main supplier: Hawker Siddeley

Type of car: No 4 Blue Line
Year of introduction: 1980
Dimensions: Length 14·78 m, height 3·568 m, width 2·819 m
Number of motored cars: 70
Average and crush capacity: 42/154
Tare and loaded weight: 27·288/37·067 tonnes
Doors: Inside sliding doors, width 1·219 m, height 1·905 m
Main supplier: Hawker Siddeley

Light Rail
Type of car: PCC Texas Cars
Year of introduction: 1945 (cars brought from Texas, original date unknown)
Dimensions: Length 14·325 m, width 2·54 m, height 3·378 m

Orange Line car built by Hawker Siddeley

Number of motored cars: 14
Average and crush capacity: 49/118
Tare and loaded weight: 17·853/25·346 tonnes
Doors: Bi-fold doors: 2 large doors 1·32 × 2·032 m, small door 0·609 × 2·032 m
Main supplier: Pullman Standard

Type of car: PCC
Year of introduction: 1941
Dimensions: Length 14·02 m, width 2·54 m, height 3·352 m
Number of motored cars: 69
Average and crush capacity: 42/130
Tare and loaded weight: 16·592/24·847 tonnes
Doors: Bi-fold doors, 1·308 × 1·987 m
Main supplier: Pullman Standard

Type of car: PCC (Picture Window)
Year of introduction: 1944
Dimensions: Length 14·02 m, width 2·54 m, height 3·352 m
Number of motored cars: 83
Average and crush capacity: 42/130
Tare and loaded weight: 16·592/24·847 tonnes
Doors: Bi-fold doors, 1·308 × 1·987 m
Main supplier: Pullman Standard

Type of car: LRV (Light Rail Vehicle)
Year of introduction: 1977
Dimensions: Length 21·64 m, width 2·698 m, height 3·454 m
Number of motored cars: 130
Average and crush capacity: 52/150
Tare and loaded weight: 38·101/46·695 tonnes

Doors: Plug type doors
Main supplier: Boeing Vertol

Traffic
Trains/track/hour: 27
Train capacity (passengers): 1060
Total passengers/track/hour (peak): 29 000
Train headways: 4½ minutes (peak); 8 minutes (off-peak)
Passenger journeys: (1982) 144·4 million

System development
A $2000 million improvement scheme is being pursued. Part of the capital comes from the fund transfer provisions of the Interstate Highway Act of 1973, part from UMTA grants.

A $792 million Southwest Corridor project, the biggest single item in the city's transit history, is relocating the Orange Line from downtown Boston to Forest Hills. The project includes removal of the old elevated track and the building of nine new stations. On the Red Line, $574 million is being invested in construction of a 5·6 km subway extension from Harvard Square to the Alewife Brook Parkway which should open for revenue service in 1983.

MBTA is continuing to study proposals for a Blue Line extension to Lynn, with accompanying commuter rail improvements, and co-operating with several other agencies in developing a multi-modal transport facility in Boston's historic South Station.

In 1982 specifications were being drafted for 58 new Red Line cars and 55 six-axle LRVs.

Bratislava
Bratislava Metropolitan

Bratislava, Czechoslovakia

Type of system: Planned metro

Government approval was given in 1977 for construction of a full metro system and the national 1981-85 Five-Year Plan includes a 9·5 km rapid transit line from Bratislava to Petrzalka.

Brussels
Société des Transports Intercommunaux de Bruxelles (STIB)

Avenue de la Toison d'Or 15, 1060 Brussels, Belgium

Telephone: (02) 512 1790
Telex: 26520
Telegrams: STIB-Bruxelles

Director General: P Appelmans

Type of system: Metro and pre-metro (light rail)

Gauge: 1435 mm
Route length: Metro, 25 km; pre-metro, 12·5 km
Number of lines: Metro, 1; pre-metro, 3
Number of stations: Metro 19
Average distance between stations: 660 m
Tunnel type: Mainly rectangular 8 m wide, 4 m high
Max gradient: 6·2%
Minimum curvature: 100 m
Electrification type: Metro, 900 V dc; pre-metro, 600 V dc

Rolling stock
Number of cars: (Metro) 90 in 45 two-car sets
Suppliers: BN Constructions Ferroviaires et Métalliques with ACEC electrical equipment
Car dimensions: Length 18·2 m, width 2·7 m, height 3·42 m
Tare weight: 31 tonnes
Braking: Regenerative, rheostatic; pneumatic and electromagnetic emergency brakes
Control: Choppers
Motors per car: 2
Motor rating: 266·2 kW
Max acceleration: 1·16 m/s²
Emergency deceleration: 1·7 m/s²
Average commercial speed: 30 km/h
Max running speed: 75 km/h
Number of seated passengers: 40
Total passenger capacity: 210
Body material: Framework in light alloy
Cars on order: 60 additional cars on order for delivery as needed

BN has also delivered type 7900 double-articulated light rail cars. A light rail car, similar to that used on Belgium's coastal light rail line, is being developed. Maximum acceleration and deceleration will be 1·35 m/s².

Traffic
Trains/track/hour: Main axis (peak hours) 20 (off-peak) 12
Branches (peak hours) 10 (off-peak) 6
Total passengers/track/hour (peak): 12 250
Passenger journeys: (1981) 210·8 million

System development
The first section of tunnel, 3·5 km long (De Brouckere—Schuman) on the east-west axis, became operative in 1969, with six stations. The same line with its extensions at one end to Tomberg and Demsey (1977) and at the other to Sainte-Catherine has operated as a full metro since September 1976. Full metro operations on this axis are planned over 15 more km by 1985.

The north-south, Petite and Grande Ceinture lines, serving 17 stations, are run on a pre-metro basis with single or two-car LRVs. A 7 km extension of Metro Line 1 was opened in October 1981 and further extensions were in hand for opening between 1983 and 1986. Pre-metro Lines 2 and 3 were also being extended and a feasibility study for conversion of Line 2 to full metro was in hand.

Bucharest

Intreprindere Metroul Bucuresti
(Bucharest Metro Enterprise, operating under the
Railway Division of the Ministry of Transport)

Str Gutemberg, 3bis Sector 5, Bucharest, Romania

Telex: 10190

Director: Tudoric Grama

Type of system: Full metro

Gauge: 1435 mm
Route length: 9·3 km
Number of lines: 1
Number of stations: 12
Average distance between stations: 1·4 km
Rail weight and type: UIC 49 (49 kg/m)
Track type: Rail laid on timber sleepers and crushed
volcanic stone ballast

Tunnel type: Open-cut rectangular box section
including both running tracks
Electrification type: 750 V dc
Signalling: Signalling and centralised elec-
trodynamic systems to control switches remotely.
Entry and exit signals transmitted automatically.
Line monitoring system by Westinghouse

Rolling stock
Supplier: Arad works
Car dimensions: Length 18·6 m (38 m coupled unit);
width 3·1 m; height 3·4 m
Capacity: 34 seats per car; 200 standing passengers
at 5 passengers/m², 300 at 8/m²
Motor rating: 185 kW
Tare weight: 36 tonnes
Minimum running curve radius: 150 m
Max speed: 80 km/h
Max acceleration: 1·35 m/s²
Average deceleration: 1 m/s²

The stock consists of permanently-coupled two-car
sets in radio communication with the control centre,

and with public address equipment. Improvements
being considered include thyristor-controlled traction systems, regenerative braking, continuous
speed control, automatic train operation and use of
aluminium in construction.

Traffic
Train headways: Peak hours 7-8 minutes, to be
reduced to 4-5 minutes
Number of passengers daily: (1981) 40 000

System development
The first section of Line 1 was opened in January
1981 and runs east-west from Republica to
Semanatoarea. Extensions from Eroilor to Iremoas
and Semanatoarea to Cringasi, totalling 9·5 km,
were to become operational by 1983, and from
Cringasi to Piata Victoriei in 1985. Design studies are
in progress for the 17 km north-south Line 2 from
Pipera to southern suburbs, which will interchange
with Line 1 at Piata Victoriei and Piata Unirii. The first
8 km of Line 2 are due to open in 1985.

Budapest

Budapesti Kozlekedési Vallalat (BKV)

Akácfa utca 15, Budapest VII, Hungary

Telephone: 422130
Telex: 226325

General Manager: József Daczó

Type of system: Full metro

Gauge: 1435 mm
Route length: 25·1 km
Number of lines: 2
Number of stations (total): 22
(in tunnel): 9
Average distance between stations: 925 m
Gradient (max): 4%
Curvature (max): 300 m
Speed (design max): 40 km/h
(average commercial): 19 km/h
Electrification type: 825 V dc, third rail
One-man operation: All trains
Signalling: Centralised traffic control

Rolling stock
Number of cars: 265, all motored in five-car sets
Main supplier: Mytischy, USSR
Car dimensions: Length 20 m, width 2·7 m
Seating capacity: 42
Tare and loaded weight: 31·5/51·7 tonnes
Doors: Pneumatic operation, 1·218 m wide
Cars on order or under delivery: 90 from Mytischy

Traffic
Trains/track/hour: 30
Train capacity (passengers): 171
Total passengers/track/hour (peak): 5130
Train headways: 2¼ minutes (peak); 4-5 minutes
(off-peak)

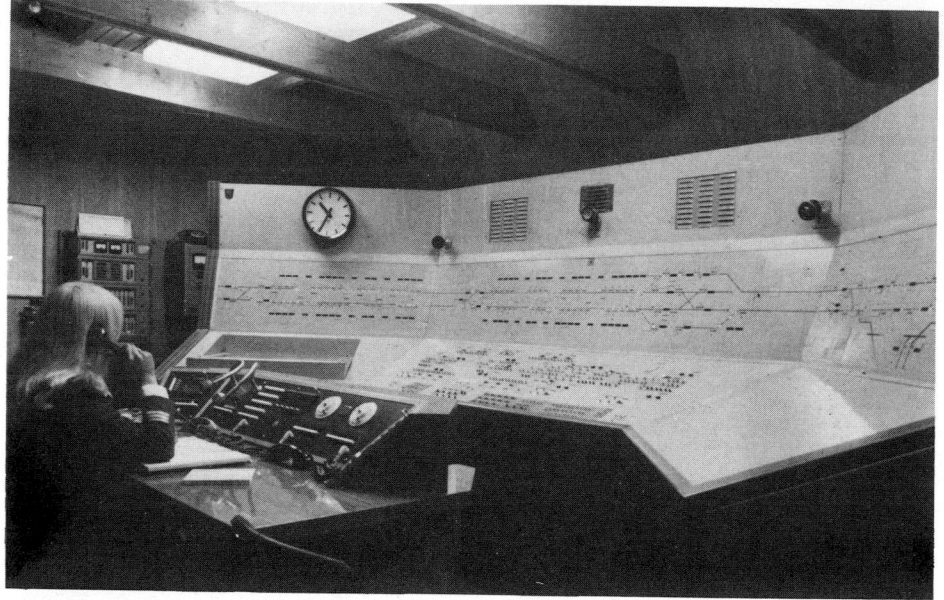

Budapest metro control centre at Deák Square

Passenger journeys: (1981) 318 million

System development
Line 2, the first of the modern metro lines running
10·1 km east-west was opened in 1972. The first 3·7
km section of the north-south line 3 between Nagyvárad Square and Deák Square opened at the end of
1976, the second 4·7 km section, Nagyvárad tés
Kobánya, in March 1980.
An 8·8 km extension of Line 3 beyond Elmunkás
tér, including 6·8 km of cut-and-cover construction,

is in progress for completion to Szilaspatak by 1989.
Construction of the 14·3 km Line 4, running almost
entirely in deep-level tubes from Bocskai on the
Danube's left bank to Ujpalota on the right bank, is
likely to start in 1987. A fifth line is also planned, with
an ultimate network length of 67·5 km in view.
BKV also runs a 97·9 km, 1 kV dc Budapest surface
suburban railway system with 43 locomotives, 223
emu power cars, 131 trailer cars and 414 freight
wagons; and the Budapest tramway system, almost
half of which is being converted to LRT standards.

Buenos Aires

Subterraneos de Buenos Aires (SBA)

Bartolomé Mitre 3342, Buenos Aires 1201 DF,
Argentina

Director General: O F Cordova

Type of system: Full metro

Gauge: 1435 mm
Route length: 34 km
Number of lines: 5
Number of stations (all in tunnel): 58
Average distance between stations: 580 m
Rail weight: Line B, 44 kg/m; other lines, 45·5 kg/m
Track type: Timber sleepers on stone ballast; con-
crete sleepers on new sections
Tunnel type: Double-track, of cut-and-cover con-
struction only in Line A and at some of the stations in
Lines B, C and D. The other lines and stations were
constructed by tunnelling. The Line A tunnel is 7·7 m
wide, and 4·45 m high from rail level; it is of rectangular section without centre supports. Line B runs
partly in tunnel of rectangular section, 8·45 m wide
by 4·65 m high, with centre supports, and partly in
tunnel with arches over each track
Gradient (max): 4%
Curvature (max): 80 m
Electrification type: Line A, 1·1 kV dc, overhead col-

Car type	Lines C, D, E		Line A	Lines A, C, D, E	Line B	
Number built	80	108	124	80	90	12
Car dimensions						
length (m)	17	17	15	17·8	17	17
width (m)	2·6	2·6	2·6	—	3·2	3·2
height (m)	2·52	2·34	3·41	—	2·6	2·6
Passenger capacity per car						
(total)	160	160	150	170	170	170
(seated)	42	40	42	41	42	42
Motors per car	4	—	2	4	2	2
Rating	116 kW	115 kW	115 kW	185 kW	109 hp	109 hp
Train composition (minimum) 2						
(max) 6						
Body material	steel	steel	steel/ wood	steel	steel	steel
Weight (tonnes)						
Motorcar	30	32	28	32	32·5	32·5
Trailer	25	21	—	31·7	—	—

lection; Line B, 600 V dc, third rail collection; Lines C,
D and E, 1·5 kV dc, overhead collection. Electrification is to be standardised with existing lines converted and new lines equipped with 750 V dc supply

Traffic
Passenger journeys: (1982) 219·8 million

System development
Discussions continue over the transfer of the system

from direct municipal to private enterprise management under a 25-year concession. The objective
is a reinvigoration of the metro.
In the first stage existing lines would be modernised with track renewal, upgrading of signalling
and new rolling stock purchases. The second stage
would see the building of two new lines (G and J)
and extension of existing lines by 11·6 km. Line G
would run from Belgrano to Crucecita (21·6 km) and
Line J from Paternal to Plaza de Mayo (10·6 km). Line
extensions planned are: Line A, Primera Junta to

Flores (2·3 km); Line B, Frederico Lacroze to Villa Urquiza (3·9 km); Line C, Retiro to the bus terminal (0·5 km) and Line E, Jose M Moreno to Parque Almirante Brown (4·9 km). Extension of Line E by 4·9 km at its northern end has already begun.

Substations, traffic and security will be controlled from a central operations room. New telephone and radio communications facilities will be installed. Cab signalling with automatic train control and automatic train stop is to be introduced, allowing peak-hour headways of 1½ minutes.

The entire rolling stock fleet will be renewed in stages. In 1982-83 40 two-car chopper-controlled units were supplied by Fiat-Materfer (for full details see under Fiat-Materfer in the Locomotives and rolling stock section).

Rolling stock
Number of cars: 494
Main suppliers: Fabricaciones Militares, Pullman Standard, General Electric (Spain), Fiat-Materfer

---

Buffalo
Niagara Frontier Transportation Authority

181 Ellicott St, Buffalo, New York 14205, USA

Telephone: (716) 855 7300
Telex: 91248

Chairman: R F Gallagher
Manager, Metro Construction: Theodore E Beck

Type of system: Light rail under construction

Gauge: 1435 mm
Route length: 10·3 km

(in tunnel): 8·37 km; includes 5·63 km in rock tunnel, 2·74 km cut-and-cover
Electrification type: 650 V dc, overhead
Method of financing: 80% Federal (UMTA); 20% State of New York
Estimated passenger volume: 10·7-11·9 million for first year of operation (1985-86)
Planned train headways: 3½ minutes (peak hours)
Planned signalling: Centrally controlled cab signalling; 100 Hz track signals

Rolling stock
Tokyu Car Corp, Japan, is to supply 26 four-axle cars each with capacity for 140 passengers, including 51 seated

System development
Work started in 1979 and construction of the eight underground stations was begun mid-1981. The surface section of the line could be ready for operation by July 1984, and the underground section should go into revenue service in April 1985. Cost of construction and equipment is expected to be $450 million.

Most of the surface section will be within a vehicular-free transit pedestrian mall, possibly the longest in the world; and the entire section, which traverses the central business district, will be fare free to stimulate retail development.

Cairo
Transport Planning Authority

Ministry of Transport, Cairo, Egypt

Technical Director: A F Lashin

Type of system: Metro under construction

Egypt's Ministries of Economy and Planning approved plans in 1978 for a Greater Cairo rapid transit railway, which will run 42 km from El Marg via the city centre to Helwan, with a complement of two urban metro lines aggregating 22 km. Current work is centred on upgrading the existing 25 km line between Bab el Louq and Helwan with renewal of track, signalling and catenary and supply by French companies of 52 electric train units. Civil engineering work on the city-centre 4·5 km tunnel section to link the existing Helwan line with the Kobri el Lamoun to El Marg line was launched in May 1982 by the 12-company Interinfra-Arabco consortium. Consultant for the project is Sofretu, France. Spie-Batignolles and CGEE-Alsthom have the tracklaying and electrification contracts, Alsthom-Atlantique, CSEE and Jeumont-Schneider the signalling and telecommunications contracts.

Calcutta
Metro Railway, Metro Rail Bhavan

33/1 Jawaharlal Nehru Road, Calcutta 700071, India

Telephone: 24 1082
Telegrams: Bhoorail, Calcutta

General Manager: K N Dasgupta
Chief Engineer: G N Phadke

Type of system: Full metro under construction

Gauge: 1676 mm
Route length: 16·43 km
(in tunnel): 15·13 km (1·1 km in twin circular tunnel; 14·03 km in rectangular reinforced concrete box construction)
Number of stations: (total) 17
(in tunnel): 15
Max gradient: 2%
Minimum curve radius: 300 m
Rail weight: UIC 60 kg/m
Track type: Ballastless track with reinforced concrete bed
Electrification type: 750 V dc, third rail
Signalling: Cab signalling with automatic train protection. Central control

Rolling stock
Cars ordered: 144 from Integral Coach Factory, Perambur, Madras, to be formed into eight-car sets, with traction equipment by the New Government Electric Factory, Bangalore. When in full operation the Metro will need 230 cars
Car dimensions: Length 19·5 m
Acceleration: 1 m/s²
Capacity per car: 60 (trailer) or 54 (power car) seated; up to 240 standing
Max speed: 80 km/h
One-man operation: All cars suitable

Traffic (estimated)
Trains/track/hour: 24
Train capacity (passengers): 2300
Total passengers/track/hour (peak): 61 440
Train headway design: 2½ minutes initially, later 1½ minutes
Passenger journeys
    (daily): 1·73 million
    (annually): 442 million

System development
The first 8·07 km of the north-south line between Dum Dum and Tollyganj is expected to start revenue service in 1984, the central section in 1987. Most of the line is being built by cut-and-cover, with only a small section by shield tunnelling. Soil conditions in Calcutta have caused engineering problems. Outer dimensions of the concrete box structure used

Calcutta metro emu by Integral Coach Factory with Bharat Heavy Electricals equipment

Pre-cast concrete box structure in course of installation

through most of the tunnel is 10 × 6 m, with the roof about 5 m below surface level. At stations the box widens to 20 m in width and 9 m in height. Most stations have a mezzanine floor for passenger entrance and ticket sales. Tunnelling from the Chitpur Yard to the Shyambazar crossing is being carried out with Soviet-built tunnel shields. All track is ballastless, on a reinforced concrete bed, employing three different types of assembly.

Total cost of the first line, including rolling stock, is estimated at Rs 5500 million at 1982 values.

An extension of Line 1 from Tollyganj southward to New Garia is planned, also an 18·3 km east-west Line 2 and another north-south route, the 27·6 km Line 3.

Calgary
City of Calgary Transportation Department

PO Box 2100, Calgary, Alberta T2P 2M5, Canada

Telephone: (403) 268 2766
Telex: 03 822 652

General Manager, Calgary Transit Division: E C Orford
Manager, Light Rail Transit Division: O Bowen

Type of system: Light rail

Gauge: 1435 mm
Route length: 12·5 km
(in tunnel): 1·43 km
Rail weight and type: 60 kg/m (R 160) girder rail; 50 kg/m (ARA· 100) T rail
Track type: 60 kg/m rail on concrete slab (direct fixation); 50 kg/m rail on ballasted concrete sleepers. Continuously welded. Parallel track centre spacing: 4000 mm
Electrification type: 600 V dc, overhead
Signalling: Block system, supplied by WABCO. Signalling can be adjusted to provide for 2½ minute headways

Rolling stock
Number of cars: 27, all motored
Main suppliers: Siemens Electric, Canada and Duewag, West Germany
Motor output: 2 × 150 kW per car
Car dimensions: Length 23·15 m, width 2·65 m, height 3·62 m
Capacity: 64 seated, 98 standing at 4/m²
Tare weight: 32·5 tonnes
Service acceleration: 1·0 m/s²
Service deceleration: 1·2 m/s²
Max speed: 80 km/h
Cars on order: 8 for South line, 48 for Northeast line and South line extension, all from Siemens and Duewag, total cost C$76 million

LRV built by Siemens and Duewag, West Germany for Calgary Transportation Department

Traffic
Passenger journeys daily: (1982) 42 000

System development
Calgary's first light rail line, the South, was completed in May 1981 at a cost of C$167 million. The city secured 58 per cent of the capital cost by debt financing and the remainder was met by the Alberta Provincial Government. A second Northeast line of 9·8 km from the city centre, costed at C$262 million, was begun in 1982 for probable completion in 1985. Also planned, but in 1983 deferred on financial grounds, are a 12·9 km Northwest line from the city centre, budgeted at C$381 million, and a 3·6 km extension of the South line at a cost of C$59 million.

Caracas
CA Metro de Caracas

Multicentro Empresarial del Este Conjunto Miranda, Torre B pisos 1 al 7, Chacao, Caracas 1060, Venezuela

Telephone: 208 2111
Telex: 24936
Telegrams: Cametro

President: J Gonzales Lander

Type of system: Planned full metro

Gauge: 1435 mm
Route length (open): 14 km
(in design): 56 km
Number of lines: 5 (2 under construction, 3 more planned)
Number of stations: 4 (first line), 50 (total planned)
Average distance between stations: 0·9 km
Gradient (max): 3·5%
Curvature (max): 225 m
Speed (design max): 80 km/h
(average commercial): 37 km/h
Rail weight and type: 54 kg/m in 18 m lengths, continuously welded

Track type: Rails on Stedef twin-block sleepers laid on concrete in tunnels and on ballast on surface sections
Tunnel type: Cut-and-cover and bored
Electrification type: 750 V dc, third rail
Signalling: Automatic signalling and train control with onboard equipment similar to that on Paris Metro cars

Rolling stock
Number of cars: 140 cars for Stage 1 with option for 102 additional cars for rest of Line 1; 136 cars for Line 2
Suppliers: Consortium led by CIMT and including Alsthom-Atlantique, ANF-Industrie, Francorail and CEM-Oerlikon
Car dimensions: Length 21·35 m, width 3·05 m, height 2·498 m
Capacity: Cars with driver's cab, 54 seats; others, 60; standing room for 120
Weight: 30 tonnes
Traction motors per car: 4 × 122 kW
Max speed: 80 km/h
Max acceleration: 1·35 m/s²
Max deceleration: 1·1 m/s²
Braking: Regenerative
Doors: 4 each side with 1·37 m openings
Car body construction: Aluminium extruded sections

System development
The contract for the initial 14 km, 14-station section of Line 1, from Propatria to Chacaito, was won by a French consortium, Frameca, and in November 1981 the group was awarded a contract to complete Line 1 and provide the additional rolling stock for a total of US $200 million. This was opened to traffic in January 1983. The group also won the US $300 million contract for construction of Line 2, including supply of 136 cars. The French companies involved, excluding those already listed for rolling stock, are: CGEE-Alsthom and Spie Batignolles (electrification); Sodeteg-TAI, Jeumont-Schneider, Alsthom-Atlantique, CSEE, Cerci and Inter-Elec (train control and communications); Spie Batignoles, Montcocol and CGEE-Alsthom (track). Much of the current civil engineering work is being done by Venezuelan and Italian companies.

The remaining 9·8 km of Line 1 from Chacaito to Palo Verde are expected to open for passenger service by mid-1986. Parts of Line 2, to run from Las Adjuntas to Silencio (16·5 km with 13 stations), are now under construction and passenger service should start by mid-1986. Line 3 from La Rinconada to the central area was still at the planning stage at the end of 1982.

Charleroi
Société des Transports Intercommunaux de Charleroi (STIC)

Chaussée de Namur, 6080 Montignies sur Sambre, Belgium

Telephone: 071 410 570

Director: F Merlin

Type of system: Light rail

Gauge: 1000 mm
Route length: 11 km (52 km planned)
Number of lines: 9 planned
Number of stations: 69 planned
Track type: SNCB-type 50 kg/m rails laid on 'Angleur' tie-plates inclined 1/20; tie-plate laid on poplar plate, 5 mm thick for sound and vibration damping. Creosoted sleepers laid at 25/18 m on straight sections, 30/18 m on curves. Type U 69 safety guard rails laid in curves, 20/40 ballast layer, 20 cm thick, laid under sleepers.

Rails welded to sections 600 m long. Switches actuated by remote control from car by electromagnetic boxes supplied with 600 V current
Electrification type: 600 V dc, overhead

Rolling stock
50 articulated bi-directional three-bogie units, of welded steel construction with four double doors on each side, ordered from BN. They are equipped with regenerative and rheostatic braking for speeds above 4 km/h, with disc brakes mounted on all axles for speeds below 4 km/h, and thyristor chopper starting equipment

Car dimensions: Overall length 22·88 m, width 2·5 m, height above rail 3·26 m
Capacity: 184, including 38 seated
Tare weight: 31·5 tonnes
Hourly rating: 456 kW

System development
In 1976 Charleroi launched a scheme to convert its tramways into a light rail network consisting of a downtown 4·3 km ring line radiating eight branches. Work on an east-west link, including the Beaux Arts-Nord section of the ring line, the radial lines to Chatelet and Gilly as far as Quatre-Bras, and a north-south link, including the Charleroi Sud-Jumet Brulotte segment of the west half-ring, could all be completed by late 1983.

Completion of the entire 52 km system and 69 stations is programmed for 1994.

Chelyabinsk

Chelyabinsk, USSR

Plans have been drafted for a 10 km line from the centre of this eastern USSR city to its north-western suburbs, construction to begin possibly in 1986.

Chicago
Chicago Transit Authority (CTA)

Merchandise Mart Plaza, PO Box 3555, Chicago, Illinois 60654, USA

Telephone: (312) 664 7200

Chairman: M A Cardilli
Executive Director: B Ford
Divisional Managers
  Operations: (Acting) J R Blaa
  Finance: P J Kole

Type of system: Full metro

Gauge: 1435 mm
Route length: 145·2 km
(in tunnel): 16·3 km
(elevated): 63·6 km
Number of lines in operation: 6: North-South, West-Northwest, West-South, Ravenswood, Evanston, Skokie
Number of stations (total): 140
(in tunnel): 20
(elevated): 65
Average distance between stations: 1·1 km
Gradient (max): 1 in 28·6 (3·5%)
Curvature (max): 27·4 m
Speed (design max): 113 km/h
  (average commercial): 40 km/h
  (averages by route range from 30-60 km/h)
Rail weight and type: 37·3 (50%), 41·4 (25%) and 47·6 (25%) kg/m flat-bottomed
Tunnel type: Single-track bored (14·2 km), cut-and-cover (1·9 km) and concrete caisson (0·2 km)
Electrification type: 600 V dc, third rail

Rolling stock
Number of cars: 1102
Main suppliers: St Louis Car, Pullman, Budd, Boeing Vertol
Main types: 6000 series (536 in service 1982); and 2400 series with Wegmann bogies
Car dimensions
6000 series: Length 14·63 m, width 2·84 m, height 3·66 m
2400 series: Length 14·63 m, width 2·84 m, height 3·66 m
Capacity
6000 series: 47, 50 or 51 seats depending on car type
2400 series: 43, 45 or 49 seats
Motors per car: 4 (both series)
Automatic train control: 6000 series, all cars except 12; 2400 series, all cars
Cars on order: 600 Series 2600 cars from Budd with option for 300 more. First two prototypes delivered March 1981, 100 will be delivered for the O'Hare Airport extension and completion is foreseen by December 1986.
  The new Budd car bodies are of stainless steel.

Boeing Vertol Type 2600 train-set

The two pairs of sliding doors on each side have 1·27 m openings and each pair of cars has 92 seats. Interior equipment includes fluorescent lighting, air-conditioning and public address system. The propulsion system consists of General Electric cam-control 110 hp traction motors and parallel drive gear boxes. New York Air Brake supplies the disc brake and Knorr the track brakes. Top speed is 112 km/h.

Traffic
Train headways: Peak hours, 3-5 minutes depending on line; off-peak, 6-15 minutes
Max line capacity (one way): theoretical capacity 1 train every 90 s
Max number of trains per hour (one way)
  24 on one route (West-Northwest)
  30 on Loop L (two routes sharing same track)
Capacity per train (seated): up to 400
  (standing): up to 800
Passenger journeys: (1981) 148·7 million

System development
Major work in progress in 1982 was a further 7·3 km extension of the Northwest line (its third since 1895) to a station beneath O'Hare Airport. The $196 million project takes the line mostly along the median strip of the Kennedy Expressway and the airport access road, then dips it underground to the airport terminal. Design of the airport and the three other 'park-and-ride' stations on the extension has been entrusted to four different firms of architects as a stimulus to new thought in transit facilities. The project is drawing $157·5 million of its funding from UMTA, $35·9 million from the Illinois DoT and $2·6 million from the city of Chicago. It was to be completed in late 1983.

The extension will be the first CTA rapid transit line to employ CTC, supplied by Union Switch & Signal, which will allow bi-directional working on each line under cab-signalling protection. This innovation was necessary because a new yard and car shop are being established near the airport, so that operation in that area will be complex.

Other capital schemes planned include a $103·5 million rehabilitation of the 85 year old downtown loop elevated system; relocation of part of the Dan Ryan line; and new yards and repair shops. The city authorities hope in 1984 to start construction of a new rapid transit line from the city centre to the south-west suburbs, which at present are not touched by a rapid transit line.

Cleveland
Greater Cleveland Regional Transit Authority

615 Superior NW St, Cleveland, Ohio 44113, USA

Telephone: (216) 516 5100

General Manager: W C Lahman
Assistant General Manager: David N Goss
Manager of Operations: J V Terange

Type of system: Full metro

Gauge: 1435 mm
Route length: 30·6 km
(in tunnel): 0·8 km
(at surface level): 29·8 km
Number of lines: 1
Number of stations: 18
(in tunnel): 2
Average distance between stations: 1·8 km

Rail weight and type: 45 kg/m ARA-A full-metro
Track type: Sleepers on ballast with continuous welded rail. Recently rebuilt sections use resilient fasteners in wood sleepers
Tunnel type: Cut-and-cover, or within structure
Electrification type: 600 V dc, overhead
Signalling: GRS three-aspect lights with automatic stop. All interlocks centrally controlled. Cab signal control will eventually be extended throughout the metro and light rail (see below) lines
Automatic control: Most westerly 6·4 km has cab signal control

Rolling stock
Number of cars: 101, all motored
Main suppliers: 72 supplied 1954-58 by St Louis Car; 29 supplied 1967 and 1970 by Pullman
Car dimensions: Pullman cars length 21·3 m, width 3·2 m
Average and crush capacity: St Louis 54/197; Pullman 81/140
Doors: Sliding, 1·27 m wide

Interior of Breda LRV

Cars on order: 60 cars from Tokyu Car at a cost of $53·2 million to replace St Louis cars. Delivery scheduled for 1984-85

Leading particulars of Tokyu cars:
Tare weight per car: 31·75 tonnes

Capacity	Double cab car	Single cab car
Seating (W1)	80	84
Normal (W2)	129	129
Crush (W3)	230	230

Car dimensions: Length 22·86 m, width 3·15 m, height 3·66 m
Max operating speed: 97 km/h
Brakes: Electro-pneumatic with dynamic brakes
Acceleration: 2·4 mph/s
Deceleration: Full service 3·0 mph/s, emergency 3·5 mph/s

Traffic
Train headways: Peak hours, 10 minutes; off-peak, 20 minutes
Passenger journeys: (1981) 10 million; (1982 estimate) 9·3 million

Type of system: Light rail

Route length: 21·2 km
Number of lines: 2
Number of stops: 29
Average distance between stops: 0·8 km
Rail weight and type: 45 kg/m ARA-B light rail
Electrification type: 600 V dc, overhead

Rolling stock
Number of cars: 68, all motored
Main suppliers: St Louis Car supplied 20 from 1946; Breda (Italy) delivered 30 of 48 new cars in 1981-82
Car dimensions: Breda cars, length 23·504 m, width 2·821 m

Artist's impression of Tokyu metro units to be delivered from February 1984

Capacity: Breda cars, 84 seated, 270 crush
Tare and loaded weight: St Louis, 17 700/24 500 kg; Breda 38 102/56 472 kg
Doors: St Louis, folding 1·47 m wide; Breda, sliding 1·249 m wide

Traffic
Train headways: Peak hours, 4 minutes; off-peak, 10 minutes

Passenger journeys: (1981) 3·86 million; (1982 estimate) 3·59 million

System development
Cleveland's full metro line links the city's central area with the airport, where the station is in the terminal building. A $ 100 million rehabilitation of the Shaker Heights light rail route was completed in 1982.

Cologne
Kolner Verkehrsbetriebe AG

Scheidtweilerstrasse 38, 5000 Cologne 41, Federal Republic of Germany

Type of system: Pre U-Bahn

Gauge: 1435 mm
Route length: 29·53 km
Number of stations: 26
Average distance between stations: 1·1 km
Electrification type: 750 V dc, overhead

Rolling stock
Number of cars: 59 articulated LRVs; 200 eight-axle trams
Car dimensions: LRVs, length 28 m, width 2·65 m, height 3·36 m
Capacity: 282, 72 seated
Tare weight: 40 tonnes
Acceleration: 1·1 m/s²
Deceleration: Normal, 1·6 m/s², emergency, 3 m/s²

System development
The first 1·4 km east-west section of a new underground tramway system for Cologne opened in

1968, between Cathedral-Hauptbahnhof and Friesenplatz. It was the first step in a project to provide segregated rights of way for some 120 km of Cologne's tramway system, by the construction of cutting and embankment and by tunnelling.

The double-track tunnel of rectangular section is internally 4·65 m high and 7·3 m wide. There are no centre supports. The tunnels are sufficiently large to accommodate full metro trains should this system be required later.

Plans have been made up to 1990, but completion of the total system of 120 km is expected to take 70 to 80 years. Park-and-ride facilities with space for 12 500 cars are planned for 35 stations.

Dallas
Dallas Area Rapid Transit (DART)

Dallas, Texas, USA

The city was due to be polled in a referendum in August 1983 for approval of a 1 per cent sales tax to fund the start of a metro. DART has drafted a 14-line, 257 km network to be built over a period of 35 years.

Denver
Regional Transportation District

Denver, Colorado, USA

Type of system: Planned light rail

A plan for a 125 km light rail network aims to have 83·6 km operational by 1995. Its financing by a sales

tax was rejected by a local referendum in 1980, but a further vote was called in November 1982.

Detroit
Southeastern Michigan Transportation Authority (SEMTA)

660 Woodward Avenue, 13th Floor, First National Building, Detroit, Michigan 48226, USA

Telephone: (313) 256 8600

General Manager: Larry E Salci
Manager of Rail Engineering: Daniel L Jones Jr

Type of system: Light rail transit (LRT). Combination of full metro (level boarding) with light rail vehicles and traction power

Gauge: 1435 mm
Route length: 24·2 km
(in tunnel): 13·7 km

Number of stations: 17
Planned start of revenue operation: Spring 1989
Estimated cost (1982 values): $890 million
Method of financing: 80% from Federal grant sources; 20% from State grant sources
Estimated passenger volume for first period of operation: 120 000 passengers/day
Planned headways: 3 minutes
Proposed electrification: 600 V dc, overhead
Signalling: Automatic train protection and automatic train supervision with manual train operation (with cab signalling) and automatic speed regulation

Rolling stock
Type of cars: Light Rail Vehicles 75-85 ft (22·86-25·9 m) long
Number required: 75 initially, 150 ultimately. First orders to be placed in 1983

System development
SEMTA's planned light rail line will service Woodward Avenue, the region's most heavily travelled corridor. That line will extend from downtown Detroit to 11 Mile Road in Royal Oak. The plan, along with a more comprehensive programme of transit development, was approved by the Michigan State Legislature for funding in 1980, and fulfilment was brought nearer in 1983 by the release of considerably increased UMTA funds for rapid transit system extensions and the Reagan Administration's withdrawal of its two-year opposition to new starts.

Construction has begun of a 5 km, 13-station people mover system in the city centre. It is the first US project to employ the linear induction motor-powered Advanced Light Rapid Transit System of UTDC, Canada.

Dnepropetrovsk

Dnepropetrovsk, USSR

Type of system: Metro under construction

Gauge: 1524 mm
Electrification type: 825 V dc

Service is due to start in 1984 on a 13 km metro line now under construction.

Dortmund
Stadtbahn Dortmund

Postfach 907, 4600 Dortmund 1, Federal Republic of
Germany

Type of system: Pré U-Bahn under construction

System development
The city plans a three-line system totalling 17·88 km.
The first 1·5 km section of the mostly underground

Line 1 opened in May 1983 and a further 8·3 km was
likely to become operational in 1984. Line 2 (6·1 km
long) and Line 3 (1·95 km long) are in course of
planning. Rolling stock consists of 30 type N8 cars
with eight axles and 12 type B6 cars with six axles.

Duisburg
Duisburger Verkehrsgesellschaft AG

Konigstrasse 30, 4100 Duisburg 1, Federal Republic
of Germany

Type of system: Pre U-Bahn

Gauge: 1435 mm
Route length: 4·9 km
Number of stations: 5
Electrification type: 750 V dc, overhead

Rolling stock
Number of cars: 18 (Cologne type B)
Supplier: Duewag/Siemens
Car dimensions: Length 26·9 m, width 2·65 m,
height 3·365 m
Motors per car: 2
Motor rating: 215 kW
Capacity: 72 seated, 112 standing (4/m²)
Doors: 4 double (1·3 m opening), 2 single (690 mm
opening)
Tare weight: 38 tonnes
Max speed: 100 km/h
Acceleration: 1·2 m/s²

Deceleration: Normal 1·3 m/s², emergency 2·7 m/s²
Cars on order: 32 additional vehicles may be needed
by 1985

System development
A 40 km, two-line pre U-Bahn network is being
created from parts of a tramway network; a further
3·1 km with four stations was being constructed in
1982. The final system will form part of the Rhine-
Ruhr Stadtbahn network eventually covering 400
km, and linking 11 cities with a total population of 16
million. Transfer from pre U-Bahn to full metro
operation is envisaged in 1986.

Dusseldorf
Rheinische Bahngesellschaft AG

Hansaallee 1, Postfach 6720, 4000 Dusseldorf-Ober-
kassel, Federal Republic of Germany

Telephone: (0211) 57761
Telex: 8582921

Type of system: Pre U-Bahn

System development
The first 1·5 km of Dusseldorf's pre U-Bahn, an
upgrading of parts of the city's tramway system,
was inaugurated in 1981 from Kennedydamm to
Heinrich-Heine-Allee (Opernhaus) and 6·1 km were

operational by the end of 1982. It is operated by B80
articulated light rail vehicles built by Duewag with
Siemens and BBC electrical equipment, and by
reconstructed tramcars.
Extensions are under way, but the city of Dusseldorf, which is financing the tunnelling, is experiencing financial difficulties and no dates have been set
for future openings.

Edmonton
Edmonton Transit

10426 81 Avenue, Edmonton, Alberta T6E 1X5,
Canada

General Manager: E V Miller

Type of system: Light rail

Gauge: 1435 mm
Route length: 9 km
(in tunnel): 1·6 km
Number of lines: 1
Number of stations (total): 6
(in tunnel): 2
Average distance between stations: 1·8 km
Rail weight and type: 100ARA (50 kg/m)
Tunnel type: Cut-and-cover and bored
Gradient (max): 3%
Curvature (max): main line 140 m, yard 25 m
Electrification type: 600 V dc, overhead

Rolling stock
Car types: 6-axle articulated motor cars, derived
from Frankfurt U2 design
Number of units: 21
Car dimensions: Length 24·3 m, width 2·65 m,
height 3·66 m
Number of doors per side: 4 double
Door width: 1·6 m
Number of passengers per car (total): 225
(seated): 64
Motors per car: 2
Motor rating: 150 kWh
Power per train (minimum): single car, 300 kW
(max): 5-car train, 1500 kW
Acceleration (max): 1·32 m/s²
Deceleration (normal service): 1·0 m/s²
(emergency): 3·0 m/s²
Max design speed: 80 km/h
Bogies (type and manufacturer): Duewag
Monomotor

Duewag Type RTE1 LRV

Brakes: Dynamic/disc/magnetic
Weight (empty): 31 tonnes
Cars on order: 20 from Duewag/Siemens (4 deli-
vered by the end of 1982)

Traffic
Max line capacity (one way): 5400 passengers
Max number of trains per hour (one way): 12
(one way-planned): 30
Train headways (currently): 12 minutes
(planned): 30 minutes

Capacity per train (passengers seated): 128
(passengers standing): 322
Passenger journeys: (1982) 5·7 million

System development
A 1 km, two-station, city-centre extension was to
open in 1983, for a cost of C$104 million. This is the
start of a planned 25 km South line, but further
progress depends on conclusion of negotiations for
a right of way over Canadian Pacific route. The first,
Northeast line made considerable use of Canadian
National infrastructure.

Erevan
Erevan Metropolitan

375010 Ploshchad Lenina, Dom Pravitelstva 2,
Erevan, USSR

Chief Executive: Ivan Georgievich Papiev
Chief Engineer: Marlen Grigorievich Artiunov

Type of system: Full metro

Gauge: 1524 mm
Route length: 7·6 km
Number of lines: 1
Number of stations: 9
Average distance between stations: 1·44 km
Electrification type: 825 V, third rail

System development
The city opened its first 7·6 km of route between

Druzhba and Sasunci David in 1981 and is proceeding with a 3·9 km extension. The initial section, of
which 5·7 km is underground, connects Erevan's
main industrial area with its most heavily populated
area via the main railway station. A 47 km network of
two lines with a common, north-south central axis
intersected by a third, east-west line, is envisaged
and is forecast to move up to 10 million passengers
a year.

Essen
Essener Verkehrs AG

Zweigertstrasse 34, Postfach 10 10 63, 4300 Essen 1, Federal Republic of Germany

Telephone: 0201 799 71
Telex: 0857 688

Type of system: Full metro (U-Stadtbahn) 14 km
Pre-metro (Pre U-Bahn) 3 km

Gauge: 1435 mm
Length in tunnel: U-Bahn 3·6 km; pre U-Bahn 3 km

Number of lines: 1 (U-Bahn)
Number of stations (total): 17
(in tunnel): 12
Average distance between stations/stops: 600 m
Rail type: S49, Ri59, NP4
Track type: Conventional sleepers on ballast
Tunnel type: Cut-and-cover; bored single track; bored stations
Electrification type: 750 V dc, overhead
One-man operation: All services
Signalling: Conventional block system by Siemens. Pre U-Bahn has point-setting by process computer
Centralised control: Central control room with train identification system and process computer for point operation

Rolling stock
Type: Cologne-type, six-axle
Main suppliers: Duewag; electrics by BBC, Kiepe and Siemens

System development
The city's objective is a 58 km U-Bahn network, of which 12·5 km will be underground, to integrate with the overall Rhine-Ruhr Stadtbahn development. The surface sections are being created largely by conversion of metre-gauge tram tracks to 1435 mm in an eight-stage programme which was absorbing an annual investment of DM950 million in 1982. The first three stages are over and two more were in progress in 1982. Completion of the first seven stages is predicted before 1990.

Frankfurt am Main
Stadtwerke Frankfurt am Main

Borneplatz 3, Postfach 4269, 6000 Frankfurt am Main 1, Federal Republic of Germany

Telephone: 0611 2131
Telex: 416411

Managing Director: Hans-Joachim Krull
Operating Manager: Helmut Oesterling

Type of system: Metro

Gauge: 1435 mm
Route length: 56 km
Number of lines in operation: 5
Number of stations (total): 61
Average distance between stations: 700 m
Rail type: S41, S49
Tunnel type: Box section, double-tracked 7·1 m wide internally and 4·8 m high, providing clearance for pantographs.

Part of the 6 km, eight-station metro tunnel, across the city from the zoo in the east to the suburb of Bockenheim in the west, scheduled for completion in 1986, has been built by a 50 metre-long shield tunnelling machine developed jointly by three construction firms hired by the city. It uses steel fibre concrete which is more cost-effective and more pressure- and crack-resistant than the spray concrete employed in the Austrian system. The machine has increased productivity, moving at a rate of about 12 metres per day. Mounted on the front of the machine are several hydraulic cutting blades, each with a width of 90 cm. These loosen the earth, which is then transported to the back of the machine by a conveyor belt. A trailing shield immediately behind the blades creates a smooth cavity, which is then lined with steel fibre concrete. The concrete is produced on-site by a cement mixer located on the maintenance trailer at the back of the machine. All operations are supervised from the construction office above ground. A monitor linked with a computer ensures precise steering of the machine, even through curves in the tunnel.
Electrification type: 600 V dc, overhead

Rolling stock
Number of cars: 127 articulated Type U2 and U3
Supplier: Duewag/Siemens/AEG-Telefunken

Type U2 light rail train-set, built by Uerdingen (under licence from Duewag) with electrical control and switching equipment from Siemens

Car dimensions: Length 24·29 m, width 2·65 m, height 3·28 m
Average capacity: 64 seated, 97 standing (4/m²)
Motors per car: 2
Motor rating: 150 kW
Max speed: 80 km/h
Tare weight: 31 tonnes
Doors: 4 double per side, 1·3 m openings, 1·9 m high. Electric drives and electromagnetic locks. Driver- or passenger-operated. Photoelectric cells for safety
Bogies: Duewag monomotor with Duewag gearboxes
Suspension: Primary, rubber chevron axle box springs; secondary, coil springs
Articulation: Duewag with double ball-bearing ring and silentbloc bearings
Wheel diameter: 720 mm
Acceleration: Average, 0-40 km/h, 1 m/s²
Deceleration: Service brake, 1·3 m/s², emergency, 3 m/s²

Traffic
Max number of trains per hour (one-way): 30

Frequency of train services: 2 minutes
Capacity per train (passengers seated): 180
(passengers standing): 420
Peak track/hour capacity: 18 000

System development
To relieve street congestion tramways are being transferred into sub-surface tunnels under the thoroughfares. Trains comprise four twin-car articulated units, with greater acceleration and overall capacity than the ordinary street cars.

Future plans include: projection of Line U across the Main river to Sachsenhausen by 1985; extensions through a four-track tunnel common to both S-Bahn and U-Bahn trains, between Hauptwache and Konstabler Wache; construction of a new U-Bahn line in tunnel from Bornheim to Hauptbahnhof with eight stations, including a junction station with the existing north-south U-Bahn line at Theaterplatz and interchange with the S-Bahn at Hauptbahnhof. The ultimate U-Bahn network extending north and south of the River Main will comprise 123 km of tunnel and segregated surface route.

Fukuoka
Municipal Transportation Bureau

Fukuoka, Japan

Superintendent: H Oishi

Type of system: Full metro

Gauge: 1067 mm
Number of lines: 2
Number of stations: 17

Electrification type: 1·5 kV dc, overhead

Rolling stock
Number of cars: 8 six-car sets
Suppliers: Kinki Sharyo, Toshiba, Hitachi, Mitsubishi
Car dimensions: Length 19·5 m (motor), 20 m (driving trailer); width 2·86 m; height 4·135 m
Average capacity per train: 312 seated, 848 crush load
Motors per car: 2
Motor rating: 150 kW, chopper-controlled

Max speed: 90 km/h
Acceleration: 0·92 m/s²
Deceleration: 0·97 m/s²

System development
The first 5·8 km from Tenjin to Muromi of a proposed 20·4 km, two-line metro system opened in 1981 and the first route is being extended to a planned length of 15·7 km. Line 2 will be 4·8 km long. Through service to Karatsu City over Japanese National Railways tracks, to be reached at Minohara, is envisaged.

Genoa
Genova Transit

Genoa, Italy

Type of system: Planned LRT

A former tramway tunnel, the Certosa, 1761 m long, which has proved unsuitable for substitute bus traffic, is being reactivated to carry a 3·85 km LRT line from Principe to Rivarolo. Work began in 1981 and nine articulated LRVs based on Zurich's Tram 2000 design were ordered from Stanga, Padua, with electrical equipment by Tecnomasio Italiano Brown Boveri. Extension of the line via the city-centre Grazie Tunnel for 4·4 km to Brignole is intended by 1985-86, and later the line may be projected to Staglieno, Foce, Begato and Sampierdarena.

Glasgow
Strathclyde Passenger Transport Executive

12 West George Street, Glasgow G2 5TR, Scotland

Telephone: 041-332 6811

Director General: A R Westwell
Underground Manager: R A Adams

Type of system: Full metro

Gauge: 1220 mm
Route length: 10·4 km (all in tunnel)
Number of lines: 1
Number of stations: 15
Average distance between stations: 710 m
Rail weight and type: 38 kg/m BS 80 A
Track type: Rails laid on concrete blocks with resilient rubber inserts, fixed to concrete bed
Max gradient: 1 in 16 (6·25%)
Minimum curve radius: 104 m on main line, 50 m in depot yard
Tunnel type: Double tubes, each of 3·35 m nominal diameter. Tunnelling was by means of shields. Depth of the tunnel top ranges from 2 to 35 m below surface; average depth is 8·84 m
Electrification type: 600 V dc, third rail
Signalling: Two-aspect colour-light signalling operated by conventional track circuits and incorporating trainstops has been used. The track-to-train control signals are by passive transponders laid in the track. There is a radio communication link between all trains and the Central Control

Rolling stock
Number of cars: 33, all motored
Main supplier: Metro-Cammell
Max number of cars per train: 2 with potential for 3
Car dimensions: Length 12·75 m, width 2·34 m, height 2·65 m
Capacity: 90 crush, 36 seated
Tare weight: 19·4 tonnes
Doors: Air-worked sliding doors

Traffic
Train headways: Peak hours, 4 minutes; off-peak, up to 8 minutes
Passenger journeys: (1981/82) 10·6 million
Trains/track/hour: 17 with potential for 27
Average schedule speed (including stops): 26 km/h

System development
In 1974, the Secretary of State for Scotland announced approval of a 75 per cent Government grant towards the modernisation of the Glasgow Underground, which opened in 1897. The project, completed in 1980, involved the rebuilding of stations with the provision of escalators; complete replacement of rolling stock and new facilities for its repair and maintenance; and new signalling and concrete slab track.

Thirty-three new cars capable of being run as two or three-car trains were built by Metro-Cammell Ltd of Birmingham and delivered between January 1978 and May 1979. They are equipped for one-man operation with automatic train operation between stations.

Buchanan Street station

Operations control room

Gorki
Ministry of Railways

Novo Basmannaya 2, Moscow 107174, USSR

Type of system: Full metro

Gauge: 1524 mm
Route length: 9·6 km
Number of lines: 1
Number of stations: 8
Average distance between stations: 1·37 km
Electrification type: 825 V, third rail

System development
Construction work on the city's first line began in 1977 and was due for completion in 1983. Under design for future construction is a 16·7 km extension with 10 stations.

Gothenburg
Goteborgs Sparvagar

PO Box 424, 401 26 Gothenburg, Sweden

General Manager: C M Elmberg

Type of system: Light rail

Gauge: 1435 mm
Route length: 119·7 km
Number of lines: 8
Rail type and weight: Vignole 43 kg/m
Minimum curve radius: 100 m
Max gradient: 4% (streets)
   2% (reserved tracks)
Electrification type: 600 V dc, with a small part at 750 V dc, overhead

Rolling stock
Number of cars: 315, all motored

Model of ASEA Type M21 LRV

Rating per car: 4 × 50 kW (types M25 and M29), 4 × 44 kW (type M28)
Capacity: 116 with 38 seats (116 with 43 seats for type M25A-V cars)
Doors: 1·57 m (double), 0·791 m (single)
Main suppliers: Hagglunds (types M25 and M29), ASJ/ASEA (type M28)
New orders: In December 1981 the Authority placed an order with ASEA for 30 prototypes of a new M21 design of six-axle LRV with an option for 50 more; to be delivered from 1984, the new model is foreseen as the system's future standard. It will have four chopper-fed 75 kW traction motors, and acceleration at 1·3 m/s² up to 30 km/h, with a maximum of 80 km/h. Seating capacity per car will be 60, with standing room for 150. Braking systems will combine regenerative, disc and emergency electromagnetic systems. The undertaking aims to renew its entire fleet at the rate of 30 vehicles a year from 1985.

Traffic
Train headways: 10 minutes on each line at peak periods; off-peak, 10-20 minutes
Passenger journeys: (1981) 90·1 million, including bus and ferry services which account for about 40% of the total
Commercial speed: 21·2 km/h

System development
New extensions are being constructed to full metro standards, with fully segregated rights of way. Following a 1·25 km projection of Line 1 from the system's eastern terminus at Vidkarr to Östra Sjukhuset

Light rail/bus interchange, Gothenburg Central station

(Eastern Hospital), opened in 1982, the remaining city-centre single-track Line 8 is being doubled, starting with the section from Central station to Gamlestadstorget.

Guadalajara
Sistema de Transporte Colectivo de la Zona Metropolitana

Estacion Mexicaltzingo, Guadalajara Jal, Mexico

Type of system: Planned full metro

Projected route length: 33 km

Number of lines: 3
Number of stations: 34
Rail weight: 48 kg/m
Electrification type: 1·5 kV dc, third rail
Planned design speed: 80 km/h max
Commercial speed: 35 km/h
Planned opening date: 1990 for full system. A 5 km first section opened in 1976, with trolleybus operation

Rolling stock
Number of cars planned: 300, to provide 150 two-car sets
Car dimensions: Length 21·5 m, width 2·6 m, height above rail 3·1 m
Capacity: 210 (56 seated)
Motors per car: 4
Motor rating: 90 kW

Hague, The
Haagsche Tramweg-Maatschappij (HTM)

Postbus 28503, 2502 KM The Hague, Netherlands

Telephone: (070) 88 92 80
Telex: 33549

Director: J B den Ouden

Type of system: Pre-metro

Gauge: 1435 mm

Route length: 5·2 km
Number of lines: 1
Electrification type: 600 V dc, overhead

Rolling stock
Cars: 65 double-articulated, chopper-controlled LRVs, type GT 3000, order completion due late 1982
Supplier: BN Constructions Ferroviaires et Métalliques
Car dimensions: Length 28·6 m, width 2·35 m, height 3·19 m
Number of motors: 8
Motor rating: 45 kW

Capacity: 77 seated, 108 standing (4·5/m²)
Doors: 5 double doors on one side only, protected by touch-sensitive edges and light-beam detection device on steps
Max speed: 70 km/h
Acceleration: 1·2 m/s²
Deceleration: Normal, 1·3 m/s²; emergency, 3-4 m/s²

System development
A new 5·2 km double-track line has been constructed as an extension of the city's 71 km tramway/light rail network.

Haifa
Municipal Corporation of Haifa

City Engineers Dept
122 Hanassi Ave, Haifa, Israel

Telephone: (4) 83765

Type of system: Funicular subway

Gauge: 1980 mm (rubber-tyred system)
Route length: 1·75 km (all in tunnel)

Number of lines: 1
Number of stations: 6 (all in tunnel)
Average distance between stations: 350 m
Track: Concrete strips with steel guide rails
Gradient (max): 15·5%
Speed (average commercial): 30 km/h
Electrification type: 1·2 kV

Rolling stock (rubber-tyred)
Number of units: 4
Car dimensions: Length 15 m, width 2·4 m, height 3·8 m

Passenger capacity per car
(total): 160
(seated): 24
Train composition: 2
Brakes: Cable

System development
This railway, which was opened in 1959, has six stations and a train every six minutes. It has a capacity of 4000 passengers per hour. It commences about ¼ mile from the harbour at Paris station, in the town-centre district, and runs in a straight line to its other terminus, Gan Haem, in the Carmel district, ascending nearly 274 m.

Hamburg
Hamburger Hochbahn Aktiengesellschaft

Steinstr 20, Postfach 10 27 20, 2000 Hamburg 1, Federal Republic of Germany

Telephone: 040 321 041
Telegrams: Hochbahn, Hamburg

Type of system: Full metro

Gauge: 1435 mm
Route length: 89·4 km
(in tunnel): 31 km
(elevated): 37 km
Number of lines: 3

Rolling stock: 841 cars
Main supplier: Linke-Hofmann-Busch

Car type	DT 1	DT 2	DT 3
Number of cars per unit	2	2	3
Set dimensions			
(length)	27·91 m	27·98 m	39·06 m
(width)	2·55 m	2·51 m	2·48 m
(height)	3·37 m	3·36 m	3·35 m
Passenger capacity			
per set (total)	276	256	365
(seated)	80	82	92
Motors per set	8	6	8
Rating	74 kWh	80 kWh	80 kWh
Acceleration (max) (m/s²)	1·14	0·8	1·2
Deceleration (emergency) (m/s²)	1·19	1·25	1·2
Brakes: Regenerative			
Weight (tonnes tare)	50·5	34·6	46·7

Number of stations (total): 80
(in tunnel): 36
(elevated): 34
Average distance between stations: 1·052 km
Rail weight and type: S49 (49 kg/m)
Track type: Conventional sleepers on ballast
Tunnel type: Bored single-track, concrete caisson,
bored double-track
Electrification type: 750 V dc, third rail
Signalling: Automatic block, with colour-light
signals
Gradient (max): 5%
Curvature (minimum): 70 m
Speed (design max): 70-80 km/h
  (average commercial): 32 km/h

Traffic
Train headways: 2-5 minutes peak; 5-10 minutes
off-peak
Trains/track/hour: 26
Train capacity (passengers): 768 (six-car set)
Total passengers/track/hour (peak): 8000
Passenger journeys (weekday): 600 000
  (annually, 1980/81): 181·3 million

System development
A 6 km extension of the U2 line from Hagenbecks
Zoo to Niendorf, with four intermediate stations, is
in progress at a likely cost of DM458·5 million
(including 48 new cars), for opening in stages between 1985 and 1987. A 3 km extension of Line U3
from Merkenstrasse to Mummelmannsberg is
expected to begin in 1984.
  An all-embracing, computer-based system of
automated control (PUSH), developed with the aid
of a grant from the Federal Ministry of Research and
Technology, is being evaluated over 10 km of Line 1.
Its functions cover driverless train operation, with

Prototype Hamburg three-phase ac U-Bahn set for probable series production 1986-87

continuous monitoring of train speed in relation to
schedule and energy consumption, and fault detection and assessment; total operating control of
trains and fixed equipment performance, including

route-setting and train despatch; and collection of
management data. The trial is being conducted with
18 cars, which are being operated without passengers.

Hanover
Hannoversche Verkehrsbetriebe (USTRA) AG

Am Hohen Ufer 6, Postfach 2540, 3000 Hanover 11,
Federal Republic of Germany

Telephone: 0511 16681
Telex: 922425
Telegrams: Ustra Hannover

Director: W Pallmann

Type of system: Pre U-Bahn

Gauge: 1435 mm
Route length: 95 km
(in tunnel): 11·4 km

Number of lines: 2
Number of stations: 59 (including 5 interchanges)
(in tunnel): 11
Average distance between stations: 680 m
Control: Traffic is controlled by the computer-based
BON system, in a project sponsored by the Federal
Ministry of Research and Technology; it is designed
for standardisation on all West German urban
transit systems. All vehicles are in radio communication with the control centre and are equipped with
on-board information displays

Rolling stock
170 thyristor-controlled, eight-axle, double-
articulated light rail vehicles by Duewag, with two
monomotor bogies, thyristor-controlled, each with

a 290 hp one-hour rating; tare weight is 38·8 tonnes,
top speed 80 km/h and passenger capacity 150. Each
vehicle has five double doors on each side.

System development
The first 7 km of Hanover's projected 90 km pre
U-Bahn system opened to traffic between Oberrick-
lingen and the Hauptbahnhof on Line A in 1975. This
line is now 18 km long, with 4 km of its inner city
length and 0·6 km at its south-western end in tunnel.
A southern extension of Line B from Kropcke to
Sarstedt was opened in September 1982.
  Line C, 20 km long with about 5 km in tunnel,
running from north-west to east and crossing the
two existing lines in the centre, was begun in 1977
and will be opened in stages between 1983 and
1987. A fourth, east-west Line D is planned.

Havana

Havana, Cuba

With the support of the Transport Ministry and
Soviet technical aid the city planning authorities
have begun planning a metro. Their conclusions

were to be presented in June 1983. Construction is
unlikely before the 1986-90 term of the next national
Five-Year Plan.

Helsinki
Helsingin Kaupunki Liikennelaitos

PO Box 242, Toinen Linja 7, 00531 Helsinki 53,
Finland

Telephone: 90 718 322
Telex: 121872

General Manager: Martti Lund

Type of system: Full metro

Gauge: 1524 mm
Route length: 11·2 km
(in tunnel): 4 km
Number of stations (total): 9
(in tunnel): 5
Average distance between stations: 1·1 km
Gradient (max): 3·5%
Curvature (minimum radius): main track 300 m,
depot area 100 m
Speed (design max): 80 km/h
  (average commercial): 43 km/h
Rail type: UIC 54 kg/m
Electrification type: 750 V, third rail
Signalling: Fully automated control of traffic and
train operation, from supervisory centres at
Hakaniemi and Herttoniemi

Rolling stock
Number of cars: 44 two-car sets

Hakaniemi station

Main suppliers: Valmet Oy (mechanical), Oy Stromberg (electrical)
Car dimensions: Two-car set, length over couplers 44·2 m, width 3·2 m, height above rail 3·7 m
Total floor area: 66 m², standing area 30 m²
Doors per side: 3
Door width: 1·4 m
Number of passengers per car (total): 200 (seated): 67
Motors per car: 4 (3-phase asynchronous motor fed by PWM-inverters)
Motor rating: 125 kW
Acceleration (max): 0-27 km/h, 1·2 m/s²; 0-80 km/h, 0·9 m/s²

Deceleration: (normal service): 80-0 km/h, 1·2 m/s² (emergency): 80-0 km/h, 1·2 m/s²
Max design speed: 90 km/h
Bogies: Air-sprung, two-motor bogies by Valmet
Brakes: Rheostatic / disc / electromagnetic track
Weight (empty): 31·6 tonnes

Traffic

Max line capacity (one way): 36 000/h (2 minute interval)
Max number of trains per hour (one way-planned): 30
Train headways (minutes): 2½ during rush hour, 5 at other times, 10 at night

Capacity per six-car train (passengers seated): 420 (passengers standing): 780

System development
The planned 51 km metro network consists of an east-west coast line and a U-line serving the inner city. The coast line of the metro connects the eastern suburbs and regional centres with the city centre and the State Railways lines. The U-line serves the inner city.
Helsinki's first metro line from Kamppi to Itakeskus was opened in 1982. The metro line will be extended from Itakeskus (the eastern urban centre) to Kontula via Myllypuro (3·1 km with two stations) by 1987.

Hiroshima
Hiroshima Electric Railway Company

Higashi Senda-machi, Naka-ku, Hiroshima, Japan

Telephone: 082 241 1191

Managing Director: Hisao Okukubo

Type of system: Light rail

Gauge: 1435 mm
Route length: 16·1 km
Number of lines: 1
Number of stops: 18
Average distance between stops: 947 m
Max gradient: 1·82%
Minimum curve radius: 161 m
Electrification type: 600 V dc, overhead

Rolling stock
Main suppliers: Kawasaki Heavy Industries, Alna Koki and others
Car dimensions and capacity
Type 1030, length 14·98 m, width 2·642 m, tare 21·5 tonnes, seats 34 (58 standing), 1 unit
Type 1050 (articulated), length 31·75 m, width 2·642 m, tare 48·9 tonnes, seats 96 (132 standing), 1 unit
Type 1060, length 15·956 m, width 2·65 m, tare 27·1 tonnes, seats 52 (68 standing), 1 unit
Type 1070 (articulated), length 30·35 m, width 2·71 m, tare 57·88 tonnes, seats 92 (92 standing), 4 units
Type 1080 (articulated), length 30·31 m, width 2·744 m, tare 57·1 tonnes, seats 76 (144 standing), 1 unit
Type 3000 (double-articulated), length 25·25 m, width 2·4 m, tare 30·1 tonnes, seats 76 (104 standing), 6 units
Type 3500 (double-articulated), length 26·3 m, width 2·47 m, tare 38·4 tonnes, seats 52 (104 standing), 1 unit

Hiroshima has been the test-bed for the prototype 3500 double-articulated unit developed by a team from Japan's Ministry of Transport and members of the Japan Railway Engineers' Association (JREA). It has been designed for through-running between the LRT and the street tramway. The vehicle consists of three air-conditioned car bodies mounted on four bogies. Bogies at each end are motored. Maximum speed is 80 km/h, acceleration 2·65 km/h/s and normal deceleration 3·5 km/h/s. Emergency deceleration can reach 4·5 km/h/s. There is independent control of the two 120 kW traction motors. The vehicle is equipped with chopper control and regenerative braking.

Traffic
Train headways: Peak hours, 5 minutes; off-peak, 15 minutes

Hong Kong
Hong Kong Mass Transit Railway Corporation

PO Box 9916, General Post Office, Hong Kong
Administration: Wai Yip Street, Kowloon Bay, Kowloon

Telephone: 3-758 5111
Telex: 86257
Telegrams: Tubes

Chairman: Wilfred Newton
Managing Director: Eric A Black
Operations Director: D B G Barraclough

Type of system: Full metro

Gauge: 1435 mm
Route length: 26·1 km
(in tunnel): 20·2 km
(elevated): 4·7 km
Number of lines: 2
Number of stations: 25
(in tunnel): 18
(elevated): 6
Average distance between stations: 1·1 km
Rail weight and type: BS rail section 90A 45 kg/m
Track type: Continuously supported FB rail; discretely supported FB rail on overhead sections of Tsuen Wan extension
Tunnel type: Bored single-track, bored double-track and cut-and-cover
Max gradient: 3%
Minimum curve radius: 300 m
One-man operation: All trains
Signalling: Route relay interlocking by WBS
Automatic control: All tracks except within depots
Centralised control: All signalling, power supply and environment systems

Rolling stock
Number of cars: Total 430, all motored
Main supplier: Metro-Cammell
Car dimensions: Length 22·75 m, width 3·096 m, height 3·7 m
Capacity: Seated 48, max standing (crush) 327
Tare and loaded weight: 39/60 tonnes (crush)
Doors: Electro-pneumatic belt-driven double sliding doors, 1·4 m wide, 1·8 m high
Motors: 4 per car 90 kW GEC
Motor suspension: Nose-suspended, axle-hung
Motor voltage: 350 V dc
Gear ratio: 82 : 15
Gear drive: Parallel helical
Brake system (service): rheostatic/air
(emergency): air
Cars on order: 26 motor and 106 trailer from Metro-Cammell, plus 128 cars for the Island Line extension. Metro-Cammell also has an option to build 18 chopper-controlled cars

Elevated section between Kowloon Bay and Ngau Tau Kok

Single-journey ticket machines at Chater station

Traffic
Train headways: Peak hours, 2-2½ minutes; off-peak, 4-10 minutes
Max number of trains per hour
(one way): 40
(planned): 30
Capacity per train: 288 seated
1962 standing
Passenger journeys: (1982) 3500 million

System development
Hong Kong's Mass Transit Railway has been

designed for the highest throughput of passengers per hour per track of any system in the world. A peak-hour volume of 800 passengers a minute is envisaged at some stations and a weekday system-wide average of 1·5 million passengers was forecast for 1983. The first 15·6 km line, the so-called Modified Initial System (MIS), including a 1·4 km crossing of the harbour in an immersed double-track tube, was completed ahead of schedule and within its budget of HK$5800 million early in 1980. A second line, the 10·5 km Tsuen Wan extension branching from the first at Prince Edward, was simi-

larly finished ahead of programme and opened in May 1982.

Construction has begun of the 12·5 km Island Line, to run initially from Western Market in the west to Chai Wan in the east, interchanging with the MIS at Admiralty. This will serve a further 13 stations. A fourth line is under consideration, to run from the west of Hong Kong Island under the harbour and via East Kowloon and the airport to Diamond Hill.

Honolulu
Honolulu Area Rapid Transit (HART)

Honolulu, Hawaii, USA

Type of system: Planned full metro

Various schemes have been canvassed, up to a 21-station route of 37 km from Pearl City to Hawaii Kai.

The favoured plan is now for a 13·4 km initial line between the International Airport and the University of Hawaii. A Federal UMTA grant for preliminary engineering work has been approved.

Houston
Metropolitan Transit Authority (METRO), Harris County

Houston, Texas, USA

Type of system: Planned full metro

Gauge: 1435 mm
Planned length: 120 km
Number of lines: 2
Number of stations: 50
Track type: Ballastless except for at-grade sections
Electrification type: 750 V dc, third-rail

Traffic
Train headways: 3½-4 minutes (peak)

System development
The decision to build the long-planned Houston Metro was taken in 1982, along with determination to fund costs locally if 75 per cent Federal funding aid were not forthcoming. Bids for construction and equipment of the first 29·3 km, 17-station line from West Belt through the city centre to Crosstimbers in the north were being called in 1983 in the hope of starting construction later in the year, with partial opening possible by mid-1987, full inauguration by 1988. To contain costs only the three-station, city-

centre section of the first line will be sub-surface; 70 per cent is to be elevated, the rest at grade. Total cost of Phase I is put at $1830 million.

Longer-term plans envisage an extension of Line 1 beyond Crosstimbers to Houston international airport. A second line would run between West and South Loops via the city centre.

From 10 contenders for supply of cars for Line 1 a joint venture by C Itoh and Hitachi, America Ltd was successful. Their bid of $139·3 million for 130 cars in two-car units compared with a METRO estimate of $153 million. Bodyshells of the chopper-controlled units will be fabricated in Japan and deliveries will begin in 1986.

Istanbul

Istanbul, Turkey

Type of system: Planned metro

Feasibility studies for construction of a 12 km metro were to be conducted in 1983. The first section would run from Dort Levant to Yenkepi; subsequent additions would connect with Yesilkoy airport and the projected Bosphorus Tunnel. In 1983 the Government transferred responsibility for the project from the city authorities to the Ministry of Public Works and allocated the equivalent of US$412 million to the project over a 10-year period.

The Electricity, Tramway and Tunnel Administration (IETT) operates a 0·573 km funicular railway linking Karakey and Galatasary. Two vehicles are operated, carrying about 25 000 passengers a day.

Istanbul funicular

Jakarta

Jakarta, Indonesia

A new rapid transit rail system is planned for Indonesia's capital city. Basically, the scheme consists of four cross-city routes and a central area circle line. (See under Indonesia.)

Karachi

Karachi, Pakistan

The Sind Regional Government is considering a proposal by Karachi's Rapid Transit Cell for construction of an 8·8 km metro line at a cost of Rs 1560 million.

Kharkov
Kharkov Metropolitan

No 29 Ulitsa Engelsa, Kharkov 310012, USSR

Chief Executive: Nikolai Yakovlevich Bessonov
Chief Engineer: Leonid Ivanovich Vstavskii

Type of system: Full metro

Gauge: 1524 mm
Route length: 17·3 km
Number of lines: 1
Number of stations: 13 (all in tunnel)
Average distance between stations: 1·44 km
Max gradient: 4%
Minimum curve radius: 300 m
Electrification type: 825 V, third rail

Rolling stock
Number of cars: 176, all motored
Car dimensions: Length 18·77 m, width 2·7 m
Capacity: 170 (44 seated)
Motors per car: 4
Motor rating: 66 kW
Doors: 4 × 1·38 m
Braking: Rheostatic
Max speed: 90 km/h
Commercial speed: 48·2 km/h
Acceleration: 1·0 m/s²
Deceleration: 1·2 m/s²
Body material: Steel
Weight: Motorcar 30 tonnes

Traffic
Train headways: Peak hours, 2½ minutes; off-peak, 6 minutes

Passenger journeys: (1980) 174·8 million
Signalling: Automatic train stop. Cab signalling, with automatic speed control. Radio-telephone communication between the central control post and trains

System development
The first 17·3 km cross-city line of the Kharkov Metro came into service in 1975. An extension was commissioned in 1978. An 11 km second line with six stations is under construction. Under study are extensions totalling 12·5 km, with 10 stations; these include a third line from Alekseevka in the north-west to Kharkov airport in the south-east, intersecting the two existing lines in the city centre. Trains are now operated as five-car sets.

Kiev
Kiev Metropolitan

Brest-Litovskii Prospekt 37a, Kiev 252055, USSR

Chief Executive: Stepan Pavlovich Kapitanyuk
Chief Engineer: Mikhail Ivanovich Mitrofanov

Type of system: Full metro

Gauge: 1524 mm
Route length: 26·2 km
Number of lines: 2
Number of stations: 21
Average distance between stations: 1·3 km
Max gradient: 4%
Minimum curve radius: 400 m

Speed (design max): 75 km/h
    (average commercial): 38 km/h
Rail type: 50 kg/m
Electrification type: 825 V, third rail
Signalling: Automatic train stop. Radio-telephone communication between trains and central control post

Rolling stock
Number of cars: 279, all motored
Car dimensions: (all) length 18·77 m, width 2·7 m
Capacity: E-type, 170 (44 seated); D-type, 164 (44 seated)
Motors per car: 4
Motor rating: D-type cars, supplied in 1960, 4 × 73 kW; E-type cars, supplied 1965-79, 4 × 66 kW
Doors: E-type, 4 × 1·38 m; D-type, 4 × 1·05 m

Braking: Rheostatic (all)

Traffic
Trains/track/hour: 30
Train capacity (passengers): 750
Total passengers/track/hour (peak): 22 500
Train headways: 2 minutes
Passenger journeys: (1980) 254·4 million

System development
The first section of the Kiev Metro was opened in 1960. Extensions of the second line at its southern end totalling 8·7 km, with seven stations, are under construction. Third and fourth lines are planned. A monorail is to be built from the new suburb of Troeshchina to the Levoberezhnaya metro station on the River Dnepr's left bank.

Kobe
Rapid Transit Department, Transportation Bureau

5-1 6 Chome, Kano-cho chuo-ku, Kobe City, Japan

Telephone: 078 831 8181

General Manager: Kenji Tsubora

Type of system: Full metro

Gauge: 1435 mm
Route length: 5·7 km
(in tunnel): 5·18 km
Number of lines: 1
Number of stations: 4
(in tunnel): 2
Average distance between stations: 1·9 km
Rail weight and type: 50 kg/m N long rail
Max gradient: 2·9%
Minimum curve radius: 300 m
Track type: Prestressed concrete and reinforced concrete sleepers with double elastic fastenings
Tunnel type: Bored single-track (shield tunnelling method), bored double-track (mountain tunnelling method and cut-and-cover)
Electrification type: 1·5 kV dc, overhead
Signalling: Cab signalling by Daido with ATC and CTC

Rolling stock
Number of cars: 32, all motored, in four-car sets, equipped with chopper control and regenerative braking
Main supplier: Kawasaki Heavy Industries
Car dimensions: Length 19 m, width 2·79 m
Capacity: 145, 56 seated
Tare and loaded weight: 35/55 tonnes
Doors: Sliding doors 1·3 m wide, 1·83 m high

Traffic
Train headways: Peak hours, 6 minutes; off-peak, 12 minutes

Kawasaki train-set of Kobe Rapid Transit Department

Passenger journeys: (1981/82) 18·6 million

System development
This important port has four surface railways, the Sanyo, Hankyu, Hanshin and Kobe Electric (besides the Japanese National Railways), whose terminal stations were until 1968 unconnected with each other by rail. With completion of its Yamate line the Kobe Rapid Railway will provide this connection.

The first 5·7 km section of an east-west transverse line from Naya to Shin-Nagata was opened in 1975. The 7·5 km Yamate line, scheduled to open 1985, will extend the existing line from Shin Nagata to

Nagata, and from Sannomiya to a new terminal at Nunobiki. Cost is put at 132 800 million yen.

A north-west extension, the Seishinenshin line, will thread three new stations from Myodani to a northern terminal at Seishin new town; it is to be completed in 1985 for revenue operation in 1986 at a cost of 59 800 million yen.

A new private railway, the Hokushin Kyuko, is planned to connect Tanigami with the Yamate line at Nunobiki.

Port Island is served by the Kobe New Transit System, employing rubber-tyred vehicles on a guideway, devised by Kawasaki.

Kuibyshev

Kuibyshev, USSR

Type of system: Planned metro

Route length: Line 1, 17·32 km

System development
A three-line network is planned for one of the USSR's fastest-expanding cities, which stretches for over 49 km along the River Volga's left bank. Its industrial centre is some 15 km distance from its business and residential complex. An 11·6 km section of the 17·3 km Line 1, the Pskov Line, is under construction and should open in 1986. This will eventually extend from Revolution Square in the

western city to the Besymyanka industrial region. Line 2, the Station Line, will run from the main station northeastward and Line 3, the Samara Line, will diverge from Line 2 at Lenin Works to cater for a new residential area on the River Samara.

Of the 13 stations on Line 1, all but one are to be underground. This line will operate four-car trains at 2-minute headways in peak hours, and is expected to deal with 22 000 passengers an hour.

Kyoto
Kyoto Transportation Bureau

48 Bojo-cho, Mibu Nakagyo-ku, Kyoto City, Japan

Telephone: 075 841 9361

General Manager: Nisuharu Nakabo

Type of system: Full metro

Gauge: 1435 mm
Route length: 6·9 km (all in tunnel)
Number of lines: 1

Number of stations: 8
Average distance between stations: 940 m
Rail weight: 60 kg/m
Track type: Sleepers on concrete with resilient pads, partly conventional sleepers on ballast
Tunnel type: Bored double-track plus some cut-and-cover
Electrification type: 1·5 kV dc, overhead
Signalling: CTC and ATC

Rolling stock
Number of cars: 36, all motored, delivered 1980, operated in four-car units

Car dimensions: Length 20 m, width 3·68 m
Capacity: 54 seated plus standees
Tare weight: 37 tonnes
Doors: 4 each side 1·3 m wide
Train capacity
(seated): 214
(standing): 604
Traction motors: 130 kW
Gear ratio: 16·99
Max speed: 105 km/h
Acceleration: 0·83 m/s²
Service braking: 0·97 m/s²
Emergency braking: 1·11 m/s²

Traffic
Train headways: Peak hours, 5 minutes; off-peak 7-9 minutes
Passenger journeys daily: (1981/82) 120 000

System development
Plans for a 45 km metro system were approved in 1971 and construction began late in 1974. The first 6·9 km section between Kyoto station and Kitaoji station opened early in 1981, when Kyoto became the seventh Japanese city to own a metro. When the second 3·6 km section reaches Takeda, in the southern part of the city, probably in 1987, it will connect with the Kyoto line of the Kinki Nippon Railway, one of four private electric railways entering Kyoto (others include the Keihan and Keihanshin Kyuko), and allow through running to Nara City. A further extension from Takeda to Misu is planned, also a second inverted horseshoe-shaped line from Naga-oka in the south-west to Rokujizo in the south-east, crossing the first at Oike.

Oike station

Lagos
Lagos Metro Authority

Lagos, Nigeria

Type of operation: Planned full metro

In September 1982 Interinfa, a subsidiary of French groups CGE and Empain-Schneider fronting 19 French companies, gained a turnkey contract worth US$952 million to build and equip a 28·5 km line from the business centre on Lagos Island to the northern suburb of Agege. After some uncertainty over payments the Government approved raising of foreign finance for the start of work in 1983. All but 1·5 km of the route will be elevated; there will be 19 stations. Electrification will be at 1·5 kV dc overhead.

The first 10 km with eight stations, to Yaba, is programmed for opening in early 1986, the whole line by the year's end. Commercial speed is planned as 40 km/h and operating capacity as 35 000/hour in each direction. Alsthom has an order for 48 cars with an option for 132 more. Similar to the design for Cairo, but air-conditioned and aluminium-bodied, they will be formed in M-T-M sets, powered with TCO 265 kW motors and arranged for a maximum speed of 100 km/h.

Long-term plans include a second line from Idimu in the north-west to Apapa in the south-west, using the first line between Yaba and Adekunle.

Leningrad
Leningradski Metropoliten

Moskovskii Prospekt 28, Leningrad 198013, USSR

Chief Executive: Victor Alexeivitch Elsukov
Chief Engineer: Konstantin Illarionovich Frolov

Type of system: Full metro

Gauge: 1524 mm
Route length: 66·1 km
(in tunnel): 66·1 km
Number of lines: 3
Number of stations: 40
(in tunnel): 38
Average distance between stations: 1·86 km
Tunnel type: The line is of deep-level tube construction, and depending on the cambresian clay formation, is at places over 60 m below surface level. Each single-track tunnel is of metal and ferro-concrete tube construction and has an internal diameter of 5·1 m
Gradient (max): 4%
Minimum curvature radius: 400 m
Speed (design max): 65 km/h
(average commercial): 40 km/h
Electrification type: 825 V, third rail
Signalling: Automatic train stop; radio-telephone communications with trains. Central control room. Automatic train operation on three lines includes programmed traffic interlocking control and automatic train operation

Rolling stock
Number of cars: 957, all motored
Rating per car: 4 × 73 kW (car type D); 4 × 66 kW (car type E)
Braking: Rheostatic
Car dimensions: Length 18·77 m, width 2·7 m
Weight: 36.2 tonnes (D); 32 tonnes (E)
Capacity: 164 (D); 170 (E). Both types 44 seats
Doors: 1·12 m wide (D); 1·38 m wide (E). Four on each car, sliding

Pushkinskaya station, Leningrad Metro

Type D cars, supplied in 1960, are gradually being replaced by the later type E cars

Traffic
Train headways: Peak hours, 1 minute 35 s; off-peak, 4 minutes
Train capacity (passengers): 1500
Total passengers/track/hour (peak): 45 000
Passenger journeys: (1981) 737·7 million

System development
Leningrad was the second Soviet city to acquire a metro, in 1955. Current extensions prolong the Moskovsko-Petrogradskaya line 6·6 km (three stations) into the northern suburbs and the Nevsko-Vasileostrovskaya line by 3·6 km (one station). A fourth line of 12 km to run from Ulitsa Kollantai to Ploschad Mira is under way.

Liège
Société des Transports Intercommunaux de Liège (STIL)

320 rue du Moulin, 4020 Bressoux, Liège, Belgium

Telephone: 430539

Director of Special Studies: O Pirson

Type of system: Planned light rail

Studies are in progress for the first line of a proposed light rail system, probably running from Guillemins railway station to Herstal in the north.

Lille
Communauté Urbaine de Lille (CUDL)

BP 749, 59034 Lille Cedex, France

Telephone: 20 06 92 08

Director of Urban Transport: B Guilleminot

Responsible agency: CUDL
Delegate contractor (overseeing the planning and
delivery of the system and the rolling stock): EPALE
(public agency for the management of the new town
of East Lille)
Prime contractor: Sofretu
General systems contractor: Matra

Type of system: Automated full metro (rubber-
tyred), VAL system

Gauge: 2060 mm between H-type guide bars. Guide
bars also used for power supply, one positive, the
other negative, insulated with moulded polyester
Route length: Line 1, 13·3 km
(in tunnel): 8·55 km
Number of stations: Line 1, 18
Track type: Track consists of precast concrete longitudinal sleepers, with track heating provided by
cables embedded in sleepers. Track equipment
specific to system's automatic controls include 170
mm wide strip carrying transmission lines;
aluminium plate contacts used for command and
control and regulation of traffic; ultrasonic trans-
ceiver at the entry and exit to every station. Track
equipment very similar to that used for Paris Metro
rubber-tyred lines; new safety devices for running
and guiding vehicles make steel security track used
in Paris unnecessary
Electrification type: 750 V dc, with collection by
shoes from guide tracks

Rolling stock
The 38 train-sets supplied by CIMT each consist of
two permanently-coupled cars, with a length per set
of 26·14 m and a height of 3·25 m. Lateral surfaces
are curved with the maximum width (2·06 m) at the
seat level. Tare weight per set is 28·635 tonnes, 30
per cent less than for modern steel-wheeled underground stock with comparable load capacity. The
light weight is achieved partly through the extensive
use of light alloys, partly because the design uses
pivoting axles with rubber-tyred wheels, instead of
conventional bogies.

Switching is achieved via 320 mm diameter guide
rollers, making it possible to do without the steel
guide wheels used on the Paris rubber-tyred stock.
In the event of a loss of pressure in the tyres, rings
mounted on the inner face of the tyres check slump
and make it possible for the train to return to the
maintenance depot without significant loss of
speed.

Service braking is electrical, but emergency braking is provided via very large discs. The axle is linked
to the body through flexible pneumatic suspension
(frequency about 1·2 Hz) which filters vibrations and
maintains a constant body floor level. Coupled with
the use of wide doors and platforms, this arrangement permits ready access for the handicapped in
wheel-chairs.

Each car is powered by two 120 kW traction
motors, providing nearly 17 kW per tonne of unla-
den weight. Coupled with good tyre grip, this permits good acceleration (1·3 m/s² up to 35 km/h under
normal loading). The set will also climb a 7 per cent
grade even with one of the cars out of working
order. The cars have chopper control and regenerative braking

System development
VAL is the first metro in the world to plan operation
of driverless trains from the start of public service.
The design of its train-sets makes no provision for
accompanying driver or conductor. Construction
was approved by the French Government in 1975
and full public service over 9 km from République
through the city centre to Quatre Cantons was
begun in May 1983 after the system had been formally inaugurated by President Mitterand in April
1983. The remaining 4 km of the line from République to CHR-B Calmette was due to open in April
1984.

General contractor for the VAL scheme has been
Matra. The Lille authority specified certain conditions which in themselves dictated the need for considerable innovation: that all cars and stations
should have a high level of comfort; that under
normal loading seats should be provided for at least
55 per cent of passengers; that a higher than usual

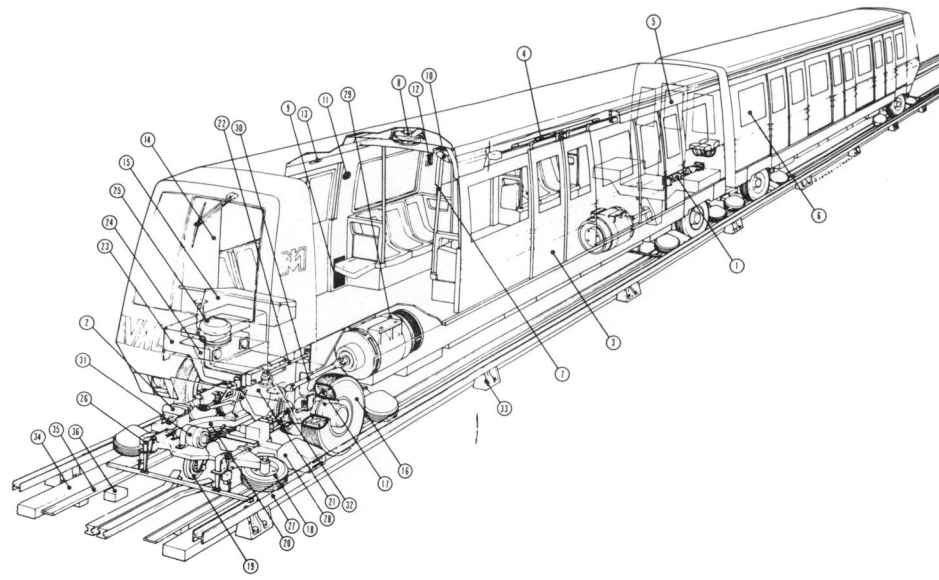

Layout of VAL unit (**1**) Grab holds (**2**) automatic coupling (**3**) entrance doors (**4**) door mechanism (**5**) door between cars
(**6**) windows (**7**) hand rails (**8**) mechanical ventilation (**9**) heating (**10**) light fixtures (**11**) PA system (**12**) emergency call
(**13**) emergency exit handle (**14**) automatic control cabinet (**15**) manual control desk (reduced speed) (**16**) tyres (**17**) safety wheel
(**18**) guide wheel (**19**) switching roller (**20**) guide frame (**21**) motor bridge (**22**) traction control linkages (**23**) frame (**24**) damper
(**25**) pneumatic suspension (**26**) cow-catcher (**27**) guide bar and energy rail (**28**) collecting shoe (**29**) traction motor
(**30**) cardan transmission (**31**) brake activation cylinder (**32**) brake disc and pad (**33**) insulator (**34**) rolling track (**35**) transmission belt (**36**) traffic regulation contact

Train alongside platform screens at Quatre Cantons station

Ticket hall, République station

commercial speed should be possible (a rated speed of 60 km/h with a maximum of 80 km/h, making possible a commercial speed of 35 km/h); that a high-frequency service (headways of 60 seconds at peak periods) must be feasible; and finally, that the design should be for a project as inexpensive as possible, taking into account that long underground sections would run through poor load-bearing, water-impregnated soil. An initial throughput capacity of 7500 passengers each way per hour is envisaged, with each train offering a normal capacity of 124 passengers and a crush loading limit of 262. Total cost was 20 per cent funded by central Government (because of VAL's role in new town development), the rest by loans and by the Verse-ment Transport, a payroll tax levied on all French towns of over 50 000 population for the support of public transport.

Matra's solution relied on two important concepts: first, that the system should be compact; and secondly, that it should be automatic, drastically reducing operating costs. The compact, small-gauge subway offered an immediate advantage in the initial civil engineering, which normally represents 70 to 75 per cent of the cost of underground railway construction. The Matra design made it necessary to build cars only 2·06 m wide, while keeping to the comfort requirements of the authorities. A lateral seat arrangement has been made possible by the large number of doors (50 per cent more than in conventional cars). Each of the three doors on each car side is 1·3 m wide, permitting easy passenger circulation. At stations passengers gather in a circulating area from which doors give access to the trains; these sliding doors open automatically when a train stops and the automated controls ensure that both trains and fixed doorways are in precise correspondence. All station operation is automated.

Construction of VAL Line 2 from Tourcoing to Haut Champs, 9 km, has been approved and may start in 1986; a branch from Roubaix to Wattrelos may be added. Connection between Lines 1 and 2 will at first be by the Mongy Tramway, which may be converted to a metro in the 1990s.

Lima

Lima, Peru

In 1982 the city was preparing to seek tenders for construction of a 45 km rapid transit system.

Lisbon

Metropolitano de Lisboa SARL (ML)

28 Av Fontes Pereira de Melo, Lisbon 1098, Portugal

Telephone: 57 5457
Telegrams: Metropolitano, Lisbon
Telex: 15681

President: Dr P Bastos
Operating Manager: A F Barros

Type of system: Full metro

Gauge: 1435 mm
Route length: 12·5 km (all in tunnel)
Number of lines: 3
Number of stations: 20
Average distance between stations: 630 m
Rail weight and type: Vignole (FB), 50 kg/m, U36 profile
Track type: Timber sleepers, normally on ballast, with resilient pads; on concrete at stations
Tunnel type: Cut-and-cover except 1 km bored double-track
Gradient (max): 4%
Curvature (max): 150 m (100 m exceptionally)
Speed (design max): 60 km/h
   (average commercial): 28 km/h
Electrification type: 750 V dc, third rail
Signalling: Automatic electric system with track circuits supplied by L M Ericsson, Sweden

Centralised control: System for signalling and points operation

Rolling stock
Number of cars: 80
Main suppliers: First supply, Linke - Hofmann - Busch / Siemens; later cars, Sorefame / Siemens
   The latest cars, of which 56 are for 1983-84 delivery, are of a completely new design 20 per cent lighter than their predecessors. With bodies of Inox stainless steel and glass fibre cab ends, the cars have rheostatic braking backed up by electro-pneumatic disc brakes. The first 20 217 kW traction motors were supplied by Alsthom-Atlantique; the rest were built under licence in Portugal by Efacec. Other electrical equipment was supplied by Siemens.
   Their monomotor bogies of MTE design are similar to those fitted to Paris Metro MF67 and 77 stock. The cars operate in permanently-coupled, two-car sets in trains of up to six cars. Passenger doors, three on each side, are 1·3 m wide; each set has 80

Car type (year introduced)	1959	1970	1981/83
Car dimensions: (length)	16·4 m	16·5 m	16 m
(width)	2·7 m	2·7 m	2·7 m
(height)	3·45 m	3·45 m	3·45 m
Passenger capacity per car			
(total)	200	200	164
(seated)	36	36	40
Motors per car	4	4	4
Rating	90 kWh	100 kWh	100 kWh
Acceleration (max)	0·9 m/s²		1·1 m/s²
Deceleration (emergency)	1·2 m/s²		1·0 m/s²

seats and standing room for 248. Maximum speed is 72 km/h, acceleration rate 1·1 m/s² and normal deceleration 1 m/s².

Traffic
Trains/track/hour: 18·4
Train headways: 3¼ minutes
Passenger journeys: (1982) 132 million

System development
Work began in 1980 on extension of Line 3 from Alvalade to Campo Grande (1·78 km) and in 1981 on a 1·37 km extension of the Sete Rios line to Estadio da Luz. Northward extension of Line 2 from Entre Campos to Lumiar, intersecting Line 3 at Campo Grande (first stage), then on to Odivelas and Loures (second stage) is likely to be finished by 1986; and southward extension of Line 2 from Rotunda to Cais do Sodre main-line railway stations with intermediate stations at Rotunda II, Rato, Restauradores and Garrett by 1987.

Lodz

Lodz, Poland

Plans for creation of a two-line pre-metro system of 21 km from the city's tramway network have been announced.

London

London Transport Executive

55 Broadway, London SW1H 0BD, England

Telephone: 01-222 5600
Telegrams: Passengers, London

Chairman: Dr Keith Bright
Managing Director (Railways): Dr T M Ridley

Gauge: 1435 mm
Route length (managed): 388 km
   (run over): 401 km
   (in tunnel): 162 km
Number of lines: 9
Number of stations: 266
Average distance between stations: 1·5 km
Rail weight and type: Running rail, 47 kg/m BH and 54 kg/m FB; conductor rail (open and sub-surface) 74 kg/m FB and 53 kg/m FB; conductor rail (tube tunnel) 64 kg/m rectangular
Track type: Conventional sleepers on ballast
Tunnel type: Bored single-track and cut-and-cover; three lines (Metropolitan, District and Circle) totalling 96 km cut-and-cover construction, remaining six lines bored tunnel. (A seventh bored tunnel, the Waterloo & City Line, is owned and operated by Southern Region of British Rail, with a design of rolling stock unique to that line; the Waterloo & City makes a passenger interchange with London Transport at Waterloo and Bank stations.)
Electrification type: 600 V dc, third rail

Signalling: Programme machine signalling is installed on the Northern and parts of other lines, and is the basis of junction signalling on the Victoria Line. The programme machines, supplied by Westinghouse Brake and Signal (UK), are used to route trains automatically at junctions and otherwise control their movements in accordance with the timetable. The timetable is carried on a roll of plastic film with punched holes providing the timetable and routing information for each train. The roll is moved forward each time the train passes the junction controlled by the machine. The holes are detected by feelers, and after comparison with the train description and with timing circuits driven by a master clock system, route-setting circuitry is energised, so that trains are automatically routed. All sections of the system which are free of junctions are controlled by colour-light signalling based on a system of track circuitry

Automatic control: The system of automatic train operation used on the Victoria Line was designed and developed by London Transport. Each train responds to safety codes transmitted through the running rails, and to high-frequency driving commands injected at pre-determined intervals on short sections of the track. The signals are picked up by coils mounted in front of the leading wheels. Trains cannot run unless the safety code is being picked up. The codes also control train speed, and will automatically stop the train if it enters a section too close to the preceding train. The Victoria Line employs no signalmen. Junctions are all set by the programme machines, and the line is supervised from a central control post at Euston

Rolling stock
Number of cars: 4267, including 2835 motored
Main supplier: Metro-Cammell
Car types: London Transport operates two categories of rolling stock: surface and tube. Surface stock is constructed to a larger loading-gauge than tube stock. Tube stock is classed by the year of introduction. There are four basic car types: the driving motor car; the non-driving motor car; the un-coupling, non-driving motor car which forms the end of a unit, and has a shunting control position enabling the unit to be driven at reduced speed; and the non-motored trailer car.
Tube stock
1938: built by the Metropolitan-Cammell and Birmingham Railway Carriage and Wagon Companies. Now used only on the Bakerloo Line.
1956/1959: unpainted aluminium stock built by Metro-Cammell and used on the Northern Line. The three 1956 trains were prototypes and have minor differences.

1960: unpainted aluminium driving motor cars built by Cravens Ltd and now in use on the Woodford-Hainault branch of the Central Line, where trains are worked automatically.

1962: unpainted aluminium stock built by Metro-Cammell, except for 169 trailer cars built by British Railways at Derby. Used on the Central Line. Very similar to the 1956/1959 tube stock.

1967: unpainted aluminium trains built by Metro-Cammell for the Victoria Line. One-man operated and incorporate automatic train control.

1972: two types, both outwardly similar to the 1967 stock. The Mk II is used on the Jubilee Line, and the Mk I on the Northern Line.

1973: built by Metro-Cammell, used on the Piccadilly Line.

Surface stock

Unpainted aluminium stock types R49 and R59 built by Metropolitan-Cammell, used on the District Line, where they are gradually being replaced.

Unpainted A60 and A62 aluminium stock built by Cravens and used on the Metropolitan main line.

Unpainted C69 aluminium stock built by Metro-Cammell originally for the Circle and Hammersmith & City lines. Entered service 1970.

Unpainted C77 aluminium stock built by Metro-Cammell for use on the Circle, Hammersmith & City and Edgware Road — Wimbledon lines. The trains are fully interchangeable with C69 stock and entered service 1978.

Unpainted D78 aluminium stock built by Metro-Cammell for the District Line. Entered service 1980. Passenger-operated doors.

Car dimensions: Tube stock

Type 1938, driving motor car, length 15·95 m, width 2·59 m; others, length 15·62 m, width 2·59 m

Type 1956, 1959 and 1962, width 2·59 m; length of driving motor car 15·93 m, others 15·62 m

Type 1960, length 15·85 m, width 2·59 m

Type 1967, width 2·64 m; length of driving motor car 16·08 m, trailer car 15·98 m

Type 1972, dimensions as type 1967

Type 1973, width 2·63 m; length of driving motor car 17·47 m, others 17·68 m

Surface stock

Type R49, length 15·57 m, width 2·72 m

Type A60 and A62, length 16·15 m, width 2·98 m

Type C69 and C77, width 2·92 m; length of driving motor car 16·03 m, trailer cars 14·94 m

Type D78, length of driving motor car 18·36 m, other cars 18·11 m

Power per train (minimum): 723 kW: 7 cars, 1938 tube stock

(max): 847 kW: 7 cars, 1972 tube stock

Acceleration (max): 1·16 m/s², 1973 tube stock

Deceleration (normal service): 1·0 m/s²

(emergency): 1·34 m/s²

Max design speed: 60 mph (96·6 km/h)

Brakes: Friction tread using two composite blocks per wheel controlled by electro-pneumatic valves with mercury switch retardation control. From 1967 onwards additional rheostatic braking on motor cars and brake blocks reduced to one per wheel on all cars. All with Westinghouse pneumatic emergency brake.

1973 tube stock and D78 has Westcode air brake and rheostatic braking with load weighting. Emergency brake is electrically controlled 'energised to release'. All brake blocks are operated by individual brake units without rigging

Cars to be ordered: Twelve prototype Tube cars with a new design of lightweight motor, steerable wheel-sets, improved suspension and probably chopper control, designed for fully automatic operation, to be evaluated with the aim of converting the Central Line to unmanned train working in the 1990s. Design bids were invited in 1983. The Greater London Council has budgeted £10·5 million for the project.

1972 Mk II type tube train at Charing Cross, Jubilee Line

Type D78 District Line car

Traffic

Train headways: 2 minutes at peak hours in central area

Passenger journeys: (1980) 559 million; (1981) 541 million; (1982) 498 million

System development

In 1982 a 5 km one-way loop extension of the Piccadilly Line beyond its present Heathrow Airport terminus was authorised, for completion by 1987. The loop will serve the sites of the proposed new terminals 4 and 5 at the airport.

Also authorised in 1982 was a £65 million LRT system from Tower Hill to the Isle of Dogs, in the dock area; work was likely to start in 1984 for a 1987 opening.

The Government intends to transfer control of London Transport from the Greater London Council to a new London Regional Transport Authority, with a Government-appointed Board of Directors, by the summer of 1984.

Los Angeles
Southern California Rapid Transit District

425 South Main St, Los Angeles, California 90013, USA

Telephone: (213) 972 6000

President: M Lewis
General Manager: J A Dyer

Type of system: Planned full metro and light rail

Gauge: 1435 mm
Length: 28·5 km

System development
With the support of a Federal UMTA grant of $25 million, contracts have been let for station and tunnel design of a metro designated the Metro Rail Project. The initial section will run from Central Los Angeles to Fairfax Avenue via Wilshire Boulevard, then north to North Hollywood. The route is primarily in tunnel with 17 stations.

In 1982 the route of a 36 km LRT between Los Angeles and Long Beach was under study. Planned to serve 31 halts at approximately 1 km spacing with 50 cars, the LRT was likely to be committed to construction in 1984 for 1987 opening. Engineering design for the $250-300 million project has been entrusted to Parsons Brinckerhoff-Kaiser.

Lvov

Lvov, USSR

Plans for construction of the first three-station, city-centre section of a metro system were approved in 1983.

Lyons

Operating authority: **Société Lyonnaise de Transports en Commun**

50 Cours Lafayette, 69003 Lyons, France

Telephone: 7 860 25 53
Telex: 330102

General Manager: Robert Bataille

Construction authority: **Société d'Economie Mixte du Métropolitain de l'Agglomération Lyonnaise (SEMALY)**

25 Cours Emile Zola, 69625 Villeurbanne Cedex, France

Telephone: 7 893 90 09
Telex: 380 801

General Manager: René Waldmann

Type of system: Rubber-tyred full metro plus rack railway
Gauge: 1435 mm (for security rails)
Route length: Metro 14 km; rack railway 0·9 km
(in tunnel): 11·8 km
Number of lines: 3
Number of stations: 20
(in tunnel): 19
Average distance between stations: 690 m
Rail type and weight: Security rails, SNCF 36 kg/m
Track type: Pneumatic rubber tyres run on 68 kg/m metal plates, with lateral guide bars from 100 × 100 × 25 mm angle iron. Security rails on RS-type concrete sleepers. Polyester insulating sleepers support guide rail, which carries power supply. Entire track system bedded in Stedef-type concrete slab
Gradient (max): 6·5%
Minimum curvature radius: 100 m
Speed (design max): 90 km/h
(average commercial): 30 km/h
Tunnel type: Cut-and-cover, 7·5 × 3·98 m
Electrification type: 750 V dc, collection from lateral bars
Signalling: Centralised traffic control
Automatic control: Automatic train operation (ATO) and automatic train control (ATC)

Rolling stock
Lines A and B
Number of cars: Total 96, including 64 motored, 32 trailers
Main suppliers: Alsthom-Atlantique
Car dimensions: Length 18 m, width 2·89 m, height 3·4 m

Laurent Bonnevay station on Line A

Capacity: 52 seated, 74 standing; crush capacity, 200
Tare weight: 79 tonnes per 3-car set
Doors: 3 double sliding doors each car side

Line C (rack and adhesion)
Number of cars: 10, all motored
Main suppliers: Alsthom-SLM (1982)
Car dimensions: Length 11·46 m, width 2·89 m, height 3·76 m
Capacity (per 2-car set): 252, of which 41% seated
Tare weight: 65·3 tonnes per 2-car set
Motors (per car): 2 × 217 kW
Max speed (rack, level): 35 km/h
(rack, 17·4%): 21 km/h
(adhesion): 80 km/h

Traffic
Trains/track/hour: 20
Total passengers/track/hour (peak): 7700
Train headways design: 1½ minutes
Train headways: Peak hours, 2 minutes 17 s; off-peak, 5 minutes

Passenger journeys: (1981) 55·3 million

System development
Under a Fr 1300 million 1980-90 investment programme, the rack-and-adhesion Line C is being lengthened by 800 km from Croix-Rousse to Hénon. In 1982 five new Type MCL80 two-car units were delivered for Line C; many of their components are interchangeable with those of the Line A and B train-sets.

Construction of the 9·2 km, 12-station Line D from St Jean to Vénissieux, which will entail an underwater crossing of the River Rhone between Wilson and University bridges and of the River Saone, has begun. Cost is estimated at Fr 2640 million. The transport authority is continuing with the same rubber-tyred technology of Lines A and B for Line D, but Line D will be built to loading-gauge and gradient parameters permitting a change to another system in the long-term future if this appears desirable. Longer-term plans envisage extension of all four lines.

Madras
Metropolitan Transport Project (Railways)

Poonamallee High Road, Madras 600 008, India

Telephone: 39394
Telegrams: Bhoorail

Chief Administrative Officer: M U Hattikudur

Type of system: Planned rapid transit

Route length: 8·5 km
Number of lines: 1
Number of stations: 11
Electrification type: 25 kV ac

System development
In 1981 government approval was still being sought for a rapid transit system for India's fourth largest city. Feasibility and other studies have been completed for a rapid transit line 21·7 km long from Kasturba Nagar to Tiruvottiyur, forming part of an inner circular rail system, and improvements to the existing metre-gauge and broad-gauge suburban railway systems. In 1983 construction of the first, mostly elevated section was authorised with finance of Rs 10 million for 1983-84.

Madrid
Cia Metropolitano de Madrid

Cavanilles 58, Madrid 7, Spain

Telephone: (91) 252 49 00

Manager: Adolfo Pool

Type of system: Full metro

Gauge: 1445 mm
Route length: 93·3 km
(in tunnel): 83 km
Number of lines: 10
Number of stations: 135
(in tunnel): 123
Average station spacing: 650 m
Rail weight and type: 45 kg/m and 54 kg/m flat-bottomed; laid in 18 m lengths on oak sleepers, with quartz ballast
Max gradient: 5%
Minimum curve radius: 90 m
Tunnel type: Double-track tunnel 6·86 m wide. The height above rail level is 4·45 m on sections of cut-and-cover construction and 4·7 m on the majority distance tunnelled by the Belgian (gallery) method. Tunnel linings are of concrete, masonry or brick

Interior of Type 5000 train-set

Electrification type: 600 V dc, overhead
Signalling: CTC with track circuits and ATO

Rolling stock
Number of cars: 818, including 625 motored
Car dimensions: Length 14·5 m, width 2·4 m (old lines); length 17·5 m, width 2·8 m (new lines 6, 7, 8, 9)
Average and crush capacities: 150/200
Tare and loaded weights: 32/50 tonnes
Doors: Automatic 2·2 m wide
Main supplier: CAF Zaragoza
Cars on order: 130 motor cars from CAF (1981)
Plans for further orders: 200 motor cars to be ordered 1982-85, all with chopper control and regenerative braking

Traffic
Train headways: Peak, 2½-3 minutes; off-peak, 3-5 minutes
Passenger journeys: (1982) 369·6 million

System development
With patronage sliding from almost 476 million passenger journeys in 1976 to 369·6 million in 1982, extension schemes have inevitably been protracted for financial reasons. In 1983 the Transport Ministry was pressing for priority rolling stock renewal on Lines 1 to 4 in preference to fresh extensions of Lines 1, 3, 7 and 8.

However, Line 8 was extended by 6·5 km from Fuencarral to Ministerios and Line 9 by 7·3 km from Herrera Oria to América in 1982; continuation of the latter south to Avenida de America was proceeding in 1983, and of Line 6 from Cuatro Caminos to Ciudad Universitaria.

Type 5000 two-car train-set built by CAF-Wesa

Manila
Light Rail Transit System Project (Metrorail)

Philcomcen Building, Ortigas Avenue, Pasig, Metro Manila, Philippines

Acting Operations Manager: Gen J V Sembrano

Type of system: Planned light rail

Length: 15 km
Max gradient: 4%
Minimum curve radius: 170 m
Electrification type: 750 V dc, overhead

System development
A 15 km elevated light rail line running above the median strips of Taft and Rizal Avenues from Pasay City to Caloocan City and passing through the central business district is being built by a Belgian/Philippine consortium for mid-1984 inauguration. The Belgian companies ACEC, BN, Tractionel and Transurb Consult are responsible for rolling stock and electro-mechanical equipment, with design and construction of the line by the Construction and Development Corporation of the Philippines. Total cost will be 2100 million pesos. The railway is to be operated as concessionaires by the Manila Electric Railroad & Light Company.

The Belgian group is supplying 64 double-articulated, eight-axle light rail vehicles each with 81 seats and standing room for 293.

Arrival at Manila of first BN-built LRV, November 1982

Construction of LRT in Rizal Avenue

Marseilles
Construction authority: Société du Métro de Marseille (SMM)

44 avenue Alexandre Dumas, 13008 Marseilles, France

Telephone: (91) 77 68 82

Director General: Henri Bochet

Operating authority: **Régie Autonome des Transports de Marseille (RTM)**

10-12 avenue Clot-Bley, 13008 Marseille

Telephone: (91) 95 92 55

Type of system: Full metro

Gauge of guideway: 2000 mm

Gauge of auxiliary rail sections: 1435 mm
Route length: 9 km
(in tunnel): 6 km
Number of lines: 1
Number of stations: 12
(in tunnel): 8
Distance between stations: 600-1000 m
Track type: 2 steel guideways for train's pneumatic tyres; 2 steel guidance rails fixed outside running guideways; 2 conventional rails for running in case

of tyre punctures and guiding through sections without guidance rails

Gradient (max): 5·5%

Curvature (minimum): 150 m

Speed (design max): 65 km/h
(average commercial): 32 km/h

Tunnel type: Bored or blasted. Double-track tunnel 7·63 m wide for plain track, 8·13 m wide through curves; twin single-track tunnels each 4·84 m wide. Concrete lined

Electrification type: 750 V dc collected by side shoes from guidance rail

Signalling: Cab signalling. Continuous speed display instruction device in all trains. Automatic operations with monitored manual drive

Centralised control: Operation of line directed from control centre. Traffic control station or computer ensures regulation of traffic by modifying interstation speeds and calculating stopping times at stations. Energy-control station ensures traction supply. Control centre also houses communications centre

Rolling stock

Main suppliers: CIMT (bodies), ANF-Industrie (bogies), TCO (traction motors), MTE (electrical equipment)

	Motor cars	Trailers
Car types	Type A	Type A
Number of units	42	21
Car dimensions		
Length (m)	16·2	15·4
Width (m)	2·6	2·6
Height (m)	3·55	3·55
Total floor area (m²)	29	30
Number of doors		
per side	3	3
Door width (m)	1·3	1·3
Number of passengers per car		
(total)	116	120
(seated)	44	48

Motors per car: 4 × 130 kW, permanently coupled in series

Acceleration (max): 1·3 m/s²

Deceleration (normal service): 1 m/s²
(emergency): 1·2-1·5 m/s²

Max design speed: 80 km/h

Tare weight: 3-car set, about 70 tonnes

Braking: Regenerative and pneumatic. Electro-pneumatic parking brake

Bogies: Bimotor with steel rail wheels and pneumatic guideway wheels, pneumatic horizontal guidance wheels. Primary suspension, rubber/metal elements; secondary suspension, pneumatic pendular type with levelling valve

Rubber-tyred metro cars

Traffic

Train headways: Peak hours, 3 minutes; off-peak, 5 minutes; evenings, 10 minutes

Passenger journeys: (1982) 132·5 million

Max number of trains per hour (one way): 16

Capacity per train (passengers seated): 136
(passengers standing): 216

System development

Operations began in November 1977 on Marseilles's first section of new metro line on a route running beneath the city centre to the north-east suburbs. Construction of a 9 km north-south, six-station Line 2 began in 1980 over a 4 km central segment between Joliette and Castellane and was scheduled for completion in 1984. This line is eventually to run from Bougainville in the north to Ste Marguerite in the south, and to interchange with the Castellane-La Rose Line 1 at French Railways' Gare St Charles and at Castellane. Completion is expected in 1986, whereafter trains on both lines will be expanded from three to four cars. Further extensions of Line 2 northward to St Louis and southward to Pont de Vivaux and Bonneveine are contemplated.

Medellin
Metro Medellin

Empresa de transporte masivo del valle de Aburrá ltda, Carrera 43b, 11a-31, 4° Piso, Apartado Aereo, 9128 Medellin, Colombia

Telephone: 326210; 326178

Chief of Administration: L E Hinestrosa M

Type of system: Planned metro

Gauge: 1435 mm

Route length: 27 km
(in tunnel): 0·8 km
(elevated): 5·4 km

Number of lines: 2

Number of stations: 24
(in tunnel): 1
(elevated): 6

Max gradient: 3·7%

Minimum curve radius: 150 m

Rail weight: 56 kg/m

Track type: Sleepers on ballast

Tunnel type: Cut and cover

Electrification type: Overhead collection

System development

Mott, Hay and Anderson International was appointed consultant for a proposed two-line rapid transit system in 1979. The north-south line, linking Bellow and Itagui, will be 22·5 km long with 19 stations. The second, east-west line will be 4 km long with six stations, including one interchange.

In December 1982 the Government authorised the US$500 million scheme. Constructors were to be selected in October 1983 with the aim of starting the project in 1984 for 1988 opening.

Melbourne
Victorian Railways (VicRail)

67 Spencer Street, Melbourne, Victoria 3000, Australia

Telephone: 6 1001
Telex: 33801
Telegrams: Railways, Melbourne

Chairman: A S Reiher
General Manager: R J Gallacher

Type of system: Suburban rail

Gauge: 1600 mm
Route length: 310 km
Number of lines: 17
Number of stations: 200
Average distance between stations: 1·55 km
Electrification type: 1·5 kV dc, overhead

Rolling stock

Number of cars: 1102

Cars on order: 200 motor cars and 100 trailers from Commonwealth Engineering for delivery 1981-87

Car dimensions: New Type M air-conditioned cars, six-car train, length 138 m

Capacity: 604 per six-car set

Train formation: MTM + MTM

Motors per car: 4 × 124 kW

Tare weight: 52 tonnes (M), 35 tonnes (T)

Acceleration (max): 0·8 m/s²

Deceleration (max): 1·1 m/s²

Max speed: 115 km/h

Doors: Power-operated

In recent years Martin and King, Melbourne, has supplied more than 100 type M stainless steel cars.

Traffic

Passenger journeys: (1981) 85 million

System development

The City Loop scheme avoids terminal turnrounds at Flinders Street station. Four single-track tunnels are being built to connect with the four major groups of suburban lines:
Eastern, passing through Burnley;
South-eastern, passing through Caulfield;
North-eastern, passing through Clifton Hill;
Northern and Western, passing through North Melbourne.

There will be three new city stations on the underground part of the system and all trains round the Loop will also pass through Flinders and Spencer Street stations, so that passengers will have the choice of five stations in the city area. In order to operate the loop trains in the direction of the predominant traffic flow in each peak period, signalling will be reversible. Each of the loops will have an effective capacity of 24 trains an hour and, in addition to the loop trains, at least another 60 trains an hour will, as a result of overall improvements to the suburban system, be able to operate to and from Flinders Street station.

The opening of the first phase of the City Loop in 1981 brought into service the two tunnels feeding the Burnley and Caulfield groups of suburban lines, and the new Museum station. The remaining two parallel tunnels in the loop, serving the Northern lines, were to be finished in 1983. The total construction programme has involved 12 km of circular tunnels, 3 km of box tunnels and 2 km of ramps linking underground and surface sections. All trains on the suburban network will have direct access to the City Loop with the exception of the Port Melbourne and St Kilda lines. Passengers using these lines and wishing to pass through the loop will have to change trains at Flinders Street.

The Melbourne Metropolitan Train Control Centre (METROL) is due to open in stages, starting with completion of the City Loop. It will then be extended over a number of years to cover the whole suburban system. L M Ericsson, Sweden, is supplying the computer-based train describer which forms the heart of the system. The system will provide a visual display to identify the position and status of all trains and signals, through links with wayside signals and signalboxes. Passenger information will be displayed on colour vdus on platforms.

Conversion of the St Kilda and Port Melbourne lines to a 1435 mm-gauge LRT is proposed at a cost of A$6 million.

(See also VicRail entry in Rail systems section)

Mexico City
Sistema de Transporte Colectivo (STC)

Organismo Público Decentralizado, Delicias 67, Mexico 1, DF, Mexico

Telephone: 521 86 20
Telex: 017 746 67

Director-General: Julian Diaz Arias
Deputy Director, Administrative: Lic Dinorah Sanabria
    Technical: Ing Juan Manuel Ramirez C

Gauge: 1995/1435 mm (rubber/steel)
Route length: 78·25 km
(in tunnel): 44·7 km
Number of lines: 5
Number of stations (total): 80
(in tunnel): 48
Average distance between stations: 881 m
Gradient (max): 7%
Curvature (max): 105 m
Speed (design max): 80 km/h
    (average commercial): 34·6 km/h
Rail weight: 35 kg/m
Track type: Concrete sleepers on ballast
Tunnel type: Concrete caisson with double track
Electrification type: 750 V dc, collected from two lateral guide bars
One-man operation: All services
Signalling: Automatic block and interlocking supplied by Jeumont Schneider (France)
Automatic control: Automatic train operation

Rolling stock
Number of cars: Total 1521, including 1014 motored (head and intermediate) and 501 trailers
Main suppliers: Alsthom, CNCF (Mexico)

Car dimensions	Motors	Trailers
(length) (m)	17·2	16·2
(width) (m)	2·5	2·5
(height) (m)	3·7	3·7
Passenger capacity per car		
(total)	170	170
(seated)	38	39

Motors per car: 4
Rating: 110 kW
Train composition (minimum): 6
    (max): 9

Tacubaya station, Mexico City Line 1

Acceleration (max): 1·35 m/s²
Deceleration (emergency): 2·25 m/s²
Brakes: Rheostatic/pneumatic
Tare and loaded weight: 'M', 22·1/34 tonnes; 'N', 26·9/38·8 tonnes; trailers, 20·6/32·5 tonnes
Doors: Sliding type, 1·3 m wide
Cars on order: 814 being built by CNCF, after completion of a 527-car order in 1983; 225 ordered from Alsthom, completion July 1983; 180 from Bombardier, also for completion by July 1983

Traffic
Train headways: Peak hours, Line 1, 1 minute 55 s; Line 2, 2 minutes 5 s; Line 3, 3 minutes 10 s; Line 4, 5 minutes 50 s; Line 5, 4½ minutes
Train capacity (passengers): 1530
Total passengers/track/hour (peak): 30 600
Passenger journeys: (1982) 1037 million

System development
The Mexico City metro system is closely modelled on the Paris Metro, its architecture and pneumatic-tyred rolling stock particularly reflecting French influence. The latter country's interest extended to a 15-year loan to assist construction, besides consultancy as to its construction. The metro operates under a computerised electronic system of traffic control.

Since its first full year of operation in 1977 the system's ridership has soared by 130 per cent, but network expansion is not keeping pace with the growth of a city likely to double in population over the next two decades because of a high birthrate and an unremitting influx of people from rural areas.

Despite the country's economic problems, extensions were continuing in 1983: a 6·5 km southern projection of Line 3 with five stations; and an 8·3 km prolongation of Line 6 with seven stations in the city's north-west. Next to come will be extensions to Line 7 (12·8 km), Line 1 (2 km) and Line 2 (3·4 km). The metro has long-range plans for enlargement of its system to 198 route-km by 1990 and to 400 km by the year 2000; the latter involves construction of as many as 14 new lines.

Miami
Metro-Dade County Transportation Administration

Suite 1700, 44 W Flagler Street, Miami, Florida 33130, USA

Telephone: (305) 579 5675

General Manager: Warren J Higgins

Type of system: Full metro

Gauge: 1435 mm
Route length: 33·8 km
(at surface level): 1·6 km
(elevated): 32·2 km
Number of lines: 1
Number of stations: 20 (in Stage 1)
Track type: Wood sleepers on ballast over reinforced concrete structure. Direct fixation fasteners with resilient pads
Max gradient: 3%
Minimum curve radius: 305 m
Electrification type: 750 V dc, third rail
One-man operation: Total
Signalling: To be installed by Union Switch & Signal Division, American Standard Company
Automatic control: Partial, with full operator override
Centralised control system: To be installed at outset

Rolling stock
Number of cars: 136, all motored

Miami Metrorail elevated structures

Main supplier: The Budd Company. Similar chopper-controlled Budd cars have been ordered for Baltimore
Car dimensions: Length 22·86 m, width 3·175 m
Capacity: 74 seated, 92 standing
Doors: 3 double-sliding doors each side, opening to 1·32 m

Motors per car: 4 (Westinghouse) × 175 hp

System development
Revenue service on the southern half of the line was scheduled to begin in late 1983, on the northern sector in December 1984. Cost of construction is put at $867 million. An additional 35·4 km is planned.

Milan
Azienda Trasporti Municipali

Foro Buonaparte 61, 20121 Milan, Italy

Telephone: 895 841; 862 041

General Manager: Dr Ing Marcello Liberatore

Construction: Design, planning and construction of new lines and extensions is carried out by Metropolitana Milanese SpA, Via del Vecchio Politecnico 8, Milan 20121

Telephone: 02 77 471
Telex: 334219

Director-General: Prof Ing Augusto Clerici

Type of system: Full metro

Gauge: 1435 mm
Route length: 35·2 km (urban); plus 11·9 km 'Adda' interurban extension of Green (No 2) Line
Number of lines: 2
Number of stations: 49 urban, Adda Line 8 (in tunnel): 43
Average distance between stations: Red Line 590 m; Green Line 800 m
Rail weight and type: 50 kg/m (UNI)
Track type: Both ballasted and slab-track
Tunnel type: Large profile, double-track tunnels 7·5 m in width and 3·9 m in height (above rail level). Tunnelling was by the 'Milan' method of cut-and-cover which permitted the resumption of surface wheeled traffic, after a minimum period of interruption, over temporary surfaces while excavation proceeded below ground. Tunnel roofs are generally 3 m below street level, allowing space between tunnel extrados and street level for pedestrian subways and public utility services. The actual tunnel is of rectangular section in cast concrete. Part of Line 2 has been built in shield driven tunnel to minimise surface traffic interference
Electrification type: Red Line 750 V dc, third rail collection and fourth rail current return; Green Line 1·5 kV dc, overhead
Signalling: Wayside light signals, cab signalling and automatic block. Suppliers, Westinghouse and SASIB (GRS)
Automatic control: Speed control, automatic train stop, and centralised traffic control over whole system

Garibaldi station on Green Line

Rolling stock
Number of cars: Red Line: 162 motored, 55 trailers; Green Line: 88 motored, 45 trailers
Main suppliers: GAI (consortium of Italian suppliers)
Car dimensions: Length 17·5 m, width 2·85 m, height 3·55 m
Tare and loaded weight: Red Line, 32/50 tonnes; Green Line, motor cars, 29·5/44 tonnes; trailers 19·2/35·5 tonnes
Max speed: 90 km/h
Doors: All sliding; Red Line, 4 × 1·3 m; Green Line, 3 × 1·3 m
Cars on order: 46

Traffic
Train headways: Peak hours, Red Line 2½ minutes; Green Line 3 minutes; off-peak, Red Line 5 minutes; Green Line 5 minutes
Passenger journeys: (1980/81) 190 million

System development
Red Line No 1 runs 20·8 km underground from the industrial north-east (Sesto Marelli) to the new residential 'Gallaratese' district in the north-west via the old centre of the city at the Piazza Duomo.

Green Line No 2 runs 14·6 km (3·1 km elevated) from the city's north-east to connect the most important railway stations of Milan. An extension, now under construction, will take it south from the Cadorna station to the Porta Genova.

The Adda Line, formerly a tram route, was brought up to full metro standards and now operates as an extension of the Green Line. It runs above ground for 11·9 km to connect Cascina Gobba with Gorgonzola, north-east of Milan.

Now under construction is a 1·8 km extension, with two stations, of the Red Line; and a 2·8 km extension of the Green Line, with four stations.

The new Yellow Line No 3, also under construction, will run 9·2 km (with 13 stations) under the old city centre at Piazza Duomo to the highly populated industrial and residential suburbs of the south-west. A number of technical problems are likely to be encountered as a result of the need to cross under the Redefossi canal and avoid disturbance of important buildings, such as the cathedral and La Scala opera house, in the city centre. To minimise those problems, tracks are being laid one above the other. With the Yellow Line and the extensions to other lines now under construction, the urban network of the Milan Metro will be increased to 54 km, with 73 stations.

Minsk
Ministry of Railways

Novo Basmannaya 2, Moscow 107174, USSR

Type of system: Full metro

Gauge: 1524 mm
Number of lines: 1
Route length: 8·6 km
Number of stations: 8
Average distance between stations: 1075 m
Max gradient: 4%
Minimum curve radius: 400 m
Electrification type: 825 V, third rail

Platforms: 100 m long

System development
The first line is due to open in 1984. Under study are extensions totalling 13·4 km, with 10 stations. Two further lines aggregating approximately 37 km are planned.

Montreal
Commission de Transport de la Communauté Urbaine de Montréal

159 St Antoine Street West, Montreal, Quebec H2Z 1H3, Canada

Telephone: (514) 877 6474
Telex: 05-825570

Chairman and General Manager: Lawrence Hanigan

Type of system: Rubber-tyred full metro

Gauge: 1435 mm
Route length: 46·8 km
Number of lines: 3
Number of stations: 51
Average distance between stations: 0·89 km
Track type: 35 kg/m security rails flanked by 254 mm-wide concrete running tracks and lateral guide bars. Max grade, 6·5%, minimum curve radius, 140 m
Tunnel type: Double-track, 7·112 m wide; concrete-lined; vertical walls; arched roof 4·9 m high at centre. About 30% cut-and-cover using single rectangular concrete section. Depth varies from 6 m to 54·8 m
Electrification type: 750 V dc
Signalling: Cab signalling with ATC and ATO

Rolling stock
Number of cars: 759 (506 motored, 253 trailers)

Typical Montreal track layout

Main suppliers: Canadian-Vickers and Bombardier
Car dimensions: Motor cars: length 17·2 m, width 2·5 m; trailers: length 16·5 m, width 2·5 m
Capacity: 160
Doors: 4 double doors on each side
Number of cars/train: 9
Average schedule speed: Line 1: 36.9 km/h; Line 2: 35.3 km/h; Line 4: 51 km/h
Cars are semi-permanently coupled in three-car sets consisting of two motor cars with a trailer in the centre. Maximum length of a nine-car train is 152·5 m. Each motor car has four 150 hp motors. Braking

is dynamic (rheostatic on older rolling stock; regenerative on newer stock). Wooden shoes act on the steel security rails at slow speeds and for emergency stops. Top speed is 72·5 km/h.

Traffic
Train headways: Line 1: 20 trains/h; Line 2: 26 trains/h; Line 4: 12 trains/h
Passenger journeys: (1982) 190 million

System development
A further 5 km extension of Line 2 from Snowdon to

Rue du Collège was completed in 1982. Elsewhere the new cross-city Line 5 was under construction, with 12 stations, over the 9·7 km from Snowdon to Saint Michel for opening in 1987 at a cost of C$360 million; this line will eventually run 20·8 km from Lafleur to Amos and serve 22 stations. A 3·5 km extension from Plamondon to Du Collège was to open in January 1984. Further plans include a new Line PAT of 7·7 km with 12 stations from Honoré Beaugrand to City of Pointe-Trembles.
(See also Addenda)

Moscow
Moskovski Metropoliten Imeni VI Lenina

5 Kolokolnikov Street, Moscow 103045, USSR

Telephone: 222 10 01

Chief Executive: Yuri Vasilievich Senyushkin
Chief Engineer: Arkadii Sergeevich Bakulin

Type of system: Full metro

Gauge: 1524 mm
Route length: 184 km
(in tunnel): 166·7 km
Number of lines: 8
Number of stations: 115
(in tunnel): 105
Average distance between stations: 1·84 km
Max gradient: 4%
Minimum curve radius: 300 m
Rail type: 50 kg/m flat-bottomed, welded up to 325 m
Tunnel type: The earlier sections were partly of cut-and-cover construction, the tunnels being double-track and of rectangular section, 7·6 m wide

by 3·9 m high from rail level. Subsequent lines (including the ring line recently built) have been largely of deep-level tube construction, each single-track tube tunnel having an internal diameter of 5·46 m. Tube lines are as much as 40 m below surface level, eg at Dynamo station
Electrification type: 825 V dc, third rail
Signalling: Automatic train stop; central control post; radiotelephone communication with all trains; cab signalling, with automatic speed control on the circle line and on a section of the Krasnopresnenski line; automatic train control on a section of the Jdanovski line

Rolling stock
Number of cars: 2967, all motored
Ratings per car: 4 × 83 kW (type G); 4 × 73 kW (type D); 4 × 66 kW (type E)
Main supplier: Mytishchi
Car dimensions: Length 18·77 m, width 2·7 m
Doors: Sliding 4 × 1·05 m wide per car (G & D); 4 × 1·38 m wide (E)
Braking: Rheostatic
Prototypes of a new series of cars which will eventually replace the G and D type cars, supplied between 1955 and 1959, have been under test since 1979.

Traffic
Train headways: Peak hours, 1 minute 20 s; off-peak, 2-4½ minutes
Passenger journeys: (1982) 2317 million
Max line capacity (one way): 88 600 passengers
Trains per hour each way (max): 45
Cars per train (max): 7
Estimated capacity per car: 170 (including 40 seated)
Average schedule speed (peak periods, including stops): 41·1 km/h

System development
Projects under way in 1983 included the new 17·9 km Serpoukhovski circle line. Extensions to be opened by 1985 include the section of the Serpoukhovski line from Dobrynskaya station to Dnepropetrovskaya station, running 13·9 km (opening 1983); a 2·8 km extension of the Serpoukhovski line from Bibliotekaimeni Lenina station (1984); a 6·4 km line beyond the Moscow river from Kashirskaya station to Orekhovo station (1984); a section from Orekhovo station to Brateevo station (3·4 km); a 1·6 km extension of the Kalinin line from Marxistskaya station to Novokuznetskaya station (1985); and a 1·3 km extension of the Serpoukhovski line from Dnepropetrovskaya station to Krasnii Mayak station (1985). Investment in 1983 would total 80·8 million roubles.

Munich
Stadtwerke Munchen Verkehrsbetriebe (SMV)

Einsteinstrasse 28, Postfach 80 18 60, 8000 Munich 80, Federal Republic of Germany

Telephone: (089) 21911
Telex: 05 22 063

Manager: A Danner

Type of system: Full metro (U-Bahn)

Gauge: 1435 mm
Route length: 32 km
Number of lines: 3
Number of stations: 37
Average distance between stations: 860 m
Tunnel type: Shield driven 5·74 m diameter, conventional tunnelling and cut-and-cover
Electrification type: 750 V dc, third rail
Signalling: Continuous automatic train control. Contract for SpDrL77 signalling and train control equipment with track circuits to Standard Elektrik Lorenz (SEL), 1980

Rolling stock
Number of cars: 388 (Type A2), 12 (Type B1)
Main suppliers: MAN/Siemens (Type A2), MBB (Type B1)
Car dimensions: Length 18 m (Type A2), 18·2 m (Type B1), width 2·9 m, height 3·55 m
Motors per car: 2 × 180 kW (A2), 2 × 188 kW three-phase (B1)
Average and crush capacity: 145/242 (49 seats per car)
Tare and loaded weight: 25·8/35·2 tonnes (4 passengers/m²)
Braking: Separately excited rheostatic brake
Max speed: 80 km/h
Average speed: 35 km/h
Doors: Sliding with 1·3 m opening; 3 per side
Cars on order: 69 Type B2
In 1983 experiments were being conducted on two train-sets with sound-absorbing powered wheel-sets manufactured by MAN under MBB licence.

Munich Type B1 train-set

Traffic
Train headways: 5 minutes
Passenger journeys (daily): Up to 600 000

System development
Construction began in 1965. Construction costs since then have exceeded DM 2000 million and to complete their medium-term programme U-Bahn authorities estimate that a further DM 1500 million will be needed.
The U-Bahn development programme has been extended from 1985 to 1992 and the projected system expanded from a planned 52 km to around 80 km. A 2·5 km section between the Hauptbahnhof

and Rotkreuzplatz on Line 1 and a 2·7 km section of Line U6 between Harras and Holzapfelkreuth were opened in April 1983. A 13·3 km east-west connection on line U5/9 is projected for completion by 1987.
In pursuance of the 1992 network plan of three main lines with 11 branches, work began in 1983 on a 7·8 km U3-South line with 8 stations from Implerstrasse to Furstenried-West and a 1·6 km U5/9-West line from Westendstrasse to Laimer Platz. Also contemplated is a 6·5 km U8-North line with 7 stations to connect with the S-Bahn system at Feldmoching. Beyond 1985 extensions are planned of the U1-West line towards Moosach, U9-East line towards Englschalking, U6-West line to Klinikum Grosshadern, and U8-South line to Harlaching.

Nagoya
Nagoya Municipal Transportation Bureau

1-1 Sannomaru 3-chome, Naka-ku, Nagoya, Japan

General Manager: K Yamada

Type of system: Full metro

Gauge: 1435 mm
Route length: 52 km
Number of lines: 4

Number of stations served: 53
Rail weight: 50 kg/m
Tunnel type: Mainly cut-and-cover
Electrification type: 600 V dc, third rail
Max gradient: 1 in 28 (3·5%)
Minimum curve radius: 125 m
Signalling: Automatic block with colour lights. Cab signalling and automatic train control introduced on one line

Rolling stock
Number of cars: 423, all motored

Car dimensions: Length 15·6 m, width 2·5 m, height 3·43 m
Motors per car: 4
Doors: 3 per side
Capacity per car: 155 (44 seated)

Traffic
Passenger journeys (daily): 744 000
Max number of trains per hour each way: 30
Number of cars per train: 3-5
Average scheduled speed: 32·8 km/h

Nantes
Société d'Economie Mixte des Transports en Commun de l'Agglomération Nantaise (SEMITAN)

110 boulevard Michelet, 44072 Nantes Cedex, France

Telephone: 40 76 60 20

President: Jacques Floch
Director: Michel Bigey

Type of system: Light rail

A five-year (1981-85) development plan adopted by

SEMITAN provides for the construction of a 1435 mm-gauge, 750-volt dc overhead light rail line between Bellevue and Halluchere, which began in January 1982. Following a change of mayor in the 1983 elections the project was halted for a month. It was resumed in June 1983, but with the rolling stock order cut from 20 to 16 cars.

Naples
Assessorato Al Trasporti

Regione Campania, Ferrovie dello Stato (FS), Naples, Italy

Construction authority: **Metropolitana Milanese (MM)**

Via del Vecchio Politecnico 8, 20121 Milan

Telephone: 02 77 471
Telex: 334219

Type of system: Full metro

Gauge: 1435 mm
Planned route length: 26·1 km
(in tunnel): 11·1 km
Number of stations: 11 (complete system 39)
Electrification type: 1·5 kV dc, overhead
Max design speed: 80 km/h

System development
The geo-physical character of Naples, which

shelves steeply away from the sea-front, poses severe metro design problems; even with a spiral loop on 170 m-radius curves the route approved by Government and city in February 1982, to run from the Piazza Garibaldi and its main-line station to Colli Aminei, will have to be graded at 5·5 per cent for 8 km. A 1·2 km section of the loop, including a stretch of 5·5 per cent gradient, has been under construction between Vanvitelli and Medaglie d'Oro since 1979.
   Naples is also served by the 140 km-long Circumvesuviana Railway (see under Italy).

Neuchâtel
Cie des Transports en Commun de Neuchatel et Environs

5 Quai Ph-Godet, 2001 Neuchatel, Switzerland

Telephone: 038 25 15 46

Director: H-P Gaze
Operating Director: D Blanchoud
Technical Director: P Moser

Type of system: Light rail

Gauge: 1000 mm
Route length: 10 km
(on own right-of-way): 10 km
Number of stations: 15
Average distance between stations: 650 m
Rail weight: 30 kg/m
Track type: Conventional sleepers on ballast
Electrification type: 630 V dc, overhead
Signalling: Simplified automatic block with cab radio on all trains; supplier Mauerhofer & Zuber (signalling) and Renens (radios)
Automatic control: Introduced 1981

Rolling stock
Number of cars: 8, including 4 motored, all put into service 1981
Main suppliers: SWS Schlieren/BBC Baden
Car dimensions: Length 18·38 m, width 2·4 m
Capacity: 88 seated, crush 220

LRV by SWS Schlieren and BBC

Tare and loaded weight: Trailers 17·3/25·5 tonnes; motor cars 25·2/33 tonnes
Doors: 2 doors each side 1·3 m wide
The company also operates three 1947 cars and four articulated cars of 1942 obtained from Genoa, Italy.

Traffic
Train headways: Peak hours, 10 minutes; off-peak, 20 minutes

Passenger journeys: (1981/82) 2·5 million

Newark
Newark City Subway, NJ Transit

McCarter Highway & Market Street, PO Box 10009, Newark, New Jersey 07101, USA

Telephone: (201) 648 7375

General Manager: G M Heinle

Type of system: Light rail

Gauge: 1435 mm
Route length: 6·9 km
(in tunnel): 2 km
Number of stations: 11
(in tunnel): 4
Rail weight and type: 100 lb (50 kg/m) TEE rail ARA type B
Track type: Conventional wood sleepers on ballast; in tunnel stations wood stub sleepers set in concrete
Tunnel type: Cut-and-cover, double-track
Signalling: Single block, track circuit system

Rolling stock
Number of cars: 26, all motored
Main supplier: St Louis Car (built 1946 for Twin City Rapid Transit, Minneapolis)
Car dimensions: Length 14·14 m, width 2·74 m
Doors: Dual bi-fold 1·42 × 1·98 m

Traffic
Train headways: Peak hours, 2 minutes; off-peak, 6 minutes
Passenger journeys: (1981) 12 000/day

Newcastle upon Tyne
Tyne and Wear Passenger Transport Executive

Cuthbert House, All Saints, Newcastle upon Tyne NE1 2DA, England

Telephone: 0632 610431
Telex: 53494

Type of system: Full metro

Director General: D P C Fletcher
Director of Engineering/Project Director (Metro): D F Howard
General Manager (Metro): P Layfield

Gauge: 1435 mm
Route length: 40·8 km
(in tunnel): 6·4 km
Number of lines: 3
Number of stations (total): 37
Average distance between stations: 1·1 km
Gradient (max): 3·3%
Curvature (max): 50 m (service line)
 210 m (main line)
Speed (design max): 80 km/h
 (average commercial): 34·3 km/h
Rail type: BS 113A
Track type: Rail laid on tied concrete sleepers in tunnels; on concrete and timber sleepers with ballast on surface sections; on PACT slab track on Byker Viaduct
Tunnel type: 4·75 m diameter to accommodate overhead electrification equipment. Mainly precast segmental concrete linings; spheroidal graphite cast iron linings in unstable ground and 7 m diameter station tunnels
Electrification type: 1·5 kV dc, overhead
Signalling: Automatic Westinghouse two-aspect lineside signals with repeaters. Inductive train stop equipment to halt trains overrunning signal
Automatic control: Philips Vetag vehicle identification system combined with microprocessors for decentralised control. Central control from South Gosforth centre

Traffic
Train headways: 3⅓ minutes in South Gosforth to Heworth section, 0730-1830; 5 minutes in central area after 1830; 10 minutes elsewhere
Passenger journeys (monthly): 3 million
Max line capacity (one way): 30 trains/h
Max number of trains per hour (one way): 24

Rolling stock
Car types: Twin articulated motor cars built by Metropolitan-Cammell. All electrical equipment is by GEC Traction; other equipment includes Duewag monomotor bogies and articulation, Westinghouse

Queen Elizabeth II bridge over River Tyne

plug doors and Westcode braking system, BSI automatic couplers and Brecknell Willis pantograph
Number of units: 90
Car dimensions: Length 27·8 m, width 2·65 m, height (overall) 3·4 m
Number of doors per side: 4
Door width: 1·3 m
Number of passengers per car (total): 270 (crush load)
 (seated): 84
Motors per car: 2
Motor rating: 185 kW continuous/205 kWh
Power per train (minimum): 360 kW
 (max): 720 kW
Acceleration (max): 1 m/s²
Deceleration (normal service): 1·3 m/s²
 (emergency): 2·3 m/s²
Max design speed: 80 km/h
Articulation: Duewag type with two body halves connected to centre bogie through ball-race assembly
Suspension: Chevron rubber between bogie frame and axle box; air springing between bogie and body
Braking: Dynamic with Metcalfe/BSI ventilated

discs on centre bogie; magnetic track brakes on all bogies for emergency use
Weight (empty): 38 tonnes

System development
The metro will eventually comprise a 55·6 km network including 14·8 km of new construction and 40·8 km of existing railway transferred from the British Rail system. Limited British Rail freight services continue to operate over parts of the system.

The initial 19 km from Haymarket, on the northern edge of the city centre, to Tynemouth, opened in 1980, was followed in May 1981 by inauguration of the 5 km branch from this route at South Gosforth to Bank Foot. In November 1981 HM the Queen formally opened the crucial city centre section and new Tyne Bridge to introduce an additional 5 km south of Haymarket via British Rail's Central station to Gateshead and Heworth. The 14 km line from St James via Wallsend to Tynemouth, intersecting with the initial system at Monument, opened in December 1982, and the final section of 13 km from Heworth to South Shields was to be inaugurated in late 1983.

New York
New York City Transit Authority (NYCTA)

370 Jay Street, Brooklyn, New York 11201, USA

Telephone: (212) 330 4566

President: John D Simpson
Chairman: Richard Ravitch
Vice-Chairmen: Laurence R Bailey, Daniel T Scannel

Type of system: Full metro

Gauge: 1435 mm
Route length: 371·1 km
(in tunnel): 220·5 km
(elevated): 150·6 km
Number of lines: 23, excluding Grand Central and Franklin shuttles
Number of stations: 458
(in tunnel): 262
(elevated): 196
Average distance between stations: 800 m
Rail type: 49·6 kg/m
Track type: According to location (conventional sleepers on ballast, sleepers on concrete with resilient pads, etc)
Tunnel type: Cut-and-cover, under-river bored tunnel, cast-iron with concrete liners, some concrete horseshoe
Electrification type: 600 V dc, third rail with contact shoe (R-10-R-44) and current collector (R-46)
Signalling: Wayside signals/train control; suppliers, Union Switch and Signal, General Railway Signal

Rolling stock
Number of cars: 6267, all motored
Year of introduction: 1948-77

NYCTA subway car

Main suppliers: St Louis Car, American Car & Foundry, Budd, Pullman-Standard
Car dimensions: A Division, length 15·65 m, width 2·67 m; B Division (except R-44s), length 18·44 m, width 3·05 m; B Division (R-44-46), length 22·86 m, width 3·05 m
Doors: Sliding doors with two panels per door opening, 6 or 8 openings per car, controlled from conduc-

tor's position. Width of R-27, R-30, R-30A, R-32, R-32A, R-38: 1·17 m/panel; all others 1·27 m/panel. Height: R-10-42, 1·88 m; R-44, 1·9 m

Cars on order
In December 1981 the Metropolitan Transportation Authority, the body created in 1967 to administer all

public transport in New York and its seven surrounding suburban counties, authorised NYCTA to embark on the most massive car orders in the history of US rapid transit. The move was stimulated by the mounting unreliability of existing equipment, which resulted in only 80 per cent fulfilment of daily scheduled services on average. The purchases formed part of a five-year, $6500 million capital improvement programme for all MTA's rail services which, since it would be financed without Federal money by local bonding and sale of tax credits, could escape Federal Buy-American requirements.

The orders for new cars total 1150 for the IRT line and 225 for the IND/BMT line. The first order for 325 R-62 IRT cars was secured by Nissho-Iwai and Kawasaki of Japan for $274·5 million, with the backing of a $126·143 million loan from the Export-Import Bank of Japan at very keen interest rates. In an even more controversial deal the $836·8 million

order for the remaining 825 IRT R-62A cars went to Bombardier of Canada, but with the help of $563 million financing from the Canadian Government at 9·7 per cent over 15 years. A $242·6 million order for 225 R-68 IND/BMT cars went to Westinghouse-Amrail. Nippon Sharyo Seizo Kaisha has a contract to supply 274 subway car chassis frames.

Traffic

Train headways: 2-4 minutes, peak; 15-20 minutes, off-peak
Passenger journeys: (1982) 938·1 million
Max number of trains per hour each way: 34
Max number of cars per train: 10 local, 11 express
Estimated capacity per car: 54 seated, 146 standing
Average schedule speed (including stops): Express trains 35 km/h; local trains 32 km/h

System development

The five-year programme approved at the end of 1981 budgeted $180 million for completion of the East 63rd Street line's extension to 21st Avenue in Queens and the Jamaica El—Southeast Queens line. Other provisions in the plan included:

	($ million)
Track and conductor rail rehabilitation	266
Welded rail and rubber seating installation for noise abatement	89
Station improvements	309
Signalling and telecommunication modernisation	500
Traction current distribution system modernisation	260
Structural renovation	199
Workshop improvements	432
Yard improvements	350

New York—New Jersey
The Port Authority Trans-Hudson Corporation (PATH)
(a subsidiary of the Port Authority of New York and New Jersey)

1 World Trade Center — 62W, New York, New York 10048, USA

Telephone: (212) 466 7662
Telex: 7687

Chairman: Alan Sagner
President: Peter C Goldmark
General Manager: Francis A Gorman

Type of system: Full metro

Gauge: 1435 mm
Route length: 22·2 km
(in tunnel): 11·9 km
Number of lines: 4
Number of stations: 13 (7 in New Jersey, 6 in New York)
(in tunnel): 10
Average distance between stations: 1·9 km
Track type: Conventional sleepers on ballast; some sections on concrete trackbed with resilient pads, with 120 lb (60 kg/m) rail
Max gradient: 4·8%
Minimum curve radius: 27·4 m
Tunnel type: Single track, mainly cast iron or concrete type construction
Electrification type: 650 V dc, third rail
Signalling: Block signal system with automatic tripper. Main suppliers, WABCO and GRS
Control centre: The John F Hoban operations control centre has overall control of all train operations: starting, switching, traction power, station monitoring and communications. The trainmaster can monitor: the position of every train on the system by train describer; the status of traction power from PATH's seven power substations, displayed on a power board; and passenger flow through each of the 13 stations, shown on 54 19-inch (0·48 m), closed circuit television screens. He is in direct and immediate communication via radio, intercom and television with all PATH units, connecting carriers and essential services. The communications team can provide immediate information to PATH passengers via the all-points public address system. Additionally, turnstiles can be closed by remote control to prevent crowding on platforms

Rolling stock
Number of cars: 41 Type K (1958); 159 Type PA-1 (1965); 44 Type PA-2 (1967); 46 Type PA-3 (1972)
Main suppliers: St Louis Car; Hawker Siddeley, Canada
Car dimensions: K type, length 15·5 m, width 2·7 m, height 3·5 m; PA type, length 15·5 m, width 2·8 m, height 3·5 m
Capacity: K type, 44 seats, crush load 200; PA-1 type, 42 seats, crush load 200 or 41 seats, crush load 197; PA-3 type, 33 seats, crush load 222
Doors: PA cars have two sets of double folding doors and K cars have three sets of single leaf doors on each side. Manually-operated end doors permit emergency passage through the train
Motors per car: 4
Motor rating: 298 kW
Acceleration (max): 4·02 km/h/s
Deceleration (normal service): 4·82 km/h/s
Max design speed: 115 km/h
Brakes: Westinghouse Air

Journal Square Transportation Center, Jersey City

John F Hoban operations control centre, Journal Square

Traffic
Max line capacity: (one way): 400 cars/h
Max number of trains per hour (one way): 40
Train headways: 3 minutes
Passenger journeys: (1982) 53 million

System development
PATH has invested over $272·4 million in acquisition, rehabilitation and modernisation of the 22·2 km rail system. The programme included purchase of a fleet of 250 new air-conditioned cars, completed in 1972 (PATH's was the first completely air-conditioned rapid transit fleet in the USA); completion of a new World Trade Center terminal in lower Manhattan in 1971 and of a new PATH Journal Square Transportation Center in Jersey City, New Jersey, in 1975.

New York

Staten Island Rapid Transit Operating Authority
(Agency of New York Metropolitan Transportation Authority)

25 Hyatt Street, Staten Island, New York 10301, USA

Telephone: (212) 447 1581

Type of system: Full metro

Chairman: Richard Ravitch
President: J D Simpson

General Superintendent: G A Duszak

Gauge: 1435 mm
Route length: 23 km
Number of stations (total): 22
Average distance between stations: 1040 m
Gradient (max): 1·9%
Speed (design max): 64 km/h (passenger), 48 km/h (freight), 48 km/h (average commercial)
Rail type: 49·6 kg/m
Electrification type: 600 V, third rail

Rolling stock
Car types: R44 motor cars

Number of units: 52
Number of passengers per car (total): 300
   (seated): 74
Motors per car: 4
Motor rating: 86 kW
Bogies: General Steel Industries, St Louis Car Division
Brakes: WABCO RT-5-C

Traffic
Max number of trains per hour (one way): 7
Capacity per train (seated): 74
   (standing): 300
Passenger journeys: 5 million

Novosibirsk

Ministry of Railways

Novo Basmannaya 2, Moscow 107174, USSR

Type of system: Full metro

Gauge: 1524 mm
Route length: 12·9 km
Number of lines: 1
Number of stations: 10
Average distance between stations: 1430 m
Electrification type: 825 V, third rail

System development
A three-line network totalling 52 km is planned. The first line, the Lenin, is under construction for 8·46 km, with eight stations, and this section is expected to open in 1985, after which part of the 74-station Kirov line will be put in hand.

Nuremberg

VAG Verkehrs-Aktiengesellschaft

Postfach 810220, 8500 Nuremberg 81, Federal Republic of Germany

Telephone: 0911 2830
Telex: 0622 249
Telegrams: VAG, Nurnberg

Chairman: Lothar Netter
Other principal officers: Dr-Ing Heinrich Dillman, Bernd-Dieter Jesinghausen, Dr Ing Wolfgang Krug

Type of system: Full metro (U-Bahn)

Gauge: 1435 mm
Route length: 14·39 km
(in tunnel): 8·86 km
Number of stations: 22
(in tunnel): 15
Average distance between stations: 685 m
Track type: Track on concrete, without ballast
Max gradient: 4%
Minimum curve radius: 100 m
Tunnel type: Cut-and-cover with some bored single-track
Electrification type: 750 V dc, third rail
Signalling: Fixed signals at stations, installed by Siemens
Centralised control: Central control room for all metro and surface operations
Speed (design max): 80 km/h
(average commercial): 32 km/h (Line U1); 29·8 km/h (Line U2)

Rolling stock
Number of cars: 49 two-car sets, aluminium-bodied, air-sprung, all motored, including 32 dc sets and 17 with three-phase ac drive

Jakobinenstrasse station, Furth

Main suppliers: MAN/Siemens
Year of introduction: 1970/71, 1975, 1979, 1980/81
Car dimensions: Two-car set, length 37·15 m, width 2·9 m, height 3·55 m
Motors per car: 4
Motor rating: 180 kW (1970-79 cars), 195 kW (1980-82 cars), 200 kW (three-phase ac drive cars)
Capacity: Average 290, crush 420
Tare and loaded weight: 51/70 tonnes
Doors: Double doors (opening outside): 1·3 m wide, 1·95 m high
Cars on order: 10 two-car sets with solid state-controlled three-phase ac motors; to be delivered 1983-84 by MAN/Siemens

Traffic
Train headways: Peak hours, 3⅓ minutes; off-peak, 5-10 minutes
Passenger journeys: (1981) 41·8 million

System development
A 43·9 km network is in course of construction. Line U1, which reached Eberhardshof in 1982, is due for completion of its final underground section to Furth in December 1985. The southern part of Line U2, from Plarrer to Schweinau, will be opened in February 1984, with final extension to its planned terminus at Rothenbach scheduled for opening in December 1986.

Omsk

Omsk, USSR

Type of system: Planned metro

Design studies are underway for the first line of a proposed metro. The line will run from the city centre to industrial and residential development areas on the left bank of the River Irtish.

Osaka

Osaka Municipal Transportation Bureau

Kujo Minami-I, Nishi-ku, Osaka 550, Japan

General Manager: Maseya Nishio

Type of system: Full metro

Gauge: 1435 mm
Route length: 90·9 km
(in tunnel): 78·3 km
(elevated): 10·5 km
Number of lines: 6
Number of stations: 73
(in tunnel): 64
Average distance between stations: 1·1 km
Rail type: 50 kg/m flat-bottomed
Max gradient: 3·5%
Minimum curve radius: 120 m
Tunnel type: Generally double-track, cut-and-cover tunnel, rectangular section, mostly in reinforced

Newtram on ICTS line

concrete with centre supports. At the city centre, parts of Lines 2 and 4 are at deep level in twin, single-track tube, internal diameter 5·7 m. The depth of rectangular tunnel below surface varies from 23 to 7·5 m

Electrification type: 750 V dc, third rail and (Line 6) 1·5 kV dc, overhead

Signalling: All lines with CTC, and automatic block signalling by Nihon Shingo and Kyosan Seisakusho. All lines with ATC

Rolling stock
Number of cars: 798, including 636 motored
Car dimensions: Length 17·7/18·9 m, height 2·84/2·89 m, width 3·74/3·75 m
Capacity: 36 to 60 seats
Main suppliers: Hitachi, Kawasaki, Kinki, Tokyu, Nihon and Alna
Doors: 3 or 4 sliding doors each side; 1·1 m and 1·3 m wide

Traffic
Train headways: 2-5 minutes at peak hours; 4-7 minutes off-peak
Passenger journeys: (1981/82) 823 million

System development
The metropolitan transport area of Osaka is served by a network of electrified lines, comprising the JNR Osaka Loop Line and 9 private railways, 5 of which have their terminals in the city centre. Between subway Lines 1 and 6, and the Hankyu and Osaka North Express railways, there is reciprocal working of trains.

Extension from Moriguchi to Dainichi, 0·6 km, on Line 2, the Tanimachi, was completed in February 1983. Other extensions in progress (scheduled opening dates in brackets) were:
Fukaebashi to Nagata, 3 km, Line 4, the Chuo (April 1985);
Nakamozu to Abiko, 5 km, Line 1, the Midosuji (April 1985);
Dobutsuen-mae to Tengachaya, 1·7 km, Line 6 (October 1986).

Adoption of a reduced profile, 4·1 m-diameter tube system is under consideration for service of outer suburban areas with lower traffic potential.

Type of system: Intermediate Capacity Transit System (ICTS)

Under the same management as the Osaka subway, the elevated ICTS came into operation between the city and Nanko Port Town in March 1981. Operating on concrete guideways, the system's 52 rubber-tyred motor cars collect current from a third rail at 600 V ac.

Gauge: 1600 mm
Number of stations: 8
Route length: 6·6 km
Average distance between stations: 900 m
Signalling: Fixed block (continuous transmission and receiving with check-in and check-out system), installed by Nihon Signal

Air-conditioned Series 10 train-set with chopper control

Line 2 extension under construction

Rolling stock
Cars: Supplied by Niigata Iron Works, the 52 motor cars are known as the 'Newtram'. Each has 24 seats with capacity for 51 standing passengers. Tare weight is 10·5 tonnes, loaded weight 15 tonnes.

Length is 8 m, width 2·3 m, height 3·15 m. Each has a sliding door on each side
Traffic
Train headways: Peak hours, 3½ minutes; off-peak, 7½ minutes

Oslo
A/S Oslo Sporveier

Økernveien 9, Oslo 6, Postbox 2857-Toyen, Norway

Telephone: 02-68 95 80
Telegrams: Sporveien

General Manager: Viggo Johannessen
Operating Manager: Rolf Gillebo

Type of system: Full metro

Gauge: 1435 mm
Route length: 48·44 km (double-track 36·8 km)
(in tunnel): approx 12 km
Number of lines: 4
Number of stations: 44
(in tunnel): 12
Average distance between stations: 900 m
Electrification type: 750 V dc, third rail
Signalling: Cab signalling controlling speeds at 15, 35 and 50 km/h in tunnel and 15, 30 and 70 km/h on surface sections. Train services operate under central traffic control at Traffic Center building at Toyen. Trains' communication equipment includes radio and telephone

Rolling stock
Number of cars: 162, all motored
Main suppliers: Strømmens Vaerksted; traction

Oslo T-Banen set on surface section

motors from NEBB (Oslo) and electrical equipment from AEG (West Berlin)
Car dimensions: Length 17 m, width 3·2 m, height above rail 3·67 m
Capacity: Total 176 (59 seated)
Motors per car: 4
Motor rating: 98 kW
Max speed: 70 km/h
Acceleration: (0-40 km/h) 1·0 m/s²
Tare weight: 29·7 tonnes

Traffic
Train headways: Peak hours in double-track tunnels, 112 s; off-peak, 3¾ minutes (actual capacity 1½ minutes in double-track tunnel, 2 minutes on branch lines)

Passenger journeys: (1982) 32·8 million

System development
The metro in the east of the city is being connected with the suburban lines by a 600 m tunnel extension between National Teatret and Sentrum. A loop at Sentrum will provide for the turning of metro trains.

Type of system: Light rail

Route length: 17·7 km
(on own right-of-way): 63%
Number of stops: 25
Average distance between stops: 740 m
Electrification type: 600 V dc

Rolling stock
Number of cars: 40, all motored four-axle vehicles of light alloy construction, delivered 1938/39

Capacity: 90 passengers

Cars on order: 25 six-axle articulated LRVs in course of 1983 delivery. Built for one-man operation they will have capacity for 140 passengers, including 70 seated. All cars are to Duewag (Dusseldorf) design. Ten are being supplied directly from Duewag and 15 under licence by Strommens Vaerksted. Traction motors come from NEBB (Oslo), electrical equipment from AEG (West Berlin) and electronics from Siemens. The light rail line runs from Ljabru, through the city centre, to Jar on the other side of the city.

Paris
Régie Autonome des Transports Parisiens (RATP)

53ter quai des Grands Augustins, 75271 Cedex 06, France

Telephone: 346 33 33
Telex: 200 000

Chairman: Claude Quin
General Manager: Philippe Essig
Operating Manager: Pierre Faucheux

Type of system: Full metro

Gauge: 1440 mm
Route length: (January 1982) 190·8 km double-track
Number of lines: 15 (13 radial, 2 circumference link lines)
Number of stations: 359
Average distance between stations: 540 m
Rail weight and type: 52 kg/m flat-bottomed in 18 m lengths; Line B: 46 and 55 kg/m in 16·5 or 18 m lengths; Line A: flat-bottomed, 60 kg/m, 144 m lengths welded in situ on underground sections; surface sections in 36 m lengths are fish-plated
Minimum curve radius: Urban systems 75 m and exceptionally 40 m, Line B 220 m, Line A 146 m
Max gradient
  Urban system: 4%
  Line A: 3·6%
  Line B: 4·08%
Tunnel type: Double-track tunnel of elliptical section, 7·1 m wide and 5·2 m high
Electrification type: 750 V dc, third rail
Signalling: All lines linked to central control and monitoring post (CCP) in Boulevard Bourdon. CCP receives all data on train movements and locations, issues appropriate instructions, and remotely controls all equipment installed along track, increasing carrying capacity on some lines by 10-15%. Automatic train operation (ATO) installed on all lines except lines 10, 3b and 7b. Braking and acceleration instructions relayed from trackside cable

Rolling stock
A total of 3510 cars was operated (2146 motored and 1364 trailers) in January 1982 providing 555 train-sets at peak hours. More than 80% of the fleet were new vehicles. By end of 1982 all old stock on lines 7, 8 and 13 was replaced by MF77 cars, of which 1000 have been ordered; 935 were in service by the end of 1982. The last of the historic Sprague stock was withdrawn in 1983.
  The first rubber-tyred trains started service on Line 11 in 1956. Four other lines are also equipped. Replacement of the first rubber-tyred cars was due for planning in early 1982. A new type of conventional steel-wheel-on-steel-rail car, the MF77, has been developed for other lines. MF77 cars are formed into five-car trains with driving motor car at each end, non-driving motor car in centre, and two intermediate trailers. Each car is 15·1 m long, with total length of five-car train, 77·5 m over couplers. Three single doors with 1·575 m openings supersede the four doors each side of previous Metro stock. Each of the three motor cars is equipped with two 270 kW traction motors built by Alsthom and CEM-Oerlikon. Chopper control provides 30% energy saving and smoother acceleration. Top speed is 100 km/h.
Cars on order: 10 five-car sets ordered in 1982 for Line 7

Traffic
Train headways: 1 minute 35 s–3 minutes 50 s depending on line
Passenger journeys: (1982) 1145 million

RATP Type MF77 train-set

System development
Two more extensions were commissioned in 1982: from Porte d'Italie to Kremlin-Bicetre (1·6 km) on Line 7 and from Chatillon-Montrouge to Chatillon II on Line 13.
  Priority extension projects up to 1987 include: Line 7 from Kremlin-Bicetre to Villejuif III (2·6 km), to be opened in 1984; Line 5 from Eglise de Pantin to Bobigny Prefecture (3·4 km), to be opened in 1984; Line 7 from Fort d'Aubervilliers northwards to La Courneuve-Quatre Routes (0·95 km); Line 4 from Porte d'Orléans to Bagneux; Line 1 from Pont de Neuilly to La Défense (1·8 km), to be ready by the end of 1987; Line 13 fron Saint-Denis Basilique to Saint-Denis University; Line 8 from Creteil-Préfecture to Creteil Parc Regional; and Line 13 bis from Asnières to Gennevilliers III (1·95 km).
  Longer term projects include extensions of Line 13 southwards to Chatillon III; Line 4 from Porte d'Orléans to Petit Bagneux; and Line 11 to Romainville.

Type of system: Regional express network (RER)

Gauge: 1435 mm
Number of lines: 3 (2 RATP, Lines A and B, 1 SNCF, Line C)
Number of stations: RATP lines, 65; SNCF line, 36
Average distance between stations: 2 km
Commercial speed: 50 km/h
Electrification type: 1·5 kV dc, overhead
Centralised control: As on Metro, each line linked to central control room for monitoring each train in service, communicating by telephone with each driver and taking appropriate measures in the event of disturbances on the network

Rolling stock
Number of cars: (1981) RATP, 589 (including 148 older models on Line B due for replacement)
Cars on order: Deliveries being made of 600 MI 79

'Interconnexion' cars for both SNCF and RATP (324 cars). Designed to operate on 1·5 kV dc or 25 kV ac supply and serve stations with varying platform heights. An improved version of the MI79, classified MI84, is to be produced in 64 four-car units to replace the type Z cars on Line A after 1984; a prototype batch of 11 has been ordered from Alsthom-Atlantique for late 1984 delivery

Traffic
Passenger journeys: (1982) 236 million

System development
The first phase of Interconnexion through service via the new underground Gare du Nord station was inaugurated in May 1983 (see under French National Railways). In 1986, the Cergy-Pontoise line will interconnect with Line A at Nanterre-Préfecture. Later there will be a direct link with the south-east suburbs via an exchange at the Gare de Lyon station. Trains arriving from Poissy will also be able to use the link with the Cergy-Pontoise line to run straight through Paris.
  It has been intended that the SNCF's south-east suburban lines (involving Corbeil, Evry and Melun) will be connected by the central tunnels Gare de Lyon — Chatelet-les-Halles — Gare du Nord (under RATP control) to the Orry-la-Ville line of the northern suburbs. This would become RER Line D serving a suburban population of one million. Orry trains will be run as far as Chatelet from 1985/86, but it is now considered doubtful that they can be accommodated in addition to Lines A and B trains over the Chatelet-Gare de Lyon double track. An additional tunnel may be necessary.
  Extension of RER Line C to serve the Vallée de Montmorency, with branches to Argenteuil and Pontoise, was finally approved by the Government in March 1982.
  Longer term plans indicate that a feeder line from Line B could serve Orly airport and that the RER could eventually grow to a network of 465 km.

Philadelphia
Southeastern Pennsylvania Transportation Authority (SEPTA)

200 West Wyoming Avenue, Philadelphia, Pennsylvania 19140, USA

Telephone: (215) 456 4000

General Manager: David L Gunn
Operations Manager: D F Feeley

Type of system: Full metro

Gauge: Market Street-Frankford 1581 mm; Broad Street, Ridge-Eighth and Camden 1435 mm
Number of lines: 2: Market Street—Frankford subway-elevated; Broad Street subway—Broad-Ridge spur
Route length: Market Street—Frankford subway-elevated 20·6 km
Broad Street subway 15·77 km
Broad-Ridge spur 2·41 km
Number of stations: Market Street—Frankford subway-elevated: 28
Broad Street subway and Broad-Ridge spur: 25
(in tunnel): 33
Average distance between stations: 0·93 km
Rail weight and type: 49·6 kg/m flat bottomed
Max gradient: 5%
Minimum curve radius: Market Street-Frankford line, 32 m; Broad Street and Ridge-Eighth lines, 49 m
Tunnel type: Double or multiple-track tunnel, of rectangular section
Electrification type: 625 V dc, third rail
Signalling: Automatic block, with colour-light signals

Rolling stock
Number of cars: 353, all motored
Main suppliers: Brill, Pressed Steel, Budd
Cars on order: 125 LRVs built by Kawasaki and assembled by Boeing-Vertol for Broad Street line.

The stainless steel vehicles, some single-cab (65 seats), some double-cab (62 seats) have a maximum capacity of 230 passengers, and a maximum speed of 88 km/h.

Traffic
Passenger journeys: (1981) 284 million
Max number of trains per hour each way: Broad St line 11, Market St line 18

Other railways: Philadelphia is also served by a system of suburban lines including a self-contained rapid transit railway, the Norristown High-speed Line, also operated by SEPTA. This electrified line runs from 69th Street terminus of the Market Street line north-west for 8·4 km to Norristown. Track gauge is 1435 mm and current supply is by top contact third rail.

Major developments sponsored by the city of Philadelphia are a 2·7 km, $300 million city-centre link to integrate commuter systems in a downtown transportation centre, due to open in 1983; and a $89 million, 15 km airport rail link, likely to be opened in 1984.

Port Authority Transit Corporation (PATCO)

Benjamin Franklin Bridge Plaza, Camden, New Jersey 08102, USA

Telephone: (609) 963 8300

President: J R Kelly
General Manager: R B Johnston
Superintendent of Transportation: R S Korach

Type of system: Full metro

Gauge: 1435 mm
Route length: 23·3 km
(in tunnel): 4·1 km
(at surface level): 15·5 km
(elevated): 3·7 km
Number of lines: 1

Number of stations: 13
(in tunnel): 6
Average distance between stations: 480 m in city, 2·4 km in suburbs
Rail weight and type: 66 kg/m continuous welded
Track type: In tunnel, sleepers encased three sides in concrete; at grade, wooden sleepers on ballast; on viaduct, no sleepers; track anchored directly to concrete deck with specially designed clips
Tunnel type: Cut-and-cover
Max gradient: 5%
Minimum curve radius: 61 m
Electrification type: 600 V dc, third rail
Signalling: Cab signals, with wayside signals at all interlockings, installed by WABCO
Automatic control: Full automation except for doors and PA announcements
Centralised control: Centre tower

Rolling stock
Car type

	1968	1980
(year introduced)		
Builder	Budd	Vickers, Canada
Number of units	75	46
Car dimensions		
(length)	20·57 m	20·57 m
(width)	3·05 m	3·05 m
(height)	3·76 m	3·76 m
Passenger capacity		
per car		
(total)	120	120
(seated)	72	80
Motors per car	4	4
Rating	116 kW	116 kW
Train composition		
(minimum): 1		
(max): 8		
Acceleration		
(max) (m/s²)	1·34	1·34
Deceleration		
(emergency) (m/s²)	1·43	1·43
Brakes: Rheostatic		
Body material: Stainless steel		
Weight (tonnes)		
motorcar	36·1/33·9	33·7

Traffic
Train headways: Morning peaks, down to 3½ minutes; evening peak, 2 minutes; off-peak, 10 minutes
Trains/track/hour: 24
Train capacity (passengers):
seated 480
standing 250
Total passengers/track/hour (peak): 17 280
Passenger journeys: (1981) 11·3 million

System development
Owned by the Delaware River Port Authority, PATCO's Lindenwold rapid transit line was completed in 1969 at a cost of $94 million. The aim was to provide suburban travellers with a fast city-centre link, as well as to improve transit facilities in the city itself. The line was designed for an overall average speed, including station stops, of 64 km/h and a maximum operating speed between stations of 120 km/h.

Three extensions are under study. The most likely would be a 9·6 km continuation from Lindenwold to Berlin and Atco, New Jersey. A proposed north-eastern extension would run 21 km from east of Broadway station in Camden to Mount Laurel, New Jersey, and would include seven stations. A southern addition would run 27·4 km from east of Broadway station to Glassboro, New Jersey, and include eight stations.

PATCO train-set supplied by Vickers, Canada

Pittsburgh
Port Authority of Allegheny County (PAT)

Beaver and Island Avenues, Pittsburgh, Pennsylvania 15233, USA

Telephone: (412) 237 7000

Chairman: James A Romanelli
Executive Director: James R Maloney

Type of system: LRT under construction

Gauge: 1580 mm
Route length: 16·89 km
(in tunnel): 2·4 km
Rail type: 57·5 kg/m RE
Electrification type: 600 V dc overhead

System development
PAT has launched conversion of its 36·2 km trolley system into a full LRT operation. Stage 1 covers the complete rebuilding (under traffic) of the 42/38 Mt Lebanon via Beechview trolley line and a section of the Shannon Library and Shannon Drake Routes 35 and 36 south of Castle Shannon; an extension to the South Hills shopping centre in Upper St Clair; a new

LRT tunnel under Washington Road in Mt Lebanon; an express entry into Pittsburgh town centre via the Panhandle railroad bridge; a town centre distribution system consisting of a subway alignment; and purchase of 55 new light rail vehicles to supplement 45 rehabilitated PCC cars. Completion is anticipated by the end of 1984.

The new section will have 17 stops with passenger shelters, 13 stations with special facilities for the handicapped, and some facilities for feeder buses, taxis, 'kiss-n-ride', 'park-n-ride', and other auxiliary services. Four stations will be located in the downtown distribution system, three of them in tunnel.

Portland
Tri-County Transportation District of Oregon (Tri-Met)

Suite 600, 421 SW 5th Street, Portland, Oregon 97204, USA

Telephone: (503) 238 4875

Director, Light Rail Project: D L Macdonald

Type of system: Light rail under construction

Gauge: 1435 mm
Route length: 24 km
Number of lines: 1
Number of stations: 26

Track type: Cwr on ballasted sleepers

Rolling stock: 26 articulated LRVs ordered from Bombardier, built under BN licence

System development
Construction began in 1982 for completion by 1985. The route follows partly existing rail right-of-way, the median strip of the Benfield freeway and streets.

Porto Alegre
Brazilian Federal Railways (RFFSA), Porto Alegre Region

Rua Voluntarios de Patria 1358, 90000 Porto Alegre, Rio Grande do Sul, Brazil

Type of system: Planned metro

Gauge: 1600 mm
Electrification type: 3 kV dc, overhead

Rolling stock
Car type: 25 four-car sets ordered from consortium of Hitachi, Nippon Sharyo and Mitsui; maximum speed 90 km/h

System development
The first 26·7 km of a proposed metropolitan railway from Porto Alegre to the municipality of Sapucaia do Sul is planned to open in 1984. The line, eventually to extend a further 15 km to Novo Hamburgo, is being fashioned largely from existing Brazilian Federal Railways (RFFSA) alignments. The project is being executed by Trensurb, an RFFSA subsidiary.

Prague
Dopravni Podniky Hlavniho Mesta Prahy (DP)

Bubenska 1, Prague 7, Czechoslovakia

Telephone: 37 25 41

Director: Eduard Straka
Deputy Director: Miroslav Mracek

Type of system: Full metro

Gauge: 1435 mm
Route length: 20 km
Number of lines: 2 (Lines A and C)
Number of stations: 23
Average distance between stations: City centre 680 m; suburbs 900 m
Tunnel type: Cut-and-cover and bored. Running tunnels, 5·1 m diameter. Deepest stations, three adjacent tunnels, each 7·8 m diameter. Over the Nulse Valley metro tunnel incorporated beneath highway on Klement Gottwald bridge, 43 m above ground level
Electrification type: 750 V dc, third rail
Signalling: Automatic block colour light

Centralised control: Radio communications with trains individually or en masse. Ericsson graph system for safety working but fully automatic system plan ed
Automatic control: Automatic train control equipment initiates brakes if signal overrun

Rolling stock
Number of cars: 138, all motored, Types Ecs and T
Main supplier: Mytyshchinsky plant, USSR
Car dimensions: (Type Ecs) length 18·81 m, width 2·67 m, height 3·662 m
Capacity: 120 with 42 seated
Motors per car: 4
Motor rating: 72 kW (Ecs), 110 kW (T)
Tare weight: 32·5 tonnes
Max speed: 90 km/h
Max acceleration: 1·2 m/s²
Max deceleration: 1·2 m/s²

Type T is an improved version of the Ecs retaining the same bogies and body structure, but with four 110 kW traction motors, battery-charging by thyristor converter, fluorescent lighting, automatic fuses and modernised electrical and pneumatic equipment.

Traffic
Train headways: Peak hours, 1½ minutes
Passenger journeys (daily): (August 1980) 600 000
Train capacity (passengers): 1000
Total passengers/track/hour (peak): 40 000

System development
The ultimate underground network will consist of three transverse lines A, B, C meeting in a city-centre triangle, supplemented by Line D. Total length will be 43 km.
    Line C is now being extended northwards for 3 km from the Sokolovska interchange with Line B to Fucikova, with an intermediate station at Vltavska. The third line, Line B, has been put in hand for about 5 km from Sokolovska to Smichovske Nadrazi. Both sections are due to open in 1985. Work has also started on a Line B extension from Smichovske Nadrazi to Unoroveho Vitezstvi, due to open 1987; and from Sokolovska to Palmovka, due to open 1990. The route of Line D has yet to be fixed. As the metro advances Prague is phasing out its tramways; by 1989 Prague intends the metro to undertake 40 per cent of the city's public transport, as against 20 per cent in 1981.

Pusan

Pusan, Republic of Korea

Type of system: Metro under construction

Gauge: 1435 mm
Route length: 23 km
Number of lines: 1
Number of stations: 28
Electrification type: 1·5 kV dc

System development
Construction began in 1980 of the first line of a planned five-line, 100 km network. Initial rolling stock requirement totals 151 cars.

Recife
Brazilian Federal Railways (RFFSA), Recife Region

Avenida Rio Capirabibe 147, 10° Andar, 50000 Recife, Brazil

Telephone: 231 2022
Telegrams: Referec 50000 Recife
Telex: 311061

Type of system: Rapid transit railway under construction

Gauge: 1600 mm
Route length: 20 km
Number of lines: 1
Electrification type: 3 kV dc

System development
A metre-gauge alignment of 16 km from Recife to Jaboatao and its 4 km Lacerde branch are being converted and electrified by GEC Transportation Projects. GEC Traction and its local licensee, Villares, are providing traction equipment for 25 four-car emus built by Santa Matilde.

Rhine-Ruhr
Stadtbahn Rhein-Ruhr GmbH

Postfach 2165, 4650 Gelsenkirchen, Federal Republic of Germany

Telephone: 02322 15141-8

Type of system: Light rail

Gauge: 1435 mm
Route length: 51·6 km
(in tunnel): 15 km
Number of stations: 66
Electrification type: 600 V dc overhead

System development
To complement the German Federal Railway's S-Bahn, a Stadtbahn network intended to cover 160 km by 1990 is being established in the area between Dusseldorf and Dortmund, which encloses Duisburg, Essen, Gelsenkirchen and Bochum.

Riga

Riga, USSR

Type of system: Planned metro

Construction is to start on a 19·9 km, 16-station

metro. The first line will link the city centre with an industrial area. The project was officially authorised in 1982.

Rio de Janeiro

Companhia do Metropolitano do Rio de Janeiro Metro

Avenue NS de Copacabana 493, Rio de Janeiro, Brazil

Telephone: 255 9292
Telex: 021021094

President: Eng C T de Souza e Mello
Planning Director: Ivan de Albuquerque Cascao

Type of system: Full metro and light rail

Gauge: 1600 mm
Metro route length: 16 km (all in tunnel)
Number of lines in operation: 2
Average distance between stations: 730 m
Gradient (max): 4%
Minimum curve radius: 500 m
Speed (design max): 100 km/h (metro car), 80 km/h (pre-metro car)
(average commercial): 35 km/h (both)
Rail type: 56·9 kg/m
Tunnel type: Mainly in cut-and-cover; Bernold system for 550 m; and New Austrian Tunnelling Method (NATM)

Electrification type: 750 V dc, third rail
Automatic control: Automatic pilot system
Centralised control: Operating control centre at Avenida President Vargas main depot and workshop houses operating computer control systems

Rolling stock
Main suppliers: Mafersa (metro cars); BN (2 prototype and 6 pre-series pre-metro cars); Cobrasma (60 production pre-metro cars). 270 metro cars on order
Number of units: 110 Type A and B; 8 PM (light rail)
Car dimensions

	A	B	PM
Length (m)	21·885	21·75	25·476
Width (m)	3·17	3·17	2·7
Height (m)	3·65	3·65	5·75
Number of doors per side	3	3	4
Door width (m)	1·9	1·9	1·3
Number of passengers per car (total)	350	377	317
(seated)	40	48	58
Motors per car	4	4	2
Motor rating (kW)	143	143	200
Power per train (minimum)	3·432	3·432	8
Acceleration (max)	1·12	1·12	1

	A	B	PM
Deceleration (normal service)	1·2	1·2	1·2
(emergency)	1·2	1·2	1·5
Max design speed (km/h)	100	100	80
Weight (empty) in tonnes	40	38	38

Braking: Regenerative / rheostatic / pneumatic; rheostatic / pneumatic / magnetic

Traffic
Frequency of services
(currently): 7 minutes
(planned): 1½ minutes
Capacity per train (passengers seated): metro cars 40, pre-metro cars 58
(passengers standing): metro cars 271, pre-metro cars 258
Passenger journeys: (1981) 5·2 million

System development
The 15·5 km pre-metro light rail line from Maria de Gracia to Pavuna was opened in 1982. Metro extensions have been authorised, of Line 1 from Botafogo to Praca Arco Verde in Copacabana and of Line 2 from Sa to Carioca. Longer-term plans envisage some 133·5 km of fresh metro and pre-metro construction.

Rome

Azienda Consortile Trasporti Laziali (ACOTRAL)

Via dei Radiotelegrafisti 42-44, 00143 Rome, Italy

Telephone: 5798

General Manager: Dr Ing Gastone Rossetti

Type of system: Full metro

Gauge: 1435 mm
Route length: 25·5 km
(in tunnel): 14·5 km
Number of lines: 2; double-track
Number of stations: 33
Average distance between stations: 670 m
Rail type: 50 kg/m Line A; 46·5 kg/m Line B
Max gradient: 4%
Minimum curve radius: 100 m
Electrification type: 1·5 kV dc, overhead
Signalling: Coded-current track circuits for continuous signal aspect repetition on board
Automatic control: Programmer monitors train movements and amends scheduled timetable accordingly
Centralised control: Traffic control by remote control from central point. All orders actuated automatically. System includes train number recognition
Communications: Line A, automatic telephone system, teleprinter network, loudspeaker system, clock system

Rolling stock
Suppliers: Breda, electrical equipment by Ercole Marelli, TIBB, Ansaldo

	Line A	Line B
Car type		
Number of cars	152	160
Car dimensions (length)	17·84 m	19·10 m
(width)	2·85 m	3·04 m
(height)	3·5 m	3·61 m
Doors per side	4	4
Door (width)	1·3 m	1·25 m
Passengers per car (total)	208	247
(seated)	32	52
Motors per car	4	4
Motor rating	110 kW	117 kW
Acceleration (max)	1·2 m/s²	1·25 m/s²
Deceleration (normal service)	1·2 m/s²	0·84 m/s²
Speed (max)	90 km/h	100 km/h

Traffic
Passenger journeys: (1982) 150 million

System development
The system was inaugurated with the opening of the 11 km Line B from Termini to Lido in 1955. After almost two decades of work prolonged by the problems of negotiating Rome's historic remains, the 14·5 km Line A was opened in February 1980. Extensions of both are in progress: of Line A by 3·7 km and three stations westward; and of Line B by 7·9 km and nine stations north-east from Rome Termini to Rebibbia. Total cost is L1240 000 million. Further extensions of both lines are planned. ACOTRAL aims to place orders in 1985-86 for 38 powered cars for the Line A extension and for 38 trailers to enlarge Line A trains from four to six cars. For the Line B extension 188 motor cars will be ordered, 106 of them with chopper control.
ACOTRAL also operates three Rome suburban rail systems.

ACOTRAL suburban rail systems

	Rome-Lido	Rome-Viterbo	Rome-Fiuggi
Gauge (mm)	1435	1435	950
Route length (km)	28·79	101·89	79·2
Electrification type (kV dc)	1·5	3	1·5
Rolling stock			
Locomotives	9	4	2
Railcars	3	10	33
Passenger coaches	48	21	42
Freight wagons	34	30	40
Rails (kg/m)	46	30, 36, 50	36
Minimum curvature radius (m)	275	100	50
Max gradient (%)	1·9	3·2	6
Max axleload (tonnes)	15	15	9·25

Rotterdam

Rotterdamse Elektrische Tram (RET)

Kleiweg 244, 3051 SN Rotterdam, Netherlands

Telephone: 010 546911
Telex: 25246

General Manager: Dr R den Besten

Type of system: Full metro/light rail (Sneltram)

Gauge: 1435 mm
Route length: 24·4 km
(in tunnel): 5 km
(elevated): 14 km
Number of stations: 22
(in tunnel): 12
Distance between stations: 550-1600 m
Rail type and weight: RT 46 kg/m
Track type: Direct fastening of rail on concrete with resilient pads, in tunnel and on viaduct; concrete sleepers on ballast on embankment
Minimum curve radius: 60 m
Max gradient: 3%
Electrification type: 750 V dc, third rail, with overhead collection at grade
One-man operation: All trains
Signalling: Cab signalling, installed by Siemens, with centralised control system

Sneltram operation with overhead current collection at Alexander station

Rolling stock
Number of units: 99 articulated two-car
Main suppliers: Werkspoor, Duewag
Car dimensions: Length 28·6 m, width 2·68 m
Capacity: 80/92 seated, 155/188 standing passengers (4·5/m²)
Tare and loaded weight: 41/64·4 tonnes
Doors: Pocket type, 1·3 m and 650 mm wide

Traffic
Train headways: Peak hours, 4 minutes
Passenger journeys: (1982) 47·5 million

Max number of trains per hour each way: 20
Line capacity: 35 000 passengers per hour

System development
Construction work is under way to add a new centre-east city line. Total length of the new line will be 18 km, with 7·1 km in tunnel. Most of the underground section has been built by open-cut sheet piling methods, using precast roof and wall sections, each 3 m long, 35 cm thick and weighing 40 tonnes. Expansion joints have been provided with a steel-rubber section. Earlier construction in Rotterdam was with the submerged tube method,

pioneered by Rotterdam engineers. 35 new cars are being delivered by Duewag for use on the new line. They are fitted with pantographs for operation on the surface-level section north of Capelsebrug, as well as a normal third rail current collector.

A further 5·8 km of the new line, from Capelsebrug to Binnenhof in the suburbs, was opened in May 1983. Here the metro becomes the Sneltram. In 1983 the east-west line was being extended from Coolhaven to Marconiplan, for completion in 1986, and the north-south line from Zalmplaat to Spijkenisse, for opening in 1985. A further Sneltram branch from Capelsebrug to De Tochten will be finished in 1984.

Sacramento
Sacramento Regional Transit District

PO Box 2110, Sacramento, California 95810, USA

Telephone: (916) 444 7591

Type of system: Light rail under construction

Gauge: 1435 mm
Route length: 30 km

Number of stations: 29

System development
Engineering began in 1982, with opening in 1985 intended. Initial rolling stock requirement will be 26 six-axle cars.

San Diego
San Diego Metropolitan Transit Development Board

620 C Street, Suite 400, San Diego, California 92101, USA

Telephone: (619) 231 1466

General Manager: T F Larwin

Type of system: Light rail

Gauge: 1435 mm
Route length: 25·2 km
Number of stations: 12
Electrification type: 600 V dc, overhead

Rolling stock
Number of cars: 24 articulated, Type U2
Main supplier: Duewag

Car dimensions: Length 23·15 m
Capacity: 64 seated, 196 standing (crush load)

Traffic
Train headways: 15 minutes
Passenger journeys daily: 11 000

System development
The route has been double-tracked. A second, 25 km line to serve the eastern suburbs is planned.

San Francisco
Bay Area Rapid Transit District (BART)

800 Madison St, Oakland, California 94607, USA

Telephone: (415) 465 4100

General Manager: C Keith Bernard

Type of system: Full metro

Gauge: 1676 mm
Route length: 115 km
(in tunnel): 37·4 km (including 6·44 km transbay tube)
(elevated): 37 km
Number of lines: 4
Number of stations: 34
(in tunnel): 14
(elevated): 13
Average distance between stations: 4 km
Gradient (max): 4%
Minimum curve radius: 120 m
Track type: Concrete sleepers on resilient pads
Tunnel type: Transbay tube: twin-section submerged caisson of steel and concrete, 7·32 m high, 14·64 m wide, designed for high resistance to seismic disturbances
Electrification type: 1 kV dc, third rail
Signalling: Safety and signalling equipment supplied by Westinghouse Corporation for high level of automatic operation and control. Twin train control computers (one for backup) are installed at Lake Merritt station, Oakland. For operation, route is divided into blocks, 61-305 m in length, each with associated speed control equipment. Local station equipment can be used to lower speeds if block ahead has not been cleared. Automatic train control system safety functions are handled entirely by equipment at each station, along wayside and on each train. Central computer supervises functions to improve operational efficiency. Westinghouse equipment includes frequency modulation for track signalling, reliable speed-coding system, multiplexing of signals and solid-state transistorised circuitry. 52 minicomputers installed later in 26 stations to provide backup train protection system are known as SORS (Sequential Occupancy Release System)

Rolling stock
Main supplier: Rohr Industries
Total number of cars: (1982) 439

Car type	1969A	1969B
Units as built	136	303
Car dimensions		
(length)	22·86 m	21·34 m
(width)	3·2 m	3·2 m
(height)	3·2 m	3·2 m
Total floor area (m²)	71·3	66·6
Doors per side	2	2
Door (width)	1·37 m	1·37 m

BART elevated track

Impression of new C-car

Passengers per car
(total)	144	144
(seated)	72	72
Motors per car	4	4
Motor rating	150 hp	150 hp
Acceleration		
(max) (m/s²)	1·34	1·34
Deceleration		
(normal service) (m/s²)	1·34	1·34
(emergency) (m/s²)	1·34	1·34
Speed (max) (km/h)	80	80
Weight (tonnes)	26·76	25·85

Brakes: Rheostatic / electro-magnetic

The A cars alone have a control cab, at one end only and with a slanted front, which makes them unsuitable for mid-train marshalling. This has proved an operational handicap, mitigated to a degree by rebuilding of wrecked A cars as B cars since 1978. BART has been able to dispense with A cars because it is running longer and fewer trains than originally planned. Reduction of the original car stock from 450 to the present 439 has resulted from several yard incidents as well as the loss of six cars in the 1979 transbay tube fire disaster.

BART has ordered from Soferval for 1984-86 delivery 150 cars of a new C type, with a flat-fronted cab at one end and chopper control, but otherwise similar to Type A. The order is valued at $184 million.

Traffic
Train headways: Peak hours, basic system 8·6-15 minutes, central business district 3·8 minutes; off-peak, basic 15 minutes, central business district 5 minutes; evening, 20 minutes
Passenger journeys: (1981/82) 53·3 million

Civic Center station

System development
Opening is expected in 1985 of the 3·75 km KE Track through the centre of Oakland, partly in tunnel, which should increase operating flexibility by simplifying removals of faulty trains from the main Oakland line and limiting service disruption when wayside equipment breaks down. The central train control computer is being replaced at a cost of $27 million.

San Juan
Department of Transportation and Public Works

Box 41269 Minillas Station, Santurce, Puerto Rico 00940, USA

Telephone: 726 6520

General Manager: Ing Edwin Cuebas

Type of system: Planned full metro

Length: 24 km double-track

System development
In 1982 alternative methods of transit were under study and the metro's construction had become unlikely.

Santiago de Chile
Metro de Santiago

Av Libertador B O'Higgins 1426, Santiago de Chile, Chile

Telephone: 88218
Telex: 40777

General Manager: Ludolf Lausen Kuhlmann
Operating Manager: Patricio Rojo T

Type of system: Full rubber-tyre metro

Gauge: 1435 mm
Route length: 25 km
(in tunnel): 20 km
(at surface level): 4 km (in open cut)
(elevated): 1 km
Number of lines: 2
Number of stations: 35
(in tunnel): 28
Gradient (max): 4·8%
Minimum curve radius: 400 m
Speed (design max): 80 km/h
(average commercial): 30 km/h
Track type: Concrete surface with 70 kg/m guide rail for rubber-tyred operation

Tunnel type: Cut-and-cover
Electrification type: 750 V dc collected from 2 lateral guide rails
One-man operation: All trains
Signalling: Centralised control system. All signalling from Jeumont-Schneider, France
Automatic control of train operation: 100% except for start order

Rolling stock
Year of introduction: 1975
Main supplier: Alsthom-Atlantique
Number of cars: 187
Train consist: Normally 3 motored cars plus 2 trailers
Motors per car: 2
Motor rating: 120 kW; 165 hp
Car dimensions: Length 16 m, width 2·6 m
Capacity: 175 (crush) with 40 seated in motored cars; 24 seats in trailers
Tare weight: 30 tonnes (motored); 24 tonnes (trailers)
Doors: 4 automatic sliding doors each side

Traffic
Train headways: Peak hours, 2½ minutes; off-peak, 4-8 minutes
Passenger journeys: (1982) 124·2 million

System development
Though the original Metro design provided for a network of 66 km with four lines, there are no immediate plans for further construction.

Santiago train-set

São Paulo
Companhia do Metropolitano de São Paulo

01304 Rua Augusta, 1626 São Paulo, Brazil

Telephone: 289 4133
Telex: 011 22013

President: Walter Bernardes Nory
Vice-President: Cantidio Salvador Filardi
Administrative Director: Waldemar Benassi
Engineering and Construction Director: Antonio Maria Claret Reis de Andrade
Finance Director: Carlos de Faro Passos

Operations Director: José Eduardo Rodrigues

Type of system: Full metro

Gauge: 1600 mm
Route length: 24·5 km
(in tunnel): 16·6 km
(elevated): 6·3 km
Number of lines: 2
Number of stations: 27
(in tunnel): 18
(elevated): 7
Average distance between stations: 980 m
Rail weight and type: AREA 57 (57 kg/m)
Track type: Continuous concrete beams in tunnels and on elevated sections; conventional concrete sleepers on surface sections
Gradient (max): 4%
Minimum curve radius: 300 m
Speed (design max): 100 km/h
(average commercial): 29 km/h (north-south), 34 km/h (east-west)
Tunnel types: Double-track cut-and-cover; single-track shield-driven bore
Electrification type: 750 V dc, third rail
Signalling and control: Automatic train supervision available, automatic train operation throughout. Both lines controlled from one centralised control centre. Automatic train operation and automatic train protection equipment by Westinghouse

Rolling stock
Number of cars: 318, all motored
Year of introduction: 1973-80 (original stock)
Main supplier: Mafersa
Car dimensions: Length 21·2 m, width 3·17 m, height 3·55 m
Doors: Sliding leaf doors with 1·3 m openings
Capacity per car: 62 seated, total 333 crush load
Motors per car: All axles motored
Motor rating: 75 kW
Acceleration (max): 1·35 m/s²
Deceleration (normal service): 1·20 m/s²
Brakes: Rheostatic
Weight empty: Motors, 32·4 tonnes
Cars on order: Delivery began in 1982 of 242 stainless steel-bodied, chopper-controlled cars by Mafersa and Cobrasma/Francorail

Traffic
Train headways: Peak hours, 2 minutes 5 s (north-south), 2¾ minutes (east-west); off-peak, 3 minutes 12 s (north-south), 4 minutes 10 s (east-west)
Passenger journeys: (1982) 347·3 million

System development
The metro opened its first section in 1974 with the eventual aim of four lines totalling 66·2 km: Line 1, cross-city, to link the northern suburb of Santana with Jabaquara in the south, with a branch to Moema, 21 km; Line 2, crossing the city east-westward from Vila Maria for 13·3 km to Casa Verde; Line 3, crossing the city from the south-west to the south-east, from Pinheiros to Via Anchieta, with a branch to Vila Bertioga (total 23·8 km); and Line 4, running from Madalena in the north-west, south-east for 8 km to join line 1 at Paraiso.

The lines at present in use are the north-south, which extends for 17·2 km, and 7·3 km of the east-west. A further 0·8 km and two additional stations of the east-west line were to open in 1983 and its extension continued.

A feasibility study for the third line has been carried out. This line will link the south-east to the south-west and interchange with the east-west Line 2 at Republica and Pedro II and with the north-south Line 1 at Luz.

New chopper-controlled train-set by Cobrasma/Francorail

Tatuaré station

Sapporo
Sapporo Metro

1-South, 14-West, Chuo-ku, Sapporo, Japan

Telephone: 011 261 5261

Managing Director: Sigeru Goto

Type of system: Full metro

Gauge and rail type
Line 1: pneumatic-tyred car 2180 mm wide. Centre-guide rail steel I-beam (310 × 446 mm). Running tracks paved with epoxy-resin plastics
Line 2: pneumatic-tyred car 2150 mm wide. Centre-guide rail steel I-beam (311 × 399 mm). Running tracks paved with steel plates
Route length: 33·1 km
(in tunnel): Line 1, 10·35 km; Line 2, 18·07 km
(elevated): Line 1, 4·67 km
Number of lines: 2
Number of stations: Line 1, 12 in tunnel, 4 elevated; Line 2, 17 in tunnel
Average distance between stations: Line 1, 0·953 km; Line 2, 1·08 km
Max gradient: Line 1: 4·3%
Line 2: 3·5%
Minimum curve radius: Line 1: 205 m
Line 2: 205 m

Type 6000 car used on Line 2

Tunnel type: Generally double-track, cut-and-cover tunnel, rectangular section, mostly reinforced concrete with centre supports. Under the Toyohira river the sections were constructed by caisson-method. Elevated section has circular aluminium shelter to protect against heavy snowfalls

Electrification type: Line 1: 750 V dc, third rail Line 2: 1·5 kV dc, overhead rigid body rail

Signalling: Full automatic train control (ATC) and centralised traffic control (CTC) supplied by Marubeni Corp and installed by Nippon Signal Co Ltd. Computerised 'Subway Total System' also installed. Main sub-systems include automatic traffic control; automatic fare collection; automatic power control; automatic car test system; automatic car operation system; and an automatic broadcasting and closed circuit television system

Automatic control: Automatic train operation (ATO) on Line 2

Rolling stock
Number of cars: 320, of which 248 motored, 72 trailers
Supplier: Marubeni Corp
Manufacturer: Kawasaki Heavy Industries

Car type	Line 1	Line 2
Units	176	144
Car dimensions		
(length)	13·8 m	18 m
(width)	3·08 m	3·08 m
(height)	3·7 m	3·9 m
Doors per side	2	3
Passengers per car		
(motor)	90	116
(trailer)	96	126
Motors per car	2	8
Motor rating	90 kW,	70 kW,
	375 V,	187·5 V,
	270 A	430 A
Max speed	70 km/h	70 km/h
Acceleration	4 km/h/s	3·5 km/h/s
Deceleration	4 km/h/s	4 km/h/s
Brakes	Electro-	Regenerative
	dynamic	and
	and	hydraulic
	hydraulic	

Traffic
Passenger journeys: (1982) 219·3 million
Max number of trains per hour: Line 1, 16; Line 2, 12
Train headways: Peak hours, Line 1: 3½-4 minutes; Line 2: 3½-4 minutes. Off-peak, Line 1: 7-7½ minutes; Line 2: 6½-7 minutes
Average speed: Line 1, 31·7 km/h; Line 2, 34·6 km/h

System development
A 7·4 km extension of the Tozai line from Shiroishi to Shin-Sapporo was opened in 1982. Construction of a new 16 km, nine-station Line 3 from Sakaemachi in the north via Susukino to Kitano was likely to start in 1983, for inauguration in 1995. Also planned is a 3 km extension of Line 2, from Kotoni to Teinehigashi.

Seoul
Seoul Metropolitan Subway Corporation
Seoul Metropolitan Government

621, 1-Ga, Taepyong-Ro, Chung-gu, Seoul, Republic of Korea

Director: Kim In Joo

Type of system: Full metro

Gauge: 1435 mm
Route length: 23·7 km
(in tunnel): 14·3 km
Number of lines: 2
Number of stations (total): 17
(in tunnel): 14
Average distance between stations: 1·39 km
Rail type: 50 kg/m
Gradient (max): 4%
Minimum curve radius: 400 m
Track type: Rail laid on timber sleepers and ballast. Track rubber-padded for protection of city's historic East and South gates
Tunnel type: Cut-and-cover. Tunnels vibration-damped near East and South gates
Electrification type: 1·5 kV dc, overhead collection (Korean National Railroad suburban trains on Line 1 dual voltage, 25 kV 50 Hz and 1·5 kV dc)

Speed (design max): 80 km/h
(average commercial): 35 km/h

Rolling stock
Number of cars: 324
Main suppliers: Early cars built in Japan; later cars built in South Korea by Daewoo with mostly imported electrical and control equipment

Car type	Motor-cars	Trailers
Car dimensions		
(length)	20·1 m	20·1 m
(width)	3·18 m	3·18 m
(height)	3·8 m	3·8 m
Doors per side	4	4
Door (width)	1·3 m	1·3 m
Passengers per car		
(total)	160*	148*
(seated)	54	48
Motors per car	4	—
Motor rating	120 kW	
	165 hp	
Acceleration (max)	0·7 m/s²	—
Deceleration		
(normal service)	1·0 m/s²	—
(emergency)	1·2 m/s²	—
Speed (max)	111 km/h	—
Brakes: Electro-pneumatic		
Weight empty		
(tons)	43·5	34·5

* peak crush load 360 persons

Cars on order: 402 by Daewoo with traction equipment by GEC Traction, including chopper control and regenerative braking, for Lines 3 and 4; 102 cars by Hyundai of South Korea, Nippon Sharyo Seizo and Mitsubishi Electric of Japan for Line 2

Traffic
Train headways: Peak hours, 3 minutes; off-peak, 4 minutes
Passenger journeys: In 1980 only 6% of journeys into and out of city centre. On completion of system, forecast of 50% or 5 million journeys daily: Line 1 1 million, Line 2 1·5 million, Line 3 1·2 million, Line 4 1·3 million

System development
The first section was opened in 1974, with the ultimate objective of a 133 km network radiating in ten directions from the city centre and its circular Line 2. A 20 km stretch of Line 2 was in use in 1982 and the remaining 28·8 km was nearing completion. Lines 3 and 4 are scheduled for opening by the end of 1984. Both lines will run broadly from north to south, Line 3 with 22 stations in its 27 km, Line 4 with 23 in 30 km.

Seville
Transportes Urbanos de Sevilla

Diego de Riano 2, Seville, Spain

Telephone: 232381

Director General: Simon Chavarri Subirat

Type of system: Metro under construction

Opening of the first 4 km section of a proposed three-line metro was planned for 1982 but has been deferred. It runs from P Nueva in the city centre to La Plata in the south-east with nine stations. Line 1 will be completed with construction of a north-east extension from P Nueva. The total system will be 27·1 km long.

The metro will operate on a 750-volt dc supply with third rail collection except in yards and shops where auxiliary pantographs will be used. A commercial speed of 30 km/h is planned with trains reaching a top speed of 75 km/h. The 1435 mm-gauge track is laid with 54 kg/m rail. Minimum curve radius is 200 m and maximum gradient 3 per cent. Cars will have an overall length of 18 m, width of 2·8 m and height of 3·4 m.

Singapore
Provisional Mass Rapid Transit Authority

1 Maritime Square 02-70, World Trade Centre, Singapore 0409

Telephone: 2735200
Telegrams: Matstudy

Type of system: Planned metro

Gauge: 1435 mm
Route length (planned): 49·7 km
Number of lines: 2
Number of stations: 35
Electrification type: 750 V dc, overhead

System development
Construction of a two-line system planned to cover eventually 73 km was approved in 1982 and contracts for Phase I, estimated to cost US$1000 million, were expected to be let in 1983. This covers 17·1 km

and 13 stations of north-south Line I, from Marina Bay to Ang Mo Kio; and the short City Hall-Outram Park section of the prospective 32·6 km, 22-station, east-west Line 2. Some 14·6 km will be underground, in both cut-and-cover and bored tunnel, and 2·5 km elevated. Phase II will complete Line 2. Further extensions to both lines aggregating 23·1 km are planned.
Rolling stock requirement for Phase I will be 48 three-car, M-T-M air-conditioned train-sets. ATO is planned.

Sofia
Construction authority: **Direction Metropolitene Aupres de Conseil Municipal de Sofia**

34 Boulevarde Dondukov, Sofia, Bulgaria

Type of system: Full metro under construction

Gauge: 1435 mm
Proposed route length: 51·9 km (by 2000)
Number of stations: 48
Average distance between stations: 1·16 km
Tunnel type: Single and double-track, prefabricated concrete sections
Electrification type: 825 V dc, third rail
Automatic control: Automatic speed control
Signalling: CTC with cab signalling

Rolling stock
Number of cars: Plans for 250 cars, all motored, for operation in two-car sets; one driving control car with one motored rear car. Train consist of up to four sets
Main suppliers: Probably Mytischy Machinery Plant, USSR
Car capacity: Crush, 270 in driving car and 300 in rear car

Traffic
Train headways: Peak hours, 2 minutes

System development
By the end of the century, Sofia's Metro will have three lines crossing the city centre. Line 1, now

under construction, will start at the Lyulin housing estate in the north-west. The first section will terminate in the city centre, but work will then continue to take the line under the Boulevarde Dondukov to Iskr station in the south-east, centre of a big industrial complex. The line will have 16 stations.
The north-south line will run 18 km from another industrial zone, Ilyantsi, beneath the main Bulgarian State Railways station and under the Boulevarde Dimitrov to reach the Mladoct housing area. It will have 17 stations. The third line will run 15·7 km beneath the Boulevarde Botevgradsko Chaussee, under the Poduyane railway station, to terminate at Knayshevo. The line will have 15 stations.
The first 7·7 km section, from Lyulin housing estate to city centre, is to open for revenue service by 1985, the remainder by 2000.

Stockholm
AB Storstockholms Lokaltrafik

Box 6301, 113 81 Stockholm, Sweden

Telephone: 08 23 65 00
Telex: 19159
Telegrams: Stocktransit

General Manager: Ingemar Backstrom
Operating Manager: Olof Holtman

Type of system: Full metro (T-Bana)

Gauge: 1435 mm
Route length: 104 km
(in tunnel): 56 km
Number of lines: 3 with branches
Number of stations (total): 94
(in tunnel): 48
Average distance between stations: 1000 m
Speed (design max): 80-90 km/h
  (average commercial): 30-40 km/h
Rail type: Flat-bottomed, 50 kg/m
Tunnel type: Concrete, rock and steel
Gradient (max): 4% (exceptional 4·8%)
Minimum curve radius: 200 m (exceptional 120 m)
Electrification type: 650-750 V, third rail
One-man operation: All trains one-man operated
with cab signalling
Signalling: Cab signalling with two speed ranges:
up to 15 and 50 km/h, with a third for higher speeds.
Signalling provides for 90 s train intervals and 30 s
stops at stations. Fixed lineside signals are installed
only at junctions. Central Control Office is linked to
all trains through radio communication

Rolling stock
Car types: C1-C12
Number of units: 887
Car dimensions: Length 17 m, width 2·7-2·8 m,
height 3·7 m
Number of doors per side: 3 × 2
Door width: 1·2 m
Number of passengers per car (total): 158
  (seated): 48

ASEA train-set at Akalla terminus

Motors per car: 4
Motor rating: 4 × 87 kW-4 × 100 kW
Power per 8-car train (minimum): 175 kN
  (max): 415 kN
Acceleration (max): 1·0-1·3 m/s²
Deceleration (normal service): 1·1 m/s²
  (emergency): 1·0 m/s²
Max design speed: 80-90 km/h
Bogies: 2 motor air-rubber-suspended, ASEA
Brakes: Electrodynamic and compressed air
Weight (empty): 23·6-30 tonnes (motor cars)
All cars (types C1-C12) are delivered by ASEA in
co-operation with the Swedish car-builder
Hagglund. Each car has three double-leaf automatic
sliding doors and each is equipped with centre buf-
fer couplers. All recently delivered cars have air
suspension and driver's cab at one end only

Cars on order: 14 chopper-controlled cars from
ASEA and Hagglund

Traffic
Train headways: Peak hours: tube 1, 2 minutes;
tube 2, 2½ minutes; tube 3, 5 minutes. Off-peak
hours: tube 1, 2²/₅-6²/₃ minutes; tube 2, 4-6²/₃
minutes; tube 3, 6-10 minutes
Passenger journeys (1982) 199 million
Max number of trains per hour (one way): 30

System development
Work is continuing on a 6·5 km section between
Vastra Skogen and Rinkeby which is due to come
into revenue operation in 1985. Another extension,
from Morby C to Taby, is scheduled for completion
in 1990.

Sverdlovsk

Sverdlovsk, USSR

Type of system: Planned metro
Gauge: 1524 mm
Electrification type: 825 V dc

System development
The Sverdlovsk metro is being designed. The first
line will be 12 km long with nine stations.

Taipei
**Transportation Planning Board, Ministry of
Communications**

240 Tunhua North Road, Taipei, Taiwan

Executive Secretary: C H Huang

Type of system: Planned metro

In 1981 the British Mass Transit Consultants Group,

consisting of seven firms, was retained to work in
co-operation with China Engineering Consultants
on proposals to build a four-line, 87 km metro by
2000. Construction is expected to begin in mid-1984
to an eight-year programme costed at T$25 800
million.

Tashkent
Tashkent Metropolitan

Ulitsa Tarasa Shevchenko 62, Tashkent 600015,
USSR

Chief Executive: Shainoyat Rakhimovich Shaab-
durakhimov
Chief Engineer: Khakim Gafurovich Gafurov

Type of system: Full metro

Gauge: 1524 mm
Route length: 15·42 km
Number of stations: 12
Average distance between stations: 1·5 km
Gradient (max): 4%

Electrification type: 825 V dc, third rail

Rolling stock
Number of cars: 75
Car dimensions
  (length): 19·2 m
  (width): 2·7 m
Doors per side: 4
Passengers per car
  (total): 170
  (seated): 44
Motors per car: 4
Motor rating: 66 kW
Brakes: Rheostatic

Traffic
Train frequencies: 20 pairs/h
Passenger journeys: (1980) 74·3 million

System development
The first underground railway to be built in an
earthquake zone, the Tashkent metro's construction
entailed special protective techniques and precautions, which satisfactorily survived the region's two
severe earthquakes in late 1980. The metro is
characterised by a higher degree of automated control than other USSR metros.
  The first line, completed in 1978, is transverse,
from the south-west to the city centre and then to
the north-east to serve a region of mass housing
construction.
  A 50 km system with three lines is planned. The
8·7 km second line will run from Pakhtakor station at
the midpoint of the first line to the eastern part of the
city; a 5·5 km section from Pakhtakor to Vokzal-
nayor, with five stations, will be opened in 1984.

Tbilisi
Tbilisi Metropolitan

Ploshchad Vokzalnaya 2, Tbilisi 38012, USSR

Chief Executive: Igor Grigoroviech Melkadze
Chief Engineer: Jondo Gerontevich Jinjikhadze

Type of system: Full metro

Gauge: 1524 mm
Route length: 18·8 km
(in tunnel): 16·4 km
Number of lines: 2
Number of stations (total): 16
(in tunnel): 9
Average distance between stations: 1·25 km

Max gradient: 4%
Minimum curve radius: 400 m
Speed (average commercial): 45·8 km/h
Electrification type: 825 V, third rail
Signalling: Automatic train stop. Radio-telephone
communication between trains and central com-
mand post

Rolling stock
Car type: E-1960
Number: 105, all motored
Car dimensions
  (length): 18·8 m
  (width): 2·7 m
  (height): 3·7 m
Doors per side: 4
Door (width): 1·38 m

Passengers per car
  (total): 170
  (seated): 44
Motors per car: 4
Motor rating: 68 kW (94 hp)
Brakes: Rheostatic

Traffic
Train headways: 2½ minutes (peak hours), 4
minutes (off-peak)
Passenger journeys: (1980) 142·5 million

System development
The first 6·3 km section of the metro came into operation in 1966. Under construction is an 8·6 km
branch from Line 1 westwards to Delisi, with four
stations. Trains are normally operated as four-car
sets, but some three-car sets were introduced in
1980.

Tehran

Société de Chemins de Fer Urbain de Téhéran et de sa Banlieu

37 Miremad Street, Tehran 15, Iran

Telephone: 838 051/5

President: M Ahmadian

Type of system: Planned full metro

Gauge: 1435 mm
Route length: 48 km
Rail weight: 52 kg/m
Track bed: Reinforced concrete
Proposed electrification: 750 V dc, third rail
Estimated passenger volume for first period of operation: 25 000 passengers/h one way

Train headways during first period of operation: approx 3 minutes

Rolling stock
Number of cars required: 800
Type of operation: Automatic and manual

System development
Work began in 1977 at Shah Nation Square, following detailed planning by Sofretu, but has been suspended since 1979.

Tianjin
Tianjin Metro

Tianjin, People's Republic of China

Deputy Chief Engineer: Wang Jinsheng

Type of system: Metro

Gauge: 1435 mm
Route length: 5 km

Number of lines: 1
Number of stations: 6
Average distance between stations: 1 km
Rail weight: 50 kg/m
Track type: Conventional, rail laid on concrete sleepers
Tunnel type: Cut-and-cover 2 m beneath surface
Max gradient: 3%
Minimum curve radius: 300 m
Electrification type: Third rail
Signalling: Automatic block with three-aspect signals

Service hours: Initial operations restricted to peak periods 0600-0900, 1630-1900

Rolling stock
Type: BJ-III
Supplier: Changchun Rolling Stock Plant
Max speed: 70 km/h
The cars are similar to those operating on the Peking metro. Trial revenue operation began in early 1980.

Lines planned: 24 km circling inner city area, with present line extended to Liutan

---

Tokyo

The present subway network in Tokyo consists of ten lines with a total length of 187·9 km of which seven lines, 131·8 km, are operated by the Teito Rapid Transit Authority.

The outer part of the city proper and its suburbs are served by seven major private railway companies.

Teito Rapid Transit Authority

19-6 Higashi Ueno, 3-Chome, Taito-Ku, Tokyo, Japan

Telephone: 03 832 2111

Director: Akiyoshi Yamada

Type of system: Full metro

Gauge: 1435 mm; 1067 mm
Route length: 136·2 km
(in tunnel): 97·3 km
(elevated): 15·9 km
Number of lines: 7
Number of stations: 123
Average distance between stations: 1 km
Rail type and weight: Main-line, 50 and 60 kg/m; sidings 30-50 kg/m
Track type: In tunnel, solid bed; at surface level, sleepers on ballast
Tunnel type: Shield driven and cut-and-cover
Max gradient: 3%
Minimum curve radius: 300 m

Rolling stock
Number of cars: 1054 motor, 234 trailers

Car type	Line 1	Line 6	Line 10
Car dimensions			
(length) (m)	18	20	20
(width) (m)	2·8	2·79	2·8
(height) (m)	3·65	3·65	3·66
Total floor area (m²)	44·6	49·8	49·5
Doors per side	3	4	4
Door (width) (m)	1·3	1·3	1·3
Passengers per side	6	8	8
Passengers per car			
(total)	145	160	160
(seated)	50	54	54
Motors per car	4	4	4
Motor rating	85 kW	100 kW	165 kW
	117 hp	137 hp	226 hp

Brakes Rheostatic

Electrification type: 600 V dc, third rail; 1·5 kV dc, overhead
Signalling: Wayside signals on four lines, cab signalling on three lines. Suppliers and installers: Kyosan Electric, Nippon Signal and Daido Signal
Automatic control: On Hibiya Line only
New cars: 46 cars (34 motored, 12 trailers) introduced 1981 on Hanzomon line
Suppliers: Mechanical, Kawasaki Heavy Industries; electrical equipment, Mitsubishi Electric and Hitachi
Car dimensions: Length 19·5 m, width 2·78 m
Capacity: Average 144, crush 210
Doors: Double sliding doors, 1·3 m wide, 1·85 m high
Plans for further orders: 152 more cars required for service in 1987

Traffic
Train headways: Peak hours, 1 minute 50 s; off-peak, 6 minutes
Passenger journeys: (1980) 1603·4 million

System development
Teito is the capital's principal metro operator. Its network includes the original Ginza line of 1927, electrified at 600 V dc. Extensions under construction in 1982 were: Yuraku-cho Line, 9 km (from Ikebukuro to Narimasu) to be completed mid-1983; 2·5 km (from Narimasu to Wako) to be completed by mid-1984; and 6·4 km (from Shintomicho to Shinkiba) to be completed early 1987.

Transportation Bureau of Tokyo Metropolitan Government

10-12-chome Yurakucho, Chiyoda-ku, Tokyo, Japan

Telephone: 03 216 1411

General Manager: Minoru Nitayama
Assistant General Manager: Misao Muramatsu
Chief Engineer: Michio Miyoshi

Type of system: Full metro

Gauge: 1067 mm; 1372 mm; 1435 mm
Route length: 54·9 km
(in tunnel): 49·3 km
Number of lines: 3
Number of stations: 60
(in tunnel): 53
Average distance between stations: 1 km
Rail weight and type: 50 kg/m T-rail
Max gradient: 3·5%
Minimum curve radius: 164 m

Car interior on TMG subway line

Track type: Conventional sleepers on ballast, sleepers on concrete and slab track
Tunnel type: Cut-and-cover, shield driven and concrete caisson
Electrification type: 1·5 kV dc, overhead
Signalling: Automatic block with three-aspect colour-light signalling and ATS, cab signalling and ATC
Lines under construction: 9·4 km extension of Line 10 to Motoyawata due to open in 1986

Traffic
Train headways: Peak hours, 2½-6 minutes; off-peak 5-11 minutes
Passenger journeys: (1981/82) 388 million

Rolling stock

Car type	Line 2	Line 5	Line 9
Units	304	246	178
Car dimensions			
(length) (m)	18	20	20
(width) (m)	2·79	2·8	2·8
(height) (m)	3·65	3·9	3·69
Doors per side	3	4	4
Passengers per car			
(total)	124	140	140
(seated)	52	54	51
Motors per car	4	4	4
Motor rating	75 kW	100 kW	145 kW
	103 hp	137 hp	200 hp
Acceleration (max)	0·98 m/s²	—	1·4 m/s²
Deceleration			
(normal service)	0·98 m/s²	—	1·6 m/s²
(emergency)	—	—	2·1 m/s²
Brakes	Rh/Pn	Rh/Pn	Rh/Pn
Weight empty (tons)			
M	31·5	32	30·2
R	—	—	34·5

Toronto
Toronto Transit Commission

1900 Yonge Street, Toronto, Ontario M4S 1Z2, Canada

Telephone: (416) 481 4252
Telex: 0622601

Chairman: Julian Porter
General Manager: R Michael Warren

Type of system: Full metro, light rail (UTDC Intermediate Capacity Transit System, under construction)

Gauge: 1495 mm
Route length: Metro 56·9 km; light rail (under construction on exclusive right-of-way) 7 km
Number of lines: Metro 2; light rail (under construction) 1
Number of stations: Metro 59 (49 in tunnel, 5 elevated, 5 at surface); light rail, 6 under construction
Average distance between stations: Metro 769 m
Rail weight and type: Metro, 115 lb (57·5 kg/m) T-rail
Track type: Metro: Open cut, conventional sleepers on ballast and concrete sleepers (on new sections) on ballast. Bored tunnel, rail laid on concrete bed; and rail laid on oversize concrete sleepers on resilient rubber pads
Tunnel type: Metro: cut-and-cover sections, steel-reinforced poured concrete box structures; 4·1 m high, 8·6 m wide in tunnel, 14·5 m wide in stations. Bored tunnels, shield driven precast concrete or cast iron linings; 4·8 m wide in tunnel, 7·2 m wide in stations
Max gradient: 3·45%
Electrification type: 570 V dc, third rail
Signalling: Automatic block and interlocking signals and wayside signals; suppliers, Siemens and General Electric Railway Signal Company, GRS, WABCO and Imperial Electric Company Division of Burwall Electric (Bloor-Danforth extensions 1980). Additional modifications to existing system by Wismer and Becker Inc in 1975
Centralised control: Centralised train despatch and control system

Mock-up of Scarborough ICTS vehicle

Rolling stock
Car types: 632 motor cars
Number of units per train: 4, 6 or 8

Traffic
Train headways: Yonge - University - Spadina line, peak hours, 2 minutes 10 s; off-peak, 3 minutes 42 s (day), 5 minutes 50 s (Sundays). Bloor-Danforth line, peak hours, 2 minutes 32 s; off-peak, 4¾ minutes (day), 5 minutes 52 s (Sundays)

Passenger journeys: (1981) 146·5 million

System development
The 7 km Scarborough light rail transit line from Kennedy station to the Scarborough Town Centre will be opened in the autumn of 1984. This is employing UTDC's Intermediate Capacity Transit System technology (see Vancouver entry), because of its promise of noise reduction, seeing that the line will be largely elevated in residential areas. It will be operated with 24 UTDC-built cars.

Rolling stock

Car type (all cars motored)	G1, 2, 3, 4	M1	H1, H2	H3	H4	H5
Number of units per train	134	36	230	6	88	138
	4·6	6·8	6·8	6·8	6·8	6·8
Car dimensions						
Length (m)	17·4	22·8	22·8	22·8	22·8	22·8
Width (m)	3·1	3·1	3·1	3·1	3·1	3·1
Height (m)	3·65	3·65	3·65	3·65	3·65	3·65
Number of doors per side	3	4	4	4	4	4
Door width (m)	1·14	1·14	1·14	1·14	1·14	1·14
Number of passengers per car (total)	223	319	319	319	319	319
(seated)	62	83	83	83	77	76
Motors per car	4	4	4	4	4	4
Motor rating (kW) (1h rating)	51	90	90/86	86½	86½	94
Acceleration (max) (m/s²)	1·25	1·25	1·25	1·25	1·25	1·25
Deceleration (normal service) (m/s²)	1·25	1·25	1·25	1·25	1·25	1·25
(emergency) (m/s²)	1·35	1·35	1·35	1·35	1·35	1·35
Bogies	GRCW	Dofasco	Dofasco	Dofasco	Dofasco	Dofasco
Brakes: rheostatic, electro-pneumatic, pneumatic service, pneumatic emergency brake	No rheostatic	All	All	Also regenerative	All	No rheostatic Regenerative
Weight (empty in tonnes) approx	85-73	60	56·5	66/68	58	66/68 (air-conditioning fitted)

Toulouse

Société d'Economie Mixte des Transports Publics de Voyageurs de l'Agglomération Toulousaine (SEMVAT)

49 rue de Gironis, 31081 Toulouse Cedex, France

Telephone: (61) 41 11 41

Telex: 521723

Director-General: Michel Montazel

Type of operation: Light rail

A commission established to determine the most effective way of improving public transport in Toulouse reported at the end of 1979 that the creation of a light rail network offered the most effective and economic solution. A three-line system totalling 28 km has been proposed. Because of city authority objection to a surface crossing of the city centre, a 2·2 km bored tube has been submitted to feasibility study. Construction cost of the initial system would be about Fr 800 million.

Tunis

Société du Métro Léger de Tunis

78 Avenue Mohamed V, Tunis, Tunisia

Telephone: 282 927; 283 734/577
Telex: 12 196

Director General: L Riahi

Type of system: Light rail

Work started in 1981 on construction of the first phase, the 8·14 km South line, of a proposed 42-station, four-line, 32 km light rail system planned to open in early 1984. Inauguration of the 6·45 km West, 7·36 km North and 4·09 km North West line is scheduled for 1985. Tunisian construction firms are collaborating with a European consortium led by Siemens, West Germany, and including MAN, Duewag, Jeumont-Schneider, Socader and Spie Batignolles. The first line will run from the main railway station to Den Den in the west.

Rolling stock
Seventy-eight chopper-controlled, eight-axle, double-articulated light rail vehicles are on order. Operating from a 750 V dc supply each 70 km/h car will have 52 seats and room for 234 standing passengers. Power will come from two chopper-controlled 220 kW motors, each serving one monomotor bogie. Rate of acceleration is 0·8 m/s² under normal load. Suppliers are Duewag, with MAN and Siemens equipment.

Turin

Consorzio Trasporti Azienda Tranvie Municipali (TTATM)

Corso Turati 19/6, Turin 10128, Italy

Telephone: 011 57641

Chairman: A Salerno
Director General: Ing L Scamardella
Operating Manager: G Biffignandi

Type of system: Light rail in construction

Gauge: 1445 mm
Route length: 31·9 km planned
Number of lines: 5 planned

Rail type: 50 kg/m
Track type: Ballasted
Electrification type: 600 V dc, overhead

Rolling stock
The new light rail transit vehicle of Turin is a six-axle single articulated vehicle, equipped with two monomotor bogies and one unpowered bogie; the rating per motor is 210 kW at 1165 rpm. The order for the first 100 vehicles was placed with Fiat in February 1981 and the delivery will be between 1983 and 1986 (pending their arrival the line is being operated by tramcars). Electrical equipment is by Ansaldo (60 vehicles) and AEG (40 vehicles).
Car dimensions: Length 28 m, width 2·5 m, height, rail to floor 850 mm

Tare weight: 39 tonnes
Wheel diameter: 680 mm
Service brakes: Electro-dynamic and disc
Emergency brakes: Electro-dynamic, disc brakes and magnetic rail brake
Max speed: 75 km/h
Service acceleration: 1·1 m/s²
Service deceleration: 1·3 m/s²
Emergency deceleration: 3 m/s²
Crush capacity: Seats 60, standing 244

System development
The first 3 km of Line 3 were opened in June 1982. The full system is expected to be operational by 1997.

Utrecht

Sneltram Utrecht

Moreelsepark 1, 3511 EP Utrecht, Netherlands

Design and construction by NV Nederlandse Spoorwegen
Operation on completion by Westnederland BV

Project Manager: J C van Hasselt

Type of system: Light rail

Gauge: 1435 mm

Route length: 17·5 km
Number of lines: 1, with branch to Nieuwegein Zuid
Track type: 46 kg/m rails on concrete sleepers. About 90% on exclusive right-of-way, with about 40 road crossings
Electrification type: 750 V dc, overhead
Signalling: None except ordinary street traffic lights
Construction timetable: Work began in 1977 with completion scheduled for 1981, but procedural difficulties have delayed opening of the first 13 km, from Utrecht Central to Nieuwegein Zuid, until December 1983

Rolling stock
Number of cars ordered: 27, all motored

Main suppliers: SIG, Switzerland; Holec (electrical equipment); BBC (traction motors)
Car output: 2 × 228 kW
Axle arrangement: Bo-Bo-Bo
Car dimensions: Length 29·8 m, width 2·65 m
Capacity: 98 seated, 160 standing

Traffic
Train headways: 7½ minutes day, 10 minutes evening on main section; alternate trains will run to IJsselstein and Nieuwegein
Planned commercial speed: 30 km/h
Estimated passenger volume for first period of operation: 21 000/day

Valencia

Valencia, Venezuela

Type of system: Planned metro under construction

Venezuela's second city has plans for a 60 km metro system with three lines intersecting in the city centre. The first 10 km line, with 11 stations, is under construction.

Vancouver

Greater Vancouver Rapid Transit Project
Urban Transit Authority of British Columbia

Suite 874, Four Bentall Centre, PO Box 49297, 1055 Dunsmuir Street, Vancouver, British Columbia V7X 1P6, Canada

Telephone: (604) 683 8401

Project Administrator: Michael J O'Connor
Committee Chairman: Jack Davis

Type of system: Light rail

Route length: Priority line, central Vancouver to New Westminster, 21·4 km
(in tunnel): 1·5 km
Track type: Mainly lightweight, pre-stressed elevated concrete guideways
Max gradient: 4%
Electrification type: 600 V dc collected by brushes from side rails (2 in vertical series) and fed to linear induction motors
Signalling: SELTRAC system with central computer control

Traffic
Estimated passenger volume for first period of operation: 8000-10 000/h/direction
Planned headways for first period of operation: 2-3 minutes

Rolling stock
Main supplier: Metro Canada (construction division of Urban Transportation Development Corporation of Ontario)
Number of cars needed: 114 in 1986; up to 200 by 1990
The lightweight cars feature linear induction motors, steerable bogies to reduce noise and vibration and wheel and track wear; an automated train control system permits headways of 1 minute

System development
Called the Advanced Light Rapid Transit (ALRT) system in Vancouver, the technology was conceived as the Intermediate Capacity Transit System (ICTS) by the UTDC. In Vancouver the line will use an existing CP Rail tunnel and will be fully grade-separated as the guideway, though using existing rights-of-way, will be elevated 5-7·5 m above ground level. Ground breaking took place for construction of the demonstration section in March 1982. This is due to open in 1986.

ICTS cars during testing

Vienna
Wiener Stadtwerke Verkehrsbetriebe

4 Favoritenstrasse 9, Postfach 40, 1041 Vienna, Austria

Telephone: 65 930

Director: Dipl-Ing Arnulf Mater
Operating Manager: Dipl-Ing Gunther Grois

Type of system: Full metro (U-Bahn)

Gauge: 1435 mm
Route length: 31 km
(in tunnel): 16·9 km
Number of lines: 3

Number of stations: 34
(in tunnel): 20
Average distance between stations: 852 m
Rail weight and type: Flat-bottomed S 48-U, 48·33 kg/m
Track type: Timber sleeper on ballast bed and sound-proofed superstructure with synthetic sleeper
Max gradient: 3·8%
Minimum curve radius: 300 m
Tunnel type: Partly single-track ring segment (steel) tunnel, covered construction; partly double-track reinforced concrete rectangular section in cut-and-cover construction
Electrification type: 750 V dc, third rail
Signalling: Continuous automatic train running control, supplied by Siemens, with centralised control

Rolling stock
Number of cars: 132
Main supplier: Simmering-Graz-Pauker
Car dimensions: Two-car sets, length 36·8 m, width 2·8 m, height 3·5 m
Tare and loaded weight: 52·6/72·87 tonnes

Traffic
Train headways: Peak hours, 3 minutes; off-peak, 10 minutes
Passenger journeys: (1981) 106·7 million

System development
Vienna's tramway system is the most extensive and the largest of Vienna's carriers, with 193 km of route. As part of the declared policy to separate public

Zentrum Kagran station, Line U1

transport from other traffic, some central tram routes are being diverted underground and converted into an U-Bahn.

Line U1, extended in 1982, now begins at the elevated Zentrum Kagran station, in the heart of a commercial complex on the Danube's east bank, and runs approximately 10 km via Praterstern southward, under the city centre and via Favoritenstrasse to Reumannplatz, just beyond the Gurtel (outer ring road). Tunnel construction was partly cut-and-cover, partly shield-driven. Line U4 was extended by 3·3 km in 1981 and now runs to Hutteldorf in the west. Line U2 is an inner city ring route. Construction of Line U3, a cross-city line, interchanging with the existing three routes, planned to run eventually from Simmering to Ottakring, will begin in 1984 from Rochusgasse to Volkstheater. Line U6 was started in 1983 over 2·6 km from Philadelphiabrucke to Gumpfendorfer Strasse.

Vienna is also served by a surface rapid transit railway, the Austrian Federal Railway's Schnellbahn. A common fare tariff applies to Vienna's Stadtbahn and Schnellbahn system.

Type of system: Light rail (Stadtbahn)

Gauge: 1435 mm
Route length: 9·8 km
(in tunnel): 1 km
(elevated): 1·9 km
Number of lines: 2
Number of stations: 11
(in tunnel): 3
(elevated): 7
Average distance between stations: 903 m
Electrification type: 750 V dc, overhead
Signalling: Magnetic train control

Rolling stock
Number of cars: Total 129, including 68 motored
Main supplier: Bombardier/Rotax
Motor output: 2 × 190 kW
Tare weight: Train (3-car set), 75·4 tonnes; motor car, 28 tonnes

Traffic
Train headways: Peak hours, 5 minutes; off-peak, 10 minutes

Warsaw
Biuro Planowania Rozwoju Warsawy

ul Stefana Batorego 16, 00-612 Warsaw, Poland

Telephone: 254321
Telex: 812374

Type of system: Full metro under construction

Gauge: 1435 mm
Route length: 90 km

Number of stations: 90
Number of lines: 4
Average distance between stations: Central area, 600-700 m; suburbs, 1300 m
Max gradient: 3·2%
Minimum curve radius: 300 m
Electrification type: 825 V dc, third rail

Traffic
Train headways: 1½ minutes
Capacity: 40 000 passengers/h
Commercial speed: 36 km/h

System development
Work was to start in August 1983 on construction of a 90 km metro system. Considerable Soviet aid will be made available for the project. First plans for a metro in Warsaw were made in 1927 and the idea has been revived several times since 1945.

The first section of the new system will be 11·9 km of Line 1 with 11 stations, to be finished by 1990; Line 1 will eventually extend for 23 km, with a total of 23 stations, entirely in tunnel, running from north to south through the city centre. All tunnels will be about 4 m below ground level. The system will be operated with six-car train-sets built in the USSR.

Washington
Washington Metropolitan Area Transit Authority

600 Fifth Street NW, Washington DC 20001, USA

Telephone: (202) 637 1234

General Manager: Carmen E Turner

Type of system: Full metro

Gauge: 1435 mm
Route length: 68·2 km
(in tunnel): 39·8 km
(at surface level): 20·6 km
(elevated): 7·8 km
Number of lines: 4 (Red, Orange, Blue, Yellow)
Number of stations: 47
(in tunnel): 31
Average distance between stations: 2 km
Rail type: 52·16 kg/m solid steel
Max gradient: 4%
Minimum curve radius: 198 m
Electrification type: 750 V dc, third rail
One-man operation: All trains
Signalling: Wayside and cab signals, installed by GRS

Crystal City station

Automatic control: Although each train carries an operator, the train is actually operated by an automatic train control (ATC) system. The operator makes station announcements, opens and closes doors and monitors passenger activity. The ATC system is made up of three sub-systems: automatic train supervision (ATS), automatic train operation (ATO), and automatic train protection (ATP). The ATS system takes information from one of two digital computers and, under order to operate an on-time high-performance rail network, can 'advise' Metro trains of speeds, spacing intervals, dwell times in stations and other performance requirements. The ATO converts signals from the ATS into operating instructions to trains. Before these directions are relayed, the ATP system comes into play as a safeguard. It can stop trains or set safe speed limits and other restructions on train operations, no matter what the ATS demands to assure on-time performance, functioning as a watchful eye over activities of ATO to protect passengers and equipment. A variety of fail-safe features has been designed into the ATC system to ensure that operating instructions are not misinterpreted, false signals are not transmitted, actual signals do not go astray, and any malfunctioning of components results in a safer, rather than more dangerous, situation. The fail-safe principle will cause a train to slow down and stop rather than run away in the event of a part failure.

Trains are monitored from a central control room in the operations headquarters building in Washington. Twelve 381-mm colour cathode-ray tubes show the train system in colour code, the position and identity of each train, and other aspects of the operating system. The communication system enables Central Control to speak to train operators and stations individually or collectively. Communications with trains underground is by 'leaky line' antenna. Operators in the control room can call up and magnify on the crts special sections of the system at will.

Rolling stock
Number of cars: 298 (operated in married pairs), all motored
Average and crush capacities: Seated 81; average standing 94; crush standing 159
Tare and loaded weight: 32·658/47·627 tonnes
Car dimensions: Length 22·8 m, width 3·04 m, height 3·2 m
Doors: Three automatic double doors per side 1981 × 1270 mm
Main supplier: Rohr Industries (deliveries beginning 1976)
Cars on order: 294 from Breda Costruzioni Ferroviarie (Pistoia, Italy), delivery under way 1983. UTDC (USA) has been awarded a contract to develop a steerable bogie design for the Metro.

Traffic
Train headways: Peak hours, Red Line 5 minutes; Blue 6 minutes; Orange 6 minutes; Yellow 6 minutes. Off-peak: Red 10 minutes; Orange/Blue/Yellow 12 minutes
Passenger journeys: (1982/83): 80·7 million

System development
The first section was opened in March 1976. Passenger volume has since grown steadily from about 20 000 per day to over 300 000.

Upon completion Metro will have 5 lines aggregating 162·5 km with 86 stations, 49 of which will be below ground. Already investment in the system totals $5000 million. In various combinations the federal government is putting up from 67 to 85% of the cost of constructing the total system. The balance is funded by two participating states, Maryland and Virginia, the District of Columbia, and other local jurisdictions. Passengers pay about 58% of the operating cost, the local jurisdictions making up most of the balance with a subsidy.

The first 5 km of the system's third route, the Yellow line from Gallery Place to National Airport, opened in April 1983, raising the total route length to 68 km. Delayed by protracted delivery of new cars, opening of the Blue Line extension to Huntington was scheduled for late 1983, and of the Red Line to Shady Grove for late 1984. An Orange Line extension to Vienna would be commissioned in 1986.

Wuppertal
Wuppertal Stadtwerke AG

Bromberger Str 39-41, 5600 Wuppertal 2, Federal Republic of Germany

Telephone: (0202) 5691
Telegrams: Stadtwerke, WPT
Telex: 8591 788

General Manager: Kurt Sunkel

Type of system: Suspended monorail

Route length: 13·3 km
Number of lines: 1
Number of stations: 19
Average distance between stations: 739 m
Gradient (max): 4%
Minimum curve radius: 75 m
Speed (design max): 80 km/h
  (average commercial): 25·1 km/h
Electrification type: 600 V dc

Rolling stock
Number of units: 28 articulated units
Car dimensions: Length 24·05 m, width 2·2 m, height 2·5 m

Doors per side: 4
Door width: 1·3 m
Number of passengers per car (total): 204
  (seated): 48
Motors per car: 4
Motor rating: 50 kW
Acceleration (max): 1·1 m/s²
Deceleration (normal service): 0·8 m/s²
  (emergency): 1·2 m/s²
Bogies: Aluminium, MAN
Brakes: E1 Disc
Weight (empty): 22·175 tonnes

Traffic
Max number of trains per hour (one way): 21
Train headways: 3 minutes
Passenger journeys: (1982) 17·3 million

Wuppertal monorail train-set

Yokohama
Yokohama Municipal Transportation Bureau

1-1 Minatocho, Naka-ku 231, Yokohama, Japan

Type of system: Full metro

Gauge: 1435 mm
Route length: 11·5 km (all in tunnel)
Number of lines: 2
Number of stations: 12
Speed (design max): 90 km/h

Electrification type: 750 V, third rail

Rolling stock
Units: 70 in five-car sets
Car dimensions: Length 18 m, width 2·78 m, height 3·54 m
Doors per side: 3
Door width: 1·3 m
Passengers per car
  (total): 145
  (seated): 52
Motors per car: 4
Motor rating: 120 kW, 165 hp

System development
This rapid transit project calls for the construction of four lines with a total length of 67·8 km. Priority was given to the important rapid transit routes 1 and 3 passing through the city's central area. The first section of Line 1 from Kami-Ohoka to Isezakichoja-machi (5·3 km) was opened to traffic in December 1972. On Line 3 construction work from Yokohama Central south to Onoe-Cho (2·75 km), was started in 1972.

The network will consist of sub-surface lines in box-type tunnel under urban Yokohama, rising to elevated tracks in the suburbs.

ADDENDA

LOCOMOTIVES AND ROLLING STOCK

Berwick
Berwick Forge & Fabricating

Berwick, Pennsylvania 18603, USA

(see also p 17)

Additional products: Prototype lightweight intermodal flatcars. An articulated four-unit skeletal frame container-carrying flatcar weighing 89 600 lb tare complete and measuring 166 feet over strikers can carry on each unit a 40-foot container with a total loaded weight of 67 500 lb. Centre of gravity with this maximum load in a 9 foot 6 inch container is 6 feet 11 inches on each end unit, 7 feet 5$^7/_{10}$ inches on each inner. From this COFC prototype a five-unit TOFC flatcar has been developed. The company has also been co-operating with American President Lines (APL) on a well car design capable of double-stacking 9 foot 6 inch containers on US transcontinental hauls as far east as Chicago. The prototype was included in a trial train of 20 five-unit articulated well cars convey-

ing 200 containers which was run for APL and its backload partner, Transway International, between Los Angeles and Chicago in July 1983.

Another innovation is FLIP (Flexible Length Intermodal Platform), a system for short-haul TOFC collection and delivery. The FLIP car system consists of short platform cars, each of which supports the rear end of a leading highway trailer and the front end of a following trailer, and a highway tractor equipped with hi-rail wheels which serves as motive power for the train. The trailer bodies serve to connect the platforms, which are not directly coupled to each other. Although the FLIP equipment operates on conventional track, it cannot be connected to or operated in the same consist with conventional railroad locomotives or cars. FLIP train consists must be limited to a maximum of 15 platforms. FLIP equipment does not comply with AAR freight car or locomotive design requirements. The Federal Railroad Administration has granted a waiver to certain FRA safety appliance, power brake and locomotive requirements for the duration of an operational test of the FLIP system on common carrier trackage. Among concerns showing interest in FLIP are Burlington Northern and the US Army, the latter for its 'fast break' military cargo concept.

Berwick articulated four-unit container flatcar

Berwick FLIP TOFC short-haul system

Dorbyl
Dorbyl Railway Products (Pty) Ltd

PO Box 229, Boksburg 1460, South Africa

(see also p 49)

Recent products: A South African Transport Services (SATS) requirement for special-purpose wagons of low tare and high payload ratio has led to several new designs. One example is the covered Type FP-1 wagon with modular constructed body sides, using pressed corrugated panels, with joints covered by pressed stanchions. The self-powered refrigeration unit circulates air at fixed temperature through ducting in the newly designed mechanical refrigeration wagon.

The emphasis is now on bulk handling wagons of all-welded design which will also meet the Association of American Railroads (AAR) Standard. One of the specifications is that the underframe horizontal forces be roughly twice that of previous requirements. The first of these wagons, Type OZL, is for conveyance of palletised boxes of fruit for export. To facilitate loading and unloading, four

sliding plug doors are provided per side, exposing any quarter of the wagon at one time.

A major breakthrough in payload/tare ratio is the iron ore gondola wagon, Type CR-1; this has a ratio of almost 4:1, whereas previous wagons normally had a ratio of 2:1. It has Scheffel High Stability (HS) bogies and air brakes, so that it is possible for the first time in South Africa to run unit trains of up to 220 wagons. It is designed with a minimum axleload of 25 tons, where previously the maximum was 18 tons.

Other recent productions are: frameless tank wagons of the parallel cylinder type and of jumbo type, which is enlarged in the centre to reduce length, while keeping the centre of gravity low; a covered grain hopper capable of discharging a 40-ton load in 20 seconds; a motor car transporter capable of transporting eight vehicles per wagon; a bulk sugar wagon with payload capacity of 52 tons; a refrigerated meat/fish wagon, which is the largest covered freight vehicle in use in South Africa; and bulk powder wagon, Type XBJ-11, with three pots, capable of discharging approximately 2 tons of cement per minute by pneumatic discharge.

In the electronic field Dorbyl Railway Products has supplied SATS with a Train Dynamics Analyser. The TDA is a computerised simulated locomotive control

Dorbyl pallet wagon for SATS

Dorbyl mechanical refrigerator wagon for SATS

panel and guides a simulated train across a video screen, showing engineers more efficient ways to use their traction and solving problems for the technical staff.

Dorbyl Railway Products started supplying locomotives from their Boksburg works in 1960, building to General Electric drawings and specifications. Over 850 locomotives have been supplied. These include diesel-hydraulics and the new SATS Class 7E1 electric locomotives, of which a contract of 50 has been delivered and another contract of 60 Type 7E3 was in production in 1983.

Dorbyl Type CR-6 ore wagon

Ganz-Mávag
Ganz-Mávag Locomotive and Railway Carriage Manufacturers and Mechanical Engineers

Budapest VIII, Hungary

(see also p 64)

Sales Manager, Railway Rolling Stock: Ferenc Tordai

Deliveries and orders 1982-83: In 1982 the company supplied 38 Type DHM 12 diesel-hydraulic locomotives of 590 kW to Bangladesh Railways. In 1983 six Class YZ-E three-car 25 kV ac electric multiple-units were built for Tunisian Railways' metre gauge; these are claimed as the world's first 25 kV ac multiple-units for metre gauge.

A repeat order of four emus following 46 similar units were manufactured for Yugoslav Railways' 1435 mm gauge, to be operated during the Sarajevo Winter Olympic Games. This contract was handled in co-operation with Ganz Electric Works. In addition, diesel-electric shunting locomotives of Type DVM 12 were built for Yugoslav Railways.

Ganz-Mávag supplied 10 Type DHM 7 diesel-hydraulic locomotives for the main lines of the Greek Railways (CH), and 20 Type DHM 13 and DHM 14 diesel-hydraulic locomotives for Tunisian National Railways (SNCFT). Other recent orders have included 100 air-conditioned passenger cars for the Tunisian National Railways and 15 two-car LRVs for Alexandria, Egypt. The factory completed its ten thousandth locomotive in 1982.

Recent developments: Ganz-Mávag has jointly with the Hungarian Ikarus Company developed a twin-unit railbus for the operation of branch lines. It is designed for powering with either a Cummins or a Ganz-Mávag 250 kW engine.

Ganz-Mávag diesel-hydraulic Bo-Bo for Tunisian National Railways

Length is 25·2 metres, weight is 26 tonnes, maximum axleload 10 tonnes, and the vehicle is designed with a maximum speed of 100 km/h. The prototype has 86 seats but their arrangement can be modified. Ganz-Mávag is to develop several versions of the railbus.

General Electric
General Electric Company

Erie, Pennsylvania 16531, USA

(see also p 66)

Deliveries and orders 1982-83: In 1982 General Electric delivered 130 B30-7A, four-axle, 3000 hp diesel-electric locomotives powered by the GE 12-cylinder diesel engine. The Sentry all-weather adhesion control system, GE-752AF traction motor, and 12-cylinder engine give the B30-7A ability to handle substantially more tonnage than many earlier four-axle, 3000 hp locomotives employing a 16-cylinder engine. Fifty-three of the B30-7As were cabless units.

The first of 39 E60C 6000 hp electric locomotives to be used by the National Railways of Mexico (NdeM) on its Queretaro Division were completed in 1982; the balance of the order was scheduled for 1983 delivery. Shipments continued on the long-term contract with NdeM for diesel-electric locomotives and kits to be assembled in NdeM's Aguascalientes workshop.

Two E60C electric locomotives were ordered by Western Fuels to haul unit coal trains 61 km from a Utah coal field to a Colorado power plant. This new rail line is the third 50 kV 60 Hz electrification in the world; it is modelled after the Black Mesa and Lake Powell operation for which General Electric supplied the motive power.

Manufacture began of an order for 64 diesel-electric locomotives for the Indonesian State Railways. Thirty-four of these 1800 hp locomotives were U18Cs with six powered axles, while the remaining 30 U18A1As have four of the six axles powered. Specially designed for reduced axleloads, the U18A1As will operate on lighter-gauge rail lines. The locomotives join a fleet of 49 U18 units currently serving the railway.

The Tunisian National Railways (SNCFT) made the largest single purchase in its history, ordering 51 diesel-electric locomotives from General Electric. During 1982, GE supplied 20 U22C 2500 hp main-line locomotives and 31 U10B switching locomotives to SNCFT.

Under licensing agreements with General Electric (USA), Krupp of West Germany and A Goninan & Co Ltd of Australia will build locomotives for the

General Electric Type U18C locomotive for Indonesian State Railways

Tanzania-Zambia Railway Authority (TAZARA) and Queensland State Railways, respectively. The 14 locomotives for TAZARA will be six-axle, 3000 hp units while the 13 Queensland locomotives in Australia will be six-axle, 2200 hp units.

General Electric do Brasil will build 23 C30-7B 3100 hp locomotives for the Carajás ore project in the East Amazon region of Brazil. The locomotives will power unit ore trains from Carajás iron mines to the port of São Luis, 890 km away.

HTC

HTC Transport Systems
An operating unit of Abercom Africa (Pty) Ltd

Barlow Street, PO Box 178, Industries West, 1401 Germiston, South Africa

Telephone: (011) 825 1212
Telex: 8-0899

Executive: Dr D J Ashby

Products: Diesel, battery and overhead trolley electric locomotives.

The company has supplied and built over 2500 locomotives for surface and underground applications since 1965; this figure includes in excess of 2000 diesel locomotives. A new generation of high-performance cardan shaft-driven diesel-hydraulic locomotives is fitted with chevron rubber suspension for low wheelflange and rail wear. These locomotives are equipped with vacuum and air train brakes.

HTC Transport Systems 15-tonne diesel-hydrostatic 60 kW locomotive

HTC Transport Systems 37-tonne 390 kW diesel-hydraulic 0-4-0

HTC diesel locomotives

Wheel arrangement	Transmission	Rated power (kW)	Max speed km/h	Total weight tonnes	No in service	Year first built	Builders		
							Mechanical parts	Engine & type	Transmission
0-4-0	Hydrostatic	60	12	15	36	1964	HTC	Air-cooled Deutz FSL912	Sunstrand/Staffa
0-4-0	Torque converter	137	30	20	52	1965	HTC	Water-cooled Cummins VT 555 L	Twin-Disc TDCC-44-511
0-6-0	Torque converter	175	25	25			HTC	Water-cooled Cummins N 855 L4	Allison CRT 5633
0-4-0	Torque converter	250	30	30	30	1961	HTC	Water-cooled Cummins NT 855 L4	Allison CRT 5633
0-4-0	Torque converter	390	45	37	6	1981	HTC	Water-cooled Cummins KTA 1150L	Clark 16000/16000
0-6-0	Torque converter	336	50	45	14	1961	HTC	Water-cooled Cummins KT 1150L	Clark 16000/8000
0-6-0	Torque converter	450	50	45	9	1963	HTC	Water-cooled Cummins KTA 1150 L	Clark 16000/16000
Bo-Bo	Torque converter	530	50	65	10	1977	HTC	Water-cooled Rolls-Royce DV 8T CA	Voith L4R4U2

Pullman Standard

200 South Michigan Avenue, Chicago, Illinois 60604, USA

(see also p 123)

Recent developments: The company is a protagonist in the development of new designs of intermodal vehicles. Its first design was a four-unit skeletal flat car, designed for loading of TOFC trailers of 40 or 48 feet by overhead cranes or mobile loaders. It consists of four platforms, two end units of 46 feet 10½ inches over end sills, two inner units of 46 feet 8 inches, each suspended by single-axle Portager bogies and semi-permanently connected by drawbars with standard couplers at each end. The four units are considered a single car, and a prototype has accumulated over 60 000 miles of in-service testing on various US railroads. The centre slot in the frame provides the torsional flexibility necessary for high-speed stability and for negotiating curves of varying radii. The cars can also convey 45 foot APL containers.

Because of railroads' desire for flexibility in loading and routing cars, the next

Single-unit Type TTX 110016 single-unit car with British Rail running gear

Single-unit Type PLWX 82 intermodal car with UIC running gear

development was to create a single-unit car with the same basic features as the four-unit car. The major difference on this Type PLWX 82 single-unit car, 50 feet 6 inches long over end sills, is the use of the UIC single-axle bogie, which eliminates the heavy sideframe assembly of the Portager truck, while retaining the high-speed performance capability.

A further refinement in this design series, Type TTX 110016, involves the application of the British Rail bogie to the basic single-unit platform. This car has also performed very well at high speeds. The various bogie designs were in 1983 being evaluated on a cost/benefit basis for final production plans.

Pullman Standard four-unit TOFC car

Youngstown Steel Door
The Youngstown Steel Door Company

Sales office: 332 South Michigan Avenue, Chicago, Illinois 60604, USA

Telephone: (312) 427 4485

2000 Bond Court, 1300 E 9th Street, Cleveland, Ohio 44114

Telephone: (216) 241 3170

President: R E Brill
Vice-President: B H Scheidler
Sales Manager: E R Johnson

Products: Backpacker lightweight intermodal railcar. The design combines reinforced side sills and seven substantial box-section cross-bearers with a low-level deck to form a well area that supports road trailers or containers at a low level to reduce the centre of gravity and the aerodynamic drag of a loaded train. The articulated three-unit vehicle is 154 feet 11⅞ inches long over striker plates and weighs approximately 107 400 lb. A substantial portion of the weight is concentrated in the side sills which have been stepped downward to provide clearance for drop frame trailers.

The tyre deck is placed at 13½ inches above the rail, providing an overall height of 14 feet 7½ inches when carrying empty 13 feet 6 inches high vans. The sides of the well are configured with a 'tyre kicker' structure to provide an 8 foot 8½ inches opening for the 8 foot trailer bogies while loading. The air brake equipment is concentrated on the end platforms of the car; all brake piping is recessed in the side sills for complete protection.

The Backpacker has been designed to accept a variety of AAR-type trailers and containers, all loaded to maximum allowable load limits. Each unit can carry any

40- or 45-foot long trailer with nose-mounted or underslung refrigerated unit. Kingpins may be set at 36 or 42 inches for nose reefer trailers. Standard 40-foot containers ride in essentially the same position as the bodies of the trailers. They are supported by permanently mounted M-F container pedestals. A single 20-foot container can be placed in the tyre deck area, eliminating the need for a separate set of special container pedestals.

Youngstown Steel Door Backpacker intermodal unit

BOGIES AND SUSPENSIONS

Ganz-Mávag
Ganz-Mávag Locomotive and Railway Carriage Manufacturers

PO Box 136, Konyves Kálmán krt 76, Budapest VIII, Hungary

(see also p 64)

Sales Manager, Railway Rolling Stock: Ferenc Tordai

Products: Bogies.
The fundamental characteristic of the Ganz-Mávag standard bogie design is the combination of flexi-coil springs and laminated rubber springs in the secondary suspension system. This arrangement is being patented in many countries.

Main features of this design are: elimination of the traditional pendulum-type bolster mechanism; elimination of all friction elements subject to wear; low turning resistance in curves, but sufficient transverse return force; achievement of appropriate oscillation characteristics for good riding quality both vertically and transversally even at high speed; high standardisation of parts in a bogie series which covers all gauges, any known type of drive or axle-hung traction motor and all types of brake used on railway rolling stock, either tread or disc; a suspension system which is maintenance-free and maintains its ride parameters for a long time.

Ganz-Mávag air-suspended bogies are produced in two versions: a motored bogie driven by two traction motors and a trailer bogie. The two bogie versions are built according to the same design principles with the use of largely similar structural members. Primary suspension and the central pivot arrangement is of standard Ganz-Mávag design.

Bogie with air suspension for New Zealand multiple-unit trains

Power bogie with disc brake

Both types of bogies are fitted with torsional air springs, which are manufactured in a light metal casting design. This type of air spring ensures in addition both vertical and transverse suspension of the carbody as well as the turning of the bogie in relation to the carbody when negotiating a curve. The bogies are equipped also with anti-roll stabiliser bar. Vibrations are damped with vertical and lateral hydraulic shock absorbers. The trailer bogies are fitted with disc brakes and the motored bogies with tread brake units with composite brake shoes.

Prototype bogie for New York City Transit Authority

Trailer bogie with tread brake units

Vickers Ruwolt
Vickers Ruwolt Division

524-582 Victoria Street, Richmond, Victoria 3121, Australia

Telephone: (03) 428 2711
Telex: 31301

Products: Freight, passenger powered and trailer bogies; cast steel bogie frames, bolsters and other castings.

Passenger, freight vehicle and locomotive bogies are designed by Vickers Ruwolt to meet specific customer requirements, overcoming specific problems with innovative solutions. For example on disc-braked bogies, a spring parking brake actuator mechanism is fitted to allow the spring parking brake to be actuated from beside the bogie, an arrangement which is thought to be unique. Vickers Ruwolt is a leader in the construction of integral bogie frame castings.

Recent contracts have included manufacture of 26 Tricotrol locomotive bogies for A Goninan and Co Ltd for a Queensland Railways contract for 13 General Electric U22C Co-Co diesel-electric locomotives; the latter are for haulage of 83 × 73-tonne unit coal trains utilising four of the new 2390 hp locomotives.

A licence agreement has been concluded with Socimi of Milan for the manufacture and marketing in Australia of the Maxiride freight and Fast ride passenger bogies; some of these fabricated bogies are going into service with State Railway Authority of New South Wales (NSW-SRA), Queensland Railways and State Transport Authority of Victoria.

To permit development of its existing range of locomotive, emu, dmu, freight and passenger bogies, the company is manufacturing a bogie frame test rig to enable full-scale static and dynamic structural tests to be carried out; the rig will be suitable for two- and three-axle bogies.

Other work executed in 1981-82 has included 184 double-deck car bogies for service on NSW-SRA's Sydney suburban system; 42 interurban commuter car bogies for service with VicRail; and prototype fabricated bogies for evaluation on narrow, standard and broad-gauge operations in three states.

ELECTRIFICATION EQUIPMENT

GEC Transmission and Distribution Projects Limited
Transportation Power Supplies Division

PO Box 27, Stafford ST17 4LN, England

Telephone: 0785 57111
Telegrams: Enelectico Stafford
Telex: 36203

Director: R K Baldwin

Products: Rectifiers for dc power supplies; power conditioning units for light rail vehicles; transistorised chopper units for driving battery-powered vehicles; battery charges for substations and multiple-unit trains; vacuum circuit breakers for 25 kV electrification; high-speed dc circuit breakers for traction supplies; ac trackside substations including EHV switchgear; traction power system studies.

Recent orders have included: power supply equipment, including rectifiers, transformers and switchgear for the Tsuen Wan extension of the Hong Kong Mass Transit Railway, contract value £10 million; power supply equipment including transformers, rectifiers, ac and dc switchgear, trackside cabling and a power system study for the Brazilian Urban Transit Authority for Recife, Brazil, contract value £3·5 million; power conversion units for Metro Canada Limited to be installed on light rail vehicles for the Intermediate Capacity Transit System at Scarborough, Ontario, contract value £2 million; supply of electrical equipment to the maglev link between Birmingham Airport and Birmingham International station, including a substation and vehicle-mounted equipment for the lifting magnets, propulsion and auxiliaries, contract value £360 000; power supply equipment for Taiwan Railway Administration West Coast main line electrification, contract value £3 million; power supply equipment for the National Railways of Zimbabwe electrification of the Harare to Dabuka section, contract value £7 million.

Constitution: The activities of GEC Rectifiers Ltd, the Traction Switchgear Division of GEC High Voltage Switchgear Ltd and the Power Transmission Division of GEC Power Engineering Ltd have been consolidated into a single new company, GEC Transmission and Distribution Projects Ltd. Its business is handled by three trading divisions: Transportation Power Supplies, for dc and ac traction substation equipment and Transidrive maglev systems; Power Systems Projects; and Power Transmission.

RAILWAY SYSTEMS

BRAZIL
Rede Ferroviaria Federal SA (RFFSA)

(see p 423)

The following are updated statistics:

Route length: 762 mm gauge, 202 km; 1000 mm gauge, 21 068 km; 1600 mm gauge, 1817 km
Electrification: 879 km at 3 kV dc

Traffic 1982

Total freight tonnes (million)	69·828
Total freight tonne-km (million)	31 686·8
Total passenger journeys (million)	14·323
Total passenger-km (million)	10 385·6

Finance 1982 (Cr million)
Revenue

Passengers	9898·7
Mail and baggage	57·1
Freight and parcels	117 990·7
Other	425 382·6
Total	553 329·1

Expenditure

Personnel	107 648·4
Materials	38 736·5
Other	483 155·0
Total	629 539·9

Locomotives
The numbers of these classes operating at the end of 1982 were as follows, and not as shown in the tables on pp 426-28:

U-12B, 28; U13-B, 48; U-20C, 156; B12, 0; G12, 168; MX-620, 71; RS-8, 19; RSD-18, 44; Baldwin C-C, 0; Whitcomb C-C, 0.

CANADA

GO Transit
Government of Ontario Transit

555 Wilson Avenue, Downsview, Ontario M3H 5Y6

Telephone: 06 217508

Chairman: L H Parson
Managing Director: A F Leach
Director, Special Projects, ALRT Programme: D A Sutherland
  Engineering and Maintenance: H W Clelland

Finance and Administration: A M Robinson
Audit and Security: J M Burwell
Services: H D Mosher
Manager, Passenger Services: F D Dormier
  Personnel: R J Desjardins

GO Transit operates under contract a commuter service over 211 route-miles of railroad-owned track in the Toronto area. At the end of 1982 its equipment comprised 32 diesel locomotives, 14 auxiliary power units and 201 passenger cars, including a fleet of bi-level cars by Hawker Siddeley Canada; in 1982 orders worth $59 million were placed for 71 more of the bi-levels.

Montreal Urban Community Transport Commission (MUCTC)
Commission de Transport de la Communauté Urbaine de Montreal

159 rue St-Antoine West, Montreal, Quebec H2Z 1H3

Telephone: (544) 877 6474
Telex: 05 825570

Chairman and General Manager: Lawrence Hanigan
General Manager, Operations: J J Bouvrette
Director, Planning: G Lafontaine
  Transportation: H Bessette
  Purchases: G Hearson
  Vehicle Maintenance: F Therrien
  Engineering: G Donato

Besides the Montreal Metro (see Rapid transit section), MUCTC is supporting CN Rail's commuter operation and its rehabilitation under a 10-year contract signed in July 1982. As a result CN Rail has undertaken a $5·6 million renovation of 14 electric locomotives, 70 passenger cars and 16 two-car mus. A similar contract was concluded with CP Rail in October 1982 and provided for rehabilitation of that system's seven diesel locomotives and 49 cars engaged in commuter service.

As yet undecided is management of the Montreal regional, steel-wheeled metro system recently drafted by COTREM, a provincial planning task force. Its first route will be Line 6, running 24 km on CN Rail infrastructure from the centre of Montreal island at Du College eastward to Pointe-aux-Trembles; construction may start in 1984, for completion by 1987. The second route to be tackled will be Line 3, from an interchange with Line 6 at the present Eastern Junction, to be renamed Cote-Vertu, to Deux-Montagnes in the north. The third line under study in 1982 was from central Montreal to Laval, and possibly further to Mirabel international airport (58 km from the city centre), if Mirabel completely replaces Dorval as Montreal's passenger airport.

INDEX

Printed and made in the United Kingdom by Netherwood Dalton & Co. Ltd., Huddersfield

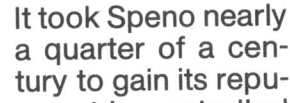
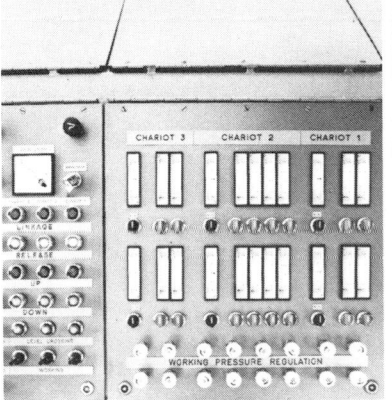

[i]

Variety in selection, excellence in performance.

Daewoo Heavy Industries' Rolling Stock Division combines variety in selection with excellence in performance to satisfy clients the world over: over 10,000 units of Daewoo Rolling Stock are riding the rails throughout Asia, Oceania, Africa and the Middle East.

Selection includes electric multiple units, diesel rail cars, passenger coaches, freight cars and wagons, locomotives, and a long list of specialty rolling stock

to meet virtually every purpose and every climatic condition. And excellence in performance is one reason for the increasing popularity of Daewoo Rolling Stock around the world.

If you're looking for rolling stock that continues to roll, and roll, and roll, maybe you should take a good look into what Daewoo has to offer. After all, we're out to keep you on the right track.

DAEWOO
DAEWOO HEAVY INDUSTRIES LTD.

SEOUL OFFICE DAEWOO CENTER BLDG. 20TH FL. 541, 5-GA, NAMDAEMOON-RO, JUNG-GU, SEOUL, KOREA C.P.O. BOX: 7955 TLX: DHILTD K23301 TEL: (752) 0211
HEAD OFFICE & FACTORY 6, MANSEOG-DONG, DONG-GU, INCHEON, KOREA TEL.: INCHEON (72) 1011-16, (72) 2011-16, TELEX: DHILTD K28473 CABLE: DHILTD INCHEON
ANYANG FACTORY 462-2, SAM-RI, EUIWANG-EUB, SIHEUNG-GUN, KYEONGGI-DO, KOREA TEL: ANYANG (3) 6171-80